Key to map pages

Shetland Islands
Lerwick
Orkney Islands
Kirkwall
Isle of Lewis
Stornoway
North Uist
Lochmaddy
South Uist
Lochboisdale
Barra
Isle of Skye
Uig
Portree
Kyle of Lochalsh
Rum
Mallaig
Gairloch
Durness
Thurso
Wick
Helmsdale
Brora
Dornoch
Ullapool
Bonar Bridge
Invergordon
Cromarty
Dingwall
Nairn
Forres
Inverness
Grantown-on-Spey
Lossiemouth
Elgin
Fraserburgh
Keith
Dufftown
Peterhead
Inverurie
Ellon
Aviemore
Fort Augustus
Newtonmore
Ballater
Banchory
Aberdeen
Braemar
Stonehaven
Fort William
Coll
Tiree
Mull
Oban
Crianlarich
Pitlochry
Forfar
Montrose
Arbroath
Dundee
Perth
St Andrews
Inveraray
Dunblane
Colonsay
Jura
Islay
Tarbert
Stirling
Alloa
Kirkaldy
Greenock
Falkirk
Edinburgh
Dunbar
Largs
Glasgow
Airdrie
Livingston
Saltcoats
East Kilbride
Lanark
Peebles
Coldstream
Berwick-upon-Tweed
Holy Island
Arran
Campbeltown
Irvine
Kilmarnock
Biggar
Galashiels
Kelso
Ayr
Cumnock
Hawick
Jedburgh
Alnwick
Girvan
Moffat
Warkworth
Thornhill
Lockerbie
Langholm
Morpeth
Dumfries
Stranraer
Wigtown
Kirkudbright
Gretna
Carlisle
Haltwhistle
Hexham
Consett
Newcastle upon Tyne
Sunderland
Wigton
Durham
Seaham
Workington
Penrith
Middlesbrough
Whitehaven
Shap
Brough
Darlington
Whitby
Seascale
Kendal
Richmond
Northallerton
Isle of Man
Douglas
Barrow-in-Furness
Lancaster
Settle
Thirsk
Helmsley
Scarborough
Ripon
Malton
Bridlington
Harrogate
York
Blackpool
Preston
Bradford
Leeds
Beverley
Southport
Bolton
Barnsley
Doncaster
Hull
Grimsby
Holyhead
Anglesey
Llandudno
Conwy
Liverpool
Manchester
Macclesfield
Sheffield
Gainsborough
Lincoln
Louth
Mablethorpe
Caernarfon
Bangor
Chester
Wrexham
Hanley
Stoke
Mansfield
Nottingham
Newark
Skegness
Boston
Porthmadog
Pwllheli
Bala
Dolgellau
Oswestry
Shrewsbury
Telford
Stafford
Derby
Grantham
Melton Mowbray
King's Lynn
Fakenham
Norwich
Great Yarmouth
Lowestoft
Welshpool
Newtown
Wolverhampton
Leicester
Coventry
Stamford
Corby
Peterborough
Ely
Swaffham
Thetford
Beccles
Aberystwyth
Aberaeron
Builth Wells
Ludlow
Kington
Worcester
Birmingham
Stratford-upon-Avon
Northampton
Cambridge
Bury St Edmunds
Aldeburgh
Ipswich
Harwich
Cardigan
St David's
Carmarthen
Brecon
Hereford
Gloucester
Cheltenham
Milton Keynes
Luton
Stevenage
Colchester
Tenby
Llanelli
Swansea
Merthyr Tydfil
Monmouth
Chepstow
Stroud
Cirencester
Oxford
Aylesbury
Watford
Hertford
Brentwood
Witham
Chelmsford
Newport
Cardiff
Bristol
Bath
Swindon
Newbury
Reading
Windsor
Woking
LONDON
Croydon
Southend-on-Sea
Chatham
Margate
Barnstaple
Bridgwater
Cheddar
Glastonbury
Devizes
Salisbury
Winchester
Guildford
Horsham
Maidstone
Ashford
Canterbury
Dover
Bideford
Bude
Gt Torrington
South Molton
Tiverton
Taunton
Chard
Yeovil
Blandford Forum
Southampton
Chichester
Lewes
Brighton
Rye
Hastings
Eastbourne
Launceston
Okehampton
Exeter
Bournemouth
Portsmouth
Camelford
Tavistock
Newton Abbot
Dorchester
Poole
Isle of Wight
Wadebridge
Newquay
Liskeard
Bodmin
Plymouth
Torquay
Redruth
Truro
St Austell
Dartmouth
Salcombe
Penzance
Helston
Falmouth
Isles of Scilly

EASYREAD NAVIGATOR Britain

www.philips-maps.co.uk

First published in 2009 by Philip's
a division of Octopus Publishing Group Ltd
www.octopusbooks.co.uk
2–4 Heron Quays London E14 4JP
An Hachette Livre UK Company
www.hachettelivre.co.uk

First edition 2009
First impression 2009

ISBN 978-1-84907-039-3

Cartography by Philip's
Copyright © 2009 Philip's

This product includes mapping data licensed from Ordnance Survey®, with the permission of the Controller of Her Majesty's Stationery Office. © Crown copyright 2009. All rights reserved. Licence number 100011710

No part of this publication may be reproduced, stored in a retrieval system or transmitted in any form or by any means, electronic, mechanical, photocopying, recording or otherwise, without the permission of the Publishers and the copyright owner.

While every reasonable effort has been made to ensure that the information compiled in this atlas is accurate, complete and up-to-date at the time of publication, some of this information is subject to change and the Publisher cannot guarantee its correctness or completeness.

The information in this atlas is provided without any representation or warranty, express or implied and the Publisher cannot be held liable for any loss or damage due to any use or reliance on the information in this atlas, nor for any errors, omissions or subsequent changes in such information.

The representation in this atlas of any road, drive or track is no evidence of the existence of a right of way.

Data for the speed cameras provided by
PocketGPSWorld.com Ltd.

Information for National Parks, Areas of Outstanding Natural Beauty, National Trails and Country Parks in Wales supplied by the Countryside Council for Wales.

Information for National Parks, Areas of Outstanding Natural Beauty, National Trails and Country Parks in England supplied by Natural England. Data for Regional Parks, Long Distance Footpaths and Country Parks in Scotland provided by Scottish Natural Heritage.

Information for Forest Parks supplied by the Forestry Commission

Information for the RSPB reserves provided by the RSPB

Gaelic name forms used in the Western Isles provided by Comhairle nan Eilean.

Data for the National Nature Reserves in England provided by Natural England. Data for the National Nature Reserves in Wales provided by Countryside Council for Wales. Darparwyd data'n ymwneud â Gwarchodfeydd Natur Cenedlaethol Cymru gan Gyngor Cefn Gwlad Cymru.

Information on the location of National Nature Reserves in Scotland was provided by Scottish Natural Heritage.

Data for National Scenic Areas in Scotland provided by the Scottish Executive Office. Crown copyright material is reproduced with the permission of the Controller of HMSO and the Queen's Printer for Scotland. Licence number C02W0003960.

Printed in China

*Navigator was the best-selling UK Road Atlas title by value in 2007/08 based on Nielsen BookScan Total Consumer Market.

Contents

II	**Key to map symbols**
III	**Save £1000** off your annual motoring costs
VI	**Why you can't rely on your SatNav alone...**
VIII	**Route planning maps**
XIV	**Distances** and journey times
1	**Road maps of Britain**
315	**Index to road maps of Britain**
370	**County and unitary authority boundaries**

Road map symbols

Symbol	Description
M25	Motorway
16 / 17	Motorway junctions – full access, restricted access
	Toll motorway
Pease Pottage Services	Motorway service area
	Motorway under construction
S	Primary route – dual, single carriageway, services
	– under construction, narrow
Cardiff	Primary destination
25 / 26	Numbered junctions – full, restricted access
	A road – dual, single carriageway
	– under construction, narrow
	B road – dual, single carriageway
	– under construction, narrow
	Minor road – dual, single carriageway
	Drive or track
	Roundabout, multi-level junction
2	Distance in miles
	Tunnel
Toll	Toll, steep gradient – points downhill
40 / 40	Speed camera – single, multiple
CLEVELAND WAY	National trail – England and Wales
GREAT GLEN WAY	Long distance footpath – Scotland
YATTON / ROPLEY	Railway with station, level crossing, tunnel
	Preserved railway with level crossing, station, tunnel
	Tramway
	National boundary
	County or unitary authority boundary
	Car ferry, catamaran
	Passenger ferry, catamaran
CALAIS 1:30	Ferry destination, journey time – hours: minutes
	Hovercraft
V / P	Internal ferry – car, passenger
	Principal airport, other airport or airfield
MENDIP HILLS	Area of outstanding natural beauty, National Forest – England and Wales, **Forest park, National park, National scenic area** – Scotland, **Regional park, National Forest**
	Woodland
	Beach – sand, shingle
KENNET AND AVON CANAL	Navigable river or canal
6 / 6	Lock, flight of locks, canal bridge number
▲965	Viewpoint, spot height – in metres
	Linear antiquity
P&R	Park and ride
29	Adjoining page number
SY 70 / 80	Ordnance Survey National Grid reference – see page 370

Tourist information

Symbol	Description
BYLAND ABBEY	Abbey or priory
WOODHENGE	Ancient monument
SEALIFE CENTRE	Aquarium or dolphinarium
CITY MUSEUM AND ART GALLERY	Art collection or museum
TATE ST IVES	Art gallery
1644	Battle site and date
ABBOTSBURY SWANNERY	Bird sanctuary or aviary
	Camping site
	Caravan site
BAMBURGH CASTLE	Castle
YORK MINSTER	Cathedral
SANDHAM MEMORIAL CHAPEL	Church of interest
	Country park
SEVEN SISTERS	– England and Wales
LOCHORE MEADOWS	– Scotland
ROYAL BATH & WEST SHOWGROUND	County show ground
MONK PARK FARM	Farm park
HILLIER GARDENS AND ARBORETUM	Garden, arboretum
ST ANDREWS	Golf course – 18-hole
TYNTESFIELD	Historic house
SS GREAT BRITAIN	Historic ship
HATFIELD HOUSE	House and garden
MUSEUM OF DARTMOOR LIFE	Local museum
HOLTON HEATH	National nature reserve
	Marina
NAT MARITIME MUSEUM	Maritime or military museum
SILVERSTONE	Motor racing circuit
CUMBERLAND PENCIL MUSEUM	Museum
	Picnic area
WEST SOMERSET RAILWAY	Preserved railway
THIRSK	Racecourse
LEAHILL TURRET	Roman antiquity
BOYTON MARSHES	RSPB reserve
THRIGBY HALL	Safari park
FREEPORT BRAINTREE	Shopping village
MILLENNIUM STADIUM	Sports venue
ALTON TOWERS	Theme park
	Tourist information centre
i	– open all year
i	– open seasonally
NATIONAL RAILWAY MUSEUM YORK	Transport collection
LEVANT MINE	World heritage site
HELMSLEY	Youth hostel
MARWELL	Zoo
SUTTON BANK VISITOR CENTRE	Other place
GLENFIDDICH DISTILLERY	of interest

Road map scale
1: 100 000 or 1.58 miles to 1 inch

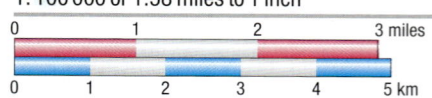

Road map scale
(Isle of Man and parts of Scotland)
1: 200 000 or 3.15 miles to 1 inch

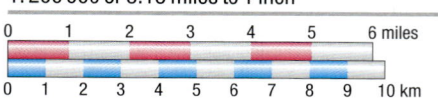

Speed Cameras

Fixed camera locations are shown using the 40 symbol. In congested areas the 40 symbol is used to show that there are two or more cameras on the road indicated.

Due to the restrictions of scale the camera locations are only approximate and cannot indicate the operating direction of the camera. Mobile camera sites, and cameras located on roads not included on the mapping are not shown. Where two or more cameras are shown on the same road, drivers are warned that this may indicate that a SPEC system is in operation. These cameras use the time taken to drive between the two camera positions to calculate the speed of the vehicle.

Jonathan Maddock / iStockphoto.com

Save £1000 off your annual motoring costs

Seven Top Tips from motoring journalist Andrew Charman

In today's cost-conscious motoring environment, is it possible to slice serious money from the cost of running a car? With the right preparation, it could well be.

Ask any motorist whether they get good value from their driving and most will likely say no – many argue that motoring has never been more expensive. Drivers fight a constant battle against many enemies including fluctuating fuel prices, aggressive tax rates and an ever-expanding epidemic of safety cameras that many believe are present to generate revenue from fines first, and slow speeds second.

Some 60% of the drivers questioned for the 2008 Annual Report on Motoring compiled by the RAC believed that rising costs were the biggest minus of running a car in Britain today. Those drivers will be surprised to hear that, in fact, motoring is getting cheaper – the report concluded that even rocketing fuel prices have not stopped the overall cost of motoring falling in the past two decades.

The RAC research concluded that such factors as cheaper purchase and maintainance prices for cars have resulted in motoring costs decreasing in real terms by 18% since 1988, despite fuel costs rising 210%. Take those fuel price rises out of the equation and motoring today is 28% cheaper than 20 years ago.

This little bit of good news, however, does not mean that you can't save money on your motoring – and I intend to show you how some simple moves could put significant cash back into your pocket each year – possibly more than £1000.

Different cars, different homes

Saving big money on your motoring costs starts even before you buy the car. The vehicle you choose and how you buy it can make a difference of thousands of pounds, as shown in the panel on page V. But have no fear, because whether you've just bought a brand-new car or have used the same vehicle for many years, you can still save a packet on your motoring costs.

Of course, I can't say exactly what you will save by following the advice in these pages – so many varying factors affect one's motoring expenses. For example, I used to live in commuter-belt Surrey. Every morning I drove my children 8 miles to school, a journey of around half an hour on congested roads. Now I live in Mid-Wales and drive my wife to work, coincidentally also around 8 miles; it takes less than 15 minutes and I use 10–15% less fuel.

Similarly, potential savings in such areas as tyre life will be affected by your car, the way you drive and the roads you drive on. What I can confidently predict, however, is that by following even some of the advice on these pages, you will leave a noticeable amount of cash in your pocket.

In order to calculate these savings, we've devised 'Mr Average Motorist'. He drives a petrol-powered car – because, despite diesel soaring in popularity in recent times, the majority of cars on today's roads still run on petrol. Our man owns a Ford Mondeo family car, which is regularly one of the UK's top ten most popular buys and averages 35mpg in fuel consumption. So, if he clocks up the national average of around 12,000 miles a year, he will use 1558 litres of fuel costing, at current prices, around £1402.

Preparation is everything

Fuel prices are the most visible and most obvious indicator of the cost of motoring today. As I write, the price of a litre of unleaded has plummeted to around 90p, having spent months steadily rising to over £1.20. But by the time you read this, prices could be soaring again and generally they are on the rise – remember that 210% figure within 20 years? We can't change fuel prices – but we can make the best use of every litre we buy.

You might think, then, that the first obvious move is to buy fuel from the cheapest source – but it's not. Before you put any fuel in your tank, you need to check that your car is in the best condition, both mechanically and otherwise, to stretch those litres. Skimping on servicing is NOT a way to save money on motoring. If your engine is not correctly tuned, it uses more fuel. In particular, clean fresh oil not only helps reduce fuel consumption but also wear caused by the friction of moving engine parts. Allow such parts to keep wearing and you could end up with a failure – and all your savings will be wiped out by an expensive repair bill. Ideally, on a petrol car you should change the oil at least once a year, and a diesel engine benefits from a change every six months.

But by far the biggest mechanical influence on fuel economy comes courtesy of what the car stands on – its tyres. Incorrectly inflated tyres, particularly containing too little pressure, leads to less mpg – and, incredibly, research by the tyre industry suggests that half of all tyres running on today's roads are under-inflated. Tyre manufacturers have calculated that for every 6psi a tyre is under-inflated, an extra 1% is added to consumption, and in roadside checks many cars have been found to have tyres under-inflated by as much as 20%.

◄ Checking your tyre pressures is simple, and could greatly improve fuel economy.

▼ Under-inflated or damaged tyres could end up costing you more than a bigger fuel bill.
Photographs courtesy of TyreSafe

Seven Top Tips to save money

1 SLOWING DOWN
average annual saving: up to £532

The first, most obvious area to watch is speed. We are always being told to slow down, but apart from the risk of paying out big money in fines having been caught by a safety camera, there's a far more obvious reason to ease back on that right-hand pedal – it saves money!

The effect is most noticeable on motorways. The national speed limit in Britain is 70mph, but on many a motorway that seems to be treated as a minimum, with traffic charging along at 80mph-plus. However, above 70mph aerodynamic drag becomes a serious issue, really eating into your fuel. If you adopt a more radical attitude, though, cruising along at 50mph instead of 70mph, your fuel costs will plummet, by an astonishing 38% in the average car.

Of course, many drivers will consider slowing down that much, particularly on a clear motorway, as a step too far, but even keeping firmly within speed limits will greatly influence your fuel costs. And there is much more you can do.

Smooth is good – don't, for example, floor the throttle the moment you see a clear stretch of road open up ahead of you. Harsh acceleration, and the resultant equally harsh braking, burns up those litres. Keep a good distance back from the car in front, so you can slow down gently when they do.

Powering around to the red line on your rev counter is another no-no – today's engines work most efficiently at speeds between 1500–2000rpm, and on modern petrol cars changing up a gear at around 2500rpm (2000rpm on a diesel) is both safe, smooth and fuel-friendly.

2 FUEL'S GOLD
average annual saving: up to £420

Find a bargain. Fuel prices charged by garages vary enormously – within a 20-mile radius of my home the differences add up to 5p per litre. And at the time of writing prices are changing almost daily. Clearly the trick is to buy from the cheapest source, but don't drive around looking for cheap prices – you could use as much as you save. Online resources, such as www.petrolprices.com, are a good way of finding out where fuel costs the least in your area, and while prices change constantly, the cheapest garages tend to remain cheapest.

When you've found your cheap supplier, try not to make a special trip to fill up – it's an unnecessary journey that uses fuel. Plan your motoring, factoring in a visit to the garage on the way to or from

Myth buster
A few motoring savings that are not always true….

? Buy your fuel from a busy garage because the fuel is used quicker, so has no time to age and lose quality

Not necessarily so – The big issue affecting fuel quality is water getting into the tanks through, for example, condensation. Garages periodically remove this water and busier garages may have less chance to do so compared to quieter rural outlets. Fuel quality depends on an individual garage's 'housekeeping' standards and there is no general standard. Also, by going to a busy garage you may lose any potential tiny saving from better-quality fuel while sitting in the queue with your engine running.

? When buying fuel in the early morning or evening, you get more for your money because in cooler conditions each litre of liquid becomes denser

False – Most garages keep their fuel in underground tanks, where temperature changes throughout the day are miniscule.

? Coasting down hills with the car in neutral saves fuel

False – At least with modern cars. Modern fuel systems cut off the supply to the engine the moment you come off the accelerator, but whether you are in gear or not a tiny amount is still used to ensure the engine does not stall. And without a gear, you have no engine braking, and less control.

? It's cheaper to get your car serviced at an independent

Not necessarily so – While independents might appear cheaper than a franchised dealer, because they don't specialize in a particular brand they don't know that brand so well, and crucially often don't possess the same level of diagnostic equipment as a franchised dealer. Therefore, tracing any faults can take significantly longer, which will be charged in service hours.

? A fast-fit supplier is the cheapest place to buy new tyres

Not necessarily so – Many franchised dealers are actively price-matching tyres to fast-fit opposition, and if you are told new tyres are needed during a service at the dealer, driving to a fast-fit supplier to find what you expect to be cheaper tyres can be an unnecessary, fuel-using journey.

▲ Recent on the scene are low-rolling-resistance tyres that extend fuel economy by causing less drag on the road surface. Photo courtesy Mercedes-Benz

▼ Neglecting servicing is not a way to save money – in fact it will end up exactly the opposite. Photo courtesy ATA

◀ Nice luggage, but leave the bags in the boot when you don't need them and you are simply adding fuel-using weight. Photo courtesy Volkswagen UK

▶ Roof racks are useful, but left atop the car when not in use, they simply ruin the aerodynamics, and the fuel economy. Photo courtesy GM UK

somewhere else. It's also prudent to visit the garage more often and only run on half a tank instead of a full one, if doing so suits your schedule, because all that extra liquid in a full tank is extra weight.

3 CUTTING DRAG
average annual saving: up to £140

Surely we can't change a car's aerodynamics? Oh yes, we can. Did you fit a roof rack to take all the extras for the family holiday last summer? Is it still bolted to the roof? The extra drag from such a large, anything-but-aerodynamic item could be costing you as much as 30% in fuel consumption.

The same goes for bike racks hung on the back of a car – they don't have the same dramatic effect as a roof rack, but they will unsettle the air ahead of them, thus affecting the aerodynamics of the rear end. Even running with your windows open harms the aerodynamics, interrupting the flow along the sides of the car. Do you tow a caravan and use those wing-mirror extensions to see around it? Well, if you haven't got the van hitched behind, take them off – they act like a couple of airbrakes.

4 AVOID THE CON
average annual saving: up to £140

Remember how it was advised to keep your windows closed for the best aerodynamics? Well, this next tip will go against the grain. Most modern cars have air-conditioning and many drivers leave it permanently switched on. But in doing so they can use up to 10% more fuel. Use the fans on cool without the system switched on, or have the window open just a little. If it's really hot, use the air-con for short periods instead of leaving it switched on and forgetting about it.

5 CLEVER FUELLING
average annual saving: up to £78

Planning ahead saves fuel and first you need to ask, 'Do I really need to make this trip?' Cars take a while to warm up during which they use the most fuel, which is why you should drive gently, avoiding stressing the engine, for the first few miles of any journey. But if said trip is merely nipping down to the shops for, say, a pint of milk, the car never has a chance to warm up, and your fuel economy suffers greatly. So for such short journeys consider walking, or perhaps cycling – it will benefit your health, as well as your car and your wallet. Alternatively, why not combine a number of short journeys in the week – visiting the family one night and doing the shopping on another – into one longer trip, perhaps popping into the garage for fuel at the same time.

Planning ahead comes into its own on longer journeys, especially if travelling to somewhere unfamiliar – you need to know exactly

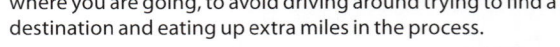

where you are going, to avoid driving around trying to find a destination and eating up extra miles in the process.

Try to avoid congestion hotspots, because sitting in traffic queues not only wastes fuel but also tries one's patience, and when the jam clears we then drive more aggressively, and less fuel-efficiently, to try and make up time. Check where the problems are likely to be – Traffic England, the Highways Agency's website (www.trafficengland.com), carries constantly updated information on traffic issues and even has a facility where one can look at the view from the roadside CCTV cameras to see how heavy the traffic is. Once in the car, listen out for traffic reports on the radio so you can plan ahead and avoid the hot spots. Don't forget to take this road atlas with you so you can use it to detour around problems.

6 PRESSURE POINTS
average annual saving: up to £42

Under-inflated tyres cause increased wear, which as well as becoming dangerous (a bald tyre will harm grip in anything but totally dry conditions, as well as further increasing fuel consumption) reduces the life of the tyre by as much as 30%. You should also check the alignment of your wheels – simply hitting a pothole or a kerb can knock the alignment out, which again will increase tyre wear.

A recent advance in tyre technology, used extensively on the new breed of 'eco' cars, is to cut the tyre's rolling resistance, which is basically the force required to move the rubber over the road. Lower-rolling-resistance tyres require less force and so aid fuel economy, by around 2.5%. Now, less rolling resistance would suggest less grip, which is not very desirable, but these tyres use silica in their construction which effectively puts the grip back. And, surprisingly, such tyres do not generally carry a big price premium over traditional counterparts.

7 CAR WEIGHTWATCHERS
average annual saving: up to £35

Of all the battles fought by motorsport car designers, two areas stand out – reducing the weight of their cars by as much as possible, and making them as smooth as possible, so they slice more efficiently through the air. Exactly the same principles apply to road cars, not for speed, but for economy, and while we would not advocate slicing bits from your car, or trying to add wings and things to a body shape honed over many hours in a wind tunnel by professionals, there are distinct steps one can take that will have major effects on efficiency.

Have you looked in the back of your car recently? Do you know what is in there? Carrying around a lot of unnecessary weight greatly affects fuel economy, and thus your motoring costs – in some cases by as much as 10%. So if you play golf and your clubs and bag live in the boot, or you've been for a day out and left the deckchairs in the car, along with the picnic basket, that weight is squeezing your wallet. Go through the car looking for those pounds that can be shed. You might not think, for example, that a glovebox full of CDs weighs very much, but it all adds up.

Out on the road
There are still big savings to be made, but the onus is now firmly on you and the way you drive the car. So, if you are a bit of a speed merchant, like to use your throttle and brakes, can't remember the last time you checked your tyre pressures, and throw your cases on the roof rack because there's no room left in the boot, following the economy regime above could save you at least £1000 in a year! But even if you are a conscientious motorist who only needs to follow a couple of these Top Tips, you could still save significant money.

◀ Whether filling up with petrol, diesel or the latest biofuels, a little preparation will make the most of your visit to the garage. Photo courtesy GM UK

▼ These graphs show how much extra you could be adding to your annual motoring costs, depending on the type of car you drive and the mileage you do. Admittedly this is a 'worst case scenario', assuming that you need to use every part of the advice in this feature, and savings will vary depending on the individual characteristics of your car and your driving environment. However even following some of the advice will save you money. (Chart based on fuel prices of 90p per litre unleaded, 99p per litre diesel)

Road warrior approximately 40,000 miles per year

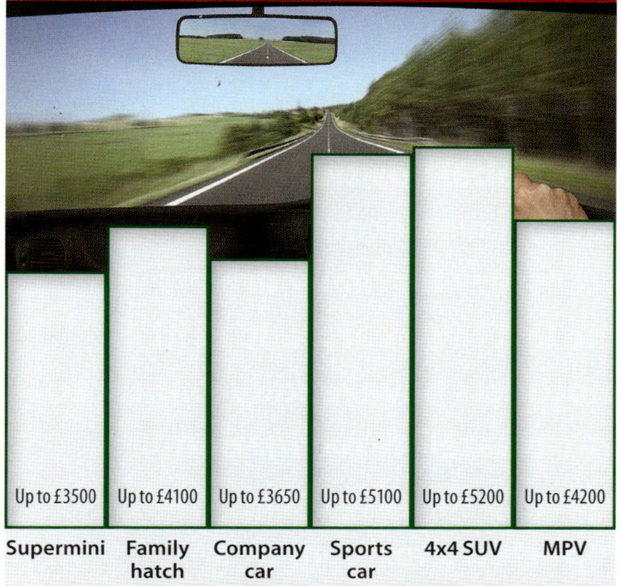

Supermini	Family hatch	Company car	Sports car	4x4 SUV	MPV
Up to £3500	Up to £4100	Up to £3650	Up to £5100	Up to £5200	Up to £4200

Professional driver approximately 22,000 miles per year

Supermini	Family hatch	Company car	Sports car	4x4 SUV	MPV
Up to £2000	Up to £2270	Up to £2000	Up to £2800	Up to £2900	Up to £2300

Family runabout approximately 12,000 miles per year

Supermini	Family hatch	Company car	Sports car	4x4 SUV	MPV
Up to £1150	Up to £1200	Up to £1100	Up to £1500	Up to £1500	Up to £1300

Just for shopping approximately 6000 miles per year

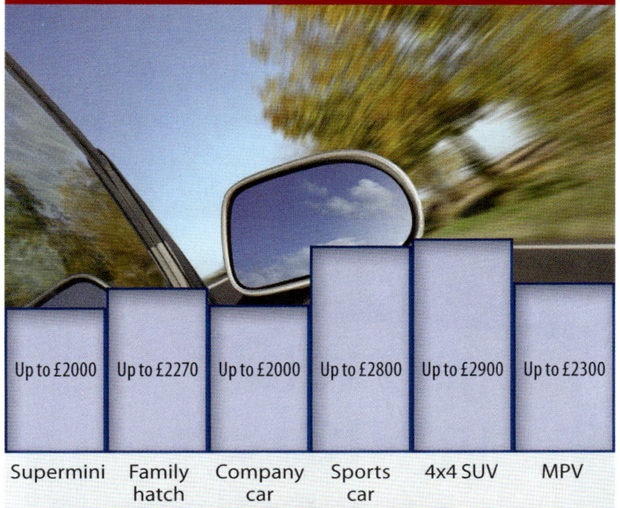

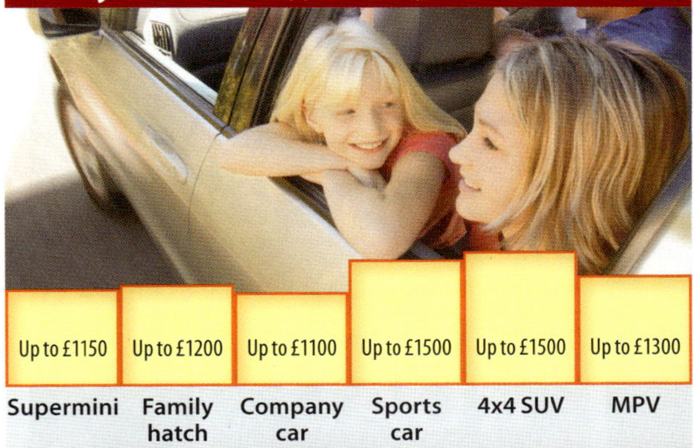

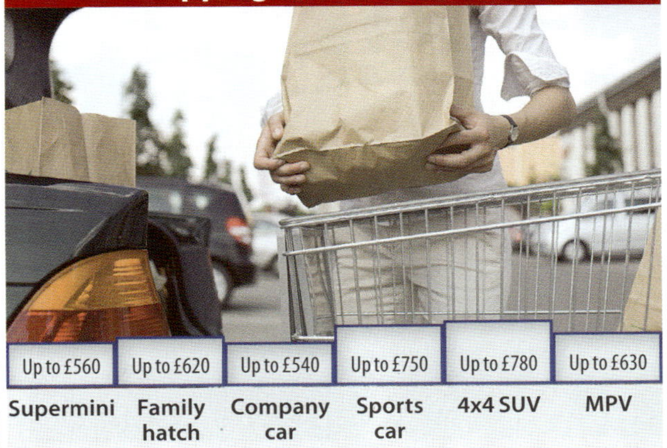

Supermini	Family hatch	Company car	Sports car	4x4 SUV	MPV
Up to £560	Up to £620	Up to £540	Up to £750	Up to £780	Up to £630

Buying a car

Most of us don't buy a new car every year, but when we do, there are thousands of pounds we can potentially save, as long as we do our homework first. Recent research by the AA found that a person spending up to £10,000 on a car could end up with a vehicle returning anything from 33 to almost 70mpg. Over a year, the difference in fuel costs for our average driver would add up to more than £700. When the AA compared the mpg figures for cars costing between £20,000 and £30,000, the potential fuel savings came close to £2000! In addition, smaller, greener cars attract lower insurance premiums, and cheaper annual road tax – depending on your model, the cost of a tax disc can vary from £0 to £400 a year.

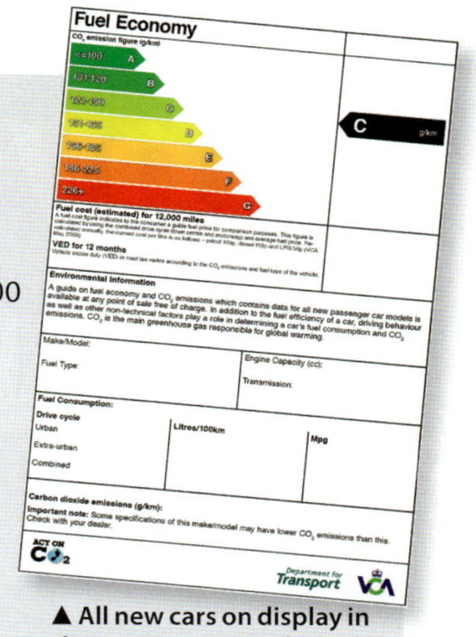

- **Think carefully before making your choice.** Do you really need a seven-seat people carrier? It might be useful on the few occasions your children bring friends home from school, but most of the time you will be carrying around extra, fuel-burning weight. Do you really want that sporty convertible? Folding roof mechanisms add weight, and as well as being less mpg-friendly to start with, performance engines encourage 'performance' driving, which gobble up those litres.

- **Many manufacturers are now producing new 'eco' versions** of their most popular models, with such refinements as low-rolling-resistance tyres, remapped engine electronics and reshaped aerodynamics to further stretch that fuel economy, and slash CO_2 emissions to levels that qualify for free road tax. But they can sometimes cost significantly more to buy than traditional counterparts.

- **The most economical cars will generally be diesel-powered.** Diesel engines travel a lot further on each litre of fuel and they produce less CO_2. But diesel fuel costs on average around 12p per litre more than the equivalent unleaded petrol – and the majority of diesel-powered cars come with a price premium over their petrol counterparts.

- **Spend time working out your annual mileage** and how far you will need to drive a diesel before you start saving money. Used-car specialist Parkers Guide recently launched a very useful fuel-cost calculator on its website (www.parkers.co.uk), which enables an instant check on how much individual car models will cost you in a year, and it can throw up surprises – for example, at current fuel prices and car list prices, a BMW 318d diesel would take close to 300,000 miles to recoup the £2790 more that it costs over the 318i petrol version.

- **Consider depreciation** when buying. Be sure to check the 'residual value' – which is an industry-quoted figure, easily found on internet sites such as Parkers, predicting how much the car will be worth after three years' use. Many factors influence such values – the make of car, its reliability, additional equipment installed, even in some cases the colour – so it's worth checking carefully to save money down the line.

Wasted fuel...

You could be using more than double the amount of fuel you need to! This chart shows how much cash you could be wasting by not attending to basic economy measures. Excess speed, for example, can increase fuel use by more than a third.

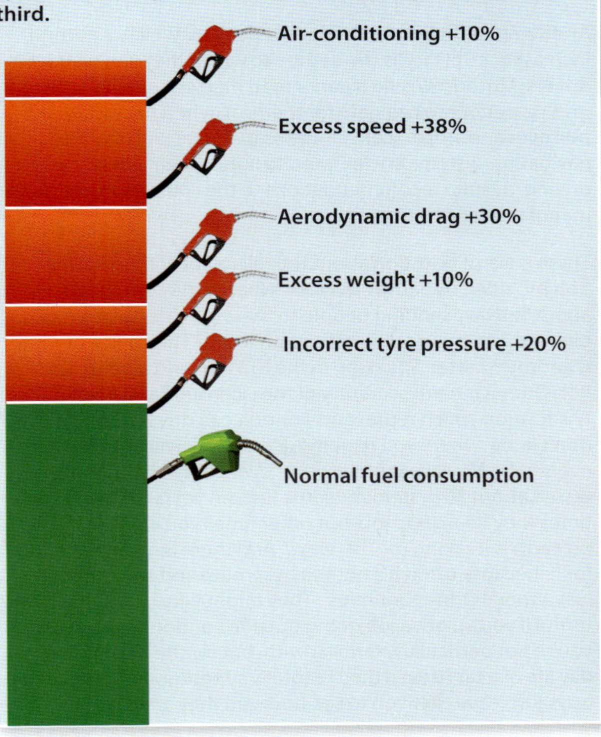

- Air-conditioning +10%
- Excess speed +38%
- Aerodynamic drag +30%
- Excess weight +10%
- Incorrect tyre pressure +20%
- Normal fuel consumption

- **Do you need to buy new?** New cars lose a significant amount of their value – sometimes 20-25% – the moment they are driven off the showroom forecourt. Yet there are many buyers who change their car every year, which adds excellent vehicles to a dealer's nearly-new selection. Many have at least a year of the manufacturer's warranty remaining – some substantially more with several makers moving to five-year and, in the case of Hyundai, seven-year warranties.

- **If you do buy used**, it's crucial to spend a little money, usually no more than £30–£40, on a vehicle data check, which will show up any irregularities in the car's history – whether it has outstanding finance owing on it, for example. This could avoid costing you a big bill, or even your car, later on.

- **Whether you buy new or used**, never accept the price stated at face value. With car sales having plummeted in the second half of 2008, dealers are desperate to sell – which puts the buyer in a very strong position to haggle over the price. Even persuading the dealer to fill the car with a tank of fuel is a significant saving at today's prices. And if you have hard cash available, this can encourage the dealer to offer you savings.

- **Shopping around for car insurance is essential**, and made easier these days thanks to a number of well-advertised internet price-comparison sites, but don't take these at face value – do your own research too. The choice of car is crucial to how much it will cost you in premiums, but insurers also like cars that are kept off the road, even better if you have a garage available. So if you have a garage full of junk with the car parked outside, why not have a clear out?

- **Also, think beyond the obvious.** If your eldest offspring has reached 17, passed their test and bought themselves an old banger to run around in, do they really need to be on the family car insurance too? If they are, it will send the premium rocketing. You might also consider taking an advanced driving course. While this will cost you money in the first place, insurers tend to give discounts to drivers with advanced qualifications, and along the way you learn driving techniques that will also help your overall economy.

- **Keeping your licence clean** can make a big difference to your insurance costs. You don't want penalty points, so don't use a handheld mobile phone at the wheel, and keep within speed limits – doing so offers a potential double saving, in fuel and insurance costs.

▲ All new cars on display in showrooms now include this chart giving the potential buyer a guide to their annual motoring cost.

▼ Careful driving really does save fuel. In the annual MPG challenge 400-mile endurance marathon, this Toyota Yaris diesel recorded 84.66mpg, almost 35% higher than its official combined fuel consumption figure. Photo courtesy Toyota GB

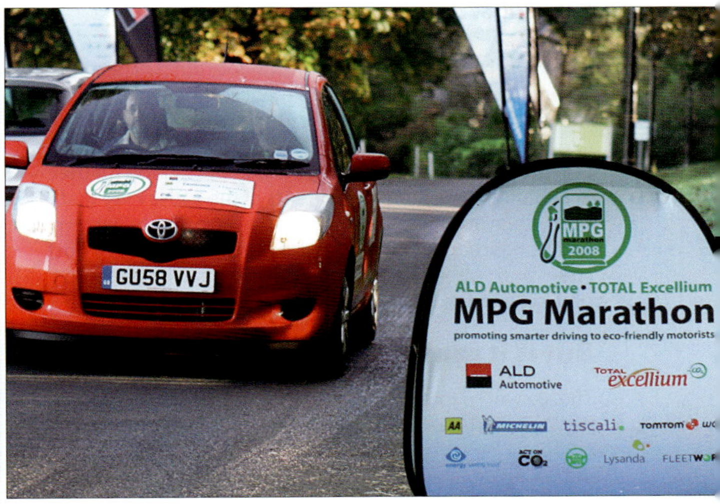

Why you can't rely on your SatNav alone

Satellite navigation aids utilizing the Global Positioning System (GPS) have become an essential accessory for many drivers in the last few years, and British motorists have readily embraced in-car satellite navigation systems despite their widely reported shortcomings.

When SatNavs first appeared in the mid 1990s, they were considered a luxury gadget and the ultimate 'boy's toy', reserved for top-of-the-range cars only. However, the situation started to change in the mid 2000s when TomTom, a software company based in Amsterdam, launched a pocket-sized, portable device aimed squarely at the mass market. Initially, the devices were relatively expensive – at around £400 – but as prices fell with improved technology and greater competition, sales started to soar and today portable SatNav units are widely available for less than £100.

In 2008, satellite navigation aids were more popular in the UK than in any other nation, with 35% of cars on UK roads carrying the technology compared with 24% for Western Europe and 16% for the United States – even Japan, where almost all new cars coming on to the market are now fitted with a SatNav, lagged behind the UK on 33%.

300,000 motorists using a SatNav said that it had caused them to have a crash or a near miss

So why is the SatNav so popular with motorists? There are several reasons: here is a device that promises to take the pressure out of driving, making getting from A to B a more relaxing experience, and saving motorists both the time and fuel costs that they would otherwise have wasted searching for their destination. The many proponents of the SatNav say that it gives them added confidence to drive into unfamiliar territory without getting lost, and that the technology's use of post codes and street names means that they can be directed to a precise location.

But is it really that simple?

The answer to that question is becoming clearer. In July 2008, the Daily Mirror reported on findings made by the insurance company Direct Line. Their research reported that a staggering 300,000 motorists using a SatNav said that it had caused them to have a crash or a near miss; 1.5 million car drivers had veered dangerously or illegally while following its directions; and 5 million drivers had been sent the wrong way down a one-way street. A spokesperson for Brake, the road safety charity, said that the organization had 'very serious concerns' about SatNavs and the effects that they had on motorists. There were fears that users were putting lives in peril by slavishly following their instructions and neglecting road safety. Barely a week goes by without a story in the national press about accidents and near misses where the blame can be attributed to drivers suspending reasonable judgement by following the directions of their satellite navigation aid.

'Some of the guys just leave them on to see how bad they are'

Another negative aspect of SatNav devices, which is getting increasing publicity, is the degree to which they can distract drivers. Motorists using a paper road map either tend to rely on a passenger to navigate for them, or, when necessary, will pull over and stop to consult the map. Those with satellite navigation systems are tempted to adjust them while they are driving, despite recommendations to the contrary made by the manufacturers themselves.

There is also a question about the reliability of the information provided by SatNav devices. What of the complaints about SatNavs sending people to the wrong destination or giving them incorrect directions en route? The choice of route is another matter. Speaking in the FT Weekend Magazine, Bob Oddy, General Secretary of the Licensed Taxi Drivers Association which represents London cab drivers, said, 'If you don't know where you're going, the SatNav will get you there eventually. My caveat is the word "eventually". I must have tested about 30 systems over the last ten years or so and sometimes they do a good job, but other times you wonder: "Why on earth is it taking me this way?" And there is no explanation for it, because often it's not the best route and sometimes it's just wrong.' Oddy continues, 'They might very occasionally be useful if you've got a job going outside London or to a suburb you're not particularly familiar with, but for the normal, everyday life of a taxi driver, they're totally superfluous. Some of the guys just leave them on to see how bad they are.'

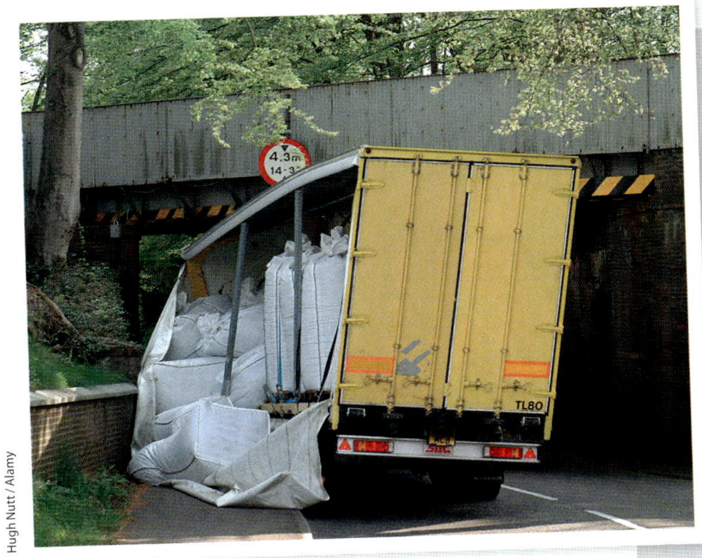

Our 10 of the best – or worst – SatNav stories, as reported in the national press:

1 Paula Ceely, 20, a student from Redditch, swore never to listen to her SatNav again after she was directed into the path of a speeding train at the Ffynnongain level crossing on the South Wales main line. Fortunately for Ceely, she had got out to close the gate behind her by the time a train smashed into her car. Miraculously, the driver and all the train passengers escaped injury too.

2 Police and rescue teams spent nine hours recovering the car of Robert Jones from Doncaster, which was left teetering on the edge of a 100 ft cliff in Todmorden, West Yorkshire, after he followed instructions from his SatNav that told him the steep, narrow footpath he was travelling down was a road.

3 A cabbie taking a fare – a daughter of Earl Spencer – from Althorp in Northamptonshire to watch Chelsea play at Stamford Bridge, in West London, ended up in Yorkshire. Rather than making the 85-mile trip to London, the driver went 146 miles in the wrong direction, ending up in the village of Stamford Bridge, in the East Riding of Yorkshire.

4 Another taxi driver, another near miss – this time with the driver stranded after following the device's instructions to drive up the River Nar near Swaffham, Norfolk. The cabbie persevered on his ill-fated journey for 200 yards before his minibus got stuck in the muddy riverbed and had to be rescued by a tractor. Keith Jarvis, owner of the Streamline taxi firm, said of the driver, 'He was in the car with his trousers rolled up. Fish were swimming around the headlights.'

5 Syrian truck driver Needet Bakimci was left red-faced after ending up 1600 miles adrift of his intended destination when driving from Turkey to Gibraltar. The driver had failed to appreciate that his SatNav had directed him to Gibraltar Point Nature Reserve near Skegness, Lincolnshire.

6 In January 2009, a 60 ft articulated lorry crashed into the country cottage of Carol and Tom Krosnar in Litton Cheney, Dorset, after the Hungarian driver was directed off a dual carriageway by his satellite navigation device. The lorry was wedged fast against the building, causing both external and internal damage to the house.

7 A Belgian truck driver blamed his electronic wayfinder after leaving a £20,000 trail of destruction in his wake in Wadebridge, Cornwall. Directed by his SatNav into an unsuitable cul-de-sac, the hapless trucker put his foot down in a panic, ending his turning manoeuvre by ploughing over a mini roundabout, getting a car trapped under his lorry, and destroying five more vehicles.

8 Lorries are becoming increasingly responsible for wreaking havoc on the roads in cases where their SatNavs have directed them in tall vehicles under low bridges, with catastrophic results. In 2007, three railway bridges within a 1-mile radius in the town of Grantham, Lincolnshire, were hit by lorries a total of 62 times.

9 From bridges getting in the way, to a bridge that was never even there – hundreds of drivers a year followed their SatNavs' instructions towards a bridge across the River Severn at Hampton Loade, Shropshire, that has never even existed. Drivers are having to make U-turns after driving miles out of their way to find that the 'bridge' is actually a ferry for foot passengers only.

10 Although some SatNav stories may make us laugh as we read of the scrapes that drivers get themselves into by blindly following the instructions from their devices, sadly every so often we come across a genuine SatNav horror story. In July 2008, a motorist confused by his satellite navigation system killed a woman after driving the wrong way along a dual carriageway and smashing into her car on the A413 in Buckinghamshire. The driver who caused the crash had misunderstood his SatNav's instructions and ignored road signs that should have made him realize his error. Sergeant Dominic Mahon of Thames Valley Police said, 'This is a tragic case that highlights the dangers of over-reliance on SatNavs.'

While SatNavs can make driving easier, safer and less stressful, serious driver errors may occur when obedience to the instructions of a digital device prevails over common sense. This may result in inconvenience to drivers and rescue workers, pollution for those who live in villages whose local roads become a rat-run for drivers on a shortcut, as well as damage to homes, railway lines and bridges – and sometimes tragic loss of life.

SatNav users beware!

Driven to distraction As SatNav technology has advanced, the temptation for manufacturers has been to cram more and more information on to the screen. As well as the mapping, most systems now show a dizzying array of extra information, such as speed limits, driving speed, locations of speed cameras, points of interest, estimated time of arrival, and traffic updates. These features are designed to help the driver, but they are all flashing up on screen while you should be concentrating on the road ahead. Other extra features, such as alternative routes, looking for local petrol stations or even simply resetting the device, can be a temptation for drivers to adjust their devices while on the move, which is potentially just as distracting and dangerous as using a mobile phone.

Out-of-date data Road networks change all the time – new roads are built, the layout of junctions are altered and side streets are made 'one-way only'. A SatNav, though, can only ever be as reliable as the mapping data it is based on. In North London, some devices will still offer to send you down Ashburton Grove, a road that was demolished several years ago to make way for Arsenal's new football stadium. 'Live' features that are now included on many devices, such as traffic information, may also be of limited reliability – quite often you will be in a queue of traffic before the device has had time to receive the latest information and warn you of a hold-up ahead. Alternatively, you may be sent on a diversion while your original route will have already cleared.

Stuck in the mud It's quite unlikely that your SatNav will be able to tell you the difference between a good-quality unclassified road and a poor one, so when you're driving through the countryside you run the risk of being directed down tracks or lanes that are really only suitable for tractors or other off-road vehicles.

An irritating bug An assumption sometimes made by SatNav systems is that the through-road is the one that goes straight ahead, when in fact you need to turn in order to follow the road.

More haste, less speed SatNavs may tell you the shortest or the fastest route to your destination, but often vehicles are sent along routes that are entirely inappropriate for them, resulting in lorries becoming stuck in small villages and providing unnecessary hazards to those towing caravans, horse boxes and trailers, for example.

Why you should always use and carry a map in your car

There are many benefits from using SatNav technology. The use of post codes can direct you door-to-door whereas a printed map can only get you as far the road you need, not the exact location, and when a SatNav is used with discretion, it can help you save time and money. But, a SatNav isn't infallible and it doesn't make you a better driver. Like all developing technologies, it has its flaws and sometimes things can go wrong.

These flaws can be compounded by the driver's over-reliance on the technology at the expense of common sense.

As a result, you should not rely on your SatNav alone and should always use it alongside a good, up-to-date road atlas.

- **By planning your route on a road atlas** before you leave, you can visualize your whole journey ahead and be confident that you are heading in the right direction.

- **When you read a paper map, you don't give up your common sense.** It's usually SatNav drivers, not map readers, who drive into rivers or get stuck in farm tracks. Road atlas users travelling alone are also far more like to pull over at the side of the road to consult their map to confirm where they are going.

- **With an atlas you can easily plan a journey** with several stops and check if there are places near to your route that you would like to visit. A SatNav is designed to get you from A to B in the quickest time possible and doesn't work as well as an atlas for leisure driving.

- **Road atlas users don't have to follow the herd.** When a SatNav gives prior warning of a traffic hold-up, hundreds of vehicles can be redirected on to the same route. A road atlas will allow the driver to choose alternatives.

- **Atlases don't lose signal, 'hang' or need recharging.** If a system crashes, it can leave hapless SatNav users high and dry – carrying an atlas means that you have a more reliable source of information to turn to in times of need.

- **It's quicker and easier to use a map when two people are travelling together.** According to Which?Computing magazine, a driver and navigator covering a set route using an atlas went a distance of 67 miles in 1 hour and 35 minutes. Using SatNav, a different car took 8 minutes longer and covered more than 70 miles to complete the same journey.

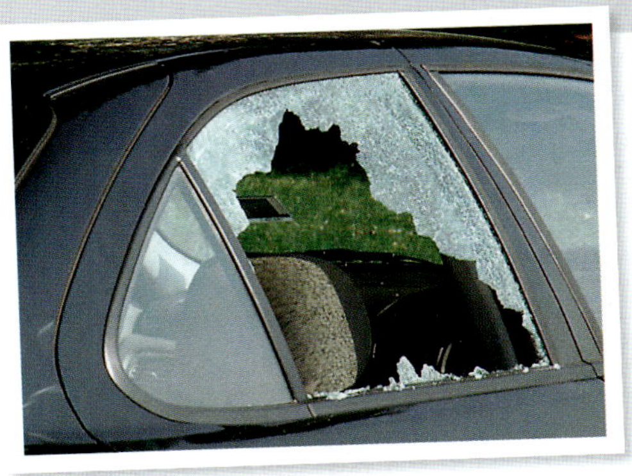

◀ It is unlikely anyone will break into your car to steal your road atlas

- **Road atlases are inexpensive,** and Philip's road atlases are updated on a regular basis using the most up-to-date data available from the Ordnance Survey. Even the most rudimentary SatNav device will cost five times as much as a good road atlas – and that's before SatNav users have to think about paying annual subscription charges to update their mapping data and other information. Making sure you have an up-to-date road atlas is much cheaper. What's more, it is unlikely anyone will break into your car to steal your road atlas!

- **Good news for truckers!** By using the new Philip's Trucker's Navigator Britain atlas, there should be no reason to get stuck under a low bridge or drive along a road that is simply unsuitable for the size of your vehicle. As well as containing the unrivalled level of detail of the highly regarded Philip's Navigator Britain atlas, this new atlas includes additional bridge-height information and indicates bridges with width and weight restrictions to help plan your journey.

So our advice to all careful drivers is this: use and enjoy your SatNav to get you from A to B, but always carry an up-to-date road atlas in your car, make a conscious effort to check every journey with your atlas before you set out to make sure you are going the best way, and don't be afraid to question your route if you're in any doubt.

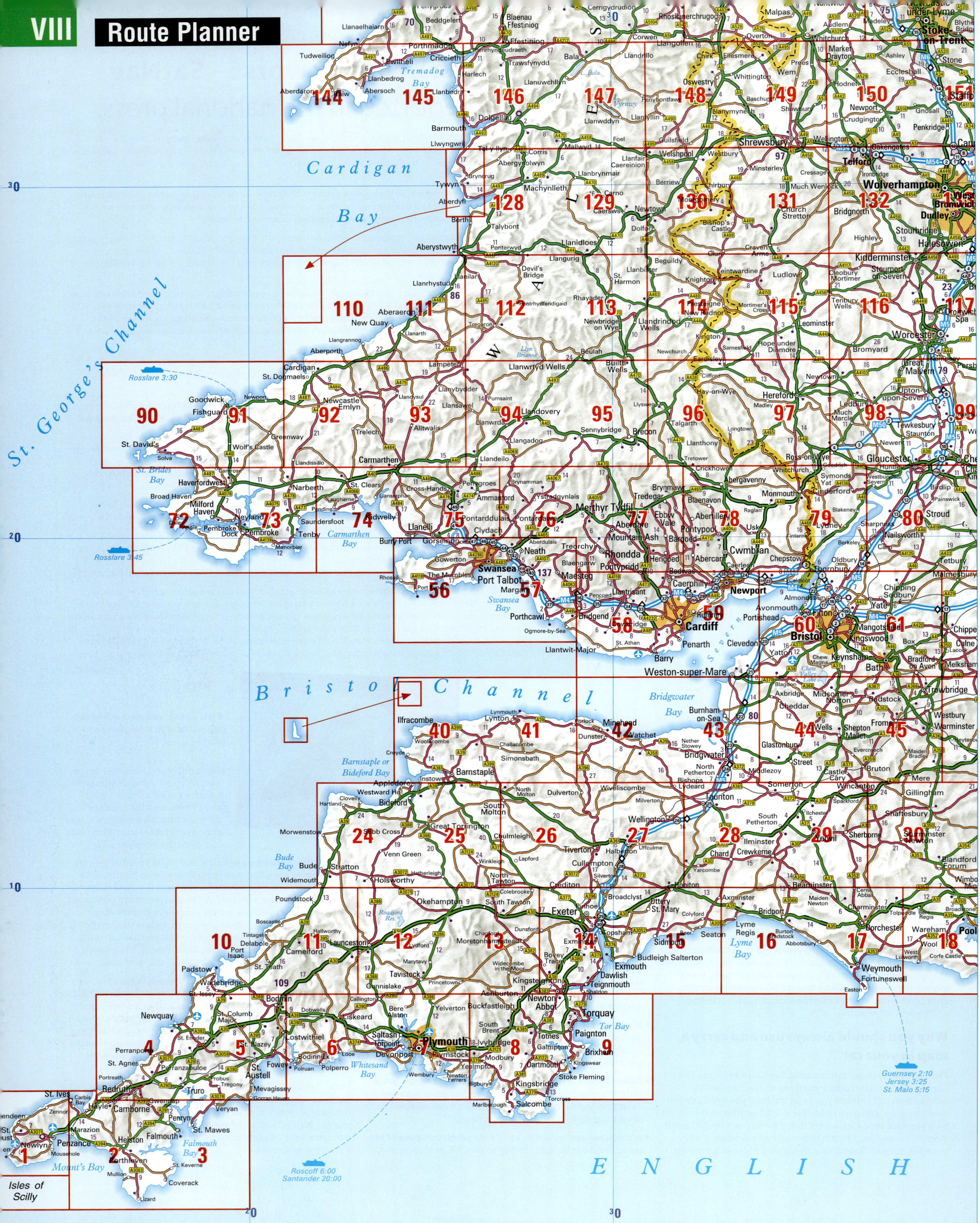
Cardigan Bay
St. George's Channel
Bristol Channel
ENGLISH
Rosslare 3:30
Rosslare 3:45
Roscoff 6:00
Santander 20:00
Guernsey 2:10
Jersey 3:25
St. Malo 5:15
Isles of Scilly
Aberystwyth
Shrewsbury
Telford
Wolverhampton
Stoke-on-Trent
Dudley
Kidderminster
Worcester
Hereford
Gloucester
Cardigan
Fishguard
St. David's
Haverfordwest
Milford Haven
Pembroke
Carmarthen
Llanelli
Swansea
Neath
Port Talbot
Merthyr Tydfil
Rhondda
Pontypridd
Caerphilly
Newport
Cardiff
Barry
Bristol
Bath
Weston-super-Mare
Ilfracombe
Barnstaple
Bideford
Taunton
Exeter
Exmouth
Torquay
Paignton
Plymouth
Newquay
Truro
Falmouth
Penzance
Weymouth
Dorchester
Yeovil
Bridgwater
Wells
Tiverton
Okehampton
Launceston
Bodmin
St. Austell
Salcombe
1 2 3 4 5 6 8 9 10 11 12 14 15 16 17 18
24 25 26 27 28 29 30
40 41 42 43 44 45
56 57 58 59 60 61
72 73 74 75 76 77 78 79 80
90 91 92 93 94 95 96 97 98 99
110 111 112 113 114 115 116 117
128 129 130 131 132
144 145 146 147 148 149 150

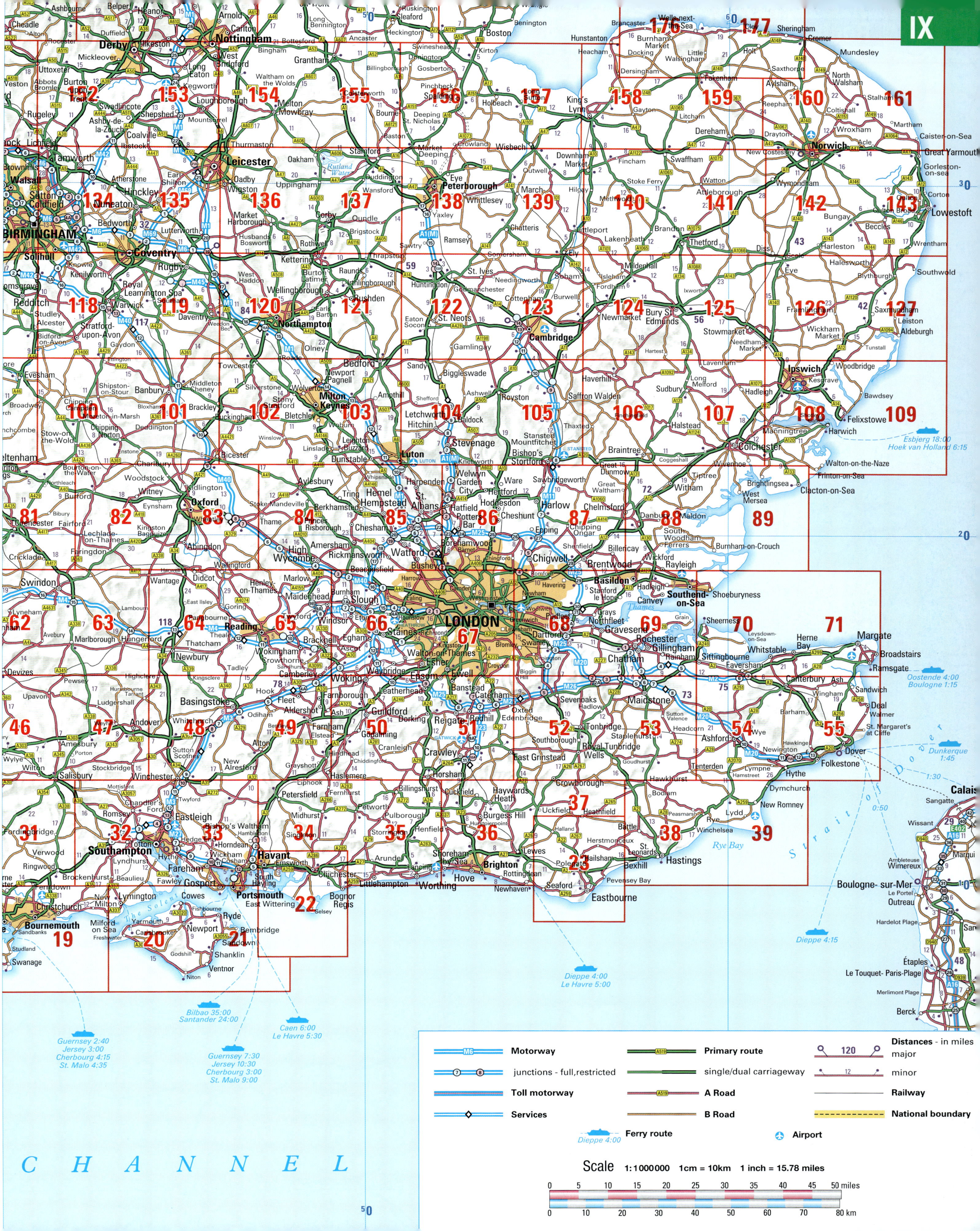
IX
CHANNEL
Strait of Dover
Motorway
junctions - full, restricted
Toll motorway
Services
Primary route
single/dual carriageway
A Road
B Road
Distances - in miles
major
minor
Railway
National boundary
Ferry route
Dieppe 4:00
Airport
Scale 1:1000000 1cm = 10km 1 inch = 15.78 miles
0 5 10 15 20 25 30 35 40 45 50 miles
0 10 20 30 40 50 60 70 80 km
Esbjerg 18:00
Hoek van Holland 6:15
Oostende 4:00
Boulogne 1:15
Dunkerque 1:45
Dieppe 4:15
Dieppe 4:00
Le Havre 5:00
Caen 6:00
Le Havre 5:30
Bilbao 35:00
Santander 24:00
Guernsey 2:40
Jersey 3:00
Cherbourg 4:15
St. Malo 4:35
Guernsey 7:30
Jersey 10:30
Cherbourg 3:00
St. Malo 9:00
LONDON
BIRMINGHAM

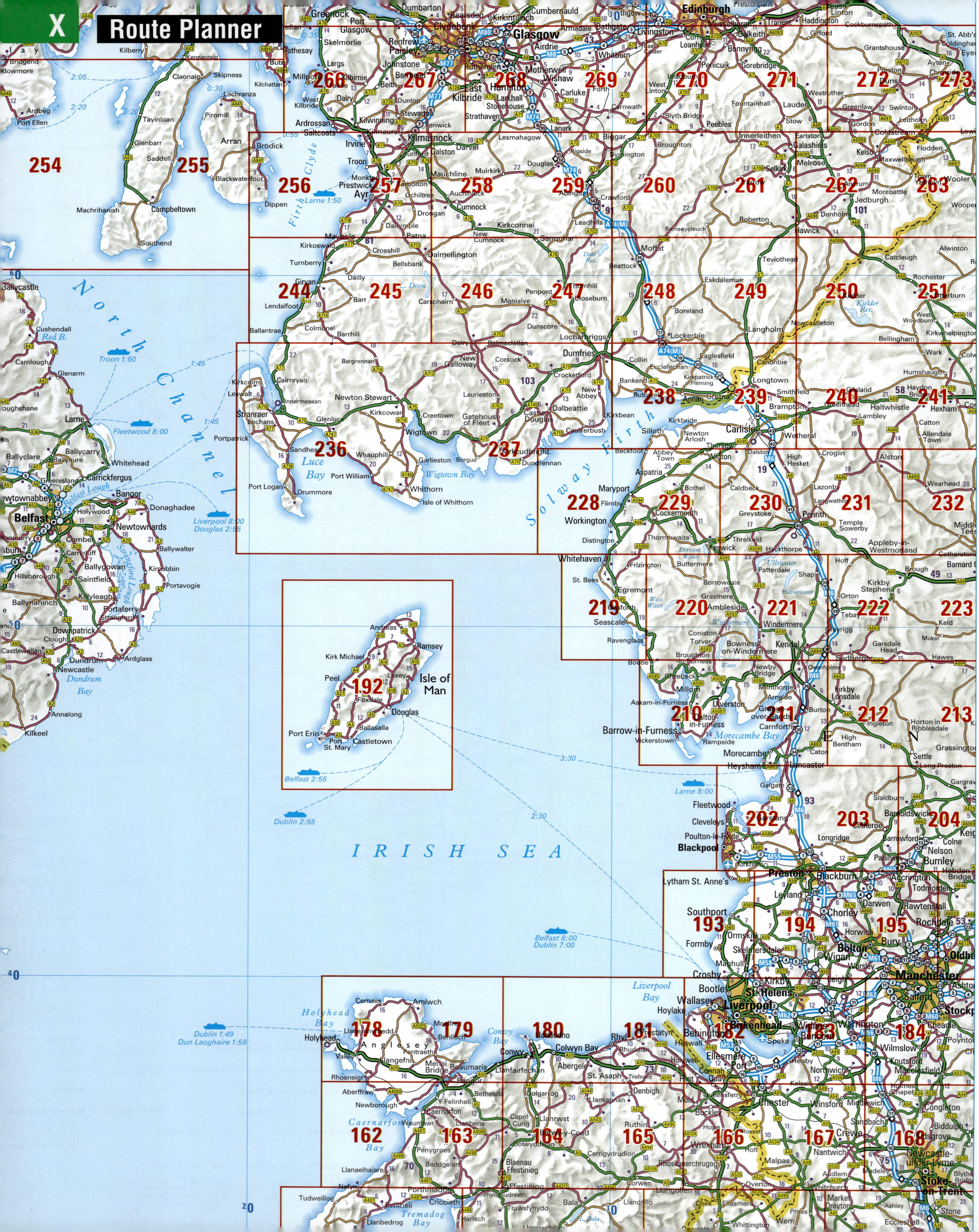

Glasgow
Edinburgh
Greenock
Paisley
Kilmarnock
Ayr
Dumfries
Carlisle
Workington
Whitehaven
Barrow-in-Furness
Lancaster
Blackpool
Preston
Southport
Liverpool
Birkenhead
Manchester
Chester
Stoke-on-Trent
Belfast
Larne
Bangor
Newtownards
Stranraer
Newton Stewart
Douglas
Isle of Man
Castletown
Peel
Ramsey
Holyhead
Anglesey
North Channel
IRISH SEA
Solway Firth
Firth of Clyde
Luce Bay
Wigtown Bay
Morecambe Bay
Caernarfon Bay
Tremadog Bay
Dundrum Bay
Arran
Campbeltown
Troon 1:50
Fleetwood 8:00
Liverpool 8:00
Douglas 2:55
Belfast 2:55
Dublin 2:55
Larne 8:00
Belfast 8:00
Dublin 7:00
Dublin 1:49
Dun Laoghaire 1:59
Larne 1:50
254
255
256
257
258
259
260
261
262
263
266
267
268
269
270
271
272
273
244
245
246
247
248
249
250
251
236
237
238
239
240
241
228
229
230
231
232
219
220
221
222
223
192
210
211
212
213
202
203
204
193
194
195
178
179
180
181
182
183
184
162
163
164
165
166
167
168

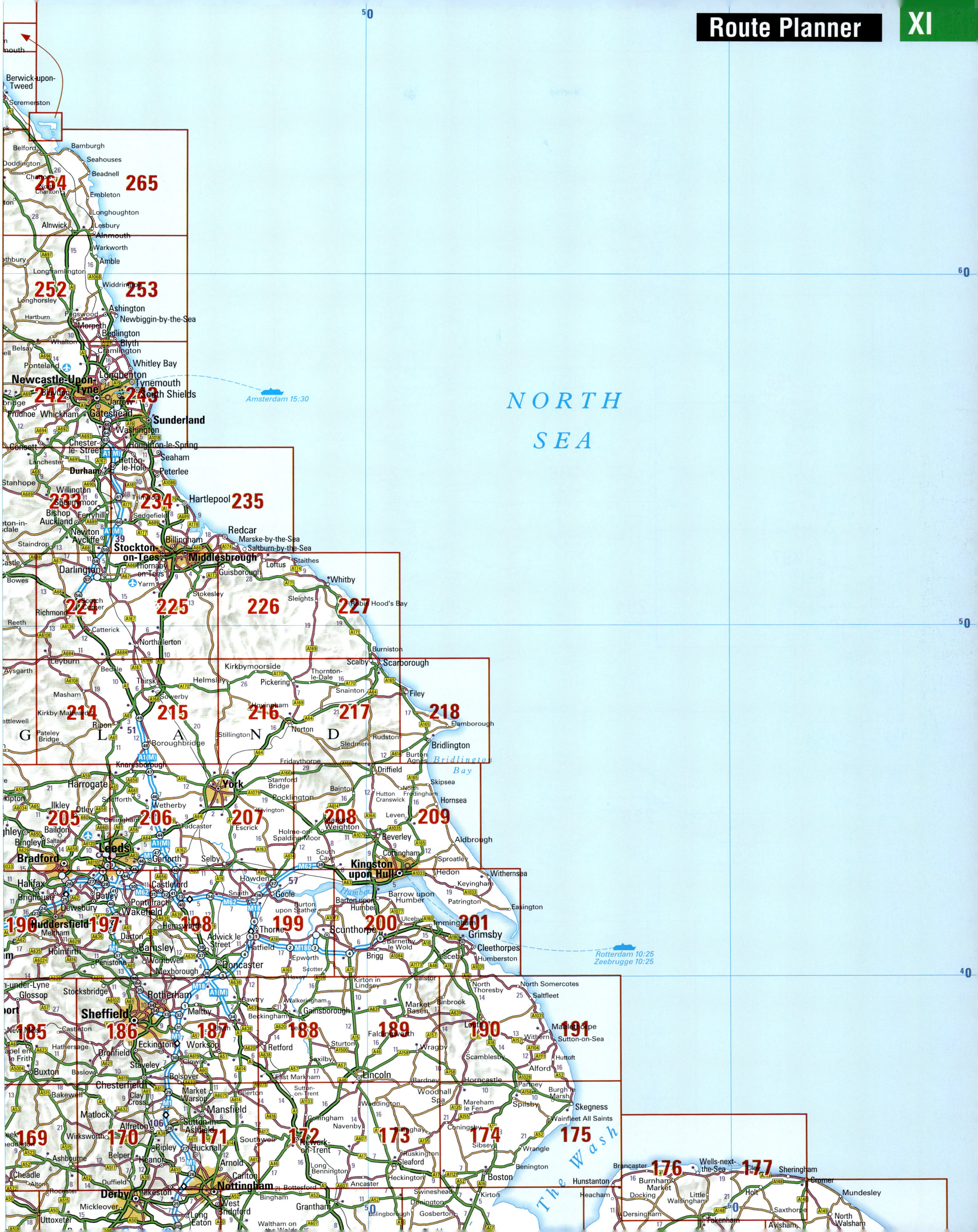
NORTH SEA
Amsterdam 15:30
Rotterdam 10:25
Zeebrugge 10:25
Berwick-upon-Tweed
Scremerston
Bamburgh
Belford
Seahouses
Beadnell
Embleton
Longhoughton
Alnwick
Lesbury
Alnmouth
Warkworth
Amble
Longframlington
Widdrington
Ashington
Newbiggin-by-the-Sea
Morpeth
Bedlington
Blyth
Cramlington
Whitley Bay
Longbenton
Tynemouth
North Shields
Newcastle-Upon-Tyne
Ponteland
Whickham
Prudhoe
Gateshead
Jarrow
Sunderland
Washington
Chester-le-Street
Houghton-le-Spring
Seaham
Peterlee
Durham
Hetton-le-Hole
Lanchester
Stanhope
Willington
Spennymoor
Bishop Auckland
Ferryhill
Sedgefield
Trimdon
Hartlepool
Newton Aycliffe
Billingham
Redcar
Marske-by-the-Sea
Saltburn-by-the-Sea
Stockton-on-Tees
Middlesbrough
Darlington
Thornaby-on-Tees
Yarm
Guisborough
Loftus
Staithes
Whitby
Robin Hood's Bay
Sleights
Staindrop
Bowes
Richmond
Scotch Corner
Catterick
Stokesley
Northallerton
Reeth
Burniston
Scalby
Scarborough
Leyburn
Aysgarth
Bedale
Thirsk
Kirkbymoorside
Pickering
Helmsley
Thornton-le-Dale
Snainton
Filey
Masham
Sowerby
Hovingham
Kirkby Malzeard
Ripon
Stillington
Norton
Flamborough
Pateley Bridge
Boroughbridge
Rudston
Sledmere
Bridlington
Burton Agnes
Bridlington Bay
Knaresborough
Fridaythorpe
Driffield
Harrogate
York
Stamford Bridge
Bainton
Skipsea
Hutton Cranswick
North Frodingham
Hornsea
Wetherby
Pocklington
Ilkley
Otley
Leven
Skipton
Collingham
Tadcaster
Escrick
Market Weighton
Beverley
Aldbrough
Baildon
Saltaire
Bingley
Leeds
Holme-on-Spalding-Moor
Cottingham
Garforth
Selby
South Cave
Sproatley
Bradford
Kingston upon Hull
Hedon
Withernsea
Halifax
Brighouse
Batley
Castleford
Howden
Goole
Snaith
Keyingham
Dewsbury
Pontefract
Wakefield
Burton upon Stather
Barton-upon-Humber
Barrow upon Humber
Patrington
Easington
Huddersfield
Hemsworth
Thorne
Scunthorpe
Immingham
Grimsby
Meltham
Holmfirth
Darton
Barnsley
Adwick le Street
Hatfield
Barnetby le Wold
Cleethorpes
Humberston
Penistone
Wombwell
Mexborough
Doncaster
Epworth
Scotter
Brigg
Laceby
Glossop
Stocksbridge
Rotherham
Kirton in Lindsey
Caistor
North Thoresby
North Somercotes
Saltfleet
Sheffield
Maltby
Bawtry
Walkeringham
Gainsborough
Market Rasen
Binbrook
Louth
Mablethorpe
Sutton-on-Sea
Withern
Castleton
Eckington
Blyth
Beckingham
Sturton
Faldingworth
Wragby
Hathersage
Bradwell
Worksop
Retford
Saxilby
Scamblesby
Huttoft
Chapel en le Frith
Buxton
Staveley
Clowne
Lincoln
Alford
Baslow
Bolsover
East Markham
Bardney
Horncastle
Partney
Burgh le Marsh
Chesterfield
Clay Cross
Market Warsop
Ollerton
Sutton-on-Trent
Woodhall Spa
Spilsby
Skegness
Bakewell
Mansfield
Waddington
Mareham le Fen
Wainfleet All Saints
Matlock
Alfreton
Sutton-in-Ashfield
Collingham
Navenby
Coningsby
Wirksworth
Ripley
Southwell
Newark-on-Trent
Billinghay
Sibsey
Wrangle
Heanor
Hucknall
Arnold
Ruskington
Sleaford
Ashbourne
Belper
Long Bennington
Benington
The Wash
Brancaster
Burnham Market
Wells-next-the-Sea
Sheringham
Cromer
Cheadle
Alton
Duffield
Heckington
Boston
Hunstanton
Nottingham
Carlton
Bottesford
Ancaster
Docking
Little Walsingham
Holt
Mundesley
Derby
Ilkeston
Rocester
West Bridgford
Bingham
Grantham
Swineshead
Donington
Kirton
Heacham
Dersingham
Fakenham
Saxthorpe
Mickleover
Long Eaton
Uttoxeter
Billingborough
Gosberton
North Walsham
Aylsham
Waltham on the Wolds
G L A N D
264 265 252 253 242 243 233 234 235 224 225 226 227 214 215 216 217 218 205 206 207 208 209 196 197 198 199 200 201 185 186 187 188 189 190 191 169 170 171 172 173 174 175 176 177
M1 M18 M62 M180 M18 A1(M) A1 A19 A64

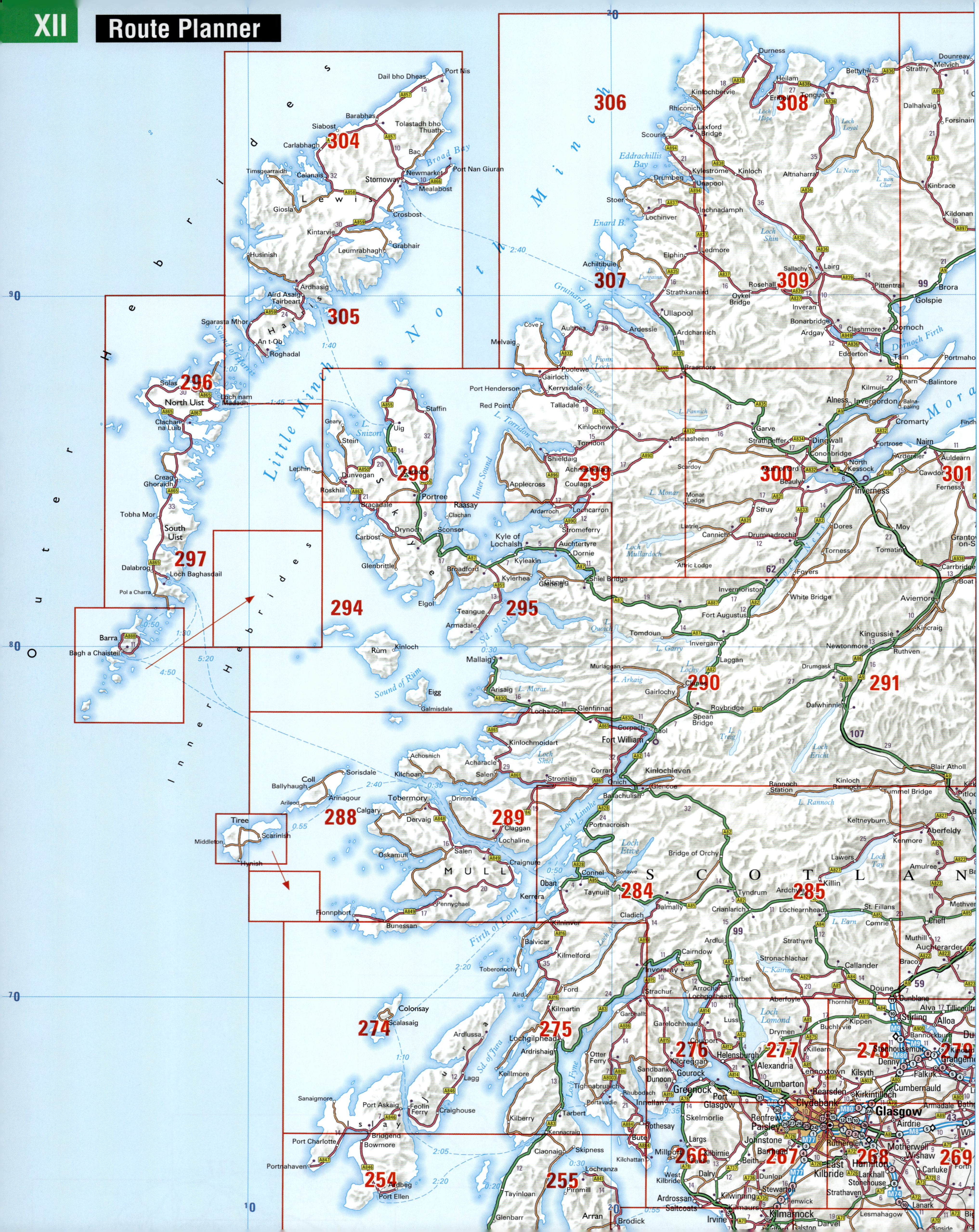
Outer Hebrides
Inner Hebrides
North Minch
Little Minch
Inner Sound
Sound of Rùm
Firth of Lorn
Moray Firth
SCOTLAND
304
305
306
307
308
309
296
297
298
299
300
301
294
295
290
291
288
289
284
285
274
275
276
277
278
279
254
255
266
267
268
269
Port Nis
Dail bho Dheas
Barabhas
Siabost
Tolastadh bho Thuath
Carlabhagh
Stornoway
Broad Bay
Port Nan Giuran
Newmarket
Mealabost
Timsgearraidh
Calanais
Lewis
Giosla
Crosbost
Kintarvie
Grabhair
Leumrabhagh
Husinish
Ardhasig
Aird Asaig
Tairbeart
Harris
Sgarasta Mhor
An t-Ob
Roghadal
Sound of Harris
Solas
North Uist
Loch nam Madadh
Clachan na Luib
Creag Ghoraidh
Tobha Mor
South Uist
Loch Baghasdail
Dalabrog
Pol a Charra
Barra
Bagh a Chaisteil
Durness
Kinlochbervie
Heilam
Eriboll
Tongue
Bettyhill
Strathy
Melvich
Dounreay
Dalhalvaig
Forsinain
Rhiconich
Laxford Bridge
Scourie
Eddrachillis Bay
Kylestrome
Drumbeg
Unapool
Kinloch
Altnaharra
Kinbrace
Kildonan
Stoer
Lochinver
Inchnadamph
Enard B.
Achiltibuie
Elphin
Ledmore
Lairg
Loch Shin
Sallachy
Rosehall
Pittentrail
Brora
Golspie
Strathkanaird
Oykel Bridge
Inveran
Bonarbridge
Ardgay
Clashmore
Dornoch
Dornoch Firth
Ullapool
Ardessie
Ardcharnich
Edderton
Tain
Portmahomack
Gruinard B.
Aultbea
Cove
Melvaig
Poolewe
Gairloch
Kerrysdale
Talladale
Braemore
Kilmuir
Fearn
Balintore
Alness
Invergordon
Cromarty
Findhorn
Port Henderson
Red Point
L. Torridon
Kinlochewe
Torridon
Achnasheen
Garve
Strathpeffer
Dingwall
Conon Bridge
Fortrose
Nairn
Auldearn
Ardersier
Cawdor
North Kessock
Inverness
Beauly
Muir of Ord
Ferness
Shieldaig
Achnashellach
Coulags
Applecross
Scardoy
Struy
Dores
Moy
Tomatin
Grantown-on-Spey
Carrbridge
Staffin
Uig
Geary
Stein
Dunvegan
Lephin
Roskhill
Skye
Portree
Bracadale
Raasay
Clachan
Drynoch
Sconser
Carbost
Kyle of Lochalsh
Kyleakin
Glenbrittle
Broadford
Kylerhea
Glenelg
Dornie
Stromeferry
Auchtertyre
Lochcarron
Ardarroch
Shiel Bridge
Elgol
Teangue
Armadale
Cannich
Drumnadrochit
Torness
Foyers
Loch Ness
Loch Mullardoch
Affric Lodge
Monar Lodge
Invermoriston
Fort Augustus
White Bridge
Aviemore
Kincraig
Kingussie
Newtonmore
Ruthven
Tomdoun
Invergarry
Laggan
L. Garry
L. Quoich
Rùm
Kinloch
Mallaig
Eigg
Galmisdale
Arisaig
Lochailort
Glenfinnan
L. Morar
L. Arkaig
Murlaggan
Gairlochy
Spean Bridge
Roybridge
Drumgask
Dalwhinnie
Loch Ericht
Corpach
Caol
Fort William
Kinlochmoidart
Achosnich
Acharacle
Salen
Kilchoan
Strontian
Corran
Onich
Kinlochleven
Glencoe
Ballachulish
Loch Linnhe
Rannoch Station
Kinloch Rannoch
L. Rannoch
Tummel Bridge
Pitlochry
Blair Atholl
Keltneybum
Aberfeldy
Kenmore
Coll
Sorisdale
Ballyhaugh
Arinagour
Arileod
Tiree
Scarinish
Middleton
Hynish
Tobermory
Drimnin
Dervaig
Calgary
Claggan
Lochaline
Oskamull
Salen
Craignure
Mull
Kerrera
Oban
Connel
Bonawe
Taynuilt
Portnacroish
Loch Etive
Bridge of Orchy
Tyndrum
Crianlarich
Dalmally
Killin
Lawers
Loch Tay
Amulree
Fionnphort
Bunessan
Pennyghael
Cladich
Ardlui
Lochearnhead
St. Fillans
Comrie
Crieff
Methven
Muthill
Auchterarder
Strathyre
Callander
Doune
Dunblane
Kilninver
Balvicar
Kilmelford
Toberonochy
Ford
Aird
Kilmartin
Inveraray
Strachur
Cairndow
Arrochar
Tarbet
Luss
Loch Lomond
Drymen
Aberfoyle
Kippen
Stirling
Alloa
Falkirk
Grangemouth
Stenhousemuir
Denny
Kilsyth
Cumbernauld
Colonsay
Scalasaig
Ardlussa
Jura
Lochgilphead
Ardrishaig
Lagg
Sd. of Jura
Kilmory
Otter Ferry
Garbhallt
Garelochhead
Helensburgh
Alexandria
Dumbarton
Balloch
Kilcreggan
Gourock
Greenock
Port Glasgow
Dunoon
Sandbank
Tighnabruaich
Rothesay
Bute
Skelmorlie
Clydebank
Glasgow
Bearsden
Kirkintilloch
Airdrie
Coatbridge
Motherwell
Paisley
Renfrew
Johnstone
Rutherglen
Hamilton
East Kilbride
Wishaw
Carluke
Larkhall
Stonehouse
Strathaven
Lanark
Sanaigmore
Port Askaig
Feolin Ferry
Craighouse
Islay
Port Charlotte
Bridgend
Bowmore
Portnahaven
Ardbeg
Port Ellen
Tarbert
Kennacraig
Skipness
Claonaig
Lochranza
Pirnmill
Arran
Tayinloan
Glenbarr
Kilchattan
Millport
Largs
West Kilbride
Kilbirnie
Dalry
Beith
Barrhead
Dunlop
Stewarton
Kilwinning
Ardrossan
Saltcoats
Irvine
Kilmarnock
Fenwick
Galston
Darvel
Lesmahagow
Brodick
Kilmaurs

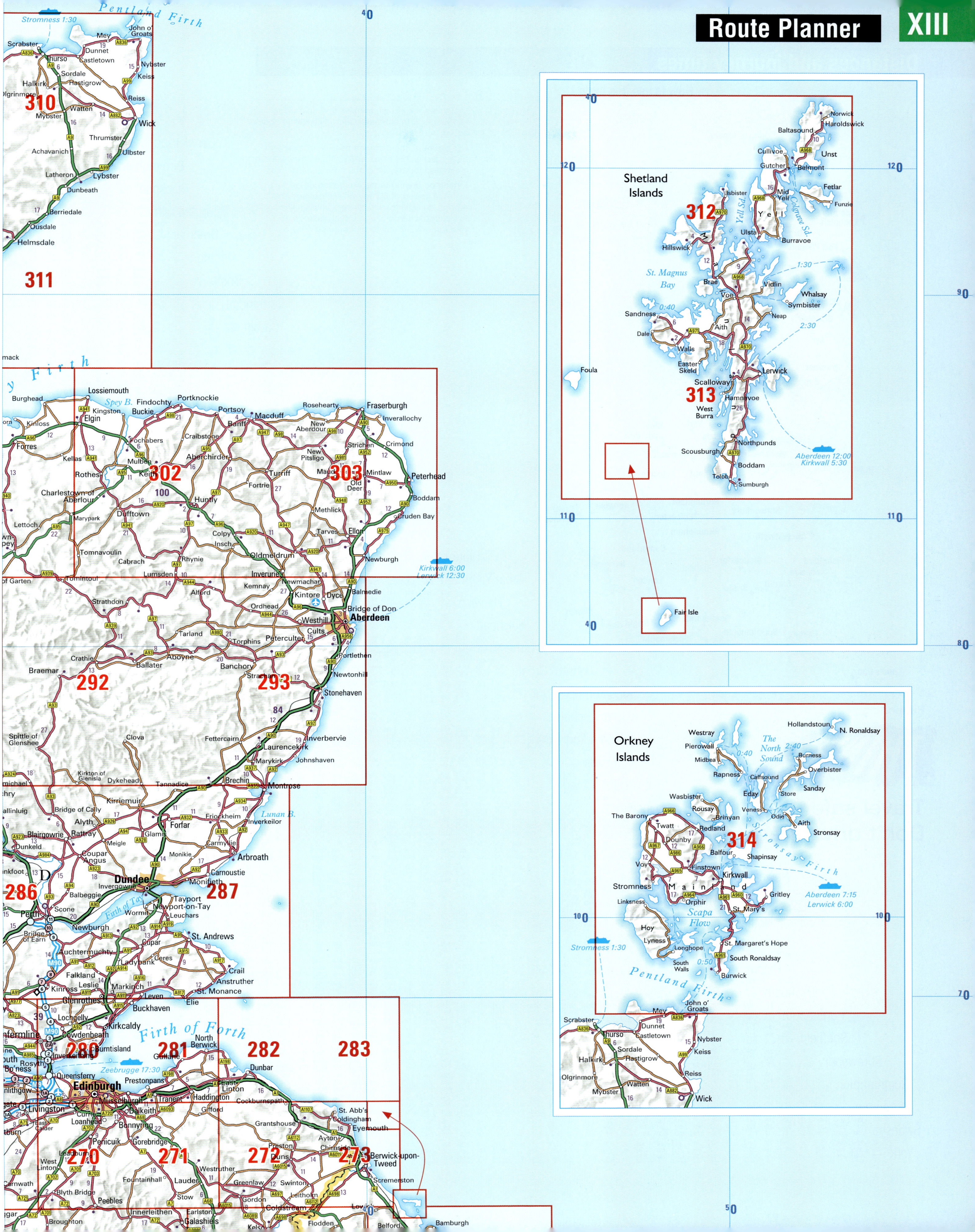

Shetland Islands
312
313
Orkney Islands
314
310
311
302
303
292
293
286
287
280
281
282
283
270
271
272
273
Pentland Firth
Firth of Forth
Firth of Tay
St. Magnus Bay
Scapa Flow
Stronsay Firth
The North Sound
Lunan B.
Spey B.
Aberdeen 12:00
Kirkwall 5:30
Aberdeen 7:15
Lerwick 6:00
Kirkwall 6:00
Lerwick 12:30
Stromness 1:30
Zeebrugge 17:30
Wick
Thurso
John o' Groats
Lerwick
Scalloway
Kirkwall
Stromness
Fair Isle
Foula
Unst
Yell
Fetlar
Whalsay
Hoy
Stronsay
Sanday
Westray
Shapinsay
South Ronaldsay
Fraserburgh
Peterhead
Elgin
Lossiemouth
Banff
Macduff
Huntly
Inverurie
Aberdeen
Stonehaven
Montrose
Arbroath
Forfar
Brechin
Dundee
Perth
St. Andrews
Kirkcaldy
Dunfermline
Edinburgh
Musselburgh
Dalkeith
Livingston
Haddington
Dunbar
North Berwick
Eyemouth
Berwick-upon-Tweed
Coldstream
Galashiels
Peebles
Bamburgh

Distances and journey times

How to use this table

Dover						390 / 4:30
Dundee					523 / 842 / 9:10	275 / 443 / 5:00
Edinburgh				56 / 90 / 1:30	462 / 744 / 8:10	219 / 352 / 4:00
Exeter			450 / 724 / 8:00	518 / 834 / 9:10	248 / 399 / 4:40	251 / 404 / 4:30
Fishguard		230 / 370 / 4:30	399 / 642 / 7:30	460 / 740 / 8:30	331 / 533 / 6:20	247 / 398 / 4:50
Fort William	486 / 782 / 9:30	560 / 901 / 10:20	144 / 232 / 3:30	127 / 204 / 3:10	596 / 959 / 11:00	357 / 575 / 7:00

Distances are shown in miles and, in italics, kilometres with estimated journey times in hours and minutes.

For example, the distance between Dover and Fishguard is 331 miles or 533 kilometres with an estimated journey time of 6 hours, 20 minutes.

Estimated driving times are based on an average speed of 60mph on Motorways and 40mph on other roads. Drivers should allow extra time when driving at peak periods or through areas likely to be congested.

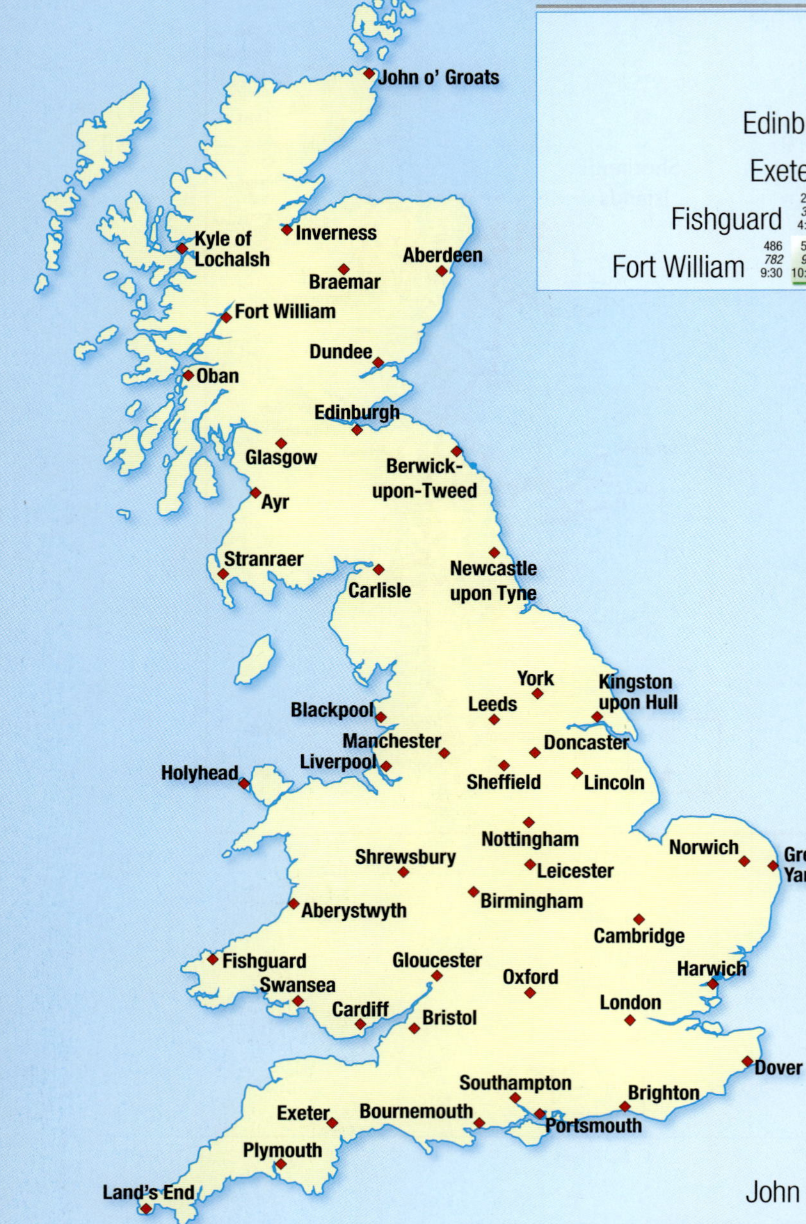

	Swansea	Stranraer	Southampton	Shrewsbury	Sheffield	Portsmouth	Plymouth	Oxford	Oban	Nottingham	Norwich	Newcastle upon Tyne	Manchester	Liverpool	Lincoln	Leicester	Leeds	Land's End	Kyle of Lochalsh	Kingston upon Hull	John o' Groats	Inverness	Holyhead	Harwich	Great Yarmouth	Gloucester	Glasgow	Fort William	Fishguard	Exeter	Edinburgh	Dundee	Dover	Doncaster	Carlisle	Cardiff	Cambridge	Bristol	Brighton	Braemar	Bournemouth	Blackpool	Birmingham	Berwick-upon-Tweed	Ayr	Aberystwyth	Aberdeen	London
Aberdeen																																																517 / 832 / 11:20
Aberystwyth																																															445 / 716 / 8:40	211 / 340 / 4:40
Ayr																																														317 / 510 / 6:10	183 / 295 / 4:20	394 / 634 / 7:20
Berwick-upon-Tweed																																													134 / 216 / 3:00	311 / 501 / 6:20	182 / 293 / 4:40	352 / 567 / 7:30
Birmingham																																												274 / 441 / 5:30	289 / 465 / 5:30	114 / 183 / 2:50	420 / 676 / 8:30	117 / 188 / 2:50
Blackpool																																											123 / 198 / 2:40	181 / 291 / 3:50	180 / 290 / 3:30	153 / 246 / 3:20	308 / 496 / 6:20	226 / 364 / 4:30
Bournemouth																																										270 / 435 / 5:00	147 / 237 / 3:10	412 / 663 / 7:50	436 / 702 / 8:00	207 / 333 / 4:30	564 / 908 / 10:20	107 / 172 / 2:40
Braemar																																									524 / 843 / 9:30	281 / 452 / 5:20	385 / 620 / 7:10	148 / 238 / 3:20	143 / 230 / 3:00	405 / 652 / 7:50	59 / 95 / 1:30	482 / 776 / 10:30
Brighton																																								534 / 859 / 9:40	92 / 148 / 2:10	286 / 460 / 5:20	163 / 262 / 3:20	409 / 658 / 7:40	446 / 718 / 8:00	253 / 407 / 5:10	573 / 922 / 10:30	52 / 84 / 1:50
Bristol																																							147 / 237 / 4:10	477 / 768 / 8:40	82 / 132 / 2:30	204 / 328 / 3:50	81 / 130 / 2:00	362 / 583 / 6:50	370 / 595 / 6:40	125 / 201 / 3:00	493 / 793 / 9:10	122 / 196 / 2:50
Cambridge																																						169 / 272 / 3:10	116 / 187 / 2:20	438 / 705 / 7:50	154 / 248 / 3:00	208 / 335 / 3:50	100 / 161 / 2:10	306 / 493 / 5:40	357 / 575 / 6:20	214 / 344 / 4:20	471 / 758 / 10:00	54 / 87 / 1:30
Cardiff																																					190 / 306 / 3:30	45 / 72 / 1:20	182 / 293 / 3:40	483 / 778 / 8:40	117 / 188 / 3:00	209 / 336 / 4:00	103 / 166 / 2:20	368 / 592 / 7:00	382 / 615 / 7:00	105 / 169 / 2:40	505 / 813 / 9:20	157 / 253 / 3:20
Carlisle																																				289 / 465 / 5:20	264 / 425 / 4:40	277 / 446 / 5:00	370 / 596 / 6:40	196 / 316 / 3:50	343 / 552 / 6:20	87 / 140 / 1:50	196 / 315 / 3:50	87 / 140 / 2:10	93 / 150 / 2:00	224 / 360 / 4:30	221 / 356 / 4:30	301 / 484 / 5:40
Doncaster																																			142 / 229 / 3:00	209 / 336 / 4:00	116 / 187 / 2:10	175 / 282 / 3:20	236 / 380 / 4:30	310 / 499 / 5:40	235 / 378 / 4:20	94 / 151 / 1:50	94 / 151 / 2:00	184 / 296 / 3:50	235 / 378 / 4:20	176 / 283 / 3:40	344 / 554 / 6:50	171 / 275 / 3:30
Dover																																		242 / 390 / 4:30	389 / 626 / 7:00	238 / 383 / 4:30	125 / 201 / 2:30	202 / 325 / 3:50	82 / 132 / 2:20	553 / 890 / 9:50	174 / 280 / 4:30	312 / 502 / 5:40	194 / 312 / 3:50	424 / 683 / 7:50	478 / 769 / 8:30	297 / 478 / 5:50	588 / 947 / 10:40	71 / 114 / 2:00
Dundee																																	523 / 842 / 9:10	275 / 443 / 5:00	152 / 245 / 3:00	441 / 710 / 8:00	406 / 654 / 7:10	430 / 692 / 7:40	517 / 832 / 9:10	52 / 84 / 1:20	495 / 797 / 8:50	239 / 385 / 4:30	349 / 562 / 6:20	113 / 182 / 2:40	117 / 188 / 2:30	376 / 605 / 7:10	67 / 108 / 1:50	448 / 721 / 8:40
Edinburgh																																56 / 90 / 1:30	462 / 744 / 8:10	219 / 352 / 4:00	96 / 154 / 2:00	385 / 620 / 7:00	345 / 555 / 6:10	373 / 600 / 6:50	456 / 734 / 8:20	91 / 146 / 2:10	439 / 707 / 8:00	183 / 295 / 3:30	292 / 470 / 5:30	57 / 92 / 1:40	73 / 117 / 1:50	320 / 515 / 6:20	125 / 201 / 3:10	390 / 628 / 7:20
Exeter																															450 / 724 / 8:00	518 / 834 / 9:10	248 / 399 / 4:40	251 / 404 / 4:30	353 / 568 / 6:20	121 / 195 / 2:30	249 / 401 / 4:30	76 / 122 / 1:40	184 / 296 / 5:00	550 / 885 / 9:40	82 / 132 / 2:20	282 / 454 / 5:10	157 / 253 / 3:10	428 / 689 / 7:50	446 / 718 / 7:50	201 / 323 / 4:10	569 / 916 / 10:20	181 / 291 / 3:40
Fishguard																														230 / 370 / 4:30	399 / 642 / 7:30	460 / 740 / 8:30	331 / 533 / 6:20	247 / 398 / 4:50	297 / 478 / 5:40	112 / 180 / 2:40	270 / 435 / 5:10	154 / 248 / 3:20	291 / 468 / 5:40	493 / 794 / 9:10	222 / 357 / 4:40	209 / 336 / 4:10	170 / 274 / 3:40	371 / 597 / 7:20	373 / 600 / 7:00	56 / 90 / 1:30	504 / 811 / 10:10	260 / 418 / 5:20
Fort William																													486 / 782 / 9:30	560 / 901 / 10:20	144 / 232 / 3:30	127 / 204 / 3:10	596 / 959 / 11:00	357 / 575 / 7:00	206 / 332 / 4:30	485 / 781 / 9:10	479 / 771 / 9:00	486 / 782 / 9:10	575 / 926 / 10:50	125 / 201 / 3:10	539 / 867 / 10:10	296 / 476 / 6:00	392 / 631 / 7:40	190 / 306 / 4:40	133 / 214 / 3:20	430 / 692 / 8:40	149 / 240 / 3:50	510 / 821 / 9:50
Glasgow																												101 / 163 / 2:50	376 / 605 / 7:10	449 / 723 / 8:00	44 / 71 / 1:20	83 / 134 / 2:00	488 / 786 / 8:40	249 / 401 / 4:40	96 / 154 / 2:10	385 / 620 / 7:00	372 / 599 / 6:40	373 / 600 / 6:50	468 / 753 / 8:30	110 / 177 / 2:30	439 / 707 / 8:00	183 / 295 / 3:40	292 / 470 / 5:30	101 / 163 / 2:40	33 / 53 / 1:10	320 / 515 / 6:20	145 / 233 / 3:30	397 / 639 / 7:30
Gloucester																											346 / 557 / 6:10	454 / 731 / 8:30	153 / 246 / 3:10	111 / 179 / 2:10	349 / 562 / 6:10	410 / 660 / 7:10	191 / 307 / 3:30	150 / 241 / 2:50	247 / 398 / 4:20	56 / 90 / 1:20	123 / 198 / 2:20	35 / 56 / 1:00	159 / 256 / 3:10	443 / 713 / 8:00	99 / 159 / 2:40	174 / 280 / 3:10	56 / 90 / 1:20	318 / 512 / 6:00	330 / 531 / 5:50	102 / 164 / 2:30	468 / 753 / 8:30	109 / 175 / 2:30
Great Yarmouth																										225 / 362 / 4:40	419 / 674 / 8:00	527 / 848 / 10:20	366 / 589 / 7:20	335 / 539 / 6:30	386 / 621 / 7:30	484 / 779 / 9:00	185 / 298 / 4:00	167 / 269 / 3:40	320 / 515 / 6:20	284 / 457 / 5:50	82 / 132 / 2:10	275 / 443 / 5:40	180 / 290 / 4:10	477 / 768 / 9:10	240 / 386 / 5:00	252 / 406 / 5:10	180 / 290 / 4:10	345 / 555 / 7:00	402 / 647 / 7:40	294 / 473 / 6:20	517 / 832 / 10:50	128 / 206 / 3:40
Harwich																									82 / 132 / 2:10	196 / 316 / 4:00	432 / 695 / 8:10	543 / 874 / 10:30	337 / 542 / 6:40	279 / 449 / 5:20	413 / 665 / 7:40	469 / 755 / 8:40	125 / 201 / 2:50	194 / 312 / 4:00	336 / 541 / 6:20	246 / 396 / 5:00	67 / 108 / 1:50	217 / 349 / 4:30	128 / 206 / 3:00	504 / 811 / 9:20	187 / 301 / 4:00	275 / 443 / 5:20	167 / 269 / 3:40	372 / 599 / 7:20	425 / 684 / 8:00	281 / 452 / 5:50	535 / 861 / 11:20	76 / 122 / 2:20
Holyhead																								349 / 562 / 7:10	334 / 538 / 7:00	191 / 307 / 4:00	330 / 531 / 6:40	438 / 705 / 8:50	167 / 269 / 4:00	282 / 454 / 5:40	333 / 536 / 6:40	394 / 634 / 7:30	360 / 580 / 7:00	181 / 291 / 3:50	231 / 372 / 4:50	216 / 348 / 5:40	270 / 435 / 5:20	206 / 332 / 4:30	334 / 538 / 6:40	426 / 686 / 8:20	288 / 463 / 5:50	141 / 227 / 3:20	148 / 238 / 3:30	311 / 501 / 6:30	305 / 491 / 6:10	111 / 179 / 2:50	439 / 707 / 8:40	269 / 433 / 5:40
Inverness																							474 / 763 / 9:40	569 / 916 / 11:00	553 / 890 / 11:00	504 / 811 / 9:30	166 / 267 / 4:00	66 / 106 / 1:40	542 / 872 / 10:30	618 / 995 / 11:30	158 / 254 / 3:50	132 / 212 / 3:20	622 / 1001 / 11:30	383 / 617 / 7:30	262 / 422 / 5:30	549 / 884 / 10:20	505 / 813 / 9:30	539 / 867 / 10:10	617 / 993 / 11:30	75 / 121 / 2:00	597 / 961 / 11:20	348 / 560 / 7:00	458 / 737 / 9:00	215 / 346 / 5:10	199 / 320 / 4:30	486 / 782 / 9:40	105 / 169 / 2:50	550 / 885 / 10:40
John o' Groats																						129 / 208 / 3:20	603 / 970 / 12:40	693 / 1116 / 14:00	677 / 1090 / 14:00	628 / 1011 / 12:30	295 / 475 / 7:10	195 / 314 / 5:00	671 / 1080 / 13:40	744 / 1197 / 14:30	285 / 459 / 7:00	259 / 417 / 6:30	746 / 1201 / 14:40	507 / 816 / 10:30	391 / 629 / 8:40	680 / 1094 / 13:30	630 / 1014 / 12:30	668 / 1075 / 13:20	741 / 1193 / 14:40	202 / 325 / 5:00	724 / 1165 / 14:20	478 / 769 / 10:00	574 / 924 / 11:50	342 / 550 / 8:10	328 / 528 / 7:40	601 / 967 / 12:40	232 / 373 / 5:50	663 / 1067 / 13:30
Kingston upon Hull																					518 / 834 / 10:50	394 / 634 / 7:50	231 / 372 / 4:50	196 / 316 / 4:10	207 / 333 / 5:20	169 / 272 / 3:10	254 / 409 / 4:50	369 / 594 / 7:20	280 / 451 / 5:30	309 / 497 / 5:40	234 / 377 / 4:30	295 / 475 / 5:30	256 / 412 / 4:50	47 / 76 / 1:10	158 / 254 / 3:00	244 / 393 / 4:40	139 / 224 / 3:10	233 / 375 / 4:20	245 / 394 / 4:40	327 / 526 / 6:10	264 / 425 / 5:00	127 / 204 / 2:30	134 / 216 / 2:50	185 / 298 / 3:50	251 / 404 / 4:40	223 / 359 / 4:40	364 / 586 / 7:20	184 / 296 / 3:50
Kyle of Lochalsh																				445 / 716 / 9:00	189 / 304 / 4:40	84 / 135 / 2:10	514 / 827 / 10:40	611 / 983 / 12:10	602 / 969 / 12:10	528 / 850 / 10:20	179 / 288 / 4:40	79 / 127 / 2:00	567 / 913 / 11:20	628 / 1011 / 12:00	216 / 348 / 5:20	186 / 299 / 4:40	671 / 1080 / 12:50	432 / 695 / 8:40	275 / 443 / 6:10	564 / 908 / 11:10	555 / 893 / 10:50	552 / 888 / 10:50	651 / 1048 / 12:40	159 / 256 / 4:00	618 / 995 / 12:10	372 / 599 / 7:50	471 / 758 / 9:40	263 / 423 / 6:20	212 / 341 / 5:10	499 / 803 / 10:20	189 / 304 / 4:50	586 / 943 / 11:40
Land's End																			763 / 1228 / 15:10	421 / 678 / 8:20	868 / 1397 / 17:20	741 / 1193 / 14:20	405 / 652 / 8:30	390 / 628 / 8:00	446 / 718 / 9:10	235 / 378 / 5:00	573 / 922 / 10:50	686 / 1104 / 13:20	353 / 568 / 7:20	123 / 198 / 3:20	574 / 924 / 10:50	642 / 1033 / 12:00	381 / 613 / 7:40	374 / 602 / 7:20	477 / 768 / 9:10	245 / 394 / 5:20	374 / 602 / 7:20	200 / 322 / 4:40	308 / 496 / 7:50	665 / 1070 / 12:30	205 / 330 / 5:20	405 / 652 / 8:00	281 / 452 / 6:00	552 / 888 / 10:40	570 / 917 / 10:50	313 / 504 / 6:50	692 / 1114 / 13:10	297 / 478 / 6:30
Leeds																		405 / 652 / 8:00	394 / 634 / 8:20	55 / 89 / 1:30	487 / 784 / 10:20	360 / 579 / 7:10	176 / 283 / 4:00	223 / 359 / 4:30	196 / 315 / 4:20	174 / 280 / 3:20	215 / 346 / 4:10	329 / 530 / 6:40	237 / 381 / 4:40	270 / 435 / 5:00	202 / 325 / 4:00	258 / 415 / 4:50	260 / 418 / 4:50	29 / 47 / 0:50	119 / 192 / 2:30	232 / 373 / 4:20	145 / 233 / 2:50	194 / 312 / 3:50	260 / 419 / 5:00	293 / 472 / 5:30	255 / 410 / 4:50	72 / 116 / 1:40	113 / 182 / 2:30	156 / 251 / 3:20	212 / 341 / 4:00	169 / 272 / 3:40	327 / 526 / 6:50	189 / 304 / 3:50
Leicester																	95 / 153 / 2:00	320 / 515 / 6:30	500 / 805 / 9:50	102 / 164 / 2:10	588 / 947 / 11:50	461 / 742 / 8:50	190 / 306 / 4:00	147 / 237 / 3:10	140 / 225 / 3:20	85 / 137 / 1:40	314 / 505 / 5:40	422 / 679 / 8:00	209 / 336 / 4:10	196 / 315 / 3:40	296 / 476 / 5:20	349 / 562 / 6:20	185 / 298 / 3:30	74 / 119 / 1:30	206 / 332 / 3:50	154 / 248 / 3:00	68 / 109 / 1:20	120 / 193 / 2:30	166 / 267 / 3:20	389 / 626 / 7:00	158 / 254 / 3:10	140 / 225 / 2:40	39 / 63 / 1:10	252 / 406 / 5:00	299 / 481 / 5:20	153 / 246 / 3:20	414 / 666 / 7:40	97 / 156 / 2:20
Lincoln																51 / 82 / 1:20	68 / 109 / 1:50	371 / 597 / 7:30	476 / 766 / 9:40	44 / 71 / 1:20	554 / 892 / 11:30	427 / 687 / 8:30	216 / 348 / 4:40	155 / 249 / 3:30	128 / 206 / 3:20	159 / 256 / 3:10	291 / 468 / 5:30	399 / 642 / 7:50	272 / 438 / 5:30	247 / 398 / 4:40	258 / 415 / 5:00	314 / 505 / 5:50	202 / 325 / 4:00	39 / 63 / 1:10	191 / 307 / 3:40	208 / 335 / 4:10	85 / 137 / 2:20	183 / 295 / 3:40	197 / 317 / 4:00	357 / 575 / 6:40	209 / 336 / 4:10	128 / 206 / 2:40	90 / 145 / 2:10	224 / 360 / 4:40	274 / 441 / 5:10	199 / 320 / 4:20	383 / 616 / 7:20	131 / 211 / 3:10
Liverpool															129 / 208 / 2:50	130 / 209 / 2:40	75 / 121 / 1:50	361 / 581 / 7:20	407 / 655 / 8:30	130 / 209 / 2:40	511 / 822 / 10:40	382 / 615 / 7:40	102 / 164 / 2:40	265 / 427 / 5:20	240 / 386 / 5:00	140 / 225 / 2:40	216 / 348 / 4:10	329 / 530 / 6:40	160 / 257 / 3:30	237 / 381 / 4:30	216 / 348 / 4:10	286 / 460 / 5:20	299 / 481 / 5:30	86 / 138 / 1:50	120 / 193 / 2:30	169 / 272 / 3:20	194 / 312 / 3:40	161 / 259 / 3:10	272 / 438 / 5:10	318 / 512 / 6:00	234 / 377 / 4:30	49 / 79 / 1:20	93 / 150 / 2:10	219 / 352 / 4:30	213 / 343 / 4:10	104 / 167 / 2:40	341 / 549 / 6:40	202 / 325 / 4:10
Manchester														35 / 56 / 1:10	84 / 135 / 2:00	92 / 148 / 2:00	40 / 64 / 1:10	361 / 581 / 7:20	406 / 654 / 8:30	95 / 153 / 2:10	500 / 805 / 10:30	373 / 600 / 7:30	124 / 200 / 3:00	228 / 367 / 4:40	212 / 341 / 4:30	126 / 203 / 2:30	215 / 346 / 4:10	329 / 530 / 6:40	197 / 317 / 4:00	236 / 380 / 4:20	215 / 346 / 4:10	285 / 459 / 5:20	276 / 444 / 5:10	61 / 98 / 1:30	119 / 192 / 2:30	183 / 295 / 3:40	165 / 266 / 3:10	161 / 259 / 3:10	257 / 414 / 4:50	318 / 512 / 6:00	227 / 365 / 4:20	48 / 77 / 1:20	80 / 129 / 2:00	196 / 315 / 4:00	212 / 341 / 4:00	129 / 208 / 3:00	340 / 547 / 6:30	185 / 298 / 3:50
Newcastle upon Tyne													132 / 212 / 2:50	168 / 270 / 3:20	159 / 256 / 3:20	187 / 301 / 3:40	92 / 148 / 2:10	498 / 802 / 9:40	318 / 512 / 7:00	132 / 212 / 2:50	395 / 636 / 8:50	268 / 431 / 5:40	272 / 438 / 5:40	308 / 496 / 6:00	281 / 452 / 5:40	266 / 428 / 4:50	148 / 238 / 3:10	253 / 407 / 5:20	329 / 529 / 6:20	364 / 586 / 6:30	110 / 177 / 2:20	166 / 267 / 3:20	358 / 576 / 6:30	114 / 183 / 2:20	57 / 92 / 1:50	325 / 523 / 6:00	241 / 388 / 4:20	299 / 481 / 5:30	352 / 567 / 6:30	201 / 323 / 4:00	347 / 558 / 6:30	129 / 208 / 2:40	207 / 333 / 4:10	64 / 103 / 1:50	149 / 240 / 3:00	257 / 414 / 5:20	235 / 378 / 4:50	286 / 460 / 5:40
Norwich												264 / 425 / 5:20	185 / 298 / 4:30	220 / 354 / 4:40	105 / 169 / 2:50	119 / 192 / 3:20	176 / 283 / 3:50	421 / 678 / 8:40	582 / 937 / 11:50	149 / 240 / 4:00	654 / 1053 / 13:30	529 / 852 / 10:30	311 / 501 / 6:40	73 / 117 / 2:00	20 / 32 / 0:40	204 / 328 / 4:10	385 / 620 / 9:00	504 / 811 / 10:00	343 / 552 / 7:00	308 / 496 / 6:00	366 / 589 / 7:00	422 / 679 / 8:00	174 / 280 / 3:50	147 / 237 / 3:20	289 / 465 / 5:40	262 / 422 / 5:20	62 / 100 / 1:50	252 / 406 / 5:10	175 / 282 / 4:00	457 / 735 / 8:40	214 / 344 / 4:40	232 / 373 / 4:50	166 / 267 / 3:50	328 / 528 / 6:40	382 / 615 / 7:20	276 / 444 / 6:00	496 / 798 / 9:40	114 / 183 / 3:30
Nottingham											130 / 209 / 3:40	157 / 253 / 3:10	73 / 118 / 1:40	98 / 158 / 2:10	35 / 56 / 1:10	25 / 40 / 0:50	70 / 113 / 1:40	345 / 555 / 7:00	479 / 771 / 9:40	90 / 145 / 2:00	557 / 896 / 11:30	430 / 692 / 8:20	185 / 298 / 4:00	150 / 241 / 3:20	153 / 246 / 3:30	110 / 177 / 2:10	293 / 472 / 5:30	401 / 646 / 7:50	220 / 354 / 4:30	221 / 356 / 4:10	262 / 422 / 4:50	328 / 528 / 6:00	205 / 330 / 3:50	43 / 69 / 1:10	194 / 312 / 3:40	172 / 277 / 3:20	83 / 134 / 1:40	145 / 233 / 3:00	193 / 311 / 3:50	353 / 568 / 6:30	183 / 295 / 3:40	111 / 179 / 2:20	50 / 80 / 1:20	221 / 356 / 4:30	274 / 441 / 5:10	164 / 264 / 3:40	393 / 633 / 7:30	122 / 196 / 2:40
Oban										390 / 628 / 7:30	492 / 792 / 9:40	233 / 375 / 4:50	307 / 494 / 6:00	308 / 496 / 6:10	387 / 623 / 7:30	419 / 674 / 7:50	307 / 494 / 6:00	665 / 1070 / 12:50	128 / 206 / 3:10	346 / 557 / 6:40	244 / 393 / 6:10	117 / 188 / 3:00	427 / 687 / 8:30	524 / 843 / 10:00	515 / 829 / 10:00	441 / 710 / 8:10	92 / 148 / 2:30	49 / 79 / 1:20	481 / 774 / 9:10	549 / 884 / 10:00	123 / 198 / 3:00	117 / 188 / 2:50	585 / 942 / 10:40	346 / 557 / 6:40	188 / 303 / 4:00	477 / 768 / 9:00	468 / 753 / 8:40	465 / 748 / 8:40	565 / 910 / 10:30	141 / 227 / 3:30	530 / 853 / 9:50	285 / 459 / 5:40	384 / 618 / 7:30	180 / 290 / 4:20	94 / 151 / 2:20	412 / 663 / 8:10	178 / 286 / 4:20	499 / 803 / 9:30
Oxford									462 / 744 / 8:30	109 / 175 / 2:10	145 / 233 / 3:50	260 / 418 / 4:50	144 / 232 / 2:50	172 / 277 / 3:20	137 / 221 / 2:50	73 / 117 / 1:30	168 / 270 / 3:10	274 / 441 / 5:40	550 / 885 / 10:40	192 / 309 / 3:40	656 / 1056 / 13:00	532 / 856 / 10:00	238 / 383 / 4:50	145 / 233 / 3:10	200 / 322 / 4:20	52 / 84 / 1:30	356 / 573 / 6:30	472 / 760 / 9:00	205 / 330 / 4:10	156 / 251 / 3:00	372 / 599 / 6:40	433 / 697 / 7:40	141 / 227 / 2:50	145 / 233 / 2:40	260 / 418 / 4:40	108 / 174 / 2:20	83 / 134 / 1:40	74 / 119 / 1:40	108 / 174 / 2:20	465 / 749 / 8:20	90 / 145 / 2:00	187 / 301 / 3:30	64 / 103 / 1:30	324 / 521 / 6:10	353 / 568 / 6:20	154 / 248 / 3:20	483 / 777 / 8:50	57 / 92 / 1:40
Plymouth								199 / 320 / 4:00	587 / 945 / 11:00	267 / 430 / 5:10	343 / 552 / 7:00	410 / 660 / 7:40	283 / 455 / 5:30	283 / 455 / 5:30	293 / 472 / 5:50	242 / 389 / 4:40	316 / 509 / 6:00	89 / 143 / 2:20	674 / 1085 / 13:10	355 / 571 / 6:40	790 / 1271 / 15:40	664 / 1069 / 12:30	328 / 528 / 6:40	309 / 497 / 6:10	365 / 588 / 7:20	157 / 253 / 3:20	495 / 797 / 9:10	595 / 958 / 11:20	264 / 425 / 5:30	46 / 74 / 1:30	496 / 798 / 9:00	552 / 888 / 10:00	300 / 483 / 5:50	297 / 478 / 5:40	399 / 642 / 7:20	167 / 269 / 3:40	293 / 472 / 5:30	122 / 196 / 2:50	224 / 361 / 6:00	587 / 945 / 10:40	128 / 206 / 3:30	328 / 528 / 6:10	203 / 327 / 4:20	474 / 763 / 9:00	492 / 792 / 9:00	237 / 382 / 5:10	615 / 990 / 11:20	218 / 351 / 4:40
Portsmouth							176 / 283 / 4:50	77 / 124 / 1:40	545 / 877 / 10:00	191 / 307 / 3:40	207 / 333 / 4:20	337 / 542 / 6:10	236 / 380 / 4:30	254 / 409 / 4:50	201 / 323 / 4:00	162 / 261 / 3:10	257 / 414 / 4:50	259 / 417 / 5:40	633 / 1019 / 12:10	269 / 433 / 5:00	737 / 1186 / 14:30	613 / 987 / 11:30	311 / 501 / 6:10	166 / 267 / 3:40	221 / 356 / 4:40	119 / 192 / 3:00	448 / 721 / 8:10	555 / 893 / 10:20	251 / 404 / 5:00	135 / 217 / 2:40	453 / 729 / 8:10	514 / 827 / 9:00	130 / 209 / 2:50	234 / 377 / 4:20	348 / 560 / 6:10	142 / 229 / 3:00	144 / 232 / 2:50	97 / 156 / 2:10	48 / 77 / 1:40	547 / 881 / 9:50	52 / 84 / 1:30	264 / 425 / 4:50	141 / 227 / 3:00	401 / 645 / 7:30	430 / 692 / 7:40	222 / 357 / 4:40	560 / 901 / 10:10	70 / 113 / 2:00
Sheffield						230 / 370 / 4:20	283 / 455 / 5:30	135 / 217 / 2:40	339 / 546 / 6:30	37 / 60 / 1:00	146 / 235 / 3:20	125 / 201 / 2:40	38 / 61 / 1:00	72 / 116 / 1:40	46 / 74 / 1:20	62 / 100 / 1:20	33 / 53 / 1:00	361 / 581 / 7:10	427 / 687 / 8:40	65 / 105 / 1:30	520 / 837 / 10:50	393 / 632 / 7:40	168 / 270 / 3:40	187 / 301 / 3:50	166 / 267 / 3:40	126 / 203 / 2:20	248 / 399 / 4:40	348 / 560 / 6:50	215 / 346 / 4:20	237 / 381 / 4:20	235 / 378 / 4:20	291 / 468 / 5:20	245 / 394 / 4:30	18 / 29 / 0:40	152 / 245 / 3:00	194 / 312 / 3:40	120 / 193 / 2:20	161 / 259 / 3:10	226 / 364 / 4:20	320 / 515 / 6:00	216 / 348 / 4:10	86 / 138 / 1:50	76 / 122 / 1:50	190 / 306 / 4:00	245 / 394 / 4:30	159 / 256 / 3:30	360 / 579 / 6:50	159 / 256 / 3:20
Shrewsbury					82 / 132 / 2:10	207 / 333 / 3:50	225 / 362 / 4:40	106 / 171 / 2:10	364 / 586 / 7:00	93 / 150 / 2:00	205 / 330 / 4:20	201 / 323 / 3:50	69 / 111 / 1:40	58 / 93 / 1:50	133 / 214 / 2:50	84 / 135 / 1:40	109 / 175 / 2:20	303 / 488 / 6:10	451 / 726 / 9:00	169 / 272 / 3:10	567 / 912 / 11:30	438 / 705 / 8:20	113 / 182 / 2:50	240 / 386 / 4:40	225 / 362 / 4:40	77 / 124 / 1:30	272 / 438 / 5:00	382 / 615 / 7:20	145 / 233 / 3:10	179 / 288 / 3:20	274 / 441 / 5:00	330 / 531 / 6:00	251 / 404 / 4:30	109 / 175 / 2:10	176 / 283 / 3:20	111 / 179 / 2:20	159 / 256 / 3:00	103 / 166 / 2:50	226 / 364 / 4:20	371 / 597 / 6:50	185 / 298 / 3:40	98 / 158 / 2:00	45 / 72 / 1:20	265 / 426 / 5:10	269 / 433 / 5:00	77 / 124 / 2:10	399 / 642 / 7:30	160 / 258 / 3:20
Southampton				185 / 298 / 4:10	199 / 320 / 3:40	21 / 34 / 0:50	151 / 243 / 4:10	64 / 103 / 1:30	530 / 853 / 9:40	176 / 283 / 3:20	206 / 332 / 4:20	324 / 521 / 5:50	221 / 356 / 4:10	239 / 385 / 4:30	204 / 328 / 4:00	137 / 220 / 2:40	232 / 373 / 4:20	228 / 367 / 5:00	618 / 995 / 12:00	256 / 412 / 4:40	723 / 1164 / 14:10	598 / 963 / 11:10	293 / 472 / 5:50	164 / 264 / 3:30	220 / 354 / 4:40	105 / 169 / 2:40	433 / 697 / 7:40	541 / 871 / 10:00	233 / 375 / 4:40	105 / 169 / 3:00	438 / 705 / 7:50	500 / 805 / 8:50	143 / 230 / 2:50	209 / 336 / 3:50	324 / 521 / 5:50	121 / 195 / 2:30	148 / 238 / 2:50	76 / 122 / 2:20	61 / 98 / 1:50	532 / 856 / 9:30	31 / 50 / 1:00	251 / 404 / 4:40	128 / 206 / 2:40	388 / 624 / 7:10	417 / 671 / 7:30	201 / 323 / 4:10	547 / 880 / 10:00	77 / 124 / 2:00
Stranraer			445 / 716 / 8:20	277 / 446 / 5:30	263 / 423 / 5:20	461 / 742 / 8:40	500 / 805 / 9:40	379 / 610 / 7:10	148 / 238 / 3:40	290 / 467 / 5:50	403 / 649 / 8:10	158 / 254 / 3:40	220 / 354 / 4:40	221 / 356 / 4:40	298 / 480 / 6:00	330 / 531 / 6:20	220 / 354 / 4:40	585 / 942 / 11:30	263 / 423 / 6:30	259 / 417 / 5:20	379 / 610 / 9:00	262 / 422 / 6:00	338 / 544 / 7:00	410 / 660 / 8:10	426 / 686 / 8:40	343 / 552 / 6:30	84 / 135 / 2:30	195 / 314 / 4:50	392 / 631 / 7:50	454 / 731 / 8:30	124 / 200 / 3:00	167 / 269 / 3:40	496 / 798 / 9:10	257 / 414 / 5:10	101 / 163 / 2:40	390 / 628 / 7:30	379 / 610 / 7:10	378 / 608 / 7:20	475 / 765 / 9:00	194 / 312 / 4:20	444 / 715 / 8:30	188 / 303 / 4:00	297 / 478 / 6:00	170 / 274 / 4:10	51 / 82 / 1:20	325 / 523 / 6:50	228 / 367 / 5:10	402 / 647 / 7:50
Swansea		417 / 671 / 7:50	161 / 259 / 3:00	118 / 190 / 2:20	217 / 349 / 4:00	182 / 293 / 3:30	206 / 332 / 4:10	141 / 227 / 2:40	506 / 815 / 9:20	192 / 309 / 3:40	301 / 485 / 6:00	347 / 559 / 6:20	187 / 301 / 3:30	195 / 314 / 3:40	233 / 375 / 4:30	177 / 285 / 3:20	248 / 399 / 4:40	285 / 459 / 6:00	594 / 956 / 11:30	264 / 425 / 4:50	696 / 1120 / 13:40	572 / 921 / 10:40	184 / 296 / 4:50	267 / 430 / 5:10	329 / 530 / 6:30	89 / 143 / 1:50	409 / 658 / 7:20	496 / 798 / 9:20	67 / 108 / 1:50	161 / 259 / 3:00	412 / 663 / 7:20	473 / 761 / 8:20	274 / 441 / 5:00	232 / 373 / 4:10	309 / 497 / 5:30	41 / 66 / 1:10	227 / 365 / 4:10	85 / 137 / 1:50	222 / 357 / 4:20	505 / 813 / 9:00	167 / 269 / 3:20	216 / 348 / 4:00	119 / 192 / 2:30	383 / 616 / 7:10	379 / 610 / 6:50	73 / 117 / 2:00	507 / 816 / 9:20	194 / 312 / 4:00
York	272 / 438 / 5:10	222 / 357 / 4:40	258 / 415 / 5:10	133 / 214 / 2:40	52 / 84 / 1:20	278 / 448 / 5:10	333 / 536 / 6:20	181 / 291 / 3:20	309 / 497 / 6:00	77 / 124 / 1:40	181 / 291 / 4:20	84 / 135 / 2:20	64 / 103 / 1:30	99 / 159 / 2:10	75 / 121 / 1:50	108 / 174 / 2:10	24 / 39 / 0:50	411 / 661 / 8:00	407 / 655 / 8:20	37 / 60 / 1:10	479 / 771 / 10:10	352 / 566 / 7:00	204 / 328 / 4:20	228 / 367 / 4:40	201 / 323 / 4:20	189 / 304 / 3:30	217 / 349 / 4:10	330 / 531 / 6:30	261 / 420 / 5:10	287 / 462 / 5:10	194 / 312 / 3:40	250 / 402 / 4:40	282 / 454 / 5:10	34 / 55 / 1:00	121 / 195 / 2:30	244 / 393 / 4:40	165 / 266 / 3:10	222 / 357 / 4:10	275 / 443 / 5:10	285 / 459 / 5:20	269 / 433 / 5:00	96 / 154 / 2:00	130 / 209 / 2:40	148 / 238 / 3:10	214 / 344 / 4:00	195 / 314 / 4:10	319 / 513 / 6:10	207 / 333 / 4:10

Supporting

THINK!

Travel safe – Don't drive tired

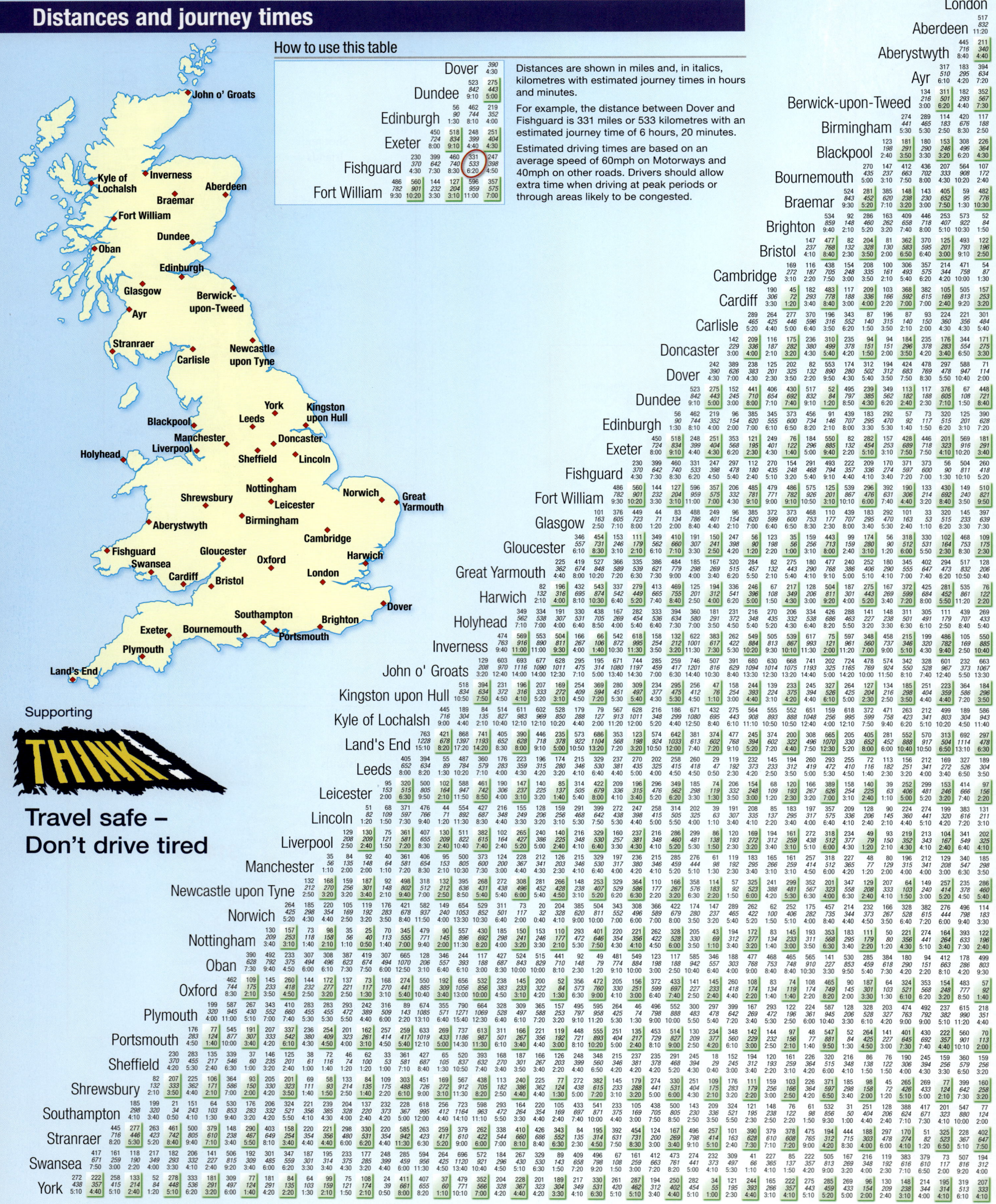

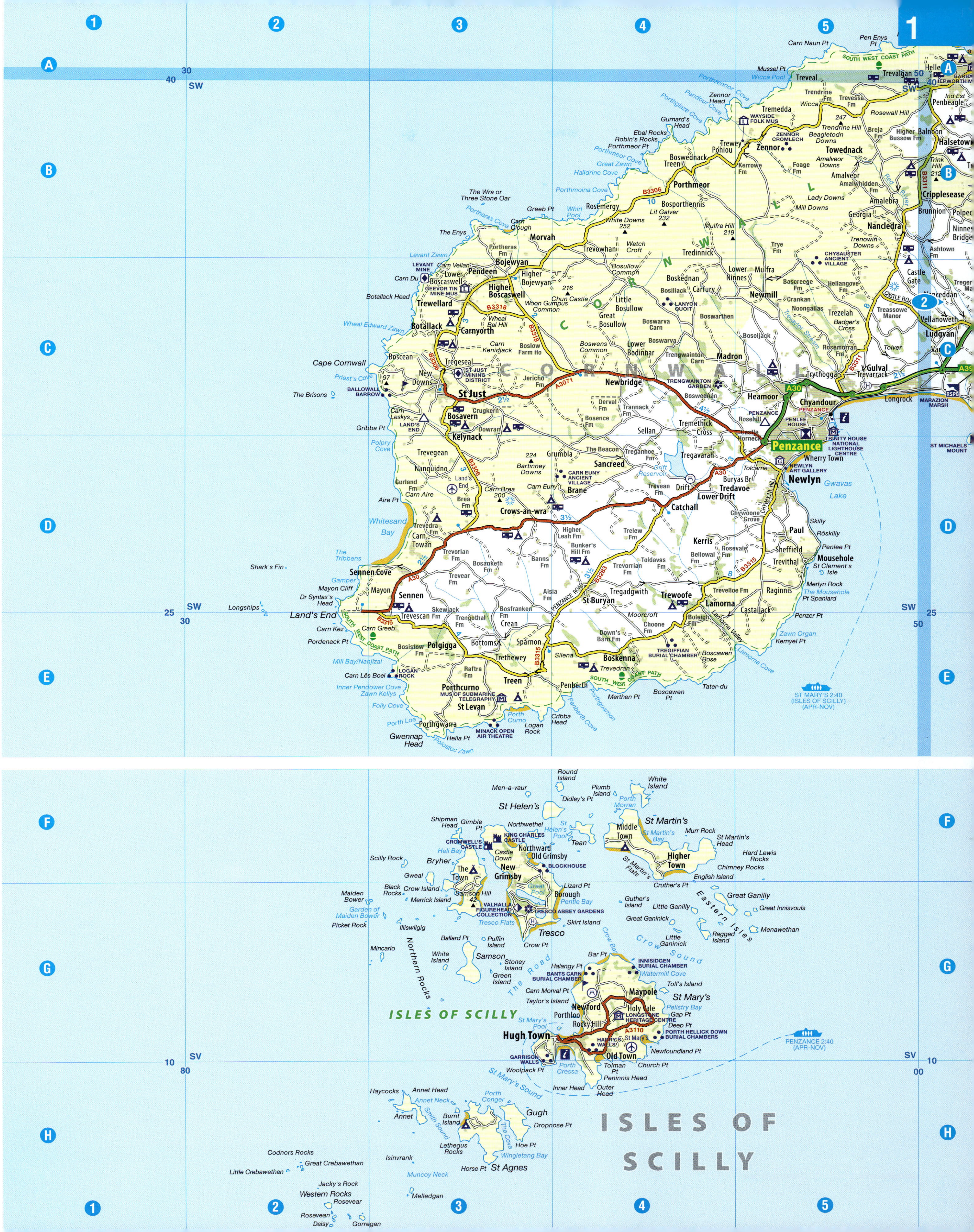
CORNWALL
Penzance
Newlyn
St Just
Land's End
Sennen
Sennen Cove
Porthcurno
St Levan
Mousehole
Lamorna
St Buryan
Zennor
Morvah
Pendeen
Botallack
Carnyorth
Trewellard
Bosavern
Kelynack
Sancreed
Newbridge
Madron
Heamoor
Gulval
Chyandour
Ludgvan
Nancledra
Towednack
Porthmeor
Treen
Polgigga
Crows-an-wra
Drift
Lower Drift
Catchall
Paul
Sheffield
Cape Cornwall
The Brisons
Longships
Whitesand Bay
Gwavas Lake
Mount's Bay
St Michael's Mount
SOUTH WEST COAST PATH
St Mary's 2:40 (Isles of Scilly) (Apr-Nov)
ISLES OF SCILLY
St Mary's
Hugh Town
Old Town
Maypole
Holy Vale
Porthloo
Newford
Tresco
New Grimsby
Old Grimsby
Bryher
The Town
St Martin's
Higher Town
Middle Town
Samson
St Agnes
Gugh
Annet
Tean
St Helen's
Round Island
White Island
Eastern Isles
Northern Rocks
Western Rocks
Bishop Rock
Crow Sound
St Mary's Sound
Smith Sound
Tresco Abbey Gardens
Penzance 2:40 (Apr-Nov)
SV
SW

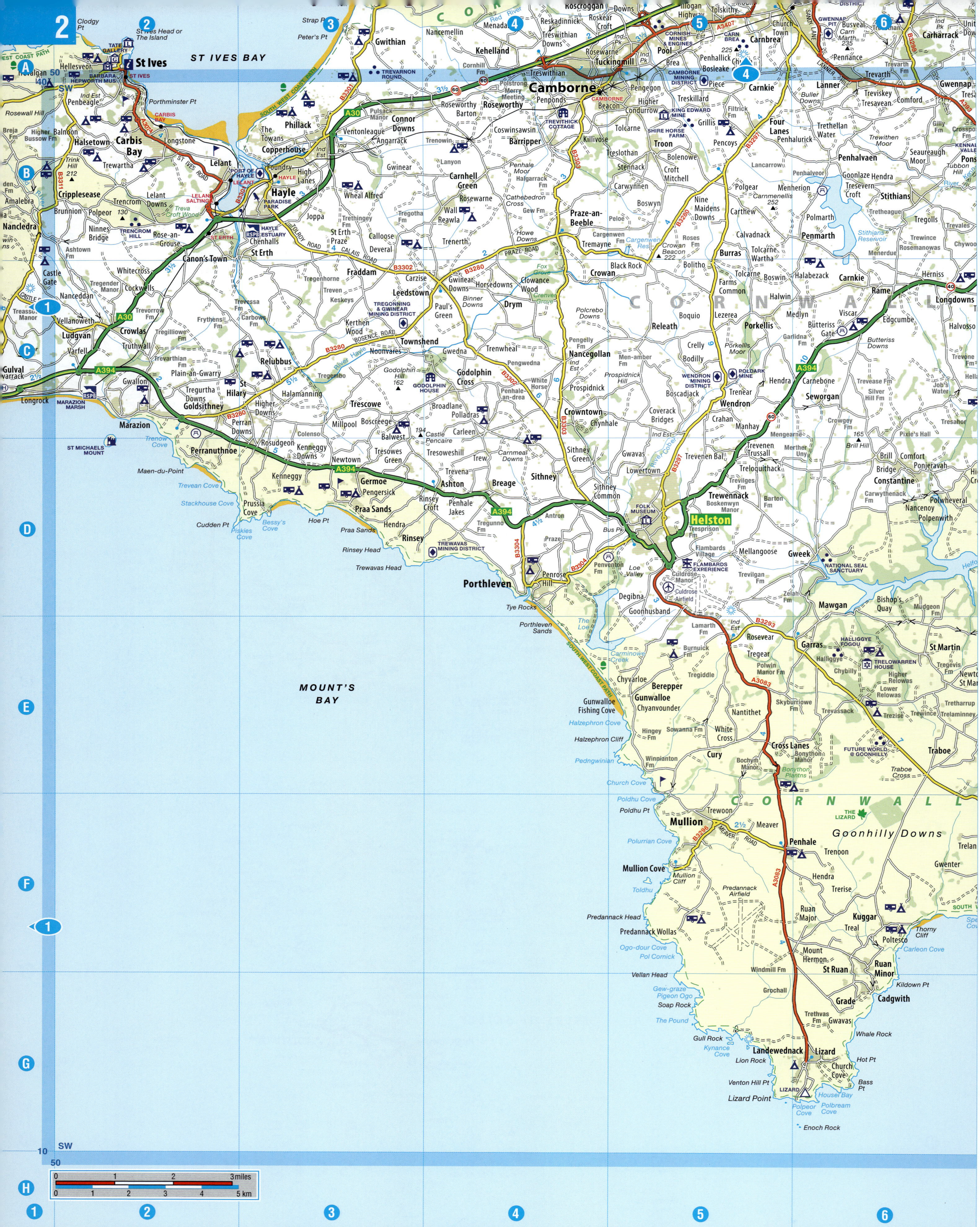
St Ives
ST IVES BAY
Carbis Bay
Lelant
Hayle
Phillack
Copperhouse
Gwithian
Camborne
Pool
Carnkie
Roseworthy
Connor Downs
Barripper
Praze-an-Beeble
Crowan
Leedstown
Townshend
Godolphin Cross
St Erth
Canon's Town
Crowlas
Ludgvan
Marazion
Perranuthnoe
Goldsithney
Relubbus
St Hilary
Germoe
Praa Sands
Ashton
Breage
Sithney
Porthleven
Helston
Wendron
Constantine
Gweek
Mawgan
Garras
St Martin
Traboe
Cury
Mullion
Mullion Cove
Cross Lanes
Penhale
Ruan Minor
Cadgwith
Grade
St Ruan
Kuggar
Lizard
Landewednack
Lizard Point
Gunwalloe
Berepper
Goonhilly Downs
MOUNT'S BAY
CORNWALL
Stithians
Penmarth
Carnkie
Porkellis
Releath
Nancegollan
Crowntown
Trewennack
Penzance
Gulval
Cripplesease
Halsetown
Nancledra
Fraddam
Drym
Trescowe
Rinsey
Hendra
Prussia Cove
Kenneggy
Rosudgeon
A30
A394
A3083
B3280
B3302
B3303
B3297
B3293
B3304
B3296
SW
0 1 2 3 miles
0 1 2 3 4 5 km

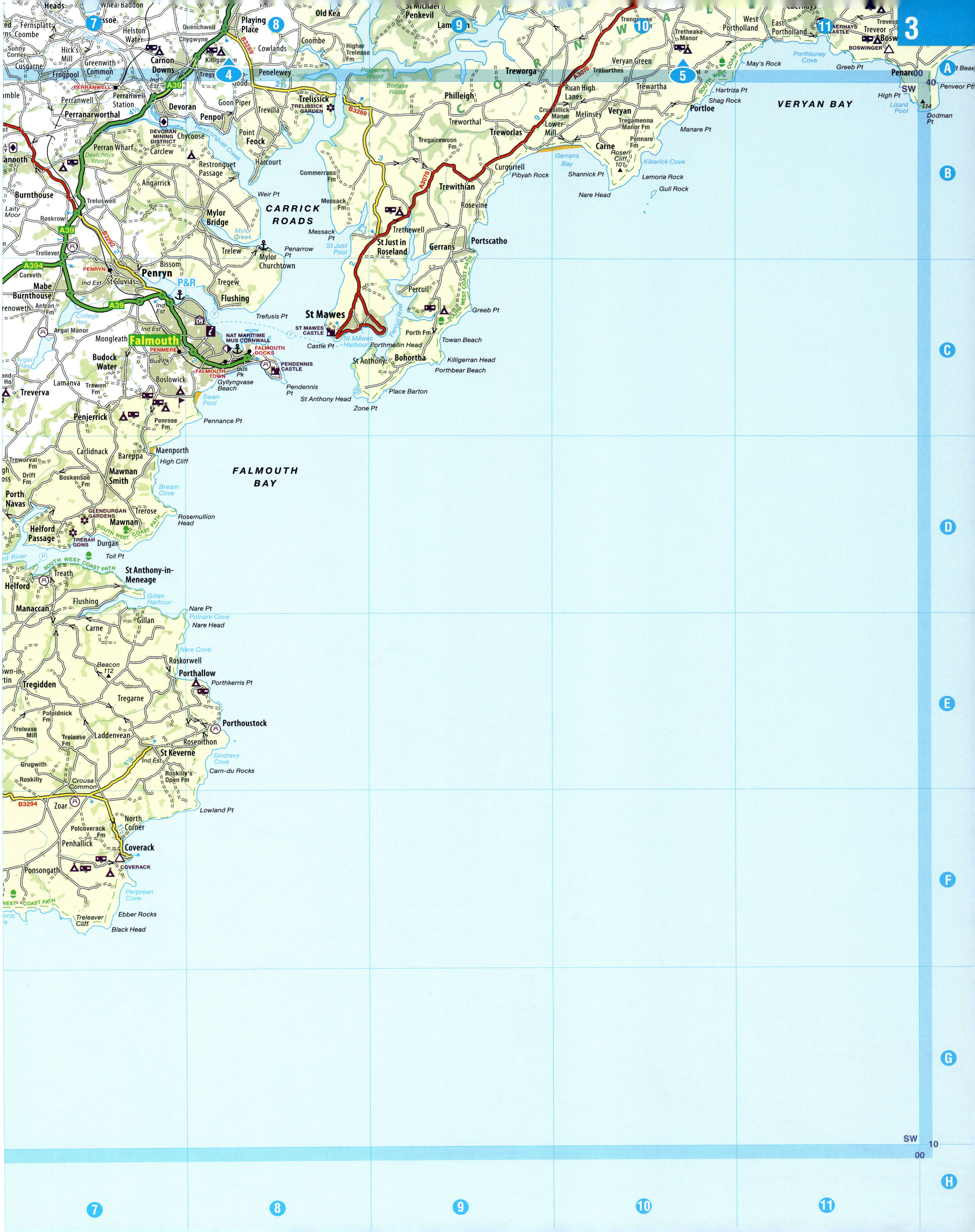
Playing Place
Old Kea
St Michael Penkevil
Lamorran
Trengrouse
West Portholland
East Portholland
Caerhays
Trevessa
Trevear
Boswinger
Quenchwell
Chygwyne
Cowlands
Coombe
Higher Trelease Fm
Ruan River
Tretheake Manor
Veryan Green
Treburthes
Portluney Cove
May's Rock
Greeb Pt
Penare
Penveor Pt
Heads
Fernsplatt
Sunny Corner
Cusgarne
Hick's Mill
Greenwithe Common
Frogpool
Helston Water
Carnon Downs
Killiganoon
Tregye
Penelewey
Polgerran Wood
Borlase Wood
Treworga
Ruan High Lanes
Trewartha
Hartriza Pt
Shag Rock
Portloe
VERYAN BAY
High Pt
Lizard Pool
Dodman Pt
Perranwell
Perranwell Station
Perranarworthal
Devoran
DEVORAN MINING DISTRICT
Goon Piper
Penpol
Chycoose
Restronguet Creek
Trelissick
TRELISSICK GARDEN
Trevilla
Point
Feock
Philleigh
Treworthal
Crugsillick Manor
Lower Mill
Melinsey
Veryan
Tregamenna Manor Fm
Treworlas
Tregairewoon Fm
Manare Pt
Carne
Roseri Cliff
Pennare Fm
Kiberick Cove
Lemoria Rock
Gull Rock
Gerrans Bay
Shannick Pt
Nare Head
Pibyah Rock
Curgurrell
Perran Wharf
Devichoys Wood
Carclew
Restronguet Passage
Harcourt
Commerrans Fm
Ponsanooth
Burnthouse
Laity Moor
Roskrow
Treluswell
Angarrick
Weir Pt
CARRICK ROADS
Messack Fm
Messack Pt
Mylor Bridge
Mylor Creek
Trewithian
Rosevine
Trethewell
St Just in Roseland
St Just Pool
Gerrans
Portscatho
Treliever
Penarrow Pt
Trelew
Mylor Churchtown
A394
Carveth
Mabe Burnthouse
Antron
PENRYN
Penryn
Bissom
St Gluvias
Ind Est
P&R
Tregew
Flushing
Percuil
Percuil River
Greeb Pt
A39
A3078
B3289
B3292
College Res
Argal Manor
Trefusis Pt
St Mawes
ST MAWES CASTLE
Castle Pt
St Mawes Harbour
Porthmellin Head
Porth Fm
Towan Beach
Mongleath
Falmouth
PENMERE
NAT MARITIME MUS CORNWALL
FALMOUTH DOCKS
PENDENNIS CASTLE
FALMOUTH TOWN
Bus Pk
Budock Water
Argal Res
Lamanva
Trewen Fm
Treverva
Boslowick
Gyllyngvase Beach
Pendennis Pt
St Anthony
Bohortha
Killigerran Head
Porthbear Beach
Place Barton
St Anthony Head
Zone Pt
Swan Pool
Penjerrick
Penrose Fm
Pennance Pt
Maenporth
High Cliff
Carlidnack
Bareppa
Treworval Fm
Drift Fm
Boskensoe Fm
Mawnan Smith
FALMOUTH BAY
Bream Cove
Porth Navas
GLENDURGAN GARDENS
Trerose
Rosemullion Head
Mawnan
SOUTH WEST COAST PATH
Helford Passage
TREBAH GDNS
Durgan
Toll Pt
Helford River
Treath
St Anthony-in-Meneage
Helford
Gillan Harbour
Flushing
Manaccan
Nare Pt
Polnare Cove
Nare Head
Gillan
Carne
Nare Cove
Beacon 112
Roskorwell
Porthallow
Porthkerris Pt
Tregidden
Tregarne
Polpidnick Fm
Trelease Mill
Trelease Fm
Laddenvean
Porthoustock
Rosenithon
St Keverne
Ind Est
Godrevy Cove
Grugwith
Roskilly's Open Fm
Carn-du Rocks
Roskilly
Crousa Common
B3294
Zoar
Lowland Pt
North Corner
Polcoverack Fm
Penhallick
Coverack
COVERACK
Ponsongath
Perprean Cove
Ebber Rocks
Treleaver Cliff
Black Head
SW
00
10
40
A
B
C
D
E
F
G
H
7
8
9
10
11
4
5

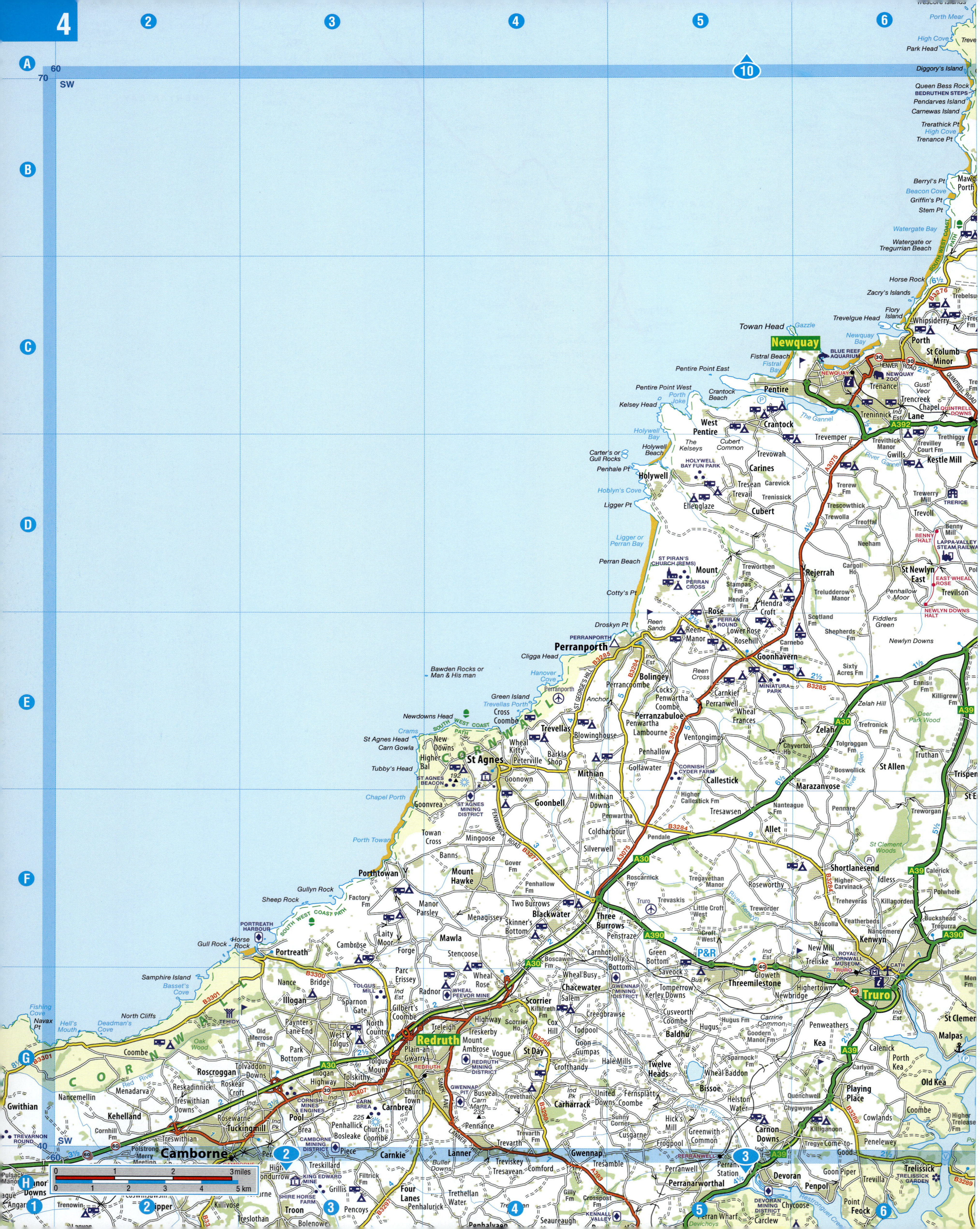
10
Porth Mear
High Cove
Park Head
Diggory's Island
Queen Bess Rock
BEDRUTHEN STEPS
Pendarves Island
Carnewas Island
Trerathick Pt
High Cove
Trenance Pt
Berryl's Pt
Beacon Cove
Griffin's Pt
Stem Pt
Mawgan Porth
Watergate Bay
Watergate or Tregurrian Beach
Horse Rock
Zacry's Islands
Flory Island
Trevelgue Head
Whipsiderry
Towan Head
Gazzle
Newquay Bay
Porth
Newquay
Fistral Beach
Fistral Bay
BLUE REEF AQUARIUM
NEWQUAY ZOO
St Columb Minor
Trenance
Pentire Point East
Pentire
Pentire Point West
Porth Joke
Crantock Beach
Kelsey Head
Crantock
The Gannel
Treninnick
Lane
Trencreek
Chapel
QUINTRELL DOWNS
West Pentire
Holywell Bay
Holywell Beach
The Kelseys
Cubert Common
Trevemper
Trevithick Manor
Trevilley Court Fm
Trethiggy Fm
Kestle Mill
Gwills
River Gannel
Carter's or Gull Rocks
Penhale Pt
Holywell
HOLYWELL BAY FUN PARK
Trevowah
Carines
Tresean
Carevick
Trevail
Trenissick
Cubert
Ellenglaze
Holywell Cove
Ligger Pt
Trerew Fm
Trewerry Mill
TRERICE
Trevoll
Trescowthick
Trewolla
Treoffal
Neeham
Ligger or Perran Bay
Perran Beach
ST PIRAN'S CHURCH (REMS)
PERRAN CROSS
Mount
Treworthen
Stampas Fm
Hendra Fm
Hendra Croft
Rejerrah
Cargoll Ho
St Newlyn East
Trerulderow Manor
Penhallow Moor
Trevilson
NEWLYN DOWNS HALT
BENNY HALT
LAPPA VALLEY STEAM RAILWAY
EAST WHEAL ROSE
Cotty's Pt
Droskyn Pt
Reen Sands
Rose
PERRAN ROUND
Lower Rose
Rosehill
Scotland Fm
Carnebo Fm
Fiddlers Green
Shepherds Fm
Newlyn Downs
PERRANPORTH
Perranporth
Reen Manor
Goonhavern
Cligga Head
Ind Est
Reen Cross
Bolingey
Perrancoombe
Sixty Acres Fm
B3285
Bawden Rocks or Man & His man
Hanover Cove
St George's Hill
MINIATURA PARK
Ennis Fm
Killigrew Fm
Green Island
Trevellas Porth
Cross Coombe
Anchor
Cocks
Penwartha Coombe
Carnkief
Perranwell
Wheal Frances
Zelah Hill
Newdowns Head
SOUTH WEST COAST PATH
Trevellas
Blowinghouse
Perranzabuloe
Penwartha
Lambourne
Ventongimps
Zelah
Trefronick Fm
Deer Park Wood
Crams
St Agnes Head
Carn Gowla
New Downs
Wheal Kitty
Higher Bal
St Agnes
Peterville
Barkla Shop
Chyverton Ho
Tolgroggan Fm
Penhallow
Truthan
Tubby's Head
ST AGNES BEACON
Goonown
Mithian
Gollawater
CORNISH CYDER FARM
Callestick
St Allen
Boswellick
Trispen
Marazanvose
Chapel Porth
Goonvrea
ST AGNES MINING DISTRICT
Goonbell
Mithian Downs
Higher Callestick Fm
Tresawsen
Nanteague Fm
Pennare
Treworgan
Penwartha Ho
Coldharbour
Pendale
B3284
Allet
Porth Towan
Town Cross
Mingoose
Silverwell
St Clement Woods
Banns
Shortlanesend
Calerick
Porthtowan
Mount Hawke
Gover Fm
Roscarrick Fm
Tregavethan Manor
Roseworthy
Higher Carvinack
Idless
Polwhele
Gullyn Rock
Sheep Rock
Factory Fm
Manor Parsley
Penhallow Fm
Two Burrows
Truro
Trevaskis
Little Croft West
River Kenwyn
Treheveras
Killagorden
Menagissey
Blackwater
Three Burrows
Trewonder
Featherbeds
Buckshead
Tregurra
PORTREATH HARBOUR
Skinner's Bottom
Penstraze
Croft West
Boscolla
Nancemere
Kenwyn
A390
Gull Rock
Horse Rock
Portreath
Laity Moor
Cambrose
Forge
Mawla
Stencoose
Carnhot
Green Bottom
P&R
Ind Est
New Mill
Treliske
ROYAL CORNWALL MUSEUM
Samphire Island
Basset's Cove
Nance
B3300
Bridge
Parc Erissey
Wheal Rose
WHEAL PEEVOR MINE
Boscawen
Jolly's Bottom
Chacewater
Wheal Busy
Saveock
GWENNAP MINING DISTRICT
Threemilestone
Gloweth
Highertown
Newbridge
Truro
Fishing Cove
Navax Pt
Hell's Mouth
Deadman's Cove
North Cliffs
Illogan
TOLGUS MILL
Sparnon Gate
Ind Est
Radnor
Gilbert's Coombe
Scorrier
Killifreth
Salem
Tomperrow
Kerley Downs
Creegbrawse
Cusveorth Coombe
Hugus
Hugus Fm
Carrine Common
Goodern Manor Fm
Penweathers
Ind Est
St Clement
Malpas
TEHIDY
Old Merrose
Paynter's Lane End
West Tolgus
North Country
Treleigh
Redruth
Highway
Treskerby
Cox Hill
Todpool
Baldhu
Kea
B3301
Coombe
Oak Wood
Park Bottom
Plain-an-Gwarry
Mount Ambrose
Vogue
St Day
Goon Gumpas
Hale Mills
Twelve Heads
Sparnock
Calenick
Porth Kea
Roscroggan
Tolvaddon Downs
Illogan Highway
Tolgus Mount
REDRUTH
REDRUTH MINING DISTRICT
Crofthandy
Wheal Baddon
Carlyon
Old Kea
Gwithian
Menadarva
Reskadinnick
Roskear Croft
Tolskithy
A3047
Church Town
GWENNAP PIT
Busveal
Carn Marth
Trevethan
Carharrack
United Downs
Fernsplatt Coombe
Bissoe
Playing Place
Nancemellin
Treswithian Downs
CORNISH MINES & ENGINES
Carn Brea
Carnbrea
Ind Pk
Sunny Corner
Hick's Mill
Helston Water
Chygwyne
Quenchwell
Coombe
Cowlands
Kehelland
Rosewarne
Tuckingmill
Pool
Brea
Penhallick
Church Coombe
Pennance
Trevarth Fm
Cusgarne
Greenwith Common
Carnon Downs
Killiganoon
Higher Trelease Fm
TREVARNON ROUND
Cornhill Fm
Treswithian
CAMBORNE MINING DISTRICT
Bosleake
Trevarth
Frogpool
Tregye
Come-to-Good
Penelewey
Polstrong
Merry Meeting
Camborne
Piece
Carnkie
Lanner
Gwennap
PERRANWELL
Devoran
A39
Trelissick
TRELISSICK GARDEN
Treskillard
KING EDWARD MINE
Buller Downs
Trevisky
Tresavean
Comford
Tresamble
Perranwell
Perran Station
Goon Piper
B3289
Grillis
Filtrick Fm
Perranarworthal
Penpol
Trevilla
SHIRE HORSE FARM
Four Lanes
Trethellan Water
Gilly Fm
Crosspost Fm
DEVORAN MINING DISTRICT
Chycoose
Point
Feock
Angarrack
Trenowin
Killivose
Troon
Pencoys
Penhalurick
KENNALL VALE
Carclew
Perran Wharf
Treslothan
Bolenowe
Penhalvean
Seaureagh
SW
60
70
40
miles
km

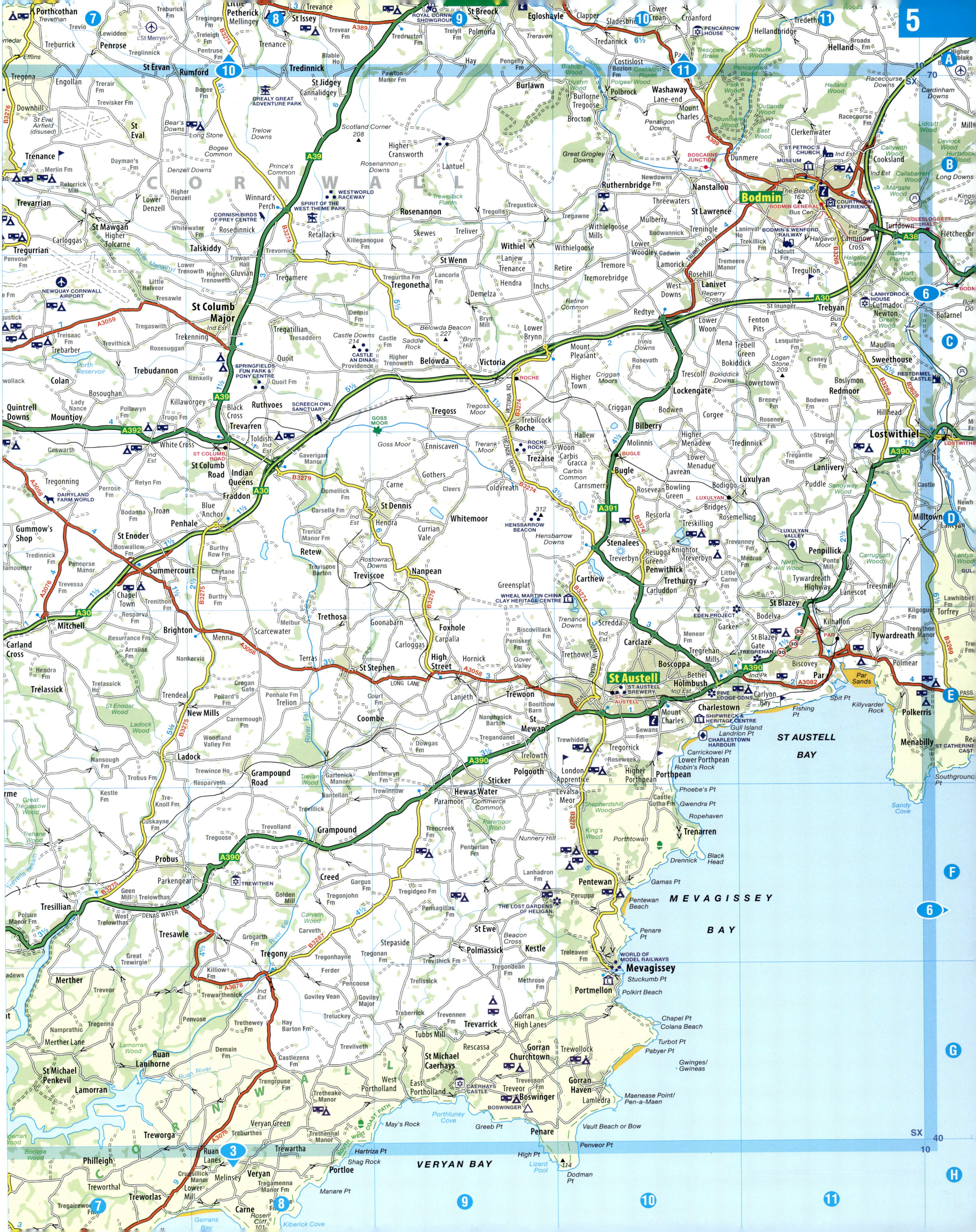
5
CORNWALL
Porthcothan
Treburrick
Penrose
St Ervan
Rumford
Little Petherick
St Issey
Trevance
Tredinnick
St Jidgey
Cannalidgey
St Breock
Polmorla
Egloshayle
Clapper
Sladesbridge
Lower Croanford
Tredethy
Hellandbridge
Helland
Pencarrow House
Burlawn
Polbrock
Washaway
Mount Charles
Costislost
Tredannick
Trerick
Clerkenwater
Bodmin
Dunmere
Nanstallon
St Lawrence
Cooksland
Turfdown
Fletchersbridge
Carminow Cross
Lanivet
Trebyan
Lostwithiel
Treverbyn
Bugle
Stenalees
Penwithick
Trethurgy
Carluddon
Eden Project
St Blazey
Par
Tywardreath
Polmear
Polkerris
Menabilly
Par Sands
Spit Pt
Biscovey
Bethel
Holmbush
Boscoppa
Carclaze
Charlestown
St Austell
St Austell Bay
Trewoon
St Mewan
Polgooth
Sticker
Hewas Water
Pentewan
Mevagissey Bay
Mevagissey
The Lost Gardens of Heligan
Portmellon
Chapel Pt
Gorran Haven
Dodman Pt
Veryan Bay
Portloe
Veryan
Ruan Lanes
St Columb Major
St Columb Road
Indian Queens
Fraddon
Summercourt
Mitchell
St Enoder
Newquay Cornwall Airport
St Mawgan
Talskiddy
Roche
Victoria
Belowda
St Wenn
Rosenannon
Withiel
Ruthernbridge
Lockengate
Bilberry
Luxulyan
Lanlivery
Penpillick
Nanpean
St Dennis
Whitemoor
St Stephen
Grampound Road
Grampound
Probus
Tresillian
Tregony
Ruan Lanihorne
St Michael Penkevil
Lamorran
Philleigh
Treworga
St Ewe
Polmassick
Kestle
Gorran Churchtown
St Michael Caerhays
Portholland
Boswinger
Penare
Trewithen
Creed
Coombe
Ladock
New Mills
Probus
Brighton
Trebudannon
Quintrell Downs
Mountjoy
Colan
Trenance
Trevarrian
Tregurrian
A30
A39
A389
A391
A390
A3058
A3078
A392
A38
B3274
B3275
B3287
B3279
B3269
SX

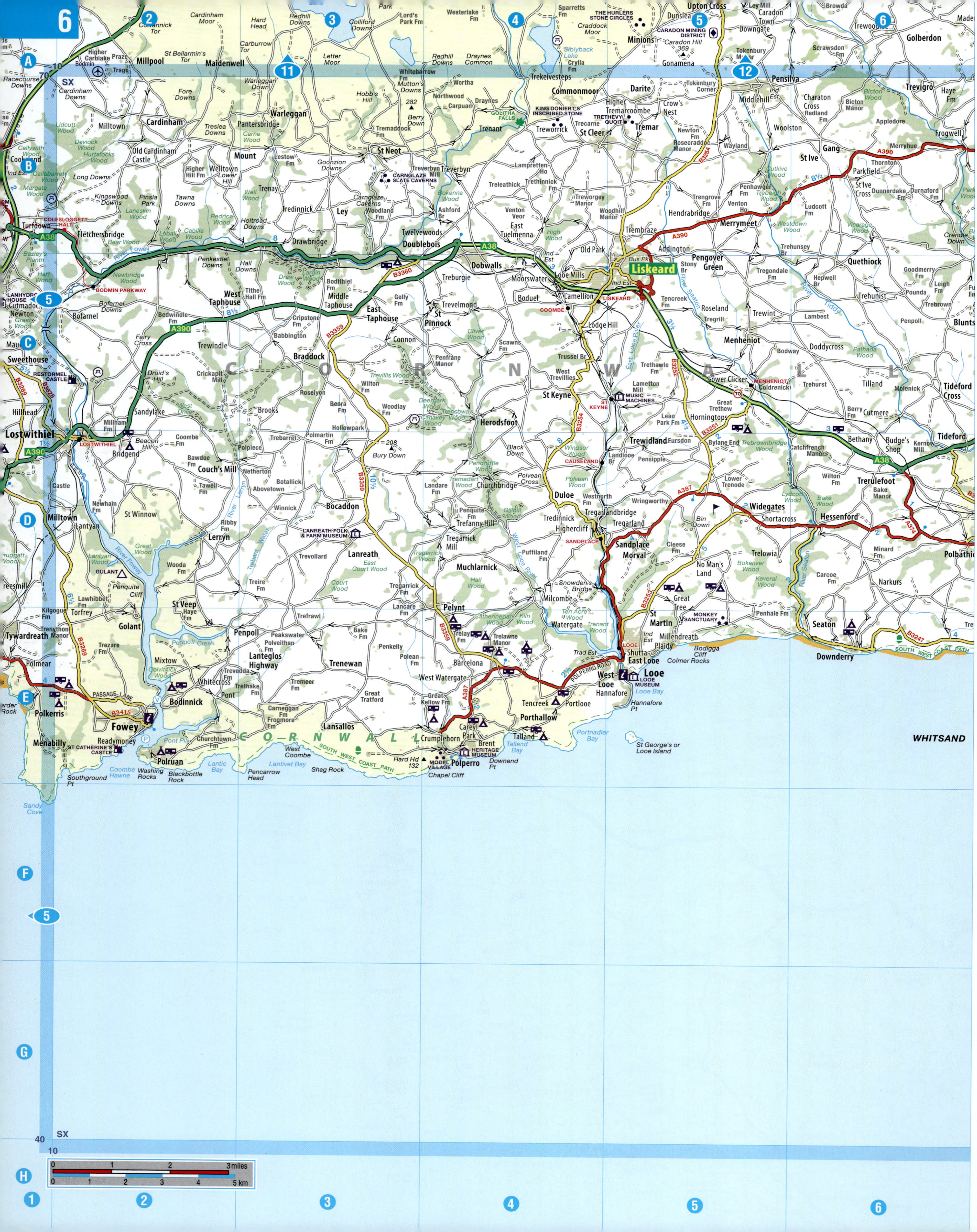

Cardinham Moor
Hard Head
Redhill Downs
Colliford Downs
Lord's Park Fm
Westerlake Fm
Sparretts
THE HURLERS STONE CIRCLES
Craddock Moor
Minions
Dunslea
Upton Cross
CARADON MINING DISTRICT
Caradon Hill
Caradon Town
Downgate
Browda
Trewoodloe
Golberdon
Made
Cornnick Tor
Carburrow Tor
St Bellarmin's Tor
Letter Moor
Redhill Downs
Draynes Common
Siblyback Lake
Crylla Fm
Gonamena
Tokenbury Manor
Higher Carblake
Prazey
Bodmin
Millpool
Maidenwell
Racecourse Downs
Warleggan Down
Whitebarrow Fm
Mutton's Downs
Wortha
Trekeivesteps
Commonmoor
Darite
Tokenbury Corner
Pensilva
Middlehill
Trevigro
Haye Fm
Cardinham Downs
Fore Downs
Hobb's Hill
Northwood
Carpuan
Draynes
GOLITHA FALLS
KING DONIERT'S INSCRIBED STONE
Higher Tremarcoombe
TRETHEVY QUOIT
Crow's Nest
Charaton Cross
Redland Fm
Bicton Manor
Bicton Wood
Appledore
Milltown
Cardinham
Treslea Downs
Pantersbridge
Warleggan
Berry Down
Tremaddock Fm
Trenant
Treworrick
St Cleer
Trecarne
Tremar
Newton Fm
Rosecraddoc Manor
Wayland
Woolston
Frogwell
Old Cardinham Castle
Mount
Lestow Fm
Goonzion Downs
St Neot
Treverbyn Mill
Treverbyn
St Ive
Gang
Merryhue
Long Downs
Higher Hill Fm
Welltown
Lower Hill
CARNGLAZE SLATE CAVERNS
Lampretten Ho
Trethinnick
Thornton
Parkfield
St Ive Cross
Dunnerdake
Durnaford Fm
Kingswood Downs
Pinsla Park
Tawna Downs
Trenay
Carnglaze Caverns
Woodland Fm
Treleathick
Treworgey Manor
Woodhill Manor
Penhawger Fm
Venton Ho
Tregrove Fm
Ludcott Fm
Tredinnick
Ley
Ashford Br
Venton Veor
East Tuelmenna
Hendrabridge
Merrymeet
Trembraze
COLESLOGGETT HALT
Turfdown
Fletchersbridge
Holtroad Downs
Twelvewoods
Doublebois
Drawbridge
Old Park
Addington
Pengover Green
Quethiock
Crendle Down
Penkestle Downs
Hall Downs
Dobwalls
Moorswater
Looe Mills
Liskeard
Stony Br
Trehunsey Br
Tregondale Fm
Hepwell Br
Goodmerry Fm
Leigh Fm
Pounda
Trebrown
Trehunist
BODMIN PARKWAY
LANHYDROCK HOUSE
Cutmadoc
Newton
Botarnel Downs
Botarnel
West Taphouse
Tithe Hall Fm
Bodithiel Fm
Middle Taphouse
Gelly Fm
East Taphouse
Treburgie
Trevelmond
St Pinnock
Boduel
Camellion
LISKEARD
COOMBE
Lodge Hill
Tencreek Fm
Roseland
Tregrill
Trewint
Lambest
Penpoll
Blunts
Bedwindle Fm
Cripstone Fm
Babbington
Connon
Menheniot
Bodway
Doddycross
Fairy Cross
Trewindle
Braddock
Penfrane Manor
Scawns Fm
Trussel Br
Trethawle Fm
Pathada Wood
Maudlin
Sweethouse
RESTORMEL CASTLE
Crickapit Mill
Roselyon
Wilton Fm
West Trevillies
Lametton Mill
MUSIC MACHINES
Lower Clicker
MENHENIOT
Coldrenick
Trehurst
Tilland
Molenick
Tideford Cross
Druid's Hill
Brooks
Beara Fm
Woodlay Fm
Deerpark Wood
Herodsfoot
St Keyne
ST KEYNE
Great Trethew
Horningtops
Lean Park Fm
Berry Down
Cutmere
Hillhead
Sandylake
Millham Fm
Hollowpark
Bethany
Budge's Shop
Kernow Mill
Tideford
Lostwithiel
LOSTWITHIEL
Beacon Hill
Bridgend
Coombe Fm
Trebarret
Polmartin Fm
208
Bury Down
Black Down
Trewidland
Fursdon
Bylane End
Catchfrench Manor
Bawdoe Fm
Couch's Mill
Polpiece
Netherton
Botallick
Abovetown
Landlooe Br
Pensipple
Trebrownbridge Wood
Lower Trenode
Wilton Fm
Trerulefoot
Bake Manor
Castle
Tawell Fm
Landare Fm
Churchbridge
Polvean Cross
Duloe
Westnorth Fm
Wringworthy
Widegates
Lycott Wood
Newham Fm
St Winnow
Milltown
Lantyan
Winnick
Bocaddon
Penquite Fm
Trefanny Hill
Tregarlandbridge
Tregarland
Bin Down
Shortacross
Hessenford
Ribby Fm
Lerryn
LANREATH FOLK & FARM MUSEUM
Tregarrick Mill
Tredinnick
Highercliff
SANDPLACE
Sandplace
Morval
Cleese Fm
Trelowia
Minard Fm
Polbathic
Lanreath
East Court Wood
Puffiland Fm
No Man's Land
Carcoe Fm
Narkurs
GULANT
Penquite Cliff
Trevollard
Muchlarnick
Wooda Fm
Treire Fm
Tregarrick Fm
Snowden's Bridge
Milcombe
Great Tree
Lawhibbet Fm
Torfrey
St Veep
Haye Fm
Lancare Fm
Pelynt
Watergate
St Martin
MONKEY SANCTUARY
Penhale Fm
Seaton
Kilgogue Fm
Golant
Penpoll
Trefrawl
Bake Fm
Trelay Fm
Trelawne Manor
Millendreath
Trenython Manor
Tywardreath
Trezare Fm
Peakswater
Polveithan Fm
Lanteglos Highway
Penkelly
Polean Fm
Barcelona
Trad Est
Shutta
East Looe
Plaidy
Bodigga Cliff
Colmer Rocks
Downderry
SOUTH WEST COAST PATH
Polmear
Mixtow
Whitecross
Trevedda
Pont
Trenewan
Tremeer Fm
West Watergate
POLPERRO ROAD
West Looe
Looe
LOOE MUSEUM
Looe Bay
Hannafore
Hannafore Pt
Polkerris
PASSAGE LANE
Bodinnick
Trethake Fm
Great Tratford
Great Kellow Fm
Tencreek
Portlooe
Fowey
Carneggan Fm
Frogmore
Lansallos
Carey Park
Porthallow
Talland
Talland Bay
Portnadler Bay
WHITSAND
Menabilly
ST CATHERINE'S CASTLE
Readymoney
Pont Pill
Churchtown Fm
Crumplehorn
Brent
HERITAGE MUSEUM
St George's or Looe Island
Polruan
West Coombe
Hard Hd
132
MODEL VILLAGE
Polperro
Downend Pt
Chapel Cliff
Coombe Hawne
Washing Rocks
Blackbottle Rock
Lantic Bay
Lantivet Bay
Pencarrow Head
Shag Rock
Southground Pt
Sandy Cove
CORNWALL
SX
0 1 2 3 miles
0 1 2 3 4 5 km

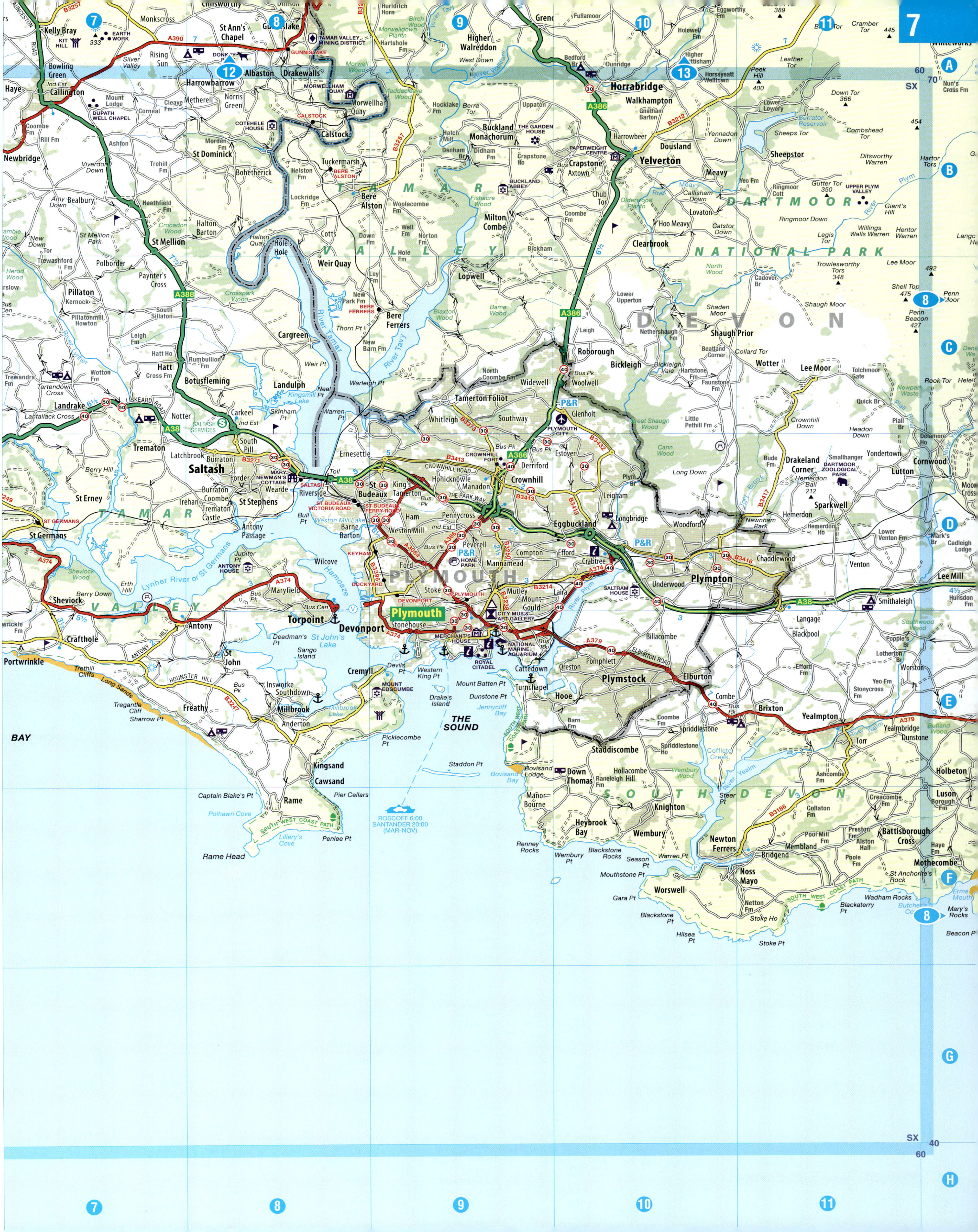
Kelly Bray
Monkscross
St Ann's Chapel
Gunnislake
Higher Walreddon
Horrabridge
Walkhampton
Callington
Harrowbarrow
Albaston
Drakewalls
Morwellham Quay
Calstock
Newbridge
St Dominick
Tuckermarsh
Bere Alston
Buckland Monachorum
Yelverton
Dousland
Sheepstor
Meavy
Milton Combe
St Mellion
Clearbrook
DARTMOOR
NATIONAL PARK
TAMAR VALLEY
Weir Quay
Lopwell
Bere Ferrers
Pillaton
DEVON
Cargreen
Shaugh Prior
Roborough
Bickleigh
Wotter
Lee Moor
Hatt
Botusfleming
Landulph
Widewell
Tamerton Foliot
Glenholt
Landrake
Notter
Carkeel
Whitleigh
Southway
Trematon
Saltash
Ernesettle
Derriford
Estover
Crownhill
Drakeland Corner
Cornwood
Lutton
St Erney
St Budeaux
Honicknowle
Manadon
Sparkwell
St Stephens
Eggbuckland
Hemerdon
St Germans
Pennycross
Weston Mill
Barne Barton
Peverell
Compton
Efford
Crabtree
Plympton
Chaddlewood
Lee Mill
Sheviock
Wilcove
Maryfield
Ford
Mannamead
Underwood
Smithaleigh
Torpoint
Antony
Devonport
Stoke
Plymouth
Mutley
Mount Gould
Laira
Stonehouse
Crafthole
PLYMOUTH
Billacombe
Langage
Blackpool
Portwrinkle
St John
Cremyll
Pomphlett
Plymstock
Elburton
Cattedown
Turnchapel
Oreston
Hooe
Combe
Brixton
Yealmpton
Freathy
Millbrook
Anderton
BAY
THE SOUND
Staddiscombe
Kingsand
Cawsand
Rame
Down Thomas
Knighton
Wembury
Heybrook Bay
Newton Ferrers
Noss Mayo
Worswell
Battisborough Cross
Holbeton
Mothecombe
Rame Head
SOUTH DEVON
ROSCOFF 6:00
SANTANDER 20:00
(MAR-NOV)
7
8
9
10
11
12
13

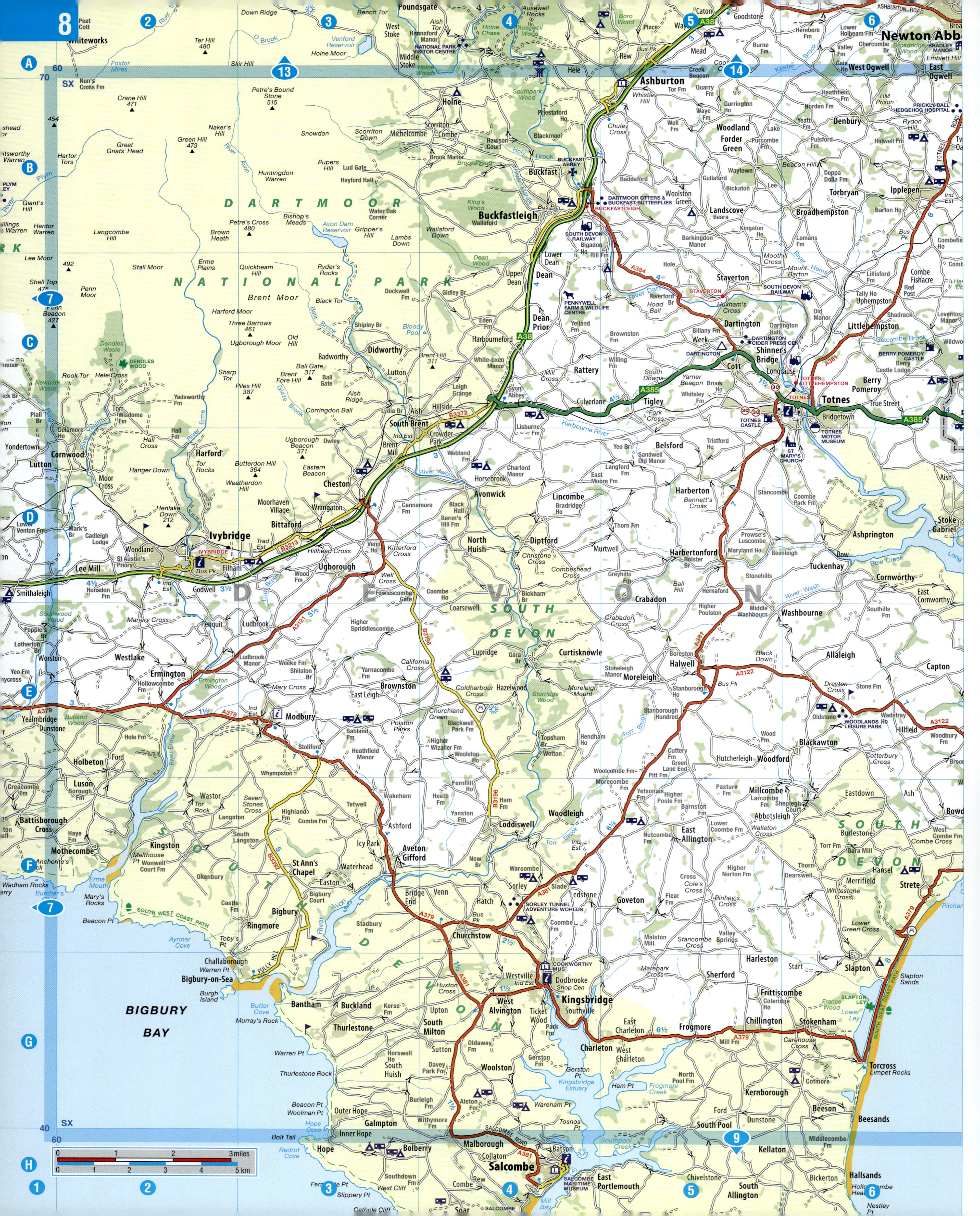
DARTMOOR
NATIONAL PARK
DEVON
SOUTH DEVON
BIGBURY BAY
Ashburton
Buckfast
Buckfastleigh
Newton Abbot
Woodland
Landscove
Broadhempston
Torbryan
Ipplepen
Denbury
Staverton
Dartington
Littlehempston
Totnes
Bridgetown
Berry Pomeroy
Shinner's Bridge
Tigley
Rattery
Dean Prior
Harbourneford
Didworthy
South Brent
Avonwick
Lincombe
Belsford
Harberton
Harbertonford
Ashprington
Tuckenhay
Cornworthy
Washbourne
Crabadon
Diptford
North Huish
Ivybridge
Bittaford
Wrangaton
Cheston
Ugborough
Harford
Cornwood
Lutton
Lee Mill
Smithaleigh
Ermington
Westlake
Modbury
Yealmbridge
Holbeton
Kingston
Battisborough Cross
Mothecombe
Ringmore
Bigbury
St Ann's Chapel
Bigbury-on-Sea
Aveton Gifford
Loddiswell
Woodleigh
Churchstow
Kingsbridge
West Alvington
Bantham
Buckland
Thurlestone
South Milton
Woolston
Malborough
Salcombe
Galmpton
Hope
Bolberry
East Portlemouth
Chivelstone
South Allington
Kellaton
Hallsands
Beesands
Torcross
Slapton
Stokenham
Chillington
Frogmore
Charleton
Sherford
Goveton
East Allington
Moreleigh
Halwell
Woodford
Blackawton
Allaleigh
Capton
Strete
Harleston
Frittiscombe
Kernborough
South Pool
Curtisknowle
Brownston
Start Bay
A38
A385
A381
A379
A3121
A3122
B3196
B3392
B3213
B3372
SX
0 1 2 3 miles
0 1 2 3 4 5 km

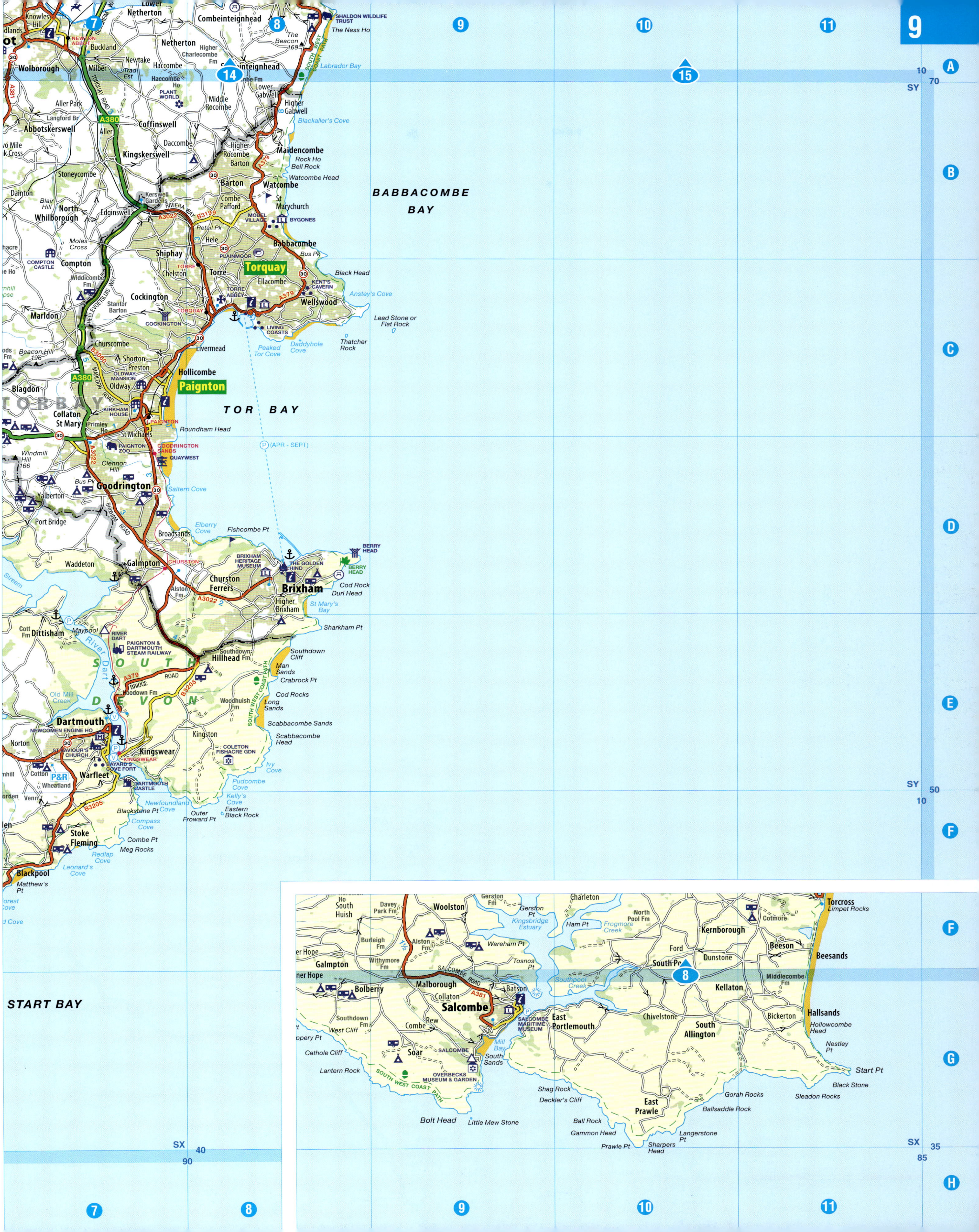

BABBACOMBE BAY
TOR BAY
START BAY
Torquay
Paignton
Brixham
Dartmouth
Salcombe
TORBAY
SOUTH DEVON
Combeinteignhead
Netherton
Buckland
Newton Abbot
Wolborough
Milber
Newtake
Haccombe
Higher Charlecombe Fm
Stokeinteignhead
SHALDON WILDLIFE TRUST
The Ness Ho
The Beacon 169
Labrador Bay
Lower Gabwell
Higher Gabwell
Middle Rocombe
PLANT WORLD
Aller Park
Langford Br
Abbotskerswell
Aller
Coffinswell
Daccombe
Kingskerswell
Two Mile Oak Cross
Stoneycombe
Higher Rocombe Barton
Maidencombe
Rock Ho
Bell Rock
Watcombe Head
Blackaller's Cove
Barton
Watcombe
Combe Pafford
St Marychurch
MODEL VILLAGE
BYGONES
Kerswell Gardens
Dainton
Blair Hill
North Whilborough
Edginswell
RIVIERA WAY
Retail Pk
Hele
Babbacombe
Bus Pk
PLAINMOOR
Moles Cross
COMPTON CASTLE
Compton
Shiphay
Chelston
TORRE
Torre
Ellacombe
KENT'S CAVERN
Black Head
Anstey's Cove
Widdicombe Fm
Cockington
TORRE ABBEY
Wellswood
Lead Stone or Flat Rock
Marldon
Stantor Barton
TORQUAY
COCKINGTON
LIVING COASTS
Thatcher Rock
Peaked Tor Cove
Daddyhole Cove
Livermead
Churscombe
Beacon Hill 196
Shorton
Preston
Hollicombe
Blagdon
OLDWAY MANSION
Oldway
KIRKHAM HOUSE
Collaton St Mary
Primley
St Michaels
PAIGNTON
Roundham Head
(APR - SEPT)
Windmill Hill 166
PAIGNTON ZOO
Clennon Hill
GOODRINGTON SANDS
QUAYWEST
Bus Pk
Goodrington
Yalberton
Saltern Cove
Port Bridge
BRIXHAM ROAD
Elberry Cove
Fishcombe Pt
Broadsands
BERRY HEAD
Waddeton
Galmpton
CHURSTON
BRIXHAM HERITAGE MUSEUM
THE GOLDEN HIND
Churston Ferrers
Alston Fm
Cod Rock
Durl Head
Higher Brixham
St Mary's Bay
Sharkham Pt
Cott Fm
Dittisham
Maypool
RIVER DART
PAIGNTON & DARTMOUTH STEAM RAILWAY
River Dart
Southdown Fm
Hillhead
Southdown Cliff
Man Sands
Crabrock Pt
Old Mill Creek
BRIDGE ROAD
Hoodown Fm
Woodhuish Fm
Cod Rocks
Long Sands
SOUTH WEST COAST PATH
Scabbacombe Sands
Scabbacombe Head
NEWCOMEN ENGINE HO
Norton
ST SAVIOUR'S CHURCH
Kingston
COLETON FISHACRE GDN
Kingswear
KINGSWEAR
BAYARD'S COVE FORT
Cotton
P&R
Wheatland
Warfleet
DARTMOUTH CASTLE
Ivy Cove
Pudcombe Cove
Kelly's Cove
Venn
Newfoundland Cove
Blackstone Pt
Compass Cove
Outer Froward Pt
Eastern Black Rock
Stoke Fleming
Combe Pt
Meg Rocks
Redlap Cove
Leonard's Cove
Blackpool
Matthew's Pt
South Huish
Davey Park Fm
Woolston
Gerston Fm
Gerston Pt
Charleton
Kingsbridge Estuary
Ham Pt
Frogmore Creek
North Pool Fm
Torcross
Limpet Rocks
Cotmore
Kernborough
Burleigh Fm
Alston Fm
Wareham Pt
Ford
Dunstone
Beeson
Beesands
Galmpton
Withymore Fm
Tosnos Pt
South Pool
Middlecombe Fm
Bolberry
Malborough
SALCOMBE ROAD
Batson
Southpool Creek
Kellaton
Collaton
Salcombe
Southdown Fm
SALCOMBE MARITIME MUSEUM
East Portlemouth
Chivelstone
South Allington
Bickerton
Hallsands
Hollowcombe Head
West Cliff
Combe
Rew
Mill Bay
South Sands
Nestley Pt
Cathole Cliff
Soar
Lantern Rock
OVERBECKS MUSEUM & GARDEN
Start Pt
Black Stone
Shag Rock
Deckler's Cliff
Gorah Rocks
Sleadon Rocks
Ballsaddle Rock
East Prawle
Bolt Head
Little Mew Stone
Ball Rock
Gammon Head
Prawle Pt
Sharpers Head
Langerstone Pt

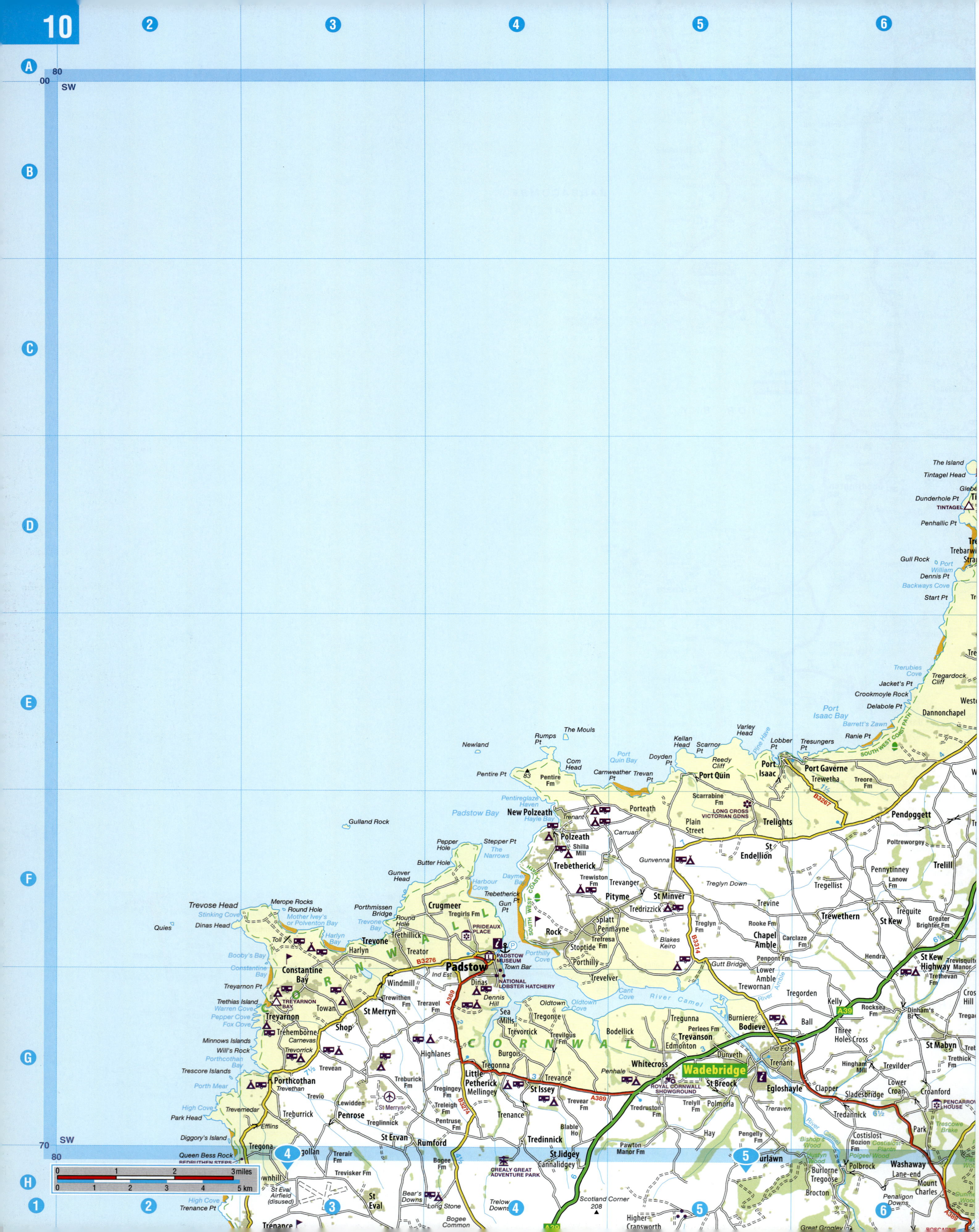

2
3
4
5
6
A
B
C
D
E
F
G
H
1
80
00
SW
70
The Island
Tintagel Head
Dunderhole Pt
TINTAGEL
Penhallic Pt
Gull Rock
Port William
Dennis Pt
Backways Cove
Start Pt
Trerubies Cove
Tregardock Cliff
Jacket's Pt
Crookmoyle Rock
Delabole Pt
Port Isaac Bay
Barrett's Zawn
Dannonchapel
Ranie Pt
SOUTH WEST COAST PATH
Varley Head
Lobber Pt
Tresungers Pt
Kellan Head
Scarnor Pt
Reedy Cliff
Doyden Pt
Port Quin Bay
Port Quin
Port Isaac
Port Gaverne
Trewetha
Treore Fm
B3267
Rumps Pt
The Mouls
Com Head
Newland
Pentire Pt
Pentire Fm
Carnweather Pt
Trevan Pt
Porteath
Scarrabine Fm
LONG CROSS VICTORIAN GDNS
Plain Street
Trelights
Pendoggett
Padstow Bay
New Polzeath
Pentireglaze Haven
Hayle Bay
Trenant
Polzeath
Carruan
Shilla Mill
Trebetherick
Gunvenna
St Endellion
Poltreworgey
Trelill
Pennytinney
Lanow Fm
Gulland Rock
Pepper Hole
Stepper Pt
The Narrows
Butter Hole
Gunver Head
Harbour Cove
Daymer Bay
Trebetherick Pt
Gun Pt
Trewiston Fm
Trevanger
Pityme
St Minver
Tredrizzick
Treglyn Down
Tregellist
Trevine
Trequite
Greater Brighter Fm
Trewethern
St Kew
Trevose Head
Stinking Cove
Merope Rocks
Round Hole
Mother Ivey's or Polventon Bay
Dinas Head
Quies
Porthmissen Bridge
Round Hole
Trevone Bay
Crugmeer
Tregirls Fm
PRIDEAUX PLACE
Harlyn Bay
Trevone
Trethillick
Toll
Harlyn
Treator
B3276
Padstow
PADSTOW MUSEUM
Town Bar
Porthilly Cove
Rock
Splatt
Penmayne
Trefresa Fm
Stoptide
Porthilly
Treglyn Fm
Blakes Keiro
Rooke Fm
Chapel Amble
Carclaze Fm
Penpont Fm
Gutt Bridge
Lower Amble
Hendra
St Kew Highway
Trevisquite Manor
Trethevan Fm
Booby's Bay
Constantine Bay
Constantine Bay
Treyarnon Pt
Windmill
Ind Est
NATIONAL LOBSTER HATCHERY
Dinas
Dennis Hill
Trevelver
Cant Cove
River Camel
Treworнan
Tregorden
Kelly
A39
Rocksea Fm
Dinham's Br
Trethias Island
Warren Cove
TREYARNON BAY
Pepper Cove
Fox Cove
Treyarnon
Towan
Trewithen Fm
St Merryn
Treravel Fm
A389
Oldtown
Oldtown Cove
Tregonce
Sea Mills
Trevilgus Fm
Trevorrick
Bodellick
Tregunna
Perlees Fm
Trevanson
Burniere
Bodieve
Ball
Three Holes Cross
Minnows Islands
Will's Rock
Porthcothan Bay
Trehemborne
Carnevas
Trevorrick
Shop
Highlanes
Burgois
CORNWALL
Edmonton
Dunveth
Ind Est
St Mabyn
Trescore Islands
Trevean
Trevena
Trethick Fm
Treburick Fm
Little Petherick
Mellingey
Tregonna
Trevance
Penhale
Whitecross
Wadebridge
Trenant
Hingham Mill
Trevilder
Porth Mear
Porthcothan
Trevethan
Trevio
Treingey Fm
Treleigh Fm
B3274
St Issey
Trevear Fm
A389
ROYAL CORNWALL SHOWGROUND
St Breock
Polmorla
Egloshayle
Clapper
Sladesbridge
Lower Croan
Croanford
PENCARROW HOUSE
High Cove
Trevemedar
Park Head
Treburrick
Lewidden
St Merryn
Penrose
Treglinnick
Pentruse Fm
Trenance
Tredruston Fm
Trelyll Fm
Treraven
Tredannick
Park
Trescowe Brake
Diggory's Island
Efflins
Blable Ho
Hay
River Camel
Costislost
Bozion Fm
Costislost Plantn
Polgeel Wood
Tregona
St Ervan
Rumford
Tredinnick
Pawton Manor Fm
Pengelly Fm
Bishop's Wood
Queen Bess Rock
BEDRUTHEN STEPS
Trerair Fm
Bogee Fm
St Jidgey
Cannalidgey
Burlorne Tregoose
Polbrock
Washaway
Lane-end
Trevisker Fm
CREALY GREAT ADVENTURE PARK
Brocton
Mount Charles
St Eval Airfield (disused)
St Eval
Bear's Downs
Long Stone
Bogee Common
Trelow Downs
Scotland Corner 208
Penaligon Downs
High Cove
Trenance Pt
Higher Cranswoth
Great Grogley
Trenance
A389
0 1 2 3 miles
0 1 2 3 4 5 km

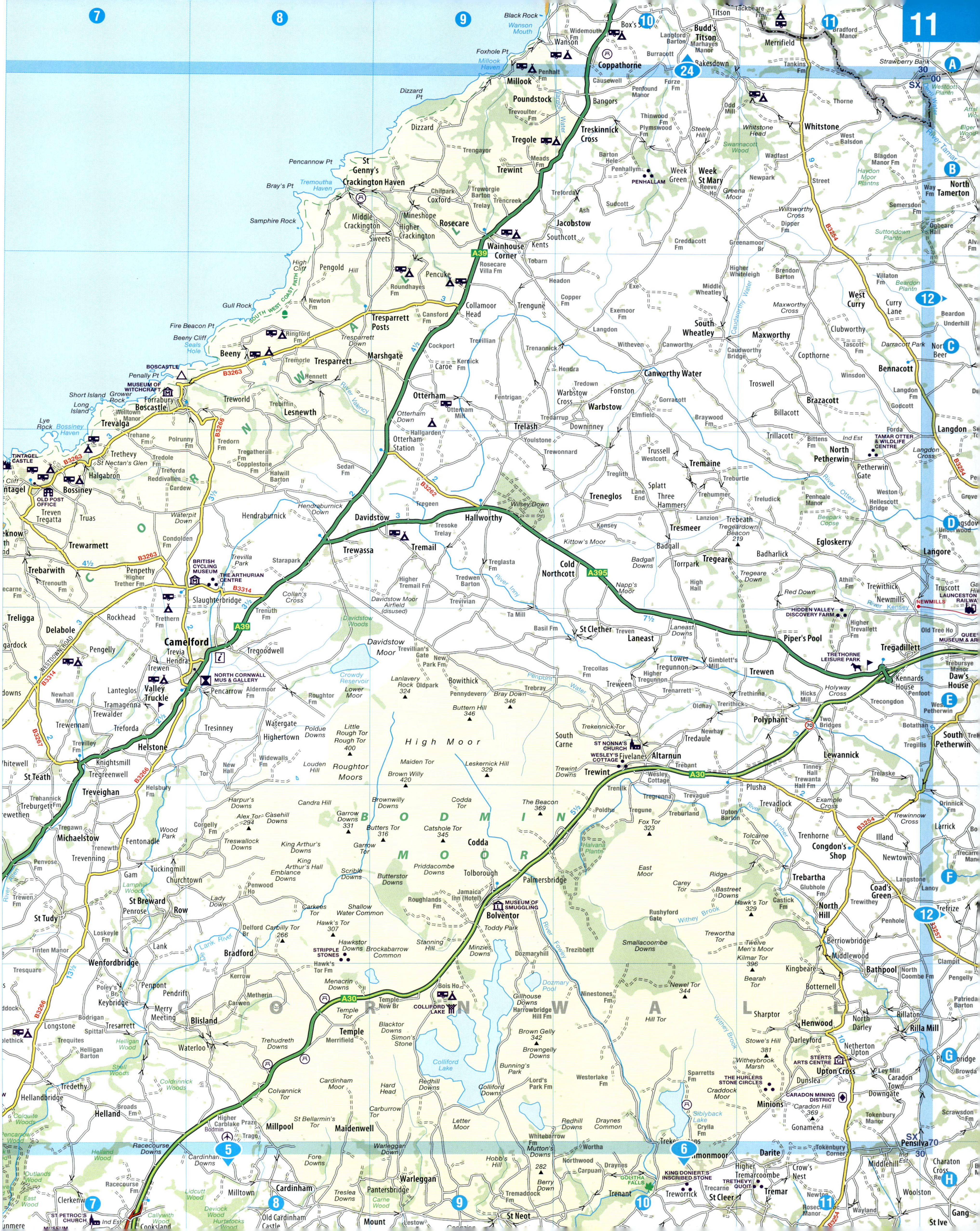
Black Rock
Wanson Mouth
Widemouth
Box's Shop
Titson
Budd's Titson
Marhayes Manor
Merrifield
Bradford Manor
Strawberry Bank
Foxhole Pt
Millook Haven
Wanson
Coppathorne
Burracott
Bakesdown
Penhalt
Millook
Poundstock
Causewell
Penfound Manor
Bangors
Dizzard Pt
Dizzard
Trevoulter Fm
Thinwood Fm
Plymswood
Odd Mill
Steele Hill
Whitestone Head
Thorne
Whitstone
West Balsdon
Treskinnick Cross
Tregole
Trengayor
Meads Fm
Barton Hele
Swannacott Wood
Wadfast
Blagdon Manor Fm
Penhallym
PENHALLAM
Week Green
Week St Mary
Reeve Ho
Greena Moor
Newpark
Street
Haydon Moor Plantns
North Tamerton
Pencannow Pt
St Genny's
Crackington Haven
Tremoutha Haven
Bray's Pt
Trewint
Treworgie Barton
Chilpark
Coxford
Trelay
Trencreek
Treforda
Sudcott
Ash
Willsworthy Cross
Dipper Fm
Somersdon Fm
Ogbeare Hall
Samphire Rock
Middle Crackington
Mineshope
Higher Crackington
Sweets
Rosecare
Jacobstow
Southcott
Wainhouse Corner
Kents
Creddacott Fm
Greenamoor Br
Suttondown Plantn
High Cliff
Pengold
Hill
Pencuke
Roundhayes Fm
Rosecare Villa Fm
Tobarn
Headon
Higher Whiteleigh
Brendon Barton
Villaton Fm
Beardon Plantn
Gull Rock
Newton Fm
SOUTH WEST COAST PATH
Collamoor Head
Trengune
Copper Fm
Exe
Middle Wheatley
Caudworthy Water
Maxworthy Cross
West Curry
Curry Lane
Beardon
Underhill
Fire Beacon Pt
Beeny Cliff
Seals Hole
Ringford Fm
Tresparrett Posts
Cansford Fm
Exemoor Fm
Langdon
South Wheatley
Maxworthy
Clubworthy
Tascott Fm
Darracott Park
Beeny
Trevillian
Trenannick
Witheven
Canworthy
Caudworthy Bridge
Copthorne
Trespparrett Down
Cockport
Trespparrett
Tremorle
Marshgate
Kernick Fm
Caroe
Hendra
Canworthy Water
Winsdon
Bennacott
BOSCASTLE
Penally Pt
MUSEUM OF WITCHCRAFT
Forrabury
Boscastle
Hennett
River Valency
Tredown
Warbstow Cross
Fonston
Troswell
Brazacott
Langdon Fm
Godcott
Short Island
Long Island
Grower Rock
Treworld
Trebiffin
Lesnewth
Otterham
Fentrigan
Warbstow
Gorracott
Billacott
Lye Rock
Bossiney Haven
Trevalga
Welltown Manor
Otterham Down
Otterham Mill
Hallgarden
Trelash
Tredarrup
Elmfield
Downinney
Braywood Fm
Langdon
Trehane Fm
Polrunny Fm
Tredorn Fm
Otterham Station
Youlstone
Trillacott
Bittens Fm
Ind Est
TAMAR OTTER & WILDLIFE CENTRE
Forda
Langdon Cross
TINTAGEL CASTLE
Trethevy
St Nectan's Glen
Tredole Fm
Tregatherall Fm
Copplestone Fm
Trewonnard
Trussell Westcott
Tremaine
North Petherwin
Petherwin Gate
Halgabron
Treforda
Reddivallen Fm
Cardew
Halwill Barton
Sedan Fm
Tregrith
Splatt
Three Hammers
Treburtle
Lane End
Trehummer
Treneglos
Treludick
Penheale Manor
River Ottery
Westcott
Hellescott Bridge
Bossiney
Tintagel
OLD POST OFFICE
Treven
Tregatta
Truas
Waterpit Down
Hendraburnick
Hendraburnick Down
Davidstow
Tregeen
Hallworthy
Wilsey Down
Kensey
Lanzion
Trebeath
Tregeardown Beacon
Tresmeer
Beerpark Copse
Underwood
Trewarmett
Condolden Fm
Tresoke
Trelay
Tremail
Trewassa
Kittow's Moor
Badgall
Egloskerry
Langore
Trebarwith
Penpethy
Higher Trether Fm
BRITISH CYCLING MUSEUM
THE ARTHURIAN CENTRE
Trevilla Park
Starapark
Treglasta Fm
Cold Northcott
Badgall Downs
Torrpark
Tregeare
Badharlick
Tregeare Down
Atthill Fm
Trewithick
Truscott
Trenouth Fm
Slaughterbridge
Collan's Cross
Higher Tremail Fm
Tredwen Barton
River Inny
Napp's Moor
High Hall
Red Down
Newmills
LAUNCESTON RAILWAY
NEWMILLS
Treligga
Rockhead
Trethern Fm
Trenuth Fm
Davidstow Moor Airfield (disused)
Trevivian
Davidstow Woods
Ta Mill
HIDDEN VALLEY DISCOVERY FARM
River Kensey
Higher Trevallett
Old Tree Ho
Delabole
Camelford
Trevia
Hendra
Tregoodwell
Davidstow Moor
Trevillian's Gate
Basil Fm
St Clether
Treven
Laneast
Laneast Downs
Piper's Pool
Tregadillett
TRETHORNE LEISURE PARK
Pengelly
Trewen
Valley Truckle
NORTH CORNWALL MUS & GALLERY
Pencarrow
Aldermoor Fm
Crowdy Reservoir
Lower Moor
Lanlavery Rock
Oldpark
New Park Fm
Bowithick
Pennydevern
Bray Down
Penpont
Trebray
Trecollas Fm
Treween
Higher Tregunnon
Lower Tregunnon
Gimblett's Mill
Trewen
Kennards House
Daw's House
Newhall Manor
Lanteglos
Tramagenna
Trewalder
Treforda
Roughton Fm
Buttern Hill
Trenarrett
Trethinna
Oldwhay
Hicks Mill
Holyway Cross
Trecongdon
Trewennan
Tresinney
Watergate
Poldue Downs
Little Rough Tor
Rough Tor
Highertown
High Moor
Trekennick Tor
South Carne
ST NONNA'S CHURCH
WESLEY'S COTTAGE
Fivelanes
Altarnun
Treriffick
Newhay
Tredaule
Polyphant
Two Bridges
Lewannick
Botathan
South Petherwin
Tregillis
Trevilley
Helstone
Knightsmill
Tregreenwell
Widewalls Fm
New Hall
Louden Hill
Roughtor Moors
Maiden Tor
Brown Willy
Leskernick Hill
Trewint Downs
Trewint
Trebant
Wesley Cottage
Tinney Hall
Trewanta Hall Fm
Treleske Ho
St Teath
Trehannick
Treburgett Fm
Treveighan
Helsbury Fm
Harpur's Downs
Candra Hill
Brownwilly Downs
Codda Tor
The Beacon
Trenlik
Poldhu
Tregune
Tregrenna
Trevague
Treburland
Plusha
Upton Barton
Trevadlock
Example Cross
Trewinnow Cross
Larrick
Trewethen
Tregawn
Michaelstow
Fentonadle
Wood Park
Corgelly Fm
Alex Tor
Casehill Downs
Garrow Downs
Butters Tor
Catshole Tor
Fox Tor
Tolcarne Tor
Trenhorne
Congdon's Shop
Illand
Trevenning
Treswallock Downs
King Arthur's Downs
King Arthur's Hall
Garrow Tor
BODMIN MOOR
Codda
Halvana Plantn
Newtown
Trecarrel Manor
Penvose Fm
Tuckingmill
Churchtown
Embiance Downs
Scribble Downs
Butterstor Downs
Priddacombe Downs
Tolborough
Palmersbridge
East Moor
Carey Tor
Ridge
Trebartha
Glubhole Fm
Langstone
Coad's Green
Trewen Fm
Gam
Lamphill Woods
Penwood Ho
Lady Down
Jamaica Inn (Hotel)
MUSEUM OF SMUGGLING
Bolventor
Roughlands Fm
Bastreet Downs
Castick Fm
North Hill
Trewithey
Treffrize
St Tudy
St Breward
Penrose
Row
Carkees Tor
Shallow Water Common
Hawk's Tor
Toddy Park
Rushyford Gate
Withey Brook
Hawk's Tor
Penhole
Loskeyle Fm
Delford Br
Carbilly Tor
Hawkstor Downs
Brockabarrow Common
Stanning Hill
Minzies Downs
Dozmaryhill
Trezibbett
Smallacoombe Downs
Treworrtha Tor
Twelve Men's Moor
Kilmar Tor
Berriowbridge
Middlewood
Clampit
Tinten Manor
Wenfordbridge
Lank
Bradford
STRIPPLE STONES
Hawk's Tor Fm
Kingbeare
Bathpool
North Coombe Fm
Pengelly
Tresquare
Penpont
Kerrow
Menacrin Downs
Bearah Tor
Poley's Br
Pendrift
Metherin
Bois Ho
Gillhouse Downs
Dozmary Pool
Ninestones Fm
Newel Tor
Botternell
Patrieda Barton
Keybridge
Merry Meeting
Carwen
Blisland
Temple New Br
COLLIFORD LAKE
Harrowbridge Hill Fm
Hill Tor
Sharptor
Henwood
North Darley
Rillaton
Rilla Mill
Longstone
Spittal
Bodrigan
Tresarrett
Temple Tor
Temple
Merrifield
Blackator Downs
Simon's Stone
Brown Gelly
Browngelly Downs
Darleyford
Stowe's Hill
Netherton
Upton
Trequites
Helligan Barton
Helligan Wood
Shell Woods
Waterloo
Trehudreth Downs
Colliford Lake
Bunning's Park
Witheybrook Marsh
STERTS ARTS CENTRE
Upton Cross
Ley Mill
Caradon Town
Dunslea
Tredethy
Hellandbridge
Coldrinnick Woods
Cardinham Moor
Hard Head
Redhill Downs
Colliford Downs
Lord's Park Fm
Westerlake Fm
Sparretts Fm
THE HURLERS STONE CIRCLES
Craddock Moor
CARADON MINING DISTRICT
Caradon Hill
Minions
Downgate
Helland
Broads Fm
Colvannick Tor
Carburrow Tor
Siblyback Lake
Gonamena
Tokenbury Manor
Scrawsdon Fm
Higher Carblake
Praze
Bodmin
Trago
Millpool
St Bellarmin's Tor
Maidenwell
Letter Moor
Redhill Downs
Draynes Common
Crylla Fm
Racecourse Downs
Cardinham Downs
Warleggan Down
Fore Downs
Hobb's Hill
Whitebarrow Fm
Mutton's Downs
Wortha
Trekeivesteps
Dranmonmoor
Darite
Tokenbury Corner
Pensilva
Middlehill
Charaton Cross
Helland Wood
Racecourse Fm
Milltown
Cardinham
Treslea Downs
Pantersbridge
Warleggan
Northwood
Carpuan
Draynes
GOLITHA FALLS
KING DONIERT'S INSCRIBED STONE
TRETHEVY QUOIT
Higher Tremarcoombe
Crow's Nest
Tremar
Woolston
East Wood
Lidcutt Wood
Deviock Wood
Hurtstocks Wood
Carne Wood
Tremaddock Fm
Berry Down
Trenant
Treworrick
Trecarne
St Cleer
Newton
Rosecraddoc Manor
Wayland
Gang
Clerkenwater
ST PETROC'S CHURCH
Ind Est
Callywith Wood
Cooksland
Old Cardinham Castle
Mount
St Neot
St Ive
A39
A395
A30
B3263
B3266
B3314
B3267
B3262
B3254
B3257
WESTDOWNS ROAD
River Tamar
River Fowey
SX 30 00
SX 30
SX 70

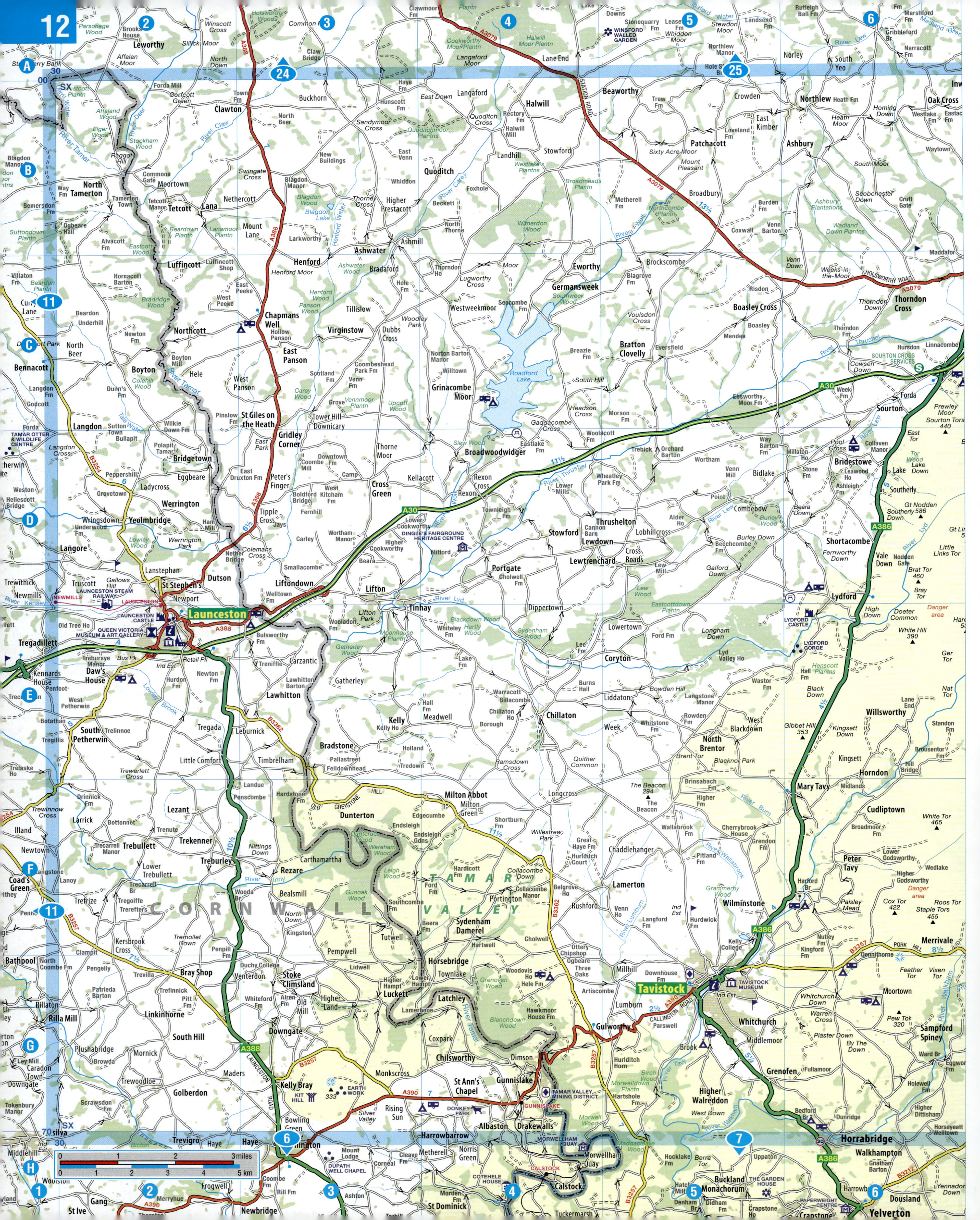
Launceston
Tavistock
CORNWALL
TAMAR VALLEY
Roadford Lake
A30
A388
A386
A3079
A390
B3257
B3362
24
25
Leworthy
Clawton
North Tamerton
Tetcott
Lana
Luffincott
Ashwater
Henford
Halwill
Beaworthy
Patchacott
Ashbury
Northlew
Quoditch
Germansweek
Broadwoodwidger
Bratton Clovelly
Boasley Cross
Thorndon Cross
Sourton
Bridestowe
Lydford
Virginstow
Chapmans Well
St Giles on the Heath
Northcott
Boyton
Bridgetown
Werrington
Yeolmbridge
St Stephen's
Dutson
Liftondown
Lifton
Tinhay
Portgate
Thrushelton
Lewdown
Lewtrenchard
Stowford
Coryton
Chillaton
Lawhitton
Kelly
Bradstone
Milton Abbot
Dunterton
Lamerton
Rezare
Horsebridge
Sydenham Damerel
Latchley
Gulworthy
Gunnislake
Calstock
Whitchurch
Mary Tavy
Peter Tavy
North Brentor
Horrabridge
Yelverton
Kelly Bray
Stoke Climsland
South Petherwin
Lezant
Trebullett
Treburley
Bray Shop
Linkinhorne
South Hill
Rilla Mill
Tregadillett
Pipers Pool
Newbridge
St Dominick
Buckland Monachorum
Dousland
Walkhampton
Merrivale
Sampford Spiney
Grenofen
Chilsworthy
Albaston
Drakewalls
St Ann's Chapel
Harrowbarrow
Bowling Green

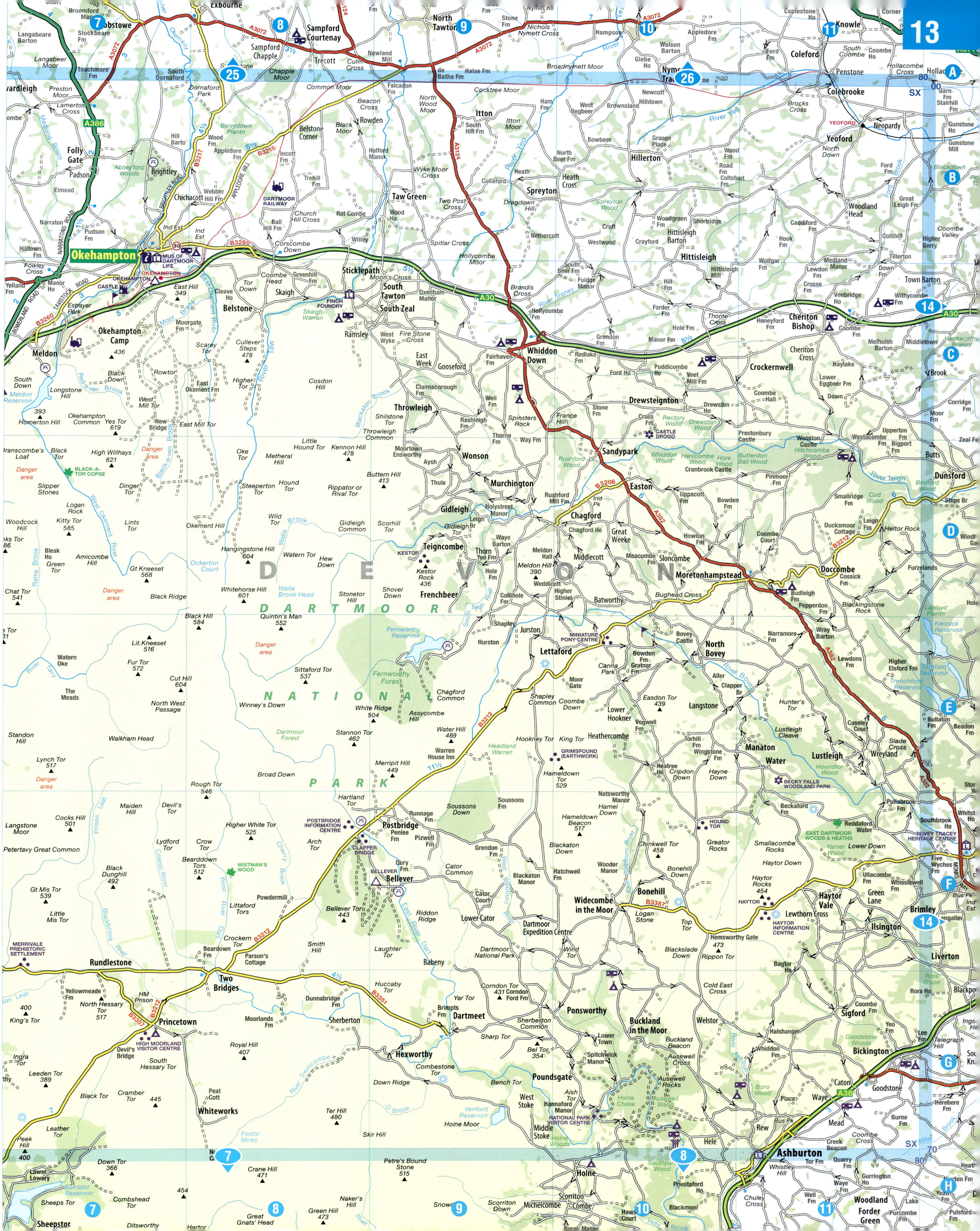
D E V O N
D A R T M O O R
N A T I O N A L
P A R K
Okehampton
Exbourne
Sampford Courtenay
North Tawton
Hatherleigh
Folly Gate
Sampford Chapple
Belstone
Sticklepath
South Zeal
South Tawton
Whiddon Down
Spreyton
Hittisleigh
Hillerton
Colebrooke
Coleford
Knowle
Yeoford
Cheriton Bishop
Crockernwell
Drewsteignton
Dunsford
Castle Drogo
Sandypark
Chagford
Gidleigh
Throwleigh
Murchington
Wonson
Easton
Moretonhampstead
Doccombe
North Bovey
Lettaford
Manaton
Lustleigh
Water
Bovey Tracey
Haytor Vale
Ilsington
Liverton
Bickington
Sigford
Ashburton
Buckland in the Moor
Widecombe in the Moor
Ponsworthy
Poundsgate
Holne
Hexworthy
Dartmeet
Postbridge
Bellever
Two Bridges
Princetown
Rundlestone
Whiteworks
Sheepstor
Meldon
Okehampton Camp
Yes Tor 619
High Willhays 621
Cut Hill 604
Great Mis Tor 539
Dartmoor Forest
Fernworthy Reservoir
Burrator Reservoir
Venford Reservoir
Hound Tor
Haytor Rocks 454
Becky Falls Woodland Park
Grimspound (Earthwork)
Postbridge Information Centre
High Moorland Visitor Centre
National Park Visitor Centre
Dartmoor Railway
Finch Foundry
Mus. of Dartmoor Life
Okehampton Castle
Wistman's Wood
A30
A38
A382
A386
A3072
A3124
B3212
B3357
B3387
B3206
B3260
B3215
B3217
B3219
B3344
River Teign
River Taw
River Bovey
East Dart River
West Dart River
River Yeo
SX
7
8
9
10
11
14
25
26
A
B
C
D
E
F
G
H
80
70

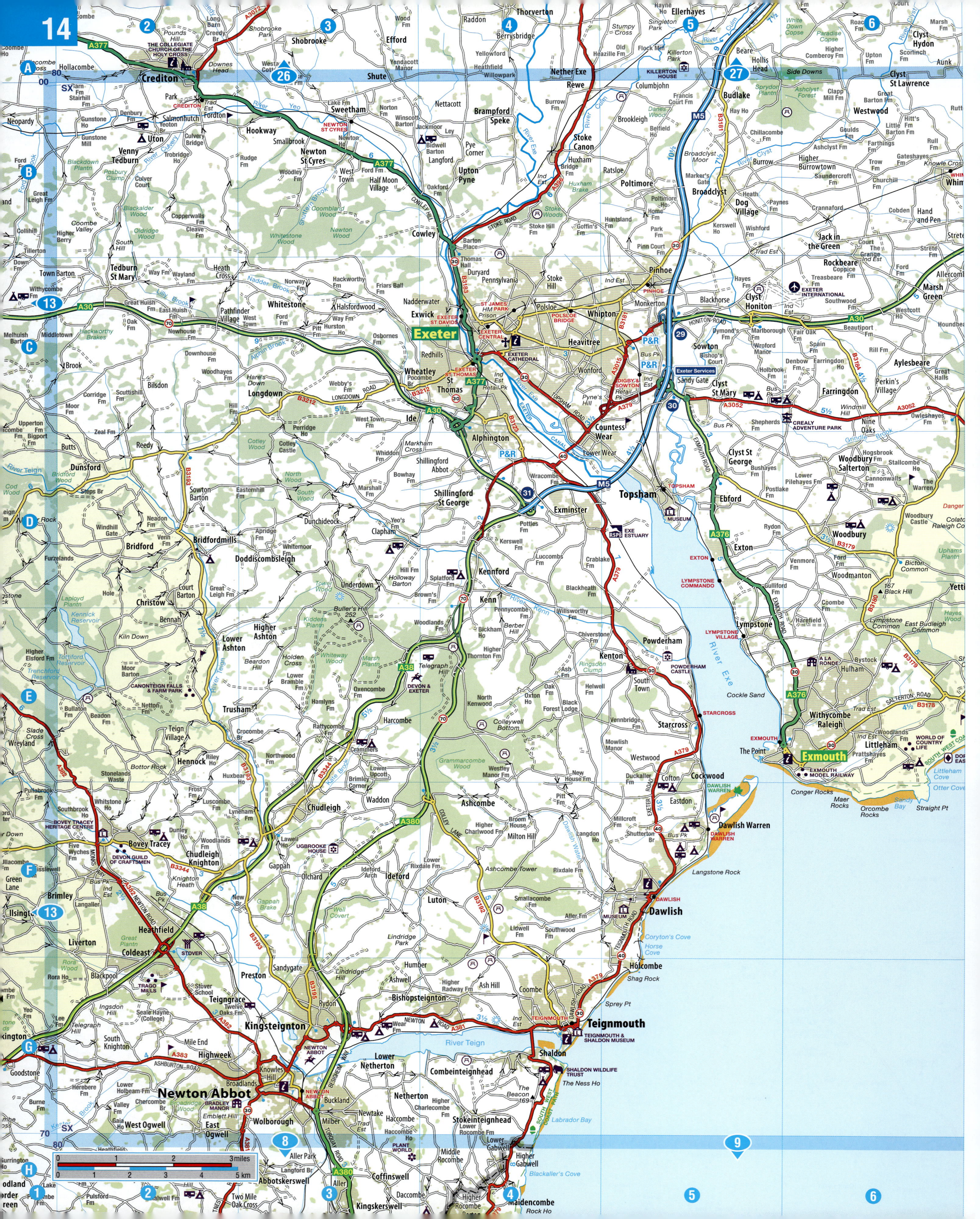
Crediton
Shobrooke
Thorverton
Nether Exe
Rewe
Sweetham
Newton St Cyres
Brampford Speke
Stoke Canon
Upton Pyne
Cowley
Budlake
St Lawrence
Westwood
Broadclyst
Dog Village
Poltimore
Pinhoe
Jack in the Green
Rockbeare
Marsh Green
Clyst Honiton
Exeter International
Whiteshill
Whitestone
Pathfinder Village
Exwick
Exeter
Heavitree
Whipton
Wonford
Sowton
Clyst St Mary
Sandy Gate
Farringdon
Aylesbeare
Redhills
Wheatley
St Thomas
Longdown
Ide
Alphington
Countess Wear
Topsham
Clyst St George
Woodbury Salterton
Woodbury
Dunsford
Bridford
Doddiscombsleigh
Shillingford St George
Exminster
Ebford
Exton
Kenford
Kenn
Christow
Lympstone
Exe Estuary
Powderham
Kenton
Lower Ashton
Higher Ashton
Trusham
Exmouth
Withycombe Raleigh
Littleham
Starcross
Cockwood
Dawlish Warren
Hennock
Chudleigh
Ashcombe
Bovey Tracey
Chudleigh Knighton
Ideford
Luton
Dawlish
Heathfield
Liverton
Coldeast
Teigngrace
Kingsteignton
Bishopsteignton
Holcombe
Teignmouth
Shaldon
Newton Abbot
Highweek
Combeinteignhead
Wolborough
Stokeinteignhead
East Ogwell
West Ogwell
Abbotskerswell
Coffinswell
Kingskerswell
Maidencombe
River Teign
River Exe
A377
A30
A38
A380
A376
A379
A3052
M5
0 1 2 3 miles
0 1 2 3 4 5 km

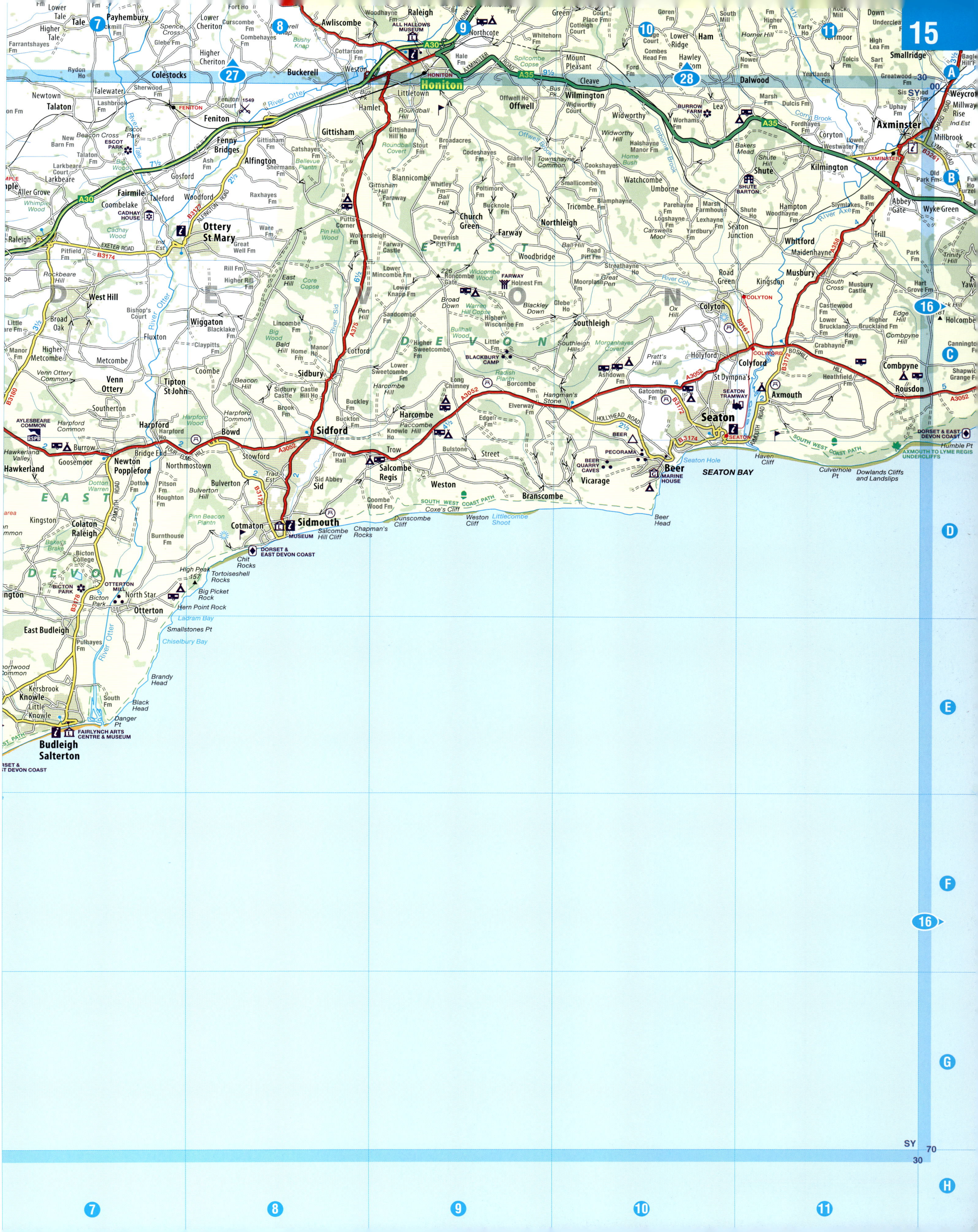

Honiton
Axminster
Ottery St Mary
Sidmouth
Sidford
Seaton
Beer
Budleigh Salterton
Colyton
Colyford
Axmouth
Feniton
Fenny Bridges
Alfington
Gittisham
Offwell
Wilmington
Widworthy
Dalwood
Shute
Kilmington
Whitford
Musbury
Rousdon
Combpyne
Northleigh
Farway
Southleigh
Branscombe
Salcombe Regis
Weston
Harcombe
Sidbury
Cotford
Tipton St John
Venn Ottery
Harpford
Newton Poppleford
Bowd
Stowford
Cotmaton
Colaton Raleigh
Otterton
North Star
East Budleigh
Knowle
Little Knowle
Kersbrook
West Hill
Wiggaton
Fluxton
Metcombe
Fairmile
Talaton
Colestocks
Buckerell
Awliscombe
Payhembury
Raleigh
Northcote
Littletown
Hamlet
Church Green
Woodbridge
Vicarage
Street
Trow
Seaton Junction
Axminster
Wyke Green
Abbey Gate
Smallridge
Holcombe
A30
A35
A375
A3052
A358
B3174
B3176
B3178
B3180
B3161
B3172
B3261
SEATON BAY
River Otter
River Sid
River Coly
River Axe
Umborne Brook
Offwell Brook
E A S T   D E V O N
SOUTH WEST COAST PATH
DORSET & EAST DEVON COAST
SEATON TRAMWAY
PECORAMA
BEER QUARRY CAVES
MARINE HOUSE
BLACKBURY CAMP
FARWAY
CADHAY HOUSE
ESCOT PARK
BICTON PARK
OTTERTON MILL
FAIRLYNCH ARTS CENTRE & MUSEUM
ALL HALLOWS MUSEUM
SHUTE BARTON
BURROW FARM
AYLESBEARE COMMON
Seaton Hole
Beer Head
Haven Cliff
Culverhole Pt
Dowlands Cliffs and Landslips
Humble Pt
AXMOUTH TO LYME REGIS UNDERCLIFFS
Weston Cliff
Littlecombe Shoot
Dunscombe Cliff
Salcombe Hill Cliff
Chapman's Rocks
Chit Rocks
High Peak
Tortoiseshell Rocks
Big Picket Rock
Hern Point Rock
Ladram Bay
Smallstones Pt
Chiselbury Bay
Brandy Head
Black Head
Danger Pt
SY
70
30
27
28
16
7
8
9
10
11
A
B
C
D
E
F
G
H

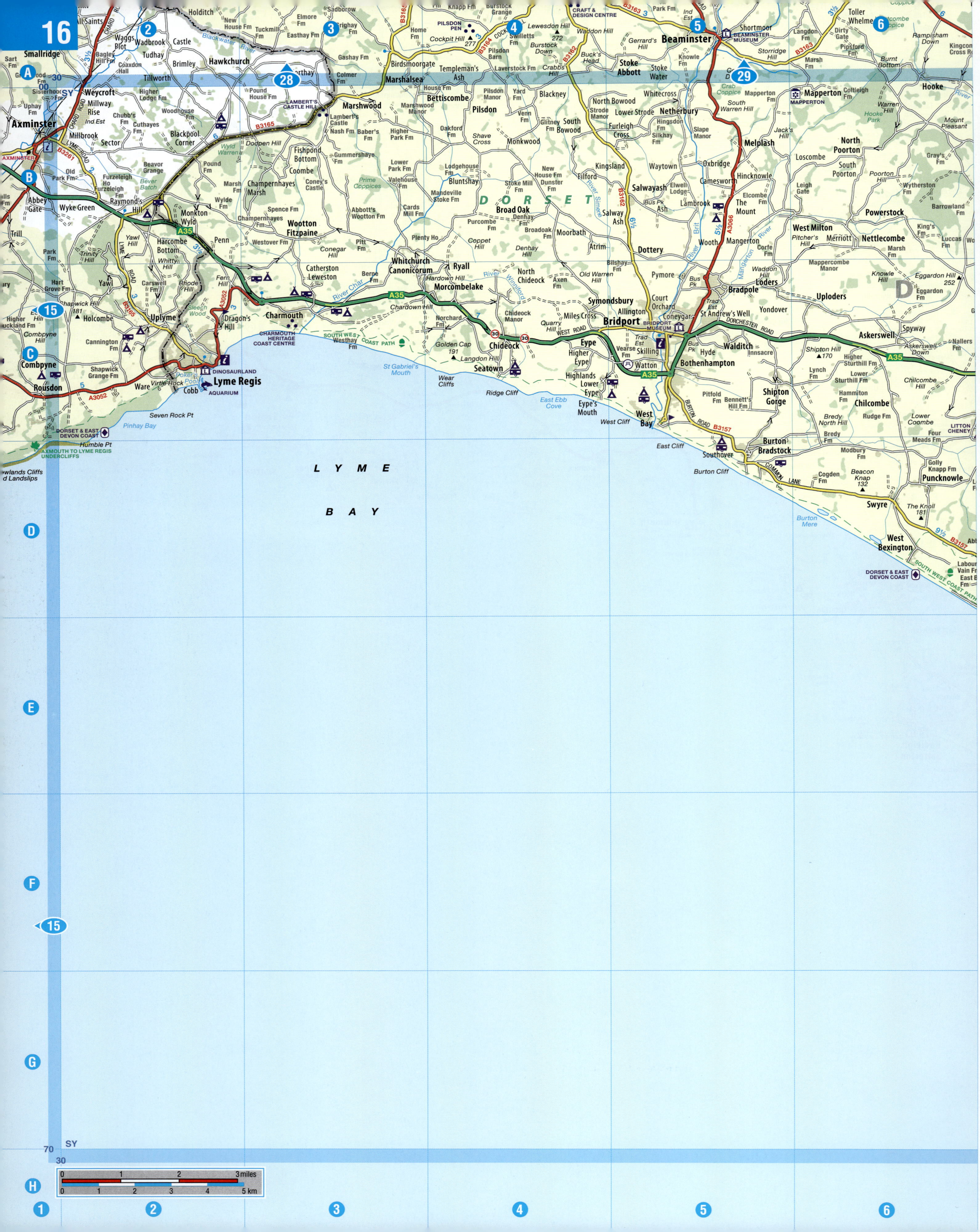
LYME BAY
DORSET
Axminster
Smallridge
Weycroft
Millbrook
Sector
Hawkchurch
Wadbrook
Tudhay
Brimley
Tillworth
Holditch
Marshwood
Birdsmoorgate
Marshalsea
Bettiscombe
Pilsdon
Blackney
Broadwindsor
Beaminster
Stoke Abbott
Netherbury
Melplash
Mapperton
Hooke
North Poorton
South Poorton
Powerstock
West Milton
Nettlecombe
Loders
Uploders
Askerswell
Salwayash
Dottery
Bradpole
Bridport
Symondsbury
Allington
Bothenhampton
Walditch
Shipton Gorge
Chilcombe
Burton Bradstock
Puncknowle
Swyre
West Bexington
West Bay
Eype
Chideock
Seatown
Morcombelake
Ryall
Whitchurch Canonicorum
Wootton Fitzpaine
Charmouth
Lyme Regis
Uplyme
Combpyne
Rousdon
Broad Oak
Monkwood
Kingsland
Waytown
Oxbridge
Camesworth
Lambrook
The Mount
Mangerton
Wooth
Pymore
Court Orchard
Coneygar
St Andrew's Well
Yondover
Spyway
Hyde
Innsacre
Wyke Green
Abbey Gate
Trill
Holcombe
Yawl
Harcombe Bottom
Penn
Monkton Wyld
Raymond's Hill
Dragon's Hill
Catherston Leweston
Fishpond Bottom
Coombe
Champernhayes Marsh
Golden Cap 191
Langdon Hill
Higher Eype
Lower Eype
Highlands
Eype's Mouth
Watton
Skilling
Ware
Cobb
Seven Rock Pt
Pinhay Bay
Humble Pt
DINOSAURLAND
AQUARIUM
CHARMOUTH HERITAGE COAST CENTRE
BRIDPORT MUSEUM
BEAMINSTER MUSEUM
MAPPERTON
PILSDON PEN
LAMBERT'S CASTLE HILL
DORSET & EAST DEVON COAST
AXMOUTH TO LYME REGIS UNDERCLIFFS
SOUTH WEST COAST PATH
St Gabriel's Mouth
Wear Cliffs
Ridge Cliff
East Ebb Cove
West Cliff
East Cliff
Burton Cliff
Burton Mere
Southover
Eggardon Hill 252
The Knoll 181
Shipton Hill 170
A35
A3052
A3066
B3157
B3162
B3163
B3164
B3165
B3261
SY
30
00
70
0 1 2 3 miles
0 1 2 3 4 5 km
A
B
C
D
E
F
G
H
1
2
3
4
5
6
15
28
29

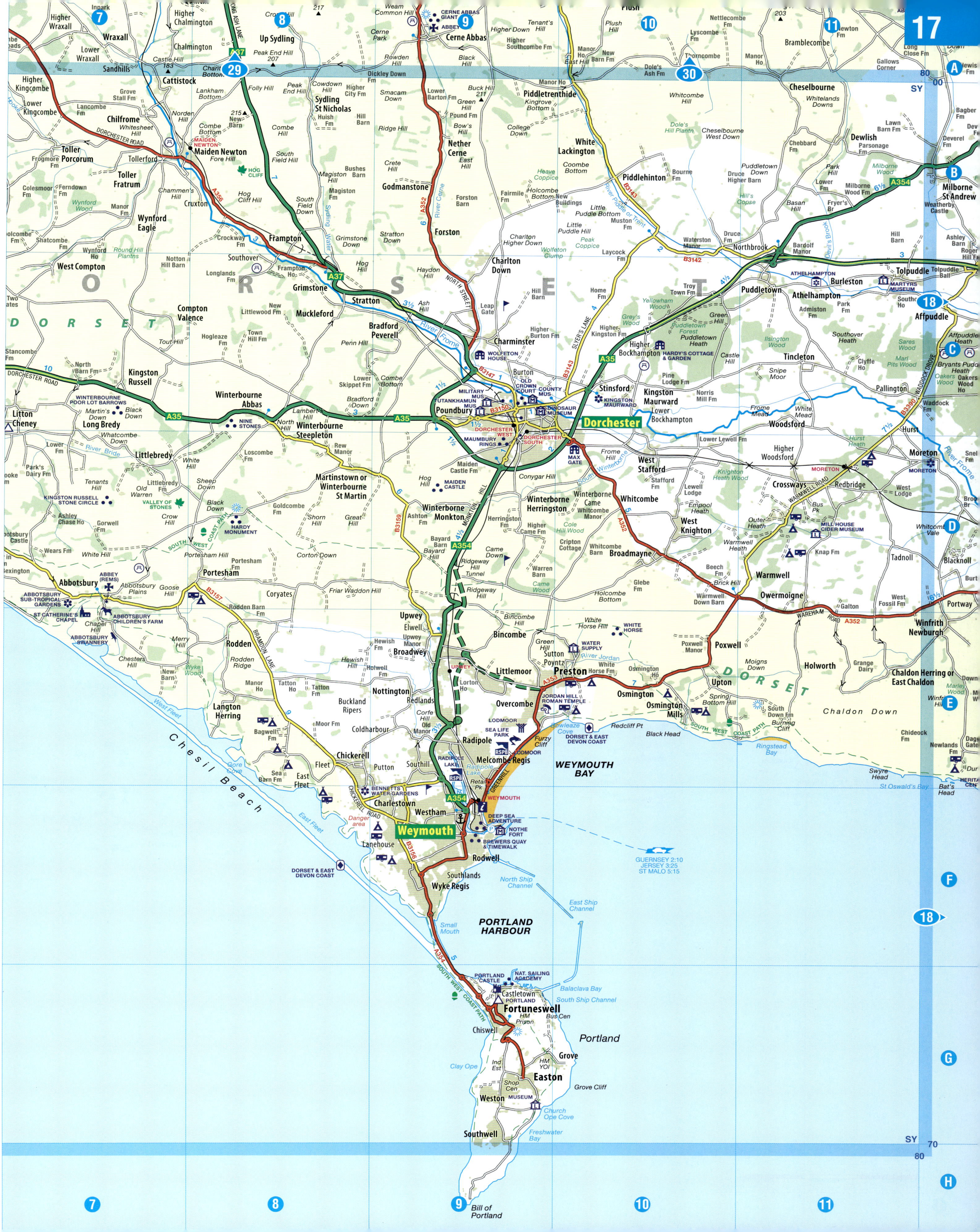
Higher Wraxall
Wraxall
Lower Wraxall
Sandhills
Higher Chalmington
Chalmington
Cattistock
Up Sydling
Cerne Abbas
Higher Kingcombe
Lower Kingcombe
Chilfrome
Toller Porcorum
Tollerford
Maiden Newton
Toller Fratrum
Wynford Eagle
Sydling St Nicholas
Nether Cerne
Godmanstone
Piddletrenthide
White Lackington
Piddlehinton
Cheselbourne
Dewlish
Milborne St Andrew
Frampton
West Compton
Forston
Charlton Down
Puddletown
Athelhampton
Tolpuddle
Burleston
Affpuddle
Compton Valence
Grimstone
Stratton
Muckleford
Bradford Peverell
Charminster
DORSET
Kingston Russell
Winterbourne Abbas
Winterbourne Steepleton
Poundbury
Dorchester
Stinsford
Kingston Maurward
Lower Bockhampton
Higher Bockhampton
Tincleton
Woodsford
Pallington
Litton Cheney
Long Bredy
Littlebredy
Martinstown or Winterbourne St Martin
West Stafford
Higher Woodsford
Crossways
Moreton
Redbridge
Winterborne Monkton
Winterborne Herringston
Whitcombe
West Knighton
Broadmayne
Warmwell
Owermoigne
Portesham
Abbotsbury
Coryates
Upwey
Bincombe
Broadwey
Littlemoor
Preston
Poxwell
Winfrith Newburgh
Rodden
Langton Herring
Nottington
Overcombe
Osmington
Osmington Mills
Upton
Holworth
Chaldon Herring or East Chaldon
Chaldon Down
Radipole
Chickerell
Fleet
East Fleet
Melcombe Regis
WEYMOUTH BAY
Charlestown
Westham
Weymouth
Rodwell
Southlands
Wyke Regis
Chesil Beach
PORTLAND HARBOUR
Castletown
Fortuneswell
Chiswell
Portland
Grove
Easton
Weston
Southwell
Bill of Portland
A37
A35
A354
A352
A353
B3157
B3159
B3143
B3142
B3390
GUERNSEY 2:10
JERSEY 3:25
ST MALO 5:15
SY

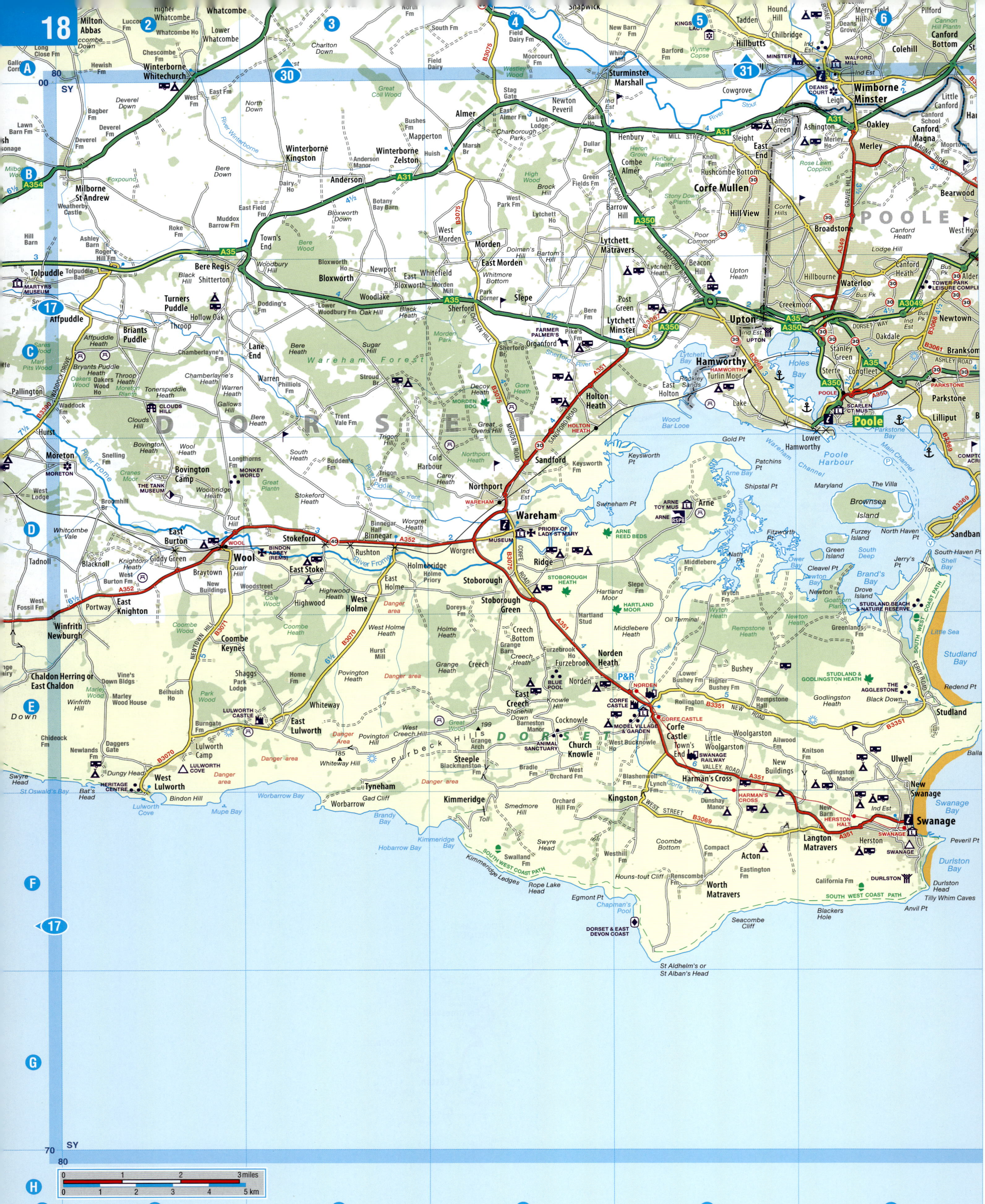
Milton Abbas
Higher Whatcombe
Whatcombe
Lower Whatcombe
Winterborne Whitechurch
Sturminster Marshall
Wimborne Minster
Colehill
Canford Bottom
Pilford
Hillbutts
Tadden
Chilbridge
Almer
Newton Peveril
Henbury
Corfe Mullen
Hill View
Broadstone
POOLE
Canford Magna
Merley
Oakley
Ashington
Lambs Green
Sleight
East End
Combe Almer
Winterborne Kingston
Winterborne Zelston
Anderson
Mapperton
Milborne St Andrew
Deverel Down
Bere Down
Muddox Barrow Fm
Town's End
Bere Regis
Shitterton
Tolpuddle
Martyrs Museum
Affpuddle
Briants Puddle
Turners Puddle
Hollow Oak
Throop
Bloxworth
Woodlake
Newport
Whitefield
East Bloxworth
Morden Mill
West Morden
Morden
East Morden
Slepe
Sherford
Lytchett Matravers
Lytchett Minster
Upton
Hamworthy
Turlin Moor
Holes Bay
Poole
Parkstone
Lilliput
Branksome
Newtown
Waterloo
Creekmoor
Oakdale
Stanley Green
Sterte
Longfleet
Canford Heath
Organford
Holton Heath
Sandford
Northport
Wareham
Wareham Forest
DORSET
Lane End
Warren
Pallington
Hurst
Moreton
Clouds Hill
Bovington Camp
The Tank Museum
Monkey World
Woolbridge Heath
Stokeford
East Burton
Wool
Bindon Abbey
East Stoke
Binnegar
Worgret
Rushton
Holmebridge
Stoborough
Stoborough Green
Ridge
Priory of Lady St Mary
Arne
Arne Reed Beds
Poole Harbour
Brownsea Island
Furzey Island
Green Island
Long Island
Round Island
Hamworthy
Lower Hamworthy
Sandbanks
South Haven Pt
Studland Bay
Studland
Little Sea
Shell Bay
Redend Pt
Winfrith Newburgh
Chaldon Herring or East Chaldon
East Knighton
Portway
West Holme
East Holme
Highwood
Coombe Keynes
Whiteway
East Lulworth
West Lulworth
Lulworth Camp
Lulworth Castle
Lulworth Cove
Durdle Door
Bat's Head
Bindon Hill
Mupe Bay
Worbarrow Bay
Worbarrow
Tyneham
Steeple
Kimmeridge
Kimmeridge Bay
Kimmeridge Ledges
Purbeck Hills
Creech
East Creech
Furzebrook
Blue Pool
Norden
Norden Heath
Corfe Castle
Church Knowle
Cocknowle
Kingston
Harman's Cross
Woolgarston
Langton Matravers
Worth Matravers
Acton
Herston
Swanage
Swanage Bay
Ulwell
New Swanage
Peveril Pt
Durlston Bay
Durlston Head
Durlston
Anvil Pt
Tilly Whim Caves
Seacombe Cliff
Winspit
Chapman's Pool
Egmont Pt
Houns-tout Cliff
St Aldhelm's or St Alban's Head
Swyre Head
Smedmore Hill
Godlington Manor
Rempstone Hall
Goathorn Plantation
Newton
Middlebere
Wych
Keysworth Pt
Patchins Pt
Shipstal Pt
Fitzworth Pt
Cleavel Pt
Studland Beach & Nature Reserve
South West Coast Path
Blackers Hole
California Fm
Dorset & East Devon Coast
Swanage Railway
Model Village & Garden
SY
80
00
70
0 1 2 3 miles
0 1 2 3 4 5 km

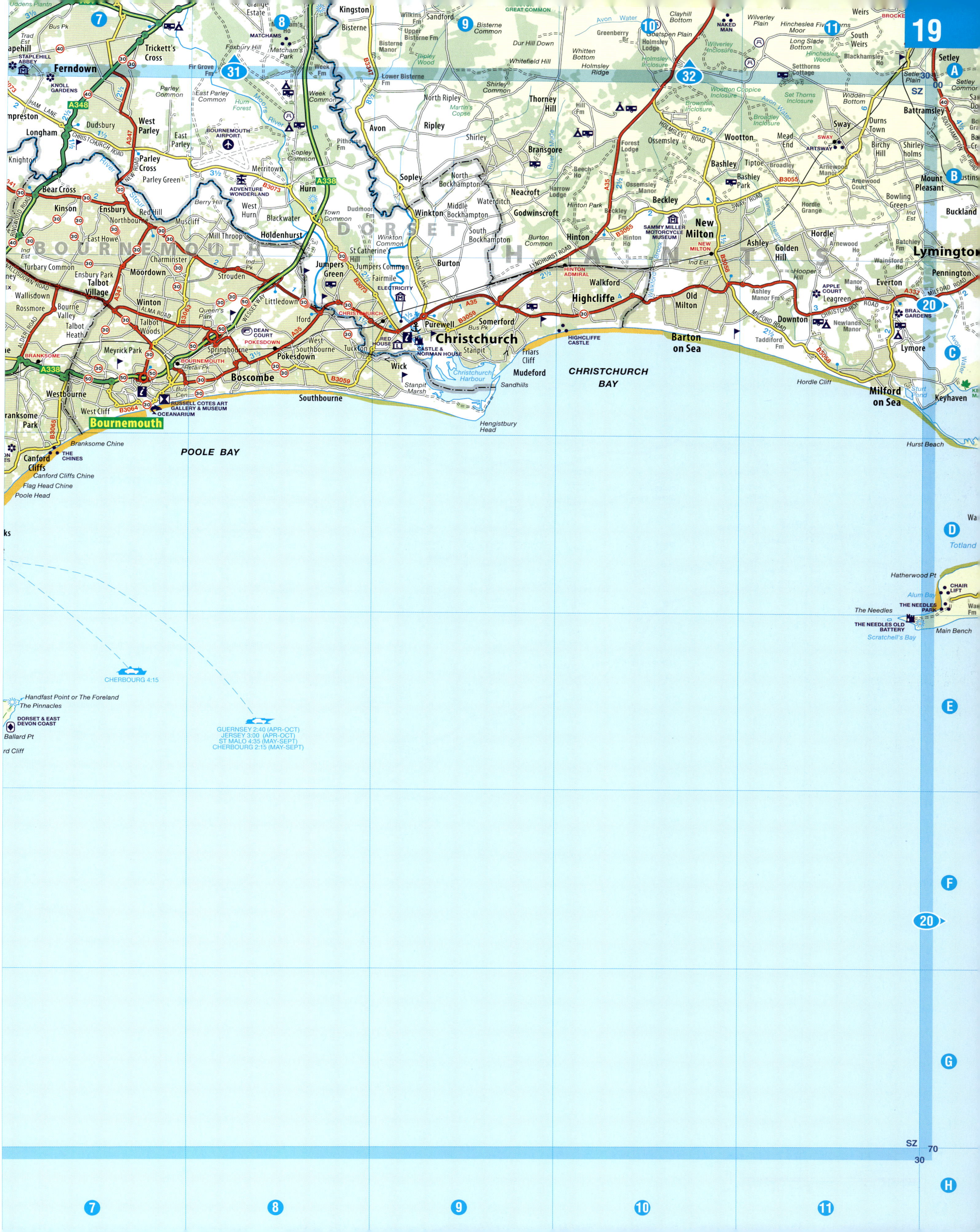
Ferndown
Trickett's Cross
West Parley
Parley Cross
Parley Green
Longham
Dudsbury
Bear Cross
Kinson
Ensbury
Northbourne
East Howe
Turbary Common
Ensbury Park
Talbot Village
Wallisdown
Rossmore
Bourne Valley
Talbot Heath
Winton
Moordown
Charminster
Strouden
Muscliff
Red Hill
Mill Throop
Holdenhurst
Queen's Park
Littledown
Iford
Springbourne
Meyrick Park
Westbourne
West Cliff
Branksome Park
Bournemouth
Boscombe
Pokesdown
West Southbourne
Southbourne
Tuckton
Wick
Christchurch
Purewell
Stanpit
Somerford
Jumpers Green
Jumpers Common
St Catherine's Hill
Fairmile
Burton
Winkton
Sopley
Avon
Ripley
North Ripley
Bisterne
Kingston
Sandford
Bisterne Common
Hurn
Merritown
East Parley Common
Parley Common
East Parley
BOURNEMOUTH AIRPORT
ADVENTURE WONDERLAND
West Hurn
Blackwater
Town Common
North Bockhampton
Middle Bockhampton
South Bockhampton
Waterditch
Neacroft
Godwinscroft
Bransgore
Thorney Hill
Shirley
Hinton
Hinton Park
Burton Common
Beckley
Ossemsley
Forest Lodge
New Milton
Ashley
Wootton
Bashley
Bashley Park
Tiptoe
Sway
Golden Hill
Hordle
Everton
Downton
Lymington
Pennington
Lymore
Keyhaven
Milford on Sea
Old Milton
Barton on Sea
Walkford
Highcliffe
HIGHCLIFFE CASTLE
Friars Cliff
Mudeford
Sandhills
Christchurch Harbour
Stanpit Marsh
Hengistbury Head
CHRISTCHURCH BAY
POOLE BAY
Hordle Cliff
Hurst Beach
Canford Cliffs
Branksome Chine
THE CHINES
Canford Cliffs Chine
Flag Head Chine
Poole Head
RUSSELL COTES ART GALLERY & MUSEUM
OCEANARIUM
DEAN COURT
POKESDOWN
CASTLE & NORMAN HOUSE
RED HOUSE
SAMMY MILLER MOTORCYCLE MUSEUM
HINTON ADMIRAL
NEW MILTON
APPLE COURT
Leagreen
Newlands Manor
Taddiford Fm
Battramsley
Setley
Mount Pleasant
Buckland
Durns Town
Birchy Hill
Shirley holms
Bowling Green
Arnewood Court
DORSET
HANTS
BOURNEMOUTH
Totland
Hatherwood Pt
Alum Bay
THE NEEDLES PARK
CHAIR LIFT
The Needles
THE NEEDLES OLD BATTERY
Scratchell's Bay
Main Bench
CHERBOURG 4:15
GUERNSEY 2:40 (APR-OCT)
JERSEY 3:00 (APR-OCT)
ST MALO 4:35 (MAY-SEPT)
CHERBOURG 2:15 (MAY-SEPT)
Handfast Point or The Foreland
The Pinnacles
DORSET & EAST DEVON COAST
Ballard Pt
A338
A348
A347
A35
A337
B3073
B3064
B3065
B3059
B3347
B3055
B3058
31
32
20
SZ
7
8
9
10
11
A
B
C
D
E
F
G
H

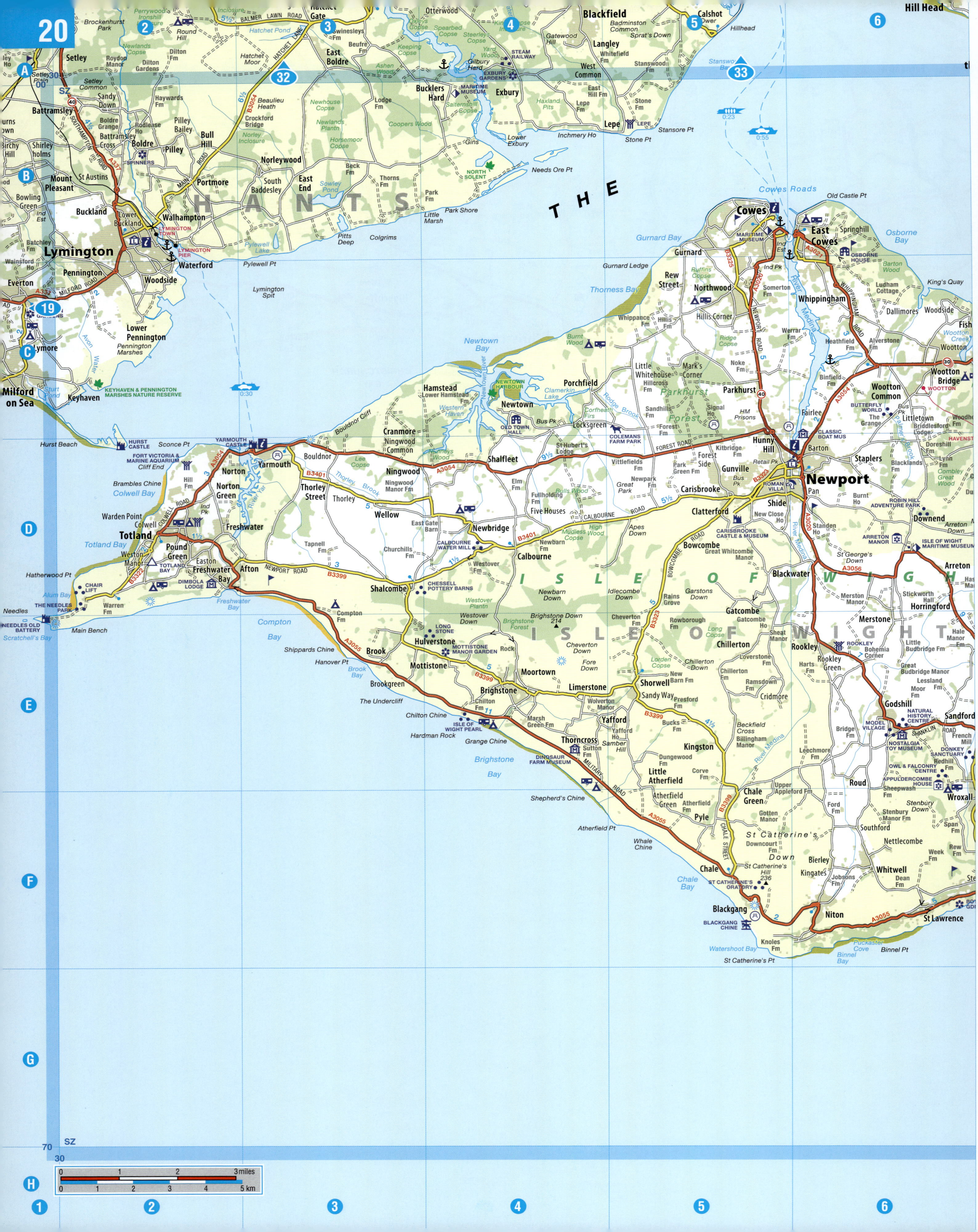

THE
HANTS
ISLE OF WIGHT
Lymington
Pennington
Woodside
Walhampton
Buckland
Lower Buckland
Waterford
Everton
Milford on Sea
Keyhaven
Lower Pennington
Pennington Marshes
Lymore
Setley
Battramsley
Boldre
Pilley
Bull Hill
Portmore
Norleywood
South Baddesley
East End
East Boldre
Beaulieu Heath
Bucklers Hard
Exbury
Lepe
Blackfield
Langley
Calshot
West Common
Hatchet Moor
Hatchet Gate
Mount Pleasant
St Austins
Bowling Green
Hurst Beach
Hurst Castle
Yarmouth
Yarmouth Castle
Norton
Norton Green
Totland
Totland Bay
Colwell Bay
Warden Point
Colwell
Freshwater
Freshwater Bay
Pound Green
Easton
Afton
Weston Manor
The Needles Park
Needles
Needles Old Battery
Scratchell's Bay
Alum Bay
Main Bench
Compton Bay
Compton Fm
Brook
Brook Bay
Hulverstone
Mottistone
Brookgreen
Brighstone
Brighstone Bay
Brighstone Down
Brighstone Forest
Shalcombe
Wellow
Thorley
Thorley Street
Bouldnor
Shalfleet
Ningwood
Ningwood Common
Cranmore
Hamstead
Newtown
Newtown Bay
Porchfield
Locksgreen
Calbourne
Newbridge
Five Houses
Moortown
Limerstone
Shorwell
Yafford
Kingston
Little Atherfield
Atherfield Green
Atherfield Pt
Pyle
Chale
Chale Green
Chale Bay
Blackgang
Blackgang Chine
Niton
St Lawrence
St Catherine's Pt
St Catherine's Down
Whitwell
Kingates
Cowes
East Cowes
Cowes Roads
Gurnard
Gurnard Bay
Rew Street
Northwood
Hillis Corner
Thorness Bay
Parkhurst
Parkhurst Forest
Whippingham
Osborne Bay
Osborne House
Wootton Bridge
Wootton Common
Fairlee
Newport
Carisbrooke
Carisbrooke Castle & Museum
Gunville
Hunny Hill
Shide
Clatterford
Bowcombe
Blackwater
Gatcombe
Chillerton
Rookley
Rookley Green
Arreton
Downend
Merstone
Horringford
Godshill
Sandford
Roud
Wroxall
Southford
Whitwell
Nettlecombe
Binnel Pt
Warren Fm
Shepherd's Chine
Whale Chine
Grange Chine
Chilton Chine
Hanover Pt
Shippards Chine
Hill Head
SZ
30
70
0 1 2 3 miles
0 1 2 3 4 5 km
A B C D E F G H
1 2 3 4 5 6

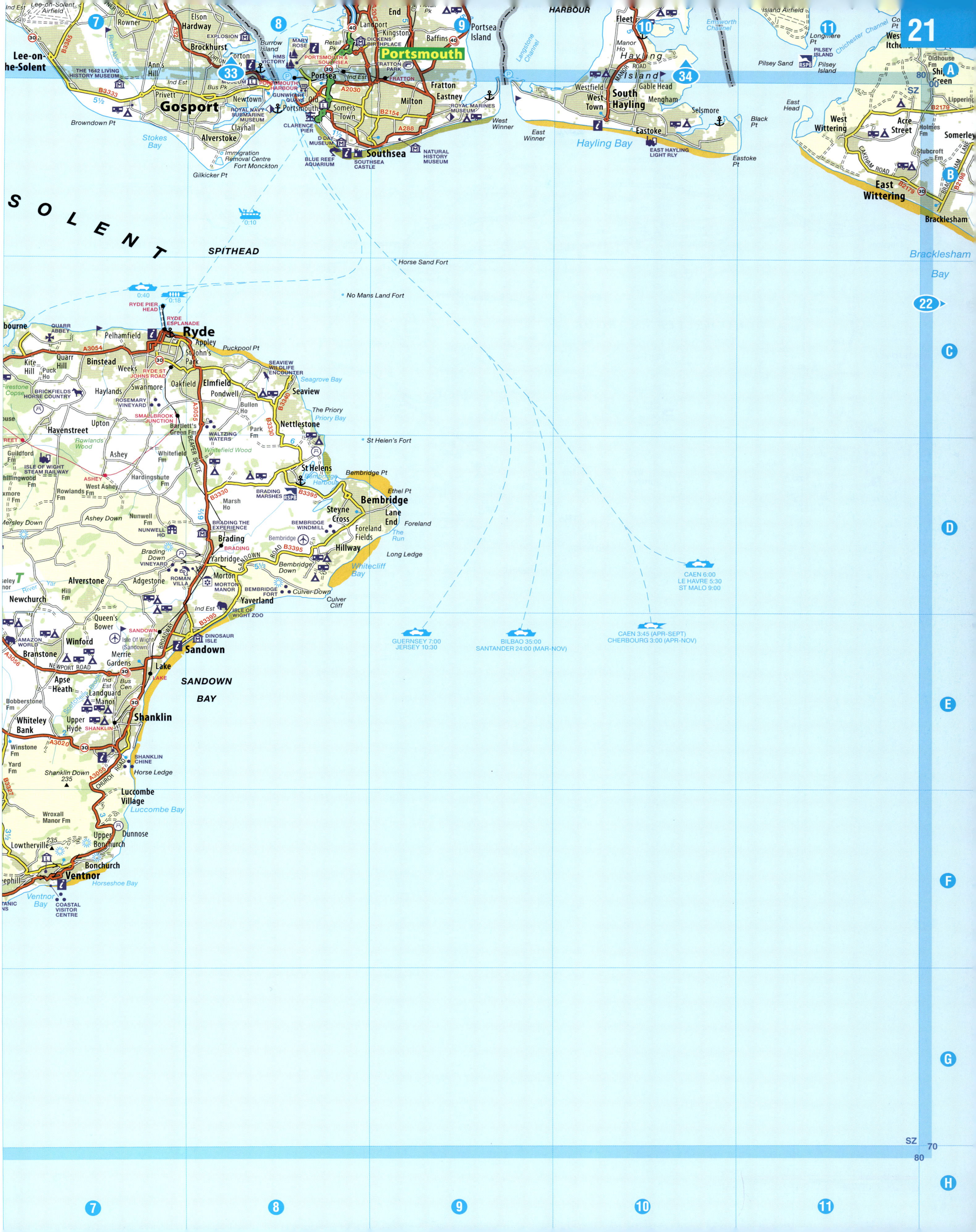
Lee-on-the-Solent
Rowner
Elson
Hardway
Brockhurst
Gosport
Alverstoke
Privett
Clayhall
Browndown Pt
Stokes Bay
Gilkicker Pt
Fort Monckton
Burrow Island
Portsmouth
Landport
Kingston
Portsea
Fratton
Milton
Eastney
Southsea
Somers Town
Baffins
Portsea Island
SOUTHSEA CASTLE
BLUE REEF AQUARIUM
D DAY MUSEUM
ROYAL MARINES MUSEUM
NATURAL HISTORY MUSEUM
ROYAL NAVY SUBMARINE MUSEUM
THE 1642 LIVING HISTORY MUSEUM
EXPLOSION
HARBOUR
Langstone Channel
Fleet
Manor Ho
Hayling Island
Westfield
West Town
South Hayling
Gable Head
Mengham
Eastoke
Selsmore
Hayling Bay
West Winner
East Winner
Black Pt
Eastoke Pt
EAST HAYLING LIGHT RLY
Emsworth Channel
Chichester Channel
Longmere Pt
Pilsey Sand
Pilsey Island
PILSEY ISLAND
East Head
West Wittering
Acre Street
Somerley
Lipperin
Stubcroft Fm
East Wittering
Bracklesham
Bracklesham Bay
SOLENT
SPITHEAD
Horse Sand Fort
No Mans Land Fort
St Helen's Fort
RYDE PIER HEAD
RYDE ESPLANADE
Ryde
Appley
St John's Park
Pelhamfield
Puckpool Pt
QUARR ABBEY
Quarr Hill
Binstead
Kite Hill
Puck Ho
Weeks
Swanmore
Haylands
Oakfield
Elmfield
Pondwell
Seaview
Seagrove Bay
SEAVIEW WILDLIFE ENCOUNTER
The Priory
Priory Bay
Nettlestone
Bullen Ho
Park Fm
Havenstreet
Upton
Ashey
Whitefield Fm
Whitefield Wood
Rowlands Wood
WALTZING WATERS
ROSEMARY VINEYARD
SMALLBROOK JUNCTION
Bartlett's Green Fm
ISLE OF WIGHT STEAM RAILWAY
Guildford Fm
Hardingshute Fm
West Ashey
Rowlands Fm
St Helens
Bembridge Harbour
Bembridge Pt
Ethel Pt
Bembridge
Lane End
Foreland
Steyne Cross
Foreland Fields
BEMBRIDGE WINDMILL
BRADING MARSHES
Marsh Ho
Nunwell Fm
NUNWELL HO
Ashey Down
BRADING THE EXPERIENCE
Brading
Brading Down
BRADING DOWN VINEYARD
Hillway
The Run
Long Ledge
Whitecliff Bay
Bembridge Down
Culver Down
Culver Cliff
Yarbridge
Morton
MORTON MANOR
ROMAN VILLA
BEMBRIDGE FORT
Yaverland
ISLE OF WIGHT ZOO
Alverstone
Adgestone
Newchurch
Hill Fm
Queen's Bower
Winford
Branstone
Merrie Gardens
Isle Of Wight (Sandown)
DINOSAUR ISLE
Sandown
SANDOWN BAY
Lake
Apse Heath
Landguard Manor
Bobberstone Fm
Whiteley Bank
Upper Hyde
Shanklin
SHANKLIN CHINE
Horse Ledge
Winstone Fm
Yard Fm
Shanklin Down 235
Luccombe Village
Luccombe Bay
Wroxall Manor Fm
Dunnose
Upper Bonchurch
Lowtherville
Bonchurch
Ventnor
Ventnor Bay
Horseshoe Bay
COASTAL VISITOR CENTRE
CAEN 6:00
LE HAVRE 5:30
ST MALO 9:00
GUERNSEY 7:00
JERSEY 10:30
BILBAO 35:00
SANTANDER 24:00 (MAR-NOV)
CAEN 3:45 (APR-SEPT)
CHERBOURG 3:00 (APR-NOV)
0:10
0:40
0:18
SZ
7
8
9
10
11
A
B
C
D
E
F
G
H
22

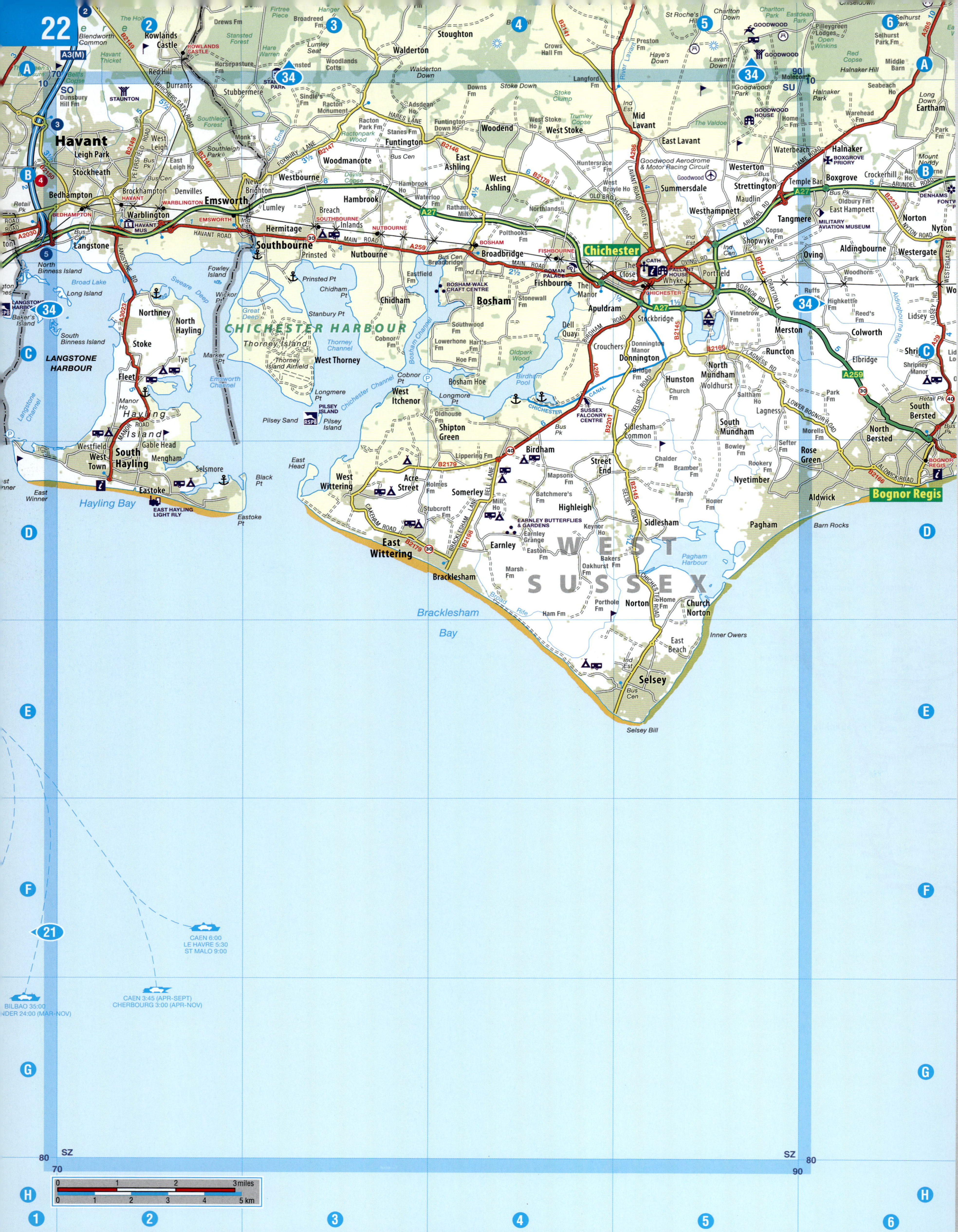
Havant
Leigh Park
Stockheath
Bedhampton
Warblington
Emsworth
Langstone
Rowlands Castle
Westbourne
Southbourne
Hermitage
Nutbourne
Woodmancote
Hambrook
Funtington
East Ashling
West Ashling
West Stoke
Woodend
Walderton
Stoughton
Mid Lavant
East Lavant
Summersdale
Westhampnett
Chichester
Fishbourne
Broadbridge
Bosham
Chidham
Apuldram
Stockbridge
Donnington
Hunston
North Mundham
Woldhurst
South Mundham
Sidlesham
Sidlesham Common
Street End
Birdham
Highleigh
Earnley
Somerley
Acre Street
West Wittering
East Wittering
Bracklesham
West Itchenor
Shipton Green
Bosham Hoe
West Thorney
Thorney Island
Northney
North Hayling
Stoke
Fleet
Hayling Island
South Hayling
West Town
Eastoke
Mengham
Selsmore
Hayling Bay
CHICHESTER HARBOUR
LANGSTONE HARBOUR
Brackesham Bay
Selsey
Selsey Bill
Church Norton
Norton
Pagham
Pagham Harbour
Nyetimber
Rose Green
Aldwick
Bognor Regis
North Bersted
South Bersted
Runcton
Merston
Colworth
Oving
Tangmere
Boxgrove
Halnaker
Westerton
Strettington
Aldingbourne
Westergate
Eartham
WEST SUSSEX
Goodwood Aerodrome & Motor Racing Circuit
CAEN 6:00
LE HAVRE 5:30
ST MALO 9:00
CAEN 3:45 (APR-SEPT)
CHERBOURG 3:00 (APR-NOV)
BILBAO 35:00
0 1 2 3 miles
0 1 2 3 4 5 km

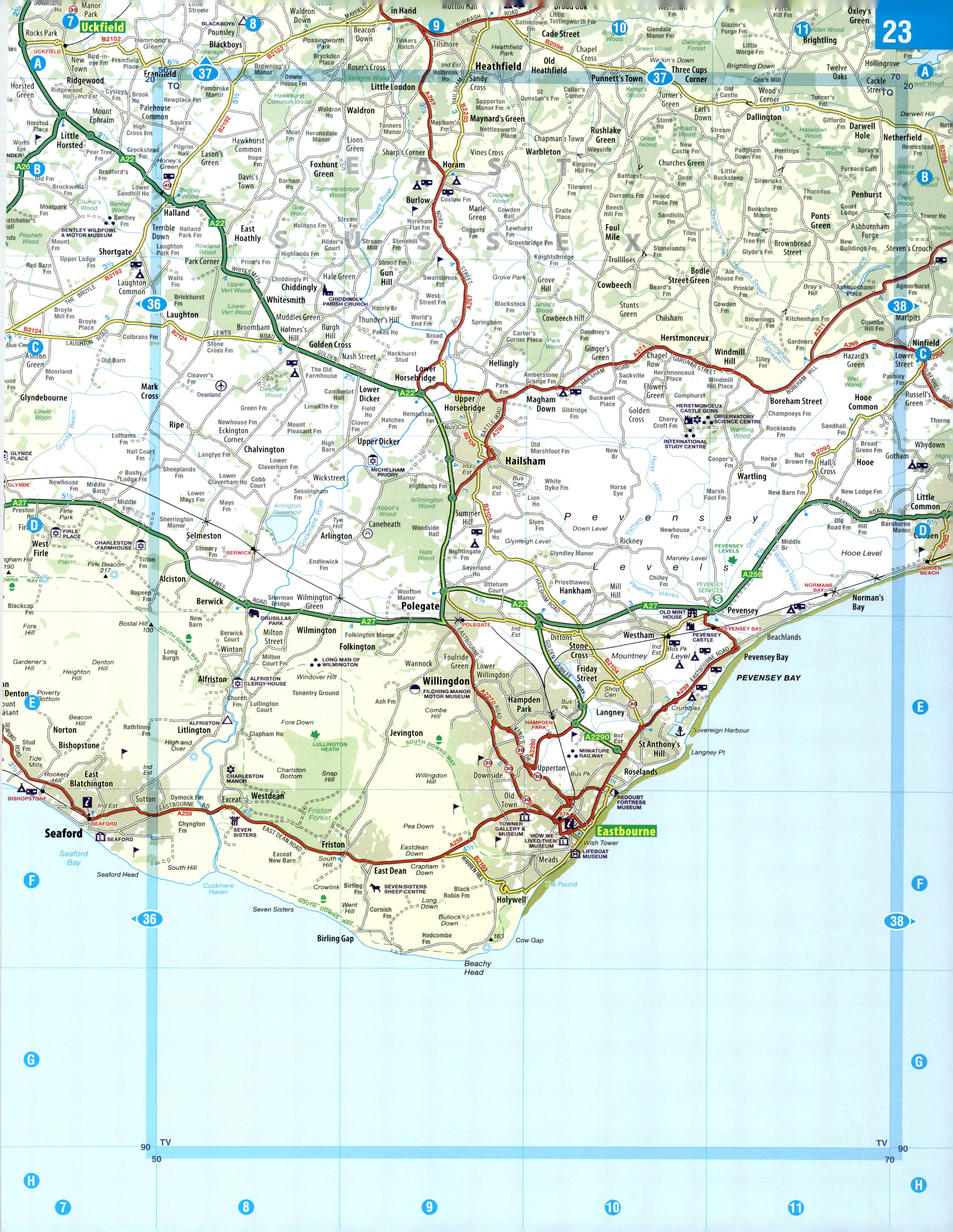
Uckfield
Manor Park
Rocks Park
New Town
Ridgewood
Horsted Green
Little Horsted
Framfield
Blackboys
Pounsley
Hammond's Green
Palehouse Common
Halland
Terrible Down
Shortgate
Laughton Common
Laughton
East Hoathly
Park Corner
Whitesmith
Chiddingly
Muddles Green
Holmes's Hill
Golden Cross
Broomham
Nash Street
Lower Horsebridge
Upper Horsebridge
Lower Dicker
Upper Dicker
Hellingly
Hailsham
Magham Down
Herstmonceux
Windmill Hill
Boreham Street
Wartling
Hooe
Hooe Common
Ninfield
Cowbeech
Stunts Green
Bodle Street Green
Foul Mile
Trolliloes
Rushlake Green
Warbleton
Heathfield
Old Heathfield
Punnett's Town
Three Cups Corner
Dallington
Darwell Hole
Netherfield
Penhurst
Brightling
Burlow
Horam
Vines Cross
Maynard's Green
Waldron
Little London
Foxhunt Green
Chalvington
Ripe
Mark Cross
Glyndebourne
Selmeston
Berwick
Alciston
West Firle
Wilmington
Polegate
Folkington
Willingdon
Jevington
Alfriston
Litlington
Westdean
Friston
East Dean
Seaford
Bishopstone
East Blatchington
Norton
Sutton
Exceat
Seaford Bay
Seaford Head
Cuckmere Haven
Seven Sisters
Birling Gap
Beachy Head
Cow Gap
Holywell
Meads
Eastbourne
Upperton
Roselands
Langney
Hampden Park
Stone Cross
Westham
Pevensey
Pevensey Bay
PEVENSEY BAY
Normans Bay
Norman's Bay
Langney Pt
Sovereign Harbour
St Anthony's Hill
Pevensey Levels
Hooe Level
Arlington
Caneheath
Hankham
Rickney
Cooden
Little Common
EAST SUSSEX
A22
A27
A259
A267
A271
A2290
A2270
A2280
A2021
B2104
B2102
B2192
B2124
B2095
B2096
B2103
36
37
38
A
B
C
D
E
F
G
H
7
8
9
10
11
TQ
TV
50
70
20
90

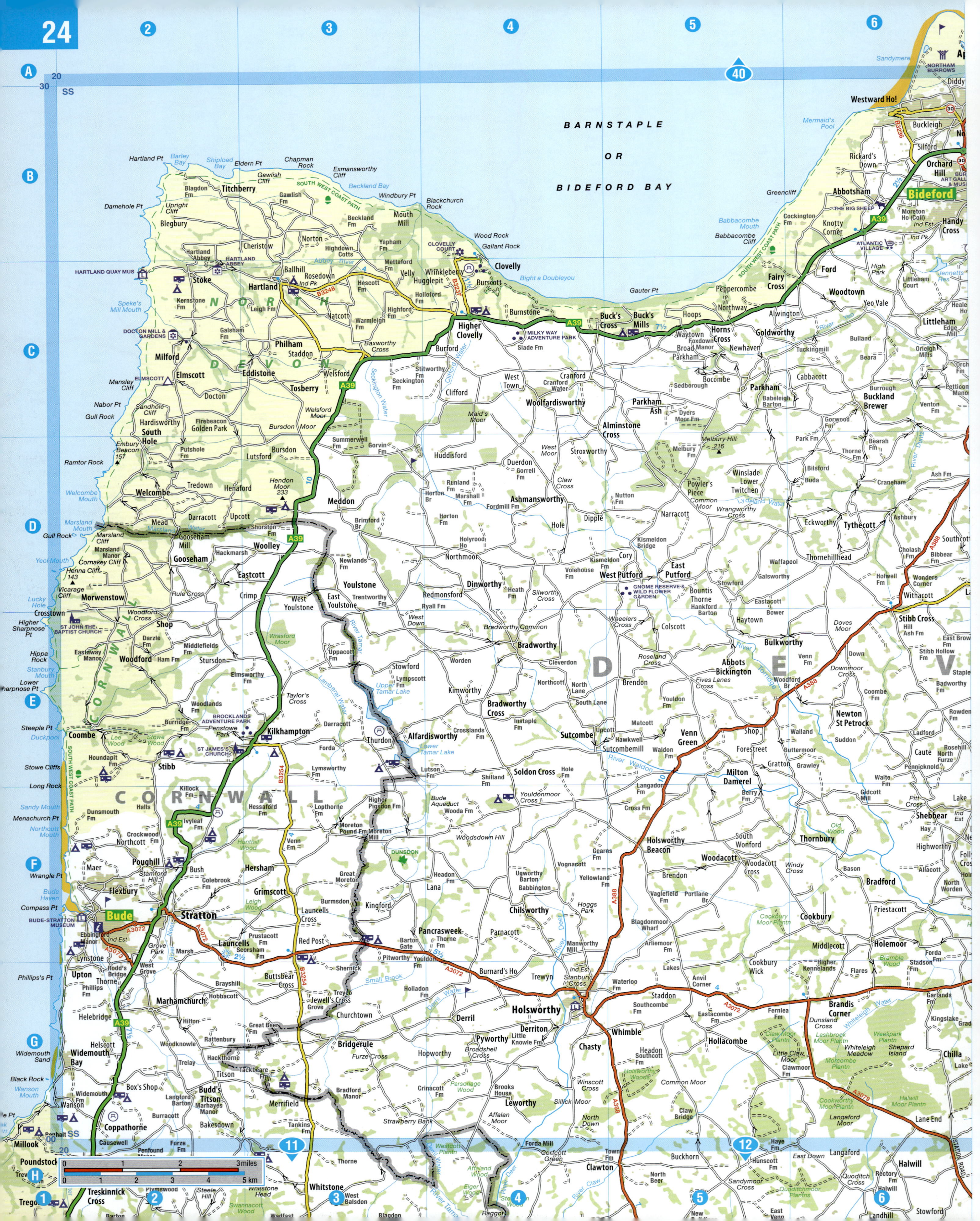

BARNSTAPLE
OR
BIDEFORD BAY
40
Westward Ho!
Northam Burrows
Bideford
Abbotsham
Orchard Hill
Handy Cross
Hartland Pt
Barley Bay
Shipload Bay
Eldern Pt
Chapman Rock
Exmansworthy Cliff
Beckland Bay
Windbury Pt
Blackchurch Rock
Titchberry
Blagdon
Damehole Pt
Blegbury
Hartland Quay Mus
Stoke
Hartland
Hartland Abbey
Cheristow
Norton
Beckland
Mouth Mill
Clovelly
Clovelly Court
Wood Rock
Gallant Rock
Bight a Doubleyou
Hugglepit
Burscott
Higher Clovelly
Burnstone
Buck's Cross
Buck's Mills
Gauter Pt
Peppercombe
Northway
Hoops
Horns Cross
Fairy Cross
Ford
Woodtown
Yeo Vale
Littleham
Goldworthy
Alwington
Parkham
Buckland Brewer
Milky Way Adventure Park
Slade Fm
Welsford
Tosberry
Philham
Eddistone
Elmscott
Milford
NORTH DEVON
South Hole
Hardisworthy
Welcombe
Mead
Darracott
Upcott
Gooseham
Woolley
Eastcott
Morwenstow
Crimp
West Youlstone
Youlstone
Shop
Woodford
Coombe
Kilkhampton
Stibb
CORNWALL
Poughill
Flexbury
Bude
Stratton
Launcells
Marhamchurch
Widemouth Bay
Upton
Coppathorne
Millook
Poundstock
Treskinnick Cross
Whitstone
Meddon
Clifford
Woolfardisworthy
Alminstone Cross
Parkham Ash
Huddisford
Ashmansworthy
Duerdon
Dipple
Narracott
East Putford
West Putford
Dinworthy
Bradworthy
Bradworthy Cross
Alfardisworthy
Sutcombe
Sutcombemill
Venn Green
Milton Damerel
Abbots Bickington
Bulkworthy
Newton St Petrock
Thornbury
Holsworthy Beacon
Woodacott
Bradford
Cookbury
Holemoor
Brandis Corner
Hollacombe
Holsworthy
Derril
Pyworthy
Chasty
Whimble
Pancrasweek
Chilsworthy
Bridgerule
Clawton
Staddon
Kingsford
Grimscott
Hersham
Thurdon
Soldon Cross
Lower Tamar Lake
Upper Tamar Lake
Stibb Cross
Withacott
Tythecott
Milford
Haytown
Forestreet
Shebbear
Halwill
Stowford
Langaford
Lane End
Chilla
11
12
3 miles
5 km

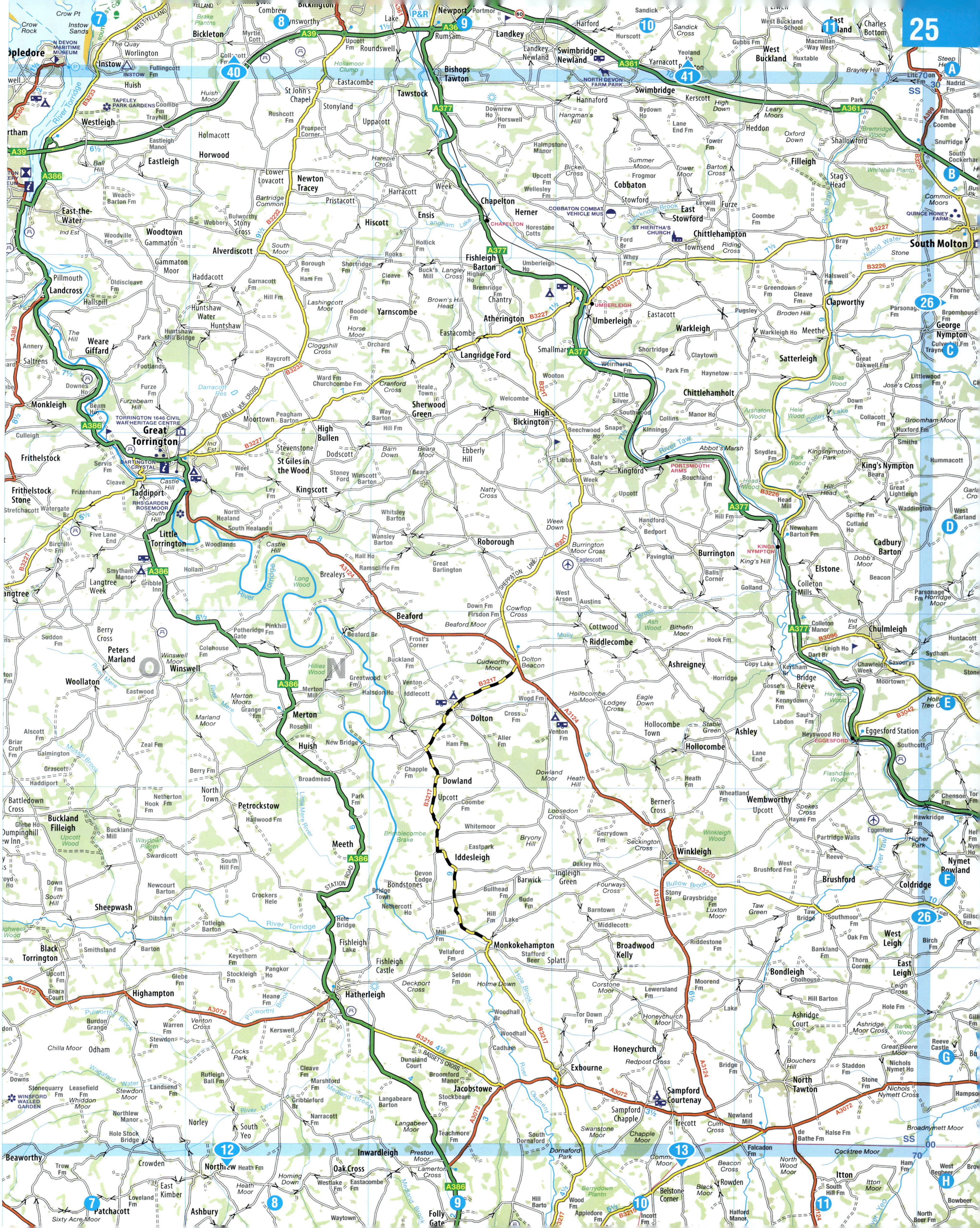
Appledore
Instow
Westleigh
Eastleigh
East-the-Water
Bideford
Woodtown
Alverdiscott
Landcross
Weare Giffard
Monkleigh
Great Torrington
Taddiport
Little Torrington
Frithelstock
Frithelstock Stone
Langtree
Peters Marland
Winswell
Woollaton
Merton
Huish
Petrockstowe
Buckland Filleigh
Sheepwash
Meeth
Black Torrington
Highampton
Hatherleigh
Jacobstowe
Inwardleigh
Northlew
Beaworthy
Patchacott
Ashbury
Exbourne
Sampford Courtenay
Honeychurch
Monkokehampton
Iddesleigh
Dowland
Dolton
Beaford
Roborough
High Bickington
Kingscott
St Giles in the Wood
High Bullen
Langridge Ford
Atherington
Umberleigh
Yarnscombe
Chapelton
Tawstock
Bishops Tawton
Barnstaple
Landkey
Swimbridge
Swimbridge Newland
Filleigh
Cobbaton
Chittlehampton
Warkleigh
Satterleigh
Chittlehamholt
Kingsford
Burrington
Chulmleigh
Riddlecombe
Ashreigney
Ashley
Hollocombe
Wembworthy
Winkleigh
Brushford
Coldridge
Broadwood Kelly
Bondleigh
North Tawton
Eggesford Station
South Molton
Clapworthy
George Nympton
King's Nympton
Cadbury Barton
Elstone
Nymet Rowland
West Leigh
East Leigh
A39
A386
A361
A377
A3124
A3072
B3227
B3217
B3220
B3226
River Torridge
River Taw
SS
70

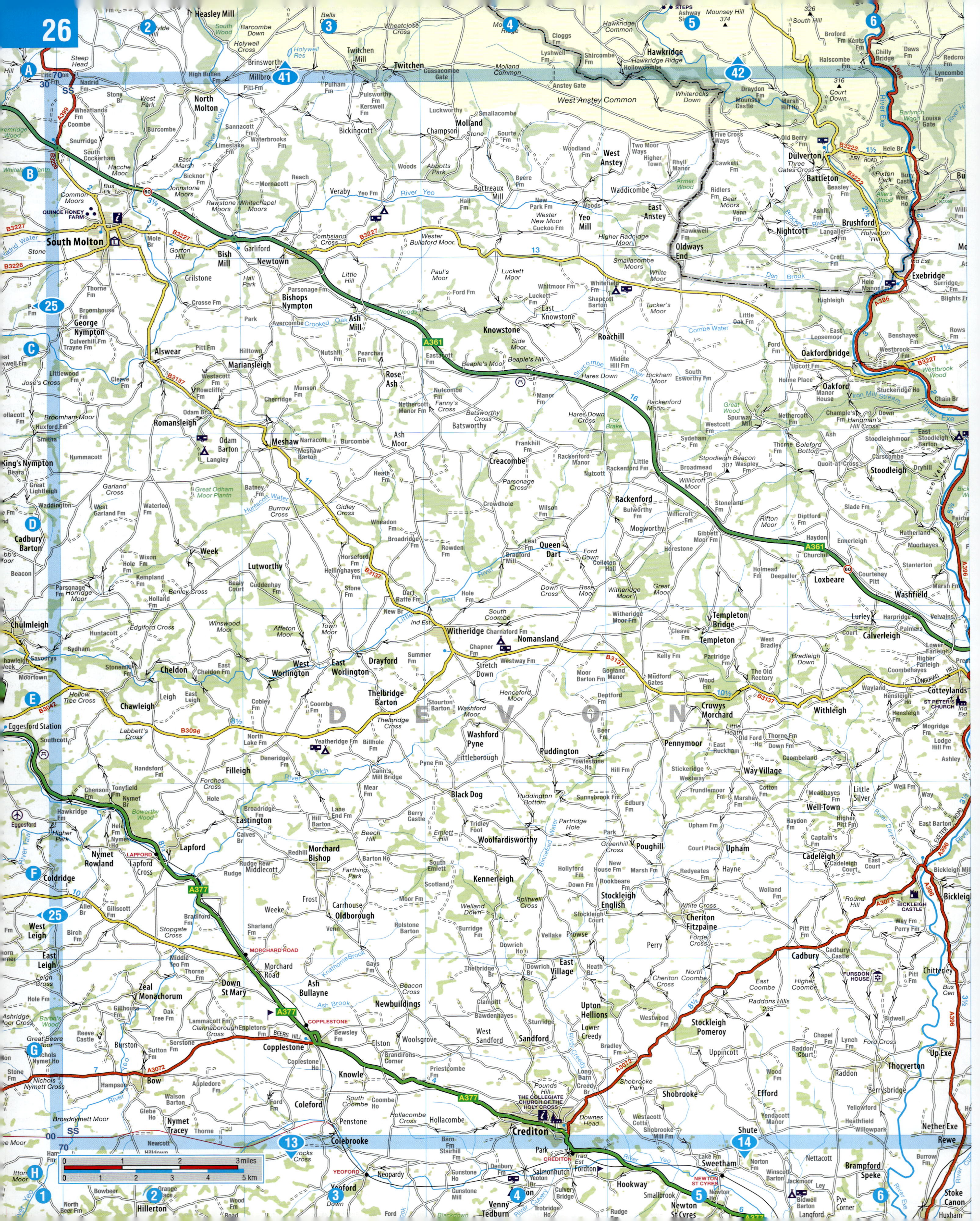

Heasley Mill
South Wood
Barcombe Down
Holywell Cross
Holywell Res
Balls
Wheatclose Cross
Twitchen Mill
Twitchen
Cussacombe Gate
Molland Common
Cloggs
Lyshwell Fm
Shircombe Fm
Hawkridge Common
Hawkridge
Hawkridge Ridge
Hollowcombe
Ashway Side
Mounsey Hill
South Hill
Broford Fm
Kents Fm
Chilly Bridge
Daws Fm
Halscombe Fm
Redcross
Lyncombe
Steep Head
High Bullen Fm
Brinsworthy
Millbrook
Pulham Fm
Pitt Fm
Nadrid
North Molton
West Park
Stony Fm
Wheatlands Fm
Coombe
Sannacott
Limeslake
Waterbrooks Fm
Pulsworthy Fm
Kerswell Fm
Bickingcott
Luckworthy
Champson
Molland
Smallacombe
Stone
Gourte Fm
Anstey Gate
West Anstey Common
Whiterocks Down
Five Cross Ways
Draydon Fm
Mounsey Castle
Marsh Hill Ho
Court Down
Old Berry Fm
Dulverton
Three Gates Cross
Battleton
Hele Br
Louisa Gate
River Exe
Snurridge
South Cockerham
Hacche Moor
East Marsh
Bicknor Fm
Johnstone Moors
Woods
Abbotts Park
Beere Fm
Woodland Fm
West Anstey
Two Moor Ways
Higher Town
Rhyll Manor
Cawkett Fm
Armer Wood
Bessley Fm
Pixton Park
Bury Castle
Common Moors
Quince Honey Farm
Mornacott
Reach
Veraby
Yeo Fm
River Yeo
Bottreaux Mill
Waddicombe
Ridlers Fm
Beer Moors
Venn Fm
Ashill Fm
Allers Wood
Weir Ho
South Molton
Rawstone Moors
Whitechapel Moors
Hall Fm
New Park Fm
Wester New Moor
Cuckoo Fm
Yeo Mill
East Anstey
Hawkwell Fm
Nightcott
Langaller
Brushford
Hulverton Hill
Stone
Mole Br
Gorton Hill
Bish Mill
Garliford
Newtown
Combsland Cross
Wester Bullaford Moor
Higher Radnidge Moor
Oldways End
Croft Fm
Smallacombe Moors
White Moor
Den Brook
Hele Manor Fm
Exebridge
Surridge Fm
Blights Fm
Grilstone
Hall Park
Little Hill
Paul's Moor
Luckett Moor
Whitmoor Fm
Whitefield Fm
Shapcott Barton
Tucker's Moor
Highleigh
Thorne Fm
Crosse Fm
Parsonage Fm
Bishops Nympton
Ford Fm
Luckett Fm
East Knowstone
Combe Water
Little Oak Fm
East Loosemoor
Benshayes Fm
Rows Fm
Broomhouse Fm
George Nympton
Culverhill Fm
Trayne Fm
Park
Avercombe
Crooked Oak
Ash Mill
Woods
Knowstone
Roachill
Ford Fm
Oakfordbridge
Westbrook Fm
Alswear
Pitt Fm
Hilltown
Nutshill Fm
Pearchay Fm
Eastacott Fm
Beaple's Moor
Beaple's Hill
Side Moor
Middle Hill Fm
Hares Down
River Bickham Moor
South Esworthy Fm
Upcott Fm
Holme Place
Oakford
Manor House
Iron Mill Stream
Stuckeridge Ho
Westbrook Wood
Chain Br
Littlewood Fm
Jose's Cross
Cleave Fm
Mariansleigh
Westacott Fm
Rowcliffe Fm
Munson Fm
Rose Ash
Nutcombe Fm
Fanny's Cross
Nethercott Manor Fm
Batsworthy Cross
Batsworthy
Manor Fm
Hares Down Cross
Fox Brake
Rackenford Moor
Great Wood
Westcott Fm
Spurway Mill
Nethercott Fm
Chample's Fm
Hangman's Hill Cross
Down
River Exe
Broomham Moor
Huxford Fm
Smitha
Cherridge
Odam Br
Romansleigh
Odam Barton
Langley
Meshaw
Narracott
Meshaw Barton
Burcombe
Ash Moor
Frankhill Fm
Creacombe
Rackenford Manor
Sydeham Fm
Stoodleigh Beacon
Thorne Fm
Coleford Bottom
East Stoodleigh Barton
Stoodleighmoor
Carscombe
Stoodleigh
Exe Valley
King's Nympton
Beara
Hummacott
Great Lightleigh
Waddington
Garland Cross
West Garland Fm
Great Odham Moor Plantn
Batney Fm
Huntacott Water
Burrow Cross
Heath Fm
Gidley Cross
Parsonage Cross
Crowdhole
Nutcott
Little Rackenford Fm
Broadmead
Waspley Fm
Willicroft Moor
Quoit-at-Cross
Drybill
Rackenford
Bulworthy Fm
Wilson Fm
Stoneland Fm
Slade Fm
Fairby
Cadbury Barton
Waterloo Fm
Wheadon Fm
Broadridge Fm
Mogworthy
Willicroft Fm
Rifton Moor
Diptford Fm
Gibbett Moor Fm
Haydon Fm
Enncrleigh
Hatherland Fm
Moorhayes
Week
Wixon Fm
Hole Fm
Kempland Fm
Lutworthy
Beaply Court
Cuddenhay Fm
Horseford Fm
Hellinghayes Fm
Rowden Fm
Bradford Mill
Queen Dart
Ford Down
Colleton Hall
Horestone
Holmead Fm
Deeppaller
Churchill
Loxbeare
Courtenay Pitt
Stanterton
Washfield
Beacon
Parsonage Fm
Horridge Moor
Holland Fm
Benley Cross
Stone Fm
Dart
Baffe Fm
Hole Fm
Down Cross
Rose Moor
Witheridge Moor
Great Moor
Marsh Fm
Templeton Bridge
Lurley
Harpridge
Velvains
Chulmleigh
Huntacott
Edgiford Cross
Winswood Moor
Affeton Moor
Town Moor
New Br
Little Dart
Ind Est
Witheridge
Charnaford Fm
South Coombe
Witheridge Moor Fm
Cleave Fm
Templeton
Court
Calverleigh
Palmers
Sydham
Savourys
Stonemill
Cheldon
Cheldon Fm
East Fm
West Worlington
East Worlington
Drayford
Summer Fm
Chapner Fm
Nomansland
Westway Fm
Stretch Down
Moor Barton Fm
Gogland Manor
Kelly Fm
Partridge Fm
West Bradley
Bradleigh Down
The Old Rectory
Lower Farleigh
Higher Farleigh
Coombehayes
Longdrag Hill
Cotteylands
Moortown
Hollow Tree Cross
Chawleigh
Leigh
East Leigh
Cobley Fm
Coombe Fm
Thelbridge Barton
Henceford Moor
Stourton Barton
Washford Moor
Mudford Gates
Wood Fm
Deptford Fm
Cruwys Morchard
Wayland
Hensleigh Ho
Withleigh
St Peter's Church
Eggesford Station
Labbett's Cross
North Lake Fm
Thelbridge Cross
Washford Pyne
Littleborough
Puddington
Beer Fm
Little Heath
Old Ford Fm
Thorne Fm
Down Fm
Pennymoor
East Ruckham
Hensleigh Fm
Mogridge Fm
Lodge Hill Fm
Ashley
Southcott
Yeatheridge Fm
Billhole Fm
Denridge Fm
Handsford Fm
Filleigh
River Dalch
Pyne Fm
Cann's Mill Bridge
Yowlestone Ho
Hill Fm
Stickeridge Fm
Westway
Coombeland
Way Village
Chenson
Tonyfield Fm
Nymet Br
Hawkridge
Bowerthy Wood
Forches Cross
Hole
Mear Fm
Black Dog
Puddington Bottom
Sunnybrook Fm
Trundlemoor Fm
Marshay Fm
Cotton Fm
Meadhayes Fm
Little Silver
Well Fm
Way
Well Town
Eggesford
Higher Park
Broadridge Fm
Eastington
Hill Barton
Lane End Fm
Berry Castle
Tridley Foot
Edbury Fm
Haydon Fm
Higher Pitt Fm
East Barton
Nymet Rowland
Lapford
Lapford Cross
Calves Br
Redhill
Morchard Bishop
Beech Hill
Emlett Hill
Woolfardisworthy
Partridge Hole
Park
Greenhill Cross
Poughill
Upham Fm
Court Place
Upham
Captain's Fm
Cadeleigh
Cadeleigh Court
East Court
Exeter Road
River Taw
Coldridge
Rudge
Rudge Rew
Middlecott
Barton Ho
Farthing Park
South Emlett
Scotland
Kennerleigh
Hollyford Fm
New House Fm
Down Fm
Marsh Fm
Redyeates Fm
Hayne
Bickleigh Mill
Bickleigh
Bickleigh Castle
Gillscott Fm
Aller Br
West Leigh
Frost
Weeke
Carrhouse
Oldborough
Moor Fm
Welland Down
Splitwell Cross
Rookbeare Fm
Stockleigh English
Stockleigh Court
Wolland Fm
White Cross
Cheriton Fitzpaine
Round Hill
Way Fm
Perry Fm
Birch Fm
Stopgate Cross
Sharland Fm
Bradiford
Morchard Road
Venn
Rolstone Barton
Burridge Fm
Vellake
Prowse
Forde Cross
Perry
Pitt Fm
Cadbury
Cadbury Castle
East Leigh
Middle Yeo Fm
Thorne Fm
Morchard Road
Knathorne Brook
Gays Fm
Thelbridge Br
Dowrich Ho
Dowrich Br
East Village
Heath Br
North Coombe
Cheriton Coombe Cross
East Coombe
Higher Coombe
Fursdon House
Pitt Fm
Chitterley
Leigh Cross
Hole Fm
Zeal Monachorum
Down St Mary
Ash Bullayne
Beacon Cross
Newbuildings
Clampitt
Bawdenhayes
Upton Hellions
Westwood Fm
Stockleigh Pomeroy
Raddons Hills
Bidwell
Bus Cen
Gillhouse
Oak Tree Fm
Lammacott Fm
Clannaborough Cross
Eppletons Fm
Copplestone
Ash Brook
West Sandford
Sturridge
Sandford
Lower Creedy
Chapel Fm
Lynch Fm
Ford Cross
Ashridge Moor Cross
Reeve Castle
Great Beere
Nichols Nymet Ho
Burston
Sutton Fm
Serstone Fm
Beers Hill
Copplestone
Bewsley Fm
Elston
Woolsgrove
Brandirons Corner
Bradley Fm
Uppincott
Raddon Court
Up Exe
Stone Fm
Nichols Nymett Cross
Bow
Hampson
Appledore Fm
Copplestone Ho
Knowle
Priestcombe
Long Barn
Creedy Br
Shobrooke Park
Shobrooke
Wood Fm
Raddon
Thorverton
Berrysbridge
Walson Barton
Glebe Ho
Ford Fm
Coleford
South Coombe
Coombe Ho
Pounds Hill
The Collegiate Church of the Holy Cross
Efford
Yellowford
Heathfield
Broadnymett Moor
Nymet Tracey
Thorne
Penstone
Hollacombe Cross
Hollacombe
Downes Head
Westacott Cotts
Shobrooke Mill Fm
Yendacott Manor
Willowpark
Nether Exe
Rewe
Newcott
Colebrooke
Crediton
Shute
Barn Fm
Stairhill Fm
Park
Trad Est
Fordton
Crediton
Lake Fm
Sweetham
Norton Fm
Winscott Barton
Nettacott
Brampford Speke
Burrow Fm
Yeoford
Neopardy
Gunstone Ho
Denbury Fm
Salmonhutch
Yeoton
Hookway
Newton St Cyres
Jackmoor
Ley
Bidwell Barton
Langford
Pye Corner
Stoke Canon
Hillerton
Grange Fm
Bowbeer
North Beer Fm
Wood Fm
Gunstone Mill
Venny Tedburn
Culvery Bridge
Smallbrook
Hooks Cross
Itton Moor
Ford
Rudge
Hulham
DEVON
A361
A377
A396
A399
A3072
A3124
B3226
B3227
B3137
B3042
B3096
B3222

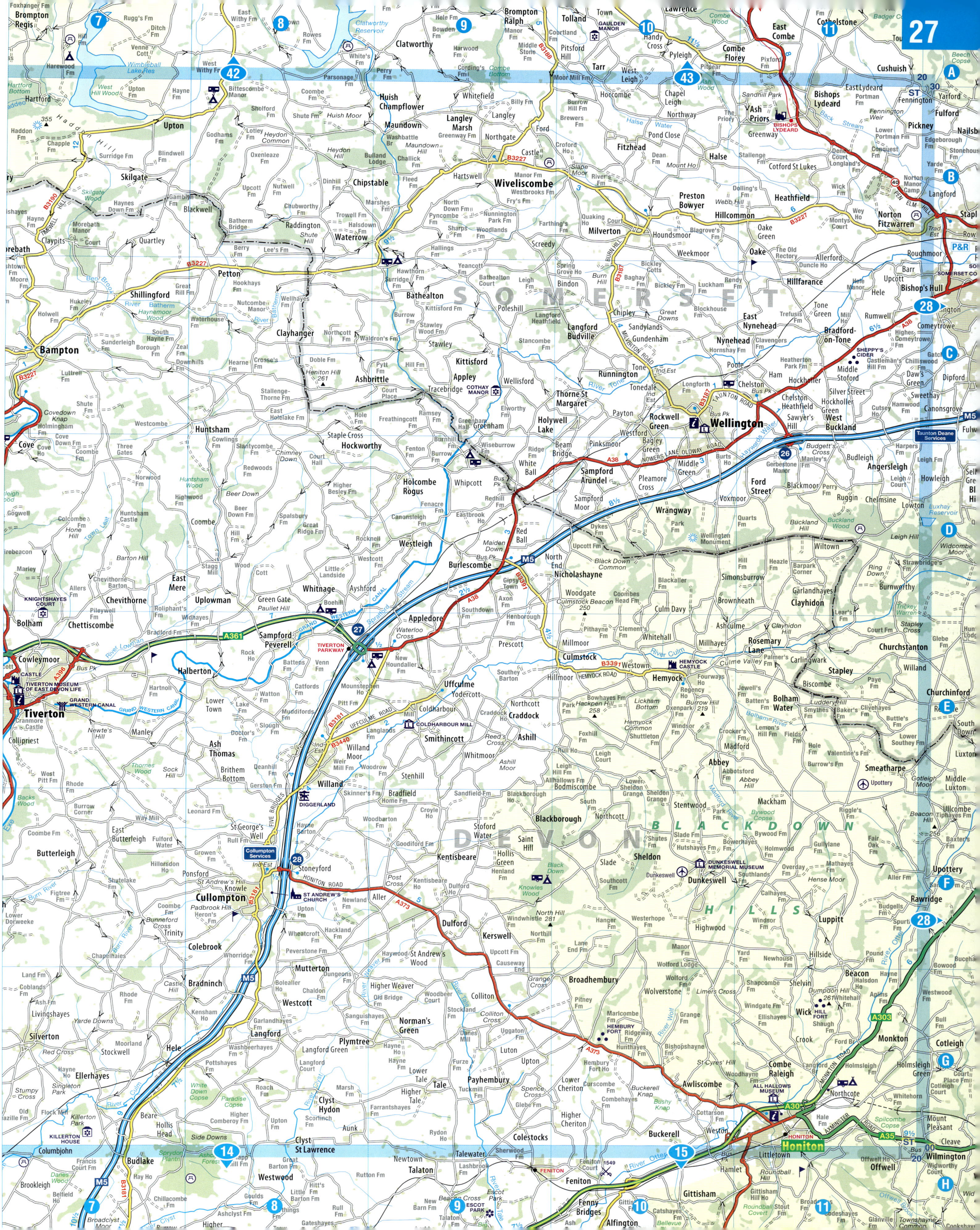
SOMERSET
DEVON
BLACKDOWN HILLS
Wiveliscombe
Wellington
Tiverton
Cullompton
Honiton
Bampton
Milverton
Bishops Lydeard
Hemyock
Uffculme
Sampford Peverell
Willand
Dunkeswell
Taunton Deane Services
Tiverton Parkway
Collumpton Services
Wellington Monument
Dunkeswell Memorial Museum
Tiverton Museum of Mid Devon Life
Grand Western Canal
Cothay Manor
Coldharbour Mill
Wimbleball Lake Res
Clatworthy Reservoir
M5
A38
A361
A373
A30
A35
B3227
B3181
B3391
B3440

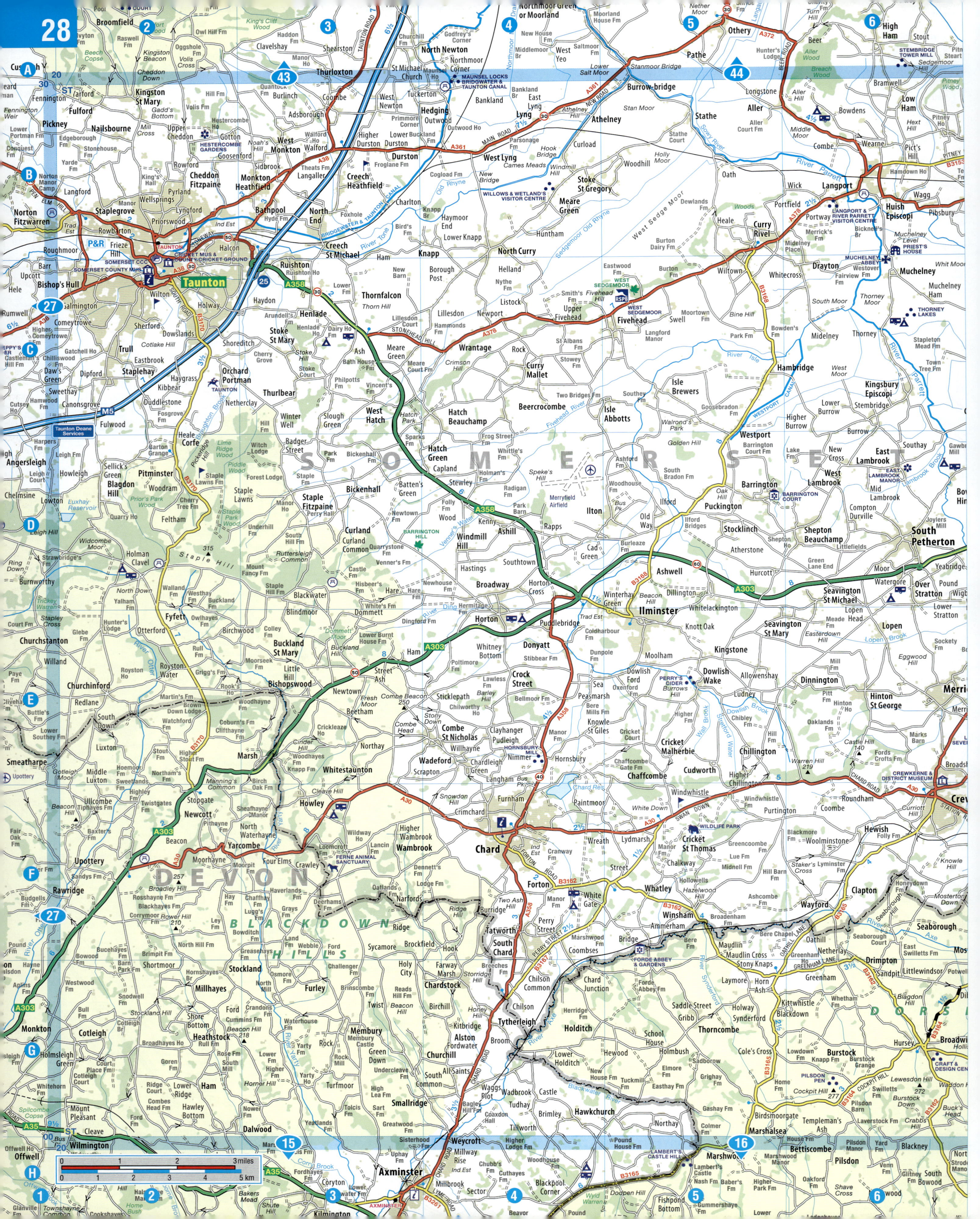
Taunton
Ilminster
Chard
Axminster
Langport
Curry Rivel
Muchelney
South Petherton
Wellington
Henlade
Hatch Beauchamp
Ilton
Ashill
Broadway
Donyatt
Horton
Combe St Nicholas
Wadeford
Crewkerne
Hinton St George
Kingsbury Episcopi
Barrington
Puckington
Shepton Beauchamp
Stoke St Gregory
Athelney
Burrow-bridge
North Curry
Thornfalcon
Bickenhall
Staple Fitzpaine
Curland
Whitestaunton
Yarcombe
Stockland
Membury
Chardstock
Hawkchurch
Tatworth
Winsham
Cricket St Thomas
Chaffcombe
Cudworth
Dowlish Wake
Kingstone
Seavington St Michael
Lopen
Drimpton
Broadwindsor
Thorncombe
Marshwood
Bettiscombe
Pilsdon
Wayford
Clapton
Seaborough
Blackdown Hills
Upottery
Churchinford
Otterford
Corfe
Pitminster
Blagdon Hill
Staplegrove
Bishop's Hull
Norton Fitzwarren
Cheddon Fitzpaine
Monkton Heathfield
Creech St Michael
Creech Heathfield
Durston
Thurloxton
North Newton
West Lyng
Othery
High Ham
Stathe
Drayton
Westport
Hambridge
Isle Abbotts
Isle Brewers
Fivehead
Swell
Beercrocombe
Curry Mallet
Wrantage
Stoke St Mary
Orchard Portman
Thurlbear
Staplehay
Trull
Fulwood
Angersleigh
Smeatharpe
Luxton
Howley
Monkton
Cotleigh
Heathstock
Millhayes
Furley
Dalwood
Wilmington
Offwell
Kilmington
Weycroft
Holditch
Churchill
Alston
Tytherleigh
South Chard
Forton
Whatley
SOMERSET
DEVON
DORSET
M5
A303
A358
A30
A378
A361
A35
Taunton Deane Services
0 1 2 3 miles
0 1 2 3 4 5 km

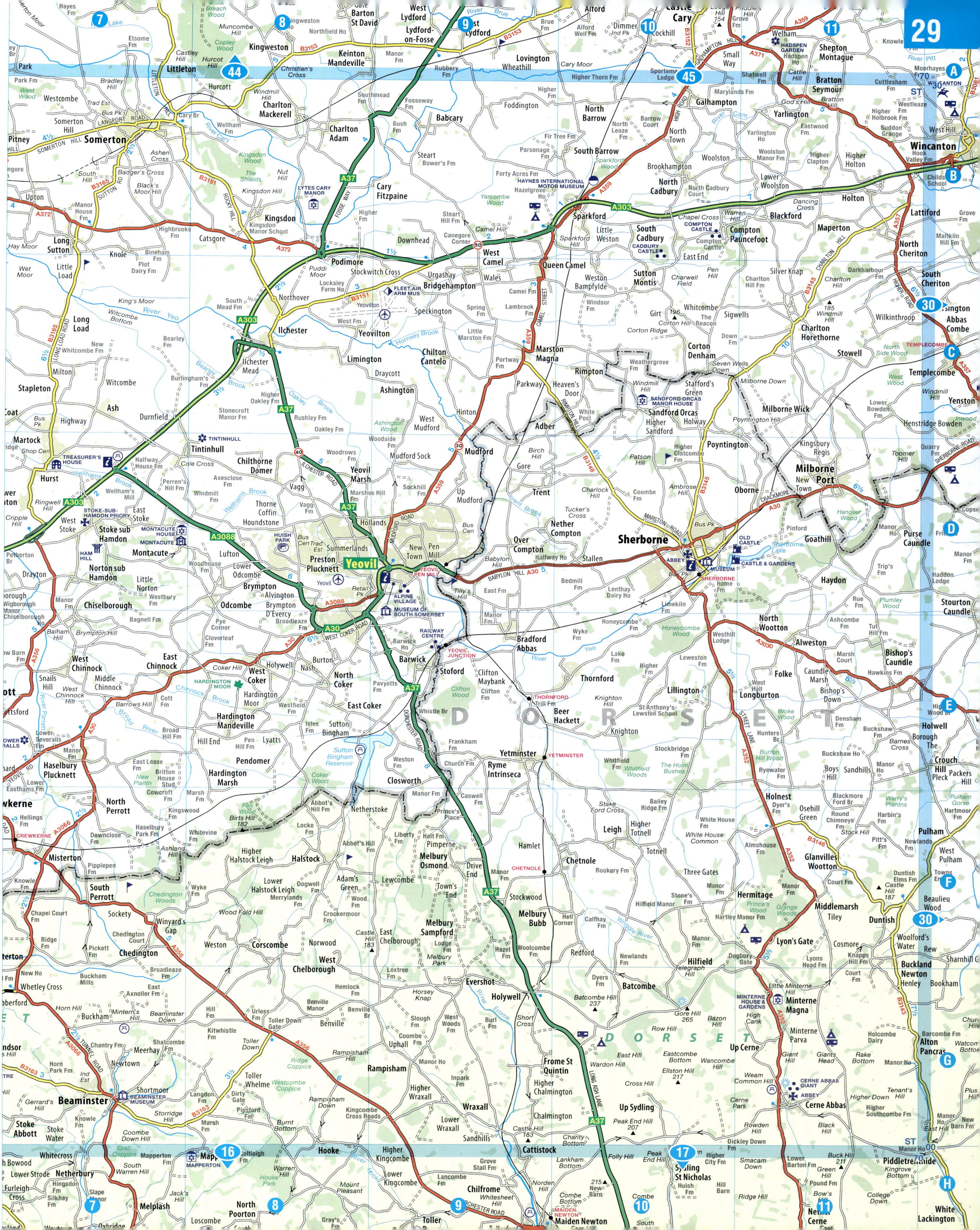
Somerton
Kingweston
Littleton
Keinton Mandeville
Lydford-on-Fosse
Castle Cary
Shepton Montague
Charlton Mackerell
Charlton Adam
Babcary
North Barrow
South Barrow
Galhampton
Yarlington
Wincanton
Cary Fitzpaine
Kingsdon
Podimore
Sparkford
Queen Camel
West Camel
South Cadbury
North Cadbury
Compton Pauncefoot
Blackford
Maperton
Holton
North Cheriton
Long Sutton
Ilchester
Yeovilton
Bridgehampton
Speckington
Marston Magna
Rimpton
Sandford Orcas
Milborne Port
Sherborne
Stalbridge
Tintinhull
Montacute
Stoke sub Hamdon
Yeovil
Preston Plucknett
Brympton
Odcombe
East Coker
West Coker
North Coker
Barwick
Stoford
Bradford Abbas
Thornford
Yetminster
Ryme Intrinseca
Leigh
Chetnole
Melbury Osmond
Melbury Sampford
Evershot
Holywell
Frome St Quintin
Cattistock
Maiden Newton
Crewkerne
Misterton
South Perrott
North Perrott
Haselbury Plucknett
Hardington Mandeville
Halstock
Corscombe
Beaminster
Netherbury
Mapperton
Hooke
Chilfrome
Sydling St Nicholas
Cerne Abbas
Up Cerne
Minterne Magna
Buckland Newton
Alton Pancras
Piddletrenthide
Hermitage
Holnest
Longburton
Folke
Lillington
Haydon
North Wootton
Purse Caundle
Stourton Caundle
Bishop's Caundle
Holwell
Pulham
Glanvilles Wootton
Dunstish
Lyon's Gate
Batcombe
Hilfield
Yenston
Templecombe
Henstridge Bowden
D O R S E T
A37
A303
A30
A359
A356
A3088
A352

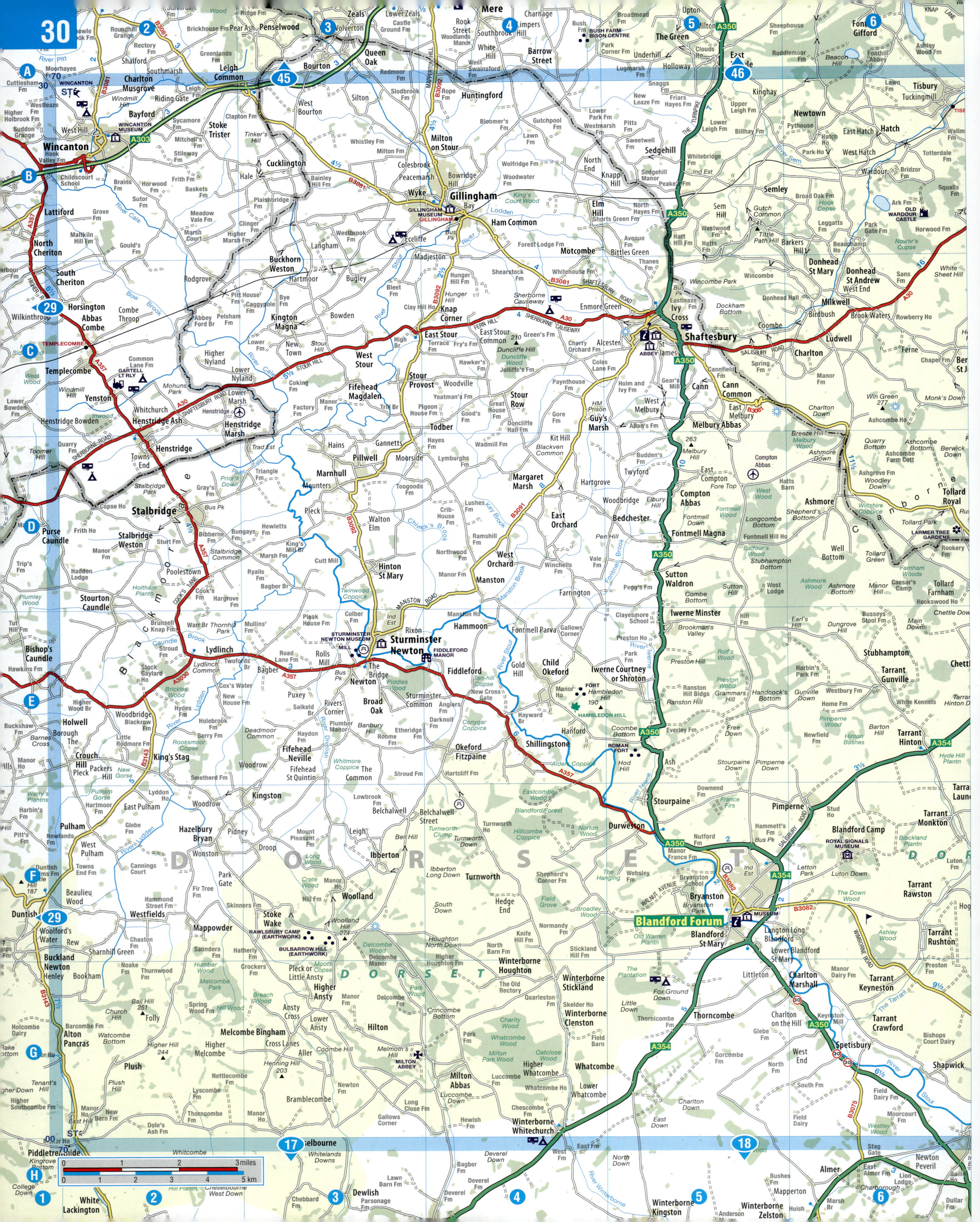
Wincanton
Gillingham
Shaftesbury
Stalbridge
Sturminster Newton
Blandford Forum
Templecombe
Henstridge
Marnhull
Hinton St Mary
Fontmell Magna
Iwerne Minster
Child Okeford
Shillingstone
Okeford Fitzpaine
Milton Abbas
Winterborne Whitechurch
Motcombe
Mere
Zeals
Penselwood
Bourton
Milton on Stour
Kington Magna
Buckhorn Weston
Cucklington
East Stour
West Stour
Stour Provost
Todber
Fifehead Magdalen
Hazelbury Bryan
Ansty
Hilton
Stourpaine
Pimperne
Spetisbury
Compton Abbas
Melbury Abbas
Cann
Ludwell
Donhead St Andrew
Donhead St Mary
Semley
Tisbury
Ashmore
Tarrant Gunville
Tarrant Hinton
Tarrant Keyneston
Tarrant Crawford
Charlton Marshall
Blandford St Mary
Bryanston
Durweston
Hanford
Hambledon Hill
Fiddleford
Manston
Margaret Marsh
East Orchard
West Orchard
Sutton Waldron
Pulham
Mappowder
Woolland
Ibberton
Turnworth
Winterborne Stickland
Winterborne Houghton
Winterborne Kingston
Winterborne Zelston
Bulbarrow Hill
Rawlsbury Camp
Alton Pancras
Buckland Newton
Plush
Whatcombe
Thornicombe
Almer
Dewlish
White Lackington
Holwell
Lydlinch
King's Stag
Purse Caundle
Stourton Caundle
Bishop's Caundle
Dunstish
Horsington
Abbas Combe
North Cheriton
South Cheriton
Lattiford
Charlton Musgrove
Bayford
Stoke Trister
Kingston
D O R S E T
A303
A30
A357
A350
A354
A3030
B3081
B3092
B3091
B3143
B3082
0 1 2 3 miles
0 1 2 3 4 5 km

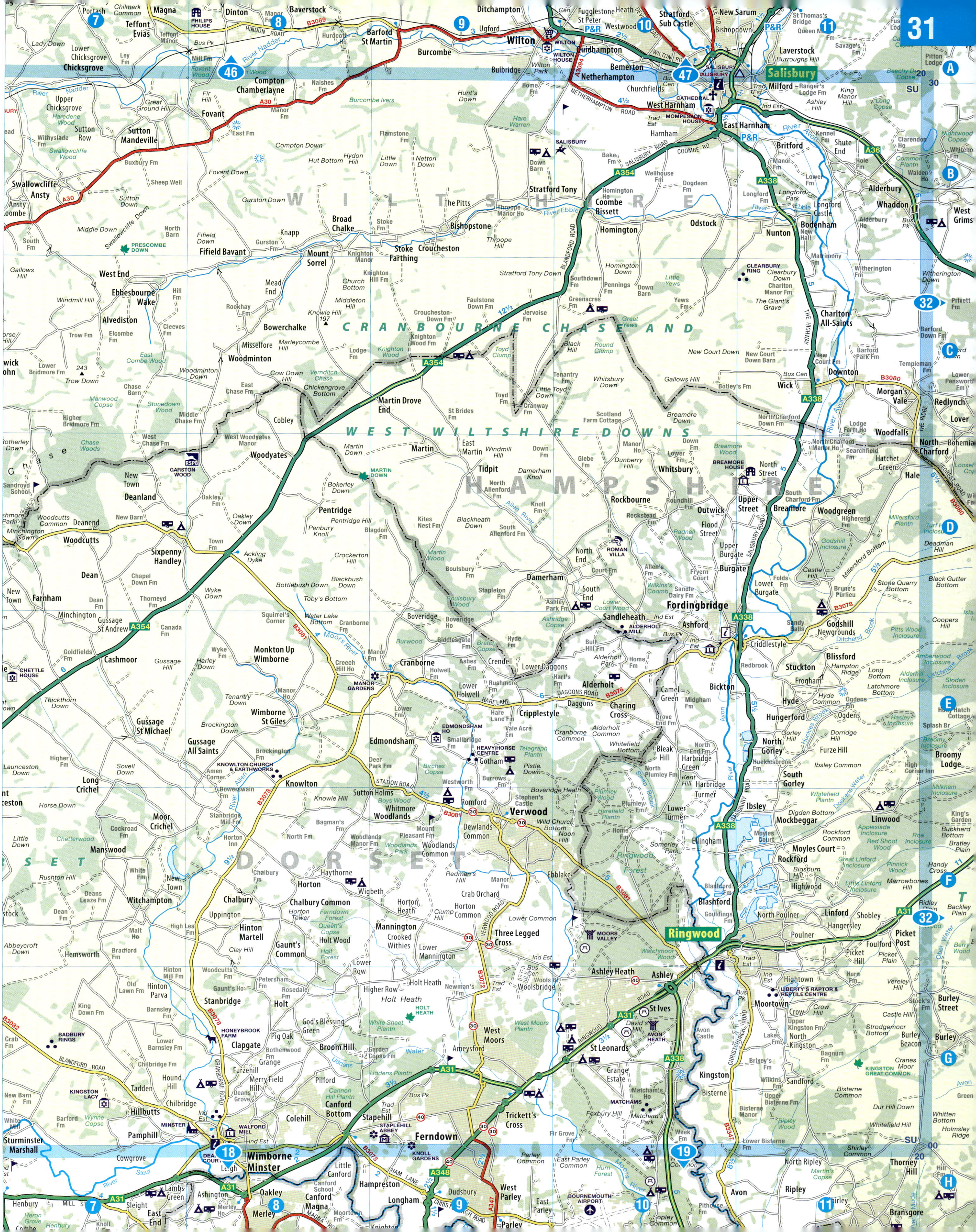

Salisbury
Wilton
Fordingbridge
Ringwood
Verwood
Ferndown
Wimborne Minster
WILTSHIRE
HAMPSHIRE
DORSET
CRANBORNE CHASE AND
WEST WILTSHIRE DOWNS
Teffont Evias
Dinton
Baverstock
Barford St Martin
Burcombe
Ditchampton
Fugglestone St Peter
Quidhampton
Bemerton
Netherhampton
Stratford Sub Castle
New Sarum
Bishopdown
Laverstock
Milford
Churchfields
West Harnham
East Harnham
Harnham
Britford
Compton Chamberlayne
Fovant
Sutton Mandeville
Swallowcliffe
Ansty
Chicksgrove
Upper Chicksgrove
Lower Chicksgrove
Broad Chalke
Bishopstone
Stratford Tony
Coombe Bissett
Homington
Odstock
Nunton
Bodenham
Alderbury
Whaddon
West Grimstead
Charlton-All-Saints
Downton
Morgan's Vale
Redlynch
Lover
Woodfalls
North Charford
Hale
Woodgreen
Breamore
Upper Street
Outwick
Whitsbury
Rockbourne
Damerham
Martin
East Martin
Tidpit
Martin Drove End
Fifield Bavant
Mount Sorrel
Stoke Farthing
Croucheston
Knapp
Ebbesbourne Wake
West End
Alvediston
Bowerchalke
Woodminton
Misselfore
Cobley
Woodyates
Pentridge
New Town
Deanland
Woodcutts
Sixpenny Handley
Dean
Farnham
Gussage St Andrew
Cashmoor
Cranborne
Boveridge
Crendell
Alderholt
Cripplestyle
Daggons
Charing Cross
Sandleheath
Ashford
Bickton
Hyde
Hungerford
North Gorley
South Gorley
Ibsley
Mockbeggar
Moyles Court
Rockford
Blashford
Linwood
Stuckton
Frogham
Godshill
Blissford
Gussage All Saints
Gussage St Michael
Monkton Up Wimborne
Wimborne St Giles
Edmondsham
Knowlton
Long Crichel
Moor Crichel
Manswood
Witchampton
Chalbury
Chalbury Common
Horton
Uppington
Hinton Martell
Gaunt's Common
Holt Wood
Mannington
Three Legged Cross
Woodlands
Woodlands Common
Dewlands Common
Ebblake
Ellingham
Ashley Heath
Ashley
St Ives
St Leonards
West Moors
Holt
Stanbridge
Hinton Parva
Clapgate
Furzehill
Colehill
Canford Bottom
Stapehill
Trickett's Cross
Hillbutts
Pamphill
Sturminster Marshall
Cowgrove
Leigh
Oakley
Merley
Canford Magna
Hampreston
Longham
Dudsbury
West Parley
Parley
Little Canford
Kingston
Bisterne
Moortown
Sandford
Poulner
North Poulner
Picket Post
Burley Street
Burley
Crow
Avon
Ripley
Sopley
Thorney Hill
Bransgore
North Ripley
A30
A36
A338
A354
A31
A348
A3094
B3089
B3080
B3078
B3081
B3072
B3073
B3347
B3082
B3078
Ringwood Forest
Moors Valley
Bournemouth Airport

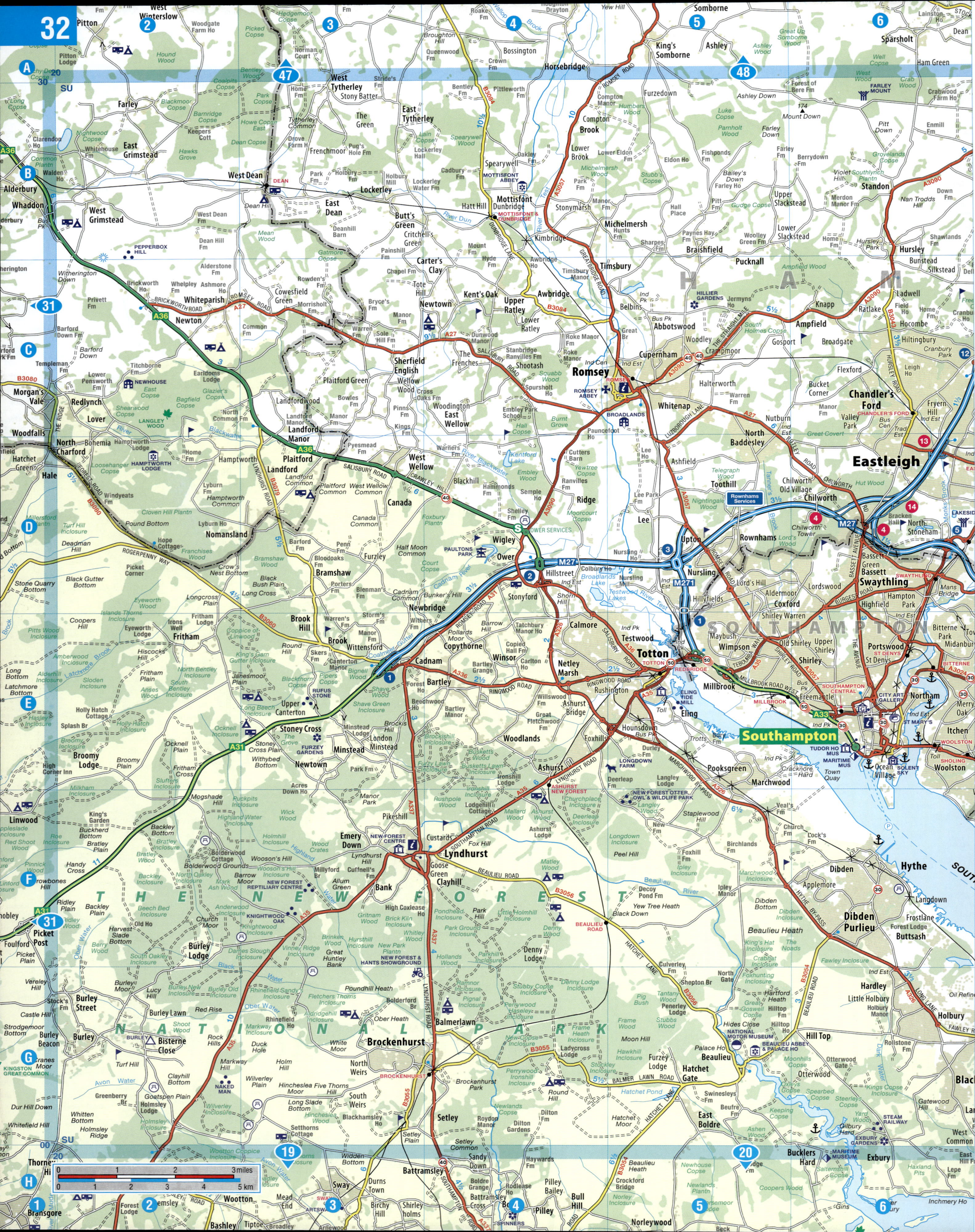
Pitton
West Winterslow
Farley
East Grimstead
West Grimstead
West Dean
Alderbury
Whaddon
Pepperbox Hill
Whiteparish
Newton
West Tytherley
East Tytherley
Lockerley
East Dean
Butt's Green
Mottisfont
Dunbridge
Mottisfont Abbey
Horsebridge
King's Somborne
Somborne
Ashley
Sparsholt
Ham Green
Compton
Brook
Michelmersh
Timsbury
Braishfield
Pucknall
Standon
Hursley
Ladwell
Knapp
Ampfield
Hiltingbury
Chandler's Ford
Eastleigh
North Baddesley
Romsey
Cupernham
Abbotswood
Whitenap
Awbridge
Kent's Oak
Upper Ratley
Newtown
Sherfield English
Plaitford
Landford
Hamptworth
Nomansland
Redlynch
Lover
Morgan's Vale
Woodfalls
North Charford
Hale
Canada
West Wellow
Wigley
Ower
Ridge
Lee
Nursling
Upton
Rownhams
Chilworth
Bassett
Swaythling
Southampton
Totton
Testwood
Calmore
Netley Marsh
Cadnam
Bartley
Copythorne
Brook
Bramshaw
Fritham
Stoney Cross
Minstead
Emery Down
Lyndhurst
Ashurst
Woodlands
Marchwood
Hythe
Dibden
Dibden Purlieu
Beaulieu
Brockenhurst
Setley
Battramsley
Sway
Pilley
Bull Hill
Norleywood
Exbury
Bucklers Hard
Holbury
Hardley
Burley
Bisterne Close
Linwood
Picket Post
Bransgore
Wootton
Bashley
Tiptoe
THE NEW FOREST NATIONAL PARK
HAMPSHIRE
Woolston
Itchen
Portswood
Shirley
Millbrook
Freemantle
Redbridge
Eling
Rushington
Ocean Village
Northam
Bitterne Park
Highfield
Hampton Park
Lordswood
Aldermoor
Coxford
Old Shirley
Upper Shirley
Nutburn
Flexford
Valley Park
Toothill
Ashfield
Great Covert
0 1 2 3 miles
0 1 2 3 4 5 km

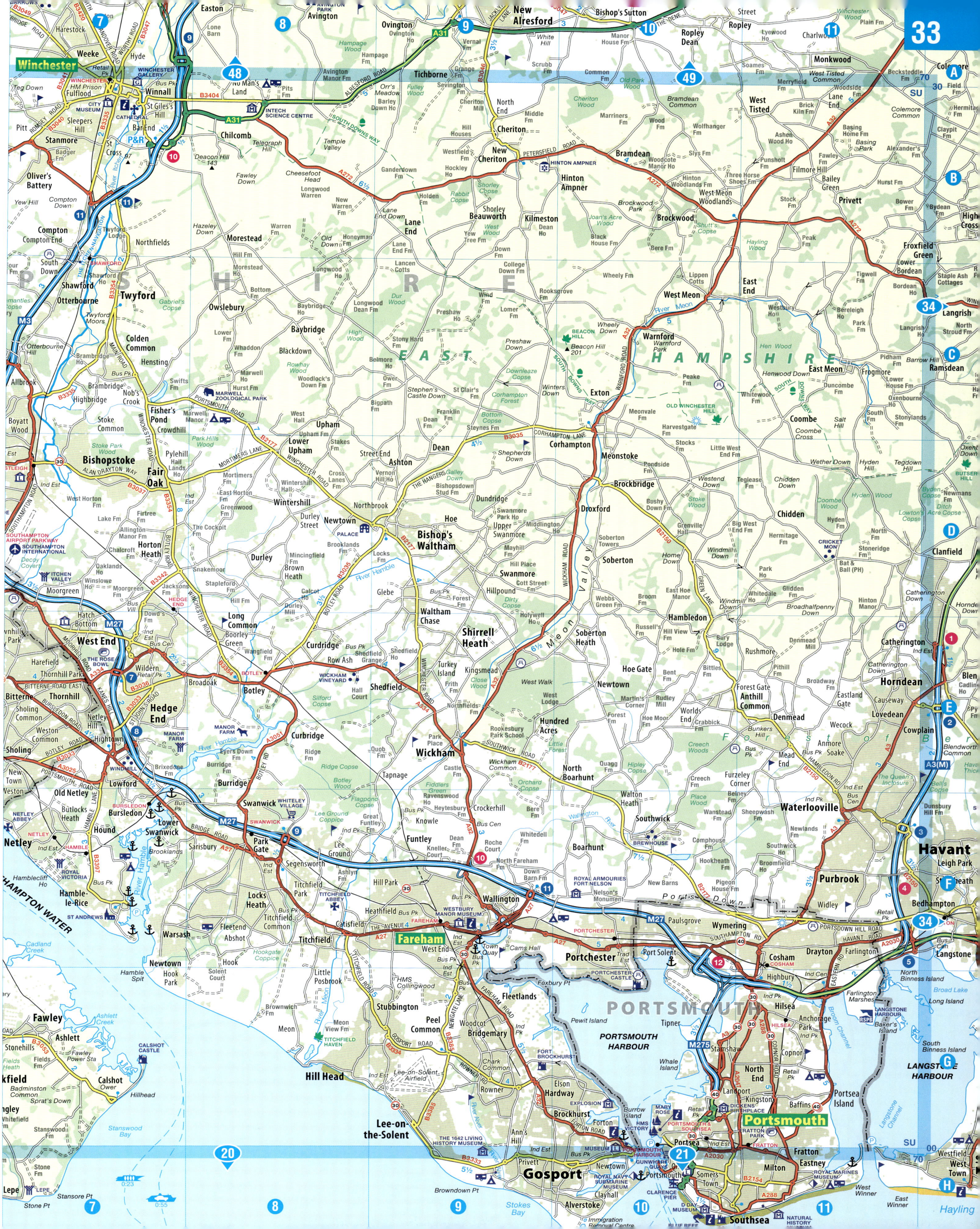
Winchester
New Alresford
Bishop's Sutton
Ropley
Tichborne
Cheriton
New Cheriton
Hinton Ampner
Bramdean
West Tisted
Privett
Twyford
Owslebury
Morestead
Chilcomb
Compton
Shawford
Otterbourne
Colden Common
Bishopstoke
Fair Oak
Upham
Durley
Bishop's Waltham
Corhampton
Meonstoke
Exton
Droxford
Soberton
Hambledon
West Meon
Warnford
East Meon
Clanfield
Horndean
Waterlooville
Havant
Purbrook
Wickham
Shedfield
Curdridge
Botley
Hedge End
West End
Netley
Hamble-le-Rice
Warsash
Titchfield
Fareham
Portchester
Cosham
Drayton
Hilsea
Portsmouth
Southsea
Gosport
Lee-on-the-Solent
Stubbington
Hill Head
Fawley
Calshot
Denmead
Rowlands Castle
Wymering
Bedhampton
Langstone
PORTSMOUTH HARBOUR
LANGSTONE HARBOUR
Portsea Island
HAMPSHIRE
EAST
Meon Valley
SOUTHAMPTON WATER
Stokes Bay
Hayling

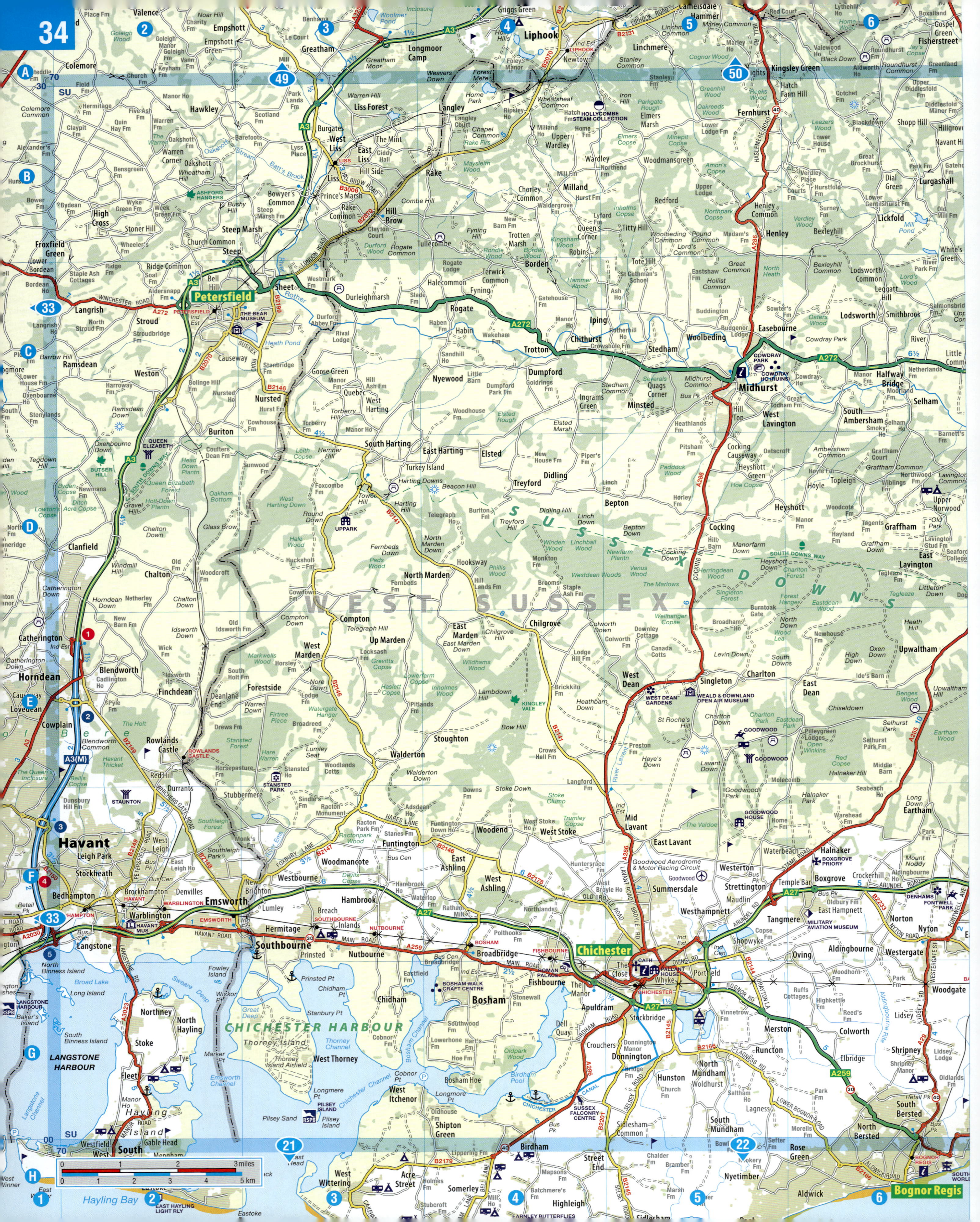

Petersfield
Liphook
Midhurst
Havant
Emsworth
Chichester
Bognor Regis
Southbourne
Bosham
Fishbourne
Westbourne
Horndean
Cowplain
Waterlooville
Rowlands Castle
Clanfield
Chalton
Buriton
Langrish
Stroud
Ramsdean
Steep
Sheet
Liss
West Liss
Greatham
Empshott
Hawkley
Rake
Hill Brow
Milland
Rogate
Trotton
Chithurst
Iping
Stedham
Woolbeding
Easebourne
Fernhurst
Henley
Lodsworth
Selham
West Lavington
Cocking
Heyshott
Graffham
Upwaltham
East Dean
Charlton
Singleton
West Dean
Chilgrove
Compton
Up Marden
West Marden
East Marden
North Marden
Harting
South Harting
East Harting
Elsted
Treyford
Didling
Bepton
Dumpford
Nyewood
Stoughton
Walderton
Funtington
West Stoke
Mid Lavant
East Lavant
Westhampnett
Tangmere
Boxgrove
Halnaker
Oving
Merston
Aldingbourne
Westergate
Woodgate
North Mundham
Hunston
Donnington
Apuldram
Birdham
Sidlesham
West Wittering
East Wittering
Bracklesham
Earnley
Selsey
Nyetimber
Pagham
Runcton
Colworth
Shripney
North Bersted
South Bersted
Westbourne
Hermitage
Lumley
Nutbourne
Prinsted
Chidham
Broadbridge
Woodmancote
Hambrook
West Ashling
East Ashling
Lavant
Strettington
Waterbeach
Westerton
Summersdale
Hayling Island
North Hayling
Northney
Langstone
Bedhampton
Warblington
Leigh Park
Stockheath
West Leigh
Denvilles
Fleet
Stoke
Thorney Island
West Thorney
CHICHESTER HARBOUR
LANGSTONE HARBOUR
Hayling Bay
WEST SUSSEX
SUSSEX DOWNS
SOUTH DOWNS WAY
UPPARK
GOODWOOD
WEST DEAN GARDENS
WEALD & DOWNLAND OPEN AIR MUSEUM
STANSTED PARK
QUEEN ELIZABETH COUNTRY PARK
COWDRAY PARK
HOLLYCOMBE STEAM COLLECTION
FISHBOURNE ROMAN PALACE
Goodwood Aerodrome & Motor Racing Circuit
A3
A3(M)
A27
A272
A286
A259
A285
B2146
B2141
B2070
SU
70
0
1
2
3 miles
4
5 km

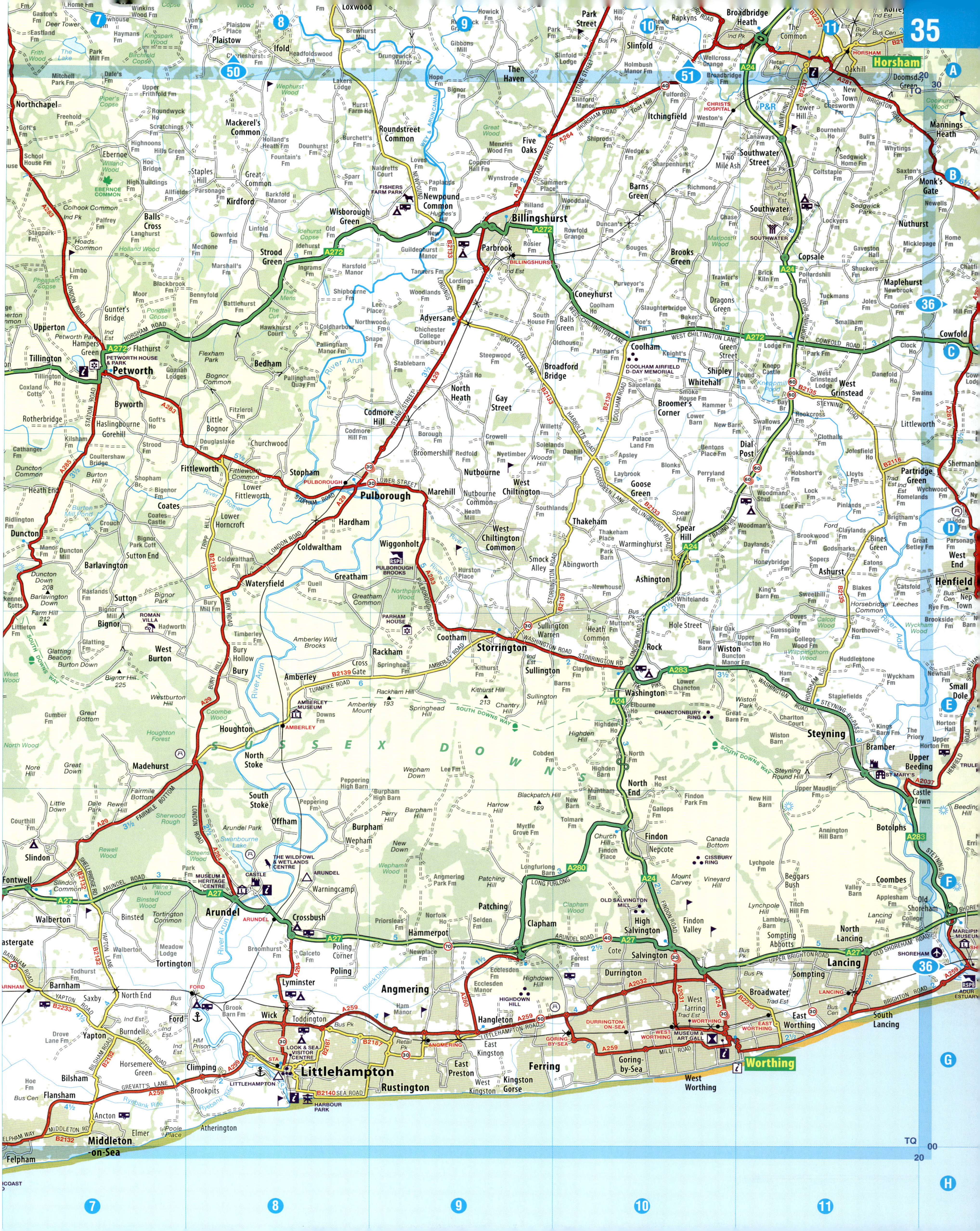
Horsham
Worthing
Petworth
Billingshurst
Pulborough
Storrington
Arundel
Littlehampton
Rustington
Angmering
Ferring
Goring-by-Sea
Lancing
Steyning
Washington
Findon
Henfield
Cowfold
Southwater
Middleton-on-Sea
SUSSEX DOWNS
South Downs Way
A24
A27
A29
A272
A283
A259
A280
A264
A281
A284
A285
A2032
A2037
B2139
B2133
50
51
36
7
8
9
10
11
A
B
C
D
E
F
G
H

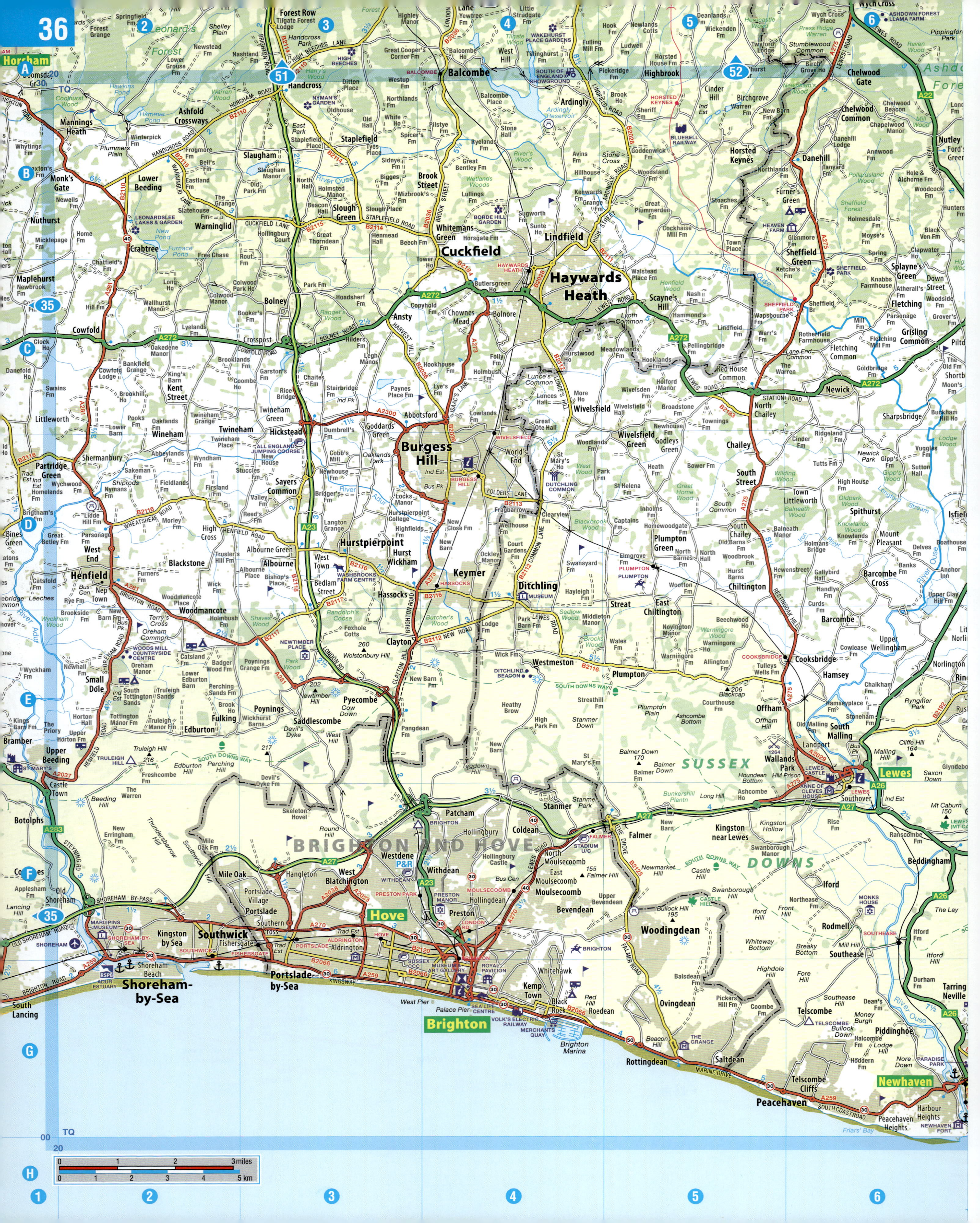
Horsham
Handcross
Balcombe
Ardingly
Highbrook
Chelwood Gate
Ashfold Crossways
Mannings Heath
Lower Beeding
Slaugham
Staplefield
Monk's Gate
Nuthurst
Warninglid
Crabtree
Slough Green
Brook Street
Whitemans Green
Cuckfield
Lindfield
Haywards Heath
Horsted Keynes
Danehill
Chelwood Common
Sheffield Green
Fletching
Maplehurst
Cowfold
Bolney
Ansty
Crosspost
Scayne's Hill
Newick
Chailey
Twineham
Hickstead
Burgess Hill
Wivelsfield
Wivelsfield Green
Wineham
Partridge Green
Shermanbury
Sayers Common
South Chailey
Hurstpierpoint
Keymer
Ditchling
Plumpton Green
Henfield
Woodmancote
Streat
East Chiltington
Chiltington
Barcombe
Small Dole
Poynings
Pyecombe
Clayton
Westmeston
Plumpton
Cooksbridge
Hamsey
Offham
Upper Beeding
Edburton
Fulking
Saddlescombe
SUSSEX
DOWNS
Lewes
South Malling
Wallands Park
Bramber
Botolphs
Patcham
Stanmer
Falmer
Kingston near Lewes
BRIGHTON AND HOVE
Coldean
Hollingbury
Westdene
Withdean
Mile Oak
West Blatchington
Hangleton
Portslade
Moulsecoomb
Woodingdean
Iford
Rodmell
Southease
Shoreham-by-Sea
Kingston by Sea
Southwick
Portslade-by-Sea
Hove
Preston
Brighton
Kemp Town
Whitehawk
Rottingdean
Ovingdean
Saltdean
Telscombe
Telscombe Cliffs
Peacehaven
Piddinghoe
Newhaven
South Lancing
Brighton Marina
0 1 2 3 miles
0 1 2 3 4 5 km

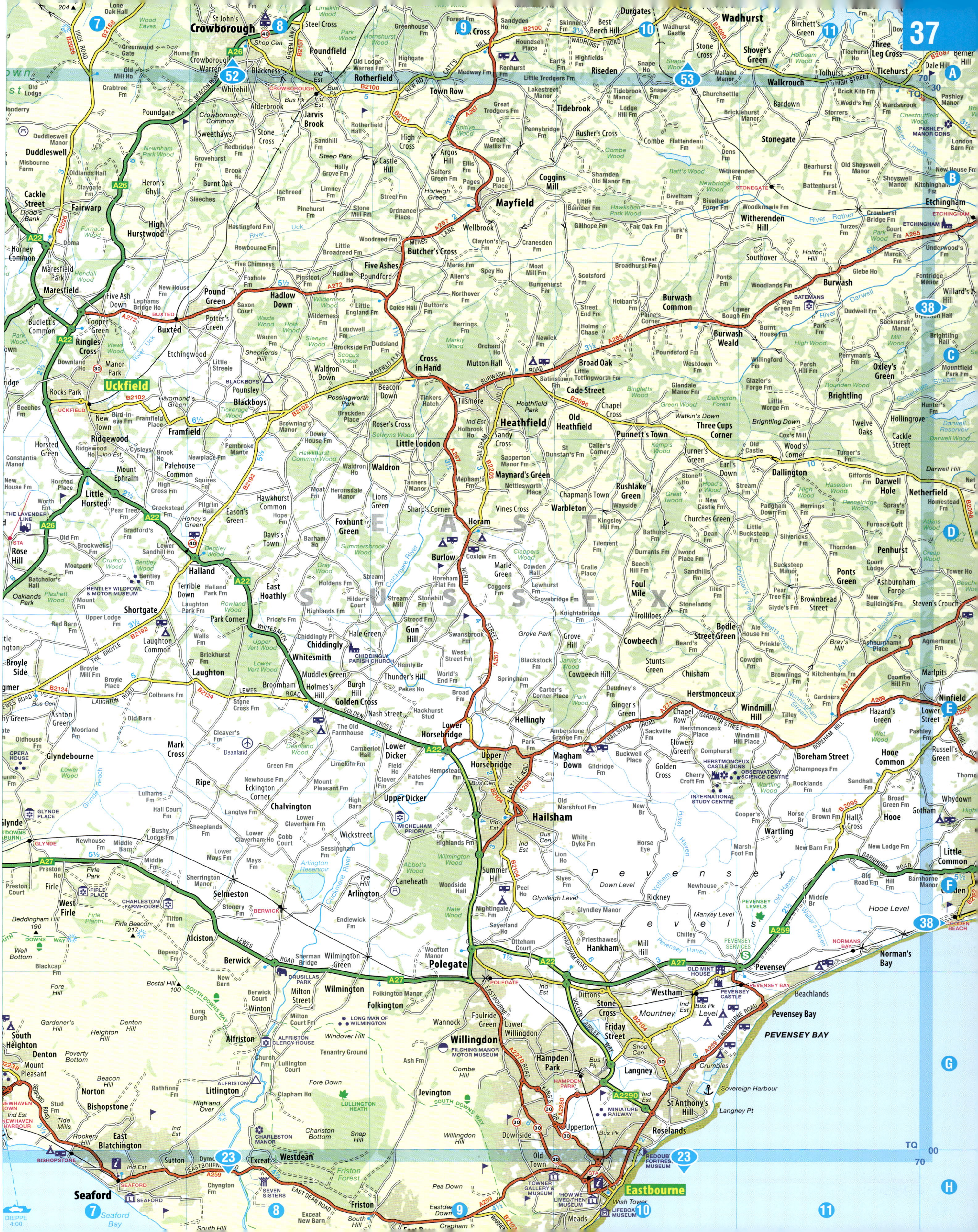
Crowborough
Wadhurst
Mayfield
Heathfield
Uckfield
Hailsham
Polegate
Eastbourne
Seaford
Pevensey
Pevensey Bay
Willingdon
Herstmonceux
Horam
Buxted
Maresfield
Jarvis Brook
Rotherfield
Five Ashes
Cross in Hand
Burwash
Burwash Common
Burwash Weald
Etchingham
Ticehurst
Wallcrouch
Stonegate
Tidebrook
Dallington
Warbleton
Rushlake Green
Punnett's Town
Three Cups Corner
Broad Oak
Cade Street
Old Heathfield
Waldron
Blackboys
Framfield
Halland
East Hoathly
Chiddingly
Whitesmith
Laughton
Golden Cross
Lower Dicker
Upper Dicker
Hellingly
Lower Horsebridge
Upper Horsebridge
Magham Down
Windmill Hill
Boreham Street
Ninfield
Hooe
Wartling
Stone Cross
Westham
Langney
Hampden Park
Jevington
Alfriston
Litlington
Berwick
Selmeston
Arlington
Wilmington
Folkington
Firle
West Firle
Glynde
Ripe
Chalvington
Norton
Bishopstone
East Blatchington
Sutton
Westdean
Exceat
Friston
East Dean
Ringles Cross
Ridgewood
Little Horsted
Shortgate
Fairwarp
High Hurstwood
Poundgate
Heron's Ghyll
Hadlow Down
Pound Green
Heathfield Park
Dudleswell
Cackle Street
Horney Common
Gun Hill
Muddles Green
Vines Cross
Foul Mile
Cowbeech
Bodle Street Green
Penhurst
Ponts Green
Netherfield
Darwell Hole
Brightling
Oxley's Green
Witherenden Hill
Three Leg Cross
Shover's Green
Stonecross
Durgates
Town Row
Mark Cross
Best Beech Hill
Riseden
Coggins Mill
Argos Hill
Butcher's Cross
Tilsmore
Sandy Cross
Maynard's Green
Little London
Horsted Green
Mount Ephraim
Palehouse Common
Eason's Green
Hawkhurst Common
Lower Willingdon
Upperton
Roselands
St Anthony's Hill
Friday Street
Mountney Level
Pevensey Levels
Normans Bay
Norman's Bay
Beachlands
Crumbles
Sovereign Harbour
Langney Pt
PEVENSEY BAY
EAST SUSSEX
A22
A26
A27
A259
A265
A267
A271
A272
A2290
B2100
B2101
B2102
B2104
B2124
B2192
B2096
B2095
Dieppe 4:00
TQ

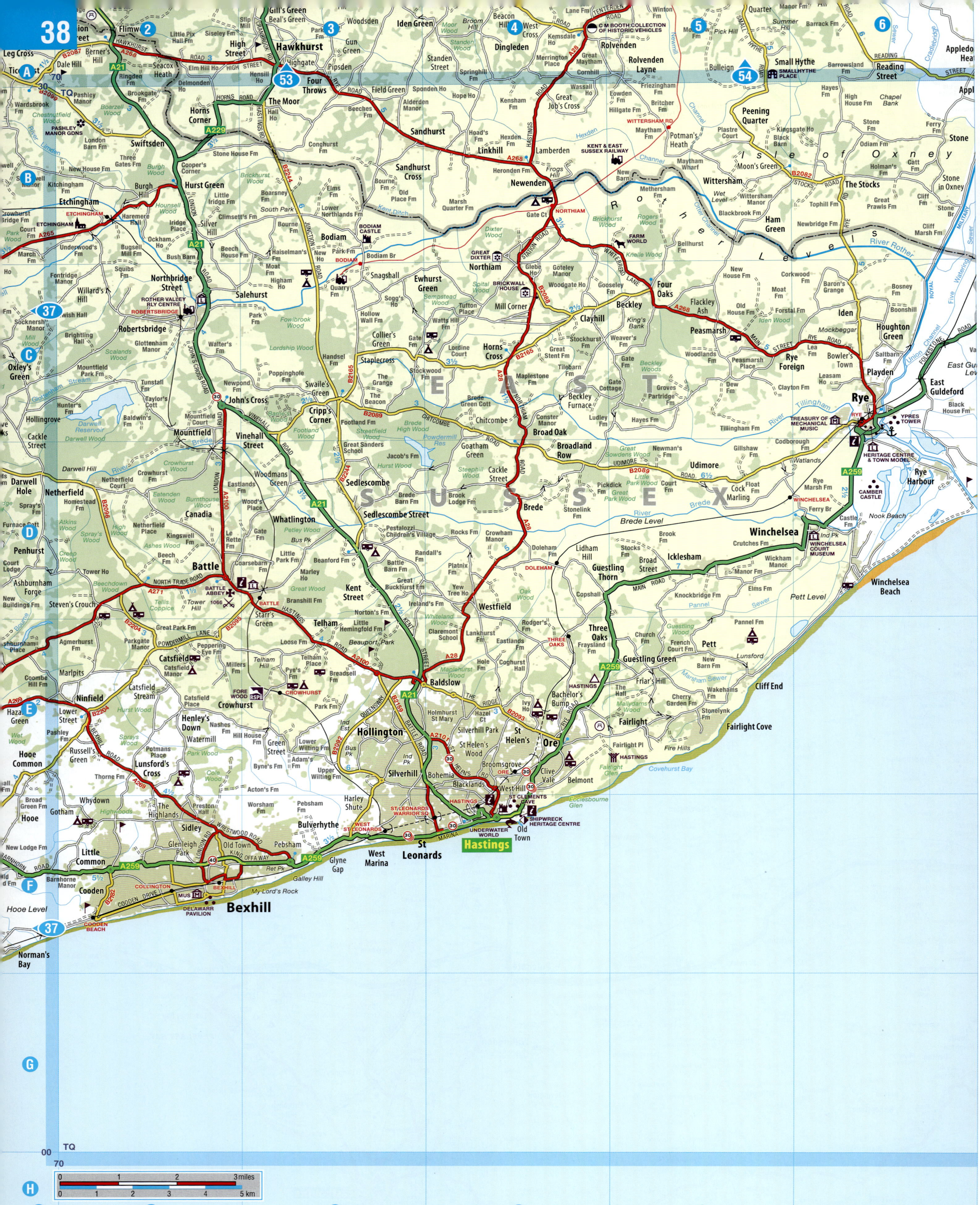
Hawkhurst
Flimwell
High Street
Four Throws
The Moor
Gun Green
Iden Green
Dingleden
Rolvenden
Rolvenden Layne
Small Hythe
Reading Street
Peening Quarter
Isle of Oxney
Wittersham
The Stocks
Stone in Oxney
Sandhurst
Sandhurst Cross
Linkhill
Newenden
Northiam
Great Dixter
Bodiam
Bodiam Castle
Salehurst
Robertsbridge
Hurst Green
Etchingham
Swiftsden
Horns Corner
Ewhurst Green
Staplecross
Cripp's Corner
John's Cross
Mountfield
Vinehall Street
Beckley
Four Oaks
Clayhill
Peasmarsh
Rye Foreign
Iden
Playden
Houghton Green
Rye
East Guldeford
Rye Harbour
Camber Castle
Broad Oak
Broadland Row
Udimore
Brede
Sedlescombe
Sedlescombe Street
Whatlington
Battle
Battle Abbey
Netherfield
Darwell Hole
Penhurst
Telham
Kent Street
Westfield
Guestling Thorn
Icklesham
Winchelsea
Winchelsea Beach
Pett Level
Three Oaks
Guestling Green
Pett
Fairlight
Fairlight Cove
Cliff End
Catsfield
Crowhurst
Ninfield
Hooe
Hooe Common
Lunsford's Cross
Sidley
Bexhill
Cooden
Little Common
Norman's Bay
Hollington
Baldslow
Silverhill
Ore
St Helen's
Hastings
St Leonards
West Marina
Glyne Gap
Bulverhythe
EAST SUSSEX
Rother Levels
River Rother
River Brede
Brede Level
Hooe Level
Covehurst Bay
A21
A28
A268
A259
A2100
A271
B2089
B2165
B2244
B2093
0 1 2 3 miles
0 1 2 3 4 5 km

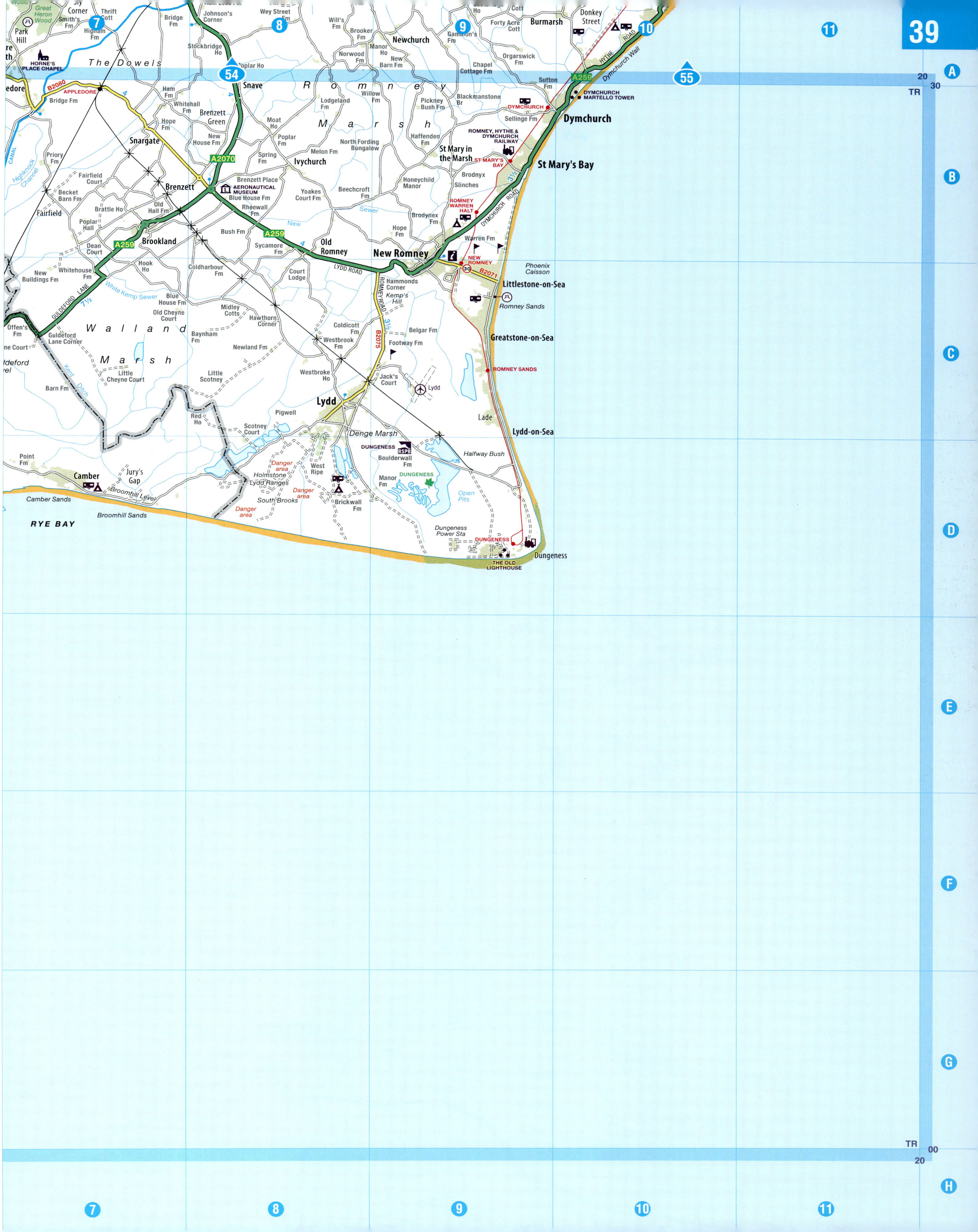
Great Heron Wood
Corner
Smith's Fm
Thrift Cott
Higham Fm
Park Hill
HORNE'S PLACE CHAPEL
The Dowels
Bridge Fm
Johnson's Corner
Stockbridge Ho
Wey Street Fm
Poplar Ho
54
Snave
Will's Fm
Brooker Fm
Norwood Fm
Manor Ho
New Barn Fm
Newchurch
Ho
Cott
Gammon's Fm
Forty Acre Cott
Burmarsh
Orgarswick Fm
Chapel Cottage Fm
Donkey Street
HYTHE ROAD
Dymchurch Wall
A259
55
Sutton Fm
DYMCHURCH MARTELLO TOWER
B2080
APPLEDORE
Bridge Fm
Ham Fm
Whitehall Fm
Brenzett Green
Hope Fm
Moat Ho
New House Fm
Snargate
A2070
Spring Fm
Poplar Fm
Romney Marsh
Lodgeland Fm
Willow Fm
Pickney Bush Fm
Blackmanstone Br
DYMCHURCH
Selling Fm
Dymchurch
North Fording Bungalow
Melon Fm
Haffenden Fm
ROMNEY, HYTHE & DYMCHURCH RAILWAY
St Mary in the Marsh
ST MARY'S BAY
St Mary's Bay
CANAL
Highknock Channel
Priory Fm
Fairfield Court
Becket Barn Fm
Fairfield
Brenzett
AERONAUTICAL MUSEUM
Blue House Fm
Brenzett Place
Ivychurch
Yoakes Court Fm
Beechcroft Fm
Honeychild Manor
Brodnyx
Slinches
Battle Ho
Old Hall Fm
Rheewall Fm
Poplar Hall
New Sewer
ROMNEY WARREN HALT
DYMCHURCH ROAD
Brodynex Fm
Hope Fm
Warren Fm
Bush Fm
A259
Sycamore Fm
Old Romney
New Romney
LYDD ROAD
Dean Court
Brookland
NEW ROMNEY
B2071
Phoenix Caisson
Littlestone-on-Sea
Hook Ho
Coldharbour Fm
Court Lodge
Hammonds Corner
Kemp's Hill
New Buildings Fm
Whitehouse Fm
White Kemp Sewer
Blue House Fm
Old Cheyne Court
Midley Cotts
Hawthorn Corner
ROMNEY ROAD
Romney Sands
GULDEFORD LANE
Walland Marsh
Offen's Fm
Guldeford Lane Corner
Baynham Fm
Coldicott Fm
Westbrook Fm
Belgar Fm
Footway Fm
B2075
Greatstone-on-Sea
ROMNEY SANDS
Newland Fm
Kent Ditch
Little Cheyne Court
Little Scotney
Westbroke Ho
Jack's Court
Lydd
Barn Fm
Lydd
Lade
Red Ho
Pigwell
Scotney Court
Denge Marsh
Lydd-on-Sea
DUNGENESS RSPB
Boulderwall Fm
Halfway Bush
Point Fm
Camber
Jury's Gap
Danger area
Holmstone
Lydd Ranges
West Ripe
Manor Fm
DUNGENESS
Open Pits
Broomhill Level
Danger area
South Brooks
Brickwall Fm
Camber Sands
Danger area
Broomhill Sands
RYE BAY
Dungeness Power Sta
DUNGENESS
Dungeness
THE OLD LIGHTHOUSE
TR
20
30
00
A
B
C
D
E
F
G
H
7
8
9
10
11

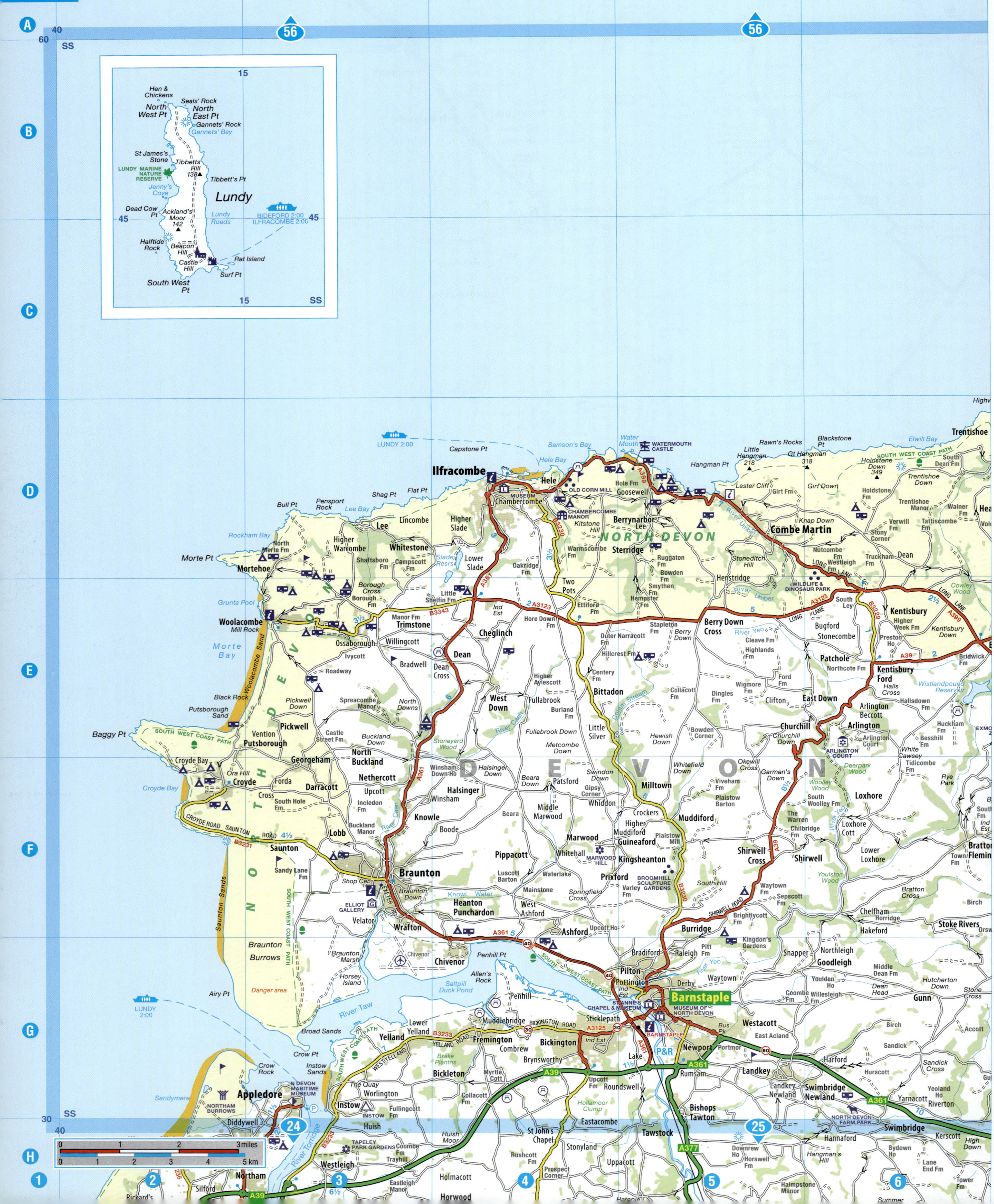
56
Lundy
Hen & Chickens
Seals' Rock
North West Pt
North East Pt
Gannets' Rock
Gannets' Bay
St James's Stone
Tibbetts Hill 138
LUNDY MARINE NATURE RESERVE
Jenny's Cove
Tibbett's Pt
Dead Cow Pt
Ackland's Moor 142
Lundy Roads
BIDEFORD 2:00 ILFRACOMBE 2:00
Halftide Rock
Beacon Hill
Castle Hill
Rat Island
Surf Pt
South West Pt
LUNDY 2:00
Capstone Pt
Samson's Bay
Hele Bay
Water Mouth
WATERMOUTH CASTLE
Rawn's Rocks
Little Hangman 218
Gt Hangman 318
Blackstone Pt
Elwill Bay
Trentishoe
Hangman Pt
Ilfracombe
Hele
MUSEUM
Chambercombe
OLD CORN MILL
Hole Fm
Goosewell
CHAMBERCOMBE MANOR
Berrynarbor
Lee
Kitstone Hill
NORTH DEVON
Lester Cliff
Girt Down
Holdstone Down 349
Combe Martin
Knap Down
Bull Pt
Pensport Rock
Shag Pt
Flat Pt
Lee Bay
Lee
Lincombe
Higher Slade
Rockham Bay
Morte Pt
Mortehoe
North Morte Fm
Higher Warcombe
Shaftsboro Fm
Whitestone
Campscott Fm
Lower Slade
Slade Resrs
Warmscombe Fm
Sterridge
Ruggaton Fm
Bowden Fm
Smythen Fm
Hempster Fm
Stoneditch Hill
Henstridge
River Umber
WILDLIFE & DINOSAUR PARK
Nutcombe Fm
Westleigh Fm
Truckham Fm
Dean
South Ley
Kentisbury
Higher Week Fm
Kentisbury Down
Grunta Pool
Borough Cross
Borough Fm
Little Shelfin Fm
Ind Est
A3123
Oakridge Fm
Two Pots
Ettiford Fm
Woolacombe
Mill Rock
Morte Bay
Manor Fm
Trimstone
Ossaborough
Willingcott
Hore Down Fm
Cheglinch
Outer Narracott Fm
Stapleton Fm
Berry Down
Berry Down Cross
River Yeo
Cleave Fm
Highlands Fm
Bugford
Stonecombe
Patchole
Northcote Fm
Kentisbury Ford
Ivycott
Bradwell
Dean
Dean Cross
Hillcrest Fm
Woolacombe Sand
Roadway
Higher Aylescott
Centery Fm
Bittadon
Collacott Fm
Dingles Fm
Wigmore Fm
Ford Fm
Clifton
East Down
Arlington Beccott
Arlington
ARLINGTON COURT
Black Rock
Putsborough Sand
Pickwell Down
Spreacombe Manor
North Downs
West Down
Fullabrook
Burland Fm
Fullabrook Down
Little Silver
Hewish Down
Bowden Corner
Churchill
Churchill Down
Baggy Pt
SOUTH WEST COAST PATH
Vention
Pickwell
Putsborough
Castle Street Fm
Buckland Down
Stoneyard Wood
Metcombe Down
Whitefield Down
Okewill Cross
Garman's Down
DEVON
Croyde Bay
Ora Hill
Croyde
Forda
Georgeham
North Buckland
Nethercott
Winsham Down Ho
Halsinger Down
Beara Down
Patsford
Swindon Down
Gipsy Corner
Whiddon
Milltown
Viveham Fm
Plaistow Barton
South Woolley Fm
Loxhore
Darracott
Upcott
Incledon Fm
Halsinger
Winsham
Middle Marwood
Crockers
Muddiford
The Warren
Chilbridge
Loxhore Cott
South Hole Fm
Knowle
Beara
Higher Muddiford
Guineaford
Plaistow Mill
CROYDE ROAD
SAUNTON ROAD
B3231
Saunton
Lobb
Buckland Manor
Boode
Marwood
Whitehall
MARWOOD HILL
Kingsheanton
Shirwell Cross
Shirwell
Lower Loxhore
Sandy Lane Fm
Braunton
Pippacott
Luscott Barton
Waterlake
Prixford
BROOMHILL SCULPTURE GARDENS
Varley Fm
South Hill
Waytown Fm
Sepscott Fm
Bratton Cross
Shop Cent
Braunton Down
Knowl Water
Heanton Punchardon
Mainstone
West Ashford
Springfield Cross
Saunton Sands
ELLIOT GALLERY
Velator
Wrafton
A361
Ashford
Upcott Ho
Burridge
Brightlycott Fm
Chelfham
Hakeford
Stoke Rivers
Braunton Burrows
Braunton Marsh
Chivenor
Chivenor
Penhill Pt
Bradiford
Raleigh
Pitt Fm
Kingdon's Gardens
Snapper
Northleigh
Goodleigh
Middle Dean Fm
Horsey Island
Allen's Rock
Pilton
Pottington
Derby
Waytown
Youlden Ho
Dean Head
Hutcherton Down
Danger area
Airy Pt
Saltpill Duck Pond
Penhill
Barnstaple
ST ANNE'S CHAPEL & MUSEUM
MUSEUM OF NORTH DEVON
Coombe Fm
Willesleigh Fm
Gunn
LUNDY 2:00
River Taw
Lower Yelland
Muddlebridge
BICKINGTON ROAD
Sticklepath
Bus Pk
Westacott
East Acland
Birch
Accott
Broad Sands
Yelland
Fremington
Bickington
Ind Est
Lake
P&R
Newport
Portmore
Sandick
Crow Pt
YELLAND ROAD
Combrew
Brynsworthy
Rumsam
Landkey
Harford
Hurscott
Sandick Cross
Crow Rock
Instow Sands
Brake Plantns
Bickleton
Myrtle Cott
A39
Upcott Fm
Roundswell
Landkey Newland
Swimbridge Newland
Yeoland Ho
Yarnacott
Riverton
Appledore
N DEVON MARITIME MUSEUM
The Quay
Worlington
Collacott Fm
Hollamoor Clump
Bishops Tawton
NORTHAM BURROWS
Sandymere
Instow
Fullingcott Fm
NORTH DEVON FARM PARK
Swimbridge
Diddywell
Huish
Eastacombe
St John's Chapel
Tawstock
Hannaford
Kerscott
24
25
River Torridge
TAPELEY PARK GARDENS
Coombe Fm
Trayhill
Huish Moor
Rushcott Fm
Stonyland
Prospect Corner
Uppacott
Downrew Ho
Horswell Fm
Hangman's Hill
Bydown Ho
Lane End Fm
Westleigh
Northam
Holmacott
Eastleigh Manor
Horwood
Halmpstone Manor
Tower Fm
Silford
Rickard's
SS
30
40
45
15
60
0 1 2 3 miles
0 1 2 3 4 5 km

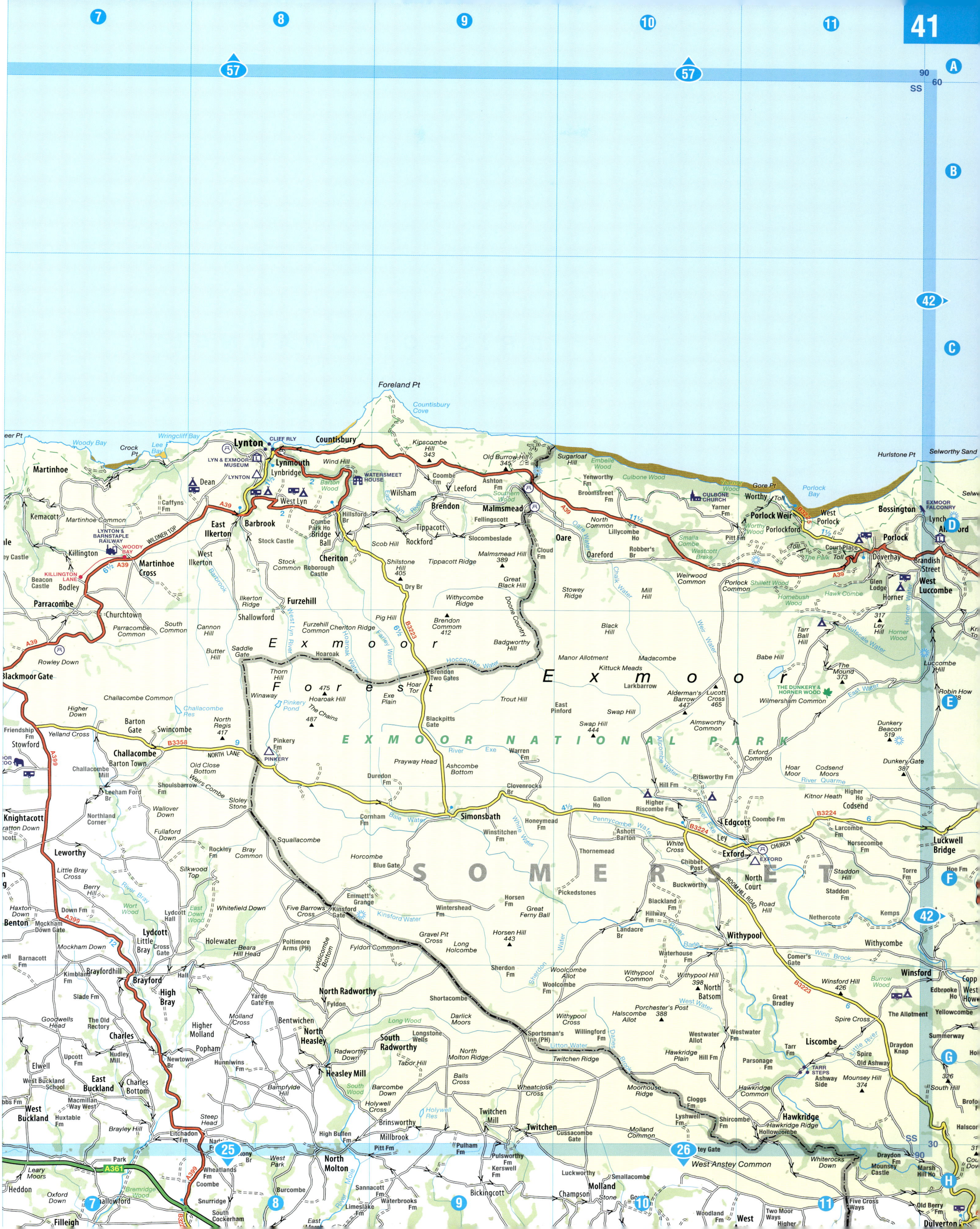

57
57
42
Foreland Pt
Countisbury Cove
Countisbury
Woody Bay
Crock Pt
Lee Bay
Wringcliff Bay
Lynton
CLIFF RLY
LYN & EXMOOR MUSEUM
Lynmouth
Lynbridge
Wind Hill
Kipscombe Hill 343
Old Burrow Hill 345
Sugarloaf Hill
Embelle Wood
Culbone Wood
Yenworthy Fm
Broomstreet Fm
CULBONE CHURCH
Yarner Fm
Gore Pt
Worthy
Porlock Bay
Hurlstone Pt
Selworthy Sand
Martinhoe
Dean
LYNTON
Barton Wood
WATERSMEET HOUSE
Coombe Fm
Leeford
Ashton Fm
Wilsham
Brendon
Malmsmead
West Lyn
Caffyns Fm
Kemacott
Martinhoe Common
LYNTON & BARNSTAPLE RAILWAY
WOODY BAY
WILDNER TOP
Killington
KILLINGTON LANE
Beacon Castle
Bodley
Martinhoe Cross
East Ilkerton
Barbrook
West Ilkerton
Stock Castle
Combe Park Ho
Bridge Ball
Hillsford Br
Cheriton
Tippacott
Rockford
Scob Hill
Fellingscott
Slocombeslade
North Common
Lillycombe Ho
Oare
Oareford
Robber's Br
Cloud Fm
Porlock Weir
Porlockford
Worthy Wood
West Porlock
Pitt Fm
Smalla Combe
Westcott Brake
Toll
Court Place
The Park
Porlock
Bossington
EXMOOR FALCONRY
Lynch
Doverhay
Brandish Street
West Luccombe
Glen Lodge
Horner
Parracombe
Churchtown
Parracombe Common
South Common
Stock Common
Roborough Castle
Shilstone Hill 405
Tippacott Ridge
Malmsmead Hill 389
Great Black Hill
Dry Br
Stowey Ridge
Mill Hill
Weirwood Common
Porlock Common
Shillett Wood
Homebush Wood
Hawk Combe
Furzehill
Ilkerton Ridge
Shallowford
Cannon Hill
Furzehill Common
Cheriton Ridge
Pig Hill
Withycombe Ridge
Brendon Common 412
Doone Country
Badgworthy Hill
Black Hill
Tarr Ball Hill
317 Ley Hill
Horner Wood
Rowley Down
Blackmoor Gate
Butter Hill
Saddle Gate
Hoaroak
Exmoor Forest
Manor Allotment
Madacombe
Kittuck Meads
Larkbarrow
Babe Hill
The Mound 373
Luccombe Hill
Thorn Hill
Winaway
475 Hoaroak Hill
Hoar Tor
Brendon Two Gates
Hoccombe Water
Exe Plain
Trout Hill
East Pinford
Alderman's Barrow 447
Lucott Cross 465
THE DUNKERY & HORNER WOOD
Wilmersham Common
Robin How
Challacombe Common
Higher Down
Challacombe Res
Pinkery Pond
The Chains 487
North Regis 417
Blackpitts Gate
Swap Hill
Swap Hill 444
Almsworthy Common
Dunkery Beacon 519
Friendship Fm
Yelland Cross
Barton Gate
Swincombe
Stowford
Challacombe
Barton Town
B3358
NORTH LANE
Pinkery Fm
PINKERY
EXMOOR NATIONAL PARK
River Exe
Warren Fm
Prayway Head
Ashcombe Bottom
Exford Common
Dunkery Gate 387
Challacombe Mill
Old Close Bottom
Weirs Combe
Duredon Fm
Clovenrocks Br
Hill Fm
Pitsworthy Fm
Hoar Moor
Codsend Moors
River Quarme
Leeham Ford Br
Shoulsbarrow Fm
Sloley Stone
Gallon Ho
Higher Riscombe Fm
Kitnor Heath
Higher Ho
Codsend
Knightacott
Northland Corner
Wallover Down
Cornham Fm
Barle Water
Simonsbath
Honeymead Fm
Pennycombe Water
Edgcott
Coombe Fm
B3224
Larcombe
Fullaford Down
Winstitchen Fm
White Water
Ashott Barton
Ley
White Cross
Exford
CHURCH HILL
Horsecombe Fm
Luckwell Bridge
Leworthy
Rockley Fm
Bray Common
Squallacombe
Horcombe
Thornemead
Chibbet Post
EXFORD
SOMERSET
Staddon Hill
Torre Fm
Hoe Fm
Little Bray Cross
Silkwood Top
Blue Gate
North Court
ROOM HILL ROAD
Staddon Fm
Buckworthy
Berry Hill
River Bray
Wort Wood
Emmett's Grange
Pickedstones
Horsen Fm
Blackland Fm
Road Hill
Haxton Down
Down Fm
Lydcott Hall
East Down Wood
Whitefield Down
Five Barrows Cross
Kinsford Gate
Kinsford Water
Wintershead Fm
Great Ferny Ball
Hillway Fm
Nethercote
Kemps
Benton
Mockham Down Gate
A399
Landacre Br
Withypool
Withycombe
Lydcott
Little Bray
Cross Gate
Holewater
Beara Hill Head
Poltimore Arms (PH)
Gravel Pit Cross
Long Holcombe
Horsen Hill 443
River Barle
Mockham Down
Fyldon Common
Waterhouse Fm
Comer's Gate
Winn Brook
Barnacott Fm
Kimbland Fm
Brayfordhill
Lyddicombe Bottom
Sherdon Fm
Woolcombe Allot
Withypool Common
Withypool Hill 398
North Batsom
Winsford Hill 426
Burrow Wood
Winsford
Brayford
Hall
High Bray
Woolcombe Fm
Slade Fm
Yarde Gate Fm
North Radworthy
Fyldon
Shortacombe
Porchester's Post 388
West Water
Great Bradley
Edbrooke Ho
The Allotment
Yellowcombe
Goodwells Head
The Old Rectory
Molland Cross
Bentwichen
Higher Molland
Long Wood
Darlick Moors
Withypool Cross
Halscombe Allot
Westwater Fm
Spire Cross
Summerway
Charles
Hudley Mill
Newtown Br
Popham
North Heasley
South Radworthy
Longstone Wells
Sportsman's Inn (PH)
Willingford Fm
Danes Brook
Westwater Allot
Tarr Fm
Liscombe
Draydon Knap
Little River
Upcott Fm
Elwell
Hunniwins Fm
Radworthy Down
North Molton Ridge
Litton Water
Twitchen Ridge
Hawkridge Plain
Hill Fm
Parsonage Fm
Spire
Old Ashway
TARR STEPS
Ashway Side
Mounsey Hill 374
South Hill
326
West Buckland School
East Buckland
Charles Bottom
Heasley Mill
Tabor Hill
Balls Cross
Bampfylde Hill
South Wood
Barcombe Down
Wheatclose Cross
Moorhouse Ridge
Hawkridge Common
Macmillan Way West
West Buckland
Huxtable Fm
Brayley Hill
Steep Head
Holywell Cross
Holywell Res
Twitchen Mill
Brinsworthy
Twitchen
Cussacombe Gate
Cloggs Fm
Lyshwell Fm
Shircombe Fm
Hawkridge
Hawkridge Ridge
Hollowcombe
Molland Common
Litchadon Fm
High Bullen Fm
Millbrook
Pitt Fm
Pulham Fm
Pulsworthy Fm
Kerswell Fm
25
26
Park
West Park
North Molton
Leary Moors
A361
Wheatlands Fm
Coombe
Burcombe
Luckworthy
Smallacombe
West Anstey Common
Whiterocks Down
Draydon Fm
Mounsey Castle
Marsh Hill Ho
Heddon
Oxford Down
Bremridge Wood
Snurridge
South Cockerham
River Mole
Sannacott Fm
Limeslake Fm
Waterbrooks Fm
Bickingcott
Champson
Molland
Stone
Woodland Fm
West
Two Moor Ways
Higher
Five Cross Ways
Old Berry Fm
Dulverton
Filleigh
SS
90
60
30
A
B
C
D
E
F
G
H
7
8
9
10
11
A39
A399
B3223
B3225

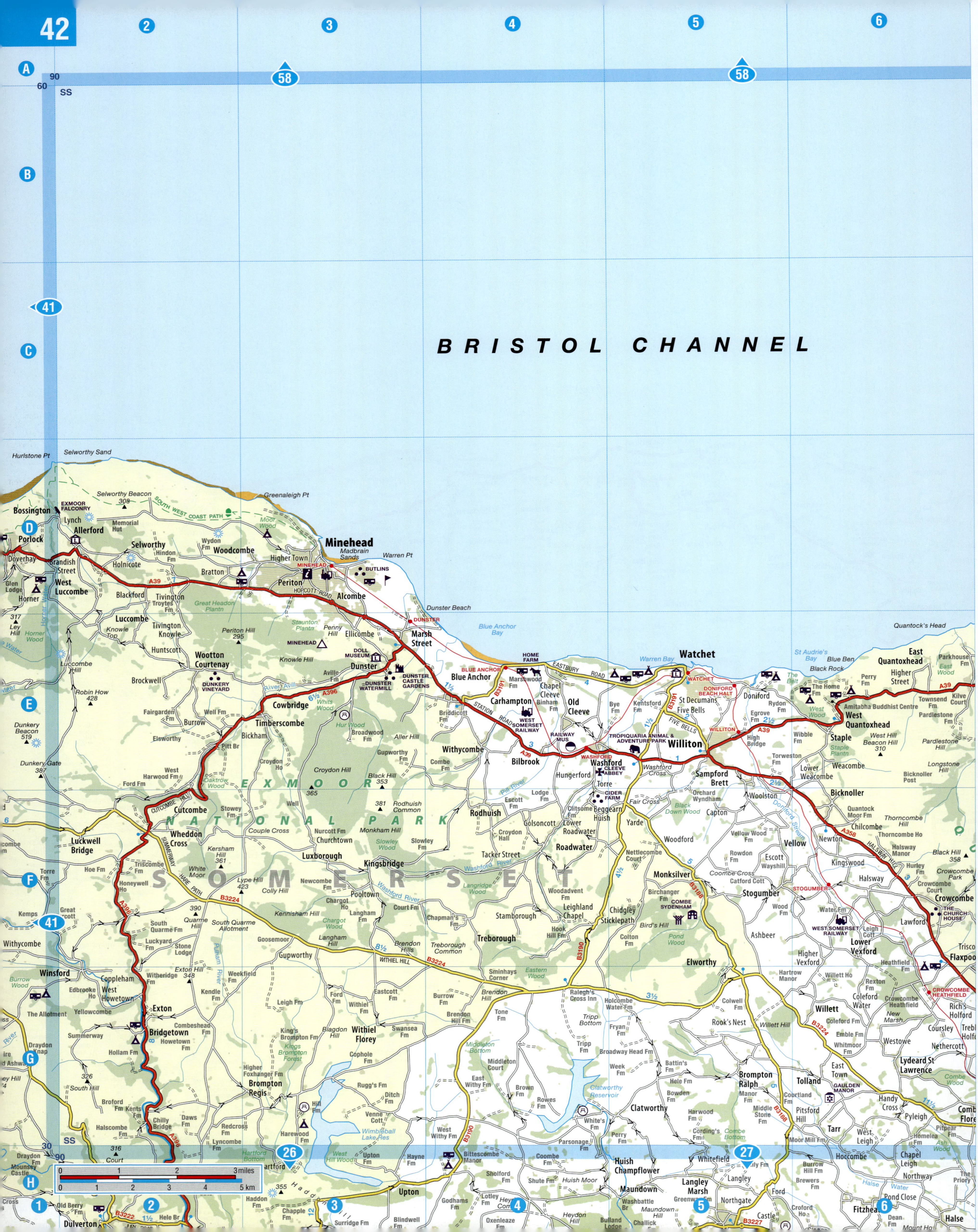
BRISTOL CHANNEL
58
41
26
27
Hurlstone Pt
Selworthy Sand
Selworthy Beacon
Greenaleigh Pt
SOUTH WEST COAST PATH
Bossington
EXMOOR FALCONRY
Lynch
Allerford
Porlock
Selworthy
Woodcombe
Minehead
Madbrain Sands
Warren Pt
BUTLINS
Higher Town
Bratton
Periton
Alcombe
Holnicote
Doverhay
Brandish Street
West Luccombe
Horner
Blackford
Tivington
Luccombe
Wootton Courtenay
DUNKERY VINEYARD
Dunster Beach
Blue Anchor Bay
Marsh Street
Dunster
DUNSTER CASTLE GARDENS
DUNSTER WATERMILL
DOLL MUSEUM
Ellicombe
Knowle Hill
Periton Hill
Timberscombe
Cowbridge
Bickham
Brockwell
Robin How 428
Dunkery Beacon 519
Dunkery Gate
Blue Anchor
HOME FARM
Marshwood
Carhampton
Chapel Cleeve
Old Cleeve
WEST SOMERSET RAILWAY
RAILWAY MUS
Withycombe
Bilbrook
Washford
CLEEVE ABBEY
Watchet
Warren Bay
EASTBURY ROAD
St Decumans
Five Bells
Doniford
DONIFORD BEACH HALT
Williton
TROPIQUARIA ANIMAL & ADVENTURE PARK
St Audrie's Bay
Blue Ben
Black Rock
Quantock's Head
East Quantoxhead
Perry Fm
Higher Street
The Home Fm
West Quantoxhead
Amitabha Buddhist Centre
Staple
Sampford Brett
Weacombe
Bicknoller
Woolston
EXMOOR NATIONAL PARK
SOMERSET
Cutcombe
Wheddon Cross
Luckwell Bridge
Luxborough
Churchtown
Kingsbridge
Rodhuish
Roadwater
Tacker Street
Treborough
Leighland Chapel
Chidgley
Sticklepath
Monksilver
COMBE SYDENHAM
Elworthy
Stogumber
Vellow
Yarde
Woodford
Capton
Halsway
Crowcombe
Kingswood
Lawford
Flaxpool
Lower Vexford
Willett
Brompton Ralph
Tolland
GAULDEN MANOR
Lydeard St Lawrence
Tarr
Clatworthy
Clatworthy Reservoir
Huish Champflower
Maundown
Langley Marsh
Withiel Florey
Brompton Regis
Wimbleball Lake Res
Upton
Exton
Bridgetown
Winsford
Withycombe
Kemps
Hoe Fm
Dulverton
Old Berry Fm
Haddon
Chapple Fm
Surridge Fm
Oxenleaze Fm
Northgate
Ford
Fitzhead
Halse
Chapel Leigh
Northway
Pond Close
Sminhays Corner
Ralegh's Cross Inn
Gupworthy
Croydon Hill
Brendon Hills
Court
Hayne
B3224
A39
A396
A358
B3190
B3191
B3188
B3227
B3222
0 1 2 3 miles
0 1 2 3 4 5 km

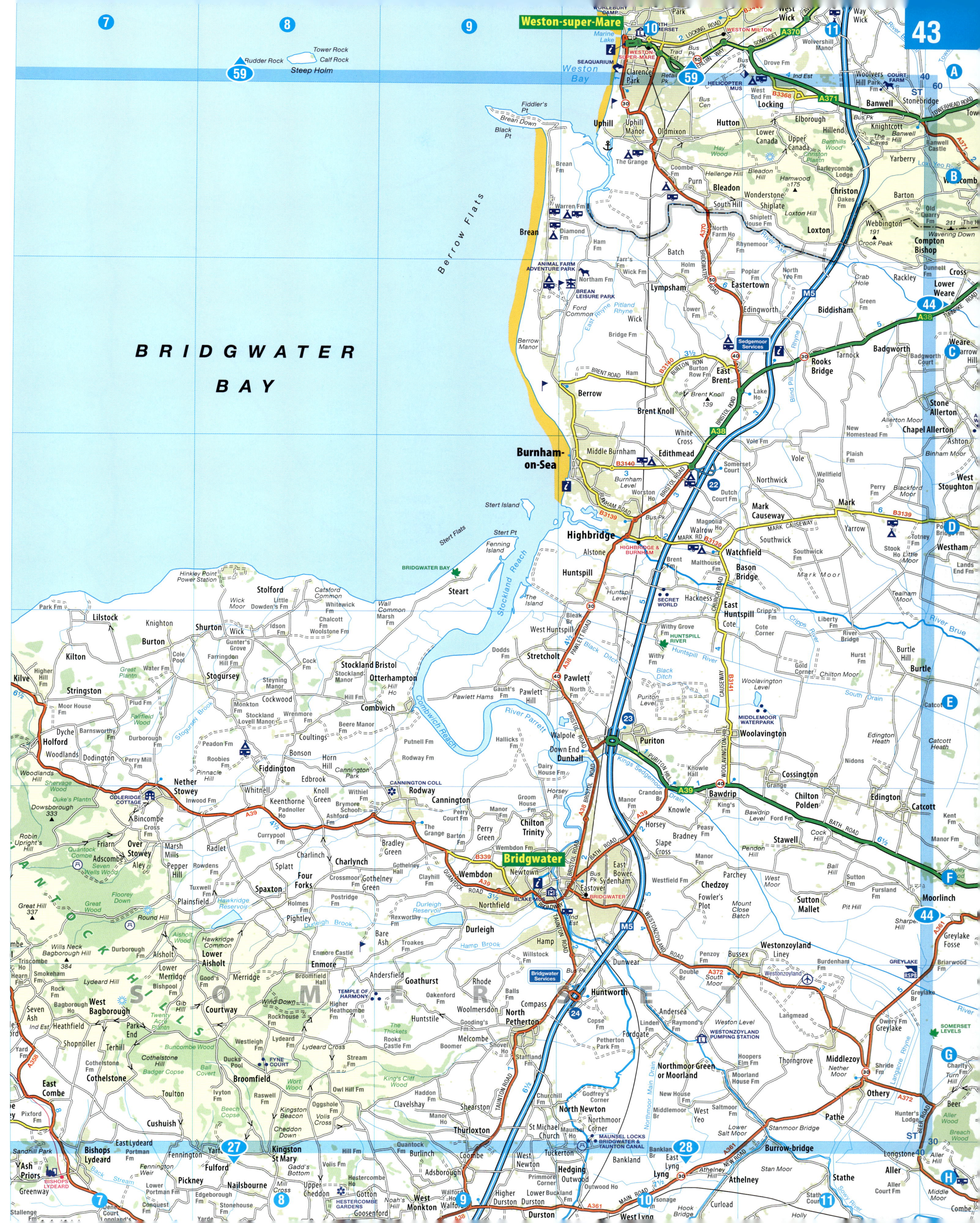
BRIDGWATER BAY
Weston-super-Mare
Steep Holm
Rudder Rock
Tower Rock
Calf Rock
Weston Bay
Brean Down
Berrow Flats
Brean
Berrow
Burnham-on-Sea
Highbridge
Stert Island
Stert Flats
Stert Pt
Fenning Island
Steart
Stockland Reach
Combwich Reach
River Parrett
Bridgwater
Uphill
Oldmixon
Hutton
Locking
Banwell
Bleadon
Loxton
Lympsham
East Brent
Brent Knoll
Edithmead
Watchfield
Bason Bridge
East Huntspill
Huntspill
Pawlett
Puriton
Woolavington
Cossington
Bawdrip
Chilton Trinity
Stretcholt
Dunball
Wembdon
Durleigh
Enmore
Goathurst
North Petherton
Huntworth
Chedzoy
Westonzoyland
Middlezoy
Othery
Burrow-bridge
Lyng
Athelney
Stathe
Aller
Moorlinch
Edington
Catcott
Chilton Polden
Stawell
Sutton Mallet
Burtle
Mark
Mark Causeway
Westham
Wedmore
Biddisham
Badgworth
Rooks Bridge
Compton Bishop
Christon
Webbington
Stolford
Stogursey
Shurton
Burton
Kilton
Lilstock
Stringston
Holford
Kilve
Nether Stowey
Over Stowey
Fiddington
Cannington
Rodway
Combwich
Otterhampton
Stockland Bristol
Spaxton
Four Forks
Charlynch
Aisholt
West Bagborough
Cothelstone
Broomfield
Kingston St Mary
Bishops Lydeard
Fulford
Nailsbourne
Pickney
Thurloxton
Durston
Hedging
Adsborough
Creech Heathfield
West Monkton
North Newton
East Combe
Cushuish
Courtway
Merridge
Lower Aisholt
Pightley
Hinkley Point Power Station
Sedgemoor Services
Bridgwater Services
River Brue
Huntspill River
King's Sedgemoor Drain
QUANTOCK HILLS
SOMERSET
M5
A38
A39
A370
A371
A372
A361
B3139
B3140
B3141
B3339
59
27
28
44

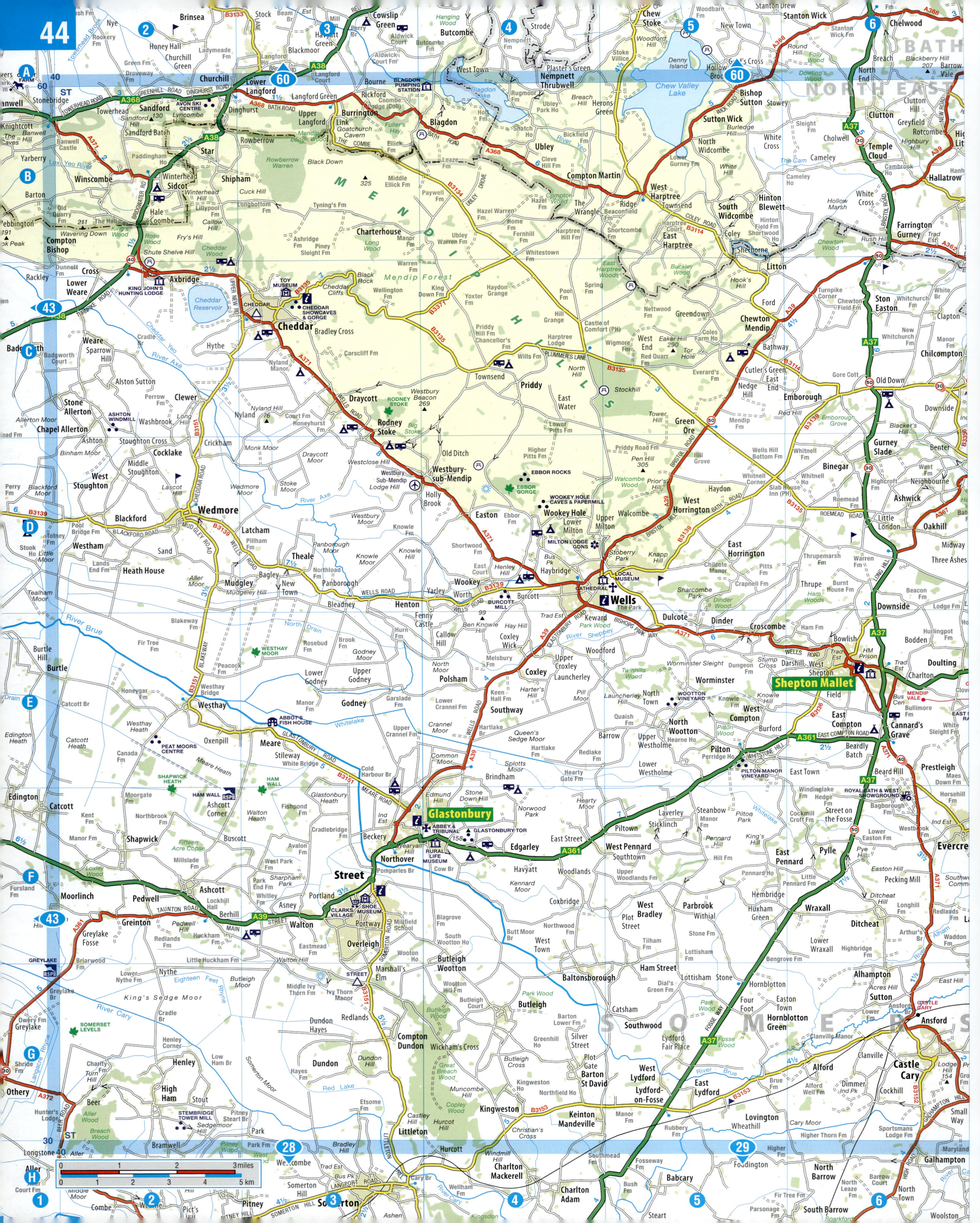
BATH
NORTH EAST
MENDIP HILLS
Mendip Forest
SOMERSET
Chew Valley Lake
Cheddar Reservoir
Churchill
Langford
Lower Langford
Sandford
Winscombe
Shipham
Star
Rowberrow
Burrington
Blagdon
Ubley
Compton Martin
West Harptree
East Harptree
Chew Stoke
Nempnett Thrubwell
Bishop Sutton
Sutton Wick
Chelwood
Clutton
Temple Cloud
Hallatrow
Hinton Blewett
Farrington Gurney
Litton
Chewton Mendip
Ston Easton
Chilcompton
Emborough
Binegar
Gurney Slade
Oakhill
Ashwick
Downside
Doulting
Shepton Mallet
Cannard's Grave
Croscombe
Dinder
Dulcote
Wells
Priddy
Westbury-sub-Mendip
Rodney Stoke
Draycott
Cheddar
Axbridge
Compton Bishop
Cross
Lower Weare
Weare
Wedmore
Blackford
Theale
Mudgley
Westham
Heath House
Wookey
Wookey Hole
Easton
Henton
Westhay
Meare
Godney
Polsham
Coxley
Glastonbury
Street
Walton
Ashcott
Shapwick
Catcott
Edington
Moorlinch
Pedwell
Greinton
Butleigh
Baltonsbridge
West Pennard
Pilton
North Wootton
Evercreech
Pylle
East Pennard
Ditcheat
Alhampton
Castle Cary
Ansford
Alford
Lovington
Wheathill
Keinton Mandeville
Kingweston
Charlton Mackerell
Charlton Adam
Babcary
Barton St David
Somerton
Compton Dundon
Littleton
Dundon
Henley
High Ham
Othery
Hurcott
Galhampton
North Barrow
South Barrow
A38
A368
A371
A39
A361
A37
A372
B3135
B3139
B3151
B3153
0 1 2 3 miles
0 1 2 3 4 5 km

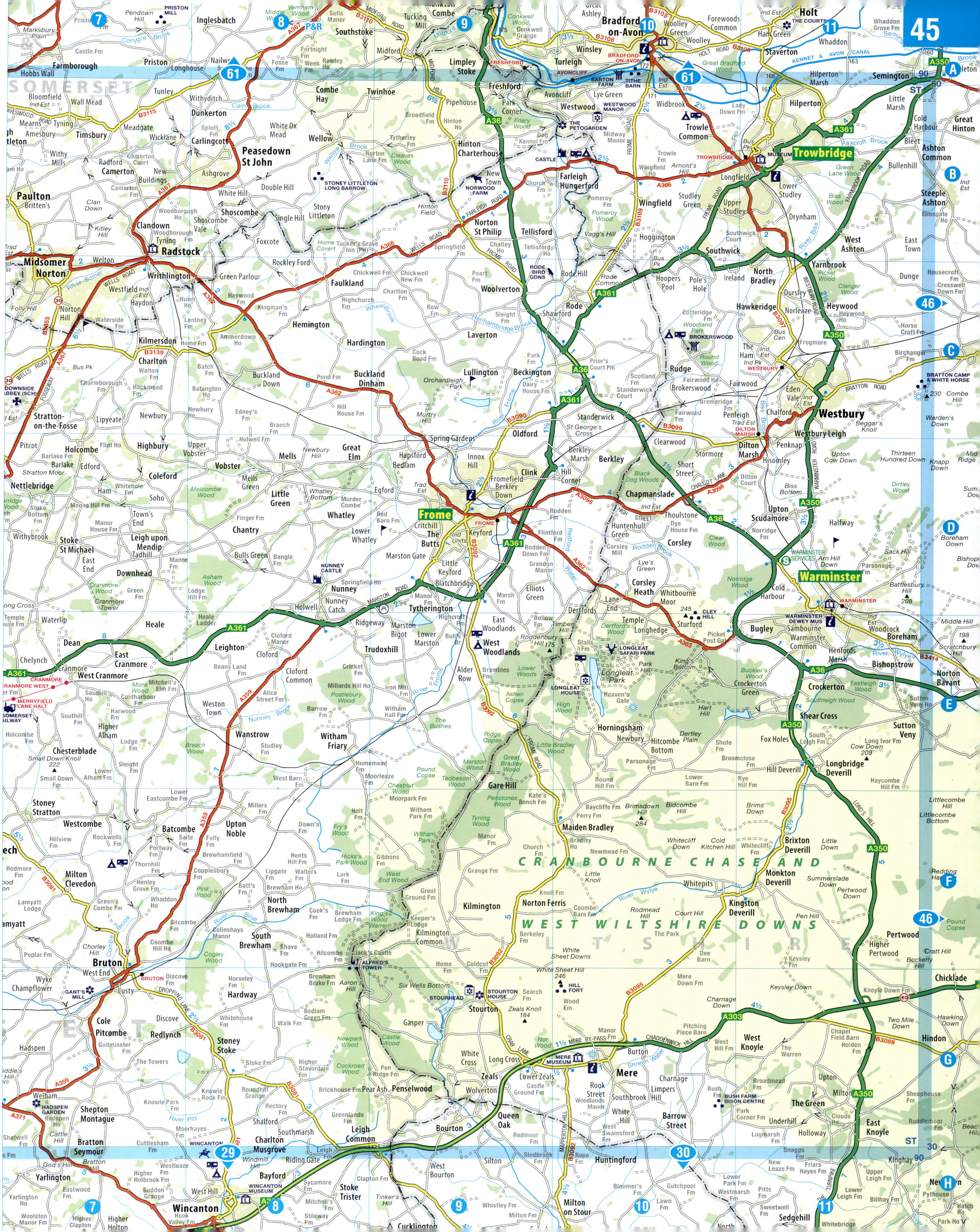
SOMERSET
CRANBOURNE CHASE AND
WEST WILTSHIRE DOWNS
WILTSHIRE
Bradford-on-Avon
Holt
Trowbridge
Westbury
Warminster
Frome
Radstock
Midsomer Norton
Paulton
Peasedown St John
Bruton
Wincanton
Mere
Inglesbatch
Southstoke
Midford
Limpley Stoke
Freshford
Winsley
Turleigh
Staverton
Semington
Hilperton
Farmborough
Priston
Tunley
Dunkerton
Timsbury
Camerton
Carlingcott
Wellow
Hinton Charterhouse
Farleigh Hungerford
Wingfield
Westwood
Avoncliff
Widbrook
Trowle Common
Shoscombe
Norton St Philip
Tellisford
Woolverton
Rode
Southwick
North Bradley
West Ashton
Yarnbrook
Heywood
Hawkeridge
Beckington
Laverton
Lullington
Hardington
Buckland Dinham
Hemington
Faulkland
Kilmersdon
Charlton
Stratton-on-the-Fosse
Holcombe
Coleford
Vobster
Mells
Great Elm
Oldford
Berkley
Standerwick
Rudge
Dilton Marsh
Chapmanslade
Corsley
Corsley Heath
Upton Scudamore
Westbury Leigh
Whatley
Chantry
Leigh upon Mendip
Stoke St Michael
Nunney
Tytherington
Marston Bigot
Trudoxhill
West Woodlands
East Woodlands
Longleat Park
Horningsham
Crockerton
Bishopstrow
Boreham
Sutton Veny
Norton Bavant
Longbridge Deverill
Hill Deverill
Brixton Deverill
Monkton Deverill
Kingston Deverill
Maiden Bradley
Gare Hill
Witham Friary
Wanstrow
Leighton
East Cranmore
West Cranmore
Chesterblade
Batcombe
Upton Noble
North Brewham
South Brewham
Milton Clevedon
Kilmington
Norton Ferris
Stourton
Zeals
Penselwood
Bourton
Charlton Musgrove
Shepton Montague
Redlynch
Stoney Stoke
Cole
Pitcombe
Yarlington
Huntingford
Milton on Stour
West Knoyle
East Knoyle
Hindon
Chicklade
Pertwood
The Green
Sedgehill
Kinghay
Queen Oak
Leigh Common
Stoke Trister
Cucklington
Bayford
Dean
Heale
Downhead
Cranmore
Pendown Hill
Castle Fm
Wall Mead
Bloomfield
Meadgate
Radford
Clandown
Welton
Writhlington
Haydon
Chilcompton
Stratton Moor
Nettlebridge
Highbury
Soho
Ham
Bullum
Upper Studley
Lower Studley
Drynham
Steeple Ashton
Great Hinton
Keevil
Littleton
Clyffe Pypard
Midway
Babington
Buckland Down
Edney's Fm
Newbury
Great Hinton
A36
A361
A350
A362
A366
A367
A303
A371
A359
B3110
B3108
B3109
B3105
B3098
B3099
B3092
B3095
B3081
B3089
B3139
B3414
61
30
29
8
9
10
11
7
46
A
B
C
D
E
F
G
H

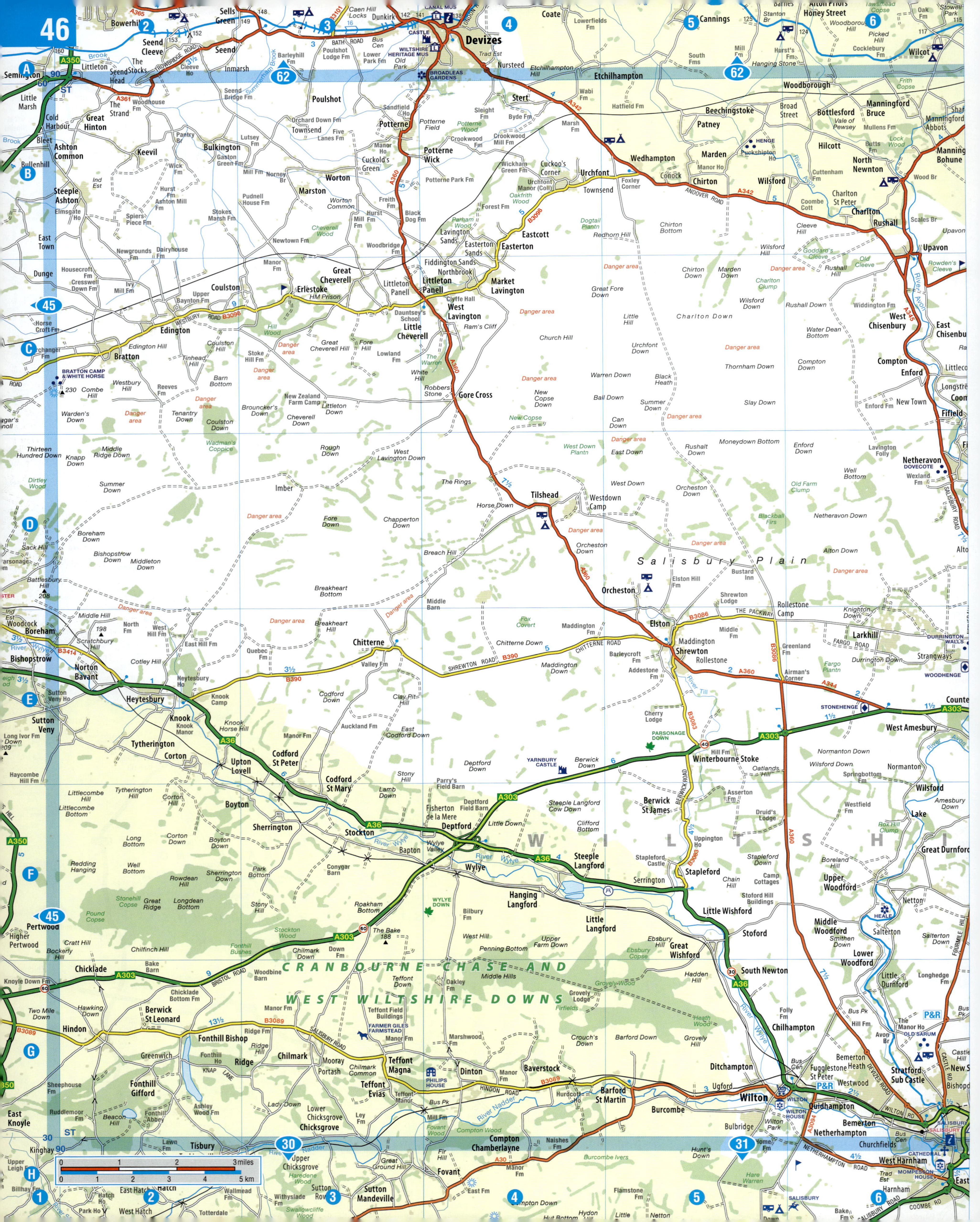

Devizes
Bowerhill
Sells Green
Seend
Seend Cleeve
Semington
Littleton
Seend Head
Inmarsh
Poulshot
Potterne
Potterne Wick
Coate
Nursteed
Etchilhampton
Cannings
Honey Street
Woodborough
Wilcot
Beechingstoke
Patney
Marden
Chirton
Conock
Wilsford
North Newnton
Manningford Bruce
Manningford Abbots
Manning Bohune
Hilcott
Charlton St Peter
Charlton
Rushall
Upavon
Wedhampton
Urchfont
Stert
Worton
Marston
Bulkington
Keevil
Great Hinton
Little Marsh
Ashton Common
Steeple Ashton
East Town
Dunge
Coulston
Erlestoke
Great Cheverell
Little Cheverell
Littleton Panell
Market Lavington
West Lavington
Easterton
Eastcott
Edington
Bratton
Gore Cross
Tilshead
Westdown Camp
Orcheston
Elston
Shrewton
Maddington
Rollestone
Larkhill
Durrington
Imber
Chitterne
Heytesbury
Norton Bavant
Bishopstrow
Boreham
Knook
Sutton Veny
Tytherington
Corton
Upton Lovell
Codford St Peter
Codford St Mary
Boyton
Sherrington
Stockton
Fisherton de la Mere
Deptford
Wylye
Bapton
Steeple Langford
Hanging Langford
Little Langford
Winterbourne Stoke
Berwick St James
Stapleford
Little Wishford
Great Wishford
Stoford
South Newton
West Amesbury
Wilsford
Lake
Great Durnford
Upper Woodford
Middle Woodford
Lower Woodford
Salisbury Plain
WILTSHIRE
CRANBOURNE CHASE AND WEST WILTSHIRE DOWNS
Chicklade
Hindon
Berwick St Leonard
Fonthill Bishop
Fonthill Gifford
Ridge
Chilmark
Teffont Magna
Teffont Evias
Dinton
Baverstock
Barford St Martin
Wilton
Burcombe
Ditchampton
Chilhampton
Quidhampton
Bemerton
Netherhampton
Stratford sub Castle
Fugglestone St Peter
Tisbury
East Knoyle
Compton Chamberlayne
Fovant
Sutton Mandeville
Chicksgrove
Upper Chicksgrove
A350
A36
A303
A360
A342
A345
A361
A3098
B3098
B390
B3086
B3083
B3089
B3414
Stonehenge
Yarnbury Castle
Danger area

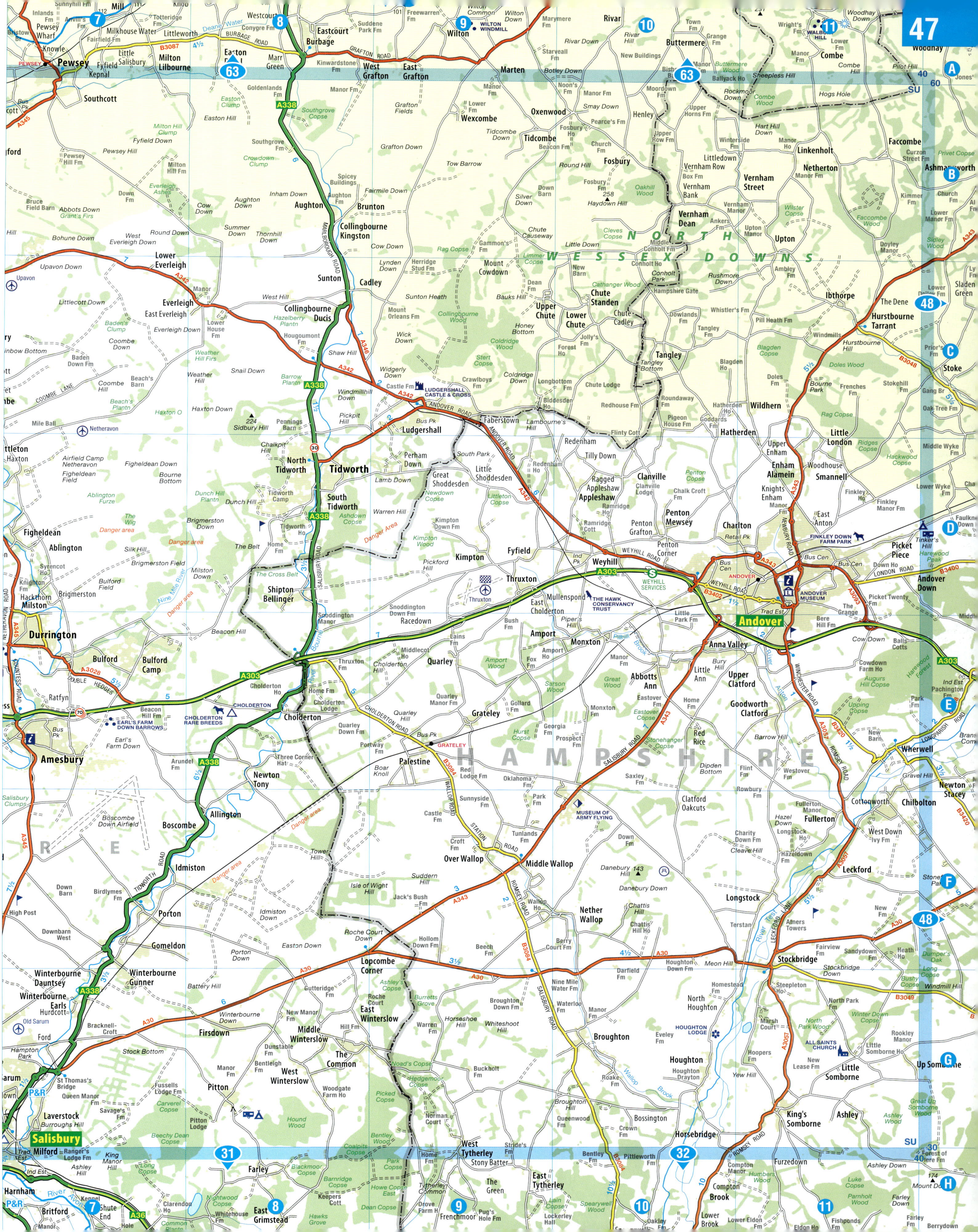
Pewsey
Southcott
Milton Lilbourne
Easton
Burbage
West Grafton
East Grafton
Wilton
Marten
Buttermere
Combe
Rivar
Oxenwood
Wexcombe
Tidcombe
Fosbury
Henley
Linkenholt
Faccombe
Vernham Row
Vernham Street
Vernham Dean
Netherton
Upton
Ibthorpe
Hurstbourne Tarrant
Aughton
Brunton
Collingbourne Kingston
Sunton
Cadley
Collingbourne Ducis
Everleigh
East Everleigh
Lower Everleigh
Upper Chute
Lower Chute
Chute Standen
Chute Cadley
Tangley
Wildhern
Hatherden
Little London
Smannell
Enham Alamein
Upper Enham
Knights Enham
Ludgershall
Tidworth
North Tidworth
South Tidworth
Perham Down
Great Shoddesden
Little Shoddesden
Faberstown
Redenham
Appleshaw
Ragged Appleshaw
Clanville
Penton Mewsey
Penton Grafton
Charlton
Kimpton
Fyfield
Weyhill
Thruxton
Mullenspond
East Cholderton
Amport
Monxton
Andover
Anna Valley
Upper Clatford
Goodworth Clatford
Abbotts Ann
Little Ann
Red Rice
Quarley
Grateley
Palestine
Cholderton
Shipton Bellinger
Figheldean
Ablington
Durrington
Bulford
Bulford Camp
Milston
Amesbury
Newton Tony
Allington
Boscombe
Idmiston
Porton
Gomeldon
Winterbourne Dauntsey
Winterbourne Gunner
Winterbourne Earls
Hurdcott
Firsdown
Middle Winterslow
West Winterslow
East Winterslow
The Common
Lopcombe Corner
Over Wallop
Middle Wallop
Nether Wallop
Broughton
Houghton
North Houghton
Longstock
Leckford
Stockbridge
Fullerton
Chilbolton
Wherwell
Little Somborne
King's Somborne
Ashley
Horsebridge
Bossington
Pitton
Farley
Laverstock
Salisbury
Milford
Britford
East Grimstead
West Tytherley
East Tytherley
Frenchmoor
Lockerley
Compton
Brook
Picket Piece
Andover Down
Newton Stacey
NORTH WESSEX DOWNS
HAMPSHIRE
A338
A342
A343
A303
A30
A345
A3057
A36
B3084
B3048
B3400
B3420
B3087
63
31
32
48

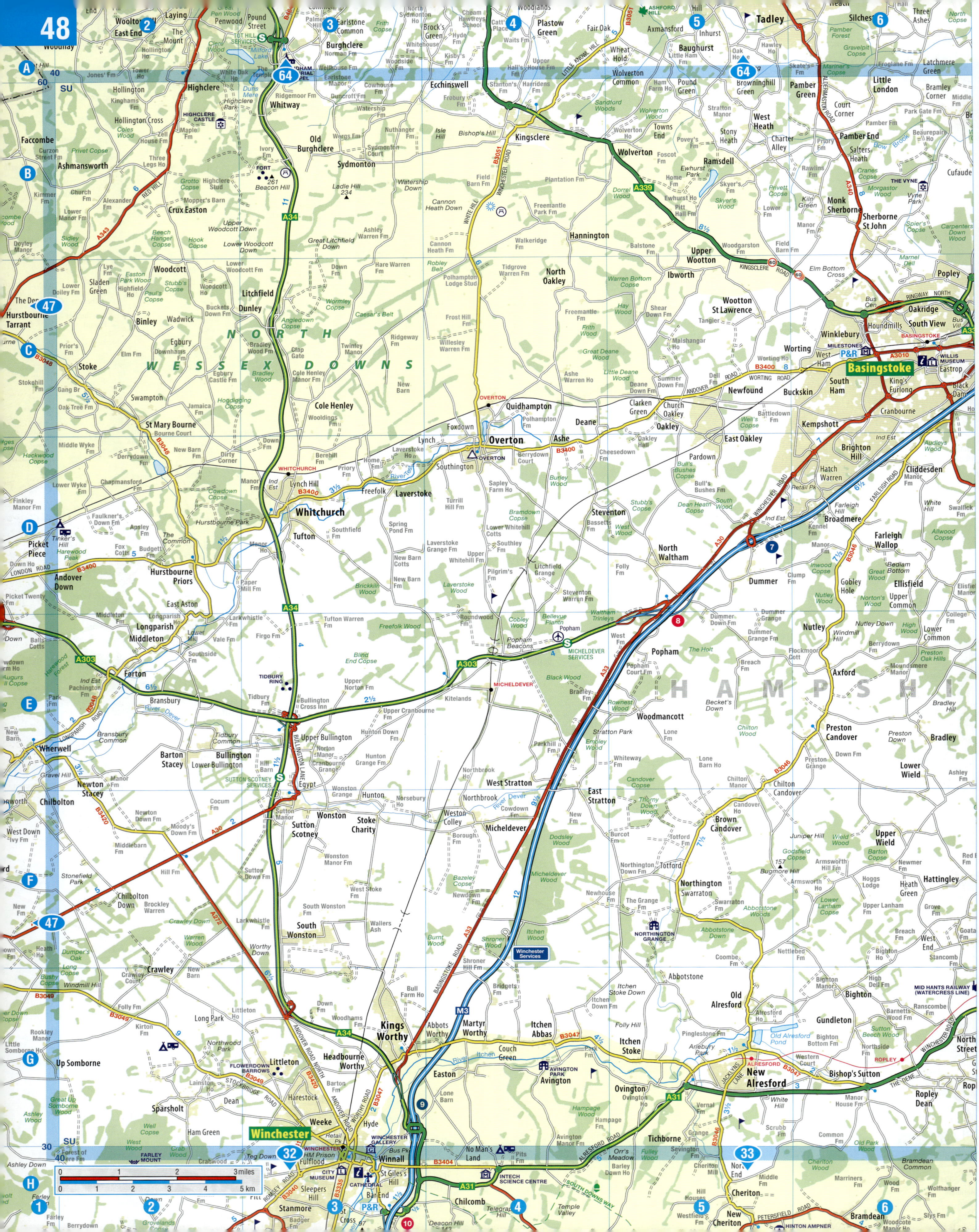

Woolton Hill
East End
Laying
The Mount
Penwood
Pound Street
Burghclere
Earlstone Common
Plastow Green
Fair Oak
Axmansford
Inhurst
Tadley
Baughurst
Silchester
Highclere
Highclere Castle
Whitway
Old Burghclere
Ecchinswell
Kingsclere
Wolverton Common
Wolverton
Pound Green
Browninghill Green
Pamber Green
Little London
Bramley Corner
Faccombe
Ashmansworth
Sydmonton
Crux Easton
Beacon Hill
Ramsdell
Charter Alley
West Heath
Pamber End
Monk Sherborne
Sherborne St John
Hannington
Upper Wootton
North Oakley
Ibworth
Wootton St Lawrence
Popley
Oakridge
South View
Woodcott
Litchfield
Dunley
Binley
Hurstbourne Tarrant
Stoke
NORTH WESSEX DOWNS
Worting
Winklebury
Basingstoke
West Ham
South Ham
Newfound
Buckskin
Kempshott
Brighton Hill
Cliddesden
Swampton
St Mary Bourne
Cole Henley
Quidhampton
Overton
Deane
Ashe
Clarken Green
Church Oakley
Oakley
East Oakley
Whitchurch
Laverstoke
Freefolk
Southington
Lynch Hill
Tufton
Steventon
North Waltham
Dummer
Farleigh Wallop
Ellisfield
Broadmere
Picket Piece
Andover Down
Hurstbourne Priors
Longparish
Middleton
Forton
Bransbury
Popham
Micheldever Services
Nutley
Axford
Woodmancott
Wherwell
Barton Stacey
Bullington
Lower Bullington
Upper Bullington
Newton Stacey
Chilbolton
Sutton Scotney Services
Sutton Scotney
Wonston
Stoke Charity
Hunton
West Stratton
East Stratton
Micheldever
Preston Candover
Bradley
Lower Wield
Chilton Candover
Brown Candover
Upper Wield
Northington
Swarraton
Hattingley
Chilbolton Down
South Wonston
Crawley
Up Somborne
Littleton
Kings Worthy
Martyr Worthy
Itchen Abbas
Itchen Stoke
Abbots Worthy
Headbourne Worthy
Avington
Old Alresford
Bighton
Gundleton
New Alresford
Bishop's Sutton
Ropley Dean
Ovington
Tichborne
Winchester
Sparsholt
Harestock
Weeke
Hyde
Easton
Fulflood
Winnall
Chilcomb
Stanmore
Cheriton
New Cheriton
Bramdean
HAMPSHIRE
A303
A34
A30
A33
M3
A339
A31
B3400

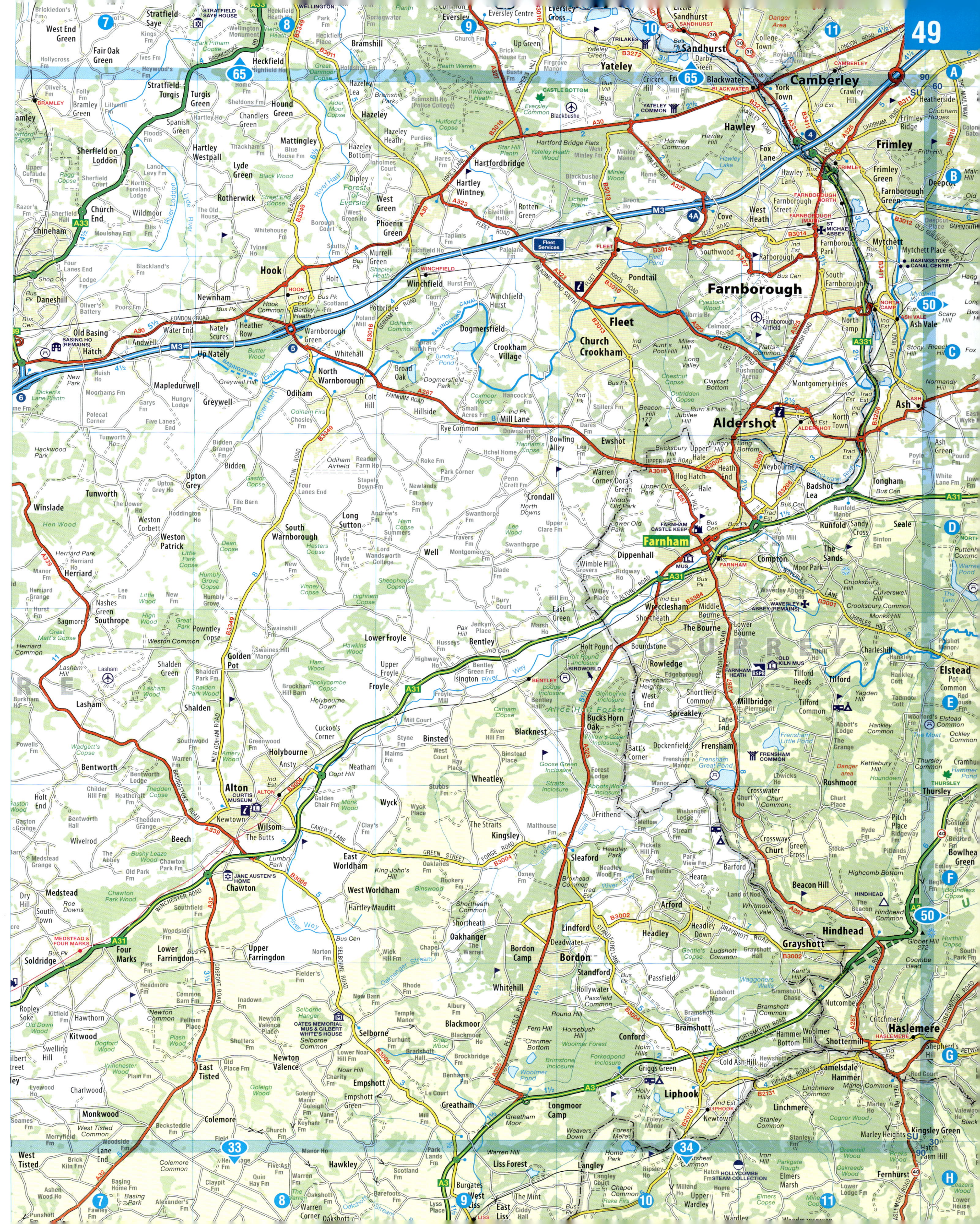

Stratfield Saye
West End Green
Fair Oak Green
Heckfield
Eversley
Eversley Centre
Eversley Cross
Sandhurst
Little Sandhurst
College Town
Bramshill
Up Green
Yateley
Camberley
Blackwater
York Town
Crawley Hill
Stratfield Turgis
Turgis Green
Hound Green
Hazeley
Hazeley Heath
Hazeley Bottom
Hawley
Frimley
Frimley Green
Sherfield on Loddon
Mattingley
Hartley Westpall
Lyde Green
Hartfordbridge
Hartley Wintney
Rotherwick
West Green
Phoenix Green
Rotten Green
Fox Lane
Cove
West Heath
Farnborough Green
Church End
Chineham
Wildmoor
Mytchett
Southwood
Farnborough Park
Hook
Winchfield
Murrell Green
Rafborough
South Farnborough
Pondtail
Farnborough
Daneshill
Newnham
Hook Common
Winchfield Hurst
Fleet
Ash Vale
Old Basing
Water End
Nately Scures
Heather Row
Warnborough Green
Potbridge
Dogmersfield
North Camp
Andwell
Up Nately
Whitehall
Crookham Village
Church Crookham
Basing Hatch
North Warnborough
Broad Oak
Montgomery Lines
Mapledurwell
Greywell
Odiham
Colt Hill
Hillside
Mill Lane
Ewshot
Aldershot
North Town
Ash
Rye Common
Bowling Alley
Upper Hale
Heath End
Weybourne
Badshot Lea
Tongham
Upton Grey
Bidden
Hale
Tunworth
Winslade
Warren Corner
Dora's Green
Crondall
Long Sutton
Weston Corbett
South Warnborough
Runfold
Seale
Weston Patrick
Farnham
Dippenhall
Compton
The Sands
Herriard
Well
Wimble Hill
Moor Park
Nashes Green
Southrope
Bagmore
Wrecclesham
Middle Bourne
The Bourne
Lower Bourne
Lower Froyle
Bentley
Holt Pound
Boundstone
Rowledge
Charleshill
SURREY
Lasham
Shalden Green
Golden Pot
Upper Froyle
Froyle
Isington
Tilford
Elstead
Shalden
Millbridge
Spreakley
Bucks Horn Oak
Binsted
Blacknest
Frensham
Holybourne
Bentworth
Alton
Neatham
Wheatley
Rushmoor
Thursley
Holt End
Wyck
Wilsom
Newtown
The Butts
Beech
Kingsley
Sleaford
Frithend
Chawton
East Worldham
West Worldham
Hartley Mauditt
Barford
Churt
Crossways
Medstead
South Town
Arford
Beacon Hill
Headley
Lindford
Bordon Camp
Bordon
Headley Down
Grayshott
Hindhead
Four Marks
Lower Farringdon
Upper Farringdon
Soldridge
Standford
Oakhanger
Whitehill
Passfield
Kitwood
Selborne
Bramshott
Conford
Haslemere
Shottermill
Newton Valence
East Tisted
Empshott
Liphook
Camelsdale
Hammer
Charlwood
Monkwood
Greatham
Longmoor Camp
Linchmere
Colemore
Kingsley Green
West Tisted
Hawkley
Liss Forest
Langley
Hatch Farm Hill
Fernhurst
Burgates
West Liss
East Liss
The Mint
Upper Wardley
Milland
M3
A31
A3
A30
A325
A287
A339
A32
A331
A323
A327
B3013
B3016
B3349
B3004
B3006
B3002

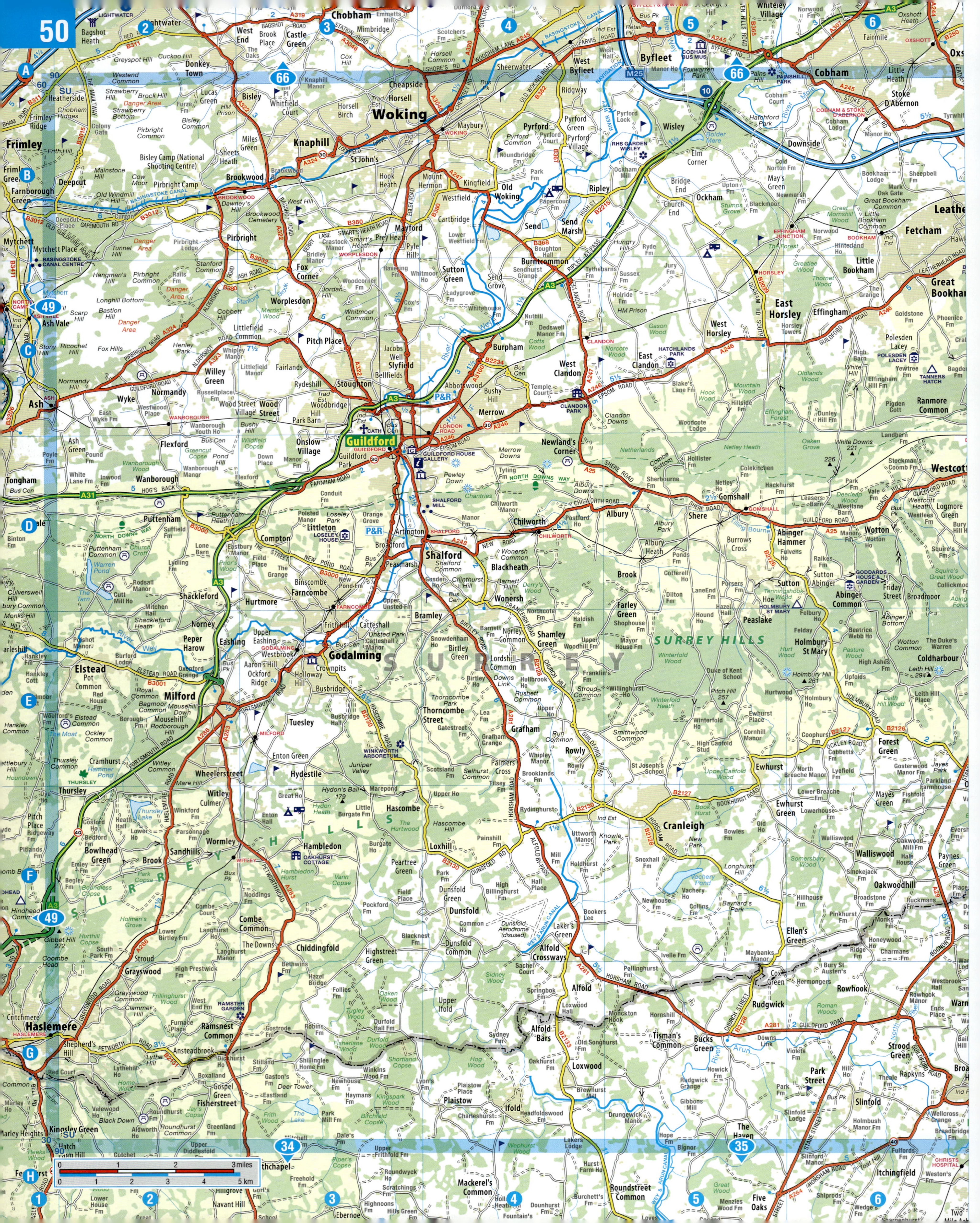
Woking
Guildford
Godalming
Haslemere
Cranleigh
Cobham
Byfleet
West Byfleet
Knaphill
Frimley
Ash
Farnborough
Pirbright
Worplesdon
Send
Ripley
Old Woking
Wisley
Ockham
East Horsley
West Horsley
Effingham
Fetcham
Great Bookham
Little Bookham
West Clandon
East Clandon
Merrow
Burpham
Shalford
Chilworth
Albury
Shere
Gomshall
Abinger Hammer
Wotton
Westcott
Bramley
Wonersh
Milford
Elstead
Witley
Chiddingfold
Hambledon
Hascombe
Dunsfold
Alfold
Loxwood
Rudgwick
Ewhurst
Peaslake
Holmbury St Mary
Compton
Puttenham
Tongham
Wanborough
Normandy
Shackleford
Farncombe
Thursley
Grayswood
Fernhurst
Ifold
Plaistow
Kirdford
Bucks Green
Forest Green
Walliswood
Oakwoodhill
Ockley
Capel
Ellen's Green
Mayford
Sutton Green
Bisley
Brookwood
Chobham
Chertsey
Ottershaw
Addlestone
Bagshot
Lightwater
Deepcut
Mytchett
Ash Vale
Aldershot
Pyrford
Sheerwater
Horsell
Send Marsh
Burntcommon
Jacobs Well
Slyfield
Stoughton
Onslow Village
Peasmarsh
Blackheath
Brook
Sandhills
Wormley
Hydestile
Busbridge
Tuesley
Grafham
Rowly
Thorncombe Street
Smithwood Common
Dunsfold Aerodrome (disused)
Alfold Crossways
Alfold Bars
Tisman's Common
Park Street
Slinfold
Rowhook
Itchingfield
Five Oaks
Kingsley Green
Camelsdale
Shottermill
Hindhead
Beacon Hill
Churt
Tilford
Crooksbury
Runfold
Seale
The Sands
Hog's Back
SURREY
SURREY HILLS
M25
M3
A3
A31
A25
A281
A24
A29
A272
A283
A286
A287
A248
A246
A247
A320
A322
A323
A324
A245
B2130
B2127
B2128
B2126
B3000
B3001
B2133
Basingstoke Canal
Wey & Arun Canal
River Wey
0 1 2 3 miles
0 1 2 3 4 5 km
1 2 3 4 5 6
A B C D E F G H
34 35 49 66

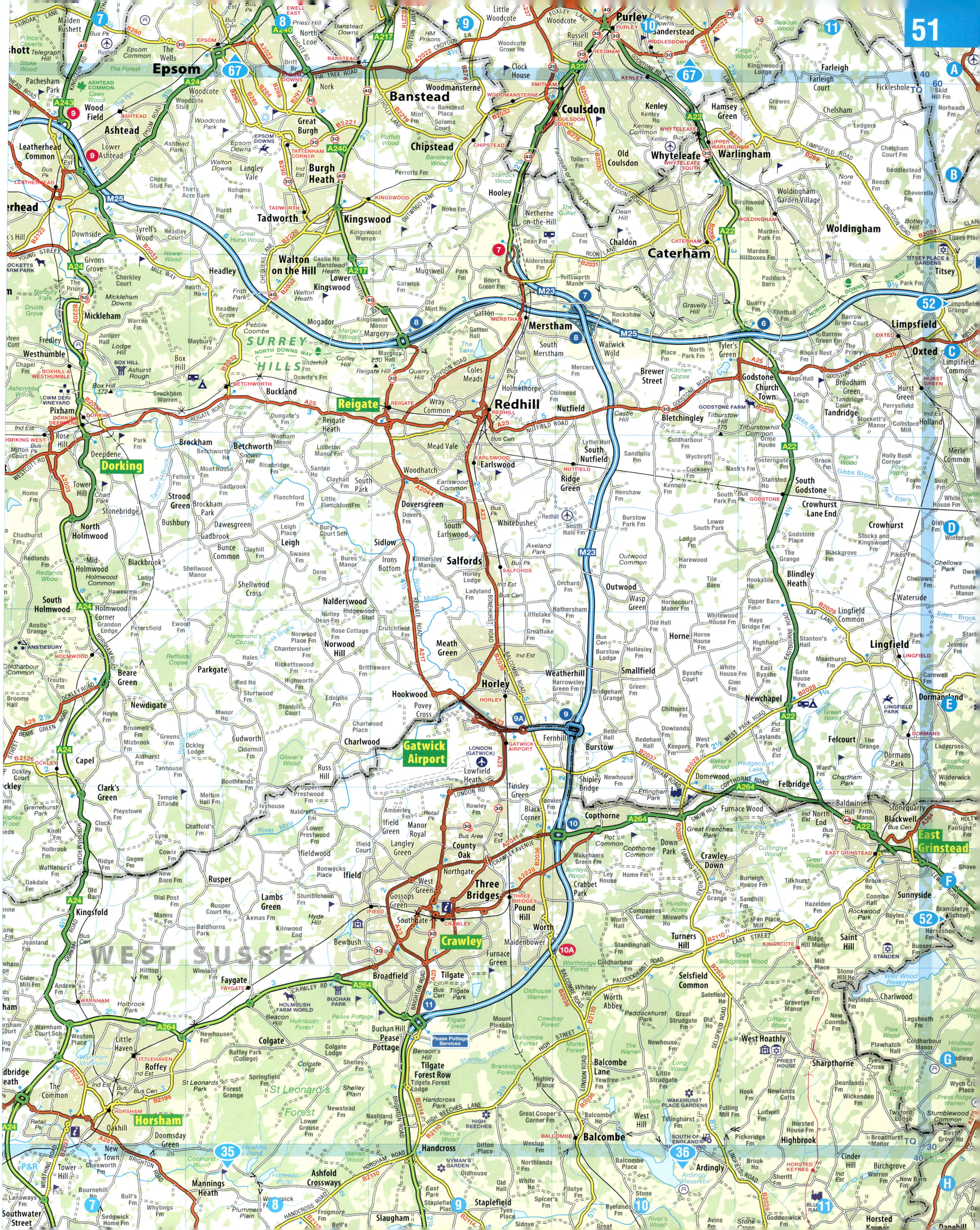

Epsom
Banstead
Purley
Coulsdon
Whyteleafe
Warlingham
Ashtead
Leatherhead
Chipstead
Burgh Heath
Tadworth
Kingswood
Woldingham
Caterham
Walton on the Hill
Merstham
Limpsfield
Oxted
SURREY HILLS
Reigate
Redhill
Nutfield
Bletchingley
Godstone
South Godstone
Dorking
Brockham
Betchworth
Earlswood
Salfords
Horley
Lingfield
Dormansland
Gatwick Airport
Burstow
Felbridge
East Grinstead
Copthorne
Crawley Down
Three Bridges
Crawley
Ifield
Pound Hill
Worth
Tilgate
Pease Pottage
Faygate
Rusper
Capel
Kingsfold
Warnham
Horsham
WEST SUSSEX
Handcross
Balcombe
Ardingly
Turners Hill
Sharpthorne
West Hoathly
Saint Hill
Sunnyside
Colgate
Mannings Heath
Ashfold Crossways
Staplefield
Slaugham
Southwater
M25
M23
A23
A24
A25
A264
A22

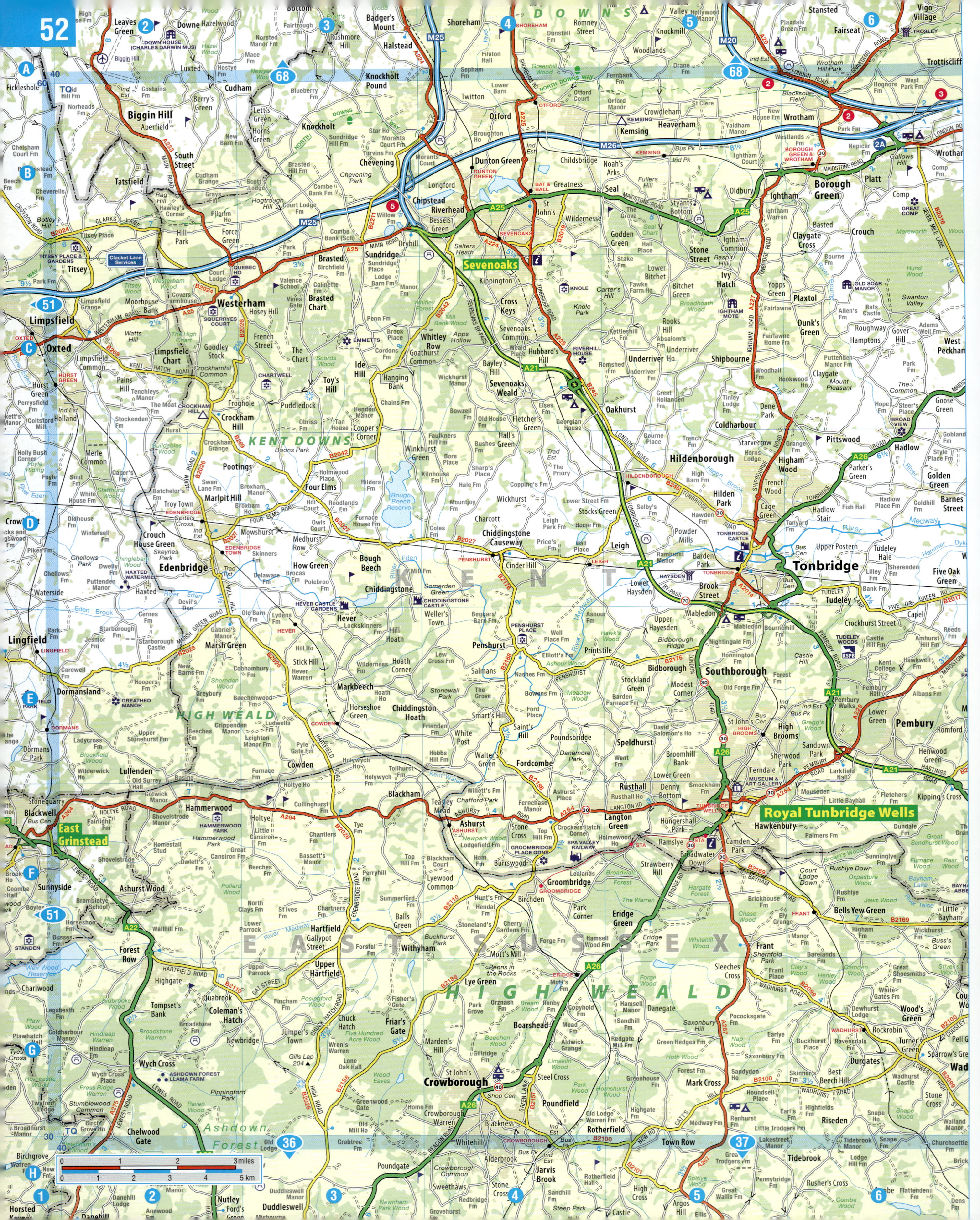

DOWNS
KENT DOWNS
KENT
HIGH WEALD
EAST SUSSEX
HIGH WEALD
Ashdown Forest
Sevenoaks
Tonbridge
Royal Tunbridge Wells
East Grinstead
Biggin Hill
Westerham
Limpsfield
Oxted
Edenbridge
Lingfield
Dormansland
Crowborough
Southborough
Hildenborough
Otford
Kemsing
Seal
Borough Green
Wrotham
Ightham
Shipbourne
Hadlow
Pembury
Penshurst
Chiddingstone
Hever
Cowden
Hartfield
Withyham
Groombridge
Frant
Mark Cross
Rotherfield
Langton Green
Rusthall
Speldhurst
Leigh
Chiddingstone Causeway
Four Elms
Crockham Hill
Sundridge
Brasted
Chevening
Knockholt
Halstead
Shoreham
Dunton Green
Riverhead
Chipstead
Tatsfield
Titsey
Ide Hill
Toy's Hill
Sevenoaks Weald
Underriver
Plaxtol
Ivy Hatch
Stone Street
Oldbury
Platt
Crouch
Fordcombe
Ashurst
Blackham
Forest Row
Wych Cross
Nutley
Duddleswell
Jarvis Brook
Town Row
Eridge Green
Lye Green
Boarshead
Hammerwood
Holtye
Sunnyside
Colemans Hatch
Upper Hartfield
Chelwood Gate
Wadhurst
Tudeley
Capel
Five Oak Green
Golden Green
Barnes Street
Vigo Village
Stansted
Fairseat
Trottiscliffe
Clacket Lane Services
Pell Green
Durgates
Tidebrook
Rusher's Cross
Bells Yew Green
Hawkenbury
Camden Park
Kipping's Cross

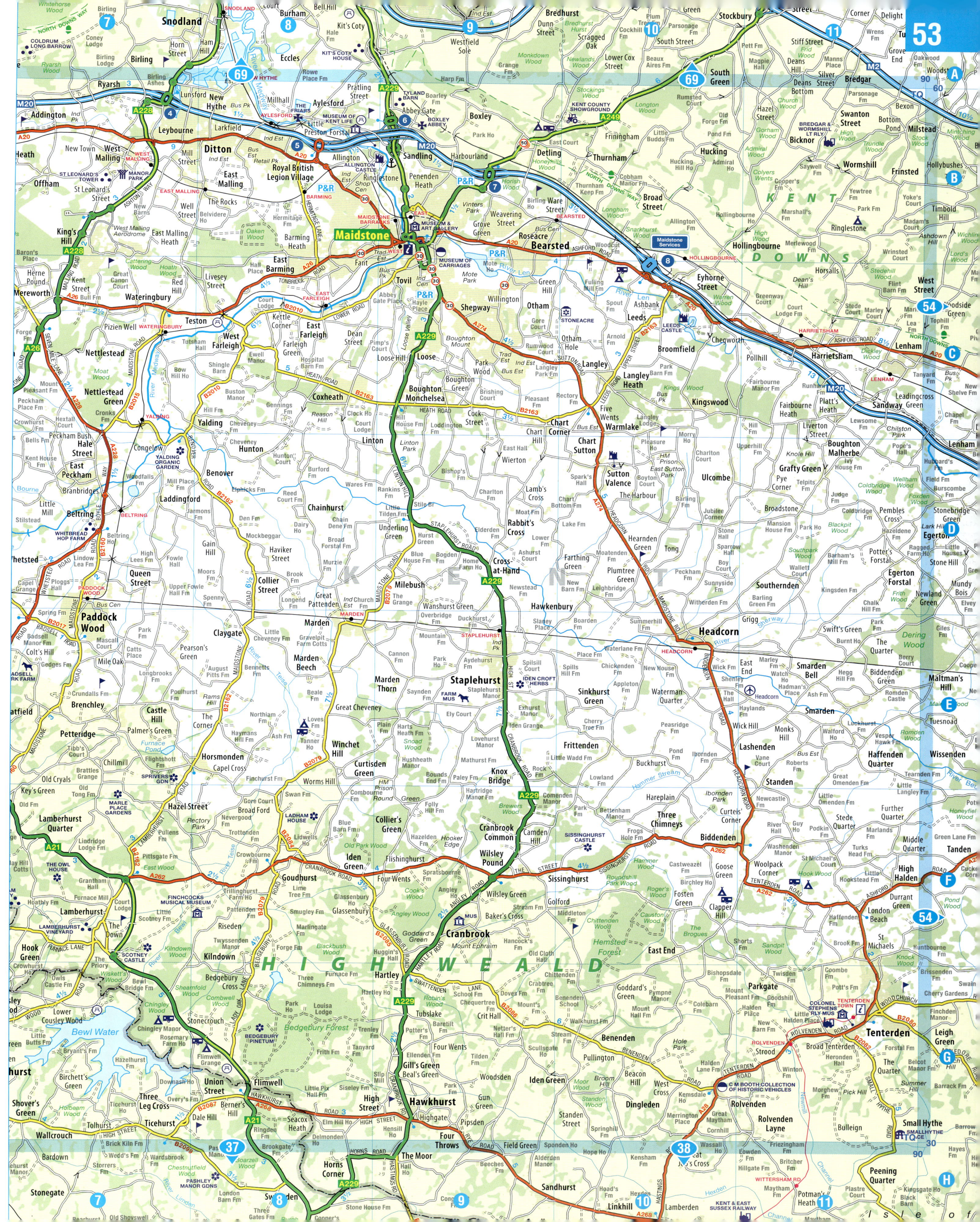
Snodland
Burham
Eccles
Kit's Coty
Westfield Sole
Bredhurst
Dunn Street
Scragged Oak
Stockbury
South Green
Bredgar
Birling
Ryarsh
Addington
Leybourne
New Hythe
Larkfield
Aylesford
Ditton
West Malling
Offham
Royal British Legion Village
East Malling
Maidstone
Sandling
Penenden Heath
Boxley
Detling
Thurnham
Bearsted
Roseacre
Grove Green
Weavering Street
Hollingbourne
Hucking
Wormshill
Frinsted
Broad Street
Ringlestone
Kent
Downs
Eyhorne Street
Harrietsham
Lenham
Sandway
Platt's Heath
Kingswood
Broomfield
Leeds
Otham
Langley
Langley Heath
Chart Sutton
Sutton Valence
Ulcombe
Boughton Malherbe
Grafty Green
Egerton
Egerton Forstal
Headcorn
Smarden
Biddenden
Frittenden
Sissinghurst
Cranbrook
Hartley
Benenden
Rolvenden
Tenterden
High Halden
St Michaels
Hawkhurst
Flimwell
Ticehurst
Wallcrouch
Stonegate
Bewl Water
Kilndown
Goudhurst
Lamberhurst
Horsmonden
Brenchley
Paddock Wood
Marden
Staplehurst
Collier Street
Laddingford
Yalding
Hunton
Linton
Coxheath
Loose
Tovil
East Farleigh
West Farleigh
Teston
Wateringbury
Mereworth
Nettlestead
East Peckham
Beltring
Hale Street
Claygate
Marden Beech
Chainhurst
Boughton Monchelsea
Wierton
Cross-at-Hand
Hawkenbury
Milebush
Winchet Hill
Curtisden Green
Knox Bridge
Cranbrook Common
Golford
Iden Green
Hazel Street
Four Throws
The Moor
Sandhurst
Linkhill
Highgate
Gill's Green
Four Wents
Tubslake
Wilsley Green
Wilsley Pound
Colliers Green
Dingleden
Pullington
Parkgate
Goddard's Green
Three Chimneys
Bettenham
Woolpack Corner
Standen
Standen Street
Horns Corner
Tolhurst
Bardown
H I G H   W E A L D

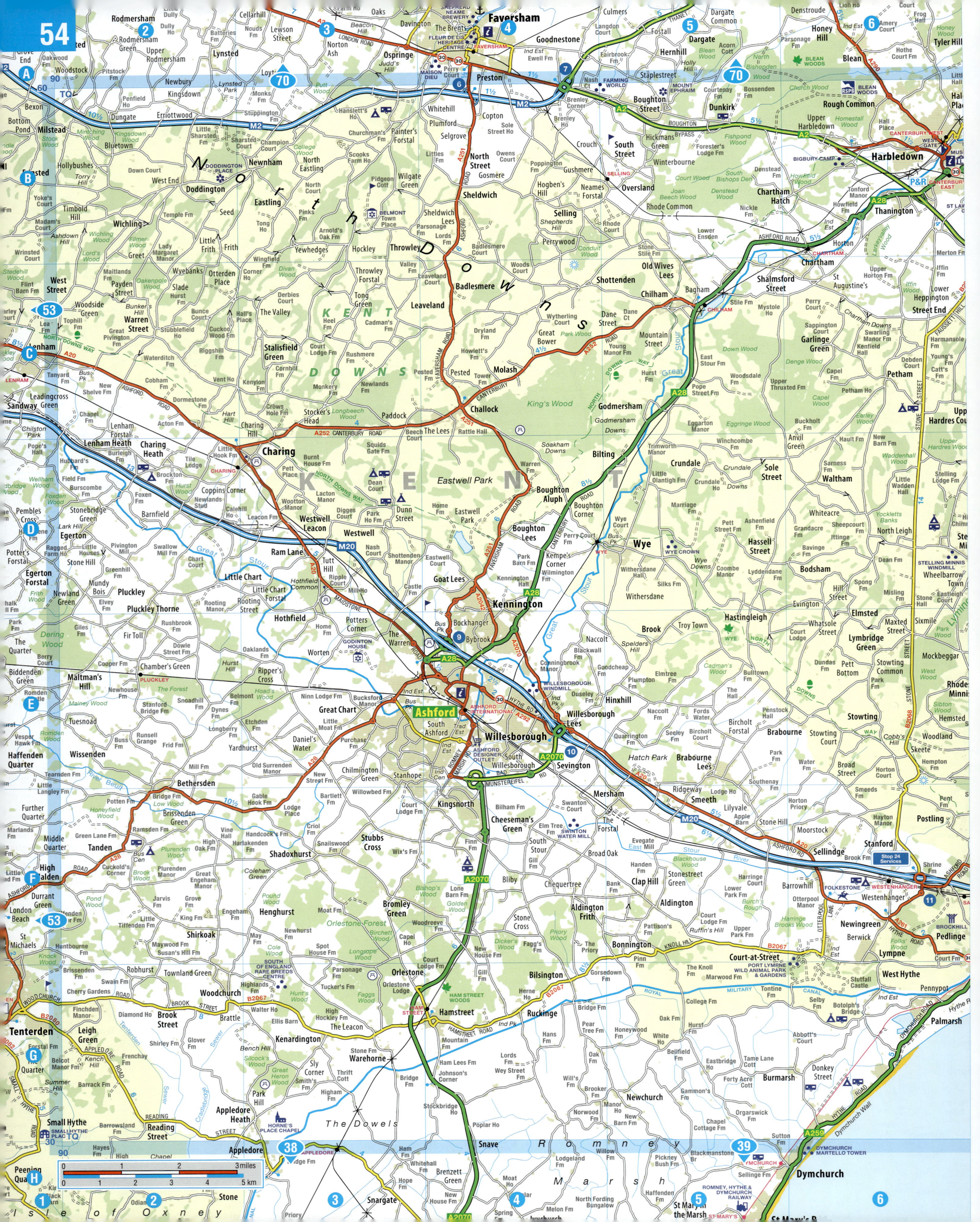
Faversham
Ospringe
Preston
Goodnestone
Dargate
Hernhill
Boughton Street
Dunkirk
Harbledown
Thanington
Chartham
Chilham
Rough Common
Blean
North Downs
Doddington
Newnham
Eastling
Throwley
Sheldwich
Badlesmere
Leaveland
Selling
Molash
Challock
Shottenden
Godmersham
Crundale
Wye
Lenham
Charing
Kent Downs
Eastwell Park
Westwell
Kennington
Boughton Aluph
Pluckley
Ashford
Willesborough
Sevington
Mersham
Smeeth
Sellindge
Brabourne
Elmsted
Stowting
Postling
Westenhanger
Newingreen
Lympne
Bethersden
Great Chart
Kingsnorth
Shadoxhurst
Bilsington
Ruckinge
Hamstreet
Orlestone
Woodchurch
Tenterden
Kenardington
Warehorne
Appledore
Snargate
Dymchurch
Burmarsh
Newchurch
Romney Marsh
Isle of Oxney
Pedlinge
West Hythe
Palmarsh
Dymchurch Wall
M2
M20
A2
A28
A20
A251
A252
A2070
A292
A259
B2067
B2068

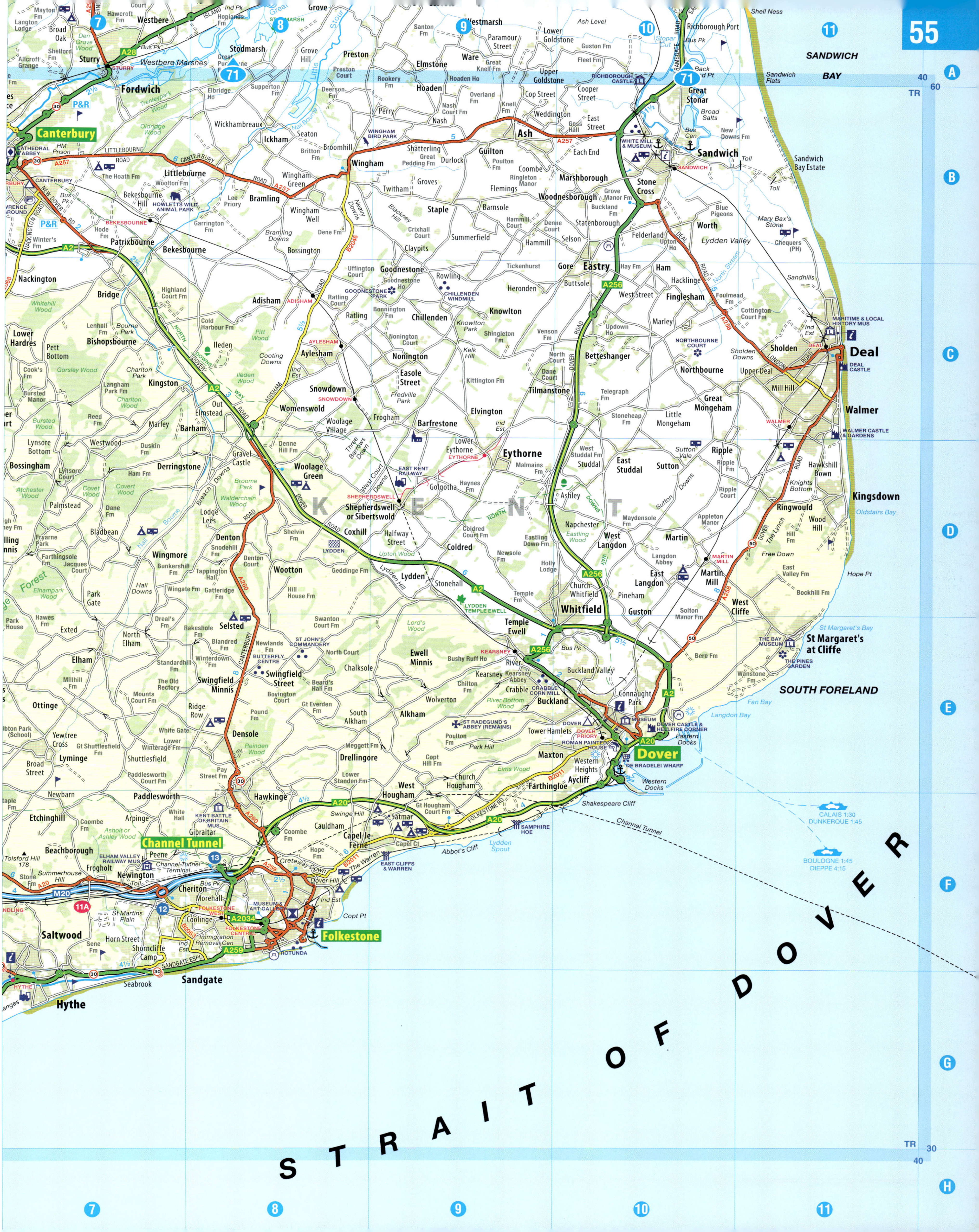

SANDWICH BAY
Canterbury
Fordwich
Sturry
Westbere
Stodmarsh
Preston
Elmstone
Wingham
Ash
Sandwich
Richborough Port
Great Stonar
Littlebourne
Bekesbourne
Patrixbourne
Bramling
Staple
Woodnesborough
Eastry
Worth
Deal
Walmer
Kingsdown
Sholden
Northbourne
Great Mongeham
Ripple
Nackington
Bridge
Bishopsbourne
Kingston
Barham
Adisham
Aylesham
Goodnestone
Chillenden
Knowlton
Nonington
Snowdown
Womenswold
Barfrestone
Eythorne
Elvington
Tilmanstone
Betteshanger
Shepherdswell or Sibertswold
Coxhill
Coldred
Lydden
Whitfield
West Langdon
Martin Mill
West Cliffe
St Margaret's at Cliffe
SOUTH FORELAND
Temple Ewell
River
Kearsney
Crabble
Buckland
Dover
Maxton
Aycliff
Farthingloe
Alkham
Ewell Minnis
Drellingore
West Hougham
Capel-le-Ferne
Hawkinge
Densole
Swingfield Minnis
Elham
Lyminge
Ottinge
Denton
Wingmore
Wootton
Selsted
Paddlesworth
Etchinghill
Beachborough
Newington
Cheriton
Folkestone
Sandgate
Hythe
Saltwood
Channel Tunnel
K E N T
STRAIT OF DOVER
CALAIS 1:30 DUNKERQUE 1:45
BOULOGNE 1:45 DIEPPE 4:15
Channel Tunnel

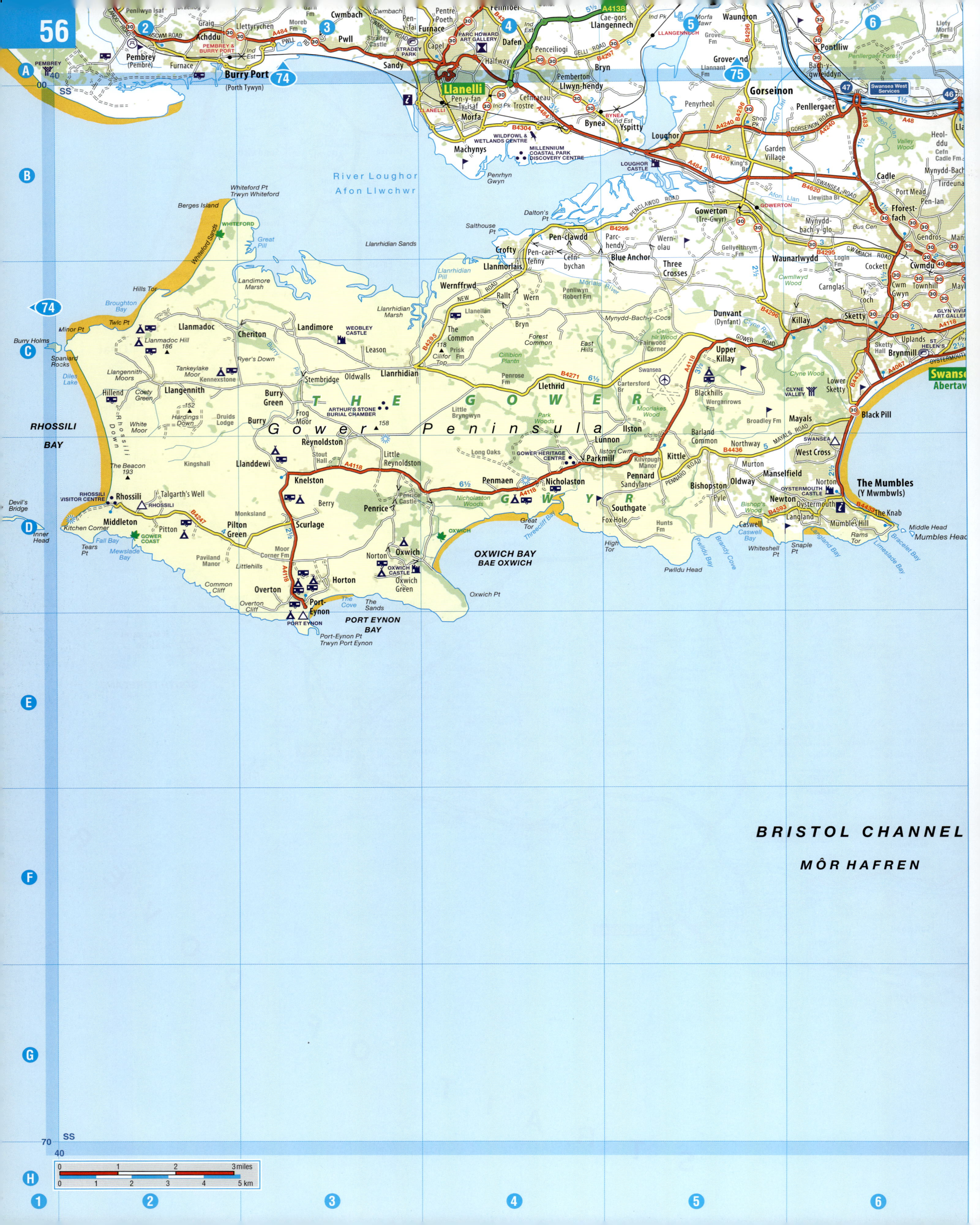

BRISTOL CHANNEL
MÔR HAFREN
Gower Peninsula
THE GOWER
GWYR
RHOSSILI BAY
OXWICH BAY
BAE OXWICH
PORT EYNON BAY
River Loughor
Afon Llwchwr
Llanelli
Burry Port
(Porth Tywyn)
Pembrey
(Pembre)
Pwll
Cwmbach
Furnace
Dafen
Sandy
Morfa
Machynys
Bynea
Llwyn-hendy
Bryn
Llangennech
Cae-gors
Loughor
Gorseinon
Penllergaer
Pontlliw
Garden Village
Gowerton
(Tre-Gwyr)
Waunarlwydd
Dunvant
(Dynfant)
Killay
Upper Killay
Sketty
Swansea
Abertawe
Black Pill
Mayals
West Cross
Norton
Oystermouth
The Mumbles
(Y Mwmbwls)
Mumbles Head
Langland
Newton
Bishopston
Murton
Kittle
Pennard
Southgate
Parkmill
Ilston
Lunnon
Nicholaston
Penmaen
Penrice
Oxwich
Oxwich Green
Horton
Port-Eynon
Overton
Scurlage
Knelston
Reynoldston
Llanddewi
Middleton
Rhossili
Pitton
Pilton Green
Llangennith
Llanmadoc
Cheriton
Landimore
Burry Green
Llanrhidian
Oldwalls
Stembridge
Crofty
Llanmorlais
Penclawdd
Wernffrwd
Llethrid
Three Crosses
Blue Anchor
Whiteford Sands
Berges Island
Burry Holms
Worms Head
Llanrhidian Sands
ARTHUR'S STONE BURIAL CHAMBER
WEOBLEY CASTLE
GOWER HERITAGE CENTRE
OXWICH CASTLE
OYSTERMOUTH CASTLE
LOUGHOR CASTLE
RHOSSILI VISITOR CENTRE
A4118
A484
A483
A4067
B4295
B4271
B4436
B4247
74
75
0 1 2 3 miles
0 1 2 3 4 5 km

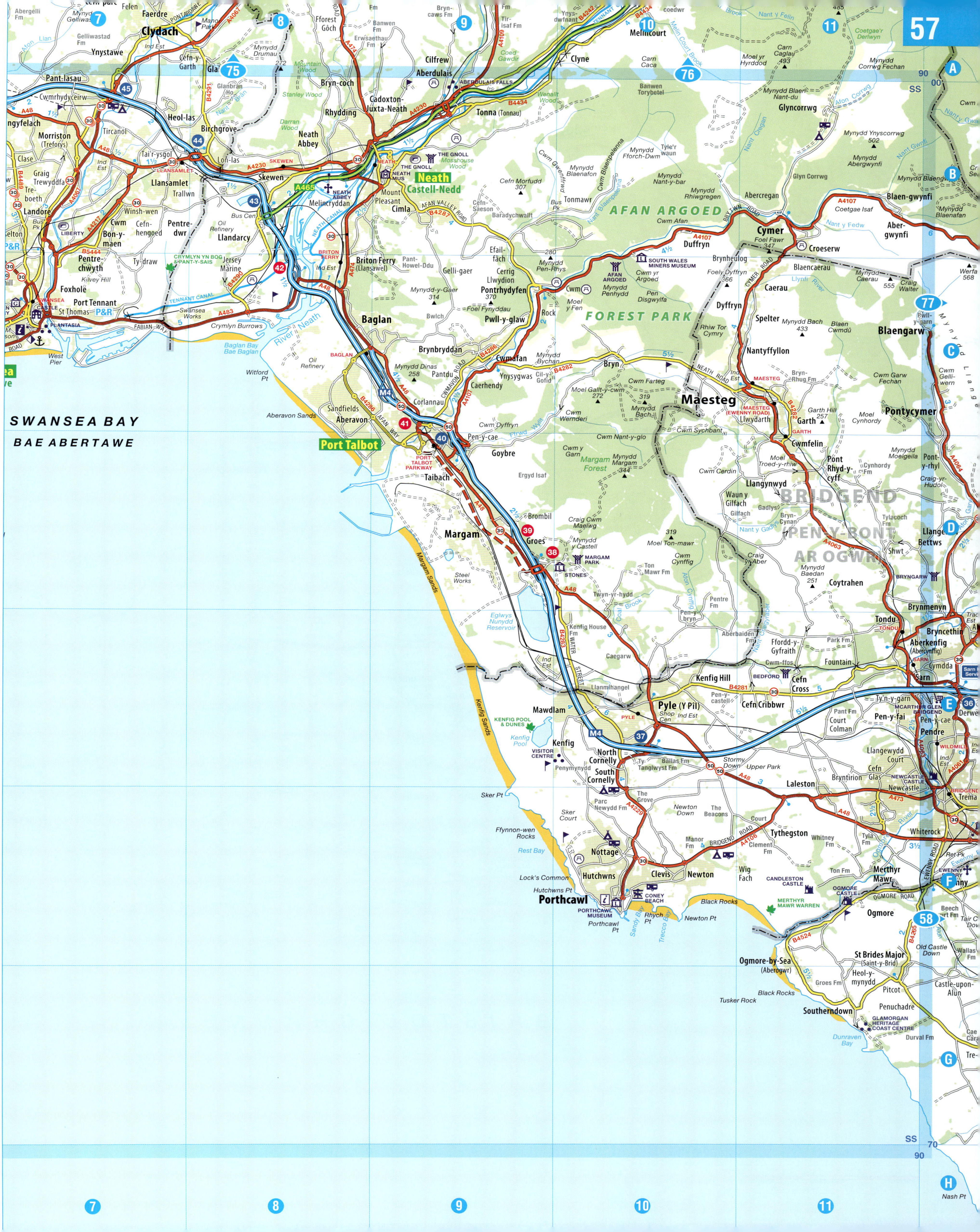
SWANSEA BAY
BAE ABERTAWE
Port Talbot
Neath
Castell-Nedd
AFAN ARGOED
FOREST PARK
BRIDGEND
(PEN-Y-BONT AR OGWR)
Clydach
Ynystawe
Morriston (Treforys)
Llansamlet
Landore
Skewen
Birchgrove
Neath Abbey
Cadoxton-Juxta-Neath
Aberdulais
Cilfrew
Tonna (Tonnau)
Clyne
Melincourt
Glyncorrwg
Cymer
Croeserw
Blaengwynfi
Aber-gwynfi
Duffryn
Caerau
Blaengarw
Pontycymer
Maesteg
Llangynwyd
Tondu
Aberkenfig
Sarn
Coytrahen
Baglan
Briton Ferry (Llansawel)
Aberavon
Taibach
Margam
Cwmafan
Pontrhydyfen
Bryn
Kenfig Hill
Pyle (Y Pil)
Cefn Cribbwr
Mawdlam
Kenfig
North Cornelly
South Cornelly
Laleston
Porthcawl
Nottage
Newton
Merthyr Mawr
Ogmore
Ogmore-by-Sea (Aberogwr)
St Brides Major (Saint-y-Brid)
Southerndown
Kenfig Sands
Margam Sands
Aberavon Sands
Rest Bay
Sker Pt
Black Rocks
Tusker Rock
Dunraven Bay
M4
A48
A465
A4107
A4063
A4229
B4283
75
76
77
58

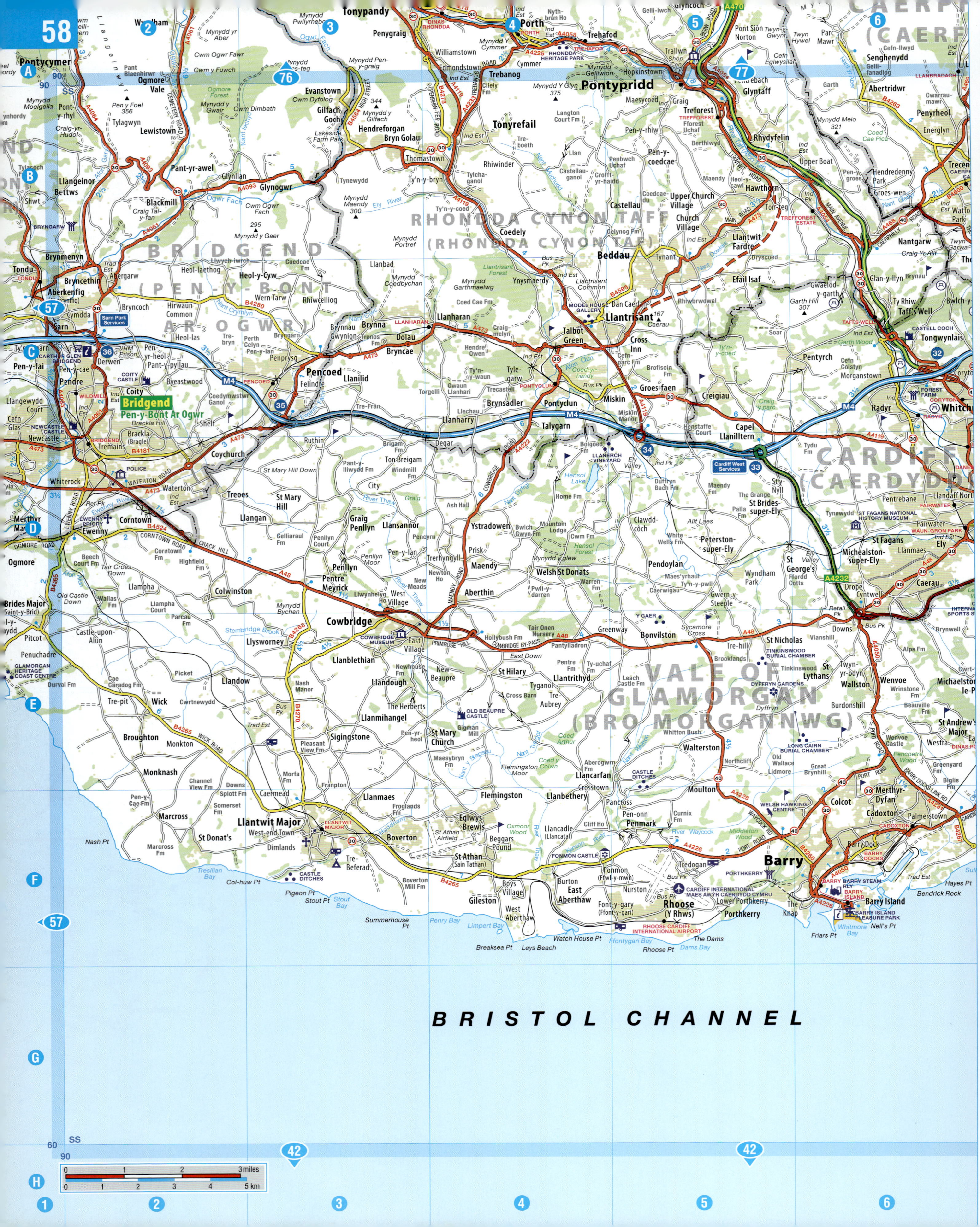
BRISTOL CHANNEL
BRIDGEND
(PEN-Y-BONT AR OGWR)
RHONDDA CYNON TAFF
(RHONDDA CYNON TAF)
VALE OF GLAMORGAN
(BRO MORGANNWG)
CARDIFF
(CAERDYDD)
Bridgend
Pen-y-Bont Ar Ogwr
Tonypandy
Porth
Pontypridd
Penygraig
Trehafod
Williamstown
Trebanog
Tonyrefail
Pontycymer
Ogmore Vale
Lewistown
Pant-yr-awel
Glynogwr
Blackmill
Llangeinor
Bettws
Brynmenyn
Tondu
Bryncethin
Aberkenfig
Heol-y-Cyw
Rhiwceiling
Pencoed
Llanilid
Brynna
Llanharan
Dolau
Bryncae
Llanharry
Talygarn
Pontyclun
Brynsadler
Miskin
Llantrisant
Beddau
Coedely
Castellau
Church Village
Upper Church Village
Llantwit Fardre
Efail Isaf
Tonteg
Hawthorn
Rhydyfelin
Treforest
Glyntaff
Maesycoed
Groes-faen
Creigiau
Capel Llanilltern
Pentyrch
Radyr
Tongwynlais
Taff's Well
Nantgarw
Whitchurch
Llandaff North
Fairwater
St Fagans
Michaelston-super-Ely
Caerau
Ely
Coity
Penyfai
Pendre
Tremains
Coychurch
Waterton
Treoes
St Mary Hill
Llangan
Ruthin
Whiterock
Merthyr Mawr
Ogmore
Ewenny
Corntown
Colwinston
Penllyn
Pentre Meyrick
Llansannor
Ystradowen
Prisk
Maendy
Aberthin
Cowbridge
Llanblethian
Llysworney
Welsh St Donats
Pendoylan
Peterston-super-Ely
St Brides-super-Ely
St George's
Wyndham Park
Drope
Bonvilston
St Nicholas
Tre-hill
Wenvoe
Wallston
St Hilary
Llantrithyd
Tre-Aubrey
St Mary Church
Llandough
Llanmihangel
Llandow
Wick
Broughton
Monknash
Marcross
St Donat's
Llantwit Major
Boverton
Llanmaes
Eglwys Brewis
St Athan
Gileston
West Aberthaw
East Aberthaw
Llancadle
Llanbethery
Flemingston
Llancarfan
Penmark
Rhoose
Fonmon
Porthkerry
Barry
Barry Island
Colcot
Cadoxton
Merthyr-Dyfan
Walterston
Moulton
St Andrew's Major
Dinas Powys
Brides Major
Pitcot
Castle-upon-Alun
Sigingstone
Nash Pt
Col-huw Pt
Summerhouse Pt
Breaksea Pt
Rhoose Pt
Friars Pt
Nell's Pt
M4
A48
A4119
A4226
A4232
A473
A4222
Sarn Park Services
Cardiff West Services
RHOOSE CARDIFF INTERNATIONAL AIRPORT
DYFFRYN GARDENS
OLD BEAUPRE CASTLE
ST FAGANS NATIONAL HISTORY MUSEUM
COWBRIDGE MUSEUM
GLAMORGAN HERITAGE COAST CENTRE
BARRY ISLAND PLEASURE PARK
0 1 2 3 miles
0 1 2 3 4 5 km

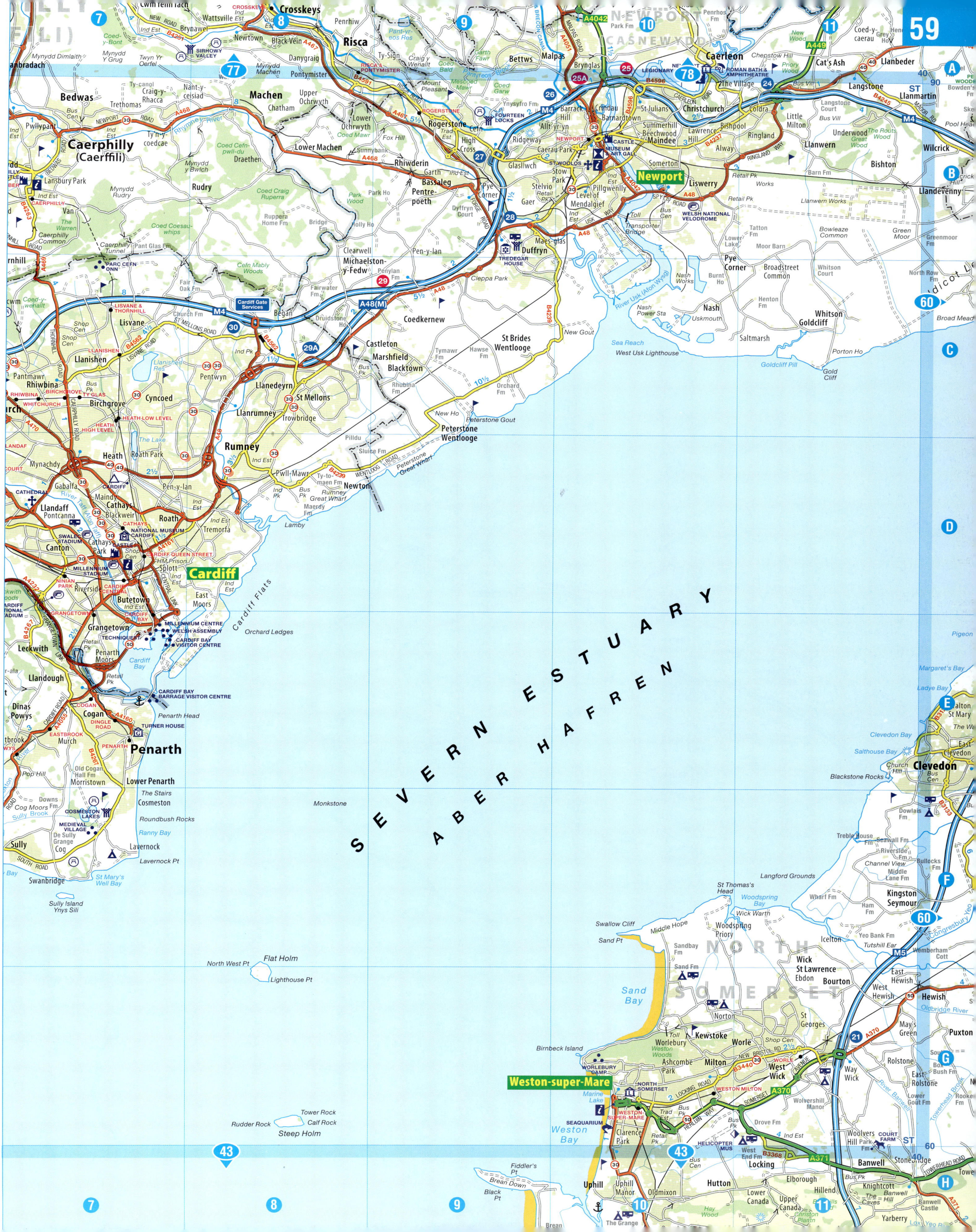
SEVERN ESTUARY
ABER HAFREN
NORTH SOMERSET
NEWPORT CASNEWYDD
Cardiff
Newport
Weston-super-Mare
Caerphilly (Caerffili)
Penarth
Clevedon
Caerleon
Risca
Crosskeys
Bedwas
Machen
Rogerstone
Bassaleg
Rhiwderin
Malpas
Bettws
Langstone
Llanmartin
Christchurch
Maindee
Liswerry
Duffryn
Michaelston-y-Fedw
Coedkernew
Castleton
Marshfield
St Brides Wentlooge
Peterstone Wentlooge
Nash
Goldcliff
Whitson
Redwick
Llandevenny
Bishton
Wilcrick
Lisvane
Llanishen
Rhiwbina
Birchgrove
Cyncoed
Pentwyn
Llanedeyrn
Llanrumney
St Mellons
Rumney
Trowbridge
Heath
Roath
Llandaff
Canton
Cathays
Butetown
Grangetown
Leckwith
Llandough
Dinas Powys
Cogan
Sully
Swanbridge
Lavernock
Lower Penarth
Cosmeston
Sully Island Ynys Sili
Flat Holm
Steep Holm
Monkstone
Orchard Ledges
Cardiff Flats
Sand Bay
Weston Bay
Worle
Kewstoke
Milton
West Wick
St Georges
Hewish
Puxton
Locking
Hutton
Uphill
Banwell
Kingston Seymour
Wick St Lawrence
Cardiff Bay
Penarth Head
Lavernock Pt
M4
M5
A48(M)
Cardiff Gate Services
77
78
60
43
7
8
9
10
11
A
B
C
D
E
F
G
H

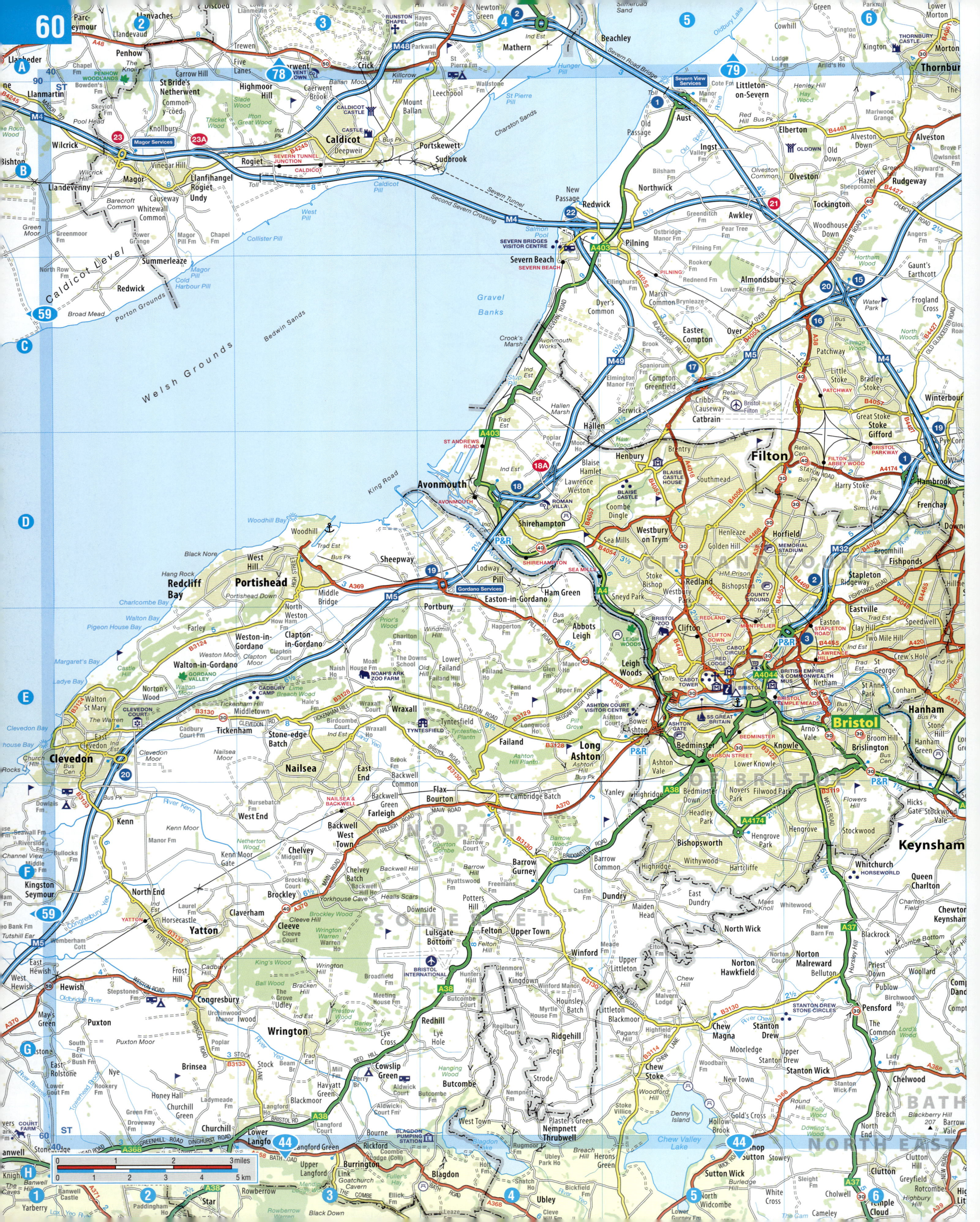
Caldicot
Magor
Rogiet
Undy
Llanmartin
Penhow
Portskewett
Sudbrook
Mathern
Beachley
Aust
Thornbury
Littleton-on-Severn
Elberton
Olveston
Tockington
Alveston
Rudgeway
Northwick
Redwick
Pilning
Severn Beach
Almondsbury
Easter Compton
Patchway
Filton
Winterbourne
Hambrook
Frenchay
Hallen
Henbury
Avonmouth
Shirehampton
Westbury on Trym
Horfield
Fishponds
Stapleton
Portishead
Redcliff Bay
Portbury
Pill
Easton-in-Gordano
Abbots Leigh
Leigh Woods
Clifton
Redland
Bristol
Bedminster
Knowle
Brislington
Hanham
Keynsham
Clevedon
Tickenham
Nailsea
Wraxall
Failand
Long Ashton
Flax Bourton
Backwell
Barrow Gurney
Dundry
Bishopsworth
Whitchurch
Yatton
Claverham
Congresbury
Wrington
Winford
Chew Magna
Chew Stoke
Stanton Drew
Pensford
Redhill
Blagdon
Burrington
Ubley
Chew Valley Lake
Welsh Grounds
Caldicot Level
Severn Tunnel
Second Severn Crossing
Gravel Banks
Bristol International
CITY AND COUNTY OF BRISTOL
NORTH SOMERSET
BATH NORTH EAST

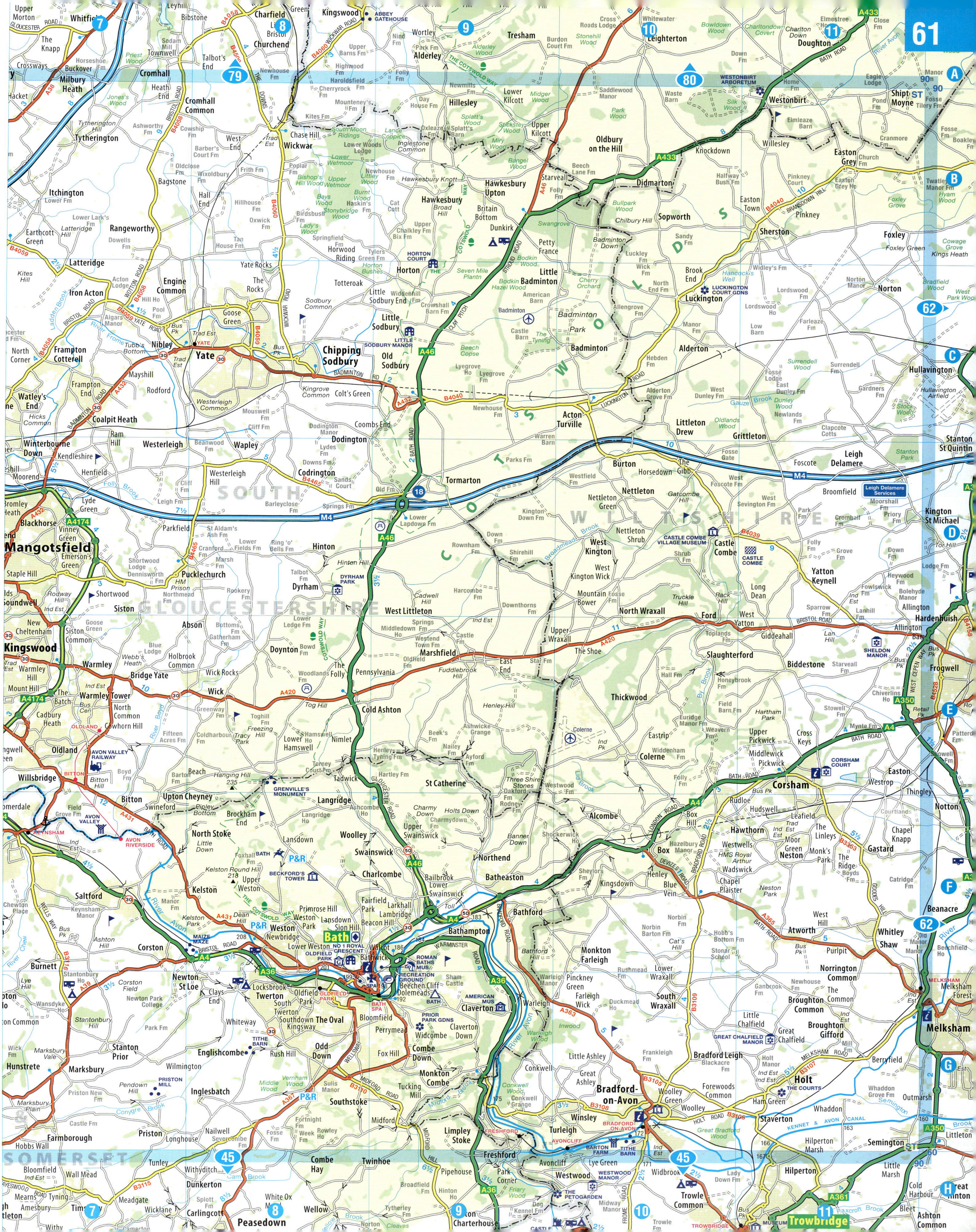

GLOUCESTERSHIRE
SOUTH
COTSWOLDS
WILTSHIRE
SOMERSET
Chipping Sodbury
Yate
Mangotsfield
Kingswood
Bath
Corsham
Melksham
Bradford-on-Avon
Trowbridge
Cromhall
Wickwar
Hawkesbury Upton
Tormarton
Marshfield
Cold Ashton
Box
Castle Combe
Luckington
Sherston
Westonbirt
Leighterton
Tresham
Alderley
Hillesley
Kingswood
Charfield
Tytherington
Iron Acton
Frampton Cotterell
Coalpit Heath
Winterbourne Down
Pucklechurch
Dyrham
Wick
Saltford
Keynsham
Batheaston
Bathampton
Bathford
Monkton Farleigh
Holt
Atworth
Neston
Lacock
Colerne
Biddestone
Slaughterford
Yatton Keynell
Grittleton
Hullavington
Stanton St Quintin
Leigh Delamere
Kington St Michael
Didmarton
Badminton
Acton Turville
Burton
Nettleton
Sopworth
Easton Grey
Norton
Foxley
Alderton
Wellow
Peasedown
Combe Hay
Freshford
Limpley Stoke
Westwood
Winsley
Staverton
Hilperton
Semington
Whitley
Shaw
Beanacre
Chippenham
Frogwell
Allington
Hardenhuish
Lower Weston
Combe Down
Odd Down
Englishcombe
Newton St Loe
Corston
Burnett
Marksbury
Farmborough
Priston
Inglesbatch
Southstoke
Midford
Monkton Combe
Claverton
Warleigh
Bitton
Upton Cheyney
North Stoke
Kelston
Langridge
Swainswick
Charlcombe
Northend
St Catherine
Nimlet
Doynton
Abson
Siston
Westerleigh
Wapley
Codrington
Dodington
Hinton
West Littleton
Pennsylvania
Thickwood
Ford
Upper Wraxall
North Wraxall
West Kington
Littleton Drew
Rangeworthy
Itchington
Latteridge
Engine Common
Nibley
Rodford
M4
A46
A4
A36
A420
A432
A433
A350
A363
A365
A361
A431
A4174
B4040
B4039
B4060
B4058
B4465
B3109
B3105
B3107
B3108
79
80
18
45
62

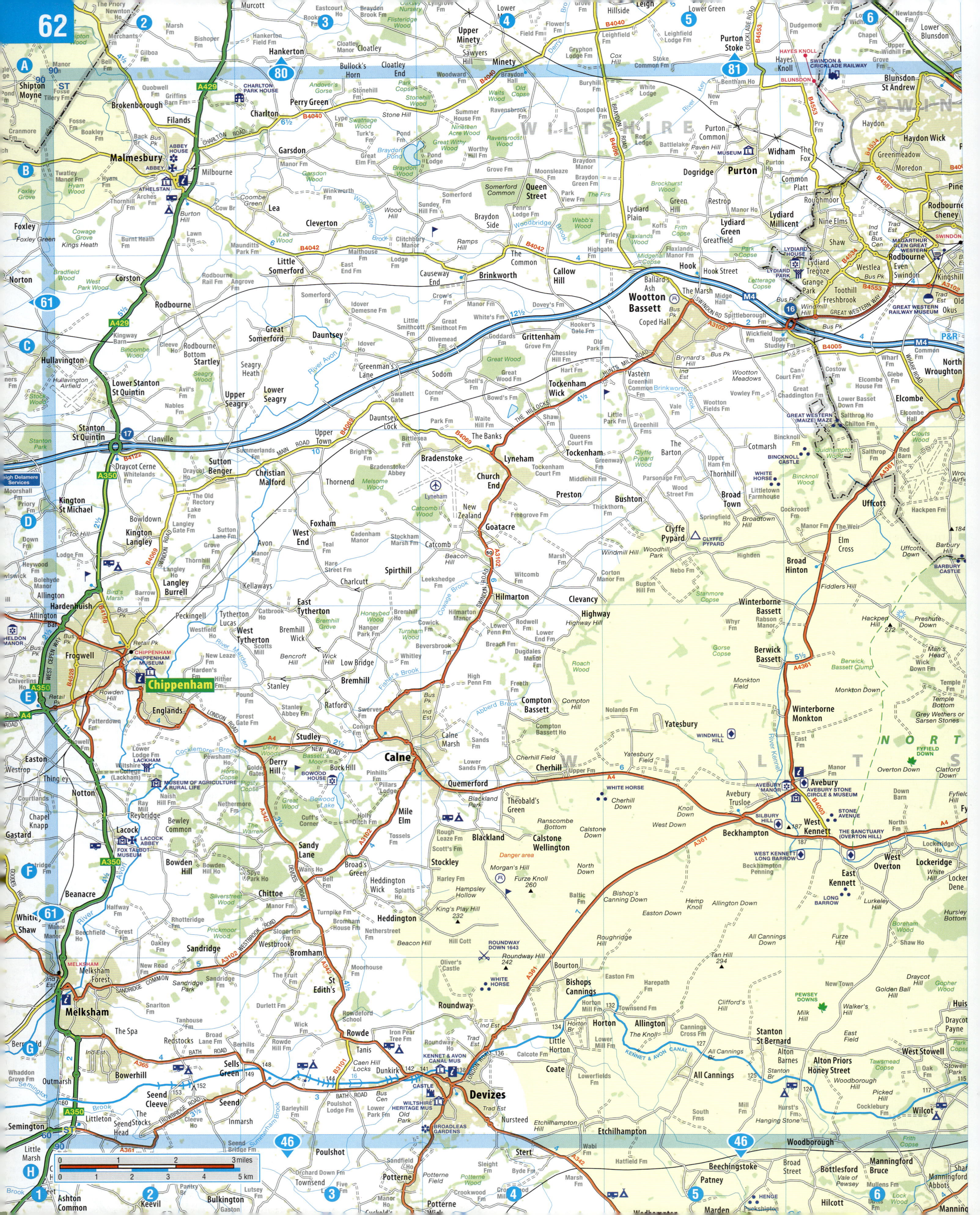

Malmesbury
Chippenham
Calne
Devizes
Melksham
Wootton Bassett
Purton
Lydiard Millicent
Lyneham
Avebury
Hilmarton
Corsham
Hullavington
Stanton St Quintin
Kington St Michael
Sutton Benger
Christian Malford
Dauntsey
Brinkworth
Little Somerford
Great Somerford
Bromham
Rowde
Seend
Bowerhill
Sandridge
Heddington
Roundway
Bishops Cannings
All Cannings
Alton Priors
Woodborough
Beckhampton
West Kennett
East Kennett
Winterbourne Monkton
Winterbourne Bassett
Broad Hinton
Uffcott
Wroughton
Swindon
Blunsdon St Andrew
Cricklade
Minety
Hankerton
Charlton
Lea
Garsdon
Cleverton
WILTSHIRE
M4
A4
A429
A350
A342
A361
A3102
Kennet & Avon Canal
Roundway Down 1643
Cherhill
Oldbury Castle
Silbury Hill
West Kennett Long Barrow
Avebury Stone Circle & Museum
Lacock Abbey
Bowood House
Chippenham Museum
Wiltshire Heritage Mus
Broadleas Gardens
Kennet & Avon Canal Mus
Lydiard House
Great Western Railway Museum
Swindon & Cricklade Railway
0 1 2 3 miles
0 1 2 3 4 5 km

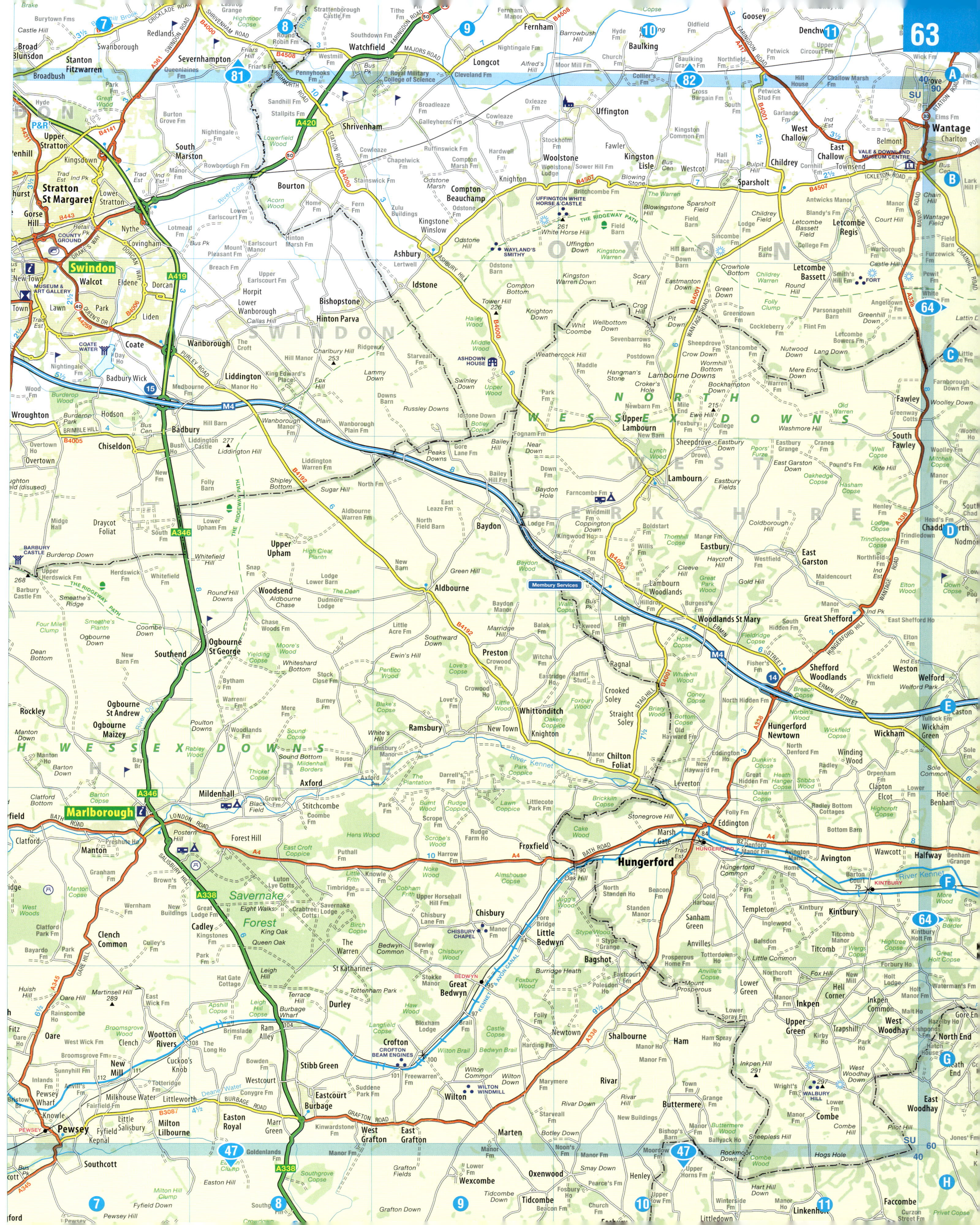
Swindon
Marlborough
Hungerford
Wantage
Stratton St Margaret
Upper Stratton
Swanborough
Watchfield
Longcot
Fernham
Baulking
Uffington
Shrivenham
South Marston
Bourton
Compton Beauchamp
Woolstone
Kingston Lisle
Sparsholt
Childrey
West Challow
East Challow
Letcombe Regis
Letcombe Bassett
Ashbury
Idstone
Bishopstone
Hinton Parva
Wanborough
Liddington
Badbury
Chiseldon
Coate
Walcot
Wroughton
Ogbourne St George
Ogbourne St Andrew
Ogbourne Maizey
Aldbourne
Baydon
Lambourn
Upper Lambourn
Eastbury
East Garston
Great Shefford
Woodlands St Mary
Shefford Woodlands
Ramsbury
Axford
Mildenhall
Preston
Whittonditch
Chilton Foliat
Froxfield
Eddington
Kintbury
Avington
Wickham
Welford
Little Bedwyn
Great Bedwyn
Shalbourne
Ham
Inkpen
Buttermere
Wilton
Burbage
Pewsey
Milton Lilbourne
Easton Royal
Savernake Forest
Manton
Oare
Clench Common
Wootton Rivers
New Mill
Southcott
Wexcombe
Oxenwood
Tidcombe
Crofton
Durley
Stibb Green
Eastcourt
West Grafton
East Grafton
Marten
Cadley
Chisbury
Bagshot
Rockley
Southend
Upper Upham
Woodsend
Draycot Foliat
Hodson
Lambourne Downs
NORTH WESSEX DOWNS
SWINDON
OXON
BERKSHIRE
WILTSHIRE
THE RIDGEWAY PATH
UFFINGTON WHITE HORSE & CASTLE
WAYLAND'S SMITHY
ASHDOWN HOUSE
Membury Services
CROFTON BEAM ENGINES
WILTON WINDMILL
WALBURY HILL
Kennet & Avon Canal
River Kennet
M4
A4
A338
A346
A419
A420
B4000
B4192
B4507
B4001
81
82
14
15
47
84
64

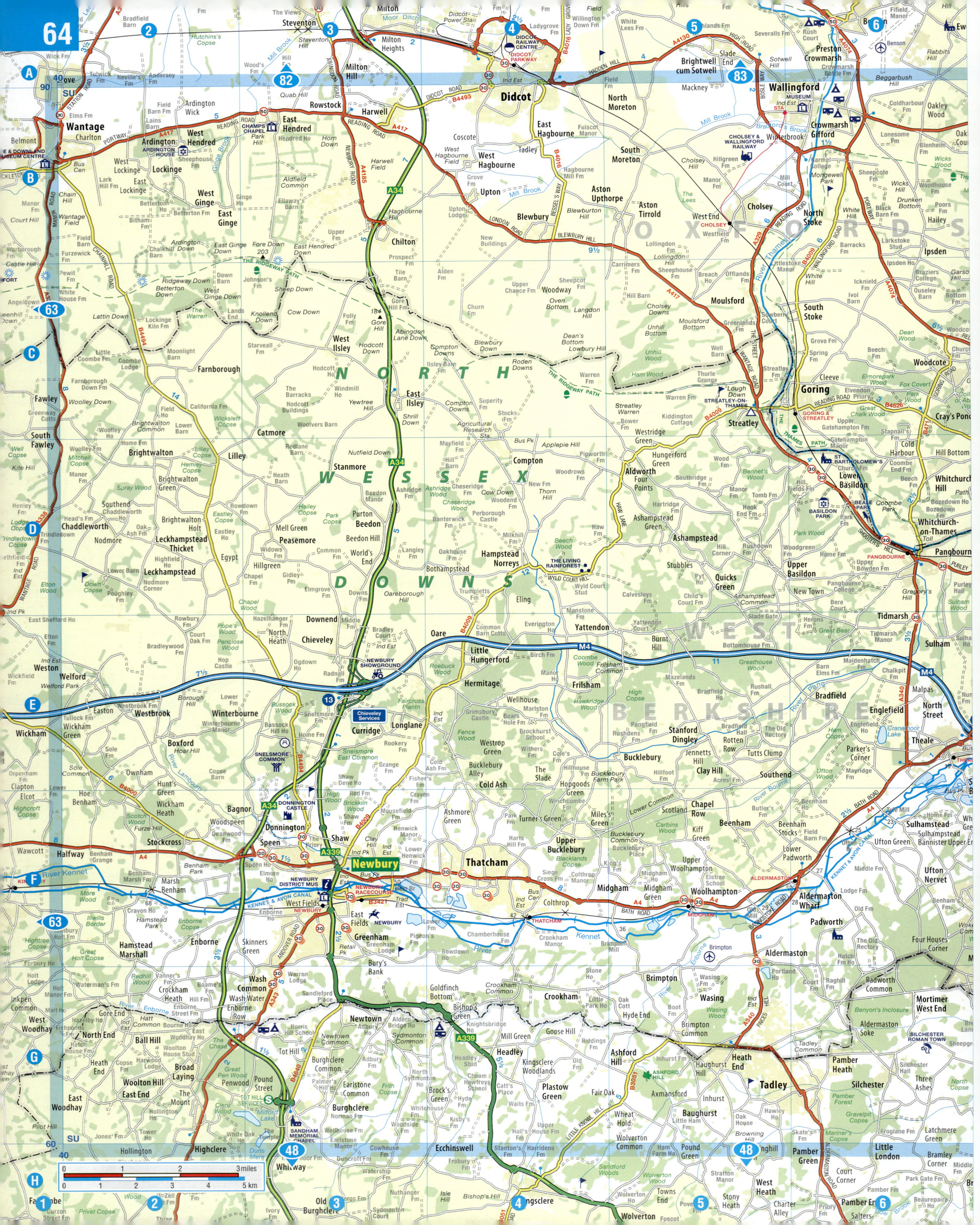
Wantage
Didcot
Wallingford
Steventon
Milton
Harwell
East Hendred
West Hendred
Ardington
Grove
Charlton
Letcombe Regis
Blewbury
Upton
Chilton
East Hagbourne
West Hagbourne
North Moreton
South Moreton
Aston Upthorpe
Aston Tirrold
Cholsey
North Stoke
South Stoke
Moulsford
Crowmarsh Gifford
Brightwell cum Sotwell
West Ilsley
East Ilsley
Compton
Chilton Foliat
Farnborough
Fawley
South Fawley
Brightwalton
Catmore
Lilley
Stanmore
Beedon
Peasemore
Chaddleworth
Leckhampstead
Leckhampstead Thicket
Hampstead Norreys
Aldworth
Streatley
Goring
Whitchurch-on-Thames
Pangbourne
Upper Basildon
Lower Basildon
Ashampstead
Yattendon
Hermitage
Frilsham
Chieveley
Curridge
Longlane
Bucklebury
Cold Ash
Thatcham
Newbury
Speen
Donnington
Shaw
Stockcross
Boxford
Winterbourne
Welford
Weston
Wickham
Easton
Westbrook
Hoe Benham
Marsh Benham
Halfway
Hamstead Marshall
Enborne
Wash Common
Woolton Hill
East Woodhay
Ball Hill
Newtown
Headley
Kingsclere Woodlands
Crookham
Midgham
Woolhampton
Brimpton
Aldermaston
Aldermaston Wharf
Padworth
Tadley
Baughurst
Pamber Heath
Silchester
Sulhamstead
Theale
Englefield
Bradfield
Southend
Tidmarsh
Sulham
Purley
Beenham
Upper Woolhampton
Chapel Row
Stanford Dingley
Burnt Hill
Ashmore Green
Upper Bucklebury
Greenham
Highclere
Whitway
Ecchinswell
NORTH WESSEX DOWNS
WEST BERKSHIRE
OXFORDSHIRE
River Thames
River Kennet
Kennet & Avon Canal
River Enborne
River Pang
River Lambourn
THE RIDGEWAY PATH
THAMES PATH
A34
A4
A339
A417
A329
A340
A343
A4074
A4130
A4185
B4009
B4000
B4494
B4016
B4493
B4526
B3421
B3051
M4
13
12
63
82
83
48
SU
0 1 2 3 miles
0 1 2 3 4 5 km

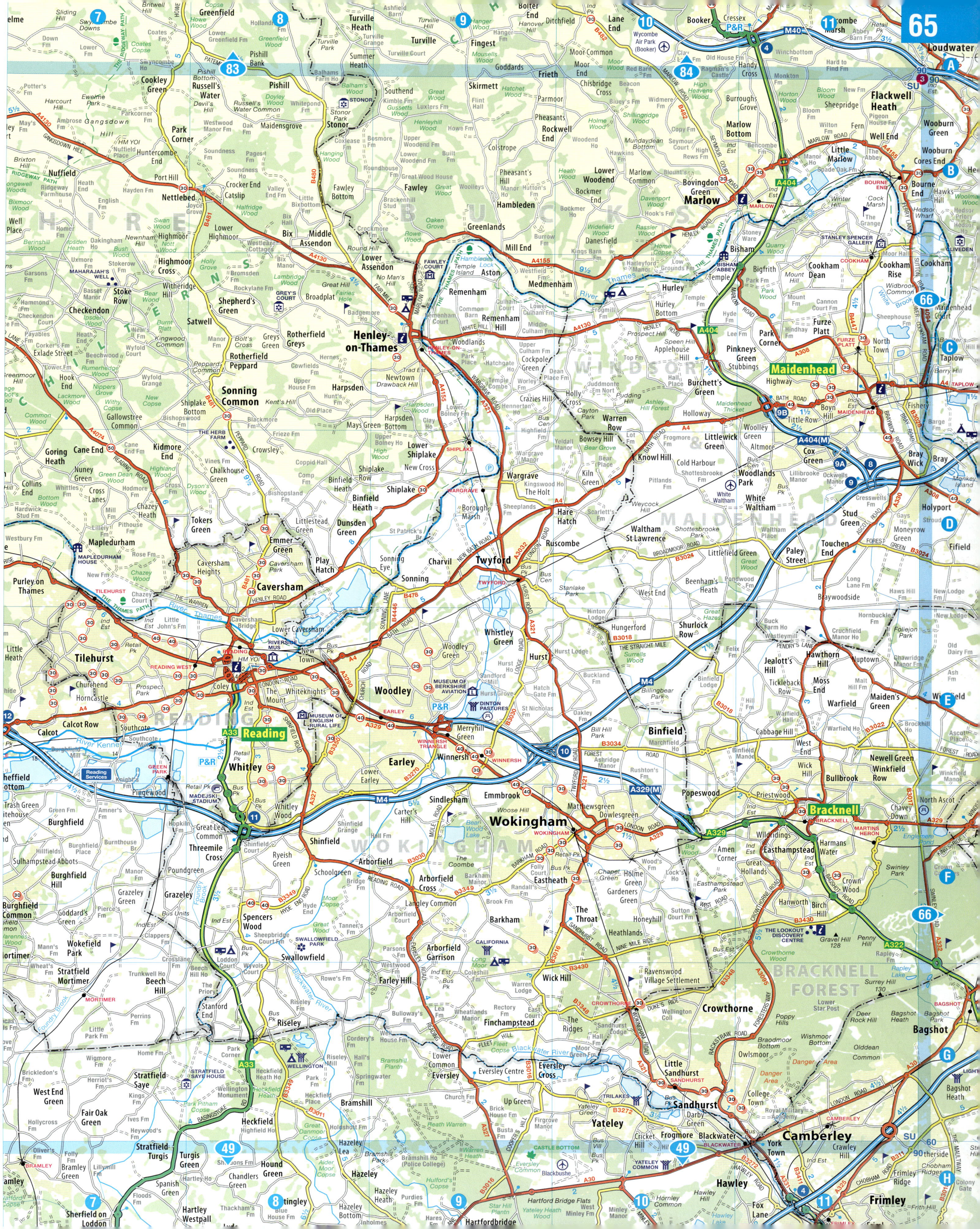
Henley-on-Thames
Marlow
Maidenhead
Reading
Wokingham
Bracknell
Twyford
Woodley
Earley
Caversham
Tilehurst
Sonning
Sonning Common
Binfield
Crowthorne
Sandhurst
Camberley
Yateley
Frimley
Bagshot
Finchampstead
Arborfield
Shinfield
Spencers Wood
Whitley
Calcot
Purley on Thames
Mapledurham
Hurley
Cookham
Bisham
Bourne End
Flackwell Heath
Wooburn Green
Taplow
Bray
Holyport
Warfield
Winkfield Row
Hawley
Blackwater
Swallowfield
Eversley
Hartley Wintney
Stratfield Mortimer
Burghfield
Wargrave
Knowl Hill
Waltham St Lawrence
White Waltham
Medmenham
Hambleden
Fingest
Turville
Stonor
Nettlebed
Checkendon
Hurst
Crowthorne
Barkham
Pangbourne
BRACKNELL FOREST
WOKINGHAM
READING
MAIDENHEAD
WINDSOR
BUCKS
CHILTERNS
M4
M40
A404(M)
A329(M)
A4
A33
A404
A329
A4130
A4155
A321
A327
A30
A322

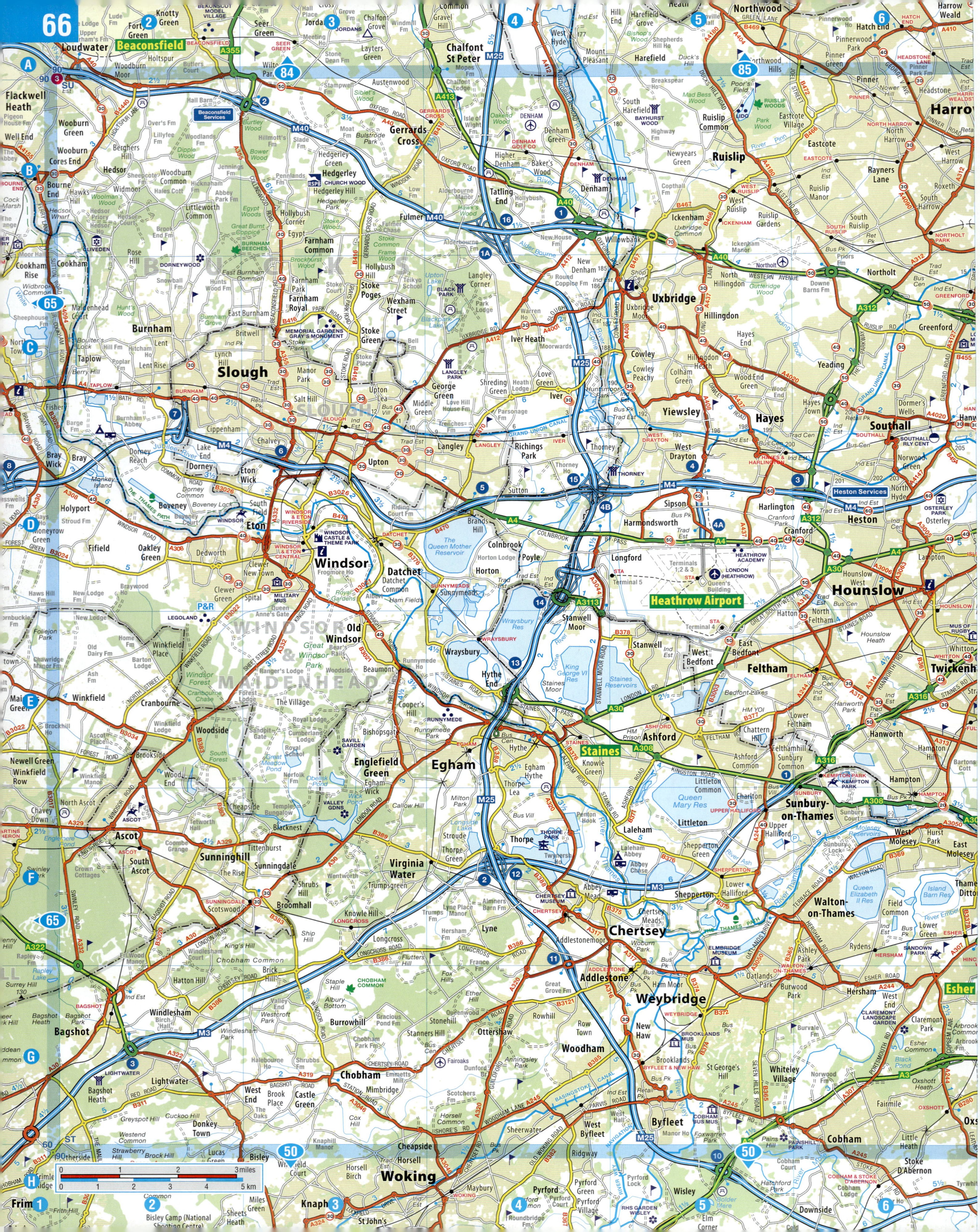

Beaconsfield
Loudwater
Flackwell Heath
Wooburn Green
Knotty Green
Seer Green
Jordans
Chalfont St Peter
Gerrards Cross
Denham
West Hyde
Harefield
Northwood
Pinner
Harrow
Ruislip
Ickenham
Uxbridge
Hillingdon
Northolt
Greenford
Yeading
Hayes
Southall
Yiewsley
West Drayton
Iver
Iver Heath
Fulmer
Farnham Common
Farnham Royal
Stoke Poges
Wexham Street
Burnham
Slough
Langley
Colnbrook
Datchet
Eton
Eton Wick
Dorney
Windsor
Old Windsor
Wraysbury
Heathrow Airport
Harlington
Cranford
Heston
Hounslow
Feltham
Bedfont
Stanwell
Ashford
Staines
Egham
Englefield Green
Thorpe
Virginia Water
Sunningdale
Sunninghill
Ascot
Winkfield
Laleham
Shepperton
Sunbury-on-Thames
Walton-on-Thames
Chertsey
Addlestone
Weybridge
Hersham
Esher
Byfleet
Woodham
Ottershaw
Chobham
Windlesham
Lightwater
Bagshot
Woking
Knaphill
Pyrford
Wisley
Cobham
Hampton
Twickenham
Whitton
Thames Ditton
Beaconsfield Services
Heston Services
Windsor Great Park
Queen Mother Reservoir
Wraysbury Res
King George VI Res
Staines Res
Queen Mary Res
Queen Elizabeth II Res
WINDSOR & MAIDENHEAD
BUCKS
M4
M25
M40
M3
A30
A4
A40
A312
A316
A308
A322
A329
A332
A320
A3
A245
A244
A412
A413
A355
0 1 2 3 miles
0 1 2 3 4 5 km

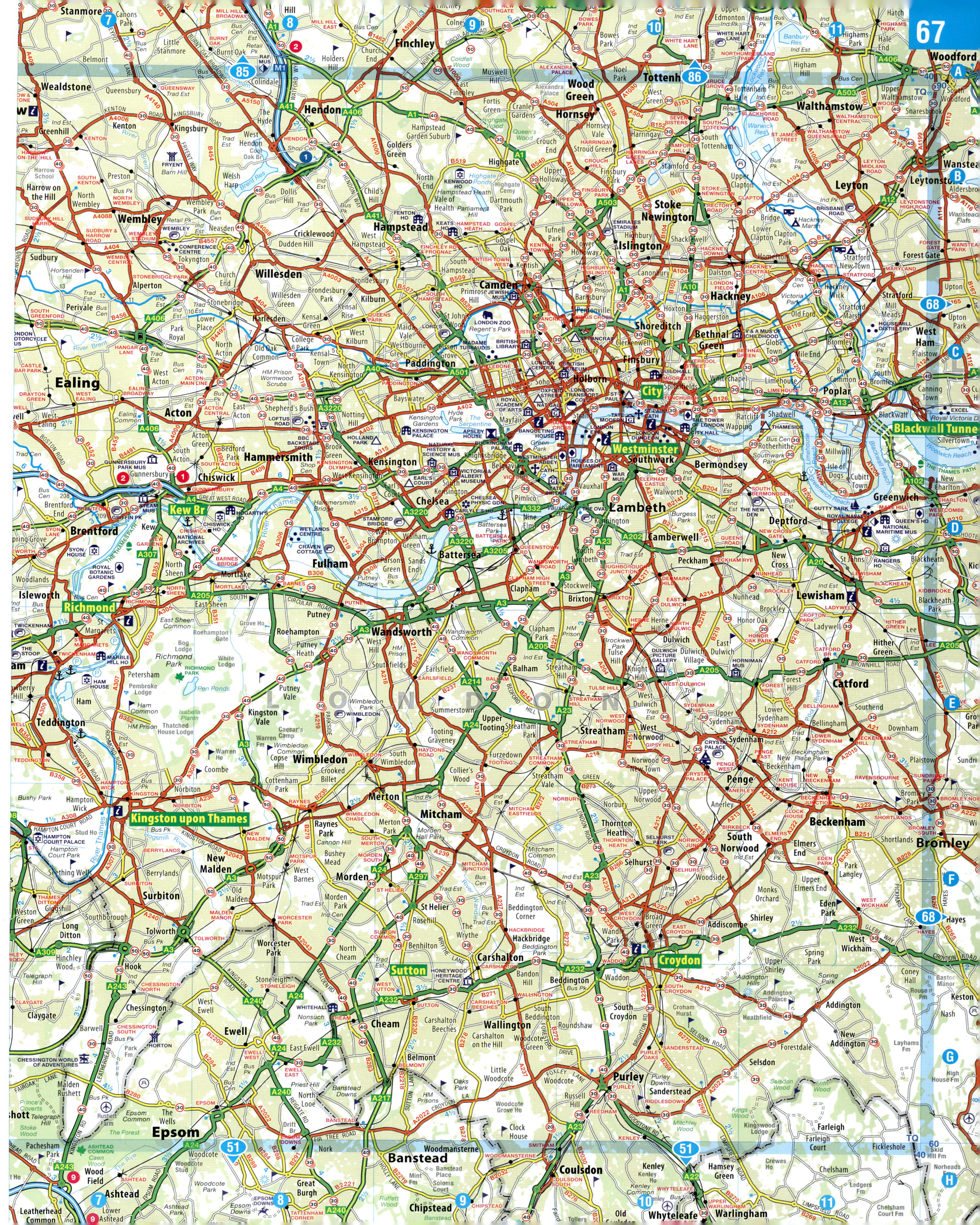
Stanmore
Finchley
Wood Green
Tottenham
Woodford
Wealdstone
Hendon
Hornsey
Walthamstow
Kenton
Kingsbury
Leyton
Harrow on the Hill
Wembley
Hampstead
Stoke Newington
Cricklewood
Islington
Sudbury
Willesden
Camden
Hackney
Stratford
Alperton
Kilburn
Shoreditch
Bethnal Green
West Ham
Ealing
Paddington
Holborn
Finsbury
Acton
City
Poplar
Blackwall Tunnel
Hammersmith
Kensington
Westminster
Southwark
Bermondsey
Chiswick
Chelsea
Kew Br
Lambeth
Greenwich
Brentford
Fulham
Camberwell
Deptford
Battersea
Peckham
Isleworth
Lewisham
Richmond
Putney
Brixton
Wandsworth
Clapham
Balham
Catford
Teddington
Streatham
Wimbledon
Norwood
Sydenham
Kingston upon Thames
Merton
Mitcham
Penge
Beckenham
Bromley
New Malden
Morden
South Norwood
Surbiton
Croydon
Sutton
Carshalton
Cheam
Ewell
Wallington
Purley
Epsom
Banstead
Coulsdon
Ashtead
Chipstead
Whyteleafe
Warlingham
LONDON

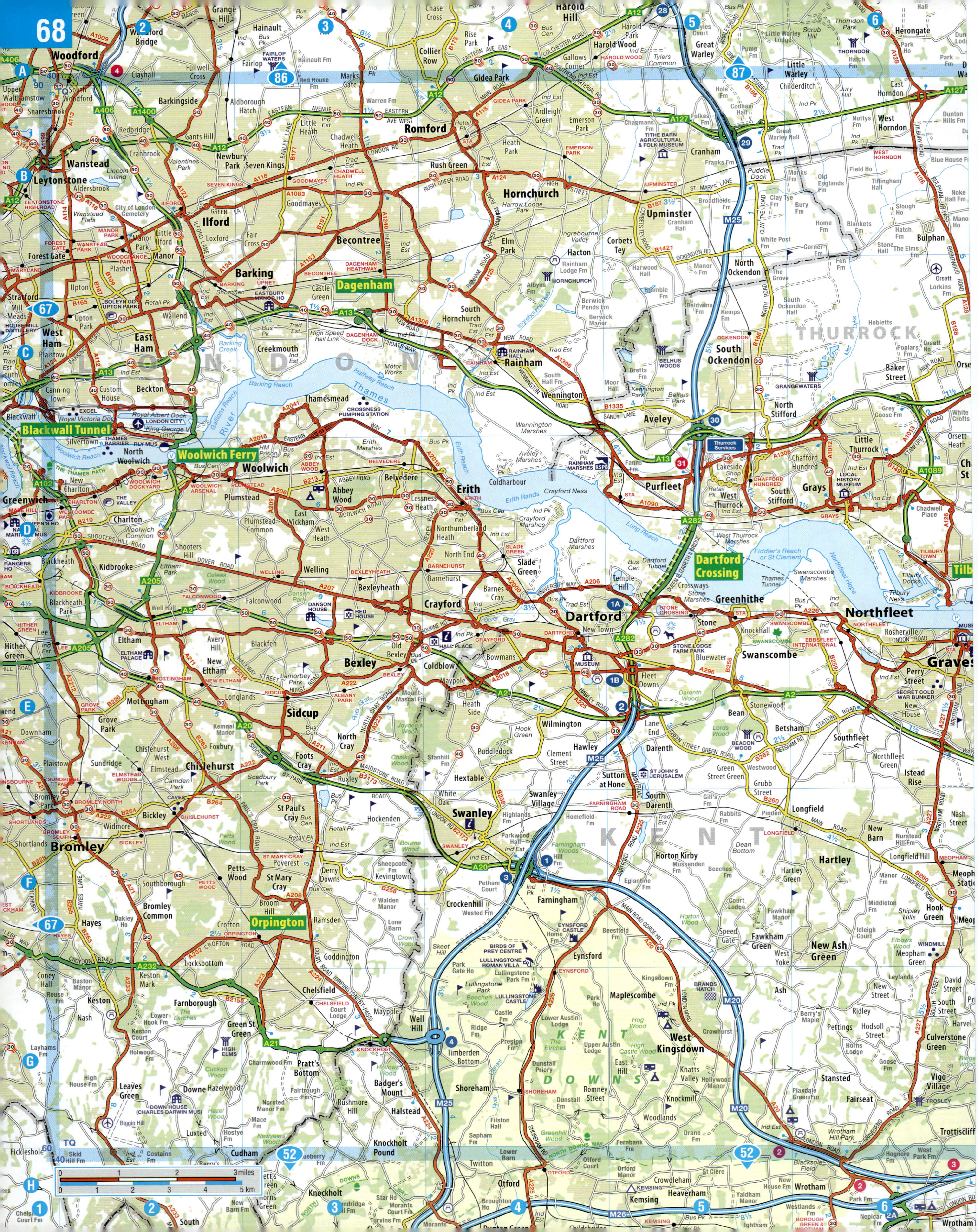

Woodford
Leytonstone
Wanstead
Ilford
Barking
Dagenham
Becontree
Romford
Gidea Park
Hornchurch
Upminster
Rainham
South Hornchurch
Elm Park
Great Warley
Little Warley
Harold Wood
Harold Hill
Cranham
North Ockendon
South Ockendon
Aveley
Purfleet
West Thurrock
Grays
Chafford Hundred
Little Thurrock
North Stifford
South Stifford
THURROCK
Stratford
West Ham
East Ham
Beckton
LONDON
Thames
Thamesmead
Blackwall Tunnel
Woolwich Ferry
Woolwich
North Woolwich
Greenwich
Charlton
Plumstead
Abbey Wood
Belvedere
Erith
Welling
Bexleyheath
Crayford
Dartford
Dartford Crossing
Greenhithe
Stone
Swanscombe
Northfleet
Bexley
Sidcup
Eltham
Chislehurst
Bromley
Orpington
St Mary Cray
St Paul's Cray
Swanley
Hextable
Wilmington
Sutton at Hone
South Darenth
Horton Kirby
Farningham
Eynsford
Shoreham
Otford
Kemsing
Knockholt
Halstead
Badger's Mount
Chelsfield
Farnborough
Keston
Hayes
West Kingsdown
Maplescombe
KENT DOWNS
KENT
Longfield
Hartley
New Ash Green
Southfleet
Betsham
Bean
Fawkham Green
Ash
Culverstone Green
Vigo Village
Wrotham
Heaverham
Crockenhill
Hawley
Darenth

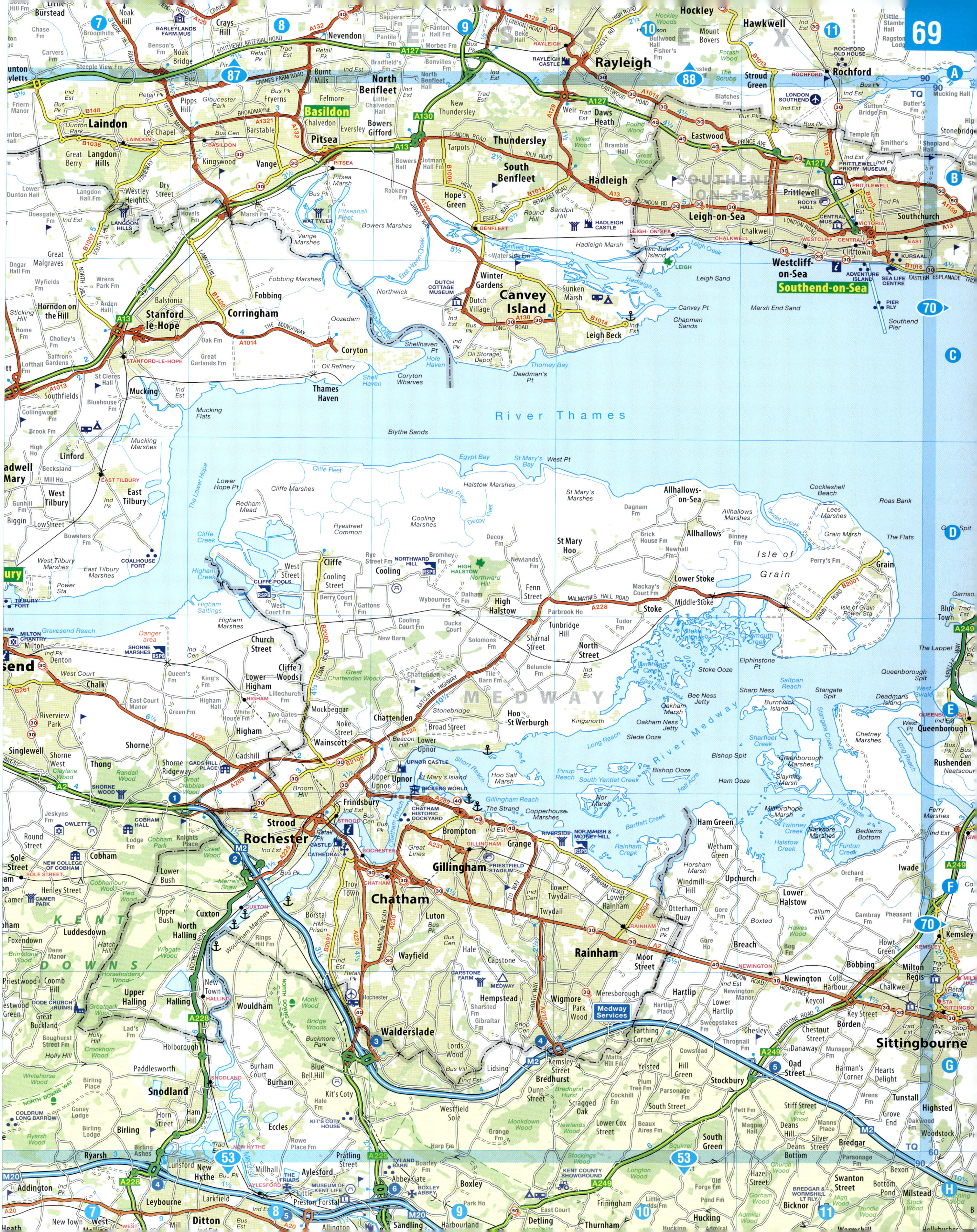
ESSEX
Rayleigh
Hockley
Hawkwell
Rochford
Basildon
Laindon
Pitsea
North Benfleet
Thundersley
South Benfleet
Hadleigh
Eastwood
Leigh-on-Sea
Prittlewell
Southchurch
Westcliff-on-Sea
Southend-on-Sea
Canvey Island
Stanford-le-Hope
Corringham
Fobbing
Coryton
Thames Haven
Linford
East Tilbury
West Tilbury
River Thames
Blythe Sands
Cliffe
Cooling
Allhallows-on-Sea
Allhallows
St Mary Hoo
High Halstow
Isle of Grain
Grain
Stoke
Lower Stoke
Middle Stoke
Hoo St Werburgh
Chattenden
Wainscott
Strood
Rochester
Chatham
Gillingham
Brompton
Rainham
Walderslade
Wouldham
Halling
Snodland
Burham
Aylesford
Sandling
Ditton
Leybourne
Cuxton
Cobham
Shorne
Higham
River Medway
MEDWAY
KENT
DOWNS
Upchurch
Newington
Sittingbourne
Milton Regis
Kemsley
Iwade
Queenborough
Rushenden
Bredhurst
Hempstead
Wigmore
Lordswood
Medway Services
M2
M20
A2
A13
A127
A130
A228
A229
A249
A289
River Thames
Sheerness
Southend Pier
Canvey Pt
Leigh Beck
Chapman Sands
Mucking
Hoo
Stoke Ooze
Sharp Ness
Kingsnorth
Bee Ness Jetty
Ham Green
Lower Halstow
Bobbing
Borden
Stockbury
Detling
Boxley
Chestnut Street
70
53
87
88

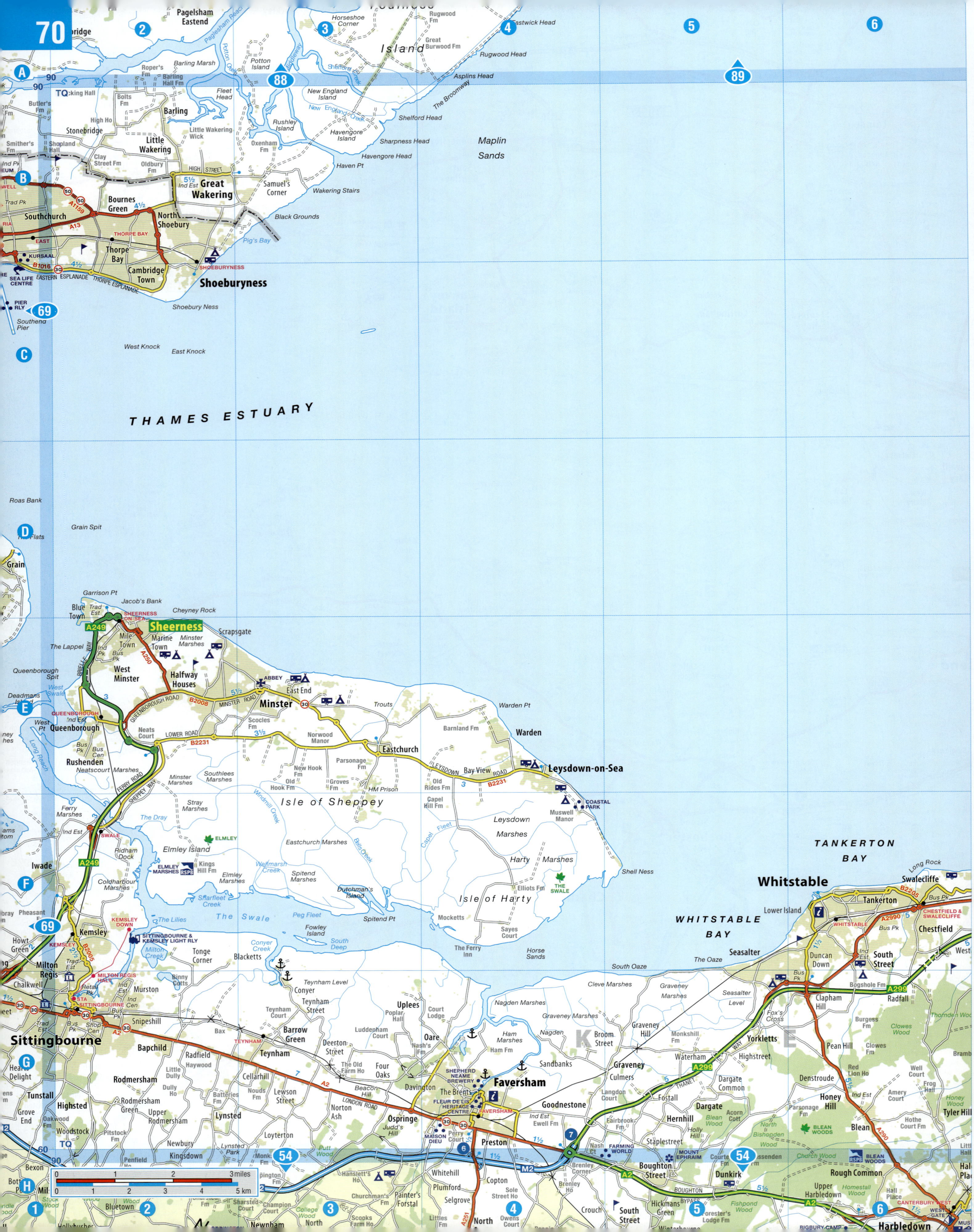
Pagelsham Eastend
Horseshoe Corner
Rugwood Fm
Eastwick Head
Island
Great Burwood Fm
Rugwood Head
Roper's Fm
Barling Marsh
Barling Hall Fm
Potton Island
88
89
Asplins Head
Fleet Head
New England Island
Bolts Fm
Butler's Fm
High Ho
Barling
Little Wakering Wick
Rushley Island
Shelford Head
Stonebridge
Smither's Fm
Shopland Hall
Little Wakering
Oxenham Fm
Havengore Island
Sharpness Head
Maplin Sands
Clay Street Fm
Oldbury Fm
Havengore Head
Haven Pt
Great Wakering
Samuel's Corner
Wakering Stairs
Southchurch
Bournes Green
North Shoebury
Black Grounds
Pig's Bay
Thorpe Bay
Cambridge Town
Shoeburyness
Shoeburyness
Sea Life Centre
Pier Rly
69
Southend Pier
Shoebury Ness
West Knock
East Knock
THAMES ESTUARY
Roas Bank
Grain Spit
Grain
Garrison Pt
Jacob's Bank
Cheyney Rock
Blue Town
Sheerness
Scrapsgate
Marine Town
Minster Marshes
Mile Town
The Lappel
West Minster
Halfway Houses
Queenborough Spit
East End
Minster
Trouts
Warden Pt
Queenborough
Neats Court
Scocles Fm
Norwood Manor
Barnland Fm
Warden
Eastchurch
Rushenden
Parsonage Fm
Leysdown-on-Sea
Bay View
New Hook Fm
Old Hook Fm
Groves Fm
HM Prison
Old Rides Fm
Capel Hill Fm
Isle of Sheppey
Muswell Manor
Coastal Park
Minster Marshes
Southlees Marshes
Stray Marshes
Ferry Marshes
The Dray
Leysdown Marshes
Elmley
Elmley Island
Eastchurch Marshes
Harty Marshes
Shell Ness
Tankerton Bay
Kings Hill Fm
Elmley Marshes
Spitend Marshes
Iwade
Ridham Dock
Coldharbour Marshes
Dutchman's Island
Elliots Fm
The Swale
Isle of Harty
Whitstable
Swalecliffe
Long Rock
Lower Island
Tankerton
Whitstable Bay
The Swale
Peg Fleet
Spitend Pt
Mocketts
Kemsley
Fowley Island
Sayes Court
Chestfield
Sittingbourne & Kemsley Light Rly
Conyer Creek
South Deep
The Ferry Inn
Horse Sands
Seasalter
The Oaze
Duncan Down
South Street
Milton Regis
Tonge Corner
Blacketts
South Oaze
Teynham Level
Cleve Marshes
Graveney Marshes
Seasalter Level
Radfall
Conyer
Murston
Teynham Street
Uplees
Court Lodge
Nagden Marshes
Clapham Hill
Sittingbourne
Snipeshill
Bax
Barrow Green
Teynham Court
Poplar Hall
Graveney Marshes
Fox's Cross
Bapchild
Teynham
Luddenham Court
Oare
Ham Marshes
Nagden
Broom Street
Graveney Hill
Monkshill Fm
Yorkletts
Radfield
Deerton Street
Ham Fm
Highstreet
Pean Hill
Rodmersham
Four Oaks
Sandbanks
Waterham
Graveney
Faversham
Culmers
Dargate Common
Denstroude
Tunstall
Highsted
Rodmersham Green
Lynsted
Davington
The Brents
Goodnestone
Fostall
Dargate
Honey Hill
Tyler Hill
Ospringe
Perry Court
Ewell Fm
Hernhill
Blean
Woodstock
Loyterton
Preston
Staplestreet
Kingsdown
Newbury
Mount Ephraim
Courte Fm
Dunkirk
Blean Woods
Bexon
Whitehill
Plumford
Copton
Boughton Street
Rough Common
Bluetown
Painter's Forstal
Selgrove
Harbledown
Newnham
North
Crouch
South Street
Hickmans Green
Upper Harbledown
0 1 2 3 miles
0 1 2 3 4 5 km

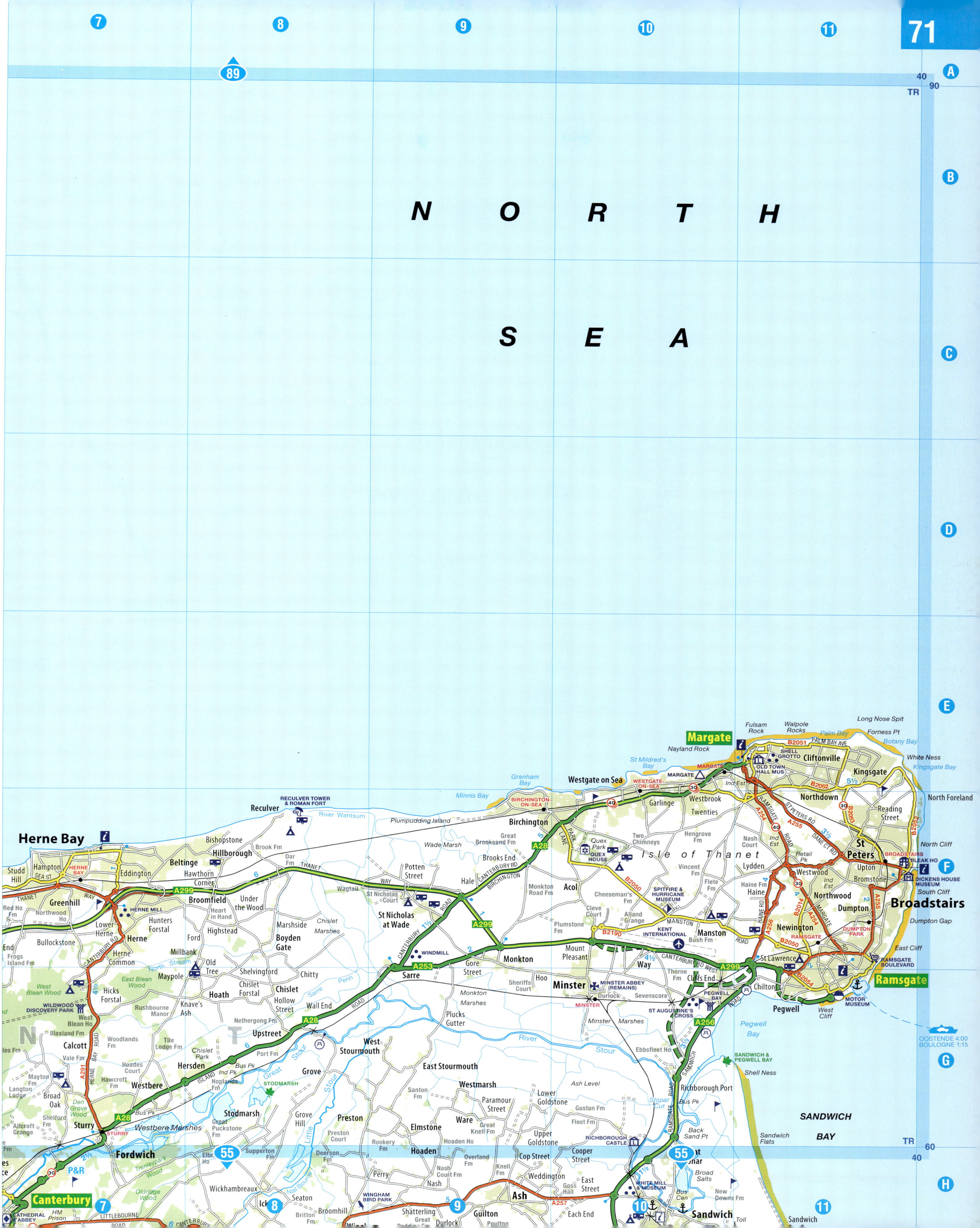
NORTH SEA
TR
Margate
Westgate on Sea
Birchington
Reculver
RECULVER TOWER & ROMAN FORT
Herne Bay
Hampton
Studd Hill
Eddington
Beltinge
Bishopstone
Hillborough
Broomfield
Herne
Greenhill
Bullockstone
Hunters Forstal
Herne Common
Lower Herne
Maypole
Highstead
Millbank
Hoath
Chislet
Marshside
Boyden Gate
St Nicholas at Wade
Sarre
Monkton
Minster
Acol
Manston
KENT INTERNATIONAL
Isle of Thanet
Garlinge
Westbrook
Twenties
Cliftonville
Northdown
Kingsgate
St Peters
Broadstairs
Reading Street
North Foreland
Northwood
Dumpton
Newington
Ramsgate
St Lawrence
Pegwell
Pegwell Bay
Cliffs End
Upstreet
West Stourmouth
East Stourmouth
Grove
Stodmarsh
Westbere
Hersden
Sturry
Fordwich
Canterbury
Calcott
Broad Oak
Preston
Elmstone
Westmarsh
Ware
Hoaden
Ash
Sandwich
SANDWICH BAY
Richborough Port
RICHBOROUGH CASTLE
Wickhambreaux
Seaton
Guilton
Weddington
Cop Street
Lower Goldstone
Upper Goldstone
WILDWOOD DISCOVERY PARK
SPITFIRE & HURRICANE MUSEUM
QUEX HOUSE
MINSTER ABBEY (REMAINS)
ST AUGUSTINE'S CROSS
DICKENS HOUSE MUSEUM
BLEAK HO
MOTOR MUSEUM
OOSTENDE 4:00
BOULOGNE 1:15
A28
A299
A253
A256
A254
A255
A257
A291
B2050
B2190
B2051
B2052
89
55

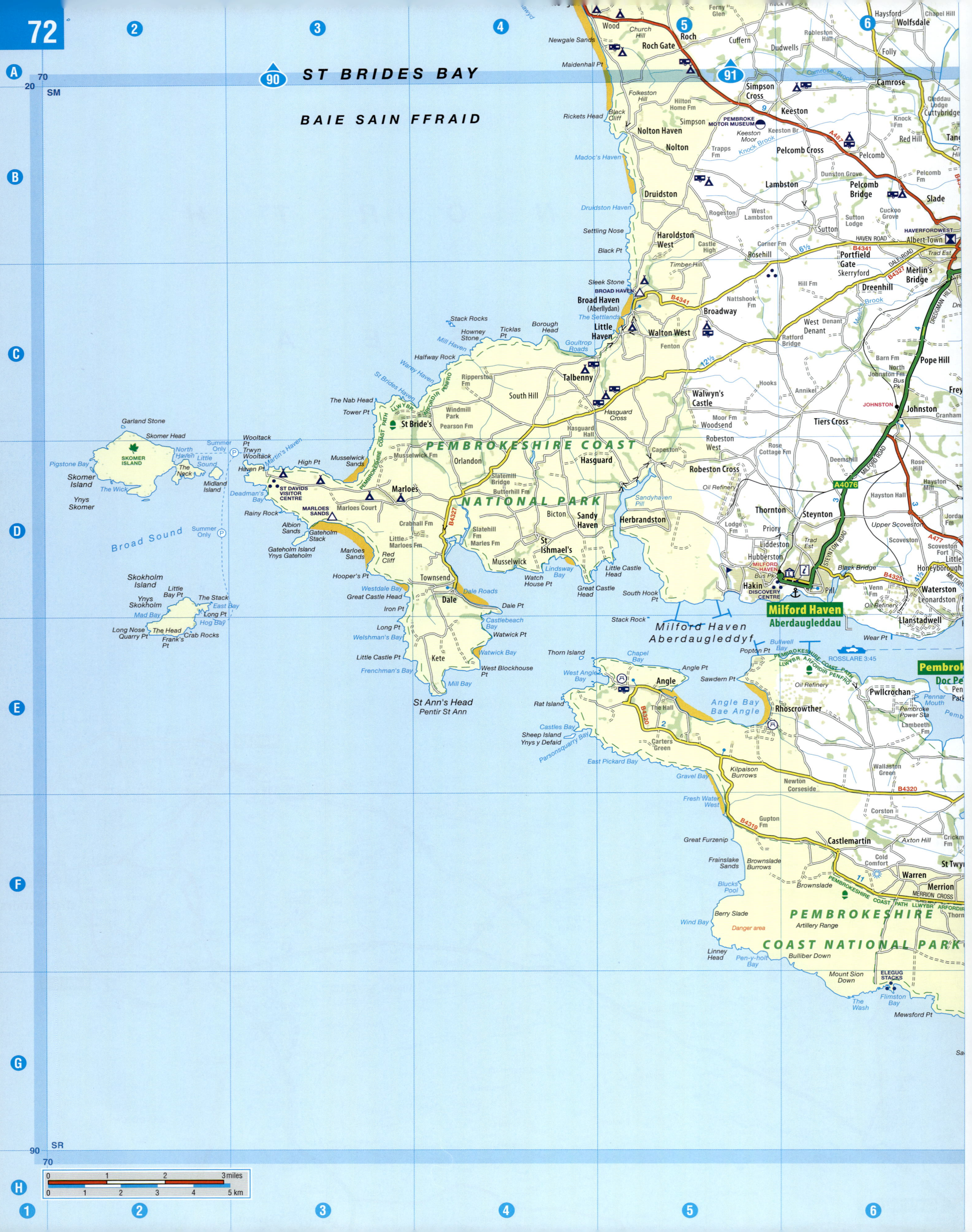
ST BRIDES BAY
BAIE SAIN FFRAID
90
91
PEMBROKESHIRE COAST NATIONAL PARK
Milford Haven
Aberdaugleddyf
Milford Haven
Aberdaugleddau
Roch
Roch Gate
Wood
Church Hill
Newgale Sands
Maidenhall Pt
Simpson Cross
Keeston
Camrose
Hayscastle
Wolfsdale
Folly
Cuffern
Dudwells
Robleston Hall
PEMBROKE MOTOR MUSEUM
Pelcomb Cross
Pelcomb
Pelcomb Bridge
Slade
Lambston
Nolton Haven
Nolton
Folkeston Hill
Rickets Head
Black Cliff
Madoc's Haven
Druidston
Druidston Haven
Settling Nose
Haroldston West
Black Pt
Sleek Stone
BROAD HAVEN
Broad Haven (Aberllydan)
The Settlands
Little Haven
Walton West
Rosehill
Portfield Gate
Merlin's Bridge
Albert Town
HAVERFORDWEST
Dreenhill
Broadway
Nattshook Fm
Skerryford
Goultrop Roads
Borough Head
Ticklas Pt
Howney Stone
Stack Rocks
Mill Haven
Halfway Rock
Warey Haven
St Brides Haven
The Nab Head
Tower Pt
St Bride's
Ripperston Fm
South Hill
Talbenny
Windmill Park
Pearson Fm
Hasguard Cross
Hasguard Hall
Hasguard
Walwyn's Castle
Moor Fm
Woodsend
Robeston West
Robeston Cross
Tiers Cross
Johnston
Pope Hill
West Denant
Ratford Bridge
Hooks
Annikel
Capeston
Oil Refinery
Thornton
Steynton
Priory
Liddeston
Hubberston
Hakin
DISCOVERY CENTRE
Pill
Waterston
Llanstadwell
Honeyborough
Garland Stone
Skomer Head
SKOMER ISLAND
North Haven
Little Sound
The Neck
Midland Island
Pigstone Bay
Skomer Island
Ynys Skomer
The Wick
Wooltack Pt
Trwyn Wooltack
Martin's Haven
Haven Pt
ST DAVIDS VISITOR CENTRE
High Pt
Musselwick Sands
Musselwick Fm
Orlandon
Marloes
MARLOES SANDS
Marloes Court
Deadman's Bay
Rainy Rock
Albion Sands
Gateholm Stack
Gateholm Island
Ynys Gateholm
Marloes Sands
Red Cliff
Crabhall Fm
Little Marloes Fm
Slatemill Bridge
Butterhill Fm
Slatehill Fm
Marles Fm
Bicton
Sandy Haven
St Ishmael's
Musselwick
Herbrandston
Sandyhaven Pill
Broad Sound
Summer Only
Skokholm Island
Ynys Skokholm
Little Bay Pt
The Stack
East Bay
Long Pt
Hog Bay
Mad Bay
Long Nose
Quarry Pt
The Head
Crab Rocks
Frank's Pt
Hooper's Pt
Westdale Bay
Great Castle Head
Townsend
Dale
Dale Roads
Dale Pt
Iron Pt
Castlebeach Bay
Watwick Pt
Long Pt
Welshman's Bay
Watwick Bay
Little Castle Pt
Kete
West Blockhouse Pt
Frenchman's Bay
Mill Bay
St Ann's Head
Pentir St Ann
Watch House Pt
Lindsway Bay
Little Castle Head
Great Castle Head
South Hook Pt
Stack Rock
Thorn Island
Chapel Bay
West Angle Bay
Angle
Angle Pt
Sawdern Pt
Popton Pt
Bullwell Bay
Angle Bay
Bae Angle
Rhoscrowther
Pwllcrochan
Rat Island
The Hall
Castles Bay
Sheep Island
Ynys y Defaid
Parsonsquarry Bay
Carters Green
East Pickard Bay
Gravel Bay
Kilpaison Burrows
Newton Corseside
Wallaston Green
Fresh Water West
Gupton Fm
Great Furzenip
Corston
Castlemartin
Axton Hill
Frainslake Sands
Brownslade Burrows
Cold Comfort
Brownslade
Warren
Merrion
Blucks Pool
Berry Slade
Wind Bay
Danger area
Artillery Range
Linney Head
Pen-y-holt Bay
Bulliber Down
Mount Sion Down
ELEGUG STACKS
Flimston Bay
The Wash
Mewsford Pt
ROSSLARE 3:45
B4341
B4327
B4320
B4319
B4325
A4076
A477
A487
SM
SR
0 1 2 3 miles
0 1 2 3 4 5 km

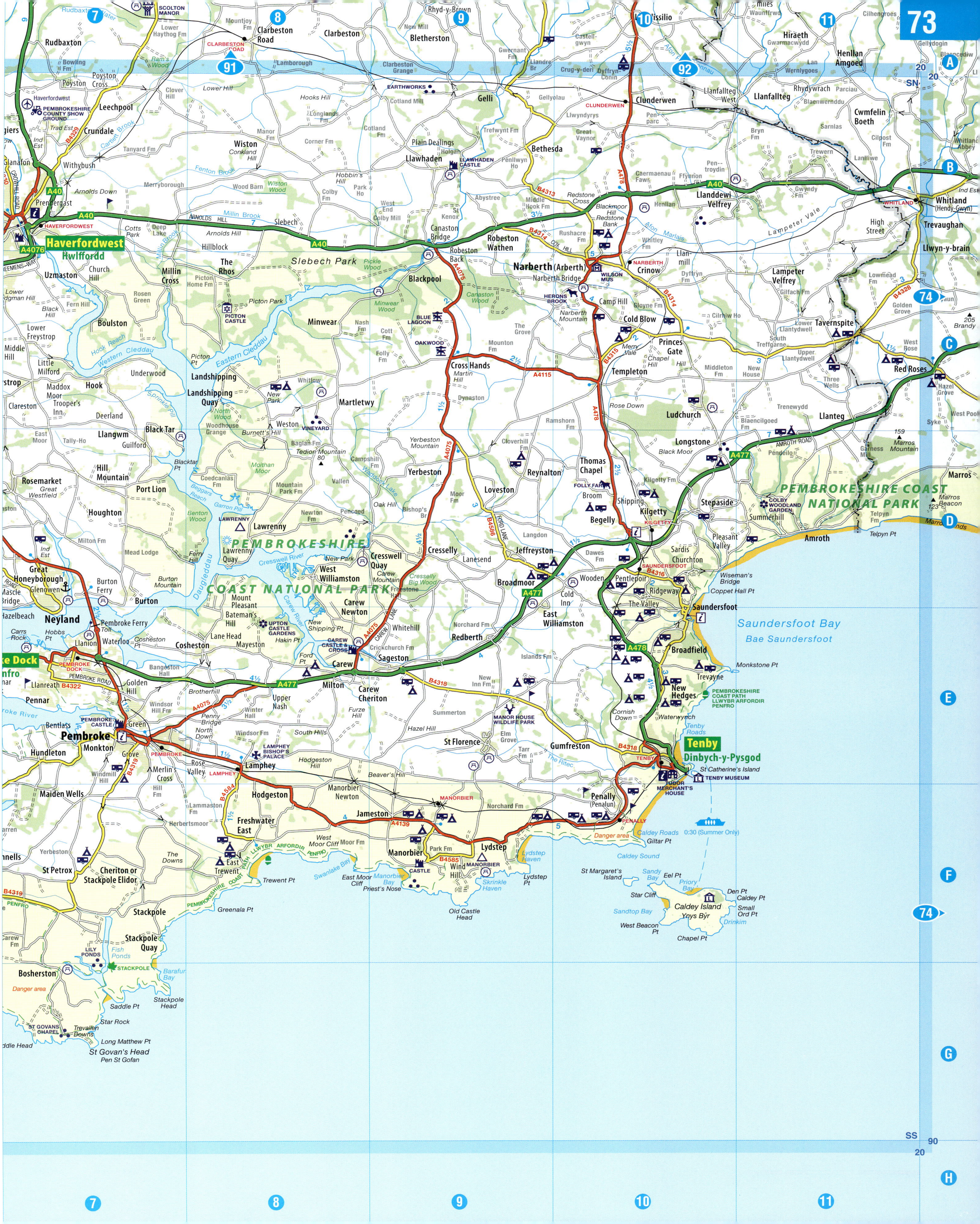

Haverfordwest
Hwlffordd
Rudbaxton
Clarbeston Road
Clarbeston
Bletherston
Clunderwen
Llanfallteg
Henllan Amgoed
Cwmfelin Boeth
Whitland
Trevaughan
Llwyn-y-brain
Gelli
Llawhaden
Bethesda
Wiston
Prendergast
Slebech
Slebech Park
Robeston Wathen
Canaston Bridge
Narberth (Arberth)
Crinow
Llanddewi Velfrey
Lampeter Velfrey
Tavernspite
Red Roses
Princes Gate
Templeton
Cross Hands
Blackpool
Minwear
Martletwy
Landshipping
Landshipping Quay
Uzmaston
Boulston
Hook
Llangwm
Black Tar
Hill Mountain
Port Lion
Rosemarket
Houghton
Lawrenny
Lawrenny Quay
Yerbeston
Reynalton
Loveston
Thomas Chapel
Begelly
Kilgetty
Stepaside
Longstone
Ludchurch
Llanteg
Amroth
Marros
Jeffreyston
Cresselly
Cresswell Quay
West Williamson
Carew Newton
Broadmoor
East Williamson
Saundersfoot
Saundersfoot Bay
Bae Saundersfoot
Sardis
Pentlepoir
Wooden
Broadfield
New Hedges
Tenby
Dinbych-y-Pysgod
Carew
Sageston
Milton
Carew Cheriton
Redberth
Whitehill
St Florence
Gumfreston
Penally
Lamphey
Hodgeston
Manorbier
Jameston
Lydstep
Freshwater East
Pembroke
Monkton
Hundleton
Maiden Wells
Neyland
Pembroke Dock
Llanion
Waterloo
Cosheston
Burton
Golden Hill
Pennar
St Petrox
Cheriton or Stackpole Elidor
Stackpole
Stackpole Quay
Bosherston
St Govan's Head
Pen St Gofan
Caldey Island
Ynys Bŷr
Caldey Sound
Giltar Pt
Old Castle Head
Manorbier Bay
Swanlake Bay
Trewent Pt
Greenala Pt
PEMBROKESHIRE COAST NATIONAL PARK
A40
A477
A478
A4075
A4115
A4139
B4318
B4314
B4316
B4585
B4584
91
92
7
8
9
10
11
A
B
C
D
E
F
G
H
74
SN
SS

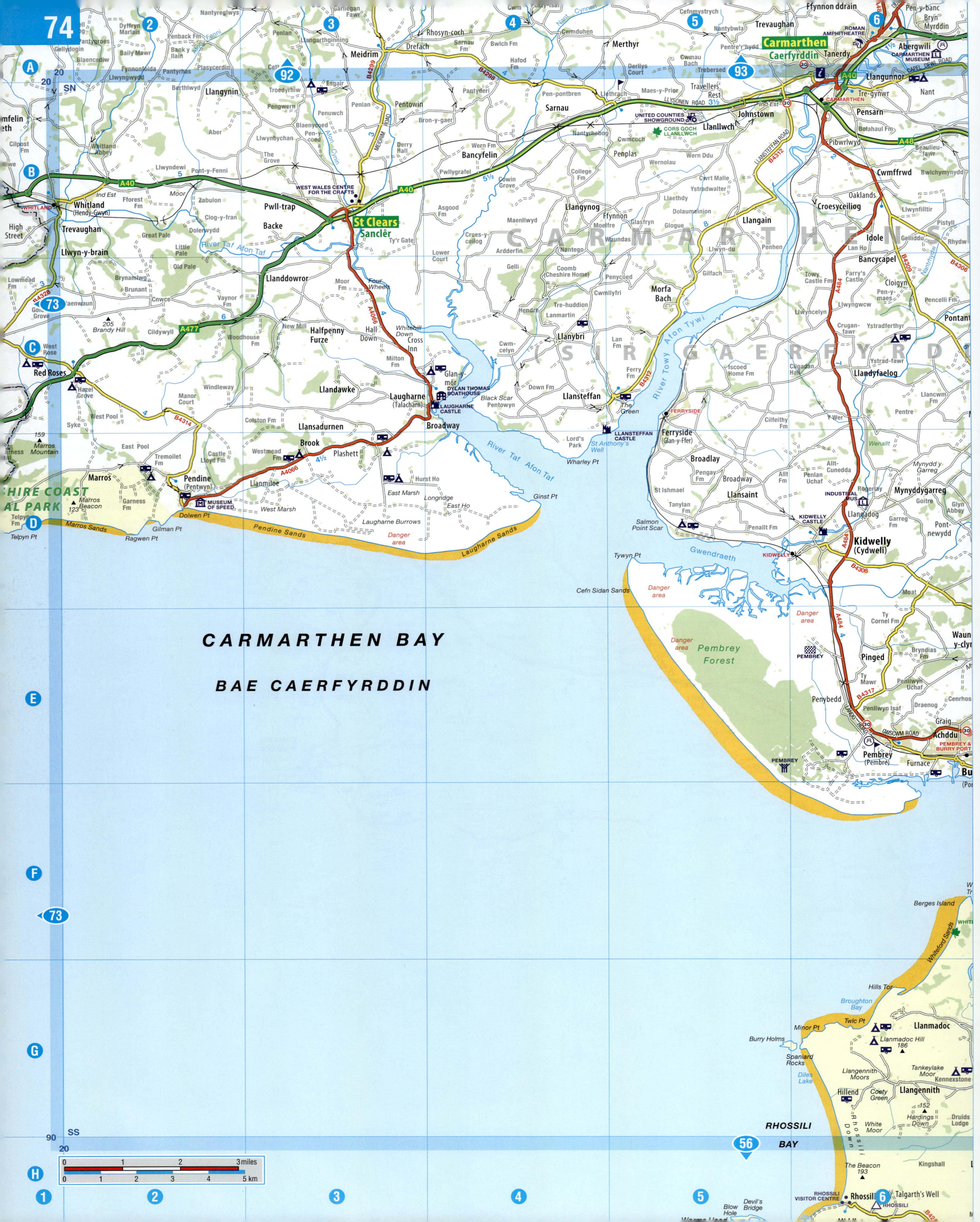
CARMARTHEN BAY
BAE CAERFYRDDIN
CARMARTHENSHIRE
SIR GAERFYRDDIN
Carmarthen
Caerfyrddin
St Clears
Sanclêr
Whitland
(Hendy-Gwyn)
Laugharne
(Talacharn)
Kidwelly
(Cydweli)
Pembrey
(Pembre)
Pendine
(Pentywyn)
Ferryside
(Glan-y-Fferi)
Meidrim
Trevaughan
Merthyr
Abergwili
Tanerdy
Llangunnor
Johnstown
Llanllwch
Sarnau
Bancyfelin
Llangynin
Pentowin
Pwll-trap
Backe
Llanddowror
Llwyn-y-brain
Red Roses
Marros
Llanmiloe
Brook
Plashett
Llansadurnen
Llandawke
Broadway
Halfpenny Furze
Llangynog
Llanybri
Llansteffan
Llangain
Morfa Bach
Croesyceiliog
Cwmffrwd
Idole
Bancycapel
Llandyfaelog
Broadlay
Llansaint
Mynyddygarreg
Pinged
Penybedd
Achddu
Furnace
Pontantwn
Llanmadoc
Llangennith
Hillend
Rhossili
RHOSSILI BAY
Pendine Sands
Laugharne Sands
Marros Sands
Cefn Sidan Sands
Pembrey Forest
River Taf Afon Taf
River Towy Afon Tywi
Gwendraeth
Ginst Pt
Tywyn Pt
Salmon Point Scar
Wharley Pt
Dolwen Pt
Gilman Pt
Ragwen Pt
Telpyn Pt
Burry Holms
Berges Island
Whiteford Sands
Broughton Bay
Hills Tor
Twlc Pt
Minor Pt
Danger area
LAUGHARNE CASTLE
DYLAN THOMAS BOATHOUSE
LLANSTEFFAN CASTLE
KIDWELLY CASTLE
MUSEUM OF SPEED
WEST WALES CENTRE FOR THE CRAFTS
UNITED COUNTIES SHOWGROUND
CORS GOCH LLANLLWCH
CARMARTHEN MUSEUM
ROMAN AMPHITHEATRE
RHOSSILI VISITOR CENTRE
A40
A48
A477
A4066
A484
B4312
B4299
B4298
B4314
B4328
B4308
B4309
B4317
SN
SS
A
B
C
D
E
F
G
H
1
2
3
4
5
6
73
92
93
56
0 1 2 3 miles
0 1 2 3 4 5 km

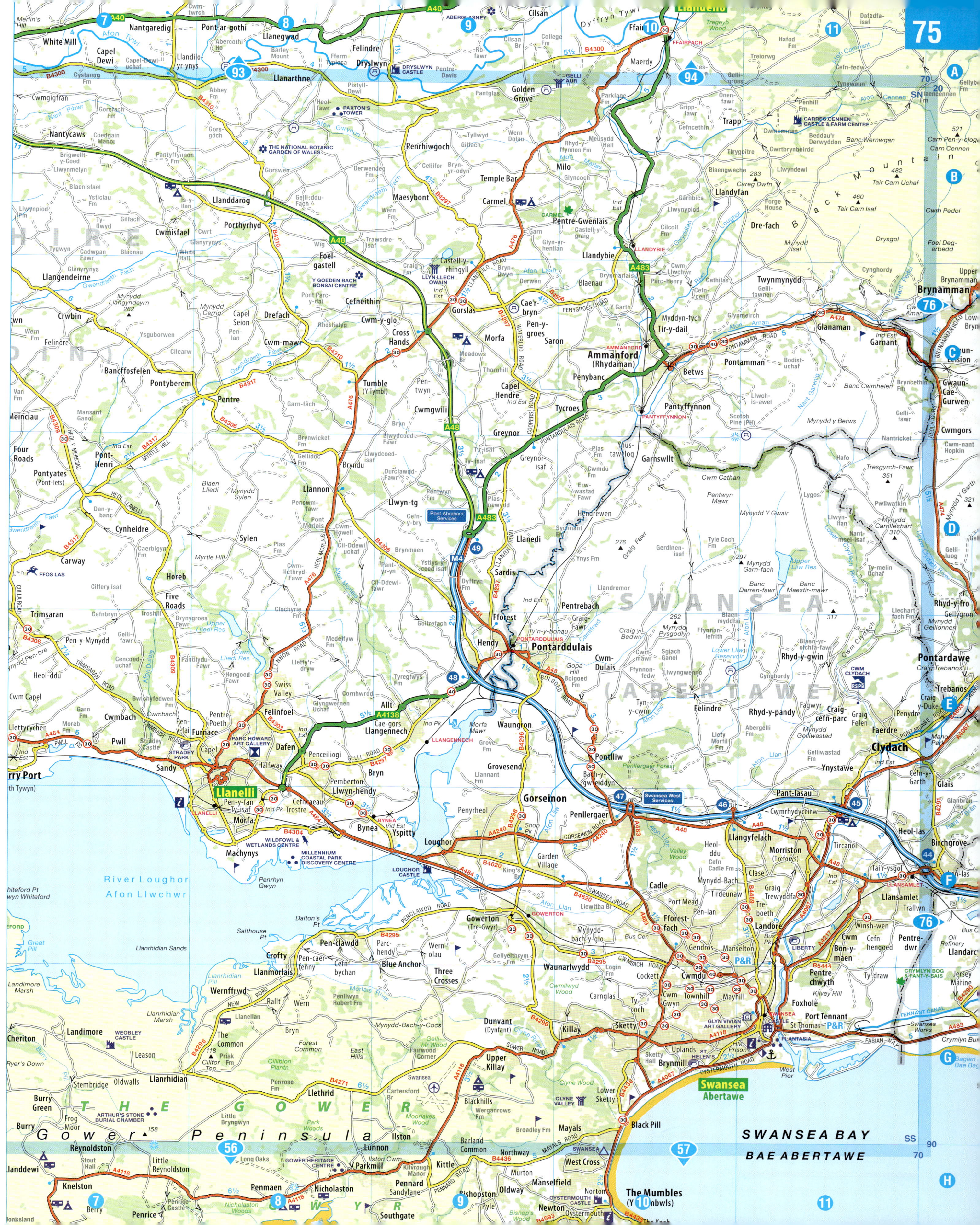
Nantgaredig
Pont-ar-gothi
Llanegwad
Felindre
Dryslwyn
Dryslwyn Castle
Aberglasney
Cilsan
Ffairfach
Llandeilo
White Mill
Capel Dewi
Llanarthne
Golden Grove
Dyffryn Tywi
Afon Tywi
Cwmgigfran
Paxton's Tower
Nantycaws
The National Botanic Garden of Wales
Penrhiwgoch
Temple Bar
Carmel
Milo
Trapp
Carreg Cennen Castle & Farm Centre
Black Mountain
Llanddarog
Maesybont
Porthyrhyd
Cwmisfael
Pentre-Gwenlais
Llandyfan
Dre-fach
Foel-gastell
Llangendeirne
Y Goeden Bach Bonsai Centre
Castell-y-rhingyll
Llyn Llech Owain
Llandybie
Cefneithin
Gorslas
Blaenau
Twynmynydd
Brynamman
Crwbin
Drefach
Cwm-y-glo
Cae'r-bryn
Glanaman
Garnant
Cross Hands
Morfa
Pen-y-groes
Saron
Ammanford (Rhydaman)
Tir-y-dail
Betws
Pontamman
Cwm-mawr
Bancffosfelen
Pontyberem
Tumble (Y Tymbl)
Capel Hendre
Penybanc
Pentre
Tycroes
Pantyffynnon
Cwmgwili
Greynor
Four Roads
Pont-Henri
Pontyates (Pont-iets)
Bryndu
Garnswllt
Llannon
Llwyn-tg
Pont Abraham Services
Cynheidre
Sylen
Llanedi
Carway
Ffos Las
Horeb
Five Roads
Sardis
Trimsaran
Pen-y-Mynydd
Fforest
Pentrebach
Swansea
Hendy
Pontarddulais
Cwm-Dulais
Rhyd-y-gwin
Pontardawe
Heol-ddu
Swiss Valley
Cwm Capel
Allt
Felinfoel
Llangennech
Waungron
Felindre
Rhyd-y-pandy
Craig-cefn-parc
Clydach
Cwmbach
Pwll
Furnace
Dafen
Pentre Poeth
Parc Howard Art Gallery
Sandy
Capel
Halfway
Penceiliogi
Bryn
Grovesend
Pontlliw
Ynystawe
Burry Port
Llanelli
Pemberton
Llwyn-hendy
Bach-y-gwreiddyn
Swansea West Services
Pant-lasau
Glais
Morfa
Bynea
Yspitty
Gorseinon
Penllergaer
Cwmrhydyceirw
Heol-las
Birchgrove
Machynys
Wildfowl & Wetlands Centre
Millennium Coastal Park Discovery Centre
Loughor
Loughor Castle
Garden Village
Llangyfelach
Morriston (Treforys)
Tirdeunaw
Llansamlet
River Loughor
Afon Llwchwr
Cadle
Port Mead
Penlan
Landore
Trallwn
Gowerton (Tre-Gwyr)
Forest-fach
Winsh-wen
Pentre-dwr
Llanrhidian Sands
Pen-clawdd
Crofty
Llanmorlais
Blue Anchor
Three Crosses
Waunarlwydd
Cockett
Cwmdu
Manselton
Bon-y-maen
Pentre-chwyth
Wernffrwd
Dunvant (Dynfant)
Killay
Sketty
Foxhole
Port Tennant
Landimore
Cheriton
Llanrhidian
Oldwalls
Upper Killay
Brynmill
Uplands
Swansea Abertawe
St Thomas
Llethrid
Blackhills
Clyne Valley
Lower Sketty
Black Pill
Burry Green
Burry
The Gower
Gower Peninsula
Reynoldston
Ilston
Lunnon
Parkmill
Kittle
Bishopston
Mayals
West Cross
Swansea Bay
Bae Abertawe
Knelston
Nicholaston
Penmaen
Pennard
Southgate
Murton
Oldway
Manselfield
Newton
Norton
Oystermouth
The Mumbles (Y Mwmbwls)
Penrice
Berry

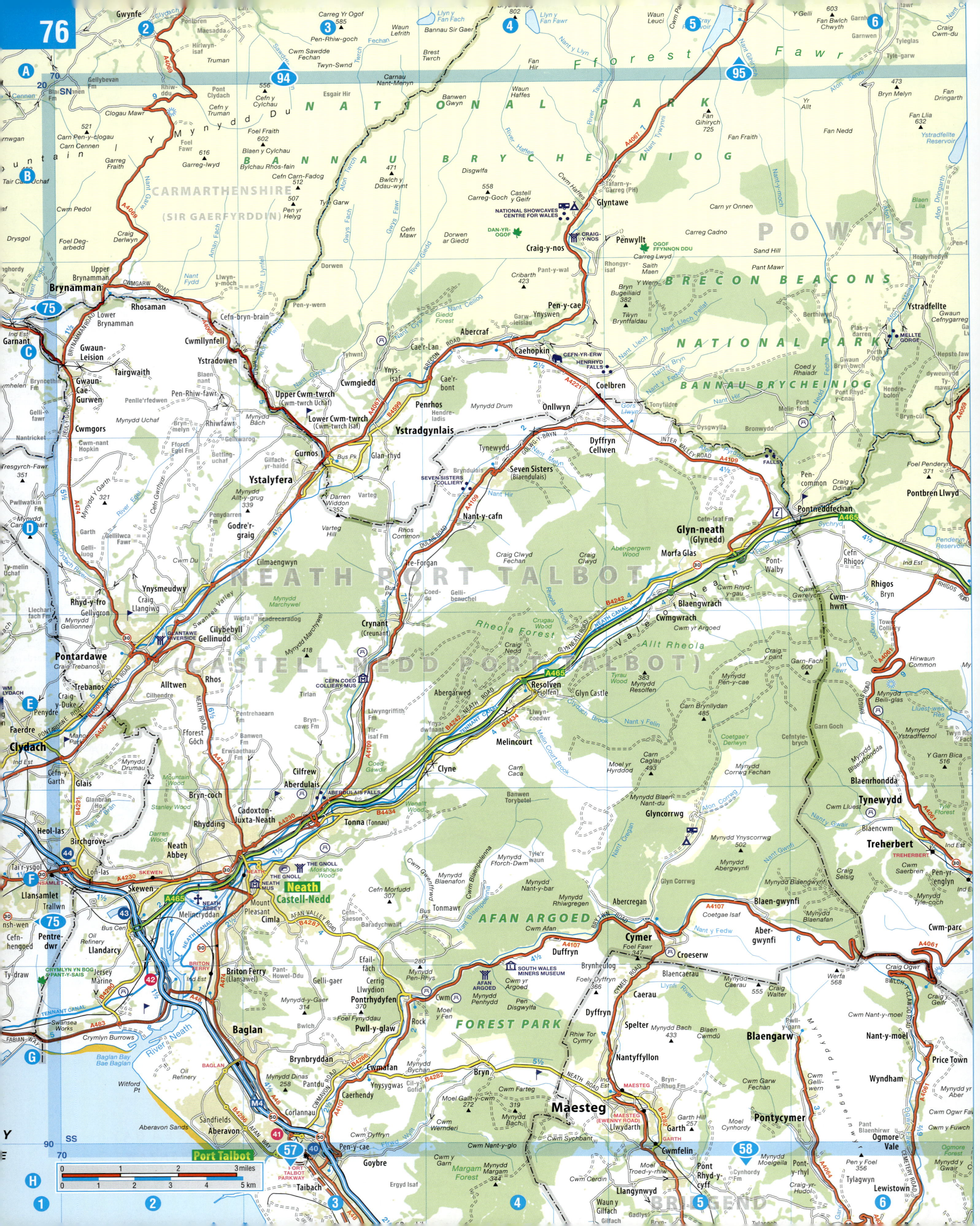

CARMARTHENSHIRE
(SIR GAERFYRDDIN)
BANNAU BRYCHEINIOG
NATIONAL PARK
Fforest Fawr
POWYS
BRECON BEACONS
NATIONAL PARK
BANNAU BRYCHEINIOG
NEATH PORT TALBOT
(CASTELL-NEDD PORT TALBOT)
Rheola Forest
Allt Rheola
AFAN ARGOED
FOREST PARK
Vale of Neath
BRIDGEND
Brynamman
Lower Brynamman
Garnant
Gwaun-Leision
Gwaun-Cae-Gurwen
Cwmgors
Rhosaman
Cwmllynfell
Ystradowen
Tairgwaith
Upper Cwm-twrch
(Cwm-twrch Uchaf)
Lower Cwm-twrch
(Cwm-twrch Isaf)
Cwmgiedd
Ystradgynlais
Gurnos
Ystalyfera
Godre'r-graig
Cilmaengwyn
Ynysmeudwy
Pontardawe
Trebanos
Alltwen
Rhos
Gellinudd
Cilybebyll
Clydach
Glais
Rhyd-y-fro
Gellygron
Craig-y-Duke
Pendyre
Faerdre
Heol-las
Birchgrove
Llansamlet
Trallwn
Lôn-las
Skewen
Neath
Castell-Nedd
Neath Abbey
Melincryddan
Cimla
Briton Ferry
(Llansawel)
Baglan
Port Talbot
Aberavon
Sandfields
Taibach
Goytre
Bryn
Maesteg
Llwydarth
Caerau
Nantyffyllon
Spelter
Cymer
Croeserw
Duffryn
Blaengarw
Pontycymer
Llangynwyd
Cwmfelin
Ogmore Vale
Lewistown
Nant-y-moel
Price Town
Wyndham
Cwm-parc
Treherbert
Tynewydd
Blaenrhondda
Blaen-gwynfi
Abergwynfi
Glyncorrwg
Abercregan
Tonmawr
Pontrhydyfen
Pwll-y-glaw
Cwmafan
Efail-fach
Cerrig Llwydion
Melincourt
Clyne
Resolven
Glyn Castle
Abergarwed
Tonna
Aberdulais
Cadoxton-Juxta-Neath
Rhydding
Bryn-coch
Cilfrew
Crynant
(Creunant)
Onllwyn
Coelbren
Dyffryn Cellwen
Seven Sisters
(Blaendulais)
Nant-y-cafn
Glyn-neath
(Glynedd)
Morfa Glas
Blaengwrach
Cwmgwrach
Pontneddfechan
Rhigos
Cwm-hwnt
Hirwaun Common
Penwyllt
Craig-y-nos
Glyntawe
Abercraf
Pen-y-cae
Caehopkin
Penrhos
Ystradfellte
Pontbren Llwyd
NATIONAL SHOWCAVES CENTRE FOR WALES
DAN-YR-OGOF
CEFN COED COLLIERY MUS
SOUTH WALES MINERS MUSEUM
ABERDULAIS FALLS
SEVEN SISTERS COLLIERY
HENRHYD FALLS
MELLTE GORGE
A465
A4067
A4109
A474
A48
M4
A4107
A4061
A4221
A4069
94
95
75
57
58
3 miles
5 km

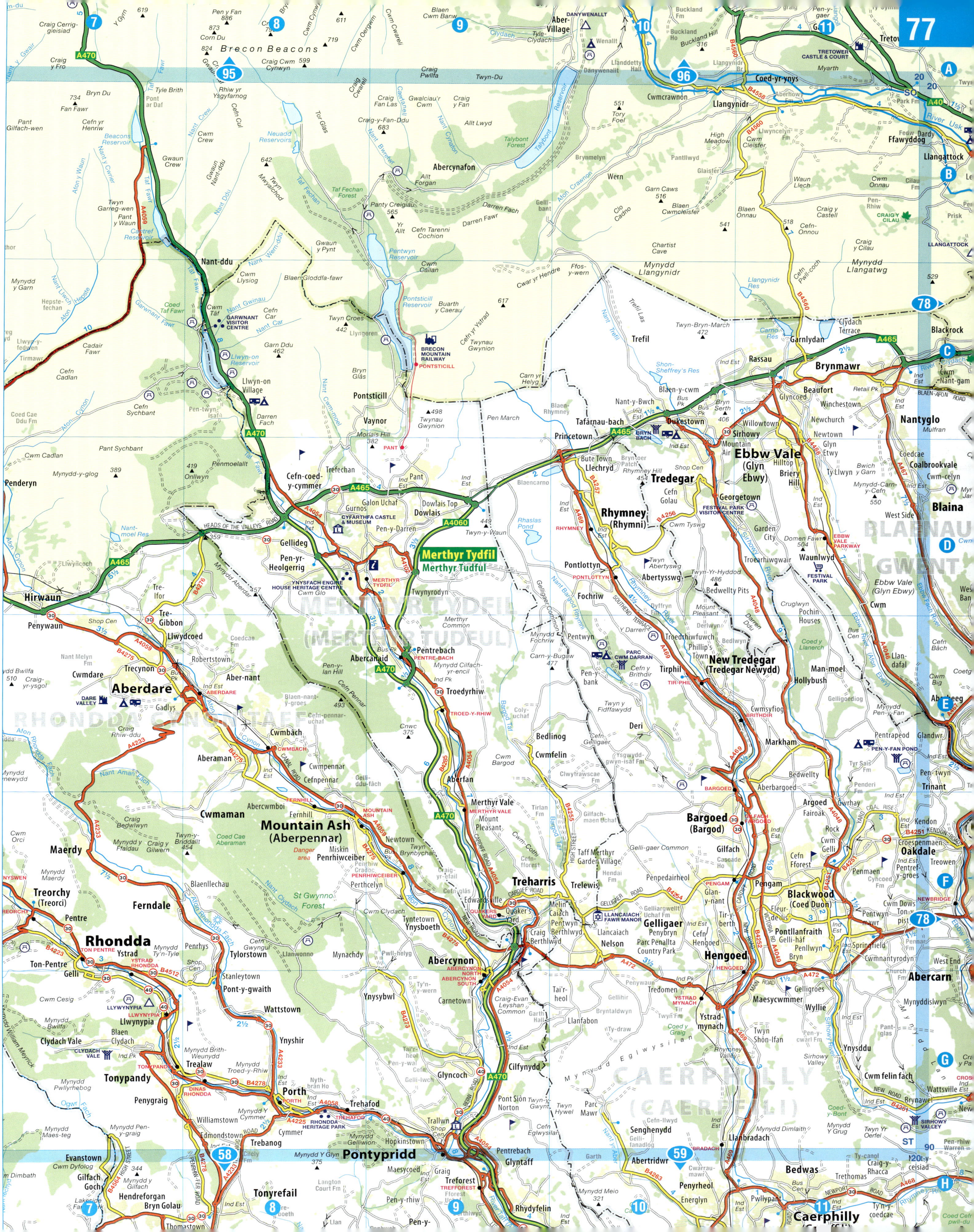
Brecon Beacons
Merthyr Tydfil
Merthyr Tudful
Aberdare
Mountain Ash
(Aberpennar)
Rhondda
Treorchy
(Treorci)
Ferndale
Maerdy
Tonypandy
Porth
Pontypridd
Tonyrefail
Treharris
Abercynon
Ebbw Vale
(Glyn
Ebwy)
Tredegar
Rhymney
(Rhymni)
New Tredegar
(Tredegar Newydd)
Bargoed
(Bargod)
Gelligaer
Hengoed
Blackwood
(Coed Duon)
Oakdale
Abercarn
Caerphilly
Brynmawr
Nantyglo
Blaina
Llangattock
Crickhowell
Hirwaun
Penderyn
Nant-ddu
Pontsticill
Vaynor
Dowlais
Troedyrhiw
Aberfan
Merthyr Vale
Llanbradach
Senghenydd
Ystrad Mynach
Bedwas
Abertridwr
Nelson
Trelewis
Bedlinog
Pontlottyn
Fochriw
Tafarnau-bach
Princetown
Dukestown
Sirhowy
Beaufort
Llangynidr
Aber-Village
Talybont Reservoir
Pentwyn Reservoir
Pontsticill Reservoir
Llwyn-on Reservoir
Cantref Reservoir
Beacons Reservoir
RHONDDA CYNON TAFF
MERTHYR TYDFIL
(MERTHYR TUDFUL)
CAERPHILLY
(CAERFFILI)
BLAENAU GWENT
Heads of the Valleys Road
Mynydd Llangynidr
Mynydd Llangatwg
Mynydd Eglwysilan
Brecon Mountain Railway
Cyfarthfa Castle & Museum
Garwnant Visitor Centre
Llancaiach Fawr Manor
Rhondda Heritage Park
Festival Park
Tretower Castle & Court
Parc Cwm Darran
A465
A470
A4059
A4054
A4060
A469
A472
A4048
A4046
A467
A4233
A4058
A40
B4560
B4558
B4275
B4276
B4255
B4254
B4278
B4512
B4223
B4256
B4257
B4263
B4251
B4591
B4560
78
58
59
95
96
7
8
9
10
11
A
B
C
D
E
F
G
H

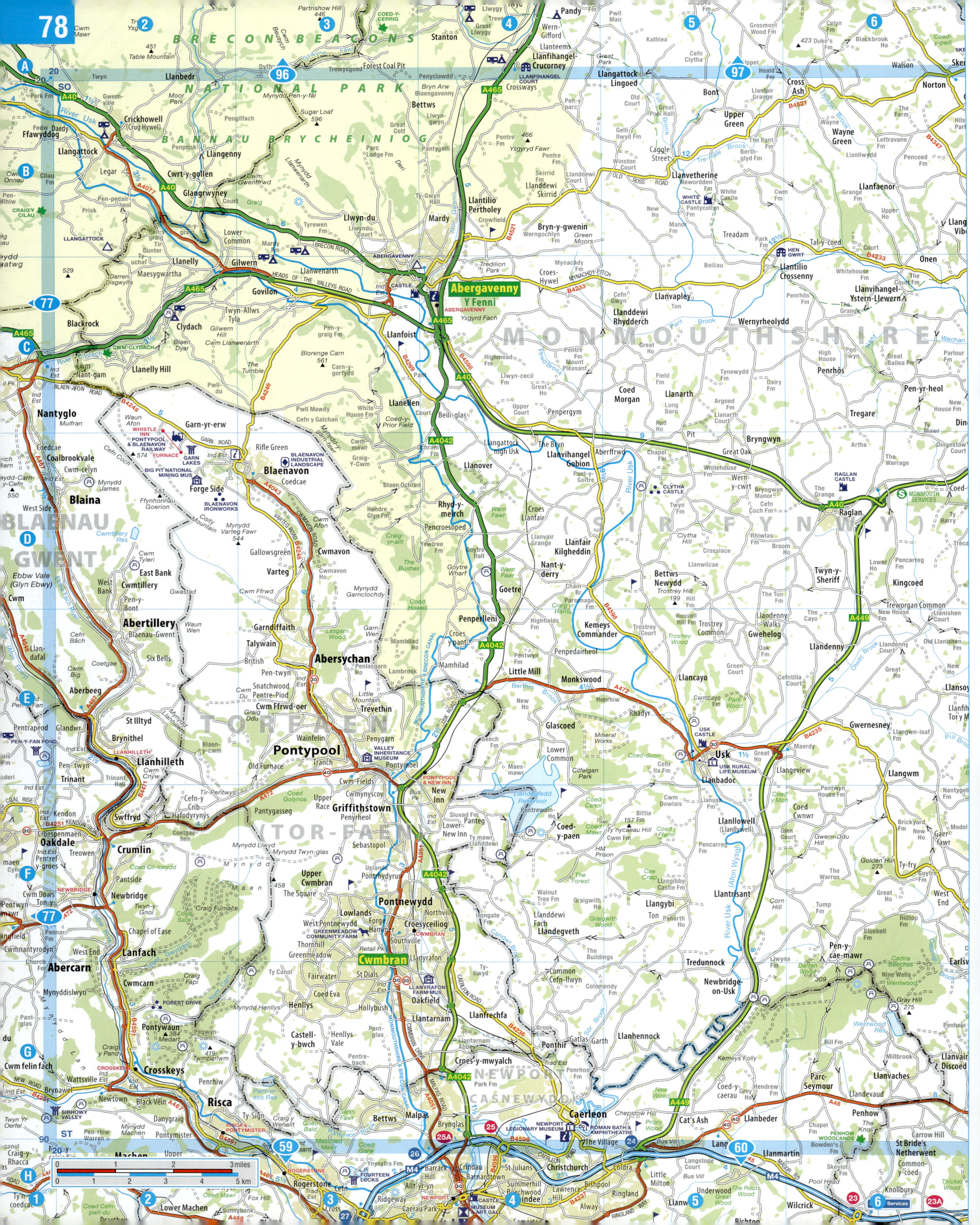
BRECON BEACONS
NATIONAL PARK
BANNAU BRYCHEINIOG
MONMOUTHSHIRE
(SIR FYNWY)
BLAENAU GWENT
TORFAEN
(TOR-FAEN)
NEWPORT
CASNEWYDD
Abergavenny
Y Fenni
Crickhowell
(Crug Hywel)
Llangattock
Llangenny
Cwrt-y-gollen
Glangrwyney
Llanbedr
Table Mountain
Sugar Loaf
596
Gilwern
Govilon
Llanelly
Maesygwartha
Clydach
Blackrock
Llanelly Hill
Nantyglo
Brynmawr
Coalbrookvale
Blaina
Blaenavon
Forge Side
Garn-yr-erw
Varteg
Cwmavon
Garndiffaith
Talywain
Abersychan
Pontypool
Griffithstown
Sebastopol
Pontnewydd
Cwmbran
Croesyceiliog
Llanyrafon
Oakfield
Llantarnam
Henllys
Upper Cwmbran
Abertillery
Six Bells
Cwmtillery
Aberbeeg
Llanhilleth
Brynithel
Swffryd
Crumlin
Newbridge
Oakdale
Pantside
Abercarn
Cwmcarn
Crosskeys
Pontywaun
Risca
Rogerstone
Bettws
Malpas
Caerleon
Christchurch
St Julians
Usk
Llanbadoc
Llangybi
Tredunnock
Newbridge-on-Usk
Llanfrechfa
Ponthir
Little Mill
Monkswood
Glascoed
Goetre
Penperlleni
Nant-y-derry
Llanover
Llanfoist
Llanellen
Mardy
Llantilio Pertholey
Bryn-y-gwenin
Llanddewi Skirrid
Llanvihangel Crucorney
Pandy
Llangattock Lingoed
Llanvetherine
Llantilio Crossenny
Llanvapley
Llanddewi Rhydderch
Coed Morgan
Llanarth
Bryngwyn
Raglan
Llanvihangel Gobion
Llanfair Kilgheddin
Kemeys Commander
Clytha Castle
Betws Newydd
Gwehelog
Llandenny
Kingcoed
Twyn-y-Sheriff
Llancayo
Gwernesney
Llangwm
Llanllowell
Llantrisant
Wernyrheolydd
Penrhos
Pen-yr-heol
Tregare
Llanvihangel-Ystern-Llewern
Llanfaenor
Cross Ash
Norton
Walson
Upper Green
Wayne Green
Bont
Llandevaud
Penhow
Llanvaches
Parc-Seymour
Llanmartin
Cat's Ash
Llanbeder
Langstone
Wern-Gifford
Llanthony
Stanton
Forest Coal Pit
Bettws
A40
A465
A4042
A449
A472
A48
M4
B4233
B4598
B4246
B4235
96
97
77
59
60
24
25
26
27
Services

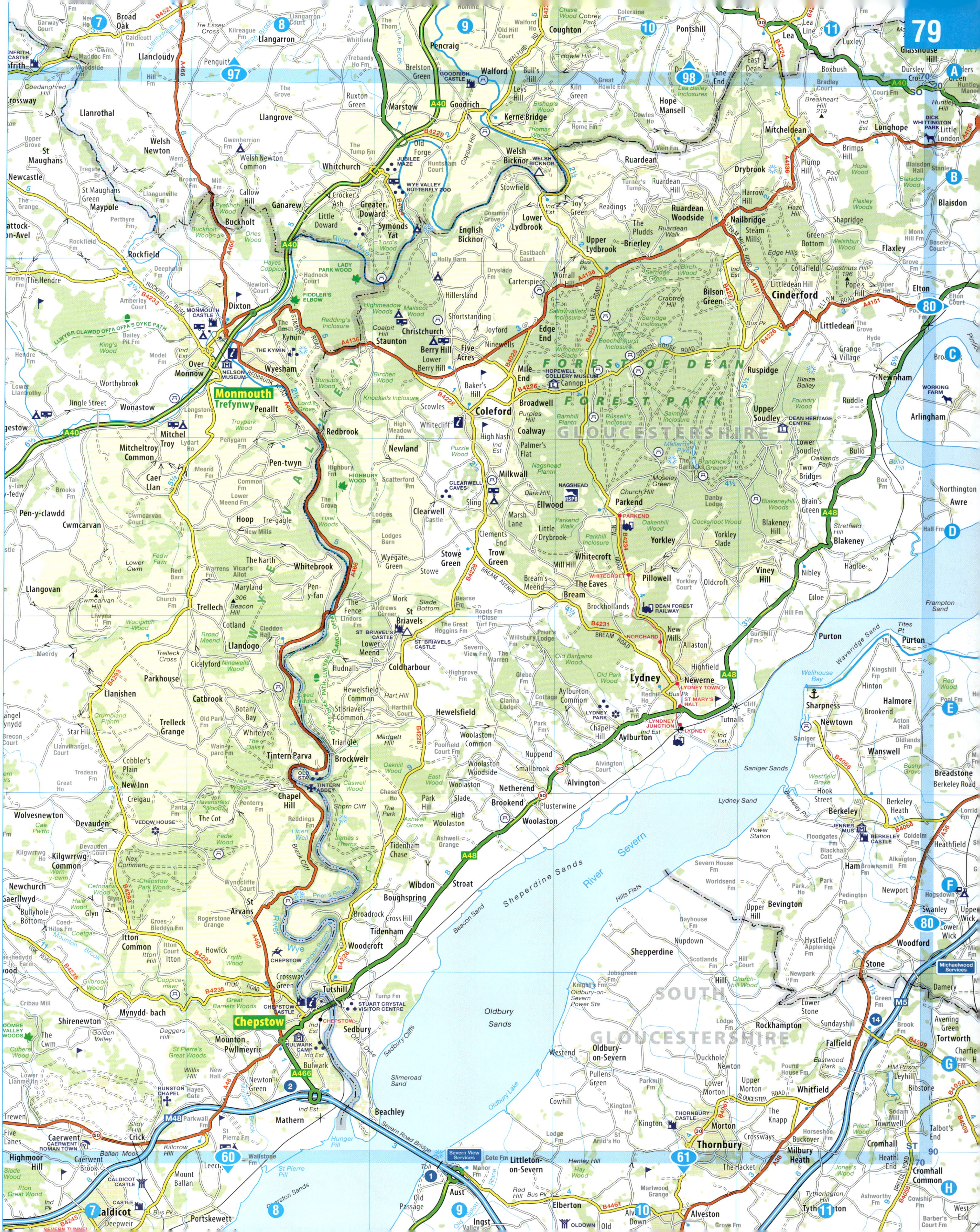

Broad Oak
Llangarron
Pencraig
Walford
Coughton
Pontshill
Lea
Llancloudy
Penguite
97
98
Goodrich
Kerne Bridge
Hope Mansell
Mitcheldean
Longhope
Llanrothal
Llangrove
Marstow
Welsh Bicknor
Ruardean
Drybrook
Welsh Newton
Whitchurch
Symonds Yat
English Bicknor
Lower Lydbrook
Ruardean Woodside
Nailbridge
St Maughans
Newcastle
Maypole
Ganarew
Buckholt
Little Dowrard
Greater Doward
Upper Lydbrook
The Pludds
Brierley
Flaxley
Rockfield
Dixton
Cinderford
Elton
Monmouth
Trefynwy
Wyesham
Staunton
Christchurch
Berry Hill
Five Acres
Edge End
Littledean
Bilson Green
Ruspidge
Newnham
Arlingham
Over Monnow
Mile End
Cannop
Broadwell
Coleford
Worthybrook
Wonastow
Penallt
Redbrook
Upper Soudley
FOREST OF DEAN
FOREST PARK
GLOUCESTERSHIRE
Mitchel Troy
Mitcheltroy Common
Newland
Coalway
Lower Soudley
Two Bridges
Caer Llan
Pen-twyn
Milkwall
Parkend
Brain's Green
Awre
Pen-y-clawdd
Cwmcarvan
Hoop
Clearwell
Ellwood
Yorkley
Blakeney
Whitebrook
Stowe Green
Trow Green
Whitecroft
Pillowell
Viney Hill
Llangovan
Trellech
Bream
The Eaves
Nibley
Etloe
Purton
Cleddon
Llandogo
St Briavels
Lower Meend
Coldharbour
New Mills
Allaston
Parkhouse
Catbrook
Hewelsfield
Lydney
Newerne
Sharpness
Halmore
Lanishen
Trelleck Grange
Tintern Parva
Brockweir
Aylburton
Tutnalls
Newtown
Wanswell
Netherend
Alvington
Woolaston
Berkeley
Wolvesnewton
Devauden
Chapel Hill
Kilgwrrwg Common
Newchurch
St Arvans
Wibdon
Stroat
Sheperdine Sands
River Severn
Bevington
Itton Common
Itton
Tidenham
Woodcroft
Woodford
Stone
Shepperdine
Mynydd-bach
Chepstow
Tutshill
Sedbury
Oldbury Sands
SOUTH GLOUCESTERSHIRE
Rockhampton
Tortworth
Shirenewton
Mounton
Pwllmeyric
Oldbury-on-Severn
Falfield
Bulwark
Whitfield
Mathern
Beachley
Severn Road Bridge
Thornbury
Morton
Crossways
Milbury Heath
Cromhall
Caerwent
Highmoor Hill
Crick
60
61
Littleton-on-Severn
Aust
Elberton
Alveston
Tytherington
Caldicot
Portskewett
Cromhall Common

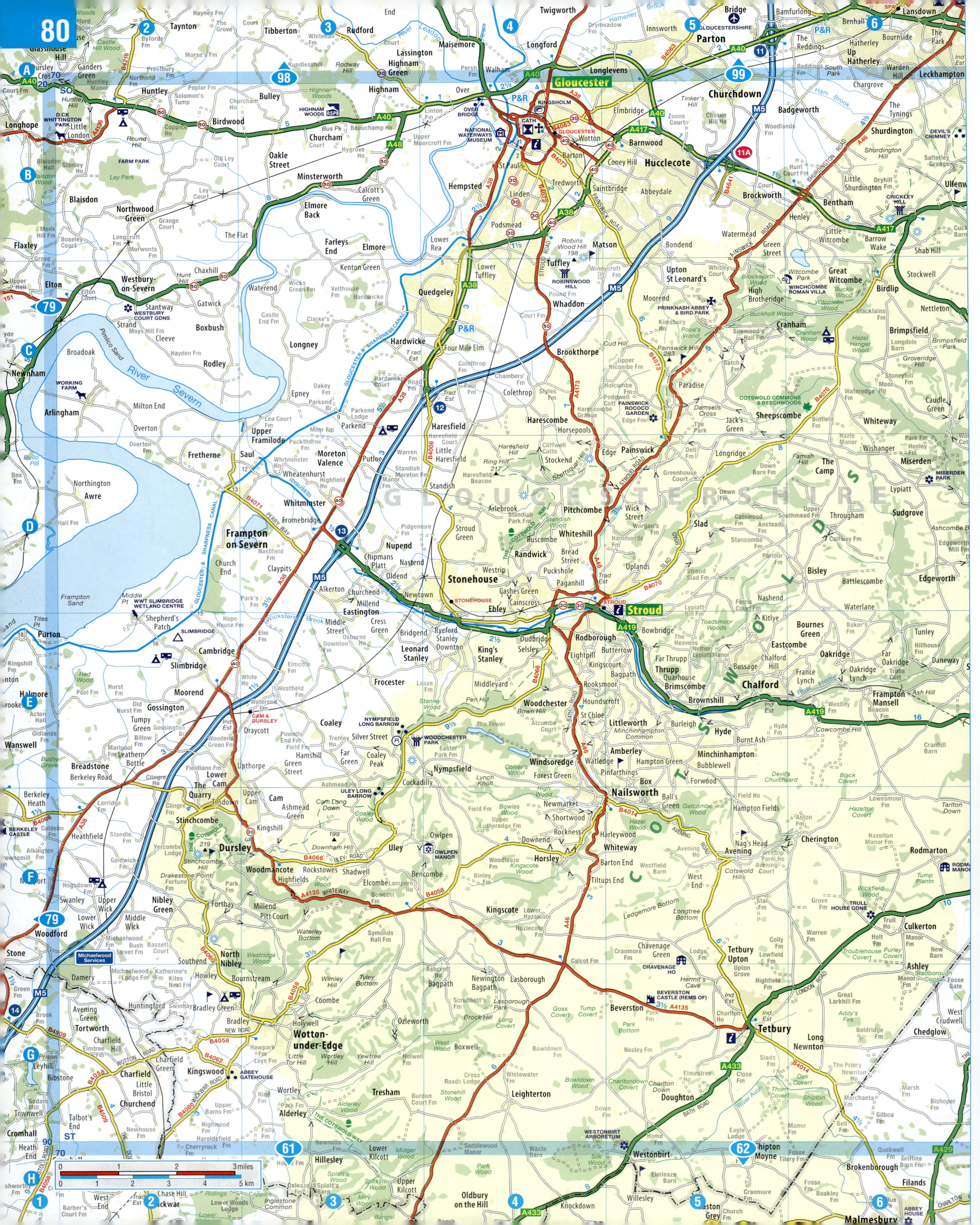
Gloucester
Stroud
GLOUCESTERSHIRE
COTSWOLDS
River Severn
Churchdown
Hucclecote
Brockworth
Bentham
Longlevens
Barnwood
Quedgeley
Hardwicke
Stonehouse
Nailsworth
Dursley
Wotton-under-Edge
Tetbury
Chalford
Painswick
Cam
Uley
Frampton on Severn
Newnham
Arlingham
Cambridge
Slimbridge
Berkeley Road
Westbury-on-Severn
Minsterworth
Longhope
Blaisdon
Flaxley
Elton
Kingswood
Charfield
Alderley
Hillesley
Leighterton
Westonbirt
Beverston
Avening
Minchinhampton
Amberley
Bisley
Sheepscombe
Cranham
Birdlip
Upton St Leonard's
Matson
Tuffley
Hempsted
Maisemore
Longford
Twigworth
Innsworth
Parton
Badgeworth
Shurdington
Leckhampton
Miserden
Sudgrove
Edgeworth
Oakridge
Eastcombe
Bussage
Brimscombe
Thrupp
Rodborough
Woodchester
Kingscote
Horsley
Cherington
Rodmarton
Culkerton
Ashley
Long Newnton
Doughton
Malmesbury
Michaelwood Services
WWT SLIMBRIDGE WETLAND CENTRE
WESTONBIRT ARBORETUM
NATIONAL WATERWAYS MUSEUM
M5
A38
A46
A419
A417
A40
A4135
A433
0 1 2 3 miles
0 1 2 3 4 5 km

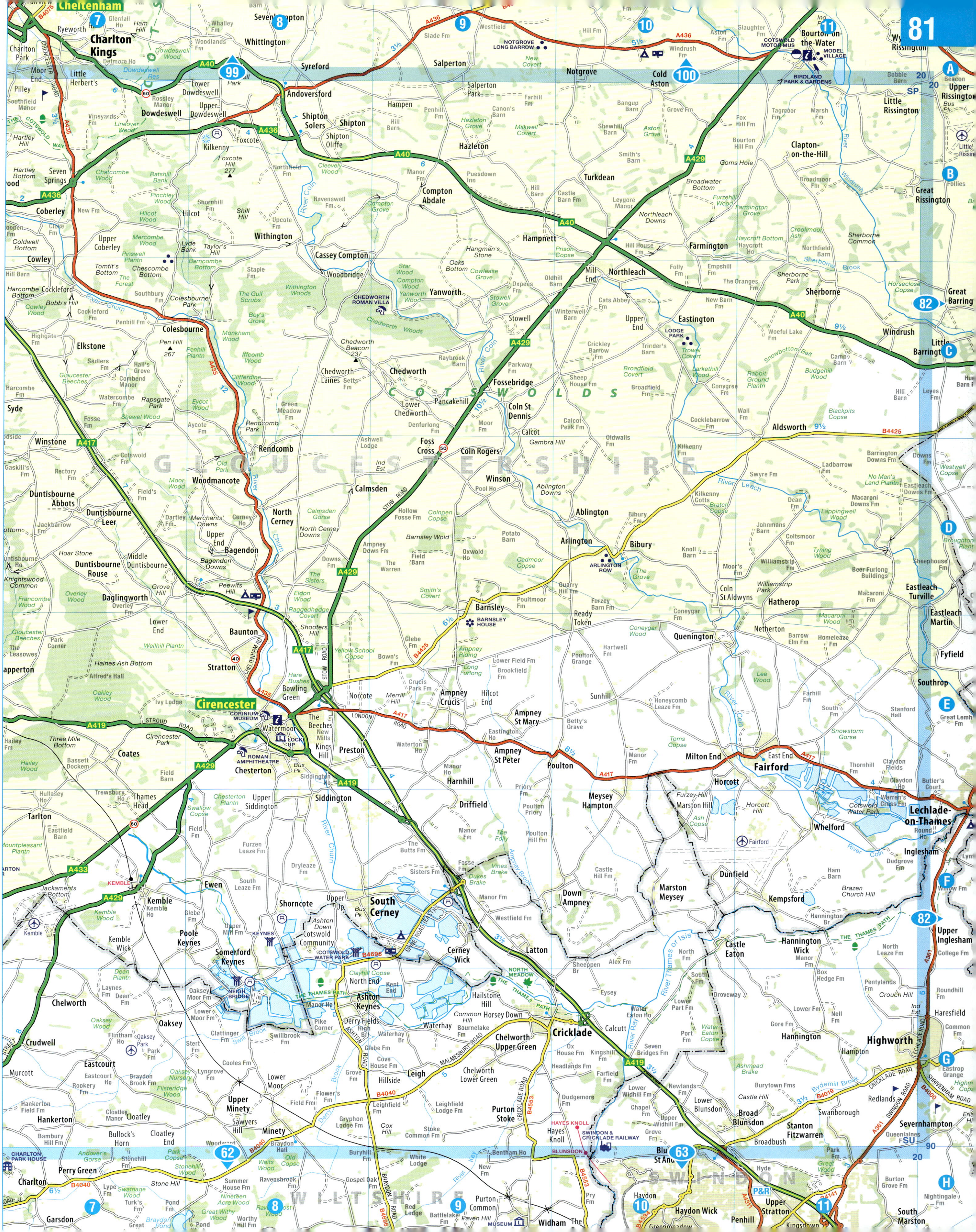
Cheltenham
Charlton Kings
Whittington
Syreford
Andoversford
Dowdeswell
Shipton
Salperton
Hazleton
Notgrove
Turkdean
Cold Aston
Bourton-on-the-Water
Little Rissington
Great Rissington
Clapton-on-the-Hill
Compton Abdale
Withington
Cassey Compton
Hampnett
Northleach
Farmington
Sherborne
Windrush
Great Barring
Little Barrington
Eastington
Chedworth
Yanworth
Stowell
Fossebridge
Coln St Dennis
COTSWOLDS
GLOUCESTERSHIRE
Colesbourne
Elkstone
Syde
Winstone
Rendcomb
Woodmancote
North Cerney
Calmsden
Coln Rogers
Winson
Ablington
Arlington
Bibury
Aldsworth
Duntisbourne Abbots
Duntisbourne Leer
Duntisbourne Rouse
Daglingworth
Bagendon
Baunton
Stratton
Barnsley
Barnsley House
Quenington
Hatherop
Coln St Aldwyns
Eastleach Turville
Eastleach Martin
Fyfield
Southrop
Cirencester
Ampney Crucis
Ampney St Mary
Ampney St Peter
Poulton
Sunhill
Milton End
Fairford
Lechlade-on-Thames
Whelford
Horcott
Preston
Chesterton
Coates
Siddington
Harnhill
Driffield
Meysey Hampton
Tarlton
Kemble
Ewen
South Cerney
Down Ampney
Marston Meysey
Kempsford
Dunfield
Poole Keynes
Somerford Keynes
Cerney Wick
Latton
Castle Eaton
Hannington Wick
Upper Inglesham
Ashton Keynes
Cricklade
Chelworth
Oaksey
Crudwell
Eastcourt
Hankerton
Minety
Upper Minety
Leigh
Purton Stoke
Hayes Knoll
Calcutt
Hannington
Highworth
Broad Blunsdon
Stanton Fitzwarren
Sevenhampton
Charlton
Perry Green
Garsdon
Widham
Blunsdon St Andrew
Haydon Wick
Upper Stratton
Penhill
South Marston
SWINDON
WILTSHIRE
A40
A436
A429
A417
A419
A435
A433
B4425
B4696
B4040
A361
B4019
THE THAMES PATH
Cotswold Water Park
Swindon & Cricklade Railway
Corinium Museum
Chedworth Roman Villa
Arlington Row
Birdland Park & Gardens
Cotswold Motor Mus
Model Village
Notgrove Long Barrow
82
62
63
99
100

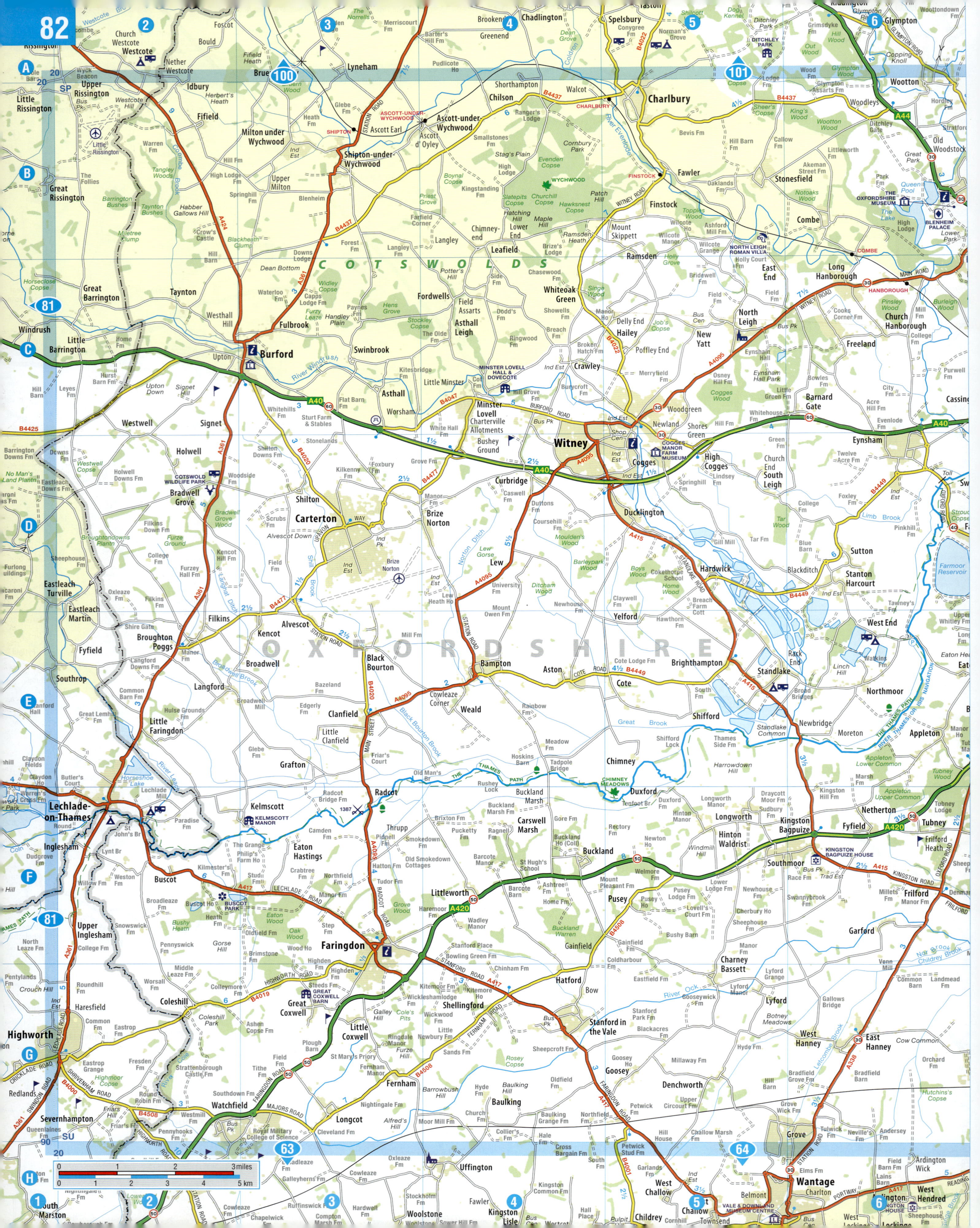
Kingham
Church Westcote
Foscott
Bould
Idbury
Fifield
Little Rissington
Great Rissington
Great Barrington
Little Barrington
Windrush
Taynton
Burford
Fulbrook
Westhall Hill
Upton
Signet
Westwell
Holwell
Bradwell Grove
Shilton
Carterton
Alvescot
Kencot
Filkins
Broughton Poggs
Eastleach Turville
Eastleach Martin
Fyfield
Southrop
Langford
Little Faringdon
Lechlade-on-Thames
Inglesham
Upper Inglesham
Buscot
Kelmscott
Eaton Hastings
Coleshill
Highworth
Great Coxwell
Faringdon
Little Coxwell
Fernham
Longcot
Watchfield
Shrivenham
Uffington
Woolstone
Baulking
Shellingford
Stanford in the Vale
Goosey
Denchworth
Hatford
Gainfield
Buckland
Littleworth
Pusey
Charney Bassett
Lyford
West Hanney
East Hanney
Grove
Wantage
West Challow
East Challow
Childrey
Kingston Lisle
Fyfield
Kingston Bagpuize
Southmoor
Hinton Waldrist
Longworth
Netherton
Tubney
Frilford
Garford
Appleton
Northmoor
Standlake
Brighthampton
Shifford
Chimney
Duxford
Aston
Cote
Bampton
Weald
Clanfield
Little Clanfield
Black Bourton
Grafton
Radcot
Buckland Marsh
Carswell Marsh
Yelford
Hardwick
Stanton Harcourt
Sutton
West End
Ducklington
Witney
Cogges
Curbridge
Lew
Brize Norton
Minster Lovell
Crawley
Hailey
New Yatt
North Leigh
East End
Freeland
Long Hanborough
Church Hanborough
Eynsham
Barnard Gate
Stanton Harcourt
South Leigh
High Cogges
Woodgreen
Newland
Asthall
Asthall Leigh
Swinbrook
Fordwells
Leafield
Ramsden
Finstock
Fawler
Charlbury
Stonesfield
Combe
Wootton
Woodstock
Glympton
Spelsbury
Chadlington
Chilson
Shorthampton
Ascott-under-Wychwood
Shipton-under-Wychwood
Milton under Wychwood
Lyneham
Fifield
Upper Milton
COTSWOLDS
OXFORDSHIRE
BLENHEIM PALACE
WYCHWOOD
A40
A361
A424
A4095
A420
A415
A417
B4437
B4022
B4477
B4020
B4449
B4019
B4508
B4000
0 1 2 3 miles
0 1 2 3 4 5 km

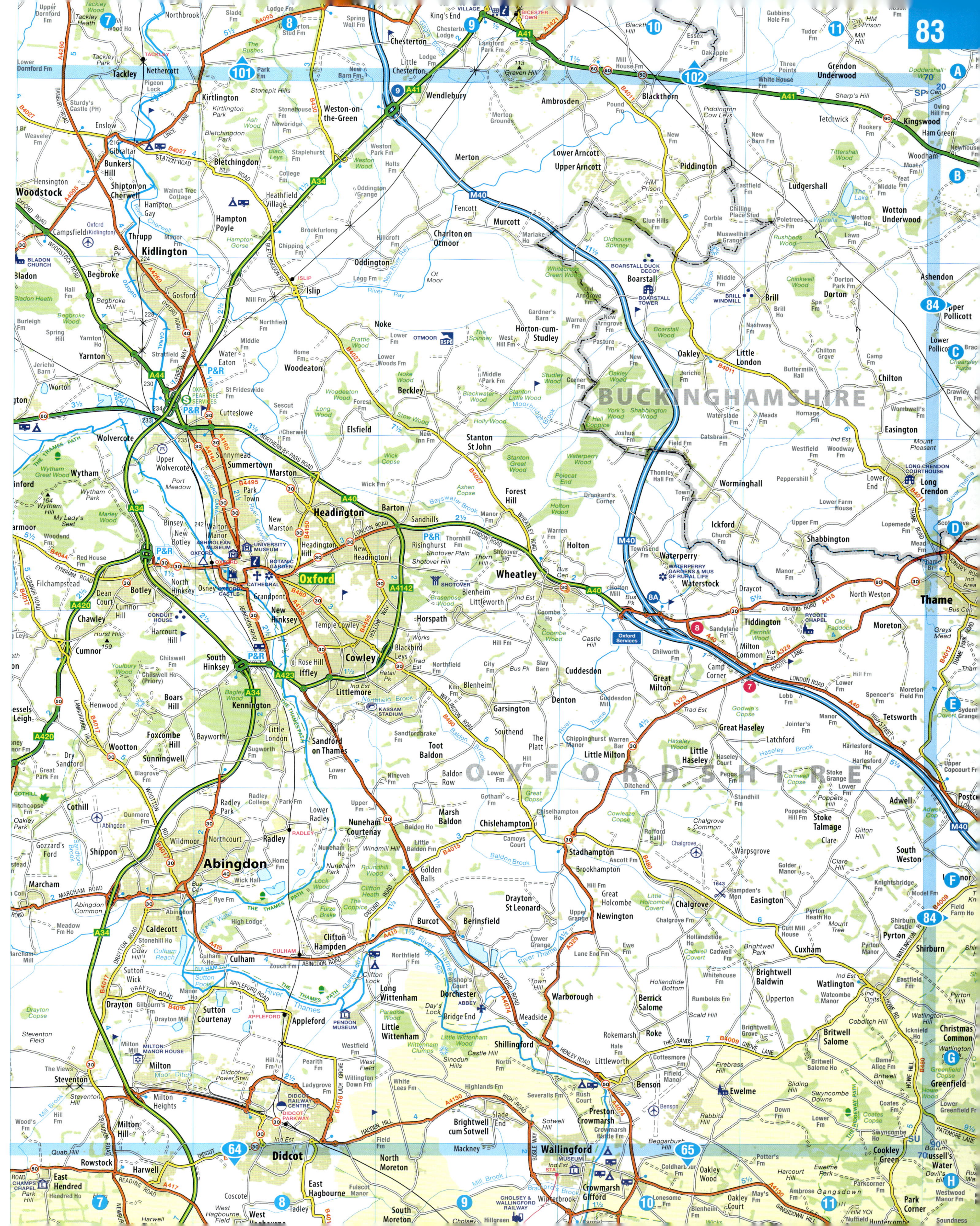
OXFORDSHIRE
BUCKINGHAMSHIRE
Oxford
Abingdon
Didcot
Wallingford
Thame
Kidlington
Woodstock
Wheatley
Headington
Cowley
Kennington
Botley
Cumnor
Wytham
Wolvercote
Yarnton
Begbroke
Tackley
Kirtlington
Bletchingdon
Islip
Oddington
Charlton on Otmoor
Noke
Beckley
Elsfield
Marston
Barton
Horspath
Garsington
Cuddesdon
Stanton St John
Forest Hill
Holton
Waterperry
Waterstock
Tiddington
Great Milton
Little Milton
Great Haseley
Chiselhampton
Stadhampton
Drayton St Leonard
Berinsfield
Dorchester
Warborough
Shillingford
Benson
Ewelme
Brightwell Baldwin
Watlington
Chalgrove
Easington
Cuxham
Pyrton
Shirburn
Tetsworth
Adwell
Stoke Talmage
Sandford on Thames
Radley
Nuneham Courtenay
Culham
Clifton Hampden
Sutton Courtenay
Appleford
Long Wittenham
Little Wittenham
Drayton
Milton
Steventon
Harwell
Rowstock
East Hendred
East Hagbourne
North Moreton
South Moreton
Brightwell cum Sotwell
Crowmarsh Gifford
Cholsey
Wendlebury
Chesterton
Bicester
Weston-on-the-Green
Ambrosden
Blackthorn
Merton
Piddington
Murcott
Fencott
Boarstall
Brill
Oakley
Little London
Worminghall
Ickford
Shabbington
Long Crendon
Chilton
Dorton
Ludgershall
Grendon Underwood
Kingswood
Wotton Underwood
Ashendon
Horton-cum-Studley
Woodeaton
Hampton Poyle
Shipton on Cherwell
Thrupp
Nethercott
Gosford
Iffley
Littlemore
Toot Baldon
Marsh Baldon
Wootton
Sunningwell
Shippon
Marcham
Caldecott
Milton Heights
Wildmoor
Northcourt
Upper Wolvercote
Summertown
Sunnymead
New Hinksey
South Hinksey
North Hinksey
Chawley
Boars Hill
Foxcombe Hill
Cothill
Dry Sandford
Filchampstead
Dean Court
Osney
Grandpont
Harcourt Hill
Headington Hill
New Headington
Sandhills
Risinghurst
Littleworth
Blackbird Leys
Denton
Southend
The Platt
Rycote Chapel
Milton Common
Camp Corner
Sydenham
Moreton
Lobb
Latchford
North Weston
Draycot
Roke
Rokemarsh
Berrick Salome
Newington
Great Holcombe
Brookhampton
Golden Balls
Burcot
Preston Crowmarsh
Mackney
Fulscot
A34
A40
A41
A44
A420
A423
A4074
A4130
A417
A415
A329
A418
A4142
B4027
B4011
B4009
B480
B4017
M40
101
102
64
65
84

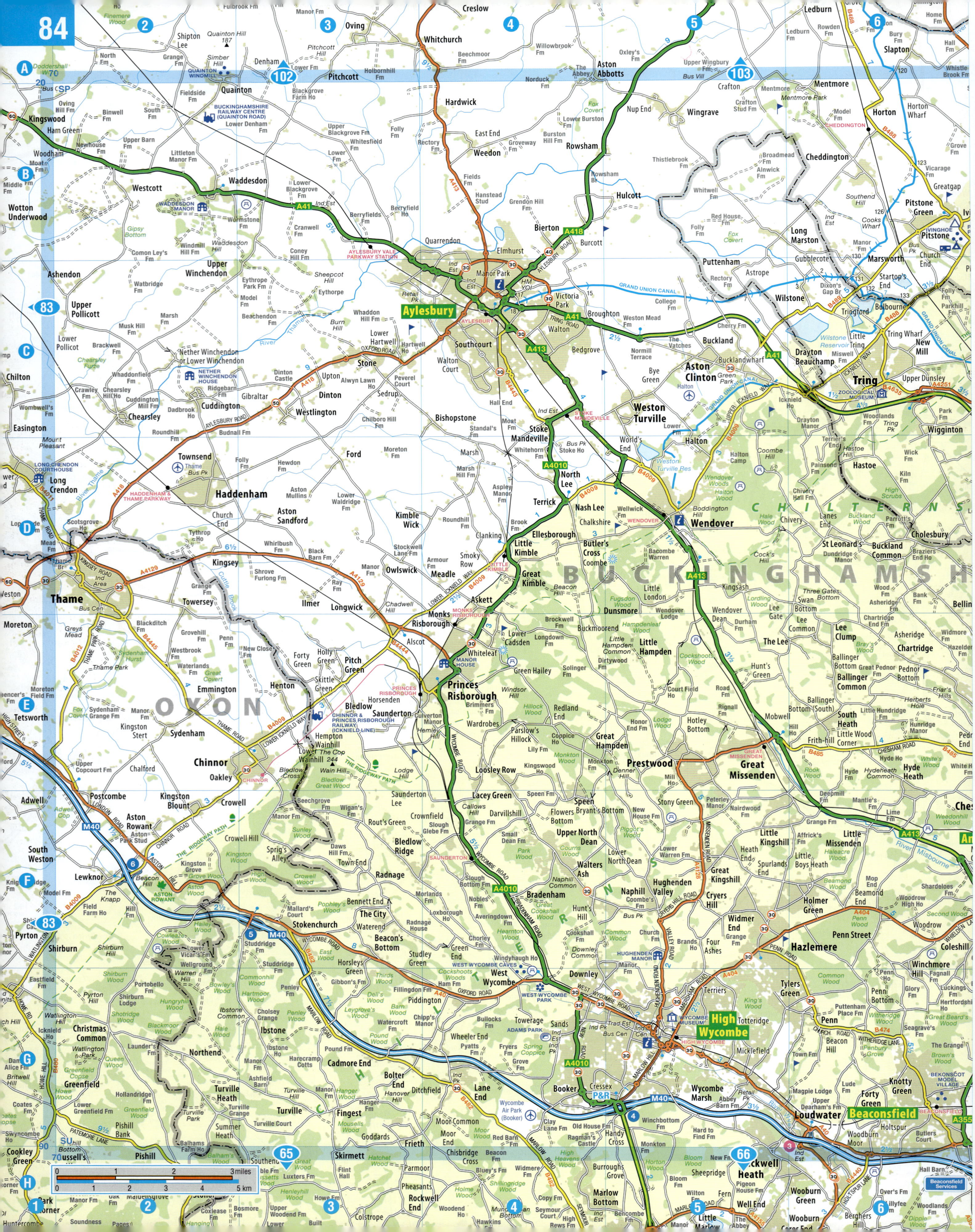

Creslow
Oving
Whitchurch
Shipton Lee
Quainton
Denham
Pitchcott
Hardwick
Aston Abbotts
Wingrave
Mentmore
Ledburn
Slapton
Horton
Cheddington
Kingswood
Ham Green
Woodham
Waddesdon
Westcott
Wotton Underwood
Weedon
Rowsham
Hulcott
Bierton
Long Marston
Pitstone Green
Pitstone
Marsworth
Puttenham
Astrope
Wilstone
Ashendon
Upper Winchendon
Upper Pollicott
Lower Pollicott
Aylesbury
Quarrendon
Elmhurst
Broughton
Buckland
Aston Clinton
Drayton Beauchamp
Tring
Chilton
Easington
Cuddington
Chearsley
Gibraltar
Dinton
Westlington
Stone
Southcourt
Bedgrove
Bishopstone
Stoke Mandeville
Weston Turville
Halton
Wigginton
Long Crendon
Townsend
Haddenham
Aston Sandford
Ford
Kimble Wick
Terrick
North Lee
Nash Lee
Wendover
Hastoe
Cholesbury
Thame
Kingsey
Towersey
Little Kimble
Great Kimble
Ellesborough
Butler's Cross
Dunsmore
Little Hampden
Owlswick
Meadle
Askett
Monks Risborough
Longwick
Ilmer
Moreton
Emmington
Henton
Forty Green
Pitch Green
Bledlow
Saunderton
Princes Risborough
Whiteleaf
Green Hailey
Great Hampden
Prestwood
Great Missenden
South Heath
Ballinger Common
Lee Common
The Lee
Swan Bottom
Sydenham
Chinnor
Oakley
Crowell
Kingston Blount
Aston Rowant
Postcombe
Tetsworth
Adwell
South Weston
Lewknor
Radnage
Bledlow Ridge
Lacey Green
Loosley Row
Speen
Upper North Dean
Walters Ash
Bradenham
Naphill
Hughenden Valley
Great Kingshill
Little Kingshill
Little Missenden
Holmer Green
Hazlemere
Penn Street
Coleshill
Winchmore Hill
Stokenchurch
Pyrton
Shirburn
Watlington
Christmas Common
Northend
Ibstone
Cadmore End
Lane End
Bolter End
West Wycombe
Downley
High Wycombe
Booker
Wycombe Marsh
Loudwater
Beaconsfield
Knotty Green
Forty Green
Penn
Tylers Green
Turville Heath
Turville
Fingest
Skirmett
Frieth
Moor Common
Greenfield
Pishill
Cookley Green
Marlow Bottom
Wooburn Green
Flackwell Heath
Handy Cross
OXON
BUCKINGHAMSHIRE
CHILTERNS
M40
A41
A413
A418
A4010
A4129
A40
A404
A355
0 1 2 3 miles
0 1 2 3 4 5 km

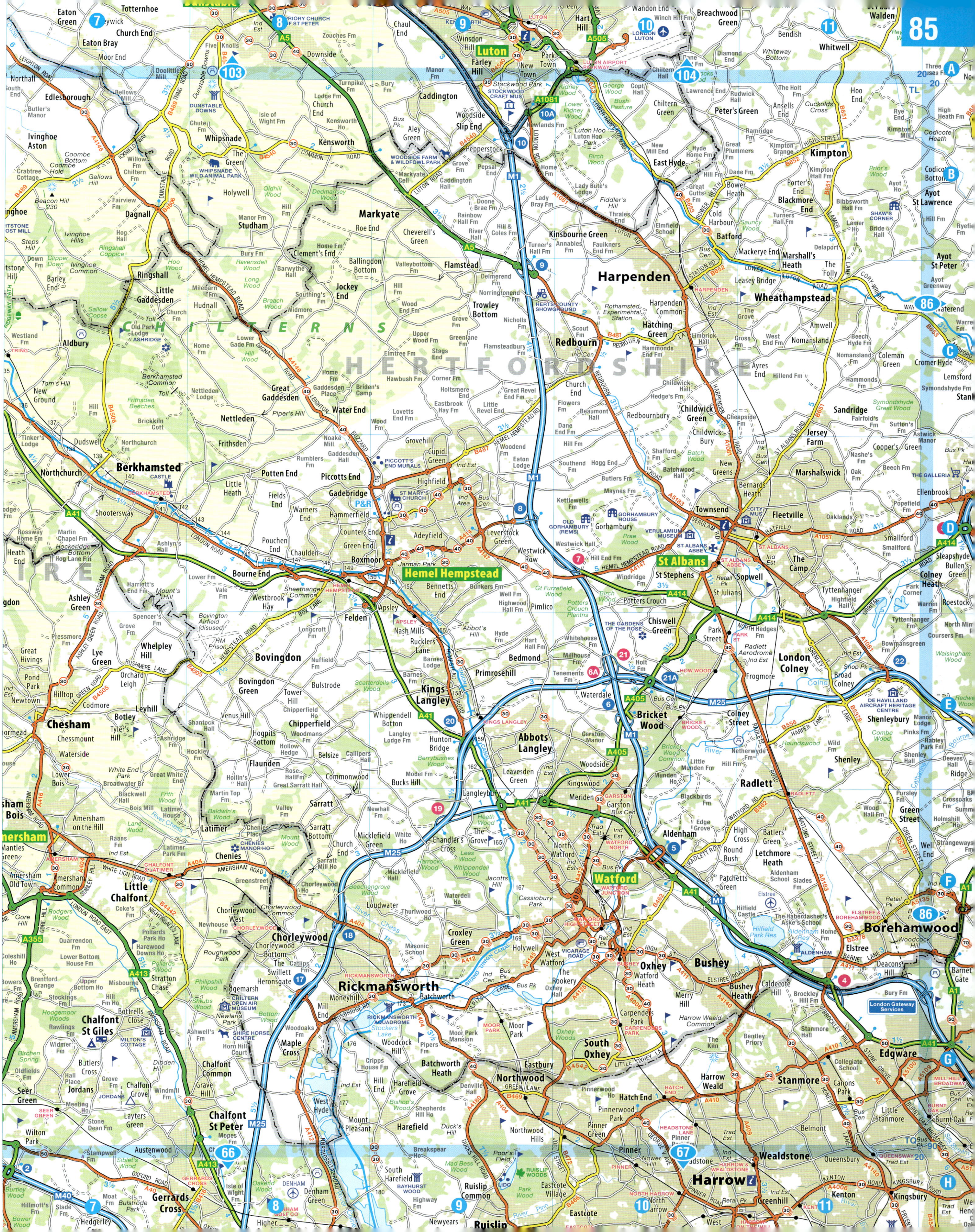
HERTFORDSHIRE
CHILTERNS
Luton
Harpenden
St Albans
Hemel Hempstead
Watford
Rickmansworth
Borehamwood
Berkhamsted
Chesham
Amersham
Harrow
Edgware
Stanmore
Bushey
Radlett
London Colney
Kings Langley
Abbots Langley
Redbourn
Wheathampstead
Markyate
Dunstable Downs
Whipsnade
Kensworth
Caddington
Flamstead
Great Gaddesden
Nettleden
Bovingdon
Chipperfield
Sarratt
Chorleywood
Little Chalfont
Chalfont St Giles
Chalfont St Peter
Gerrards Cross
Northwood
Ruislip
Pinner
Oxhey
South Oxhey
Bricket Wood
Park Street
Shenley
Elstree
Kimpton
Whitwell
Sandridge
Fleetville
Marshalswick
Leverstock Green
Aldbury
Ivinghoe
Edlesborough
Dagnall
Studham
Wealdstone
Kenton
Kingsbury
Harefield
Denham
M1
M25
A41
A5
A414
A405
A1
M40

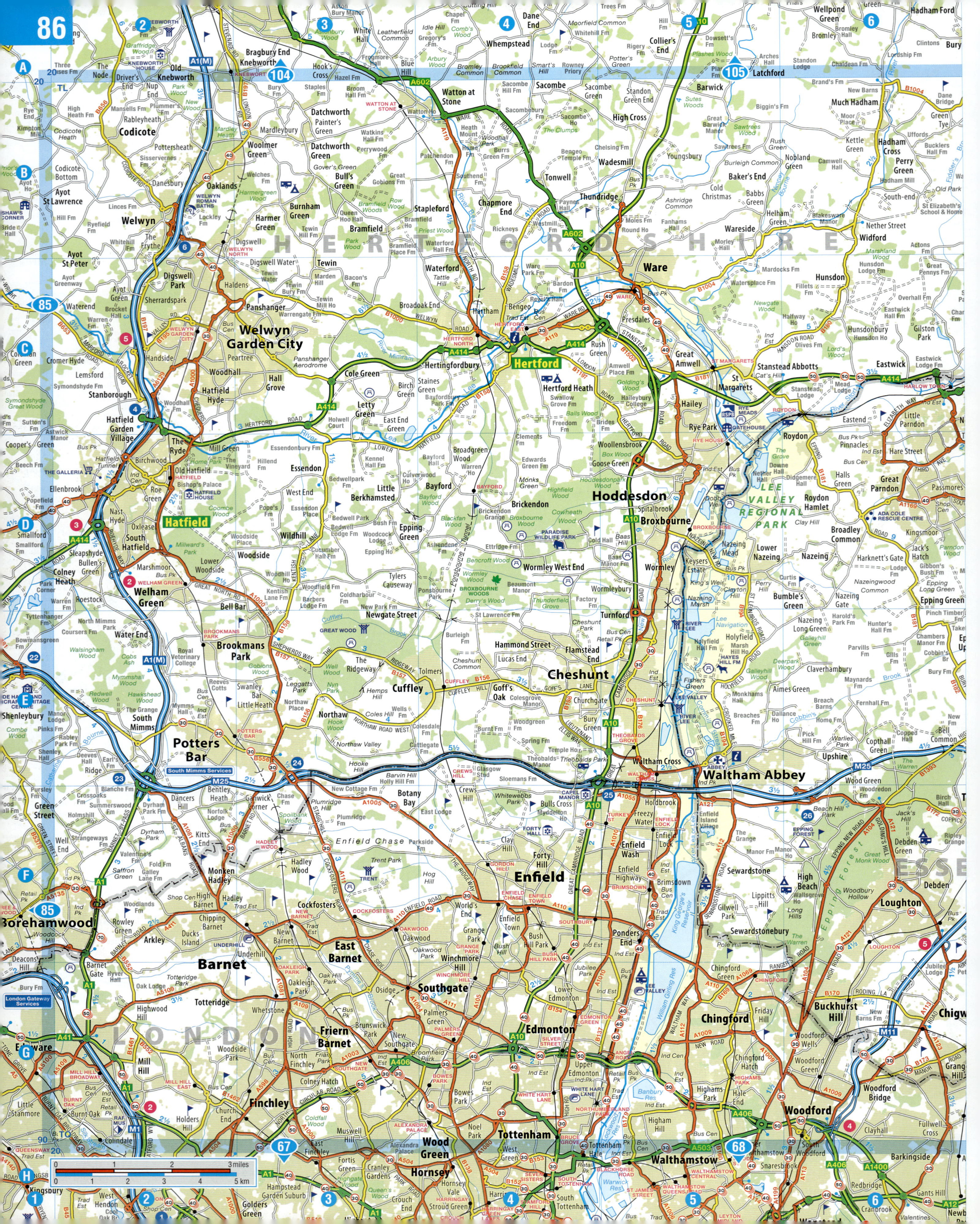
HERTFORDSHIRE
LONDON
ESSEX
Welwyn Garden City
Hertford
Hatfield
Ware
Hoddesdon
Broxbourne
Cheshunt
Waltham Abbey
Potters Bar
Enfield
Borehamwood
Barnet
East Barnet
Friern Barnet
Finchley
Southgate
Edmonton
Tottenham
Wood Green
Hornsey
Walthamstow
Chingford
Woodford
Loughton
Buckhurst Hill
Welwyn
Codicote
Knebworth
Digswell Park
Welham Green
Brookmans Park
Cuffley
Goff's Oak
Stanstead Abbotts
St Margarets
Roydon
Nazeing
Epping Green
Essendon
Little Berkhamsted
Bayford
Brickendon
Wormley
Turnford
Waltham Cross
Ponders End
Cockfosters
Hadley Wood
Monken Hadley
High Barnet
Totteridge
Whetstone
Edgware
Mill Hill
Kingsbury
Lee Valley Regional Park
King George's Reservoir
William Girling Reservoir
Epping Forest
0 1 2 3 miles
0 1 2 3 4 5 km

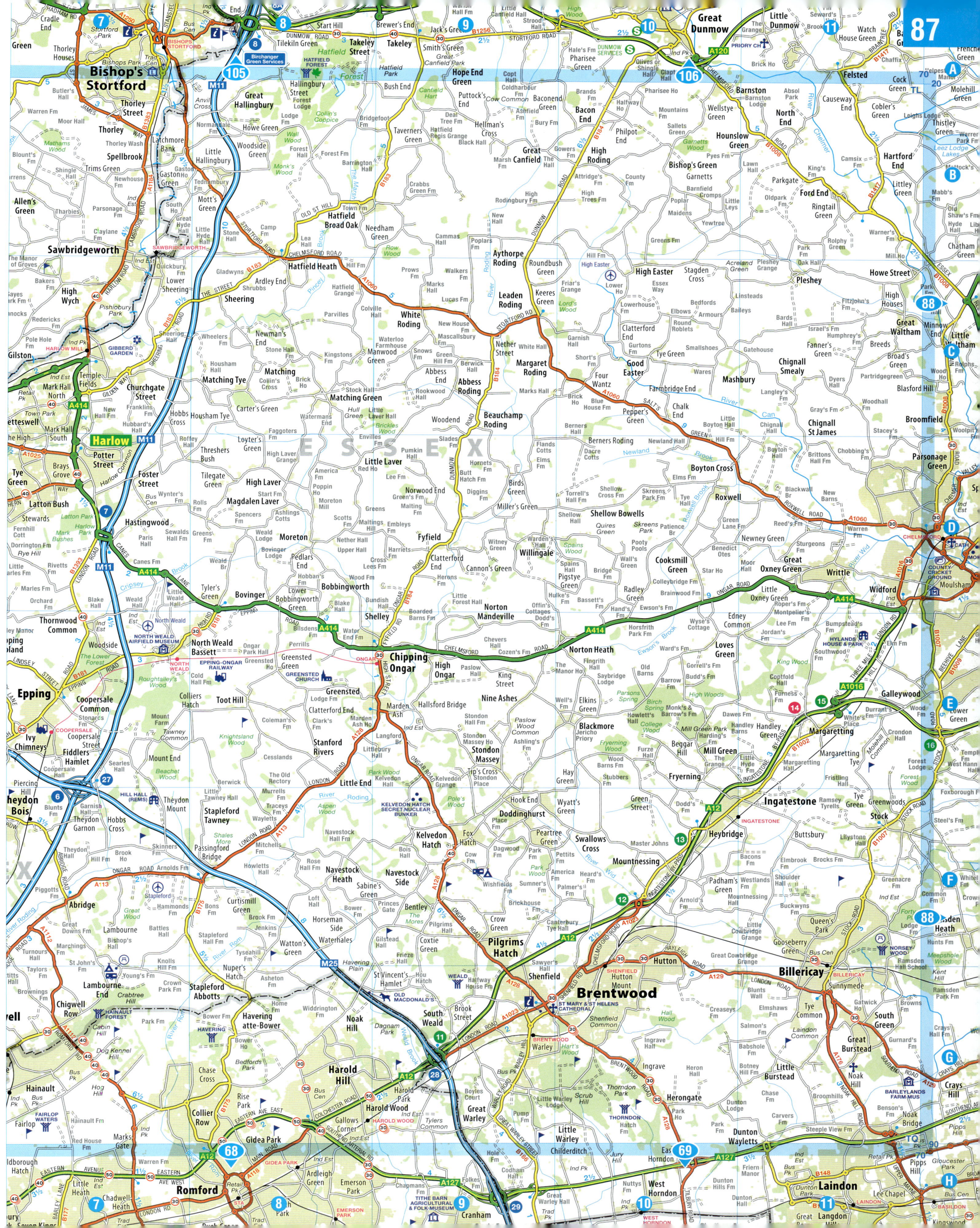
Bishop's Stortford
Great Dunmow
Felsted
Sawbridgeworth
Harlow
Epping
Chipping Ongar
Brentwood
Billericay
Ingatestone
Romford
Harold Hill
Hatfield Heath
Leaden Roding
High Easter
Pleshey
Writtle
Laindon
E S S E X

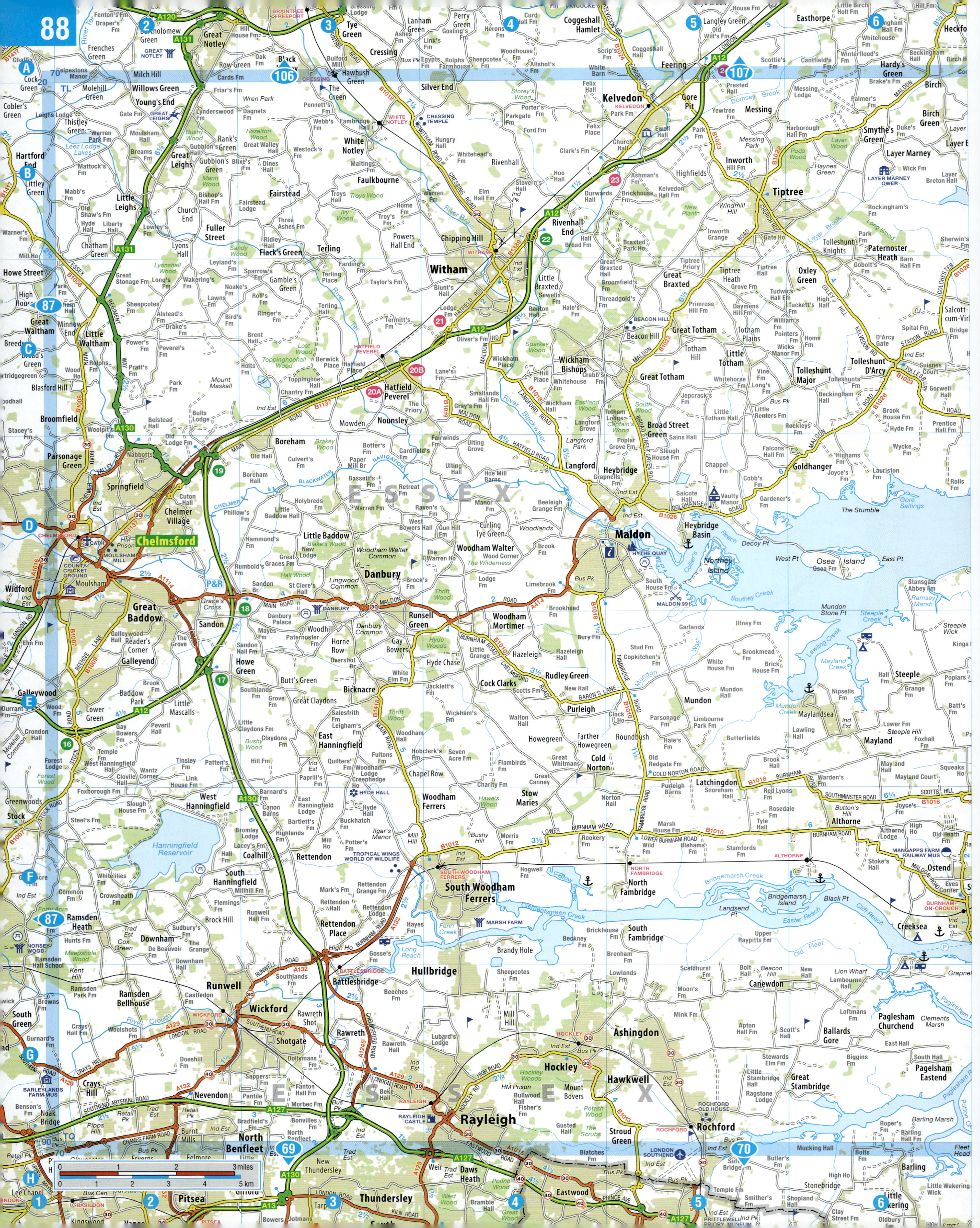
ESSEX
Chelmsford
Witham
Maldon
Tiptree
Kelvedon
Coggeshall Hamlet
Feering
Hatfield Peverel
Boreham
Danbury
Great Baddow
Springfield
Broomfield
Great Waltham
Little Waltham
Terling
Fairstead
White Notley
Silver End
Rivenhall
Great Braxted
Great Totham
Little Totham
Tolleshunt D'Arcy
Tolleshunt Major
Tolleshunt Knights
Goldhanger
Heybridge
Heybridge Basin
Langford
Woodham Mortimer
Woodham Walter
Woodham Ferrers
South Woodham Ferrers
Purleigh
Cold Norton
Latchingdon
Mundon
Maylandsea
Mayland
Steeple
Althorne
Burnham-on-Crouch
Creeksea
North Fambridge
South Fambridge
Hullbridge
Battlesbridge
Rettendon
East Hanningfield
West Hanningfield
South Hanningfield
Hanningfield Reservoir
Bicknacre
Sandon
Galleyend
Galleywood
Stock
Billericay
Ramsden Heath
Runwell
Wickford
Shotgate
Rawreth
Rayleigh
Hockley
Hawkwell
Ashingdon
Canewdon
Rochford
Eastwood
Thundersley
Pitsea
North Benfleet
Nevendon
Crays Hill
Osea Island
Northey Island
The Stumble
Blackwater
River Crouch
Paglesham Churchend
Paglesham Eastend
Ballards Gore
Great Stambridge
Stow Maries
Hazeleigh
Rudley Green
Cock Clarks
Little Baddow
Great Notley
Black Notley
Cressing
Faulkbourne
Inworth
Messing
Layer Marney
Birch
Salcott-cum-Virley
A12
A130
A131
A120
A414
A132
A127
A129
B1018
B1010
B1012
106
107
87
69
70
0 1 2 3 miles
0 1 2 3 4 5 km

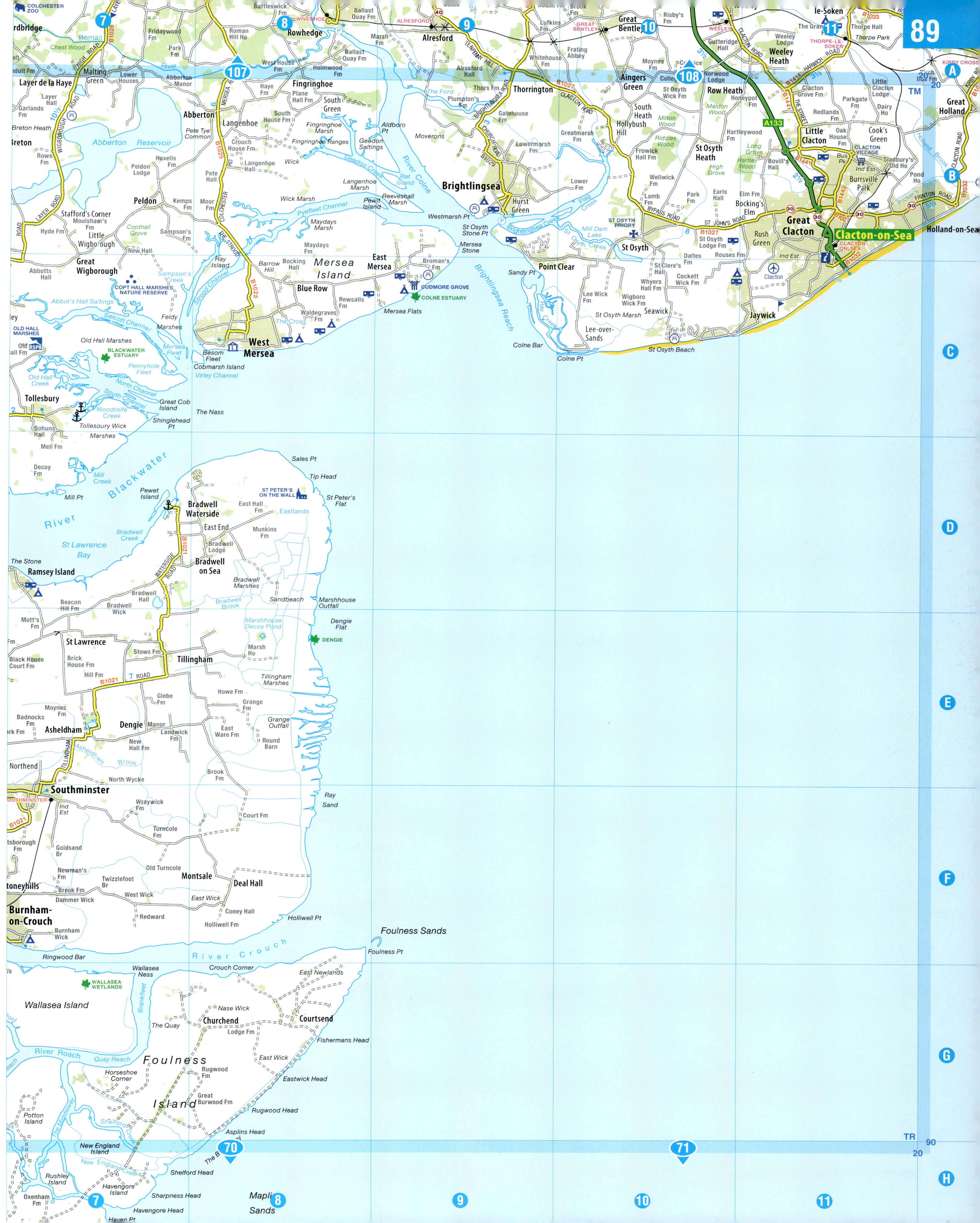
COLCHESTER ZOO
Layer de la Haye
Malting Green
Abberton
Abberton Reservoir
Langenhoe
Peldon
Fingringhoe
Rowhedge
Wivenhoe
Alresford
Thorrington
Great Bentley
Weeley
Weeley Heath
Aingers Green
Row Heath
Little Clacton
St Osyth Heath
Brightlingsea
Hurst Green
Point Clear
St Osyth
Great Clacton
Clacton-on-Sea
Holland-on-Sea
Great Holland
Jaywick
Seawick
Lee-over-Sands
Colne Point
St Osyth Beach
Colne Bar
Sandy Pt
Brightlingsea Reach
St Osyth Marsh
Mersea Island
East Mersea
West Mersea
Mersea Flats
CUDMORE GROVE
COLNE ESTUARY
River Colne
Geedon Saltings
Pyefleet Channel
Strood Channel
Great Wigborough
Little Wigborough
COPT HALL MARSHES NATURE RESERVE
BLACKWATER ESTUARY
OLD HALL MARSHES
Tollesbury
Tollesbury Wick Marshes
Salcott Channel
Cobmarsh Island
Virley Channel
North Channel
South Channel
Shinglehead Pt
The Nass
Sales Pt
Tip Head
ST PETER'S ON THE WALL
St Peter's Flat
Bradwell Waterside
East End
Bradwell on Sea
River Blackwater
St Lawrence Bay
Ramsey Island
St Lawrence
Tillingham
Tillingham Marshes
Dengie
DENGIE
Dengie Flat
Asheldham
Southminster
Ray Sand
Montsale
Deal Hall
Holliwell Pt
Burnham-on-Crouch
Foulness Sands
Foulness Pt
River Crouch
WALLASEA WETLANDS
Wallasea Island
Churchend
Courtsend
Fishermans Head
Foulness Island
River Roach
Potton Island
New England Island
Havengore Island
Rushley Island
Shelford Head
Sharpness Head
Havengore Head
Maplin Sands
Asplins Head
Rugwood Head
Eastwick Head
A133
B1027
B1025
B1021
B1029
B1032
TM
TR
107
108
70
71
7
8
9
10
11
A
B
C
D
E
F
G
H

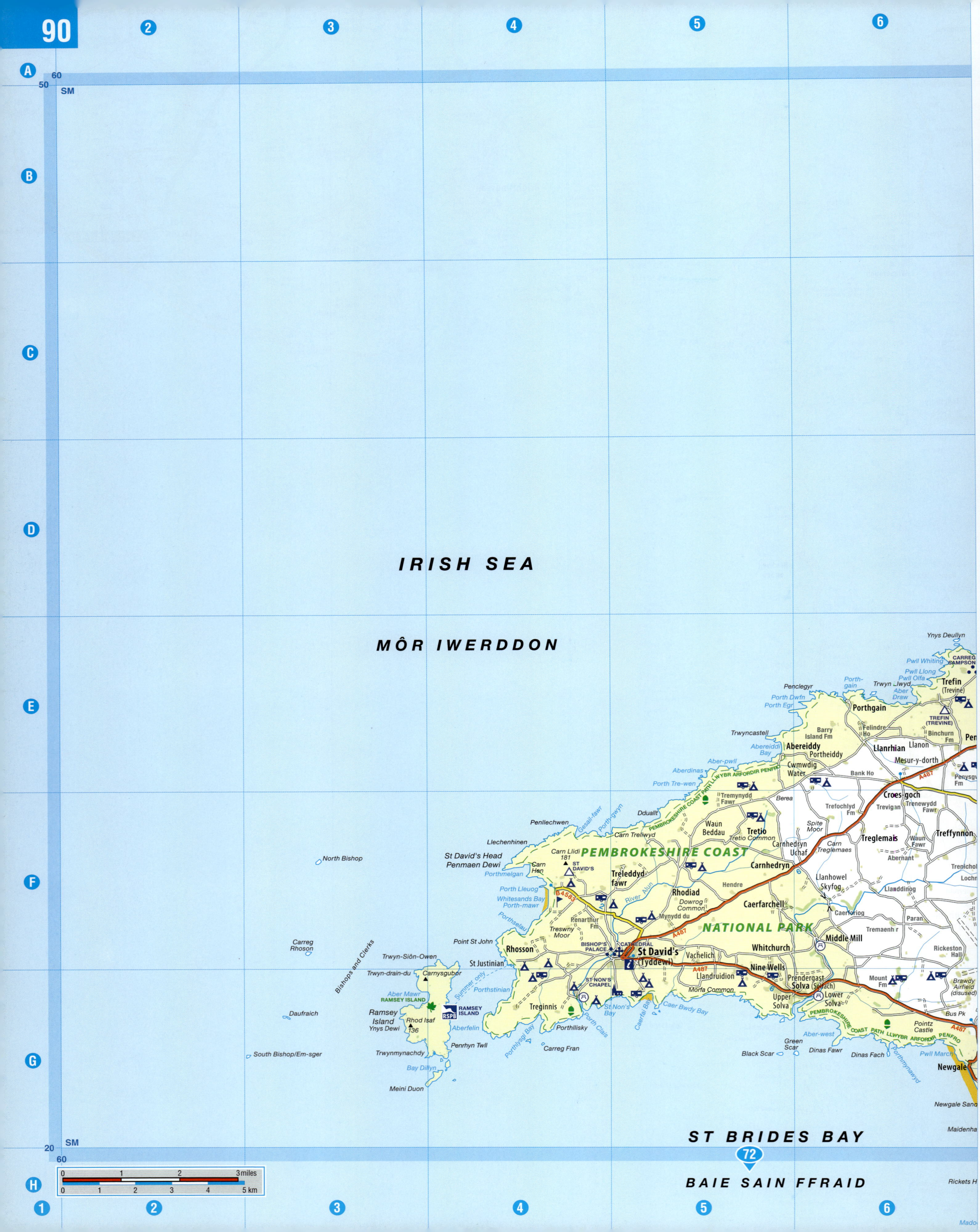

IRISH SEA
MÔR IWERDDON
ST BRIDES BAY
BAIE SAIN FFRAID
72
PEMBROKESHIRE COAST
NATIONAL PARK
PEMBROKESHIRE COAST PATH LLWYBR ARFORDIR PENFRO
SM
Ynys Deullyn
Pwll Whiting
CARREG SAMPSON
Pwll Llong
Pwll Olfa
Trefin
(Trevine)
Porthgain
Porth Dwfn
Porth Egr
Penclegyr
Trwyn Llwyd
Aber Draw
TREFIN (TREVINE)
Felindre Ho
Binchurn Fm
Trwyncastell
Barry Island Fm
Abereiddi Bay
Abereiddy
Portheiddy
Llanrhian
Llanon
Mesur-y-dorth
Aber-pwll
Cwmwdig Water
Aberdinas
Porth Tre-wen
Bank Ho
Penysgwarn Fm
A487
Croes-goch
Trevigan
Trenewydd Fawr
Tremynydd Fawr
Berea
Trefochlyd Fm
Dduallt
Penllechwen
Gesail-fawr
Porth-gwyn
Waun Beddau
Tretio
Tretio Common
Spite Moor
Treglemais
Waun Fawr
Treffynnon
Carn Treliwyd
Llechenhinen
Carn Llidi
181
Carnhedryn Uchaf
Carn Treglemaes
Abernant
St David's Head
Penmaen Dewi
Carn Hen
ST DAVID'S
Porthmelgan
Treleddyd-fawr
Carnhedryn
Trenichol
Hendre
Llanhowel
Skyfog
Llaundinog
Porth Lleuog
Whitesands Bay
Porth-mawr
B4583
River Alun
Rhodiad
Dowrog Common
Caerfarchell
Porthselau
Mynydd du
Caerforiog
Paran
Treswny Moor
Penarthur Fm
Tremaenhir
North Bishop
Point St John
Middle Mill
Carreg Rhoson
BISHOP'S PALACE
CATHEDRAL
Rhosson
St David's
(Tyddewi)
Vachelich
Whitchurch
Rickeston Hall
Bishops and Clerks
Trwyn-Siôn-Owen
Trwyn-drain-du
Carnysgubor
St Justinian
Summer only
Porthstinian
Llandruidion
Nine Wells
Prendergast
Solva
Mount Fm
Brawdy Airfield (disused)
ST NON'S CHAPEL
Morfa Common
Upper Solva
Lower Solva
Aber Mawr
RAMSEY ISLAND
RSPB
Treginnis
St Non's Bay
Caerfai Bay
Caer Bwdy Bay
Bus Pk
Daufraich
Ramsey Island
Ynys Dewi
Rhod Isaf
136
Aberfelin
Porthllisky
Porth Clais
Pointz Castle
Porthlysgi Bay
Aber-west
Penrhyn Twll
Carreg Fran
Green Scar
Black Scar
Dinas Fawr
Dinas Fach
Pwll March
South Bishop/Em-sger
Trwynmynachdy
Porthmynawyd
Newgale
Bay Dillyn
Meini Duon
Newgale Sands
Maidenhall
Rickets H
0 1 2 3 miles
0 1 2 3 4 5 km

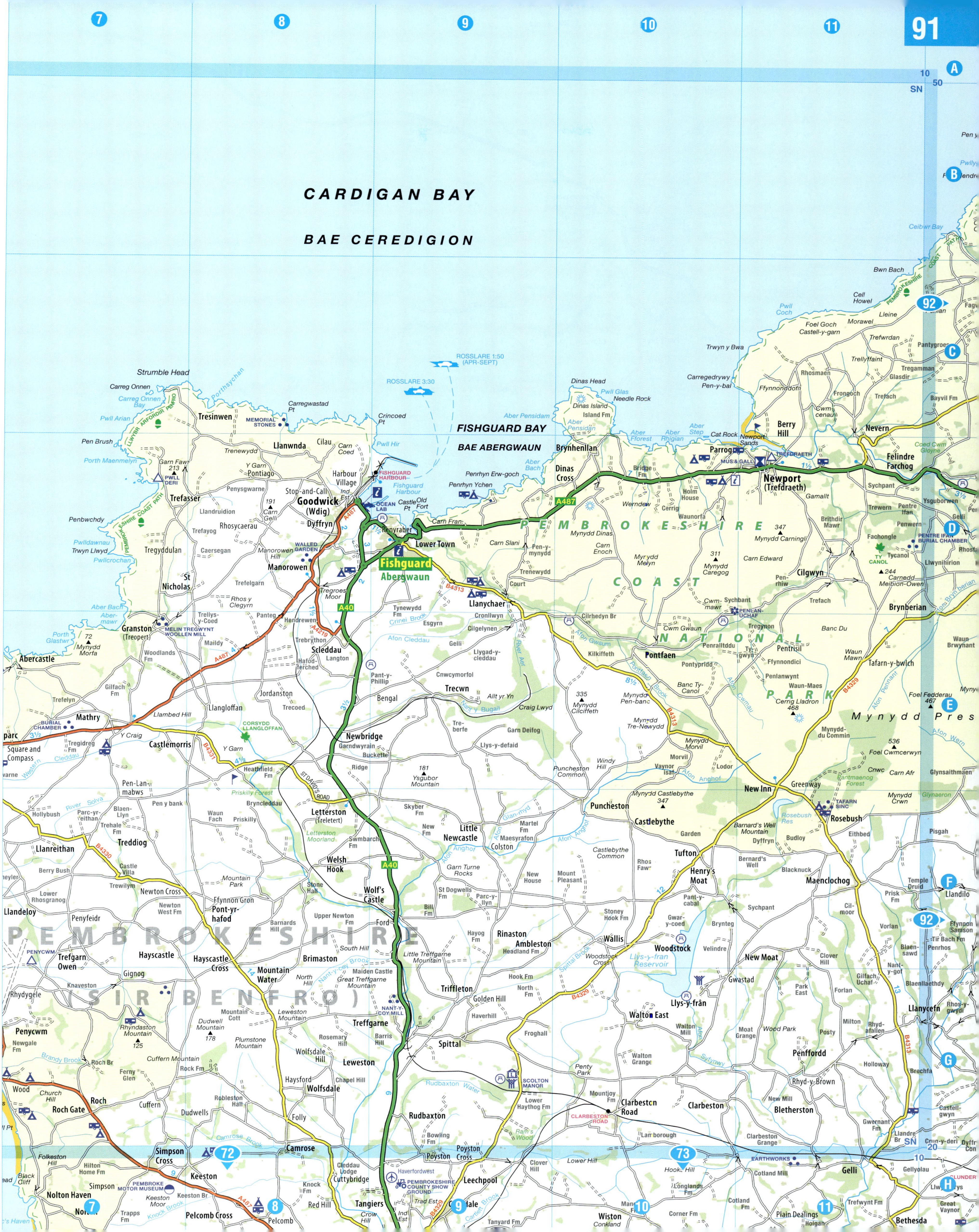
CARDIGAN BAY
BAE CEREDIGION
FISHGUARD BAY
BAE ABERGWAUN
ROSSLARE 3:30
ROSSLARE 1:50 (APR-SEPT)
Strumble Head
Carreg Onnen
Carreg Onnen Bay
Pwll Arian
Pen Brush
Porth Maenmelyn
Tresinwen
MEMORIAL STONES
Carregwastad Pt
Llanwnda
Cilau
Carn Coed
Crincoed Pt
Pwll Hir
Trenewydd
Y Garn Pontiago
Garn Fawr 213
PWLL DERI
Trefasser
Penysgwarne
Stop-and-Call
Goodwick (Wdig)
Harbour Village
FISHGUARD HARBOUR
Fishguard Harbour
OCEAN LAB
Castle Pt
Old Fort
Dyffryn
Llandruidion
Rhosycaerau
Penbwchdy
Pwlldawnau
Trwyn Llwyd
Pwllcrochan
Tregyddulan
Trefayog
Caersegan
Manorowen Hill
Manorowen
WALLED GARDEN
St Nicholas
Trefelgarn
Rhos y Clegyrn
Tregroes Moor
Fishguard
Abergwaun
Lower Town
Penyraber
Carn Fran
Aber Bach
Abermawr
Porth Glastwr
Granston (Treopert)
MELIN TREGWYNT WOOLLEN MILL
Trellys-y-Coed
Panteg
Hendrewen
Trebrython
Scleddau
Langton
Hafod-Ferched
Maildy
Mynydd Morfa 72
Abercastle
Woodlands Fm
Trefelyn
Gilfach Fm
Mathry
BURIAL CHAMBER
Llambed Hill
Llangloffan
Jordanston
Trecoed
CORSYDD LLANGLOFFAN
Square and Compass
Tregidreg Fm
Y Craig
Castlemorris
Y Garn
Heathfield Fm
Priskilly Forest
Brynycleddau
Pen-Lan-mabws
Pen y bank
Waun Fach
Priskilly
Hollybush
Parc-yr-eithan
Blaen-Llyn
Trehale Fm
Treddiog
Llanreithan
Berry Bush
Castle Villa
Trewilym
Newton Cross
Mountain Park
Ffynnon Gron
Pont-yr-hafod
Newton West Fm
Lower Rhosgranog
Llandeloy
Penyfeidr
PEMBROKESHIRE
(SIR BENFRO)
PENYCWM
Trefgarn Owen
Hayscastle
Hayscastle Cross
Gignog
Knaveston
Rhydygele
Penycwm
Newgale Fm
Rhyndaston Mountain 125
Cuffern Mountain
Ferny Glen
Roch Br
Rock Fm
Church Hill
Roch Gate
Roch
Cuffern
Robleston Hall
Dudwells
Simpson Cross
Keeston
Folkeston Hill
Hilton Home Fm
Simpson
PEMBROKE MOTOR MUSEUM
Keeston Moor
Keeston Br
Nolton Haven
Black Cliff
Pelcomb Cross
Pelcomb
Trapps Fm
Camrose
Camrose Brook
Knock Fm
Red Hill
Cleddau Lodge
Cuttybridge
Tangiers
Crow Hill
Haverfordwest
PEMBROKESHIRE COUNTY SHOW GROUND
Trad Est
Leechpool
Poyston
Poyston Cross
Bowling Fm
Rudbaxton
Rudbaxton Water
Folly
Hayford
Wolfsdale
Wolfsdale Hill
Chapel Hill
Leweston
Leweston Mountain
Rosemary Hill
Barris Hill
Treffgarne
NANT-Y-COY MILL
Spittal
Mountain Cott
Dudwell Mountain 178
Plumstone Mountain
North Hill
Maiden Castle
Great Treffgarne Mountain
Brimaston
South Hill
Mountain Water
Barnards Hill
Upper Newton Fm
Ford
Little Treffgarne Mountain
Wolf's Castle
Stone Hall
Welsh Hook
Swmbarch Fm
Letterston (Treletert)
Letterston Moorland
Ridge
Skyber Fm
New Fm
Little Newcastle
Martel Fm
Maesyrafon
Colston
Garn Turne Rocks
St Dogwells Fm
Parc-y-llyn
Bill Fm
Hayog Fm
Rinaston
Ambleston
Headland Fm
Triffleton
Golden Hill
Haverhill
North Fm
Hook Fm
Froghall
SCOLTON MANOR
Lower Haythog Fm
Penty Park
Mountjoy Fm
Clarbeston Road
CLARBESTON ROAD
Clarbeston
Lamborough
Clover Hill
Lower Hill
Wiston
Conkland
Tanyard Fm
Mynydd Dinas
Ysgubor Mountain 181
Newbridge
Garndwyrain
Buckette
Bengal
Pant-y-Phillip
Cnwcymorfol
Trecwn
Allt yr Yn
Craig Lwyd
Tre-berfe
Garn Deifog
Llys-y-defaid
Tynewydd Fm
Esgyrn
Gelli
Llygad-y-cleddau
Afon Cleddau
Crinei Brook
Cilgelynen
Cronllwyn
Llanychaer
Court
Trenewydd
Pen-y-mynydd
Carn Slani
Carn Enoch
Penrhyn Erw-goch
Penrhyn Ychen
Aber Pensidan
Dinas Head
Dinas Island
Island Fm
Pwll Glas
Needle Rock
Brynhenllan
Dinas Cross
Aber Fforest
Aber Rhigian
Aber Step
Bridge Fm
Werndew
Holm House
Cerrig
Waunorfa
PEMBROKESHIRE COAST NATIONAL PARK
Myrydd Melyn
Mynydd Caregog 311
Cwm-mawr
Sychbant
PENLAN-UCHAF
Cilrhedyn Br
Afon Gwaun
Kilkiffeth
Pontfaen
Cwm Gwaun
Penrallt-ddu
Tregynon
Tŷ-gwyn
Pontyprìdd
Banc Ty-Canol
Mynydd Pen-banc
Mynydd Cilciffeth 335
Mynydd Tre-Newydd
Mynydd Morvil
Morvil
Vaynor Isaf
Afon Angof
Lodor
Windy Hill
Puncheston Common
Puncheston
Mynydd Castlebythe 347
Castlebythe
Castlebythe Common
Rhos Fawr
Mount Pleasant
New House
Tufton
Henry's Moat
Garden
Pant-y-cabal
Gwar-y-coed
Stoney Hook Fm
Wallis
Woodstock
Woodstock Cross
Llys-y-fran Reservoir
Llys-y-frân
Walton East
Walton Mill
Walton Grange
Velindre
Brynteg
Sychpant
Bernard's Well
Blacknuck
Maenclochog
New Moat
Gwastad
Clover Hill
Park East
Moat Grange
Wood Park
Posty
Penffordd
Rhyd-y-Brown
New Mill
Bletherston
Clarbeston Grange
Cotland Mill
Cotland Fm
Gelli
Plain Dealings
Holgan
EARTHWORKS
Hook Hill
Longlands Fm
Corner Fm
Manor
Newport (Trefdraeth)
Parrog
Newport Sands
Berry Hill
Cat Rock
Carregedrywy
Pen-y-bal
Trwyn y Bwa
Pwll Coch
Cell Howel
Bwn Bach
Ceibwr Bay
Lleine
Morawel
Foel Goch
Castell-y-garn
Trefwrdan
Trellyffaint
Rhosmaen
Ffynnondofn
Frongoch
Cwm-cenau
Glasdir
Tregamman
Trefach
Pantygroes
Bayvil Fm
Nevern
Felindre Farchog
Coed Cwm Gloyne
Sychpant
Gamallt
Mynydd Carningli 347
Carn Edward
Brithdir Mawr
Pen-rhiw
Cilgwyn
Trewern
Pentre Ifan
Penwern
PENTRE IFAN BURIAL CHAMBER
Fachongle
TY CANOL
Tycanol
Carnedd Meibion-Owen 244
Llwynihirion
Rhosfach
Ysguborwen
Trefach
Banc Du
Brynberian
Waun Mawr
Pentrisil
Ffynnondici
Penlanwynt
Waun-Maes
Cerrig Lladron 468
Tafarn-y-bwlch
Waun Brwynant
Foel Feddrau 467
Mynydd Presely
Mynydd-du Commin
Foel Cwmcerwyn 536
Cnwc
Carn Afr
Glynsaithmaen
Mynydd Crwn
Pantmaenog Forest
Glynaeron
Greenway
New Inn
TAFARN SINC
Rosebush
Rosebush Res
Barnard's Well Mountain
Dyffryn
Budloy
Eithbed
Pisgah
Temple Druid
Prisk Fm
Llandilo
Vorlan
Cil-moor
Blaen-sawd
Nant-y-gof
Gilfach Uchaf
Blaenllaethdy
Forlan
Ffynnon Samson
Tir Bach Fm
Penrhos
Llanycefn
Rhos-y-gwydd
Milton
Rhyd-afallen
Holloway
Brechfa
Castell-gwyn
Gwernant Fm
Llandre Br
Gellyolau
Crug-y-deri
Dyffryn
Llwyn
Trefwynt Fm
Great Vaynor
Bethesda
A487
A40
A4219
B4313
B4329
B4330
B4331
A4330
STDAVIDS ROAD
92
72
73
7
8
9
10
11
SN
10
20
50
A
B
C
D
E
F
G
H

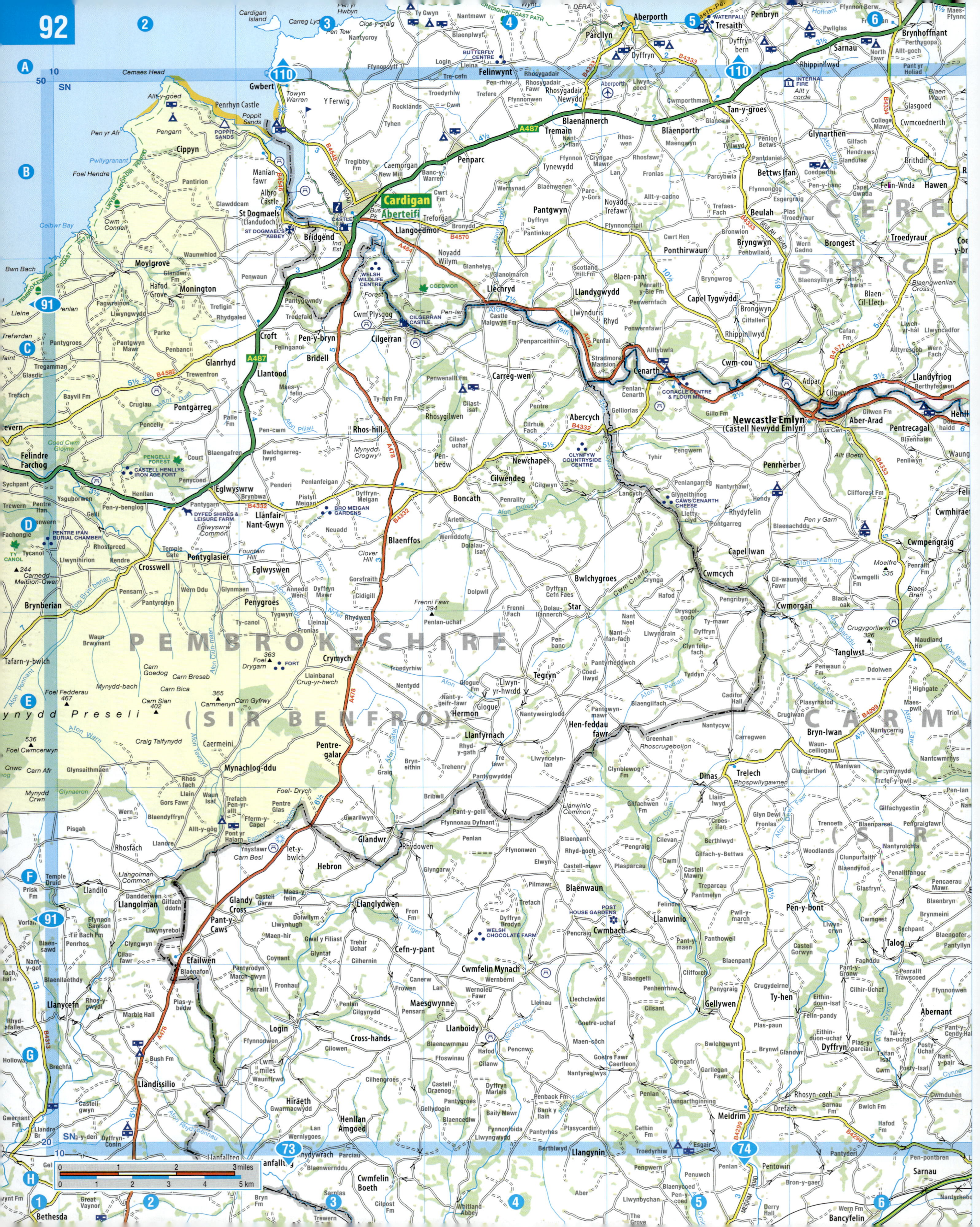
Cardigan Island
Cemaes Head
Gwbert
Cardigan
Aberteifi
Penparc
Tremain
Blaenannerch
Aberporth
Parcllyn
Tresaith
Penbryn
Sarnau
Brynhoffnant
Tan-y-groes
Felinwynt
Glynarthen
Bettws Ifan
Beulah
Brongest
Troedyraur
Ponthirwaun
Pentwyn
Capel Tygwydd
Llandygwydd
Llechryd
Cilgerran
Cwm Plysgog
Welsh Wildlife Centre
Cilgerran Castle
Cenarth
Adpar
Newcastle Emlyn
(Castell Newydd Emlyn)
Aber-Arad
Pentrecagal
Llandyfriog
Cwm-cou
Rhippinllwyd
St Dogmaels
(Llandudoch)
St Dogmael's Abbey
Bridgend
Moylgrove
Monington
Croft
Pen-y-bryn
Bridell
Glanrhyd
Llantood
Pontgarreg
Rhos-hill
Carreg-wen
Abercych
Newchapel
Cilwendeg
Boncath
Blaenffos
Felindre Farchog
Pentre Ifan Burial Chamber
Castell Henllys Iron Age Fort
Eglwyswrw
Llanfair-Nant-Gwyn
Pontyglasier
Crosswell
Eglwyswen
Brynberian
Penygroes
Crymych
Bwlchygroes
Star
Tegryn
Cwmcych
Cwmorgan
Capel Iwan
Penrherber
Tanglwst
PEMBROKESHIRE
(SIR BENFRO)
Mynydd Preseli
Foel Drygarn
Foel Cwmcerwyn
Pentre-galar
Mynachlog-ddu
Hermon
Glogue
Llanfyrnach
Hen-feddau fawr
Bryn-Iwan
Trelech
Dinas
Glandwr
Hebron
Rhydowen
Blaenwaun
Llanwinio
Cwmbach
Pen-y-bont
Talog
Llanglydwen
Cefn-y-pant
Cwmfelin Mynach
Welsh Chocolate Farm
Llangolman
Glandy Cross
Pant-y-Caws
Efailwen
Llanycefn
Llandissilio
Login
Cross-hands
Maesgwynne
Llanboidy
Hiraeth
Henllan Amgoed
Llangynin
Meidrim
Drefach
Gellywen
Ty-hen
Dyffryn
Abernant
Cwmfelin Boeth
Bethesda
Sarnau
Bancyfelin
Pentowin
CARM
(SIR
CERE
(SIR CE
1
2
3
4
5
6
A
B
C
D
E
F
G
H
110
91
73
74
0 1 2 3 miles
0 1 2 3 4 5 km

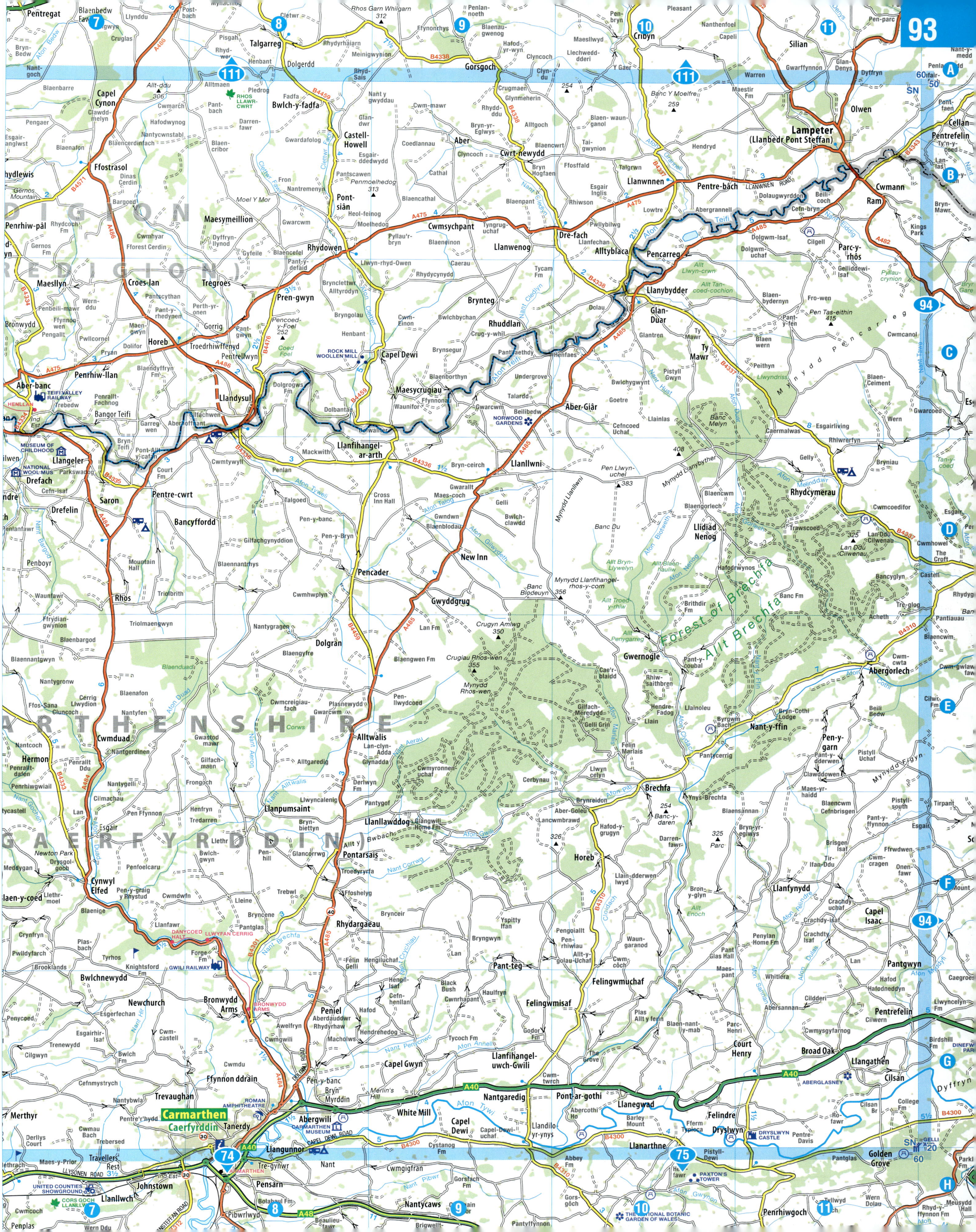
Pentregat
Blaenbedw Fawr
Talgarreg
Dolgerdd
Rhydyrhalarn
Rhos Garn Whilgarn 312
Ffynonrhys
Blaenau-gwenog
Gorsgoch
Cribyn
Pen-bryn
Pleasant
Nanthenfoel
Capeli
Silian
Ram-parc
Capel Cynon
Bwlch-y-fadfa
Castell-Howell
Aber
Cwrt-newydd
Rhos Llawr-Cwrt
Lampeter
(Llanbedr Pont Steffan)
Olwen
Cellan
Pentrefelin
Ffostrasol
Llanwnnen
Pentre-bach
Cwmann
Ram
Penrhiw-pâl
Maesymeillion
Pont-siân
Cwmsychpant
Llanwenog
Dre-fach
Alltyblaca
Pencarreg
Cilgell
Parc-y-rhôs
Rhydowen
Maesllyn
Croes-lan
Tregroes
Pren-gwyn
Llanybydder
Glan-Duar
Ty Mawr
Brynteg
Rhuddlan
Horeb
Troedrhiwffenyd
Capel Dewi
Rock Mill Woollen Mill
Penrhiw-llan
Aber-banc
Henllan
Teifi Valley Railway
Llandysul
Maescrugiau
Aber-Giâr
Norwood Gardens
Bangor Teifi
Llangeler
Drefach
Museum of Childhood
National Wool Mus
Llanfihangel-ar-arth
Llanllwni
Pentre-cwrt
Saron
Bancyffordd
Drefelin
Llidiad Nenog
Rhydcymerau
New Inn
Pencader
Gwyddgrug
Rhos
Dolgran
Forest of Brechfa
Allt Brechfa
Gwernogle
Abergorlech
Cwmduad
Alltwalis
Nant-y-ffin
Hermon
Brechfa
Llanpumsaint
Llanllawddog
Pontarsais
Horeb
Cynwyl Elfed
Llanfynydd
Capel Isaac
Rhydargaeau
Pant-teg
Felingwmuchaf
Bwlchnewydd
Newchurch
Bronwydd Arms
Peniel
Felingwmisaf
Pantgwyn
Pentrefelin
Court Henry
Broad Oak
Llangathen
Cilsan
Gwili Railway
Danycoed Halt
Llwyfan Cerrig
Capel Gwyn
Llanfihangel-uwch-Gwili
Ffynnon ddrain
Trevaughan
Carmarthen
Caerfyrddin
Abergwili
Carmarthen Museum
White Mill
Capel Dewi
Nantgaredig
Pont-ar-gothi
Llanegwad
Felindre
Dryslwyn
Dryslwyn Castle
Aberglasney
Merthyr
Tanerdy
Llangunnor
Llanarthne
Golden Grove
Johnstown
Pensarn
Llanllwch
United Counties Showground
Paxton's Tower
The National Botanic Garden of Wales
Penrhiwgoch
Nantycaws
CEREDIGION
CARMARTHENSHIRE
SIR GAERFYRDDIN
Mynydd Pencarreg
Mynydd Llanybyther
A40
A48
A475
A485
A486
A484
B4459
B4336
B4338
B4337
B4310
B4300
B4301

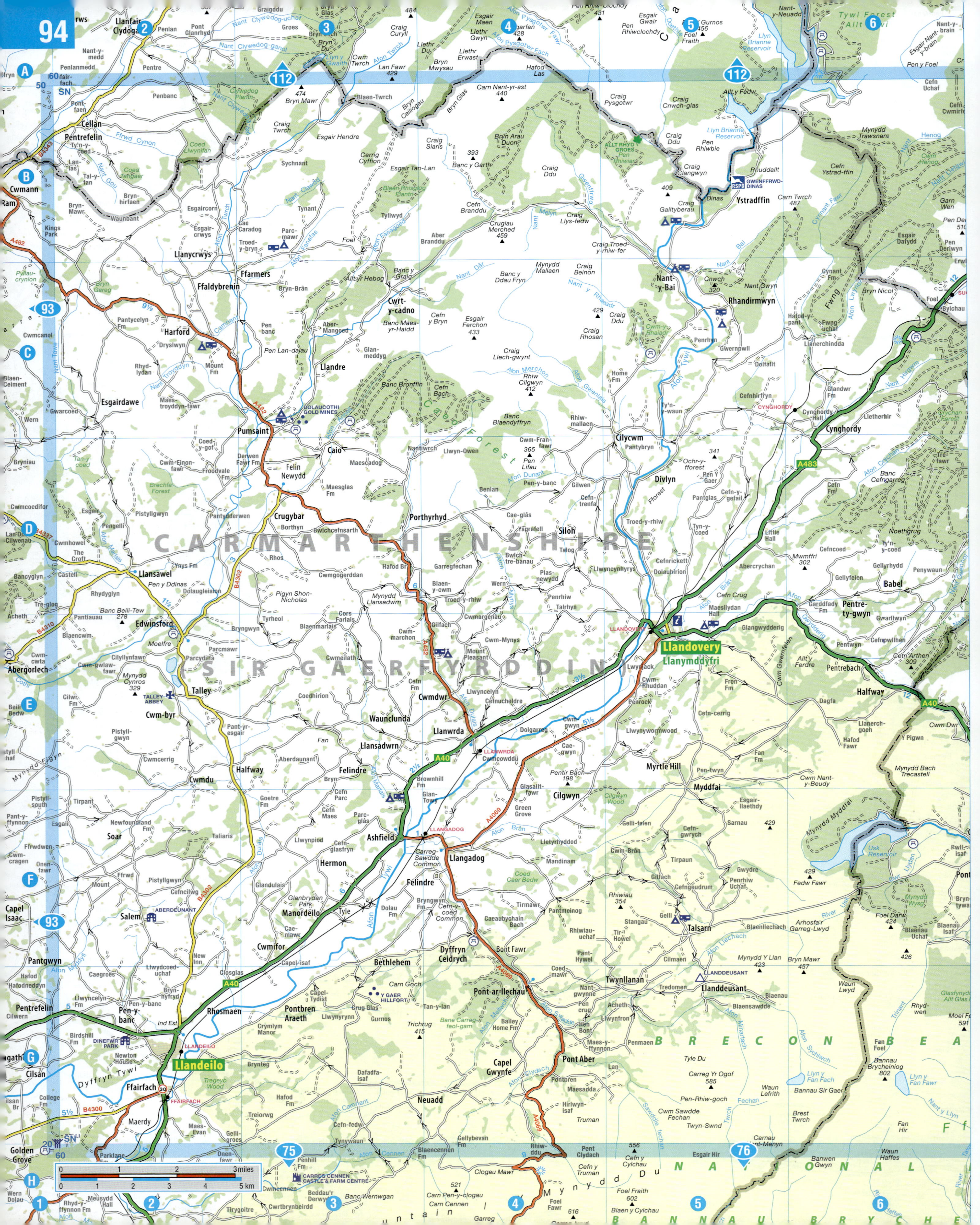
CARMARTHENSHIRE
(SIR GAERFYRDDIN)
BRECON BEACONS NATIONAL PARK
BANNAU BRYCHEINIOG
Llandovery
Llanymddyfri
Llandeilo
Llangadog
Llanwrda
Llansawel
Talley
Pumsaint
Caio
Cilycwm
Rhandirmwyn
Ystradffin
Nant-y-Bai
Myddfai
Llanddeusant
Bethlehem
Ffairfach
Cynghordy
Halfway
Salem
Cwmann
Ffarmers
Harford
Llanycrwys
Ffaldybrenin
Crugybar
Porthyrhyd
Siloh
Myrtle Hill
Twynllanan
Talsarn
Pont-ar-llechau
Capel Gwynfe
Pont Aber
Llyn Brianne Reservoir
Usk Reservoir
Tywi Forest
Crychan Forest
Dolaucothi Gold Mines
Talley Abbey
Dinefwr Park
Carreg Cennen Castle & Farm Centre
A40
A482
A483
A4069
B4302
B4300
112
93
75
76
SN
0 1 2 3 miles
0 1 2 3 4 5 km

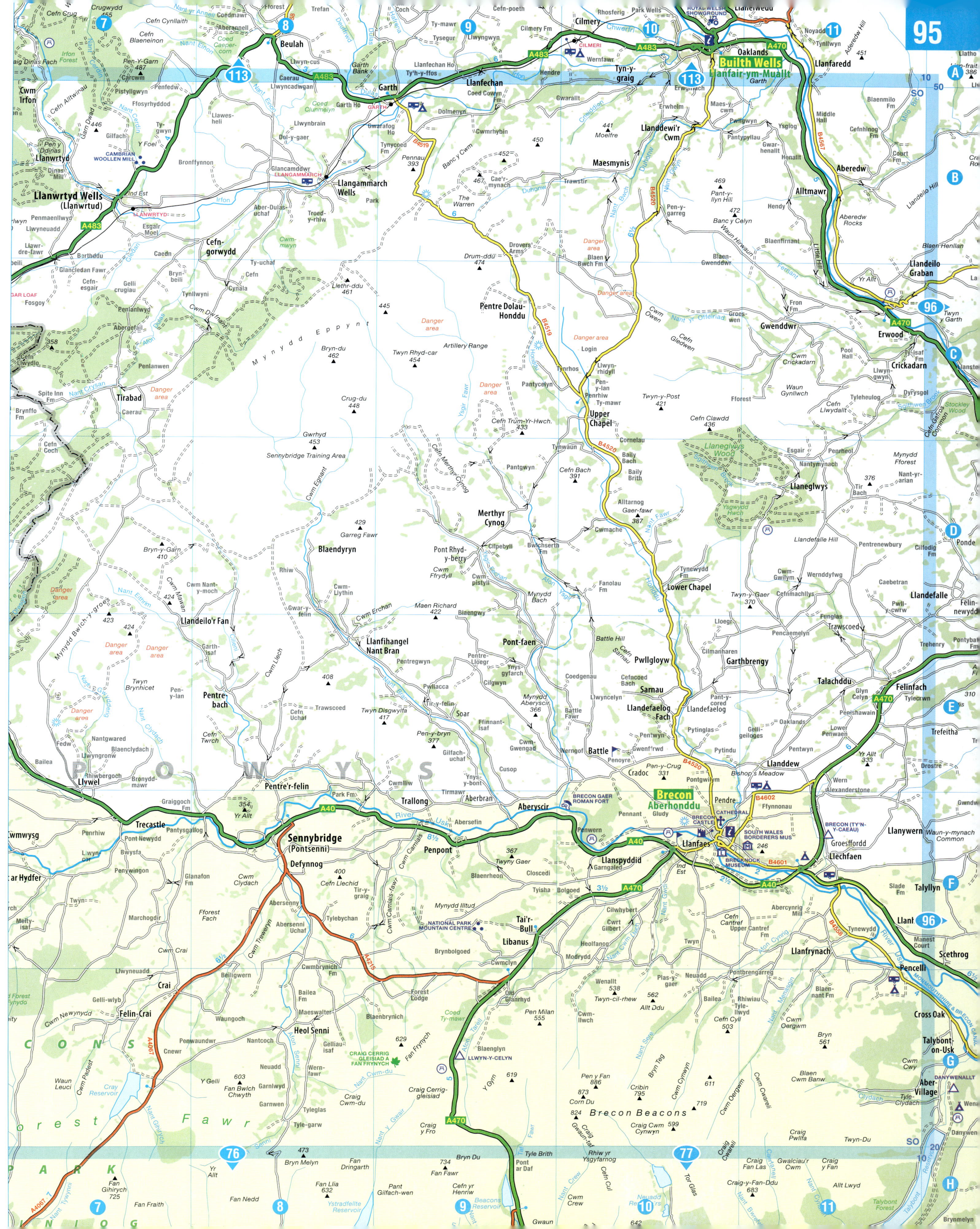
Builth Wells
Llanfair-ym-Muallt
Llanwrtyd Wells
(Llanwrtud)
Beulah
Garth
Llanfechan
Cilmery
Llangammarch Wells
Maesmynis
Llanddewi'r Cwm
Aberedw
Alltmawr
Llanfaredd
Oaklands
Erwood
Crickadarn
Gwenddwr
Llandeilo Graban
Pentre Dolau-Honddu
Upper Chapel
Lower Chapel
Merthyr Cynog
Blaendyryn
Llandeilo'r Fan
Llanfihangel Nant Bran
Pont-faen
Pwllgloyw
Sarnau
Garthbrengy
Llandefaelog Fach
Llaneglwys
Talachddu
Felinfach
Llanddew
Llandefalle
Battle
Brecon
Aberhonddu
Llanfaes
Llanspyddid
Aberyscir
Trallong
Penpont
Sennybridge
(Pontsenni)
Defynnog
Trecastle
Llywel
Pentre'r-felin
Pentre-bach
Tirabad
Cefn-gorwydd
Libanus
Tai'r-Bull
Heol Senni
Felin-Crai
Crai
Llanfrynach
Pencelli
Scethrog
Talybont-on-Usk
Llechfaen
Talyllyn
Llanywern
Cross Oak
Aber-Village
Mynydd Eppynt
Sennybridge Training Area
Artillery Range
Danger area
Brecon Beacons
Fforest Fawr
POWYS
A40
A470
A483
A4067
A4215
B4519
B4520
B4567
B4602
B4601
B4558
River Usk
Irfon
CAMBRIAN WOOLLEN MILL
BRECON GAER ROMAN FORT
BRECKNOCK MUSEUM
SOUTH WALES BORDERERS MUS
CATHEDRAL
BRECON CASTLE
NATIONAL PARK MOUNTAIN CENTRE
CRAIG CERRIG GLEISIAD A FAN FRYNYCH
LLWYN-Y-CELYN
Cray Reservoir
Beacons Reservoir
Fan Frynych
Fan Gihirych
Fan Nedd
Fan Llia
Pen Milan
113
76
77
96

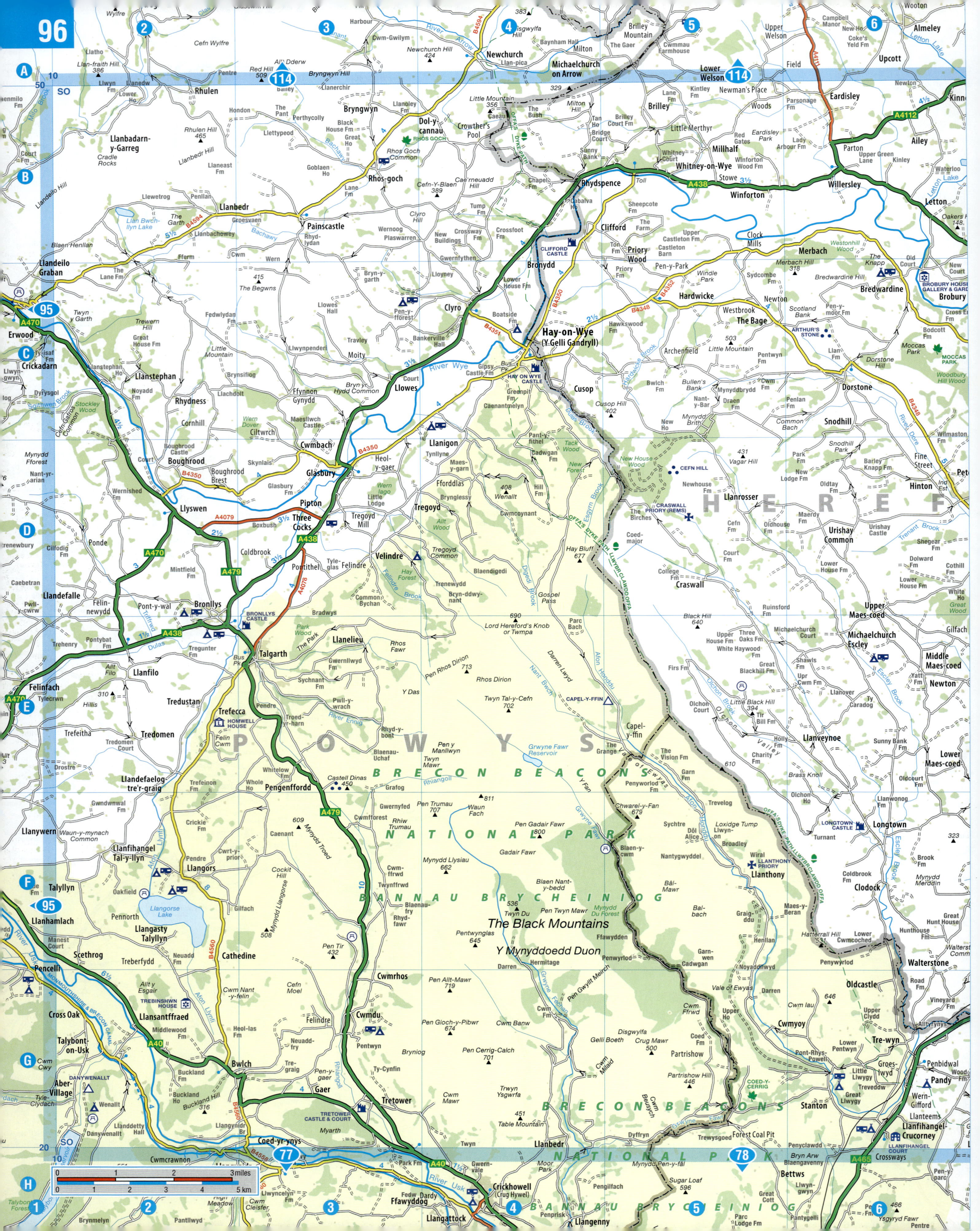

Hay-on-Wye (Y Gelli Gandryll)
Talgarth
Bronllys
Glasbury
Clyro
Three Cocks
Llyswen
Boughrood
Painscastle
Rhos-goch
Newchurch
Michaelchurch on Arrow
Rhydspence
Whitney-on-Wye
Winforton
Willersley
Eardisley
Clifford
Bredwardine
Dorstone
Cusop
Llanigon
Velindre
Felindre
Craswall
Longtown
Llanthony
Llanveynoe
Walterstone
Oldcastle
Pandy
Llanfihangel Crucorney
Crickhowell (Crug Hywel)
Llangattock
Tretower
Bwlch
Cwmdu
Llangors
Llangorse Lake
Llanfihangel Tal-y-llyn
Talyllyn
Pennorth
Cathedine
Scethrog
Pencelli
Talybont-on-Usk
Aber-Village
Llanhamlach
Trefecca
Pengenffordd
Llanelieu
Llanfilo
Tredustan
Tredomen
Llandefaelog tre'r-graig
Llanywern
Llandefalle
Llanstephan
Erwood
Crickadarn
Llandeilo Graban
Llanbedr
Rhulen
Llanbadarn-y-Garreg
Bryngwyn
Llowes
Bronydd
Hardwicke
Merbach
Brobury
Snodhill
Michaelchurch Escley
Longtown
Clodock
Llanbedr
Bettws
Stanton
Cwmyoy
Tre-wyn
Hay Bluff 677
Lord Hereford's Knob or Twmpa 690
Gospel Pass
Capel-y-ffin
Waun Fach 811
Pen y Gadair Fawr 800
Pen Allt-Mawr 719
Pen Cerrig-Calch 701
Table Mountain 451
Sugar Loaf 596
Mynydd Troed 609
The Black Mountains
Y Mynyddoedd Duon
P O W Y S
H E R E F
BRECON BEACONS
NATIONAL PARK
BANNAU BRYCHEINIOG
River Wye
River Usk
Offa's Dyke Path
A438
A470
A479
A4078
A4079
A40
A465
B4350
B4351
B4352
B4348
B4594
B4560
B4558
A4111
A4112
95
114
77
78
0 1 2 3 miles
0 1 2 3 4 5 km

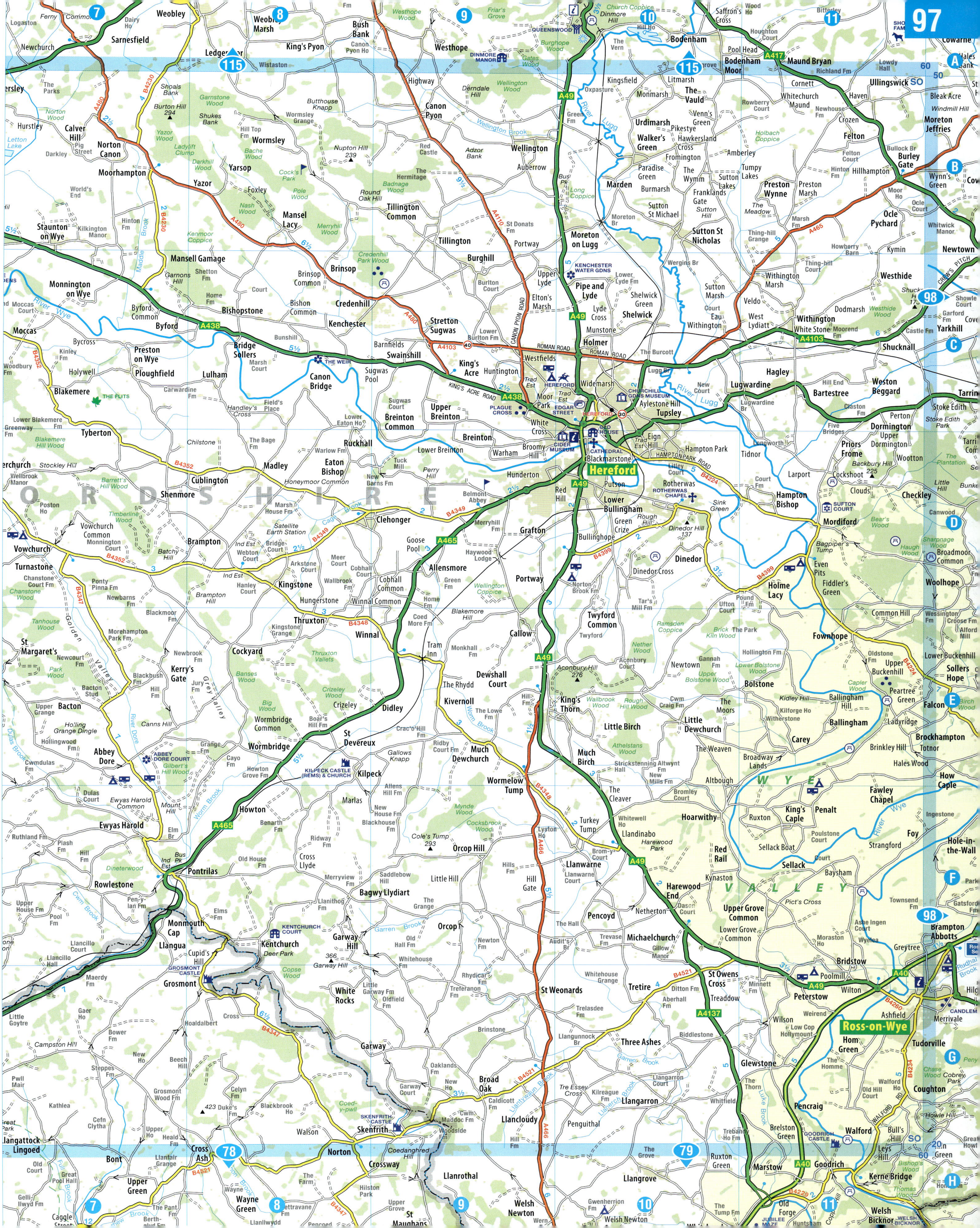
Hereford
Ross-on-Wye
Weobley
Sarnesfield
King's Pyon
Canon Pyon
Westhope
Wellington
Bodenham
Maund Bryan
Ullingswick
Moreton Jeffries
Felton
Burley Gate
Marden
Sutton St Nicholas
Moreton on Lugg
Tillington
Burghill
Brinsop
Credenhill
Mansel Lacy
Yazor
Moorhampton
Norton Canon
Staunton on Wye
Monnington on Wye
Mansell Gamage
Bishopstone
Byford
Moccas
Preston on Wye
Bridge Sollers
Kenchester
Stretton Sugwas
Swainshill
King's Acre
Holmer
Shelwick
Pipe and Lyde
Withington
Shucknall
Lugwardine
Bartestree
Tupsley
Hampton Park
Hagley
Weston Beggard
Dormington
Mordiford
Hampton Bishop
Checkley
Lower Bullingham
Rotherwas
Dinedor
Holme Lacy
Fownhope
Woolhope
Breinton
Upper Breinton
Canon Bridge
Blakemere
Tyberton
Madley
Cublington
Shenmore
Eaton Bishop
Ruckhall
Clehonger
Kingstone
Thruxton
Allensmore
Grafton
Callow
Twyford Common
Kerry's Gate
Cockyard
Vowchurch
Turnastone
St Margaret's
Bacton
Abbey Dore
Wormbridge
Kilpeck
Didley
St Devereux
Kivernoll
Much Dewchurch
Wormelow Tump
Much Birch
King's Thorn
Little Birch
Little Dewchurch
Carey
Ballingham
Bolstone
Brockhampton
How Caple
Fawley Chapel
King's Caple
Penalt
Sellack
Hoarwithy
Harewood End
Pencoyd
Michaelchurch
Tretire
St Owens Cross
Peterstow
Bridstow
Wilton
Ewyas Harold
Pontrilas
Rowlestone
Howton
Orcop Hill
Bagwy Llydiart
Orcop
Garway Hill
Kentchurch
Grosmont
Monmouth Cap
Llangua
White Rocks
Garway
Broad Oak
Skenfrith
Llancloudy
Llangarron
St Weonards
Three Ashes
Glewstone
Goodrich
Walford
Kerne Bridge
Pencraig
Marstow
Welsh Bicknor
Welsh Newton
Llangrove
Llanrothal
Crossway
Norton
Cross Ash
Upper Green
Bont
Lingoed
Llangattock Lingoed
Wye Valley
Golden Valley
A49
A438
A465
A4103
A417
A4137
A466
A40
B4349
B4352
B4348
B4399
B4224
B4347
B4521
B4230
B4234
B4230
115
98
78
79
7
8
9
10
11

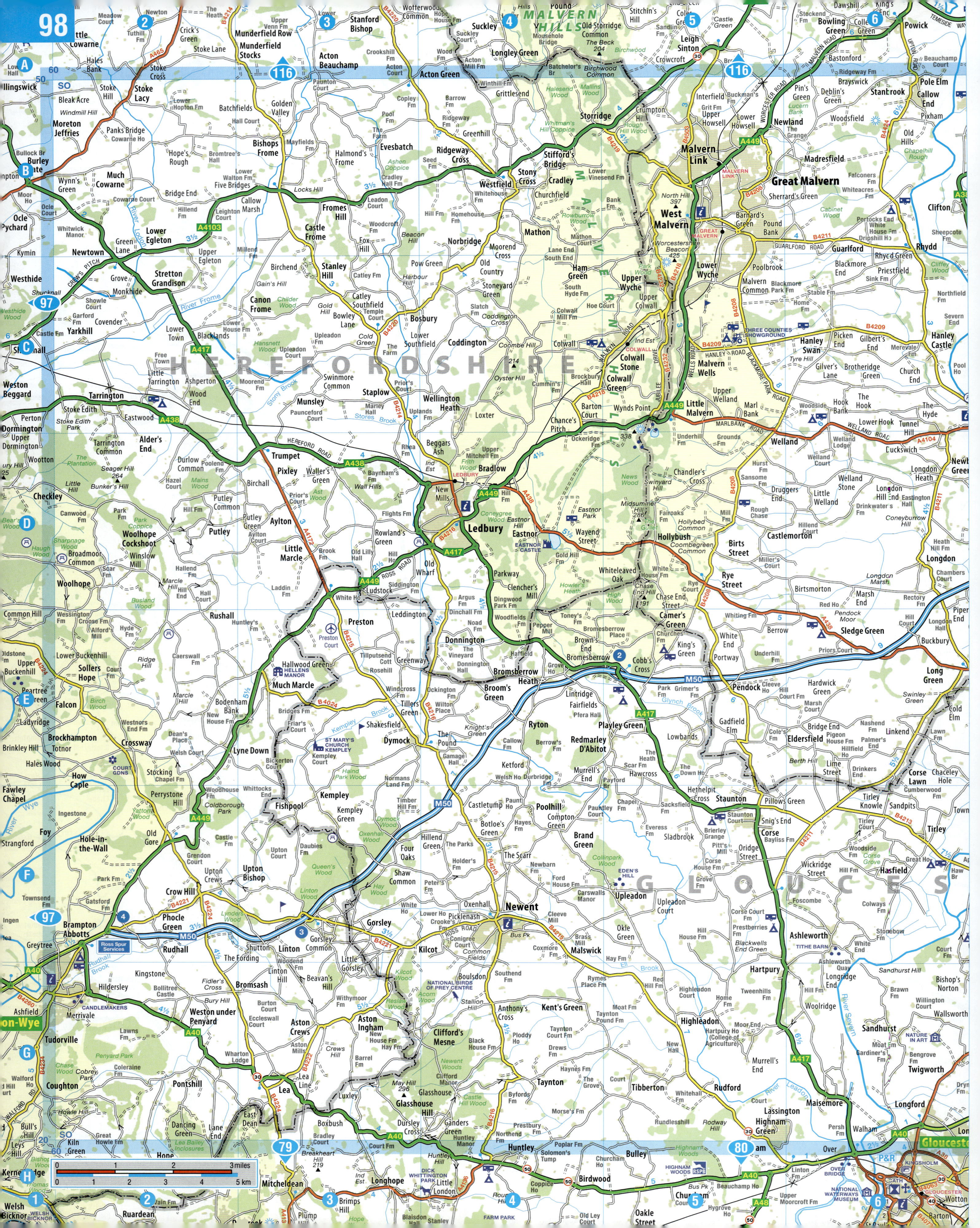
HEREFORDSHIRE
GLOUCES
MALVERN HILLS
Great Malvern
Malvern Link
West Malvern
Malvern Wells
Little Malvern
Ledbury
Newent
Welland
Upton Bishop
Much Marcle
Bromyard
Stoke Lacy
Bishops Frome
Castle Frome
Cradley
Colwall
Tarrington
Trumpet
Dymock
Kempley
Ross Spur Services
Weston under Penyard
Huntley
Highleadon
Hartpury
Maisemore
Gloucester
Staunton
Corse
Ashleworth
Sandhurst
Mitcheldean
Longhope
Birdwood
Tibberton
Rudford
Taynton
Bromsberrow Heath
Redmarley D'Abitot
Eastnor
Hollybush
Castlemorton
Birtsmorton
Pendock
Eldersfield
Upleadon
Kilcot
Gorsley
Linton
Fownhope
Woolhope
Putley
Aylton
Pixley
Much Cowarne
Acton Beauchamp
Suckley
Storridge
Mathon
Coddington
Wellington Heath
Bosbury
Munsley
Staplow
Stretton Grandison
Lower Eglelton
Yarkhill
Weston Beggard
Dormington
Mordiford
Checkley
Brockhampton
How Caple
Hole-in-the-Wall
Brampton Abbotts
Rudhall
Bromsash
Aston Ingham
Clifford's Mesne
Lea
Coughton
Pontshill
M50
A449
A417
A438
A4103
A40
A48
A4172
B4215
B4216
B4221
B4224
B4208
B4211
B4209
B4218
B4219
B4220
B4214
B4232
B4213
B4211
0 1 2 3 miles
0 1 2 3 4 5 km

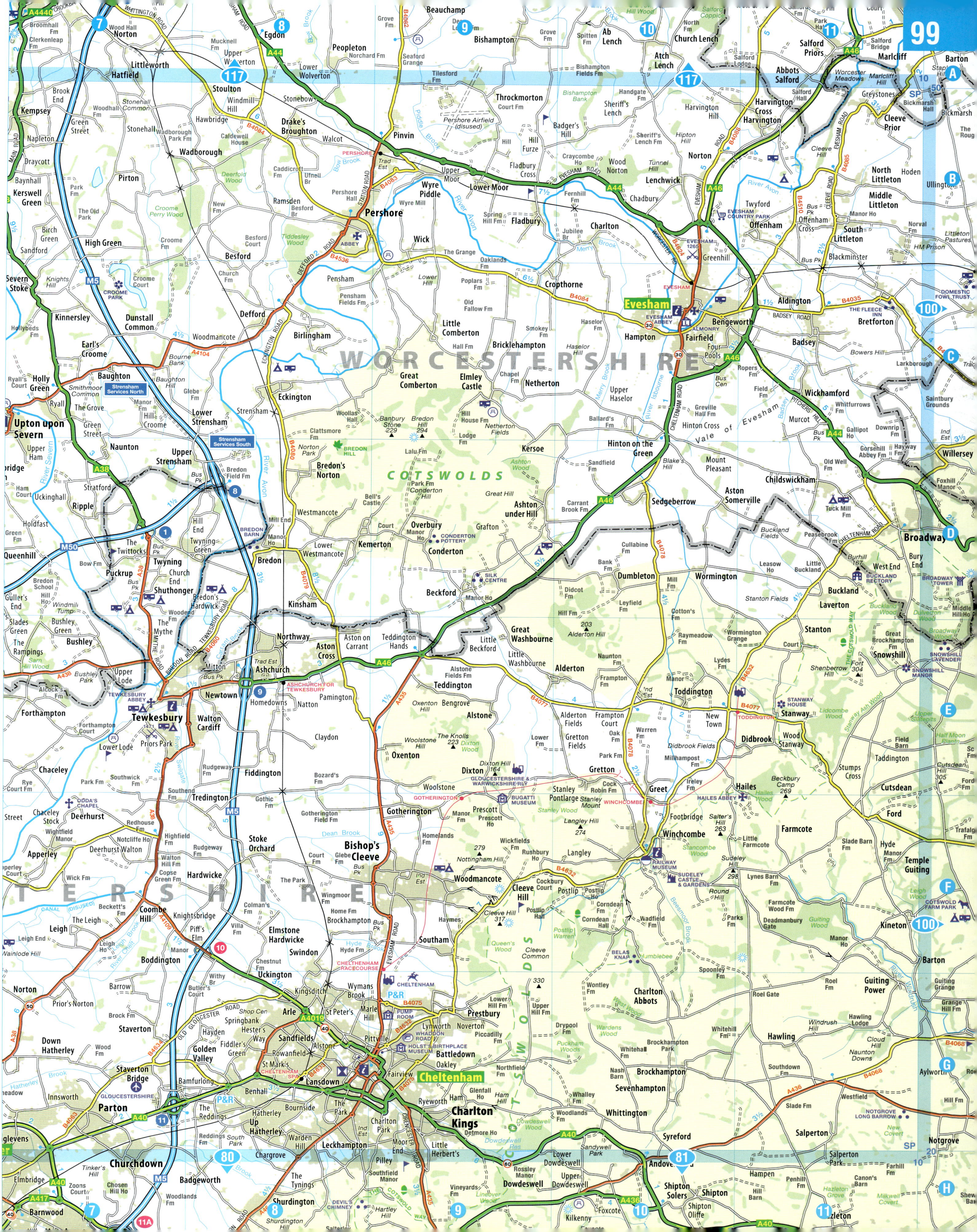
WORCESTERSHIRE
COTSWOLDS
Vale of Evesham
Evesham
Pershore
Tewkesbury
Cheltenham
Bishop's Cleeve
Winchcombe
Broadway
Charlton Kings
Upton upon Severn
Kempsey
Norton
Littleworth
Hatfield
Stoulton
Wadborough
Pirton
Drake's Broughton
Pinvin
Wyre Piddle
Fladbury
Cropthorne
Peopleton
Bishampton
Throckmorton
Ab Lench
Church Lench
Atch Lench
Harvington
Abbots Salford
Salford Priors
Marlcliff
Cleeve Prior
North Littleton
Middle Littleton
South Littleton
Offenham
Bretforton
Badsey
Aldington
Bengeworth
Hampton
Wickhamford
Childswickham
Willersey
Charlton
Lenchwick
Chadbury
Besford
Defford
Birlingham
Eckington
Great Comberton
Little Comberton
Elmley Castle
Bricklehampton
Netherton
Kersoe
Ashton under Hill
Sedgeberrow
Hinton on the Green
Aston Somerville
Bredon's Norton
Bredon
Kemerton
Overbury
Conderton
Beckford
Kinsham
Northway
Ashchurch
Aston Cross
Teddington
Alderton
Great Washbourne
Little Washbourne
Dumbleton
Wormington
Buckland
Laverton
Stanton
Snowshill
Stanway
Toddington
Didbrook
Hailes
Greet
Gretton
Dixton
Alstone
Oxenton
Woolstone
Gotherington
Stoke Orchard
Tredington
Walton Cardiff
Deerhurst
Apperley
Coombe Hill
Boddington
Uckington
Elmstone Hardwicke
Swindon
Prestbury
Southam
Cleeve Hill
Charlton Abbots
Sudeley Castle
Guiting Power
Kineton
Temple Guiting
Ford
Cutsdean
Hawling
Brockhampton
Sevenhampton
Whittington
Syreford
Andoversford
Shipton
Dowdeswell
Churchdown
Parton
Staverton
Down Hatherley
Leckhampton
Shurdington
Badgeworth
Kinnersley
Severn Stoke
Ripple
Twyning
Shuthonger
Bushley
Forthampton
Chaceley
Leigh
Norton
Hasfield
M5
M50
A44
A46
A435
A438
A40
A4019
B4084
B4035
B4632
B4077
B4078
B4080
B4079
B4104
A4104

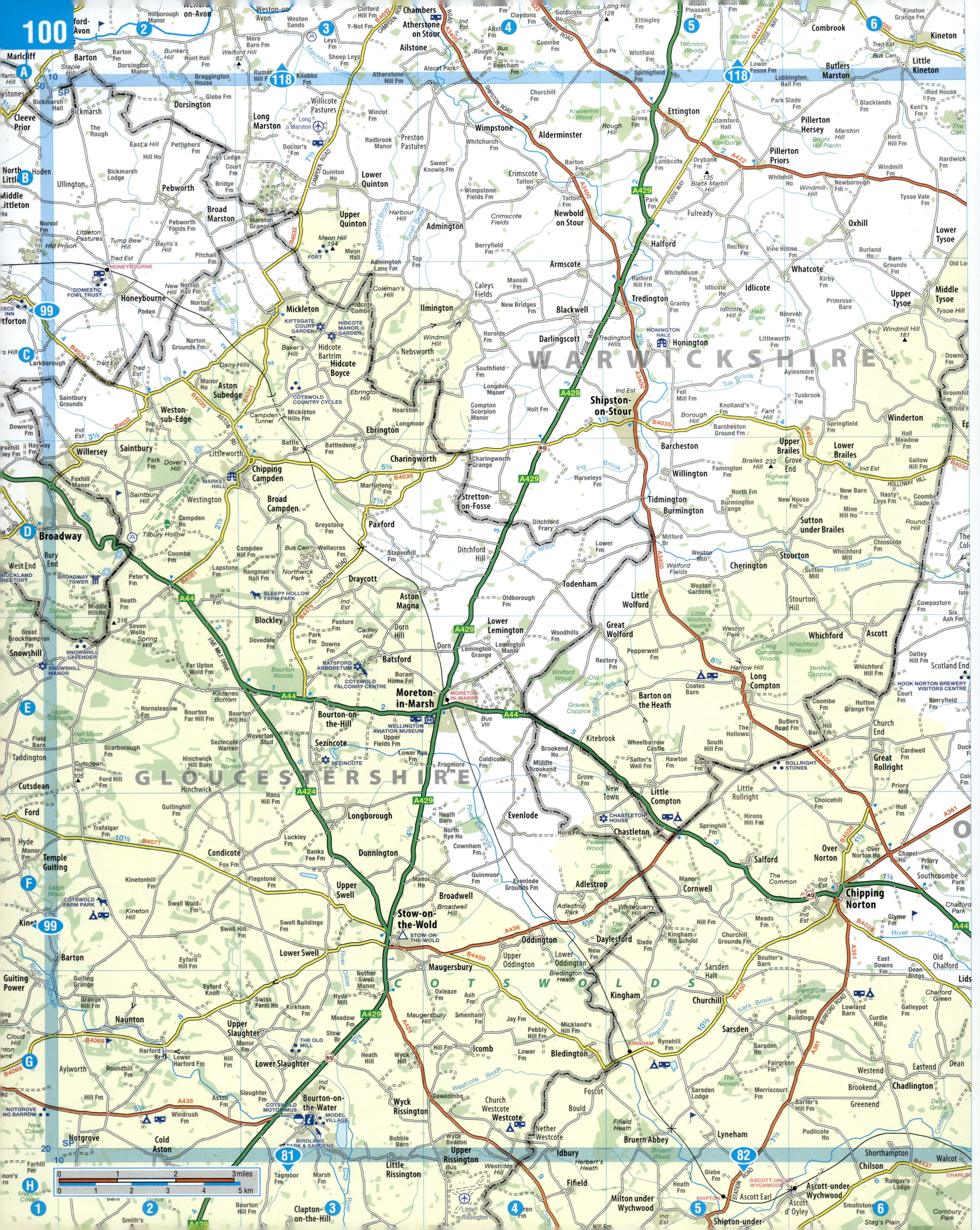
WARWICKSHIRE
GLOUCESTERSHIRE
COTSWOLDS
Marlcliff
Barton
Cleeve Prior
Bickmarsh
Dorsington
Long Marston
Pebworth
Ullington
Broad Marston
Honeybourne
Mickleton
Hidcote Bartrim
Hidcote Boyce
Ilmington
Admington
Upper Quinton
Lower Quinton
Wimpstone
Alderminster
Ettington
Atherstone on Stour
Ailstone
Preston Pastures
Newbold on Stour
Armscote
Blackwell
Darlingscott
Tredington
Halford
Idlicote
Whatcote
Pillerton Hersey
Pillerton Priors
Butlers Marston
Combrook
Kineton
Little Kineton
Oxhill
Lower Tysoe
Middle Tysoe
Upper Tysoe
Honington
Shipston-on-Stour
Barcheston
Willington
Tidmington
Burmington
Cherington
Stourton
Sutton under Brailes
Upper Brailes
Lower Brailes
Winderton
Weston-sub-Edge
Aston Subedge
Saintbury
Willersey
Chipping Campden
Broad Campden
Ebrington
Charingworth
Paxford
Stretton-on-Fosse
Broadway
Snowshill
Blockley
Draycott
Aston Magna
Batsford
Moreton-in-Marsh
Bourton-on-the-Hill
Sezincote
Todenham
Little Wolford
Great Wolford
Lower Lemington
Barton on the Heath
Long Compton
Whichford
Ascott
Little Rollright
Great Rollright
Kitebrook
Little Compton
Chastleton
Evenlode
Longborough
Donnington
Condicote
Upper Swell
Broadwell
Stow-on-the-Wold
Lower Swell
Maugersbury
Adlestrop
Oddington
Daylesford
Salford
Over Norton
Chipping Norton
Cornwell
Kingham
Churchill
Sarsden
Icomb
Bledington
Foscot
Bould
Wyck Rissington
Church Westcote
Nether Westcote
Bruern Abbey
Lyneham
Idbury
Fifield
Milton under Wychwood
Upper Rissington
Little Rissington
Bourton-on-the-Water
Upper Slaughter
Lower Slaughter
Naunton
Temple Guiting
Guiting Power
Cutsdean
Taddington
Ford
Barton
Aylworth
Notgrove
Cold Aston
Clapton-on-the-Hill
Chadlington
Shorthampton
Chilson
Ascott-under-Wychwood
Shipton-under-
Ascott Earl
Ascott d'Oyley
Walcot
Westend
Eastend
Dean
A44
A429
A424
A436
A3400
A422
A361
B4035
B4632
B4081
B4450
B4068
B4077
B4026
B4437
118
99
81
82
0 1 2 3 miles
0 1 2 3 4 5 km

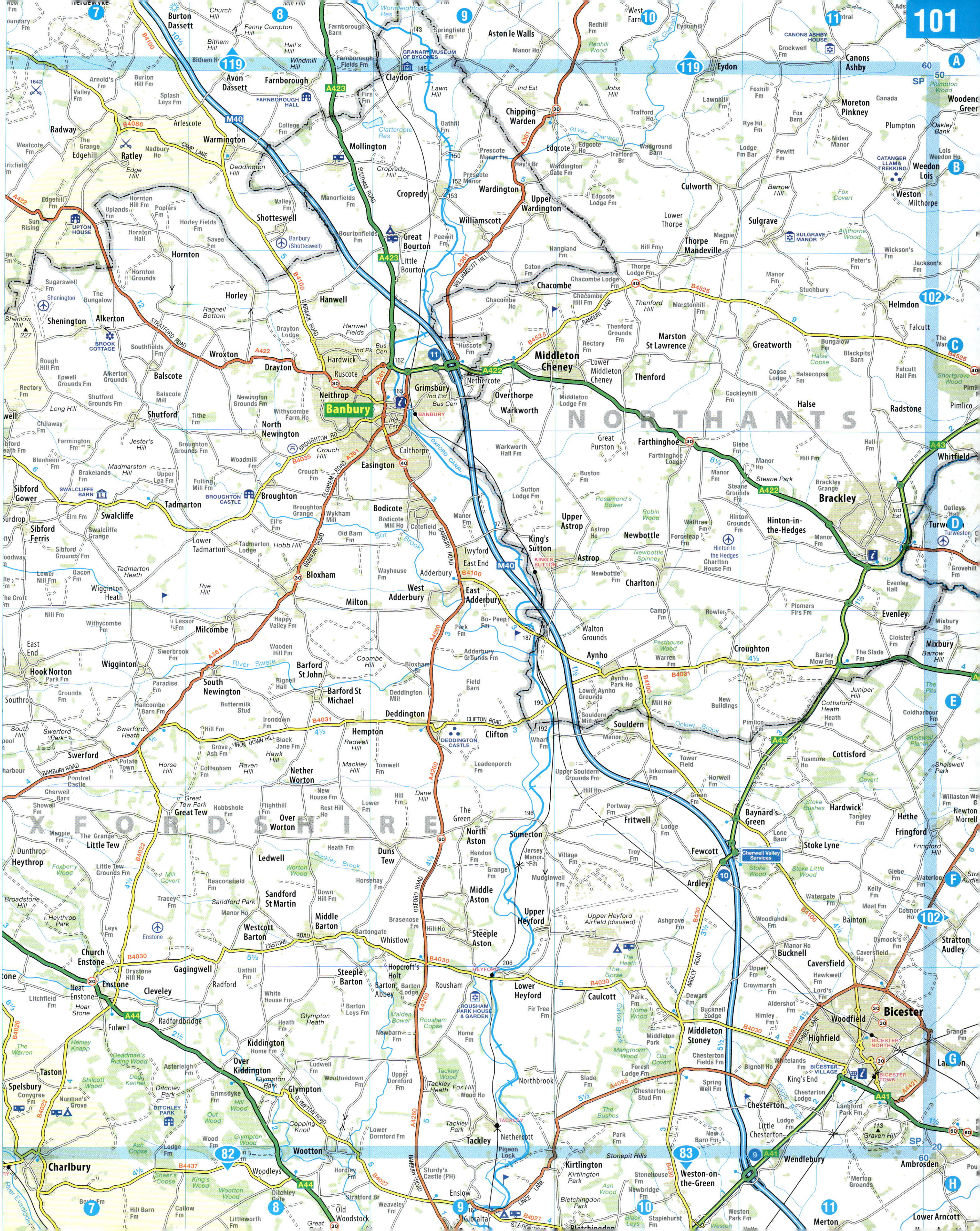
NORTHANTS
OXFORDSHIRE
Banbury
Burton Dassett
Avon Dassett
Farnborough
Claydon
Aston le Walls
Eydon
Canons Ashby
Moreton Pinkney
Radway
Ratley
Warmington
Mollington
Cropredy
Wardington
Chipping Warden
Edgcote
Culworth
Sulgrave
Weedon Lois
Weston
Shotteswell
Great Bourton
Little Bourton
Williamscott
Upper Wardington
Thorpe Mandeville
Hornton
Horley
Hanwell
Chacombe
Helmdon
Shenington
Alkerton
Wroxton
Drayton
Hardwick
Ruscote
Neithrop
Grimsbury
Nethercote
Middleton Cheney
Marston St Lawrence
Greatworth
Thenford
Balscote
Shutford
North Newington
Overthorpe
Warkworth
Farthinghoe
Halse
Radstone
Brackley
Whitfield
Turweston
Sibford Gower
Sibford Ferris
Swalcliffe
Tadmarton
Lower Tadmarton
Broughton
Easington
Calthorpe
Bodicote
Twyford
King's Sutton
Upper Astrop
Astrop
Newbottle
Charlton
Hinton-in-the-Hedges
Bloxham
Milton
Adderbury
West Adderbury
East Adderbury
Evenley
Milcombe
Wigginton
Hook Norton
South Newington
Barford St John
Barford St Michael
Aynho
Croughton
Mixbury
Deddington
Hempton
Clifton
Souldern
Swerford
Nether Worton
Over Worton
Great Tew
Little Tew
Cottisford
Hardwick
Hethe
Fringford
Fritwell
Fewcott
Ardley
Baynard's Green
Stoke Lyne
North Aston
Somerton
Duns Tew
Ledwell
Sandford St Martin
Middle Aston
Upper Heyford
Westcott Barton
Middle Barton
Steeple Aston
Church Enstone
Enstone
Neat Enstone
Cleveley
Gagingwell
Radford
Steeple Barton
Rousham
Lower Heyford
Caulcott
Middleton Stoney
Bucknell
Caversfield
Bicester
Woodfield
Highfield
Fulwell
Radfordbridge
Kiddington
Over Kiddington
Glympton
Taston
Spelsbury
Charlbury
Wootton
Woodleys
Tackley
Nethercott
Northbrook
Kirtlington
Chesterton
Little Chesterton
Weston-on-the-Green
Wendlebury
Ambrosden
Enslow
Gibraltar
Bletchingdon
Hopcroft's Holt
Whistlow
Dunthrop
Heythrop
Cherwell Valley Services
Stratton Audley
Lower Arncott
M40
A423
A422
A361
A4260
A43
A44
A41
A4095
B4100
B4035
B4031
B4030
B4525
B4027
119
102
82
83
A
B
C
D
E
F
G
H

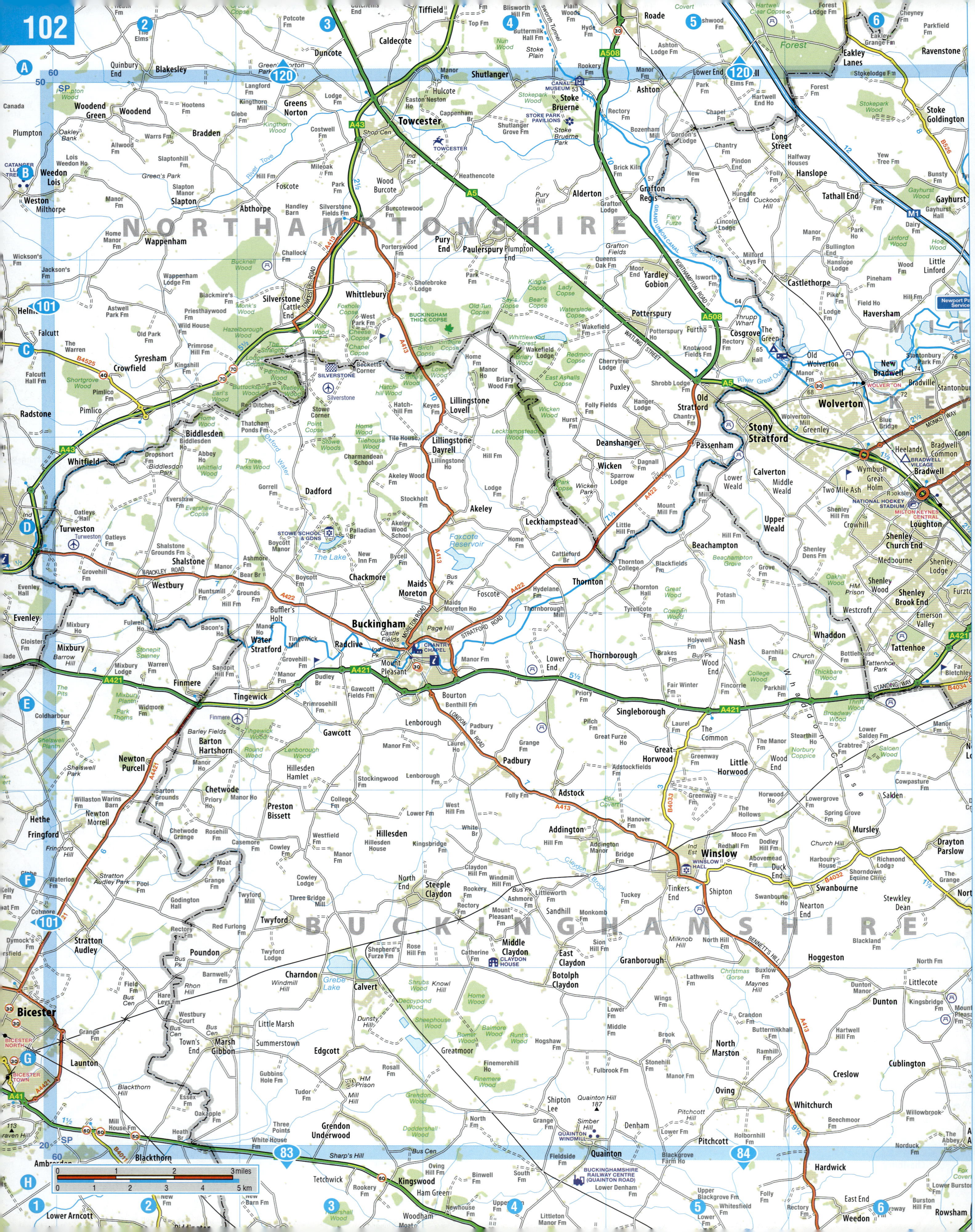
NORTHAMPTONSHIRE
BUCKINGHAMSHIRE
Towcester
Buckingham
Winslow
Bicester
Stony Stratford
Wolverton
Blakesley
Duncote
Caldecote
Tiffield
Shutlanger
Stoke Bruerne
Roade
Ashton
Hulcote
Greens Norton
Woodend
Bradden
Weedon Lois
Weston
Slapton
Abthorpe
Wappenham
Silverstone
Whittlebury
Syresham
Crowfield
Radstone
Biddlesden
Whitfield
Turweston
Evenley
Mixbury
Westbury
Shalstone
Dadford
Chackmore
Maids Moreton
Foscote
Akeley
Leckhampstead
Lillingstone Lovell
Lillingstone Dayrell
Pury End
Paulerspury
Alderton
Grafton Regis
Yardley Gobion
Potterspury
Cosgrove
Deanshanger
Wicken
Passenham
Old Stratford
Puxley
Castlethorpe
Hanslope
Long Street
Haversham
Calverton
Upper Weald
Beachampton
Thornton
Nash
Thornborough
Whaddon
Water Stratford
Radclive
Tingewick
Finmere
Gawcott
Lenborough
Padbury
Adstock
Addington
Singleborough
Great Horwood
Little Horwood
Mursley
Swanbourne
Granborough
Hillesden
Preston Bissett
Chetwode
Barton Hartshorn
Newton Purcell
Hethe
Fringford
Stratton Audley
Poundon
Twyford
Charndon
Calvert
Steeple Claydon
Middle Claydon
East Claydon
Botolph Claydon
Marsh Gibbon
Edgcott
Launton
Grendon Underwood
Quainton
Oving
Pitchcott
North Marston
Whitchurch
Creslow
Cublington
Dunton
Hoggeston
Hardwick
Kingswood
Blackthorn
Weedon
Rowsham
Newport Pagnell Services
A5
A43
A413
A422
A421
A508
A4421
A41
B4525
B4033
B4032
M1
0 1 2 3 miles
0 1 2 3 4 5 km

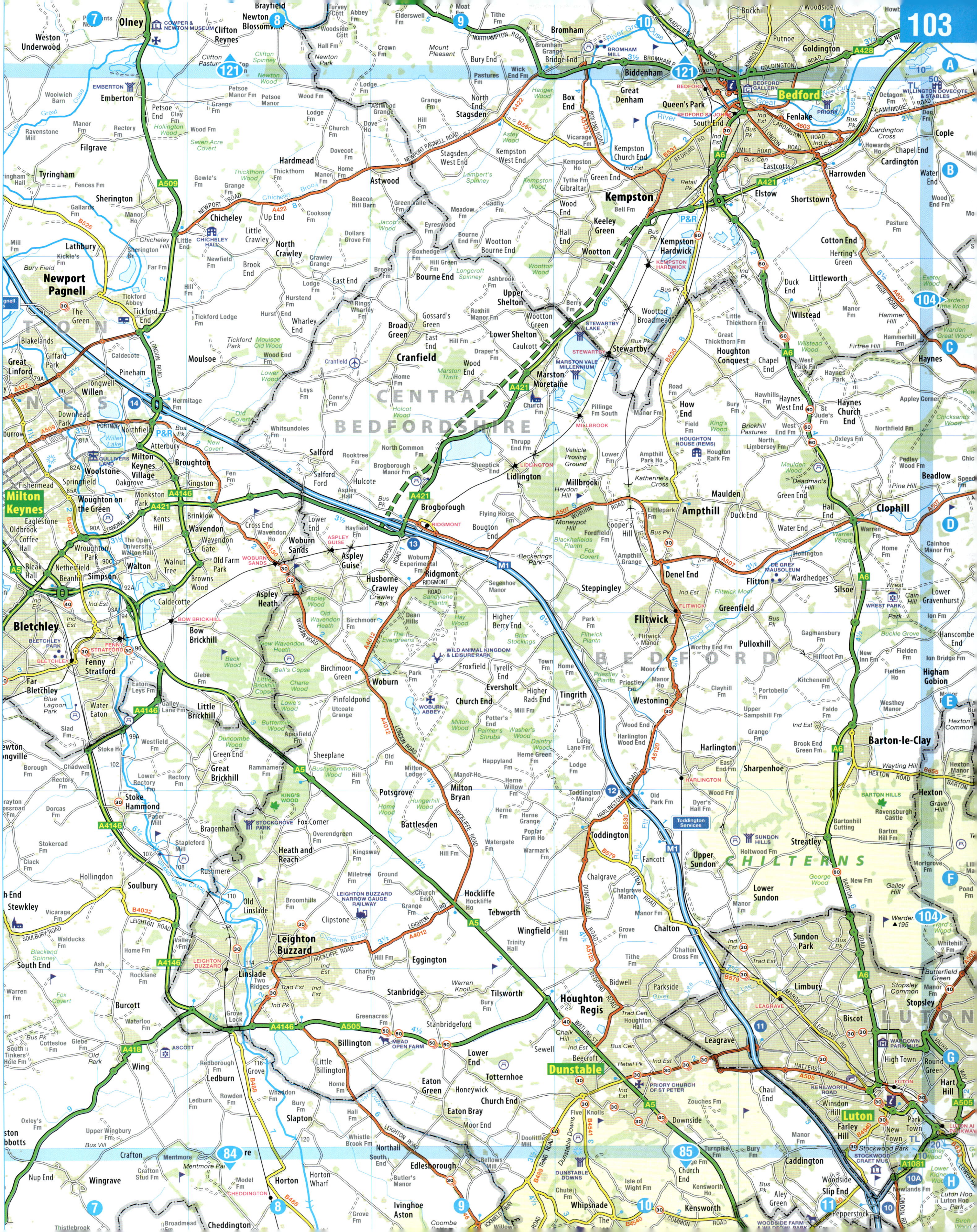
Olney
Bedford
Kempston
Cranfield
CENTRAL BEDFORDSHIRE
BEDFORD
Milton Keynes
Bletchley
Newport Pagnell
Woburn
Woburn Sands
Ampthill
Flitwick
Clophill
Barton-le-Clay
Toddington
Leighton Buzzard
Houghton Regis
Dunstable
Luton
CHILTERNS
Wing
Cheddington
Ivinghoe Aston
Whipsnade
Caddington
Stewartby
Marston Moretaine
Lidlington
Shefford
Haynes
Cardington
Elstow
Wilstead
Silsoe
Harlington
Streatley
Sundon Park
Leagrave
Stopsley
Eaton Bray
Totternhoe
Stanbridge
Tilsworth
Hockliffe
Heath and Reach
Soulbury
Linslade
Great Brickhill
Little Brickhill
Bow Brickhill
Aspley Guise
Aspley Heath
Ridgmont
Brogborough
Husborne Crawley
Sherington
Chicheley
North Crawley
Astwood
Hardmead
Emberton
Filgrave
Tyringham
Clifton Reynes
Bromham
Biddenham
Great Denham
Stagsden
M1
A5
A6
A421
A507
A4146
A509
A422
A428
A505

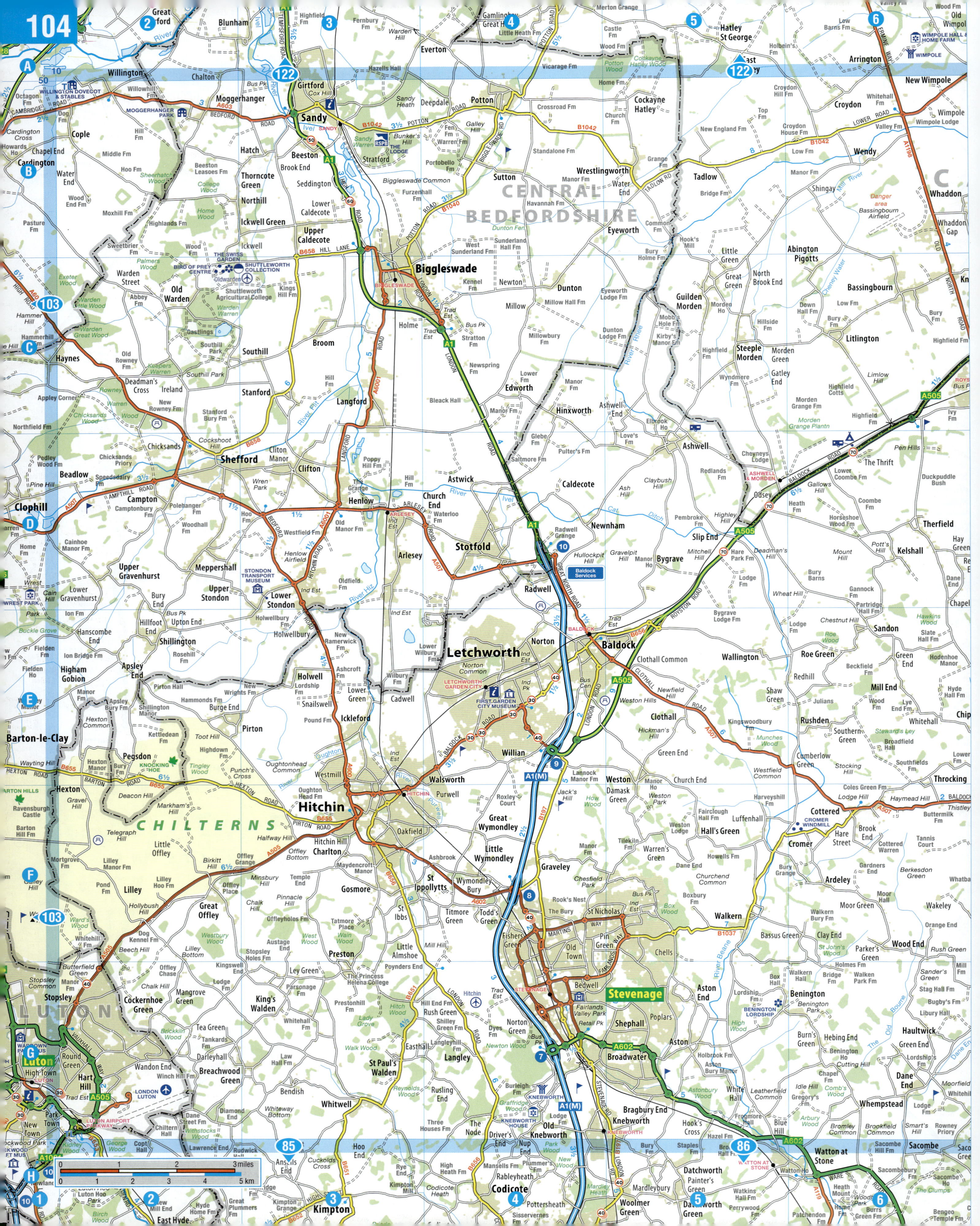

CENTRAL BEDFORDSHIRE
CHILTERNS
LUTON
Sandy
Biggleswade
Potton
Letchworth
Hitchin
Baldock
Stevenage
Shefford
Luton
Ashwell
Royston Road
Girtford
Blunham
Willington
Moggerhanger
Cople
Cardington
Haynes
Old Warden
Southill
Broom
Stanford
Langford
Henlow
Clifton
Arlesey
Stotfold
Radwell
Norton
Astwick
Edworth
Hinxworth
Caldecote
Newnham
Bygrave
Dunton
Eyeworth
Wrestlingworth
Cockayne Hatley
Tadlow
Sutton
Everton
Gamlingay
Hatley St George
East Hatley
Arrington
Croydon
Wendy
Shingay
Whaddon
Abington Pigotts
Bassingbourn
Litlington
Steeple Morden
Guilden Morden
Kelshall
Therfield
Sandon
Wallington
Rushden
Clothall
Weston
Graveley
Great Wymondley
Little Wymondley
Willian
Walsworth
Purwell
Ickleford
Pirton
Holwell
Pegsdon
Hexton
Barton-le-Clay
Lilley
Great Offley
Little Offley
Charlton
St Ippollytts
Gosmore
Preston
King's Walden
St Paul's Walden
Langley
Knebworth
Codicote
Kimpton
Whitwell
Breachwood Green
Shephall
Broadwater
Aston
Walkern
Benington
Cromer
Cottered
Ardeley
Watton at Stone
Sacombe
Woolmer Green
Datchworth
Clophill
Campton
Chicksands
Meppershall
Upper Stondon
Lower Stondon
Shillington
Upper Gravenhurst
Lower Gravenhurst
Higham Gobion
Apsley End
Ireland
Northill
Ickwell Green
Thorncote Green
Beeston
Hatch
Upper Caldecote
Lower Caldecote
Stratford
A1
A1(M)
A505
A507
A600
A6001
A602
A603
A6
B1042
B658
B655
B656
B651
B1037
B197
B1040
0 1 2 3 miles
0 1 2 3 4 5 km

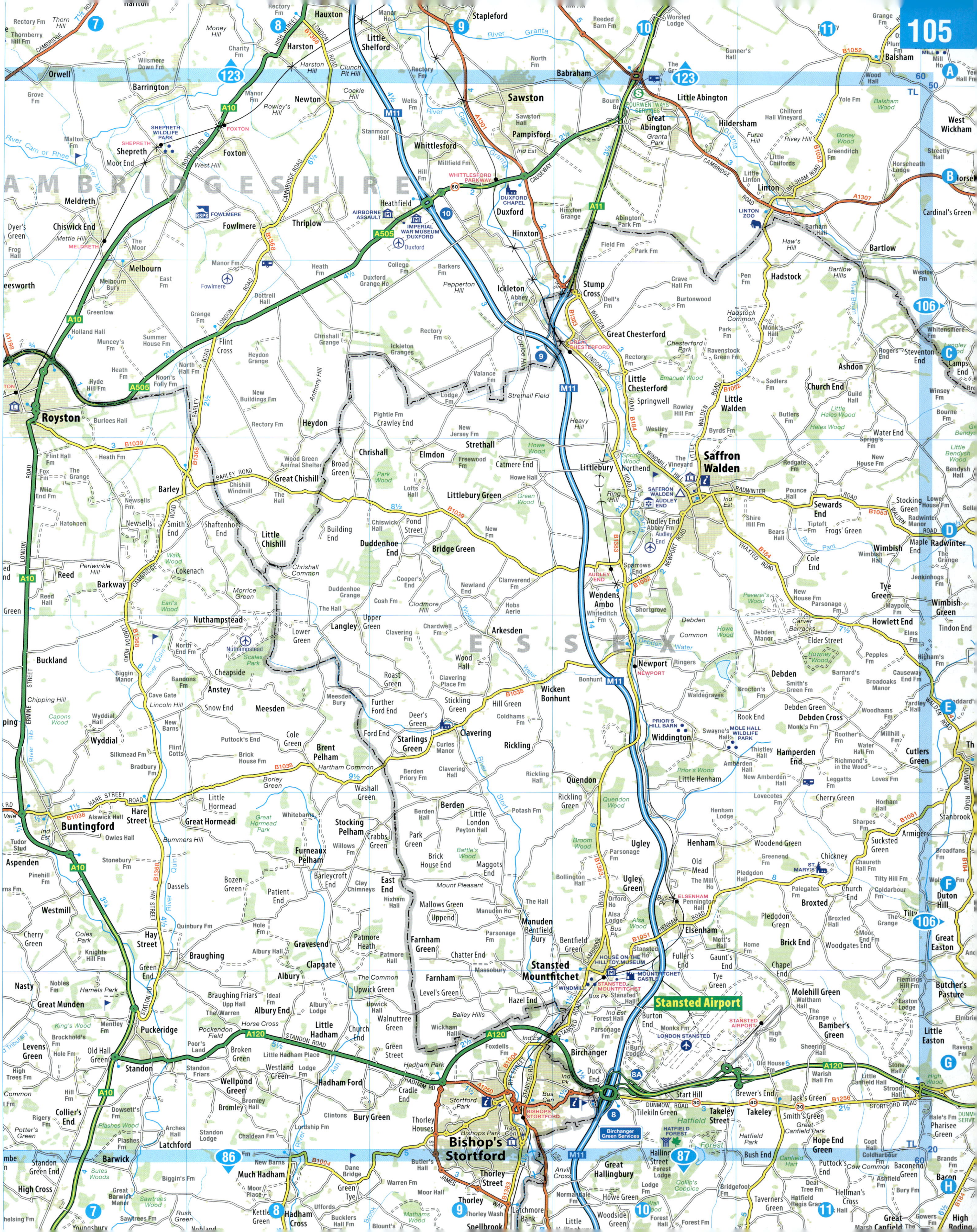

CAMBRIDGESHIRE
ESSEX
Orwell
Barrington
Harston
Little Shelford
Stapleford
Babraham
Balsham
Newton
Sawston
Little Abington
Great Abington
Hildersham
Shepreth
Foxton
Pampisford
Whittlesford
West Wickham
Meldreth
Fowlmere
Thriplow
Heathfield
Duxford
Hinxton
Linton
Chiswick End
Melbourn
Ickleton
Stump Cross
Hadstock
Bartlow
Great Chesterford
Little Chesterford
Ashdon
Royston
Heydon
Chrishall
Elmdon
Strethall
Littlebury
Saffron Walden
Little Walden
Barley
Great Chishill
Little Chishill
Littlebury Green
Duddenhoe End
Bridge Green
Audley End
Sewards End
Radwinter
Wimbish
Reed
Barkway
Nuthampstead
Langley
Wendens Ambo
Newport
Arkesden
Debden
Buckland
Anstey
Meesden
Clavering
Wicken Bonhunt
Widdington
Wyddial
Brent Pelham
Starlings Green
Rickling
Quendon
Hamperden End
Buntingford
Great Hormead
Stocking Pelham
Berden
Furneaux Pelham
Ugley
Henham
Broxted
Aspenden
Westmill
Braughing
Gravesend
Manuden
Elsenham
Stansted Mountfitchet
Stansted Airport
Great Munden
Albury
Farnham
Puckeridge
Standon
Little Hadham
Birchanger
Takeley
Hadham Ford
Bishop's Stortford
Great Hallingbury
Much Hadham
Thorley
Thorley Street
Great Easton
Little Easton
A10
A505
A11
A120
M11
A1301
B1368
B1039
B1038
B1383
B1052
B1051
B1004
B1256

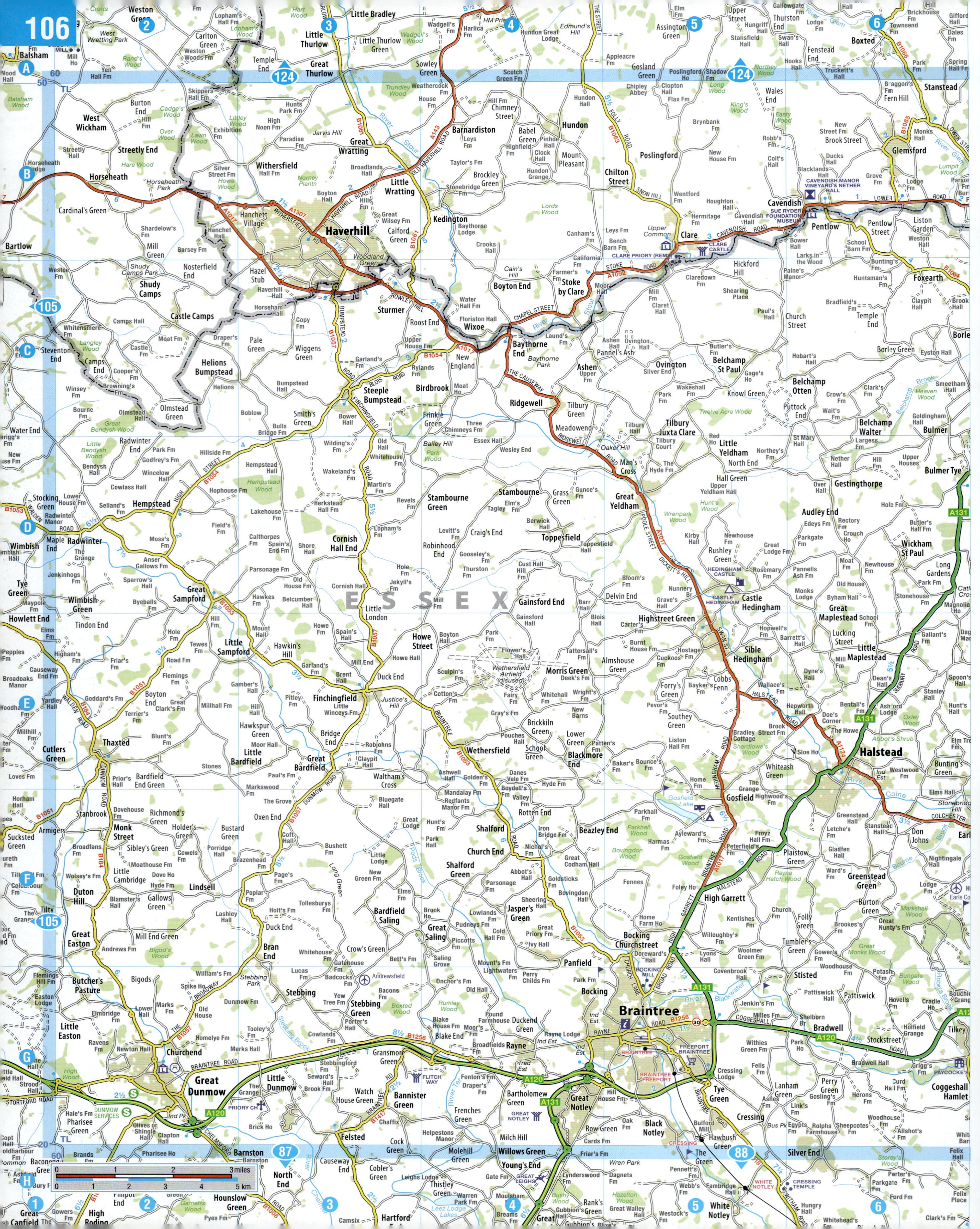
ESSEX
Balsham
Weston Green
Little Bradley
Little Thurlow
Great Thurlow
Little Thurlow Green
Sowley Green
Barnardiston
Hundon
Chilton Street
Poslingford
Clare
Cavendish
Glemsford
Boxted
Stanstead
Pentlow
Liston Garden
Foxearth
West Wickham
Streetly End
Horseheath
Withersfield
Great Wratting
Little Wratting
Kedington
Haverhill
Hanchett Village
Calford Green
Stoke by Clare
Boyton End
Mount Pleasant
Babel Green
Brockley Green
Cardinal's Green
Bartlow
Shudy Camps
Castle Camps
Sturmer
Wixoe
Water End
Baythorne End
Ashen
Ovington
Belchamp St Paul
Belchamp Otten
Borley Green
Borley
Steventon End
Helions Bumpstead
Steeple Bumpstead
Birdbrook
New England
Ridgewell
Tilbury Green
Tilbury Juxta Clare
Little Yeldham
Belchamp Walter
Bulmer
Bulmer Tye
Olmstead Green
Smith's Green
Hempstead
Radwinter
Wimbish
Wimbish Green
Stambourne Green
Stambourne
Great Yeldham
Gestingthorpe
Audley End
Toppesfield
Cornish Hall End
Great Sampford
Little Sampford
Little London
Howe Street
Gainsford End
Castle Hedingham
Sible Hedingham
Great Maplestead
Little Maplestead
Wickham St Paul
Howlett End
Tindon End
Finchingfield
Wethersfield
Morris Green
Highstreet Green
Thaxted
Cutlers Green
Little Bardfield
Great Bardfield
Bridge End
Waltham's Cross
Shalford
Church End
Shalford Green
Beazley End
Gosfield
Halstead
Monk Street
Lindsell
Duton Hill
Great Easton
Bardfield Saling
Great Saling
Jasper's Green
Panfield
Bocking Churchstreet
High Garrett
Stisted
Greenstead Green
Stebbing
Stebbing Green
Bocking
Braintree
Bradwell
Coggeshall Hamlet
Little Easton
Butcher's Pasture
Churchend
Great Dunmow
Little Dunmow
Bannister Green
Rayne
Great Notley
Black Notley
Tye Green
Cressing
Felsted
Barnston
North End
Willows Green
Young's End
Silver End
White Notley
Hartford End
High Roding
Great Canfield
Hounslow Green
124
105
87
88
A120
A131
A1017
A1307
A143
A1092
B1054
B1057
B1053
B1256
B1051
B1058
B1065
B1063
B1061
B1052
B1008
B1066
B1417
A1124
A1017
0 1 2 3 miles
0 1 2 3 4 5 km

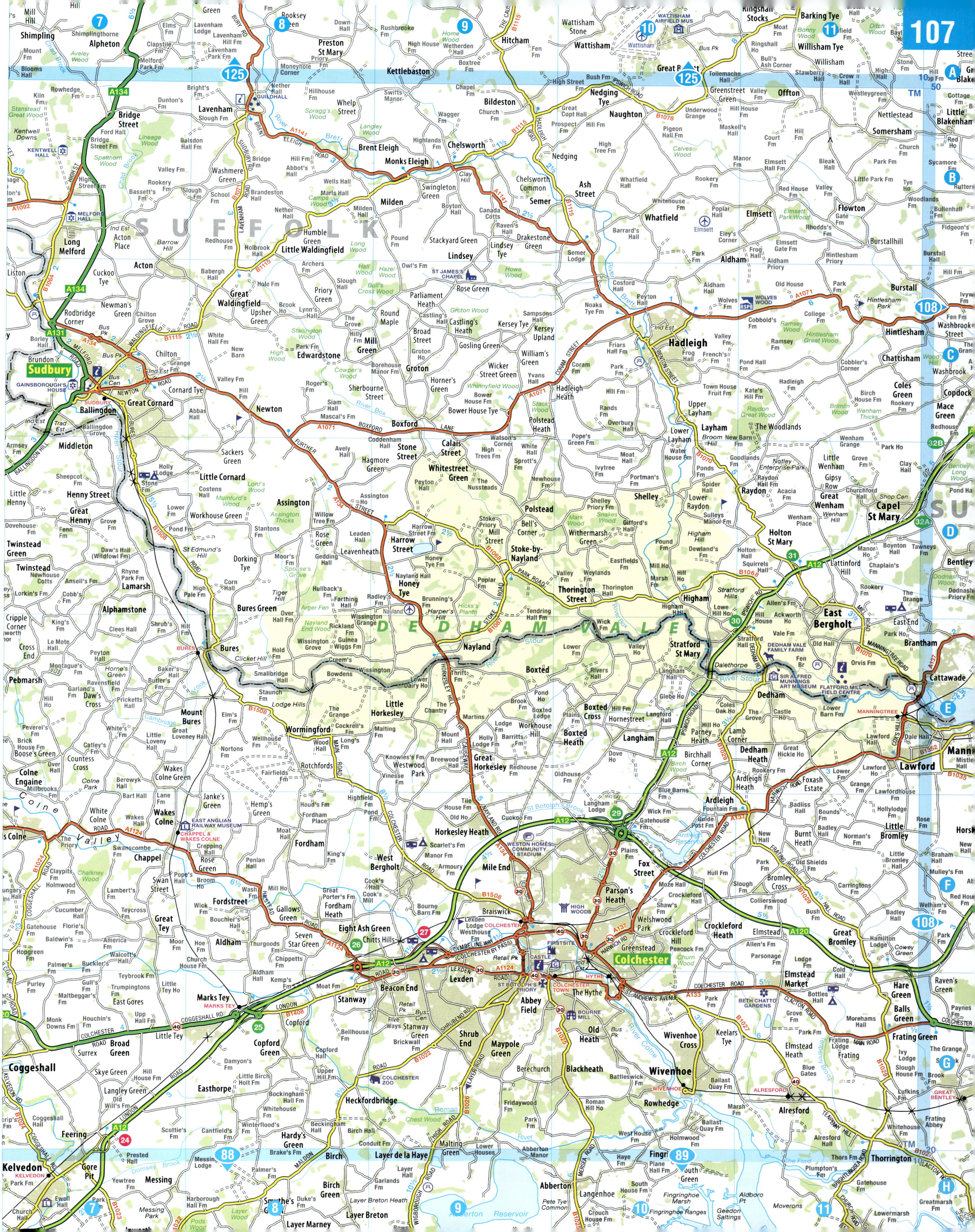
SUFFOLK
DEDHAM VALE
Sudbury
Colchester
Hadleigh
Long Melford
Lavenham
Kettlebaston
Hitcham
Wattisham
Bildeston
Chelsworth
Monks Eleigh
Brent Eleigh
Milden
Lindsey
Kersey
Great Waldingfield
Little Waldingfield
Acton
Chilton
Great Cornard
Newton
Boxford
Edwardstone
Groton
Polstead
Layham
Raydon
Holton St Mary
Capel St Mary
East Bergholt
Brantham
Cattawade
Manningtree
Mistley
Lawford
Dedham
Stratford St Mary
Higham
Shelley
Stoke-by-Nayland
Nayland
Leavenheath
Assington
Bures
Wormingford
Little Horkesley
Great Horkesley
Boxted
Langham
Ardleigh
Mile End
West Bergholt
Fordham
Aldham
Eight Ash Green
Marks Tey
Stanway
Lexden
Wivenhoe
Rowhedge
Alresford
Frating Green
Great Bromley
Elmstead Market
Thorrington
Abberton
Layer de la Haye
Birch
Coggeshall
Kelvedon
Feering
Messing
Chappel
Wakes Colne
Earls Colne
Pebmarsh
Alphamstone
Lamarsh
Twinstead
Middleton
Henny Street
Great Henny
Ballingdon
Hintlesham
Chattisham
Burstall
Aldham
Elmsett
Whatfield
Naughton
Nedging Tye
Offton
Somersham
Little Blakenham
Flowton
Washbrook
Copdock
Wenham
Tattingstone

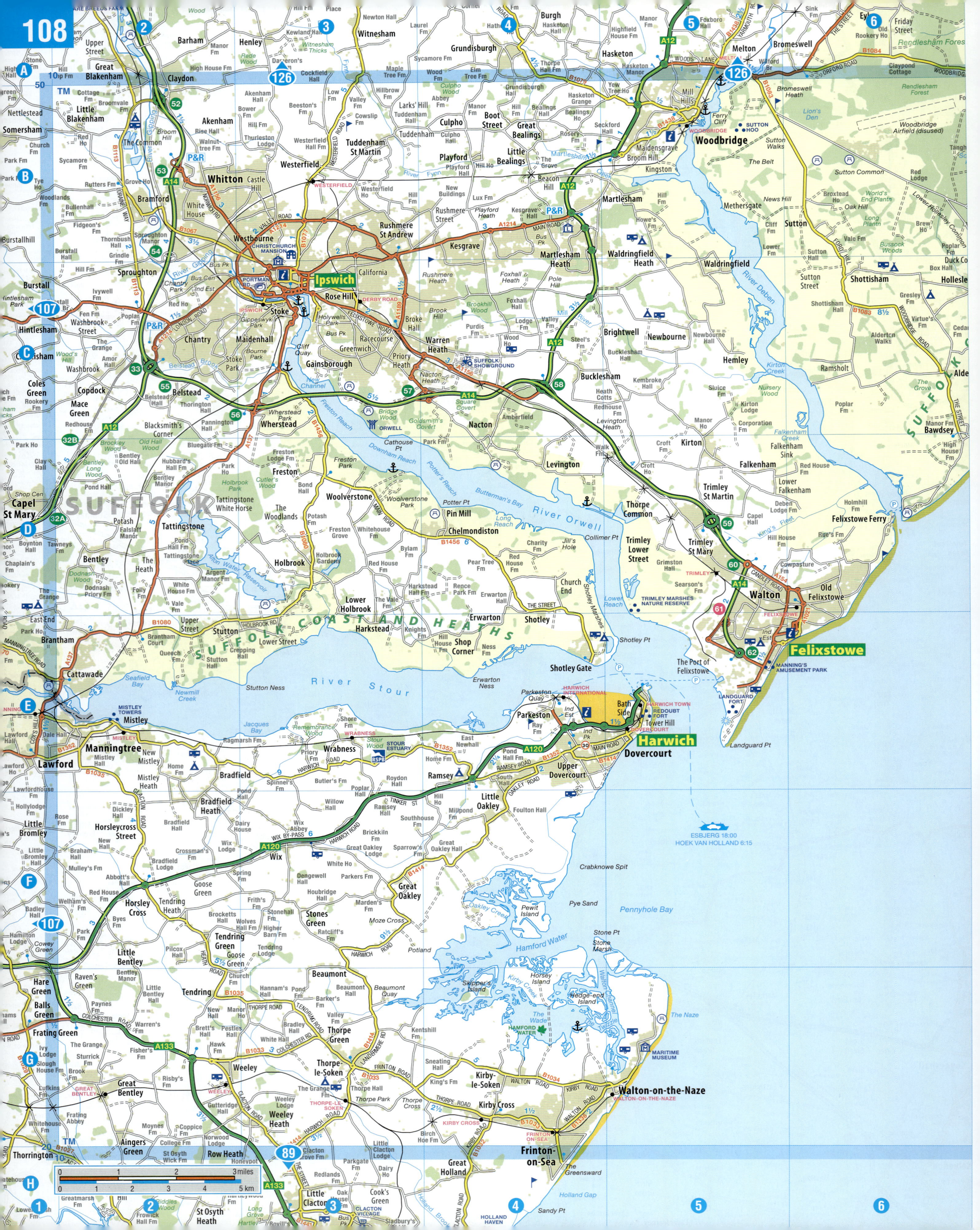

Ipswich
Felixstowe
Harwich
Dovercourt
Woodbridge
Walton-on-the-Naze
Frinton-on-Sea
Manningtree
Mistley
Lawford
Great Bentley
Weeley
Thorpe-le-Soken
Kirby-le-Soken
Kirby Cross
Great Oakley
Little Oakley
Ramsey
Wrabness
Bradfield
Wix
Tendring
Beaumont
Thorpe Green
Great Holland
Little Clacton
Shotley Gate
Holbrook
Tattingstone
Brantham
Cattawade
Stutton
Woolverstone
Chelmondiston
Pin Mill
Levington
Nacton
Kesgrave
Martlesham
Martlesham Heath
Rushmere St Andrew
Westerfield
Whitton
Claydon
Bramford
Sproughton
Westbourne
Rose Hill
Gainsborough
Belstead
Wherstead
Freston
Capel St Mary
Bentley
Copdock
Hintlesham
Burstall
Melton
Bromeswell
Sutton
Shottisham
Hemley
Newbourne
Brightwell
Bucklesham
Kirton
Falkenham
Trimley St Martin
Trimley St Mary
Walton
Old Felixstowe
Felixstowe Ferry
Waldringfield
Tuddenham St Martin
Culpho
Playford
Grundisburgh
Great Bealings
Little Bealings
Witnesham
Henley
Barham
Akenham
River Stour
River Orwell
River Deben
SUFFOLK
SUFFOLK COAST AND HEATHS
Hamford Water
Pennyhole Bay
The Naze
Landguard Pt
ESBJERG 18:00
HOEK VAN HOLLAND 6:15
A12
A14
A120
A133
A137

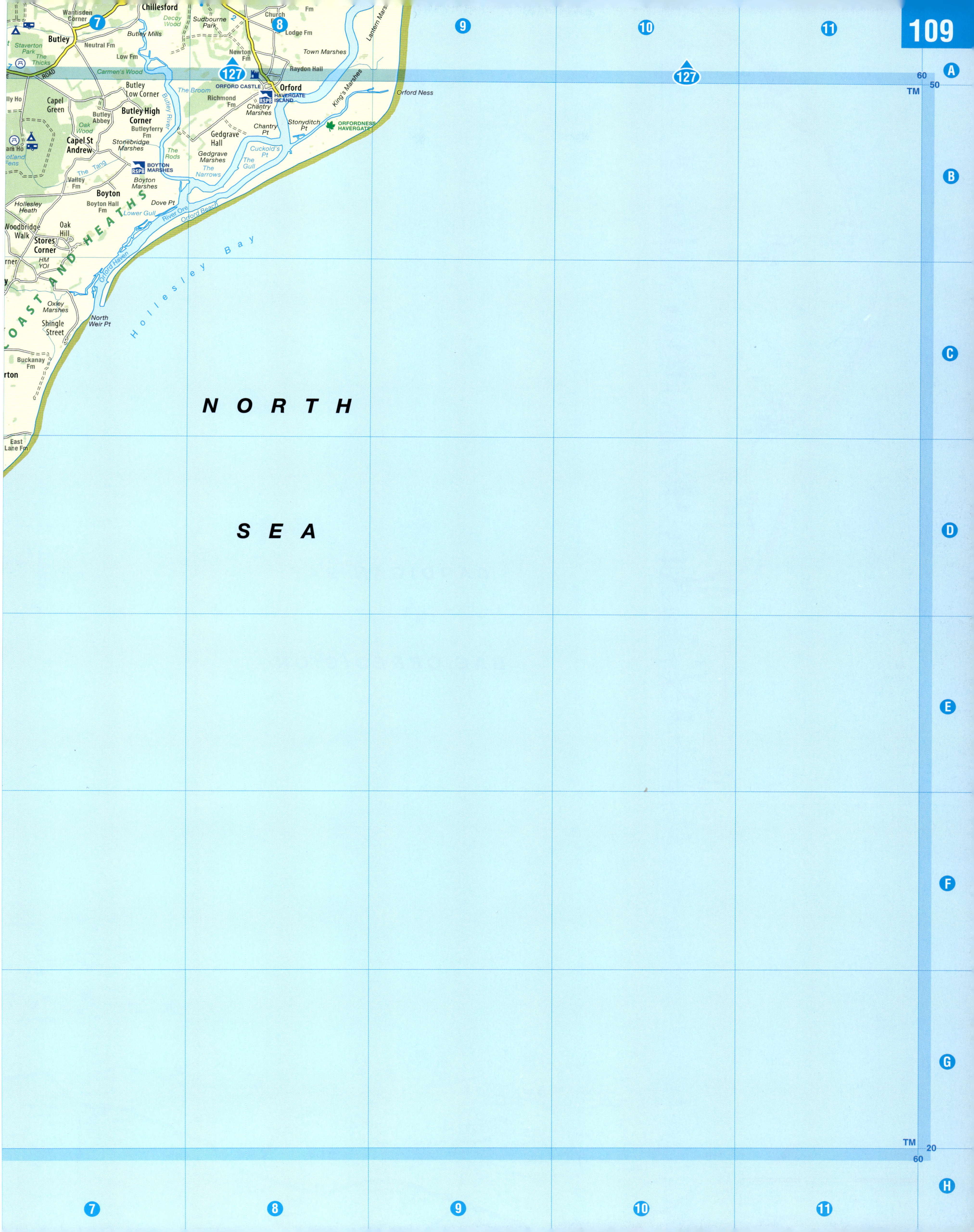
Wantisden Corner
Chillesford
Decoy Wood
Sudbourne Park
Church Fm
Fm
Lodge Fm
Butley
Staverton Park
The Thicks
Neutral Fm
Butley Mills
Low Fm
Newton Fm
Town Marshes
Lantern Marshes
Carmen's Wood
Raydon Hall
ROAD
127
ORFORD CASTLE
Orford
HAVERGATE ISLAND
Orford Ness
King's Marshes
Butley Low Corner
Butley River
The Broom
Richmond Fm
Chantry Marshes
Capel Green
Butley Abbey
Butley High Corner
Butleyferry Fm
Oak Wood
Capel St Andrew
Stonebridge Marshes
The Rods
Gedgrave Hall
Chantry Pt
Stonyditch Pt
ORFORDNESS-HAVERGATE
Gedgrave Marshes
Cuckold's Pt
The Narrows
The Gull
The Tang
BOYTON MARSHES
Valley Fm
Boyton Marshes
Boyton
Boyton Hall Fm
Dove Pt
Lower Gull
River Ore
Orford Beach
Hollesley Heath
Woodbridge Walk
Oak Hill
Stores Corner
HM YOI
COAST AND HEATHS
Orford Haven
Hollesley Bay
Oxley Marshes
Shingle Street
North Weir Pt
Buckanay Fm
East Lane Fm
NORTH SEA
7
8
9
10
11
A
B
C
D
E
F
G
H
TM
60
50
20

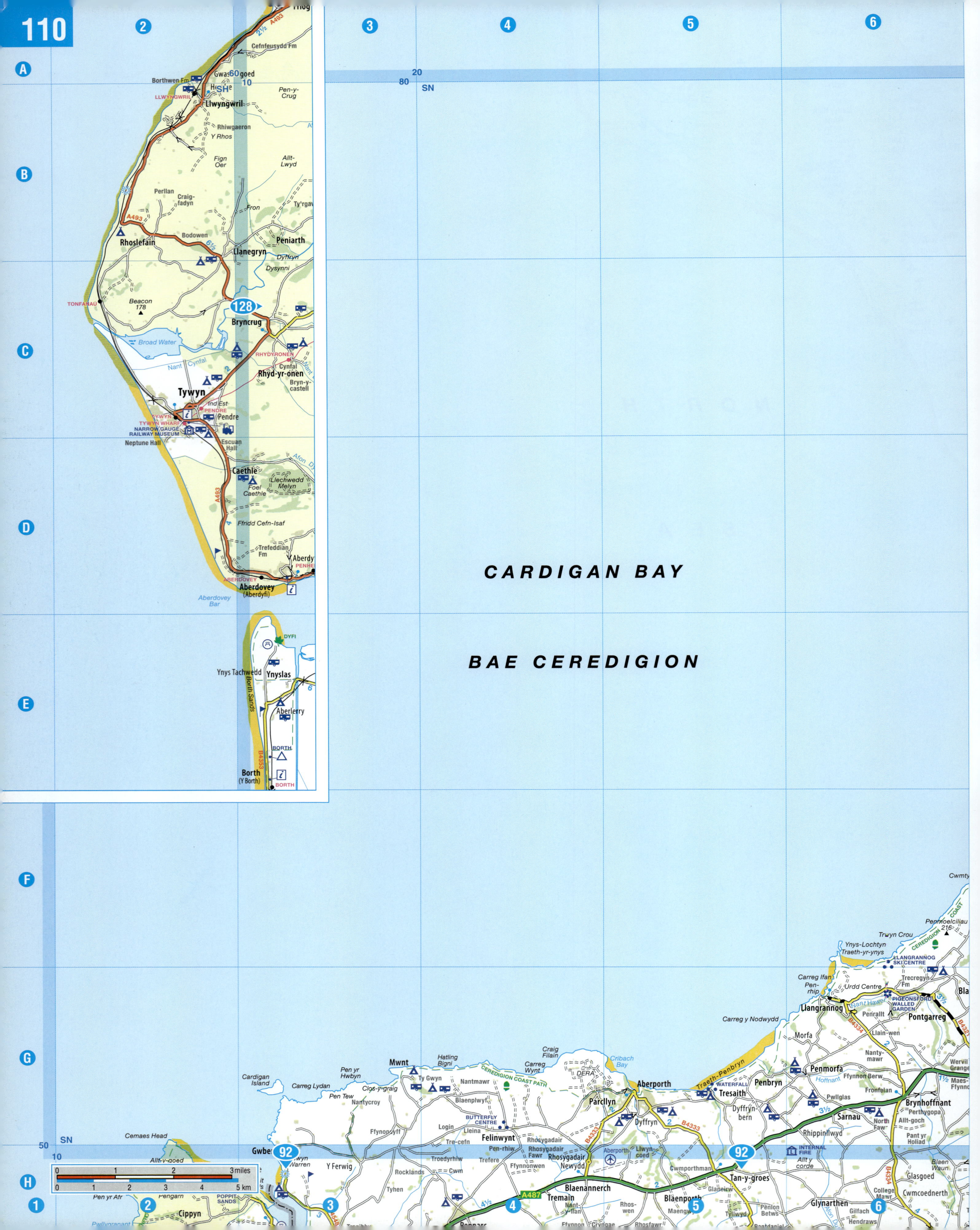
CARDIGAN BAY
BAE CEREDIGION
Cefnfeusydd Fm
Borthwen Fm
Gwastadgoed
LLWYNGWRIL
Llwyngwril
Pen-y-Crug
Rhiwgaeron
Y Rhos
Fign Oer
Allt-Lwyd
Perllan
Craig-fadyn
Fron
Ty'rgaw
A493
Rhoslefain
Bodowen
Llanegryn
Peniarth
Dyffryn
Dysynni
TONFANAU
Beacon 178
128
Bryncrug
Broad Water
Nant Cynfal
RHYDYRONEN
Cynfal
Rhyd-yr-onen
Bryn-y-castell
Tywyn
Ind Est
PENDRE
Pendre
TYWYN
TYWYN WHARF
NARROW GAUGE RAILWAY MUSEUM
Neptune Hall
Escuan Hall
Afon Dyfi
Caethle
Foel Caethle
Llechwedd Melyn
Ffridd Cefn-Isaf
Trefeddian Fm
ABERDOVEY
Aberdovey
(Aberdyfi)
Aberdovey Bar
DYFI
Ynys Tachwedd
Ynyslas
Borth Sands
Aberlerry
BORTH
B4353
Borth
(Y Borth)
20
80
SN
Cwmtydu
Penmoelciliau 216
Trwyn Crou
Ynys-Lochtyn
Traeth-yr-ynys
CEREDIGION COAST
LLANGRANNOG SKI CENTRE
Carreg Ifan
Pen-rhip
Urdd Centre
Trecregyn Fm
PIGEONSFORD WALLED GARDEN
Nant Hawen
Llangrannog
Penrallt
Pontgarreg
B4334
Carreg y Nodwydd
Morfa
Llain-wen
Nanty-mawr
Penmorfa
Hoffnant
Ffynnon Berw
Fronfelan
Brynhoffnant
Perthygopa
Sarnau
North Faw
Allt-goch
Pant yr Holiad
Rhippinllwyd
Wervil Grange
Maes-Ffynnon
Cardigan Island
Carreg Lydan
Pen yr Hwbyn
Mwnt
Hatling Bigni
Pen Tew
Clos-y-graig
Nantycroy
Ty Gwyn
Nantmawr
CEREDIGION COAST PATH
Craig Filain
Carreg Wynt
DERA
Cribach Bay
Aberporth
Traeth-Penbryn
WATERFALL
Tresaith
Penbryn
Pwllglas
Dyffryn-bern
Blaenplwyf
Parcllyn
Dyffryn
B4333
BUTTERFLY CENTRE
Ffynonyyff
Login
Lleina
Tre-cefn
Felinwynt
Rhosygadair
Pen-rhiw
Rhosygadair Fawr
Rhosygadair Newydd
Llwyn-coed
INTERNAL FIRE
Allt y corde
Cemaes Head
Allt-y-goed
Gwbert
Warren
92
Y Ferwig
Troedyrhiw
Trefere
Cwm
Ffynnonwen
Cwmporthman
Tan-y-groes
Blaen Waun
Glasgoed
Rocklands
Tyhen
A487
Tremain
Blaenannerch
Nant-y-llan
Rhos-wen
Blaenporth
Glaneirw
Maengwyn
Tyllwyd
Penlon Betws
Glynarthen
College Mawr
Cwmcoednerth
Gilfach
Hendraws
Pen yr Afr
Pengarn
POPPIT SANDS
Cippyn
Pwllygranant
Penparc
Ffynnon Grygae
Rhosfawr
SN
50
10
0 1 2 3 miles
0 1 2 3 4 5 km
A B C D E F G H
1 2 3 4 5 6

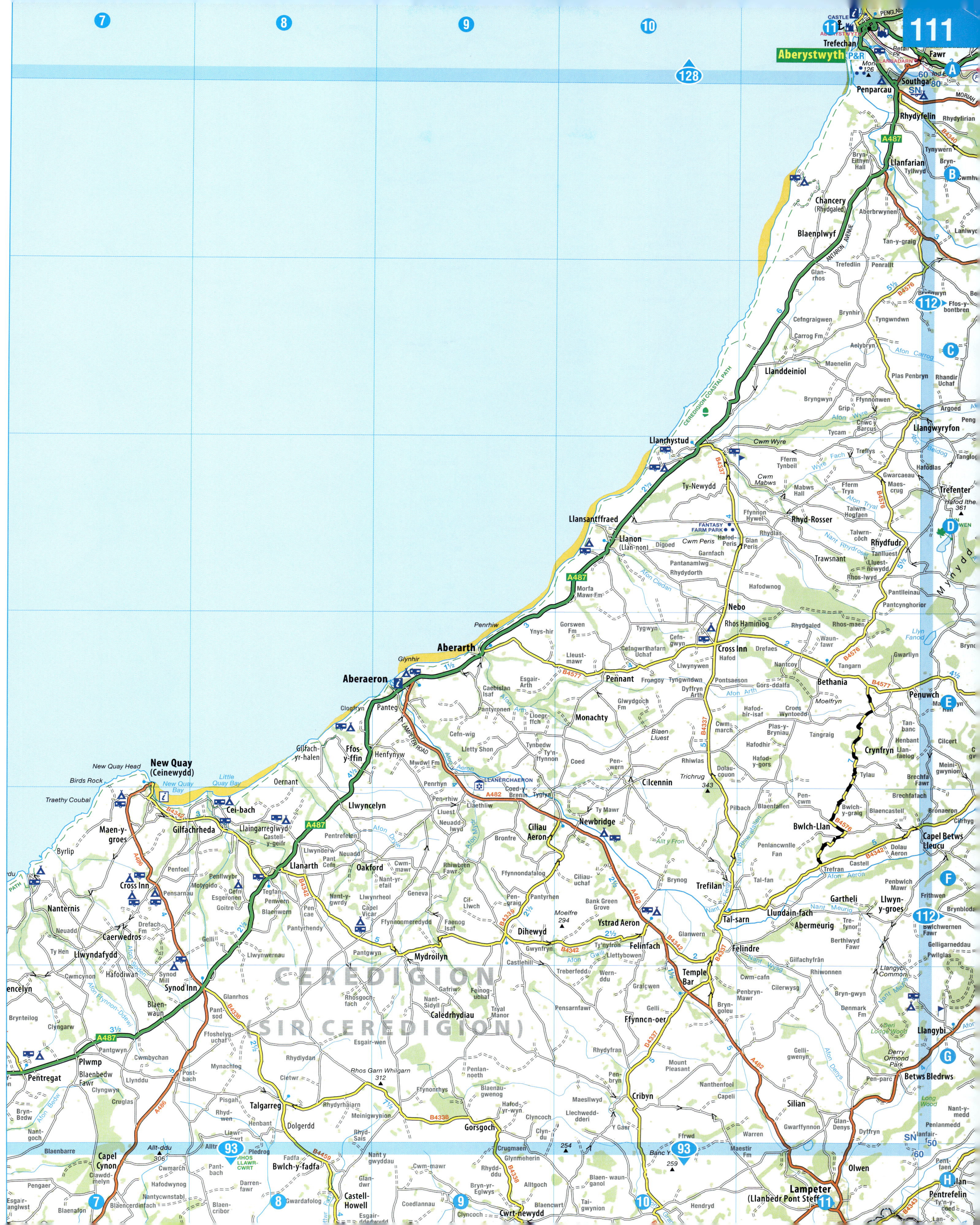

Aberystwyth
Trefechan
Penparcau
Southgate
Rhydyfelin
Llanfarian
Chancery (Rhydgaled)
Blaenplwyf
Llanddeiniol
Llangwyryfon
CEREDIGION COASTAL PATH
Llanrhystud
Ty-Newydd
Rhyd-Rosser
Llansantffraed
Llanon (Llan-non)
FANTASY FARM PARK
Rhydfudr
Trawsnant
Mynydd
Nebo
Rhos Haminiog
Aberarth
Cross Inn
Bethania
Aberaeron
Pennant
Monachty
Penuwch
Crynfryn
Cilcennin
Bwlch-Llan
Ffos-y-ffin
Henfynyw
LLANERCHAERON
New Quay Head
New Quay (Ceinewydd)
Birds Rock
Traethy Coubal
Little Quay Bay
Oernant
Cei-bach
Gilfachrheda
Llaingarreglwyd
Llwyncelyn
Ciliau Aeron
Newbridge
Capel Betws Lleucu
Maen-y-groes
Byrlip
Cross Inn
Llanarth
Oakford
Trefilan
Tal-sarn
Llundain-fach
Gartheli
Llwyn-y-groes
Abermeurig
Nanternis
Caerwedros
Llwyndafydd
Dihewyd
Ystrad Aeron
Felinfach
Felindre
Mydroilyn
Temple Bar
Synod Inn
Hafodiwan
Blaen-waun
CEREDIGION
(SIR CEREDIGION)
Caledrhydiau
Ffynnon-oer
Llangybi
Plwmp
Pentregat
Talgarreg
Gorsgoch
Cribyn
Silian
Betws Bledrws
Capel Cynon
Bwlch-y-fadfa
Castell-Howell
Crugmaen
Olwen
Lampeter (Llanbedr Pont Steffan)
Cwrt-newydd
Pentrefelin
A487
B4577
B4337
A482
B4342
A485
B4576
B4338
A486
B4459
B4343
7
8
9
10
11
128
112
93

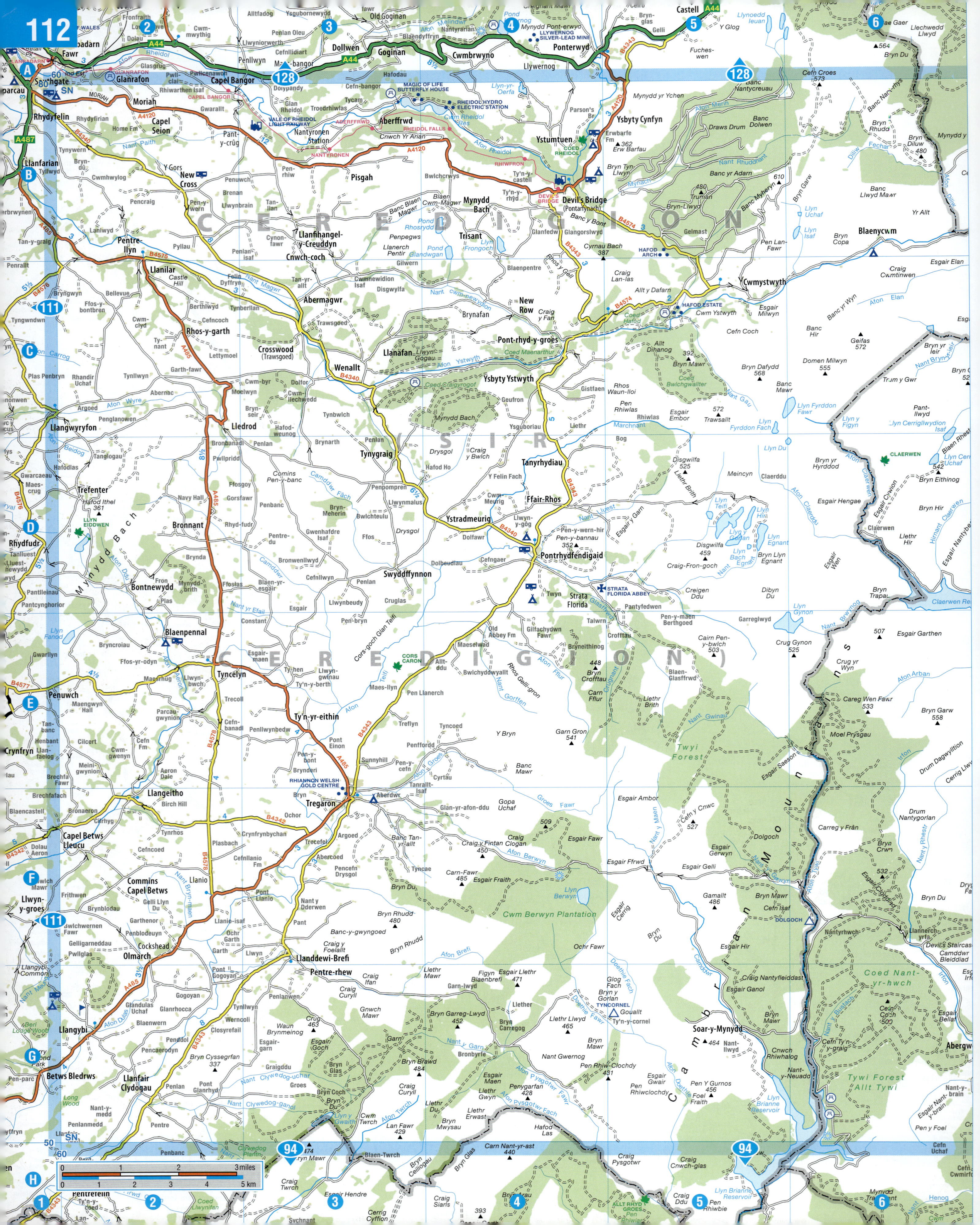

Penparcau
Rhydyfelin
Llanfarian
Capel Bangor
Glanrafon
Moriah
Capel Seion
Dollwen
Goginan
Cwmbrwyno
Ponterwyd
Castell
Old Goginan
Nantyronen Station
Aberffrwd
Pisgah
New Cross
Pentre-llyn
Llanilar
Llanfihangel-y-Creuddyn
Cnwch-coch
Abermagwr
Trisant
Mynydd Bach
Devil's Bridge (Pontarfynach)
Ystumtuen
Ysbyty Cynfyn
Cwmystwyth
Blaenycwm
Pont-rhyd-y-groes
Ysbyty Ystwyth
Llanafan
Wenallt
Crosswood (Trawsgoed)
Rhos-y-garth
Llangwyryfon
Lledrod
Tynygraig
Tanyrhydiau
Ystradmeurig
Ffair-Rhos
Pontrhydfendigaid
Strata Florida
Swyddffynnon
Trefenter
Bronnant
Bontnewydd
Rhydfudr
Blaenpennal
Tyncelyn
Penuwch
Ty'n-yr-eithin
Tregaron
Llangeitho
Capel Betws Lleucu
Commins Capel Betws
Llanio
Olmarch
Llanddewi-Brefi
Pentre-rhew
Llangybi
Betws Bledrws
Llanfair Clydogau
Soar-y-Mynydd
Crynfryn
Llwyn-y-groes
C E R E D I G I O N
S I R
C E R E D I G I O N
Cambrian Mountains
Mynydd Bach
Cwm Berwyn Plantation
Twyi Forest
Coed Nant-yr-hwch
Tywi Forest Allt Tywi
Llyn Brianne Reservoir
Claerwen Reservoir
Llyn Teifi
Llyn Egnant
Llyn Berwyn
Cors Caron
Strata Florida Abbey
Rhiannon Welsh Gold Centre
Hafod Estate
Vale of Rheidol Light Railway
Rheidol Hydro Electric Station
Magic of Life Butterfly House
Llywernog Silver-Lead Mine
A44
A487
A485
A4120
B4340
B4343
B4574
B4575
B4576
B4577
B4578
B4342
128
111
94
0 1 2 3 miles
0 1 2 3 4 5 km

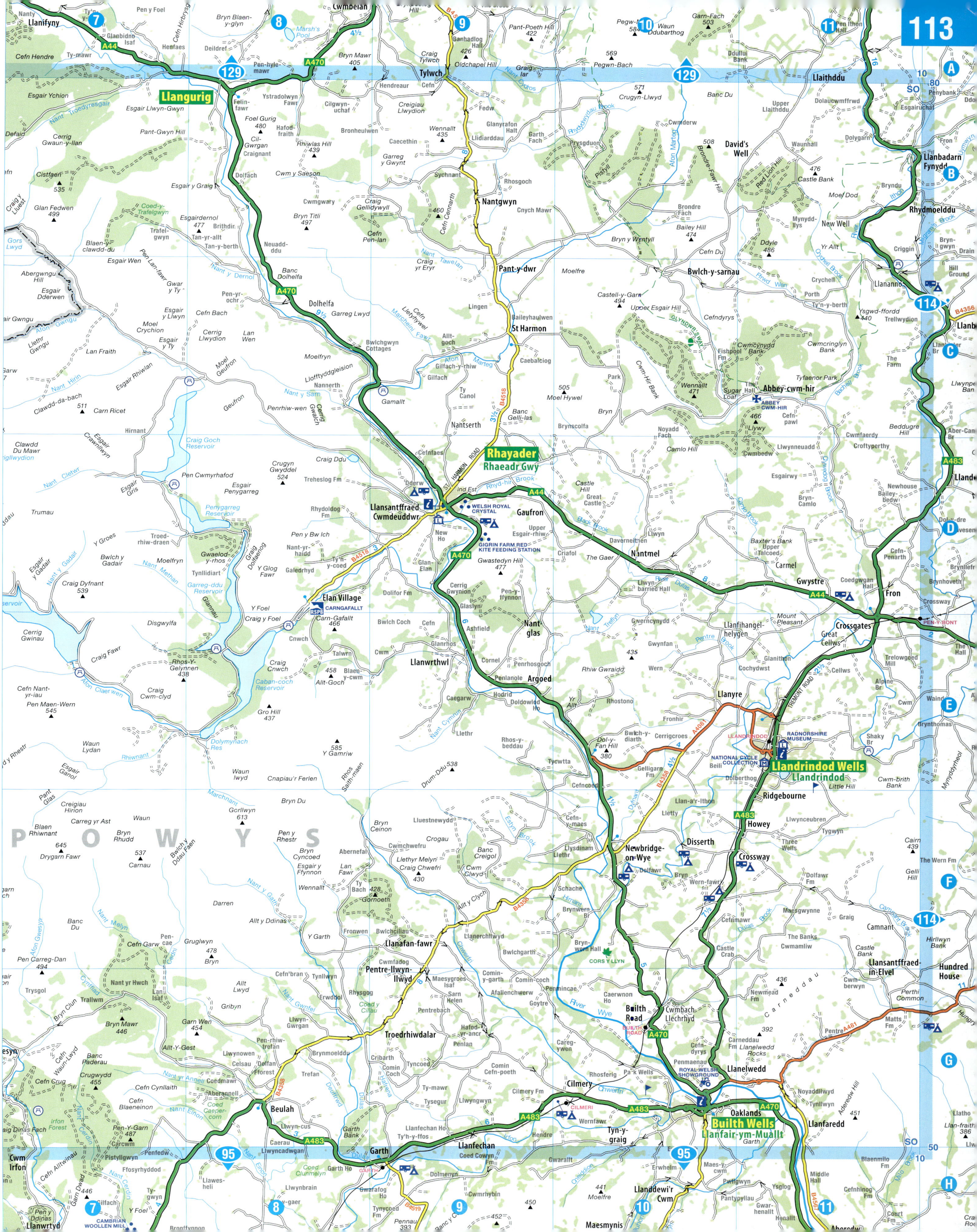

Llanifyny
Llangurig
Tylwch
Nantgwyn
Pant-y-dwr
St Harmon
Llaithddu
Llanbadarn Fynydd
Rhydmoelddu
David's Well
Bwlch-y-sarnau
Abbey-cwm-hir
Rhayader
Rhaeadr Gwy
Llansantffraed Cwmdeuddwr
Gaufron
Elan Village
Nantmel
Gwystre
Crossgates
Llanwrthwl
Nantglas
Argoed
Llanyre
Llandrindod Wells
Llandrindod
Ridgebourne
Howey
Disserth
Newbridge-on-Wye
Crossway
Llanafan-fawr
Pentre-llwyn-llwyd
Troedrhiwdalar
Beulah
Garth
Cilmery
Builth Road
Llanelwedd
Builth Wells
Llanfair-ym-Muallt
Llanfaredd
Llanfechan
Llanwrtyd
Llansantffraed-in-Elvel
Hundred House
Craig Goch Reservoir
Pen-y-garreg Reservoir
Garreg-ddu Reservoir
Caban-coch Reservoir
P O W Y S
A44
A470
A483
A4081
B4518
B4358
B4356
B4519
B4567
A481

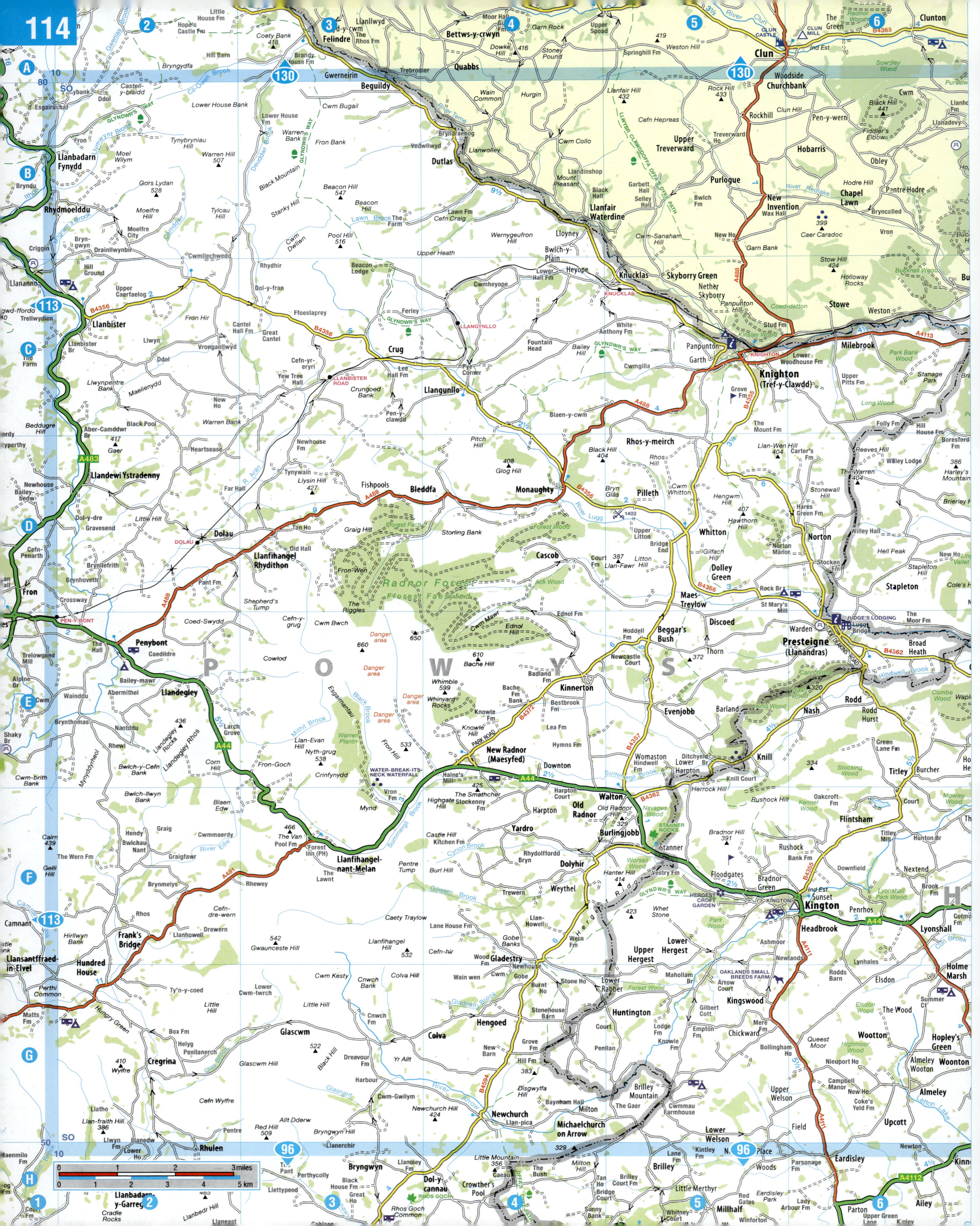
Felindre
Bettws-y-crwyn
Quabbs
Beguildy
Gwerneirin
Clun
Clunton
Woodside
Churchbank
Rockhill
Pen-y-wern
Hobarris
Obley
Chapel Lawn
Pentre Hodre
New Invention
Purlogue
Upper Treverward
Cwm Collo
Llanfair Waterdine
Dutlas
Llanbadarn Fynydd
Rhydmoelddu
Llanbister
Llanananno
Crug
Llangunllo
Knucklas
Skyborry Green
Stowe
Weston
Milebrook
Knighton (Tref-y-Clawdd)
Panpunton
Garth
Rhos-y-meirch
Pilleth
Whitton
Norton
Stapleton
Monaughty
Bleddfa
Llandewi Ystradenny
Dolau
Llanfihangel Rhydithon
Fron
Radnor Forest
Cascob
Dolley Green
Maes-Treylow
Discoed
Beggar's Bush
Presteigne (Llanandras)
Broad Heath
Kinnerton
Evenjobb
Nash
Rodd
Penybont
Llandegley
POWYS
New Radnor (Maesyfed)
Walton
Old Radnor
Burlingjobb
Knill
Titley
Flintsham
Llanfihangel-nant-Melan
Yardro
Dolyhir
Weythel
Kington
Lyonshall
Headbrook
Frank's Bridge
Hundred House
Gladestry
Upper Hergest
Lower Hergest
Huntington
Kingswood
Hengoed
Colva
Glascwm
Cregrina
Wootton
Almeley
Newchurch
Michaelchurch on Arrow
Upcott
Eardisley
Rhulen
Bryngwyn
Dol-y-cannau
Brilley
Millhalf
Llanbadarn-y-Garreg
Holme Marsh
Hopley's Green
Stanner
A44
A488
A483
A481
A4113
A4111
A4112
B4356
B4355
B4357
B4362
B4372
B4594
B4363
113
130
96

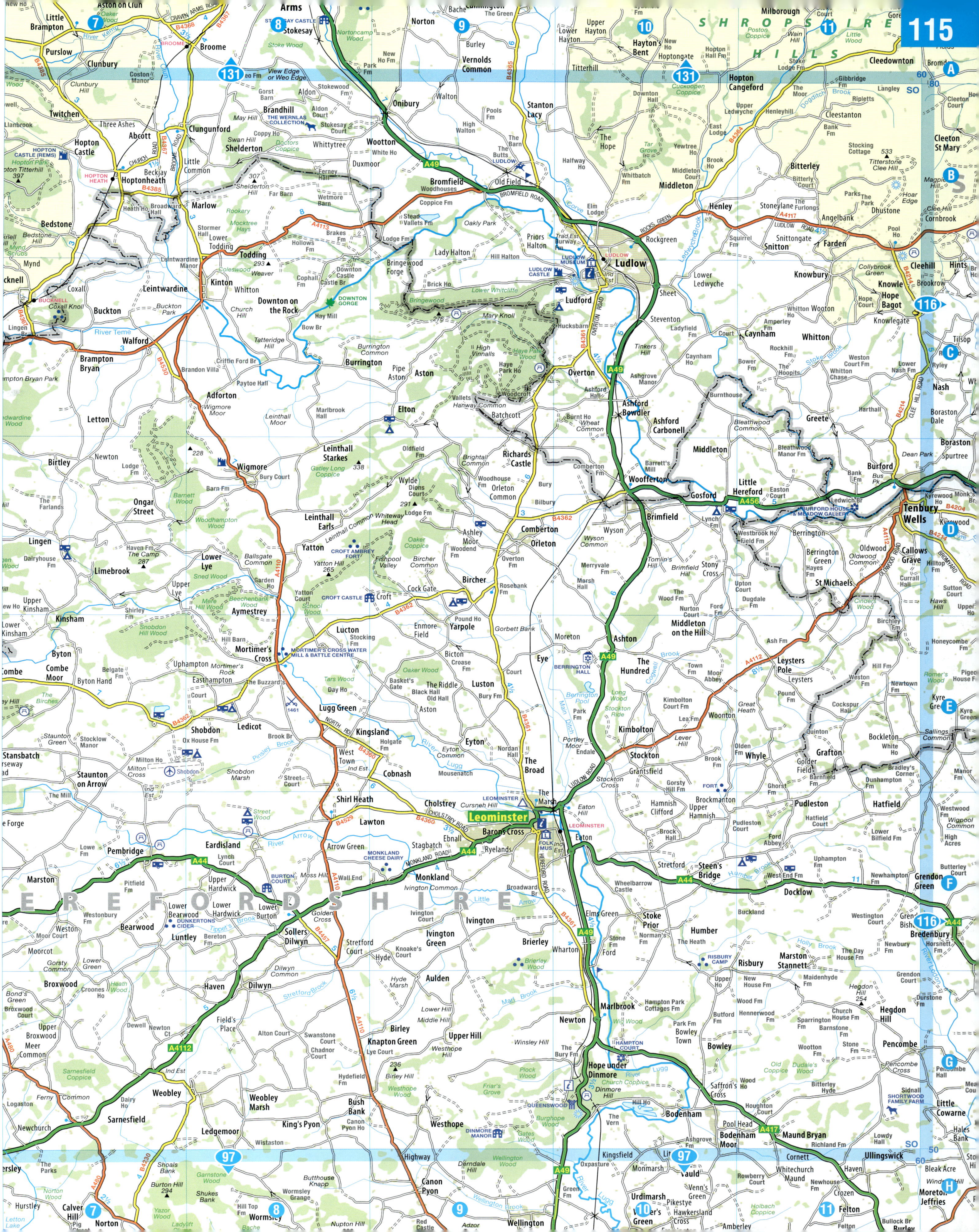
SHROPSHIRE HILLS
HEREFORDSHIRE
Ludlow
Leominster
Tenbury Wells
Little Brampton
Purslow
Clunbury
Twitchen
Hopton Castle
Hoptonheath
Abcott
Clungunford
Shelderton
Broome
Bedstone
Bucknell
Leintwardine
Kinton
Buckton
Walford
Brampton Bryan
Adforton
Letton
Wigmore
Birtley
Lingen
Limebrook
Kinsham
Byton
Combe Moor
Lower Lye
Aymestrey
Mortimer's Cross
Shobdon
Ledicot
Lugg Green
Kingsland
Pembridge
Eardisland
Staunton on Arrow
Lyonshall
Marston
Bearwood
Luntley
Dilwyn
Sollers Dilwyn
Haven
Weobley
Weobley Marsh
Sarnesfield
Ledgemoor
King's Pyon
Canon Pyon
Norton
Onibury
Stokesay
Wootton
Bromfield
Aldon
Brandhill
Whittytree
Duxmoor
Marlow
Todding
Downton on the Rock
Burrington
Aston
Elton
Pipe Aston
Leinthall Starkes
Leinthall Earls
Yatton
Croft
Lucton
Yarpole
Bircher
Eye
Luston
Orleton
Comberton
Richards Castle
Batchcott
Ashford Bowdler
Ashford Carbonell
Overton
Ludford
Woofferton
Brimfield
Gosford
Little Hereford
Middleton on the Hill
Ashton
Kimbolton
Stockton
The Broad
Cholstrey
Ebnall
Barons Cross
Monkland
Stretford
Ivington
Ivington Green
Brierley
Aulden
Birley
Knapton Green
Upper Hill
Westhope
Newton
Hope under Dinmore
Bodenham
Bodenham Moor
Marlbrook
Stoke Prior
Humber
Risbury
Marston Stannett
Docklow
Pudleston
Hatfield
Grafton
Whyle
Leysters
Leysters Pole
Woonton
Burford
Boraston
Nash
Greete
Middleton
Caynham
Whitton
Knowbury
Farden
Snitton
Bitterley
Henley
Hopton Cangeford
Cleedownton
Hayton's Bent
Stanton Lacy
The Hope
Cleeton St Mary
Knowle
Hope Bagot
Cleehill
Hopton Cangeford
Bowley
Pencombe
Hegdon Hill
Little Cowarne
Maund Bryan
Ullingswick
Wellington
Urdimarsh
Moreton Jeffries
Steen's Bridge
Grendon Green
Bredenbury
St Michaels
Callows Grave
Kyre Green
Berrington
Oldwood
A49
A44
A4112
A4110
A456
A417
131
97
116

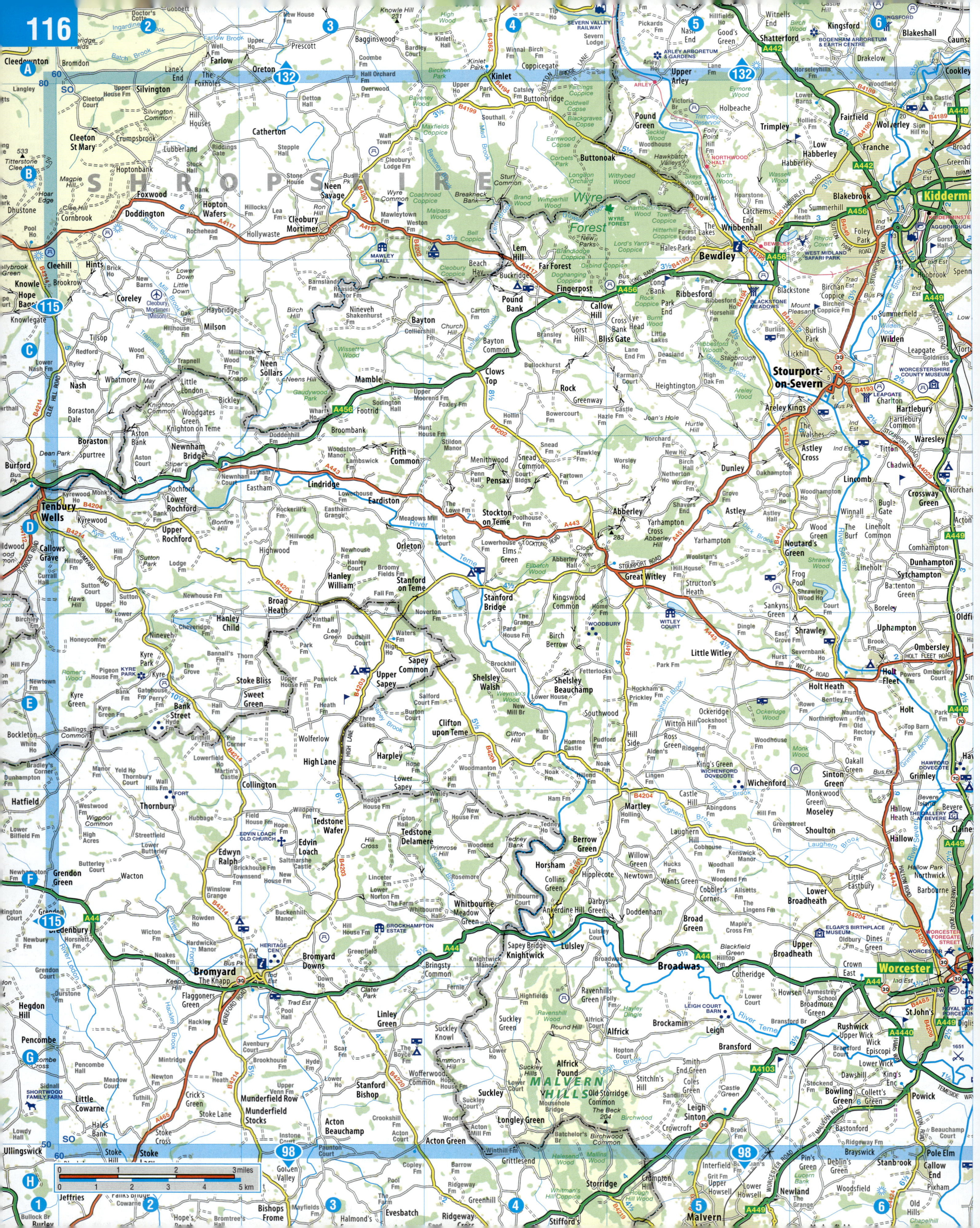
SHROPSHIRE
Wyre Forest
MALVERN HILLS
Cleedownton
Silvington
Cleeton St Mary
Oreton
Farlow
Prescott
Kinlet
Buttonoak
Catherton
Hopton Wafers
Doddington
Cleobury Mortimer
Neen Savage
Hollywaste
Far Forest
Bewdley
Wribbenhall
Kidderminster
Blakebrook
Stourport-on-Severn
Areley Kings
Bayton
Bayton Common
Mamble
Clows Top
Rock
Milson
Neen Sollars
Nash
Tenbury Wells
Kyrewood
Eastham
Lindridge
Eardiston
Pensax
Stockton on Teme
Abberley
Astley
Dunley
Great Witley
Orleton
Stanford on Teme
Stanford Bridge
Hanley William
Hanley Child
Upper Rochford
Lower Rochford
Newnham Bridge
Broad Heath
Kyre Green
Bank Street
Stoke Bliss
Sweet Green
Upper Sapey
Sapey Common
Shelsley Walsh
Shelsley Beauchamp
Clifton upon Teme
Little Witley
Holt Heath
Holt Fleet
Ombersley
Hartlebury
Crossway Green
Wichenford
Martley
Hallow
Grimley
Collington
High Lane
Harpley
Thornbury
Edwyn Ralph
Tedstone Wafer
Tedstone Delamere
Edvin Loach
Whitbourne
Horsham
Berrow Green
Knightwick
Lulsley
Broadwas
Bromyard
The Knapp
Bromyard Downs
Bringsty Common
Linley Green
Suckley
Alfrick
Alfrick Pound
Leigh
Bransford
Powick
Worcester
Crown East
Lower Broadheath
Upper Broadheath
Broad Green
Doddenham
Stanford Bishop
Munderfield Row
Munderfield Stocks
Acton Beauchamp
Acton Green
Longley Green
Leigh Sinton
Storridge
Cradley
Malvern
Stoke Lacy
Golden Valley
Pencombe
Little Cowarne
Hegdon Hill
Hatfield
Grendon Green
Bredenbury
Evesbatch
Bishops Frome
Stifford's
Newland
Stanbrook
Callow End
A44
A443
A456
A4117
A451
A449
A442
A4103
A465
B4204
B4202
B4203
B4214
B4220
A4440
SO
60
80
50
115
132
98
0 1 2 3 miles
0 1 2 3 4 5 km

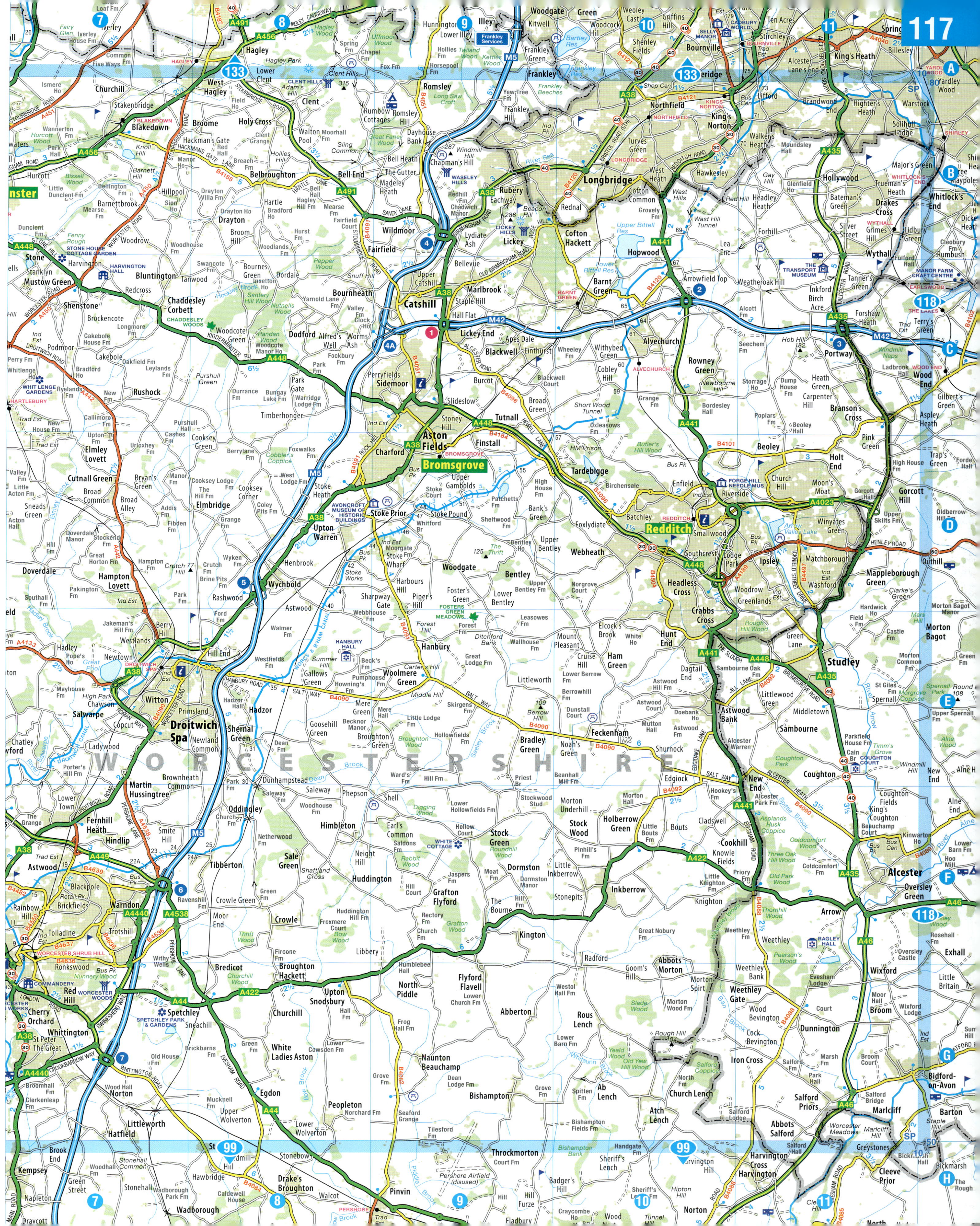
WORCESTERSHIRE
Bromsgrove
Redditch
Droitwich Spa
Catshill
Aston Fields
Stoke Prior
Upton Warren
Wychbold
Hagley
West Hagley
Blakedown
Churchill
Clent
Belbroughton
Fairfield
Wildmoor
Rubery
Frankley
Longbridge
Northfield
King's Norton
Bournville
Hollywood
Alvechurch
Hopwood
Cofton Hackett
Barnt Green
Lickey
Lickey End
Marlbrook
Blackwell
Burcot
Tardebigge
Finstall
Sidemoor
Charford
Chaddesley Corbett
Harvington
Stone
Shenstone
Rushock
Elmley Lovett
Cutnall Green
Hampton Lovett
Doverdale
Elmbridge
Dodford
Woodcote Green
Hanbury
Woolmere Green
Feckenham
Astwood Bank
Studley
Sambourne
Coughton
Alcester
Arrow
Wixford
Broom
Dunnington
Bidford-on-Avon
Salford Priors
Abbots Salford
Harvington
Iron Cross
Inkberrow
Abbots Morton
Rous Lench
Ab Lench
Church Lench
Atch Lench
Flyford Flavell
North Piddle
Upton Snodsbury
Naunton Beauchamp
Bishampton
Abberton
Throckmorton
Kington
Grafton Flyford
Dormston
Stock Wood
Himbleton
Huddington
Tibberton
Oddingley
Crowle
Bredicot
Broughton Hackett
Churchill
White Ladies Aston
Egdon
Peopleton
Spetchley
Whittington
Norton
Littleworth
Hatfield
Kempsey
Wadborough
Drake's Broughton
Pinvin
Fernhill Heath
Hindlip
Martin Hussingtree
Salwarpe
Ombersley
Warndon
Blackpole
Ipsley
Matchborough
Headless Cross
Crabbs Cross
Webheath
Bentley
Upper Bentley
Woodgate
Portway
Wythall
Tanworth
Beoley
Weatherley
Cookhill
Weethley
Great Alne
Oversley Green
Exhall
Kinwarton
Greystones
Barton
Marlcliff
Cleeve Prior
Radford
Kitwell
Illey
Romsley
Bell End
Drayton
Harvington Hall
Hanbury Hall
Avoncroft Museum of Historic Buildings
Forge Mill Needle Museum
Spetchley Park & Gardens
Ragley Hall
M5
M42
A38
A448
A441
A435
A422
A44
A46
A491
A456
A4023
B4090
B4091
B4096

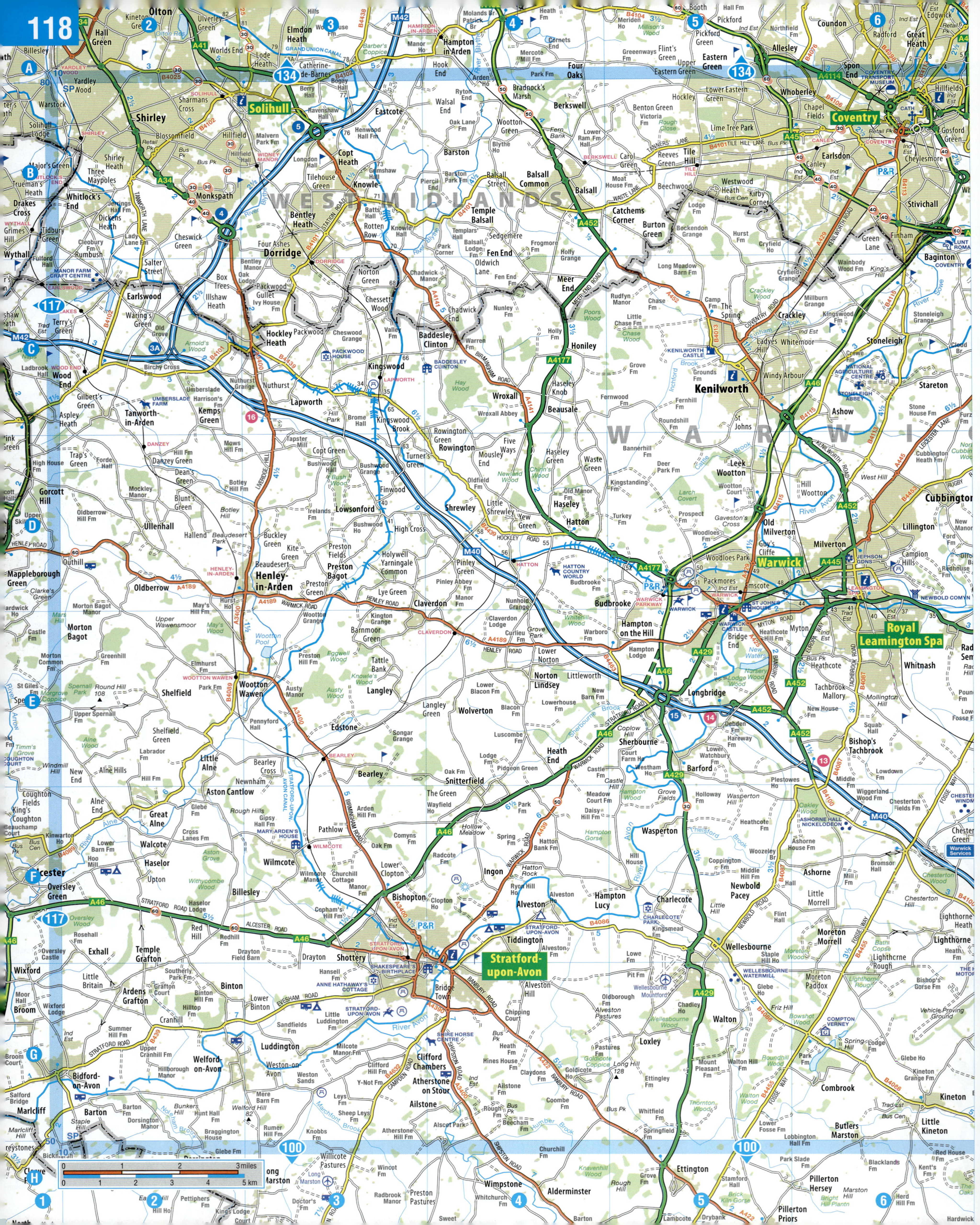
Solihull
Shirley
Coventry
Kenilworth
Warwick
Royal Leamington Spa
Stratford-upon-Avon
Henley-in-Arden
WEST MIDLANDS
W A R W I C K
Hampton in Arden
Balsall Common
Dorridge
Knowle
Hockley Heath
Lapworth
Tanworth-in-Arden
Wootton Wawen
Claverdon
Hatton
Cubbington
Lillington
Whitnash
Wellesbourne
Ettington
Alderminster
Wimpstone
Clifford Chambers
Bidford-on-Avon
Welford-on-Avon
Luddington
Shottery
Tiddington
Alveston
Charlecote
Barford
Sherbourne
Longbridge
Hampton on the Hill
Budbrooke
Stoneleigh
Baginton
Finham
Earlsdon
Allesley
Berkswell
Meriden
Earlswood
Mappleborough Green
Oldberrow
Morton Bagot
Aston Cantlow
Wilmcote
Snitterfield
Bearley
Ardens Grafton
Binton
Temple Grafton
Exhall
Wixford
Marcliff
Barton
M42
M40
A46
A452
A429
A3400
A4189
0 1 2 3 miles
0 1 2 3 4 5 km

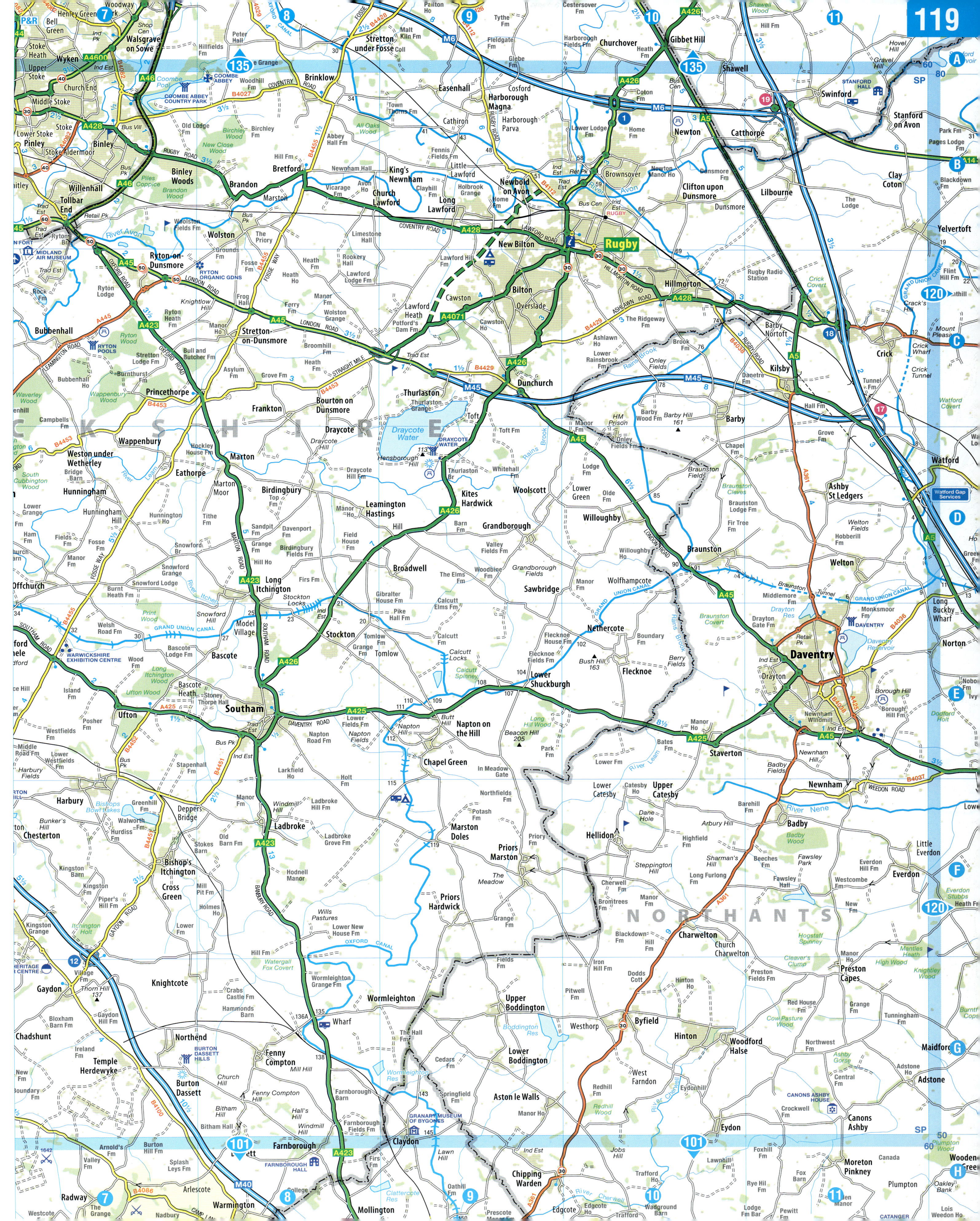
Henley Green
Woodway
Walsgrave on Sowe
Bell Green
Stoke Heath
Wyken
Upper Stoke
Church End
Middle Stoke
Lower Stoke
Pinley
Stoke Aldermoor
Binley
Binley Woods
Willenhall
Tollbar End
Brandon
Wolston
Ryton-on-Dunsmore
Bubbenhall
Brinklow
Stretton under Fosse
Easenhall
Harborough Magna
Harborough Parva
Cosford
Churchover
Gibbet Hill
Shawell
Swinford
Stanford on Avon
Catthorpe
Newton
Clifton upon Dunsmore
Lilbourne
Clay Coton
Yelvertoft
Bretford
King's Newnham
Church Lawford
Long Lawford
Little Lawford
Newbold on Avon
Brownsover
Rugby
New Bilton
Bilton
Hillmorton
Cawston
Lawford Heath
Overslade
Dunchurch
Thurlaston
Stretton-on-Dunsmore
Princethorpe
Frankton
Bourton on Dunsmore
Draycote
Draycote Water
Barby
Kilsby
Crick
Watford
Ashby St Ledgers
Welton
Braunston
Willoughby
Woolscott
Kites Hardwick
Grandborough
Sawbridge
Leamington Hastings
Broadwell
Marton
Eathorpe
Hunningham
Weston under Wetherley
Wappenbury
Birdingbury
Long Itchington
Offchurch
Stockton
Bascote
Southam
Ufton
Napton on the Hill
Lower Shuckburgh
Flecknoe
Nethercote
Wolfhampcote
Daventry
Drayton
Norton
Long Buckby Wharf
Staverton
Newnham
Badby
Upper Catesby
Lower Catesby
Hellidon
Priors Marston
Marston Doles
Priors Hardwick
Chapel Green
Ladbroke
Harbury
Chesterton
Deppers Bridge
Bishop's Itchington
Cross Green
Charwelton
Everdon
Little Everdon
Preston Capes
Byfield
Hinton
Woodford Halse
Upper Boddington
Lower Boddington
Westhorp
Wormleighton
Fenny Compton
Northend
Burton Dassett
Temple Herdewyke
Knightcote
Gaydon
Chadshunt
Aston le Walls
Eydon
Canons Ashby
Moreton Pinkney
Adstone
Maidford
Claydon
Farnborough
Chipping Warden
Warmington
Mollington
Radway
Arlescote
Edgcote
Plumpton
WARWICKSHIRE
NORTHANTS
M6
M45
M40
A45
A423
A426
A425
A428
A5
A361
Grand Union Canal
Oxford Canal
River Avon
River Leam
River Nene

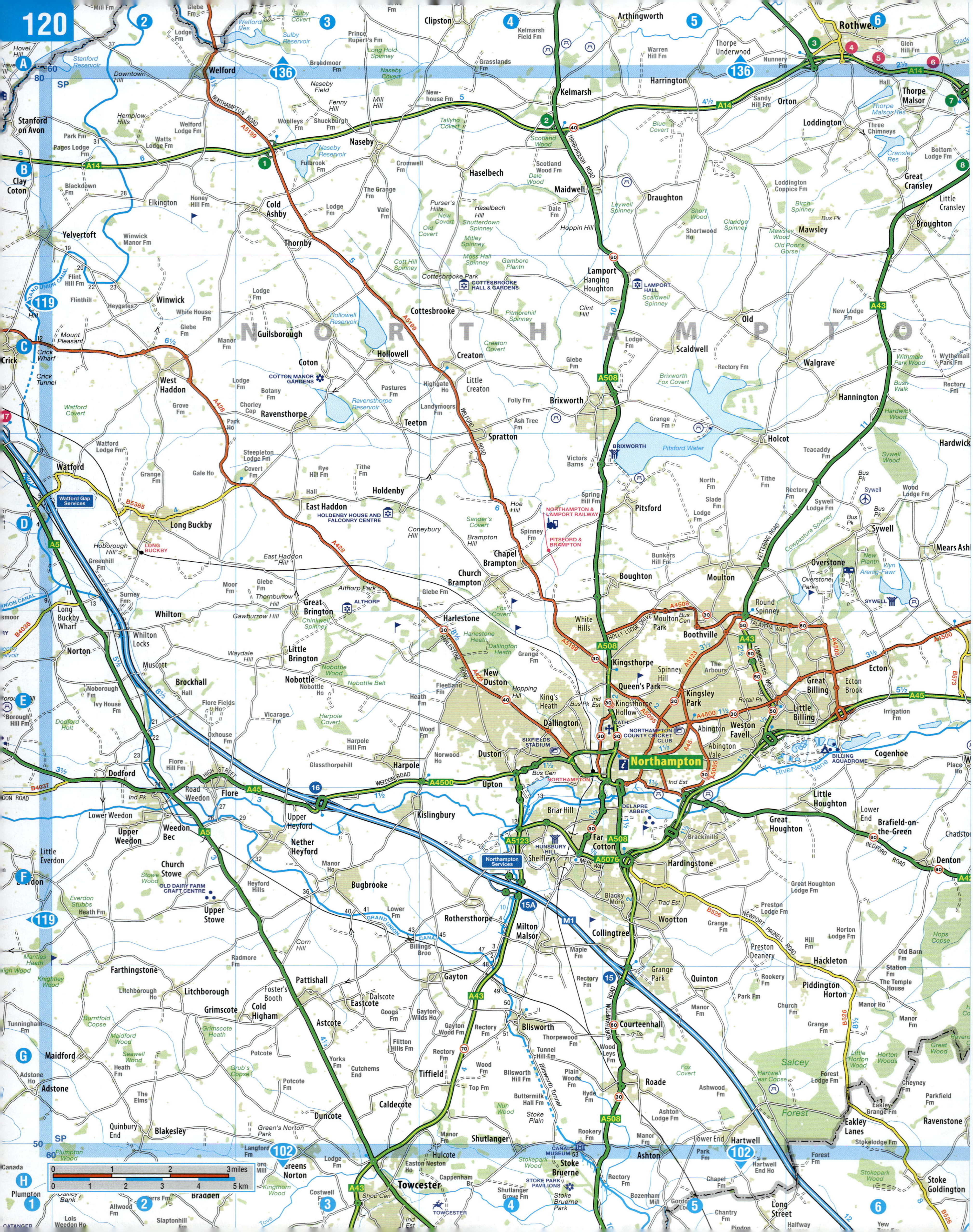
NORTHAMPTON
Northampton
Welford
Naseby
Clipston
Kelmarsh
Arthingworth
Harrington
Rothwell
Orton
Loddington
Thorpe Malsor
Stanford on Avon
Clay Coton
Elkington
Yelvertoft
Cold Ashby
Thornby
Haselbech
Maidwell
Draughton
Lamport
Hanging Houghton
Old
Scaldwell
Walgrave
Hannington
Broughton
Mawsley
Great Cransley
Little Cransley
Winwick
Guilsborough
Cottesbrooke
Hollowell
Creaton
Little Creaton
Coton
West Haddon
Ravensthorpe
Teeton
Spratton
Brixworth
Holcot
Pitsford Water
Pitsford
Watford
Long Buckby
East Haddon
Holdenby
Chapel Brampton
Church Brampton
Boughton
Moulton
Sywell
Overstone
Hardwick
Mears Ashby
Whilton
Great Brington
Little Brington
Harlestone
Norton
Long Buckby Wharf
Muscott
Brockhall
Nobottle
New Duston
Kingsthorpe
Boothville
Queen's Park
Kingsley Park
Great Billing
Little Billing
Ecton
Dallington
Duston
Abington
Weston Favell
Cogenhoe
Dodford
Weedon Bec
Upper Weedon
Lower Weedon
Flore
Upper Heyford
Nether Heyford
Harpole
Kislingbury
Upton
Briar Hill
Far Cotton
Hardingstone
Great Houghton
Little Houghton
Brafield-on-the-Green
Denton
Little Everdon
Church Stowe
Upper Stowe
Bugbrooke
Rothersthorpe
Milton Malsor
Collingtree
Wootton
Quinton
Hackleton
Piddington
Horton
Farthingstone
Litchborough
Pattishall
Gayton
Grimscote
Cold Higham
Eastcote
Astcote
Blisworth
Courteenhall
Tiffield
Roade
Maidford
Adstone
Blakesley
Duncote
Caldecote
Shutlanger
Towcester
Stoke Bruerne
Ashton
Hartwell
Greens Norton
Salcey Forest
Ravenstone
Eakley Lanes
Stoke Goldington
Long Street
Northampton Services
Watford Gap Services
Pitsford Reservoir
Hollowell Reservoir
Ravensthorpe Reservoir
Naseby Reservoir
Sulby Reservoir
Welford Res
Stanford Reservoir
Thorpe Malsor Res
Cransley Res
Sywell Res
COTTESBROOKE HALL & GARDENS
COTTON MANOR GARDENS
LAMPORT HALL
HOLDENBY HOUSE AND FALCONRY CENTRE
ALTHORP
NORTHAMPTON & LAMPORT RAILWAY
PITSFORD & BRAMPTON
NORTHAMPTON COUNTY CRICKET CLUB
SIXFIELDS STADIUM
BILLING AQUADROME
DELAPRE ABBEY
HUNSBURY HILL
OLD DAIRY FARM CRAFT CENTRE
CANAL MUSEUM
STOKE PARK PAVILIONS
TOWCESTER
GRAND UNION CANAL
River Nene
A14
A5199
A508
A43
A428
A4500
A45
A5
M1
A5123
A5076
A4508
B5385
B526
HARBOROUGH ROAD
KETTERING ROAD
WELFORD ROAD
HARLESTONE ROAD
WEEDON ROAD
NEWPORT PAGNELL ROAD
NORTHAMPTON ROAD
BEDFORD ROAD
MERE WAY
TALAVERA WAY
HOLLY LODGE DRIVE
SP
0 1 2 3 miles
0 1 2 3 4 5 km
136
119
102

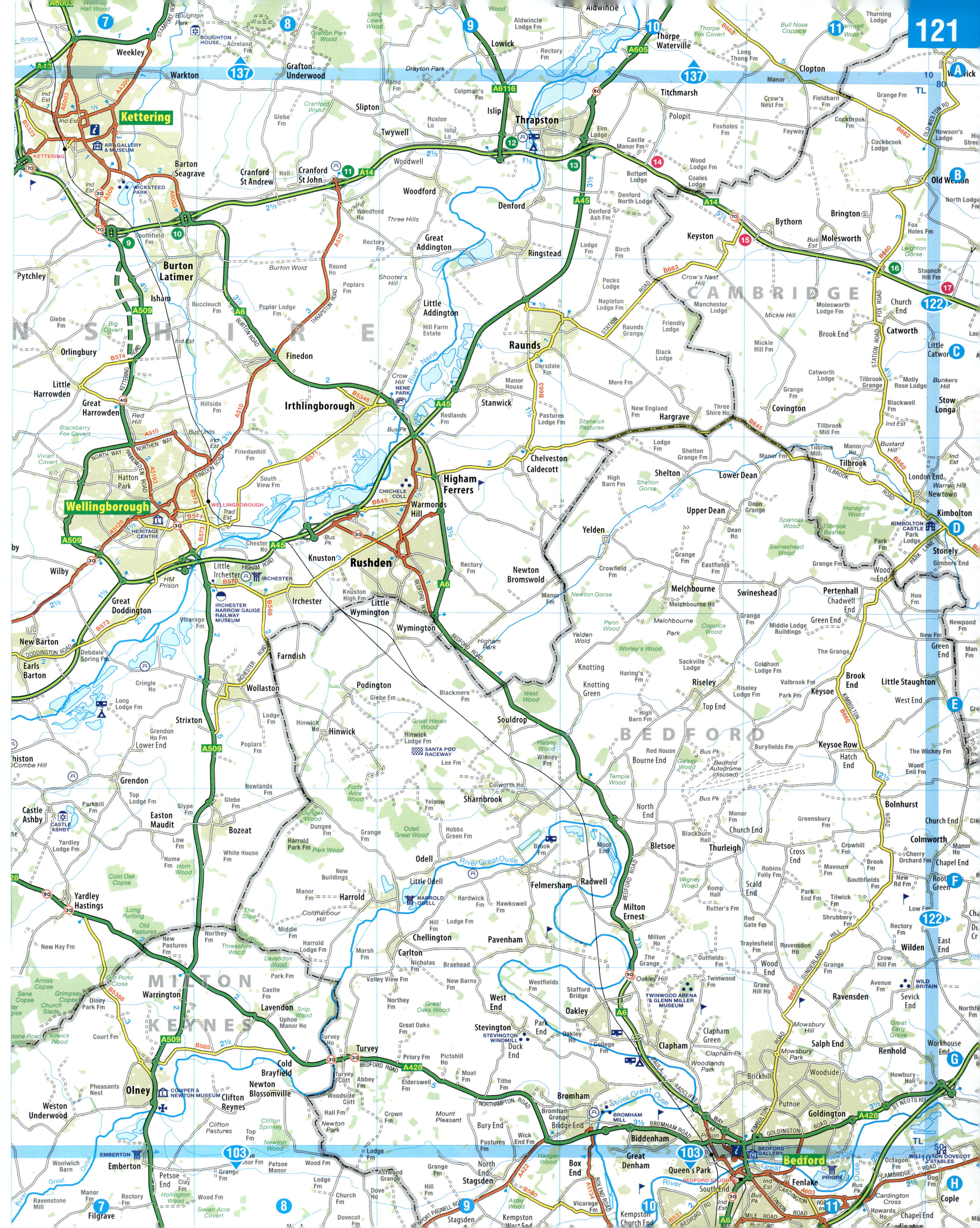
Kettering
Weekley
Warkton
Grafton Underwood
Boughton House
Slipton
Twywell
Islip
Thrapston
Lowick
Drayton Park
Aldwincle
Titchmarsh
Thorpe Waterville
Clopton
Polopit
Barton Seagrave
Cranford St Andrew
Cranford St John
Woodford
Denford
Ringstead
Keyston
Bythorn
Brington
Molesworth
Burton Latimer
Great Addington
Little Addington
Isham
Pytchley
Orlingbury
Finedon
Raunds
CAMBRIDGE
Catworth
Little Harrowden
Great Harrowden
Irthlingborough
Stanwick
Hargrave
Covington
Wellingborough
Higham Ferrers
Chelveston
Caldecott
Shelton
Lower Dean
Upper Dean
Tilbrook
Kimbolton
Rushden
Knuston
Yelden
Newton Bromswold
Little Irchester
Irchester
Wilby
Great Doddington
Little Wymington
Wymington
Melchbourne
Swineshead
Pertenhall
New Barton
Earls Barton
Farndish
Podington
Wollaston
Knotting
Knotting Green
Riseley
Souldrop
Little Staughton
Keysoe
Brook End
Strixton
Hinwick
BEDFORD
Keysoe Row
Grendon
Sharnbrook
Bolnhurst
Castle Ashby
Easton Maudit
Bozeat
Odell
North End
Bletsoe
Thurleigh
Colmworth
Harrold
Felmersham
Radwell
Milton Ernest
Yardley Hastings
Chellington
Carlton
Pavenham
Wilden
MILTON KEYNES
Warrington
Lavendon
Oakley
West End
Stevington
Clapham
Ravensden
Olney
Cold Brayfield
Turvey
Newton Blossomville
Clifton Reynes
Bromham
Biddenham
Goldington
Putnoe
Emberton
Great Denham
Queen's Park
Bedford
Stagsden
Kempston
Fenlake
Cople
Weston Underwood
Filgrave
River Great Ouse
River Nene
A14
A6
A45
A509
A428
A605
A6116
137
122
103

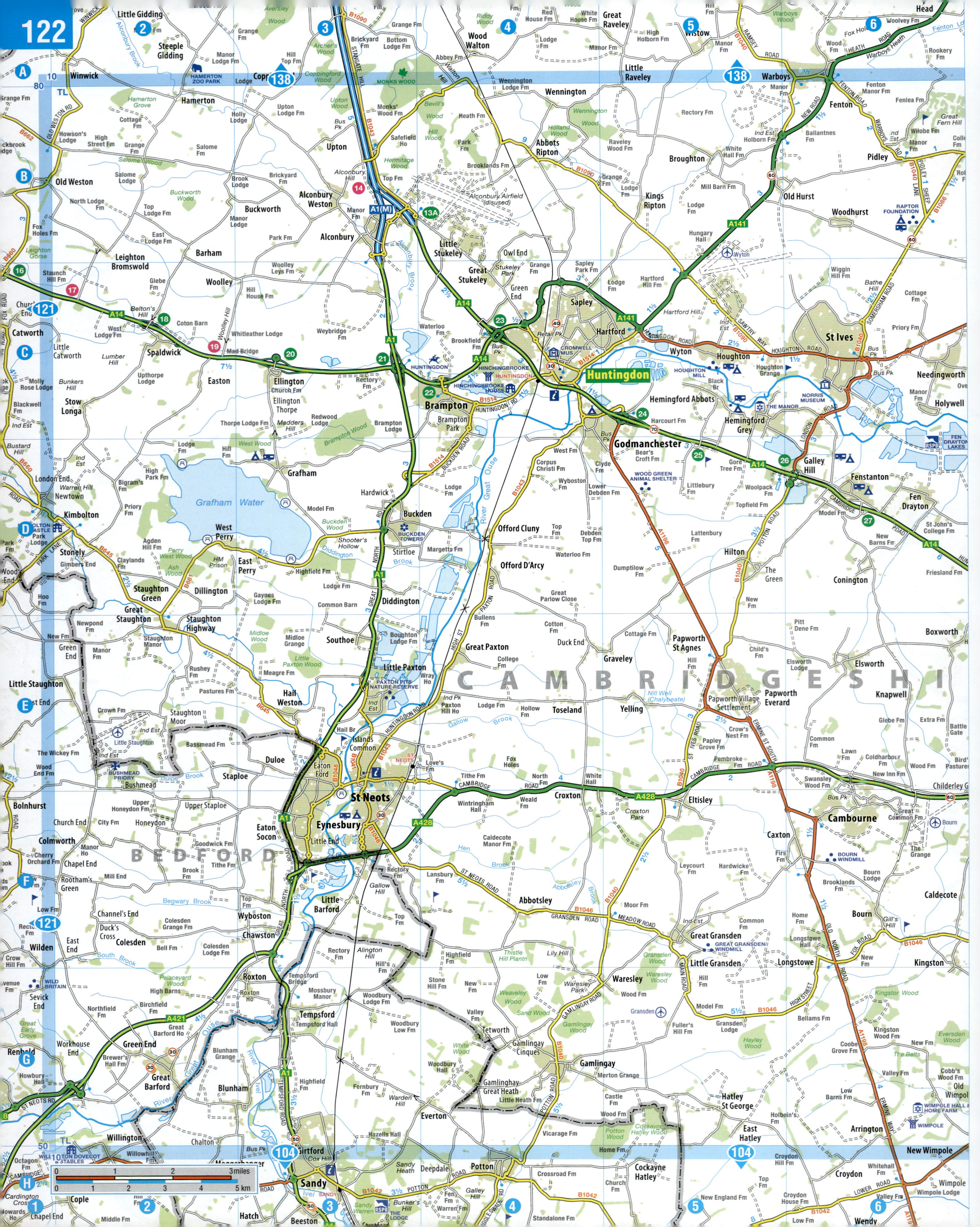

Little Gidding
Steeple Gidding
Winwick
Hamerton Zoo Park
Copmanford
Hamerton
Old Weston
Leighton Bromswold
Barham
Woolley
Buckworth
Alconbury Weston
Alconbury
Upton
Alconbury Airfield (disused)
Little Stukeley
Great Stukeley
Wood Walton
Monks Wood
Wennington
Abbots Ripton
Kings Ripton
Little Raveley
Great Raveley
Wistow
Broughton
Warboys
Fenton
Pidley
Old Hurst
Woodhurst
Raptor Foundation
Wyton
Hartford
Sapley
Huntingdon
Hinchingbrooke House
Brampton
Brampton Park
Godmanchester
Hemingford Abbots
Hemingford Grey
Houghton
Houghton Mill
St Ives
Norris Museum
Needingworth
Holywell
Fen Drayton Lakes
Fenstanton
Fen Drayton
Galley Hill
Hilton
Conington
Catworth
Spaldwick
Easton
Stow Longa
Ellington
Ellington Thorpe
Grafham
Grafham Water
West Perry
East Perry
Kimbolton
Stonely
Dillington
Staughton Green
Great Staughton
Staughton Highway
Buckden
Buckden Towers
Stirtloe
Diddington
Offord Cluny
Offord D'Arcy
Southoe
Great Paxton
Little Paxton
Paxton Pits Nature Reserve
Toseland
Graveley
Yelling
Papworth St Agnes
Papworth Everard
Papworth Village Settlement
Elsworth
Boxworth
Knapwell
Little Staughton
Hail Weston
Staughton Moor
Duloe
Staploe
Bushmead
Upper Staploe
Eaton Ford
St Neots
Eynesbury
Eaton Socon
Little End
Croxton
Eltisley
Cambourne
Caxton
Bourn
Caldecote
Kingston
Abbotsley
Great Gransden
Little Gransden
Longstowe
Waresley
Gamlingay
Gamlingay Cinques
Gamlingay Great Heath
Tetworth
Everton
Potton
Cockayne Hatley
Hatley St George
East Hatley
Croydon
Arrington
Wimpole
New Wimpole
Wendy
Little Barford
Wyboston
Chawston
Roxton
Tempsford
Blunham
Great Barford
Willington
Sandy
Beeston
Colmworth
Wilden
Bolnhurst
Renhold
Colesden
BEDFORD
CAMBRIDGESHIRE
A1
A1(M)
A14
A141
A428
A421
A1198
B1043
B1090
B1514
B1040
B1046
B1041
B1042
B1048
B645
B660
B661
B662

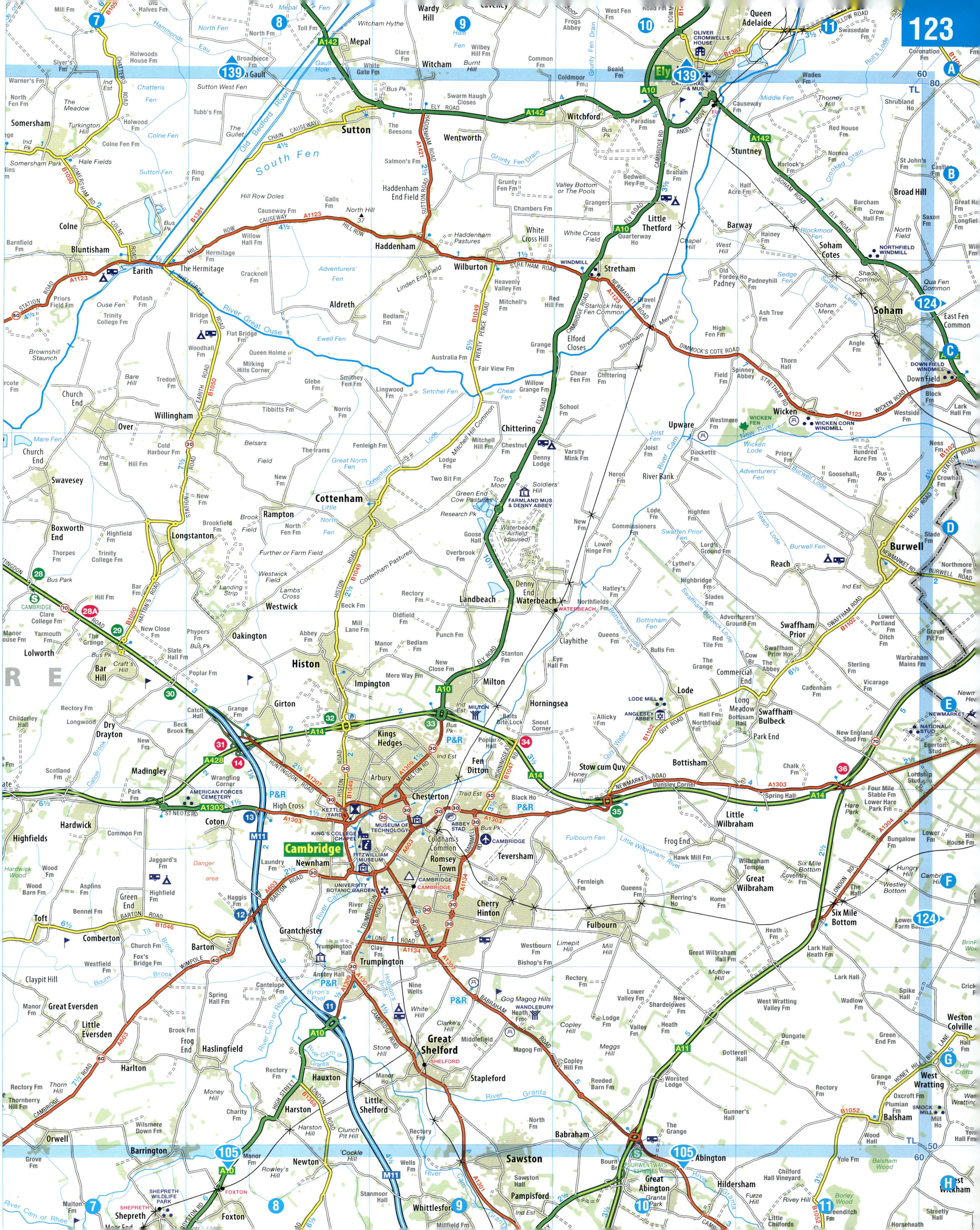

Mill Fm
Halves Fm
Hammonds Eau
North Fen
North Fm
Toll Fm
Mepal
Witcham Hythe
Wardy Hill
Coveney
Frogs Abbey
West Fen Fm
Queen Adelaide
Swasedale Fm
Oliver Cromwell's House
Ely
Witcham
Wilbey Hill Fm
Burnt Hill
Common Fm
Coldmoor Fm
Beald Fm
Witchford
Sutton
Sutton West Fen
Broadpiece Fm
Gault
Chatteris
Somersham
Somersham Park
The Meadow
Turkington Hill
Holwood Fm
Colne Fen Fm
Colne Fen
Hale Fields
Sutton Fen
The Gullet
Old Bedford River
South Fen
The Beesons
Wentworth
Grunty Fen Drain
Salmon's Fm
Haddenham End Field
Sutton Road
Haddenham Road
Paradise Fm
Red House Fm
Stuntney
Nornea Fm
Crooked Drain
Harlock's Fm
Shrubland Ho
St John's Fm
Broad Hill
Barcham Fm
Crow Hall Fm
Saxon Fm
North Field
Northfield Windmill
Barway
Hainey Fm
Soham Cotes
Blockmoor Fen
Little Thetford
Quarterway Ho
Chapel Hill
White Cross Field
Valley Bottom or The Pools
Grangers Fm
Chambers Fm
White Cross Hill
Grunty Fen Fm
Bedwell Hey Fm
Braham Fm
Half Acre Fm
Hill Row Doles
Galls Fm
North Hill
Causeway Fm
Colne
Bluntisham
Barnfield Fm
Earth
The Hermitage
Hermitage Fm
Willow Hall Fm
Haddenham
Haddenham Pastures
Wilburton
Stretham
Windmill
Heavenly Valley Fm
Mitchell's Fm
Red Hill Fm
Starlock Hay Fen Common
Gravel Fm
West Hill
Old Fordey Ho
Padney
Padneyhill Fen
Sedge Fen
Shade Common
Soham
Qua Fen Common
East Fen Common
Soham Mere
Ash Tree Fm
High Fen Fm
Angle Fm
Dimmock's Cote Road
Thorn Hall
Spinney Abbey
Down Field Windmill
Down Field
Block Fm
Lark Hall Fm
Westside Fm
Wicken
Wicken Fen
Wicken Corn Windmill
Wicken Lode
Westmere Fm
Upware
Joist Fen
Joist Fm
Ducketts Fm
Priory Fm
Hundred Acre Fm
Gooseshall Fm
Adventurers' Fen
Burwell Lode
Priors Field Fm
Potash Fm
Ouse Fen
Trinity College Fm
Bridge Fm
Flat Bridge Fm
River Great Ouse
Crackwell Fm
Adventurers' Fen
Linden End Field
Aldreth
Bedlam Fm
Ewell Fen
Brownshill Staunch
Woodhall Fm
Queen Holme
Milking Hills Corner
Australia Fm
Twenty Pence Road
Grange Fm
Elford Closes
Chear Fen Fm
Chittering Fm
Bare Hill
Tredon Fm
Glebe Fm
Smithey Fen Fm
Lingwood Fm
Setchel Fen
Fair View Fm
Chear Fen
Willow Grange Fm
School Fm
Church End
Willingham
Tibbitts Fm
Norris Fm
Chittering
Over
Mare Fen
Cold Harbour Fm
Belsars Field
The Irams
Fenleigh Fm
Mitchell Hill Common
Mitchell Hill Fm
Chestnut Fm
Varsity Mink Fm
Denny Lodge
Church End
Swavesey
Hill Fm
Great North Fen
New Fm
Lodge Fm
Two Bit Fm
Top Moor
Soldiers' Hill
Farmland Mus & Denny Abbey
Heron Fm
River Bank
Green End
Cow Pastures
Research Pk
Cottenham
Little North Fen
Rampton
North Fen Fm
Brookfield Fm
Brook Field
Boxworth End
Highfield Fm
Longstanton
Thorpes Fm
Trinity College Fm
Further or Farm Field
Waterbeach Airfield (disused)
Goose Hall
Overbrook Fm
Cottenham Pastures
Lode Fm
Highfen Fm
New Fm
Lower Hinge Fm
Commissioners Fm
Swaffen Prior Fen
Lord's Ground Fm
Reach Lode
Burwell Fen
Burwell
Reach
Slade Fm
Northmore Fm
Bus Park
Landing Strip
Westwick Field
Lambs' Cross
Westwick
Rectory Fm
Landbeach
Denny End
Waterbeach
Hatley's Fm
Northfields Fm
Highbridge Fm
Slades Fm
Adventurers' Ground Fm
Swaffham Prior
Lower Portland Fm
Ditch Fm
Gravel Pit Fm
Cambridge Services
Clare College Fm
Manor House Fm
Yarmouth Fm
The Grange
Lolworth
New Close Fm
Slate Hall Fm
Phypers Fm
Oakington
Abbey Fm
Beck Fm
Mill Lane Fm
Oldfield Fm
Punch Fm
Clayhithe
Bottisham Fen
Queens Fm
Red Tile Fm
Bulls Fm
Swaffham Prior Ho
Cow Br
The Abbey
Warbraham Mains Fm
Sterling Fm
Craft's Hill
Bar Hill
Poplar Fm
Histon
Manor Fm
Bedlam Fm
New Close Fm
Mere Way Fm
Stanton Fm
Eye Hall Fm
The Grange
Commercial End
Lode
Cadenham Fm
Vicarage Fm
Impington
Milton
Horningsea
Lode Mill
Anglesey Abbey
Long Meadow
Swaffham Bulbeck
Rectory Fm
Childerley Hall
Longwood
Catch Hall
Grange Fm
Girton
Kings Hedges
Milton
Baits Bite Lock
Snout Corner
Allicky Fm
Quy Water
Bottisham Hall
Northfield Fm
Hall Fm
Park End
New England Stud Fm
Newmarket
National Stud
Egerton Stud
Dry Drayton
Beck Brook Fm
New Fm
Poplar Hall
Fen Ditton
Stow cum Quy
Honey Hill
Bottisham
Chalk Fm
Lordship Stud
Madingley
Wrangling Corner
Arbury
Chesterton
Trad Est
Black Ho
Dunsley Corner
Spring Hall
Four Mile Stable Fm
Lower Hare Park Fm
Hare Park
Scotland Fm
Park Fm
American Forces Cemetery
High Cross
Kettle's Yard
Abbey Stad
Little Wilbraham
Coton
Hardwick
Highfields
Common Fm
King's College Chapel
Museum of Technology
Coldham's Common
Cambridge Airport
Fulbourn Fen
Little Wilbraham River
Frog End
Hawk Mill Fm
Wilbraham Temple
Great Wilbraham
Six Mile Bottom Coventry Fm
Bungalow Fm
Lower Fm
Hill House Fm
Hardwick Wood
Wood Fm
Wood Barn Fm
Asplins Fm
Jaggard's Fm
Danger area
Laundry Fm
Newnham
Cambridge
Fitzwilliam Museum
University Botanic Garden
Cambridge
Romsey Town
Teversham
Fernleigh Fm
Queens Fm
Herring's Ho
Home Fm
The Hall
Six Mile Bottom
Westley Bottom
Hungry Hill
Highfield Fm
Green End
Haggis Fm
River Fm
Cherry Hinton
Fulbourn
Heath Fm
Lower Farm Barn
Toft
Comberton
Bennel Fm
Barton Road
Grantchester
Trumpington Road
Long Road
Westbourn Fm
Limepit Hill
Mill Hill
Great Wilbraham Hall Fm
Lark Hall Heath Fm
Church Fm
Fox's Bridge Fm
Barton
Trumpington Hall
Clay Fm
Trumpington
Bishop's Fm
Westfield Fm
Bourn Brook
Wimpole Road
Rectory Fm
Mutlow Hill
Lark Hall
Claypit Hill
Anstey Hall
Cantelupe Fm
Byron's Pool
Nine Wells
Gog Magog Hills
Wandlebury
Lower Valley Fm
Shardelowes Fm
New Fm
West Wratting Valley Fm
Wadlow Fm
Spike Hall
Manor Fm
Great Eversden
Little Eversden
Spring Hall Fm
White Hill
Clarke's Hill
Middlefield
Heath Fm
Lodge Fm
Copley Hill
Valley Fm
Heath Fm
Dungate Fm
Green End Fm
Weston Colville
Brook Fm
Frog End
Haslingfield
Harlton
Stone Hill
Great Shelford
Magog Fm
Meggs Hill
Dotterell Hall
Copley Hill Fm
Shelford
Stapleford
Reeded Barn Fm
Worsted Lodge
Grange Fm
West Wratting
Oxcroft Fm
Rectory Fm
Thorn Hill
Rectory Fm
Thornberry Hill Fm
Money Hill
Hauxton
Manor Ho
Little Shelford
River Granta
Gunner's Hall
Plumian Fm
Smock Mill
Balsham
Mill Ho
West Wratting
Charity Fm
Harston
Harston Hill
Clunch Pit Hill
Rectory Fm
North Fm
The Grange
Babraham
Wood Hall
Orwell
Wilsmere Down Fm
Barrington
Manor Fm
Newton
Cockle Hill
Rowley's Hill
Wells Fm
River Cam
Sawston
Sawston Hall
Pampisford
Bourn Br
Fourwentways Services
Abington
Great Abington
Granta Park
Hildersham
Chilford Hall Vineyard
Furze Hill
Rivey Hill
Yole Fm
Balsham Wood
Borley Wood
Grove Fm
Malton Fm
Shepreth Wildlife Park
Shepreth
Foxton
River Cam or Rhee
Stanmoor Hall
Whittlesford
Millfield Fm
Ind Est
Little Chilfords
Meenditch Fm
Streetly Hall
Horseheath
West Wickham
A10
A14
A142
A1123
A1303
A1134
A1307
A1309
A1301
A428
A603
A11
A1304
A505
M11
B1049
B1050
B1381
B1040
B1046
B1047
B1102
B1368
B1052
B1382
B1085
B1104

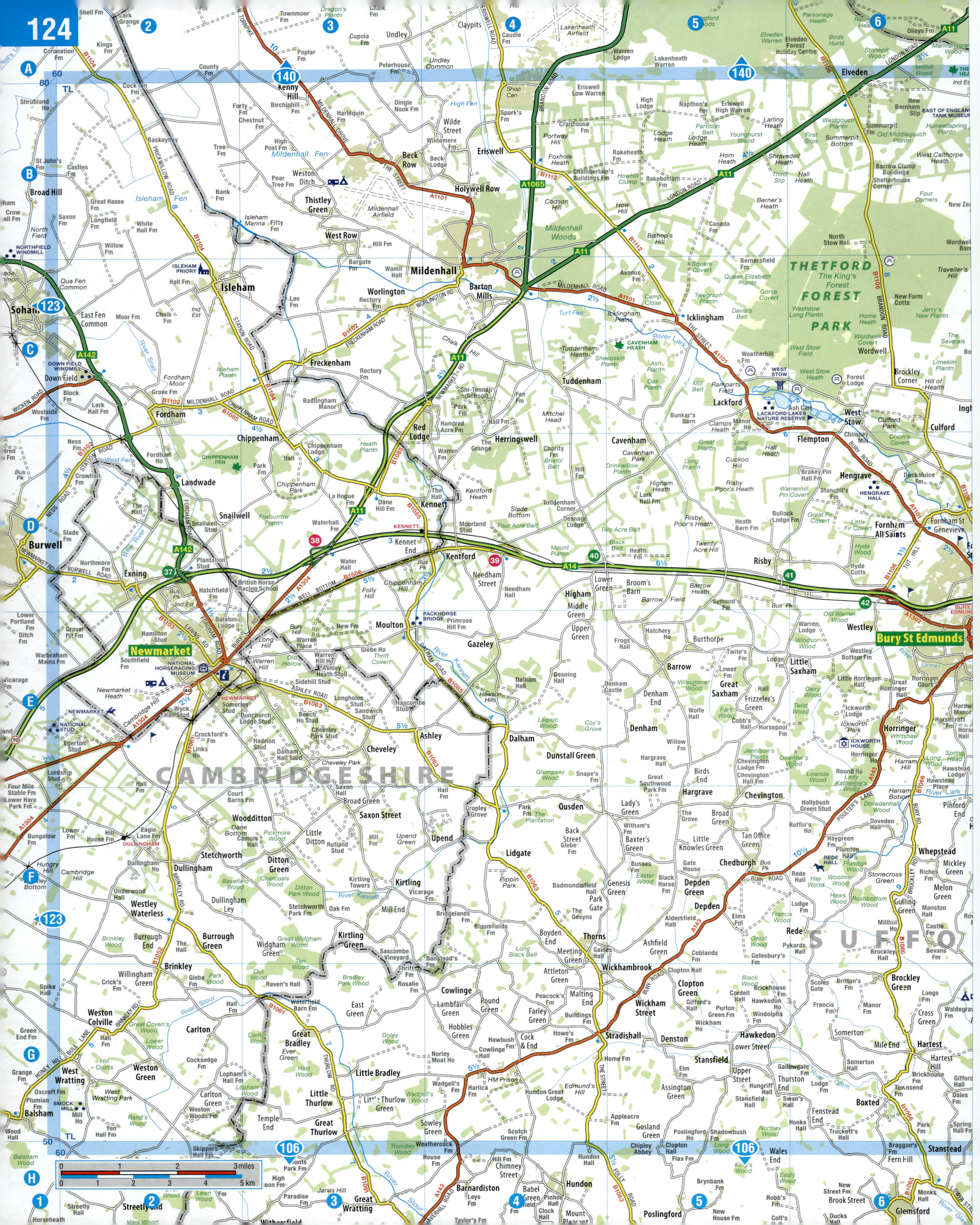

CAMBRIDGESHIRE
SUFFOLK
THETFORD FOREST PARK
The King's Forest
Newmarket
Bury St Edmunds
Mildenhall
Isleham
Soham
Burwell
Fordham
Freckenham
Worlington
Barton Mills
Icklingham
Tuddenham
Cavenham
Herringswell
Kentford
Kennett
Red Lodge
Chippenham
Snailwell
Landwade
Exning
Moulton
Gazeley
Higham
Risby
Flempton
Hengrave
Lackford
West Stow
Culford
Wordwell
Elveden
Eriswell
Holywell Row
Beck Row
West Row
Kenny Hill
Thistley Green
Barrow
Burthorpe
Denham
Dalham
Ashley
Cheveley
Saxon Street
Woodditton
Dullingham
Stetchworth
Ditton Green
Kirtling
Kirtling Green
Upend
Lidgate
Ousden
Dunstall Green
Hargrave
Chevington
Chedburgh
Depden
Wickhambrook
Stradishall
Denston
Stansfield
Hawkedon
Rede
Whepstead
Brockley Green
Hartest
Boxted
Cowlinge
Great Bradley
Little Bradley
Great Thurlow
Little Thurlow
Carlton
Brinkley
Burrough Green
Westley Waterless
Weston Colville
West Wratting
Balsham
Horringer
Westley
Little Saxham
Great Saxham
Fornham All Saints
Fornham St Genevieve
Hundon
Poslingford
Barnardiston
Great Wratting
Glemsford
Stanstead
Wales End

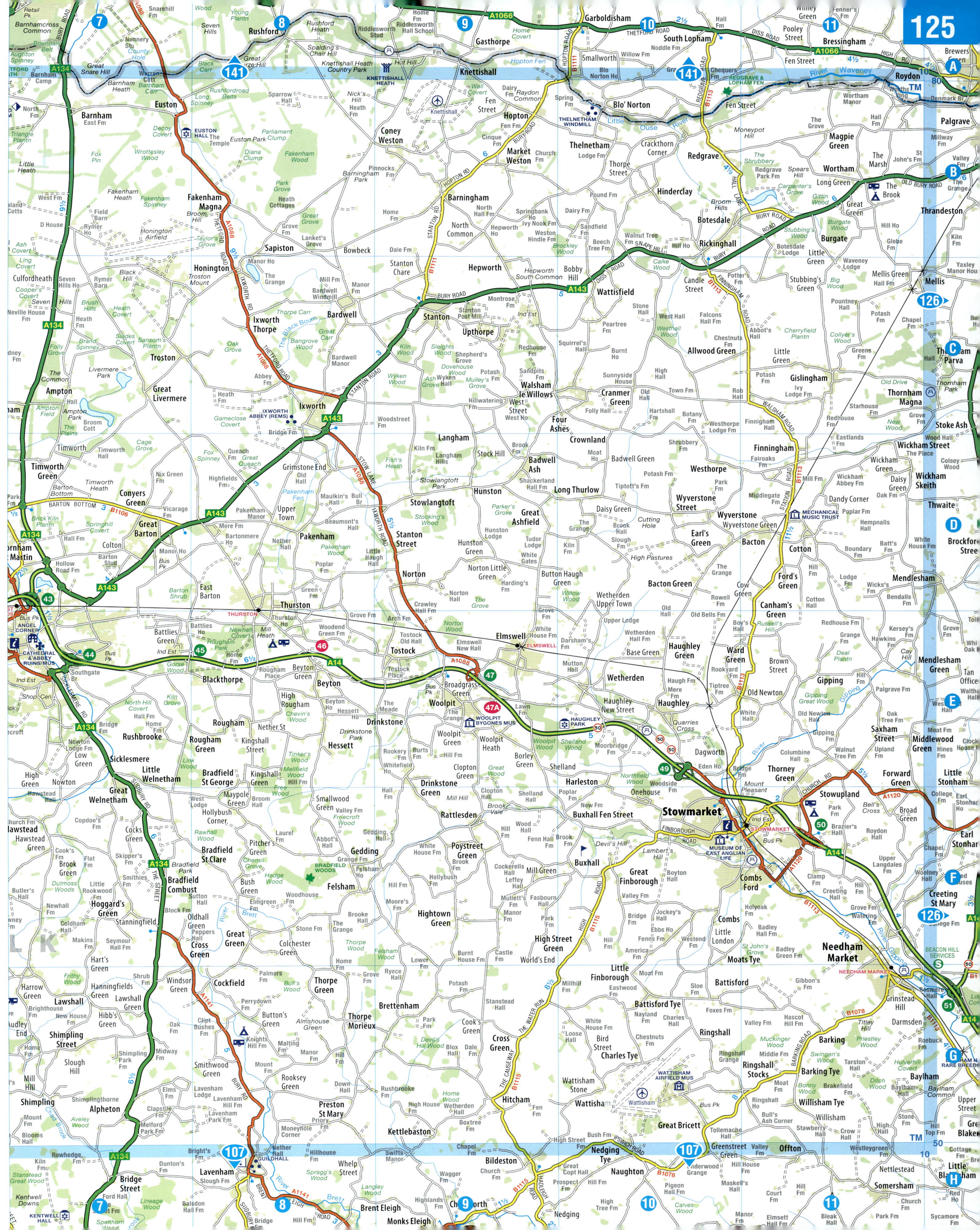
Rushford
Knettishall
Gasthorpe
Garboldisham
South Lopham
Bressingham
Roydon
Blo' Norton
Redgrave
Palgrave
Barnham
Euston
Coney Weston
Hopton
Market Weston
Thelnetham
Hinderclay
Wortham
Magpie Green
Fakenham Magna
Barningham
Botesdale
Rickinghall
Burgate
Thrandeston
Sapiston
Honington
Hepworth
Wattisfield
Mellis
Ixworth Thorpe
Bardwell
Stanton
Upthorpe
Allwood Green
Gislingham
Troston
Great Livermere
Walsham le Willows
Cranmer Green
Thornham Magna
Ampton
Ixworth
Four Ashes
Crownland
Finningham
Stoke Ash
Langham
Badwell Ash
Westhorpe
Wickham Street
Timworth Green
Conyers Green
Great Barton
Stowlangtoft
Hunston
Great Ashfield
Long Thurlow
Wyverstone Street
Wyverstone
Pakenham
Stanton Street
Cotton
Bacton
Norton
Bacton Green
Mendlesham
Thurston
Elmswell
Tostock
Beyton
Haughley Green
Ward Green
Blackthorpe
Woolpit
Wetherden
Haughley
Old Newton
Gipping
Mendlesham Green
Rougham
Drinkstone
Rushbrooke
Hessett
Sicklesmere
Great Welnetham
Little Welnetham
Harleston
Stowmarket
Stowupland
Buxhall Fen Street
Gedding
Felsham
Buxhall
Great Finborough
Combs Ford
Creeting St Mary
Bradfield St Clare
Bradfield Combust
Hightown Green
Combs
Needham Market
Cockfield
Thorpe Green
Brettenham
Little Finborough
Battisford
Lawshall
Shimpling Street
Ringshall
Barking
Charles Tye
Hitcham
Wattisham
Ringshall Stocks
Baylham
Preston St Mary
Alpheton
Kettlebaston
Great Bricett
Offton
Bildeston
Lavenham
Nedging Tye
Naughton
Somersham
Brent Eleigh
Monks Eleigh
A134
A143
A1088
A14
A1066
A1120
A1141
B1113
B1115
B1078

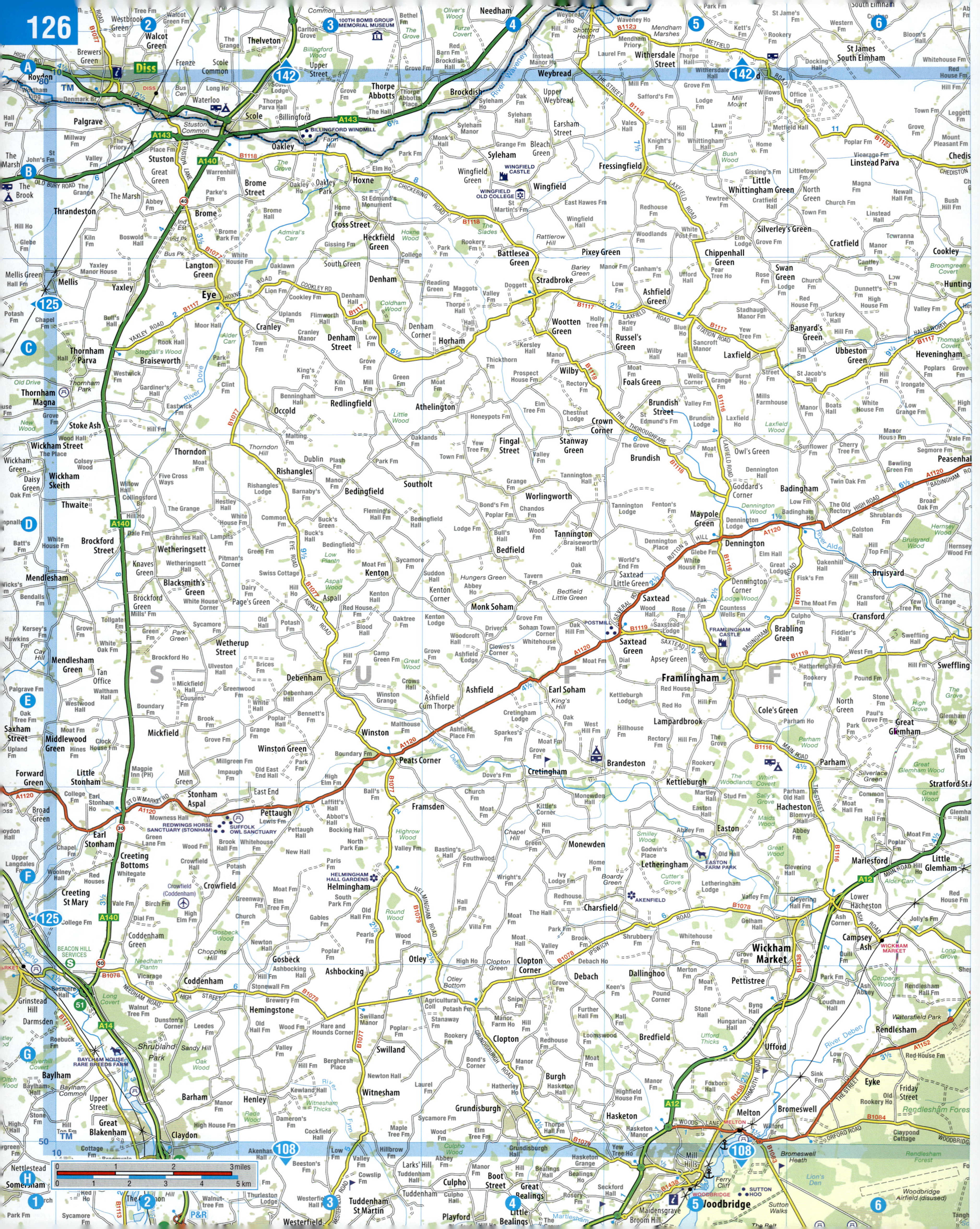
Diss
Roydon
Palgrave
Walcot Green
Thelveton
Scole
Billingford
Oakley
Thorpe Abbotts
Brockdish
Needham
Weybread
Withersdale Street
Mendham
St James South Elmham
Syleham
Wingfield
Fressingfield
Hoxne
Stuston
Brome
Brome Street
Thrandeston
Langton Green
Mellis
Yaxley
Eye
Cross Street
Heckfield Green
Denham
Battlesea Green
Stradbroke
Pixey Green
Chippenhall Green
Silverley's Green
Cratfield
Linstead Parva
Little Whittingham Green
Cookley
Cranley
Denham Street
Horham
Wootten Green
Wilby
Laxfield
Ubbeston Green
Heveningham
Braiseworth
Thornham Parva
Thornham Magna
Occold
Redlingfield
Athelington
Brundish Street
Foals Green
Crown Corner
Stoke Ash
Wickham Street
Thorndon
Rishangles
Bedingfield
Southolt
Fingal Street
Stanway Green
Brundish
Worlingworth
Badingham
Peasenhall
Wickham Skeith
Thwaite
Brockford Street
Wetheringsett
Bedfield
Tannington
Maypole Green
Dennington
Bruisyard
Mendlesham
Blacksmith's Green
Kenton
Aspall
Monk Soham
Saxtead
Cransford
Brabling Green
Wetherup Street
Framlingham
Saxtead Green
Sweffling
Mendlesham Green
Debenham
Ashfield
Earl Soham
Lampardbrook
Great Glemham
Saxham Street
Middlewood Green
Mickfield
Winston
Peats Corner
Cretingham
Brandeston
Kettleburgh
Parham
Hacheston
Forward Green
Little Stonham
Stonham Aspal
Pettaugh
Framsden
Easton
Earl Stonham
Creeting Bottoms
Crowfield
Helmingham
Monewden
Letheringham
Marlesford
Little Glemham
Creeting St Mary
Charsfield
Campsey Ash
Coddenham
Gosbeck
Ashbocking
Otley
Clopton Corner
Debach
Dallinghoo
Wickham Market
Pettistree
Hemingstone
Swilland
Clopton
Bredfield
Rendlesham
Ufford
Baylham
Barham
Henley
Witnesham
Burgh
Grundisburgh
Hasketon
Eyke
Great Blakenham
Claydon
Melton
Bromeswell
Tuddenham St Martin
Culpho
Great Bealings
Little Bealings
Playford
Woodbridge
Westerfield
Somersham
A140
A143
A1120
A12
A14
A1152
B1077
B1078
B1116
B1117
B1118
B1119
B1123
B1079
B1438
B1084
SUFFOLK OWL SANCTUARY
REDWINGS HORSE SANCTUARY (STONHAM)
HELMINGHAM HALL GARDENS
FRAMLINGHAM CASTLE
EASTON FARM PARK
BAYLHAM HOUSE RARE BREEDS FARM
100TH BOMB GROUP MEMORIAL MUSEUM
BILLINGFORD WINDMILL
WINGFIELD CASTLE
WINGFIELD OLD COLLEGE
AKENFIELD
SUTTON HOO
River Waveney
River Deben
River Dove
River Alde
0 1 2 3 miles
0 1 2 3 4 5 km

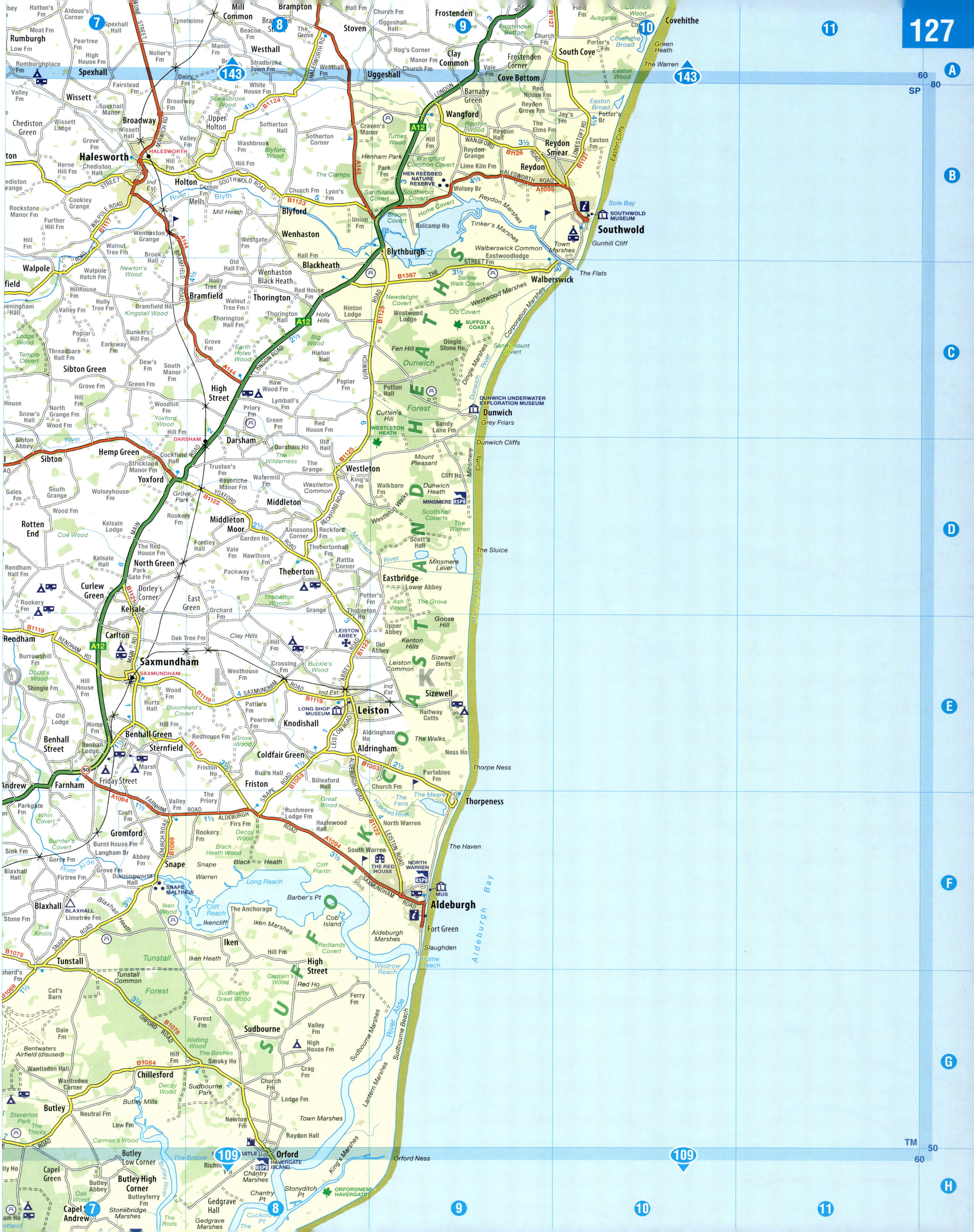
Rumburgh
Spexhall
Wissett
Halesworth
Holton
Westhall
Brampton
Stoven
Uggeshall
Frostenden
Covehithe
South Cove
Cove Bottom
Wangford
Reydon
Reydon Smear
Southwold
SOUTHWOLD MUSEUM
Sole Bay
Gunhill Cliff
Walberswick
The Flats
Blythburgh
Blyford
Wenhaston
Blackheath
Thorington
Bramfield
Walpole
Sibton Green
Sibton
Hemp Green
Yoxford
Darsham
High Street
Dunwich
DUNWICH UNDERWATER EXPLORATION MUSEUM
Grey Friars
Dunwich Cliffs
Dunwich Forest
Westleton
MINSMERE RSPB
The Sluice
Minsmere Level
Middleton
Middleton Moor
Theberton
Eastbridge
North Green
Kelsale
Carlton
Saxmundham
Curlew Green
Rendham
Benhall Green
Benhall Street
Sternfield
Farnham
Friday Street
Leiston
LONG SHOP MUSEUM
LEISTON ABBEY
Sizewell
Knodishall
Coldfair Green
Aldringham
Thorpe Ness
Thorpeness
The Meare
Friston
Snape
SNAPE MALTINGS
Gromford
Blaxhall
Tunstall
Tunstall Forest
Iken
North Warren
The Haven
Aldeburgh
Fort Green
Slaughden
Aldeburgh Bay
Sudbourne
High Street
Chillesford
Butley
Orford
Orford Ness
HAVERGATE ISLAND
King's Marshes
Capel St Andrew
Butley High Corner
Boyton
SUFFOLK COAST AND HEATHS
SUFFOLK
A12
A144
A1094
A1095
B1122
B1125
B1119
B1121
B1069
B1078
B1084
B1387
B1123
B1124
B1126
B1127
B1353
143
109
SP
TM
60
50
80
A
B
C
D
E
F
G
H
7
8
9
10
11

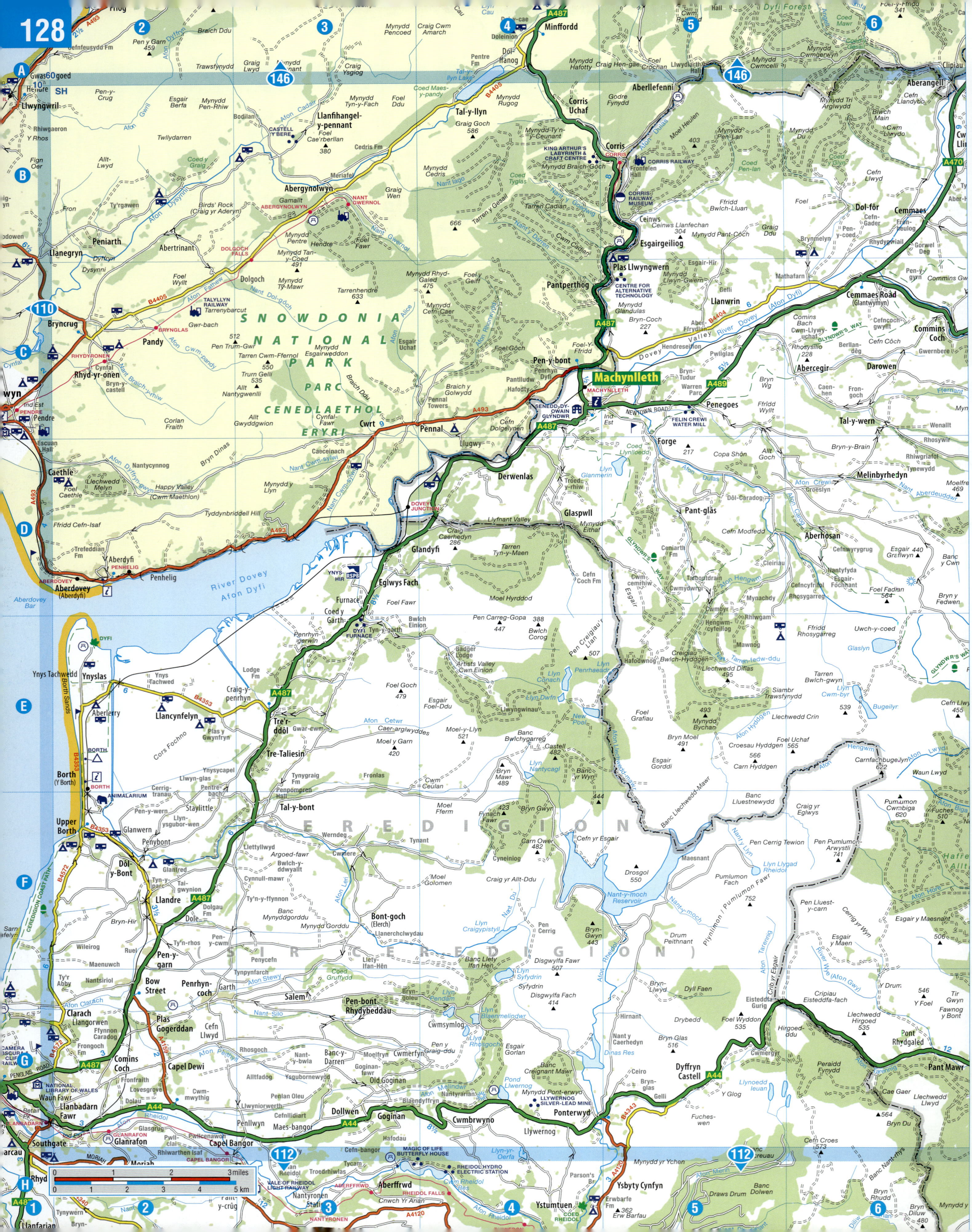
Minffordd
Dolgellau
Talyllyn Lake
Tal-y-llyn
Llanfihangel-y-pennant
Abergynolwyn
Corris Uchaf
Corris
Aberllefenni
Aberangell
Llwyngwril
Peniarth
Llanegryn
Dolgoch
Bryncrug
Pandy
Rhyd-yr-onen
Tywyn
Pendre
Caethle
Happy Valley
Aberdyfi
Aberdovey (Aberdyfi)
Penhelig
SNOWDONIA NATIONAL PARK
PARC CENEDLAETHOL ERYRI
Cwrt
Pennal
Pen-y-bont
Machynlleth
Esgairgeiliog
Plas Llwyngwern
Centre for Alternative Technology
Pantperthog
Llanwrin
Cemmaes Road (Glantwymyn)
Cemmaes
Dol-fôr
Commins Coch
Abercegir
Darowen
Penegoes
Forge
Tal-y-wern
Melinbyrhedyn
Derwenlas
Glaspwll
Pant-glâs
Aberhosan
Glandyfi
Eglwys Fach
River Dovey
Afon Dyfi
Furnace
Ynyslas
Ynys Tachwedd
Borth Sands
Llancynfelyn
Tre'r-ddôl
Tre-Taliesin
Borth (Y Borth)
Upper Borth
Tal-y-bont
CEREDIGION
SIR CEREDIGION
Dôl-y-Bont
Llandre
Bont-goch (Elerch)
Nant-y-moch Reservoir
Plynlimon / Pumlumon Fawr
Pen-y-garn
Bow Street
Penrhyn-coch
Salem
Pen-bont Rhydybeddau
Clarach
Llangorwen
Plas Gogerddan
Capel Dewi
Comins Coch
Waun Fawr
Llanbadarn Fawr
Southgate
Glanrafon
Capel Bangor
Dollwen
Goginan
Cwmbrwyno
Ponterwyd
Dyffryn Castell
Pant Mawr
Aberffrwd
Ystumtuen
Ysbyty Cynfyn
Nantyronen Station
Rheidol Falls
A487
A493
A470
A489
A44
B4405
B4404
B4353
B4572
A4120
146
110
112
3 miles
5 km

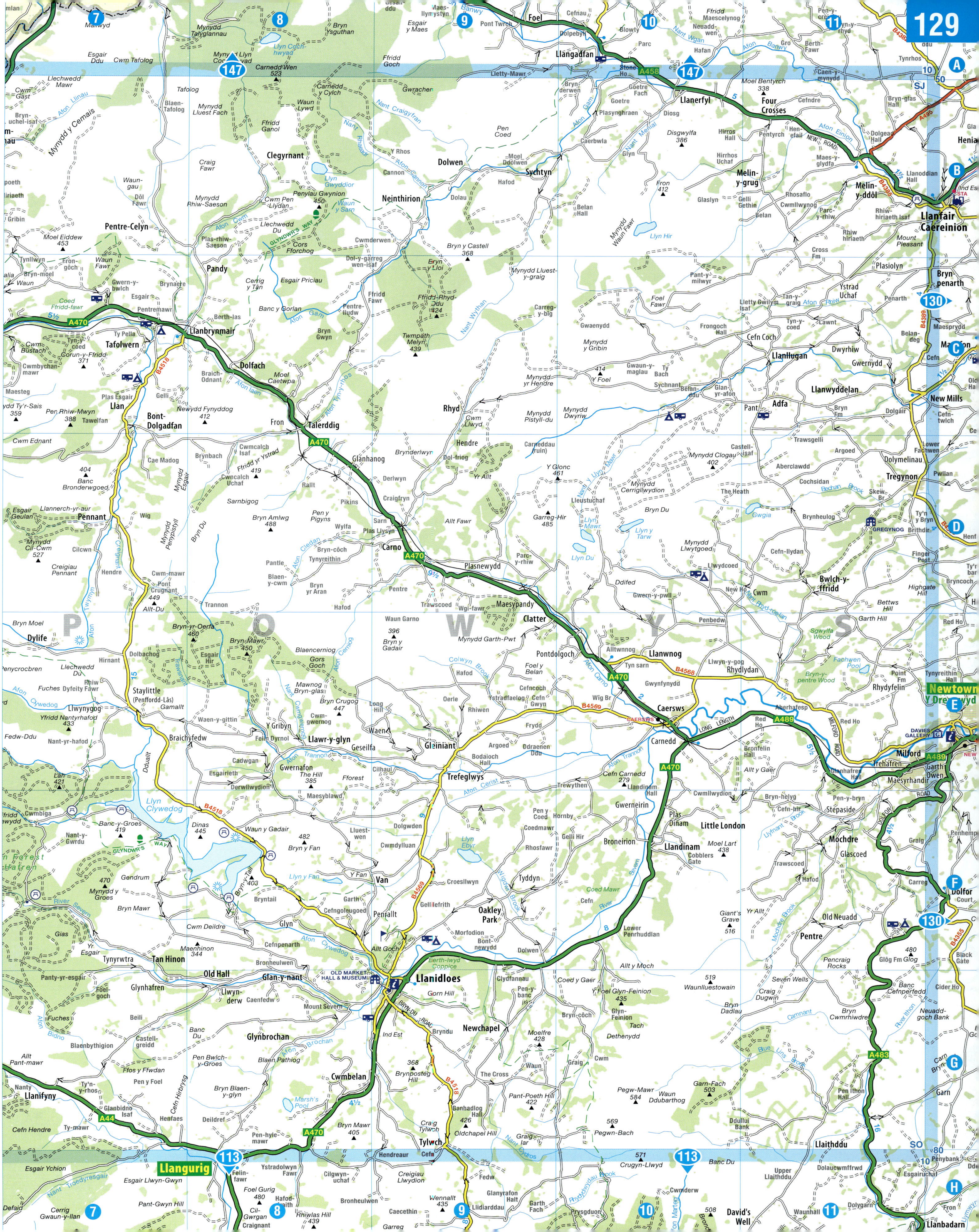
Foel
Llangadfan
Llanerfyl
Four Crosses
Llanfair Caereinion
Melin-y-ddôl
Melin-y-grug
Dolwen
Sychtyn
Neinthirion
Clegyrnant
Pentre-Celyn
Pandy
Llanbrynmair
Tafolwern
Dolfach
Talerddig
Bont-Dolgadfan
Llan
Rhyd
Llanllugan
Llanwyddelan
Adfa
New Mills
Tregynon
Pennant
Carno
Clatter
Maesypandy
Llanwnog
Pontdolgoch
Rhydlydan
Caersws
Carnedd
Newtown
Y Drenewydd
Milford
Dylife
Staylittle
Llawr-y-glyn
Trefeglwys
Gleiniant
Llyn Clywedog
Van
Llanidloes
Oakley Park
Little London
Llandinam
Mochdre
Stepaside
Dolfor
Tan Hinon
Old Hall
Glan-y-nant
Newchapel
Cwmbelan
Llanifyny
Llangurig
Tylwch
Llaithddu
Llanbadarn
David's Well
Pentre
A470
A458
A489
A483
A44
B4518
B4568
B4569
B4389
B4355
POWYS
Glyndŵr's Way
147
130
113
SJ
SO

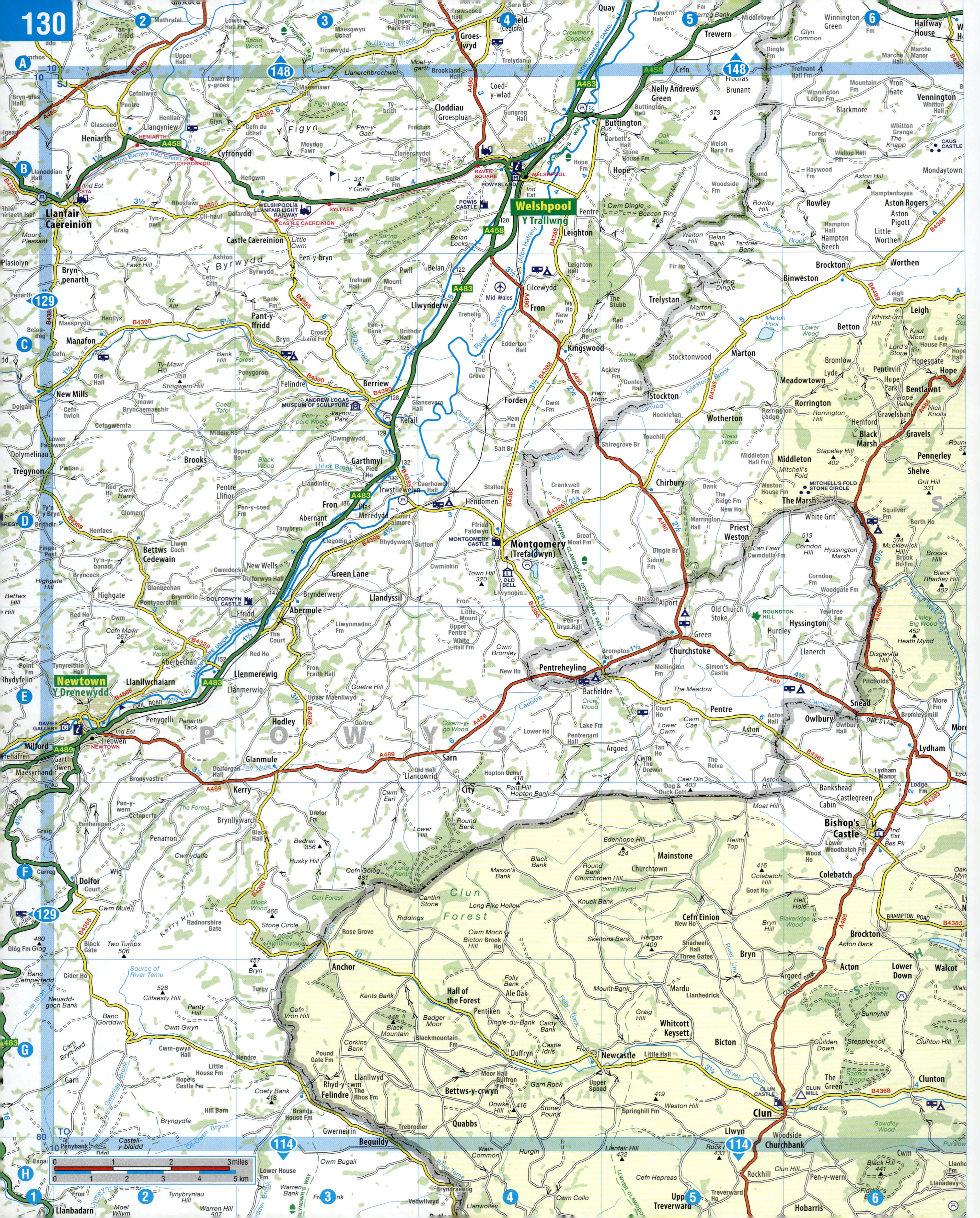
Welshpool
Y Trallwng
Newtown
Y Drenewydd
Montgomery
(Trefaldwyn)
Bishop's Castle
Clun
Llanfair Caereinion
Castle Caereinion
Heniarth
Cyfronydd
Buttington
Leighton
Kingswood
Forden
Berriew
Garthmyl
Fron
Abermule
Llanmerewig
Kerry
Sarn
Churchstoke
Chirbury
Marton
Worthen
Brockton
Lydham
Snead
Pentreheyling
Bacheldre
Mainstone
Newcastle
Bettws-y-crwyn
Felindre
Anchor
Beguildy
Dolfor
Tregynon
Manafon
New Mills
Bettws Cedewain
Llandyssil
Hodley
Glanmule
Trelystan
Hope
Rowley
Stockton
Wotherton
Middleton
Priest Weston
Hyssington
Owlbury
Pentre
Aston
Colebatch
Acton
Walcot
Clunton
Churchbank
Trewern
Nelly Andrews Green
Halfway House
Clun Forest
P O W Y S
A458
A483
A490
A489
B4385
B4386
B4388
B4390
B4368
A488
Montgomery Canal
Offa's Dyke Path
River Severn
148
129
114
1 2 3 4 5 6
A B C D E F G H
0 1 2 3 miles
0 1 2 3 4 5 km

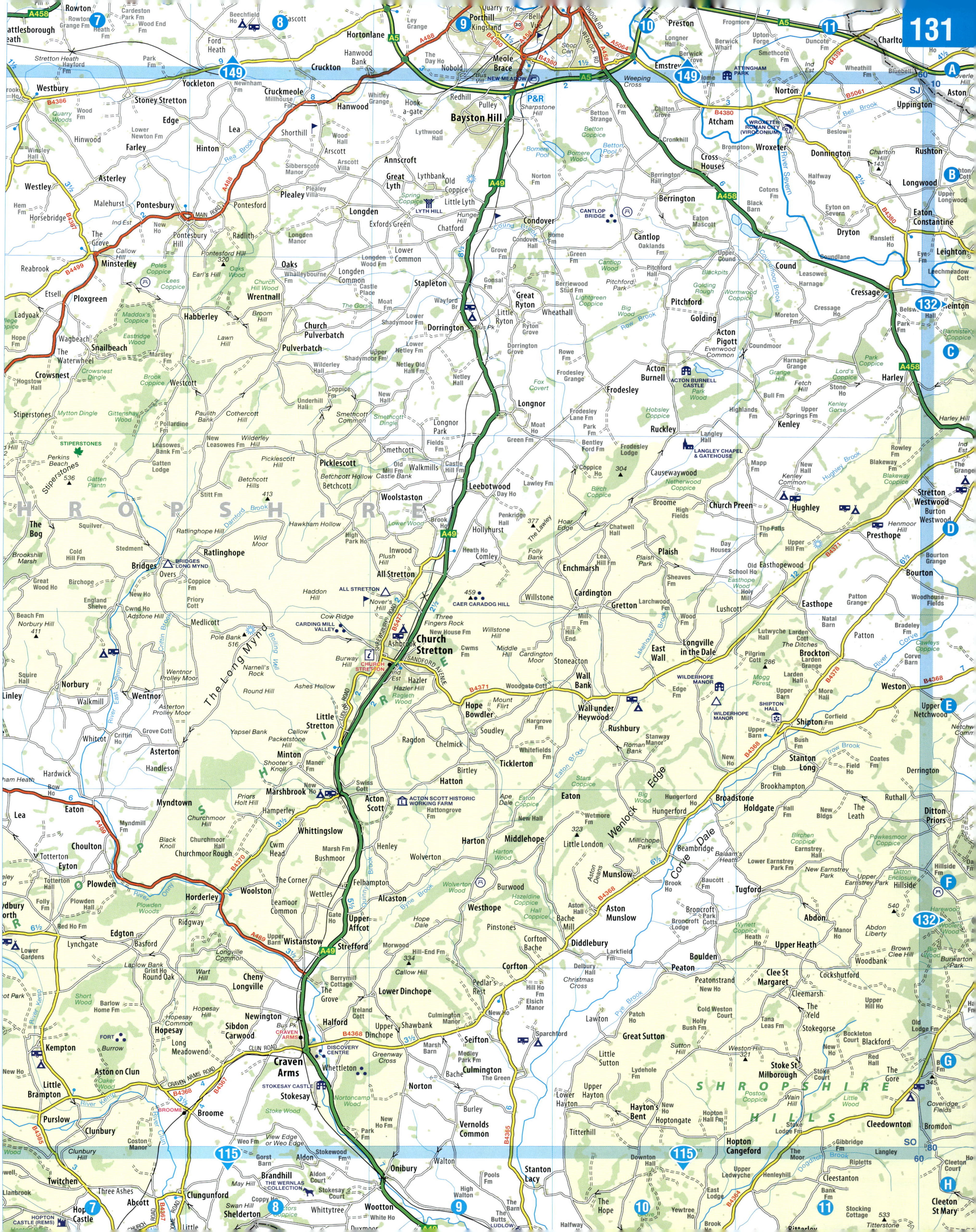
Rowton
Porthill
Kingsland
Belle Vue
Meole Brace
Preston
Emstrey
Attingham Park
Norton
Atcham
Wroxeter
Uppington
Wattlesborough Heath
Westbury
Yockleton
Stoney Stretton
Edge
Cruckton
Cruckmeole
Hanwood
Bayston Hill
Hinwood
Farley
Lea
Hinton
Shorthill
Arscott
Annscroft
Great Lyth
Lythbank
Lyth Hill
Little Lyth
Condover
Cantlop
Berrington
Cross Houses
Donnington
Rushton
Longwood
Eaton Constantine
Dryton
Leighton
Westley
Asterley
Pontesbury
Pontesford
Plealey
Longden
Exfords Green
Chatford
Minsterley
Radlith
Oaks
Cound
Cressage
Reabrook
Etsell
Ploxgreen
Wrentnall
Stapleton
Great Ryton
Pitchford
Golding
Acton Pigott
Habberley
Church Pulverbatch
Pulverbatch
Dorrington
Little Ryton
Wheathall
Snailbeach
Crowsnest
Westcott
Acton Burnell
Acton Burnell Castle
Frodesley
Harley
Stiperstones
Longnor
Ruckley
Kenley
Stiperstones
Picklescott
Smethcott
Walkmills
Leebotwood
Langley Chapel & Gatehouse
Causewaywood
Church Preen
Hughley
Stretton Westwood
SHROPSHIRE
The Bog
Woolstaston
Hollyhurst
Presthope
Ratlinghope
Bridges
All Stretton
Enchmarsh
Plaish
Cardington
Gretton
Lushcott
Easthope
Bourton
Caer Caradog Hill
Willstone
Church Stretton
Hope Bowdler
East Wall
Longville in the Dale
Brockton
Patton
Norbury
Wentnor
The Long Mynd
Wall Bank
Wall under Heywood
Weston
Linley
Walkmill
Little Stretton
Ragdon
Chelmick
Rushbury
Shipton
Whitcot
Asterton
Minton
Ticklerton
Stanton Long
Hatton
Acton Scott
Acton Scott Historic Working Farm
Eaton
Broadstone
Holdgate
Ditton Priors
Myndtown
Marshbrook
Wenlock Edge
Hungerford
Choulton
Whittingslow
Harton
Middlehope
Little London
Corve Dale
Plowden
Horderley
Woolston
Alcaston
Westhope
Munslow
Tugford
Abdon
Edgton
Wistanstow
Strefford
Upper Affcot
Diddlebury
Aston Munslow
Upper Heath
Boulden
Peaton
Cheny Longville
Corfton
Clee St Margaret
Kempton
Hopesay
Newington
Sibdon Carwood
Halford
Craven Arms
Lower Dinchope
Seifton
Great Sutton
Aston on Clun
Little Brampton
Stokesay Castle
Stokesay
Culmington
Norton
Stoke St Milborough
Purslow
Clunbury
Broome
Vernolds Common
Hayton's Bent
Cleedownton
Hopton Cangeford
Twitchen
Onibury
Aldon
Walton
Stanton Lacy
Clungunford
Abcott
Brandhill
The Wernlas Collection
Shelderton
Wootton
Hopton Castle
Cleeton St Mary
SHROPSHIRE HILLS
A5
A49
A458
A488
B4368
B4370
B4371
B4371
B5477
A4113

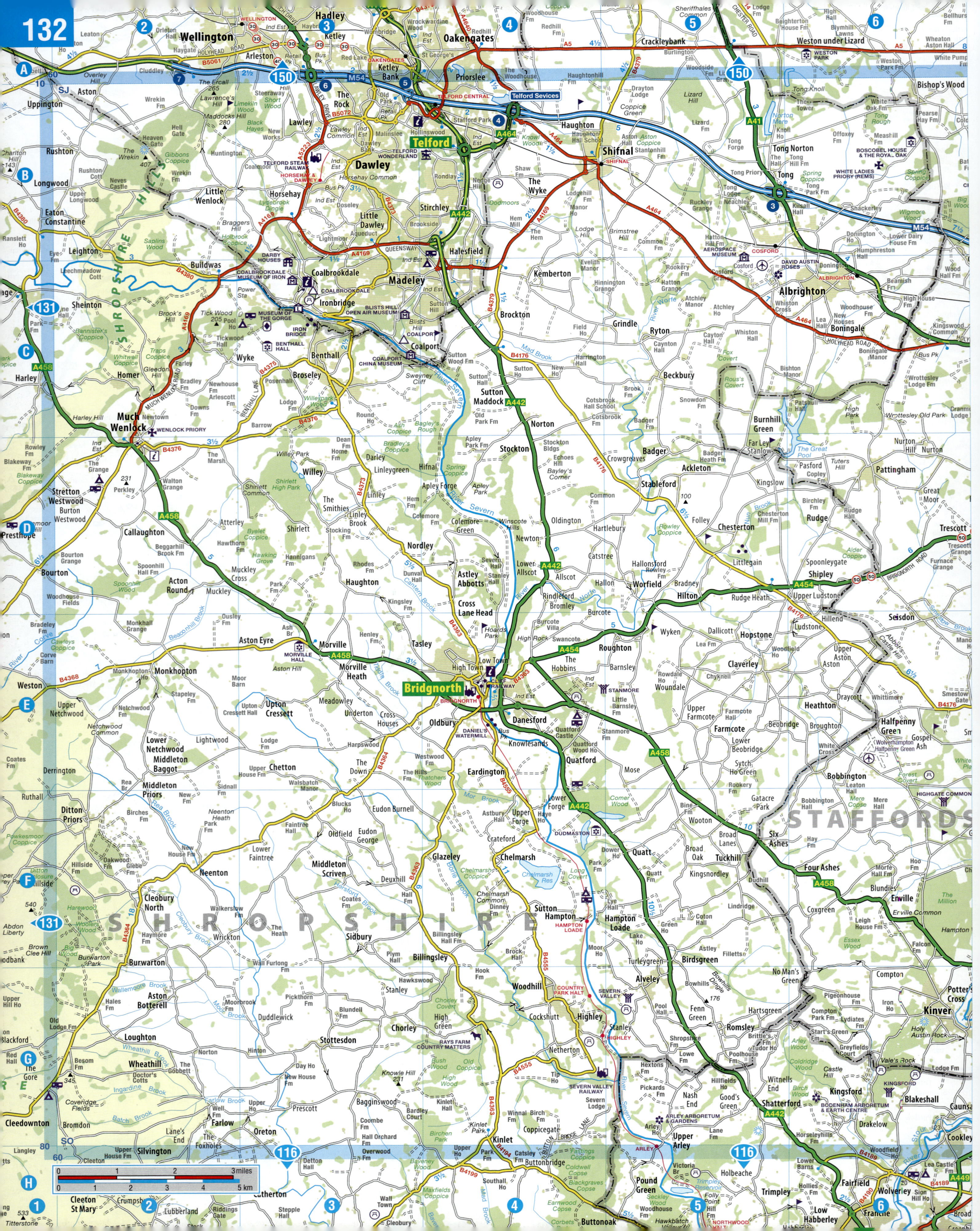
Wellington
Hadley
Oakengates
Crackleybank
Weston under Lizard
Telford
Dawley
Shifnal
Tong
Madeley
Coalbrookdale
Ironbridge
Albrighton
Boningale
Much Wenlock
Broseley
Bridgnorth
Kinver
Cleobury North
Highley
Shatterford
Wolverley
Kinlet
STAFFORDS
S H R O P S H I R E
SHROPSHIRE HILLS
M54
A5
A442
A458
A454
A464
A4169
A41
A449
B4176
B4363
B4364
B4555
150
131
116

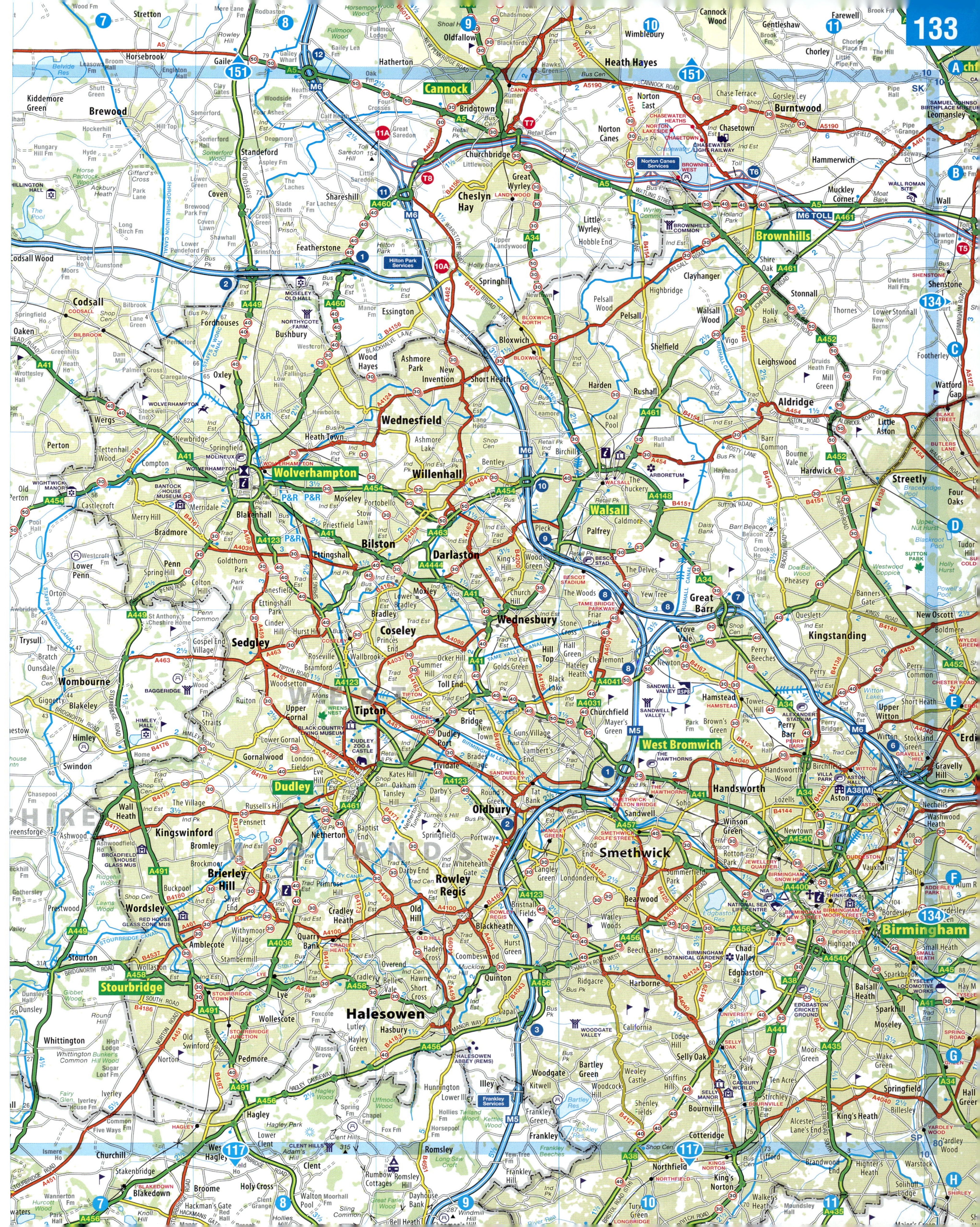
Cannock
Wolverhampton
Walsall
Brownhills
Stourbridge
Dudley
West Bromwich
Birmingham
Halesowen
Smethwick
Wednesfield
Willenhall
Bilston
Darlaston
Wednesbury
Tipton
Coseley
Sedgley
Oldbury
Rowley Regis
Brierley Hill
Kingswinford
Wordsley
Wombourne
Codsall
Brewood
Cheslyn Hay
Great Wyrley
Norton Canes
Heath Hayes
Burntwood
Aldridge
Streetly
Great Barr
Kingstanding
Handsworth
Sandwell
Bearwood
Harborne
Edgbaston
Selly Oak
Bournville
Northfield
Hagley
Romsley
Blakedown
Amblecote
Pensnett
Quarry Bank
Cradley Heath
Lye
Pedmore
Essington
Shareshill
Featherstone
Bloxwich
Pelsall
Rushall
Shenstone
Little Aston
Four Oaks
Erdington
Aston
Balsall Heath
Moseley
Kings Norton
Tettenhall
Perton
Penn
Wall Heath
Himley
Swindon
Fordhouses
Bushbury
Oxley
Short Heath
New Invention
Coven
Standeford
Hatherton
Churchbridge
Bridgtown
Chasetown
Hammerwich
Stonnall
Walsall Wood
Clayhanger
Shelfield
Leighswood
Wednesbury
Hamstead
Perry Barr
Winson Green
Ladywood
Quinton
Woodgate
Blackheath
Old Hill
Cradley
Hasbury
Illey
Frankley
Longbridge
Rubery
Wollaston
Whittington
Kinver
West Midlands

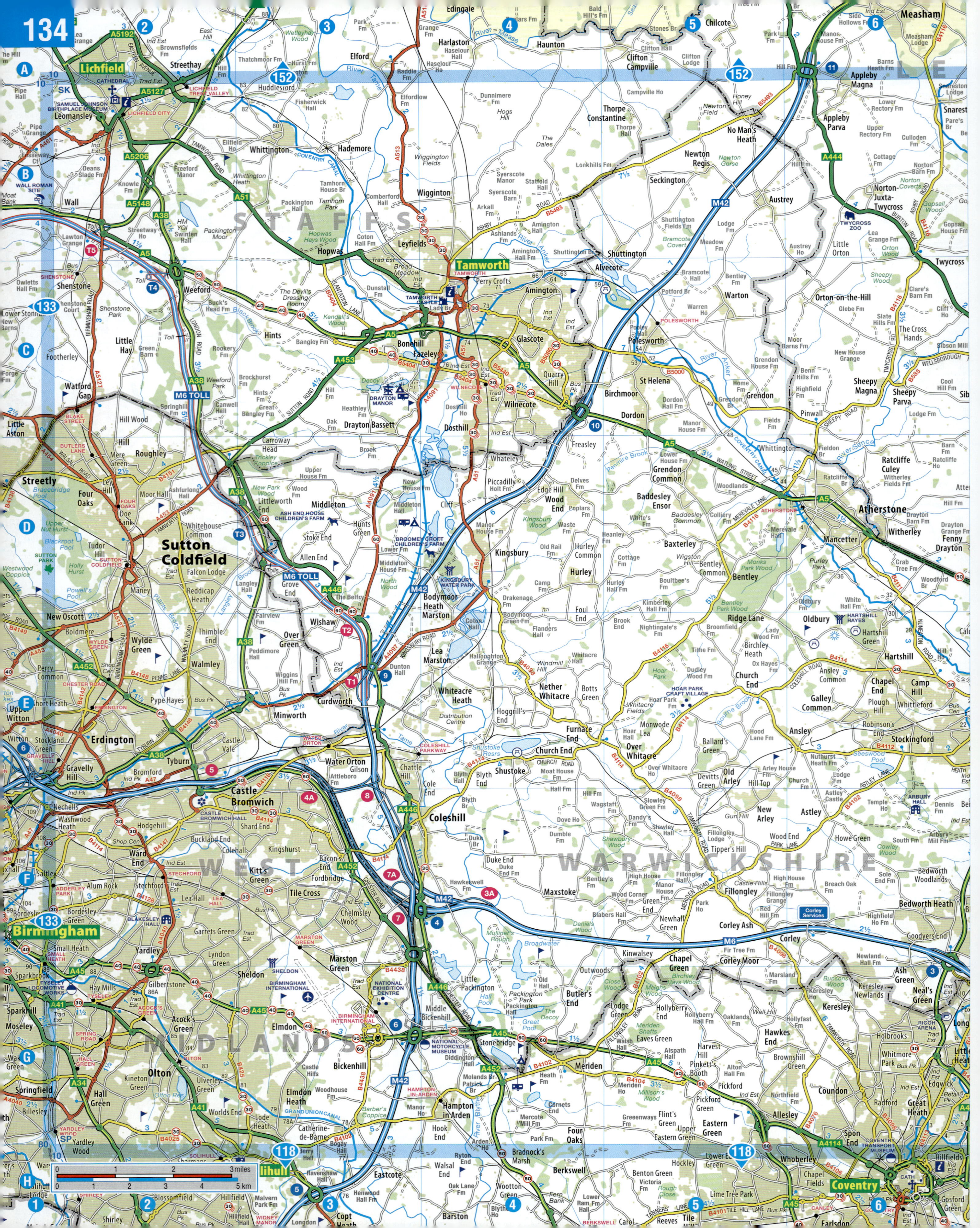

Lichfield
Tamworth
Sutton Coldfield
Birmingham
Coventry
STAFFS
WEST MIDLANDS
WARWICKSHIRE
Atherstone
Measham
Polesworth
Coleshill
Castle Bromwich
Erdington
Kingsbury
Fillongley
Meriden
Hampton in Arden
Solihull
Olton
Yardley
Streetly
Shenstone
Whittington
Hopwas
Fazeley
Wilnecote
Dordon
Baddesley Ensor
Mancetter
Hartshill
Ansley
Corley
Keresley
Shustoke
Water Orton
Curdworth
Minworth
Wishaw
Middleton
Drayton Bassett
Elford
Harlaston
Haunton
Clifton Campville
Chilcote
Appleby Magna
Snarestone
Twycross
Sheepy Magna
Grendon
Warton
Austrey
Newton Regis
Seckington
Shuttington
Alvecote
Amington
Wigginton
Hademore
Streethay
Wall
Weeford
Hints
Canwell
Footherley
Stonebridge
Bickenhill
Elmdon
Marston Green
Sheldon
Kinwalsey
Maxstoke
Whitacre Heath
Nether Whitacre
Over Whitacre
Furnace End
Church End
Astley
New Arley
Old Arley
Chapel End
Galley Common
Stockingford
Fenny Drayton
Witherley
Ratcliffe Culey
Sheepy Parva
Little Orton
Orton-on-the-Hill
Norton-Juxta-Twycross
Pinwall
Fillongley
Berkswell
Balsall Common
Allesley
Eastern Green
Whoberley
Great Heath
M6 TOLL
M42
M6
A5
A38
A446
A452
A45
A444
A51
A453
0 1 2 3 miles
0 1 2 3 4 5 km
152
133
118

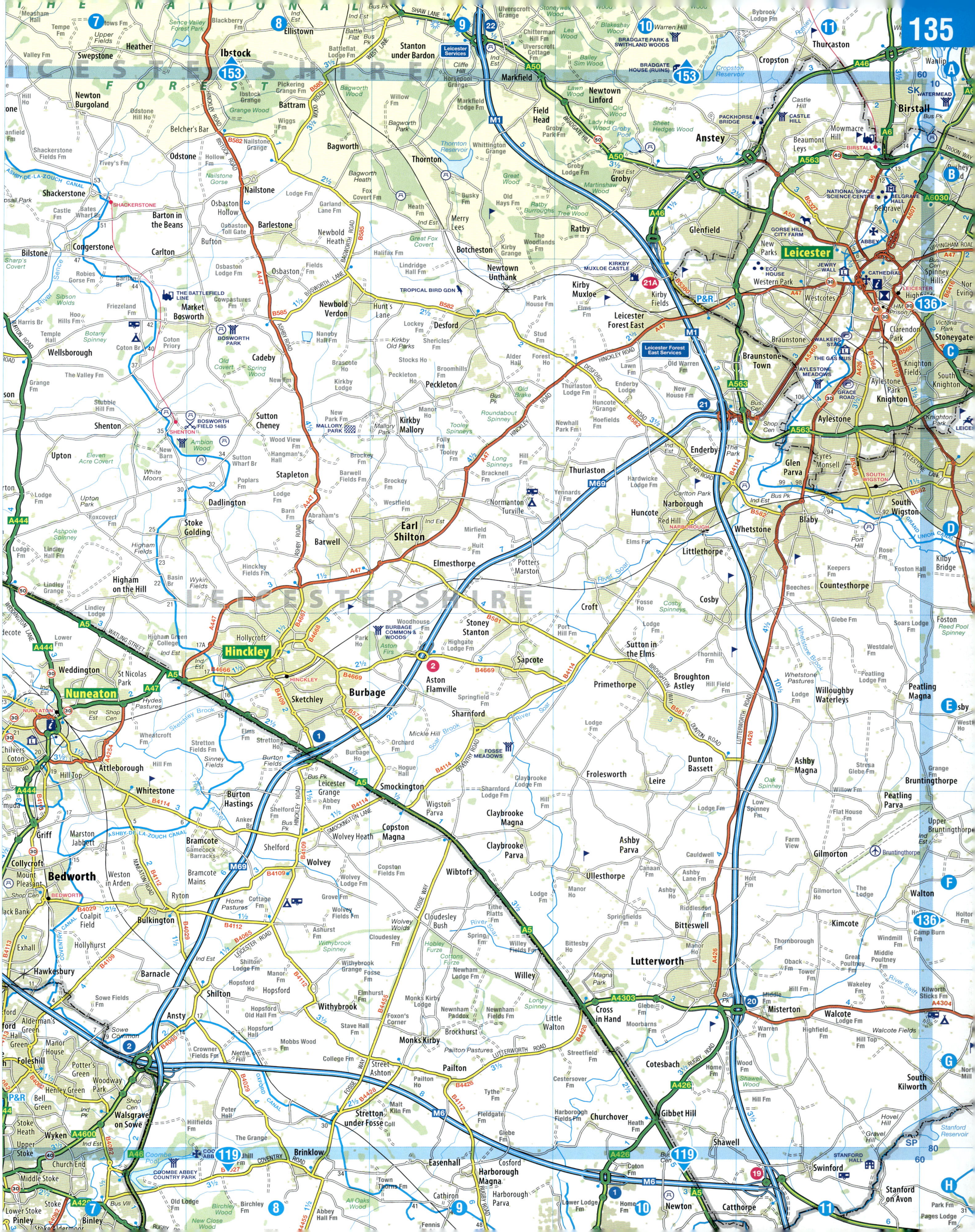
LEICESTERSHIRE
THE NATIONAL FOREST
Leicester
Hinckley
Nuneaton
Bedworth
Lutterworth
Ibstock
Market Bosworth
Earl Shilton
Burbage
Birstall
Anstey
Glenfield
Groby
Ratby
Kirby Muxloe
Braunstone Town
Aylestone
Knighton
Stoneygate
Glen Parva
Blaby
Enderby
Narborough
Whetstone
South Wigston
Countesthorpe
Cosby
Croft
Thurlaston
Desford
Newbold Verdon
Barlestone
Nailstone
Bagworth
Thornton
Markfield
Field Head
Stanton under Bardon
Thurcaston
Cropston
Newtown Linford
Botcheston
Newtown Unthank
Peckleton
Kirkby Mallory
Sutton Cheney
Cadeby
Shenton
Upton
Dadlington
Stapleton
Barwell
Stoke Golding
Higham on the Hill
Elmesthorpe
Stoney Stanton
Sapcote
Aston Flamville
Sharnford
Sketchley
Smockington
Wigston Parva
Wolvey
Copston Magna
Claybrooke Magna
Claybrooke Parva
Frolesworth
Leire
Ashby Parva
Ullesthorpe
Dunton Bassett
Ashby Magna
Broughton Astley
Sutton in the Elms
Primethorpe
Willoughby Waterleys
Peatling Magna
Peatling Parva
Gilmorton
Kimcote
Walton
Bruntingthorpe
Bitteswell
Misterton
Walcote
Cotesbach
South Kilworth
Shawell
Swinford
Catthorpe
Stanford on Avon
Gibbet Hill
Churchover
Pailton
Monks Kirby
Withybrook
Shilton
Ansty
Bulkington
Barnacle
Wolvey Heath
Burton Hastings
Attleborough
Whitestone
Weddington
Congerstone
Shackerstone
Odstone
Carlton
Osbaston
Wellsborough
Sheepy
Bilstone
Barton in the Beans
Newton Burgoland
Swepstone
Heather
Battram
Hollycroft
Wibtoft
Willey
Little Walton
Cross in Hand
Brinklow
Easenhall
Harborough Magna
Stretton under Fosse
Walsgrave on Sowe
Wyken
Binley
Foleshill
Hawkesbury
Exhall
Keresley
Ryton
Weston in Arden
Collycroft
Griff
Marston Jabbett
Bramcote
Shelford
Leicester Forest East
Kirby Fields
Huncote
Littlethorpe
Thurlaston
Normanton Turville
Potters Marston
Kilby Bridge
Foston
Catthorpe
Newton
M1
M69
M6
A5
A47
A46
A50
A426
A4303
A444
A447
Thornton Reservoir
Cropston Reservoir
Stanford Reservoir
BOSWORTH FIELD 1485
THE BATTLEFIELD LINE
NATIONAL SPACE SCIENCE CENTRE
BRADGATE HOUSE (RUINS)
KIRBY MUXLOE CASTLE
Leicester Forest East Services
Leicester Services
MALLORY PARK
TROPICAL BIRD GDN
ASHBY-DE-LA-ZOUCH CANAL
COVENTRY CANAL
OXFORD CANAL
GRAND UNION CANAL
River Soar
River Swift

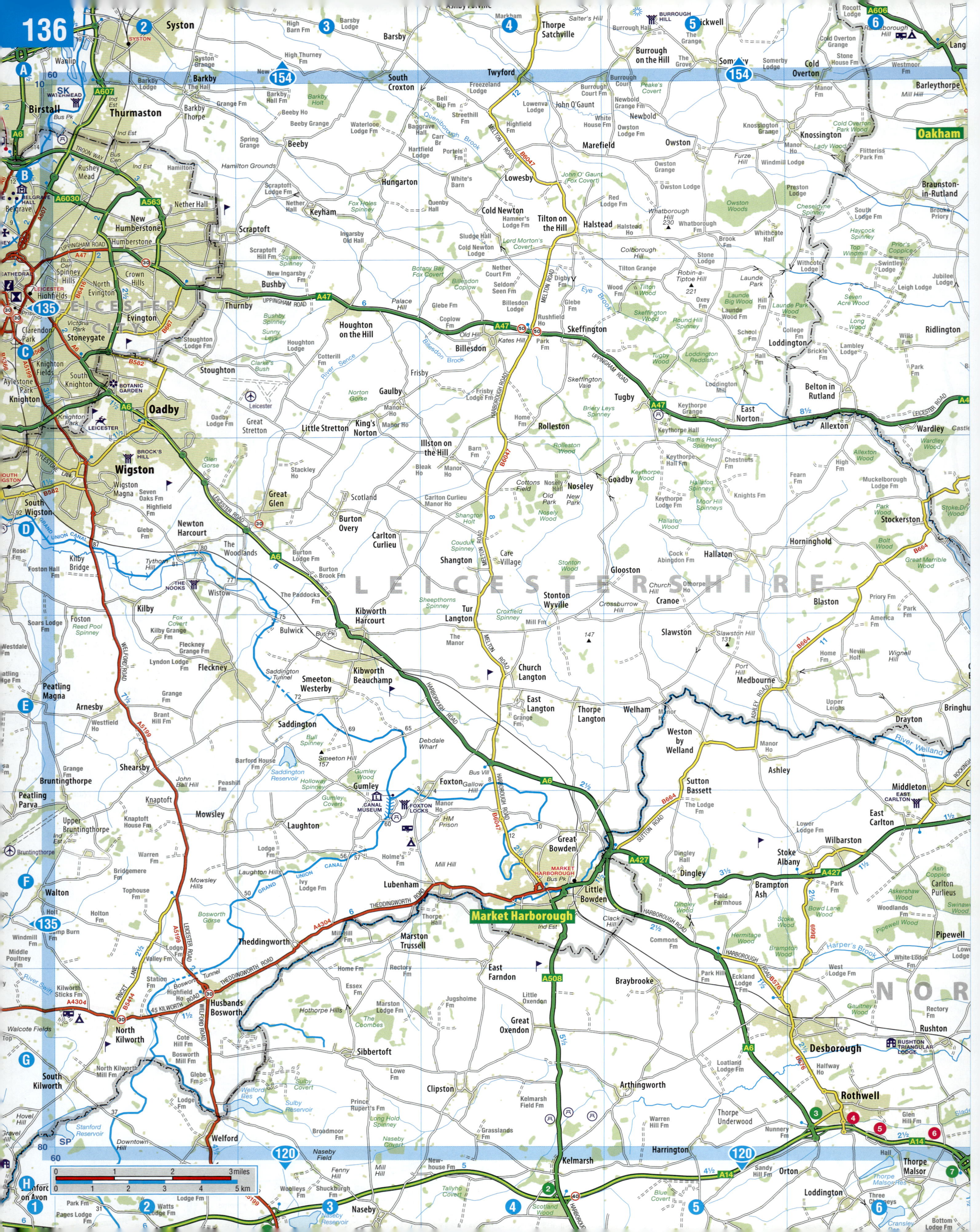
LEICESTERSHIRE
LEICESTER CITY
Syston
Birstall
Thurmaston
Barkby
Barsby
South Croxton
Twyford
Thorpe Satchville
Burrough on the Hill
Somerby
Cold Overton
Oakham
Barleythorpe
Knossington
Owston
Marefield
Lowesby
Hungarton
Beeby
Keyham
Scraptoft
New Humberstone
Humberstone
Belgrave
Evington
Thurnby
Bushby
Houghton on the Hill
Cold Newton
Tilton on the Hill
Halstead
Skeffington
Billesdon
Loddington
Ridlington
Stoneygate
Knighton
Oadby
Stoughton
Gaulby
King's Norton
Little Stretton
Great Stretton
Tugby
East Norton
Belton in Rutland
Allexton
Wardley
Rolleston
Illston on the Hill
Noseley
Goadby
Wigston
Great Glen
Burton Overy
Carlton Curlieu
Scotland
Shangton
Hallaton
Horninghold
Stockerston
South Wigston
Newton Harcourt
Kilby Bridge
Kilby
Fleckney
Wistow
Kibworth Harcourt
Kibworth Beauchamp
Smeeton Westerby
Tur Langton
Stonton Wyville
Glooston
Cranoe
Blaston
Slawston
Church Langton
East Langton
Thorpe Langton
Welham
Medbourne
Drayton
Peatling Magna
Arnesby
Saddington
Shearsby
Foxton
Gumley
Mowsley
Laughton
Lubenham
Great Bowden
Market Harborough
Little Bowden
Weston by Welland
Sutton Bassett
Ashley
Dingley
Stoke Albany
Wilbarston
Brampton Ash
East Carlton
Middleton
Bruntingthorpe
Peatling Parva
Walton
Theddingworth
Marston Trussell
East Farndon
Husbands Bosworth
North Kilworth
South Kilworth
Sibbertoft
Great Oxendon
Braybrooke
Desborough
Rushton
Clipston
Arthingworth
Rothwell
Welford
Kelmarsh
Harrington
Naseby
Orton
Thorpe Malsor
Loddington
Pipewell
A6
A47
A427
A508
A4304
A14
A606
A5199
B6047
B664
154
135
120

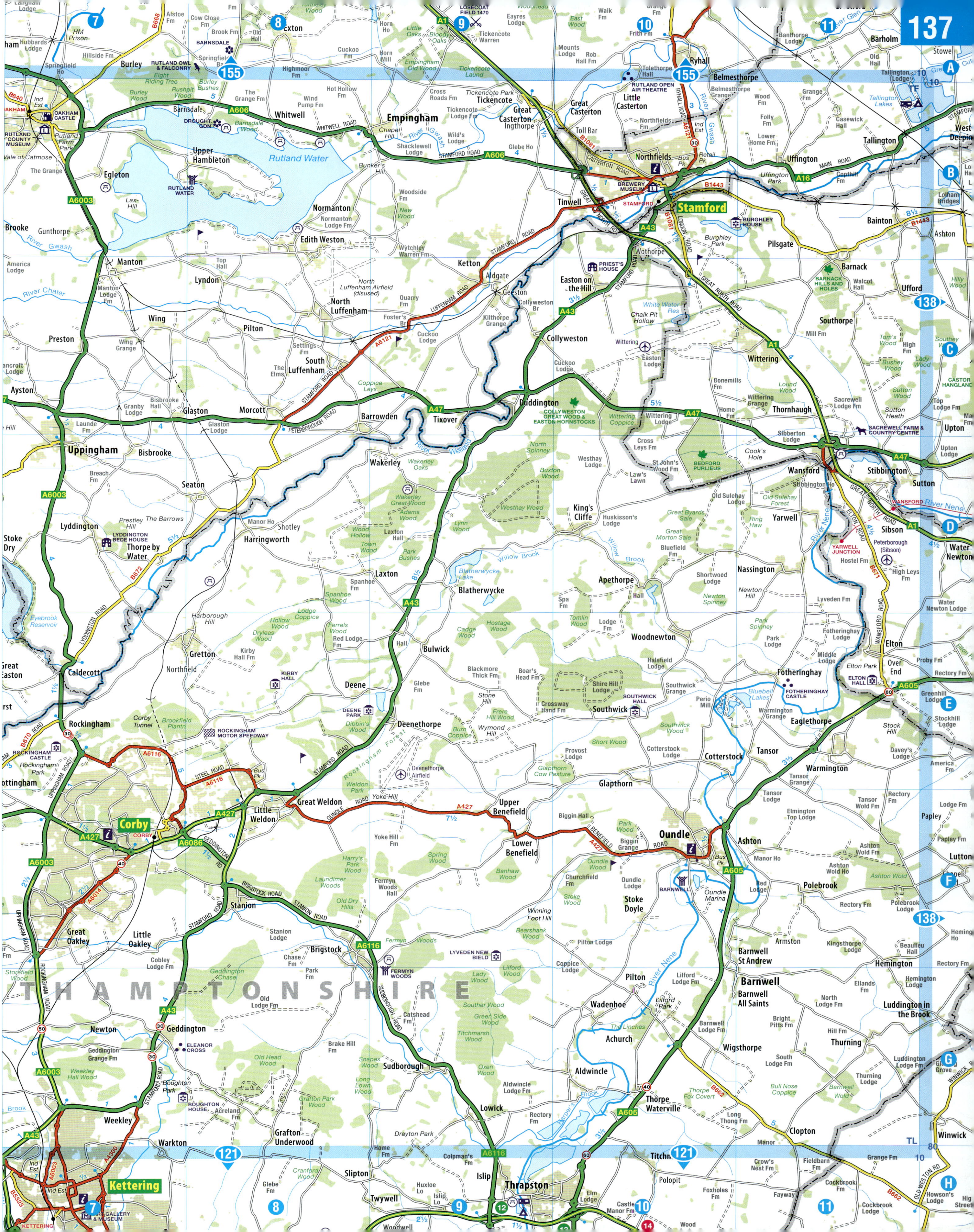
Stamford
Empingham
Rutland Water
Upper Hambleton
Egleton
Burley
Whitwell
Normanton
Edith Weston
Manton
Lyndon
Ketton
Tinwell
Great Casterton
Little Casterton
Ryhall
Uffington
Tallington
Barnack
Ufford
Bainton
Pilsgate
Southorpe
Wittering
Thornhaugh
Wansford
Stibbington
Sutton
Sibson
Yarwell
Nassington
Apethorpe
Woodnewton
Elton
Fotheringhay
Tansor
Cotterstock
Warmington
Eaglethorpe
Oundle
Ashton
Polebrook
Barnwell
Hemington
Luddington in the Brook
Thurning
Wigsthorpe
Clopton
Pilton
Stoke Doyle
Wadenhoe
Achurch
Aldwincle
Thorpe Waterville
Titchmarsh
Thrapston
Islip
Lowick
Sudborough
Brigstock
Stanion
Great Weldon
Little Weldon
Upper Benefield
Lower Benefield
Corby
Great Oakley
Little Oakley
Geddington
Newton
Weekley
Warkton
Kettering
Grafton Underwood
Slipton
Twywell
Rockingham
Caldecott
Gretton
Deene
Deenethorpe
Bulwick
Blatherwycke
Laxton
Harringworth
Wakerley
Seaton
Uppingham
Bisbrooke
Glaston
Morcott
Barrowden
Tixover
Duddington
Collyweston
Easton on the Hill
Aldgate
Geeston
South Luffenham
North Luffenham
Pilton
Wing
Preston
Ayston
Lyddington
Thorpe by Water
King's Cliffe
Southwick
Glapthorn
Fotheringhay Castle
Burghley House
Rockingham Castle
Rockingham Motor Speedway
Kirby Hall
Deene Park
Lyveden New Bield
Barnwell
River Nene
River Welland
River Gwash
River Chater
A1
A43
A47
A427
A605
A606
A6003
A6116
A6121
A16
Northamptonshire
Hemington
Barnwell All Saints

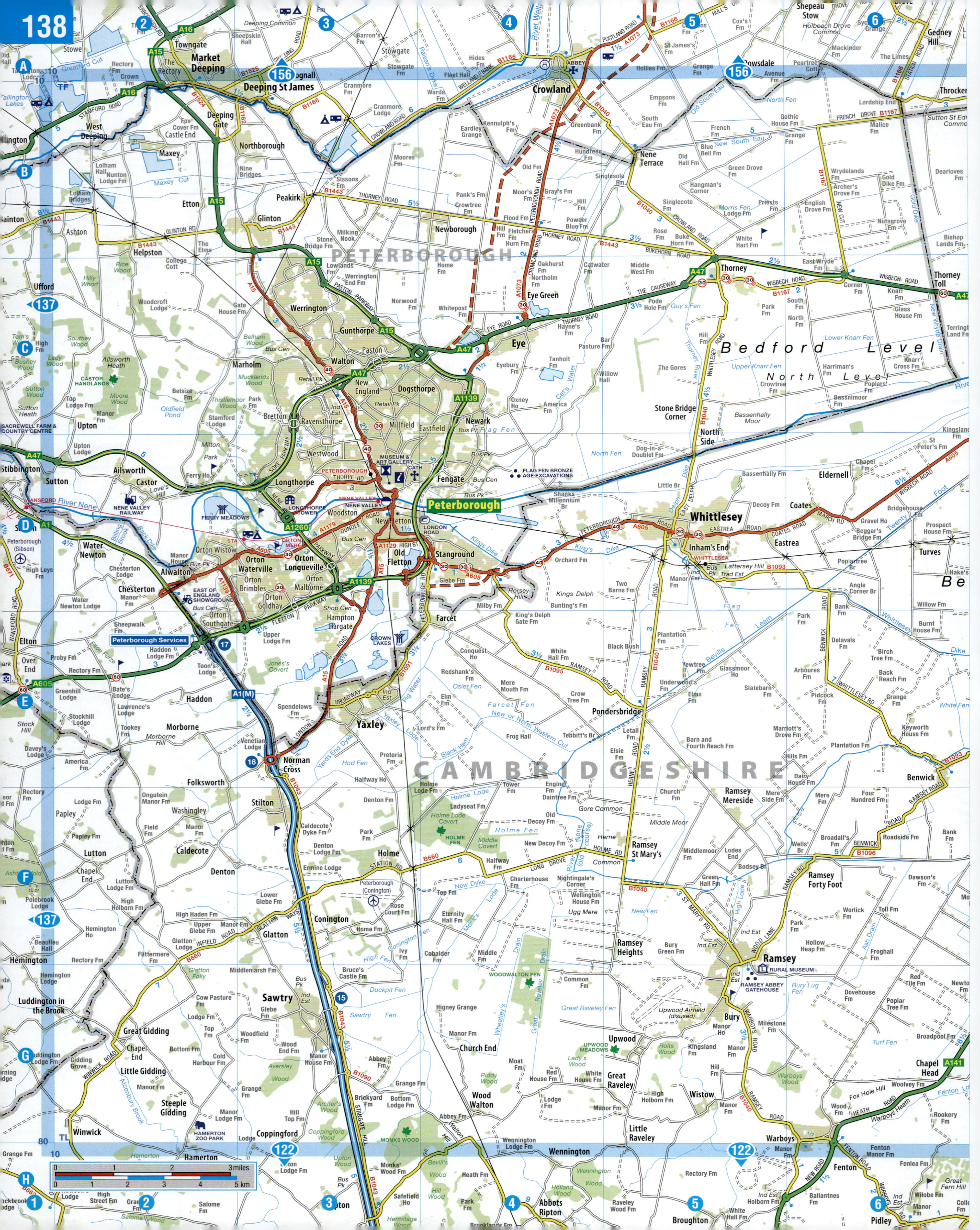

Market Deeping
Deeping St James
Deeping Gate
Towngate
West Deeping
Maxey
Northborough
Crowland
Nene Terrace
Thorney
Thorney Toll
Peakirk
Glinton
Etton
Helpston
Ashton
Ufford
Newborough
Eye Green
Eye
PETERBOROUGH
Werrington
Gunthorpe
Paston
Walton
Marholm
New England
Dogsthorpe
Millfield
Eastfield
Newark
Ravensthorpe
Bretton
Westwood
Longthorpe
Fengate
Peterborough
Woodston
New Fletton
Old Fletton
Stanground
Orton Wistow
Orton Waterville
Orton Longueville
Orton Malborne
Orton Brimbles
Orton Goldhay
Orton Southgate
Alwalton
Chesterton
Castor
Ailsworth
Sutton
Upton
Stibbington
Water Newton
Elton
Hampton Hargate
Farcet
Yaxley
Norman Cross
Haddon
Morborne
Folksworth
Stilton
Washingley
Caldecote
Denton
Lutton
Papley
Holme
Conington
Glatton
Sawtry
Great Gidding
Little Gidding
Steeple Gidding
Winwick
Hamerton
Coppingford
Luddington in the Brook
Hemington
Wood Walton
Church End
Great Raveley
Little Raveley
Upwood
Bury
Ramsey
Ramsey Heights
Ramsey St Mary's
Ramsey Mereside
Ramsey Forty Foot
Pondersbridge
Whittlesey
Inham's End
Eastrea
Coates
Turves
Eldernell
North Side
Stone Bridge Corner
Benwick
Wistow
Warboys
Fenton
Pidley
Abbots Ripton
Broughton
Wennington
Chapel Head
Bedford Level
North Level
CAMBRIDGESHIRE
Peterborough Services
Ferry Meadows
Nene Valley Railway
Flag Fen Bronze Age Excavations
Crown Lakes
Rural Museum
Ramsey Abbey Gatehouse
Woodwalton Fen
Upwood Meadows
Monks Wood
Hamerton Zoo Park
Sacrewell Farm & Country Centre
Castor Hanglands
Peterborough (Conington)
Peterborough (Sibson)
3 miles
5 km

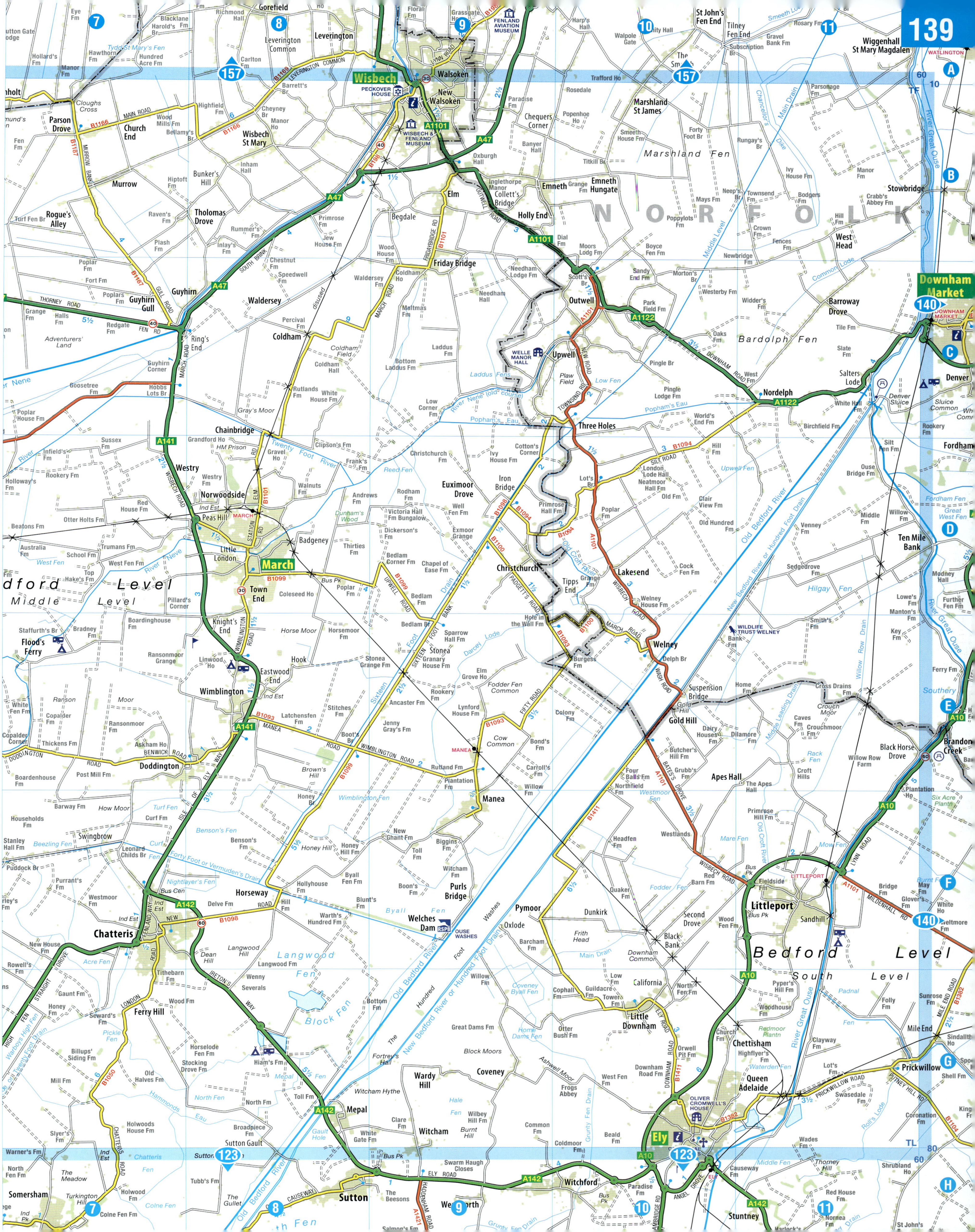
Wisbech
Walsoken
New Walsoken
Leverington
Leverington Common
Wisbech St Mary
Parson Drove
Church End
Murrow
Guyhirn
Guyhirn Gull
Rogue's Alley
Tholomas Drove
Elm
Begdale
Friday Bridge
Coldham
Waldersey
Emneth
Emneth Hungate
Holly End
Outwell
Upwell
Three Holes
Marshland St James
Marshland Fen
NORFOLK
Downham Market
Barroway Drove
Bardolph Fen
Nordelph
Stowbridge
Denver
Fordham
Ten Mile Bank
Hilgay Fen
Welney
Lakesend
Christchurch
Euximoor Drove
Iron Bridge
Tipps End
Gold Hill
Suspension Bridge
Apes Hall
Brandon Creek
Southery
Littleport
Sandhill
Bedford Level
South Level
Middle Level
Chainbridge
Westry
Norwoodside
Peas Hill
March
Town End
Little London
Badgeney
Knight's End
Wimblington
Eastwood End
Hook
Doddington
Manea
Horseway
Chatteris
Flood's Ferry
Swingbrow
Welches Dam
Ouse Washes
Pymoor
Oxlode
Dunkirk
Black Bank
Little Downham
California
Langwood Fen
Block Fen
Ferry Hill
Mepal
Witcham
Wardy Hill
Coveney
Witchford
Sutton
Sutton Gault
Ely
Queen Adelaide
Prickwillow
Chettisham
Stuntney
Somersham
Old Bedford River
New Bedford River or Hundred Foot River
River Great Ouse
River Nene
Twenty Foot River
Sixteen Foot Drain
Forty Foot or Vermuden's Drain
Popham's Eau
Middle Level Main Drain
Peckover House
Wisbech & Fenland Museum
Fenland Aviation Museum
Welle Manor Hall
Oliver Cromwell's House
Wildlife Trust Welney
A47
A141
A142
A1101
A1122
A10
B1098
B1099
B1101
B1093
B1094
B1100
B1411
B1382
B1050
B1166
B1167
B1169
157
123
140
60
80
TF
TL

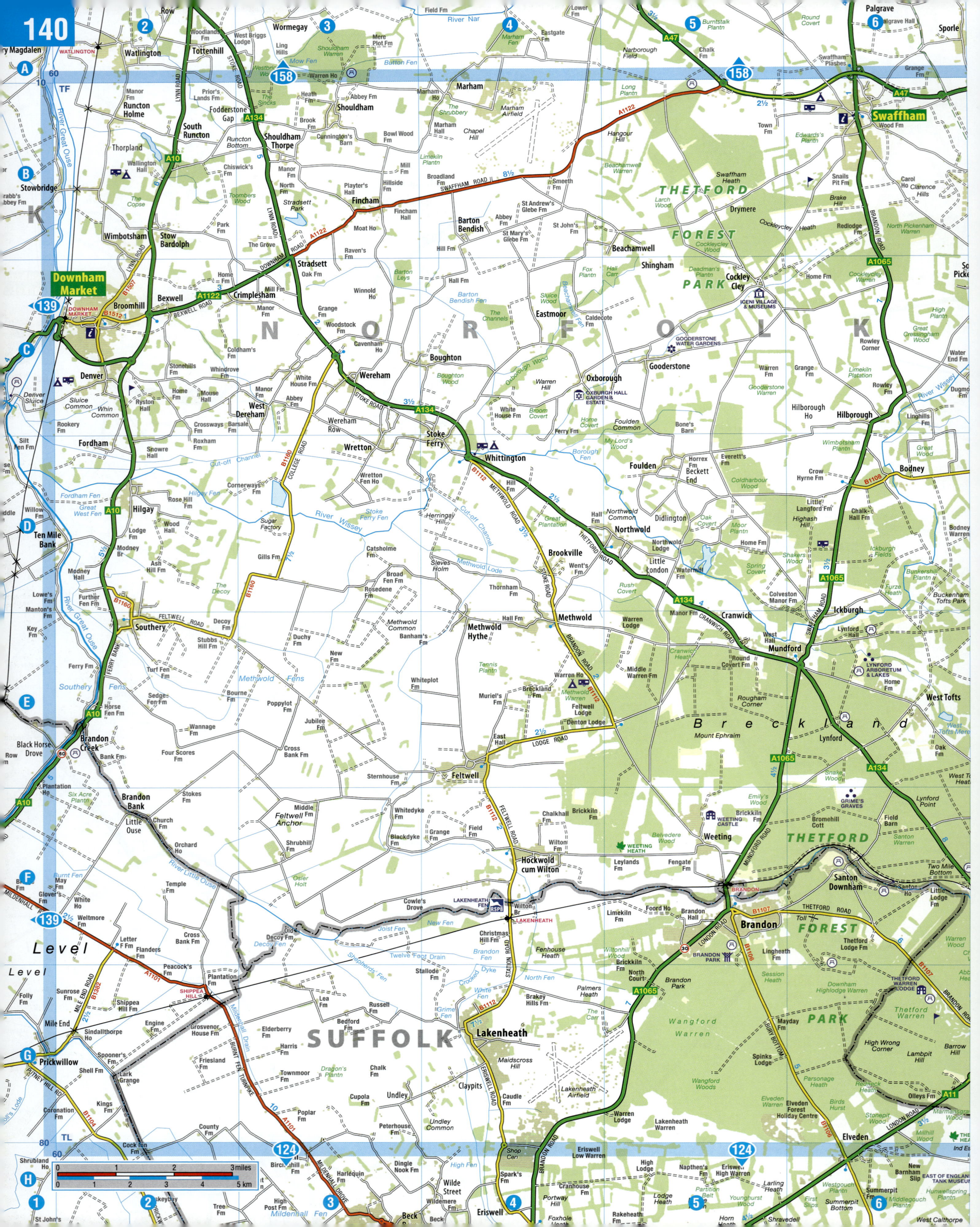

Downham Market
Swaffham
NORFOLK
SUFFOLK
THETFORD FOREST PARK
Breckland
Watlington
Tottenhill
Wormegay
Marham
Narborough Field
Palgrave
Sporle
Runcton Holme
South Runcton
Shouldham
Shouldham Thorpe
Fincham
Barton Bendish
Beachamwell
Shingham
Drymere
Cockley Cley
Stow Bardolph
Wimbotsham
Stowbridge
Stradsett
Crimplesham
Bexwell
Broomhill
Denver
Fordham
West Dereham
Wereham
Wretton
Stoke Ferry
Whittington
Boughton
Oxborough
Eastmoor
Gooderstone
Foulden
Hilborough
Bodney
Northwold
Didlington
Little London
Brookville
Methwold
Methwold Hythe
Cranwich
Mundford
Ickburgh
Lynford
West Tofts
Hilgay
Ten Mile Bank
Southery
Brandon Creek
Brandon Bank
Little Ouse
Feltwell
Feltwell Anchor
Hockwold cum Wilton
Weeting
Santon Downham
Brandon
Lakenheath
Prickwillow
Mile End
Elveden
Eriswell
Wilde Street
Shippea Hill
River Great Ouse
River Wissey
River Little Ouse
Cut-off Channel
Methwold Fens
Level
A10
A134
A1122
A1065
A47
A1101
A11
B1112
B1106
B1107
B1160
B1507
B1512
B1104
B1382
139
158
124
TF
TL

0 1 2 3 miles
0 1 2 3 4 5 km

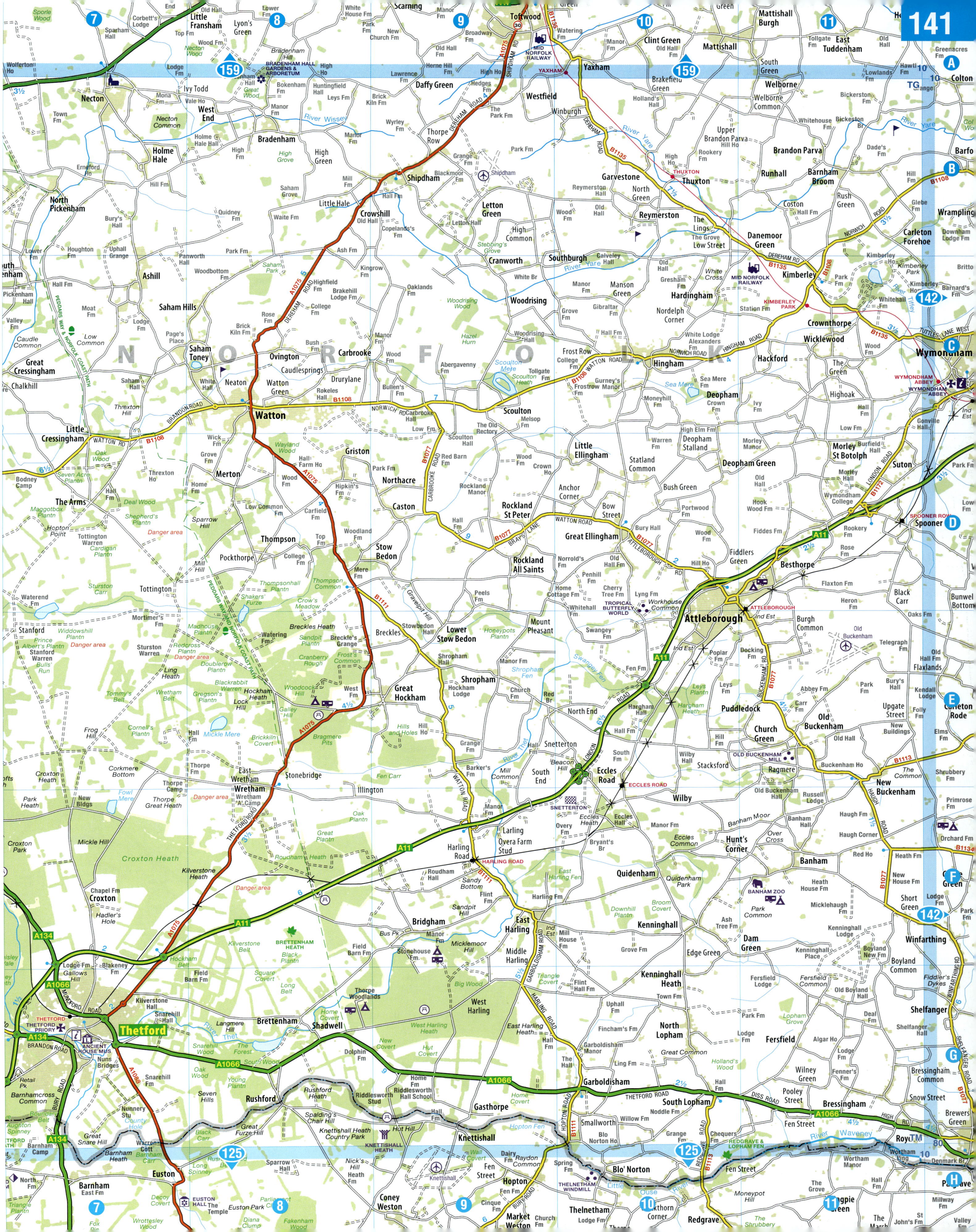
NORFOLK
Watton
Thetford
Attleborough
Wymondham
Shipdham
Yaxham
Garvestone
Hingham
Kimberley
Mattishall
Necton
Bradenham
Saham Toney
Ovington
Carbrooke
Scoulton
Deopham
Griston
Merton
Caston
Great Ellingham
Rockland St Peter
Rockland All Saints
Little Ellingham
Thompson
Stow Bedon
Tottington
Great Hockham
Shropham
Wretham
Stonebridge
Illington
Snetterton
Eccles Road
Quidenham
Kenninghall
Banham
New Buckenham
Old Buckenham
Puddledock
Besthorpe
Wicklewood
Crownthorpe
Morley St Botolph
Suton
Spooner Row
Brettenham
Shadwell
Rushford
Gasthorpe
Knettishall
Garboldisham
South Lopham
North Lopham
Fersfield
Bressingham
Winfarthing
Shelfanger
Blo' Norton
Hopton
Euston
Barnham
Coney Weston
Redgrave
Croxton
East Harling
West Harling
Bridgham
Larling
Harling Road
Watton Green
Little Cressingham
Great Cressingham
Ashill
Holme Hale
North Pickenham
Cranworth
Woodrising
Southburgh
Reymerston
Thuxton
Westfield
Letton Green
Thorpe Row
Daffy Green
Tottington
Mid Norfolk Railway
Snetterton
Banham Zoo
Euston Hall
A11
A1066
A1075
A134
B1108
B1077
B1111
B1113
B1135
B1172
TG

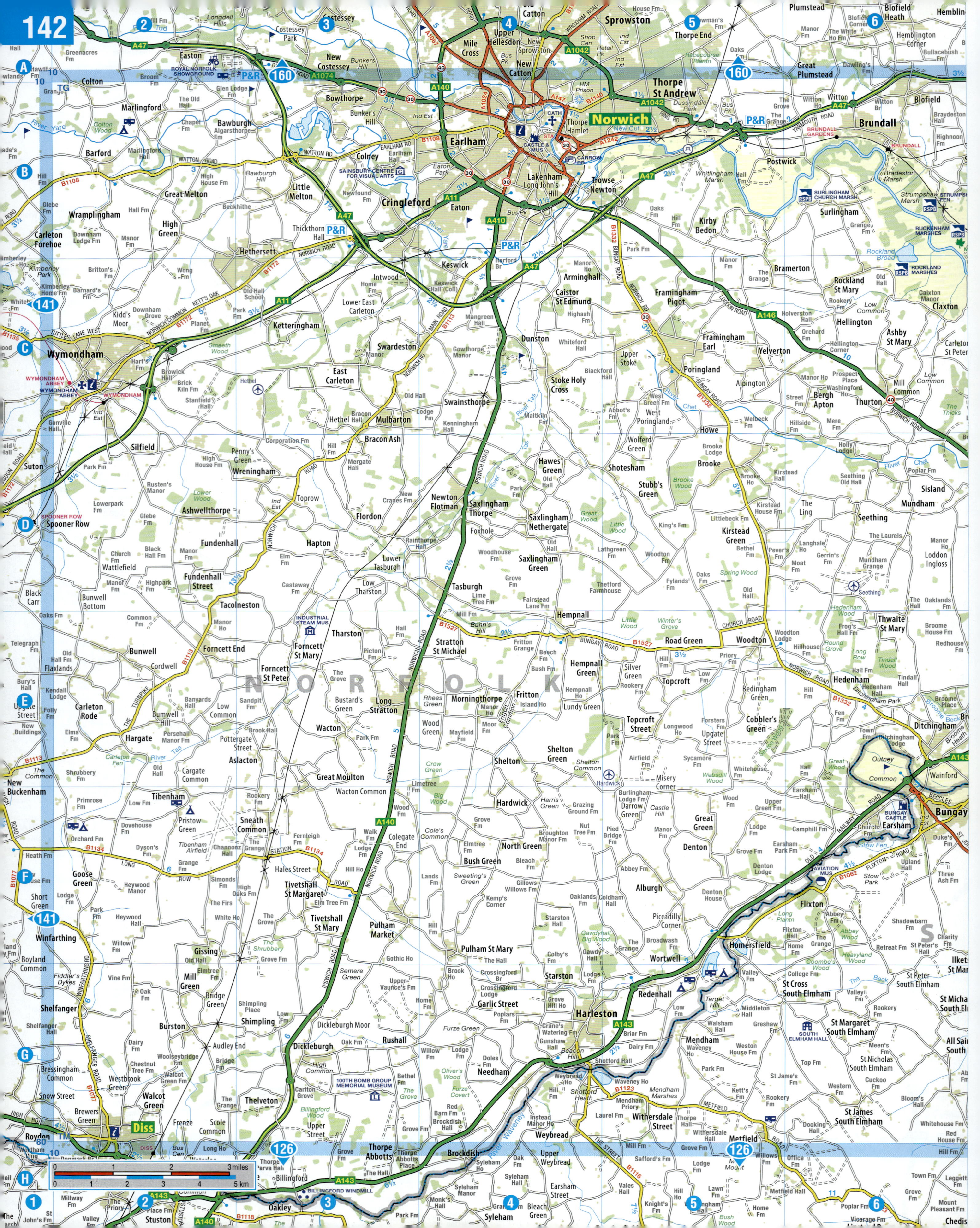
NORFOLK
Norwich
Costessey
New Costessey
Easton
Colton
Marlingford
Bawburgh
Bowthorpe
Earlham
Colney
Barford
Great Melton
Little Melton
Cringleford
Eaton
Lakenham
Trowse Newton
Hethersett
Wramplingham
Carleton Forehoe
Keswick
Intwood
Ketteringham
Wymondham
Swardeston
East Carleton
Mulbarton
Bracon Ash
Swainsthorpe
Dunston
Arminghall
Caistor St Edmund
Stoke Holy Cross
Framingham Pigot
Framingham Earl
Poringland
Upper Stoke
Shotesham
Silfield
Suton
Wreningham
Ashwellthorpe
Spooner Row
Fundenhall
Hapton
Flordon
Newton Flotman
Saxlingham Thorpe
Saxlingham Nethergate
Saxlingham Green
Tasburgh
Tacolneston
Forncett End
Forncett St Mary
Forncett St Peter
Tharston
Stratton St Michael
Long Stratton
Morningthorpe
Fritton
Hempnall
Hempnall Green
Woodton
Bunwell
Carleton Rode
Hargate
Wacton
Aslacton
Great Moulton
Tibenham
Sneath Common
Tivetshall St Margaret
Tivetshall St Mary
Pulham Market
Pulham St Mary
Shelton
Hardwick
Topcroft
Topcroft Street
Bedingham Green
Hedenham
Ditchingham
Bungay
Earsham
Denton
Alburgh
Harleston
Redenhall
Wortwell
Homersfield
Flixton
Mendham
Needham
Rushall
Dickleburgh
Thelveton
Shimpling
Burston
Gissing
Winfarthing
Shelfanger
Diss
Roydon
Scole
Brockdish
Thorpe Abbotts
Weybread
Withersdale Street
Metfield
Billingford
Oakley
Syleham
Stuston
Sprowston
Thorpe St Andrew
Thorpe End
Great Plumstead
Brundall
Blofield
Postwick
Surlingham
Kirby Bedon
Bramerton
Rockland St Mary
Claxton
Hellington
Ashby St Mary
Yelverton
Alpington
Bergh Apton
Thurton
Howe
Brooke
Kirstead Green
Seething
Mundham
Sisland
Thwaite St Mary
Woodton
Road Green
St Cross South Elmham
St Margaret South Elmham
St James South Elmham
Wainford
New Buckenham

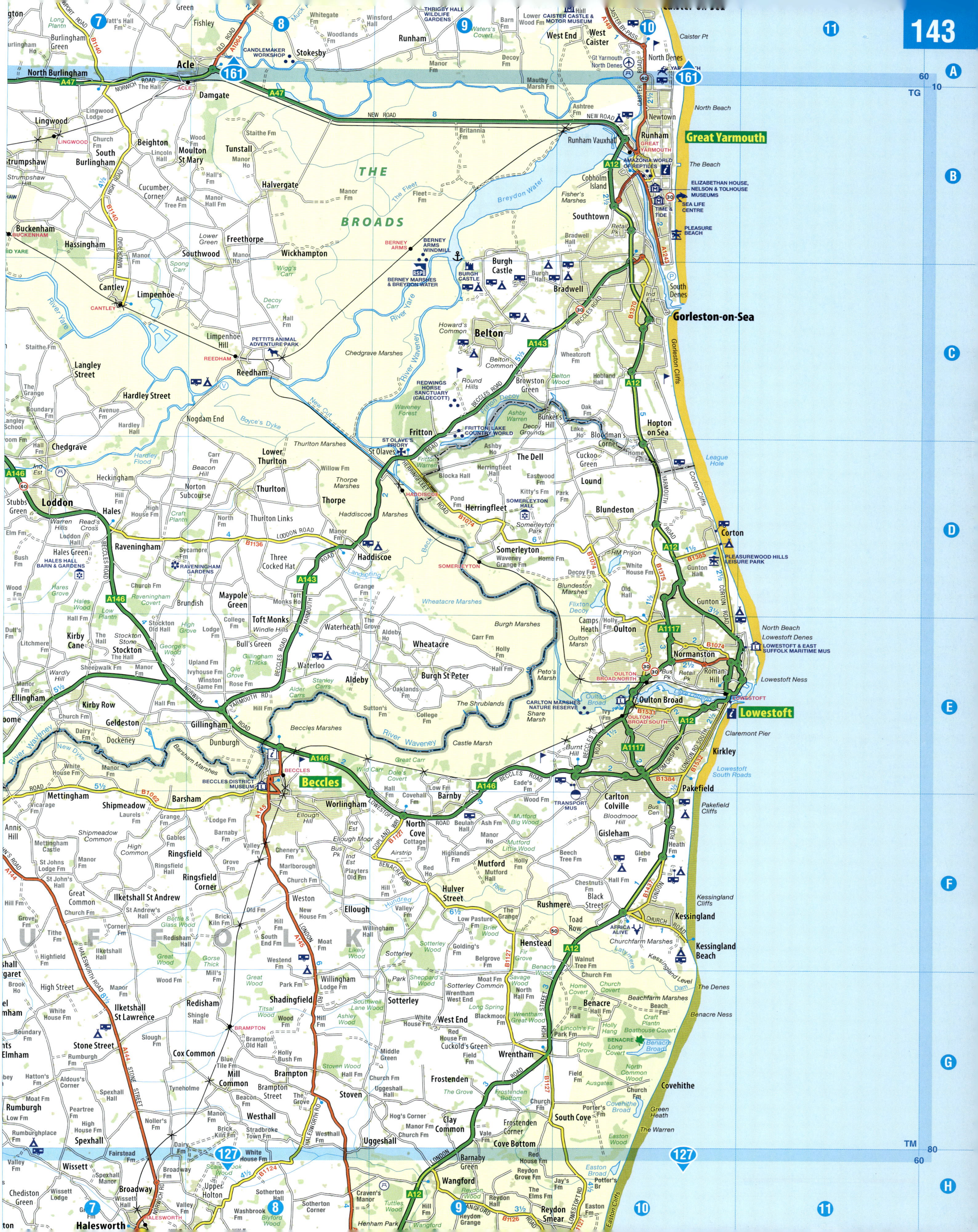
Great Yarmouth
Lowestoft
Beccles
Gorleston-on-Sea
THE BROADS
Acle
Damgate
Lingwood
Beighton
Moulton St Mary
Tunstall
Halvergate
Stokesby
Runham
West Caister
Caister Pt
North Denes
North Beach
Newtown
The Beach
Cobholm Island
Southtown
Breydon Water
Burgh Castle
Bradwell
Belton
Wickhampton
Freethorpe
Southwood
Hassingham
Buckenham
Strumpshaw
Cantley
Limpenhoe
Reedham
Langley Street
Hardley Street
Chedgrave
Loddon
Hales
Heckingham
Norton Subcourse
Thurlton
Lower Thurlton
Thorpe
Haddiscoe
St Olaves
Fritton
Hopton on Sea
The Dell
Herringfleet
Somerleyton
Lound
Blundeston
Corton
Gunton
Oulton
Oulton Broad
Normanston
Lowestoft Ness
Kirkley
Pakefield
Carlton Colville
Gisleham
Kessingland
Kessingland Beach
Benacre
Benacre Ness
Covehithe
South Cove
Wrentham
Henstead
Rushmere
Mutford
Barnby
North Cove
Worlingham
Aldeby
Wheatacre
Burgh St Peter
Toft Monks
Stockton
Kirby Cane
Raveningham
Ellingham
Kirby Row
Geldeston
Gillingham
Dockeney
Mettingham
Shipmeadow
Barsham
Ringsfield
Ringsfield Corner
Ilketshall St Andrew
Redisham
Weston
Ellough
Sotterley
Shadingfield
Willingham
Brampton
Stoven
Uggeshall
Westhall
Cox Common
Ilketshall St Lawrence
Stone Street
Spexhall
Wissett
Halesworth
Holton
Wangford
Reydon
Reydon Smear
Frostenden
Clay Common
Cove Bottom
SUFFOLK
River Waveney
River Yare
New Cut
Haddiscoe Marshes
Beccles Marshes
Chedgrave Marshes
The Warren
The Denes
Claremont Pier
Lowestoft Denes
Pleasurewood Hills Leisure Park
Africa Alive
Carlton Marshes Nature Reserve
Transport Mus
Berney Arms
Pettits Animal Adventure Park
Raveningham Gardens
Hales Hall Barn & Gardens
Elizabethan House, Nelson & Tolhouse Museums
Sea Life Centre
Pleasure Beach
Lowestoft & East Suffolk Maritime Mus
Beccles District Museum
A47
A143
A146
A12
A1117
A145
A144
TG
TM
60
10
80
127
161

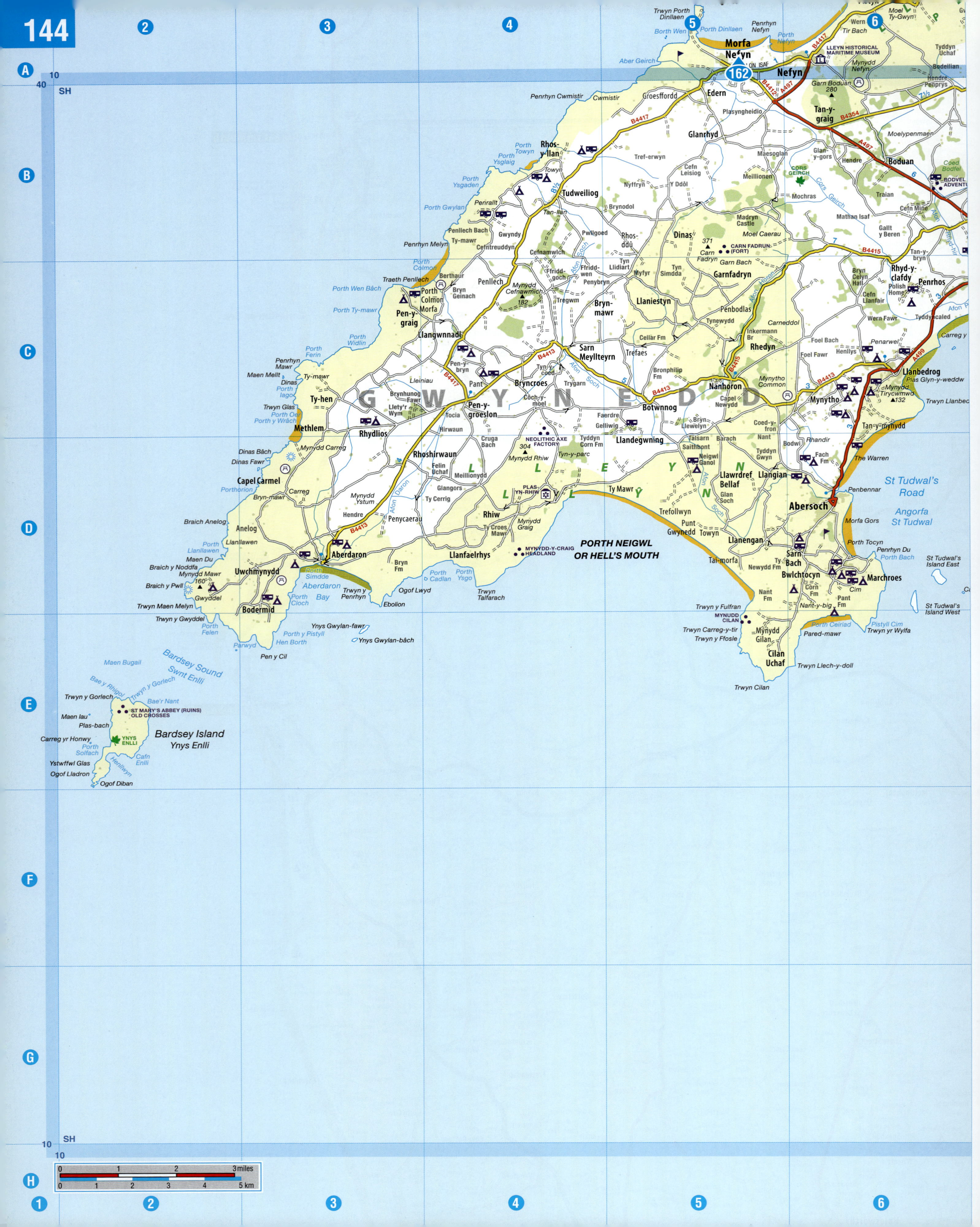
Trwyn Porth Dinllaen
Borth Wen
Porth Dinllaen
Penrhyn Nefyn
Porth Nefyn
Morfa Nefyn
Nefyn
162
Aber Geirch
LLEYN HISTORICAL MARITIME MUSEUM
Mynydd Nefyn
Tir Bach
Wern
Moel Ty-Gwyn
Tyddyn Uchaf
Garn Boduan
280
Tan-y-graig
Edern
Groesffordd
Penrhyn Cwmistir
Cwmistir
Plasyngheidio
Glanrhyd
Tref-erwyn
Maesoglan
Glan-y-gors
Hendre
Boduan
Moelypenmaen
CORS GEIRCH
Mochras
Traian
Cefn Mine
Mathan Isaf
Gallt y Beren
Rhos-y-llan
Porth Towyn
Porth Ysglaig
Towyn
Porth Ysgaden
Tudweiliog
Cefn Leisiog
Nyffryn
Y Ddôl
Meillionen
Porth Gwylan
Penrallt
Tan-llan
Brynodol
Madryn Castle
Moel Caerau
Penllech Bach
Ty-mawr
Gwyndy
Pwllgoed
Rhos-ddû
Dinas
371
Carn Fadryn
CARN FADRUN (FORT)
Garn Bach
Penrhyn Melyn
Cefntreuddyn
Cefnamwlch
Tyn Llidiart
Tyn Simdda
Garnfadryn
Porth Colmon
Traeth Penllech
Berthaur
Penllech
Ffridd-goch
Ffridd-wen
Penybryn
Myfyr
Porth Wen Bâch
Porth Colmon
Morfa
Bryn Geinach
Mynydd Cefnamwlch
182
Tregwm
Bryn-mawr
Llaniestyn
Penbodlas
Porth Ty-mawr
Pen-y-graig
Tynewydd
Carneddol
Inkermann Br
Llangwnnadl
Porth Widlin
Porth Ferin
Penrhyn Mawr
Maen Mellt
Dinas
Porth Iago
Ty-mawr
Pen-y-bryn
Sarn Meyllteyrn
Trefaes
Cellar Fm
Rhedyn
Foel Bach
Foel Fawr
Henllys
Penarwel
Llanbedrog
Plas Glyn-y-weddw
Ty-hen
Lleiniau
Pant
Tyn-y-coed
Bryncroes
Trygarn
Bronphilip Fm
Nanhoron
Mynytho Common
Mynydd Tirycwmwd
132
Trwyn Llanbedrog
Mynytho
Trwyn Glas
Porth Oer
Porth y Wrâch
Brynhunog Fawr
Llety'r Wym
Pen-y-groeslon
Coch-y-moel
Botwnnog
Capel Newydd
G W Y N E D D
Methlem
Rhydlios
Tocia
Faerdre
Gelliwig
Bryn-Llewelyn
Coed-y-fron
Tan-y-mynydd
Hirwaun
NEOLITHIC AXE FACTORY
Tyddyn Corn Fm
Llandegwning
Yalsarn
Barach
Nant
Rhandir
Dinas Bâch
Dinas Fawr
Mynydd Carreg
Rhoshirwaun
Cruga Bach
304
Mynydd Rhiw
Tyn-y-parc
Saithbont
Neigwl Ganol
Tyddyn Gwyn
Bodwi
Fach Fm
The Warren
Capel Carmel
Porthorion
Felin Uchaf
Meillionydd
Llawrdref Bellaf
Llangian
St Tudwal's Road
Carreg
Bryn-mawr
Mynydd Ystum
Glangors
Ty Cerrig
PLAS YN-RHIW
Ty Mawr
Glan Soch
Penbennar
Abersoch
Angorfa St Tudwal
L L E Y N
Braich Anelog
Anelog
Hendre
Penycaerau
Rhiw
Ty Croes Mawr
Mynydd Graig
Trefollwyn
Punt Gwynedd
Towyn
Morfa Gors
Porth Tocyn
Penrhyn Du
Porth Bach
Porth Llanllawen
Llanllawen
Aberdaron
MYNYDD-Y-CRAIG HEADLAND
PORTH NEIGWL OR HELL'S MOUTH
Llanengan
Sarn Bach
St Tudwal's Island East
Maen Du
Braich y Noddfa
Mynydd Mawr
160
Braich y Pwll
Uwchmynydd
Porth Simdde
Aberdaron Bay
Bryn Fm
Llanfaelrhys
Porth Cadlan
Porth Ysgo
Tal-y-morfa
Newydd Fm
Ty-Bach
Bwlchtocyn
Marchroes
Cim
Gwyddel
Trwyn Maen Melyn
Bodermid
Porth Cloch
Trwyn y Penrhyn
Ogof Lwyd
Ebolion
Trwyn Talfarach
Nant Fm
Corn Fm
Nant-y-big
Pant Fm
Trwyn y Gwyddel
Porth Felen
Parwyd
Porth y Pistyll
Hen Borth
Ynys Gwylan-fawr
Ynys Gwylan-bâch
Trwyn y Fulfran
MYNYDD CILAN
Trwyn Carreg-y-tir
Trwyn y Ffosle
Mynydd Gilan
Porth Ceiriad
Pared-mawr
Pistyll Cim
Trwyn yr Wylfa
St Tudwal's Island West
Pen y Cil
Cilan Uchaf
Trwyn Llech-y-doll
Trwyn Cilan
Maen Bugail
Bardsey Sound
Swnt Enlli
Bae y Rhigol
Trwyn y Gorlech
Trwyn y Gorlech
Bae'r Nant
ST MARY'S ABBEY (RUINS)
OLD CROSSES
Maen Iau
Plas-bach
Carreg yr Honwy
YNYS ENLLI
Bardsey Island
Ynys Enlli
Porth Solfach
Cafn Enlli
Henllwyn
Ystwffwl Glas
Ogof Lladron
Ogof Diban
B4417
B4412
A497
B4354
B4415
B4413
A499
B4411
Afon Soch
Afon Daron
Cors Geirch
SH
10
40
A
B
C
D
E
F
G
H
1
2
3
4
5
6
0
1
2
3 miles
0
1
2
3
4
5 km

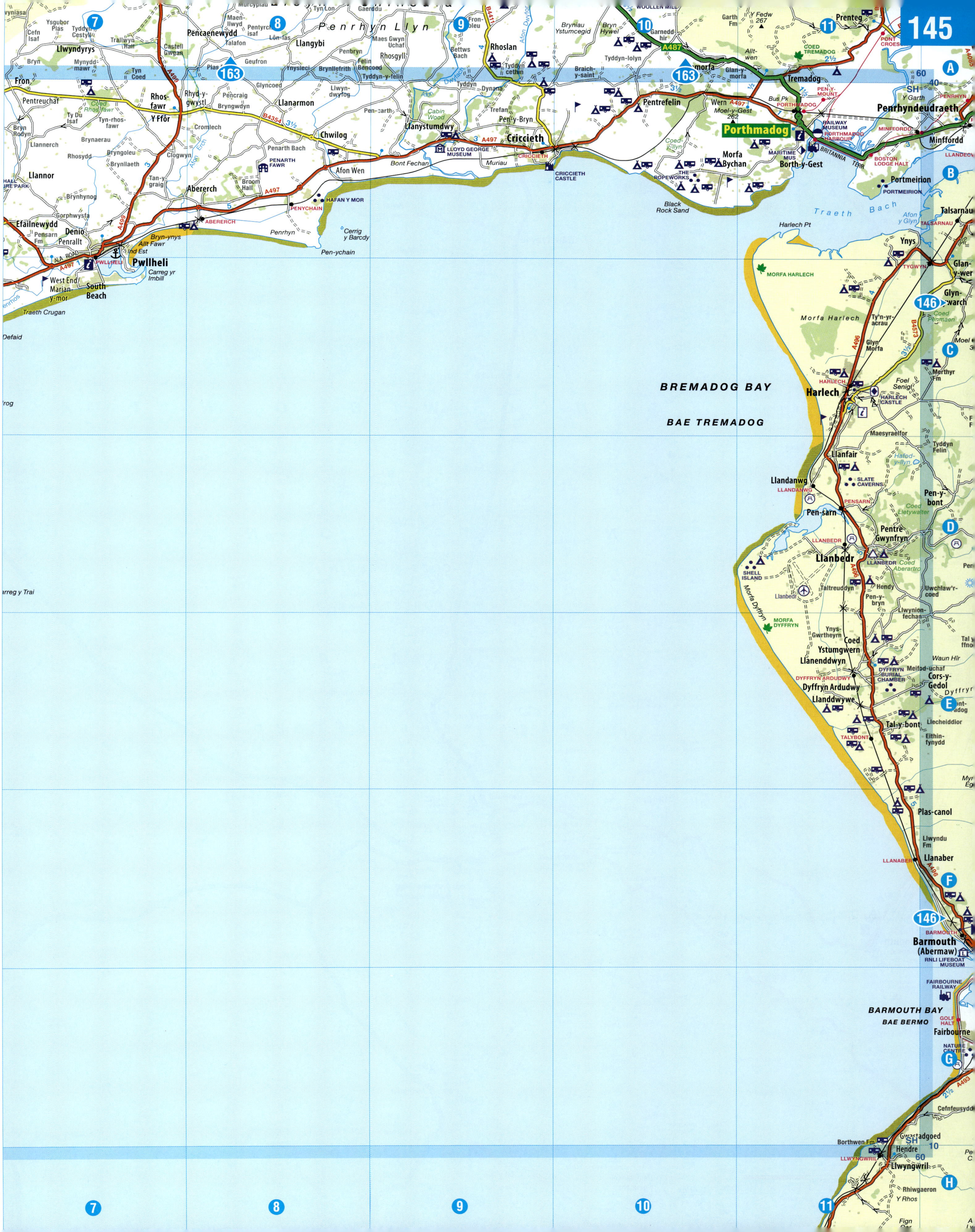
Penrhyn Llŷn
Llwyndyrys
Pencaenewydd
Llangybi
Rhoslan
Tremadog
Prenteg
Porthmadog
Penrhyndeudraeth
Minffordd
Borth-y-Gest
Morfa Bychan
Portmeirion
Pentrefelin
Criccieth
Criccieth Castle
Llanystumdwy
Lloyd George Museum
Chwilog
Afon Wen
Llanarmon
Y Ffôr
Rhos-fawr
Abererch
Pwllheli
South Beach
West End/Marian-y-mor
Denio
Efailnewydd
Llannor
Penrhos
Traeth Crugan
Black Rock Sand
Traeth Bach
Harlech Pt
Morfa Harlech
Talsarnau
Ynys
Glyn-y-wer
Harlech
Harlech Castle
Bremadog Bay
Bae Tremadog
Llanfair
Llandanwg
Pen-sarn
Llanbedr
Shell Island
Morfa Dyffryn
Llanenddwyn
Dyffryn Ardudwy
Llanddwywe
Tal-y-bont
Plas-canol
Llanaber
Barmouth (Abermaw)
RNLI Lifeboat Museum
Barmouth Bay
Bae Bermo
Fairbourne
Fairbourne Railway
Llwyngwril
Hendre
Rhiwgaeron
A497
A487
A496
A499
B4354
163
146
7
8
9
10
11
A
B
C
D
E
F
G
H

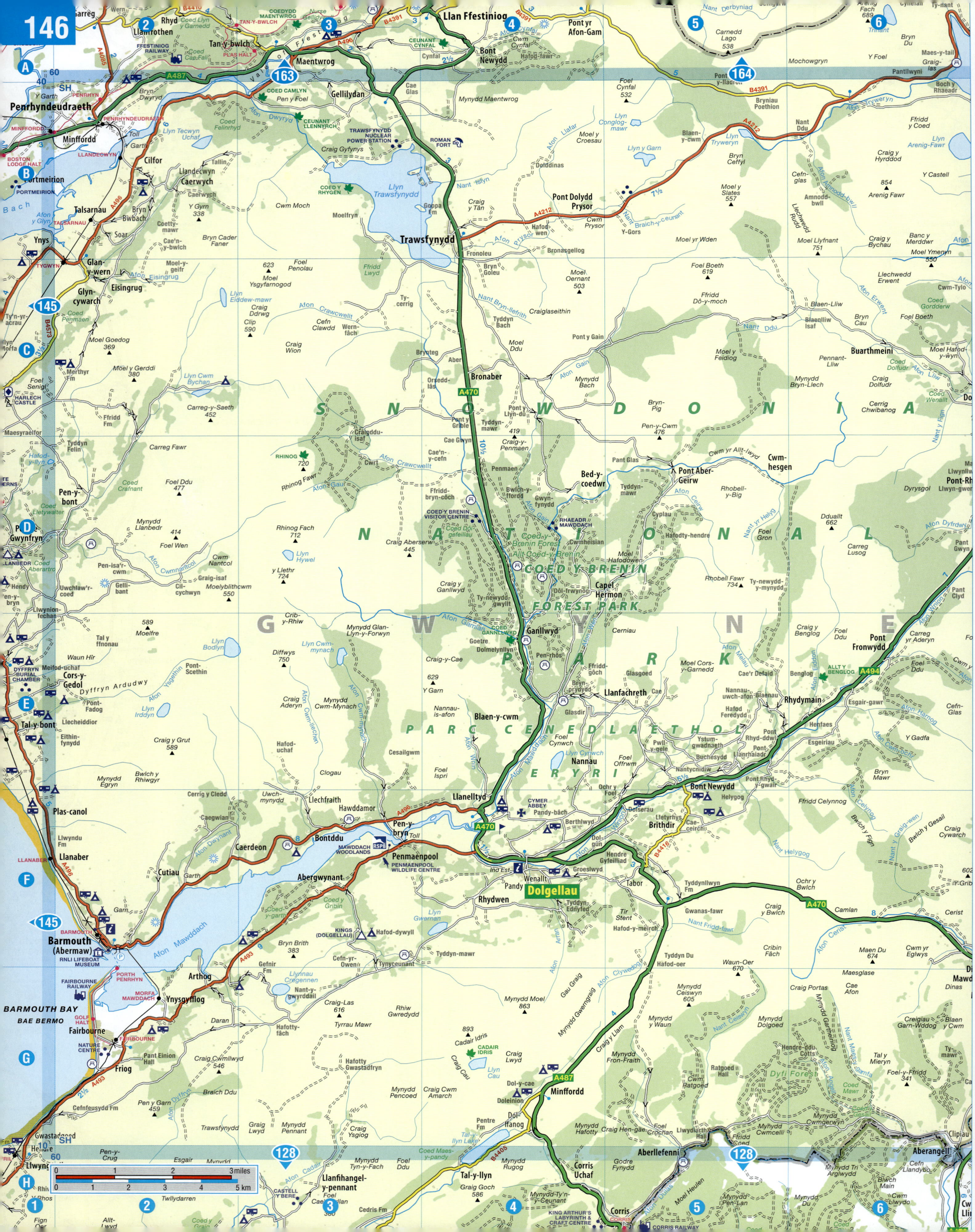
Llan Ffestiniog
Maentwrog
Penrhyndeudraeth
Minffordd
Portmeirion
Talsarnau
Harlech
Trawsfynydd
Llyn Trawsfynydd
Pont Dolydd Prysor
Gellilydan
Bronaber
Coed y Brenin Forest Park
Ganllwyd
Llanfachreth
Rhydymain
Llanelltyd
Dolgellau
Barmouth (Abermaw)
Fairbourne
Arthog
Penmaenpool
Bontddu
Abergwynant
Cadair Idris
Tal-y-llyn
Minffordd
Corris Uchaf
Corris
Aberllefenni
Aberangell
Brithdir
Bont Newydd
Llanaber
Tal-y-bont
Dyffryn Ardudwy
Barmouth Bay
Bae Bermo
Snowdonia National Park
Parc Cenedlaethol Eryri
Gwynedd
A470
A487
A496
A494
A4212
B4391
0 1 2 3 miles
0 1 2 3 4 5 km

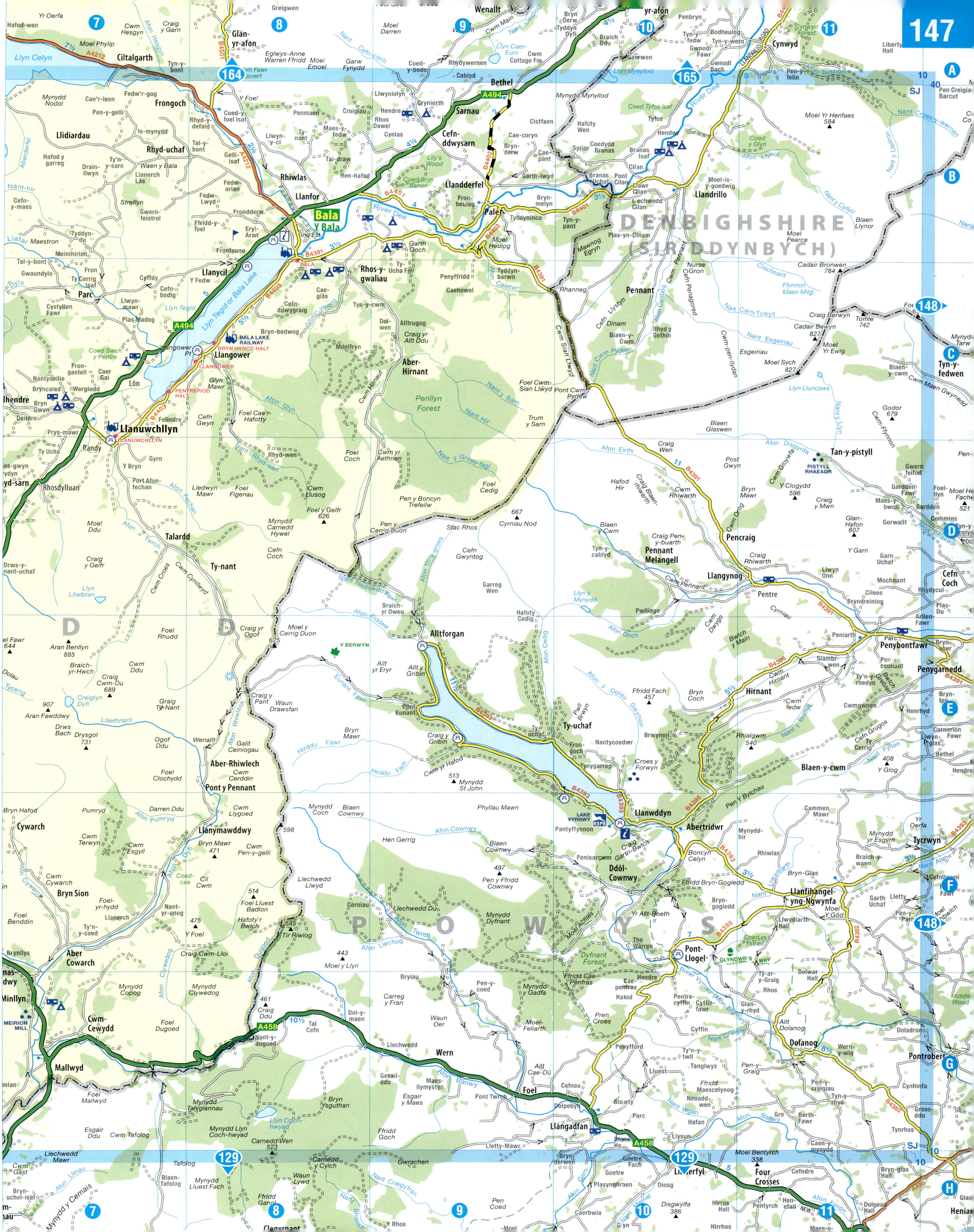
DENBIGHSHIRE
(SIR DDYNBYCH)
P O W Y S
Bala
Y Bala
Llyn Tegid or Bala Lake
BALA LAKE RAILWAY
Llanuwchllyn
Llangower
Llanycil
Llanfor
Rhiwlas
Frongoch
Rhyd-uchaf
Lliidiardau
Ciltalgarth
Llyn Celyn
Moel Phylip
Glân-yr-afon
Bethel
Sarnau
Cefn-ddwysarn
Llandderfel
Pale
Llandrillo
Cynwyd
Rhos-y-gwaliau
Aber-Hirnant
Penllyn Forest
Pennant
Tan-y-pistyll
PISTYLL RHAEADR
Pencraig
Pennant Melangell
Llangynog
Pentre
Penybontfawr
Penygarnedd
Hirnant
Blaen-y-cwm
Alltforgan
Y BERWYN
Lake Vyrnwy
Llanwddyn
Abertridwr
Ddôl-Cownwy
Llanfihangel-yng-Ngwynfa
Pont-Llogel
Dolanog
Pontrobert
Ty-uchaf
Tycrwyn
Talardd
Ty-nant
Aran Benllyn
885
Aran Fawddwy
907
Aber-Rhiwlech
Pont y Pennant
Llanymawddwy
Cywarch
Bryn Sion
Aber Cowarch
Minllyn
Cwm-Cewydd
Mallwyd
Wern
Foel
Llangadfan
Llanerfyl
Four Crosses
Dinas-Mawddwy
MEIRION MILL
Rhosdylluan
Parc
Pandy
Cadair Berwyn
827
Moel Sych
Cadair Bronwen
784
Cyrniau Nod
667
Moel y Cerrig Duon
Cwm Hirnant
Lake Vyrnwy RSPB
Glyndŵr's Way
A494
A458
A4212
B4391
B4401
B4402
B4403
B4393
B4396
B4395
B4382
B4501
164
165
129
148
7
8
9
10
11
A
B
C
D
E
F
G
H
SJ

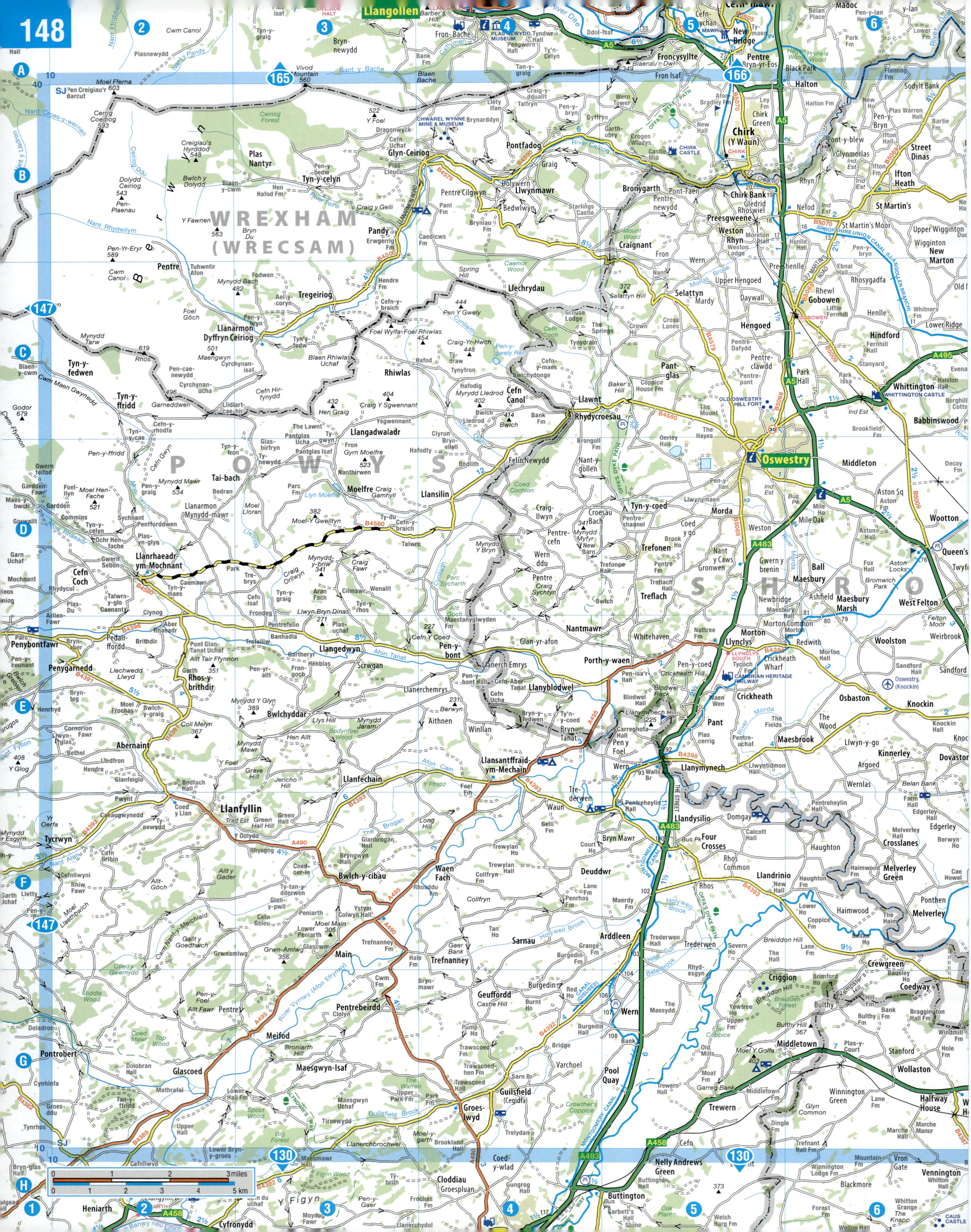
WREXHAM
(WRECSAM)
POWYS
SHROPSHIRE
Llangollen
Chirk (Y Waun)
Chirk Castle
Oswestry
Glyn-Ceiriog
Pontfadog
Llanarmon Dyffryn Ceiriog
Llansilin
Llangadwaladr
Rhydycroesau
Llanrhaeadr-ym-Mochnant
Llangedwyn
Pen-y-bont
Llansantffraid-ym-Mechain
Llanfyllin
Llanfechain
Llanymynech
Four Crosses
Llandysilio
Meifod
Guilsfield (Cegidfa)
Welshpool
Buttington
Trewern
Middletown
Criggion
Arddleen
Sarnau
Llandrinio
Crosslanes
Melverley
Knockin
Kinnerley
Maesbrook
Pant
Crickheath
Morton
Maesbury Marsh
West Felton
Woolston
Whittington
Whittington Castle
Gobowen
Weston Rhyn
St Martin's
Hindford
Selattyn
Trefonen
Morda
Middleton
Babbinswood
Ifton Heath
Halton
Froncysyllte
Pentre
Glascoed
Pontrobert
Bwlch-y-cibau
Deuddwr
Nantmawr
Porth-y-waen
Llanyblodwel
Bryngwyn
Moel Fferna 603
Vivod Mountain 560
Offa's Dyke Path
Montgomery Canal
Shropshire Union Canal (Llangollen Branch)
165
166
147
130
A5
A483
A495
A490
A458
B4396
B4580
B4393
B4398
B4500
B4579
B4392
0 1 2 3 miles
0 1 2 3 4 5 km

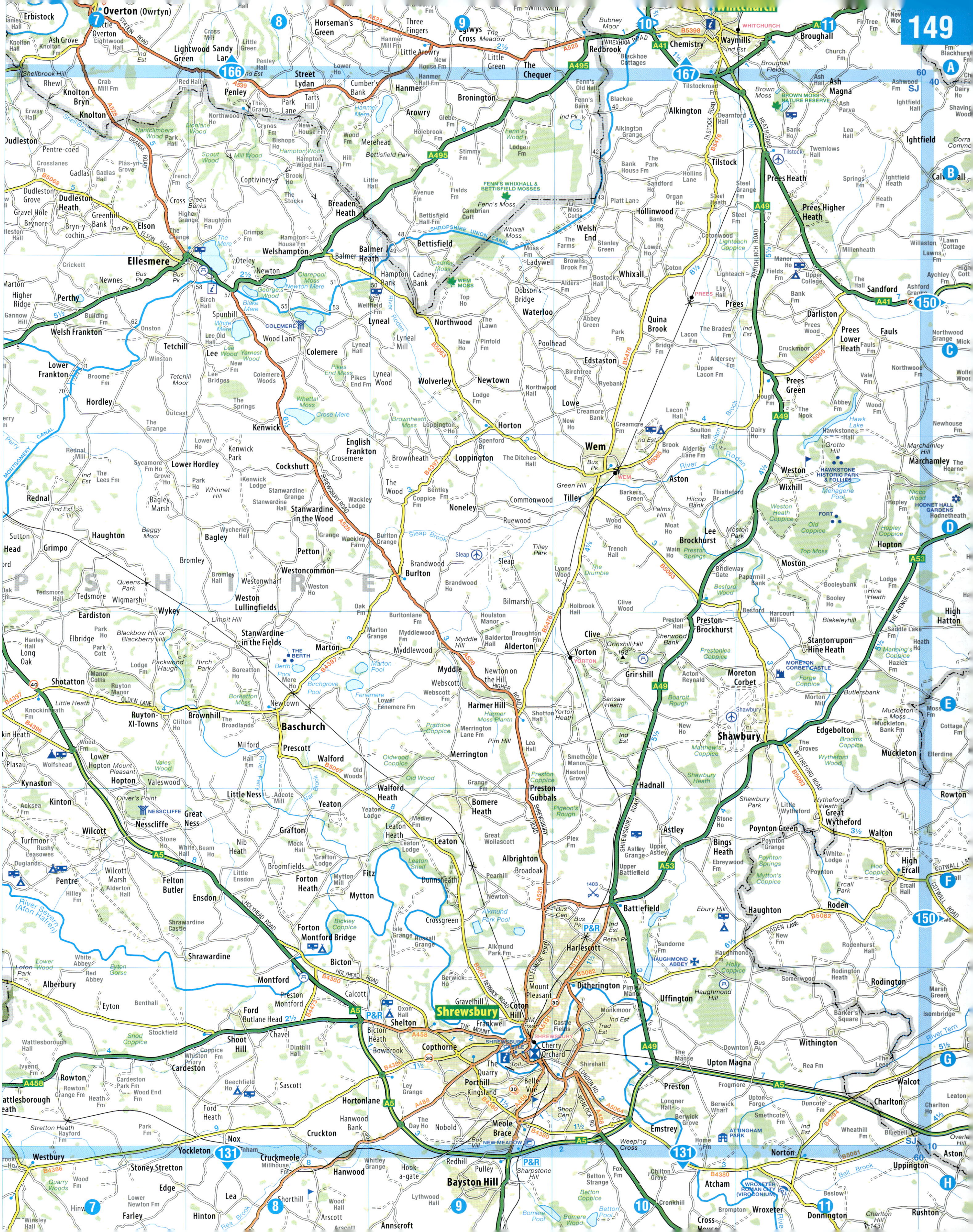
Overton (Owrtyn)
Erbistock
Horseman's Green
Three Fingers
Eglwys Cross
Whitchurch
Chemistry
Waymills
Broughall
Redbrook
Lightwood Green
Sandy Lane
Penley
Street Lydan
Hanmer
Bronington
The Chequer
Alkington
Tilstock
Ash Magna
Ightfield
Knolton
Knolton Bryn
Dudleston
Dudleston Heath
Arowry
Prees Heath
Prees Higher Heath
Elson
Ellesmere
Breaden Heath
Welshampton
Balmer Heath
Bettisfield
Welsh End
Hollinwood
Whixall
Sandford
Perthy
Welsh Frankton
Colemere
Lyneal
Northwood
Waterloo
Quina Brook
Prees
Darliston
Fauls
Prees Lower Heath
Tetchill
Lee
Wood Lane
Edstaston
Prees Green
Lower Frankton
Hordley
Wolverley
Newtown
Horton
Lowe
Kenwick
English Frankton
Cockshutt
Loppington
Wem
Weston
Wixhall
Marchamley
Lower Hordley
Stanwardine in the Wood
Noneley
Tilley
Aston
Rednal
Haughton
Grimpo
Bagley
Petton
Brockhurst
Hopton
Moston
Burlton
Sleap
Weston Lullingfields
Wykey
Eardiston
Bilmarsh
Preston Brockhurst
High Hatton
Stanwardine in the Fields
Marton
Myddlewood
Alderton
Clive
Yorton
Stanton upon Hine Heath
Myddle
Grinshill
Moreton Corbet
Shotatton
Ruyton-XI-Towns
Brownhill
Baschurch
Harmer Hill
Shawbury
Edgebolton
Muckleton
Prescott
Walford
Merrington
Hadnall
Kynaston
Kinton
Hopton
Little Ness
Yeaton
Walford Heath
Bomere Heath
Preston Gubbals
Wilcott
Nesscliffe
Great Ness
Grafton
Leaton
Astley
Poynton Green
Great Wytheford
Walton
Pentre
Felton Butler
Ensdon
Fitz
Mytton
Albrighton
Bings Heath
Rowton
High Ercall
Forton Heath
Battlefield
Haughton
Roden
Shrawardine
Montford Bridge
Harlescott
Bicton
Alberbury
Montford
Ditherington
Uffington
Rodington
Ford
Shelton
Shrewsbury
Withington
Rowton
Cardeston
Shoot Hill
Copthorne
Upton Magna
Walcot
Porthill
Kingsland
Belle Vue
Preston
Charlton
Hortonlane
Emstrey
Meole Brace
Nox
Cructon
Westbury
Yockleton
Cruckmeole
Hanwood
Redhill
Bayston Hill
Atcham
Norton
Uppington
Stoney Stretton
Edge
Lea
Hinton
Farley
Annscroft
Wroxeter
Donnington
Rushton
SHROPSHIRE

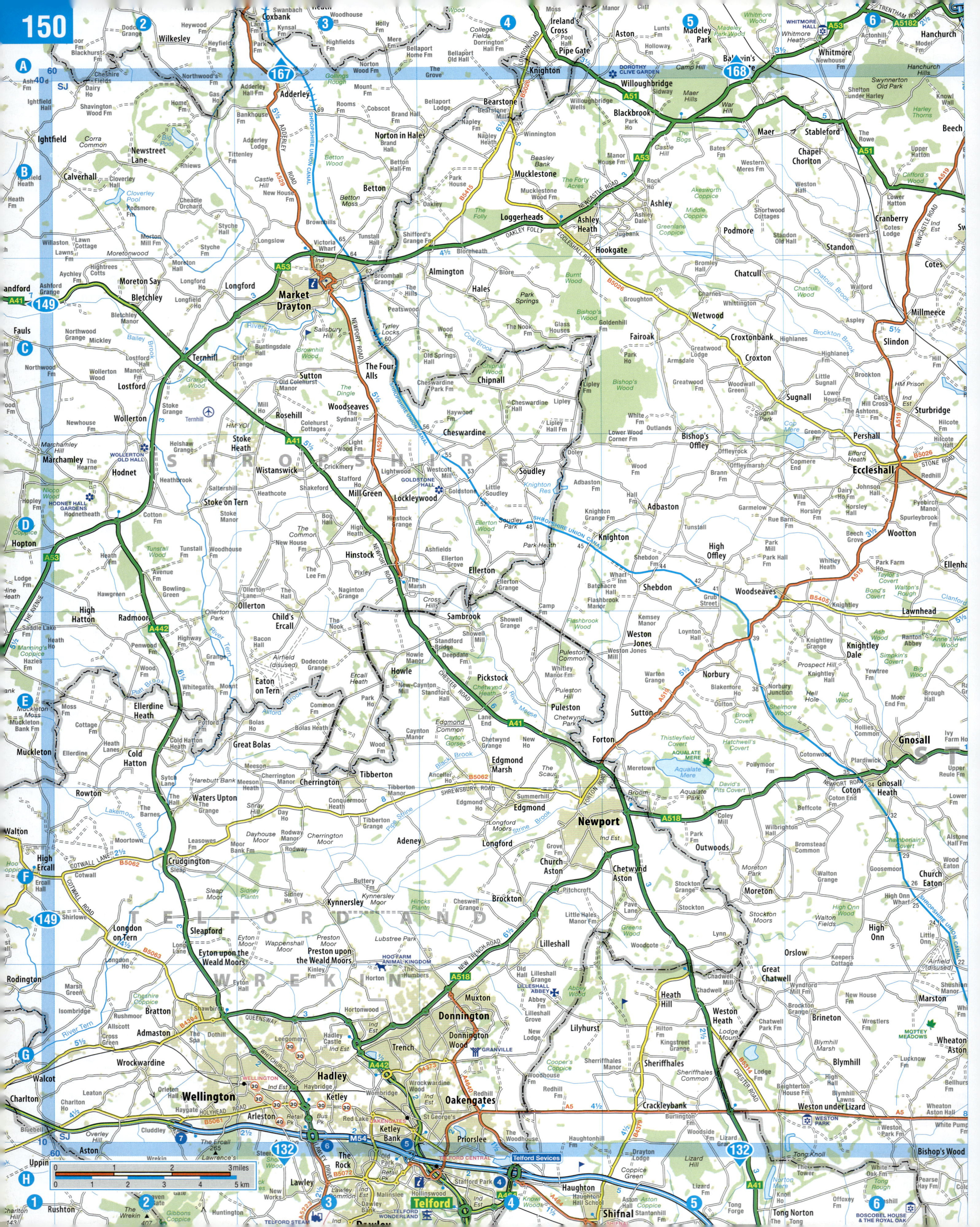

Market Drayton
Newport
Wellington
Telford
Oakengates
Donnington
Hadley
Eccleshall
Gnosall
Shifnal
Hodnet
Ternhill
Adderley
Bearstone
Mucklestone
Loggerheads
Ashley
Ashley Heath
Hookgate
Knighton
Willoughbridge
Maer
Chapel Chorlton
Stableford
Cranberry
Standon
Chatcull
Croxton
Croxtonbank
Fairoak
Wetwood
Slindon
Millmeece
Sturbridge
Pershall
Sugnall
Bishop's Offley
High Offley
Woodseaves
Adbaston
Knighton
Shebdon
Soudley
Cheswardine
Chipnall
Almington
Hales
Lockleywood
Hinstock
Ellerton
Sambrook
Pickstock
Howle
Puleston
Forton
Norbury
Weston Jones
Sutton
Knightley Dale
Lawnhead
Wootton
Edgmond
Tibberton
Cherrington
Great Bolas
Child's Ercall
Ollerton
Stoke Heath
Stoke on Tern
Wistanswick
Rosehill
Woodseaves
Sutton
Lostford
Wollerton
Marchamley
Hopton
High Hatton
Radmore
Ellerdine Heath
Muckleton
Cold Hatton
Eaton on Tern
Rowton
Waters Upton
Crudgington
High Ercall
Sleapford
Longdon on Tern
Eyton upon the Weald Moors
Preston upon the Weald Moors
Kynnersley
Adeney
Longford
Church Aston
Chetwynd Aston
Brockton
Lilleshall
Muxton
Lilyhurst
Heath Hill
Weston Heath
Sheriffhales
Crackleybank
Weston under Lizard
Great Chatwell
Orslow
High Onn
Church Eaton
Moreton
Outwoods
Brineton
Blymhill
Marston
Wrockwardine
Admaston
Bratton
Rodington
Walcot
Charlton
Arleston
Ketley
Ketley Bank
Priorslee
Haughton
Lawley
Dawley
Rushton
Aston
Uppin
Calverhall
Ightfield
Newstreet Lane
Moreton Say
Bletchley
Longford
Faulsl
Mickley
Radmore
Norton in Hales
Betton
Tunstall
Podmore
Whitmore
Hanchurch
Madeley Park
Aston
Ireland's Cross
Pipe Gate
Wilkesley
Coxbank
SHROPSHIRE
TELFORD AND WREKIN
A53
A41
A442
A518
A519
A529
A51
A5
A4640
M54
B5026
B5415
B5062
B5063
B5405
B4379
B4394
B5061
167
168
149
132
Shropshire Union Canal
River Tern
Aqualate Mere
0 1 2 3 miles
0 1 2 3 4 5 km

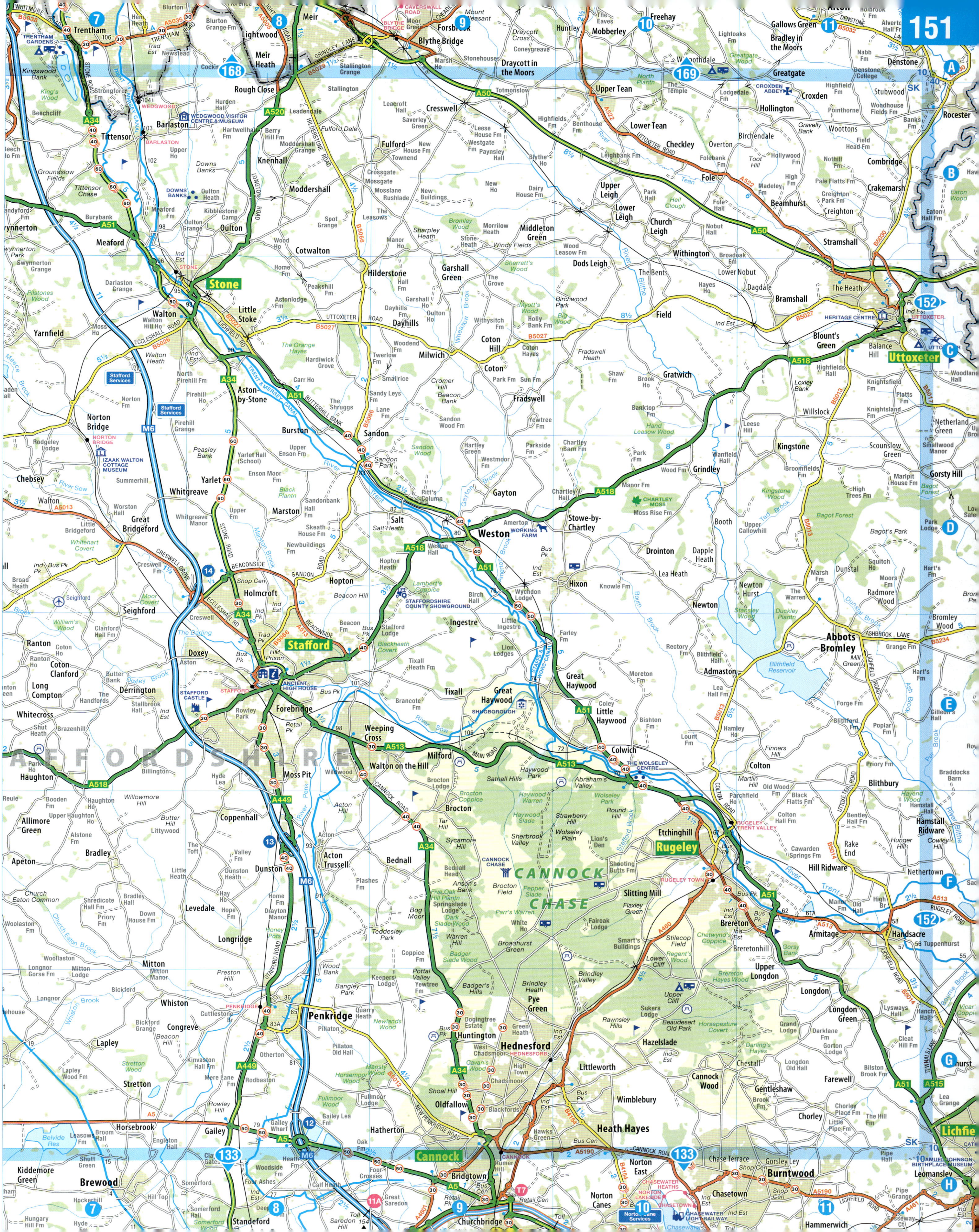

Trentham
Blurton
Meir
Meir Heath
Lightwood
Forsbrook
Blythe Bridge
Draycott in the Moors
Mobberley
Freehay
Huntley
Gallows Green
Bradley in the Moors
Denstone
Rocester
Rough Close
Stallington Grange
Cresswell
Upper Tean
Lower Tean
Hollington
Croxden
Tittensor
Barlaston
WEDGWOOD VISITOR CENTRE & MUSEUM
Knenhall
Fulford
Checkley
Overton
Fole
Combridge
Crakemarsh
Moddershall
Upper Leigh
Lower Leigh
Church Leigh
Beamhurst
Creighton
Stramshall
Meaford
Oulton
Cotwalton
Middleton Green
Withington
Dods Leigh
Stone
Hilderstone
Garshall Green
The Heath
Bramshall
Uttoxeter
Walton
Little Stoke
Dayhills
Field
Yarnfield
Milwich
Coton Hill
Coton
Blount's Green
Balance Hill
Aston-by-Stone
Gratwich
Fradswell
Norton Bridge
IZAAK WALTON COTTAGE MUSEUM
Burston
Sandon
Willslock
Kingstone
Chebsey
Yarlet
Whitgreave
Marston
Gayton
Grindley
Gorsty Hill
Great Bridgeford
Salt
Weston
Stowe-by-Chartley
Drointon
Hopton
Holmcroft
Hixon
Newton
Abbots Bromley
Seighford
Ingestre
Stafford
STAFFORDSHIRE COUNTY SHOWGROUND
Ranton
Coton Clanford
Doxey
Derrington
Long Compton
Tixall
Great Haywood
Little Haywood
Admaston
Forebridge
Whitecross
Weeping Cross
Milford
Walton on the Hill
Colwich
Colton
Blithbury
Haughton
Moss Pit
Brocton
STAFFORDSHIRE
Allimore Green
Coppenhall
Acton Trussell
Bednall
Etchinghill
Rugeley
Hamstall Ridware
Hill Ridware
Bradley
Dunston
CANNOCK CHASE
Apeton
Levedale
Slitting Mill
Brereton
Armitage
Handsacre
Longridge
Mitton
Whiston
Congreve
Penkridge
Huntington
Hednesford
Upper Longdon
Longdon
Longdon Green
Hazelslade
Lapley
Stretton
Littleworth
Cannock Wood
Gentleshaw
Farewell
Wimblebury
Chorley
Horsebrook
Gailey
Heath Hayes
Cannock
Bridgtown
Norton East
Burntwood
Chasetown
Kiddemore Green
Brewood
Standeford
Churchbridge
Norton Canes
Hammerwich
Leomansley
Lichfield
M6
A34
A51
A50
A518
A513
A449
A5

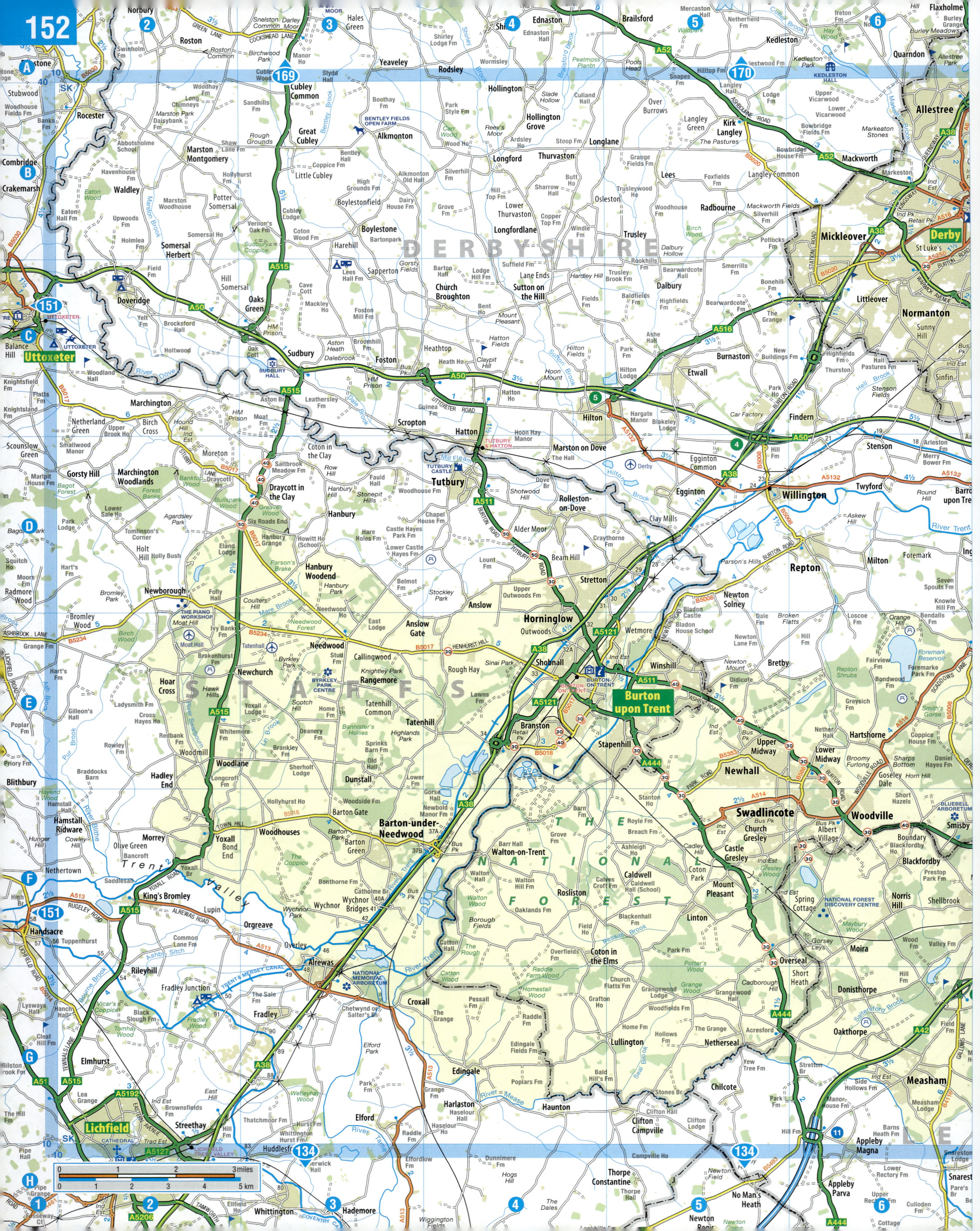
DERBYSHIRE
STAFFS
THE NATIONAL FOREST
Derby
Burton upon Trent
Uttoxeter
Lichfield
Swadlincote
Tutbury
Mickleover
Allestree
Normanton
Littleover
Willington
Repton
Hilton
Etwall
Egginton
Stretton
Horninglow
Winshill
Stapenhill
Branston
Newhall
Woodville
Measham
Hatton
Sudbury
Doveridge
Rocester
Marchington
Barton-under-Needwood
Alrewas
Fradley
Walton-on-Trent
Rosliston
Linton
Overseal
Moira
Donisthorpe
Oakthorpe
Netherseal
Lullington
Croxall
Edingale
Elford
Harlaston
Clifton Campville
Appleby Magna
Kedleston
Quarndon
Mackworth
Brailsford
Longford
Boylestone
Cubley
Marston Montgomery
Yoxall
Hamstall Ridware
King's Bromley
Handsacre
Armitage
Streethay
Whittington
Hademore
Thorpe Constantine
No Man's Heath
Newton Regis
Chilcote
Findern
Stenson
Twyford
Milton
Foremark
Bretby
Hartshorne
Castle Gresley
Church Gresley
Blackfordby
Smisby
Dunstall
Tatenhill
Rangemore
Anslow
Hanbury
Draycott in the Clay
Newborough
Hoar Cross
Needwood
Scropton
Foston
Church Broughton
Sutton on the Hill
Dalbury
Radbourne
Burnaston
Rolleston-on-Dove
Marston on Dove
A38
A50
A511
A515
A444
A5121
A513
A516
A52
A5127
A5192
A51
A5206
B5017
B5018
B5016
B5234
B5008
B5353
Trent
River Dove
River Mease
Trent & Mersey Canal
National Memorial Arboretum
Tutbury Castle
Sudbury Hall
Kedleston Hall
National Forest Discovery Centre
169
170
151
134
0 1 2 3 miles
0 1 2 3 4 5 km

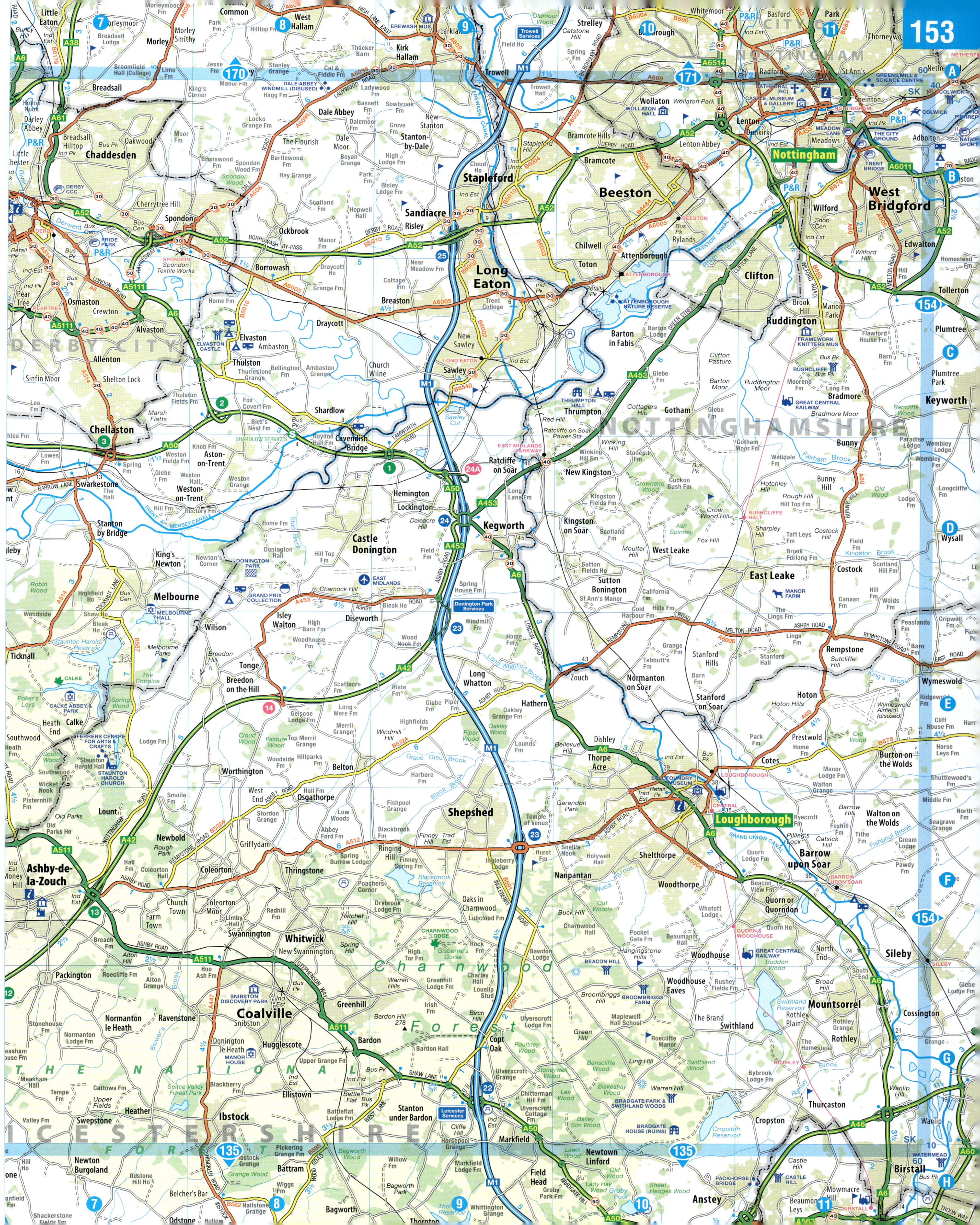
Nottingham
NOTTINGHAM
West Bridgford
Beeston
Stapleford
Long Eaton
Sandiacre
Risley
Chilwell
Toton
Attenborough
Clifton
Ruddington
Edwalton
Tollerton
Plumtree
Keyworth
Bradmore
Bunny
Gotham
Barton in Fabis
Thrumpton
Ratcliffe on Soar
Kegworth
Kingston on Soar
West Leake
East Leake
Costock
Wysall
Rempstone
Normanton on Soar
Stanford on Soar
Hathern
Zouch
Long Whatton
Diseworth
Castle Donington
Hemington
Lockington
Shardlow
Aston-on-Trent
Weston-on-Trent
Melbourne
Isley Walton
Breedon on the Hill
Tonge
Worthington
Belton
Osgathorpe
Shepshed
Loughborough
Dishley
Thorpe Acre
Cotes
Prestwold
Hoton
Burton on the Wolds
Walton on the Wolds
Barrow upon Soar
Quorn or Quorndon
Woodhouse
Woodhouse Eaves
Woodthorpe
Nanpantan
Shelthorpe
Sileby
Mountsorrel
Rothley
Swithland
Thurcaston
Cropston
Anstey
Birstall
Wanlip
Cossington
Newtown Linford
Markfield
Copt Oak
Whitwick
Coalville
Thringstone
Griffydam
Coleorton
Swannington
Ashby-de-la-Zouch
Packington
Ravenstone
Ibstock
Heather
Hugglescote
Bardon
Stanton under Bardon
Ellistown
Swepstone
Normanton le Heath
Newton Burgoland
Bagworth
Ticknall
Calke
Smisby
Lount
Newbold
Derby
DERBY CITY
Chaddesden
Spondon
Alvaston
Chellaston
Allenton
Elvaston
Thulston
Borrowash
Ockbrook
Draycott
Breaston
Swarkestone
Stanton by Bridge
Kirk Hallam
Dale Abbey
Stanton-by-Dale
West Hallam
Trowell
Strelley
Bilborough
Wollaton
Lenton
Radford
NOTTINGHAMSHIRE
LEICESTERSHIRE
DERBYSHIRE
Charnwood Forest
THE NATIONAL FOREST
M1
A50
A52
A6
A42
A453
A511
A512
A46
A60
A6006
Donington Park Services
Leicester Services
Trowell Services
East Midlands Airport
Donington Park
Calke Abbey & Park
Staunton Harold Reservoir
Attenborough Nature Reserve
Great Central Railway
Swithland Reservoir
Cropston Reservoir
Bradgate Park & Swithland Woods
Beacon Hill
Mount St Bernard Abbey
170
171
135
154

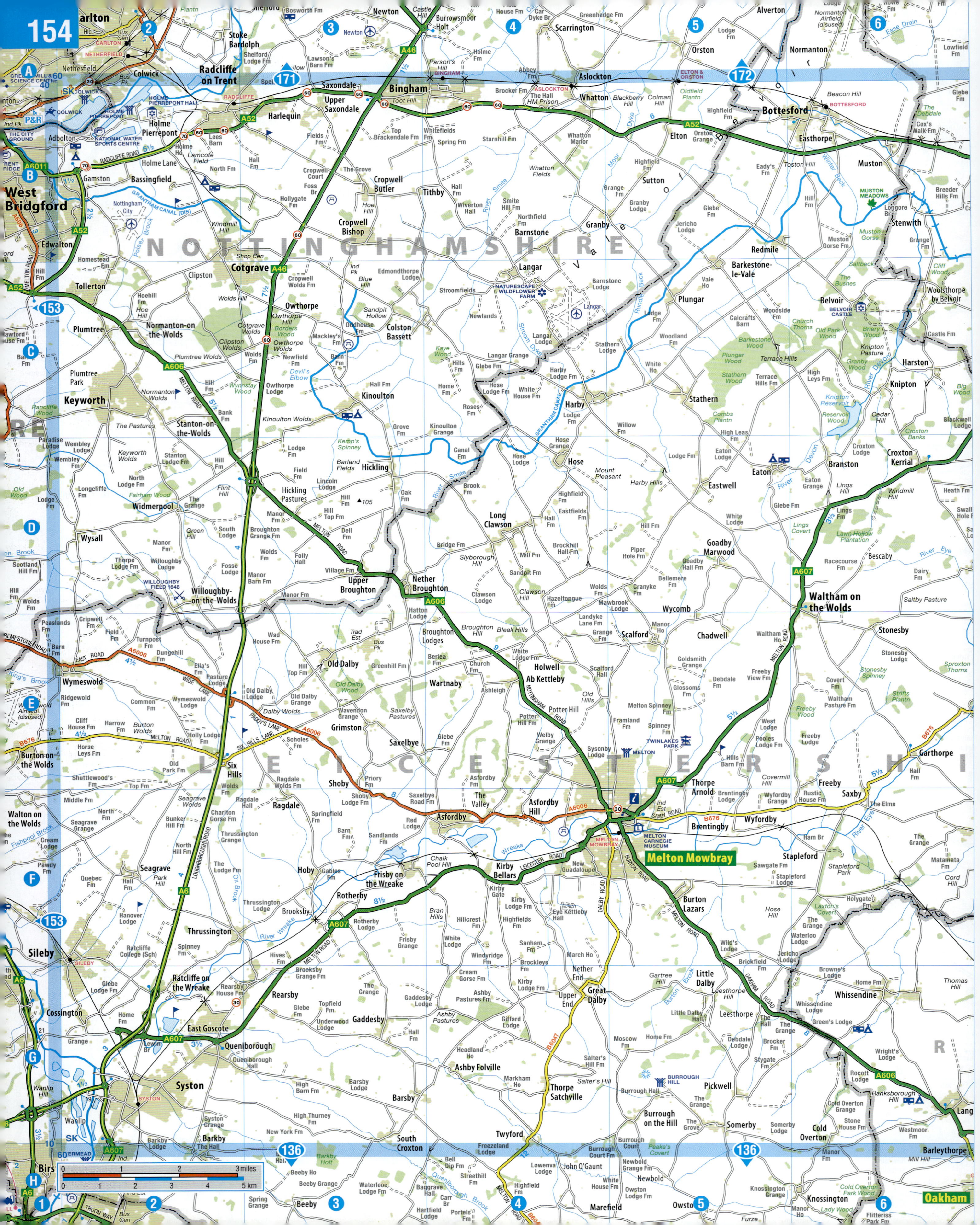

NOTTINGHAMSHIRE
LEICESTERSHIRE
Vale of Belvoir
West Bridgford
Radcliffe on Trent
Holme Pierrepont
Bingham
Saxondale
Upper Saxondale
Aslockton
Whatton
Orston
Elton
Bottesford
Easthorpe
Muston
Normanton
Alverton
Scarrington
Stoke Bardolph
Newton
Burrowsmoor Holt
Gamston
Bassingfield
Holme Lane
Edwalton
Tollerton
Cotgrave
Clipston
Cropwell Butler
Cropwell Bishop
Tithby
Barnstone
Langar
Granby
Sutton
Redmile
Barkestone-le-Vale
Plungar
Belvoir
Woolsthorpe by Belvoir
Stenwith
Harston
Knipton
Branston
Croxton Kerrial
Eaton
Eastwell
Stathern
Harby
Hose
Plumtree
Normanton-on-the-Wolds
Owthorpe
Colston Bassett
Kinoulton
Keyworth
Stanton-on-the-Wolds
Hickling
Widmerpool
Wysall
Long Clawson
Upper Broughton
Nether Broughton
Willoughby-on-the-Wolds
Goadby Marwood
Waltham on the Wolds
Wycomb
Chadwell
Scalford
Stonesby
Wymeswold
Old Dalby
Wartnaby
Holwell
Ab Kettleby
Grimston
Saxelbye
Burton on the Wolds
Six Hills
Shoby
Asfordby
Asfordby Hill
Thorpe Arnold
Brentingby
Freeby
Saxby
Wyfordby
Garthorpe
Melton Mowbray
Walton on the Wolds
Ragdale
Hoby
Seagrave
Kirby Bellars
Frisby on the Wreake
Rotherby
Stapleford
Burton Lazars
Sileby
Thrussington
Ratcliffe on the Wreake
Rearsby
Cossington
Gaddesby
Great Dalby
Little Dalby
Whissendine
East Goscote
Queniborough
Syston
Ashby Folville
Thorpe Satchville
Pickwell
Barsby
Burrough on the Hill
Somerby
Cold Overton
Twyford
South Croxton
Barkby
Barleythorpe
Oakham
Knossington
Owston
Marefield
Beeby
A46
A52
A606
A607
A6006
B676
171
172
153
136

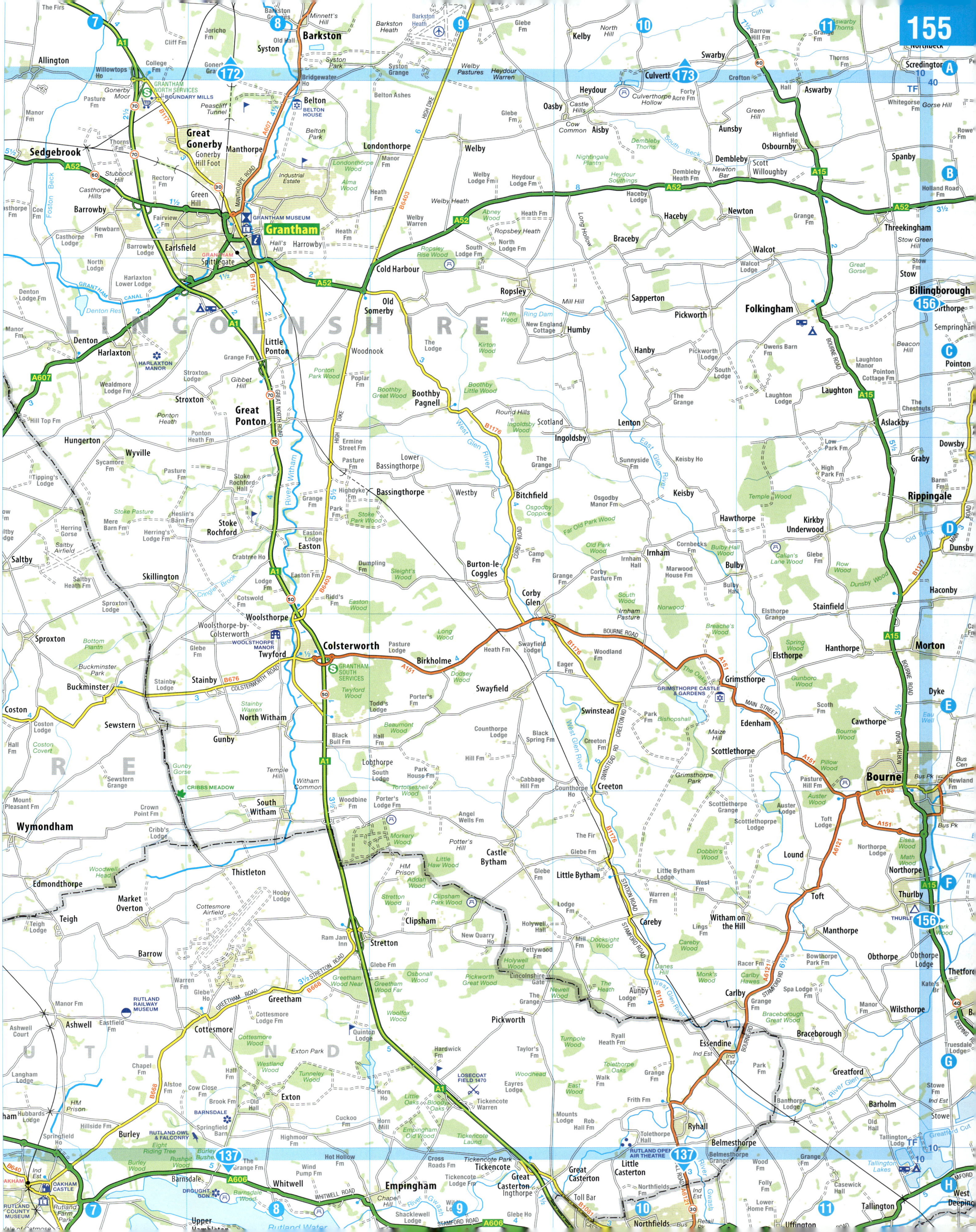

LINCOLNSHIRE
RUTLAND
Grantham
Grantham Museum
Great Gonerby
Manthorpe
Londonthorpe
Belton
Belton House
Barkston
Syston
Allington
Sedgebrook
Barrowby
Earlsfield
Spittlegate
Harrowby
Harlaxton
Harlaxton Manor
Denton
Denton Res
Grantham Canal
Little Ponton
Great Ponton
Stroxton
Hungerton
Wyville
Stoke Rochford
Saltby
Skillington
Woolsthorpe
Woolsthorpe-by-Colsterworth
Woolsthorpe Manor
Colsterworth
Twyford
Stainby
Buckminster
Sproxton
Coston
Sewstern
Gunby
North Witham
South Witham
Wymondham
Edmondthorpe
Thistleton
Market Overton
Teigh
Barrow
Cottesmore
Ashwell
Burley
Oakham
Oakham Castle
Rutland County Museum
Rutland Railway Museum
Greetham
Exton
Whitwell
Empingham
Rutland Water
Stretton
Clipsham
Pickworth
Tickencote
Great Casterton
Little Casterton
Ryhall
Belmesthorpe
Essendine
Carlby
Careby
Little Bytham
Castle Bytham
Swinstead
Creeton
Corby Glen
Burton-le-Coggles
Bitchfield
Bassingthorpe
Boothby Pagnell
Old Somerby
Cold Harbour
Ropsley
Humby
Ingoldsby
Lenton
Keisby
Hanby
Folkingham
Pickworth
Sapperton
Walcot
Braceby
Haceby
Newton
Welby
Oasby
Heydour
Aisby
Culverthorpe
Kelby
Swarby
Aswarby
Aunsby
Osbournby
Dembleby
Scott Willoughby
Spanby
Threekingham
Stow
Billingborough
Pointon
Laughton
Aslackby
Dowsby
Rippingale
Kirkby Underwood
Dunsby
Hawthorpe
Irnham
Bulby
Haconby
Stainfield
Morton
Hanthorpe
Elsthorpe
Grimsthorpe
Grimsthorpe Castle & Gardens
Edenham
Scottlethorpe
Cawthorpe
Dyke
Bourne
Toft
Lound
Manthorpe
Witham on the Hill
Thurlby
Northorpe
Obthorpe
Wilsthorpe
Braceborough
Greatford
Barholm
Stowe
Tallington
Uffington
Northfields
Scredington
Swayfield
Birkholme
Losecoat Field 1470
Rutland Open Air Theatre
Barnsdale
A1
A52
A15
A151
A606
A607
A6121
B1174
B1176
B6403
B676
B668
B1193
7
8
9
10
11
172
173
137
156
A
B
C
D
E
F
G
H

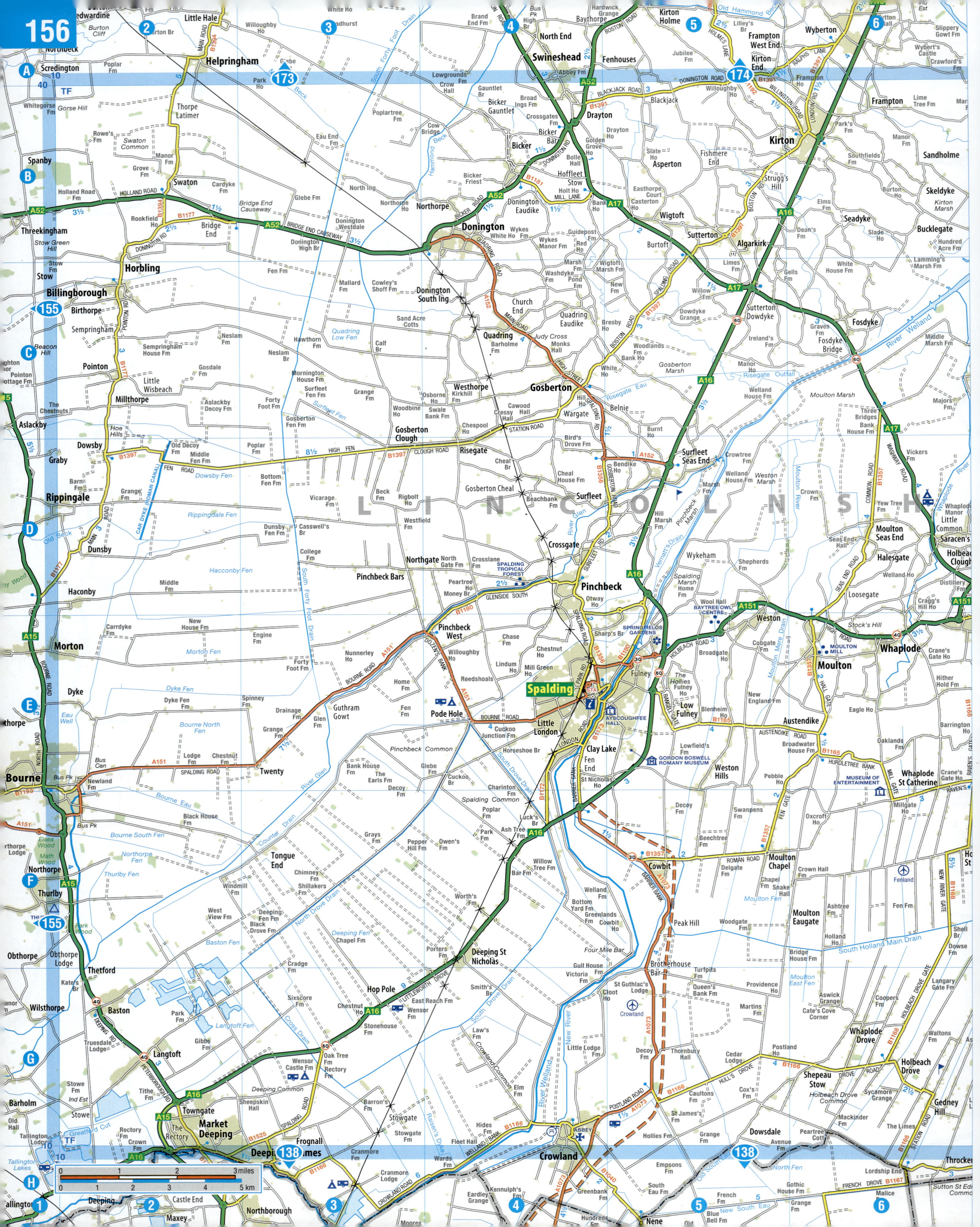
LINCOLNSHIRE
Spalding
Bourne
Market Deeping
Crowland
Donington
Swineshead
Kirton
Gosberton
Pinchbeck
Surfleet
Moulton
Whaplode
Helpringham
Horbling
Billingborough
Rippingale
Morton
Deeping St Nicholas
Cowbit
Weston
Fosdyke
Algarkirk
Sutterton
Wigtoft
Quadring
Langtoft
Baston
Thurlby
Haconby
Dunsby
Pointon
Sempringham
Aslackby
Dowsby
Swaton
Bicker
Frampton
Wyberton
Moulton Chapel
Whaplode Drove
Holbeach Drove
Gedney Hill
Twenty
Tongue End
Pode Hole
Pinchbeck West
Little London
Weston Hills
Surfleet Seas End
Gosberton Clough
Risegate
Northorpe
Deeping Fen
Bourne North Fen
Dyke Fen
Haconby Fen
Baston Fen
Moulton Marsh
River Welland
River Glen
South Holland Main Drain
A15
A16
A17
A52
A151
A152
A1073
B1166
B1397
173
174
155
138
0 1 2 3 miles
0 1 2 3 4 5 km

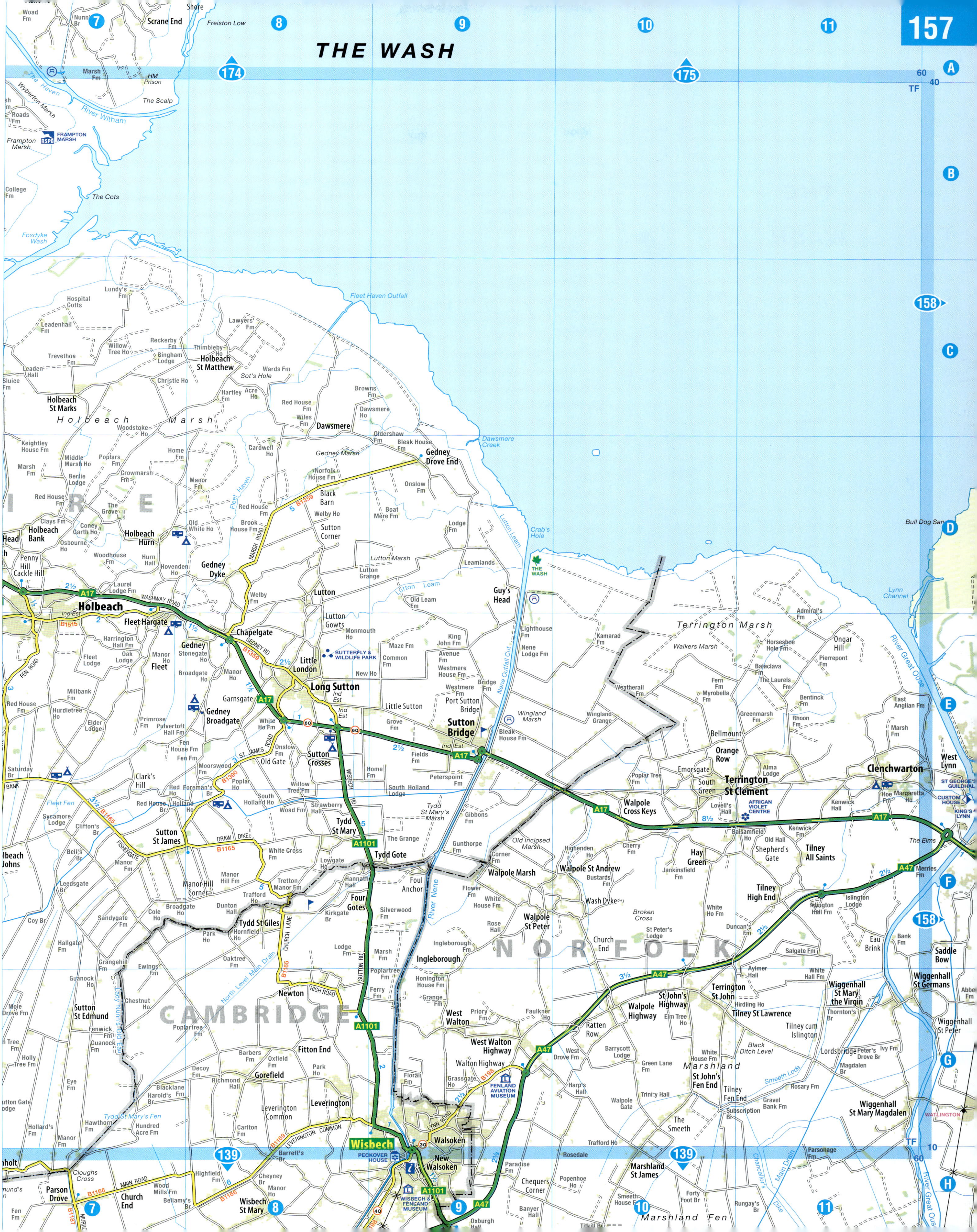
THE WASH
174
175
158
139
TF
60
40
10
A
B
C
D
E
F
G
H
7
8
9
10
11
Shore
Scrane End
Freiston Low
Nunn Br
Woad Fm
Marsh Fm
HM Prison
The Haven
Wyberton Marsh
The Scalp
River Witham
Roads Fm
FRAMPTON MARSH
RSPB
Frampton Marsh
College Fm
The Cots
Fosdyke Wash
Fleet Haven Outfall
Lundy's Fm
Hospital Cotts
Leadenhall Fm
Lawyers' Fm
Reckerby Fm
Thimbleby Ho
Willow Tree Ho
Bingham Lodge
Holbeach St Matthew
Trevethoe Fm
Wards Fm
Leaden Hall
Sot's Hole
Sluice Fm
Christie Ho
Hartley Fm
Acre Ho
Browns Fm
Holbeach St Marks
Red House Fm
Dawsmere Ho
Wiles Fm
Dawsmere
Holbeach
Marsh
Woodstoke Ho
Oldershaw Fm
Keightley House Fm
Cardwell Ho
Bleak House Fm
Dawsmere Creek
Home Fm
Gedney Marsh
Gedney Drove End
Middle Marsh Ho
Poplars Fm
Marsh Fm
Crowmarsh Fm
Norfolk House Fm
Bertie Lodge
Manor Fm
Onslow Fm
Black Barn
Red House Fm
Fleet Haven
Red House Fm
The Grove
B1359
Boat Mere Fm
Welby Ho
Clays Fm
Coney Garth Ho
Old White Ho
Brook House Fm
Lodge Fm
Crab's Hole
Bull Dog Sand
Holbeach Bank
Holbeach Hurn
Sutton Corner
Lutton Leam
Osbourne Ho
MARSH ROAD
Penny Hill
Woodhouse Fm
Hurn Hall
Gedney Dyke
Lutton Marsh
Lutton Grange
Leamlands
THE WASH
Cackle Hill
Hovenden Ho
Laurel Lodge Fm
A17
Welby Fm
Lutton
Guy's Head
Lynn Channel
Holbeach
WASHWAY ROAD
Lutton Leam
Old Leam Fm
Ind Est
Fleet Hargate
Chapelgate
Lutton Gowts
Lighthouse Fm
Terrington Marsh
Admiral's Fm
B1515
Harrington Hall Fm
Monmouth Ho
King John Fm
Kamarad Fm
GEDNEY RD
Gedney
Stonegate Ho
BUTTERFLY & WILDLIFE PARK
Maze Fm
Avenue Fm
Nene Lodge Fm
Walkers Marsh
Horseshoe Hole Fm
Ongar Hill
Oak Lodge
Fleet Lodge
Manor Ho
Fleet
Little London
Common Fm
Westmere House Fm
Nene Outfall Cut
Pierrepont Fm
FEN ROAD
Broadgate Ho
Manor Ho
New Ho
Bridge Fm
Balaclava Fm
River Great Ouse
Long Sutton
Westmere Fm
Weatherall Fm
Fern Fm
The Laurels Fm
Millbank Fm
Garnsgate
Ind Est
Port Sutton Bridge
Myrobella Fm
Bentinck Fm
East Anglian Fm
Red House Fm
Hurdletree Ho
Gedney Broadgate
Little Sutton
Wingland Marsh
Wingland Grange
Greenmarsh Fm
Rhoon Fm
Elder Lodge
Primrose Fm
White Ho Fm
Grove Fm
Sutton Bridge
Bleak House Fm
Marsh Fm
Pulvertoft Hall Fm
Fen House Fm
St JAMES ROAD
Onslow Fm
Sutton Crosses
Fields Fm
Bellmount
Orange Row
West Lynn
Clenchwarton
Saturday Br
Fen Fm
Old Gate
Ind Est
Alma Lodge
Moorswood Fm
WISBECH RD
Home Fm
Peterspoint Fm
Poplar Tree Fm
Emorsgate
ST GEORGE'S GUILDHALL
Clark's Hill
B1390
Poplar Ho
South Green
Terrington St Clement
Hoe Fm
Margaretta Ho
CUSTOM HOUSE
KING'S LYNN
BANK
Red Foreman's Br
Willow Tree Fm
South Holland Lodge
Walpole Cross Keys
Kenwick Hall
Fleet Fen
B1165
Red House Br
Holland Ho
South Holland Ho
Strawberry Hall
Lovell's Hall
AFRICAN VIOLET CENTRE
Sycamore Lodge
Clifton's Br
Wood Fm
Tydd St Mary
Tydd St Mary's Marsh
Gibbons Fm
Balsamfield Ho
Kenwick Fm
The Elms
Sutton St James
DRAW DIKE
A1101
The Grange
Old Inclosed Marsh
Old Hall Fm
Tilney All Saints
Holbeach St Johns
Bell's Br
FISHERGATE
White Cross Fm
Gunthorpe Fm
Highenden Ho
Cherry Fm
Shepherd's Gate
Manor Fm
B1165
Lowgate Ho
Tydd Gote
Corner Fm
Hay Green
Manor Hill Fm
Hannath Hall
Walpole Marsh
Walpole St Andrew
Jankinsfield Fm
A47
Merries Fm
Leedsgate Fm
Manor Hill Corner
Tretton Manor Fm
Foul Anchor
Bustards Fm
Tilney High End
Trafford Ho
Flower Fm
Dunton Hall
Four Gotes
White House Fm
Wash Dyke
Broken Cross
White Ho Fm
Islington Hall Fm
Islington Lodge
Broadgate Ho
River Nene
Coy Br
Sandygate Fm
Cole Ho
Tydd St Giles
Kirkgate Br
Silverwood Fm
Walpole St Peter
Duncan's Fm
Park Ho
Hornfield Ho
CHURCH LANE
Rose Hall
St Peter's Lodge
Bank Fm
Eau Brink
Hallgate Fm
Church End
NORFOLK
Salgate Fm
Saddle Bow
Grangehill Fm
Ewings Fm
Oaktree Fm
Lodge Fm
Marsh Fm
Ingleborough Fm
Ingleborough
Aylmer Hall
White Hall Fm
Wiggenhall St Germans
Guanock Ho
North Level Main Drain
SUTTON ROAD
B1165
Poplartree Fm
Honington House Fm
A47
Terrington St John
Wiggenhall St Mary the Virgin
Mole Drove Fm
Lady Nunn's Old Eau
Chestnut Ho
Newton
HIGH ROAD
Ferry Fm
Grange Fm
St John's Highway
Walpole Highway
Elm Tree Ho
Hirdling Ho
Tilney St Lawrence
Thornton's Br
Sutton St Edmund
CAMBRIDGE
A1101
West Walton
Priory Fm
Faulkner Ho
Ratten Row
Tilney cum Islington
Wiggenhall St Peter
Fenwick Fm
Poplartree Fm
Guanock Fm
West Walton Highway
A47
West Drove Fm
Barrycott Lodge
Black Ditch Level
Lordsbridge
Peter's Drove Br
Ivy Fm
Holly Tree Fm
Barbers Fm
Oxfield Fm
Fitton End
Park Ho
Walton Highway
B198
White House Fm
Green Lane Fm
Marshland
Magdalen Br
Decoy Fm
Gorefield
Grassgate Ho
Floral Fm
FENLAND AVIATION MUSEUM
Harp's Hall
St John's Fen End
Smeeth Lode
Rosary Fm
Eye Fm
Richmond Hall
Blacklane Fm
Harold's Br
Walpole Gate
Trinity Hall
Tilney Fen End
Gravel Bank Fm
Leverington Common
Leverington
LYNN ROAD
The Smeeth
Subscription Br
Wiggenhall St Mary Magdalen
WATLINGTON
Tydd St Mary's Fen
Hawthorn Fm
Hundred Acre Fm
Carlton Fm
Hollard's Fm
Manor Fm
B1169
LEVERINGTON COMMON
Walsoken
Trafford Ho
Wisbech
Rosedale
Parsonage Fm
Chancellor's
Main Drain
Barrett's Br
PECKOVER HOUSE
New Walsoken
Paradise Fm
Marshland St James
Cloughs Cross
Highfield Fm
Cheyney Br
Chequers Corner
Popenhoe Ho
MAIN ROAD
Wood Mills Fm
Manor Ho
WISBECH & FENLAND MUSEUM
Smeeth House Fm
Forty Foot Br
Rungay's Br
Parson Drove
B1166
Church End
Bellamy's Br
Wisbech St Mary
B1166
Banyer Hall
Marshland Fen
Dyke
River Great Ouse
Fen Fm
B1187
MURROW
Oxburgh Hall
Titkill Br

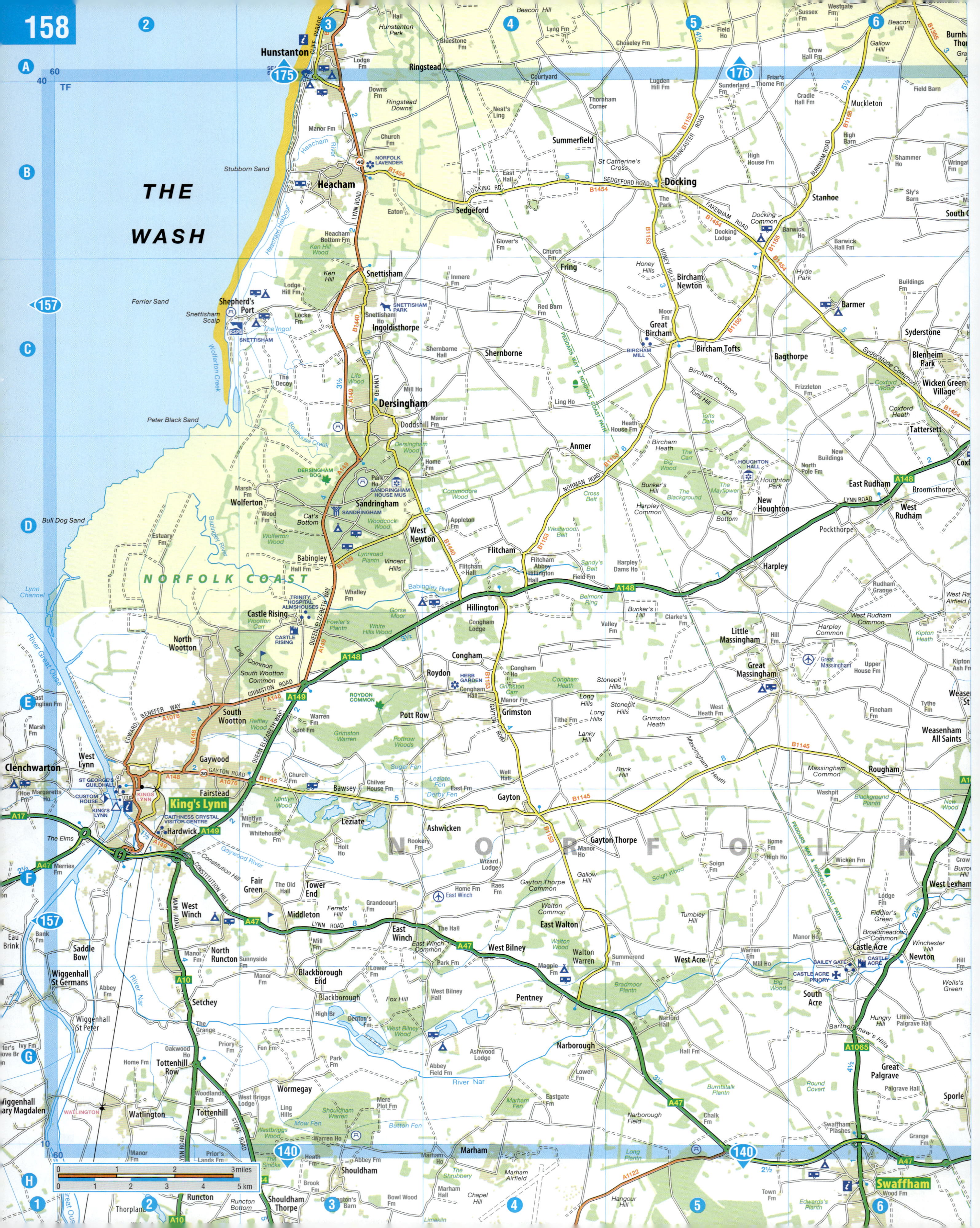
THE WASH
Hunstanton
Heacham
Snettisham
Shepherd's Port
Ingoldisthorpe
Dersingham
Sandringham
Wolferton
West Newton
Babingley
Castle Rising
North Wootton
South Wootton
Gaywood
King's Lynn
West Lynn
Clenchwarton
Fairstead
Hardwick
NORFOLK COAST
Ringstead
Sedgeford
Docking
Summerfield
Fring
Shernborne
Stanhoe
Barmer
Syderstone
Bircham Newton
Great Bircham
Bircham Tofts
Bagthorpe
Anmer
Flitcham
Hillington
Congham
Roydon
Grimston
Pott Row
Bawsey
Leziate
Gayton
Ashwicken
Gayton Thorpe
East Rudham
West Rudham
New Houghton
Harpley
Little Massingham
Great Massingham
Rougham
Weasenham All Saints
Castle Acre
Newton
South Acre
West Acre
East Walton
West Bilney
East Winch
Middleton
West Winch
Tower End
Fair Green
Pentney
Narborough
Great Palgrave
Sporle
Swaffham
Marham
Shouldham
Shouldham Thorpe
Wormegay
Tottenhill
Tottenhill Row
Watlington
Setchey
North Runcton
Saddle Bow
Wiggenhall St Germans
Wiggenhall St Peter
Runcton
N O R F O L K
Stubborn Sand
Ferrier Sand
Peter Black Sand
Bull Dog Sand
Snettisham Scalp
River Great Ouse
River Nar
Gaywood River
Babingley River
PEDDARS WAY & NORFOLK COAST PATH
A148
A149
A47
A10
A17
A1065
A1122
B1454
B1153
B1145
B1155
B1440
B1439
B1355
157
175
176
140
0 1 2 3 miles
0 1 2 3 4 5 km

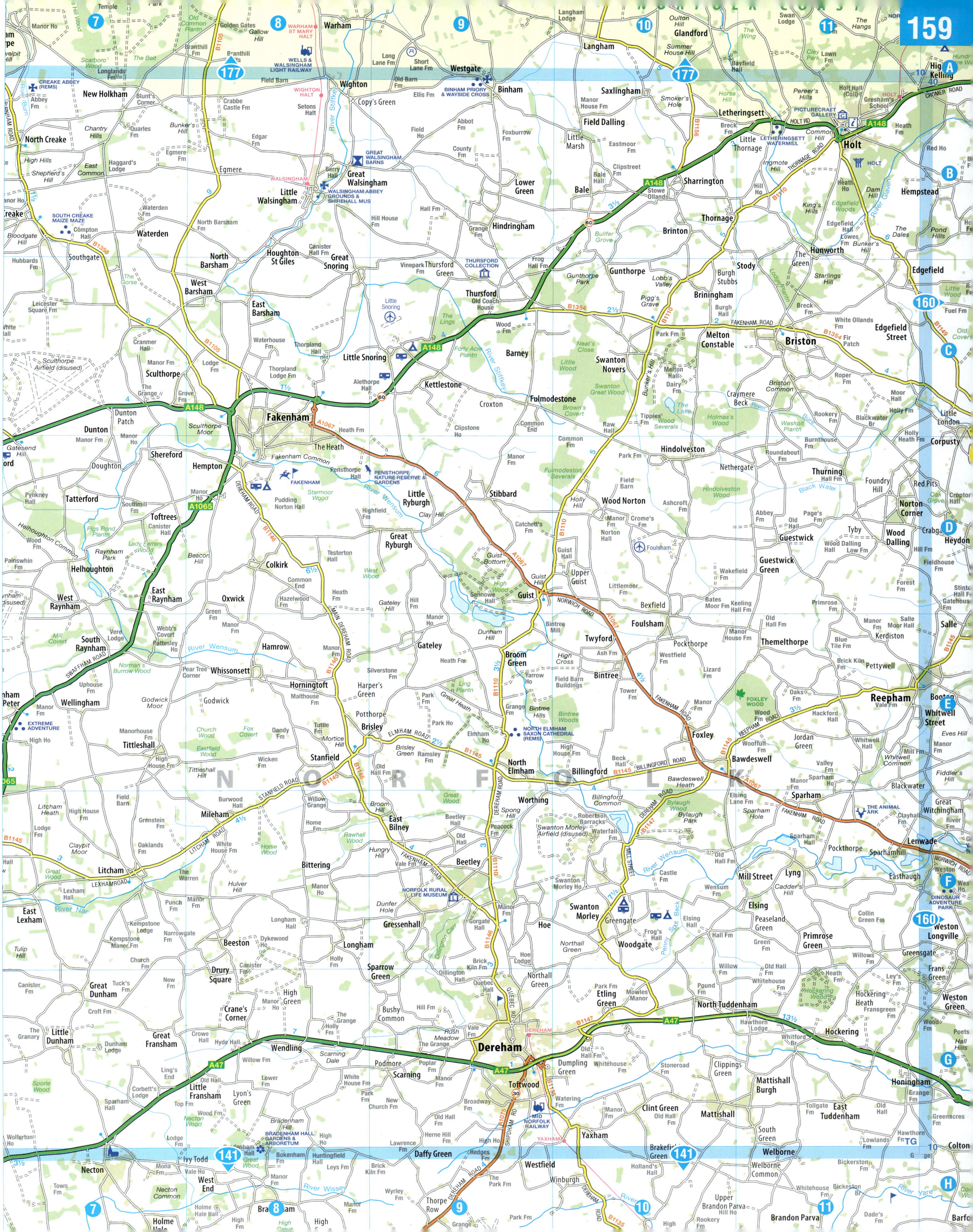

Warham
Wells & Walsingham Light Railway
Westgate
Binham Priory & Wayside Cross
Binham
Langham
Glandford
Saxlingham
Field Dalling
Letheringsett
Holt
Creake Abbey (Rems)
New Holkham
North Creake
Wighton
Great Walsingham
Little Walsingham
Walsingham Abbey Grounds & Shirehall Mus
Egmere
Lower Green
Bale
Sharrington
Thornage
Hempstead
Waterden
South Creake Maize Maze
Houghton St Giles
Great Snoring
Thursford
Thursford Collection
Hindringham
Brinton
Hunworth
Stody
Gunthorpe
Briningham
Edgefield
North Barsham
West Barsham
East Barsham
Southgate
Little Snoring
Barney
Melton Constable
Briston
Edgefield Street
Sculthorpe
Kettlestone
Fulmodestone
Croxton
Swanton Novers
Fakenham
Dunton
Shereford
Hempton
The Heath
Fakenham Common
Pensthorpe Nature Reserve & Gardens
Little Ryburgh
Stibbard
Wood Norton
Hindolveston
Thurning
Tatterford
Toftrees
Great Ryburgh
Helhoughton
Colkirk
Guist
Foulsham
Guestwick
Guestwick Green
Wood Dalling
Heydon
Corpusty
West Raynham
East Raynham
Oxwick
Twyford
Bintree
South Raynham
Hamrow
Gateley
Broom Green
Themelthorpe
Salle
Reepham
Whissonsett
Horningtoft
Wellingham
Godwick
Harper's Green
Brisley
North Elmham Saxon Cathedral (Rems)
North Elmham
Billingford
Foxley
Bawdeswell
Tittleshall
Stanfield
Mileham
Worthing
Sparham
Great Witchingham
The Animal Ark
Lenwade
Litcham
East Bilney
Beetley
Bittering
Norfolk Rural Life Museum
Swanton Morley
Lyng
Mill Street
Elsing
Weston Longville
East Lexham
Gressenhall
Hoe
Greengate
Woodgate
Beeston
Longham
Sparrow Green
Great Dunham
Little Dunham
Great Fransham
Wendling
Dereham
Dumpling Green
North Tuddenham
Hockering
Honingham
Little Fransham
Scarning
Toftwood
Mid Norfolk Railway
Yaxham
Mattishall
Clint Green
East Tuddenham
Welborne
Necton
Ivy Todd
Bradenham Hall Gardens & Arboretum
Daffy Green
Westfield
Thorpe Row
Brandon Parva
Colton
NORFOLK
A148
A1067
A1065
A47
B1105
B1110
B1145
B1146
B1147
B1135

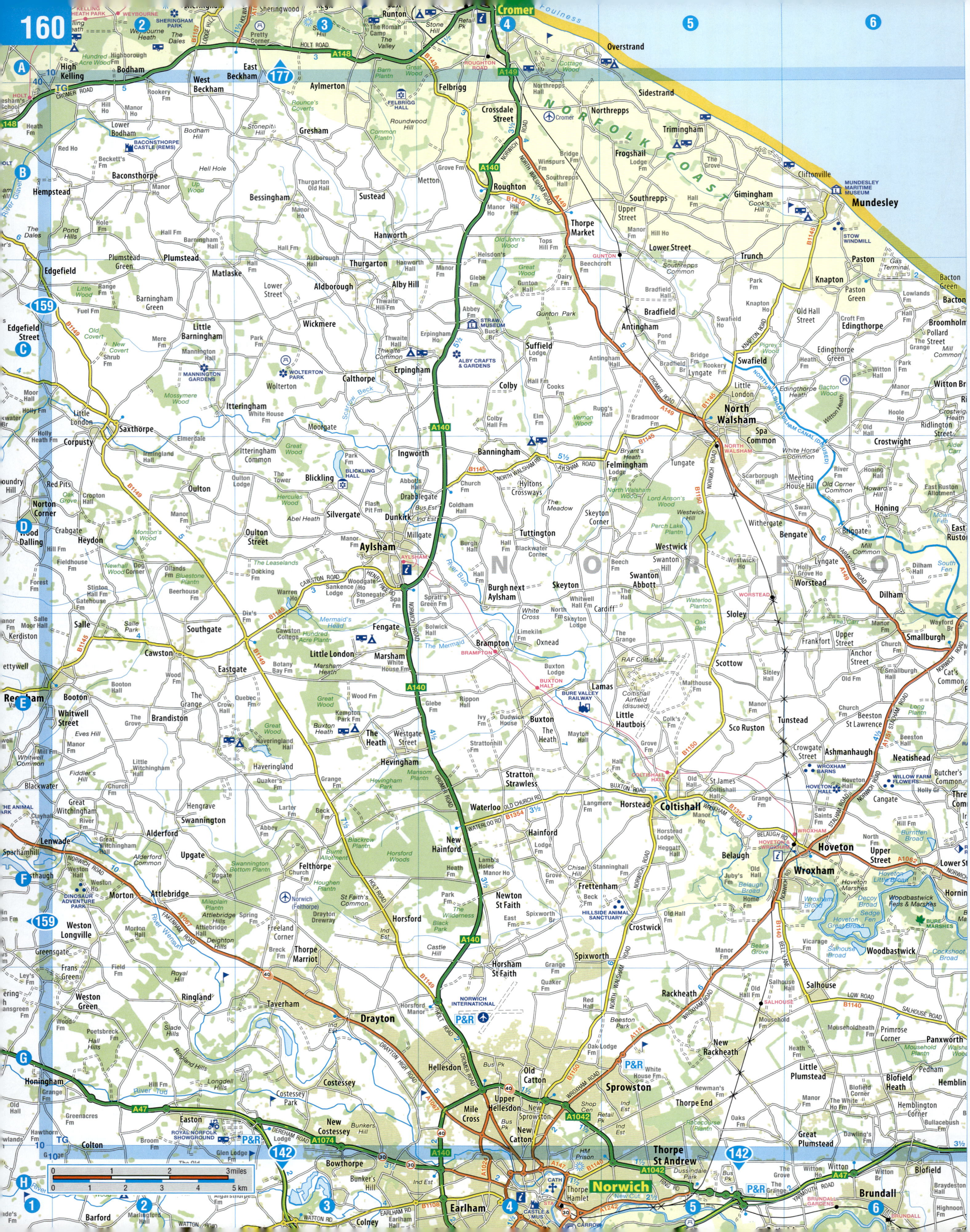
Cromer
Overstrand
Sidestrand
Northrepps
Trimingham
Mundesley
Gimingham
Southrepps
Roughton
Felbrigg
Aylmerton
West Beckham
East Beckham
Bodham
High Kelling
Gresham
Baconsthorpe
Hempstead
Bessingham
Sustead
Metton
Hanworth
Thurgarton
Aldborough
Alby Hill
Plumstead
Matlaske
Edgefield
Edgefield Street
Barningham Green
Little Barningham
Wickmere
Erpingham
Calthorpe
Wolterton
Itteringham
Saxthorpe
Corpusty
Little London
Colby
Suffield
Thorpe Market
Antingham
Bradfield
Knapton
Paston
Bacton
Trunch
Swafield
North Walsham
Spa Common
Felmingham
Banningham
Ingworth
Blickling
Aylsham
Millgate
Burgh next Aylsham
Tuttington
Skeyton
Westwick
Swanton Abbott
Worstead
Dilham
Smallburgh
Heydon
Salle
Cawston
Southgate
Eastgate
Reepham
Booton
Whitwell Street
Brandiston
Marsham
Brampton
Oxnead
Buxton
Lamas
Little Hautbois
Scottow
Sloley
Tunstead
Sco Ruston
Ashmanhaugh
Neatishead
Coltishall
Horstead
Hevingham
Stratton Strawless
Hainford
Frettenham
Crostwick
Spixworth
Rackheath
Horsham St Faith
Newton St Faith
Horsford
Felthorpe
Swannington
Alderford
Attlebridge
Morton
Weston Longville
Ringland
Taverham
Drayton
Hellesdon
Costessey
New Costessey
Easton
Honingham
Old Catton
Sprowston
Thorpe End
Thorpe St Andrew
Norwich
Earlham
Colney
Bowthorpe
Hoveton
Wroxham
Belaugh
Salhouse
Woodbastwick
Panxworth
Little Plumstead
Great Plumstead
Blofield Heath
Brundall
Blofield
NORFOLK COAST
NORFOLK
A140
A148
A149
A1151
A1067
A47
A1042
B1145
B1149
B1150
B1354
B1436
B1140
3 miles
5 km

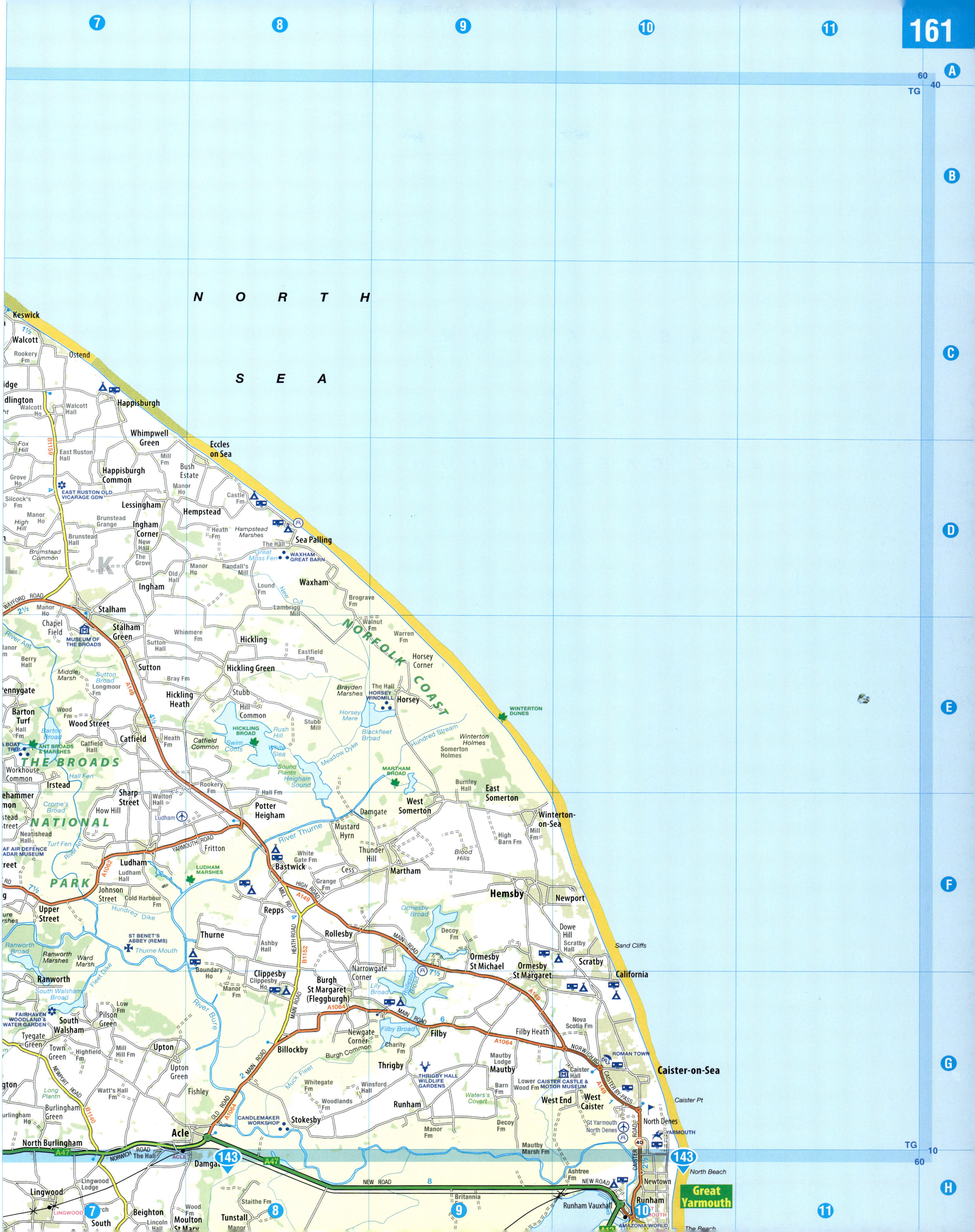

NORTH SEA
NORFOLK COAST
THE BROADS
NATIONAL PARK
Keswick
Walcott
Ostend
Happisburgh
Whimpwell Green
Eccles on Sea
Happisburgh Common
Bush Estate
EAST RUSTON OLD VICARAGE GDN
Lessingham
Hempstead
Sea Palling
Hampstead Marshes
WAXHAM GREAT BARN
Ingham Corner
Ingham
Waxham
Stalham
Stalham Green
MUSEUM OF THE BROADS
Hickling
Hickling Green
Horsey Corner
Horsey
HORSEY WINDMILL
Sutton
Hickling Heath
Stubb
Hill Common
HICKLING BROAD
WINTERTON DUNES
Winterton Holmes
Somerton Holmes
Wood Street
Catfield
Catfield Common
Barton Turf
ANT BROADS & MARSHES
Irstead
Sharp Street
How Hill
Potter Heigham
MARTHAM BROAD
East Somerton
West Somerton
Damgate
Winterton-on-Sea
Ludham
LUDHAM MARSHES
Fritton
Bastwick
Mustard Hyrn
Thunder Hill
Martham
Hemsby
Newport
Repps
Upper Street
Thurne
ST BENET'S ABBEY (REMS)
Rollesby
Ormesby St Michael
Ormesby St Margaret
Scratby
California
Sand Cliffs
Ranworth
Clippesby
Burgh St Margaret (Fleggburgh)
Filby
Filby Heath
South Walsham
FAIRHAVEN WOODLAND & WATER GARDEN
Upton
Billockby
Thrigby
THRIGBY HALL WILDLIFE GARDENS
Mauthy
CAISTER CASTLE & MOTOR MUSEUM
ROMAN TOWN
Caister-on-Sea
Caister Pt
West Caister
West End
Runham
Fishley
Stokesby
CANDLEMAKER WORKSHOP
Acle
North Burlingham
Burlingham Green
North Denes
Damgate
Newtown
North Beach
Great Yarmouth
Runham Vauxhall
Lingwood
Beighton
Tunstall
Moulton St Mary
AMAZONIA WORLD
The Beach
A47
A149
A1064
A1062
B1152
B1159
B1140
143

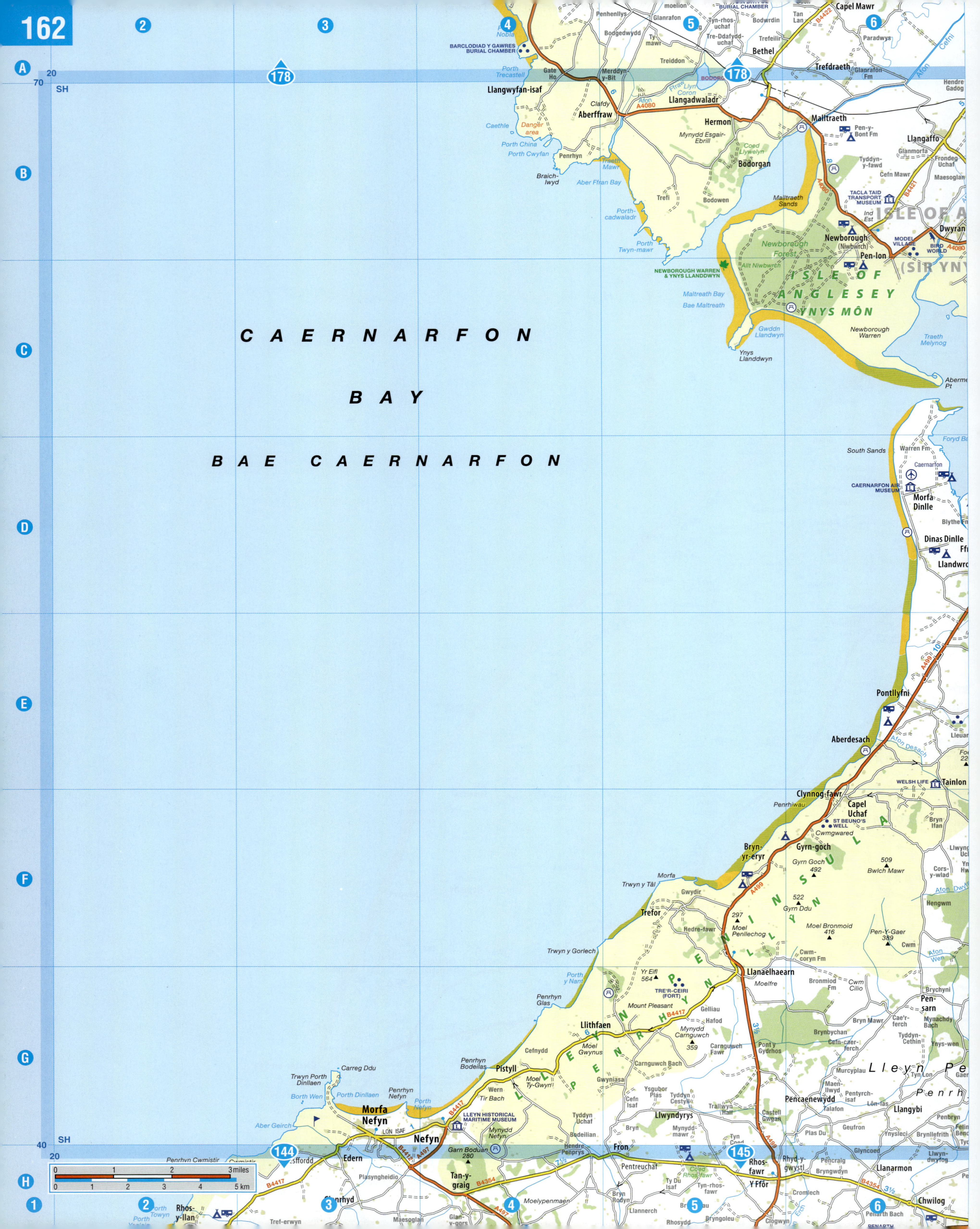
CAERNARFON
BAY
BAE CAERNARFON
ISLE OF ANGLESEY
YNYS MÔN
LLEYN PENINSULA
BARCLODIAD Y GAWRES BURIAL CHAMBER
Porth Trecastell
Llangwyfan-isaf
Aberffraw
Llangadwaladr
Hermon
Malltraeth
Bodorgan
Bethel
Trefdraeth
Capel Mawr
Llangaffo
Newborough
(Niwbwrch)
Pen-lon
Dwyran
Malltraeth Sands
Newborough Forest
NEWBOROUGH WARREN & YNYS LLANDDWYN
Malltreath Bay
Bae Maltreath
Ynys Llanddwyn
Newborough Warren
Abermenai Pt
TACLA TAID TRANSPORT MUSEUM
MODEL VILLAGE
BIRD WORLD
Porth Cwyfan
Porth China
Aber Ffraw Bay
Porth-cadwaladr
Porth Twyn-mawr
South Sands
Warren Fm
Caernarfon
CAERNARFON AIR MUSEUM
Morfa Dinlle
Dinas Dinlle
Llandwrog
Pontllyfni
Aberdesach
Clynnog-fawr
Capel Uchaf
ST BEUNO'S WELL
Tainlon
WELSH LIFE
Gyrn-goch
Bryn-yr-eryr
Trefor
Trwyn y Tâl
Trwyn y Gorlech
Llanaelhaearn
Yr Eifl 564
TRE'R-CEIRI (FORT)
Llithfaen
Pistyll
Porth y Nant
Penrhyn Glas
Morfa Nefyn
Nefyn
LLEYN HISTORICAL MARITIME MUSEUM
Edern
Porth Dinllaen
Trwyn Porth Dinllaen
Carreg Ddu
Aber Geirch
Garn Boduan 280
Tan-y-graig
Fron
Rhos-fawr
Y Ffôr
Llwyndyrys
Pencaenewydd
Llangybi
Llanarmon
Chwilog
Rhydyclafdy
Rhos-y-llan
0 1 2 3 miles
0 1 2 3 4 5 km
178
144
145
SH
A
B
C
D
E
F
G
H
1
2
3
4
5
6

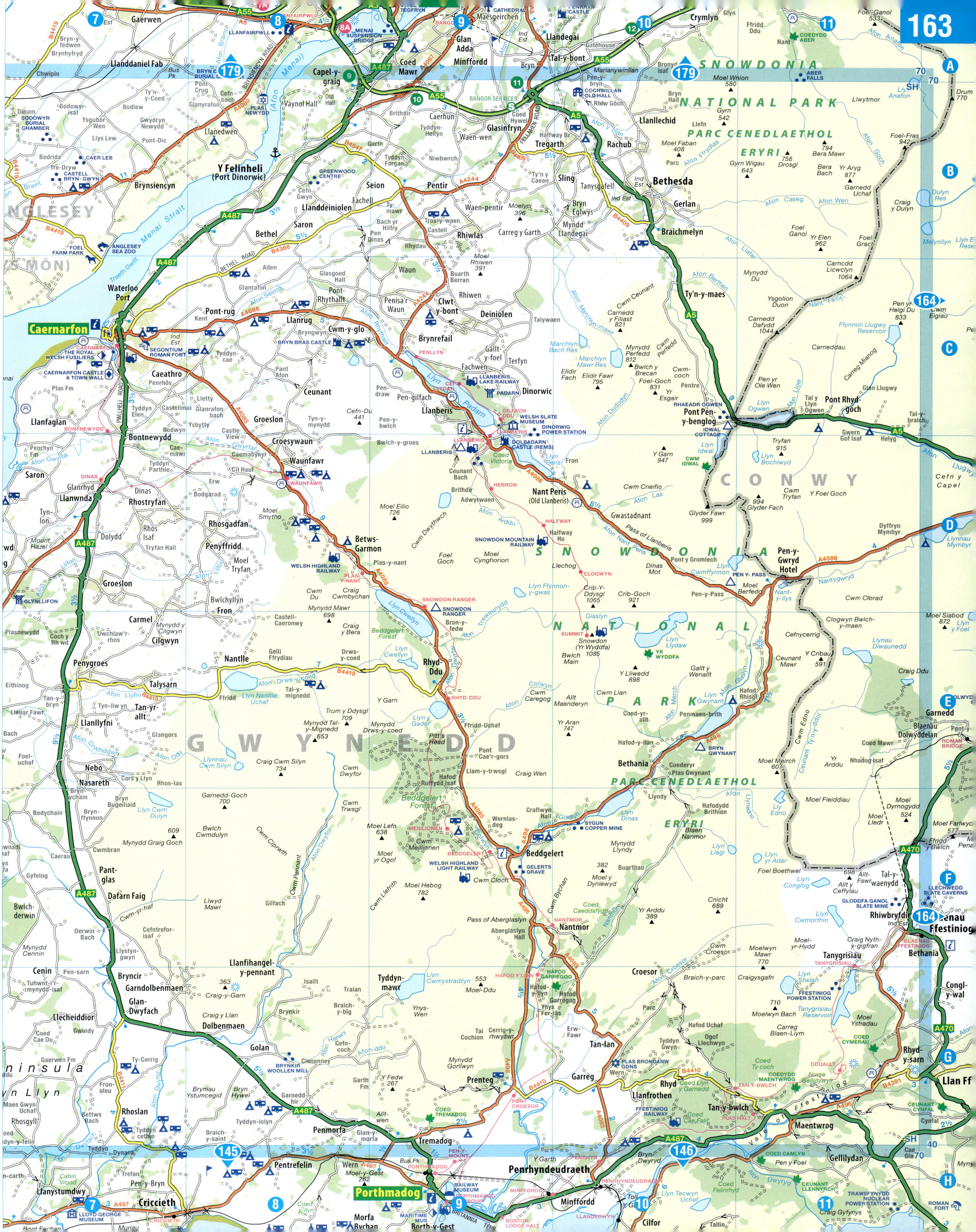
SNOWDONIA NATIONAL PARK
PARC CENEDLAETHOL ERYRI
GWYNEDD
CONWY
ANGLESEY
Menai Strait
Caernarfon
Y Felinheli (Port Dinorwic)
Llanddaniel Fab
Gaerwen
Brynsiencyn
Capel-y-graig
Glan Adda
Maesgeirchen
Minffordd
Llandegai
Tal-y-bont
Crymlyn
Bethesda
Gerlan
Rachub
Tregarth
Glasinfryn
Caerhun
Waen-wen
Llanllechid
Bethel
Saron
Llanddeiniolen
Pentir
Seion
Fachell
Waen-pentir
Rhiwlas
Sling
Tanysgafell
Bryn Eglwys
Mynydd Llandegai
Braichmelyn
Waterloo Port
Pont-rug
Llanrug
Cwm-y-glo
Clwt-y-bont
Deiniolen
Brynrefail
Fachwen
Dinorwic
Llanberis
Nant Peris (Old Llanberis)
Caeathro
Ceunant
Groeslon
Croesywaun
Waunfawr
Bontnewydd
Llanfaglan
Saron
Glanrhyd
Llanwnda
Dinas
Rhostryfan
Rhosgadfan
Penyffridd
Moel Tryfan
Betws-Garmon
Groeslon
Carmel
Cilgwyn
Fron
Penygroes
Nantlle
Talysarn
Tan-yr-allt
Llanllyfni
Nebo
Nasareth
Rhyd-Ddu
Pitt's Head
Beddgelert
Nantmor
Aberglaslyn Hall
Pass of Aberglaslyn
Bethania
Llanfihangel-y-pennant
Garndolbenmaen
Bryncir
Glan-Dwyfach
Dolbenmaen
Golan
Pant-glas
Dafarn Faig
Llecheiddior
Rhoslan
Penmorfa
Tremadog
Pentrefelin
Criccieth
Porthmadog
Penrhyndeudraeth
Minffordd
Prenteg
Garreg
Tan-lan
Llanfrothen
Rhyd
Croesor
Tan-y-bwlch
Maentwrog
Gellilydan
Blaenau Ffestiniog
Tanygrisiau
Rhiwbryfdir
Congl-y-wal
Rhyd-y-sarn
Llan Ff
Garnedd
Pen-y-Gwryd Hotel
Pen-y-Pass
Pont Pen-y-benglog
Pont Rhyd-goch
Ty'n-y-maes
Snowdon (Yr Wyddfa) 1085
Glyder Fawr 999
Glyder Fach 994
Tryfan 915
Carnedd Dafydd 1044
Carnedd Llewelyn 1064
Y Garn 947
Y Lliwedd 898
Moel Hebog 782
Moel Siabod 872
Cnicht 689
Moelwyn Mawr 770
Moelwyn Bach 710
Mynydd Mawr 698
Moel Eilio 726
Llyn Padarn
Llyn Cwellyn
Llyn Ogwen
Llyn Gwynant
Llyn Dinas
Llynnau Mymbyr
Llyn Trawsfynydd
Caernarfon Castle & Town Wall
Welsh Highland Railway
Snowdon Mountain Railway
Llanberis Lake Railway
Welsh Slate Museum
Dolbadarn Castle
Ffestiniog Railway
A55
A487
A4085
A4086
A5
A498
A4244
A470
A496
B4418
B4410
B4366
B4547
B4409
B4411
B4391
179
164
145
146

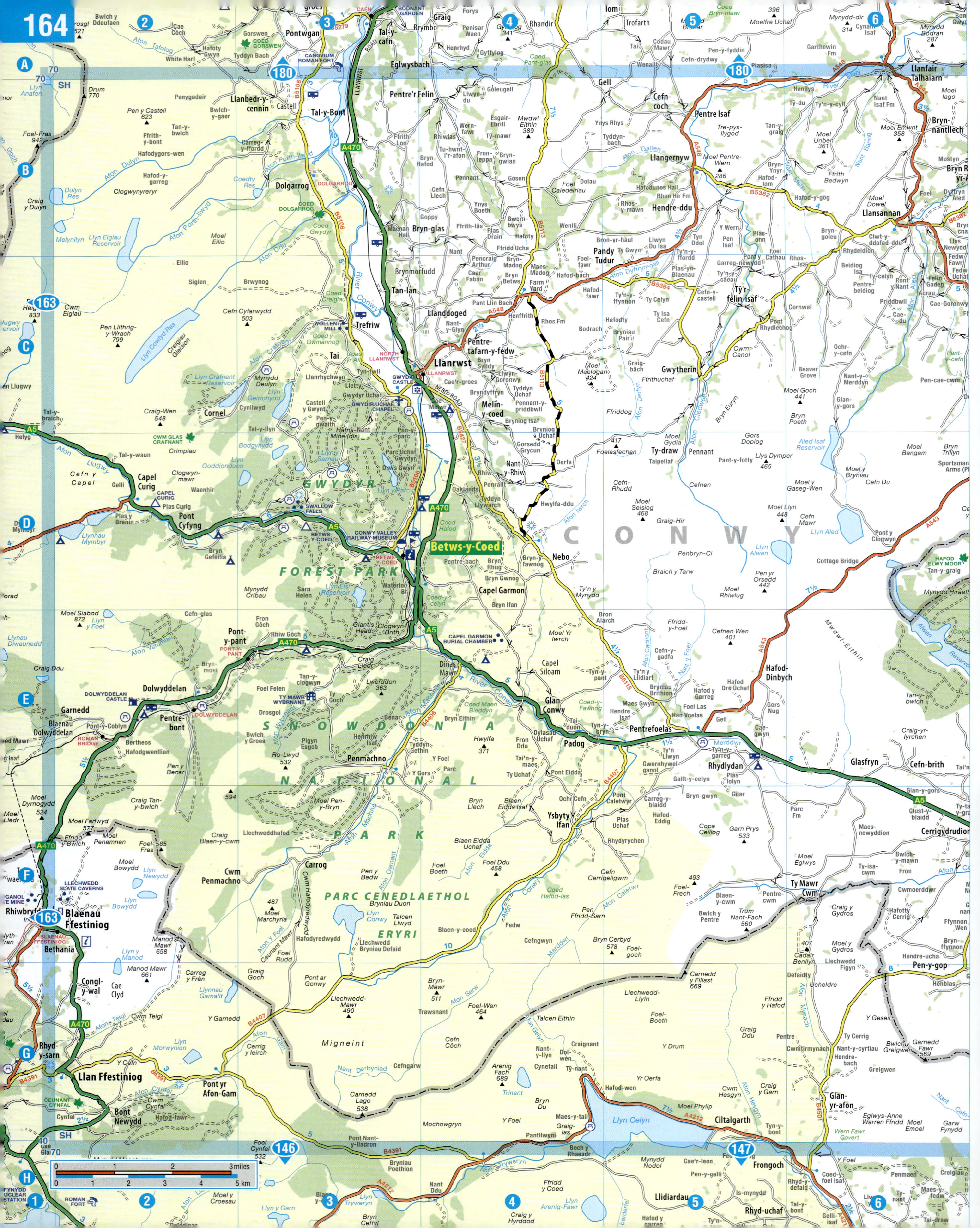

180
Pontwgan
Tal-y-cafn
Graig
Eglwysbach
Rhandir
Trofarth
Gell
Llanfair Talhaiarn
Llanbedr-y-cennin
Tal-y-Bont
Pentre'r Felin
Cefn-coch
Pentre Isaf
Bryn-nantllech
Dolgarrog
Llangernyw
Hendre-ddu
Llansannan
Bryn-glas
Tan-lan
Pandy Tudur
Llanddoged
Trefriw
Pentre-tafarn-y-fedw
Llanrwst
Tŷ'r-felin-isaf
Gwytherin
163
Tai
Cornel
Melin-y-coed
Capel Curig
GWYDYR
Pont Cyfyng
Nebo
Betws-y-Coed
FOREST PARK
Capel Garmon
CONWY
Pont-y-pant
Dolwyddelan
Garnedd
Pentre-bont
Dinas Mawr
Capel Siloam
Glan Conwy
Pentrefoelas
Padog
Rhydlydan
Glasfryn
Cefn-brith
Hafod-Dinbych
SNOWDONIA
NATIONAL
PARK
Penmachno
Ysbyty Ifan
Cerrigydrudion
Carrog
Cwm Penmachno
Blaenau Ffestiniog
Bethania
PARC CENEDLAETHOL
ERYRI
Ty Mawr
Cwm
Pen-y-gop
Congl-y-wal
Migneint
Rhyd-y-sarn
Llan Ffestiniog
Pont yr Afon-Gam
Llyn Celyn
Ciltalgarth
Glan-yr-afon
Bont Newydd
146
147
Frongoch
Llidiardau
Rhyd-uchaf
A5
A470
A548
A543
A4212
B4391
B4407
B4406
B5106
B5113
B5427
0 1 2 3 miles
0 1 2 3 4 5 km

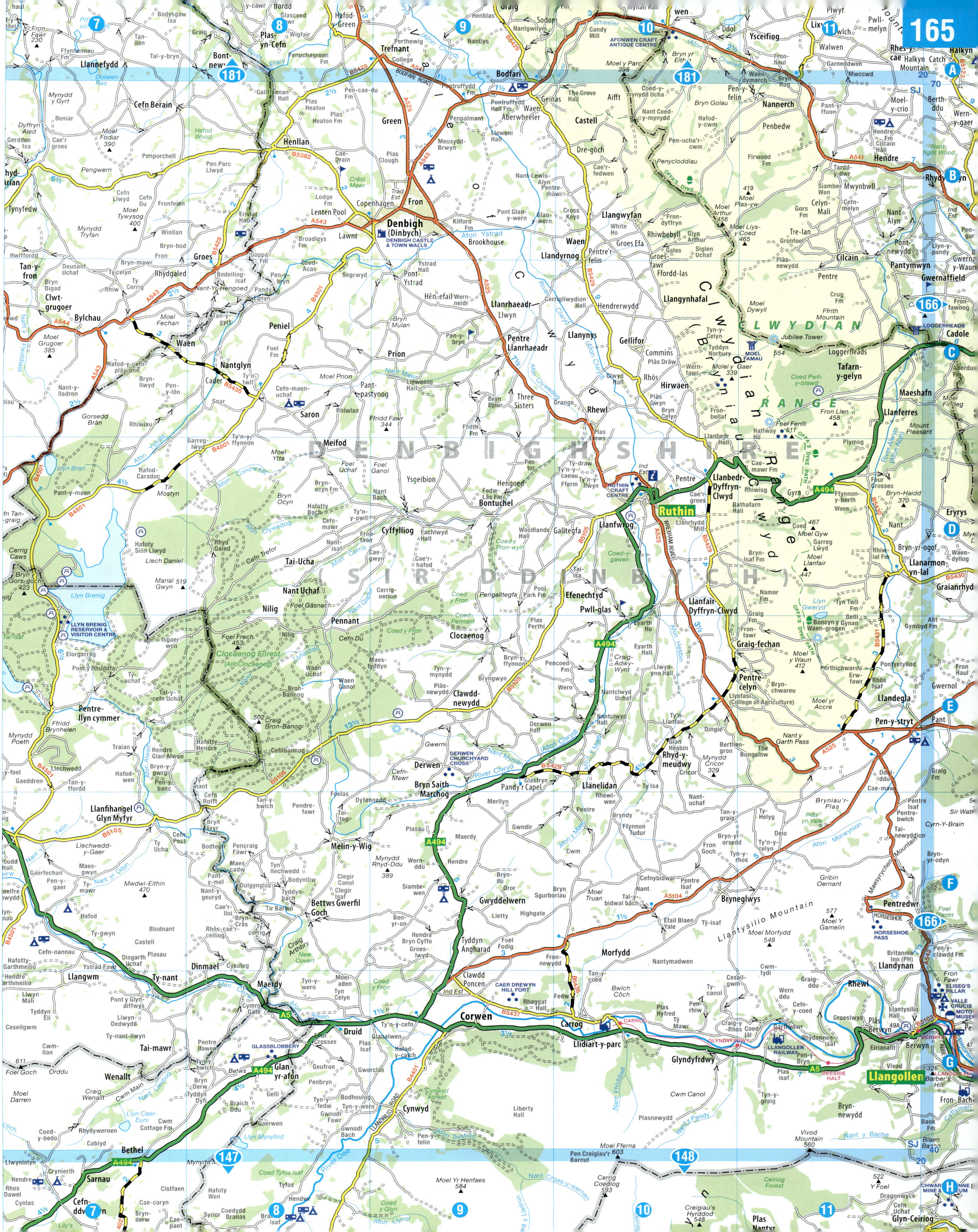
DENBIGHSHIRE
(SIR DDINBYCH)
Vale of Clwyd
Clwydian Range
(Bryniau Clwyd)
CLWYDIAN RANGE
Denbigh (Dinbych)
DENBIGH CASTLE & TOWN WALLS
Ruthin
RUTHIN CRAFT CENTRE
Llangollen
Corwen
Bodfari
Trefnant
Henllan
Llannefydd
Cefn Berain
Lawnt
Groes
Rhydgaled
Bylchau
Waen
Nantglyn
Saron
Peniel
Prion
Llanrhaeadr
Pentre Llanrhaeadr
Llanynys
Rhewl
Gellifor
Hirwaen
Llandyrnog
Llangwyfan
Llangynhafal
Llanbedr-Dyffryn-Clwyd
Llanfwrog
Efenechtyd
Pwll-glas
Llanfair Dyffryn-Clwyd
Graig-fechan
Pentre-celyn
Llandegla
Pen-y-stryt
Clocaenog
Clawdd-newydd
Cyffylliog
Bontuchel
Derwen
Bryn Saith Marchog
Llanelidan
Rhyd-y-meudwy
Melin-y-Wig
Betws Gwerfil Goch
Gwyddelwern
Tyddyn Angharad
Clawdd Poncen
Cynwyd
Carrog
Llidiart-y-parc
Glyndyfrdwy
Bryneglwys
Morfydd
Maerdy
Druid
Glan-yr-afon
Dinmael
Ty-nant
Llangwm
Tai-mawr
Bethel
Sarnau
Wenallt
Llanfihangel Glyn Myfyr
Pentre-llyn cymmer
Cerrigydrudion
Nilig
Pennant
Nant Uchaf
Tai-Ucha
Clocaenog Forest
(Allt Clocaenog)
Llyn Brenig
LLYN BRENIG RESERVOIR & VISITOR CENTRE
Moel Famau 554
Jubilee Tower
Cilcain
Nannerch
Caerwys
Ysceifiog
Halkyn
Rhydymwyn
Gwernaffield
Pantymwyn
Cadole
Loggerheads
Tafarn-y-gelyn
Maeshafn
Llanferres
Eryrys
Llanarmon-yn-Ial
Graianrhyd
Gwernol
Rhewl
Llandynan
Pentredwr
HORSESHOE PASS
ELISEG'S PILLAR
VALLE CRUCIS
LLANGOLLEN RAILWAY
Llantysilio Mountain
CAER DREWYN HILL FORT
DERWEN CHURCHYARD CROSS
AFONWEN CRAFT ANTIQUE CENTRE
Afonwen
Aifft
Geinas
Castell
Dre-goch
Waen
Llanrhaeadr
Aberwheeler
Kilford
Brookhouse
Three Sisters
Offa's Dyke Path
River Clwyd
River Dee
A494
A541
A543
A525
A5
A5104
B5105
B5429
B5437
B5436
B4401
B5430
B5431
B5428
B5382
B4501
B5435
147
148
166
181

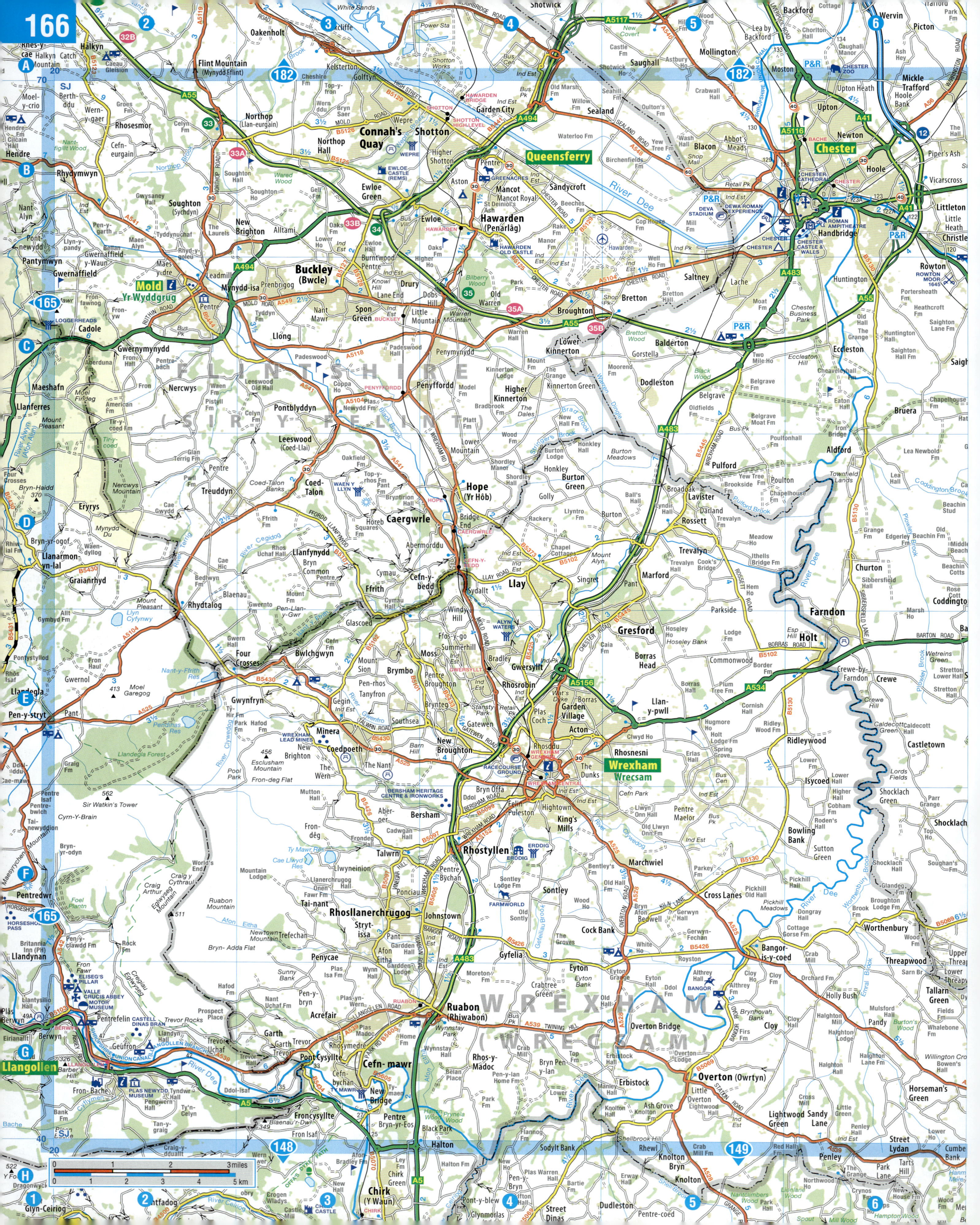
Halkyn
Oakenholt
Flint Mountain (Mynydd Fflint)
Northop (Llan-eurgain)
Northop Hall
Connah's Quay
Shotton
Queensferry
Garden City
Sealand
Saughall
Mollington
Backford
Wervin
Picton
Upton
Chester
Newton
Hoole
Vicarscross
Littleton
Rhosesmor
Rhydymwyn
Hendre
Soughton (Sychdyn)
New Brighton
Alltami
Ewloe
Ewloe Green
Aston
Pentre
Mancot
Mancot Royal
Sandycroft
Hawarden (Penarlâg)
River Dee
Blacon
Handbridge
Mold
Yr Wyddgrug
Gwernaffield
Pantymwyn
Mynydd-isa
Buckley (Bwcle)
Drury
Spon Green
Nant Mawr
Little Mountain
Broughton
Bretton
Saltney
Lache
Huntington
Rowton
Cadole
Llong
Gwernymynydd
Penymynydd
Lower Kinnerton
Higher Kinnerton
Balderton
Dodleston
Eccleston
Maeshafn
Llanferres
Nercwys
Pontblyddyn
Penyffordd
F L I N T S H I R E
(S I R Y F F L I N T)
Leeswood (Coed-Llai)
Treuddyn
Coed-Talon
Hope (Yr Hôb)
Caergwrle
Lower Mountain
Burton Green
Pulford
Lavister
Rossett
Aldford
Bruera
Eryrys
Llanarmon-yn-Ial
Graianrhyd
Llanfynydd
Ffrith
Cefn-y-bedd
Llay
Marford
Trevalyn
Churton
Farndon
Rhydtalog
Four Crosses
Bwlchgwyn
Moss
Gwersyllt
Gresford
Borras Head
Holt
Crewe-by-Farndon
Crewe
Llandegla
Pen-y-stryt
Gwynfryn
Minera
Coedpoeth
Brymbo
Tanyfron
Southsea
New Broughton
Rhosrobin
Acton
Llan-y-pwll
Wrexham
Wrecsam
Rhosnesni
Ridleywood
Castletown
Bersham
Rhostyllen
Sontley
Marchwiel
Bowling Bank
Shocklach
Talwrn
Rhosllanerchrugog
Johnstown
Cross Lanes
Bangor-is-y-coed
Worthenbury
Threapwood
Penycae
Gyfelia
Eyton
Ruabon (Rhiwabon)
W R E X H A M
(W R E C S A M)
Overton Bridge
Cloy
Overton (Owrtyn)
Llangollen
Trevor
Garth
Pont Cysyllte
Cefn-mawr
Rhos-y-Madoc
Erbistock
New Bridge
Froncysyllte
Halton
Chirk (Y Waun)
Penley
Knolton
Dudleston
Glyn-Ceiriog
0 1 2 3 miles
0 1 2 3 4 5 km

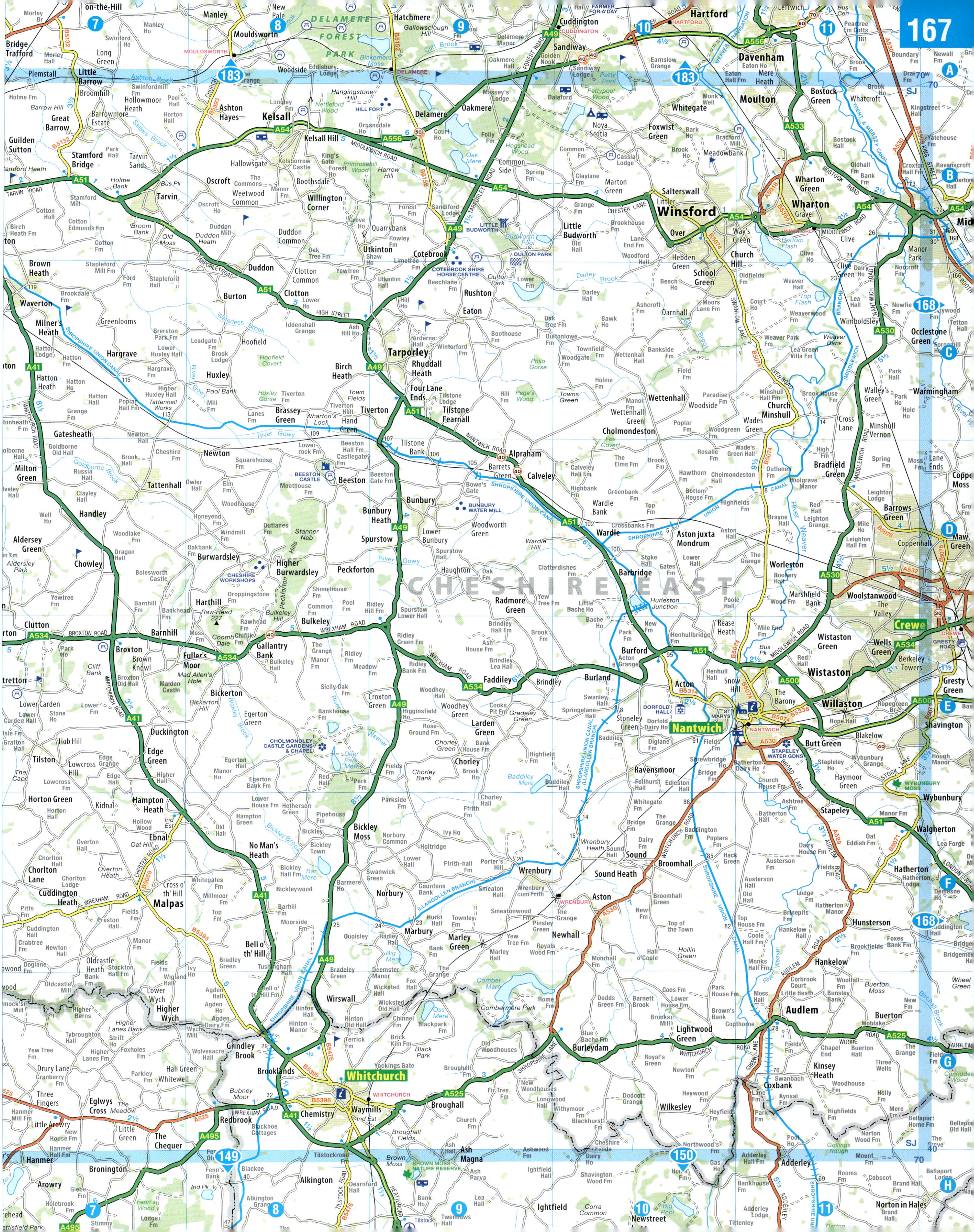
CHESHIRE EAST
DELAMERE FOREST PARK
Kelsall
Tarvin
Tarporley
Winsford
Davenham
Moulton
Wharton
Hartford
Cuddington
Sandiway
Delamere
Oakmere
Little Budworth
Cotebrook
Eaton
Rushton
Beeston
Bunbury
Alpraham
Calveley
Wardle
Barbridge
Nantwich
Crewe
Willaston
Wistaston
Shavington
Audlem
Wrenbury
Malpas
Whitchurch
Chemistry
Broughall
Burleydam
Cholmondeston
Church Minshull
Minshull Vernon
Warmingham
Worleston
Acton
Burland
Faddiley
Bulkeley
Broxton
Barnhill
Clutton
Tattenhall
Waverton
Handley
Duckington
Hampton Heath
No Man's Heath
Bickley Moss
Marbury
Norbury
Grindley Brook
Redbrook
Ightfield
Adderley
Newhall
Aston
Sound
Hankelow
Hunsterson
Hatherton
Walgherton
Stapeley
Wybunbury
A49
A51
A54
A41
A534
A530
A500
A525
A556
A533
A495
BEESTON CASTLE
CHOLMONDELEY CASTLE GARDENS & CHAPEL
OULTON PARK
COTEBROOK SHIRE HORSE CENTRE
BUNBURY WATER MILL
STAPELEY WATER GDNS
BROWN MOSS NATURE RESERVE
CHESHIRE WORKSHOPS
SHROPSHIRE UNION CANAL
LLANGOLLEN BRANCH
River Weaver
River Gowy
183
168
149
150

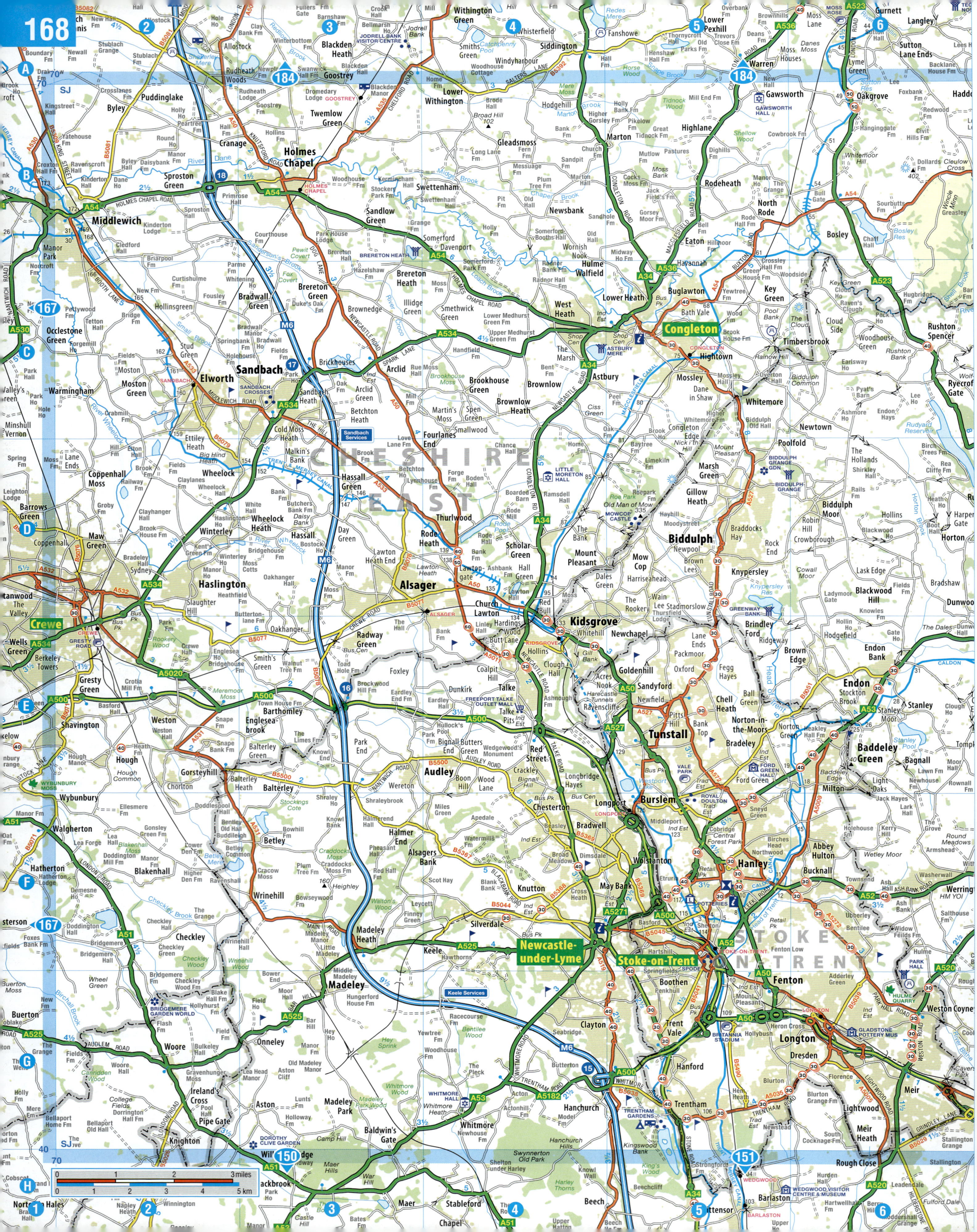
Sandbach
Holmes Chapel
Middlewich
Elworth
Congleton
Crewe
Alsager
Kidsgrove
Biddulph
Tunstall
Burslem
Hanley
Stoke-on-Trent
Newcastle-under-Lyme
Longton
Fenton
Madeley
Audley
Haslington
Wheelock
Goostrey
Swettenham
Astbury
Mow Cop
Endon
Baddeley Green
Bucknall
Trentham
Meir
Clayton
Keele
Silverdale
Woore
Betley
Wybunbury
Shavington
Weston
Hough
Wistaston
Warmingham
Brereton Heath
Somerford
Marton
Timbersbrook
Rushton Spencer
Bosley
Gawsworth
Withington Green
Lower Withington
Twemlow Green
Cranage
Sproston Green
Byley
Knutton
Chesterton
Wolstanton
Bradwell
Talke
Red Street
Goldenhill
Sandyford
Smallthorne
Milton
Werrington
Hanford
Hanchurch
Whitmore
Baldwin's Gate
Onneley
Checkley
Blakenhall
Walgherton
Hatherton
Balterley
Barthomley
Englesea-brook
Radway Green
Church Lawton
Scholar Green
Rode Heath
Thurlwood
Hassall Green
Arclid
Brookhouse Green
Brownlow Heath
Hulme Walfield
Buglawton
Mossley
Whitemore
Knypersley
Brown Edge
Norton-in-the-Moors
CHESHIRE EAST
STOKE-ON-TRENT
M6
A34
A50
A500
A51
A52
A53
A54
A523
A527
A534
A5020
0 1 2 3 miles
0 1 2 3 4 5 km

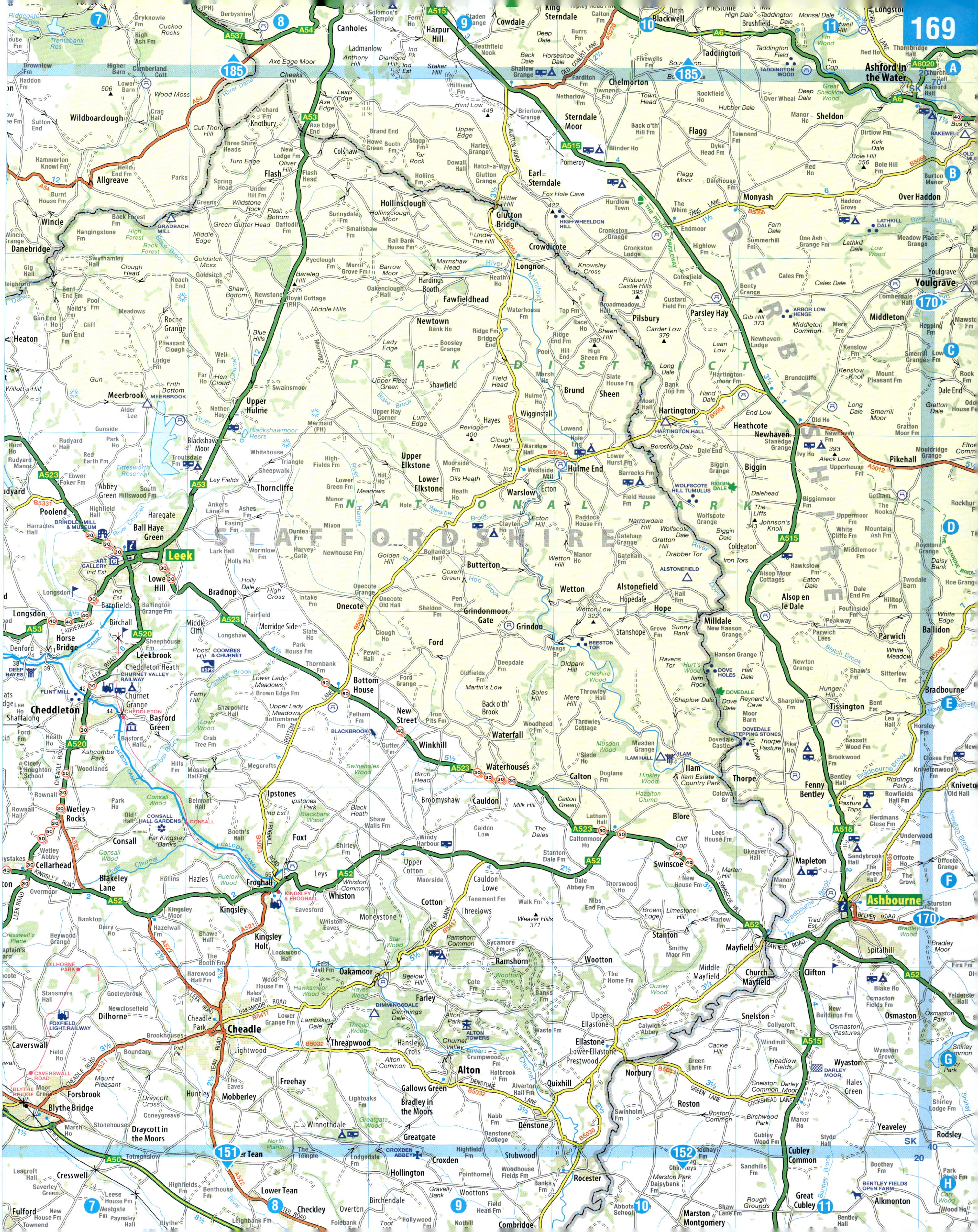

PEAK DISTRICT NATIONAL PARK
STAFFORDSHIRE
DERBYSHIRE
Leek
Cheadle
Ashbourne
Ashford in the Water
Youlgrave
Hartington
Longnor
Warslow
Hulme End
Alstonefield
Wetton
Ilam
Waterhouses
Cauldon
Ipstones
Froghall
Kingsley
Cheddleton
Alton
Denstone
Rocester
Mayfield
Clifton
Fenny Bentley
Tissington
Parwich
Biggin
Monyash
Flagg
Chelmorton
Taddington
Earl Sterndale
Glutton Bridge
Crowdicote
Hollinsclough
Flash
Allgreave
Wincle
Danebridge
Meerbrook
Upper Hulme
Bradnop
Onecote
Butterton
Grindon
Upper Elkstone
Lower Elkstone
Sheen
Brund
Pilsbury
Middleton
Newhaven
Pikehall
Ballidon
Bradbourne
Mapleton
Thorpe
Blore
Swinscoe
Calton
Winkhill
Bottom House
Whiston
Oakamoor
Farley
Ramshorn
Cotton
Threapwood
Freehay
Mobberley
Draycott in the Moors
Forsbrook
Blythe Bridge
Dilhorne
Caverswall
Cellarhead
Wetley Rocks
Consall
Blakeley Lane
Kingsley Holt
Hollington
Croxden
Checkley
Lower Tean
Upper Tean
Stubwood
Marston Montgomery
Great Cubley
Cubley Common
Roston
Norbury
Ellastone
Snelston
Wyaston
Yeaveley
Rodsley
Osmaston
Spitalhill
Church Mayfield
Stanton
Wootton
Quixhill
Gallows Green
Bradley in the Moors
Greatgate
Winnothdale
Ball Haye Green
Lowe Hill
Horse Bridge
Longsdon
Leekbrook
Basford Green
Birchall
Poolend
Heaton
Gratton
A515
A523
A53
A52
A50
A54
A537
A6
A520
A521
A522
A5012
B5053
B5054
B5032
B5417
185
170
151
152

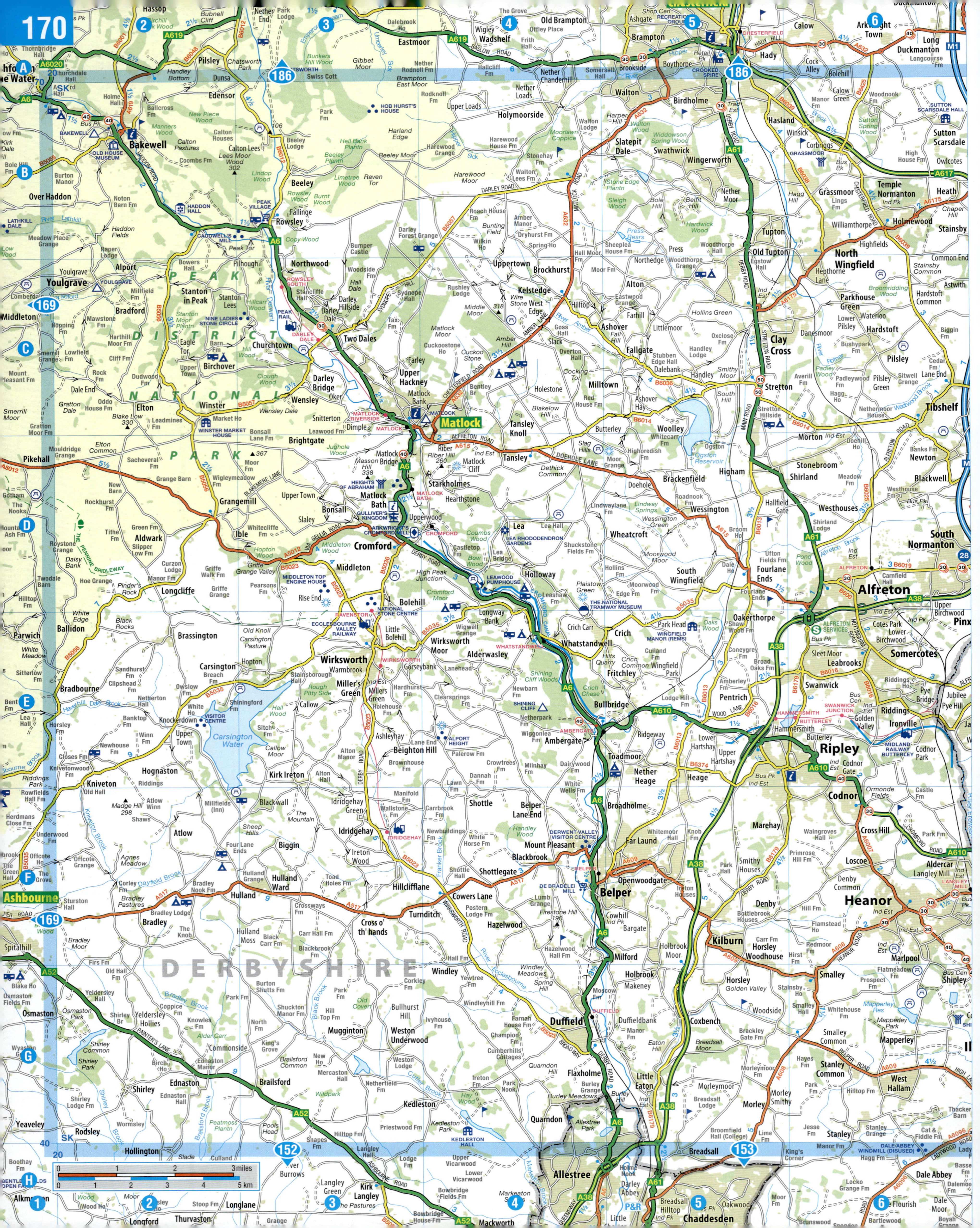
Hassop
Bubnell Cliff
Nether End
Park Lodge
Dalebrook Ho
Eastmoor
The Grove
Wigley
Old Brampton
Offley Place
Wadshelf
Brampton
Ashgate
Calow
Arkwright Town
Long Duckmanton
Hady
Cock Alley
Bolehill
Pilsley
Chatsworth Park
Handley Bottom
Dunsa
Edensor
Bunkers Hill Wood
Swiss Cott
Gibbet Moor
Nether Rodnoll Fm
Brampton East Moor
Hallcliff Fm
Nether Chanderhill
Somersall Hall
Brookside
Boythorpe
Holmesfield
Nether Loads
Walton
Birdholme
Calow Green
Woodnook Fm
Sutton Scarsdale Hall
Bakewell
Old House Museum
Ballcross Fm
Manners Wood
New Piece Wood
Calton Houses
Calton Pastures
Calton Lees
Coombs Fm
Lees Moor Wood
Beeley Lodge
Hob Hurst's House
Park Fm
Harland Edge
Rodknoll Fm
Upper Loads
Holymoorside
Harewood House Fm
Harewood Grange
Beeley Moor
Harper Hill
Slatepit Dale
Walton Lodge Fm
Widdowson Spring Wood
Swathwick
Wingerworth
Hasland
Winsick
Corbriggs
Grassmoor
Temple Normanton
Sutton Scarsdale
Owlcotes
Heath
Chapel Hill
Over Haddon
Burton Manor
Noton Barn Fm
Haddon Hall
Beeley
Rowsley
Peak Village
Fallinge
Burnt Wood
Raven Tor
Harewood Moor
Darley Road
Holmewood
Stainsby
Lathkill Dale
Meadow Place Grange
Haddon Fields
Peak Tor
Copy Wood
Darley Forest Grange
Bunting Field
Amber Manor
Dryhurst Fm
Spring Ho
Roach House Fm
Press
Tupton
Old Tupton
North Wingfield
Highfields
Hepthorne Lane
Williamthorpe
Common End
Stainsby Common
Astwith
Youlgrave
Alport
Pilhough
Northwood
Bowers Hall
Stanton in Peak
Stanton Lees
Raper Lodge
Bradford
Middleton
Peak District National Park
Rowsley South
Stancliffe Hall
Darley Hillside
Darley Dale
Two Dales
Peak Rail
Woodside Fm
Hall Moor
Sydnope Hall
Rushley Lodge
Uppertown
Brockhurst
Kelstedge
West Edge
Middle Moor
Hilltop
Ashover
Alton
Eastwood Grange
Farhill
Northedge
Littlemoor
Parkhouse Green
Lower Pilsley
Waterloo
Hardstoft
Hollins Green
Oxclose Fm
Clay Cross
Danesmoor
Nine Ladies Stone Circle
Harthill Moor Fm
Mawstone Fm
Cliff Fm
Churchtown
Eagle Tor
Birchover
Upper Town
Matlock Ho
Cuckoostone Ho
Cuckoo Stone
Amber Hill
Slack
Overton Hall
Fallgate
Stubben Edge Hall
Dalebank
Handley
Smithy Moor
Pilsley
Stretton
Tibshelf
Farley
Upper Hackney
Matlock Bank
Darley Bridge
Oker
Wensley
Winster
Wensley Dale
Snitterton
Dale End
Oddo House Fm
Elton
Gratton Dale
Leadmines Fm
Winster Market House
Market Ho
Bentley Br
Holestone
Milltown
Red House Fm
Blakelow Hill
Ashover Hay
Woolley
Ogston Reservoir
Higham
Morton
Doehill
Banks Fm
Newton
Matlock
Matlock Riverside
Dimple
Brightgate
Bonsall Lane Fm
Tansley Knoll
Tansley
Dethick Common
Butterley
Slag Hills
Moor Grange
Highoredish Fm
Brackenfield
Stonebroom
Shirland
Blackwell
Pikehall
Mouldridge Grange
Elton Common
Sacheveral Fm
Grange Barn
Wigleymeadow Fm
Masson Hill
Matlock Bath
Riber
Riber Hill
Matlock Cliff
Starkholmes
Hearthstone
Doehole
Lindwaylane Fm
Roadnook Fm
Wessington
Hallfield Gate
Westhouses
Shirland Lodge
Gotham
The Nooks
Rockhurst Fm
New Barn
Grangemill
Upper Town
Bonsall
Heights of Abraham
Gulliver's Kingdom
Slaley
Upperwood
Lea
Lea Hall
Lea Rhododendron Gardens
Wheatcroft
Wessington Green
Broom Ho
South Normanton
Tithe Fm
Green Fm
Aldwark
Slipper Low Fm
Ible
Whitecliffe Fm
Arkwright's Cromford Mill
Cromford
Castletop Fm
Shuckstone Fields Fm
Moorwood Moor
Ufton Fields Fm
Fourlane Ends
Alfreton
Roystone Grange
Daisy Bank
Twodale Barn
Hoe Grange
The Pennine Bridleway
Curzon Lodge
Manor Fm
Pinder's Rock
Longcliffe
Griffe Walk Fm
Griffe Grange
Griffe Grange Valley
Hopton Wood
Middleton
Middleton Top Engine House
Pearsons Fm
Rise End
High Peak Junction
Leawood Pumphouse
Holloway
Hollins Fm
Plaistow Green
South Wingfield
Edge Fm
The National Tramway Museum
Oakerthorpe
Camfield Fm
Upper Birchwood
Pinxton
Hilltop Fm
White Edge Fm
Ballidon
Black Rocks
Brassington
Old Knoll
Carsington Pasture
Bolehill
National Stone Centre
Ravenstor
Ecclesbourne Valley Railway
Little Bolehill
Longway Bank
Wigwell Grange
Wirksworth Moor
Alderwasley
Whatstandwell
Crich Carr
Crich
Park Head
Wingfield Manor
Shaw Wood Fm
Conneygrey Fm
Cotes Park
Lower Birchwood
Somercotes
Parwich
White Meadow
Sitterlow Fm
Sandhurst Fm
Clipshead Fm
Bradbourne
Carsington
Breach Fm
Hopton
Stainsborough Hall
Wirksworth
Warmbrook
Gorseybank
Lanehead
Shining Cliff Woods
Hilts Quarry
Crich Common
Culland Fm
Wingfield Park
Fritchley
Broad Oaks Fm
Riddings
Sleet Moor
Leabrooks
Swanwick
Pye Bridge
Jubilee
Bent Fm
Lea Hall
Netherton Fm
Owslow Fm
White Fm
Shiningford
Carsington Water
Visitor Centre
Knockerdown
Hall Wood
Rough Pitty Side
Callow
Miller's Green
Millers Green
Holehouse
Hardhurst Fm
Clearsprings Fm
Newburn Fm
Shining Cliff
Netherpark Fm
Crich Chase
Bullbridge
Lodge Hill Fm
Amberley Fm
Pentrich
Hammersmith
Butterley
Swanwick Junction
Golden Valley
Ironville
Midland Railway Butterley
Codnor Park
Horsley Fm
Banktop Fm
Winn Fm
Upper Town
Sitch Fm
Callow Moor
Ashleyhay
Beighton Hill
Alport Height
Wigwell Lee
Ambergate
Ridgeway
Lower Hartshay
Upper Hartshay
Ripley
Newhouse Fm
Closes Fm
Knivetonwood Fm
Hognaston
Ridgings Park
Rowfields Hall Fm
Kniveton
Old Hall
Madge Hill
Atlow Winn
Shaws
Kirk Ireton
Alton Hall
Alton Manor
Brownhouse Fm
Palerow Fm
Crowtrees Fm
Minnay Fm
Dairywood Fm
White Wells Fm
Toadmoor
Nether Heage
Heage
Codnor Gate
Codnor
Ormonde Fields
Castle Fm
Herdsmans Close Fm
Millfields (Inn)
Blackwall
The Mountain
Idridgehay Green
Manifold Fm
Wallstone Fm
Carrbrook Fm
Lawn Fm
Dannah Fm
Shottle
Belper Lane End
Broadholme
Marehay
Waingroves Hall
Cross Hill
Park Fm
Underwood Fm
Atlow
Sheep Hills
Biggin
Idridgehay
Newbuildings Fm
White Horse Fm
Handley Wood
Mount Pleasant
Derwent Valley Visitor Centre
Whitemoor Hall
Knob Fm
Far Laund
Smithy Houses
Primrose Hill Fm
Loscoe
Aldercar
Langley Mill
Offcote Grange
Agnes Meadow
Four Lane Ends
Ireton Wood
Hulland Grange
Hulland Ward
Toad Holes Fm
Hillcliffaane
Shottle Hall
Shottlegate
Blackbrook
Openwoodgate
Belper
Ireton Houses
Denby Common
Heanor
Ashbourne
Sturston Hall
Corley Fm
Bradley Pastures
Bradley Nook Fm
Hulland
Dayfield Brook
Crossways Fm
Turnditch
Cowers Lane
Postern Lodge Fm
Hazelwood
De Bradelei Mill
Lumb Grange
Firestone Hill
Cowhill
Bargate
Denby
Bottlebrook Houses
Hill Fm
Flamstead Ho
Bradley
Bradley Lodge
The Knob
Hulland Moss
Carr Hall Fm
Black Carr Fm
Cross o' th' hands
Hazelwood Hall Fm
Milford
Holbrook Moor
Kilburn
Horsley Woodhouse
Carr Fm
Redmoor Fm
Marlpool
Spitalhill
Bradley Moor
Firs Fm
Old Hall Fm
Blackbrook Fm
Derbyshire
Hall Fm
Windley
Yewtree Fm
Corkley Fm
Windley Meadows
Spring Hill
Holbrook
Makeney
Horsley
Smalley
Prospect Fm
Flatmeadow Fm
Shipley
Osmaston Fields Fm
Osmaston
Yeldersley Hall
Coppice Fm
Shirley Br
Yeldersley Hollies
Burton Shutts Fm
Park Fm
Old Covert
Bullhurst Hill
Windleyhill Fm
Moscow Fm
Duffield
Duffieldbank
Golden Valley
Woodside
Smalley Hall
Whitehouse Fm
Mapperley Park
Osmaston Park
Knowles Fm
North Fm
Shuckton Manor Fm
Black Brook
Hill Top Fm
Mugginton
Ivyhouse Fm
Weston Underwood
Farnah House Fm
Champion Fm
Manor Fm
Brackley Gate Fm
Smalley Common
Mapperley
Shirley Common
Shirley Park
King's Grove
Commonside
Ednaston Manor Fm
Brailsford Common
New Fm
Weston Lodge
Cumberhills Cottages
Eaton Hill
Breadsall Moor
Morleymoor Fm
Hayes Fm
Stanley Common
Wyaston
Birch Fm
Shirley
Ednaston
Ednaston Hall
Brailsford
Mercaston Hall
Netherfield Fm
Quarndon Hill
Flaxholme
Burley Grange
Little Eaton
Morleymoor
Morley Smithy
West Hallam
Hilltop Fm
Shirley Lodge Fm
Wildpark
Kedleston
Ireton Fm
Park Nook
Burley Meadows
Breadsall Lodge
Morley
Thacker Barn
Yeaveley
Rodsley
Wormsley
Peatmoss Plantn
Pools Head
Priestwood Fm
Kedleston Park
Quarndon
Allestree Park
Jesse Fm
Stanley
Stanley Grange
Cat & Fiddle Fm
Hollington
Slade
Culland
Snapes Fm
Hilltop Fm
Kedleston Hall
Langley Hall
Breadsall
Manor Fm
King's Corner
Dale Abbey Windmill (Disused)
Hagg Fm
Boothay Fm
Longford
Burrows
Langley Green
Kirk Langley
The Pastures
Lodge Fm
Upper Vicarwood
Lower Vicarwood
Bowbridge Fields Fm
Markeaton
Allestree
Darley Abbey
Breadsall Hilltop
Chaddesden
Oakwood
Dale Abbey
Locko Grange Fm
Moor Fm
Dale Moor
Flourish
Alkmonton
Wood Ho
Moor Fm
Bradley
Stoop Fm
Longlane
Thurvaston
Grange
Bowbridge House Fm
Mackworth
Little
Brunswood
Bartlewood
DERBYSHIRE

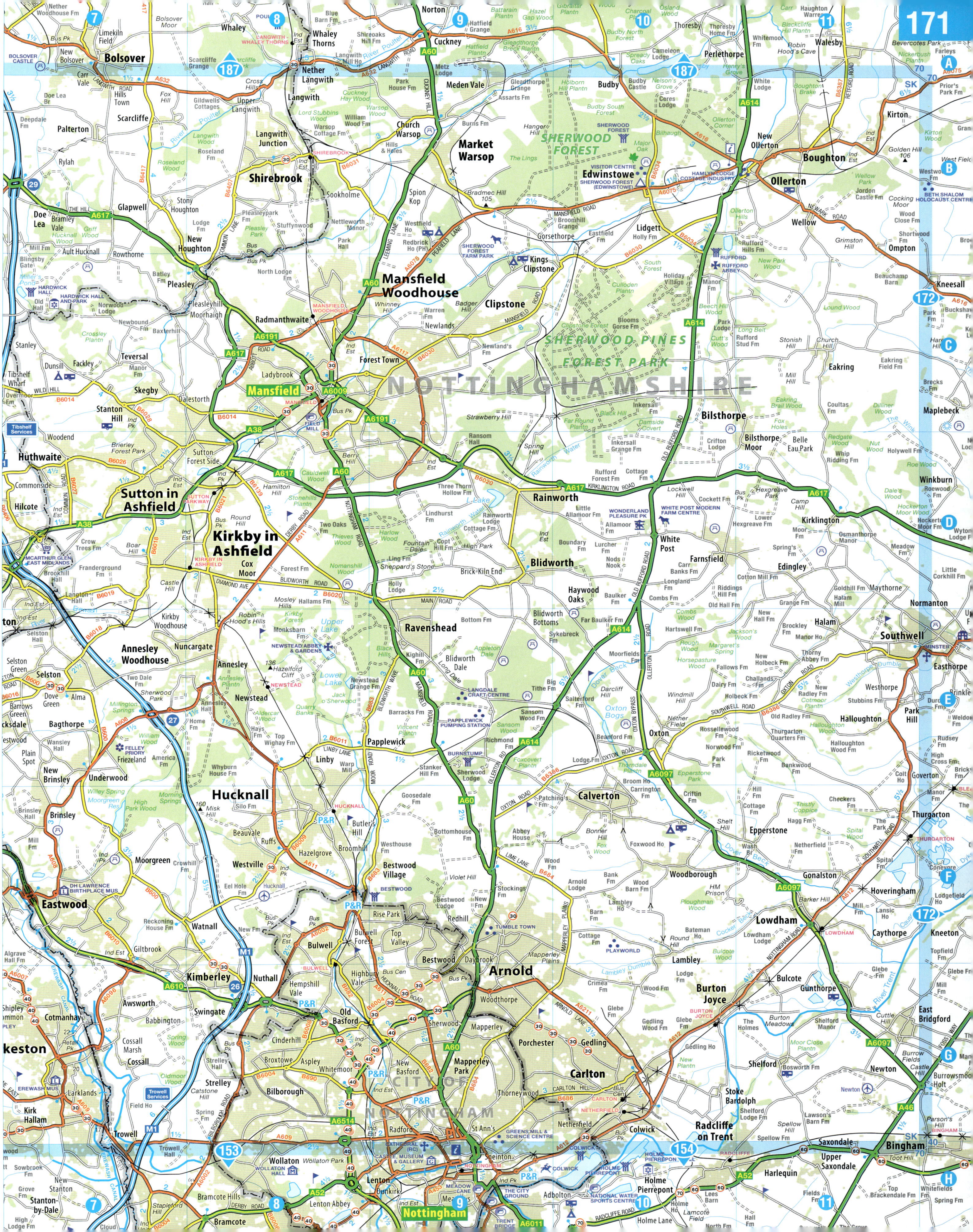
NOTTINGHAMSHIRE
SHERWOOD FOREST
SHERWOOD PINES FOREST PARK
CITY OF NOTTINGHAM
Bolsover
Whaley
Whaley Thorns
Nether Langwith
Langwith
Norton
Cuckney
Meden Vale
Budby
Thoresby
Perlethorpe
Walesby
Boughton
Ollerton
New Ollerton
Kirton
Edwinstowe
Market Warsop
Church Warsop
Shirebrook
Langwith Junction
Scarcliffe
Palterton
Glapwell
New Houghton
Pleasley
Mansfield Woodhouse
Clipstone
Kings Clipstone
Lidgett
Wellow
Ompton
Kneesall
Radmanthwaite
Forest Town
Mansfield
Teversal
Skegby
Stanton Hill
Huthwaite
Sutton in Ashfield
Kirkby in Ashfield
Rainworth
Blidworth
Bilsthorpe
Eakring
Kirklington
Farnsfield
Edingley
Halam
Southwell
Ravenshead
Annesley Woodhouse
Annesley
Newstead
Papplewick
Linby
Hucknall
Calverton
Oxton
Epperstone
Woodborough
Lowdham
Gonalston
Hoveringham
Thurgarton
Caythorpe
Lambley
Burton Joyce
Arnold
Bestwood Village
Bulwell
Eastwood
Kimberley
Nuthall
Awsworth
Cotmanhay
Ilkeston
Strelley
Bilborough
Carlton
Gedling
Netherfield
Colwick
Radcliffe on Trent
Bingham
Shelford
Newton
Holme Pierrepont
Nottingham
West Bridgford
Beeston
Trowell
Stapleford
Bramcote
Wollaton
Lenton
Mapperley
Sherwood
Basford
Aspley
A60
A617
A614
A6097
A38
A611
A608
A610
A6514
A52
A46
A616
M1
187
172
153
154
SK

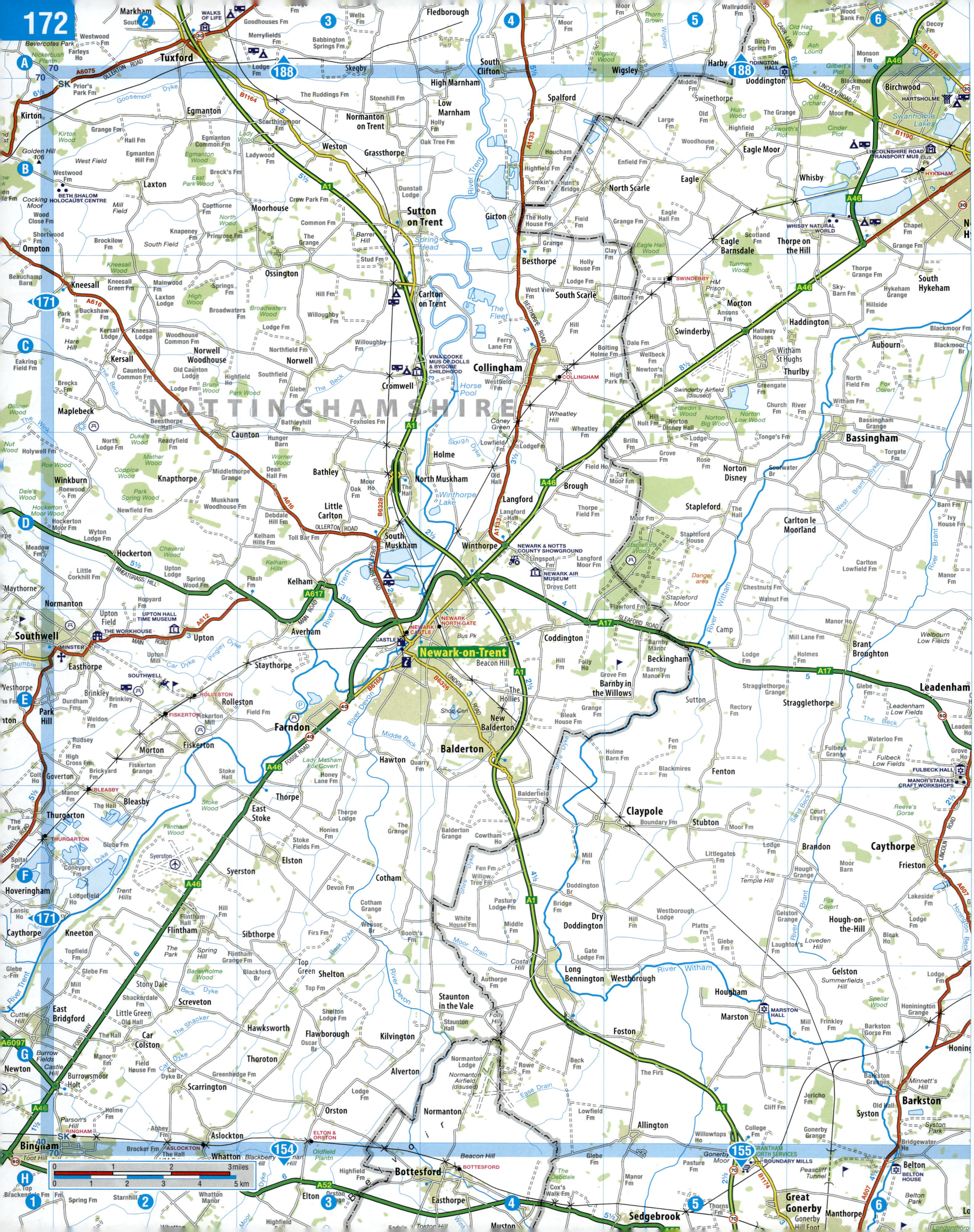
Markham
Tuxford
Fledborough
South Clifton
Wigsley
Harby
Doddington
188
Skegby
High Marnham
Low Marnham
Spalford
Kirton
Egmanton
Normanton on Trent
Weston
Grassthorpe
Eagle Moor
Birchwood
Laxton
North Scarle
Eagle
Whisby
Sutton on Trent
Girton
Moorhouse
Ompton
Eagle Barnsdale
Thorpe on the Hill
Besthorpe
Ossington
Kneesall
171
South Scarle
Morton
Carlton on Trent
South Hykeham
Haddington
Swinderby
Kersall
Norwell
Norwell Woodhouse
Collingham
Cromwell
Witham St Hughs
Thurlby
Aubourn
NOTTINGHAMSHIRE
Maplebeck
Caunton
Holme
Bassingham
Winkburn
Knapthorpe
Bathley
North Muskham
Brough
Norton Disney
Langford
Little Carlton
Stapleford
Carlton le Moorland
South Muskham
Winthorpe
Hockerton
Kelham
Normanton
Southwell
Upton
Averham
Coddington
Newark-on-Trent
Beckingham
Staythorpe
Brant Broughton
Easthorpe
Rolleston
Barnby in the Willows
Leadenham
Farndon
New Balderton
Balderton
Stragglethorpe
Morton
Fiskerton
Hawton
Bleasby
Thorpe
Fenton
Claypole
Stubton
Thurgarton
East Stoke
Elston
Brandon
Caythorpe
Syerston
Cotham
Hoveringham
Dry Doddington
Kneeton
Flintham
Sibthorpe
Hough-on-the-Hill
Long Bennington
Westborough
Shelton
Hougham
Marston
Screveton
East Bridgford
Staunton in the Vale
Hawksworth
Flawborough
Kilvington
Car Colston
Foston
Thoroton
Alverton
Newton
Scarrington
Orston
Normanton
Allington
Barkston
Syston
Bingham
Aslockton
Whatton
154
155
Bottesford
Elton
Easthorpe
Sedgebrook
Great Gonerby
Manthorpe
Belton
A46
A1
A17
A52
A616
A617
A612
A6097
A607
B1164
B6325
B6326
B6166
B1190
B1378
B1174

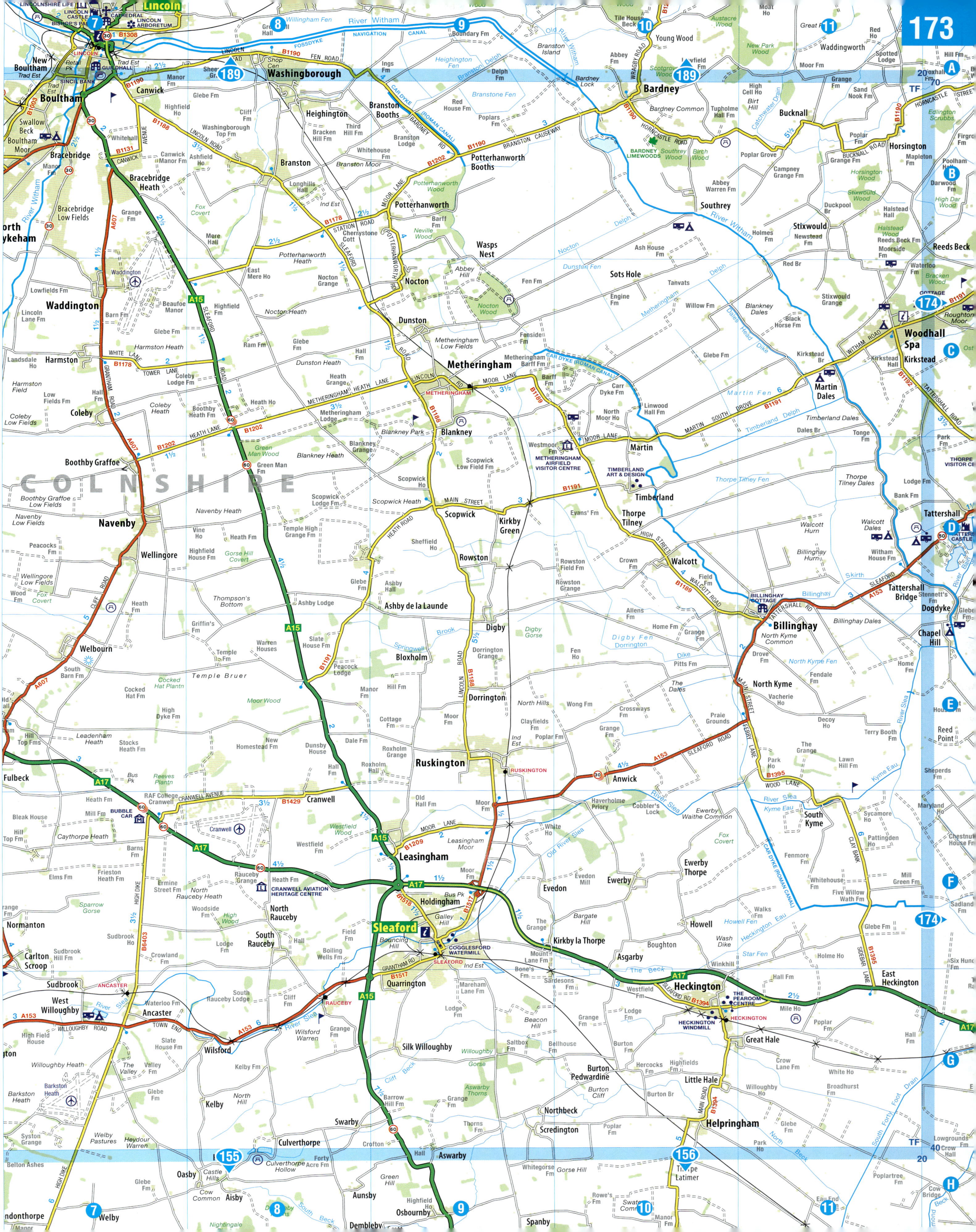

Lincoln
LINCOLNSHIRE LIFE
LINCOLN CASTLE
CATHEDRAL
LINCOLN ARBORETUM
BISHOP'S PALACE
New Boultham
Boultham
Swallow Beck
Boultham Moor
Bracebridge
Bracebridge Heath
Bracebridge Low Fields
North Hykeham
Canwick
Washingborough
Heighington
Branston
Branston Booths
Potterhanworth
Potterhanworth Booths
Bardney
Bucknall
Horsington
Southrey
Stixwould
Woodhall Spa
Kirkstead
Waddington
Harmston
Coleby
Boothby Graffoe
Navenby
Wellingore
Welbourn
Fulbeck
Nocton
Dunston
Metheringham
Blankney
Martin
Martin Dales
Timberland
Thorpe Tilney
Walcott
Scopwick
Kirkby Green
Rowston
Digby
Ashby de la Launde
Bloxholm
Dorrington
Ruskington
North Kyme
Billinghay
Tattershall
Tattershall Bridge
Dogdyke
Chapel Hill
Anwick
South Kyme
Cranwell
Leasingham
Sleaford
Holdingham
North Rauceby
South Rauceby
Quarrington
Evedon
Ewerby
Ewerby Thorpe
Howell
Kirkby la Thorpe
Asgarby
Heckington
Great Hale
East Heckington
Little Hale
Helpringham
Burton Pedwardine
Scredington
Northbeck
Silk Willoughby
Swarby
Aswarby
Aunsby
Osbournby
Spanby
Culverthorpe
Wilsford
Kelby
Ancaster
Sudbrook
West Willoughby
Carlton Scroop
Normanton
Welby
Oasby
Aisby
Threekingham
Thorpe Latimer
Dembleby
LINCOLNSHIRE
River Witham
River Slea
A15
A17
A153
A607
B1188
B1189
B1191
B1202
B1395
B1429
189
155
156
174

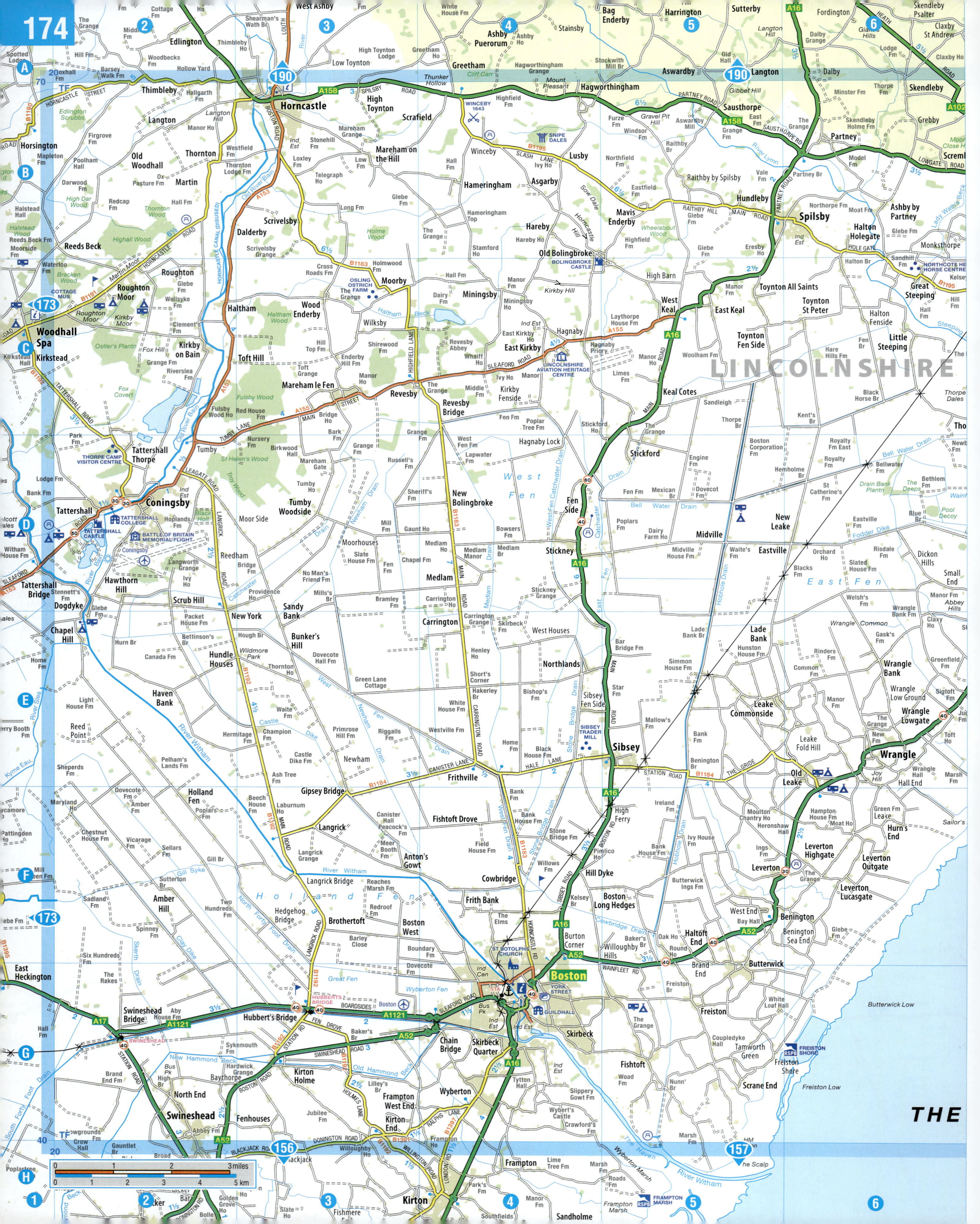

LINCOLNSHIRE
THE
Horncastle
Woodhall Spa
Kirkstead
Coningsby
Tattershall
Tattershall Thorpe
Tattershall Bridge
Spilsby
Boston
Sibsey
Stickney
Stickford
Midville
Eastville
New Leake
Wrangle
Old Leake
Leverton
Benington
Butterwick
Freiston
Fishtoft
Skirbeck
Wyberton
Frampton
Kirton
Kirton End
Kirton Holme
Swineshead
Swineshead Bridge
North End
Hubbert's Bridge
Langrick
Langrick Bridge
Gipsey Bridge
Frithville
Carrington
Medlam
New Bolingbroke
Revesby
Revesby Bridge
Mareham le Fen
Mareham on the Hill
Moorby
Wilksby
Miningsby
East Kirkby
Hagnaby
West Keal
East Keal
Keal Cotes
Old Bolingbroke
Hareby
Hameringham
Asgarby
Lusby
Winceby
Hagworthingham
Mavis Enderby
Raithby by Spilsby
Hundleby
Halton Holegate
Toynton All Saints
Toynton St Peter
Toynton Fen Side
Great Steeping
Little Steeping
Greetham
Ashby Puerorum
Bag Enderby
Harrington
Sutterby
Aswardby
Langton
Sausthorpe
Partney
Dalby
Skendleby
Grebby
Ashby by Partney
Edlington
Thimbleby
Thornton
Martin
Old Woodhall
Langton
Horsington
Reeds Beck
Roughton
Roughton Moor
Kirkby on Bain
Haltham
Wood Enderby
Toft Hill
High Toynton
Scrafield
Scrivelsby
Dalderby
Tumby
Tumby Woodside
Moor Side
Hawthorn Hill
Dogdyke
Chapel Hill
Scrub Hill
New York
Sandy Bank
Bunker's Hill
Hundle Houses
Haven Bank
Reed Point
Holland Fen
Amber Hill
Brothertoft
Boston West
Hedgehog Bridge
Anton's Gowt
Cowbridge
Frith Bank
Fishtoft Drove
Hill Dyke
Boston Long Hedges
Willoughby Hills
Haltoft End
Brand End
Burton Corner
Chain Bridge
Skirbeck Quarter
Bicker
Fenhouses
Bayhorpe
East Heckington
Fen Side
Northlands
West Fen
East Fen
Holland Fen
Lade Bank
Leake Commonside
Wrangle Bank
Wrangle Lowgate
Leverton Highgate
Leverton Outgate
Leverton Lucasgate
Freiston Shore
Scrane End
Sandholme
Fishmere
Butterwick Low
Freiston Low
River Witham
The Haven
Hobhole Drain
Horncastle Canal (disused)
River Bain
A16
A52
A17
A1121
A155
A153
A158
B1183
B1192
B1184
190
173
156
157

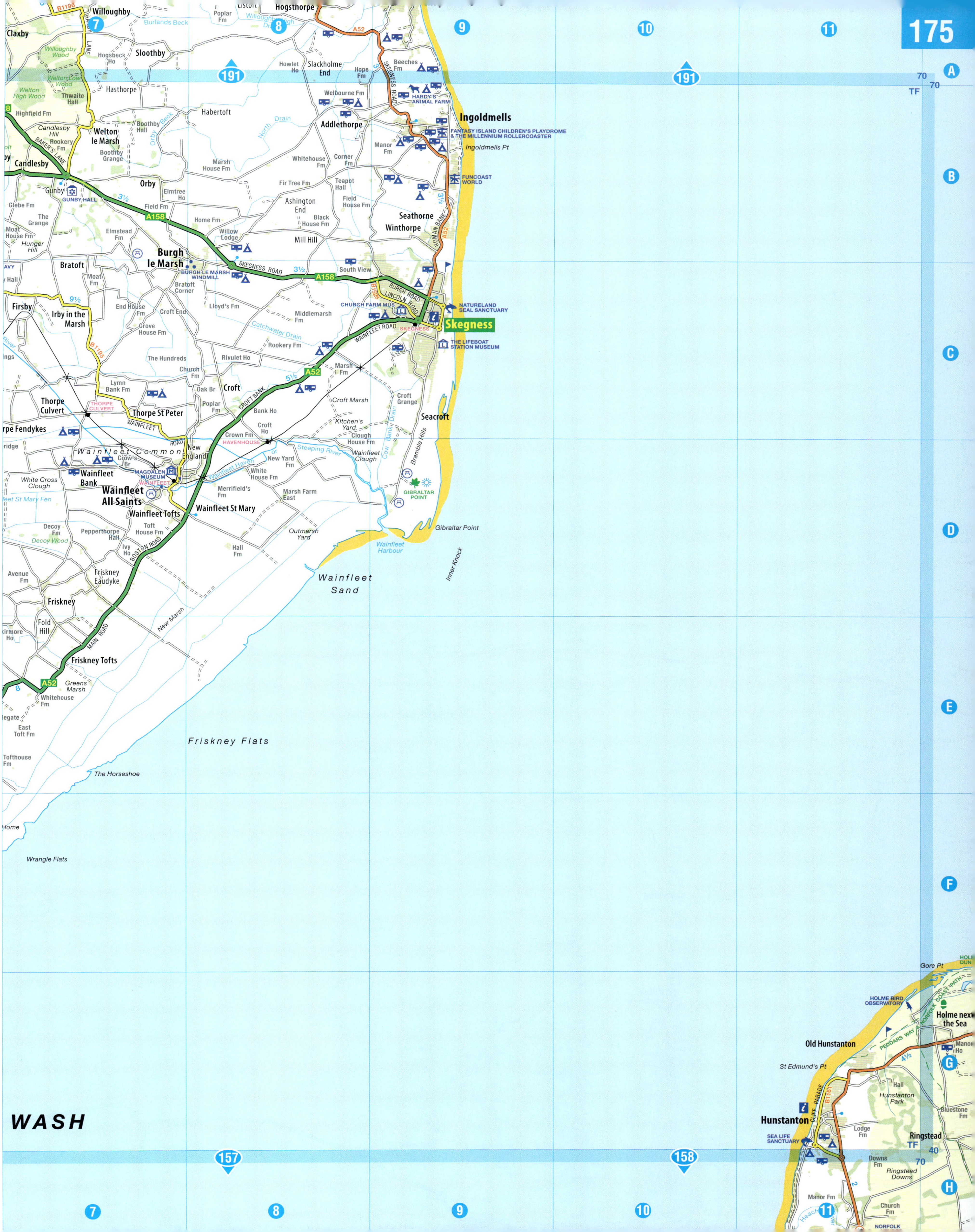
Willoughby
Claxby
Willoughby Wood
Hogsbeck Ho
Sloothby
Burlands Beck
Poplar Fm
Hogsthorpe
Howlet Ho
Slackholme End
Hope Fm
Beeches Fm
191
Welton Low Wood
Welton High Wood
Thwaite Hall
Hasthorpe
Welbourne Fm
HARDY'S ANIMAL FARM
SKEGNESS ROAD
Highfield Fm
Habertoft
Boothby Hall
North Drain
Addlethorpe
Ingoldmells
FANTASY ISLAND CHILDREN'S PLAYDROME & THE MILLENNIUM ROLLERCOASTER
Ingoldmells Pt
Candlesby Hill
Welton le Marsh
Rookery Fm
BAKER'S LANE
Boothby Grange
Marsh House Fm
Whitehouse Fm
Corner Fm
Manor Fm
Candlesby
Gunby
GUNBY HALL
Orby
Elmtree Ho
Fir Tree Fm
Teapot Hall
FUNCOAST WORLD
Glebe Fm
Field Fm
Ashington End
Field House Fm
The Grange
A158
Home Fm
Black House Fm
Seathorne
Winthorpe
ROMAN BANK
Moat House Fm
Elmstead Fm
Willow Lodge
Mill Hill
Hunger Hill
Burgh le Marsh
Bratoft
SKEGNESS ROAD
BURGH LE MARSH WINDMILL
South View
Moat Fm
Bratoft Corner
BURGH ROAD
LINCOLN ROAD
NATURELAND SEAL SANCTUARY
Firsby
Irby in the Marsh
End House Fm
Croft End
Lloyd's Fm
Middlemarsh Fm
CHURCH FARM MUS
Skegness
SKEGNESS
WAINFLEET ROAD
Grove House Fm
Catchwater Drain
Rookery Fm
THE LIFEBOAT STATION MUSEUM
B1195
The Hundreds
Rivulet Ho
Church Fm
Marsh Fm
A52
Lymn Bank Fm
Oak Br
Croft
CROFT BANK
Croft Grange
Thorpe Culvert
THORPE CULVERT
Thorpe St Peter
Poplar Fm
Croft Marsh
Bank Ho
Seacroft
rpe Fendykes
WAINFLEET ROAD
Croft Ho
Kitchen's Yard
Cow Bank Drain
Crown Fm
HAVENHOUSE
Clough House Fm
Bramble Hills
New England
Wainfleet Common
Crow's Br
Steeping River
New Yard Fm
Wainfleet Clough
Wainfleet Bank
MAGDALEN MUSEUM
WAINFLEET
Wainfleet Haven
White House Fm
White Cross Clough
Wainfleet All Saints
Merrifield's Fm
Marsh Farm East
GIBRALTAR POINT
leet St Mary Fen
Wainfleet Tofts
Wainfleet St Mary
Decoy Fm
Decoy Wood
Pepperthorpe Hall
Toft House Fm
Outmarsh Yard
Gibraltar Point
Ivy Ho
BOSTON ROAD
Hall Fm
Wainfleet Harbour
Inner Knock
Avenue Fm
Friskney Eaudyke
Wainfleet Sand
Friskney
Fold Hill
MAIN ROAD
New Marsh
Friskney Tofts
Greens Marsh
Whitehouse Fm
East Toft Fm
Friskney Flats
Tofthouse Fm
The Horseshoe
Home
Wrangle Flats
WASH
Gore Pt
HOLME BIRD OBSERVATORY
Holme next the Sea
NORFOLK COAST PATH
PEDDARS WAY
Old Hunstanton
St Edmund's Pt
Hall
Hunstanton Park
CLIFF PARADE
B1161
Bluestone Fm
Hunstanton
SEA LIFE SANCTUARY
Lodge Fm
Ringstead
Downs Fm
Ringstead Downs
Manor Fm
Church Fm
NORFOLK
157
158
TF
70
40
A
B
C
D
E
F
G
H
7
8
9
10
11

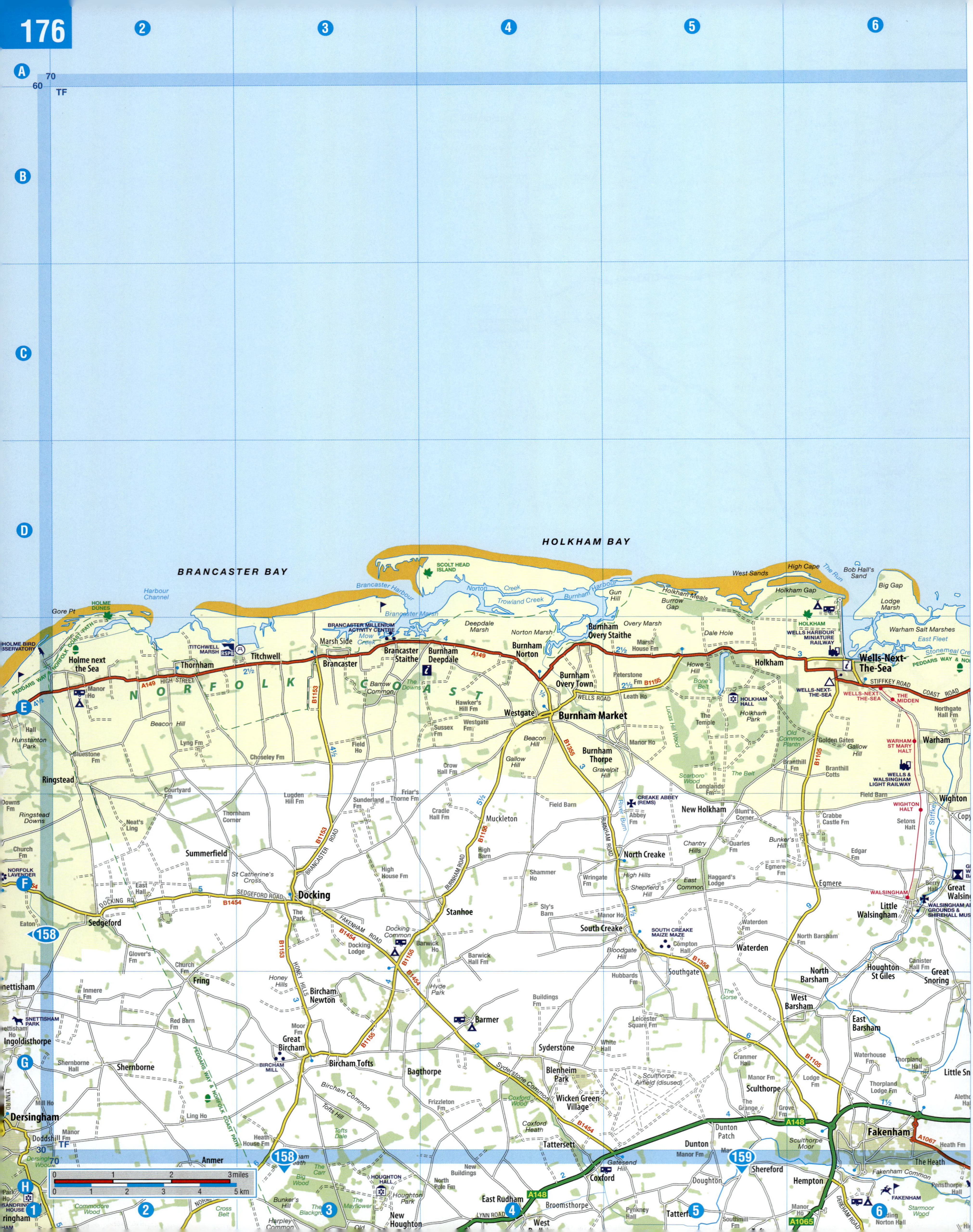
HOLKHAM BAY
BRANCASTER BAY
SCOLT HEAD ISLAND
Harbour Channel
Brancaster Harbour
Norton Creek
Trowland Creek
Burnham Harbour
Gore Pt
HOLME DUNES
HOLME BIRD OBSERVATORY
Holme next the Sea
PEDDARS WAY & NORFOLK COAST PATH
TITCHWELL MARSH
Thornham
Titchwell
Brancaster
BRANCASTER MILLENIUM ACTIVITY CENTRE
Marsh Side
Brancaster Staithe
Burnham Deepdale
Deepdale Marsh
Norton Marsh
Burnham Norton
Burnham Overy Staithe
Overy Marsh
Gun Hill
Holkham Meals
Burrow Gap
West Sands
High Cape
The Run
Bob Hall's Sand
Big Gap
Holkham Gap
Lodge Marsh
Warham Salt Marshes
East Fleet
Stonemeal Creek
Dale Hole
HOLKHAM
WELLS HARBOUR MINIATURE RAILWAY
Wells-Next-The-Sea
Holkham
HOLKHAM HALL
Holkham Park
Burnham Overy Town
Burnham Market
Westgate
Burnham Thorpe
NORFOLK COAST
A149
B1153
B1155
B1355
B1454
B1105
B1454
A148
A1065
A1067
Hunstanton Park
Ringstead
Sedgeford
Docking
Stanhoe
Summerfield
Fring
Bircham Newton
Great Bircham
Bircham Tofts
BIRCHAM MILL
Bagthorpe
Barmer
Syderstone
Blenheim Park
Wicken Green Village
Tattersett
Coxford
East Rudham
Broomsthorpe
New Houghton
HOUGHTON HALL
Anmer
Shernborne
SNETTISHAM PARK
Ingoldisthorpe
Dersingham
NORFOLK LAVENDER
Muckleton
North Creake
South Creake
SOUTH CREAKE MAIZE MAZE
CREAKE ABBEY (REMS)
New Holkham
Waterden
Egmere
North Barsham
West Barsham
East Barsham
Sculthorpe
Fakenham
Dunton
Shereford
Hempton
The Heath
Houghton St Giles
Great Snoring
Little Walsingham
Great Walsingham
WALSINGHAM
Wighton
Warham
WELLS & WALSINGHAM LIGHT RAILWAY
Sculthorpe Airfield (disused)
Sculthorpe Moor
FAKENHAM
158
159
0 1 2 3 miles
0 1 2 3 4 5 km

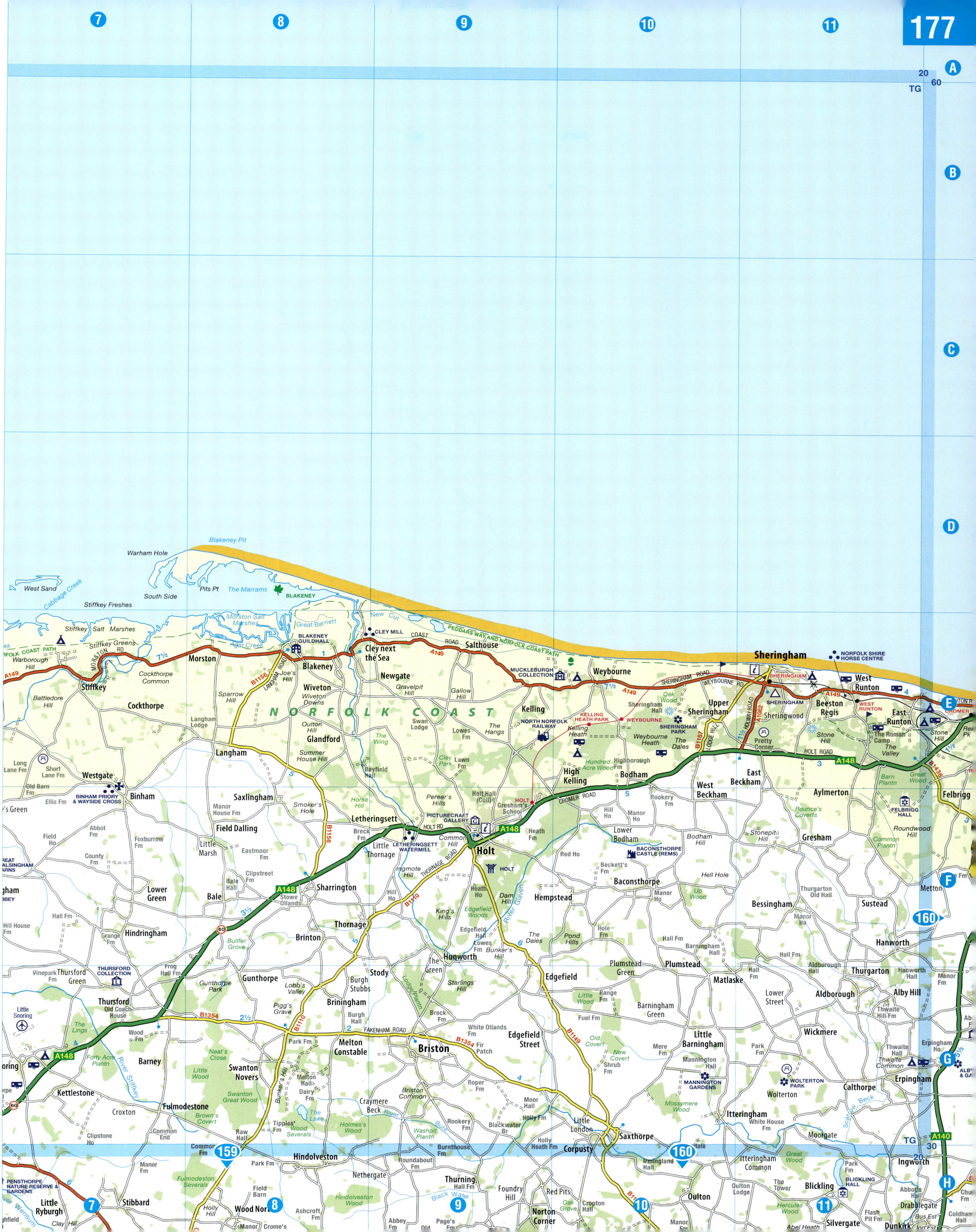
Blakeney Pit
Warham Hole
West Sand
Cabbage Creek
South Side
Pits Pt
The Marrams
BLAKENEY
Stiffkey Freshes
Stiffkey Salt Marshes
Morston Salt Marshes
Great Barnett
Agar Creek
BLAKENEY GUILDHALL
CLEY MILL
New Cut
PEDDARS WAY AND NORFOLK COAST PATH
Warborough Hill
Stiffkey Greens
Morston
Blakeney
Cley next the Sea
Salthouse
Stiffkey
Cockthorpe Common
Cockthorpe
Battledore Hill
Sparrow Hill
Joe's Hill
Wiveton
Wiveton Downs
Newgate
Gravelpit Hill
Gallow Hill
MUCKLEBURGH COLLECTION
Weybourne
Sheringham
NORFOLK SHIRE HORSE CENTRE
West Runton
Beeston Regis
East Runton
NORFOLK COAST
Langham Lodge
Oulton Hill
Glandford
Swan Lodge
Lowes Fm
The Hangs
Kelling
NORTH NORFOLK RAILWAY
KELLING HEATH PARK
Kelling Heath
WEYBOURNE
Sheringham Hall
Oak Wood
SHERINGHAM PARK
Upper Sheringham
Sheringwood
Weybourne Heath
The Dales
Pretty Corner
Stone Hill
The Roman Camp
The Valley
Langham
Summer House Hill
The Wing
Cley Park
Lawn Fm
Hundred Acre Wood
Highborough Fm
High Kelling
Bodham
East Beckham
West Beckham
Aylmerton
Felbrigg
Westgate
Long Lane Fm
Short Lane Fm
Old Barn Fm
BINHAM PRIORY & WAYSIDE CROSS
Binham
Ellis Fm
Saxlingham
Manor House Fm
Smoker's Hole
Bayfield Hall
Horse Hill
Pereer's Hills
Holt Hall (Coll)
Gresham's School
Letheringsett
PICTURECRAFT GALLERY
HOLT RD
Field Dalling
Breck Fm
LETHERINGSETT WATERMILL
Little Thornage
Common Hill
Holt
Heath Fm
Red Ho
Lower Bodham
BACONSTHORPE CASTLE (REMS)
Bodham Hill
Stonepit Hill
Gresham
Rounce's Coverts
FELBRIGG HALL
Roundwood Hill
Common Plantn
Abbot Fm
Field Ho
Foxburrow Fm
County Fm
Little Marsh
Eastmoor Fm
Clipstreet Fm
Bale Hall
Bale
Lower Green
Stowe Ollands
Sharrington
Ingmote Hill
Hill Ho
Heath Ho
Dam Hill
Hempstead
Beckett's Fm
Baconsthorpe
Manor Ho
Up Wood
Hell Hole
Thurgarton Old Hall
Bessingham
Sustead
Metton
Hall Fm
Hill House Fm
Grange Fm
Hindringham
Bullfer Grove
Brinton
Thornage
King's Hills
Edgefield Woods
Edgefield Hall
Lowes Fm
Bunker's Hill
The Dales
Pond Hills
Hole Fm
Hall Fm
Barningham Hall
Manor Ho
Hanworth
Vinepark Fm
Thursford Green
THURSFORD COLLECTION
Frog Hall Fm
Gunthorpe Park
Gunthorpe
Lobb's Valley
Burgh Stubbs
Stody
The Green
Hunworth
Starlings' Hill
Edgefield
Plumstead Green
Plumstead
Matlaske
Thurgarton
Hanworth Hall
Manor Fm
Little Snoring
Thursford
Old Coach House
The Lings
Pigg's Grave
Briningham
Burgh Hall
Breck Fm
Little Wood
Range Fm
Barningham Green
Lower Street
Aldborough
Alby Hill
Thwaite Hill Fm
Wood Fm
Forty Acre Plantn
River Stiffkey
Barney
Park Fm
FAKENHAM ROAD
Melton Constable
Briston
White Ollands Fm
Fir Patch
Edgefield Street
Fuel Fm
Old Covert
New Covert
Shrub Fm
Little Barningham
Mere Fm
Mannington Hall
MANNINGTON GARDENS
Park Fm
Wickmere
WOLTERTON PARK
Wolterton
Thwaite Hall
Thwaite Common
Erpingham Ho
Erpingham
Calthorpe
Kettlestone
Neat's Close
Little Wood
Swanton Novers
Swanton Great Wood
Bunker's Hill
Melton Hall
Dairy Fm
Briston Common
Roper Fm
Moor Hall
Mossymere Wood
Itteringham
Scarrow Beck
Croxton
Fulmodestone
Brown's Covert
Craymere Beck
River
The Lake
Holmes's Wood
Rookery Fm
Washpit Plantn
Blackwater Br
Holly Fm
Little London
Saxthorpe
White House Fm
Moorgate
Clipstone Ho
Common End
Raw Hall
Tipples' Fm
Wood Severals
Burnthouse Fm
Holly Heath Fm
Corpusty
Hale
Irmingland Hall
Itteringham Common
Great Wood
Park Fm
Ingworth
Manor Fm
Common Fm
Park Fm
Hindolveston
Roundabout Fm
Nethergate
Thurning Hall Fm
Foundry Hill
Red Pits
Oak Grove
Crofton Hall
Oulton
Oulton Lodge
The Tower
Blickling
BLICKLING HALL
Abbots Hall
Drabblegate
PENSTHORPE NATURE RESERVE & GARDENS
Little Ryburgh
Stibbard
Fulmodeston Severals
Field Barn
Hindolveston Wood
Holly Hill
Wood Norton
Ashcroft Fm
Black Water
Norton Corner
Hercules Wood
Silvergate
Flash Pit Fm
Dunkirk
Colby Hall
River Wensum
Clay Hill
Crome's
Abbey Fm
Page's Fm
Abel Heath
Bus Est
River Glaven
Lodge Plantn
A149
A148
A1082
A140
B1156
B1110
B1354
B1149
B1157
B1436
SHERINGHAM ROAD
WEYBOURNE RD
HOLWAY ROAD
LODGE HILL
CROMER ROAD
HOLT ROAD
THORNAGE ROAD
LANGHAM ROAD
MORSTON RD
COAST ROAD
TG
20
60
30
159
160

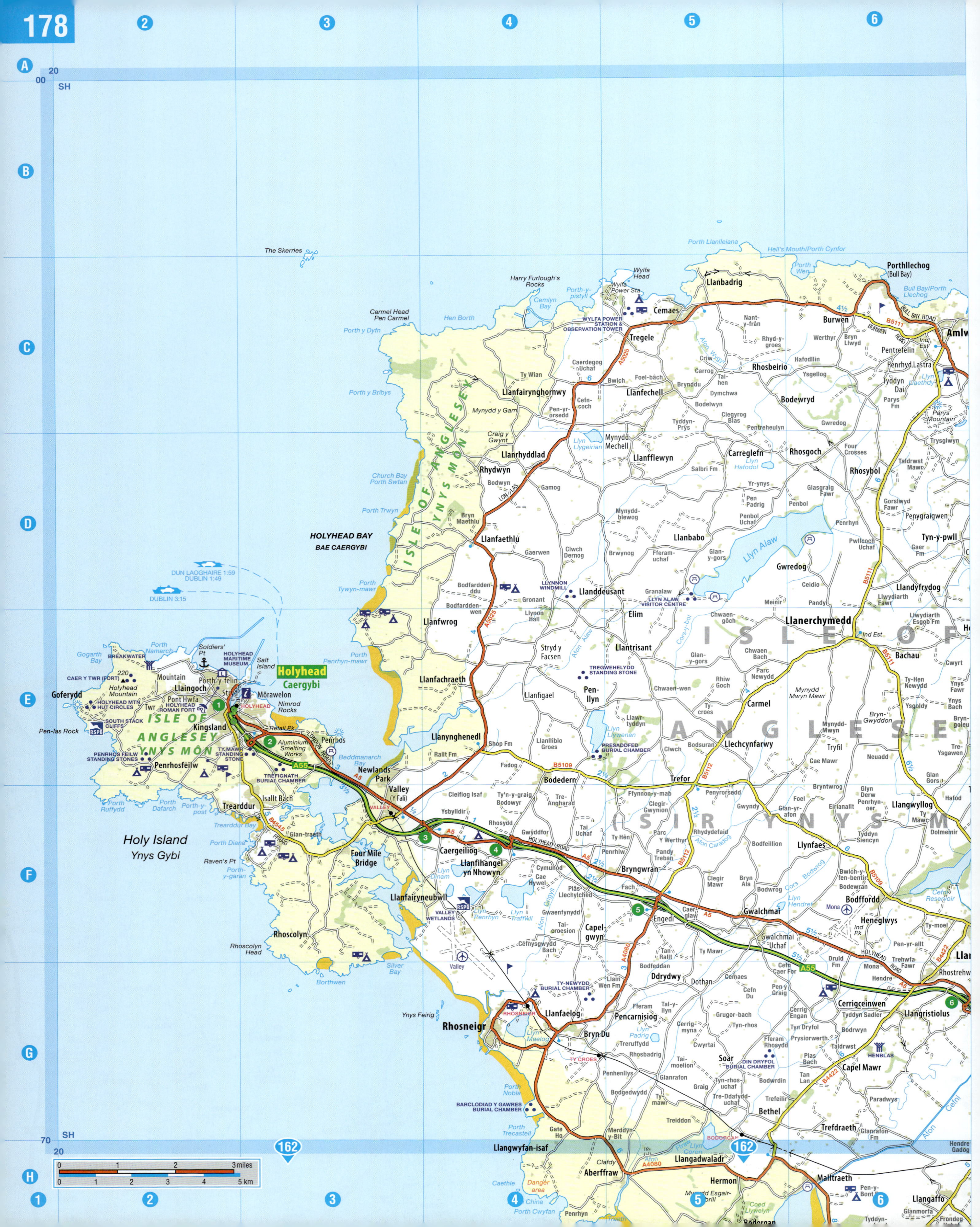

The Skerries
Porth Llanlleiana
Hell's Mouth/Porth Cynfor
Porthllechog (Bull Bay)
Bull Bay/Porth Llechog
Harry Furlough's Rocks
Wylfa Head
Wylfa Power Sta
Llanbadrig
Porth Wen
Cemlyn Bay
Porth-y-pistyll
Cemaes
Burwen
Amlwch
Carmel Head
Pen Carmel
Hen Borth
Porth y Dyfn
WYLFA POWER STATION & OBSERVATION TOWER
Tregele
Nant-y-frân
Rhyd-y-groes
Werthyr
Bryn Llwyd
Pentrefelin
Penrhyd Lastra
Caerdegog Uchaf
Hafodllin
Rhosbeirio
Ysgellog
Tyddyn Dai
Ty Wian
Llanfairynghornwy
Bwlch
Foel-bâch
Brynddu
Carrog
Tai-hen
Llanfechell
Porth y Bribys
Mynydd y Garn
Pen-yr-orsedd
Cefn-coch
Dymchwa
Bodelwyn
Bodewryd
Parys Fm
Parys Mountain
Clegyrog Blas
Gwredog
Craig y Gwynt
Tyddyn-Prys
Pentreheulyn
Trysglwyn
Llanrhyddlad
Mynydd Mechell
Llyn Llygeirian
Llanfflewyn
Carreglefn
Llyn Hafodol
Rhosgoch
Four Crosses
Taldrwst Mawr
Church Bay
Porth Swtan
Rhydwyn
Salbri Fm
Rhosybol
Bodwyn
Gamog
Yr-ynys
Glasgraig Fawr
Gorslwyd Fawr
Pen Padrig
Penbol
Penygraigwen
Porth Trwyn
Bryn Maethlu
Mynydd-blewog
Penbol Uchaf
Penrhyn
HOLYHEAD BAY
BAE CAERGYBI
Llanfaethlu
Llanbabo
Pwllcoch Uchaf
Tyn-y-pwll
Gaerwen
Clwch Dernog
Brwynog
Fferam-uchaf
Glan-y-gors
Llyn Alaw
Gwredog
Gaer Fm
ISLE OF ANGLESEY
YNYS MÔN
DUN LAOGHAIRE 1:59
DUBLIN 1:49
DUBLIN 3:15
Porth Tywyn-mawr
Bodfardden-ddu
LLYNNON WINDMILL
Llanddeusant
Granalaw
LLYN ALAW VISITOR CENTRE
Meinir
Ceidio
Pandy
Llandyfrydog
Llwydiarth Fawr
Gronant
Bodfardden-wen
Llynon Hall
Elim
Chwaen-goch
Llanerchymedd
Llwydiarth Esgob Fm
Llanfwrog
Porth Namarch
Gogarth Bay
BREAKWATER
Soldiers' Pt
HOLYHEAD MARITIME MUSEUM
Salt Island
Porth Penrhyn-mawr
Stryd y Facsen
Llantrisant
Glan-y-gors
Chwaen Bach
Ind Est
Bachau
Cwyrt
Holyhead
Caergybi
CAER Y TWR (FORT)
Holyhead Mountain
Mountain
Llaingoch
Porth-y-felin
Llanfachraeth
TREGWEHELYDD STANDING STONE
Parc Newydd
Ty-Hen Newydd
Goferydd
HOLYHEAD MTN HUT CIRCLES
Twr
Pont Hwfa
HOLYHEAD ROMAN FORT
Stryd
Môrawelon
Nimrod Rocks
Llanfigael
Pen-llyn
Chwaen-wen
Rhiw Goch
Mynydd Mwyn Mawr
Carmel
Ysgoldy
Bryn-Gwyddon
SOUTH STACK CLIFFS
ISLE OF ANGLESEY
YNYS MÔN
Kingsland
Retail Pk
Penrhos
Ty-croes
Llawr-tyddyn
Pen-las Rock
Aluminium Smelting Works
Beddmanarch Bay
Llanynghenedl
Llyn Llywenan
Llanllibio Groes
Shop Fm
Bodsuran
Llechcynfarwy
Mynydd-Mwyn
Tryfil
Penrhosfeilw
PENRHOS FEILW STANDING STONES
TY-MAWR STANDING STONE
TREFIGNATH BURIAL CHAMBER
Newlands Park
Rallt Fm
PRESADDFED BURIAL CHAMBER
Clwch
Cae Mawr
Neuadd
Fadog
Bodedern
Trefor
Valley (Y Fali)
Isallt Bach
Cleifiog Isaf
Ty'n-y-graig
Bodowyr
Tre-Angharad
Flynnon-y-mab
Penyrorsedd
Bryntwrog
Glyn Derw
Penrhyn-oer
Llangwyllog
Porth Ruffydd
Porth Dafarch
Porth-y-post
Trearddur
Ysbyldir
Clegir-Gwynion
Gwyndy
Foel
Glan-yr-afon
Eirianallt
Trearddur Bay
Glan-traeth
Rhosydd
Tai Uchaf
Rhydydefaid
Tyddyn Siencyn
Holy Island
Ynys Gybi
Porth Diana
Gwyddfor
Ty Hên
Parc
Y Werthyr
Bodfeilion
Llynfaes
Raven's Pt
Porth-y-garan
Four Mile Bridge
Caergeiliog
Llanfihangel yn Nhowyn
Penrhiw
Pandy Treban
Bryngwran
Clegir Mawr
Bryn Ala
Bwlch-y-fen-bentir
Bodewran
Cymunod
Cae Hywel
Plâs-Llechylched
Fach
Bodwrog
Llyn Hendref
Bodffordd
Llyn Dinam
Llanfairyneubwll
VALLEY WETLANDS
Llyn Penrhyn
Llyn Traffwll
Gwaenfynydd
Engedi
Caer-glaw
Gwalchmai
Mona
Heneglwys
Rhoscolyn
Tai-croesion
Capel-gwyn
Gwalchmai Uchaf
Pen-yr-allt
Rhoscolyn Head
Cefnysgwydd Bach
Tan Rallt
Ty Mawr
Cefn Cae For
Druid Fm
Trehwfa Fawr
Silver Bay
Borthwen
Valley
Bodfeddan
Ddrydwy
Dothan
Cemaes
Mona
Hendre
Rhostrehwfa
TY-NEWYDD BURIAL CHAMBER
Llain Wen Fm
Cefn Du
Pen-y-Graig
Cerrigceinwen
Ynys Feirig
RHOSNEIGR
Llanfaelog
Fferam
Tal-y-llyn
Pencarnisiog
Grugor-bach
Cerrig Engan
Tyddyn Sadler
Llangristiolus
Rhosneigr
Bryn Du
Llyn Maelog
Llyn Padrig
Cerrig-mynn
Tyn-rhos
Tyn Dryfol
Bodrwyn
Treruffydd
Cwyrtai
Fferam Rhosydd
Prysiorwerth
Rhosbadrig
Taldrwst
HENBLAS
TY CROES
Tai-moelion
Soar
DIN DRYFOL BURIAL CHAMBER
Plas Bach
Capel Mawr
Penhenllys
Glanrafon
Graig
Tyn-rhos-uchaf
Bodwrdin
Tan Lan
Porth Nobla
Bodgedwydd
Ty mawr
Tre-Ddafydd-uchaf
Trefeilir
Paradwys
BARCLODIAD Y GAWRES BURIAL CHAMBER
Bethel
Treiddon
Porth Trecastell
Gate Ho
Merddyn-y-Bit
BODORGAN
Trefdraeth
Glanrafon Fm
Afon Cefni
Hendre Gadog
Llangwyfan-isaf
Clafdy
Ffraw
Llyn Coron
Aberffraw
Llangadwaladr
Hermon
Malltraeth
Pen-y-Bont
Caethle
Danger area
China
Porth Cwyfan
Mynydd Esgair-Forill
Coed Llywelyn
Llangaffo
Glanmorfa
Frondeg
Penrhyn
Bodorgan
Tyddyn-
ISLE OF ANGLESEY
(SIR YNYS MÔN)
Llangefni
A5
A55
A5025
B5109
B5111
B5112
A4080
B4545
B4422
HOLYHEAD ROAD
LONDON ROAD
LÔN LAS
BULL BAY ROAD
BURWEN ROAD
162
SH
00
20
70
0 1 2 3 miles
0 1 2 3 4 5 km
A
B
C
D
E
F
G
H
1
2
3
4
5
6

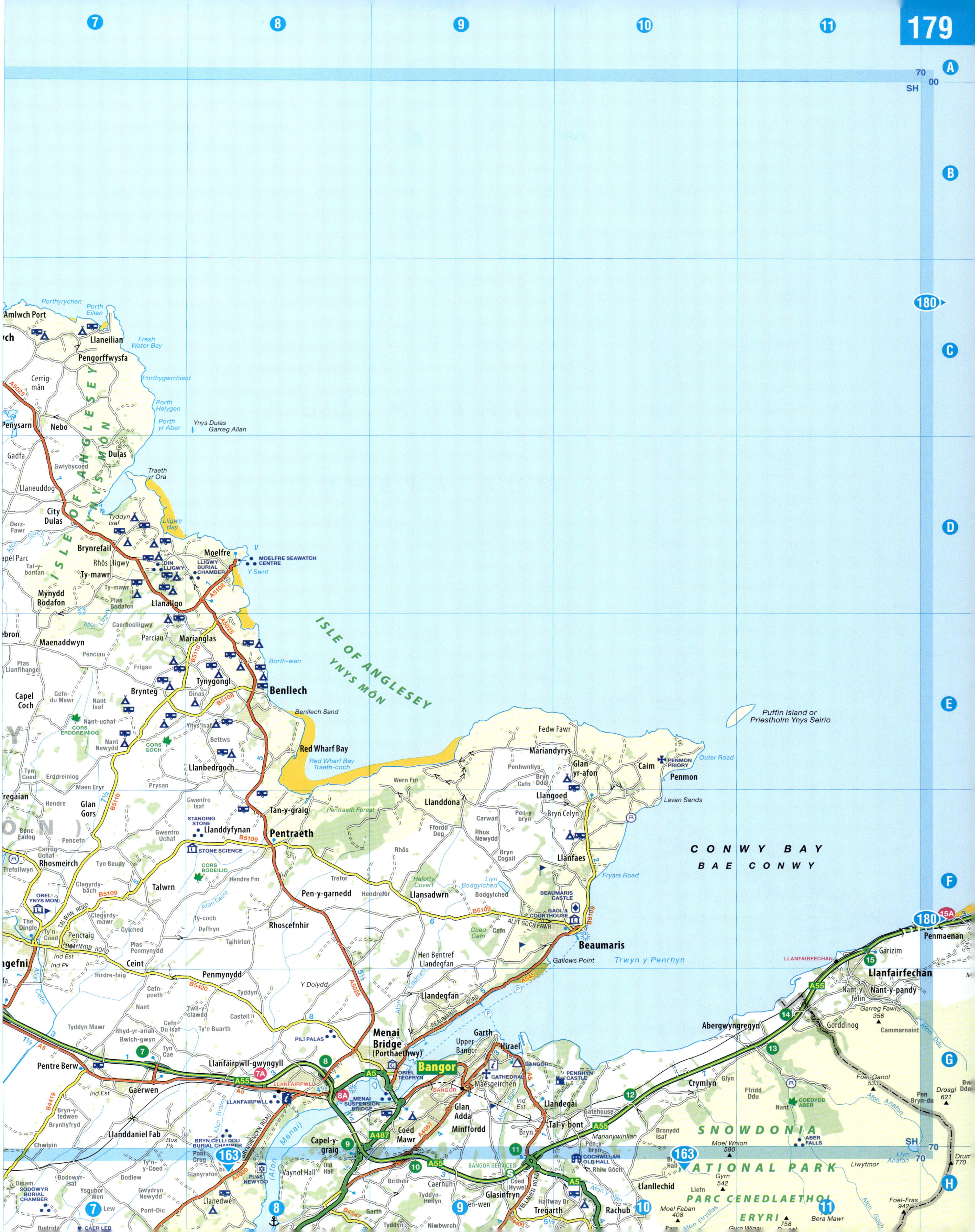
7
8
9
10
11
A
B
C
D
E
F
G
H
180
163
SH
70
00
Amlwch Port
Porthyrychen
Porth Eilian
Llaneilian
Fresh Water Bay
Pengorffwysfa
Cerrig-mân
Porthygwichiaid
Porth Helygen
Porth yr Aber
Ynys Dulas
Garreg Allan
Penysarn
Nebo
Gadfa
Dulas
Gwlybycoed
Traeth yr Ora
Llaneuddog
City Dulas
Derz-Fawr
Tyddyn Isaf
Lligwy Bay
Brynrefail
Rhôs Lligwy
Moelfre
MOELFRE SEAWATCH CENTRE
Y Swnt
LLIGWY BURIAL CHAMBER
DIN LLIGWY
Ty-mawr
Tal-y-bontan
Mynydd Bodafon
Plas Bodafon
Llanallgo
ISLE OF ANGLESEY
YNYS MÔN
Caerhosliggwy
Parciau
Marianglas
Maenaddwyn
Penciau
Borth-wen
Plas Llanfihangel
Frigan
Tynygongl
Benllech
Capel Coch
Cefn-du Mawr
Nant Isaf
Brynteg
Dinas
Benllech Sand
Nant-uchaf
CORS ERDDREINIOG
Ynys Isaf
Bettws
Nant Newydd
CORS GOCH
Red Wharf Bay
Red Wharf Bay Traeth-coch
Llanbedrgoch
Tyn Coed
Erddreiniog
Maen Eryr
Prysan
Hendre
Glan Gors
Gwenfro Isaf
Tan-y-graig
Pentraeth Forest
STANDING STONE
Llanddyfnan
Gwenfro Uchaf
Pentraeth
Bonc Fadog
Pencefn
Carrog Uchaf
Rhosmeirch
STONE SCIENCE
CORS BODEILIO
Tyn Beudy
Trefollwyn
Hendre Fm
Clegyrdy-bach
Talwrn
ORIEL YNYS MON
The Dingle
Clegyrdy-mawr
Afon Ceint
Tŷ-coch
Dyffryn
Rhoscefnhir
Pencraig
Gylched
Plas Penmynydd
Taihirion
Ceint
Ind Est
Ind Pk
Hirdre-faig
Penmynydd
Cefn-poeth
Nant
Twll-y-clawdd
Tyddyn
Castell
Cefn Du Isaf
Ty'n Buarth
Tyddyn Mawr
Rhyd-yr-arian
Bwlch-gwyn
Tyn Cae
PILI PALAS
Pentre Berw
Llanfairpwll-gwyngyll
LLANFAIRPWLL
Gaerwen
Ind Est
Bryn-y-fedwen
Brynhyfryd
Llanddaniel Fab
Chwilpin
Bus Pk
BRYN CELLI DDU BURIAL CHAMBER
Pont Crug
PLAS NEWYDD
Afon Menai
Glanyrafon
Ty'n-y-Coed
Bodwyr-isaf
Bodlew
Gwydryn Newydd
Dinam
BODOWYR BURIAL CHAMBER
Ysgubor Wen
Lew
Pont-Dic
Llanedwen
Bodrida
CAER LEB
Y Dolydd
Trefor
Hendrefor
Pen-y-garnedd
Rhôs
Wern Fm
Llanddona
Ffordd Deg
Carwad
Rhos Newydd
Pen-y-bryn
Bryn Cogail
Hafotty Covert
Llyn Bodgylched
Bodgylched
Llansadwrn
Coed Cefn
Cefn
ALLT GOCH FAWR
Hen Bentref Llandegfan
Llandegfan
BEAUMARIS ROAD
Menai Bridge (Porthaethwy)
MENAI SUSPENSION BRIDGE
ORIEL TEGFRYN
Bangor
Upper Bangor
Garth
Hirael
CATHEDRAL
Maesgeirchen
BANGOR
Glan Adda
Minffordd
Coed Mawr
Capel-y-graig
Vaynol Hall
Old Hall
Brithdir
Caerhun
Tyddyn-Hellyn
Glasinfryn
Pen-wen
Garth
Tyddyn
Niwbwrch
BANGOR SERVICES
Fedw Fawr
Mariandyrys
Penhwnllys
Bryn Ddol
Glan-yr-afon
Cefn
Llangoed
Bryn Celyn
Llanfaes
BEAUMARIS CASTLE
GAOL & COURTHOUSE
Beaumaris
Gallows Point
Trwyn y Penrhyn
Caim
PENMON PRIORY
Penmon
Outer Road
Lavan Sands
Puffin Island or Priestholm Ynys Seiriol
Fryars Road
CONWY BAY
BAE CONWY
PENRHYN CASTLE
Llandegai
Ind Est
Bryn
Tal-y-bont
Gatehouse
Marianywinllan
Pen-y-bryn
COCHWILLAN OLD HALL
Rhiw Goch
Coed Hywel
Halfway Br
Tregarth
FELLINHELI ROAD
Rachub
Llanllechid
Abergwyngregyn
Crymlyn
Glyn
Ffridd Ddu
Bronydd Isaf
Moel Wnion 580
Gyrn 542
Llefn
SNOWDONIA
NATIONAL PARK
PARC CENEDLAETHOL ERYRI
ABER FALLS
COEDYDD ABER
Moel Faban 408
Gyrn Wigau
Nant
Afon Anafon
Llyn Anafon
Llwytmor
Bera Mawr
758
Foel-Ganol 533
Gorddinog
Cammarnaint
Garreg Fawr 356
Nant-y-felin
Nant-y-pandy
Llanfairfechan
LLANFAIRFECHAN
Garizim
Penmaenan
Pen Bryn-du
Drosgl 621
Foel-Fras 942
Afon Ddu
A5025
A5108
B5110
B5109
B5108
B5420
A5
A55
A4080
B4419
A487
A4087
A545
A4244
B4547
B4409
7A
8A
15A
7
8
9
10
11
12
13
14
15

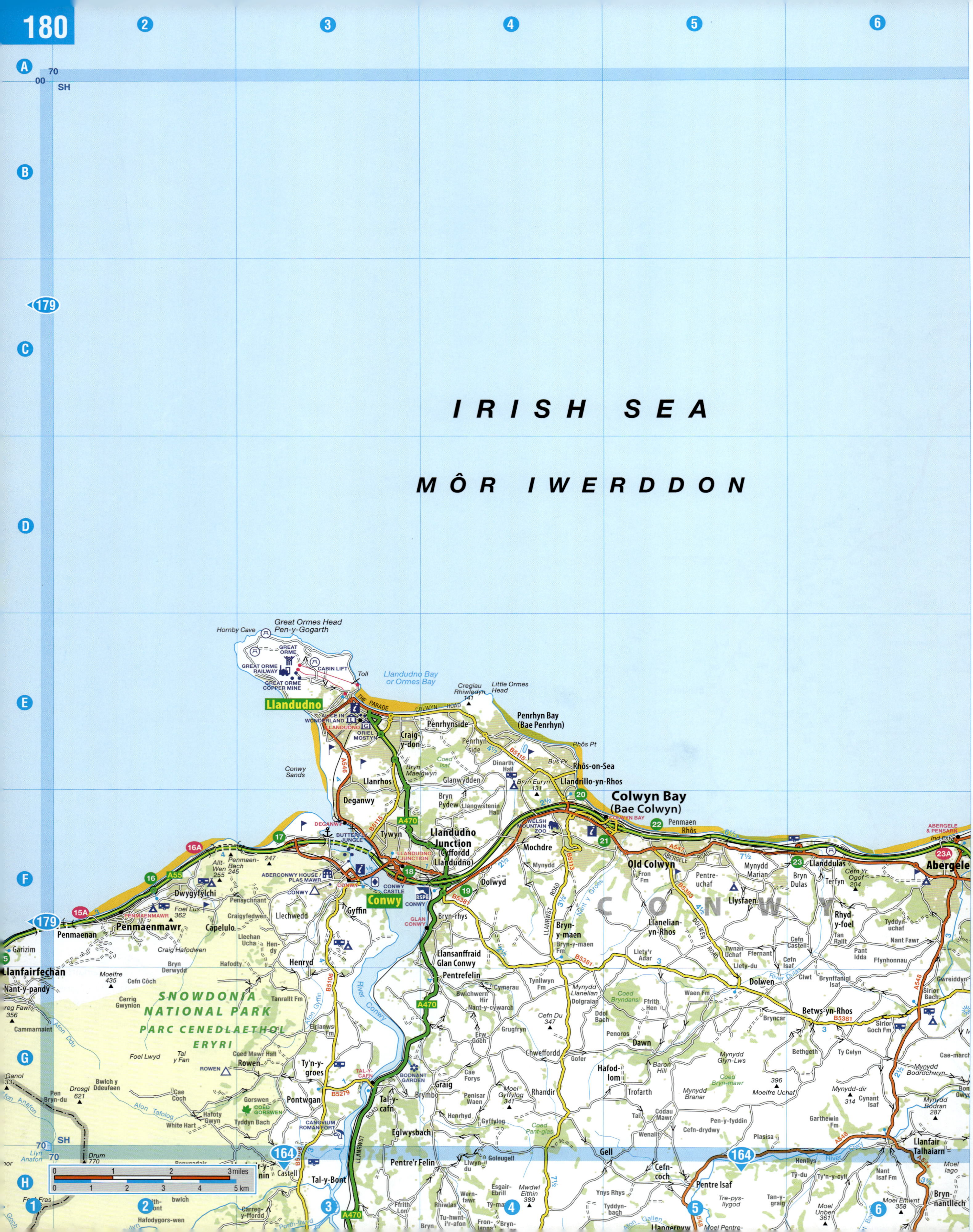

IRISH SEA
MÔR IWERDDON
Great Ormes Head
Pen-y-Gogarth
Hornby Cave
GREAT ORME
CABIN LIFT
GREAT ORME RAILWAY
GREAT ORME COPPER MINE
Toll
Llandudno Bay or Ormes Bay
Llandudno
THE PARADE
COLWYN ROAD
Cregiau Rhiwledyn 141
Little Ormes Head
Penrhyn Bay (Bae Penrhyn)
Rhôs Pt
Penrhynside
Craig-y-don
Bus Pk
Rhôs-on-Sea
Llandrillo-yn-Rhos
Conwy Sands
Llanrhos
Deganwy
Glanwydden
Bryn Pydew
Colwyn Bay (Bae Colwyn)
Penmaen Rhôs
Llandudno Junction (Cyffordd Llandudno)
Tywyn
Mochdre
Old Colwyn
Llanddulas
Abergele
Mynydd Marian
Llysfaen
Dolwyd
Conwy
CONWY CASTLE
CONWY
Gyffin
Llechwedd
Dwygyfylchi
Penmaenmawr
Penmaenan
Capelulo
Llanfairfechan
Nant-y-pandy
Garizim
SNOWDONIA NATIONAL PARK
PARC CENEDLAETHOL ERYRI
Henryd
Llansanffraid Glan Conwy
Pentrefelin
Bryn-y-maen
Llanelian-yn-Rhos
Dolwen
Betws-yn-Rhos
Rhyd-y-foel
Dawn
Hafod-lom
Trofarth
Rowen
Ty'n-y-groes
Pontwgan
Tal-y-cafn
Eglwysbach
Graig
Brymbo
Rhandir
Gell
Pentre Isaf
Llanfair Talhaiarn
Pentre'r Felin
Tal-y-Bont
Cefn-coch
River Conwy
A55
A470
A546
A547
A548
B5115
B5113
B5381
B5106
B5279
CONWY

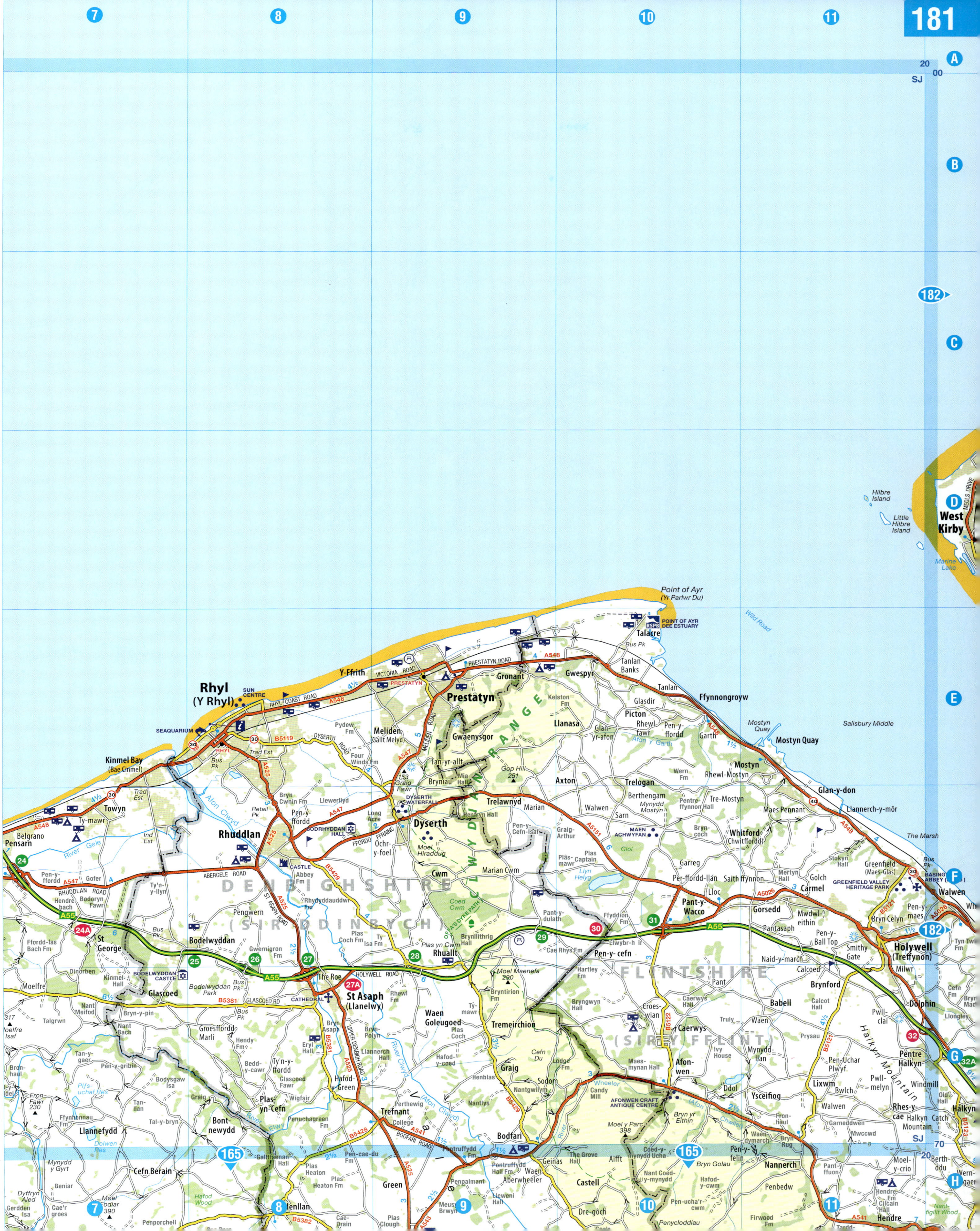
7
8
9
10
11
A
B
C
D
E
F
G
H
SJ
182
165
Hilbre Island
Little Hilbre Island
West Kirby
Marine Lake
Point of Ayr
(Yr Parlwr Du)
POINT OF AYR DEE ESTUARY
Talacre
Wild Road
Tanlan Banks
Tanlan
Gwespyr
Gronant
Ffynnongroyw
Salisbury Middle
Mostyn Quay
Picton
Glasdir
Llanasa
Kelston Fm
Rhyl
(Y Rhyl)
SUN CENTRE
SEAQUARIUM
Y-Ffrith
PRESTATYN ROAD
VICTORIA ROAD
RHYL COAST ROAD
Prestatyn
Meliden
(Gallt Melyd)
Gwaenysgor
Tan-yr-allt
Gop Hill
Axton
Trelogan
Berthengam
Mostyn
Rhewl-Mostyn
Garth
Kinmel Bay
(Bae Cinmel)
Towyn
Ty-mawr
Belgrano
Pensarn
Rhuddlan
Dyserth
DYSERTH WATERFALL
Trelawnyd
Marian
Walwen
Sarn
MAEN ACHWYFAN
Whitford
(Chwitffordd)
Glan-y-don
Llannerch-y-môr
Maes Pennant
The Marsh
Greenfield
(Maes-Glas)
GREENFIELD VALLEY HERITAGE PARK
BASINGWERK ABBEY
Walwen
Carmel
Golch
Garreg
Per-ffordd-llân
Saith ffynnon
Lloc
Pant-y-Wacco
Gorsedd
Pantasaph
Mwdwl-eithin
Pen-y-maes
Bryn Celyn
Holywell
(Treffynon)
Milwr
Dolphin
Pentre Halkyn
Halkyn
Halkyn Mountain
Rhes-y-cae
Windmill
Lixwm
Brynford
Calcoed
Babell
Naid-y-march
Smithy Gate
DENBIGHSHIRE
(SIR DDINBYCH)
FLINTSHIRE
(SIR Y FFLINT)
CLWYDIAN RANGE
OFFA'S DYKE PATH
Marian Cwm
Cwm
Moel Hiraddug
Ochr-y-foel
Bodelwyddan
BODELWYDDAN CASTLE
St George
Kinmel Hall
Moelfre
Glascoed
St Asaph
(Llanelwy)
CATHEDRAL
The Roe
Rhuallt
Waen
Goleugoed
Tremeirchion
Moel Maenefa
Graig
Sodom
Cefn Du
Caerwys
Afon-wen
AFONWEN CRAFT ANTIQUE CENTRE
Ysceifiog
Ddol
Pen-y-cefn
Llwybr-h
Cae Rhys Fm
Bodfari
Trefnant
Plas yn-Cefn
Bont-newydd
Llannefydd
Cefn Berain
Henllan
Green
Aberwheeler
Castell
Dre-goch
Aifft
Nannerch
Penbedw
Hendre
Moel-y-crio
Llyn Helyg
Glol
Coed Cwm
A55
A548
A547
A525
A5151
A541
A543
B5119
B5381
B5382
B5428
B5429
B5122
B5121
B5123
B5026
A5026

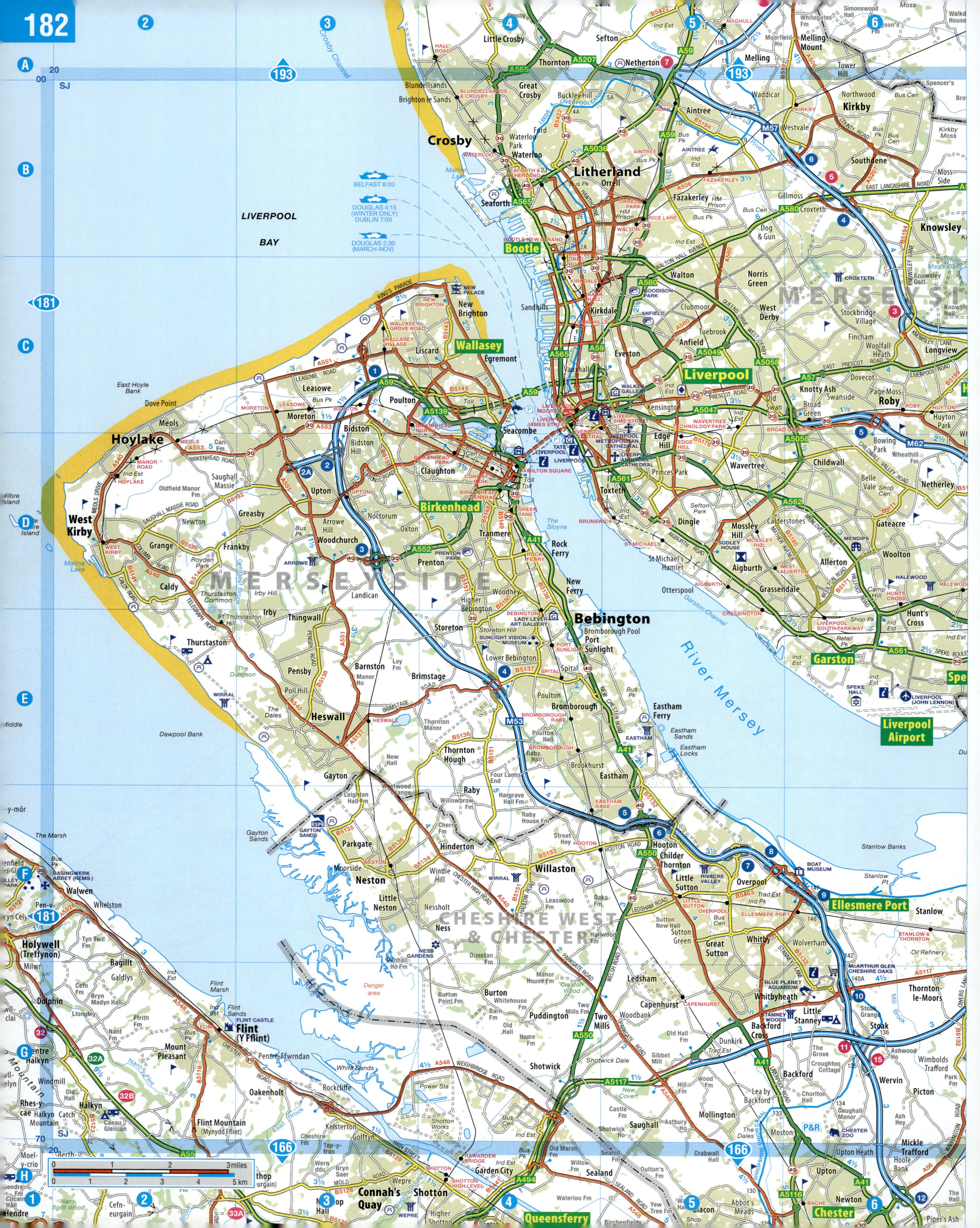

LIVERPOOL BAY
MERSEYSIDE
CHESHIRE WEST & CHESTER
River Mersey
Crosby
Litherland
Bootle
Wallasey
Liverpool
Birkenhead
Bebington
Hoylake
West Kirby
Heswall
Neston
Ellesmere Port
Garston
Liverpool Airport
Knowsley
Kirkby
Chester
Flint (Y Fflint)
Holywell (Treffynon)
Connah's Quay
Queensferry
Shotton
BELFAST 8:00
DOUGLAS 4:15 (WINTER ONLY)
DUBLIN 7:00
DOUGLAS 2:30 (MARCH-NOV)
M53
M57
M62
A41
A550
A5117
0 1 2 3 miles
0 1 2 3 4 5 km

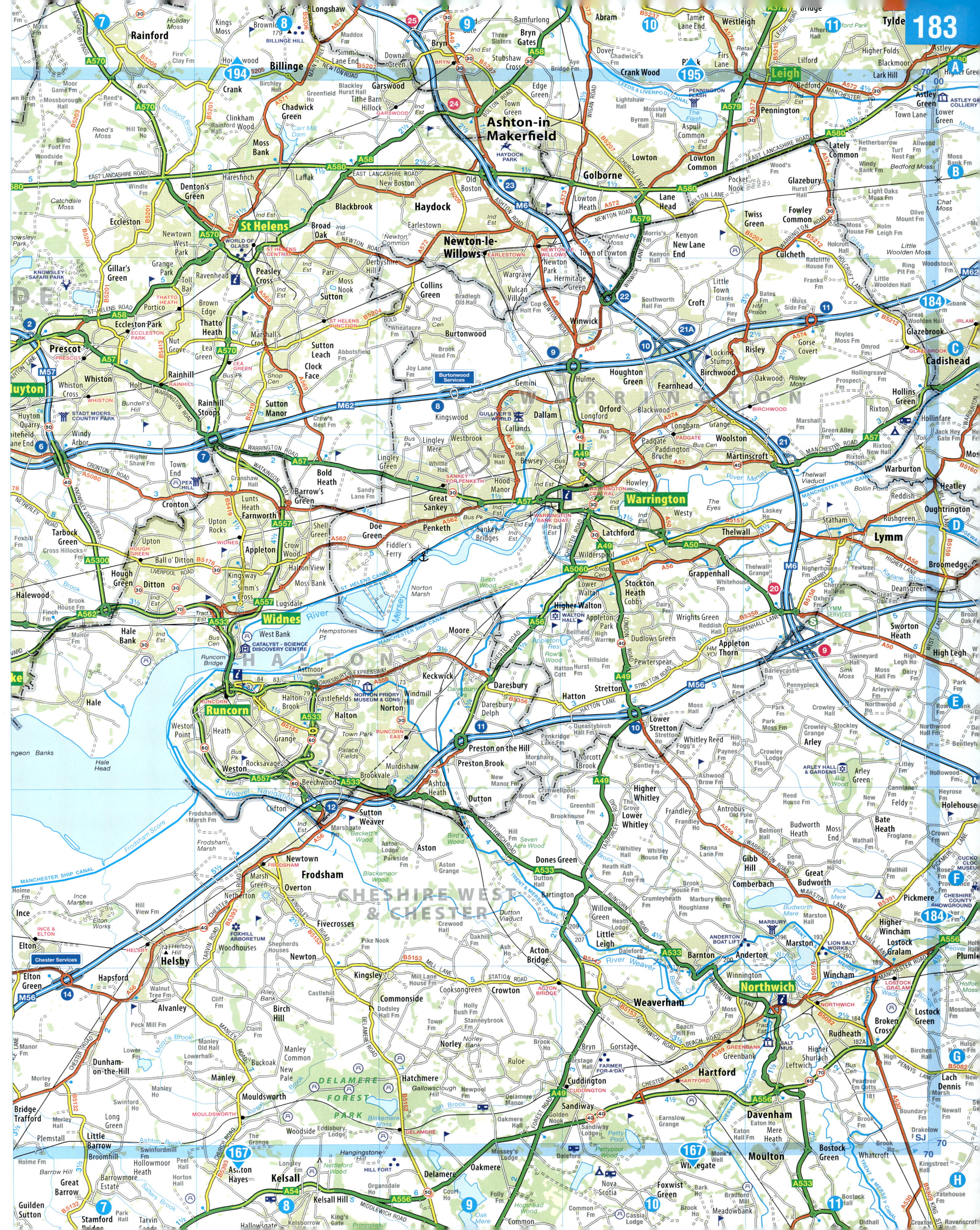
Rainford
Billinge
Ashton-in-Makerfield
Golborne
Leigh
Haydock
St Helens
Newton-le-Willows
Prescot
Huyton
Rainhill
Widnes
Warrington
Runcorn
Lymm
Frodsham
Helsby
Northwich
Weaverham
Hartford
Davenham
Moulton
Kelsall
Delamere
Culcheth
Birchwood
Thelwall
Grappenhall
Stockton Heath
Daresbury
Preston Brook
Sutton Weaver
Dutton
Little Leigh
Barnton
Anderton
Marston
Wincham
Rudheath
Cuddington
Sandiway
Mouldsworth
Manley
Alvanley
Kingsley
Crowton
Acton Bridge
Norley
Hale
Halewood
Cronton
Farnworth
Penketh
Great Sankey
Burtonwood
Winwick
Croft
Glazebury
Risley
Woolston
Latchford
Appleton Thorn
High Legh
Arley
Antrobus
Comberbach
Great Budworth
Pickmere
Lostock Gralam
Broken Cross
WARRINGTON
HALTON
CHESHIRE WEST & CHESTER
DELAMERE FOREST PARK
MANCHESTER SHIP CANAL
River Mersey
River Weaver

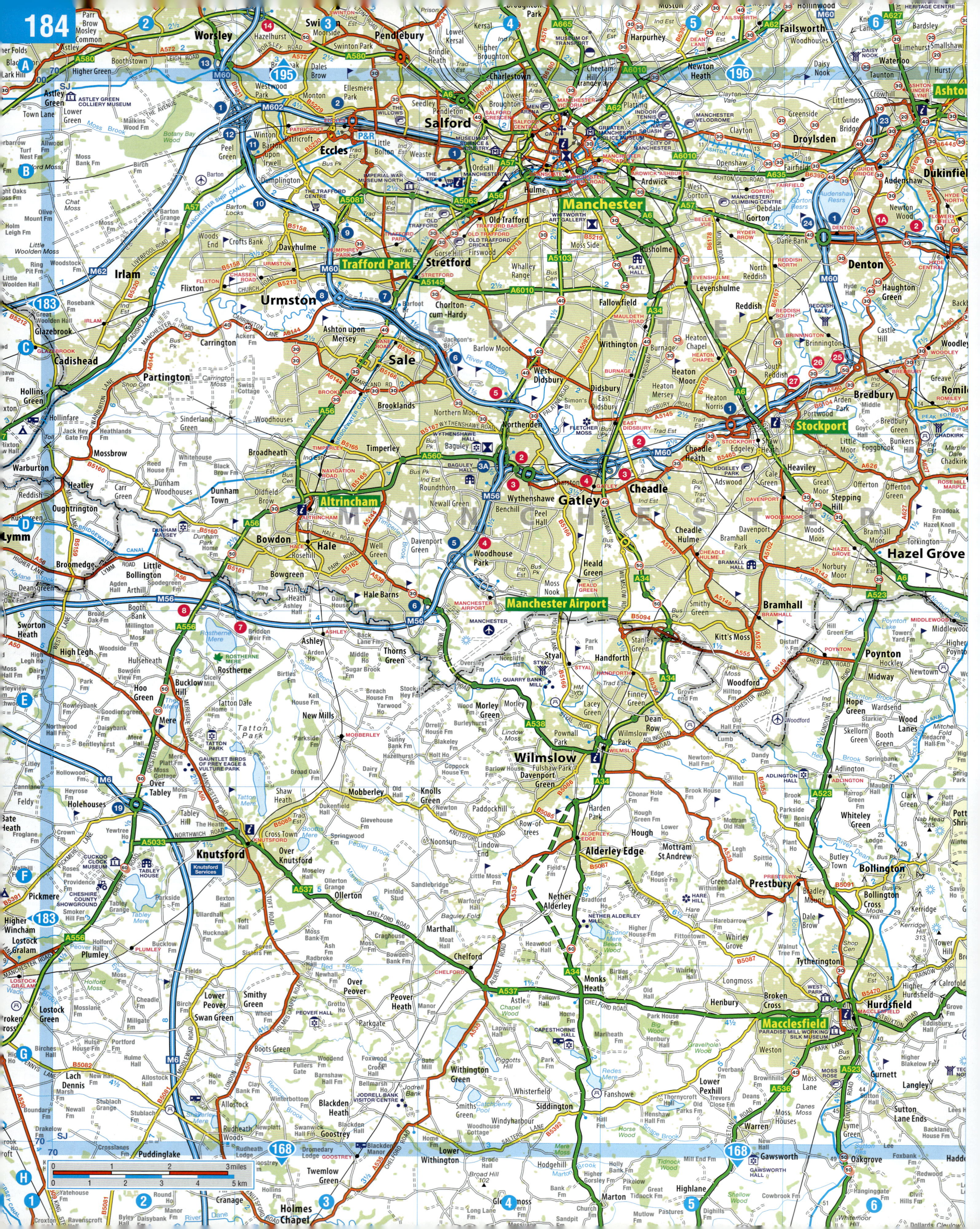
Worsley
Pendlebury
Swinton
Salford
Eccles
Manchester
Trafford Park
Old Trafford
Stretford
Failsworth
Droylsden
Ashton
Dukinfield
Denton
Irlam
Urmston
Davyhulme
Flixton
Chorlton-cum-Hardy
Fallowfield
Levenshulme
Reddish
Glazebrook
Cadishead
Partington
Carrington
Sale
Withington
Didsbury
West Didsbury
Brooklands
Northenden
Stockport
Bredbury
Timperley
Altrincham
Cheadle
Gatley
Heaton Moor
Hale
Bowdon
Wythenshawe
Warburton
Lymm
Broomedge
Heatley
Manchester Airport
Cheadle Hulme
Hazel Grove
Bramhall
Poynton
Styal
Handforth
Ashley
Rostherne
Mere
Mobberley
Wilmslow
Knutsford
Alderley Edge
Nether Alderley
Prestbury
Bollington
Macclesfield
Chelford
Plumley
Pickmere
Lostock Gralam
Over Peover
Lower Peover
Siddington
Henbury
Goostrey
Gawsworth
Lower Withington
Holmes Chapel
GREATER MANCHESTER
M60
M56
M6
M62
A34
A6
A538
A537
A556
195
196
183
168
0 1 2 3 miles
0 1 2 3 4 5 km

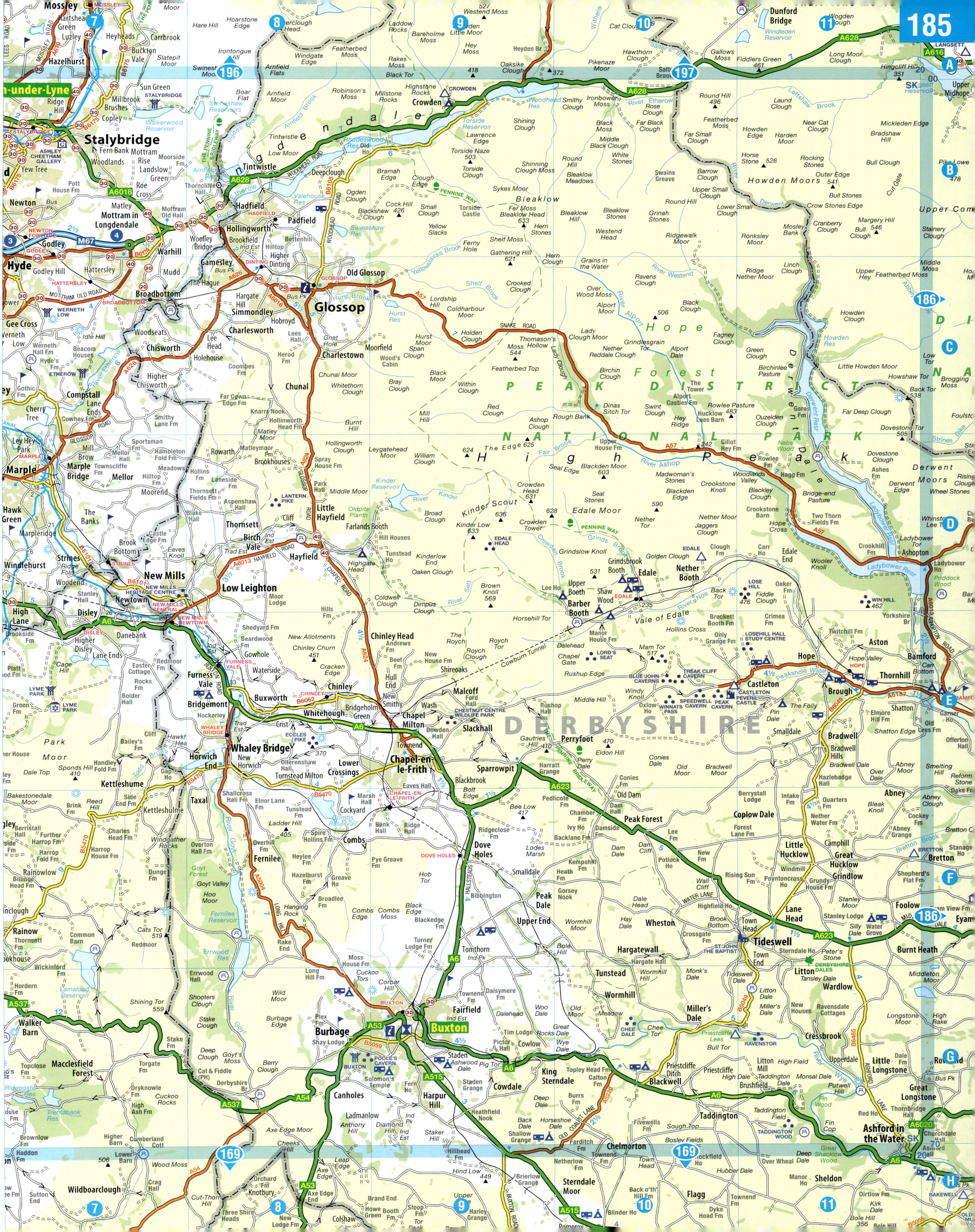

Mossley
Hazelhurst
Stalybridge
Dukinfield
Hyde
Godley
Newton
Mottram in Longdendale
Hattersley
Broadbottom
Gee Cross
Werneth Low
Compstall
Marple
Marple Bridge
Mellor
Strines
New Mills
Newtown
Disley
High Lane
Hadfield
Padfield
Tintwistle
Hollingworth
Gamesley
Dinting
Glossop
Old Glossop
Simmondley
Charlesworth
Chisworth
Charlestown
Chunal
Low Leighton
Hayfield
Little Hayfield
Birch Vale
Thornsett
Chinley
Chinley Head
Buxworth
Whaley Bridge
Bridgemont
Furness Vale
Horwich End
Chapel-en-le-Frith
Chapel Milton
Slackhall
Sparrowpit
Dove Holes
Peak Dale
Kettleshulme
Taxal
Fernilee
Combs
Burbage
Buxton
Fairfield
Harpur Hill
Cowdale
King Sterndale
Chelmorton
Sterndale Moor
Flagg
Taddington
Priestcliffe
Blackwell
Wormhill
Tunstead
Millers Dale
Tideswell
Litton
Wardlow
Cressbrook
Little Longstone
Great Longstone
Ashford in the Water
Sheldon
Peak Forest
Bradwell
Hope
Castleton
Edale
Barber Booth
Upper Booth
Nether Booth
Aston
Thornhill
Bamford
Brough
Hathersage
Little Hucklow
Great Hucklow
Grindlow
Foolow
Eyam
Wheston
Hargatewall
Bretton
Abney
Ladybower Reservoir
Derwent Reservoir
Howden Reservoir
Woodhead Reservoir
Torside Reservoir
Rhodeswood Reservoir
Valehouse Reservoir
Bottoms Reservoir
Longdendale
Crowden
Kinder Scout
Kinder Reservoir
Edale Moor
Bleaklow
Howden Moors
Vale of Edale
Mam Tor
Lose Hill
Win Hill
PEAK DISTRICT NATIONAL PARK
DERBYSHIRE
High Peak
Hope Forest
Derwent Dale
Macclesfield Forest
Wildboarclough
Goyt Valley
Errwood Reservoir
Fernilee Reservoir
Combs Reservoir
Speedwell Cavern
Peak Cavern
Treak Cliff Cavern
Blue John Cavern
Peveril Castle
Poole's Cavern
Winnats Pass
Snake Road
Cowburn Tunnel
A57
A628
A624
A6
A623
A53
A54
A537
A515
A6187
A6013
A6016
A6018
A560
A626
A6101
B6062
B5470
M67
196
197
186
169

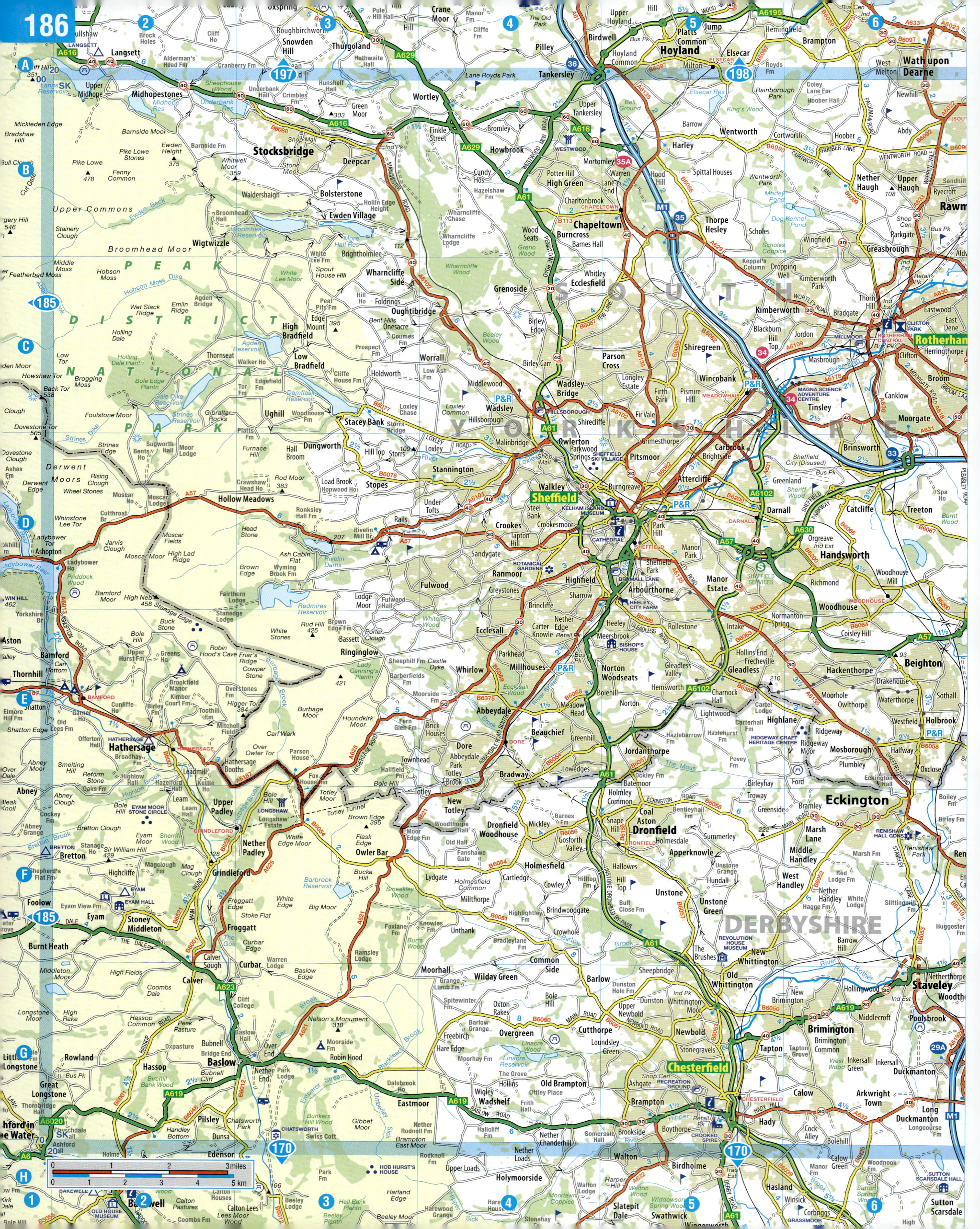

Langsett
Midhopestones
Stocksbridge
Deepcar
Bolsterstone
Ewden Village
Wortley
Thurgoland
Tankersley
Hoyland
Elsecar
Wath upon Dearne
Brampton
Wentworth
Chapeltown
High Green
Grenoside
Ecclesfield
Oughtibridge
Wharncliffe Side
Worrall
High Bradfield
Low Bradfield
Dungworth
Stannington
Wadsley Bridge
Kimberworth
Rotherham
Tinsley
Brinsworth
Catcliffe
Treeton
Darnall
Handsworth
Woodhouse
Beighton
Sheffield
Crookes
Walkley
Fulwood
Ecclesall
Millhouses
Beauchief
Dore
Totley
Bradway
Norton
Hackenthorpe
Mosborough
Halfway
Eckington
Killamarsh
Dronfield
Coal Aston
Unstone
Apperknowle
Marsh Lane
Ridgeway
Holmesfield
Barlow
Chesterfield
Old Whittington
New Whittington
Staveley
Brimington
Tapton
Calow
Duckmanton
Hady
Brampton
Walton
Birdholme
Hasland
Holymoorside
Wadshelf
Overgreen
Baslow
Calver
Curbar
Froggatt
Grindleford
Nether Padley
Upper Padley
Hathersage
Bamford
Thornhill
Ashopton
Eyam
Stoney Middleton
Foolow
Great Longstone
Hassop
Rowland
Pilsley
Edensor
Beeley
Bakewell
Owler Bar
PEAK DISTRICT NATIONAL PARK
SOUTH YORKSHIRE
DERBYSHIRE
Broomhead Moor
Upper Commons
Hollow Meadows
Stanage Edge
Big Moor
M1
A57
A61
A616
A629
A6102
A625
A623
A619
A6
197
198
185
170
0 1 2 3 miles
0 1 2 3 4 5 km

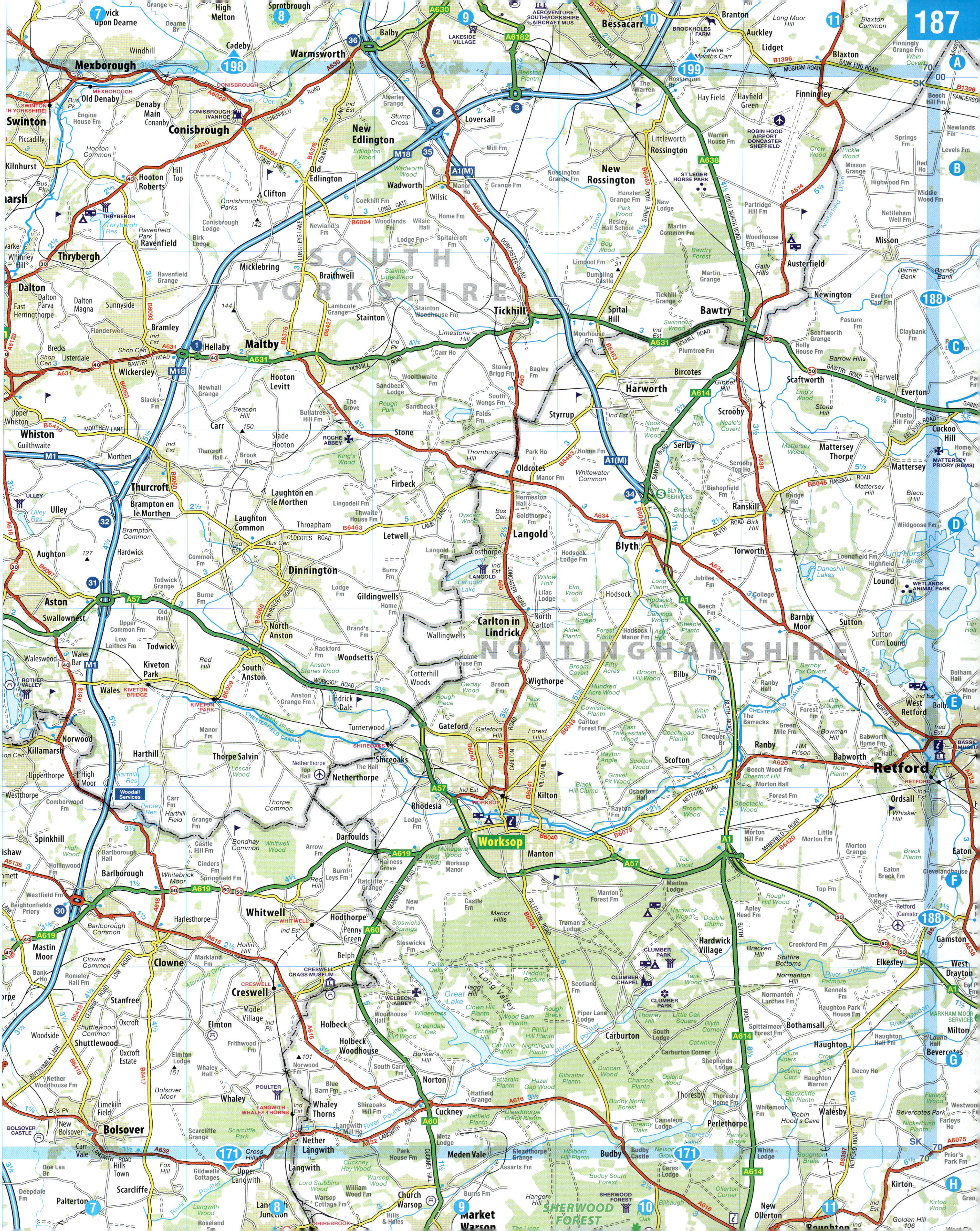
Mexborough
Conisbrough
Swinton
Old Denaby
Denaby Main
Conanby
Kilnhurst
Hooton Roberts
Old Edlington
New Edlington
Edlington Wood
Warmsworth
Balby
Loversall
Wadworth
Wilsic
High Melton
Cadeby
Sprotbrough
Clifton
Thrybergh
Ravenfield
Dalton
Dalton Parva
Dalton Magna
East Herringthorpe
Sunnyside
Bramley
Flanderwell
Wickersley
Hellaby
Maltby
Micklebring
Braithwell
Stainton
Tickhill
Spital Hill
Bessacarr
Branton
Auckley
Lidget
Blaxton
Finningley
Rossington
New Rossington
Littleworth
Austerfield
Misson
Newington
Bawtry
Bircotes
Harworth
Scaftworth
Everton
Styrrup
Serlby
Scrooby
Mattersey
Mattersey Thorpe
Ranskill
Torworth
Blyth
Hodsock
Barnby Moor
Sutton
Sutton Cum Lound
Lound
Bilby
Ranby
Babworth
Retford
Ordsall
Eaton
Gamston
West Drayton
Milton
Elkesley
Bevercotes
Haughton
Walesby
Perlethorpe
Thoresby
Budby
Carburton
Clumber Park
Hardwick Village
Manton
Worksop
Kilton
Shireoaks
Rhodesia
Gateford
Wigthorpe
Carlton in Lindrick
North Carlton
Langold
Oldcotes
Letwell
Firbeck
Stone
Woodsetts
Gildingwells
Dinnington
Throapham
Laughton en le Morthen
Laughton Common
North Anston
South Anston
Todwick
Kiveton Park
Wales
Harthill
Thorpe Salvin
Netherthorpe
Turnerwood
Lindrick Dale
Whitwell
Barlborough
Clowne
Creswell
Elmton
Holbeck
Norton
Cuckney
Nether Langwith
Langwith
Meden Vale
Market Warsop
Church Warsop
Whaley Thorns
Bolsover
Palterton
Scarcliffe
Stanfree
Shuttlewood
Oxcroft
Mastin Moor
Killamarsh
Norwood
Aston
Swallownest
Aughton
Ulley
Thurcroft
Brampton en le Morthen
Whiston
Morthen
Carr
Hooton Levitt
Slade Hooton
SOUTH YORKSHIRE
NOTTINGHAMSHIRE
SHERWOOD FOREST
M18
M1
A1(M)
A1
A57
A60
A614
A631
A634
A638
A619
A616
ROCHE ABBEY
WELBECK ABBEY
CRESWELL CRAGS MUSEUM
CLUMBER CHAPEL
ROBIN HOOD AIRPORT DONCASTER SHEFFIELD
ST LEGER HORSE PARK
MATTERSEY PRIORY (REMS)
WETLANDS ANIMAL PARK
BROCKHOLES FARM
LAKESIDE VILLAGE
AEROVENTURE SOUTH YORKSHIRE AIRCRAFT MUS
Woodall Services
BLYTH SERVICES
Great Lake
Langold Lake
Long Valley

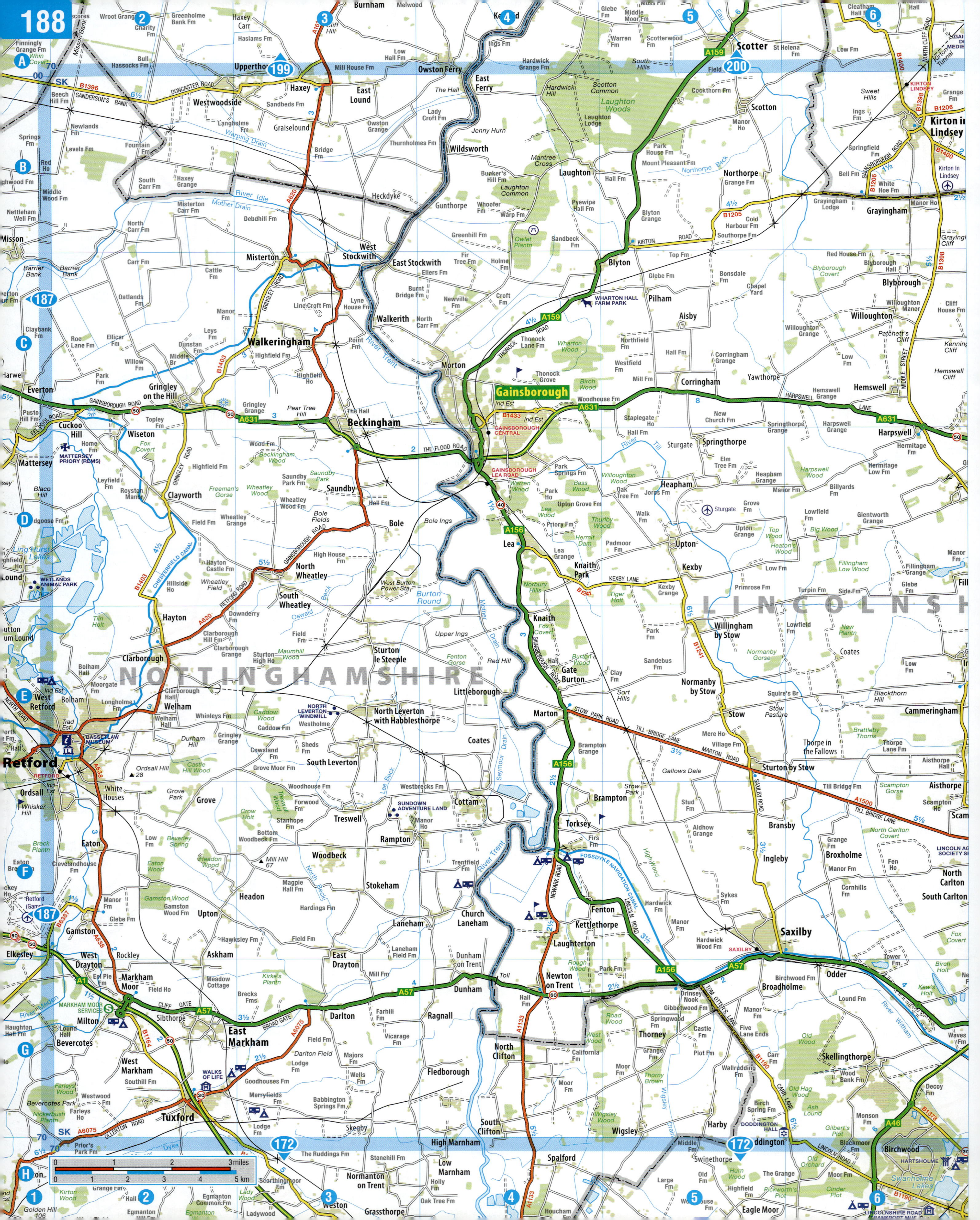
Scotter
Kirton in Lindsey
Haxey
Upperthorpe
Westwoodside
East Lound
Owston Ferry
East Ferry
Wildsworth
Graiselound
Laughton
Scotton
Northorpe
Grayingham
Blyton
Misterton
West Stockwith
East Stockwith
Walkeringham
Walkerith
Morton
Gainsborough
Corringham
Hemswell
Harpswell
Pilham
Aisby
Willoughton
Blyborough
Everton
Gringley on the Hill
Beckingham
Wiseton
Cuckoo Hill
Mattersey
Clayworth
Saundby
Bole
Lea
Knaith Park
Kexby
Upton
Heapham
Springthorpe
Sturgate
North Wheatley
South Wheatley
Hayton
Clarborough
Welham
Retford
West Retford
Bolham
Ordsall
Knaith
Gate Burton
Marton
Littleborough
Sturton le Steeple
North Leverton with Habblesthorpe
South Leverton
Coates
Willingham by Stow
Normanby by Stow
Stow
Cammeringham
Sturton by Stow
Thorpe in the Fallows
Aisthorpe
Brampton
Torksey
Cottam
Treswell
Rampton
Grove
Eaton
Woodbeck
Headon
Upton
Stokeham
Laneham
Church Laneham
Fenton
Kettlethorpe
Laughterton
Newton on Trent
Saxilby
Ingleby
Bransby
Broxholme
North Carlton
South Carlton
Gamston
Elkesley
West Drayton
Askham
East Drayton
Dunham
Markham Moor
Milton
Darlton
Ragnall
East Markham
Bevercotes
West Markham
Tuxford
Fledborough
North Clifton
South Clifton
Thorney
Wigsley
Harby
Broadholme
Odder
Skellingthorpe
Birchwood
High Marnham
Low Marnham
Normanton on Trent
Spalford
Skegby
Grassthorpe
Weston
Doddington
NOTTINGHAMSHIRE
LINCOLNSHIRE
River Trent
River Idle
Chesterfield Canal
Fossdyke Navigation Canal
A159
A631
A156
A620
A57
A1
A638
A1133
A1500
B1403
B1241
B1205
B1400
B1396
199
200
187
172
0 1 2 3 miles
0 1 2 3 4 5 km

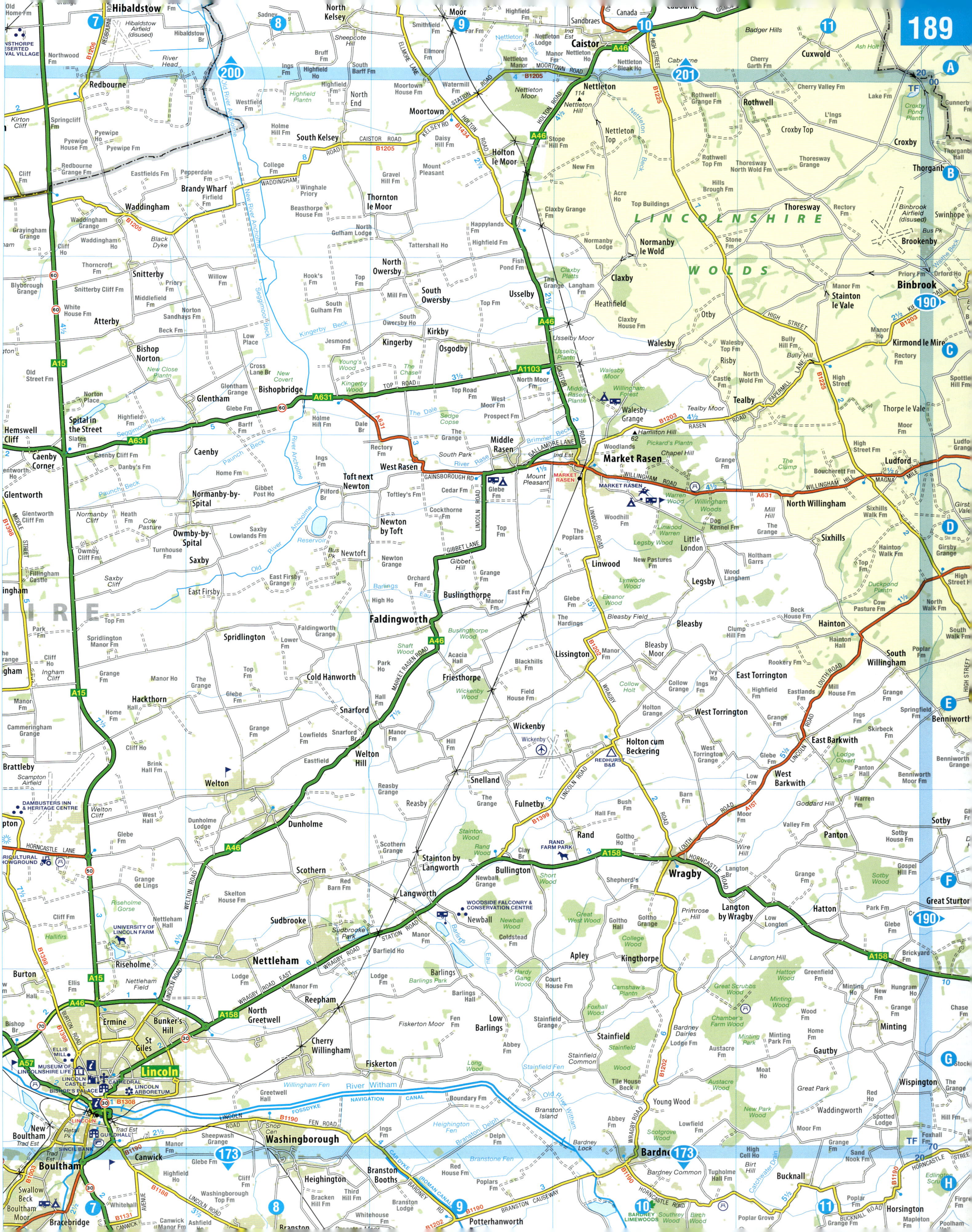
Hibaldstow
North Kelsey
Moor
Caistor
Nettleton
Cuxwold
Rothwell
Redbourne
Moortown
South Kelsey
Holton le Moor
Croxby
Thorganby
Brandy Wharf
Waddingham
Thornton le Moor
LINCOLNSHIRE
Thoresway
Swinhope
Normanby le Wold
Brookenby
Snitterby
North Owersby
Claxby
WOLDS
Binbrook
South Owersby
Usselby
Stainton le Vale
Atterby
Otby
Kirkby
Kingerby
Osgodby
Walesby
Kirmond le Mire
Bishop Norton
Bishopbridge
Glentham
Tealby
Spital in the Street
Middle Rasen
Walesby Grange
Thorpe le Vale
Hemswell Cliff
Caenby Corner
Caenby
West Rasen
Market Rasen
Ludford
Toft next Newton
Glentworth
Normanby-by-Spital
Owmby-by-Spital
North Willingham
Newton by Toft
Sixhills
Saxby
Newtoft
Little London
Linwood
Legsby
Buslingthorpe
Faldingworth
Spridlington
Bleasby
Hainton
Lissington
South Willingham
Cold Hanworth
Friesthorpe
Hackthorn
East Torrington
West Torrington
Snarford
Benniworth
Wickenby
Holton cum Beckering
East Barkwith
Welton Hill
Brattleby
Snelland
West Barkwith
Welton
Fulnetby
Dunholme
Sotby
Rand
Panton
Stainton by Langworth
Scothern
Bullington
Wragby
Langworth
Langton by Wragby
Hatton
Great Sturton
Sudbrooke
Riseholme
Nettleham
Apley
Kingthorpe
Burton
Barlings
Reepham
Low Barlings
Minting
North Greetwell
Ermine
Bunker's Hill
Stainfield
St Giles
Cherry Willingham
Gautby
Lincoln
Fiskerton
Wispington
River Witham
Waddingworth
New Boultham
Washingborough
Young Wood
Bardney
Boultham
Canwick
Branston Booths
Heighington
Bucknall
Horsington
Bracebridge
Potterhanworth
Branston

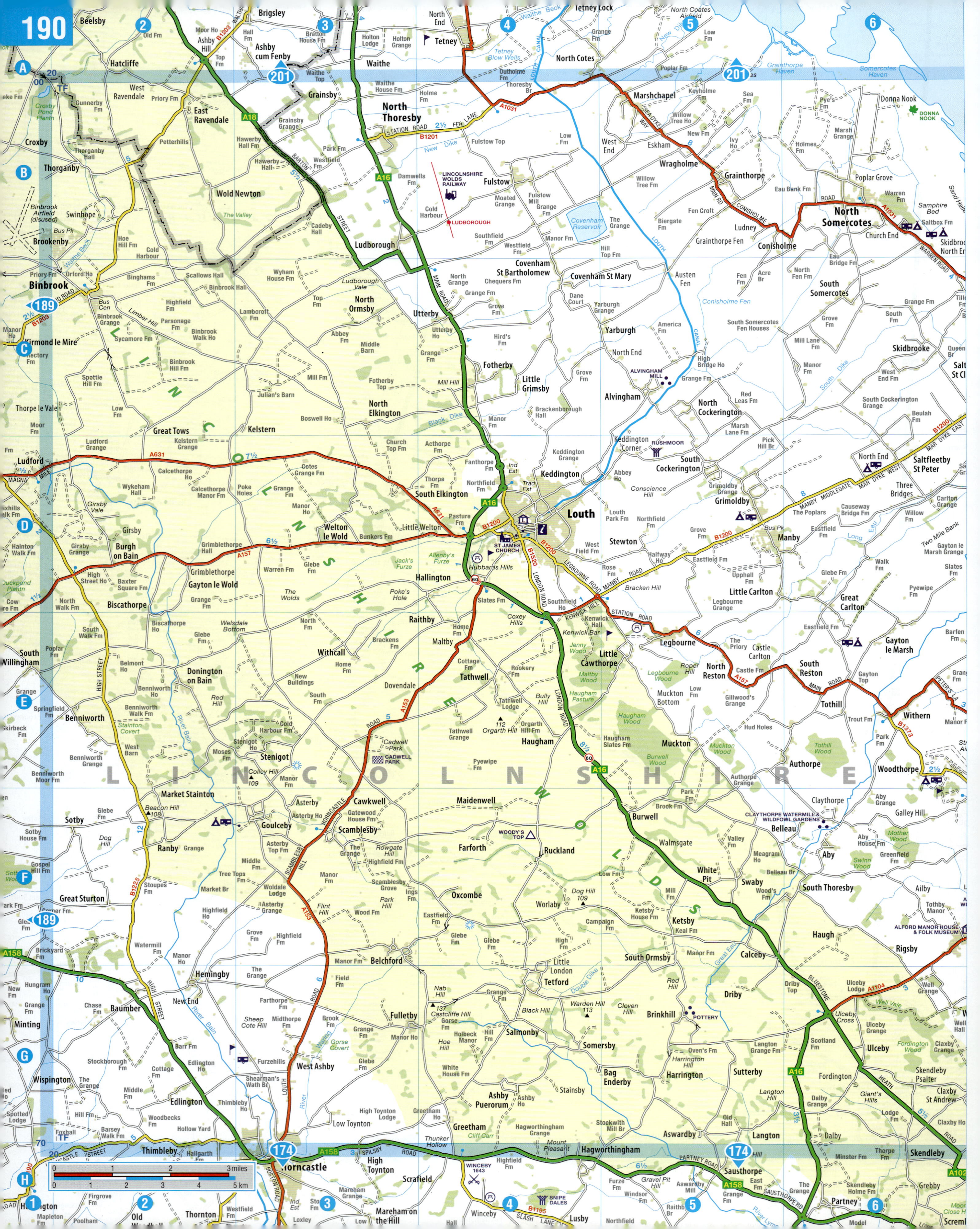
Beelsby
Brigsley
Tetney Lock
North Coates Airfield
Ashby Hill
Ashby cum Fenby
North End
Tetney
Holton Lodge
Holton Grange
North Cotes
Hatcliffe
Waithe
Marshchapel
Donna Nook
DONNA NOOK
West Ravendale
East Ravendale
Grainsby
North Thoresby
Croxby
Thorganby
Wold Newton
Fulstow
LINCOLNSHIRE WOLDS RAILWAY
LUDBOROUGH
Covenham Reservoir
Eskham
Wragholme
Grainthorpe
Grainthorpe Haven
Somercotes Haven
North Somercotes
Binbrook Airfield (disused)
Swinhope
Brookenby
Binbrook
Ludborough
Covenham St Bartholomew
Covenham St Mary
Grainthorpe Fen
Conisholme
Ludney
Church End
Skidbrooke North End
North Ormsby
Utterby
Yarburgh
South Somercotes
Kirmond le Mire
Fotherby
Little Grimsby
Alvingham
ALVINGHAM MILL
North Cockerington
Skidbrooke
North Elkington
Thorpe le Vale
Great Tows
Kelstern
Ludford
Keddington
Keddington Corner
RUSHMOOR
South Cockerington
Saltfleetby St Peter
South Elkington
Louth
Grimoldby
Three Bridges
Welton le Wold
Little Welton
ST JAMES CHURCH
Stewton
Manby
Burgh on Bain
Gayton le Wold
Hallington
Biscathorpe
Little Carlton
Great Carlton
Raithby
Legbourne
Gayton le Marsh
Withcall
Maltby
Little Cawthorpe
North Reston
South Reston
South Willingham
Donington on Bain
Tathwell
Dovendale
Tothill
Withern
Benniworth
Haugham
Mucknton
Mucknton Wood
Authorpe
Stenigot
CADWELL PARK
Woodthorpe
LINCOLNSHIRE
WOLDS
Market Stainton
Cawkwell
Maidenwell
Burwell
Claythorpe
CLAYTHORPE WATERMILL & WILDFOWL GARDENS
Belleau
Sotby
Goulceby
Asterby
Scamblesby
Farforth
Ruckland
Walmsgate
Aby
Ranby
White Pit
Swaby
South Thoresby
Great Sturton
Oxcombe
Worlaby
Ketsby
Haugh
Rigsby
ALFORD MANOR HOUSE & FOLK MUSEUM
Hemingby
Belchford
Tetford
South Ormsby
Calceby
Driby
Baumber
Fulletby
Salmonby
Brinkhill
POTTERY
Ulceby Cross
Minting
Somersby
Ulceby
Wispington
West Ashby
Bag Enderby
Harrington
Sutterby
Fordington
Skendleby Psalter
Claxby St Andrew
Edlington
Ashby Puerorum
Greetham
Aswardby
Langton
Thimbleby
Horncastle
High Toynton
Hagworthingham
Sausthorpe
Skendleby
Scrafield
WINCEBY 1643
SNIPE DALES
Partney
Old
Thornton
Mareham on the Hill
Winceby
Lusby
Grebby
A18
A16
A1031
A631
A157
A153
A158
A1104
B1200
B1203
B1201
B1225
B1520
B1373
B1195
189
201
174
60
0 1 2 3 miles
0 1 2 3 4 5 km

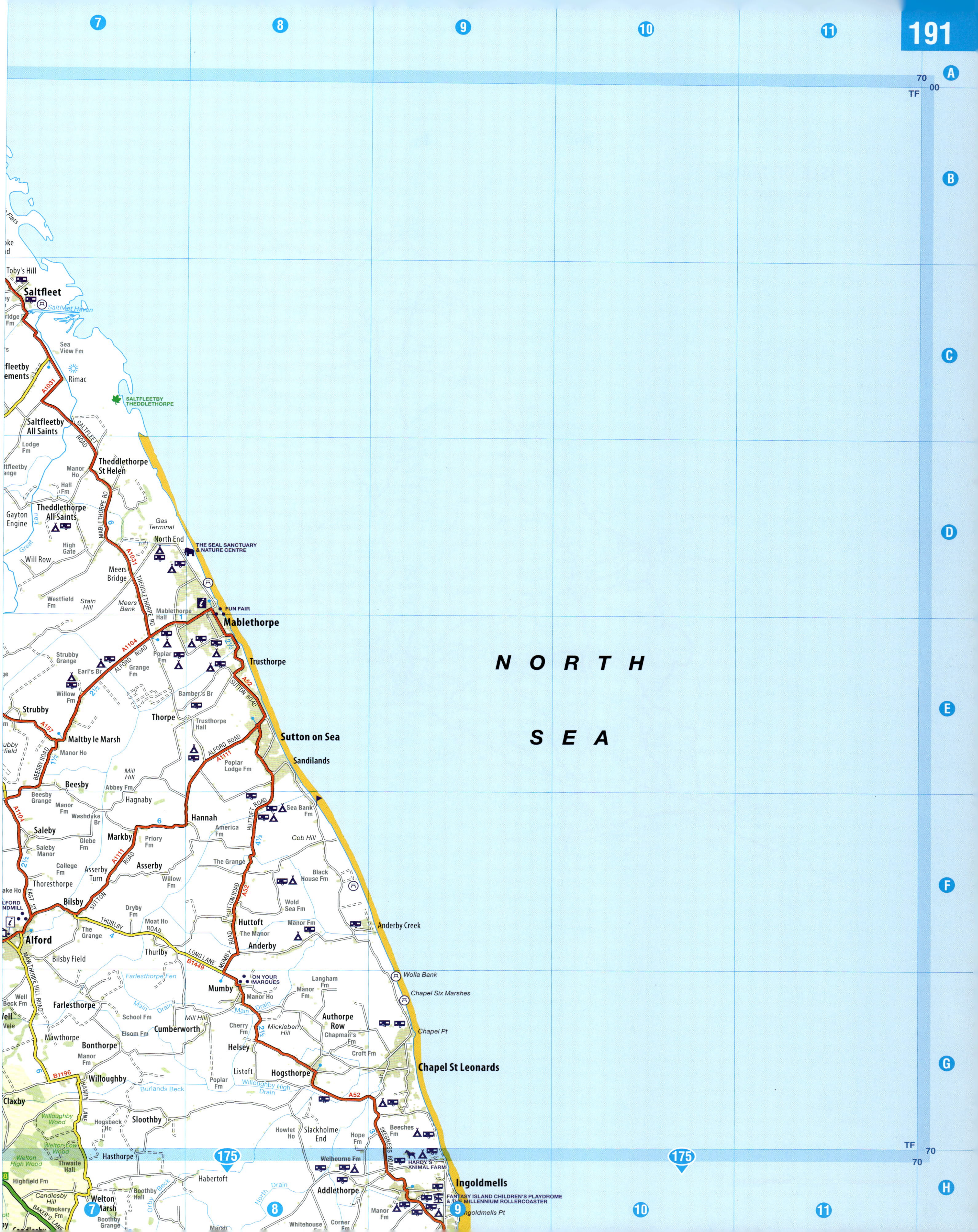
NORTH SEA
Toby's Hill
Saltfleet
Saltfleet Haven
Sea View Fm
Rimac
SALTFLEETBY THEDDLETHORPE
Saltfleetby All Saints
Lodge Fm
SALTFLEET ROAD
Theddlethorpe St Helen
Manor Ho
Hall Fm
Theddlethorpe All Saints
Gayton Engine
MABLETHORPE RD
Gas Terminal
North End
THE SEAL SANCTUARY & NATURE CENTRE
High Gate
Will Row
Meers Bridge
Westfield Fm
Stain Hill
Meers Bank
THEDDLETHORPE RD
Mablethorpe Hall
FUN FAIR
Mablethorpe
Strubby Grange
ALFORD ROAD
Poplar Fm
Trusthorpe
Earl's Br
Grange Fm
Willow Fm
Bamber's Br
SUTTON ROAD
Strubby
Thorpe
Trusthorpe Hall
Maltby le Marsh
Sutton on Sea
Manor Ho
ALFORD ROAD
Sandilands
BEESBY ROAD
Poplar Lodge Fm
Mill Hill
Beesby
Abbey Fm
Beesby Grange
Hagnaby
Manor Fm
Washdyke Br
Sea Bank Fm
Hannah
HUTTOFT ROAD
Saleby
America Fm
Cob Hill
Glebe Fm
Markby
Priory Fm
Saleby Manor
The Grange
College Fm
Asserby Turn
Asserby
Black House Fm
Thoresthorpe
Willow Fm
EAST ST
Bilsby
SUTTON ROAD
Dryby Fm
Wold Sea Fm
Alford
The Grange
THURLBY
Moat Ho ROAD
Huttoft
Manor Fm
Anderby Creek
The Manor
Thurlby
LONG LANE
MUMBY ROAD
Anderby
Bilsby Field
MAWTHORPE HILL ROAD
Farlesthorpe Fen
ON YOUR MARQUES
Wolla Bank
Mumby
Langham Fm
Manor Fm
Chapel Six Marshes
Well Beck Fm
Farlesthorpe
Main Drain
Manor Ho
School Fm
Mill Hill
Authorpe Row
Cherry Fm
Mickleberry Hill
Chapman's Fm
Chapel Pt
Elsom Fm
Cumberworth
Mawthorpe
Bonthorpe
Helsey
Croft Fm
Manor Fm
Chapel St Leonards
Listoft
Hogsthorpe
Willoughby
Poplar Fm
Willoughby High Drain
Burlands Beck
HANBY LANE
Claxby
Willoughby Wood
Sloothby
Hogsbeck Ho
Howlet Ho
Slackholme End
Hope Fm
Beeches Fm
SKEGNESS ROAD
Welton Low Wood
Welton High Wood
Thwaite Hall
Hasthorpe
Welbourne Fm
HARDY'S ANIMAL FARM
Highfield Fm
Habertoft
Ingoldmells
Candlesby Hill
Rookery Fm
Welton le Marsh
Boothby Hall
Addlethorpe
FANTASY ISLAND CHILDREN'S PLAYDROME & THE MILLENNIUM ROLLERCOASTER
Ingoldmells Pt
Boothby Grange
Manor Fm
Corner Fm
Whitehouse
Marsh
BAKER'S LANE
A1031
A1104
A157
A52
A1111
B1449
B1196
175
TF

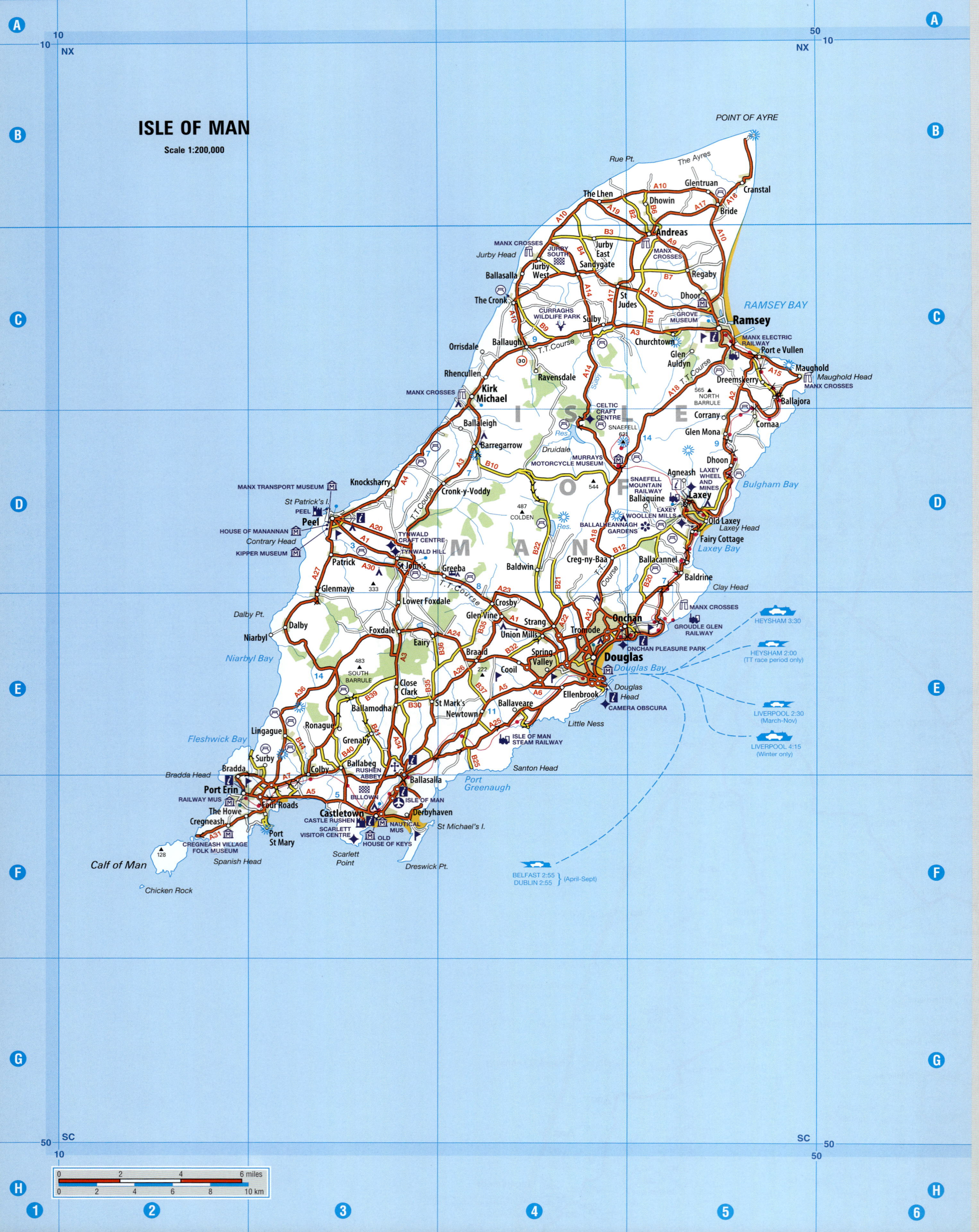

ISLE OF MAN
Scale 1:200,000
POINT OF AYRE
Rue Pt.
The Ayres
Glentruan
Cranstal
The Lhen
Dhowin
Bride
Andreas
Jurby East
Jurby West
Jurby Head
MANX CROSSES
JURBY SOUTH
Sandygate
Regaby
Ballasalla
Dhoor
St Judes
The Cronk
CURRAGHS WILDLIFE PARK
GROVE MUSEUM
RAMSEY BAY
Ramsey
Sulby
Churchtown
MANX ELECTRIC RAILWAY
Port e Vullen
Orrisdale
Ballaugh
T.T.Course
Glen Auldyn
Maughold
Maughold Head
Rhencullen
Ravensdale
Dreemskerry
Kirk Michael
565 NORTH BARRULE
Ballajora
Ballaleigh
ISLE OF MAN
CELTIC CRAFT CENTRE
SNAEFELL
Corrany
Cornaa
Glen Mona
Barregarrow
Druidale
Dhoon
MURRAYS MOTORCYCLE MUSEUM
Agneash
LAXEY WHEEL AND MINES
Bulgham Bay
Knocksharry
SNAEFELL MOUNTAIN RAILWAY
Laxey
MANX TRANSPORT MUSEUM
Cronk-y-Voddy
Ballaquine
St Patrick's I.
PEEL
Peel
487 COLDEN
LAXEY WOOLLEN MILLS
Old Laxey
Laxey Head
HOUSE OF MANANNAN
Contrary Head
KIPPER MUSEUM
TYNWALD CRAFT CENTRE
TYNWALD HILL
BALLALHEANNAGH GARDENS
Fairy Cottage
Laxey Bay
Patrick
St John's
Greeba
Baldwin
Creg-ny-Baa
Ballacannel
Glenmaye
333
Baldrine
Clay Head
Lower Foxdale
Crosby
MANX CROSSES
Dalby Pt.
Dalby
Glen Vine
Strang
Onchan
HEYSHAM 3:30
GROUDLE GLEN RAILWAY
Niarbyl
Foxdale
Union Mills
Tromode
ONCHAN PLEASURE PARK
Eairy
HEYSHAM 2:00 (TT race period only)
Niarbyl Bay
Braaid
Spring Valley
Douglas
483 SOUTH BARRULE
222
Cooil
Douglas Bay
Close Clark
Ellenbrook
Douglas Head
CAMERA OBSCURA
St Mark's
Ballaveare
LIVERPOOL 2:30 (March-Nov)
Ballamodha
Newtown
Little Ness
Lingague
Ronague
ISLE OF MAN STEAM RAILWAY
LIVERPOOL 4:15 (Winter only)
Fleshwick Bay
Grenaby
Surby
Ballabeg
RUSHEN ABBEY
Santon Head
Bradda Head
Bradda
Colby
Ballasalla
Port Greenaugh
Port Erin
BILLOWN
ISLE OF MAN
RAILWAY MUS
Four Roads
The Howe
Castletown
Derbyhaven
Cregneash
CASTLE RUSHEN
NAUTICAL MUS
St Michael's I.
SCARLETT VISITOR CENTRE
OLD HOUSE OF KEYS
CREGNEASH VILLAGE FOLK MUSEUM
Port St Mary
Scarlett Point
128
Calf of Man
Spanish Head
Dreswick Pt.
BELFAST 2:55
DUBLIN 2:55
(April-Sept)
Chicken Rock
NX
SC
0 2 4 6 miles
0 2 4 6 8 10 km

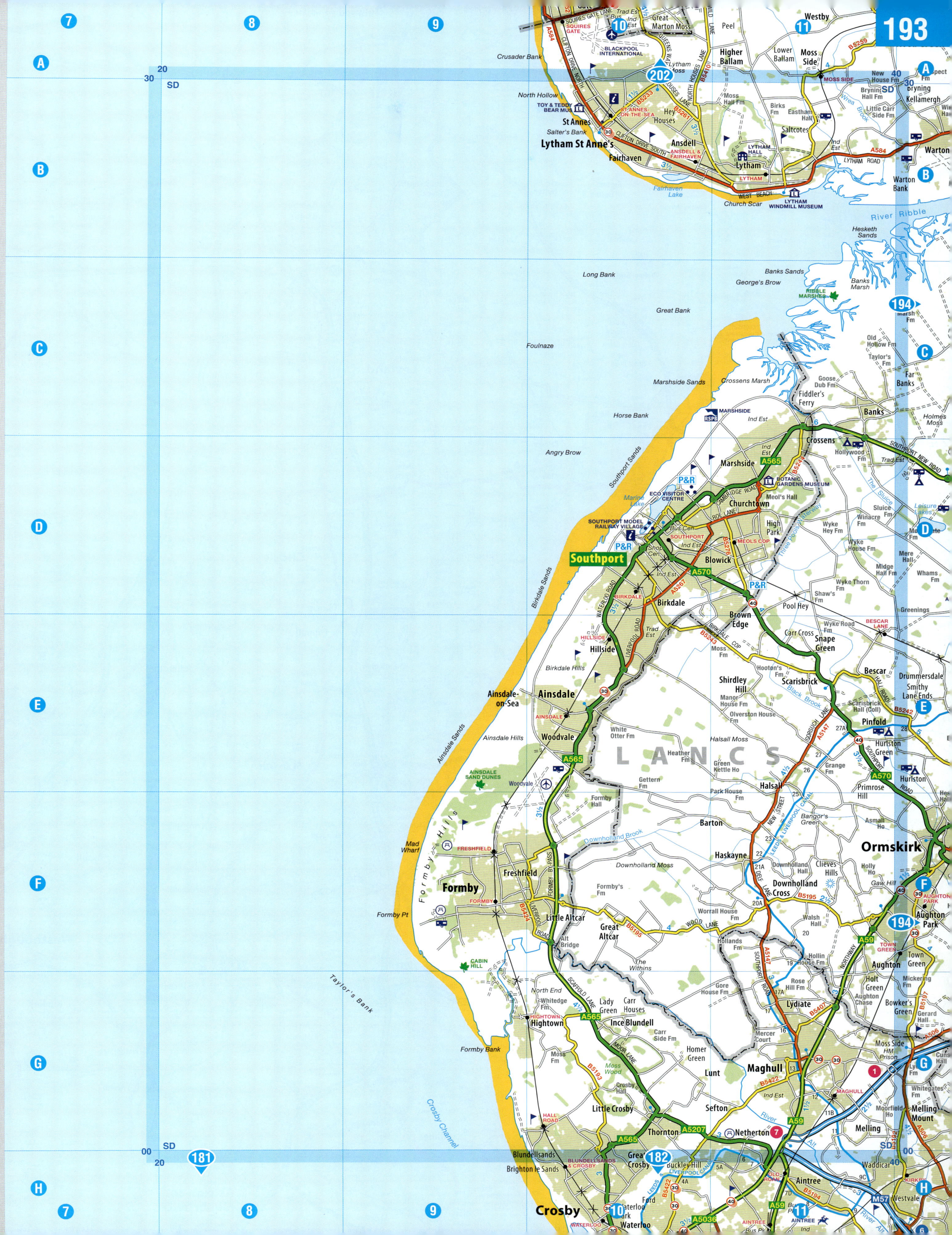
Lytham St Anne's
St Annes
Ansdell
Fairhaven
Lytham
Warton
Westby
Peel
Great Marton Moss
Higher Ballam
Lower Ballam
Moss Side
Saltcotes
Blackpool International
Crusader Bank
North Hollow
Salter's Bank
Church Scar
Lytham Windmill Museum
River Ribble
Hesketh Sands
Banks Sands
George's Brow
Banks Marsh
Long Bank
Great Bank
Foulnaze
Marshside Sands
Crossens Marsh
Horse Bank
Angry Brow
Southport Sands
Fiddler's Ferry
Banks
Crossens
Marshside
Churchtown
Southport
Blowick
Birkdale
Birkdale Sands
Birkdale Hills
Hillside
Ainsdale
Ainsdale-on-Sea
Ainsdale Sands
Ainsdale Hills
Woodvale
Formby Hills
Mad Wharf
Freshfield
Formby
Formby Pt
Little Altcar
Great Altcar
Taylor's Bank
Formby Bank
Crosby Channel
Hightown
Ince Blundell
Little Crosby
Thornton
Blundellsands
Brighton le Sands
Crosby
Great Crosby
Waterloo
Netherton
Aintree
Sefton
Lunt
Maghull
Lydiate
Melling
Melling Mount
Waddicar
Westvale
Ormskirk
Aughton
Aughton Park
Town Green
Downholland Cross
Haskayne
Barton
Halsall
Scarisbrick
Shirdley Hill
Snape Green
Brown Edge
Pool Hey
Bescar
Pinfold
Hurlston Green
Primrose Hill
Drummersdale
Smithy Lane Ends
Holmes Moss
L A N C S
Downholland Moss
Halsall Moss
Leeds & Liverpool Canal
River Alt
Moss Side
SD
202
194
181
182

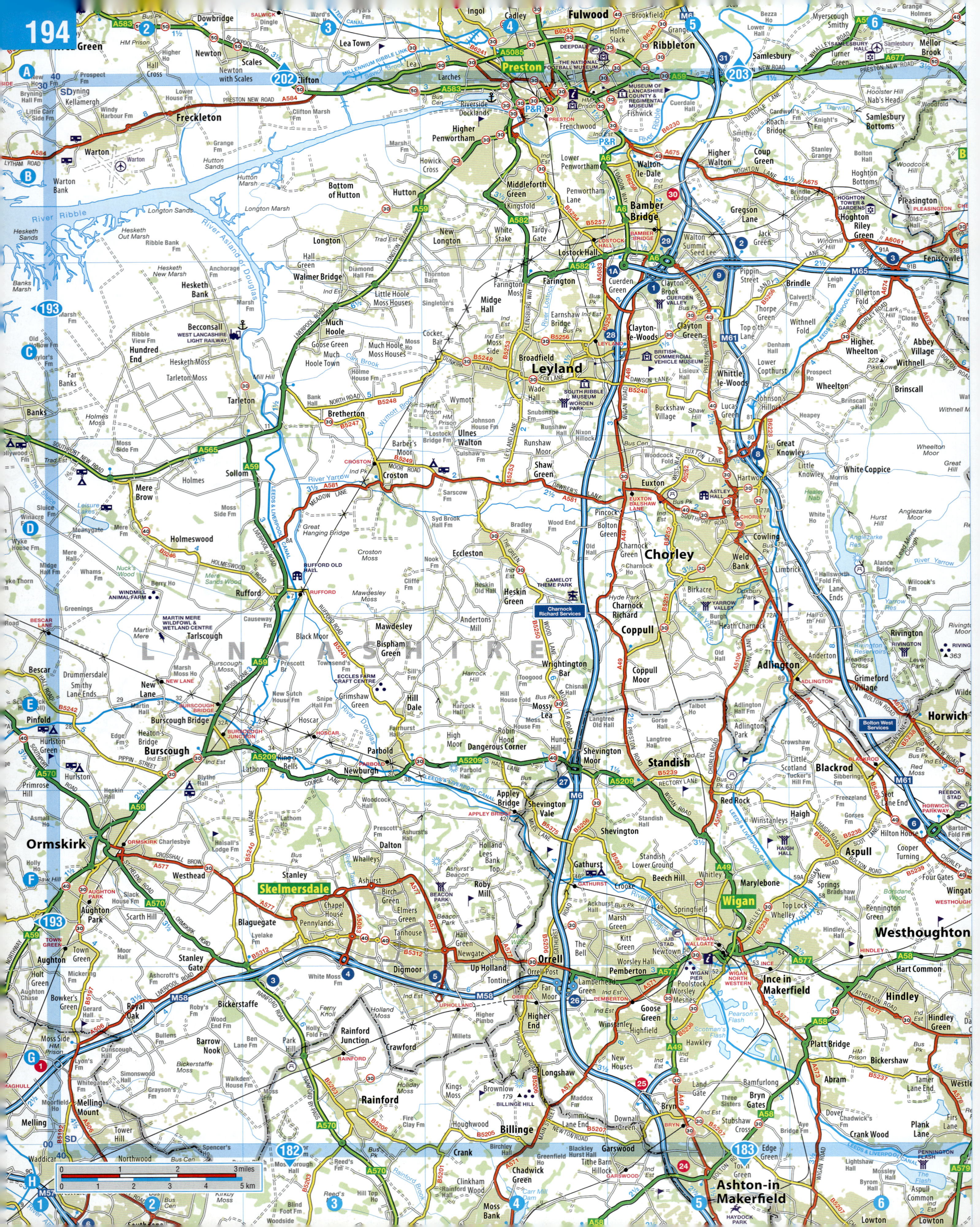
Preston
Fulwood
Ribbleton
Ingol
Cadley
Lea Town
Larches
Ashton-on-Ribble
Penwortham
Higher Penwortham
Middleforth Green
Kingsfold
Walton-le-Dale
Bamber Bridge
Higher Walton
Samlesbury
Samlesbury Bottoms
Mellor Brook
Freckleton
Warton
Warton Bank
Newton
Clifton
Scales
River Ribble
Hutton
Bottom of Hutton
Longton
New Longton
Walmer Bridge
Hesketh Bank
Hesketh Sands
Much Hoole
Becconsall
Tarleton
Bretherton
Croston
Ulnes Walton
Midge Hall
Farington
Lostock Hall
Leyland
Broadfield
Clayton-le-Woods
Clayton Green
Whittle-le-Woods
Wheelton
Brinscall
Higher Wheelton
Withnell
Abbey Village
Gregson Lane
Coupe Green
Hoghton
Riley Green
Feniscowles
Pleasington
Euxton
Chorley
Astley Hall
Buckshaw Village
Heath Charnock
Charnock Richard
Coppull
Coppull Moor
Adlington
Anderton
Rivington
Grimeford Village
Horwich
Blackrod
Standish
Shevington
Shevington Moor
Appley Bridge
Wrightington Bar
Eccleston
Heskin Green
Mawdesley
Bispham Green
Rufford
Holmeswood
Sollom
Mere Brow
Banks
Burscough
Burscough Bridge
New Lane
Pinfold
Hurlston Green
Ormskirk
Aughton
Aughton Park
Westhead
Lathom
Newburgh
Parbold
Dangerous Corner
Dalton
Skelmersdale
Up Holland
Orrell
Pemberton
Wigan
Ince in Makerfield
Hindley
Hindley Green
Westhoughton
Aspull
Haigh
Marylebone
Platt Bridge
Abram
Bryn
Ashton-in-Makerfield
Garswood
Billinge
Rainford
Rainford Junction
Crawford
Bickerstaffe
Stanley Gate
Royal Oak
Melling Mount
Melling
Haydock Park
LANCASHIRE
M6
M61
M65
M58
A59
A6
A49
A5209
A577
A570
A58
A565
A581
A582
A583
A584
A675
A674
A673
A571
A5085
Bolton West Services
Charnock Richard Services
202
203
193
183
182
0 1 2 3 miles
0 1 2 3 4 5 km

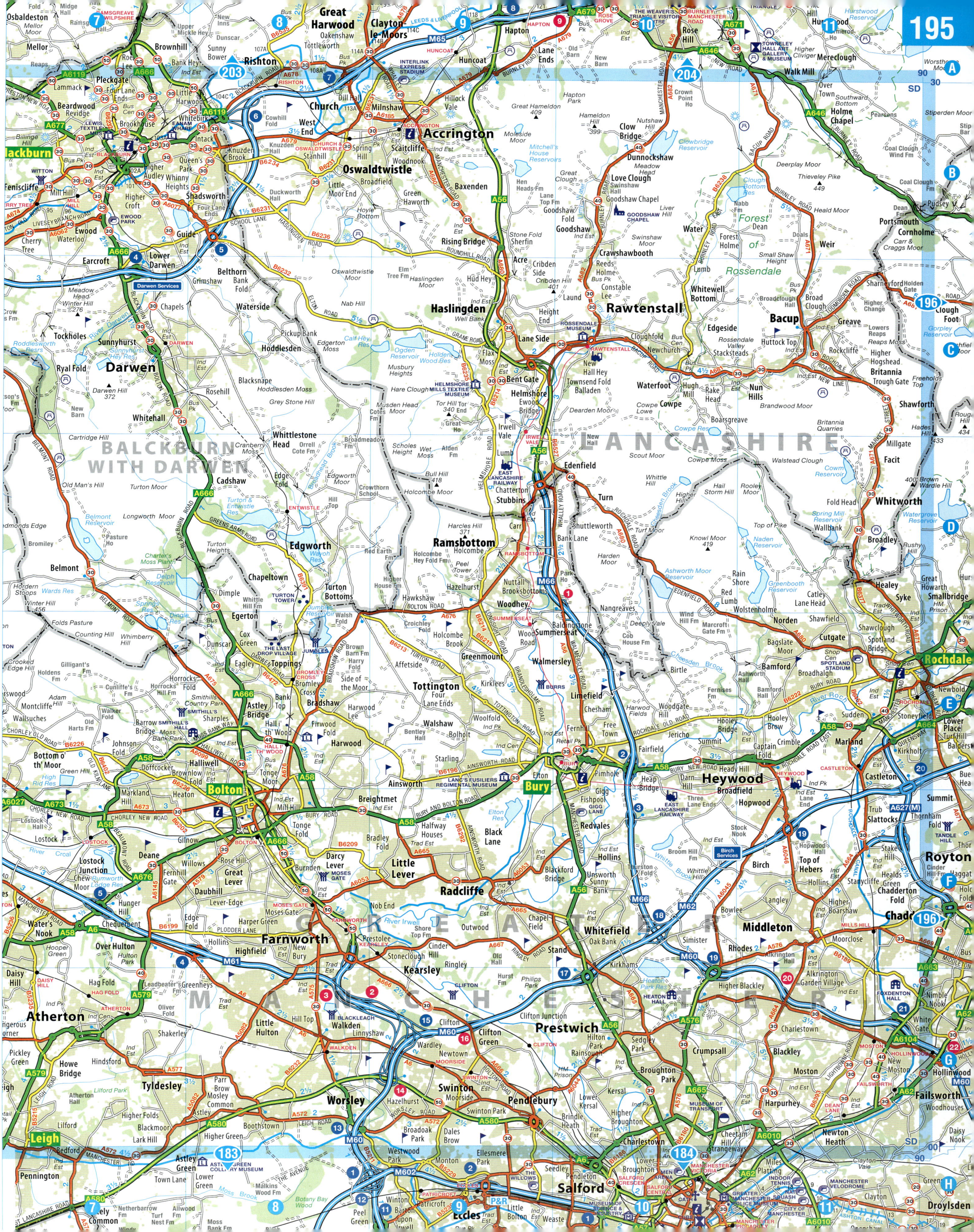
LANCASHIRE
BALCKBURN WITH DARWEN
GREATER MANCHESTER
Blackburn
Accrington
Oswaldtwistle
Great Harwood
Clayton-le-Moors
Rishton
Church
Darwen
Haslingden
Rawtenstall
Bacup
Whitworth
Rochdale
Ramsbottom
Edgworth
Tottington
Bolton
Bury
Heywood
Middleton
Radcliffe
Whitefield
Prestwich
Farnworth
Kearsley
Little Lever
Walkden
Worsley
Swinton
Pendlebury
Salford
Eccles
Atherton
Tyldesley
Leigh
Royton
Failsworth
Droylsden
Haslingden Moor
Forest of Rossendale
Helmshore
Edenfield
Summerseat
Horwich
Westhoughton
Hapton
Huncoat
Oakenshaw
Belmont
Egerton
Turton Bottoms
Harwood
Ainsworth
Halliwell
Little Hulton
Clifton
Walshaw
Simister
Higher Blackley
Crumpsall
Moston
Newton Heath
Cheetham
Broughton
Irlams o' th' Height
Pennington
Stacksteads
Shawforth
Britannia
Healey
Norden
Bamford
Castleton
Hopwood
Birch
Alkrington Garden Village
Chadderton
M65
M66
M60
M61
M62
M602
A56
A58
A666
A676
A680
A681
A6
A580
A579
A671
A646
A6119
A627(M)
A663
A6010
A62

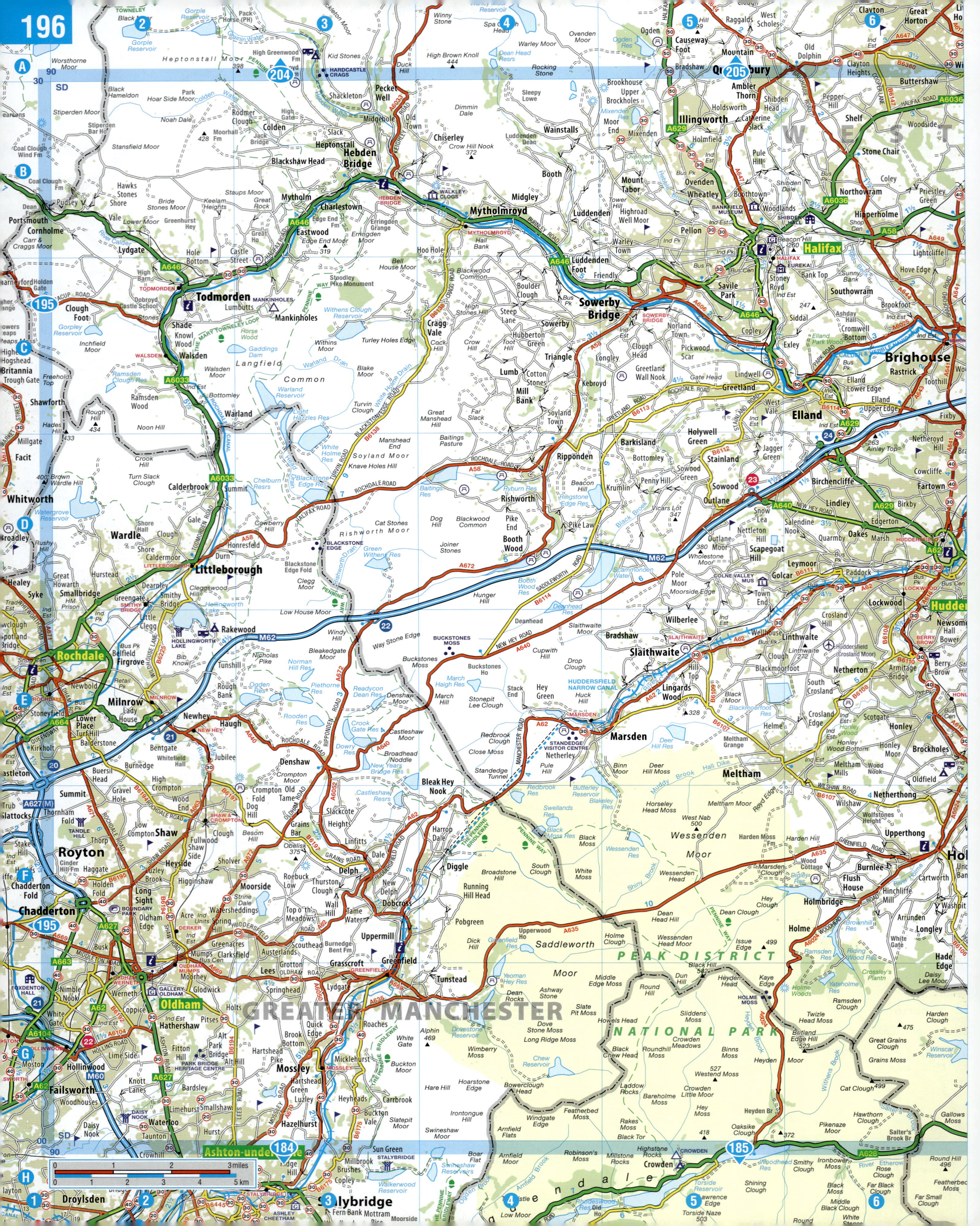

Todmorden
Hebden Bridge
Mytholmroyd
Sowerby Bridge
Halifax
Brighouse
Elland
Queensbury
Illingworth
Rochdale
Littleborough
Milnrow
Royton
Oldham
Chadderton
Shaw
Delph
Diggle
Uppermill
Greenfield
Mossley
Stalybridge
Slaithwaite
Marsden
Meltham
Holmfirth
Ripponden
Rishworth
Walsden
Whitworth
Wardle
Failsworth
Droylsden
Ashton-under-Lyne
Lindley
Golcar
Linthwaite
Netherton
Honley
Holmbridge
Saddleworth Moor
Wessenden Moor
PEAK DISTRICT NATIONAL PARK
GREATER MANCHESTER
WEST
M62
A58
A646
A629
A640
A62
A635
A672
A6033
Soyland Moor
Rishworth Moor
Langfield Common
Hollingworth Lake
Heptonstall
Mankinholes
Blackstone Edge
Standedge
Huddersfield Narrow Canal
0 1 2 3 miles
0 1 2 3 4 5 km

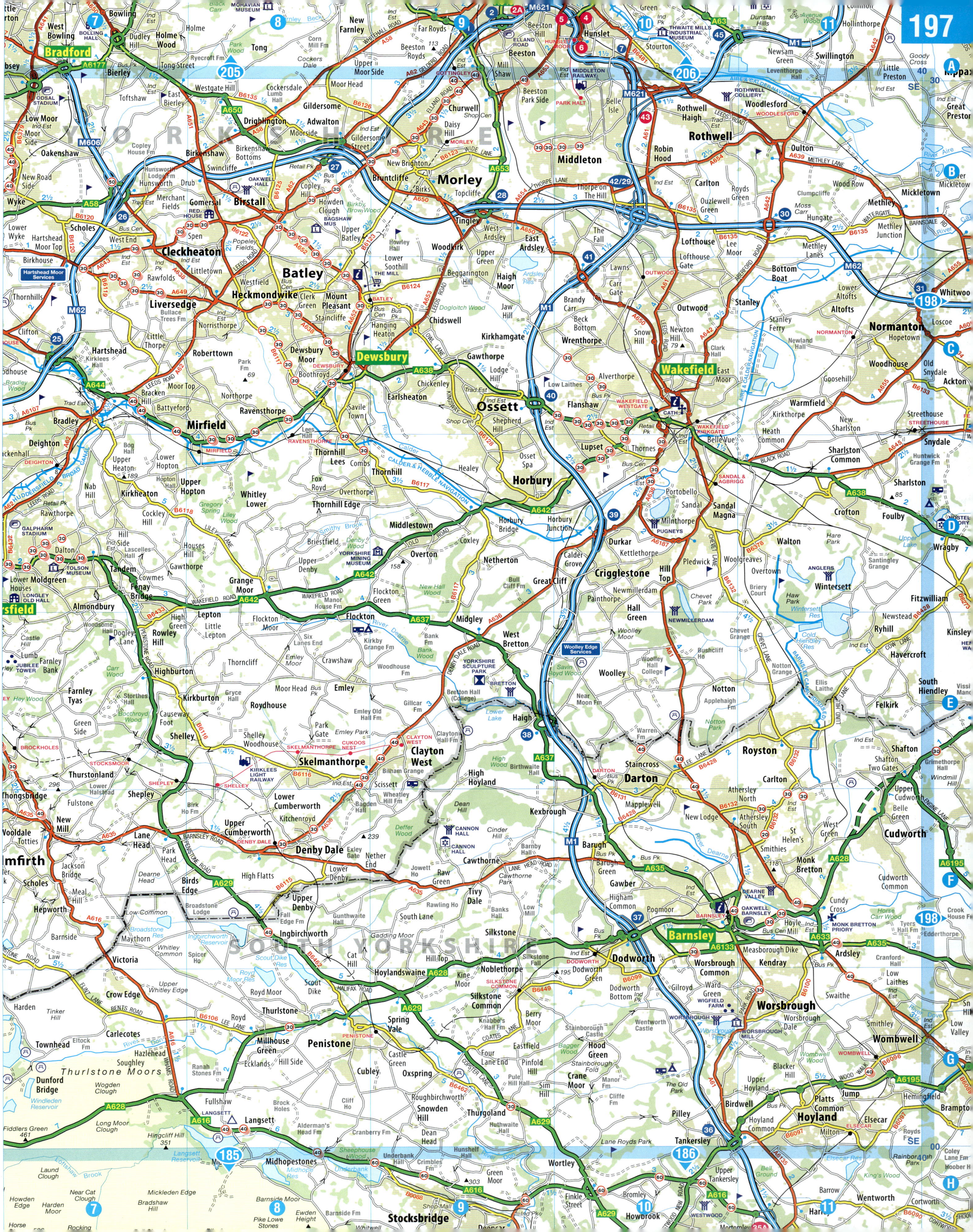
YORKSHIRE
SOUTH YORKSHIRE
Bradford
Bowling
Bierley
Tong
Drighlington
Gildersome
Morley
Middleton
Rothwell
Oulton
Woodlesford
Methley
Birkenshaw
Birstall
Gomersal
Cleckheaton
Batley
Heckmondwike
Liversedge
Dewsbury
Ossett
Horbury
Mirfield
Ravensthorpe
Thornhill
Wakefield
Normanton
Altofts
Stanley
Outwood
Lofthouse
Sandal Magna
Crofton
Walton
Crigglestone
Netherton
Middlestown
Flockton
Lepton
Kirkburton
Shelley
Skelmanthorpe
Clayton West
High Hoyland
Darton
Royston
Carlton
Cudworth
Barnsley
Dodworth
Worsbrough
Wombwell
Hoyland
Denby Dale
Penistone
Thurlstone
Thurlstone Moors
Langsett
Stocksbridge
Silkstone
Hoylandswaine
Oxspring
Thurgoland
Tankersley
Midhopestones
Holmfirth
Hepworth
New Mill
Almondbury
Fitzwilliam
Havercroft
Ryhill
Felkirk
Shafton
Grimethorpe
Whitwood
Flanshaw
Alverthorpe
Chickenley
Earlsheaton
Kexbrough
Barugh
Mapplewell
Staincross
Woolley
West Bretton
Haigh

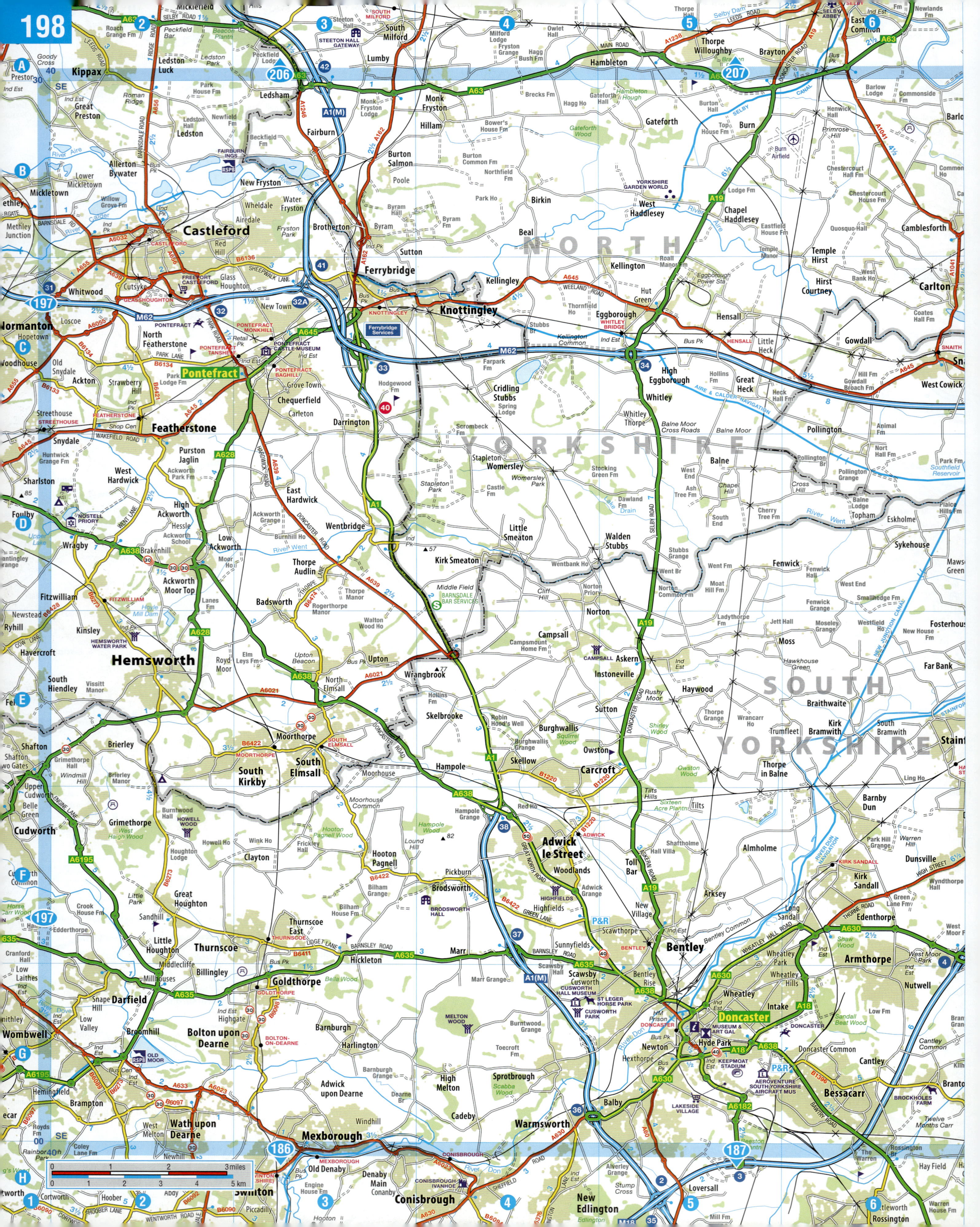
Kippax
Castleford
Ferrybridge
Knottingley
Pontefract
Featherstone
Hemsworth
South Kirkby
South Elmsall
Adwick le Street
Bentley
Doncaster
Cudworth
Darfield
Wombwell
Goldthorpe
Thurnscoe
Bolton upon Dearne
Mexborough
Conisbrough
Swinton
Wath upon Dearne
Bessacarr
Armthorpe
Carcroft
Askern
Snaith
Carlton
Hensall
Kellington
Hambleton
Brayton
Selby
Sherburn in Elmet
Ledsham
Ledston
Fairburn
Brotherton
Knottingley
Whitley
Norton
Campsall
Kirk Smeaton
Wentbridge
Darrington
Ackworth Moor Top
Fitzwilliam
Sutton
Burghwallis
Owston
Skellow
Hampole
Hooton Pagnell
Clayton
Barnburgh
High Melton
Sprotbrough
Warmsworth
Balby
Hexthorpe
Edenthorpe
Kirk Sandall
Dunsville
Barnby Dun
Thorpe in Balne
Kirk Bramwith
Braithwaite
Fenwick
Moss
Sykehouse
Pollington
Balne
Gowdall
West Cowick
Temple Hirst
Hirst Courtney
Camblesforth
Chapel Haddlesey
West Haddlesey
Birkin
Gateforth
Burn
NORTH YORKSHIRE
SOUTH YORKSHIRE
A1(M)
M62
A1
A19
A638
A635
A630
M18
206
207
197
186
187
0 1 2 3 miles
0 1 2 3 4 5 km

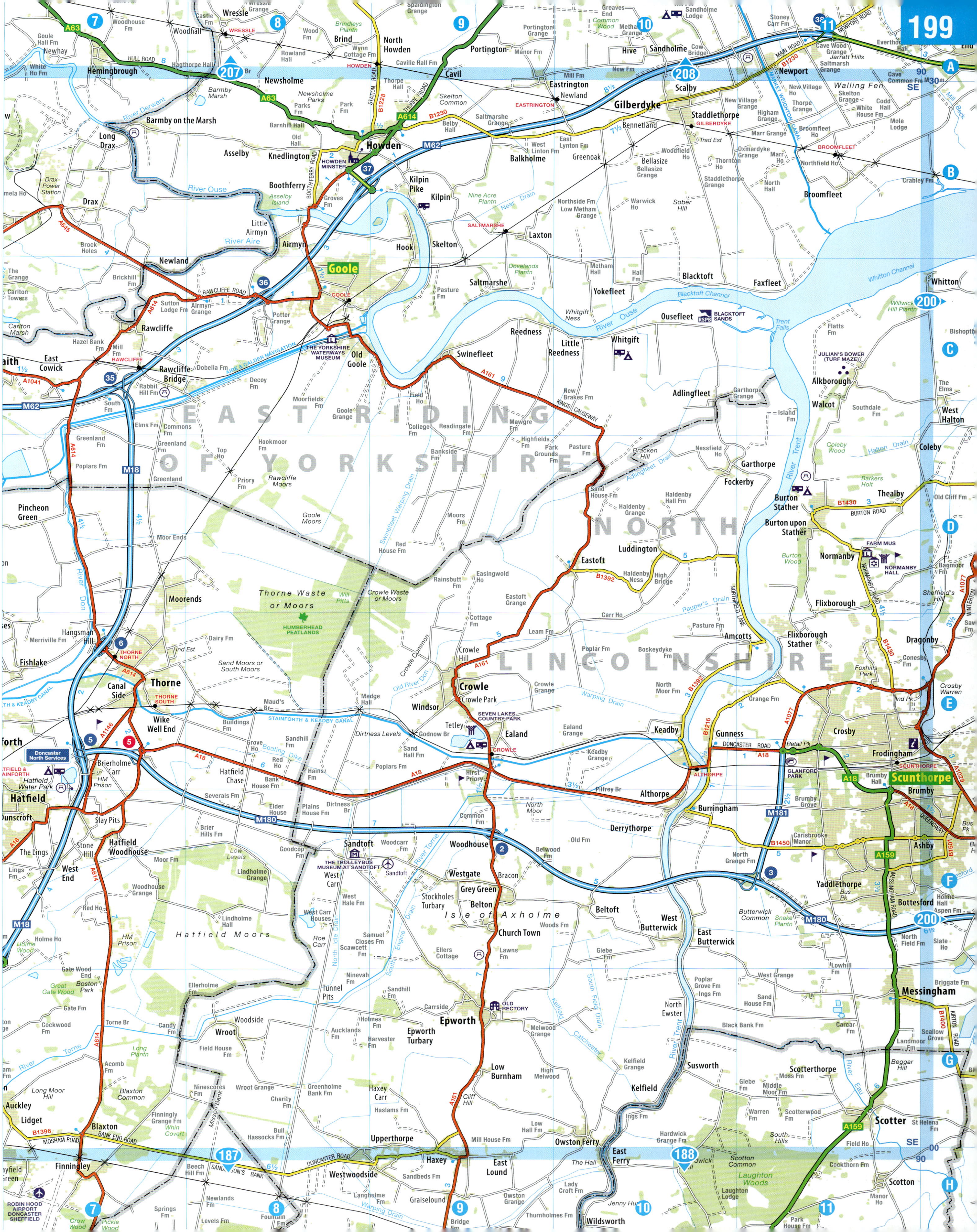
EAST RIDING OF YORKSHIRE
NORTH LINCOLNSHIRE
Isle of Axholme
Hatfield Moors
Thorne Waste or Moors
Crowle Waste or Moors
Goole Moors
Howden
Goole
Gilberdyke
Scunthorpe
Thorne
Hatfield
Crowle
Epworth
Messingham
Scotter
Haxey
Finningley
Blaxton
Hemingbrough
Wressle
Newsholme
Barmby on the Marsh
Asselby
Knedlington
Boothferry
Airmyn
Hook
Skelton
Kilpin
Saltmarshe
Laxton
Eastrington
Newport
Scalby
Balkholme
Portington
Cavil
Hive
Sandholme
Broomfield
Blacktoft
Yokefleet
Faxfleet
Whitton
Ousefleet
Whitgift
Reedness
Little Reedness
Swinefleet
Old Goole
Rawcliffe
Rawcliffe Bridge
Newland
Drax
Long Drax
Adlingfleet
Garthorpe
Fockerby
Luddington
Eastoft
Amcotts
Alkborough
Walcot
West Halton
Coleby
Thealby
Burton Stather
Burton upon Stather
Normanby
Flixborough
Flixborough Stather
Dragonby
Gunness
Keadby
Althorpe
Burringham
Derrythorpe
Crosby
Frodingham
Brumby
Ashby
Yaddlethorpe
Bottesford
Moorends
Fishlake
Hangsman Hill
Canal Side
Wike Well End
Brierholme Carr
Hatfield Woodhouse
Stone Hill
West End
The Lings
Dunscroft
Slay Pits
Sandtoft
Westgate
Grey Green
Belton
Bracon
Woodhouse
Church Town
Beltoft
West Butterwick
East Butterwick
North Ewster
Susworth
Kelfield
Scotterthorpe
Owston Ferry
East Ferry
Low Burnham
Upperthorpe
Westwoodside
Graiselound
Wroot
Windsor
Ealand
Tetley
Crowle Park
Auckley
Lidget
Wildsworth
East Lound
River Ouse
River Aire
River Don
River Trent
River Torne
Whitton Channel
Blacktoft Channel
Stainforth & Keadby Canal
Aire & Calder Navigation
Market Weighton Canal
Trent Falls
M62
M18
M180
M181
A63
A614
A161
A18
A1077
A159
A1029
A645
A1041
A1146
B1230
B1228
B1392
B1430
B1450
B1396
B1400
THE YORKSHIRE WATERWAYS MUSEUM
THE TROLLEYBUS MUSEUM AT SANDTOFT
HUMBERHEAD PEATLANDS
SEVEN LAKES COUNTRY PARK
OLD RECTORY
JULIAN'S BOWER (TURF MAZE)
NORMANBY HALL
FARM MUS
BLACKTOFT SANDS
RSPB
ROBIN HOOD AIRPORT DONCASTER SHEFFIELD
Doncaster North Services
207
208
187
188
200
SE
90
00

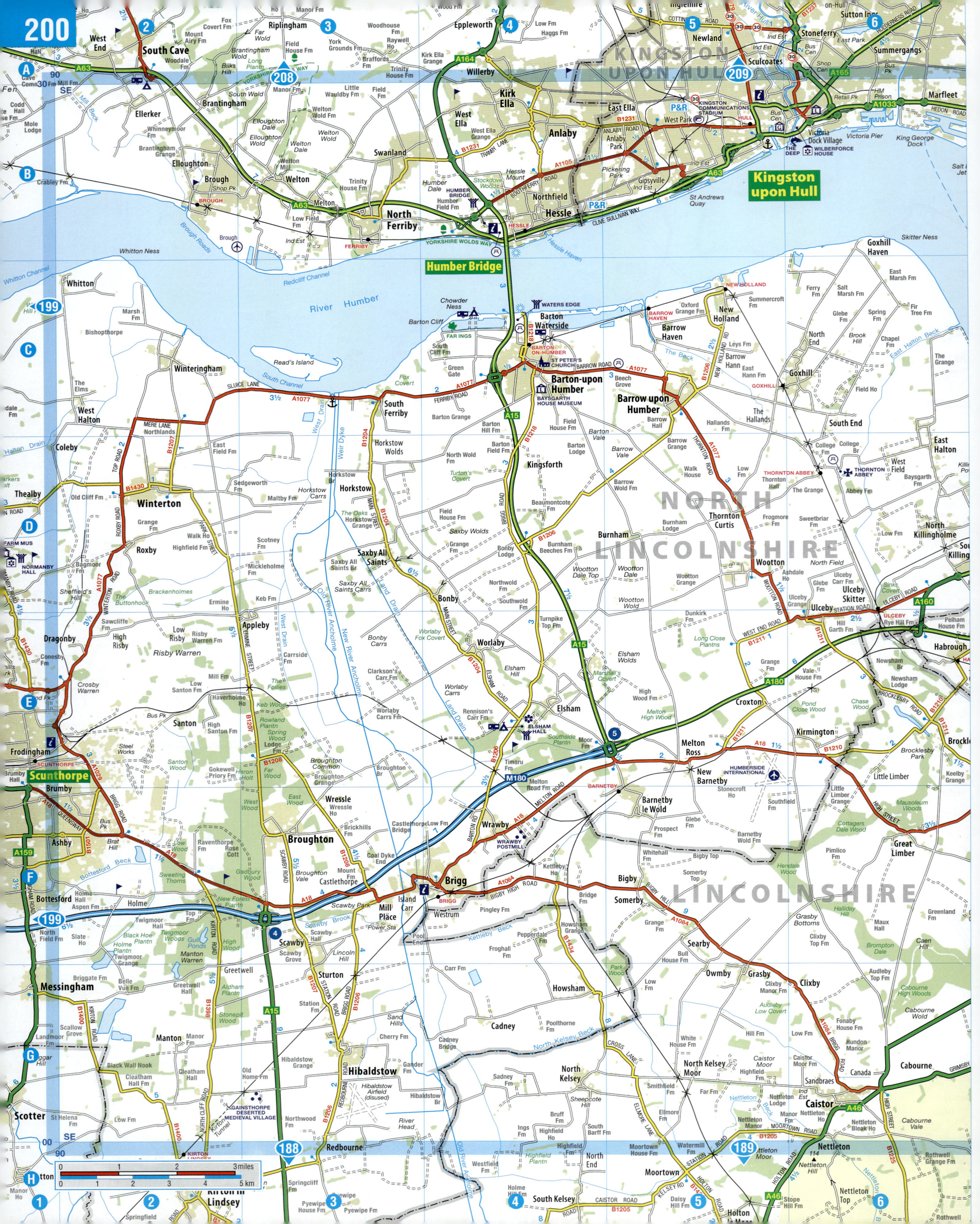
Kingston upon Hull
KINGSTON UPON HULL
Humber Bridge
River Humber
NORTH LINCOLNSHIRE
LINCOLNSHIRE
South Cave
West End
Riplingham
Eppleworth
Willerby
Kirk Ella
West Ella
Anlaby
East Ella
Newland
Sculcoates
Stoneferry
Sutton Ings
Summergangs
Marfleet
Victoria Dock Village
Victoria Pier
King George Dock
THE DEEP
WILBERFORCE HOUSE
KINGSTON COMMUNICATIONS STADIUM
Brantingham
Ellerker
Elloughton
Brough
Welton
Melton
Swanland
North Ferriby
Hessle
Northfield
Anlaby Park
Pickering Park
Gipsyville
St Andrews Quay
CLIVE SULLIVAN WAY
YORKSHIRE WOLDS WAY
Whitton Ness
Whitton Channel
Redcliff Channel
Whitton
Read's Island
South Channel
Winteringham
West Halton
Coleby
Thealby
Winterton
Roxby
Dragonby
Frodingham
Scunthorpe
Brumby
Ashby
Bottesford
Messingham
Scotter
Manton
Appleby
Santon
Broughton
Wressle
Horkstow
South Ferriby
Saxby All Saints
Bonby
Worlaby
Elsham
Barton Waterside
Barton-upon Humber
BAYSGARTH HOUSE MUSEUM
ST PETER'S CHURCH
WATERS EDGE
Chowder Ness
Barton Cliff
FAR INGS
Kingsforth
Barrow upon Humber
Barrow Haven
New Holland
Goxhill
Goxhill Haven
Skitter Ness
South End
East Halton
Thornton Curtis
THORNTON ABBEY
Burnham
Wootton
Ulceby
Ulceby Skitter
North Killingholme
Habrough
Croxton
Kirmington
HUMBERSIDE INTERNATIONAL
Melton Ross
New Barnetby
Barnetby le Wold
Wrawby
Brigg
Castlethorpe
Scawby
Sturton
Hibaldstow
Redbourne
Cadney
Howsham
Bigby
Somerby
Searby
Owmby
Grasby
Clixby
Great Limber
Cabourne
Caistor
Nettleton
North Kelsey
North Kelsey Moor
Moortown
South Kelsey
Holton le Moor
Kirton in Lindsey
GAINSTHORPE DESERTED MEDIEVAL VILLAGE
Hibaldstow Airfield (disused)
Risby Warren
Crosby Warren
Old River Ancholme
New River Ancholme
Land Drain
A63
A164
A1105
A165
A1033
A1077
A15
A18
A180
A160
A159
A1084
A1029
A46
M180
B1231
B1206
B1204
B1218
B1207
B1208
B1430
B1211
B1210
B1205
B1398
B1400
B1434
B1225
0 1 2 3 miles
0 1 2 3 4 5 km

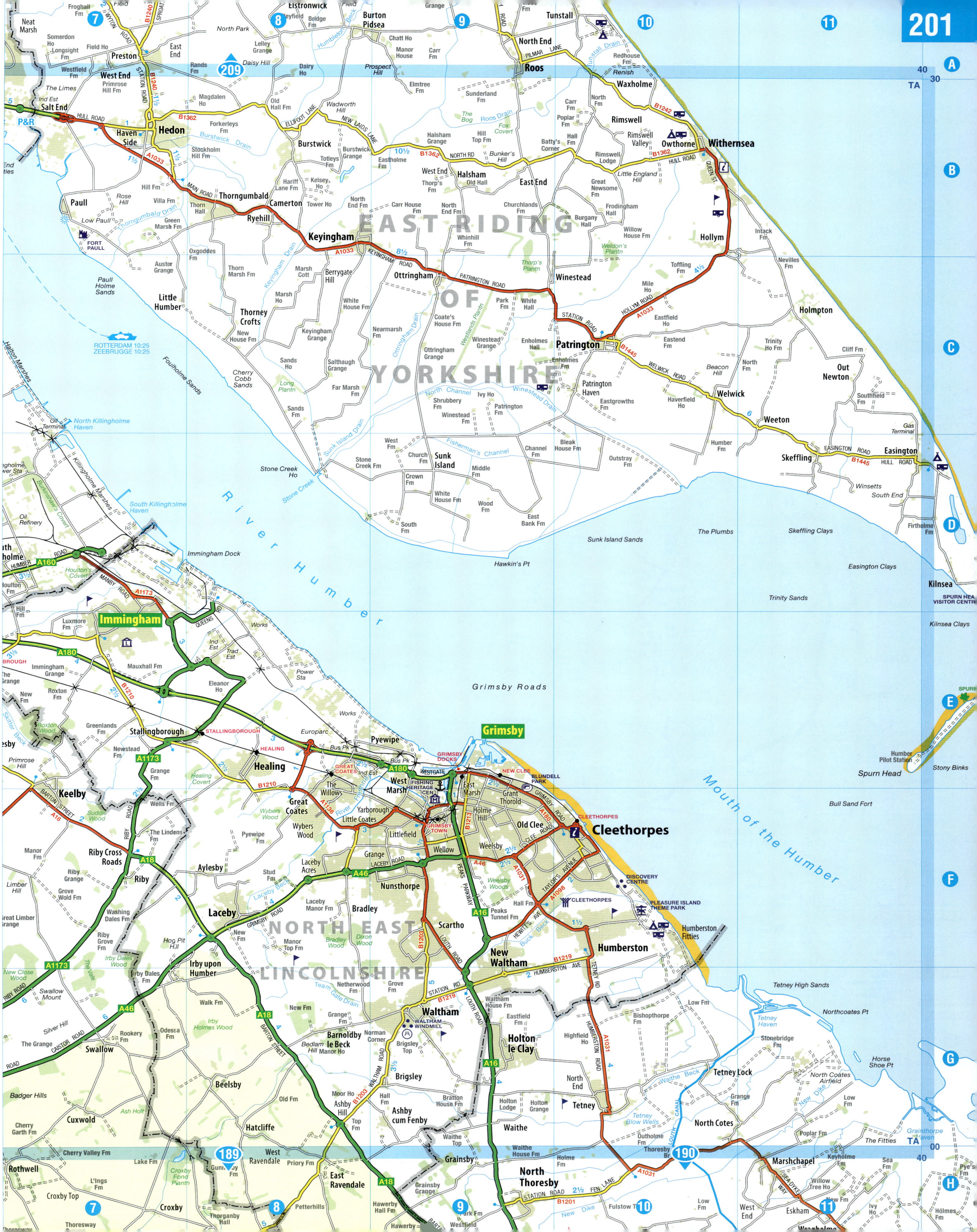
EAST RIDING
OF
YORKSHIRE
NORTH EAST
LINCOLNSHIRE
River Humber
Mouth of the Humber
Grimsby Roads
Hedon
Preston
Salt End
Haven Side
Paull
Thorngumbald
Ryehill
Keyingham
Burstwick
Camerton
Ottringham
Roos
Tunstall
North End
Waxholme
Rimswell
Owthorne
Withernsea
Halsham
East End
Hollym
Winestead
Patrington
Patrington Haven
Welwick
Weeton
Holmpton
Out Newton
Skeffling
Easington
Kilnsea
Sunk Island
Spurn Head
Burton Pidsea
Immingham
Immingham Dock
Stallingborough
Healing
Keelby
Riby
Riby Cross Roads
Aylesby
Laceby
Great Coates
Pyewipe
Grimsby
West Marsh
Cleethorpes
Old Clee
Weelsby
Scartho
New Waltham
Humberston
Humberston Fitties
Waltham
Holton le Clay
Tetney
Tetney Lock
North Cotes
Marshchapel
North Thoresby
Grainsby
Barnoldby le Beck
Brigsley
Ashby cum Fenby
Irby upon Humber
Beelsby
Hatcliffe
Cuxwold
Swallow
Rothwell
Croxby
East Ravendale
West Ravendale
Waithe
Nunsthorpe
Bradley
Little Coates
Littlefield
Yarborough
Wellow
ROTTERDAM 10:25
ZEEBRUGGE 10:25
A1033
B1362
B1445
A180
A160
A1173
A18
A46
A16
A1031
A1098
B1210
B1219
B1203
B1201
209
189
190

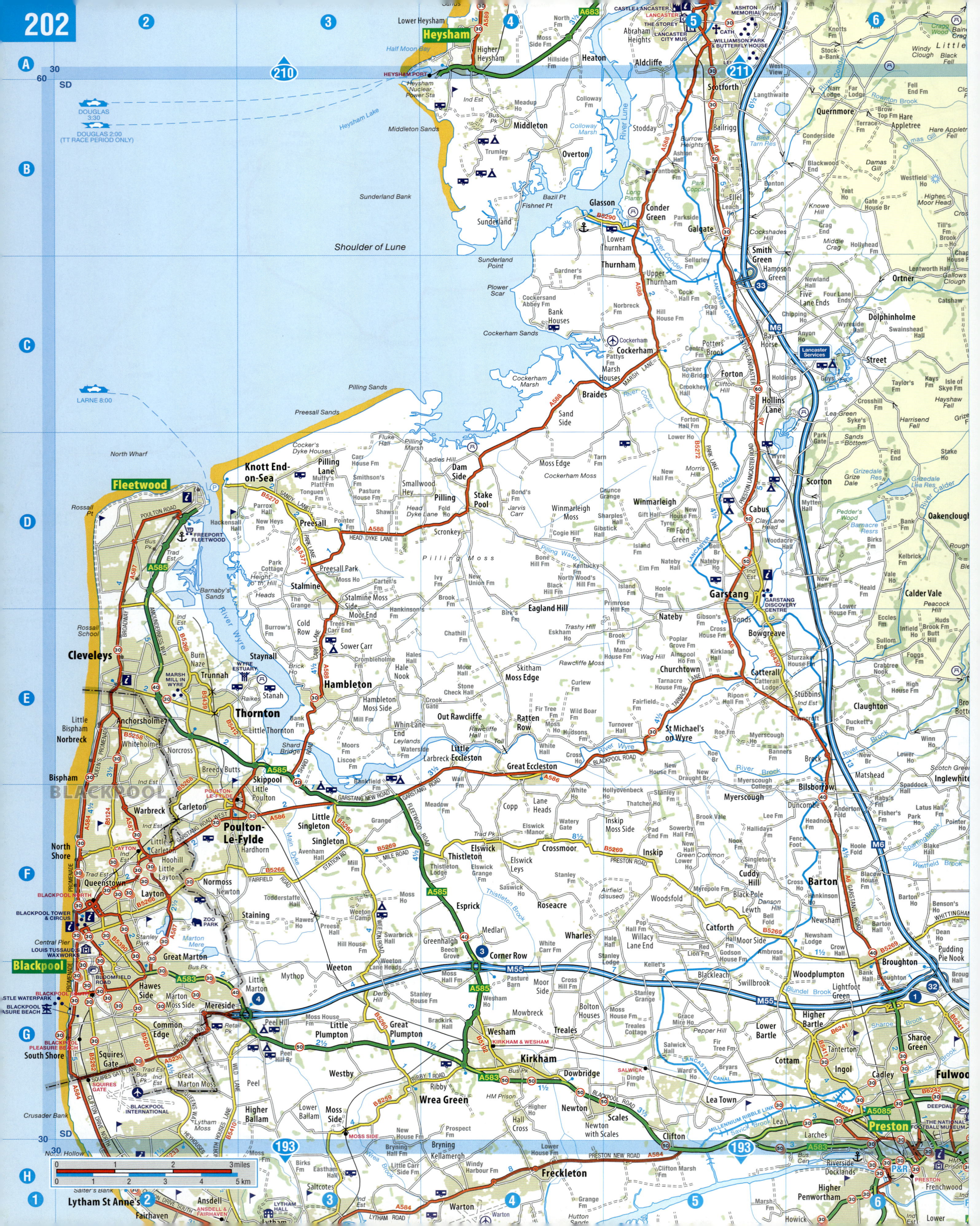
Heysham
Lower Heysham
Half Moon Bay
Heysham Port
Heysham Nuclear Power Sta
DOUGLAS 3:30
DOUGLAS 2:00 (TT RACE PERIOD ONLY)
Heysham Lake
Middleton Sands
Middleton
Overton
Sunderland Bank
Sunderland
Shoulder of Lune
Sunderland Point
Plover Scar
Cockerham Sands
Cockersand Abbey Fm
Bank Houses
Cockerham
Cockerham Marsh
Glasson
Lower Thurnham
Thurnham
Conder Green
Galgate
Aldcliffe
Scotforth
Bailrigg
Lancaster
Heaton
Quernmore
Smith Green
Ortner
Dolphinholme
Lancaster Services
Forton
Hollins Lane
Street
Scorton
Cabus
Garstang
Garstang Discovery Centre
Bowgreave
Catterall
Claughton
Calder Vale
Oakenclough
Pilling Sands
Preesall Sands
LARNE 8:00
North Wharf
Fleetwood
Rossall Pt
Knott End-on-Sea
Pilling Lane
Preesall
Pilling
Stake Pool
Dam Side
Braides
Sand Side
Pilling Moss
Winmarleigh
Winmarleigh Moss
Nateby
Stalmine
Preesall Park
Cleveleys
Thornton
Hambleton
Staynall
Stanah
Trunnah
Anchorsholme
Little Bispham
Norbreck
Bispham
Out Rawcliffe
Little Eccleston
Great Eccleston
Ratten Row
St Michael's on Wyre
Churchtown
Eagland Hill
Skitham Moss Edge
BLACKPOOL
Poulton-Le-Fylde
Carleton
Warbreck
Singleton
Little Singleton
Thistleton
Elswick
Crossmoor
Inskip
Myerscough
Bilsborrow
Barton
Broughton
Woodplumpton
Catforth
Roseacre
Esprick
Wharles
Layton
North Shore
Queenstown
Blackpool
Blackpool Tower & Circus
Central Pier
Louis Tussaud's Waxworks
Normoss
Staining
Great Marton
Marton Mere
Zoo Park
Weeton
Greenhalgh
Corner Row
Little Marton
Hawes Side
Marton Moss Side
Mereside
Common Edge
South Shore
Squires Gate
Blackpool International
Great Marton Moss
Little Plumpton
Great Plumpton
Wesham
Kirkham
Treales
Westby
Peel
Ribby
Wrea Green
Dowbridge
Newton
Scales
Newton with Scales
Clifton
Lea Town
Higher Bartle
Lower Bartle
Cottam
Ingol
Sharoe Green
Cadley
Fulwood
Preston
Larches
Riversdale
Higher Penwortham
Higher Ballam
Lower Ballam
Moss Side
Bryning
Kellamergh
Freckleton
Warton
Lytham St Anne's
Ansdell
Fairhaven
Crusader Bank
M6
M55
A6
A585
A583
A588
A586
0 1 2 3 miles
0 1 2 3 4 5 km

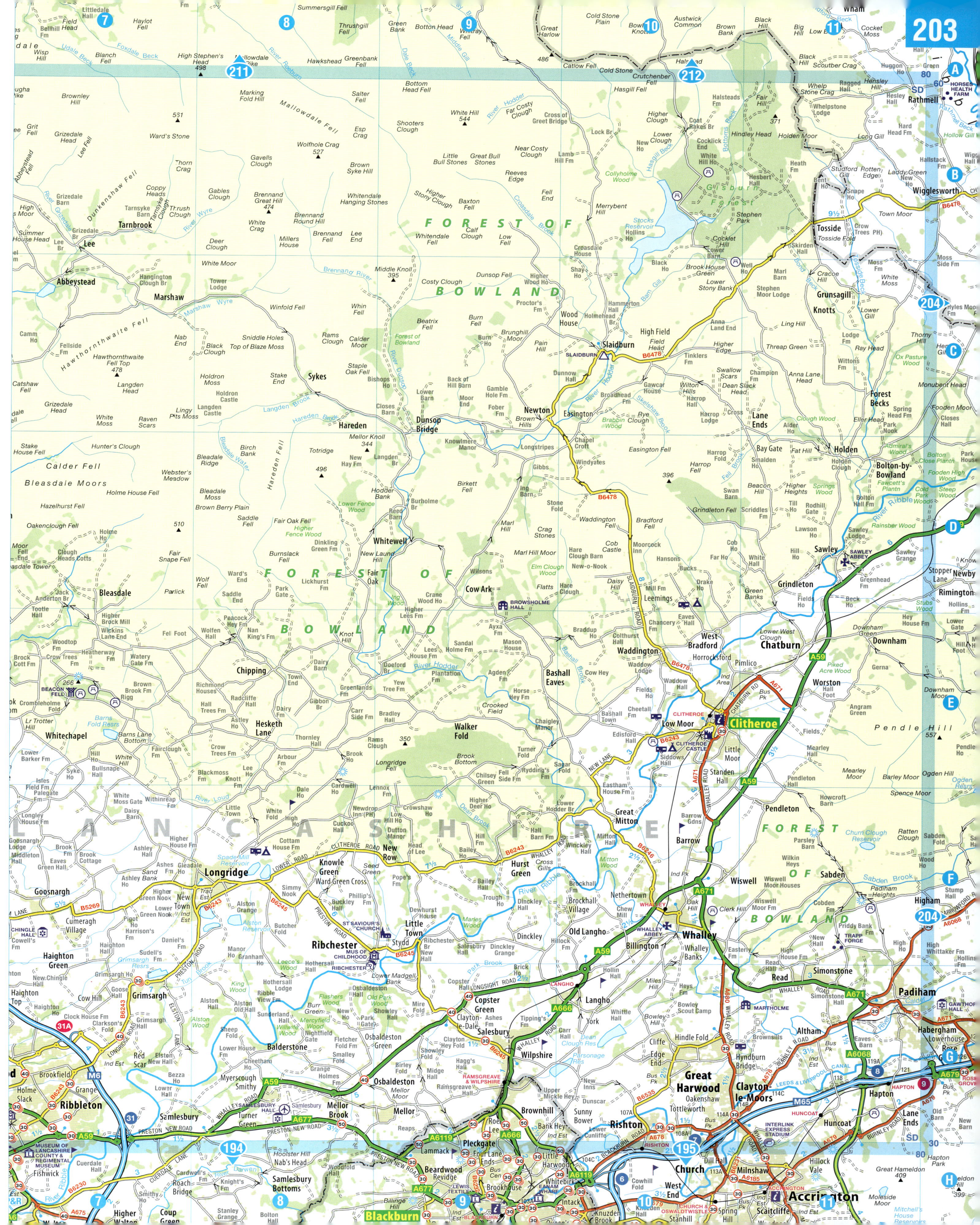
FOREST OF BOWLAND
FOREST OF BOWLAND
LANCASHIRE
FOREST OF BOWLAND
Clitheroe
Slaidburn
Newton
Dunsop Bridge
Whitewell
Chipping
Longridge
Ribchester
Whalley
Great Harwood
Clayton-le-Moors
Accrington
Blackburn
Rishton
Church
Padiham
Read
Simonstone
Sabden
Pendleton
Pendle Hill
Chatburn
Downham
Waddington
West Bradford
Grindleton
Sawley
Bolton-by-Bowland
Holden
Tosside
Wigglesworth
Rathmell
Gisburn Forest
Stocks Reservoir
Hurst Green
Great Mitton
Barrow
Wiswell
Billington
Langho
Wilpshire
Salesbury
Mellor
Osbaldeston
Balderstone
Grimsargh
Goosnargh
Ribbleton
Samlesbury
Pleckgate
Hesketh Lane
Bashall Eaves
Walker Fold
Cow Ark
Sykes
Hareden
Bleasdale
Calder Fell
Bleasdale Moors
Tarnbrook
Lee
Abbeystead
Marshaw
Whitechapel
Haighton Green
Easington
Knotts
Grunsagill
Forest Becks
Low Moor
B6478
B6243
B6245
B6246
B5269
B6535
A59
A671
A666
A677
A6119
A678
A680
A679
A6068
M6
M65
River Hodder
River Ribble
Longsight Road
Whalley Road
Slaidburn Road
Clitheroe Road
Preston Road
Preston New Road
211
212
194
195
204

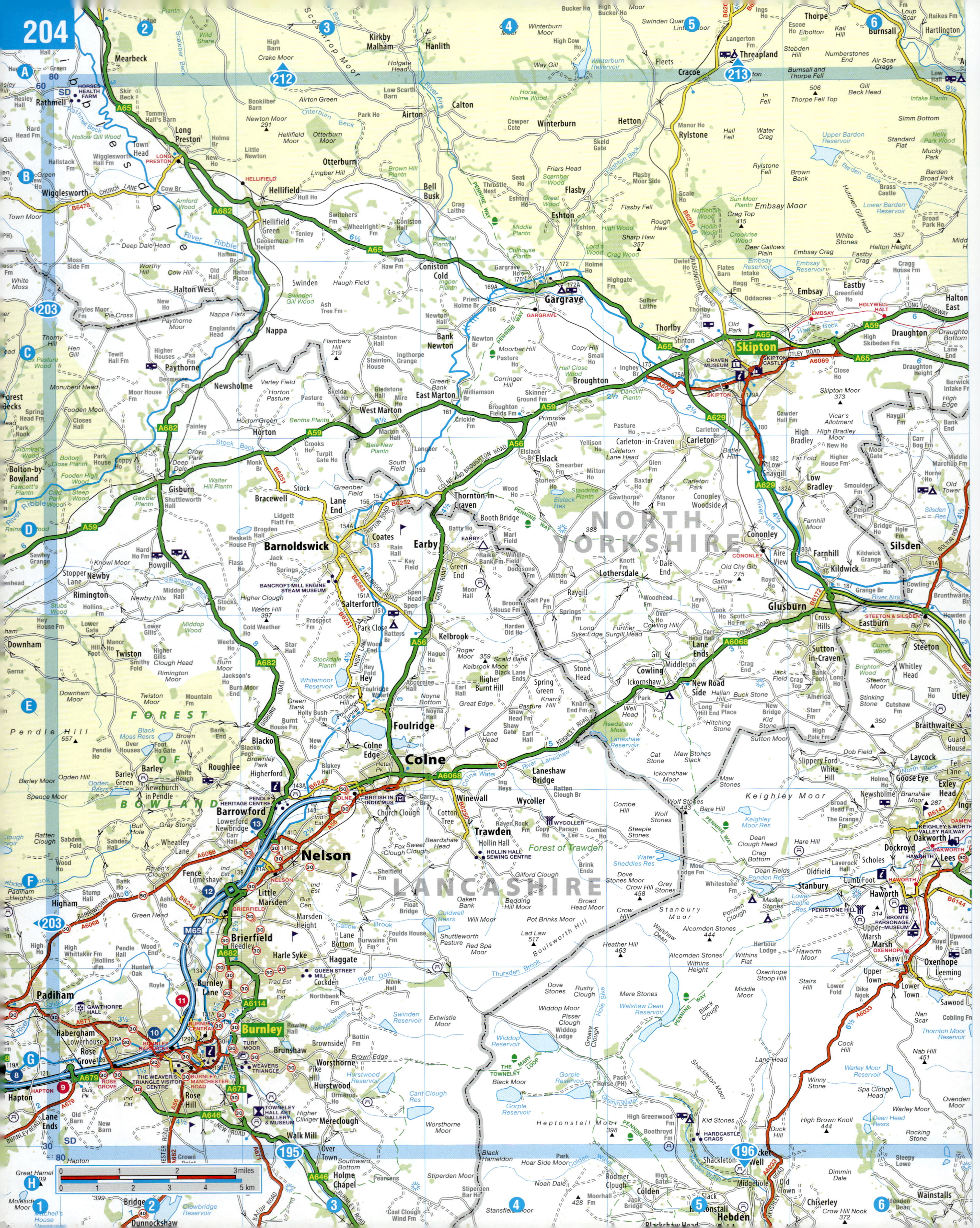
NORTH YORKSHIRE
LANCASHIRE
FOREST OF BOWLAND
Forest of Trawden
Skipton
Nelson
Colne
Burnley
Barnoldswick
Earby
Gargrave
Gisburn
Barrowford
Brierfield
Padiham
Glusburn
Cononley
Embsay
Hellifield
Long Preston
Settle
Malham
Kirkby Malham
Airton
Calton
Winterburn
Hetton
Rylstone
Cracoe
Threapland
Flasby
Eshton
Bell Busk
Coniston Cold
Otterburn
Swinden
Nappa
Paythorne
Newsholme
Horton
West Marton
East Marton
Broughton
Thornton-in-Craven
Elslack
Carleton-in-Craven
Lothersdale
Cowling
Kelbrook
Salterforth
Foulridge
Laneshaw Bridge
Trawden
Winewall
Wycoller
Haworth
Oxenhope
Stanbury
Oakworth
Silsden
Kildwick
Farnhill
Sutton-in-Craven
Eastburn
Steeton
Draughton
Thorlby
Stirton
Rimington
Downham
Twiston
Barley
Roughlee
Higham
Fence
Harle Syke
Haggate
Worsthorne
Hurstwood
Cliviger
Walk Mill
Habergham
Rose Grove
Hapton
Wigglesworth
Rathmell
Mearbeck
Bolton-by-Bowland
Sawley
Pendle Hill 557
Boulsworth Hill
Keighley Moor
Embsay Moor
Barden Moor
Pennine Way
River Ribble
River Aire
A65
A59
A56
A682
A6068
A629
A6131
A646
A671
A679
A6114
M65
B6251
B6252
B6383
B6247
B6250
B6478
B6265
B6143
B6144
PENNINE WAY
SKIPTON CASTLE
CRAVEN MUSEUM
BANCROFT MILL ENGINE STEAM MUSEUM
BRITISH IN INDIA MUS
PENDLE HERITAGE CENTRE
HOLLIN HALL SEWING CENTRE
WYCOLLER
QUEEN STREET MILL
GAWTHORPE HALL
THE WEAVERS' TRIANGLE VISITOR CENTRE
TOWNELEY HALL ART GALLERY & MUSEUM
BRONTE PARSONAGE MUSEUM
KEIGHLEY & WORTH VALLEY RAILWAY
203
212
213
195
196
0 1 2 3 miles
0 1 2 3 4 5 km

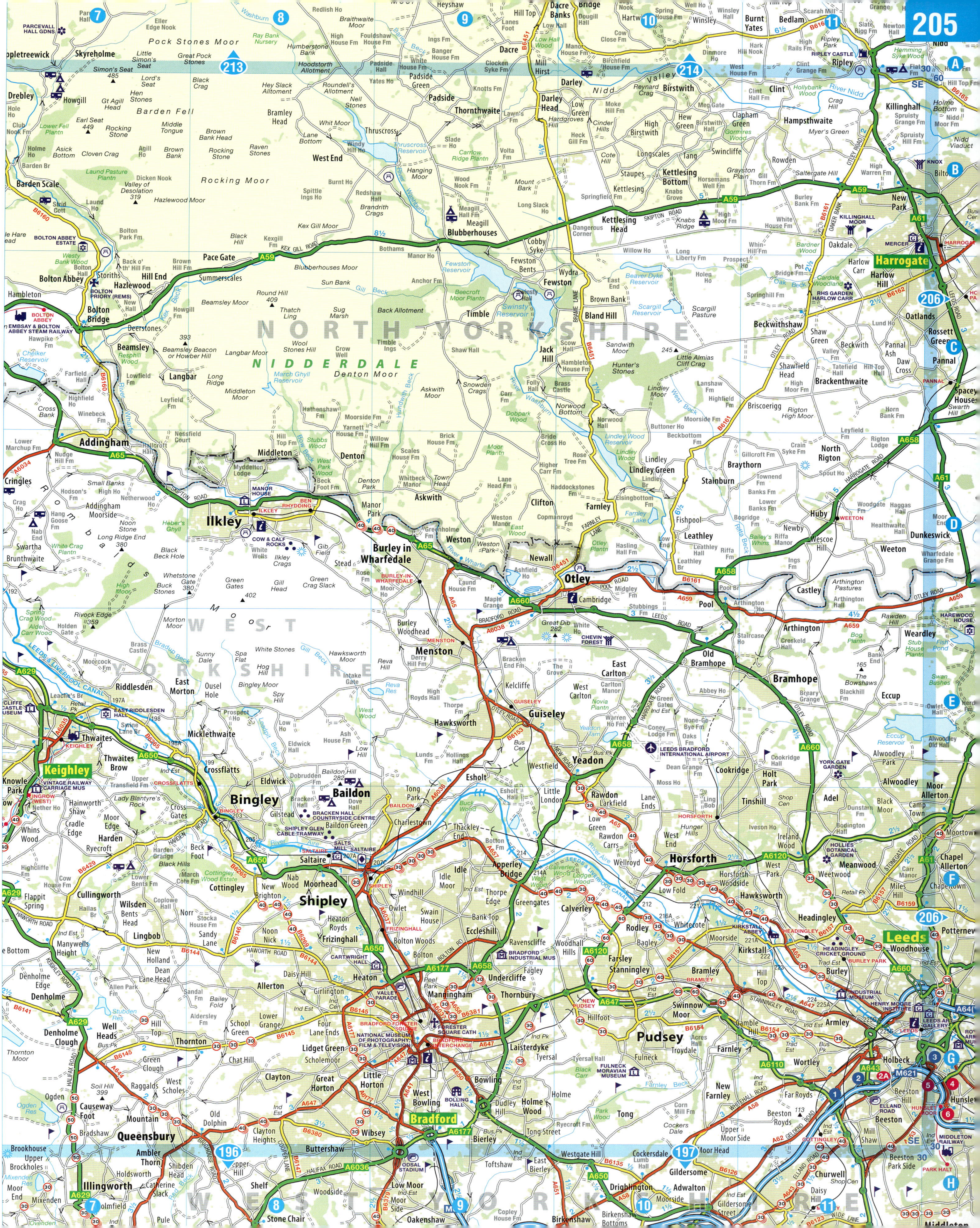
NORTH YORKSHIRE
NIDDERDALE
WEST YORKSHIRE
Rombalds Moor
Pock Stones Moor
Barden Fell
Rocking Moor
Denton Moor
Harrogate
Ripley
Killinghall
Pannal
Hampsthwaite
Birstwith
Darley
Dacre
Dacre Banks
Summerbridge
Thornthwaite
Padside
Kettlesing
Kettlesing Head
Kettlesing Bottom
Blubberhouses
Fewston
Timble
Beckwithshaw
Brackenthwaite
Stainburn
Braythorn
Huby
Weeton
Dunkeswick
Lindley Green
Farnley
Newall
Otley
Pool
Arthington
Castley
Bramhope
Eccup
Adel
Alwoodley
Moortown
Chapel Allerton
Leeds
Headingley
Burley
Kirkstall
Armley
Horsforth
Rawdon
Yeadon
Guiseley
Menston
Burley in Wharfedale
Askwith
Denton
Middleton
Ilkley
Addingham
Bolton Abbey
Bolton Bridge
Hazlewood
Beamsley
Langbar
Draughton
Barden Scale
Drebley
Howgill
Skyreholme
Appletreewick
Pace Gate
Riddlesden
East Morton
Keighley
Thwaites Brow
Crossflatts
Bingley
Baildon
Shipley
Saltaire
Cottingley
Cullingworth
Wilsden
Harden
Denholme
Thornton
Allerton
Heaton
Manningham
Bradford
Idle
Thackley
Eccleshill
Apperley Bridge
Calverley
Rodley
Farsley
Pudsey
Stanningley
Bramley
Thornbury
Undercliffe
Wibsey
Queensbury
Illingworth
Horton
Clayton
Tong
Holme Wood
Drighlington
Gildersome
Churwell
Beeston
Holbeck
Hunslet
Morley
Tyersal
Fulneck
Farnley
Wortley
Oakenshaw
Buttershaw
Tinshill
Cookridge
Holt Park
Leeds Bradford International Airport
Hawksworth
Esholt
Charlestown
Low Fold
Hawksworth
Whitcote
A59
A61
A65
A658
A660
A6120
A629
A650
A647
A6177
A6036
A641
A64
A62
B6451
B6161
B6160
B6265
M621
206
213
214
196
197

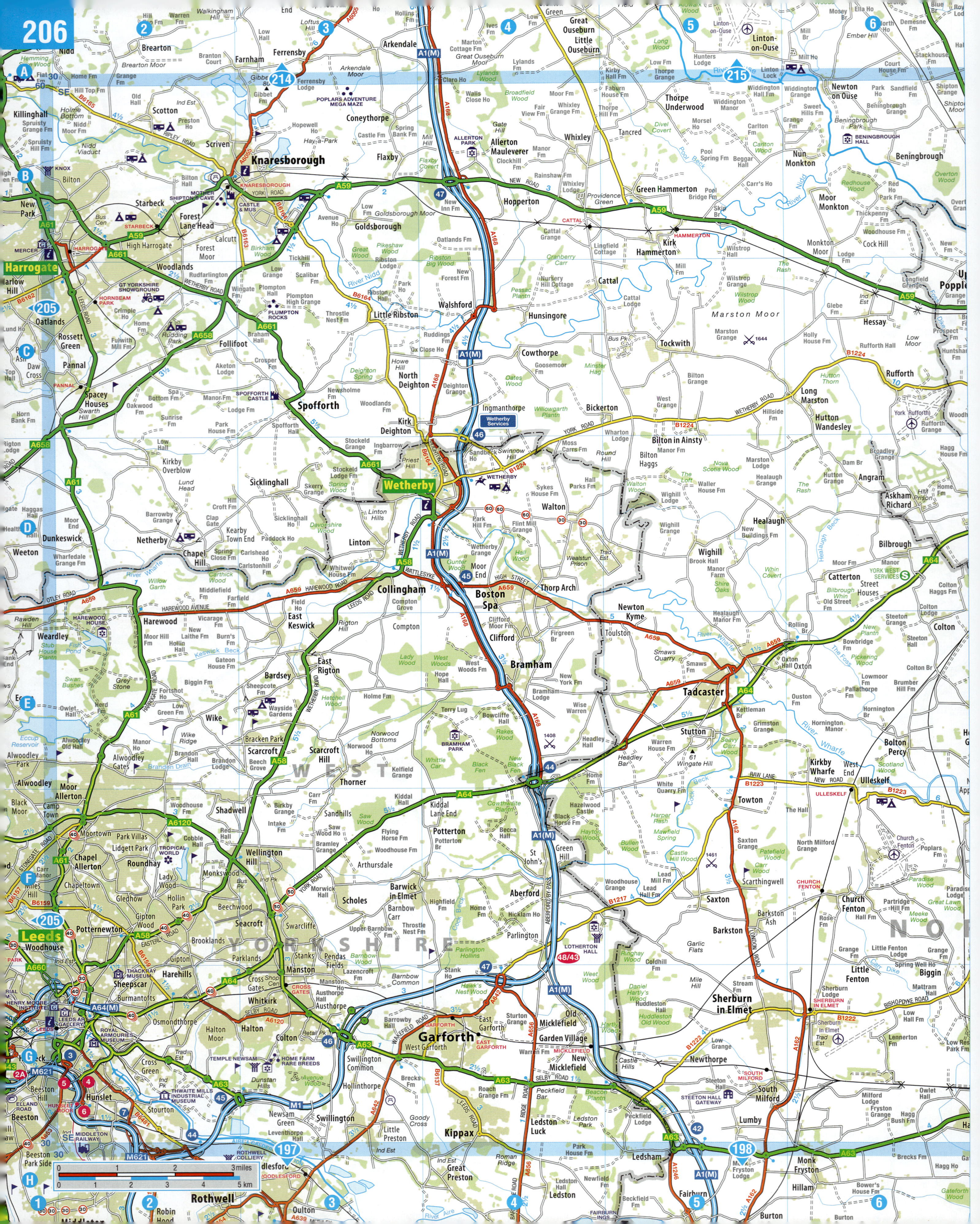
Knaresborough
Harrogate
Wetherby
Spofforth
Boston Spa
Collingham
Tadcaster
Bramham
Garforth
Leeds
Sherburn in Elmet
Kippax
Rothwell
Green Hammerton
Kirk Hammerton
Marston Moor
Long Marston
Hutton Wandesley
Bilbrough
Ulleskelf
Church Fenton
South Milford
Monk Fryston
Aberford
Barwick in Elmet
Scholes
Thorner
Bardsey
East Keswick
Harewood
Sicklinghall
Linton
Follifoot
Pannal
Beningbrough
Nun Monkton
Whixley
Little Ouseburn
Arkendale
Ferrensby
Farnham
Brearton
Scotton
Scriven
Starbeck
Chapel Allerton
Roundhay
Moortown
Alwoodley
Seacroft
Whitkirk
Colton
Halton
Osmondthorpe
Swillington
Micklefield
Ledsham
Ledston
Fairburn
Newthorpe
Saxton
Towton
Stutton
Newton Kyme
Clifford
Thorp Arch
Walton
Cattal
Hunsingore
Cowthorpe
Tockwith
Bickerton
Hopperton
Allerton Mauleverer
Flaxby
Goldsborough
Coneythorpe
Walshford
Little Ribston
North Deighton
Kirk Deighton
WEST YORKSHIRE
A1(M)
A59
A64
A61
A58
A659
M1
0 1 2 3 miles
0 1 2 3 4 5 km

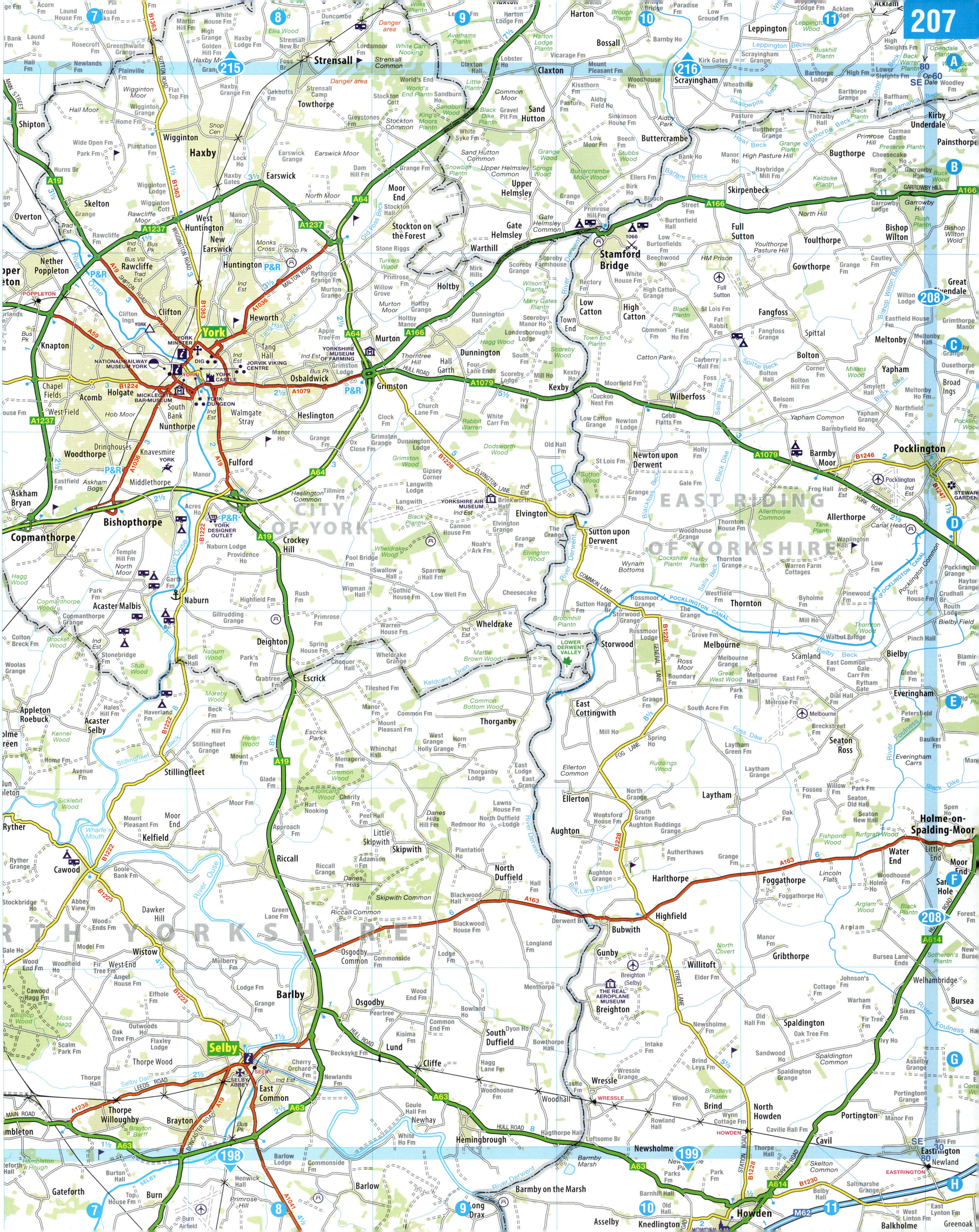
York
Selby
Strensall
Haxby
Wigginton
Earswick
Skelton
Shipton
Overton
Nether Poppleton
Rawcliffe
Clifton
Huntington
Heworth
Osbaldwick
Acomb
Holgate
Knapton
Woodthorpe
Dringhouses
Askham Bryan
Copmanthorpe
Bishopthorpe
Fulford
Heslington
Grimston
Murton
Dunnington
Kexby
Elvington
Wheldrake
Escrick
Naburn
Deighton
Crockey Hill
Stamford Bridge
Full Sutton
Fangfoss
Wilberfoss
Pocklington
Yapham
Meltonby
Allerthorpe
Melbourne
Thornton
Storwood
Sutton upon Derwent
Newton upon Derwent
East Cottingwith
Thorganby
Ellerton
Aughton
Laytham
Seaton Ross
Everingham
Bielby
Holme-on-Spalding-Moor
Harlthorpe
Foggathorpe
Highfield
Bubwith
Gunby
Breighton
Willitoft
Gribthorpe
Spaldington
Wressle
North Howden
Howden
Newsholme
Portington
Cavil
Eastrington
Barmby on the Marsh
Hemingbrough
Cliffe
Lund
South Duffield
North Duffield
Skipwith
Riccall
Barlby
Osgodby
Stillingfleet
Kelfield
Cawood
Wistow
Acaster Malbis
Acaster Selby
Appleton Roebuck
Thorpe Willoughby
Brayton
Barlow
Burn
Gateforth
Leppington
Scrayingham
Claxton
Harton
Bossall
Sand Hutton
Upper Helmsley
Gate Helmsley
Warthill
Holtby
Stockton on the Forest
Moor End
Skirpenbeck
Buttercrambe
Bugthorpe
Kirby Underdale
Youlthorpe
Bishop Wilton
Gowthorpe
Low Catton
High Catton
Spittal
Bolton
Barmby Moor
CITY OF YORK
EAST RIDING OF YORKSHIRE
NORTH YORKSHIRE
A19
A64
A1079
A166
A163
A63
A1237
A59
A1036
A614
B1228
B1222
B1223
B1363
B1224
B1246
B1247
M62

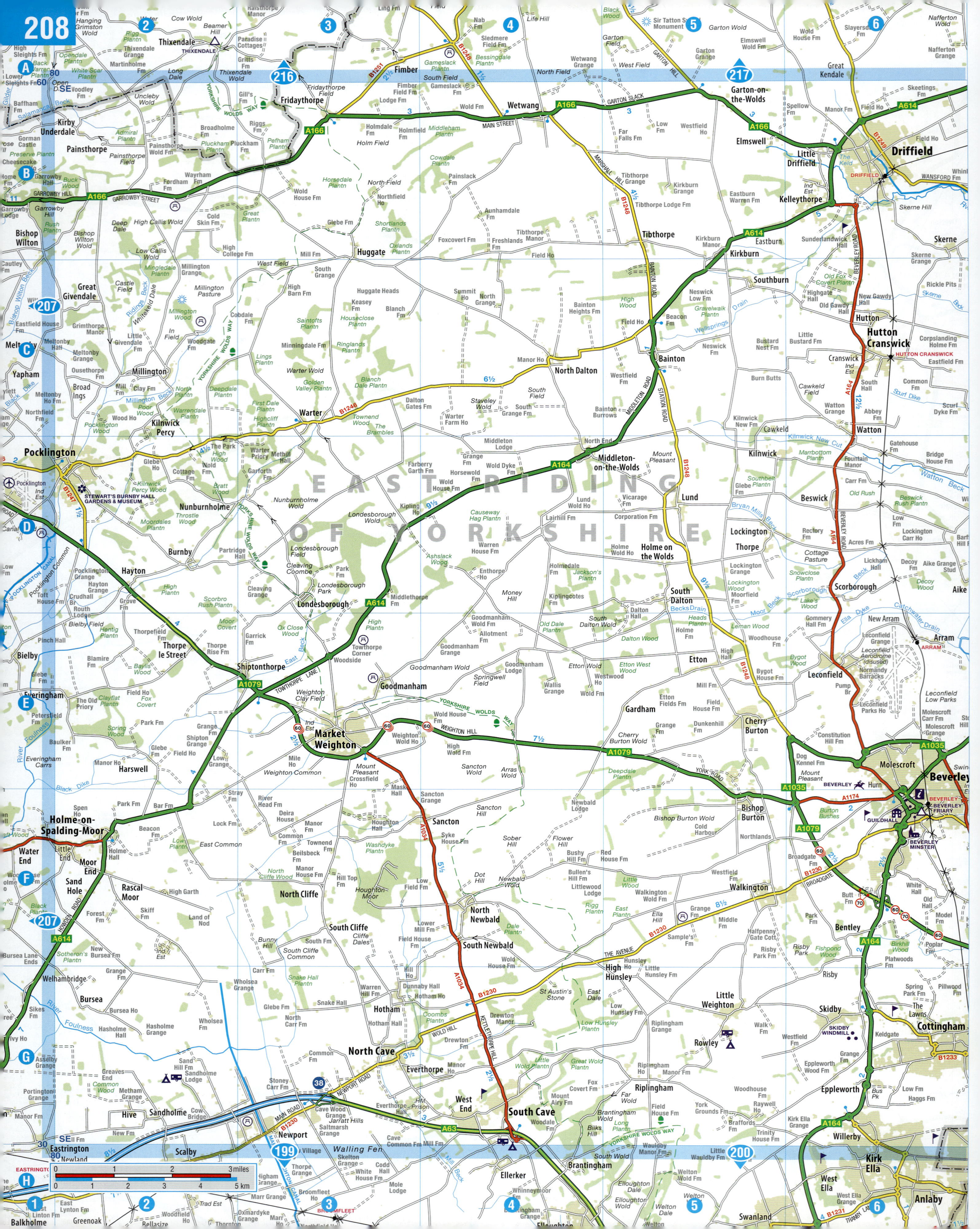

EAST RIDING OF YORKSHIRE
Driffield
Beverley
Pocklington
Market Weighton
Holme-on-Spalding-Moor
Cottingham
Fridaythorpe
Wetwang
Fimber
Thixendale
Garton-on-the-Wolds
Kirby Underdale
Bishop Wilton
Great Givendale
Millington
Huggate
Warter
North Dalton
Bainton
Tibthorpe
Kirkburn
Southburn
Hutton Cranswick
Watton
Kilnwick
Middleton-on-the-Wolds
Lund
Lockington
Beswick
Scorborough
Leconfield
Arram
Etton
South Dalton
Holme on the Wolds
Cherry Burton
Bishop Burton
Walkington
Molescroft
Londesborough
Goodmanham
Shiptonthorpe
Hayton
Burnby
Nunburnholme
Kilnwick Percy
Yapham
Everingham
Harswell
Thorpe le Street
Bielby
Sancton
North Newbald
South Newbald
North Cliffe
South Cliffe
Hotham
North Cave
South Cave
Everthorpe
West End
Newport
Gilberdyke
Eastrington
Sandholme
Hive
Bursea
Welhambridge
Ellerker
Brantingham
Riplingham
Rowley
Little Weighton
High Hunsley
Skidby
Eppleworth
Willerby
Kirk Ella
West Ella
Anlaby
Swanland
Bentley
Risby
Balkholme
YORKSHIRE WOLDS WAY
A166
A614
A164
A1079
A1035
A63
A1034
B1248
B1246
B1230
B1251
216
217
207
199
200
STEWART'S BURNBY HALL GARDENS & MUSEUM
SKIDBY WINDMILL
BEVERLEY MINSTER
GUILDHALL
0 1 2 3 miles
0 1 2 3 4 5 km

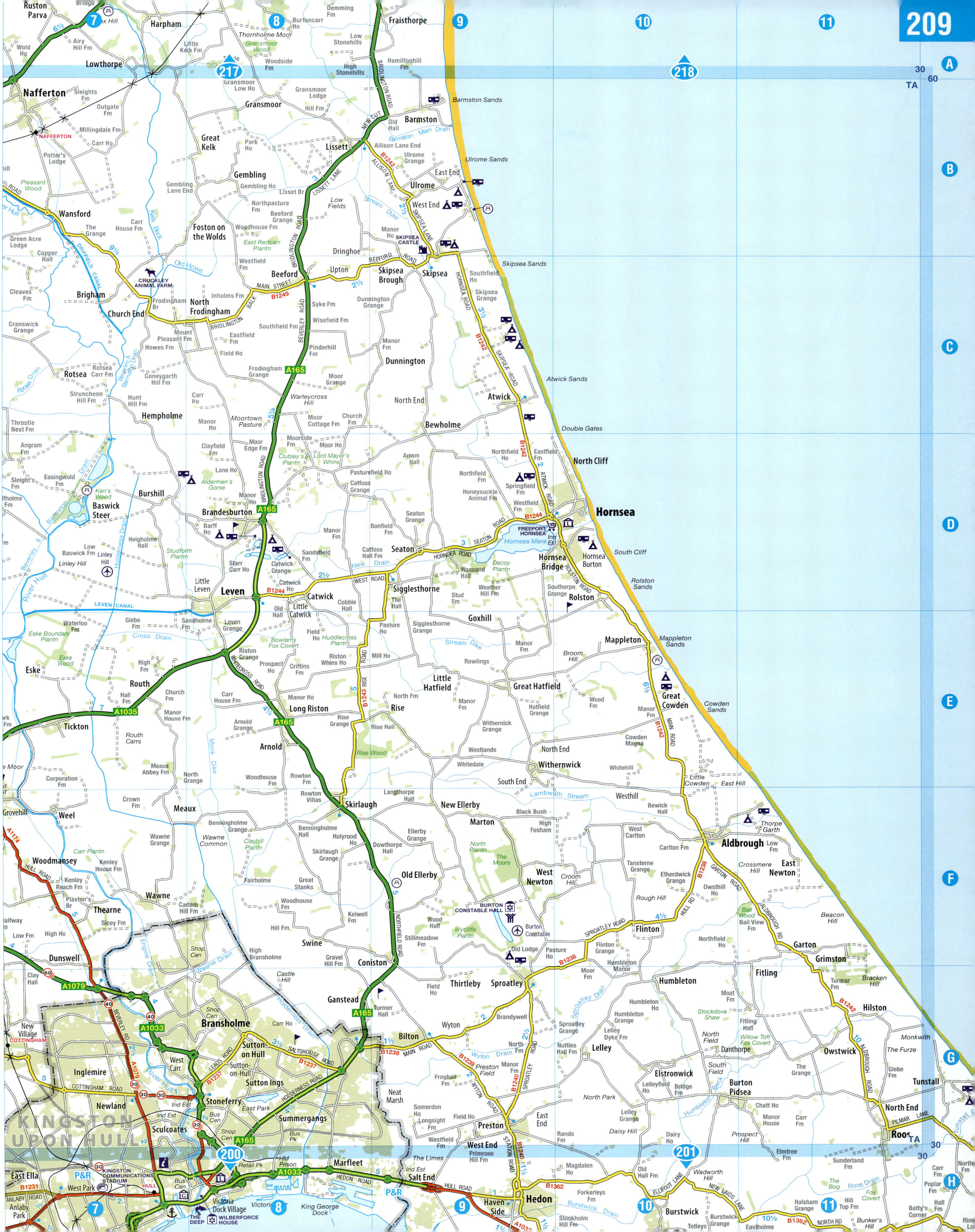
Ruston Parva
Harpham
Fraisthorpe
Lowthorpe
Nafferton
Gransmoor
Barmston
Barmston Sands
Great Kelk
Lissett
Gembling
Ulrome
Ulrome Sands
Wansford
Foston on the Wolds
Skipsea
Skipsea Castle
Skipsea Brough
Skipsea Sands
Beeford
Brigham
Church End
North Frodingham
Cruckley Animal Farm
Rotsea
Dunnington
Atwick
Atwick Sands
Hempholme
Bewholme
Double Gates
North Cliff
Burshill
Baswick Steer
Brandesburton
Hornsea
Freeport Hornsea
Hornsea Mere
Hornsea Bridge
Hornsea Burton
South Cliff
Seaton
Leven
Leven Canal
Catwick
Sigglesthorne
Rolston
Rolston Sands
Goxhill
Mappleton
Mappleton Sands
Eske
Routh
Little Hatfield
Great Hatfield
Great Cowden
Cowden Sands
Tickton
Long Riston
Rise
Arnold
Withernwick
Meaux
Skirlaugh
New Ellerby
Marton
Aldbrough
East Newton
Weel
Woodmansey
Old Ellerby
West Newton
Wawne
Thearne
Burton Constable Hall
Flinton
Garton
Grimston
Dunswell
Swine
Coniston
Thirtleby
Sproatley
Humbleton
Fitling
Hilston
Ganstead
Bransholme
Bilton
Wyton
Lelley
Owstwick
Sutton-on-Hull
Sutton Ings
Inglemire
Elstronwick
Burton Pidsea
Tunstall
Newland
Stoneferry
Summergangs
Preston
North End
Sculcoates
Kingston upon Hull
Roos
Marfleet
Salt End
West End
East Ella
West Park
Anlaby Park
Victoria Dock Village
The Deep
Wilberforce House
Kingston Communications Stadium
Hedon
Haven Side
Burstwick
King George Dock
A165
A1035
A1079
A1033
A1174
B1242
B1249
B1244
B1243
B1238
B1237
B1239
B1240
B1362
B1231
217
218
200
201
TA

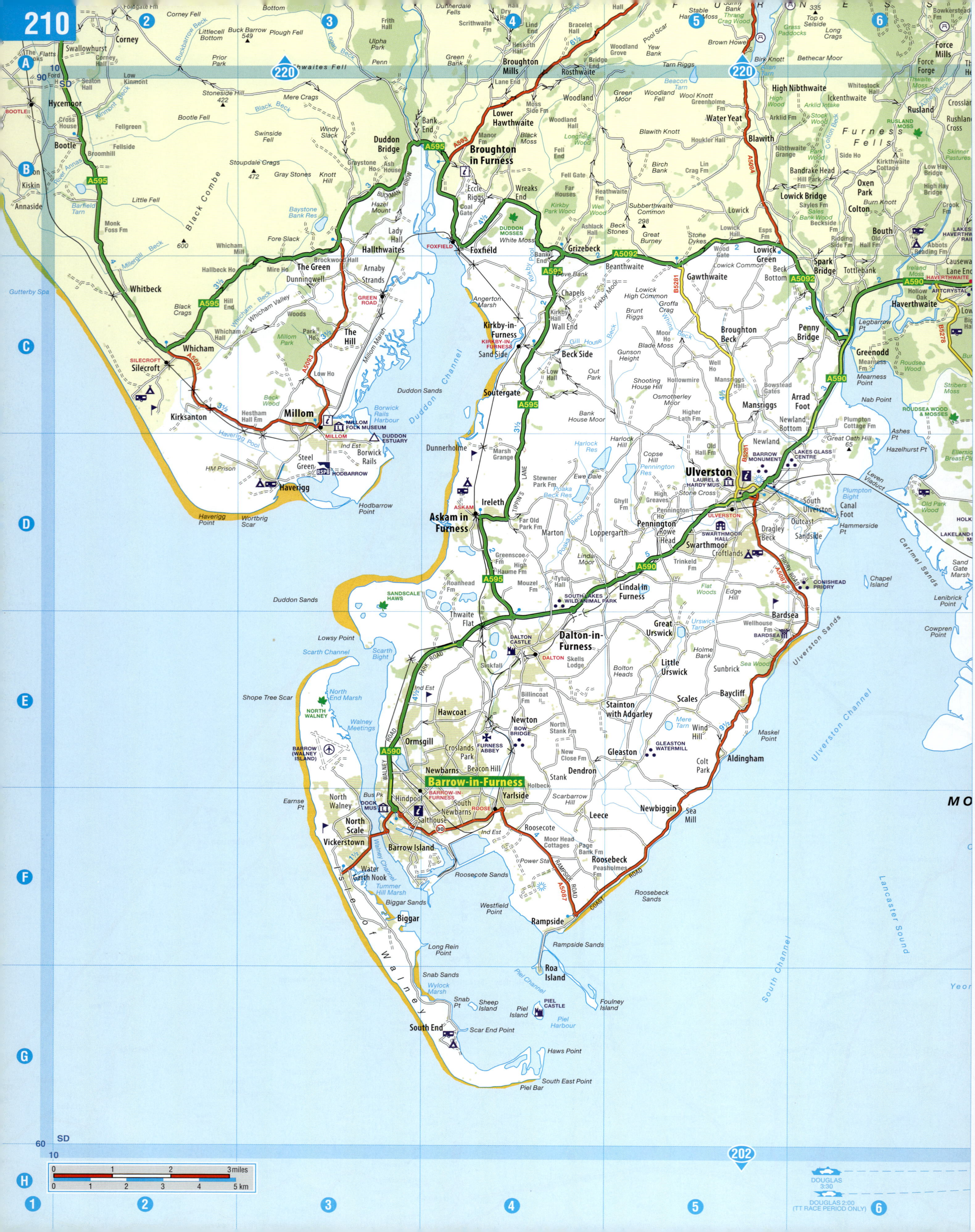

220
202
SD
Corney
Swallowhurst
Hycemoor
Bootle
Kiskin
Annaside
Whitbeck
Whicham
Silecroft
Kirksanton
Millom
Haverigg
The Green
The Hill
Duddon Bridge
Broughton Mills
Broughton in Furness
Foxfield
Hallthwaites
Kirkby-in-Furness
Sand Side
Soutergate
Grizebeck
Gawthwaite
Lowick Green
Lowick Bridge
Spark Bridge
Penny Bridge
Greenodd
Broughton Beck
Mansriggs
Arrad Foot
Newland
Ulverston
Swarthmoor
Pennington
Ireleth
Askam in Furness
Lindal in Furness
Dalton-in-Furness
Great Urswick
Little Urswick
Bardsea
Baycliff
Scales
Stainton with Adgarley
Gleaston
Aldingham
Dendron
Newbiggin
Leece
Roosebeck
Rampside
Roa Island
Yarlside
Barrow-in-Furness
Newbarns
Ormsgill
Hawcoat
Newton
North Walney
North Scale
Vickerstown
Barrow Island
Biggar
South End
Isle of Walney
Haverthwaite
Water Yeat
Blawith
High Nibthwaite
Rusland
Oxen Park
Colton
Bouth
Furness Fells
Black Combe
Duddon Sands
Duddon Channel
Ulverston Sands
Ulverston Channel
South Channel
Lancaster Sound
Piel Island
Piel Castle
Furness Abbey
A590
A595
A5092
A5093
A5087
A5084
B5281
A593
0 1 2 3 miles
0 1 2 3 4 5 km
DOUGLAS 3:30
DOUGLAS 2:00 (TT RACE PERIOD ONLY)

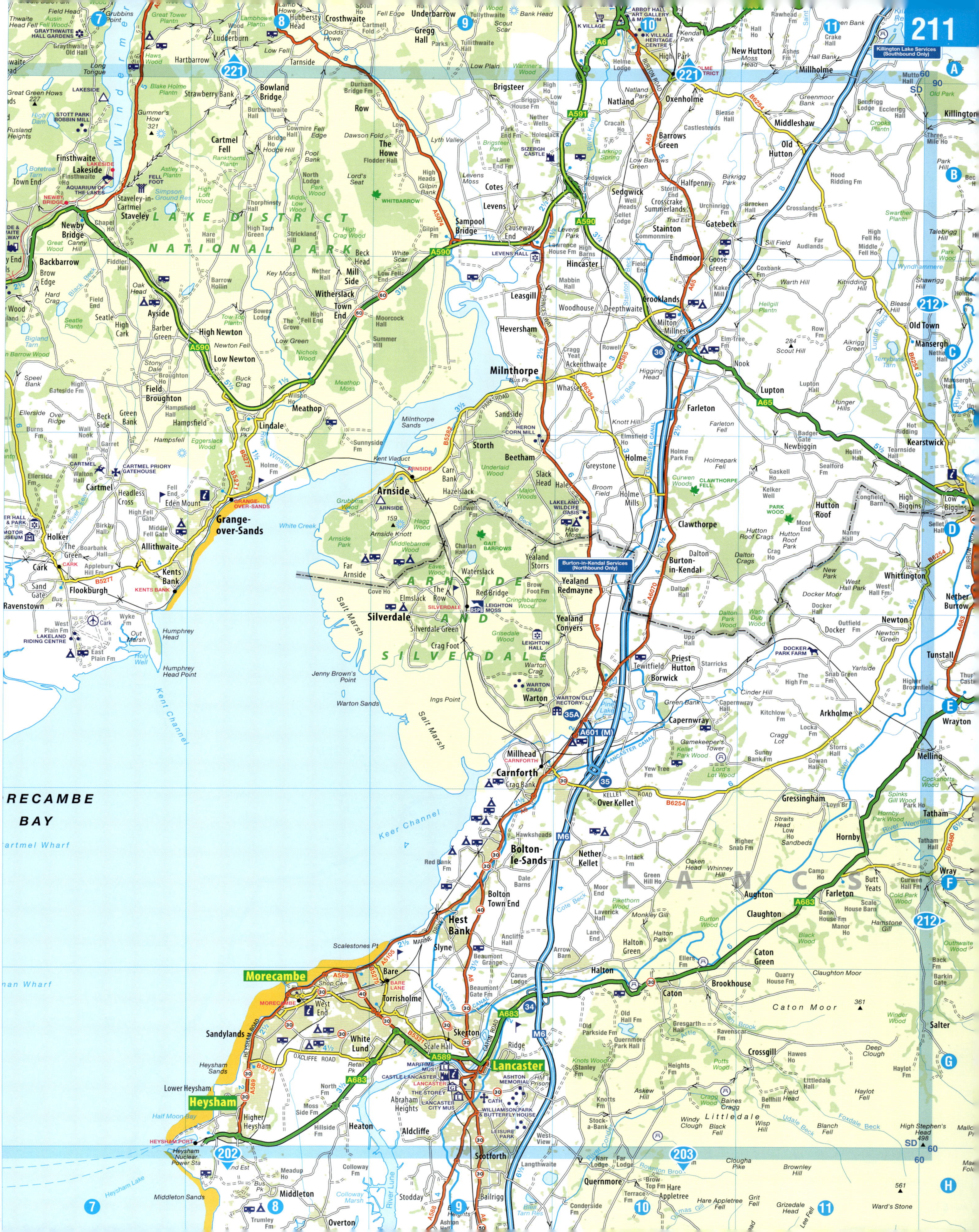

Killington Lake Services (Southbound Only)
Burton-in-Kendal Services (Northbound Only)
LAKE DISTRICT NATIONAL PARK
ARNSIDE AND SILVERDALE
MORECAMBE BAY
Kent Channel
Keer Channel
Salt Marsh
Windermere
Lakeside
Finsthwaite
Newby Bridge
Staveley-in-Cartmel
Backbarrow
Ayside
High Newton
Low Newton
Field Broughton
Lindale
Meathop
Grange-over-Sands
Cartmel
Allithwaite
Kents Bank
Flookburgh
Cark
Holker
Ravenstown
Humphrey Head
Humphrey Head Point
Witherslack
Levens
Sampool Bridge
Levens Hall
Brigsteer
Natland
Oxenholme
Barrows Green
Sedgwick
Stainton
Endmoor
Crooklands
Milton
Hincaster
Heversham
Leasgill
Milnthorpe
Sandside
Storth
Beetham
Arnside
Arnside Knott
Far Arnside
Silverdale
Yealand Conyers
Yealand Redmayne
Burton-in-Kendal
Holme
Clawthorpe
Hutton Roof
Priest Hutton
Borwick
Warton
Carnforth
Over Kellet
Nether Kellet
Bolton-le-Sands
Hest Bank
Slyne
Bare
Morecambe
Torrisholme
Sandylands
Heysham
Lower Heysham
Middleton
Overton
Heaton
Aldcliffe
Lancaster
Skerton
Scotforth
Halton
Caton
Brookhouse
Caton Moor
Claughton
Aughton
Gressingham
Hornby
Wray
Farleton
Tatham
Melling
Wrayton
Arkholme
Whittington
Tunstall
Newton
Kearstwick
Lupton
Farleton
Mansergh
Old Town
Middleshaw
Old Hutton
Millholme
Killington
Lambrigg
Crosthwaite
Underbarrow
Strawberry Bank
Bowland Bridge
Cartmel Fell
Halton Green
Quernmore
Littledale
Salter
A590
A591
A6
A65
A683
A589
A601 (M)
M6
B6254
B5277
B5282
B5321
B5273
221
212
203
202

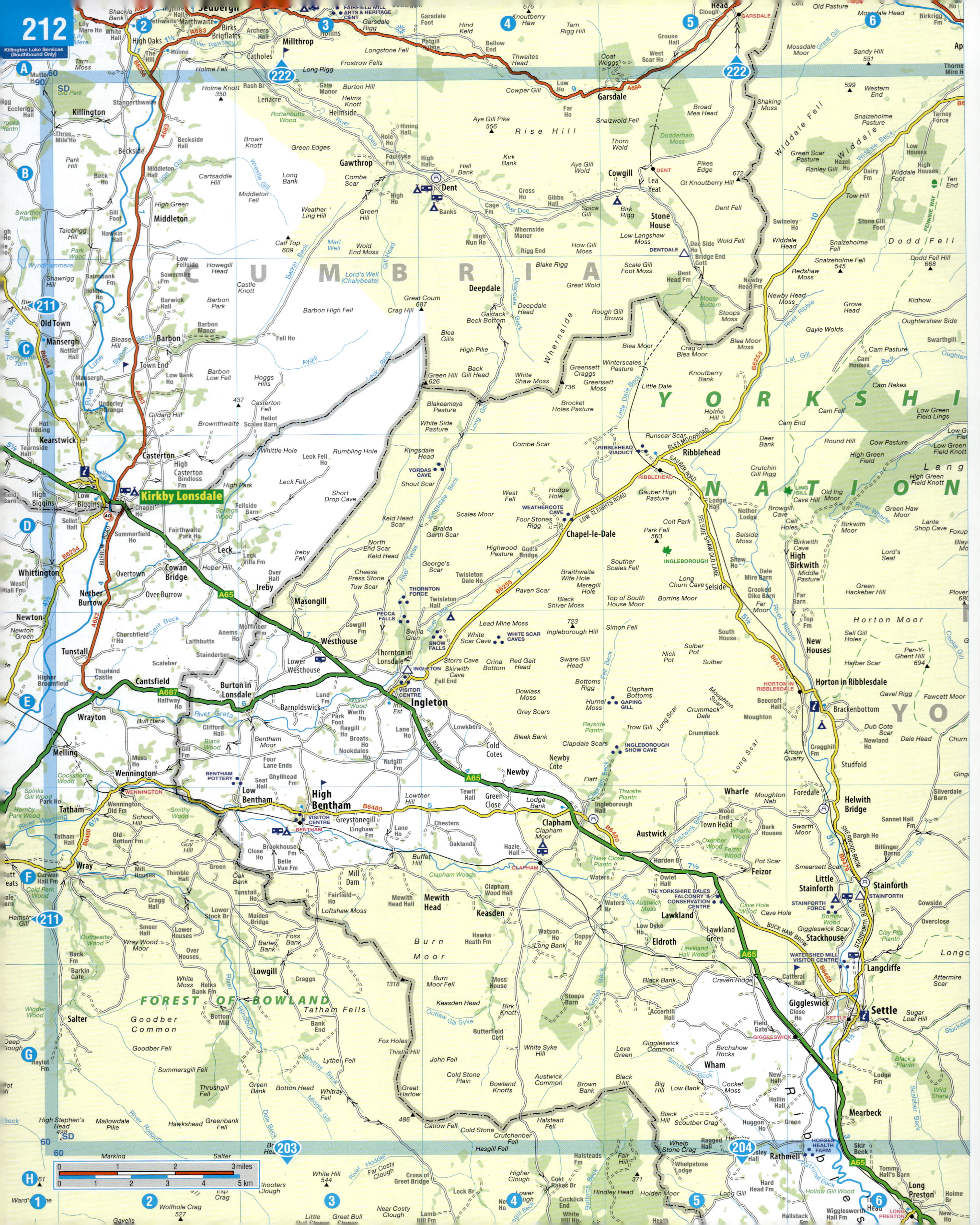
Killington Lake Services (Southbound Only)
Sedbergh
Millthrop
Hollins
Marthwaite
Birks
Brigflatts
Catholes
Frostrow Fells
Garsdale
Garsdale Head
Killington
Middleton
Old Town
Mansergh
Barbon
Casterton
Kirkby Lonsdale
Kearstwick
High Biggins
Low Biggins
Whittington
Nether Burrow
Over Burrow
Cowan Bridge
Leck
Ireby
Masongill
Westhouse
Lower Westhouse
Thornton in Lonsdale
Ingleton
Burton in Lonsdale
Cantsfield
Tunstall
Newton
Wrayton
Melling
Wennington
Tatham
Wray
Low Bentham
High Bentham
Clapham
Newby
Austwick
Lawkland
Eldroth
Keasden
Mewith Head
Lowgill
Salter
Deepdale
Dent
Gawthrop
Cowgill
Stone House
Ribblehead
Chapel-le-Dale
Selside
Horton in Ribblesdale
Helwith Bridge
Stainforth
Little Stainforth
Stackhouse
Langcliffe
Giggleswick
Settle
Wharfe
Feizor
Rathmell
Mearbeck
Long Preston
Wham
C U M B R I A
Y O R K S H I R E   D A L E S   N A T I O N A L   P A R K
FOREST OF BOWLAND
Whernside
Rise Hill
Widdale Fell
Dodd Fell
Horton Moor
Burn Moor
Tatham Fells
Goodber Common
Gaping Gill
White Scar Caves
Ingleborough Show Cave
Ingleborough Hill 723
Ribblehead Viaduct
Yordas Cave
Thornton Force
Pecca Falls
Snow Falls
A683
A684
A65
A687
B6254
B6255
B6480
B6479
B6478
Blea Moor Road
Low Sleights Road
Bentham Pottery
The Yorkshire Dales Falconry & Conservation Centre
Watershed Mill Visitor Centre
Horses Health Farm
211
222
203
204
0 1 2 3 miles
0 1 2 3 4 5 km

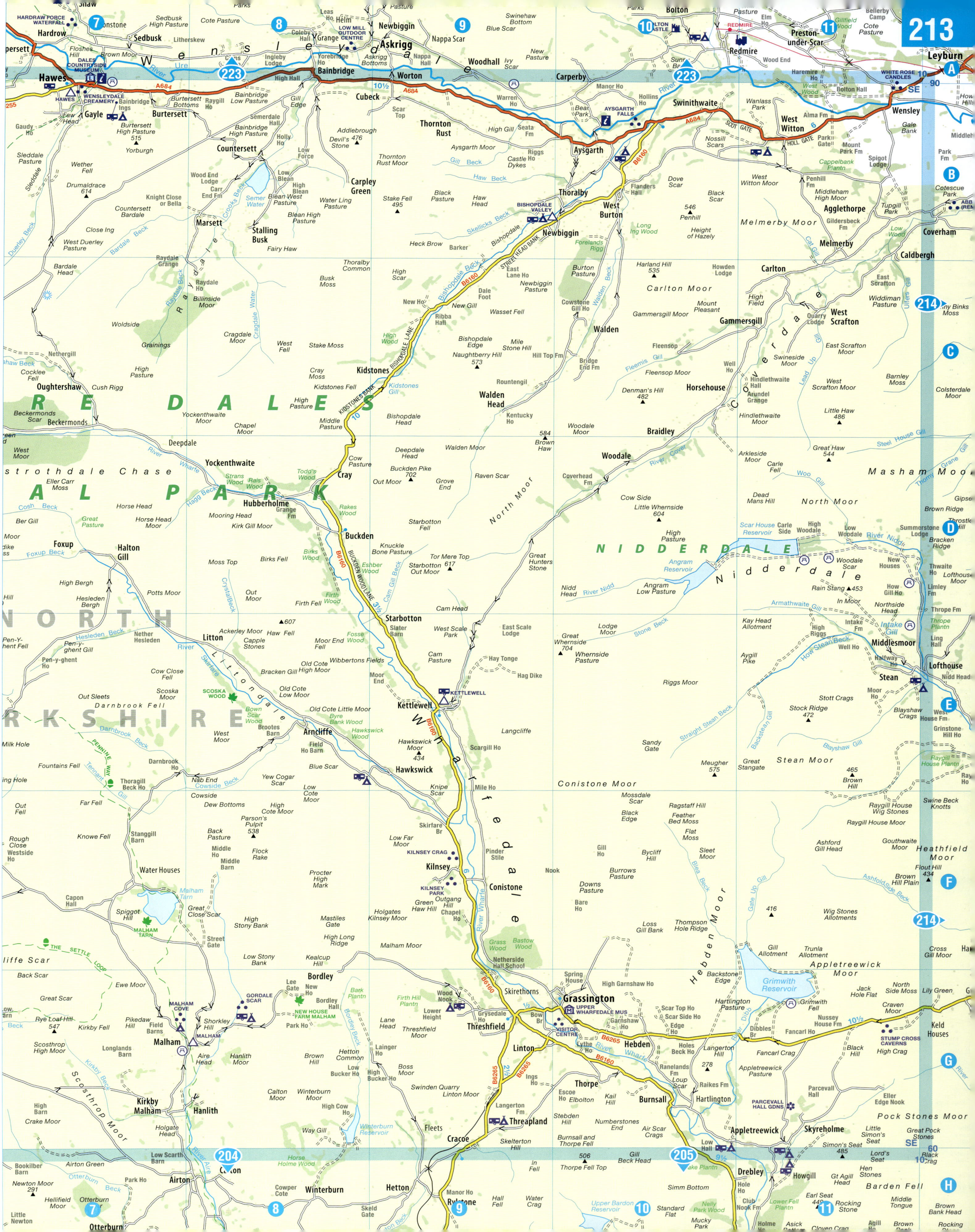
Hardraw Force Waterfall
Hardrow
Sedbusk
Hawes
Dales Countryside Museum
Wensleydale Creamery
Gayle
Burtersett
Askrigg
Bainbridge
Worton
Cubeck
Nappa Scar
Woodhall
Carperby
Aysgarth
Aysgarth Falls
Swinithwaite
Redmire
Preston-under-Scar
Leyburn
Wensley
West Witton
Thoralby
West Burton
Newbiggin
Countersett
Semer Water
Marsett
Stalling Busk
Carpley Green
Thornton Rust
Raydale
Walden
Walden Head
Carlton
Carlton Moor
West Scrafton
Gammersgill
Horsehouse
Braidley
Woodale
Coverdale
Melmerby
Coverham
Caldbergh
Kidstones
Cray
Hubberholme
Buckden
Yockenthwaite
Deepdale
Oughtershaw
Beckermonds
Foxup
Halton Gill
Litton
Littondale
Starbotton
Kettlewell
Arncliffe
Hawkswick
Kilnsey
Conistone
Wharfedale
Grassington
Threshfield
Linton
Hebden
Thorpe
Burnsall
Hartlington
Appletreewick
Skyreholme
Cracoe
Rylstone
Hetton
Winterburn
Airton
Calton
Kirkby Malham
Malham
Malham Tarn
Malham Cove
Gordale Scar
Hanlith
Otterburn
Bordley
Lofthouse
Middlesmoor
Stean
Ramsgill
Nidderdale
Angram Reservoir
Scar House Reservoir
Grimwith Reservoir
Stump Cross Caverns
Parcevall Hall Gdns
Drebley
Howgill
Barden Fell
Pock Stones Moor
Masham Moor
Great Whernside
Buckden Pike
Conistone Moor
Hebden Moor
Appletreewick Moor
Fountains Fell
Pen-y-ghent
Yorkshire Dales National Park
North Yorkshire
Langstrothdale Chase
A684
B6160
B6265
223
214
204
205

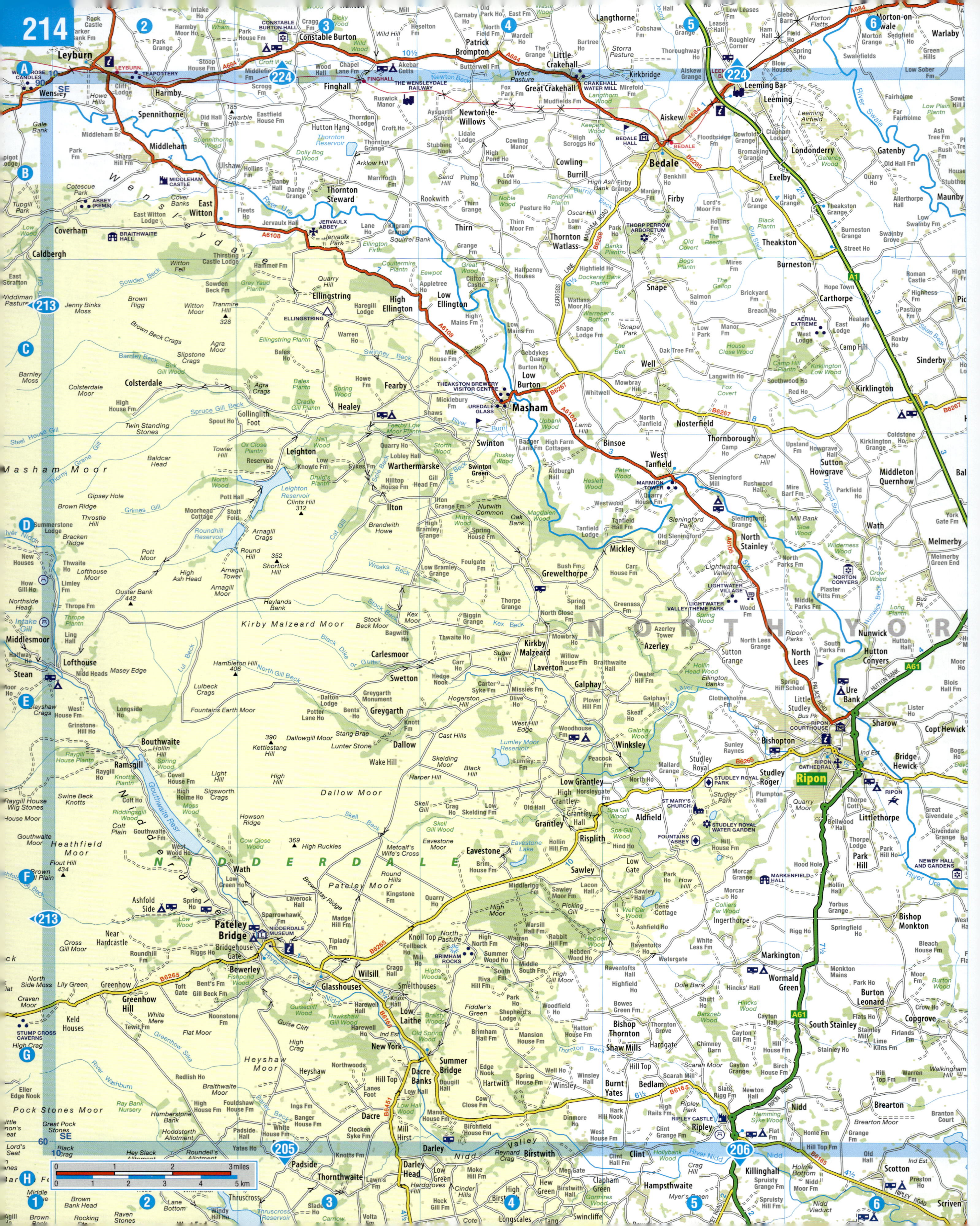
Leyburn
Wensley
Harmby
Spennithorne
Middleham
Constable Burton
Finghall
Patrick Brompton
Newton-le-Willows
Little Crakehall
Great Crakehall
Kirkbridge
Langthorne
Aiskew
Bedale
Leeming Bar
Leeming
Londonderry
Gatenby
Exelby
Firby
Morton-on-Swale
Warlaby
Maunby
Coverham
Caldbergh
East Witton
Thornton Steward
Thirn
Cowling
Burrill
Thornton Watlass
Theakston
Burneston
Snape
Carthorpe
Sinderby
Kirklington
Ellingstring
High Ellington
Low Ellington
Masham
Fearby
Healey
Colsterdale
Swinton
Warthermarske
Ilton
Well
Nosterfield
Thornborough
West Tanfield
Binsoe
Sutton Howgrave
Middleton Quernhow
Wath
Melmerby
Mickley
Grewelthorpe
North Stainley
Kirkby Malzeard
Laverton
Azerley
Galphay
Carlesmoor
Swetton
Greygarth
Dallow
Winksley
Sutton Grange
North Lees
Nunwick
Hutton Conyers
Ure Bank
Sharow
Copt Hewick
Bridge Hewick
Ripon
Bishopton
Studley Roger
Littlethorpe
Grantley
Risplith
Aldfield
Sawley
Eavestone
Park Hill
Bishop Monkton
Markington
Wormald Green
Burton Leonard
Copgrove
South Stainley
Bishop Thornton
Shaw Mills
Hardgate
Bedlam
Burnt Yates
Ripley
Nidd
Brearton
Scotton
Killinghall
Clint
Hampsthwaite
Birstwith
Darley
Dacre
Dacre Banks
Summer Bridge
New York
Low Laithe
Wilsill
Glasshouses
Pateley Bridge
Bewerley
Wath
Ramsgill
Bouthwaite
Lofthouse
Middlesmoor
Stean
Greenhow
Greenhow Hill
Keld Houses
Padside
Thornthwaite
Darley Head
Masham Moor
Kirkby Malzeard Moor
Dallow Moor
Heathfield Moor
Pateley Moor
Heyshaw Moor
Pock Stones Moor
NIDDERDALE
NORTH YOR
Leighton Reservoir
Roundhill Reservoir
Gouthwaite Reservoir
River Ure
River Nidd
River Swale
Wensleydale
A684
A6108
B6267
B6268
B6265
B6165
B6451
A61
A1
THE WENSLEYDALE RAILWAY
JERVAULX ABBEY
MIDDLEHAM CASTLE
CONSTABLE BURTON HALL
BEDALE HALL
THORP PERROW ARBORETUM
THEAKSTON BREWERY VISITOR CENTRE
MARMION TOWER
LIGHTWATER VALLEY THEME PARK
NORTON CONYERS
STUDLEY ROYAL PARK
STUDLEY ROYAL WATER GARDEN
FOUNTAINS ABBEY
RIPON CATHEDRAL
MARKENFIELD HALL
NEWBY HALL AND GARDENS
BRIMHAM ROCKS
NIDDERDALE MUSEUM
STUMP CROSS CAVERNS
RIPLEY CASTLE
224
213
205
206
0 1 2 3 miles
0 1 2 3 4 5 km

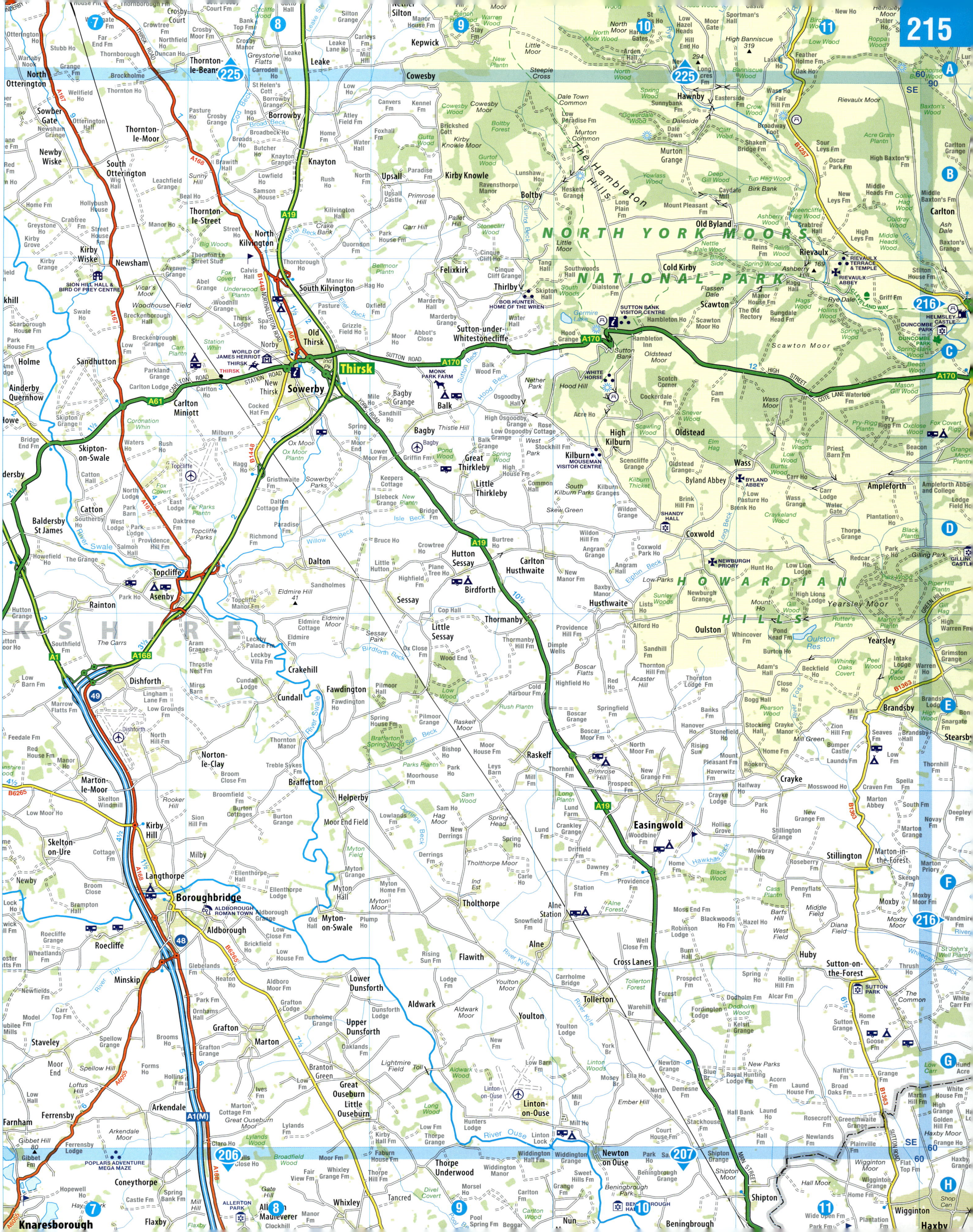
NORTH YORK MOORS NATIONAL PARK
HOWARDIAN HILLS
The Hambleton Hills
Thirsk
Sowerby
Old Thirsk
Thornton-le-Beans
Thornton-le-Moor
Thornton-le-Street
North Kilvington
South Kilvington
Knayton
Borrowby
Leake
Cowesby
Kepwick
Silton
Upsall
Kirby Knowle
Boltby
Felixkirk
Thirlby
Sutton-under-Whitestonecliffe
Sutton Bank
Hambleton
Cold Kirby
Old Byland
Rievaulx
Hawnby
Murton Grange
Scawton
Oldstead
High Kilburn
Kilburn
Wass
Byland Abbey
Ampleforth
Coxwold
Oulston
Yearsley
Brandsby
Stearsby
Crayke
Easingwold
Stillington
Marton-in-the-Forest
Moxby
Huby
Sutton-on-the-Forest
Tollerton
Alne
Youlton
Linton-on-Ouse
Newton on Ouse
Shipton
Beningbrough
Wigginton
Haxby
Nun Monkton
Whixley
Thorpe Underwood
Great Ouseburn
Little Ouseburn
Upper Dunsforth
Lower Dunsforth
Aldwark
Flawith
Tholthorpe
Myton-on-Swale
Helperby
Brafferton
Raskelf
Thormanby
Little Sessay
Sessay
Birdforth
Hutton Sessay
Carlton Husthwaite
Husthwaite
Dalton
Crakehill
Cundall
Fawdington
Norton-le-Clay
Dishforth
Rainton
Asenby
Topcliffe
Baldersby St James
Catton
Skipton-on-Swale
Carlton Miniott
Sandhutton
Newsham
Kirby Wiske
South Otterington
North Otterington
Newby Wiske
Sowber Gate
Marton-le-Moor
Kirby Hill
Langthorpe
Boroughbridge
Aldborough
Roecliffe
Skelton-on-Ure
Milby
Minskip
Grafton
Marton
Staveley
Arkendale
Ferrensby
Farnham
Coneythorpe
Flaxby
Knaresborough
Allerton Mauleverer
Helmsley
Bagby
Balk
Great Thirkleby
Little Thirkleby
Bagby
Thirsk
A19
A170
A168
A61
A1
A1(M)
B1448
B6265
B1363
B1257
River Swale
River Ouse
River Kyle
Sutton Park
Newburgh Priory
Shandy Hall
World of James Herriot
Sutton Bank Visitor Centre
Rievaulx Terrace & Temple
Rievaulx Abbey
Byland Abbey
Duncombe Park
Helmsley Castle
Aldborough Roman Town
Sion Hill Hall & Bird of Prey Centre
Poplars Adventure Mega Maze
Monk Park Farm
Mouseman Visitor Centre
Bob Hunter Home of the Wren
White Horse

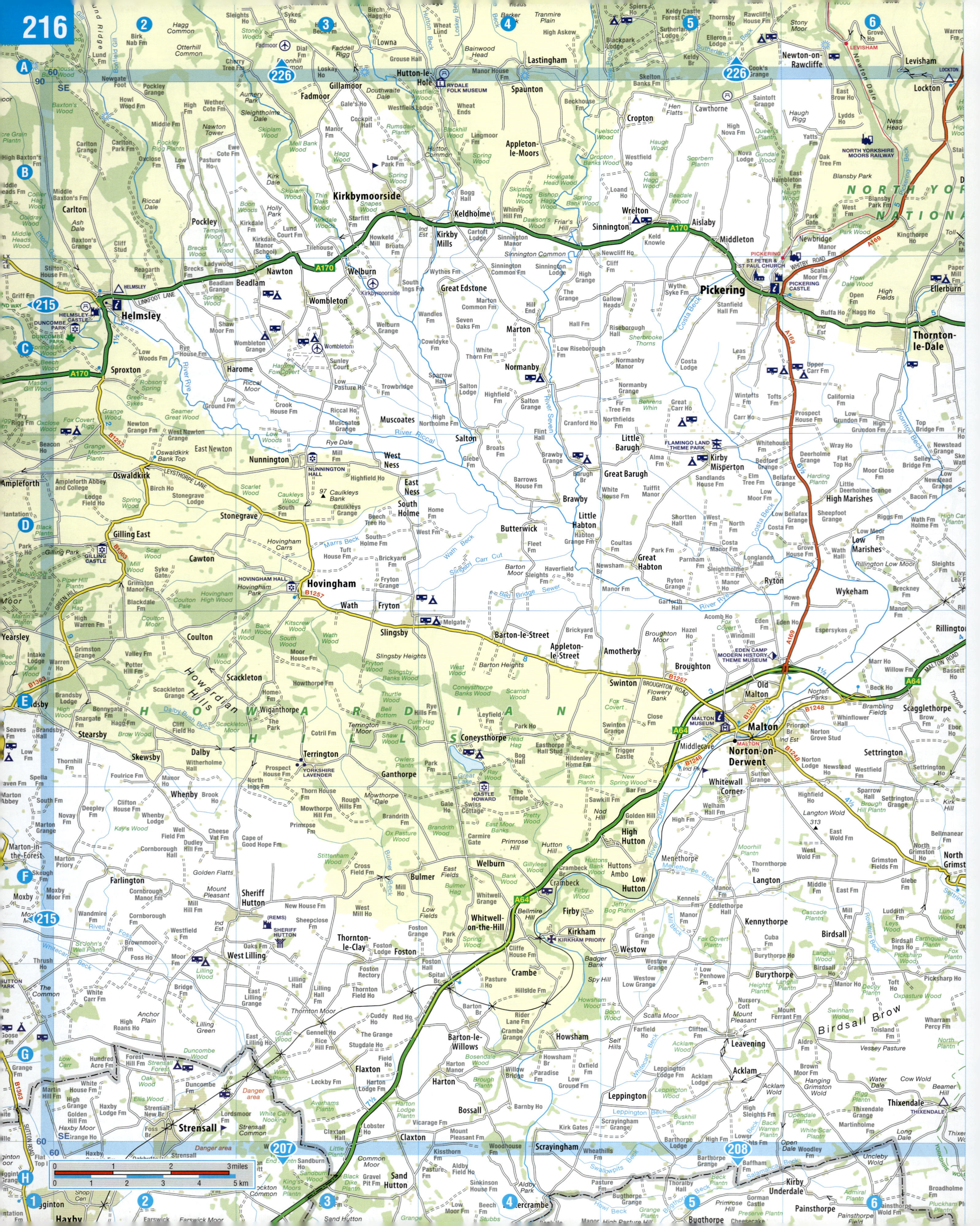
Helmsley
Kirkbymoorside
Pickering
Malton
Norton-on-Derwent
Old Malton
Hovingham
Slingsby
Nawton
Beadlam
Wombleton
Harome
Sproxton
Oswaldkirk
Ampleforth
Gilling East
Cawton
Coulton
Stonegrave
Nunnington
West Ness
East Ness
South Holme
Salton
Muscoates
Great Edstone
Marton
Normanby
Sinnington
Wrelton
Aislaby
Middleton
Cropton
Lastingham
Spaunton
Appleton-le-Moors
Hutton-le-Hole
Gillamoor
Fadmoor
Keldholme
Kirkby Mills
Welburn
Carlton
Pockley
Newton-on-Rawcliffe
Levisham
Lockton
Thornton-le-Dale
Ellerburn
Newbridge
Kirby Misperton
Great Barugh
Little Barugh
Brawby
Little Habton
Great Habton
Butterwick
Ryton
Wykeham
High Marishes
Low Marishes
Rillington
Scagglethorpe
Settrington
Swinton
Broughton
Amotherby
Appleton-le-Street
Barton-le-Street
Wath
Fryton
Terrington
Coneysthorpe
Ganthorpe
Welburn
Bulmer
Whitwell-on-the-Hill
Crambe
Firby
Kirkham
Westow
Huttons Ambo
High Hutton
Low Hutton
Menethorpe
Langton
Kennythorpe
Birdsall
Burythorpe
Leavening
Acklam
Thixendale
Howsham
Barton-le-Willows
Harton
Bossall
Flaxton
Claxton
Sand Hutton
Scrayingham
Leppington
Stearsby
Dalby
Skewsby
Whenby
Brandsby
Yearsley
Scackleton
Farlington
Sheriff Hutton
West Lilling
Thornton-le-Clay
Foston
Strensall
Kirby Underdale
Painsthorpe
Bugthorpe
Whitwell Corner
Howardian Hills
HOWARDIAN
NORTH YORK MOORS NATIONAL PARK
Birdsall Brow
A170
A169
A64
B1257
B1363
B1248
215
226
207
208
NUNNINGTON HALL
CASTLE HOWARD
KIRKHAM PRIORY
MALTON MUSEUM
EDEN CAMP MODERN HISTORY THEME MUSEUM
FLAMINGO LAND THEME PARK
PICKERING CASTLE
RYEDALE FOLK MUSEUM
HELMSLEY CASTLE
DUNCOMBE PARK
GILLING CASTLE
HOVINGHAM HALL
NORTH YORKSHIRE MOORS RAILWAY
SHERIFF HUTTON
Danger area
0 1 2 3 miles
0 1 2 3 4 5 km

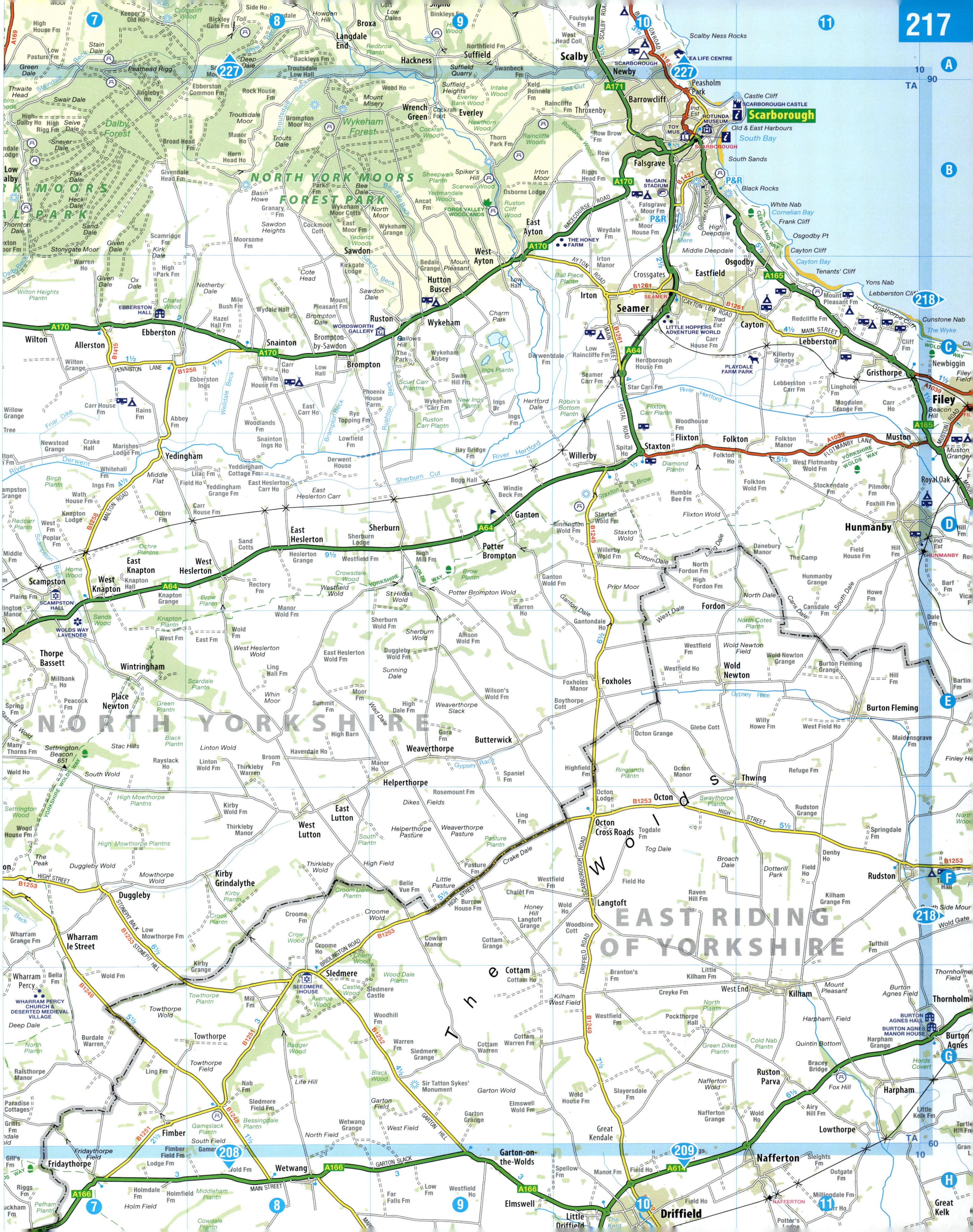

NORTH YORK MOORS FOREST PARK
NORTH YORKSHIRE
EAST RIDING OF YORKSHIRE
The Wolds
Scarborough
Scalby
Newby
Scalby Ness Rocks
Sea Life Centre
Peasholm Park
Castle Cliff
Scarborough Castle
Old & East Harbours
South Bay
South Sands
Black Rocks
White Nab
Cornelian Bay
Frank Cliff
Osgodby Pt
Cayton Cliff
Cayton Bay
Tenants' Cliff
Yons Nab
Lebberston Cliff
Gristhorpe Cliff
Cunstone Nab
The Wyke
Filey
Newbiggin
Gristhorpe
Lebberston
Cayton
Osgodby
Eastfield
Crossgates
Seamer
Irton
East Ayton
West Ayton
Falsgrave
Barrowcliff
Throxenby
Hackness
Suffield
Everley
Wrench Green
Broxa
Langdale End
Dalby Forest
Wykeham Forest
Sawdon
Hutton Buscel
Wykeham
Ruston
Brompton-by-Sawdon
Brompton
Snainton
Ebberston
Allerston
Wilton
Yedingham
Scampston
West Knapton
East Knapton
West Heslerton
East Heslerton
Sherburn
Potter Brompton
Ganton
Willerby
Staxton
Flixton
Folkton
Muston
Hunmanby
Fordon
Wold Newton
Foxholes
Burton Fleming
Thwing
Octon
Octon Cross Roads
Rudston
Langtoft
Cottam
Kilham
Thornholme
Burton Agnes
Harpham
Ruston Parva
Lowthorpe
Nafferton
Driffield
Little Driffield
Elmswell
Garton-on-the-Wolds
Wetwang
Fimber
Fridaythorpe
Towthorpe
Sledmere
Sledmere House
Sledmere Castle
Wharram le Street
Wharram Percy Church & Deserted Medieval Village
Duggleby
Kirby Grindalythe
West Lutton
East Lutton
Helperthorpe
Weaverthorpe
Butterwick
Wintringham
Thorpe Bassett
Place Newton
Settrington Beacon
Scampston Hall
Wolds Way Lavender
Sir Tatton Sykes' Monument
Great Kendale
Great Kelk
Little Kelk
River Derwent
River Hertford
Sherburn Cut
Gypsey Race
A64
A165
A170
A171
A166
A614
A1039
B1249
B1253
B1248
B1251
B1252
B1261
B1258
B1415
227
218
208
209
TA

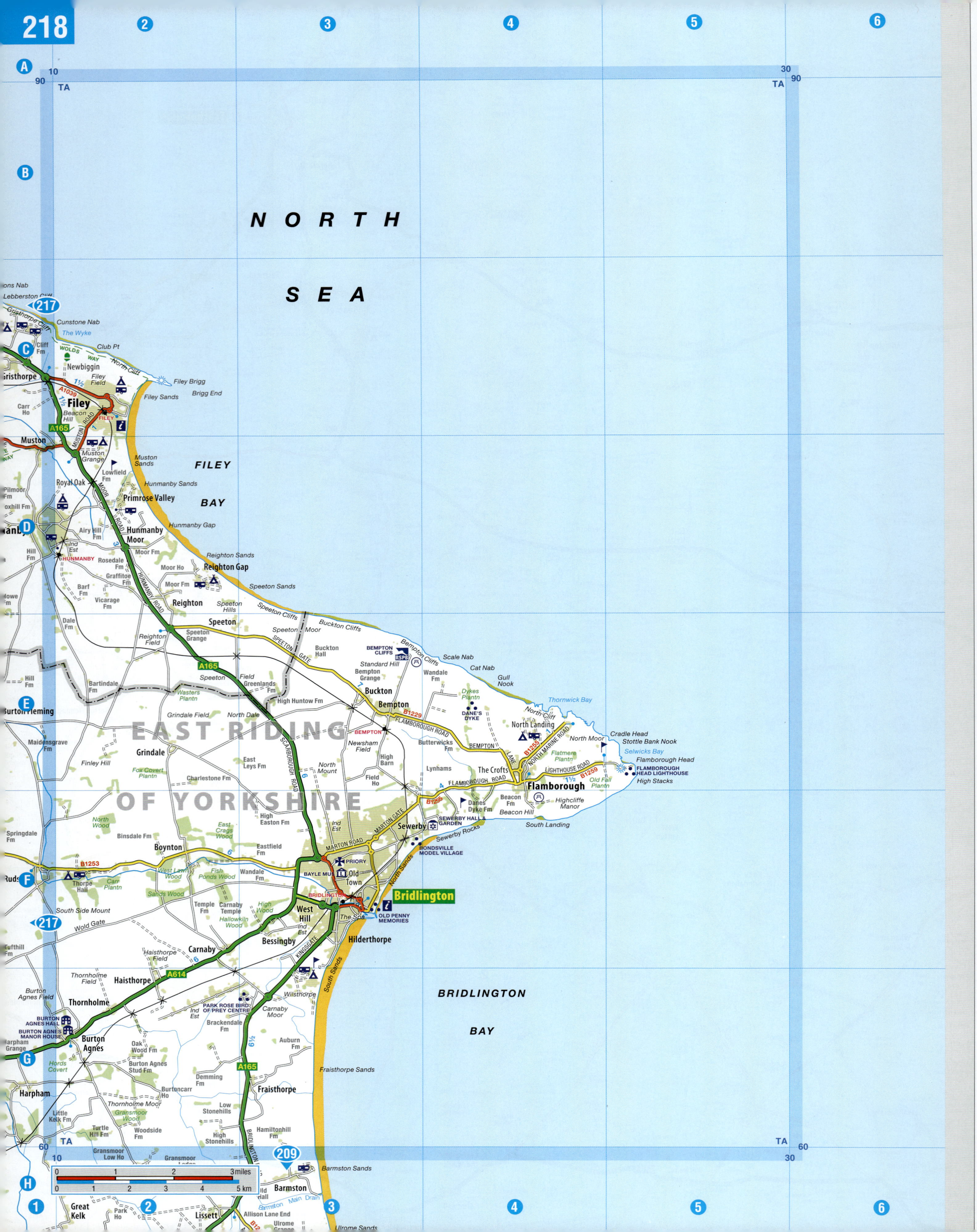

NORTH SEA
FILEY BAY
BRIDLINGTON BAY
EAST RIDING OF YORKSHIRE
217
209
Lebberston Cliff
Cunstone Nab
The Wyke
Club Pt
Newbiggin
North Cliff
Filey Brigg
Brigg End
Filey Sands
Filey Field
Filey
Gristhorpe
Beacon Hill
A1039
A165
Muston
Muston Grange
Muston Sands
Lowfield Fm
Royal Oak
Hunmanby Sands
Primrose Valley
Hunmanby Gap
Humanby Moor
Airy Hill Fm
HUNMANBY
Moor Fm
Rosedale Fm
Reighton Sands
Reighton Gap
Graffitoe Fm
Moor Ho
Moor Fm
Speeton Sands
Barf Fm
Vicarage Fm
Reighton
Speeton Hills
Speeton Cliffs
Speeton
Speeton Grange
Reighton Field
Speeton Moor
Buckton Cliffs
Buckton Hall
BEMPTON CLIFFS
RSPB
Bempton Cliffs
Scale Nab
Cat Nab
Gull Nook
Standard Hill
Bempton Grange
Wandale Fm
Dykes Plantn
DANE'S DYKE
Thornwick Bay
North Cliff
North Landing
North Moor
Cradle Head
Stottle Bank Nook
Selwicks Bay
Flamborough Head
FLAMBOROUGH HEAD LIGHTHOUSE
High Stacks
Flatmere Plantn
LIGHTHOUSE ROAD
NORTH MARINE ROAD
B1255
B1259
Old Fall Plantn
Flamborough
The Crofts
Highcliffe Manor
Beacon Fm
Beacon Hill
South Landing
Buckton
Bempton
B1229
BEMPTON
FLAMBOROUGH ROAD
Butterwicks Fm
Newsham Field
High Barn
Lynhams
Field Ho
North Mount
Field Greenlands Fm
High Huntow Fm
Bartindale Fm
Wasters Plantn
Grindale Field
North Dale
Grindale
Maidensgrave Fm
Finley Hill
Fox Covert Plantn
Charlestone Fm
East Leys Fm
SCARBOROUGH ROAD
High Easton Fm
Ind Est
MARTON GATE
Danes Dyke Fm
B1255
Sewerby
SEWERBY HALL & GARDEN
Sewerby Rocks
BONDSVILLE MODEL VILLAGE
North Wood
East Craggs Wood
Binsdale Fm
Boynton
Eastfield Fm
MARTON ROAD
PRIORY
BAYLE MUS
Old Town
North Sands
B1253
Springdale Fm
West Lawn Wood
Fish Ponds Wood
Wandale Fm
Thorpe Hall
Carr Plantn
Sands Wood
BRIDLINGTON
Bridlington
OLD PENNY MEMORIES
The Spa
West Hill
Ind Est
Temple Fm
Carnaby Temple
Hallowkiln Wood
High Wood
South Side Mount
Wold Gate
Bessingby
KINGSGATE
Hilderthorpe
Haisthorpe Field
Carnaby
Thornholme Field
Haisthorpe
A614
South Sands
Wilsthorpe
Burton Agnes Field
Thornholme
BURTON AGNES HALL
BURTON AGNES MANOR HOUSE
PARK ROSE BIRD OF PREY CENTRE
Ind Est
Carnaby Moor
Brackendale Fm
Burton Agnes
Oak Wood Fm
Auburn Fm
Hords Covert
Burton Agnes Stud Fm
A165
Fraisthorpe Sands
Demming Fm
Harpham
Burtoncarr Ho
Fraisthorpe
Thornholme Moor
Gransmoor Wood
Little Kelk Fm
Low Stonehills
Turtle Hill Fm
Woodside Fm
High Stonehills
Hamiltonhill Fm
BRIDLINGTON ROAD
Gransmoor Low Ho
Gransmoor Lodge
Barmston Sands
Barmston
Barmston Main Drain
Allison Lane End
Great Kelk
Park Ho
Lissett
Ulrome Grange
Ulrome Sands
TA
0 1 2 3 miles
0 1 2 3 4 5 km

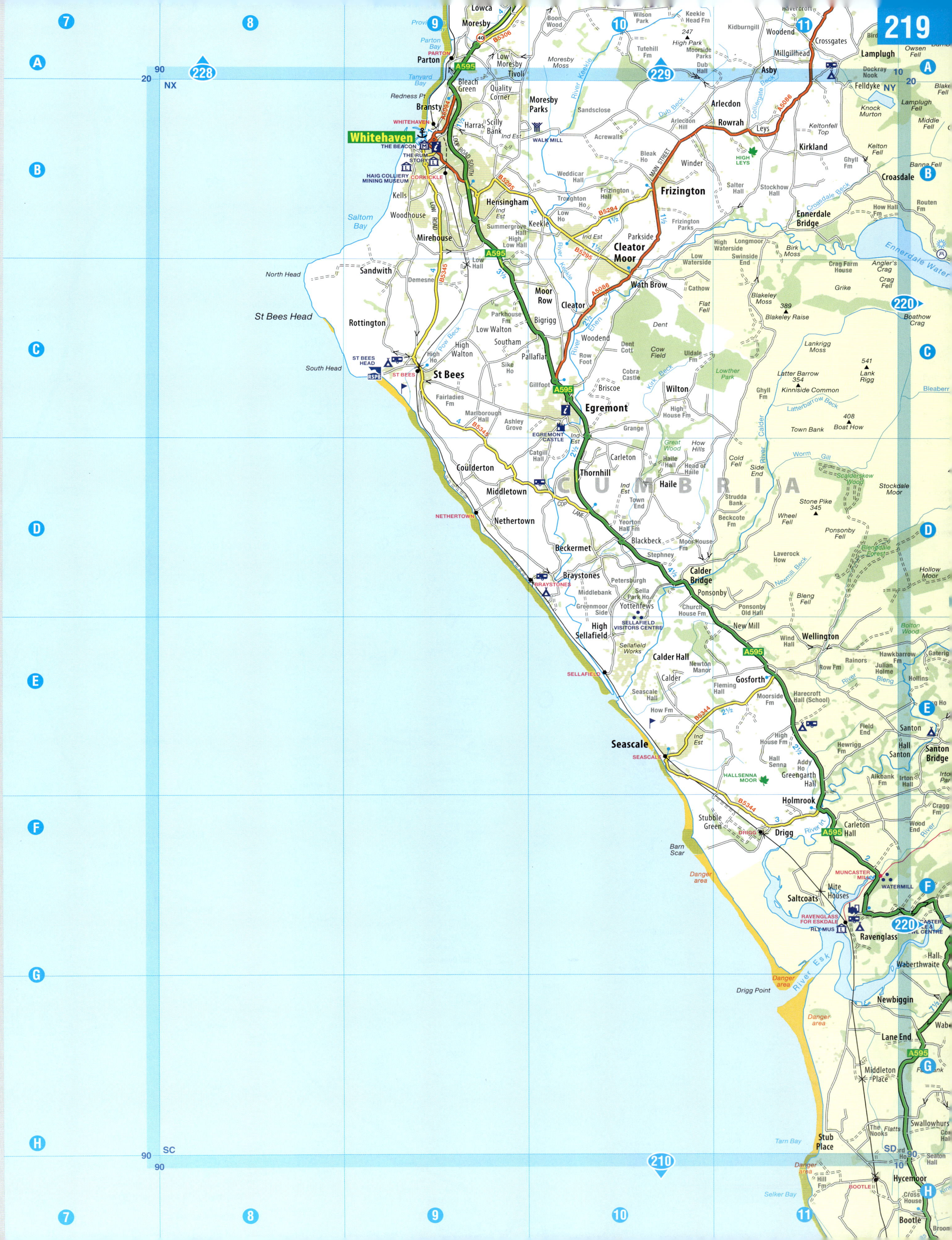

Whitehaven
THE BEACON
THE RUM STORY
HAIG COLLIERY MINING MUSEUM
CORKICKLE
WHITEHAVEN
Redness Pt
Tanyard Bay
Parton Bay
Parton
PARTON
Lowca
Moresby
Bransty
Bleach Green
Quality Corner
Low Moresby
Tivoli
Harras
Scilly Bank
Moresby Parks
Moresby Moss
Boon Wood
Wilson Park
Keekle Head Fm
247
High Park
Moorside Parks
Dub Hall
Tutehill Fm
Kidburngill
Woodend
Havercroft
Crossgates
Millgillhead
Lamplugh
Asby
Dockray Nook
Felldyke
Owsen Fell
Blake Fell
Lamplugh Fell
Knock Murton
Middle Fell
Arlecdon
Arlecdon Hill
Rowrah
Leys
Keltonfell Top
Kelton Fell
Kirkland
Ghyll Fm
Banna Fell
Croasdale
Sandsclose
WALK MILL
Acrewalls
Bleak Ho
Winder
HIGH LEYS
Frizington
Frizington Hall
Frizington Parks
Weddicar Hall
Troughton Ho
Salter Hall
Stockhow Hall
Ennerdale Bridge
Croasdale Beck
How Hall Fm
Routen Fm
Enerdale Water
Kells
Woodhouse
Saltom Bay
Hensingham
Summergrove Hall
Keekle
Low Ho
Mirehouse
High Low Hall
Parkside
Cleator Moor
Wath Brow
High Waterside
Longmoor
Swinside End
Low Waterside
Birk Moss
Crag Farm House
Angler's Crag
Crag Fell
Grike
North Head
Sandwith
Demesne
Low Hall
Moor Row
Cleator
Cathow
Flat Fell
Blakeley Moss
389
Blakeley Raise
Boathow Crag
St Bees Head
Rottington
Parkhouse Fm
Low Walton
Bigrigg
Woodend
Dent
Southam
High Walton
Pallaflat
Dent Cott
Cow Field
Uldale Fm
Lankrigg Moss
541
Lank Rigg
ST BEES HEAD
RSPB
South Head
ST BEES
St Bees
High Ho
Sike Ho
Row Foot
Cobra Castle
Gillfoot
Briscoe
Wilton
Lowther Park
Ghyll Fm
Latter Barrow
354
Kinniside Common
Fairladies Fm
Egremont
High House Fm
Marlborough Hall
Ashley Grove
EGREMONT CASTLE
Grange
Town Bank
408
Boat How
Catgill Hall
Great Wood
How Hills
Haile Hall
Head of Haile
Cold Fell
Side End
Coulderton
Carleton
Thornhill
Haile
Middletown
C U M B R I A
Strudda Bank
Stone Pike
345
Stockdale Moor
Wheel Fell
Beckcote Fm
Ponsonby Fell
NETHERTOWN
Nethertown
Yeorton Hall Fm
Blackbeck
Moorhouse Fm
Laverock How
Blengdale Forest
Beckermet
Stephney
Calder Bridge
Ponsonby
Braystones
BRAYSTONES
Petersburgh
Middlebank
Sella Park Ho
Bleng Fell
Hollow Moor
Greenmoor Side
Yottenfews
Church House Fm
Ponsonby Old Hall
High Sellafield
SELLAFIELD VISITORS CENTRE
New Mill
Wind Hall
Wellington
Sellafield Works
Calder Hall
Newton Manor
Rainors
Hawkbarrow
Julian Holme
SELLAFIELD
Calder
Fleming Hall
Gosforth
Row Fm
Seascale Hall
Moorside Fm
Harecroft Hall (School)
How Fm
Field End
Santon
Seascale
SEASCALE
High House Fm
Ind Est
Hewrigg Fm
Hall Santon
Santon Bridge
Hall Senna
Addy Ho
HALLSENNA MOOR
Greengarth Hall
Aikbank Fm
Irton Hall
Holmrook
Stubble Green
DRIGG
Drigg
Carleton Hall
Barn Scar
Danger area
MUNCASTER MILL
WATERMILL
Mite Houses
Saltcoats
RAVENGLASS FOR ESKDALE
RLY MUS
Ravenglass
Waberthwaite
Drigg Point
River Esk
Newbiggin
Lane End
Middleton Place
Tarn Bay
Stub Place
Swallowhurst
Seaton Hall
Hycemoor
Hill Fm
BOOTLE
Selker Bay
Cross House
Bootle
A595
A5086
B5295
B5294
B5345
B5344
LOW ROAD
MAIN STREET
COP LANE
NX
NY
SC
SD
228
229
210
220

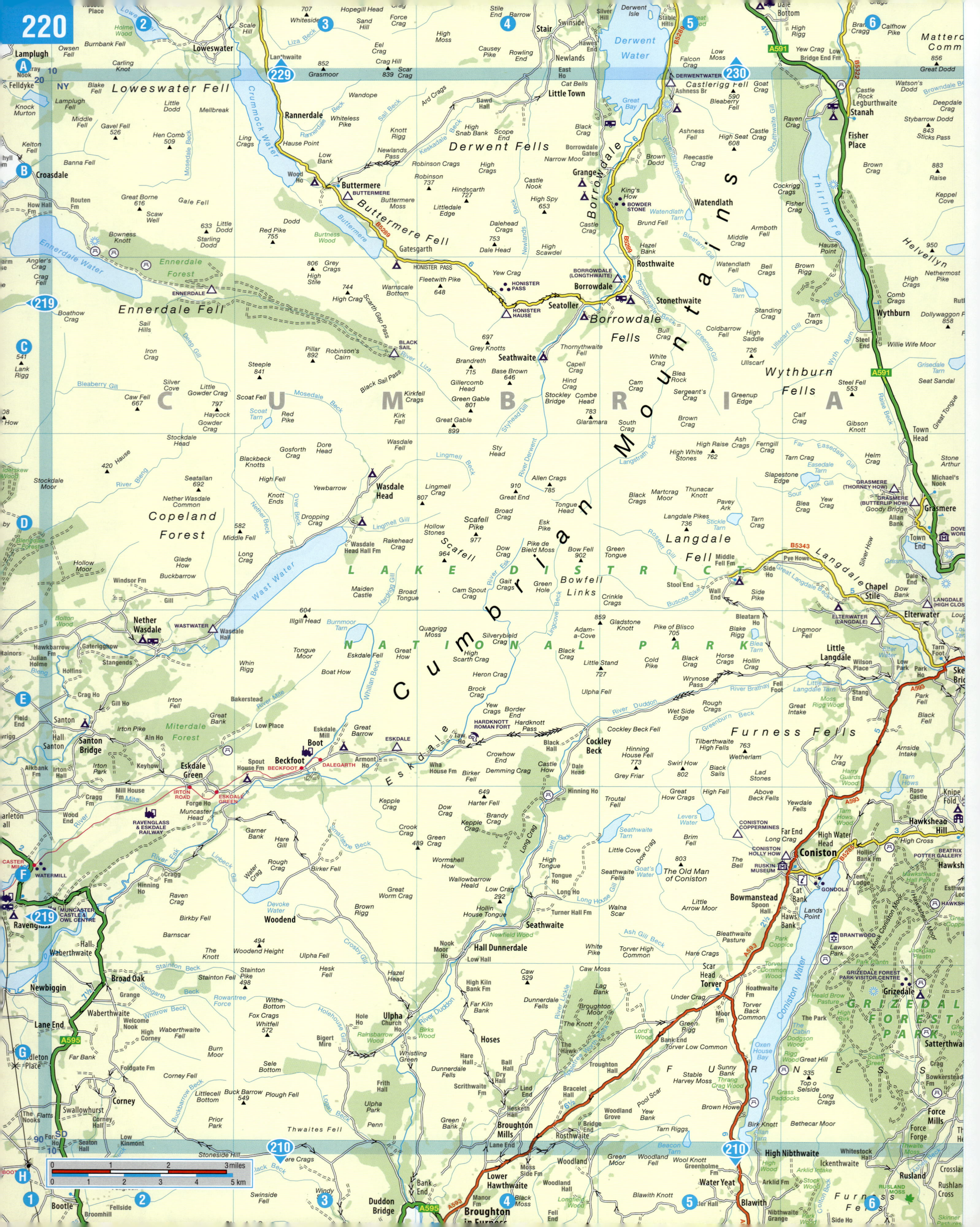
Lamplugh
Loweswater
Loweswater Fell
Crummock Water
Rannerdale
Buttermere
Buttermere Fell
Gatesgarth
Derwent Fells
Derwent Water
Castlerigg Fell
Little Town
Newlands
Grange
Borrowdale
Rosthwaite
Stonethwaite
Seatoller
Seathwaite
Borrowdale Fells
Watendlath
Thirlmere
Helvellyn
Wythburn
Wythburn Fells
Fisher Place
Stanah
Ennerdale Water
Ennerdale Forest
Ennerdale Fell
Croasdale
C U M B R I A
Cumbrian Mountains
Copeland Forest
Wast Water
Wasdale Head
Nether Wasdale
Scafell Pike
Scafell
Great End
Bowfell
Crinkle Crags
Langdale Pikes
Langdale Fell
Langdale
Chapel Stile
Elterwater
Grasmere
Little Langdale
L A K E D I S T R I C T
N A T I O N A L P A R K
Eskdale
Eskdale Green
Beckfoot
Boot
Santon Bridge
Miterdale Forest
Cockley Beck
Hardknott Pass
Furness Fells
Coniston
The Old Man of Coniston
Coniston Water
Torver
Hawkshead
Grizedale
G R I Z E D A L E F O R E S T P A R K
Seathwaite
Hall Dunnerdale
Ulpha
Hoses
Broughton Mills
Woodend
Broad Oak
Waberthwaite
Newbiggin
Lane End
Ravenglass
Corney
Bootle
Duddon Bridge
Broughton in Furness
Lower Hawthwaite
Water Yeat
Blawith
High Nibthwaite
Rusland
Satterthwaite
Force Mills
Thwaites Fell
A591
A593
A595
B5289
B5343
229
230
219
210
0 1 2 3 miles
0 1 2 3 4 5 km

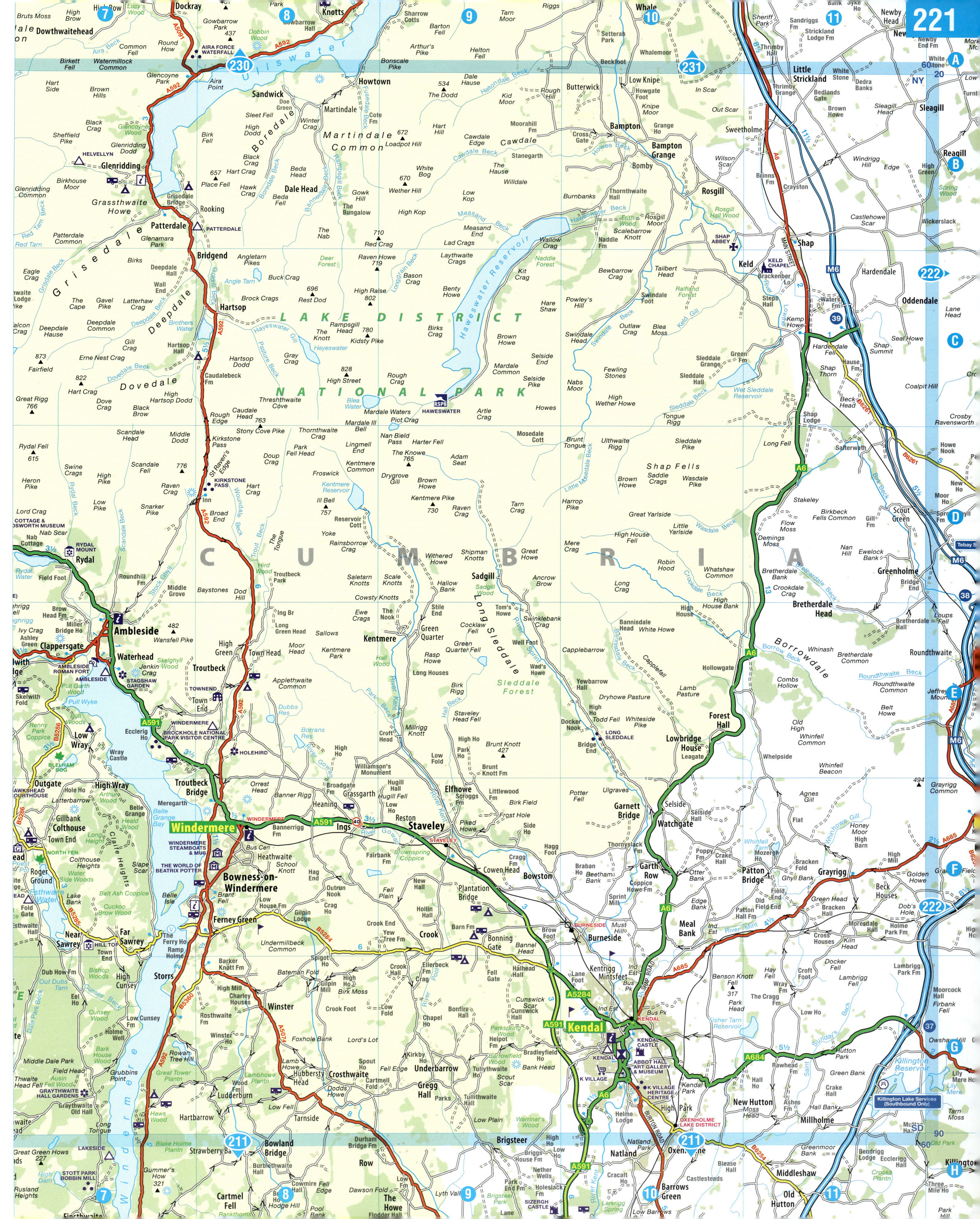
LAKE DISTRICT NATIONAL PARK
CUMBRIA
Ullswater
Haweswater Reservoir
Windermere
Ambleside
Rydal
Clappersgate
Waterhead
Troutbeck
Troutbeck Bridge
Windermere
Bowness-on-Windermere
Ferney Green
Staveley
Ings
Kentmere
Sadgill
Long Sleddale
Shap
Keld
Bampton
Bampton Grange
Rosgill
Patterdale
Glenridding
Grisedale
Deepdale
Dovedale
Hartsop
Kirkstone Pass
Martindale Common
Howtown
Sandwick
Bretherdale Head
Borrowdale
Forest Hall
Lowbridge House
Garnett Bridge
Selside
Watchgate
Patton Bridge
Grayrigg
Kendal
Burneside
Meal Bank
Natland
Oxenholme
Brigsteer
Crook
Underbarrow
Crosthwaite
Winster
Bowland Bridge
Cartmel Fell
Storrs
Near Sawrey
Far Sawrey
High Wray
Low Wray
Outgate
Middleshaw
Old Hutton
Killington Reservoir
Killington Lake Services (Southbound Only)
Tebay
Greenholme
Roundthwaite
Oddendale
Hardendale
Little Strickland
Sleagill
Reagill
Crosby Ravensworth
Whale
Dockray
Sleddale Forest
Wet Sleddale Reservoir
Shap Fells
M6
A6
A591
A592
A5284
A684
A685
B5284
B6261
B6260
B5286
B5285
230
231
222
211

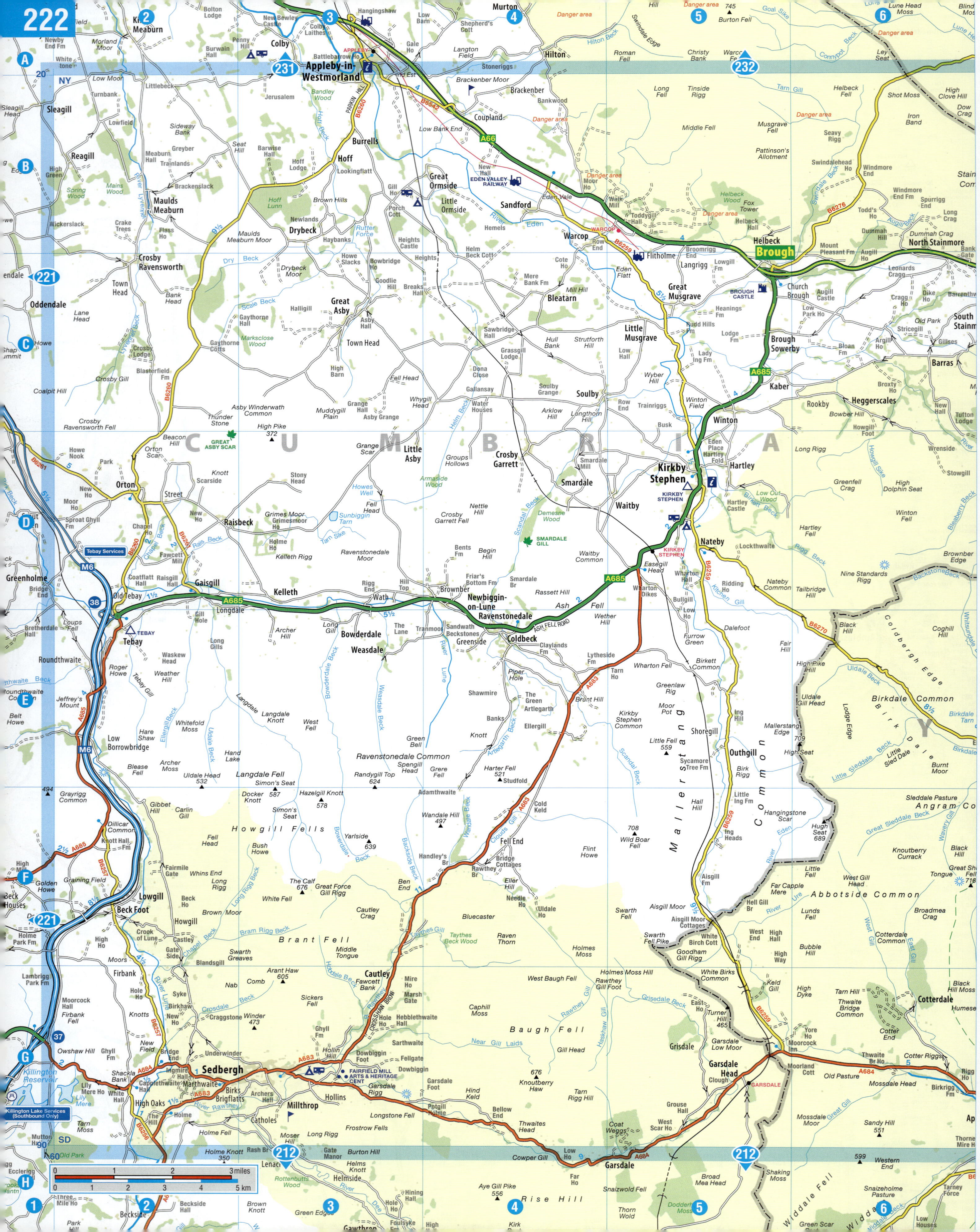
Appleby-in-Westmorland
Brough
Kirkby Stephen
Sedbergh
Tebay
Orton
Ravenstonedale
Newbiggin-on-Lune
Gaisgill
Kelleth
Old Tebay
Crosby Ravensworth
Great Asby
Little Asby
Crosby Garrett
Soulby
Winton
Hartley
Nateby
Waitby
Smardale
Great Musgrave
Little Musgrave
Warcop
Sandford
Great Ormside
Little Ormside
Drybeck
Hoff
Burrells
Colby
Murton
Hilton
Brackenber
Coupland
Flitholme
Bleatarn
Church Brough
Brough Sowerby
Kaber
Barras
North Stainmore
South Stainmore
Heggerscales
Rookby
Outhgill
Shoregill
Garsdale Head
Garsdale
Grisdale
Cotterdale
Cautley
Firbank
Lowgill
Beck Foot
Millthrop
Howgill
Bowderdale
Weasdale
Greenside
Coldbeck
Raisbeck
Sleagill
Reagill
Maulds Meaburn
Oddendale
Greenholme
Roundthwaite
Low Borrowbridge
C U M B R I A
Howgill Fells
Ravenstonedale Common
Brant Fell
Baugh Fell
Rise Hill
Mallerstang Common
Abbotside Common
Birkdale Common
Wild Boar Fell
Great Asby Scar
Smardale Gill
Tebay Services
Killington Reservoir
Killington Lake Services (Southbound Only)
Eden Valley Railway
Fairfield Mill Arts & Heritage Cent
Kirkby Stephen
Appleby
Warcop
Garsdale
Sunbiggin Tarn
River Eden
River Lune
River Rawthey
M6
A66
A685
A683
A684
B6260
B6259
B6270
B6276
B6261
B6257
B6255
B6542
NY
SD
231
232
221
212
1
2
3
4
5
6
A
B
C
D
E
F
G
H
0 1 2 3 miles
0 1 2 3 4 5 km

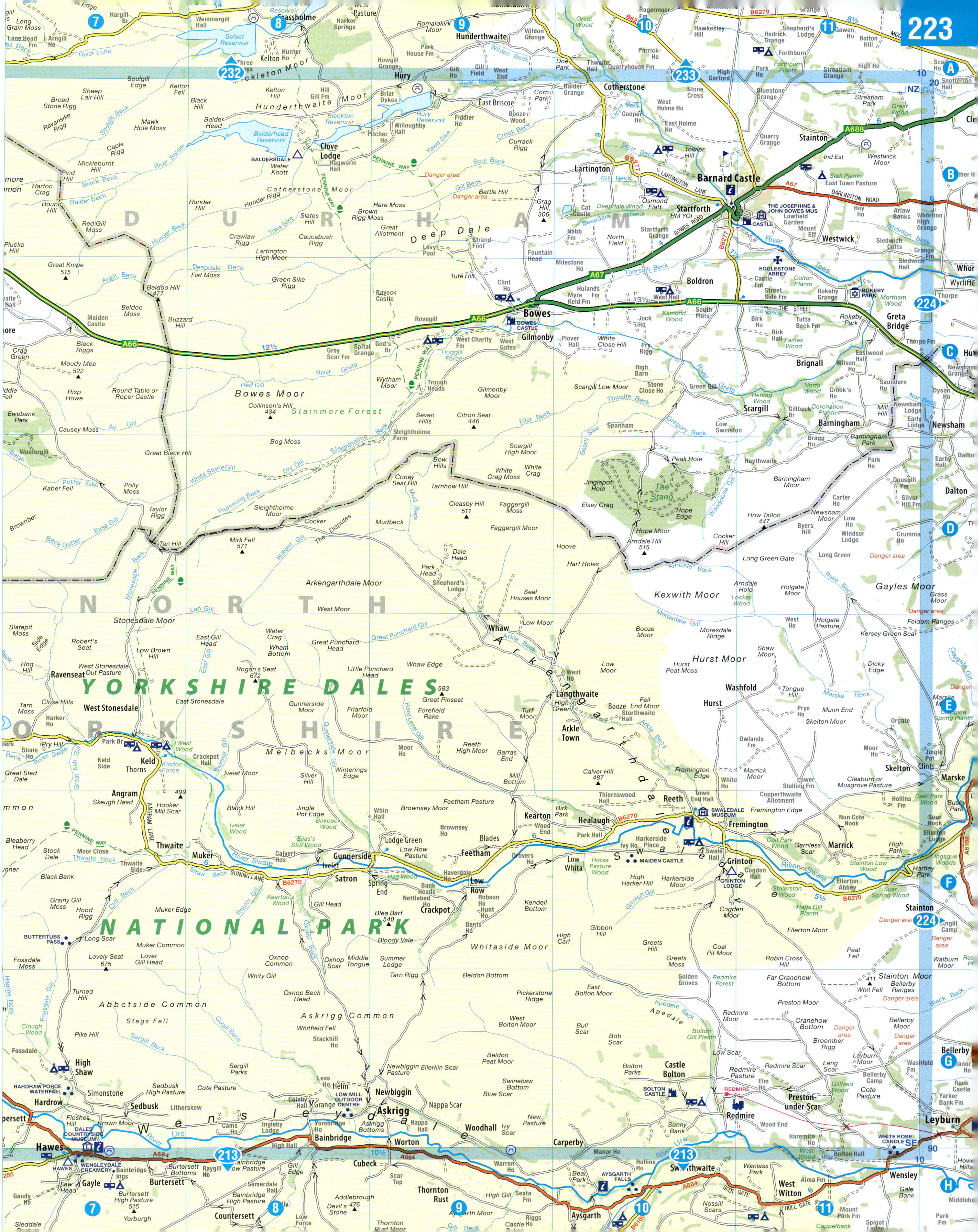

DURHAM
NORTH YORKSHIRE
YORKSHIRE DALES NATIONAL PARK
Barnard Castle
Startforth
Lartington
Cotherstone
Hunderthwaite
Romaldkirk
Grassholme
Selset Reservoir
Grassholme Reservoir
Balderhead Reservoir
Blackton Reservoir
Hury Reservoir
Hury
Clove Lodge
Cotherstone Moor
Deep Dale
Bowes
Bowes Castle
Gilmonby
Boldron
Rokeby Park
Greta Bridge
Brignall
Scargill
Barningham
Newsham
Dalton
Stainton
Westwick
Whorlton
Wycliffe
Egglestone Abbey
The Josephine & John Bowes Mus
Bowes Moor
Stainmore Forest
Gods Bridge
Pennine Way
Tan Hill
Keld
Thwaite
Muker
Angram
Ravenseat
West Stonesdale
Stonesdale Moor
Arkengarthdale Moor
Whaw
Langthwaite
Arkle Town
Booze
Reeth
Healaugh
Fremington
Grinton
Marrick
Marske
Skelton
Hurst
Washfold
Gunnerside
Ivelet
Satron
Low Row
Feetham
Kearton
Crackpot
Melbecks Moor
Whitaside Moor
Low Whita
Maiden Castle
Swaledale Museum
Grinton Lodge
Butter Tubs Pass
High Shaw
Hardrow
Hardraw Force Waterfall
Simonstone
Sedbusk
Hawes
Dales Countryside Museum
Wensleydale Creamery
Gayle
Burtersett
Askrigg
Askrigg Common
Abbotside Common
Newbiggin
Helm
Bainbridge
Worton
Woodhall
Carperby
Aysgarth
Aysgarth Falls
Swinithwaite
West Witton
Wensley
Castle Bolton
Bolton Castle
Redmire
Preston-under-Scar
Leyburn
Bellerby
Cubeck
Thornton Rust
Countersett
Wensleydale
River Tees
River Greta
River Swale
River Ure
River Balder
A66
A67
A688
A684
B6277
B6270
B6279
Kexwith Moor
Hurst Moor
Gayles Moor
Danger area

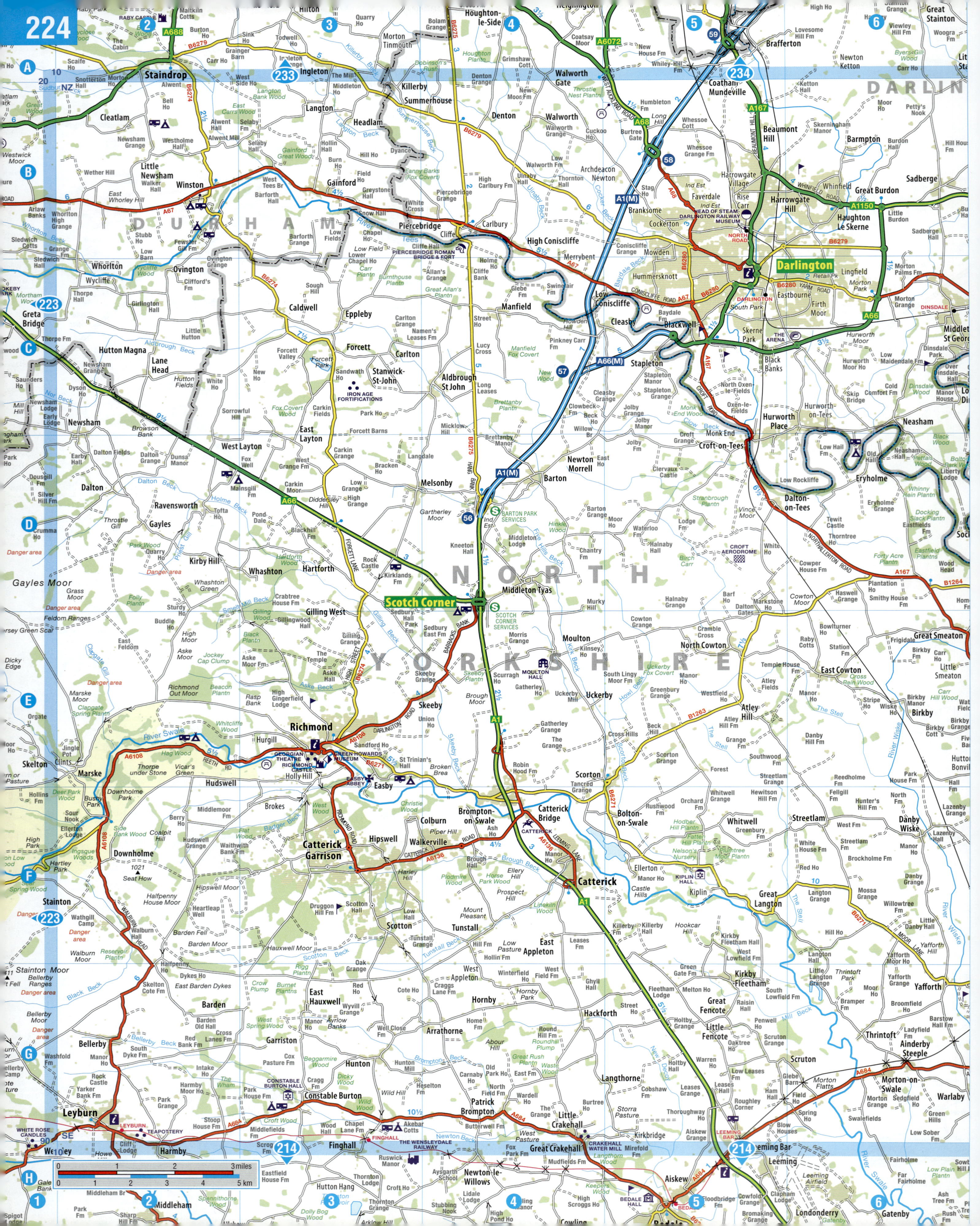
DURHAM
NORTH YORKSHIRE
DARLIN
Staindrop
Ingleton
Killerby
Summerhouse
Houghton-le-Side
Denton
Walworth
Brafferton
Coatham Mundeville
Barmpton
Sadberge
Great Burdon
Haughton Le Skerne
Cleatlam
Headlam
Gainford
Winston
Little Newsham
Piercebridge
Carlbury
High Coniscliffe
Darlington
Cockerton
Harrowgate Hill
Whorlton
Wycliffe
Ovington
Greta Bridge
Caldwell
Eppleby
Forcett
Carlton
Stanwick-St-John
Aldbrough St John
Low Coniscliffe
Cleasby
Blackwell
Stapleton
Hutton Magna
Lane Head
Newsham
East Layton
West Layton
Melsonby
Barton
Newton Morrell
Croft-on-Tees
Hurworth Place
Neasham
Eryholme
Dalton-on-Tees
Dalton
Ravensworth
Gayles
Kirby Hill
Whashton
Hartforth
Scotch Corner
Middleton Tyas
Gilling West
Moulton
North Cowton
East Cowton
Great Smeaton
Uckerby
Atley Hill
Birkby
Richmond
Skeeby
Easby
Hudswell
Marske
Skelton
Scorton
Bolton-on-Swale
Catterick Bridge
Brompton-on-Swale
Colburn
Hipswell
Catterick Garrison
Downholme
Catterick
Great Langton
Danby Wiske
Streetlam
Whitwell
Kiplin
Stainton
Scotton
Tunstall
East Appleton
Hornby
Hackforth
Kirkby Fleetham
Great Fencote
Little Fencote
Yafforth
Thrintoft
Ainderby Steeple
Morton-on-Swale
Scruton
Warlaby
Barden
Bellerby
Leyburn
Harmby
Garriston
Hunton
Constable Burton
Finghall
Patrick Brompton
Arrathorne
Langthorne
Little Crakehall
Great Crakehall
Kirkbridge
Leeming Bar
Leeming
Aiskew
Bedale
Newton-le-Willows
Middleham
Londonderry
Gatenby
A1(M)
A1
A66
A66(M)
A67
A68
A167
A6108
A684
A6136
B6275
B6274
B6279
B6280
B6271
B1263
0 1 2 3 miles
0 1 2 3 4 5 km

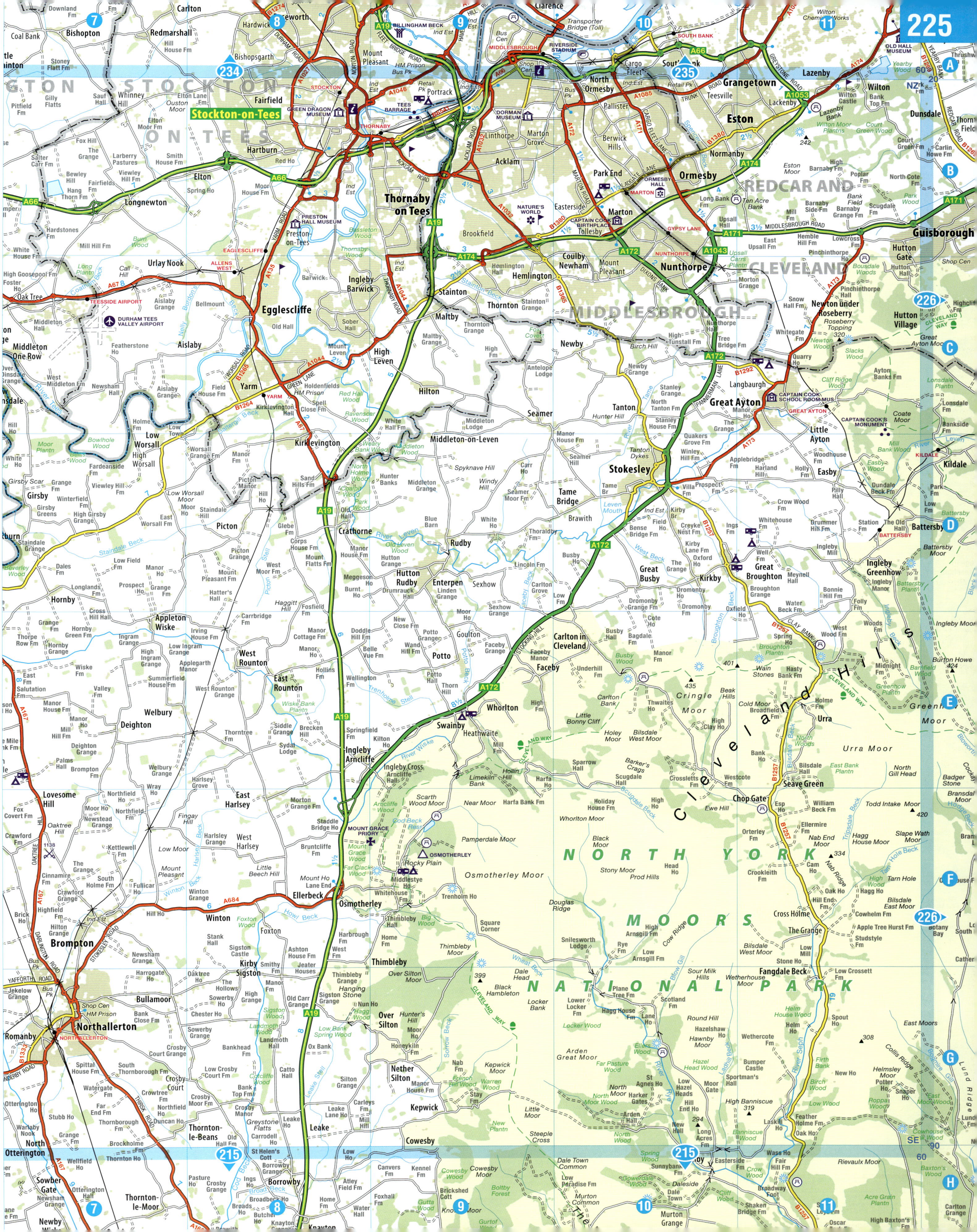

Stockton-on-Tees
STOCKTON ON TEES
MIDDLESBROUGH
REDCAR AND CLEVELAND
Thornaby on Tees
Eston
Ormesby
Grangetown
Guisborough
Nunthorpe
Marton
Acklam
Hemlington
Ingleby Barwick
Eaglescliffe
Yarm
Kirklevington
Great Ayton
Stokesley
Hutton Rudby
Crathorne
Great Broughton
Kildale
Ingleby Greenhow
Carlton in Cleveland
Swainby
Osmotherley
Ingleby Arncliffe
Brompton
Northallerton
Romanby
North Otterington
Thornton-le-Moor
Cleveland Hills
NORTH YORK MOORS NATIONAL PARK
Osmotherley Moor
Urra Moor
Chop Gate
Seave Green
Fangdale Beck
The Grange
Teesside Airport
Durham Tees Valley Airport
Appleton Wiske
West Rounton
East Rounton
Welbury
Deighton
East Harlsey
West Harlsey
Ellerbeck
Kirby Sigston
Bullamoor
Over Silton
Nether Silton
Kepwick
Cowesby
Leake
Borrowby
Knayton

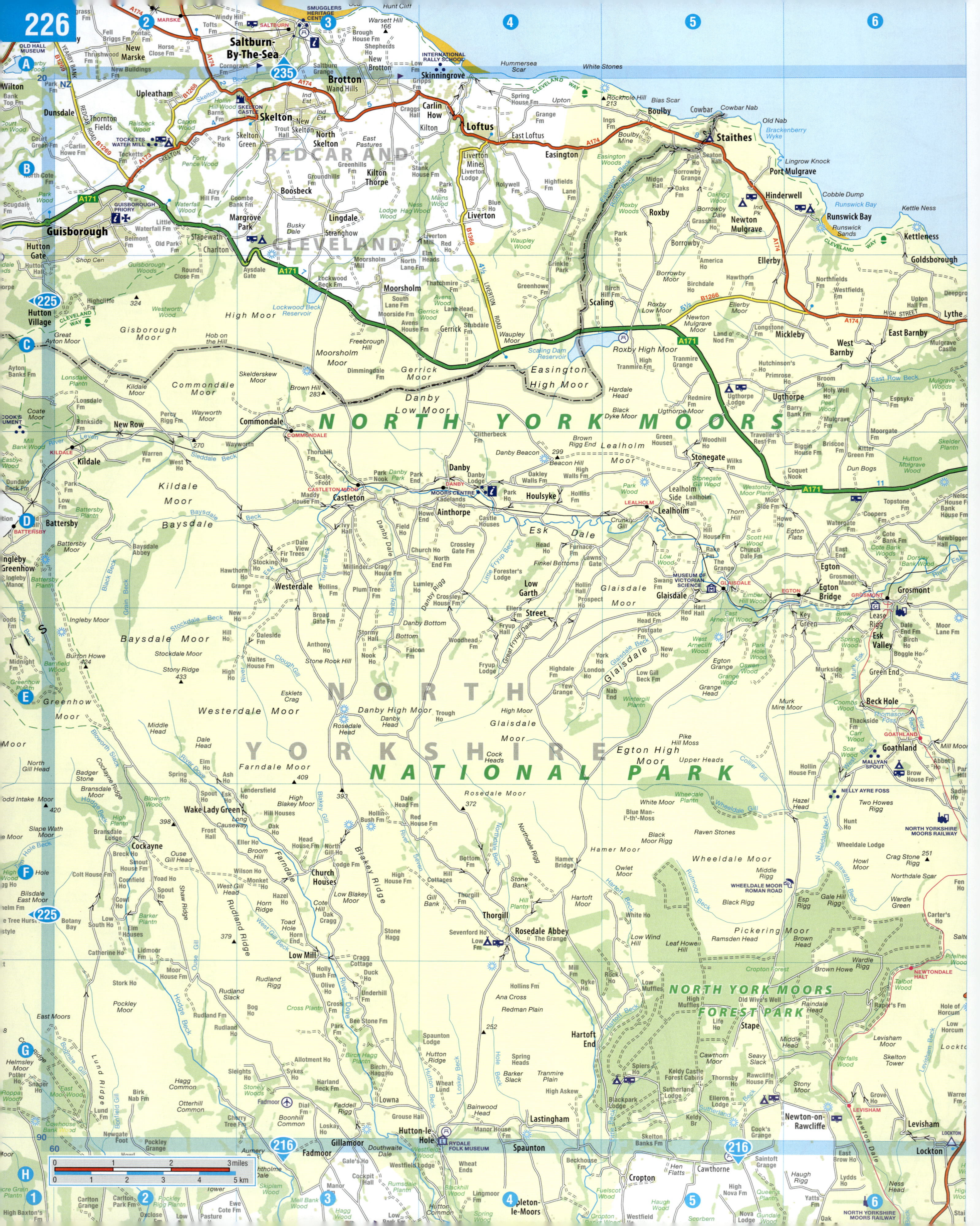
Saltburn-By-The-Sea
Marske
Smugglers Heritage Centre
Brotton
Skinningrove
International Rally School
Hummersea Scar
White Stones
Upleatham
New Marske
Skelton
Skelton Green
North Skelton
Carlin How
Loftus
East Loftus
Boulby
Cowbar
Cowbar Nab
Staithes
Old Nab
Brackenberry Wyke
Lingrow Knock
Port Mulgrave
Hinderwell
Cobble Dump
Runswick Bay
Kettle Ness
Kettleness
Goldsborough
Lythe
East Barnby
West Barnby
Mickleby
Ellerby
Newton Mulgrave
Roxby
Easington
Liverton
Liverton Mines
Kilton Thorpe
Lingdale
Stanghow
Boosbeck
Margrove Park
Guisborough
Guisborough Priory
Hutton Gate
Hutton Village
Dunsdale
Wilton
Tocketts Water Mill
REDCAR AND CLEVELAND
Moorsholm
Gerrick
Scaling
Scaling Dam Reservoir
Lockwood Beck Reservoir
Roxby High Moor
Easington High Moor
Gisborough Moor
Commondale Moor
Commondale
Kildale
Kildale Moor
Baysdale
Battersby
Ingleby Greenhow
Danby Low Moor
Danby
Danby Beacon
The Moors Centre
Castleton
Ainthorpe
Houlsyke
Lealholm
Lealholm Moor
Stonegate
Ugthorpe
Glaisdale
Glaisdale Moor
Museum of Victorian Science
Egton
Egton Bridge
Grosmont
Esk Valley
Green End
Beck Hole
Goathland
Mallyan Spout
Nelly Ayre Foss
North Yorkshire Moors Railway
Esk Dale
Low Garth
Street
Westerdale
Westerdale Moor
Baysdale Moor
Danby High Moor
Rosedale Head
Rosedale Moor
NORTH YORK MOORS
NORTH YORKSHIRE NATIONAL PARK
Egton High Moor
Wheeldale Moor
Wheeldale Moor Roman Road
Hamer Moor
Pickering Moor
NORTH YORK MOORS FOREST PARK
Farndale Moor
Wake Lady Green
Church Houses
Blakey Ridge
Cockayne
Farndale
Rudland Ridge
Low Mill
Thorgill
Rosedale Abbey
The Grange
Hartoft End
Stape
Newton-on-Rawcliffe
Newtondale Halt
Levisham
Lockton
Lastingham
Hutton-le-Hole
Ryedale Folk Museum
Gillamoor
Fadmoor
Spaunton
Cropton
Cawthorne
Appleton-le-Moors
Lund Ridge
Bransdale
Helmsley Moor
A171
A174
B1366
B1266
B1268
B1269
A173
216
225
235
0 1 2 3 miles
0 1 2 3 4 5 km

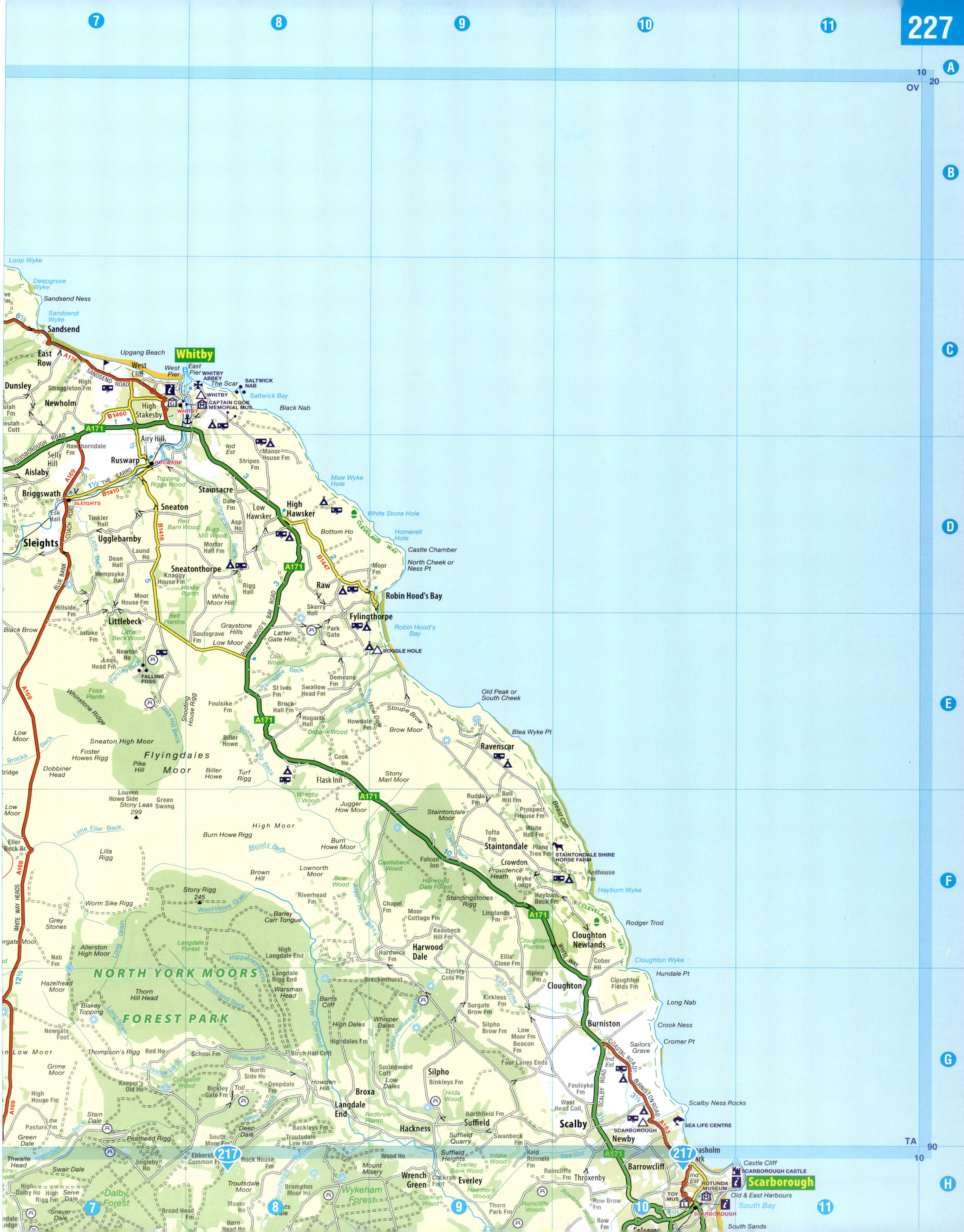
7
8
9
10
11
A
B
C
D
E
F
G
H
OV
TA
Loop Wyke
Deepgrove Wyke
Sandsend Ness
Sandsend Wyke
Sandsend
Upgang Beach
Whitby
East Row
West Cliff
West Pier
East Pier
WHITBY ABBEY
The Scar
SALTWICK NAB
Saltwick Bay
Black Nab
Dunsley
Straggleton Fm
SANDSEND ROAD
Newholm
High Stakesby
WHITBY
CAPTAIN COOK MEMORIAL MUS
B1460
A171
A174
Airy Hill
Hawthorndale Fm
Selly Hill
Ruswarp
RUSWARP
Aislaby
GUISBOROUGH ROAD
A169
THE CARRS
B1410
Briggswath
SLEIGHTS
Esk Hall
Topping Riggs Wood
Stainsacre
Ind Est
Manor House Fm
Stripes Fm
Maw Wyke Hole
Sneaton
Dale Fm
Low Hawsker
High Hawsker
White Stone Hole
Tinkler Hall
Red Barn Wood
Rigg Mill Wood
Asp Ho
Bottom Ho
CLEVELAND WAY
Homerell Hole
Sleights
Ugglebarnby
Laund Ho
Mortar Hall Fm
Castle Chamber
North Cheek or Ness Pt
B1416
B1447
Dean Hall
Hempsyke Hall
Sneatonthorpe
Knaggy House Fm
Haxby Plantn
Moor Fm
Raw
Robin Hood's Bay
BLUE BANK
COACH ROAD
Little Beck
Rigg Hall
Moor House Fm
White Moor Hill
Skerry Hall
Fylingthorpe
Hillside Fm
Littlebeck
Belt Plantns
Graystone Hills
Robin Hood's Bay
Black Brow
Intake Fm
Little Beck Wood
Soulsgrave Fm
Low Moor
Latter Gate Hills
Park Gate
BOGGLE HOLE
Newton Ho
Leas Head Fm
Oak Wood
ROBIN HOOD'S BAY ROAD
FALLING FOSS
Ramsdale Beck
Demesne Fm
Foss Plantn
St Ives Fm
Swallow Head Fm
Whinstone Ridge
Shooting House Rigg
Foulsike Fm
Brock Hall Fm
Old Peak or South Cheek
Stoupe Brow
Hogarth Hall
Howdale Fm
How Dale
Brow Moor
Oxbank Wood
Blea Wyke Pt
Low Moor
Biller Howe
Ravenscar
Sneaton High Moor
Foster Howes Rigg
Flyingdales Moor
Cook Ho
Brocka Beck
Pike Hill
Dobbiner Head
Biller Howe
Turf Rigg
Flask Inn
Stony Marl Moor
Rudda Fm
Bell Hill Fm
Louven Howe Side
Green Swang
Stony Leas 299
Wragby Wood
Jugger Howe Moor
Staintondale Moor
Prospect House Fm
Beast Cliff
Low Moor
High Moor
White Hall Fm
Little Eller Beck
Burn Howe Rigg
Bloody Beck
Burn Howe Moor
Tofta Fm
Staintondale
Plane Tree Fm
STAINTONDALE SHIRE HORSE FARM
Eller Beck Br
Lilla Rigg
Castlebeck Wood
Falcon Inn
Crowdon
Providence Heath
Redhouse
Lownorth Moor
Brown Hill
Scar Wood
Harwood Dale Forest
Wyke Lodge
Hayburn Wyke
Stony Rigg 245
Woof Howe Gran
Riverhead Fm
Hayburn Beck Fm
Worm Sike Rigg
Chapel Fm
Standingstones Rigg
Barley Carr Tongue
Moor Cottage Fm
Linglands Fm
Rodger Trod
Grey Stones
Keasbeck Hill Fm
Cloughton Newlands
Allerston High Moor
Langdale Forest
High Langdale End
Harwood Dale
Ellis' Close Fm
Cloughton Plantns
Nab Fm
Hipperley Beck
Langdale Rigg End
Hardwick Fm
Cober Hill
Cloughton Wyke
NORTH YORK MOORS
Thirley Cote Fm
Ripley's Fm
Cloughton Fields Fm
Hundale Pt
Hazelhead Moor
Thorn Hill Head
Warsman Head
Breckenhurst
Cloughton
WHITE WAY
WHITE WAY HEADS
Stockland Beck
Barns Cliff
Kirkless Fm
Long Nab
Blakey Topping
FOREST PARK
River Derwent
Whisper Dales
Surgate Brow Fm
Newgate Foot
High Dales
Silpho Brow Fm
Low Moor Fm
Burniston
Crook Ness
Highdales Fm
Beacon Fm
Cromer Pt
Low Moor
Thompson's Rigg
Red Ho
School Fm
Black Beck
Birch Hall Cott
Four Lanes Ends
Sailors' Grave
COASTAL ROAD
Grime Moor
Springwood Cott
Silpho
Ind Est
North Side Ho
Binkleys Fm
Keeper's Old Ho
Crosscliff Wood
Deepdale Fm
Low Dales
Howden Hill
Broxa
Foulsyke Fm
BURNISTON ROAD
High House Fm
Bickley Gate Fm
Toll
Hilda Wood
SCALBY ROAD
Scalby Ness Rocks
Langdale End
West Head Coll
Stain Dale
Redbrow Plantn
Northfield Fm
Suffield
Scalby
SEA LIFE CENTRE
Pasture Fm
Low Fm
Deep Dale
Backleys Fm
Hackness
SCARBOROUGH
Green Dale
Peathead Rigg
South Moor Fm
Troutsdale Low Hall
Suffield Quarry
Swanbeck Fm
Newby
A165
Thwaite Head
Jingleby Ho
Ebberston Common Fm
217
Rock House Fm
Wood Ho
Suffield Heights
Intake Wood
Keld Runnels Fm
Sea Cut
Barrowcliff
Castle Cliff
SCARBOROUGH CASTLE
Swair Dale
Mount Misery
Everley Bank Wood
Raincliffe Fm
Throxenby
Scarborough
Troutsdale Moor
Wrench Green
Cockrah Foot
Everley
Ind Est
ROTUNDA MUSEUM
Old & East Harbours
Dalby Ho
High Rigg Fm
Seive Dale
Brompton Moor Ho
Wykeham Forest
Hawthorn Wood
TOY MUS
South Bay
Dalby Forest
Sneverdale
Manor Ho
Cockrah Wood
Thorn Park Fm
Raincliffe Woods
Row Brow Fm
SCARBOROUGH
Broad Head Fm
Row Fm
South Sands
Hern Head Ho
10
90
20

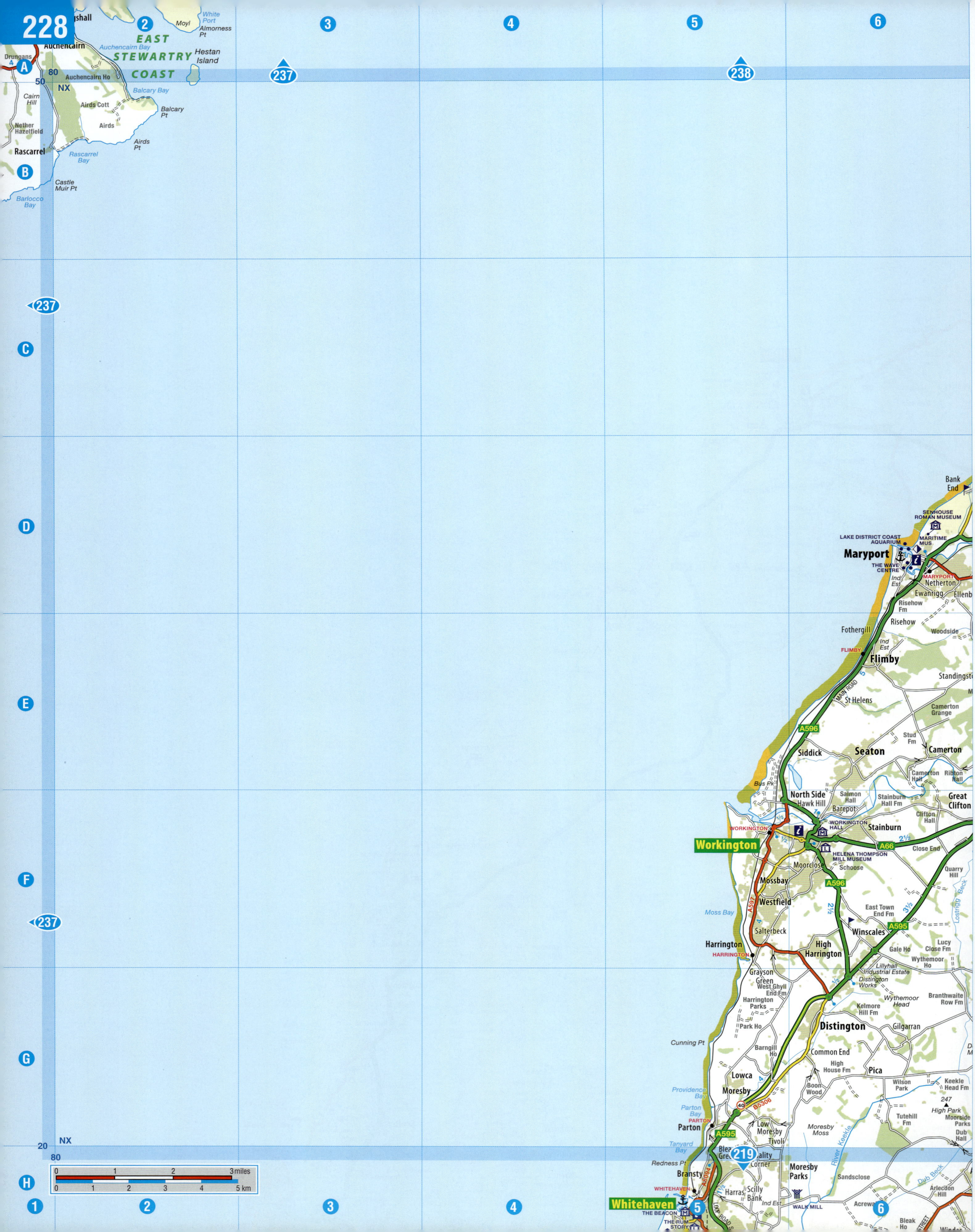
EAST
STEWARTRY
COAST
Drungans
Auchencairn
Auchencairn Bay
Moyl
White Port
Almorness Pt
Hestan Island
Auchencairn Ho
Balcary Bay
Cairn Hill
Airds Cott
Airds
Balcary Pt
Nether Hazelfield
Airds Pt
Rascarrel
Rascarrel Bay
Castle Muir Pt
Barlocco Bay
NX
237
238
Bank End
SENHOUSE ROMAN MUSEUM
LAKE DISTRICT COAST AQUARIUM
MARITIME MUS
Maryport
THE WAVE CENTRE
MARYPORT
Netherton
Ewanrigg
Ind Est
Risehow Fm
Risehow
Woodside
Fothergill
FLIMBY
Flimby
Standingstone
St Helens
MAIN ROAD
Camerton Grange
A596
Stud Fm
Siddick
Seaton
Camerton
Camerton Hall
Ribton Hall
Bus Pk
North Side
Hawk Hill
Salmon Hall
Barepot
Stainburn Hall Fm
Great Clifton
Clifton Hall
WORKINGTON HALL
Stainburn
WORKINGTON
Workington
A66
Close End
HELENA THOMPSON MILL MUSEUM
Schoose
Moorclose
Mossbay
Quarry Hill
Westfield
East Town End Fm
Moss Bay
A597
A595
Lostrigg Beck
Salterbeck
Winscales
Harrington
HARRINGTON
High Harrington
Gale Ho
Lucy Close Fm
Wythemoor Ho
Grayson Green
Lillyhall Industrial Estate
Distington Works
West Ghyll End Fm
Harrington Parks
Wythemoor Head
Branthwaite Row Fm
Kelmore Hill Fm
Park Ho
Distington
Gilgarran
Cunning Pt
Barngill Ho
Common End
High House Fm
Pica
Lowca
Wilson Park
Keekle Head Fm
Moresby
Providence Bay
Boon Wood
B5306
247
High Park
Parton Bay
Moorside Parks
PARTON
Tutehill Fm
Parton
Low Moresby
Moresby Moss
Dub Hall
Tanyard Bay
Tivoli
River Keekle
219
Redness Pt
Corner
Moresby Parks
Bransty
Sandsclose
Dub Beck
WHITEHAVEN
Harras
Scilly Bank
Arlecdon Hill
Whitehaven
Ind Est
WALK MILL
Acrewalls
THE BEACON
THE RUM STORY
Bleak Ho
A B C D E F G H
1 2 3 4 5 6
50
80
20
0 1 2 3 miles
0 1 2 3 4 5 km

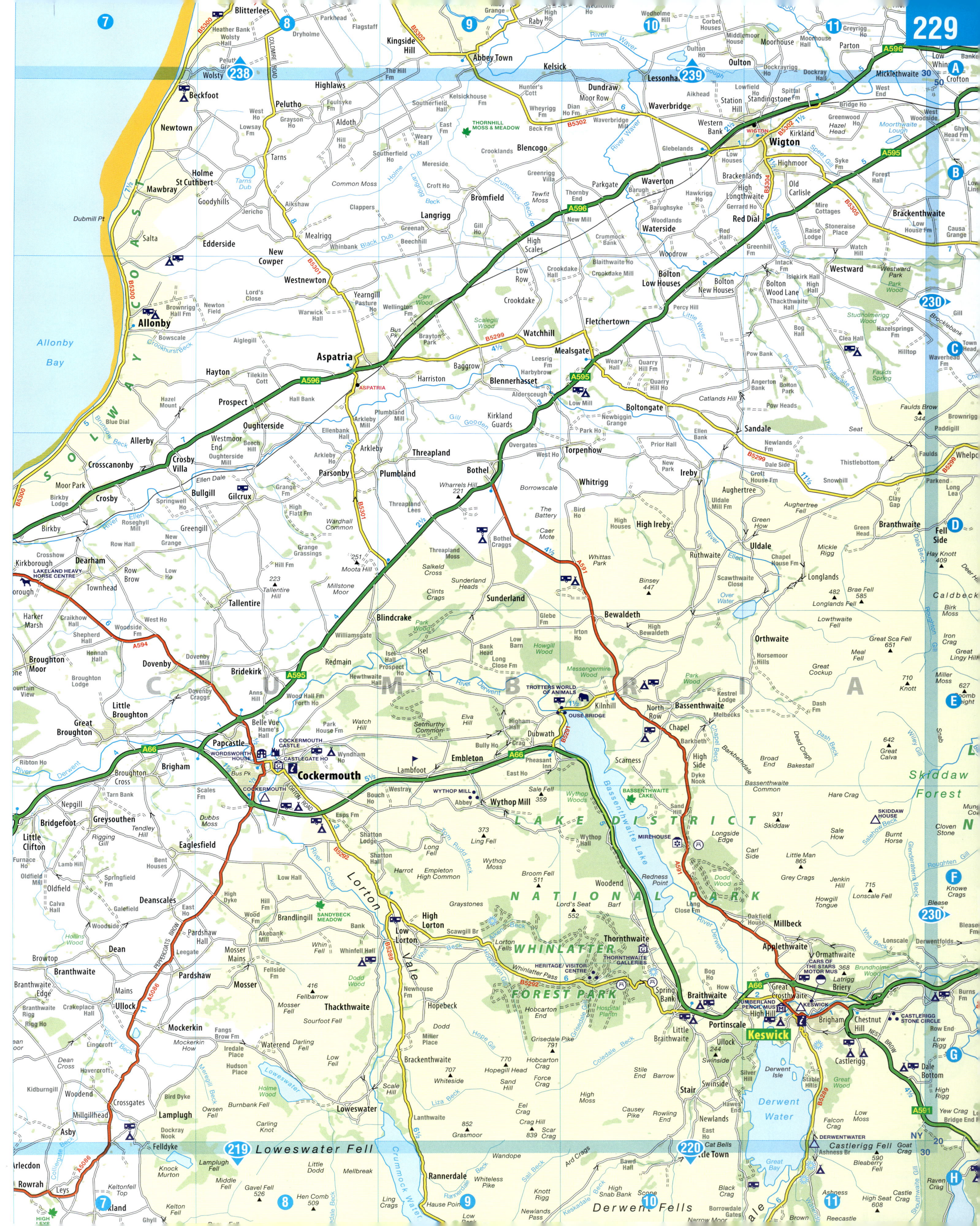
Blitterlees
Heather Bank
Wolsty Hall
Wolsty
Beckfoot
Newtown
Dryholme
Parkhead
Flagstaff
Kingside Hill
Abbey Town
Raby
Kelsick
Corbet Houses
Middlemoor House
Moorhouse
Oulton
Parton
Micklethwaite
Crofton
Highlaws
Pelutho
Foulsyke Fm
Aldoth
Southerfield Hall
Kelsickhouse Fm
Hunter's Cott
Dundraw
Moor Row
Wheyrigg Fm
Dian Ho Fm
Waverbridge Mill
Waverbridge
Lessonhall
Aikhead
Station Hill
Lowfield Ho
Standingstone
Spittal Fm
Dockray Hall
Western Bank
Wigton
Kirkland
Greenwood Ho
Hazel Head
Moorthwaite Lough
West Woodside
Ghyll Head Fm
Thornhill Moss & Meadow
Beck Fm
Crooklands
Blencogo
Glebelands
Low Houses
Highmoor
Old Carlisle
Syke Fm
Forest Hall
Tarns
Tarns Dub
Holme St Cuthbert
Mawbray
Goodyhills
Jericho
Common Moss
Croft Ho
Mereside
Greenrigg Villa
Tewfit Moss
Thornby End
Parkgate
Waverton
Brackenlands
High Longthwaite
Gerrard Ho
Mire Cottages
Brackenthwaite
Dubmill Pt
Salta
Aikshaw
Clappers
Langrigg
Bromfield
New Mill
Barugh
Barughsyke
Hawkrigg Ho
Red Dial
Stoneraise Place
Raise Lodge
Causa Grange
Edderside
Mealrigg
Greenah
Whinbank
Beechhill
Gill Ho
High Scales
Woodlands
Waterside
Crummock Bank
Red Hall
Greenhill Fm
Watch Hill
New Cowper
Westnewton
Woodrow
Crookdake Hall
Blaithwaite Ho
Crookdake Mill
Low Row
Bolton Low Houses
Bolton New Houses
Intack Fm
Islekirk Hall
Bolton Wood Lane
Thackthwaite Hall
Westward
Westward Park
Park Wood
Lord's Close
Brownrigg Hall Fm
Newton Field
Yearngill Pasture Ho
Wellington Fm
Carr Wood
Crookdake
Percy Hill
Allonby
Bowscale
Warwick Hall
Aiglegill
Bus Pk
Brayton Park
Scalegill Wood
Watchhill
Fletchertown
Studholmerigg Wood
Hazelsprings Fm
Hilltop
Clea Hall
Bog Hall
Allonby Bay
Aspatria
Baggrow
Mealsgate
Leesrig Fm
Harbybrow
Weary Hall
Quarry Hill Fm
Pow Bank
Waverhead Fm
Hayton
Tilekiln Cott
Harriston
Blennerhasset
Aldersceugh
Low Mill
Quarry Hill Ho
Angerton Bank
Bolton Park
Catlands Hill
Faulds Spring
Hazel Mount
Prospect
Hall Bank
Plumbland Mill
Kirkland Guards
Boltongate
Pow Heads
Faulds Brow
Blue Dial
Oughterside
Ellenbank
Arkleby Mill
Newbiggin Grange
Park Ho
Ellen Bank
Sandale
Seat
Brownrigg
Paddigill
Allerby
Westmoor End
Oughterside Mill
Beech Hill
Arkleby Hall
Arkleby
Threapland
Overgates
West Ho
Torpenhow
Prior Hall
Newlands Fm
Dale Side
Faulds
Whelpo
Crosscanonby
Crosby Villa
Ellen Dale
Arkleby Ho
Parsonby
Plumbland
Bothel
Whitrigg
New Park
Ireby
Croft House Fm
Snowbill
Thistlebottom
Moor Park
Birkby Lodge
Crosby
Bullgill
Gilcrux
Grange Fm
Wharrels Hill 221
Borrowscale
Aughertree
Parkend
Long Lea
Springwell Ho
High Flatt Fm
Threapland Lees
The Battery
Bird Ho
Uldale Mill Fm
Aughertree Fell
Clay Gap
Birkby
Roseghyll Mill
Greengill
Wardhall Common
Caer Mote
High Houses
High Ireby
Green How
Green Head
Branthwaite
Fell Side
Row Hall
New Grange
Grange Grassings
Bothel Craggs
Ruthwaite
Uldale
Mickle Rigg
Crosshow
Kirkborough
Dearham
Lakeland Heavy Horse Centre
251 Moota Hill
Threapland Moss
Whittas Park
Chapel House Fm
Hay Knott 409
Hill Fm
Salkeld Cross
Row Brow
Low Ho
Townhead
223 Tallentire Hill
Millstone Moor
Sunderland Heads
Binsey 447
Scawthwaite Close
Longlands
Clints Crags
Over Water
482 Longlands Fell
Brae Fell 585
Caldbeck
Tallentire
Blindcrake
Sunderland
Glebe Fm
Bewaldeth
High Bewaldeth
Harker Marsh
Craikhow Hall
Woodside Fm
West Ho
Shepherd Hall
Park Wood
Irton Ho
Orthwaite
Lowthwaite Fell
Birk Moss
Iron Crag
Great Sca Fell 651
Great Lingy Hill
Hennah Hall
Williamsgate
Low Barn
Bank Head
Isel Hall
Isel
Howgill Wood
Long Close Fm
Horsemoor Hills
Meal Fell
Broughton Moor
Dovenby
Dovenby Mill
Bridekirk
Redmain
Prospect Ho
Messengermire Wood
Park Wood
Great Cockup
Miller Moss
Broughton Lodge
Hewthwaite Hall
River Derwent
Trotters World of Animals
Kestrel Lodge
710 Knott
627
Dovenby Craggs
Anns Hill
Wood Hall Fm
Forth Ho
Ouse Bridge
Kilnhill
North Row
Bassenthwaite
Melbecks
Dash Fm
Little Broughton
Elva Hill
Setmurthy Common
Higham Hall
Dubwath
Chapel
Great Broughton
Belle Vue
Hame's Hall
Park House Fm
Watch Hill
Papcastle
Cockermouth Castle
Wordsworth House
Castlegate Ho
Wyndham Ho
Bully Ho
Crag
Embleton
Pheasant Inn
Scarness
Barkbeth
High Side
Dyke Nook
Barkbethdale
Broad End
Bakestall
642 Great Calva
Ribton Ho
Brigham
Cockermouth
Lambfoot
East Ho
Bassenthwaite Common
Skiddaw Forest
Broughton Cross
Tarn Bank
Scales Fm
Westray
Bouch Ho
Wythop Mill
Abbey
Wythop Mill
Sale Fell 359
Wythop Woods
Bassenthwaite Lake
Sand Hill
Hare Crag
Nepgill
Bridgefoot
Greysouthen
Tendley Hill
Dubbs Moss
Esps Fm
Lake District National Park
931 Skiddaw
Skiddaw House
Little Clifton
Rigging Gill
Eaglesfield
Shatton Lodge
373 Ling Fell
Wythop Hall
Mirehouse
Longside Edge
Carl Side
Sale How
Cloven Stone
Burnt Horse
Furnace Ho
Lamb Hill
Bent Houses
Shatton Hall
Long Fell
Wythop Moss
Little Man 865
Oldfield Ho
Springfield Fm
Harrot
Empleton High Common
Redness Point
Dodd Wood
Grey Crags
Jenkin Hill
715 Lonscale Fell
Knowe Crags
Oldfield
Low Hall
Broom Fell 511
Woodend
Calva Hall
Galefield
High Dyke
Hill Fm
Deanscales
East Ho
Brandlingill
Sandybeck Meadow
Lorton Vale
Graystones
Lord's Seat 552
Barf
Long Close Fm
Howgill Tongue
Blease Fell
Woodside
Wood Fm
Akebank Mill
Bank
High Lorton
Low Lorton
Scawgill Br
Oakfield House
Millbeck
Hollins Wood
Pardshaw Hall
Dean
Leegate
Mosser Mains
Whin Fell
Whinfell Hall
Lorton Fells
Whinlatter Forest Park
Thornthwaite
Thornthwaite Galleries
Applethwaite
Ormathwaite
Lonscale
Derwentfolds
Browtop
Branthwaite
Pardshaw
Mosser
Fellside Fm
Dodd Wood
Heritage/Visitor Centre
Whinlatter Pass
Cars of the Stars Motor Mus
368 Latrigg
Briery
Brundholme Wood
Branthwaite Edge
Mains
416 Fellbarrow
Thackthwaite
Newhouse Fm
Hopebeck
Hobcarton End
Spring Bank
Braithwaite
Cumberland Pencil Mus
Great Crosthwaite
Keswick
Brigham
Chestnut Hill
Castlerigg Stone Circle
Burns Fm
Rigg Ho
Branthwaite Rigg
Crakeplace Hall
Ullock
Mosser Fell
Sourfoot Fell
Dodd
High Hill
Portinscale
Row End
Mockerkin
Fangs Brow Fm
Waterend
Darling Fell
Miller Place
Grisedale Pike 791
Hospital Plantn
Little Braithwaite
Keswick
Low Rigg
Lingcroft
Mockerkin How
Iredale Place
Ullock
244 Swinside
Castlerigg
Dean Cross
Havercroft
Hudson Place
Low Fell
Brackenthwaite
770 Hopegill Head
Hobcarton Crag
Stile End
Barrow
Derwent Isle
Dale Bottom
Kidburngill
Woodend
Crossgates
Holme Wood
Loweswater
Scale Hill
707 Whiteside
Sand Hill
Force Crag
High Moss
Silver Hill
Swinside
Stable Hills
Great Wood
High Rigg
Millgillhead
Lamplugh
Bird Dyke
Owsen Fell
Burnbank Fell
Loweswater
Eel Crag
Causey Pike
Rowling End
Stair
Derwent Water
Yew Crag
Bridge End Fm
Asby
Dockray Nook
Carling Knot
Lanthwaite
852 Grasmoor
Crag Hill 839
Scar Crag
Newlands
Hawes End
Falcon Crag
Low Moss
Felldyke
Loweswater Fell
Castlerigg Fell
Goat Crag
Arlecdon
Lamplugh Fell
Little Dodd
Mellbreak
Crummock Water
Wandope
Ard Crags
Bawd Hall
Little Town
Cat Bells
Derwentwater
Ashness Br
Great Bay
590 Bleaberry Fell
Rowrah
Knock Murton
Middle Fell
Rannerdale
Whiteless Pike
Black Crag
Raven Crag
Leys
Keltonfell Top
Gavel Fell 526
Hen Comb 509
Knott Rigg
High Snab Bank
Scope
Ashness
High Seat 608
Castle Crag
Kelton Fell
Ling Crags
Hause Point
Newlands Pass
Derwent Fells
Borrowdale Gates
Reecastle
Brown
Solway Coast
Cumbria
Skiddaw Forest

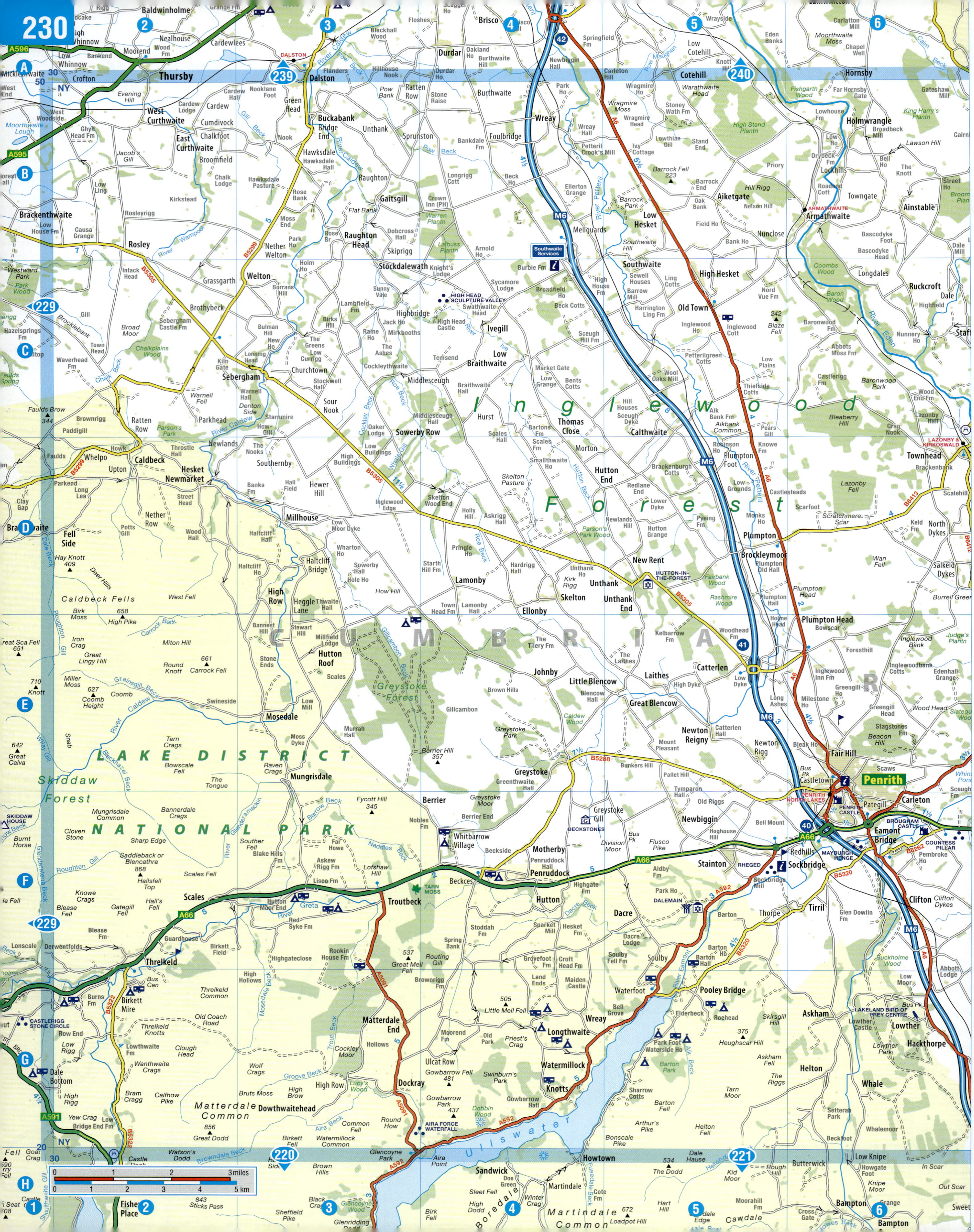
Baldwinholme
Thursby
Dalston
Durdar
Brisco
Carleton
Wreay
Cotehill
Hornsby
Holmwrangle
Armathwaite
Ainstable
West Curthwaite
East Curthwaite
Cardew
Cardewlees
Crofton
Buckabank
Hawksdale
Raughton
Gaitsgill
Raughton Head
Stockdalewath
Brackenthwaite
Rosley
Welton
Sebergham
High Hesket
Low Hesket
Southwaite
Southwaite Services
Old Town
Aiketgate
Ivegill
Low Braithwaite
Middlesceugh
Sowerby Row
Inglewood Forest
Calthwaite
Thomas Close
Hutton End
Plumpton
Brockleymoor
New Rent
Unthank
Skelton
Ellonby
Lamonby
Whelpo
Caldbeck
Hesket Newmarket
Millhouse
Upton
Fell Side
Haltcliff Bridge
High Row
Hutton Roof
Catterlen
Laithes
Johnby
Little Blencow
Great Blencow
Newton Reigny
Plumpton Head
Mosedale
Mungrisdale
Greystoke
Greystoke Forest
Berrier
Penruddock
Motherby
Newbiggin
Stainton
Sockbridge
Penrith
Eamont Bridge
Clifton
Fair Hill
Pategill
Scales
Threlkeld
Troutbeck
Hutton
Dacre
Tirril
Pooley Bridge
Askham
Lowther
Hackthorpe
Helton
Whale
Bampton
Matterdale End
Dockray
Watermillock
Wreay
Longthwaite
Howtown
Sandwick
Martindale
Ullswater
Dowthwaitehead
Matterdale Common
Martindale Common
CUMBRIA
LAKE DISTRICT NATIONAL PARK
Skiddaw Forest
Caldbeck Fells
A6
A66
A592
A5091
A591
B5305
B5288
B5320
M6
239
240
229
220
221
0 1 2 3 miles
0 1 2 3 4 5 km

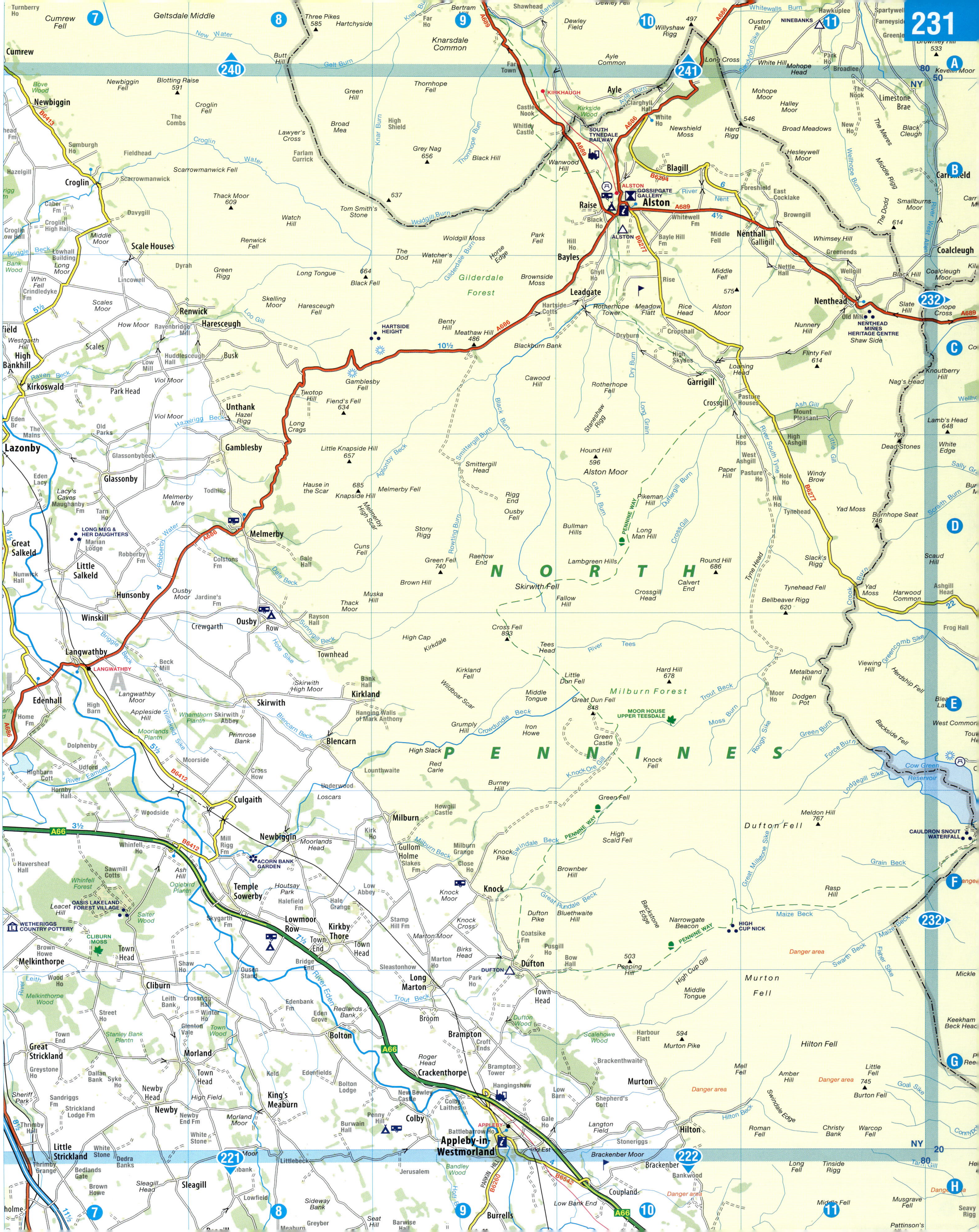

Cumrew
Croglin
Renwick
Kirkoswald
Lazonby
Glassonby
Gamblesby
Unthank
Melmerby
Great Salkeld
Little Salkeld
Hunsonby
Winskill
Langwathby
Edenhall
Ousby
Skirwith
Kirkland
Blencarn
Culgaith
Newbiggin
Milburn
Temple Sowerby
Kirkby Thore
Knock
Dufton
Long Marton
Cliburn
Bolton
Morland
Great Strickland
Little Strickland
King's Meaburn
Newby
Sleagill
Colby
Appleby-in-Westmorland
Murton
Hilton
Brackenber
Coupland
Burrells
Alston
Nenthead
Nenthall
Garrigill
Leadgate
Bayles
Raise
Ayle
Blagill
Alston Moor
Gilderdale Forest
Knarsdale Common
Milburn Forest
Dufton Fell
Murton Fell
Hilton Fell
NORTH PENNINES
Cross Fell 893
Great Dun Fell 848
Little Dun Fell
Knock Fell
Cow Green Reservoir
Cauldron Snout Waterfall
Moor House Upper Teesdale
High Cup Nick
Pennine Way
Long Meg & Her Daughters
Lacy's Caves
Acorn Bank Garden
Oasis Lakeland Forest Village
Wetheriggs Country Pottery
Cliburn Moss
Hartside Height
South Tynedale Railway
Gossipgate Gallery
Nenthead Mines Heritage Centre
Kirkhaugh
A686
A689
A66
B6412
B6413
B6277
B6294
B6260
B6542
River Eden
River Tees
River South Tyne
240
241
232
221
222
NY
A
B
C
D
E
F
G
H
7
8
9
10
11

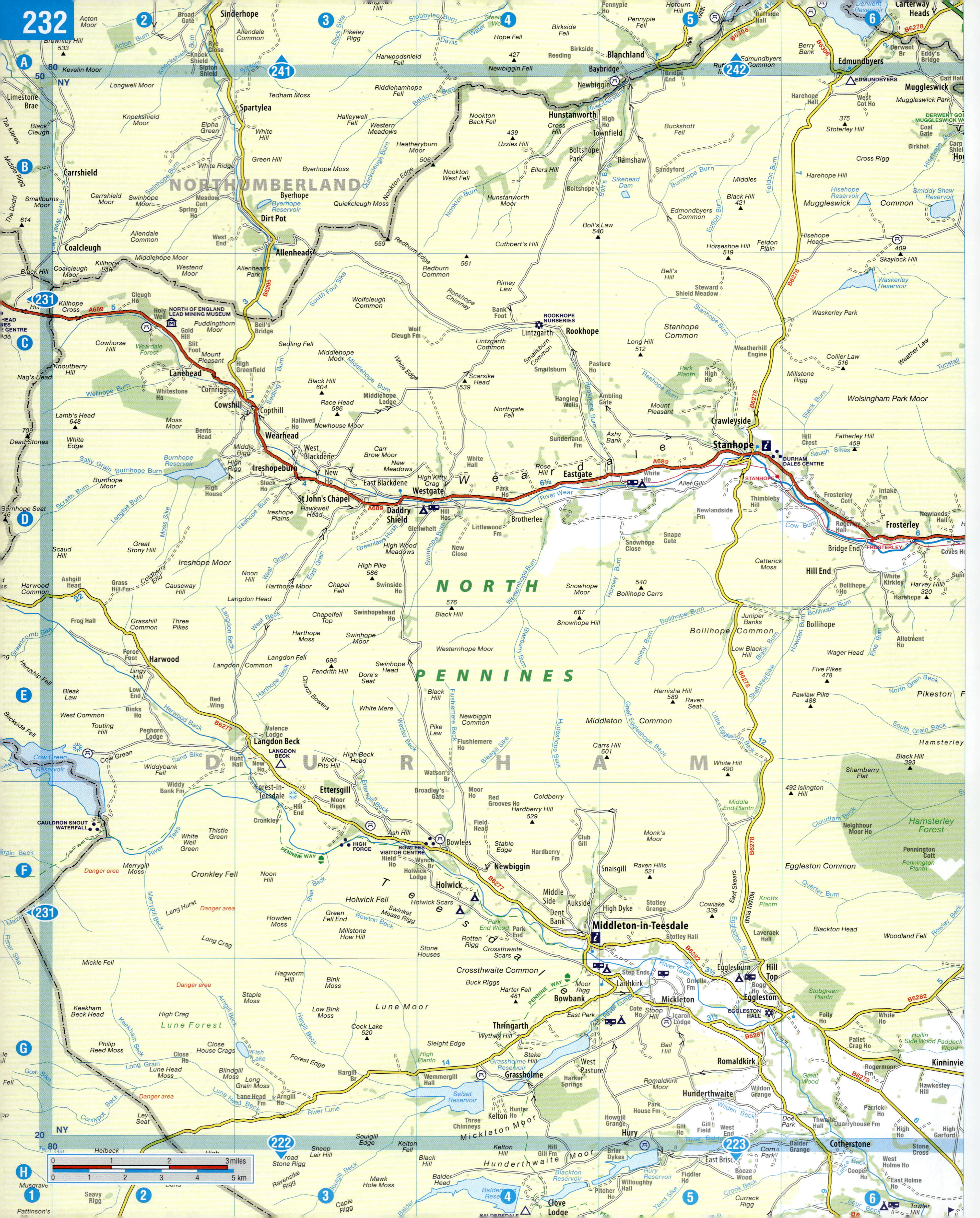
NORTHUMBERLAND
NORTH PENNINES
DURHAM
Weardale
Teesdale
Sinderhope
Allendale Common
Acton Moor
Broad Gate
Kevelin Moor
Longwell Moor
Limestone Brae
Knockshield Moor
Spartylea
Tedham Moss
Pikeley Rigg
Harwoodshield Fell
Riddlehamhope Fell
Halleywell Fell
Western Meadows
Heatheryburn Moor
Byerhope Moss
Byerhope
Byerhope Reservoir
Dirt Pot
Quickcleugh Moss
Carrshield
Carrshield Moor
Swinhope Moor
Smallburns Moor
Allendale Common
Coalcleugh
Allenheads
Allenheads Park
Middlehope Moor
Westend Moor
Killhope Cross
Killhope Law
NORTH OF ENGLAND LEAD MINING MUSEUM
Puddingthorn Moor
Cowhorse Hill
Weardale Forest
Knoutberry Hill
Nag's Head
Lanehead
Cornriggs
Cowshill
Copthill
Wearhead
Lamb's Head 648
Dead Stones
White Edge
Burnhope Reservoir
Burnhope Moor
Ireshopeburn
St John's Chapel
Ireshope Plains
Ireshope Moor
Great Stony Hill
Harwood Common
Frog Hall
Grasshill Common
Three Pikes
Harwood
Langdon Head
Langdon Common
Langdon Fell
Fendrith Hill
Dora's Seat
Bleak Law
West Common
Touting Hill
Langdon Beck
Cow Green Reservoir
CAULDRON SNOUT WATERFALL
Widdybank Fell
Forest-in-Teesdale
Ettersgill
HIGH FORCE
BOWLEES VISITOR CENTRE
Bowlees
PENNINE WAY
Cronkley Fell
Merrygill Moss
Danger area
Newbiggin
Holwick
Holwick Fell
Holwick Scars
Middleton-in-Teesdale
Mickle Fell
Keekham Beck Head
High Crag
Lune Forest
Lune Moor
Philip Reed Moss
Close House Craggs
Long Grain Moss
Lune Head Moss
Cock Lake 520
Thringarth
Grassholme
Grassholme Reservoir
Selset Reservoir
Kelton Ho
Mickleton Moor
Hunderthwaite Moor
Hury
Hury Reservoir
Blackton Reservoir
Balderhead Reservoir
Clove Lodge
Romaldkirk
Hunderthwaite
Cotherstone
Eggleston
EGGLESTON HALL
Laithkirk
Mickleton
Bowbank
Crossthwaite Common
Eggleston Common
Hamsterley Forest
Kinninvie
Blackton Head
Woodland Fell
Westgate
Daddry Shield
Eastgate
Rookhope
ROOKHOPE NURSERIES
Lintzgarth
Stanhope
DURHAM DALES CENTRE
Frosterley
Bridge End
Hill End
Crawleyside
Stanhope Common
Wolsingham Park Moor
Waskerley Reservoir
Waskerley Park
Muggleswick
Muggleswick Common
Edmundbyers
Edmundbyers Common
Blanchland
Baybridge
Newbiggin
Hunstanworth
Hunstanworth Moor
Townfield
Ramshaw
Boltshope Park
Nookton Edge
Redburn Common
Wolfcleugh Common
Middlehope Moor
Black Hill 604
Race Head 586
Newhouse Moor
Chapel Fell
High Pike 586
Swinside Ho
Black Hill
Westernhope Moor
Snowhope Moor
Snowhope Hill 607
Bollihope Common
Bollihope Carrs
Middleton Common
Carrs Hill 601
White Hill 490
Harnisha Hill 589
Raven Seat
Five Pikes 478
Pawlaw Pike 488
Pikeston Fell
Hamsterley
Shornberry Flat
Islington Hill
Monk's Moor
Raven Hills 521
Snaisgill
Stotley Hall
Cowlake 339
ROMAN ROAD
Harter Fell 481
A689
B6277
B6278
B6295
B6306
B6282
B6281
231
241
242
222
223
NY
A
B
C
D
E
F
G
H
1
2
3
4
5
6
0
1
2
3 miles
4
5 km

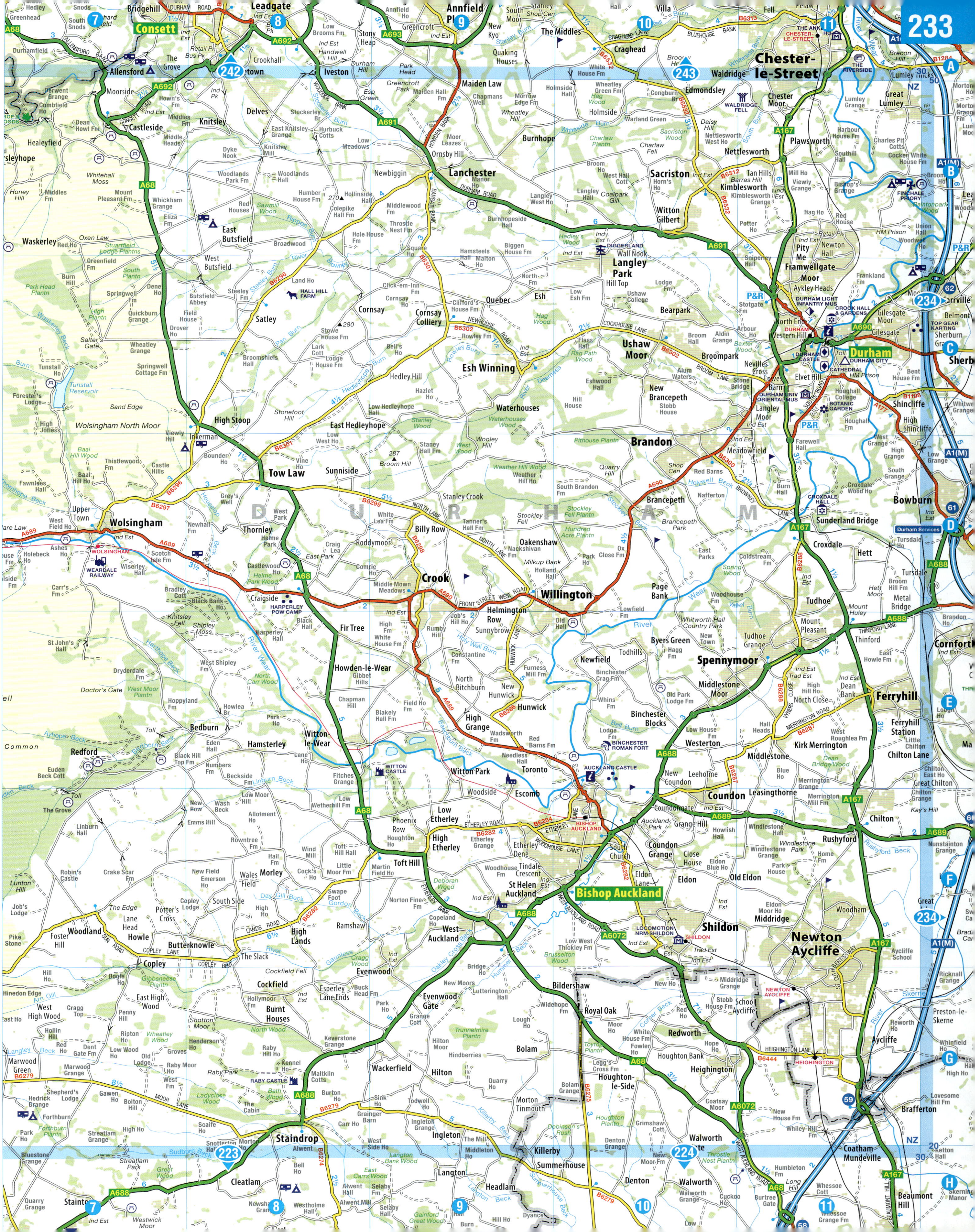
Consett
Leadgate
Annfield Plain
Chester-le-Street
Lanchester
Sacriston
Kimblesworth
Witton Gilbert
Langley Park
Esh Winning
Ushaw Moor
Durham
Brandon
Waterhouses
Tow Law
Wolsingham
Crook
Willington
Brancepeth
Spennymoor
Ferryhill
Tudhoe
Coundon
Bishop Auckland
West Auckland
Shildon
Newton Aycliffe
Heighington
Evenwood
Cockfield
Staindrop
Hamsterley
Witton-le-Wear
Toft Hill
Wackerfield
Royal Oak
Bolam
Redworth
Killerby
Summerhouse
Denton
Walworth
Headlam
Langton
Ingleton
Cleatlam
Staindrop
Satley
Cornsay
Cornsay Colliery
Quebec
Esh
Bearpark
Framwellgate Moor
Pity Me
Sherburn
Shincliffe
Bowburn
Croxdale
Sunderland Bridge
Hett
Chilton
Rushyford
Middlestone Moor
Kirk Merrington
Westerton
Binchester Blocks
Hunwick
High Grange
Toronto
Escomb
Witton Park
Etherley Dene
High Etherley
Low Etherley
St Helen Auckland
Eldon
Middridge
Woodland
Copley
Butterknowle
Morley
Howden-le-Wear
Fir Tree
Billy Row
Stanley Crook
Sunniside
Oakenshaw
Helmington Row
Redford
Bedburn
Thornley
Wolsingham North Moor
Waskerley
Castleside
Allensford
Knitsley
Delves
Iveston
Maiden Law
Burnhope
Edmondsley
Nettlesworth
DURHAM

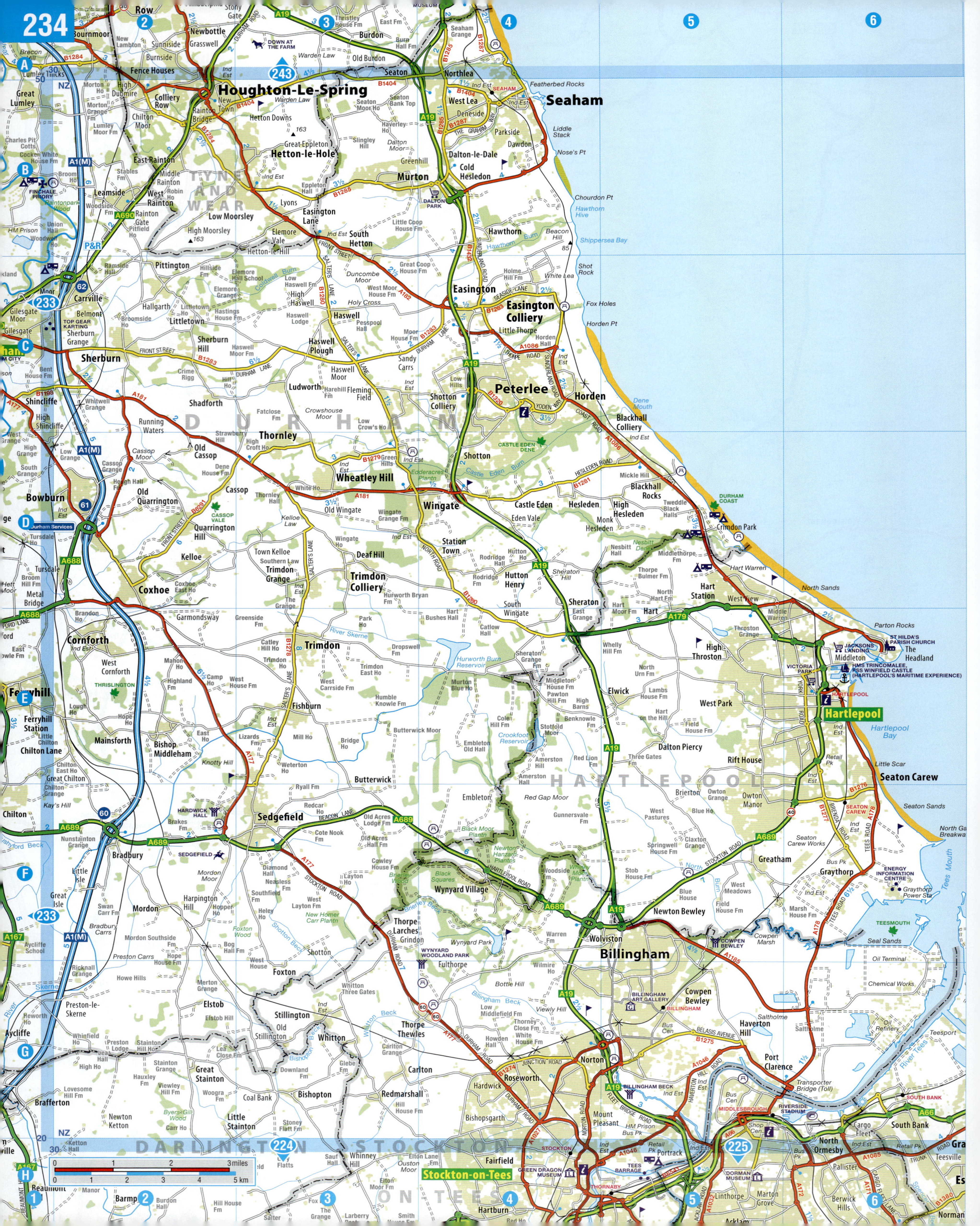

Houghton-Le-Spring
Seaham
Hetton-le-Hole
Murton
Dalton-le-Dale
Cold Hesledon
Easington Lane
South Hetton
Hawthorn
Easington
Easington Colliery
Peterlee
Horden
Blackhall Colliery
Shotton
Wheatley Hill
Thornley
Wingate
Castle Eden
Hesleden
Blackhall Rocks
Crimdon Park
Hart
Hartlepool
Seaton Carew
Greatham
Graythorp
Billingham
Wolviston
Norton
Stockton-on-Tees
Port Clarence
Haverton Hill
Sedgefield
Trimdon
Fishburn
Bishop Middleham
Trimdon Colliery
Coxhoe
Cornforth
Kelloe
Cassop
Sherburn
Sherburn Hill
Shincliffe
Bowburn
Pittington
Carrville
Ferryhill
Chilton
Bradbury
Mordon
Wynyard Village
Thorpe Thewles
Carlton
Redmarshall
Bishopton
Great Stainton
Little Stainton
Stillington
Whitton
Elstob
Foxton
Fairfield
Roseworth
Hardwick
Bishopsgarth
Middleton
West Park
Dalton Piercy
Elwick
High Throston
Newton Bewley
Cowpen Bewley
North Ormesby
South Bank
Middlesbrough
D U R H A M
H A R T L E P O O L
T Y N E A N D W E A R
D A R L I N G T O N
S T O C K T O N O N T E E S

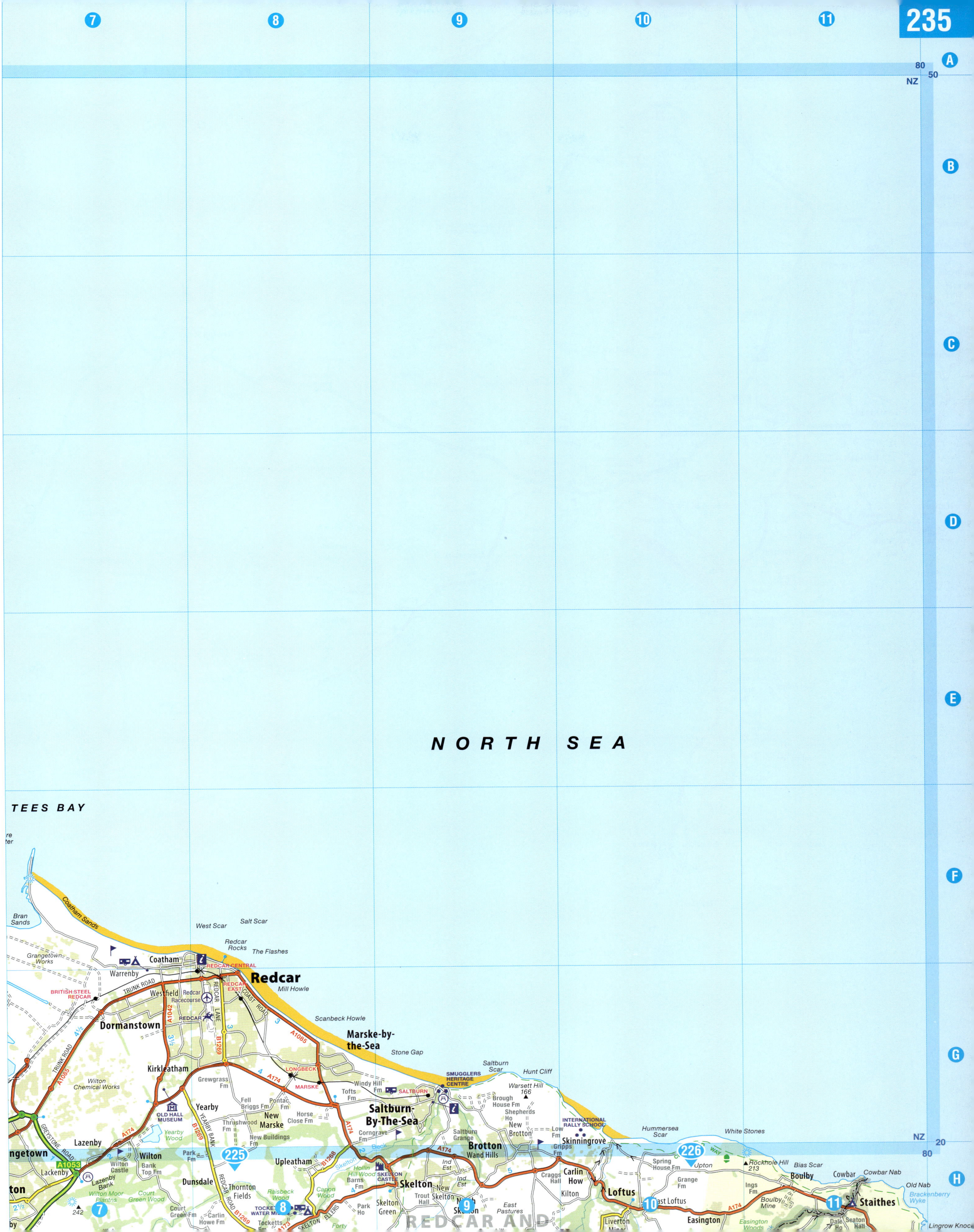

NORTH SEA
TEES BAY
Coatham Sands
Bran Sands
West Scar
Salt Scar
Redcar Rocks
The Flashes
Grangetown Works
Coatham
Warrenby
REDCAR CENTRAL
Redcar
Mill Howle
REDCAR EAST
BRITISH STEEL REDCAR
TRUNK ROAD
Westfield
Redcar Racecourse
REDCAR LANE
COAST ROAD
Dormanstown
Scanbeck Howle
Marske-by-the-Sea
Stone Gap
Kirkleatham
LONGBECK
MARSKE
Wilton Chemical Works
Grewgrass Fm
Windy Hill Fm
SALTBURN
SMUGGLERS HERITAGE CENTRE
Saltburn Scar
Hunt Cliff
Warsett Hill 166
Tofts Fm
Fell Briggs Fm
Pontac Fm
OLD HALL MUSEUM
Yearby
YEARBY BANK
Yearby Wood
New Marske
Horse Close Fm
Thrushwood Fm
New Buildings Fm
Saltburn-By-The-Sea
Corngrave Fm
Brough House Fm
Shepherds Ho
New Brotton
INTERNATIONAL RALLY SCHOOL
Skinningrove
Saltburn Grange
Brotton
Wand Hills
Low Fm
Gripps Fm
Hummersea Scar
White Stones
Lazenby
Wilton
Wilton Castle
Bank Top Fm
Lackenby
Lazenby Bank
Wilton Moor Plantns
Court Green Wood
GREYSTONE ROAD
Park Fm
Dunsdale
Upleatham
Thornton Fields
Raisbeck Wood
Capon Wood
Court Green Fm
Carlin Howe Fm
TOCKETTS WATER MILL
Tocketts
SKELTON ELLERS
Forty
Skelton
Hollin Hill Wood
Barns Fm
SKELTON CASTLE
Park Ho
Skelton Green
Trout Hall
New Skelton
Ind Est
North Skelton
East Pastures
Craggs Hall
Carlin How
Kilton
Loftus
East Loftus
Liverton Mines
Easington
Spring House Fm
Upton
Grange Fm
Rockhole Hill 213
Bias Scar
Boulby
Ings Fm
Boulby Mine
Easington Woods
Cowbar
Cowbar Nab
Staithes
Old Nab
Brackenberry Wyke
Dale Ho
Seaton Hall
Lingrow Knock
REDCAR AND
A1053
A174
A1085
A1042
B1269
B1268
A173
225
226
NZ
80
50
20

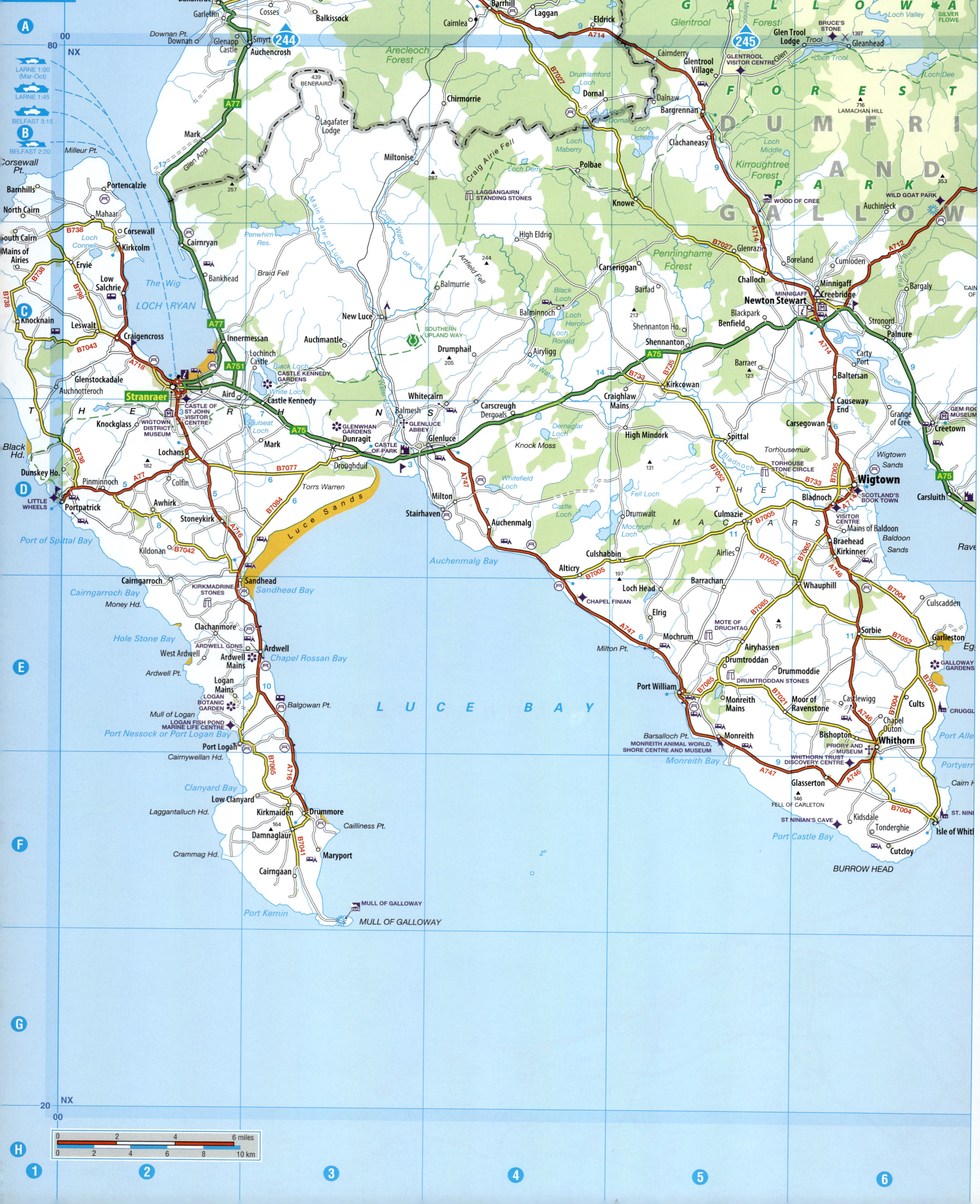
Ballantrae Bay
Ballantrae
Garleffin
Heronsford
Glen Tig
Cosses
Balkissock
Water of Tig
Barrhill
Cairnlea
Laggan
Clauchrie
Eldrick
Palgowan
Loch Enoch
Glentrool
Forest
GALLOWAY
SILVER FLOWE
Loch Valley
Glen Trool Lodge
BRUCE'S STONE
Gleanhead
Loch Trool
Loch Dee
GLENTROOL VISITOR CENTRE
Glentrool Village
Cairnderry
Downan Pt.
Downan
Glenapp Castle
Smyrt
Auchencrosh
244
245
Arecleoch Forest
Drumlamford Loch
Dornal
Dalnaw
Bargrennan
FOREST
DUMFRIES AND GALLOWAY
PARK
LAMACHAN HILL
BENERAIRD
LARNE 1:00 (Mar-Oct)
LARNE 1:45
BELFAST 3:15
BELFAST 2:20
Milleur Pt.
Corsewall Pt.
Mark
Glen App
Lagafater Lodge
Chirmorrie
Miltonise
Craig Airie Fell
Loch Derry
Polbae
Loch Maberry
Loch Ochiltree
Clachaneasy
Loch Middle
Kirroughtree Forest
WOOD OF CREE
WILD GOAT PARK
Auchinleck
Barnhills
Portencalzie
North Cairn
Mahaar
Corsewall
Kirkcolm
South Cairn
Mains of Airies
Loch Connell
Cairnryan
Penwhirn Res.
Main Water of Luce
Cross Water of Luce
LAGGANGAIRN STANDING STONES
High Eldrig
Knowe
Artfield Fell
Ervie
Low Salchrie
Bankhead
Braid Fell
Balmurrie
Penninghame Forest
Carseriggan
Glenrazie
Boreland
Cumloden
Bargaly
The Wig
LOCH RYAN
Barfad
Black Loch
Balminnoch
Minnigaff
Creebridge
Newton Stewart
Blackpark
Benfield
Knocknain
Leswalt
Craigencross
Innermessan
Auchmantle
New Luce
SOUTHERN UPLAND WAY
Loch Heron
Loch Ronald
Airyligg
Shennanton Ho.
Shennanton
Stronord
Palnure
Carty Port
Glenstockadale
Auchnotteroch
Lochinch Castle
Black Loch
CASTLE KENNEDY GARDENS
Drumphail
Barraer
Baltersan
Stranraer
CASTLE OF ST JOHN VISITOR CENTRE
Aird
White Loch
Castle Kennedy
Whitecairn
Carscreugh
Dergoals
Craighlaw Mains
Kirkcowan
Causeway End
Grange of Cree
Creetown
GEM ROCK MUSEUM
Knockglass
WIGTOWN DISTRICT MUSEUM
Soulseat Loch
Mark
GLENWHAN GARDENS
Dunragit
Balmesh
GLENLUCE ABBEY
Glenluce
CASTLE OF PARK
Dernaglar Loch
Knock Moss
High Mindork
Carsegowan
Spittal
Torhousemuir
TORHOUSE STONE CIRCLE
Wigtown Sands
Wigtown
Carsluith
Black Hd.
Lochans
Colfin
Droughduil
Torrs Warren
Whitefield Loch
Fell Loch
SCOTLAND'S BOOK TOWN
Bladnoch
Dunskey Ho.
LITTLE WHEELS
Pinminnoch
Portpatrick
Awhirk
Stoneykirk
Luce Sands
Milton
Stairhaven
Castle Loch
Drumwalt
Mochrum Loch
Culmazie
MACHARS
VISITOR CENTRE
Mains of Baldoon
Baldoon Sands
Port of Spittal Bay
Kildonan
Auchenmalg
Braehead
Kirkinner
Auchenmalg Bay
Culshabbin
Airlies
Cairngarroch
Sandhead
Alticry
Loch Head
Barrachan
Whauphill
Cairngarroch Bay
KIRKMADRINE STONES
Sandhead Bay
Money Hd.
CHAPEL FINIAN
Elrig
Culscadden
Clachanmore
MOTE OF DRUCHTAG
Sorbie
Hole Stone Bay
West Ardwell
ARDWELL GDNS
Ardwell
Ardwell Mains
Chapel Rossan Bay
Mochrum
Milton Pt.
Airyhassen
Garlieston
Ardwell Pt.
Drumtroddan
Drummoddie
GALLOWAY GARDENS
Logan Mains
DRUMTRODDAN STONES
LOGAN BOTANIC GARDEN
Balgowan Pt.
LUCE BAY
Port William
Monreith Mains
Moor of Ravenstone
Castlewigg
Cults
CRUGGLETON
Mull of Logan
LOGAN FISH POND MARINE LIFE CENTRE
Chapel Outon
Port Nessock or Port Logan Bay
Barsalloch Pt.
MONREITH ANIMAL WORLD, SHORE CENTRE AND MUSEUM
Monreith
Bishopton
Port Allen
Port Logan
PRIORY AND MUSEUM
Whithorn
Cairnywellan Hd.
Monreith Bay
WHITHORN TRUST DISCOVERY CENTRE
Port Yerrock
Clanyard Bay
Glasserton
Cairn Hd.
Low Clanyard
FELL OF CARLETON
Laggantalluch Hd.
Kirkmaiden
Drummore
ST NINIAN'S CAVE
Kidsdale
Tonderghie
Isle of Whithorn
Damnaglaur
Cailliness Pt.
Port Castle Bay
Crammag Hd.
Maryport
Cutcloy
Cairngaan
BURROW HEAD
MULL OF GALLOWAY
Port Kemin
NX
0 2 4 6 miles
0 2 4 6 8 10 km

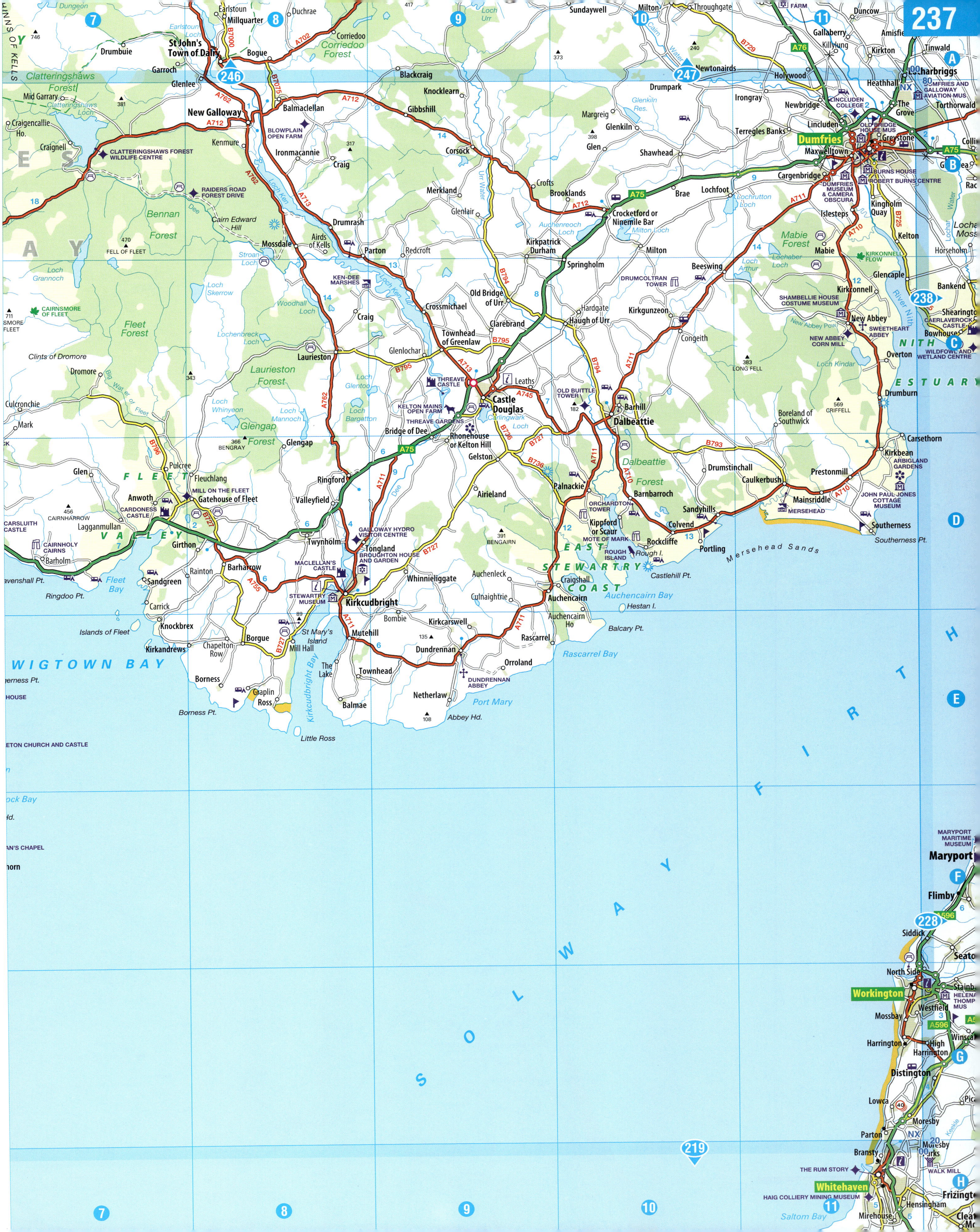
Dungeon
Earlstoun
Millquarter
Duchrae
St John's Town of Dalry
Corriedoo
Corriedoo Forest
Drumbuie
Bogue
Garroch
Glenlee
246
Clatteringshaws Forest
Mid Garrary
Clatteringshaws Loch
Craigencallie Ho.
New Galloway
Balmaclellan
Blackcraig
Knocklearn
Gibbshill
Craignell
CLATTERINGSHAWS FOREST WILDLIFE CENTRE
Kenmure
BLOWPLAIN OPEN FARM
Ironmacannie
Craig
Corsock
RAIDERS ROAD FOREST DRIVE
Bennan Forest
Cairn Edward Hill
Merkland
Glenlair
Drumrash
Mossdale
Airds of Kells
Parton
Redcroft
FELL OF FLEET
Loch Grannoch
Loch Skerrow
Stroan Loch
KEN-DEE MARSHES
Loch Ken
CAIRNSMORE OF FLEET
Woodhall Loch
Craig
Crossmichael
Fleet Forest
Lochenbreck Loch
Townhead of Greenlaw
Clints of Dromore
Laurieston
Glenlochar
Dromore
Laurieston Forest
Loch Whinyeon
Glengap Forest
Culcronchie
Mark
BENGRAY
Glengap
THREAVE CASTLE
KELTON MAINS OPEN FARM
THREAVE GARDENS
Bridge of Dee
Castle Douglas
Leaths
Carlingwark Loch
Rhonehouse or Kelton Hill
Gelston
Airieland
Pulcree
Fleuchlang
Glen
FLEET
MILL ON THE FLEET
Gatehouse of Fleet
Anwoth
Ringford
Valleyfield
CARDONESS CASTLE
CAIRNHARROW
CARSLUITH CASTLE
Lagganmullan
VALLEY
Girthon
CAIRNHOLY CAIRNS
Barholm
Twynholm
GALLOWAY HYDRO VISITOR CENTRE
Tongland
BROUGHTON HOUSE AND GARDEN
MACLELLAN'S CASTLE
Rainton
Barharrow
Sandgreen
Fleet Bay
Ringdoo Pt.
Carrick
STEWARTRY MUSEUM
Kirkcudbright
Whinnieliggate
Auchenleck
Culnaightrie
BENGAIRN
Knockbrex
Islands of Fleet
Kirkandrews
St Mary's Isle
Borgue
Mill Hall
Mutehill
Bombie
Kirkcarswell
Dundrennan
Rascarrel
Chapelton Row
WIGTOWN BAY
Borness
Kirkcudbright Bay
The Lake
Townhead
Orroland
DUNDRENNAN ABBEY
Balmae
Netherlaw
Port Mary
Abbey Hd.
Ross
Borness Pt.
Little Ross
Sundaywell
Milton
Throughgate
Newtonairds
247
Drumpark
Irongray
Holywood
Margreig
Glenkiln Res.
Glenkiln
Glen
Shawhead
Terregles Banks
Crofts
Brooklands
Auchenreoch Loch
Crocketford or Ninemile Bar
Milton Loch
Milton
Brae
Lochfoot
Lochrutton Loch
Kirkpatrick Durham
Springholm
Old Bridge of Urr
Clarebrand
Hardgate
Haugh of Urr
DRUMCOLTRAN TOWER
Kirkgunzeon
Beeswing
Loch Arthur
Lochaber Loch
Congeith
OLD BUITTLE TOWER
Barhill
Dalbeattie
Dalbeattie Forest
LONG FELL
Boreland of Southwick
CRIFFELL
Drumstinchall
Caulkerbush
Palnackie
Barnbarroch
ORCHARDTON TOWER
Kippford or Scaur
MOTE OF MARK
ROUGH ISLAND
Rough I.
Rockcliffe
Colvend
Sandyhills
Portling
EAST STEWARTRY COAST
Castlehill Pt.
Craigshall
Auchencairn
Auchencairn Bay
Hestan I.
Auchencairn Ho
Balcary Pt.
Rascarrel Bay
Mersehead Sands
Prestonmill
Mainsriddle
MERSEHEAD
Southerness
Southerness Pt.
Duncow
Gallaberry
Killylung
Amisfield
Kirkton
Tinwald
Heathhall
Locharbriggs
DUMFRIES AND GALLOWAY AVIATION MUS
Torthorwald
LINCLUDEN COLLEGE
Newbridge
The Grove
Lincluden
OLD BRIDGE HOUSE MUS
Dumfries
Greystone
Maxwelltown
BURNS HOUSE
ROBERT BURNS CENTRE
Cargenbridge
DUMFRIES MUSEUM & CAMERA OBSCURA
Islesteps
Kingholm Quay
Mabie Forest
Mabie
Kelton
KIRKCONNELL FLOW
Glencaple
Kirkconnell
River Nith
238
SHAMBELLIE HOUSE COSTUME MUSEUM
New Abbey
SWEETHEART ABBEY
NEW ABBEY CORN MILL
Loch Kindar
Bankend
Shearington
CAERLAVEROCK CASTLE
Bowhouse
WILDFOWL AND WETLAND CENTRE
Overton
NITH ESTUARY
Drumburn
Carsethorn
Kirkbean
ARBIGLAND GARDENS
JOHN PAUL JONES COTTAGE MUSEUM
SOLWAY FIRTH
MARYPORT MARITIME MUSEUM
Maryport
Flimby
228
Siddick
North Side
Workington
HELENA THOMPSON MUS
Westfield
Mossbay
Harrington
High Harrington
Distington
Lowca
Moresby
Parton
Bransty
THE RUM STORY
Whitehaven
HAIG COLLIERY MINING MUSEUM
WALK MILL
Hensingham
Mirehouse
Saltom Bay
219

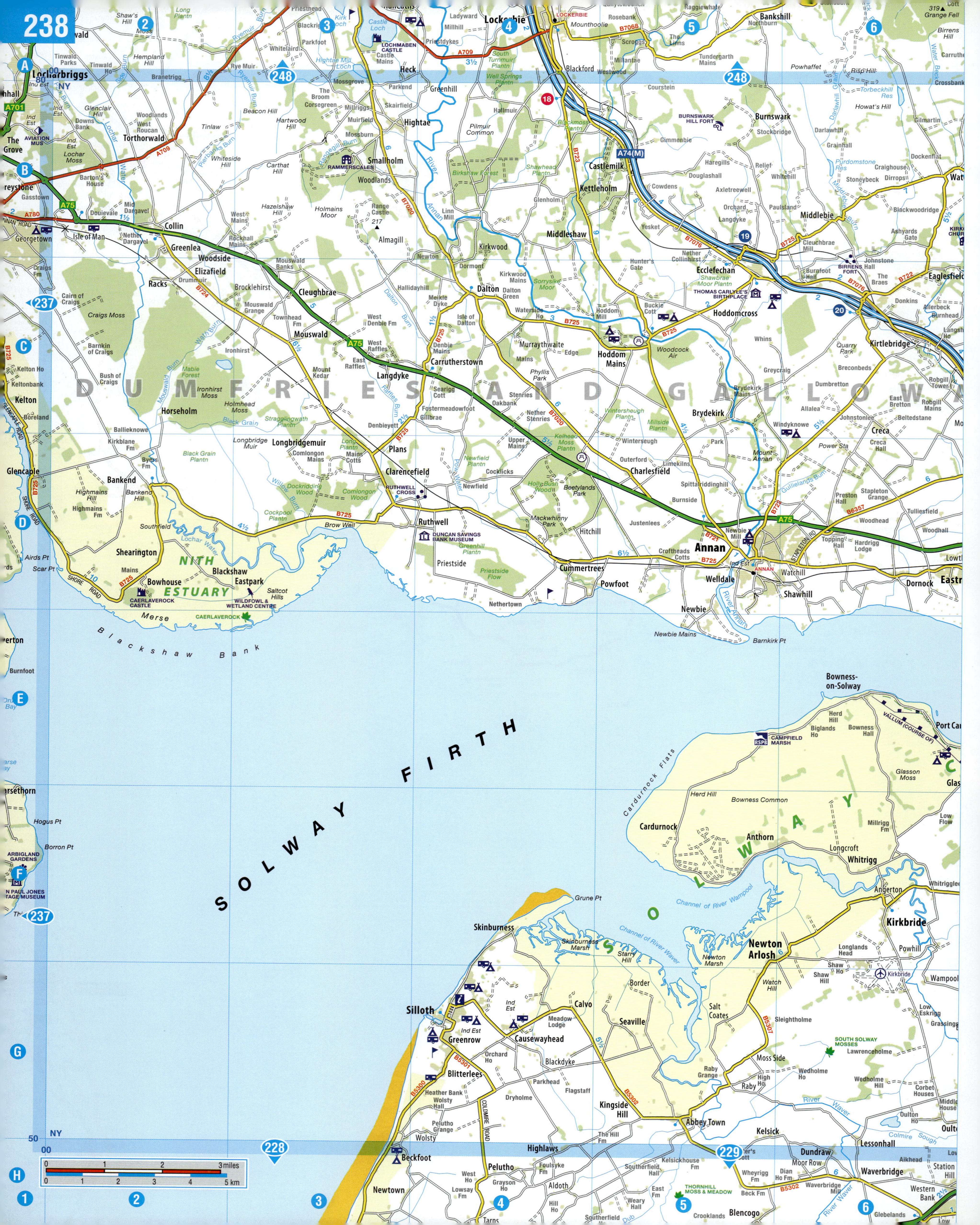
DUMFRIES AND GALLOWAY
SOLWAY FIRTH
NITH ESTUARY
SOLWAY
Blackshaw Bank
Cardurnock Flats
Channel of River Wampool
Channel of River Waver
Lockerbie
Lochmaben Castle
Heck
Hightae
Smallholm
Rammerscales
Woodlands
Castlemilk
Kettleholm
Middleshaw
Kirkwood
Dalton
Ecclefechan
Thomas Carlyle's Birthplace
Hoddomcross
Hoddom Mains
Burnswark
Middlebie
Eaglesfield
Kirtlebridge
Brydekirk
Creca
Charlesfield
Annan
Welldale
Shawhill
Dornock
Newbie
Powfoot
Cummertrees
Ruthwell
Duncan Savings Bank Museum
Ruthwell Cross
Clarencefield
Plans
Longbridgemuir
Carrutherstown
Langdyke
Mouswald
Cleughbrae
Collin
Greenlea
Woodside
Elizafield
Racks
Isle of Man
Georgetown
Locharbriggs
Torthorwald
Kelton
Glencaple
Bankend
Shearington
Blackshaw
Eastpark
Bowhouse
Caerlaverock Castle
Wildfowl & Wetland Centre
Caerlaverock
Horseholm
Bowness-on-Solway
Campfield Marsh
Cardurnock
Anthorn
Whitrigg
Kirkbride
Newton Arlosh
Skinburness
Grune Pt
Silloth
Greenrow
Causewayhead
Calvo
Seaville
Blitterlees
Beckfoot
Abbey Town
Kingside Hill
Highlaws
Pelutho
Newtown
Blencogo
Dundraw
Waverbridge
Lessonhall
Kelsick
Salt Coates
South Solway Mosses
Thornhill Moss & Meadow
Southerness
Arbigland Gardens
John Paul Jones Cottage Museum
A75
A74(M)
A709
A701
B725
B7020
B724
B723
B722
B7076
B6357
B5302
B5300
B5301
B5307
237
248
228
229
NY
0 1 2 3 miles
0 1 2 3 4 5 km

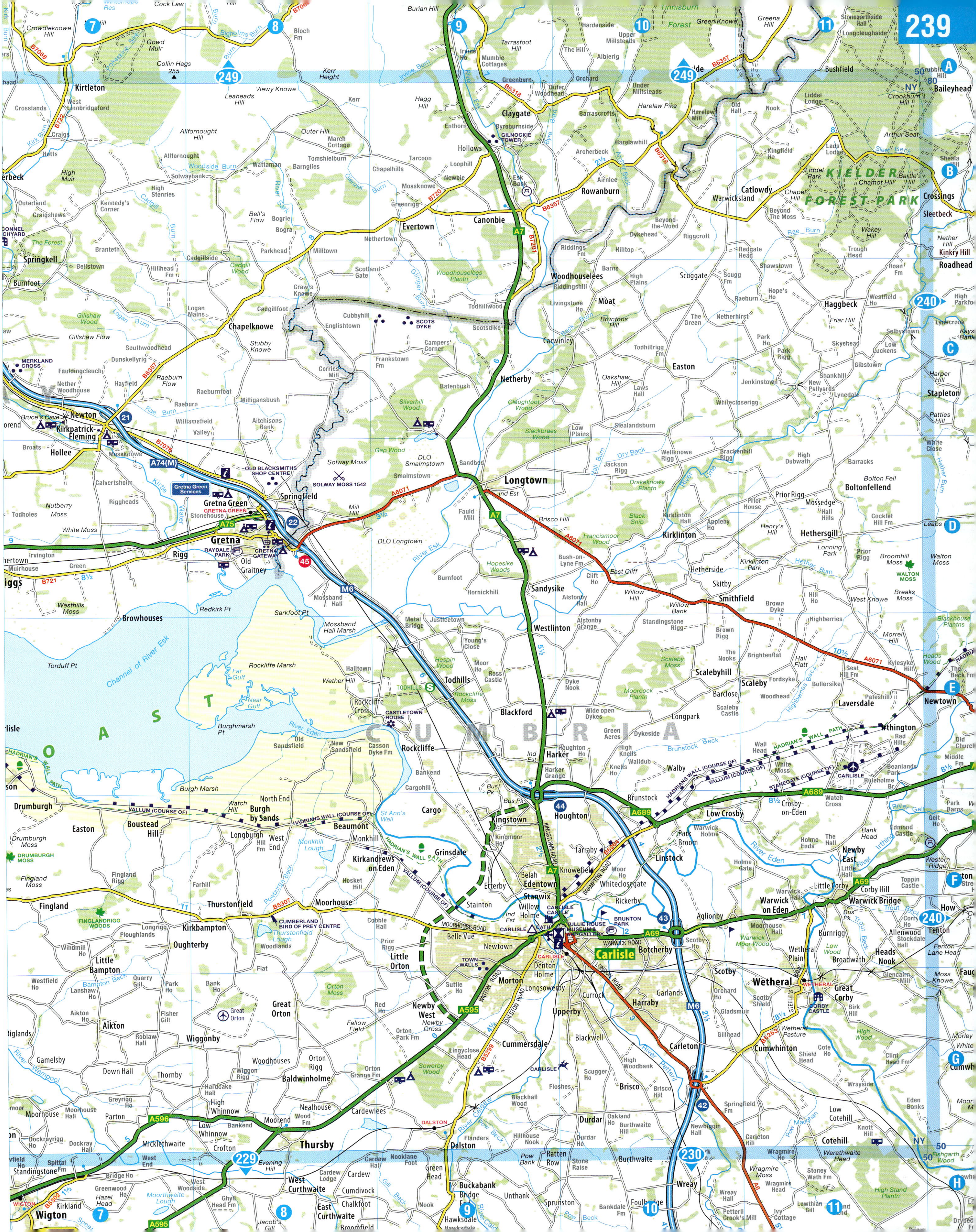

Kirtleton
Crowdieknowe Hill
Collin Hags 255
Kerr Height
Burian Hill
Tinnisburn Forest
Greena Hill
Stonegarthside Hall
Bushfield
Baileyhead
Claygate
Gilnockie Tower
Hollows
Canonbie
Rowanburn
Catlowdy
Warwicksland
KIELDER FOREST PARK
Crossings
Sleetbeck
Evertown
Milltown
Springkell
Burnfoot
Chapelknowe
Woodhouselees
Moat
Scuggate
Haggbeck
Roadhead
Kinkry Hill
Scots Dyke
Carwinley
Netherby
Easton
Stapleton
Newton
Kirkpatrick-Fleming
Hollee
Gretna Green
Gretna Green Services
Old Blacksmiths Shop Centre
Solway Moss 1542
Springfield
Gretna
Rigg
Old Graitney
Longtown
Kirklinton
Hethersgill
Bolton Fell
Boltonfellend
Smithfield
Sandysike
Westlinton
Browhouses
Redkirk Pt
Torduff Pt
Sarkfoot Pt
Rockliffe Marsh
Channel of River Esk
Burghmarsh Pt
Todhills
Blackford
Rockcliffe
Castletown House
Scaleby
Scalebyhill
Laversdale
Irthington
Newtown
CUMBRIA
SOLWAY COAST
Harker
Houghton
Brunstock
Crosby-on-Eden
Low Crosby
Linstock
Drumburgh
Burgh by Sands
Boustead Hill
Beaumont
Kirkandrews on Eden
Grinsdale
Cargo
Kingstown
Vallum (course of)
Hadrian's Wall Path
Fingland
Thurstonfield
Moorhouse
Kirkbampton
Oughterby
Little Bampton
Little Orton
Great Orton
Aikton
Wiggonby
Newby West
Morton
Stanwix
Carlisle
Botcherby
Tullie House Museum & Art Gallery
Carlisle Castle
Brunton Park
Harraby
Scotby
Wetheral
Great Corby
Corby Castle
Warwick on Eden
Warwick Bridge
Heads Nook
Upperby
Blackwell
Cummersdale
Carleton
Cumwhinton
Brisco
Durdar
Orton Rigg
Baldwinholme
Thursby
Dalston
Buckabank
Wreay
Cotehill
Wigton
Kirkland
West Curthwaite
East Curthwaite
M6
A7
A74(M)
A6071
A689
A69
A595
A596

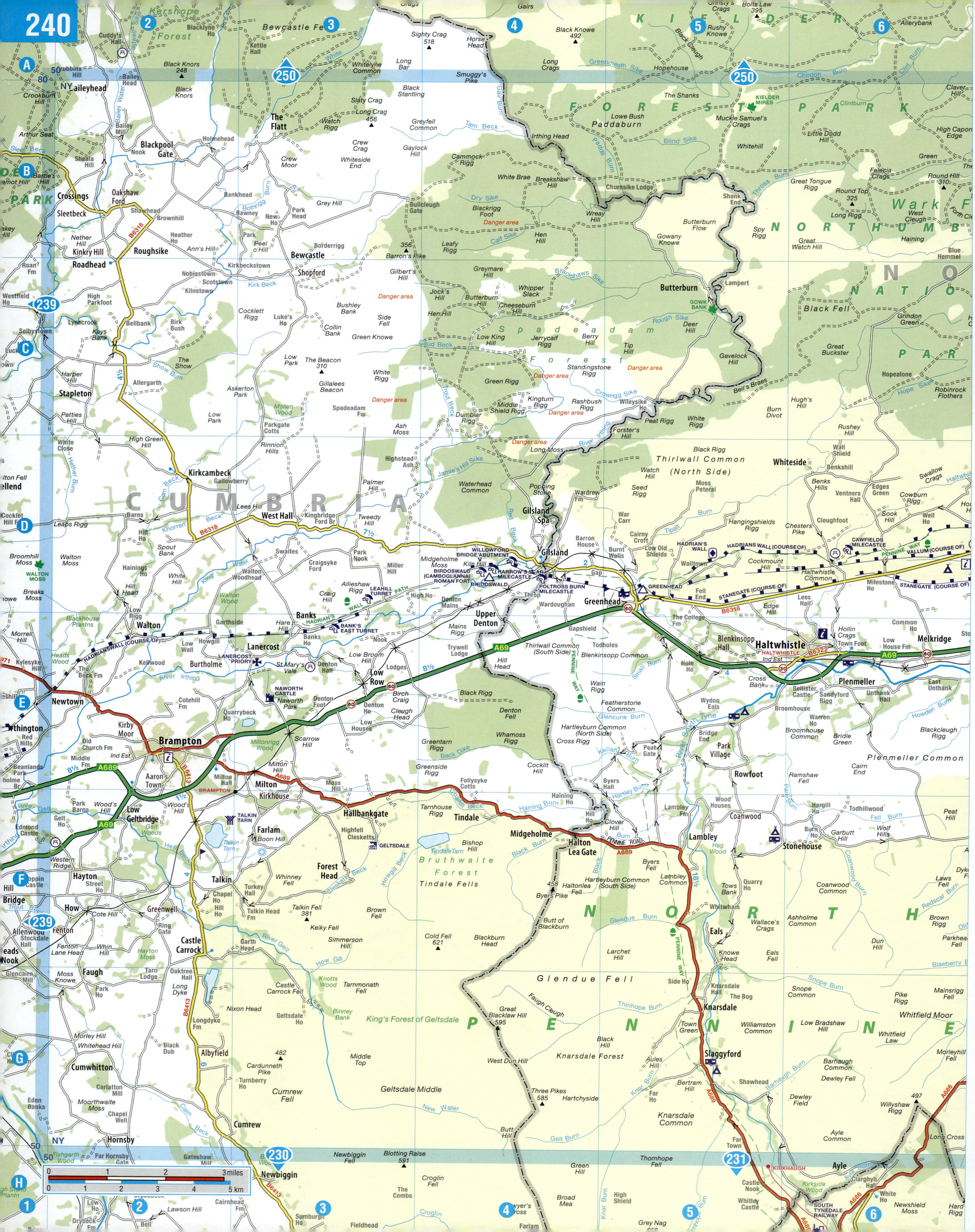
Kershope Forest
Bewcastle Fells
Kielder Forest Park
Northumberland National Park
Wark Forest
Spadeadam Forest
Cumbria
Bruthwaite Forest
Tindale Fells
North Pennines
Glendue Fell
Knarsdale Forest
King's Forest of Geltsdale
Geltsdale Middle
Plenmeller Common
Whitfield Moor
Thirlwall Common (North Side)
Thirlwall Common (South Side)
Blenkinsopp Common
Hartleyburn Common (North Side)
Hartleyburn Common (South Side)
Butterburn
Bewcastle
Shopford
Roadhead
Roughshike
Crossings
Sleetbeck
Kinkry Hill
Blackpool Gate
The Flatt
Stapleton
Kirkcambeck
West Hall
Gilsland
Greenhead
Haltwhistle
Melkridge
Plenmeller
Upper Denton
Banks
Walton
Lanercost
Burtholme
Newtown
Brampton
Milton
Kirkhouse
Hallbankgate
Tindale
Midgeholme
Halton Lea Gate
Lambley
Coanwood
Stonehouse
Rowfoot
Park Village
Farlam
Talkin
Hayton
How
Castle Carrock
Faugh
Cumwhitton
Hornsby
Cumrew
Newbiggin
Albyfield
Knarsdale
Slaggyford
Eals
Whiteside
Low Row
Low Geltbridge
Aaron's Town
Greenwell
Forest Head
A69
A689
B6318
B6413
B6322
A686
HADRIAN'S WALL (COURSE OF)
STANEGATE (COURSE OF)
VALLUM (COURSE OF)
PENNINE WAY
SOUTH TYNEDALE RAILWAY
Danger area
BIRDOSWALD
LANERCOST PRIORY
NAWORTH CASTLE
TALKIN TARN
GELTSDALE
Kirkhaugh
Ayle
Sighty Crag 518
Black Knowe 492
Cold Fell 621
Great Blacklaw Hill 595
Three Pikes 585
Blotting Raise 591
0 1 2 3 miles
0 1 2 3 4 5 km

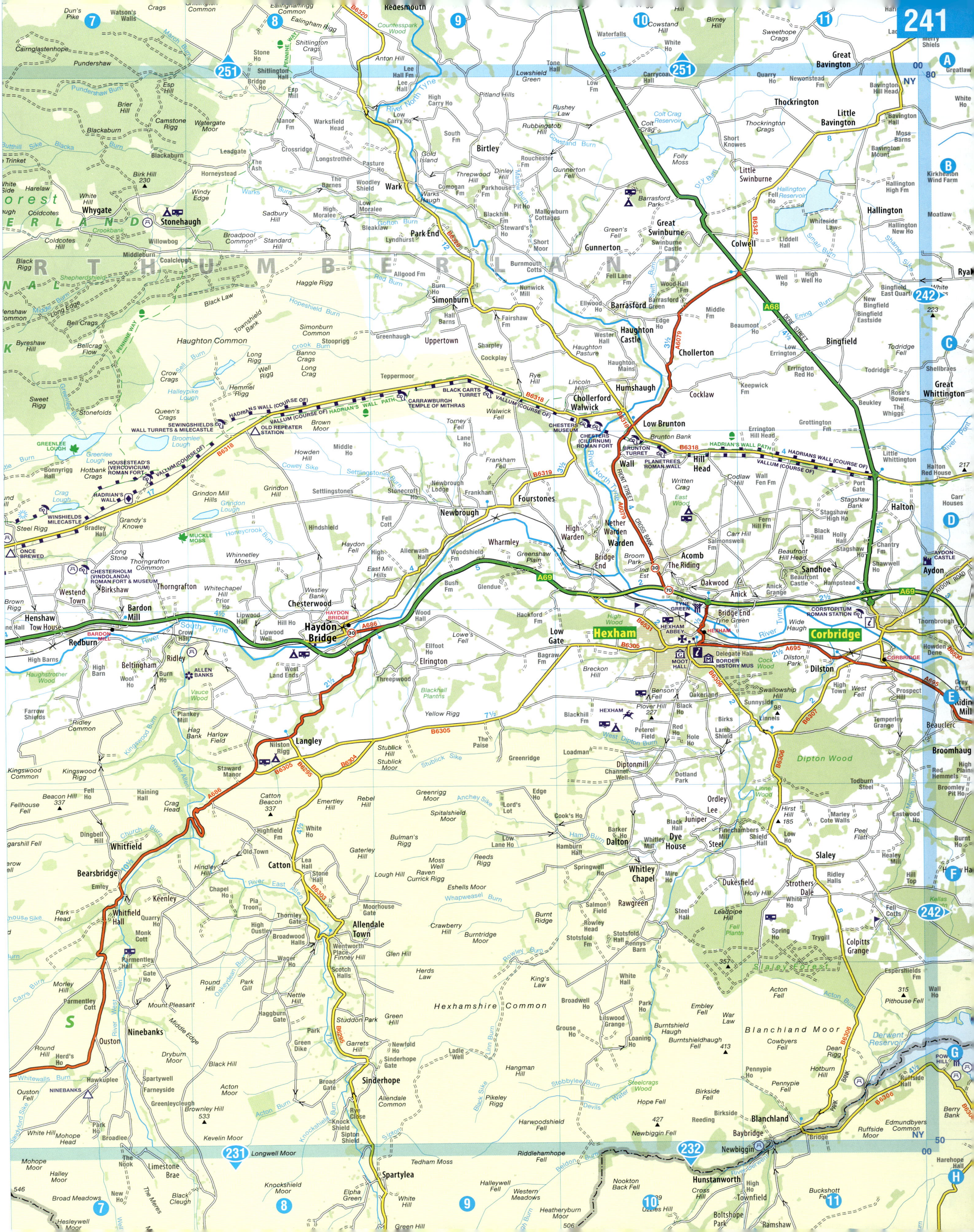
NORTHUMBERLAND
Hexham
Corbridge
Haydon Bridge
Bardon Mill
Redesmouth
Wark
Park End
Simonburn
Birtley
Barrasford
Gunnerton
Great Swinburne
Colwell
Great Bavington
Little Bavington
Thockrington
Hallington
Bingfield
Chollerton
Humshaugh
Haughton Castle
Chollerford
Walwick
Low Brunton
Wall
Hill Head
Acomb
Sandhoe
Aydon
Halton
Great Whittington
Fourstones
Newbrough
Wharmley
Warden
Bridge End
Oakwood
Anick
Dilston
Beaufront Castle
Stonehaugh
Whygate
Haughton Common
Hadrian's Wall (course of)
Vallum (course of)
Hadrian's Wall Path
Chesters Museum
Chesters (Cilurnum) Roman Fort
Housesteads (Vercovicium) Roman Fort
Chesterholm (Vindolanda) Roman Fort & Museum
Carrawburgh Temple of Mithras
Black Carts Turret
Brunton Turret
Planetrees Roman Wall
Sewingshields Wall Turrets & Milecastle
Winshields Milecastle
Once Brewed
Twice Brewed
Henshaw
Redburn
Beltingham
Ridley
Allen Banks
Langley
Elrington
Chesterwood
Thorngrafton
Westend Town
Whitfield
Bearsbridge
Keenley
Catton
Allendale Town
Ninebanks
Ouston
Sinderhope
Spartylea
Whitley Chapel
Dalton
Dye House
Juniper
Steel
Slaley
Dukesfield
Rawgreen
Blanchland
Blanchland Moor
Baybridge
Newbiggin
Hunstanworth
Hexhamshire Common
Dipton Wood
Diptonmill
Slaley Forest
Derwent Reservoir
Colt Crag Reservoir
Hallington Reservoir
Corstopitum Roman Station
Hexham Abbey
Border History Mus
Moot Hall
A68
A69
A686
A695
A6079
B6318
B6319
B6320
B6342
B6305
B6306
B6307
B6295
B6303
B6304
B6531
Dere Street
River North Tyne
River South Tyne
River Tyne
River Allen
River East Allen
River West Allen
Pennine Way
251
231
232
242

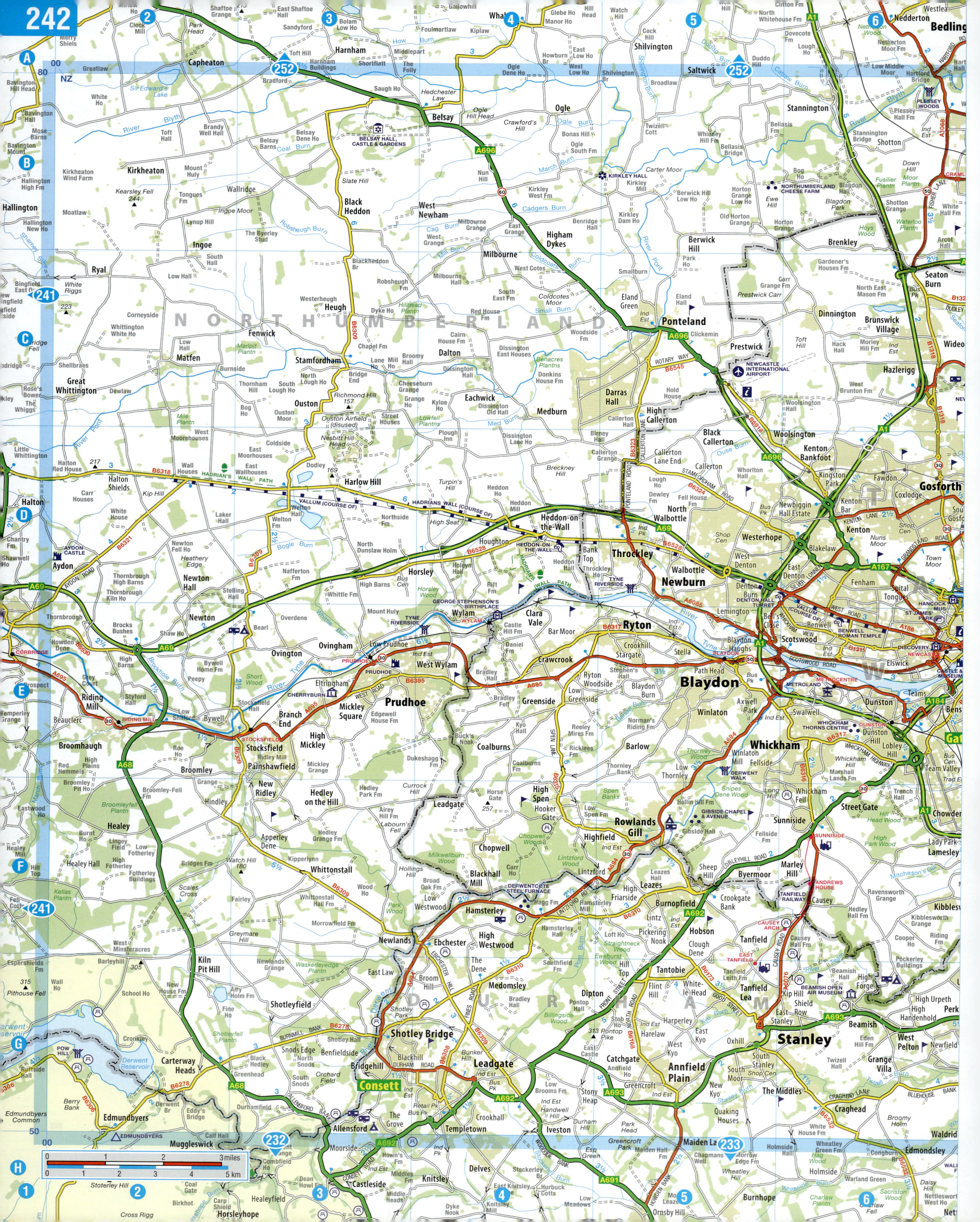
NORTHUMBERLAND
DURHAM
Capheaton
Belsay
Ogle
Shilvington
Saltwick
Bedlington
Stannington
Kirkheaton
Black Heddon
West Newham
Higham Dykes
Milbourne
Berwick Hill
Hallington
Ryal
Ingoe
Heugh
Fenwick
Matfen
Stamfordham
Ponteland
Prestwick
Dinnington
Brunswick Village
Hazlerigg
Great Whittington
Ouston
Dalton
Eachwick
Medburn
Darras Hall
High Callerton
Black Callerton
Woolsington
Kenton Bankfoot
Gosforth
Harlow Hill
Halton
Halton Shields
Heddon-on-the-Wall
North Walbottle
Westerhope
Kenton
Throckley
Newburn
Walbottle
Aydon
Newton Hall
Newton
Horsley
Wylam
Clara Vale
Ryton
Ovington
Ovingham
Prudhoe
West Wylam
Crawcrook
Blaydon
Greenside
Winlaton
Whickham
Dunston
Scotswood
Fenham
Riding Mill
Broomhaugh
Stocksfield
Bromley
Mickley Square
High Mickley
New Ridley
Hedley on the Hill
Coalburns
Leadgate
High Spen
Rowlands Gill
Sunniside
Street Gate
Marley Hill
Byermoor
Healey
Whittonstall
Chopwell
Blackhall Mill
Hamsterley
Burnopfield
Newlands
Ebchester
High Westwood
Medomsley
Hobson
Tanfield
Tantobie
Dipton
Kiln Pit Hill
Shotleyfield
Shotley Bridge
Leadgate
Consett
Catchgate
Annfield Plain
Stanley
Tanfield Lea
Carterway Heads
Edmundbyers
Muggleswick
Allensford
Templetown
Iveston
Castleside
Knitsley
Delves
Beamish
Craghead
The Middles
Kibblesworth
Lamesley
Burnhope
A68
A69
A696
A1
A692
A693
A694
A695
A691
B6318
B6309
B6395
B6310
B6278
NEWCASTLE INTERNATIONAL AIRPORT
BELSAY HALL, CASTLE & GARDENS
KIRKLEY HALL
HADRIAN'S WALL PATH
GEORGE STEPHENSON'S BIRTHPLACE
TYNE RIVERSIDE
DERWENT WALK
GIBSIDE CHAPEL & AVENUE
TANFIELD RAILWAY
BEAMISH OPEN AIR MUSEUM
METROCENTRE
Derwent Reservoir
River Tyne
River Blyth
0 1 2 3 miles
0 1 2 3 4 5 km

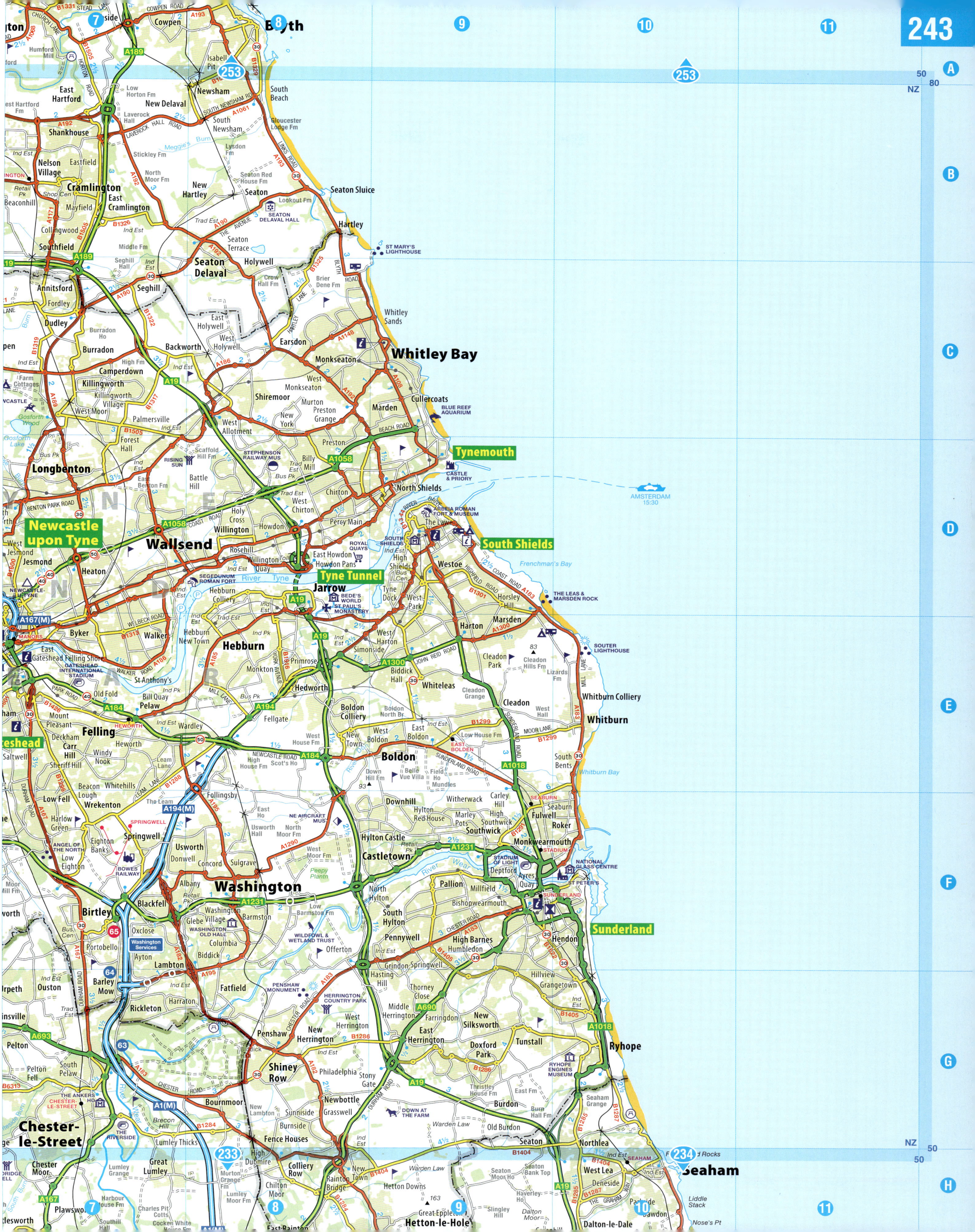
Blyth
Cowpen
Newsham
South Newsham
South Beach
Cramlington
East Cramlington
Shankhouse
East Hartford
Nelson Village
Seaton Sluice
Hartley
New Hartley
Seaton
Seaton Delaval
Holywell
Seghill
Annitsford
Dudley
Burradon
Backworth
Earsdon
Whitley Bay
Monkseaton
Whitley Sands
Cullercoats
Marden
Shiremoor
Killingworth
Camperdown
Longbenton
Palmersville
Forest Hall
Preston
Tynemouth
North Shields
Chirton
Percy Main
Howdon
Willington
Wallsend
Newcastle upon Tyne
Jesmond
Heaton
Byker
Walker
Tyne Tunnel
Jarrow
Hebburn
South Shields
Westoe
Harton
Marsden
Cleadon
Whitburn
Whitburn Colliery
Boldon
East Boldon
West Boldon
Whiteleas
Simonside
Pelaw
Felling
Heworth
Wardley
Gateshead
Usworth
Washington
Castletown
Hylton Castle
Fulwell
Roker
Monkwearmouth
Southwick
Sunderland
Pallion
Millfield
Hendon
High Barnes
Humbledon
Grangetown
Ryhope
Tunstall
Silksworth
Doxford Park
Farringdon
East Herrington
New Herrington
Penshaw
Fatfield
Shiney Row
Philadelphia
Newbottle
Burdon
Seaton
Northlea
Seaham
Dalton-le-Dale
Hetton-le-Hole
Fence Houses
Chester-le-Street
Great Lumley
Birtley
Lambton
Rickleton
Harraton
Ouston
Pelton
Springwell
Wrekenton
Low Fell
Eighton Banks
Sunniside
Burnside
Colliery Row
Rainton Bridge
New Town
Amsterdam 15:30
Frenchman's Bay
Whitburn Bay
Souter Lighthouse
St Mary's Lighthouse
Seaton Delaval Hall
Blue Reef Aquarium
Castle & Priory
Arbeia Roman Fort & Museum
The Leas & Marsden Rock
Segedunum Roman Fort
Bede's World St Paul's Monastery
Stephenson Railway Mus
Washington Old Hall
Wildfowl & Wetland Trust
Penshaw Monument
Herrington Country Park
Ryhope Engines Museum
National Glass Centre
Stadium of Light
A19
A1(M)
A194(M)
A167(M)
A1058
A1231
A1018
A690
A184
A183
A1300

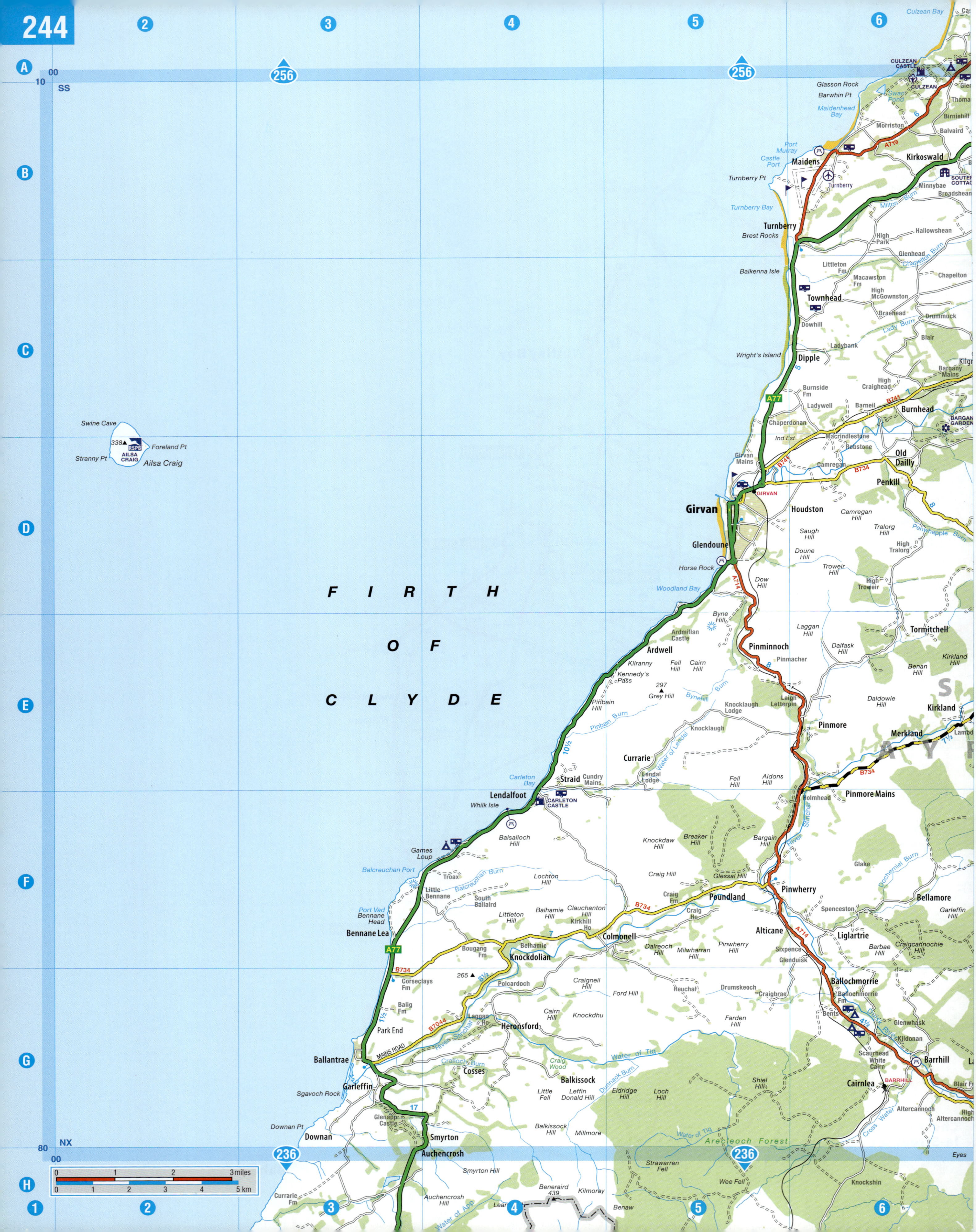

FIRTH OF CLYDE
Ailsa Craig
Swine Cave
Foreland Pt
Stranny Pt
338
RSPB
AILSA CRAIG
256
236
Culzean Bay
CULZEAN CASTLE
Glasson Rock
Barwhin Pt
Maidenhead Bay
Swan Pond
Morriston
Port Murray
Castle Port
Maidens
Turnberry Pt
Turnberry
Turnberry Bay
Brest Rocks
Balkenna Isle
Kirkoswald
Minnybae
Balvaird
Birniehill
Broadshean
Milton Burn
Hallowshean
High Park
Glenhead
Chapelton Burn
Chapelton
Littleton Fm
Macawston Fm
High McGownston
Townhead
Braehead
Drummuck
Lady Burn
Dowhill
Blair
Ladybank
Wright's Island
Dipple
Bargany Mains
Burnside Fm
High Craighead
Ladywell
Barneil
Burnhead
Chaperdonan
Ind Est
Macrindlestone
Robstone
Old Dailly
Camregan
Penkill
Girvan Mains
Girvan
GIRVAN
Houdston
Camregan Hill
Saugh Hill
Tralorg Hill
High Tralorg
Penwhapple Burn
Glendoune
Doune Hill
Horse Rock
Troweir Hill
High Troweir
Dow Hill
Woodland Bay
Byne Hill
Ardmillan Castle
Ardwell
Laggan Hill
Pinminnoch
Pinmacher
Dalfask Hill
Tormitchell
Kirkland Hill
Benan Hill
Kilranny
Kennedy's Pass
Fell Hill
Cairn Hill
297
Grey Hill
Byne Hill Burn
Laigh Letterpin
Knocklaugh Lodge
Knocklaugh
Daldowie Hill
Kirkland
Pinmore
Merkland
Pinbain Hill
Pinbain Burn
Currarie
Water of Lendal
Lendal Lodge
Fell Hill
Aldons Hill
Carleton Bay
Straid
Cundry Mains
Lendalfoot
Whilk Isle
CARLETON CASTLE
Holmhead
Pinmore Mains
Balsalloch Hill
Knockdaw Hill
Breaker Hill
Bargain Hill
River Stinchar
Games Loup
Troax
Lochton Hill
Craig Hill
Glessal Hill
Glake
Balcreuchan Port
Balcreuchan Burn
Little Bennane
South Ballaird
Craig Fm
Poundland
Pinwherry
Bellamore
Port Vad
Bennane Head
Littleton Hill
Balhamie Hill
Clauchanton Hill
Kirkhill Ho
Craig Ho
Spenceston
Garleffin Hill
Bennane Lea
Belhamie
Colmonell
Alticane
Liglartrie
Bougang Fm
Knockdolian
Dalreoch Hill
Milwharran Hill
Pinwherry Hill
Sixpence
Glenduisk
Barbae Hill
Craigcannochie Hill
Corseclays Fm
265
Polcardoch
Craigneil Hill
Ford Hill
Reuchal
Drumskeoch
Craigbrae
Ballochmorrie
Balig Fm
Cairn Hill
Knockdhu
Farden Hill
Bents
Glenwhask
Park End
Laggan Ho
Heronsford
Kildonan
Duisk River
Mains Road
Water of Tig
Scaurhead
White Cairn
Barrhill
Ballantrae
Crailloch Burn
Cosses
Craig Wood
Balkissock
Dunnack Burn
Shiel Hill
Cairnlea
BARRHILL
Blair
Garleffin
Sgavoch Rock
Little Fell
Leffin
Donald Hill
Eldridge Hill
Loch Hill
Altercannoch
Glenapp Castle
Cross Water
Downan Pt
Downan
Balkissock Hill
Millmore
Arecleoch Forest
Smyrton
Auchencrosh
Eyes
Strawarren Fell
Smyrton Hill
Wee Fell
Knockshin
Beneraird
439
Kilmoray
Currarie Fm
Auchencrosh Hill
Water of App
Benaw
A77
A714
A719
B734
B741
B7044
SS
NX
00
10
80
3 miles
5 km

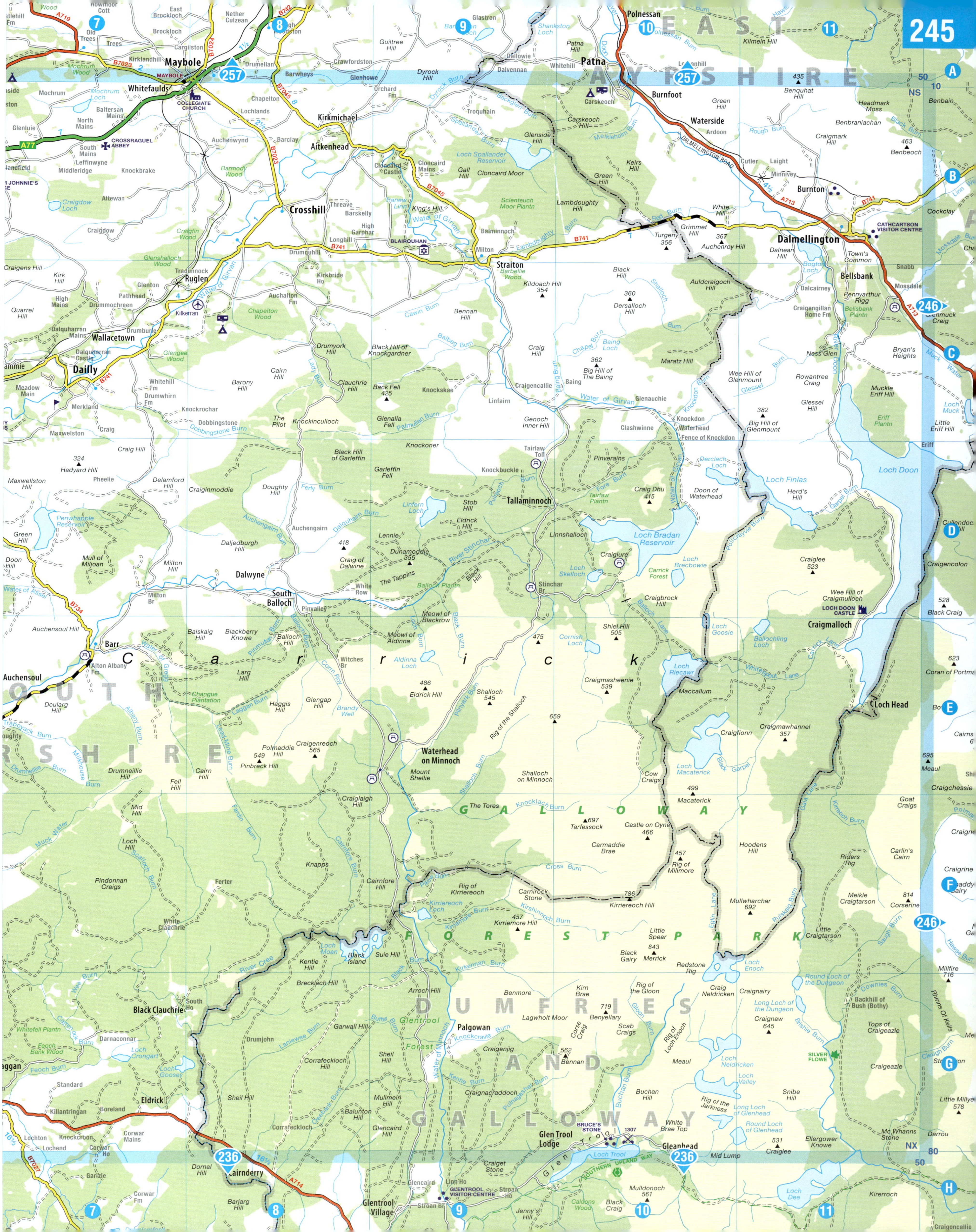
EAST AYRSHIRE
SOUTH AYRSHIRE
Carrick
GALLOWAY FOREST PARK
DUMFRIES AND GALLOWAY
Maybole
Whitefaulds
COLLEGIATE CHURCH
CROSSRAGUEL ABBEY
Kirkmichael
Aitkenhead
Crosshill
Cloncaird Castle
Kirkoswald
Patna
Polnessan
Burnfoot
Waterside
Dalmellington
CATHCARTSON VISITOR CENTRE
Bellsbank
Burnton
Straiton
BLAIRQUHAN
Milton
Ruglen
Kilkerran
Wallacetown
Daily
Dalquharran Castle
Dalwyne
South Balloch
Barr
Alton Albany Fm
Auchensoul
Tallaminnoch
Stinchar Br
Loch Bradan Reservoir
Loch Doon
LOCH DOON CASTLE
Craigmalloch
Loch Head
Loch Finlas
Loch Riecawr
Loch Macaterick
Loch Enoch
Loch Moan
Black Island
Waterhead on Minnoch
Mount Shellie
Palgowan
Glentrool Forest
Glen Trool Lodge
BRUCE'S STONE
Loch Trool
Glenhead
SOUTHERN UPLAND WAY
Glentrool Village
GLENTROOL VISITOR CENTRE
Cairnderry
Black Clauchrie
Eldrick
Merrick 843
Mullwharchar 692
Shalloch on Minnoch
Tarfessock 697
Kirriereoch Hill 786
Benyellary 719
Rhinns of Kells
SILVER FLOWE
Craiglee 523
Bennan 562
Cornish Loch
Shiel Hill 505
Craigmasheenie 539
Eldrick Hill 486
Polmaddie Hill 549
Craigenreoch 565
Back Fell 425
Big Hill of The Baing 362
Dersalloch Hill 360
Turgeny 356
Kildoach Hill 354
Water of Girvan
River Stinchar
River Cree
Water of Minnoch
Dyrock Hill
Glenauchie
Genoch Inner Hill
Knockdon
Fence of Knockdon
Big Hill of Glenmount 382
Wee Hill of Craigmulloch
Cairnfore Hill
Rig of Kirriereoch
Kirriereoch Hill
Kentie Hill
Suie Hill
Garwall Hill
Drumjohn
Corrafeckloch Hill
Craigenjig
Craignacraddoch
Mulldonoch 561
Caldons Wood
Jenny's Hill
Stroan Br
Glencaird Hill
Mid Lump
Craiglee 531
A77
A713
A714
B741
B7023
B7045
B734
B7027
DALMELLINGTON ROAD
246
236
257
NS
NX

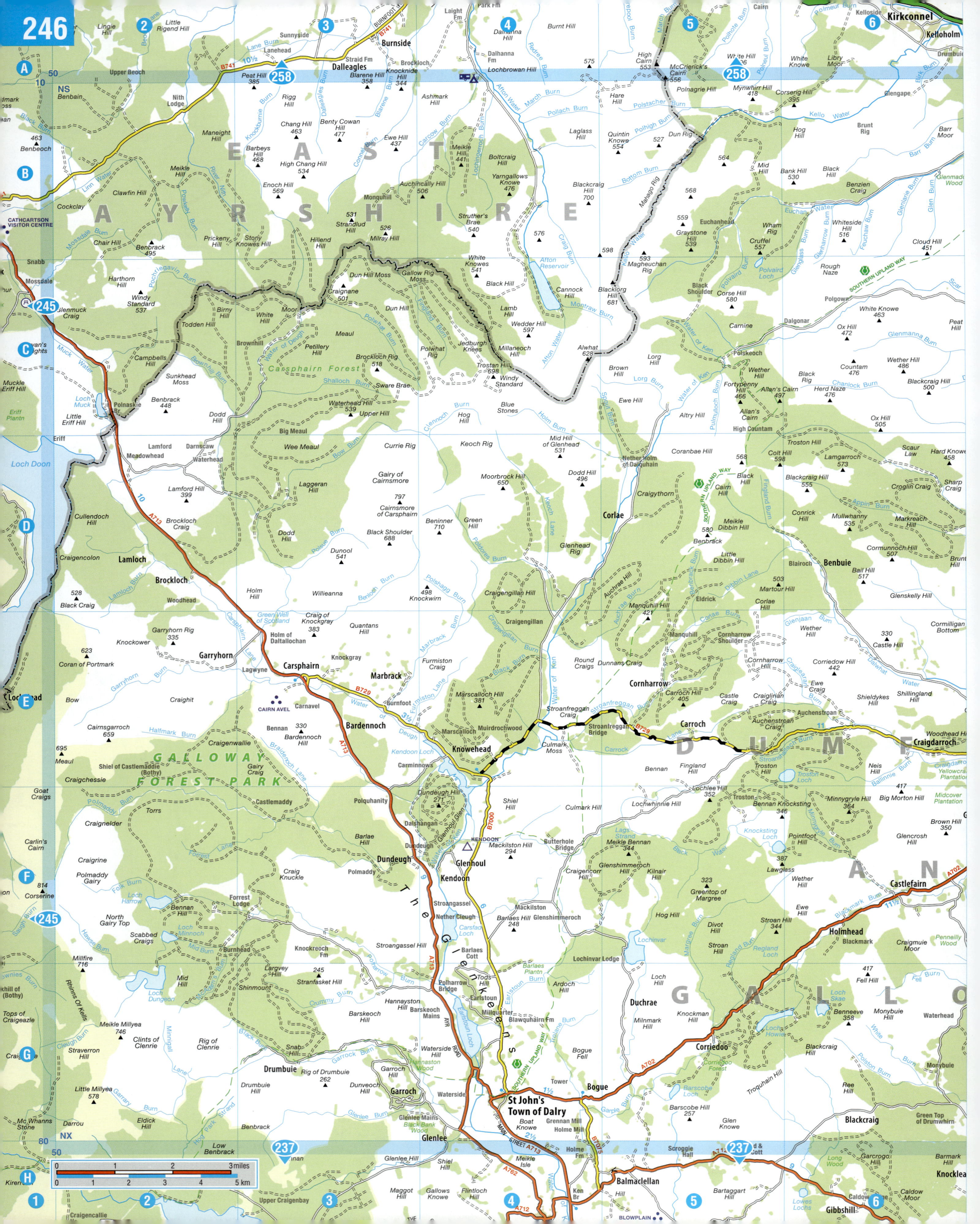
EAST AYRSHIRE
DUMFRIES AND GALLOWAY
GALLOWAY FOREST PARK
Carsphairn Forest
The Glenkens
Kirkconnel
Kelloholm
Dalleagles
Burnside
Lanehead
Sunnyside
Little Rigend Hill
Lingie Hill
Upper Beoch
Peat Hill 385
Blarene Hill 358
Knocknide Hill 344
Rigg Hill
Nith Lodge
Benbain
Benbeoch
Maneight Hill
Barbeys Hill 468
Chang Hill 463
Benty Cowan Hill 477
High Chang Hill 534
Ewe Hill 437
Ashmark Hill
Meikle Hill 441
Boltcraig Hill
Auchincally Hill 506
Enoch Hill 569
Clawfin Hill
Cockclay
Yarngallows Knowe 476
Monguhill
Struther's Brae 540
Strandlud Hill 531
Milray Hill 526
Hillend Hill
Chair Hill
Benbrack 495
Prickeny Hill
Stony Knowes Hill
Snabb
Mossdale
Harthorn Hill
Windy Standard 537
Craignane 501
Dun Hill Moss
Gallow Rig Moss
Dun Hill
Meaul
Petillery Hill
Brocklach Rig 518
Polwhat Rig
Jedburgh Knees
Millaneoch Hill
Trostan Hill 698
Windy Standard
Wedder Hill 597
Lamb Hill
White Knowes 541
Black Hill
Afton Reservoir
Cannock Hill
Blacklorg Hill 681
Alwhat 628
Blackcraig Hill 700
Laglass Hill
Quintin Knowe 554
Dun Rig
Hare Hill
High Cairn 553
McCririck's Cairn 556
Polnagrie Hill
Mynwhirr Hill 418
White Hill 526
Corserig Hill 395
Glengape
Hog Hill
Brunt Rig
Barr Moor
Bank Hill 530
Black Hill
Mid Hill
Benzien Craig
Euchanhead
Graystone Hill 539
Wham Rig
Cruffel 557
Whiteside Hill 516
Cloud Hill 451
Magheuchan Rig 593
Black Shoulder
Corse Hill 580
Rough Naze
Polgown
Carnine
Dalgonar
White Knowe 463
Ox Hill 472
Peat Hill
Polskeoch
Wether Hill 486
Countam 476
Blackcraig Hill 500
Fortypenny Hill 466
Allan's Cairn 497
Herd Naze 476
Black Rig
Allan's Cairn
High Countam
Ox Hill 505
Lorg Hill
Brown Hill
Ewe Hill
Altry Hill
Todden Hill
Birny Hill
White Hill
Moor
Brownhill
Campbells Hill
Sunkhead Moss
Benbrack 448
Dodd Hill
Polnaskie Br
Loch Muck
Little Eriff Hill
Muckle Eriff Hill
Eriff Plantn
Eriff
Loch Doon
Lamford
Darnscaw
Meadowhead
Waterhead
Waterhead Hill 539
Swatre Brae
Upper Hill
Big Meaul
Wee Meaul
Currie Rig
Hog Hill
Keoch Rig
Blue Stones
Mid Hill of Glenhead 531
Lamford Hill 399
Laggeran Hill
Gairy of Cairnsmore
Cairnsmore of Carsphairn 797
Moorbrock Hill 650
Dodd Hill 496
Green Hill
Beninner 710
Black Shoulder 688
Brockloch Craig
Cullendoch Hill
Craigencolon
Lamloch
Brockloch
Woodhead
Dodd Hill
Dunool 541
Glenhead Rig
Corlae
Craigythorn
Nether Holm of Dalquhain
Coranbae Hill
Cairn Hill
Black Hill
Meikle Dibbin Hill
Benbrack 580
Little Dibbin Hill
Colt Hill 598
Troston Hill
Lamgarroch 573
Scaur Law
Hard Knowe 458
Blackcraig Hill 555
Croglin Craig
Sharp Craig
Conrick Hill
Mullwhanny 535
Markreach Hill
Cormunnoch Hill 507
Blairoch
Benbuie
Bail Hill 517
Glenskelly Hill
Martour Hill 503
Corlae Hill
Eldrick
Auchrae Hill
Manquhill Hill 421
Manquhill
Cornharrow Shoulder
Wether Hill
Castle Hill 330
Cormilligan Bottom
Corriedow Hill 442
Cornharrow Hill
Craigengillan Hill
Craigengillan
Knockwirn 498
Willieanna
Holm Hill
Black Craig 528
Garryhorn Rig 335
Green Well of Scotland
Craig of Knockgray 383
Quantans Hill
Holm of Daltallochan
Knockower
Coran of Portmark 623
Garryhorn
Lagwyne
Carsphairn
Knockgray
Marbrack
Furmiston Craig
Round Craigs
Dunnans Craig
Cornharrow
Carroch Hill 405
Castle Craig
Craiglinan Craig
Ewe Craig
Shieldykes Hill
Shillingland Hill
Bow
Craight
Cairn Avel
Carnavel
Burnfoot
Marscalloch Hill 381
Stroanfreggan Craig
Stroanfreggan Bridge
Carroch
Auchenstroan
Auchenstroan Craig
Woodhead Hill
Craigdarroch
Cairnsgarroch 659
Bennan 330
Bardennoch Hill
Bardennoch
Marscalloch
Muirdrochwood
Knowehead
Culmark Moss
Bennan
Fingland Hill
Troston Hill
Neis Hill
Meaul 695
Shiel of Castlemaddie (Bothy)
Gairy Craig
Craigenwallie
Craigchessie
Carminnows
Kendoon Loch
Dundeugh Hill 271
Shiel Hill
Culmark Hill
Lochwhinnie Hill
Lochlee Hill 352
Troston
Bennan Knocksting 346
Minnygryle Hill 364
Big Morton Hill 417
Goat Craigs
Castlemaddy
Polquhanity
Torrs
Craignelder
Dalshangan
Glenhoul Glen
Kendoon
Mackilston Hill 294
Butterhole Bridge
Meikle Bennan 344
Glenshimmeroch Hill
Kilnair Hill
Craigencorr Hill
Knocksting Loch
Pointfoot Hill
Brown Hill 350
Glencrosh Hill
Carlin's Cairn
Craigrine
Polmaddy Gairy
Barlae Hill
Dundeugh
Glenhoul
Kendoon
Polmaddy
Craig Knuckle
Greentop of Margree 323
Lawglass 387
Wether Hill
Castlefairn
Corserine 814
Loch Harrow
Forrest Lodge
Bennan Hill
North Gairy Top
Loch Minnoch
Strongassel
Nether Cleugh
Mackilston
Barlaes Hill 248
Glenshimmeroch
Hog Hill
Divot Hill
Ewe Hill
Stroan Hill 344
Holmhead
Blackmark
Scabbed Craigs
Burnhead
Knockreoch Fm
Stroangassel Hill
Carsfad Loch
Barlaes Cott
Lochinvar
Lochinvar Lodge
Stroan Hill
Regland Loch
Craigmuie Moor
Millfire 716
Mid Hill
Largvey Hill
Stranfasket Hill 245
Shinmount
Loch Dungeon
Polharrow Bridge
Tods Hill
Earlstoun
Earlstoun Loch
Ardoch Hill
Loch Hill
Duchrae
Fell Hill 417
Rhinns Of Kells
Hannayston Hill
Barskeoch Mains
Barskeoch Hill
Millquarter
Blawquhairn Fm
Milnmark Hill
Knockman Hill
Loch Skae
Benneeve 358
Monybuie Hill
Waterhead
Meikle Millyea 746
Clints of Clenrie
Rig of Clenrie
Straverron Hill
Snab Hill
Waterside Hill
Hannaston Wood
Bogue Fell
Corriedoo
Loch Howie
Blackcraig Hill
Monybuie
Little Millyea 578
Drumbuie
Rig of Drumbuie 262
Dunveoch Hill
Garroch Hill
Garroch
Waterside
Tower
Bogue
Barscobe Loch
Troquhain Hill
Ree Hill
Drumbuie Hill
Mo Whanns Stone
Darrou
Eldrick Hill
Benbrack
Glenlee Mains
Black Bank Wood
Glenlee
St John's Town of Dalry
Boat Knowe
Grennan Mill
Holme Mill
Barscobe Hill 257
Glen Knowe
Blackcraig
Green Top of Drumwhirn
Low Benbrack
Glenlee Hill
Shiel Hill
Holme Fm
Meikle Isle
Scroggie Hall
Barmark Hill
Garcrogo Hill
Long Wood
Knocklea
Upper Craigenbay
Maggot Hill
Gallows Knowe
Flintloch Hill
Ken Br
Balmaclellan
Bartaggart Hill
Lowes Loch
Caldow Moor
Gibbshill
Blowplain
Craigencallie
Kendoon
Southern Upland Way
Cathcartson Visitor Centre
A713
A702
A712
A762
B741
B729
B7000
B7075
245
258
237
0 1 2 3 miles
0 1 2 3 4 5 km

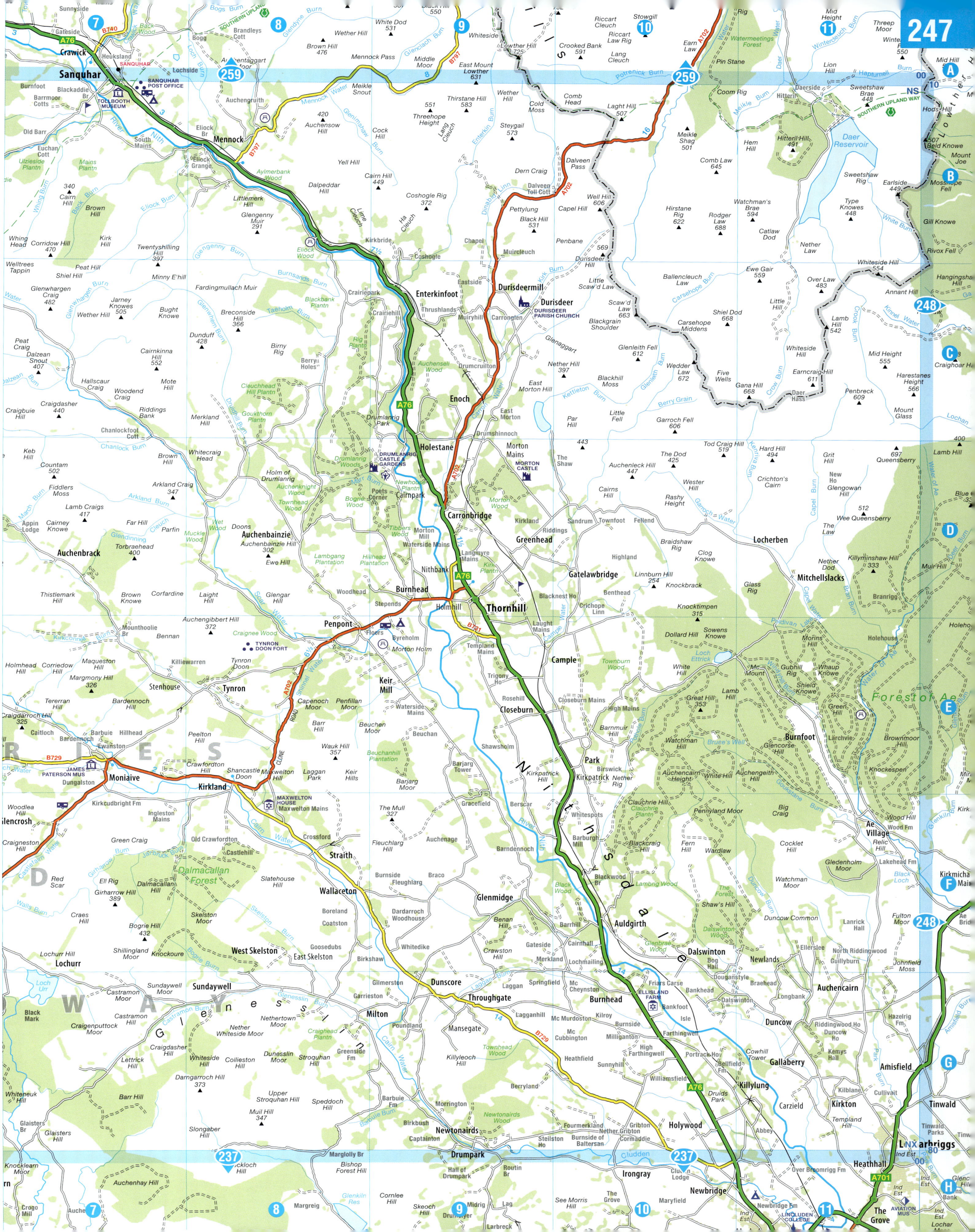
Sanquhar
Crawick
Gateside
Heuksland
Sanquhar Post Office
Tollbooth Museum
Burnfoot
Blackaddie
Barrmoor Cotts
Old Barr
Euchan Cott
Mennock
Mennock Pass
Elliock Grange
South Mains
Auchengruith
Brandleys Cott
Southern Upland Way
Wether Hill
Brown Hill 476
White Dod 531
Whiteside
Middle Moor
East Mount Lowther 631
Lowther Hill 725
Crooked Bank 591
Riccart Cleuch
Riccart Law Rig
Lang Cleuch
Stowgill
Earn Law
Watermeetings Forest
Pin Stane
Mid Height
Threep Moor
Mid Hill
Daerside
Sweetshaw Brae 448
Daer Reservoir
Hitteril Hill 491
Hem Hill
Comb Law 645
Meikle Shag 501
Laght Hill 507
Comb Head
Wether Hill
Cold Moss
Steygail 573
Thirstane Hill 583
Threehope Height
Auchensow Hill
Cock Hill
Yell Hill
Cairn Hill 449
Dalpeddar Hill
Coshogle Rig 372
Dern Craig
Dalveen Pass
Dalveen Toll Cott
Pettylung
Black Hill 531
Capel Hill
Well Hill 606
Penbane
Durisdeer Hill
Little Scaw'd Law
Scaw'd Law 663
Blackgrain Shoulder
Durisdeermill
Durisdeer
Durisdeer Parish Church
Carronglen
Glenaggart
Nether Hill 397
East Morton Hill
Blackhill Moss
Glenleith Fell 612
Wedder Law 672
Five Wells
Gana Hill 668
Carsehope Middens
Shiel Dod 668
Ballencleuch Law
Ewe Gair 559
Little Hill
Over Law 483
Whiteside Hill 554
Annant Hill
Lamb Hill 542
Whiteside Hill
Earncraig Hill 611
Daer Hass
Mid Height 555
Harestanes Height 566
Penbreck 609
Mount Glass
Craighoar Hill
Hirstane Rig 622
Rodger Law 688
Watchman's Brae 594
Catlaw Dod
Nether Law
Type Knowes 448
Sweetshaw Rig
Earlside 449
Mosshope Fell
Gill Knowe
Rivox Fell
Hangingshaw Hill
Beld Knowe
Mount Joe
Hods Hill
Littlemerk Hill
Glengenny Muir 291
Cairn Hill 340
Brown Hill
Kirk Hill
Whing Head
Corridow Hill 470
Twentyshilling Hill 397
Peat Hill
Shiel Hill
Minny E'hill
Welltrees Tappin
Glenwhargen Craig 482
Jarney Knowes 505
Wether Hill
Bught Knowe
Fardingmullach Muir
Breconside Hill 366
Dunduff 428
Birny Rig
Berry Holes
Peat Craig
Dalzean Snout 407
Cairnkinna Hill 552
Mote Hill
Hallscaur Craig
Woodend Craig
Craigbuie Hill
Craigdasher 440
Riddings Bank
Chanlockfoot Cott
Merkland Hill
Keb Hill
Countam 502
Brown Hill
Whitecraig Head
Holm of Drumlanrig
Arkland Craig 347
Fiddlers Moss
Lamb Craigs 417
Appin Lodge
Cairney Knowe
Far Hill
Parfin
Auchenbrack
Torbraehead 400
Doons
Auchenbainzie
Auchenbainzie Hill 302
Ewe Hill
Thistlemark Hill
Brown Knowe
Corfardine
Laight Hill
Glengar Hill
Kirkbride
Coshogle
Chapel
Muircleuch
Enterkinfoot
Crairiepark
Crairiehill
Thrushlands
Eastside
Muiryhill
Drumcruilton
Enoch
East Morton
Drumlanrig Park
Holestane
Drumshinnoch
Morton Mains
Morton Castle
Drumlanrig Castle & Gardens
Poets Corner
Cairnpark
Carronbridge
Kirkland
Riddings
Greenhead
Morton Mill
Waterside Mains
Langmyre Mains
Nithbank
Burnhead
Thornhill
Holmhill
Stepends
Penpont
Floors
Byreholm
Morton Holm
Templand Mains
Laught Mains
Cample
Blacknest Ho
Gatelawbridge
Benthead
Crichope Linn
Highland
Sandrum
Townfoot
Fellend
The Shaw
Auchenleck Hill 447
Cairns Hill
The Dod 425
Tod Craig Hill 519
Hard Hill 494
Wester Hill
Rashy Height
Crichton's Cairn
Grit Hill
Queensberry 697
New Ho Glengowan Hill
Wee Queensberry 512
Braidshaw Rig
Clog Knowe
Locherben
The Law
Nether Dod
Killyminshaw Hill 333
Mitchellslacks
Linnburn Hill 254
Knockbrack
Glass Rig
Knocktimpen 315
Dollard Hill
Sowens Knowe
Holehouse
Loch Ettrick
White Hill
Mc Mount
Morins Hill
Gubhill Rig
Whaup Knowe
Shield Knowe
Lamb Hill
Great Hill 353
Green Hill
Forest of Ae
Larchvie
Burnfoot
Glencorse Hill
Brownmoor Hill
Knockespen
Watchman Hill
Auchencairn Height
White Hill
Auchengeith Hill
Auchenguttie Hill
Big Craig
Ae Village
Wood Hill
Wood Fm
Relic Hill
Lakehead Fm
Cocklet Hill
Gledenholm Moor
Watchman Moor
Kirkmichael Mains
Duncow Common
Lanrick Hall
Fulton Moor
North Riddingwood
Johnfield Moss
Guillyburn
Auchencairn
Duncow
Riddingwood Ho
Duncow Ho
Kemys Hall
Hazelrig Fm
Amisfield
Gallaberry
Cowhill Tower
Kilblane
Cullivait
Kirkton
Templand Hill
Tinwald
Tinwald Parks
Locharbriggs
Heathhall
Ind Est
Over Broomrigg Fm
The Grove
Aviation Mus
Linkluden College
Newbridge Fm
Newbridge
Irongray
Cluden Lodge
Maryfield
See Morris Hill
The Grove
Holywood
Abbey
Killylung
Druids Park
Carzield
Williamsfield
Bellfield
Portrack Ho
High Farthingwell
Farthingwell
Milliganton
Burnside
Kilroy
Mc Murdoston
Mc Cubbington
Heathfield
Sunnyhill
Berryland
Fourmerkland
Nether Gribton
Gribton
Cormaddie
Burnside of Balterson
Steilston Ho
Cluden
Keir Mill
Waterside Mains
Penfillan Moor
Capenoch Moor
Barr Hill
Beuchen Moor
Beuchan
Beuchanhill Plantation
Rosehill
Closeburn
Closeburn Mains
High Mains
Barnmuir Hill
Trigony Ho
Shawsholm
Park
Birswick
Kirkpatrick
Kirkpatrick Hill
Nether Rig
Whitespots
Clauchrie Hill
Pennyland Moor
Fern Hill
Wardlaw
Blackcraig Hill
Barburgh Mill
Blackwood Br
Black Wood
Barrhill
Auldgirth
Shaw's Hill
Cairnhall
Lochmailing
Dalswinton
Bog Hall
Douganstyle
Newlands
Ellerslee
Braehead
Longbank
Dalswinton
Friars Carse
Ellisland Farm
Bankhead
Bankfoot
Isle
Burnhead
Mc Cheynston
Springfield
Laggan
Merkland
Gateside
Crawston Hill
Benan Hill
Glenmidge
Dardarroch Woodhouse
Whitedike
Barjarg Tower
Barjarg Moor
Gracefield
Berscar
Barndennoch
Auchenage
Fleuchlarg Hill
The Mull 327
Braco
Burnside
Fleughlarg
Nithsdale
Laggan Park
Keir Hills
Wauk Hill 357
Maxwelton Hill
Maxwelton House
Maxwelton Mains
Shancastle Doon
Crawfordton Hill
Kirkland
Moniaive
James Paterson Mus
Dungalston
Ewanston
Bardennoch
Barbuie
Hillhead
Peelton Hill
Caitloch
Craigdarroch Hill 325
Tererran Hill
Bardennoch Hill
Margmony Hill 326
Maquestion Hill
Stenhouse
Tynron
Tynron Doon
Tynron Doon Fort
Killiewarren
Bennan
Auchengibbert Hill 372
Mounthoolie Br
Holmhead Hill
Corriedow Hill
Woodlea Hill
Glencrosh
Craigneston Hill
Kirkcudbright Fm
Ingleston Mains
Green Craig
Old Crawfordton
Castlehill
Crossford
Straith
Slatehouse Hill
Wallaceton
Dalmacallan Forest
Dalmacallan Hill
Ell Rig
Girharrow Hill 389
Red Scar
Craes Hill
Bogrie Hill 432
Skelston Moor
Shillingland Moor
Knockoure
West Skelston
East Skelston
Goosedubs
Boreland
Coatston
Birkshaw
Lochurr Hill
Lochurr
Loch Urr
Sundaywell Moor
Sundaywell
Castramon Moor
Castramon Hill
Black Mark
Craigenputtock Moor
Glenesslin
Nethertown Moor
Nether Whiteside Moor
Craigdasher Hill
Whiteside Hill
Collieston Hill
Dunesslin Moor
Stroquhan Hill
Greenside Fm
Craighead Plantn
Milton
Garrieston
Gilmerston
Dunscore
Throughgate
Lagganhill
Poundland
Mansegate
Killyleoch Hill
Townhead Wood
Lettrick Hill
Whiteneuk Hill
Barr Hill
Darngarroch Hill 373
Upper Stroquhan Hill
Speddoch Hill
Muil Hill 347
Barbuie Fm
Morrington
Newtonairds Wood
Birkbush
Captainton
Newtonairds
Drumpark
Glaisters Br
Glaisters Hill
Slongaber Hill
Marglolly Br
Bishop Forest Hill
Hall of Drumpark
Routin Br
Knocklearn Moor
Auchenhay Hill
Crogo Mill
Cornlee Hill
Skeoch Hill
Midrig
Margreig
Glenkiln Res
Lag
Larbreck
A76
A702
A701
B740
B797
B729
B731
259
248
237
NS
00
10
80

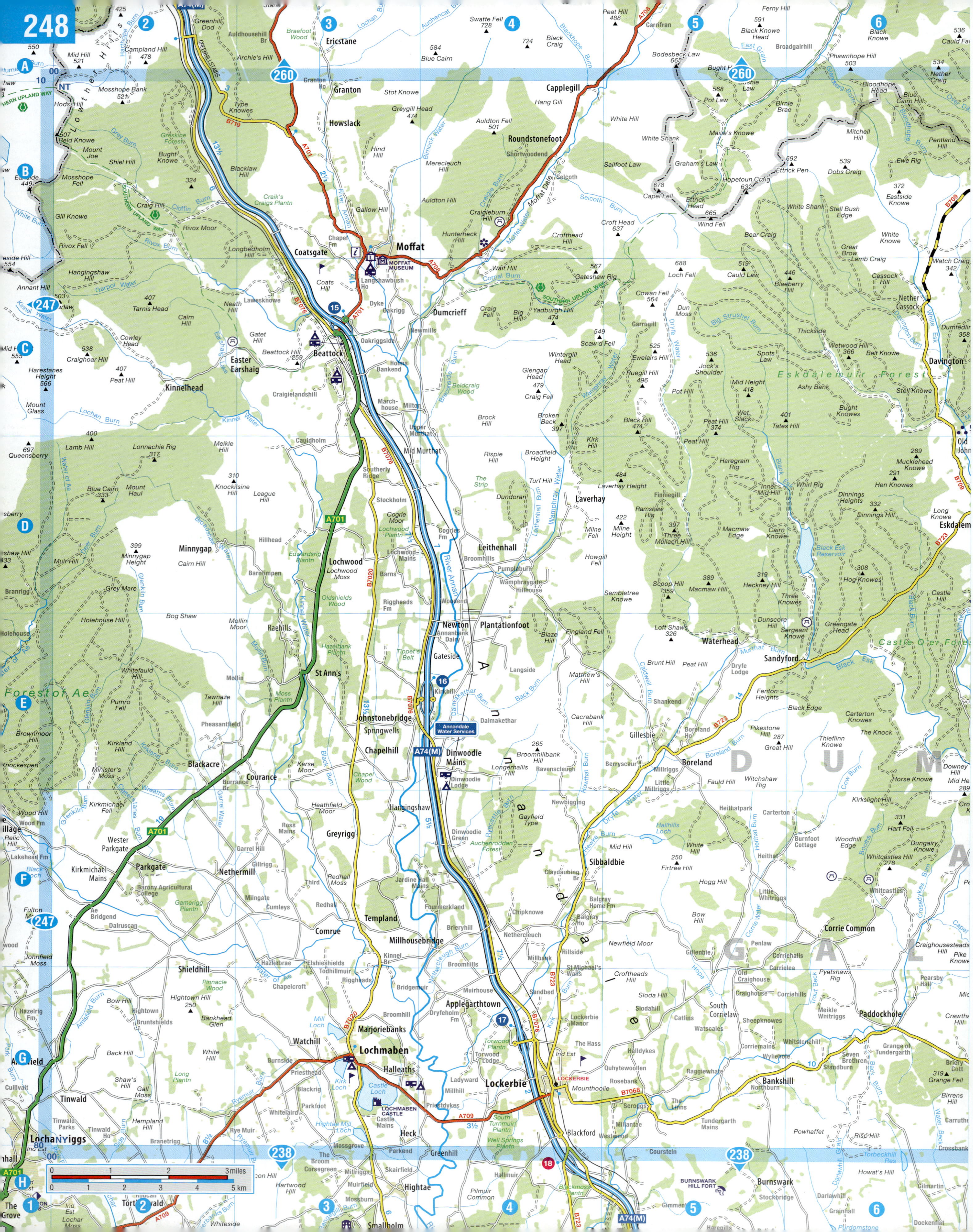

Ericstane
Granton
Howslack
Capplegill
Roundstonefoot
Shortwoodend
Selcoth
Moffat
MOFFAT MUSEUM
Coatsgate
Chapel Fm
Langshawbush Ho
Dumcrieff
Beattock
Easter Earshaig
Kinnelhead
Craigielandshill
Mid Murthat
Laverhay
Leithenhall
Minnygap
Lochwood
Newton
Plantationfoot
Gateside
St Ann's
Johnstonebridge
Springwells
Annandale Water Services
Chapelhill
Dinwoodie Mains
Blackacre
Courance
Greyrigg
Parkgate
Nethermill
Templand
Comrie
Millhousebridge
Applegarthtown
Marjoriebanks
Lochmaben
Halleaths
LOCHMABEN CASTLE
Lockerbie
Heck
Greenhill
Hightae
Smallholm
Shieldhill
Watchill
Tinwald
Sibbaldbie
Boreland
Sandyford
Waterhead
Eskdalemuir Forest
Davington
Corrie Common
Paddockhole
Bankshill
Burnswark
BURNSWARK HILL FORT
Forest of Ae
Kirkmichael Mains
Wester Parkgate
Wamphray Water
River Annan
Annandale
Black Esk Reservoir
Castle O'er Forest
Southern Upland Way
A701
A74(M)
A708
A709
B7068
B723
B7076
B7020
B719
260
247
238
DUM
GAL
0 1 2 3 miles
0 1 2 3 4 5 km

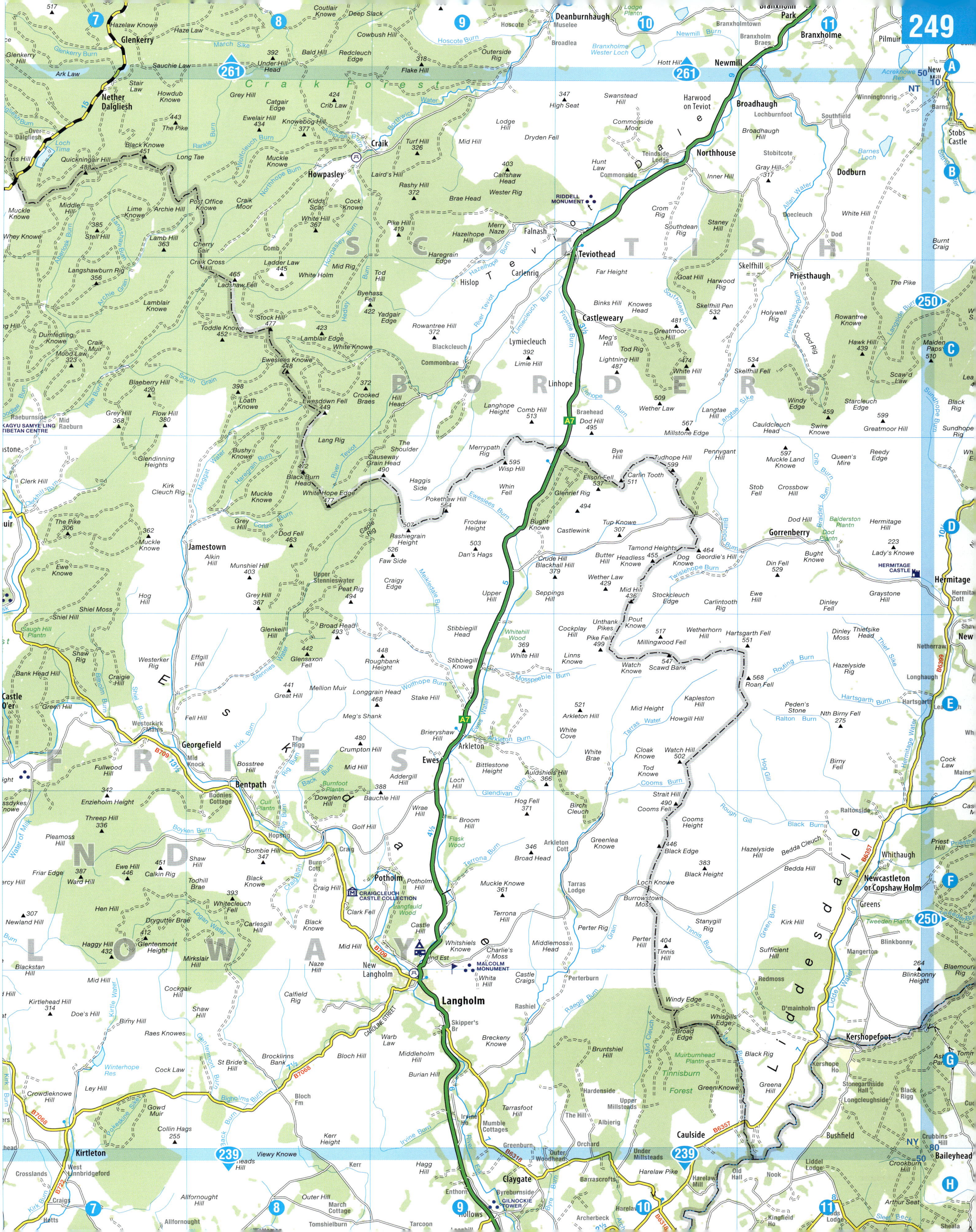
Glenkerry
Hazelaw Knowe
Haze Law
Coutlair Knowe
Deep Slack
Cowbush Hill
Deanburnhaugh
Muselee
Hoscote
Hoscote Burn
Broadlea
Branxholm Park
Branxholmtown
Branxholm Braes
Branxholme
Pilmuir
Newmill
Hott Hill
Branxholme Wester Loch
Newmill Burn
March Sike
392 Under Hill Head
Redcleuch Edge
Bald Hill
318 Flake Hill
Outerside Rig
Glenkerry Burn
Sauchie Law
Ark Law
Stair Law
Nether Dalgliesh
Craik Forest
Grey Hill
Catgair Edge
424 Crib Law
Howdub Knowe
443 The Pike
Ewelair Hill 434
Knowebog Hill 377
Borthwick Water
Craik
Turf Hill 326
Lodge Hill
Mid Hill
Dryden Fell
347 High Seat
Swanstead Hill
Harwood on Teviot
Broadhaugh
Lochburnfoot
Winningtonrig
Southfield
Stobs Castle
Commonside Moor
Broadhaugh Hill
Stobitcote
Northhouse
Teindside Lodge
Barnes Loch
Dodburn
Gray Hill 317
Inner Hill
Hunt Law
Commonside
Black Knowe 451
Long Tae
Quickningair Hill 488
Muckle Knowe
Howpasley
Laird's Hill
403 Calfshaw Head
Wester Rig
Rashy Hill 372
Brae Head
RIDDELL MONUMENT
Allan Water
Crom Rig
Southdean Rig
Staney Hill
Doecleuch
White Hill
Dod
Burnt Craig
Middle Hill
Lime Knowe
Archie Hill
Post Office Knowe
Craik Moor
Kidds Scar
Cock Knowe
White Hill 367
Pike Hill 419
Merry Naze
Hazelhope Hill
Falnash
Teviothead
Muckle Knowe
Whey Knowe
385 Stell Hill
Lamb Hill 363
Cherry Cair
Comb
Haregrain Edge
Craik Cross Hill
Ladder Law 445
Mid Rig
White Holm
Tod Hill
Hislop
Carlenrig
Far Height
Goat Hill
Harwood Rig
Skelfhill
Priesthaugh
The Pike
Langshawburn Rig 356
465 Ladshaw Fell
Byehass Fell 422
Yadgair Edge
Binks Hill
Knowes Head
Skelfhill Pen 532
Holywell Rig
Lamblair Knowe
Stock Hill 477
Toddle Knowe 452
423 Lamblair Edge
White Knowe
Rowantree Hill 372
Blackcleuch
Lymiecleuch
Castleweary
Meg's Hill
481 Greatmoor Hill
Rowantree Knowe
Hawk Hill 439
Maiden Paps 510
Dumfedling Knowe
Craik Muir
Mood Law 323
Eweslees Knowe 448
Commonbrae
392 Limie Hill
Lightning Hill 487
Tod Rig
474 White Hill
534 Skelfhill Fell
Dod Rig
Scaw'd Law
Blaeberry Hill 420
398 Loath Knowe
372 Crooked Braes
Ewesdown Fell 449
Hill Head
Linhope
509 Wether Law
Langtae Hill
Windy Edge
Starcleuch Edge
Black Rig
Raeburnside
Mid Raeburn
Grey Hill 368
Flow Hill 380
Langhope Height
Comb Hill 513
Braehead
Dod Hill 495
567 Millstone Edge
Cauldcleuch Head
459 Swire Knowe
599 Greatmoor Hill
Sundhope Rig
KAGYU SAMYE LING TIBETAN CENTRE
Glendinning Heights
Bushy Knowe
Lang Rig
The Shoulder
Causeway Grain Head 490
Merrypath Rig
595 Wisp Hill
Bye Hill
Tudhope Hill 599
Pennygant Hill
597 Muckle Land Knowe
Queen's Mire
Reedy Edge
Clerk Hill
Kirk Cleuch Rig
472 Black Burn Head
White Hope Edge 477
Haggis Side
Whin Fell
Elson Fell 537
Carlin Tooth 511
Glenrief Rig
Stob Fell
Crossbow Hill
Muckle Knowe
Poketha Hill 564
494
The Pike 306
362 Muckle Knowe
Grey Hill
Dod Fell 463
Cadgie Rig
507
Frodaw Height
Bught Knowe
Castlewink
Tup Knowe 307
Dod Hill
Gorrenberry
Balderston Plantn
Hermitage Hill
Jamestown
Alkin Hill
Rashiegrain Height
526 Faw Side
503 Dan's Hags
Crude Hill
Blackhall Hill 379
Butter Hill
Headless Knowe
Tamond Heights 455
Dog Knowe
464 Geordie's Hill
Din Fell 529
Bught Knowe
223 Lady's Knowe
Ewe Knowe
Munshiel Hill 403
Upper Stenneswater
Craigy Edge
Upper Hill
Seppings Hill
Wether Law 429
Mid Hill 436
Stockcleuch Edge
Carlintooth Rig
Ewe Hill
Dinley Fell
Graystone Hill
HERMITAGE CASTLE
Hermitage
Hog Hill
Grey Hill 367
Peat Rig 494
Shiel Moss
Shiel Hill
Saugh Hill Plantn
Glenkeil Hill
Broad Head 493
Stibbiegill Head
Whitehill Wood
369 White Hill
Cockplay Hill
Unthank Pikes
Pike Fell 499
Pout Knowe
517 Millingwood Fell
Wetherhorn Hill
Hartsgarth Fell 551
Dinley Moss
Thiefsike Head
Shaw Rig
Westerker Rig
Effgill Hill
442 Glensaxon Fell
448 Roughbank Height
Stibbiegill Knowe
Linns Knowe
Watch Knowe
547 Scawd Bank
568 Roan Fell
Hazelyside Rig
Netherraw
Longhaugh
Bank Head Hill
Craigie Hill
441 Great Hill
Mellion Muir
Longgrain Head 468
Stake Hill
521 Arkleton Hill
Mid Height
Kapleston Hill
Howgill Hill
Peden's Stone
Nth Birny Fell 275
Hartsgarth
Castle O'er
Green Hill
Fell Hill
Meg's Shank
Brieryshaw Hill
Arkleton
White Cove
White Brae
Westerkirk Mains
Georgefield
Mid Knock
The Rigg
480 Crumpton Hill
Ewes
Bittlestone Height
Cloak Knowe
Watch Hill 502
Birny Fell
Cock Law
Fullwood Hill
Bosstree Hill
Bentpath
Mid Hill
Addergill Hill
Loch Hill
Auldshiels Hill 366
Tod Knowe
342 Enzieholm Height
Boonies Cottage
Burnfoot Plantn
Dowglen Hill
388 Bauchle Hill
Glendivan
Strait Hill
490 Cooms Fell
Threep Hill 336
Hog Fell 371
Birch Cleuch
Wrae Hill
Cooms Height
Raltonside
Pleamoss Hill
Golf Hill
Broom Hill
Hopsrig
Bombie Hill 347
Craig
Flask Wood
Greenlea Knowe
346 Broad Head
Arkleton Cott
446 Black Edge
Hazelyside Hill
Bedda Cleuch
Bedda Hill
Priest Hill
Whithaugh
Friar Edge
387 Ward Hill
Ewe Hill 446
451 Calkin Rig
Shaw Hill
Todhill Brae
Black Knowe
Burn Cott
Craig Hill
Potholm
Potholm Hill
383 Black Height
Loch Knowe
Tarras Lodge
Muckle Knowe 361
Newcastleton or Copshaw Holm
CRAIGCLEUCH CASTLE COLLECTION
Whitecleuch Fell 393
Burrowstown Moss
Greens
307 Newland Hill
Hen Hill
Drygutter Brae
Carlesgill Hill
Clark Fell
Langfauld Wood
Black Knowe
Castle Hill
Terrona Hill
Perter Rig
Stanygill Rig
Kirk Hill
412 Glentenmont Height
Haggy Hill 432
Mirkslair Hill
Mid Hill
Whitshiels Knowe
Charlie's Moss
Middlemoss Head
Perter Hill
404 Tinnis Hill
Sufficient Hill
Blinkbonny
Mangerton
Blackstan Hill
Naze Hill
New Langholm
MALCOLM MONUMENT
Whita Hill
Castle Craigs
Perterburn
264 Blinkbonny Height
Mid Hill
Cockgair Hill
Calfield Rig
Langholm
Rashiel
Redmoss
Kirtlehead Hill 314
Doe's Hill
Shaw Hill
CAROLINE STREET
Skipper's Br
Windy Edge
D'mainholm
Whisgills Edge
Birny Hill
Warb Law
Breckeny Knowe
Broad Edge
Kershopefoot
Raes Knowes
Bloch Hill
Bruntshiel Hill
Muirburnhead Plantn
Black Rig
Winterhope Res
Cock Law
St Bride's Hill
Brocklinns Bank
Middleholm Hill
Burian Hill
Tinnisburn Forest
Kershope Ho
Greena Hill
Stonegarthside Hall
Ley Hill
Crowdieknowe Hill
Bloch Fm
Hardenside
Green Knowe
Longcleughside
Black Rigg
Gowd Muir
Irvine Ho
Mumble Cottages
Tarrasfoot Hill
Upper Millsteads
The Hill
Albierig
Collin Hags 255
Kerr Height
Orchard
Caulside
Bushfield
Crubbins Hill
Kirtleton
West Linnbridgeford
Viewy Knowe
Kerr
Hagg Hill
Greenburn
Outer Woodhead
Under Millsteads
Baileyhead
Crosslands
Claygate
Barrascrofts
Harelaw Pike
Harelaw Mill
Old Hall
Nook
Liddel Lodge
Crookburn Hill
Craigs
Allfornought Hill
Outer Hill
March Cottage
Enthorn
Byreburnside
GILNOCKIE TOWER
Hollows
Archerbeck
Harelaw
Kingfield Ho
Arthur Seat
Tarcoon
Tomshielburn
Allfornought
Hatts
Eskdalemuir
S C O T T I S H
B O R D E R S
D U M F R I E S
A N D
G A L L O W A Y
Teviotdale
Ewes Dale
Liddesdale
Eskdale
A7
B709
B7068
B6357
B6399
B6318
B722
261
239
250

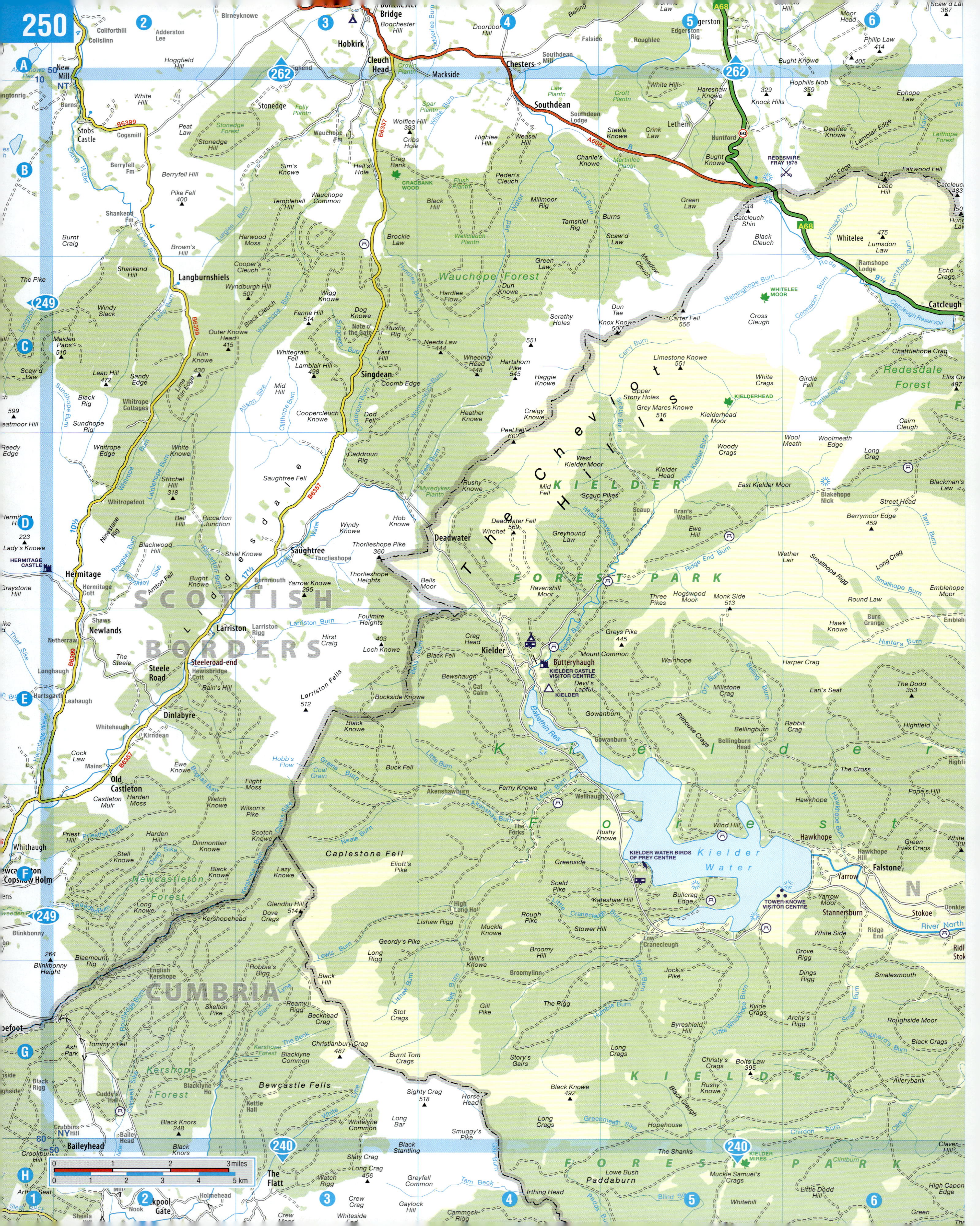

SCOTTISH
BORDERS
CUMBRIA
The Cheviot Hills
KIELDER FOREST PARK
Kielder Forest
Wauchope Forest
Redesdale Forest
Newcastleton Forest
Kershope Forest
Kielder Water
Bakethin Res
Liddesdale
Hobkirk
Cleuch Head
Bonchester Bridge
Chesters
Southdean
Mackside
Stonedge
Stobs Castle
Langburnshiels
Singdean
Saughtree
Deadwater
Kielder
Butteryhaugh
KIELDER CASTLE VISITOR CENTRE
Hermitage
HERMITAGE CASTLE
Newlands
Steele Road
Larriston
Steeleroad-end
Dinlabyre
Old Castleton
Whitehaugh
Copshaw Holm
Falstone
Yarrow
Stannersburn
Hawkhope
Stokoe
TOWER KNOWE VISITOR CENTRE
KIELDER WATER BIRDS OF PREY CENTRE
Whitelee
Catcleugh
Catcleugh Reservoir
Carter Fell 556
Peel Fell 602
Deadwater Fell 569
Caplestone Fell
Bewcastle Fells
Larriston Fells 512
Baileyhead
The Flatt
Paddaburn
Lowe Bush
REDESMIRE FRAY 1575
CRAGBANK WOOD
WHITELEE MOOR
KIELDERHEAD
KIELDER MIRES
A68
A6088
B6357
B6399
River Rede
River North Tyne
Lewis Burn
Hermitage Water
Liddel Water
Jed Water
262
249
240
1 miles 2 3
1 2 3 4 5 km

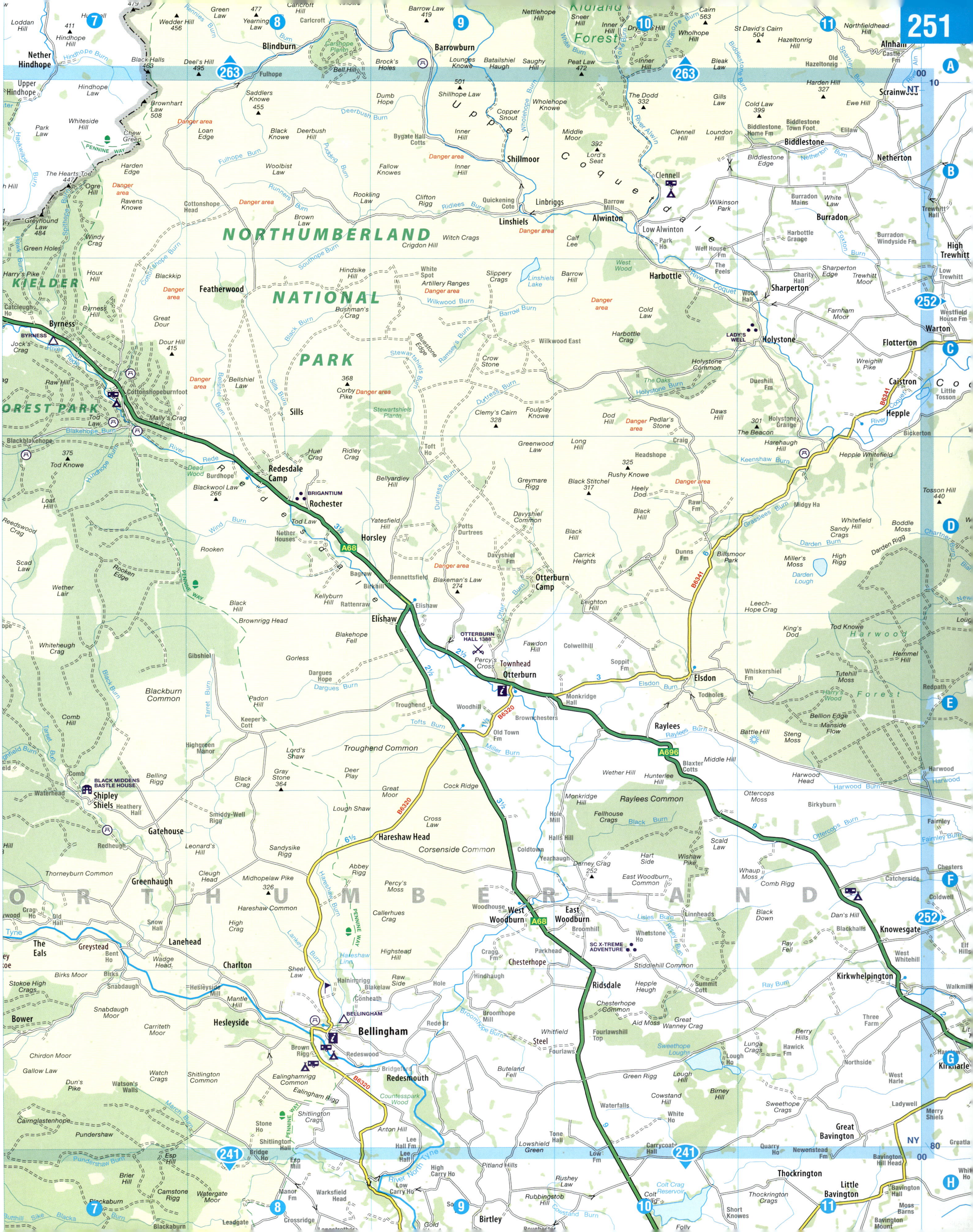
NORTHUMBERLAND
NATIONAL
PARK
KIELDER
FOREST PARK
Upper Coquetdale
Kidland Forest
N O R T H U M B E R L A N D
263
252
241
Loddan Hill
Nether Hindhope
Upper Hindhope
Hindhope Hill
Hindhope Law
Whiteside Hill
Park Law
The Hearts Toe 447
Ogre Hill
Harden Edge
Ravens Knowe
Black Halls 463
Brownhart Law 508
Chew Green
PENNINE WAY
Wedder Hill 456
Deel's Hill 495
Green Law
Yearning Law
Blindburn
Fulhope
Carlcroft
Saddlers Knowe 455
Loan Edge
Danger area
Brock's Holes
Bell Hill
Barrow Law 419
Barrowburn
Lounges Knowe
Batailshiel Haugh
Saughy Hill
Nettlehope Hill
Shillhope Law 501
Dumb Hope
Deerbush Burn
Copper Snout
Wholehope Knowe
Inner Hill
Bygate Hall Cotts
Black Knowe
Deerbush Hill
Woolbist Law
Fallow Knowes
Inner Hill
Shillmoor
Rookling Law
Clifton Rigg
Quickening Cote
Linbriggs
Linshiels
Cottonshope Head
Brown Law
Witch Crags
Crigdon Hill
Sneer Hill
Inner Hill
Dryhope Hill
Wholhope Hill
Cairn 563
Peat Law 472
Inner Hill
Middle Moor
Lord's Seat 392
The Dodd 332
River Alwine
Clennell
Clennell Hill
Barrow Mill
Alwinton
Low Alwinton
Park Ho
Calf Lee
St David's Cairn 504
Hazeltonrig Hill
Northfieldhead Hill
Alnham
Castle Fm
Old Hazeltonrig
Bleak Law
Harden Hill 327
Scrainwood
Gills Law
Cold Law 399
Ewe Hill
Biddlestone Home Fm
Biddlestone Town Foot
Biddlestone
Biddlestone Edge
Netherton
Lounden Hill
Burradon Mains
White Law
Wilkinson Park
Burradon
Trewhitt Hall
High Trewhitt
Low Trewhitt
Harbottle Grange
Burradon Windyside Fm
Well House Fm
The Peels
Harbottle
West Wood
Barrow Hill
Linshiels Lake
Slippery Crags
Hindsike Hill
White Spot
Artillery Ranges
Wilkwood Burn
Barrow Burn
Charity Hall
Sharperton
Sharperton Edge
Trewhitt Moor
Wood Hall
Farnham Moor
Warton
Westfield House Fm
Flotterton
Greyhound Law 484
Windy Crag
Green Holes
Harry's Pike
Houx Hill
Blackkip
Featherwood
Byrness Hill
Catcleugh
Byrness
Jock's Crag
Great Dour
Dour Hill 415
Raw Hill
Cottonshopeburnfoot
Mally's Crag
Tod Law
Blakehope Burn
Blackblakehope
Tod Knowe 375
Bushman's Crag
Bluestone Edge
Wilkwood East
Harbottle Crag
Cold Law
LADY'S WELL
Holystone
Holystone Common
Crow Stone
The Oaks
Holystone Burn
Dueshill Fm
Wreighill Pike
Caistron
Little Tosson
Hepple
Bellshiel Law
Corby Pike 368
Sills
Stewartshiels Plantn
Clemy's Cairn 328
Foulplay Knowe
Dod Hill
Pedlar's Stone
Daws Hill
The Beacon 301
Holystone Grange
Bickerton
Harehaugh Hill
Hepple Whitefield
Craig
Headshope
Greenwood Law
Long Hill
Rushy Knowe 325
Keenshaw Burn
Tosson Hill 440
Huel Crag
Ridley Crag
Toft Ho
Redesdale Camp
Burdhope
Dead Wood
River Rede
Blackwood Law 266
BRIGANTIUM
Rochester
Bellyardley Hill
Greymare Rigg
Black Stitchel 317
Heely Dod
Raw Fm
Midgy Ha
Grasslees Burn
Loaf Hill
Reedswood Crag
Wind Burn
Tod Law
Nether Houses
Yatesfield Hill
Horsley
Potts Durtrees
Davyshiel Common
Black Hill
Black Hill
Whitefield Hill
Sandy Crags
Boddle Moss
Darden Burn
Darden Rigg
Rooken
Rooken Edge
Scad Law
Wether Lair
A68
Bagraw
Birkhill
Bennettsfield
Davyshiel
Blakeman's Law 274
Otterburn Camp
Carrick Heights
Dunns Fm
Billsmoor Park
B6341
Miller's Moss
High Rigg
Darden Lough
Black Hill
Kellyburn Hill
Rattenraw
Elishaw
Leighton Hill
Leech-Hope Crag
Brownrigg Head
Blakehope Fell
OTTERBURN HALL 1388
Percy's Cross
Townhead
Otterburn
Fawdon Hill
Colwellhill
Soppit Fm
Elsdon
Elsdon Burn
King's Dod
Tod Knowe
Harwood
Hemmel Hill
Tutehill Moss
Redpath
Whiteheugh Crag
Gibshiel
Gorless
Dargues Hope
Dargues Burn
Blackburn Common
Padon Hill
Troughend
Woodhill
Monkridge Hall
Todholes
Whiskershiel Fm
Harry's Wood
Forest
Bellion Edge
Manside Flow
Comb Hill
Keeper's Cott
Tofts Burn
Browchesters
Old Town Fm
Raylees
Raylees Burn
Battle Hill
Steng Moss
B6320
Miller Burn
A696
Highgreen Manor
Lord's Shaw
Troughend Common
Gray Stone 364
Deer Play
Black Crag
Belling Rigg
BLACK MIDDENS BASTLE HOUSE
Shipley Shiels
Heathery Hall
Comb
Waterhead
Great Moor
Cock Ridge
Wether Hill
Hunterlee Hill
Blaxter Cotts
Middle Hill
Harwood Head
Harwood Burn
Monkridge Hill
Raylees Common
Ottercops Moss
Birkyburn
Smiddy-Well Rigg
Lough Shaw
Cross Law
Hole Mill
Fellhouse Crags
Black Burn
Ottercops Burn
Fairnley
Gatehouse
Leonard's Hill
Redheugh
Hareshaw Head
Corsenside Common
Halls Hill
Scald Law
Sandysike Rigg
Coldtown
Yearhaugh
Hart Side
Wishaw Pike
Darney Crag 252
Thorneyburn Common
Greenhaugh
Cleugh Head
Midhopelaw Pike 326
Abbey Rigg
Percy's Moss
East Woodburn Common
Whaup Moss
Comb Rigg
Chesters
Catcherside
Coldwell
Hareshaw Common
Hareshaw Burn
Callerhues Crag
Woodhouse
West Woodburn
East Woodburn
Broomhill
Linnheads
Black Down
Dan's Hill
Blackhalls
Knowesgate
Crag Ho
Old Hall
Snow Hall
High Crag
Lisles Burn
Whetstone Ho
Ray Fell
West Whitehill
Tyne
The Eals
Greystead
Bent Ho
Lanehead
Wadge Head
Charlton
Highstead Hill
Hareshaw Linn
Cragg Fm
Parkhead
Chesterhope
SC X-TREME ADVENTURE
Stiddlehill Common
Birks Moor
Birks
Snabdaugh
Sheel Law
Halningrigg
Blakelaw
Raw Side
Hole
Hindhaugh
Ridsdale
Hepple Heugh
Summit Cott
Ray Burn
Kirkwhelpington
Walkmill
Stokoe High Crags
Hesleyside Mill
Mantle Hill
Conheath
Bower
Snabdaugh Moor
Carriteth Moor
Hesleyside
BELLINGHAM
Bellingham
Rede Br
Broomhope Mill
Broomhope Burn
Chesterhope Common
Aid Moss
Great Wanney Crag
Three Farm
Whitfield Steel
Fourlaws
Fourlawshill Top
Sweethope Loughs
Lunga Crags
Berry Hills
Hawick Fm
Northside
Chirdon Moor
Brown Rigg
Redeswood
Bridgeford
Redesmouth
Lough Ho
Gallow Law
Dun's Pike
Watson's Walls
Watch Crags
Shitlington Common
Ealinghamrigg Common
Ealingham Rigg
Buteland Fell
Green Rigg
Lough Hill
Birney Hill
West Harle
Kirkharle
March Burn
Countesspark Wood
Shitlington Crags
Waterfalls
Cowstand Hill
White Ho
Sweethope Crags
Ladywell
Merry Shiels
Cairnglastenhope
Pundershaw
Stone Ho
Shitlington Hall
Anton Hill
Lee Hill Fm
Lee Hall
Tone Hall
Lowshield Green
Great Bavington
Greatla
Pundershaw Burn
Esp Hill
Bridge Ho
Esp Mill
River North Tyne
High Carry Ho
Pitland Hills
Low Fm
Carrycoats Hall
Quarry Ho
Newonstead Fm
Thockrington
Bavington Hill Head
Brier Hill
Camstone Rigg
Watergate Moor
Manor Fm
Warksfield Head
Low Carry Ho
Rushey Law
Colt Crag Reservoir
Thockrington Crags
Little Bavington
Bavington Hall
Blackaburn
Leadgate
Crossridge
Birtley
Rubbingstob Hill
Colt Crag
Short Knowes
Moss Barns
Bavington Mount
Folly
Gold
NT
NY
00
10
80
A
B
C
D
E
F
G
H
7
8
9
10
11

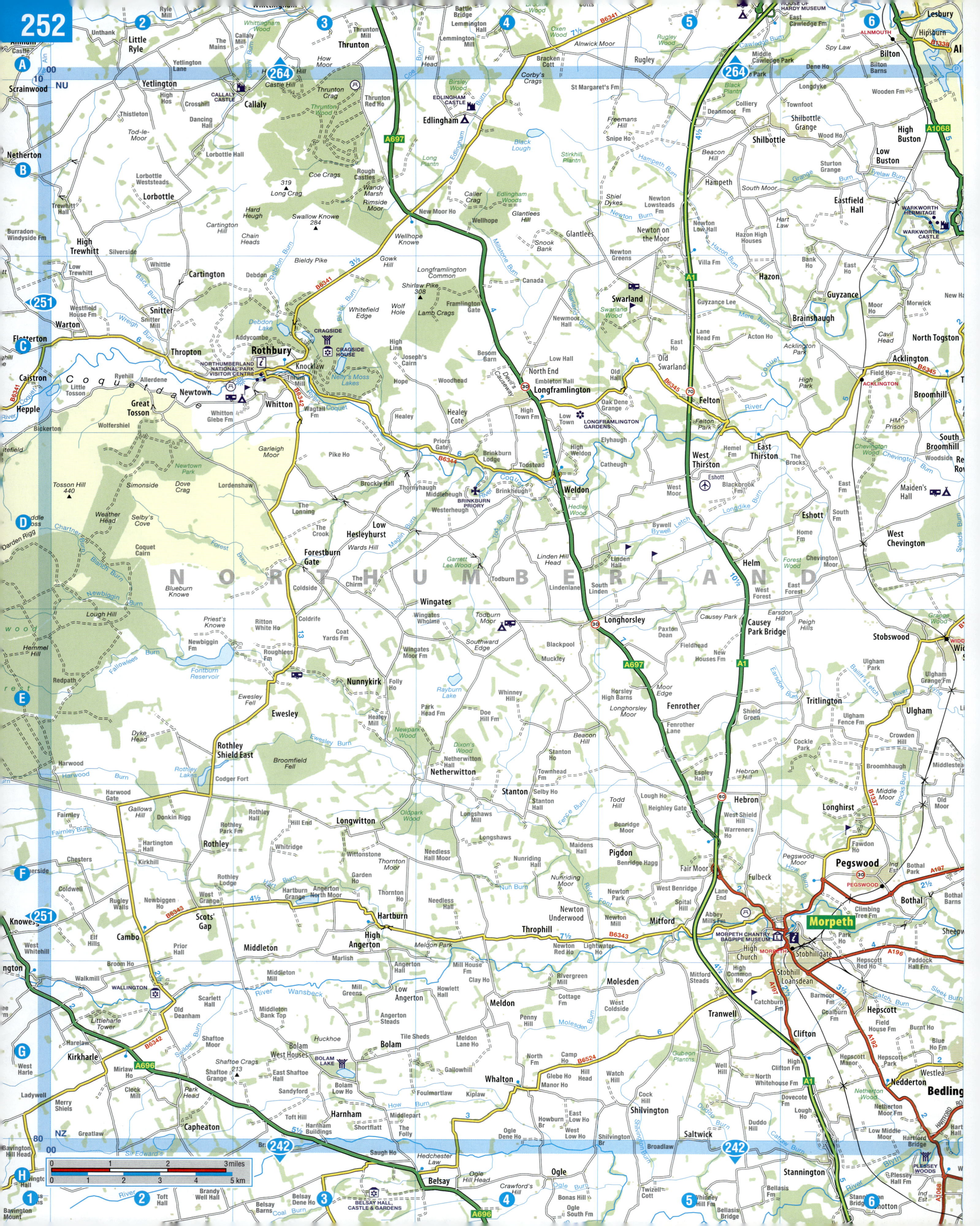

NORTHUMBERLAND
Rothbury
Morpeth
Longframlington
Longhorsley
Felton
Warkworth Castle
Warkworth Hermitage
Alnwick Moor
Lesbury
Hipsburn
Alnmouth
Bilton
Shilbottle
Edlingham
Edlingham Castle
Callaly Castle
Callaly
Yetlington
Thrunton
Whittingham Wood
Little Ryle
Netherton
Lorbottle
Cartington
Snitter
Thropton
Warton
Flotterton
Caistron
Hepple
Newtown
Great Tosson
Whitton
Cragside
Cragside House
Northumberland National Park Visitor Centre
Coquetdale
Weldon
Brinkburn Priory
Longframlington Gardens
Swarland
Guyzance
Brainshaugh
Acklington
North Togston
Broomhill
South Broomhill
West Thirston
East Thirston
Eshott
Helm
West Chevington
Causey Park Bridge
Stobswood
Tritlington
Ulgham
Longhirst
Pegswood
Bothal
Hebron
Fenrother
Pigdon
Mitford
Netherwitton
Stanton
Wingates
Nunnykirk
Ewesley
Forestburn Gate
Hesleyhurst
Rothley Shield East
Rothley
Longwitton
Cambo
Wallington
Scots' Gap
Middleton
Hartburn
High Angerton
Meldon
Bolam
Whalton
Throphill
Shilvington
Saltwick
Tranwell
Clifton
Hepscott
Stobhill
Morpeth Chantry Bagpipe Museum
Kirkharle
Capheaton
Harnham
Belsay
Belsay Hall, Castle & Gardens
Ogle
Stannington
Nedderton
Bedlington
Plessey Woods
Fontburn Reservoir
Simonside
Tosson Hill 440
A697
A1
A696
B6341
B6342
B6343
B6344
B6345
B6524
A1068
A192
A196
A197
B1337
264
251
242
0 1 2 3 miles
0 1 2 3 4 5 km

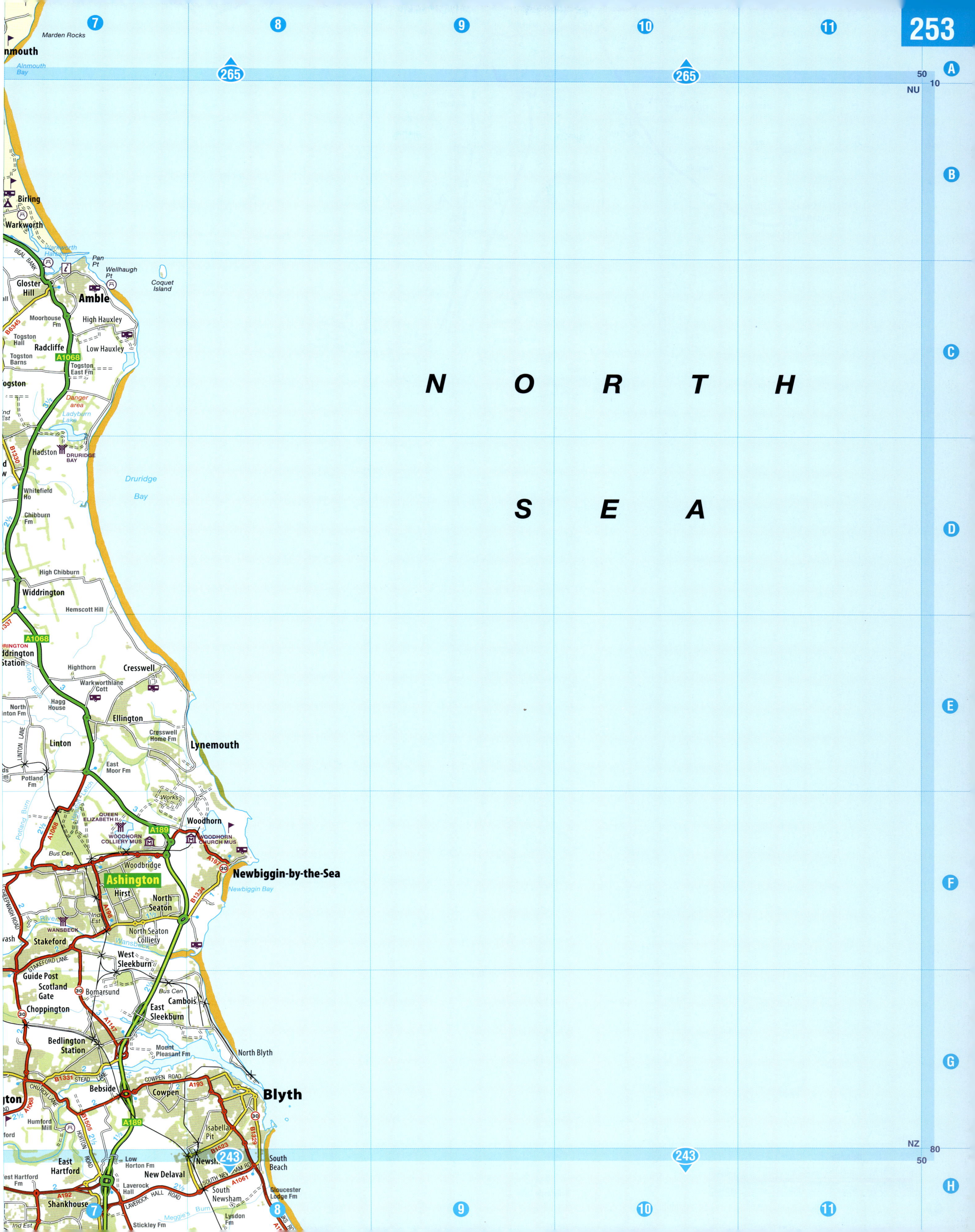
NORTH SEA
Marden Rocks
Alnmouth Bay
Birling
Warkworth
Warkworth Harbour
Pan Pt
Wellhaugh Pt
Coquet Island
Gloster Hill
Amble
Moorhouse Fm
High Hauxley
Togston Hall
Radcliffe
Low Hauxley
Togston Barns
A1068
Togston East Fm
Danger area
Ladyburn Lake
B1330
Hadston
DRURIDGE BAY
Druridge Bay
Whitefield Ho
Chibburn Fm
High Chibburn
Widdrington
Hemscott Hill
A1068
Highthorn
Cresswell
Warkworthlane Cott
Hagg House
Ellington
North Linton Fm
Cresswell Home Fm
Linton
Lynemouth
LINTON LANE
Potland Fm
East Moor Fm
Works
QUEEN ELIZABETH II
A189
Woodhorn
WOODHORN COLLIERY MUS
WOODHORN CHURCH MUS
Potland Burn
A1068
Bus Cen
Woodbridge
Ashington
Newbiggin-by-the-Sea
Newbiggin Bay
Hirst
North Seaton
B1334
Ind Est
A196
WANSBECK
North Seaton Colliery
Wansbeck
Stakeford
STAKEFORD LANE
West Sleekburn
Guide Post
Scotland Gate
Bomarsund
Bus Cen
Cambois
Choppington
East Sleekburn
A1147
Bedlington Station
Mount Pleasant Fm
North Blyth
B1331
STEAD LANE
COWPEN ROAD
A193
CHURCH LANE
Bebside
Cowpen
Blyth
A1068
Humford Mill
B1505
A189
HORTON ROAD
Isabella Pit
B1329
B1523
Low Horton Fm
East Hartford
Newsham
South Beach
New Delaval
SOUTH NEWSHAM RD
A1061
East Hartford Fm
Laverock Hall
LAVEROCK HALL ROAD
South Newsham
Gloucester Lodge Fm
A192
Shankhouse
Meggie's Burn
Lysdon Fm
Ind Est
Stickley Fm
265
243
NU
NZ
50
10
80
7
8
9
10
11
A
B
C
D
E
F
G
H

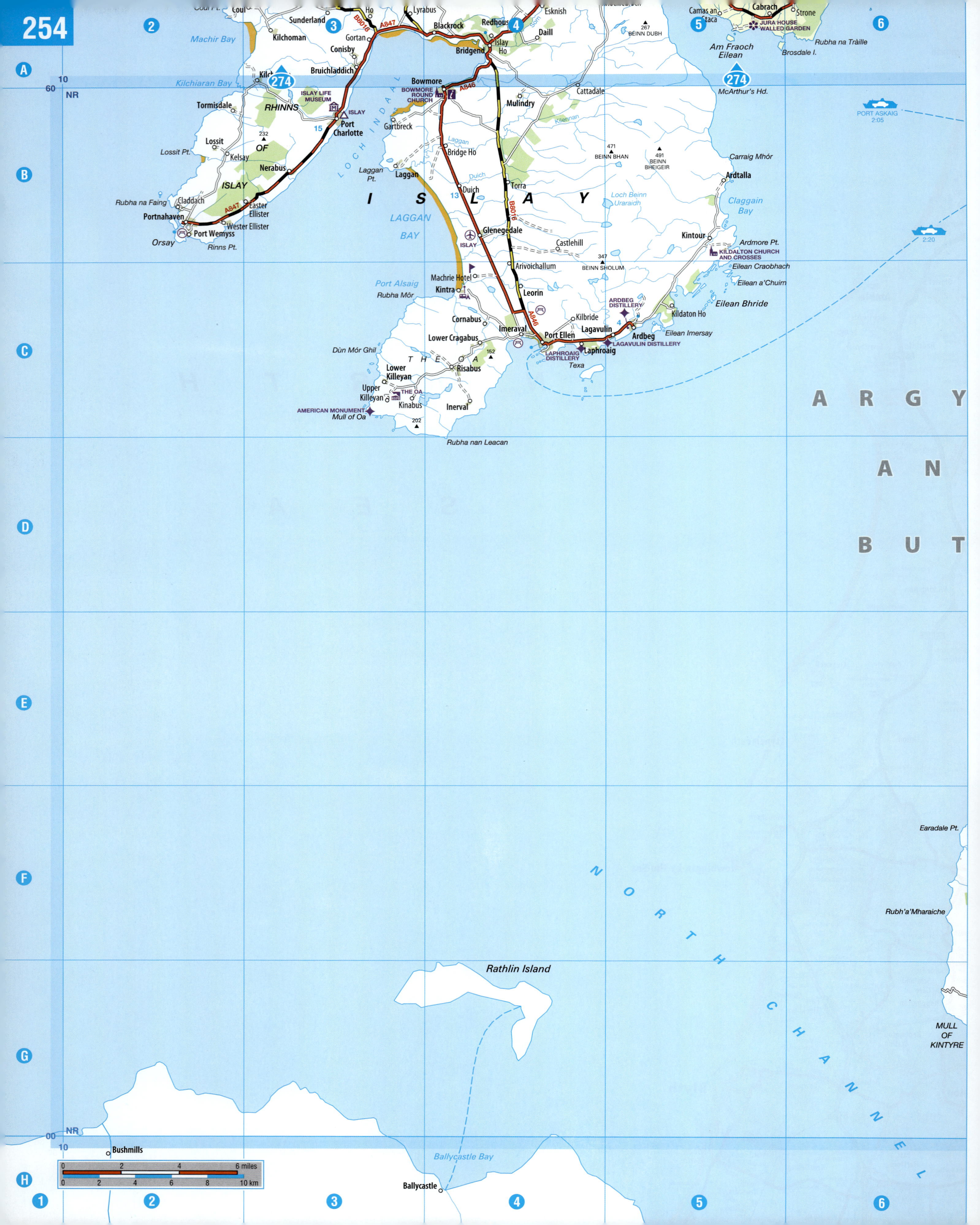
Machir Bay
Sunderland
Kilchoman
Gortan
Conisby
Bruichladdich
Kilchiaran Bay
Lyrabus
Blackrock
Redhouse
Esknish
Daill
Islay Ho
Bridgend
Bowmore
BOWMORE ROUND CHURCH
ISLAY LIFE MUSEUM
Tormisdale
RHINNS
OF
ISLAY
Port Charlotte
Gartbreck
LOCH INDAAL
Lossit
Lossit Pt.
Kelsay
Nerabus
Rubha na Faing
Claddach
Portnahaven
Port Wemyss
Orsay
Rinns Pt.
Easter Ellister
Wester Ellister
Laggan Pt.
Laggan
Bridge Ho
Duich
I S L A Y
LAGGAN BAY
Glenegedale
ISLAY
Machrie Hotel
Kintra
Port Alsaig
Rubha Mòr
Mulindry
Cattadale
Torra
Castlehill
Arivoichallum
Leorin
Loch Beinn Uraraidh
BEINN DUBH
BEINN BHAN
BEINN BHEIGEIR
BEINN SHOLUM
Cornabus
Lower Cragabus
Imeraval
Port Ellen
Kilbride
Lagavulin
Ardbeg
ARDBEG DISTILLERY
LAGAVULIN DISTILLERY
Laphroaig
LAPHROAIG DISTILLERY
Texa
Dùn Mór Ghil
T H E O A
Risabus
Lower Killeyan
Upper Killeyan
THE OA
Kinabus
Inerval
AMERICAN MONUMENT
Mull of Oa
Rubha nan Leacan
Camas an Staca
Cabrach
Strone
JURA HOUSE WALLED GARDEN
Am Fraoch Eilean
Brosdale I.
Rubha na Tràille
McArthur's Hd.
PORT ASKAIG 2:05
Carraig Mhór
Ardtalla
Claggain Bay
Kintour
Ardmore Pt.
KILDALTON CHURCH AND CROSSES
Eilean Craobhach
Eilean a'Chuirn
Eilean Bhride
Kildaton Ho
Eilean Imersay
2:20
A R G Y
A N
B U T
Earadale Pt.
Rubh'a'Mharaiche
MULL OF KINTYRE
N O R T H C H A N N E L
Rathlin Island
Bushmills
Ballycastle Bay
Ballycastle
0 2 4 6 miles
0 2 4 6 8 10 km

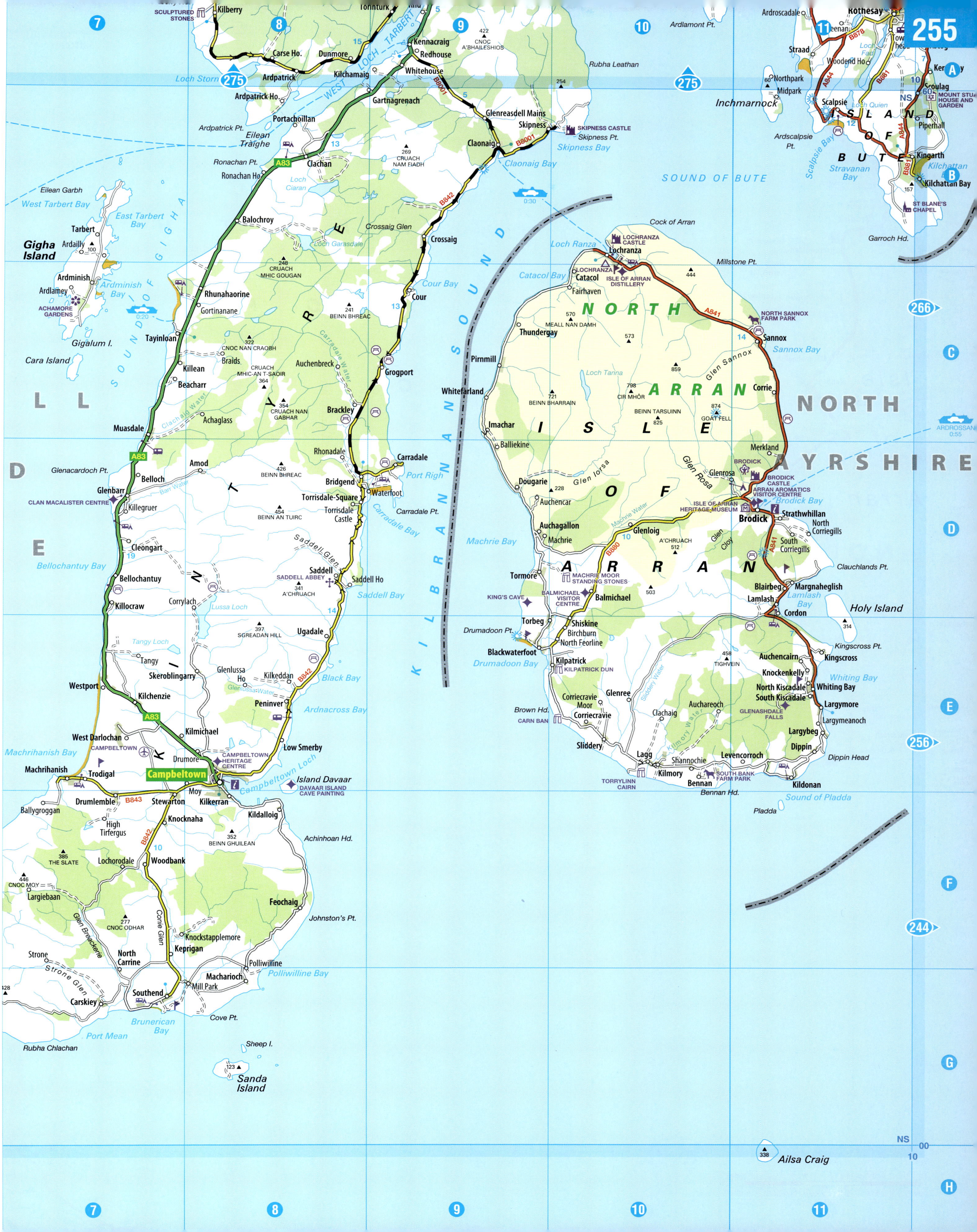

Kilberry
SCULPTURED STONES
Carse Ho.
Dunmore
Kennacraig
Redhouse
Whitehouse
Kilchamaig
Ardpatrick
Ardpatrick Ho.
Loch Stornoway
275
WEST LOCH TARBERT
Gartnagrenach
CNOC A'BHAILESHIOS
Rubha Leathan
Ardlamont Pt.
Glenreasdell Mains
Skipness
SKIPNESS CASTLE
Skipness Pt.
Skipness Bay
Claonaig
Claonaig Bay
Portachoillan
Ardpatrick Pt.
Eilean Traighe
Ronachan Pt.
Ronachan Ho.
Clachan
Loch Ciaran
CRUACH NAM FIADH
Eilean Garbh
West Tarbert Bay
East Tarbert Bay
Tarbert
Ardailly
Gigha Island
Ardminish
Ardlamey
Ardminish Bay
ACHAMORE GARDENS
Balochroy
Crossaig Glen
Crossaig
Loch Garasdale
CRUACH MHIC GOUGAN
Rhunahaorine
Gortinanane
Cour Bay
Cour
BEINN BHREAC
Tayinloan
Gigalum I.
Cara Island
SOUND OF GIGHA
CNOC NAN CRAOBH
Braids
Killean
Beacharr
CRUACH MHIC-AN T-SAOIR
Auchenbreck
Carradale Water
Grogport
Clachaig Water
Achaglass
CRUACH NAN GABHAR
Brackley
Muasdale
Rhonadale
Carradale
Port Righ
Amod
BEINN BHREAC
Glenacardoch Pt.
Belloch
Barr Water
Glenbarr
CLAN MACALISTER CENTRE
Killegruer
Bridgend
Torrisdale-Square
Waterfoot
Torrisdale Castle
Carradale Pt.
Carradale Bay
BEINN AN TUIRC
Saddell Glen
Cleongart
Bellochantuy Bay
Bellochantuy
Saddell
SADDELL ABBEY
A'CHRUACH
Saddell Ho
Saddell Bay
Killocraw
Corrylach
Lussa Loch
SGREADAN HILL
Ugadale
Tangy Loch
Tangy
Skeroblingarry
Glenlussa Ho
Kilkeddan
Black Bay
Westport
Kilchenzie
Peninver
Ardnacross Bay
West Darlochan
Kilmichael
Low Smerby
Machrihanish Bay
CAMPBELTOWN
Machrihanish
Trodigal
Drumore
CAMPBELTOWN HERITAGE CENTRE
Campbeltown
Campbeltown Loch
Island Davaar
DAVAAR ISLAND CAVE PAINTING
Ballygroggan
Drumlemble
Stewarton
Moy
Kilkerran
Kildalloig
High Tirfergus
Knocknaha
BEINN GHUILEAN
Achinhoan Hd.
THE SLATE
Lochorodale
Woodbank
CNOC MOY
Largiebaan
Feochaig
CNOC ODHAR
Glen Breackerie
Conie Glen
Johnston's Pt.
Knockstapplemore
Keprigan
Strone
North Carrine
Polliwilline
Polliwilline Bay
Strone Glen
Machariooch
Mill Park
Southend
Carskiey
Brunerican Bay
Cove Pt.
Port Mean
Rubha Chlachan
Sheep I.
Sanda Island
KINTYRE
KILBRANNAN SOUND
Cock of Arran
LOCHRANZA CASTLE
Lochranza
Loch Ranza
Catacol Bay
Catacol
ISLE OF ARRAN DISTILLERY
Fairhaven
Millstone Pt.
NORTH ARRAN
MEALL NAN DAMH
Thundergay
A841
NORTH SANNOX FARM PARK
Sannox
Sannox Bay
Loch Tanna
Glen Sannox
Pirnmill
Whitefarland
BEINN BHARRAIN
CIR MHÒR
Corrie
BEINN TARSUINN
GOAT FELL
Imachar
Balliekine
ISLE OF ARRAN
Glen Iorsa
Glen Rosa
Merkland
BRODICK
Glenrosa
BRODICK CASTLE
ARRAN AROMATICS VISITOR CENTRE
Brodick Bay
Dougarie
Auchencar
ISLE OF ARRAN HERITAGE MUSEUM
Brodick
Strathwhillan
North Corriegills
Machrie Water
Auchagallon
Machrie
Glenloig
A'CHRUACH
Glen Cloy
South Corriegills
Machrie Bay
Clauchlands Pt.
Tormore
MACHRIE MOOR STANDING STONES
KING'S CAVE
BALMICHAEL VISITOR CENTRE
Balmichael
Margnaheglish
Blairbeg
Lamlash
Lamlash Bay
Cordon
Holy Island
Torbeg
Drumadoon Pt.
Shiskine
Birchburn
North Feorline
Blackwaterfoot
Drumadoon Bay
Kilpatrick
KILPATRICK DUN
TIGHVEIN
Auchencairn
Kingscross Pt.
Kingscross
Knockenkelly
Whiting Bay
North Kiscadale
South Kiscadale
Sliddery Water
Glenree
Corriecravie Moor
Corriecravie
Brown Hd.
CARN BAN
Clachaig
Auchareoch
GLENASHDALE FALLS
Largymore
Largymeanoch
Kilmory Water
Largybeg
Dippin
Dippin Head
Sliddery
Lagg
Shannochie
Levencorroch
Kilmory
Bennan
SOUTH BANK FARM PARK
Kildonan
TORRYLINN CAIRN
Bennan Hd.
Sound of Pladda
Pladda
Ardroscadale
Rothesay
Straad
Woodend Ho
Northpark
Midpark
Inchmarnock
Scalpsie
Loch Quien
MOUNT STUART HOUSE AND GARDEN
Scoulag
ISLAND OF BUTE
Piperhall
Ardscalpsie Pt.
Scalpsie Bay
Kingarth
Kilchattan
Stravanan Bay
Kilchattan Bay
ST BLANE'S CHAPEL
Garroch Hd.
SOUND OF BUTE
NORTH AYRSHIRE
ARDROSSAN 0:55
Ailsa Craig
266
256
244
A83
A841
B842
B843
B8001
B880
B881
A844
B878

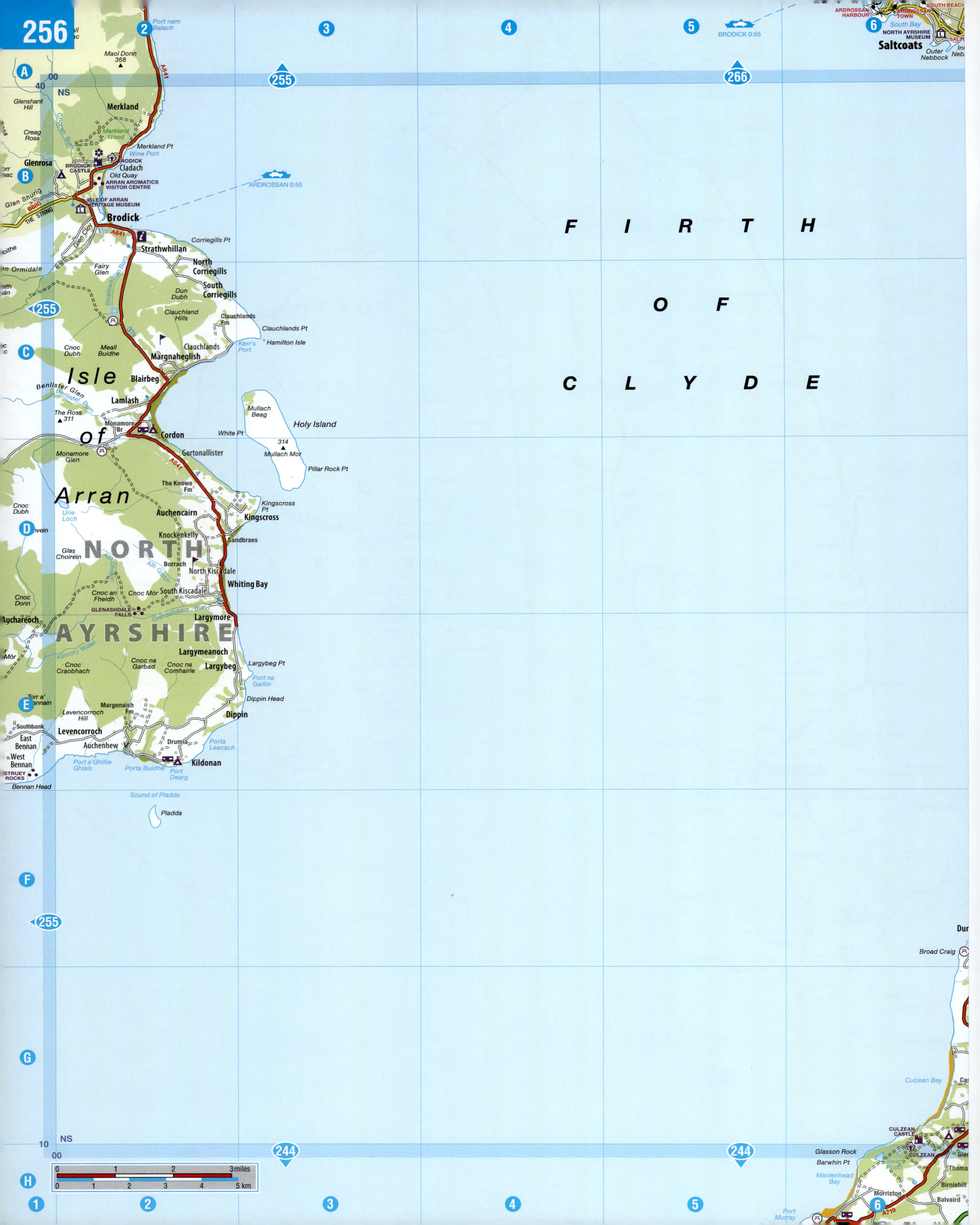
FIRTH OF CLYDE
Isle of Arran
NORTH AYRSHIRE
Port nam Balach
Maol Donn 368
Glenshant Hill
Merkland
Merkland Wood
Creag Rosa
Merkland Pt
Wine Port
Glenrosa
BRODICK CASTLE
Cladach
Old Quay
ARRAN AROMATICS VISITOR CENTRE
ISLE OF ARRAN HERITAGE MUSEUM
Glen Shurig
THE STRING
Brodick
ARDROSSAN 0:55
Glen Cloy
Corriegills Pt
Strathwhillan
Strathwhillan Burn
North Corriegills
Fairy Glen
South Corriegills
Dun Dubh
Clauchland Hills
Clauchlands Fm
Clauchlands Pt
Kerr's Port
Hamilton Isle
Clauchlands
Cnoc Dubh
Meall Buidhe
Margnaheglish
Blairbeg
Benlister Glen
Benlister Burn
Lamlash
The Ross 311
Monamore Br
Cordon
Mullach Beag
Holy Island
White Pt
314 Mullach Mor
Pillar Rock Pt
Monamore Glen
Gortonallister
The Knowe Fm
Kingscross Pt
Kingscross
Auchencairn
Urie Loch
Cnoc Dubh
Knockenkelly
Sandbraes
Glas Choirein
Borrach
Allt Garbh
North Kiscadale
Whiting Bay
Cnoc an Fheidh
Cnoc Mòr
South Kiscadale
Cnoc Donn
GLENASHDALE FALLS
Glenashdale Burn
Largymore
Auchareoch
Kilmory Water
Largymeanoch
Cnoc Craobhach
Cnoc na Garbad
Cnoc na Comhairle
Largybeg
Largybeg Pt
Port na Gaillin
Dippin Head
Margenaish Fm
Dippin
Levencorroch Hill
Southbank
Levencorroch
East Bennan
Auchenhew
Drumla
Porta Leacach
West Bennan
STRUEY ROCKS
Port a' Ghillie Ghlais
Porta Buidhe
Port Dearg
Kildonan
Bennan Head
Sound of Pladda
Pladda
A841
B880
BRODICK 0:55
ARDROSSAN HARBOUR
ARDROSSAN TOWN
SOUTH BEACH
South Bay
NORTH AYRSHIRE MUSEUM
Saltcoats
Outer Nebbock
Broad Craig
Culzean Bay
CULZEAN CASTLE
CULZEAN
Glasson Rock
Barwhin Pt
Maidenhead Bay
Morriston
Thomaston
Birniehill
Balvaird
Port Murray
A719
NS
255
266
244
0 1 2 3 miles
0 1 2 3 4 5 km

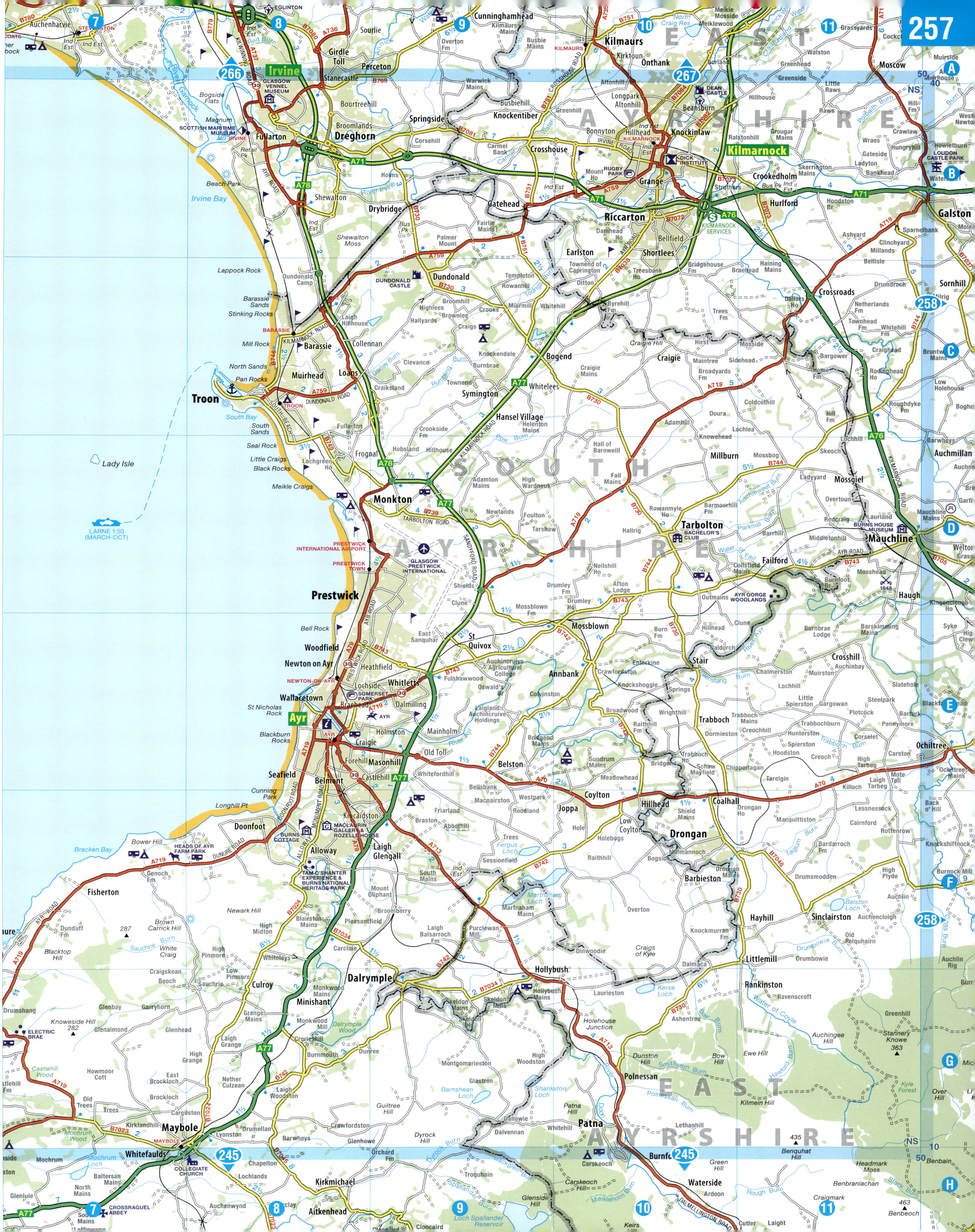
EAST AYRSHIRE
SOUTH AYRSHIRE
Irvine
Kilmaurs
Kilmarnock
Dreghorn
Springside
Crosshouse
Riccarton
Galston
Hurlford
Troon
Barassie
Muirhead
Symington
Monkton
Prestwick
Ayr
Tarbolton
Mauchline
Annbank
Mossblown
Drongan
Coylton
Dalrymple
Maybole
Patna
Irvine Bay
Lady Isle
LARNE 1:50 (MARCH-OCT)
GLASGOW PRESTWICK INTERNATIONAL
Ochiltree
Sinclairston
Hollybush
Kirkmichael
Crosshill
Dundonald
Dundonald Castle
Catrine
A71
A77
A78
A70
A719
A76
A713
Doonfoot
Alloway
Heads of Ayr Farm Park
Fisherton
Culroy
Minishant
Polnessan
Waterside
Dunure Road
Crossraguel Abbey
Whitefaulds
Cumnock

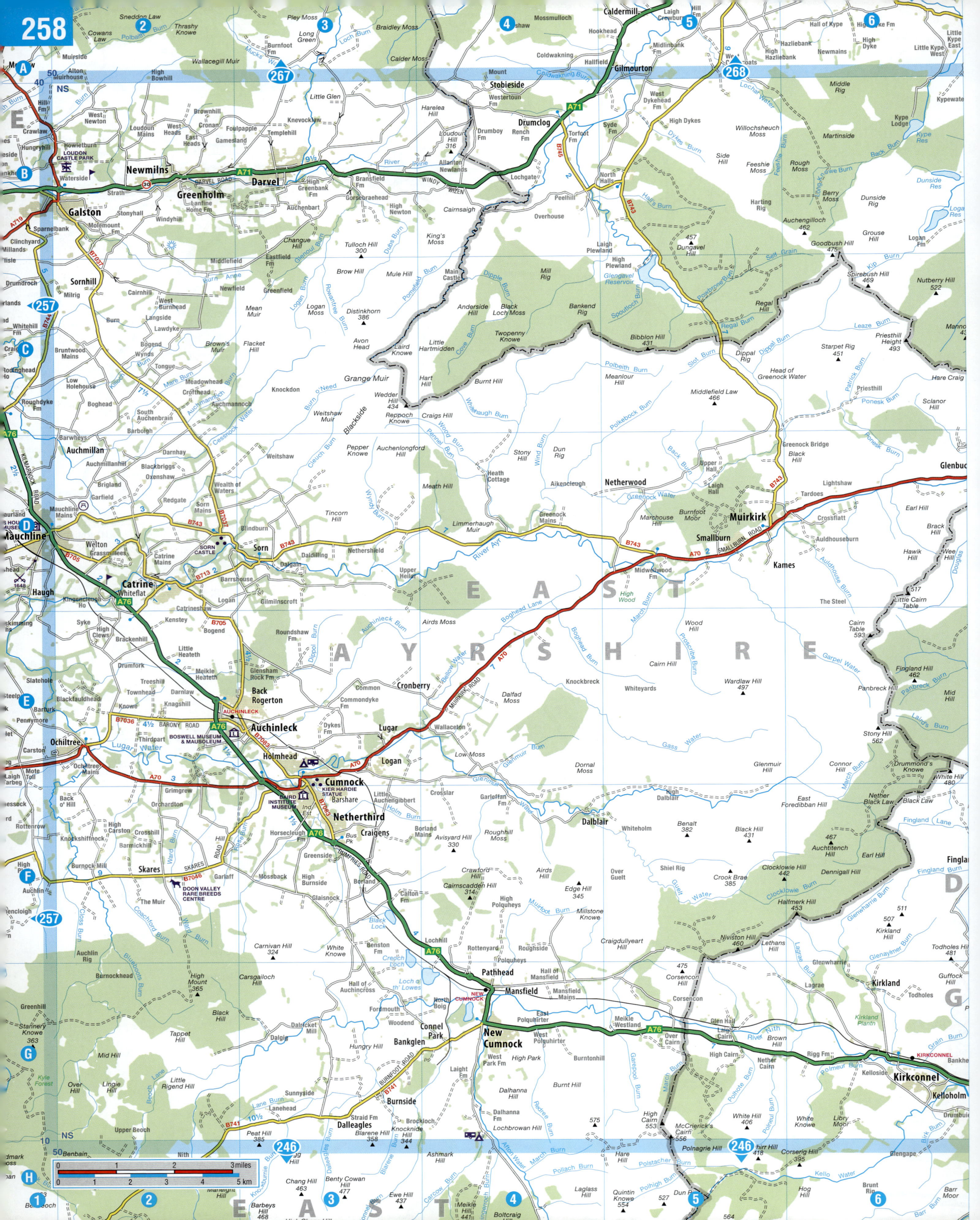
EAST AYRSHIRE
Galston
Newmilns
Greenholm
Darvel
Drumclog
Gilmourton
Stobieside
Caldermill
Mauchline
Catrine
Sorn
Muirkirk
Smallburn
Kames
Netherwood
Auchinleck
Ochiltree
Cumnock
Netherthird
Logan
Lugar
Cronberry
Skares
New Cumnock
Mansfield
Pathhead
Kirkconnel
Kelloholm
Dalblair
Glenbuck
Glengavel Reservoir
River Ayr
A71
A70
A76
B743
B705
B7036
B741
267
268
257
246

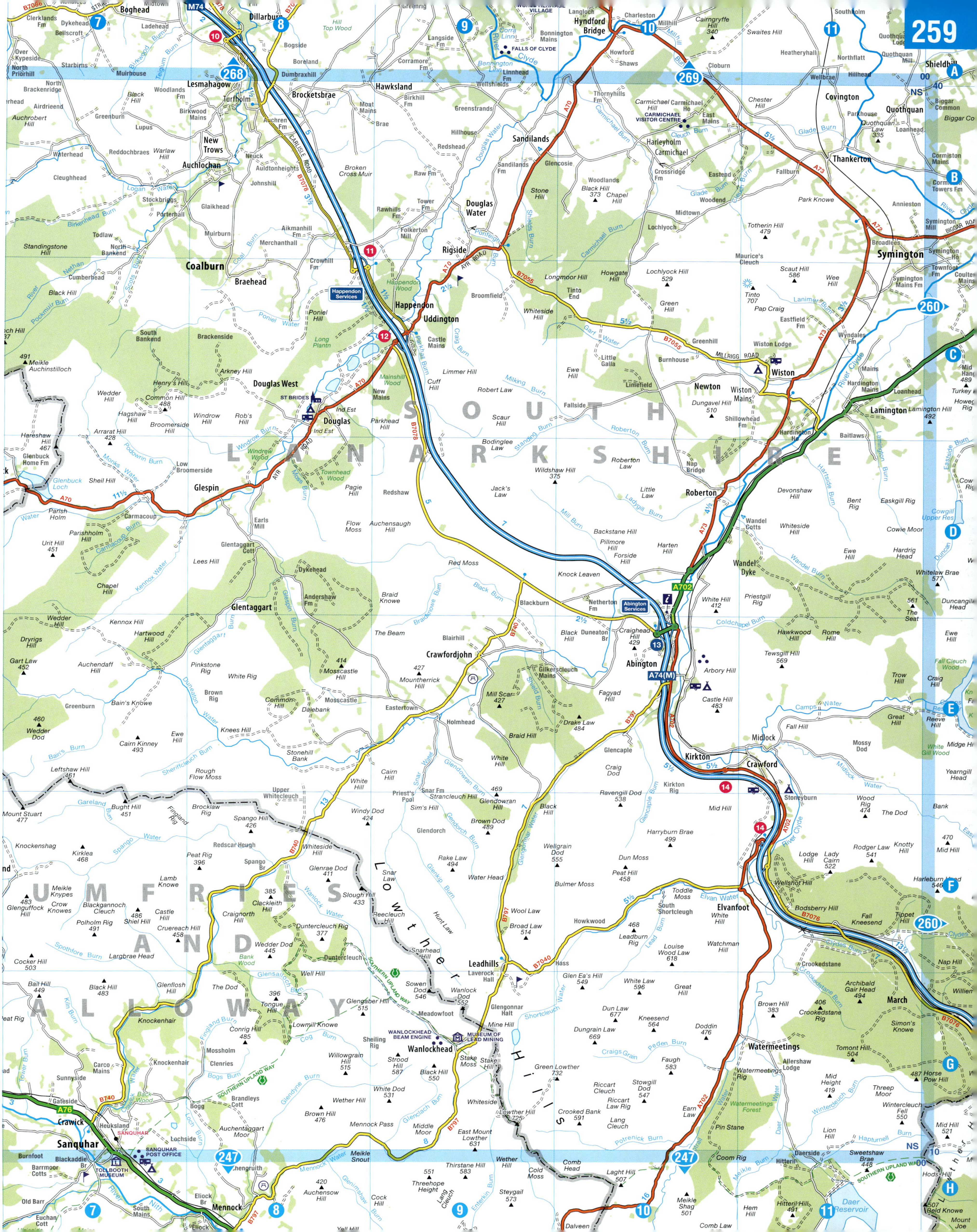
SOUTH LANARKSHIRE
DUMFRIES AND GALLOWAY
Lowther Hills
Boghead
Dillarburn
Clerklands Fm
Dykehead
Bellscroft
Ladehead
Over Kypeside
North Priorhill
Starbirns
Muirhouse
Lesmahagow
Turfholm
Dumbraxhill
Brocketsbrae
Hawksland
North Brackenridge
Airdrieend
Auchrobert Hill
Black Hill
Woodlands Fm
Birkwood Mains
Greenburn
Lupus
New Trows
Auchren Fm
Moat Mains
Birkhill Fm
Brae
Greenstrands
Hillhouse
Redshead
Waterhead
Reddochbraes
Warlaw Hill
Auchlochan
Neuck
Auldtonheights
Broken Cross Muir
Raw Fm
Cleughhead
Logan Water
Johnshill
Stockbriggs
Porterhall
Glaikhead
Tower Fm
Rawhills Fm
Douglas Water
Birkenhead Burn
Todlaw
Muirburn
Aikmanhill Fm
Merchanthall
Folkerton Mill
Rigside
Standingstone Hill
North Bankend
Coalburn
Braehead
Crowhill Fm
Cumberhead
Nethan
Black Hill
Happendon Services
Happendon Wood
Happendon
Uddington
Broomfield
Poniel Hill
Poniel Water
Long Plantn
Castle Mains
South Bankend
Brackenside
Meikle Auchinstilloch
491
Arkney Hill
Henry's Hill
Douglas West
Mainshill Wood
New Mains
Limmer Hill
Cuff Hill
Wedder Hill
Common Hill 488
St Brides
Ind Est
Douglas
Parkhead Hill
Hagshaw Hill
Windrow Hill
Rob's Hill
Broomerside Hill
Arrarat Hill 428
Hareshaw Hill 467
Glenbuck Home Fm
Glenbuck Loch
Windrow Burn
Windrew Wood
Townhead Wood
Low Broomerside
Shiel Hill
Glespin
Pagie Hill
Redshaw
Parish Holm
Carmacoup
Parishholm Hill
Earls Mill
Flow Moss
Auchensaugh Hill
Urit Hill 451
Glentaggart Cott
Lees Hill
Dykehead
Kennox Water
Chapel Hill
Andershaw Fm
Braid Knowe
Glentaggart
Wedder Hill
Kennox Hill
Hartwood Hill
The Beam
Drygrigs Hill
Blairhill
Crawfordjohn
Gart Law 452
Auchendaff Hill
Pinkstone Rig
White Rig
414 Mosscastle Hill
427 Mountherrick Hill
Brown Rig
Common Hill
Mosscastle
Dalebank
Easterton
Greenburn
Bain's Knowe
460 Wedder Dod
Cairn Kinney 493
Ewe Hill
Knees Hill
Stonehill Bank
Bain's Burn
Leftshaw Hill 461
Rough Flow Moss
Upper Whitecleuch
Mount Stuart 477
Gareland Burn
Bught Hill 451
Brocklaw Rig
Spango Hill 426
Knockenshag
Kirklea 468
Peat Rig 396
Redscar Heugh
Whiteside Hill
Meikle Knypes
Crow Knowes
Blackgannoch Cleuch
483 Glenguffock Hill
486 Shiel Hill
Castle Hill
Polholm Rig 491
Crairgnorth Hill
Cruereach Hill 458
385 Clackleith Hill
Glenrae Dod 411
Duntercleuch Rig 377
Wedder Dod 445
Cocker Hill 503
Largbrae Head
Bank Wood
Duntercleuch
Ball Hill 449
Black Hill 483
Glenflosh Hill
The Dod
396 Tongue Hill
Well Hill
Knockenhair
Conrig Hill 485
Mossholm
Clenries
Knockenhair
Carco Mains
Sunnyside
Gateside
Crawick
Heuksland
Sanquhar
Sanquhar Post Office
Tollbooth Museum
Burnfoot
Blackaddie
Barrmoor Cotts
Old Barr
South Mains
Euchan Cott
Eliock
Eliock Br
Mennock
Lochside
Auchentaggart Moor
Brandleys Cott
Bogg
Southern Upland Way
Wanlockhead
Wanlockhead Beam Engine
Museum of Lead Mining
Willowgrain Hill 515
Shieling Rig
Strood Hill 587
Black Hill 550
White Dod 531
Brown Hill 476
Wether Hill
Mennock Pass
Middle Moor
East Mount Lowther 631
Whiteside
Lowther Hill 725
Glengaber Hill 515
Sowen Dod 546
Wanlock Dod 552
Meadowfoot
Lowmill Knowe
Leadhills
Laverock Hall
Glengonnar Halt
Mine Hill
Stake Moss
Stake Hill
Sim's Hill
Priest's Pool
Snar Fm
Strancleuch Hill
Windy Dod 424
Glendorch
Rake Law 494
Water Head
Snar Law
Slough Hill 433
Reecleuch Hill
Hunt Law
Snarhead Hill
Cairn Hill
White Hill
Holmhead
Mill Scar 427
Gilkerscleuch Mains
Fagyad Hill
Drake Law 484
Braid Hill
Glencaple
Craig Dod
469 Glendowran Hill
Brown Dod 489
Black Hill
Ravengill Dod 538
Wellgrain Dod 555
Dun Moss
Peat Hill 458
Bulmer Moss
Wool Law
Broad Law 514
Howkwood
468 Leadburn Rig
Louise Wood Law 618
Watchman Hill
Hass
Glen Ea's Hill 549
White Law 596
Great Hill
Dun Law 677
Kneesend 564
Doddin 476
Dungrain Law 669
Craigs Grain
Peden Burn
Green Lowther 732
Faugh 583
Riccart Cleuch
Stowgill Dod 547
Riccart Law Rig
Crooked Bank 591
Lang Cleuch
Earn Law
Potrenick Burn
Thirstane Hill 583
Comb Head
Cold Moss
Laght Hill 507
Steygail 573
Threehope Height
551
420 Auchensow Hill
Cock Hill
Meikle Snout
Meikle Shag 501
Hem Hill
Coom Rig
Daerside
Hitteril
Hitteril Hill 491
Daer Reservoir
Sweetshaw Brae 448
Hods Hill
507 Beld Knowe
Mount Joe
Comb Law
Dalveen
Pin Stane
Watermeetings Forest
Watermeetings Rig
Watermeetings
Allershaw Lodge
Tomont Hill 504
Mid Height 419
Threep Moor
Wintercleuch Fell 550
Mid Hill 521
Lion Hill
Hapturnell Burn
487 Horse Pow Hill
Simon's Knowe
406 Crookedstane Rig
Brown Hill 383
Archibald Gair Head 494
March
Crookedstane
Fall Kneesend
Tippet Hill
Bodsberry Hill
Harleburn Head 546
Elvanfoot
White Hill
Toddle Moss
South Shortcleugh
Elvan Water
Wellshot Hill
Lodge Hill
Lady Cairn 522
Rodger Law 541
Knotty Hill
470 Mid Hill
The Dod
Wood Rig 474
Harryburn Brae 499
Mid Hill
Kirkton Rig
Stoneyburn
Crawford
Kirkton
Midlock
Mossy Dod
Fall Hill
Great Hill
Reeve Hill
Midge Hill
Yearngill Head
Bank
Castle Hill 483
Arbory Hill
Abington
Abington Services
Craighead Hill 429
Black Hill
Duneaton Br
Tewsgill Hill 569
Hawkwood Hill
Rome Hill
Ewe Hill
Trow Hill
Craig Hill
White Hill 412
Priestgill Rig
Netherton Fm
Blackburn
Knock Leaven
Red Moss
Pillmore Hill
Forside Hill
Backstane Hill
Harten Hill
Wandel Dyke
Wandel Cotts
Whiteside Hill
Ewe Hill
Hardrig Head
Whitelaw Brae 577
561 The Seat
Duncangill Head
Cowie Moor
Jack's Law
Little Law
Roberton
Devonshaw Hill
Bent Rig
Easkgill Rig
Wildshaw Hill 375
Roberton Law
Nap Bridge
Bodinglee Law
Scaur Hill
Robert Law
Fallside
Dungavel Hill 510
Shillowhead Fm
Hardington Ho
Baitlaws
Lamington
Lamington Hill 492
Newton
Wiston Mains
Wiston
Wiston Lodge
Millrigg Road
Burnhouse
Limefield
Little Galla
Ewe Hill
Greenhill
Hardington Mains
Loanhead
Mains
Whiteside Hill
Green Hill
Eastfield Fm
Wyndales Fm
Pap Craig
Tinto 707
Tinto End
Howgate Hill
Longmoor Hill
Lochlyoch Hill 529
Scaut Hill 586
Wee Hill
Maurice's Cleuch
Lochlyoch
Midtown
Stone Hill
Woodlands
Black Hill 373
Chapel Hill
Glencosie
Sandilands
Sandilands Fm
Woodend
Eastend
Crossridge Fm
Harleyholm
Carmichael
Carmichael Hill
Carmichael Ho
Carmichael Visitor Centre
East Mains
Thornyhills Fm
Howford
Shaws
Hyndford Bridge
Charleston
Langloch
Millhill
Cairngryffe Hill 340
Bonnington Mains
Falls of Clyde
Corra Linn
Bonnington Linn
Linnhead Fm
Wellshields
Langside Fm
Corramore Fm
Boreland
Bogside
Top Wood
Greenrig
Cloburn
Wellbrae
Covington
Quothquan
Parkhouse
Quothquan Law 335
Chester Hill
Thankerton
Fallburn
Park Knowe
Totherin Hill 479
Annieston
Symington
Symington Mill
Broadlees
Symington Ho
Townfoot Fm
Symington Mains Fm
Southholm
Swaites Hill
Heatheryhall
Northflatt
Quothquan Mill
Shieldhill
Biggar Common
Biggar Co
Loanhead
Cormiston Mains
Cormiston Towers Fm
Hillhead
Cowgill Upper Res
Camps Water
Fall Cleuch Wood
White Gill Wood
River Clyde
Clyde
M74
A74(M)
A70
A73
A72
A702
B7078
B7055
B7076
B797
B740
B7040
B7066
Ayr Road
Carlisle Road
NS
00
40
10
268
269
260
247

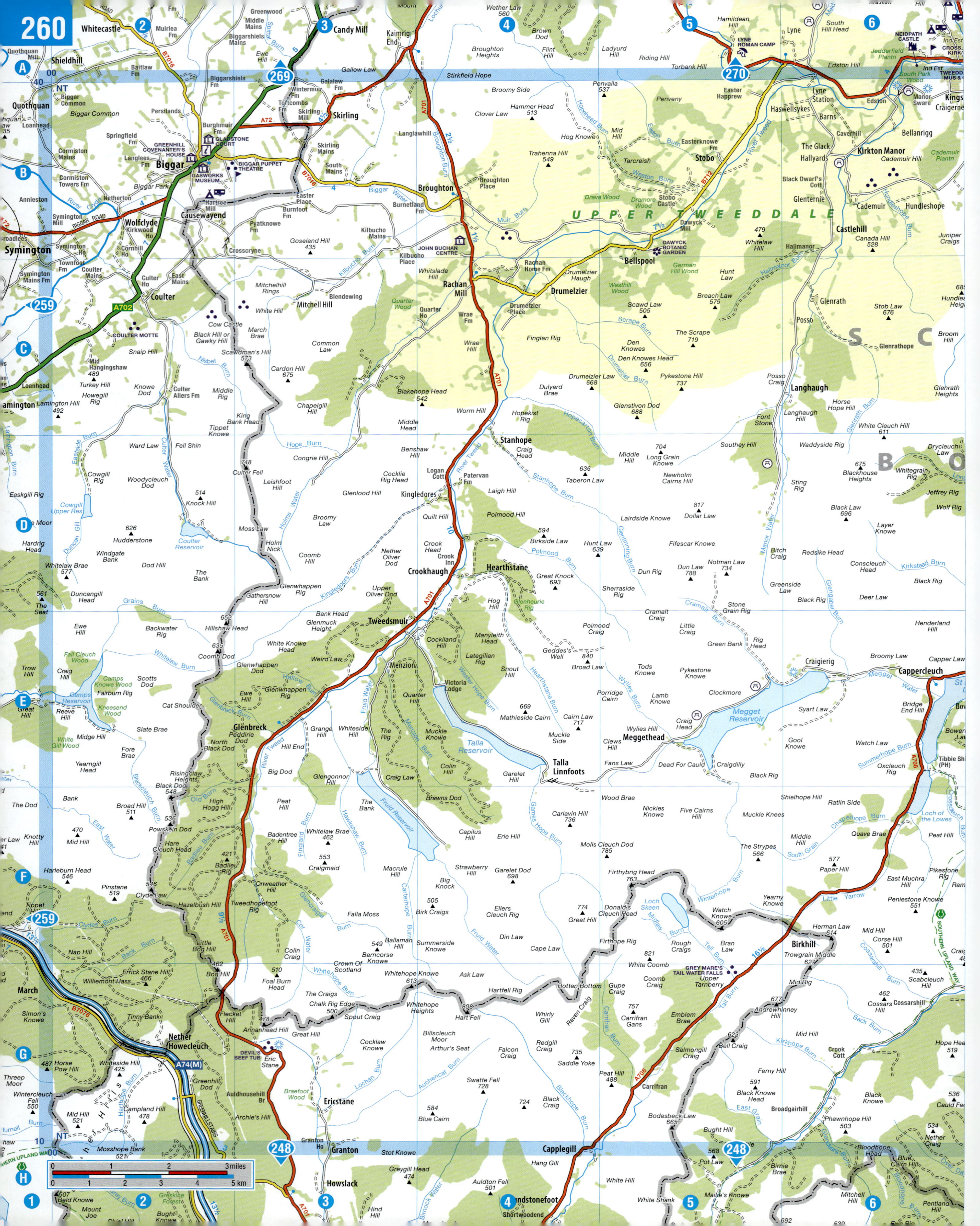
Whitecastle
Candy Mill
Kaimrig End
Weather Law 560
Hamildean Hill
Lyne
LYNE ROMAN CAMP
South Hill Head
NEIDPATH CASTLE
Jedderfield Plantn
Quothquan
Shieldhill
Biggar Common
Biggar
GREENHILL COVENANTER'S HOUSE
GLADSTONE COURT
BIGGAR PUPPET THEATRE
GASWORKS MUSEUM
Skirling
Broughton
Broughton Heights
Stirkfield Hope
Penvalla 537
Broomy Side
Hammer Head 513
Clover Law
Easter Happrew
Penveny
Lyne Station
Haswellsykes
Barns
Manor Sware
Kings
Edston
Cavehill
Bellanrigg
Kirkton Manor
Cademuir Hill
Hallyards
Stobo
Stobo Castle
Dawyck Mill
DAWYCK BOTANIC GARDEN
Bellspool
U P P E R   T W E E D D A L E
Trahenna Hill 549
Tarcreish
Dreva Wood
Black Dwarf's Cott
Glenternie
Cademuir
Hundleshope
Castlehill
Canada Hill 528
Juniper Craigs
Whitelaw Hill 479
Hallmanor
Symington
Wolfclyde
Causewayend
Crosscryne
Goseland Hill 435
Kilbucho Mains
JOHN BUCHAN CENTRE
Kilbucho Place
Rachan Mill
Rachan Home Fm
Drumelzier Haugh
Drumelzier
Whitslade Hill
Coulter
COULTER MOTTE
Mitchell Hill
Blendewing
Quarter Wood
Wrae Fm
Drumelzier Place
Scawd Law 505
Breach Law 575
Glenrath
Stob Law 676
Posso
Glenrathope
The Scrape 719
Den Knowes Head 656
Pykestone Hill 737
Drumelzier Law 668
Glenstivon Dod 688
Langhaugh
Lamington
Culter Fell 748
Hopekist Rig
Stanhope
Middle Hill
Long Grain Knowe 704
Taberon Law 636
Newholm Cairns Hill
Southey Hill
Waddyside Rig
White Cleuch Hill 611
Blackhouse Heights 675
Whitegrain Rig
Jeffrey Rig
Wolf Rig
Logan Cott
Paterván Fm
Laigh Hill
Kingledores
Glenlood Hill
Polmood Hill
Dollar Law 817
Lairdside Knowe
Black Law 696
Coulter Reservoir
Hudderstone 626
Birkside Law 594
Hunt Law 639
Fifescar Knowe
Crook Inn
Crookhaugh
Hearthstane
Great Knock 693
Dun Rig
Dun Law 788
Notman Law 734
Redside Head
Consceuch Head
Black Rig
Tweedsmuir
Glenwhappen Rig
Upper Oliver Dod
Manylieth Head
Polmood Craig
Cramalt Craig
Stone Grain Rig
Craigierig
Cappercleuch
Menzion
Victoria Lodge
Geddes's Well
Broad Law 840
Tods Knowe
Pykestone Knowe
Clockmore
Megget Reservoir
Glenbreck
Talla Reservoir
Talla Linnfoots
Mathieside Cairn 669
Cairn Law 717
Meggethead
Wylies Hill
Fans Law
Dead For Cauld
Craigdilly
Fruid Reservoir
Broad Hill 511
Badlieu Rig 421
Badentree Hill
Whitelaw Brae 462
Craigmaid 553
Molls Cleuch Dod 785
Firthybrig Head 763
The Strypes 566
Paper Hill 577
Garelet Dod 698
Great Hill 774
Donald's Cleuch Head
Loch Skeen
Birkhill
Herman Law 614
Trowgrain Middle 627
Ellers Cleuch Rig
Hart Fell 808
Hartfell Rig
Whitehope Knowe 613
Chalk Rig Edge 500
Spout Craig
Carrifran Gans 757
GREY MARE'S TAIL WATER FALLS
Bell Craig 623
Erickstane Hill
DEVIL'S BEEF TUB
Nether Howecleuch
Ericstane
Swatte Fell 728
Capplegill
Granton
Stot Knowe
Greygill Head 474
Howslack
Auldton Fell 501
Lindstonefoot
Shortwoodend
Moffat Water
River Tweed
A701
A702
A72
A708
A74(M)
B7016
B712
B7076
0 1 2 3 miles
0 1 2 3 4 5 km

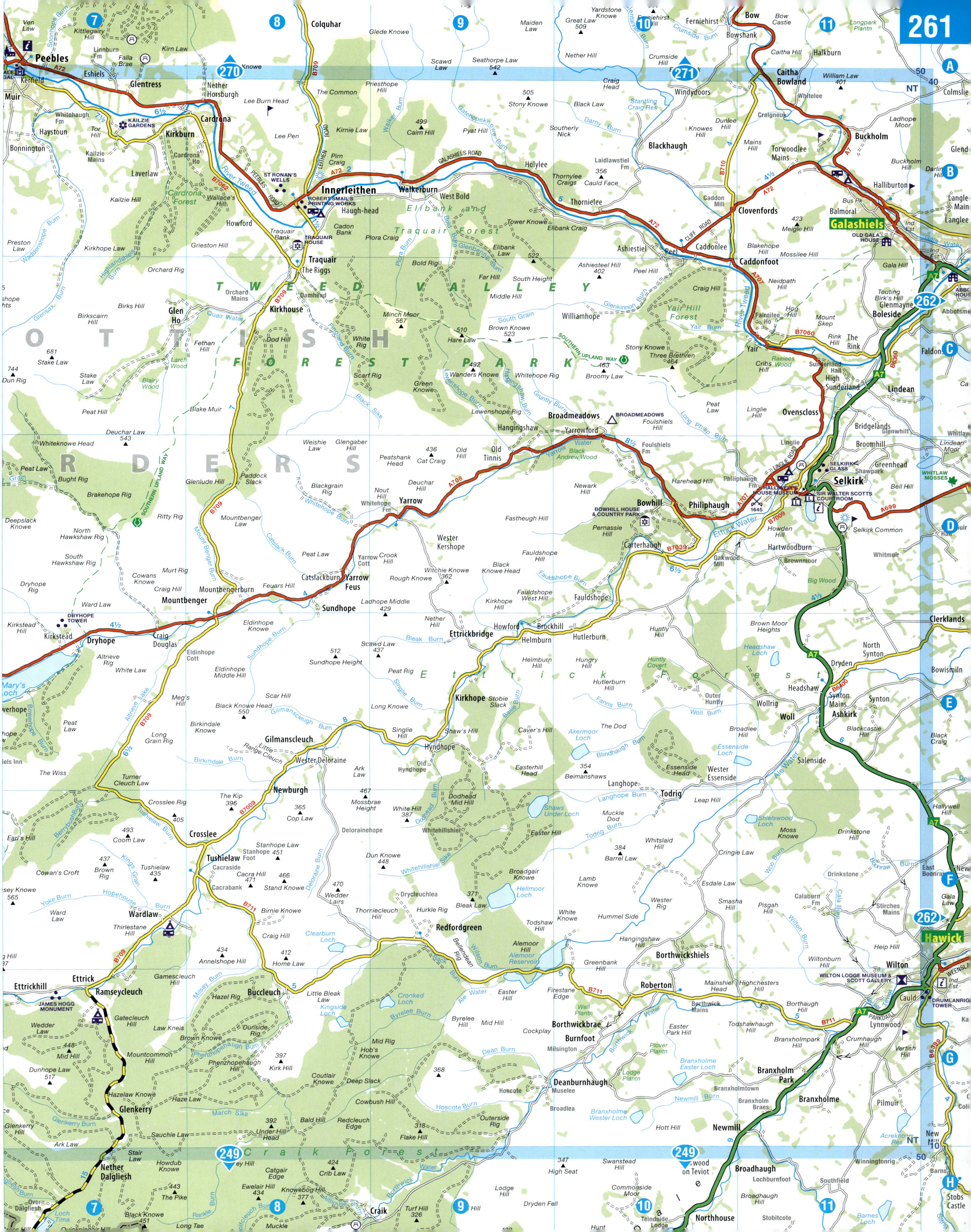
Peebles
Eshiels
Glentress
Kerfield
Cardrona
Kirkburn
Haystoun
Bonnington
Kailzie Gardens
Kailzie Mains
Laverlaw
Kailzie Hill
Cardrona Forest
Colquhar
Glede Knowe
Scawd Law
Seathorpe Law
Maiden Law
Great Law
Yardstone Knowe
Ferniehirst
Bow
Bow Castle
Bowshank
Caitha Hill
Halkburn
Longpark Plantn
Caitha Bowland
William Law
Colmslie
Windydoors
Whitelee
Nether Horsburgh
Lee Burn Head
The Common
Priesthope Hill
Stony Knowe
Black Law
Craig Head
Stantling Craig Res
Lee Pen
Kirnie Law
Cairn Hill
Pyat Hill
Southerly Nick
Blackhaugh
Knowes Hill
Dunlee Hill
Mains Hill
Torwoodlee Mains
Buckholm
Ladhope Moor
Glend
Buckholm Hill
Pirn Craig
Galashiels Road
Holylee
Laidlawstiel Fm
Thornylee Craigs
Cauld Face
St Ronan's Wells
Innerleithen
Walkerburn
West Bold
Thorniele
Caddon Mill
Clovenfords
Halliburton
Balmoral
Galashiels
Old Gala House
Langlee
Robert Smail's Printing Works
Haugh-head
Elibank and Traquair Forest
Tower Knowe
Elibank Craig
Meigle Hill
Mossilee Hill
Howford
Traquair Bank
Traquair House
Cadon Bank
Plora Craig
Elibank Law
Ashiestiel
Peel
Caddonlee
Blakehope Hill
Gala Hill
Preston Law
Kirkhope Law
Grieston Hill
Traquair
The Riggs
Bold Rig
Ashiestiel Hill
Peel Hill
Caddonfoot
Orchard Rig
Tweed Valley
Far Hill
South Height
Middle Hill
Craig Hill
Neidpath Hill
Orchard Mains
Oamhead
Kirkhouse
Glen Ho
Birks Hill
Birkscairn Hill
Quair Water
Minch Moor
Williamhope
Yair Hill Forest
Fairnilee Ho
Hog Hill
Mount Skep
Touting Birk's Hill
Glenmayne
Boleside
Abbotsford
Tweed Valley
Hare Law
Brown Knowe
South Grain
Southern Upland Way
Stony Knowe
Three Brethren
Yair
Rink Hill
The Rink
Faldonside
Fethan Hill
Dod Hill
White Rig
Stake Law
Dun Rig
Stake Law
Larch Wood
Blairy Wood
Scarf Rig
Wanders Knowe
Whitehope Rig
Broomy Law
Cribs Hill
Sunderland Hall
High Sunderland
Lindean
Green Knowe
Peat Hill
Blake Muir
Lewenshope Rig
Hangingshaw
Broadmeadows
Yarrowford
Foulshiels Hill
Foulshiels Fm
Peat Law
Linglie Hill
Ovenscloss
Bridgelands
Broomhill
Greenhead
Shawpark
Whitlaw Mosses
Lindean Moor
Whiteknowe Head
Deuchar Law
Weishie Law
Glengaber Hill
Peatshank Head
Cat Craig
Old Hill
Old Tinnis
Black Andrew Wood
Harehead Hill
Philiphaugh
Linglie
Selkirk Glass
Selkirk
Halliwell's House Museum
Sir Walter Scott's Courtroom
Bell Hill
Peat Law
Bught Rig
Brakehope Rig
Glenlude Hill
Paddock Slack
Blackgrain Rig
Nout Hill
Whitehope Fm
Yarrow
Deuchar Hill
Newark Hill
Bowhill
Bowhill House & Country Park
Philiphaugh
Ettrick Water
Selkirk Common
Deepslack Knowe
North Hawkshaw Rig
South Hawkshaw Rig
Ritty Rig
Mountberger Law
Fastheugh Hill
Pernassie Hill
Carterhaugh
Howden Hill
Hartwoodburn
Brownmoor
Whitmuir
Wester Kershope
Oakwood Mill
Big Wood
Dryhope Rig
Cowans Knowe
Craig Hill
Murt Rig
Mountbengerburn
Mountbenger
Peat Law
Yarrow Cott
Crook Hill
Catslackburn
Yarrow Feus
Rough Knowe
Witchie Knowe
Black Knowe Head
Fauldshope Hill
Fauldshope
Feuars Hill
Sundhope
Ladhope Middle
Kirkhope Hill
Fauldshope West Hill
Ward Law
Dryhope Tower
Kirkstead Hill
Kirkstead
Dryhope
Craig Douglas
Eldinhope Knowe
Nether Hill
Ettrickbridge
Howford
Brockhill
Helmburn
Hutlerburn
Huntly Hill
Brown Moor Heights
Clerklands
St Mary's Loch
Altrieve Rig
White Law
Eldinhope Cott
Eldinhope Middle Hill
Sundhope Height
Scawd Law
Peat Rig
Helmburn Hill
Hungry Hill
Huntly Covert
Headshaw Loch
North Synton
Dryden
Bowismiln
Ettrick Forest
Hutlerburn Hill
Headshaw
Synton Mains
Synton
Outer Huntly
Wollrig
Woll
Ashkirk
Meg's Hill
Scar Hill
Black Knowe Head
Long Knowe
Kirkhope
Stobie Slack
Fanns Burn
Woll Burn
Peat Law
Birkindale Knowe
Gilmanscleuch
Singlie Hill
Shaw's Hill
Caver's Hill
Akermoor Loch
The Dod
Broadlee Hill
Blackcastle Hill
Black Craig
Long Grain Rig
Little Range Cleuch
Wester Deloraine
Hyndhope
Old Hyndhope
Essenside Loch
Salenside
The Wiss
Turner Cleuch Law
Ark Law
Easterhill Head
Belmanshaws
Essenside Head
Wester Essenside
Newburgh
The Kip
Mossbrae Height
Dodhead Mid Hill
Langhope
Todrig
Leap Hill
Hallywell Hill
Crosslee Rig
Cop Law
White Hill
Shaws Under Loch
Langhope Burn
Earl's Hill
Coom Law
Crosslee
Deloraineshope
Whitehillshiel
Easter Hill
Muckle Dod
Shielswood Loch
Moss Knowe
Drinkstone Hill
Tushielaw
Stanhope Law
Stanhope Foot
Whitslaid Hill
Cringie Law
Brown Rig
Cowan's Croft
Cacraside
Cacra Hill
Stand Knowe
Dun Knowe
Barrel Law
Drinkstone
East Boonraw
Cacrabank
Broadgair Knowe
Lamb Knowe
Esdale Law
Hellmoor Loch
Wester Lairs
Drycleuchlea
Bleak Law
Wester Rig
Smasha Hill
Calaburn Fm
Gala Law
Stirches Mains
Ward Law
Wardlaw
Birnie Knowe
Thorniecleuch Hill
Hurkle Rig
Redfordgreen
White Knowe
Hummel Side
Pisgah Hill
Thirlestane Hill
Craig Hill
Clearburn Loch
Todshaw Hill
Hangingshaw Hill
Alemoor Hill
Alemoor Reservoir
Heip Hill
Hawick
Annelshope Hill
Home Law
Borthwickshiels
Wiltonburn Hill
Wilton
Greenbank Hill
Wilton Lodge Museum & Scott Gallery
Ettrickhill
Ettrick
Ramseycleuch
Gamescleuch Hill
Buccleuch
Little Bleak Law
Easter Hill
Firestane Edge
Roberton
Mainshiel Head
Highchesters Hill
Drumlanrig Tower
James Hogg Monument
Hazel Rig
Kingside Loch
Crooked Loch
Borthwick Mains
Borthwick Hill
Cauld
Gatecleuch Hill
Law Kneis
Dunside Rig
Byrelee Hill
Mid Hill
Well Plantn
Borthwickbrae
Easter Park Hill
Todshawhaugh Hill
Lynnwood
Wedder Law
Mid Hill
Brown Knowe
Mid Rig
Hob's Knowe
Cockplay
Burnfoot
Milsington
Plover Plantn
Branxholmpark Hill
Crumhaugh Hill
Vertish Hill
Mountcommon Hill
Phenzhopehaugh Hill
Dean Burn
Branxholme Easter Loch
Dunhope Law
Kirk Hill
Coutlair Knowe
Deep Slack
Lodge Plantn
Deanburnhaugh
Muselee
Branxholm Park
Hazelaw Knowe
Haze Law
Hoscote
Branxholmtown
Branxholme
Glenkerry
Cowbush Hill
Hoscote Burn
Broadlea
Newmill Burn
Branxholm Braes
Pilmuir
March Sike
Bald Hill
Redcleuch Edge
Outerside Rig
Branxholme Wester Loch
Glenkerry Hill
Under Hill Head
Flake Hill
Hott Hill
Newmill
Acreknowe Res
New Mill
Ark Law
Sauchie Law
Stair Law
Craik Forest
Swanstead Hill
Howdub Knowe
Crib Law
High Seat
Broadhaugh
Lochburnfoot
Winningtonrig
Nether Dalgliesh
Catgair Edge
Ewelair Hill
The Pike
Knowebog Hill
Lodge Hill
Commonside Moor
Branxholme Wester Loch
Broadhaugh Hill
Southfield
Barnes
Stobs Castle
Over Dalgliesh
Black Knowe
Craik
Turf Hill
Dryden Fell
Teindside Lodge
Northhouse
Stobicote
Long Tae
Muckle
River Tweed
Leithen Water
Yarrow Water
Ettrick Water
Ale Water
Borthwick Water
Southern Upland Way
Tweed Valley Forest Park
Borders

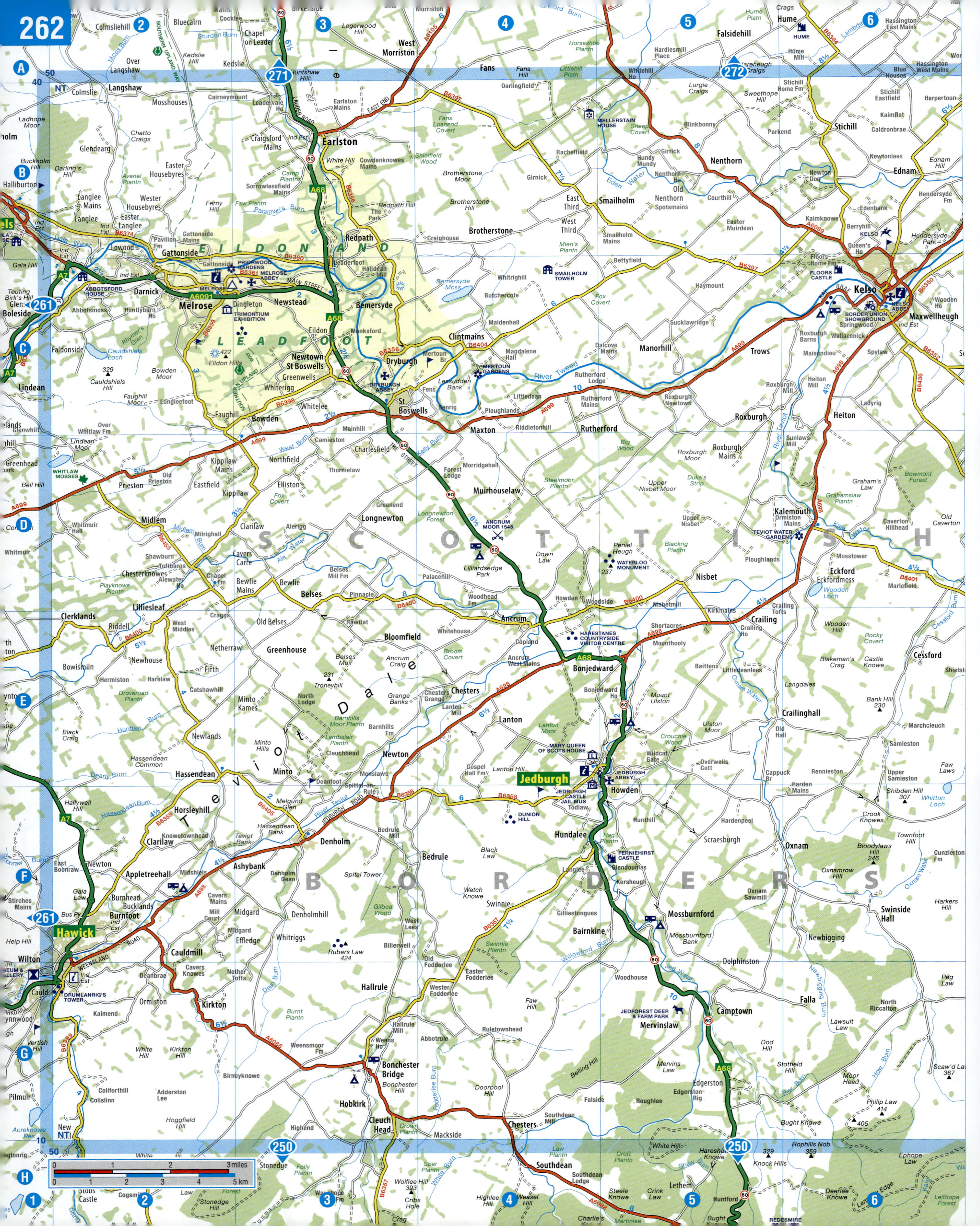
Colmslie
Bluecairn
Chapel on Leader
Legerwood Hill
West Morriston
Fans
Falsidehill
Hume
Crags
Hardiesmill Place
Langshaw
Over Langshaw
Kedslie
Colmslie
Mosshouses
Cairneymount
Leadervale Ho
Huntshaw Hill
Earlston Mains
Darlingfield
Whitehill Ho
Lurgie Craigs
Sweethope Hill
Stichill
Harpertoun
Kaimflat
Caldronbrae
Ladhope Moor
Chatto Craigs
Craigsford Mains
Earlston
Glendearg
Mellerstain House
Blinkbonny
Parkend
Rachelfield
Girrick
Hundy Mundy
Nenthorn
Newtonlees
Ednam
Buckholm Hill
Halliburton
Darling's Hill
Easter Housebyres
White Hill
Cowdenknowes Mains
Shielfield Wood
Brotherstone Moor
Girnick
Eden Water
Newton Don
Old Nenthorn
Courthill
Edenbank
Langlee Mains
Langlee
Wester Housebyres
Easter Langlee
Sorrowlessfield Mains
Redpath Hill
The Park
Brotherstone Hill
East Third
West Third
Smailholm
Smailholm Mains
Nenthorn Spotsmains
Easter Muirdean
Kaimknowe
Berryhill
Kelso
Hendersyde Park
Pavilion
Gattonside Mains
Gattonside
Redpath
Craighouse
Brotherstone
Bettyfield
Queen's Ho
Floors Home Fm
Floors Castle
Lowood
Eildon and Leadfoot
Leaderfoot
Priorwood Gardens
Melrose Abbey
Halidean Mill
Whitrighill
Smailholm Tower
Haymount
Gala Hill
Abbotsford House
Darnick
Melrose
Newstead
Bemersyde
Bemersyde Moss
Butchercote
Fox Covert
Maxwellheugh
Boleside
Abbotsmoss
Huntlyburn
Dingleton
Trimontium Exhibition
Eildon
Maidenhall
Sucklawridge
Border Union Showground
Springwood
Wooden Ho
Faldonside
Cauldshiels Loch
Monksford
Newtown St Boswells
Clintmains
Magdalene Hall
Dalcove Mains
Manorhill
Trows
Roxburgh Barns
Wallacenick
Spylaw
Eildon Hills
Dryburgh
Dryburgh Abbey
Mertoun Br
Mertoun Gardens
River Tweed
Rutherford Lodge
Maisendieu
Lindean
Cauldshiels Hill
Bowden Moor
Greenwells
Whiterigg
Faughill Moor
Longlee foot
Whitelee
Fens
St Boswells
Lessudden Bank
Littledean
Rutherford Mains
Roxburgh Mill
Roxburgh Newtown
Heiton Mill
Roxburgh
Heiton
Ladyrig
Faughill
Bowden
Benrig
Ploughlands
Riddleton hill
Maxton
Rutherford
Sunlaws Mill
Over Whitlaw Fm
Lindean Moor
Camieston
Mainhill
Charlesfield
Big Wood
Roxburgh Moor
Roxburgh Mains
Greenhead
Whitlaw Mosses
Prieston
Old Prieston
Kippilaw Mains
Northfield
Thornielaw
Forest Lodge
Morridgehall
Muirhouselaw
Steelmoor Plantn
Upper Nisbet Moor
Duke's Strip
Graham's Law
Bowmont Forest
Bell Hill
Eastfield
Kippilaw
Elliston
Fox Covert
Greenend
Longnewton Forest
Longnewton
Ancrum Moor 1545
Grahamslaw Plantn
Kalemouth
Ormiston Mains
Teviot Water Gardens
Old Caverton
Caverton Hillhead
Midlem
Mirighall
Clarilaw
Alerigg
Scottish
Upper Nisbet
Peniel Heugh
Blackrig Plantn
Ploughlands
Whitmuir Hall
Whitmuir
Shawburn
Toftbarns
Cavers Carre
Ale Water
Lilliardsedge Park
Down Law
Waterloo Monument
Mosstower
Eckford
Eckfordmoss
Marlefield
Chesterknowes
Alewater Ho
Playknowe Plantn
Chapel Fm
Bewlie Mains
Bewlie
Belses Mill Fm
Palacehill
Nisbet
Wooden Loch
Lilliesleaf
Belses
Pinnacle
Woodhead Fm
Howden
Woodside
Nisbetmill
Kirkmains
Crailing Tofts
Clerklands
Riddell
West Middles
Craggs
Old Belses
Rawflat
Ancrum
Shortacres
Crailing
Crailing Ho
Wooden Hill
Rocky Covert
Newhouse
Netherraw
Greenhouse
Bloomfield
Whitehouse
Harestanes Countryside Visitor Centre
Copland
Mounthooly
Cessford
Bowismiln
Firth
Belses Muir
Ancrum Craig
Broom Covert
Ancrum West Mains
Bonjedward
Baittens
Littledeanlees
Blakeman's Crag
Castle Knowe
Hermiston
Harelaw
Troneyhill
Bonjedward Ho
Langdales
Bank Hill
Catshawhill
Minto Kames
North Lodge
Grange Banks
Chesters Grange
Chesters
Mount Ulston
Oxnam Water
Droveroad Plantn
Teviot Dale
Barnhills Moor Plantn
Barnhills Fm
Lanton Mill
Lanton
Crailinghall
Marchcleuch
Black Craig
Huntaw Burn
Newlands
Minto Hills
Lambslair Plantn
Lanton Moor
Ulston Moor
Old Hall
Samieston
Cleuchhead
Newton
Mary Queen of Scots House
Crouchie Wood
Wildcat Gate
Overwells Cott
Hassendean Common
Minto
Deanfoot
Monslaws
Gospel Hall Fm
Lanton Hill
Jedburgh
Jedburgh Abbey
Howden
Cappuck Br
Rennieston
Harden Mains
Upper Samieston
Faw Laws
Hassendean
Jedburgh Castle Jail Mus
Shibden Hill
Whitton Loch
Hallywell Hill
Horsleyhill
Melgund Glen
Spittal-on-Rule
Todlaw
Dunion Hill
Hassendean Bank
River Teviot
Bedrule Mill
Hundalee
Hunthill
Hardenpeel
Crook Knowes
Townfoot Hill
Clarilaw
Knowetownhead
Teviot Bank
Denholm
Scraesburgh
Oxnam
Bloodylaws Hill
Cunzierton Fm
East Boonraw
Newton
Ashybank
Bedrule
Black Law
Ferniehirst Castle
Glendouglas
Oxnamrow Hill
Appletreehall
Midshiels
Denholm Dean
Spittal Tower
Kersheugh
Oxnam Sawmill
Gala Law
Burnhead
Cavers Mains
Bucklands
Burnfoot
Mill Court
Midgard
Denholmhill
Gilboa Wood
Watch Knowe
Swinnie
Gilliestongues
Mossburnford
Swinside Hall
Harkers Hill
Hawick
Effledge
Whitriggs
West Lees
Bairnkine
Mossburnford Bank
Newbigging
Cauldmill
Rubers Law
Billerwell
Swinnie Plantn
Willowford Burn
Wilton
Drumlanrig's Tower
Deanbrae
Cavers Knowes
Nether Tofts
Old Fodderlee
Easter Fodderlee
Woodhouse
Dolphinston
Jed Water
Peg Law
Hallrule
Wester Fodderlee
Faw Hill
Camptown
Falla
North Riccalton
Kaimend
Ormiston
Kirkton
Burnt Plantn
Jedforest Deer & Farm Park
Mervinslaw
Lawsuit Law
Hallrule Mill
Ruletownhead
Weens Ho
Abbotrule
Dod Hill
Vertish Hill
White Hill
Kirkton Hill
Weensmoor Fm
Bonchester Bridge
Belling Hill
Mervins Law
Stotfield Hill
Moor Head
Scaw'd Law
Birneyknowe
Bonchester Hill
Doorpool Hill
Edgerston
Edgerston Rig
Philip Law
Pilmuir
Coliforthill
Colislinn
Adderston Lee
Hobkirk
Falside
Roughlee
Hoggfield Hill
Highend
Cleuch Head
Mackside
Chesters
Southdean Mill
Bught Knowe
Hophills Nob
New
Acreknowe Res
White Hill
Harestanes Knowe
Knock Hills
Ephope Law
Stonedge
Folly Plantn
Spar Plantn
Wolfiee Hill
Law Plantn
Southdean
Croft Plantn
Southdean Lodge
Steele Knowe
Crink Law
Lethem
Deerlee Knowe
Stobs Castle
Cogsmill
Stonedge Hill
Cribs Hole
Highlee Hill
Weasel Hill
Huntford
Charlie's
Martinlee
Redesmire
Craig
Bught
Leithope Forest
Lamb Edge
3 miles
5 km

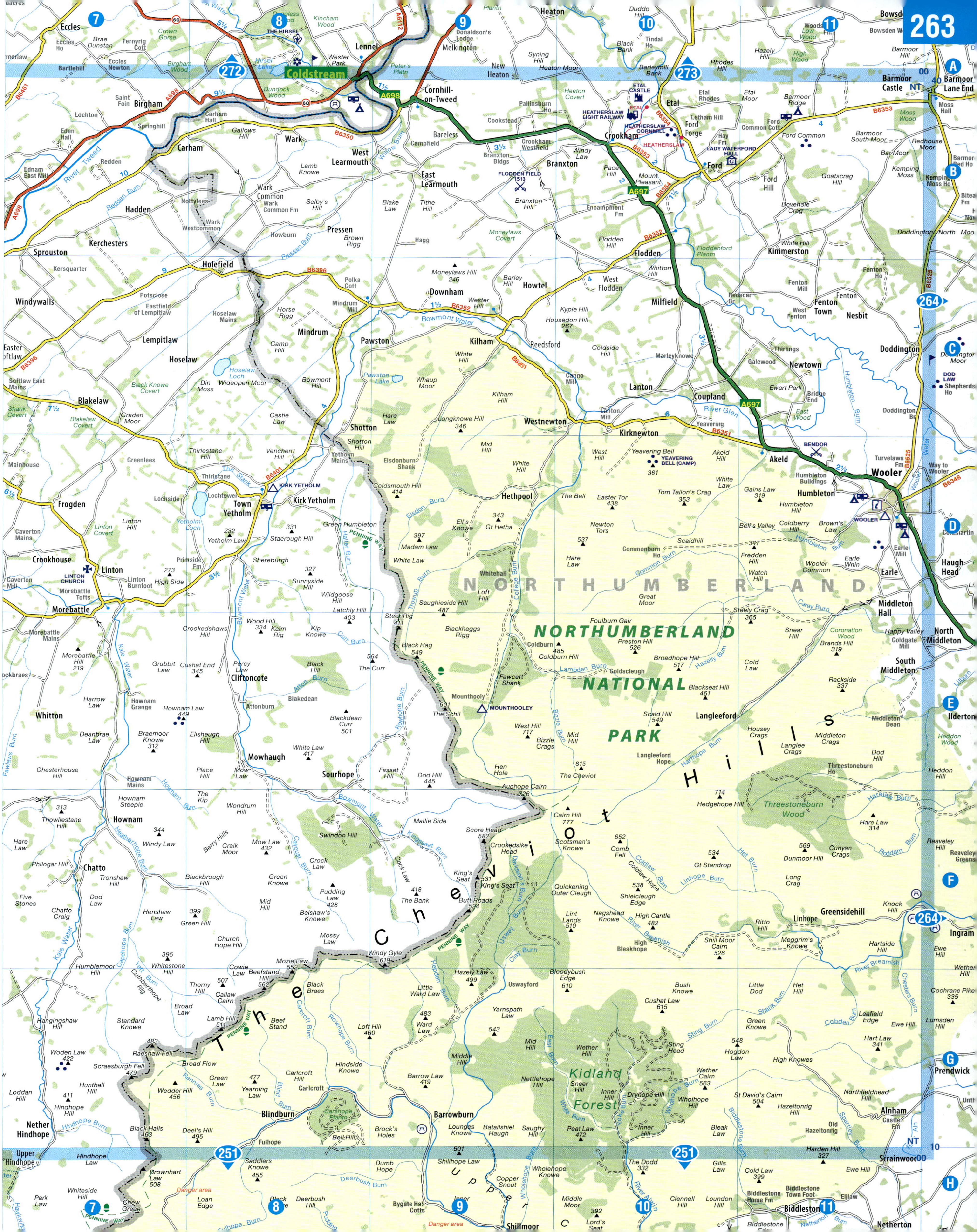
Coldstream
Cornhill-on-Tweed
Eccles
Birgham
Carham
Wark
Lennel
Melkington
Heaton
New Heaton
Etal
Etal Castle
Ford
Ford Forge
Crookham
Branxton
Flodden Field 1513
Flodden
Kimmerston
Milfield
Doddington
Fenton Town
Nesbit
Lanton
Coupland
Kirknewton
Westnewton
Kilham
Akeld
Wooler
Humbleton
Earle
Middleton Hall
North Middleton
South Middleton
Langleeford
Ilderton
Ingram
Greensidehill
Linhope
Alnham
Prendwick
Netherton
Biddlestone
Scrainwood
Shillmoor
Barrowburn
Blindburn
Nether Hindhope
Upper Hindhope
Kidland Forest
The Cheviot Hills
The Cheviot
815
NORTHUMBERLAND
NORTHUMBERLAND NATIONAL PARK
Hedgehope Hill
714
Yeavering Bell
361
Tom Tallon's Crag
Kirk Yetholm
Town Yetholm
Yetholm Loch
Linton
Morebattle
Frogden
Crookhouse
Hownam
Chatto
Whitton
Mowhaugh
Sourhope
Cliftoncote
Pawston
Mindrum
Downham
Howtel
Holefield
Sprouston
Hadden
Kerchesters
Lempitlaw
Hoselaw
Windywalls
Blakelaw
Shotton
Hethpool
Pressen
Learmouth
Windy Gyle
619
Pennine Way
Bowmont Water
College Burn
River Glen
River Breamish
River Tweed
Coquet
Usway Burn
Threestoneburn Wood
A697
A698
B6350
B6351
B6352
B6353
B6396
B6401
B6525
B6348
272
273
264
251
7
8
9
10
11
A
B
C
D
E
F
G
H

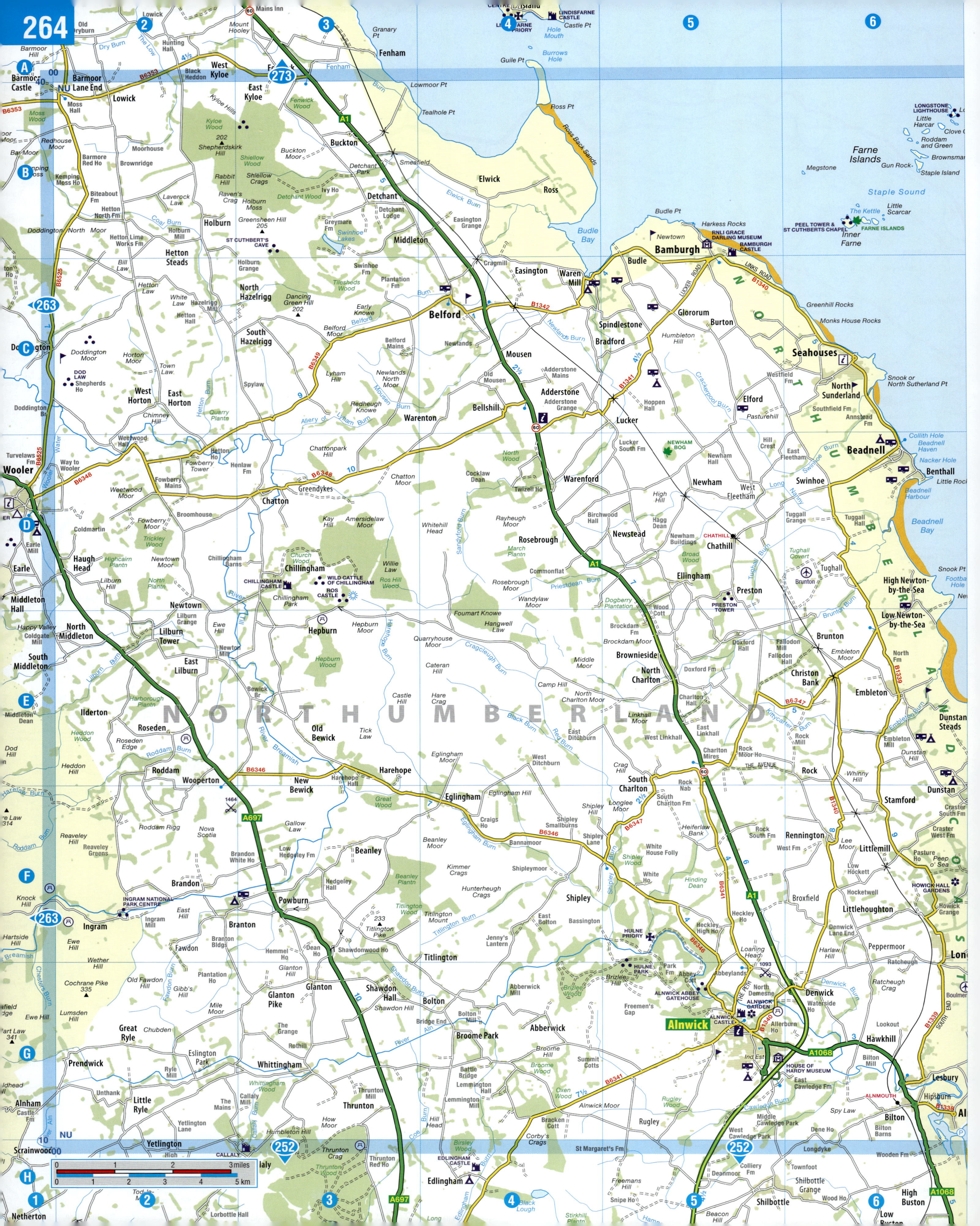
NORTHUMBERLAND
NORTHUMBERLAND COAST
Farne Islands
Staple Sound
Inner Farne
FARNE ISLANDS
LONGSTONE LIGHTHOUSE
Brownsman
Staple Island
Megstone
Gun Rock
Little Harcar
Clove C
Roddam and Green
The Kettle
Little Scarcar
PEEL TOWER & ST CUTHBERTS CHAPEL
LINDISFARNE CASTLE
Castle Pt
Hole Mouth
Burrows Hole
Guile Pt
Ross Pt
Ross Back Sands
Granary Pt
Fenham
Lowmoor Pt
Tealhole Pt
Budle Pt
Budle Bay
Harkess Rocks
RNLI GRACE DARLING MUSEUM
BAMBURGH CASTLE
Bamburgh
Newtown
Budle
Waren Mill
Easington
Belford
Buckton
Detchant
Middleton
Elwick
Ross
Lowick
West Kyloe
East Kyloe
Fenwick
Barmoor Castle
Barmoor Lane End
Holburn
Hetton Steads
North Hazelrigg
South Hazelrigg
Doddington
West Horton
East Horton
Wooler
Chatton
Chillingham
CHILLINGHAM CASTLE
WILD CATTLE OF CHILLINGHAM
ROS CASTLE
Hepburn
Lilburn Tower
East Lilburn
North Middleton
South Middleton
Middleton Hall
Earle
Ilderton
Roseden
Roddam
Wooperton
Old Bewick
New Bewick
Harehope
Eglingham
Beanley
Brandon
Powburn
Branton
Ingram
INGRAM NATIONAL PARK CENTRE
Glanton
Glanton Pike
Shawdon Hall
Bolton
Titlington
Broome Park
Abberwick
Whittingham
Great Ryle
Little Ryle
Prendwick
Alnham
Yetlington
Callaly
Thrunton
Edlingham
EDLINGHAM CASTLE
Netherton
Scrainwood
Alnwick
ALNWICK CASTLE
ALNWICK GARDEN
ALNWICK ABBEY GATEHOUSE
HULNE PRIORY
HULNE PARK
HOUSE OF HARDY MUSEUM
Rugley
Shilbottle
Denwick
Lesbury
Hipsburn
Alnmouth
Bilton
High Buston
Hawkhill
Littlehoughton
Longhoughton
HOWICK HALL GARDENS
Littlemill
Rennington
Stamford
Dunstan
Rock
Embleton
Christon Bank
Brunton
Low Newton-by-the-Sea
High Newton-by-the-Sea
Tughall
Preston
PRESTON TOWER
Ellingham
Chathill
Newham
Beadnell
Beadnell Bay
Swinhoe
Benthall
Seahouses
North Sunderland
Elford
Burton
Glororum
Spindlestone
Bradford
Lucker
Adderstone
Mousen
Bellshill
Warenton
Warenford
Newstead
Rosebrough
NEWHAM BOG
Brownieside
North Charlton
South Charlton
Shipley
Bassington
Dunstan Steads
Craster
Snook Pt
Greenhill Rocks
Monks House Rocks
Snook or North Sutherland Pt
Collith Hole
Nacker Hole
Football Hole
A1
A697
A1068
B6353
B6525
B6348
B6349
B1342
B1341
B1340
B1339
B6347
B6346
B6341
B1338
263
273
252
1 2 3 4 5 6
A B C D E F G H
0 1 2 3 miles
0 1 2 3 4 5 km

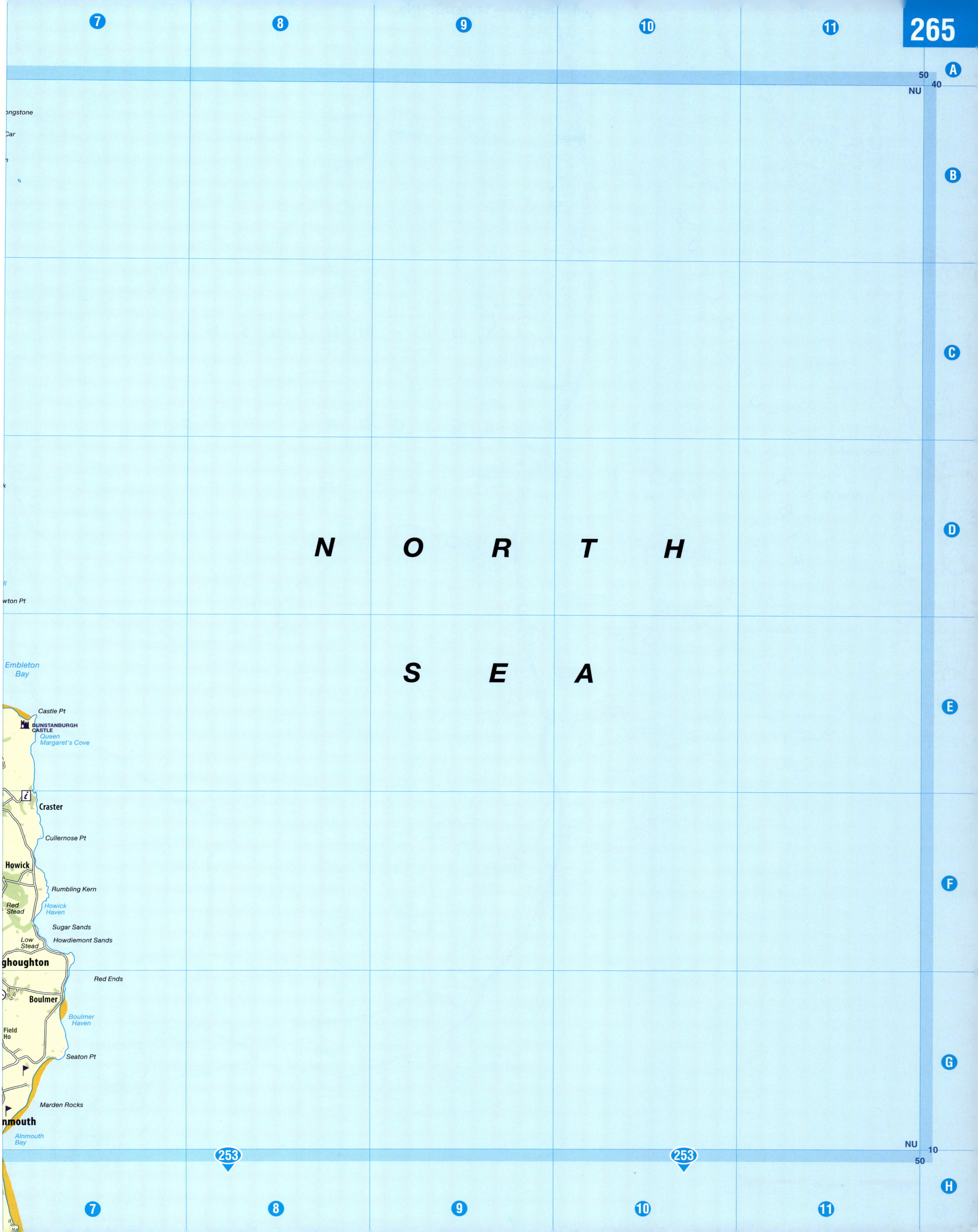
NORTH SEA
Embleton Bay
Castle Pt
DUNSTANBURGH CASTLE
Queen Margaret's Cove
Craster
Cullernose Pt
Howick
Rumbling Kern
Red Stead
Howick Haven
Sugar Sands
Low Stead
Howdiemont Sands
Red Ends
Boulmer
Boulmer Haven
Field Ho
Seaton Pt
Marden Rocks
Alnmouth Bay
NU
50
40
10
253
253
7
8
9
10
11
A
B
C
D
E
F
G
H

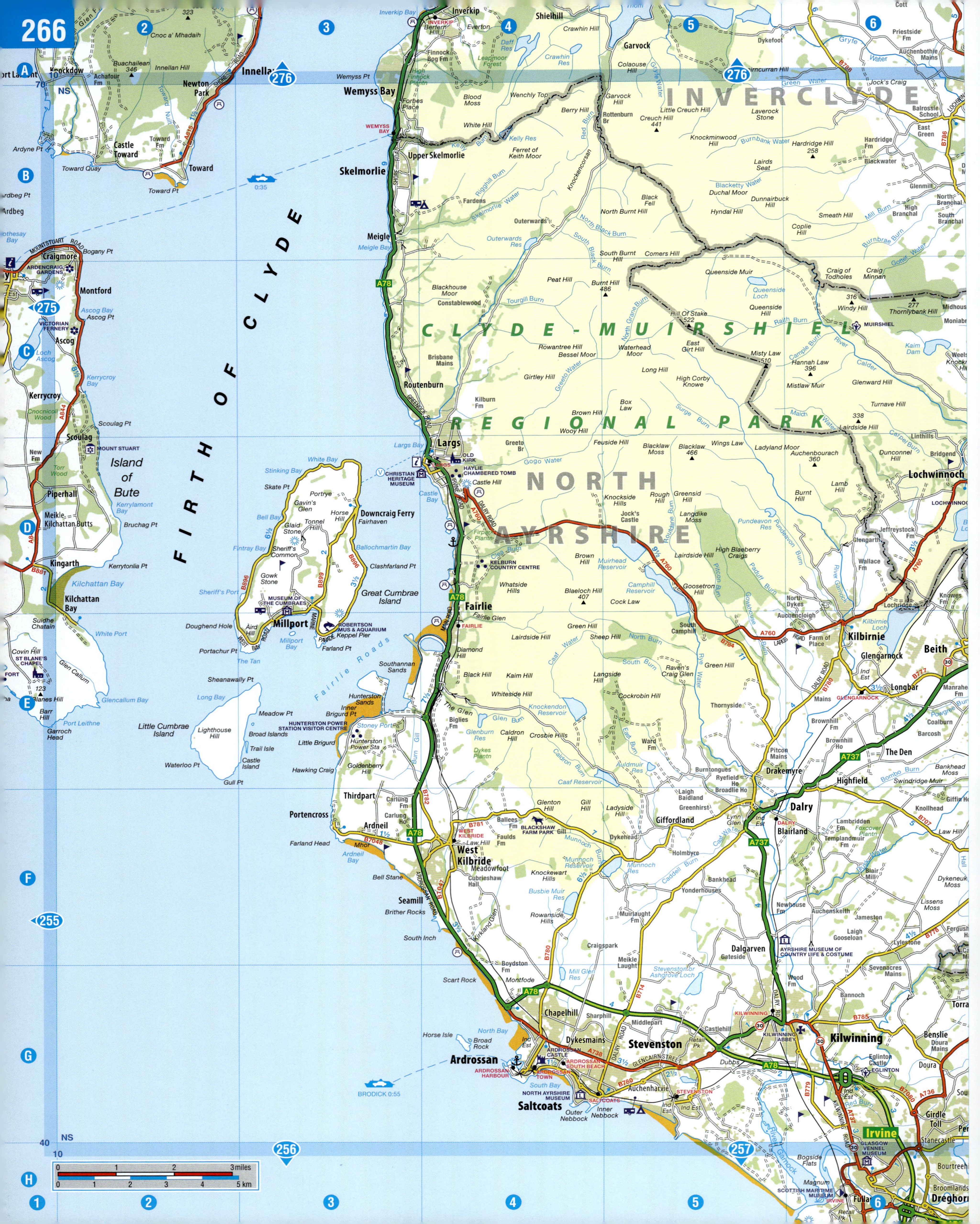
FIRTH OF CLYDE
INVERCLYDE
CLYDE-MUIRSHIEL REGIONAL PARK
NORTH AYRSHIRE
Island of Bute
Great Cumbrae Island
Little Cumbrae Island
Inverkip
Wemyss Bay
Skelmorlie
Upper Skelmorlie
Meigle
Largs
Fairlie
Millport
Portencross
Ardneil
West Kilbride
Seamill
Ardrossan
Saltcoats
Stevenston
Kilwinning
Irvine
Dalry
Kilbirnie
Beith
Glengarnock
Longbar
Lochwinnoch
Garvock
Shielhill
Innellan
Toward
Castle Toward
Craigmore
Montford
Ascog
Kerrycroy
Scoulag
Piperhall
Kingarth
Kilchattan Bay
Drakemyre
Blairland
Dalgarven
Chapelhill
Dykesmains
Auchenharvie
Highfield
The Den
Giffordland
Fullarton
Dreghorn
A78
A760
A737
B780
B714
Brodick 0:55
0:35
255
256
257
275
276
0 1 2 3 miles
0 1 2 3 4 5 km

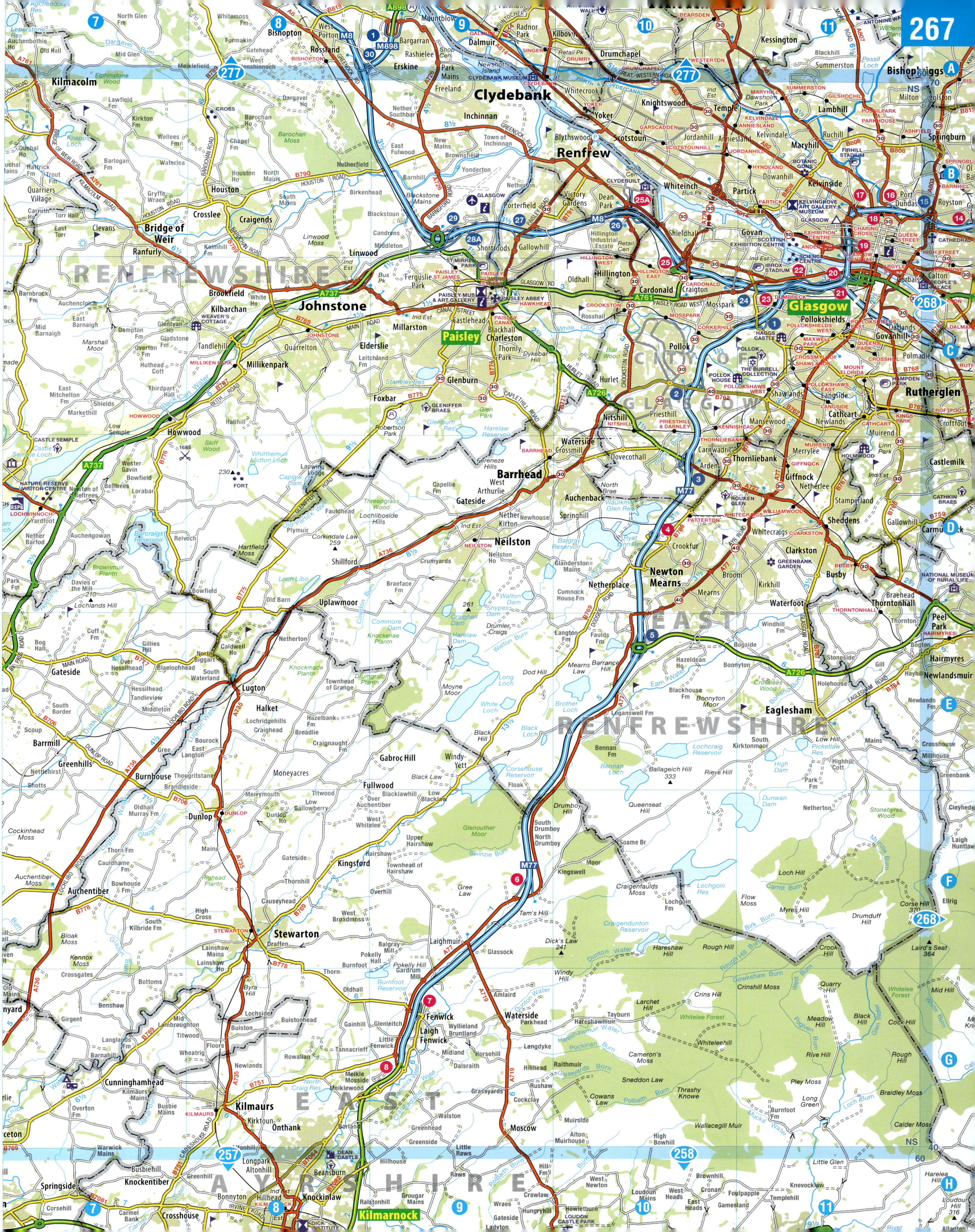
Glasgow
Paisley
Kilmarnock
Clydebank
Renfrew
Johnstone
Barrhead
Neilston
Newton Mearns
Eaglesham
Rutherglen
Stewarton
Kilmaurs
Dunlop
Lugton
Uplawmoor
Kilmacolm
Bridge of Weir
Houston
Kilbarchan
Howwood
Elderslie
Linwood
Erskine
Bishopton
Dalmuir
Knightswood
Scotstoun
Partick
Govan
Cardonald
Pollok
Pollokshields
Giffnock
Clarkston
Busby
Thornliebank
Cathcart
Castlemilk
Carmunnock
Fenwick
Laigh Fenwick
Waterside
Moscow
Kingsford
Burnhouse
Auchentiber
Cunninghamhead
Crosshouse
Knockentiber
Knockinlaw
Springside
Barrmill
Gateside
Caldwell
Halket
RENFREWSHIRE
EAST RENFREWSHIRE
CITY OF GLASGOW
EAST AYRSHIRE
M8
M77
M898
A737
A736
A726
A735
A77
A719
A761
B775
277
257
258
268

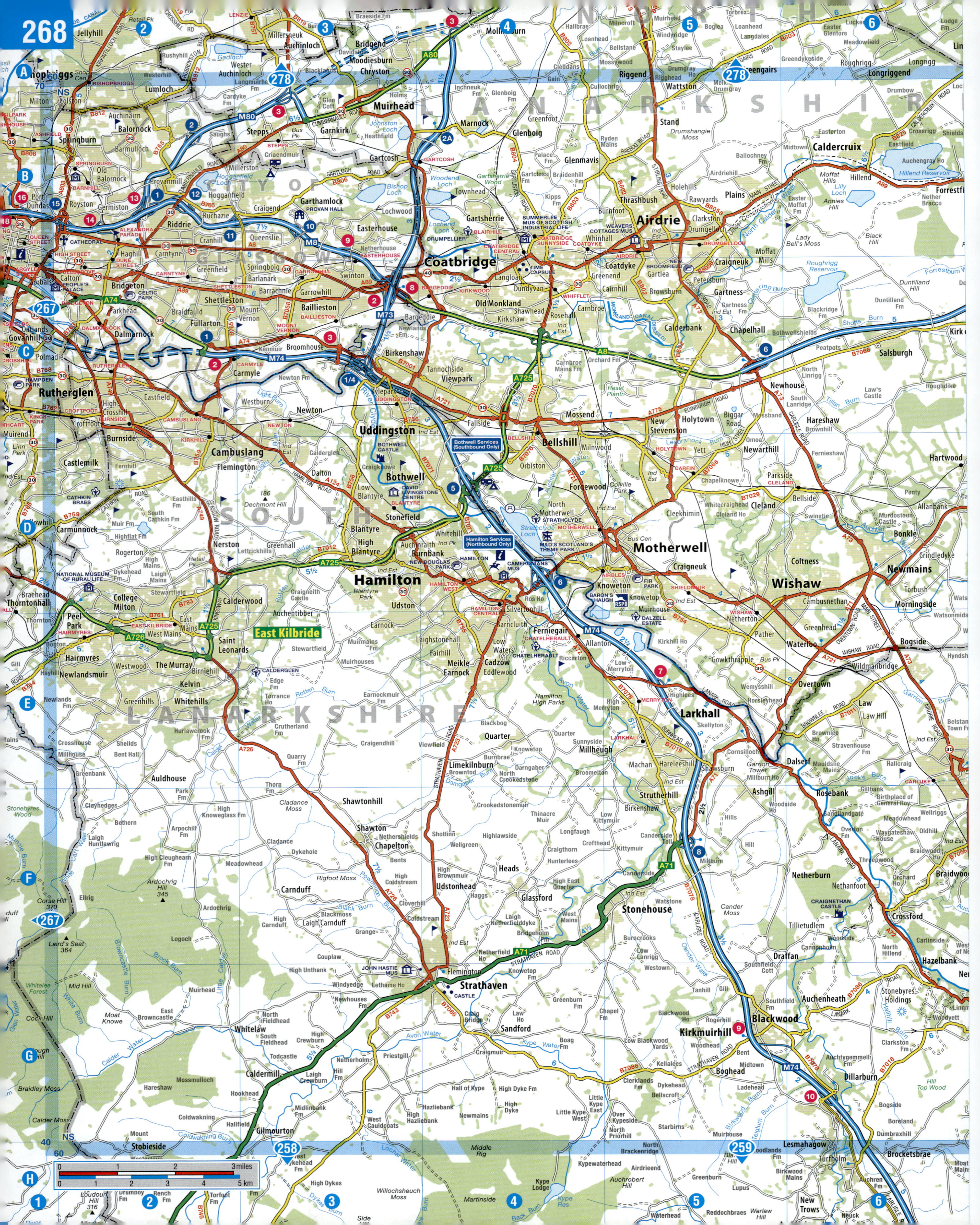
NORTH LANARKSHIRE
GLASGOW
SOUTH LANARKSHIRE
Springburn
Riddrie
Stepps
Muirhead
Chryston
Moodiesburn
Glenboig
Glenmavis
Gartcosh
Garnkirk
Baillieston
Coatbridge
Airdrie
Plains
Caldercruix
Calderbank
Chapelhall
Salsburgh
Newhouse
Holytown
Bellshill
Uddingston
Viewpark
Bothwell
Rutherglen
Cambuslang
Carmyle
Castlemilk
Carmunnock
Blantyre
Hamilton
Motherwell
Wishaw
Newmains
Cleland
Craigneuk
Overtown
Larkhall
Dalserf
Rosebank
Netherburn
Stonehouse
Strathaven
Blackwood
Kirkmuirhill
Lesmahagow
Auchenheath
Crossford
East Kilbride
Thorntonhall
Waterfoot
Eaglesham
Chapelton
Sandford
Glassford
Quarter
Ashgill
Shotts
Carluke
Bogside
Braidwood
Brocketsbrae
Hazelbank
Stonebyres Holdings
Whitelaw
Caldermill
Gilmourton
Auldhouse
Jackton
Nerston
High Blantyre
Stonefield
Burnbank
Newton
Halfway
Flemington
Kirkton
Mossend
Newarthill
Carfin
Fortissat
Greengairs
Longriggend
Wattston
Riggend
Forrestfield
Hillend Reservoir
Strathclyde Loch
Avon Water
River Clyde
Calder Water
Black Burn
M74
M73
M8
M80
A71
A72
A73
A74
A80
A89
A721
A723
A725
A726
A8
0 1 2 3 miles
0 1 2 3 4 5 km

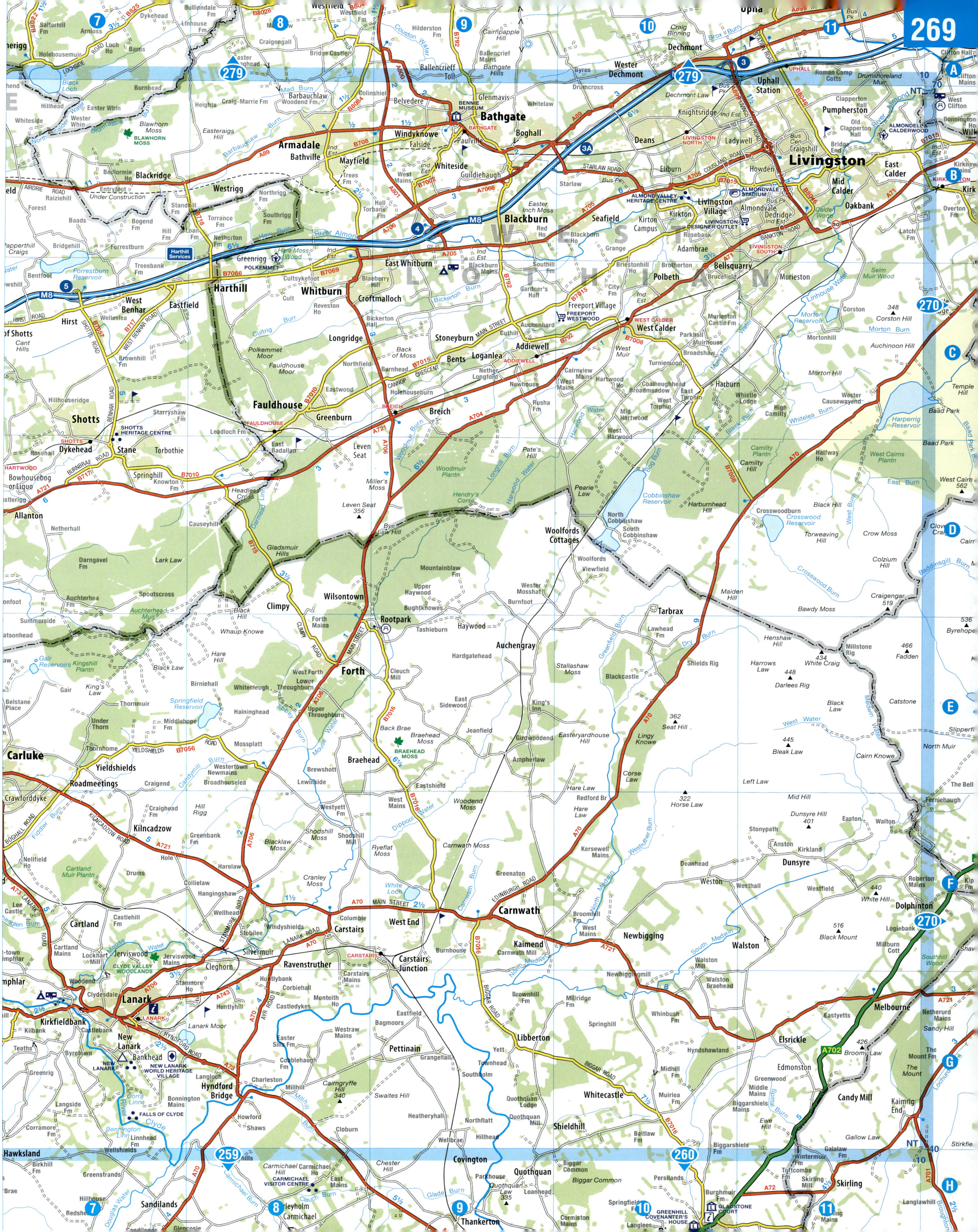
Bathgate
Armadale
Bathville
Livingston
Uphall Station
Dechmont
Wester Dechmont
Deans
Ladywell
Knightsridge
Eliburn
Howden
Craigshill
Mid Calder
East Calder
Oakbank
Kirkton Campus
Livingston Village
Almondvale
Dedridge
Seafield
Blackburn
Whitburn
Harthill
Eastfield
West Benhar
Hirst
Shotts
Dykehead
Stane
Fauldhouse
Greenburn
Longridge
Stoneyburn
Addiewell
Loganlea
Bents
Breich
West Calder
Polbeth
Bellsquarry
Murieston
Harburn
Blackridge
Westrigg
Whiteside
Mayfield
Boghall
Croftmalloch
East Whitburn
Leven Seat
Tarbrax
Auchengray
Woolfords Cottages
Wilsontown
Forth
Rootpark
Climpy
Braehead
Carluke
Yieldshields
Roadmeetings
Kilncadzow
Carstairs
Carstairs Junction
West End
Carnwath
Kaimend
Cartland
Lanark
Kirkfieldbank
New Lanark
Hyndford Bridge
Ravenstruther
Pettinain
Libberton
Whitecastle
Newbigging
Walston
Dunsyre
Dolphinton
Elsrickle
Candy Mill
Skirling
Covington
Thankerton
Quothquan
Carmichael
Sandilands
Hawksland
Shieldhill
Allanton
Cobbinshaw Reservoir
Harperrig Reservoir
WEST LOTHIAN
M8
A70
A71
A706
A721
A73
A702
279
270
260
259

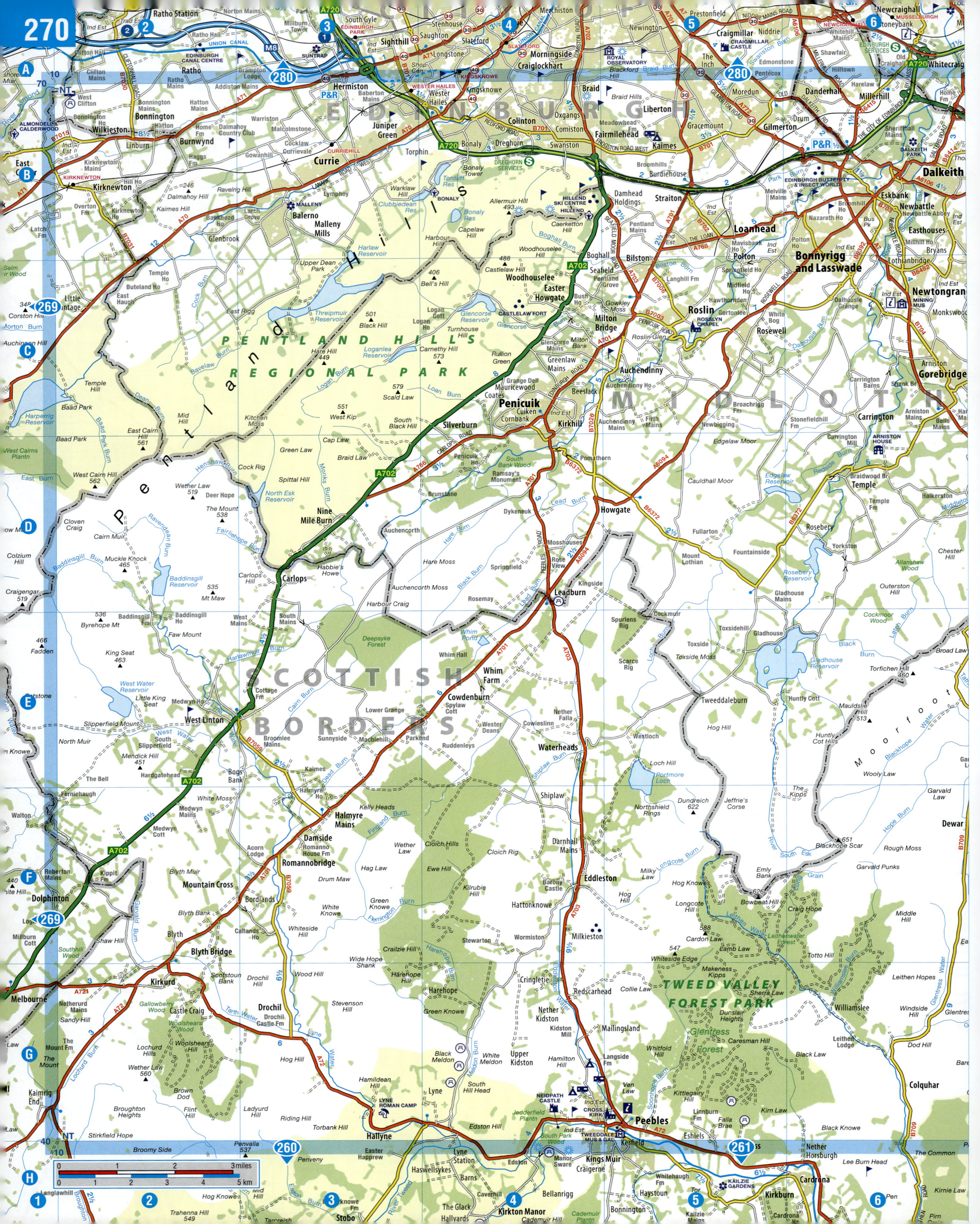

EDINBURGH
Ratho Station
Ratho
Hermiston
Sighthill
Longstone
Slateford
Merchiston
Morningside
Craiglockhart
Newington
Prestonfield
Craigmillar
Niddrie
Newcraighall
Whitecraig
Juniper Green
Colinton
Oxgangs
Liberton
Gilmerton
Danderhall
Millerhill
Dalkeith
Eskbank
Newbattle
Easthouses
Currie
Balerno
Malleny Mills
Bonnington
Wilkieston
Burnwynd
Kirknewton
East Calder
Straiton
Loanhead
Bilston
Bonnyrigg and Lasswade
Newtongrange
Gorebridge
Roslin
Rosewell
Milton Bridge
Auchendinny
Penicuik
Silverburn
Woodhouselee
Easter Howgate
Kirkhill
Howgate
Carrington
Temple
Pentland Hills
PENTLAND HILLS REGIONAL PARK
M I D L O T H I A N
SCOTTISH BORDERS
Carlops
Nine Mile Burn
Leadburn
Whim Farm
Cowdenburn
West Linton
Waterheads
Halmyre Mains
Romannobridge
Mountain Cross
Eddleston
Blyth Bridge
Dolphinton
Kirkurd
Drochil
Lyne
Hallyne
Peebles
Cardrona
Kirkburn
Kings Muir
Kirkton Manor
Stobo
Melbourne
Colquhar
Dewar
Moorfoot
TWEED VALLEY FOREST PARK
280
269
260
261
A720
A702
A701
A703
A72
A721
A6094
B6372
M8

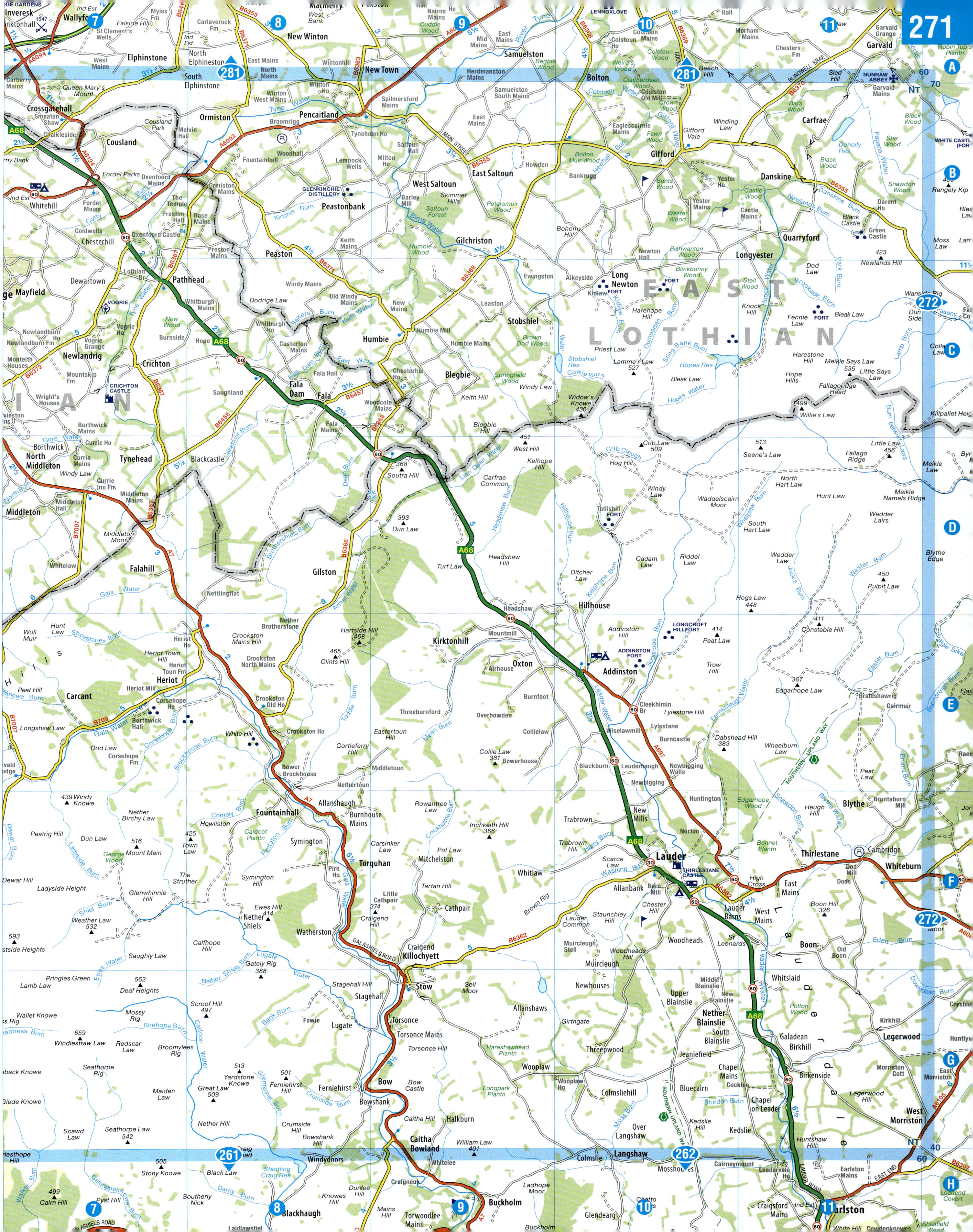
Inveresk
Wallyford
Elphinstone
New Winton
Macmerry
Samuelston
Bolton
Morham
Garvald
Crossgatehall
Ormiston
Pencaitland
New Town
Cousland
Gifford
Carfrae
Danskine
East Saltoun
West Saltoun
Whitehill
Peastonbank
Gilchriston
Quarryford
Longyester
Peaston
Pathhead
Dewartown
Mayfield
Long Newton
EAST
LOTHIAN
Newlandrig
Crichton
Humbie
Stobshiel
Blegbie
Fala Dam
Fala
CRICHTON CASTLE
Tynehead
North Middleton
Middleton
Falahill
Gilston
Hillhouse
Kirktonhill
Oxton
Addinston
Heriot
Carcant
Fountainhall
Allanshaugh
Symington
Torquhan
Lauder
THIRLESTANE CASTLE
Thirlestane
Whiteburn
Blythe
Watherston
Cathpair
Killochyett
Stow
Stagehall
Lugate
Torsonce
Wooplaw
Threepwood
Bow
Bowshank
Caitha Bowland
Langshaw
Colmslie
Kedslie
Nether Blainslie
Legerwood
Birkenside
West Morriston
Blackhaugh
Buckholm
Earlston
Boon
Whitslaid
Lauderdale
GALASHIELS ROAD
SOUTHERN UPLAND WAY
A68
A7
A697
B6355
B6368
B6362

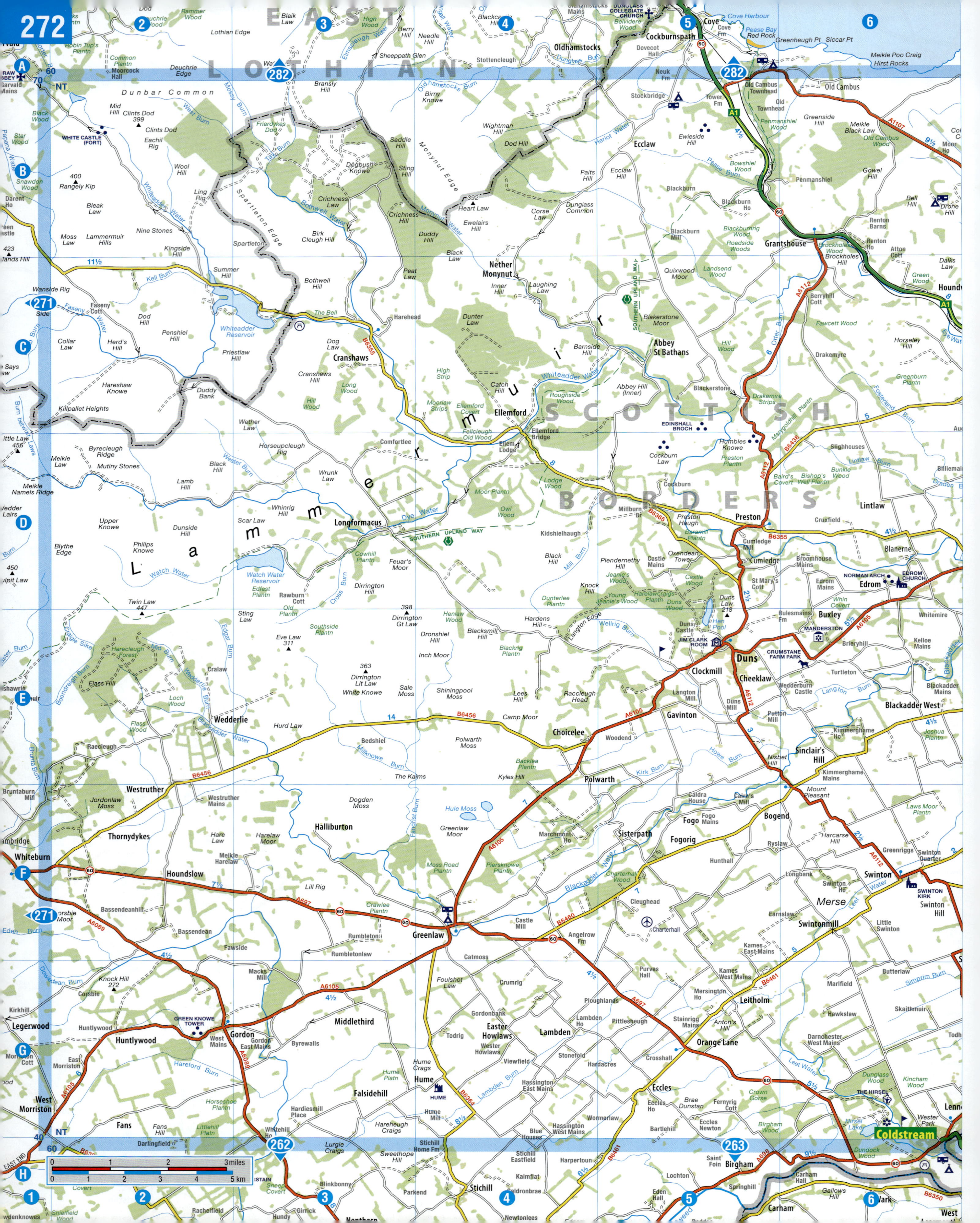
EAST LOTHIAN
SCOTTISH BORDERS
Lammermuir
Cockburnspath
Cove
Oldhamstocks
Dunbar Common
Stottencleugh
Old Cambus
Ecclaw
Grantshouse
Penmanshiel
Cranshaws
Whiteadder Reservoir
Ellemford
Abbey St Bathans
Longformacus
Preston
Lintlaw
Duns
Clockmill
Cheeklaw
Edrom
Blanerne
Buxley
Gavinton
Wedderlie
Westruther
Choicelee
Polwarth
Thornydykes
Whiteburn
Houndslow
Halliburton
Sisterpath
Fogo
Fogorig
Bogend
Sinclair's Hill
Swinton
Swintonmill
Merse
Blackadder West
Greenlaw
Gordon
Huntlywood
Legerwood
Middlethird
Easter Howlaws
Lambden
Leitholm
Orange Lane
Eccles
Hume
Falsidehill
Fans
West Morriston
Stichill
Birgham
Coldstream
Carham
Watch Water
Dye Water
Blackadder Water
Whiteadder Water
Southern Upland Way
A1
A6112
A6105
A697
A6089
B6355
B6456
B6460
B6461
B6364
B6365
B6438
A1107
B6350
282
271
262
263
0 1 2 3 miles
0 1 2 3 4 5 km

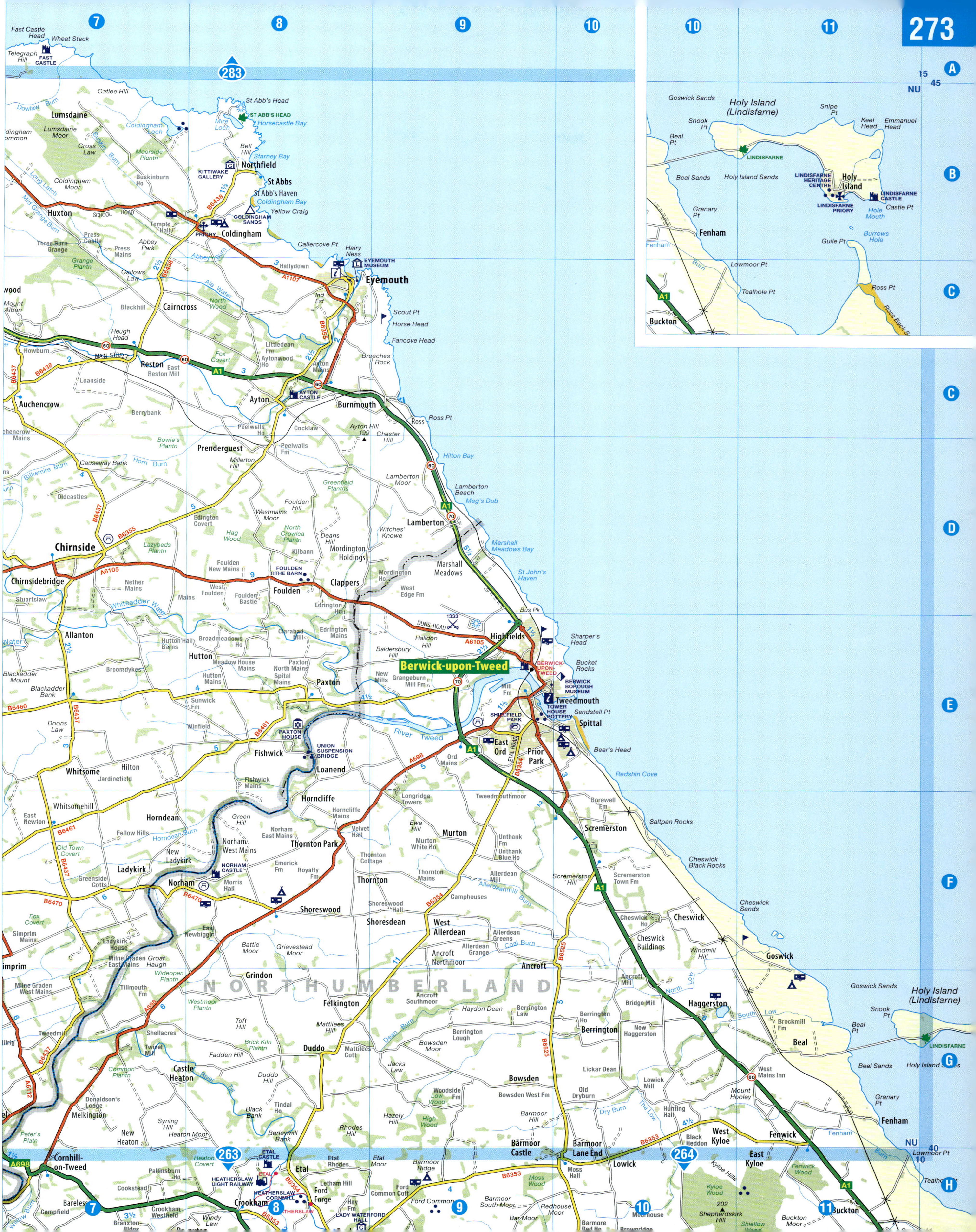
Fast Castle Head
Wheat Stack
Telegraph Hill
FAST CASTLE
Oatlee Hill
St Abb's Head
ST ABB'S HEAD
Horsecastle Bay
Mire Loch
Lumsdaine
Lumsdaine Moor
Coldingham Loch
Cross Law
Moorside Plantn
Bell Hill
Starney Bay
KITTIWAKE GALLERY
Northfield
St Abbs
St Abb's Haven
Coldingham Bay
COLDINGHAM SANDS
Yellow Craig
Buskinburn Ho
Coldingham Moor
Long Latch
Mid Grange Burn
Huxton
SCHOOL ROAD
Temple Hall
PRIORY
Coldingham
Three Burn Grange
Press Castle
Press Mains
Abbey Park
Abbey Burn
Grange Plantn
Gallows Law
Callercove Pt
Hairy Ness
EYEMOUTH MUSEUM
Hallydown
A1107
Eyemouth
Ale Water
North Wood
Ind Est
Mount Alban
Blackhill
Cairncross
Scout Pt
Horse Head
Fancove Head
Heugh Head
Howburn
MAIN STREET
Reston
East Reston Mill
Fox Covert
Littledean Fm
Aytonwood Ho
Ayton Mains
Breeches Rock
Loanside
Auchencrow
Berrybank
Ayton
AYTON CASTLE
Burnmouth
Ross
Ross Pt
Peelwalls Ho
Cocklaw
Ayton Hill 199
Chester Hill
Bowie's Plantn
Prenderguest
Peelwalls Fm
Millerton Hill
Hilton Bay
Causeway Bank
Horn Burn
Billiemire Burn
Oldcastles
Lamberton Moor
Greenfield Plantns
Lamberton Beach
Meg's Dub
Foulden Hill
Westmains Moor
Edington Covert
Hag Wood
North Crowlea Plantn
Witches' Knowe
Lamberton
Deans Hill
Kilbann
Mordington Holdings
Marshall Meadows Bay
Chirnside
Lazybeds Plantn
Foulden New Mains
FOULDEN TITHE BARN
Marshall Meadows
St John's Haven
Chirnsidebridge
Nether Mains
Mordington Ho
Clappers
Stuartslaw
West Foulden
Foulden Bastle
Fouldon
West Edge Fm
Whiteadder Water
Edrington Ho
Mains
Bus Pk
DUNS ROAD
Allanton
Hutton Hall Barns
Broadmeadows Ho
Clarabad Mill
Edrington Mains
Halidon Hill
Highfields
Sharper's Head
Hutton
Meadow House Mains
Baldersbury Hill
Berwick-upon-Tweed
BERWICK-UPON-TWEED
Bucket Rocks
Blackadder Mount
Broomdykes
Hutton Mains
Paxton North Mains
Spital Mains
Paxton
New Mills
Grangeburn Mill Fm
Mill Fm
BERWICK BOROUGH MUSEUM
Blackadder Bank
Sunwick Fm
Tweedmouth
TOWER HOUSE POTTERY
Sandstell Pt
Doons Law
Winfield
PAXTON HOUSE
SHIELFIELD PARK
Spittal
River Tweed
East Ord
Bear's Head
UNION SUSPENSION BRIDGE
Fishwick
Ord Mains
ETAL ROAD
Prior Park
Whitsome
Hilton
Jardinefield
Loanend
Redshin Cove
Fishwick Mains
Horncliffe
Longridge Towers
Tweedmouthmoor
Borewell Fm
Whitsomehill
Horncliffe Mains
Saltpan Rocks
Horndean
Green Hill
Velvet Hall
East Newton
Norham East Mains
Ewe Hill
Murton
Scremerston
Fellow Hills
Horndean Burn
Norham West Mains
Thornton Park
Murton White Ho
Unthank Fm
Unthank Blue Ho
Old Town Covert
New Ladykirk
Thornton Cottage
Cheswick Black Rocks
Ladykirk
NORHAM CASTLE
Emerick Fm
Royalty Fm
Thornton
Thornton Mains
Allerdean Mill
Scremerston Hill
Scremerston Town Fm
Greenside Cotts
Norham
Morris Hall
Allerdeanmill Burn
Camphouses
Shoreswood Hall
Shoreswood
Cheswick Sands
Fox Covert
East Newbiggin
Shoresdean
West Allerdean
Cheswick Ho
Cheswick
Simprim Mains
Ladykirk House
Battle Moor
Grievestead Moor
Allerdean Greens
Allerdean Grange
Coal Burn
Cheswick Buildings
Windmill Hill
Goswick
Milne Graden East Mains
Groat Haugh
Ancroft Northmoor
Ancroft
Simprim
Widdepen Plantn
Grindon
Ancroft Mill
Tillmouth Fm
NORTHUMBERLAND
North Low
Goswick Sands
Milne Graden West Mains
Westmoor Plantn
Felkington
Ancroft Southmoor
Haydon Dean
Berrington Law
Bridge Mill
Haggerston
Holy Island (Lindisfarne)
Tweedmill
Toft Hill
Berrington Ho
Snook Pt
Shellacres
Mattilees Hill
Dean Burn
Berrington Lough
Berrington
New Haggerston
South Low
Brockmill Fm
Beal Pt
Brick Kiln Plantn
Bowsden Moor
Beal
LINDISFARNE
Twizel Mill
Fadden Hill
Duddo
Mattilees Cott
Castle Heaton
Common Plantn
Jacks Law
Lickar Dean
Beal Sands
Holy Island Sands
Duddo Hill
Bowsden
West Mains Inn
Lowick Mill
Tindal Ho
Woodside Fm
Low Wood
Bowsden West Fm
Old Dryburn
Dry Burn
The Low
Mount Hooley
Granary Pt
Donaldson's Lodge
Black Bank
Hazely Hill
High Wood
Barmoor Hill
Hunting Hall
Melkington
Rhodes Hill
Fenham
Peter's Plantn
New Heaton
Syning Hill
Heaton Moor
Barleymill Bank
Barmoor Castle
Barmoor Lane End
Black Heddon
West Kyloe
Fenwick
Cornhill-on-Tweed
Heaton Covert
ETAL CASTLE
Etal
Etal Rhodes
Etal Moor
Barmoor Ridge
Lowick
Kyloe Hills
East Kyloe
Fenwick Wood
Lowmoor Pt
Pallinsburn Ho
HEATHERSLAW LIGHT RAILWAY
HEATHERSLAW CORNMILL
Letham Hill
Ford Forge
Ford Fm
Common Cott
Moss Hall
Moss Wood
Kyloe Wood
Tealhow Pt
Cookstead
Ford Common
Barmoor South Moor
Redhouse Moor
Shepherdskirk Hill
Bareless
Campfield
Crookham Westfield
Crookham
Windy Law
Hay Fm
LADY WATERFORD HALL
Bar Moor
Moorhouse
Buckton Moor
Buckton
Shiellow Wood
Branxton Ridge
Barmoore Red Ho
Goswick Sands
Holy Island (Lindisfarne)
Snipe Pt
Keel Head
Emmanuel Head
Beal Pt
LINDISFARNE HERITAGE CENTRE
Holy Island
LINDISFARNE CASTLE
LINDISFARNE PRIORY
Castle Pt
Hole Mouth
Granary Pt
Burrows Hole
Guile Pt
Lowmoor Pt
Tealhole Pt
Ross Pt
Ross Back Sands
Buckton
NU

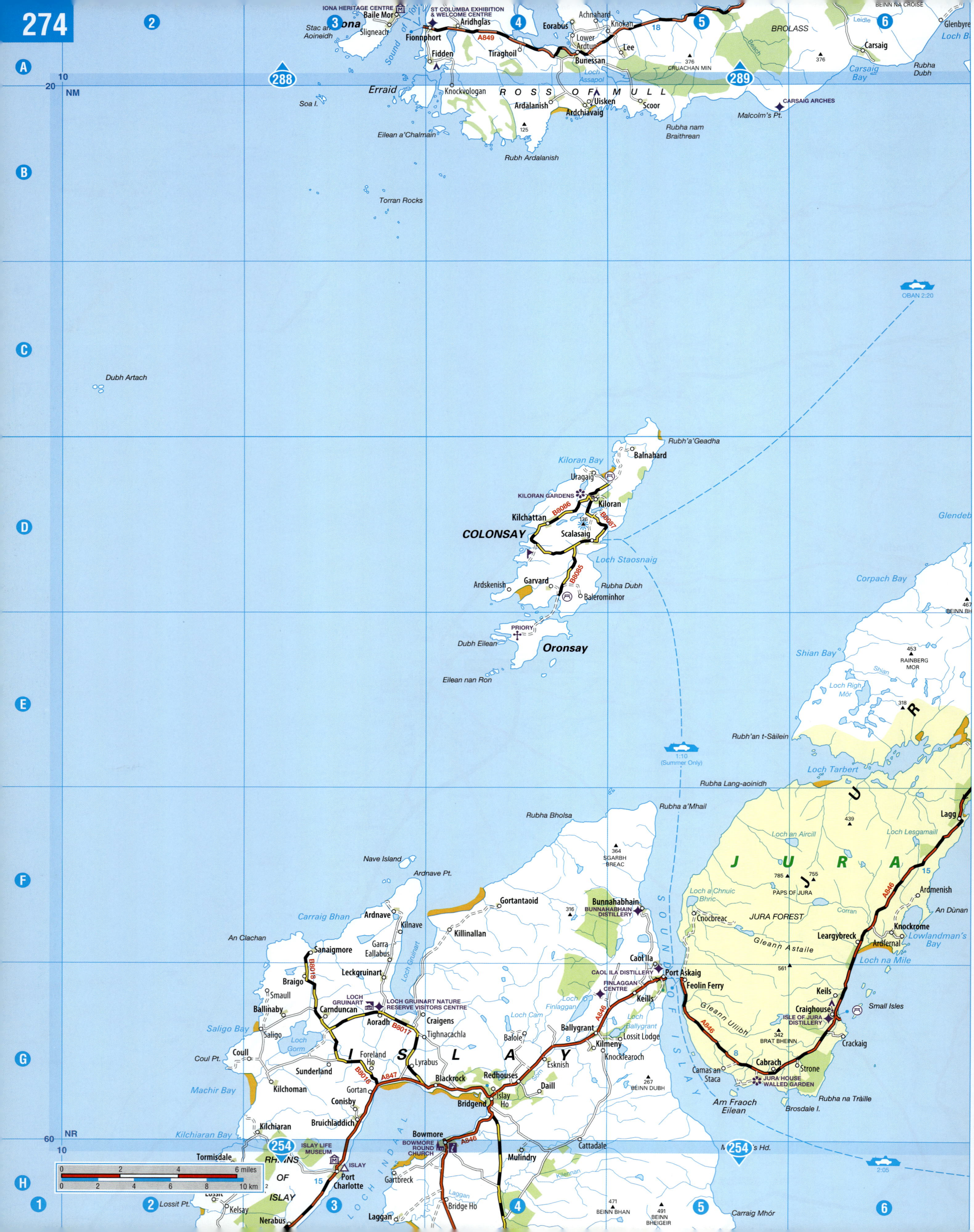
IONA HERITAGE CENTRE
Baile Mor
Stac an Aoineidh
Iona
Sligneach
Sound of Iona
ST COLUMBA EXHIBITION & WELCOME CENTRE
Aridhglas
Fionnphort
Fidden
A849
Tiraghoil
Eorabus
Achnahard
Knokan
Lower Ardtun
Lee
Bunessan
BROLASS
376
CRUACHAN MIN
Leidle
Carsaig
Glenbyre
Loch Buie
BEINN NA CROISE
Carsaig Bay
Rubha Dubh
288
289
Erraid
Knockvologan
ROSS OF MULL
Loch Assapol
Uisken
Scoor
Ardalanish
Ardchiavaig
Soa I.
CARSAIG ARCHES
Malcolm's Pt.
125
Eilean a'Chalmain
Rubha nam Braithrean
Rubh Ardalanish
Torran Rocks
OBAN 2:20
Dubh Artach
Rubh'a'Geadha
Balnahard
Kiloran Bay
Uragaig
KILORAN GARDENS
Kiloran
B8086
B8087
Kilchattan
136
COLONSAY
Scalasaig
Loch Staosnaig
Glendebadel
B8085
Ardskenish
Garvard
Rubha Dubh
Balerominhor
Corpach Bay
467
PRIORY
Dubh Eilean
Oronsay
Shian Bay
453
RAINBERG MOR
Eilean nan Ron
Loch Righ Mòr
318
Rubh'an t-Sàilein
1:10 (Summer Only)
Loch Tarbert
Rubha Lang-aoinidh
Rubha a'Mhail
Rubha Bholsa
Lagg
439
Loch an Aircil
Loch Lesgamaill
364
SGARBH BREAC
Nave Island
Ardnave Pt.
JURA
785
755
PAPS OF JURA
A846
Ardmenish
Loch a'Chnuic Bhric
Gortantaoid
316
Bunnahabhain
BUNNAHABHAIN DISTILLERY
Cnocbreac
JURA FOREST
Corran
An Dùnan
Knockrome
Carraig Bhan
Ardnave
Kilnave
Killinallan
Leargybreck
Lowlandman's Bay
An Clachan
Garra Eallabus
Gleann Astaile
Ardfernal
Loch na Mile
Sanaigmore
B8018
Caol Ila
561
Leckgruinart
Loch Gruinart
CAOL ILA DISTILLERY
Port Askaig
Braigo
FINLAGGAN CENTRE
Feolin Ferry
Keils
Smaull
LOCH GRUINART
LOCH GRUINART NATURE RESERVE VISITORS CENTRE
Keills
Small Isles
Ballinaby
Carnduncan
Craigens
Loch Finlaggan
Gleann Ullibh
Craighouse
Aoradh
B8017
Loch Cam
ISLE OF JURA DISTILLERY
Saligo Bay
Saligo
Tighnacachla
Ballygrant
Loch Ballygrant
342
BRAT BHEINN
Loch Gorm
Lossit Lodge
Crackaig
Coull
Balole
Kilmeny
Coul Pt.
ISLAY
Foreland Ho
Esknish
Knockfearoch
Cabrach
Sunderland
Lyrabus
Camas an Staca
Strone
B8016
A847
Blackrock
Redhouses
JURA HOUSE WALLED GARDEN
Kilchoman
Gortan
267
BEINN DUBH
Machir Bay
Islay Ho
Daill
Rubha na Tràille
Conisby
Bridgend
Am Fraoch Eilean
Brosdale I.
Bruichladdich
SOUND OF ISLAY
NR
60
10
Kilchiaran
Kilchiaran Bay
Bowmore
BOWMORE ROUND CHURCH
ISLAY LIFE MUSEUM
254
Cattadale
M's Hd.
Tormisdale
RHINNS OF ISLAY
ISLAY
Mulindry
2:05
Port Charlotte
LOCH INDAAL
Gartbreck
Kilennan
Laggan
471
BEINN BHAN
491
BEINN BHEIGEIR
Carraig Mhór
Lossit Pt.
Lossit
Kelsay
Bridge Ho
Nerabus
0 2 4 6 miles
0 2 4 6 8 10 km

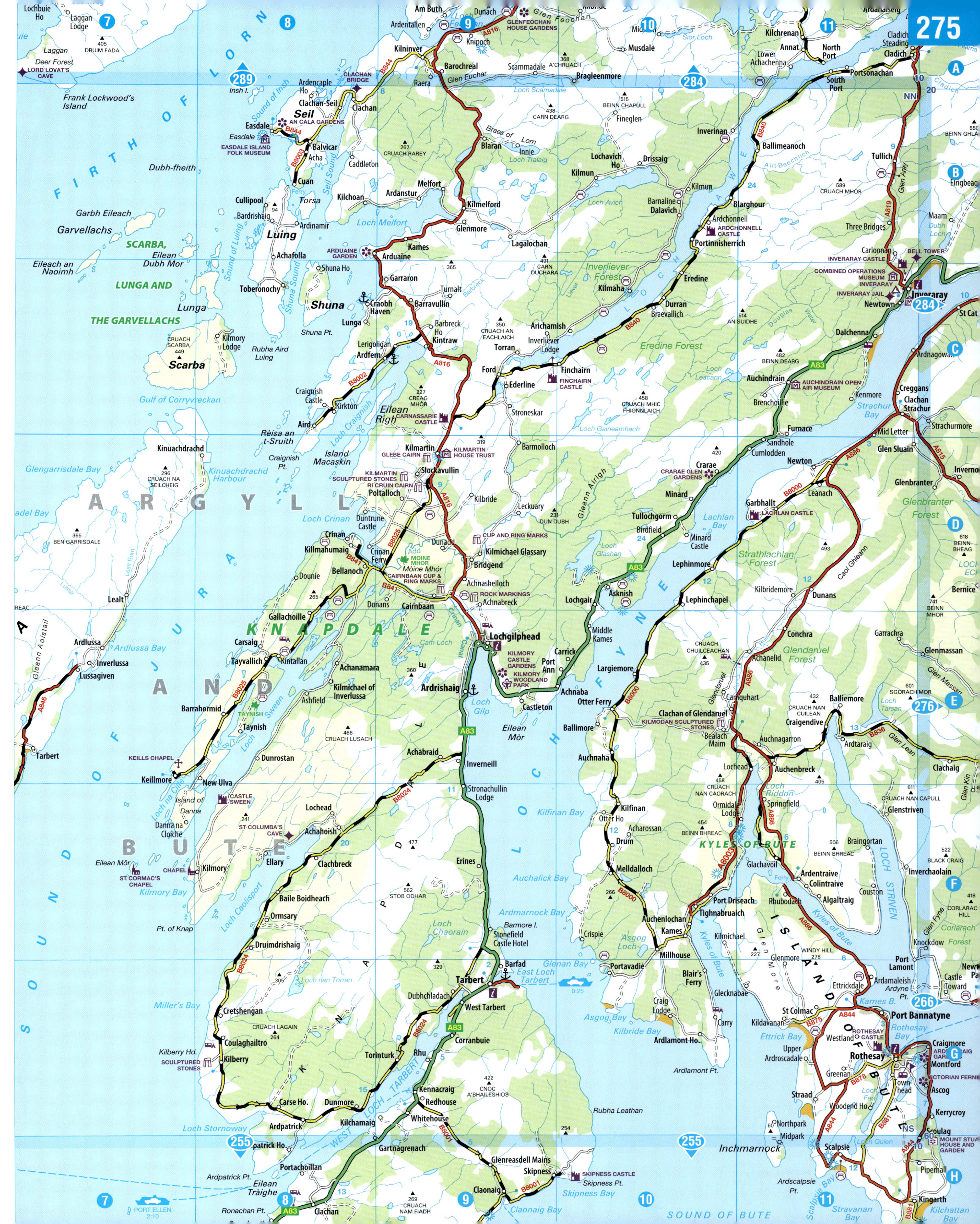

FIRTH OF LORN
SOUND OF JURA
ARGYLL AND BUTE
KNAPDALE
LOCH FYNE
LOCH AWE
ISLAND OF BUTE
KYLES OF BUTE
SOUND OF BUTE
LOCH STRIVEN
WEST LOCH TARBERT
Lochbuie Ho
Laggan Lodge
Laggan
Deer Forest
LORD LOVAT'S CAVE
405 DRUIM FADA
Frank Lockwood's Island
Insh I.
Sound of Insh
Seil
AN CALA GARDENS
Easdale
EASDALE ISLAND FOLK MUSEUM
Ardencaple Ho
Clachan-Seil
CLACHAN BRIDGE
Clachan
Balvicar
Acha
Cuan
Torsa
Seil Sound
Dubh-fheith
Garbh Eileach
Garvellachs
Cullipool
Bardrishaig
Luing
Ardinamir
Achafolla
SCARBA, LUNGA AND THE GARVELLACHS
Eilean Dubh Mor
Eileach an Naoimh
Lunga
Toberonochy
Shuna Sound
Shuna
Shuna Ho
Shuna Pt.
Cruach Scarba 449
Scarba
Kilmory Lodge
Rubha Aird Luing
Gulf of Corryvreckan
Am Buth
Ardentallen
Dunach
GLENFEOCHAN HOUSE GARDENS
Glen Feochan
Kilninver
Knipoch
Barochreal
Raera
Scammadale
Glen Euchar
Bragleenmore
Loch Scamadale
Braes of Lorn
Blaran
Innie
Loch Tralaig
CRUACH RAREY
Caddleton
Melfort
Kilchoan
Ardanstur
Kilmelford
Loch Melfort
Glenmore
ARDUAINE GARDEN
Arduaine
Kames
Lagalochan
Garraron
Turnalt
Craobh Haven
Barravullin
Lunga
Lerigoligan
Ardfern
Barbreck Ho
Kintraw
CRUACH AN EACHLAICH
Torran
Arichamish
Inverliever Lodge
Ford
Finchairn
FINCHAIRN CASTLE
Ederline
Stroneskar
CREAG MHÒR
Craignish Castle
Kirkton
Aird
Loch Craignish
Eilean Righ
CARNASSARIE CASTLE
Barmolloch
Kinuachdrachd
Kinuachdrachd Harbour
CRUACH NA SEILCHEIG
Rèisa an t-Sruith
Craignish Pt.
Island Macaskin
Kilmartin
GLEBE CAIRN
KILMARTIN HOUSE TRUST
KILMARTIN SCULPTURED STONES
RI CRUIN CAIRN
Slockavullin
Poltalloch
Kilbride
Leckuary
DUN DUBH
Glengarrisdale Bay
Loch Crinan
Duntrune Castle
Crinan
Killmahumaig
Crinan Ferry
MOINE MHOR
Mòine Mhòr
CAIRNBAAN CUP & RING MARKS
Dunadd
CUP AND RING MARKS
Kilmichael Glassary
Bridgend
Achnashelloch
ROCK MARKINGS
Achnabreck
Bellanoch
Dunans
Cairnbaan
Dounie
BEN GARRISDALE
Lealt
Lealt Burn
Gallachoille
Carsaig
Tayvallich
Kintallan
Achanamara
Cam Loch
Crinan Canal
Lochgilphead
KILMORY CASTLE GARDENS
KILMORY WOODLAND PARK
Ardrishaig
Loch Gilp
Castleton
Kilmichael of Inverlussa
Ashfield
Ardlussa
Ardlussa Bay
Inverlussa
Lussagiven
Gleann Aoistail
Barrahormid
TAYNISH
Taynish
Loch Sween
CRUACH LUSACH
Achabraid
Inverneill
Stronachullin Lodge
Eilean Mòr
Tarbert
KEILLS CHAPEL
Keillmore
Dunrostan
New Ulva
CASTLE SWEEN
Island of Danna
Danna na Cloiche
Loch na Cille
ST COLUMBA'S CAVE
Lochead
Achahoish
Clachbreck
Ellary
Eilean Mòr
ST CORMAC'S CHAPEL
CHAPEL
Kilmory
Kilmory Bay
Baile Boidheach
Ormsary
Loch Caolisport
Pt. of Knap
Druimdrishaig
Miller's Bay
Cretshengan
CRUACH LAGAIN
Coulaghailtro
Kilberry Hd.
SCULPTURED STONES
Kilberry
Carse Ho.
Dunmore
Loch Stornoway
Ardpatrick
Ardpatrick Ho.
Ardpatrick Pt.
Portachoillan
Eilean Traighe
Ronachan Pt.
Clachan
PORT ELLEN 2:10
STOB ODHAR
Erines
Kilfinan Bay
Auchalick Bay
Ardmarnock Bay
Loch Chaorain
Barmore I.
Stonefield Castle Hotel
Barfad
East Loch Tarbert
Glenan Bay
Tarbert
West Tarbert
Dubhchladach
Loch nan Torran
Corranbuie
Torinturk
Rhu
Kennacraig
Redhouse
Whitehouse
Kilchamaig
CNOC A'BHAILESHIOS
Gartnagrenach
Glenreasdell Mains
Skipness
SKIPNESS CASTLE
Skipness Pt.
Skipness Bay
Claonaig
Claonaig Bay
CRUACH NAM FIADH
Rubha Leathan
Inchmarnock
Dalchenna
Midhouse
Musdale
Slor Loch
A'CHRUACH
BEINN CHAPULL
Fineglen
CARN DEARG
Lochavich Ho
Drissaig
Kilmun
Loch Avich
Barnaline
Dalavich
Inverliever Forest
Kilmaha
CARN DUCHARA
Kilchrenan
Annat
North Port
Lower Achachenna
Portsonachan
South Port
Inverinan
Ballimeanoch
Allt Beochlich
Kilmun
Blarghour
Ardchonnell
ARDCHONNELL CASTLE
Portinnisherrich
Eredine
Durran
Braevallich
Eredine Forest
AN SUIDHE
Douglas Water
Cladich
Cladich Steading
Tullich
Glen Aray
CRUACH MHOR
Three Bridges
Maam
Carloonan
BELL TOWER
INVERARAY CASTLE
COMBINED OPERATIONS MUSEUM INVERARAY
INVERARAY JAIL
Inveraray
Newtown
St Cat
BEINN DEARG
Auchindrain
AUCHINDRAIN OPEN AIR MUSEUM
Brenchoillie
Loch Leacann
CRUACH MHIC FHIONNLAIGH
Loch Gaineamhach
Kenmore
Strachur Bay
Creggans
Clachan Strachur
Strachurmore
Ardnagowan
Furnace
Mid Letter
Glen Slain
Sandhole
Cumlodden
Newton
Cramalt
CRARAE GLEN GARDENS
Crarae
Minard
Leanach
Glenbranter
Glenbranter Forest
Garbhallt
LACHLAN CASTLE
Tullochgorm
Birdfield
Lachlan Bay
Minard Castle
Loch Glashan
Gleann Airigh
Lephinmore
Strathlachlan Forest
Lephinchapel
Kilbridemore
Caol Ghleann
Dunans
Bernice
BEINN MHOR
Lochgair
Asknish
Middle Kames
Carrick
Port Ann
Achnaba
Largiemore
Otter Ferry
Conchra
CRUACH CHUILCEACHAN
Achanelid
Glendaruel Forest
Garrachra
Glenmassan
Glen Massan
SGORACH MOR
Camquhart
CRUACH NAN CUILEAN
Balliemore
Loch Tarsan
Craigendive
Clachan of Glendaruel
KILMODAN SCULPTURED STONES
Bealach Maim
Ballimore
Auchnaha
Auchnagarron
Ardtaraig
Glen Lean
Lochead
Auchenbreck
Clachaig
CRUACH NAN CAORACH
Loch Riddon
Springfield
CRUACH NAN CAPULL
Glenstriven
Kilfinan
Otter Ho
Acharossan
Ormidale Lodge
BEINN BHREAC
Drum
Glachavoil
Braingortan
BEINN BHREAC
BLACK CRAIG
Inverchaolain
Melldalloch
Ardentraive
Colintraive
Couston
Rhubodach
Algaltraig
Port Driseach
Tighnabruaich
Crispie
Asgog Loch
Auchenlochan
Kames
Kilmichael
Glen More
Glenmore
WINDY HILL
Knockdow
Port Lamont
Glen Fyne
CORLARACH HILL
Corlarach Forest
Portavadie
Millhouse
Blair's Ferry
Ettrickdale
Ardamaleish
Ardyne Pt.
Castle Toward
Asgog Bay
Craig Lodge
Glecknabae
Kilbride Bay
Carry
Kames B.
Port Bannatyne
St Colmac
Kildavanan
Ettrick Bay
Rothesay Bay
ROTHESAY CASTLE
Westland
Rothesay
Upper Ardroscadale
Craigmore
Montford
VICTORIAN FERNERY
Greenan
Town-head
Ascog
Straad
Loch Fad
Woodend Ho
Kerrycroy
Ardlamont Ho.
Ardlamont Pt.
Northpark
Midpark
Loch Quien
Scalpsie
MOUNT STUART HOUSE AND GARDEN
Ascog
Ardscalpsie Pt.
Scalpsie Bay
Stravanan Bay
Piperhall
Kingarth
Kilchattan Bay

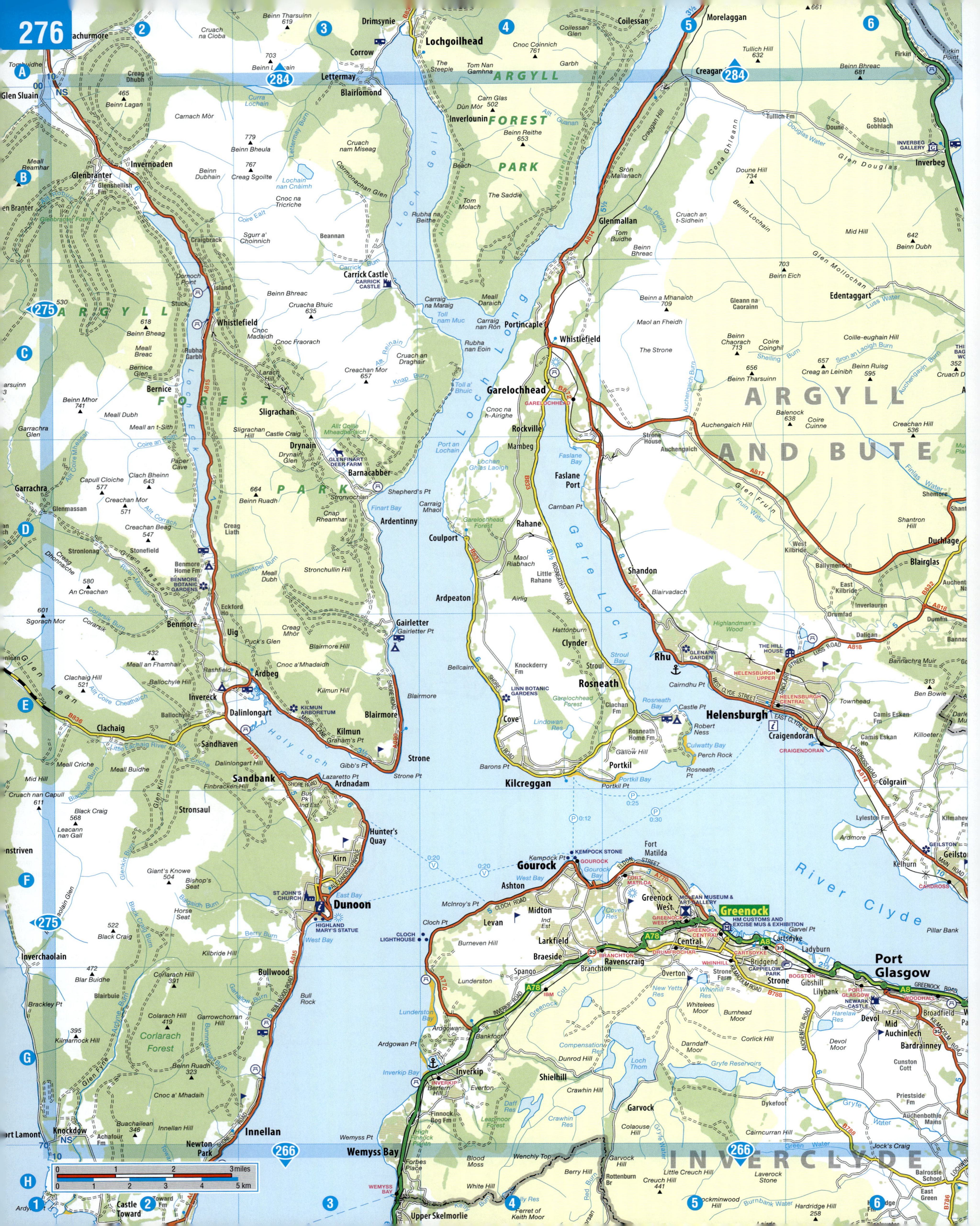
ARGYLL FOREST PARK
ARGYLL AND BUTE
INVERCLYDE
Lochgoilhead
Drimsynie
Lettermay
Blairimond
Corrow
Coilessan
Morelaggan
Creagan
Tullich Hill 632
Beinn Bhreac 681
Inverbeg
Glen Douglas
Doune Hill 734
Mid Hill
Edentaggart
Luss Water
Glenbranter
Invernoaden
Strachur
Whistlefield
Stuck
Beinn Bheag
Loch Eck
Sligrachan
Drynain
Barnacabber
Ardentinny
Coulport
Ardpeaton
Gairletter
Blairmore
Kilmun
Strone
Benmore
Uig
Ardbeg
Inverchaolain
Dalinlongart
Clachaig
Sandhaven
Sandbank
Stronsaul
Ardnadam
Hunter's Quay
Kirn
Dunoon
Bullwood
Innellan
Toward
Castle Toward
Holy Loch
Loch Long
Loch Goil
Carrick Castle
Portincaple
Garelochhead
Rockville
Mambeg
Faslane Port
Rahane
Clynder
Rosneath
Kilcreggan
Cove
Portkil
Shandon
Rhu
Helensburgh
Craigendoran
Colgrain
Gare Loch
Blairglas
Duchlage
Kilbride
Gourock
Ashton
Greenock
Port Glasgow
River Clyde
Cloch Pt
Levan
Larkfield
Braeside
Branchton
Ravenscraig
Spango
Inverkip
Wemyss Bay
Upper Skelmorlie
Shielhill
Garvock
Loch Thom
Kelburn
Strone
Devol
Auchinlech
Bardrainney
Corlarach Forest
Knockdow
Newton Park
284
275
266
0 1 2 3 miles
0 1 2 3 4 5 km

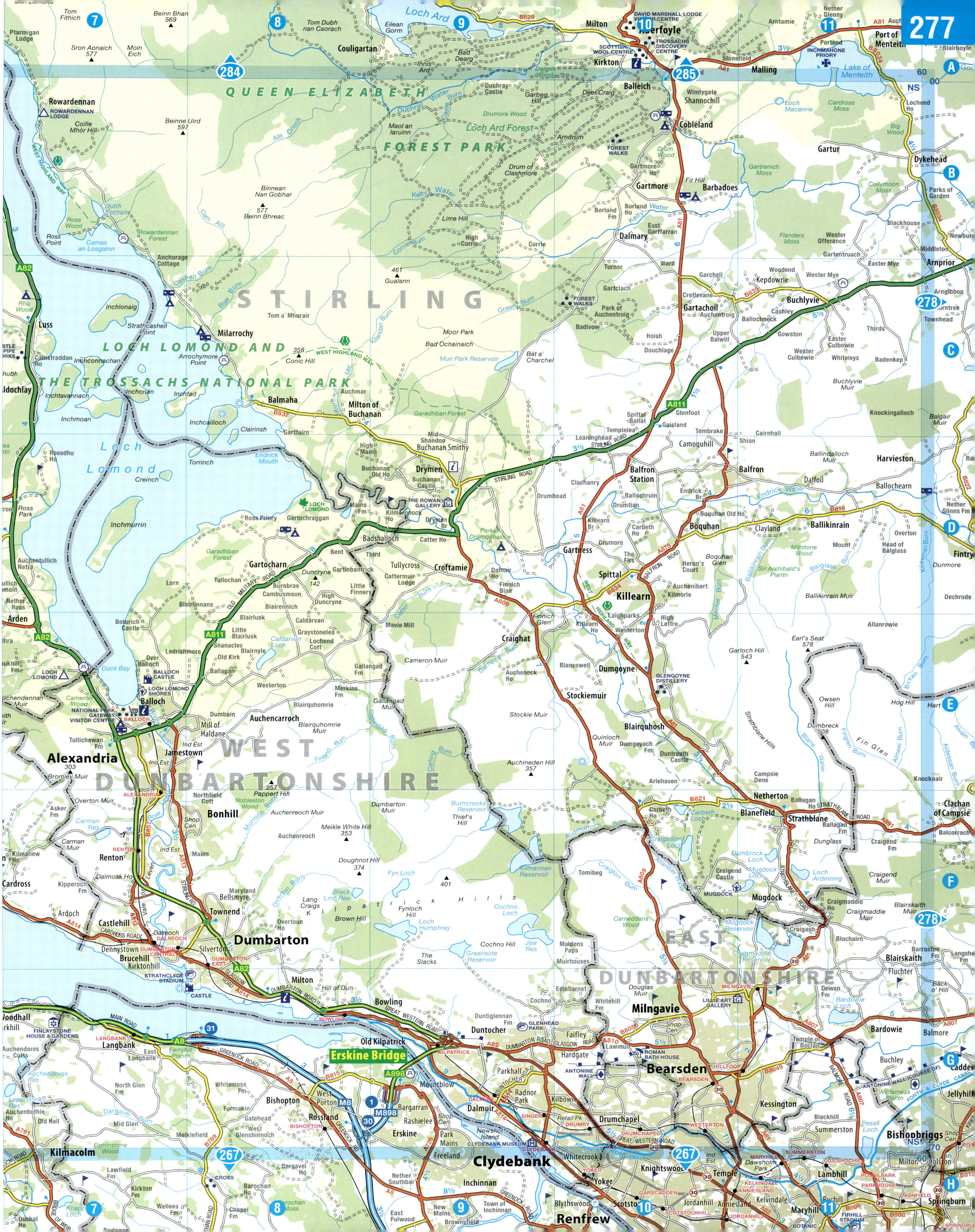

QUEEN ELIZABETH FOREST PARK
STIRLING
LOCH LOMOND AND THE TROSSACHS NATIONAL PARK
WEST DUNBARTONSHIRE
EAST DUNBARTONSHIRE
Loch Lomond
Loch Ard
Lake of Menteith
Aberfoyle
Milton
Kinlochard
Kirkton
Balleich
Port of Menteith
Malling
Cobleland
Gartmore
Barbadoes
Dalmary
Gartur
Dykehead
Arnprior
Buchlyvie
Gartachoil
Rowardennan
Luss
Milarrochy
Balmaha
Milton of Buchanan
Drymen
Croftamie
Gartocharn
Balfron
Balfron Station
Boquhan
Ballikinrain
Harvieston
Fintry
Killearn
Gartness
Spittal
Craighat
Dumgoyne
Stockiemuir
Blairquhosh
Blanefield
Strathblane
Netherton
Mugdock
Milngavie
Bearsden
Balloch
Alexandria
Jamestown
Bonhill
Renton
Cardross
Dumbarton
Milton
Bowling
Old Kilpatrick
Erskine Bridge
Duntocher
Dalmuir
Clydebank
Langbank
Bishopton
Erskine
Kilmacolm
Renfrew
Yoker
Knightswood
Drumchapel
Kessington
Bishopbriggs
Springburn
Maryhill
Balmore
Bardowie
Blairskaith
Inchmurrin
Inchcailloch
Kilpatrick Hills
Campsie Dene
Blane Water
Endrick Water
Loch Ard Forest
Queen Elizabeth Forest Park
West Highland Way
Antonine Wall
284
285
278
267
A
B
C
D
E
F
G
H
7
8
9
10
11

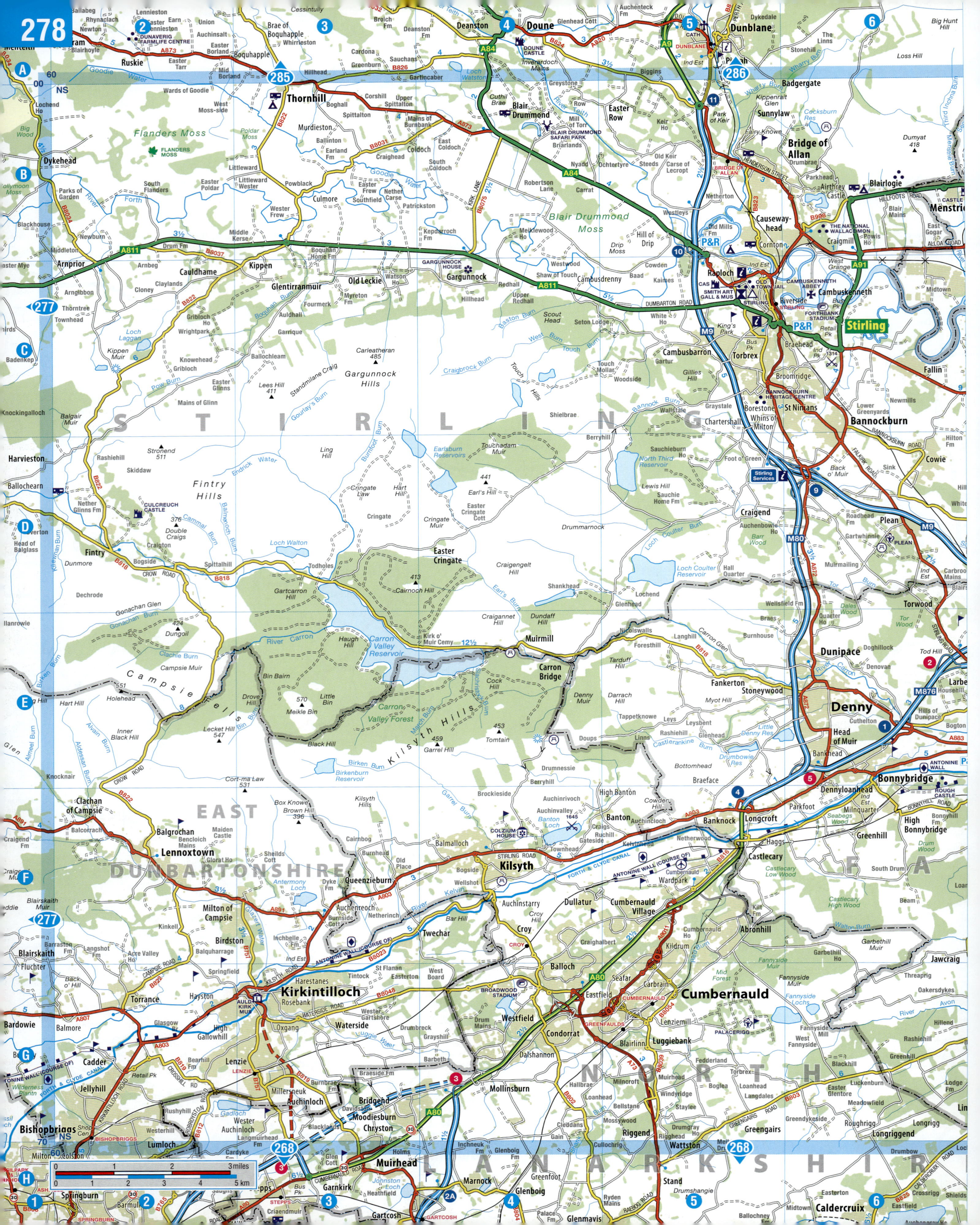

Deanston
Doune
Doune Castle
Dunblane
Bridge of Allan
Badgergate
Sunnylaw
Blairlogie
Menstrie
Thornhill
Flanders Moss
Ruskie
Boquhapple
Dykehead
Arnprior
Kippen
Cauldhame
Gargunnock
Old Leckie
Blair Drummond
Blair Drummond Moss
Blair Drummond Safari Park
Cambusdrenny
Raploch
Cornton
Causewayhead
Craigmill
Cambuskenneth
Stirling
Riverside
Braehead
King's Park
Torbrex
Cambusbarron
Broomridge
St Ninians
Whins of Milton
Bannockburn
Fallin
Cowie
Plean
Gargunnock Hills
Fintry Hills
Fintry
Culcreuch Castle
Stronend 511
Touchadam Muir
Earl's Hill
Cringate Muir
Easter Cringate
Craigengelt Hill
Carron Valley Reservoir
Carron Valley Forest
Carron Bridge
Kilsyth Hills
Campsie Fells
Lecket Hill 547
Meikle Bin
Garrel Hill
Tomtain
Muirmill
Dundaff Hill
Dunipace
Denny
Torwood
Stoneywood
Fankerton
Head of Muir
Bonnybridge
Dennyloanhead
High Bonnybridge
Banknock
Longcroft
Castlecary
Haggs
Kilsyth
Queenzieburn
Lennoxtown
Milton of Campsie
Clachan of Campsie
Balgrochan
Birdston
Twechar
Croy
Dullatur
Cumbernauld Village
Cumbernauld
Abronhill
Condorrat
Westfield
Balloch
Kirkintilloch
Waterside
Lenzie
Auchinloch
Torrance
Bishopbriggs
Cadder
Jellyhill
Bardowie
Blairskaith
Mollinsburn
Moodiesburn
Chryston
Muirhead
Garnkirk
Marnock
Glenboig
Stand
Greengairs
Riggend
Caldercruix
Wattston
Longriggend
Jawcraig
Greenhill
Luggiebank
Lenziemill
Stirling
East Dunbartonshire
North Lanarkshire
Falkirk
Antonine Wall (course of)
Forth & Clyde Canal

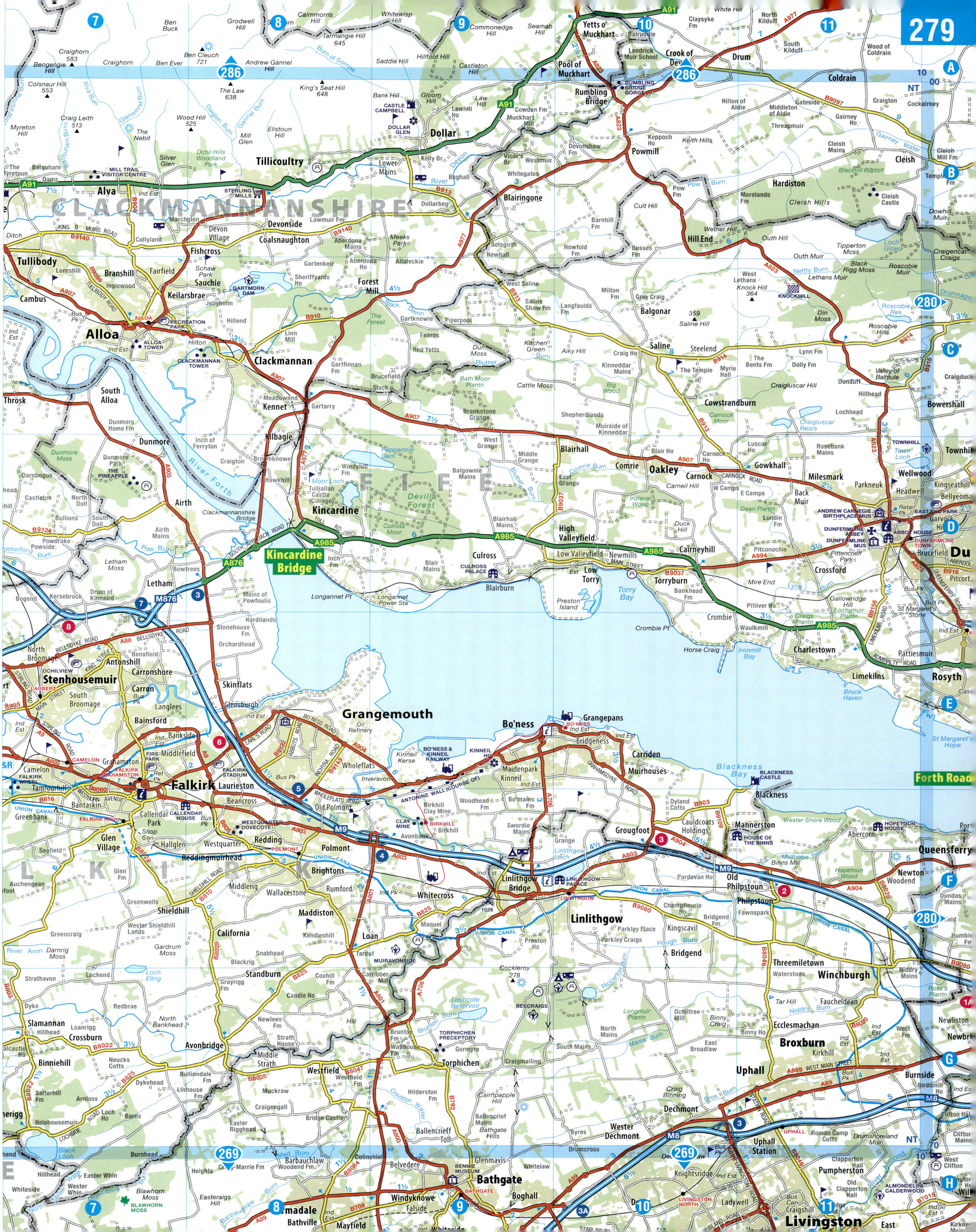
CLACKMANNANSHIRE
FIFE
Alloa
Tullibody
Alva
Tillicoultry
Dollar
Clackmannan
Kincardine
Kincardine Bridge
Culross
Dunfermline
Saline
Oakley
Comrie
High Valleyfield
Cairneyhill
Crossford
Limekilns
Charlestown
Rosyth
Torryburn
Grangemouth
Bo'ness
Falkirk
Stenhousemuir
Larbert
Carronshore
Polmont
Linlithgow
Linlithgow Bridge
Blackness
Queensferry
Forth Road
Winchburgh
Broxburn
Uphall
Livingston
Bathgate
Torphichen
Avonbridge
Westfield
Whitecross
Maddiston
California
Shieldhill
Brightons
Reddingmuirhead
Wallacestone
Standburn
Slamannan
Dechmont
Blairhall
Airth
Letham
Dunmore
South Alloa
Menstrie
Cambus
Fishcross
Sauchie
Coalsnaughton
Devonside
Forest Mill
Blairingone
Powmill
Crook of Devon
Yetts o' Muckhart
Pool of Muckhart
Cleish
Hill End
Gowkhall
Carnock
Milesmark
Philpstoun
Threemiletown
Kingscavil
Bridgend
Carriden
Muirhouses
Skinflats
Laurieston
Camelon
Bainsford
Glen Village
Hallglen
Redding
Westquarter
Union Canal
River Forth
A91
A907
A977
A985
A876
A905
A9
A803
A904
A706
A89
A899
M9
M876
M8
286
280
269

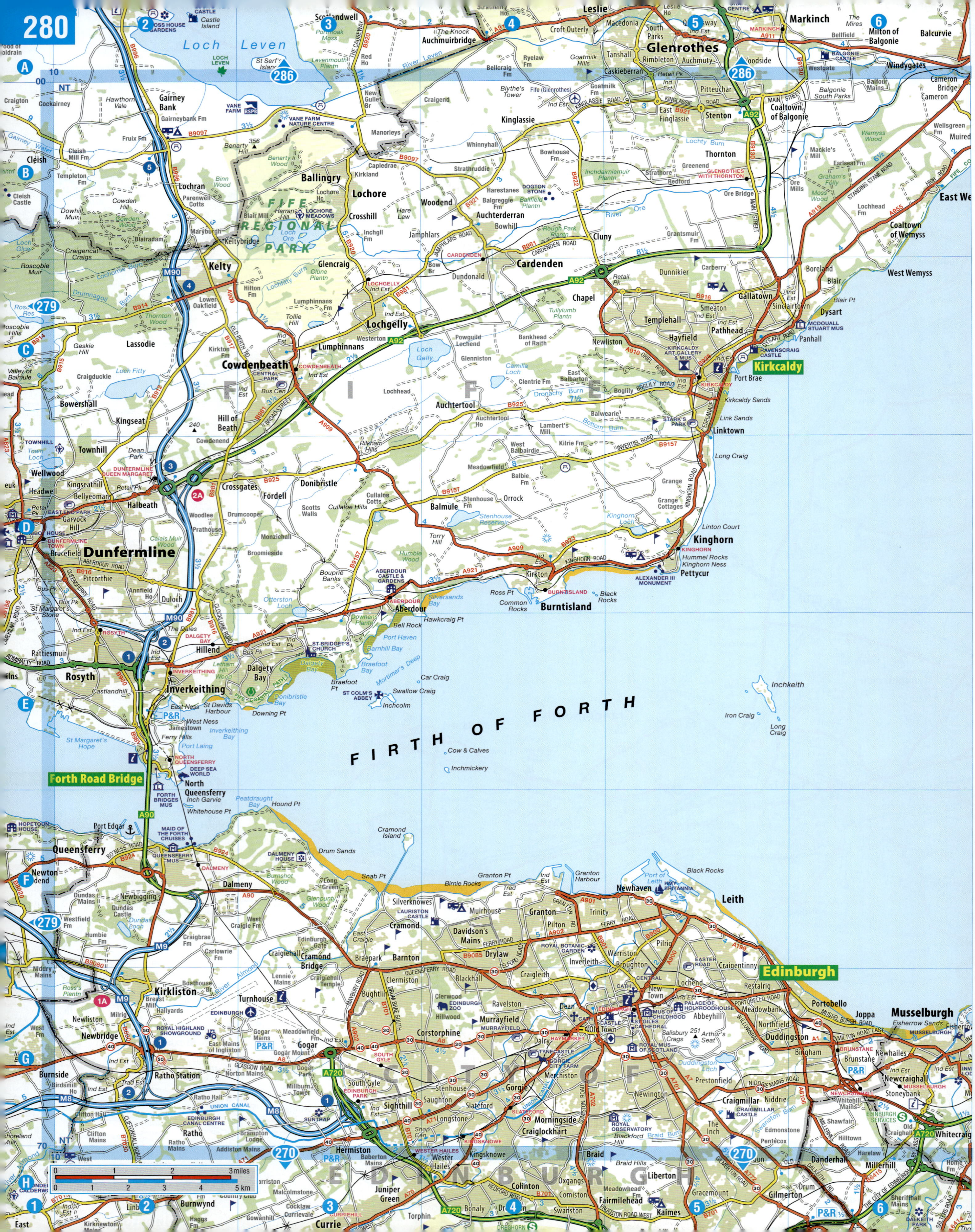
Loch Leven
Scotlandwell
Leslie
Glenrothes
Markinch
Milton of Balgonie
Balcurvie
Windygates
Cameron Bridge
Coaltown of Balgonie
Auchmuirbridge
Kinglassie
Stenton
Thornton
Gairney Bank
Cleish
Ballingry
Lochore
Crosshill
Woodend
Auchterderran
Bowhill
Cluny
Lochore Meadows Fife Regional Park
Kelty
Lochgelly
Cardenden
Chapel
Lumphinnans
Cowdenbeath
Gallatown
Dysart
Templehall
Hayfield
Pathhead
Kirkcaldy
Port Brae
Kirkcaldy Sands
Linktown
East Wemyss
Coaltown of Wemyss
West Wemyss
FIFE
Lassodie
Kingseat
Hill of Beath
Auchtertool
Townhill
Crossgates
Donibristle
Fordell
Halbeath
Dunfermline
Balmule
Orrock
Kinghorn
Pettycur
Burntisland
Aberdour
Kirkton
Rosyth
Inverkeithing
Hillend
Dalgety Bay
North Queensferry
Forth Road Bridge
FIRTH OF FORTH
Inchkeith
Inchcolm
Cramond Island
Queensferry
Dalmeny
Newhaven
Leith
Edinburgh
Granton
Trinity
Pilton
Davidson's Mains
Cramond
Barnton
Kirkliston
Ratho Station
Ratho
Corstorphine
Murrayfield
Gorgie
Merchiston
Morningside
Portobello
Joppa
Musselburgh
Duddingston
Craigmillar
Liberton
Colinton
Juniper Green
Currie
Dalkeith
Gilmerton
EDINBURGH
CITY OF EDINBURGH

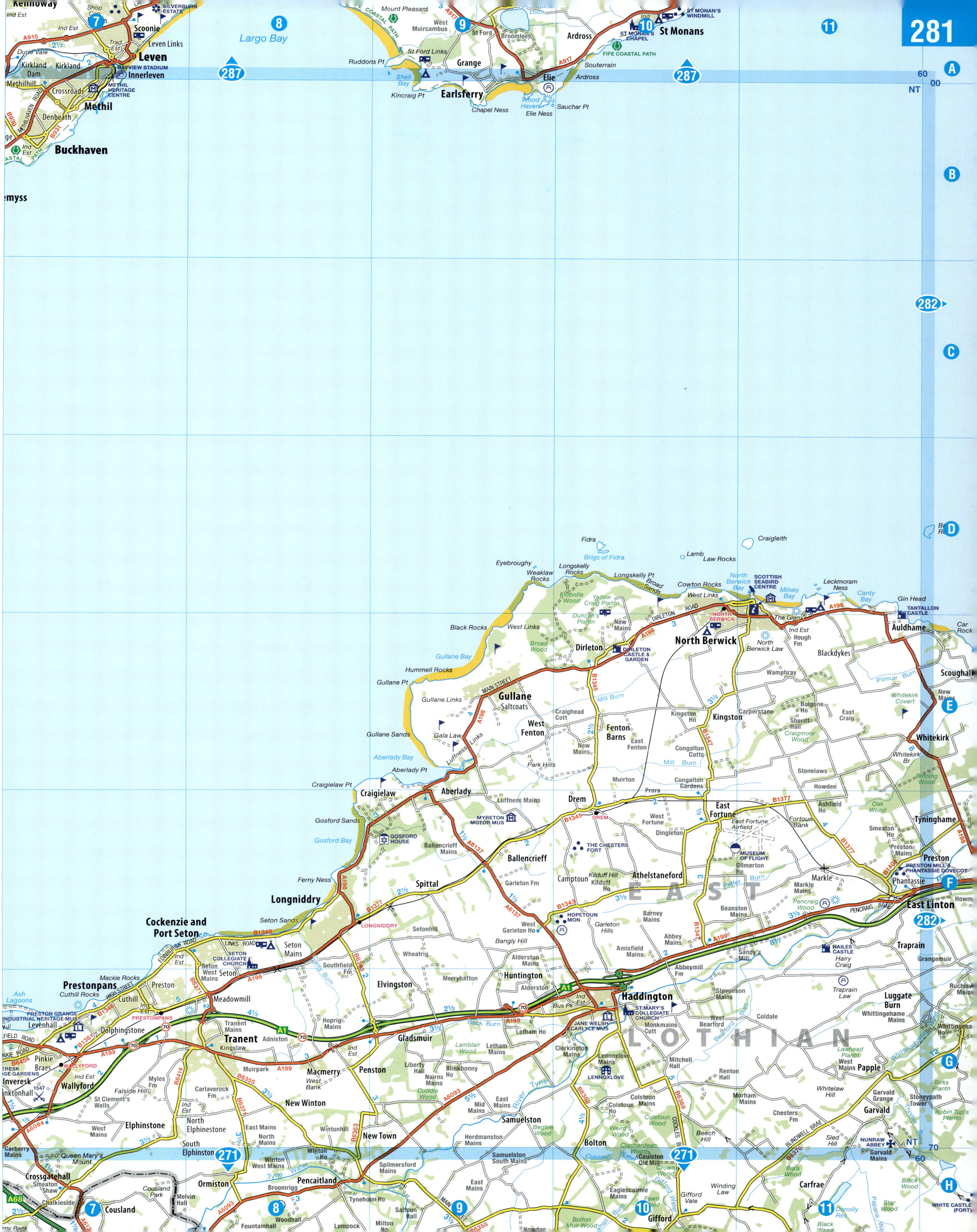
Leven
Methil
Buckhaven
Sconoie
Leven Links
Innerleven
Kirkland
Methilhill
Denbeath
Largo Bay
Earlsferry
Elie
Grange
St Monans
Ardross
Kincraig Pt
Chapel Ness
Elie Ness
Sauchar Pt
Shell Bay
FIFE COASTAL PATH
Fidra
Brigs of Fidra
Craigleith
Lamb
Eyebroughy
North Berwick
Dirleton
Gullane
Gullane Bay
Gullane Sands
Aberlady Bay
Aberlady
Craigielaw
Gosford Sands
Gosford Bay
Longniddry
Cockenzie and Port Seton
Prestonpans
Tranent
Haddington
East Linton
Drem
East Fortune
Athelstaneford
Kingston
Whitekirk
Tyninghame
Auldhame
Scoughall
Ballencrieff
Spittal
Elvingston
Gladsmuir
Macmerry
Penston
New Winton
Samuelston
Bolton
Gifford
Pencaitland
Ormiston
Elphinstone
Wallyford
Cousland
Crossgatehall
Traprain
Garvald
Pappie
Luggate Burn
Carfrae
Fenton Barns
West Fenton
Markle
Preston
Phantassie
TANTALLON CASTLE
SCOTTISH SEABIRD CENTRE
MUSEUM OF FLIGHT
EAST
LOTHIAN

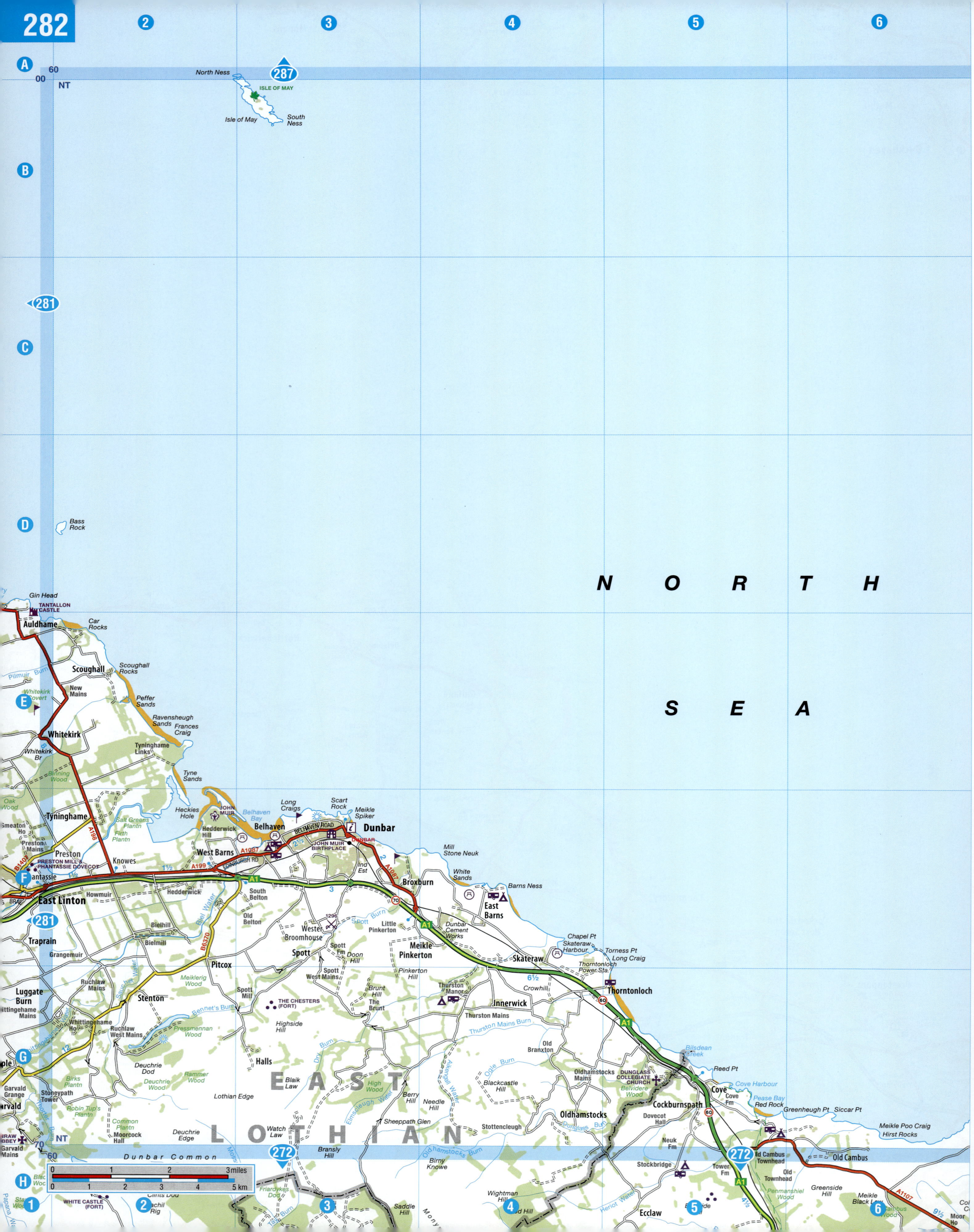

287
281
272
North Ness
Isle of May
South Ness
ISLE OF MAY
Bass Rock
NORTH SEA
Gin Head
TANTALLON CASTLE
Auldhame
Car Rocks
Scoughall
Scoughall Rocks
Pilmuir Burn
New Mains
Peffer Sands
Whitekirk Covert
Whitekirk
Whitekirk Br
Ravensheugh Sands
Frances Craig
Tyninghame Links
Binning Wood
Tyne Sands
Oak Wood
Tyninghame
Heckies Hole
JOHN MUIR
Belhaven Bay
Hedderwick Hill
Salt Greens Plantn
Firth Plantn
Preston Mains
Preston
PRESTON MILL & PHANTASSIE DOVECOT
Knowes
West Barns
Long Craigs
Scart Rock
Meikle Spiker
Belhaven
BELHAVEN ROAD
Dunbar
JOHN MUIR BIRTHPLACE
DUNBAR
EDINBURGH RD
Ind Est
Mill Stone Neuk
White Sands
Barns Ness
Broxburn
East Barns
Howmuir
Hedderwick
South Belton
East Linton
Old Belton
Bielhill
Bielmill
Biel Water
Traprain
Grangemuir
Wester Broomhouse
Spott Burn
Little Pinkerton
Dunbar Cement Works
Chapel Pt
Skateraw Harbour
Torness Pt
Long Craig
Thorntonloch Power Sta.
Meikle Pinkerton
Skateraw
Spott
Spott Fm
Doon Hill
Pitcox
Pinkerton Hill
Crowhill
Thorntonloch
Ruchlaw Mains
Meiklerig Wood
Spott West Mains
Spott Mill
Brunt Hill
The Brunt
Thurston Manor
Innerwick
Luggate Burn
Whittingehame Mains
Stenton
Bennet's Burn
THE CHESTERS (FORT)
Highside Hill
Thurston Mains
Thurston Mains Burn
Whittingehame Ho
Ruchlaw West Mains
Pressmennan Wood
Old Branxton
Bilsdean Creek
Halls
Deuchrie Dod
Rammer Wood
Deuchrie Wood
Birks Plantn
Blaik Law
High Wood
Oldhamstocks Mains
DUNGLASS COLLEGIATE CHURCH
Belvidere Wood
Reed Pt
Cove
Cove Harbour
Cove Fm
Blackcastle Hill
Pease Bay
Red Rock
Garvald Grange
Stoneypath Tower
Lothian Edge
Berry Hill
Needle Hill
Allengall Water
Cockburnspath
Greenheugh Pt
Siccar Pt
Robin Tup's Plantn
Common Plantn
Moorcock Hall
Deuchrie Edge
Watch Law
Eimscleugh Water
Sheeppath Glen
Stottencleugh
Oldhamstocks
Dunglass Burn
Dovecot Hall
Meikle Poo Craig
Hirst Rocks
EAST LOTHIAN
Garvald Mains
Dunbar Common
Bransly Hill
Birny Knowe
Neuk Fm
Old Cambus Townhead
Old Cambus
Stockbridge
Tower Fm
Old Townhead
Greenside Hill
Penmanshiel Wood
Wightman Hill
Heriot Water
Meikle Black Law
A1107
Friardykes Dod
Saddle Hill
Ecclaw
WHITE CASTLE (FORT)
Moor Ho
A1
A1087
A199
A198
B6370
B1407
Monynut Water
0 1 2 3 miles
0 1 2 3 4 5 km

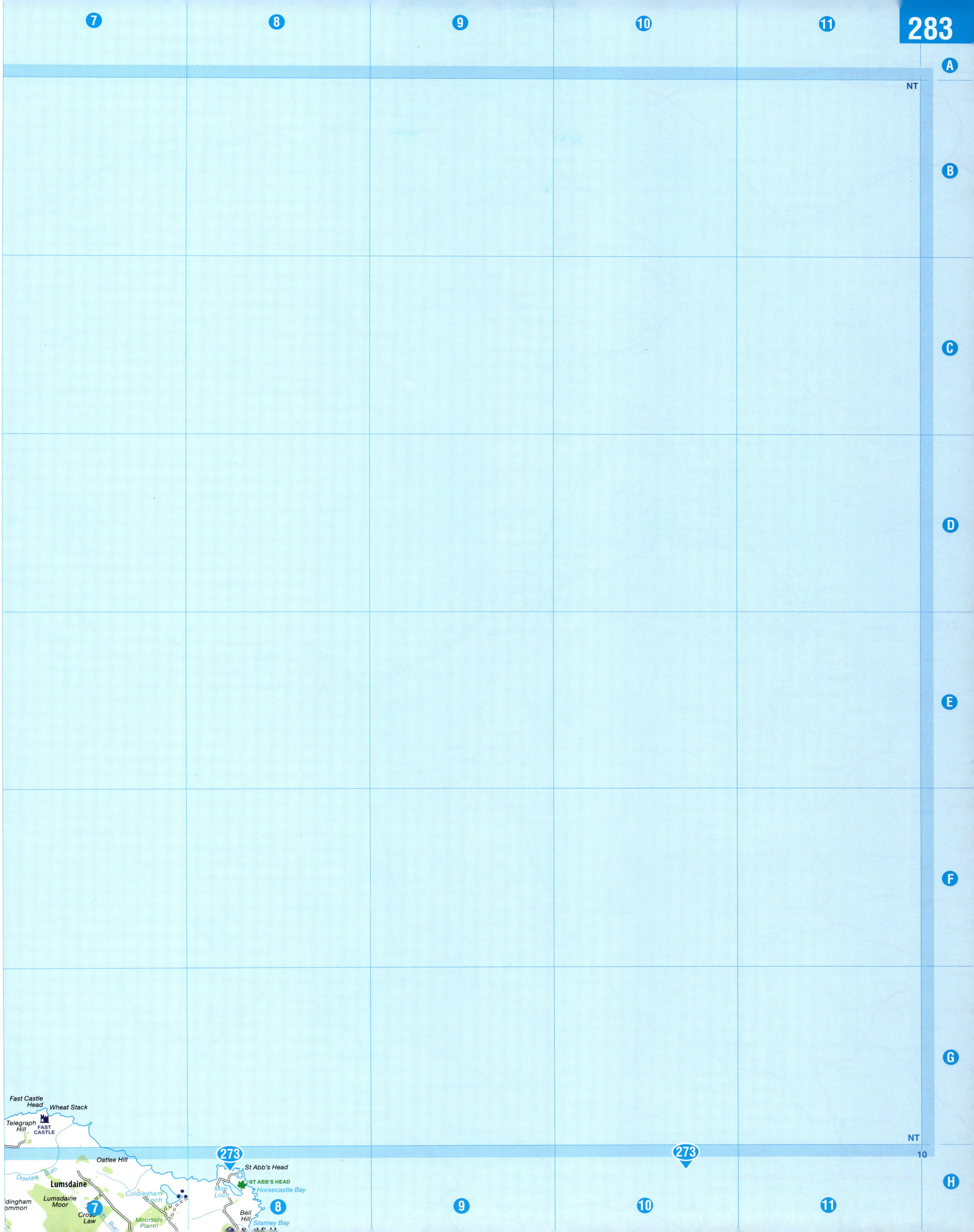

7
8
9
10
11
A
B
C
D
E
F
G
H
NT
NT
10
Fast Castle Head
Wheat Stack
Telegraph Hill
FAST CASTLE
Oatlee Hill
Dowlaw Burn
Lumsdaine
Lumsdaine Moor
Coldingham Loch
Moorside Plantn
Law
273
273
St Abb's Head
ST ABB'S HEAD
Horsecastle Bay
Mire Loch
Bell Hill
Starney Bay

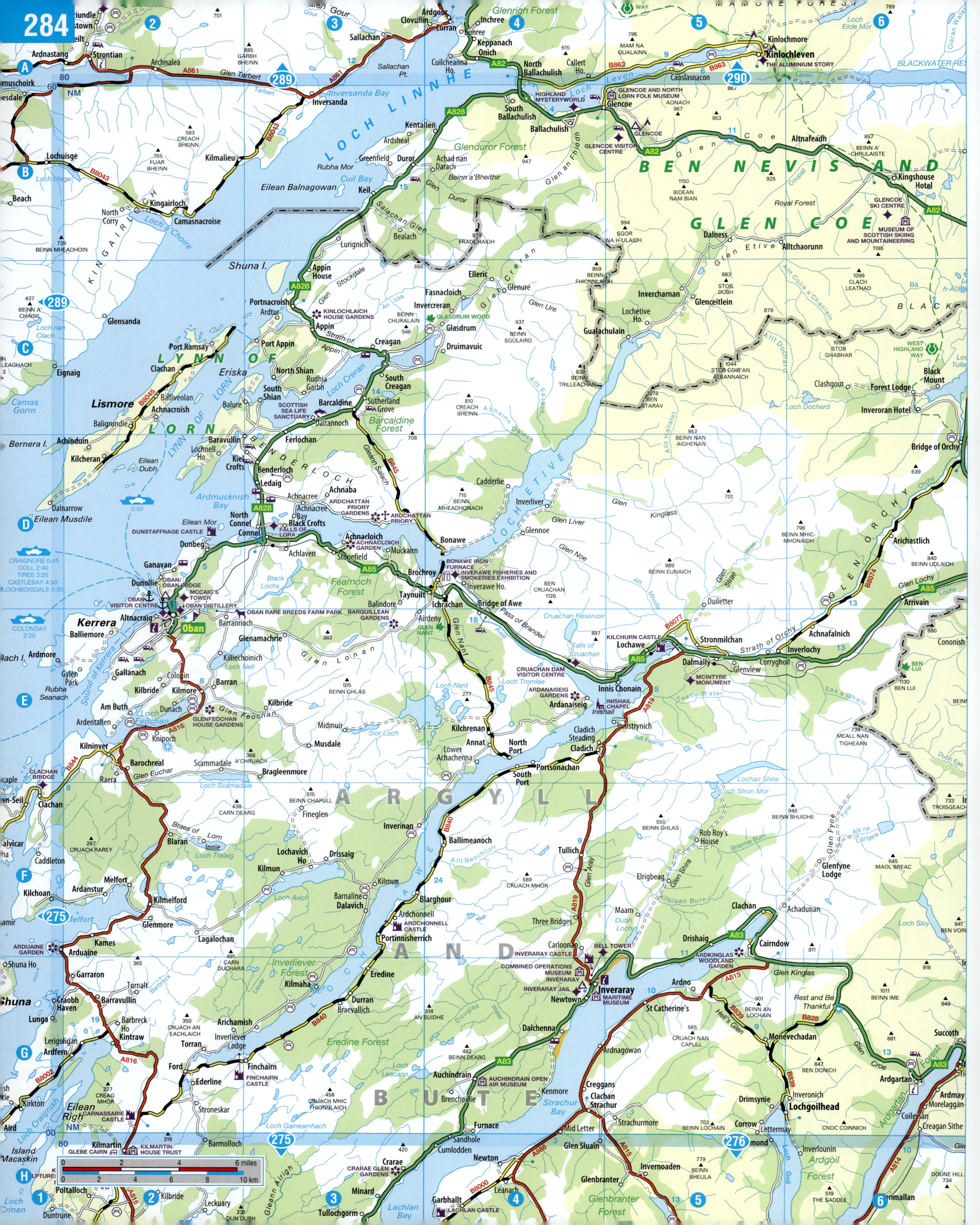

LOCH LINNHE
BEN NEVIS AND GLEN COE
LYNN OF LORN
ARGYLL AND BUTE
Ardnastang
Strontian
Inversanda
Ardgour
Clovullin
Corran
Inchree
Glenrigh Forest
Keppanach
Onich
Kinlochmore
Kinlochleven
THE ALUMINIUM STORY
BLACKWATER RES
Caolasnacon
North Ballachulish
South Ballachulish
Ballachulish
Glencoe
GLENCOE AND NORTH LORN FOLK MUSEUM
HIGHLAND MYSTERYWORLD
GLENCOE VISITOR CENTRE
Altnafeadh
Kingshouse Hotel
GLENCOE SKI CENTRE
MUSEUM OF SCOTTISH SKIING AND MOUNTAINEERING
Kentallen
Duror
Glenduror Forest
Kilmalieu
Lochuisge
Kingairloch
Camasnacroise
Eilean Balnagowan
Keil
Cuil Bay
Shuna I.
Lurignich
Bealach
Appin House
Portnacroish
KINLOCHLAICH HOUSE GARDENS
Appin
Port Appin
Glensanda
Port Ramsay
Lismore
Achnacroish
Baligrundle
Achinduin
Kilcheran
Eilean Musdile
Eriska
North Shian
South Shian
SCOTTISH SEA LIFE SANCTUARY
Barcaldine
Dalrannoch
Barcaldine Forest
Creagan
South Creagan
Sutherland Grove
Fasnacloich
Invercreran
Glasdrum
Druimavuic
GLASDRUM WOOD
Elleric
Glenure
Dalness
Alltchaorunn
Inverchaorann
Glenceitlein
Lochetive Ho.
Gualachulain
Clashgour
Forest Lodge
Inveroran Hotel
Bridge of Orchy
Black Mount
WEST HIGHLAND WAY
Ferlochan
Baravullin
Benderloch
Ledaig
Kiel Crofts
Achnacree
Achnaba
ARDCHATTAN PRIORY GARDENS
ARDCHATTAN PRIORY
North Connel
Connel
Black Crofts
FALLS OF LORA
DUNSTAFFNAGE CASTLE
Dunbeg
Ganavan
Dunollie
OBAN/OBAN LODGE
MCCAIG'S TOWER
OBAN DISTILLERY
OBAN VISITOR CENTRE
Oban
Kerrera
Achnacloich
ACHNACLOICH GARDEN
Muckairn
Stonefield
Achlaven
Fearnoch Forest
Bonawe
BONAWE IRON FURNACE
INVERAWE FISHERIES AND SMOKERIES EXHIBITION
Inverawe Ho.
Brochroy
Taynuilt
Ichrachan
Bridge of Awe
Pass of Brander
Cadderlie
Inverliver
Glennoe
Loch Etive
Glen Kinglass
Archastlich
Arrivain
Duiletter
Stronmilchan
Achnafalnich
Inverlochy
Dalmally
Glenview
Corryghoil
MCINTYRE MONUMENT
KILCHURN CASTLE
Lochawe
CRUACHAN DAM VISITOR CENTRE
Falls of Cruachan
ARDANAISEIG GARDENS
Ardanaiseig
Innis Chonain
INISHAIL CHAPEL
Innistrynich
Cladich
Portsonachan
South Port
Kilchrenan
Annat
North Port
Lower Achachenna
OBAN RARE BREEDS FARM PARK
BARGUILLEAN GARDENS
Balindore
Airdeny
GLEN NANT
Barranrioch
Glenamachrie
Killiechoinich
Glen Lonan
Altnacraig
Balliemore
Ardmore
Gylen Park
Gallanach
Colgin
Kilbride
Kilmore
Barran
Am Buth
Dunach
GLENFEOCHAN HOUSE GARDENS
Ardentallen
Knipoch
Kilninver
Barochreal
Musdale
Midmuir
Scammadale
Bragleenmore
Raera
Clachan
CLACHAN BRIDGE
Blaran
Innie
Fineglen
Inverinan
Ballimeanoch
Lochavich Ho
Drissaig
Kilmun
Barnaline
Dalavich
Blarghour
Ardchonnell
ARDCHONNELL CASTLE
Portinnisherrich
Tullich
Elrigbeag
Rob Roy's House
Glenfyne Lodge
Achadunan
Clachan
Drishaig
Cairndow
ARDKINGLAS WOODLAND GARDEN
Maam
Three Bridges
Carloonan
BELL TOWER
INVERARAY CASTLE
COMBINED OPERATIONS MUSEUM
INVERARAY JAIL
Inveraray
MARITIME MUSEUM
Newtown
Ardno
St Catherine's
Rest and Be Thankful
Glen Kinglas
Monevechadan
Succoth
Ardgartan
Ardmay
Drimsynie
Lochgoilhead
Inveronich
Carrick
Lettermay
Coilessan
Creagan Sithe
Ardgoil Forest
Kilchoan
Melfort
Ardanstur
Kilmelford
Glenmore
Kames
Arduaine
ARDUAINE GARDEN
Lagalochan
Garraron
Turnalt
Barravullin
Craobh Haven
Lunga
Barbreck Ho
Kintraw
Lerigoligan
Ardfern
Arichamish
Inverliever Lodge
Inverliever Forest
Kilmaha
Eredine
Eredine Forest
Durran
Braevallich
Torran
Ford
Ederline
Finchairn
FINCHAIRN CASTLE
Stroneskar
Kirkton
Eilean Righ
CARNASSARIE CASTLE
Kilmartin
GLEBE CAIRN
KILMARTIN HOUSE TRUST
Barmolloch
Dalchenna
Ardnagowan
Auchindrain
AUCHINDRAIN OPEN AIR MUSEUM
Brenchoillie
Kenmore
Creggans
Clachan
Strachur
Strachur Bay
Strachurmore
Mid Letter
Furnace
Sandhole
Cumlodden
Newton
Glen Shira
Glen Aray
Glen Fyne
Glen Shira
Glen Sluain
Invernoaden
Glenbranter
Glenbranter Forest
Leanach
Garbhallt
LACHLAN CASTLE
Lachlan Bay
Minard
Crarae
CRARAE GLEN GARDENS
Tullochgorm
Leckuary
Kilbride
Poltalloch
Duntrune
Loch Crinan
Island Macaskin
Shuna
Rubha Seanach
Glen Euchar
Glen Feochan
Glen Nant
Glen Liver
Glen Noe
Glen Strae
Glen Orchy
Glen Etive
Glen Creran
Glen Ure
Loch Awe
Loch Fyne
Loch Creran
Loch Nell
Loch Avich
Loch Scammadale
Loch Tralaig
Loch Nant
Loch Tromlee
Loch Shira
Loch Eck
Loch Goil
CRAIGNURE 0:45
COLL 2:40
TIREE 3:20
CASTLEBAY 4:50
LOCHBOISDALE 5:20
COLONSAY 2:20

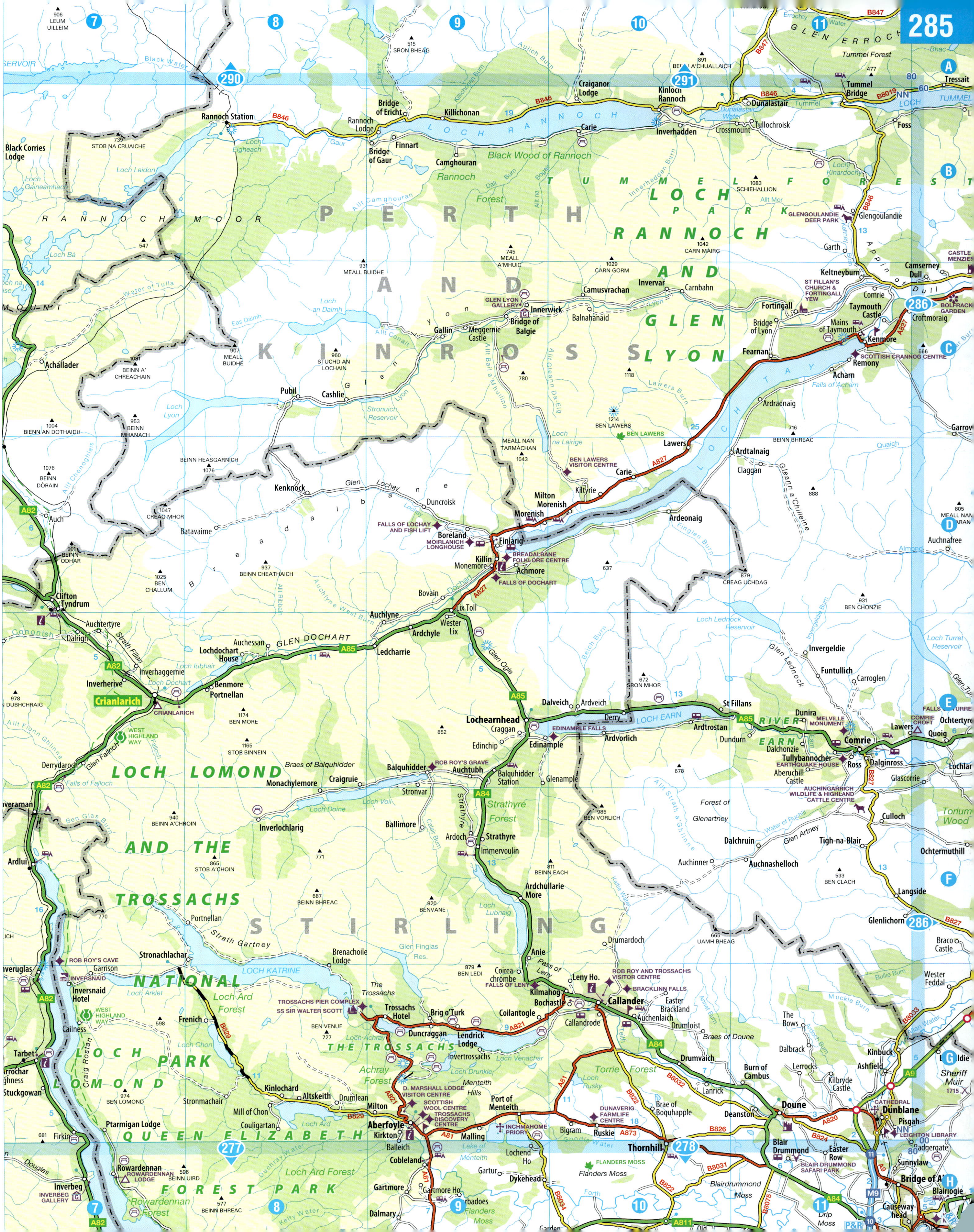

RANNOCH MOOR
Rannoch Station
Loch Laidon
Black Corries Lodge
STOB NA CRUAICHE
Bridge of Ericht
Killichonan
LOCH RANNOCH
Bridge of Gaur
Finnart
Camghouran
Black Wood of Rannoch
Rannoch Forest
Carie
Craiganor Lodge
Kinloch Rannoch
Dunalastair
Inverhadden
Crossmount
Tullochroisk
Tummel Bridge
Tressait
Foss
GLEN ERROCHTY
Tummel Forest
LOCH TUMMEL
SCHIEHALLION
TUMMEL FOREST PARK
LOCH RANNOCH AND GLEN LYON
GLENGOULANDIE DEER PARK
Glengoulandie
CARN MAIRG
Garth
Keltneyburn
Camserney
Dull
CASTLE MENZIES
ST FILLAN'S CHURCH & FORTINGALL YEW
Fortingall
Comrie
Taymouth Castle
Croftmoraig
Bridge of Lyon
Mains of Taymouth
Kenmore
SCOTTISH CRANNOG CENTRE
Remony
Acharn
Falls of Acharn
Fearnan
Ardradnaig
BEN LAWERS
BEN LAWERS VISITOR CENTRE
Lawers
Ardtalnaig
Claggan
Carie
Kiltyrie
Milton Morenish
Morenish
Ardeonaig
Finlarig
Killin
BREADALBANE FOLKLORE CENTRE
Achmore
FALLS OF DOCHART
FALLS OF LOCHAY AND FISH LIFT
Boreland
MOIRLANICH LONGHOUSE
Monemore
Duncroisk
Kenknock
Glen Lochay
Batavaime
Breadalbane
PERTH AND KINROSS
GLEN LYON GALLERY
Innerwick
Bridge of Balgie
Gallin
Meggernie Castle
Camusvrachan
Balnahanaid
Inververvar
Carnbahn
Pubil
Cashlie
Stronuich Reservoir
Loch Lyon
Loch an Daimh
MEALL BUIDHE
STUCHD AN LOCHAIN
BEINN A' CHREACHAIN
Achallader
BEINN MHANACH
BIENN AN DOTHAIDH
BEINN DÒRAIN
Auch
CREAG MHOR
BEINN ODHAR
BEN CHALLUM
BEINN CHEATHAICH
BEINN HEASGARNICH
MEALL NAN TARMACHAN
Loch na Lairige
CREAG UCHDAG
BEN CHONZIE
Auchnafree
Loch Lednock Reservoir
Invergeldie
Funtullich
Carroglen
Glen Lednock
Loch Turret Reservoir
Clifton
Tyndrum
Auchtertyre
Dalrigh
Strath Fillan
Bovain
Lix Toll
Auchlyne
Wester Lix
Ardchyle
GLEN DOCHART
Auchessan
Lochdochart House
Ledcharrie
Loch Iubhair
Inverhaggernie
Inverherive
Crianlarich
CRIANLARICH
Benmore
Portnellan
BEN MORE
STOB BINNEIN
Glen Ogle
Lochearnhead
Craggan
Edinchip
Edinample
EDINAMPLE FALLS
Dalveich
Ardveich
Derry
LOCH EARN
Ardvorlich
Ardtrostan
St Fillans
Dundurn
RIVER EARN
Dunira
MELVILLE MONUMENT
Dalchonzie
Comrie
Lawers
Ochtertyre
Quoig
Tullybannocher
EARTHQUAKE HOUSE
Ross
Dalginross
Aberuchill Castle
Glascorrie
AUCHINGARRICH WILDLIFE & HIGHLAND CATTLE CENTRE
Culloch
Forest of Glenartney
Glen Artney
Dalchruin
Tigh-na-Blair
Auchinner
Auchnashelloch
BEN CLACH
Ochtermuthill
Langside
Glenlichorn
Torlum Wood
WEST HIGHLAND WAY
Glen Falloch
Derrydaroch
Falls of Falloch
LOCH LOMOND AND THE TROSSACHS NATIONAL PARK
Braes of Balquhidder
Balquhidder
ROB ROY'S GRAVE
Auchtubh
Balquhidder Station
Glenample
Monachylemore
Craigruie
Stronvar
Loch Voil
Loch Doine
Inverlochlarig
Ballimore
Strathyre
Strathyre Forest
Ardoch
Immervoulin
BEN VORLICH
BEINN A' CHROIN
STOB A' CHOIN
BEINN EACH
Ardchullarie More
Loch Lubnaig
BEINN BHREAC
BENVANE
STIRLING
Ardlui
Portnellan
Strath Gartney
Glen Finglas Res.
Brenachoile Lodge
Stronachlachar
LOCH KATRINE
ROB ROY'S CAVE
Inversnaid
Garrison
Inversnaid Hotel
Loch Arklet
Loch Ard Forest
TROSSACHS PIER COMPLEX
SS SIR WALTER SCOTT
The Trossachs
Trossachs Hotel
Brig o'Turk
BEN VENUE
BEN LEDI
Coirea-chrombe
FALLS OF LENY
Pass of Leny
Anie
Drumardoch
ROB ROY AND TROSSACHS VISITOR CENTRE
BRACKLINN FALLS
Leny Ho.
Kilmahog
Bochastle
Callander
Callandrode
Coilantogle
Duncraggan
Lendrick Lodge
Loch Venachar
Invertrossachs
THE TROSSACHS
Achray Forest
Loch Achray
Loch Drunkie
Menteith Hills
D. MARSHALL LODGE VISITOR CENTRE
SCOTTISH WOOL CENTRE
TROSSACHS DISCOVERY CENTRE
Aberfoyle
Kirkton
Milton
Drumlean
Altskeith
Kinlochard
Loch Ard
Couligartan
Mill of Chon
Stronmachair
Frenich
Loch Chon
Tarbet
Arrochar
Stuckgowan
Cailness
LOCH LOMOND
BEN LOMOND
Ptarmigan Lodge
Firkin
Rowardennan
ROWARDENNAN LODGE
Inverbeg
INVERBEG GALLERY
QUEEN ELIZABETH FOREST PARK
Loch Ard Forest
Rowardennan Forest
BEINN UIRD
BEINN BHREAC
Balleich
Cobleland
Gartmore
Gartmore Ho
Dalmary
Flanders Moss
Port of Menteith
Lake of Menteith
INCHMAHOME PRIORY
Malling
Lochend Ho
Gartur
Dykehead
Bigram
Ruskie
DUNAVERIG FARMLIFE CENTRE
FLANDERS MOSS
Flanders Moss
Thornhill
Blairdrummond Moss
BLAIR DRUMMOND SAFARI PARK
Blair Drummond
Torrie Forest
Brae of Boquhapple
Lanrick
Deanston
Doune
Drumvaich
Burn of Cambus
Easter Brackland
Auchenlaich
Drumloist
Braes of Doune
The Bows
Dalbrack
Lerrocks
Kilbryde Castle
Kinbuck
Ashfield
Dunblane
CATHEDRAL
LEIGHTON LIBRARY
Pisgah
Sheriff Muir
Sunnylaw
Easter Row
Bridge of Allan
Blairlogie
Causewayhead
Braco Castle
Wester Feddal
UAMH BHEAG
SRON MHOR

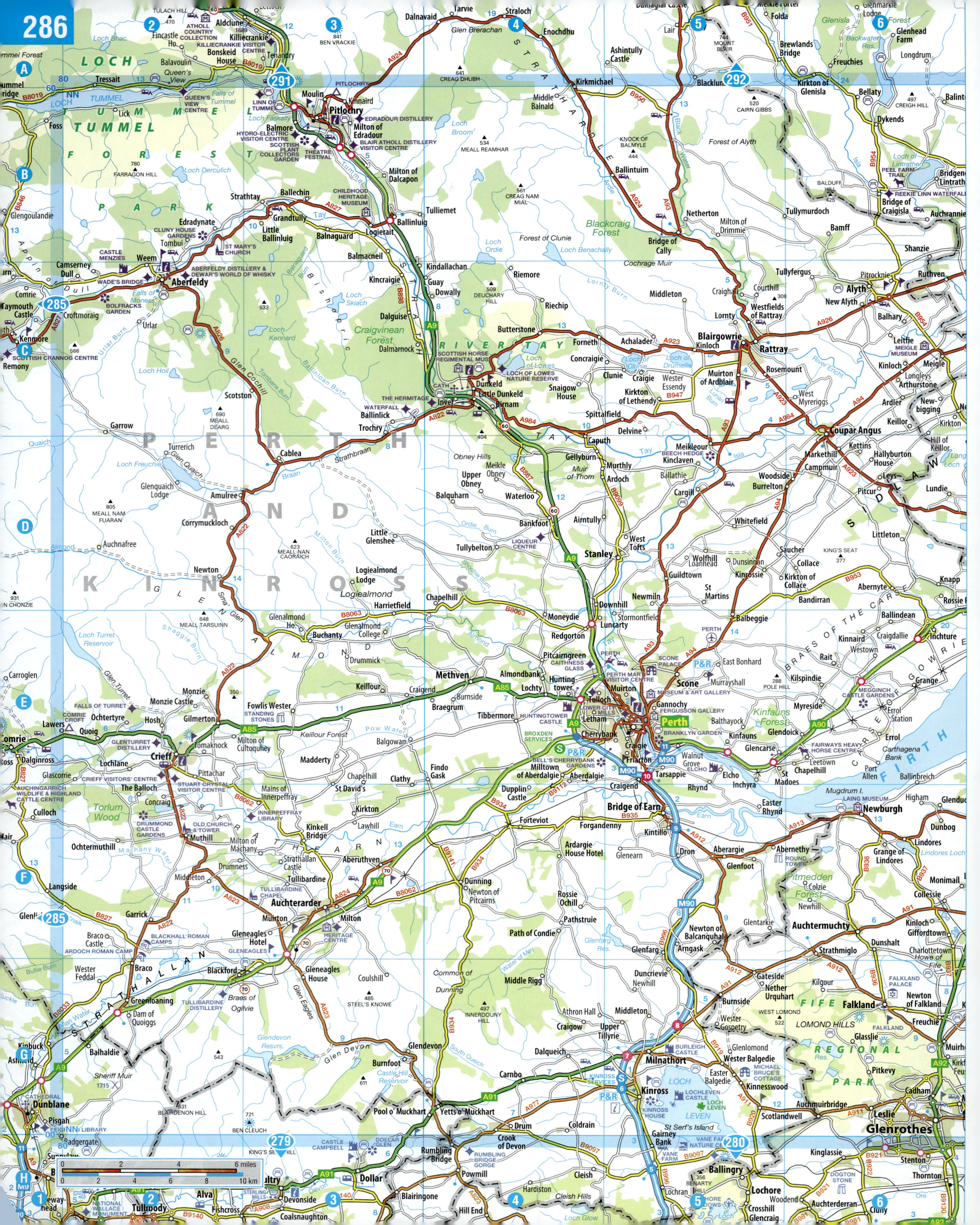

285
291
292
279
280
LOCH TUMMEL
TUMMEL FOREST PARK
PERTH AND KINROSS
GLEN ALMOND
STRATHEARN
STRATHALLAN
STRATH TAY
RIVER TAY
FIRTH OF TAY
CARSE OF GOWRIE
SIDLAW
FIFE REGIONAL PARK
LOMOND HILLS
Pitlochry
Moulin
Aldclune
Killiecrankie
Tenandry
Dalnavaid
Straloch
Enochdhu
Kirkmichael
Blacklunans
Ashintully Castle
Forest of Alyth
Bridge of Cally
Blairgowrie
Rattray
Alyth
New Alyth
Coupar Angus
Meigle
Kinloch
Ballinluig
Logierait
Grandtully
Strathtay
Aberfeldy
Weem
Kenmore
Croftmoraig
Dalguise
Dunkeld
Birnam
Inver
Caputh
Murthly
Stanley
Bankfoot
Amulree
Corrymuckloch
Glenquaich Lodge
Newton
Harrietfield
Buchanty
Methven
Almondbank
Luncarty
Redgorton
Scone
Perth
Bridge of Earn
Kintillo
Aberargie
Abernethy
Newburgh
Errol
Inchture
St Madoes
Glencarse
Kinfauns
Rait
Crieff
Gilmerton
Monzie
Muthill
Comrie
Auchterarder
Aberuthven
Dunning
Forteviot
Forgandenny
Gleneagles Hotel
Blackford
Braco
Greenloaning
Dunblane
Glendevon
Yetts o' Muckhart
Pool o' Muckhart
Dollar
Tillicoultry
Alva
Tullibody
Milnathort
Kinross
Loch Leven
Scotlandwell
Auchtermuchty
Strathmiglo
Falkland
Freuchie
Leslie
Glenrothes
Ballingry
Lochore
Kelty
Drum
Crook of Devon
Rumbling Bridge
Powmill
Cleish
Path of Condie
Glenfarg
Arngask
Glenfoot

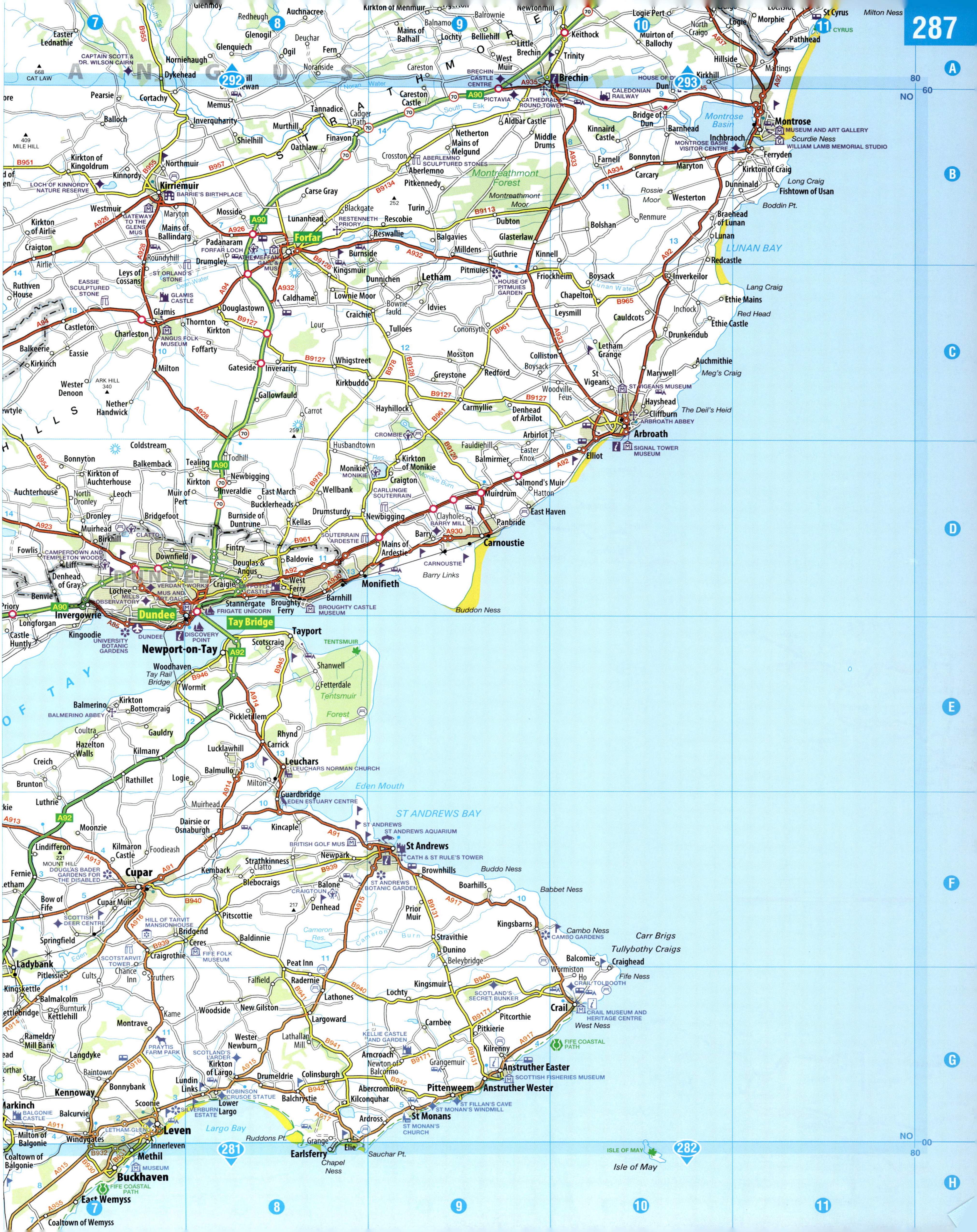
A N G U S
S T R A T H M O R E
Kirriemuir
Forfar
Brechin
Montrose
Montrose Basin
Arbroath
Carnoustie
Monifieth
Dundee
Tay Bridge
Newport-on-Tay
Tayport
Broughty Ferry
Invergowrie
Letham
Friockheim
Inverkeilor
Lunan Bay
St Cyrus
Glamis
Tentsmuir Forest
Leuchars
Eden Mouth
St Andrews Bay
St Andrews
Cupar
Crail
Anstruther Easter
Anstruther Wester
Pittenweem
St Monans
Elie
Earlsferry
Largo Bay
Leven
Methil
Buckhaven
East Wemyss
Isle of May
Fife Ness
Buddon Ness
Carr Brigs
Kingsbarns
Ladybank
Kennoway
Lower Largo
Lundin Links
A90
A92
A91
A94
A930
A917
A915
Scurdie Ness
Red Head
Lang Craig
Barry Links
Montreathmont Forest
Carnoustie
Arbroath Abbey
Signal Tower Museum
Scottish Fisheries Museum
Crail Museum and Heritage Centre
St Andrews Aquarium
British Golf Mus
Cath & St Rule's Tower
St Andrews Botanic Garden
Fife Coastal Path
Isle of May
292
293
281
282
7
8
9
10
11
A
B
C
D
E
F
G
H

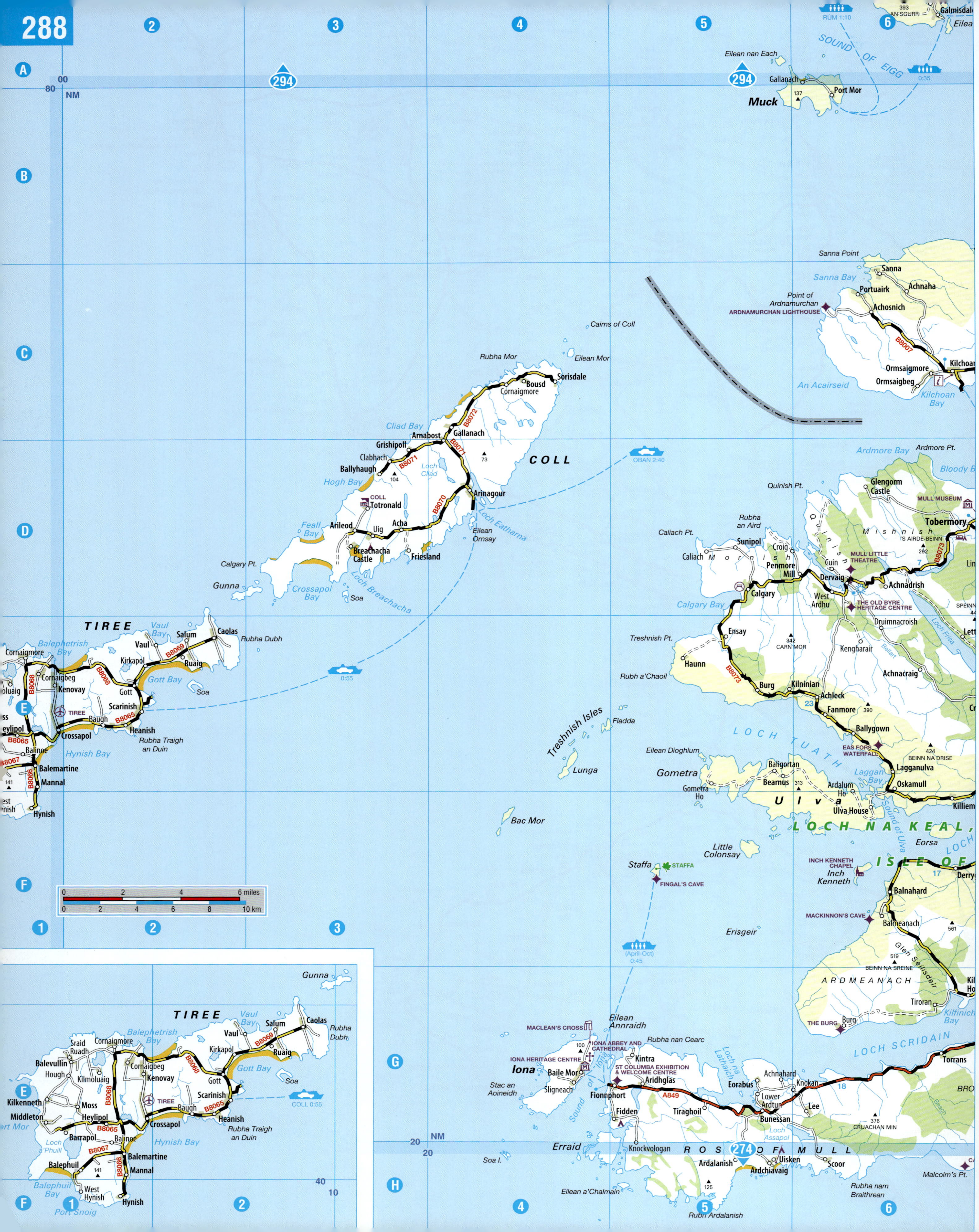

294
Eilean nan Each
Gallanach
Port Mor
Muck
137
SOUND OF EIGG
RUM 1:10
0:35
393
AN SGURR
Galmisdale
Sanna Point
Sanna Bay
Sanna
Portuairk
Achnaha
Point of Ardnamurchan
ARDNAMURCHAN LIGHTHOUSE
Achosnich
B8007
Ormsaigmore
Ormsaigbeg
Kilchoan
Kilchoan Bay
An Acairseid
Cairns of Coll
Eilean Mor
Rubha Mor
Sorisdale
Bousd
Cornaigmore
B8072
Cliad Bay
Arnabost
Gallanach
Grishipoll
Clabhach
Ballyhaugh
B8071
Loch Cliad
104
73
COLL
Hogh Bay
Arinagour
COLL
Totronald
B8070
Feall Bay
Arileod
Uig
Acha
Eilean Ornsay
Loch Eatharna
Breachacha Castle
Friesland
Calgary Pt.
Gunna
Crossapol Bay
Soa
Loch Breachacha
OBAN 2:40
0:55
TIREE
Vaul Bay
Salum
Caolas
Rubha Dubh
Balephetrish Bay
Cornaigmore
Vaul
B8069
Kirkapol
Ruaig
Cornaigbeg
B8068
Kenovay
Gott Bay
Soa
Gott
Scarinish
TIREE
Baugh
B8065
Heanish
Rubha Traigh an Duin
Crossapol
Hynish Bay
Balinoe
Balemartine
Mannal
B8066
B8067
141
Hynish
Ardmore Bay
Ardmore Pt.
Bloody Bay
Quinish Pt.
Glengorm Castle
MULL MUSEUM
Tobermory
Mishnish
Rubha an Aird
Caliach Pt.
Sunipol
Croig
Quinish
Caliach
Mornish
Penmore Mill
MULL LITTLE THEATRE
Cuin
Dervaig
Achnadrish
B8073
Calgary
West Ardhu
THE OLD BYRE HERITAGE CENTRE
Calgary Bay
Druimnacroish
Loch Frisa
Treshnish Pt.
Ensay
342
CARN MOR
Kengharair
Haunn
Achnacraig
Rubh a'Chaoil
Burg
Kilninian
Achleck
Fanmore
390
Treshnish Isles
Fladda
LOCH TUATH
Ballygown
Lunga
Eilean Dioghlum
EAS FORS WATERFALL
424
BEINN NA DRISE
Gometra
Baligortan
Laggan Bay
Lagganulva
Bearnus
313
Ardalum Ho
Oskamull
Gometra Ho
Ulva
Ulva House
Killiemor
Bac Mor
LOCH NA KEAL
Sound of Ulva
Eorsa
Little Colonsay
INCH KENNETH CHAPEL
Inch Kenneth
ISLE OF
Staffa
STAFFA
FINGAL'S CAVE
Balnahard
MACKINNON'S CAVE
Balmeanach
561
Erisgeir
(April-Oct) 0:45
519
BEINN NA SREINE
Glen Seilisdeir
ARDMEANACH
Tiroran
THE BURG
Burg
Kilfinichen Bay
Eilean Annraidh
MACLEAN'S CROSS
100
IONA ABBEY AND CATHEDRAL
Rubha nan Cearc
IONA HERITAGE CENTRE
Kintra
Iona
ST COLUMBA EXHIBITION & WELCOME CENTRE
Aridhglas
Loch na Lathaich
Achnahard
LOCH SCRIDAIN
Torrans
Baile Mor
Stac an Aoineidh
Sligneach
Fionnphort
A849
Eorabus
Knockan
Lower Ardtun
18
Sound of Iona
Fidden
Tiraghoil
Bunessan
Lee
376
CRUACHAN MIN
Loch Assapol
Erraid
Knockvologan
ROSS OF MULL
274
Uisken
Scoor
Soa I.
Ardalanish
Ardchiavaig
125
Malcolm's Pt.
Eilean a'Chalmain
Rubha nam Braithrean
Rubh Ardalanish
0 2 4 6 miles
0 2 4 6 8 10 km
00
80
NM
20
TIREE
Gunna
Vaul Bay
Caolas
Salum
Balephetrish Bay
Rubha Dubh
Sraid Ruadh
Cornaigmore
Vaul
Kirkapol
B8069
Ruaig
Balevullin
Cornaigbeg
B8068
Hough
Kilmoluaig
Kenovay
Gott Bay
Gott
Soa
Kilkenneth
TIREE
Scarinish
Moss
B8068
Baugh
B8065
COLL 0:55
Middleton
Heylipol
B8065
Heanish
Port Mor
Crossapol
Rubha Traigh an Duin
Barrapol
Balinoe
Hynish Bay
Loch a'Phuill
B8067
Balephuil
141
Balemartine
B8066
Mannal
Balephuil Bay
West Hynish
Hynish
Port Snoig
40
10

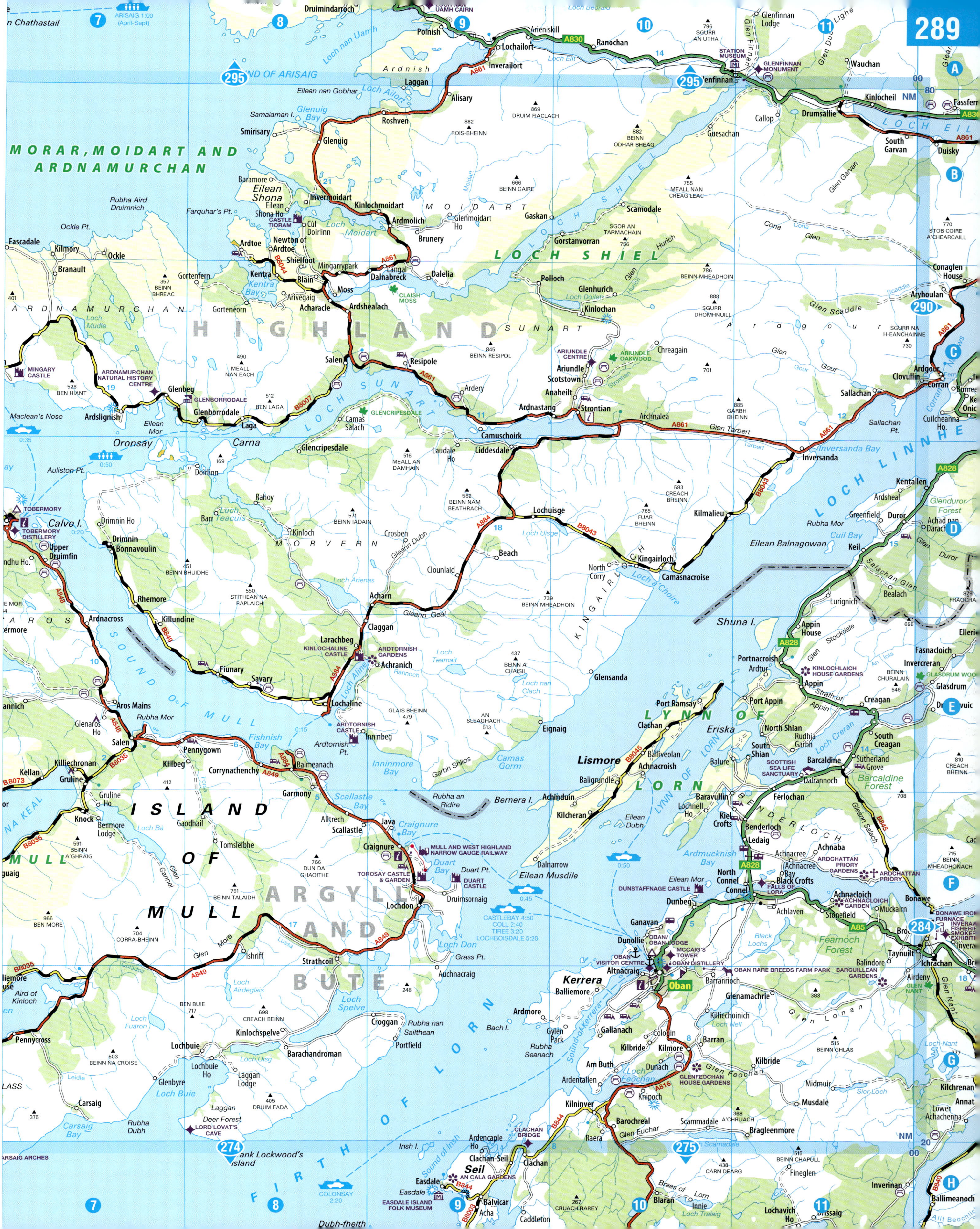
MORAR, MOIDART AND ARDNAMURCHAN
HIGHLAND
ARGYLL AND BUTE
ISLAND OF MULL
LOCH SHIEL
LOCH LINNHE
SOUND OF MULL
FIRTH OF LORN
LYNN OF LORN
SOUND OF ARISAIG
LOCH SUNART
MOIDART
ARDNAMURCHAN
SUNART
Ardgour
MORVERN
KINGAIRLOCH
BENDERLOCH
ARISAIG 1:00 (April-Sept)
Druimindarroch
Polnish
Lochailort
Inverailort
Arieniskill
Ranochan
Glenfinnan
Glenfinnan Lodge
GLENFINNAN MONUMENT
STATION MUSEUM
Wauchan
Kinlocheil
Fassfern
Drumsallie
Callop
Guesachan
South Garvan
Duisky
Laggan
Ardnish
Alisary
Roshven
Glenuig
Samalaman I.
Smirisary
Eilean nan Gobhar
Loch Ailort
Glenuig Bay
Baramore
Eilean Shona
Invermoidart
Kinlochmoidart
Ardmolich
Glenmoidart Ho
Brunery
Gaskan
Scamodale
Gorstanvorran
Rubha Aird Druimnich
Farquhar's Pt.
Ockle Pt.
Fascadale
Kilmory
Ockle
Branault
Gortenfern
Kentra
Kentra Bay
Ardtoe
Newton of Ardtoe
Shielfoot
Cul Doirlinn
CASTLE TIORAM
Mingarrypark
Langal
Dalnabreck
Dalelia
Blain
Arivegaig
Moss
Acharacle
Ardshealach
CLAISH MOSS
Polloch
Glenhurich
Kinlochan
Gorteneorn
Salen
Resipole
ARIUNDLE CENTRE
ARIUNDLE OAKWOOD
Chreagain
Ariundle
Scotstown
Anaheilt
Strontian
Ardnastang
Ardery
MINGARY CASTLE
ARDNAMURCHAN NATURAL HISTORY CENTRE
Glenbeg
GLENBORRODALE
Glenborrodale
Ardslignish
Maclean's Nose
Laga
Camas Salach
GLENCRIPESDALE
Camuschoirk
Archnalea
Glen Tarbert
Conaglen House
Aryhoulan
Ardgour
Clovullin
Corran
Sallachan
Sallachan Pt.
Cuilcheanna Ho.
Inversanda
Inversanda Bay
Oronsay
Carna
Glencripesdale
Liddesdale
Laudale Ho
Auliston Pt.
Doirlinn
TOBERMORY
TOBERMORY DISTILLERY
Calve I.
Drimnin Ho
Drimnin
Bonnavoulin
Upper Druimfin
Rahoy
Barr
Loch Teacuis
Kinloch
Crosben
Lochuisge
Loch Uisge
Kilmalieu
Kingairloch
Camasnacroise
North Corry
Beach
Clounlaid
Rhemore
Killundine
Ardnacross
Acharn
Claggan
Gleann Geal
Larachbeg
KINLOCHALINE CASTLE
ARDTORNISH GARDENS
Achranich
Fiunary
Savary
Lochaline
Aros Mains
Glenaros Ho
Rubha Mor
Salen
Killiechronan
Gruline
Kellan
Pennygown
Killbeg
Corrynachenchy
Fishnish Bay
Balmeanach
ARDTORNISH CASTLE
Ardtornish Pt.
Inninbeg
Innimore Bay
Garbh Shlios
Camas Gorm
Eignaig
Glensanda
Kentallen
Ardsheal
Duror
Greenfield
Keil
Cuil Bay
Eilean Balnagowan
Lurignich
Bealach
Shuna I.
Appin House
Portnacroish
Ardtur
KINLOCHLAICH HOUSE GARDENS
Appin
Fasnacloich
Invercreran
Glasdrum
Creagan
Port Appin
Port Ramsay
Clachan
Lismore
Eriska
North Shian
South Shian
Rudha Garbh
SCOTTISH SEA LIFE SANCTUARY
Barcaldine
Barcaldine Forest
Dalrannoch
South Creagan
Balliveolan
Achnacroish
Baligrundle
Achinduin
Kilcheran
Bernera I.
Rubha an Ridire
Balure
Baravullin
Ferlochan
Lochnell Ho
Kiel Crofts
Benderloch
Ledaig
Achnacree
Achnaba
ARDCHATTAN PRIORY GARDENS
ARDCHATTAN PRIORY
Bonawe
North Connel
Connel
Black Crofts
FALLS OF LORA
DUNSTAFFNAGE CASTLE
Dunbeg
Achnacloich
ACHNACLOICH GARDEN
Muckairn
Achlaven
Stonefield
Taynuilt
Fearnoch Forest
Ganavan
Dunollie
OBAN VISITOR CENTRE
MCCAIG'S TOWER
OBAN DISTILLERY
Oban
Kerrera
Balliemore
Altnacraig
OBAN RARE BREEDS FARM PARK
BARGUILLEAN GARDENS
Barranrioch
Glenamachrie
Ardmore
Gylen Park
Gallanach
Kilbride
Kilmore
Barran
Am Buth
Dunach
GLENFEOCHAN HOUSE GARDENS
Glen Feochan
Ardentallen
Kilninver
Barochreal
Scammadale
Bragleenmore
Knipoch
Glen Euchar
Raera
CLACHAN BRIDGE
Clachan-Seil
Clachan
Seil
AN CALA GARDENS
Easdale
EASDALE ISLAND FOLK MUSEUM
Balvicar
Acha
Caddleton
Ardencaple Ho
Insh I.
Blaran
Braes of Lorn
Innie
Loch Tralaig
Lochavich Ho
Finegeln
Inverinan
Ballimeanoch
Kilchrenan
Annat
Lower Achachenna
Musdale
Midmuir
Ichrachan
Airdeny
Balindore
GLEN NANT
Glen Nant
Glen Lonan
Killiechoinich
Knock
Benmore Lodge
Gruline Ho
Gaodhail
Tomsleibhe
Glen Cannel
Craignure
Craignure Bay
MULL AND WEST HIGHLAND NARROW GAUGE RAILWAY
TOROSAY CASTLE & GARDEN
DUART CASTLE
Duart Pt.
Duart Bay
Druimsornaig
Lochdon
Loch Don
Grass Pt.
Auchnacraig
Java
Scallastle
Alltrech
Scallastle Bay
Garmony
Eilean Musdile
Dalnarrow
Eilean Dubh
Ardmucknish Bay
Strathcoil
Ishriff
Glen More
Loch Spelve
Croggan
Rubha nan Sailthean
Portfield
Barachandroman
Kinlochspelve
Lochbuie
Lochbuie Ho
Laggan Lodge
Loch Uisg
Glenbyre
Loch Buie
Carsaig
Carsaig Bay
Rubha Dubh
Laggan Deer Forest
LORD LOVAT'S CAVE
Pennycross
Aird of Kinloch
Loch Fuaron
Rubha Seanach
Bach I.
CASTLEBAY 4:50
COLL 2:40
TIREE 3:20
LOCHBOISDALE 5:20
COLONSAY 2:20
Dubh-fheith
Frank Lockwood's Island
CARSAIG ARCHES
A830
A861
A884
A848
A849
A828
A85
A816
B8007
B8043
B8044
B8035
B8045
B845
B844
B849
B8073
295
290
284
274
275

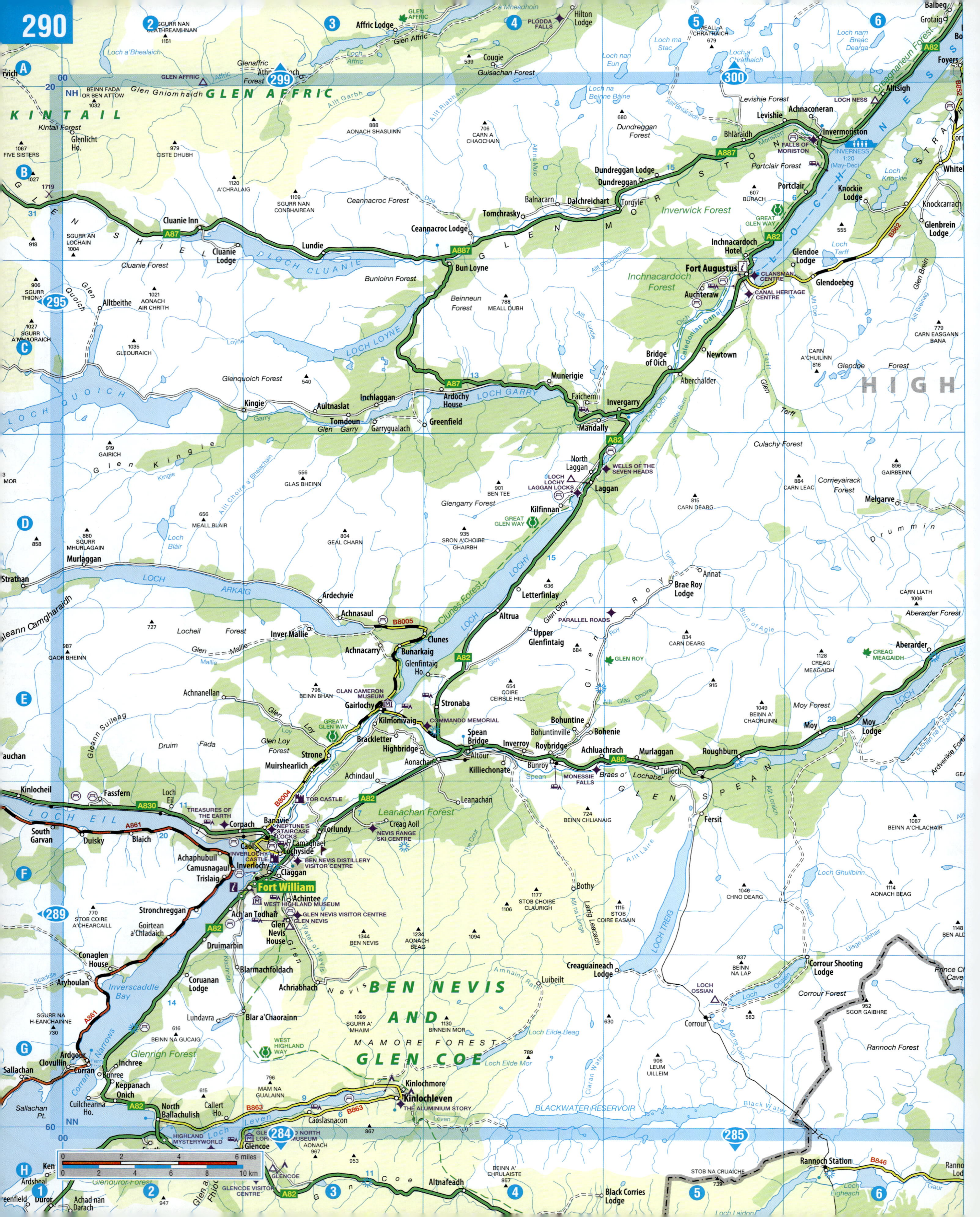
KINTAIL
GLEN AFFRIC
Affric Lodge
Glen Affric
Loch a'Bhealaich
Glenaffric
Athnamulloch
Forest
299
300
Cougie
Guisachan Forest
Hilton Lodge
PLODDA FALLS
Loch ma Stac
Loch nan Eun
Loch na Beinne Bàine
Levishie Forest
Levishie
Achnaconeran
Bhlaraidh
Invermoriston
FALLS OF MORISTON
INVERNESS 1:20 (May-Dec)
Portclair Forest
Portclair
Knockie Lodge
Glenbrein Lodge
Knockcarrach
Whitebridge
Foyers
Alltsigh
LOCH NESS
Grotaig
Balbeg
Dundreggan Lodge
Dundreggan
Dundreggan Forest
Balnacarn
Dalchreichart
Torgyle
Tomchrasky
Inverwick Forest
GLEN MORISTON
Ceannacroc Forest
Ceannacroc Lodge
Cluanie Inn
Cluanie Lodge
LOCH CLUANIE
Cluanie Forest
Lundie
Bun Loyne
Bunloinn Forest
Beinneun Forest
MEALL DUBH
Inchnacardoch Hotel
Fort Augustus
Inchnacardoch Forest
CLANSMAN CENTRE
CANAL HERITAGE CENTRE
Auchteraw
Glendoe Lodge
Glendoebeg
Caledonian Canal
Bridge of Oich
Newtown
Aberchalder
LOCH LOYNE
Glenquoich Forest
LOCH QUOICH
Kingie
Aultnaslat
Inchlaggan
Ardochy House
LOCH GARRY
Munerigie
Faichem
Invergarry
Mandally
Tomdoun
Glen Garry
Garrygualach
Greenfield
Glen Kingie
GLAS BHEINN
BEN TEE
North Laggan
LOCH LOCHY
LAGGAN LOCKS
WELLS OF THE SEVEN HEADS
Laggan
Kilfinnan
Glengarry Forest
GREAT GLEN WAY
Culachy Forest
Corrieyairack Forest
Melgarve
CARN DEARG
Murlaggan
Strathan
LOCH ARKAIG
Ardechive
Achnasaul
Locheil Forest
Inver Mallie
Glen Mallie
Achnacarry
Clunes
Bunarkaig
Glenfintaig Ho.
Clunes Forest
LOCH LOCHY
Letterfinlay
Altrua
Brae Roy Lodge
Annat
Glen Gloy
PARALLEL ROADS
Upper Glenfintaig
Glen Roy
GLEN ROY
Aberarder Forest
Aberarder
CREAG MEAGAIDH
LOCH LAGGAN
Moy Forest
Moy
Moy Lodge
CLAN CAMERON MUSEUM
Gairlochy
Kilmonivaig
COMMANDO MEMORIAL
Stronaba
Spean Bridge
Bohuntine
Bohuntinville
Bohenie
Inverroy
Roybridge
Achluachrach
Murlaggan
Roughburn
Tulloch
Glen Loy Forest
Strone
Brackletter
Highbridge
Aonachan
Altour
Killiechonate
Bunroy
MONESSIE FALLS
Braes o' Lochaber
GLEN SPEAN
Muirshearlich
Achindaul
TOR CASTLE
Leanachan
Leanachan Forest
Kinlocheil
Fassfern
LOCH EIL
TREASURES OF THE EARTH
Corpach
Banavie
NEPTUNE'S STAIRCASE LOCKS
Caol
Lochyside
Torlundy
Creag Aoil
NEVIS RANGE SKI CENTRE
INVERLOCHY CASTLE
Inverlochy
BEN NEVIS DISTILLERY VISITOR CENTRE
Claggan
South Garvan
Duisky
Blaich
Achaphubuil
Camusnagaul
Trislaig
Fort William
Achintee
WEST HIGHLAND MUSEUM
GLEN NEVIS VISITOR CENTRE
Ach'an Todhair
Glen Nevis House
Stronchreggan
Goirtean a'Chladaich
Druimarbin
BEN NEVIS
AONACH BEAG
Fersit
LOCH TREIG
Loch Ghuilbinn
Bothy
CHNO DEARG
Conaglen House
Aryhoulan
Inverscaddle Bay
Coruanan Lodge
Blarmachfoldach
Achriabhach
BEN NEVIS AND MAMORE FOREST GLEN COE
Creaguaineach Lodge
Luibeilt
Corrour Shooting Lodge
Corrour Forest
LOCH OSSIAN
Corrour
Lundavra
Blar a'Chaorainn
Loch Eilde Beag
Loch Eilde Mor
Rannoch Forest
Glenrigh Forest
WEST HIGHLAND WAY
Ardgour
Clovullin
Corran
Sallachan
Inchree
Bunree
Keppanach
Onich
Cuilcheanna Ho.
North Ballachulish
Callert Ho.
Kinlochmore
Kinlochleven
THE ALUMINIUM STORY
LOCH LEVEN
Caolasnacon
BLACKWATER RESERVOIR
Glencoe
GLENCOE
GLENCOE VISITOR CENTRE
Altnafeadh
Black Corries Lodge
Rannoch Station
284
285
289
295
0 2 4 6 miles
0 2 4 6 8 10 km

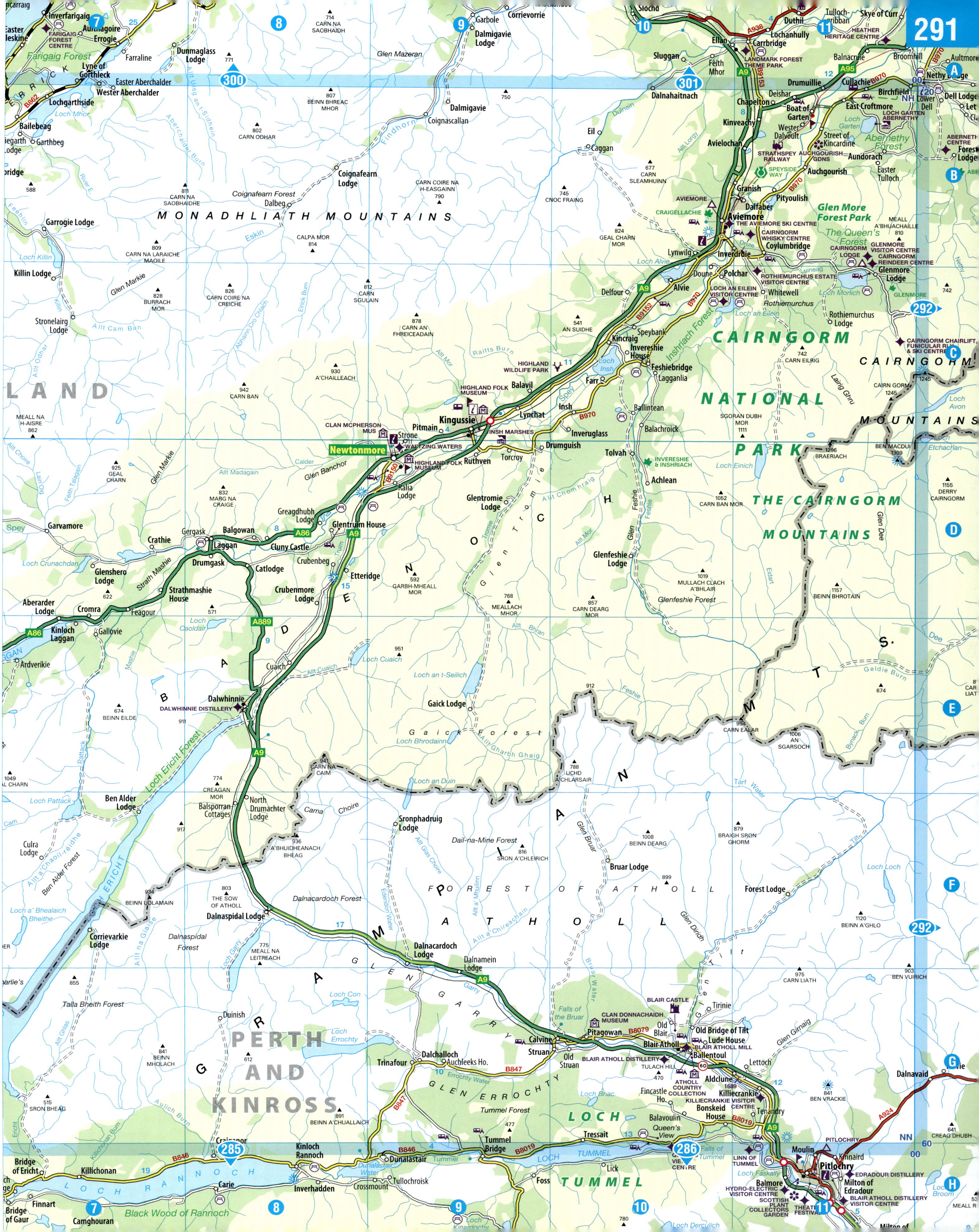
MONADHLIATH MOUNTAINS
CAIRNGORM NATIONAL PARK
THE CAIRNGORM MOUNTAINS
CAIRNGORM MOUNTAINS
FOREST OF ATHOLL
GRAMPIAN MOUNTAINS
PERTH AND KINROSS
GLEN GARRY
GLEN ERROCHTY
LOCH TUMMEL
LOCH RANNOCH
Inverfarigaig
Aultnagoire
Errogie
Farigaig Forest
Dunmaglass Lodge
Farraline
Lyne of Gorthleck
Easter Aberchalder
Wester Aberchalder
Lochgarthside
Loch Mhor
Bailebeag
Garthbeg
Garrogie Lodge
Loch Killin
Killin Lodge
Stronelairg Lodge
Glen Markie
Coignafearn Forest
Dalbeg
Coignafearn Lodge
Coignascallan
Dalmigavie
Dalmigavie Lodge
Garbole
Corrievorrie
Glen Mazeran
Findhorn
Slochd
Sluggan
Dalnahaitnach
Ellan
Carrbridge
Landmark Forest Theme Park
Lochanhully
Duthil
Tulloch
Skye of Curr
Heather Heritage Centre
Balnacruie
Broomhill
Nethy Bridge
Drumuillie
Cullachie
Deishar
Chapelton
Boat of Garten
Wester Dalvoult
Kinveachy
Avielochan
Street of Kincardine
Abernethy Forest
Aundorach
Auchgourish
Easter Tulloch
Strathspey Railway
Speyside Way
Granish
Dalfaber
Aviemore
Craigellachie
The Aviemore Ski Centre
Cairngorm Whisky Centre
Coylumbridge
Glen More Forest Park
The Queen's Forest
Glenmore Visitor Centre
Cairngorm Reindeer Centre
Glenmore Lodge
Loch Morlich
Rothiemurchus Estate Visitor Centre
Rothiemurchus
Rothiemurchus Lodge
Whitewell
Inverdruie
Polchar
Doune
Lynwilg
Loch Alvie
Alvie
Loch an Eilein Visitor Centre
Loch an Eilein
Delfour
Speybank
Kincraig
Inveresie House
Inshriach Forest
Feshiebridge
Lagganlia
Highland Wildlife Park
Loch Insh
Farr
Insh
Inveruglass
Balavil
Lynchat
Kingussie
Highland Folk Museum
Insh Marshes
Ruthven
Torcroy
Drumguish
Tolvah
Ballintean
Balachroick
Inveresie & Inshriach
Achlean
Loch Einich
Cairngorm Chairlift, Funicular Rly & Ski Centre
Carn Eilrig
Sgoran Dubh Mor
Braeriach
Ben Macdui
Carn Ban Mor
Derry Cairngorm
Glen Dee
Glen Feshie
Glenfeshie Lodge
Glenfeshie Forest
Mullach Clach a' Bhlair
Beinn Bhrotain
Carn Dearg Mor
Meallach Mhor
Glen Tromie
Glentromie Lodge
Newtonmore
Clan Macpherson Mus.
Strone
Pitmain
Waltzing Waters
Ralia Lodge
Glen Banchor
Greagdhubh Lodge
Balgowan
Gergask
Laggan
Cluny Castle
Crubenbeg
Glentruim House
Etteridge
Crathie
Garvamore
Loch Crunachdan
Glenshero Lodge
Drumgask
Catlodge
Strath Mashie
Strathmashie House
Crubenmore Lodge
Aberarder Lodge
Cromra
Feagour
Loch Caoldair
Kinloch Laggan
Gallovie
Ardverikie
Loch Cuaich
Cuaich
Dalwhinnie
Dalwhinnie Distillery
Loch an t-Seilich
Gaick Lodge
Gaick Forest
Loch Bhrodainn
Loch an Duin
Loch Ericht Forest
Loch Pattack
Ben Alder Lodge
Balsporran Cottages
North Drumachter Lodge
Culra Lodge
Ben Alder Forest
Loch a' Bhealaich Bheithe
Corrievarkie Lodge
Dalnaspidal Lodge
Dalnaspidal Forest
The Sow of Atholl
Sronphadruig Lodge
Dail-na-Mine Forest
Dalnacardoch Forest
Dalnacardoch Lodge
Dalnamein Lodge
Glen Bruar
Bruar Lodge
Forest Lodge
Loch Loch
Glen Tilt
Falls of the Bruar
Blair Castle
Clan Donnachaidh Museum
Tirinie
Calvine
Struan
Old Struan
Pitagowan
Old Blair
Old Bridge of Tilt
Lude House
Blair Atholl
Blair Atholl Watermill
Ballentoul
Blair Atholl Distillery
Tulach Hill
Aldclune
Killiecrankie
Killiecrankie Visitor Centre
Atholl Country Collection
Fincastle Ho.
Bonskeid House
Tenandry
Lettoch
Dalnavaid
Ben Vrackie
Loch Bhac
Balavoulin
Queen's View
Tressait
Falls of Tummel
Tummel Forest
Tummel Bridge
Loch Con
Loch Errochty
Dalchalloch
Auchleeks Ho.
Trinafour
Duinish
Talla Bheith Forest
Craiganour
Kinloch Rannoch
Dunalastair
Dunalastair Water
Tullochroisk
Crossmount
Inverhadden
Carie
Killichonan
Bridge of Ericht
Finnart
Bridge of Gaur
Camghouran
Black Wood of Rannoch
Foss
Lick
Loch Faskally
Linn of Tummel
Balmore
Hydro-Electric Visitor Centre
Scottish Plant Collectors Garden
Moulin
Pitlochry
Kinnaird
Edradour Distillery
Milton of Edradour
Blair Atholl Distillery Visitor Centre
Pitlochry Festival Theatre
A9
A86
A889
A938
A95
B9153
B970
B9152
B847
B846
B8019
B8079
A924

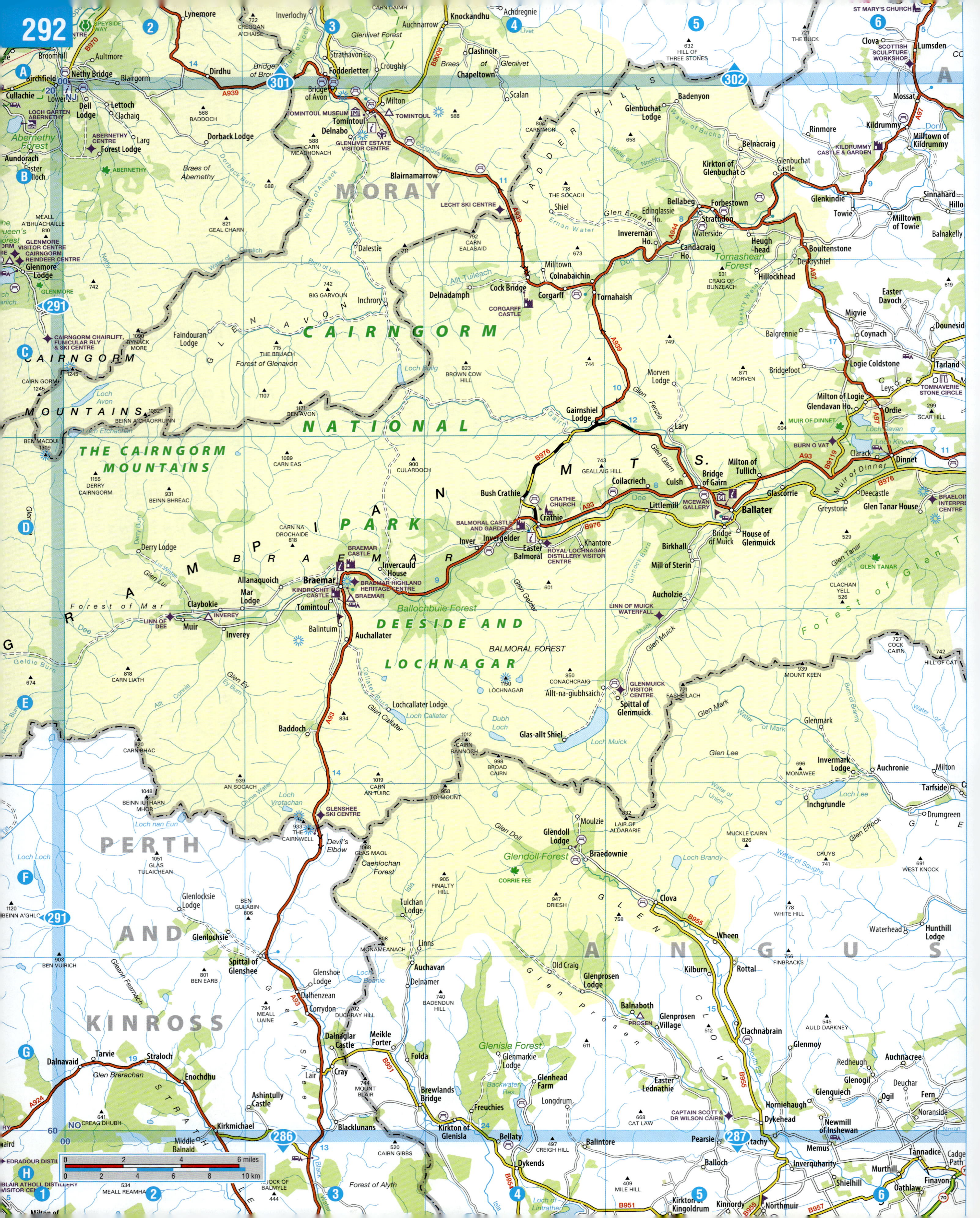
MORAY
CAIRNGORM
NATIONAL
PARK
CAIRNGORM MOUNTAINS
THE CAIRNGORM MOUNTAINS
GRAMPIAN MTS.
BRAEMAR
DEESIDE AND LOCHNAGAR
BALMORAL FOREST
LADDER HILLS
PERTH AND KINROSS
ANGUS
GLEN CLOVA
GLEN PROSEN
STRATH ARDLE
Forest of Glen Tanar
301
302
291
286
287
Nethy Bridge
Boat of Garten
Abernethy Forest
Glenmore
Tomintoul
Tomintoul Museum
Glenlivet Forest
Glenlivet Estate Visitor Centre
Bridge of Avon
Delnabo
Chapeltown
Knockandhu
Lecht Ski Centre
Cairngorm Chairlift, Funicular Rly & Ski Centre
Cairn Gorm 1245
Ben Macdui 1309
Forest of Glenavon
Loch Avon
Cock Bridge
Corgarff
Corgarff Castle
Colnabaichin
Tornahaish
Strathdon
Kildrummy
Kildrummy Castle & Garden
Lumsden
Scottish Sculpture Workshop
Tornashean Forest
Glenkindie
Towie
Gairnshiel Lodge
Bush Crathie
Crathie
Crathie Church
Balmoral Castle and Gardens
Easter Balmoral
Royal Lochnagar Distillery Visitor Centre
Inver
Invergelder
Invercauld House
Braemar Castle
Braemar Highland Heritage Centre
Kindrochit Castle
Ballochbuie Forest
Linn of Dee
Inverey
Muir
Derry Lodge
Auchallater
Lochcallater Lodge
Loch Callater
Lochnagar 1150
Loch Muick
Glas-allt Shiel
Spittal of Glenmuick
Glenmuick Visitor Centre
Allt-na-giubhsaich
Linn of Muick Waterfall
Mount Keen 939
Ballater
Bridge of Gairn
McEwan Gallery
Bridge of Muick
Glen Tanar House
Glen Tanar
Dinnet
Muir of Dinnet
Loch Kinord
Burn o Vat
Ordie
Logie Coldstone
Tarland
Tomnaverie Stone Circle
Glenshee Ski Centre
The Cairnwell 933
Devil's Elbow
Glas Maol 1068
Caenlochan Forest
Spittal of Glenshee
Glenshee Lodge
Dalhenzean
Corrydon
Dalnaglar Castle
Cray
Glenisla Forest
Glenmarkie Lodge
Glenhead Farm
Brewlands Bridge
Kirkton of Glenisla
Glendoll Lodge
Glendoll Forest
Corrie Fee
Braedownie
Clova
Glenprosen Lodge
Glenprosen Village
Balnaboth
Kirriemuir
Captain Scott & Dr Wilson Cairn
Dykehead
Pearsie
Memus
Kirkmichael
Ashintully Castle
Enochdhu
Straloch
Tarvie
Dalnavaid
Blair Atholl Distillery
Edradour Distillery
Inchgrundle
Invermark Lodge
Tarfside
Glen Esk
Auchronie
Edzell
Finavon
Tannadice
0 2 4 6 miles
0 2 4 6 8 10 km

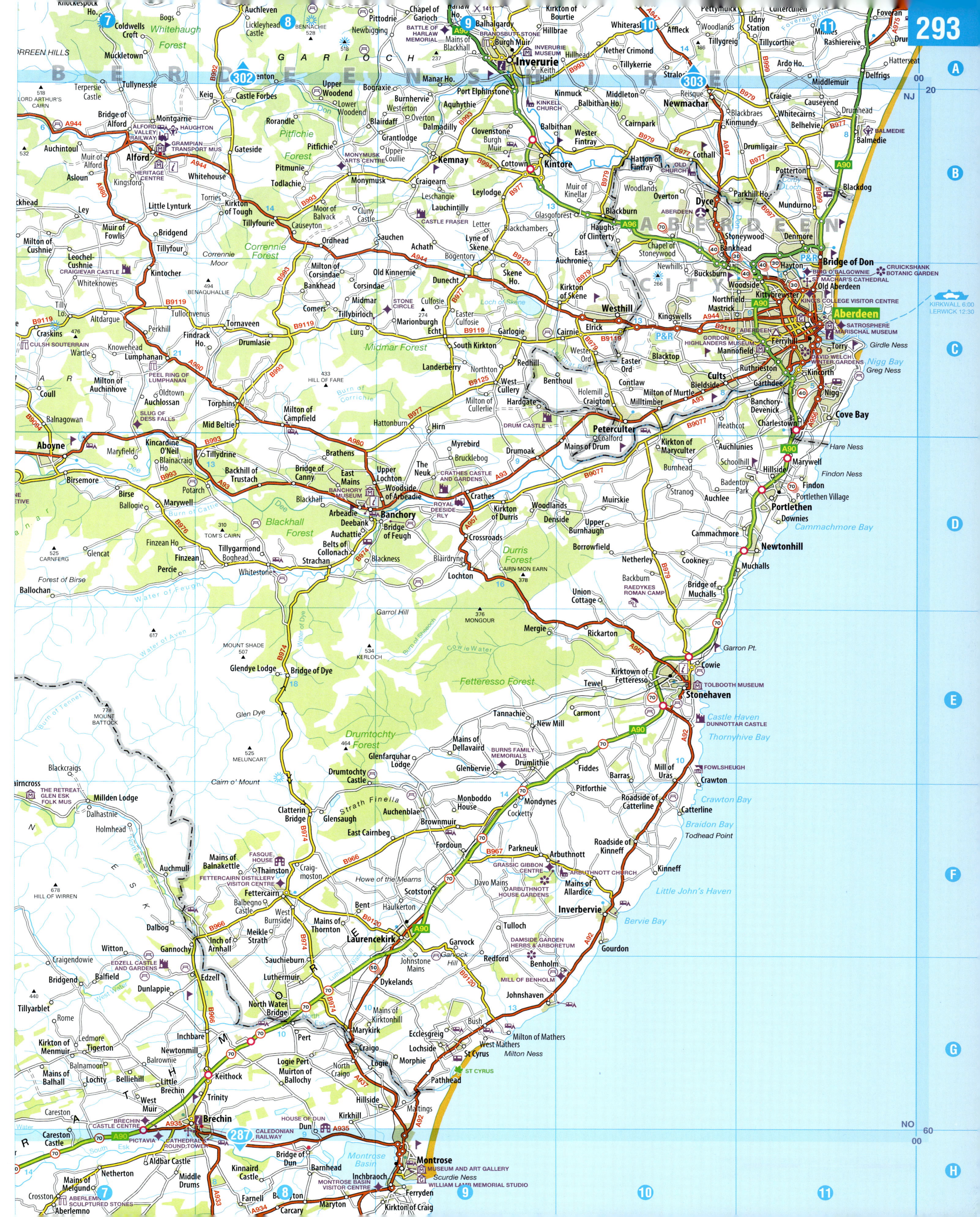
ABERDEENSHIRE
ABERDEEN CITY
Aberdeen
Inverurie
Kintore
Kemnay
Alford
Dyce
Newmachar
Westhill
Peterculter
Cults
Bridge of Don
Banchory
Aboyne
Portlethen
Newtonhill
Stonehaven
Inverbervie
Laurencekirk
Fettercairn
Brechin
Montrose
Edzell
Marykirk
St Cyrus
Johnshaven
Cove Bay
Blackdog
Balmedie
Fetteresso Forest
Drumtochty Forest
Durris Forest
Blackhall Forest
Midmar Forest
Pitfichie Forest
Corrennie Forest
Whitehaugh Forest
Nigg Bay
Cammachmore Bay
Crawton Bay
Braidon Bay
Bervie Bay
Little John's Haven
Castle Haven
Thornyhive Bay
Girdle Ness
Greg Ness
Hare Ness
Findon Ness
Garron Pt.
Todhead Point
Milton Ness
Scurdie Ness
Montrose Basin
Strath Finella
Howe of the Mearns
KIRKWALL 6:00
LERWICK 12:30
NJ
NO
302
303
287

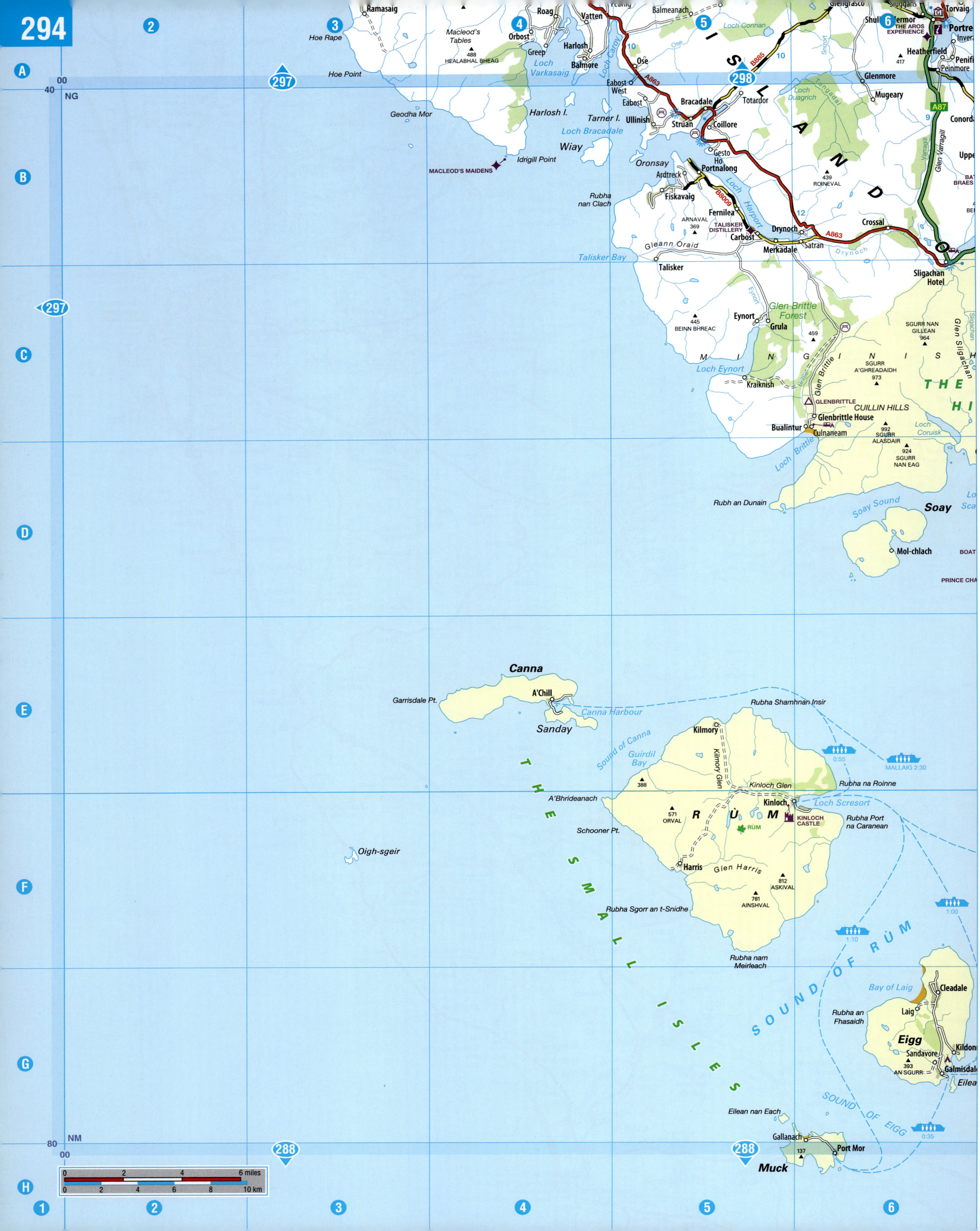
Ramasaig
Hoe Rape
Hoe Point
Macleod's Tables
488
HEALABHAL BHEAG
Roag
Vatten
Orbost
Greep
Harlosh
Balmore
Loch Varkasaig
Loch Caroy
Balmeanach
Loch Connan
Ose
Eabost West
Eabost
A863
B885
I S L A N D
Geodha Mor
Harlosh I.
Tarner I.
Ullinish
Bracadale
Totardor
Struan
Coillore
Loch Bracadale
Wiay
Idrigill Point
MACLEOD'S MAIDENS
Oronsay
Gesto
Ho
Ardtreck
Portnalong
Rubha nan Clach
Fiskavaig
B8009
Loch Harport
Fernilea
ARNAVAL
369
TALISKER DISTILLERY
Carbost
Drynoch
Merkadale
Satran
Crossal
Gleann Oraid
Talisker Bay
Talisker
Sligachan Hotel
Glen Brittle Forest
Eynort
Grula
445
BEINN BHREAC
459
Loch Eynort
Kraiknish
M I N G I N I S
SGURR NAN GILLEAN
964
SGURR A'GHREADAIDH
973
Glen Sligachan
Glen Brittle
THE
GLENBRITTLE
CUILLIN HILLS
Glenbrittle House
Bualintur
Culnaneam
992
SGURR ALASDAIR
924
SGURR NAN EAG
Loch Coruisk
Loch Brittle
Rubh an Dunain
Soay Sound
Soay
Mol-chlach
Lochalsh Glendale
Glenmore
Mugeary
Heatherfield
Portree
Torvaig
THE AROS EXPERIENCE
A87
Conordan
Glen Varragill
439
ROINEVAL
Canna
A'Chill
Garrisdale Pt.
Canna Harbour
Sanday
Rubha Shamhnan Insir
Kilmory
Sound of Canna
Guirdil Bay
Kilmory Glen
0:55
MALLAIG 2:30
388
Kinloch Glen
Rubha na Roinne
A'Bhrideanach
Kinloch
Loch Scresort
571
ORVAL
R Ù M
KINLOCH CASTLE
RÙM
Rubha Port na Caranean
Schooner Pt.
Oigh-sgeir
THE SMALL ISLES
Harris
Glen Harris
812
ASKIVAL
781
AINSHVAL
Rubha Sgorr an t-Snidhe
1:00
1:10
Rubha nam Meirleach
SOUND OF RÙM
Bay of Laig
Cleadale
Laig
Rubha an Fhasaidh
Eigg
Sandavore
393
AN SGURR
Galmisdale
SOUND OF EIGG
Eilean nan Each
Gallanach
137
Port Mor
Muck
0:35
0 2 4 6 miles
0 2 4 6 8 10 km
NG
NM
A B C D E F G H
1 2 3 4 5 6
297
298
288

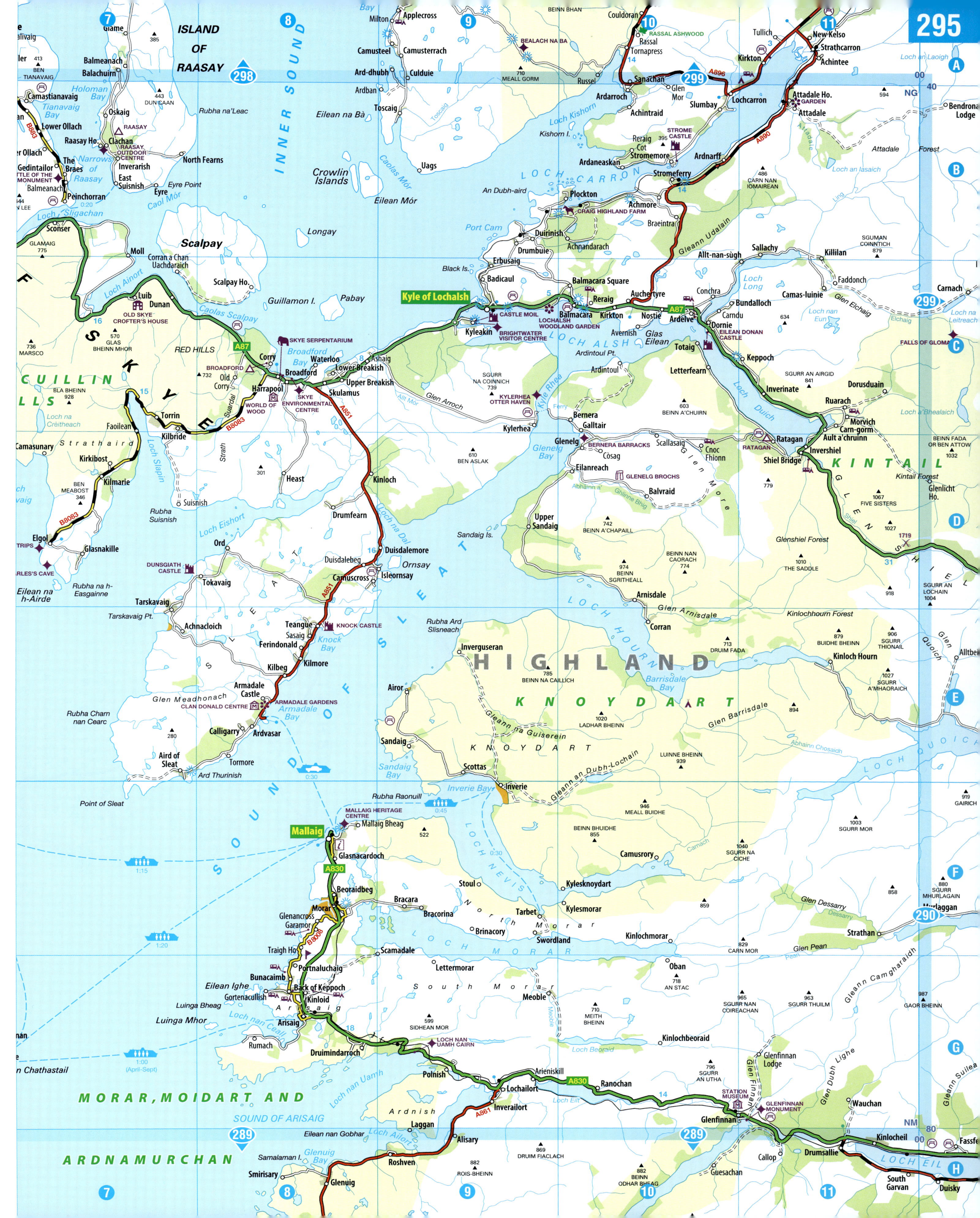
ISLAND OF RAASAY
INNER SOUND
Applecross
Milton
Camusteel
Camusterrach
Ard-dhubh
Culduie
Ardban
Toscaig
Eilean na Bà
Crowlin Islands
Caolas Mòr
Eilean Mór
Uags
BEALACH NA BA
MEALL GORM
Couldoran
RASSAL ASHWOOD
Rassal
Tornapress
Russel
Sanachan
Glen Mor
Ardarroch
Achintraid
Slumbay
Lochcarron
Loch Kishorn
Kishorn I.
Reraig
Cot
Stromemore
STROME CASTLE
Ardaneaskan
Ardnarff
Stromeferry
LOCH CARRON
Tullich
New Kelso
Strathcarron
Achintee
Kirkton
Attadale Ho.
GARDEN
Attadale
Bendronaig Lodge
Attadale Forest
Loch an Laoigh
Loch an Iasaich
CARN NAN IOMAIREAN
Plockton
CRAIG HIGHLAND FARM
Achmore
Braeintra
Duirinish
Achnandarach
Drumbuie
Erbusaig
Badicaul
Port Cam
An Dubh-aird
Kyle of Lochalsh
Kyleakin
CASTLE MOIL
BRIGHTWATER VISITOR CENTRE
LOCHALSH WOODLAND GARDEN
Balmacara Square
Balmacara
Reraig
Kirkton
Auchertyre
Nostie
Ardelve
Avernish
Glas Eilean
Dornie
EILEAN DONAN CASTLE
Totaig
Conchra
Bundalloch
Carndu
Gleann Udalain
Allt-nan-sùgh
Sallachy
Killilan
Faddonch
Camas-luinie
Glen Elchaig
Loch Long
Carnach
SGUMAN COINNTICH
FALLS OF GLOMACH
Keppoch
Letterfearn
Inverinate
Ruarach
Dorusduain
Morvich
Carn-gorm
Ault a'chruinn
Invershiel
Shiel Bridge
Ratagan
KINTAIL
Kintail Forest
Glenlicht Ho.
FIVE SISTERS
GLEN SHIEL
Glenshiel Forest
THE SADDLE
SGURR AN AIRGID
BEINN FADA OR BEN ATTOW
Loch a'Bhealaich
Loch Duich
Ardintoul
Ardintoul Pt.
LOCH ALSH
Kyle Rhea
KYLERHEA OTTER HAVEN
Kylerhea
Glen Arroch
SGURR NA COINNICH
BEINN A'CHUIRN
Bernera
Galltair
Glenelg
BERNERA BARRACKS
Glenelg Bay
Scallasaig
Cosag
Eilanreach
GLENELG BROCHS
Balvraid
Cnoc Fhionn
Glen More
Upper Sandaig
Sandaig Is.
BEINN A'CHAPAILL
BEINN SGRITHEALL
BEINN NAN CAORACH
Arnisdale
Glen Arnisdale
Corran
LOCH HOURN
Kinlochhourn Forest
DRUIM FADA
BUIDHE BHEINN
SGURR THIONAIL
Kinloch Hourn
SGURR A'MHAORAICH
SGURR AN LOCHAIN
Glen Quoich
Alltbeithe
Scalpay
Scalpay Ho.
Longay
Guillamon I.
Pabay
Caolas Scalpay
Moll
Corran a Chan Uachdaraich
Loch Ainort
Luib
Dunan
OLD SKYE CROFTER'S HOUSE
GLAS BHEINN MHOR
MARSCO
RED HILLS
SKYE
CUILLIN HILLS
BLA BHEINN
Broadford
Broadford Bay
SKYE SERPENTARIUM
Corry
Old Corry
Waterloo
Ashaig
Lower Breakish
Upper Breakish
Harrapool
Skulamus
SKYE ENVIRONMENTAL CENTRE
WORLD OF WOOD
BROADFORD
Torrin
Kilbride
Strathaird
Loch Slapin
Camasunary
Kirkibost
Kilmarie
BEN MEABOST
Elgol
Glasnakille
Loch na Creitheach
Faoilean
Strath
BEN ASLAK
Heast
Kinloch
Suisnish
Rubha Suisnish
Loch Eishort
Drumfearn
Loch na Dal
Ord
Duisdalemore
Duisdaleheg
Camuscross
Isleornsay
Ornsay
DUNSGAITH CASTLE
Tokavaig
Tarskavaig
Tarskavaig Pt.
Achnacloich
SLEAT
Teangue
Sasaig
KNOCK CASTLE
Knock Bay
Ferindonald
Kilbeg
Kilmore
Armadale Castle
ARMADALE GARDENS
CLAN DONALD CENTRE
Armadale Bay
Glen Meadhonach
Rubha Chàrn nan Cearc
Calligarry
Ardvasar
Aird of Sleat
Tormore
Ard Thurinish
Point of Sleat
Eilean na h-Airde
Rubha na h-Easgainne
Rubha Ard Slisneach
SOUND OF SLEAT
Inverguseran
HIGHLAND
BEINN NA CAILLICH
Barrisdale Bay
KNOYDART
Airor
LADHAR BHEINN
Gleann na Guiserein
Glen Barrisdale
Sandaig
Sandaig Bay
Scottas
Inverie
Inverie Bay
Gleann an Dubh-Lochain
LUINNE BHEINN
MEALL BUIDHE
BEINN BHUIDHE
Rubha Raonuill
LOCH QUOICH
SGURR MOR
GAIRICH
MALLAIG HERITAGE CENTRE
Mallaig
Mallaig Bheag
Glasnacardoch
SOUND OF SLEAT
LOCH NEVIS
Camusrory
SGURR NA CICHE
Stoul
Kylesknoydart
Kylesmorar
Beoraidbeg
Morar
Bracara
Bracorina
Brinacory
North Morar
Tarbet
Swordland
Kinlochmorar
Glenancross
Garamor
Traigh Ho
Scamadale
LOCH MORAR
Lettermorar
Oban
AN STAC
CARN MOR
Glen Dessarry
Strathan
SGURR MHURLAGAIN
Glen Pean
Portnaluchaig
Bunacaimb
Eilean Ighe
Back of Keppoch
Gortenacullish
Kinloid
Arisaig
Luinga Bheag
Luinga Mhor
Loch nan Ceall
Rumach
Druimindarroch
South Morar
Meoble
SIDHEAN MOR
MEITH BHEINN
SGURR NAN COIREACHAN
SGURR THUILM
Gleann Camgharaidh
GAOR BHEINN
Kinlochbeoraid
Loch Beoraid
LOCH NAN UAMH CAIRN
Glenfinnan Lodge
Gleann Dubh Lighe
Gleann Suileag
Polnish
Arieniskill
Lochailort
Ranochan
Inverailort
SGURR AN UTHA
STATION MUSEUM
GLENFINNAN MONUMENT
Glenfinnan
Wauchan
Kinlocheil
Fassfern
Loch Eil
Drumsallie
Callop
Guesachan
South Garvan
Duisky
Loch nan Uamh
Ardnish
Laggan
Loch Ailort
Alisary
Roshven
DRUIM FIACLACH
ROIS-BHEINN
BEINN ODHAR BHEAG
MORAR, MOIDART AND SOUND OF ARISAIG
ARDNAMURCHAN
Eilean nan Gobhar
Samalaman I.
Glenuig Bay
Smirisary
Glenuig
Rubha Chathastail
Raasay Ho.
Clachan
RAASAY OUTDOOR CENTRE
Inverarish
North Fearns
East Suisnish
Eyre
Eyre Point
Caol Mòr
Narrows of Raasay
The Braes
Gedintailor
Balmeanach
Peinchorran
Loch Sligachan
Sconser
GLAMAIG
Balmeanach
Balachuirn
Glame
DUN CAAN
Rubha na'Leac
Holoman Bay
Camastianavaig
Tianavaig Bay
Oskaig
Lower Ollach
Upper Ollach
RAASAY
A87
A890
A896
A851
A830
A861
B883
B8083
B8008
298
299
289
290

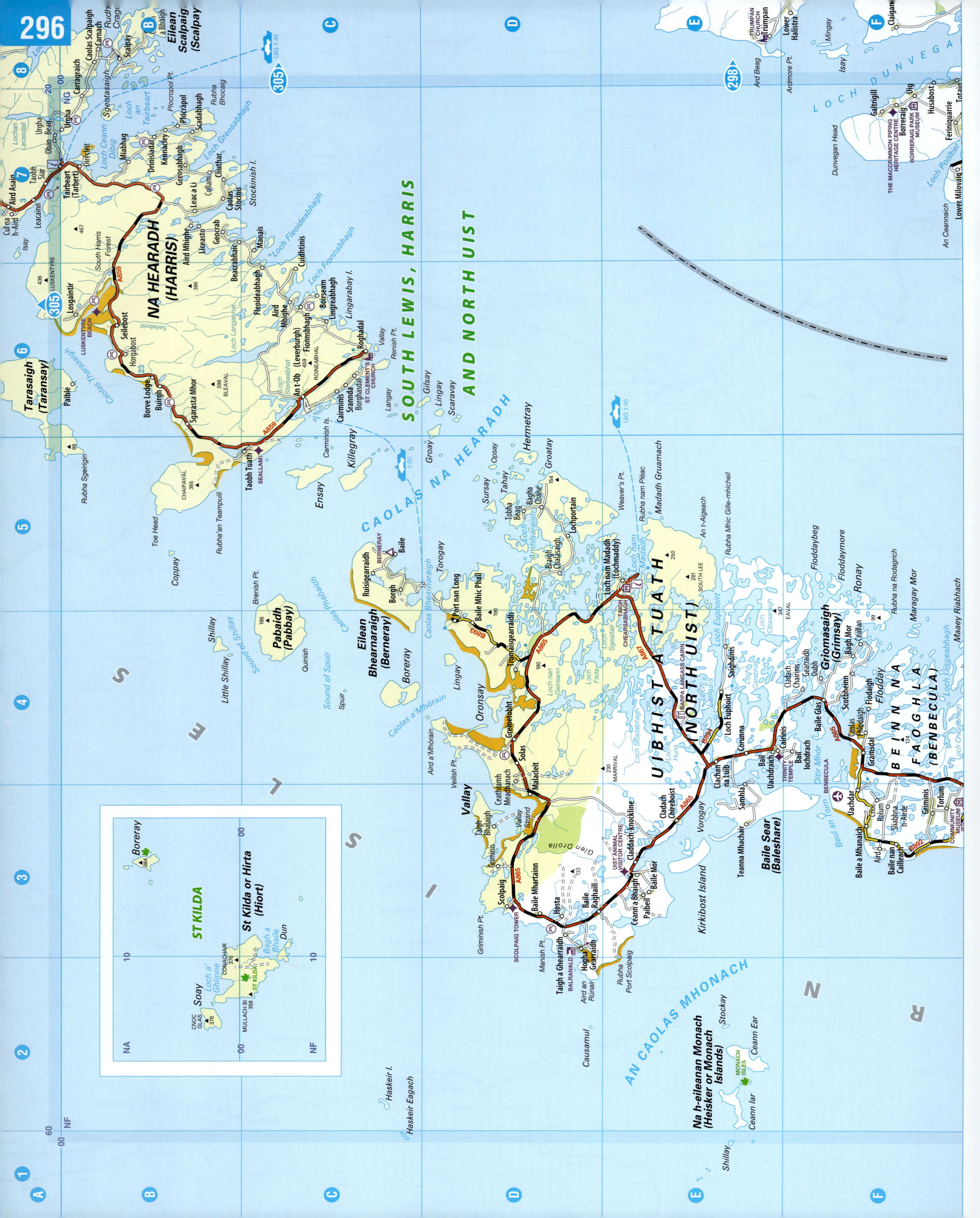
SOUTH LEWIS, HARRIS
AND NORTH UIST
NA HEARADH
(HARRIS)
UIBHIST A TUATH
(NORTH UIST)
CAOLAS NA HEARADH
AN CAOLAS MHONACH
LOCH DUNVEGA
BEINN NA FAOGHLA
(BENBECULA)
Eilean Scalpaig
(Scalpay)
Tarasaigh
(Taransay)
Eilean Bhearnaraigh
(Berneray)
Pabaidh
(Pabbay)
Griomasaigh
(Grimsay)
Baile Sear
(Baleshare)
Na h-eileanan Monach
(Heisker or Monach Islands)
ST KILDA
St Kilda or Hirta
(Hiort)
Boreray
Soay
Tairbeart
(Tarbert)
An t-Ob
(Leverburgh)
Loch nam Madadh
(Lochmaddy)
Taobh Tuath
Roghadal
Seilebost
Losgaintir
Sgarasta Mhor
Borve Lodge
Buirgh
Horgabost
Fionnsbhagh
Port nan Long
Baile Mhic Phail
Grenetobht
Solas
Malacleit
Scolpaig
Baile Mhartainn
Hosta
Claddach Kirkibost
Clachan na Luib
Cairinis
Baile Glas
Loch Euphoirt
Vallay
Valley Strand
Oronsay
Boreray
Lingay
Kirkibost Island
Killegray
Ensay
Haskeir I.
Haskeir Eagach
Shillay
Little Shillay
Sound of Pabbay
Sound of Harris
A859
A865
A867
B893
B894
305
298
UIG 1:40
UIG 1:45
BALRANALD
SCOLPAIG TOWER
UIST ANIMAL VISITOR CENTRE
BARPA LANGASS CARN
TAIGH CHEARSABHAGH
ST CLEMENT'S CHURCH
LUSKENTYRE BEACH
SEALLAM!
TRINITY TEMPLE
MONACH ISLES
THE MACCRIMMON PIPING HERITAGE CENTRE
BORRERAIG PARK MUSEUM
BENBECULA
Uig
Dunvegan Head
TRUMPAN CHURCH
Trumpan
Isay
Mingay
Claigan
NA
NF
NG
ATLANTIC

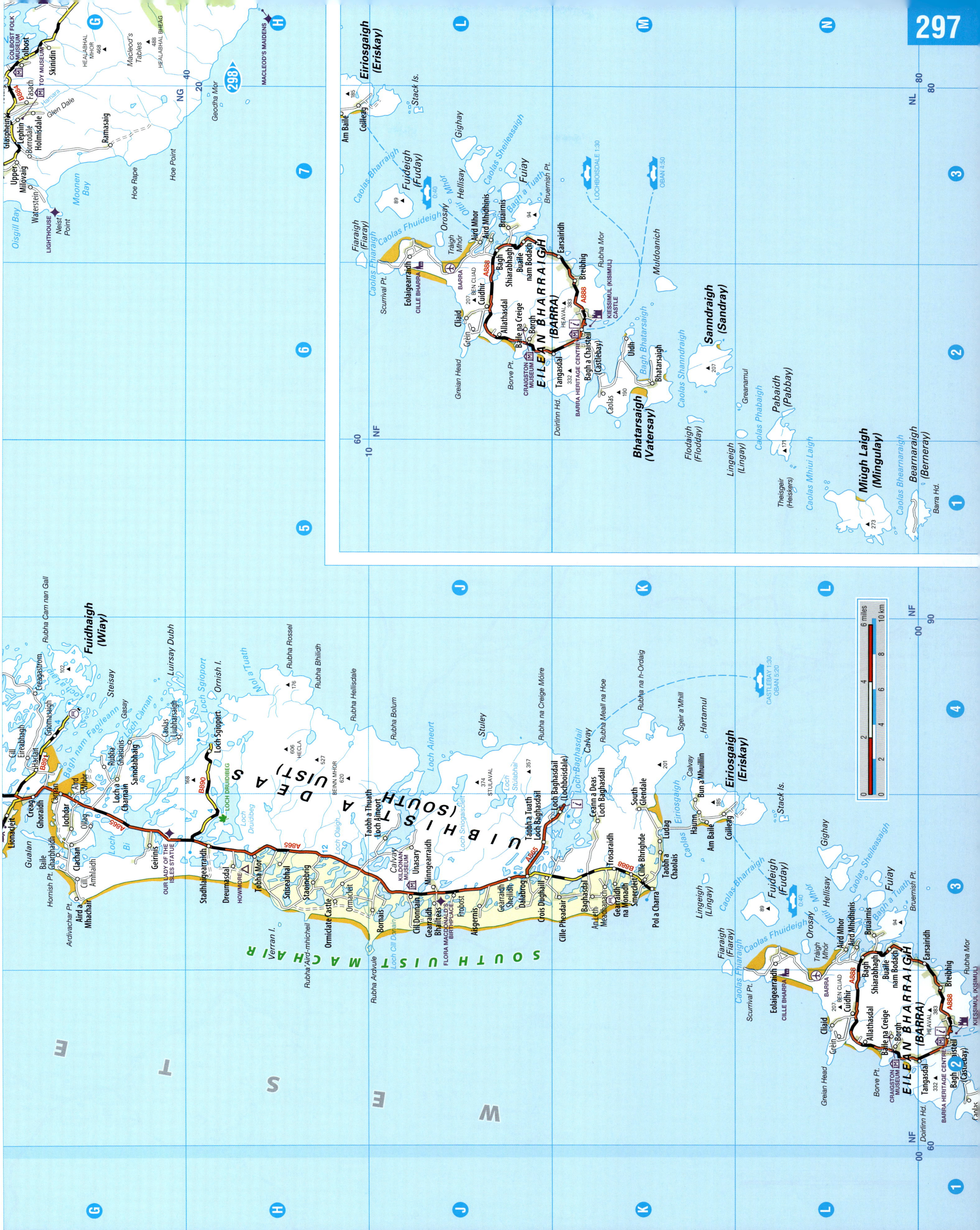
UIBHIST A DEAS (SOUTH UIST)
SOUTH UIST MACHAIR
EILEAN BHARRAIGH (BARRA)
Eiriosgaigh (Eriskay)
Fuideigh (Fuday)
Bhatarsaigh (Vatersay)
Sanndraigh (Sandray)
Pabaidh (Pabbay)
Miùgh Laigh (Mingulay)
Bearnaraigh (Berneray)
Fuidhaigh (Wiay)
Loch Baghasdail (Lochboisdale)
Bagh a Chaisteil (Castlebay)
Loch Sgioport
Loch Aineort
Loch Druidibeg
Hecla
Beinn Mhòr
Stuley
Calvay
Hellisay
Gighay
Lingeigh (Lingay)
Flodaigh (Flodday)
Muldoanich
Caolas Bharraigh
Caolas Phabaigh
Caolas Sanndraigh
Caolas Mhiùi Laigh
Caolas Bhearnaraigh
Barra Hd.
Stack Is.
Neist Point
Moonen Bay
Hoe Point
Hoe Rape
Waterstein
Glen Dale
Ramasaig
Colbost
Skinidin
Macleod's Tables
Macleod's Maidens
Oisgill Bay
Craigston Museum
Barra Heritage Centre
Kilbride
Kildonan Museum
Flora MacDonald's Birthplace
Our Lady of the Isles Statue
Kiessimul (Kisimul) Castle
Lochboisdale 1:30
Oban 4:50
Castlebay 1:30
Oban 5:20
A865
A888
B888
B890
0 2 4 6 8 10 km
0 2 4 6 miles
298
W E S T

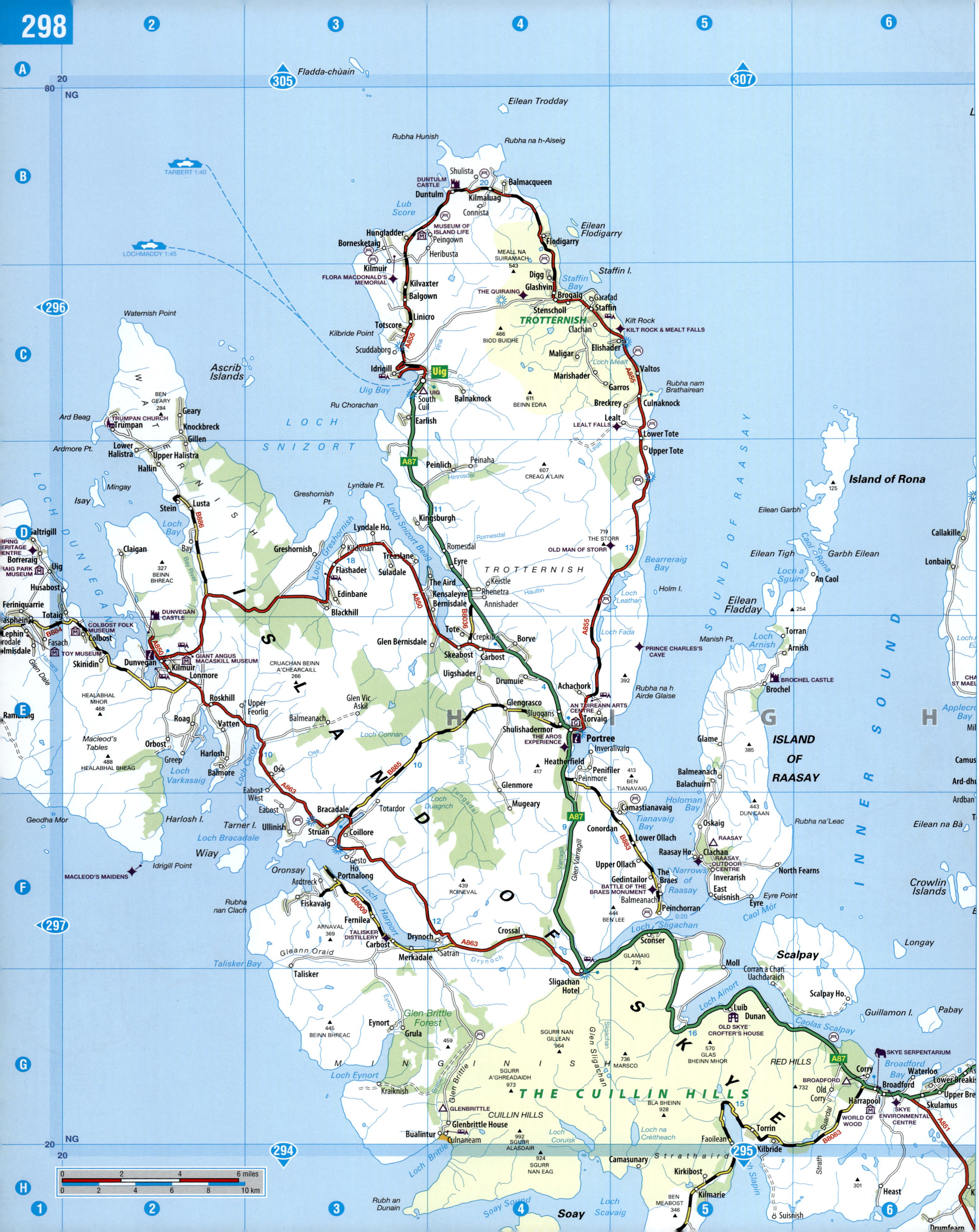

Fladda-chùain
305
307
Eilean Trodday
Rubha Hunish
Rubha na h-Aiseig
TARBERT 1:40
LOCHMADDY 1:45
Shulista
Duntulm Castle
Duntulm
Balmacqueen
Kilmaluag
Connista
Lub Score
Museum of Island Life
Hungladder
Peingown
Borneskętaig
Heribusta
Eilean Flodigarry
Flodigarry
Meall na Suiramach 543
Kilmuir
Flora MacDonald's Memorial
Staffin I.
Digg
Staffin Bay
Kilvaxter
Glashvin
The Quiraing
Balgown
Brogaig
Garafad
Staffin
Stenscholl
296
Waternish Point
Linicro
Kilt Rock
Totscore
Trotternish
Kilt Rock & Mealt Falls
Kilbride Point
Clachan
466 Biod Buidhe
Elishader
Scuddaborg
Maligar
Loch Mealt
Ascrib Islands
Idrigill
Uig
Valtos
Marishader
Rubha nam Brathairean
Uig Bay
Garros
South Cuil
Balnaknock
Ru Chorachan
611 Beinn Edra
Breckrey
Culnaknock
Ben Geary 284
Geary
Trumpan Church
Trumpan
Earlish
Lealt
Ard Beag
Knockbreck
Lealt Falls
Lower Tote
Gillen
Loch
Snizort
Lower Halistra
Upper Halistra
Ardmore Pt.
Hallin
Upper Tote
A87
Peinlich
Peinaha
607 Creag a' Lain
Mingay
Island of Rona
Isay
Lyndale Pt.
125
Stein
Lusta
Greshornish Pt.
Kingsburgh
Eilean Garbh
Loch Bay
Lyndale Ho.
719 The Storr
Galtrigill
Claigan
Greshornish
Kildonan
Romesdal
Old Man of Storr
Callakille
Garbh Eilean
Eilean Tigh
Borreraig
Uig
327 Beinn Bhreac
Flashader
Treaslane
Suladale
Trotternish
Lonbain
Husabost
Edinbane
The Aird
Keistle
Bearreraig Bay
An Caol
Holm I.
Kensaleyre
Rhenetra
Bernisdale
Annishader
Feriniquarrie
Totaig
Blackhill
Eilean Fladday
254
Dunvegan Castle
Colbost Folk Museum
Colbost
Tote
Glen Bernisdale
Borve
Loch Fada
Torran
Manish Pt.
Fasach
Toy Museum
Skinidin
Dunvegan
Kilmuir
Giant Angus MacAskill Museum
Cruachan Beinn a' Chearcaill 266
Skeabost
Carbost
Prince Charles's Cave
Arnish
Uigshader
Drumuie
Lonmore
Achachork
392
Brochel Castle
Brochel
Healabhal Mhor 468
Roskhill
Glen Vic Askil
Rubha na h Airde Glaise
Upper Feorlig
Glengrasco
An Tuireann Arts Centre
Torvaig
Balmeanach
Sluggans
Roag
Vatten
Loch Connan
Shulishadermor
Portree
Island of Raasay
Macleod's Tables
The Aros Experience
Inverailvaig
Glame
Orbost
385
Harlosh
Heatherfield
488 Healabhal Bheag
Greep
Ose
417
Penifiler
413 Ben Tianavaig
Balmeanach
Balachuirn
Loch Varkasaig
Balmore
Peinmore
Eabost West
Glenmore
Camastianavaig
443 Dun Caan
Eabost
Bracadale
Totardor
Mugeary
Holoman Bay
Geodha Mor
Harlosh I.
Tarner I.
Ullinish
Struan
Coillore
Tianavaig Bay
Oskaig
Rubha na' Leac
Eilean na Bà
Loch Bracadale
Conordan
Raasay
Wiay
Gesto Ho.
Lower Ollach
Raasay Ho.
Clachan
Raasay Outdoor Centre
Idrigill Point
Macleod's Maidens
Oronsay
Portnalong
Upper Ollach
The Braes
Inverarish
North Fearns
Ardtreck
Gedintailor
Narrows of Raasay
Crowlin Islands
Battle of the Braes Monument
East Suisnish
Eyre Point
Fiskavaig
439 Roineval
Balmeanach
Eyre
Rubha nan Clach
Fernilea
Peinchorran
Caol Mór
297
Arnaval 369
Talisker Distillery
444 Ben Lee
Loch Sligachan
Crossal
Longay
Carbost
Drynoch
Gleann Oraid
Sconser
Talisker Bay
Merkadale
Satran
Drynoch
Glamaig 775
Scalpay
Moll
Talisker
Sligachan Hotel
Corran a Chan Uachdaraich
Scalpay Ho.
Loch Ainort
Glen Brittle Forest
Luib
Dunan
Pabay
Eynort
Guillamon I.
445 Beinn Bhreac
Grula
Sgurr nan Gillean 964
Old Skye Crofter's House
Caolas Scalpay
459
570 Glas Bheinn Mhor
736 Marsco
Skye Serpentarium
Red Hills
Broadford Bay
Loch Eynort
Waterloo
Sgurr a' Ghreadaidh 973
Corry
Broadford
Lower Breakish
Kraiknish
The Cuillin Hills
732
Old Corry
Harrapool
Skulamus
Glenbrittle
Bla Bheinn 928
Skye Environmental Centre
World of Wood
Cuillin Hills
Glenbrittle House
Torrin
Loch Coruisk
Loch na Creitheach
Bualintur
Culnaneam
992 Sgurr Alasdair
Faoilean
Kilbride
294
924 Sgurr nan Eag
Camasunary
Strathaird
295
Kirkibost
Strath
301
Heast
Loch Brittle
Ben Meabost 346
Kilmarie
Loch Slapin
Rubh an Dunain
Soay Sound
Soay
Loch Scavaig
Suisnish
Drumfearn
0 2 4 6 miles
0 2 4 6 8 10 km

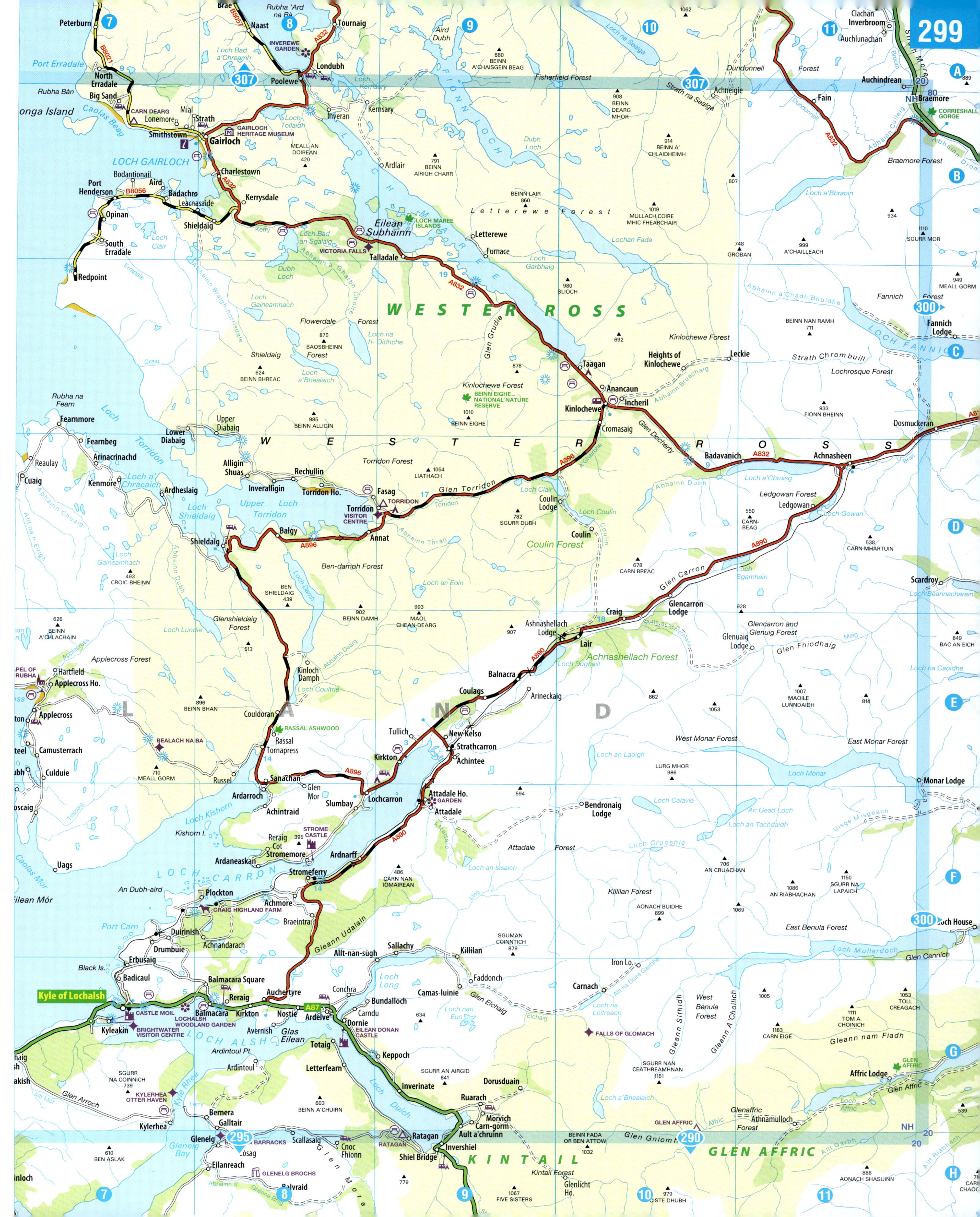
Peterburn
Rubha 'Ard na Bà
Naast
Tournaig
Aird Dubh
Clachan
Inverbroom
Auchlunachan
Port Erradale
INVEREWE GARDEN
Loch Bad a'Chreamh
680 BEINN A'CHAISGEIN BEAG
Fisherfield Forest
Dundonnell
Forest
Auchindrean
North Erradale
Londubh
Poolewe
Achneigie
Strath na Sealga
Rubha Bàn
Big Sand
Kernsary
Inveran
908 BEINN DEARG MHOR
Fain
Braemore
CORRIESHALLOCH GORGE
Longa Island
Caolas Beag
CARN DEARG
Lonemore
Mial
Strath
Smithstown
Gairloch
GAIRLOCH HERITAGE MUSEUM
Loch Tollaidh
MEALL AN DOIREAN 420
Dubh Loch
914 BEINN A' CHLAIDHEIMH
Braemore Forest
LOCH GAIRLOCH
Charlestown
Ardlair
791 BEINN AIRIGH CHARR
Bodantionail
Port Henderson
Aird
Badachro
Leacnasaide
Opinan
Kerrysdale
807
Loch a'Bhraoin
BEINN LAIR 860
Letterewe Forest
1019 MULLACH COIRE MHIC FHEARCHAIR
934
Shieldaig
Kerry
Eilean Subhainn
LOCH MAREE ISLANDS
Letterewe
Lochan Fada
1110 SGURR MOR
South Erradale
Loch Bad an Sgalaig
VICTORIA FALLS
Talladale
Furnace
Loch Garbhaig
748 GROBAN
999 A'CHAILLEACH
Redpoint
Dubh Loch
980 SLIOCH
949 MEALL GORM
Loch Gaineamhach
WESTER ROSS
Flowerdale Forest
Loch na h-Dìdhche
875 BAOSBHEINN
Forest
Fannich
Forest
692
BEINN NAN RAMH 711
Fannich Lodge
LOCH FANNICH
Kinlochewe Forest
Glen Grudie
Shieldaig
Forest
Craig
Heights of Kinlochewe
Leckie
Strath Chrombuill
Taagan
624 BEINN BHREAC
878
Loch a'Bhealaich
Lochrosque Forest
Kinlochewe Forest
Anancaun
BEINN EIGHE NATIONAL NATURE RESERVE
Incheril
Rubha na Fearn
Kinlochewe
933 FIONN BHEINN
Loch
1010 BEINN EIGHE
985 BEINN ALLIGIN
Fearnmore
Upper Diabaig
Cromasaig
Glen Docherty
Dosmuckeran
Lower Diabaig
WESTER ROSS
Fearnbeg
Torridon
Badavanich
Achnasheen
Arinacrinachd
Reaulay
Alligin Shuas
Torridon Forest
1054 LIATHACH
Rechullin
Loch a'Chroisg
Cuaig
Kenmore
Loch a' Chracaich
Ardheslaig
Inveralligin
Torridon Ho.
Fasag
Glen Torridon
Loch Clair
Coulin Lodge
Abhainn Dubh
Ledgowan Forest
Ledgowan
Loch Shieldaig
Upper Loch Torridon
TORRIDON
Torridon VISITOR CENTRE
782 SGURR DUBH
Loch Coulin
550 CARN-BEAG
Loch Gowan
Balgy
Annat
Coulin
Coulin Forest
538 CARN MHARTUIN
Shieldaig
Loch Gaineamhach
493 CROIC-BHEINN
Ben-damph Forest
678 CARN BREAC
Glen Carron
Loch Sgamhain
Scardroy
Loch Beannacharain
BEN SHIELDAIG 439
Loch an Eoin
Loch Damh
626 BEINN A'CHLACHAIN
Glenshieldaig Forest
Loch Lundie
902 BEINN DAMH
993 MAOL CHEAN-DEARG
907
Ashnashellach Lodge
Craig
Glencarron Lodge
928
Glencarron and Glenuig Forest
Glenuaig Lodge
849 BAC AN EICH
Applecross Forest
513
Lair
Glen Fhiodhaig
Kinloch Damph
Achnashellach Forest
Loch Dughaill
Loch na Caoidhe
Hartfield
Applecross Ho.
Loch Coultrie
Balnacra
Coulags
Arineckaig
862
1053
1007 MAOILE LUNNDAIDH
814
896 BEINN BHAN
Couldoran
Applecross
RASSAL ASHWOOD
Rassal
Tornapress
Tullich
New Kelso
Strathcarron
Achintee
Kirkton
West Monar Forest
East Monar Forest
Loch an Laoigh
LURG MHOR 986
Loch Monar
Monar Lodge
BEALACH NA BA
Camusterrach
Culduie
710 MEALL GORM
Russel
Sanachan
Glen Mor
Slumbay
Lochcarron
Attadale Ho. GARDEN
Attadale
594
Bendronaig Lodge
Loch Calavie
An Gead Loch
Loch an Tachdaidh
Ardarroch
Achintraid
Loch Kishorn
Kishorn I.
Reraig
Cot
Stromemore
395 STROME CASTLE
Ardnarff
Attadale
Forest
Loch Cruoshie
Uags
Ardaneaskan
LOCH CARRON
Stromeferry
486 CARN NAN IOMAIREAN
Loch an Iasaich
706 AN CRUACHAN
1150 SGURR NA LAPAICH
1086 AN RIABHACHAN
Caolas Mòr
An Dubh-aird
Eilean Mór
Plockton
CRAIG HIGHLAND FARM
Achmore
Killilan Forest
AONACH BUIDHE 899
1069
Port Cam
Duirinish
Drumbuie
Achnandarach
Braeintra
Gleann Udalain
SGUMAN COINNTICH 879
East Benula Forest
Loch House
Loch Mullardoch
Glen Cannich
Erbusaig
Sallachy
Killilan
Allt-nan-sùgh
Black Is.
Badicaul
Balmacara Square
Loch Long
Faddoch
Iron Lo.
Carnach
Kyle of Lochalsh
CASTLE MOIL
Balmacara
LOCHALSH WOODLAND GARDEN
Reraig
Kirkton
Auchertyre
Conchra
Camas-luinie
Glen Elchaig
Loch na Leitreach
West Benula Forest
Gleann Sithidh
Gleann a Choilich
1005
1053 TOLL CREAGACH
1111 TOM A CHOINICH
Kyleakin
BRIGHTWATER VISITOR CENTRE
Avernish
Nostie
Ardelve
Bundalloch
Carndu
Dornie
EILEAN DONAN CASTLE
634
Loch nan Eun
FALLS OF GLOMACH
1183 CARN EIGE
Gleann nam Fiadh
LOCH ALSH
Glas Eilean
Totaig
Ardintoul Pt.
Ardintoul
Keppoch
Letterfearn
SGURR NA COINNICH 739
KYLERHEA OTTER HAVEN
Glen Arroch
Kyle Rhea
Inverinate
SGURR AN AIRGID 841
Dorusduain
SGURR NAN CEATHREAMHNAN 1151
Affric Lodge
GLEN AFFRIC
Glen Affric
Loch Duich
Loch a'Bhealaich
603 BEINN A'CHUIRN
Ruarach
Morvich
Carn-gorm
Aultachruinn
Glenaffric Forest
Athnamulloch
Loch Affric
539
Kylerhea
Bernera
Galltair
Glenelg
BARRACKS
Scallasaig
Glen More
RATAGAN
Ratagan
GLEN AFFRIC
BEINN FADA OR BEN ATTOW 1032
Glen Gniomh
GLEN AFFRIC
610 BEN ASLAK
Glenelg Bay
Eilanreach
Cnoc Fhionn
Shiel Bridge
Invershiel
KINTAIL
Kintail Forest
Glenlicht Ho.
888 AONACH SHASUINN
GLENELG BROCHS
Balvraid
779
1067 FIVE SISTERS
979 CISTE DHUBH
7 8 9 10 11
A B C D E F G H
307 300 295 290
NH 20 80

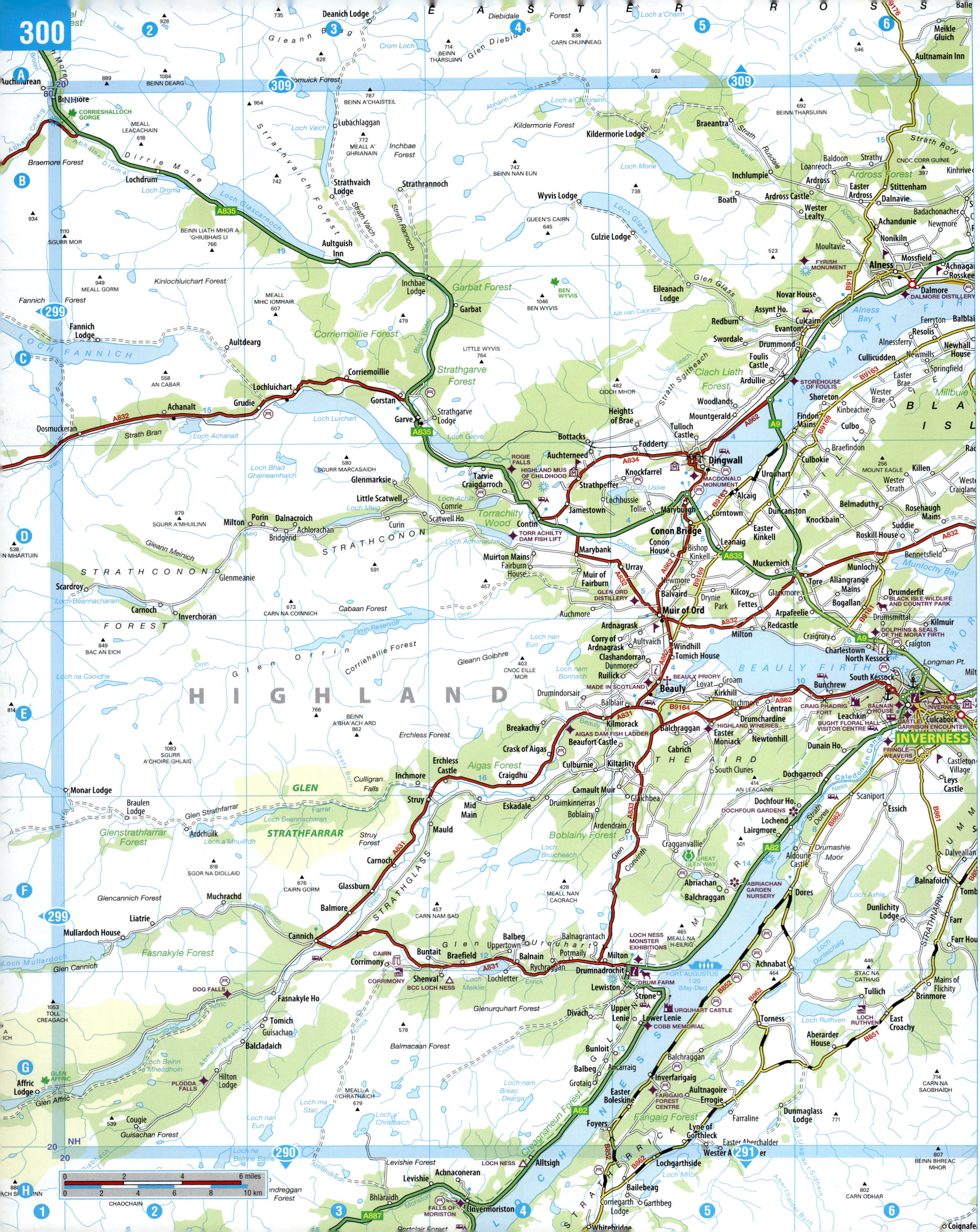
E A S T E R R O S S
309
299
290
291
HIGHLAND
INVERNESS
Dingwall
Alness
Conon Bridge
Muir of Ord
Beauly
Drumnadrochit
Invermoriston
Cannich
Garve
Strathpeffer
Evanton
Dalmore
Maryburgh
Kirkhill
Lentran
Drumchardine
Charlestown
North Kessock
South Kessock
Kilmuir
Craigton
Culcabock
Dochgarroch
Dores
Foyers
Inverfarigaig
Whitebridge
Alltsigh
Lewiston
Milton
Strone
Balnain
Buntait
Struy
Kiltarlity
Kilmorack
Beaufort Castle
Eskadale
Culburnie
Aigas Forest
Strathconon
STRATH CONON FOREST
Glen Orrin
Orrin Reservoir
GLEN STRATHFARRAR
Glenstrathfarrar Forest
Loch Luichart
Loch Fannich
Loch Glascarnoch
Loch Mullardoch
Loch Ness
Beauly Firth
Cromarty Firth
Glen Affric
Affric Lodge
Fasnakyle Forest
Tomich
Guisachan
Glen Urquhart
Urquhart Castle
Caledonian Canal
Abriachan
Torness
Essich
Leys Castle
Castleton Village
Aberarder House
East Croachy
Brinmore
Farr
Mains of Flichity
Tullich
Dunlichity Lodge
Balnafoich
Dalveallan
A9
A82
A831
A832
A833
A834
A835
A862
A887
B851
B852
B862
B9163
B9164
B9169
B9176
Lochdrum
Dirrie More
Braemore Forest
Aultguish Inn
Inchbae Lodge
Garbat
Garbat Forest
Corriemoillie Forest
Strathgarve Forest
Lochluichart
Grudie
Achanalt
Dosmuckeran
Gorstan
Contin
Tarvie
Jamestown
Marybank
Urray
Tore
Munlochy
Killen
Culbokie
Findon Mains
Ardullie
Foulis Castle
Drummond
Swordale
Kildermorie Lodge
Wyvis Lodge
Ben Wyvis
Fannich Lodge
Milton
Porin
Dalnacroich
Scardroy
Invercroran
Monar Lodge
Braulen Lodge
Muchrachd
Liatrie
Mullardoch House
Hilton Lodge
Cougie
Guisachan Forest
Levishie
Bhlaraidh
Achnaconeran
Lochgarthside
Balchraggan
Erchless Castle
Inchmore
Mauld
Carnoch
Glassburn
Balmore
Corrimony
Shenval
Lochletter
0 2 4 6 miles
0 2 4 6 8 10 km

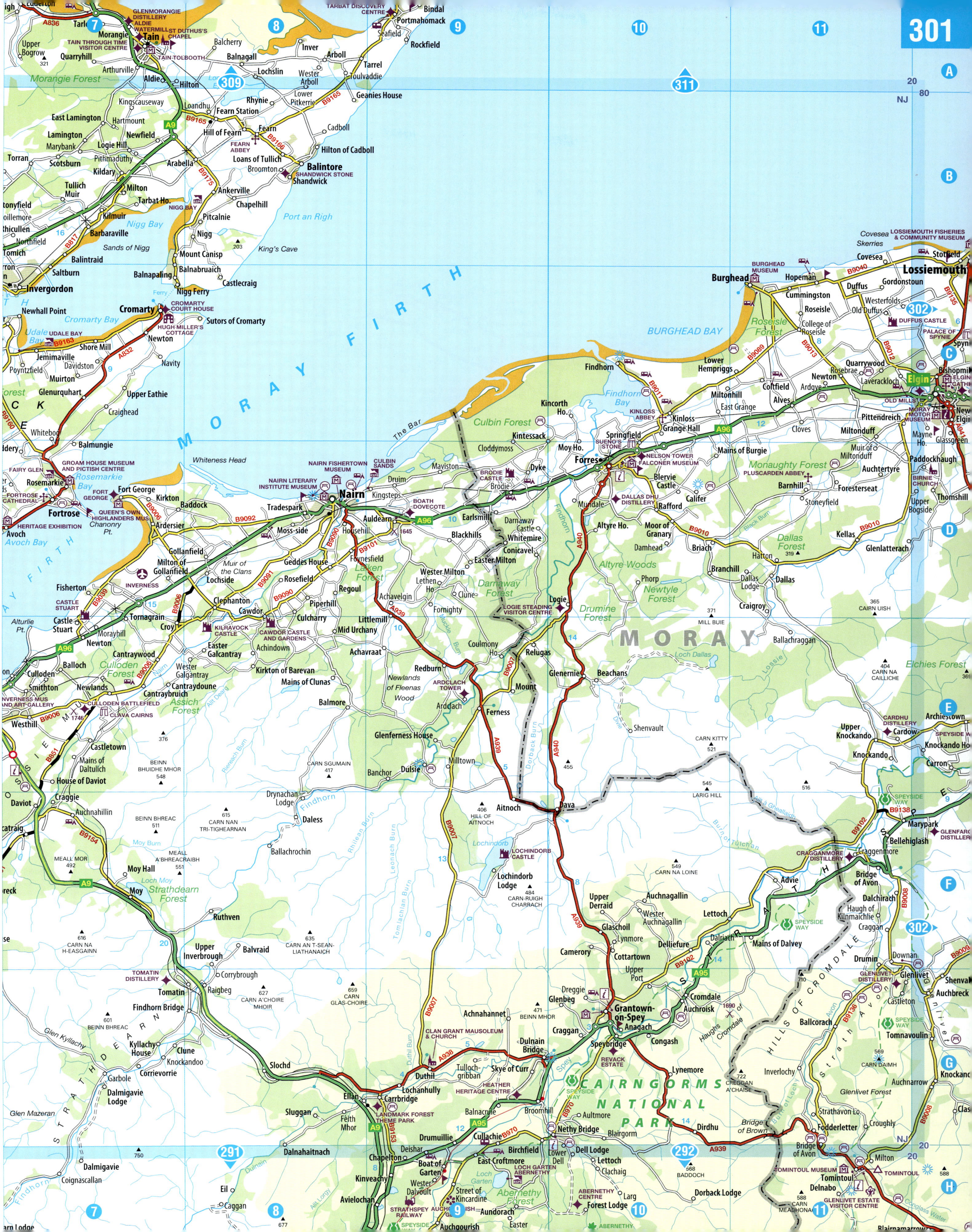
MORAY FIRTH
MORAY
CAIRNGORMS NATIONAL PARK
BURGHEAD BAY
Cromarty Bay
Nigg Bay
Port an Righ
Avoch Bay
Tain
Portmahomack
Balintore
Invergordon
Cromarty
Fortrose
Rosemarkie
Fort George
Nairn
Forres
Findhorn
Kinloss
Burghead
Lossiemouth
Elgin
Grantown-on-Spey
Carrbridge
Boat of Garten
Nethy Bridge
Tomintoul
Dava
Ferness
Cawdor
Ardersier
Culloden
Inverness
Kilravock Castle
Cawdor Castle and Gardens
Brodie Castle
Culbin Forest
Roseisle Forest
Monaughty Forest
Dallas Forest
Altyre Woods
Newtyle Forest
Drumine Forest
Culloden Forest
Assich Forest
Strathdearn Forest
Abernethy Forest
Lochindorb
Lochindorb Castle
Hills of Cromdale
Speyside Way
Glenlivet
Glenlivet Forest
Tomnavoulin
Marypark
Advie
Cromdale
Dulnain Bridge
Duthil
Slochd
Tomatin
Moy
Findhorn Bridge
Dalmigavie
Culbin Sands
Whiteness Head
King's Cave
Sutors of Cromarty
Nigg Ferry
Hilton of Cadboll
Geanies House
Tarbat Ness
A9
A96
A939
A940
A95
A938
B9006
B9090
B9091
B9101
B9007
B9010
B9089
B9013
B9012
B9040
B9135
B9102
B9138
B9008
B9136
B9009
B970
B9153
B9154
B851
B9163
B9165
B9166
B9175
B817
A832
A836
A941
291
292
302
309
311
7
8
9
10
11
A
B
C
D
E
F
G
H
NJ

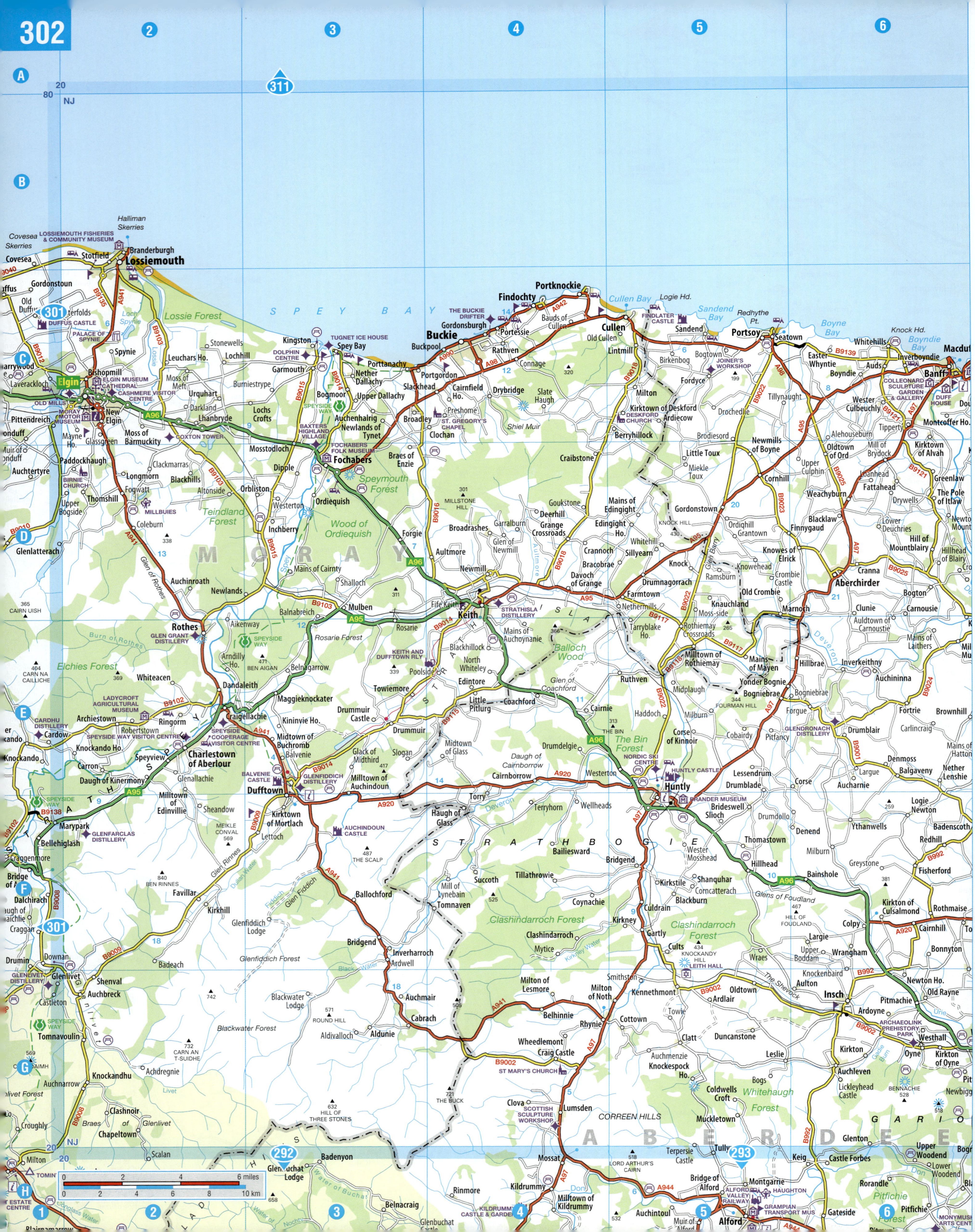
SPEY BAY
MORAY
STRATHBOGIE
ABERDEENSHIRE
Lossiemouth
Branderburgh
Covesea
Gordonstoun
Duffus
Elgin
Lossie Forest
Spynie
Bishopmill
New Elgin
Lhanbryde
Fochabers
Speymouth Forest
Kingston
Garmouth
Spey Bay
Portgordon
Buckie
Findochty
Portknockie
Cullen
Cullen Bay
Logie Hd.
Sandend
Sandend Bay
Portsoy
Boyne Bay
Banff
Macduff
Keith
Rothes
Dufftown
Craigellachie
Charlestown of Aberlour
Huntly
Aberchirder
Insch
Alford
Lumsden
Rhynie
Glenlivet
Tomnavoulin
Bin Forest
Clashindarroch Forest
Teindland Forest
Wood of Ordiequish
Elchies Forest
Blackwater Forest
Glenfiddich Forest
Balloch Wood
Correen Hills
Milltown of Rothiemay
Ardlair
Kennethmont
Leith Hall
A96
A95
A98
A941
A920
A97
A944
301
311
292
293
0 2 4 6 miles
0 2 4 6 8 10 km

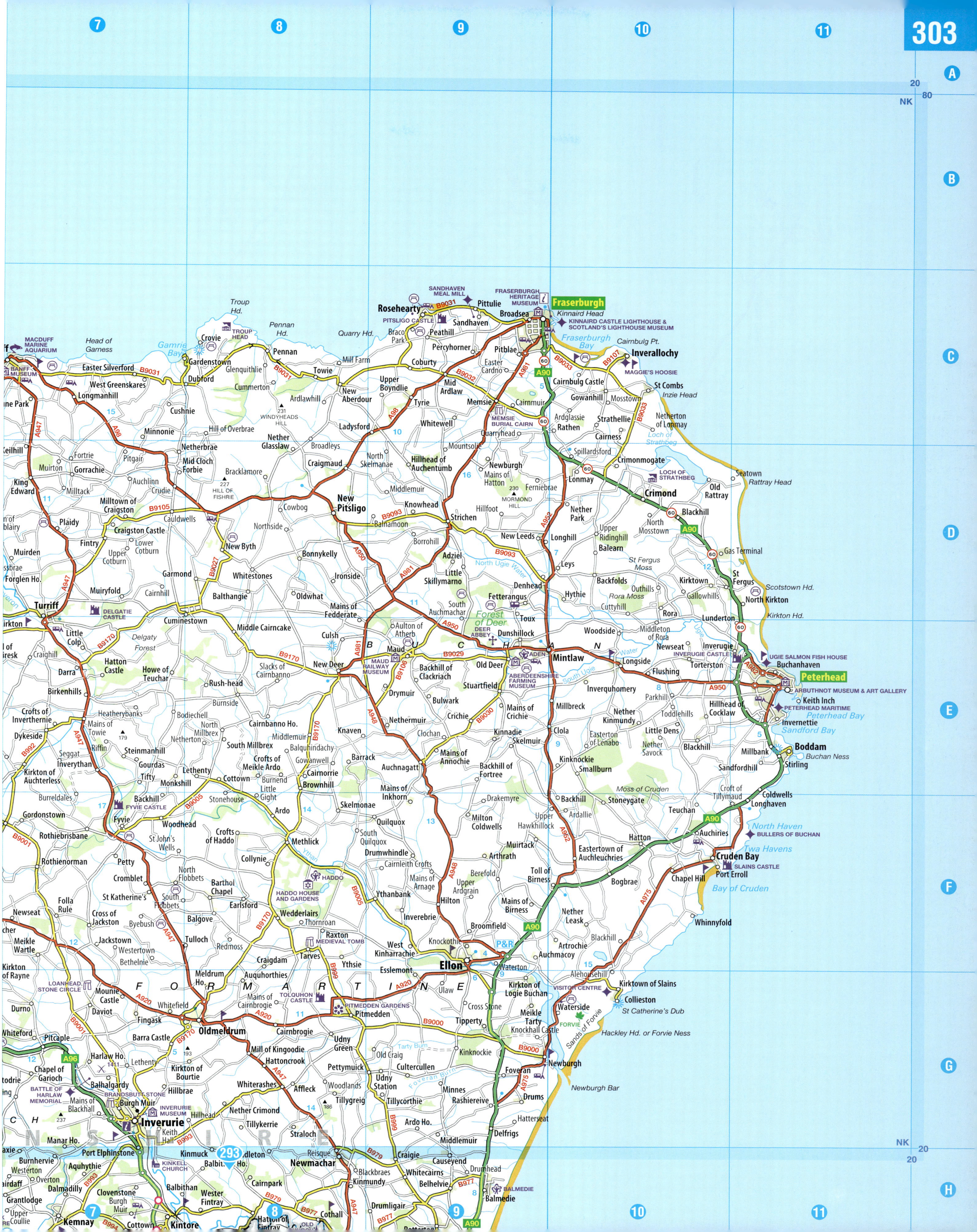
7
8
9
10
11
A
B
C
D
E
F
G
H
NK
20
80
Troup Hd.
Pennan Hd.
Quarry Hd.
Head of Garness
MACDUFF MARINE AQUARIUM
BANFF MUSEUM
Gamrie Bay
Crovie
TROUP HEAD
Gardenstown
Pennan
Easter Silverford
Dubford
Glenquithlie
Towie
Mill Farm
West Greenskares
Cummerton
Longmanhill
New Aberdour
Ardlawhill
Cushnie
231 WINDYHEADS HILL
Minnonie
Hill of Overbrae
Nether Glasslaw
Netherbrae
Fortrie
Gorrachie
Muirton
Pitgair
Mid Cloch Forbie
Bracklamore
Broadleys
Craigmaud
King Edward
Milltack
Auchlinn
Crudie
227 HILL OF FISHRIE
Milltown of Craigston
Cauldwells
Cowbog
Plaidy
Fintry
Craigston Castle
Lower Cotburn
Upper Cotburn
Northside
New Byth
Muirden
Forglen Ho.
Garmond
Whitestones
Bonnykelly
Muiryfold
Cairnhill
Balthangie
Oldwhat
Turriff
DELGATIE CASTLE
Cuminestown
Middle Cairncake
Little Colp
Delgaty Forest
Hatton Castle
Craighill
Darra
Howe of Teuchar
Slacks of Cairnbanno
Rush-head
Birkenhills
Burnside
Crofts of Inverthernie
Heatherybanks
Bodiechell
Mains of Towie
North Millbrex
Netherton
Cairnbanno Ho.
Middlemuir
Dykeside
Riffin
South Millbrex
Balquhindachy
Steinmanhill
Seggat
Inverythan
Gourdas
Crofts of Meikle Ardo
Gowanwell
Kirkton of Auchterless
Tifty
Lethenty
Cottown
Burnend
Cairnorrie
Monkshill
Little Gight
Brownhill
Burreldales
Backhill
FYVIE CASTLE
Stonehouse
Ardo
Gordonstown
Fyvie
Woodhead
Rothiebrisbane
St John's Wells
Crofts of Haddo
Methlick
Rothienorman
Petty
North Flobbets
Collynie
Cromblet
South Flobbets
Barthol Chapel
HADDO HOUSE AND GARDENS
HADDO
Folla Rule
St Katherine's
Earlsford
Newseat
Cross of Jackston
Byebush
Balgove
Wedderlairs
Thornroan
Meikle Wartle
Jackstown
Tulloch
Westertown
Redmoss
Bethelnie
Craigdam
Tarves
Kirkton of Rayne
Meldrum Ho.
Auquhorthies
LOANHEAD STONE CIRCLE
Mounie Castle
Mains of Cairnbrogie
TOLQUHON CASTLE
Durno
Daviot
Whitefield
Fingask
Oldmeldrum
PITMEDDEN GARDENS
Pitmedden
Whiteford
Pitcaple
Barra Castle
Cairnbrogie
Udny Green
Harlaw Ho.
193
Lethenty
Mill of Kingoodie
Chapel of Garioch
Kirkton of Bourtie
Hattoncrook
Balhalgardy
Hillbrae
Whiterashes
Affleck
BATTLE OF HARLAW MEMORIAL
BRANDSBUTT STONE
Mains of Blackhall
Burgh Muir
Inverurie
INVERURIE MUSEUM
Hillhead
Nether Crimond
Tillykerrie
Keith Hall
Manar Ho.
Straloch
Port Elphinstone
Kinmuck
293
Burnhervie
Westerton
Aquhythie
KINKELL CHURCH
Balbithan Ho.
Newmachar
Reisque
Overton
Dalmadilly
Cairnpark
Clovenstone
Burgh Muir
Balbithan
Wester Fintray
Grantlodge
Upper Coullie
Kemnay
Cottown
Kintore
Hatton of Fintray
Cothall
Rosehearty
SANDHAVEN MEAL MILL
Pittulie
FRASERBURGH HERITAGE MUSEUM
Fraserburgh
Kinnaird Head
KINNAIRD CASTLE LIGHTHOUSE & SCOTLAND'S LIGHTHOUSE MUSEUM
PITSLIGO CASTLE
Sandhaven
Broadsea
Braco Park
Peathill
Fraserburgh Bay
Cairnbulg Pt.
Percyhorner
Pitblae
Inverallochy
Coburty
Easter Cardno
MAGGIE'S HOOSIE
Upper Boyndlie
Mid Ardlaw
Cairnbulg Castle
Tyrie
Memsie
Cairnmuir
Gowanhill
Mosstown
St Combs
Inzie Head
MEMSIE BURIAL CAIRN
Ardglassie
Rathen
Strathellie
Whitewell
Ladysford
Netherton of Lonmay
Quarryhead
Cairness
Loch of Strathbeg
Mountsolie
Spillardsford
North Skelmanae
Hillhead of Auchentumb
Newburgh
Mains of Hatton
Lonmay
Crimonmogate
LOCH OF STRATHBEG
Seatown
Rattray Head
Middlemuir
230 MORMOND HILL
Ferniebrae
Crimond
Old Rattray
New Pitsligo
Knowhead
Hillfoot
Nether Park
Blackhill
Balnamoon
Strichen
Upper Ridinghill
North Mosstown
New Leeds
Longhill
Balearn
Gas Terminal
Borrohill
Adziel
St Fergus Moss
Little Skillymarno
Leys
Kirktown
St Fergus
Ironside
Denhead
Backfolds
Outhills
Scotstown Hd.
Hythie
Rora Moss
Gallowhills
North Kirkton
Mains of Fedderate
South Auchmachar
Fetterangus
Cuttyhill
Rora
Forest of Deer
Kirkton Hd.
Toux
Lunderton
Culsh
Aulton of Atherb
DEER ABBEY
Dunshillock
Woodside
Middleton of Rora
Maud
Newseat
Inverugie
B U C H A N
MAUD RAILWAY MUSEUM
Backhill of Clackriach
Old Deer
ADEN
Mintlaw
Longside
INVERUGIE CASTLE
UGIE SALMON FISH HOUSE
Buchanhaven
New Deer
Torterston
Flushing
Peterhead
ABERDEENSHIRE FARMING MUSEUM
Stuartfield
Inverquhomery
ARBUTHNOT MUSEUM & ART GALLERY
Drymuir
Parkhill
Keith Inch
Bulwark
Millbreck
Nether Kinmundy
Hillhead of Cocklaw
PETERHEAD MARITIME
Peterhead Bay
Mains of Crichie
Toddlehills
Invernettie
Nethermuir
Crichie
Sandford Bay
Knaven
Clochan
Kinnadie
Clola
Easterton of Lenabo
Little Dens
Skelmuir
Nether Savock
Blackhill
Boddam
Millbank
Buchan Ness
Barrack
Mains of Annochie
Kinknockie
Smallburn
Auchnagatt
Backhill of Fortree
Sandfordhill
Stirling
Mains of Inkhorn
Moss of Cruden
Croft of Tillymaud
Coldwells
Skelmonae
Drakemyre
Backhill
Stoneygate
Teuchan
Longhaven
Ardallie
Quilquox
South Quilquox
Milton Coldwells
Upper Hawkhillock
Auchiries
North Haven
BULLERS OF BUCHAN
Drumwhindle
Hatton
Muirtack
Eastertown of Auchleuchries
Cruden Bay
Twa Havens
Cairnleith Crofts
Arthrath
SLAINS CASTLE
Mains of Arnage
Berefold
Toll of Birness
Chapel Hill
Port Erroll
Upper Ardgrain
Bogbrae
Bay of Cruden
Ythanbank
Hilton
Mains of Birness
Inverebrie
Nether Leask
Whinnyfold
Broomfield
Raxton
MEDIEVAL TOMB
Knockothie
Blackhill
P&R
Artrochie
West Kinharrachie
Ythsie
Auchmacoy
Ellon
Esslemont
Waterton
Alehousehill
Kirktown of Slains
Kirkton of Logie Buchan
Ulaw
VISITOR CENTRE
Collieston
St Catherine's Dub
Cross Stone
Waterside
Meikle Tarty
FORVIE
Knockhall Castle
Sands of Forvie
Hackley Hd. or Forvie Ness
Tipperty
Tarty Burn
Old Craig
Kinknockie
Newburgh
Culterculen
Foveran Burn
Pettymuick
Foveran
Udny Station
Minnes
Newburgh Bar
Woodlands
Drums
Tillycorthie
Rashieiceive
Tillygreig
186
Hatterseat
Ardo Ho.
Delfrigs
Middlemuir
Craigie
Causeyend
Blackbraes
Whitecairns
Drumhead
Kinmundy
Belhelvie
BALMEDIE
Balmedie
Drumligair
Potterton
F O R M A R T I N E
A B E R D E E N S H I R E
A90
A96
A98
A947
A950
A952
A948
A981
A920
A975
A982
B9031
B9032
B9033
B9107
B9093
B9105
B9027
B9170
B9029
B9106
B9030
B9005
B9000
B9001
B992
B999
B979
B977
B993
B994

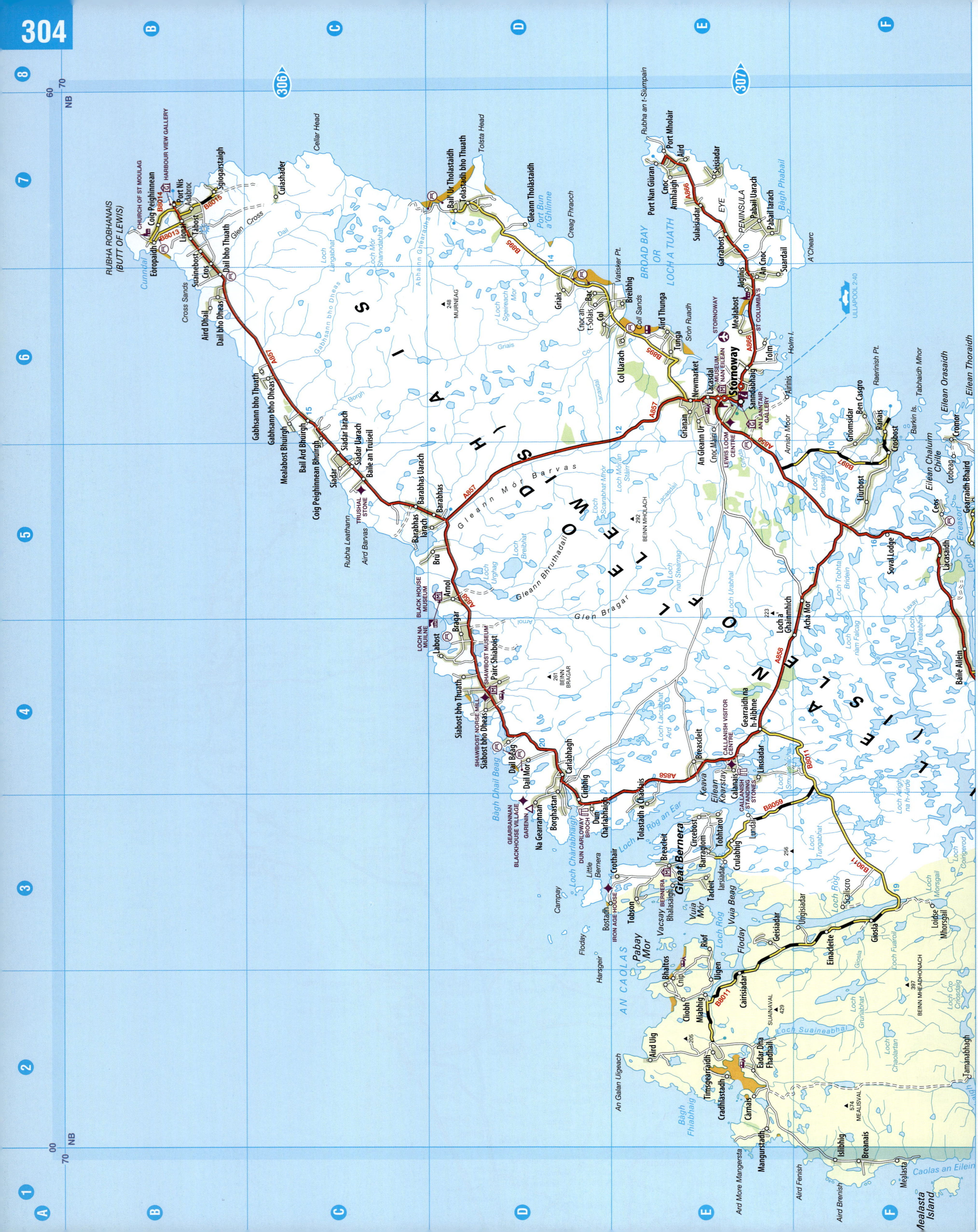
ISLE OF LEWIS (LEODHAS)
Stornoway
RUBHA ROBHANAIS (BUTT OF LEWIS)
Eoropaidh
Port Nis
Sgiogarstaigh
Dail bho Thuath
Dail bho Dheas
Cross Sands
Cellar Head
Culashader
Tolsta Head
Tolastadh bho Thuath
Gleann Tholàstaidh
Port Bun a'Ghlinne
Creag Fhraoch
Rubha an t-Siumpain
Port Mholair
Port Nan Giùran
EYE PENINSULA
Bàgh Phabail
Pabail Iarach
Pabail Uarach
Garabost
An Cnoc
Suardail
A'Chearc
Aiginis
ST COLUMBA'S
Mealabost
Holm I.
Tolm
ULLAPOOL 2:40
BROAD BAY OR LOCH A TUATH
Vatisker Pt.
Breibhig
Griais
Col
Col Uarach
Aird Thunga
Tunga
Sròn Ruadh
STORNOWAY
Newmarket
Lacasdal
MUSEUM NAN EILEAN
AN LANNTAIR GALLERY
LEWIS LOOM CENTRE
Sanndabhaig
Airinis
Arnish Moor
Raerinish Pt.
Ben Casgro
Grimsiadar
Ranais
Crosbost
Barkin Is.
Tabhaidh Mhòr
Eilean Orasaidh
Eilean Thoraidh
Cromor
Eilean Chaluim Chille
Gearraidh Bhaird
Liurbost
Loch Eireasort
Lacasaidh
Soval Lodge
Baile Ailein
Grianan
An Gleann Ùr
Cnoc Màiri
Gleann Mòr Barvas
BEINN MHOLACH
Gleann Bhruthadail
Glen Bragar
Barabhas
Barabhas Uarach
Barabhas Iarach
TRUSHAL STONE
Rubha Leathann
Aird Barvas
Siadar
Siadar Uarach
Siadar Iarach
Baile an Truiseil
Gabhsann bho Thuath
Gabhsann bho Dheas
Mealabost Bhuirgh
Bail Àrd Bhuirgh
Coig Peighinnean Bhuirgh
Brù
Arnol
BLACK HOUSE MUSEUM
LOCH NA MUILNE
Labost
Bragar
SHAWBOST MUSEUM
Pàirc Shiabost
Siabost bho Thuath
Siabost bho Dheas
SHAWBOST NORSE MILL
BEINN BRAGAR
Dail Beag
Dail Mòr
Bàgh Dhail Beag
Carlabhagh
Borghastan
GEARRANNAN BLACKHOUSE VILLAGE
Na Gearrannan
Loch Chàrlabhaigh
Càrlabhagh
DUN CARLOWAY BROCH
Dùn Chàrlabhaigh
Tolastadh a Chaolais
Breascleit
CALLANISH VISITOR CENTRE
Calanais
CALLANISH STANDING STONES
Linsiadar
Gearraidh na h-Aibhne
Loch a' Ghainmhich
Acha Mòr
Great Bernera
Little Bernera
Breacleit
Bostadh
IRON AGE HOUSE
Tobson
Vacsay
Pabay Mòr
Campay
Floday
Harsgeir
AN CAOLAS
Bhaltos
Cnip
Uigen
Riof
Cliobh
Miabhig
Cairisiadar
SUAINAVAL
Loch Suaineabhal
Aird Uig
An Galan Uigeach
Timsgearraidh
Cradhlastadh
Eadar Dha Fhadhail
Càrnais
Bàgh Fhiabhaig
MEALISVAL
Manurstadh
Ard More Mangersta
Aird Feinish
Aird Brenish
Islibhig
Breanais
Mealasta
Mealasta Island
Caolas an Eilein
Einacleite
Giosla
Ungisiadar
Geisiadar
BEINN MHEADHONACH
Loch Ròg
Scaliscro
Tamanabhagh
Crulabhig
Iarsiadar
Tacleit
Lundal
Keava
Eilean Kearstay
B8011
B8059
A858
A857
A859
B897
A866
B895
B8014
B8013
B8015
306
307
NB

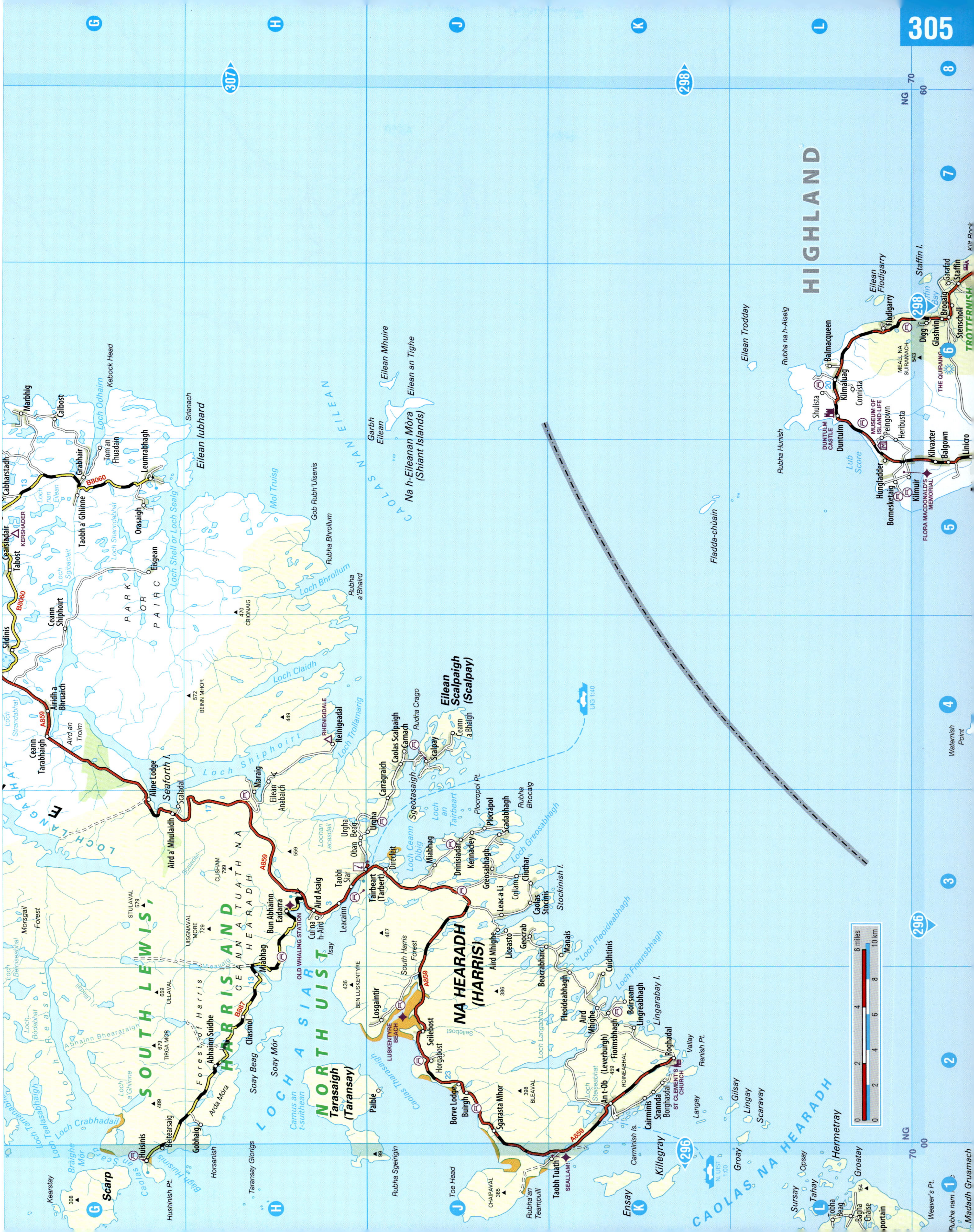
HIGHLAND
SOUTH LEWIS,
HARRIS AND
NORTH UIST
NA HEARADH (HARRIS)
CEANN A TUATH NA HEARADH
PARK OR PAIRC
LOCH A SIAR
CAOLAS NAN EILEAN
CAOLAS NA HEARADH
LOCH LANGABHAT
Na h-Eileanan Mòra (Shiant Islands)
Eilean Scalpaigh (Scalpay)
Tarasaigh (Taransay)
Scarp
Eilean Iubhard
Eilean Mhuire
Eilean an Tighe
Garbh Eilean
Eilean Trodday
Eilean Flodigarry
Staffin I.
Fladda-chùain
Rubha Hunish
Rubha na h-Aiseig
Lub Score
Kebock Head
Srianach
Gob Rubh'Uisenis
Rubha Bhrollum
Rubha a'Bhaird
Rudha Crago
Rubha Bhocaig
Stockinish I.
Loch Shell or Loch Seaforth
Loch Shiphoirt
Loch Claidh
Loch Bhrollum
Mol Truisg
Loch Trollamarig
Loch Odhairn
Loch Tarbeart
Loch Ceann Dibig
Loch Greosabhagh
Loch Fleoideabhagh
Loch Fionnsbhagh
Lingarabay I.
Seaforth I.
Kershader
Rhenigidale
Old Whaling Station
Luskentyre Beach
Seallam!
St Clement's Church
Duntulm Castle
Museum of Island Life
Flora MacDonald's Memorial
The Quiraing
Trotternish
Cabharstadh
Marbhig
Calbost
Grabhair
Tom an Fhuadain
Leumrabhagh
Orasaigh
Eisgean
Taobh a' Ghlinne
Tabost
Gearraidh
Ceann Shiphoirt
Sildinis
Airidh a Bhruaich
Ceann Tarabhaigh
Aline Lodge
Aird a' Mhulaidh
Bogha Glas
Maraig
Reinigeadal
Caolas Scalpaigh
Carnach
Carragraich
Scalpay
Ceann a Bhaigh
Sgeotasaigh
Urgha
Urgha Beag
Tairbeart (Tarbert)
Diraclett
Aird Asaig
Bun Abhainn Eadarra
Miabhag
Cliasmol
Abhainn Suidhe
Huisinis
Bealach a' Chaolais
Crabhadail
Gobhaig
Losgaintir
Seilebost
Horgabost
Borve Lodge
Buirgh
Sgarasta Mhor
Taobh Tuath
An t-Ob (Leverburgh)
Fionnsbhagh
Roghadal
Ceann a Bhaigh
Kennavay
Drinisiadar
Greosabhagh
Plocrapol
Scadabhagh
Collam
Cluthar
Caolas Stocinis
Aird Mhighe
Lìceasto
Geocrab
Beacravik
Manais
Cuidhtinis
Fleoideabhagh
Boirseam
Lingreabhagh
Strond
Grosebay
Quidinish
Renish Pt.
Killegray
Ensay
Langay
Gilsay
Lingay
Scaravay
Groay
Hermetray
Opsay
Tahay
Sursay
Groatay
Toe Head
Rubha Sgeirigin
Rubha an Teampuill
Hushinish Pt.
Kearstay
Soay Beag
Soay Mòr
Isay
Taransay Glorigs
Horsanish
Duntulm
Shulista
Kilmaluag
Balmacqueen
Connista
Heribusta
Peingown
Flodigarry
Digg
Glashvin
Brogaig
Stenscholl
Staffin
Garafad
Kilt Rock
Hungladder
Kilmuir
Kilvaxter
Balgown
Linicro
Borneskitaig
Waternish Point
Weaver's Pt.
Madadh Gruamach
Staffin Bay
Meall na Suiramach 543
Stulaval 579
Clisham 799
Uisgnaval More 729
Ulaval 659
Tirga Mor 679
Beinn Mhor 572
Crionaig 470
Ben Luskentyre
Bleaval 398
Roineabhal 460
Chaipaval 365
Forest of Harris
Morsgail Forest
South Harris Forest
A859
B887
B8060
A855
Uig 1:40
N. Uist 1:00
G
H
J
K
L
1
2
3
4
5
6
7
8
NG
60
70
00
296
298
307
0
2
4
6
8
10 km
6 miles

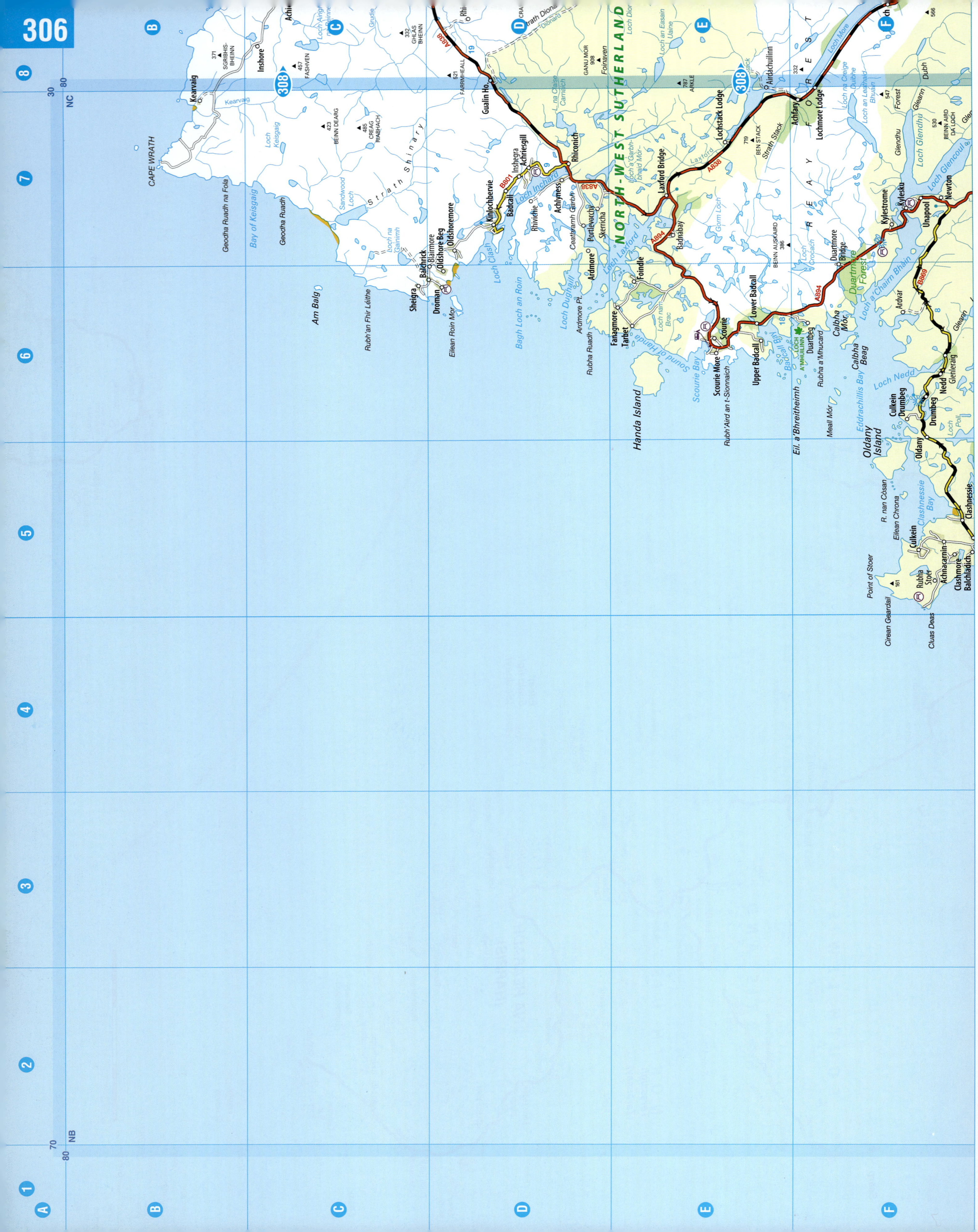

CAPE WRATH
Kearvaig
Inshore
SGRIBHIS-BHEINN
FASHVEN
Bay of Keisgaig
Loch Keisgaig
Geodha Ruadh
Geodha Ruadh na Fola
BEINN DEARG
CREAG RIABHACH
Strath Shinary
Sandwood Loch
Loch na Gainimh
GHLAS BHEINN
FARMHEALL
Am Balg
Rubh'an Fhir Lèithe
Sheigra
Balchrick
Blairmore
Oldshore Beg
Oldshoremore
Droman
Eilean Roin Mor
Kinlochbervie
Badcall
Inshegra
Achriesgill
Loch Inchard
Loch Clash
Rhiconich
Gualin Ho.
Rhivichie
Achlyness
Portlevorchy
Skerricha
Ardmore
Ardmore Pt.
Ceathramh Garbh
Bagh Loch an Roin
Loch Dùghaill
Loch Laxford
Rubha Ruadh
Foindle
Fanagmore
Tarbet
Sound of Handa
Handa Island
Loch nam Brac
Scourie
Scourie More
Scourie Bay
Rubh'Aird an t-Sionnaich
Badnabay
Laxford Bridge
Gorm Loch
NORTH-WEST SUTHERLAND
Foinaven
GANU MOR
Strath Dionard
ARKLE
Loch Stack
Lochstack Lodge
BEN STACK
Strath Stack
Airdachuilinn
Achfary
Lochmore Lodge
Loch More
REAY FOREST
Lower Badcall
Upper Badcall
Badcall Bay
Eil. a' Bhreitheimh
LOCH A'MHUILINN
Duartbeg
Rubha a'Mhucard
BEINN AUSKAIRD
Duartmore Bridge
Duartmore Forest
Calbha Mor
Calbha Beag
Eddrachillis Bay
Meall Mòr
Oldany Island
Oldany
Kylestrome
Kylesku
Unapool
Newton
Loch Glencoul
Loch Glendhu
Glendhu Forest
Loch a'Chàirn Bhàin
Ardvar
Loch Nedd
Nedd
Glenleraig
Drumbeg
Culkein Drumbeg
Loch Poll
Clashnessie
Clashnessie Bay
Eilean Chrona
R. nan Cosan
Culkein
Achnacarnin
Rubha Stoer
Point of Stoer
Clashmore
Balchladich
Cirean Geardail
Cluas Deas
A838
A894
B801
B869
308
NC
NB
A
B
C
D
E
F
1
2
3
4
5
6
7
8

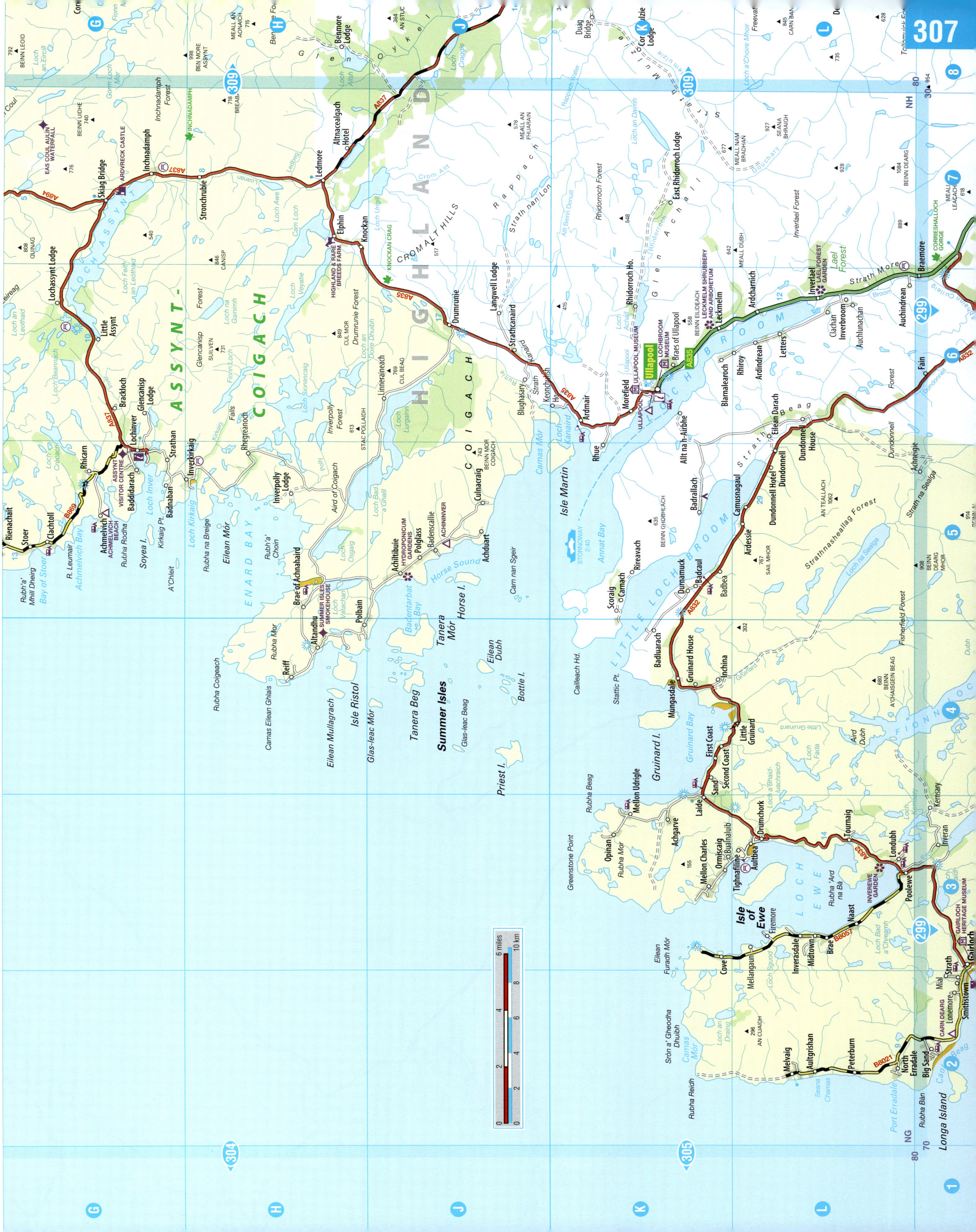
Ullapool
LOCH BROOM
LITTLE LOCH BROOM
LOCH EWE
Isle of Ewe
Summer Isles
Tanera Mór
Tanera Beg
Isle Ristol
Priest I.
Gruinard I.
Isle Martin
Horse I.
Eilean Dubh
Bottle I.
ENARD BAY
Gruinard Bay
Annat Bay
Horse Sound
Badentarbat Bay
HIGHLAND
COIGACH
ASSYNT
CROMALT HILLS
Lochinver
Achiltibuie
Polbain
Altandhu
Reiff
Polglass
Badenscallie
Achduart
Culnacraig
Inverkirkaig
Strathan
Badnaban
Baddidarach
Achmelvich
Clachtoll
Stoer
Rienachait
Little Assynt
Lochassynt Lodge
Skiag Bridge
Inchnadamph
Stronchrubie
Ledmore
Elphin
Knockan
Drumrunie
Strathcanaird
Ardmair
Rhue
Morefield
Braes of Ullapool
Leckmelm
Ardcharnich
Inverlael
Braemore
Auchindrean
Letters
Ardindrean
Rhiroy
Blarnalearoch
Allt na h-Airbhe
Badrallach
Scoraig
Durnamuck
Badcaul
Ardessie
Camusnagaul
Dundonnell
Badluarach
Mungasdale
Gruinard House
Inchina
Little Gruinard
First Coast
Second Coast
Sand
Laide
Mellon Udrigle
Opinan
Achgarve
Mellon Charles
Ormiscaig
Bualnaluib
Aultbea
Tighnafiline
Drumchork
Tournaig
Poolewe
Londubh
Inverasdale
Midtown
Brae
Naast
Cove
Mellangaun
Melvaig
Aultgrishan
Peterburn
North Erradale
Big Sand
Gairloch
Strath
Smithstown
Lonemore
Kernsary
Inveran
Fain
Achneigie
Eilean Darach
Dundonnell House
Dundonnell Hotel
Clachan
Inverbroom
Auchlunachan
Leckmelm Shrubbery and Arboretum
Lael Forest Garden
Corrieshalloch Gorge
Inverewe Garden
Gairloch Heritage Museum
Ullapool Museum
Lochbroom Museum
Knockan Crag
Highland & Rare Breeds Farm
Ardvreck Castle
Assynt Visitor Centre
Achmelvich Beach
Summer Isles Smokehouse
Hydroponicum Gardens
Achininver
Eas Coul Aulin Waterfall
Stornoway 2:40
A835
A837
A832
A894
B869
B8021
B8057
Rubha Reidh
Greenstone Point
Rubha Coigeach
Cailleach Hd.
Rubha Beag
Longa Island
309
304
305
299
6 miles
10 km

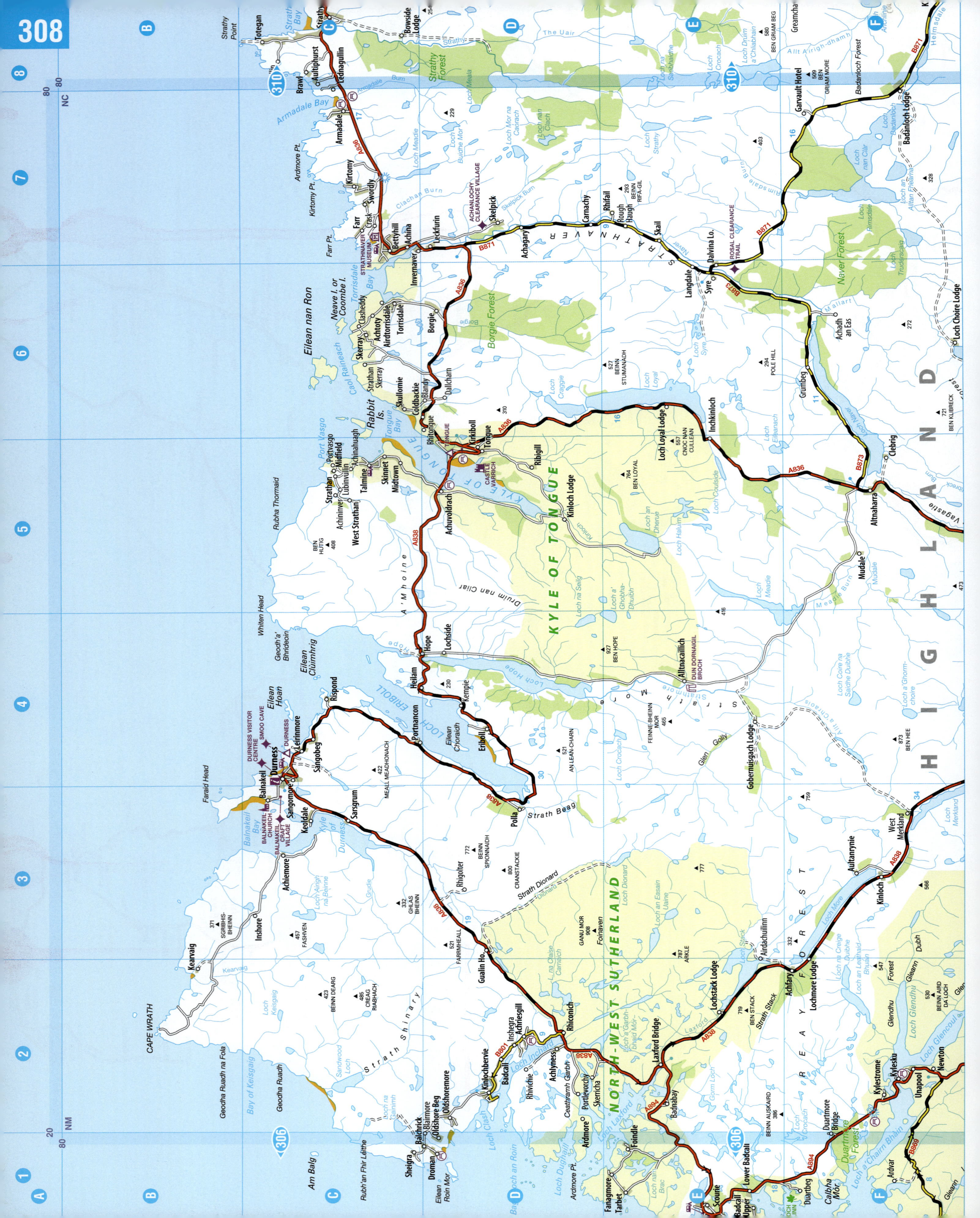
CAPE WRATH
Faraid Head
Whiten Head
Strathy Point
Armadale Bay
Kirtomy Pt.
Farr Pt.
Eilean nan Ron
Neave I. or Coombe I.
Rabbit Is.
Tongue Bay
Port Vasgo
Rubha Thormaid
Eilean Hoan
Eilean Choraidh
Eilean Cluimhrig
LOCH ERIBOLL
Loch Hope
Kyle of Durness
Balnakeil Bay
Bay of Keisgaig
Am Balg
Loch Inchard
Loch Laxford
Loch Dughaill
Ardmore Pt.
KYLE OF TONGUE
NORTH-WEST SUTHERLAND
HIGHLAND
REAY FOREST
STRATHNAVER
Borgie Forest
Naver Forest
Strathy Forest
Badanloch Forest
Durness
Balnakeil
Sangomore
Keoldale
Leirinmore
Sangobeg
Rispond
Portnancon
Heilam
Hope
Lochside
Kempie
Eriboll
Polla
Achiemore
Inshore
Kearvaig
Rhiconich
Achriesgill
Inshegra
Kinlochbervie
Badcall
Oldshoremore
Oldshore Beg
Blairmore
Balchrick
Sheigra
Droman
Laxford Bridge
Achfary
Lochmore Lodge
Kylestrome
Kylesku
Unapool
Newton
Scourie
Tongue
Talmine
Skinnet
Midtown
Melness
Achuvoldrach
Kinloch Lodge
Ribigill
Rhitongue
Coldbackie
Skullomie
Dalcharn
Borgie
Torrisdale
Skerray
Invernaver
Bettyhill
Achina
Farr
Swordly
Kirtomy
Armadale
Lednagullin
Aultiphurst
Brawl
Strathy
Totegan
Skelpick
Achagary
Carnachy
Rhifail
Skail
Dalvina Lo.
Syre
Langdale
Grumbeg
Altnaharra
Clebrig
Inchkinloch
Loch Loyal Lodge
Mudale
Altnacaillich
Gobernuisgach Lodge
West Merkland
Aultanrynie
Kinloch
Garvault Hotel
Badanloch Lodge
Loch Choire Lodge
BEN HOPE 927
BEN LOYAL 764
BEN HEE 873
BEN KLIBRECK 721
ARKLE 787
FOINAVEN
CRANSTACKIE 800
A838
A836
B871
B873
A894
B801
B869
306
310

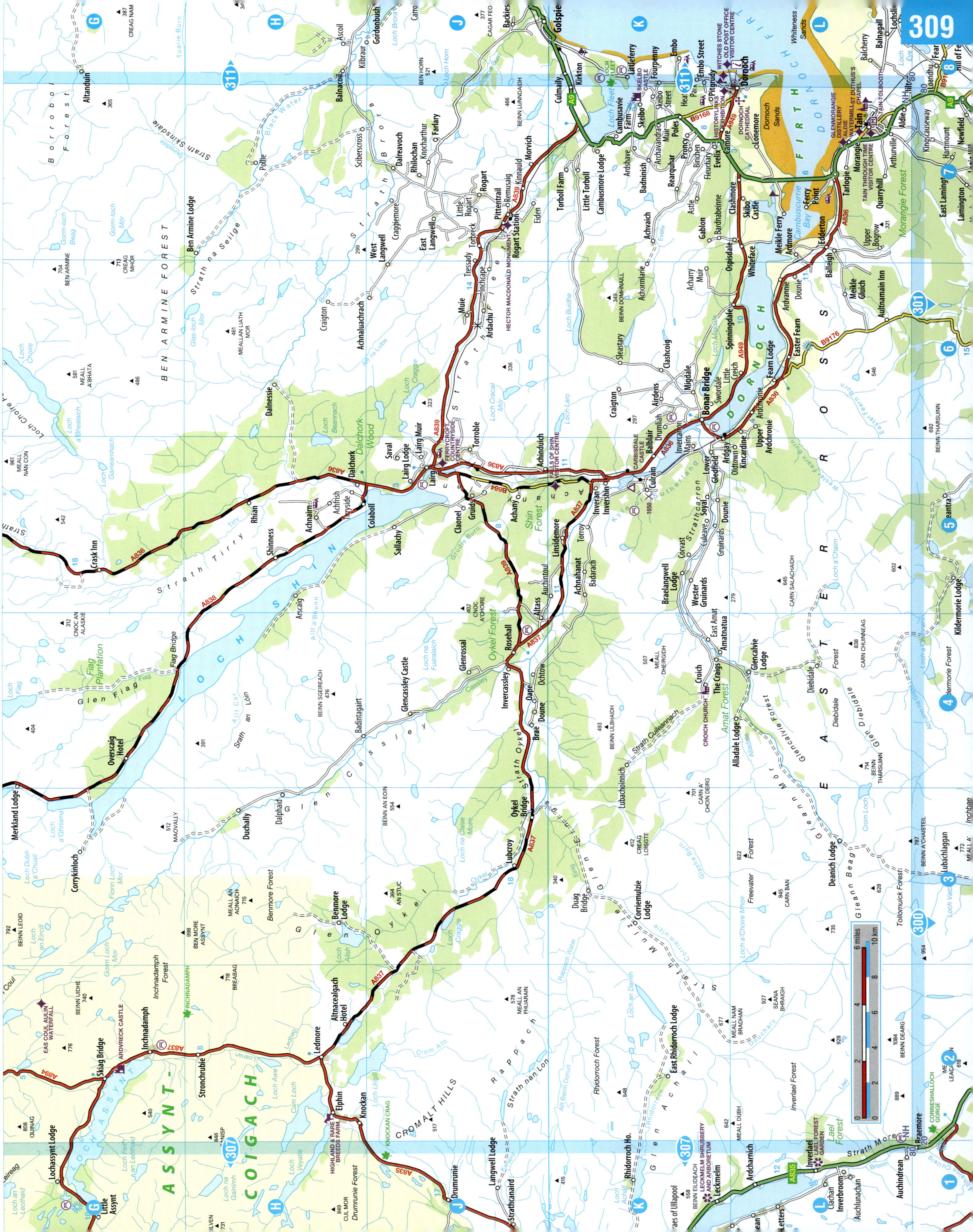
Golspie
Dornoch
Dornoch Firth
Embo
Skelbo
Tain
Edderton
Bonar Bridge
Ardgay
Spinningdale
Clashmore
Lairg
Rogart
Pittentrail
Achany
Invershin
Culrain
Rosehall
Invercassley
Oykel Bridge
Lubcroy
Altnacealgach Hotel
Ledmore
Inchnadamph
Skiag Bridge
Lochassynt Lodge
Elphin
Knockan
Drumrunie
Strathcanaird
Langwell Lodge
Rhidorroch Ho.
Leckmelm
Ardcharnich
Inverlael
Inverbroom
Auchindrean
Aultnamain Inn
Loch Shin
Overscaig Hotel
Merkland Lodge
Crask Inn
Dalchork Wood
Shin Forest
Oykel Forest
Amat Forest
Glencalvie Lodge
Alladale Lodge
Deanich Lodge
Strath Oykel
Strath Carron
Glen Cassley
Glen Einig
Glen Achall
Strath Mulzie
Strath Fleet
Strath Tirry
Strath na Seilge
Ben Armine Forest
Borrobol Forest
Assynt - Coigach
Cromalt Hills
Rhidorroch Forest
Freevater Forest
Inverlael Forest
Easter Ross
Morangie Forest
Strath More
A836
A837
A838
A839
A835
A9
A949
A894
B9176
B9168
B864
311
307
301
300
6 miles
10 km

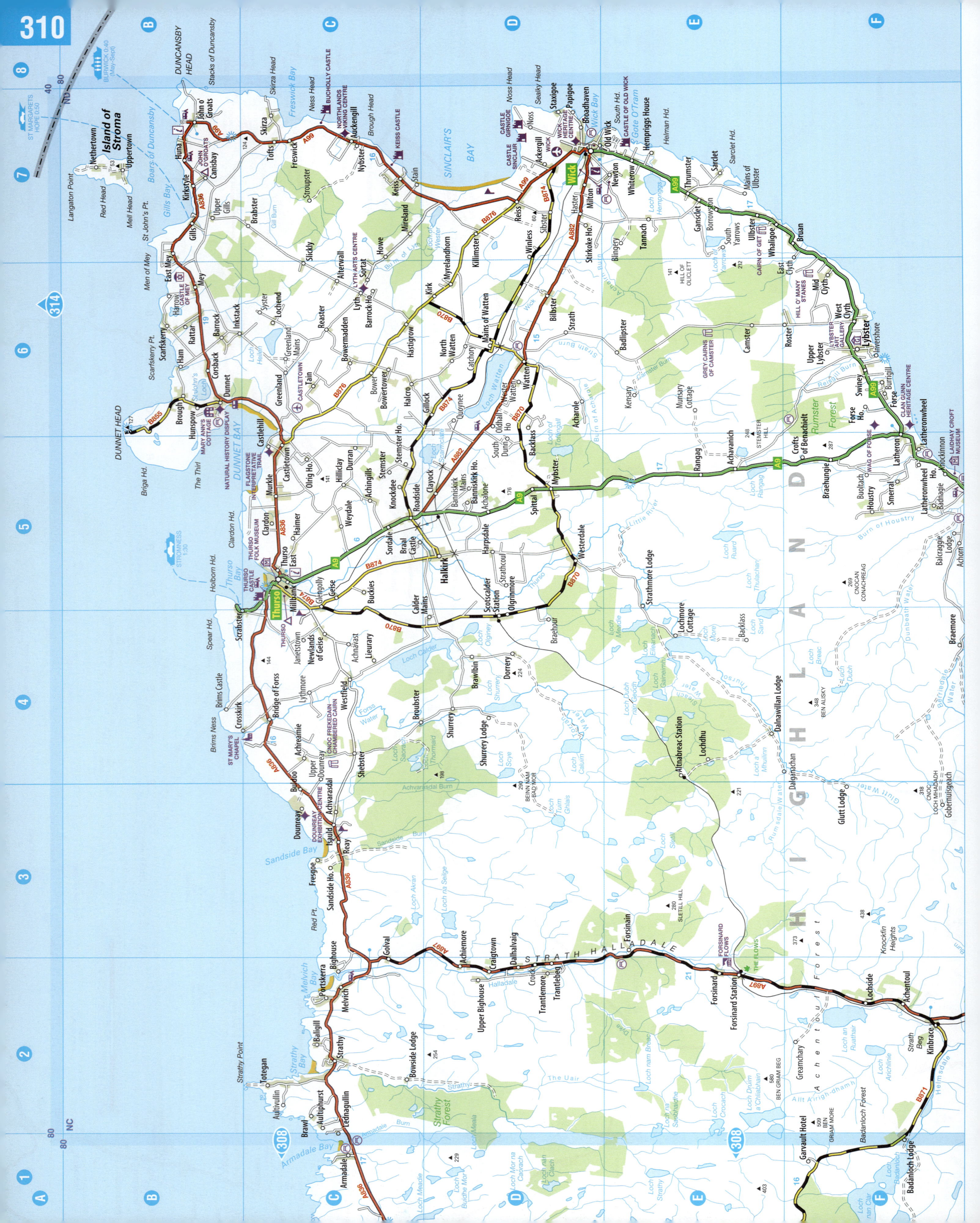
DUNCANSBY HEAD
Stacks of Duncansby
Island of Stroma
John o' Groats
Canisbay
Huna
Freswick
Auckengill
Keiss
Wick
Thurso
Castletown
Dunnet
DUNNET HEAD
DUNNET BAY
SINCLAIR'S BAY
Mey
Barrock
Lyth
Killimster
Reiss
Watten
Loch Watten
Bilbster
Thrumster
Lybster
Latheron
Dunbeath
Halkirk
Georgemas
Scotscalder Station
Westerdale
Altnabreac Station
Dalnawillan Lodge
Dounreay
Reay
Melvich
Portskerra
Strathy
Armadale
Forsinard
Forsinard Station
Kinbrace
Achentoul
STRATH HALLADALE
Sandside Bay
Armadale Bay
Strathy Forest
Rumster Forest
HIGHLAND
A9
A99
A836
A882
A897
B870
B874
B876
B855
B871

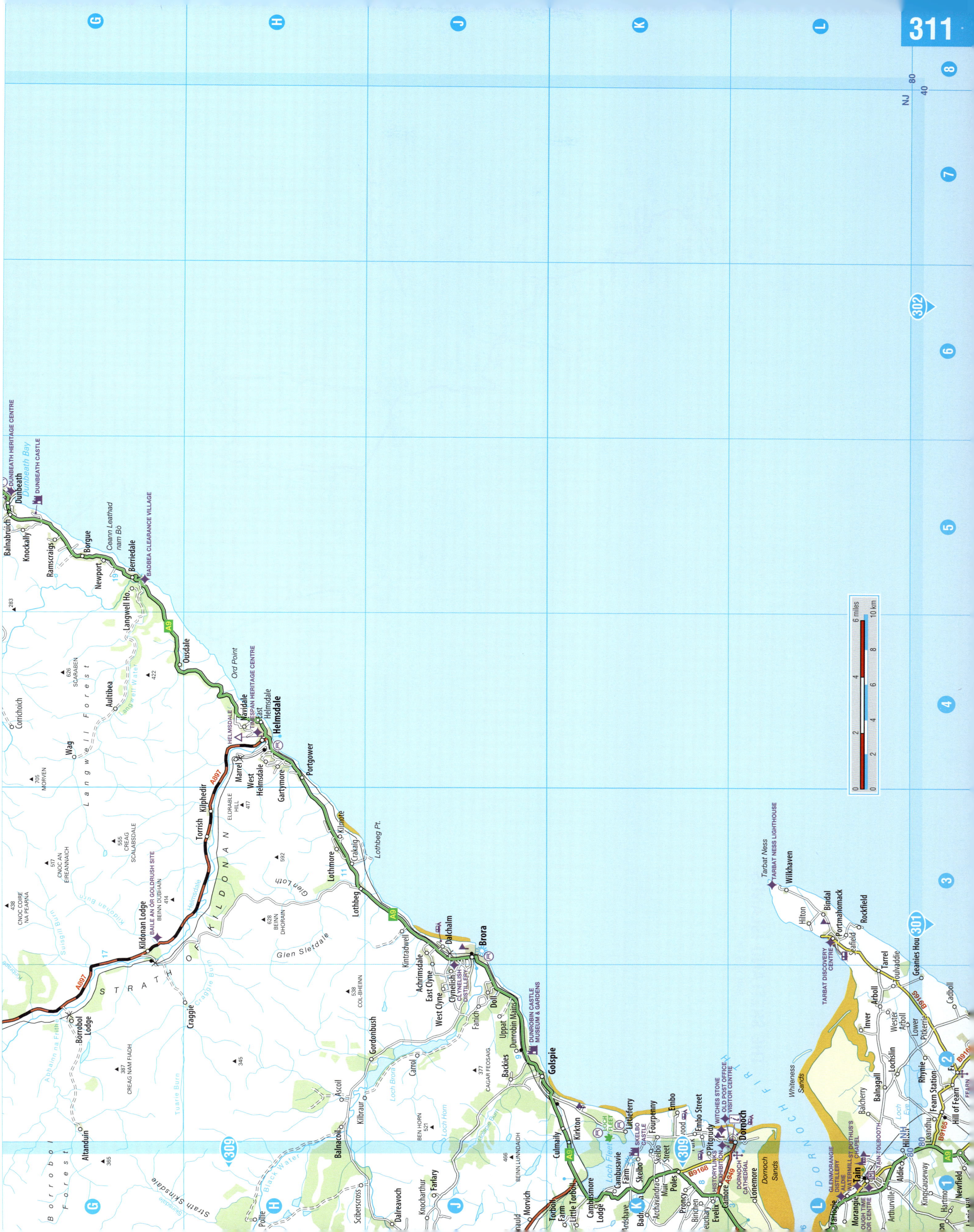

DUNBEATH HERITAGE CENTRE
Dunbeath
Dunbeath Bay
DUNBEATH CASTLE
Balnabruich
Knockally
Ramscraigs
Borgue
Ceann Leathad nam Bò
Newport
Berriedale
BADBEA CLEARANCE VILLAGE
Langwell Ho.
Langwell Water
L a n g w e l l F o r e s t
SCARABEN
Aultibea
Corrichoich
Wag
MORVEN
Ousdale
Ord Point
TIMESPAN HERITAGE CENTRE
HELMSDALE
Navidale
East Helmsdale
Helmsdale
Marrel
West Helmsdale
Gartymore
Portgower
EILDRABLE HILL
Kilphedir
Torrish
A897
A9
CREAG SCALABSDALE
CNOC AN EIREANNAICH
CNOC COIRE NA FEARNA
BAILE AN ÒR GOLDRUSH SITE
BEINN DUBHAIN
Kildonan Lodge
Kildonan Burn
Suisgill Burn
S T R A T H O F K I L D O N A N
Glen Loth
Lothmore
Kilmote
Crakaig
Lothbeg Pt.
Lothbeg
BEINN DHORAIN
Glen Sletdale
Kintradwell
Dalchalm
Brora
Achrimsdale
East Clyne
West Clyne
Clynelish
CLYNELISH DISTILLERY
COL-BHEINN
Doll
Fanich
Uppat
Dunrobin Mains
DUNROBIN CASTLE MUSEUM & GARDENS
Golspie
Backies
CAGAR FEOSAIG
Carrol
Loch Brora
Gordonbush
Craggie
Craggie Burn
Borrobol Lodge
Abhainn na Frithe
CREAG NAM FIADH
Tuarie Burn
Altanduin
B o r r o b o l F o r e s t
Strath Skinsdale
Black Water
Polie
Sciberscross
Dalreavoch
Ascoil
Kilbraur
Balnacoil
BEN HORN
Loch Horn
Knocharthur
Farlary
BEINN LUNNDAIDH
Morvich
Culmaily
Kirkton
Loch Fleet
Littleferry
Torboll Farm
Little Torboll
Cambusmore Lodge
Cambusavie Farm
Skelbo
SKELBO CASTLE
Skelbo Street
Fourpenny
Embo
Embo Street
Achavandra Muir
Poles
Proncy
Pitgrudy
WITCHES STONE
OLD POST OFFICE VISITOR CENTRE
HISTORYLINKS EXHIBITION
DORNOCH CATHEDRAL
Dornoch
Evelix
Camore
Lonemore
Dornoch Sands
B9168
A949
D O R N O C H F I R T H
Whiteness Sands
Tarbat Ness
TARBAT NESS LIGHTHOUSE
Wilkhaven
Hilton
Bindal
Portmahomack
Rockfield
TARBAT DISCOVERY CENTRE
Seafield
Tarrel
Arboll
Inver
Wester Arboll
Lower Pitkerrie
Geanies Hou
Cadboll
Balcherry
Balnagall
Lochslin
Rhynie
Fearn Station
Hill of Fearn
FEARN
Loandhu
Kingscauseway
Arthurville
Aldie
Hill
Tain
TAIN THROUGH TIME VISITOR CENTRE
GLENMORANGIE DISTILLERY
ALDIE WATERMILL
ST DUTHUS'S CHAPEL
TAIN TOLBOOTH
Morangie
Tarlogie
Hartmo
Newfield
B9165
B9166
309
301
302
NJ
NH
0 2 4 6 miles
0 2 4 6 8 10 km

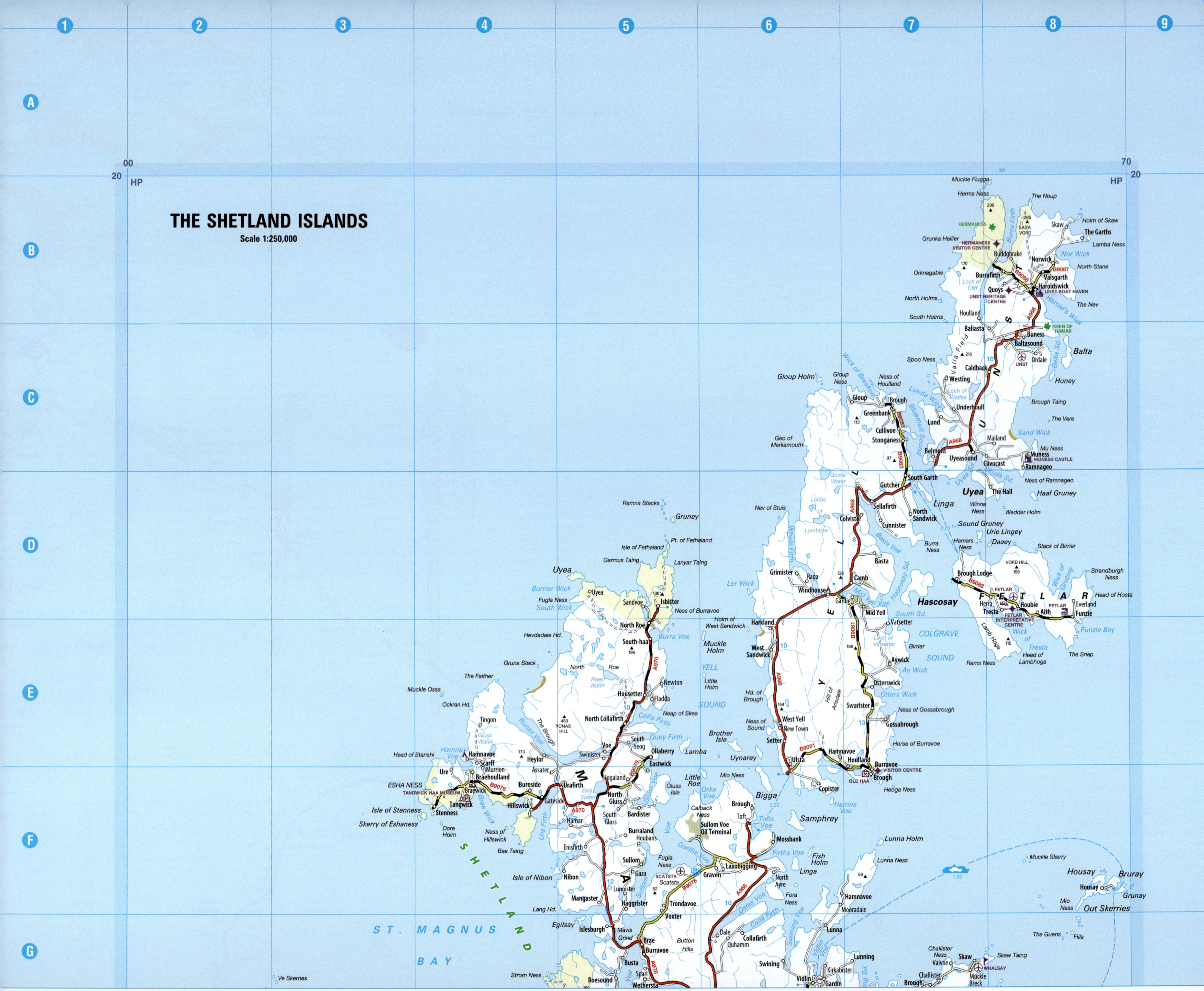

THE SHETLAND ISLANDS
Scale 1:250,000
UNST
YELL
FETLAR
MAINLAND
Muckle Flugga
Herma Ness
The Noup
Hermaness
Hermaness Visitor Centre
Skaw
Holm of Skaw
The Garths
Lamba Ness
Burra Firth
Saxa Vord
Grunka Hellier
Buddabrake
Norwick
Nor Wick
North Stane
Orknagable
Burrafirth
Valsgarth
Haroldswick
Quoys
Unst Heritage Centre
Unst Boat Haven
North Holms
The Nev
South Holms
Houlland
Baliasta
Keen of Hamar
Buness
Baltasound
Balta
Spoo Ness
Ordale
Unst
Caldback
Westing
Huney
Gloup Holm
Gloup Ness
Ness of Houlland
Brough Taing
Gloup
Brough
Greenbank
Underhoull
The Vere
Lund
Cullivoe
Stonganess
Geo of Markamouth
Mailand
Sand Wick
Belmont
Uyeasound
Mu Ness
Muness
Muness Castle
Clivocast
Ramnageo
South Garth
Gutcher
Uyea
The Hall
Ness of Ramnageo
Haaf Gruney
Linga
Nev of Stuis
Sellafirth
Colvister
North Sandwick
Cunnister
Wedder Holm
Sound Gruney
Urie Lingey
Daaey
Stack of Birrier
Ramna Stacks
Gruney
Isle of Fethaland
Pt. of Fethaland
Garmus Taing
Lanyar Taing
Uyea
Basta
Brough Lodge
Vord Hill
Strandburgh Ness
Head of Hosta
Grimister
Camb
Hascosay
Houbie
Tresta
Aith
Everland
Funzie
Funzie Bay
Burrier Wick
Fugla Ness
South Wick
Sandvoe
Isbister
Ness of Burravoe
Windhouse
Gardie
Mid Yell
Harkland
Holm of West Sandwick
West Sandwick
North Roe
South-haa
Burra Voe
Muckle Holm
Vatsetter
Hevdadale Hd.
COLGRAVE SOUND
Lamb Hoga
Head of Lambhoga
The Snap
Rams Ness
Gruna Stack
Aywick
The Faither
Roer Water
Newton
Little Holm
YELL SOUND
Otterswick
Muckle Ossa
Ockran Hd.
Housetter
Fladda
Hd. of Brough
Swarister
Tingon
North Collafirth
Ness of Gossabrough
Gossabrough
Ronas Hill
Brother Isle
Head of Stanshi
Hamnavoe
Heylor
Voe
Ollaberry
Lamba
Uynarey
Setter
West Yell
New Town
Horse of Burravoe
Ure
Braehoulland
Assater
Swinister
Eastwick
Ulsta
Houlland
Burravoe
Old Haa
ESHA NESS
Tangwick Haa Museum
Braewick
Burnside
Urafirth
Hogaland
Little Roe
Mio Ness
Bigga
Copister
Heoga Ness
Tangwick
Isle of Stenness
Stenness
Skerry of Eshaness
Hillswick
Gateside
North Gluss
Gluss Isle
Calback Ness
Sullom Voe Oil Terminal
Samphrey
Dore Holm
Ness of Hillswick
Hamar
Bardister
Toft
Mossbank
Lunna Holm
Baa Taing
Burraland
Houbans
Firths Voe
Fish Holm
Lunna Ness
Enisfirth
Sullom
Fugla Ness
Graven
Laxobigging
Linga
Muckle Skerry
Isle of Nibon
Nibon
Gaza
Scatsta
North Ayre
Hamnavoe
Housay
Bruray
Grunay
Mangaster
Lunnister
Haggrister
Trondavoe
Fora Ness
Mooradale
Out Skerries
Lang Hd.
Egilsay
Islesburgh
Mavis Grind
Voxter
Lunna
The Guens
Filla
ST. MAGNUS BAY
SHETLAND
Brae
Burravoe
Button Hills
Dale
Quhamm
Collafirth
Lunning
Chaillister Ness
Skaw
Skaw Taing
Vaivoe
WHALSAY
Busta
Swining
Kirkabister
Vidlin
Gardin
Roesound
Spari
Wethersta
Strom Ness
Muckle Breck
Ve Skerries
A968
A970
B9081
B9082
B9083
B9086
B9087
B9088
B9076
B9078
B9079
HP

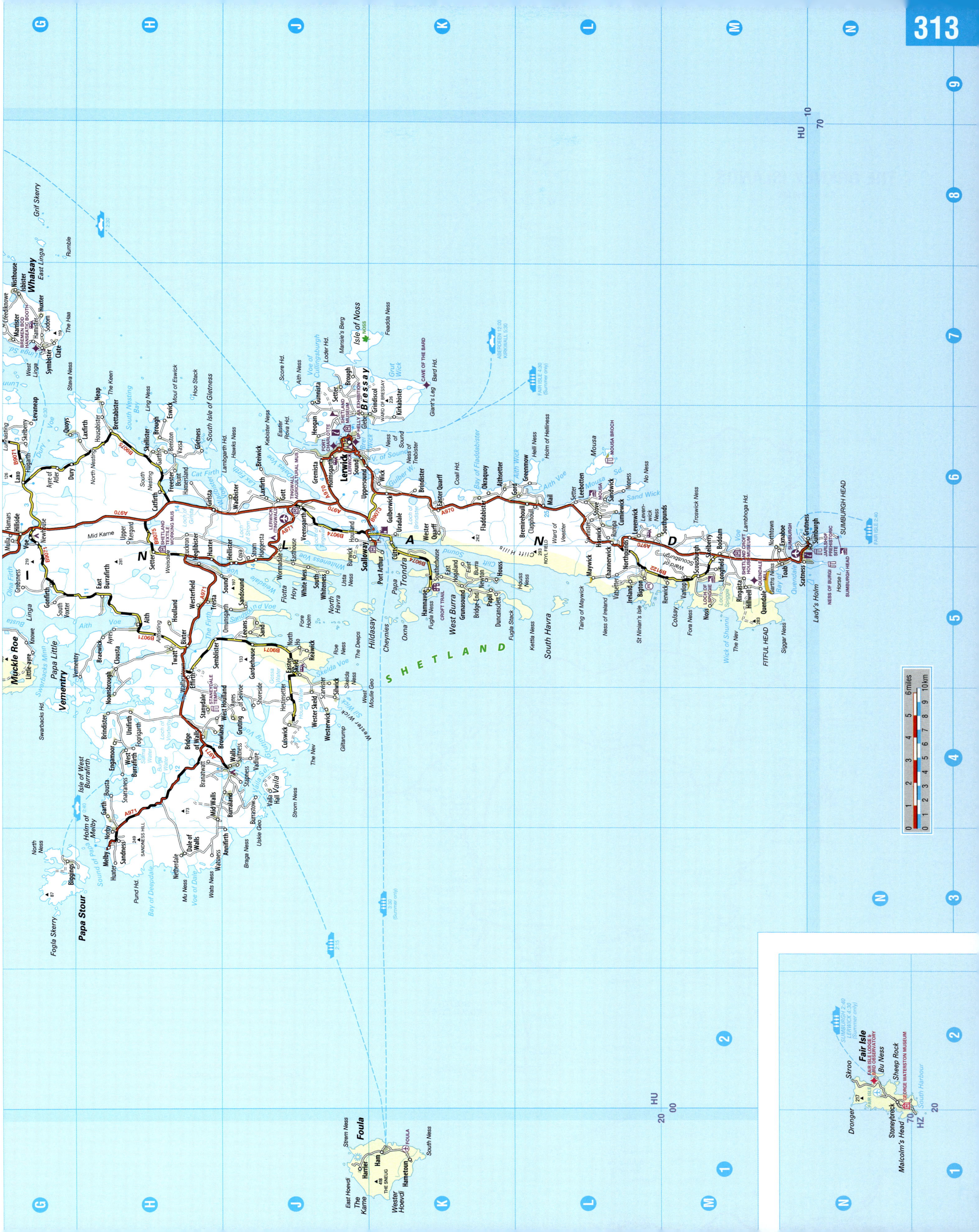
SHETLAND
Lerwick
Bressay
Isle of Noss
Scalloway
Whalsay
Muckle Roe
Papa Little
Vementry
Papa Stour
Vaila
West Burra
Trondra
Hildasay
Oxna
Papa
South Havra
Mousa
Foula
Fair Isle
Sumburgh
SUMBURGH HEAD
FITFUL HEAD
Lady's Holm
Sandwick
Levenwick
Boddam
Quendale
Bigton
Walls
Sandness
Melby
Aith
Voe
Tingwall
Gott
Whiteness
Weisdale
Sand
Skeld
Reawick
Hamnavoe
Cunningsburgh
Fladdabister
Gulberwick
Brindister
Girlsta
Brettabister
Laxo
Vidlin
Dury
Treswick Ness
No Ness
A970
A971
B9071
B9074
B9075
SHETLAND MUSEUM
JARLSHOF PREHISTORIC SITE
MOUSA BROCH
CROFT TRAIL
CAVE OF THE BARD
GEORGE WATERSTON MUSEUM
ABERDEEN 12:00
KIRKWALL 5:30
FAIR ISLE 2:40
HU
HZ
G
H
J
K
L
M
N
1
2
3
4
5
6
7
8
9
0 1 2 3 4 5 6 miles
0 1 2 3 4 5 6 7 8 9 10 km

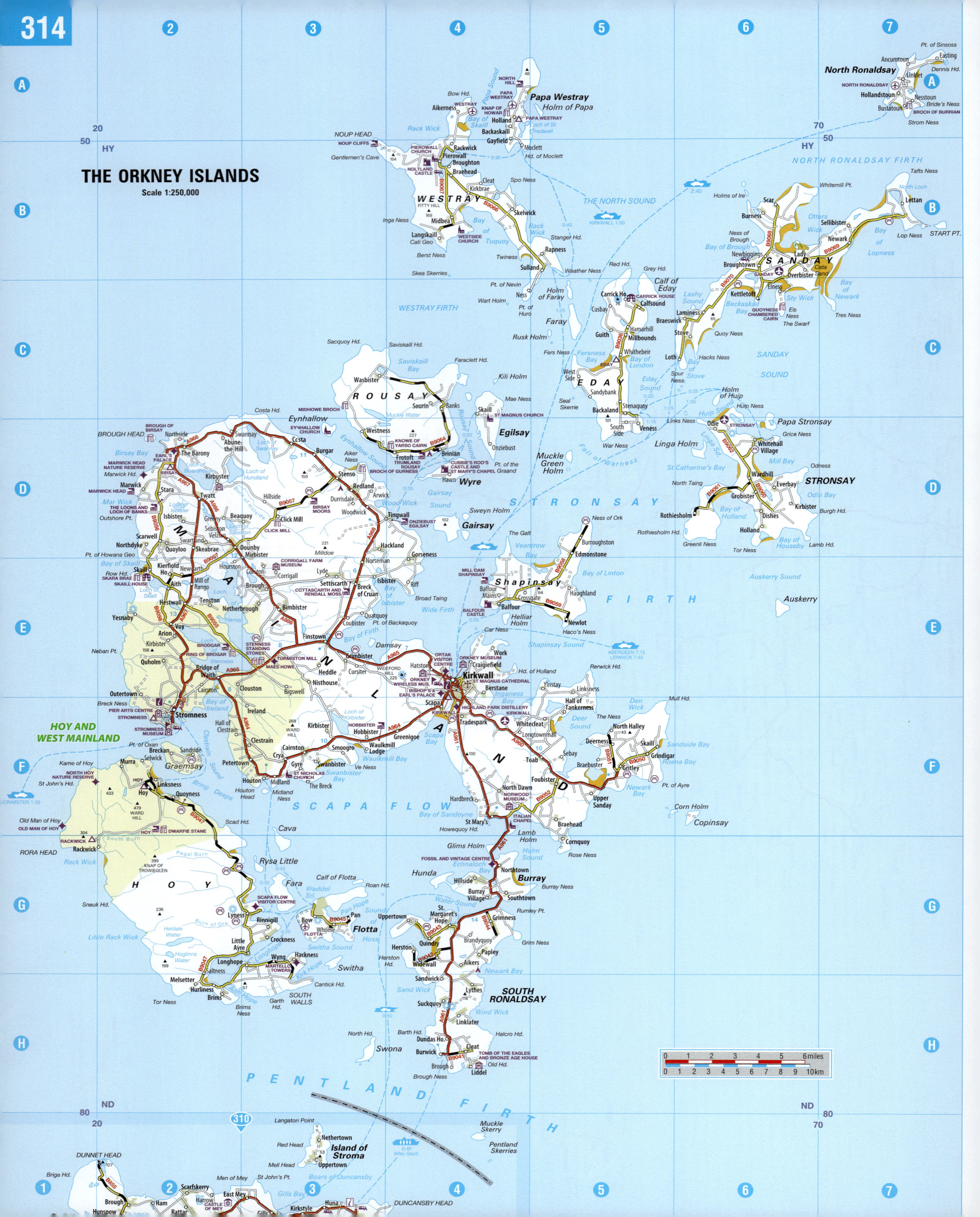
THE ORKNEY ISLANDS
Scale 1:250,000
HOY AND WEST MAINLAND
Papa Westray
Holm of Papa
WESTRAY
Westray Firth
Noup Head
North Ronaldsay
North Ronaldsay Firth
SANDAY
Sanday Sound
EDAY
Calf of Eday
Faray
Holm of Faray
ROUSAY
Egilsay
Wyre
Gairsay
Eynhallow
Eynhallow Sound
Papa Stronsay
STRONSAY
Linga Holm
Muckle Green Holm
Shapinsay
Shapinsay Sound
Auskerry
STRONSAY FIRTH
MAINLAND
Kirkwall
Stromness
Finstown
Dounby
Birsay
Brough Head
Marwick Head
Evie
Tingwall
St Mary's
Deerness
Copinsay
Graemsay
HOY
Lyness
Longhope
Rackwick
Old Man of Hoy
Flotta
Fara
Cava
Rysa Little
Switha
SCAPA FLOW
Burray
SOUTH RONALDSAY
St Margaret's Hope
Burwick
Swona
PENTLAND FIRTH
Muckle Skerry
Pentland Skerries
Island of Stroma
Dunnet Head
Duncansby Head
Lamb Holm
Glims Holm
Hunda
Helliar Holm
Rothiesholm
Wide Firth
Bay of Firth
Bay of Skaill
Skara Brae
Ring of Brodgar
Stenness Standing Stones
Maes Howe
St Magnus Cathedral
Bishop's & Earl's Palace
Highland Park Distillery
Italian Chapel
Scapa Flow Visitor Centre
Tomb of the Eagles and Bronze Age House
Dwarfie Stane
Noltland Castle
Brough of Birsay
Earl's Palace
Broch of Gurness
Midhowe Broch
Knowe of Yarso Cairn
Balfour Castle
Quoyness Chambered Cairn
Broch of Burrian
Orkney Museum
Orkney Wireless Mus.
Stromness Museum
Pier Arts Centre
Orkney Visitor Centre
Corrigall Farm Museum
Kirbuster Farm Museum
Martello Towers
A965
A966
A967
A964
A961
A986
B9057
B9055
B9047
B9045
B9041
B9044
B9043
Scrabster 1:30
Aberdeen 7:15
Lerwick 7:45
Kirkwall 1:50
0 1 2 3 4 5 6 miles
0 1 2 3 4 5 6 7 8 9 10km
HY
ND
310

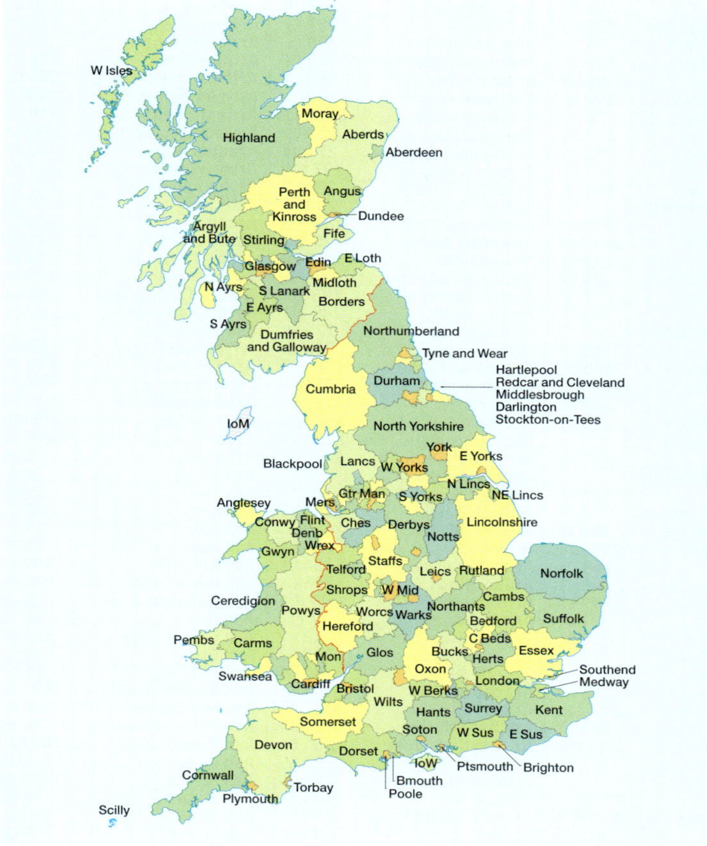

Abbreviations used in the index

Abbreviation	Name
Aberdeen	Aberdeen City
Aberds	Aberdeenshire
Ald	Alderney
Anglesey	Isle of Anglesey
Angus	Angus
Argyll	Argyll and Bute
Bath	Bath and North East Somerset
Bedford	Bedford
Bl Gwent	Blaenau Gwent
Blackburn	Blackburn with Darwen
Blackpool	Blackpool
Bmouth	Bournemouth
Borders	Scottish Borders
Brack	Bracknell
Bridgend	Bridgend
Brighton	City of Brighton and Hove
Bristol	City and County of Bristol
Bucks	Buckinghamshire
C Beds	Central Bedfordshire
Caerph	Caerphilly
Cambs	Cambridgeshire
Cardiff	Cardiff
Carms	Carmarthenshire
Ceredig	Ceredigion
Ches E	Cheshire East
Ches W	Cheshire West and Chester
Clack	Clackmannanshire
Conwy	Conwy
Corn	Cornwall
Cumb	Cumbria
Darl	Darlington
Denb	Denbighshire
Derby	City of Derby
Derbys	Derbyshire
Devon	Devon
Dorset	Dorset
Dumfries	Dumfries and Galloway
Dundee	Dundee City
Durham	Durham
E Ayrs	East Ayrshire
E Dunb	East Dunbartonshire
E Loth	East Lothian
E Renf	East Renfrewshire
E Sus	East Sussex
E Yorks	East Riding of Yorkshire
Edin	City of Edinburgh
Essex	Essex
Falk	Falkirk
Fife	Fife
Flint	Flintshire
Glasgow	City of Glasgow
Glos	Gloucestershire
Gtr Man	Greater Manchester
Guern	Guernsey
Gwyn	Gwynedd
Halton	Halton
Hants	Hampshire
Hereford	Herefordshire
Herts	Hertfordshire
Highld	Highland
Hrtlpl	Hartlepool
Hull	Hull
IoM	Isle of Man
IoW	Isle of Wight
Invclyd	Inverclyde
Jersey	Jersey
Kent	Kent
Lancs	Lancashire
Leicester	City of Leicester
Leics	Leicestershire
Lincs	Lincolnshire
London	Greater London
Luton	Luton
M Keynes	Milton Keynes
M Tydf	Merthyr Tydfil
Mbro	Middlesbrough
Medway	Medway
Mers	Merseyside
Midloth	Midlothian
Mon	Monmouthshire
Moray	Moray
N Ayrs	North Ayrshire
N Lincs	North Lincolnshire
N Lanark	North Lanarkshire
N Som	North Somerset
N Yorks	North Yorkshire
NE Lincs	North East Lincolnshire
Neath	Neath Port Talbot
Newport	City and County of Newport
Norf	Norfolk
Northants	Northamptonshire
Northumb	Northumberland
Nottingham	City of Nottingham
Notts	Nottinghamshire
Orkney	Orkney
Oxon	Oxfordshire
Pboro	Peterborough
Pembs	Pembrokeshire
Perth	Perth and Kinross
Plym	Plymouth
Poole	Poole
Powys	Powys
Ptsmth	Portsmouth
Reading	Reading
Redcar	Redcar and Cleveland
Renfs	Renfrewshire
Rhondda	Rhondda Cynon Taff
Rutland	Rutland
S Ayrs	South Ayrshire
S Glos	South Gloucestershire
S Lanark	South Lanarkshire
S Yorks	South Yorkshire
Scilly	Scilly
Shetland	Shetland
Shrops	Shropshire
Slough	Slough
Som	Somerset
Soton	Southampton
Staffs	Staffordshire
Southend	Southend-on-Sea
Stirling	Stirling
Stockton	Stockton-on-Tees
Stoke	Stoke-on-Trent
Suff	Suffolk
Sur	Surrey
Swansea	Swansea
Swindon	Swindon
T&W	Tyne and Wear
Telford	Telford & Wrekin
Thurrock	Thurrock
Torbay	Torbay
Torf	Torfaen
V Glam	The Vale of Glamorgan
W Berks	West Berkshire
W Dunb	West Dunbartonshire
W Isles	Western Isles
W Loth	West Lothian
W Mid	West Midlands
W Sus	West Sussex
W Yorks	West Yorkshire
Warks	Warwickshire
Warr	Warrington
Wilts	Wiltshire
Windsor	Windsor and Maidenhead
Wokingham	Wokingham
Worcs	Worcestershire
Wrex	Wrexham
York	City of York

Index to road maps of Britain

How to use the index

Example **Blatherwycke** Northants **137** D9

- grid square
- page number
- county or unitary authority

A

Aaron's Hill Sur 50 E3
Aaron's Town Cumb 240 E2
Ab Kettleby Leics 154 E4
Ab Lench Worcs 117 G10
Abbas Combe Som 30 C2
Abberley Worcs 116 D5
Abberton Essex 89 B8
Abberton Worcs 117 G9
Abberwick Northumb 264 G4
Abbess End Essex 87 C9
Abbess Roding Essex 87 C9
Abbey Devon 27 E10
Abbey-cwm-hir Powys 113 C11
Abbey Dore Hereford 97 E7
Abbey Field Essex 107 G9
Abbey Gate Kent 53 B9
Abbey Green Shrops 149 C10
Abbey Green Staffs 169 D7
Abbey Hey Gtr Man 184 B5
Abbey Hulton Stoke 168 F6
Abbey Mead Sur 66 F4
Abbey St Bathans Borders 272 C5
Abbey Town Cumb 238 G5
Abbey Village Lancs 194 C6
Abbey Wood London 68 D3
Abbeycwmhir Powys 113 C11
Abbeydale Glos 80 B5
Abbeydale S Yorks 186 E4
Abbeydale Park S Yorks 186 E4
Abbeyhill Edin 280 G5
Abbeystead Lancs 203 C7
Abbots Bickington Devon 24 E5
Abbots Bromley Staffs 151 E11
Abbots Langley Herts 85 E9
Abbots Leigh N Som 60 E4
Abbot's Meads W Ches 166 B5
Abbots Morton Worcs 117 F10
Abbots Ripton Cambs 122 B4
Abbots Salford Warks 117 G11
Abbots Worthy Hants 48 G3
Abbotsbury Dorset 17 D7
Abbotsford W Sus 36 C4
Abbotsham Devon 24 B6
Abbotskerswell Devon 9 B7
Abbotsleigh Devon 8 F6
Abbotsley Cambs 122 F4
Abbotstone Hants 48 G5
Abbotswood Hants 32 C5
Abbotswood Sur 50 C4
Abbotts Ann Hants 47 E10
Abcott Shrops 115 B7
Abdon Shrops 131 F11
Abdy S Yorks 186 B6
Aber Ceredig 93 B9
Aber-Arad Carms 92 D6
Aber-banc Ceredig 93 C7
Aber Cowarch Gwyn 147 F7
Aber-Giâr Carms 93 C10
Aber-gwynfi Neath 57 B11
Aber-Hirnant Gwyn 147 C9
Aber miwl = Abermule Powys 130 E3
Aber-nant Rhondda 77 E8
Aber-oer Wrex 166 F3
Aber-Rhiwlech Gwyn 147 E8
Aber-Village Powys 96 G2
Aberaeron Ceredig 111 E9
Aberaman Rhondda 77 E8
Aberangell Gwyn 146 G6
Aberarder Highld 290 E6
Aberarder House Highld 300 G6
Aberarder Lodge Highld 291 E7
Aberargie Perth 286 F5
Aberarth Ceredig 111 E9
Aberavon Neath 57 C8
Aberbargoed Caerph 77 E11
Aberbechan Powys 130 E2
Aberbeeg Bl Gwent 78 E2
Aberbran Powys 95 F9
Abercanaid M Tydf 77 E9
Abercarn Caerph 78 G2
Abercastle Pembs 91 E7
Abercegir Powys 128 C6
Aberchalder Highld 290 C5
Aberchirder Aberds 302 D6
Abercorn W Loth 279 F11
Abercraf Powys 76 C4
Abercregan Neath 57 B11
Abercrombie Fife 287 G9
Abercwmboi Rhondda 77 F8
Abercych Pembs 92 C4
Abercynafon Powys 77 B9
Abercynffig = Aberkenfig Bridgend 57 E11
Abercynon Rhondda 77 F9
Aberdâr = Aberdare Rhondda 77 E7
Aberdalgie Perth 286 E4
Aberdare = Aberdâr Rhondda 77 E7
Aberdaron Gwyn 144 D3
Aberdeen Aberdeen 293 C11
Aberdesach Gwyn 162 E6
Aberdour Fife 280 D3
Aberdovey = Aberdyfi Gwyn 128 D2
Aberdulais Neath 76 E3
Aberdyfi = Aberdovey Gwyn 128 D2
Aberedw Powys 95 B11
Abereiddy Pembs 90 E5
Abererch Gwyn 145 B7
Aberfan M Tydf 77 E9
Aberfeldy Perth 286 C2
Aberffraw Anglesey 162 B5
Aberffrwd Ceredig 112 B3
Aberffrwd Mon 78 D5
Aberford W Yorks 206 F4
Aberfoyle Stirl 285 G9
Abergarw Bridgend 58 C2
Abergarwed Neath 76 E4
Abergavenny Mon 78 C3
Abergele Conwy 180 F6
Abergorlech Carms 93 E11
Abergwaun = Fishguard Pembs 91 D9
Abergwesyn Powys 113 G7
Abergwili Carms 93 G8
Abergwynant Gwyn 146 F3
Abergwynfi Neath 57 B11
Abergwyngregyn Gwyn 179 G11
Abergynolwyn Gwyn 128 B3
Aberhosan Powys 128 D6
Aberkenfig = Abercynffig Bridgend 57 E11
Aberlady E Loth 281 E9
Aberlemno Angus 287 B9
Aberlerry Ceredig 128 E2
Aberllefenni Gwyn 128 B5
Aberllydan = Broad Haven Pembs 72 C5
Aberllynfi = Three Cocks Powys 96 D3
Abermagwr Ceredig 112 C3
Abermaw = Barmouth Gwyn 146 F2
Abermeurig Ceredig 111 F11
Abermorddu Flint 166 D4
Abermule = Aber-miwl Powys 130 E3
Abernaint Powys 148 E2
Abernant Carms 92 G6
Abernant Powys 130 D3
Abernethy Perth 286 F5
Abernyte Perth 286 D6
Aberogwr = Ogmore by Sea V Glam 57 F11
Aberpennar = Mountain Ash Rhondda 77 F8
Aberporth Ceredig 110 G5
Aberriw = Berriew Powys 130 C3
Abersoch Gwyn 144 D6
Abersychan Torf 78 E3
Abertawe = Swansea Swansea 56 C6
Aberteifi = Cardigan Ceredig 92 B3
Aberthin V Glam 58 D4
Abertillery Bl Gwent 78 E2
Abertridwr Caerph 58 B6
Abertridwr Powys 147 F10
Abertrinant Gwyn 128 B2
Abertysswg Caerph 77 D10
Aberuchill Castle Perth 285 E11
Aberuthven Perth 286 F3
Aberyscir Powys 95 F9
Aberystwyth Ceredig 111 A11
Abhainn Suidhe W Isles 305 H2
Abingdon Oxon 83 F7
Abinger Common Sur 50 D6
Abinger Hammer Sur 50 D5
Abington Northants 120 E5
Abington S Lnrk 259 E10
Abington Pigotts Cambs 104 C6
Abington Vale Northants 120 E5
Abingworth W Sus 35 D10
Ablington Glos 81 D10
Ablington Wilts 47 D7
Abney Derbys 185 F11
Aboyne Aberds 293 D7
Abraham Heights Lancs 211 G9
Abram Gtr Man 194 G6
Abriachan Highld 300 F5
Abridge Essex 87 F7
Abronhill N Lnrk 278 F5
Abshot Hants 33 F8
Abson S Glos 61 E8
Abthorpe Northants 102 B2
Abune-the-Hill Orkney 314 D2
Aby Lincs 190 F6
Acaster Malbis York 207 D7
Acaster Selby N Yorks 207 E7
Accrington Lancs 195 B9
Acha Argyll 275 B8
Acha Argyll 288 D3
Acha Mor W Isles 304 F5
Achabraid Argyll 275 E9
Achachork Highld 298 E4
Achad nan Darach Highld 284 B4
Achadh an Eas Highld 308 F6
Achadunan Argyll 284 F5
Achafolla Argyll 275 B8
Achagary Highld 308 D7
Achaglass Argyll 255 C8
Achahoish Argyll 275 F8
Achalader Perth 286 C5
Achallader Argyll 285 C7
Achalone Highld 310 D5
Ach'an Todhair Highld 290 F2
Achanalt Highld 300 C2
Achanamara Argyll 275 E8
Achandunie Highld 300 B6
Achanelid Argyll 275 E11
Achany Highld 309 J5
Achaphubuil Highld 290 F2
Acharacle Highld 289 C8
Acharn Highld 289 D9
Acharn Perth 285 C11
Acharole Highld 310 D6
Acharossan Argyll 275 F10
Acharry Muir Highld 309 K6
Achath Aberds 293 B9
Achavanich Highld 310 E5
Achavelgin Highld 301 D9
Achavraat Highld 301 E9
Achddu Carms 74 E6
Achdregnie Moray 302 G2
Achduart Highld 307 J5
Achentoul Highld 310 F2
Achfary Highld 306 F7
Achfrish Highld 309 H5
Achgarve Highld 307 K3
Achiemore Highld 308 C3
Achiemore Highld 310 D2
A'Chill Highld 294 E4
Achiltibuie Highld 307 J5
Achina Highld 308 C7
Achinahuagh Highld 308 C5
Achindaul Highld 290 E3
Achindown Highld 301 E8
Achinduich Highld 309 J5
Achinduin Argyll 289 F10
Achingills Highld 310 C5
Achininver Highld 308 C5
Achintee Highld 290 F3
Achintee Highld 299 E9
Achintraid Highld 295 B10
Achlaven Argyll 289 F11
Achlean Highld 291 D10
Achleck Argyll 288 E6
Achlorachan Highld 300 D3
Achluachrach Highld 290 E4
Achlyness Highld 306 D7
Achmelvich Highld 307 G5
Achmore Highld 295 B10
Achmore Stirl 285 D9
Achnaba Argyll 275 E10
Achnaba Argyll 289 F11
Achnabat Highld 300 F5
Achnabreck Argyll 275 D9
Achnacarnin Highld 306 F5
Achnacarry Highld 290 E3
Achnacloich Argyll 289 F11
Achnacloich Highld 295 E7
Achnaconeran Highld 290 B6
Achnacraig Argyll 288 E6
Achnacree Argyll 289 F11
Achnacree Bay Argyll 289 F11
Achnacroish Argyll 289 E10
Achnadrish Argyll 288 D6
Achnafalnich Argyll 284 E6
Achnagarron Highld 300 C6
Achnaha Highld 288 C6
Achnahanat Highld 309 K5
Achnahannet Highld 301 G9
Achnahard Argyll 288 G5
Achnairn Highld 309 H5
Achnaluachrach Highld 309 J6
Achnandarach Highld 295 B10
Achnanellan Highld 290 E2
Achnasaul Highld 290 E3
Achnasheen Highld 299 D11
Achnashelloch Argyll 275 D9
Achnavast Highld 310 C4
Achneigie Highld 299 B10
Achormlarie Highld 309 K6
Achorn Highld 310 F5
Achosnich Highld 288 C6
Achranich Highld 289 E9
Achreamie Highld 310 C4
Achriabhach Highld 290 G3
Achriesgill Highld 306 D7
Achrimsdale Highld 311 J3
Achtoty Highld 308 C6
Achurch Northants 137 G10
Achuvoldrach Highld 308 D5
Achvaich Highld 309 K7
Achvarasdal Highld 310 C3
Ackenthwaite Cumb 211 C10
Ackergill Highld 310 D7
Acklam M'bro 225 B9
Acklam N Yorks 216 G5
Ackleton Shrops 132 D5
Acklington Northumb 252 C6
Ackton W Yorks 198 C2
Ackworth Moor Top W Yorks 198 D2
Acle Norf 161 G8
Acock's Green W Mid 134 G2
Acol Kent 71 F10
Acomb Northumb 241 D10
Acomb York 207 C7
Acre Gtr Man 196 F2
Acre Lancs 195 C9
Acre Street W Sus 21 B11
Acrefair Wrex 166 G3
Acres Nook Staffs 168 E4
Acton Dorset 18 F5
Acton E Ches 167 E10
Acton London 67 C8
Acton Shrops 130 G6
Acton Staffs 168 G4
Acton Suff 107 C7
Acton Worcs 116 D6
Acton Wrex 166 E4
Acton Beauchamp Hereford 116 G3
Acton Bridge W Ches 183 F9
Acton Burnell Shrops 131 C10
Acton Green Hereford 116 G3
Acton Green London 67 D8
Acton Pigott Shrops 131 C10
Acton Place Suff 107 B7
Acton Reynald Shrops 149 E10
Acton Round Shrops 132 D2
Acton Scott Shrops 131 F9
Acton Trussell Staffs 151 F8
Acton Turville S Glos 61 C10
Adabroc W Isles 304 B7
Adambrae W Loth 269 A10
Adam's Green Dorset 29 F8
Adbaston Staffs 150 D5
Adber Dorset 29 C9
Adbolton Notts 154 B2
Adderbury Oxon 101 D9
Adderley Shrops 150 B3
Adderley Green Stoke 168 G6
Adderstone Northumb 264 C4
Addiewell W Loth 269 C9
Addingham W Yorks 205 D7
Addingham Moorside W Yorks 205 D7
Addington Bucks 102 F4
Addington Corn 6 B5
Addington Kent 53 B7
Addington London 67 G11
Addinston Borders 271 E10
Addiscombe London 67 F10
Addlestone Sur 66 G5
Addlestonemoor Sur 66 F4
Addlethorpe Lincs 175 B8
Adel W Yorks 205 F11
Adeney Telford 150 F4
Adeyfield Herts 85 D9
Adfa Powys 129 C11
Adforton Hereford 115 C8
Adgestone I o W 21 D7
Adisham Kent 55 C8
Adlestrop Glos 100 F4
Adlingfleet E Yorks 199 C10
Adlington E Ches 184 E6
Adlington Lancs 194 E6
Adlington Park Lancs 194 E5
Admaston Staffs 151 E10
Admaston Telford 150 G2
Admington Warks 100 B4
Adpar Ceredig 92 C6
Adsborough Som 28 B3
Adscombe Som 43 F7
Adstock Bucks 102 E4
Adstone Northants 119 G11
Adswood Gtr Man 184 D5
Adversane W Sus 35 C9
Advie Highld 301 F11
Adwalton W Yorks 197 B8
Adwell Oxon 83 F11
Adwick le Street S Yorks 198 F4
Adwick upon Dearne S Yorks 198 G3
Adziel Aberds 303 D9
Ae Dumfries 247 F11
Ae Village Dumfries 247 F11
Affetside Gtr Man 195 E9
Affleck Aberds 303 G8
Affpuddle Dorset 18 C2
Affric Lodge Highld 299 G11
Afon Eitha Wrex 166 F3
Afon-wen Flint 181 G10
Afon Wen Gwyn 145 B8
Afton I o W 20 D2
Agar Nook Leics 153 G9
Agbrigg W Yorks 197 D10
Aggborough Worcs 116 B6
Agglethorpe N Yorks 213 B11
Aglionby Cumb 239 F10
Agneash I o M 192 D5
Aifft Denb 165 B10
Aigburth Mers 182 D5
Aiginis W Isles 304 E6
Aike E Yorks 209 D7
Aikenway Moray 302 E2
Aikerness Orkney 314 A4
Aikers Orkney 314 G4
Aiketgate Cumb 230 B5
Aikton Cumb 239 G7
Ailby Lincs 190 F6
Ailey Hereford 96 B6
Ailstone Warks 118 G4
Ailsworth P'boro 138 D2
Aimes Green Essex 86 E5
Ainderby Quernhow N Yorks 215 C7
Ainderby Steeple N Yorks 224 G6
Aingers Green Essex 108 G2
Ainley Top W Yorks 196 D6
Ainsdale Mers 193 E10
Ainsdale-on-Sea Mers 193 E9
Ainstable Cumb 230 B6
Ainsworth Gtr Man 195 E9
Ainthorpe N Yorks 226 D4
Aintree Mers 182 B5
Aird Argyll 275 C8
Aird Dumfries 236 C2
Aird Highld 299 B7
Aird W Isles 296 F3
Aird W Isles 304 E7
Aird a Mhachair W Isles 297 G3
Aird a' Mhulaidh W Isles 305 G3
Aird Asaig W Isles 305 H3
Aird Dhail W Isles 304 B6
Aird Mhòr W Isles 297 G4
Aird Mhidhinis W Isles 297 L3
Aird Mhighe W Isles 296 C6
Aird Mhighe W Isles 305 J3
Aird Mhor W Isles 297 L3
Aird of Sleat Highld 295 E7
Aird Thunga W Isles 304 E6
Aird Uig W Isles 304 E2
Airdachuilinn Highld 306 E7
Airdens Highld 309 K6
Airdeny Argyll 289 G11
Airdrie N Lnrk 268 B5
Airds of Kells Dumfries 237 B8
Airdtorrisdale Highld 308 C6
Aire View N Yorks 204 D5
Airedale W Yorks 198 B3
Airidh a Bhruaich W Isles 305 G4
Airieland Dumfries 237 D9
Airinis W Isles 304 E6
Airlie Angus 287 B7
Airlies Dumfries 236 D5
Airmyn E Yorks 199 B8
Airntully Perth 286 D4
Airor Highld 295 E9
Airth Falk 279 D7
Airthrey Castle Stirl 278 B6
Airton N Yorks 204 B4
Airy Hill N Yorks 227 D7
Airyhassen Dumfries 236 E5
Airyligg Dumfries 236 C4
Aisby Lincs 155 B10
Aisby Lincs 188 C5
Aisgernis W Isles 297 J3
Aish Devon 8 C3
Aish Devon 8 D6
Aisholt Som 43 F7
Aiskew N Yorks 214 B5
Aislaby N Yorks 216 B5
Aislaby N Yorks 227 D7
Aislaby Stockton 225 C8
Aisthorpe Lincs 188 E6
Aith Orkney 314 E2
Aith Shetland 312 D8
Aith Shetland 313 H5
Aithnen Powys 148 E4
Aithsetter Shetland 313 K6
Aitkenhead S Ayrs 245 B8
Aitnoch Highld 301 F9
Akeld Northumb 263 D11
Akeley Bucks 102 D4
Akenham Suff 108 B2
Albany T & W 243 F7
Albaston Corn 12 G4
Alberbury Shrops 149 G7
Albert Town Pembs 72 B6
Albert Village Leics 152 F6
Albourne W Sus 36 D3
Albourne Green W Sus 36 D3
Albrighton Shrops 132 C6
Albrighton Shrops 149 F9
Albro Castle Ceredig 92 B3
Alburgh Norf 142 F5
Albury Herts 105 G8
Albury Sur 50 D5
Albury End Herts 105 G8
Albury Heath Sur 50 D5
Alby Hill Norf 160 C3
Albyfield Cumb 240 G2
Alcaig Highld 300 D5
Alcaston Shrops 131 F9
Alcester Dorset 30 C5
Alcester Warks 117 F11
Alcester Lane's End W Mid 133 G11
Alciston E Sus 23 D8
Alcombe Som 42 D3
Alcombe Wilts 61 F10
Alconbury Cambs 122 B3
Alconbury Weston Cambs 122 B3
Aldbar Castle Angus 287 B9
Aldborough N Yorks 215 F8
Aldborough Norf 160 C3
Aldborough Hatch London 68 B3
Aldbourne Wilts 63 D9
Aldbrough E Yorks 209 F10
Aldbrough St John N Yorks 224 C4
Aldbury Herts 85 C7
Aldcliffe Lancs 211 G9
Aldclune Perth 291 G11

Aldeburgh Suff 127 F9
Aldeby Norf 143 E8
Aldenham Herts 85 F10
Alder Forest Gtr Man 184 B3
Alder Moor Staffs 152 D4
Alder Row Som 45 E9
Alderbrook E Sus 37 B8
Alderbury Wilts 31 B11
Aldercar Derbys 170 F6
Alderford Norf 160 F2
Alderholt Dorset 31 E10
Alderley Glos 80 G3
Alderley Edge E Ches 184 F4
Alderman's Green W Mid 135 G7
Aldermaston W Berks 64 F5
Aldermaston Soke W Berks 64 G6
Aldermaston Wharf W Berks 64 F6
Alderminster Warks 100 B4
Aldermoor Soton 32 D5
Alderney Poole 18 C6
Alder's End Hereford 98 C2
Aldersbrook London 68 B2
Aldersey Green W Ches 167 D7
Aldershawe Staffs 134 B2
Aldershot Hants 49 C11
Alderton Glos 99 E10
Alderton Northants 102 B4
Alderton Shrops 149 E9
Alderton Suff 108 C6
Alderton Wilts 61 C10
Alderton Fields Glos 99 E10
Alderwasley Derbys 170 E4
Aldfield N Yorks 214 F5
Aldford W Ches 166 D6
Aldgate Rutland 137 C9
Aldham Essex 107 F8
Aldham Suff 107 B10
Aldie Highld 309 L7
Aldingbourne W Sus 22 B6
Aldingham Cumb 210 E5
Aldington Kent 54 F5
Aldington Worcs 99 C11
Aldington Frith Kent 54 F4
Aldivalloch Moray 302 G3
Aldochlay Argyll 277 C7
Aldon Shrops 115 B8
Aldoth Cumb 229 B8
Aldourie Castle Highld 300 F6
Aldreth Cambs 123 C8
Aldridge W Mid 133 C11
Aldringham Suff 127 E8
Aldrington Brighton 36 F3
Aldsworth Glos 81 C11
Aldunie Moray 302 G3
Aldwark Derbys 170 D2
Aldwark N Yorks 215 G9
Aldwarke S Yorks 186 C6
Aldwick W Sus 22 D6
Aldwincle Northants 137 G10
Aldworth W Berks 64 D5
Ale Oak Shrops 130 G4
Alehouseburn Aberds 302 C6
Alehousehill Aberds 303 G10
Alexandria W Dunb 277 F7
Aley Som 43 F7
Aley Green C Beds 85 B9
Alfardisworthy Devon 24 E3
Alfington Devon 15 B8
Alfold Sur 50 G4
Alfold Bars W Sus 50 G4
Alfold Crossways Sur 50 F4
Alford Aberds 293 B7
Alford Lincs 191 F7
Alford Som 44 G6
Alfred's Well Worcs 117 C8
Alfreton Derbys 170 D6
Alfrick Worcs 116 G4
Alfrick Pound Worcs 116 G4
Alfriston E Sus 23 E8
Algakirk Lincs 156 B5
Algaltraig Argyll 275 F11
Algarkirk Lincs 156 B5
Alhampton Som 44 G6
Aline Lodge W Isles 305 G3
Alisary Highld 289 B9
Alkborough N Lincs 199 C11
Alkerton Glos 80 D3
Alkerton Oxon 101 C7
Alkham Kent 55 E9
Alkington Shrops 149 B10
Alkmonton Derbys 152 B3
Alkrington Garden Village Gtr Man 195 G11
All Cannings Wilts 62 G5
All Saints Devon 28 G4
All Saints South Elmham Suff 142 G6
All Stretton Shrops 131 D9
Alladale Lodge Highld 309 L4
Allaleigh Devon 8 E6
Allanaquoich Aberds 292 D3
Allanbank Borders 271 F10
Allanbank N Lnrk 268 D6
Allangrange Mains Highld 300 D6
Allanshaugh Borders 271 F8
Allanshaws Borders 271 G9
Allanton Borders 273 E7
Allanton N Lnrk 269 D7
Allanton S Lnrk 268 E4
Allaston Glos 79 E10
Allathasdal W Isles 297 L2
Allbrook Hants 33 C7
Allen End Warks 134 D3
Allendale Town Northumb 241 F8
Allenheads Northumb 232 B3
Allens Green Herts 87 B7
Allensford Durham 242 G3
Allensmore Hereford 97 D9
Allenton Derby 153 C7
Allenwood Cumb 239 F11
Aller Devon 9 B7
Aller Devon 27 F9
Aller Dorset 30 G3
Aller Som 28 B6
Aller Park Devon 9 B7
Allerby Cumb 229 D7
Allerford Som 27 B11
Allerford Som 42 D2
Allerston N Yorks 217 C7
Allerthorpe E Yorks 207 D11
Allerton Mers 182 D6
Allerton W Yorks 205 G8
Allerton Bywater W Yorks 198 B2
Allerton Mauleverer N Yorks 206 B4
Allesley W Mid 134 G6
Allestree Derby 152 B6
Allet Corn 4 F5
Allexton Leics 136 C6
Allgreave E Ches 169 B7
Allhallows Medway 69 D10
Allhallows-on-Sea Medway 69 D10
Alligin Shuas Highld 299 D8
Allimore Green Staffs 151 F7
Allington Kent 53 B8
Allington Lincs 172 G5
Allington Wilts 47 F8
Allington Wilts 61 D11
Allington Wilts 62 G5
Allington Bar Wilts 61 E11
Allithwaite Cumb 211 D7
Alloa Clack 279 C7
Allonby Cumb 229 C7
Allostock W Ches 184 G2
Alloway S Ayrs 257 F8
Allowenshay Som 28 E5
Allscot Shrops 132 D4
Allscott Telford 150 G2
Allt Carms 75 E9
Allt-na-giubhsaich Aberds 292 E4
Allt na h-Airbhe Highld 307 K6
Allt-nan-sùgh Highld 295 C11
Allt-yr-yn Newport 59 B9
Alltami Flint 166 B3
Alltbeithe Highld 290 C2
Alltchaorunn Highld 284 B5
Alltforgan Powys 147 E9
Alltmawr Powys 95 B11
Alltnacaillich Highld 308 E4
Alltrech Argyll 289 F8
Alltsigh Highld 290 B6
Alltwalis Carms 93 E8
Alltwen Neath 76 E2
Alltyblaca Ceredig 93 B10
Allwood Green Suff 125 C10
Alma Notts 171 E7
Almagill Dumfries 238 B3
Almeley Hereford 114 G6
Almeley Wooton Hereford 114 G6
Almer Dorset 18 B4
Almholme S Yorks 198 F5
Almington Staffs 150 C4
Alminstone Cross Devon 24 C4
Almondbank Perth 286 E4
Almondbury W Yorks 197 D7
Almondsbury S Glos 60 C6
Almondvale W Loth 269 B11
Almshouse Green Essex 106 E5
Alne N Yorks 215 F9
Alne End Warks 118 F2
Alne Hills Warks 118 E2
Alne Station N Yorks 215 F10
Alness Highld 300 C6
Alnessferry Highld 300 C6
Alnham Northumb 263 G11
Alnmouth Northumb 264 G6
Alnwick Northumb 264 G5
Alperton London 67 C7
Alphamstone Essex 107 D7
Alpheton Suff 125 G7
Alphington Devon 14 C4
Alpington Norf 142 C5
Alport Derbys 170 C2
Alport Powys 130 D5
Alpraham E Ches 167 D9
Alresford Essex 107 G11
Alrewas Staffs 152 F3
Alsager E Ches 168 D3
Alsagers Bank Staffs 168 F4
Alscot Bucks 84 E4
Alsop en le Dale Derbys 169 D11
Alston Cumb 231 B10
Alston Devon 28 G4
Alston Sutton Som 44 C2
Alstone Glos 99 E9
Alstone Glos 99 G8
Alstone Som 43 D10
Alstonefield Staffs 169 D10
Alswear Devon 26 C2
Alt Gtr Man 196 G2
Alt Hill Gtr Man 196 G2
Altandhu Highld 307 H4
Altanduin Highld 311 G2
Altarnun Corn 11 E10
Altass Highld 309 J4
Altbough Hereford 97 E10
Altdargue Aberds 293 C7
Alterwall Highld 310 C6
Altham Lancs 203 G11
Althorne Essex 88 F6
Althorpe N Lincs 199 F10
Alticane S Ayrs 244 F6
Alticry Dumfries 236 D4
Altmore Windsor 65 D11
Altnabreac Station Highld 310 E4
Altnacealgach Hotel Highld 307 H7
Altnacraig Argyll 289 G10
Altnafeadh Highld 284 B6
Altnaharra Highld 308 F5
Altofts W Yorks 197 C11
Alton Derbys 170 C5
Alton Hants 49 F8
Alton Staffs 169 G9
Alton Wilts 47 D7
Alton Barnes Wilts 62 G6
Alton Pancras Dorset 30 G2
Alton Priors Wilts 62 G6
Altonhill E Ayrs 257 B10
Altonside Moray 302 D2
Altour Highld 290 E4
Altrincham Gtr Man 184 D3
Altrua Highld 290 E4
Altskeith Stirl 285 G8
Altyre Ho Moray 301 D10
Alum Rock W Mid 134 F2
Alva Clack 279 B7
Alvanley W Ches 183 G7
Alvaston Derby 153 C7
Alvechurch Worcs 117 C10
Alvecote Warks 134 C4
Alvediston Wilts 31 C7
Alveley Shrops 132 G5
Alverdiscott Devon 25 B8
Alverstoke Hants 21 B8
Alverstone I o W 21 D7
Alverthorpe W Yorks 197 C10
Alverton Notts 172 G3
Alves Moray 301 C11
Alvescot Oxon 82 E3
Alveston S Glos 60 B6
Alveston Warks 118 F4
Alveston Down S Glos 60 B6
Alveston Hill Warks 118 G4
Alvie Highld 291 C10
Alvingham Lincs 190 C5
Alvington Glos 79 E10
Alvington Som 29 D8
Alwalton Cambs 138 D2
Alway Newport 59 B10
Alweston Dorset 29 E11
Alwington Devon 24 C6
Alwinton Northumb 251 B10
Alwoodley W Yorks 205 E11
Alwoodley Gates W Yorks 206 E2
Alwoodley Park W Yorks 205 E11
Alyth Perth 286 C6
Am Baile W Isles 297 K3
Am Buth Argyll 289 G10
Amalebra Corn 1 B5
Amalveor Corn 1 B5
Amatnatua Highld 309 K4
Ambaston Derbys 153 C8
Amber Hill Lincs 174 F2
Ambergate Derbys 170 E4
Amberley Glos 80 E5
Amberley Hereford 97 B10
Amberley W Sus 35 E8
Amble Northumb 253 C7
Amblecote W Mid 133 F7
Ambler Thorn W Yorks 196 B5
Ambleside Cumb 221 E7
Ambleston Pembs 91 F10
Ambrosden Oxon 83 B10
Amcotts N Lincs 199 E11
Amen Corner Brack 65 F10
Amersham Bucks 85 F7
Amersham Common Bucks 85 F7
Amersham Old Town Bucks 85 F7
Amersham on the Hill Bucks 85 F7
Amerton Staffs 151 D9
Amesbury Bath 45 B7
Amesbury Wilts 47 E7
Ameysford Dorset 31 G9
Amington Staffs 134 C4
Amisfield Dumfries 247 G11
Amlwch Anglesey 178 C6
Amlwch Port Anglesey 179 C7
Ammanford = Rhydaman Carms 75 C10
Ammerham Som 28 F5
Amod Argyll 255 D8
Amotherby N Yorks 216 E4
Ampfield Hants 32 C6
Ampleforth N Yorks 215 D11
Ampney Crucis Glos 81 E9
Ampney St Mary Glos 81 E9
Ampney St Peter Glos 81 E9
Amport Hants 47 E9
Ampthill C Beds 103 D10
Ampton Suff 125 C7
Amroth Pembs 73 D11
Amulree Perth 286 D2
Amwell Herts 85 C11
An Caol Highld 298 D6
An Cnoc W Isles 304 E6
An Gleann Ur W Isles 304 E6
An Leth Meadhanach W Isles 297 K3
An t-Ob W Isles 296 C6
Anagach Highld 301 G10
Anaheilt Highld 289 C10
Anancaun Highld 299 C10
Ancarraig Highld 300 G4
Ancaster Lincs 173 G7
Anchor Shrops 130 G3
Anchor Corner Norf 141 D10
Anchor Street Norf 160 E6
Anchorage Park Ptsmth 33 G11
Anchorsholme Blkpool 202 E2
Ancoats Gtr Man 184 B5
Ancroft Northumb 273 F9
Ancroft Northmoor Northumb 273 F9
Ancrum Borders 262 E4
Ancton W Sus 35 G7
Ancumton Orkney 314 A7
Anderby Lincs 191 F8
Anderby Creek Lincs 191 F8
Andersea Som 43 G10
Andersfield Som 43 G8
Anderson Dorset 18 B3
Anderton Corn 7 E8
Anderton Lancs 194 E6
Anderton W Ches 183 F10
Andertons Mill Lancs 194 E4
Andover Hants 47 D11
Andover Down Hants 47 D11
Andoversford Glos 81 B8
Andreas I o M 192 C5
Andwell Hants 49 C7
Anelog Gwyn 144 D3
Anerley London 67 F10
Anfield Mers 182 C5
Angarrack Corn 2 B3
Angarrick Corn 3 B7
Angelbank Shrops 115 B11
Angersleigh Som 27 D11
Angerton Cumb 238 F6
Angle Pembs 72 E5
Angmering W Sus 35 G9
Angram N Yorks 206 D6
Angram N Yorks 223 F7
Anick Northumb 241 D11
Anie Stirl 285 F9
Ankerdine Hill Worcs 116 F4
Ankerville Highld 301 B8
Anlaby E Yorks 200 B4
Anlaby Park Hull 200 B5
Anmer Norf 158 D4
Anmore Hants 33 E11
Anna Valley Hants 47 E10
Annan Dumfries 238 D5
Annaside Cumb 210 B1
Annat Argyll 284 E4
Annat Highld 290 D5
Annat Highld 299 D8
Annbank S Ayrs 257 E10
Annesley Notts 171 E8
Annesley Woodhouse Notts 171 E7
Annfield Plain Durham 242 G5
Anniesland Glasgow 267 B10
Annifirth Shetland 313 J3
Annis Hill Suff 143 F7
Annishader Highld 298 D4
Annitsford T & W 243 C7
Ann's Hill Hants 33 G9
Annscroft Shrops 131 B9
Annwell Place Derbys 152 F6
Ansdell Lancs 193 B10
Ansells End Herts 85 B11
Ansford Som 44 G6
Ansley Warks 134 E5
Ansley Common Warks 134 E6
Anslow Staffs 152 D4
Anslow Gate Staffs 152 D3
Ansteadbrook Sur 50 G2
Anstey Herts 105 E8
Anstey Leics 135 B10
Anstruther Easter Fife 287 G9
Anstruther Wester Fife 287 G9
Ansty Hants 49 E8
Ansty W Sus 36 C3
Ansty Warks 135 G7
Ansty Wilts 31 B7
Ansty Coombe Wilts 31 B7
Ansty Cross Dorset 30 G3
Anthill Common Hants 33 E10
Anthony Corn 7 E7
Anthony's Cross Glos 98 G4
Anthorn Cumb 238 F5
Antingham Norf 160 C5
Anton's Gowt Lincs 174 F3
Antonshill Falk 279 E7
Antony Corn 7 E7
Antony Passage Corn 7 D8
Antrobus W Ches 183 F10
Anvil Green Kent 54 D6
Anvilles W Berks 63 F10
Anwick Lincs 173 E10
Anwoth Dumfries 237 D7
Aonachan Highld 290 E4
Aoradh Argyll 274 G3
Apedale Staffs 168 F4
Aperfield London 52 B2
Apes Dale Worcs 117 C9
Apes Hall Cambs 139 E11
Apethorpe Northants 137 D10
Apeton Staffs 151 F7
Apley Lincs 189 F10
Apley Forge Shrops 132 D4
Apperknowle Derbys 186 F5
Apperley Glos 99 F7
Apperley Bridge W Yorks 205 F9
Apperley Dene Northumb 242 F3
Appersett N Yorks 223 G7
Appin Argyll 289 E11
Appin House Argyll 289 E11
Appleby N Lincs 200 E3
Appleby-in-Westmorland Cumb 231 G9
Appleby Magna Leics 134 B6
Appleby Parva Leics 134 B6
Applecross Highld 299 E7
Applecross Ho Highld 299 E7
Appledore Devon 27 E9
Appledore Devon 40 G3
Appledore Kent 39 B7
Appledore Heath Kent 54 G3
Appleford Oxon 83 G8
Applegarthtown Dumfries 248 G4
Applehouse Hill Windsor 65 C10
Applemore Hants 32 F5
Appleshaw Hants 47 D10
Applethwaite Cumb 229 F11
Appleton Halton 183 D8
Appleton Oxon 82 E6
Appleton-le-Moors N Yorks 216 B4
Appleton-le-Street N Yorks 216 E4
Appleton Park Warr 183 E10
Appleton Roebuck N Yorks 207 E7
Appleton Thorn Warr 183 E10
Appleton Wiske N Yorks 225 E7
Appletreehall Borders 262 F2
Appletreewick N Yorks 213 G11
Appley I o W 21 C8
Appley Som 27 C9
Appley Bridge Lancs 194 F4
Apse Heath I o W 21 E7
Apsey Green Suff 126 E5
Apsley Herts 85 D9
Apsley End C Beds 104 E2
Apuldram W Sus 22 C4
Aqueduct Telford 132 B3
Aquhythie Aberds 293 B9
Arabella Highld 301 B8
Arbeadie Aberds 293 D8
Arberth = Narberth Pembs 73 C10
Arbirlot Angus 287 C10
Arboll Highld 311 L2
Arborfield Wokingham 65 F9
Arborfield Cross Wokingham 65 F9
Arborfield Garrison Wokingham 65 F9
Arbourthorne S Yorks 186 D5
Arbroath Angus 287 C10
Arbury Cambs 123 E8
Arbuthnott Aberds 293 F9
Archavandra Muir Highld 309 K7
Archdeacon Newton Darl 224 B5
Archenfield Hereford 96 C5
Archiestown Moray 302 E2
Archnalea Highld 289 C10
Arclid E Ches 168 C3
Arclid Green E Ches 168 C3
Ard-dhubh Highld 299 E7
Ardachu Highld 309 J6
Ardailly Argyll 255 B7
Ardalanish Argyll 274 B4
Ardallie Aberds 303 F10
Ardalum Ho Argyll 288 F6
Ardamaleish Argyll 275 G11
Ardanaiseig Argyll 284 E4
Ardaneaskan Highld 295 B10
Ardanstur Argyll 275 B9
Ardargie House Hotel Perth 286 F4
Ardarroch Highld 295 B10
Ardban Highld 295 B9
Ardbeg Argyll 254 C5
Ardbeg Argyll 276 E3
Ardcharnich Highld 307 L6
Ardchiavaig Argyll 274 B4
Ardchonnell Argyll 275 B10
Ardchronie Highld 309 L6
Ardchuilk Highld 300 F2
Ardchullarie More Stirl 285 F9
Ardchyle Stirl 285 E9
Ardclach Highld 301 E9
Arddleen Powys 148 F5
Ardechvie Highld 290 D3
Ardeley Herts 104 F6
Ardelve Highld 295 C10
Arden Argyll 277 E7
Arden E Renf 267 D10
Arden Park Gtr Man 184 C6
Ardencaple Ho Argyll 275 B8
Ardendrain Highld 300 F5
Ardens Grafton Warks 118 G2
Ardentallen Argyll 289 G10
Ardentinny Argyll 276 D3
Ardentraive Argyll 275 F11
Ardeonaig Stirl 285 D10
Ardersier Highld 301 D7
Ardery Highld 289 C9
Ardessie Highld 307 L5
Ardfern Argyll 275 C9
Ardfernal Argyll 274 F6
Ardgartan Argyll 284 G6
Ardgay Highld 309 K5
Ardglassie Aberds 303 C10
Ardgour Highld 290 G2
Ardgye Moray 301 C11
Ardheslaig Highld 299 D7
Ardiecow Moray 302 C5
Ardinamir Argyll 275 B8
Ardindrean Highld 307 L6
Ardingly W Sus 36 B4
Ardington Oxon 64 B2
Ardington Wick Oxon 64 B2
Ardintoul Highld 295 C10
Ardlair Aberds 302 G5
Ardlair Highld 299 B9
Ardlamey Argyll 255 C7
Ardlamont Ho Argyll 275 G10
Ardlawhill Aberds 303 C8
Ardleigh Essex 107 F11
Ardleigh Green London 68 B4
Ardleigh Heath Essex 107 E10
Ardler Perth 286 C6
Ardley Oxon 101 F10
Ardley End Essex 87 C8
Ardlui Argyll 285 F7
Ardlussa Argyll 275 E7
Ardmair Highld 307 K6
Ardmay Argyll 284 G6
Ardmenish Argyll 274 F6
Ardminish Argyll 255 C7
Ardmolich Highld 289 B9
Ardmore Argyll 289 G9
Ardmore Highld 306 D7
Ardmore Highld 309 L7
Ardnacross Argyll 289 E7
Ardnadam Argyll 276 F3
Ardnagowan Argyll 284 G4
Ardnagrask Highld 300 E5
Ardnarff Highld 295 B10
Ardnastang Highld 289 C10
Ardnave Argyll 274 F3
Ardneil N Ayrs 266 F3
Ardno Argyll 284 G5
Ardo Aberds 303 F8
Ardo Ho Aberds 303 G9
Ardoch Argyll 277 F7
Ardoch Perth 286 D4
Ardoch Stirl 285 F9
Ardochy House Highld 290 C4
Ardoyne Aberds 302 G6
Ardpatrick Argyll 275 G8
Ardpatrick Ho Argyll 255 B8
Ardpeaton Argyll 276 D4
Ardradnaig Perth 285 C11
Ardrishaig Argyll 275 E9
Ardross Fife 287 G9
Ardross Highld 300 B6
Ardross Castle Highld 300 B6
Ardrossan N Ayrs 266 G4
Ardshave Highld 309 K7
Ardsheal Highld 289 D11
Ardshealach Highld 289 C8
Ardskenish Argyll 274 D4
Ardsley S Yorks 197 F11
Ardslignish Highld 289 C7
Ardtalla Argyll 254 B5
Ardtalnaig Perth 285 D11
Ardtaraig Argyll 275 E11
Ardtoe Highld 289 B8
Ardtreck Highld 294 B5
Ardtrostan Perth 285 E10
Ardtur Argyll 289 E11
Arduaine Argyll 275 B8
Ardullie Highld 300 C5
Ardvannie Highld 309 L6
Ardvar Highld 306 F6
Ardvasar Highld 295 E8
Ardveich Stirl 285 E10
Ardverikie Highld 291 E7
Ardvorlich Perth 285 E10
Ardwell Dumfries 236 E3
Ardwell Moray 302 F3
Ardwell S Ayrs 244 E5
Ardwell Mains Dumfries 236 E3
Ardwick Gtr Man 184 B5
Areley Kings Worcs 116 C6
Arford Hants 49 F10
Argoed Caerph 77 F11
Argoed Powys 113 E9
Argoed Powys 130 E5
Argoed Shrops 130 G6
Argoed Shrops 148 E6
Argos Hill E Sus 37 B9
Arichamish Argyll 275 C10
Arichastlich Argyll 284 D6
Aridhglas Argyll 288 G5
Arieniskill Highld 295 G9
Arileod Argyll 288 D3
Arinacrinachd Highld 299 D7
Arinagour Argyll 288 D4
Arion Orkney 314 E2
Arisaig Highld 295 G8
Ariundle Highld 289 C10
Arivegaig Highld 289 C8
Arivoichallum Argyll 254 C4
Arkendale N Yorks 215 G7
Arkesden Essex 105 E9
Arkholme Lancs 211 E11
Arkle Town N Yorks 223 E10
Arkleby Cumb 229 D8
Arkleton Dumfries 249 E9
Arkley London 86 F2
Arksey S Yorks 198 F5
Arkwright Town Derbys 186 G6
Arle Glos 99 G8
Arlebrook Glos 80 D4
Arlecdon Cumb 219 B10
Arlescote Warks 101 B7
Arlesey C Beds 104 D3
Arleston Telford 150 G3
Arley E Ches 183 E11
Arley Green E Ches 183 E11
Arlingham Glos 80 C2
Arlington Devon 40 E6
Arlington E Sus 23 D8
Arlington Glos 81 D10
Arlington Beccott Devon 40 E6
Armadale Highld 308 C7
Armadale W Loth 269 B8
Armadale Castle Highld 295 E8
Armathwaite Cumb 230 B6
Armigers Essex 105 F11
Arminghall Norf 142 C5
Armitage Staffs 151 F11
Armitage Bridge W Yorks 196 E6
Armley W Yorks 205 G11
Armscote Warks 100 C4
Armsdale Staffs 150 C5
Armshead Staffs 168 F6
Armston Northants 137 F11
Armthorpe S Yorks 198 F6
Arnabost Argyll 288 D4
Arnaby Cumb 210 C3
Arncliffe N Yorks 213 E8
Arncroach Fife 287 G9
Arndilly Ho Moray 302 E2
Arne Dorset 18 D5
Arnesby Leics 136 E2
Arngask Perth 286 F5
Arnisdale Highld 295 D10
Arnish Highld 298 E5
Arniston Midloth 270 C6
Arnol W Isles 304 D5
Arnold E Yorks 209 E8
Arnold Notts 171 F9
Arno's Vale Bristol 60 E6
Arnprior Stirl 278 C2
Arnside Cumb 211 D9
Aros Mains Argyll 289 E7
Arowry Wrex 149 B9
Arpafeelie Highld 300 D6
Arpinge Kent 55 F7
Arrad Foot Cumb 210 C6
Arram E Yorks 208 E6
Arrathorne N Yorks 224 G4
Arreton I o W 20 D6
Arrington Cambs 122 G6
Arrivain Argyll 284 D6
Arrochar Argyll 284 G6
Arrow Warks 117 F11
Arrow Green Hereford 115 F8
Arrowe Hill Mers 182 D3
Arrowfield Top Worcs 117 C10
Arrunden W Yorks 196 F6
Arscaig Highld 309 H5
Arscott Shrops 131 B8
Arthill E Ches 184 D2
Arthington W Yorks 205 E11
Arthingworth Northants 136 G5
Arthog Gwyn 146 G2
Arthrath Aberds 303 F9
Arthursdale W Yorks 206 F3
Arthurstone Perth 286 C6
Arthurville Highld 309 L7
Artington Sur 50 D3
Artrochie Aberds 303 F10
Arundel W Sus 35 F8
Arwick Orkney 314 D3
Aryhoulan Highld 290 G2
Asby Cumb 229 G7
Ascog Argyll 266 C2
Ascoil Highld 311 H2
Ascot Windsor 66 F2
Ascott Warks 100 E6
Ascott d'Oyley Oxon 82 B4
Ascott Earl Oxon 82 B3
Ascott-under-Wychwood Oxon 82 B4
Asenby N Yorks 215 D7
Asfordby Leics 154 F4
Asfordby Hill Leics 154 F4
Asgarby Lincs 173 F10
Asgarby Lincs 174 B4
Ash Devon 8 F6
Ash Dorset 30 E5
Ash Kent 55 B9
Ash Kent 68 G5
Ash Som 28 C3
Ash Som 29 C7
Ash Sur 49 C11
Ash Bank Staffs 168 F6
Ash Bullayne Devon 26 G3
Ash Green Sur 50 D2
Ash Green Warks 134 F6
Ash Grove Wrex 166 G5
Ash Hill Devon 14 G4
Ash Magna Shrops 149 B11
Ash Mill Devon 26 C3
Ash Moor Devon 26 D3
Ash Parva Shrops 149 B11
Ash Priors Som 27 B11
Ash Street Suff 107 B10
Ash Thomas Devon 27 E8
Ash Vale Sur 49 C11
Ashaig Highld 295 C8
Ashampstead W Berks 64 D5
Ashampstead Green W Berks 64 D5
Ashansworth Hants 48 B2
Ashbank Kent 53 C10
Ashbeer Som 42 F5
Ashbocking Suff 126 G3
Ashbourne Derbys 169 F11
Ashbrittle Som 27 C9
Ashbrook Shrops 131 E9
Ashburnham Forge E Sus 23 B11
Ashburton Devon 8 B5
Ashbury Devon 12 B6
Ashbury Oxon 63 C9
Ashby N Lincs 200 F2
Ashby by Partney Lincs 174 B6
Ashby cum Fenby NE Lincs 201 G9
Ashby de la Launde Lincs 173 D9
Ashby-de-la-Zouch Leics 153 F7
Ashby Folville Leics 154 G4
Ashby Hill NE Lincs 201 G8
Ashby Magna Leics 135 E11
Ashby Parva Leics 135 F10
Ashby Puerorum Lincs 190 G4
Ashby St Ledgers Northants 119 D11
Ashby St Mary Norf 142 C6
Ashchurch Glos 99 E8
Ashcombe Devon 14 F4
Ashcombe Park N Som 59 G10
Ashcott Som 44 F2
Ashcott Corner Som 44 F2
Ashculme Devon 27 E10
Ashdon Essex 105 C11
Ashe Hants 48 D4
Asheldham Essex 89 E7
Ashen Essex 106 C4
Ashendon Bucks 84 C2
Asheridge Bucks 84 E6
Ashey I o W 21 D7
Ashfield Argyll 275 E8
Ashfield Carms 94 F3
Ashfield Hants 32 D5
Ashfield Hereford 97 G11
Ashfield Shrops 148 D6
Ashfield Stirl 285 G11
Ashfield Suff 126 E4
Ashfield Cum Thorpe Suff 126 E4
Ashfield Green Suff 124 F5
Ashfield Green Suff 126 C5
Ashfields Shrops 150 D4
Ashfold Crossways W Sus 36 B2
Ashfold Side N Yorks 214 F2
Ashford Devon 8 F3
Ashford Devon 40 F4
Ashford Hants 31 E10
Ashford Kent 54 E4
Ashford Sur 66 E5
Ashford Bowdler Shrops 115 C10
Ashford Carbonell Shrops 115 C10
Ashford Common Sur 66 E5
Ashford Hill Hants 64 G5
Ashford in the Water Derbys 185 G11
Ashgate Derbys 186 G5
Ashgill S Lnrk 268 F5
Ashgrove Bath 45 B8
Ashiestiel Borders 261 B10
Ashill Devon 27 E9
Ashill Norf 141 C7
Ashill Som 28 D4
Ashingdon Essex 88 G5
Ashington Northumb 253 F7
Ashington Poole 18 B6

Ash – Bal 317

Ashington Som 29 C9
Ashington W Sus 35 D10
Ashington End Lincs 175 B8
Ashintully Castle Perth 292 G3
Ashkirk Borders 261 E11
Ashlett Hants 33 G7
Ashleworth Glos 98 F6
Ashley Cambs 124 E3
Ashley Devon 25 E10
Ashley Dorset 31 G10
Ashley E Ches 184 E3
Ashley Glos 80 G6
Ashley Hants 19 B11
Ashley Hants 47 G11
Ashley Kent 55 D10
Ashley Northants 136 E5
Ashley Staffs 150 B5
Ashley Wilts 61 F10
Ashley Dale Staffs 150 B5
Ashley Down Bristol 60 D5
Ashley Green Bucks 85 D7
Ashley Heath Ches 184 D3
Ashley Heath Dorset 31 G10
Ashley Heath Staffs 150 B4
Ashley Moor Hereford 115 D9
Ashley Park Sur 66 F6
Ashleyhay Derbys 170 E3
Ashmanhaugh Norf 160 E6
Ashmansworth Hants 48 B2
Ashmansworthy Devon 24 D4
Ashmead Green Glos 80 F3
Ashmill Devon 12 B3
Ashmore Dorset 30 D6
Ashmore Green W Berks 64 F4
Ashmore Lake W Mid 133 D9
Ashmore Park W Mid 133 C9
Ashnashellach Lodge Highld 299 E10
Ashopton Derbys 185 D11
Ashorne Warks 118 F6
Ashover Derbys 170 C4
Ashover Hay Derbys 170 C5
Ashow Warks 118 C6
Ashperton Hereford 98 C2
Ashprington Devon 8 D6
Ashreigney Devon 25 E10
Ashridge Court Devon 25 G11
Ashtead Sur 51 B7
Ashton Corn 2 D4
Ashton Hants 33 D9
Ashton Hereford 115 E10
Ashton Invclyd 276 F4
Ashton Northants 102 B5
Ashton Northants 137 F11
Ashton P'boro 138 B2
Ashton Som 44 D2
Ashton Common Wilts 45 B11
Ashton Gate Bristol 60 E5
Ashton Green E Sus 23 C7
Ashton Hayes W Ches 167 B8
Ashton Heath Halton 183 F9
Ashton-in-Makerfield Gtr Man 183 B9
Ashton Keynes Wilts 81 G8
Ashton under Hill Worcs 99 D9
Ashton-under-Lyne Gtr Man 184 B6
Ashton upon Mersey Gtr Man 184 C3
Ashton Vale Bristol 60 E5
Ashurst Hants 32 E4
Ashurst Kent 52 F4
Ashurst Lancs 194 F3
Ashurst W Sus 35 D11
Ashurst Bridge Hants 32 E4
Ashurst Wood W Sus 52 F2
Ashvale Bl Gwent 77 C10
Ashwater Devon 12 B3
Ashwell Devon 14 G3
Ashwell Herts 104 D5
Ashwell Rutland 155 G7
Ashwell Som 28 D5
Ashwell End Herts 104 C5
Ashwellthorpe Norf 142 D2
Ashwick Som 44 D6
Ashwicken Norf 158 F4
Ashwood Staffs 133 F7
Ashybank Borders 262 F2
Askam in Furness Cumb 210 D4
Askern S Yorks 198 E5
Askerswell Dorset 16 C6
Askerton Hill Lincs 172 F4
Askett Bucks 84 D4
Askham Cumb 230 G6
Askham Notts 188 G2
Askham Bryan York 207 D7
Askham Richard York 206 D6
Asknish Argyll 275 D10
Askrigg N Yorks 223 G8
Askwith N Yorks 205 D9
Aslackby Lincs 155 C11
Aslacton Norf 142 E3
Aslockton Notts 154 B4
Asloun Aberds 293 B7
Asney Som 44 F3
Aspall Suff 126 D3
Aspatria Cumb 229 C8
Aspenden Herts 105 F7
Asperton Lincs 156 B5
Aspley Nottingham 171 G8
Aspley Staffs 150 C6
Aspley Guise C Beds 103 D8
Aspley Heath C Beds 103 D8
Aspley Heath Warks 117 C11
Aspull Gtr Man 194 F6
Aspull Common Gtr Man 183 B10
Assater Shetland 312 F4
Asselby E Yorks 199 B8
Asserby Lincs 191 F7
Asserby Turn Lincs 191 F7
Assington Suff 107 D8
Assington Green Suff 124 G5
Assynt Ho Highld 300 C5
Astbury E Ches 168 C4
Astcote Northants 120 G3
Asterby Lincs 190 F3
Asterley Shrops 131 B7
Asterton Shrops 131 E7
Asthall Oxon 82 C3
Asthall Leigh Oxon 82 C4
Astle E Ches 184 G4
Astle Highld 309 K7
Astley Gtr Man 195 G8
Astley Shrops 149 F10
Astley Warks 134 F6
Astley Worcs 116 D5
Astley Abbotts Shrops 132 D4
Astley Bridge Gtr Man 195 E8
Astley Cross Worcs 116 D6
Astley Green Gtr Man 184 B2
Astmoor Halton 183 E8
Aston Derbys 152 C3
Aston Derbys 185 E11
Aston E Ches 167 F10
Aston Flint 166 B4
Aston Hereford 115 C9
Aston Hereford 115 E9
Aston Herts 104 G5
Aston Oxon 82 E4
Aston Powys 130 E5
Aston S Yorks 187 D7
Aston Shrops 132 E6
Aston Shrops 149 D10
Aston Staffs 151 E7
Aston Staffs 168 G3
Aston Telford 132 B2
Aston W Ches 183 F9
Aston W Mid 133 F11
Aston Wokingham 65 C9
Aston Abbotts Bucks 102 G6
Aston Bank Worcs 116 C2
Aston Botterell Shrops 132 G2
Aston-by-Stone Staffs 151 C8
Aston Cantlow Warks 118 F2
Aston Clinton Bucks 84 C5
Aston Crews Hereford 98 G3
Aston Cross Glos 99 E8
Aston End Herts 104 G5
Aston Eyre Shrops 132 E3
Aston Fields Worcs 117 D9
Aston Flamville Leics 135 E9
Aston Ingham Hereford 98 G3
Aston juxta Mondrum E Ches 167 D11
Aston le Walls Northants 119 G9
Aston Magna Glos 100 D3
Aston Munslow Shrops 131 F10
Aston on Carrant Glos 99 E8
Aston on Clun Shrops 131 G7
Aston-on-Trent Derbys 153 D8
Aston Pigott Shrops 130 B6
Aston Rogers Shrops 130 B6
Aston Rowant Oxon 84 F2
Aston Sandford Bucks 84 D3
Aston Somerville Worcs 99 D10
Aston Square Shrops 148 D6
Aston Subedge Glos 100 C2
Aston Tirrold Oxon 64 B5
Aston Upthorpe Oxon 64 B5
Astrop Northants 101 D10
Astrope Herts 84 C5
Astwick C Beds 104 D4
Astwith Derbys 170 C6
Astwood M Keynes 103 B9
Astwood Worcs 117 D8
Astwood Worcs 117 F7
Astwood Bank Worcs 117 E10
Aswarby Lincs 173 G9
Aswardby Lincs 190 G5
Atch Lench Worcs 117 G10
Atcham Shrops 131 B10
Athelhampton Dorset 17 C11
Athelington Suff 126 C4
Athelney Som 28 B4
Athelstaneford E Loth 281 F10
Atherfield Green I o W 20 F5
Atherington Devon 25 C9
Atherington W Sus 35 G8
Athersley North S Yorks 197 F11
Athersley South S Yorks 197 F11
Atherstone Som 28 D5
Atherstone Warks 134 D6
Atherstone on Stour Warks 118 G4
Atherton Gtr Man 195 G7
Athnamulloch Highld 299 G11
Athron Hall Perth 286 G4
Atley Hill N Yorks 224 E5
Atlow Derbys 170 F2
Attadale Highld 295 B11
Attadale Ho Highld 295 B11
Attenborough Notts 153 B10
Atterbury M Keynes 103 D7
Atterby Lincs 189 C7
Attercliffe S Yorks 186 D5
Atterley Shrops 132 D2
Atterton Leics 135 D7
Attleborough Norf 141 D10
Attleborough Warks 135 E7
Attlebridge Norf 160 F2
Attleton Green Suff 124 G4
Atwick E Yorks 209 C9
Atworth Wilts 61 F11
Auberrow Hereford 97 B9
Aubourn Lincs 172 C6
Auch Argyll 285 D7
Auchagallon N Ayrs 255 D9
Auchallater Aberds 292 E3
Auchareoch N Ayrs 255 E10
Aucharnie Aberds 302 E6
Auchattie Aberds 293 D8
Auchavan Angus 292 G3
Auchbreck Moray 302 G2
Auchenback E Renf 267 D10
Auchenbainzie Dumfries 247 D8
Auchenblae Aberds 293 F9
Auchenbrack Dumfries 247 D7
Auchenbreck Argyll 255 C8
Auchenbreck Argyll 275 E11
Auchencairn Dumfries 237 D9
Auchencairn Dumfries 247 G11
Auchencairn N Ayrs 256 D2
Auchencairn Ho Dumfries 237 D10
Auchencar N Ayrs 255 D9
Auchencarroch W Dunb 277 E8
Auchencrosh S Ayrs 236 B3
Auchencrow Borders 273 C7
Auchendinny Midloth 270 C5
Auchengray S Lnrk 269 E9
Auchenhalrig Moray 302 C3
Auchenharvie N Ayrs 266 G5
Auchenheath S Lnrk 268 G6
Auchenhew N Ayrs 256 E2
Auchenlaich Stirl 285 G10
Auchenleck Dumfries 237 D9
Auchenlochan Argyll 275 F10
Auchenmalg Dumfries 236 D4
Auchenreoch E Dunb 278 F3
Auchensoul S Ayrs 245 E7
Auchentibber S Lnrk 268 E3
Auchentiber N Ayrs 267 F7
Auchertyre Highld 295 C10
Auchessan Stirl 285 E8
Auchgourish Highld 291 B11
Auchinairn E Dunb 268 B2
Auchindrain Argyll 284 G4
Auchindrean Highld 307 L6
Auchininna Aberds 302 E6
Auchinleck Dumfries 236 B6
Auchinleck E Ayrs 258 E3
Auchinloch N Lnrk 278 G3
Auchinner Perth 285 F10
Auchinraith S Lnrk 268 D3
Auchinroath Moray 302 D2
Auchinstarry N Lnrk 278 F4
Auchintoul Aberds 293 B7
Auchintoul Highld 309 K5
Auchiries Aberds 303 F10
Auchlee Aberds 293 D10
Auchleeks Ho Perth 291 G9
Auchleven Aberds 302 G6
Auchlinn Aberds 303 D7
Auchlochan S Lnrk 259 B8
Auchlossan Aberds 293 C7
Auchlunachan Highld 307 L6
Auchlunies Aberds 293 D10
Auchlyne Stirl 285 E9
Auchmacoy Aberds 303 F9
Auchmair Moray 302 G3
Auchmantle Dumfries 236 C3
Auchmenzie Aberds 302 G5
Auchmillan E Ayrs 258 D2
Auchmithie Angus 287 C10
Auchmore Highld 300 D4
Auchmuirbridge Fife 286 G6
Auchmull Angus 293 F7
Auchnacraig Argyll 289 G9
Auchnacree Angus 292 G6
Auchnafree Perth 286 D2
Auchnagallin Highld 301 F10
Auchnagarron Argyll 275 E11
Auchnagatt Aberds 303 E9
Auchnaha Argyll 275 E10
Auchnahillin Highld 301 F7
Auchnarrow Moray 302 G2
Auchnashelloch Perth 285 F11
Auchnotteroch Dumfries 236 C1
Aucholzie Aberds 292 D5
Auchrannie Angus 286 B6
Auchroisk Highld 301 G10
Auchronie Angus 292 E6
Auchterarder Perth 286 F3
Auchteraw Highld 290 C5
Auchterderran Fife 280 B4
Auchterhouse Angus 287 D7
Auchtermuchty Fife 286 F6
Auchterneed Highld 300 D4
Auchtertool Fife 280 C4
Auchtertyre Moray 301 D11
Auchtertyre Stirl 285 E7
Auchtubh Stirl 285 E9
Auckengill Highld 310 C7
Auckley S Yorks 199 G7
Audenshaw Gtr Man 184 B6
Audlem E Ches 167 G11
Audley Staffs 168 E3
Audley End Essex 105 D10
Audley End Essex 106 D6
Audley End Norf 142 G2
Audley End Suff 125 G7
Auds Aberds 302 C6
Aughertree Cumb 229 D11
Aughton E Yorks 207 F10
Aughton Lancs 193 F11
Aughton Lancs 211 F10
Aughton S Yorks 187 D7
Aughton Wilts 47 B8
Aughton Park Lancs 194 F2
Aukside Durham 232 F4
Auldearn Highld 301 D9
Aulden Hereford 115 G9
Auldgirth Dumfries 247 F10
Auldhame E Loth 281 E11
Auldhouse S Lnrk 268 E2
Auldtown of Carnoustie Aberds 302 E6
Ault a'chruinn Highld 295 C11
Ault Hucknall Derbys 171 B7
Aultanrynie Highld 308 F3
Aultbea Highld 307 L3
Aultdearg Highld 300 C2
Aultgrishan Highld 307 L2
Aultguish Inn Highld 300 B3
Aultibea Highld 311 G4
Aultiphurst Highld 310 C2
Aultivullin Highld 310 C2
Aultmore Highld 301 G10
Aultmore Moray 302 D4
Aultnagoire Highld 300 G5
Aultnamain Inn Highld 309 L6
Aultnaslat Highld 290 C3
Aulton Aberds 302 G6
Aulton of Atherb Aberds 303 E9
Aultvaich Highld 300 E5
Aunby Lincs 155 G10
Aundorach Highld 291 B11
Aunk Devon 27 G8
Aunsby Lincs 155 B10
Auquhorthies Aberds 303 G8
Aust S Glos 60 B5
Austen Fen Lincs 190 C5
Austendike Lincs 156 E5
Austenwood Bucks 66 B3
Austerfield S Yorks 187 C11
Austerlands Gtr Man 196 F3
Austhorpe W Yorks 206 G3
Austrey Warks 134 B5
Austwick N Yorks 212 F5
Authorpe Lincs 190 E6
Authorpe Row Lincs 191 G8
Avebury Wilts 62 F6
Avebury Trusloe Wilts 62 F5
Aveley Thurrock 68 C5
Avening Glos 80 F5
Avening Green S Glos 80 G2
Averham Notts 172 E3
Avernish Highld 295 C10
Avery Hill London 68 E2
Aveton Gifford Devon 8 F3
Avielochan Highld 291 B11
Aviemore Highld 291 B10
Avington Hants 48 G4
Avington W Berks 63 F11
Avoch Highld 301 D7
Avon Hants 19 B8
Avon Wilts 62 D3
Avon Dassett Warks 101 B8
Avonbridge Falk 279 G8
Avoncliff Wilts 45 B10
Avonmouth Bristol 60 D4
Avonwick Devon 8 D4
Awbridge Hants 32 C4
Awhirk Dumfries 236 D2
Awkley S Glos 60 B5
Awliscombe Devon 27 G10
Awre Glos 80 D2
Awsworth Notts 171 G7
Axbridge Som 44 C2
Axford Hants 48 E6
Axford Wilts 63 F8
Axmansford Hants 64 G5
Axminster Devon 15 B11
Axmouth Devon 15 C11
Axton Flint 181 E10
Axtown Devon 7 B10
Axwell Park T & W 242 E5
Aycliff Kent 55 E10
Aycliffe Durham 233 G11
Aydon Northumb 242 D2
Aykley Heads Durham 233 C11
Aylburton Glos 79 E10
Aylburton Common Glos 79 E10
Ayle Northumb 231 B10
Aylesbeare Devon 14 C6
Aylesbury Bucks 84 C4
Aylesby NE Lincs 201 F8
Aylesford Kent 53 B8
Aylesham Kent 55 C8
Aylestone Leicester 135 C11
Aylestone Hill Hereford 97 C10
Aylestone Park Leicester 135 C11
Aylmerton Norf 160 B3
Aylsham Norf 160 D3
Aylton Hereford 98 D3
Aylworth Glos 100 G2
Aymestrey Hereford 115 D8
Aynho Northants 101 E10
Ayot Green Herts 86 C2
Ayot St Lawrence Herts 85 B11
Ayot St Peter Herts 86 B2
Ayr S Ayrs 257 E8
Ayre of Atler Shetland 313 G6
Ayres Shetland 313 H5
Ayres End Herts 85 C11
Ayres of Selivoe Shetland 313 J4
Ayres Quay T & W 243 F9
Aysgarth N Yorks 213 B10
Ayshford Devon 27 D8
Ayside Cumb 211 C7
Ayston Rutland 137 C7
Aythorpe Roding Essex 87 B9
Ayton Borders 273 C8
Ayton T & W 243 F7
Ayton Castle Borders 273 C8
Aywick Shetland 312 E7
Azerley N Yorks 214 E5

B

Babbacombe Torbay 9 B8
Babbington Notts 171 G7
Babbinswood Shrops 148 C6
Babbs Green Herts 86 B5
Babcary Som 29 B9
Babel Carms 94 D6
Babel Green Suff 106 B4
Babell Flint 181 G11
Babeny Devon 13 F9
Babingley Norf 158 D3
Babraham Cambs 123 G10
Babworth Notts 187 E11
Bac W Isles 304 D6
Bach-y-gwreiddyn Swansea 75 E10
Bachau Anglesey 178 E6
Bache Shrops 131 G9
Bache Mill Shrops 131 F10
Bacheldre Powys 130 E4
Bachelor's Bump E Sus 38 E4
Back of Keppoch Highld 295 G8
Back o' th' Brook Staffs 169 E9
Back Muir Fife 279 D11
Back Rogerton E Ayrs 258 E3
Back Street Suff 124 F4
Backaland Orkney 314 C5
Backaskaill Orkney 314 A4
Backbarrow Cumb 211 C7
Backbower Gtr Man 185 C7
Backburn Aberds 293 D10
Backe Carms 74 B3
Backfolds Aberds 303 D10
Backford W Ches 182 G6
Backford Cross W Ches 182 G5
Backhill Aberds 303 F10
Backhill Aberds 303 F7
Backhill of Clackriach Aberds 303 E9
Backhill of Fortree Aberds 303 E9
Backhill of Trustach Aberds 293 D8
Backies Highld 311 J2
Backlass Highld 310 D6
Backlass Highld 310 E4
Backwell N Som 60 F3
Backwell Common N Som 60 F3
Backwell Green N Som 60 F3
Backworth T & W 243 C8
Bacon End Essex 87 B10
Baconend Green Essex 87 B10
Bacon's End W Mid 134 F3
Baconsthorpe Norf 160 B2
Bacton Hereford 97 E7
Bacton Norf 160 C6
Bacton Suff 125 D11
Bacton Green Norf 160 C6
Bacton Green Suff 125 D10
Bacup Lancs 195 C11
Badachonacher Highld 300 B6
Badachro Highld 299 B7
Badanloch Lodge Highld 308 F7
Badarach Highld 309 K5
Badavanich Highld 299 D11
Badbea Highld 307 K5
Badbury Swindon 63 C7
Badbury Wick Swindon 63 C7
Badby Northants 119 F11
Badcall Highld 306 D7
Badcaul Highld 307 K5
Baddeley Edge Stoke 168 E6
Baddeley Green Stoke 168 E6
Baddesley Clinton Warks 118 C4
Baddesley Ensor Warks 134 D5
Baddidarach Highld 307 G5
Baddoch Aberds 292 E3
Baddock Highld 301 D7
Baddow Park Essex 88 E2
Badeach Moray 302 F2
Badenscallie Highld 307 J5
Badenscoth Aberds 303 F7
Badentoy Park Aberds 293 D11
Badenyon Aberds 292 B5
Badgall Corn 11 D10
Badgeney Cambs 139 D8
Badger Shrops 132 D5
Badger Street Som 28 D3
Badgergate Stirl 278 B5
Badger's Hill Worcs 99 B10
Badger's Mount Kent 68 G3
Badgeworth Glos 80 B6
Badgworth Som 43 C11
Badharlick Corn 11 D11
Badicaul Highld 295 C9
Badingham Suff 126 D6
Badintagairt Highld 309 H4
Badlesmere Kent 54 C4
Badlipster Highld 310 E6
Badluarach Highld 307 K4
Badminton S Glos 61 C10
Badnaban Highld 307 G5
Badnabay Highld 306 E7
Badnagie Highld 310 F5
Badninish Highld 309 K7
Badrallach Highld 307 K5
Badsey Worcs 99 C11
Badshalloch W Dunb 277 D9
Badshot Lea Sur 49 D11
Badsworth W Yorks 198 E3
Badwell Ash Suff 125 D9
Badwell Green Suff 125 D10
Badworthy Devon 8 C3
Bae Cinmel = Kinmel Bay Conwy 181 E7
Bae Colwyn = Colwyn Bay Conwy 180 F4
Bae Penrhyn = Penrhyn Bay Conwy 180 E4
Baffins Ptsmth 33 G11
Bag Enderby Lincs 190 G5
Bagber Dorset 30 E3
Bagby N Yorks 215 C9
Bagby Grange N Yorks 215 C9
Bagendon Glos 81 D8
Bagginswood Shrops 132 G3
Baggrow Cumb 229 C9
Bàgha Chàise W Isles 296 D5
Bagh a Chaisteil W Isles 297 M2
Bagh Mor W Isles 296 F4
Bagh Shiarabhagh W Isles 297 L3
Bagham Kent 54 C5
Baghasdal W Isles 297 K3
Bagillt Flint 182 F2
Baginton Warks 118 C6
Baglan Neath 57 C8
Bagley Shrops 149 D8
Bagley Som 44 D3
Bagley W Yorks 205 F10
Bagley Green Som 27 D10
Bagley Marsh Shrops 149 D7
Bagmore Hants 49 E7
Bagnall Staffs 168 E6
Bagnor W Berks 64 F3
Bagpath Glos 80 E5
Bagpath Glos 80 G4
Bagshaw Derbys 185 E9
Bagshot Sur 66 G2
Bagshot Wilts 63 F10
Bagshot Heath Sur 66 G2
Bagslate Moor Gtr Man 195 E11
Bagstone S Glos 61 B7
Bagthorpe Norf 158 C5
Bagthorpe Notts 171 E7
Baguley Gtr Man 184 D4
Bagworth Leics 135 B8
Bagwy Llydiart Hereford 97 F8
Bagwyllydiart Hereford 97 F8
Bail Àrd Bhuirgh W Isles 304 C6
Bail' Iochdrach W Isles 296 F4
Bail Uachdraich W Isles 296 E4
Bail' Ur Tholastaidh W Isles 304 D7
Bailbrook Bath 61 F9
Baildon W Yorks 205 F9
Baildon Green W Yorks 205 F8
Baile W Isles 296 C5
Baile a Mhanaich W Isles 296 F3
Baile Ailein W Isles 304 F4
Baile an Truiseil W Isles 304 C5
Baile Boidheach Argyll 275 F8
Baile Gharbhaidh W Isles 297 G3
Baile Glas W Isles 296 F4
Baile Mhartainn W Isles 296 D3
Baile Mhic Phail W Isles 296 D4
Baile Mor Argyll 288 G4
Baile Mor W Isles 296 E3
Baile na Creige W Isles 297 L2
Baile nan Cailleach W Isles 296 F3
Baile Raghaill W Isles 296 D3
Bailebeag Highld 291 B7
Bailey Green Hants 33 B11
Baileyhead Cumb 240 B2
Bailiesward Aberds 302 F4
Bailiff Bridge W Yorks 196 C6
Baillieston Glasgow 268 C3
Bailrigg Lancs 202 B5
Bainbridge N Yorks 223 G8
Bainsford Falk 279 E7
Bainshole Aberds 302 F6
Bainton E Yorks 208 C5
Bainton Oxon 101 F11
Bainton P'boro 137 B11
Baintown Fife 287 G7
Bairnkine Borders 262 F5
Baker Street Thurrock 68 C6
Baker's Cross Kent 53 F9
Bakers End Herts 86 B5
Baker's Hill Glos 79 C9
Baker's Wood Bucks 66 B4
Bakesdown Corn 24 G2
Bakestone Moor Derbys 187 F8
Bakewell Derbys 170 B2
Bala = Y Bala Gwyn 147 B8
Balachroick Highld 291 C10
Balachuirn Highld 298 E5
Balance Hill Staffs 151 C11
Balavil Highld 291 C9
Balavoulin Perth 291 G10
Balbeg Highld 300 F4
Balbeg Highld 300 G4
Balbeggie Perth 286 E5
Balbegno Castle Aberds 293 F8
Balbithan Aberds 293 B9
Balbithan Ho Aberds 293 B10
Balblair Highld 300 E5
Balblair Highld 301 C7
Balblair Highld 309 K5
Balby S Yorks 198 G5
Balcherry Highld 311 L2
Balchladich Highld 306 F5
Balchraggan Highld 300 E5
Balchraggan Highld 300 F5
Balchraggan Highld 300 G5
Balchrick Highld 306 D6
Balchrystie Fife 287 G8
Balcladaich Highld 300 G2
Balcombe W Sus 51 G10
Balcombe Lane W Sus 51 G10
Balcomie Fife 287 F10
Balcraggie Lodge Highld 310 F5
Balcurvie Fife 287 G7
Baldersby N Yorks 215 D7
Baldersby St James N Yorks 215 D7
Balderstone Gtr Man 196 E2
Balderstone Lancs 203 G8
Balderton Notts 172 E4
Balderton W Ches 166 C5
Baldhu Corn 4 G5
Baldingstone Gtr Man 195 E10
Baldinnie Fife 287 F8
Baldock Herts 104 E4
Baldon Row Oxon 83 E9
Baldoon Highld 300 B6
Baldovie Dundee 287 D8
Baldrine I o M 192 D5
Baldslow E Sus 38 E3
Baldwin I o M 192 D4
Baldwinholme Cumb 239 G8
Baldwin's Gate Staffs 168 G3
Baldwins Hill W Sus 51 F11
Bale Norf 159 B10
Balearn Aberds 303 D10
Balemartine Argyll 288 E1
Balephuil Argyll 288 E1
Balerno Edin 270 B3
Balerominhor Argyll 274 D4
Balevullin Argyll 288 E1
Balfield Angus 293 G7
Balfour Orkney 314 E4
Balfour Mains Orkney 314 E4
Balfron Stirl 277 D10
Balfron Station Stirl 277 D10
Balgaveny Aberds 302 E6
Balgavies Angus 287 B9
Balgonar Fife 279 C10
Balgove Aberds 303 F8
Balgowan Highld 291 D8
Balgowan Perth 286 E3
Balgown Highld 298 C3
Balgrennie Aberds 292 C6
Balgrochan E Dunb 278 F2
Balgy Highld 299 D8
Balhaldie Stirl 286 G2
Balhalgardy Aberds 303 G7
Balham London 67 E9
Balhary Perth 286 C6
Baliasta Shetland 312 C8
Baligill Highld 310 C2
Baligortan Argyll 288 E5
Baligrundle Argyll 289 E10
Balindore Argyll 289 F11
Balinoe Argyll 288 E1
Balintore Angus 286 B6
Balintore Highld 301 B8
Balintraid Highld 301 B7
Balintuim Aberds 292 E3
Balk N Yorks 215 C9
Balk Field Notts 188 E2
Balkeerie Angus 287 C7
Balkemback Angus 287 D7
Balkholme E Yorks 199 B9
Balkissock S Ayrs 244 G4
Ball Corn 10 G6
Ball Shrops 148 D6
Ball Green Stoke 168 E5
Ball Haye Green Staffs 169 D7
Ball Hill Hants 64 G2
Ball o'Ditton Halton 183 D7
Ballabeg I o M 192 E3
Ballacannel I o M 192 D5
Ballachraggan Moray 301 E11
Ballachrochin Highld 301 F8
Ballachulish Highld 284 B4
Balladen Lancs 195 C10
Ballajora I o M 192 C5
Ballaleigh I o M 192 D4
Ballamodha I o M 192 E3
Ballantrae S Ayrs 244 G3
Ballaquine I o M 192 D5
Ballard's Ash Wilts 62 C5
Ballards Gore Essex 88 G6
Ballard's Green Warks 134 E5
Ballasalla I o M 192 C4
Ballasalla I o M 192 E3
Ballater Aberds 292 D5
Ballathie Perth 286 D5
Ballaugh I o M 192 C4
Ballaveare I o M 192 E4
Ballcorach Moray 301 G11
Ballechin Perth 286 B3
Balleich Stirl 277 B10
Balleigh Highld 309 L7
Ballencrieff E Loth 281 F9
Ballencrieff Toll W Loth 279 G9
Ballentoul Perth 291 G10
Ballhill Devon 24 C3
Ballidon Derbys 170 E2
Balliekine N Ayrs 255 D9
Balliemore Argyll 275 E11
Balliemore Argyll 289 G10
Ballikinrain Stirl 277 D11
Ballimeanoch Argyll 284 F4
Ballimore Argyll 275 E10
Ballimore Stirl 285 F9
Ballinaby Argyll 274 G3
Ballinbreich Fife 286 E6
Ballindean Perth 286 E6
Ballingdon Suff 107 C7
Ballingdon Bottom Herts 85 C8
Ballinger Bottom Bucks 84 E6
Ballinger Bottom (South) Bucks 84 E6
Ballinger Common Bucks 84 E6
Ballingham Hereford 97 E11
Ballingham Hill Hereford 97 E11
Ballingry Fife 280 B3
Ballinlick Perth 286 C3
Ballinluig Perth 286 B3
Ballintean Highld 291 C10
Ballintuim Perth 286 B5
Balliveolan Argyll 289 E10
Balloch Angus 287 B7
Balloch Highld 301 E7
Balloch N Lnrk 278 G4
Balloch W Dunb 277 E7
Ballochan Aberds 293 D7
Ballochearn Stirl 277 D11
Ballochford Moray 302 F3
Ballochmorrie S Ayrs 244 G6
Ballogie Aberds 293 D7
Balls Cross W Sus 35 B7
Balls Green E Sus 52 F3
Balls Green Essex 107 G11
Ball's Green Glos 80 F5
Balls Green W Sus 35 C10
Balls Hill W Mid 133 E9
Ballygown Argyll 288 E6
Ballygrant Argyll 274 G4
Ballygroggan Argyll 255 F7
Ballyhaugh Argyll 288 D3
Balmacara Highld 295 C10
Balmacara Square Highld 295 C10
Balmaclellan Dumfries 237 B8
Balmacneil Perth 286 B3
Balmacqueen Highld 298 B4
Balmae Dumfries 237 E8
Balmaha Stirl 277 C8
Balmalcolm Fife 287 G7
Balmalloch N Lnrk 278 F4
Balmeanach Argyll 288 F6
Balmeanach Argyll 289 E8
Balmeanach Highld 295 B7
Balmeanach Highld 298 E3
Balmeanach Highld 298 E5
Balmedie Aberds 293 B11
Balmer Shrops 149 C8
Balmer Heath Shrops 149 C8

318 Bal – Bee

Balmerino Fife 287 E7
Balmerlawn Hants 32 G4
Balmesh Dumfries 236 D3
Balmichael N Ayrs 255 D10
Balminnoch Dumfries 236 C4
Balmirmer Angus 287 D9
Balmoral Borders 261 B11
Balmore E Dunb 278 G2
Balmore Highld 298 E2
Balmore Highld 300 F3
Balmore Highld 301 E8
Balmore Perth 286 B3
Balmule Fife 280 D4
Balmullo Fife 287 E8
Balmungie Highld 301 D7
Balmurrie Dumfries 236 C4
Balnaboth Angus 292 G5
Balnabreich Moray 302 D3
Balnabruaich Highld 301 C7
Balnabruich Highld 311 G5
Balnacarn Highld 290 B4
Balnacoil Highld 311 H2
Balnacra Highld 299 E9
Balnacruie Highld 301 G9
Balnafoich Highld 300 F6
Balnagall Highld 311 L2
Balnagowan Aberds 293 C7
Balnagrantach Highld 300 F4
Balnaguard Perth 286 B3
Balnahanaid Perth 285 C10
Balnahard Argyll 274 D5
Balnahard Argyll 288 F6
Balnain Highld 300 F4
Balnakeil Highld 308 C3
Balnakelly Aberds 293 B7
Balnaknock Highld 298 C4
Balnamoon Aberds 303 D9
Balnamoon Angus 293 G7
Balnapaling Highld 301 C7
Balne N Yorks 198 D5
Balnoon Corn 2 B2
Balochroy Argyll 255 B8
Balole Argyll 274 G4
Balone Fife 287 F8
Balornock Glasgow 268 B2
Balquharn Perth 286 D4
Balquhidder Stirl 285 E9
Balquhidder Station Stirl 285 E9
Balquhindachy Aberds 303 E8
Balrownie Angus 293 G7
Balsall W Mid 118 B4
Balsall Common W Mid 118 B4
Balsall Heath W Mid 133 G11
Balsall Street W Mid 118 B4
Balsam Cambs 123 G11
Balscote Oxon 101 C7
Balscott Oxon 101 C7
Balsham Cambs 123 G11
Balsporran Cottages Highld 291 F8
Balstonia Thurrock 69 C7
Baltasound Shetland 312 C8
Balterley Staffs 168 E3
Balterley Green Staffs 168 E3
Balterley Heath Staffs 168 E2
Baltersan Dumfries 236 C6
Balthangie Aberds 303 D8
Balthayock Perth 286 E5
Baltonsborough Som 44 G4
Balure Argyll 289 E11
Balvaird Highld 300 D5
Balvenie Moray 302 E3
Balvicar Argyll 275 B8
Balvraid Highld 295 D10
Balvraid Highld 301 F8
Balwest Corn 2 C3
Bamber Bridge Lancs 194 B5
Bamber's Green Essex 105 G11
Bamburgh Northumb 264 C5
Bamff Perth 286 B6
Bamford Derbys 186 E2
Bamford Gtr Man 195 E11
Bamfurlong Glos 99 G8
Bamfurlong Gtr Man 194 G5
Bampton Cumb 221 B10
Bampton Devon 27 C7
Bampton Oxon 82 E4
Bampton Grange Cumb 221 B10
Banavie Highld 290 F3
Banbury Oxon 101 C9
Banc-y-Darren Ceredig 128 G3
Bancffosfelen Carms 75 C7
Banchor Highld 301 E9
Banchory Aberds 293 D8
Banchory-Devenick Aberds 293 C11
Bancycapel Carms 74 B6
Bancyfelin Carms 74 B4
Bancyffordd Carms 93 D8
Bandirran Perth 286 D6
Bandonhill London 67 G9
Bandrake Head Cumb 210 B6
Banff Aberds 302 C6
Bangor Gwyn 179 G9
Bangor is y coed = Bangor on Dee Wrex 166 F5
Bangor on Dee = Bangor-is-y-coed Wrex 166 F5
Bangor Teifi Ceredig 93 C7
Bangors Corn 11 B10
Banham Norf 141 F11
Bank Hants 32 F3
Bank End Cumb 210 B3
Bank End Cumb 228 D6
Bank Fold Blkburn 195 C8
Bank Hey Blkburn 203 G9
Bank Houses Lancs 202 C4
Bank Lane Gtr Man 195 D9
Bank Newton N Yorks 204 C4
Bank Street Worcs 116 E2
Bank Top Gtr Man 195 E8
Bank Top Lancs 194 F4
Bank Top Stoke 168 E5
Bank Top T & W 242 D4
Bank Top W Yorks 196 C6
Bank Top W Yorks 205 F9
Bankend Dumfries 238 D2
Bankfoot Perth 286 D4
Bankglen E Ayrs 258 G4
Bankhead Aberdeen 293 B10
Bankhead Aberds 293 C8
Bankhead Dumfries 236 C2
Bankhead Falk 278 E6
Bankhead S Lnrk 269 G7
Bankland Som 28 B4
Banknock Falk 278 F5
Banks Cumb 240 E3
Banks Lancs 193 C11
Banks Orkney 314 C4
Bank's Green Worcs 117 D9
Bankshead Shrops 130 F6
Bankshill Dumfries 248 G5
Bankside Falk 279 E7
Banners Gate W Mid 133 D11
Banningham Norf 160 D4
Banniskirk Ho Highld 310 D5
Banniskirk Mains Highld 310 D5
Bannister Green Essex 106 G3
Bannockburn Stirl 278 C5
Banns Corn 4 F4
Banstead Sur 51 B8
Bantam Grove W Yorks 197 B9
Bantaskin Falk 279 F7
Bantham Devon 8 G3
Banton N Lnrk 278 F5
Banwell N Som 43 B11
Banyard's Green Suff 126 C5
Bapchild Kent 70 G2
Baptist End W Mid 133 F8
Bapton Wilts 46 F3
Bar End Hants 33 B7
Bar Hill Cambs 123 E7
Bar Hill Staffs 168 G3
Bar Moor T & W 242 E4
Barabhas W Isles 304 D5
Barabhas Iarach W Isles 304 D5
Barabhas Uarach W Isles 304 C5
Barachandroman Argyll 289 G8
Baramore Highld 289 B8
Barassie S Ayrs 257 C8
Baravullin Argyll 289 F10
Barbadoes Stirl 277 B11
Barbaraville Highld 301 B7
Barbauchlaw W Loth 269 B8
Barber Booth Derbys 185 E10
Barber Green Cumb 211 C7
Barber's Moor Lancs 194 D3
Barbican Plym 7 E9
Barbieston S Ayrs 257 F10
Barbon Cumb 212 C2
Barbourne Worcs 116 F6
Barbreck Ho Argyll 275 C9
Barbridge E Ches 167 D10
Barbrook Devon 41 D8
Barby Northants 119 C10
Barby Nortoft Northants 119 C11
Barcaldine Argyll 289 E11
Barcelona Corn 6 E4
Barcheston Warks 100 D5
Barclose Cumb 239 E10
Barcombe E Sus 36 E6
Barcombe Cross E Sus 36 D6
Barcroft W Yorks 204 F6
Barden N Yorks 224 G2
Barden Park Kent 52 D5
Barden Scale N Yorks 205 B7
Bardennoch Dumfries 246 E3
Bardfield End Green Essex 106 E2
Bardfield Saling Essex 106 F3
Bardister Shetland 312 F5
Bardnabeinne Highld 309 K7
Bardney Lincs 173 B10
Bardon Leics 153 G8
Bardon Mill Northumb 241 E7
Bardowie E Dunb 277 G11
Bardown E Sus 37 B11
Bardrainney Invclyd 276 G6
Bardrishaig Argyll 275 B8
Bardsea Cumb 210 E6
Bardsey W Yorks 206 E3
Bardsley Gtr Man 196 G2
Bardwell Suff 125 C8
Bare Lancs 211 G9
Bare Ash Som 43 F9
Bareless Northumb 263 B9
Barepot Cumb 228 F6
Bareppa Corn 3 D7
Barfad Argyll 275 G9
Barfad Dumfries 236 C5
Barford Norf 142 B2
Barford Sur 49 F11
Barford Warks 118 E5
Barford St John Oxon 101 E8
Barford St Martin Wilts 46 G5
Barford St Michael Oxon 101 E8
Barfrestone Kent 55 C9
Bargaly Dumfries 236 C6
Bargarran Renfs 277 G9
Bargate Derbys 170 F5
Bargeddie N Lnrk 268 C4
Bargoed Caerph 77 F10
Bargrennan Dumfries 236 B5
Barham Cambs 122 B2
Barham Kent 55 C8
Barham Suff 126 G2
Barharrow Dumfries 237 D8
Barhill Dumfries 237 C10
Barholm Dumfries 237 D7
Barholm Lincs 155 G11
Barkby Leics 136 B2
Barkby Thorpe Leics 136 B2
Barkers Green Shrops 149 D10
Barkers Hill Wilts 30 B6
Barkestone-le-Vale Leics 154 C5
Barkham Wokingham 65 F9
Barking London 68 C2
Barking Suff 125 G11
Barking Tye Suff 125 G11
Barkingside London 68 B2
Barkisland W Yorks 196 D5
Barkla Shop Corn 4 E4
Barkston Lincs 172 G6
Barkston N Yorks 206 F5
Barkston Ash N Yorks 206 F5
Barkway Herts 105 D7
Barlake Som 45 D7
Barlanark Glasgow 268 C3
Barland Powys 114 E5
Barland Common Swansea 56 D5
Barlaston Staffs 151 B7
Barlavington W Sus 35 D7
Barlborough Derbys 187 F7
Barlby N Yorks 207 G8
Barlestone Leics 135 B8
Barley Herts 105 D7
Barley Lancs 204 E2
Barley End Bucks 85 C7
Barley Green Lancs 204 E2
Barley Mow T & W 243 G7
Barleycroft End Herts 105 F8
Barleythorpe Rutland 136 B6
Barling Essex 70 B2
Barlings Lincs 189 G9
Barlow Derbys 186 G4
Barlow N Yorks 198 B6
Barlow T & W 242 E5
Barlow Moor Gtr Man 184 C4
Barmby Moor E Yorks 207 D11
Barmby on the Marsh E Yorks 199 B7
Barmer Norf 158 C6
Barming Heath Kent 53 B8
Barmolloch Argyll 275 D9
Barmoor Castle Northumb 263 B11
Barmoor Lane End Northumb 264 B2
Barmouth = Abermaw Gwyn 146 F2
Barmpton Darl 224 B6
Barmston E Yorks 209 B9
Barmston T & W 243 F8
Barmulloch Glasgow 268 B2
Barnaby Green Suff 127 B9
Barnacabber Argyll 276 D3
Barnack P'boro 137 B11
Barnacle Warks 135 G7
Barnaline Argyll 275 B10
Barnard Castle Durham 223 B11
Barnard Gate Oxon 82 C6
Barnardiston Suff 106 B4
Barnard's Green Worcs 98 B5
Barnardtown Newport 59 B10
Barnbarroch Dumfries 237 D10
Barnbow Carr W Yorks 206 F3
Barnburgh S Yorks 198 G3
Barnby Suff 143 F9
Barnby Dun S Yorks 198 F6
Barnby in the Willows Notts 172 E5
Barnby Moor Notts 187 E11
Barncluith S Lnrk 268 E4
Barndennoch Dumfries 247 F9
Barne Barton Plym 7 D8
Barnehurst London 68 D4
Barnes Cray London 68 D4
Barnes Hall S Yorks 186 B4
Barnes Street Kent 52 D6
Barnet London 86 F2
Barnet Gate London 86 F2
Barnetby le Wold N Lincs 200 F5
Barnett Brook E Ches 167 G10
Barnettbrook Worcs 117 B7
Barney Norf 159 C9
Barnfield Kent 54 D2
Barnfields Hereford 97 C9
Barnfields Staffs 169 D7
Barnham Suff 125 B7
Barnham W Sus 35 G7
Barnham Broom Norf 141 B11
Barnhead Angus 287 B10
Barnhill Dundee 287 D8
Barnhill Moray 301 D11
Barnhill W Ches 167 E7
Barnhills Dumfries 236 B1
Barningham Durham 223 C11
Barningham Suff 125 B9
Barningham Green Norf 160 C2
Barnmoor Green Warks 118 E3
Barnoldby le Beck NE Lincs 201 G8
Barnoldswick Lancs 204 D3
Barnoldswick N Yorks 212 E3
Barns Borders 260 B6
Barns Green W Sus 35 B10
Barnsbury London 67 C10
Barnsdale Rutland 137 B8
Barnside W Yorks 197 F7
Barnsley Glos 81 D9
Barnsley S Yorks 197 F10
Barnsley Shrops 132 E5
Barnsole Kent 55 B9
Barnstaple Devon 40 G5
Barnston Essex 87 B10
Barnston Mers 182 E3
Barnstone Notts 154 B4
Barnt Green Worcs 117 C10
Barnton Edin 280 F3
Barnton W Ches 183 F10
Barnwell Northants 137 G10
Barnwell All Saints Northants 137 G10
Barnwell St Andrew Northants 137 F10
Barnwood Glos 80 B5
Barochreal Argyll 289 G10
Barons Cross Hereford 115 F9
Barr Highld 289 D8
Barr S Ayrs 245 E7
Barr Som 27 C11
Barr Common W Mid 133 D11
Barra Castle Aberds 303 G7
Barrachan Dumfries 236 E5
Barrachnie Glasgow 268 C3
Barrack Aberds 303 E8
Barrack Hill Newport 59 B10
Barraer Dumfries 236 C5
Barraglom W Isles 304 E3
Barrahormid Argyll 275 E8
Barran Argyll 289 G10
Barranrioch Argyll 289 G10
Barrapol Argyll 288 E1
Barras Aberds 293 E10
Barras Cumb 222 C6
Barrasford Northumb 241 C10
Barravullin Argyll 275 C9
Barregarrow I o M 192 D4
Barrets Green E Ches 167 D9
Barrhead E Renf 267 D9
Barrhill S Ayrs 244 G6
Barrington Cambs 105 B7
Barrington Som 28 D5
Barripper Corn 2 B4
Barrmill N Ayrs 267 E7
Barrock Highld 310 B6
Barrock Ho Highld 310 C6
Barrow Glos 99 G7
Barrow Lancs 203 F10
Barrow Rutland 155 F7
Barrow S Yorks 186 B5
Barrow Shrops 132 C3
Barrow Som 44 E5
Barrow Suff 124 E5
Barrow Bridge Gtr Man 195 E7
Barrow Burn Northumb 263 G9
Barrow Common N Som 60 F4
Barrow Green Kent 70 G3
Barrow Gurney N Som 60 F4
Barrow Hann N Lincs 200 C5
Barrow Haven N Lincs 200 C5
Barrow Hill Derbys 186 F6
Barrow Hill Dorset 18 B5
Barrow-in-Furness Cumb 210 F4
Barrow Island Cumb 210 F3
Barrow Nook Lancs 194 G2
Barrow Street Wilts 45 G10
Barrow upon Humber N Lincs 200 C5
Barrow upon Soar Leics 153 F11
Barrow upon Trent Derbys 153 D7
Barrow Vale Bath 60 G6
Barrow Wake Glos 80 B6
Barroway Drove Norf 139 C11
Barrowburn Northumb 263 G9
Barrowby Lincs 155 B7
Barrowcliff N Yorks 217 B10
Barrowden Rutland 137 C8
Barrowford Lancs 204 F3
Barrowhill Kent 54 F6
Barrowmore Estate W Ches 167 B7
Barrows Green Cumb 211 B10
Barrows Green E Ches 167 D11
Barrow's Green Mers 183 D8
Barrows Green Notts 171 E7
Barry Angus 287 D9
Barry V Glam 58 F6
Barry Dock V Glam 58 F6
Barry Island V Glam 58 F6
Barsby Leics 154 G3
Barsham Suff 143 F7
Barshare E Ayrs 258 F3
Barstable Essex 69 B8
Barston W Mid 118 B4
Bartestree Hereford 97 C11
Barthol Chapel Aberds 303 F8
Bartholomew Green Essex 106 G4
Barthomley E Ches 168 E3
Bartington W Ches 183 F10
Bartley Hants 32 E4
Bartley Green W Mid 133 G10
Bartlow Cambs 105 B11
Barton Cambs 123 F8
Barton Glos 80 B4
Barton Glos 99 F11
Barton I o W 20 D6
Barton Lancs 193 F11
Barton Lancs 202 F6
Barton N Som 43 B11
Barton N Yorks 224 D4
Barton Oxon 83 D9
Barton Torbay 9 B8
Barton W Ches 166 E6
Barton Warks 118 G2
Barton Abbey Oxon 101 G9
Barton Bendish Norf 140 B4
Barton Court Hereford 98 C4
Barton End Glos 80 F4
Barton Gate Devon 41 E7
Barton Gate Staffs 152 F3
Barton Green Staffs 152 F3
Barton Hartshorn Bucks 102 E2
Barton Hill Bristol 60 E6
Barton Hill N Yorks 216 G4
Barton in Fabis Notts 153 C10
Barton in the Beans Leics 135 B7
Barton-le-Clay C Beds 103 E11
Barton-le-Street N Yorks 216 E4
Barton-le-Willows N Yorks 216 G4
Barton Mills Suff 124 C4
Barton on Sea Hants 19 C10
Barton on the Heath Warks 100 E5
Barton St David Som 44 G4
Barton Seagrave Northants 121 B7
Barton Stacey Hants 48 E2
Barton Town Devon 41 E7
Barton Turf Norf 161 E7
Barton Turn Staffs 152 F4
Barton-under-Needwood Staffs 152 F3
Barton-upon-Humber N Lincs 200 C4
Barton Upon Irwell Gtr Man 184 B3
Barton Waterside N Lincs 200 C4
Bartonsham Hereford 97 D10
Barugh S Yorks 197 F10
Barugh Green S Yorks 197 F10
Barway Cambs 123 B10
Barwell Leics 135 D8
Barwell London 67 G7
Barwick Devon 25 F9
Barwick Herts 86 B5
Barwick Som 29 E9
Barwick in Elmet W Yorks 206 F3
Baschurch Shrops 149 E8
Bascote Warks 119 E8
Bascote Heath Warks 119 E7
Base Green Suff 125 E10
Basford Shrops 131 F7
Basford Staffs 168 F5
Basford Green Staffs 169 E7
Bashall Eaves Lancs 203 E9
Bashley Hants 19 B10
Bashley Park Hants 19 B10
Basildon Essex 69 B8
Basingstoke Hants 48 C6
Baslow Derbys 186 G3
Bason Bridge Som 43 D10
Bassaleg Newport 59 B9
Bassenthwaite Cumb 229 E10
Bassett S Yorks 186 E3
Bassett Soton 32 D6
Bassett Green Soton 32 D6
Bassingbourn Cambs 104 C6
Bassingfield Notts 154 B2
Bassingham Lincs 172 C6
Bassingthorpe Lincs 155 D9
Bassus Green Herts 104 F6
Basta Shetland 312 D7
Basted Kent 52 B6
Baston Lincs 156 G2
Bastonford Worcs 116 G6
Bastwick Norf 161 F8
Baswich Staffs 151 E8
Baswick Steer E Yorks 209 D7
Batavaime Stirl 285 D8
Batch Som 43 B10
Batchcott Shrops 115 C9
Batchfields Hereford 98 B3
Batchley Worcs 117 D10
Batchworth Herts 85 G9
Batchworth Heath Herts 85 G9
Batcombe Dorset 29 G10
Batcombe Som 45 F7
Bate Heath E Ches 183 F11
Bateman's Green Worcs 117 B11
Bateman's Hill Pembs 73 E8
Batemoor S Yorks 186 E5
Batford Herts 85 B10
Bath Bath 61 F8
Bath Side Essex 108 E5
Bath Vale E Ches 168 C5
Bathampton Bath 61 F9
Bathealton Som 27 C9
Batheaston Bath 61 F9
Bathford Bath 61 F9
Bathgate W Loth 269 B9
Bathley Notts 172 D3
Bathpool Corn 11 G11
Bathpool Som 28 B3
Bathville W Loth 269 B8
Bathway Som 44 C5
Bathwick Bath 61 F9
Batlers Green Herts 85 F11
Batley W Yorks 197 C8
Batley Carr W Yorks 197 C8
Batsford Glos 100 E3
Batson Devon 9 G9
Batsworthy Devon 26 D4
Batten's Green Som 28 D3
Battenton Green Worcs 116 D6
Battersby N Yorks 225 D11
Battersea London 67 D9
Battisborough Cross Devon 7 F11
Battisford Suff 125 G11
Battisford Tye Suff 125 G10
Battle E Sus 38 D2
Battle Powys 95 E10
Battle Hill T & W 243 D8
Battledown Glos 99 G9
Battledown Cross Devon 25 F7
Battlefield Shrops 149 F10
Battlesbridge Essex 88 G3
Battlescombe Glos 80 D6
Battlesden C Beds 103 F9
Battlesea Green Suff 126 B4
Battleton Som 26 B6
Battlies Green Suff 125 E7
Battram Leics 135 B8
Battramsley Hants 20 B2
Battramsley Cross Hants 20 B2
Batt's Corner Hants 49 E10
Battyeford W Yorks 197 C7
Batworthy Devon 13 D10
Bauds of Cullen Moray 302 C4
Baugh Argyll 288 E2
Baughton Worcs 99 C7
Baughurst Hants 48 B5
Baulking Oxon 82 G4
Baumber Lincs 190 G2
Baunton Glos 81 E8
Baverstock Wilts 46 G4
Bawburgh Norf 142 B3
Bawdeswell Norf 159 E10
Bawdrip Som 43 F10
Bawdsey Suff 108 C6
Bawsey Norf 158 F3
Bawtry S Yorks 187 C11
Baxenden Lancs 195 B9
Baxterley Warks 134 D5
Baxter's Green Suff 124 F5
Bay Dorset 30 B4
Bay Highld 298 D2
Bay Gate Lancs 203 D11
Bay Horse Lancs 202 C5
Bay View Kent 70 E4
Baybridge Hants 33 C8
Baybridge Northumb 241 G11
Baycliff Cumb 210 E5
Baydon Wilts 63 D9
Bayford Herts 86 D4
Bayford Som 30 B2
Bayles Cumb 231 C10
Bayley's Hill Kent 52 C4
Baylham Suff 126 G2
Baylis Green Worcs 117 C11
Baynard's Green Oxon 101 F10
Baynhall Worcs 99 B7
Baysham Hereford 97 F11
Bayston Hill Shrops 131 B9
Bayswater London 67 C9
Baythorne End Essex 106 C4
Baythorpe Lincs 174 G2
Bayton Worcs 116 C3
Bayton Common Worcs 116 C4
Bayworth Oxon 83 E8
Beach Highld 289 D9
Beach S Glos 61 E8
Beach Hay Worcs 116 C4
Beachampton Bucks 102 D5
Beachamwell Norf 140 B5
Beachans Moray 301 E10
Beacharr Argyll 255 C7
Beachborough Kent 55 F7
Beachlands E Sus 23 E11
Beachley Glos 79 G9
Beacon Corn 2 B5
Beacon Devon 27 F11
Beacon Devon 28 F2
Beacon Down E Sus 37 C9
Beacon End Essex 107 G9
Beacon Hill Bath 61 F9
Beacon Hill Bucks 84 G6
Beacon Hill Cumb 210 E4
Beacon Hill Dorset 18 C5
Beacon Hill Essex 88 C5
Beacon Hill Kent 53 G10
Beacon Hill Notts 172 E4
Beacon Hill Suff 108 B4
Beacon Hill Sur 49 F11
Beacon Lough T & W 243 F7
Beaconhill Northumb 243 B7
Beacon's Bottom Bucks 84 F3
Beaconsfield Bucks 66 B2
Beaconside Staffs 151 E8
Beacrabhaic W Isles 305 J3
Beadlam N Yorks 216 C3
Beadlow C Beds 104 D2
Beadnell Northumb 264 D6
Beaford Devon 25 E9
Beal N Yorks 198 B4
Beal Northumb 273 G11
Bealach Highld 289 D11
Bealach Maim Argyll 275 E10
Bealbury Corn 7 B7
Beal's Green Kent 53 G9
Bealsmill Corn 12 F3
Beam Bridge Som 27 D10
Beam Hill Staffs 152 D4
Beambridge Shrops 131 F10
Beamhurst Staffs 151 B11
Beamhurst Lane Staffs 151 B11
Beaminster Dorset 29 G7
Beamish Durham 242 G6
Beamond End Bucks 84 F6
Beamsley N Yorks 205 C7
Bean Kent 68 E5
Beanacre Wilts 62 F2
Beancross Falk 279 F8
Beanhill M Keynes 103 D7
Beanley Northumb 264 F3
Beansburn E Ayrs 257 B10
Beanthwaite Cumb 210 C4
Beaquoy Orkney 314 D3
Bear Cross Bmouth 19 B7
Beard Hill Som 44 E6
Beardly Batch Som 44 E6
Beardwood Blkburn 195 B7
Beare Devon 27 G7
Beare Green Sur 51 E7
Bearley Warks 118 E3
Bearley Cross Warks 118 E3
Bearnus Argyll 288 E5
Bearpark Durham 233 C10
Bearsbridge Northumb 241 F7
Bearsden E Dunb 277 G10
Bearsted Kent 53 B9
Bearstone Shrops 150 B4
Bearwood Hereford 115 F7
Bearwood Poole 18 B6
Bearwood W Mid 133 F10
Beasley Staffs 168 F4
Beattock Dumfries 248 C3
Beauchamp Roding Essex 87 C9
Beauchief S Yorks 186 E4
Beauclerc Northumb 242 E2
Beaudesert Warks 118 D3
Beaufort Bl Gwent 77 C11
Beaufort Castle Highld 300 E5
Beaulieu Hants 32 G5
Beaulieu Wood Dorset 30 F2
Beauly Highld 300 E5
Beaumaris Anglesey 179 F10
Beaumont Cumb 239 F8
Beaumont Essex 108 G3
Beaumont Windsor 66 E3
Beaumont Hill Darl 224 B5
Beaumont Leys Leicester 135 B11
Beausale Warks 118 C4
Beauvale Notts 171 F8
Beauworth Hants 33 B9
Beavan's Hill Hereford 98 G3
Beaworthy Devon 12 B5
Beazley End Essex 106 F4
Bebington Mers 182 E4
Bebside Northumb 253 G7
Beccles Suff 143 E8
Becconsall Lancs 194 C2
Beck Bottom Cumb 210 C5
Beck Bottom W Yorks 197 C10
Beck Foot Cumb 222 F2
Beck Foot W Yorks 205 F8
Beck Head Cumb 211 C8
Beck Hole N Yorks 226 E6
Beck Houses Cumb 221 F11
Beck Row Suff 124 B3
Beck Side Cumb 210 C4
Beck Side Cumb 211 C7
Beckbury Shrops 132 C5
Beckces Cumb 230 F4
Beckenham London 67 F11
Beckermet Cumb 219 D10
Beckermonds N Yorks 213 C7
Beckery Som 44 F3
Beckett End Norf 140 D5
Beckfoot Cumb 220 E3
Beckfoot Cumb 229 B7
Beckford Worcs 99 D9
Beckhampton Wilts 62 F5
Beckingham Lincs 172 E5
Beckingham Notts 188 D3
Beckington Som 45 C10
Beckjay Shrops 115 B7
Beckley E Sus 38 C5
Beckley Hants 19 B10
Beckley Oxon 83 C9
Beckley Furnace E Sus 38 C4
Beckside Cumb 212 B2
Beckton London 68 C2
Beckwith N Yorks 205 C11
Beckwithshaw N Yorks 205 C11
Becontree London 68 B3
Bed-y-coedwr Gwyn 146 D4
Bedale N Yorks 214 B5
Bedburn Durham 233 E8
Bedchester Dorset 30 D5
Beddau Rhondda 58 B5
Beddgelert Gwyn 163 F9
Beddingham E Sus 36 F6
Beddington London 67 G10
Beddington Corner London 67 F9
Bedfield Suff 126 D4
Bedford Beds 121 G11
Bedford Gtr Man 183 B11
Bedford Park London 67 D8
Bedgebury Cross Kent 53 G8
Bedgrove Bucks 84 C4
Bedham W Sus 35 C8
Bedhampton Hants 22 B2
Bedingfield Suff 126 D3
Bedingham Green Norf 142 E5
Bedlam N Yorks 214 G5
Bedlam Som 45 D9
Bedlam Street W Sus 36 D3
Bedlar's Green Essex 105 G10
Bedlington Northumb 253 G7
Bedlington Station Northumb 253 G7
Bedlinog M Tydf 77 E9
Bedminster Bristol 60 E5
Bedminster Down Bristol 60 F5
Bedmond Herts 85 E9
Bednall Staffs 151 F9
Bednall Head Staffs 151 F9
Bedrule Borders 262 F4
Bedstone Shrops 115 B7
Bedwas Caerph 59 B7
Bedwell Herts 104 G4
Bedwell Wrex 166 F5
Bedwellty Caerph 77 E11
Bedwellty Pits Bl Gwent 77 D11
Bedwlwyn Wrex 148 B4
Bedworth Warks 135 F7
Bedworth Heath Warks 134 F6
Bedworth Woodlands Warks 134 F6
Beeby Leics 136 B3
Beech Hants 49 F7
Beech Staffs 151 B7
Beech Hill Gtr Man 194 F5
Beech Hill W Berks 65 G7
Beech Lanes W Mid 133 F10
Beechcliff Staffs 151 B7
Beechcliffe W Yorks 205 E7
Beechen Cliff Bath 61 G9
Beechingstoke Wilts 46 B5
Beechwood Halton 183 E8
Beechwood Newport 59 B10
Beechwood W Mid 118 B5
Beechwood W Yorks 206 F2
Beecroft C Beds 103 G10
Beedon W Berks 64 D3
Beedon Hill W Berks 64 D3
Beeford E Yorks 209 C8
Beeley Derbys 170 B3
Beelsby NE Lincs 201 G8
Beenham W Berks 64 F5
Beenham Stocks W Berks 64 F5
Beenham's Heath Windsor 65 D10
Beeny Corn 11 C8
Beer Devon 15 D10
Beer Som 44 G2
Beer Hackett Dorset 29 E9
Beercrocombe Som 28 C4
Beesands Devon 8 G6
Beesby Lincs 191 E7
Beeslack Midloth 270 C4
Beeson Devon 8 G6
Beeston C Beds 104 B3
Beeston Norf 159 F8
Beeston Notts 153 B10
Beeston W Ches 167 D8
Beeston W Yorks 205 G11
Beeston Hill W Yorks 205 G11
Beeston Park Side W Yorks 197 B9

Beeston Regis Norf 177 E11
Beeston Royds W Yorks 205 G11
Beeston St Lawrence Norf 160 E6
Beeswing Dumfries 237 C10
Beetham Cumb 211 D9
Beetham Som 28 E3
Beetley Norf 159 F9
Beffcote Staffs 150 F6
Began Cardiff 59 C8
Begbroke Oxon 83 C7
Begdale Cambs 139 B9
Begelly Pembs 73 D10
Beggar Hill Essex 87 E10
Beggarington Hill W Yorks 197 C9
Beggars Ash Hereford 98 D4
Beggar's Bush Powys 114 E5
Beggars Bush W Sus 35 F11
Beggars Pound V Glam 58 F4
Beggearn Huish Som 42 F4
Beguildy Powys 114 B3
Beighton Norf 143 B7
Beighton S Yorks 186 E6
Beighton Hill Derbys 170 E3
Beili-glas Mon 78 C4
Beitearsaig W Isles 305 G1
Beith N Ayrs 266 E6
Bekesbourne Kent 55 B7
Bekesbourne Hill Kent 55 B7
Belah Cumb 239 F9
Belan Powys 130 C4
Belaugh Norf 160 F5
Belbins Hants 32 C5
Belbroughton Worcs 117 B8
Belchalwell Dorset 30 F3
Belchalwell Street Dorset 30 F3
Belchamp Otten Essex 106 C6
Belchamp St Paul Essex 106 C5
Belchamp Walter Essex 106 C6
Belcher's Bar Leics 135 B8
Belchford Lincs 190 F3
Beleybridge Fife 287 F9
Belfield Gtr Man 196 E2
Belford Northumb 264 C4
Belgrano Conwy 181 F7
Belgrave Leicester 135 B11
Belgrave Staffs 134 C4
Belgrave W Ches 166 C5
Belgravia London 67 D9
Belhaven E Loth 282 F3
Belhelvie Aberds 293 B11
Belhinnie Aberds 302 G4
Bell Bar Herts 86 D3
Bell Busk N Yorks 204 B4
Bell Common Essex 86 E6
Bell End Worcs 117 B8
Bell Green London 67 E11
Bell Green W Mid 135 G7
Bell Heath Worcs 117 B9
Bell Hill Hants 34 C2
Bell o' th' Hill W Ches 167 F8
Bellabeg Aberds 292 B5
Bellamore S Ayrs 244 F6
Bellanoch Argyll 275 D8
Bellanrigg Borders 260 B6
Bellasize E Yorks 199 B10
Bellaty Angus 286 B6
Belle Eau Park Notts 171 D11
Belle Green S Yorks 197 F11
Belle Isle W Yorks 197 B10
Belle Vale Mers 182 D6
Belle Vale W Mid 133 G9
Belle Vue Cumb 229 E8
Belle Vue Cumb 239 F9
Belle Vue Gtr Man 184 B5
Belle Vue S Yorks 198 G5
Belle Vue Shrops 149 G9
Belle Vue W Yorks 197 D10
Belleau Lincs 190 F6
Bellehiglash Moray 301 F11
Bellerby N Yorks 224 G2
Bellever Devon 13 F9
Bellevue Worcs 117 C9
Bellfield E Ayrs 257 B10
Bellfields Sur 50 C3
Belliehill Angus 293 G7
Bellingdon Bucks 84 D6
Bellingham London 67 E11
Bellingham Northumb 251 G8
Bellmount Norf 157 E10
Belloch Argyll 255 D7
Bellochantuy Argyll 255 D7
Bell's Close T & W 242 E5
Bell's Corner Suff 107 D9
Bells Yew Green E Sus 52 F6
Bellsbank E Ayrs 245 C11
Bellshill N Lnrk 268 C4
Bellshill Northumb 264 C4
Bellside N Lnrk 268 D6
Bellsmyre W Dunb 277 F8
Bellspool Borders 260 B5
Bellsquarry W Loth 269 C10
Belluton Bath 60 G6
Bellyeoman Fife 280 D2
Belmaduthy Highld 300 D6
Belmesthorpe Rutland 155 G10
Belmont Blkburn 195 D7
Belmont Durham 234 C2
Belmont E Sus 38 E4
Belmont London 67 G9
Belmont London 85 G11
Belmont Oxon 63 B11
Belmont S Ayrs 257 E8
Belmont Shetland 312 C7
Belnacraig Aberds 292 B5
Belnagarrow Moray 302 E3
Belnie Lincs 156 C5
Belowda Corn 5 C9
Belper Derbys 170 F4
Belper Lane End Derbys 170 F4
Belph Derbys 187 F8
Belsay Northumb 242 B4
Belses Borders 262 D3
Belsford Devon 8 D5
Belsize Herts 85 E8
Belstead Suff 108 C2
Belston S Ayrs 257 E9
Belstone Devon 13 C8
Belstone Corner Devon 13 B8
Belthorn Blkburn 195 C8
Beltinge Kent 71 F7
Beltingham Northumb 241 E7
Beltoft N Lincs 199 F10
Belton Leics 153 E8
Belton Lincs 155 B8
Belton N Lincs 199 F9
Belton Norf 143 C9
Belton in Rutland Rutland 136 C6
Beltring Kent 53 D7
Belts of Collonach Aberds 293 D8
Belvedere London 68 D3
Belvedere W Loth 269 B9
Belvoir Leics 154 C6
Bembridge I o W 21 D8
Bemersyde Borders 262 C3
Bemerton Wilts 46 G6
Bemerton Heath Wilts 46 G6
Bempton E Yorks 218 E3
Ben Alder Lodge Highld 291 F7
Ben Armine Lodge Highld 309 H7
Ben Casgro W Isles 304 F6
Ben Rhydding W Yorks 205 D8
Benacre Suff 143 G10
Benbuie Dumfries 246 D6
Benchill Gtr Man 184 D4
Bencombe Glos 80 F3
Benderloch Argyll 289 F11
Bendish Herts 104 G3
Bendronaig Lodge Highld 299 F10
Benenden Kent 53 G10
Benfield Dumfries 236 C5
Benfieldside Durham 242 G3
Bengal Pembs 91 E9
Bengate Norf 160 D6
Bengeo Herts 86 C4
Bengeworth Worcs 99 C10
Bengrove Glos 99 E9
Benhall Glos 99 G8
Benhall Green Suff 127 E7
Benhall Street Suff 127 E7
Benhilton London 67 F9
Benholm Aberds 293 G10
Beningbrough N Yorks 206 B6
Benington Herts 104 G5
Benington Lincs 174 F5
Benington Sea End Lincs 174 F6
Benllech Anglesey 179 E8
Benmore Argyll 276 E2
Benmore Stirl 285 E8
Benmore Lodge Argyll 289 F7
Benmore Lodge Highld 309 H3
Bennacott Corn 11 C11
Bennah Devon 14 E2
Bennan N Ayrs 255 E10
Bennane Lea S Ayrs 244 F3
Bennetland E Yorks 199 B10
Bennetsfield Highld 300 D6
Bennett End Bucks 84 F3
Bennetts End Herts 85 D9
Benniworth Lincs 190 E2
Benover Kent 53 D8
Bensham T & W 242 E6
Benslie N Ayrs 266 G6
Benson Oxon 83 G10
Benston Shetland 313 H6
Bent Aberds 293 F8
Bent Gate Lancs 195 C9
Benter Som 44 D6
Bentfield Bury Essex 105 F9
Bentfield Green Essex 105 F10
Bentgate Gtr Man 196 E2
Benthall Northumb 264 D6
Benthall Shrops 132 C3
Bentham Glos 80 B6
Benthoul Aberdeen 293 C10
Bentilee Stoke 168 F6
Bentlass Pembs 73 E7
Bentlawnt Shrops 130 C6
Bentley E Yorks 208 F6
Bentley Essex 87 F9
Bentley Hants 49 E9
Bentley S Yorks 198 F5
Bentley Suff 108 D2
Bentley W Mid 133 D9
Bentley Warks 134 D5
Bentley Worcs 117 D9
Bentley Common Warks 134 D5
Bentley Heath Herts 86 F2
Bentley Heath W Mid 118 B3
Bentley Rise S Yorks 198 G5
Benton Devon 41 F7
Benton Green W Mid 118 B5
Bentpath Dumfries 249 E8
Bents W Loth 269 C9
Bents Head W Yorks 205 F7
Bentwichen Devon 41 G8
Bentworth Hants 49 E7
Benvie Dundee 287 D7
Benville Dorset 29 G8
Benwell T & W 242 E6
Benwick Cambs 138 E6
Beobridge Shrops 132 E5
Beoley Worcs 117 D11
Beoraidbeg Highld 295 F8
Bepton W Sus 34 D5
Berden Essex 105 F9
Bere Alston Devon 7 B8
Bere Ferrers Devon 7 C9
Bere Regis Dorset 18 C2
Berechurch Essex 107 G9
Berefold Aberds 303 F9
Berepper Corn 2 E5
Bergh Apton Norf 142 C6
Berghers Hill Bucks 66 B2
Berhill Som 44 F2
Berinsfield Oxon 83 F9
Berkeley Glos 79 F11
Berkeley Heath Glos 79 F11
Berkeley Road Glos 80 E2
Berkeley Towers E Ches 167 E11
Berkhamsted Herts 85 D7
Berkley Som 45 D10
Berkley Down Som 45 D9
Berkley Marsh Som 45 D10
Berkswell W Mid 118 B4
Bermondsey London 67 D10
Bermuda Warks 135 F7
Bernards Heath Herts 85 D11
Bernera Highld 295 C10
Berner's Cross Devon 25 F10
Berner's Hill E Sus 53 G8
Berners Roding Essex 87 D10
Bernice Argyll 276 C2
Bernisdale Highld 298 D4
Berrick Salome Oxon 83 G10
Berriedale Highld 311 G5
Berrier Cumb 230 F3
Berriew = Aberriw Powys 130 C3
Berrington Northumb 273 G10
Berrington Shrops 131 B10
Berrington Worcs 115 D11
Berrington Green Worcs 115 D11
Berriowbridge Corn 11 F11
Berrow Som 43 C10
Berrow Worcs 98 E5
Berrow Green Worcs 116 F4
Berry Swansea 56 D3
Berry Brow W Yorks 196 E6
Berry Cross Devon 25 E7
Berry Down Cross Devon 40 E5
Berry Hill Glos 79 C9
Berry Hill Pembs 91 C11
Berry Hill Stoke 168 F6
Berry Hill Worcs 117 E7
Berry Moor S Yorks 197 G9
Berry Pomeroy Devon 8 C6
Berryfield Wilts 61 G11
Berrygate Hill E Yorks 201 C8
Berryhillock Moray 302 C5
Berrylands London 67 F7
Berrynarbor Devon 40 D5
Berry's Green London 52 B2
Berrysbridge Devon 26 G6
Bersham Wrex 166 F4
Berstane Orkney 314 E4
Berth-ddu Flint 166 B2
Berthengam Flint 181 F10
Berwick E Sus 23 D8
Berwick Kent 54 F6
Berwick S Glos 60 C5
Berwick Bassett Wilts 62 E5
Berwick Hill Northumb 242 B5
Berwick Hills M'bro 225 B10
Berwick St James Wilts 46 F5
Berwick St John Wilts 30 C6
Berwick St Leonard Wilts 46 G2
Berwick-upon-Tweed Northumb 273 E9
Berwick Wharf Shrops 149 G10
Berwyn Denb 165 G11
Bescaby Leics 154 D6
Bescar Lancs 193 E11
Bescot W Mid 133 D10
Besford Shrops 149 E11
Besford Worcs 99 C8
Bessacarr S Yorks 198 G6
Bessels Green Kent 52 B4
Bessels Leigh Oxon 83 E7
Besses o' th' Barn Gtr Man 195 F10
Bessingby E Yorks 218 F3
Bessingham Norf 160 B3
Best Beech Hill E Sus 52 G6
Besthorpe Norf 141 D11
Besthorpe Notts 172 C4
Bestwood Nottingham 171 G9
Bestwood Village Notts 171 F9
Beswick E Yorks 208 D6
Beswick Gtr Man 184 B5
Betchcott Shrops 131 D8
Betchton Heath E Ches 168 C3
Betchworth Sur 51 D8
Bethania Ceredig 111 E11
Bethania Gwyn 163 E10
Bethania Gwyn 164 F2
Bethany Corn 6 D6
Bethel Anglesey 178 G5
Bethel Corn 5 E10
Bethel Gwyn 147 B9
Bethel Gwyn 163 B8
Bethelnie Aberds 303 F7
Bethersden Kent 54 E2
Bethesda Gwyn 163 B10
Bethesda Pembs 73 B9
Bethlehem Carms 94 F3
Bethnal Green London 67 C10
Betley Staffs 168 F3
Betley Common Staffs 168 F2
Betsham Kent 68 E6
Betteshanger Kent 55 C10
Bettiscombe Dorset 16 B3
Bettisfield Wrex 149 B9
Betton Shrops 130 C6
Betton Shrops 150 B3
Betton Strange Shrops 131 B10
Bettws Bridgend 58 B2
Bettws Mon 78 B3
Bettws Newport 78 G3
Bettws Cedewain Powys 130 D2
Bettws Gwerfil Goch Denb 165 F8
Bettws Ifan Ceredig 92 B6
Bettws Newydd Mon 78 D5
Bettws-y-crwyn Shrops 130 G4
Bettyhill Highld 308 C7
Betws Bridgend 57 D11
Betws Carms 75 C10
Betws Bledrws Ceredig 111 G11
Betws-Garmon Gwyn 163 D8
Betws Ifan Ceredig 92 B6
Betws-y-Coed Conwy 164 D4
Betws-yn-Rhos Conwy 180 G6
Beulah Ceredig 92 B5
Beulah Powys 113 G8
Bevendean Brighton 36 F4
Bevercotes Notts 187 G11
Bevere Worcs 116 F6
Beverley E Yorks 208 F6
Beverston Glos 80 G5
Bevington Glos 79 F11
Bewaldeth Cumb 229 E10
Bewbush W Sus 51 F8
Bewcastle Cumb 240 C3
Bewdley Worcs 116 B5
Bewerley N Yorks 214 G3
Bewholme E Yorks 209 C9
Bewley Common Wilts 62 F2
Bewlie Borders 262 D3
Bewlie Mains Borders 262 D3
Bewsey Warr 183 D9
Bexfield Norf 159 D10
Bexhill E Sus 38 F2
Bexley London 68 E3
Bexleyheath London 68 D3
Bexleyhill W Sus 34 B6
Bexon Kent 53 B11
Bexwell Norf 140 C2
Beyton Suff 125 E8
Beyton Green Suff 125 E8
Bhalasaigh W Isles 304 E3
Bhaltos W Isles 304 E2
Bhatarsaigh W Isles 297 M2
Bhlàraidh Highld 290 B5
Bibstone S Glos 79 G11
Bibury Glos 81 D10
Bicester Oxon 101 G11
Bickenhall Som 28 D3
Bickenhill W Mid 134 G3
Bicker Lincs 156 B4
Bicker Bar Lincs 156 B4
Bicker Gauntlet Lincs 156 B4
Bickershaw Gtr Man 194 G6
Bickerstaffe Lancs 194 G2
Bickerton Devon 9 G11
Bickerton E Ches 167 E8
Bickerton N Yorks 206 C5
Bickford Staffs 151 G7
Bickham Som 42 E3
Bickingcott Devon 26 B3
Bickington Devon 13 G11
Bickington Devon 40 G4
Bickleigh Devon 7 C10
Bickleigh Devon 26 F6
Bickleton Devon 40 G4
Bickley London 68 F2
Bickley W Ches 167 F8
Bickley Worcs 116 C2
Bickley Moss W Ches 167 F8
Bickley Town W Ches 167 F8
Bickleywood W Ches 167 F8
Bickmarsh Warks 100 B2
Bicknacre Essex 88 E3
Bicknoller Som 42 F6
Bicknor Kent 53 B11
Bickton Hants 31 E11
Bicton Hereford 115 E9
Bicton Pembs 72 D4
Bicton Shrops 130 G5
Bicton Shrops 149 F8
Bicton Heath Shrops 149 G9
Bidborough Kent 52 E5
Bidden Hants 49 D8
Biddenden Kent 53 F11
Biddenden Green Kent 53 E11
Biddenham Beds 103 B10
Biddestone Wilts 61 E11
Biddick T & W 243 F8
Biddick Hall T & W 243 E9
Biddisham Som 43 C11
Biddlesden Bucks 102 C2
Biddlestone Northumb 251 B11
Biddulph Staffs 168 D5
Biddulph Moor Staffs 168 D6
Bideford Devon 25 B7
Bidford-on-Avon Warks 118 G2
Bidlake Devon 12 D5
Bidston Mers 182 C3
Bidston Hill Mers 182 D3
Bidwell C Beds 103 G10
Bielby E Yorks 207 E11
Bieldside Aberdeen 293 C10
Bierley I o W 20 F6
Bierley W Yorks 205 G9
Bierton Bucks 84 B4
Big Mancot Flint 166 B4
Big Sand Highld 299 B7
Bigbury Devon 8 F3
Bigbury-on-Sea Devon 8 G3
Bigby Lincs 200 F5
Bigfrith Windsor 65 C11
Biggar Cumb 210 F3
Biggar S Lnrk 260 B2
Biggar Road N Lnrk 268 C5
Biggin Derbys 169 D11
Biggin Derbys 170 F3
Biggin N Yorks 206 F6
Biggin Thurrock 69 D7
Biggin Hill London 52 B2
Biggings Shetland 313 G3
Biggleswade C Beds 104 C3
Bighouse Highld 310 C2
Bighton Hants 48 G6
Biglands Cumb 239 G7
Bignall End Staffs 168 E4
Bignor W Sus 35 E7
Bigods Essex 106 G2
Bigram Stirl 285 G10
Bigrigg Cumb 219 C10
Bigswell Orkney 314 E3
Bigton Shetland 313 L5
Bilberry Corn 5 C10
Bilborough Nottingham 171 G8
Bilbrook Som 42 E4
Bilbrook Staffs 133 C7
Bilbrough N Yorks 206 D6
Bilbster Highld 310 D6
Bilby Notts 187 E10
Bildershaw Durham 233 G10
Bildeston Suff 107 B9
Bill Quay T & W 243 E7
Billacombe Plym 7 E10
Billacott Corn 11 C11
Billericay Essex 87 G11
Billesdon Leics 136 C4
Billesley W Mid 133 G11
Billesley Warks 118 F2
Billesley Common W Mid 133 G11
Billingborough Lincs 156 C2
Billinge Mers 194 G4
Billingford Norf 126 B3
Billingford Norf 159 E10
Billingham Stockton 234 G5
Billinghay Lincs 173 E11
Billingley S Yorks 198 G2
Billingshurst W Sus 35 B9
Billingsley Shrops 132 F4
Billington C Beds 103 G8
Billington Lancs 203 F10
Billington Staffs 151 E7
Billockby Norf 161 G8
Billy Mill T & W 243 D8
Billy Row Durham 233 D9
Bilmarsh Shrops 149 D9
Bilsborrow Lancs 202 F6
Bilsby Lincs 191 F7
Bilsby Field Lincs 191 F7
Bilsdon Devon 14 C2
Bilsham W Sus 35 G7
Bilsington Kent 54 G4
Bilson Green Glos 79 C11
Bilsthorpe Notts 171 C10
Bilsthorpe Moor Notts 171 D11
Bilston Midloth 270 C5
Bilston W Mid 133 D9
Bilstone Leics 135 B7
Bilting Kent 54 D5
Bilton E Yorks 209 G9
Bilton N Yorks 206 B2
Bilton Northumb 264 G6
Bilton Warks 119 C9
Bilton Haggs N Yorks 206 D5
Bilton in Ainsty N Yorks 206 D5
Bimbister Orkney 314 E3
Binbrook Lincs 190 C2
Binchester Blocks Durham 233 E10
Bincombe Dorset 17 E9
Bincombe Som 43 F7
Bindal Highld 311 L3
Bindon Som 27 C10
Binegar Som 44 D6
Bines Green W Sus 35 D11
Binfield Brack 65 E10
Binfield Heath Oxon 65 D8
Bingfield Northumb 241 C11
Bingham Edin 280 G6
Bingham Notts 154 B4
Bingley W Yorks 205 F8
Bings Heath Shrops 149 F10
Binham Norf 159 B9
Binley Hants 48 C2
Binley W Mid 119 B7
Binley Woods Warks 119 B7
Binnegar Dorset 18 D3
Binniehill Falk 279 G7
Binscombe Sur 50 D3
Binsey Oxon 83 D7
Binsoe N Yorks 214 D4
Binstead Hants 49 E9
Binstead I o W 21 C7
Binsted Hants 49 E9
Binsted W Sus 35 F7
Binton Warks 118 G2
Bintree Norf 159 E10
Binweston Shrops 130 C6
Birch Essex 88 B6
Birch Gtr Man 195 F11
Birch Acre Worcs 117 C11
Birch Berrow Worcs 116 E4
Birch Cross Staffs 152 C2
Birch Green Essex 88 B6
Birch Green Herts 86 C3
Birch Green Lancs 194 F3
Birch Green Worcs 99 B7
Birch Heath W Ches 167 C8
Birch Hill Brack 65 F11
Birch Hill W Ches 183 G8
Birch Vale Derbys 185 D8
Birchall Hereford 98 D3
Birchall Staffs 169 E7
Bircham Newton Norf 158 C5
Bircham Tofts Norf 158 C5
Birchan Coppice Worcs 116 C6
Birchanger Essex 105 G10
Birchburn N Ayrs 255 E10
Birchden E Sus 52 F4
Birchencliffe W Yorks 196 D6
Birchend Hereford 98 C3
Birchendale Staffs 151 B11
Bircher Hereford 115 D9
Birches Green W Mid 134 E2
Birches Head Stoke 168 F5
Birchett's Green E Sus 53 G7
Birchfield Highld 301 G9
Birchfield W Mid 133 E11
Birchgrove Cardiff 59 D7
Birchgrove E Sus 36 B6
Birchgrove Swansea 57 B8
Birchhall Corner Essex 107 E10
Birchill Devon 28 G4
Birchills W Mid 133 D10
Birchington Kent 71 F9
Birchley Heath Warks 134 E5
Birchmoor Warks 134 C5
Birchmoor Green C Beds 103 E8
Bircholt Forstal Kent 54 E5
Birchover Derbys 170 C2
Birchwood Herts 86 D2
Birchwood Lincs 172 B6
Birchwood Som 28 E2
Birchwood Warr 183 C10
Birchy Hill Hants 19 B11
Bircotes Notts 187 C10
Bird Street Suff 125 G10
Birdbrook Essex 106 C4
Birdbush Wilts 30 C6
Birdfield Argyll 275 D10
Birdforth N Yorks 215 D9
Birdham W Sus 22 D4
Birdholme Derbys 170 B5
Birdingbury Warks 119 D8
Birdlip Glos 80 C6
Birds Edge W Yorks 197 F8
Birds End Suff 124 E5
Birds Green Essex 87 D9
Birdsall N Yorks 216 F6
Birdsgreen Shrops 132 F5
Birdsmoorgate Dorset 28 G5
Birdston E Dunb 278 F3
Birdwell S Yorks 197 G10
Birdwood Glos 80 B2
Birgham Borders 263 B7
Birichen Highld 309 K7
Birkacre Lancs 194 D5
Birkby Cumb 229 D7
Birkby N Yorks 224 E6
Birkby W Yorks 196 D6
Birkdale Mers 193 D10
Birkenbog Aberds 302 C5
Birkenhead Mers 182 D4
Birkenhills Aberds 303 E7
Birkenshaw N Lnrk 268 C3
Birkenshaw S Lnrk 268 F5
Birkenshaw W Yorks 197 B8
Birkenshaw Bottoms W Yorks 197 B8
Birkenside Borders 271 G11
Birkett Mire Cumb 230 G2
Birkhall Aberds 292 D5
Birkhill Angus 287 D7
Birkhill Borders 260 F6
Birkhill Borders 271 G11
Birkholme Lincs 155 E9
Birkhouse W Yorks 197 C7
Birkin N Yorks 198 B4
Birks Cumb 222 G3
Birks W Yorks 197 B9
Birkshaw Northumb 241 D7
Birley Hereford 115 G9
Birley Carr S Yorks 186 C4
Birley Edge S Yorks 186 C4
Birleyhay Derbys 186 E5
Birling Kent 69 G7
Birling Northumb 252 B6
Birling Gap E Sus 23 F9
Birlingham Worcs 99 C8
Birmingham W Mid 133 F11
Birnam Perth 286 C4
Birniehill S Lnrk 268 E2
Birse Aberds 293 D7
Birsemore Aberds 293 D7
Birstall Leics 135 B11
Birstall W Yorks 197 B8
Birstall Smithies W Yorks 197 B8
Birstwith N Yorks 205 B10
Birthorpe Lincs 156 C2
Birtle Gtr Man 195 E10
Birtley Hereford 115 D7
Birtley Northumb 241 B9
Birtley Shrops 131 E9
Birtley T & W 243 F7
Birtley Green Sur 50 E4
Birts Street Worcs 98 D5
Birtsmorton Worcs 98 D6
Bisbrooke Rutland 137 D7
Biscathorpe Lincs 190 D2
Biscombe Som 27 E11
Biscot Luton 103 G11
Biscovey Corn 5 E11
Bish Mill Devon 26 B2
Bisham Windsor 65 C10
Bishampton Worcs 117 G9
Bishon Common Hereford 97 C8
Bishop Auckland Durham 233 F10
Bishop Burton E Yorks 208 F5
Bishop Kinkell Highld 300 D5
Bishop Middleham Durham 234 E2
Bishop Monkton N Yorks 214 F6
Bishop Norton Lincs 189 C7
Bishop Sutton Bath 44 B5
Bishop Thornton N Yorks 214 G5
Bishop Wilton E Yorks 207 B11
Bishopbridge Lincs 189 C8
Bishopbriggs E Dunb 278 G2
Bishopdown Wilts 47 G7
Bishopmill Moray 302 C2
Bishops Cannings Wilts 62 G4
Bishop's Castle Shrops 130 F6
Bishop's Caundle Dorset 29 E11
Bishop's Cleeve Glos 99 F9
Bishop's Down Dorset 29 E11
Bishops Frome Hereford 98 B3
Bishops Green Essex 87 B10
Bishop's Green W Berks 64 G4
Bishop's Hull Som 28 C2
Bishop's Itchington Warks 119 F7
Bishops Lydeard Som 27 B11
Bishops Norton Glos 98 G6
Bishops Nympton Devon 26 C3
Bishop's Offley Staffs 150 D5
Bishop's Quay Corn 2 D6
Bishop's Stortford Herts 105 G9
Bishop's Sutton Hants 48 G6
Bishop's Tachbrook Warks 118 E6
Bishops Tawton Devon 40 G5
Bishop's Waltham Hants 33 D9
Bishops Wood Staffs 132 B6
Bishopsbourne Kent 55 C7
Bishopsgarth Stockton 234 G4
Bishopsgate Sur 66 E3
Bishopsteignton Devon 14 G4
Bishopstoke Hants 33 D7
Bishopston Bristol 60 D5
Bishopston Swansea 56 D5
Bishopstone Bucks 84 C4
Bishopstone E Sus 23 E7
Bishopstone Hereford 97 C8
Bishopstone Kent 71 F8
Bishopstone Swindon 63 C8
Bishopstone Wilts 31 B9
Bishopstrow Wilts 45 E11
Bishopswood Som 28 E3
Bishopsworth Bristol 60 F5
Bishopthorpe York 207 D7
Bishopton Darl 234 G3
Bishopton Dumfries 236 E6
Bishopton N Yorks 214 E6
Bishopton Renfs 277 G8
Bishopton Warks 118 F3
Bishopwearmouth T & W 243 F9
Bishpool Newport 59 B10
Bishton Newport 59 B11
Bishton Staffs 151 E10
Bisley Glos 80 D6
Bisley Sur 50 B3
Bisley Camp Sur 50 B2
Bispham Blkpool 202 E2
Bispham Green Lancs 194 E3
Bissoe Corn 4 G5
Bissom Corn 3 C7
Bisterne Hants 31 G10
Bisterne Close Hants 32 G2
Bitchet Green Kent 52 C5
Bitchfield Lincs 155 D9
Bittadon Devon 40 E4
Bittaford Devon 8 D3
Bittering Norf 159 F8
Bitterley Shrops 115 B11
Bitterne Soton 33 E7
Bitterne Park Soton 32 E6
Bitterscote Staffs 134 C4
Bitteswell Leics 135 F10
Bittles Green Dorset 30 C5
Bitton S Glos 61 F7
Bix Oxon 65 B8
Bixter Shetland 313 H5
Blaby Leics 135 D11
Black Bank Cambs 139 F10
Black Bank Warks 135 F7
Black Banks Darl 224 C5
Black Barn Lincs 157 D8
Black Bourton Oxon 82 E3
Black Callerton T & W 242 D5
Black Carr Norf 141 D11
Black Clauchrie S Ayrs 245 G7
Black Corner W Sus 51 F9
Black Corries Lodge Highld 284 B6
Black Crofts Argyll 289 F11
Black Cross Corn 5 C8
Black Dam Hants 48 C6
Black Dog Devon 26 F4
Black Heddon Northumb 242 B3
Black Hill W Yorks 204 E6
Black Horse Drove Cambs 139 E11
Black Lake W Mid 133 E9
Black Lane Gtr Man 195 F9
Black Marsh Shrops 130 D6
Black Moor Lancs 194 E3
Black Moor W Yorks 205 F11
Black Mount Argyll 284 C6
Black Notley Essex 106 G5
Black Park Wrex 166 G4
Black Pill Swansea 56 C6
Black Pole Lancs 202 F5
Black Rock Brighton 36 G4
Black Rock Corn 2 C5
Black Street Suff 143 F10
Black Tar Pembs 73 D7
Black Torrington Devon 25 F7
Black Vein Caerph 78 G2
Blackacre Dumfries 248 E2
Blackadder West Borders 272 E6
Blackawton Devon 8 E6
Blackbeck Cumb 219 D10
Blackborough Devon 27 F9
Blackborough Norf 158 G3
Blackborough End Norf 158 G3
Blackboys E Sus 37 C8
Blackbraes Aberds 293 B10
Blackbrook Derbys 170 F4
Blackbrook Derbys 185 E9
Blackbrook Mers 183 B8
Blackbrook Staffs 150 B5
Blackbrook Sur 51 D7
Blackburn Aberds 293 B10
Blackburn Aberds 302 F5
Blackburn Blkburn 195 B7
Blackburn S Yorks 186 C5
Blackburn W Loth 269 B9
Blackcastle Midloth 271 D8
Blackchambers Aberds 293 B9
Blackcraig Dumfries 246 G6
Blackcraigs Angus 293 E7
Blackden Heath E Ches 184 G3
Blackditch Oxon 82 D6
Blackdog Aberds 293 B11
Blackdown Dorset 28 G5
Blackdown Hants 33 C8
Blackdown Warks 118 D6
Blackdyke Cumb 238 G4
Blackdykes E Loth 281 E11
Blacker Hill S Yorks 197 G11
Blacketts Kent 70 F2
Blackfell T & W 243 F7
Blackfen London 68 E3
Blackfield Hants 32 G6
Blackford Cumb 239 E9
Blackford Dumfries 248 G4
Blackford Perth 286 G2
Blackford Shrops 131 G11
Blackford Som 29 B11
Blackford Som 42 D2
Blackford Som 44 D2
Blackford Bridge Gtr Man 195 F10

320 Bla – Bow

Blackfordby Leics 152 F6
Blackfords Staffs 151 G9
Blackgang I o W 20 F5
Blackgate Angus 287 B8
Blackhall Aberds 293 D8
Blackhall Edin 280 G4
Blackhall Renfs 267 C9
Blackhall Colliery Durham 234 D5
Blackhall Mill T & W 242 F4
Blackhall Rocks Durham 234 D5
Blackham E Sus 52 F3
Blackhaugh Borders 261 B10
Blackheath Essex 107 G10
Blackheath London 67 D11
Blackheath Suff 127 C8
Blackheath Sur 50 D4
Blackheath W Mid 133 F9
Blackheath Park London 68 D2
Blackhill Aberds 303 D10
Blackhill Aberds 303 E10
Blackhill Aberds 303 F10
Blackhill Durham 242 G3
Blackhill Hants 32 D4
Blackhill Highld 298 D3
Blackhillock Moray 302 E4
Blackhills Highld 301 D9
Blackhills Moray 302 D2
Blackhills Swansea 56 C5
Blackhorse Devon 14 C5
Blackhorse S Glos 61 D7
Blackird Leys Oxon 83 E9
Blackjack Lincs 156 B5
Blackland Wilts 62 F4
Blacklands E Sus 38 E4
Blacklands Hereford 98 C2
Blacklaw Aberds 302 D6
Blackleach Lancs 202 G5
Blackley Gtr Man 195 G11
Blackley W Yorks 196 D6
Blacklunans Perth 292 G3
Blackmarstone Hereford 97 D10
Blackmill Bridgend 58 B2
Blackminster Worcs 99 C11
Blackmoor Bath 60 G5
Blackmoor Gtr Man 195 G7
Blackmoor Hants 49 G9
Blackmoor N Som 60 G3
Blackmoor Som 27 D11
Blackmoor Gate Devon 41 E7
Blackmoorfoot W Yorks 196 E5
Blackmore Essex 87 E10
Blackmore Shrops 130 B6
Blackmore End Essex 106 E4
Blackmore End Herts 85 B11
Blackmore End Worcs 98 C6
Blackness Aberds 293 D8
Blackness E Sus 52 G4
Blackness Falk 279 F11
Blacknest Hants 49 E9
Blacknest Windsor 66 F3
Blacknoll Dorset 18 D2
Blacko Lancs 204 E3
Blackoe Shrops 149 B10
Blackpark Dumfries 236 C5
Blackpole Worcs 117 F7
Blackpool Blkpool 202 F2
Blackpool Devon 7 E11
Blackpool Devon 9 F7
Blackpool Devon 14 G2
Blackpool Pembs 73 C9
Blackpool Gate Cumb 240 B2
Blackridge W Loth 269 B7
Blackrock Argyll 274 G4
Blackrock Bath 60 F6
Blackrock Mon 78 C2
Blackrod Gtr Man 194 E6
Blackshaw Dumfries 238 D2
Blackshaw Head W Yorks 196 B3
Blackshaw Moor Staffs 169 D8
Blacksmith's Corner Suff 108 C2
Blacksmith's Green Suff 126 D2
Blacksnape Blkburn 195 C8
Blackstone W Sus 36 D2
Blackstone Worcs 116 C5
Blackthorn Oxon 83 B10
Blackthorpe Suff 125 E8
Blacktoft E Yorks 199 C10
Blacktop Aberdeen 293 C10
Blacktown Newport 59 C9
Blackwall Derbys 170 F3
Blackwall London 67 C11
Blackwall Tunnel London 67 C11
Blackwater Corn 4 F4
Blackwater Dorset 19 B8
Blackwater Hants 49 B11
Blackwater I o W 20 D6
Blackwater Norf 159 E11
Blackwater Som 28 D3
Blackwater Lodge Moray 302 G3
Blackwaterfoot N Ayrs 255 E9
Blackweir Cardiff 59 D7
Blackwell Cumb 239 G10
Blackwell Darl 224 C5
Blackwell Derbys 170 D6
Blackwell Derbys 185 G10
Blackwell Devon 27 B8
Blackwell W Sus 51 F11
Blackwell Warks 100 C4
Blackwell Worcs 117 C9
Blackwood Caerph 77 F11
Blackwood S Lnrk 268 G5
Blackwood Warr 183 C10
Blackwood Hill Staffs 168 D6
Blacon W Ches 166 B5
Bladbean Kent 55 D7
Blades N Yorks 223 F9
Bladnoch Dumfries 236 D6
Bladon Oxon 82 C6
Blaen-Cil-Llech Ceredig 92 C6
Blaen Clydach Rhondda 77 G7
Blaen-gwynfi Neath 57 B11
Blaen-pant Ceredig 92 C5
Blaen-waun Carms 92 F4
Blaen-waun Ceredig 111 G7
Blaen-y-coed Carms 92 F6
Blaen-y-cwm Bl Gwent 77 C10
Blaen-y-Cwm Denb 147 C10
Blaen-y-cwm Gwyn 146 E4
Blaen-y-cwm Powys 147 E11
Blaenannerch Ceredig 92 B4
Blaenau Carms 75 C10
Blaenau Flint 166 D2
Blaenau Dolwyddelan Conwy 164 E2
Blaenau Ffestiniog Gwyn 164 F2
Blaenau-Gwent Bl Gwent 78 E2
Blaenavon Torf 78 D3
Blaenbedw Fawr Ceredig 111 G7
Blaencaerau Bridgend 57 C11
Blaencelyn Ceredig 111 G7
Blaencwm Rhondda 76 F6
Blaendulais = Seven Sisters Neath 76 D4
Blaendyryn Powys 95 D8
Blaenffos Pembs 92 D3
Blaengarw Bridgend 76 G6
Blaengwrach Neath 76 D5
Blaengwynfi Neath 57 B11
Blaenllechau Rhondda 77 F8
Blaenpennal Ceredig 112 E2
Blaenplwyf Ceredig 111 B11
Blaenporth Ceredig 92 B5
Blaenrhondda Rhondda 76 E6
Blaenwaun Carms 92 F4
Blaenycwm Ceredig 112 B6
Blagdon N Som 44 B4
Blagdon Torbay 9 C7
Blagdon Hill Som 28 D2
Blagill Cumb 231 B10
Blaguegate Lancs 194 F3
Blaich Highld 290 F2
Blain Highld 289 C8
Blaina Bl Gwent 78 D2
Blainacraig Ho Aberds 293 D7
Blair Fife 280 C6
Blair Atholl Perth 291 G10
Blair Drummond Stirl 278 B4
Blairbeg N Ayrs 256 C2
Blairburn Fife 279 D9
Blairdaff Aberds 293 B8
Blairdryne Aberds 293 D9
Blairglas Argyll 276 D6
Blairgorm Highld 301 G10
Blairgowrie Perth 286 C5
Blairhall Fife 279 D10
Blairhill N Lnrk 268 B4
Blairingone Perth 279 B9
Blairland N Ayrs 266 F6
Blairlinn N Lnrk 278 G5
Blairlogie Stirl 278 B6
Blairlomond Argyll 276 B3
Blairmore Argyll 276 E3
Blairmore Highld 306 D6
Blairnamarrow Moray 292 B4
Blairquhosh Stirl 277 E10
Blair's Ferry Argyll 275 G10
Blairskaith E Dunb 277 F11
Blaisdon Glos 80 B2
Blaise Hamlet Bristol 60 D5
Blake End Essex 106 G4
Blakebrook Worcs 116 B6
Blakedown Worcs 117 B7
Blakelands M Keynes 103 C7
Blakelaw Borders 263 C7
Blakelaw T & W 242 D6
Blakeley Staffs 133 E7
Blakeley Lane Staffs 169 F7
Blakelow E Ches 167 E11
Blakemere Hereford 97 C7
Blakenall Heath W Mid 133 C10
Blakeney Glos 79 D11
Blakeney Norf 177 E8
Blakenhall E Ches 168 F2
Blakenhall W Mid 133 D8
Blakeshall Worcs 132 G6
Blakesley Northants 120 G2
Blanchland Northumb 241 G11
Bland Hill N Yorks 205 C10
Blandford Camp Dorset 30 F6
Blandford Forum Dorset 30 F5
Blandford St Mary Dorset 30 F5
Blandy Highld 308 D6
Blanefield Stirl 277 F11
Blanerne Borders 272 D6
Blank Bank Staffs 168 F4
Blankney Lincs 173 C9
Blantyre S Lnrk 268 D3
Blar a'Chaorainn Highld 290 G3
Blaran Argyll 275 B9
Blarghour Argyll 275 B10
Blarmachfoldach Highld 290 G2
Blarnalearoch Highld 307 K6
Blasford Hill Essex 88 C2
Blashford Hants 31 F11
Blaston Leics 136 D6
Blatchbridge Som 45 D9
Blatherwycke Northants 137 D9
Blawith Cumb 210 B5
Blaxhall Suff 127 F7
Blaxton S Yorks 199 G7
Blaydon T & W 242 E5
Blaydon Burn T & W 242 E5
Blaydon Haughs T & W 242 E5
Bleach Green Cumb 219 B9
Bleach Green Suff 126 B4
Bleadney Som 44 D3
Bleadon N Som 43 B10
Bleak Acre Hereford 98 B2
Bleak Hall M Keynes 103 D7
Bleak Hey Nook Gtr Man 196 F4
Bleak Hill Hants 31 E10
Blean Kent 70 G6
Bleasby Lincs 189 E10
Bleasby Notts 172 F2
Bleasby Moor Lincs 189 E10
Bleasdale Lancs 203 D7
Bleatarn Cumb 222 C4
Blebocraigs Fife 287 F8
Bleddfa Powys 114 D4
Bledington Glos 100 G4
Bledlow Bucks 84 E3
Bledlow Ridge Bucks 84 F3
Bleet Wilts 45 B11
Blegbie E Loth 271 C9
Blegbury Devon 24 B2
Blencarn Cumb 231 E8
Blencogo Cumb 229 B9
Blendworth Hants 34 E2
Blenheim Oxon 83 D9
Blenheim Oxon 83 E9
Blenheim Park Norf 158 C6
Blenkinsopp Hall Northumb 240 E5
Blennerhasset Cumb 229 C9
Blervie Castle Moray 301 D10
Bletchingdon Oxon 83 B8
Bletchingley Sur 51 C10
Bletchley M Keynes 103 E7
Bletchley Shrops 150 C2
Bletherston Pembs 91 G11
Bletsoe Beds 121 F10
Blewbury Oxon 64 B4
Bliby Kent 54 F4
Blickling Norf 160 D3
Blidworth Notts 171 D9
Blidworth Bottoms Notts 171 E9
Blidworth Dale Notts 171 E9
Blindburn Northumb 263 G8
Blindcrake Cumb 229 E8
Blindley Heath Sur 51 D11
Blindmoor Som 28 E3
Blingery Highld 310 E7
Blisland Corn 11 G8
Bliss Gate Worcs 116 C4
Blissford Hants 31 E11
Blisworth Northants 120 G4
Blithbury Staffs 151 E11
Blitterlees Cumb 238 G4
Blo' Norton Norf 125 B10
Blockley Glos 100 D3
Blofield Norf 142 B6
Blofield Heath Norf 160 G6
Bloodman's Corner Suff 143 D10
Bloomfield Bath 45 B7
Bloomfield Bath 61 G8
Bloomfield Borders 262 E3
Bloomfield W Mid 133 E9
Bloomsbury London 67 C10
Blore Staffs 150 C4
Blore Staffs 169 F10
Bloreheath Staffs 150 B4
Blossomfield W Mid 118 B2
Blount's Green Staffs 151 C11
Blowick Mers 193 D11
Blowinghouse Corn 4 E4
Bloxham Oxon 101 D8
Bloxholm Lincs 173 E9
Bloxwich W Mid 133 C9
Bloxworth Dorset 18 C3
Blubberhouses N Yorks 205 B9
Blue Anchor Corn 5 D8
Blue Anchor Som 42 E4
Blue Anchor Swansea 56 B4
Blue Bell Hill Kent 69 G8
Blue Hill Herts 104 G5
Blue Row Essex 89 C8
Blue Town Kent 70 D2
Blue Vein Wilts 61 F10
Bluebell Telford 149 G11
Bluecairn Borders 271 G10
Bluetown Kent 54 B2
Bluewater Kent 68 E5
Blughasary Highld 307 J6
Blundellsands Mers 182 B4
Blundeston Suff 143 D10
Blundies Staffs 132 F6
Blunham C Beds 122 G3
Blunsdon St Andrew Swindon 62 B6
Bluntington Worcs 117 C7
Bluntisham Cambs 123 C7
Blunts Corn 6 C6
Blunt's Green Warks 118 D2
Blurton Stoke 168 G5
Blyborough Lincs 188 C6
Blyford Suff 127 B8
Blymhill Staffs 150 G6
Blymhill Lawns Staffs 150 G6
Blyth Borders 270 F2
Blyth Northumb 253 G8
Blyth Notts 187 D10
Blyth Bridge Borders 270 F2
Blyth End Warks 134 E4
Blythburgh Suff 127 B9
Blythe Borders 271 F11
Blythe Bridge Staffs 169 G7
Blythe Marsh Staffs 169 G7
Blythswood Renfs 267 B10
Blyton Lincs 188 C5
Boarhills Fife 287 F9
Boarhunt Hants 33 F10
Boars Hill Oxon 83 E7
Boarsgreave Lancs 195 C10
Boarshead E Sus 52 G4
Boarstall Bucks 83 C10
Boasley Cross Devon 12 C5
Boat of Garten Highld 291 B11
Boath Highld 300 B5
Bobbing Kent 69 F11
Bobbington Staffs 132 E6
Bobbingworth Essex 87 D8
Bobby Hill Suff 125 C10
Boblainy Highld 300 F4
Bocaddon Corn 6 D3
Bochastle Stirl 285 G10
Bockhanger Kent 54 E4
Bocking Essex 106 G5
Bocking Churchstreet Essex 106 F5
Bocking's Elm Essex 89 B11
Bockleton Worcs 115 E11
Bockmer End Bucks 65 B10
Bocombe Devon 24 C5
Bodantionail Highld 299 B7
Boddam Aberds 303 E11
Boddam Shetland 313 M5
Bodden Som 44 E6
Boddington Glos 99 F7
Bodedern Anglesey 178 E4
Bodellick Corn 10 G5
Bodelva Corn 5 E11
Bodelwyddan Denb 181 F8
Bodenham Hereford 115 G10
Bodenham Wilts 31 B11
Bodenham Bank Hereford 98 E2
Bodenham Moor Hereford 115 G10
Bodermid Gwyn 144 D3
Bodewryd Anglesey 178 C5
Bodfari Denb 181 G9
Bodffordd Anglesey 178 F6
Bodham Norf 177 E10
Bodiam E Sus 38 B3
Bodicote Oxon 101 D9
Bodiechell Aberds 303 E7
Bodieve Corn 10 G5
Bodiggo Corn 5 D10
Bodilly Corn 2 C5
Bodinnick Corn 6 E2
Bodle Street Green E Sus 23 C11
Bodley Devon 41 D7
Bodmin Corn 5 B11
Bodmiscombe Devon 27 F10
Bodney Norf 140 D6
Bodorgan Anglesey 162 B5
Bodsham Kent 54 D6
Boduan Gwyn 144 B6
Boduel Corn 6 C4
Bodwen Corn 5 C10
Bodymoor Heath Warks 134 D4
Bofarnel Corn 6 C2
Bogallan Highld 300 D6
Bogbrae Aberds 303 F10
Bogend Borders 272 F5
Bogend Notts 171 F7
Bogend S Ayrs 257 C9
Bogentory Aberds 293 C9
Boghall Midloth 270 B4
Boghall W Loth 269 B9
Boghead Aberds 293 D8
Boghead S Lnrk 268 G5
Bogmoor Moray 302 C3
Bogniebrae Aberds 302 E5
Bogniebrae Aberds 302 E6
Bognor Regis W Sus 22 D6
Bograxie Aberds 293 B9
Bogs Aberds 302 G5
Bogs Bank Borders 270 E3
Bogside N Lnrk 268 E6
Bogthorn W Yorks 204 F6
Bogton Aberds 302 D6
Bogtown Aberds 302 C5
Bogue Dumfries 246 G4
Bohemia E Sus 38 E4
Bohemia Wilts 32 D2
Bohenie Highld 290 E4
Bohetherick Corn 7 B8
Bohortha Corn 3 C9
Bohuntine Highld 290 E4
Bohuntinville Highld 290 E4
Boirseam W Isles 296 C6
Bojewyan Corn 1 C3
Bokiddick Corn 5 C11
Bolahaul Fm Carms 74 B6
Bolam Durham 233 G9
Bolam Northumb 252 G3
Bolam West Houses Northumb 252 G3
Bolas Heath Telford 150 E3
Bolberry Devon 9 G8
Bold Heath Mers 183 D8
Boldmere W Mid 134 E2
Boldon T & W 243 E9
Boldon Colliery T & W 243 E8
Boldre Hants 20 B2
Boldron Durham 223 C10
Bole Notts 188 D3
Bole Hill Derbys 186 G4
Bolehall Staffs 134 C4
Bolehill Derbys 170 E3
Bolehill Derbys 186 G6
Bolehill S Yorks 186 E5
Bolenowe Corn 2 B5
Boleside Borders 261 C11
Boley Park Staffs 134 B2
Bolham Devon 27 E7
Bolham Notts 188 E2
Bolham Water Devon 27 E11
Bolholt Gtr Man 195 E9
Bolingey Corn 4 E5
Bolitho Corn 2 C5
Bollihope Durham 232 E6
Bollington E Ches 184 F6
Bollington Cross E Ches 184 F6
Bolney W Sus 36 C3
Bolnhurst Beds 121 F11
Bolnore W Sus 36 C4
Bolshan Angus 287 B10
Bolsover Derbys 187 G7
Bolsterstone S Yorks 186 B3
Bolstone Hereford 97 E11
Boltby N Yorks 215 B9
Bolter End Bucks 84 G3
Bolton Cumb 231 G8
Bolton E Loth 281 G10
Bolton E Yorks 207 C11
Bolton Gtr Man 195 F8
Bolton Northumb 264 G4
Bolton W Yorks 205 F9
Bolton Abbey N Yorks 205 C7
Bolton Bridge N Yorks 205 C7
Bolton-by-Bowland Lancs 203 D11
Bolton Green Lancs 194 D5
Bolton Houses Lancs 202 G4
Bolton-le-Sands Lancs 211 F9
Bolton Low Houses Cumb 229 C10
Bolton New Houses Cumb 229 C10
Bolton-on-Swale N Yorks 224 F5
Bolton Percy N Yorks 206 E6
Bolton Town End Lancs 211 F9
Bolton upon Dearne S Yorks 198 G3
Bolton Wood Lane Cumb 229 C11
Bolton Woods W Yorks 205 F9
Boltonfellend Cumb 239 D11
Boltongate Cumb 229 C10
Boltshope Park Durham 232 B4
Bolventor Corn 11 F9
Bomarsund Northumb 253 G7
Bombie Dumfries 237 D9
Bomby Cumb 221 B10
Bomere Heath Shrops 149 F9
Bon-y-maen Swansea 57 B7
Bonaly Edin 270 B4
Bonar Bridge Highld 309 K6
Bonawe Argyll 284 D4
Bonby N Lincs 200 D4
Boncath Pembs 92 D4
Bonchester Bridge Borders 262 G3
Bonchurch I o W 21 F7
Bond End Staffs 152 F2
Bondend Glos 80 B5
Bondleigh Devon 25 G11
Bondman Hays Leics 135 B9
Bonds Lancs 202 E5
Bondstones Devon 25 F9
Bonehill Devon 13 F10
Bonehill Staffs 134 C3
Bo'ness Falk 279 E9
Bonhill W Dunb 277 F7
Boningale Shrops 132 C6
Bonjedward Borders 262 E5
Bonkle N Lnrk 268 D6
Bonnavoulin Highld 289 D7
Bonning Gate Cumb 221 F9
Bonnington Borders 261 B7
Bonnington Edin 270 B2
Bonnington Kent 54 F5
Bonnybank Fife 287 G7
Bonnybridge Falk 278 E6
Bonnykelly Aberds 303 D8
Bonnyrigg and Lasswade Midloth 270 B6
Bonnyton Aberds 302 F6
Bonnyton Angus 287 B10
Bonnyton Angus 287 D7
Bonnyton E Ayrs 257 B10
Bonsall Derbys 170 D3
Bonskeid House Perth 291 G10
Bonson Som 43 E8
Bont Mon 78 B5
Bont-Dolgadfan Powys 129 C7
Bont Fawr Carms 94 F4
Bont goch = Elerch Ceredig 128 F3
Bont-newydd Conwy 181 G8
Bont Newydd Gwyn 146 E5
Bont Newydd Gwyn 164 G2
Bontddu Gwyn 146 F3
Bonthorpe Lincs 191 G7
Bontnewydd Ceredig 112 D2
Bontnewydd Gwyn 163 D7
Bontuchel Denb 165 D9
Bonvilston = Tresimwn V Glam 58 E5
Boode Devon 40 F4
Booker Bucks 84 G4
Bookham Dorset 30 G2
Booleybank Shrops 149 D11
Boon Borders 271 F11
Boon Hill Staffs 168 E4
Boorley Green Hants 33 E8
Boosbeck Redcar 226 B3
Boose's Green Essex 106 E6
Boot Cumb 220 E3
Boot Street Suff 108 B4
Booth Staffs 151 D10
Booth W Yorks 196 B4
Booth Bank E Ches 184 D2
Booth Bridge Lancs 204 D4
Booth Green E Ches 184 E6
Booth Wood W Yorks 196 D4
Boothby Graffoe Lincs 173 D7
Boothby Pagnell Lincs 155 C9
Boothen Stoke 168 G5
Boothferry E Yorks 199 B8
Boothgate Derbys 170 F5
Boothroyd W Yorks 197 C8
Boothsdale W Ches 167 B8
Boothstown Gtr Man 195 G8
Boothtown W Yorks 196 B5
Boothville Northants 120 E5
Bootle Cumb 210 B2
Bootle Mers 182 B4
Booton Norf 160 E2
Boots Green W Ches 184 G3
Booze N Yorks 223 E10
Boquhan Stirl 277 D10
Boquio Corn 2 C5
Boraston Shrops 116 D2
Boraston Dale Shrops 116 C2
Borden Kent 69 G11
Borden W Sus 34 C4
Border Cumb 238 G5
Bordesley W Mid 133 F11
Bordesley Green W Mid 134 F2
Bordlands Borders 270 F3
Bordley N Yorks 213 G8
Bordon Hants 49 F10
Bordon Camp Hants 49 F9
Boreham Essex 88 D3
Boreham Wilts 45 E11
Boreham Street E Sus 23 C11
Borehamwood Herts 85 F11
Boreland Dumfries 236 C5
Boreland Dumfries 248 E5
Boreland Fife 280 C6
Boreland Stirl 285 D9
Boreland of Southwick Dumfries 237 C11
Boreley Worcs 116 D6
Borestone Stirl 278 C5
Borgh W Isles 296 C5
Borgh W Isles 297 L2
Borghasdal W Isles 296 C6
Borghastan W Isles 304 D4
Borgie Highld 308 D6
Borgue Dumfries 237 E8
Borgue Highld 311 G5
Borley Essex 106 C6
Borley Green Essex 106 C6
Borley Green Suff 125 E9
Bornais W Isles 297 J3
Bornesketaig Highld 298 B3
Borness Dumfries 237 E8
Borough Scilly 1 G3
Borough Green Kent 52 B6
Borough Marsh Wokingham 65 D9
Borough Park Staffs 134 B4
Borough Post Som 28 C4
Boroughbridge N Yorks 215 F7
Borras Wrex 166 E4
Borras Head Wrex 166 E5
Borreraig Highld 296 F7
Borrobol Lodge Highld 311 G2
Borrodale Highld 297 G7
Borrohill Aberds 303 D9
Borrowash Derbys 153 C8
Borrowby N Yorks 215 B8
Borrowby N Yorks 226 B5
Borrowdale Cumb 220 C5
Borrowfield Aberds 293 D10
Borrowston Highld 310 E7
Borrowstoun Mains Falk 279 E9
Borstal Medway 69 F8
Borth = Y Borth Ceredig 128 E2
Borth-y-Gest Gwyn 145 B11
Borthwick Midloth 271 D7
Borthwickbrae Borders 261 G10
Borthwickshiels Borders 261 F10
Borve Highld 298 E4
Borve Lodge W Isles 305 J2
Borwick Lancs 211 E10
Borwick Rails Cumb 210 D3
Bosavern Corn 1 C3
Bosbury Hereford 98 C3
Boscadjack Corn 2 C5
Boscastle Corn 11 C8
Boscean Corn 1 C3
Boscombe Bmouth 19 C8
Boscombe Wilts 47 F8
Boscomoor Staffs 151 G8
Boscoppa Corn 5 E10
Boscreege Corn 2 C3
Bosham W Sus 22 C4
Bosham Hoe W Sus 22 C4
Bosherston Pembs 73 G7
Boskednan Corn 1 C4
Boskenna Corn 1 E4
Bosleake Corn 4 G3
Bosley E Ches 168 B6
Boslowick Corn 3 C7
Boslymon Corn 5 C11
Bosoughan Corn 5 C7
Bosporthennis Corn 1 B4
Bossall N Yorks 216 G4
Bossiney Corn 11 D7
Bossingham Kent 54 D6
Bossington Hants 47 G10
Bossington Kent 55 B8
Bossington Som 41 D11
Bostadh W Isles 304 D3
Bostock Green W Ches 167 B11
Boston Lincs 174 G4
Boston Long Hedges Lincs 174 F5
Boston Spa W Yorks 206 D4
Boston West Lincs 174 F3
Boswednack Corn 1 B4
Boswin Corn 2 C5
Boswinger Corn 5 G9
Boswyn Corn 2 B5
Botallack Corn 1 C3
Botany Bay London 86 F3
Botany Bay Mon 79 E8
Botcherby Cumb 239 F10
Botcheston Leics 135 B9
Botesdale Suff 125 B10
Bothal Northumb 252 F6
Bothampstead W Berks 64 D4
Bothamsall Notts 187 G11
Bothel Cumb 229 D9
Bothenhampton Dorset 16 C5
Bothwell S Lnrk 268 D4
Bothy Highld 290 F4
Botley Bucks 85 E7
Botley Hants 33 E8
Botley Oxon 83 D7
Botloe's Green Glos 98 F4
Botolph Claydon Bucks 102 G4
Botolphs W Sus 35 F11
Bottacks Highld 300 C4
Botternell Corn 11 G11
Bottesford Leics 154 B6
Bottesford N Lincs 199 F11
Bottisham Cambs 123 E10
Bottlesford Wilts 46 B6
Bottom Boat W Yorks 197 C11
Bottom House Staffs 169 E8
Bottom o' th' Moor Gtr Man 195 E7
Bottom of Hutton Lancs 194 B3
Bottom Pond Kent 53 B11
Bottomcraig Fife 287 E7
Bottomley W Yorks 196 D5
Bottoms Corn 1 E3
Bottreaux Mill Devon 26 B4
Bottrells Close Bucks 85 G7
Botts Green Warks 134 E4
Botusfleming Corn 7 C8
Botwnnog Gwyn 144 C5
Bough Beech Kent 52 D3
Boughrood Powys 96 D2
Boughrood Brest Powys 96 D2
Boughspring Glos 79 F9
Boughton Lincs 173 F10
Boughton Norf 140 C3
Boughton Northants 120 D5
Boughton Notts 171 B11
Boughton W Ches 166 B6
Boughton Aluph Kent 54 D4
Boughton Corner Kent 54 D4
Boughton Green Kent 53 C9
Boughton Heath W Ches 166 B6
Boughton Lees Kent 54 D4
Boughton Malherbe Kent 53 D11
Boughton Monchelsea Kent 53 C9
Boughton Street Kent 54 B5
Bougton End C Beds 103 D9
Boulby Redcar 226 B5
Bould Oxon 100 G4
Boulden Shrops 131 F10
Boulder Clough W Yorks 196 C4
Bouldnor I o W 20 D3
Bouldon Shrops 131 F10
Boulmer Northumb 265 G7
Boulsdon Glos 98 G4
Boulston Pembs 73 C7
Boultenstone Aberds 292 B6
Boultham Lincs 173 B7
Boultham Moor Lincs 173 B7
Boulton Derbys 153 C7
Boulton Moor Derbys 153 C7
Boundary Leics 152 F6
Boundary Staffs 169 G7
Boundstone Sur 49 E10
Bountis Thorne Devon 24 D5
Bourn Cambs 122 F6
Bournbrook W Mid 133 G10
Bourne Lincs 155 E11
Bourne N Som 44 B3
Bourne End Beds 121 E10
Bourne End Bucks 65 B11
Bourne End C Beds 103 C9
Bourne End Herts 85 D8
Bourne Vale W Mid 133 D11
Bourne Valley Poole 19 C7
Bournemouth Bmouth 19 C7
Bournes Green Glos 80 E6
Bournes Green Sthend 70 B2
Bournes Green Worcs 117 C8
Bournheath Worcs 117 C9
Bournmoor Durham 243 G8
Bournside Glos 99 G8
Bournstream Glos 80 G2
Bournville W Mid 133 G10
Bourton Bucks 102 E4
Bourton Dorset 45 G9
Bourton N Som 59 G11
Bourton Oxon 63 B8
Bourton Shrops 131 D11
Bourton Wilts 62 G4
Bourton on Dunsmore Warks 119 C8
Bourton-on-the-Hill Glos 100 E3
Bourton-on-the-Water Glos 100 G3
Bourtreehill N Ayrs 257 B8
Bousd Argyll 288 C4
Bousta Shetland 313 H4
Boustead Hill Cumb 239 F7
Bouth Cumb 210 B6
Bouthwaite N Yorks 214 E2
Bouts Worcs 117 F10
Bovain Stirl 285 D9
Boveney Bucks 66 D2
Boveridge Dorset 31 E9
Boverton V Glam 58 F3
Bovey Tracey Devon 14 F2
Bovingdon Herts 85 E8
Bovingdon Green Bucks 65 B10
Bovingdon Green Herts 85 E8
Bovinger Essex 87 D8
Bovington Camp Dorset 18 D2
Bow Borders 271 G9
Bow Devon 8 D6
Bow Devon 26 G2
Bow Orkney 314 G3
Bow Oxon 82 G4
Bow Brickhill M Keynes 103 E8
Bow Broom S Yorks 187 B7
Bow Common London 67 C11
Bow of Fife Fife 287 F7
Bow Street Ceredig 128 G2
Bow Street Norf 141 D10
Bowbank Durham 232 G4
Bowbeck Suff 125 B8
Bowbridge Glos 80 E5
Bowbrook Shrops 149 G9
Bowburn Durham 234 D2
Bowcombe I o W 20 D5
Bowd Devon 15 C8
Bowden Borders 262 C3
Bowden Devon 8 F6
Bowden Dorset 30 C3
Bowden Hill Wilts 62 F2
Bowdens Som 28 B6
Bowderdale Cumb 222 E3
Bowdon Gtr Man 184 D3
Bower Highld 310 C6
Bower Northumb 251 G7
Bower Ashton Bristol 60 E5
Bower Heath Herts 85 B10
Bower Hinton Som 29 D7
Bower House Tye Suff 107 C9
Bowerchalke Wilts 31 C8
Bowerhill Wilts 62 G2
Bowerhope Borders 261 E7
Bowermadden Highld 310 C6
Bowers Staffs 150 B6
Bowers Gifford Essex 69 B9
Bowershall Fife 279 C11
Bowertower Highld 310 C6
Bowes Durham 223 C9
Bowes Park London 86 G4
Bowgreave Lancs 202 E5
Bowgreen Gtr Man 184 D3
Bowhill Borders 261 D10

Bow – Bro 321

Bowhill Fife 280 B4
Bowhouse Dumfries 238 D2
Bowhousebog or Liquo N Lnrk 269 D7
Bowing Park Mers 182 D6
Bowismiln Borders 262 E2
Bowithick Corn 11 E9
Bowker's Green Lancs 194 G2
Bowland Bridge Cumb 211 B8
Bowldown Wilts 62 D2
Bowlee Gtr Man 195 F10
Bowlees Durham 232 F4
Bowler's Town E Sus 38 C6
Bowley Hereford 115 G10
Bowley Lane Hereford 98 C3
Bowley Town Hereford 115 G10
Bowlhead Green Sur 50 F2
Bowling W Dunb 277 G9
Bowling W Yorks 205 G9
Bowling Alley Hants 49 D9
Bowling Bank Wrex 166 F5
Bowling Green Corn 5 D10
Bowling Green Corn 12 G3
Bowling Green Glos 81 E8
Bowling Green Hants 19 B11
Bowling Green Shrops 150 D2
Bowling Green W Mid 133 F8
Bowling Green Worcs 116 G6
Bowlish Som 44 E6
Bowmans Kent 68 E4
Bowmanstead Cumb 220 F6
Bowmore Argyll 254 B4
Bowness-on-Solway Cumb 238 E6
Bowness-on-Windermere Cumb 221 F8
Bowridge Hill Dorset 30 B4
Bowrie-fauld Angus 287 C9
Bowsden Northumb 273 G9
Bowsey Hill Windsor 65 C10
Bowshank Borders 271 G9
Bowside Lodge Highld 310 C2
Bowston Cumb 221 F9
Bowthorpe Norf 142 B3
Bowyer's Common Hants 34 B3
Box Glos 80 E5
Box Wilts 61 F10
Box End Beds 103 B10
Box Hill Sur 51 C7
Box Hill Wilts 61 F10
Box Trees W Mid 118 C2
Boxbush Glos 80 C2
Boxbush Glos 98 G3
Boxford Suff 107 C9
Boxford W Berks 64 E2
Boxgrove W Sus 22 B6
Boxley Kent 53 B9
Boxmoor Herts 85 D9
Box's Shop Corn 24 G2
Boxted Essex 107 E9
Boxted Suff 124 G6
Boxted Cross Essex 107 E10
Boxted Heath Essex 107 E10
Boxwell Glos 80 G4
Boxworth Cambs 122 E6
Boxworth End Cambs 123 D7
Boyatt Wood Hants 32 C6
Boyden End Suff 124 F4
Boyden Gate Kent 71 F8
Boyland Common Norf 141 G11
Boylestone Derbys 152 B3
Boylestonfield Derbys 152 B3
Boyn Hill Windsor 65 C11
Boyndie Aberds 302 C6
Boynton E Yorks 218 F2
Boys Hill Dorset 29 E11
Boys Village V Glam 58 F4
Boysack Angus 287 C10
Boysack Angus 287 C9
Boythorpe Derbys 186 G5
Boyton Corn 12 C2
Boyton Suff 109 B7
Boyton Wilts 46 F3
Boyton Cross Essex 87 D10
Boyton End Essex 106 E2
Boyton End Suff 106 C4
Bozeat Northants 121 F8
Bozen Green Herts 105 F8
Brù W Isles 304 D5
Braaid I o M 192 E4
Braal Castle Highld 310 C5
Brabling Green Suff 126 E5
Brabourne Kent 54 E5
Brabourne Lees Kent 54 E5
Brabster Highld 310 C7
Bracadale Highld 294 B5
Bracara Highld 295 F9
Braceborough Lincs 155 G11
Bracebridge Lincs 173 B7
Bracebridge Heath Lincs 173 B7
Bracebridge Low Fields Lincs 173 B7
Braceby Lincs 155 B10
Bracewell Lancs 204 D3
Bracken Bank W Yorks 204 F6
Bracken Hill W Yorks 197 C7
Bracken Park W Yorks 206 E3
Brackenber Cumb 222 B4
Brackenbottom N Yorks 212 E6
Brackenfield Derbys 170 D5
Brackenhall W Yorks 197 D7
Brackenlands Cumb 229 B11
Brackenthwaite Cumb 229 B11
Brackenthwaite Cumb 229 G9
Brackenthwaite N Yorks 205 C11
Brackla = Bragle Bridgend 58 D2
Bracklamore Aberds 303 D8
Bracklesham W Sus 22 D4
Brackletter Highld 290 E3
Brackley Argyll 255 C8
Brackley Northants 101 D11
Brackloch Highld 307 G6
Bracknell Brack 65 F11
Braco Perth 286 G2
Braco Castle Perth 286 F2
Braco Park Aberds 303 C9
Bracobrae Moray 302 D5
Bracon N Lincs 199 F9
Bracon Ash Norf 142 D3
Bracorina Highld 295 F9
Bradaford Devon 12 C3
Bradbourne Derbys 170 E2
Bradbury Durham 234 F2
Bradda I o M 192 F2
Bradden Northants 102 B2
Braddock Corn 6 C3
Braddocks Hay Staffs 168 D5
Bradeley Stoke 168 E5
Bradeley Green E Ches 167 G8
Bradenham Bucks 84 F4
Bradenham Norf 141 B8
Bradenstoke Wilts 62 D4
Brades Village W Mid 133 E9
Bradfield Devon 27 F9
Bradfield Essex 108 E2
Bradfield Norf 160 C5
Bradfield W Berks 64 E6
Bradfield Combust Suff 125 F7
Bradfield Green E Ches 167 D11
Bradfield Heath Essex 108 F2
Bradfield St Clare Suff 125 F8
Bradfield St George Suff 125 E8
Bradford Corn 11 F8
Bradford Derbys 170 C2
Bradford Devon 24 F6
Bradford Gtr Man 184 B5
Bradford Northumb 264 C5
Bradford W Yorks 205 G9
Bradford Abbas Dorset 29 E9
Bradford Leigh Wilts 61 G10
Bradford-on-Avon Wilts 61 G10
Bradford-on-Tone Som 27 C11
Bradford Peverell Dorset 17 C9
Bradgate S Yorks 186 C6
Bradiford Devon 40 G5
Brading I o W 21 D8
Bradley Derbys 170 F2
Bradley Glos 80 G3
Bradley Hants 48 E6
Bradley NE Lincs 201 F8
Bradley Staffs 151 F7
Bradley W Mid 133 D8
Bradley W Yorks 197 C7
Bradley Wrex 166 E4
Bradley Cross Som 44 C3
Bradley Fold Gtr Man 195 F9
Bradley Green Glos 80 G2
Bradley Green Som 43 F9
Bradley Green W Ches 167 F8
Bradley Green Warks 134 C5
Bradley Green Worcs 117 E9
Bradley in the Moors Staffs 169 G9
Bradley Mills W Yorks 197 D7
Bradley Mount E Ches 184 F6
Bradley Stoke S Glos 60 C6
Bradlow Hereford 98 D4
Bradmore Notts 153 C11
Bradmore W Mid 133 D7
Bradney Shrops 132 D5
Bradney Som 43 F10
Bradninch Devon 27 G8
Bradnock's Marsh W Mid 118 B4
Bradnop Staffs 169 D8
Bradnor Green Hereford 114 F5
Bradpole Dorset 16 C5
Bradshaw Gtr Man 195 E8
Bradshaw Staffs 168 D6
Bradshaw W Yorks 196 E5
Bradshaw W Yorks 205 G7
Bradstone Devon 12 E3
Bradville M Keynes 102 C6
Bradwall Green E Ches 168 C3
Bradway S Yorks 186 E4
Bradwell Derbys 185 E11
Bradwell Devon 40 E3
Bradwell Essex 106 G6
Bradwell M Keynes 102 D6
Bradwell Norf 143 C10
Bradwell Staffs 168 F4
Bradwell Common M Keynes 102 D6
Bradwell Grove Oxon 82 D2
Bradwell Hills Derbys 185 E11
Bradwell on Sea Essex 89 D8
Bradwell Waterside Essex 89 D7
Bradworthy Devon 24 E4
Bradworthy Cross Devon 24 E4
Brae Dumfries 237 B10
Brae Highld 307 L3
Brae Highld 309 J4
Brae Shetland 312 G5
Brae of Achnahaird Highld 307 H5
Brae of Boquhapple Stirl 285 G10
Brae Roy Lodge Highld 290 D5
Braeantra Highld 300 B5
Braebuster Orkney 314 F5
Braedownie Angus 292 F4
Braeface Falk 278 E5
Braefield Highld 300 F4
Braefindon Highld 300 D6
Braegrum Perth 286 E4
Braehead Dumfries 236 D6
Braehead Orkney 314 B4
Braehead Orkney 314 F5
Braehead S Ayrs 257 E8
Braehead S Lnrk 259 C8
Braehead S Lnrk 267 D11
Braehead S Lnrk 269 E9
Braehead Stirl 278 C6
Braehead of Lunan Angus 287 B10
Braehoulland Shetland 312 F4
Braehour Highld 310 D4
Braehungie Highld 310 F5
Braeintra Highld 295 B10
Braelangwell Lodge Highld 309 K5
Braemar Aberds 292 D3
Braemore Highld 299 B11
Braemore Highld 310 F4
Braepark Edin 280 F3
Braes Enzie Moray 302 D3
Braes of Ullapool Highld 307 K6
Braeside Invclyd 276 F4
Braeswick Orkney 314 C6
Braevallich Argyll 275 C10
Braewick Shetland 312 F4
Braewick Shetland 313 H5
Brafferton Darl 233 G11
Brafferton N Yorks 215 E8
Brafield-on-the-Green Northants 120 F6
Bragar W Isles 304 D4
Bragbury End Herts 104 G5
Bragenham Bucks 103 F8
Bragle = Brackla Bridgend 58 D2
Bragleenmore Argyll 289 G11
Braichmelyn Gwyn 163 B10
Braichyfedw Powys 129 E7
Braid Edin 280 G4
Braides Lancs 202 C4
Braidfauld Glasgow 268 C2
Braidley N Yorks 213 C10
Braids Argyll 255 C8
Braidwood S Lnrk 268 F6
Braigh Chalasaigh W Isles 296 D5
Braigo Argyll 274 G3
Brailsford Derbys 170 G3
Brailsford Green Derbys 170 G3
Braingortan Argyll 275 F11
Brain's Green Glos 79 D11
Brainshaugh Northumb 252 C6
Braintree Essex 106 G5
Braiseworth Suff 126 C2
Braishfield Hants 32 B5
Braiswick Essex 107 F9
Braithwaite Cumb 229 G10
Braithwaite S Yorks 198 E6
Braithwaite W Yorks 204 E6
Braithwell S Yorks 187 C8
Brakefield Green Norf 141 B10
Brakenhill W Yorks 198 D2
Bramber W Sus 35 E11
Bramblecombe Dorset 30 G3
Brambridge Hants 33 C7
Bramcote Notts 153 B10
Bramcote Warks 135 F8
Bramcote Hills Notts 153 B10
Bramcote Mains Warks 135 F8
Bramdean Hants 33 B10
Bramerton Norf 142 C5
Bramfield Herts 86 B3
Bramfield Suff 127 C7
Bramford Suff 108 B2
Bramford W Mid 133 E8
Bramhall Gtr Man 184 D5
Bramhall Moor Gtr Man 184 D6
Bramhall Park Gtr Man 184 D5
Bramham W Yorks 206 E4
Bramhope W Yorks 205 E11
Bramley Derbys 186 F6
Bramley Hants 48 B6
Bramley S Yorks 187 C7
Bramley Sur 50 D4
Bramley W Yorks 205 F10
Bramley Corner Hants 48 B6
Bramley Green Hants 49 B7
Bramley Head N Yorks 205 B8
Bramley Vale Derbys 171 B7
Bramling Kent 55 B8
Brampford Speke Devon 14 B4
Brampton Cambs 122 C4
Brampton Cumb 231 G9
Brampton Cumb 240 E2
Brampton Derbys 186 G5
Brampton Hereford 97 D8
Brampton Lincs 188 F4
Brampton Norf 160 E4
Brampton S Yorks 198 G2
Brampton Suff 143 G8
Brampton Abbotts Hereford 98 F2
Brampton Ash Northants 136 F5
Brampton Bryan Hereford 115 C7
Brampton en le Morthen S Yorks 187 D7
Brampton Park Cambs 122 C4
Brampton Street Suff 143 G8
Bramshall Staffs 151 C11
Bramshaw Hants 32 D3
Bramshill Hants 65 G8
Bramshott Hants 49 G10
Bramwell Som 28 B6
Bran End Essex 106 F3
Branatwatt Shetland 313 H4
Branault Highld 289 C7
Branbridges Kent 53 D7
Brancaster Norf 176 E3
Brancaster Staithe Norf 176 E3
Brancepeth Durham 233 D10
Branch End Northumb 242 E3
Branchill Moray 301 D10
Branchton Invclyd 276 F4
Brand End Lincs 174 F5
Brand Green Glos 98 F4
Brand Green Hereford 98 C5
Branderburgh Moray 302 B2
Brandesburton E Yorks 209 D8
Brandeston Suff 126 E4
Brandhill Shrops 115 B8
Brandis Corner Devon 24 G6
Brandish Street Som 42 D2
Brandiston Norf 160 E2
Brandlingill Cumb 229 F8
Brandon Durham 233 D10
Brandon Lincs 172 F6
Brandon Northumb 264 F2
Brandon Suff 140 F5
Brandon Warks 119 B8
Brandon Bank Cambs 140 F2
Brandon Creek Norf 140 E2
Brandon Parva Norf 141 B11
Brands Hill Windsor 66 D4
Brandsby N Yorks 215 E11
Brandwood Shrops 149 D9
Brandwood End W Mid 117 B11
Brandy Carr W Yorks 197 C10
Brandy Hole Essex 88 F4
Brandy Wharf Lincs 189 B8
Brandyquoy Orkney 314 G4
Brane Corn 1 D4
Branksome Darl 224 B5
Branksome Poole 18 C6
Branksome Park Poole 19 C7
Bransbury Hants 48 E2
Bransby Lincs 188 F5
Branscombe Devon 15 D9
Bransford Worcs 116 G5
Bransgore Hants 19 B9
Branshill Clack 279 C7
Bransholme Hull 209 G8
Branson's Cross Worcs 117 C11
Branston Leics 154 D6
Branston Lincs 173 B8
Branston Staffs 152 E4
Branston Booths Lincs 173 B9
Branstone I o W 21 E7
Bransty Cumb 219 B9
Brant Broughton Lincs 172 E6
Brantham Suff 108 E2
Branthwaite Cumb 229 D11
Branthwaite Cumb 229 G7
Branthwaite Edge Cumb 229 G7
Brantingham E Yorks 200 B2
Branton Northumb 264 F2
Branton S Yorks 198 G6
Branton Green N Yorks 215 G8
Branxholm Park Borders 261 G11
Branxholme Borders 261 G11
Branxton Northumb 263 B9
Brascote Leics 135 C8
Brassey Green W Ches 167 C8
Brassington Derbys 170 E2
Brasted Kent 52 C3
Brasted Chart Kent 52 C3
Brathens Aberds 293 D8
Bratoft Lincs 175 B7
Brattle Kent 54 G2
Brattleby Lincs 188 E6
Bratton Som 42 D2
Bratton Telford 150 G2
Bratton Wilts 46 C2
Bratton Clovelly Devon 12 C5
Bratton Fleming Devon 40 F6
Bratton Seymour Som 29 B11
Braughing Herts 105 F7
Braughing Friars Herts 105 G8
Braulen Lodge Highld 300 F2
Braunston Northants 119 D10
Braunston-in-Rutland Rutland 136 B6
Braunstone Leics 135 C11
Braunstone Town Leicester 135 C11
Braunton Devon 40 F3
Brawby N Yorks 216 D4
Brawith N Yorks 225 D10
Brawl Highld 310 C2
Brawlbin Highld 310 D4
Bray Windsor 66 D2
Bray Shop Corn 12 G2
Bray Wick Windsor 65 D11
Braybrooke Northants 136 G5
Braydon Side Wilts 62 B4
Brayford Devon 41 G7
Brayfordhill Devon 41 G7
Brays Grove Essex 87 D7
Braystones Cumb 219 D10
Brayswick Worcs 98 B6
Braythorn N Yorks 205 D10
Brayton N Yorks 207 G8
Braytown Dorset 18 D2
Braywoodside Windsor 65 D11
Brazacott Corn 11 C11
Brazenhill Staffs 151 E7
Brea Corn 4 G3
Breach Bath 60 G6
Breach Kent 69 F10
Breach W Sus 22 B3
Breachacha Castle Argyll 288 D3
Breachwood Green Herts 104 G2
Breacleit W Isles 304 E3
Bread Street Glos 80 D4
Breaden Heath Shrops 149 B8
Breadsall Derbys 153 B7
Breadsall Hilltop Derby 153 B7
Breadstone Glos 80 E2
Breage Corn 2 D4
Breakachy Highld 300 E4
Brealeys Devon 25 D8
Bream Glos 79 D10
Breamore Hants 31 D11
Bream's Meend Glos 79 D9
Brean Som 43 B9
Breanais W Isles 304 F1
Brearley W Yorks 196 B4
Brearton N Yorks 214 G6
Breascleit W Isles 304 E4
Breaston Derbys 153 C9
Brechfa Carms 93 E10
Brechin Angus 293 G7
Breck of Cruan Orkney 314 E3
Breckan Orkney 314 F2
Breckles Norf 141 E9
Breckrey Highld 298 C5
Brecks S Yorks 187 C7
Brecon Powys 95 F10
Bredbury Gtr Man 184 C6
Bredbury Green Gtr Man 184 D6
Brede E Sus 38 D4
Bredenbury Hereford 116 F2
Bredfield Suff 126 G5
Bredgar Kent 69 G11
Bredhurst Kent 69 G9
Bredicot Worcs 117 G8
Bredon Worcs 99 D8
Bredon's Hardwick Worcs 99 D8
Bredon's Norton Worcs 99 D8
Bredwardine Hereford 96 C6
Breedon on the Hill Leics 153 E8
Breeds Essex 87 C11
Breedy Butts Lancs 202 E2
Breibhig W Isles 297 M2
Breibhig W Isles 304 E6
Breich W Loth 269 C9
Breightmet Gtr Man 195 F8
Breighton E Yorks 207 G10
Breinton Hereford 97 D9
Breinton Common Hereford 97 C9
Breiwick Shetland 313 J6
Brelston Green Hereford 97 G11
Bremhill Wilts 62 E3
Bremhill Wick Wilts 62 E3
Bremirehoull Shetland 313 L6
Brenachoile Lodge Stirl 285 G8
Brenchley Kent 53 E7
Brenchoillie Argyll 284 G4
Brendon Devon 24 E5
Brendon Devon 24 F5
Brendon Devon 41 D9
Brenkley T & W 242 B6
Brent Corn 6 E4
Brent Eleigh Suff 107 B8
Brent Knoll Som 43 C10
Brent Mill Devon 8 D3
Brent Pelham Herts 105 E8
Brentford London 67 D7
Brentford End London 67 D7
Brentingby Leics 154 F5
Brentry Bristol 60 D5
Brentwood Essex 87 G9
Brenzett Kent 39 B8
Brenzett Green Kent 39 B8
Brereton Staffs 151 F11
Brereton Cross Staffs 151 F11
Brereton Green E Ches 168 C3
Brereton Heath E Ches 168 C4
Breretonhill Staffs 151 F11
Bressingham Norf 141 G11
Bressingham Common Norf 141 G11
Bretby Derbys 152 E5
Bretford Warks 119 B8
Bretforton Worcs 99 C11
Bretherdale Head Cumb 221 E11
Bretherton Lancs 194 C3
Brettabister Shetland 313 H6
Brettenham Norf 141 G8
Brettenham Suff 125 G9
Bretton Derbys 186 F2
Bretton Flint 166 C5
Bretton P'boro 138 C3
Brewer Street Sur 51 C10
Brewer's End Essex 105 G11
Brewers Green Norf 142 G2
Brewlands Bridge Angus 292 G3
Brewood Staffs 133 B7
Briach Moray 301 D10
Briants Puddle Dorset 18 C2
Briar Hill Northants 120 F4
Brick End Essex 105 F11
Brick Hill Sur 66 G3
Brick House End Essex 105 F9
Brick Houses S Yorks 186 E4
Brick-kiln End Notts 171 D9
Brickendon Herts 86 D4
Bricket Wood Herts 85 E10
Brickfields Worcs 117 F7
Brickhill Beds 121 G11
Brickhouses E Ches 168 C3
Brickkiln Green Essex 106 E4
Bricklehampton Worcs 99 C9
Bride I o M 192 B5
Bridekirk Cumb 229 E8
Bridell Pembs 92 C3
Bridestowe Devon 12 D6
Brideswell Aberds 302 F5
Bridford Devon 14 D2
Bridfordmills Devon 14 D2
Bridge Corn 2 D6
Bridge Corn 4 G3
Bridge Kent 55 C7
Bridge Som 28 F5
Bridge Ball Devon 41 D8
Bridge End Beds 121 G10
Bridge End Cumb 230 B3
Bridge End Devon 8 F3
Bridge End Durham 232 D6
Bridge End Essex 106 E3
Bridge End Flint 166 D4
Bridge End Hereford 98 B2
Bridge End Lincs 156 B2
Bridge End Northumb 241 D10
Bridge End Northumb 241 E10
Bridge End Oxon 83 G9
Bridge-End Shetland 313 K5
Bridge End Sur 50 B5
Bridge End Warks 118 E5
Bridge End Worcs 98 E6
Bridge Green Essex 105 D9
Bridge Green Norf 142 G2
Bridge Hewick N Yorks 214 E6
Bridge Ho Argyll 254 B4
Bridge of Alford Aberds 293 B7
Bridge of Allan Stirl 278 B5
Bridge of Avon Moray 301 F11
Bridge of Avon Moray 301 G11
Bridge of Awe Argyll 284 E4
Bridge of Balgie Perth 285 C9
Bridge of Cally Perth 286 B5
Bridge of Canny Aberds 293 D8
Bridge of Craigisla Angus 286 B6
Bridge of Dee Dumfries 237 D9
Bridge of Don Aberdeen 293 B11
Bridge of Dun Angus 287 B10
Bridge of Dye Aberds 293 E8
Bridge of Earn Perth 286 F5
Bridge of Ericht Perth 285 B9
Bridge of Feugh Aberds 293 D9
Bridge of Forss Highld 310 C4
Bridge of Gairn Aberds 292 D5
Bridge of Gaur Perth 285 B9
Bridge of Lyon Perth 285 C11
Bridge of Muchalls Aberds 293 D10
Bridge of Muick Aberds 292 D5
Bridge of Oich Highld 290 C5
Bridge of Orchy Argyll 284 D6
Bridge of Waith Orkney 314 E2
Bridge of Walls Shetland 313 H4
Bridge of Weir Renfs 267 B7
Bridge Reeve Devon 25 E11
Bridge Sollers Hereford 97 C8
Bridge Street Suff 107 B7
Bridge Town Warks 118 G4
Bridge Trafford W Ches 183 G7
Bridge Yate S Glos 61 E7
Bridgefoot Aberds 292 C6
Bridgefoot Angus 287 D7
Bridgefoot Cumb 229 F7
Bridgehampton Som 29 C9
Bridgehill Durham 242 G3
Bridgeholm Green Derbys 185 E8
Bridgehouse Gate N Yorks 214 F3
Bridgelands Borders 261 C11
Bridgemary Hants 33 G9
Bridgemere E Ches 168 F2
Bridgemont Derbys 185 E8
Bridgend Aberds 293 B7
Bridgend Aberds 302 F5
Bridgend Angus 293 G7
Bridgend Argyll 255 D8
Bridgend Argyll 274 G4
Bridgend Argyll 275 D9
Bridgend Corn 6 D2
Bridgend Cumb 221 C7
Bridgend Devon 7 F11
Bridgend Fife 287 F7
Bridgend Glos 80 E4
Bridgend Highld 300 D3
Bridgend Invclyd 276 F5
Bridgend Moray 302 F3
Bridgend N Lnrk 278 G3
Bridgend Pembs 92 B3
Bridgend W Loth 279 F10
Bridgend = Pen-y-Bont ar-ogwr Bridgend 58 C2
Bridgend of Lintrathen Angus 286 B6
Bridgeness Falk 279 E10
Bridgerule Devon 24 G3
Bridges Corn 5 D10
Bridges Shrops 131 D7
Bridgeton Glasgow 268 C2
Bridgetown Corn 12 D2
Bridgetown Devon 8 C6
Bridgetown Som 42 G2
Bridgetown Staffs 133 B9
Bridgham Norf 141 F9
Bridgnorth Shrops 132 E4
Bridgtown Staffs 133 B9
Bridgwater Som 43 F10
Bridlington E Yorks 218 F3
Bridport Dorset 16 C5
Bridstow Hereford 97 G11
Brierfield Lancs 204 F2
Brierholme Carr S Yorks 199 E7
Brierley Glos 79 B10
Brierley Hereford 115 F9
Brierley S Yorks 198 E2
Brierley Hill W Mid 133 F8
Brierton Hrtlpl 234 E5
Briery Cumb 229 G11
Briery Hill Bl Gwent 77 D11
Briestfield W Yorks 197 D8
Brig o'Turk Stirl 285 G9
Brigflatts Cumb 222 G2
Brigg N Lincs 200 F3
Brigg N Lincs 200 F4
Briggate Norf 160 D6
Briggswath N Yorks 227 D7
Brigham Cumb 229 E7
Brigham Cumb 229 G11
Brigham E Yorks 209 C7
Brighouse W Yorks 196 C6
Brighstone I o W 20 E4
Brightgate Derbys 170 D3
Brighthampton Oxon 82 E5
Brightholmlee S Yorks 186 B3
Brightley Devon 13 B7
Brightling E Sus 37 C11
Brightlingsea Essex 89 B9
Brighton Brighton 36 G4
Brighton Corn 5 E8
Brighton Hill Hants 48 D6
Brighton le Sands Mers 182 B4
Brightons Falk 279 F8
Brightside S Yorks 186 D5
Brightwalton W Berks 64 D2
Brightwalton Green W Berks 64 D2
Brightwalton Holt W Berks 64 D2
Brightwell Suff 108 C4
Brightwell Baldwin Oxon 83 F11
Brightwell cum Sotwell Oxon 83 G9
Brigmerston Wilts 47 D7
Brignall Durham 223 C11
Brigsley NE Lincs 201 G9
Brigsteer Cumb 211 B9
Brigstock Northants 137 F8
Brill Bucks 83 C11
Brill Corn 2 D6
Brilley Hereford 96 B5
Brilley Mountain Powys 114 G5
Brimaston Pembs 91 G8
Brimfield Hereford 115 D10
Brimington Derbys 186 G6
Brimington Common Derbys 186 G6
Brimley Devon 13 F11
Brimley Devon 28 G4
Brimps Hill Glos 79 B11
Brimpsfield Glos 80 C6
Brimpton W Berks 64 G5
Brimpton Common W Berks 64 G5
Brims Orkney 314 H2
Brims Castle Highld 310 B4
Brimscombe Glos 80 E5
Brimsdown London 86 F5
Brimstage Mers 182 E4
Brinacory Highld 295 F9
Brincliffe S Yorks 186 D4
Brind E Yorks 207 G10
Brindham Som 44 E4
Brindister Shetland 313 H4
Brindister Shetland 313 K6
Brindle Lancs 194 C6
Brindle Heath Gtr Man 195 G10
Brindley E Ches 167 E9
Brindley Ford Stoke 168 E5
Brindwoodgate Derbys 186 F4
Brineton Staffs 150 G6
Bringewood Forge Hereford 115 C9
Bringhurst Leics 136 E6
Bringsty Common Hereford 116 F4
Brington Cambs 121 B11
Brinian Orkney 314 D4
Briningham Norf 159 C10
Brinkhill Lincs 190 G5
Brinkley Cambs 124 G2
Brinkley Notts 172 E2
Brinkley Hill Hereford 97 E11
Brinklow M Keynes 103 D8
Brinklow Warks 119 B8
Brinkworth Wilts 62 C4
Brinmore Highld 300 G6
Brinnington Gtr Man 184 C6
Brinscall Lancs 194 C6
Brinsea N Som 60 G2
Brinsford Staffs 133 B8
Brinsley Notts 171 F7
Brinsop Hereford 97 C8
Brinsop Common Hereford 97 C8
Brinsworth S Yorks 186 D6
Brinsworthy Devon 41 G9
Brinton Norf 159 B10
Brisco Cumb 239 G10
Briscoe Cumb 219 C10
Briscoerigg N Yorks 205 C11
Brisley Norf 159 E8
Brislington Bristol 60 E6
Brissenden Green Kent 54 F2
Bristnall Fields W Mid 133 F9
Bristol Bristol 60 E5
Briston Norf 159 C11
Britain Bottom S Glos 61 B9
Britannia Lancs 195 C11
Britford Wilts 31 B11
Brithdir Caerph 77 E11
Brithdir Ceredig 92 B6
Brithdir Gwyn 146 F5
Brithem Bottom Devon 27 E8
British Torf 78 E3
Briton Ferry = Llansawel Neath 57 C8
Britten's Bath 45 B7
Britwell Slough 66 C3
Britwell Salome Oxon 83 G11
Brixham Torbay 9 D8
Brixton Devon 7 E11
Brixton London 67 D10
Brixton Deverill Wilts 45 F11
Brixworth Northants 120 C4
Brize Norton Oxon 82 D4
Broad Alley Worcs 117 D7
Broad Blunsdon Swindon 81 G11
Broad Campden Glos 100 D3
Broad Carr W Yorks 196 D5
Broad Chalke Wilts 31 B8
Broad Clough Lancs 195 C11
Broad Colney Herts 85 E11
Broad Common Worcs 117 D7
Broad Ford Kent 53 F8
Broad Green C Beds 103 C9
Broad Green Cambs 124 F3
Broad Green Essex 105 D8
Broad Green Essex 107 G7
Broad Green London 67 F10
Broad Green Mers 182 C6
Broad Green Suff 124 F5
Broad Green Suff 125 F11
Broad Green Worcs 116 F5
Broad Green Worcs 117 C9
Broad Haven = Aberllydan Pembs 72 C5
Broad Heath Powys 114 E6
Broad Heath Staffs 151 D7
Broad Heath Worcs 116 D3
Broad Hill Cambs 123 B11
Broad Hinton Wilts 62 D6
Broad Ings E Yorks 208 C2
Broad Lane Corn 4 G3
Broad Lanes Shrops 132 F5
Broad Laying Hants 64 G2
Broad Layings Hants 64 G2
Broad Marston Worcs 100 B2
Broad Meadow Staffs 168 F4
Broad Oak Carms 93 G11
Broad Oak Cumb 220 G2
Broad Oak Dorset 30 E3
Broad Oak E Sus 37 C10
Broad Oak E Sus 38 D4
Broad Oak Hants 49 C9
Broad Oak Hereford 97 G9
Broad Oak Kent 54 F4
Broad Oak Kent 71 G7
Broad Oak Mers 183 B8
Broad Oak Shrops 132 F5
Broad Parkham Devon 24 C5
Broad Street E Sus 38 D5
Broad Street Kent 53 B10
Broad Street Kent 54 E6
Broad Street Kent 55 E7
Broad Street Medway 69 E9

Broad Street Suff 107 C9
Broad Street Wilts 46 B6
Broad Street Green Essex 88 D5
Broad Tenterden Kent 53 G11
Broad Town Wilts 62 D5
Broadbottom Gtr Man 185 C7
Broadbridge W Sus 22 B4
Broadbridge Heath W Sus 50 G6
Broadbury Devon 12 B5
Broadbush Swindon 81 G11
Broadclyst Devon 14 B5
Broadfield Gtr Man 195 E10
Broadfield Invclyd 276 G6
Broadfield Lancs 194 C4
Broadfield Lancs 195 B8
Broadfield Pembs 73 E10
Broadfield W Sus 51 G9
Broadford Highld 295 C8
Broadford Sur 50 D3
Broadford Bridge W Sus 35 C9
Broadgate Hants 32 C6
Broadgrass Green Suff 125 E9
Broadgreen Wood Herts 86 D4
Broadhalgh Gtr Man 195 E11
Broadham Green Sur 51 C11
Broadhaugh Borders 249 B10
Broadhaven Highld 310 D7
Broadheath Gtr Man 184 D3
Broadhembury Devon 27 G10
Broadhempston Devon 8 B6
Broadholm Derbys 170 F4
Broadholme Derbys 170 F5
Broadholme Lincs 188 G5
Broadland Row E Sus 38 D4
Broadlands Devon 14 G3
Broadlane Corn 2 C4
Broadlay Carms 74 D5
Broadley Lancs 195 D11
Broadley Moray 302 C3
Broadley Common Essex 86 D6
Broadleys Aberds 303 C8
Broadmayne Dorset 17 D10
Broadmeadows Borders 261 C10
Broadmere Hants 48 D6
Broadmoor Pembs 73 D9
Broadmoor Sur 50 D6
Broadmoor Common Hereford 98 D2
Broadmore Green Worcs 116 G6
Broadoak Dorset 16 B4
Broadoak Glos 80 C2
Broadoak Hants 33 E8
Broadoak Shrops 149 F9
Broadoak Wrex 166 D5
Broadoak End Herts 86 C4
Broadoak Park Gtr Man 195 G9
Broadplat Oxon 65 C8
Broadrashes Moray 302 D4
Broadrock Glos 79 F8
Broad's Green Essex 87 C11
Broad's Green Wilts 62 F3
Broadsands Torbay 9 D7
Broadsea Aberds 303 C9
Broadshard Som 28 E6
Broadstairs Kent 71 F11
Broadstone Kent 53 D11
Broadstone Mon 79 E8
Broadstone Poole 18 B6
Broadstone Shrops 131 F10
Broadstreet Common Newport 59 C11
Broadwas Worcs 116 F5
Broadwater Herts 104 G4
Broadwater W Sus 35 G11
Broadwater Down Kent 52 F5
Broadwaters Worcs 116 B6
Broadwath Cumb 239 F11
Broadway Carms 74 D3
Broadway Carms 74 D5
Broadway Pembs 72 C5
Broadway Som 28 D4
Broadway Suff 127 B7
Broadway Worcs 99 D11
Broadway Lands Hereford 97 E11
Broadwell Glos 79 C9
Broadwell Glos 100 F4
Broadwell Oxon 82 E3
Broadwell Warks 119 D9
Broadwey Dorset 17 E9
Broadwindsor Dorset 28 G6
Broadwood Kelly Devon 25 F10
Broadwoodwidger Devon 12 D4
Brobury Hereford 96 C6
Brochel Highld 298 E5
Brochroy Argyll 284 D4
Brock Lancs 202 E6
Brock Hill Essex 88 F2
Brockamin Worcs 116 G5
Brockbridge Hants 33 D10
Brockdish Norf 126 B4
Brockencote Worcs 117 C7
Brockenhurst Hants 32 G4
Brocketsbrae S Lnrk 259 B8
Brockfield Devon 28 F4
Brockford Green Suff 126 D2
Brockford Street Suff 126 D2
Brockhall Northants 120 E2
Brockhall Village Lancs 203 F10
Brockham Sur 51 D7
Brockham End Bath 61 F8
Brockham Park Sur 51 D8
Brockhampton Glos 99 F8
Brockhampton Glos 99 G10
Brockhampton Hants 22 B2
Brockhampton Hereford 97 E11
Brockhampton Green Dorset 30 F2
Brockhill Borders 261 E9
Brockholes W Yorks 197 E7
Brockhollands Glos 79 D10
Brockhurst Derbys 170 C4
Brockhurst Hants 33 G10
Brockhurst Warks 135 G9
Brocklebank Cumb 230 C2
Brocklehirst Dumfries 238 C3
Brocklesby Lincs 200 E6
Brockley London 67 E11
Brockley N Som 60 F3
Brockley Corner Suff 124 C6
Brockley Green Suff 106 B4
Brockley Green Suff 124 G6
Brockleymoor Cumb 230 D5
Brockloch Dumfries 246 D2
Brockmanton Hereford 115 F10
Brockmoor W Mid 133 F8
Brock's Green Hants 64 G4
Brock's Watering Norf 142 E2
Brockscombe Devon 12 C5
Brockton Shrops 130 C6
Brockton Shrops 130 F6
Brockton Shrops 131 E11
Brockton Shrops 132 C4
Brockton Staffs 150 C6
Brockton Telford 150 F4
Brockweir Glos 79 E8
Brockwell Som 42 E2
Brockwood Hants 33 B10
Brockworth Glos 80 B5
Brocton Corn 5 B10
Brocton Staffs 151 F9
Brodick N Ayrs 256 B2
Brodie Moray 301 D9
Brodiesord Aberds 302 C5
Brodsworth S Yorks 198 F4
Brogaig Highld 298 C4
Brogborough C Beds 103 D9
Broke Hall Suff 108 C3
Broken Cross E Ches 184 G6
Broken Cross W Ches 183 G11
Broken Green Herts 105 G8
Brokenborough Wilts 62 B2
Brokerswood Wilts 45 C10
Brokes N Yorks 224 F3
Brombil Neath 57 D9
Bromborough Mers 182 E4
Bromborough Pool Mers 182 E4
Bromdon Shrops 132 G2
Brome Suff 126 B2
Brome Street Suff 126 B3
Bromesberrow Glos 98 E4
Bromesberrow Heath Glos 98 E4
Bromeswell Suff 126 G6
Bromfield Cumb 229 B9
Bromfield Shrops 115 B9
Bromford W Mid 134 E2
Bromham Beds 121 G10
Bromham Wilts 62 F3
Bromley Herts 105 G8
Bromley London 67 C11
Bromley London 68 F2
Bromley S Yorks 186 B4
Bromley Shrops 132 D4
Bromley Shrops 149 D8
Bromley W Mid 133 F8
Bromley Common London 68 F2
Bromley Cross Essex 107 F11
Bromley Cross Gtr Man 195 E8
Bromley Green Kent 54 F3
Bromley Hall Staffs 150 C5
Bromley Heath S Glos 61 D7
Bromley Park London 67 F11
Bromley Wood Staffs 152 E2
Bromlow Shrops 130 C6
Brompton London 67 D9
Brompton Medway 69 F9
Brompton N Yorks 217 C8
Brompton N Yorks 225 F7
Brompton Shrops 131 B10
Brompton-by-Sawdon N Yorks 217 C8
Brompton-on-Swale N Yorks 224 F4
Brompton Ralph Som 42 G5
Brompton Regis Som 42 G3
Bromsash Hereford 98 G2
Bromsberrow Heath Glos 98 E4
Bromsgrove Worcs 117 C9
Bromstead Common Staffs 150 F6
Bromstead Heath Staffs 150 F6
Bromstone Kent 71 F11
Bromyard Hereford 116 G3
Bromyard Downs Hereford 116 F3
Bronaber Gwyn 146 C4
Broncroft Shrops 131 F10
Brondesbury London 67 C8
Brondesbury Park London 67 C8
Broneirion Powys 129 F10
Brongest Ceredig 92 B6
Brongwyn Ceredig 92 C5
Bronington Wrex 149 B9
Bronllys Powys 96 D2
Bronnant Ceredig 112 D2
Bronwydd Ceredig 93 C7
Bronwydd Arms Carms 93 G8
Bronydd Powys 96 B4
Bronygarth Shrops 148 B5
Brook Carms 74 D3
Brook Devon 12 G5
Brook Devon 14 C2
Brook Hants 32 B4
Brook Hants 32 E3
Brook I o W 20 E3
Brook Kent 54 E5
Brook Sur 50 D5
Brook Sur 50 F2
Brook Bottom Gtr Man 185 D7
Brook Bottom Gtr Man 196 G3
Brook Bottom Lancs 202 E6
Brook End Beds 121 E11
Brook End C Beds 104 B3
Brook End Cambs 121 C11
Brook End Herts 104 F6
Brook End M Keynes 103 C8
Brook End Wilts 61 C10
Brook End Worcs 99 B7
Brook Green London 67 D8
Brook Green Suff 125 F7
Brook Hill Hants 32 E3
Brook Hill Notts 153 C11
Brook Place Sur 66 G3
Brook Street Essex 87 G9
Brook Street Kent 52 D5
Brook Street Kent 54 G2
Brook Street Suff 106 B6
Brook Street W Sus 36 B4
Brook Waters Wilts 30 C6
Brooke Norf 142 D5
Brooke Rutland 136 B6
Brookenby Lincs 190 B2
Brookend Glos 79 E11
Brookend Glos 79 F9
Brookend Oxon 100 G6
Brookfield Derbys 185 B8
Brookfield Lancs 203 G7
Brookfield M'bro 225 B9
Brookfield Renfs 267 C8
Brookfoot W Yorks 196 C6
Brookgreen I o W 20 E3
Brookhampton Oxon 83 F10
Brookhampton Shrops 131 E11
Brookhampton Som 29 B10
Brookhouse Blkburn 195 B7
Brookhouse Denb 165 B9
Brookhouse E Ches 184 F6
Brookhouse Lancs 211 G10
Brookhouse S Yorks 187 D8
Brookhouse W Yorks 196 B5
Brookhouse Green E Ches 168 C4
Brookhouses Derbys 185 D8
Brookhouses Staffs 169 G7
Brookhurst Mers 182 E4
Brookland Kent 39 B7
Brooklands Dumfries 237 B10
Brooklands Gtr Man 184 C3
Brooklands Shrops 167 G8
Brooklands Sur 66 G5
Brooklands W Yorks 206 F2
Brookleigh Devon 14 B5
Brookmans Park Herts 86 E2
Brookpits W Sus 35 G8
Brookrow Shrops 116 C2
Brooks Corn 6 C3
Brooks Powys 130 D2
Brooks End Kent 71 F9
Brooks Green W Sus 35 C10
Brooksbottoms Gtr Man 195 D9
Brooksby Leics 154 F3
Brookside Brack 66 E2
Brookside Derbys 186 G5
Brookside Telford 132 B3
Brookthorpe Glos 80 C4
Brookvale Halton 183 E8
Brookville Norf 140 D4
Brookwood Sur 50 B2
Broom C Beds 104 C3
Broom Cumb 231 G9
Broom Devon 28 G4
Broom E Renf 267 D10
Broom Pembs 73 D10
Broom S Yorks 186 C5
Broom Warks 117 G11
Broom Green Norf 159 E9
Broom Hill Bristol 60 E6
Broom Hill Dorset 31 G8
Broom Hill Durham 242 G4
Broom Hill London 68 F3
Broom Hill Suff 108 B5
Broom Hill Worcs 117 B8
Broom Street Kent 70 G4
Broombank Worcs 116 C3
Broome Norf 143 E7
Broome Shrops 131 D10
Broome Shrops 131 G8
Broome Worcs 117 B8
Broome Park Northumb 264 G4
Broomedge Warr 184 D2
Broomer's Corner W Sus 35 C10
Broomershill W Sus 35 D9
Broomfield Aberds 303 F9
Broomfield Cumb 230 B2
Broomfield Essex 88 D2
Broomfield Kent 53 C10
Broomfield Kent 71 F7
Broomfield Som 43 G8
Broomfield Wilts 61 D11
Broomfields Shrops 149 F8
Broomfleet E Yorks 199 B11
Broomhall E Ches 167 F10
Broomhall Windsor 66 F3
Broomhall Green E Ches 167 F10
Broomham E Sus 23 C8
Broomhaugh Northumb 242 E2
Broomhill Borders 261 D11
Broomhill Bristol 60 D6
Broomhill Highld 301 G9
Broomhill Kent 55 B8
Broomhill Norf 140 C2
Broomhill Northumb 252 C6
Broomhill Notts 171 F8
Broomhill S Yorks 198 G2
Broomhill W Ches 167 B7
Broomhill Bank Kent 52 E5
Broomholm Norf 160 C6
Broomhouse Glasgow 268 C3
Broomlands N Ayrs 257 B8
Broomley Northumb 242 E2
Broompark Durham 233 C10
Broomridge Stirl 278 C6
Broom's Barn Suff 124 D5
Broom's Green Glos 98 E4
Broomsgrove E Sus 38 E4
Broomsthorpe Norf 158 D6
Broomton Highld 301 B8
Broomy Hill Hereford 97 D9
Broomy Lodge Hants 32 E2
Broomyshaw Staffs 169 F9
Brora Highld 311 J3
Broseley Shrops 132 C3
Brotherhouse Bar Lincs 156 G5
Brotheridge Green Worcs 98 C6
Brotherlee Durham 232 D4
Brotherstone Borders 262 B4
Brothertoft Lincs 174 F3
Brotherton N Yorks 198 B3
Brothybeck Cumb 230 C2
Brotton Redcar 226 B3
Broubster Highld 310 C4
Brough Cumb 222 C5
Brough Derbys 185 E11
Brough E Yorks 200 B2
Brough Highld 310 B6
Brough Notts 172 D4
Brough Orkney 314 H4
Brough Orkney 314 E3
Brough Shetland 312 C7
Brough Shetland 312 F6
Brough Shetland 312 F7
Brough Shetland 313 G7
Brough Shetland 313 H6
Brough Shetland 313 J7
Brough Lodge Shetland 312 D7
Brough Sowerby Cumb 222 C5
Broughall Shrops 167 G9
Broughton Borders 260 B4
Broughton Bucks 84 C4
Broughton Cambs 122 B5
Broughton Edin 280 F5
Broughton Flint 166 C4
Broughton Hants 47 G10
Broughton Lancs 202 F6
Broughton M Keynes 103 C7
Broughton N Lincs 200 F3
Broughton N Yorks 204 C4
Broughton N Yorks 216 E5
Broughton Northants 120 B6
Broughton Orkney 314 B4
Broughton Oxon 101 D8
Broughton Shrops 132 E6
Broughton Staffs 150 C5
Broughton V Glam 58 E2
Broughton Astley Leics 135 E10
Broughton Beck Cumb 210 C5
Broughton Common N Lincs 200 E3
Broughton Common Wilts 61 G11
Broughton Cross Cumb 229 E7
Broughton Gifford Wilts 61 G11
Broughton Green Worcs 117 E9
Broughton Hackett Worcs 117 G8
Broughton in Furness Cumb 210 B4
Broughton Lodges Leics 154 E4
Broughton Mills Cumb 220 G4
Broughton Moor Cumb 228 E6
Broughton Park Gtr Man 195 G10
Broughton Poggs Oxon 82 E2
Broughtown Orkney 314 B6
Broughty Ferry Dundee 287 D8
Brow Edge Cumb 211 C7
Browhouses Dumfries 239 D7
Browland Shetland 313 H4
Brown Bank N Yorks 205 C10
Brown Candover Hants 48 F5
Brown Edge Lancs 193 E11
Brown Edge Mers 183 C8
Brown Edge Staffs 168 E6
Brown Heath Hants 33 D8
Brown Heath W Ches 167 B7
Brown Knowl W Ches 167 E7
Brown Lees Staffs 168 D5
Brown Moor W Yorks 206 G3
Brown Street Suff 125 E11
Brownber Cumb 222 D4
Brownbread Street E Sus 23 B11
Brownedge E Ches 168 C3
Brownheath Devon 27 D10
Brownheath Shrops 149 D9
Brownheath Common Worcs 117 E7
Brownhill Aberds 302 E6
Brownhill Aberds 303 E8
Brownhill Blkburn 203 G9
Brownhill Shrops 149 E8
Brownhills Fife 287 F9
Brownhills Shrops 150 B3
Brownhills W Mid 133 B10
Brownieside Northumb 264 E5
Browninghill Green Hants 48 B5
Brownlow E Ches 168 C4
Brownlow Mers 194 G4
Brownlow Fold Gtr Man 195 E8
Brownlow Heath E Ches 168 C4
Brownmuir Aberds 293 F9
Brown's Bank E Ches 167 G10
Brown's End Glos 98 E4
Brown's Green W Mid 133 E10
Browns Wood M Keynes 103 D8
Brownshill Glos 80 E5
Brownshill Green W Mid 134 G6
Brownside Lancs 204 G3
Brownsover Warks 119 B10
Brownston Devon 8 E3
Browsburn N Lnrk 268 C5
Browston Green Norf 143 C9
Browtop Cumb 229 G7
Broxa N Yorks 227 G8
Broxbourne Herts 86 D5
Broxburn E Loth 282 F3
Broxburn W Loth 279 G11
Broxfield Northumb 264 F6
Broxholme Lincs 188 F6
Broxted Essex 105 F11
Broxton W Ches 167 E7
Broxtowe Nottingham 171 G8
Broxwood Hereford 115 G7
Broyle Side E Sus 23 C7
Bruairnis W Isles 297 L3
Bruan Highld 310 F7
Bruar Lodge Perth 291 F10
Brucefield Fife 280 D2
Brucehill W Dunb 277 F7
Bruche Warr 183 D10
Brucklebog Aberds 293 D9
Bruera W Ches 166 C6
Bruern Abbey Oxon 100 G5
Bruichladdich Argyll 274 G3
Bruisyard Suff 126 D6
Brumby N Lincs 199 F11
Brunant Powys 130 B5
Brund Staffs 169 C10
Brundall Norf 142 B6
Brundish Norf 143 D7
Brundish Suff 126 D5
Brundish Street Suff 126 C5
Brundon Suff 107 C7
Brunery Highld 289 B9
Brunnion Corn 2 B2
Brunshaw Lancs 204 G3
Brunstane Edin 280 G6
Brunstock Cumb 239 F10
Brunswick Gtr Man 184 B4
Brunswick Park London 86 G3
Brunswick Village T & W 242 C6
Brunt Hamersland Shetland 313 H6
Bruntcliffe W Yorks 197 B9
Brunthwaite W Yorks 205 D7
Bruntingthorpe Leics 136 F2
Brunton Fife 287 E7
Brunton Northumb 264 E6
Brunton Wilts 47 B8
Brushes Gtr Man 185 B7
Brushfield Derbys 185 G11
Brushford Devon 25 F11
Brushford Som 26 B6
Bruton Som 45 G7
Bryans Midloth 270 C6
Bryan's Green Worcs 117 D7
Bryanston Dorset 30 F5
Bryant's Bottom Bucks 84 F5
Brydekirk Dumfries 238 C5
Bryher Scilly 1 G3
Brymbo Conwy 180 G4
Brymbo Wrex 166 E3
Brympton Som 29 D8
Brympton D'Evercy Som 29 D8
Bryn Caerph 77 F11
Bryn Carms 75 E8
Bryn Gtr Man 194 G5
Bryn Gwyn 179 G9
Bryn Neath 57 C10
Bryn Powys 130 C3
Bryn Rhondda 76 D5
Bryn Shrops 130 F5
Bryn Swansea 56 C4
Bryn W Ches 183 G10
Bryn Bwbach Gwyn 146 B2
Bryn-coch Neath 57 B8
Bryn Celyn Anglesey 179 F10
Bryn Celyn Flint 181 F11
Bryn Common Flint 166 D3
Bryn Du Anglesey 178 G4
Bryn Dulas Conwy 180 F6
Bryn Eglwys Gwyn 163 B10
Bryn Gates Gtr Man 194 G5
Bryn-glas Conwy 164 B4
Bryn Golau Rhondda 58 B3
Bryn-henllan Pembs 91 D10
Bryn-Iwan Carms 92 E6
Bryn-mawr Gwyn 144 C4
Bryn Mawr Powys 148 F5
Bryn Myrddin Carms 93 G8
Bryn-nantllech Conwy 164 B6
Bryn-newydd Denb 165 G11
Bryn Offa Wrex 166 F4
Bryn Pen-y-lan Wrex 166 G4
Bryn-penarth Powys 130 C2
Bryn Pydew Conwy 180 F4
Bryn Rhyd-yr-Arian Conwy 165 B7
Bryn-rhys Conwy 180 F4
Bryn Saith Marchog Denb 165 E9
Bryn Sion Gwyn 147 F7
Bryn Tanat Powys 148 E4
Bryn-y-cochin Shrops 149 B7
Bryn-y-gwenin Mon 78 B4
Bryn-y-maen Conwy 180 F4
Bryn-yr-Eos Wrex 166 G3
Bryn-yr-eryr Gwyn 162 F5
Bryn-yr-ogof Denb 165 D11
Brynafan Ceredig 112 C4
Brynamman Carms 76 C2
Brynawel Caerph 77 G11
Brynberian Pembs 92 D2
Brynbryddan Neath 57 C9
Bryncae Rhondda 58 C3
Bryncethin Bridgend 58 C2
Brynbryddan Neath 57 C9
Bryncae Rhondda 58 C3
Bryncethin Bridgend 58 C2
Bryncir Gwyn 163 G7
Bryncoch Bridgend 58 C2
Bryncroes Gwyn 144 C4
Bryncrug Gwyn 128 C2
Brynderwen Powys 130 D3
Bryndu Carms 75 D8
Bryneglwys Denb 165 F10
Brynford Flint 181 G11
Brynglas Newport 59 B10
Brynglas Sta Gwyn 128 C2
Bryngwran Anglesey 178 F4
Bryngwyn Ceredig 92 B5
Bryngwyn Mon 78 D5
Bryngwyn Powys 96 B3
Brynhenllan Pembs 91 D10
Brynheulog Bridgend 57 C11
Brynhoffnant Ceredig 110 G6
Bryniau Denb 181 E9
Bryning Lancs 194 B2
Brynithel Bl Gwent 78 E2
Brynllywarch Powys 130 F3
Brynmawr Bl Gwent 77 C11
Brynmenyn Bridgend 58 B2
Brynmill Swansea 56 C6
Brynmorfudd Conwy 164 C4
Brynna Rhondda 58 C3
Brynnau Gwynion Rhondda 58 C3
Brynore Shrops 149 B7
Brynrefail Anglesey 179 D7
Brynrefail Gwyn 163 C9
Brynsadler Rhondda 58 C4
Brynsiencyn Anglesey 163 B7
Brynsworthy Devon 40 G4
Brynteg Anglesey 179 E7
Brynteg Ceredig 93 C9
Brynteg Wrex 166 E4
Bryntirion Bridgend 57 E11
Buaile nam Bodach W Isles 297 L3
Bualintur Highld 294 C6
Bualnaluib Highld 307 K3
Buarthmeini Gwyn 146 C6
Bubbenhall Warks 119 C7
Bubblewell Glos 80 E5
Bubnell Derbys 186 G2
Bubwith E Yorks 207 F10
Buccleuch Borders 261 G8
Buchan Hill W Sus 51 G9
Buchanan Smithy Stirl 277 D9
Buchanhaven Aberds 303 E11
Buchanty Perth 286 E3
Buchley E Dunb 277 G11
Buchlyvie Stirl 277 C11
Buck Hill Wilts 62 E3
Buckabank Cumb 230 B3
Buckbury Worcs 98 E6
Buckden Cambs 122 D3
Buckden N Yorks 213 D8
Buckenham Norf 143 B7
Buckerell Devon 27 G10
Bucket Corner Hants 32 C6
Buckfast Devon 8 B4
Buckfastleigh Devon 8 B4
Buckham Dorset 29 G7
Buckhaven Fife 281 B7
Buckholm Borders 261 B11
Buckholt Mon 79 B8
Buckhorn Devon 12 B3
Buckhorn Weston Dorset 30 C3
Buckhurst Kent 53 E10
Buckhurst Hill Essex 86 G6
Buckie Moray 302 C4
Buckies Highld 310 C5
Buckingham Bucks 102 E3
Buckland Bucks 84 C5
Buckland Devon 8 G3
Buckland Devon 14 G3
Buckland Glos 99 D11
Buckland Hants 20 B2
Buckland Herts 105 E7
Buckland Kent 55 E10
Buckland Oxon 82 F4
Buckland Sur 51 C8
Buckland Brewer Devon 24 C6
Buckland Common Bucks 84 D6
Buckland Dinham Som 45 C9
Buckland Down Som 45 C8
Buckland End W Mid 134 F2
Buckland Filleigh Devon 25 F7
Buckland in the Moor Devon 13 G10
Buckland Marsh Oxon 82 F4
Buckland Monachorum Devon 7 B9
Buckland Newton Dorset 29 F11
Buckland Ripers Dorset 17 E8
Buckland St Mary Som 28 E3
Buckland Valley Kent 55 E10
Bucklands Borders 262 F2
Bucklandwharf Bucks 84 C5
Bucklebury W Berks 64 E5
Bucklebury Alley W Berks 64 E4
Bucklegate Lincs 156 B6
Buckleigh Devon 24 B6
Bucklerheads Angus 287 D8
Bucklers Hard Hants 20 B4
Bucklesham Suff 108 C4
Buckley = Bwcle Flint 166 C3
Buckley Green Warks 118 D3
Buckley Hill Mers 182 B4
Bucklow Hill E Ches 184 E2
Buckminster Leics 155 E7
Buckmoorend Bucks 84 E4
Bucknall Lincs 173 B11
Bucknall Stoke 168 F6
Bucknell Oxon 101 F11
Bucknell Shrops 115 C7
Buckoak W Ches 183 G8
Buckover S Glos 79 G11
Buckpool Moray 302 C4
Buckpool W Mid 133 F7
Buckridge Worcs 116 C4
Buck's Cross Devon 24 C4
Bucks Green W Sus 50 G5
Bucks Hill Herts 85 E9
Bucks Horn Oak Hants 49 E10
Buck's Mills Devon 24 C5
Bucksburn Aberdeen 293 C10
Buckskin Hants 48 C6
Buckton E Yorks 218 E3
Buckton Hereford 115 C7
Buckton Northumb 264 B3
Buckton Vale Gtr Man 196 G3
Buckworth Cambs 122 B2
Budbrooke Warks 118 D5
Budby Notts 171 B10
Buddgbrake Shetland 312 B8
Buddileigh Staffs 168 F3
Budd's Titson Corn 24 G2
Bude Corn 24 F2
Budge's Shop Corn 6 D6
Budlake Devon 14 B5
Budle Northumb 264 B5
Budleigh Som 27 D11
Budleigh Salterton Devon 15 E7
Budlett's Common E Sus 37 C7
Budock Water Corn 3 C7
Budworth Heath W Ches 183 F11
Buersil Head Gtr Man 196 E2
Buerton E Ches 167 G11
Buffler's Holt Bucks 102 D3
Bufton Leics 135 B8
Bugbrooke Northants 120 F3
Bugford Devon 40 E6
Bughtlin Edin 280 G3
Buglawton E Ches 168 C5
Bugle Corn 5 D10
Bugle Gate Worcs 116 D6
Bugley Dorset 30 C3
Bugley Wilts 45 E11
Bugthorpe E Yorks 207 B11
Building End Essex 105 D8
Buildwas Shrops 132 C2
Builth Road Powys 113 G10
Builth Wells Powys 113 G10
Buirgh W Isles 305 J2
Bulbourne Herts 84 C6
Bulbridge Wilts 46 G5
Bulby Lincs 155 D11
Bulcote Notts 171 G11
Buldoo Highld 310 C3
Bulford Wilts 47 E7
Bulford Camp Wilts 47 E7
Bulkeley E Ches 167 E8
Bulkeley Hall Shrops 168 G2
Bulkington Warks 135 F7
Bulkington Wilts 46 B2
Bulkworthy Devon 24 E5
Bull Bay = Porthllechog Anglesey 178 C6
Bull Hill Hants 20 B2
Bullamoor N Yorks 225 G7
Bullbridge Derbys 170 E5
Bullbrook Brack 65 F11
Bulleign Kent 53 G11
Bullenhill Wilts 45 B11
Bullen's Green Herts 86 D2
Bulley Glos 80 B3
Bullgill Cumb 229 D7
Bullhurst Hill Derbys 170 G3
Bullinghope Hereford 97 D10
Bullington Hants 48 E3
Bullington Lincs 189 F9
Bullo Glos 79 D11
Bullock's Horn Wilts 81 G7
Bullockstone Kent 71 F7
Bulls Cross London 86 F4
Bull's Green Herts 86 B3
Bull's Green Norf 143 E8
Bulls Green Som 45 D8
Bull's Hill Hereford 97 G11
Bullwood Argyll 276 G3
Bullyhole Bottom Mon 79 F7
Bulmer Essex 106 C6
Bulmer N Yorks 216 F3
Bulmer Tye Essex 106 D6
Bulphan Thurrock 68 B6
Bulstrode Herts 85 E8
Bulthy Shrops 148 G6
Bulverhythe E Sus 38 F3
Bulwark Aberds 303 E9
Bulwark Mon 79 G8
Bulwell Nottingham 171 F8
Bulwell Forest Nottingham 171 F8
Bulwick Leics 136 E3
Bulwick Northants 137 E9
Bumble's Green Essex 86 D6
Bumwell Hill Norf 142 E2
Bun Abhainn Eadarra W Isles 305 H3
Bun a'Mhuillin W Isles 297 K3
Bun Loyne Highld 290 C4
Bunacaimb Highld 295 G8
Bunarkaig Highld 290 E3
Bunbury E Ches 167 D9
Bunbury Heath E Ches 167 D9
Bunce Common Sur 51 D8
Bunchrew Highld 300 E6
Bundalloch Highld 295 C10
Buness Shetland 312 C8
Bunessan Argyll 288 G5
Bungay Suff 142 F6
Bunker's Hill Cambs 139 B8
Bunkers Hill Gtr Man 184 D6
Bunker's Hill Lincs 174 E3
Bunker's Hill Lincs 189 G7
Bunker's Hill Norf 142 B3
Bunkers Hill Oxon 83 B7
Bunker's Hill Suff 143 C10
Bunloit Highld 300 G5
Bunnahabhain Argyll 274 F5
Bunny Notts 153 D11
Bunny Hill Notts 153 D11
Bunree Highld 290 G2
Bunroy Highld 290 E4
Bunsley Bank E Ches 167 G11
Bunstead Hants 32 C6
Buntait Highld 300 F3
Buntingford Herts 105 F7
Bunting's Green Essex 106 E6
Bunwell Norf 142 E2
Bunwell Bottom Norf 142 D2
Buoltach Highld 310 F5
Burbage Derbys 185 G8
Burbage Leics 135 E8
Burbage Wilts 63 G8
Burcher Hereford 114 E6
Burchett's Green Windsor 65 C10
Burcombe Wilts 46 G5
Burcot Oxon 83 F9
Burcot Worcs 117 C9
Burcote Shrops 132 D4
Burcott Bucks 84 B4
Burcott Bucks 103 G7
Burcott Som 44 D4
Burdiehouse Edin 270 B5
Burdon T & W 243 G9
Burdonshill V Glam 58 E6
Burdrop Oxon 101 D7
Bures Suff 107 E8
Bures Green Suff 107 D8
Burford Devon 24 C4
Burford E Ches 167 E10
Burford Oxon 82 C3
Burford Shrops 115 D11
Burford Som 44 E5

Burg Argyll 288 E5
Burg Argyll 288 G6
Burgar Orkney 314 D3
Burgate Hants 31 D11
Burgate Suff 125 B11
Burgates Hants 34 B3
Burge End Herts 104 E2
Burgedin Powys 148 G4
Burgess Hill W Sus 36 D4
Burgh Suff 126 G4
Burgh by Sands Cumb 239 F8
Burgh Castle Norf 143 B9
Burgh Common Norf 141 E11
Burgh Heath Sur 51 B8
Burgh Hill E Sus 23 C8
Burgh Hill E Sus 38 B2
Burgh le Marsh Lincs 175 B8
Burgh Muir Aberds 293 B9
Burgh Muir Aberds 303 G7
Burgh next Aylsham Norf 160 D4
Burgh on Bain Lincs 190 D2
Burgh St Margaret = Fleggburgh Norf 161 G8
Burgh St Peter Norf 143 E9
Burgh Stubbs Norf 159 C10
Burghclere Hants 64 G3
Burghclere Common Hants 64 G3
Burghead Moray 301 C11
Burghfield W Berks 65 F7
Burghfield Common W Berks 64 F6
Burghfield Hill W Berks 65 F7
Burghill Hereford 97 C9
Burghwallis S Yorks 198 E4
Burgois Corn 10 G4
Burham Kent 69 G8
Burham Court Kent 69 G8
Buriton Hants 34 C2
Burland E Ches 167 E10
Burlawn Corn 10 G5
Burleigh Brack 65 E11
Burleigh Glos 80 E5
Burlescombe Devon 27 D9
Burleston Dorset 17 C11
Burlestone Devon 8 F6
Burley Hants 32 G2
Burley Rutland 155 G7
Burley Shrops 131 G9
Burley W Yorks 205 G11
Burley Beacon Hants 32 G2
Burley Gate Hereford 97 B11
Burley in Wharfedale W Yorks 205 D9
Burley Lawn Hants 32 G2
Burley Lodge Hants 32 F2
Burley Street Hants 32 G2
Burley Woodhead W Yorks 205 E9
Burleydam E Ches 167 G10
Burlinch Som 28 B3
Burlingham Green Norf 161 G7
Burlingjobb Powys 114 F5
Burlish Park Worcs 116 C6
Burlorne Tregoose Corn 5 B10
Burlow E Sus 23 B9
Burlton Shrops 149 D9
Burmantofts W Yorks 206 G2
Burmarsh Hereford 97 B10
Burmarsh Kent 54 G5
Burmington Warks 100 D5
Burn N Yorks 198 B5
Burn Bridge N Yorks 206 C2
Burn Naze Lancs 202 E2
Burn of Cambus Stirl 285 G11
Burnage Gtr Man 184 C5
Burnard's Ho Devon 24 G4
Burnaston Derbys 152 C5
Burnbank S Lnrk 268 D4
Burnby E Yorks 208 D2
Burncross S Yorks 186 B4
Burndell W Sus 35 G7
Burnden Gtr Man 195 F8
Burnedge Gtr Man 196 E2
Burnend Aberds 303 E8
Burneside Cumb 221 F10
Burness Orkney 314 B6
Burneston N Yorks 214 B6
Burnett Bath 61 F7
Burnfoot Borders 261 G10
Burnfoot Borders 262 F2
Burnfoot Dumfries 239 C7
Burnfoot Dumfries 247 E11
Burnfoot E Ayrs 245 B10
Burnfoot N Lnrk 268 B5
Burnfoot Perth 286 G3
Burngreave S Yorks 186 D5
Burnham Bucks 66 C2
Burnham N Lincs 200 D5
Burnham Deepdale Norf 176 E4
Burnham Green Herts 86 B3
Burnham Market Norf 176 E4
Burnham Norton Norf 176 E4
Burnham-on-Crouch Essex 88 F6
Burnham-on-Sea Som 43 D10
Burnham Overy Staithe Norf 176 E4
Burnham Overy Town Norf 176 E4
Burnham Thorpe Norf 176 E5
Burnhead Aberds 293 D10
Burnhead Borders 262 F2
Burnhead Dumfries 247 D9
Burnhead Dumfries 247 G10
Burnhead S Ayrs 244 C6
Burnhervie Aberds 293 B9
Burnhill Green Staffs 132 C5
Burnhope Durham 233 B9
Burnhouse N Ayrs 267 E7
Burnhouse Mains Borders 271 F8
Burniere Corn 10 G5
Burniestrype Moray 302 C3
Burniston N Yorks 227 G10
Burnlee W Yorks 196 F6
Burnley Lancs 204 G2
Burnley Lane Lancs 204 G2
Burnley Wood Lancs 204 G2
Burnmouth Borders 273 C9
Burnopfield Durham 242 F5
Burnrigg Cumb 239 F11
Burn's Green Herts 104 G6
Burnsall N Yorks 213 G10
Burnside Aberds 303 E8
Burnside Angus 287 B9
Burnside E Ayrs 258 G3
Burnside Fife 286 G5
Burnside Perth 286 E4
Burnside S Lnrk 268 C2
Burnside Shetland 312 F4
Burnside T & W 243 G8
Burnside W Loth 279 G11
Burnside of Duntrune Angus 287 D8
Burnstone Devon 24 C4
Burnswark Dumfries 238 B5
Burnt Ash Glos 80 E5
Burnt Heath Derbys 186 F2
Burnt Heath Essex 107 F11
Burnt Hill W Berks 64 E5
Burnt Houses Durham 233 G8
Burnt Mills Essex 88 G2
Burnt Oak E Sus 37 B8
Burnt Oak London 86 G2
Burnt Tree W Mid 133 E9
Burnt Yates N Yorks 214 G5
Burntcommon Sur 50 C4
Burntheath Derbys 152 C4
Burnthouse Corn 3 B7
Burntisland Fife 280 D4
Burnton E Ayrs 245 B11
Burnturk Fife 287 G7
Burntwood Staffs 133 B11
Burntwood Green Staffs 133 B11
Burntwood Pentre Flint 166 C3
Burnworthy Som 27 D11
Burnwynd Edin 270 B2
Burpham Sur 50 C4
Burpham W Sus 35 F8
Burradon Northumb 251 B11
Burradon T & W 243 C7
Burrafirth Shetland 312 B8
Burraland Shetland 312 F5
Burraland Shetland 313 J4
Burras Corn 2 C5
Burrastow Shetland 313 J4
Burraton Corn 7 D8
Burraton Coombe Corn 7 D8
Burravoe Shetland 312 F7
Burravoe Shetland 312 G5
Burray Village Orkney 314 G4
Burreldales Aberds 303 F7
Burrells Cumb 222 B3
Burrelton Perth 286 D6
Burridge Devon 28 F4
Burridge Devon 40 F5
Burridge Hants 33 E8
Burrigill Highld 310 F6
Burrill N Yorks 214 B4
Burringham N Lincs 199 F10
Burrington Devon 25 D10
Burrington Hereford 115 C8
Burrington N Som 44 B3
Burrough End Cambs 124 F2
Burrough Green Cambs 124 F2
Burrough on the Hill Leics 154 G5
Burroughs Grove Bucks 65 B11
Burroughston Orkney 314 D5
Burrow Devon 14 B5
Burrow Som 28 C6
Burrow Som 42 E2
Burrow-bridge Som 28 B5
Burrowbridge Som 43 G11
Burrowhill Sur 66 G3
Burrows Cross Sur 50 D5
Burrowsmoor Holt Notts 172 G2
Burrsville Park Essex 89 B11
Burrswood Kent 52 F4
Burry Swansea 56 C3
Burry Green Swansea 56 C3
Burry Port = Porth Tywyn Carms 74 E6
Burscott Devon 24 C4
Burscough Lancs 194 E2
Burscough Bridge Lancs 194 E2
Bursdon Devon 24 D3
Bursea E Yorks 208 G2
Burshill E Yorks 209 D7
Bursledon Hants 33 F7
Burslem Stoke 168 F5
Burstall Suff 107 C11
Burstallhill Suff 107 B11
Burstock Dorset 28 G6
Burston Devon 26 G2
Burston Norf 142 G2
Burston Staffs 151 C8
Burstow Sur 51 E10
Burstwick E Yorks 201 B8
Burtersett N Yorks 213 B7
Burtholme Cumb 240 E2
Burthorpe Suff 124 E5
Burthwaite Cumb 230 B4
Burtle Som 43 E11
Burtle Hill Som 43 E11
Burtoft Lincs 156 B5
Burton Dorset 17 C9
Burton Dorset 19 C9
Burton Lincs 189 G7
Burton Northumb 264 C5
Burton Pembs 73 D7
Burton Som 29 E8
Burton Som 43 E7
Burton V Glam 58 F4
Burton W Ches 167 C8
Burton W Ches 182 G4
Burton Wilts 45 G10
Burton Wilts 61 D10
Burton Wrex 166 D5
Burton Agnes E Yorks 218 G2
Burton Bradstock Dorset 16 D5
Burton Corner Lincs 174 F4
Burton Dassett Warks 119 G7
Burton End Cambs 106 B2
Burton End Essex 105 G10
Burton Ferry Pembs 73 D7
Burton Fleming E Yorks 217 E11
Burton Green Essex 106 F6
Burton Green W Mid 118 B5
Burton Green Wrex 166 D4
Burton Hastings Warks 135 E8
Burton-in-Kendal Cumb 211 D10
Burton in Lonsdale N Yorks 212 E3
Burton Joyce Notts 171 G10
Burton Latimer Northants 121 C8
Burton Lazars Leics 154 F5
Burton-le-Coggles Lincs 155 D9
Burton Leonard N Yorks 214 G6
Burton Manor Staffs 151 E8
Burton on the Wolds Leics 153 E11
Burton Overy Leics 136 D3
Burton Pedwardine Lincs 173 G10
Burton Pidsea E Yorks 209 G10
Burton Salmon N Yorks 198 B3
Burton Stather N Lincs 199 D11
Burton upon Stather N Lincs 199 D11
Burton upon Trent Staffs 152 E5
Burton Westwood Shrops 132 D2
Burtonwood Warr 183 C9
Burwardsley W Ches 167 D8
Burwarton Shrops 132 F2
Burwash E Sus 37 C11
Burwash Common E Sus 37 C10
Burwash Weald E Sus 37 C10
Burwell Cambs 123 D11
Burwell Lincs 190 F5
Burwen Anglesey 178 C6
Burwick Orkney 314 H4
Burwick Shetland 313 J5
Burwood Shrops 131 F9
Burwood Park Sur 66 G6
Bury Cambs 138 G5
Bury Gtr Man 195 E10
Bury Som 26 B6
Bury W Sus 35 E8
Bury End Beds 121 G9
Bury End C Beds 104 E2
Bury End Worcs 99 D11
Bury Green Herts 86 E4
Bury Green Herts 105 G8
Bury Hollow W Sus 35 E8
Bury Park Luton 103 G11
Bury St Edmunds Suff 125 E7
Buryas Br Corn 1 D4
Burybank Staffs 151 B7
Bury's Bank W Berks 64 F3
Burythorpe N Yorks 216 G5
Busbiehill N Ayrs 257 B9
Busbridge Sur 50 E3
Busby E Renf 267 D11
Buscot Oxon 82 F2
Buscott Som 44 F2
Bush Aberds 293 G9
Bush Corn 24 F2
Bush Bank Hereford 115 G9
Bush Crathie Aberds 292 D4
Bush End Essex 87 B9
Bush Estate Norf 161 D8
Bush Green Norf 141 D10
Bush Green Norf 142 F4
Bush Green Suff 125 F8
Bush Hill Park London 86 F4
Bushbury Sur 51 D7
Bushbury W Mid 133 C8
Bushby Leics 136 C3
Bushey Dorset 18 E5
Bushey Herts 85 G10
Bushey Ground Oxon 82 D4
Bushey Heath Herts 85 G11
Bushey Mead London 67 F8
Bushfield Cumb 249 G11
Bushley Worcs 99 E7
Bushley Green Worcs 99 E7
Bushmead Beds 122 E2
Bushmoor Shrops 131 F8
Bushton Wilts 62 D5
Bushy Common Norf 159 G9
Bushy Hill Sur 50 C4
Busk Cumb 231 C8
Busk Gtr Man 196 F2
Buslingthorpe Lincs 189 D9
Bussage Glos 80 E5
Bussex Som 43 F11
Busta Shetland 312 G5
Bustard Green Essex 106 F2
Bustard's Green Norf 142 E3
Bustatoun Orkney 314 A7
Busveal Corn 4 G4
Butcher's Common Norf 160 E6
Butcher's Cross E Sus 37 B9
Butcher's Pasture Essex 106 G2
Butcombe N Som 60 G4
Bute Town Caerph 77 D10
Butetown Cardiff 59 D7
Butlane Head Shrops 149 G8
Butleigh Som 44 G4
Butleigh Wootton Som 44 G4
Butler's Cross Bucks 84 D4
Butlers Cross Bucks 85 G7
Butler's End Warks 134 G4
Butler's Hill Notts 171 F8
Butlers Marston Warks 118 G6
Butlersbank Shrops 149 E11
Butley Suff 127 G7
Butley High Corner Suff 109 B7
Butley Low Corner Suff 109 B7
Butley Town E Ches 184 F6
Butlocks Heath Hants 33 F7
Butt Green E Ches 167 E11
Butt Lane Staffs 168 E4
Butt Yeats Lancs 211 F11
Butter Bank Staffs 151 E7
Butterburn Cumb 240 C5
Buttercrambe N Yorks 207 B10
Butteriss Gate Corn 2 C6
Butterknowle Durham 233 F8
Butterleigh Devon 27 F7
Butterley Derbys 170 C4
Butterley Derbys 170 E6
Buttermere Cumb 220 B3
Buttermere Wilts 63 G10
Butterrow Glos 80 E5
Butters Green Staffs 168 E4
Buttershaw W Yorks 196 B6
Butterstone Perth 286 C4
Butterton Staffs 168 G4
Butterton Staffs 169 D9
Butterwick Cumb 221 B10
Butterwick Durham 234 F3
Butterwick Lincs 174 G5
Butterwick N Yorks 216 D4
Butterwick N Yorks 217 E9
Butteryhaugh Northumb 250 E4
Buttington Powys 130 B5
Button Haugh Green Suff 125 D9
Buttonbridge Shrops 116 B4
Buttonoak Worcs 116 B5
Button's Green Suff 125 G8
Butts Devon 14 D2
Butt's Green Essex 88 E3
Butts Green Essex 105 E9
Butt's Green Hants 32 B4
Buttsash Hants 32 F6
Buttsbear Cross Corn 24 G3
Buttsbury Essex 87 F11
Buttsole Kent 55 C10
Buxhall Suff 125 F10
Buxhall Fen Street Suff 125 F10
Buxley Borders 272 E6
Buxted E Sus 37 C7
Buxton Derbys 185 G9
Buxton Norf 160 E4
Buxworth Derbys 185 E8
Bwcle = Buckley Flint 166 C3
Bwlch Flint 181 G11
Bwlch Powys 96 G2
Bwlch-derwin Gwyn 163 F7
Bwlch-Llan Ceredig 111 F11
Bwlch-newydd Carms 93 G7
Bwlch-y-cibau Powys 148 F3
Bwlch-y-cwm Cardiff 58 C6
Bwlch-y-fadfa Ceredig 93 B8
Bwlch-y-ffridd Powys 129 D11
Bwlch-y-Plain Powys 114 B4
Bwlch-y-sarnau Powys 113 C10
Bwlchgwyn Wrex 166 E3
Bwlchnewydd Carms 93 G7
Bwlchtocyn Gwyn 144 D6
Bwlchyddar Powys 148 E3
Bwlchygroes Pembs 92 D4
Bwlchyllyn Gwyn 163 D8
Bybrook Kent 54 E4
Bycross Hereford 97 C7
Bye Green Bucks 84 C5
Byeastwood Bridgend 58 C2
Byebush Aberds 303 F7
Byerhope Northumb 232 B3
Byermoor T & W 242 F5
Byers Green Durham 233 E10
Byfield Northants 119 G10
Byfleet Sur 66 G5
Byford Hereford 97 C7
Byford Common Hereford 97 C7
Bygrave Herts 104 D5
Byker T & W 243 E7
Byland Abbey N Yorks 215 D10
Bylchau Conwy 165 C7
Byley W Ches 168 B2
Bynea Carms 56 B4
Byram N Yorks 198 B3
Byrness Northumb 251 C7
Bythorn Cambs 121 B11
Byton Hereford 115 E7
Byton Hand Hereford 115 E7
Bywell Northumb 242 E2
Byworth W Sus 35 C7

C

Cabbacott Devon 24 C6
Cabbage Hill Brack 65 E11
Cabharstadh W Isles 304 F5
Cabin Shrops 130 F6
Cablea Perth 286 D3
Cabourne Lincs 200 G6
Cabrach Argyll 274 G5
Cabrach Moray 302 G3
Cabrich Highld 300 E5
Cabus Lancs 202 D5
Cackle Hill Lincs 157 D7
Cackle Street E Sus 23 B11
Cackle Street E Sus 37 B7
Cackle Street E Sus 38 D4
Cackleshaw W Yorks 204 F6
Cad Green Som 28 D4
Cadbolt Highld 301 B8
Cadbury Devon 26 G6
Cadbury Barton Devon 25 D11
Cadbury Heath S Glos 61 E7
Cadder E Dunb 278 G2
Cadderlie Argyll 284 D4
Caddington C Beds 85 B9
Caddleton Argyll 275 B8
Caddonfoot Borders 261 C10
Caddonlee Borders 261 B10
Cade Street E Sus 37 C10
Cadeby Leics 135 C8
Cadeby S Yorks 198 G4
Cadeleigh Devon 26 F6
Cademuir Borders 260 B6
Cader Denb 165 C8
Cadger Path Angus 287 B8
Cadgwith Corn 2 G6
Cadham Fife 286 G6
Cadishead Gtr Man 184 C2
Cadle Swansea 56 B6
Cadley Lancs 202 G6
Cadley Wilts 47 C8
Cadley Wilts 63 F8
Cadmore End Bucks 84 G3
Cadnam Hants 32 E3
Cadney N Lincs 200 G4
Cadney Bank Wrex 149 C9
Cadole Flint 166 C2
Cadoxton V Glam 58 F6
Cadoxton-Juxta-Neath Neath 57 B9
Cadshaw Blkburn 195 D8
Cadwell Herts 104 E3
Cadzow S Lnrk 268 E4
Cae Clyd Gwyn 164 G2
Cae-gors Carms 75 E9
Caeathro Gwyn 163 C7
Caehopkin Powys 76 C4
Caemorgan Ceredig 92 B3
Caenby Lincs 189 D8
Caenby Corner Lincs 189 D7
Cae'r-bont Powys 76 C4
Cae'r-bryn Carms 75 C9
Caer-Estyn Wrex 166 D4
Caer-Farchell Pembs 90 F5
Cae'r-Lan Powys 76 C4
Caer Llan Mon 79 D7
Caerau Bridgend 57 C11
Caerau Cardiff 58 D6
Caerau Park Newport 59 B9
Caerdeon Gwyn 146 F2
Caerfarchell Pembs 90 F5
Caerffili = Caerphilly Caerph 59 B7
Caerfyrddin = Carmarthen Carms 93 G8
Caergeiliog Anglesey 178 F4
Caergwrle Flint 166 D4
Caergybi = Holyhead Anglesey 178 E2
Caerhendy Neath 57 C9
Caerhun Gwyn 163 B9
Caerleon Newport 78 G4
Caermead V Glam 58 F3
Caermeini Pembs 92 E2
Caernarfon Gwyn 163 C7
Caerphilly = Caerffili Caerph 59 B7
Caersws Powys 129 E10
Caerwedros Ceredig 111 F7
Caerwent Mon 79 G7
Caerwent Brook Mon 60 B3
Caerwych Gwyn 146 B2
Caerwys Flint 181 G10
Caethle Gwyn 128 D2
Cage Green Kent 52 D5
Caggan Highld 291 B10
Caggle Street Mon 78 B5
Cailness Stirl 285 G7
Caim Anglesey 179 E10
Cainscross Glos 80 D4
Caio Carms 94 D3
Cairinis W Isles 296 E4
Cairisiadar W Isles 304 E2
Cairminis W Isles 296 C6
Cairnbaan Argyll 275 D9
Cairnbanno Ho Aberds 303 E8
Cairnborrow Aberds 302 E4
Cairnbrogie Aberds 303 G8
Cairnbulg Castle Aberds 303 C10
Cairncross Angus 292 F6
Cairncross Borders 273 C7
Cairnderry Dumfries 236 B5
Cairndow Argyll 284 F5
Cairness Aberds 303 C10
Cairneyhill Fife 279 D10
Cairnfield Ho Moray 302 C4
Cairngaan Dumfries 236 F3
Cairngarroch Dumfries 236 E2
Cairnhill Aberds 302 F6
Cairnhill Aberds 303 D7
Cairnhill N Lnrk 268 C5
Cairnie Aberds 293 C10
Cairnie Aberds 302 E4
Cairnlea S Ayrs 244 G6
Cairnleith Crofts Aberds 303 F9
Cairnmuir Aberds 303 C9
Cairnorrie Aberds 303 E8
Cairnpark Aberds 293 B10
Cairnpark Dumfries 247 D9
Cairnryan Dumfries 236 C2
Cairnton Orkney 314 F3
Cairston Orkney 314 E2
Caister-on-Sea Norf 161 G10
Caistor Lincs 200 G6
Caistor St Edmund Norf 142 C4
Caistron Northumb 251 C11
Caitha Bowland Borders 271 G9
Cakebole Worcs 117 C7
Calais Street Suff 107 D9
Calanais W Isles 304 E4
Calbost W Isles 305 G6
Calbourne I o W 20 D4
Calceby Lincs 190 F5
Calcoed Flint 181 G11
Calcot Glos 81 C9
Calcot W Berks 65 E7
Calcot Row W Berks 65 E7
Calcott Kent 71 G7
Calcott Shrops 149 G8
Calcott's Green Glos 80 B3
Calcutt N Yorks 206 B2
Calcutt Wilts 81 G10
Caldback Shetland 312 C8
Caldbeck Cumb 230 D2
Caldbergh N Yorks 213 B11
Caldecote Cambs 122 F6
Caldecote Cambs 138 F2
Caldecote Herts 104 D4
Caldecote Northants 120 G3
Caldecote Warks 135 E7
Caldecote Hill Herts 85 G11
Caldecott Northants 121 D9
Caldecott Oxon 83 F7
Caldecott Rutland 137 E7
Caldecotte M Keynes 103 D7
Calder Cumb 219 E10
Calder Bridge Cumb 219 D10
Calder Grove W Yorks 197 D10
Calder Hall Cumb 219 E10
Calder Mains Highld 310 D4
Calder Vale Lancs 202 D6
Calderbank N Lnrk 268 C5
Calderbrook Gtr Man 196 D2
Caldercruix N Lnrk 268 B6
Caldermill S Lnrk 268 G3
Caldermoor Gtr Man 196 D2
Calderstones Mers 182 D6
Calderwood S Lnrk 268 D2
Caldhame Angus 287 C8
Caldicot = Cil-y-coed Mon 60 B3
Caldmore W Mid 133 D10
Caldwell Derbys 152 F5
Caldwell N Yorks 224 C3
Caldy Mers 182 D2
Cale Green Gtr Man 184 D5
Caledrhydiau Ceredig 111 G9
Calenick Corn 4 G6
Caleys Fields Worcs 100 C4
Calf Heath Staffs 133 B8
Calford Green Suff 106 B3
Calfsound Orkney 314 C5
Calgary Argyll 288 D5
Caliach Argyll 288 D5
Califer Moray 301 D10
California Cambs 139 G10
California Falk 279 F8
California Norf 161 G10
California Suff 108 C3
California W Mid 133 G10
Calke Derbys 153 E7
Callakille Highld 298 D6
Callaly Northumb 252 B3
Callander Stirl 285 G10
Callandrode Stirl 285 G10
Callands Warr 183 C9
Callaughton Shrops 132 D2
Callendar Park Falk 279 F7
Callert Ho Highld 290 G2
Callerton T & W 242 D5
Callerton Lane End T & W 242 D5
Callestick Corn 4 E5
Calligarry Highld 295 E8
Callington Corn 7 B7
Callingwood Staffs 152 E3
Calloose Corn 2 B3
Callop Highld 289 B11
Callow Derbys 170 E3
Callow Hereford 97 E9
Callow End Worcs 98 B6
Callow Hill Mon 79 B8
Callow Hill Som 44 E4
Callow Hill Wilts 62 C4
Callow Hill Worcs 116 C4
Callow Marsh Hereford 98 B3
Callows Grave Worcs 115 D11
Calmore Hants 32 E4
Calmsden Glos 81 D8
Calne Wilts 62 E4
Calne Marsh Wilts 62 E4
Calow Derbys 186 G6
Calow Green Derbys 170 B6
Calrofold E Ches 184 G6
Calshot Hants 33 G7
Calstock Corn 7 B8
Calstone Wellington Wilts 62 F4
Calthorpe Norf 160 C3
Calthorpe Oxon 101 D9
Calthwaite Cumb 230 C5
Calton Glasgow 268 C2
Calton N Yorks 204 B4
Calton Staffs 169 E10
Calton Lees Derbys 170 B3
Calvadnack Corn 2 B5
Calveley E Ches 167 D9
Calver Derbys 186 G2
Calver Hill Hereford 97 B7
Calver Sough Derbys 186 F2
Calverhall Shrops 150 B2
Calverleigh Devon 26 E6
Calverley W Yorks 205 F10
Calvert Bucks 102 G3
Calverton M Keynes 102 D5
Calverton Notts 171 F10
Calvine Perth 291 G10
Calvo Cumb 238 G4
Cam Glos 80 F3
Camaghael Highld 290 F3
Camas an Staca Argyll 274 G5
Camas-luinie Highld 295 C11
Camas Salach Highld 289 C8
Camasnacroise Highld 289 D10
Camastianavaig Highld 295 B7
Camasunary Highld 295 D7
Camault Muir Highld 300 E5
Camb Shetland 312 D7
Camber E Sus 39 D7
Camberley Sur 65 G11
Camberwell London 67 D10
Camblesforth N Yorks 199 B7
Cambo Northumb 252 F2
Cambois Northumb 253 G8
Camborne Corn 4 G3
Cambourne Cambs 122 F6
Cambridge Borders 271 F11
Cambridge Cambs 123 F9
Cambridge Glos 80 E3
Cambridge W Yorks 205 D10
Cambridge Batch N Som 60 F4
Cambridge Town Sthend 70 C2
Cambrose Corn 4 F3
Cambus Clack 279 C7
Cambusavie Farm Highld 309 K7
Cambusbarron Stirl 278 C5
Cambusdrenny Stirl 278 C5
Cambuskenneth Stirl 278 C6
Cambuslang S Lnrk 268 D2
Cambusmore Lodge Highld 309 K7
Cambusnethan N Lnrk 268 D6
Camden London 67 C9
Camden Hill Kent 53 F9
Camden Park Kent 52 F5
Camel Green Dorset 31 E10
Cameley Bath 44 B6
Camelford Corn 11 E8
Camelon Falk 279 E7
Camelsdale Sur 49 G11
Camer Kent 69 F7
Cameron Fife 280 B6
Cameron Bridge Fife 280 B6
Camerory Highld 301 F10
Camer's Green Worcs 98 D5
Camerton Bath 45 B7
Camerton Cumb 228 E6
Camerton E Yorks 201 B8
Camghouran Perth 285 B9
Cammachmore Aberds 293 D11
Cammeringham Lincs 188 E6
Camnant Powys 113 F11
Camoquhill Stirl 277 D10
Camore Highld 309 K7
Camp Lincs 172 E5
Camp Corner Oxon 83 E10
Camp Hill N Yorks 214 C6
Camp Hill Pembs 73 C10
Camp Hill W Yorks 196 D5
Camp Hill Warks 134 E6
Camp Town W Yorks 206 F2
Campbeltown Argyll 255 E8
Camperdown T & W 243 C7
Camphill Derbys 185 F11
Campion Hills Warks 118 D6
Campions Essex 87 C7
Cample Dumfries 247 E9
Campmuir Perth 286 D6
Camps End Cambs 106 C2
Camps Heath Suff 143 E10
Campsall S Yorks 198 E4
Campsea Ashe Suff 126 F6
Campsey Ash Suff 126 F6
Campsfield Oxon 83 B7
Campton C Beds 104 D2
Camptoun E Loth 281 F10
Camptown Borders 262 G5
Camquhart Argyll 275 E10
Camrose Pembs 91 G8
Camserney Perth 286 C2
Camster Highld 310 E6
Camuschoirk Highld 289 C9
Camuscross Highld 295 D8
Camusnagaul Highld 290 F2
Camusnagaul Highld 307 L5
Camusrory Highld 295 F10
Camusteel Highld 299 E7
Camusterrach Highld 299 E7
Camusvrachan Perth 285 C10
Canada Hants 32 D3
Canada Lincs 200 G6
Canadia E Sus 38 D2
Canal Foot Cumb 210 D6
Canal Side S Yorks 199 E7
Canbus Clack 279 C7
Candacraig Ho Aberds 292 B5
Candle Street Suff 125 C10
Candlesby Lincs 175 B7
Candy Mill S Lnrk 269 G11
Cane End Oxon 65 D7
Caneheath E Sus 23 D9
Canewdon Essex 88 G5
Canford Bottom Dorset 31 G8
Canford Cliffs Poole 19 D7
Canford Heath Poole 18 C6
Canford Magna Poole 18 B6
Cangate Norf 160 F6
Canham's Green Suff 125 D11
Canholes Derbys 185 G8
Canisbay Highld 310 B7
Canklow S Yorks 186 C6
Canley W Mid 118 B6
Cann Dorset 30 C5
Cann Common Dorset 30 C5
Cannalidgey Corn 5 B8
Cannard's Grave Som 44 E6
Cannich Highld 300 F3
Canning Town London 68 C2
Cannington Som 43 F9
Cannock Staffs 133 B9
Cannock Wood Staffs 151 G10
Cannon's Green Essex 87 D9
Cannop Glos 79 C10
Canon Bridge Hereford 97 C8
Canon Frome Hereford 98 C3
Canon Pyon Hereford 97 B9
Canonbie Dumfries 239 B9
Canonbury London 67 C10
Canons Ashby Northants 119 G11
Canons Park London 85 G11
Canon's Town Corn 2 B2
Canonsgrove Som 28 C2
Canterbury Kent 54 B6
Cantley Norf 143 C7
Cantley S Yorks 198 G6
Cantlop Shrops 131 B10
Canton Cardiff 59 D7
Cantraybruich Highld 301 E7
Cantraydoune Highld 301 E7
Cantraywood Highld 301 E7
Cantsfield Lancs 212 E2
Canvey Island Essex 69 C9
Canwick Lincs 173 B7
Canworthy Water Corn 11 C10
Caol Highld 290 F3
Caol Ila Argyll 274 F5

Caolas Argyll 288 E2
Caolas W Isles 297 M2
Caolas Fhlodaigh W Isles 296 F4
Caolas Liubharsaigh W Isles 297 G4
Caolas Scalpaigh W Isles 305 J4
Caolas Stocinis W Isles 305 J3
Caoslasnacon Highld 290 G3
Capel Carms 75 E8
Capel Kent 52 E6
Capel Sur 51 E7
Capel Bangor Ceredig 128 G3
Capel Betws Lleucu Ceredig 112 F2
Capel Carmel Gwyn 144 D3
Capel Coch Anglesey 179 E7
Capel Cross Kent 53 E8
Capel Curig Conwy 164 D2
Capel Cynon Ceredig 93 B7
Capel Dewi Carms 93 G9
Capel Dewi Ceredig 93 C9
Capel Dewi Ceredig 128 G2
Capel Garmon Conwy 164 D4
Capel Green Suff 109 B7
Capel-gwyn Anglesey 178 F4
Capel Gwyn Carms 93 G9
Capel Gwynfe Carms 94 G4
Capel Hendre Carms 75 C9
Capel Hermon Gwyn 146 D4
Capel Isaac Carms 93 F11
Capel Iwan Carms 92 D5
Capel-le-Ferne Kent 55 F8
Capel Llanilltern Cardiff 58 C5
Capel Mawr Anglesey 178 G6
Capel Newydd = Newchapel Pembs 92 D4
Capel Parc Anglesey 178 D6
Capel St Andrew Suff 109 B7
Capel St Mary Suff 107 D11
Capel Seion Carms 75 C8
Capel Seion Ceredig 112 B2
Capel Siloam Conwy 164 E4
Capel Tygwydd Ceredig 92 C5
Capel Uchaf Gwyn 162 F6
Capel-y-ffin Powys 96 E5
Capel-y-graig Gwyn 163 B8
Capelulo Conwy 180 F2
Capenhurst W Ches 182 G5
Capernwray Lancs 211 E10
Capheaton Northumb 252 G2
Capland Som 28 D4
Cappercleuch Borders 260 E6
Capplegill Dumfries 248 B4
Capstone Medway 69 F9
Captain Fold Gtr Man 195 E11
Capton Devon 8 E6
Capton Som 42 F5
Caputh Perth 286 D4
Car Colston Notts 172 G2
Caradon Town Corn 11 G11
Carbis Corn 5 D10
Carbis Bay Corn 2 B2
Carbost Highld 294 B5
Carbost Highld 298 E4
Carbrain N Lnrk 278 G5
Carbrook S Yorks 186 D5
Carbrooke Norf 141 C9
Carburton Notts 187 G10
Carcant Borders 271 E7
Carcary Angus 287 B10
Carclaze Corn 5 E10
Carclew Corn 3 B7
Carcroft S Yorks 198 E4
Cardenden Fife 280 C4
Cardeston Shrops 149 G7
Cardew Cumb 230 B2
Cardewlees Cumb 239 G8
Cardiff Cardiff 59 D7
Cardigan = Aberteifi Ceredig 92 B3
Cardinal's Green Cambs 106 B2
Cardington Beds 103 B11
Cardington Shrops 131 D10
Cardinham Corn 6 B2
Cardonald Glasgow 267 C10
Cardow Moray 301 E11
Cardrona Borders 261 B8
Cardross Argyll 276 F6
Cardurnock Cumb 238 F5
Care Village Leics 136 D4
Careby Lincs 155 F10
Careston Angus 293 G7
Careston Castle Angus 287 B9
Carew Pembs 73 E8
Carew Cheriton Pembs 73 E8
Carew Newton Pembs 73 E8
Carey Hereford 97 E11
Carey Park Corn 6 E4
Carfin N Lnrk 268 D5
Carfrae E Loth 271 B11
Carfury Corn 1 C4
Cargate Common Norf 142 E2
Cargenbridge Dumfries 237 B11
Cargill Perth 286 D5
Cargo Cumb 239 F9
Cargo Fleet M'bro 234 G6
Cargreen Corn 7 C8
Carham Northumb 263 B8
Carhampton Som 42 E4
Carharrack Corn 4 G4
Carie Perth 285 B10
Carie Perth 285 D10
Carines Corn 4 D5
Carisbrooke I o W 20 D5
Cark Cumb 211 D7
Carkeel Corn 7 C8
Carlabhagh W Isles 304 D4
Carland Cross Corn 5 E7
Carlbury N Yorks 224 B4
Carlby Lincs 155 G11
Carlecotes S Yorks 197 G7
Carleen Corn 2 C4
Carlenrig Borders 249 C9
Carlesmoor N Yorks 214 E3
Carleton Cumb 219 D10
Carleton Cumb 230 F6
Carleton Cumb 239 G10
Carleton Lancs 202 F2
Carleton N Yorks 204 D5
Carleton W Yorks 198 C3
Carleton Forehoe Norf 141 B11
Carleton Hall Cumb 219 F11
Carleton-in-Craven N Yorks 204 D5
Carleton Rode Norf 142 E2
Carleton St Peter Norf 142 C6
Carley Hill T & W 243 F9
Carlidnack Corn 3 D7
Carlin How Redcar 226 B4
Carlincraig Aberds 302 E6
Carlingcott Bath 45 B7
Carlinghow W Yorks 197 C8
Carlingwark Devon 27 E11
Carlisle Cumb 239 F10
Carloggas Corn 5 B7
Carloggas Corn 5 E9
Carloonan Argyll 284 F4
Carlops Borders 270 D3
Carlton Beds 121 F9
Carlton Cambs 124 G2
Carlton Leics 135 C7
Carlton N Yorks 198 C6
Carlton N Yorks 213 C11
Carlton N Yorks 216 B2
Carlton N Yorks 224 C3
Carlton Notts 171 G10
Carlton S Yorks 197 E11
Carlton Stockton 234 G3
Carlton Suff 127 E7
Carlton W Yorks 197 B10
Carlton Colville Suff 143 F10
Carlton Curlieu Leics 136 D3
Carlton Green Cambs 124 G2
Carlton Husthwaite N Yorks 215 D9
Carlton in Cleveland N Yorks 225 E10
Carlton in Lindrick Notts 187 E9
Carlton le Moorland Lincs 172 D6
Carlton Miniott N Yorks 215 C7
Carlton on Trent Notts 172 C3
Carlton Purlieus Northants 136 F6
Carlton Scroop Lincs 172 G6
Carluddon Corn 5 D10
Carluke S Lnrk 268 E6
Carlyon Bay Corn 5 E11
Carmarthen = Caerfyrddin Carms 93 G8
Carmel Anglesey 178 E5
Carmel Carms 75 B9
Carmel Flint 181 F11
Carmel Gwyn 163 E7
Carmel Powys 113 D11
Carmichael S Lnrk 259 B10
Carminow Cross Corn 5 B11
Carmont Aberds 293 E10
Carmunnock Glasgow 268 D2
Carmyle Glasgow 268 C2
Carmyllie Angus 287 C9
Carn Arthen Corn 2 B5
Carn Brea Village Corn 4 G3
Carn-gorm Highld 295 C11
Carn Towan Corn 1 D3
Carnaby E Yorks 218 F2
Carnach Highld 299 G10
Carnach Highld 307 K5
Carnach W Isles 305 J4
Carnachy Highld 308 D7
Càrnais W Isles 304 E2
Càrnan W Isles 297 G3
Carnbahn Perth 285 C10
Carnbee Fife 287 G9
Carnbo Perth 286 G4
Carnbrea Corn 4 G3
Carnbroe N Lnrk 268 C4
Carndu Highld 295 C10
Carnduff S Lnrk 268 F3
Carnduncan Argyll 274 G3
Carne Corn 3 B10
Carne Corn 3 E7
Carne Corn 5 D9
Carnebone Corn 2 C6
Carnedd Powys 129 E10
Carnetown Rhondda 77 G9
Carnforth Lancs 211 E10
Carnforth Lancs 211 E9
Carnglas Swansea 56 C6
Carnhedryn Pembs 90 F6
Carnhedryn Uchaf Pembs 90 F5
Carnhell Green Corn 2 B4
Carnhot Corn 4 F4
Carnkie Corn 2 B5
Carnkie Corn 2 C6
Carnkief Corn 4 E5
Carno Powys 129 D9
Carnoch Highld 300 D2
Carnoch Highld 300 F3
Carnock Fife 279 D10
Carnon Downs Corn 4 G5
Carnousie Aberds 302 D6
Carnoustie Angus 287 D9
Carnsmerry Corn 5 D10
Carntyne Glasgow 268 B2
Carnwadric E Renf 267 D10
Carnwath S Lnrk 269 F9
Carnyorth Corn 1 C3
Caroe Corn 11 C9
Carol Green W Mid 118 B5
Carpalla Corn 5 E9
Carpenders Park Herts 85 G10
Carpenter's Hill Worcs 117 C11
Carperby N Yorks 213 B10
Carpley Green N Yorks 213 B8
Carr Gtr Man 195 D9
Carr S Yorks 187 C8
Carr Bank Cumb 211 D9
Carr Cross Lancs 193 E11
Carr Gate W Yorks 197 C10
Carr Green Gtr Man 184 D2
Carr Hill T & W 243 E7
Carr Houses Mers 193 G10
Carr Vale Derbys 171 B7
Carradale Argyll 255 D9
Carragraich W Isles 305 J3
Carrbridge Highld 301 G9
Carrbrook Gtr Man 196 G3
Carreg-wen Pembs 92 C4
Carreg y Garth Gwyn 163 B9
Carreglefn Anglesey 178 D5
Carrhouse Devon 26 F3
Carrick Argyll 275 E10
Carrick Dumfries 237 D7
Carrick Fife 287 E8
Carrick Castle Argyll 276 C3
Carrick Ho Orkney 314 C5
Carriden Falk 279 E10
Carrington Gtr Man 184 C2
Carrington Lincs 174 E4
Carrington Midloth 270 C6
Carrington Nottingham 171 G9
Carroch Dumfries 246 E5
Carrog Conwy 164 F3
Carrog Denb 165 G10
Carroglen Perth 285 E11
Carrol Highld 311 J2
Carron Falk 279 E7
Carron Moray 302 E2
Carron Bridge Stirl 278 E4
Carronbridge Dumfries 247 D9
Carronshore Falk 279 E7
Carrot Angus 287 C8
Carrow Hill Mon 78 G6
Carroway Head Staffs 134 D3
Carrshield Northumb 232 B2
Carrutherstown Dumfries 238 C4
Carrville Durham 234 C2
Carry Argyll 275 G10
Carsaig Argyll 275 E8
Carsaig Argyll 289 G7
Carscreugh Dumfries 236 D4
Carse Gray Angus 287 B8
Carse Ho Argyll 275 G8
Carsegowan Dumfries 236 D6
Carseriggan Dumfries 236 C5
Carsethorn Dumfries 237 D11
Carshalton London 67 G9
Carshalton Beeches London 67 G9
Carshalton on the Hill London 67 G9
Carsington Derbys 170 E3
Carskiey Argyll 255 G7
Carsluith Dumfries 236 D6
Carsphairn Dumfries 246 E3
Carstairs S Lnrk 269 F8
Carstairs Junction S Lnrk 269 F9
Carswell Marsh Oxon 82 F4
Cartbridge Sur 50 B4
Carter Knowle S Yorks 186 E4
Carterhaugh Borders 261 D10
Carter's Clay Hants 32 C4
Carter's Green Essex 87 C8
Carter's Hill Wokingham 65 F9
Carterspiece Glos 79 C9
Carterton Oxon 82 D3
Carterway Heads Northumb 242 G2
Carthamartha Corn 12 F3
Carthew Corn 2 B5
Carthew Corn 5 D10
Carthorpe N Yorks 214 C6
Cartington Northumb 252 C2
Cartland S Lnrk 269 F7
Cartledge Derbys 186 F4
Cartmel Cumb 211 D7
Cartmel Fell Cumb 211 B8
Cartsdyke Invclyd 276 F5
Cartworth W Yorks 196 F6
Carty Port Dumfries 236 C6
Carway Carms 75 D7
Carwinley Cumb 239 C10
Carwynnen Corn 2 B5
Cary Fitzpaine Som 29 B9
Carzantic Corn 12 E3
Carzield Dumfries 247 G11
Carzise Corn 2 C3
Cas Mael = Puncheston Pembs 91 F10
Cascob Powys 114 D4
Cashes Green Glos 80 D4
Cashlie Perth 285 C8
Cashmoor Dorset 31 E7
Cassey Compton Glos 81 C9
Cassington Oxon 83 C7
Cassop Durham 234 D2
Castallack Corn 1 D5
Castell Conwy 164 B3
Castell Denb 165 B10
Castell-Howell Ceredig 93 B8
Castell nedd = Neath Neath 57 B8
Castell Newydd Emlyn = Newcastle Emlyn Carms 92 C6
Castell-y-bwch Torf 78 G3
Castell-y-rhingyll Carms 75 C9
Castellau Rhondda 58 B5
Casterton Cumb 212 D2
Castle Devon 28 G4
Castle Som 27 B9
Castle Acre Norf 158 F6
Castle Ashby Northants 121 F7
Castle Bolton N Yorks 223 G10
Castle Bromwich W Mid 134 F2
Castle Bytham Lincs 155 F9
Castle Caereinion Powys 130 B3
Castle Camps Cambs 106 C2
Castle Carlton Lincs 190 E5
Castle Carrock Cumb 240 F2
Castle Cary Som 44 G6
Castle Combe Wilts 61 D10
Castle Donington Leics 153 D8
Castle Douglas Dumfries 237 C9
Castle Eaton Swindon 81 F10
Castle Eden Durham 234 D4
Castle End P'boro 138 B2
Castle Fields Shrops 149 G10
Castle Forbes Aberds 293 B8
Castle Frome Hereford 98 B3
Castle Gate Corn 1 C5
Castle Green London 68 C3
Castle Green S Yorks 197 G9
Castle Green Sur 66 G3
Castle Gresley Derbys 152 F5
Castle Heaton Northumb 273 G8
Castle Hedingham Essex 106 D5
Castle Hill E Sus 37 B9
Castle Hill Gtr Man 184 C6
Castle Hill Kent 53 E7
Castle Hill Suff 108 B3
Castle Hill Worcs 116 F5
Castle Huntly Perth 287 E7
Castle Kennedy Dumfries 236 D3
Castle O'er Dumfries 248 E6
Castle Rising Norf 158 E3
Castle Street W Yorks 196 C3
Castle Stuart Highld 301 E7
Castle Toward Argyll 266 B2
Castle Town W Sus 36 E2
Castle-upon-Alun V Glam 58 E2
Castle Vale W Mid 134 E2
Castlebythe Pembs 91 F10
Castlecary N Lnrk 278 F5
Castle Craig Borders 270 G2
Castlecraig Highld 301 C8
Castlecroft Staffs 133 D7
Castlefairn Dumfries 246 F6
Castlefields Halton 183 E8
Castleford W Yorks 198 B2
Castlegreen Shrops 130 F6
Castlehead Renfs 267 C9
Castlehill Argyll 254 B4
Castlehill Borders 260 B6
Castlehill Highld 310 C5
Castlehill S Ayrs 257 E9
Castlehill W Dunb 277 F7
Castlemaddy Dumfries 246 F3
Castlemartin Pembs 72 F6
Castlemilk Dumfries 238 B5
Castlemilk Glasgow 268 D2
Castlemorris Pembs 91 E8
Castlemorton Worcs 98 D5
Castlerigg Cumb 229 G11
Castleside Durham 233 B7
Castlethorpe M Keynes 102 C6
Castlethorpe N Lincs 200 F3
Castleton Angus 287 C7
Castleton Argyll 275 E9
Castleton Derbys 185 E11
Castleton Gtr Man 195 E11
Castleton Moray 301 G11
Castleton N Yorks 226 D3
Castleton Newport 59 C9
Castleton Village Highld 300 E6
Castletown Cumb 230 E6
Castletown Dorset 17 G9
Castletown Highld 301 E7
Castletown Highld 310 C5
Castletown I o M 192 F3
Castletown Staffs 151 E8
Castletown T & W 243 F9
Castletown W Ches 166 E6
Castletump Glos 98 F4
Castleweary Borders 249 C10
Castlewigg Dumfries 236 E6
Castley N Yorks 205 D11
Castling's Heath Suff 107 C9
Caston Norf 141 D9
Castor P'boro 138 D2
Caswell Swansea 56 D5
Cat Bank Cumb 220 F6
Cat Hill S Yorks 197 F8
Catacol N Ayrs 255 C10
Catbrain S Glos 60 C5
Catbrook Mon 79 E8
Catch Flint 182 G2
Catchall Corn 1 D4
Catchems Corner W Mid 118 B4
Catchems End Worcs 116 B5
Catchgate Durham 242 G5
Catchory Highld 310 D6
Catcleugh Northumb 250 C6
Catcliffe S Yorks 186 D6
Catcomb Wilts 62 D4
Catcott Som 43 F11
Caterham Sur 51 B10
Catfield Norf 161 E7
Catfirth Shetland 313 H6
Catford London 67 E11
Catforth Lancs 202 F5
Cathays Cardiff 59 D7
Cathays Park Cardiff 59 D7
Cathcart Glasgow 267 C11
Cathedine Powys 96 F2
Catherine-de-Barnes W Mid 134 G3
Catherine Slack W Yorks 196 B5
Catherington Hants 33 E11
Catherton Shrops 116 B3
Cathiron Warks 119 B9
Catholes Cumb 222 G3
Cathpair Borders 271 F9
Catisfield Hants 33 F8
Catley Lane Head Gtr Man 195 D11
Catley Southfield Hereford 98 C3
Catlodge Highld 291 D8
Catlowdy Cumb 239 B11
Catmere End Essex 105 D9
Catmore W Berks 64 C3
Caton Devon 13 G11
Caton Lancs 211 G10
Caton Green Lancs 211 F10
Catrine E Ayrs 258 D2
Cat's Ash Newport 78 G5
Cat's Common Norf 160 E6
Cats Edge Staffs 169 E7
Cat's Hill Cross Staffs 150 C6
Catsfield E Sus 38 E2
Catsfield Stream E Sus 38 E2
Catsgore Som 29 B8
Catsham Som 44 G5
Catshaw S Yorks 197 G8
Catshill W Mid 133 B11
Catshill Worcs 117 C9
Catslackburn Borders 261 D8
Catslip Oxon 65 B8
Catstree Shrops 132 D4
Cattadale Argyll 274 G4
Cattal N Yorks 206 C4
Cattawade Suff 108 E2
Cattedown Plym 7 E9
Catterall Lancs 202 E5
Catterick N Yorks 224 F4
Catterick Bridge N Yorks 224 F4
Catterick Garrison N Yorks 224 F3
Catterlen Cumb 230 E5
Catterline Aberds 293 F10
Catterton N Yorks 206 D6
Catteshall Sur 50 E3
Catthorpe Leics 119 B11
Cattistock Dorset 17 B7
Cattle End Northants 102 C3
Catton N Yorks 215 D7
Catton Northumb 241 F8
Catwick E Yorks 209 D8
Catworth Cambs 121 C11
Caudle Green Glos 80 C6
Caudlesprings Norf 141 C8
Caulcott C Beds 103 C9
Caulcott Oxon 101 G10
Cauld Borders 261 G11
Cauldcoats Holdings Falk 279 F10
Cauldcots Angus 287 C10
Cauldhame Stirl 278 C2
Cauldmill Borders 262 G2
Cauldon Staffs 169 F9
Cauldon Lowe Staffs 169 F9
Cauldwells Aberds 303 D7
Caulkerbush Dumfries 237 D11
Caulside Dumfries 249 G10
Caundle Marsh Dorset 29 E11
Caunsall Worcs 132 G6
Caunton Notts 172 D2
Causeway Hants 33 E11
Causeway Hants 34 C2
Causeway Mon 60 B2
Causeway End Cumb 210 C6
Causeway End Cumb 211 B9
Causeway End Dumfries 236 C6
Causeway End Essex 87 B11
Causeway End Wilts 62 C4
Causeway Foot W Yorks 197 E7
Causeway Foot W Yorks 205 G7
Causeway Green W Mid 133 F9
Causewayend S Lnrk 260 B2
Causewayhead Cumb 238 G4
Causewayhead Stirl 278 B6
Causewaywood Shrops 131 D10
Causey Durham 242 F6
Causey Park Bridge Northumb 252 E5
Causeyend Aberds 293 B11
Causeyton Aberds 293 B8
Caute Devon 24 E6
Cautley Cumb 222 G3
Cavendish Suff 106 B6
Cavendish Bridge Leics 153 D8
Cavenham Suff 124 D5
Cavers Carre Borders 262 D3
Caversfield Oxon 101 F11
Caversham Reading 65 E8
Caversham Heights Reading 65 D8
Caverswall Staffs 169 G7
Cavil E Yorks 207 G11
Cawdor Highld 301 D8
Cawkeld E Yorks 208 C5
Cawkwell Lincs 190 F3
Cawood N Yorks 207 F7
Cawsand Corn 7 E8
Cawston Norf 160 E2
Cawston Warks 119 C9
Cawthorne N Yorks 216 B5
Cawthorne S Yorks 197 F9
Cawthorpe Lincs 155 E11
Cawton N Yorks 216 D2
Caxton Cambs 122 F6
Caynham Shrops 115 C11
Caythorpe Lincs 172 F6
Caythorpe Notts 171 F11
Cayton N Yorks 217 C11
Ceallan W Isles 296 F4
Ceann a Bhàigh W Isles 305 J4
Ceann a Bhaigh W Isles 296 E3
Ceann a Deas Loch Baghasdail W Isles 297 K3
Ceann Shiphoirt W Isles 305 G4
Ceann Tarabhaigh W Isles 305 G4
Ceannacroc Lodge Highld 290 B4
Cearsiadair W Isles 304 F5
Ceathramh Meadhanach W Isles 296 D4
Cefn Newport 59 B9
Cefn Powys 148 G5
Cefn Berain Conwy 165 B7
Cefn-brith Conwy 164 E6
Cefn-bryn-brain Carms 76 C2
Cefn-bychan Swansea 56 B4
Cefn-bychan Wrex 166 G3
Cefn Canol Powys 148 C4
Cefn-coch Conwy 164 B5
Cefn Coch Powys 129 C10
Cefn Coch Powys 148 D2
Cefn-coed-y-cymmer M Tydf 77 D9f
Cefn Cribbwr Bridgend 57 E11
Cefn Cross Bridgend 57 E11
Cefn-ddwysarn Gwyn 147 B9
Cefn Einion Shrops 130 F5
Cefn-eurgain Flint 166 B2
Cefn Fforest Caerph 77 F11
Cefn Glas Bridgend 57 E11
Cefn Golau Bl Gwent 77 D10
Cefn-gorwydd Powys 95 B8
Cefn Hengoed Caerph 77 F10
Cefn-hengoed Swansea 57 B7
Cefn Llwyd Ceredig 128 G2
Cefn-mawr Wrex 166 G3
Cefn Rhigos Rhondda 76 D6
Cefn-y-bedd Flint 166 D4
Cefn-y-Crib Torf 78 F2
Cefn-y-Garth Swansea 76 E2
Cefn-y-pant Carms 92 F3
Cefncaeau Carms 56 B4
Cefneithin Carms 75 C9
Cefnpennar Rhondda 77 E8
Cegidfa = Guilsfield Powys 148 G4
Cei-bach Ceredig 111 F8
Ceinewydd = New Quay Ceredig 111 F7
Ceint Anglesey 179 F7
Ceinws Powys 128 B5
Cellan Ceredig 94 B2
Cellarhead Staffs 169 F7
Cellarhill Kent 70 G3
Celyn-Mali Flint 165 B11
Cemaes Anglesey 178 C5
Cemmaes Powys 128 B6
Cemmaes Road = Glantwymyn Powys 128 C6
Cenarth Carms 92 C5
Cenin Gwyn 163 F7
Central Invclyd 276 F5
Central Milton Keynes M Keynes 102 D6
Ceos W Isles 304 F5
Ceres Fife 287 F8
Ceri = Kerry Powys 130 F2
Cerne Abbas Dorset 29 G11
Cerney Wick Glos 81 F9
Cerrig Llwydion Neath 57 C9
Cerrig-mân Anglesey 179 C7
Cerrigceinwen Anglesey 178 G6
Cerrigydrudion Conwy 165 F7
Cess Norf 161 F8
Cessford Borders 262 E6
Ceunant Gwyn 163 C8
Chaceley Glos 99 E7
Chaceley Hole Glos 98 E6
Chaceley Stock Glos 99 F7
Chacewater Corn 4 G4
Chackmore Bucks 102 D3
Chacombe Northants 101 C9
Chad Valley W Mid 133 F10
Chadbury Worcs 99 B10
Chadderton Gtr Man 196 F2
Chadderton Fold Gtr Man 195 F11
Chaddesden Derby 153 B7
Chaddesley Corbett Worcs 117 C7
Chaddlehanger Devon 12 F5
Chaddlewood Plym 7 D11
Chaddleworth W Berks 64 D2
Chadkirk Gtr Man 184 D6
Chadlington Oxon 100 G6
Chadshunt Warks 118 G6
Chadsmoor Staffs 151 G9
Chadstone Northants 121 F7
Chadwell Leics 154 E5
Chadwell Shrops 150 G5
Chadwell End Beds 121 D11
Chadwell Heath London 68 B3
Chadwell St Mary Thurrock 68 D6
Chadwick Worcs 116 D6
Chadwick End W Mid 118 C4
Chadwick Green Mers 183 B8
Chaffcombe Som 28 E5
Chafford Hundred Thurrock 68 D5
Chagford Devon 13 D10
Chailey E Sus 36 D5
Chain Bridge Lincs 174 G4
Chainbridge Cambs 139 C8
Chainhurst Kent 53 D8
Chalbury Dorset 31 F8
Chalbury Common Dorset 31 F8
Chaldon Sur 51 B10
Chaldon Herring or East Chaldon Dorset 17 E11
Chale I o W 20 F5
Chale Green I o W 20 F5
Chalfont Common Bucks 85 G8
Chalfont Grove Bucks 85 G7
Chalfont St Giles Bucks 85 G7
Chalfont St Peter Bucks 85 G8
Chalford Glos 80 E5
Chalford Oxon 84 E2
Chalford Wilts 45 C11
Chalford Hill Glos 80 E5
Chalgrave C Beds 103 F10
Chalgrove Oxon 83 F10
Chalk Kent 69 E7
Chalk End Essex 87 C10
Chalkfoot Cumb 230 B2
Chalkhill Norf 141 C7
Chalkhouse Green Oxon 65 D8
Chalkshire Bucks 84 D4
Chalksole Kent 55 E9
Chalkway Som 28 F5
Chalkwell Kent 69 G11
Chalkwell Sthend 69 B11
Challaborough Devon 8 G3
Challacombe Devon 41 E7
Challister Shetland 312 G7
Challoch Dumfries 236 C5
Challock Kent 54 C4
Chalmington Dorset 29 G9
Chalton C Beds 103 F10
Chalton Hants 34 D2
Chalvedon Essex 69 B8
Chalvey Slough 66 D3
Chalvington E Sus 23 D8
Chambercombe Devon 40 D4
Chamber's Green Kent 54 E2
Champson Devon 26 B4
Chance Inn Fife 287 F7
Chancery = Rhydgaled Ceredig 111 B11
Chance's Pitch Hereford 98 C4
Chandler's Cross Herts 85 F9
Chandler's Cross Worcs 98 D5
Chandler's Ford Hants 32 C6
Chandlers Green Hants 49 B8
Channel Tunnel Kent 55 F7
Channel's End Beds 122 F2
Channerwick Shetland 313 L6
Chantry Devon 25 C9
Chantry Som 45 D8
Chantry Suff 108 C2
Chapel Corn 4 C6
Chapel Cumb 229 E10
Chapel Fife 280 C5
Chapel Allerton Som 44 C2
Chapel Allerton W Yorks 206 F2
Chapel Amble Corn 10 F5
Chapel Brampton Northants 120 D4
Chapel Chorlton Staffs 150 B6
Chapel Cleeve Som 42 E4
Chapel Cross E Sus 37 C10
Chapel-en-le-Frith Derbys 185 E9
Chapel End Beds 103 B11
Chapel End Beds 122 F2
Chapel End C Beds 103 C11
Chapel End Cambs 138 G2
Chapel End E Ches 167 G11
Chapel End Essex 105 G11
Chapel End Northants 138 F2
Chapel End Warks 134 E6
Chapel Field Gtr Man 195 F9
Chapel Field Norf 161 E7
Chapel Fields W Mid 118 B6
Chapel Fields York 207 C7
Chapel Green Herts 104 D6
Chapel Green Warks 119 E9
Chapel Green Warks 134 F5
Chapel Haddlesey N Yorks 198 B5
Chapel Head Cambs 138 G6
Chapel Hill Aberds 303 F10
Chapel Hill Glos 79 E10
Chapel Hill Lincs 174 E2
Chapel Hill Mon 79 F8
Chapel Hill N Yorks 206 D2
Chapel House Lancs 194 F3
Chapel Knapp Wilts 61 F11
Chapel Lawn Shrops 114 B6
Chapel-le-Dale N Yorks 212 D4
Chapel Leigh Som 27 B10
Chapel Mains Borders 271 G11
Chapel Milton Derbys 185 E9
Chapel of Garioch Aberds 303 G7
Chapel of Stoneywood Aberdeen 293 B10
Chapel on Leader Borders 271 G11
Chapel Outon Dumfries 236 E6
Chapel Plaister Wilts 61 F10
Chapel Row E Sus 23 C10
Chapel Row Essex 88 E3
Chapel Row W Berks 64 F5
Chapel St Leonards Lincs 191 G9
Chapel Stile Cumb 220 D6
Chapel Town Corn 5 D7
Chapelgate Lincs 157 E8
Chapelhall N Lnrk 268 C5
Chapelhill Dumfries 248 E3
Chapelhill Highld 301 B8
Chapelhill N Ayrs 266 G4
Chapelhill Perth 286 D4
Chapelhill Perth 286 E3
Chapelhill Perth 286 E6
Chapelknowe Dumfries 239 C8
Chapels Blkburn 195 C7
Chapels Cumb 210 C4
Chapelthorpe W Yorks 197 D10
Chapelton Angus 287 C10
Chapelton Devon 25 B9
Chapelton Highld 291 B11
Chapelton S Lnrk 268 F3
Chapelton Row Dumfries 237 E8
Chapeltown Blkburn 195 D8
Chapeltown Moray 302 G2
Chapeltown S Yorks 186 B5
Chapeltown W Yorks 206 F2
Chapman's Hill Worcs 117 B9
Chapman's Town E Sus 23 B10
Chapmans Well Devon 12 C3
Chapmanslade Wilts 45 D10
Chapmore End Herts 86 B4
Chappel Essex 107 F7
Charaton Cross Corn 6 B6
Charcott Kent 52 D4
Chard Som 28 F4
Chard Junction Dorset 28 G4
Chardleigh Green Som 28 E4
Chardstock Devon 28 G4
Charfield S Glos 80 G2
Charfield Green S Glos 80 G2
Charfield Hill S Glos 80 G2
Charford Worcs 117 D9
Chargrove Glos 80 B6
Charing Kent 54 D3
Charing Cross Dorset 31 E10

Charing Heath Kent 54 D2
Charing Hill Kent 54 C3
Charingworth Glos 100 D4
Charlbury Oxon 82 B5
Charlcombe Bath 61 F8
Charlcutt Wilts 62 D3
Charlecote Warks 118 F5
Charlemont W Mid 133 E10
Charles Devon 41 G7
Charles Bottom Devon 41 G7
Charles Tye Suff 125 G10
Charlesfield Borders 262 D3
Charlesfield Dumfries 238 D5
Charleshill Sur 49 E11
Charleston Angus 287 C7
Charleston Renfs 267 C9
Charlestown Aberdeen 293 C11
Charlestown Corn 5 E10
Charlestown Derbys 185 C8
Charlestown Dorset 17 F9
Charlestown Fife 279 E11
Charlestown Gtr Man 195 G10
Charlestown Gtr Man 195 G11
Charlestown Highld 299 B8
Charlestown Highld 300 E6
Charlestown W Yorks 196 B3
Charlestown W Yorks 205 F9
Charlestown of Aberlour Moray 302 E2
Charlesworth Derbys 185 C8
Charleton Devon 8 G5
Charlinch Som 43 F8
Charlottetown Fife 286 F6
Charlton Hants 47 D11
Charlton Herts 104 F3
Charlton London 68 D2
Charlton Northants 101 D10
Charlton Northumb 251 F8
Charlton Oxon 64 B2
Charlton Redcar 226 B2
Charlton Som 28 B3
Charlton Som 44 E6
Charlton Som 45 C7
Charlton Sur 66 F5
Charlton Telford 149 G11
Charlton W Sus 34 E5
Charlton Wilts 30 C6
Charlton Wilts 46 B6
Charlton Wilts 62 B3
Charlton Worcs 99 B10
Charlton Worcs 116 C6
Charlton Abbots Glos 99 G10
Charlton Adam Som 29 B8
Charlton-All-Saints Wilts 31 C11
Charlton Down Dorset 17 C9
Charlton Horethorne Som 29 C11
Charlton Kings Glos 99 G9
Charlton Mackrell Som 29 B8
Charlton Marshall Dorset 30 G5
Charlton Musgrove Som 30 B2
Charlton on Otmoor Oxon 83 B9
Charlton on the Hill Dorset 30 G5
Charlton Park Glos 99 G9
Charlton St Peter Wilts 46 B6
Charltonbrook S Yorks 186 B4
Charlwood E Sus 51 G11
Charlwood Hants 49 G7
Charlwood Sur 51 E8
Charlynch Som 43 F8
Charminster Bmouth 19 C8
Charminster Dorset 17 C9
Charmouth Dorset 16 C3
Charnage Wilts 45 G10
Charndon Bucks 102 G3
Charnes Staffs 150 C5
Charney Bassett Oxon 82 G5
Charnock Green Lancs 194 D5
Charnock Hall S Yorks 186 E5
Charnock Richard Lancs 194 D5
Charsfield Suff 126 F5
Chart Corner Kent 53 C9
Chart Hill Kent 53 D9
Chart Sutton Kent 53 D10
Charter Alley Hants 48 B5
Charterhouse Som 44 B3
Chartershall Stirl 278 C6
Charterville Allotments Oxon 82 C4
Chartham Kent 54 C6
Chartham Hatch Kent 54 B6
Chartridge Bucks 84 E6
Charvil Wokingham 65 D9
Charwelton Northants 119 F10
Chase Cross London 87 G8
Chase End Street Worcs 98 D5
Chase Hill S Glos 61 B8
Chase Terrace Staffs 133 B10
Chasetown Staffs 133 B10
Chastleton Oxon 100 F4
Chasty Devon 24 G4
Chat Hill W Yorks 205 G8
Chatburn Lancs 203 E11
Chatcull Staffs 150 C5
Chatford Shrops 131 B9
Chatham Caerph 59 B8
Chatham Medway 69 F9
Chatham Green Essex 88 B2
Chathill Northumb 264 D5
Chatley Worcs 117 E7
Chattenden Medway 69 E9
Chatter End Essex 105 F9
Chatteris Cambs 139 F7
Chatterley Staffs 168 E4
Chattern Hill Sur 66 E5
Chatterton Lancs 195 D9
Chattisham Suff 107 C11
Chattle Hill Warks 134 E3
Chatto Borders 263 F7
Chatton Northumb 264 D3
Chaul End C Beds 103 G11
Chaulden Herts 85 D8
Chavel Shrops 149 G8
Chavenage Green Glos 80 F5
Chavey Down Brack 65 F11
Chawleigh Devon 26 E2
Chawley Oxon 83 E7
Chawson Worcs 117 E7
Chawston Beds 122 F3
Chawton Hants 49 F8
Chaxhill Glos 80 C2
Chazey Heath Oxon 65 D7
Cheadle Gtr Man 184 D5
Cheadle Staffs 169 G8
Cheadle Heath Gtr Man 184 D5
Cheadle Hulme Gtr Man 184 D5
Cheadle Park Staffs 169 G8
Cheam London 67 G8
Cheapside Herts 105 E8
Cheapside Sur 50 B4
Cheapside Windsor 66 F2
Chearsley Bucks 84 C2
Chebsey Staffs 151 D7
Checkendon Oxon 65 C7
Checkley E Ches 168 F2
Checkley Hereford 97 D11
Checkley Staffs 151 B10
Checkley Green E Ches 168 F2
Chedburgh Suff 124 F5
Cheddar Som 44 C3
Cheddington Bucks 84 B6
Cheddleton Staffs 169 E7
Cheddleton Heath Staffs 169 E7
Cheddon Fitzpaine Som 28 B2
Chedglow Wilts 80 G6
Chedgrave Norf 143 D7
Chedington Dorset 29 F7
Chediston Suff 127 B7
Chediston Green Suff 127 B7
Chedworth Glos 81 C9
Chedworth Laines Glos 81 C8
Chedzoy Som 43 F10
Cheeklaw Borders 272 E5
Cheeseman's Green Kent 54 F4
Cheetam Hill Gtr Man 195 G10
Cheglinch Devon 40 E4
Chegworth Kent 53 C10
Cheldon Devon 26 E2
Chelfham Devon 40 F6
Chelford E Ches 184 G4
Chell Heath Stoke 168 E5
Chellaston Derby 153 C7
Chellington Beds 121 F9
Chells Herts 104 F5
Chelmarsh Shrops 132 F4
Chelmer Village Essex 88 D2
Chelmick Shrops 131 E9
Chelmondiston Suff 108 D4
Chelmorton Derbys 169 B10
Chelmsford Essex 88 D2
Chelmsine Som 27 D11
Chelmsley Wood W Mid 134 F3
Chelsea London 67 D9
Chelsfield London 68 G3
Chelsham Sur 51 B11
Chelston Som 27 C11
Chelston Torbay 9 C7
Chelston Heathfield Som 27 C11
Chelsworth Suff 107 B9
Chelsworth Common Suff 107 B9
Cheltenham Glos 99 G8
Chelveston Northants 121 D9
Chelvey N Som 60 F3
Chelvey Batch N Som 60 F3
Chelwood Bath 60 G6
Chelwood Common E Sus 36 B6
Chelwood Gate E Sus 36 B6
Chelworth Wilts 81 G7
Chelworth Lower Green Wilts 81 G9
Chelworth Upper Green Wilts 81 G9
Chelynch Som 45 E7
Chemistry Shrops 167 G8
Cheney Longville Shrops 131 G8
Chenhalls Corn 2 B3
Chenies Bucks 85 F8
Cheny Longville Shrops 131 G8
Chepstow Mon 79 G8
Chequerbent Gtr Man 195 F7
Chequerfield W Yorks 198 C3
Chequers Corner Norf 139 B9
Chequertree Kent 54 F4
Cherhill Wilts 62 E4
Cherington Glos 80 F6
Cherington Warks 100 D5
Cheriston Devon 24 B3
Cheriton Devon 41 D8
Cheriton Hants 33 B9
Cheriton Kent 55 F7
Cheriton Swansea 56 C3
Cheriton Bishop Devon 13 C11
Cheriton Cross Devon 13 C11
Cheriton Fitzpaine Devon 26 F5
Cheriton or Stackpole Elidor Pembs 73 F7
Cherrington Telford 150 E3
Cherry Burton E Yorks 208 E5
Cherry Green Essex 105 F11
Cherry Green Herts 105 F7
Cherry Hinton Cambs 123 F9
Cherry Orchard Shrops 149 G9
Cherry Orchard Worcs 117 G7
Cherry Tree Blkburn 195 B7
Cherry Tree Gtr Man 185 C7
Cherry Willingham Lincs 189 G8
Cherrybank Perth 286 E5
Cherrytree Hill Derby 153 B7
Chertsey Sur 66 F4
Chertsey Meads Sur 66 F5
Cheselbourne Dorset 17 B11
Chesham Bucks 85 E7
Chesham Gtr Man 195 E10
Chesham Bois Bucks 85 F7
Cheshunt Herts 86 E5
Chesley Kent 69 G11
Cheslyn Hay Staffs 133 B9
Chessetts Wood Warks 118 C3
Chessington London 67 G7
Chessmount Bucks 85 E7
Chestall Staffs 151 G11
Chester W Ches 166 B6
Chester-le-Street Durham 243 G7
Chester Moor Durham 233 B11
Chesterblade Som 45 E7
Chesterfield Derbys 186 G5
Chesterfield Staffs 134 B2
Chesterhill Midloth 271 B7
Chesterhope Northumb 251 F9
Chesterknowes Borders 262 D2
Chesters Borders 262 E4
Chesters Borders 262 G4
Chesterton Cambs 123 E9
Chesterton Cambs 138 D2
Chesterton Glos 81 E8
Chesterton Oxon 101 G11
Chesterton Shrops 132 D5
Chesterton Staffs 168 F4
Chesterton Warks 118 F6
Chesterton Green Warks 118 F6
Chesterwood Northumb 241 D8
Chestfield Kent 70 F6
Chestnut Hill Cumb 229 G11
Chestnut Street Kent 69 G11
Cheston Devon 8 D3
Cheswardine Shrops 150 D4
Cheswell Telford 150 F4
Cheswick Northumb 273 F10
Cheswick Buildings Northumb 273 F10
Cheswick Green W Mid 118 B2
Chetnole Dorset 29 F10
Chettiscombe Devon 27 E7
Chettisham Cambs 139 G10
Chettle Dorset 31 E7
Chetton Shrops 132 E3
Chetwode Bucks 102 F2
Chetwynd Aston Telford 150 F5
Cheveley Cambs 124 E3
Chevening Kent 52 B3
Cheverell's Green Herts 85 B9
Chevin End W Yorks 205 E9
Chevington Suff 124 F5
Chevithorne Devon 27 D7
Chew Magna Bath 60 G5
Chew Moor Gtr Man 195 F7
Chew Stoke Bath 60 G5
Chewton Keynsham Bath 61 F7
Chewton Mendip Som 44 C5
Cheylesmore W Mid 118 B6
Chichacott Devon 13 B8
Chicheley M Keynes 103 B8
Chichester W Sus 22 C5
Chickenley W Yorks 197 C9
Chickerell Dorset 17 E8
Chicklade Wilts 46 G2
Chickney Essex 105 F11
Chicksands C Beds 104 D2
Chicksgrove Wilts 46 G3
Chickward Hereford 114 G5
Chidden Hants 33 D11
Chiddingfold Sur 50 F3
Chiddingly E Sus 23 C8
Chiddingstone Kent 52 D3
Chiddingstone Causeway Kent 52 D4
Chiddingstone Hoath Kent 52 E3
Chideock Dorset 16 C4
Chidgley Som 42 F4
Chidham W Sus 22 C3
Chidswell W Yorks 197 C9
Chieveley W Berks 64 E3
Chignall St James Essex 87 D11
Chignall Smealy Essex 87 C11
Chigwell Essex 86 G6
Chigwell Row Essex 87 G7
Chilbolton Hants 47 F11
Chilbolton Down Hants 48 F2
Chilbridge Dorset 31 G7
Chilcomb Hants 33 B8
Chilcombe Dorset 16 C6
Chilcombe Som 42 F6
Chilcompton Som 44 C6
Chilcote Leics 152 G5
Child Okeford Dorset 30 E4
Childer Thornton W Ches 182 F5
Childerditch Essex 68 B6
Childerley Gate Cambs 123 F7
Childrey Oxon 63 B11
Child's Ercall Shrops 150 E3
Child's Hill London 67 B8
Childsbridge Kent 52 B5
Childswickham Worcs 99 D11
Childwall Mers 182 D6
Childwick Bury Herts 85 C10
Childwick Green Herts 85 C10
Chilfrome Dorset 17 B7
Chilgrove W Sus 34 E4
Chilham Kent 54 C5
Chilhampton Wilts 46 G5
Chilla Devon 24 G6
Chillaton Devon 12 E4
Chillenden Kent 55 C9
Chillerton I o W 20 E5
Chillesford Suff 127 G7
Chillingham Northumb 264 D3
Chillington Devon 8 G5
Chillington Som 28 E5
Chillmill Kent 53 E7
Chilmark Wilts 46 G3
Chilmington Green Kent 54 E3
Chilsham E Sus 23 C10
Chilson Oxon 82 B4
Chilson Som 28 G4
Chilson Common Som 28 G4
Chilsworthy Corn 12 G4
Chilsworthy Devon 24 F4
Chiltern Green Beds 85 B10
Chilthorne Domer Som 29 D8
Chiltington E Sus 36 D5
Chilton Bucks 83 C11
Chilton Durham 233 F11
Chilton Kent 71 G11
Chilton Oxon 64 B3
Chilton Suff 107 C7
Chilton Candover Hants 48 E5
Chilton Cantelo Som 29 C9
Chilton Foliat Wilts 63 E10
Chilton Lane Durham 234 E2
Chilton Moor T & W 234 B2
Chilton Polden Som 43 F11
Chilton Street Suff 106 B5
Chilton Trinity Som 43 F9
Chilvers Coton Warks 135 E7
Chilwell Notts 153 B10
Chilworth Hants 32 D6
Chilworth Sur 50 D4
Chilworth Old Village Hants 32 D6
Chimney Oxon 82 E5
Chimney-end Oxon 82 B4
Chimney Street Suff 106 B4
Chineham Hants 49 C7
Chingford London 86 G5
Chingford Green London 86 G5
Chingford Hatch London 86 G5
Chinley Derbys 185 E8
Chinley Head Derbys 185 E9
Chinnor Oxon 84 E3
Chipley Som 27 C10
Chipmans Platt Glos 80 D3
Chipnall Shrops 150 C4
Chippenhall Green Suff 126 B5
Chippenham Cambs 124 D3
Chippenham Wilts 62 E2
Chipperfield Herts 85 E8
Chipping Herts 105 E7
Chipping Lancs 203 E8
Chipping Barnet London 86 F2
Chipping Campden Glos 100 D3
Chipping Hill Essex 88 B4
Chipping Norton Oxon 100 F6
Chipping Ongar Essex 87 E8
Chipping Sodbury S Glos 61 C8
Chipping Warden Northants 101 B9
Chipstable Som 27 B8
Chipstead Kent 52 B3
Chipstead Sur 51 B9
Chirbury Shrops 130 D5
Chirk = Y Waun Wrex 148 B5
Chirk Bank Shrops 148 B5
Chirk Green Wrex 148 B5
Chirmorrie S Ayrs 236 B4
Chirnside Borders 273 D7
Chirnsidebridge Borders 273 D7
Chirton T & W 243 D8
Chirton Wilts 46 B5
Chisbridge Cross Bucks 65 B10
Chisbury Wilts 63 F9
Chiselborough Som 29 E7
Chiseldon Swindon 63 D7
Chiserley W Yorks 196 B4
Chislehampton Oxon 83 F9
Chislehurst London 68 E2
Chislehurst West London 68 E2
Chislet Kent 71 G8
Chislet Forstal Kent 71 G8
Chiswell Dorset 17 G9
Chiswell Green Herts 85 E10
Chiswick London 67 D8
Chiswick End Cambs 105 B7
Chisworth Derbys 185 C7
Chitcombe E Sus 38 C4
Chithurst W Sus 34 C4
Chittering Cambs 123 C9
Chitterley Devon 26 G6
Chitterne Wilts 46 E3
Chittlehamholt Devon 25 C11
Chittlehampton Devon 25 B10
Chittoe Wilts 62 F3
Chitts Hills Essex 107 F9
Chitty Kent 71 G8
Chivelstone Devon 9 G10
Chivenor Devon 40 G4
Chivery Bucks 84 D6
Chobham Sur 66 G3
Choicelee Borders 272 E4
Cholderton Wilts 47 E8
Cholesbury Bucks 84 D6
Chollerford Northumb 241 C10
Chollerton Northumb 241 C10
Cholmondeston E Ches 167 C10
Cholsey Oxon 64 B5
Cholstrey Hereford 115 F9
Cholwell Bath 44 B6
Chop Gate N Yorks 225 F11
Choppington Northumb 253 G7
Chopwell T & W 242 F4
Chorley E Ches 167 E9
Chorley Lancs 194 D5
Chorley Shrops 132 G3
Chorley Staffs 151 G11
Chorley Common W Sus 34 B4
Chorleywood Herts 85 F8
Chorleywood Bottom Herts 85 F8
Chorleywood West Herts 85 F8
Chorlton E Ches 168 E2
Chorlton-cum-Hardy Gtr Man 184 C4
Chorlton Lane W Ches 167 F7
Choulton Shrops 131 F7
Chowdene T & W 243 F7
Chowley W Ches 167 D7
Chownes Mead W Sus 36 C4
Chreagain Highld 289 C10
Chrishall Essex 105 D8
Christchurch Cambs 139 D9
Christchurch Dorset 19 C9
Christchurch Glos 79 C9
Christchurch Newport 59 B10
Christian Malford Wilts 62 D3
Christleton W Ches 166 B6
Christmas Common Oxon 84 G2
Christon N Som 43 B11
Christon Bank Northumb 264 E6
Christow Devon 14 D2
Chryston N Lnrk 278 G3
Chub Tor Devon 7 B10
Chuck Hatch E Sus 52 G3
Chudleigh Devon 14 F3
Chudleigh Knighton Devon 14 F2
Chulmleigh Devon 25 E11
Chunal Derbys 185 C8
Church Lancs 195 B8
Church Aston Telford 150 F4
Church Brampton Northants 120 D4
Church Brough Cumb 222 C5
Church Broughton Derbys 152 C4
Church Charwelton Northants 119 F10
Church Clough Lancs 204 F3
Church Common Hants 34 B2
Church Coombe Corn 4 G3
Church Cove Corn 2 G6
Church Crookham Hants 49 C10
Church Eaton Staffs 150 F6
Church End Beds 121 G12
Church End Beds 122 F2
Church End Bucks 84 B6
Church End Bucks 84 D2
Church End C Beds 85 B8
Church End C Beds 103 E9
Church End C Beds 103 G9
Church End C Beds 104 D3
Church End C Beds 122 G3
Church End Cambs 121 C11
Church End Cambs 123 C7
Church End Cambs 123 D7
Church End Cambs 138 G4
Church End Cambs 139 B7
Church End E Yorks 209 C7
Church End Essex 88 B2
Church End Essex 105 C11
Church End Essex 105 F11
Church End Essex 106 F4
Church End Glos 80 D2
Church End Glos 99 D7
Church End Hants 49 B7
Church End Herts 85 C10
Church End Herts 85 F8
Church End Herts 104 E5
Church End Herts 105 G8
Church End Lincs 156 C4
Church End Lincs 190 B6
Church End London 67 C8
Church End London 86 G2
Church End Norf 157 F10
Church End Oxon 82 D5
Church End Oxon 100 E6
Church End Suff 108 D4
Church End Sur 50 B5
Church End W Mid 119 B7
Church End Warks 134 E4
Church End Warks 134 E5
Church End Wilts 62 D4
Church End Worcs 98 C6
Church Enstone Oxon 101 G7
Church Fenton N Yorks 206 F6
Church Green Devon 15 B9
Church Green Norf 141 E11
Church Gresley Derbys 152 F5
Church Hanborough Oxon 82 C6
Church Hill Pembs 73 C7
Church Hill Staffs 151 G10
Church Hill W Ches 167 C10
Church Hill W Mid 133 D9
Church Hill Worcs 117 D11
Church Hougham Kent 55 E9
Church Houses N Yorks 226 F3
Church Knowle Dorset 18 E4
Church Laneham Notts 188 F4
Church Langton Leics 136 E4
Church Lawford Warks 119 B8
Church Lawton E Ches 168 D4
Church Leigh Staffs 151 B10
Church Lench Worcs 117 G10
Church Mayfield Staffs 169 G11
Church Minshull E Ches 167 C11
Church Norton W Sus 22 D5
Church Oakley Hants 48 C5
Church Preen Shrops 131 D10
Church Pulverbatch Shrops 131 C8
Church Stowe Northants 120 F2
Church Street Essex 106 C5
Church Street Kent 69 E8
Church Stretton Shrops 131 E9
Church Town Corn 4 G3
Church Town Leics 153 F7
Church Town N Lincs 199 F9
Church Town Sur 51 C11
Church Village Rhondda 58 B5
Church Warsop Notts 171 B9
Church Westcote Glos 100 G4
Church Whitfield Kent 55 D10
Church Wilne Derbys 153 C8
Churcham Glos 80 B3
Churchbank Shrops 114 B6
Churchbridge Corn 6 D4
Churchbridge Staffs 133 B9
Churchdown Glos 80 B5
Churchend Essex 89 G8
Churchend Essex 106 G2
Churchend Glos 80 D3
Churchend Reading 65 E7
Churchend S Glos 80 G2
Churches Green E Sus 23 B10
Churchfield Hereford 98 B4
Churchfield W Mid 133 E10
Churchfields Wilts 31 B10
Churchgate Herts 86 E4
Churchgate Street Essex 87 C7
Churchill Devon 28 G4
Churchill Devon 40 E5
Churchill N Som 44 B2
Churchill Oxon 100 G5
Churchill Worcs 117 B7
Churchill Worcs 117 G8
Churchill Green N Som 60 G2
Churchinford Som 28 E2
Churchmoor Rough Shrops 131 F8
Churchover Warks 135 G10
Churchstanton Som 27 E11
Churchstoke Powys 130 E5
Churchstow Devon 8 F4
Churchton Pembs 73 D10
Churchtown Corn 11 F7
Churchtown Cumb 230 C3
Churchtown Derbys 170 C3
Churchtown Devon 24 G3
Churchtown Devon 41 E7
Churchtown I o M 192 C5
Churchtown Lancs 202 E5
Churchtown Mers 193 D11
Churchtown Shrops 130 F5
Churchtown Som 42 F3
Churchwood W Sus 35 D8
Churnet Grange Staffs 169 E7
Churnsike Lodge Northumb 240 B5
Churscombe Torbay 9 C7
Churston Ferrers Torbay 9 D8
Churt Sur 49 F11
Churton W Ches 166 D6
Churwell W Yorks 197 B9
Chute Cadley Wilts 47 C10
Chute Standen Wilts 47 C10
Chweffordd Conwy 180 G4
Chwilog Gwyn 145 B8
Chwitffordd = Whitford Flint 181 F10
Chyandour Corn 1 C5
Chyanvounder Corn 2 E5
Chycoose Corn 3 B8
Chynhale Corn 2 C4
Chynoweth Corn 2 C2
Chyvarloe Corn 2 E5
Cicelyford Mon 79 E8
Cil y coed = Caldicot Mon 60 B3
Cilan Uchaf Gwyn 144 E5
Cilau Pembs 91 D8
Cilcain Flint 165 B11
Cilcennin Ceredig 111 E10
Cilcewydd Powys 130 C4
Cilfor Gwyn 146 B2
Cilfrew Neath 76 E3
Cilfynydd Rhondda 77 G9
Cilgerran Pembs 92 C3
Cilgwyn Carms 94 F4
Cilgwyn Ceredig 92 C6
Cilgwyn Gwyn 163 E7
Cilgwyn Pembs 91 D11
Ciliau Aeron Ceredig 111 F9
Cill Amhlaidh W Isles 297 G3
Cill Donnain W Isles 297 J3
Cill Eireabhagh W Isles 297 G4
Cille Bhrighde W Isles 297 K3
Cille Pheadair W Isles 297 K3
Cilmaengwyn Neath 76 D2
Cilmery Powys 113 G10
Cilsan Carms 93 G11
Ciltalgarth Gwyn 164 G5
Ciltwrch Powys 96 C3
Cilwendeg Pembs 92 D4
Cilybebyll Neath 76 E2
Cilycwm Carms 94 D5
Cimla Neath 57 B9
Cinder Hill Gtr Man 195 F9
Cinder Hill Kent 52 D4
Cinder Hill W Mid 133 E8
Cinder Hill W Sus 36 B5
Cinderford Glos 79 C11
Cinderhill Derbys 170 F5
Cinderhill Nottingham 171 G8
Cinnamon Brow Warr 183 C10
Cippenham Slough 66 C2
Cippyn Pembs 92 B2
Circebost W Isles 304 E3
Cirencester Glos 81 E8
Ciribhig W Isles 304 D3
City London 67 C10
City Powys 130 F4
City V Glam 58 D3
City Dulas Anglesey 179 D7
Clabhach Argyll 288 D3
Clachaig Argyll 276 E2
Clachaig Highld 292 B2
Clachaig N Ayrs 255 E10
Clachan Argyll 255 B8
Clachan Argyll 275 B8
Clachan Argyll 284 F5
Clachan Argyll 289 E10
Clachan Highld 295 B7
Clachan Highld 298 C4
Clachan Highld 307 L6
Clachan W Isles 297 G3
Clachan na Luib W Isles 296 E4
Clachan of Campsie E Dunb 278 F2
Clachan of Glendaruel Argyll 275 E10
Clachan-Seil Argyll 275 B8
Clachan Strachur Argyll 284 G4
Clachaneasy Dumfries 236 B5
Clachanmore Dumfries 236 E2
Clachbreck Argyll 275 F8
Clachnabrain Angus 292 G5
Clachtoll Highld 307 G5
Clackmannan Clack 279 C8
Clackmarras Moray 302 D2
Clacton-on-Sea Essex 89 B11
Cladach N Ayrs 256 B2
Cladach Chairinis W Isles 296 F4
Cladach Chireboist W Isles 296 E3
Claddach Argyll 254 B2
Claddach-knockline W Isles 296 E3
Cladich Argyll 284 E4
Cladich Steading Argyll 284 E4
Cladswell Worcs 117 F10
Claggan Highld 289 E8
Claggan Highld 290 F3
Claggan Perth 285 D11
Claigan Highld 298 D2
Claines Worcs 117 F7
Clandown Bath 45 B7
Clanfield Hants 33 D11
Clanfield Oxon 82 E3
Clanking Bucks 84 D4
Clanville Hants 47 D10
Clanville Som 44 G6
Clanville Wilts 62 D2
Claonaig Argyll 255 B9
Claonel Highld 309 J5
Clap Hill Kent 54 F5
Clapgate Dorset 31 G8
Clapgate Herts 105 G8
Clapham Beds 121 G10
Clapham Devon 14 D3
Clapham London 67 D9
Clapham N Yorks 212 F4
Clapham W Sus 35 F9
Clapham Green Beds 121 G10
Clapham Green N Yorks 205 B10
Clapham Hill Kent 70 G6
Clapham Park London 67 E9
Clapper Corn 10 G6
Clapper Hill Kent 53 F10
Clappers Borders 273 D8
Clappersgate Cumb 221 E7
Clapphoull Shetland 313 L6
Clapton Som 28 F6
Clapton Som 44 C6
Clapton W Berks 63 E11
Clapton in Gordano N Som 60 E3
Clapton-on-the-Hill Glos 81 B11
Clapton Park London 67 B11
Clapworthy Devon 25 C11
Clara Vale T & W 242 E4
Clarach Ceredig 128 G2
Clarack Aberds 292 D6
Clarbeston Pembs 91 G10
Clarbeston Road Pembs 91 G10
Clarborough Notts 188 E2
Clardon Highld 310 C5
Clare Oxon 83 F11
Clare Suff 106 B5
Clarebrand Dumfries 237 C9
Claregate W Mid 133 C7
Claremont Park Sur 66 G6
Claremount W Yorks 196 B5
Clarence Park N Som 59 G10
Clarencefield Dumfries 238 D3
Clarendon Park Leicester 135 C11
Clareston Pembs 73 C7
Clarilaw Borders 262 D3
Clarilaw Borders 262 F2
Clark Green E Ches 184 F6
Clarken Green Hants 48 C5
Clark's Green Sur 51 F7
Clark's Hill Lincs 157 E7
Clarksfield Gtr Man 196 G2
Clarkston E Renf 267 D11
Clarkston N Lnrk 268 B5
Clase Swansea 57 B7
Clashandorran Highld 300 E5
Clashcoig Highld 309 K6
Clasheddy Highld 308 C6
Clashgour Argyll 284 C6
Clashindarroch Aberds 302 F4
Clashmore Highld 306 F5
Clashmore Highld 309 L7
Clashnessie Highld 306 F5
Clashnoir Moray 302 G2
Clate Shetland 313 G7
Clatford Wilts 63 F7
Clatford Oakcuts Hants 47 F10
Clathy Perth 286 F3
Clatt Aberds 302 G5
Clatter Powys 129 E9
Clatterford I o W 20 D5
Clatterford End Essex 87 C10
Clatterford End Essex 87 D9
Clatterford End Essex 87 E8
Clatterin Bridge Aberds 293 F8
Clatto Fife 287 F8
Clatworthy Som 42 G5
Clauchlands N Ayrs 256 C2
Claughton Lancs 202 E6
Claughton Lancs 211 F11
Claughton Mers 182 D4
Clavelshay Som 43 G9
Claverdon Warks 118 E3
Claverham N Som 60 F2
Claverhambury Essex 86 E6
Clavering Essex 105 E9
Claverley Shrops 132 E5
Claverton Bath 61 G9
Claverton Down Bath 61 G9
Clawdd-côch V Glam 58 D5
Clawdd-newydd Denb 165 E9
Clawdd Poncen Denb 165 G9
Clawthorpe Cumb 211 D10
Clawton Devon 12 B3
Claxby Lincs 189 C10
Claxby Lincs 191 G7
Claxby St Andrew Lincs 191 G7

326 Cla – Con

Claxton N Yorks 216 G3
Claxton Norf 142 C6
Clay Common Suff 143 G9
Clay Coton Northants 119 B11
Clay Cross Derbys 170 C5
Clay End Herts 104 F6
Clay Hill Bristol 60 E6
Clay Hill London 86 F4
Clay Hill W Berks 64 E5
Clay Lake Lincs 156 E5
Clay Mills Derbys 152 D5
Claybokie Aberds 292 D2
Claybrooke Magna Leics 135 F9
Claybrooke Parva Leics 135 F9
Claydon Glos 99 E8
Claydon Oxon 119 G9
Claydon Suff 126 G2
Claygate Dumfries 239 B9
Claygate Kent 52 C6
Claygate Kent 53 E8
Claygate Sur 67 G7
Claygate Cross Kent 52 B6
Clayhall Hants 21 B8
Clayhall London 86 G6
Clayhanger Devon 27 C8
Clayhanger Som 28 E4
Clayhanger W Mid 133 C10
Clayhidon Devon 27 D11
Clayhill E Sus 38 C4
Clayhill Hants 32 F4
Clayhithe Cambs 123 E10
Clayholes Angus 287 D9
Clayland Stirl 277 D11
Clayock Highld 310 D5
Claypit Hill Cambs 123 G7
Claypits Devon 27 B7
Claypits Glos 80 D3
Claypits Kent 55 B9
Claypits Suff 140 G4
Claypole Lincs 172 F5
Clays End Bath 61 G8
Claythorpe Lincs 190 F6
Clayton Gtr Man 184 B5
Clayton S Yorks 198 F3
Clayton Staffs 168 G5
Clayton W Sus 36 E3
Clayton W Yorks 205 G8
Clayton Brook Lancs 194 C5
Clayton Green Lancs 194 C5
Clayton Heights W Yorks 205 G8
Clayton-le-Dale Lancs 203 G9
Clayton-le-Moors Lancs 203 G10
Clayton-le-Woods Lancs 194 C5
Clayton West W Yorks 197 E9
Clayworth Notts 188 D2
Cleadale Highld 294 G6
Cleadon T & W 243 E9
Cleadon Park T & W 243 E9
Clearbrook Devon 7 B10
Clearwell Glos 79 D9
Clearwell Newport 59 B9
Clearwood Wilts 45 D10
Cleasby N Yorks 224 C5
Cleat Orkney 314 B4
Cleat Orkney 314 H4
Cleatlam Durham 224 B2
Cleator Cumb 219 C10
Cleator Moor Cumb 219 B10
Cleave Devon 28 G2
Clebrig Highld 308 F5
Cleckheaton W Yorks 197 B7
Cleddon Mon 79 E8
Clee St Margaret Shrops 131 G11
Cleedownton Shrops 131 G11
Cleehill Shrops 115 B11
Cleekhimin N Lnrk 268 D5
Cleemarsh Shrops 131 G11
Cleestanton Shrops 115 B11
Cleethorpes NE Lincs 201 F10
Cleeton St Mary Shrops 116 B2
Cleeve Glos 80 C2
Cleeve N Som 60 F3
Cleeve Oxon 64 C6
Cleeve Hill Glos 99 F9
Cleeve Prior Worcs 99 B11
Cleghorn S Lnrk 269 F8
Clegyrnant Powys 129 B8
Clehonger Hereford 97 D9
Cleirwy = Clyro Powys 96 C4
Cleish Perth 279 B11
Cleland N Lnrk 268 D5
Clement Street Kent 68 E4
Clement's End C Beds 85 B8
Clemens End Glos 79 C9
Clench Wilts 63 G7
Clench Common Wilts 63 F7
Clencher's Mill Hereford 98 D4
Clenchwarton Norf 157 E11
Clennell Northumb 251 B10
Clent Worcs 117 B8
Cleobury Mortimer Shrops 116 B3
Cleobury North Shrops 132 F2
Cleongart Argyll 255 D7
Clephanton Highld 301 D8
Clerk Green W Yorks 197 C8
Clerkenwater Corn 5 B11
Clerkenwell London 67 C10
Clerklands Borders 262 E2
Clermiston Edin 280 G3
Clestrain Orkney 314 F3
Cleuch Head Borders 262 G3
Cleughbrae Dumfries 238 C3
Clevancy Wilts 62 D5
Clevans Renfs 267 B7
Clevedon N Som 60 E2
Cleveley Oxon 101 G7
Cleveleys Lancs 202 E2
Cleverton Wilts 62 B3
Clevis Bridgend 57 F10
Clewer Som 44 C2
Clewer Green Windsor 66 D2
Clewer New Town Windsor 66 D3
Clewer Village Windsor 66 D3
Cley next the Sea Norf 177 E8
Cliaid W Isles 297 L2
Cliasmol W Isles 305 H2
Cliburn Cumb 231 G7
Click Mill Orkney 314 D3
Cliddesden Hants 48 D6
Cliff Derbys 185 D8
Cliff Warks 134 D4
Cliff End E Sus 38 E5
Cliff End W Yorks 196 D6
Cliffburn Angus 287 C10
Cliffe Lancs 203 G10
Cliffe Medway 69 D8
Cliffe N Yorks 207 G9
Cliffe N Yorks 224 B4
Cliffe Woods Medway 69 E8
Clifford Devon 24 C4
Clifford Hereford 96 B4
Clifford W Yorks 206 E4
Clifford Chambers Warks 118 G3
Clifford's Mesne Glos 98 G4
Cliffs End Kent 71 G10
Clifftown Sthend 69 B11
Clifton Bristol 60 E5
Clifton C Beds 104 D3
Clifton Cumb 230 F6
Clifton Derbys 169 G11
Clifton Devon 40 E5
Clifton Gtr Man 195 G9
Clifton Lancs 202 G5
Clifton N Yorks 205 D9
Clifton Northumb 252 G6
Clifton Nottingham 153 C11
Clifton Oxon 101 E9
Clifton S Yorks 186 C6
Clifton S Yorks 187 B8
Clifton Stirl 285 D7
Clifton W Ches 183 F8
Clifton W Yorks 197 C7
Clifton Worcs 98 B6
Clifton York 207 C7
Clifton Campville Staffs 152 G5
Clifton Green Gtr Man 195 G9
Clifton Hampden Oxon 83 F8
Clifton Junction Gtr Man 195 G9
Clifton Maybank Dorset 29 E9
Clifton Moor York 207 B7
Clifton Reynes M Keynes 121 G8
Clifton upon Dunsmore Warks 119 B10
Clifton upon Teme Worcs 116 E4
Cliftoncote Borders 263 E8
Cliftonville Kent 71 E11
Cliftonville N Lnrk 268 B4
Cliftonville Norf 160 B6
Climping W Sus 35 G8
Climpy S Lnrk 269 D8
Clink Som 45 D9
Clinkham Wood Mers 183 B8
Clint N Yorks 205 B11
Clint Green Norf 159 G10
Clintmains Borders 262 C4
Clints N Yorks 224 E2
Cliobh W Isles 304 E2
Clipiau Gwyn 146 G6
Clippesby Norf 161 G8
Clippings Green Norf 159 G10
Clipsham Rutland 155 F9
Clipston Northants 136 G4
Clipston Notts 154 C2
Clipstone C Beds 103 F8
Clitheroe Lancs 203 E10
Cliton Manor C Beds 104 D3
Cliuthar W Isles 305 J3
Clive Shrops 149 E10
Clive W Ches 167 B11
Clive Green W Ches 167 C11
Clive Vale E Sus 38 E4
Clivocast Shetland 312 C8
Clixby Lincs 200 G6
Cloatley Wilts 81 G7
Cloatley End Wilts 81 G7
Clocaenog Denb 165 E9
Clochan Aberds 303 E9
Clochan Moray 302 C4
Clock Face Mers 183 C8
Clock House London 67 G9
Clock Mills Hereford 96 B5
Clockmill Borders 272 E5
Cloddiau Powys 130 B4
Cloddymoss Moray 301 D9
Clodock Hereford 96 F6
Cloford Som 45 E8
Cloford Common Som 45 E8
Cloigyn Carms 74 C6
Clola Aberds 303 E10
Clophill C Beds 103 D11
Clopton Northants 137 G11
Clopton Suff 126 G4
Clopton Corner Suff 126 G4
Clopton Green Suff 124 G5
Clopton Green Suff 125 E9
Close Clark I o M 192 E3
Close House Durham 233 F10
Closeburn Dumfries 247 E9
Closworth Som 29 E9
Clothall Herts 104 E5
Clothall Common Herts 104 E5
Clotton W Ches 167 C8
Clotton Common W Ches 167 C8
Cloud Side Staffs 168 C6
Cloudesley Bush Warks 135 F9
Clouds Hereford 97 D11
Clough Gtr Man 196 D2
Clough Gtr Man 196 F2
Clough W Yorks 196 E5
Clough Dene Durham 242 F5
Clough Foot W Yorks 196 C2
Clough Hall Staffs 168 E4
Clough Head W Yorks 196 C5
Cloughfold Lancs 195 C10
Cloughton N Yorks 227 G10
Cloughton Newlands N Yorks 227 F10
Clounlaid Highld 289 D9
Clousta Shetland 313 H5
Clouston Orkney 314 E2
Clova Aberds 302 G4
Clova Angus 292 F5
Clove Lodge Durham 223 B8
Clovelly Devon 24 C4
Clovenfords Borders 261 B10
Clovenstone Aberds 293 B9
Cloves Moray 301 C11
Clovullin Highld 290 G2
Clow Bridge Lancs 195 B10
Clowance Wood Corn 2 C4
Clowne Derbys 187 F7
Clows Top Worcs 116 C4
Cloy Wrex 166 G5
Cluanie Inn Highld 290 B2
Cluanie Lodge Highld 290 B2
Clubmoor Mers 182 C5
Clubworthy Corn 11 C11
Cluddley Telford 150 G2
Clun Shrops 130 G6
Clunbury Shrops 131 G7
Clunderwen Carms 73 B10
Clune Highld 301 D9
Clune Highld 301 G7
Clunes Highld 290 E4
Clungunford Shrops 115 B7
Clunie Aberds 302 D6
Clunie Perth 286 C5
Clunton Shrops 130 G6
Cluny Fife 280 B4
Cluny Castle Aberds 293 B8
Cluny Castle Highld 291 D8
Clutton Bath 44 B6
Clutton W Ches 167 E7
Clutton Hill Bath 44 B6
Clwt-grugoer Conwy 165 C7
Clwt-y-bont Gwyn 163 C9
Clwydyfagwyr M Tydf 77 D8
Clydach Mon 78 C2
Clydach Swansea 75 E11
Clydach Terrace Powys 77 C11
Clydach Vale Rhondda 77 G7
Clydebank W Dunb 277 G9
Clyffe Pypard Wilts 62 D5
Clynder Argyll 276 E4
Clyne Neath 76 E4
Clynelish Highld 311 J2
Clynnog-fawr Gwyn 162 F6
Clyro = Cleirwy Powys 96 C4
Clyst Honiton Devon 14 C5
Clyst Hydon Devon 27 G8
Clyst St George Devon 14 D5
Clyst St Lawrence Devon 27 G8
Clyst St Mary Devon 14 C5
Cnìp W Isles 304 E2
Cnoc Amhlaigh W Isles 304 E7
Cnoc an t-Solais W Isles 304 D6
Cnoc Fhionn Highld 295 D10
Cnoc Màiri W Isles 304 E6
Cnoc Rolum W Isles 296 F3
Cnocbreac Argyll 274 F5
Cnwch-coch Ceredig 112 B3
Coachford Aberds 302 E4
Coad's Green Corn 11 F11
Coal Aston Derbys 186 F5
Coal Bank Darl 234 G3
Coal Pool W Mid 133 C10
Coalbrookdale Telford 132 C3
Coalbrookvale Bl Gwent 77 D11
Coalburn S Lnrk 259 C8
Coalburns T & W 242 E4
Coalcleugh Northumb 232 B2
Coaley Glos 80 E3
Coaley Peak Glos 80 E3
Coalford Aberds 293 D10
Coalhall E Ayrs 257 F10
Coalhill Essex 88 F3
Coalmoor Telford 132 B3
Coalpit Field Warks 135 F7
Coalpit Heath S Glos 61 C7
Coalpit Hill Staffs 168 E4
Coalport Telford 132 C3
Coalsnaughton Clack 279 B8
Coaltown of Balgonie Fife 280 B5
Coaltown of Wemyss Fife 280 B6
Coalville Leics 153 G8
Coalway Glos 79 C9
Coanwood Northumb 240 F5
Coarsewell Devon 8 E4
Coat Som 29 C7
Coatbridge N Lnrk 268 C4
Coatdyke N Lnrk 268 C5
Coate Swindon 63 C7
Coate Wilts 62 G4
Coates Cambs 138 D6
Coates Glos 81 E7
Coates Lancs 204 D3
Coates Lincs 188 E6
Coates Midloth 270 C4
Coates Notts 188 E4
Coates W Sus 35 D7
Coatham Redcar 235 F7
Coatham Mundeville Darl 233 G11
Coatsgate Dumfries 248 B3
Cobairdy Aberds 302 E5
Cobbaton Devon 25 B10
Cobbler's Corner Worcs 116 F5
Cobbler's Green Norf 142 E5
Cobbler's Plain Mon 79 E7
Cobbs Warr 183 D10
Cobb's Cross Glos 98 E5
Cobbs Fenn Essex 106 E5
Cobby Syke N Yorks 205 B9
Coberley Glos 81 B7
Cobhall Common Hereford 97 D9
Cobham Kent 69 F7
Cobham Sur 66 G6
Cobleland Stirl 277 B10
Cobler's Green Essex 87 B11
Cobley Dorset 31 C8
Cobley Hill Worcs 117 C10
Cobnash Hereford 115 E9
Cobridge Stoke 168 F5
Cobscot Shrops 150 B3
Coburty Aberds 303 C9
Cock and End Suff 124 G4
Cock Alley Derbys 186 G6
Cock Bank Wrex 166 F5
Cock Bevington Warks 117 G11
Cock Bridge Aberds 292 C4
Cock Clarks Essex 88 E4
Cock Gate Hereford 115 D9
Cock Green Essex 87 B11
Cock Hill N Yorks 206 B6
Cock Marling E Sus 38 D5
Cock Street Kent 53 C9
Cock Street Suff 107 D9
Cockadilly Glos 80 E4
Cockayne N Yorks 226 F2
Cockburnspath Borders 282 G5
Cockden Lancs 204 G3
Cockenzie and Port Seton E Loth 281 F8
Cocker Bar Lancs 194 C4
Cockerham Lancs 202 C5
Cockermouth Cumb 229 E8
Cockernhoe Herts 104 G2
Cockernhoe Green Herts 104 G2
Cockersdale W Yorks 197 B8
Cockerton Darl 224 B5
Cockett Swansea 56 C6
Cocketty Aberds 293 F9
Cockfield Durham 233 G8
Cockfield Suff 125 G8
Cockfosters London 86 F3
Cockhill Som 44 G6
Cocking W Sus 34 D5
Cocking Causeway W Sus 34 D5
Cockington Torbay 9 C7
Cocklake Som 44 D2
Cocklaw Northumb 241 C10
Cockleford Glos 81 C7
Cockley Beck Cumb 220 E4
Cockley Cley Norf 140 C5
Cockley Hill W Yorks 197 D7
Cocknowle Dorset 18 E4
Cockpole Green Wokingham 65 C9
Cocks Corn 4 E5
Cocks Green Suff 125 F7
Cockshead Ceredig 112 F2
Cockshoot Hereford 97 D11
Cockshutford Shrops 131 F11
Cockshutt Shrops 132 G4
Cockshutt Shrops 149 D8
Cockthorpe Norf 177 E7
Cockwells Corn 2 C2
Cockwood Devon 14 E5
Cockwood Som 43 E8
Cockyard Derbys 185 F8
Cockyard Hereford 97 E8
Codda Corn 11 F9
Coddenham Suff 126 G2
Coddenham Green Suff 126 F2
Coddington Hereford 98 C4
Coddington Notts 172 E4
Coddington W Ches 167 D7
Codford St Mary Wilts 46 F3
Codford St Peter Wilts 46 F3
Codicote Herts 86 B2
Codicote Bottom Herts 86 B2
Codmore Bucks 85 E7
Codmore Hill W Sus 35 C9
Codnor Derbys 170 F6
Codnor Breach Derbys 170 F6
Codnor Gate Derbys 170 E6
Codnor Park Derbys 170 E6
Codrington S Glos 61 D8
Codsall Staffs 133 C7
Codsall Wood Staffs 132 B6
Codsend Som 41 F11
Coed Cwnwr Mon 78 F6
Coed Eva Torf 78 G3
Coed Llai = Leeswood Flint 166 D3
Coed Mawr Gwyn 179 G9
Coed Morgan Mon 78 C5
Coed-Talon Flint 166 D3
Coed-y-bryn Ceredig 93 C7
Coed-y-caerau Newport 78 G5
Coed-y-fedw Mon 78 D6
Coed y Garth Ceredig 128 E3
Coed y go Shrops 148 D5
Coed-y-paen Mon 78 F4
Coed-y-parc Gwyn 163 B10
Coed-y-wlad Powys 130 B4
Coed-yr-ynys Powys 96 G3
Coed Ystumgwern Gwyn 145 E11
Coedcae Bl Gwent 77 D11
Coedcae Torf 78 D3
Coedely Rhondda 58 B4
Coedkernew Newport 59 C9
Coedpoeth Wrex 166 E3
Coedway Powys 148 G6
Coelbren Powys 76 C4
Coffee Hall M Keynes 103 D7
Coffinswell Devon 9 B7
Cofton Devon 14 E5
Cofton Common W Mid 117 B10
Cofton Hackett Worcs 117 B10
Cog V Glam 59 F7
Cogan V Glam 59 E7
Cogenhoe Northants 120 E6
Cogges Oxon 82 D5
Coggeshall Essex 106 G6
Coggeshall Hamlet Essex 107 G7
Coggins Mill E Sus 37 B9
Coig Peighinnean W Isles 304 B7
Coig Peighinnean Bhuirgh W Isles 304 C6
Coignafearn Lodge Highld 291 B8
Coignascallan Highld 291 B9
Coilacriech Aberds 292 D5
Coilantogle Stirl 285 G9
Coilessan Argyll 284 G6
Coilleag W Isles 297 K3
Coillemore Highld 300 B6
Coillore Highld 294 B5
Coirea-chrombe Stirl 285 G9
Coisley Hill S Yorks 186 E6
Coity Bridgend 58 C2
Cokenach Herts 105 D7
Cokhay Green Derbys 152 D5
Col W Isles 304 D6
Col Uarach W Isles 304 E6
Colaboll Highld 309 H5
Colan Corn 5 C7
Colaton Raleigh Devon 15 D7
Colbost Highld 298 E2
Colburn N Yorks 224 F3
Colby Cumb 231 G9
Colby I o M 192 E3
Colby Norf 160 C4
Colchester Essex 107 F10
Colchester Green Suff 125 F8
Colcot V Glam 58 F6
Cold Ash W Berks 64 F4
Cold Ash Hill Hants 49 G10
Cold Ashby Northants 120 B3
Cold Ashton S Glos 61 E9
Cold Aston Glos 81 B10
Cold Blow Pembs 73 C10
Cold Brayfield M Keynes 121 G8
Cold Christmas Herts 86 B5
Cold Cotes N Yorks 212 E4
Cold Elm Glos 98 E6
Cold Hanworth Lincs 189 E8
Cold Harbour Dorset 18 D4
Cold Harbour Herts 85 B10
Cold Harbour Kent 69 G11
Cold Harbour Lincs 155 C9
Cold Harbour Oxon 64 D6
Cold Harbour Wilts 45 B11
Cold Harbour Wilts 45 D11
Cold Harbour Windsor 65 D10
Cold Hatton Telford 150 E2
Cold Hatton Heath Telford 150 E2
Cold Hesledon Durham 234 B4
Cold Hiendley W Yorks 197 E11
Cold Higham Northants 120 G3
Cold Inn Pembs 73 D10
Cold Kirby N Yorks 215 C10
Cold Moss Heath E Ches 168 C3
Cold Newton Leics 136 B4
Cold Northcott Corn 11 D10
Cold Norton Essex 88 E4
Cold Overton Leics 154 G6
Cold Row Lancs 202 E3
Cold Well Staffs 151 G11
Coldbackie Highld 308 D6
Coldbeck Cumb 222 E4
Coldblow London 68 E4
Coldbrook Powys 96 D3
Coldean Brighton 36 F4
Coldeast Devon 14 G2
Coldeaton Derbys 169 D10
Colden W Yorks 196 B3
Colden Common Hants 33 C7
Coldfair Green Suff 127 E8
Coldham Cambs 139 C8
Coldham Staffs 133 B7
Coldham's Common Cambs 123 F9
Coldharbour Corn 4 F5
Coldharbour Devon 27 E9
Coldharbour Dorset 17 E9
Coldharbour Glos 79 E9
Coldharbour Kent 52 C5
Coldharbour London 68 D4
Coldharbour Sur 50 E6
Coldingham Borders 273 B8
Coldmeece Staffs 151 C7
Coldoch Stirl 278 B3
Coldra Newport 59 B11
Coldrain Perth 286 G4
Coldred Kent 55 D9
Coldridge Devon 25 F11
Coldstream Angus 287 D7
Coldstream Borders 263 B8
Coldvreath Corn 5 D9
Coldwaltham W Sus 35 D8
Coldwells Aberds 303 E11
Coldwells Croft Aberds 302 G5
Cole Som 45 G7
Cole End Essex 105 D11
Cole End Warks 134 F3
Cole Green Herts 86 C3
Cole Green Herts 105 E8
Cole Henley Hants 48 C3
Cole Park London 67 E7
Colebatch Shrops 130 F6
Colebrook Devon 27 F8
Colebrooke Devon 13 B11
Coleburn Moray 302 D2
Coleby Lincs 173 C7
Coleby N Lincs 199 D11
Coleford Devon 26 G3
Coleford Glos 79 C9
Coleford Som 45 D7
Coleford Water Som 42 G6
Colegate End Norf 142 F3
Colehall W Mid 134 F2
Colehill Dorset 31 G8
Coleman Green Herts 85 C11
Coleman's Hatch E Sus 52 G3
Colemere Shrops 149 C8
Colemore Hants 49 G8
Colemore Green Shrops 132 D4
Coleorton Leics 153 F8
Coleorton Moor Leics 153 F8
Colerne Wilts 61 E10
Cole's Cross Dorset 28 G5
Coles Green Suff 107 C11
Cole's Green Suff 126 E5
Coles Green Worcs 116 G5
Coles Meads Sur 51 C9
Colesbourne Glos 81 C7
Colesbrook Dorset 30 B4
Colesden Beds 122 F2
Coleshill Bucks 85 F7
Coleshill Oxon 82 G2
Coleshill Warks 134 F4
Colestocks Devon 27 G9
Colethrop Glos 80 C4
Coley Bath 44 B5
Coley Reading 65 E8
Coley W Yorks 196 B6
Colfin Dumfries 236 D2
Colgate W Sus 51 G8
Colgrain Argyll 276 E6
Colham Green London 66 C5
Colindale London 67 B8
Colinsburgh Fife 287 G8
Colinton Edin 270 B4
Colintraive Argyll 275 F11
Colkirk Norf 159 D8
Collace Perth 286 D6
Collafield Glos 79 C11
Collafirth Shetland 312 G6
Collam W Isles 305 J3
Collamoor Head Corn 11 C9
Collaton Devon 9 G9
Collaton St Mary Torbay 9 D7
College Milton S Lnrk 268 D2
College of Roseisle Moray 301 C11
College Park London 67 C8
College Town Brack 65 G11
Collennan S Ayrs 257 C8
Collessie Fife 286 F6
Colleton Mills Devon 25 D11
Collett's Br Norf 139 B9
Collett's Green Worcs 116 G6
Collier Row London 87 G8
Collier Street Kent 53 D8
Collier's End Herts 105 G7
Collier's Green E Sus 38 C3
Collier's Green Kent 53 F9
Colliers Hatch Essex 87 E8
Collier's Wood London 67 E9
Colliery Row T & W 234 B2
Collieston Aberds 303 G10
Collin Dumfries 238 B2
Collingbourne Ducis Wilts 47 C8
Collingbourne Kingston Wilts 47 B8
Collingham Notts 172 C4
Collingham W Yorks 206 D3
Collington Hereford 116 E2
Collingtree Northants 120 F5
Collingwood Northumb 243 B7
Collins End Oxon 65 D7
Collins Green Warr 183 C9
Collins Green Worcs 116 F4
Collipriest Devon 27 E7
Colliston Angus 287 C10
Colliton Devon 27 G9
Collycroft Warks 135 F7
Collyhurst Gtr Man 195 G11
Collynie Aberds 303 F8
Collyweston Northants 137 C9
Colmonell S Ayrs 244 F4
Colmslie Borders 262 B2
Colmsliehill Borders 271 G10
Colmworth Beds 122 F2
Coln Rogers Glos 81 D9
Coln St Aldwyns Glos 81 D10
Coln St Dennis Glos 81 C9
Colnabaichin Aberds 292 C4
Colnbrook Slough 66 D4
Colne Cambs 123 B7
Colne Lancs 204 E3
Colne Bridge W Yorks 197 C7
Colne Edge Lancs 204 E3
Colne Engaine Essex 107 E7
Colnefields Cambs 123 B7
Colney Norf 142 B3
Colney Hatch London 86 G3
Colney Heath Herts 86 D2
Colney Street Herts 85 E11
Cologin Argyll 289 G10
Colpitts Grange Northumb 241 F11
Colpy Aberds 302 F6
Colquhar Borders 270 G6
Colscott Devon 24 E5
Colshaw Staffs 169 B8
Colsterdale N Yorks 214 C2
Colsterworth Lincs 155 E8
Colston E Dunb 268 B2
Colston Pembs 91 F9
Colston Bassett Notts 154 C3
Colstrope Bucks 65 B9
Colt Hill Hants 49 C8
Colt Park Cumb 210 E5
Coltfield Moray 301 C11
Colthouse Cumb 221 F7
Colthrop W Berks 64 F4
Coltishall Norf 160 F5
Coltness N Lnrk 268 D6
Colton Cumb 210 B6
Colton N Yorks 206 E6
Colton Norf 142 B2
Colton Staffs 151 E11
Colton Suff 125 D7
Colton W Yorks 206 G3
Colton Hills Staffs 133 D8
Colt's Green S Glos 61 C8
Colt's Hill Kent 52 E6
Columbia T & W 243 F8
Columbjohn Devon 14 B5
Colva Powys 114 G4
Colvend Dumfries 237 D10
Colvister Shetland 312 D7
Colwall Hereford 98 C4
Colwall Green Hereford 98 C4
Colwall Stone Hereford 98 C5
Colwell I o W 20 D2
Colwell Northumb 241 B11
Colwich Staffs 151 E10
Colwick Notts 171 G10
Colwinston = Tregolwyn V Glam 58 D2
Colworth W Sus 22 C6
Colwyn Bay = Bae Colwyn Conwy 180 F4
Colychurch Bridgend 58 D2
Colyford Devon 15 C10
Colyton Devon 15 C10
Colzie Fife 286 F6
Combe Devon 7 E10
Combe Devon 8 B4
Combe Devon 9 G9
Combe E Sus 37 B10
Combe Hereford 114 E6
Combe Oxon 82 B6
Combe Som 28 B6
Combe W Berks 63 G11
Combe Almer Dorset 18 B5
Combe Common Sur 50 F3
Combe Down Bath 61 G9
Combe Fishacre Devon 8 C6
Combe Florey Som 43 G7
Combe Hay Bath 45 B8
Combe Martin Devon 40 D5
Combe Moor Hereford 115 E7
Combe Pafford Torbay 9 B8
Combe Raleigh Devon 27 G11
Combe St Nicholas Som 28 E4
Combe Throop Som 30 C2
Combebow Devon 12 D5
Combeinteignhead Devon 14 G4
Comberbach W Ches 183 F10
Comberford Staffs 134 B3
Comberton Cambs 123 F7
Comberton Hereford 115 D9
Combpyne Devon 15 C11
Combrew Devon 40 G4
Combridge Staffs 151 B11
Combrook Warks 118 G6
Combs Derbys 185 F8
Combs Suff 125 F10
Combs W Yorks 197 D8
Combs Ford Suff 125 F11
Combwich Som 43 E9
Come-to-Good Corn 4 G6
Comers Aberds 293 C8
Comeytrowe Som 28 C2
Comford Corn 2 B6
Comfort Corn 2 D6
Comhampton Worcs 116 D6
Comins Coch Ceredig 128 G2
Comiston Edin 270 B4
Comley Shrops 131 D9
Commercial End Cambs 123 E11
Commins Denb 165 C10
Commins Capel Betws Ceredig 112 F2
Commins Coch Powys 128 C6
Common Cefn-llwyn Mon 78 G4
Common Edge Blkpool 202 G2
Common End Cumb 228 G6
Common End Derbys 170 C6
Common Hill Hereford 97 E11
Common Moor Corn 6 B4
Common Platt Wilts 62 B6
Common Side Derbys 170 F6
Common Side Derbys 186 F4
Common Side W Ches 167 B9
Common-y-coed Mon 60 B2
Commondale N Yorks 226 C3
Commonmoor Corn 6 B4
Commonside Derbys 170 G2
Commonside Notts 171 D7
Commonside W Ches 183 G8
Commonwood Herts 85 E8
Commonwood Shrops 149 D9
Commonwood Wrex 166 E5
Comp Kent 52 B6
Compass Som 43 G9
Compstall Gtr Man 185 C7
Compton Derbys 169 F11
Compton Devon 9 C7
Compton Hants 32 B4
Compton Hants 33 B7
Compton Plym 7 D9
Compton Staffs 132 G6
Compton Sur 49 D11
Compton Sur 50 D3
Compton W Berks 64 D4
Compton W Mid 133 D7
Compton W Sus 34 E3
Compton W Yorks 206 E3
Compton Wilts 46 C6
Compton Abbas Dorset 30 D5
Compton Abdale Glos 81 B9
Compton Bassett Wilts 62 E4
Compton Beauchamp Oxon 63 B9
Compton Bishop Som 43 B11
Compton Chamberlayne Wilts 31 B8
Compton Common Bath 60 G6
Compton Dando Bath 60 G6
Compton Dundon Som 44 G3
Compton Durville Som 28 D6
Compton End Hants 33 B7
Compton Green Glos 98 F4
Compton Greenfield S Glos 60 C5
Compton Martin Bath 44 B4
Compton Pauncefoot Som 29 B10
Compton Valence Dorset 17 C7
Comrie Fife 279 D10
Comrie Highld 300 D4
Comrie Perth 285 C11
Comrie Perth 285 E11
Comrue Dumfries 248 F3
Conaglen House Highld 290 G2
Conanby S Yorks 187 B7
Conchra Argyll 275 E11
Conchra Highld 295 C10
Concord T & W 243 F8
Concraig Perth 286 F2
Concraigie Perth 286 C5
Conder Green Lancs 202 B5

Conderton Worcs 99 D9
Condicote Glos 100 F3
Condorrat N Lnrk 278 G4
Condover Shrops 131 B9
Coney Hall London 67 G11
Coney Hill Glos 80 B5
Coney Weston Suff 125 B9
Coneyhurst W Sus 35 C10
Coneysthorpe N Yorks 216 E4
Coneythorpe N Yorks 206 B3
Conford Hants 49 G10
Congash Highld 301 G10
Congdon's Shop Corn 11 F11
Congeith Dumfries 237 C10
Congelow Kent 53 D7
Congerstone Leics 135 B7
Congham Norf 158 E4
Congl-y-wal Gwyn 164 G2
Congleton E Ches 168 C5
Congleton Edge E Ches 168 C5
Congresbury N Som 60 G2
Congreve Staffs 151 G8
Conham Bristol 60 E6
Conicavel Moray 301 D9
Coningsby Lincs 174 D2
Conington Cambs 122 D6
Conington Cambs 138 F3
Conisbrough S Yorks 187 B8
Conisby Argyll 274 G3
Conisholme Lincs 190 B6
Coniston Cumb 220 F6
Coniston E Yorks 209 F9
Coniston Cold N Yorks 204 B4
Conistone N Yorks 213 F9
Conkwell Wilts 61 G9
Connage Moray 302 C4
Connah's Quay Flint 166 B3
Connel Argyll 289 F11
Connel Park E Ayrs 258 G4
Conniburrow M Keynes 103 D7
Connista Highld 298 B4
Connon Corn 6 C3
Connor Downs Corn 2 B3
Conock Wilts 46 B5
Conon Bridge Highld 300 D5
Conon House Highld 300 D5
Cononish Stirl 285 E7
Cononley N Yorks 204 D5
Cononley Woodside N Yorks 204 D5
Cononsyth Angus 287 C9
Conordan Highld 295 B7
Conquermoor Heath Telford 150 F3
Consall Staffs 169 F7
Consett Durham 242 G4
Constable Burton N Yorks 224 G3
Constable Lee Lancs 195 C10
Constantine Corn 2 D6
Constantine Bay Corn 10 G3
Contin Highld 300 D4
Contlaw Aberdeen 293 C10
Conwy Conwy 180 F3
Conyer Kent 70 G3
Conyers Green Suff 125 D7
Cooden E Sus 38 F2
Cooil I o M 192 E4
Cookbury Devon 24 F6
Cookbury Wick Devon 24 F5
Cookham Windsor 65 B11
Cookham Dean Windsor 65 C11
Cookham Rise Windsor 65 C11
Cookhill Worcs 117 F11
Cookley Suff 126 B6
Cookley Worcs 132 G6
Cookley Green Oxon 83 G11
Cookney Aberds 293 D10
Cookridge W Yorks 205 E11
Cook's Green Essex 89 B11
Cook's Green Suff 125 G9
Cooksbridge E Sus 36 E6
Cooksey Corner Worcs 117 D8
Cooksey Green Worcs 117 D8
Cookshill Staffs 168 G6
Cooksland Corn 5 B11
Cooksmill Green Essex 87 D10
Cooksongreen W Ches 183 G9
Coolham W Sus 35 C10
Cooling Medway 69 D9
Cooling Street Medway 69 E8
Coolinge Kent 55 F8
Coomb Hill Kent 69 G7
Coombe Bucks 84 D4
Coombe Corn 4 G2
Coombe Corn 4 G5
Coombe Corn 4 G6
Coombe Corn 5 E9
Coombe Corn 6 C4
Coombe Corn 24 E2
Coombe Devon 14 G4
Coombe Devon 27 D8
Coombe Glos 80 G3
Coombe Hants 33 C11
Coombe Kent 55 B9
Coombe London 67 E8
Coombe Som 28 B3
Coombe Som 28 F6
Coombe Wilts 30 C5
Coombe Wilts 47 C7
Coombe Bissett Wilts 31 B10
Coombe Dingle Bristol 60 D5
Coombe Hill Glos 99 F7
Coombe Keynes Dorset 18 E2
Coombes W Sus 35 F11
Coombesdale Staffs 150 B6
Coombeswood W Mid 133 F9
Coombs End S Glos 61 C9
Coombses Som 28 F4
Cooper Street Kent 55 B10
Cooper Turning Gtr Man 194 F6
Cooper's Corner Kent 52 D3
Cooper's Green E Sus 37 C7
Cooper's Green Herts 85 D11
Cooper's Hill C Beds 103 D10
Cooper's Hill Sur 66 E3
Coopersale Common Essex 87 E7
Coopersale Street Essex 87 E7
Cootham W Sus 35 E9
Cop Street Kent 55 B9
Copcut Worcs 117 E7
Copdock Suff 108 C2
Coped Hall Wilts 62 C5
Copenhagen Denb 165 B8
Copford Essex 107 G8
Copford Green Essex 107 G8
Copgrove N Yorks 214 G6
Copister Shetland 312 F6
Cople Beds 104 B2
Copley Durham 233 F7
Copley Gtr Man 185 B7
Copley W Yorks 196 C5
Copley Hill W Yorks 197 B8
Coplow Dale Derbys 185 F11
Copmanthorpe York 207 D7
Copmere End Staffs 150 D6
Copnor Ptsmth 33 G11
Copp Lancs 202 F4
Coppathorne Corn 24 G2
Coppenhall E Ches 168 D2
Coppenhall Staffs 151 F8
Coppenhall Moss E Ches 168 D2
Copperhouse Corn 2 B3
Coppice Gtr Man 196 G2
Coppicegate Shrops 132 G4
Coppingford Cambs 138 G3
Coppins Corner Kent 54 D2
Coppleham Som 42 G2
Copplestone Devon 26 G3
Coppull Lancs 194 E5
Coppull Moor Lancs 194 E5
Copsale W Sus 35 C11
Copse Hill London 67 E8
Copster Green Lancs 203 G9
Copster Hill Gtr Man 196 G2
Copston Magna Warks 135 F9
Copt Green Warks 118 D3
Copt Heath W Mid 118 B3
Copt Hewick N Yorks 214 E6
Copt Oak Leics 153 G9
Copthall Green Essex 86 E6
Copthill Durham 232 C3
Copthorne Corn 11 C11
Copthorne E Ches 167 G11
Copthorne Shrops 149 G9
Copthorne Sur 51 F10
Coptiviney Shrops 149 B8
Copton Kent 54 B4
Copy's Green Norf 159 B8
Copythorne Hants 32 E4
Corbets Tey London 68 B5
Corbridge Northumb 241 E11
Corbriggs Derbys 170 B6
Corby Northants 137 F7
Corby Glen Lincs 155 E9
Corby Hill Cumb 239 F11
Cordon N Ayrs 256 C2
Cordwell Norf 142 E2
Coreley Shrops 116 C2
Cores End Bucks 66 B2
Corfe Som 28 D2
Corfe Castle Dorset 18 E5
Corfe Mullen Dorset 18 B5
Corfton Shrops 131 F9
Corfton Bache Shrops 131 F9
Corgarff Aberds 292 C4
Corgee Corn 5 C10
Corhampton Hants 33 C10
Corlae Dumfries 246 D5
Corlannau Neath 57 C9
Corley Warks 134 F6
Corley Ash Warks 134 F5
Corley Moor Warks 134 F5
Cornaa I o M 192 D5
Cornabus Argyll 254 C4
Cornaigbeg Argyll 288 E1
Cornaigmore Argyll 288 C4
Cornaigmore Argyll 288 E1
Cornard Tye Suff 107 C8
Cornbank Midloth 270 C4
Cornbrook Shrops 116 B2
Corncatterach Aberds 302 F5
Cornel Conwy 164 C2
Corner Row Lancs 202 F4
Cornett Hereford 97 B11
Corney Cumb 220 G2
Cornforth Durham 234 E2
Cornharrow Dumfries 246 E5
Cornhill Aberds 302 D5
Cornhill Powys 96 C2
Cornhill Stoke 168 E5
Cornhill-on-Tweed Northumb 263 B9
Cornholme W Yorks 196 B2
Cornish Hall End Essex 106 D3
Cornquoy Orkney 314 G5
Cornriggs Durham 232 C2
Cornsay Durham 233 C8
Cornsay Colliery Durham 233 C9
Cornton Stirl 278 B5
Corntown Highld 300 D5
Corntown V Glam 58 D2
Cornwell Oxon 100 F5
Cornwood Devon 8 D2
Cornworthy Devon 8 D6
Corpach Highld 290 F2
Corpusty Norf 160 C2
Corran Highld 290 G2
Corran Highld 295 E10
Corran a Chan Uachdaraich Highld 295 C7
Corranbuie Argyll 275 G9
Corrany I o M 192 D5
Corrichoich Highld 311 G4
Corrie N Ayrs 255 C11
Corrie Common Dumfries 248 F6
Corriecravie N Ayrs 255 E10
Corriecravie Moor N Ayrs 255 E10
Corriedoo Dumfries 246 G5
Corriegarth Lodge Highld 291 B7
Corriemoillie Highld 300 C3
Corriemulzie Lodge Highld 309 K3
Corrievarkie Lodge Perth 291 F7
Corrievorrie Highld 301 G7
Corrigall Orkney 314 E3
Corrimony Highld 300 F3
Corringham Lincs 188 C5
Corringham Thurrock 69 C8
Corris Gwyn 128 B5
Corris Uchaf Gwyn 128 B4
Corrour Highld 290 G5
Corrour Shooting Lodge Highld 290 G6
Corrow Argyll 284 G5
Corry Highld 295 C8
Corry of Ardnagrask Highld 300 E5
Corrybrough Highld 301 G8
Corrydon Perth 292 G3
Corryghoil Argyll 284 E5
Corrykinloch Highld 309 G3
Corrylach Argyll 255 D8
Corrymuckloch Perth 286 D2
Corrynachenchy Argyll 289 E8
Cors-y-Gedol Gwyn 145 E11
Corsback Highld 310 B6
Corscombe Dorset 29 F8
Corse Aberds 302 E6
Corse Glos 98 F5
Corse Lawn Worcs 98 E6
Corse of Kinnoir Aberds 302 E5
Corsewall Dumfries 236 C2
Corsham Wilts 61 E11
Corsindae Aberds 293 C8
Corsley Wilts 45 D10
Corsley Heath Wilts 45 D10
Corsock Dumfries 237 B9
Corston Bath 61 F7
Corston Orkney 314 E3
Corston Wilts 62 C2
Corstorphine Edin 280 G3
Cortachy Angus 287 B7
Corton Suff 143 D10
Corton Wilts 46 E2
Corton Denham Som 29 C10
Cortworth S Yorks 186 B6
Coruanan Lodge Highld 290 G2
Corunna W Isles 296 E4
Corvast Highld 309 K5
Corwen Denb 165 G9
Cory Devon 24 D5
Coryates Dorset 17 D8
Coryton Cardiff 58 C6
Coryton Devon 12 E5
Coryton Thurrock 69 C8
Côsag Highld 295 D10
Cosby Leics 135 E10
Coscote Oxon 64 B4
Coseley W Mid 133 E8
Cosford Warks 119 B9
Cosgrove Northants 102 C5
Cosham Ptsmth 33 F11
Cosheston Pembs 73 E8
Cosmeston V Glam 59 F7
Cosmore Dorset 29 F11
Cossall Notts 171 G7
Cossall Marsh Notts 171 G7
Cosses S Ayrs 244 G4
Cossington Leics 154 G2
Cossington Som 43 E11
Costa Orkney 314 D3
Costessey Norf 160 G3
Costessey Park Norf 160 G3
Costhorpe Notts 187 D9
Costislost Corn 10 G6
Costock Notts 153 D11
Coston Leics 154 E6
Coston Norf 141 B11
Coswinsawsin Corn 2 B4
Cote Oxon 82 E4
Cote Som 43 E10
Cote W Sus 35 F10
Cotebrook W Ches 167 B9
Cotehill Cumb 239 G11
Cotes Cumb 211 B9
Cotes Leics 153 E11
Cotes Staffs 150 C6
Cotes Heath Staffs 150 C6
Cotes Park Derbys 170 E6
Cotesbach Leics 135 G10
Cotford St Lukes Som 27 B11
Cotgrave Notts 154 B2
Cothall Aberds 293 B10
Cotham Bristol 60 E5
Cotham Notts 172 F3
Cothelstone Som 43 G7
Cotheridge Worcs 116 G5
Cotherstone Durham 223 B10
Cothill Oxon 83 F7
Cotland Mon 79 E8
Cotleigh Devon 28 G2
Cotmanhay Derbys 171 G7
Cotmarsh Wilts 62 D5
Cotmaton Devon 15 D8
Coton Cambs 123 F8
Coton Northants 120 C3
Coton Shrops 149 C10
Coton Staffs 134 B3
Coton Staffs 150 E6
Coton Staffs 151 C9
Coton Clanford Staffs 151 E7
Coton Hayes Staffs 151 C9
Coton Hill Shrops 149 G9
Coton Hill Staffs 151 C9
Coton in the Clay Staffs 152 D3
Coton in the Elms Derbys 152 F4
Coton Park Derbys 152 F5
Cotonwood Shrops 149 B10
Cotonwood Staffs 150 E6
Cotswold Community Wilts 81 F8
Cott Devon 8 C5
Cottam E Yorks 217 F9
Cottam Lancs 202 G6
Cottam Notts 188 F4
Cottartown Highld 301 F10
Cottenham Cambs 123 D8
Cottenham Park London 67 F8
Cotterdale N Yorks 222 G6
Cottered Herts 104 F6
Cotterhill Woods S Yorks 187 E9
Cotteridge W Mid 117 B10
Cotterstock Northants 137 E10
Cottesbrooke Northants 120 C4
Cottesmore Rutland 155 G8
Cotteylands Devon 26 E6
Cottingham E Yorks 208 G6
Cottingham Northants 136 E6
Cottingley W Yorks 205 F8
Cottisford Oxon 101 E11
Cotton Staffs 169 F9
Cotton Suff 125 D11
Cotton End Beds 103 B11
Cotton End Northants 120 F5
Cotton Stones W Yorks 196 C4
Cotton Tree Lancs 204 F4
Cottonworth Hants 47 F11
Cottown Aberds 293 B9
Cottown Aberds 302 G5
Cottown Aberds 303 E8
Cotts Devon 7 B8
Cottwood Devon 25 E10
Cotwall Telford 150 F2
Cotwalton Staffs 151 B8
Coubister Orkney 314 E3
Couch Green Hants 48 G4
Couch's Mill Corn 6 D2
Coughton Hereford 97 G11
Coughton Warks 117 E11
Coughton Fields Warks 117 F11
Cougie Highld 300 G2
Coulaghailtro Argyll 275 G8
Coulags Highld 299 E9
Coulby Newham M'bro 225 B10
Coulderton Cumb 219 D9
Couldoran Highld 299 E8
Couligartan Stirl 285 G8
Coulin Highld 299 D10
Coulin Lodge Highld 299 D10
Coull Aberds 293 C7
Coull Argyll 274 G3
Coulmony Ho Highld 301 E9
Coulport Argyll 276 D4
Coulsdon London 51 B9
Coulshill Perth 286 G3
Coulston Wilts 46 C3
Coulter S Lnrk 260 C2
Coultings Som 43 E8
Coulton N Yorks 216 E2
Coultra Fife 287 E7
Cound Shrops 131 C11
Coundlane Shrops 131 B11
Coundmoor Shrops 131 C11
Coundon Durham 233 F10
Coundon W Mid 134 G6
Coundon Grange Durham 233 F10
Coundongate Durham 233 F10
Counters End Herts 85 D8
Countersett N Yorks 213 B8
Countess Wilts 47 E7
Countess Cross Essex 107 E7
Countess Wear Devon 14 D4
Countesthorpe Leics 135 D11
Countisbury Devon 41 D8
County Oak W Sus 51 F9
Coup Green Lancs 194 B5
Coupar Angus Perth 286 C6
Coupland Cumb 222 B4
Coupland Northumb 263 C10
Cour Argyll 255 C9
Courance Dumfries 248 E3
Coursley Som 42 G6
Court-at-Street Kent 54 F5
Court Barton Devon 14 D2
Court Colman Bridgend 57 E11
Court Corner Hants 48 B6
Court Henry Carms 93 G11
Court House Green W Mid 135 G7
Courteenhall Northants 120 G5
Courthill Perth 286 C5
Courtsend Essex 89 G8
Courtway Som 43 G8
Cousland Midloth 271 B7
Cousley Wood E Sus 53 G7
Couston Argyll 275 F11
Cova Shetland 313 J5
Cove Argyll 276 E4
Cove Borders 282 G5
Cove Devon 27 D7
Cove Hants 49 B11
Cove Highld 307 K3
Cove Bay Aberdeen 293 C11
Cove Bottom Suff 127 B9
Covehithe Suff 143 G10
Coven Staffs 133 B8
Coven Heath Staffs 133 C8
Coven Lawn Staffs 133 B8
Covender Hereford 98 C2
Coveney Cambs 139 G9
Covenham St Bartholomew Lincs 190 C4
Covenham St Mary Lincs 190 C4
Coventry W Mid 118 B6
Coverack Corn 3 F7
Coverack Bridges Corn 2 C5
Coverham N Yorks 214 B2
Covesea Moray 301 B11
Covingham Swindon 63 B7
Covington Cambs 121 C11
Covington S Lnrk 259 B11
Cow Ark Lancs 203 D9
Cow Green Suff 125 D11
Cow Hill Lancs 203 G7
Cow Roast Herts 85 C7
Cowan Bridge Lancs 212 D2
Cowbar Redcar 226 B5
Cowbeech E Sus 23 C10
Cowbeech Hill E Sus 23 C10
Cowbit Lincs 156 F5
Cowbog Aberds 303 D8
Cowbridge Lincs 174 F4
Cowbridge Som 42 E3
Cowbridge = Y Bont-Faen V Glam 58 E3
Cowcliffe W Yorks 196 D6
Cowdale Derbys 185 G9
Cowden Kent 52 E3
Cowdenbeath Fife 280 C3
Cowdenburn Borders 270 E4
Cowen Head Cumb 221 F9
Cowers Lane Derbys 170 F4
Cowes I o W 20 B5
Cowesby N Yorks 215 B9
Cowesfield Green Wilts 32 C3
Cowfold W Sus 36 C2
Cowgill Cumb 212 B5
Cowgrove Dorset 18 B5
Cowhill Derbys 170 F5
Cowhill S Glos 79 G10
Cowhorn Hill S Glos 61 E7
Cowie Aberds 293 E10
Cowie Stirl 278 D6
Cowlands Corn 4 G6
Cowleaze Corner Oxon 82 E4
Cowley Derbys 186 F4
Cowley Devon 14 B4
Cowley Glos 81 C7
Cowley London 66 C5
Cowley Oxon 83 E8
Cowley Peachy London 66 C5
Cowleymoor Devon 27 E7
Cowling Lancs 194 D5
Cowling N Yorks 204 E5
Cowling N Yorks 214 B4
Cowlinge Suff 124 G4
Cowlow Derbys 185 G9
Cowmes W Yorks 197 D7
Cowpe Lancs 195 C10
Cowpen Northumb 253 G7
Cowpen Bewley Stockton 234 G5
Cowplain Hants 33 E11
Cowshill Durham 232 C3
Cowslip Green N Som 60 G3
Cowstrandburn Fife 279 C10
Cowthorpe N Yorks 206 C4
Cox Common Suff 143 G8
Cox Green Gtr Man 195 E8
Cox Green Sur 50 G5
Cox Green Windsor 65 D11
Cox Hill Corn 4 G4
Cox Moor Notts 171 D8
Coxall Hereford 115 C7
Coxbank E Ches 167 G11
Coxbench Derbys 170 G5
Coxbridge Som 44 F4
Coxford Corn 11 B9
Coxford Norf 158 D6
Coxford Soton 32 D5
Coxgreen Staffs 132 F6
Coxheath Kent 53 C8
Coxhill Kent 55 D8
Coxhoe Durham 234 D2
Coxley Som 44 E4
Coxley W Yorks 197 D9
Coxley Wick Som 44 E4
Coxlodge T & W 242 D6
Coxpark Corn 12 G4
Coxtie Green Essex 87 F9
Coxwold N Yorks 215 D10
Coychurch Bridgend 58 D2
Coylton S Ayrs 257 E10
Coylumbridge Highld 291 B11
Coynach Aberds 292 C6
Coynachie Aberds 302 F4
Coytrahen Bridgend 57 D11
CoytrahÛn Bridgend 57 D11
Crab Orchard Dorset 31 F9
Crabadon Devon 8 E5
Crabbet Park W Sus 51 F10
Crabble Kent 55 E9
Crabbs Cross Worcs 117 E10
Crabbs Green Herts 105 F9
Crabgate Norf 159 D11
Crabtree Plym 7 D10
Crabtree W Sus 36 B2
Crabtree Green Wrex 166 G4
Crackaig Argyll 274 G6
Crackenedge W Yorks 197 C8
Crackenthorpe Cumb 231 G9
Crackington Haven Corn 11 B8
Crackley Staffs 168 E4
Crackley Warks 118 C5
Crackleybank Shrops 150 G5
Crackpot N Yorks 223 F9
Crackthorn Corner Suff 125 B10
Cracoe N Yorks 213 G9
Cracow Moss E Ches 168 F2
Cracow Moss Staffs 168 F3
Craddock Devon 27 E9
Cradhlastadh W Isles 304 E2
Cradle Edge W Yorks 205 F7
Cradle End Herts 105 G9
Cradley Hereford 98 B4
Cradley W Mid 133 G8
Cradley Heath W Mid 133 F8
Cradoc Powys 95 E10
Crafthole Corn 7 E7
Crafton Bucks 84 B5
Crag Bank Lancs 211 E9
Crag Foot Lancs 211 E9
Cragg Hill W Yorks 205 F10
Cragg Vale W Yorks 196 C4
Craggan Highld 301 G10
Craggan Moray 301 F11
Craggan Stirl 285 E9
Cragganvallie Highld 300 F5
Craggenmore Moray 301 F11
Craggie Highld 301 F7
Craggie Highld 311 H2
Craggiemore Highld 309 J7
Craghead Durham 242 G6
Crahan Corn 2 C5
Crai Powys 95 G7
Craibstone Moray 302 D4
Craichie Angus 287 C9
Craig Dumfries 237 B8
Craig Dumfries 237 C8
Craig Highld 299 E10
Craig Berthlwyd M Tydf 77 F9
Craig Castle Aberds 302 G4
Craig-cefn-parc Swansea 75 E11
Craig Douglas Borders 261 E7
Craig Llangiwg Neath 76 D2
Craig-llwyn Shrops 148 D4
Craig Lodge Argyll 275 G10
Craig-moston Aberds 293 F8
Craig Penllyn V Glam 58 D3
Craig-y-don Conwy 180 E3
Craig-y-Duke Swansea 76 E2
Craig-y-nos Powys 76 B4
Craig-y-penrhyn Ceredig 128 E3
Craig-y-Rhacca Caerph 59 B7
Craiganor Lodge Perth 285 B10
Craigdallie Perth 286 E6
Craigdam Aberds 303 F8
Craigdarroch Dumfries 246 E6
Craigdarroch Highld 300 D4
Craigdhu Highld 300 E4
Craigearn Aberds 293 B9
Craigellachie Moray 302 E2
Craigencallie Ho Dumfries 237 B7
Craigencross Dumfries 236 C2
Craigend Borders 271 F9
Craigend Glasgow 268 B3
Craigend Perth 286 E3
Craigend Perth 286 E5
Craigend Stirl 278 D5
Craigendive Argyll 275 E11
Craigendoran Argyll 276 E6
Craigendowie Angus 293 G7
Craigends Renfs 267 B8
Craigens Argyll 274 G3
Craigens E Ayrs 258 F3
Craigentinny Edin 280 G5
Craigerne Borders 261 B7
Craighall Perth 286 C5
Craighat Stirl 277 E9
Craighead Fife 287 G10
Craighead Highld 301 C7
Craighill Aberds 303 E7
Craighlaw Mains Dumfries 236 C5
Craighouse Argyll 274 G6
Craigie Aberds 293 B11
Craigie Dundee 287 D8
Craigie Perth 286 C5
Craigie Perth 286 E5
Craigie S Ayrs 257 C10
Craigie S Ayrs 257 E8
Craigiefield Orkney 314 E4
Craigiehall Edin 280 F3
Craigielaw E Loth 281 F9
Craigierig Borders 260 E6
Craigleith Edin 280 G4
Craiglockhart Edin 280 G4
Craigmalloch E Ayrs 245 E11
Craigmaud Aberds 303 D8
Craigmill Stirl 278 B6
Craigmillar Edin 280 G5
Craigmore Argyll 266 B2
Craignant Shrops 148 B5
Craignell Dumfries 237 B7
Craigneuk N Lnrk 268 C5
Craigneuk N Lnrk 268 D5
Craignish Castle Argyll 275 C8
Craignure Argyll 289 F9
Craigo Angus 293 G8
Craigow Perth 286 G4
Craigrory Highld 300 E6
Craigrothie Fife 287 F7
Craigroy Moray 301 D11
Craigruie Stirl 285 E8
Craig's End Essex 106 D4
Craigsford Mains Borders 262 B3
Craigshall Dumfries 237 D10
Craigshill W Loth 269 B11
Craigside Durham 233 D8
Craigston Castle Aberds 303 D7
Craigton Aberdeen 293 C10
Craigton Angus 287 B7
Craigton Angus 287 D9
Craigton Glasgow 267 C10
Craigton Highld 300 E6
Craigton Highld 309 H6
Craigton Highld 309 K6
Craigtown Highld 310 D2
Craik Borders 249 B8
Crail Fife 287 G10
Crailing Borders 262 E5
Crailinghall Borders 262 E5
Crakaig Highld 311 H3
Crakehill N Yorks 215 E8
Crakemarsh Staffs 151 B11
Crambe N Yorks 216 G4
Crambeck N Yorks 216 F4
Cramhurst Sur 50 E2
Cramlington Northumb 243 B7
Cramond Edin 280 F3
Cramond Bridge Edin 280 F3
Crampmoor Hants 32 C5
Cranage E Ches 168 B3
Cranberry Staffs 150 B6
Cranborne Dorset 31 E9
Cranbourne Brack 66 E2
Cranbourne Hants 48 C6
Cranbrook Kent 53 F9
Cranbrook London 68 B2
Cranbrook Common Kent 53 F9
Crane Moor S Yorks 197 G10
Crane's Corner Norf 159 G8
Cranfield C Beds 103 C9
Cranford Devon 24 C4
Cranford London 66 D6
Cranford St Andrew Northants 121 B8
Cranford St John Northants 121 B8
Cranham Glos 80 C5
Cranham London 68 B5
Cranhill Glasgow 268 B2
Cranhill Warks 118 G2
Crank Mers 183 B8
Crank Wood Gtr Man 194 G6
Crankwood Gtr Man 194 G6
Cranleigh Sur 50 F5
Cranley Suff 126 C3
Cranley Gardens London 67 B9
Cranmer Green Suff 125 C10
Cranmore I o W 20 D3
Cranmore Som 45 E7
Cranna Aberds 302 D6
Crannich Argyll 289 E7
Crannoch Moray 302 D4
Cranoe Leics 136 D5
Cransford Suff 126 E6
Cranshaws Borders 272 C3
Cranstal I o M 192 B5
Cranswick E Yorks 208 C6
Crantock Corn 4 C5
Cranwell Lincs 173 F8
Cranwich Norf 140 E5
Cranworth Norf 141 C9
Craobh Haven Argyll 275 C8
Crapstone Devon 7 B10
Crarae Argyll 275 D10
Crask Highld 308 C7
Crask Inn Highld 309 G5
Crask of Aigas Highld 300 E4
Craskins Aberds 293 C7
Craster Northumb 265 F7
Craswall Hereford 96 D5
Crateford Shrops 132 F4
Crateford Staffs 133 B8
Cratfield Suff 126 B6
Crathes Aberds 293 D9
Crathie Aberds 292 D4
Crathie Highld 291 D7
Crathorne N Yorks 225 D8
Craven Arms Shrops 131 G8
Crawcrook T & W 242 E4
Crawford Lancs 194 G3
Crawford S Lnrk 259 E11
Crawforddyke S Lnrk 269 F7
Crawfordjohn S Lnrk 259 E9
Crawick Dumfries 259 G7
Crawley Devon 28 F3
Crawley Hants 48 G2
Crawley Oxon 82 C4
Crawley W Sus 51 F9
Crawley Down W Sus 51 F10
Crawley End Essex 105 C8
Crawley Hill Sur 65 G11
Crawleyside Durham 232 C5
Crawshaw W Yorks 197 E8
Crawshawbooth Lancs 195 B10
Crawton Aberds 293 F10
Cray N Yorks 213 D8
Cray Perth 292 G3
Crayford London 68 E4
Crayke N Yorks 215 E11
Craymere Beck Norf 159 C11
Crays Hill Essex 88 G2
Cray's Pond Oxon 64 C6
Crazies Hill Wokingham 65 C9
Creacombe Devon 26 D4
Creag Aoil Highld 290 F3
Creag Ghoraidh W Isles 297 G3
Creagan Argyll 289 E11
Creagan Sithe Argyll 284 G6
Creagastrom W Isles 297 G4
Creaguaineach Lodge Highld 290 G5
Creaksea Essex 88 F6
Creamore Bank Shrops 149 C10
Crean Corn 1 E3
Creaton Northants 120 C4
Creca Dumfries 238 C6
Credenhill Hereford 97 C9
Crediton Devon 26 G4
Creebridge Dumfries 236 C6
Creech Dorset 18 E4
Creech Bottom Dorset 18 E4
Creech Heathfield Som 28 B3
Creech St Michael Som 28 B3
Creed Corn 5 F8
Creediknowe Shetland 312 G7
Creegbrawse Corn 4 G4
Creekmoor Poole 18 C6
Creekmouth London 68 C3
Creeksea Essex 88 F6
Creeting Bottoms Suff 126 F2
Creeting St Mary Suff 125 F11
Creeton Lincs 155 E10
Creetown Dumfries 236 D6
Creg-ny-Baa I o M 192 D4
Creggans Argyll 284 G4
Cregneash I o M 192 F2
Cregrina Powys 114 G2
Creich Fife 287 E7
Creigau Mon 79 F7
Creighton Staffs 151 B11
Creigiau Cardiff 58 C5
Crelly Corn 2 C5
Cremyll Corn 7 E9
Crendell Dorset 31 E9
Crepkill Highld 298 E4
Creslow Bucks 102 G6
Cress Green Glos 80 E3
Cressage Shrops 131 C11
Cressbrook Derbys 185 G11
Cresselly Pembs 73 D9
Cressex Bucks 84 G4
Cressing Essex 106 G5
Cresswell Northumb 253 E7
Cresswell Staffs 151 B9
Cresswell Quay Pembs 73 D9
Creswell Derbys 187 G8
Creswell Staffs 151 D7
Creswell Staffs 151 D8
Creswell Green Staffs 151 G11
Cretingham Suff 126 E4
Cretshengan Argyll 275 G8
Creunant = Crynant Neath 76 E3
Crewe E Ches 168 D2
Crewe W Ches 166 E6
Crewe-by-Farndon W Ches 166 E6
Crewgarth Cumb 231 E8
Crewgreen Powys 148 F6
Crewkerne Som 28 F6
Crews Hill London 86 F4
Crew's Hole Bristol 60 E6
Crewton Derby 153 C7
Crianlarich Stirl 285 E7

Cribbs Causeway S Glos 60 C5
Cribden Side Lancs 195 C9
Cribyn Ceredig 111 G10
Criccieth Gwyn 145 B9
Crich Derbys 170 E5
Crich Carr Derbys 170 E4
Crichie Aberds 303 E9
Crichton Midloth 271 C7
Crick Mon 79 G7
Crick Northants 119 C11
Crickadarn Powys 95 C11
Cricket Hill Hants 65 G10
Cricket Malherbie Som 28 E5
Cricket St Thomas Som 28 F5
Crickham Som 44 D2
Crickheath Shrops 148 E5
Crickheath Wharf Shrops 148 E5
Crickhowell Powys 78 B2
Cricklade Wilts 81 G10
Cricklewood London 67 B8
Crickmery Shrops 150 D3
Crick's Green Hereford 116 G2
Criddlestyle Hants 31 E11
Cridling Stubbs N Yorks 198 C4
Cridmore I o W 20 E5
Crieff Perth 286 E2
Criggan Corn 5 C10
Criggion Powys 148 F5
Crigglestone W Yorks 197 D10
Crimble Gtr Man 195 E11
Crimchard Som 28 F4
Crimdon Park Durham 234 D5
Crimond Aberds 303 D10
Crimonmogate Aberds 303 D10
Crimp Corn 24 D3
Crimplesham Norf 140 C3
Crimscote Warks 100 B4
Crinan Argyll 275 D8
Crinan Ferry Argyll 275 D8
Crindau Newport 59 B10
Crindledyke N Lnrk 268 D6
Cringleford Norf 142 B3
Cringles W Yorks 204 D6
Cringletie Borders 270 G4
Crinow Pembs 73 C10
Cripple Corner Essex 107 E7
Cripplesease Corn 2 B2
Cripplestyle Dorset 31 E9
Cripp's Corner E Sus 38 C3
Crispie Argyll 275 F10
Crist Derbys 185 E8
Crit Hall Kent 53 G9
Critchell's Green Hants 32 B3
Critchill Som 45 D9
Critchmere Sur 49 G11
Crizeley Hereford 97 E8
Croanford Corn 10 G6
Croasdale Cumb 219 B11
Crobeag W Isles 304 F5
Crock Street Som 28 E4
Crockenhill Kent 68 F4
Crocker End Oxon 65 B8
Crockerhill Hants 33 F9
Crockerhill W Sus 22 B6
Crockernwell Devon 13 C11
Crockers Devon 40 F5
Crocker's Ash Hereford 79 B8
Crockerton Wilts 45 E11
Crockerton Green Wilts 45 E11
Crocketford or Ninemile Bar Dumfries 237 B10
Crockey Hill York 207 D8
Crockham Heath W Berks 64 G2
Crockham Hill Kent 52 C2
Crockhurst Street Kent 52 E6
Crockleford Heath Essex 107 F10
Crockleford Hill Essex 107 F10
Crockness Orkney 314 G3
Croes-goch Pembs 87 E11
Croes-Hywel Mon 78 C4
Croes-lan Ceredig 93 C7
Croes Llanfair Mon 78 D4
Croes-wian Flint 181 G10
Croes-y-mwyalch Torf 78 G4
Croes y pant Mon 78 E4
Croesau Bach Shrops 148 D4
Croeserw Neath 57 B11
Croesor Gwyn 163 G10
Croespenmaen Caerph 77 F11
Croesyceiliog Carms 74 B6
Croesyceiliog Torf 78 F4
Croesywaun Gwyn 163 D8
Croft Hereford 115 D9
Croft Leics 135 D10
Croft Lincs 175 C8
Croft Pembs 92 C3
Croft Warr 183 C10
Croft Mitchell Corn 2 B5
Croft of Tillymaud Aberds 303 F11
Croft-on-Tees N Yorks 224 D5
Croftamie Stirl 277 D9
Croftfoot S Lnrk 268 C2
Crofthandy Corn 4 G4
Croftlands Cumb 210 D5
Croftmalloch W Loth 269 C8
Croftmoraig Perth 285 C11
Crofton Cumb 239 G8
Crofton London 68 F2
Crofton W Yorks 197 D11
Crofton Wilts 63 G9
Crofts Dumfries 237 B9
Crofts Bank Gtr Man 184 B3
Crofts of Benachielt Highld 310 F5
Crofts of Haddo Aberds 303 F8
Crofts of Inverthernie Aberds 303 E7
Crofts of Meikle Ardo Aberds 303 E8
Crofty Swansea 56 B4
Croggan Argyll 289 G9
Croglin Cumb 231 B7
Croich Highld 309 K4
Croick Highld 310 D2
Croig Argyll 288 D5
Crois Dughaill W Isles 297 J3
Cromarty Highld 301 C7
Cromasaig Highld 299 C10
Crombie Fife 279 D10
Crombie Castle Aberds 302 D5
Cromblet Aberds 303 F7
Cromdale Highld 301 G10
Cromer Herts 104 F5
Cromer Norf 160 A4
Cromer-Hyde Herts 86 C2
Cromford Derbys 170 D3
Cromhall S Glos 79 G11
Cromhall Common S Glos 61 B7
Cromor W Isles 304 F6
Crompton Fold Gtr Man 196 F2
Cromra Highld 291 D7
Cromwell Notts 172 C3
Cromwell Bottom W Yorks 196 C6
Cronberry E Ayrs 258 E4
Crondall Hants 49 D9
Cronk-y-Voddy I o M 192 D4
Cronton Mers 183 D7
Crook Cumb 221 G9
Crook Devon 27 G11
Crook Durham 233 D9
Crook of Devon Perth 286 G4
Crookdake Cumb 229 C9
Crooke Gtr Man 194 F5
Crooked Billet London 67 E8
Crooked Soley Wilts 63 E10
Crooked Withies Dorset 31 F9
Crookedholm E Ayrs 257 B11
Crookes S Yorks 186 D4
Crookesmoor S Yorks 186 D4
Crookfur E Renf 267 D10
Crookgate Bank Durham 242 F5
Crookhall Durham 242 G4
Crookham Northumb 263 B10
Crookham W Berks 64 G4
Crookham Village Hants 49 C9
Crookhaugh Borders 260 D4
Crookhill T & W 242 E5
Crookhouse Borders 263 D7
Crooklands Cumb 211 C10
Crookston Glasgow 267 C10
Cropredy Oxon 101 B9
Cropston Leics 153 G11
Cropthorne Worcs 99 C9
Cropton N Yorks 216 B5
Cropwell Bishop Notts 154 B3
Cropwell Butler Notts 154 B3
Cros W Isles 304 B7
Crosben Highld 289 D9
Crosbost W Isles 304 F5
Crosby Cumb 229 D7
Crosby I o M 192 E4
Crosby Mers 182 B4
Crosby N Lincs 199 E11
Crosby Court N Yorks 225 G7
Crosby Garrett Cumb 222 D4
Crosby-on-Eden Cumb 239 F11
Crosby Ravensworth Cumb 222 C2
Crosby Villa Cumb 229 D7
Croscombe Som 44 E5
Crosemere Shrops 149 D8
Crosland Edge W Yorks 196 E6
Crosland Hill W Yorks 196 E6
Crosland Moor W Yorks 196 D6
Croslands Park Cumb 210 E4
Cross Devon 40 F3
Cross Devon 40 G6
Cross Shrops 149 B7
Cross Som 44 C2
Cross Ash Mon 78 B6
Cross-at-Hand Kent 53 D9
Cross Bank Worcs 116 C4
Cross Coombe Corn 4 E4
Cross End Beds 121 F11
Cross End Essex 107 E7
Cross End M Keynes 103 D8
Cross Gate W Sus 35 E8
Cross Gates W Yorks 205 F7
Cross Gates W Yorks 206 G3
Cross Green Devon 12 D3
Cross Green Staffs 133 B8
Cross Green Suff 124 G6
Cross Green Suff 125 F7
Cross Green Suff 125 G9
Cross Green Telford 150 G2
Cross Green W Yorks 206 G2
Cross Green Warks 119 F7
Cross Hands Carms 75 C9
Cross-hands Carms 92 G3
Cross Hands Pembs 73 C9
Cross Heath Staffs 168 F4
Cross Hill Corn 10 G6
Cross Hill Derbys 170 F6
Cross Hill Glos 79 F9
Cross Hills N Yorks 204 E6
Cross Holme N Yorks 225 F11
Cross Houses Shrops 131 B10
Cross Houses Shrops 132 E3
Cross in Hand E Sus 37 C9
Cross in Hand Leics 135 G10
Cross Inn Carms 74 C3
Cross Inn Ceredig 111 E10
Cross Inn Ceredig 111 F7
Cross Inn Rhondda 58 C5
Cross Keys Kent 52 C4
Cross Keys Wilts 61 E11
Cross Lane E Ches 167 C11
Cross Lane Head Shrops 132 D4
Cross Lanes Corn 2 E5
Cross Lanes Dorset 30 G3
Cross Lanes N Yorks 215 F10
Cross Lanes Oxon 65 D7
Cross Lanes Wrex 166 F5
Cross Llyde Hereford 97 F8
Cross o' th' hands Derbys 170 F3
Cross o' th' Hill W Ches 167 F7
Cross Oak Powys 96 G2
Cross of Jackston Aberds 303 F7
Cross Roads Devon 12 D5
Cross Roads W Yorks 204 F6
Cross Stone Aberds 303 G9
Cross Street Suff 126 B3
Cross Town E Ches 184 F3
Crossaig Argyll 255 B9
Crossal Highld 294 B6
Crossapol Argyll 288 E1
Crossbrae Aberds 302 D6
Crossburn Falk 279 G7
Crossbush W Sus 35 F8
Crosscanonby Cumb 229 D7
Crosscrake Cumb 211 B10
Crossdale Street Norf 160 B4
Crossens Mers 193 D11
Crossflatts W Yorks 205 E8
Crossford Fife 279 D11
Crossford S Lnrk 268 F6
Crossgate Lincs 156 D4
Crossgate Orkney 314 E4
Crossgate Staffs 151 B8
Crossgatehall E Loth 271 B7
Crossgates Cumb 229 G7
Crossgates Fife 280 D2
Crossgates N Yorks 217 C10
Crossgates Powys 113 E11
Crossgill Cumb 231 C10
Crossgill Lancs 211 G11
Crossgreen Shrops 149 F9
Crosshands Carms 92 G3
Crosshill E Ayrs 257 E11
Crosshill Fife 280 B3
Crosshill S Ayrs 245 B8
Crosshouse E Ayrs 257 B9
Crossings Cumb 240 B2
Crosskeys Caerph 78 G2
Crosskirk Highld 310 B4
Crosslands Cumb 210 B6
Crosslanes Shrops 148 F6
Crosslee Borders 261 F8
Crosslee Renfs 267 B8
Crossley Hall W Yorks 205 G8
Crossmichael Dumfries 237 C9
Crossmill E Renf 267 D10
Crossmoor Lancs 202 F4
Crossmount Perth 285 B11
Crosspost W Sus 36 C3
Crossroads Aberds 293 D9
Crossroads E Ayrs 257 C11
Crossroads Fife 281 B7
Crossroads Angus 287 B9
Crosstown Corn 24 D2
Crosstown V Glam 58 F4
Crosswater Sur 49 F11
Crossway Hereford 98 E2
Crossway Mon 78 B6
Crossway Powys 113 F11
Crossway Green Mon 79 G8
Crossway Green Worcs 116 D6
Crossways Dorset 17 D11
Crossways Kent 68 D5
Crossways Mon 96 G6
Crossways S Glos 79 G11
Crossways Sur 49 F11
Crosswell = Ffynnongroes Pembs 92 D2
Crosswood Ceredig 112 C3
Crosthwaite Cumb 221 G8
Croston Lancs 194 D3
Crostwick Norf 160 F5
Crostwight Norf 160 D6
Crothair W Isles 304 E3
Crouch Kent 52 B6
Crouch Kent 54 B5
Crouch End London 67 B9
Crouch Hill Dorset 30 E2
Crouch House Green Kent 52 D2
Croucheston Wilts 31 B9
Crouchers W Sus 22 C4
Croughly Moray 301 G11
Croughton Northants 101 E10
Crovie Aberds 303 C8
Crow Hants 31 G11
Crow Edge S Yorks 197 G7
Crow Green Essex 87 F9
Crow Hill Hereford 98 F2
Crow Nest W Yorks 205 F8
Crow Wood Halton 183 D8
Crowan Corn 2 C4
Crowborough E Sus 52 G4
Crowborough Staffs 168 D6
Crowborough Warren E Sus 52 G4
Crowcombe Som 42 F6
Crowcroft Worcs 116 G5
Crowden Derbys 185 B9
Crowden Devon 12 B5
Crowder Park Devon 8 D4
Crowdhill Hants 33 C7
Crowdicote Derbys 169 B10
Crowdleham Kent 52 B5
Crowdon N Yorks 227 F9
Crowell Oxon 84 F2
Crowell Hill Oxon 84 F3
Crowfield Northants 102 C2
Crowfield Suff 126 F2
Crowgate Street Norf 160 E6
Crowgreaves Shrops 132 D4
Crowhill M Keynes 102 D6
Crowhill Gtr Man 184 B6
Crowhole Derbys 186 F4
Crowhurst E Sus 38 E3
Crowhurst Sur 51 D11
Crowhurst Lane End Sur 51 D11
Crowland Lincs 156 G4
Crowlas Corn 2 C2
Crowle N Lincs 199 E9
Crowle Worcs 117 F8
Crowle Green Worcs 117 F8
Crowle Hill N Lincs 199 E9
Crowle Park N Lincs 199 E9
Crowmarsh Gifford Oxon 64 B6
Crown Corner Suff 126 C5
Crown East Worcs 116 G6
Crown Hills Leicester 136 C2
Crown Wood Brack 65 F11
Crownfield Bucks 84 F4
Crownhill Plym 7 D9
Crownland Suff 125 D10
Crownpits Sur 50 E3
Crownthorpe Norf 141 C11
Crowntown Corn 2 C4
Crows-an-wra Corn 1 D3
Crow's Green Essex 106 F3
Crow's Nest Corn 6 B5
Crowshill Norf 141 B8
Crowsley Oxon 65 D8
Crowsnest Shrops 131 C7
Crowther's Pool Powys 96 B4
Crowthorne Brack 65 G10
Crowton W Ches 183 G9
Croxall Staffs 152 G3
Croxby Lincs 189 B11
Croxby Top Lincs 189 B11
Croxdale Durham 233 D11
Croxden Staffs 151 B11
Croxley Green Herts 85 F9
Croxteth Mers 182 B6
Croxton Cambs 122 E4
Croxton N Lincs 200 E5
Croxton Norf 141 F7
Croxton Norf 159 C9
Croxton Staffs 150 C5
Croxton Green E Ches 167 E8
Croxton Kerrial Leics 154 D6
Croxtonbank Staffs 150 C5
Croy Highld 301 E7
Croy N Lnrk 278 F4
Croyde Devon 40 F2
Croyde Bay Devon 40 F2
Croydon Cambs 104 B6
Croydon London 67 F10
Crozen Hereford 97 B11
Crubenbeg Highld 291 D8
Crubenmore Lodge Highld 291 D8
Cruckmeole Shrops 131 B8
Cruckton Shrops 149 G8
Cruden Bay Aberds 303 F10
Crudgington Telford 150 F2
Crudie Aberds 303 D7
Crudwell Wilts 81 G7
Crug Powys 114 C3
Crugmeer Corn 10 F4
Crugybar Carms 94 D3
Cruise Hill Worcs 117 E10
Crulabhig W Isles 304 E3
Crumlin Caerph 78 F2
Crumplehorn Corn 6 E4
Crumpsall Gtr Man 195 G10
Crumpsbrook Shrops 116 B2
Crumpton Hill Worcs 98 B5
Crundale Kent 54 D5
Crundale Pembs 73 B7
Cruwys Morchard Devon 26 E5
Crux Easton Hants 48 B2
Cruxton Dorset 17 B8
Crwbin Carms 75 C7
Crya Orkney 314 F3
Cryers Hill Bucks 84 F5
Crymlyn Gwyn 179 G10
Crymych Pembs 92 E3
Crynant = Creunant Neath 76 E3
Crynfryn Ceredig 111 E11
Cuaich Highld 291 E8
Cuaig Highld 299 D7
Cuan Argyll 275 B8
Cubbington Warks 118 D6
Cubeck N Yorks 213 B9
Cubert Corn 4 D5
Cubitt Town London 67 D11
Cubley S Yorks 197 G8
Cubley Common Derbys 152 B3
Cublington Bucks 102 G6
Cublington Hereford 97 D8
Cuckfield W Sus 36 B4
Cucklington Som 30 B3
Cuckney Notts 187 G9
Cuckold's Green Suff 143 G9
Cuckold's Green Wilts 46 B3
Cuckoo Green Suff 143 D10
Cuckoo Hill Notts 188 C2
Cuckoo Tye Suff 107 C7
Cuckoo's Corner Hants 49 E8
Cuckoo's Corner Wilts 46 B4
Cuckoo's Knob Wilts 63 G7
Cuckron Shetland 313 H6
Cucumber Corner Norf 143 B7
Cuddesdon Oxon 83 E10
Cuddington Bucks 84 C2
Cuddington W Ches 183 G10
Cuddington Heath W Ches 167 F7
Cuddy Hill Lancs 202 F5
Cudham London 52 B2
Cudlipptown Devon 12 F6
Cudliptown Devon 12 F6
Cudworth S Yorks 197 F11
Cudworth Som 28 E5
Cudworth Sur 51 E8
Cudworth Common S Yorks 197 F11
Cuerden Green Lancs 194 C5
Cuerdley Cross Warr 183 D8
Cufaude Hants 48 B6
Cuffern Pembs 91 G7
Cuffley Herts 86 E4
Cuiashader W Isles 304 C7
Cuidhir W Isles 297 L2
Cuidhtinis W Isles 296 C6
Cuiken Midloth 270 C4
Cuilcheanna Ho Highld 290 G2
Cuin Argyll 288 D6
Cul na h-Aird W Isles 305 H3
Cùl Doirlinn Highld 289 B8
Culbo Highld 300 C6
Culbokie Highld 300 D6
Culburnie Highld 300 E4
Culcabock Highld 300 E6
Culcairn Highld 300 C6
Culcharry Highld 301 D8
Culcheth Warr 183 B11
Culcronchie Dumfries 237 C7
Culdrain Aberds 302 F5
Culduie Highld 299 E7
Culeave Highld 309 K5
Culford Suff 124 D6
Culfordheath Suff 125 C7
Culfosie Aberds 293 C9
Culgaith Cumb 231 F8
Culham Oxon 83 F8
Culkein Highld 306 F5
Culkein Drumbeg Highld 306 F6
Culkerton Glos 80 F6
Cullachie Highld 301 G9
Cullen Moray 302 C5
Cullercoats T & W 243 C9
Cullicudden Highld 300 C6
Cullingworth W Yorks 205 F7
Cullipool Argyll 275 B8
Cullivoe Shetland 312 C7
Culloch Perth 285 F11
Culloden Highld 301 E7
Cullompton Devon 27 F8
Culm Davy Devon 27 D10
Culmaily Highld 311 K2
Culmazie Dumfries 236 D5
Culmer Sur 50 F2
Culmers Kent 70 G5
Culmington Shrops 131 G9
Culmore Stirl 278 B3
Culmstock Devon 27 E10
Culnacraig Highld 307 J5
Culnaightrie Dumfries 237 D9
Culnaknock Highld 298 C5
Culnaneam Highld 294 C6
Culpho Suff 108 B4
Culra Lodge Highld 291 F7
Culrain Highld 309 K5
Culross Fife 279 D9
Culroy S Ayrs 257 G8
Culscadden Dumfries 236 E6
Culsh Aberds 292 D5
Culsh Aberds 303 E8
Culshabbin Dumfries 236 D5
Culswick Shetland 313 J4
Cultercullen Aberds 303 G9
Cults Aberdeen 293 C10
Cults Aberds 302 F5
Cults Dumfries 236 E6
Cults Fife 287 G7
Culverlane Devon 8 C4
Culverstone Green Kent 68 G6
Culverthorpe Lincs 173 G8
Culworth Northants 101 B10
Culzie Lodge Highld 300 B5
Cumberlow Green Herts 104 E6
Cumbernauld N Lnrk 278 G5
Cumbernauld Village N Lnrk 278 F5
Cumber's Bank Wrex 149 B8
Cumberworth Lincs 191 G8
Cumdivock Cumb 230 B2
Cumeragh Village Lancs 203 F7
Cuminestown Aberds 303 D8
Cumledge Borders 272 D5
Cumlewick Shetland 313 L6
Cumlodden Argyll 275 D11
Cumloden Dumfries 236 C6
Cummersdale Cumb 239 G9
Cummerton Aberds 303 C8
Cummertrees Dumfries 238 D4
Cummingston Moray 301 C11
Cumnock E Ayrs 258 E3
Cumnor Oxon 83 E7
Cumnor Hill Oxon 83 D7
Cumrew Cumb 240 G2
Cumwhinton Cumb 239 G10
Cumwhitton Cumb 240 G2
Cundall N Yorks 215 E8
Cundy Cross S Yorks 197 F11
Cundy Hos S Yorks 186 B4
Cunninghamhead N Ayrs 267 G7
Cunnister Shetland 312 D7
Cupar Fife 287 F7
Cupar Muir Fife 287 F7
Cupernham Hants 32 C5
Cupid Green Herts 85 D9
Cupid's Hill Mon 97 F8
Curbar Derbys 186 G3
Curborough Staffs 152 G2
Curbridge Hants 33 E8
Curbridge Oxon 82 D4
Curdridge Hants 33 E8
Curdworth Warks 134 E3
Curgurrell Corn 3 B9
Curin Highld 300 D3
Curland Som 28 D3
Curland Common Som 28 D3
Curlew Green Suff 127 D7
Curling Tye Green Essex 88 D4
Curload Som 28 B4
Currarie S Ayrs 244 E5
Currian Vale Corn 5 D9
Curridge W Berks 64 E3
Currie Edin 270 B3
Currock Cumb 239 G10
Curry Lane Corn 11 C11
Curry Mallet Som 28 C4
Curry Rivel Som 28 B5
Cursiter Orkney 314 E3
Curteis' Corner Kent 53 F11
Curtisden Green Kent 53 E8
Curtisknowle Devon 8 E4
Curtismill Green Essex 87 F8
Cury Corn 2 E5
Cusbay Orkney 314 C5
Cusgarne Corn 4 G5
Cushnie Aberds 303 C7
Cushuish Som 43 G7
Cusop Hereford 96 C4
Custards Hants 32 F3
Custom House London 68 C2
Cusveorth Coombe Corn 4 G5
Cusworth S Yorks 198 G4
Cutcloy Dumfries 236 F6
Cutcombe Som 42 F2
Cutgate Gtr Man 195 E11
Cuthill E Loth 281 G7
Cutiau Gwyn 146 F2
Cutlers Green Essex 105 E11
Cutler's Green Som 44 C5
Cutmadoc Corn 5 C11
Cutmere Corn 6 C6
Cutnall Green Worcs 117 D7
Cutsdean Glos 99 E11
Cutsyke W Yorks 198 C2
Cutteslowe Oxon 83 C8
Cutthorpe Derbys 186 G4
Cuttiford's Door Som 28 E4
Cutts Shetland 313 K6
Cuttybridge Pembs 72 B6
Cuttyhill Aberds 303 D10
Cuxham Oxon 83 F11
Cuxton Medway 69 F8
Cuxwold Lincs 201 G7
Cwm Bl Gwent 77 D11
Cwm Denb 181 F9
Cwm Neath 57 C10
Cwm Powys 129 D11
Cwm Powys 130 E5
Cwm Shrops 114 B6
Cwm Swansea 57 B7
Cwm-byr Carms 94 E2
Cwm Capel Carms 75 E7
Cwm-celyn Bl Gwent 78 D2
Cwm-Cewydd Gwyn 147 G7
Cwm-cou Ceredig 92 C5
Cwm Dows Caerph 78 F2
Cwm-Dulais Swansea 75 E10
Cwm-felin-fach Caerph 77 G11
Cwm Ffrwd-oer Torf 78 E3
Cwm-Fields Torf 78 E3
Cwm Gelli Caerph 77 F11
Cwm Gwyn Swansea 56 C6
Cwm Head Shrops 131 F8
Cwm-hesgen Gwyn 146 D5
Cwm-hwnt Rhondda 76 D6
Cwm Irfon Powys 95 B7
Cwm-Llinau Powys 128 B6
Cwm-mawr Carms 75 C8
Cwm-miles Carms 92 G3
Cwm Nant-gam Bl Gwent 78 C2
Cwm-parc Rhondda 77 F7
Cwm Penmachno Conwy 164 F3
Cwm Plysgog Ceredig 92 C3
Cwm-twrch Isaf Powys 76 C3
Cwm-twrch Uchaf Powys 76 C3
Cwm-y-glo Carms 75 C9
Cwm-y-glo Gwyn 163 C8
Cwmafan Neath 57 C9
Cwmaman Rhondda 77 F8
Cwmann Carms 93 B11
Cwmavon Torf 78 D3
Cwmbâch Rhondda 77 E8
Cwmbach Carms 75 E7
Cwmbach Carms 92 F5
Cwmbach Powys 96 D3
Cwmbach Rhondda 77 E8
Cwmbach Llechrhyd Powys 113 G10
Cwmbelan Powys 129 G8
Cwmbran Torf 78 G3
Cwmbrwyno Ceredig 128 G4
Cwmcarn Caerph 78 G2
Cwmcarvan Mon 79 D7
Cwmcoednerth Ceredig 92 B6
Cwmcrawnon Powys 77 B10
Cwmcych Carms 92 D5
Cwmdare Rhondda 77 E7
Cwmdu Carms 94 E2
Cwmdu Powys 96 G3
Cwmdu Swansea 56 C6
Cwmduad Carms 93 E7
Cwmdwr Carms 94 E4
Cwmerfyn Ceredig 128 G3
Cwmfelin Bridgend 57 D11
Cwmfelin M Tydf 77 E9
Cwmfelin Boeth Carms 73 B11
Cwmfelin Mynach Carms 92 G4
Cwmffrwd Carms 74 B6
Cwmgiedd Powys 76 C3
Cwmgors Neath 76 C2
Cwmgwili Carms 75 C9
Cwmgwrach Neath 76 E5
Cwmhiraeth Carms 92 D6
Cwmifor Carms 94 F3
Cwmisfael Carms 75 B7
Cwmllynfell Neath 76 C2
Cwmnantyrodyn Caerph 77 F11
Cwmorgan Pembs 92 E5
Cwmparc Rhondda 77 F7
Cwmpengraig Carms 92 D6
Cwmpennar Rhondda 77 E8
Cwmrhos Powys 96 G3
Cwmrhydyceirw Swansea 57 B7
Cwmsychpant Ceredig 93 B9
Cwmsyfiog Caerph 77 E11
Cwmsymlog Ceredig 128 G4
Cwmtillery Bl Gwent 78 D2
Cwmwdig Water Pembs 90 E6
Cwmwysg Powys 95 F7
Cwmynyscoy Torf 78 F3
Cwmyoy Mon 96 G5
Cwmystwyth Ceredig 112 C5
Cwrt Gwyn 128 C3
Cwrt-newydd Ceredig 93 B9
Cwrt-y-cadno Carms 94 C3
Cwrt-y-gollen Powys 78 B2
Cydweli = Kidwelly Carms 74 D6
Cyffordd Llandudno = Llandudno Junction Conwy 180 F3
Cyffylliog Denb 165 D9
Cyfronydd Powys 130 B2
Cymau Flint 166 D3
Cymdda Bridgend 58 C2
Cymer Neath 57 B11
Cymmer Rhondda 77 G8
Cyncoed Cardiff 59 C7
Cynghordy Carms 94 C6
Cynheidre Carms 75 D7
Cynonville Neath 57 B10
Cyntwell Cardiff 58 D6
Cynwyd Denb 165 G9
Cynwyl Elfed Carms 93 F7
Cywarch Gwyn 147 F7

D

Daccombe Devon 9 B8
Dacre Cumb 230 F5
Dacre N Yorks 214 G3
Dacre Banks N Yorks 214 G3
Daddry Shield Durham 232 D3
Dadford Bucks 102 D3
Dadlington Leics 135 D8
Dafarn Faig Gwyn 163 F7
Dafen Carms 75 E8
Daffy Green Norf 141 B9
Dagdale Staffs 151 C11
Dagenham London 68 C3
Daggons Dorset 31 E10
Daglingworth Glos 81 D7
Dagnall Bucks 85 B7
Dagtail End Worcs 117 E10
Dagworth Suff 125 E10
Dail Beag W Isles 304 D4
Dail bho Dheas W Isles 304 B6
Dail bho Thuath W Isles 304 B6
Dail Mor W Isles 304 D4
Daill Argyll 274 G4
Dailly S Ayrs 245 C7
Dainton Devon 9 B7
Dairsie or Osnaburgh Fife 287 F8
Daisy Green Suff 125 D10
Daisy Green Suff 125 D11
Daisy Hill Gtr Man 195 G7
Daisy Hill W Yorks 197 B9
Daisy Hill W Yorks 205 G8
Daisy Nook Gtr Man 196 G2
Dalabrog W Isles 297 J3
Dalavich Argyll 275 B10
Dalbeattie Dumfries 237 C10
Dalbeg Highld 291 B8
Dalblair E Ayrs 258 F4
Dalbog Angus 293 F7
Dalbrack Stirl 285 G11
Dalbury Derbys 152 C5
Dalby I o M 192 E3
Dalby Lincs 190 G6
Dalby N Yorks 216 E2
Dalchalloch Perth 291 G9
Dalchalm Highld 311 J3
Dalchenna Argyll 284 G4
Dalchirach Moray 301 F11
Dalchonzie Perth 285 E11
Dalchork Highld 309 H5
Dalchreichart Highld 290 B4
Dalchruin Perth 285 F11
Dalderby Lincs 174 B2
Dale Cumb 230 C6
Dale Gtr Man 196 F3
Dale Pembs 72 D4
Dale Shetland 312 G6
Dale Abbey Derbys 153 B8
Dale Bottom Cumb 229 G11
Dale Brow E Ches 184 F6
Dale End Derbys 170 C2
Dale End N Yorks 204 D5
Dale Head Cumb 221 B8
Dale Hill E Sus 53 G7
Dale Hill E Sus 53 G8
Dale Moor Derbys 153 B8
Dale of Walls Shetland 313 H3
Dalebank Derbys 170 C5
Dalelia Highld 289 C9
Dales Brow Gtr Man 195 G9
Dales Green Staffs 168 D5
Daless Highld 301 F8
Dalestie Moray 292 B3
Dalestorth Notts 171 C8
Dalfaber Highld 291 B11
Dalfoil Stirl 277 D11
Dalganachan Highld 310 E4
Dalgarven N Ayrs 266 F5
Dalgety Bay Fife 280 E3
Dalginross Perth 285 E11
Dalguise Perth 286 C3
Dalhalvaig Highld 310 D2
Dalham Suff 124 E4
Dalhastnie Angus 293 F7
Dalhenzean Perth 292 G3
Dalinlongart Argyll 276 E2
Dalkeith Midloth 270 B6
Dallam Warr 183 C9
Dallas Moray 301 D11
Dallas Lodge Moray 301 D11
Dallcharn Highld 308 D6
Dalleagles E Ayrs 258 G3
Dallicott Shrops 132 E5
Dallimores I o W 20 C6
Dallinghoo Suff 126 G5
Dallington E Sus 23 B11
Dallington Northants 120 E4
Dallow N Yorks 214 E3
Dalmadilly Aberds 293 B9
Dalmally Argyll 284 E5
Dalmarnock Glasgow 268 C2
Dalmarnock Perth 286 C3
Dalmary Stirl 277 B10
Dalmellington E Ayrs 245 B11
Dalmeny Edin 280 F2
Dalmigavie Highld 291 B9
Dalmigavie Lodge Highld 301 G7
Dalmilling S Ayrs 257 E9
Dalmore Highld 300 C6
Dalmuir W Dunb 277 G9
Dalnabreck Highld 289 C8
Dalnacardoch Lodge Perth 291 F9
Dalnacroich Highld 300 D3
Dalnaglar Castle Perth 292 G3
Dalnahaitnach Highld 301 G8
Dalnamein Lodge Perth 291 G9
Dalnarrow Argyll 289 F9
Dalnaspidal Lodge Perth 291 F8
Dalnavaid Perth 292 G2
Dalnavie Highld 300 B6
Dalnaw Dumfries 236 B5

Dalnawillan Lodge Highld 310 E4
Dalness Highld 284 B5
Dalnessie Highld 309 H6
Dalphaid Highld 309 H3
Dalqueich Perth 286 G4
Dalrannoch Argyll 289 E11
Dalreavoch Highld 309 J7
Dalriach Highld 301 F10
Dalrigh Stirl 285 E7
Dalry Edin 280 G4
Dalry N Ayrs 266 F5
Dalrymple E Ayrs 257 G9
Dalscote Northants 120 G3
Dalserf S Lnrk 268 E6
Dalshannon N Lnrk 278 G4
Dalston Cumb 239 G9
Dalston London 67 C10
Dalswinton Dumfries 247 F10
Dalton Cumb 211 D10
Dalton Dumfries 238 C4
Dalton Lancs 194 F3
Dalton N Yorks 215 D8
Dalton N Yorks 224 D2
Dalton Northumb 241 F10
Dalton Northumb 242 C4
Dalton S Lnrk 268 D3
Dalton S Yorks 187 C7
Dalton W Yorks 197 D7
Dalton-in-Furness Cumb 210 E4
Dalton-le-Dale Durham 234 B4
Dalton Magna S Yorks 187 C7
Dalton-on-Tees N Yorks 224 D5
Dalton Parva S Yorks 187 C7
Dalton Piercy Hrtlpl 234 E5
Dalveallan Highld 300 F6
Dalveich Stirl 285 E10
Dalvina Lo Highld 308 E6
Dalwey Telford 132 B3
Dalwhinnie Highld 291 E8
Dalwood Devon 28 G3
Dalwyne S Ayrs 245 D8
Dam Green Norf 141 F11
Dam Head W Yorks 196 B6
Dam Mill Staffs 133 C7
Dam of Quoiggs Perth 286 G2
Dam Side Lancs 202 D4
Damask Green Herts 104 F5
Damems W Yorks 204 F6
Damerham Hants 31 D10
Damery Glos 80 G2
Damgate Norf 143 B8
Damgate Norf 161 F9
Damhead Moray 301 D10
Damhead Holdings Midloth 270 B5
Damnaglaur Dumfries 236 F3
Damside Borders 270 F3
Dan Caerlan Rhondda 58 C5
Danaway Kent 69 G11
Danbury Essex 88 E3
Danbury Common Essex 88 E3
Danby N Yorks 226 D4
Danby Wiske N Yorks 224 F6
Dancers Hill Herts 86 F2
Dancing Green Hereford 98 G2
Dandaleith Moray 302 E2
Danderhall Midloth 270 B6
Dandy Corner Suff 125 D11
Dane Bank Gtr Man 184 B6
Dane End Herts 104 G6
Dane in Shaw E Ches 168 C5
Dane Street Kent 54 C5
Danebank E Ches 185 E7
Danebridge E Ches 169 B7
Danegate E Sus 52 G5
Danehill E Sus 36 B6
Danemoor Green Norf 141 B11
Danes Moss E Ches 184 G6
Danesbury Herts 86 B2
Danesfield Bucks 65 C10
Danesford Shrops 132 E4
Daneshill Hants 49 C7
Danesmoor Derbys 170 C6
Daneway Glos 80 E6
Dangerous Corner Gtr Man 195 G7
Dangerous Corner Lancs 194 E4
Daniel's Water Kent 54 E3
Danna na Cloiche Argyll 275 F7
Dannonchapel Corn 10 E6
Danskine E Loth 271 B11
Danthorpe E Yorks 209 G10
Danygraig Caerph 78 G2
Danzey Green Warks 118 D2
Dapple Heath Staffs 151 D10
Darby End W Mid 133 F9
Darby Green Hants 65 G10
Darbys Green Worcs 116 F4
Darby's Hill W Mid 133 F9
Darcy Lever Gtr Man 195 F8
Dardy Powys 78 B2
Darenth Kent 68 E5
Daresbury Halton 183 E9
Daresbury Delph Halton 183 E9
Darfield S Yorks 198 G2
Darfoulds Notts 187 F9
Dargate Kent 70 G5
Dargate Common Kent 70 G5
Darite Corn 6 B5
Darkland Moray 302 C2
Darland Wrex 166 D5
Darlaston W Mid 133 D9
Darlaston Green W Mid 133 D9
Darley N Yorks 205 B10
Darley Shrops 132 D3
Darley Abbey Derby 153 B7
Darley Bridge Derbys 170 C3
Darley Dale Derbys 170 C3
Darley Green Warks 118 C3
Darley Head N Yorks 205 B9
Darley Hillside Derbys 170 C3
Darleyford Corn 11 G11
Darleyhall Herts 104 G2
Darlingscott Warks 100 C4
Darlington Darl 224 C5
Darliston Shrops 149 C11
Darlton Notts 188 G3
Darmsden Suff 125 G11
Darn Hill Gtr Man 195 E10
Darnall S Yorks 186 D5
Darnaway Castle Moray 301 D9
Darnford Staffs 134 B2
Darnhall W Ches 167 C10
Darnhall Mains Borders 270 F4
Darnick Borders 262 C2
Darowen Powys 128 C6
Darra Aberds 303 E7
Darracott Devon 24 D2
Darracott Devon 40 F3
Darras Hall Northumb 242 C5
Darrington W Yorks 198 D3
Darrow Green Norf 142 F5
Darsham Suff 127 D8
Darshill Som 44 E6
Dartford Kent 68 E4
Dartford Crossing Kent 68 D5
Dartington Devon 8 C5
Dartmeet Devon 13 G9
Dartmouth Devon 9 E7
Dartmouth Park London 67 B9
Darton S Yorks 197 F10
Darvel E Ayrs 258 B3
Darvillshill Bucks 84 F4
Darwell Hole E Sus 23 B11
Darwen Blkburn 195 C7
Dassels Herts 105 F7
Datchet Windsor 66 D3
Datchet Common Windsor 66 D3
Datchworth Herts 86 B3
Datchworth Green Herts 86 B3
Daubhill Gtr Man 195 F8
Daugh of Kinermony Moray 302 E2
Dauntsey Wilts 62 C3
Dauntsey Lock Wilts 62 C3
Dava Moray 301 F10
Davenham W Ches 183 G11
Davenport E Ches 168 B4
Davenport Gtr Man 184 D5
Davenport Green E Ches 184 F4
Davenport Green Gtr Man 184 D4
Daventry Northants 119 E11
David Street Kent 68 G6
David's Well Powys 113 B11
Davidson's Mains Edin 280 F4
Davidston Highld 301 C7
Davidstow Corn 11 D9
Davington Dumfries 248 C6
Davington Kent 70 G4
Daviot Aberds 303 G7
Daviot Highld 301 F7
Davis's Town E Sus 23 B8
Davo Mains Aberds 293 F9
Davoch of Grange Moray 302 D4
Davyhulme Gtr Man 184 B3
Daw Cross N Yorks 205 C11
Daw End W Mid 133 C10
Dawdon Durham 234 B4
Dawesgreen Sur 51 D8
Dawker Hill N Yorks 207 F7
Dawley Telford 132 B3
Dawley Bank Telford 132 B3
Dawlish Devon 14 F5
Dawlish Warren Devon 14 F5
Dawn Conwy 180 G5
Daw's Cross Essex 107 E7
Daw's Green Som 27 C11
Daws Heath Essex 69 B10
Daw's House Corn 12 E2
Dawshill Worcs 116 G6
Dawsmere Lincs 157 C8
Day Green E Ches 168 D3
Dayhills Staffs 151 C9
Dayhouse Bank Worcs 117 B9
Daylesford Glos 100 F4
Daywall Shrops 148 C5
Ddol Flint 181 G10
Ddôl Cownwy Powys 147 F10
Ddrydwy Anglesey 178 G5
De Beauvoir Town London 67 C10
Deacons Hill Herts 85 F11
Deadman's Cross C Beds 104 C2
Deadman's Green Staffs 151 B10
Deadwater Hants 49 F10
Deadwater Northumb 250 D4
Deaf Hill Durham 234 D3
Deal Kent 55 C11
Deal Hall Essex 89 F8
Dean Cumb 229 F7
Dean Devon 8 C4
Dean Devon 40 D6
Dean Devon 40 E4
Dean Devon 41 D8
Dean Dorset 31 D7
Dean Edin 280 G4
Dean Hants 33 D9
Dean Hants 48 G2
Dean Lancs 195 B11
Dean Oxon 100 G6
Dean Som 45 E7
Dean Bank Durham 233 E11
Dean Court Oxon 83 D7
Dean Cross Devon 40 E4
Dean Head S Yorks 197 G9
Dean Lane Head W Yorks 205 G7
Dean Park Renfs 267 B10
Dean Prior Devon 8 C4
Dean Row E Ches 184 E5
Dean Street Kent 53 C8
Deanburnhaugh Borders 261 G9
Deane Gtr Man 195 F7
Deane Hants 48 C4
Deanend Dorset 31 D7
Deanich Lodge Highld 309 L3
Deanland Dorset 31 D7
Deanlane End W Sus 34 E2
Deans W Loth 269 B10
Deans Bottom Kent 69 G11
Dean's Green Warks 118 D2
Deans Hill Kent 69 G11
Deanscales Cumb 229 F7
Deansgreen E Ches 183 D11
Deanshanger Northants 102 D5
Deanston Stirl 285 G11
Dearham Cumb 229 D7
Dearnley Gtr Man 196 D2
Debach Suff 126 G4
Debdale Gtr Man 184 B5
Debden Essex 86 F6
Debden Essex 105 E11
Debden Cross Essex 105 E11
Debden Green Essex 86 F6
Debden Green Essex 105 E11
Debenham Suff 126 E3
Deblin's Green Worcs 98 B6
Dechmont W Loth 279 G10
Deckham T & W 243 E7
Deddington Oxon 101 E9
Dedham Essex 107 E11
Dedham Heath Essex 107 E11
Dedridge W Loth 269 B11
Dedworth Windsor 66 D2
Deebank Aberds 293 D8
Deecastle Aberds 292 D6
Deene Northants 137 E8
Deenethorpe Northants 137 E9
Deepcar S Yorks 186 B3
Deepclough Derbys 185 B8
Deepcut Sur 50 B2
Deepdale C Beds 104 B4
Deepdale Cumb 212 C4
Deepdale N Yorks 213 D7
Deepdene Sur 51 D7
Deepfields W Mid 133 E8
Deeping Gate Lincs 138 B2
Deeping St James Lincs 138 B3
Deeping St Nicholas Lincs 156 F4
Deepthwaite Cumb 211 C10
Deepweir Mon 60 B3
Deerhill Moray 302 D4
Deerhurst Glos 99 F7
Deerhurst Walton Glos 99 F7
Deerland Pembs 73 C7
Deerness Orkney 314 F5
Deer's Green Essex 105 E9
Deerstones N Yorks 205 C7
Deerton Street Kent 70 G3
Defford Worcs 99 C8
Defynnog Powys 95 F8
Deganwy Conwy 180 F3
Degar V Glam 58 D4
Degibna Corn 2 D5
Deighton N Yorks 225 E7
Deighton W Yorks 197 D7
Deighton York 207 E8
Deiniolen Gwyn 163 C9
Deishar Highld 291 B11
Delabole Corn 11 E7
Delamere W Ches 167 B9
Delfour Highld 291 C10
Delfrigs Aberds 303 G9
Dell Lodge Highld 292 B2
Dell Quay W Sus 22 C4
Delliefure Highld 301 F10
Delly End Oxon 82 C5
Delnabo Moray 292 B3
Delnadamph Aberds 292 C4
Delnamer Angus 292 G3
Delph Gtr Man 196 F3
Delves Durham 233 B8
Delvin End Essex 106 D5
Delvine Perth 286 C5
Dembleby Lincs 155 B10
Demelza Corn 5 C9
Denaby Main S Yorks 187 B7
Denbeath Fife 281 B7
Denbigh Denb 165 B9
Denbury Devon 8 B6
Denby Derbys 170 F5
Denby Bottles Derbys 170 F5
Denby Common Derbys 170 F6
Denby Dale W Yorks 197 F8
Denchworth Oxon 82 G5
Dendron Cumb 210 E4
Dene Park Kent 52 C5
Denel End C Beds 103 D10
Denend Aberds 302 F6
Deneside Durham 234 B4
Denford Northants 121 B9
Denford Staffs 169 E7
Dengie Essex 89 E7
Denham Bucks 66 B4
Denham Bucks 102 G5
Denham Suff 124 E5
Denham Suff 126 C3
Denham Corner Suff 126 C3
Denham End Suff 124 E5
Denham Green Bucks 66 B4
Denham Street Suff 126 C3
Denhead Aberds 303 D9
Denhead Fife 287 F8
Denhead of Arbilot Angus 287 C9
Denhead of Gray Dundee 287 D7
Denholm Borders 262 F3
Denholme W Yorks 205 G7
Denholme Clough W Yorks 205 G7
Denholme Edge W Yorks 205 G7
Denholme Gate W Yorks 205 G7
Denholmhill Borders 262 F3
Denio Gwyn 145 B7
Denmead Hants 33 E11
Denmore Aberdeen 293 B11
Denmoss Aberds 302 E6
Dennington Suff 126 D5
Dennington Corner Suff 126 D5
Dennington Hall Suff 126 D5
Denny Falk 278 E6
Denny Bottom Kent 52 F5
Denny End Cambs 123 D9
Denny Lodge Hants 32 F4
Dennyloanhead Falk 278 E6
Dennystown W Dunb 277 F7
Denshaw Gtr Man 196 E3
Denside Aberds 293 D10
Densole Kent 55 E8
Denston Suff 124 G5
Denstone Staffs 169 G9
Denstroude Kent 70 G6
Dent Cumb 212 B4
Dent Bank Durham 232 F4
Denton Cambs 138 F2
Denton Darl 224 B4
Denton E Sus 23 E7
Denton Gtr Man 184 B6
Denton Kent 55 D8
Denton Kent 69 E7
Denton Lincs 155 C7
Denton N Yorks 205 D8
Denton Norf 142 F5
Denton Northants 120 F6
Denton Oxon 83 E9
Denton Burn T & W 242 D5
Denton Holme Cumb 239 G10
Denton's Green Mers 183 B7
Denver Norf 140 C2
Denvilles Hants 22 B2
Denwick Northumb 264 G6
Deopham Norf 141 C11
Deopham Green Norf 141 D10
Deopham Stalland Norf 141 D10
Depden Suff 124 F5
Depden Green Suff 124 F5
Deppers Bridge Warks 119 F7
Deptford London 67 D11
Deptford T & W 243 F9
Deptford Wilts 46 F4
Derby Derbys 153 B7
Derby Devon 40 G5
Derbyhaven I o M 192 F3
Derbyshire Hill Mers 183 C8
Dereham Norf 159 G9
Dergoals Dumfries 236 D4
Deri Caerph 77 E10
Derriford Plym 7 D9
Derril Devon 24 G4
Derringstone Kent 55 D8
Derrington Shrops 132 E2
Derrington Staffs 151 E7
Derriton Devon 24 G4
Derry Stirl 285 E10
Derry Downs London 68 F3
Derry Fields Wilts 81 G8
Derry Hill Wilts 62 E3
Derry Lodge Aberds 292 D2
Derrydaroch Stirl 285 E7
Derryguaig Argyll 288 F6
Derrythorpe N Lincs 199 F10
Dersingham Norf 158 C3
Dertfords Wilts 45 D10
Dervaig Argyll 288 D6
Derwen Bridgend 58 C2
Derwen Denb 165 E9
Derwenlas Powys 128 D4
Desborough Northants 136 G6
Desford Leics 135 C9
Deskryshiel Aberds 292 B6
Detchant Northumb 264 B3
Detling Kent 53 B9
Deuchar Angus 292 G6
Deuddwr Powys 148 F4
Deuxhill Shrops 132 F3
Devauden Mon 79 F7
Deveral Corn 2 B3
Devil's Bridge = Pontarfynach Ceredig 112 B4
Devitts Green Warks 134 E5
Devizes Wilts 62 G4
Devol Invclyd 276 G6
Devon Village Clack 279 B8
Devonport Plym 7 E9
Devonside Clack 279 B8
Devoran Corn 3 B7
Dewar Borders 270 F6
Dewartown Midloth 271 C7
Dewes Green Essex 105 E9
Dewlands Common Dorset 31 F9
Dewlish Dorset 17 B11
Dewsbury W Yorks 197 C8
Dewsbury Moor W Yorks 197 C8
Dewshall Court Hereford 97 E9
Dhoon I o M 192 D5
Dhoor I o M 192 C5
Dhowin I o M 192 B5
Dhustone Shrops 115 B11
Dial Green W Sus 34 B6
Dial Post W Sus 35 D11
Dibberford Dorset 29 G7
Dibden Hants 32 F6
Dibden Purlieu Hants 32 F6
Dickens Heath W Mid 118 B2
Dickleburgh Norf 142 G3
Dickleburgh Moor Norf 142 G3
Dickon Hills Lincs 174 D6
Didbrook Glos 99 E11
Didcot Oxon 64 B4
Diddington Cambs 122 D3
Diddlebury Shrops 131 F10
Diddywell Devon 25 B7
Didley Hereford 97 E9
Didling W Sus 34 D4
Didlington Norf 140 D5
Didmarton Glos 61 B10
Didsbury Gtr Man 184 C4
Didworthy Devon 8 C3
Diebidale Highld 309 L4
Digbeth W Mid 133 F11
Digby Lincs 173 E9
Digg Highld 298 C4
Diggle Gtr Man 196 F4
Diglis Worcs 116 G6
Digmoor Lancs 194 F3
Digswell Herts 86 B3
Digswell Park Herts 86 C2
Digswell Water Herts 86 C3
Dihewyd Ceredig 111 F9
Dilham Norf 160 D6
Dilhorne Staffs 169 G7
Dill Hall Lancs 195 B8
Dillarburn S Lnrk 268 G6
Dillington Cambs 122 D2
Dillington Som 28 D5
Dilston Northumb 241 E11
Dilton Marsh Wilts 45 D11
Dilwyn Hereford 115 G8
Dimlands V Glam 58 F3
Dimmer Som 44 G6
Dimple Derbys 170 C3
Dimple Gtr Man 195 D8
Dimsdale Staffs 168 F4
Dimson Corn 12 G4
Dinas Carms 92 E5
Dinas Corn 10 G4
Dinas Gwyn 144 B5
Dinas Gwyn 163 D7
Dinas Cross Pembs 91 D10
Dinas Dinlle Gwyn 162 D6
Dinas-Mawddwy Gwyn 147 G7
Dinas Mawr Conwy 164 E4
Dinas Powys V Glam 59 E7
Dinbych y Pysgod = Tenby Pembs 73 E10
Dinckley Lancs 203 F9
Dinder Som 44 E5
Dinedor Hereford 97 D10
Dinedor Cross Hereford 97 D10
Dines Green Worcs 116 F6
Dingestow Mon 79 C7
Dinghurst N Som 44 B2
Dingle Mers 182 D5
Dingleden Kent 53 G10
Dingleton Borders 262 C2
Dingley Northants 136 F5
Dingwall Highld 300 D5
Dinlabyre Borders 250 E2
Dinmael Conwy 165 G8
Dinnet Aberds 292 D6
Dinnington S Yorks 187 D8
Dinnington Som 28 E6
Dinnington T & W 242 C6
Dinorwic Gwyn 163 C9
Dinton Bucks 84 C3
Dinton Wilts 46 G4
Dinwoodie Mains Dumfries 248 E4
Dinworthy Devon 24 D4
Dipford Som 28 C2
Dipley Hants 49 B8
Dippenhall Sur 49 D10
Dippertown Devon 12 E4
Dippin N Ayrs 256 E2
Dipple Devon 24 D4
Dipple Moray 302 D3
Dipple S Ayrs 244 C6
Diptford Devon 8 D4
Dipton Durham 242 G5
Diptonmill Northumb 241 E10
Dirdhu Highld 301 G10
Direcleit W Isles 305 J3
Dirleton E Loth 281 E10
Dirt Pot Northumb 232 B3
Discoed Powys 114 E5
Discove Som 45 G7
Diseworth Leics 153 E9
Dishes Orkney 314 D6
Dishforth N Yorks 215 E7
Dishley Leics 153 E10
Disley E Ches 185 E7
Diss Norf 126 B2
Disserth Powys 113 F10
Distington Cumb 228 G6
Ditchampton Wilts 46 G5
Ditcheat Som 44 F6
Ditchfield Bucks 84 G4
Ditchford Hill Worcs 100 D4
Ditchingham Norf 142 E6
Ditchling E Sus 36 D4
Ditherington Shrops 149 G10
Ditteridge Wilts 61 F10
Dittisham Devon 9 E7
Ditton Halton 183 D7
Ditton Kent 53 B8
Ditton Green Cambs 124 F3
Ditton Priors Shrops 132 F2
Dittons E Sus 23 E10
Divach Highld 300 G4
Divlyn Carms 94 D5
Dixton Glos 99 E9
Dixton Mon 79 C8
Dizzard Corn 11 B9
Dobcross Gtr Man 196 F3
Dobs Hill Flint 166 C4
Dobson's Bridge Shrops 149 C9
Dobwalls Corn 6 C4
Doc Penfro = Pembroke Dock Pembs 73 E7
Doccombe Devon 13 D11
Dochfour Ho Highld 300 F6
Dochgarroch Highld 300 E6
Dockeney Norf 143 E7
Dockenfield Sur 49 E10
Docker Lancs 211 E11
Docking Norf 158 B5
Docklow Hereford 115 F11
Dockray Cumb 230 G3
Dockroyd W Yorks 204 F6
Docton Devon 24 C2
Dodbrooke Devon 8 G4
Dodburn Borders 249 B11
Doddenham Worcs 116 F5
Doddinghurst Essex 87 F9
Doddington Cambs 139 E7
Doddington Kent 54 B2
Doddington Lincs 188 G6
Doddington Northumb 263 C11
Doddington Shrops 116 B2
Doddiscombsleigh Devon 14 D3
Doddshill Norf 158 C3
Doddycross Corn 6 C6
Dodford Northants 120 E2
Dodford Worcs 117 C8
Dodington S Glos 61 C9
Dodington Som 43 E7
Dodleston W Ches 166 C5
Dodmarsh Hereford 97 C11
Dods Leigh Staffs 151 C10
Dodscott Devon 25 D8
Dodworth S Yorks 197 F10
Dodworth Bottom S Yorks 197 G10
Dodworth Green S Yorks 197 G10
Doe Bank W Mid 134 D2
Doe Green Warr 183 D9
Doe Lea Derbys 171 B7
Doehole Derbys 170 D5
Doffcocker Gtr Man 195 E7
Dog & Gun Mers 182 B5
Dog Hill Gtr Man 196 F3
Dog Village Devon 14 B5
Dogdyke Lincs 174 D2
Dogingtree Estate Staffs 151 G9
Dogley Lane W Yorks 197 E7
Dogmersfield Hants 49 C9
Dogridge Wilts 62 B5
Dogsthorpe P'boro 138 C3
Doirlinn Highld 289 D8
Dol-fôr Powys 128 B6
Dol-ffanog Gwyn 146 G4
Dôl-y-Bont Ceredig 128 F2
Dol-y-cannau Powys 96 B3
Dolanog Powys 147 G11
Dolau Powys 114 D2
Dolau Rhondda 58 C3
Dolbenmaen Gwyn 163 G8
Dole Ceredig 128 F2
Dolemeads Bath 61 G9
Doley Staffs 150 D4
Dolfach Powys 129 C8
Dolfor Powys 130 F2
Dolgarrog Conwy 164 B3
Dolgellau Gwyn 146 F4
Dolgerdd Ceredig 111 G8
Dolgoch Gwyn 128 C3
Dolgran Carms 93 E8
Dolhelfa Powys 113 C8
Dolhendre Gwyn 147 C7
Doll Highld 311 J2
Dollar Clack 279 B9
Dolley Green Powys 114 D5
Dollis Hill London 67 B8
Dollwen Ceredig 128 G3
Dolphin Flint 181 G11
Dolphingstone E Loth 281 G7
Dolphinholme Lancs 202 C6
Dolphinston Borders 262 F5
Dolphinton S Lnrk 270 F2
Dolton Devon 25 E9
Dolwen Conwy 180 G5
Dolwen Powys 129 B9
Dolwyd Conwy 180 F4
Dolwyddelan Conwy 164 E2
Dolydd Gwyn 163 D7
Dolyhir Powys 114 F4
Dolymelinau Powys 129 D11
Dolywern Wrex 148 B4
Domewood Sur 51 E10
Domgay Powys 148 F5
Dommett Som 28 E3
Don Johns Essex 106 F6
Doncaster S Yorks 198 G5
Doncaster Common S Yorks 198 G6
Dones Green W Ches 183 F10
Donhead St Andrew Wilts 30 C6
Donhead St Mary Wilts 30 C6
Donibristle Fife 280 D3
Doniford Som 42 E5
Donington Lincs 156 B4
Donington Shrops 132 C6
Donington Eaudike Lincs 156 B4
Donington le Heath Leics 153 G8
Donington on Bain Lincs 190 E2
Donington South Ing Lincs 156 C4
Donisthorpe Leics 152 G6
Donkey Street Kent 54 G6
Donkey Town Sur 66 G2
Donna Nook Lincs 190 B6
Donnington Glos 100 F3
Donnington Hereford 98 E4
Donnington Shrops 131 B11
Donnington Telford 150 G4
Donnington W Berks 64 F3
Donnington W Sus 22 C5
Donnington Wood Telford 150 G4
Donwell T & W 243 F7
Donyatt Som 28 E4
Doomsday Green W Sus 35 B11
Doonfoot S Ayrs 257 F8
Dora's Green Hants 49 D10
Dorback Lodge Highld 292 B2
Dorcan Swindon 63 C7
Dorchester Dorset 17 C9
Dorchester Oxon 83 G9
Dordale Worcs 117 C8
Dordon Warks 134 C5
Dore S Yorks 186 E4
Dores Highld 300 F5
Dorking Sur 51 D7
Dorking Tye Suff 107 D8
Dorley's Corner Suff 127 D7
Dormans Park Sur 51 E11
Dormansland Sur 52 E2
Dormanstown Redcar 235 G7
Dormer's Wells London 66 C6
Dormington Hereford 97 C11
Dormston Worcs 117 F9
Dorn Glos 100 E4
Dorn Hill Worcs 100 E3
Dornal S Ayrs 236 B4
Dorney Bucks 66 D2
Dorney Reach Bucks 66 D2
Dornie Highld 295 C10
Dornoch Highld 309 L7
Dornock Dumfries 238 D6
Dorrery Highld 310 D4
Dorridge W Mid 118 B3
Dorrington Lincs 173 E9
Dorrington Shrops 131 C9
Dorsington Warks 100 B2
Dorstone Hereford 96 C6
Dorton Bucks 83 C11
Dorusduain Highld 295 C11
Doseley Telford 132 B3
Dosmuckeran Highld 300 C2
Dosthill Staffs 134 C4
Dosthill Staffs 134 D4
Dothan Anglesey 178 G5
Dothill Telford 150 G2
Dottery Dorset 16 B5
Double Hill Bath 45 B8
Doublebois Corn 6 C3
Dougarie N Ayrs 255 D9
Doughton Glos 80 G5
Doughton Norf 159 D7
Douglas I o M 192 E4
Douglas S Lnrk 259 C8
Douglas & Angus Dundee 287 D8
Douglas Water S Lnrk 259 B9
Douglas West S Lnrk 259 C8
Douglastown Angus 287 C8
Doulting Som 44 E6
Dounby Orkney 314 D2
Doune Highld 291 C10
Doune Highld 309 J4
Doune Stirl 285 G11
Doune Park Aberds 303 C7
Douneside Aberds 292 C6
Dounie Argyll 275 D8
Dounie Highld 309 K5
Dounie Highld 309 L6
Dounreay Highld 310 C3
Doura N Ayrs 266 G6
Dousland Devon 7 B10
Dovaston Shrops 149 E7
Dove Green Notts 171 E7
Dove Holes Derbys 185 F9
Dove Point Mers 182 C2
Dovecot Mers 182 C6
Dovecothall Glasgow 267 D10
Dovenby Cumb 229 E7
Dovendale Lincs 190 E4
Dover Gtr Man 194 G6
Dover Kent 55 E10
Dovercourt Essex 108 E5
Doverdale Worcs 117 D7
Doverhay Som 41 D11
Doveridge Derbys 152 C2
Doversgreen Sur 51 D9
Dowally Perth 286 C4
Dowanhill Glasgow 267 B11
Dowbridge Lancs 202 G4
Dowdeswell Glos 81 B7
Dowe Hill Norf 161 F10
Dowlais M Tydf 77 D10
Dowlais Top M Tydf 77 D9
Dowland Devon 25 E9
Dowles Worcs 116 B5
Dowlesgreen Wokingham 65 F10
Dowlish Ford Som 28 E5
Dowlish Wake Som 28 E5
Down Ampney Glos 81 F10
Down End Som 43 E10
Down Field Cambs 124 C2
Down Hall Cumb 239 G7
Down Hatherley Glos 99 G7
Down Park W Sus 51 F10
Down St Mary Devon 26 G2
Down Street E Sus 36 C6
Down Thomas Devon 7 E10
Downall Green Gtr Man 194 G5
Downan Moray 301 F11
Downan S Ayrs 244 G3
Downcraig Ferry N Ayrs 266 D3
Downderry Corn 6 E6
Downe London 68 G2
Downend Glos 80 F4
Downend I o W 20 D6
Downend S Glos 60 D6
Downend W Berks 64 D3
Downfield Dundee 287 D7
Downgate Corn 11 G11
Downgate Corn 12 G3
Downham Essex 88 F2
Downham Lancs 203 E11
Downham London 67 E11
Downham Northumb 263 C9
Downham Market Norf 140 C2
Downhead Som 29 B9
Downhead Som 45 D7
Downhead Park M Keynes 103 C7
Downhill Corn 5 B7
Downhill Perth 286 D4
Downhill T & W 243 F9
Downholland Cross Lancs 193 F11
Downholme N Yorks 224 F2
Downicary Devon 12 C3
Downies Aberds 293 D11
Downinney Corn 11 C10
Downley Bucks 84 G4
Downs V Glam 58 E6
Downside C Beds 103 G10
Downside E Sus 23 E9
Downside N Som 60 F3
Downside Som 44 D6
Downside Sur 50 B6
Downside Sur 51 B7
Downton Hants 19 C11
Downton Powys 114 E4
Downton Shrops 149 G10
Downton Wilts 31 C11
Downton on the Rock Hereford 115 C8
Dowsby Lincs 156 D2
Dowsdale Lincs 156 G5
Dowslands Som 28 C2
Dowthwaitehead Cumb 230 G3
Doxey Staffs 151 E8
Doxford Park T & W 243 G9
Doynton S Glos 61 E8
Drabblegate Norf 160 D4
Draethen Newport 59 B8
Draffan S Lnrk 268 F5

330 Dra – Eas

Dragley Beck Cumb 210 D5
Dragonby N Lincs 200 E2
Dragons Green W Sus 35 C10
Drakehouse S Yorks 186 E6
Drakeland Corner Devon 7 D11
Drakelow Worcs 132 G6
Drakemyre Aberds 303 F9
Drakemyre N Ayrs 266 E5
Drake's Broughton Worcs 99 B8
Drakes Cross Worcs 117 B11
Drakestone Green Suff 107 B9
Drakewalls Corn 12 G4
Draughton N Yorks 204 C6
Draughton Northants 120 B5
Drawbridge Corn 6 B3
Drax N Yorks 199 B7
Draycot Oxon 83 D10
Draycot Cerne Wilts 62 D2
Draycot Fitz Payne Wilts 62 G6
Draycot Foliat Swindon 63 D7
Draycote Warks 119 C8
Draycott Derbys 153 C8
Draycott Glos 80 E2
Draycott Glos 100 D3
Draycott Shrops 132 E6
Draycott Som 29 C8
Draycott Som 44 C3
Draycott Worcs 99 B7
Draycott in the Clay Staffs 152 D3
Draycott in the Moors Staffs 169 G7
Drayford Devon 26 E3
Drayton Leics 136 E6
Drayton Lincs 156 B4
Drayton Norf 160 G3
Drayton Northants 119 E11
Drayton Oxon 83 G7
Drayton Oxon 101 C8
Drayton Ptsmth 33 F11
Drayton Som 28 C6
Drayton Som 29 D7
Drayton Warks 118 F3
Drayton Worcs 117 B8
Drayton Bassett Staffs 134 C3
Drayton Beauchamp Bucks 84 C6
Drayton Parslow Bucks 102 F6
Drayton St Leonard Oxon 83 F10
Dre-fach Carms 75 B11
Dre-fach Ceredig 93 B10
Dre-gôch Denb 165 B10
Drebley N Yorks 205 B7
Dreemskerry I o M 192 C5
Dreenhill Pembs 72 C6
Drefach Carms 75 C8
Drefach Carms 92 G5
Drefach Carms 93 D7
Drefelin Carms 93 D7
Dreggie Highld 301 G10
Dreghorn Edin 270 B4
Dreghorn N Ayrs 257 B9
Drellingore Kent 55 E8
Drem E Loth 281 F10
Dresden Stoke 168 G6
Dreumasdal W Isles 297 H3
Drewsteignton Devon 13 C10
Driby Lincs 190 G5
Driffield E Yorks 208 B6
Driffield Glos 81 F9
Drift Corn 1 D4
Drigg Cumb 219 F11
Drighlington W Yorks 197 B8
Drimnin Highld 289 D7
Drimnin Ho Highld 289 D7
Drimpton Dorset 28 F6
Drimsynie Argyll 284 G5
Dringhoe E Yorks 209 C9
Dringhouses York 207 D7
Drinisiadar W Isles 305 J3
Drinkstone Suff 125 E9
Drinkstone Green Suff 125 E9
Drishaig Argyll 284 F5
Drissaig Argyll 275 B10
Drive End Dorset 29 F9
Driver's End Herts 86 B2
Drochedlie Aberds 302 C5
Drochil Borders 270 G3
Drointon Staffs 151 D10
Droitwich Spa Worcs 117 E7
Droman Highld 306 D6
Dromore Dumfries 237 C7
Dron Perth 286 F5
Dronfield Derbys 186 F5
Dronfield Woodhouse Derbys 186 F4
Drongan E Ayrs 257 F10
Dronley Angus 287 D7
Droop Dorset 30 F3
Drope Cardiff 58 D6
Dropping Well S Yorks 186 C5
Droughduil Dumfries 236 D3
Droxford Hants 33 D10
Droylsden Gtr Man 184 B6
Drub W Yorks 197 B7
Druggers End Worcs 98 D5
Druid Denb 165 G8
Druidston Pembs 72 B5
Druim Highld 301 D9
Druimarbin Highld 290 F2
Druimavuic Argyll 284 C4
Druimdrishaig Argyll 275 F8
Druimindarroch Highld 295 G8
Druimkinnerras Highld 300 F4
Druimnacroish Argyll 288 E6
Druimsornaig Argyll 289 F9
Druimyeon More Argyll 255 B7
Drum Argyll 275 F10
Drum Edin 270 B6
Drum Perth 286 G4
Drumardoch Stirl 285 F10
Drumbeg Highld 306 F6
Drumblade Aberds 302 E5
Drumblair Aberds 302 E6
Drumbuie Dumfries 246 G3
Drumbuie Highld 295 B9
Drumburgh Cumb 239 F7
Drumburn Dumfries 237 C11
Drumchapel Glasgow 277 G10
Drumchardine Highld 300 E5
Drumchork Highld 307 L3
Drumclog S Lnrk 258 B4
Drumdelgie Aberds 302 E4
Drumderfit Highld 300 D6
Drumdollo Aberds 302 F6
Drumeldrie Fife 287 G8
Drumelzier Borders 260 C4
Drumfearn Highld 295 D8
Drumgask Highld 291 D8
Drumgelloch N Lnrk 268 B5
Drumgley Angus 287 B8
Drumgreen Angus 292 F6
Drumguish Highld 291 D9
Drumhead Aberds 293 B11
Drumin Moray 301 F11
Drumindorsair Highld 300 E4
Drumlasie Aberds 293 C8
Drumlean Stirl 285 G8
Drumlemble Argyll 255 F7
Drumliah Highld 309 K6
Drumligair Aberds 293 B11
Drumlithie Aberds 293 E9
Drumloist Stirl 285 G10
Drummersdale Lancs 193 E11
Drummick Perth 286 E3
Drummoddie Dumfries 236 E5
Drummond Highld 300 C6
Drummore Dumfries 236 F3
Drummuir Moray 302 E3
Drummuir Castle Moray 302 E3
Drumnadrochit Highld 300 G5
Drumnagorrach Moray 302 D5
Drumness Perth 286 F2
Drumoak Aberds 293 D9
Drumore Argyll 255 E8
Drumpark Dumfries 247 G9
Drumpellier N Lnrk 268 B4
Drumphail Dumfries 236 C4
Drumrash Dumfries 237 B8
Drumrunie Highld 307 J6
Drumry W Dunb 277 G10
Drums Aberds 303 G9
Drumsallie Highld 289 B11
Drumsmittal Highld 300 E6
Drumstinchall Dumfries 237 D10
Drumsturdy Angus 287 D8
Drumtochty Castle Aberds 293 F8
Drumtroddan Dumfries 236 E5
Drumuie Highld 298 E4
Drumuillie Highld 301 G9
Drumvaich Stirl 285 G10
Drumwalt Dumfries 236 D5
Drumwhindle Aberds 303 F9
Drunkendub Angus 287 C10
Drury Flint 166 C3
Drury Lane Wrex 167 G7
Drury Square Norf 159 F8
Drurylane Norf 141 C8
Dry Doddington Lincs 172 F4
Dry Drayton Cambs 123 E7
Dry Hill Hants 49 F7
Dry Sandford Oxon 83 E7
Dry Street Essex 69 B7
Drybeck Cumb 222 B3
Drybridge Moray 302 C4
Drybridge N Ayrs 257 B9
Drybrook Glos 79 B10
Dryburgh Borders 262 C3
Dryden Borders 261 E11
Dryhill Kent 52 B3
Dryhope Borders 261 E7
Drylaw Edin 280 F4
Drym Corn 2 C4
Drymen Stirl 277 D9
Drymere Norf 140 B5
Drymuir Aberds 303 E9
Drynachan Lodge Highld 301 F8
Drynain Argyll 276 D3
Drynham Wilts 45 B11
Drynie Park Highld 300 D5
Drynoch Highld 294 B6
Dryslwyn Carms 93 G11
Dryton Shrops 131 B11
Drywells Aberds 302 D6
Duag Bridge Highld 309 K3
Duartbeg Highld 306 F6
Duartmore Bridge Highld 306 F6
Dubbs Cross Devon 12 C3
Dubford Aberds 303 C8
Dubhchladach Argyll 275 G9
Dublin Suff 126 D3
Dubton Angus 287 B9
Dubwath Cumb 229 E9
Duchally Highld 309 H3
Duchlage Argyll 276 D6
Duchrae Dumfries 246 G5
Duck Corner Suff 109 C7
Duck End Beds 103 C11
Duck End Beds 121 G9
Duck End Bucks 102 F5
Duck End Cambs 122 E4
Duck End Essex 105 G10
Duck End Essex 106 E3
Duck End Essex 106 F3
Duckend Green Essex 106 G4
Duckhole S Glos 79 G10
Duckington W Ches 167 E7
Ducklington Oxon 82 D5
Duckmanton Derbys 186 G6
Duck's Cross Beds 122 F2
Ducks Island London 86 F2
Duckswich Worcs 98 D6
Dudbridge Glos 80 E4
Dudden Hill London 67 B8
Duddenhoe End Essex 105 D9
Duddingston Edin 280 G5
Duddington Northants 137 C9
Duddlestone Som 28 C2
Duddleswell E Sus 37 B7
Duddlewick Shrops 132 G3
Duddo Northumb 273 G8
Duddon W Ches 167 C8
Duddon Bridge Cumb 210 B3
Duddon Common W Ches 167 B8
Dudleston Shrops 148 B6
Dudleston Grove Shrops 149 B7
Dudleston Heath (Criftins) Shrops 149 B7
Dudley T & W 243 C7
Dudley W Mid 133 E8
Dudley Hill W Yorks 205 G9
Dudley Port W Mid 133 E9
Dudley Wood W Mid 133 F8
Dudley's Fields W Mid 133 C9
Dudlows Green Warr 183 E10
Dudsbury Dorset 19 B7
Dudswell Herts 85 D7
Dudwells Pembs 91 G8
Duerdon Devon 24 D4
Duffield Derbys 170 G4
Duffieldbank Derbys 170 G5
Duffryn Neath 57 B10
Duffryn Newport 59 B9
Duffryn Shrops 130 G4
Dufftown Moray 302 F3
Duffus Moray 301 C11
Dufton Cumb 231 F9
Duggleby N Yorks 217 F7
Duich Argyll 254 B4
Duiletter Argyll 284 D5
Duinish Perth 291 G8
Duirinish Highld 295 B9
Duisdalebeg Highld 295 D8
Duisdalemore Highld 295 D9
Duisky Highld 290 F2
Duke End Warks 134 F4
Dukesfield Northumb 241 F10
Dukestown Bl Gwent 77 C10
Dukinfield Gtr Man 184 B6
Dulas Anglesey 179 D7
Dulcote Som 44 E5
Dulford Devon 27 F9
Dull Perth 286 C2
Dullatur N Lnrk 278 F4
Dullingham Cambs 124 F2
Dullingham Ley Cambs 124 F2
Dulnain Bridge Highld 301 G9
Duloch Fife 280 D2
Duloe Beds 122 E3
Duloe Corn 6 D4
Dulsie Highld 301 E9
Dulverton Som 26 B6
Dulwich London 67 E10
Dulwich Village London 67 E10
Dumbarton W Dunb 277 F7
Dumbleton Glos 99 D10
Dumcrieff Dumfries 248 C4
Dumfries Dumfries 237 B11
Dumgoyne Stirl 277 E10
Dummer Hants 48 D5
Dumpford W Sus 34 C4
Dumpinghill Devon 24 F6
Dumpling Green Norf 159 G10
Dumplington Gtr Man 184 B3
Dumpton Kent 71 F11
Dun Angus 287 B10
Dun Charlabhaigh W Isles 304 D3
Dunach Argyll 289 G10
Dunadd Argyll 275 D9
Dunain Ho Highld 300 E6
Dunalastair Perth 285 B11
Dunan Highld 295 C7
Dunans Argyll 275 D11
Dunans Argyll 275 D9
Dunball Som 43 E10
Dunbar E Loth 282 F3
Dunbeath Highld 311 G5
Dunbeg Argyll 289 F10
Dunblane Stirl 285 G11
Dunbog Fife 286 F6
Dunbridge Hants 32 B4
Duncansclett Shetland 313 K5
Duncanston Highld 300 D5
Duncanstone Aberds 302 G5
Dunchideock Devon 14 D3
Dunchurch Warks 119 C9
Duncombe Lancs 202 F6
Duncote Northants 120 G3
Duncow Dumfries 247 G11
Duncraggan Stirl 285 G9
Duncrievie Perth 286 G5
Duncroisk Stirl 285 D9
Duncton W Sus 35 D7
Dundas Ho Orkney 314 H4
Dundee Dundee 287 D8
Dundeugh Dumfries 246 F3
Dundon Som 44 G3
Dundon Hayes Som 44 G3
Dundonald Fife 280 C4
Dundonald S Ayrs 257 C9
Dundonnell Highld 307 L5
Dundonnell Hotel Highld 307 L5
Dundonnell House Highld 307 L6
Dundraw Cumb 229 B10
Dundreggan Highld 290 B5
Dundreggan Lodge Highld 290 B5
Dundrennan Dumfries 237 E9
Dundridge Hants 33 D9
Dundry N Som 60 F5
Dundurn Perth 285 E11
Dundyvan N Lnrk 268 C4
Dunecht Aberds 293 C9
Dunfermline Fife 279 D11
Dunfield Glos 81 F10
Dunford Bridge S Yorks 197 G7
Dungate Kent 54 B2
Dunge Wilts 45 C11
Dungeness Kent 39 D9
Dungworth S Yorks 186 D3
Dunham Notts 188 G4
Dunham-on-the-Hill W Ches 183 G7
Dunham on Trent Notts 188 G4
Dunham Town Gtr Man 184 D2
Dunham Woodhouses Gtr Man 184 D2
Dunhampstead Worcs 117 E8
Dunhampton Worcs 116 D6
Dunholme Lincs 189 F8
Dunino Fife 287 F9
Dunipace Falk 278 E6
Dunira Perth 285 E11
Dunkeld Perth 286 C4
Dunkerton Bath 45 B8
Dunkeswell Devon 27 F10
Dunkeswick N Yorks 206 D2
Dunkirk Cambs 139 F10
Dunkirk Kent 54 B5
Dunkirk Norf 160 D4
Dunkirk Nottingham 153 B11
Dunkirk S Glos 61 B9
Dunkirk Staffs 168 E4
Dunkirk W Ches 182 G5
Dunkirk Wilts 62 G3
Dunk's Green Kent 52 C6
Dunlappie Angus 293 G7
Dunley Hants 48 C3
Dunley Worcs 116 D5
Dunlichity Lodge Highld 300 F6
Dunlop E Ayrs 267 F8
Dunmaglass Lodge Highld 300 G5
Dunmere Corn 5 B10
Dunmore Argyll 275 G8
Dunmore Falk 279 D7
Dunmore Highld 300 E5
Dunn Street Kent 54 D3
Dunn Street Kent 69 G9
Dunnerholme Cumb 210 D4
Dunnet Highld 310 B6
Dunnichen Angus 287 C9
Dunnikier Fife 280 C5
Dunninald Angus 287 B11
Dunning Perth 286 F4
Dunnington E Yorks 209 C9
Dunnington Warks 117 G11
Dunnington York 207 C9
Dunningwell Cumb 210 C3
Dunnockshaw Lancs 195 B10
Dunnose I o W 21 F7
Dunnsheath Shrops 149 F9
Dunollie Argyll 289 F10
Dunoon Argyll 276 F3
Dunragit Dumfries 236 D3
Dunrobin Mains Highld 311 J2
Dunrostan Argyll 275 E8
Duns Borders 272 E5
Duns Tew Oxon 101 F9
Dunsa Derbys 186 G2
Dunsby Lincs 156 D2
Dunscar Gtr Man 195 E8
Dunscore Dumfries 247 G9
Dunscroft S Yorks 199 F7
Dunsdale Redcar 226 B2
Dunsden Green Oxon 65 D8
Dunsfold Sur 50 F4
Dunsfold Common Sur 50 F4
Dunsfold Green Sur 50 F4
Dunsford Devon 14 D2
Dunsford Sur 50 F4
Dunshalt Fife 286 F6
Dunshillock Aberds 303 E9
Dunsill Notts 171 C7
Dunsinnan Perth 286 D5
Dunskey Ho Dumfries 236 D2
Dunslea Corn 11 G11
Dunsley N Yorks 227 C7
Dunsley Staffs 133 G7
Dunsmore Bucks 84 D5
Dunsmore Warks 119 B10
Dunsop Bridge Lancs 203 C9
Dunstable C Beds 103 G10
Dunstal Staffs 151 D11
Dunstall Staffs 152 E3
Dunstall Common Worcs 99 C7
Dunstall Green Suff 124 E4
Dunstall Hill W Mid 133 C8
Dunstan Northumb 265 F7
Dunstan Steads Northumb 264 E6
Dunster Som 42 E3
Dunston Derbys 186 G5
Dunston Lincs 173 C9
Dunston Norf 142 C4
Dunston Staffs 151 F8
Dunston T & W 242 E6
Dunston Heath Staffs 151 F8
Dunston Hill T & W 242 E6
Dunstone Devon 7 E11
Dunstone Devon 8 G5
Dunsville S Yorks 198 F6
Dunswell E Yorks 209 F7
Dunsyre S Lnrk 269 F11
Dunterton Devon 12 F3
Dunthrop Oxon 101 F7
Duntisbourne Abbots Glos 81 D7
Duntisbourne Leer Glos 81 D7
Duntisbourne Rouse Glos 81 D7
Duntish Dorset 29 F11
Duntocher W Dunb 277 G9
Dunton Bucks 102 G6
Dunton C Beds 104 C4
Dunton Norf 159 C7
Dunton Bassett Leics 135 E10
Dunton Green Kent 52 B4
Dunton Patch Norf 159 C7
Dunton Wayletts Essex 87 G11
Duntrune Castle Argyll 275 D8
Duntulm Highld 298 B4
Dunure S Ayrs 257 F7
Dunvant = Dynfant Swansea 56 C5
Dunvegan Highld 298 E2
Dunveth Corn 10 G5
Dunwear Som 43 F10
Dunwich Suff 127 C9
Dunwood Staffs 168 D6
Dupplin Castle Perth 286 F4
Durdar Cumb 239 G10
Durgan Corn 3 D7
Durgates E Sus 52 G6
Durham Durham 233 C11
Durisdeer Dumfries 247 C9
Durisdeermill Dumfries 247 C9
Durkar W Yorks 197 D10
Durleigh Som 43 F9
Durleighmarsh W Sus 34 C3
Durley Hants 33 D8
Durley Wilts 63 G8
Durley Street Hants 33 D8
Durlock Kent 55 B9
Durlow Common Hereford 98 D2
Durn Gtr Man 196 D2
Durnamuck Highld 307 K5
Durness Highld 308 C4
Durnfield Som 29 C7
Durno Aberds 303 G7
Durns Town Hants 19 B11
Duror Highld 289 D11
Durran Argyll 275 C10
Durran Highld 310 C5
Durrant Green Kent 53 F11
Durrants Hants 22 B2
Durrington W Sus 35 F10
Durrington Wilts 47 E7
Durrisdale Orkney 314 D3
Dursley Glos 80 F3
Dursley Wilts 45 C11
Dursley Cross Glos 98 G3
Durston Som 28 B3
Durweston Dorset 30 F5
Dury Shetland 313 G6
Duryard Devon 14 C4
Duston Northants 120 E4
Dutch Village Essex 69 C9
Duthil Highld 301 G9
Dutlas Powys 114 B4
Duton Hill Essex 106 F2
Dutson Corn 12 D2
Dutton Ches 183 F9
Duxford Cambs 105 B9
Duxford Oxon 82 F5
Duxmoor Shrops 115 B8
Dwygyfylchi Conwy 180 F2
Dwyran Anglesey 162 B6
Dwyrhiw Powys 129 C11
Dyce Aberdeen 293 B10
Dyche Som 43 E7
Dye House Northumb 241 F10
Dyer's Common S Glos 60 C5
Dyer's Green Cambs 105 B7
Dyffryn Bridgend 57 C11
Dyffryn Carms 92 G6
Dyffryn Ceredig 110 G5
Dyffryn Pembs 91 D8
Dyffryn Ardudwy Gwyn 145 E11
Dyffryn-bern Ceredig 110 G5
Dyffryn Castell Ceredig 128 G5
Dyffryn Ceidrych Carms 94 F4
Dyffryn Cellwen Neath 76 D5
Dyke Lincs 156 E2
Dyke Moray 301 D9
Dykehead Angus 292 G5
Dykehead N Lnrk 269 D7
Dykehead Stirl 277 B11
Dykelands Aberds 293 G9
Dykends Angus 286 B6
Dykeside Aberds 303 E7
Dykesmains N Ayrs 266 G5
Dylife Powys 129 E7
Dymchurch Kent 39 B9
Dymock Glos 98 E4
Dynfant = Dunvant Swansea 56 C5
Dyrham S Glos 61 D8
Dysart Fife 280 C6
Dyserth Denb 181 F9

E

Eabost Highld 294 B5
Eabost West Highld 298 E3
Each End Kent 55 B10
Eachway Worcs 117 B9
Eachwick Northumb 242 C4
Eadar Dha Fhadhail W Isles 304 E2
Eagland Hill Lancs 202 D4
Eagle Lincs 172 B5
Eagle Barnsdale Lincs 172 B5
Eagle Moor Lincs 172 B5
Eagle Tor Derbys 170 C2
Eaglesfield Cumb 229 F7
Eaglesfield Dumfries 238 C6
Eaglesham E Renf 267 E11
Eaglestone M Keynes 103 D7
Eaglethorpe Northants 137 E11
Eagley Gtr Man 195 E8
Eairy I o M 192 E3
Eakley Lanes M Keynes 120 G6
Eakring Notts 171 C11
Ealand N Lincs 199 E9
Ealing London 67 C7
Eals Northumb 240 F5
Eamont Bridge Cumb 230 F6
Earby Lancs 204 D3
Earcroft Blkburn 195 C7
Eardington Shrops 132 E4
Eardisland Hereford 115 F8
Eardisley Hereford 96 B6
Eardiston Shrops 149 D7
Eardiston Worcs 116 D3
Earith Cambs 123 C7
Earl Shilton Leics 135 D9
Earl Soham Suff 126 E4
Earl Sterndale Derbys 169 B9
Earl Stonham Suff 126 F2
Earle Northumb 263 D11
Earlestown Mers 183 B9
Earley Wokingham 65 E9
Earlham Norf 142 B4
Earlish Highld 298 C3
Earls Barton Northants 121 E7
Earls Colne Essex 107 F7
Earl's Common Worcs 117 F9
Earl's Court London 67 D9
Earl's Croome Worcs 99 C7
Earl's Down E Sus 23 B10
Earl's Green Suff 125 D10
Earlsdon W Mid 118 B6
Earlsferry Fife 281 B9
Earlsfield Lincs 155 B8
Earlsfield London 67 E9
Earlsford Aberds 303 F8
Earlsheaton W Yorks 197 C9
Earlsmill Moray 301 D9
Earlston Borders 262 B3
Earlston E Ayrs 257 B10
Earlstone Common Hants 64 G3
Earlswood Mon 79 F7
Earlswood Sur 51 D9
Earlswood Warks 118 C2
Earnley W Sus 22 D4
Earnock S Lnrk 268 E3
Earnshaw Bridge Lancs 194 C4
Earsairidh W Isles 297 M3
Earsdon T & W 243 C8
Earsham Norf 142 F6
Earsham Street Suff 126 B4
Earswick York 207 B8
Eartham W Sus 22 B6
Earthcott Green S Glos 61 B7
Easby N Yorks 224 E3
Easby N Yorks 225 D11
Easdale Argyll 275 B8
Easebourne W Sus 34 C5
Easenhall Warks 119 B9
Eashing Sur 50 E2
Easington Bucks 83 C11
Easington Durham 234 C4
Easington E Yorks 201 D11
Easington Lancs 203 C10
Easington Northumb 264 C4
Easington Oxon 83 F11
Easington Oxon 101 D9
Easington Redcar 226 B4
Easington Colliery Durham 234 C4
Easington Lane T & W 234 B3
Easingwold N Yorks 215 F10
Easole Street Kent 55 C9
Eason's Green E Sus 23 B8
Eassie Angus 287 C7
East Aberthaw V Glam 58 F4
East Acton London 67 C8
East Adderbury Oxon 101 D9
East Allington Devon 8 F5
East Amat Highld 309 K4
East Anstey Devon 26 B5
East Anton Hants 47 D11
East Appleton N Yorks 224 F4
East Ardsley W Yorks 197 B10
East Ashling W Sus 22 B4
East Aston Hants 48 D2
East Auchronie Aberds 293 C10
East Ayton N Yorks 217 B9
East Bank Bl Gwent 78 D2
East Barkwith Lincs 189 E11
East Barming Kent 53 C8
East Barnby N Yorks 226 C6
East Barnet London 86 F3
East Barns E Loth 282 F4
East Barsham Norf 159 C8
East Barton Suff 125 D8
East Beach W Sus 22 E5
East Beckham Norf 177 E11
East Bedfont London 66 E5
East Bergholt Suff 107 D11
East Bierley W Yorks 197 B7
East Bilney Norf 159 F9
East Blackdene Durham 232 D3
East Blatchington E Sus 23 E7
East Bloxworth Dorset 18 C3
East Boldon T & W 243 E9
East Boldre Hants 32 G5
East Bower Som 43 F10
East Bonhard Perth 286 E5
East Brent Som 43 C11
East Bridgford Notts 171 G11
East Briscoe Durham 223 B9
East Buckland Devon 41 G7
East Budleigh Devon 15 E7
East Burnham Bucks 66 C3
East Burrafirth Shetland 313 H5
East Burton Dorset 18 D2
East Butsfield Durham 233 B8
East Butterleigh Devon 27 F7
East Butterwick N Lincs 199 F10
East Cairnbeg Aberds 293 F9
East Calder W Loth 269 B11
East Carleton Norf 142 C3
East Carlton Northants 136 F6
East Carlton W Yorks 205 E10
East Chaldon or Chaldon Herring Dorset 17 E11
East Challow Oxon 63 B11
East Charleton Devon 8 G5
East Chelborough Dorset 29 F9
East Chiltington E Sus 36 D5
East Chinnock Som 29 E7
East Chisenbury Wilts 46 C6
East Cholderton Hants 47 D9
East Clandon Sur 50 C5
East Claydon Bucks 102 F4
East Clevedon N Som 60 E2
East Clyne Highld 311 J3
East Clyth Highld 310 F7
East Coker Som 29 E8
East Combe Som 43 G7
East Common N Yorks 207 G8
East Compton Dorset 30 D5
East Compton Som 44 E6
East Cornworthy Devon 8 D6
East Cottingwith E Yorks 207 E10
East Cowes I o W 20 B6
East Cowick E Yorks 199 C7
East Cowton N Yorks 224 E6
East Cramlington Northumb 243 B7
East Cranmore Som 45 E7
East Creech Dorset 18 E4
East Croachy Highld 300 G6
East Croftmore Highld 291 B11
East Curthwaite Cumb 230 B2
East Dean E Sus 23 F9
East Dean Glos 98 G3
East Dean Hants 32 B3
East Dean W Sus 34 E6
East Dene S Yorks 186 C6
East Denton T & W 242 D6
East Didsbury Gtr Man 184 C5
East Down Devon 40 E6
East Drayton Notts 188 F3
East Dulwich London 67 E10
East Dundry N Som 60 F5
East Ella Hull 200 B5
East End Beds 122 F2
East End Bucks 84 B4
East End C Beds 103 C9
East End Dorset 18 B5
East End E Yorks 201 B9
East End E Yorks 209 B9
East End E Yorks 209 G9
East End Essex 89 D8
East End Glos 81 E11
East End Hants 20 B3
East End Hants 33 C11
East End Hants 64 G2
East End Herts 105 F9
East End Kent 53 E11
East End Kent 53 F10
East End Kent 70 E3
East End M Keynes 103 C8
East End N Som 60 E3
East End Oxon 82 C5
East End Oxon 101 D9
East End Oxon 101 E7
East End S Glos 61 E9
East End Som 29 B10
East End Som 44 C5
East End Som 45 D7
East End Suff 108 E2
East End Suff 126 F3
East End Green Herts 86 C3
East Everleigh Wilts 47 C8
East Ewell Sur 67 G8
East Farleigh Kent 53 C8
East Farndon Northants 136 F4
East Fen Common Cambs 124 C2
East Ferry Lincs 188 B4
East Fields W Berks 64 F3
East Finchley London 67 B9
East Finglassie Fife 280 B5
East Firsby Lincs 189 D8
East Fleet Dorset 17 E8
East Fortune E Loth 281 F10
East Garforth W Yorks 206 G4
East Garston W Berks 63 D11
East Gateshead T & W 243 E7
East Ginge Oxon 64 B2
East Gores Essex 107 G7
East Goscote Leics 154 G2
East Grafton Wilts 63 G9
East Grange Moray 301 C10
East Green Hants 49 E9
East Green Suff 124 G3
East Green Suff 127 D8
East Grimstead Wilts 32 B2
East Grinstead W Sus 51 F11
East Guldeford E Sus 38 C6
East Haddon Northants 120 D3
East Hagbourne Oxon 64 B4
East Halton N Lincs 200 D6
East Ham London 68 C2
East Hampnett W Sus 22 B6
East Hanney Oxon 82 G6
East Hanningfield Essex 88 E3
East Hardwick W Yorks 198 D3
East Harling Norf 141 F9
East Harlsey N Yorks 225 F8
East Harnham Wilts 31 B10
East Harptree Bath 44 B5
East Hartford Northumb 243 B7
East Harting W Sus 34 D3
East Hatch Wilts 30 B6
East Hatley Cambs 122 G5
East Hauxwell N Yorks 224 G3
East Heckington Lincs 173 G11
East Hedleyhope Durham 233 C9
East Helmsdale Highld 311 H4
East Hendred Oxon 64 B3
East Herringthorpe S Yorks 187 C7
East Herrington T & W 243 G9
East Heslerton N Yorks 217 D8
East Hewish N Som 59 G11
East Hill Kent 68 G5
East Hoathly E Sus 23 B8
East Hogaland Shetland 313 K5
East Holme Dorset 18 D3
East Holton Dorset 18 C5
East Holywell Northumb 243 C8
East Horndon Essex 68 B6
East Horrington Som 44 D5
East Horsley Sur 50 C5
East Horton Northumb 264 C2
East Howdon T & W 243 D8
East Howe Bmouth 19 B7
East Huntspill Som 43 E10
East Hyde C Beds 85 B10
East Ilkerton Devon 41 D8
East Ilsley W Berks 64 C3
East Keal Lincs 174 C5
East Kennett Wilts 62 F6
East Keswick W Yorks 206 E3
East Kilbride S Lnrk 268 E2
East Kimber Devon 12 B5
East Kingston W Sus 35 G9
East Kirkby Lincs 174 C4
East Knapton N Yorks 217 D7
East Knighton Dorset 18 D2
East Knowstone Devon 26 C4
East Knoyle Wilts 45 G11
East Kyloe Northumb 264 B3
East Kyo Durham 242 G5
East Lambrook Som 28 D6
East Lamington Highld 301 B7
East Langdon Kent 55 D10

East Langton Leics 136 E4
East Langwell Highld 309 J7
East Lavant W Sus 22 B5
East Lavington W Sus 34 D6
East Law Northumb 242 G3
East Layton N Yorks 224 D3
East Leake Notts 153 D11
East Learmouth Northumb 263 B9
East Leigh Devon 8 E3
East Leigh Devon 25 F11
East Lexham Norf 159 F7
East Lilburn Northumb 264 E2
East Linton E Loth 281 F11
East Liss Hants 34 B3
East Lockinge Oxon 64 B2
East Loftus Redcar 226 B4
East Looe Corn 6 E5
East Lound N Lincs 188 B3
East Lulworth Dorset 18 E3
East Lutton N Yorks 217 F8
East Lydeard Som 27 B11
East Lydford Som 44 G5
East Lyng Som 28 B4
East Mains Aberds 293 D8
East Mains Borders 271 F11
East Mains S Lnrk 268 E2
East Malling Kent 53 B8
East Malling Heath Kent 53 B7
East March Angus 287 D8
East Marden W Sus 34 E4
East Markham Notts 188 G2
East Marsh NE Lincs 201 E9
East Martin Hants 31 D9
East Marton N Yorks 204 C4
East Melbury Dorset 30 C5
East Meon Hants 33 C11
East Mere Devon 27 D7
East Mersea Essex 89 C9
East Mey Highld 310 B7
East Molesey Sur 67 F7
East Moor W Yorks 197 C10
East Moors Cardiff 59 D8
East Morden Dorset 18 B4
East Morton W Yorks 205 E7
East Moulsecoomb Brighton 36 F4
East Ness N Yorks 216 D3
East Newton E Yorks 209 F11
East Newton N Yorks 216 D2
East Norton Leics 136 C5
East Nynehead Som 27 C11
East Oakley Hants 48 C5
East Ogwell Devon 14 G2
East Orchard Dorset 30 D4
East Ord Northumb 273 E9
East Panson Devon 12 C3
East Parley Dorset 19 B8
East Peckham Kent 53 D7
East Pennard Som 44 F5
East Perry Cambs 122 D3
East Portholland Corn 5 G9
East Portlemouth Devon 9 G9
East Prawle Devon 9 G10
East Preston W Sus 35 G9
East Pulham Dorset 30 F2
East Putford Devon 24 D5
East Quantoxhead Som 42 E6
East Rainton T & W 234 B2
East Ravendale NE Lincs 190 B2
East Raynham Norf 159 D7
East Rhidorroch Lodge Highld 307 K7
East Rigton W Yorks 206 E3
East Rolstone N Som 59 G11
East Rounton N Yorks 225 E8
East Row N Yorks 227 C7
East Rudham Norf 158 D6
East Runton Norf 177 E11
East Ruston Norf 160 D6
East Saltoun E Loth 271 B9
East Sheen London 67 D8
East Skelston Dumfries 247 F8
East Sleekburn Northumb 253 G7
East Somerton Norf 161 F9
East Stanley Durham 242 G6
East Stockwith Lincs 188 C3
East Stoke Dorset 18 D3
East Stoke Notts 172 F3
East Stoke Som 29 D7
East Stour Dorset 30 C4
East Stour Common Dorset 30 C4
East Stourmouth Kent 71 G9
East Stowford Devon 25 B10
East Stratton Hants 48 F4
East Street Kent 55 B10
East Street Som 44 F4
East Studdal Kent 55 D10
East Suisnish Highld 295 B7
East Taphouse Corn 6 C3
East-the-Water Devon 25 B7
East Third Borders 262 B4
East Thirston Northumb 252 D5
East Tilbury Thurrock 69 D7
East Tisted Hants 49 G8
East Torrington Lincs 189 E10
East Town Som 42 G6
East Town Som 44 E6
East Town Wilts 45 B11
East Trewent Pembs 73 F8
East Tuddenham Norf 159 G11
East Tuelmenna Corn 6 B4
East Tytherley Hants 32 B3
East Tytherton Wilts 62 E3
East Village Devon 26 F4
East Village V Glam 58 E3
East Wall Shrops 131 E10
East Walton Norf 158 F4
East Water Som 44 C4
East Week Devon 13 C9
East Wellow Hants 32 C4
East Wemyss Fife 280 B6
East Whitburn W Loth 269 B9
East Wickham London 68 D3
East Williamston Pembs 73 E9
East Winch Norf 158 F3
East Winterslow Wilts 47 G8
East Wittering W Sus 21 B11
East Witton N Yorks 214 B2
East Woodburn Northumb 251 F10
East Woodhay Hants 64 G2
East Woodlands Som 45 E9
East Worldham Hants 49 F8
East Worlington Devon 26 E3
East Worthing W Sus 35 G11
East Wretham Norf 141 E8
East Youlstone Devon 24 D3
Eastacombe Devon 25 B8
Eastacombe Devon 25 C9
Eastacott Devon 25 C10
Eastbourne Darl 224 C6
Eastbourne E Sus 23 F10
Eastbridge Suff 127 D9
Eastbrook Som 28 C2
Eastbrook V Glam 59 E7
Eastburn E Yorks 208 B5
Eastburn W Yorks 204 E6
Eastburn Br W Yorks 204 E6
Eastbury London 85 G9
Eastbury W Berks 63 D10
Eastby N Yorks 204 C6
Eastchurch Kent 70 E3
Eastcombe Glos 80 E5
Eastcote London 66 B6
Eastcote Northants 120 G3
Eastcote W Mid 118 B3
Eastcote Village London 66 B6
Eastcott Corn 24 D3
Eastcott Wilts 46 B4
Eastcotts Beds 103 B11
Eastcourt Wilts 63 G8
Eastcourt Wilts 81 G7
Eastdon Devon 14 F5
Eastdown Devon 8 F6
Eastend Essex 86 C6
Eastend Oxon 100 G6
Easter Aberchalder Highld 291 B7
Easter Ardross Highld 300 B6
Easter Balgedie Perth 286 G5
Easter Balmoral Aberds 292 D4
Easter Boleskine Highld 300 G5
Easter Brackland Stirl 285 G10
Easter Brae Highld 300 C6
Easter Cardno Aberds 303 C9
Easter Compton S Glos 60 C5
Easter Cringate Stirl 278 D4
Easter Culfosie Aberds 293 C9
Easter Davoch Aberds 292 C6
Easter Earshaig Dumfries 248 C2
Easter Ellister Argyll 254 B3
Easter Fearn Highld 309 L6
Easter Galcantray Highld 301 E8
Easter Housebyres Borders 262 B2
Easter Howgate Midloth 270 C4
Easter Howlaws Borders 272 G4
Easter Kinkell Highld 300 D5
Easter Knox Angus 287 D9
Easter Langlee Borders 262 B2
Easter Lednathie Angus 292 G5
Easter Milton Highld 301 D9
Easter Moniack Highld 300 E5
Easter Ord Aberdeen 293 C10
Easter Quarff Shetland 313 K6
Easter Rhynd Perth 286 F5
Easter Row Stirl 278 B5
Easter Silverford Aberds 303 C7
Easter Skeld Shetland 313 J5
Easter Softlaw Borders 263 C7
Easter Tulloch Highld 291 B11
Easter Whyntie Aberds 302 C6
Eastergate W Sus 22 B6
Easterhouse Glasgow 268 B3
Eastern Green W Mid 134 G5
Easterside M'bro 225 B10
Easterton Wilts 46 C4
Easterton of Lenabo Aberds 303 E10
Easterton Sands Wilts 46 B4
Eastertown Som 43 C10
Eastertown of Auchleuchries Aberds 303 F10
Eastfield Borders 262 D2
Eastfield Bristol 60 D5
Eastfield N Lnrk 269 C7
Eastfield N Lnrk 278 G4
Eastfield N Yorks 217 C10
Eastfield Northumb 243 B7
Eastfield P'boro 138 D4
Eastfield S Lnrk 268 C2
Eastfield S Yorks 197 G9
Eastfield Hall Northumb 252 B6
Eastgate Durham 232 D5
Eastgate Norf 160 E2
Eastgate P'boro 138 D4
Easthall Herts 104 G3
Eastham Mers 182 E5
Eastham Worcs 116 D3
Eastham Ferry Mers 182 E5
Easthampstead Brack 65 F11
Easthampton Hereford 115 E8
Eastheath Norf 159 F11
Eastheath Wokingham 65 F10
Easthope Shrops 131 D11
Easthopewood Shrops 131 D11
Easthorpe Essex 107 G8
Easthorpe Leics 154 B6
Easthorpe Notts 172 E2
Easthouse Shetland 313 J5
Easthouses Midloth 270 B6
Easting Orkney 314 A7
Eastington Devon 26 F2
Eastington Glos 80 D3
Eastington Glos 81 C10
Eastland Gate Hants 33 E11
Eastleach Martin Glos 82 D2
Eastleach Turville Glos 81 D11
Eastleigh Devon 25 B7
Eastleigh Hants 32 D6
Eastling Kent 54 B3
Eastmoor Derbys 186 G4
Eastmoor Norf 140 C4
Eastney Ptsmth 21 B9
Eastnor Hereford 98 D4
Eastoft N Lincs 199 D10
Eastoke Hants 21 B10
Easton Bristol 60 E6
Easton Cambs 122 C2
Easton Cumb 239 C10
Easton Cumb 239 F7
Easton Devon 8 F3
Easton Devon 13 D10
Easton Dorset 17 G9
Easton Hants 48 G4
Easton I o W 20 D2
Easton Lincs 155 D8
Easton Norf 160 G2
Easton Som 44 D4
Easton Suff 126 F5
Easton W Berks 64 E2
Easton Wilts 61 E11
Easton Grey Wilts 61 B11
Easton in Gordano N Som 60 D4
Easton Maudit Northants 121 F7
Easton on the Hill Northants 137 C10
Easton Royal Wilts 63 G8
Easton Town Som 44 G5
Easton Town Wilts 61 B11
Eastover Som 43 F10
Eastpark Dumfries 238 D2
Eastrea Cambs 138 D5
Eastriggs Dumfries 238 D6
Eastrington E Yorks 199 B9
Eastrip Wilts 61 E10
Eastrop Hants 48 C6
Eastry Kent 55 C10
Eastville Bristol 60 E6
Eastville Lincs 174 D6
Eastwell Leics 154 D5
Eastwell Park Kent 54 D4
Eastwick Herts 86 C6
Eastwick Shetland 312 F5
Eastwood Hereford 98 C2
Eastwood Notts 171 F7
Eastwood S Yorks 186 C6
Eastwood Sthend 69 B10
Eastwood W Yorks 196 B3
Eastwood End Cambs 139 E8
Eastwood Hall Notts 171 F7
Eathorpe Warks 119 D7
Eaton Ches 168 B5
Eaton Hereford 115 F10
Eaton Leics 154 D5
Eaton Norf 142 B4
Eaton Notts 188 F2
Eaton Oxon 82 E6
Eaton Shrops 131 F10
Eaton Shrops 131 F7
Eaton W Ches 167 C9
Eaton Bishop Hereford 97 D8
Eaton Bray C Beds 103 G9
Eaton Constantine Shrops 131 B11
Eaton Ford Cambs 122 E3
Eaton Green C Beds 103 G9
Eaton Hastings Oxon 82 F3
Eaton Mascott Shrops 131 B10
Eaton on Tern Shrops 150 E3
Eaton Socon Cambs 122 F3
Eaton upon Tern Shrops 150 E3
Eau Brink Norf 157 F11
Eau Withington Hereford 97 C10
Eaves Green W Mid 134 G5
Eavestone N Yorks 214 F4
Ebberly Hill Devon 25 D9
Ebberston N Yorks 217 C7
Ebbesbourne Wake Wilts 31 C7
Ebblake Hants 31 F10
Ebbw Vale Bl Gwent 77 D11
Ebchester Durham 242 F4
Ebdon N Som 59 G11
Ebernoe W Sus 35 B7
Ebford Devon 14 D5
Ebley Glos 80 D4
Ebnal W Ches 167 F7
Ebnall Hereford 115 F9
Ebreywood Shrops 149 F10
Ebrington Glos 100 C3
Ecchinswell Hants 48 B4
Ecclaw Borders 272 B5
Eccle Riggs Cumb 210 B4
Ecclefechan Dumfries 238 C5
Eccles Borders 272 G5
Eccles Gtr Man 184 B3
Eccles Kent 69 G8
Eccles on Sea Norf 161 D8
Eccles Road Norf 141 E10
Ecclesall S Yorks 186 E4
Ecclesfield S Yorks 186 C5
Ecclesgreig Aberds 293 G9
Eccleshall Staffs 150 D6
Eccleshill W Yorks 205 F9
Ecclesmachan W Loth 279 G11
Eccleston Lancs 194 D4
Eccleston Mers 183 B7
Eccleston W Ches 166 C6
Eccleston Park Mers 183 C7
Eccliffe Dorset 30 B3
Eccup W Yorks 205 E11
Echt Aberds 293 C9
Eckford Borders 262 D6
Eckfordmoss Borders 262 D6
Eckington Derbys 186 F6
Eckington Worcs 99 C8
Eckington Corner E Sus 23 D8
Ecklands S Yorks 197 G8
Eckworthy Devon 24 D6
Ecton Northants 120 E6
Ecton Staffs 169 D9
Ecton Brook Northants 120 E6
Edale Derbys 185 D10
Edale End Derbys 185 D11
Edbrook Som 43 E8
Edburton W Sus 36 E2
Edderside Cumb 229 B7
Edderton Highld 309 L7
Eddington Kent 71 F7
Eddington W Berks 63 F10
Eddistone Devon 24 C3
Eddleston Borders 270 F4
Eddlewood S Lnrk 268 E4
Eden Mount Cumb 211 D8
Eden Park London 67 F11
Eden Vale Durham 234 D4
Eden Vale Wilts 45 C11
Edenbridge Kent 52 D2
Edenfield Lancs 195 D9
Edenhall Cumb 231 E7
Edenham Lincs 155 E11
Edensor Derbys 170 B2
Edentaggart Argyll 276 C6
Edenthorpe S Yorks 198 F6
Edentown Cumb 239 F9
Ederline Argyll 275 C9
Edern Gwyn 144 B5
Edford Som 45 D7
Edgarley Som 44 F4
Edgbaston W Mid 133 G11
Edgcote Northants 101 B10
Edgcott Bucks 102 G3
Edgcott Som 41 F10
Edgcumbe Corn 2 C6
Edge Glos 80 D4
Edge Shrops 131 B7
Edge End Glos 79 C9
Edge End Lancs 203 G10
Edge Fold Blkburn 195 D8
Edge Fold Gtr Man 195 F8
Edge Green Gtr Man 183 B9
Edge Green Norf 141 F10
Edge Green W Ches 167 E7
Edge Hill Mers 182 C5
Edge Hill Warks 134 D4
Edge Mount S Yorks 186 C3
Edgebolton Shrops 149 E11
Edgefield Norf 159 C11
Edgefield Street Norf 159 C11
Edgehill Warks 101 B7
Edgeley Gtr Man 184 D5
Edgerley Shrops 148 F6
Edgerston Borders 262 G5
Edgerton W Yorks 196 D6
Edgeside Lancs 195 C10
Edgeworth Glos 80 D6
Edginswell Devon 9 B7
Edgiock Worcs 117 E10
Edgmond Telford 150 F4
Edgmond Marsh Telford 150 E4
Edgton Shrops 131 F7
Edgware London 85 G11
Edgwick W Mid 134 G6
Edgworth Blkburn 195 D8
Edham Borders 262 B6
Edial Staffs 133 B11
Edinample Stirl 285 E9
Edinbane Highld 298 D3
Edinburgh Edin 280 G5
Edinchip Stirl 285 E9
Edingale Staffs 152 G4
Edingight Ho Moray 302 D5
Edinglassie Ho Aberds 292 B5
Edingley Notts 171 D11
Edingthorpe Norf 160 C6
Edingthorpe Green Norf 160 C6
Edington Som 43 F11
Edington Wilts 46 C2
Edingworth Som 43 C11
Edintore Moray 302 E4
Edistone Devon 24 C2
Edith Weston Rutland 137 B8
Edithmead Som 43 D10
Edlaston Derbys 169 G11
Edlesborough Bucks 85 B7
Edlingham Northumb 252 B4
Edlington Lincs 190 G2
Edmondsham Dorset 31 E9
Edmondsley Durham 233 B10
Edmondstown Rhondda 77 G8
Edmondthorpe Leics 155 F7
Edmonston S Lnrk 269 G11
Edmonstone Orkney 314 D5
Edmonton Corn 10 G5
Edmonton London 86 G4
Edmundbyers Durham 242 G2
Ednam Borders 262 B6
Ednaston Derbys 170 G2
Edney Common Essex 87 E11
Edradynate Perth 286 B2
Edrom Borders 272 D6
Edstaston Shrops 149 C10
Edstone Warks 118 E3
Edvin Loach Hereford 116 F3
Edwalton Notts 153 B11
Edwardstone Suff 107 C8
Edwardsville M Tydf 77 F9
Edwinsford Carms 94 E2
Edwinstowe Notts 171 B10
Edworth C Beds 104 C4
Edwyn Ralph Hereford 116 F2
Edzell Angus 293 G7
Efail-fôch Neath 57 B9
Efail Isaf Rhondda 58 C5
Efailnewydd Gwyn 145 B7
Efailwen Carms 92 F2
Efenechtyd Denb 165 D10
Effingham Sur 50 C6
Effirth Shetland 313 H5
Effledge Borders 262 F3
Efflinch Staffs 152 F3
Efford Devon 26 G5
Efford Plym 7 D10
Egbury Hants 48 C2
Egdon Worcs 117 G8
Egerton Gtr Man 195 E8
Egerton Kent 54 D2
Egerton Forstal Kent 53 D11
Egerton Green E Ches 167 E8
Egford Som 45 D9
Eggbeare Corn 12 D2
Eggborough N Yorks 198 C5
Eggbuckland Plym 7 D10
Eggesford Station Devon 25 E11
Eggington C Beds 103 F9
Egginton Derbys 152 D5
Egginton Common Derbys 152 D5
Egglesburn Durham 232 G5
Egglescliffe Stockton 225 C8
Eggleston Durham 232 G5
Egham Sur 66 E4
Egham Hythe Sur 66 E4
Egham Wick Sur 66 E3
Egleton Rutland 137 B7
Eglingham Northumb 264 F4
Egloshayle Corn 10 G5
Egloskerry Corn 11 D11
Eglwys-Brewis V Glam 58 F4
Eglwys Cross Wrex 167 G7
Eglwys Fach Ceredig 128 D3
Eglwysbach Conwy 180 G4
Eglwyswen Pembs 92 D3
Eglwyswrw Pembs 92 D2
Egmanton Notts 172 B2
Egmere Norf 159 B8
Egremont Cumb 219 C10
Egremont Mers 182 C4
Egton N Yorks 226 D6
Egton Bridge N Yorks 226 D6
Egypt Bucks 66 B3
Egypt Hants 48 E3
Egypt W Berks 64 D2
Egypt W Yorks 205 G7
Eiden Highld 309 J7
Eight Ash Green Essex 107 F8
Eighton Banks T & W 243 F7
Eign Hill Hereford 97 D10
Eignaig Highld 289 E9
Eil Highld 291 B10
Eilanreach Highld 295 D10
Eildon Borders 262 C3
Eilean Anabaich W Isles 305 H4
Eilean Darach Highld 307 L6
Eilean Shona Ho Highld 289 B8
Eileanach Lodge Highld 300 C5
Einacleite W Isles 304 F3
Einsiob = Evenjobb Powys 114 E5
Eisgean W Isles 305 G5
Eisingrug Gwyn 146 C2
Elan Village Powys 113 D8
Eland Green Northumb 242 C5
Elberton S Glos 60 B6
Elborough N Som 43 B11
Elbridge Shrops 149 E7
Elbridge W Sus 22 C6
Elburton Plym 7 E10
Elcho Perth 286 E5
Elcock's Brook Worcs 117 E10
Elcombe Glos 80 F3
Elcombe Swindon 62 C6
Elcot W Berks 63 F11
Eldene Swindon 63 C7
Elder Street Essex 105 E11
Eldernell Cambs 138 D6
Eldersfield Worcs 98 E6
Elderslie Renfs 267 C8
Eldon Durham 233 F10
Eldon Lane Durham 233 F10
Eldrick S Ayrs 245 G7
Eldroth N Yorks 212 F5
Eldwick W Yorks 205 E8
Elemore Vale T & W 234 B3
Elerch = Bont-goch Ceredig 128 F3
Elfhowe Cumb 221 F9
Elford Northumb 264 C5
Elford Staffs 152 G3
Elford Closes Cambs 123 C10
Elgin Moray 302 C2
Elgol Highld 295 D7
Elham Kent 55 E7
Eliburn W Loth 269 B10
Elie Fife 287 G8
Elim Anglesey 178 D5
Eling Hants 32 E5
Eling W Berks 64 D4
Elishader Highld 298 C5
Elishaw Northumb 251 D9
Elizafield Dumfries 238 C2
Elkesley Notts 187 F11
Elkington Northants 120 B2
Elkins Green Essex 87 E10
Elkstone Glos 81 C7
Ellacombe Torbay 9 C8
Ellan Highld 301 G8
Elland W Yorks 196 C6
Elland Lower Edge W Yorks 196 C6
Elland Upper Edge W Yorks 196 C6
Ellary Argyll 275 F8
Ellastone Staffs 169 G10
Ellel Lancs 202 B5
Ellemford Borders 272 C4
Ellenborough Cumb 228 D6
Ellenbrook Herts 86 D2
Ellenbrook I o M 192 E4
Ellenglaze Corn 4 D5
Ellenhall Staffs 150 D6
Ellen's Green Sur 50 F5
Ellerbeck N Yorks 225 F8
Ellerburn N Yorks 216 C6
Ellerby N Yorks 226 C5
Ellerdine Telford 150 E2
Ellerdine Heath Telford 150 E2
Ellerhayes Devon 27 G7
Elleric Argyll 284 C4
Ellerker E Yorks 200 B2
Ellerton E Yorks 207 F10
Ellerton N Yorks 224 F5
Ellerton Shrops 150 D4
Ellesborough Bucks 84 D4
Ellesmere Shrops 149 C8
Ellesmere Park Gtr Man 184 B3
Ellesmere Port W Ches 182 F6
Ellicombe Som 42 E3
Ellingham Hants 31 F10
Ellingham Norf 143 E7
Ellingham Northumb 264 D5
Ellingstring N Yorks 214 C3
Ellington Cambs 122 C3
Ellington Northumb 253 E7
Ellington Thorpe Cambs 122 C3
Elliot Angus 287 D10
Elliots Green Som 45 D9
Elliot's Town Caerph 77 E10
Ellisfield Hants 48 D6
Elliston Borders 262 D3
Ellistown Leics 153 G8
Ellon Aberds 303 F9
Ellonby Cumb 230 D4
Ellough Suff 143 F8
Elloughton E Yorks 200 B2
Ellwood Glos 79 D9
Elm Cambs 139 B9
Elm Corner Sur 50 B5
Elm Cross Wilts 62 D6
Elm Hill Dorset 30 B4
Elm Park London 68 B4
Elmbridge Glos 80 B5
Elmbridge Worcs 117 D8
Elmdon Essex 105 D9
Elmdon W Mid 134 G3
Elmdon Heath W Mid 134 G3
Elmer W Sus 35 G7
Elmers End London 67 F11
Elmers Green Lancs 194 F3
Elmers Marsh W Sus 34 B5
Elmesthorpe Leics 135 D9
Elmfield I o W 21 C8
Elmhurst Bucks 84 B4
Elmhurst Staffs 152 G2
Elmley Castle Worcs 99 C9
Elmley Lovett Worcs 117 D7
Elmore Glos 80 B3
Elmore Back Glos 80 B3
Elms Green Hereford 115 F10
Elms Green Worcs 116 D4
Elmscott Devon 24 C2
Elmsett Suff 107 B11
Elmslack Lancs 211 D9
Elmstead Essex 107 F11
Elmstead London 68 E2
Elmstead Heath Essex 107 G11
Elmstead Market Essex 107 G11
Elmsted Kent 54 E6
Elmsthorpe Leics 135 D9
Elmstone Kent 71 G9
Elmstone Hardwicke Glos 99 F8
Elmswell E Yorks 208 B5
Elmswell Suff 125 E9
Elmton Derbys 187 G8
Elness Orkney 314 C6
Elphin Highld 307 H7
Elphinstone E Loth 281 G7
Elrick Aberds 293 C10
Elrig Dumfries 236 E5
Elrigbeag Argyll 284 F5
Elrington Northumb 241 E9
Elscar S Yorks 197 G11
Elsdon Hereford 114 G6
Elsdon Northumb 251 E10
Elsecar S Yorks 186 B5
Elsecar S Yorks 197 G11
Elsenham Essex 105 F10
Elsenham Sta Essex 105 F10
Elsfield Oxon 83 C8
Elsham N Lincs 200 E4
Elsing Norf 159 F11
Elslack N Yorks 204 D4
Elson Hants 33 G10
Elson Shrops 149 B7
Elsrickle S Lnrk 269 G11
Elstead Sur 50 E2
Elsted W Sus 34 D4
Elsthorpe Lincs 155 E11
Elstob Durham 234 G2
Elston Devon 26 G3
Elston Notts 172 F3
Elston Wilts 46 E5
Elstone Devon 25 D11
Elstow Beds 103 B11
Elstree Herts 85 F11
Elstronwick E Yorks 209 G10
Elswick Lancs 202 F4
Elswick T & W 242 E6
Elswick Leys Lancs 202 F4
Elsworth Cambs 122 E6
Elterwater Cumb 220 E6
Eltham London 68 E2
Eltisley Cambs 122 F5
Elton Cambs 137 E11
Elton Derbys 170 C2
Elton Glos 80 C2
Elton Gtr Man 195 E9
Elton Hereford 115 C9
Elton Notts 154 B5
Elton Stockton 225 B8
Elton W Ches 183 F7
Elton Green W Ches 183 G7
Elton's Marsh Hereford 97 C9
Eltringham Northumb 242 E3
Elvanfoot S Lnrk 259 F11
Elvaston Derbys 153 C8
Elveden Suff 124 B6
Elvet Hill Durham 233 C11
Elvingston E Loth 281 G9
Elvington Kent 55 C9
Elvington York 207 D9
Elwell Devon 41 G7
Elwell Dorset 17 E9
Elwick Hrtlpl 234 E5
Elwick Northumb 264 B4
Elworth E Ches 168 C2
Elworthy Som 42 G5
Ely Cambs 139 G10
Ely Cardiff 58 D6
Emberton M Keynes 103 B7
Embleton Cumb 229 E9
Embleton Durham 234 F4
Embleton Northumb 264 E6
Embo Highld 311 K2
Embo Street Highld 311 K2
Emborough Som 44 C6
Embsay N Yorks 204 C6
Emerson Park London 68 B4
Emerson Valley M Keynes 102 E6
Emerson's Green S Glos 61 D7
Emery Down Hants 32 F3
Emley W Yorks 197 E8
Emmbrook Wokingham 65 F9
Emmer Green Reading 65 D8
Emmett Carr Derbys 187 F7
Emmington Oxon 84 E2
Emneth Norf 139 B9
Emneth Hungate Norf 139 B10
Emorsgate Norf 157 E10
Empingham Rutland 137 B8
Empshott Hants 49 G9
Empshott Green Hants 49 G8
Emscote Warks 118 D5
Emstrey Shrops 149 G10
Emsworth Hants 22 B2
Enborne W Berks 64 F2
Enborne Row W Berks 64 G2
Enchmarsh Shrops 131 D10
Enderby Leics 135 D10
Endmoor Cumb 211 C10
Endon Staffs 168 E6
Endon Bank Staffs 168 E6
Energlyn Caerph 58 B6
Enfield London 86 F4
Enfield Worcs 117 D10
Enfield Highway London 86 F5
Enfield Lock London 86 F5
Enfield Town London 86 F4
Enfield Wash London 86 F5
Enford Wilts 46 C6
Engamoor Shetland 313 H4
Engedi Anglesey 178 F5
Engine Common S Glos 61 C7
Englefield W Berks 64 E6
Englefield Green Sur 66 E3
Englesea-brook E Ches 168 E3
English Bicknor Glos 79 B9
English Frankton Shrops 149 D9
Englishcombe Bath 61 G8
Engollan Corn 10 G3
Enham Alamein Hants 47 D11
Enis Devon 25 B9
Enisfirth Shetland 312 F5
Enmore Som 43 G8
Enmore Field Hereford 115 E9
Enmore Green Dorset 30 C5
Ennerdale Bridge Cumb 219 B11
Enniscaven Corn 5 D9
Enoch Dumfries 247 C9
Enochdhu Perth 292 G2
Ensay Argyll 288 E5
Ensbury Bmouth 19 B7
Ensbury Park Bmouth 19 C7
Ensdon Shrops 149 F8
Ensis Devon 25 B9
Enslow Oxon 83 B7
Enstone Oxon 101 G7
Enterkinfoot Dumfries 247 C9
Enterpen N Yorks 225 D9
Enton Green Sur 50 E3
Enville Staffs 132 F6
Eolaigearraidh W Isles 297 L3
Eorabus Argyll 288 G5
Eòropaidh W Isles 304 B7
Epney Glos 80 C3
Epperstone Notts 171 F11
Epping Essex 87 E7
Epping Green Essex 86 D6
Epping Green Herts 86 D3
Epping Upland Essex 86 E6
Eppleby N Yorks 224 C3
Eppleworth E Yorks 208 G6
Epsom Sur 67 G8
Epwell Oxon 101 C7
Epworth N Lincs 199 G9
Epworth Turbary N Lincs 199 G9
Erbistock Wrex 166 G5
Erbusaig Highld 295 C9
Erchless Castle Highld 300 E4
Erdington W Mid 134 E2
Eredine Argyll 275 C10
Eriboll Highld 308 D4
Ericstane Dumfries 260 G3
Eridge Green E Sus 52 F5
Erines Argyll 275 F9
Eriswell Suff 124 B4
Erith London 68 D4
Erlestoke Wilts 46 C3
Ermine Lincs 189 G7
Ermington Devon 8 E2
Ernesettle Plym 7 D8
Erpingham Norf 160 C3
Erriottwood Kent 54 B2
Errogie Highld 300 G5
Errol Perth 286 E6
Errol Station Perth 286 E6
Erskine Renfs 277 G9
Erskine Bridge Renfs 277 G9
Ervie Dumfries 236 C2
Erwarton Suff 108 E4
Erwood Powys 95 C11
Eryholme N Yorks 224 D6
Eryrys Denb 166 D2
Escomb Durham 233 E9
Escott Som 42 F5
Escrick N Yorks 207 E8
Esgairdawe Carms 94 C2
Esgairgeiliog Powys 128 B5
Esgyryn Conwy 180 F4
Esh Durham 233 C9
Esh Winning Durham 233 C9
Esher Sur 66 G6
Eshiels Borders 261 B7
Esholt W Yorks 205 E9
Eshott Northumb 252 D6
Eshton N Yorks 204 B4
Esk Valley N Yorks 226 E6
Eskadale Highld 300 F4
Eskbank Midloth 270 B6
Eskdale Green Cumb 220 E2
Eskdalemuir Dumfries 249 D7
Eske E Yorks 209 E7
Eskham Lincs 190 B5
Eskholme S Yorks 198 D6
Esknish Argyll 274 G4
Eslington Park Northumb 264 G2

Esperley Lane Ends Durham 233 G8
Esprick Lancs 202 F4
Essendine Rutland 155 G10
Essendon Herts 86 D3
Essich Highld 300 F6
Essington Staffs 133 C9
Esslemont Aberds 303 G9
Eston Redcar 225 B11
Estover Plym 7 D10
Eswick Shetland 313 H6
Etal Northumb 263 B10
Etchilhampton Wilts 62 G4
Etchingham E Sus 38 B2
Etchinghill Kent 55 F7
Etchinghill Staffs 151 F10
Etchingwood E Sus 37 C8
Etherley Dene Durham 233 F9
Ethie Castle Angus 287 C10
Ethie Mains Angus 287 C10
Etling Green Norf 159 G10
Etloe Glos 79 D11
Eton Windsor 66 D3
Eton Wick Windsor 66 D2
Etruria Stoke 168 F5
Etsell Shrops 131 C7
Etterby Cumb 239 F9
Etteridge Highld 291 D8
Ettersgill Durham 232 F3
Ettiley Heath E Ches 168 C2
Ettingshall W Mid 133 D8
Ettingshall Park W Mid 133 D8
Ettington Warks 100 B5
Etton E Yorks 208 E5
Etton P'boro 138 B2
Ettrick Borders 261 G7
Ettrickbridge Borders 261 E9
Ettrickdale Argyll 275 G11
Ettrickhill Borders 261 G7
Etwall Derbys 152 C5
Etwall Common Derbys 152 C5
Eudon Burnell Shrops 132 F3
Eudon George Shrops 132 F3
Euston Suff 125 B7
Euximoor Drove Cambs 139 D9
Euxton Lancs 194 D5
Evanstown Bridgend 58 B3
Evanton Highld 300 C6
Eve Hill W Mid 133 E8
Evedon Lincs 173 F9
Evelix Highld 309 K7
Even Pits Hereford 97 D11
Even Swindon Swindon 62 B6
Evendine Hereford 98 C5
Evenjobb = Einsiob Powys 114 E5
Evenley Northants 101 E11
Evenlode Glos 100 F4
Evenwood Durham 233 G9
Evenwood Gate Durham 233 G9
Everbay Orkney 314 D6
Evercreech Som 44 F6
Everdon Northants 119 F11
Everingham E Yorks 208 E2
Everland Shetland 312 D8
Everleigh Wilts 47 C8
Everley N Yorks 217 B9
Eversholt C Beds 103 E9
Evershot Dorset 29 G9
Eversley Essex 69 B8
Eversley Hants 65 G9
Eversley Centre Hants 65 G9
Eversley Cross Hants 65 G9
Everthorpe E Yorks 208 G4
Everton C Beds 122 G4
Everton Hants 19 C11
Everton Mers 182 C5
Everton Notts 187 C11
Evertown Dumfries 239 B9
Evesbatch Hereford 98 B3
Evesham Worcs 99 C10
Evington Kent 54 D6
Evington Leicester 136 C2
Ewanrigg Cumb 228 D6
Ewden Village S Yorks 186 B3
Ewell Sur 67 G8
Ewell Minnis Kent 55 E9
Ewelme Oxon 83 G10
Ewen Glos 81 F8
Ewenny V Glam 58 D2
Ewerby Lincs 173 F10
Ewerby Thorpe Lincs 173 F10
Ewes Dumfries 249 E9
Ewesley Northumb 252 E3
Ewhurst Sur 50 E5
Ewhurst Green E Sus 38 C3
Ewhurst Green Sur 50 F5
Ewloe Flint 166 B4
Ewloe Green Flint 166 B3
Ewood Blkburn 195 B7
Ewood Bridge Lancs 195 C9
Eworthy Devon 12 C5
Ewshot Hants 49 D10
Ewyas Harold Hereford 97 F7
Exbourne Devon 25 G10
Exbury Hants 20 B4
Exceat E Sus 23 F8
Exebridge Devon 26 C6
Exelby N Yorks 214 B5
Exeter Devon 14 C4
Exford Som 41 F11
Exfords Green Shrops 131 B9
Exhall Warks 118 F2
Exhall Warks 135 F7
Exlade Street Oxon 65 C7
Exley W Yorks 196 C5
Exley Head W Yorks 204 F6
Exminster Devon 14 D4
Exmouth Devon 14 E6
Exnaboe Shetland 313 M5
Exning Suff 124 D2
Exted Kent 55 E7
Exton Devon 14 D5
Exton Hants 33 C10
Exton Rutland 155 G8
Exton Som 42 G2
Exwick Devon 14 C4
Eyam Derbys 186 F2
Eydon Northants 119 G10
Eye Hereford 115 E9
Eye P'boro 138 C4
Eye Suff 126 C2
Eye Green P'boro 138 C4
Eyemouth Borders 273 C8
Eyeworth C Beds 104 B4
Eyhorne Street Kent 53 C10
Eyke Suff 126 G6
Eynesbury Cambs 122 F3
Eynort Highld 294 C5
Eynsford Kent 68 F4
Eynsham Oxon 82 D6
Eype Dorset 16 C5
Eyre Highld 295 B7
Eyre Highld 298 D4
Eyres Monsell Leicester 135 D11
Eythorne Kent 55 D9
Eyton Hereford 115 E9
Eyton Shrops 131 F7
Eyton Shrops 149 G7
Eyton Wrex 166 G4
Eyton on Severn Shrops 131 B11
Eyton upon the Weald Moors Telford 150 G3

F

Faberstown Wilts 47 C9
Faccombe Hants 47 B11
Faceby N Yorks 225 E9
Fachell Gwyn 163 B8
Fachwen Gwyn 163 C9
Facit Lancs 195 D11
Fackley Notts 171 C7
Faddiley E Ches 167 E9
Faddonch Highld 295 C11
Fadmoor N Yorks 216 B3
Faerdre Swansea 75 E11
Fagley W Yorks 205 G9
Fagwyr Swansea 75 E11
Faichem Highld 290 C4
Faifley W Dunb 277 G10
Failand N Som 60 E4
Failford S Ayrs 257 D11
Failsworth Gtr Man 195 G11
Fain Highld 299 B11
Faindouran Lodge Moray 292 C2
Fair Cross London 68 B3
Fair Green Norf 158 F3
Fair Hill Cumb 230 E6
Fair Moor Northumb 252 F5
Fair Oak Hants 33 D7
Fair Oak Hants 64 G5
Fair Oak Lancs 203 D8
Fair Oak Green Hants 65 G7
Fairbourne Gwyn 146 G2
Fairbourne Heath Kent 53 C11
Fairburn N Yorks 198 B3
Fairburn House Highld 300 D4
Fairfield Clack 279 C7
Fairfield Derbys 185 G9
Fairfield Gtr Man 184 B6
Fairfield Gtr Man 195 E10
Fairfield Kent 39 B7
Fairfield Mers 182 C5
Fairfield Stockton 225 B8
Fairfield Worcs 99 C10
Fairfield Worcs 117 B8
Fairfield Park Bath 61 F9
Fairfields Glos 98 E4
Fairford Glos 81 E11
Fairhaven Lancs 193 B10
Fairhaven N Ayrs 255 C10
Fairhill S Lnrk 268 E4
Fairlands Sur 50 C3
Fairlee I o W 20 C6
Fairlie N Ayrs 266 D4
Fairlight E Sus 38 E5
Fairlight Cove E Sus 38 E5
Fairlop London 87 G7
Fairmile Devon 15 B7
Fairmile Dorset 19 C9
Fairmile Sur 66 G6
Fairmilehead Edin 270 B4
Fairoak Caerph 77 F11
Fairoak Staffs 150 C5
Fairseat Kent 68 G6
Fairstead Essex 88 B3
Fairstead Norf 158 F2
Fairview Glos 99 G9
Fairwarp E Sus 37 B7
Fairwater Cardiff 58 D6
Fairwater Torf 78 G3
Fairwood Wilts 45 C10
Fairy Cottage I o M 192 D5
Fairy Cross Devon 24 C6
Fakenham Norf 159 D8
Fakenham Magna Suff 125 B8
Fala Midloth 271 C8
Fala Dam Midloth 271 C8
Falahill Borders 271 D7
Falcon Hereford 98 E2
Falcon Lodge W Mid 134 D2
Falconwood London 68 D3
Falcutt Northants 101 C11
Faldingworth Lincs 189 E9
Faldonside Borders 262 C2
Falfield Fife 287 G8
Falfield S Glos 79 G11
Falkenham Suff 108 D5
Falkenham Sink Suff 108 D5
Falkirk Falk 279 F7
Falkland Fife 286 G6
Falla Borders 262 G6
Fallgate Derbys 170 C5
Fallin Stirl 278 C6
Fallinge Derbys 170 B3
Fallings Heath W Mid 133 D9
Fallowfield Gtr Man 184 C5
Fallside N Lnrk 268 C4
Falmer E Sus 36 F5
Falmouth Corn 3 C8
Falnash Borders 249 B9
Falsgrave N Yorks 217 B10
Falside W Loth 269 B9
Falsidehill Borders 272 G3
Falstone Northumb 250 F6
Fanagmore Highld 306 E6
Fancott C Beds 103 F10
Fangdale Beck N Yorks 225 G11
Fangfoss E Yorks 207 C11
Fanich Highld 311 J2
Fankerton Falk 278 E5
Fanmore Argyll 288 E6
Fanner's Green Essex 87 C11
Fannich Lodge Highld 300 C2
Fans Borders 272 G2
Fanshowe E Ches 184 G5
Fant Kent 53 B8
Faoilean Highld 295 C7
Far Arnside Cumb 211 D8
Far Bank S Yorks 198 E6
Far Banks Lancs 194 C2
Far Bletchley M Keynes 103 E7
Far Coton Leics 135 C7
Far Cotton Northants 120 F4
Far End Cumb 220 F6
Far Forest Worcs 116 C4
Far Green Glos 80 E3
Far Hoarcross Staffs 152 E2
Far Laund Derbys 170 F5
Far Ley Staffs 132 D5
Far Moor Gtr Man 194 G4
Far Oakridge Glos 80 E6
Far Royds W Yorks 205 G11
Far Sawrey Cumb 221 F7
Far Thrupp Glos 80 E5
Farcet Cambs 138 E4
Farden Shrops 115 B11
Fareham Hants 33 F9
Farewell Staffs 151 G11
Farforth Lincs 190 F4
Farhill Derbys 170 C5
Faringdon Oxon 82 F3
Farington Lancs 194 B4
Farington Moss Lancs 194 C4
Farlam Cumb 240 F3
Farlands Booth Derbys 185 D9
Farlary Highld 309 J7
Farleigh N Som 60 F3
Farleigh Sur 67 G11
Farleigh Court Sur 67 G11
Farleigh Green Kent 53 C8
Farleigh Hungerford Som 45 B10
Farleigh Wallop Hants 48 D6
Farleigh Wick Wilts 61 G10
Farlesthorpe Lincs 191 G7
Farleton Cumb 211 C10
Farleton Lancs 211 F11
Farley Bristol 60 E2
Farley Derbys 170 C3
Farley Shrops 131 B7
Farley Shrops 132 C2
Farley Staffs 169 G9
Farley Wilts 32 B2
Farley Green Suff 124 G4
Farley Green Sur 50 D5
Farley Hill Luton 103 G11
Farley Hill Wokingham 65 G8
Farleys End Glos 80 B3
Farlington N Yorks 216 F2
Farlington Ptsmth 33 F11
Farlow Shrops 132 G2
Farm Town Leics 153 F7
Farmborough Bath 61 G7
Farmbridge End Essex 87 C10
Farmcote Glos 99 F11
Farmcote Shrops 132 E5
Farmington Glos 81 B10
Farmoor Oxon 82 D6
Farms Common Corn 2 C5
Farmtown Moray 302 D5
Farnah Green Derbys 170 F4
Farnborough Hants 49 C11
Farnborough London 68 G2
Farnborough W Berks 64 C2
Farnborough Warks 101 B8
Farnborough Green Hants 49 B11
Farnborough Park Hants 49 B11
Farnborough Street Hants 49 B11
Farncombe Sur 50 E3
Farndish Beds 121 E8
Farndon Notts 172 E3
Farndon W Ches 166 E6
Farnell Angus 287 B10
Farnham Dorset 31 D7
Farnham Essex 105 G9
Farnham N Yorks 215 G7
Farnham Suff 127 E7
Farnham Sur 49 D10
Farnham Common Bucks 66 C3
Farnham Green Essex 105 F9
Farnham Park Bucks 66 C3
Farnham Royal Bucks 66 C3
Farnhill N Yorks 204 D6
Farningham Kent 68 F4
Farnley N Yorks 205 D10
Farnley W Yorks 205 G11
Farnley Bank W Yorks 197 E7
Farnley Tyas W Yorks 197 E7
Farnsfield Notts 171 D10
Farnworth Gtr Man 195 F8
Farnworth Halton 183 D8
Farr Highld 291 C10
Farr Highld 300 F6
Farr Highld 308 C7
Farr House Highld 300 F6
Farraline Highld 300 G5
Farringdon Devon 14 C6
Farringdon T & W 243 G9
Farrington Dorset 30 D4
Farrington Gurney Bath 44 B6
Farsley W Yorks 205 F10
Farsley Beck Bottom W Yorks 205 F10
Farther Howegreen Essex 88 E4
Farthing Corner Medway 69 G10
Farthing Green Kent 53 D10
Farthinghoe Northants 101 D10
Farthingloe Kent 55 E9
Farthingstone Northants 120 F2
Fartown W Yorks 196 D6
Farway Devon 15 B9
Farway Marsh Devon 28 G4
Fasach Highld 297 G7
Fasag Highld 299 D8
Fascadale Highld 289 B7
Faslane Port Argyll 276 D4
Fasnacloich Argyll 284 C4
Fasnakyle Ho Highld 300 G3
Fassfern Highld 290 F2
Fatfield T & W 243 G8
Fattahead Aberds 302 D6
Faucheldean W Loth 279 G11
Faugh Cumb 240 G2
Faughill Borders 262 C2
Fauld Staffs 152 D3
Fauldhouse W Loth 269 C8
Fauldiehill Angus 287 D9
Fauldshope Borders 261 D10
Faulkbourne Essex 88 B3
Faulkland Som 45 C8
Fauls Shrops 149 C11
Faverdale Darl 224 B5
Faversham Kent 70 G4
Favillar Moray 302 F2
Fawdington N Yorks 215 E8
Fawdon Northumb 264 F2
Fawdon T & W 242 D6
Fawfieldhead Staffs 169 C9
Fawkham Green Kent 68 F5
Fawler Oxon 63 B10
Fawler Oxon 82 B5
Fawley Bucks 65 B9
Fawley Hants 33 G7
Fawley W Berks 63 C11
Fawley Bottom Bucks 65 B8
Fawley Chapel Hereford 97 F11
Faxfleet E Yorks 199 C11
Faygate W Sus 51 G8
Fazakerley Mers 182 B5
Fazeley Staffs 134 C4
Feagour Highld 291 D7
Fearby N Yorks 214 C3
Fearn Highld 301 B8
Fearn Lodge Highld 309 L6
Fearn Station Highld 301 B8
Fearnan Perth 285 C11
Fearnbeg Highld 299 D7
Fearnhead Warr 183 C10
Fearnmore Highld 299 C7
Fearnville W Yorks 206 F2
Featherstone Staffs 133 B8
Featherstone W Yorks 198 C2
Featherwood Northumb 251 C8
Feckenham Worcs 117 E10
Fedw Fawr Anglesey 179 E10
Feering Essex 107 G7
Feetham N Yorks 223 F9
Fegg Hayes Stoke 168 E5
Fèith Mhor Highld 301 G8
Feizor N Yorks 212 F5
Felbridge Sur 51 F11
Felbrigg Norf 160 B4
Felcourt Sur 51 E11
Felden Herts 85 E8
Felderland Kent 55 B10
Feldy E Ches 183 F11
Felhampton Shrops 131 F8
Felin-Crai Powys 95 G7
Felin Newydd Carms 94 D3
Felin-newydd Powys 96 D2
Felin Newydd = New Mills Powys 129 C11
Felin Puleston Wrex 166 F4
Felin-Wnda Ceredig 92 B6
Felindre Carms 75 C7
Felindre Carms 93 D7
Felindre Carms 93 G11
Felindre Carms 94 E3
Felindre Carms 94 F4
Felindre Ceredig 111 F10
Felindre Powys 96 D3
Felindre Powys 96 G3
Felindre Powys 130 C3
Felindre Powys 130 G3
Felindre Rhondda 58 C3
Felindre Swansea 75 E10
Felindre Farchog Pembs 92 D2
Felinfach Ceredig 111 F10
Felinfach Powys 95 E11
Felinfoel Carms 75 E8
Felingwmisaf Carms 93 G10
Felingwmuchaf Carms 93 G10
Felinwynt Ceredig 110 G4
Felixkirk N Yorks 215 C9
Felixstowe Suff 108 E5
Felixstowe Ferry Suff 108 D6
Felkington Northumb 273 G8
Felkirk W Yorks 197 E11
Fell End Cumb 222 F4
Fell Lane W Yorks 204 E6
Fell Side Cumb 230 D2
Felldyke Cumb 219 B11
Fellgate T & W 243 E8
Felling T & W 243 E7
Felling Shore T & W 243 E7
Fellside T & W 242 E5
Felmersham Beds 121 F9
Felmingham Norf 160 D5
Felmore Essex 69 B8
Felpham W Sus 35 H7
Felsham Suff 125 F8
Felsted Essex 106 G3
Feltham London 66 E6
Feltham Som 28 D2
Felthamhill London 66 E5
Felthorpe Norf 160 F3
Felton Hereford 97 B11
Felton N Som 60 F4
Felton Northumb 252 C5
Felton Butler Shrops 149 F7
Feltwell Norf 140 E4
Fen Ditton Cambs 123 E9
Fen Drayton Cambs 122 D6
Fen End Lincs 156 E4
Fen End W Mid 118 B4
Fen Side Lincs 174 D4
Fen Street Norf 141 G11
Fen Street Suff 125 B11
Fen Street Suff 125 B9
Fenay Bridge W Yorks 197 D7
Fence Lancs 204 F2
Fence Houses T & W 243 G8
Fencott Oxon 83 B9
Fengate Norf 160 E3
Fengate P'boro 138 D4
Fenham Northumb 273 G11
Fenham T & W 242 D6
Fenhouses Lincs 174 G3
Feniscliffe Blkburn 195 B7
Feniscowles Blkburn 194 B6
Feniton Devon 15 B8
Fenlake Beds 103 B11
Fenn Green Shrops 132 G5
Fenn Street Medway 69 D9
Fennington Som 27 B11
Fenn's Bank Wrex 149 B10
Fenny Bentley Derbys 169 E11
Fenny Bridges Devon 15 B8
Fenny Castle Som 44 E4
Fenny Compton Warks 119 G8
Fenny Drayton Leics 134 D6
Fenny Stratford M Keynes 103 E7
Fenrother Northumb 252 E5
Fenstanton Cambs 122 D6
Fenstead End Suff 124 G6
Fenton Cambs 122 B6
Fenton Cumb 240 F2
Fenton Lincs 172 E5
Fenton Lincs 188 F4
Fenton Northumb 263 C11
Fenton Stoke 168 G5
Fenton Barns E Loth 281 E10
Fenton Low Stoke 168 F5
Fenton Pits Corn 5 C11
Fenton Town Northumb 263 C11
Fentonadle Corn 11 F7
Fenwick E Ayrs 267 G9
Fenwick Northumb 242 C3
Fenwick Northumb 273 G11
Fenwick S Yorks 198 D5
Feochaig Argyll 255 F8
Feock Corn 3 B8
Feolin Ferry Argyll 274 G5
Ferguslie Park Renfs 267 C9
Ferindonald Highld 295 E8
Feriniquarrie Highld 296 F7
Ferlochan Argyll 289 E11
Fern Angus 292 G6
Fern Bucks 65 B11
Fern Bank Gtr Man 185 B7
Fern Hill Suff 106 B6
Ferndale Kent 52 E5
Ferndale Rhondda 77 F7
Ferndown Dorset 31 G9
Ferne Wilts 30 C6
Ferness Highld 301 E9
Ferney Green Cumb 221 F8
Fernham Oxon 82 G3
Fernhill Gtr Man 195 E10
Fernhill Rhondda 77 F8
Fernhill W Sus 51 E10
Fernhill Gate Gtr Man 195 F7
Fernhill Heath Worcs 117 F7
Fernhurst W Sus 34 B5
Fernie Fife 287 F7
Ferniebrae Aberds 303 D9
Ferniegair S Lnrk 268 E4
Ferniehirst Borders 271 G8
Fernilea Highld 294 B5
Fernilee Derbys 185 F8
Fernsplatt Corn 4 G5
Ferrensby N Yorks 215 G7
Ferring W Sus 35 G9
Ferry Hill Cambs 139 G7
Ferry Point Highld 309 L7
Ferrybridge W Yorks 198 C3
Ferryden Angus 287 B11
Ferryhill Aberdeen 293 C11
Ferryhill Durham 233 E11
Ferryhill Station Durham 234 E2
Ferryside = Glan-y-Ffer Carms 74 C5
Ferryton Highld 300 C6
Fersfield Norf 141 G11
Fersit Highld 290 F5
Feshiebridge Highld 291 C10
Fetcham Sur 50 B6
Fetterangus Aberds 303 D9
Fettercairn Aberds 293 F8
Fetterdale Fife 287 E8
Fettes Highld 300 D5
Fewcott Oxon 101 F10
Fewston N Yorks 205 C9
Fewston Bents N Yorks 205 C9
Ffair-Rhos Ceredig 112 D4
Ffairfach Carms 94 G2
Ffaldybrenin Carms 94 C2
Ffarmers Carms 94 C3
Ffawyddog Powys 78 B2
Ffodun = Forden Powys 130 C4
Ffont y gari = Font y gary V Glam 58 F5
Ffordd-las Denb 165 C10
Ffordd-y-Gyfraith Bridgend 57 E11
Fforddlas Powys 96 D4
Fforest Carms 75 E9
Fforest-fach Swansea 56 B6
Fforest Gôch Neath 76 E2
Ffos-y-ffin Ceredig 111 E8
Ffos-y-go Wrex 166 E4
Ffostrasol Ceredig 93 B7
Ffridd Powys 130 D3
Ffrith Wrex 166 D3
Ffrwd Gwyn 163 D7
Ffwl y mwn = Fonmon V Glam 58 F4
Ffynnon Carms 74 B5
Ffynnon ddrain Carms 93 G8
Ffynnon Gron Pembs 91 F8
Ffynnon Gynydd Powys 96 C3
Ffynnon-oer Ceredig 111 G10
Ffynnongroes = Crosswell Pembs 92 D2
Ffynnongroyw Flint 181 E10
Fickleshole Sur 67 G11
Fidden Argyll 288 G5
Fiddes Aberds 293 E10
Fiddington Glos 99 E8
Fiddington Som 43 E8
Fiddington Sands Wilts 46 C4
Fiddleford Dorset 30 E4
Fiddler' Green Norf 141 D10
Fiddler's Ferry Mers 193 C11
Fiddler's Ferry Warr 183 D9
Fiddler's Green Glos 99 G8
Fiddler's Green Hereford 97 D11
Fiddlers Hamlet Essex 87 E7
Field Hereford 114 G6
Field Som 44 E6
Field Staffs 151 C10
Field Assarts Oxon 82 C4
Field Broughton Cumb 211 C7
Field Common Sur 66 F6
Field Dalling Norf 159 B10
Field Green Kent 38 B3
Field Head Leics 135 B9
Fields End Herts 85 D8
Field's Place Hereford 115 G8
Fife Keith Moray 302 D4
Fifehead Magdalen Dorset 30 C3
Fifehead Neville Dorset 30 E3
Fifehead St Quintin Dorset 30 E3
Fifield Oxon 82 B2
Fifield Wilts 46 C6
Fifield Windsor 66 D2
Fifield Bavant Wilts 31 B8
Figheldean Wilts 47 D7
Filands Wilts 62 B2
Filby Norf 161 G9
Filby Heath Norf 161 G9
Filchampstead Oxon 83 D7
Filey N Yorks 218 C2
Filgrave M Keynes 103 B7
Filham Devon 8 D2
Filkins Oxon 82 E2
Filleigh Devon 25 B11
Filleigh Devon 26 E2
Fillingham Lincs 188 D6
Fillongley Warks 134 F5
Filmore Hill Hants 33 B11
Filton S Glos 60 D6
Filwood Park Bristol 60 F5
Fimber E Yorks 217 G7
Finavon Angus 287 B8
Fincastle Ho Perth 291 G10
Finchairn Argyll 275 C10
Fincham Mers 182 C6
Fincham Norf 140 B3
Finchampstead Wokingham 65 G9
Finchdean Hants 34 E2
Finchingfield Essex 106 E3
Finchley London 86 G3
Findern Derbys 152 C6
Findhorn Moray 301 C10
Findhorn Bridge Highld 301 G8
Findo Gask Perth 286 E4
Findochty Moray 302 C4
Findon Aberds 293 D11
Findon W Sus 35 F10
Findon Mains Highld 300 C6
Findon Valley W Sus 35 F10
Findrack Ho Aberds 293 C8
Fine Street Hereford 96 D6
Finedon Northants 121 C8
Fineglen Argyll 275 B10
Fingal Street Suff 126 D4
Fingask Aberds 303 G7
Fingerpost Worcs 116 C4
Fingest Bucks 84 G3
Finghall N Yorks 214 B3
Fingland Cumb 239 F7
Fingland Dumfries 259 F7
Finglesham Kent 55 C10
Fingringhoe Essex 107 G10
Finham W Mid 118 B6
Finkle Street S Yorks 186 B4
Finlarig Stirl 285 D9
Finmere Oxon 102 E2
Finnart Perth 285 B9
Finney Green E Ches 184 E5
Finney Green Staffs 168 F3
Finningham Suff 125 D11
Finningley S Yorks 187 B11
Finnygaud Aberds 302 D5
Finsbury London 67 C10
Finsbury Park London 67 B10
Finstall Worcs 117 D9
Finsthwaite Cumb 211 B7
Finstock Oxon 82 B5
Finstown Orkney 314 E3
Fintry Aberds 303 D7
Fintry Dundee 287 D8
Fintry Stirl 278 D2
Finwood Warks 118 D3
Finzean Aberds 293 D8
Finzean Ho Aberds 293 D7
Fionnphort Argyll 288 G5
Fionnsbhagh W Isles 296 C6
Fir Toll Kent 54 E2
Fir Tree Durham 233 E8
Fir Vale S Yorks 186 C5
Firbank Cumb 222 G2
Firbeck S Yorks 187 D9
Firby N Yorks 214 B5
Firby N Yorks 216 F4
Firemore Highld 307 L3
Firgrove Gtr Man 196 E2
Firkin Argyll 285 G7
Firle E Sus 23 D7
Firs Lane Gtr Man 194 G6
First Coast Highld 307 K4
Firsby Lincs 175 C7
Firsdown Wilts 47 G8
Firswood Gtr Man 184 B4
Firth Borders 262 E2
Firth Moor Darl 224 C6
Firth Park S Yorks 186 C5
Firwood Fold Gtr Man 195 E8
Fishbourne I o W 21 C7
Fishbourne W Sus 22 C4
Fishburn Durham 234 E3
Fishcross Clack 279 B7
Fisher Place Cumb 220 B6
Fisherford Aberds 302 F6
Fishermead M Keynes 103 D7
Fisherrow E Loth 280 G6
Fishers Green Herts 104 F4
Fisher's Pond Hants 33 C7
Fishersgate Brighton 36 F3
Fisherstreet W Sus 50 G3
Fisherton Highld 301 D7
Fisherton S Ayrs 257 F7
Fisherton de la Mere Wilts 46 F4
Fisherwick Staffs 134 B3
Fishery Windsor 65 C11
Fishguard = Abergwaun Pembs 91 D9
Fishlake S Yorks 199 E7
Fishleigh Devon 25 F8
Fishleigh Barton Devon 25 C9
Fishleigh Castle Devon 25 F8
Fishley Norf 161 G8
Fishley W Mid 133 C10
Fishmere End Lincs 156 B5
Fishponds Bristol 60 D6
Fishpool Glos 98 F3
Fishpool Gtr Man 195 F10
Fishpool N Yorks 205 D10
Fishpools Powys 114 D3
Fishtoft Lincs 174 G5
Fishtoft Drove Lincs 174 F4
Fishtown of Usan Angus 287 B11
Fishwick Borders 273 E8
Fishwick Lancs 194 B5
Fiskavaig Highld 294 B5
Fiskerton Lincs 189 G8
Fiskerton Notts 172 E2
Fitling E Yorks 209 G11
Fittleton Wilts 46 D6
Fittleworth W Sus 35 D8
Fitton End Cambs 157 G8
Fitton Hill Gtr Man 196 G2
Fitz Shrops 149 F8
Fitzhead Som 27 B10
Fitzwilliam W Yorks 198 D2
Fiunary Highld 289 E8
Five Acres Glos 79 C9
Five Ash Down E Sus 37 C7
Five Ashes E Sus 37 C9
Five Bells Som 42 E5
Five Bridges Hereford 98 B3
Five Houses I o W 20 D4
Five Lane Ends Lancs 202 C6
Five Lanes Mon 78 G6
Five Oak Green Kent 52 D6
Five Oaks W Sus 35 B9
Five Roads Carms 75 D7
Five Ways Warks 118 D4
Five Wents Kent 53 C10
Fivecrosses W Ches 183 F8
Fivehead Som 28 C5
Fivelanes Corn 11 E10
Fixby W Yorks 196 C6
Flackley Ash E Sus 38 C5
Flack's Green Essex 88 B3
Flackwell Heath Bucks 65 B11
Fladbury Worcs 99 B9
Fladbury Cross Worcs 99 B9
Fladda Shetland 312 E5
Fladdabister Shetland 313 K6
Flagg Derbys 169 B10
Flaggoners Green Hereford 116 G2
Flamborough E Yorks 218 E4
Flamstead Herts 85 C9
Flamstead End Herts 86 E4
Flansham W Sus 35 G7
Flanshaw W Yorks 197 C10
Flappit Spring W Yorks 205 F7
Flasby N Yorks 204 B4
Flash Staffs 169 B8
Flashader Highld 298 D3
Flask Inn N Yorks 227 E8
Flathurst W Sus 35 C7
Flaunden Herts 85 E8
Flawborough Notts 172 G3
Flawith N Yorks 215 F9
Flax Bourton N Som 60 F4
Flax Moss Lancs 195 C9
Flaxby N Yorks 206 B3
Flaxholme Derbys 170 G4
Flaxlands Norf 142 E2
Flaxley Glos 79 B11
Flaxpool Som 42 F6
Flaxton N Yorks 216 G3
Fleckney Leics 136 E2
Flecknoe Warks 119 E10
Fledborough Notts 188 G4
Fleet Dorset 17 E8
Fleet Hants 22 C2
Fleet Hants 49 C10
Fleet Lincs 157 E7
Fleet Downs Kent 68 E5
Fleet Hargate Lincs 157 E7
Fleetend Hants 33 F8
Fleetlands Hants 33 G9
Fleets N Yorks 213 G9
Fleetville Herts 85 D11
Fleetwood Lancs 202 D2
Fleggburgh = Burgh St Margaret Norf 161 G8
Fleming Field Durham 234 C3
Flemings Kent 55 B9
Flemingston V Glam 58 E4
Flemington S Lnrk 268 D3
Flemington S Lnrk 268 G4
Flempton Suff 124 D6
Fleoideabhagh W Isles 296 C6
Fletcher's Green Kent 52 C4
Fletchersbridge Corn 6 B2
Fletchertown Cumb 229 C10
Fletching E Sus 36 C6

Fle – Gar 333

Fletching Common E Sus 36 C6
Fleuchary Highld 309 K7
Fleuchlang Dumfries 237 D8
Fleur-de-lis Caerph 77 F11
Flexbury Corn 24 F2
Flexford Hants 32 C6
Flexford Sur 50 D2
Flimby Cumb 228 E6
Flimwell E Sus 53 G8
Flint Flint 182 G2
Flint Cross Cambs 105 C8
Flint Hill Durham 242 G5
Flint Mountain = Mynydd Fflint Flint 182 G2
Flintham Notts 172 F2
Flinton E Yorks 209 F10
Flint's Green W Mid 134 G5
Flintsham Hereford 114 F6
Flishinghurst Kent 53 F9
Flitcham Norf 158 D4
Flitholme Cumb 222 B5
Flitton C Beds 103 D11
Flitwick C Beds 103 D10
Flixborough N Lincs 199 D11
Flixborough Stather N Lincs 199 E11
Flixton Gtr Man 184 C2
Flixton N Yorks 217 D10
Flixton Suff 142 F6
Flockton W Yorks 197 E8
Flockton Green W Yorks 197 D8
Flockton Moor W Yorks 197 E8
Flodaigh W Isles 296 F4
Flodden Northumb 263 B10
Flodigarry Highld 298 B4
Flood Street Hants 31 D10
Floodgates Hereford 114 F5
Flood's Ferry Cambs 139 E7
Flookburgh Cumb 211 D7
Flordon Norf 142 D3
Flore Northants 120 E2
Florence Stoke 168 G6
Flotterton Northumb 251 C11
Flowers Bottom Bucks 84 F4
Flowers Green E Sus 23 C10
Flowery Field Gtr Man 184 B6
Flowton Suff 107 B11
Fluchter E Dunb 277 G11
Flugarth Shetland 313 G6
Flush House W Yorks 196 F6
Flushdyke W Yorks 197 C9
Flushing Aberds 303 E10
Flushing Corn 3 C8
Flushing Corn 3 D7
Flyford Flavell Worcs 117 G9
Foals Green Suff 126 C5
Fobbing Thurrock 69 C8
Fochabers Moray 302 D3
Fochriw Caerph 77 D10
Fockerby N Lincs 199 D10
Fodderletter Moray 301 G11
Fodderstone Gap Norf 140 B3
Fodderty Highld 300 D5
Foddington Som 29 B9
Foel Powys 147 G9
Foel-gastell Carms 75 C8
Foffarty Angus 287 C8
Foggathorpe E Yorks 207 F11
Foggbrook Gtr Man 184 D6
Fogo Borders 272 F5
Fogorig Borders 272 F5
Fogrigarth Shetland 313 H4
Fogwatt Moray 302 D2
Foindle Highld 306 E6
Fold Head Lancs 195 D11
Fold Hill Lincs 175 E7
Folda Angus 292 G3
Foldrings S Yorks 186 C3
Fole Staffs 151 B10
Foleshill W Mid 135 G7
Foley Park Worcs 116 B6
Folke Dorset 29 E11
Folkestone Kent 55 F8
Folkingham Lincs 155 C11
Folkington E Sus 23 E9
Folksworth Cambs 138 F2
Folkton N Yorks 217 D11
Folla Rule Aberds 303 F7
Folley Shrops 132 D5
Follifoot N Yorks 206 C2
Follingsby T & W 243 E8
Folly Dorset 30 G2
Folly Pembs 91 G8
Folly Cross Devon 25 F7
Folly Gate Devon 13 B7
Folly Green Essex 106 F6
Fonmon = Ffwl-y-mwn V Glam 58 F4
Fonston Corn 11 C10
Font-y-gary = Ffont-y-gari V Glam 58 F5
Fonthill Bishop Wilts 46 G2
Fonthill Gifford Wilts 46 G2
Fontmell Magna Dorset 30 D5
Fontmell Parva Dorset 30 E4
Fontwell W Sus 35 F7
Foodieash Fife 287 F7
Foolow Derbys 185 F11
Footbridge Glos 99 F10
Footherley Staffs 134 C2
Footrid Worcs 116 C3
Foots Cray London 68 E3
Forbestown Aberds 292 B5
Force Forge Cumb 220 G6
Force Green Kent 52 B2
Force Mills Cumb 220 G6
Forcett N Yorks 224 C3
Ford Argyll 275 C9
Ford Bucks 84 D3
Ford Derbys 186 E6
Ford Devon 8 E2
Ford Devon 8 G5
Ford Devon 24 C6
Ford Devon 28 G2
Ford Glos 99 F11
Ford Hereford 115 F10
Ford Kent 71 F8
Ford Mers 182 B4
Ford Northumb 263 B10
Ford Pembs 91 F9
Ford Plym 7 D9
Ford Shrops 149 G8
Ford Som 27 B9
Ford Som 44 C5
Ford Staffs 169 E9
Ford W Sus 35 G7
Ford Wilts 47 G7
Ford Wilts 61 E10
Ford End Essex 87 B11
Ford End Essex 105 E9
Ford Forge Northumb 263 B10
Ford Green Lancs 202 D5
Ford Green Stoke 168 E5
Ford Heath Shrops 149 G8
Ford Hill Northumb 263 B11
Ford Street Som 27 D11
Forda Devon 12 C6
Forda Devon 40 F3
Fordbridge W Mid 134 F3
Fordcombe Kent 52 E4
Fordell Fife 280 D3
Forden = Ffodun Powys 130 C4
Forder Corn 7 D8
Forder Green Devon 8 B5
Fordgate Som 43 G10
Fordham Cambs 124 C2
Fordham Essex 107 F8
Fordham Norf 140 D2
Fordham Heath Essex 107 F8
Fordhouses W Mid 133 C8
Fordingbridge Hants 31 E10
Fordington Lincs 190 G6
Fordley T & W 243 C7
Fordon E Yorks 217 D10
Fordoun Aberds 293 F9
Ford's Green E Sus 36 B6
Ford's Green Suff 125 D11
Fordstreet Essex 107 F8
Fordton Devon 14 B2
Fordwater Devon 28 G4
Fordwells Oxon 82 C4
Fordwich Kent 55 B7
Fordyce Aberds 302 C5
Forebridge Staffs 151 E8
Foredale N Yorks 212 F6
Forehill S Ayrs 257 E8
Foreland Fields I o W 21 D9
Foreland Ho Argyll 274 G3
Foremark Derbys 152 D6
Forest Lodge Argyll 284 C6
Forest Lodge Highld 292 B2
Forest Lodge Perth 291 F11
Forest Becks Lancs 203 C11
Forest Coal Pit Mon 96 G5
Forest Gate Hants 33 E10
Forest Gate London 68 C2
Forest Green Glos 80 E4
Forest Green Sur 50 E6
Forest Hall Cumb 221 E10
Forest Hall T & W 243 D7
Forest Head Cumb 240 F3
Forest Hill London 67 E11
Forest Hill Oxon 83 D9
Forest Hill Wilts 63 F8
Forest Holme Lancs 195 B10
Forest-in-Teesdale Durham 232 F3
Forest Lane Head N Yorks 206 B2
Forest Mill Clack 279 C9
Forest Moor N Yorks 206 B2
Forest Row E Sus 52 G2
Forest Side I o W 20 D5
Forest Town Notts 171 C9
Forestburn Gate Northumb 252 D3
Forestdale London 67 G11
Foresterseat Moray 301 D11
Forestreet Devon 24 E5
Forestside W Sus 34 E3
Forewoods Common Wilts 61 G10
Forfar Angus 287 B8
Forgandenny Perth 286 F4
Forge Corn 4 F3
Forge Powys 128 D5
Forge Hammer Torf 78 F3
Forge Side Torf 78 D2
Forgewood N Lnrk 268 D4
Forgie Moray 302 D3
Forglen Ho Aberds 302 D6
Forgue Aberds 302 E6
Forhill Worcs 117 B11
Formby Mers 193 F10
Forncett End Norf 142 E2
Forncett St Mary Norf 142 E3
Forncett St Peter Norf 142 E3
Forneth Perth 286 C4
Fornham All Saints Suff 124 D6
Fornham St Genevieve Suff 124 D6
Fornham St Martin Suff 125 D7
Fornighty Highld 301 D9
Forrabury Corn 11 C7
Forres Moray 301 D10
Forrest Lodge Dumfries 246 F3
Forrestfield N Lnrk 269 B7
Forry's Green Essex 106 E5
Forsbrook Staffs 169 G7
Forse Highld 310 F6
Forse Ho Highld 310 F6
Forshaw Heath Warks 117 C11
Forsinain Highld 310 E3
Forsinard Highld 310 E2
Forsinard Station Highld 310 E2
Forstal Kent 53 B8
Forston Dorset 17 B9
Fort Augustus Highld 290 C5
Fort George Highld 301 D7
Fort Matilda Invclyd 276 F5
Fort William Highld 290 F3
Forteviot Perth 286 F4
Forth S Lnrk 269 E8
Forth Road Bridge Edin 280 F2
Forthampton Glos 99 E7
Forthay Glos 80 F2
Fortingall Perth 285 C11
Fortis Green London 67 B9
Forton Hants 33 G10
Forton Hants 48 E2
Forton Lancs 202 C5
Forton Shrops 149 F8
Forton Som 28 F4
Forton Staffs 150 E5
Forton Heath Shrops 149 F8
Fortrie Aberds 302 E6
Fortrie Aberds 303 D7
Fortrose Highld 301 D7
Fortuneswell Dorset 17 G9
Forty Green Bucks 84 E3
Forty Green Bucks 84 G6
Forty Hill London 86 F4
Forward Green Suff 125 F11
Forwood Glos 80 E5
Fosbury Wilts 47 B10
Foscot Oxon 100 G4
Foscote Bucks 102 D4
Foscote Northants 102 B3
Foscote Wilts 61 D11
Fosdyke Lincs 156 C6
Fosdyke Bridge Lincs 156 C6
Foss Perth 285 B11
Foss Cross Glos 81 D9
Fossebridge Glos 81 C9
Fostall Kent 70 G5
Fosten Green Kent 53 F10
Foster Street Essex 87 D7
Fosterhouses S Yorks 199 E7
Foster's Booth Northants 120 G3
Foster's Green Worcs 117 D9
Foston Derbys 152 C3
Foston Leics 136 D2
Foston Lincs 172 G5
Foston N Yorks 216 F3
Foston on the Wolds E Yorks 209 B8
Fotherby Lincs 190 C4
Fothergill Cumb 228 E6
Fotheringhay Northants 137 E11
Foubister Orkney 314 F5
Foul Anchor Cambs 157 F9
Foul End Warks 134 E4
Foul Mile E Sus 23 B10
Foulbridge Cumb 230 B4
Foulby W Yorks 197 D11
Foulden Borders 273 D8
Foulden Norf 140 D5
Foulford Hants 31 F11
Foulis Castle Highld 300 C5
Foulride Green E Sus 23 E9
Foulridge Lancs 204 E3
Foulsham Norf 159 E10
Foundry Corn 2 B3
Foundry Hill Norf 159 D11
Fountain Bridgend 57 E11
Fountainhall Borders 271 F8
Four Ashes Bucks 84 F5
Four Ashes Staffs 132 F6
Four Ashes Staffs 133 B8
Four Ashes Suff 125 C10
Four Ashes W Mid 118 B3
Four Crosses Powys 129 B11
Four Crosses Powys 148 F5
Four Crosses Staffs 133 B9
Four Crosses Wrex 166 E3
Four Elms Devon 28 F3
Four Elms Kent 52 D3
Four Foot Som 44 G5
Four Forks Som 43 F8
Four Gates Gtr Man 194 F6
Four Gotes Cambs 157 F9
Four Houses Corner W Berks 64 F6
Four Lane End S Yorks 197 G9
Four Lane Ends Blkburn 195 B7
Four Lane Ends Gtr Man 195 E9
Four Lane Ends W Ches 167 C9
Four Lane Ends W Yorks 205 G8
Four Lanes Corn 2 B5
Four Marks Hants 49 G7
Four Mile Bridge Anglesey 178 F3
Four Mile Elm Glos 80 C4
Four Oaks E Sus 38 C5
Four Oaks Glos 98 F3
Four Oaks Kent 70 G3
Four Oaks W Mid 134 D2
Four Oaks W Mid 134 G4
Four Oaks Park W Mid 134 D2
Four Points W Berks 64 D5
Four Pools Worcs 99 C10
Four Roads Carms 74 D6
Four Roads I o M 192 F3
Four Throws Kent 38 B3
Four Wantz Essex 87 C10
Four Wents Kent 53 F9
Fourlane Ends Derbys 170 D5
Fourlanes End E Ches 168 D4
Fourpenny Highld 311 K2
Fourstones Northumb 241 D9
Fovant Wilts 31 B8
Foveran Aberds 303 G9
Fowey Corn 6 E2
Fowler's Plot Som 43 F10
Fowley Common Warr 183 B11
Fowlis Angus 287 D7
Fowlis Wester Perth 286 E3
Fowlmere Cambs 105 B8
Fownhope Hereford 97 E11
Fox Corner C Beds 103 F8
Fox Corner Sur 50 C3
Fox Hatch Essex 87 F9
Fox Hill Bath 61 G9
Fox Hill Hereford 98 B3
Fox Hole Swansea 56 D5
Fox Holes Wilts 45 E11
Fox Lane Hants 49 B11
Fox Royd W Yorks 197 D8
Fox Street Essex 107 F10
Foxash Estate Essex 107 E11
Foxbar Renfs 267 C9
Foxbury London 68 E2
Foxcombe Hill Oxon 83 E7
Foxcote Glos 81 B8
Foxcote Som 45 B8
Foxdale I o M 192 E3
Foxdown Hants 48 C4
Foxearth Essex 106 C6
Foxendown Kent 69 F7
Foxfield Cumb 210 B4
Foxford W Mid 135 G7
Foxham Wilts 62 D3
Foxhills Hants 32 E4
Foxhole Corn 5 E9
Foxhole Norf 142 D4
Foxhole Swansea 57 C7
Foxholes N Yorks 217 E10
Foxhunt Green E Sus 23 B8
Foxley Hereford 97 B8
Foxley Norf 159 E10
Foxley Staffs 168 E3
Foxley Wilts 61 B11
Foxlydiate Worcs 117 D10
Foxt Staffs 169 F8
Foxton Cambs 105 B8
Foxton Durham 234 F3
Foxton Leics 136 E4
Foxton N Yorks 225 F8
Foxup N Yorks 213 D7
Foxwist Green W Ches 167 B10
Foxwood Shrops 116 B2
Foy Hereford 97 F11
Foyers Highld 300 G4
Foynesfield Highld 301 D8
Fraddam Corn 2 C3
Fraddon Corn 5 D8
Fradley Staffs 152 G3
Fradley Junction Staffs 152 G2
Fradswell Staffs 151 C9
Fraisthorpe E Yorks 218 G3
Framfield E Sus 37 C7
Framingham Earl Norf 142 C5
Framingham Pigot Norf 142 C5
Framlingham Suff 126 E5
Frampton Dorset 17 B8
Frampton Lincs 156 B6
Frampton Cotterell S Glos 61 C7
Frampton Court Glos 99 E10
Frampton End S Glos 61 C7
Frampton Mansell Glos 80 E6
Frampton on Severn Glos 80 D2
Frampton West End Lincs 174 G3
Framsden Suff 126 F3
Framwellgate Moor Durham 233 C11
France Lynch Glos 80 E6
Franche Worcs 116 B6
Frandley W Ches 183 F10
Frankby Mers 182 D2
Frankfort Norf 160 E6
Franklands Gate Hereford 97 B10
Frankley Worcs 133 G9
Frankley Green Worcs 133 G9
Frankley Hill Worcs 117 B9
Frank's Bridge Powys 114 F2
Frankton Warks 119 C8
Frankwell Shrops 149 G9
Frans Green Norf 160 G2
Frant E Sus 52 F5
Fraserburgh Aberds 303 C9
Frating Essex 107 G11
Frating Green Essex 107 G11
Fratton Ptsmth 21 B9
Freasley Warks 134 D4
Freathy Corn 7 E8
Frecheville S Yorks 186 E5
Freckenham Suff 124 C3
Freckleton Lancs 194 B2
Fredley Sur 51 C7
Free Town Gtr Man 195 E10
Freebirch Derbys 186 G4
Freeby Leics 154 E6
Freefolk Hants 48 D3
Freehay Staffs 169 G8
Freeland Oxon 82 C6
Freeland Renfs 267 B9
Freeland Corner Norf 160 F3
Freemantle Soton 32 E6
Freeport Village W Loth 269 C10
Freester Shetland 313 H6
Freethorpe Norf 143 B8
Freezy Water London 86 F5
Freiston Lincs 174 G5
Freiston Shore Lincs 174 G5
Fremington Devon 40 G4
Fremington N Yorks 223 F10
French Street Kent 52 C3
Frenchay S Glos 60 D6
Frenchbeer Devon 13 D9
Frenches Green Essex 106 G4
Frenchmoor Hants 32 B3
Frenchwood Lancs 194 B4
Frenich Stirl 285 G8
Frensham Sur 49 E10
Frenze Norf 142 G2
Fresgoe Highld 310 C3
Freshbrook Swindon 62 C6
Freshfield Mers 193 F9
Freshford Bath 61 G9
Freshwater I o W 20 D2
Freshwater Bay I o W 20 D2
Freshwater East Pembs 73 F8
Fressingfield Suff 126 B5
Freston Suff 108 D3
Freswick Highld 310 C7
Fretherne Glos 80 D2
Frettenham Norf 160 F4
Freuchie Fife 286 G6
Freuchies Angus 292 G4
Freystrop Pembs 73 C7
Friar Park W Mid 133 E10
Friarn Som 43 F7
Friars Cliff Dorset 19 C9
Friar's Gate E Sus 52 G3
Friar's Hill E Sus 38 E5
Friarton Perth 286 E5
Friday Bridge Cambs 139 C9
Friday Hill London 86 G5
Friday Street E Sus 23 E10
Friday Street Suff 126 G6
Friday Street Suff 127 E7
Friday Street Sur 50 D6
Fridaythorpe E Yorks 208 B3
Friendly W Yorks 196 C5
Friern Barnet London 86 G3
Friesland Argyll 288 D3
Friesthorpe Lincs 189 E9
Frieston Lincs 172 F6
Frieth Bucks 84 G3
Frieze Hill Som 28 B2
Friezeland Notts 171 E7
Frilford Oxon 82 F6
Frilford Heath Oxon 82 F6
Frilsham W Berks 64 E4
Frimley Sur 49 B11
Frimley Green Sur 49 B11
Frimley Ridge Sur 49 B11
Frindsbury Medway 69 E8
Fring Norf 158 C4
Fringford Oxon 102 F2
Friningham Kent 53 B10
Frinkle Green Essex 106 C4
Frinsted Kent 53 B11
Frinton-on-Sea Essex 108 G4
Friockheim Angus 287 C9
Friog Gwyn 146 G2
Frisby Leics 136 C4
Frisby on the Wreake Leics 154 F3
Friskney Lincs 175 D7
Friskney Eaudyke Lincs 175 D7
Friskney Tofts Lincs 175 E7
Friston E Sus 23 F8
Friston Suff 127 E8
Fritchley Derbys 170 E5
Frith Kent 54 B2
Frith Bank Lincs 174 F4
Frith Common Worcs 116 D3
Frith-hill Bucks 84 E6
Frith Hill Sur 50 E3
Fritham Hants 32 E2
Frithelstock Devon 25 D7
Frithelstock Stone Devon 25 D7
Frithend Hants 49 F10
Frithsden Herts 85 D8
Frithville Lincs 174 E4
Frittenden Kent 53 E10
Frittiscombe Devon 8 G6
Fritton Norf 142 E4
Fritton Norf 143 C9
Fritton Norf 161 F8
Fritwell Oxon 101 F10
Frizinghall W Yorks 205 F8
Frizington Cumb 219 B10
Frizzeler's Green Suff 124 E5
Frobost W Isles 297 J3
Frocester Glos 80 E3
Frochas Powys 148 G5
Frodesley Shrops 131 C10
Frodingham N Lincs 199 E11
Frodsham W Ches 183 F8
Frog End Cambs 123 F10
Frog End Cambs 123 G8
Frog Moor Swansea 56 C3
Frog Pool Worcs 116 D5
Frogden Borders 263 D7
Froggatt Derbys 186 F2
Froghall Staffs 169 F8
Frogham Hants 31 E11
Frogham Kent 55 C9
Froghole Kent 52 C2
Frogholt Kent 55 F7
Frogland Cross S Glos 60 C6
Frogmore Devon 8 G5
Frogmore Hants 33 C11
Frogmore Hants 49 B10
Frogmore Herts 85 E11
Frognal S Ayrs 257 D8
Frognall Lincs 156 G3
Frogpool Corn 4 G5
Frogs' Green Essex 105 D11
Frogshail Norf 160 B5
Frogwell Corn 6 B6
Frolesworth Leics 135 E10
Frome St Quintin Dorset 29 G9
Fromebridge Glos 80 D3
Fromefield Som 45 D9
Fromes Hill Hereford 98 B3
Fromington Hereford 97 B10
Fron Denb 165 B9
Fron Gwyn 145 B7
Fron Gwyn 163 D8
Fron Powys 113 D11
Fron Powys 129 C8
Fron Powys 130 C4
Fron Powys 130 D3
Fron Shrops 148 B5
Fron-Bache Denb 166 G2
Fron-dêg Wrex 166 F3
Fron Isaf Wrex 166 G3
Froncysyllte Wrex 166 G3
Frongoch Gwyn 147 B8
Frost Devon 26 F3
Frost Hill N Som 60 G2
Frost Row Norf 141 C10
Frostenden Suff 143 G9
Frostenden Corner Suff 143 G9
Frosterley Durham 232 D6
Frostlane Hants 32 F6
Frotoft Orkney 314 D4
Froxfield C Beds 103 E9
Froxfield Wilts 63 F9
Froxfield Green Hants 34 B2
Froyle Hants 49 E9
Fryern Hill Hants 32 C6
Fryerning Essex 87 E10
Fryerns Essex 69 B8
Fryton N Yorks 216 E3
Fugglestone St Peter Wilts 46 G6
Fulbeck Lincs 172 E6
Fulbeck Northumb 252 F5
Fulbourn Cambs 123 F10
Fulbrook Oxon 82 C3
Fulflood Hants 33 B7
Fulford Som 28 B2
Fulford Staffs 151 B9
Fulford York 207 D8
Fulham London 67 D8
Fulking W Sus 36 E2
Full Sutton E Yorks 207 B10
Fullabrook Devon 40 E4
Fullarton Glasgow 268 C2
Fullarton N Ayrs 257 B8
Fuller Street Essex 88 B2
Fuller's End Essex 105 F10
Fuller's Moor W Ches 167 E7
Fullerton Hants 47 F11
Fulletby Lincs 190 G3
Fullshaw S Yorks 197 G8
Fullwell Cross London 86 G6
Fullwood E Ayrs 267 E8
Fullwood Gtr Man 196 F2
Fulmer Bucks 66 B3
Fulmodestone Norf 159 C9
Fulneck W Yorks 205 G10
Fulnetby Lincs 189 F9
Fulney Lincs 156 E5
Fulready Warks 100 B5
Fulshaw Park E Ches 184 E4
Fulstone W Yorks 197 F7
Fulstow Lincs 190 B4
Fulthorpe Stockton 234 G4
Fulwell Oxon 101 G7
Fulwell T & W 243 F9
Fulwood Lancs 202 G6
Fulwood S Yorks 186 D4
Fulwood Som 28 C2
Fundenhall Norf 142 D3
Fundenhall Street Norf 142 D2
Funtington W Sus 22 B3
Funtley Hants 33 F9
Funtullich Perth 285 E11
Funzie Shetland 312 D8
Furley Devon 28 G3
Furnace Argyll 284 G4
Furnace Carms 74 E6
Furnace Carms 75 E8
Furnace Ceredig 128 D3
Furnace Highld 299 B9
Furnace End Warks 134 E4
Furnace Green W Sus 51 F9
Furnace Wood W Sus 51 F11
Furneaux Pelham Herts 105 F8
Furner's Green E Sus 36 B6
Furness Vale Derbys 185 E8
Furneux Pelham Herts 105 F8
Furnham Som 28 F4
Further Ford End Essex 105 E9
Further Quarter Kent 53 F11
Furtho Northants 102 C5
Furze Devon 25 B10
Furze Hill Hants 31 E11
Furze Platt Windsor 65 C11
Furzebrook Dorset 18 E4
Furzedown Hants 32 B5
Furzedown London 67 E9
Furzehill Devon 41 D8
Furzehill Dorset 31 G8
Furzeley Corner Hants 33 E11
Furzey Lodge Hants 32 G5
Furzley Hants 32 D3
Furzton M Keynes 102 D6
Fyfett Som 28 E2
Fyfield Essex 87 D9
Fyfield Glos 82 E2
Fyfield Hants 47 D9
Fyfield Oxon 82 F6
Fyfield Wilts 63 F7
Fyfield Wilts 63 G7
Fylingthorpe N Yorks 227 D8
Fyning W Sus 34 C4
Fyvie Aberds 303 F7

G

Gabalfa Cardiff 59 D7
Gabhsann bho Dheas W Isles 304 C6
Gabhsann bho Thuath W Isles 304 C6
Gable Head Hants 21 B10
Gablon Highld 309 K7
Gabroc Hill E Ayrs 267 E9
Gadbrook Sur 51 D8
Gaddesby Leics 154 G3
Gadebridge Herts 85 D8
Gadfa Anglesey 179 D7
Gadfield Elm Worcs 98 E5
Gadlas Shrops 149 B7
Gadlys Rhondda 77 E7
Gadshill Kent 69 E8
Gaer Newport 59 B9
Gaer Powys 96 G3
Gaer-fawr Mon 78 F6
Gaerllwyd Mon 78 F6
Gaerwen Anglesey 179 G7
Gagingwell Oxon 101 F8
Gaick Lodge Highld 291 E9
Gailey Staffs 151 G8
Gailey Wharf Staffs 151 G8
Gain Hill Kent 53 D8
Gainfield Oxon 82 F4
Gainford Durham 224 B3
Gainsborough Lincs 188 C4
Gainsborough Suff 108 C3
Gainsford End Essex 106 D4
Gairletter Argyll 276 E3
Gairloch Highld 299 B8
Gairlochy Highld 290 E3
Gairney Bank Perth 280 B2
Gairnshiel Lodge Aberds 292 C4
Gaisgill Cumb 222 D2
Gaitsgill Cumb 230 B3
Galadean Borders 271 G11
Galashiels Borders 261 B11
Galdlys Flint 182 G2
Gale Gtr Man 196 D2
Galgate Lancs 202 B5
Galhampton Som 29 B10
Gallaberry Dumfries 247 G11
Gallachoille Argyll 275 E8
Gallanach Argyll 288 C4
Gallanach Argyll 289 G10
Gallanach Highld 294 G6
Gallantry Bank E Ches 167 E8
Gallatown Fife 280 C5
Galley Common Warks 134 E6
Galley Hill Cambs 122 D6
Galley Hill Lincs 190 F6
Galleyend Essex 88 E2
Galleywood Essex 88 E2
Galligill Cumb 231 B11
Gallin Perth 285 C9
Gallovie Highld 291 E7
Gallowfauld Angus 287 C8
Gallowhill Glasgow 267 D11
Gallowhill Renfs 267 B9
Gallowhills Aberds 303 D10
Gallows Corner London 87 G8
Gallows Green Essex 106 F2
Gallows Green Essex 107 F8
Gallows Green Staffs 169 G9
Gallows Green Worcs 117 E8
Gallows Inn Derbys 171 G7
Gallowsgreen Torf 78 D3
Gallowstree Common Oxon 65 C7
Gallt Melyd = Meliden Denb 181 E9
Gallt-y-foel Gwyn 163 C9
Galltair Highld 295 C10
Galltegfa Denb 165 D10
Gallypot Street E Sus 52 F3
Galmington Som 28 C2
Galmisdale Highld 294 G6
Galmpton Devon 8 G3
Galmpton Torbay 9 D7
Galon Uchaf M Tydf 77 D9
Galphay N Yorks 214 E5
Galston E Ayrs 258 B2
Galtrigill Highld 296 F7
Gam Corn 11 F7
Gamble Hill W Yorks 205 G11
Gamble's Green Essex 88 C3
Gamblesby Cumb 231 D8
Gamelsby Cumb 239 G7
Gamesley Derbys 185 C8
Gamlingay Cambs 122 G4
Gamlingay Cinques Cambs 122 G4
Gamlingay Great Heath Cambs 122 G4
Gammaton Devon 25 B7
Gammaton Moor Devon 25 C7
Gammersgill N Yorks 213 C11
Gamston Notts 154 B2
Gamston Notts 188 F2
Ganarew Hereford 79 B8
Ganavan Argyll 289 F10
Ganders Green Glos 98 G4
Gang Corn 6 B6
Ganllwyd Gwyn 146 E4
Gannetts Dorset 30 D3
Gannochy Angus 293 F7
Gannochy Perth 286 E5
Gansclet Highld 310 E7
Ganstead E Yorks 209 G9
Ganthorpe N Yorks 216 E3
Ganton N Yorks 217 D9
Gants Hill London 68 B2
Ganwick Corner Herts 86 F3
Gaodhail Argyll 289 F8
Gappah Devon 14 F3
Garafad Highld 298 C4
Garamor Highld 295 F8
Garbat Highld 300 C4
Garbhallt Argyll 275 D11
Garboldisham Norf 141 G10
Garbole Highld 301 G7
Garden City Bl Gwent 77 D11
Garden City Flint 166 B4
Garden Village S Yorks 186 B3
Garden Village Swansea 56 B5
Garden Village W Yorks 206 G4
Garden Village Wrex 166 E4
Gardeners Green Wokingham 65 F10
Gardenstown Aberds 303 C7
Garderhouse Shetland 313 J5
Gardham E Yorks 208 E5
Gardie Shetland 312 D7
Gardin Shetland 312 G6
Gare Hill Som 45 E9
Garelochhead Argyll 276 C4
Garford Oxon 82 F6
Garforth W Yorks 206 G4
Gargrave N Yorks 204 C4
Gargunnock Stirl 278 C4
Garizim Conwy 179 F11
Garker Corn 5 E10
Garlandhayes Devon 27 D11
Garlands Cumb 239 G10
Garleffin S Ayrs 244 G3
Garlic Street Norf 142 G4
Garlieston Dumfries 236 E6
Garliford Devon 26 B3
Garlinge Kent 71 F10
Garlinge Green Kent 54 C6
Garlogie Aberds 293 C9
Garmelow Staffs 150 D5
Garmond Aberds 303 D8
Garmondsway Durham 234 E2
Garmony Argyll 289 E8
Garmouth Moray 302 C3
Garmston Shrops 132 B2
Garn Powys 130 G2
Garn-swllt Swansea 75 D10
Garn-yr-erw Torf 78 C2
Garnant Carms 75 C11
Garndiffaith Torf 78 E3
Garndolbenmaen Gwyn 163 G7
Garnedd Conwy 164 E2
Garnett Bridge Cumb 221 F10
Garnetts Essex 87 B10
Garnfadryn Gwyn 144 C5
Garnkirk N Lnrk 268 B3

Garnlydan Bl Gwent 77 C11
Garnsgate Lincs 157 E8
Garnswllt Swansea 75 D10
Garra Eallabus Argyll 274 F3
Garrabost W Isles 304 E7
Garrachra Argyll 275 E11
Garralburn Moray 302 D4
Garraron Argyll 275 C9
Garras Corn 2 E6
Garreg Flint 181 F10
Garreg Gwyn 163 G10
Garrets Green W Mid 134 F2
Garrick Perth 286 F2
Garrigill Cumb 231 C10
Garrison Stirl 285 G7
Garriston N Yorks 224 G3
Garroch Dumfries 246 G3
Garrogie Lodge Highld 291 B7
Garros Highld 298 C4
Garrow Perth 286 C2
Garrowhill Glasgow 268 C3
Garrygualach Highld 290 C3
Garryhorn Dumfries 246 E2
Garsdale Cumb 212 B4
Garsdale Head Cumb 222 G5
Garsdon Wilts 62 B3
Garshall Green Staffs 151 C9
Garsington Oxon 83 E9
Garstang Lancs 202 D5
Garston Herts 85 F10
Garston Mers 182 E6
Garswood Mers 183 B9
Gartachoil Stirl 277 C10
Gartbreck Argyll 254 B3
Gartcosh N Lnrk 268 B3
Garth Bridgend 57 C11
Garth Ceredig 128 G2
Garth Flint 181 E10
Garth Gwyn 179 G9
Garth Newport 59 B9
Garth Newport 78 G4
Garth Perth 285 B11
Garth Powys 95 B9
Garth Powys 114 C5
Garth Shetland 313 H4
Garth Shetland 313 H6
Garth Wrex 166 G3
Garth Owen Powys 130 E2
Garth Row Cumb 221 F10
Garth Trevor Wrex 166 G3
Garthamlock Glasgow 268 B3
Garthbeg Highld 291 B7
Garthbrengy Powys 95 E10
Garthdee Aberdeen 293 C11
Gartheli Ceredig 111 F11
Garthmyl Powys 130 D3
Garthorpe Leics 154 E6
Garthorpe N Lincs 199 D11
Gartlea N Lnrk 268 C5
Gartloch Glasgow 268 B3
Gartly Aberds 302 F5
Gartmore Stirl 277 B10
Gartmore Ho Stirl 277 B10
Gartnagrenach Argyll 255 B8
Gartness N Lnrk 268 C5
Gartness Stirl 277 D10
Gartocharn W Dunb 277 D8
Garton E Yorks 209 F11
Garton-on-the-Wolds E Yorks 208 B5
Gartsherrie N Lnrk 268 B4
Gartur Stirl 277 B11
Gartymore Highld 311 H4
Garvald E Loth 281 G11
Garvamore Highld 291 D7
Garvard Argyll 274 D4
Garvault Hotel Highld 308 F7
Garve Highld 300 C3
Garvestone Norf 141 B10
Garvock Aberds 293 F9
Garvock Invclyd 276 G5
Garvock Hill Fife 280 D2
Garway Hereford 97 G9
Garway Hill Hereford 97 F8
Gaskan Highld 289 B9
Gasper Wilts 45 G9
Gastard Wilts 61 F11
Gasthorpe Norf 141 G9
Gaston Green Essex 87 B7
Gatacre Park Shrops 132 F5
Gatcombe I o W 20 D5
Gate Burton Lincs 188 E4
Gate Helmsley N Yorks 207 B9
Gateacre Mers 182 D6
Gatebeck Cumb 211 B10
Gateford Notts 187 E9
Gateford Common Notts 187 E9
Gateforth N Yorks 198 B5
Gatehead E Ayrs 257 B9
Gatehouse Northumb 251 F7
Gatehouse of Fleet Dumfries 237 D8
Gatelawbridge Dumfries 247 D10
Gateley Norf 159 E9
Gatenby N Yorks 214 B6
Gatesgarth Cumb 220 B3
Gateshead T & W 243 E7
Gatesheath W Ches 167 C7
Gateside Aberds 293 B8
Gateside Angus 287 C8
Gateside Dumfries 248 E4
Gateside E Renf 267 D9
Gateside Fife 286 G5
Gateside N Ayrs 267 E7
Gateside Shetland 312 F4
Gatewen Wrex 166 E4
Gatherley Devon 12 E3
Gathurst Gtr Man 194 F4
Gatlas Newport 78 G4
Gatley End Gtr Man 184 D4
Gatley End Cambs 104 C5
Gatton Sur 51 C9
Gattonside Borders 262 B2
Gatwick Glos 80 C2
Gatwick Airport W Sus 51 E9
Gaufron Powys 113 D9
Gaulby Leics 136 C3
Gauldry Fife 287 E7
Gauntons Bank E Ches 167 F9
Gaunt's Common Dorset 31 F8
Gaunt's Earthcott S Glos 60 C6
Gaunt's End Essex 105 F10
Gautby Lincs 189 G11
Gavinton Borders 272 E5
Gawber S Yorks 197 F10
Gawcott Bucks 102 E3
Gawsworth E Ches 168 B5
Gawthorpe W Yorks 197 C9
Gawthorpe W Yorks 197 D7
Gawthrop Cumb 212 B3
Gawthwaite Cumb 210 C5
Gay Bowers Essex 88 E3
Gay Street W Sus 35 C9
Gaydon Warks 119 G7
Gayfield Orkney 314 A4
Gayhurst M Keynes 103 B7
Gayle N Yorks 213 B7
Gayles N Yorks 224 D2
Gayton Mers 182 E3
Gayton Norf 158 F4
Gayton Northants 120 G4
Gayton Staffs 151 D9
Gayton Engine Lincs 191 D7
Gayton le Marsh Lincs 190 E6
Gayton le Wold Lincs 190 D2
Gayton Thorpe Norf 158 F4
Gaywood Norf 158 E2
Gaza Shetland 312 F5
Gazeley Suff 124 E4
Geàrraidh Sheilidh W Isles 297 J3
Geanies House Highld 301 B8
Gearraidh Bhailteas W Isles 297 J3
Gearraidh Bhaird W Isles 304 F5
Gearraidh Dubh W Isles 296 F4
Gearraidh na h-Aibhne W Isles 304 E4
Gearraidh na Monadh W Isles 297 K3
Geary Highld 298 C2
Geat Wolford Warks 100 E4
Geddes House Highld 301 D8
Gedding Suff 125 F9
Geddington Northants 137 G7
Gedgrave Hall Suff 109 B8
Gedintailor Highld 295 B7
Gedling Notts 171 G10
Gedney Lincs 157 E8
Gedney Broadgate Lincs 157 E8
Gedney Drove End Lincs 157 D9
Gedney Dyke Lincs 157 D8
Gedney Hill Lincs 156 G6
Gee Cross Gtr Man 185 C7
Geeston Rutland 137 C9
Gegin Wrex 166 E3
Geilston Argyll 276 F6
Geinas Denb 165 B9
Geirinis W Isles 297 G3
Geise Highld 310 C5
Geisiadar W Isles 304 E3
Geldeston Norf 143 E7
Gell Conwy 164 B5
Gelli Pembs 73 B9
Gelli Rhondda 77 G7
Gelli-gaer Neath 57 C9
Gelli-hôf Caerph 77 F11
Gellideg M Tydf 77 D8
Gellifor Denb 165 C10
Gelligaer Caerph 77 F10
Gelligroes Caerph 77 G11
Gellilydan Gwyn 146 B3
Gellinud Neath 76 E2
Gellinudd Neath 76 E2
Gellyburn Perth 286 D4
Gellygron Neath 76 E2
Gellywen Carms 92 G5
Gelsmoor Leics 153 F8
Gelston Dumfries 237 D9
Gelston Lincs 172 G6
Gembling E Yorks 209 B8
Gemini Warr 183 C9
Gendros Swansea 56 B6
Genesis Green Suff 124 F4
Gentleshaw Staffs 151 G11
Geocrab W Isles 305 J3
George Green Bucks 66 C4
George Nympton Devon 26 C2
Georgefield Dumfries 249 E7
Georgeham Devon 40 F3
Georgetown Bl Gwent 77 D10
Georgia Corn 1 B5
Gergask Highld 291 D8
Gerlan Gwyn 163 B10
Germansweek Devon 12 C4
Germiston Glasgow 268 B2
Germoe Corn 2 D3
Gernon Bushes Essex 87 E7
Gerrans Corn 3 B9
Gerrard's Bromley Staffs 150 C5
Gerrards Cross Bucks 66 B4
Gerrick Redcar 226 C4
Geseilfa Powys 129 E8
Gestingthorpe Essex 106 D6
Gesto Ho Highld 294 B5
Geuffordd Powys 148 G4
Geufron Denb 166 G2
Gib Heath W Mid 133 F11
Gibb Hill W Ches 183 F10
Gibbet Hill W Mid 118 C6
Gibbet Hill Warks 135 G10
Gibbshill Dumfries 237 B9
Gibraltar Beds 103 B10
Gibraltar Bucks 84 C3
Gibraltar Kent 55 F8
Gibralter Oxon 83 B7
Gibshill Invclyd 276 G6
Gibsmere Notts 172 F2
Giddeahall Wilts 61 E11
Giddy Green Dorset 18 D2
Gidea Park London 68 B4
Gidleigh Devon 13 D9
Giffard Park M Keynes 103 C7
Giffnock E Renf 267 D11
Gifford E Loth 271 B10
Giffordland N Ayrs 266 F5
Giffordtown Fife 286 F6
Gigg Gtr Man 195 F10
Giggetty Staffs 133 E7
Giggleswick N Yorks 212 G6
Giggshill Sur 67 F7
Gignog Pembs 91 G7
Gilberdyke E Yorks 199 B10
Gilbert Street Hants 49 G7
Gilbert's Coombe Corn 4 G3
Gilbert's End Worcs 98 C6
Gilbert's Green Warks 118 C2
Gilbertstone W Mid 134 G2
Gilchriston E Loth 271 B9
Gilcrux Cumb 229 D8
Gildersome W Yorks 197 B8
Gildersome Street W Yorks 197 B8
Gildingwells S Yorks 187 D9
Gilesgate Durham 233 C11
Gilesgate Moor Durham 233 C11
Gileston V Glam 58 F4
Gilfach Caerph 77 F11
Gilfach Hereford 96 E6
Gilfach Goch Rhondda 58 B3
Gilfachrheda Ceredig 111 F8
Gilgarran Cumb 228 G6
Gill N Yorks 204 E5
Gillamoor N Yorks 216 B3
Gillan Corn 3 E7
Gillar's Green Mers 183 B7
Gillbank Cumb 221 F7
Gillbent Gtr Man 184 E5
Gillen Highld 298 D2
Gillesbie Dumfries 248 E5
Gilling East N Yorks 216 D2
Gilling West N Yorks 224 D3
Gillingham Dorset 30 B4
Gillingham Medway 69 F9
Gillingham Norf 143 E8
Gillmoss Mers 182 B6
Gillock Highld 310 D6
Gillow Heath Staffs 168 D5
Gills Highld 310 B7
Gill's Green Kent 53 G9
Gillway Staffs 134 C4
Gilmanscleuch Borders 261 E8
Gilmerton Edin 270 B5
Gilmerton Perth 286 E2
Gilmonby Durham 223 C9
Gilmorton Leics 135 F11
Gilmourton S Lnrk 268 G3
Gilnow Gtr Man 195 F8
Gilroyd S Yorks 197 G10
Gilsland Northumb 240 D4
Gilsland Spa Cumb 240 D4
Gilson Warks 134 E3
Gilstead W Yorks 205 F8
Gilston Borders 271 D8
Gilston Herts 86 C6
Gilston Park Herts 86 C6
Giltbrook Notts 171 F7
Gilver's Lane Worcs 98 C6
Gilwell Park Essex 86 F5
Gilwern Mon 78 C2
Gimingham Norf 160 B5
Ginclough E Ches 185 F7
Ginger's Green E Sus 23 C10
Giosla W Isles 304 F3
Gipping Suff 125 E11
Gipsey Bridge Lincs 174 F3
Gipsy Row Suff 107 D11
Gipsyville Hull 200 B5
Gipton W Yorks 206 F2
Gipton Wood W Yorks 206 F2
Girdle Toll N Ayrs 266 G6
Girlington W Yorks 205 G8
Girlsta Shetland 313 H6
Girsby Lincs 190 D2
Girsby N Yorks 225 D7
Girt Som 29 C10
Girtford C Beds 104 B3
Girtford C Beds 122 G3
Girthon Dumfries 237 D8
Girton Cambs 123 E8
Girton Notts 172 B4
Girvan S Ayrs 244 D5
Gisburn Lancs 204 D2
Gisleham Suff 143 F10
Gislingham Suff 125 C11
Gissing Norf 142 F2
Gittisham Devon 15 B8
Givons Grove Sur 51 C7
Glachavoil Argyll 275 F11
Glack of Midthird Moray 302 E3
Glackmore Highld 300 D6
Gladestry Powys 114 F4
Gladsmuir E Loth 281 G9
Glaichbea Highld 300 F5
Glais Swansea 76 E2
Glaisdale N Yorks 226 D5
Glame Highld 298 E5
Glamis Angus 287 C7
Glan Adda Gwyn 179 G9
Glan-Conwy Conwy 164 E4
Glan-Duar Carms 93 C10
Glan-Dwyfach Gwyn 163 G7
Glan Gors Anglesey 179 F7
Glan-rhyd Gwyn 163 D7
Glan-rhyd Powys 76 D3
Glan-traeth Anglesey 178 F3
Glan-y-don Flint 181 F11
Glan y Ffer = Ferryside Carms 74 C5
Glan-y-llyn Rhondda 58 C6
Glan-y-môr Carms 74 C4
Glan-y-nant Caerph 77 F10
Glan-y-nant Powys 129 G8
Glan-y-wern Gwyn 146 C2
Glan-yr-afon Anglesey 179 E10
Glan-yr-afon Flint 181 E10
Glan-yr-afon Gwyn 164 G6
Glan-yr-afon Gwyn 165 G8
Glan-yr-afon Shrops 148 E4
Glanafon Pembs 73 B7
Glanaman Carms 75 C11
Glandford Norf 177 E8
Glandwr Caerph 78 E2
Glandwr Pembs 92 F3
Glandy Cross Carms 92 F2
Glandyfi Ceredig 128 D3
Glangrwyney Powys 78 B2
Glanhanog Powys 129 D8
Glanmule Powys 130 E3
Glanrafon Ceredig 128 G2
Glanrhyd Gwyn 144 B5
Glanrhyd Pembs 92 C2
Glantlees Northumb 252 B4
Glanton Northumb 264 G3
Glanton Pike Northumb 264 G3
Glantwymyn = Cemmaes Road Powys 128 C6
Glanvilles Wootton Dorset 29 F11
Glanwern Ceredig 128 F2
Glanwydden Conwy 180 E4
Glapthorn Northants 137 E10
Glapwell Derbys 171 B7
Glas-allt Shiel Aberds 292 E4
Glasbury Powys 96 D3
Glaschoil Highld 301 F10
Glascoed Denb 181 G7
Glascoed Mon 78 E4
Glascoed Powys 129 F11
Glascoed Powys 148 G2
Glascoed Wrex 166 E3
Glascorrie Aberds 292 D5
Glascorrie Perth 286 E2
Glascote Staffs 134 C4
Glascwm Powys 114 G3
Glasdir Flint 181 E10
Glasdrum Argyll 284 C4
Glasfryn Conwy 164 E6
Glasgoed Ceredig 92 B6
Glasgoforest Aberds 293 B10
Glasgow Glasgow 267 B11
Glashvin Highld 298 C4
Glasinfryn Gwyn 163 B9
Glasllwch Newport 59 B9
Glasnacardoch Highld 295 F8
Glasnakille Highld 295 D7
Glasphein Highld 297 G7
Glaspwll Powys 128 D4
Glass Houghton W Yorks 198 C2
Glassburn Highld 300 F3
Glassenbury Kent 53 F8
Glasserton Dumfries 236 F6
Glassford S Lnrk 268 F4
Glassgreen Moray 302 C2
Glasshouse Glos 98 G4
Glasshouse Hill Glos 98 G4
Glasshouses N Yorks 214 G3
Glasslie Fife 286 G6
Glasson Cumb 228 D6
Glasson Cumb 239 E7
Glasson Lancs 202 B4
Glassonby Cumb 231 D7
Glasterlaw Angus 287 B9
Glaston Rutland 137 C7
Glastonbury Som 44 F4
Glatton Cambs 138 F3
Glazebrook Warr 183 C11
Glazebury Warr 183 B11
Glazeley Shrops 132 F4
Gleadless S Yorks 186 E5
Gleadless Valley S Yorks 186 E5
Gleadmoss E Ches 168 B4
Gleadsmoss E Ches 168 B4
Gleanhead Dumfries 245 G10
Gleann Tholàstaidh W Isles 304 D7
Gleaston Cumb 210 E5
Glebe Hants 33 D9
Glebe Shetland 313 J6
Glebe T & W 243 F8
Glecknabae Argyll 275 G11
Gledhow W Yorks 206 F2
Gledrid Shrops 148 B5
Gleiniant Powys 129 E9
Glemsford Suff 106 B6
Glen Dumfries 237 B10
Glen Dumfries 237 D7
Glen Auldyn I o M 192 C5
Glen Bernisdale Highld 298 E4
Glen Ho Borders 261 C7
Glen Mona I o M 192 D5
Glen Mor Highld 295 B10
Glen Nevis House Highld 290 F3
Glen of Newmill Moray 302 D4
Glen Parva Leics 135 D11
Glen Sluain Argyll 275 D11
Glen Tanar House Aberds 292 D6
Glen Trool Lodge Dumfries 245 G10
Glen Vic Askil Highld 298 E3
Glen Village Falk 279 F7
Glen Vine I o M 192 E4
Glenallachie Moray 302 E2
Glenalmond College Perth 286 E3
Glenalmond Ho Perth 286 E3
Glenamachrie Argyll 289 G11
Glenample Stirl 285 E9
Glenancross Highld 295 F8
Glenapp Castle S Ayrs 244 G3
Glenaros Ho Argyll 289 E7
Glenbarr Argyll 255 D7
Glenbeg Highld 289 C7
Glenbeg Highld 301 G10
Glenbervie Aberds 293 E9
Glenboig N Lnrk 268 B4
Glenborrodale Highld 289 C8
Glenbranter Argyll 276 B2
Glenbreck Borders 260 E3
Glenbrein Lodge Highld 290 B6
Glenbrittle House Highld 294 C6
Glenbrook Edin 270 B2
Glenbuchat Castle Aberds 292 B5
Glenbuchat Lodge Aberds 292 B5
Glenbuck E Ayrs 259 D7
Glenburn Renfs 267 C9
Glenbyre Argyll 289 G7
Glencalvie Lodge Highld 309 L4
Glencanisp Lodge Highld 307 G6
Glencaple Dumfries 237 C11
Glencarron Lodge Highld 299 D10
Glencarse Perth 286 E5
Glencassley Castle Highld 309 J4
Glencat Aberds 293 D7
Glenceitlein Highld 284 C5
Glencoe Highld 284 B4
Glencraig Fife 280 B3
Glencripesdale Highld 289 D8
Glencrosh Dumfries 247 F7
Glendavan Ho Aberds 292 C6
Glendearg Borders 262 B2
Glendevon Perth 286 G3
Glendoe Lodge Highld 290 C6
Glendoebeg Highld 290 C6
Glendoick Perth 286 E6
Glendoll Lodge Angus 292 F4
Glendoune S Ayrs 244 D5
Glenduckie Fife 286 F6
Glendye Lodge Aberds 293 E8
Gleneagles Hotel Perth 286 F3
Gleneagles House Perth 286 G3
Glenearn Perth 286 F5
Glenegedale Argyll 254 B4
Glenelg Highld 295 D10
Glenernie Moray 301 E10
Glenfarg Perth 286 F5
Glenfarquhar Lodge Aberds 293 E9
Glenferness House Highld 301 E9
Glenfeshie Lodge Highld 291 D10
Glenfiddich Lodge Moray 302 F3
Glenfield Leics 135 B10
Glenfinnan Highld 295 G10
Glenfinnan Lodge Highld 295 G11
Glenfintaig Ho Highld 290 E4
Glenfoot Perth 286 F5
Glenfyne Lodge Argyll 284 F6
Glengap Dumfries 237 D8
Glengarnock N Ayrs 266 E6
Glengolly Highld 310 C5
Glengorm Castle Argyll 288 D6
Glengoulandie Perth 285 B11
Glengrasco Highld 298 E4
Glenhead Farm Angus 292 G4
Glenholt Plym 7 C10
Glenhoul Dumfries 246 F4
Glenhurich Highld 289 C10
Glenkerry Borders 261 G7
Glenkiln Dumfries 237 B10
Glenkindie Aberds 292 B6
Glenlair Dumfries 237 B9
Glenlatterach Moray 301 D11
Glenlee Dumfries 246 G4
Glenleigh Park E Sus 38 F2
Glenleraig Highld 306 F6
Glenlichorn Perth 285 F11
Glenlicht Ho Highld 290 B2
Glenlivet Moray 301 G11
Glenlochar Dumfries 237 C9
Glenlochsie Perth 292 F2
Glenlocksie Lodge Perth 292 F2
Glenloig N Ayrs 255 D10
Glenlomond Perth 286 G5
Glenluce Dumfries 236 D4
Glenlussa Ho Argyll 255 E8
Glenmallan Argyll 276 B5
Glenmark Angus 292 E6
Glenmarkie Lodge Angus 292 G4
Glenmarksie Highld 300 D3
Glenmavis N Lnrk 268 B4
Glenmavis W Loth 269 B9
Glenmaye I o M 192 E3
Glenmayne Borders 261 C11
Glenmeanie Highld 300 D2
Glenmidge Dumfries 247 F9
Glenmoidart Ho Highld 289 B9
Glenmore Argyll 275 B9
Glenmore Argyll 275 G11
Glenmore Highld 298 E4
Glenmore Lodge Highld 291 C11
Glenmoy Angus 292 G6
Glennoe Argyll 284 D4
Glenogil Angus 292 G6
Glenowen Pembs 73 D7
Glenprosen Lodge Angus 292 G4
Glenprosen Village Angus 292 G5
Glenquaich Lodge Perth 286 D2
Glenquiech Angus 292 G6
Glenquithlie Aberds 303 C8
Glenrath Borders 260 C6
Glenrazie Dumfries 236 C5
Glenreasdell Mains Argyll 255 B9
Glenree N Ayrs 255 E10
Glenridding Cumb 221 B7
Glenrosa N Ayrs 256 B2
Glenrossal Highld 309 J4
Glenrothes Fife 286 G6
Glensanda Highld 289 E10
Glensaugh Aberds 293 F8
Glensburgh Falk 279 E8
Glenshero Lodge Highld 291 D7
Glenshoe Lodge Perth 292 G3
Glenstockadale Dumfries 236 C2
Glenstriven Argyll 275 F11
Glentaggart S Lnrk 259 D8
Glentarkie Perth 286 F5
Glenternie Borders 260 B6
Glentham Lincs 189 C8
Glentirranmuir Stirl 278 C3
Glenton Aberds 302 G6
Glentress Borders 261 B7
Glentromie Lodge Highld 291 D9
Glentrool Village Dumfries 236 B5
Glentruan I o M 192 B5
Glentruim House Highld 291 D8
Glentworth Lincs 188 D6
Glenuaig Lodge Highld 299 E11
Glenuig Highld 289 B8
Glenure Argyll 284 C4
Glenurquhart Highld 301 C7
Glenview Argyll 284 E5
Glespin S Lnrk 259 D8
Gletness Shetland 313 H6
Glewstone Hereford 97 G11
Glinton P'boro 138 B3
Globe Town London 67 C11
Glodwick Gtr Man 196 G2
Glogue Pembs 92 E4
Glooston Leics 136 D4
Glororum Northumb 264 C5
Glossop Derbys 185 C8
Gloster Hill Northumb 253 C7
Gloucester Glos 80 B4
Gloup Shetland 312 C7
Gloweth Corn 4 G5
Glusburn N Yorks 204 E6
Glutt Lodge Highld 310 F3
Glutton Bridge Staffs 169 B9
Gluvian Corn 5 C8
Glympton Oxon 101 G8
Glyn Mon 79 F7
Glyn Powys 129 F8
Glyn Castle Neath 76 E4
Glyn-Ceiriog Wrex 148 B4
Glyn-cywarch Gwyn 146 C2
Glyn Etwy Bl Gwent 77 D11
Glyn-neath = Glynedd Neath 76 D5
Glynarthen Ceredig 92 B6
Glynbrochan Powys 129 G8
Glyncoch Rhondda 77 G9
Glyncoed Bl Gwent 77 C11
Glyncorrwg Neath 57 B11
Glynde E Sus 23 D7
Glyndebourne E Sus 23 C7
Glyndyfrdwy Denb 165 G10
Glyne Gap E Sus 38 F3
Glynedd = Glyn neath Neath 76 D5
Glynhafren Powys 129 G7
Glynllan Bridgend 58 B2
Glynmorlas Shrops 148 B6
Glynogwr Bridgend 58 B3
Glyntaff Rhondda 58 B5
Glyntawe Powys 76 B4
Gnosall Staffs 150 E6
Gnosall Heath Staffs 150 E6
Goadby Leics 136 D4
Goadby Marwood Leics 154 D5
Goat Lees Kent 54 D4
Goatacre Wilts 62 D4
Goatham Green E Sus 38 C4
Goathill Dorset 29 D11
Goathland N Yorks 226 E6
Goathurst Som 43 G9
Goathurst Common Kent 52 C3
Gobernuisgach Lodge Highld 308 E4
Gobernuisgeach Highld 310 F3
Gobhaig W Isles 305 H2
Gobley Hole Hants 48 D6
Gobowen Shrops 148 C6
Godalming Sur 50 E3
Goddards Bucks 84 G3
Goddard's Corner Suff 126 D5
Goddard's Green Kent 53 G10
Goddard's Green W Berks 65 F7
Goddards' Green W Sus 36 C3
Godden Green Kent 52 B5
Goddington London 68 F3
Godley Gtr Man 185 B7
Godley Hill Gtr Man 185 C7
Godleybrook Staffs 169 G7
Godleys Green E Sus 36 D5
Godmanchester Cambs 122 C4
Godmanstone Dorset 17 B9
Godmersham Kent 54 C5
Godney Som 44 E3
Godolphin Cross Corn 2 C4
Godre'r-graig Neath 76 D3
God's Blessing Green Dorset 31 G8
Godshill Hants 31 E11
Godshill I o W 20 E6
Godstone Sur 51 C10
Godswinscroft Hants 19 B9
Godwell Devon 8 D2
Godwick Norf 159 E8
Godwinscroft Hants 19 B9
Goferydd Anglesey 178 E2
Goff's Oak Herts 86 E4
Gogar Edin 280 G3
Goginan Ceredig 128 G3
Goirtean a'Chladaich Highld 290 F2
Golan Gwyn 163 G8
Golant Corn 6 E2
Golberdon Corn 12 G2
Golborne Gtr Man 183 B10
Golcar W Yorks 196 D6
Golch Flint 181 F11
Gold Hill Dorset 30 E4
Gold Hill Norf 139 E10
Goldcliff Newport 59 C11
Golden Balls Oxon 83 F9
Golden Cross E Sus 23 C10
Golden Cross E Sus 23 C8
Golden Green Kent 52 D6
Golden Grove Carms 75 B9
Golden Hill Bristol 60 D5
Golden Hill Hants 19 B11
Golden Hill Pembs 73 E7
Golden Hill Pembs 91 G9
Golden Park Devon 24 C2
Golden Pot Hants 49 E8
Golden Valley Derbys 170 E6
Golden Valley Glos 99 G8
Golden Valley Hereford 98 B3
Goldenhill Stoke 168 E5
Golder Field Hereford 115 E11
Golders Green London 67 B9
Goldfinch Bottom W Berks 64 G4
Goldhanger Essex 88 D6
Golding Shrops 131 C10
Goldington Beds 121 G11
Gold's Cross Bath 60 G5
Golds Green W Mid 133 E9
Goldsborough N Yorks 206 B3
Goldsborough N Yorks 226 C6
Goldsithney Corn 2 C2
Goldstone Shrops 150 D4
Goldthorn Park W Mid 133 D8
Goldthorpe S Yorks 198 G3
Goldworthy Devon 24 C5
Golford Kent 53 F9
Golftyn Flint 182 G3
Golgotha Kent 55 D9
Gollanfield Highld 301 D8
Gollawater Corn 4 E5
Gollinglith Foot N Yorks 214 C3
Golly Wrex 166 D4
Golsoncott Som 42 F4
Golspie Highld 311 J2
Golval Highld 310 C2
Golynos Torf 78 E3
Gomeldon Wilts 47 F7
Gomersal W Yorks 197 B8
Gometra Ho Argyll 288 E5
Gomshall Sur 50 D5
Gonalston Notts 171 F11
Gonamena Corn 11 G11
Gonerby Hill Foot Lincs 155 B8
Gonfirth Shetland 313 G5
Good Easter Essex 87 C10
Gooderstone Norf 140 C5
Goodleigh Devon 40 G6
Goodley Stock Kent 52 C2
Goodmanham E Yorks 208 E3
Goodmayes London 68 B3
Goodnestone Kent 55 C9
Goodnestone Kent 70 G4
Goodrich Hereford 79 B9
Goodrington Torbay 9 D7
Good's Green Worcs 132 G5
Goodshaw Lancs 195 B10
Goodshaw Chapel Lancs 195 B10
Goodshaw Fold Lancs 195 B10
Goodstone Devon 13 G11
Goodwick = Wdig Pembs 91 D8
Goodworth Clatford Hants 47 E11
Goodyers End Warks 134 F6
Goodyhills Cumb 229 B8
Goom's Hill Worcs 117 G10
Goon Gumpas Corn 4 G4
Goon Piper Corn 3 B8
Goonabarn Corn 5 E9
Goonbell Corn 4 F4
Goonhavern Corn 4 E5
Goonhusband Corn 2 D5
Goonlaze Corn 2 B6
Goonown Corn 4 E4
Goonvrea Corn 4 F4
Goose Eye W Yorks 204 E6
Goose Green Cumb 211 C10
Goose Green Essex 108 F2
Goose Green Gtr Man 194 G5
Goose Green Hants 32 F4
Goose Green Herts 86 D5
Goose Green Kent 52 C6
Goose Green Kent 53 F10
Goose Green Lancs 194 C3
Goose Green Norf 142 F2
Goose Green S Glos 61 C8
Goose Green W Sus 34 C3
Goose Green W Sus 35 D10
Goose Hill Hants 64 G4
Goose Pool Hereford 97 D9
Gooseberry Green Essex 87 F11
Gooseford Devon 13 C9
Gooseham Mill Devon 24 D2
Goosehill W Yorks 197 C11
Goosehill Green Worcs 117 E8
Goosemoor Staffs 150 F6
Goosemoor Green Staffs 151 G11
Goosenford Som 28 B2
Goosewell Devon 40 D5
Goosey Oxon 82 G5
Goosnargh Lancs 203 F7
Goostrey E Ches 184 G3
Gorbals Glasgow 267 C11
Gorcott Hill Warks 117 D11
Gord Shetland 313 L6
Gorddinog Conwy 179 G11
Gordon Borders 272 G2
Gordonbush Highld 311 J2
Gordonsburgh Moray 302 C4
Gordonstoun Moray 301 C11
Gordonstown Aberds 302 D5
Gordonstown Aberds 303 F7
Gore Dorset 29 D9
Gore Kent 55 B10
Gore Cross Wilts 46 C4
Gore End Hants 64 G2
Gore Pit Essex 88 B5
Gore Street Kent 71 F9
Gorebridge Midloth 270 C6
Gorefield Cambs 157 G8
Gorehill W Sus 35 C7
Gorgie Edin 280 G4
Gorhambury Herts 85 D10
Goring Oxon 64 C6
Goring-by-Sea W Sus 35 G10
Goring Heath Oxon 65 D7
Gorleston-on-Sea Norf 143 C10

Gornalwood W Mid 133 E8
Gorrachie Aberds 303 D7
Gorran Churchtown Corn 5 G9
Gorran Haven Corn 5 G10
Gorran High Lanes Corn 5 G9
Gorrenberry Borders 249 D11
Gorrig Ceredig 93 C8
Gorse Covert Warr 183 C11
Gorse Hill Gtr Man 184 B4
Gorse Hill Swindon 63 B7
Gorsedd Flint 181 F11
Gorseinon Swansea 56 B5
Gorseness Orkney 314 E4
Gorsethorpe Notts 171 B9
Gorseybank Derbys 170 E3
Gorsgoch Ceredig 111 G9
Gorslas Carms 75 C9
Gorsley Glos 98 F3
Gorsley Common Hereford 98 F3
Gorsley Ley Staffs 133 B11
Gorst Hill Worcs 116 C4
Gorstage W Ches 183 G10
Gorstan Highld 300 C3
Gorstanvorran Highld 289 B10
Gorstella W Ches 166 C5
Gorsteyhill E Ches 168 E2
Gorsty Hill Staffs 151 D11
Gorstyhill Staffs 168 E2
Gortan Argyll 274 G3
Gortantaoid Argyll 274 F4
Gortenacullish Highld 295 G8
Gorteneorn Highld 289 C8
Gortenfern Highld 289 C8
Gortinanane Argyll 255 C8
Gorton Gtr Man 184 B5
Gortonallister N Ayrs 256 D2
Gosbeck Suff 126 F3
Gosberton Lincs 156 C4
Gosberton Cheal Lincs 156 D4
Gosberton Clough Lincs 156 D3
Goscote W Mid 133 C10
Goseley Dale Derbys 152 E6
Gosfield Essex 106 F5
Gosford Hereford 115 D10
Gosford Oxon 83 C7
Gosford Green W Mid 118 B6
Gosforth Cumb 219 E11
Gosforth T & W 242 D6
Gosforth Valley Derbys 186 F4
Gosland Green Suff 124 G5
Gosling Green Suff 107 C9
Gosmere Kent 54 B4
Gosmore Herts 104 F3
Gospel Ash Staffs 132 E6
Gospel End Village Staffs 133 E7
Gospel Green W Sus 50 G2
Gospel Oak London 67 B9
Gosport Hants 21 B8
Gosport Hants 32 C5
Gossabrough Shetland 312 E7
Gossard's Green C Beds 103 C9
Gossington Glos 80 E2
Gossops Green W Sus 51 F9
Goswick Northumb 273 F11
Gotham Dorset 31 E9
Gotham E Sus 38 F2
Gotham Notts 153 C10
Gothelney Green Som 43 F9
Gotherington Glos 99 F9
Gothers Corn 5 D9
Gott Argyll 288 E2
Gott Shetland 313 J6
Gotton Som 28 B2
Goudhurst Kent 53 F8
Goukstone Moray 302 D4
Goulceby Lincs 190 F3
Goulton N Yorks 225 E9
Gourdas Aberds 303 E7
Gourdon Aberds 293 F10
Gourock Invclyd 276 F4
Govan Glasgow 267 B11
Govanhill Glasgow 267 C11
Gover Hill Kent 52 C6
Goverton Notts 172 E2
Goveton Devon 8 F5
Govilon Mon 78 C3
Gowanhill Aberds 303 C10
Gowanwell Aberds 303 E8
Gowdall E Yorks 198 C6
Gowerton = Tre-Gwyr Swansea 56 B5
Gowhole Derbys 185 E8
Gowkhall Fife 279 D11
Gowkthrapple N Lnrk 268 E5
Gowthorpe E Yorks 207 C11
Goxhill E Yorks 209 E9
Goxhill N Lincs 200 C6
Goxhill Haven N Lincs 200 B6
Goybre Neath 57 D9
Goytre Neath 57 D9
Gozzard's Ford Oxon 83 F7
Grabhair W Isles 305 G5
Graby Lincs 155 D11
Gracca Corn 5 D10
Gracemount Edin 270 B5
Grade Corn 2 G6
Graffham W Sus 34 D6
Grafham Cambs 122 D3
Grafham Sur 50 E4
Grafton Hereford 97 D9
Grafton N Yorks 215 G8
Grafton Oxon 82 E3
Grafton Shrops 149 F8
Grafton Worcs 99 D9
Grafton Worcs 115 E11
Grafton Flyford Worcs 117 F9
Grafton Regis Northants 102 B5
Grafton Underwood Northants 137 G8
Grafty Green Kent 53 D11
Grahamston Falk 279 E7
Graianrhyd Denb 166 D2
Graig Carms 74 E6
Graig Conwy 180 G4
Graig Denb 181 G9
Graig Rhondda 58 B5
Graig Wrex 148 B4
Graig-Fawr Swansea 75 E10
Graig-fechan Denb 165 E10
Graig Felen Swansea 75 E11
Graig Penllyn V Glam 58 D3
Graig Trewyddfa Swansea 57 B7
Grain Medway 69 D11
Grains Bar Gtr Man 196 F3
Grainsby Lincs 190 B3
Grainthorpe Lincs 190 B5
Grainthorpe Fen Lincs 190 B5
Graiselound N Lincs 188 B3
Grampound Corn 5 F8
Grampound Road Corn 5 E8
Gramsdal W Isles 296 F4
Granborough Bucks 102 F5
Granby Notts 154 B5
Grandborough Warks 119 D9
Grandpont Oxon 83 D8
Grandtully Perth 286 B3
Grange Cumb 220 B5
Grange Dorset 31 G8
Grange E Ayrs 257 B10
Grange Fife 287 G8
Grange Halton 183 E8
Grange Lancs 203 G7
Grange Medway 69 F9
Grange Mers 182 D2
Grange N Yorks 223 G8
Grange NE Lincs 201 F9
Grange Perth 286 E6
Grange Warr 183 C10
Grange Crossroads Moray 302 D4
Grange Estate Dorset 31 G10
Grange Hall Moray 301 C10
Grange Hill Durham 233 F10
Grange Hill Essex 86 G6
Grange Moor W Yorks 197 D8
Grange of Cree Dumfries 236 D6
Grange of Lindores Fife 286 F6
Grange-over-Sands Cumb 211 D8
Grange Park London 86 F4
Grange Park Mers 183 C7
Grange Park Northants 120 F5
Grange Park Swindon 62 C6
Grange Villa Durham 242 G6
Grange Village Glos 79 C11
Grangemill Derbys 170 D2
Grangemouth Falk 279 E8
Grangemuir Fife 287 G9
Grangepans Falk 279 E10
Grangetown Cardiff 59 E7
Grangetown Redcar 235 G7
Grangetown T & W 243 G10
Granish Highld 291 B11
Gransmoor E Yorks 209 B8
Gransmore Green Essex 106 G3
Granston = Treopert Pembs 91 E7
Grant Thorold NE Lincs 201 F9
Grantchester Cambs 123 F8
Grantham Lincs 155 B8
Grantley N Yorks 214 F4
Grantley Hall N Yorks 214 F4
Grantlodge Aberds 293 B9
Granton Dumfries 248 B3
Granton Edin 280 F4
Grantown Aberds 302 D5
Grantown-on-Spey Highld 301 G10
Grantsfield Hereford 115 E10
Grantshouse Borders 272 B6
Graplin Dumfries 237 E8
Grappenhall Warr 183 D10
Grasby Lincs 200 G5
Grasmere Cumb 220 D6
Grass Green Essex 106 D4
Grasscroft Gtr Man 196 G3
Grassendale Mers 182 D5
Grassgarth Cumb 221 F8
Grassgarth Cumb 230 C2
Grassholme Durham 232 G4
Grassington N Yorks 213 G10
Grassmoor Derbys 170 B6
Grassthorpe Notts 172 B3
Grasswell T & W 243 G8
Grateley Hants 47 E9
Gratton Devon 24 E5
Gratwich Staffs 151 C10
Gravel W Ches 167 B11
Gravel Castle Kent 55 D8
Gravel Hill Bucks 85 G8
Gravel Hole Gtr Man 196 F2
Gravel Hole Shrops 149 B7
Graveley Cambs 122 E4
Graveley Herts 104 F4
Gravelhill Shrops 149 G9
Gravelly Hill W Mid 134 E2
Gravels Shrops 130 D6
Gravelsbank Shrops 130 C6
Graven Shetland 312 F6
Graveney Kent 70 G5
Gravenhunger Moss Shrops 168 G2
Gravesend Herts 105 F8
Gravesend Kent 68 E6
Grayingham Lincs 188 B6
Grayrigg Cumb 221 F11
Grays Thurrock 68 D6
Grayshott Hants 49 F11
Grayson Green Cumb 228 F5
Grayswood Sur 50 G2
Graythorp Hrtlpl 234 F6
Grazeley Wokingham 65 F7
Grazeley Green W Berks 65 F7
Greagdhubh Lodge Highld 291 D8
Greamchary Highld 310 F2
Greasbrough S Yorks 186 B6
Greasby Mers 182 D3
Greasley Notts 171 F7
Great Abington Cambs 105 B10
Great Addington Northants 121 B9
Great Alne Warks 118 F2
Great Altcar Lancs 193 F10
Great Amwell Herts 86 C5
Great Asby Cumb 222 C3
Great Ashfield Suff 125 D9
Great Ashley Wilts 61 G10
Great Ayton N Yorks 225 C11
Great Baddow Essex 88 E2
Great Bardfield Essex 106 E3
Great Barford Beds 122 G2
Great Barrington Glos 82 C2
Great Barrow W Ches 167 B7
Great Barton Suff 125 D7
Great Barugh N Yorks 216 D4
Great Bavington Northumb 251 G11
Great Bealings Suff 108 B4
Great Bedwyn Wilts 63 G9
Great Bentley Essex 108 G2
Great Berry Essex 69 B7
Great Billing Northants 120 E6
Great Bircham Norf 158 C5
Great Blakenham Suff 126 G2
Great Blencow Cumb 230 E5
Great Bolas Telford 150 E2
Great Bookham Sur 50 C6
Great Bosullow Corn 1 C4
Great Bourton Oxon 101 B9
Great Bowden Leics 136 F4
Great Bower Kent 54 C4
Great Bradley Suff 124 G3
Great Braxted Essex 88 C5
Great Bricett Suff 125 G10
Great Brickhill Bucks 103 E8
Great Bridge W Mid 133 E9
Great Bridgeford Staffs 151 D7
Great Brington Northants 120 D3
Great Bromley Essex 107 F11
Great Broughton Cumb 229 E7
Great Broughton N Yorks 225 D10
Great Buckland Kent 69 G7
Great Budworth W Ches 183 F11
Great Burdon Darl 224 B6
Great Burgh Sur 51 B8
Great Burstead Essex 87 G11
Great Busby N Yorks 225 D10
Great Canfield Essex 87 B9
Great Carlton Lincs 190 D6
Great Casterton Rutland 137 B10
Great Casterton Rutland 137 B9
Great Cellws Powys 113 E11
Great Chalfield Wilts 61 G11
Great Chart Kent 54 E3
Great Chatwell Staffs 150 G5
Great Chell Stoke 168 E5
Great Chesterford Essex 105 C10
Great Cheveney Kent 53 E8
Great Cheverell Wilts 46 C3
Great Chilton Durham 233 E11
Great Chishill Cambs 105 D8
Great Clacton Essex 89 B11
Great Claydons Essex 88 E3
Great Cliff W Yorks 197 D10
Great Clifton Cumb 228 F6
Great Coates NE Lincs 201 F8
Great Comberton Worcs 99 C9
Great Common Suff 143 F7
Great Common W Sus 35 B8
Great Corby Cumb 239 G11
Great Cornard Suff 107 C7
Great Cowden E Yorks 209 E10
Great Coxwell Oxon 82 G3
Great Crakehall N Yorks 224 G4
Great Cransley Northants 120 B6
Great Cressingham Norf 141 C7
Great Crosby Mers 182 B4
Great Crosthwaite Cumb 229 G11
Great Cubley Derbys 152 B3
Great Dalby Leics 154 G4
Great Denham Beds 103 B10
Great Doddington Northants 121 E7
Great Doward Hereford 79 B9
Great Dunham Norf 159 G7
Great Dunmow Essex 106 G2
Great Durnford Wilts 46 F6
Great Easton Essex 106 F2
Great Easton Leics 136 E6
Great Eccleston Lancs 202 E4
Great Edstone N Yorks 216 C4
Great Ellingham Norf 141 D10
Great Elm Som 45 D8
Great Eppleton T & W 234 B3
Great Eversden Cambs 123 G7
Great Fencote N Yorks 224 G5
Great Finborough Suff 125 F10
Great Fransham Norf 159 G7
Great Gaddesden Herts 85 C8
Great Gate Staffs 169 G9
Great Gidding Cambs 138 G2
Great Givendale E Yorks 208 C2
Great Glemham Suff 126 E6
Great Glen Leics 136 D3
Great Gonerby Lincs 155 B7
Great Gransden Cambs 122 F5
Great Green Cambs 104 C5
Great Green Norf 142 F5
Great Green Suff 125 B11
Great Green Suff 125 F8
Great Green Suff 126 B2
Great Habton N Yorks 216 D5
Great Hale Lincs 173 G10
Great Hallingbury Essex 87 B8
Great Hampden Bucks 84 E4
Great Harrowden Northants 121 C7
Great Harwood Lancs 203 G10
Great Haseley Oxon 83 E10
Great Hatfield E Yorks 209 E9
Great Haywood Staffs 151 E10
Great Haywood Staffs 151 E9
Great Heath W Mid 134 G6
Great Heck N Yorks 198 C5
Great Henny Essex 107 D7
Great Hinton Wilts 46 B2
Great Hivings Bucks 85 E7
Great Hockham Norf 141 E9
Great Holcombe Oxon 83 F10
Great Holland Essex 89 B12
Great Hollands Brack 65 F11
Great Holm M Keynes 102 D6
Great Honeyborough Pembs 73 D7
Great Horkesley Essex 107 E9
Great Hormead Herts 105 F7
Great Horton W Yorks 205 G8
Great Horwood Bucks 102 E5
Great Houghton Northants 120 F5
Great Houghton S Yorks 198 F2
Great Howarth Gtr Man 196 D2
Great Hucklow Derbys 185 F11
Great Job's Cross Kent 38 B4
Great Kelk E Yorks 209 B8
Great Kendale E Yorks 217 G10
Great Kimble Bucks 84 D4
Great Kingshill Bucks 84 F5
Great Langton N Yorks 224 F5
Great Lea Common Reading 65 F8
Great Leighs Essex 88 B2
Great Lever Gtr Man 195 F8
Great Limber Lincs 200 F6
Great Linford M Keynes 103 C7
Great Livermere Suff 125 C7
Great Longstone Derbys 186 G2
Great Lumley Durham 233 B11
Great Lyth Shrops 131 B9
Great Malgraves Thurrock 69 C7
Great Malvern Worcs 98 B5
Great Maplestead Essex 106 E6
Great Marton Blkpool 202 F2
Great Marton Moss Blkpool 202 G2
Great Massingham Norf 158 E5
Great Melton Norf 142 B2
Great Milton Oxon 83 E10
Great Missenden Bucks 84 E5
Great Mitton Lancs 203 F10
Great Mongeham Kent 55 C10
Great Moor Gtr Man 184 D6
Great Moor Staffs 132 D6
Great Moulton Norf 142 E3
Great Munden Herts 105 G7
Great Musgrave Cumb 222 C5
Great Ness Shrops 149 F7
Great Notley Essex 106 G4
Great Oak Mon 78 D5
Great Oakley Essex 108 F3
Great Oakley Northants 137 F7
Great Offley Herts 104 F2
Great Ormside Cumb 222 B4
Great Orton Cumb 239 G8
Great Ouseburn N Yorks 215 G8
Great Oxendon Northants 136 G4
Great Oxney Green Essex 87 D11
Great Palgrave Norf 158 G6
Great Parndon Essex 86 D6
Great Pattenden Kent 53 E8
Great Paxton Cambs 122 E4
Great Plumpton Lancs 202 G3
Great Plumstead Norf 160 G6
Great Ponton Lincs 155 C8
Great Preston W Yorks 198 B2
Great Purston Northants 101 D10
Great Raveley Cambs 138 G5
Great Rissington Glos 81 B11
Great Rollright Oxon 100 E6
Great Ryburgh Norf 159 D9
Great Ryle Northumb 264 G2
Great Ryton Shrops 131 C9
Great Saling Essex 106 F4
Great Salkeld Cumb 231 D7
Great Sampford Essex 106 D2
Great Sankey Warr 183 D9
Great Saredon Staffs 133 B9
Great Saxham Suff 124 E5
Great Shefford W Berks 63 E11
Great Shelford Cambs 123 G9
Great Shoddesden Hants 47 D9
Great Smeaton N Yorks 224 E6
Great Snoring Norf 159 C8
Great Somerford Wilts 62 C3
Great Stainton Darl 234 G2
Great Stambridge Essex 88 G5
Great Staughton Cambs 122 E2
Great Steeping Lincs 174 C6
Great Stoke S Glos 60 C6
Great Stonar Kent 55 B10
Great Stretton Leics 136 C3
Great Strickland Cumb 231 G7
Great Stukeley Cambs 122 C4
Great Sturton Lincs 190 F2
Great Sutton Shrops 131 G10
Great Sutton W Ches 182 F5
Great Swinburne Northumb 241 B10
Great Tew Oxon 101 F7
Great Tey Essex 107 F7
Great Thirkleby N Yorks 215 D9
Great Thurlow Suff 124 G3
Great Torrington Devon 25 D7
Great Tosson Northumb 252 C2
Great Totham Essex 88 C5
Great Tows Lincs 190 C2
Great Tree Corn 6 D5
Great Urswick Cumb 210 E5
Great Wakering Essex 70 B2
Great Waldingfield Suff 107 C8
Great Walsingham Norf 159 B8
Great Waltham Essex 87 C11
Great Warley Essex 87 G9
Great Washbourne Glos 99 E9
Great Weeke Devon 13 D10
Great Weldon Northants 137 F8
Great Welnetham Suff 125 F7
Great Wenham Suff 107 D11
Great Whittington Northumb 242 C2
Great Wigborough Essex 89 C7
Great Wilbraham Cambs 123 F10
Great Wilne Derbys 153 C8
Great Wishford Wilts 46 F5
Great Witchingham Norf 160 E2
Great Witcombe Glos 80 C6
Great Witley Worcs 116 D5
Great Wolford Warks 100 E4
Great Wratting Suff 106 B3
Great Wymondley Herts 104 F4
Great Wyrley Staffs 133 B9
Great Wytheford Shrops 149 F11
Great Yarmouth Norf 143 B10
Great Yeldham Essex 106 D5
Greater Doward Hereford 79 B9
Greatfield Wilts 62 B5
Greatford Lincs 155 G11
Greatgap Bucks 84 B6
Greatgate Staffs 169 G9
Greatham Hants 49 G9
Greatham Hrtlpl 234 F5
Greatham W Sus 35 D8
Greatmoor Bucks 102 G4
Greatness Kent 52 B4
Greatstone-on-Sea Kent 39 C9
Greatworth Northants 101 C11
Greave Gtr Man 184 C6
Greave Lancs 195 C11
Grebby Lincs 174 B6
Greeba I o M 192 D4
Green Denb 165 B9
Green Pembs 73 E7
Green Powys 130 E5
Green Bank Cumb 211 C7
Green Bottom Corn 4 F5
Green Bottom Glos 79 B11
Green Close N Yorks 212 F4
Green Clough W Yorks 205 G7
Green Crize Hereford 97 D10
Green Cross Sur 49 F11
Green Down Devon 28 G3
Green End Beds 103 B10
Green End Beds 121 E11
Green End Beds 122 E2
Green End Beds 122 G2
Green End Bucks 84 F4
Green End Bucks 103 E8
Green End C Beds 103 D11
Green End Cambs 122 C4
Green End Cambs 123 F7
Green End Herts 85 D8
Green End Herts 104 E5
Green End Herts 104 E6
Green End Herts 104 G6
Green End Herts 105 F7
Green End Lancs 204 D4
Green End N Yorks 226 E6
Green End Warks 134 F5
Green Gate Devon 27 D8
Green Hailey Bucks 84 E4
Green Hammerton N Yorks 206 B5
Green Haworth Lancs 195 B9
Green Head Cumb 230 B3
Green Heath Staffs 151 G9
Green Hill Kent 53 C9
Green Hill Lincs 155 B8
Green Hill W Yorks 206 F4
Green Hill Wilts 62 B5
Green Lane Devon 13 F11
Green Lane Hereford 98 B2
Green Lane Powys 130 D3
Green Lane Warks 117 E11
Green Lane Warks 118 B6
Green Moor S Yorks 186 B3
Green Ore Som 44 C5
Green Parlour Bath 45 C8
Green Quarter Cumb 221 E9
Green St Green London 68 G3
Green Side W Yorks 197 E7
Green Side W Yorks 205 G11
Green Street E Sus 38 E3
Green Street Essex 87 F10
Green Street Glos 80 B5
Green Street Glos 80 E3
Green Street Herts 85 F11
Green Street Herts 105 G9
Green Street W Sus 35 C10
Green Street Worcs 99 B7
Green Street Worcs 99 C7
Green Street Green Kent 68 E5
Green Street Green London 68 G3
Green Tye Herts 86 B6
Greenacres Gtr Man 196 F2
Greenan Argyll 275 G11
Greenbank Falk 279 F7
Greenbank Shetland 312 C7
Greenbank W Ches 183 G10
Greenburn W Loth 269 C8
Greencroft Durham 242 G5
Greendale E Ches 184 F5
Greendikes Northumb 264 D3
Greendown Som 44 C5
Greendykes Northumb 264 D3
Greenend N Lnrk 268 C4
Greenend Oxon 100 G6
Greenfaulds N Lnrk 278 G5
Greenfield C Beds 103 E11
Greenfield Glasgow 268 C2
Greenfield Gtr Man 196 G3
Greenfield Highld 289 D11
Greenfield Highld 290 C4
Greenfield Oxon 84 G2
Greenfield = Maes-Glas Flint 181 F11
Greenfoot N Lnrk 268 B4
Greenford London 66 C6
Greengairs N Lnrk 278 G5
Greengarth Hall Cumb 219 E11
Greengate Gtr Man 196 D2
Greengate Norf 159 F10
Greengates W Yorks 205 F9
Greengill Cumb 229 D8
Greenhalgh Lancs 202 F4
Greenhall S Lnrk 268 D3
Greenham Dorset 28 G6
Greenham Som 27 C9
Greenham W Berks 64 F3
Greenhaugh Northumb 251 F7
Greenhead Borders 261 D11
Greenhead Dumfries 247 D9
Greenhead N Lnrk 268 E6
Greenhead Northumb 240 D5
Greenhead Staffs 169 F7
Greenheys Gtr Man 195 G8
Greenhill Dumfries 238 B4
Greenhill Durham 234 B3
Greenhill Falk 278 F6
Greenhill Hereford 98 B4
Greenhill Kent 71 F7
Greenhill Leics 153 G8
Greenhill London 67 B7
Greenhill S Yorks 186 E4
Greenhill Worcs 99 B10
Greenhill Worcs 116 B6
Greenhill Bank Shrops 149 B7
Greenhillocks Derbys 170 F6
Greenhills N Ayrs 267 F7
Greenhills S Lnrk 268 E2
Greenhithe Kent 68 E5
Greenholm E Ayrs 258 B2
Greenholme Cumb 221 D11
Greenhouse Borders 262 E3
Greenhow N Yorks 214 G2
Greenhow Hill N Yorks 214 G2
Greenigoe Orkney 314 F4
Greenland Highld 310 C6
Greenland S Yorks 186 D5
Greenland Mains Highld 310 C6
Greenlands Bucks 65 B9
Greenlands Worcs 117 D11
Greenlaw Aberds 302 D6
Greenlaw Borders 272 F4
Greenlaw Mains Midloth 270 C4
Greenlea Dumfries 238 B2
Greenley M Keynes 102 C6
Greenloaning Perth 286 G2
Greenlooms W Ches 167 C7
Greenman's Lane Wilts 62 C3
Greenmeadow Swindon 62 B6
Greenmeadow Torf 78 F3
Greenmount Gtr Man 195 E9
Greenmow Shetland 313 L6
Greenoak E Yorks 199 B10
Greenock Invclyd 276 F5
Greenock West Invclyd 276 F5
Greenodd Cumb 210 C6
Greenrigg W Loth 269 C8
Greenrow Cumb 238 G4
Greens Borders 249 F11
Greens Norton Northants 102 B3
Greensforge Staffs 133 F7
Greensgate Norf 160 F2
Greenside Cumb 222 E4
Greenside Derbys 186 F5
Greenside Gtr Man 184 B6
Greenside T & W 242 E4
Greenside W Yorks 197 D7
Greensidehill Northumb 263 F11
Greensplat Corn 5 D9
Greenstead Essex 107 F10
Greenstead Green Essex 106 F6
Greensted Essex 87 E8
Greensted Green Essex 87 E8
Greenstreet Green Suff 107 B10
Greenway Hereford 98 E4
Greenway Pembs 91 E11
Greenway Som 27 B11
Greenway V Glam 58 E5
Greenway Worcs 116 C4
Greenwell Cumb 240 F2
Greenwells Borders 262 C3
Greenwich London 67 D11
Greenwich Suff 108 C3
Greenwich Wilts 46 G2
Greenwith Common Corn 4 G5
Greenwoods Essex 87 F11
Greeny Orkney 314 D2
Greep Highld 298 E2
Greet Glos 99 E10
Greet Kent 54 B2
Greete Shrops 115 C11
Greetham Lincs 190 G4
Greetham Rutland 155 G8
Greetland W Yorks 196 C5
Greetland Wall Nook W Yorks 196 C5
Greetwell N Lincs 200 G2
Gregg Hall Cumb 221 G9
Gregson Lane Lancs 194 B5
Gregynog Powys 129 D11
Greinetobht W Isles 296 D4
Grèin W Isles 297 L2
Greinton Som 44 F2
Gremista Shetland 313 J6
Grenaby I o M 192 E3
Grendon Northants 121 E7
Grendon Warks 134 C5
Grendon Bishop Hereford 115 F11
Grendon Common Warks 134 D5
Grendon Green Hereford 115 F11
Grendon Underwood Bucks 102 G3
Grenofen Devon 12 G5
Grenoside S Yorks 186 C4
Greosabhagh W Isles 305 J3
Gresford Wrex 166 E5
Gresham Norf 160 B3
Greshornish Highld 298 D3
Gressenhall Norf 159 F9
Gressingham Lancs 211 F11
Gresty Green E Ches 168 E2
Greta Bridge Durham 223 C11
Gretna Dumfries 239 D8
Gretna Green Dumfries 239 D8
Gretton Glos 99 E10
Gretton Northants 137 E7
Gretton Shrops 131 D10
Gretton Fields Glos 99 E10
Grewelthorpe N Yorks 214 D4
Grey Green N Lincs 199 F9
Greyfield Bath 44 B6
Greygarth N Yorks 214 E3
Greylake Som 43 G11
Greylake Fosse Som 44 F2
Greynor Carms 75 D9
Greynor-isaf Carms 75 D9
Greyrigg Dumfries 248 F3
Greys Green Oxon 65 C8
Greysouthen Cumb 229 F7
Greystead Northumb 251 F7
Greystoke Cumb 230 E4
Greystoke Gill Cumb 230 F4
Greystone Aberds 292 D6
Greystone Aberds 302 F6
Greystone Angus 287 C9
Greystone Cumb 211 D10
Greystone Dumfries 237 B11
Greystonegill N Yorks 212 F3
Greystones S Yorks 186 D4
Greystones Warks 99 B11
Greytree Hereford 97 F11
Greywell Hants 49 C8
Griais W Isles 304 D6
Grianan W Isles 304 E6
Gribb Dorset 28 G5
Gribthorpe E Yorks 207 F11
Gridley Corner Devon 12 C3
Griff Warks 135 F7
Griffins Hill W Mid 133 G10
Griffithstown Torf 78 F3
Griffydam Leics 153 F8
Grigg Kent 53 E11
Griggs Green Hants 49 G10
Grillis Corn 2 B5
Grilstone Devon 26 C2
Grimbister Orkney 314 E3
Grimblethorpe Lincs 190 D2
Grimeford Village Lancs 194 E6
Grimes Hill Worcs 117 B11
Grimesthorpe S Yorks 186 C5
Grimethorpe S Yorks 198 F2
Griminis W Isles 296 D3
Griminis W Isles 296 F3
Grimister Shetland 312 D6
Grimley Worcs 116 E6
Grimness Orkney 314 G4
Grimoldby Lincs 190 D5
Grimpo Shrops 149 D7
Grimsargh Lancs 203 G7
Grimsbury Oxon 101 C9
Grimsby NE Lincs 201 E9
Grimscote Northants 120 G3
Grimscott Corn 24 F3
Grimshaw Blkburn 195 C8
Grimshaw Green Lancs 194 E3
Grimsthorpe Lincs 155 E10
Grimston E Yorks 209 F11
Grimston Leics 154 E3
Grimston Norf 158 E4
Grimston York 207 C8
Grimstone Dorset 17 C8
Grimstone End Suff 125 D8
Grinacombe Moor Devon 12 C4
Grindale E Yorks 218 E2
Grindigar Orkney 314 F5
Grindiscol Shetland 313 K6
Grindle Shrops 132 C5
Grindleford Derbys 186 F2
Grindleton Lancs 203 D11
Grindley Staffs 151 D10
Grindley Brook Shrops 167 G8
Grindlow Derbys 185 F11
Grindon Northumb 273 G8
Grindon Staffs 169 E9
Grindon Stockton 234 F3
Grindon T & W 243 G9
Grindonmoor Gate Staffs 169 E9
Grindsbrook Booth Derbys 185 D10
Gringley on the Hill Notts 188 C2
Grinsdale Cumb 239 F9
Grinshill Shrops 149 E10
Grinstead Hill Suff 125 G11
Grinton N Yorks 223 F10
Griomasaigh W Isles 297 G4
Griomsidar W Isles 304 F5
Grisdale Cumb 222 G5
Grishipoll Argyll 288 D3
Grisling Common E Sus 36 C6
Gristhorpe N Yorks 217 C11
Griston Norf 141 D8
Gritley Orkney 314 F5
Grittenham Wilts 62 C4
Grittlesend Hereford 98 B4
Grittleton Wilts 61 C11
Grizebeck Cumb 210 C4
Grizedale Cumb 220 G6
Groam Highld 300 E5
Grobister Orkney 314 D6
Grobsness Shetland 313 G5
Groby Leics 135 B10
Groes Conwy 165 C8
Groes Neath 57 D9
Groes Efa Denb 165 B10
Groes-faen Rhondda 58 C5
Groes-fawr Denb 165 B10
Groes-lwyd Mon 96 G6
Groes-lwyd Powys 148 G4
Groes-wen Caerph 58 B6
Groesffordd Gwyn 144 B5
Groesffordd Powys 95 F11
Groesffordd Marli Denb 181 G8
Groeslon Gwyn 163 C8
Groeslon Gwyn 163 D7
Groespluan Powys 130 B4
Grogport Argyll 255 C9
Gromford Suff 127 F7
Gronant Flint 181 E9
Gronwen Shrops 148 D5
Groombridge E Sus 52 F4
Grosmont Mon 97 G8
Grosmont N Yorks 226 D6
Gross Green Warks 119 F7
Grotaig Highld 300 G4
Groton Suff 107 C9
Grotton Gtr Man 196 G3

336 Gro – Har

Grougfoot Falk 279 F10
Grove Bucks 103 G8
Grove Dorset 17 G10
Grove Hereford 98 C2
Grove Kent 71 G8
Grove Notts 188 F2
Grove Oxon 82 G6
Grove Pembs 73 E7
Grove End Kent 69 G11
Grove End Warks 100 D6
Grove End Warks 134 D3
Grove Green Kent 53 B9
Grove Hill E Sus 23 C10
Grove Hill Kent 71 G8
Grove Park London 67 D8
Grove Park London 68 E2
Grove Town W Yorks 198 C3
Grove Vale W Mid 133 E10
Grovehill E Yorks 208 F6
Grovehill Herts 85 D9
Groves Kent 55 B9
Grovesend Swansea 75 E9
Grub Street Staffs 150 D5
Grubb Street Kent 68 F5
Grudie Highld 300 C3
Gruids Highld 309 J5
Gruinard House Highld 307 K4
Gruinards Highld 309 K5
Grula Highld 294 C5
Gruline Argyll 289 E7
Gruline Ho Argyll 289 F7
Grumbeg Highld 308 F6
Grumbla Corn 1 D4
Grunasound Shetland 313 K5
Grundisburgh Suff 126 G4
Grunsagill Lancs 203 C11
Gruting Shetland 313 J4
Grutness Shetland 313 N6
Gryn Goch Gwyn 162 F6
Gualachulain Highld 284 C5
Gualin Ho Highld 308 D3
Guard House W Yorks 204 E6
Guardbridge Fife 287 F8
Guarlford Worcs 98 B6
Guay Perth 286 C4
Gubbion's Green Essex 88 B2
Gubblecote Herts 84 C6
Guesachan Highld 289 B10
Guestling Green E Sus 38 E5
Guestling Thorn E Sus 38 D4
Guestwick Norf 159 D11
Guestwick Green Norf 159 D11
Guide Blkburn 195 B8
Guide Bridge Gtr Man 184 B6
Guide Post Northumb 253 F7
Guilden Morden Cambs 104 C5
Guilden Sutton W Ches 166 B6
Guildford Sur 50 D3
Guildford Park Sur 50 D3
Guildiehaugh W Loth 269 B9
Guildtown Perth 286 D5
Guilford Pembs 73 D7
Guilsborough Northants 120 C3
Guilsfield = Cegidfa Powys 148 G4
Guilthwaite S Yorks 187 D7
Guilton Kent 55 B9
Guineaford Devon 40 F5
Guisachan Highld 300 G3
Guisborough Redcar 226 B2
Guiseley W Yorks 205 E9
Guist Norf 159 D9
Guith Orkney 314 C5
Guiting Power Glos 99 G11
Gulberwick Shetland 313 K6
Gullane E Loth 281 E9
Guller's End Worcs 99 D7
Gulling Green Suff 124 F6
Gullom Holme Cumb 231 F9
Gulval Corn 1 C5
Gulworthy Devon 12 G4
Gumfreston Pembs 73 E10
Gumley Leics 136 E3
Gummow's Shop Corn 5 D7
Gun Green Kent 53 G9
Gun Hill E Sus 23 C9
Gunby E Yorks 207 F10
Gunby Lincs 155 E8
Gunby Lincs 175 B7
Gundenham Som 27 C10
Gundleton Hants 48 G6
Gunn Devon 40 G6
Gunnersbury London 67 D7
Gunnerside N Yorks 223 F9
Gunnerton Northumb 241 C10
Gunness N Lincs 199 E10
Gunnislake Corn 12 G4
Gunnista Shetland 313 J7
Guns Village W Mid 133 E9
Gunstone Staffs 133 C7
Gunter's Bridge W Sus 35 C7
Gunthorpe Lincs 188 B4
Gunthorpe Norf 159 C10
Gunthorpe Notts 171 G11
Gunthorpe P'boro 138 C3
Gunthorpe Rutland 137 B7
Gunton Suff 143 D10
Gunville I o W 20 D5
Gunwalloe Corn 2 E5
Gunwalloe Fishing Cove Corn 2 E5
Gupworthy Som 42 F3
Gurnard I o W 20 B5
Gurnett E Ches 184 G6
Gurney Slade Som 44 D6
Gurnos M Tydf 77 D8
Gurnos Powys 76 D3
Gushmere Kent 54 B4
Gussage All Saints Dorset 31 E8
Gussage St Andrew Dorset 31 E7
Gussage St Michael Dorset 31 E7
Gustard Wood Herts 85 B11
Guston Kent 55 E10
Gutcher Shetland 312 D7
Guthram Gowt Lincs 156 E3
Guthrie Angus 287 B9
Guyhirn Cambs 139 C7
Guyhirn Gull Cambs 139 C7
Guy's Cliffe Warks 118 D5
Guy's Head Lincs 157 D9
Guy's Marsh Dorset 30 C4
Guyzance Northumb 252 C6
Gwaelod-y-garth Cardiff 58 C6
Gwaenysgor Flint 181 E9
Gwalchmai Anglesey 178 F5
Gwalchmai Uchaf Anglesey 178 F5
Gwallon Corn 2 C2
Gwastad Pembs 91 G10
Gwastadgoed Gwyn 145 G11
Gwastadnant Gwyn 163 D10
Gwaun-Cae-Gurwen Neath 76 C2
Gwaun-Leision Neath 76 C2
Gwavas Corn 2 D5
Gwavas Corn 2 G6
Gwbert Ceredig 92 B3
Gwedna Corn 2 C4
Gweek Corn 2 D6
Gwehelog Mon 78 E5
Gwenddwr Powys 95 C11
Gwennap Corn 2 B6
Gwenter Corn 2 F6
Gwern y brenin Shrops 148 D6
Gwern-y-Steeple V Glam 58 D5
Gwernaffield-y-Waun Flint 166 C2
Gwernafon Powys 129 E8
Gwerneirin Powys 129 F10
Gwerneirin Powys 130 G3
Gwernesney Mon 78 E6
Gwernogle Carms 93 E10
Gwernol Denb 166 E2
Gwernydd Powys 129 C11
Gwernymynydd Flint 166 C2
Gwersyllt Wrex 166 E4
Gwespyr Flint 181 E10
Gwills Corn 4 D6
Gwinear Corn 2 B3
Gwinear Downs Corn 2 C4
Gwithian Corn 2 A3
Gwredog Anglesey 178 D6
Gwrhay Caerph 77 F11
Gwyddelwern Denb 165 F9
Gwyddgrug Carms 93 D9
Gwynfryn Wrex 166 E3
Gwystre Powys 113 D11
Gwytherin Conwy 164 C5
Gyfelia Wrex 166 F4
Gyffin Conwy 180 F3
Gylen Park Argyll 289 G10
Gyre Orkney 314 F3
Gyrn Denb 165 D11
Gyrn-goch Gwyn 162 F6

H

Habberley Shrops 131 C7
Habberley Worcs 116 B6
Habergham Lancs 204 G2
Habertoft Lincs 175 B8
Habin W Sus 34 C4
Habrough NE Lincs 200 E6
Haccombe Devon 14 G3
Haceby Lincs 155 B10
Hacheston Suff 126 F6
Hack Green E Ches 167 F10
Hackbridge London 67 F9
Hackenthorpe S Yorks 186 E6
Hackford Norf 141 C11
Hackforth N Yorks 224 G4
Hackland Orkney 314 D3
Hackleton Northants 120 F6
Hacklinge Kent 55 C10
Hackman's Gate Worcs 117 B7
Hackness N Yorks 227 G9
Hackness Orkney 314 G3
Hackness Som 43 D10
Hackney London 67 C10
Hackney Wick London 67 C11
Hackthorn Lincs 189 E7
Hackthorn Wilts 47 D7
Hackthorpe Cumb 230 G6
Haclait W Isles 297 G4
Haconby Lincs 156 D2
Hacton London 68 B4
Haddacott Devon 25 C8
Hadden Borders 263 B7
Haddenham Bucks 84 D2
Haddenham Cambs 123 B9
Haddenham End Field Cambs 123 B9
Haddington E Loth 281 G10
Haddington Lincs 172 C6
Haddiscoe Norf 143 D8
Haddoch Aberds 302 E5
Haddon Cambs 138 E2
Haddon E Ches 169 B7
Hade Edge W Yorks 196 F6
Hademore Staffs 134 B3
Haden Cross W Mid 133 F9
Hadfield Derbys 185 B8
Hadham Cross Herts 86 B6
Hadham Ford Herts 105 G8
Hadleigh Essex 69 B10
Hadleigh Suff 107 C10
Hadleigh Heath Suff 107 C9
Hadley London 86 F2
Hadley Telford 150 G3
Hadley Worcs 117 E7
Hadley Castle Telford 150 G3
Hadley End Staffs 152 E2
Hadley Wood London 86 F3
Hadlow Kent 52 D6
Hadlow Down E Sus 37 C8
Hadlow Stair Kent 52 D6
Hadnall Shrops 149 F10
Hadspen Som 45 G7
Hadstock Essex 105 C11
Hadston Northumb 253 D7
Hady Derbys 186 G5
Hadzor Worcs 117 E8
Haffenden Quarter Kent 53 E11
Hafod Swansea 57 C7
Hafod-Dinbych Conwy 164 E5
Hafod Grove Pembs 92 C2
Hafod-lom Conwy 180 G5
Hafod-y-Green Denb 181 G8
Hafodiwan Ceredig 111 G7
Hafodyrynys Bl Gwent 78 F2
Hag Fold Gtr Man 195 G7
Haggate Gtr Man 196 F2
Haggate Lancs 204 F3
Haggbeck Cumb 239 C11
Haggersta Shetland 313 J5
Haggerston London 67 C10
Haggerston Northumb 273 G10
Hagginton Hill Devon 40 D5
Haggrister Shetland 312 F5
Haggs Falk 278 F5
Haghill Glasgow 268 B2
Hagley Hereford 97 C11
Hagley Worcs 133 G8
Hagloe Glos 79 D11
Hagmore Green Suff 107 D9
Hagnaby Lincs 174 C4
Hagnaby Lincs 191 F7
Hagnaby Lock Lincs 174 D4
Hague Bar Derbys 185 D7
Hagworthingham Lincs 174 B4
Haigh Gtr Man 194 F6
Haigh S Yorks 197 E9
Haigh Moor W Yorks 197 C9
Haighton Green Lancs 203 G7
Haighton Top Lancs 203 G7
Hail Weston Cambs 122 E3
Haile Cumb 219 D10
Hailes Glos 99 E10
Hailey Herts 86 C5
Hailey Oxon 64 B6
Hailey Oxon 82 C5
Hailsham E Sus 23 D9
Hailstone Hill Wilts 81 G9
Haimer Highld 310 C5
Haimwood Powys 148 F6
Hainault London 87 G7
Haine Kent 71 F11
Hainford Norf 160 F4
Hains Dorset 30 D3
Hainton Lincs 189 E11
Hainworth W Yorks 205 F7
Hainworth Shaw W Yorks 205 F7
Hairmyres S Lnrk 268 E2
Haisthorpe E Yorks 218 G2
Hakeford Devon 40 F6
Hakin Pembs 72 D5
Halabezack Corn 2 C6
Halam Notts 171 E11
Halamanning Corn 2 C3
Halbeath Fife 280 D2
Halberton Devon 27 E8
Halcon Som 28 B2
Halcro Highld 310 C6
Haldens Herts 86 C2
Hale Cumb 211 D10
Hale Gtr Man 184 D3
Hale Halton 183 E7
Hale Hants 31 D11
Hale Kent 71 F9
Hale Medway 69 F9
Hale Som 30 B3
Hale Sur 49 D10
Hale Bank Halton 183 E7
Hale Barns Gtr Man 184 D3
Hale Coombe N Som 44 B2
Hale End London 86 G5
Hale Green E Sus 23 C9
Hale Mills Corn 4 G5
Hale Nook Lancs 202 E3
Hale Street Kent 53 D7
Halecommon W Sus 34 C4
Hales Norf 143 D7
Hales Staffs 150 C4
Hales Bank Hereford 116 G2
Hales Green Derbys 169 G11
Hales Green Norf 143 D7
Hales Park Worcs 116 B5
Hales Place Kent 54 B6
Hales Street Norf 142 F3
Hales Wood Hereford 98 E2
Halesfield Telford 132 C4
Halesgate Lincs 156 D6
Halesowen W Mid 133 G9
Halesworth Suff 127 B7
Halewood Mers 183 D7
Half Moon Village Devon 14 B3
Halford Shrops 131 G8
Halford Warks 100 B5
Halfpenny Cumb 211 B10
Halfpenny Furze Carms 74 C3
Halfpenny Green Staffs 132 E6
Halfway Carms 75 E8
Halfway Carms 94 E2
Halfway Carms 94 E6
Halfway S Yorks 186 E6
Halfway W Berks 64 F2
Halfway Wilts 45 D11
Halfway Bridge W Sus 34 C6
Halfway House Shrops 148 G6
Halfway Houses Gtr Man 195 F9
Halfway Houses Kent 70 E2
Halfway Street Kent 55 D9
Halgabron Corn 11 D7
Halifax W Yorks 196 B5
Halkburn Borders 271 G9
Halket E Ayrs 267 E8
Halkirk Highld 310 D5
Halkyn = Helygain Flint 182 G2
Halkyn Mountain Flint 182 G2
Hall Bower W Yorks 196 E6
Hall Broom S Yorks 186 D3
Hall Cross Lancs 202 G4
Hall Dunnerdale Cumb 220 F4
Hall End Beds 103 B10
Hall End C Beds 103 D11
Hall End Lincs 174 E6
Hall End S Glos 61 B8
Hall End Warks 134 C5
Hall Flat Worcs 117 C9
Hall Garth York 207 C9
Hall Green E Ches 168 D4
Hall Green Essex 106 D5
Hall Green Lancs 194 C3
Hall Green Lancs 194 F4
Hall Green W Mid 133 E10
Hall Green W Mid 134 G2
Hall Green W Mid 135 G7
Hall Green W Yorks 197 D10
Hall Green Wrex 167 G7
Hall Grove Herts 89 C8
Hall i' th' Wood Gtr Man 195 E8
Hall of Clestrain Orkney 314 F2
Hall of Tankerness Orkney 314 F5
Hall of the Forest Shrops 130 G4
Hall Santon Cumb 220 E2
Hall Waberthwaite Cumb 220 F2
Hallam Fields Derbys 153 B9
Halland E Sus 23 B8
Hallaton Leics 136 D5
Hallatrow Bath 44 B6
Hallbankgate Cumb 240 F3
Halleaths Dumfries 248 G3
Hallen S Glos 60 C5
Hallend Warks 118 D2
Hallew Corn 5 D10
Hallfield Gate Derbys 170 D5
Hallgarth Durham 234 C2
Hallglen Falk 279 F7
Halliburton Borders 261 B11
Halliburton Borders 272 F3
Hallin Highld 298 D2
Halling Medway 69 G8
Hallingbury Street Essex 87 B8
Hallington Lincs 190 D4
Hallington Northumb 241 B11
Halliwell Gtr Man 195 E8
Hallon Shrops 132 D5
Hallonsford Shrops 132 D5
Halloughton Notts 171 E11
Hallow Worcs 116 F6
Hallow Heath Worcs 116 F6
Hallowes Derbys 186 F5
Hallowsgate W Ches 167 B8
Hallrule Borders 262 G3
Halls E Loth 282 G3
Hall's Cross E Sus 23 D11
Halls Green Essex 86 D6
Hall's Green Herts 104 F5
Hall's Green Kent 52 D4
Hallsands Devon 9 G11
Hallsford Bridge Essex 87 E9
Hallspill Devon 25 C7
Hallthwaites Cumb 210 B3
Hallwood Green Glos 98 E3
Hallworthy Corn 11 D9
Hallyards Borders 260 B6
Hallyburton House Perth 286 D6
Hallyne Borders 270 G3
Halmer End Staffs 168 F3
Halmond's Frome Hereford 98 B3
Halmore Glos 79 E11
Halmyre Mains Borders 270 F3
Halnaker W Sus 22 B6
Halsall Lancs 193 E11
Halse Northants 101 C11
Halse Som 27 B10
Halsetown Corn 2 B2
Halsfordwood Devon 14 C3
Halsham E Yorks 201 B9
Halsinger Devon 40 F4
Halstead Essex 106 E6
Halstead Kent 68 G3
Halstead Leics 136 B4
Halstock Dorset 29 F8
Halsway Som 42 F6
Haltcliff Bridge Cumb 230 D3
Halterworth Hants 32 C5
Haltham Lincs 174 C2
Haltoft End Lincs 174 F5
Halton Bucks 84 C5
Halton Halton 183 E8
Halton Lancs 211 G10
Halton Northumb 241 D11
Halton W Yorks 206 G2
Halton Wrex 148 B6
Halton Barton Corn 7 B8
Halton Brook Halton 183 E8
Halton East N Yorks 204 C6
Halton Fenside Lincs 174 C6
Halton Gill N Yorks 213 D7
Halton Green Lancs 211 F10
Halton Holegate Lincs 174 B6
Halton Lea Gate Northumb 240 F5
Halton Moor W Yorks 206 G2
Halton Shields Northumb 242 D2
Halton View Halton 183 D8
Halton West N Yorks 204 C2
Haltwhistle Northumb 240 E6
Halvergate Norf 143 B8
Halvosso Corn 2 C6
Halwell Devon 8 E5
Halwill Devon 12 B4
Halwill Junction Devon 24 G6
Halwin Corn 2 C5
Ham Devon 28 G2
Ham Glos 79 F11
Ham Glos 99 G9
Ham Highld 310 B6
Ham Kent 55 C10
Ham London 67 E7
Ham Plym 7 D9
Ham Shetland 313 K1
Ham Som 27 C11
Ham Som 28 B3
Ham Som 28 E3
Ham Som 45 D7
Ham Wilts 63 G10
Ham Common Dorset 30 B4
Ham Green Bucks 83 B11
Ham Green Hants 48 G2
Ham Green Hereford 98 C4
Ham Green Kent 38 B5
Ham Green Kent 69 F10
Ham Green N Som 60 D4
Ham Green Wilts 61 G11
Ham Green Worcs 117 E10
Ham Hill Kent 69 G8
Ham Moor Sur 66 G5
Ham Street Som 44 G5
Hamar Shetland 312 F5
Hamarhill Orkney 314 C5
Hamars Shetland 313 G6
Hamble-le-Rice Hants 33 F7
Hambleden Bucks 65 B9
Hambledon Hants 33 E10
Hambledon Sur 50 F3
Hambleton Lancs 202 E3
Hambleton N Yorks 205 C7
Hambleton N Yorks 207 G7
Hambleton Moss Side Lancs 202 E3
Hambridge Som 28 C5
Hambrook S Glos 60 D6
Hambrook W Sus 22 B3
Hameringham Lincs 174 B4
Hamerton Cambs 122 B2
Hametoun Shetland 313 K1
Hamilton S Lnrk 268 D3
Hamister Shetland 313 G7
Hamlet Dorset 29 F9
Hammer W Sus 49 G11
Hammer Bottom Hants 49 G11
Hammerfield Herts 85 D8
Hammerpot W Sus 35 F9
Hammersmith Derbys 170 E5
Hammersmith London 67 D8
Hammerwich Staffs 133 B11
Hammerwood E Sus 52 F2
Hammill Kent 55 B9
Hammond Street Herts 86 E4
Hammoon Dorset 30 E4
Hamnavoe Shetland 312 E4
Hamnavoe Shetland 312 E6
Hamnavoe Shetland 312 F6
Hamnavoe Shetland 313 K5
Hamnish Clifford Hereford 115 F10
Hamp Som 43 F10
Hampden Park E Sus 23 E10
Hampen Glos 81 B9
Hamperden End Essex 105 E11
Hamperley Shrops 131 F8
Hampers Green W Sus 35 C7
Hampeth Northumb 252 B5
Hampnett Glos 81 B10
Hampole S Yorks 198 E4
Hampreston Dorset 19 B7
Hampsfield Cumb 211 C8
Hampson Green Lancs 202 C5
Hampstead London 67 B9
Hampstead Garden Suburb London 67 B9
Hampstead Norreys W Berks 64 D4
Hampsthwaite N Yorks 205 B11
Hampton Kent 71 F7
Hampton London 66 F6
Hampton Shrops 132 F4
Hampton Swindon 81 G11
Hampton Worcs 99 C10
Hampton Bank Shrops 149 C9
Hampton Beech Shrops 130 B6
Hampton Bishop Hereford 97 D11
Hampton Fields Glos 80 F5
Hampton Gay Oxon 83 B7
Hampton Green Glos 80 E5
Hampton Green W Ches 167 F8
Hampton Hargate P'boro 138 E3
Hampton Heath W Ches 167 F7
Hampton Hill London 66 E6
Hampton in Arden W Mid 134 G4
Hampton Loade Shrops 132 F5
Hampton Lovett Worcs 117 D7
Hampton Lucy Warks 118 F5
Hampton Magna Warks 118 D5
Hampton on the Hill Warks 118 E5
Hampton Park Hereford 97 D10
Hampton Park Soton 32 D6
Hampton Poyle Oxon 83 B8
Hampton Wick London 67 F7
Hamptons Kent 52 C6
Hamptworth Wilts 32 D2
Hamrow Norf 159 E8
Hamsey E Sus 36 E6
Hamsey Green London 51 B10
Hamshill Glos 80 E3
Hamstall Ridware Staffs 152 F2
Hamstead I o W 20 C4
Hamstead W Mid 133 E10
Hamstead Marshall W Berks 64 F2
Hamsterley Durham 233 E8
Hamsterley Durham 242 F4
Hamstreet Kent 54 G4
Hamworthy Poole 18 C5
Hanbury Staffs 152 D3
Hanbury Worcs 117 E9
Hanbury Woodend Staffs 152 D3
Hanby Lincs 155 C10
Hanchett Village Suff 106 B3
Hanchurch Staffs 168 G4
Hand Green W Ches 167 C8
Handbridge W Ches 166 B6
Handcross W Sus 36 B3
Handforth E Ches 184 E5
Handless Shrops 131 E7
Handley Derbys 170 C5
Handley W Ches 167 D7
Handley Green Essex 87 E11
Handsacre Staffs 151 F11
Handside Herts 86 C2
Handsworth S Yorks 186 D6
Handsworth W Mid 133 E10
Handsworth Wood W Mid 133 E11
Handy Cross Bucks 84 G5
Handy Cross Devon 24 B6
Handy Cross Som 42 G6
Hanford Dorset 30 E4
Hanford Stoke 168 G5
Hangersley Hants 31 F11
Hanging Bank Kent 52 C3
Hanging Heaton W Yorks 197 C9
Hanging Houghton Northants 120 C5
Hanging Langford Wilts 46 F4
Hangingshaw Borders 261 C9
Hangingshaw Dumfries 248 F4
Hangleton Brighton 36 F3
Hangleton W Sus 35 G9
Hangsman Hill S Yorks 199 E7
Hanham S Glos 60 E6
Hanham Green S Glos 60 E6
Hankelow E Ches 167 F11
Hankerton Wilts 81 G7
Hankham E Sus 23 D10
Hanley Stoke 168 F5
Hanley Castle Worcs 98 C6
Hanley Child Worcs 116 E3
Hanley Swan Worcs 98 C6
Hanley William Worcs 116 D3
Hanlith N Yorks 213 G8
Hanmer Wrex 149 B9
Hannaford Devon 25 B10
Hannafore Corn 6 E5
Hannah Lincs 191 F8
Hanningfields Green Suff 125 G7
Hannington Hants 48 B4
Hannington Northants 120 C6
Hannington Swindon 81 G11
Hannington Wick Swindon 81 F11
Hanscombe End C Beds 104 E2
Hansel Devon 8 F6
Hansel Village S Ayrs 257 C9
Hansley Cross Staffs 169 G9
Hanslope M Keynes 102 B6
Hanthorpe Lincs 155 E11
Hanwell London 67 C7
Hanwell Oxon 101 C8
Hanwood Shrops 131 B8
Hanwood Bank Shrops 149 G8
Hanworth Brack 65 F11
Hanworth London 66 E6
Hanworth Norf 160 B3
Happendon S Lnrk 259 C9
Happisburgh Norf 161 C7
Happisburgh Common Norf 161 D7
Hapsford Som 45 D9
Hapsford W Ches 183 G7
Hapton Lancs 203 G11
Hapton Norf 142 D3
Hararden = Penarlëg Flint 166 B4
Harberton Devon 8 D5
Harbertonford Devon 8 D5
Harbledown Kent 54 B6
Harborne W Mid 133 G10
Harborough Magna Warks 119 B9
Harborough Parva Warks 119 B9
Harbottle Northumb 251 C10
Harbour Heights E Sus 36 G6
Harbour Village Pembs 91 D8
Harbourland Kent 53 B9
Harbourneford Devon 8 C4
Harbours Hill Worcs 117 D9
Harbridge Hants 31 E10
Harbridge Green Hants 31 E10
Harburn W Loth 269 C10
Harbury Warks 119 F7
Harby Leics 154 C4
Harby Notts 188 G5
Harcombe Devon 14 E3
Harcombe Devon 15 C9
Harcourt Corn 3 B8
Harcourt Hill Oxon 83 E7
Hardbreck Orkney 314 F4
Hardeicke Glos 80 C4
Harden S Yorks 197 G7
Harden W Mid 133 C10
Harden W Yorks 205 F7
Harden Park E Ches 184 F4
Hardendale Cumb 221 C11
Hardenhuish Wilts 62 E2
Hardgate Aberds 293 C9
Hardgate Dumfries 237 C10
Hardgate N Yorks 214 G5
Hardgate W Dunb 277 G10
Hardham W Sus 35 D8
Hardhorn Lancs 202 F3
Hardingham Norf 141 C10
Hardings Booth Staffs 169 C9
Hardings Wood Staffs 168 E4
Hardingstone Northants 120 F5
Hardington Som 45 C8
Hardington Mandeville Som 29 E8
Hardington Marsh Som 29 F8
Hardington Moor Som 29 E8
Hardiston Perth 279 B11
Hardisworthy Devon 24 C2
Hardley Hants 32 G6
Hardley Street Norf 143 C7
Hardmead M Keynes 103 B8
Hardrow N Yorks 223 G7
Hardstoft Derbys 170 C6
Hardstoft Common Derbys 170 C6
Hardway Hants 33 G10
Hardway Som 45 G8
Hardwick Bucks 84 B4
Hardwick Cambs 122 D3
Hardwick Cambs 123 F7
Hardwick Norf 142 F4
Hardwick Norf 158 F2
Hardwick Northants 121 D7
Hardwick Oxon 82 D5
Hardwick Oxon 101 C8
Hardwick Oxon 101 F11
Hardwick S Yorks 187 D7
Hardwick Shrops 131 E7
Hardwick Stockton 234 G4
Hardwick W Mid 133 D11
Hardwick Green Worcs 98 E6
Hardwick Village Notts 187 F10
Hardwicke Glos 80 C3
Hardwicke Glos 99 F8
Hardwicke Hereford 96 C5
Hardy's Green Essex 107 G8
Hare Som 28 D3
Hare Appletree Lancs 202 B6
Hare Edge Derbys 186 G4
Hare Green Essex 107 G11
Hare Hatch Wokingham 65 D10
Hare Street Essex 86 D6
Hare Street Herts 104 F6
Hare Street Herts 105 F7
Hareby Lincs 174 B4
Harecroft W Yorks 205 F7
Hareden Lancs 203 C8
Harefield London 85 G9
Harefield Soton 33 E7
Harefield Grove London 85 G9
Haregate Staffs 169 D7
Harehill Derbys 152 B3
Harehills W Yorks 206 G2
Harehope Borders 270 G4
Harehope Northumb 264 E3
Harelaw Durham 242 G5
Hareleeshill S Lnrk 268 E5
Hareplain Kent 53 F10
Haresceugh Cumb 231 C8
Harescombe Glos 80 C4
Haresfield Glos 80 C4
Haresfield Swindon 82 G2
Haresfinch Mers 183 B8
Hareshaw N Lnrk 268 C6
Hareshaw Head Northumb 251 F9
Harestanes E Dunb 278 G3
Harestock Hants 48 G3
Harewood W Yorks 206 D2
Harewood End Hereford 97 F10
Harewood Hill W Yorks 204 F6
Harford Carms 94 C2
Harford Devon 8 D2
Harford Devon 40 G6
Hargate Norf 142 E2
Hargate Hill Derbys 185 C8
Hargatewall Derbys 185 F10
Hargrave Northants 121 C10
Hargrave Suff 124 F5
Hargrave W Ches 167 C7
Harker Cumb 239 E9
Harker Marsh Cumb 229 E7
Harkland Shetland 312 E6
Harknett's Gate Essex 86 D6
Harkstead Suff 108 E3
Harlaston Staffs 152 G4
Harlaw Ho Aberds 303 G7
Harlaxton Lincs 155 C7
Harle Syke Lancs 204 F3
Harlech Gwyn 145 C11
Harlequin Notts 154 B3
Harlescott Shrops 149 F10
Harlesden London 67 C8
Harlesthorpe Derbys 187 F7
Harleston Devon 8 F5
Harleston Norf 142 G4
Harleston Suff 125 F10
Harlestone Northants 120 E4
Harley S Yorks 186 B5
Harley Shrops 131 C11
Harley Shute E Sus 38 F3
Harleyholm S Lnrk 259 B10
Harleywood Glos 80 F4
Harling Road Norf 141 F9
Harlington C Beds 103 E10
Harlington London 66 D5
Harlington S Yorks 198 G3
Harlosh Highld 298 E2
Harlow Essex 86 C6
Harlow Carr N Yorks 205 C11
Harlow Green T & W 243 F7
Harlow Hill N Yorks 205 C11
Harlow Hill Northumb 242 D3
Harlthorpe E Yorks 207 F10
Harlton Cambs 123 G7
Harlyn Corn 10 F3
Harman's Corner Kent 69 G11
Harman's Cross Dorset 18 E5
Harmans Water Brack 65 F11
Harmby N Yorks 214 B2
Harmer Green Herts 86 B3
Harmer Hill Shrops 149 E9
Harmondsworth London 66 D5
Harmston Lincs 173 C7
Harnage Shrops 131 C11
Harnham Northumb 242 B3
Harnham Wilts 31 B10
Harnham Wilts 31 B11
Harnhill Glos 81 E9
Harold Hill London 87 G8
Harold Park London 87 G9
Harold Wood London 87 G8
Haroldston West Pembs 72 B5
Haroldswick Shetland 312 B8
Harome N Yorks 216 C2
Harpenden Herts 85 C10
Harpenden Common Herts 85 C10
Harper Green Gtr Man 195 F8
Harperley Durham 242 G5
Harper's Gate Staffs 169 D7
Harper's Green Norf 159 E8
Harpford Devon 15 C7
Harpham E Yorks 217 G11
Harpley Norf 158 D5
Harpley Worcs 116 E3
Harpole Northants 120 E3
Harpsdale Highld 310 D5
Harpsden Oxon 65 C9
Harpsden Bottom Oxon 65 C9
Harpswell Lincs 188 D6
Harpton Powys 114 F4
Harpur Hill Derbys 185 G9
Harpurhey Gtr Man 195 G11
Harraby Cumb 239 G10
Harracott Devon 25 B9
Harrapool Highld 295 C8

Har – Her 337

Harras Cumb 219 B9
Harraton T & W 243 G7
Harrier Shetland 313 J1
Harrietfield Perth 286 E3
Harrietsham Kent 53 C11
Harringay London 67 B10
Harrington Cumb 228 F5
Harrington Lincs 190 G5
Harrington Northants 136 G5
Harringworth Northants 137 D8
Harris Highld 294 F5
Harriseahead Staffs 168 D5
Harriston Cumb 229 C9
Harrogate N Yorks 206 C2
Harrold Beds 121 F8
Harrop Dale Gtr Man 196 F4
Harrow Highld 310 B6
Harrow London 67 B7
Harrow Green Suff 125 G7
Harrow Hill Glos 79 B10
Harrow on the Hill London 67 B7
Harrow Street Suff 107 D9
Harrow Weald London 85 G11
Harrowbarrow Corn 7 B7
Harrowbeer Devon 7 B10
Harrowby Lincs 155 B8
Harrowden Beds 103 B11
Harrowgate Hill Darl 224 B5
Harrowgate Village Darl 224 B5
Harry Stoke S Glos 60 D6
Harston Cambs 123 G8
Harston Leics 154 C6
Harswell E Yorks 208 E2
Hart Hrtlpl 234 E5
Hart Common Gtr Man 194 F6
Hart Hill Luton 104 G2
Hart Station Hrtlpl 234 D5
Hartbarrow Cumb 221 G8
Hartburn Northumb 252 F3
Hartburn Stockton 225 B8
Hartcliffe Bristol 60 F5
Hartest Suff 124 G6
Hartest Hill Suff 124 G6
Hartfield E Sus 52 F3
Hartfield Highld 299 E7
Hartford Cambs 122 C5
Hartford Som 27 B7
Hartford W Ches 183 G10
Hartford End Essex 87 B11
Hartfordbeach W Ches 183 G10
Hartfordbridge Hants 49 B9
Hartforth N Yorks 224 D3
Hartgrove Dorset 30 D4
Hartham Herts 86 C4
Harthill N Lnrk 269 C8
Harthill S Yorks 187 E7
Harthill W Ches 167 D8
Hartington Derbys 169 C10
Hartland Devon 24 C3
Hartle Worcs 117 B8
Hartlebury Shrops 132 D4
Hartlebury Worcs 116 C6
Hartlebury Common Worcs 116 C6
Hartlepool Hrtlpl 234 E6
Hartley Cumb 222 D5
Hartley Kent 53 G9
Hartley Kent 68 F6
Hartley Northumb 243 B8
Hartley Plym 7 D9
Hartley Green Kent 68 F6
Hartley Green Staffs 151 D9
Hartley Mauditt Hants 49 F8
Hartley Westpall Hants 49 B7
Hartley Wintney Hants 49 B9
Hartlington N Yorks 213 G10
Hartlip Kent 69 G10
Hartmoor Dorset 30 C3
Hartmount Highld 301 B7
Hartoft End N Yorks 226 G5
Harton N Yorks 216 G4
Harton Shrops 131 F9
Harton T & W 243 E9
Hartpury Glos 98 F5
Hart's Green Suff 125 F7
Hart's Hill W Mid 133 F8
Hartsgreen Shrops 132 G5
Hartshead W Yorks 197 C7
Hartshead Green Gtr Man 196 G3
Hartshead Moor Side W Yorks 197 C7
Hartshead Moor Top W Yorks 197 B7
Hartshead Pike Gtr Man 196 G3
Hartshill Stoke 168 F5
Hartshill Warks 134 E6
Hartshill Green Warks 134 E6
Hartshorne Derbys 152 E6
Hartsop Cumb 221 C8
Hartswell Som 27 B9
Hartwell Northants 120 G5
Hartwell Staffs 151 B8
Hartwith N Yorks 214 G4
Hartwood Lancs 194 D5
Hartwood N Lnrk 268 D6
Hartwoodburn Borders 261 D11
Harvel Kent 68 G6
Harvest Hill W Mid 134 G5
Harvieston Stirl 277 D11
Harvills Hawthorn W Mid 133 E9
Harvington Worcs 99 B11
Harvington Worcs 117 C7
Harvington Cross Worcs 99 B11
Harvington Hill Worcs 99 B10
Harwell Notts 187 C11
Harwell Oxon 64 B3
Harwich Essex 108 E5
Harwood Durham 232 E2
Harwood Gtr Man 195 E8
Harwood Dale N Yorks 227 F9
Harwood Lee Gtr Man 195 E8
Harwood on Teviot Borders 249 B10
Harworth Notts 187 C10
Hasbury W Mid 133 G9
Hascombe Sur 50 E3
Haselbech Northants 120 B4
Haselbury Plucknett Som 29 E7
Haseley Warks 118 D4
Haseley Green Warks 118 D4
Haseley Knob Warks 118 C4
Haselor Warks 118 F2
Hasfield Glos 98 F6
Hasguard Pembs 72 D5
Haskayne Lancs 193 F11
Hasketon Suff 126 G4
Hasland Derbys 170 B5
Haslemere Sur 50 G2
Haslingbourne W Sus 35 C7
Haslingden Lancs 195 C9
Haslingfield Cambs 123 G8
Haslington E Ches 168 D2
Hasluck's Green W Mid 118 B2
Hassall E Ches 168 D3
Hassall Green E Ches 168 D3
Hassell Street Kent 54 D5
Hassendean Borders 262 E2
Hassingham Norf 143 B7
Hassocks W Sus 36 D3
Hassop Derbys 186 G2
Haster Highld 310 D7
Hasthorpe Lincs 175 B7
Hastigrow Highld 310 C6
Hasting Hill T & W 243 G9
Hastingleigh Kent 54 E5
Hastings E Sus 38 F4
Hastings Som 28 D4
Hastingwood Essex 87 D7
Hastoe Herts 84 D6
Haston Shrops 149 E10
Haswell Durham 234 C3
Haswell Moor Durham 234 C3
Haswell Plough Durham 234 C3
Haswellsykes Borders 260 B6
Hatch C Beds 104 B3
Hatch Devon 8 F4
Hatch Hants 49 C7
Hatch Wilts 30 B6
Hatch Beauchamp Som 28 C4
Hatch Bottom Hants 33 E7
Hatch End Beds 121 E11
Hatch End London 85 G10
Hatch Farm Hill W Sus 34 B6
Hatch Green Som 28 D4
Hatch Warren Hants 48 D6
Hatchet Gate Hants 32 G5
Hatchet Green Hants 31 D11
Hatching Green Herts 85 C10
Hatchmere W Ches 183 G9
Hatcliffe NE Lincs 201 G8
Hateley Heath W Mid 133 E10
Hatfield Hereford 115 F11
Hatfield Herts 86 D2
Hatfield S Yorks 199 F7
Hatfield Worcs 117 G7
Hatfield Broad Oak Essex 87 B8
Hatfield Chase S Yorks 199 E8
Hatfield Garden Village Herts 86 D2
Hatfield Heath Essex 87 B8
Hatfield Hyde Herts 86 C2
Hatfield Peverel Essex 88 C3
Hatfield Woodhouse S Yorks 199 F7
Hatford Oxon 82 G4
Hatherden Hants 47 C10
Hatherleigh Devon 25 G8
Hatherley Glos 99 G8
Hathern Leics 153 E9
Hatherop Glos 81 D11
Hathersage Derbys 186 E2
Hathersage Booths Derbys 186 E2
Hathershaw Gtr Man 196 G2
Hatherton E Ches 167 F11
Hatherton Staffs 151 G9
Hatley St George Cambs 122 G5
Hatston Orkney 314 E4
Hatt Corn 7 C7
Hatt Hill Hants 32 B4
Hatterseat Aberds 303 G9
Hattersley Gtr Man 185 C7
Hattingley Hants 48 F6
Hatton Aberds 303 F10
Hatton Angus 287 D9
Hatton Derbys 152 D4
Hatton Lincs 189 F11
Hatton London 66 D5
Hatton Moray 301 D11
Hatton Shrops 131 E9
Hatton Warks 118 D4
Hatton Warr 183 E9
Hatton Castle Aberds 303 E7
Hatton Grange Shrops 132 C5
Hatton Heath W Ches 167 C7
Hatton Hill Sur 66 G2
Hatton of Fintray Aberds 293 B10
Hatton Park Northants 121 D7
Hattonburn Aberds 293 C9
Hattoncrook Aberds 303 G8
Hattonknowe Borders 270 F4
Haugh E Ayrs 257 D11
Haugh Gtr Man 196 E2
Haugh Lincs 190 F6
Haugh-head Borders 261 B8
Haugh Head Northumb 264 D2
Haugh of Glass Moray 302 F4
Haugh of Kilnmaichlie Moray 301 F11
Haugh of Urr Dumfries 237 C10
Haugham Lincs 190 E4
Haughland Orkney 314 E5
Haughley Suff 125 E10
Haughley Green Suff 125 E10
Haughley New Street Suff 125 E10
Haughs of Clinterty Aberdeen 293 B10
Haughton E Ches 167 D9
Haughton Notts 187 G11
Haughton Powys 148 F6
Haughton Shrops 132 B4
Haughton Shrops 132 D3
Haughton Shrops 149 D7
Haughton Shrops 149 F11
Haughton Staffs 151 E7
Haughton Castle Northumb 241 C10
Haughton Green Gtr Man 184 C6
Haughton Le Skerne Darl 224 B6
Haughurst Hill W Berks 64 G5
Haulkerton Aberds 293 F9
Haultwick Herts 104 G6
Haunn Argyll 288 E5
Haunn W Isles 297 K3
Haunton Staffs 152 G4
Hauxton Cambs 123 G8
Havannah E Ches 168 C5
Havant Hants 22 B2
Haven Hereford 97 B11
Haven Hereford 115 G8
Haven Bank Lincs 174 E2
Haven Side E Yorks 201 B7
Havenstreet I o W 21 C7
Havercroft W Yorks 197 E11
Haverfordwest = Hwlffordd Pembs 73 B7
Haverhill Suff 106 B3
Haverigg Cumb 210 D3
Havering-atte-Bower London 87 G8
Haveringland Norf 160 E3
Haversham M Keynes 102 C6
Haverthwaite Cumb 210 C6
Haverton Hill Stockton 234 G5
Haviker Street Kent 53 D8
Havyatt Som 44 F4
Havyatt Green N Som 60 G3
Hawarden = Penarlâg Flint 166 B4
Hawbridge Worcs 99 B8
Hawbush Green Essex 106 G5
Hawcoat Cumb 210 E4
Hawcross Glos 98 E5
Hawddamor Gwyn 146 F3
Hawen Ceredig 92 B6
Hawes N Yorks 213 B7
Hawes' Green Norf 142 D4
Hawes Side Blkpool 202 G2
Hawford Worcs 116 E6
Hawgreen Shrops 150 D2
Hawick Borders 262 F2
Hawk Green Gtr Man 185 D7
Hawk Hill Cumb 228 F6
Hawkchurch Devon 28 G4
Hawkcombe Som 41 D11
Hawkedon Suff 124 G5
Hawkenbury Kent 52 F5
Hawkenbury Kent 53 E10
Hawkeridge Wilts 45 C11
Hawkerland Devon 15 D7
Hawkersland Cross Hereford 97 B10
Hawkes End W Mid 134 G6
Hawkesbury S Glos 61 B9
Hawkesbury Warks 135 G7
Hawkesbury Upton S Glos 61 B9
Hawkesley W Mid 117 B10
Hawkhill Northumb 264 G6
Hawkhope Northumb 250 F6
Hawkhurst Kent 53 G9
Hawkhurst Common E Sus 23 B8
Hawkinge Kent 55 F8
Hawkin's Hill Essex 106 E3
Hawkley Gtr Man 194 G5
Hawkley Hants 34 B2
Hawkridge Som 41 G11
Hawks Green Staffs 151 G9
Hawks Hill Bucks 66 B2
Hawk's Hill Sur 51 B7
Hawks Stones W Yorks 196 B2
Hawksdale Cumb 230 B3
Hawkshaw Blkburn 195 D9
Hawkshead Cumb 221 F7
Hawkshead Hill Cumb 220 F6
Hawksland S Lnrk 259 B8
Hawkspur Green Essex 106 E3
Hawkswick N Yorks 213 E9
Hawksworth Notts 172 G3
Hawksworth W Yorks 205 E9
Hawksworth W Yorks 205 F11
Hawkwell Essex 88 G4
Hawley Hants 49 B11
Hawley Kent 68 E4
Hawley Bottom Devon 28 G2
Hawley Lane Hants 49 B11
Hawling Glos 99 G11
Hawn Orkney 314 D4
Hawnby N Yorks 215 B10
Hawne W Mid 133 G9
Haworth W Yorks 204 F6
Haws Bank Cumb 220 F6
Hawstead Suff 125 F7
Hawstead Green Suff 125 F7
Hawthorn Durham 234 B4
Hawthorn Hants 49 G7
Hawthorn Rhondda 58 B6
Hawthorn Wilts 61 F11
Hawthorn Corner Kent 71 F8
Hawthorn Hill Brack 65 E11
Hawthorn Hill Lincs 174 D2
Hawthorns Staffs 168 F4
Hawthorpe Lincs 155 D10
Hawton Notts 172 E3
Haxby York 207 B8
Haxey N Lincs 188 B3
Haxey N Lincs 199 G9
Haxey Carr N Lincs 199 G9
Haxted Sur 52 D2
Haxton Wilts 46 D6
Hay Corn 10 G5
Hay Field S Yorks 187 B10
Hay Green Essex 87 E10
Hay Green Herts 104 D6
Hay Green Norf 157 F10
Hay Mills W Mid 134 G2
Hay-on-Wye Powys 96 C4
Hay Street Herts 105 F7
Haybridge Shrops 116 C2
Haybridge Som 44 D4
Haybridge Telford 150 G3
Hayden Glos 99 G8
Haydock Mers 183 B9
Haydon Bath 45 C7
Haydon Dorset 29 D11
Haydon Som 28 C3
Haydon Som 44 D5
Haydon Swindon 62 B6
Haydon Bridge Northumb 241 E8
Haydon Wick Swindon 62 B6
Haye Corn 7 B7
Haye Fm Corn 6 B6
Hayes London 66 C6
Hayes London 68 F2
Hayes Staffs 169 C9
Hayes End London 66 C5
Hayes Knoll Wilts 81 G10
Hayes Town London 66 C6
Hayfield Derbys 185 D8
Hayfield Fife 280 C5
Hayfield Green S Yorks 187 B11
Haygate Telford 150 G2
Haygrass Som 28 C2
Hayhill E Ayrs 257 F11
Hayhillock Angus 287 C9
Haylands I o W 21 C7
Hayle Corn 2 B3
Hayley Green W Mid 133 G8
Haymoor End Som 28 B4
Haymoor Green E Ches 167 E11
Hayne Devon 26 F5
Haynes C Beds 103 C11
Haynes Church End C Beds 103 C11
Haynes West End C Beds 103 C11
Hayscastle Pembs 91 F7
Hayscastle Cross Pembs 91 G8
Haysford Pembs 91 G8
Hayshead Angus 287 C10
Hayston E Dunb 278 G2
Haystoun Borders 261 B7
Haythorne Dorset 31 F8
Hayton Aberdeen 293 C11
Hayton Cumb 229 C8
Hayton Cumb 240 F2
Hayton E Yorks 208 D2
Hayton Notts 188 E2
Hayton's Bent Shrops 131 G10
Haytor Vale Devon 13 F11
Haytown Devon 24 E5
Haywards Heath W Sus 36 C4
Haywood S Lnrk 269 E9
Haywood S Yorks 198 E5
Haywood Oaks Notts 171 D10
Hazard's Green E Sus 23 C11
Hazel End Essex 105 G9
Hazel Grove Gtr Man 184 D6
Hazel Street Kent 53 B11
Hazel Street Kent 53 F7
Hazel Stub Suff 106 C3
Hazelbank S Lnrk 268 F6
Hazelbeach Pembs 72 E6
Hazelbury Bryan Dorset 30 F2
Hazeleigh Essex 88 E4
Hazeley Hants 49 B8
Hazeley Bottom Hants 49 B9
Hazeley Heath Hants 49 B9
Hazeley Lea Hants 49 B8
Hazelgrove Notts 171 F8
Hazelhurst Gtr Man 195 D9
Hazelhurst Gtr Man 195 G9
Hazelhurst Gtr Man 196 G3
Hazelslack Cumb 211 D9
Hazelslade Staffs 151 G10
Hazelton Glos 81 B9
Hazelton Walls Fife 287 E7
Hazelwood Derbys 170 F4
Hazelwood Devon 8 E4
Hazelwood London 68 G2
Hazlehead S Yorks 197 G7
Hazlemere Bucks 84 F5
Hazler Shrops 131 E9
Hazlerigg T & W 242 C6
Hazles Staffs 169 F8
Hazlescross Staffs 169 F8
Hazleton Glos 81 B9
Hazlewood N Yorks 205 C7
Hazon Northumb 252 C5
Heacham Norf 158 B3
Head of Muir Falk 278 E6
Headbourne Worthy Hants 48 G3
Headbrook Hereford 114 F6
Headcorn Kent 53 E10
Headingley W Yorks 205 F11
Headington Oxon 83 D8
Headington Hill Oxon 83 D8
Headlam Durham 224 B3
Headless Cross Cumb 211 D7
Headless Cross Worcs 117 D10
Headley Hants 49 F10
Headley Hants 64 G4
Headley Sur 51 C8
Headley Down Hants 49 F10
Headley Heath Worcs 117 B11
Headley Park Bristol 60 F5
Headon Devon 24 G5
Headon Notts 188 F2
Heads S Lnrk 268 F4
Heads Nook Cumb 239 F11
Headshaw Borders 261 E11
Headstone London 66 B6
Headwell Fife 279 D11
Heady Hill Gtr Man 195 E10
Heage Derbys 170 E5
Healaugh N Yorks 206 D5
Healaugh N Yorks 223 F10
Heald Green Gtr Man 184 D4
Healds Green Gtr Man 195 F11
Heale Devon 40 D6
Heale Som 28 B5
Heale Som 28 D2
Heale Som 45 E7
Healey Gtr Man 195 D11
Healey N Yorks 214 C3
Healey Northumb 242 F2
Healey W Yorks 197 C8
Healey W Yorks 197 D9
Healey Cote Northumb 252 C4
Healey Hall Northumb 242 F2
Healeyfield Durham 233 B7
Healing NE Lincs 201 E8
Heamoor Corn 1 C5
Heaning Cumb 221 F8
Heanish Argyll 288 E2
Heanor Derbys 170 F6
Heanor Gate Derbys 170 F6
Heanton Punchardon Devon 40 F4
Heap Bridge Gtr Man 195 E10
Heapham Lincs 188 D5
Hearn Hants 49 F10
Hearnden Green Kent 53 D10
Hearthstane Borders 260 D4
Hearthstone Derbys 170 D4
Hearts Delight Kent 69 G11
Heasley Mill Devon 41 G8
Heast Highld 295 D8
Heath Cardiff 59 D7
Heath Derbys 170 B6
Heath Halton 183 E8
Heath and Reach C Beds 103 F8
Heath Charnock Lancs 194 E5
Heath Common W Sus 35 E10
Heath Common W Yorks 197 D11
Heath Cross Devon 13 B10
Heath Cross Devon 14 C2
Heath End Bucks 84 F5
Heath End Bucks 85 D7
Heath End Derbys 153 E7
Heath End Hants 64 G2
Heath End Hants 64 G5
Heath End S Glos 61 B7
Heath End Sur 49 D10
Heath End W Mid 133 C10
Heath End W Sus 35 D7
Heath End Warks 118 E4
Heath Green Hants 48 F6
Heath Green Worcs 117 C11
Heath Hayes Staffs 151 G10
Heath Hill Shrops 150 G5
Heath House Som 44 D2
Heath Lanes Telford 150 E2
Heath Park London 68 B4
Heath Side Kent 68 E4
Heath Town W Mid 133 D8
Heathcot Aberds 293 C10
Heathcote Derbys 169 C10
Heathcote Shrops 150 D3
Heathcote Warks 118 E6
Heather Leics 153 G7
Heather Row Hants 49 C8
Heathercombe Devon 13 E10
Heatherfield Highld 298 E4
Heatherside Sur 50 B2
Heatherwood Park Highld 311 K2
Heatherybanks Aberds 303 E7
Heathfield Cambs 105 B9
Heathfield Devon 14 F2
Heathfield E Sus 37 C9
Heathfield Glos 80 F2
Heathfield Hants 33 F9
Heathfield Lincs 189 C10
Heathfield N Yorks 214 F2
Heathfield S Ayrs 257 E9
Heathfield Som 27 B11
Heathfield Som 43 G7
Heathfield Village Oxon 83 B8
Heathhall Dumfries 237 B11
Heathlands Wokingham 65 F10
Heathrow Airport London 66 D5
Heathstock Devon 28 G2
Heathton Shrops 132 E6
Heathtop Derbys 152 C4
Heathwaite Cumb 221 F8
Heathwaite N Yorks 225 E9
Heatley Staffs 151 D11
Heatley Warr 184 D2
Heaton Gtr Man 195 F7
Heaton Lancs 211 G8
Heaton Staffs 169 C7
Heaton T & W 243 D7
Heaton W Yorks 205 G8
Heaton Chapel Gtr Man 184 C5
Heaton Mersey Gtr Man 184 C5
Heaton Moor Gtr Man 184 C5
Heaton Norris Gtr Man 184 C5
Heaton Royds W Yorks 205 F8
Heaton Shay W Yorks 205 F8
Heaton's Bridge Lancs 194 E2
Heaven's Door Som 29 C10
Heaverham Kent 52 B5
Heaviley Gtr Man 184 D6
Heavitree Devon 14 C4
Hebburn T & W 243 E8
Hebburn Colliery T & W 243 D8
Hebburn New Town T & W 243 E8
Hebden N Yorks 213 G10
Hebden Bridge W Yorks 196 B3
Hebden Green W Ches 167 B10
Hebing End Herts 104 G6
Hebron Anglesey 179 E7
Hebron Carms 92 F3
Hebron Northumb 252 F5
Heck Dumfries 248 G3
Heckdyke N Lincs 188 B3
Heckfield Hants 65 G8
Heckfield Green Suff 126 B3
Heckfordbridge Essex 107 G8
Heckingham Norf 143 D7
Heckington Lincs 173 G10
Heckmondwike W Yorks 197 C8
Heddington Wilts 62 F3
Heddington Wick Wilts 62 F3
Heddle Orkney 314 E3
Heddon Devon 25 B11
Heddon-on-the-Wall Northumb 242 D4
Hedenham Norf 142 E6
Hedge End Dorset 30 F4
Hedge End Hants 33 E7
Hedgehog Bridge Lincs 174 F3
Hedgerley Bucks 66 B3
Hedgerley Green Bucks 66 B3
Hedgerley Hill Bucks 66 B3
Hedging Som 28 B4
Hedley Hill Durham 233 C9
Hedley on the Hill Northumb 242 F3
Hednesford Staffs 151 G9
Hedon E Yorks 201 B7
Hedsor Bucks 66 B2
Hedworth T & W 243 E8
Heelands M Keynes 102 D6
Heeley S Yorks 186 E5
Hegdon Hill Hereford 115 G11
Heggerscales Cumb 222 C6
Heggle Lane Cumb 230 D3
Heglibister Shetland 313 H5
Heighington Darl 233 G11
Heighington Lincs 173 B8
Heighley Staffs 168 F3
Height End Lancs 195 C9
Heightington Worcs 116 C5
Heights Gtr Man 196 F3
Heights of Brae Highld 300 C5
Heights of Kinlochewe Highld 299 C10
Heilam Highld 308 C4
Heiton Borders 262 C6
Helbeck Cumb 222 B5
Hele Devon 12 C2
Hele Devon 13 G10
Hele Devon 27 G7
Hele Devon 40 D4
Hele Som 27 C11
Hele Torbay 9 B8
Helebridge Corn 24 G2
Helensburgh Argyll 276 E5
Helford Corn 3 D7
Helford Passage Corn 3 D7
Helham Green Herts 86 B5
Helhoughton Norf 159 D7
Helions Bumpstead Essex 106 C3
Hell Corner W Berks 63 G11
Hellaby S Yorks 187 C8
Helland Corn 11 G7
Helland Som 28 C4
Hellandbridge Corn 11 G7
Hellesdon Norf 160 G4
Hellesveor Corn 2 A2
Hellidon Northants 119 F10
Hellifield N Yorks 204 B3
Hellifield Green N Yorks 204 B3
Hellingly E Sus 23 C9
Hellington Norf 142 C6
Hellister Shetland 313 J5
Hellman's Cross Essex 87 B9
Helm N Yorks 223 G8
Helm Northumb 252 D5
Helmburn Borders 261 E9
Helmdon Northants 101 C11
Helme W Yorks 196 E5
Helmingham Suff 126 F3
Helmington Row Durham 233 D9
Helmsdale Highld 311 H4
Helmshore Lancs 195 C9
Helmside Cumb 212 B3
Helmsley N Yorks 216 C2
Helperby N Yorks 215 F8
Helperthorpe N Yorks 217 E9
Helpringham Lincs 173 G10
Helpston P'boro 138 B2
Helsby W Ches 183 F7
Helscott Corn 24 G2
Helsey Lincs 191 G8
Helston Corn 2 D5
Helston Water Corn 4 G5
Helstone Corn 11 E7
Helton Cumb 230 G6
Helwith Bridge N Yorks 212 F6
Helygain = Halkyn Flint 182 G2
Hem Heath Stoke 168 G5
Hemblington Norf 160 G6
Hemblington Corner Norf 160 G6
Hembridge Som 44 F5
Hemel Hempstead Herts 85 D9
Hemerdon Devon 7 D11
Hemford Shrops 130 C6
Hemingbrough N Yorks 207 G9
Hemingby Lincs 190 G2
Hemingfield S Yorks 197 G11
Hemingford Abbots Cambs 122 C5
Hemingford Grey Cambs 122 C5
Hemingstone Suff 126 G3
Hemington Leics 153 D9
Hemington Northants 137 F11
Hemington Som 45 C8
Hemley Suff 108 C5
Hemlington M'bro 225 C10
Hemp Green Suff 127 D7
Hempholme E Yorks 209 C7
Hempnall Norf 142 E4
Hempnall Green Norf 142 E4
Hempriggs House Highld 310 E7
Hemp's Green Essex 107 F8
Hempshill Vale Notts 171 G8
Hempstead Essex 106 D2
Hempstead Medway 69 G9
Hempstead Norf 160 B2
Hempstead Norf 161 D8
Hempsted Glos 80 B4
Hempton Norf 159 D8
Hempton Oxon 101 E8
Hempton Wainhill Oxon 84 E3
Hemsby Norf 161 F9
Hemsted Kent 54 E6
Hemswell Lincs 188 C6
Hemswell Cliff Lincs 188 D6
Hemsworth Dorset 31 F7
Hemsworth S Yorks 186 E5
Hemsworth W Yorks 198 E2
Hemyock Devon 27 E10
Hen Bentref Llandegfan Anglesey 179 G9
Hên-efail Denb 165 C9
Hen-feddau fawr Pembs 92 E4
Henaford Devon 24 D2
Henbrook Worcs 117 D8
Henbury Bristol 60 D5
Henbury Dorset 18 B5
Henbury E Ches 184 G5
Hendomen Powys 130 D4
Hendon London 67 B8
Hendon T & W 243 F10
Hendra Corn 2 B6
Hendra Corn 2 C5
Hendra Corn 2 D3
Hendra Corn 2 F6
Hendra Corn 5 C9
Hendra Corn 5 D9
Hendra Corn 11 E7
Hendra Croft Corn 4 D5
Hendrabridge Corn 6 B5
Hendraburnick Corn 11 D8
Hendre Flint 165 B11
Hendre Gwyn 110 B2
Hendre Powys 129 D9
Hendre-ddu Conwy 164 B5
Hendredenny Park Caerph 58 B6
Hendreforgan Rhondda 58 B3
Hendrerwydd Denb 165 C10
Hendrewen Swansea 75 D10
Hendy Carms 75 E9
Hendy-Gwyn Carms 74 B2
Hendy Gwyn = Whitland Carms 73 B11
Heneglwys Anglesey 178 F6
Henfield S Glos 61 D7
Henfield W Sus 36 D2
Henford Devon 12 C3
Henfords Marsh Wilts 45 E11
Henghurst Kent 54 F3
Hengoed Caerph 77 F10
Hengoed Denb 165 D9
Hengoed Powys 114 G4
Hengoed Shrops 148 C5
Hengrave Norf 160 F2
Hengrave Suff 124 D6
Hengrove Bristol 60 F6
Hengrove Park Bristol 60 F5
Henham Essex 105 F10
Heniarth Powys 130 B2
Henlade Som 28 C3
Henleaze Bristol 60 D5
Henley Dorset 29 G11
Henley Glos 80 B6
Henley Shrops 115 B10
Henley Shrops 131 F9
Henley Som 44 G2
Henley Suff 126 G3
Henley W Sus 34 B5
Henley Wilts 47 B10
Henley Wilts 61 F10
Henley Common W Sus 34 B5
Henley Green W Mid 135 G7
Henley-in-Arden Warks 118 D3
Henley-on-Thames Oxon 65 C9
Henley Street Kent 69 F7
Henley's Down E Sus 38 E2
Henllan Ceredig 93 C7
Henllan Denb 165 B8
Henllan Amgoed Carms 92 G3
Henlle Shrops 148 C6
Henllys Torf 78 G3
Henllys Vale Torf 78 G3
Henlow C Beds 104 D3
Hennock Devon 14 E2
Henny Street Essex 107 D7
Henryd Conwy 180 G3
Henry's Moat Pembs 91 F10
Hensall N Yorks 198 C5
Henshaw Northumb 241 E7
Henshaw W Yorks 205 E10
Hensingham Cumb 219 B9
Hensington Oxon 83 B7
Henstead Suff 143 F9
Hensting Hants 33 C7
Henstridge Devon 40 E5
Henstridge Som 30 D2
Henstridge Ash Som 30 C2
Henstridge Bowden Som 29 C11
Henstridge Marsh Som 30 C2
Henton Oxon 84 E3
Henton Som 44 D3
Henwood Corn 11 G11
Henwood Oxon 83 E7
Henwood Green Kent 52 E6
Heogan Shetland 313 J6
Heol-ddu Carms 75 E7
Heol-ddu Swansea 56 B6
Heol-laethog Bridgend 58 C2
Heol-las Bridgend 58 C2
Heol-las Swansea 57 B7
Heol Senni Powys 95 G8
Heol-y-gaer Powys 96 D3
Heol-y-mynydd V Glam 57 G11
Heolgerrig M Tydf 77 D8
Hepburn Northumb 264 E3
Hepple Northumb 251 C11
Hepscott Northumb 252 G6
Hepthorne Lane Derbys 170 C6
Heptonstall W Yorks 196 B3
Hepworth Suff 125 C9
Hepworth W Yorks 197 F7
Herbrandston Pembs 72 D5
Hereford Hereford 97 C10
Heribusta Highld 298 B4
Heriot Borders 271 E7
Hermiston Edin 280 G3
Hermit Hill S Yorks 197 G10
Hermit Hole W Yorks 205 F7
Hermitage Borders 250 D2
Hermitage Dorset 29 F10
Hermitage W Berks 64 E4
Hermitage W Sus 22 B3
Hermitage Green Mers 183 C10
Hermon Anglesey 162 B5
Hermon Carms 93 E7
Hermon Carms 94 F3

338 Her – Hol

Hermon Pembs 92 E4
Herne Kent 71 F7
Herne Bay Kent 71 F7
Herne Common Kent 71 F7
Herne Hill London 67 E10
Herne Pound Kent 53 C7
Herner Devon 25 B9
Hernhill Kent 70 G5
Herniss Corn 2 C6
Herodsfoot Corn 6 C4
Heron Cross Stoke 168 G5
Heronden Kent 55 C9
Herongate Essex 87 G10
Heron's Ghyll E Sus 37 B7
Herons Green Bath 44 B5
Heronsford S Ayrs 244 G4
Heronsgate Herts 85 G8
Heronston Bridgend 58 D2
Herra Shetland 312 D8
Herriard Hants 49 D7
Herringfleet Suff 143 D9
Herring's Green Beds 103 C11
Herringswell Suff 124 C4
Herringthorpe S Yorks 186 C6
Hersden Kent 71 G8
Hersham Corn 24 F3
Hersham Sur 66 G6
Herstmonceux E Sus 23 C10
Herston Dorset 18 F6
Herston Orkney 314 G4
Hertford Herts 86 C4
Hertford Heath Herts 86 C4
Hertingfordbury Herts 86 C4
Hesket Newmarket Cumb 230 D2
Hesketh Bank Lancs 194 C2
Hesketh Lane Lancs 203 E8
Hesketh Moss Lancs 194 C2
Heskin Green Lancs 194 D4
Hesleden Durham 234 D4
Hesleyside Northumb 251 G8
Heslington York 207 C8
Hessay York 206 C6
Hessenford Corn 6 D6
Hessett Suff 125 E8
Hessle E Yorks 200 B4
Hessle W Yorks 198 D2
Hest Bank Lancs 211 F9
Hester's Way Glos 99 G8
Hestinsetter Shetland 313 J4
Heston London 66 D6
Hestwall Orkney 314 E2
Heswall Mers 182 E3
Hethe Oxon 101 F11
Hethel Norf 142 C3
Hethelpit Cross Glos 98 F5
Hethersett Norf 142 C3
Hethersgill Cumb 239 D11
Hetherside Cumb 239 D10
Hetherson Green W Ches 167 F8
Hethpool Northumb 263 D9
Hett Durham 233 D11
Hetton N Yorks 204 B5
Hetton Downs T & W 234 B3
Hetton-le-Hill T & W 234 B3
Hetton-le-Hole T & W 234 B3
Hetton Steads Northumb 264 B2
Heugh Northumb 242 C3
Heugh-head Aberds 292 B5
Heveningham Suff 126 C6
Hever Kent 52 E3
Heversham Cumb 211 C9
Hevingham Norf 160 E3
Hew Green N Yorks 205 B10
Hewas Water Corn 5 F9
Hewelsfield Glos 79 E9
Hewelsfield Common Glos 79 E8
Hewer Hill Cumb 230 D3
Hewish N Som 60 G2
Hewish Som 28 F6
Hewood Dorset 28 G5
Heworth T & W 243 E7
Heworth York 207 C8
Hexham Northumb 241 E10
Hextable Kent 68 E4
Hexthorpe S Yorks 198 G5
Hexton Herts 104 E2
Hexworthy Devon 13 G9
Hey Lancs 204 E3
Hey Green W Yorks 196 E4
Hey Houses Lancs 193 B10
Heybridge Essex 88 D5
Heybridge Essex 87 F10
Heybridge Basin Essex 88 D5
Heybrook Bay Devon 7 F10
Heydon Cambs 105 C8
Heydon Norf 160 D2
Heydour Lincs 155 B10
Heyheads Gtr Man 196 G3
Heylipol Argyll 288 E1
Heylor Shetland 312 E4
Heyope Powys 114 C4
Heyrod Gtr Man 185 B7
Heysham Lancs 211 G8
Heyshaw N Yorks 214 G3
Heyshott W Sus 34 D5
Heyshott Green W Sus 34 D5
Heyside Gtr Man 196 F2
Heytesbury Wilts 46 E2
Heythrop Oxon 101 F7
Heywood Gtr Man 195 E11
Heywood Wilts 45 C11
Hibaldstow N Lincs 200 G3
Hibb's Green Suff 125 G7
Hickford Hill Essex 106 C5
Hickleton S Yorks 198 F3
Hickling Norf 161 E8
Hickling Notts 154 D3
Hickling Green Norf 161 E8
Hickling Heath Norf 161 E8
Hickling Pastures Notts 154 D3
Hickmans Green Kent 54 B5
Hicks Forstal Kent 71 G7
Hicks Gate Bath 60 F6
Hick's Mill Corn 4 G5
Hickstead W Sus 36 C3
Hidcote Bartrim Glos 100 C3
Hidcote Boyce Glos 100 C3
Hifnal Shrops 132 D4
Higginshaw Gtr Man 196 F2
High Ackworth W Yorks 198 D2
High Angerton Northumb 252 F3
High Bankhill Cumb 231 C7
High Banton N Lnrk 278 E4
High Barn Lincs 174 C5
High Barnes T & W 243 F9
High Barnet London 86 F2
High Beach Essex 86 F6
High Bentham N Yorks 212 F3
High Bickington Devon 25 C10
High Biggins Cumb 212 D2
High Birkwith N Yorks 212 D5
High Birstwith N Yorks 205 B10
High Blantyre S Lnrk 268 D3
High Bonnybridge Falk 278 F6
High Bradfield S Yorks 186 C3
High Bradley N Yorks 204 D6
High Bray Devon 41 G7
High Brooms Kent 52 E5
High Brotheridge Glos 80 C5
High Bullen Devon 25 C8
High Buston Northumb 252 B6
High Callerton Northumb 242 C5
High Cark Cumb 211 C7
High Casterton Cumb 212 D2
High Catton E Yorks 207 C10
High Church Northumb 252 F5
High Cogges Oxon 82 D5
High Common Norf 141 B9
High Coniscliffe Darl 224 B4
High Crompton Gtr Man 196 F2
High Cross Cambs 123 F8
High Cross Corn 2 D6
High Cross E Sus 37 B9
High Cross Hants 34 B2
High Cross Herts 85 F10
High Cross Herts 86 B5
High Cross Newport 59 B9
High Cross W Sus 36 D2
High Cross Warks 118 D3
High Crosshill S Lnrk 268 C2
High Cunsey Cumb 221 G7
High Dubmire T & W 234 B2
High Dyke Durham 232 F5
High Easter Essex 87 C10
High Eggborough N Yorks 198 C5
High Eldrig Dumfries 236 C4
High Ellington N Yorks 214 C3
High Ercall Telford 149 F11
High Etherley Durham 233 F9
High Ferry Lincs 174 F5
High Field Lancs 203 C10
High Flatts W Yorks 197 F8
High Forge Durham 242 G6
High Friarside Durham 242 F5
High Gallowhill E Dunb 278 G2
High Garrett Essex 106 F5
High Grange Durham 233 E9
High Grantley N Yorks 214 F4
High Green Cumb 221 E8
High Green Norf 141 B8
High Green Norf 142 B2
High Green Norf 159 G8
High Green S Yorks 186 B4
High Green Shrops 132 G4
High Green Suff 125 E7
High Green W Yorks 197 E7
High Green Worcs 99 B7
High Halden Kent 53 F11
High Halstow Medway 69 D9
High Ham Som 44 G2
High Handenhold Durham 242 G6
High Harrington Cumb 228 F6
High Harrogate N Yorks 206 B2
High Haswell Durham 234 C3
High Hatton Shrops 150 E2
High Hauxley Northumb 253 C7
High Hawsker N Yorks 227 D8
High Heath Shrops 150 D3
High Heath W Mid 133 C10
High Hesket Cumb 230 C5
High Hesleden Durham 234 D5
High Hill Cumb 229 G11
High Houses Essex 87 C11
High Hoyland S Yorks 197 E9
High Hunsley E Yorks 208 F4
High Hurstwood E Sus 37 B7
High Hutton N Yorks 216 F5
High Ireby Cumb 229 D10
High Kelling Norf 177 E10
High Kilburn N Yorks 215 D10
High Lands Durham 233 F8
High Lane Gtr Man 185 D7
High Lane Worcs 116 E3
High Lanes Corn 2 B3
High Laver Essex 87 D8
High Legh E Ches 184 E2
High Leven Stockton 225 C8
High Littleton Bath 44 B6
High Longthwaite Cumb 229 B11
High Lorton Cumb 229 F9
High Marishes N Yorks 216 D6
High Marnham Notts 188 G4
High Melton S Yorks 198 G4
High Mickley Northumb 242 E3
High Mindork Dumfries 236 D5
High Moor Derbys 187 E7
High Moor Lancs 194 E4
High Moorsley T & W 234 B2
High Nash Glos 79 C9
High Newton Cumb 211 C8
High Newton-by-the-Sea Northumb 264 D6
High Nibthwaite Cumb 210 B5
High Oaks Cumb 222 G2
High Offley Staffs 150 D5
High Ongar Essex 87 E9
High Onn Staffs 150 F6
High Onn Wharf Staffs 150 F6
High Park Cumb 221 G10
High Park Mers 193 D11
High Risby N Lincs 200 E2
High Roding Essex 87 B10
High Rougham Suff 125 E8
High Row Cumb 230 D3
High Row Cumb 230 G3
High Salvington W Sus 35 F10
High Scales Cumb 229 B9
High Sellafield Cumb 219 E10
High Shaw N Yorks 223 G7
High Shields T & W 243 D9
High Shincliffe Durham 233 C11
High Side Cumb 229 E10
High Southwick T & W 243 F9
High Spen T & W 242 F4
High Stakesby N Yorks 227 C7
High Stoop Durham 233 C8
High Street Corn 5 E9
High Street Kent 53 G8
High Street Pembs 73 B11
High Street Suff 107 B7
High Street Suff 127 C8
High Street Suff 127 F8
High Street Suff 143 G7
High Street Green Suff 125 F10
High Sunderland Borders 261 C11
High Throston Hrtlpl 234 E5
High Tirfergus Argyll 255 F7
High Town Luton 103 G11
High Town Shrops 132 E4
High Town Staffs 151 G9
High Toynton Lincs 174 B3
High Trewhitt Northumb 252 B2
High Urpeth Durham 242 G6
High Valleyfield Fife 279 D10
High Walton Cumb 219 C9
High Warden Northumb 241 D10
High Water Head Cumb 220 F6
High Westwood Durham 242 F4
High Whinnow Cumb 239 G8
High Woolaston Glos 79 F9
High Worsall N Yorks 225 D7
High Wray Cumb 221 F7
High Wych Herts 87 C7
High Wycombe Bucks 84 G5
Higham Derbys 170 D5
Higham Fife 286 F6
Higham Kent 69 E8
Higham Lancs 204 F2
Higham S Yorks 197 F10
Higham Suff 107 D10
Higham Suff 124 E4
Higham Common S Yorks 197 F10
Higham Dykes Northumb 242 B4
Higham Ferrers Northants 121 D9
Higham Gobion C Beds 104 E2
Higham Hill London 86 G5
Higham on the Hill Leics 135 D7
Higham Wood Kent 52 D5
Highampton Devon 25 G7
Highams Park London 86 G5
Highbridge Cumb 230 C3
Highbridge Hants 33 C7
Highbridge Highld 290 E3
Highbridge Som 43 D10
Highbridge W Mid 133 C10
Highbrook W Sus 51 G11
Highburton W Yorks 197 E7
Highbury London 67 B10
Highbury Ptsmth 33 G11
Highbury Som 45 D7
Highbury Vale Nottingham 171 G8
Highclere Hants 64 G2
Highcliffe Derbys 186 F2
Highcliffe Dorset 19 C10
Higher Alham Som 45 E7
Higher Ansty Dorset 30 G3
Higher Ashton Devon 14 E3
Higher Audley Blkburn 195 B7
Higher Bal Corn 4 E4
Higher Ballam Lancs 202 G3
Higher Bartle Lancs 202 G6
Higher Bebington Mers 182 D4
Higher Berry End C Beds 103 E9
Higher Blackley Gtr Man 195 G10
Higher Boarshaw Gtr Man 195 F11
Higher Bockhampton Dorset 17 C10
Higher Bojewyan Corn 1 C3
Higher Boscaswell Corn 1 C3
Higher Brixham Torbay 9 D8
Higher Broughton Gtr Man 195 G10
Higher Burrow Som 28 C6
Higher Burwardsley W Ches 167 D8
Higher Chalmington Dorset 29 G9
Higher Cheriton Devon 27 G10
Higher Chillington Som 28 E5
Higher Chisworth Derbys 185 C7
Higher Clovelly Devon 24 C4
Higher Condurrow Corn 2 B5
Higher Crackington Corn 11 B9
Higher Cransworth Corn 5 B9
Higher Croft Blkburn 195 B7
Higher Denham Bucks 66 B4
Higher Dinting Derbys 185 C8
Higher Disley E Ches 185 E7
Higher Downs Corn 2 C3
Higher Durston Som 28 B3
Higher End Gtr Man 194 G4
Higher Folds Gtr Man 195 G7
Higher Gabwell Torbay 9 B8
Higher Green Gtr Man 195 G8
Higher Halstock Leigh Dorset 29 F8
Higher Heysham Lancs 211 G8
Higher Hogshead Lancs 195 C11
Higher Holton Som 29 B11
Higher Hurdsfield E Ches 184 G6
Higher Kingcombe Dorset 16 B6
Higher Kinnerton Flint 166 C4
Higher Land Corn 12 G3
Higher Marsh Som 30 C2
Higher Melcombe Dorset 30 G2
Higher Menadew Corn 5 D10
Higher Molland Devon 41 G8
Higher Muddiford Devon 40 F5
Higher Nyland Dorset 30 C2
Higher Penwortham Lancs 194 B4
Higher Pertwood Wilts 45 F11
Higher Porthpean Corn 5 E10
Higher Poynton E Ches 184 E6
Higher Prestacott Devon 12 B3
Higher Rads End C Beds 103 E9
Higher Ridge Shrops 149 C7
Higher Rocombe Barton Devon 9 B8
Higher Row Dorset 31 G8
Higher Runcorn Halton 183 E8
Higher Sandford Dorset 29 C10
Higher Shotton Flint 166 B4
Higher Shurlach W Ches 183 G11
Higher Slade Devon 40 D4
Higher Street Som 42 E6
Higher Tale Devon 27 G9
Higher Tolcarne Corn 5 B7
Higher Totnell Dorset 29 F10
Higher Town Corn 5 C10
Higher Town Scilly 1 F4
Higher Town Som 42 D3
Higher Tremarcoombe Corn 6 B5
Higher Vexford Som 42 F6
Higher Walreddon Devon 12 G5
Higher Walton Lancs 194 B5
Higher Walton Warr 183 D9
Higher Wambrook Som 28 F3
Higher Warcombe Devon 40 D3
Higher Weaver Devon 27 G9
Higher Whatcombe Dorset 30 G4
Higher Wheelton Lancs 194 C6
Higher Whitley W Ches 183 E10
Higher Wincham W Ches 183 F11
Higher Woodsford Dorset 17 D11
Higher Wraxall Dorset 29 G9
Higher Wych W Ches 167 G7
Highercliff Corn 6 D4
Higherford Lancs 204 E3
Highertown Corn 4 G6
Highertown Corn 11 E8
Highfield E Yorks 207 F10
Highfield Glos 79 E10
Highfield Gtr Man 194 G5
Highfield Gtr Man 195 F8
Highfield Herts 85 D9
Highfield N Ayrs 266 E6
Highfield Oxon 101 G11
Highfield S Yorks 186 D5
Highfield Soton 32 E6
Highfield T & W 242 F4
Highfields Cambs 123 F7
Highfields Derbys 170 B6
Highfields Essex 88 B5
Highfields Glos 80 F3
Highfields Leicester 136 C2
Highfields Northumb 273 E9
Highfields S Yorks 198 F4
Highfields Staffs 151 E8
Highgate E Sus 52 G2
Highgate Kent 53 G9
Highgate London 67 B9
Highgate Powys 130 D2
Highgate S Yorks 198 G3
Highgate W Mid 133 F11
Highlane Derbys 186 E6
Highlane E Ches 168 B5
Highlanes Corn 10 G4
Highlanes Staffs 150 C5
Highlaws Cumb 229 B8
Highleadon Glos 98 G5
Highleigh W Sus 22 D4
Highley Shrops 132 G4
Highmoor Cumb 229 B11
Highmoor Oxon 65 B8
Highmoor Cross Oxon 65 C8
Highmoor Hill Mon 60 B3
Highnam Glos 80 B3
Highnam Green Glos 98 G5
Highoak Norf 141 C11
Highridge Bristol 60 F5
Highroad Well Moor W Yorks 196 B5
Highstead Kent 71 F8
Highsted Kent 70 G2
Highstreet Kent 70 G5
Highstreet Green Essex 106 E5
Highstreet Green Sur 50 F3
Hightae Dumfries 238 B3
Highter's Heath W Mid 117 B11
Hightown E Ches 168 C5
Hightown Hants 31 G11
Hightown Mers 193 G10
Hightown Soton 33 E7
Hightown W Yorks 197 C7
Hightown Wrex 166 F4
Hightown Green Suff 125 F9
Hightown Heights W Yorks 197 C7
Highway Corn 4 G4
Highway Hereford 97 B9
Highway Som 29 C7
Highway Wilts 62 D4
Highway Windsor 65 C11
Highweek Devon 14 G2
Highwood Devon 27 F10
Highwood Dorset 18 D3
Highwood Essex 87 E10
Highwood Hants 31 F11
Highwood Worcs 116 D3
Highwood Hill London 86 G2
Highworth Swindon 82 G2
Highworthy Devon 24 F6
Hilborough Norf 140 C6
Hilborough Ho Norf 140 C6
Hilcot Glos 81 B7
Hilcot End Glos 81 E9
Hilcote Derbys 171 D7
Hilcott Wilts 46 B6
Hilden Park Kent 52 D5
Hildenborough Kent 52 D5
Hildersham Cambs 105 B10
Hildersley Hereford 98 G2
Hilderstone Staffs 151 C8
Hilderthorpe E Yorks 218 F3
Hilfield Dorset 29 F10
Hilgay Norf 140 D2
Hill S Glos 79 G10
Hill W Mid 134 D2
Hill Warks 119 D9
Hill Bottom Oxon 64 D6
Hill Brow W Sus 34 B3
Hill Chorlton Staffs 150 B5
Hill Common Norf 161 E8
Hill Corner Som 45 D10
Hill Croome Worcs 99 C7
Hill Dale Lancs 194 E3
Hill Deverill Wilts 45 E11
Hill Dyke Lincs 174 F4
Hill End Durham 232 D6
Hill End Fife 279 B10
Hill End Glos 99 D8
Hill End London 85 G8
Hill End N Yorks 205 C7
Hill End Som 29 E8
Hill End Worcs 117 E8
Hill Furze Worcs 99 B9
Hill Gate Hereford 97 F9
Hill Green Essex 105 E9
Hill Green Kent 69 G10
Hill Head Hants 33 G8
Hill Head Northumb 241 D10
Hill Hoath Kent 52 E3
Hill Hook W Mid 134 C2
Hill Houses Shrops 116 B2
Hill Mountain Pembs 73 D7
Hill of Beath Fife 280 C3
Hill of Drip Stirl 278 B5
Hill of Fearn Highld 301 B8
Hill of Keillor Angus 286 C6
Hill of Mountblairy Aberds 302 D6
Hill of Overbrae Aberds 303 C8
Hill Park Hants 33 F9
Hill Park Kent 52 B2
Hill Ridware Staffs 151 F11
Hill Side Hants 34 B3
Hill Side S Yorks 197 G8
Hill Side W Yorks 197 D7
Hill Side Worcs 116 E5
Hill Somersal Derbys 152 C2
Hill Street Kent 54 D6
Hill Top Derbys 186 F5
Hill Top Durham 232 G5
Hill Top Durham 233 C10
Hill Top Durham 242 G5
Hill Top Gtr Man 195 G8
Hill Top Hants 32 G6
Hill Top N Yorks 214 G3
Hill Top N Yorks 214 G5
Hill Top Notts 171 F7
Hill Top S Yorks 186 C5
Hill Top S Yorks 186 D3
Hill Top S Yorks 187 B7
Hill Top S Yorks 197 F9
Hill Top Staffs 133 B7
Hill Top W Mid 133 E9
Hill Top W Sus 34 C5
Hill Top W Yorks 196 E5
Hill Top W Yorks 197 D10
Hill Top W Yorks 205 G11
Hill Top W Yorks 205 G7
Hill Top Warks 134 E5
Hill Top Warks 135 E7
Hill View Dorset 18 B5
Hill Wood W Mid 134 C2
Hill Wootton Warks 118 D6
Hillam N Yorks 198 B4
Hillbeck Cumb 222 B5
Hillblock Pembs 73 B8
Hillborough Kent 71 F8
Hillbourne Poole 18 C6
Hillbrae Aberds 302 E6
Hillbrae Aberds 303 G7
Hillbutts Dorset 31 G7
Hillcliffe Warr 183 D10
Hillclifflane Derbys 170 F3
Hillcommon Som 27 B11
Hillcross Derbys 152 C6
Hilldyke Lincs 174 F4
Hillend Fife 280 E2
Hillend N Lnrk 268 B6
Hillend N Som 43 B11
Hillend Shrops 132 E6
Hillend Swansea 56 C2
Hillend Green Glos 98 F4
Hillersland Glos 79 C9
Hillerton Devon 13 B10
Hillesden Bucks 102 F3
Hillesden Hamlet Bucks 102 E3
Hillesley Glos 61 B9
Hillfarance Som 27 C11
Hillfarrance Som 27 C11
Hillfield Devon 8 E6
Hillfield W Mid 118 B2
Hillfields S Glos 60 D6
Hillfields W Mid 118 B6
Hillfoot Aberds 303 D9
Hillfoot W Yorks 205 G10
Hillfoot End C Beds 104 E2
Hillgreen W Berks 64 D3
Hillgrove W Sus 34 B6
Hillhampton Hereford 97 B11
Hillhead Aberds 302 F5
Hillhead Aberds 303 G8
Hillhead Corn 5 C11
Hillhead Devon 9 E8
Hillhead E Ayrs 257 B10
Hillhead S Ayrs 257 F10
Hillhead of Auchentumb Aberds 303 D9
Hillhead of Blairy Aberds 302 D6
Hillhead of Cocklaw Aberds 303 E10
Hillhouse Borders 271 D10
Hilliard's Cross Staffs 152 G3
Hilliclay Highld 310 C5
Hillingdon London 66 C5
Hillingdon Heath London 66 C5
Hillington Glasgow 267 C10
Hillington Norf 158 D4
Hillis Corner I o W 20 C5
Hillmoor Devon 27 E10
Hillmorton Warks 119 C10
Hillock Vale Lancs 195 B9
Hillockhead Aberds 292 B6
Hillockhead Aberds 292 C5
Hillpool Worcs 117 B7
Hillpound Hants 33 D9
Hills Town Derbys 171 B7
Hillsborough S Yorks 186 C4
Hillside Aberds 293 D11
Hillside Angus 293 G9
Hillside Devon 8 C4
Hillside Devon 27 F11
Hillside Hants 49 C9
Hillside Mers 193 E10
Hillside Orkney 314 G4
Hillside Orkney 314 D3
Hillside Shetland 313 G6
Hillside Shrops 131 F11
Hillside Wilts 81 G9
Hillstreet Hants 32 D4
Hillswick Shetland 312 F4
Hilltop Bl Gwent 77 D11
Hilltop Bucks 85 E7
Hilltop Derbys 170 C4
Hillview T & W 243 G9
Hillway I o W 21 D8
Hillwell Shetland 313 M5
Hillyfields Hants 32 D5
Hilmarton Wilts 62 D4
Hilperton Wilts 45 B11
Hilperton Marsh Wilts 45 B11
Hilsea Ptsmth 33 G11
Hilston E Yorks 209 G11
Hiltingbury Hants 32 C6
Hilton Aberds 303 F9
Hilton Borders 273 E7
Hilton Cambs 122 D5
Hilton Cumb 231 G10
Hilton Derbys 152 C4
Hilton Dorset 30 G3
Hilton Durham 233 G9
Hilton Highld 309 L7
Hilton Highld 311 L3
Hilton Shrops 132 D5
Hilton Staffs 133 B11
Hilton Stockton 225 C9
Hilton House Gtr Man 194 F6
Hilton Lodge Highld 300 G2
Hilton of Cadboll Highld 301 B8
Hilton Park Gtr Man 195 G10
Himbleton Worcs 117 F8
Himley Staffs 133 E7
Hincaster Cumb 211 C10
Hinchley Wood Sur 67 F7
Hinchliffe Mill W Yorks 196 F6
Hinchwick Glos 100 E2
Hinckley Leics 135 E8
Hinderclay Suff 125 B10
Hinderton W Ches 182 F4
Hinderwell N Yorks 226 B5
Hindford Shrops 148 C6
Hindhead Sur 49 F11
Hindle Fold Lancs 203 G10
Hindley Gtr Man 194 G6
Hindley Northumb 242 F2
Hindley Green Gtr Man 194 G6
Hindlip Worcs 117 F7
Hindolveston Norf 159 D10
Hindon Wilts 46 G2
Hindpool Cumb 210 F3
Hindringham Norf 159 B9
Hindsford Gtr Man 195 G7
Hingham Norf 141 C10
Hinstock Shrops 150 D3
Hintlesham Suff 107 C11
Hinton Glos 79 E11
Hinton Hants 19 B10
Hinton Hereford 96 D6
Hinton Northants 119 G10
Hinton S Glos 61 D8
Hinton Shrops 131 B8
Hinton Som 29 C9
Hinton Ampner Hants 33 B9
Hinton Blewett Bath 44 B5
Hinton Charterhouse Bath 45 B9
Hinton Cross Worcs 99 C10
Hinton-in-the-Hedges Northants 101 D11
Hinton Martell Dorset 31 F8
Hinton on the Green Worcs 99 C10
Hinton Parva Dorset 31 G7
Hinton Parva Swindon 63 C8
Hinton St George Som 28 E6
Hinton St Mary Dorset 30 D3
Hinton Waldrist Oxon 82 F5
Hints Shrops 116 C2
Hints Staffs 134 C3
Hinwick Beds 121 E8
Hinwood Shrops 131 B7
Hinxhill Kent 54 E5
Hinxton Cambs 105 B9
Hinxworth Herts 104 C4
Hipperholme W Yorks 196 B6
Hipplecote Worcs 116 F4
Hipsburn Northumb 264 G6
Hipswell N Yorks 224 F3
Hirael Gwyn 179 G9
Hiraeth Carms 92 G3
Hirn Aberds 293 C9
Hirnant Powys 147 E11
Hirst N Lnrk 269 C7
Hirst Northumb 253 F7
Hirst Courtney N Yorks 198 C6
Hirwaen Denb 165 C10
Hirwaun Rhondda 77 D7
Hirwaun Common Bridgend 58 C2
Hiscott Devon 25 B8
Hislop Borders 249 C9
Hisomley Wilts 45 D11
Histon Cambs 123 E8
Hitcham Suff 125 G9
Hitchill Dumfries 238 D4
Hitchin Herts 104 F3
Hitchin Hill Herts 104 F3
Hitcombe Bottom Wilts 45 E10
Hither Green London 67 E11
Hittisleigh Devon 13 C10
Hittisleigh Barton Devon 13 B10
Hive E Yorks 208 G2
Hixon Staffs 151 D10
Hoaden Kent 55 B9
Hoar Cross Staffs 152 E2
Hoarwithy Hereford 97 F10
Hoath Kent 71 G8
Hoath Corner Kent 52 E3
Hob Hill W Ches 167 E7
Hobarris Shrops 114 B6
Hobbister Orkney 314 F3
Hobble End Staffs 133 B10
Hobbles Green Suff 124 G4
Hobbs Cross Essex 87 C7
Hobbs Cross Essex 87 F7
Hobbs Wall Bath 61 G7
Hobkirk Borders 262 G3
Hobroyd Derbys 185 C8
Hobson Durham 242 F5
Hoby Leics 154 F3
Hoccombe Som 27 B10
Hockenden London 68 F3
Hockerill Herts 105 G9
Hockering Norf 159 G11
Hockering Heath Norf 159 G11
Hockerton Notts 172 D2
Hockholler Som 27 C11
Hockholler Green Som 27 C11
Hockley E Ches 184 E6
Hockley Essex 88 G4
Hockley Kent 54 B3
Hockley Staffs 134 C4
Hockley W Mid 118 B5
Hockley Heath W Mid 118 C3
Hockliffe C Beds 103 F9
Hockwold cum Wilton Norf 140 F4
Hockworthy Devon 27 D8
Hocombe Hants 32 C6
Hoddesdon Herts 86 D5
Hoddlesden Blkburn 195 C8
Hoddom Mains Dumfries 238 C5
Hoddomcross Dumfries 238 C5
Hoden Worcs 99 B11
Hodgefield Staffs 168 E6
Hodgehill E Ches 168 B4
Hodgehill W Mid 134 F2
Hodgeston Pembs 73 F8
Hodley Powys 130 E3
Hodnet Shrops 150 D2
Hodnetheath Shrops 150 D2
Hodsock Notts 187 D10
Hodsoll Street Kent 68 G6
Hodson Swindon 63 C7
Hodthorpe Derbys 187 F8
Hoe Hants 33 D9
Hoe Norf 159 F9
Hoe Sur 50 D5
Hoe Benham W Berks 64 F2
Hoe Gate Hants 33 E10
Hoff Cumb 222 B3
Hoffleet Stow Lincs 156 B4
Hog Hatch Sur 49 D10
Hogaland Shetland 312 F5
Hogben's Hill Kent 54 B4
Hogganfield Glasgow 268 B2
Hoggard's Green Suff 125 F7
Hoggeston Bucks 102 G6
Hoggington Wilts 45 B10
Hoggrill's End Warks 134 E4
Hogha Gearraidh W Isles 296 D3
Hoghton Lancs 194 B6
Hoghton Bottoms Lancs 194 B6
Hogley Green W Yorks 196 F6
Hognaston Derbys 170 E2
Hogpits Bottom Herts 85 E8
Hogsthorpe Lincs 191 G8
Hogstock Dorset 31 F7
Holbeach Lincs 157 E7
Holbeach Bank Lincs 157 D7
Holbeach Clough Lincs 156 D6
Holbeach Drove Lincs 156 G6
Holbeach Hurn Lincs 157 D7
Holbeach St Johns Lincs 156 F6
Holbeach St Marks Lincs 157 C7
Holbeach St Matthew Lincs 157 C8
Holbeache Worcs 116 B5
Holbeck Notts 187 G8
Holbeck W Yorks 205 G11
Holbeck Woodhouse Notts 187 G8
Holberrow Green Worcs 117 F10
Holbeton Devon 8 E2
Holborn London 67 C10
Holborough Kent 69 G8
Holbrook Derbys 170 G5
Holbrook S Yorks 186 E6
Holbrook Suff 108 D3
Holbrook Common S Glos 61 E7
Holbrook Moor Derbys 170 F5
Holbrooks W Mid 134 G6
Holburn Northumb 264 B2
Holbury Hants 32 G6
Holcombe Devon 14 G5
Holcombe Gtr Man 195 D9

Hol – Hur 339

Holcombe Som 45 D7
Holcombe Brook Gtr Man 195 E9
Holcombe Rogus Devon 27 D9
Holcot Northants 120 D5
Holdbrook London 86 F5
Holden Lancs 203 D11
Holden Fold Gtr Man 196 F2
Holdenby Northants 120 D3
Holdenhurst Bmouth 19 B8
Holder's Green Essex 106 F2
Holders Hill London 86 G2
Holdfast Worcs 99 D7
Holdgate Shrops 131 F11
Holdingham Lincs 173 F9
Holditch Dorset 28 G4
Holdsworth W Yorks 196 B5
Holdworth S Yorks 186 C3
Hole Devon 24 D4
Hole W Yorks 204 F6
Hole Bottom W Yorks 196 C2
Hole-in-the-Wall Hereford 98 F2
Hole Street W Sus 35 E10
Holefield Borders 263 C8
Holehills N Lnrk 268 B5
Holehouse Derbys 185 C8
Holehouses E Ches 184 F2
Holemill Aberdeen 293 C10
Holemoor Devon 24 F6
Hole's Hole Devon 7 B8
Holestane Dumfries 247 D9
Holestone Derbys 170 C4
Holewater Devon 41 F8
Holford Som 43 E7
Holgate York 207 C7
Holker Cumb 211 D7
Holkham Norf 176 E5
Hollacombe Devon 24 G5
Hollacombe Devon 26 G4
Hollacombe Hill Devon 7 E10
Holland Orkney 314 D6
Holland Orkney 314 A4
Holland Sur 52 C2
Holland Fen Lincs 174 F2
Holland Lees Lancs 194 F4
Holland-on-Sea Essex 89 B12
Hollands Som 29 D9
Hollandstoun Orkney 314 A7
Hollee Dumfries 239 D7
Hollesley Suff 109 C7
Hollicombe Torbay 9 C7
Hollies Common Staffs 150 E6
Hollin Hall Lancs 204 F4
Hollin Park W Yorks 206 F2
Hollinfare Warr 183 C11
Hollingbourne Kent 53 B10
Hollingbury Brighton 36 F4
Hollingdean Brighton 36 F4
Hollingdon Bucks 103 F7
Hollingrove E Sus 37 C11
Hollingthorpe W Yorks 197 D10
Hollington Derbys 152 B4
Hollington E Sus 38 E3
Hollington Hants 48 B2
Hollington Staffs 151 B11
Hollington Cross Hants 48 B2
Hollington Grove Derbys 152 B4
Hollingwood Derbys 186 G6
Hollingworth Gtr Man 185 B8
Hollins Cumb 222 G3
Hollins Derbys 186 G4
Hollins Gtr Man 195 F10
Hollins Gtr Man 195 F11
Hollins Gtr Man 195 F8
Hollins Staffs 168 D6
Hollins Staffs 168 E4
Hollins Staffs 169 F7
Hollins End S Yorks 186 E5
Hollins Green Warr 183 C11
Hollins Lane Lancs 202 C5
Hollins Lane Shrops 149 B10
Hollinsclough Staffs 169 B9
Hollinsgreen E Ches 168 C2
Hollinswood Telford 132 B4
Hollinthorpe W Yorks 206 G3
Hollinwood Gtr Man 196 G2
Hollinwood Shrops 149 B10
Hollis Green Devon 27 F9
Hollis Head Devon 27 G7
Hollocombe Devon 25 E10
Hollocombe Town Devon 25 E10
Hollow Brook Bath 60 G5
Hollow Meadows S Yorks 186 D2
Hollow Oak Dorset 18 C2
Hollow Street Kent 71 G8
Holloway Derbys 170 D4
Holloway Wilts 45 G11
Holloway Windsor 65 C10
Holloway Hill Sur 50 E3
Hollowell Northants 120 C3
Hollowmoor Heath W Ches 167 B7
Hollows Dumfries 239 B9
Holly Bank W Mid 133 C11
Holly Brook Som 44 D4
Holly Bush Wrex 166 G6
Holly Cross Windsor 65 C10
Holly End Norf 139 B9
Holly Green Bucks 84 E3
Holly Green Worcs 99 C7
Holly Hill N Yorks 224 E3
Hollyberry End W Mid 134 G5
Hollybush Caerph 77 E11
Hollybush E Ayrs 257 G9
Hollybush Stoke 168 G5
Hollybush Torf 78 G3
Hollybush Worcs 98 D5
Hollybush Corner Bucks 66 B3
Hollybush Corner Suff 125 F8
Hollybush Hill Bucks 66 C3
Hollybush Hill Essex 89 B10
Hollybushes Kent 54 B2
Hollycroft Leics 135 E8
Hollyhurst Shrops 131 D9
Hollyhurst Warks 135 F7
Hollym E Yorks 201 B10
Hollywaste Shrops 116 B2
Hollywater Hants 49 G10
Hollywood Worcs 117 B11
Holmacott Devon 25 B8
Holman Clavel Som 28 D2
Holmbridge W Yorks 196 F6
Holmbury St Mary Sur 50 E6
Holmbush Corn 5 E10
Holmbush Dorset 28 G5
Holmcroft Staffs 151 D8
Holme C Beds 104 C3
Holme Cambs 138 F3
Holme Cumb 211 D10
Holme N Lincs 200 F2
Holme N Yorks 215 C7
Holme Notts 172 D4
Holme W Yorks 196 F6
Holme W Yorks 205 G9
Holme Chapel Lancs 195 B11
Holme Green C Beds 104 C3
Holme Green N Yorks 207 E7
Holme Green Wokingham 65 F10
Holme Hale Norf 141 B7
Holme Hill NE Lincs 201 F9
Holme Lacy Hereford 97 D11
Holme Lane Notts 154 B2
Holme Marsh Hereford 114 G6
Holme Mills Cumb 211 D10
Holme next the Sea Norf 176 E2
Holme-on-Spalding-Moor E Yorks 208 F2
Holme on the Wolds E Yorks 208 D5
Holme Pierrepont Notts 154 B2
Holme St Cuthbert Cumb 229 B8
Holme Slack Lancs 203 G7
Holme Wood W Yorks 205 G9
Holmebridge Dorset 18 D3
Holmer Hereford 97 C10
Holmer Green Bucks 84 F6
Holmes Lancs 194 D2
Holmes Chapel E Ches 168 B3
Holmesdale Derbys 186 F5
Holmesfield Derbys 186 F4
Holmes's Hill E Sus 23 C8
Holmeswood Lancs 194 D2
Holmethorpe Sur 51 C9
Holmewood Derbys 170 B6
Holmfield W Yorks 196 B5
Holmfirth W Yorks 196 F6
Holmhead Angus 293 F7
Holmhead Dumfries 246 F6
Holmhead E Ayrs 258 E3
Holmhill Dumfries 247 D9
Holmisdale Highld 297 G7
Holmley Common Derbys 186 F5
Holmpton E Yorks 201 C11
Holmrook Cumb 219 F11
Holmsgarth Shetland 313 J6
Holmside Durham 233 B10
Holmsleigh Green Devon 28 G2
Holmston S Ayrs 257 E9
Holmwood Corner Sur 51 E7
Holmwrangle Cumb 230 B6
Holne Devon 8 B4
Holnest Dorset 29 E11
Holnicote Som 42 D2
Holsworthy Devon 24 G4
Holsworthy Beacon Devon 24 F5
Holt Dorset 31 G8
Holt Hants 49 C8
Holt Mers 183 C7
Holt Norf 159 B11
Holt Wilts 61 G11
Holt Worcs 116 E6
Holt Wrex 166 E6
Holt End Hants 49 F7
Holt End Worcs 117 D11
Holt Fleet Worcs 116 E6
Holt Green Lancs 193 G11
Holt Head W Yorks 196 E5
Holt Heath Dorset 31 G9
Holt Heath Worcs 116 E6
Holt Hill Kent 53 B8
Holt Hill Staffs 152 D2
Holt Park W Yorks 205 E11
Holt Pound Hants 49 E10
Holt Wood Dorset 31 F8
Holtby York 207 C9
Holton Oxon 83 D10
Holton Som 29 B11
Holton Suff 127 B7
Holton cum Beckering Lincs 189 E10
Holton Heath Dorset 18 C4
Holton le Clay Lincs 201 G9
Holton le Moor Lincs 189 B9
Holton St Mary Suff 107 D11
Holts Gtr Man 196 G3
Holtspur Bucks 84 G6
Holtye E Sus 52 F3
Holway Dorset 28 G5
Holway Dorset 29 C10
Holway Flint 181 F11
Holway Som 28 C2
Holwell Dorset 30 E2
Holwell Herts 104 E3
Holwell Leics 154 E4
Holwell Oxon 82 D2
Holwell Som 45 D8
Holwellbury C Beds 104 E3
Holwick Durham 232 F4
Holworth Dorset 17 E11
Holy City Devon 28 G3
Holy Cross T & W 243 D8
Holy Cross Worcs 117 B8
Holy Island Northumb 273 B11
Holy Vale Scilly 1 G4
Holybourne Hants 49 E8
Holyfield Essex 86 E5
Holyhead = Caergybi Anglesey 178 E2
Holylee Borders 261 B9
Holymoorside Derbys 170 B4
Holyport Windsor 65 D11
Holystone Northumb 251 C11
Holytown N Lnrk 268 C5
Holywell C Beds 85 B8
Holywell Cambs 122 C6
Holywell Corn 4 D5
Holywell Dorset 29 G9
Holywell E Sus 23 F9
Holywell Glos 80 G3
Holywell Hereford 97 C7
Holywell Herts 85 F9
Holywell Northumb 243 C8
Holywell Som 29 E8
Holywell Warks 118 D3
Holywell = Treffynnon Flint 181 F11
Holywell Green W Yorks 196 D5
Holywell Lake Som 27 C10
Holywell Row Suff 124 B4
Holywood Dumfries 247 G10
Hom Green Hereford 97 G11
Homedowns Glos 99 E8
Homer Shrops 132 C2
Homer Green Mers 193 G10
Homersfield Suff 142 F5
Homerton London 67 B11
Homington Wilts 31 B10
Honey Hall N Som 60 G2
Honey Hill Kent 70 G6
Honey Street Wilts 62 G6
Honey Tye Suff 107 D9
Honeyborne Worcs 100 C2
Honeychurch Devon 25 G10
Honeydon Beds 122 F2
Honeyhill Wokingham 65 F10
Honeystreet Wilts 62 G6
Honeywick C Beds 103 G9
Honicknowle Plym 7 D9
Honiley Warks 118 C4
Honing Norf 160 D6
Honingham Norf 160 G2
Honington Lincs 172 G6
Honington Suff 125 C8
Honington Warks 100 C5
Honiton Devon 27 G11
Honkley Wrex 166 D4
Honley W Yorks 196 E6
Honley Moor W Yorks 196 E6
Honnington Telford 150 F4
Honor Oak London 67 E11
Honor Oak Park London 67 E11
Honresfeld Gtr Man 196 D2
Hoo Kent 71 G9
Hoo End Herts 85 B11
Hoo Green E Ches 184 E2
Hoo Hole W Yorks 196 B4
Hoo Meavy Devon 7 B10
Hoo St Werburgh Medway 69 E9
Hoober S Yorks 186 B6
Hoobrook Worcs 116 C6
Hood Green S Yorks 197 G10
Hood Hill S Yorks 186 B5
Hood Manor Warr 183 D9
Hooe E Sus 23 D11
Hooe Plym 7 E10
Hooe Common E Sus 23 C11
Hoofield W Ches 167 C8
Hoohill Blkpool 202 F2
Hook Cambs 139 E8
Hook Devon 28 F4
Hook E Yorks 199 B9
Hook Hants 33 F8
Hook Hants 49 C8
Hook London 67 G7
Hook Pembs 73 C7
Hook Wilts 62 C5
Hook-a-gate Shrops 131 B9
Hook Bank Worcs 98 C6
Hook End Essex 87 F9
Hook End Oxon 65 C7
Hook End W Mid 134 G4
Hook Green Kent 53 F7
Hook Green Kent 68 F6
Hook Heath Sur 50 B3
Hook Norton Oxon 101 E7
Hook Park Hants 33 G7
Hook Street Glos 79 F11
Hook Street Wilts 62 C5
Hooke Dorset 16 B6
Hooker Gate T & W 242 F4
Hookgate Staffs 150 B4
Hook's Cross Herts 104 G5
Hooksway W Sus 34 D4
Hookway Devon 14 B3
Hookwood Sur 51 E9
Hoole W Ches 166 B6
Hoole Bank W Ches 166 B6
Hooley Sur 51 B9
Hooley Bridge Gtr Man 195 E11
Hooley Brow Gtr Man 195 E11
Hooley Hill Gtr Man 184 B6
Hoop Mon 79 D8
Hoopers Pool Wilts 45 C10
Hoops Devon 24 C5
Hooton W Ches 182 F5
Hooton Levitt S Yorks 187 C8
Hooton Pagnell S Yorks 198 F3
Hooton Roberts S Yorks 187 B7
Hop Pole Lincs 156 G3
Hopcroft's Holt Oxon 101 F9
Hope Derbys 185 E11
Hope Devon 9 G8
Hope Highld 308 D4
Hope Powys 130 B5
Hope Shrops 130 C6
Hope Staffs 169 D10
Hope = Yr Hôb Flint 166 D4
Hope Bagot Shrops 115 C11
Hope Bowdler Shrops 131 E9
Hope End Green Essex 105 G11
Hope Green E Ches 184 E6
Hope Mansell Hereford 79 B10
Hope Park Shrops 130 C6
Hope under Dinmore Hereford 115 G10
Hopebeck Cumb 229 G9
Hopedale Staffs 169 D10
Hopeman Moray 301 C11
Hope's Green Essex 69 B9
Hope's Rough Hereford 98 B2
Hopesay Shrops 131 G7
Hopesgate Shrops 130 C6
Hopetown W Yorks 197 C11
Hopgoods Green W Berks 64 F4
Hopkinstown Rhondda 77 G9
Hopley's Green Hereford 114 G6
Hopperton N Yorks 206 B4
Hopsford Warks 135 G8
Hopstone Shrops 132 E5
Hopton Derbys 170 E3
Hopton Shrops 149 D11
Hopton Shrops 149 E7
Hopton Staffs 151 D8
Hopton Suff 125 B9
Hopton Cangeford Shrops 131 G10
Hopton Castle Shrops 115 B7
Hopton Heath Staffs 151 D9
Hopton on Sea Norf 143 D10
Hopton Wafers Shrops 116 B2
Hoptonbank Shrops 116 B2
Hoptongate Shrops 131 G10
Hoptonheath Shrops 115 B7
Hopwas Staffs 134 B3
Hopwood Gtr Man 195 F11
Hopwood Worcs 117 B10
Hopworthy Devon 24 G4
Horam E Sus 23 B9
Horbling Lincs 156 B2
Horbury W Yorks 197 D9
Horbury Bridge W Yorks 197 D9
Horbury Junction W Yorks 197 D10
Horcott Glos 81 E11
Horden Durham 234 C4
Horderley Shrops 131 F8
Hordle Hants 19 B11
Hordley Shrops 149 C7
Horeb Carms 75 D7
Horeb Carms 93 F10
Horeb Ceredig 93 C7
Horeb Flint 166 D3
Horfield Bristol 60 D6
Horgabost W Isles 305 J2
Horham Suff 126 C4
Horkesley Heath Essex 107 F9
Horkstow N Lincs 200 D3
Horkstow Wolds N Lincs 200 D3
Horley Oxon 101 C8
Horley Sur 51 E9
Horn Ash Dorset 28 G5
Horn Hill Som 43 E8
Horn Street Kent 55 F7
Horn Street Kent 69 G7
Hornblotton Som 44 G5
Hornblotton Green Som 44 G5
Hornby Lancs 211 F11
Hornby N Yorks 224 G4
Hornby N Yorks 225 D7
Horncastle Lincs 174 B3
Horncastle Reading 65 E7
Hornchurch London 68 B4
Horncliffe Northumb 273 F8
Horndean Borders 273 F7
Horndean Hants 34 E2
Horndon Devon 12 F6
Horndon on the Hill Thurrock 69 C7
Horne Sur 51 E10
Horne Row Essex 88 E3
Horner Som 41 D11
Horner's Green Suff 107 C9
Hornestreet Essex 107 E10
Horney Common E Sus 37 B7
Hornick Corn 5 E9
Horniehaugh Angus 292 G6
Horning Norf 160 F6
Horninghold Leics 136 D6
Horninglow Staffs 152 D4
Horningsea Cambs 123 E9
Horningsham Wilts 45 E10
Horningtoft Norf 159 E8
Horningtops Corn 6 C5
Horns Corner Kent 38 B2
Horns Cross Devon 24 C5
Horns Cross E Sus 38 C4
Horns Green Kent 52 B3
Hornsbury Som 28 E4
Hornsby Cumb 240 G2
Hornsea E Yorks 209 D10
Hornsea Bridge E Yorks 209 D10
Hornsea Burton E Yorks 209 D10
Hornsey London 67 B10
Hornsey Vale London 67 B10
Hornton Oxon 101 B7
Horpit Swindon 63 C8
Horrabridge Devon 7 B10
Horringer Suff 124 E6
Horringford I o W 20 D6
Horrocks Fold Gtr Man 195 E8
Horrocksford Lancs 203 E10
Horsalls Kent 53 C11
Horse Bridge Staffs 169 E7
Horsebridge Devon 12 G4
Horsebridge Hants 47 G10
Horsebridge Shrops 131 B7
Horsebrook Devon 8 D4
Horsebrook Staffs 151 G7
Horsecastle N Som 60 F2
Horsedown Wilts 61 D10
Horsedowns Corn 2 C4
Horsehay Telford 132 B3
Horseheath Cambs 106 B2
Horseholm Dumfries 238 C2
Horsehouse N Yorks 213 C10
Horseley Heath W Mid 133 E9
Horsell Sur 50 B3
Horsell Birch Sur 50 B3
Horseman Side Essex 87 F8
Horseman's Green Wrex 166 G6
Horsemere Green W Sus 35 G7
Horsenden Bucks 84 E3
Horsepools Glos 80 C4
Horseway Cambs 139 F8
Horseway Head Hereford 114 E6
Horsey Norf 161 E9
Horsey Som 43 F10
Horsey Corner Norf 161 E9
Horsey Down Wilts 81 G9
Horsford Norf 160 F3
Horsforth W Yorks 205 F10
Horsforth Woodside W Yorks 205 F10
Horsham W Sus 51 G7
Horsham Worcs 116 F4
Horsham St Faith Norf 160 F4
Horshoe Green Kent 52 E3
Horsington Lincs 173 B11
Horsington Som 30 C2
Horsley Derbys 170 G5
Horsley Glos 80 F4
Horsley Northumb 242 D3
Horsley Northumb 251 D8
Horsley Cross Essex 108 F2
Horsley Hill T & W 243 D9
Horsley Woodhouse Derbys 170 G5
Horsleycross Street Essex 108 F2
Horsleyhill Borders 262 F2
Horsleyhope Durham 233 B7
Horsleys Green Bucks 84 F3
Horsmonden Kent 53 E7
Horspath Oxon 83 E9
Horstead Norf 160 F5
Horsted Green E Sus 23 B7
Horsted Keynes W Sus 36 B5
Horton Bucks 84 B6
Horton Dorset 31 F8
Horton Kent 54 B6
Horton Lancs 204 C3
Horton Northants 120 G6
Horton S Glos 61 C9
Horton Shrops 149 D9
Horton Som 28 E4
Horton Staffs 168 D6
Horton Swansea 56 D3
Horton Telford 150 G3
Horton Wilts 62 G5
Horton Windsor 66 D4
Horton Common Dorset 31 F9
Horton Cross Som 28 D4
Horton-cum-Studley Oxon 83 C9
Horton Green W Ches 167 F7
Horton Heath Dorset 31 F9
Horton Heath Hants 33 D7
Horton in Ribblesdale N Yorks 212 E6
Horton Kirby Kent 68 F5
Horton Wharf Bucks 84 B6
Hortonlane Shrops 149 G8
Hortonwood Telford 150 G3
Horwich Gtr Man 194 E6
Horwich End Derbys 185 E8
Horwood Devon 25 B8
Horwood Riding S Glos 61 B8
Hoscar Lancs 194 E3
Hose Leics 154 D4
Hoselaw Borders 263 C8
Hoses Cumb 220 G4
Hosey Hill Kent 52 C3
Hosh Perth 286 E2
Hosta W Isles 296 D3
Hoswick Shetland 313 L6
Hotham E Yorks 208 G3
Hothfield Kent 54 D3
Hotley Bottom Bucks 84 E5
Hoton Leics 153 E11
Hotwells Bristol 60 E5
Houbans Shetland 312 F5
Houbie Shetland 312 D8
Houdston S Ayrs 244 D5
Hough Argyll 288 E1
Hough E Ches 168 E2
Hough E Ches 184 F5
Hough Green Halton 183 D7
Hough-on-the-Hill Lincs 172 F6
Hough Side W Yorks 205 G10
Hougham Lincs 172 G5
Houghton Cambs 122 C5
Houghton Cumb 239 F10
Houghton Hants 47 G10
Houghton Northumb 242 D4
Houghton Pembs 73 D7
Houghton W Sus 35 E8
Houghton Bank Darl 233 G10
Houghton Conquest C Beds 103 C10
Houghton Green E Sus 38 C6
Houghton Green Warr 183 C10
Houghton-le-Side Darl 233 G10
Houghton-le-Spring T & W 234 B2
Houghton on the Hill Leics 136 C3
Houghton Regis C Beds 103 G10
Houghton St Giles Norf 159 B8
Houghwood Mers 194 G4
Houlland Shetland 312 B7
Houlland Shetland 312 F7
Houlland Shetland 313 H5
Houlland Shetland 313 J6
Houlsyke N Yorks 226 D4
Hound Hants 33 F7
Hound Green Hants 49 B8
Hound Hill Dorset 31 G7
Houndmills Hants 48 C6
Houndscroft Glos 80 E5
Houndslow Borders 272 F2
Houndsmoor Som 27 B10
Houndstone Som 29 D8
Houndwood Borders 272 C6
Hounsdown Hants 32 E5
Hounsley Batch N Som 60 G4
Hounslow London 66 D6
Hounslow Green Essex 87 B11
Hounslow West London 66 D6
Hourston Orkney 314 E2
Housabister Shetland 313 H6
Housay Shetland 312 F8
House of Daviot Highld 301 E7
House of Glenmuick Aberds 292 D5
Househill Highld 301 D8
Houses Hill W Yorks 197 D7
Housetter Shetland 312 E5
Housham Tye Essex 87 C8
Houss Shetland 313 K5
Houston Renfs 267 B8
Houstry Highld 310 F5
Houton Orkney 314 F3
Hove Brighton 36 G3
Hove Edge W Yorks 196 C6
Hoveringham Notts 171 F11
Hoveton Norf 160 F6
Hovingham N Yorks 216 D3
How Cumb 240 F2
How Caple Hereford 98 E2
How End C Beds 103 C10
How Green Kent 52 D3
How Hill Norf 161 F7
How Wood Herts 85 E10
Howbeck Bank E Ches 167 F11
Howbrook S Yorks 186 B4
Howden Borders 262 E5
Howden E Yorks 199 B8
Howden W Loth 269 B11
Howden Clough W Yorks 197 B8
Howden-le-Wear Durham 233 E9
Howdon T & W 243 D8
Howdon Pans T & W 243 D8
Howe Highld 310 C7
Howe N Yorks 214 C6
Howe Norf 142 C5
Howe Bridge Gtr Man 195 G7
Howe Green Essex 88 E2
Howe Green Essex 87 B8
Howe Green Warks 134 F6
Howe of Teuchar Aberds 303 E7
Howe Street Essex 87 C11
Howe Street Essex 106 E3
Howegreen Essex 88 E4
Howell Lincs 173 F10
Howey Powys 113 F11
Howford Borders 261 B8
Howford Borders 261 E9
Howgate Cumb 228 G5
Howgate Midloth 270 D4
Howgill Cumb 222 F2
Howgill Lancs 204 D2
Howgill N Yorks 205 B7
Howick Mon 79 F8
Howick Northumb 265 F7
Howick Cross Lancs 194 B4
Howle Durham 233 F7
Howle Telford 150 E3
Howleigh Som 28 D2
Howlett End Essex 105 E11
Howley Glos 80 G2
Howley Som 28 F3
Howley Warr 183 D10
Hownam Borders 263 F7
Hownam Mains Borders 263 E7
Howpasley Borders 249 B8
Howsen Worcs 116 G5
Howsham N Lincs 200 G4
Howsham N Yorks 216 G4
Howslack Dumfries 248 B3
Howt Green Kent 69 F11
Howtel Northumb 263 C9
Howton Hereford 97 F8
Howtown Cumb 221 B8
Howwood Renfs 267 C7
Hoxne Suff 126 B3
Hoxton London 67 C10
Hoy Orkney 314 F2
Hoylake Mers 182 D2
Hoyland S Yorks 197 G11
Hoyland Common S Yorks 197 G11
Hoylandswaine S Yorks 197 G9
Hoyle W Sus 34 D6
Hoyle Mill S Yorks 197 F11
Hubbard's Hill Kent 52 C4
Hubberholme N Yorks 213 D8
Hubberston Pembs 72 D5
Hubbersty Head Cumb 221 G8
Hubberton Green W Yorks 196 C4
Hubbert's Bridge Lincs 174 G3
Huby N Yorks 205 D11
Huby N Yorks 215 F11
Hucclecote Glos 80 B5
Hucking Kent 53 B10
Hucknall Notts 171 F8
Hud Hey Lancs 195 C9
Huddersfield W Yorks 196 D6
Huddington Worcs 117 F8
Huddisford Devon 24 D4
Huddlesford Staffs 134 B3
Hudnall Herts 85 C8
Hudnalls Glos 79 E8
Hudswell N Yorks 224 E3
Hudswell Wilts 61 F11
Huggate E Yorks 208 B3
Hugglepit Devon 24 C4
Hugglescote Leics 153 G8
Hugh Mill Lancs 195 C10
Hugh Town Scilly 1 G4
Hughenden Valley Bucks 84 F5
Hughley Shrops 131 D11
Hugus Corn 4 G5
Huish Devon 25 B7
Huish Devon 25 E8
Huish Wilts 62 G6
Huish Champflower Som 27 B9
Huish Episcopi Som 28 B6
Huisinis W Isles 305 G1
Hulcote C Beds 103 D8
Hulcote Northants 102 B4
Hulcott Bucks 84 B5
Hull End Derbys 185 E9
Hulland Derbys 170 F2
Hulland Moss Derbys 170 F3
Hulland Ward Derbys 170 F3
Hullavington Wilts 61 C11
Hullbridge Essex 88 G4
Hulme Gtr Man 184 B4
Hulme Staffs 168 F6
Hulme Warr 183 C10
Hulme End Staffs 169 D10
Hulme Walfield E Ches 168 B4
Hulseheath E Ches 184 E2
Hulver Street Suff 143 F9
Hulverstone I o W 20 E3
Humber Devon 14 G3
Humber Hereford 115 F10
Humber Bridge N Lincs 200 C4
Humberston NE Lincs 201 F10
Humberston Fitties NE Lincs 201 F10
Humberstone Leicester 136 B2
Humbie E Loth 271 C9
Humble Green Suff 107 B8
Humbledon T & W 243 F9
Humbleton E Yorks 209 G10
Humbleton Northumb 263 D11
Humby Lincs 155 C10
Hume Borders 272 G4
Hummersknott Darl 224 C5
Humshaugh Northumb 241 C10
Huna Highld 310 B7
Huncoat Lancs 203 G11
Huncote Leics 135 D10
Hundalee Borders 262 F4
Hundall Derbys 186 F5
Hunderthwaite Durham 232 G5
Hunderton Hereford 97 D9
Hundle Houses Lincs 174 E3
Hundleby Lincs 174 B5
Hundleshope Borders 260 B6
Hundleton Pembs 73 E7
Hundon Suff 106 B4
Hundred Acres Hants 33 E9
Hundred End Lancs 194 C2
Hundred House Powys 114 G2
Hungarton Leics 136 B3
Hungate W Yorks 197 B11
Hunger Hill Gtr Man 195 F7
Hunger Hill Lancs 194 E4
Hungerford Hants 31 E11
Hungerford Shrops 131 F10
Hungerford Som 42 E4
Hungerford W Berks 63 F10
Hungerford Windsor 65 E10
Hungerford Green W Berks 64 D5
Hungerford Newtown W Berks 63 E11
Hungershall Park Kent 52 F5
Hungerstone Hereford 97 D8
Hungerton Lincs 155 D7
Hungladder Highld 298 B3
Hungreyhatton Shrops 150 D3
Hunmanby N Yorks 217 D11
Hunmanby Moor N Yorks 218 D2
Hunningham Warks 119 D7
Hunningham Hill Warks 119 D7
Hunnington Worcs 133 G9
Hunny Hill I o W 20 D5
Hunsdon Herts 86 C6
Hunsdonbury Herts 86 C6
Hunsingore N Yorks 206 C4
Hunslet W Yorks 206 G2
Hunslet Carr W Yorks 206 G2
Hunsonby Cumb 231 D7
Hunspow Highld 310 B6
Hunstanton Norf 175 G11
Hunstanworth Durham 232 B5
Hunsterson E Ches 167 F11
Hunston Suff 125 D9
Hunston W Sus 22 C5
Hunston Green Suff 125 D9
Hunstrete Bath 60 G6
Hunsworth W Yorks 197 B7
Hunt End Worcs 117 E10
Huntenhull Green Wilts 45 D10
Huntercombe End Oxon 65 B7
Hunters Forstal Kent 71 F7
Hunter's Quay Argyll 276 F3
Huntham Som 28 B4
Hunthill Lodge Angus 292 F6
Hunting-tower Perth 286 E4
Huntingdon Cambs 122 C4
Huntingfield Suff 126 C6
Huntingford Dorset 45 G10
Huntingford S Glos 80 G2
Huntington E Loth 281 F9
Huntington Hereford 97 C9
Huntington Hereford 114 G5
Huntington Staffs 151 G9
Huntington Telford 132 B3
Huntington W Ches 166 C6
Huntington York 207 B8
Huntley Glos 80 B2
Huntley Staffs 169 G8
Huntly Aberds 302 F5
Huntlywood Borders 272 G2
Hunton Hants 48 F3
Hunton Kent 53 D8
Hunton N Yorks 224 G3
Hunton Bridge Herts 85 E9
Hunt's Corner Norf 141 F11
Hunt's Cross Mers 182 D6
Hunt's Green Bucks 84 E5
Hunt's Green W Berks 64 E2
Hunts Green Warks 134 D3
Hunt's Hill Bucks 84 F4
Hunt's Lane Leics 135 C9
Huntscott Som 42 E2
Huntsham Devon 27 C8
Huntshaw Devon 25 C8
Huntshaw Water Devon 25 C8
Huntspill Som 43 D10
Huntstile Som 43 G9
Huntworth Som 43 G10
Hunwick Durham 233 E9
Hunworth Norf 159 B11
Hurcott Som 28 D5
Hurcott Som 29 B8
Hurcott Worcs 117 B7
Hurdcott Wilts 47 G7
Hurdley Powys 130 E5
Hurdsfield E Ches 184 G6
Hurgill N Yorks 224 E3
Hurlet Glasgow 267 C10
Hurley Warks 134 D4

340 Hur – Kep

Hurley Windsor 65 C10
Hurley Bottom Windsor 65 C10
Hurley Common Warks 134 D4
Hurlford E Ayrs 257 B11
Hurliness Orkney 314 H2
Hurlston Lancs 194 E2
Hurlston Green Lancs 193 E11
Hurn Dorset 19 B8
Hurn E Yorks 208 E6
Hurn's End Lincs 174 F6
Hursey Dorset 28 G6
Hursley Hants 32 B6
Hurst Cumb 230 C4
Hurst Dorset 17 C11
Hurst Gtr Man 196 G2
Hurst N Yorks 223 E10
Hurst Som 29 D7
Hurst Wokingham 65 E9
Hurst Green E Sus 38 B2
Hurst Green Essex 89 B9
Hurst Green Lancs 203 F9
Hurst Green Sur 51 C11
Hurst Green W Mid 133 F9
Hurst Hill W Mid 133 E8
Hurst Park Sur 66 F6
Hurst Wickham W Sus 36 D3
Hurstbourne Priors Hants 48 D2
Hurstbourne Tarrant Hants 47 C11
Hurstead Gtr Man 196 D2
Hurstley Hereford 97 B7
Hurstpierpoint W Sus 36 D3
Hurstwood Lancs 204 G3
Hurtmore Sur 50 D3
Hurworth-on-Tees Darl 224 C6
Hurworth Place Darl 224 D5
Hury Durham 223 B9
Husabost Highld 298 D2
Husbands Bosworth Leics 136 G2
Husbandtown Angus 287 D8
Husborne Crawley C Beds 103 D9
Husthwaite N Yorks 215 D10
Hut Green N Yorks 198 C5
Hutcherleigh Devon 8 E5
Hutchesontown Glasgow 267 C11
Hutchwns Bridgend 57 F10
Huthwaite Notts 171 D7
Hutlerburn Borders 261 E10
Huttock Top Lancs 195 C11
Huttoft Lincs 191 F8
Hutton Borders 273 E9
Hutton Cumb 230 F4
Hutton E Yorks 208 C6
Hutton Essex 87 F10
Hutton Lancs 194 B3
Hutton N Som 43 B11
Hutton Bonville N Yorks 224 E6
Hutton Buscel N Yorks 217 C9
Hutton Conyers N Yorks 214 E6
Hutton Cranswick E Yorks 208 C6
Hutton End Cumb 230 D4
Hutton Gate Redcar 225 B11
Hutton Hang N Yorks 214 B3
Hutton Henry Durham 234 D4
Hutton-le-Hole N Yorks 226 G4
Hutton Magna Durham 224 C2
Hutton Mount Essex 87 G10
Hutton Roof Cumb 211 D11
Hutton Roof Cumb 230 E3
Hutton Rudby N Yorks 225 D9
Hutton Sessay N Yorks 215 D9
Hutton Village Redcar 225 C11
Hutton Wandesley N Yorks 206 C6
Huttons Ambo N Yorks 216 F5
Huxham Devon 14 B4
Huxham Green Som 44 F5
Huxley W Ches 167 C8
Huxter Shetland 313 G7
Huxter Shetland 313 H3
Huxter Shetland 313 H5
Huxton Borders 273 B7
Huyton Mers 182 C6
Huyton Park Mers 182 C6
Huyton Quarry Mers 183 C7
Hwlffordd = Haverfordwest Pembs 73 B7
Hycemoor Cumb 210 B1
Hyde Glos 80 E5
Hyde Glos 99 F11
Hyde Gtr Man 184 B6
Hyde Hants 31 E11
Hyde Hants 48 G3
Hyde Hereford 115 F9
Hyde Chase Essex 88 E4
Hyde End W Berks 64 G5
Hyde Heath Bucks 84 E6
Hyde Lea Staffs 151 E8
Hyde Park S Yorks 198 G5
Hydestile Sur 50 E3
Hylton Castle T & W 243 F9
Hylton Red House T & W 243 F9
Hyltons Crossways Norf 160 D4
Hyndburn Bridge Lancs 203 G10
Hyndford Bridge S Lnrk 269 G8
Hyndhope Borders 261 E9
Hynish Argyll 288 F1
Hyssington Powys 130 E6
Hystfield Glos 79 F11
Hythe Hants 32 F6
Hythe Kent 55 G7
Hythe Som 44 C2
Hythe Sur 66 E4
Hythe End Windsor 66 E4
Hythie Aberds 303 D10
Hyton Cumb 210 B1

I

Iarsiadar W Isles 304 E3
Ibberton Dorset 30 F3
Ible Derbys 170 D2
Ibsley Hants 31 F11
Ibstock Leics 153 G8
Ibstone Bucks 84 G3
Ibthorpe Hants 47 C11
Ibworth Hants 48 C5
Icelton N Som 59 F11
Ichrachan Argyll 284 D4
Ickburgh Norf 140 E6
Ickenham London 66 B5
Ickenthwaite Cumb 210 B6
Ickford Bucks 83 D11
Ickham Kent 55 B8
Ickleford Herts 104 E3
Icklesham E Sus 38 D5
Ickleton Cambs 105 C9
Icklingham Suff 124 C5
Ickornshaw N Yorks 204 E5
Ickwell C Beds 104 B3
Ickwell Green C Beds 104 B3
Icomb Glos 100 G4
Icy Park Devon 8 F3
Idbury Oxon 82 B2
Iddesleigh Devon 25 F9
Ide Devon 14 C3
Ide Hill Kent 52 C3
Ideford Devon 14 F3
Iden E Sus 38 C6
Iden Green Kent 53 F8
Iden Green Kent 53 G10
Idle W Yorks 205 F9
Idle Moor W Yorks 205 F9
Idless Corn 4 F6
Idlicote Warks 100 C5
Idmiston Wilts 47 F7
Idole Carms 74 B6
Idridgehay Derbys 170 F3
Idridgehay Green Derbys 170 F3
Idrigill Highld 298 C3
Idstone Oxon 63 C9
Idvies Angus 287 C9
Iet-y-bwlch Carms 92 F3
Iffley Oxon 83 E8
Ifield W Sus 51 F8
Ifield Green W Sus 51 F9
Ifieldwood W Sus 51 F8
Ifold W Sus 50 G4
Iford Bmouth 19 C8
Iford E Sus 36 F6
Ifton Heath Shrops 148 B6
Ightfield Shrops 149 B11
Ightfield Heath Shrops 149 B11
Ightham Kent 52 B5
Igtham Common Kent 52 B5
Iken Suff 127 F8
Ilam Staffs 169 E10
Ilchester Som 29 C8
Ilchester Mead Som 29 C8
Ilderton Northumb 264 E2
Ileden Kent 55 C8
Ilford London 68 B2
Ilford Som 28 D5
Ilfracombe Devon 40 D4
Ilkeston Derbys 171 G7
Ilketshall St Andrew Suff 143 F7
Ilketshall St Lawrence Suff 143 G7
Ilketshall St Margaret Suff 142 F6
Ilkley W Yorks 205 D8
Illand Corn 11 F11
Illey W Mid 133 G9
Illidge Green E Ches 168 C3
Illington Norf 141 F8
Illingworth W Yorks 196 B5
Illogan Corn 4 G3
Illogan Highway Corn 4 G3
Illshaw Heath W Mid 118 C2
Illston on the Hill Leics 136 D4
Ilmer Bucks 84 D3
Ilmington Warks 100 C4
Ilminster Som 28 E5
Ilsington Devon 13 F11
Ilston Swansea 56 C5
Ilton N Yorks 214 D3
Ilton Som 28 D5
Imachar N Ayrs 255 C9
Imber Wilts 46 D3
Imeraval Argyll 254 C4
Immervoulin Stirl 285 F9
Immingham NE Lincs 201 E7
Impington Cambs 123 E8
Ince W Ches 183 F7
Ince Blundell Mers 193 G10
Ince in Makerfield Gtr Man 194 G5
Inch of Arnhall Aberds 293 F8
Inchbae Lodge Highld 300 C4
Inchbare Angus 293 G8
Inchberry Moray 302 D3
Inchbraoch Angus 287 B11
Inchbrook Glos 80 E4
Inchcape Highld 309 J6
Incheril Highld 299 C10
Inchgrundle Angus 292 F6
Inchina Highld 307 K4
Inchinnan Renfs 267 B9
Inchkinloch Highld 308 E5
Inchlaggan Highld 290 C3
Inchlumpie Highld 300 B5
Inchmore Highld 300 E3
Inchmore Highld 300 E5
Inchnacardoch Hotel Highld 290 B5
Inchnadamph Highld 307 G7
Inchock Angus 287 C10
Inchree Highld 290 G2
Inchrory Moray 292 C3
Inchs Corn 5 C9
Inchture Perth 286 E6
Inchyra Perth 286 E5
Indian Queens Corn 5 D8
Inerval Argyll 254 C4
Ingatestone Essex 87 F11
Ingbirchworth S Yorks 197 F8
Ingerthorpe N Yorks 214 F5
Ingestre Staffs 151 E9
Ingham Lincs 188 E6
Ingham Norf 161 D7
Ingham Suff 125 C7
Ingham Corner Norf 161 D7
Ingleborough Norf 157 F9
Ingleby Derbys 152 D6
Ingleby Lincs 188 F5
Ingleby Arncliffe N Yorks 225 E8
Ingleby Barwick Stockton 225 C9
Ingleby Cross N Yorks 225 E9
Ingleby Greenhow N Yorks 225 D11
Ingleigh Green Devon 25 F10
Inglemire Hull 209 G7
Inglesbatch Bath 61 G8
Inglesham Swindon 82 F2
Ingleton Durham 233 G9
Ingleton N Yorks 212 E3
Inglewhite Lancs 202 E6
Ingmanthorpe N Yorks 206 C4
Ingoe Northumb 242 C2
Ingol Lancs 202 G6
Ingoldisthorpe Norf 158 C3
Ingoldmells Lincs 175 B9
Ingoldsby Lincs 155 C10
Ingon Warks 118 F4
Ingram Northumb 264 F2
Ingrams Green W Sus 34 C4
Ingrave Essex 87 G10
Ingrow W Yorks 205 F7
Ings Cumb 221 F8
Ingst S Glos 60 B5
Ingthorpe Rutland 137 B9
Ingworth Norf 160 D3
Inham's End Cambs 138 D5
Inhurst Hants 64 G5
Inkberrow Worcs 117 F10
Inkerman Durham 233 D8
Inkersall Derbys 186 G6
Inkersall Green Derbys 186 G6
Inkford Worcs 117 C11
Inkpen W Berks 63 G11
Inkpen Common W Berks 63 G11
Inkstack Highld 310 B6
Inlands W Sus 22 B3
Inmarsh Wilts 62 G2
Inn Cumb 221 D8
Innellan Argyll 276 G3
Inner Hope Devon 9 G8
Innerleithen Borders 261 B8
Innerleven Fife 287 G7
Innermessan Dumfries 236 C2
Innerwick E Loth 282 G4
Innerwick Perth 285 C9
Innie Argyll 275 B9
Inninbeg Highld 289 E8
Innis Chonain Argyll 284 E5
Innistrynich Argyll 284 E5
Innox Hill Som 45 D9
Innsworth Glos 99 G7
Insch Aberds 302 G6
Insh Highld 291 C10
Inshegra Highld 306 D7
Inshore Highld 308 C3
Inskip Lancs 202 F5
Inskip Moss Side Lancs 202 F5
Instoneville S Yorks 198 E5
Instow Devon 40 G3
Insworke Corn 7 E8
Intack Blkburn 195 B8
Intake S Yorks 186 E5
Intake S Yorks 198 G5
Intake W Yorks 205 F10
Interfield Worcs 98 B5
Intwood Norf 142 C3
Inver Aberds 292 D4
Inver Highld 311 L2
Inver Perth 286 C4
Inver Mallie Highld 290 E3
Inverailort Highld 295 G9
Inveraldie Angus 287 D8
Inveralivaig Highld 298 E4
Inveralligin Highld 299 D8
Inverallochy Aberds 303 C10
Inveran Highld 309 K5
Inveraray Argyll 284 G4
Inverarish Highld 295 B7
Inverarity Angus 287 C8
Inverarnan Stirl 285 F7
Inverasdale Highld 307 L3
Inverawe Ho Argyll 284 D4
Inverbeg Argyll 276 B6
Inverbervie Aberds 293 F10
Inverboyndie Aberds 302 C6
Inverbroom Highld 307 L6
Invercarron Mains Highld 309 K5
Invercassley Highld 309 J4
Invercauld House Aberds 292 D3
Inverchaolain Argyll 275 F11
Invercharnan Highld 284 C5
Inverchoran Highld 300 D2
Invercreran Argyll 284 C4
Inverdruie Highld 291 B11
Inverebrie Aberds 303 F9
Invereck Argyll 276 E2
Inverernan Ho Aberds 292 B5
Invereshie House Highld 291 C10
Inveresk E Loth 280 G6
Inverey Aberds 292 E2
Inverfarigaig Highld 300 G5
Invergarry Highld 290 C5
Invergelder Aberds 292 D4
Invergeldie Perth 285 E11
Invergordon Highld 301 C7
Invergowrie Perth 287 D7
Inverguseran Highld 295 E9
Inverhadden Perth 285 B10
Inverhaggernie Stirl 285 E7
Inverharroch Moray 302 F3
Inverherive Stirl 285 E7
Inverie Highld 295 F9
Inverinan Argyll 275 B10
Inverinate Highld 295 C11
Inverkeilor Angus 287 C10
Inverkeithing Fife 280 E2
Inverkeithny Aberds 302 E6
Inverkip Invclyd 276 G4
Inverkirkaig Highld 307 H5
Inverlael Highld 307 L6
Inverleith Edin 280 F4
Inverliever Lodge Argyll 275 C9
Inverliver Argyll 284 D4
Inverlochlarig Stirl 285 F8
Inverlochy Argyll 284 E5
Inverlochy Highld 290 F3
Inverlochy Moray 301 G11
Inverlounin Argyll 276 B4
Inverlussa Argyll 275 E7
Invermark Lodge Angus 292 E6
Invermoidart Highld 289 B8
Invermoriston Highld 290 B6
Invernaver Highld 308 C7
Inverneill Argyll 275 E9
Inverness Highld 300 E6
Invernettie Aberds 303 E11
Invernoaden Argyll 276 B2
Inveronich Argyll 284 G6
Inveroran Hotel Argyll 284 C6
Inverpolly Lodge Highld 307 H5
Inverquharity Angus 287 B8
Inverquhomery Aberds 303 E10
Inverroy Highld 290 E4
Inversanda Highld 289 D11
Invershiel Highld 295 D11
Invershin Highld 309 K5
Invershore Highld 310 F6
Inversnaid Hotel Stirl 285 G7
Invertrossachs Stirl 285 G9
Inverugie Aberds 303 E11
Inveruglas Argyll 285 G7
Inveruglass Highld 291 C10
Inverurie Aberds 303 G7
Invervar Perth 285 C10
Inverythan Aberds 303 E7
Inwardleigh Devon 13 B7
Inwood Shrops 131 D9
Inworth Essex 88 B5
Iochdar W Isles 297 G3
Iping W Sus 34 C5
Ipplepen Devon 8 B6
Ipsden Oxon 64 B6
Ipsley Worcs 117 D11
Ipstones Staffs 169 F8
Ipswich Suff 108 C3
Irby Mers 182 E3
Irby in the Marsh Lincs 175 C7
Irby upon Humber NE Lincs 201 G7
Irchester Northants 121 D8
Ireby Cumb 229 D10
Ireby Lancs 212 D3
Ireland C Beds 104 C2
Ireland Orkney 314 F3
Ireland Shetland 313 L5
Ireland Wilts 45 C10
Ireland Wood W Yorks 205 F11
Ireland's Cross Shrops 168 G2
Ireleth Cumb 210 D4
Ireshopeburn Durham 232 D3
Ireton Wood Derbys 170 F3
Irlam Gtr Man 184 C2
Irlams o' th' Height Gtr Man 195 G9
Irnham Lincs 155 D10
Iron Acton S Glos 61 C7
Iron Bridge Cambs 139 D9
Iron Cross Warks 117 G11
Iron Lo Highld 299 G10
Ironbridge Telford 132 C3
Irongray Dumfries 237 B11
Ironmacannie Dumfries 237 B8
Irons Bottom Sur 51 D9
Ironside Aberds 303 D8
Ironville Derbys 170 E6
Irstead Norf 161 E7
Irstead Street Norf 161 F7
Irthington Cumb 239 E11
Irthlingborough Northants 121 C8
Irton N Yorks 217 C10
Irvine N Ayrs 257 B8
Irwell Vale Lancs 195 C9
Isabella Pit Northumb 253 G8
Isallt Bach Anglesey 178 F3
Isauld Highld 310 C3
Isbister Orkney 314 E3
Isbister Orkney 314 D2
Isbister Shetland 312 D5
Isbister Shetland 313 G7
Isel Cumb 229 E9
Isfield E Sus 36 D6
Isham Northants 121 C7
Ishriff Argyll 289 F8
Isington Hants 49 E9
Island Carr N Lincs 200 F3
Islands Common Cambs 122 E3
Islay Ho Argyll 274 G4
Isle Abbotts Som 28 C5
Isle Brewers Som 28 C5
Isle of Axholme N Lincs 199 F9
Isle of Dogs London 67 D11
Isle of Man Dumfries 238 B2
Isle of Whithorn Dumfries 236 F6
Isleham Cambs 124 C2
Isleornsay Highld 295 D9
Islesburgh Shetland 312 G5
Islesteps Dumfries 237 B11
Isleworth London 67 D7
Isley Walton Leics 153 D8
Islibhig W Isles 304 F1
Islington London 67 C10
Islington Telford 150 E4
Islip Northants 121 B9
Islip Oxon 83 C8
Isombridge Telford 150 G2
Istead Rise Kent 68 F6
Isycoed Wrex 166 E6
Itchen Soton 32 E6
Itchen Abbas Hants 48 G4
Itchen Stoke Hants 48 G5
Itchingfield W Sus 35 B10
Itchington S Glos 61 B7
Itteringham Norf 160 C2
Itteringham Common Norf 160 D3
Itton Devon 13 B9
Itton Mon 79 F7
Itton Common Mon 79 F7
Ivegill Cumb 230 C4
Ivelet N Yorks 223 F8
Iver Bucks 66 C4
Iver Heath Bucks 66 C4
Iverley Staffs 133 G7
Iveston Durham 242 G4
Ivinghoe Bucks 84 B6
Ivinghoe Aston Bucks 85 B7
Ivington Hereford 115 F9
Ivington Green Hereford 115 F9
Ivy Chimneys Essex 86 E6
Ivy Cross Dorset 30 C5
Ivy Hatch Kent 52 C5
Ivy Todd Norf 141 B7
Ivybridge Devon 8 D2
Ivychurch Kent 39 B8
Iwade Kent 69 F11
Iwerne Courtney or Shroton Dorset 30 E5
Iwerne Minster Dorset 30 E5
Iwood N Som 60 G3
Ixworth Suff 125 C8
Ixworth Thorpe Suff 125 C8

J

Jack Green Lancs 194 B5
Jack Hayes Staffs 168 F6
Jack Hill N Yorks 205 C10
Jack in the Green Devon 14 B6
Jackfield Telford 132 C3
Jack's Green Essex 105 G11
Jack's Green Glos 80 D5
Jack's Hatch Essex 86 D6
Jacksdale Notts 170 E6
Jackson Bridge W Yorks 197 F7
Jackstown Aberds 303 F7
Jacobs Well Sur 50 C3
Jacobstow Corn 11 B9
Jacobstowe Devon 25 G9
Jagger Green W Yorks 196 D5
Jameston Pembs 73 F9
Jamestown Dumfries 249 D8
Jamestown Highld 300 D4
Jamestown W Dunb 277 E7
Jamphlars Fife 280 B4
Janetstown Highld 310 C4
Janke's Green Essex 107 F8
Jarrow T & W 243 D8
Jarvis Brook E Sus 37 B8
Jasper's Green Essex 106 F4
Java Argyll 289 F9
Jaw Hill W Yorks 197 C9
Jawcraig Falk 278 F6
Jaywick Essex 89 C11
Jealott's Hill Brack 65 E11
Jeaniefield Borders 271 G10
Jedburgh Borders 262 E5
Jedurgh Borders 262 F5
Jeffreyston Pembs 73 D9
Jellyhill E Dunb 278 G2
Jemimaville Highld 301 C7
Jennetts Hill W Berks 64 E5
Jennyfield N Yorks 205 B11
Jericho Gtr Man 195 E10
Jersey Farm Herts 85 D11
Jersey Marine Neath 57 C8
Jerviswood S Lnrk 269 F7
Jesmond T & W 243 D7
Jevington E Sus 23 E9
Jewell's Cross Corn 24 G3
Jingle Street Mon 79 C7
Jockey End Herts 85 C8
Jodrell Bank E Ches 184 G3
John O'Gaunt Leics 136 B4
John O'Gaunts W Yorks 197 B11
John o'Groats Highld 310 B7
Johnby Cumb 230 E4
John's Cross E Sus 38 C2
Johnshaven Aberds 293 G9
Johnson Fold Gtr Man 195 E7
Johnson Street Norf 161 F7
Johnson's Hillock Lancs 194 C5
Johnston Pembs 72 C6
Johnstone Renfs 267 C8
Johnstone Mains Aberds 293 F9
Johnstonebridge Dumfries 248 E3
Johnstown Carms 74 B6
Johnstown Wrex 166 F4
Jolly's Bottom Corn 4 F5
Joppa Corn 2 B3
Joppa Edin 280 G6
Joppa S Ayrs 257 F10
Jordan Green Norf 159 E11
Jordanhill Glasgow 267 B10
Jordans Bucks 85 G7
Jordanston Pembs 91 E8
Jordanthorpe S Yorks 186 E5
Jordon S Yorks 186 C6
Joyford Glos 79 C9
Joy's Green Glos 79 B10
Jubilee Gtr Man 196 E2
Jubilee Notts 170 E6
Jugbank Staffs 150 B5
Jump S Yorks 197 G11
Jumpers Common Dorset 19 C8
Jumpers Green Dorset 19 C8
Jumper's Town E Sus 52 G3
Junction N Yorks 204 D6
Juniper Northumb 241 F10
Juniper Green Edin 270 B3
Jurby East I o M 192 C4
Jurby West I o M 192 C4
Jurston Devon 13 E9
Jury's Gap E Sus 39 D7

K

Kaber Cumb 222 C5
Kaimend S Lnrk 269 F9
Kaimes Edin 270 B5
Kaimrig End Borders 269 G11
Kalemouth Borders 262 D6
Kame Fife 287 G7
Kames Argyll 275 B9
Kames Argyll 275 F10
Kames E Ayrs 258 D5
Kates Hill W Mid 133 E9
Kea Corn 4 G6
Keadby N Lincs 199 E10
Keal Cotes Lincs 174 C5
Kearby Town End N Yorks 206 D2
Kearnsey Kent 55 E9
Kearsley Gtr Man 195 F9
Kearstwick Cumb 212 C2
Kearton N Yorks 223 F9
Kearvaig Highld 306 B7
Keasden N Yorks 212 F4
Kebroyd W Yorks 196 C4
Keckwick Halton 183 E9
Keddington Lincs 190 D4
Keddington Corner Lincs 190 D5
Kedington Suff 106 B4
Kedleston Derbys 170 G4
Kedslie Borders 271 G11
Keekle Cumb 219 B10
Keelars Tye Essex 107 G11
Keelby Lincs 201 E7
Keele Staffs 168 F4
Keeley Green Beds 103 B10
Keelham W Yorks 205 G7
Keenley Northumb 241 F7
Keenthorne Som 43 F8
Keeres Green Essex 87 C9
Keeston Pembs 72 B6
Keevil Wilts 46 B2
Kegworth Leics 153 D9
Kehelland Corn 4 G2
Keig Aberds 293 B8
Keighley W Yorks 205 E7
Keil Highld 289 D11
Keilarsbrae Clack 279 C7
Keilhill Aberds 303 D7
Keillmore Argyll 275 E7
Keillor Perth 286 C6
Keillour Perth 286 E3
Keills Argyll 274 G5
Keils Argyll 274 G6
Keinton Mandeville Som 44 G4
Keir Mill Dumfries 247 E9
Keisby Lincs 155 D10
Keiss Highld 310 C7
Keistle Highld 298 D4
Keith Moray 302 D4
Keith Hall Aberds 303 G7
Keith Inch Aberds 303 E11
Keithock Angus 293 G8
Kelbrook Lancs 204 E4
Kelby Lincs 173 G8
Kelcliffe W Yorks 205 E9
Keld Cumb 221 C11
Keld N Yorks 223 E7
Keld Houses N Yorks 214 G2
Keldholme N Yorks 216 B4
Kelfield N Lincs 199 G10
Kelfield N Yorks 207 F7
Kelham Notts 172 D3
Kelhurn Argyll 276 F6
Kellacott Devon 12 D4
Kellamergh Lancs 194 B2
Kellan Argyll 289 E7
Kellas Angus 287 D8
Kellas Moray 301 D11
Kellaton Devon 9 G11
Kellaways Wilts 62 D3
Kelleth Cumb 222 D3
Kelleythorpe E Yorks 208 B5
Kelleythorpe E Yorks 208 B6
Kelling Norf 177 E9
Kellingley N Yorks 198 C4
Kellington N Yorks 198 C5
Kelloe Durham 234 D2
Kelloholm Dumfries 258 G6
Kells Cumb 219 B9
Kelly Corn 10 G6
Kelly Devon 12 E3
Kelly Bray Corn 12 G3
Kelmarsh Northants 120 B4
Kelmscott Oxon 82 F3
Kelsale Suff 127 D7
Kelsall W Ches 167 B8
Kelsall Hill W Ches 167 B8
Kelsay Argyll 254 B2
Kelshall Herts 104 D6
Kelsick Cumb 238 G5
Kelso Borders 262 C6
Kelstedge Derbys 170 C4
Kelstern Lincs 190 C3
Kelsterton Flint 182 G3
Kelston Bath 61 F8
Keltneyburn Perth 285 C11
Kelton Dumfries 237 B11
Kelton Durham 232 G4
Kelty Fife 280 C2
Keltybridge Fife 280 B2
Kelvedon Essex 88 B5
Kelvedon Hatch Essex 87 F9
Kelvin S Lnrk 268 E2
Kelvindale Glasgow 267 B11
Kelvinside Glasgow 267 B11
Kelynack Corn 1 D3
Kemacott Devon 41 D7
Kemback Fife 287 F8
Kemberton Shrops 132 C4
Kemble Glos 81 F7
Kemble Wick Glos 81 F7
Kemerton Worcs 99 D8
Kemeys Commander Mon 78 E4
Keminchams E Ches 168 B4
Kemnay Aberds 293 B9
Kemp Town Brighton 36 G4
Kempe's Corner Kent 54 D4
Kempie Highld 308 D4
Kempley Glos 98 F3
Kempley Green Glos 98 F3
Kemps Green Warks 118 C2
Kempsey Worcs 99 B7
Kempsford Glos 81 F11
Kempshott Hants 48 C6
Kempston Beds 103 B10
Kempston Church End Beds 103 B10
Kempston Hardwick Beds 103 C10
Kempston West End Beds 103 B9
Kempton Shrops 131 G7
Kemsing Kent 52 B4
Kemsley Kent 70 F2
Kemsley Street Kent 69 G10
Kenardington Kent 54 G3
Kenchester Hereford 97 C8
Kencot Oxon 82 E3
Kendal Cumb 221 G10
Kendal End Worcs 117 C10
Kendleshire S Glos 61 D7
Kendon Caerph 77 F11
Kendoon Dumfries 246 F4
Kendray S Yorks 197 F11
Kenfig Bridgend 57 E10
Kenfig Hill Bridgend 57 E10
Kengharair Argyll 288 E6
Kenilworth Warks 118 C5
Kenknock Stirl 285 D8
Kenley London 51 B10
Kenley Shrops 131 C11
Kenmore Argyll 284 G4
Kenmore Highld 299 D7
Kenmore Perth 285 C11
Kenmure Dumfries 237 B8
Kenn Devon 14 D4
Kenn N Som 60 F2
Kenn Moor Gate N Som 60 F2
Kennacley W Isles 305 J3
Kennacraig Argyll 275 G9
Kennards House Corn 11 E11
Kenneggy Corn 2 D3
Kenneggy Downs Corn 2 D3
Kennerleigh Devon 26 F4
Kennet Clack 279 C8
Kennet End Suff 124 D4
Kennethmont Aberds 302 G5
Kennett Cambs 124 D3
Kennford Devon 14 D4
Kenninghall Norf 141 F10
Kenninghall Heath Norf 141 G10
Kennington Kent 54 E4
Kennington London 67 D10
Kennington Oxon 83 E8
Kennoway Fife 287 G7
Kenny Som 28 D4
Kenny Hill Suff 124 B3
Kennythorpe N Yorks 216 F5
Kenovay Argyll 288 E1
Kensal Green London 67 C8
Kensal Rise London 67 C8
Kensal Town London 67 C8
Kensaleyre Highld 298 D4
Kensary Highld 310 E6
Kensington London 67 D9
Kensington Mers 182 C5
Kensworth C Beds 85 B8
Kensworth Common C Beds 85 B8
Kent Street E Sus 38 D3
Kent Street Kent 53 C7
Kent Street W Sus 36 C2
Kentallen Highld 284 B4
Kentchurch Hereford 97 F8
Kentford Suff 124 D4
Kentisbeare Devon 27 F9
Kentisbury Devon 40 E6
Kentisbury Ford Devon 40 E6
Kentish Town London 67 C9
Kentmere Cumb 221 E9
Kenton Devon 14 E5
Kenton London 67 B7
Kenton Suff 126 D3
Kenton T & W 242 D6
Kenton Bankfoot T & W 242 D6
Kenton Bar T & W 242 D6
Kenton Corner Suff 126 D4
Kenton Green Glos 80 C3
Kentra Highld 289 C8
Kentrigg Cumb 221 G10
Kents Corn 11 B9
Kents Bank Cumb 211 D7
Kent's Green Glos 98 G4
Kents Hill M Keynes 103 D7
Kent's Oak Hants 32 C4
Kenwick Shrops 149 C8
Kenwick Park Shrops 149 D8
Kenwyn Corn 4 F6
Kenyon Warr 183 B10
Keoldale Highld 308 C3
Keonchulish Ho Highld 307 K6
Kepdowrie Stirl 277 C11
Kepnal Wilts 63 G7
Keppanach Highld 290 G2
Keppoch Highld 295 C11
Keprigan Argyll 255 F7
Kepwick N Yorks 225 G9

Kerchesters Borders 263 B7
Kerdiston Norf 159 E11
Keresforth Hill S Yorks 197 F10
Keresley W Mid 134 G6
Keresley Newlands Warks 134 G6
Kerfield Borders 270 G5
Kerley Downs Corn 4 G5
Kernborough Devon 8 G5
Kerne Bridge Hereford 79 B9
Kernsary Highld 299 B8
Kerridge E Ches 184 F6
Kerridge-end E Ches 184 F6
Kerris Corn 1 D4
Kerry = Ceri Powys 130 F2
Kerry Hill Staffs 168 F6
Kerrycroy Argyll 266 C2
Kerry's Gate Hereford 97 E7
Kerrysdale Highld 299 B8
Kersal Gtr Man 195 G10
Kersall Notts 172 C2
Kersbrook Cross Corn 12 F2
Kerscott Devon 25 B10
Kersey Suff 107 C10
Kersey Tye Suff 107 C9
Kersey Upland Suff 107 C9
Kershopefoot Cumb 249 G11
Kersoe Worcs 99 D9
Kerswell Devon 27 F9
Kerswell Green Worcs 99 B7
Kerthen Wood Corn 2 C3
Kesgrave Suff 108 B4
Kessingland Suff 143 F10
Kessingland Beach Suff 143 F10
Kessington E Dunb 277 G11
Kestle Corn 5 F9
Kestle Mill Corn 5 D7
Keston London 68 G2
Keston Mark London 68 F2
Keswick Cumb 229 G11
Keswick Norf 142 C4
Keswick Norf 161 C7
Kete Pembs 72 E4
Ketford Glos 98 E4
Ketley Telford 150 G3
Ketley Bank Telford 150 G3
Ketsby Lincs 190 F5
Kettering Northants 121 B7
Ketteringham Norf 142 C3
Kettins Perth 286 D6
Kettle Corner Kent 53 C8
Kettle Green Herts 86 B6
Kettlebaston Suff 125 G9
Kettlebridge Fife 287 G7
Kettlebrook Staffs 134 C4
Kettleburgh Suff 126 E5
Kettlehill Fife 287 G7
Kettleholm Dumfries 238 B4
Kettleness N Yorks 226 B6
Kettleshulme E Ches 185 F7
Kettleshume E Ches 185 F7
Kettlesing N Yorks 205 B10
Kettlesing Bottom N Yorks 205 B10
Kettlesing Head N Yorks 205 B10
Kettlestone Norf 159 C9
Kettlethorpe Lincs 188 F4
Kettlethorpe W Yorks 197 D10
Kettletoft Orkney 314 C6
Kettlewell N Yorks 213 E9
Ketton Rutland 137 C9
Kevingtown London 68 F3
Kew London 67 D7
Kew Bridge London 67 D7
Keward Som 44 E4
Kewstoke N Som 59 G10
Kexbrough S Yorks 197 F9
Kexby Lincs 188 D5
Kexby York 207 C10
Key Green E Ches 168 C5
Key Green N Yorks 226 E6
Key Street Kent 69 G11
Keybridge Corn 11 G7
Keycol Kent 69 G11
Keyford Som 45 D9
Keyham Leics 136 B3
Keyhaven Hants 20 C2
Keyingham E Yorks 201 B8
Keymer W Sus 36 D4
Keynsham Bath 61 F7
Key's Green Kent 53 F7
Keysers Estate Essex 86 D5
Keysoe Beds 121 E11
Keysoe Row Beds 121 E11
Keyston Cambs 121 B10
Keyworth Notts 154 C2
Khantore Aberds 292 D4
Kibbear Som 28 C2
Kibblesworth T & W 242 F6
Kibworth Beauchamp Leics 136 E3
Kibworth Harcourt Leics 136 E3
Kidbrooke London 68 D2
Kidburngill Cumb 229 G7
Kiddal Lane End W Yorks 206 F4
Kiddemore Green Staffs 133 B7
Kidderminster Worcs 116 B6
Kiddington Oxon 101 G8
Kidd's Moor Norf 142 C2
Kidlington Oxon 83 C7
Kidmore End Oxon 65 D7
Kidnal W Ches 167 F7
Kidsdale Dumfries 236 F6
Kidsgrove Staffs 168 E4
Kidstones N Yorks 213 C9
Kidwelly = Cydweli Carms 74 D6
Kiel Crofts Argyll 289 F11
Kielder Northumb 250 E4
Kierfiold Ho Orkney 314 E2
Kiff Green W Berks 64 F5
Kilbagie Fife 279 D8
Kilbarchan Renfs 267 C8
Kilbeg Highld 295 E8
Kilberry Argyll 275 G8
Kilbirnie N Ayrs 266 E6
Kilbowie W Dunb 277 G10
Kilbraur Highld 311 H2
Kilbride Argyll 254 C4
Kilbride Argyll 275 D9
Kilbride Argyll 289 G10
Kilbride Argyll 289 G11
Kilbride Highld 295 C7
Kilbridemore Argyll 275 D11
Kilbryde Castle Stirl 285 G11
Kilburn Angus 292 G5
Kilburn Derbys 170 F5
Kilburn London 67 C9
Kilburn N Yorks 215 D10
Kilby Leics 136 D2
Kilby Bridge Leics 136 D2
Kilchamaig Argyll 275 G9
Kilchattan Argyll 274 D4
Kilchattan Bay Argyll 266 E2
Kilchenzie Argyll 255 E7
Kilcheran Argyll 289 F10
Kilchiaran Argyll 274 G3
Kilchoan Argyll 275 B8
Kilchoan Highld 288 C6
Kilchoman Argyll 274 G3
Kilchrenan Argyll 284 E4
Kilconquhar Fife 287 G8
Kilcot Glos 98 F3
Kilcoy Highld 300 D5
Kilcreggan Argyll 276 E4
Kildale N Yorks 226 D2
Kildalloig Argyll 255 F8
Kildary Highld 301 B7
Kildaton Ho Argyll 254 C5
Kildavanan Argyll 275 G11
Kildermorie Lodge Highld 300 B5
Kildonan Dumfries 236 D2
Kildonan Highld 298 D3
Kildonan N Ayrs 256 E2
Kildonan Lodge Highld 311 G3
Kildonnan Highld 294 G6
Kildrum N Lnrk 278 F5
Kildrummy Aberds 292 B6
Kildwick N Yorks 204 D6
Kilfinan Argyll 275 F10
Kilfinnan Highld 290 D4
Kilgetty Pembs 73 D10
Kilgour Fife 286 G6
Kilgrammie S Ayrs 245 C7
Kilgwrrwg Common Mon 79 F7
Kilhallon Corn 5 E11
Kilham E Yorks 217 G11
Kilham Northumb 263 C9
Kilkeddan Argyll 255 E8
Kilkenneth Argyll 288 E1
Kilkenny Glos 81 B8
Kilkerran Argyll 255 F8
Kilkhampton Corn 24 E3
Killamarsh Derbys 187 E7
Killaworgey Corn 5 C8
Killay Swansea 56 C6
Killbeg Argyll 289 E8
Killean Argyll 255 C7
Killearn Stirl 277 D10
Killegruer Argyll 255 D7
Killen Highld 300 D6
Killerby Darl 224 B3
Killichonan Perth 285 B9
Killiechoinich Argyll 289 G10
Killiechonate Highld 290 E4
Killiechronan Argyll 289 E7
Killiecrankie Perth 291 G11
Killiemor Argyll 288 F6
Killiemore House Argyll 288 G6
Killilan Highld 295 B11
Killimster Highld 310 D7
Killin Stirl 285 D9
Killin Lodge Highld 291 C7
Killinallan Argyll 274 F4
Killingbeck W Yorks 206 G2
Killinghall N Yorks 205 B11
Killington Cumb 212 B2
Killington Devon 41 D7
Killingworth T & W 243 C7
Killingworth Moor T & W 243 C7
Killingworth Village T & W 243 C7
Killivose Corn 2 B4
Killmahumaig Argyll 275 D8
Killochyett Borders 271 F9
Killocraw Argyll 255 D7
Killundine Highld 289 E7
Killylung Dumfries 247 G11
Kilmacolm Invclyd 267 B7
Kilmaha Argyll 275 C10
Kilmahog Stirl 285 G10
Kilmalieu Highld 289 D10
Kilmaluag Highld 298 B4
Kilmany Fife 287 E7
Kilmarie Highld 295 D7
Kilmarnock E Ayrs 257 B10
Kilmaron Castle Fife 287 F7
Kilmartin Argyll 275 D9
Kilmaurs E Ayrs 267 G8
Kilmelford Argyll 275 B9
Kilmeny Argyll 274 G4
Kilmersdon Som 45 C7
Kilmeston Hants 33 B9
Kilmichael Argyll 255 E7
Kilmichael Argyll 275 F10
Kilmichael Glassary Argyll 275 D9
Kilmichael of Inverlussa Argyll 275 E8
Kilmington Devon 15 B11
Kilmington Wilts 45 F9
Kilmington Common Wilts 45 F9
Kilmoluaig Argyll 288 E1
Kilmonivaig Highld 290 E3
Kilmorack Highld 300 E4
Kilmore Argyll 289 G10
Kilmore Highld 295 E8
Kilmory Argyll 275 F8
Kilmory Highld 289 B7
Kilmory Highld 294 E5
Kilmory N Ayrs 255 E10
Kilmory Lodge Argyll 275 C8
Kilmote Highld 311 H3
Kilmuir Highld 298 B3
Kilmuir Highld 298 E2
Kilmuir Highld 300 E6
Kilmuir Highld 301 B7
Kilmun Argyll 275 B10
Kilmun Argyll 276 E3
Kiln Green Hereford 79 B10
Kiln Green Wokingham 65 D10
Kiln Pit Hill Northumb 242 G2
Kilnave Argyll 274 F3
Kilncadzow S Lnrk 269 F7
Kilndown Kent 53 G8
Kilnhill Cumb 229 E10
Kilnhurst S Yorks 187 B7
Kilninian Argyll 288 E5
Kilninver Argyll 289 G10
Kilnsea E Yorks 201 D12
Kilnsey N Yorks 213 F9
Kilnwick E Yorks 208 D5
Kilnwick Percy E Yorks 208 C2
Kiloran Argyll 274 D4
Kilpatrick N Ayrs 255 E10
Kilpeck Hereford 97 E8
Kilphedir Highld 311 H3
Kilpin E Yorks 199 B9
Kilpin Pike E Yorks 199 B9
Kilrenny Fife 287 G9
Kilsby Northants 119 C11
Kilspindie Perth 286 E6
Kilsyth N Lnrk 278 F4
Kiltarlity Highld 300 E5
Kilton Notts 187 F9
Kilton Redcar 226 B4
Kilton Som 43 E7
Kilton Thorpe Redcar 226 B3
Kiltyrie Perth 285 D10
Kilvaxter Highld 298 C3
Kilve Som 43 E7
Kilvington Notts 172 G3
Kilwinning N Ayrs 266 G6
Kimberley Norf 141 C11
Kimberley Notts 171 G8
Kimberworth S Yorks 186 C6
Kimberworth Park S Yorks 186 C6
Kimble Wick Bucks 84 D4
Kimblesworth Durham 233 B11
Kimbolton Cambs 121 D11
Kimbolton Hereford 115 E10
Kimbridge Hants 32 B4
Kimcote Leics 135 F11
Kimmeridge Dorset 18 F4
Kimmerston Northumb 263 B11
Kimpton Hants 47 D9
Kimpton Herts 85 B11
Kimworthy Devon 24 E4
Kinabus Argyll 254 C3
Kinbeachie Highld 300 C6
Kinbrace Highld 310 F2
Kinbuck Stirl 285 G11
Kincaidston S Ayrs 257 F9
Kincaple Fife 287 F8
Kincardine Fife 279 D8
Kincardine Highld 309 L6
Kincardine Bridge Falk 279 D8
Kincardine O'Neil Aberds 293 D7
Kinclaven Perth 286 D5
Kincorth Aberdeen 293 C11
Kincorth Ho Moray 301 C10
Kincraig Highld 291 C10
Kincraigie Perth 286 C3
Kindallachan Perth 286 C3
Kine Moor S Yorks 197 G9
Kineton Glos 99 F11
Kineton Warks 118 G6
Kineton Green W Mid 134 G2
Kinfauns Perth 286 E5
King Edward Aberds 303 D7
King Sterndale Derbys 185 G9
King Street Essex 87 E9
Kingairloch Highld 289 D10
Kingarth Argyll 255 B11
Kingates I o W 20 F6
Kingbeare Corn 11 G11
Kingcoed Mon 78 D6
Kingdown N Som 60 G4
Kingerby Lincs 189 C9
Kingfield Sur 50 B4
Kingford Devon 24 F3
Kingford Devon 25 D10
Kingham Oxon 100 G5
Kinghay Wilts 30 B5
Kingholm Quay Dumfries 237 B11
Kinghorn Fife 280 D5
Kingie Highld 290 C3
Kinglassie Fife 280 B4
Kingledores Borders 260 D4
Kingoodie Perth 287 E7
King's Acre Hereford 97 C9
King's Bromley Staffs 152 F2
King's Caple Hereford 97 F11
King's Cliffe Northants 137 D10
Kings Clipstone Notts 171 C10
King's Coughton Warks 117 F11
King's Dyke Cambs 138 D4
King's End Oxon 101 G11
King's End Worcs 116 G6
King's Furlong Hants 48 C6
King's Green Glos 98 E5
King's Green Worcs 116 E5
King's Heath Northants 120 E4
King's Heath W Mid 133 G11
Kings Hedges Cambs 123 E9
Kings Hill Glos 81 E8
King's Hill Kent 53 C7
King's Hill W Mid 133 D9
Kings Langley Herts 85 E9
King's Lynn Norf 158 E2
King's Meaburn Cumb 231 G8
King's Mills Derbys 153 D8
King's Mills Wrex 166 F4
Kings Moss Mers 194 G4
Kings Muir Borders 261 B7
King's Newnham Warks 119 B9
King's Newton Derbys 153 D7
King's Norton Leics 136 C3
King's Norton W Mid 117 B11
King's Nympton Devon 25 D11
King's Pyon Hereford 115 G8
Kings Ripton Cambs 122 B5
King's Somborne Hants 47 G11
King's Stag Dorset 30 E2
King's Stanley Glos 80 E4
King's Sutton Northants 101 D9
King's Tamerton Plym 7 D9
King's Thorn Hereford 97 E10
King's Walden Herts 104 G3
Kings Worthy Hants 48 G3
Kingsand Corn 7 E8
Kingsash Bucks 84 D5
Kingsbarns Fife 287 F9
Kingsbridge Devon 8 G4
Kingsbridge Som 42 F3
Kingsburgh Highld 298 D3
Kingsbury London 67 B8
Kingsbury Warks 134 D4
Kingsbury Episcopi Som 28 C6
Kingsbury Regis Som 29 D11
Kingscauseway Highld 301 B7
Kingscavil W Loth 279 F10
Kingsclere Hants 48 B4
Kingsclere Woodlands Hants 64 G4
Kingscote Glos 80 F4
Kingscott Devon 25 D8
Kingscourt Glos 80 E4
Kingscross N Ayrs 256 D2
Kingsditch Glos 99 G8
Kingsdon Som 29 B8
Kingsdown Kent 54 B2
Kingsdown Kent 55 D11
Kingsdown Swindon 63 B7
Kingsdown Wilts 61 F10
Kingseat Fife 280 C2
Kingseathill Fife 280 D2
Kingsett Devon 12 E6
Kingsey Bucks 84 D2
Kingsfield Hereford 97 B10
Kingsfold Lancs 194 B4
Kingsfold W Sus 51 F7
Kingsford Aberds 293 B7
Kingsford E Ayrs 267 F8
Kingsford Worcs 132 G6
Kingsforth N Lincs 200 D4
Kingsgate Kent 71 E11
Kingshall Green Suff 125 E8
Kingshall Street Suff 125 E8
Kingsheanton Devon 40 F5
Kingshill Glos 80 F3
Kingshill Swindon 62 C6
Kingsholm Glos 80 B4
Kingshouse Hotel Highld 284 B6
Kingshurst W Mid 134 F3
Kingside Hill Cumb 238 G5
Kingskerswell Devon 9 B7
Kingskettle Fife 287 G7
Kingsknowe Edin 280 G4
Kingsland Anglesey 178 E2
Kingsland Hereford 115 E8
Kingsland London 67 C10
Kingsland Shrops 149 G9
Kingsley Hants 49 F9
Kingsley Staffs 169 F8
Kingsley W Ches 183 G9
Kingsley Green W Sus 49 G11
Kingsley Holt Staffs 169 F8
Kingsley Moor Staffs 169 F7
Kingsley Park Northants 120 E5
Kingslow Shrops 132 D5
Kingsmead Hants 33 E9
Kingsmoor Essex 86 D6
Kingsmuir Angus 287 C8
Kingsmuir Fife 287 G9
Kingsnordley Shrops 132 F5
Kingsnorth Kent 54 F4
Kingstanding W Mid 133 E11
Kingsteignton Devon 14 G3
Kingsteps Highld 301 D9
Kingsthorpe Northants 120 E5
Kingsthorpe Hollow Northants 120 E5
Kingston Cambs 122 F6
Kingston Devon 8 F2
Kingston Devon 9 E8
Kingston Dorset 18 F5
Kingston Dorset 30 F3
Kingston E Loth 281 E10
Kingston Gtr Man 184 B6
Kingston Hants 31 G11
Kingston I o W 20 E5
Kingston Kent 55 C7
Kingston M Keynes 103 D8
Kingston Moray 302 C3
Kingston Ptsmth 33 G11
Kingston Suff 108 B5
Kingston Bagpuize Oxon 82 F6
Kingston Blount Oxon 84 F2
Kingston by Sea W Sus 36 G2
Kingston Deverill Wilts 45 F10
Kingston Gorse W Sus 35 G9
Kingston Lisle Oxon 63 B10
Kingston Maurward Dorset 17 C10
Kingston near Lewes E Sus 36 F5
Kingston on Soar Notts 153 D10
Kingston Park T & W 242 D6
Kingston Russell Dorset 17 C7
Kingston St Mary Som 28 B2
Kingston Seymour N Som 60 F2
Kingston Stert Oxon 84 E2
Kingston upon Hull Hull 200 B5
Kingston upon Thames London 67 F7
Kingston Vale London 67 E8
Kingstone Hereford 97 D8
Kingstone Hereford 98 G2
Kingstone S Yorks 197 F10
Kingstone Som 28 E5
Kingstone Staffs 151 D11
Kingstone Winslow Oxon 63 B9
Kingstown Cumb 239 F9
Kingsway Bath 61 G8
Kingsway Halton 183 D8
Kingswear Devon 9 E7
Kingswells Aberdeen 293 C10
Kingswinford W Mid 133 F7
Kingswood Bucks 83 B11
Kingswood Essex 69 B8
Kingswood Glos 80 G2
Kingswood Hereford 114 G5
Kingswood Herts 85 E10
Kingswood Kent 53 C10
Kingswood Powys 130 C4
Kingswood S Glos 60 E6
Kingswood Som 42 F6
Kingswood Sur 51 B8
Kingswood Warks 118 C3
Kingswood Warr 183 C9
Kingswood Brook Warks 118 C3
Kingswood Common Staffs 132 C6
Kingswood Common Worcs 116 D4
Kingthorpe Lincs 189 F10
Kington Hereford 114 F5
Kington S Glos 79 G10
Kington Worcs 117 F9
Kington Langley Wilts 62 D2
Kington Magna Dorset 30 C3
Kington St Michael Wilts 62 D2
Kingussie Highld 291 C9
Kingweston Som 44 G4
Kinhrive Highld 301 B7
Kininvie Ho Moray 302 E3
Kinkell Bridge Perth 286 F3
Kinknockie Aberds 303 E10
Kinknockie Aberds 303 G9
Kinkry Hill Cumb 240 B2
Kinlet Shrops 132 G4
Kinloch Fife 286 F6
Kinloch Highld 289 D8
Kinloch Highld 294 F5
Kinloch Highld 295 D8
Kinloch Highld 308 F3
Kinloch Perth 286 C5
Kinloch Perth 286 C6
Kinloch Damph Highld 299 E8
Kinloch Hourn Highld 295 E11
Kinloch Laggan Highld 291 E7
Kinloch Lodge Highld 308 D5
Kinloch Rannoch Perth 285 B10
Kinlochan Highld 289 C10
Kinlochard Stirl 285 G8
Kinlochbeoraid Highld 295 G10
Kinlochbervie Highld 306 D7
Kinlocheil Highld 289 B11
Kinlochewe Highld 299 C10
Kinlochleven Highld 290 G3
Kinlochmoidart Highld 289 B9
Kinlochmorar Highld 295 F10
Kinlochmore Highld 290 G3
Kinlochspelve Argyll 289 G8
Kinloid Highld 295 G8
Kinloss Moray 301 C10
Kinmel Bay = Bae Cinmel Conwy 181 E7
Kinmuck Aberds 293 B10
Kinmundy Aberds 293 B10
Kinnadie Aberds 303 E9
Kinnaird Perth 286 B3
Kinnaird Perth 286 E6
Kinnaird Castle Angus 287 B10
Kinnauld Highld 309 J7
Kinneff Aberds 293 F10
Kinneil Falk 279 E9
Kinnelhead Dumfries 248 C2
Kinnell Angus 287 B10
Kinnerley Shrops 148 E6
Kinnersley Hereford 96 B6
Kinnersley Worcs 99 C7
Kinnerton Powys 114 E4
Kinnerton Green Flint 166 C4
Kinnesswood Perth 286 G5
Kinninvie Durham 233 G7
Kinnordy Angus 287 B7
Kinoulton Notts 154 C3
Kinross Perth 286 G5
Kinrossie Perth 286 D5
Kinsbourne Green Herts 85 B10
Kinsey Heath E Ches 167 G11
Kinsham Hereford 115 E7
Kinsham Worcs 99 D8
Kinsley W Yorks 198 E2
Kinson Bmouth 19 B7
Kintallan Argyll 275 E8
Kintbury W Berks 63 F11
Kintessack Moray 301 C9
Kintillo Perth 286 F5
Kintocher Aberds 293 C7
Kinton Hereford 115 C8
Kinton Shrops 149 F7
Kintore Aberds 293 B9
Kintour Argyll 254 B5
Kintra Argyll 254 C4
Kintra Argyll 288 G5
Kintradwell Highld 311 J3
Kintraw Argyll 275 C9
Kinuachdrachd Argyll 275 D8
Kinveachy Highld 291 B11
Kinver Staffs 132 G6
Kinwalsey Warks 134 F5
Kip Hill Durham 242 G6
Kiplin N Yorks 224 F5
Kippax W Yorks 206 G4
Kippen Stirl 278 C3
Kippford or Scaur Dumfries 237 D10
Kippilaw Borders 262 D2
Kippilaw Mains Borders 262 D2
Kipping's Cross Kent 52 F6
Kippington Kent 52 C4
Kirbister Orkney 314 E2
Kirbister Orkney 314 D6
Kirbister Orkney 314 F3
Kirbuster Orkney 314 D2
Kirby Bedon Norf 142 B5
Kirby Bellars Leics 154 F4
Kirby Cane Norf 143 E7
Kirby Corner W Mid 118 B5
Kirby Cross Essex 108 G4
Kirby Fields Leics 135 C10
Kirby Green Norf 143 E7
Kirby Grindalythe N Yorks 217 F8
Kirby Hill N Yorks 215 F7
Kirby Hill N Yorks 224 D2
Kirby Knowle N Yorks 215 B9
Kirby-le-Soken Essex 108 G4
Kirby Misperton N Yorks 216 D5
Kirby Moor Cumb 240 E2
Kirby Muxloe Leics 135 C10
Kirby Row Norf 143 E7
Kirby Sigston N Yorks 225 G8
Kirby Underdale E Yorks 208 B2
Kirby Wiske N Yorks 215 C7
Kirdford W Sus 35 B8
Kirk Highld 310 D6
Kirk Bramwith S Yorks 198 E6
Kirk Deighton N Yorks 206 C3
Kirk Ella E Yorks 200 B4
Kirk Hallam Derbys 171 G7
Kirk Hammerton N Yorks 206 B5
Kirk Ireton Derbys 170 E3
Kirk Langley Derbys 152 B5
Kirk Merrington Durham 233 E11
Kirk Michael I o M 192 C4
Kirk of Shotts N Lnrk 268 C6
Kirk Sandall S Yorks 198 F6
Kirk Smeaton N Yorks 198 D4
Kirk Yetholm Borders 263 D8
Kirkabister Shetland 312 G6
Kirkabister Shetland 313 K6
Kirkandrews Dumfries 237 E8
Kirkandrews-on-Eden Cumb 239 F9
Kirkapol Argyll 288 E2
Kirkbampton Cumb 239 F8
Kirkbean Dumfries 237 D11
Kirkborough Cumb 229 D7
Kirkbrae Orkney 314 B4
Kirkbride Cumb 238 F6
Kirkbridge N Yorks 224 G5
Kirkbuddo Angus 287 C9
Kirkburn Borders 261 B7
Kirkburn E Yorks 208 B5
Kirkburton W Yorks 197 E7
Kirkby Lincs 189 C9
Kirkby Mers 182 B6
Kirkby N Yorks 225 D10
Kirkby Fenside Lincs 174 C4
Kirkby Fleetham N Yorks 224 G5
Kirkby Green Lincs 173 D9
Kirkby Hill N Yorks 215 F7
Kirkby in Ashfield Notts 171 D8
Kirkby-in-Furness Cumb 210 C4
Kirkby la Thorpe Lincs 173 F10
Kirkby Lonsdale Cumb 212 D2
Kirkby Malham N Yorks 213 G7
Kirkby Mallory Leics 135 C9
Kirkby Malzeard N Yorks 214 E4
Kirkby Mills N Yorks 216 B4
Kirkby on Bain Lincs 174 C2
Kirkby Overblow N Yorks 206 D2
Kirkby Stephen Cumb 222 D5
Kirkby Thore Cumb 231 F8
Kirkby Underwood Lincs 155 D11
Kirkby Wharfe N Yorks 206 E6
Kirkby Woodhouse Notts 171 E7
Kirkbymoorside N Yorks 216 B3
Kirkcaldy Fife 280 C5
Kirkcambeck Cumb 240 D2
Kirkcarswell Dumfries 237 E9
Kirkcolm Dumfries 236 C2
Kirkconnel Dumfries 258 G6
Kirkconnell Dumfries 237 C11
Kirkcowan Dumfries 236 C5
Kirkcudbright Dumfries 237 D8
Kirkdale Mers 182 C4
Kirkfieldbank S Lnrk 269 G7
Kirkforthar Feus Fife 286 G6
Kirkgunzeon Dumfries 237 C10
Kirkham Lancs 202 G4
Kirkham N Yorks 216 F4
Kirkhamgate W Yorks 197 C9
Kirkhams Gtr Man 195 F10
Kirkharle Northumb 252 G2
Kirkheaton Northumb 242 B2
Kirkheaton W Yorks 197 D7
Kirkhill Angus 293 G8
Kirkhill E Renf 267 D11
Kirkhill Highld 300 E5
Kirkhill Midloth 270 C4
Kirkhill Moray 302 F2
Kirkhill W Loth 279 G11
Kirkholt Gtr Man 195 E11
Kirkhope Borders 261 E9
Kirkhouse Borders 261 C8
Kirkhouse Cumb 240 F3
Kirkiboll Highld 308 D5
Kirkibost Highld 295 D7
Kirkinch Angus 287 C7
Kirkinner Dumfries 236 D6
Kirkintilloch E Dunb 278 G3
Kirkland Cumb 219 B11
Kirkland Cumb 229 B11
Kirkland Cumb 231 E8
Kirkland Dumfries 247 E8
Kirkland Dumfries 258 G6
Kirkland S Ayrs 244 E6
Kirkland Guards Cumb 229 C9
Kirkleatham Redcar 235 G7
Kirklees Gtr Man 195 E9
Kirklevington Stockton 225 D8
Kirkley Suff 143 E10
Kirklington N Yorks 214 C6
Kirklington Notts 171 D11
Kirklinton Cumb 239 D10
Kirkliston Edin 280 G2
Kirkmaiden Dumfries 236 F3
Kirkmichael Perth 286 B4
Kirkmichael S Ayrs 245 B8
Kirkmichael Mains Dumfries 248 F2
Kirkmuirhill S Lnrk 268 G5
Kirknewton Northumb 263 C10
Kirknewton W Loth 270 B2
Kirkney Aberds 302 F5
Kirkoswald Cumb 231 C7
Kirkoswald S Ayrs 244 B6
Kirkpatrick Dumfries 247 E10
Kirkpatrick Durham Dumfries 237 B9
Kirkpatrick-Fleming Dumfries 239 C7
Kirksanton Cumb 210 C2
Kirkshaw N Lnrk 268 C4
Kirkstall W Yorks 205 F11
Kirkstead Borders 261 E7
Kirkstead Lincs 173 C11
Kirkstile Aberds 302 F5
Kirkstyle Highld 310 B7
Kirkthorpe W Yorks 197 C11
Kirkton Aberds 302 E6
Kirkton Aberds 302 G6
Kirkton Angus 286 C6
Kirkton Angus 287 C8
Kirkton Angus 287 D8
Kirkton Argyll 275 C8
Kirkton Borders 262 G2
Kirkton Dumfries 247 G11
Kirkton Fife 280 D4
Kirkton Fife 287 E7
Kirkton Highld 295 C10
Kirkton Highld 299 E9
Kirkton Highld 301 D7
Kirkton Highld 309 K7
Kirkton Perth 286 F3
Kirkton S Lnrk 259 E10
Kirkton Stirl 285 G9
Kirkton W Loth 269 B10
Kirkton Manor Borders 260 B6
Kirkton of Airlie Angus 287 B7
Kirkton of Auchterhouse Angus 287 D7
Kirkton of Auchterless Aberds 303 E7
Kirkton of Barevan Highld 301 E8
Kirkton of Bourtie Aberds 303 G8
Kirkton of Collace Perth 286 D5
Kirkton of Craig Angus 287 B11
Kirkton of Culsalmond Aberds 302 F6
Kirkton of Durris Aberds 293 D9
Kirkton of Glenbuchat Aberds 292 B5
Kirkton of Glenisla Angus 292 G4
Kirkton of Kingoldrum Angus 287 B7
Kirkton of Largo Fife 287 G8
Kirkton of Lethendy Perth 286 C5
Kirkton of Logie Buchan Aberds 303 G9
Kirkton of Maryculter Aberds 293 D10
Kirkton of Menmuir Angus 293 G7
Kirkton of Monikie Angus 287 D9
Kirkton of Oyne Aberds 302 G6
Kirkton of Rayne Aberds 302 G6
Kirkton of Skene Aberds 293 C10
Kirkton of Tough Aberds 293 B8
Kirktonhill Borders 271 E9
Kirktonhill W Dunb 277 G7
Kirktoun E Ayrs 267 G8
Kirktown Aberds 303 D10
Kirktown of Alvah Aberds 302 C6
Kirktown of Deskford Moray 302 C5
Kirktown of Fetteresso Aberds 293 E10
Kirktown of Mortlach Moray 302 F3
Kirktown of Slains Aberds 303 G10
Kirkurd Borders 270 G2
Kirkwall Orkney 314 E4
Kirkwhelpington Northumb 251 G11
Kirkwood Dumfries 238 B4
Kirkwood N Lnrk 268 C4
Kirmington N Lincs 200 E6
Kirmond le Mire Lincs 189 C11
Kirn Argyll 276 F3
Kirriemuir Angus 287 B7
Kirstead Green Norf 142 D5
Kirtlebridge Dumfries 238 C6
Kirtleton Dumfries 249 G7
Kirtling Cambs 124 F3
Kirtling Green Cambs 124 F3
Kirtlington Oxon 83 B7
Kirtomy Highld 308 C7
Kirton Lincs 156 B6
Kirton Notts 171 B11
Kirton Suff 108 D5
Kirton Campus W Loth 269 B10
Kirton End Lincs 174 G3
Kirton Holme Lincs 174 G3
Kirton in Lindsey N Lincs 188 B6
Kiskin Cumb 210 B1
Kislingbury Northants 120 F3
Kit Hill Dorset 30 D4
Kitbridge Devon 28 G4
Kitchenroyd W Yorks 197 F8

342 Kit – Led

Kite Green Warks 118 D3
Kite Hill I o W 21 C7
Kitebrook Warks 100 E4
Kites Hardwick Warks 119 D9
Kitlye Glos 80 E5
Kit's Coty Kent 69 G8
Kitt Green Gtr Man 194 F5
Kittisford Som 27 C9
Kittle Swansea 56 D5
Kitts End Herts 86 F2
Kitt's Green W Mid 134 F3
Kitt's Moss Gtr Man 184 E5
Kittwhistle Dorset 28 G5
Kittybrewster Aberdeen 293 C11
Kitwell W Mid 133 G9
Kitwood Hants 49 G7
Kivernoll Hereford 97 E9
Kiveton Park S Yorks 187 E7
Knaith Lincs 188 E4
Knaith Park Lincs 188 D4
Knap Corner Dorset 30 C4
Knaphill Sur 50 B3
Knapp Hants 32 C6
Knapp Perth 286 D6
Knapp Som 28 B4
Knapp Wilts 31 B8
Knapp Hill Wilts 30 B5
Knapthorpe Notts 172 D2
Knaptoft Leics 136 F2
Knapton Norf 160 C6
Knapton York 207 C7
Knapton Green Hereford 115 G8
Knapwell Cambs 122 E6
Knaresborough N Yorks 206 B3
Knarsdale Northumb 240 G5
Knatts Valley Kent 68 G5
Knauchland Moray 302 D5
Knaven Aberds 303 E8
Knave's Ash Kent 71 G7
Knaves Green Suff 126 D2
Knavesmire York 207 D7
Knayton N Yorks 215 B8
Knebworth Herts 104 G5
Knedlington E Yorks 199 B8
Kneesall Notts 172 C2
Kneesworth Cambs 104 C6
Kneeton Notts 172 F2
Knelston Swansea 56 D3
Knenhall Staffs 151 B8
Knettishall Suff 141 G9
Knightacott Devon 41 F7
Knightcote Warks 119 G7
Knightcott N Som 43 B11
Knightley Staffs 150 D6
Knightley Dale Staffs 150 E6
Knighton Devon 7 F10
Knighton Dorset 29 E10
Knighton Leicester 135 C11
Knighton Oxon 63 B9
Knighton Poole 18 B6
Knighton Som 43 E7
Knighton Staffs 150 D4
Knighton Staffs 168 G2
Knighton Wilts 63 E9
Knighton Worcs 117 F10
Knighton = Tref-y-Clawdd Powys 114 C5
Knighton Fields Leicester 135 C11
Knighton on Teme Worcs 116 C2
Knightor Corn 5 D10
Knight's End Cambs 139 E8
Knights Enham Hants 47 D11
Knight's Hill London 67 E10
Knightsbridge Glos 99 F7
Knightsbridge London 67 D9
Knightsmill Corn 11 E7
Knightsridge W Loth 269 B10
Knightswood Glasgow 267 B10
Knightwick Worcs 116 F4
Knill Hereford 114 E5
Knipe Fold Cumb 220 F6
Knipoch Argyll 289 G10
Knipton Leics 154 C6
Knitsley Durham 233 B8
Kniveton Derbys 170 E2
Knocharthur Highld 309 J7
Knock Argyll 289 F7
Knock Cumb 231 F9
Knock Moray 302 D5
Knockally Highld 311 G5
Knockan Highld 307 H7
Knockandhu Moray 302 G2
Knockando Moray 301 E11
Knockando Ho Moray 302 E2
Knockandoo Highld 301 G7
Knockbain Highld 300 D6
Knockbreck Highld 298 C2
Knockbrex Dumfries 237 E7
Knockcarrach Highld 290 B6
Knockdee Highld 310 C5
Knockdolian S Ayrs 244 F4
Knockdow Argyll 276 G2
Knockdown Glos 61 B10
Knockenbaird Aberds 302 G6
Knockenkelly N Ayrs 256 D2
Knockentiber E Ayrs 257 B9
Knockerdown Derbys 170 E2
Knockespock Ho Aberds 302 G5
Knockfarrel Highld 300 D5
Knockglass Dumfries 236 D2
Knockhall Kent 68 E5
Knockhall Castle Aberds 303 G9
Knockholt Kent 52 B3
Knockholt Pound Kent 52 B3
Knockie Lodge Highld 290 B6
Knockin Shrops 148 E6
Knockin Heath Shrops 149 E7
Knockinlaw E Ayrs 257 B10
Knockinnon Highld 310 F5
Knocklaw Northumb 252 C3
Knocklearn Dumfries 237 B9
Knocklearoch Argyll 274 G4
Knockmill Kent 68 G5
Knocknaha Argyll 255 F7
Knocknain Dumfries 236 C1
Knockothie Aberds 303 F9
Knockrome Argyll 274 F6
Knocksharry I o M 192 D3
Knockstapplemore Argyll 255 F7
Knockvologan Argyll 274 B4
Knodishall Suff 127 E8
Knokan Argyll 288 G6
Knole Som 29 B7
Knoll Green Som 43 F8
Knoll Top N Yorks 214 F3
Knollbury Mon 60 B2
Knolls Green E Ches 184 F4
Knolton Wrex 149 B7
Knolton Bryn Wrex 149 B7
Knook Wilts 46 E2
Knossington Leics 136 B6
Knotbury Staffs 169 B8
Knott End-on-Sea Lancs 202 D3
Knott Lanes Gtr Man 196 G2
Knott Oak Som 28 E5
Knotting Beds 121 E10
Knotting Green Beds 121 E10
Knottingley W Yorks 198 C4
Knotts Cumb 230 G4
Knotts Lancs 203 C11
Knotty Ash Mers 182 C6
Knotty Corner Devon 24 B6
Knotty Green Bucks 84 G6
Knowbury Shrops 115 C11
Knowe Dumfries 236 B5
Knowe Shetland 313 G5
Knowefield Cumb 239 F10
Knowehead Aberds 293 C7
Knowehead Aberds 302 D5
Knowehead Dumfries 246 E4
Knowes E Loth 282 F2
Knowes of Elrick Aberds 302 D6
Knowesgate Northumb 251 F11
Knoweton N Lnrk 268 D5
Knowetop N Lnrk 268 D5
Knowhead Aberds 303 D9
Knowl Bank Staffs 168 F3
Knowl Green Essex 106 C5
Knowl Hill Windsor 65 D10
Knowl Wall Staffs 151 B7
Knowl Wood W Yorks 196 C2
Knowle Bristol 60 E6
Knowle Devon 15 E7
Knowle Devon 26 G3
Knowle Devon 27 F8
Knowle Devon 40 F3
Knowle Hants 33 F9
Knowle Shrops 115 C11
Knowle Som 43 F10
Knowle W Mid 118 B3
Knowle Wilts 63 G7
Knowle Fields Worcs 117 F10
Knowle Green Lancs 203 F8
Knowle Green Sur 66 E4
Knowle Grove W Mid 118 B3
Knowle Hill Sur 66 F3
Knowle Park W Yorks 205 E7
Knowle St Giles Som 28 E4
Knowlegate Shrops 115 C11
Knowles Hill Devon 14 G3
Knowlesands Shrops 132 E4
Knowlton Dorset 31 E8
Knowlton Kent 55 C9
Knowsley Mers 182 B6
Knowsthorpe W Yorks 206 G2
Knowstone Devon 26 C4
Knox Bridge Kent 53 E9
Knucklas Powys 114 C5
Knuston Northants 121 D8
Knutsford E Ches 184 F3
Knutton Staffs 168 F4
Knuzden Brook Lancs 195 B8
Knypersley Staffs 168 D5
Kraiknish Highld 294 C5
Krumlin W Yorks 196 D5
Kuggar Corn 2 F6
Kyle of Lochalsh Highld 295 C9
Kyleakin Highld 295 C9
Kylepark N Lnrk 268 C3
Kylerhea Highld 295 C9
Kylesknoydart Highld 295 F10
Kylesku Highld 306 F7
Kylesmorar Highld 295 F10
Kylestrome Highld 306 F7
Kyllachy House Highld 301 G7
Kymin Hereford 97 B11
Kymin Mon 79 C8
Kynaston Hereford 97 F10
Kynaston Shrops 149 E7
Kynnersley Telford 150 F3
Kyre Worcs 116 E2
Kyre Green Worcs 116 E2
Kyre Magna Worcs 116 E2
Kyre Park Worcs 116 E2
Kyrewood Worcs 116 D2

L

Labost W Isles 304 D4
Lacasaidh W Isles 304 F5
Lacasdal W Isles 304 E6
Laceby NE Lincs 201 F8
Laceby Acres NE Lincs 201 F8
Lacey Green Bucks 84 F4
Lacey Green E Ches 184 E4
Lach Dennis W Ches 184 G2
Lache W Ches 166 C5
Lackenby Redcar 225 B11
Lackford Suff 124 C5
Lacock Wilts 62 F2
Ladbroke Warks 119 F8
Laddenvean Corn 3 E7
Laddingford Kent 53 D7
Lade Kent 39 C9
Lade Bank Lincs 174 E5
Ladies Riggs N Yorks 214 F2
Ladmanlow Derbys 185 G8
Ladock Corn 5 E7
Ladwell Hants 32 C6
Lady Orkney 314 B6
Lady Green Mers 193 G10
Lady Hall Cumb 210 B3
Lady Halton Shrops 115 B9
Lady House Gtr Man 196 E2
Lady Park T & W 242 F6
Lady Wood W Yorks 206 F2
Ladybank Fife 287 F7
Ladybrook Notts 171 C8
Ladyburn Invclyd 276 F6
Ladycross Corn 12 D2
Ladyes Hill Warks 118 C5
Ladykirk Borders 273 F7
Ladyoak Shrops 131 C7
Ladyridge Hereford 97 E11
Lady's Green Suff 124 F5
Ladysford Aberds 303 C9
Ladywell London 67 E11
Ladywell Shrops 149 C9
Ladywell W Loth 269 B10
Ladywood Telford 132 C3
Ladywood W Mid 133 F11
Ladywood Worcs 117 E7
Laffak Mers 183 B8
Laga Highld 289 C8
Lagafater Lodge Dumfries 236 B3
Lagalochan Argyll 275 B9
Lagavulin Argyll 254 C5
Lagg Argyll 274 F6
Lagg N Ayrs 255 E10
Laggan Argyll 254 B3
Laggan Highld 289 B9
Laggan Highld 290 D4
Laggan Highld 291 D8
Laggan S Ayrs 245 G7
Laggan Lodge Argyll 289 G8
Lagganlia Highld 291 C10
Lagganmullan Dumfries 237 D7
Lagganulva Argyll 288 E6
Lagness W Sus 22 C5
Laide Highld 307 K3
Laig Highld 294 G6
Laigh Carnduff S Lnrk 268 F3
Laigh Fenwick E Ayrs 267 G9
Laigh Glengall S Ayrs 257 F8
Laighmuir E Ayrs 267 F9
Laighstonehall S Lnrk 268 E4
Laindon Essex 69 B7
Lair Highld 299 E10
Lair Perth 292 G3
Laira Plym 7 D10
Lairg Highld 309 J5
Lairg Lodge Highld 309 J5
Lairg Muir Highld 309 J5
Lairgmore Highld 300 F5
Laisterdyke W Yorks 205 G9
Laithes Cumb 230 E5
Laithkirk Durham 232 G5
Laity Moor Corn 4 F3
Lake Devon 12 D6
Lake Devon 24 F6
Lake Devon 40 G5
Lake I o W 21 E7
Lake Poole 18 C5
Lake Wilts 46 F6
Lake End Bucks 66 D2
Lakenham Norf 142 B4
Lakenheath Suff 140 G4
Laker's Green Sur 50 F4
Lakesend Norf 139 D10
Lakeside Cumb 211 B7
Lakeside Thurrock 68 D5
Lakeside Worcs 117 D11
Laleham Sur 66 F5
Laleston = Trelales Bridgend 57 F11
Lamanva Corn 3 C7
Lamarsh Essex 107 D7
Lamas Norf 160 E4
Lamb Corner Essex 107 E10
Lambden Borders 272 G4
Lamberden Kent 38 B4
Lamberhead Green Gtr Man 194 G4
Lamberhurst Kent 53 F7
Lamberhurst Quarter Kent 53 F7
Lamberton Borders 273 D9
Lambert's End W Mid 133 E9
Lambeth London 67 D10
Lambfair Green Suff 124 G4
Lambfoot Cumb 229 E9
Lambhill Glasgow 267 B11
Lambley Northumb 240 F5
Lambley Notts 171 F10
Lambourn W Berks 63 D10
Lambourn Woodlands W Berks 63 D10
Lambourne Corn 4 E5
Lambourne Essex 87 F7
Lambourne End Essex 87 G7
Lambridge Bath 61 F9
Lamb's Cross Kent 53 D9
Lambs' Green Dorset 18 B5
Lambs Green W Sus 51 F8
Lambston Pembs 72 B6
Lambton T & W 243 G7
Lamellion Corn 6 C4
Lamerton Devon 12 F5
Lamesley T & W 243 F7
Laminess Orkney 314 C6
Lamington Highld 301 B7
Lamington S Lnrk 259 C11
Lamlash N Ayrs 256 C2
Lamledra Corn 5 G10
Lamloch Dumfries 246 D2
Lammack Blkburn 195 B7
Lamonby Cumb 230 D4
Lamorick Corn 5 C10
Lamorna Corn 1 E4
Lamorran Corn 5 G7
Lampardbrook Suff 126 E5
Lampeter = Llanbedr Pont Steffan Ceredig 93 B11
Lampeter Velfrey Pembs 73 C11
Lamphey Pembs 73 E8
Lamplugh Cumb 229 G7
Lamport Northants 120 C5
Lampton London 66 D6
Lamyatt Som 45 F7
Lana Devon 12 B2
Lana Devon 24 F4
Lanark S Lnrk 269 G7
Lancaster Lancs 211 G9
Lanchester Durham 233 B9
Lancing W Sus 35 G11
Land Gate Gtr Man 194 G5
Landbeach Cambs 123 D9
Landcross Devon 25 C7
Landerberry Aberds 293 C9
Landewednack Corn 2 G6
Landford Wilts 32 D3
Landford Manor Wilts 32 C3
Landfordwood Wilts 32 C3
Landguard Manor I o W 21 E7
Landhill Devon 12 B4
Landican Mers 182 D3
Landimore Swansea 56 C3
Landkey Devon 40 G5
Landkey Newland Devon 40 G5
Landore Swansea 57 B7
Landport E Sus 36 E6
Landport Ptsmth 33 G10
Landrake Corn 7 C7
Landscove Devon 8 B5
Landshipping Pembs 73 C8
Landshipping Quay Pembs 73 C8
Landslow Green Gtr Man 185 B7
Landulph Corn 7 C8
Landwade Suff 124 D2
Landywood Staffs 133 B9
Lane Corn 4 C6
Lane Bottom Lancs 204 F3
Lane Bottom W Yorks 205 F7
Lane End Bucks 84 G4
Lane-end Corn 5 B10
Lane End Cumb 220 G2
Lane End Derbys 170 C6
Lane End Devon 24 G6
Lane End Dorset 18 C3
Lane End Flint 166 C3
Lane End Glos 79 B10
Lane End Hants 33 B11
Lane End Hants 33 B9
Lane End I o W 21 D9
Lane End Kent 68 E5
Lane End Lancs 204 D3
Lane End S Yorks 186 B5
Lane End Sur 49 E10
Lane End W Yorks 204 F6
Lane End Wilts 45 D10
Lane Ends Cumb 210 C6
Lane Ends Derbys 152 C4
Lane Ends E Ches 168 D2
Lane Ends E Ches 185 E7
Lane Ends Gtr Man 185 C7
Lane Ends Lancs 194 D6
Lane Ends Lancs 203 C11
Lane Ends Lancs 203 G11
Lane Ends N Yorks 204 E5
Lane Ends Stoke 168 E5
Lane Ends W Yorks 205 F10
Lane Green Staffs 133 C7
Lane Head Derbys 185 F11
Lane Head Durham 224 C2
Lane Head Gtr Man 183 B10
Lane Head Pembs 73 E8
Lane Head W Mid 133 C9
Lane Head W Yorks 197 F7
Lane Heads Lancs 202 F4
Lane Side Lancs 195 C9
Laneast Corn 11 E10
Laneham Notts 188 F4
Lanehead Durham 232 C2
Lanehead Northumb 251 F7
Lanehouse Dorset 17 F9
Lanercost Cumb 240 E3
Lanes End Bucks 84 D6
Lane's End Shrops 132 G2
Lanescot Corn 5 D11
Lanesend Pembs 73 D9
Lanesfield W Mid 133 D8
Laneshaw Bridge Lancs 204 E4
Laney Green Staffs 133 B9
Lanfach Caerph 78 F2
Langaford Devon 12 B4
Langage Devon 7 E11
Langal Highld 289 C9
Langaller Som 28 B3
Langar Notts 154 C4
Langbank Renfs 277 G7
Langbar N Yorks 205 C7
Langbaurgh N Yorks 225 C11
Langburnshiels Borders 250 C2
Langcliffe N Yorks 212 G6
Langdale Highld 308 E6
Langdale End N Yorks 227 G8
Langdon Corn 12 D2
Langdon Beck Durham 232 E3
Langdon Hills Essex 69 B7
Langdown Hants 32 F6
Langdyke Dumfries 238 C3
Langdyke Fife 287 G7
Langenhoe Essex 89 B8
Langford C Beds 104 C3
Langford Devon 14 B4
Langford Devon 27 G8
Langford Essex 88 D4
Langford Notts 172 D4
Langford Oxon 82 E2
Langford Som 28 B2
Langford Budville Som 27 C10
Langford Green Devon 27 G8
Langford Green N Som 44 B3
Langham Dorset 30 B3
Langham Essex 107 E10
Langham Norf 177 E8
Langham Rutland 154 G6
Langham Som 28 E4
Langham Suff 125 C9
Langhaugh Borders 260 C6
Langho Lancs 203 G10
Langholm Dumfries 249 G9
Langholme N Lincs 188 B3
Langhope Borders 261 E10
Langland Swansea 56 D6
Langlee Borders 262 B2
Langlee Mains Borders 262 B2
Langleeford Northumb 263 E10
Langlees Falk 279 E7
Langley Derbys 170 F6
Langley E Ches 184 G6
Langley Essex 105 D8
Langley Glos 99 F10
Langley Gtr Man 195 F11
Langley Hants 32 G6
Langley Herts 104 G4
Langley Kent 53 C10
Langley Northumb 241 E8
Langley Oxon 82 B4
Langley Slough 66 D4
Langley Som 27 B9
Langley W Mid 133 F9
Langley W Sus 34 B4
Langley Warks 118 E3
Langley Burrell Wilts 62 D2
Langley Common Derbys 152 B5
Langley Common Wokingham 65 F9
Langley Corner Bucks 66 C4
Langley Green Derbys 152 B5
Langley Green Essex 107 G7
Langley Green W Mid 133 F9
Langley Green W Sus 51 F9
Langley Green Warks 118 E3
Langley Heath Kent 53 C10
Langley Marsh Som 27 B9
Langley Mill Derbys 170 F6
Langley Moor Durham 233 C11
Langley Park Durham 233 C10
Langley Street Norf 143 C7
Langley Vale Sur 51 B8
Langleybury Herts 85 E9
Langloan N Lnrk 268 C4
Langney E Sus 23 E10
Langold Notts 187 D9
Langore Corn 12 D2
Langport Som 28 B6
Langrick Lincs 174 F3
Langrick Bridge Lincs 174 F3
Langridge Bath 61 F8
Langridge Ford Devon 25 C9
Langrigg Cumb 222 C5
Langrigg Cumb 229 B9
Langrish Hants 34 C2
Langsett S Yorks 197 G8
Langshaw Borders 262 B2
Langside Glasgow 267 C11
Langside Perth 285 F11
Langskaill Orkney 314 B4
Langstone Devon 13 E10
Langstone Hants 22 C2
Langstone Newport 78 G5
Langthorne N Yorks 224 G5
Langthorpe N Yorks 215 F7
Langthwaite N Yorks 223 E10
Langtoft E Yorks 217 F10
Langtoft Lincs 156 G2
Langton Durham 224 B3
Langton Lincs 174 B2
Langton Lincs 190 G5
Langton N Yorks 216 F5
Langton by Wragby Lincs 189 F11
Langton Green Kent 52 F4
Langton Green Suff 126 C2
Langton Herring Dorset 17 E8
Langton Long Blandford Dorset 30 F5
Langton Matravers Dorset 18 F6
Langtree Devon 25 D7
Langtree Week Devon 25 D7
Langwathby Cumb 231 E7
Langwell Ho Highld 311 G5
Langwell Lodge Highld 307 J6
Langwith Derbys 171 B8
Langwith Junction Derbys 171 B8
Langworth Lincs 189 F9
Lanham Green Essex 106 G5
Lanivet Corn 5 C10
Lanjeth Corn 5 E9
Lanjew Corn 5 C9
Lank Corn 11 F7
Lanlivery Corn 5 D11
Lanner Corn 2 B6
Lanreath Corn 6 D3
Lanrick Stirl 285 G10
Lansallos Corn 6 E3
Lansbury Park Caerph 59 B7
Lansdown Bath 61 F8
Lansdown Glos 99 G8
Lanstephan Corn 12 D2
Lanteglos Corn 11 E7
Lanteglos Highway Corn 6 E3
Lanton Borders 262 E4
Lanton Northumb 263 C10
Lantuel Corn 5 B9
Lantyan Corn 6 D2
Lapal W Mid 133 G9
Lapford Devon 26 F2
Lapford Cross Devon 26 F2
Laphroaig Argyll 254 C4
Lapley Staffs 151 G7
Lapworth Warks 118 C3
Larachbeg Highld 289 E8
Larbert Falk 279 E7
Larbreck Lancs 202 E4
Larches Lancs 202 G6
Larden Green E Ches 167 E9
Larg Highld 292 B2
Largie Aberds 302 F6
Largiebaan Argyll 255 F7
Largiemore Argyll 275 E10
Largoward Fife 287 G8
Largs N Ayrs 266 D4
Largue Aberds 302 E6
Largybeg N Ayrs 256 E3
Largymeanoch N Ayrs 256 E2
Largymore N Ayrs 256 E2
Lark Hill Gtr Man 195 G7
Larkfield Invclyd 276 F4
Larkfield Kent 53 B8
Larkfield W Yorks 205 F10
Larkhall Bath 61 F9
Larkhall S Lnrk 268 E5
Larkhill Wilts 46 E6
Larklands Derbys 171 G7
Larks' Hill Suff 108 B3
Larling Norf 141 F9
Larport Hereford 97 D11
Larrick Corn 12 F2
Larriston Borders 250 E2
Lartington Durham 223 B10
Lary Aberds 292 C5
Lasborough Glos 80 G4
Lasham Hants 49 E7
Lashenden Kent 53 E10
Lask Edge Staffs 168 D6
Lassington Glos 98 G5
Lassodie Fife 280 C2
Lastingham N Yorks 226 G4
Latcham Som 44 D2
Latchbrook Corn 7 D8
Latchford Herts 105 G7
Latchford Oxon 83 E11
Latchford Warr 183 D10
Latchingdon Essex 88 E5
Latchley Corn 12 G4
Latchmere Green Hants 64 G6
Latchmore Bank Essex 87 B7
Lately Common Warr 183 B11
Lathallan Mill Fife 287 G8
Lathbury M Keynes 103 B7
Latheron Highld 310 F5
Latheronwheel Highld 310 F5
Latheronwheel Ho Highld 310 F5
Lathom Lancs 194 E3
Lathones Fife 287 G8
Latimer Bucks 85 F8
Latteridge S Glos 61 C7
Lattiford Som 29 B11
Lattinford Hill Suff 107 D11
Latton Wilts 81 F9
Latton Bush Essex 87 D7
Lauchintilly Aberds 293 B9
Laudale Ho Highld 289 D9
Lauder Borders 271 F10
Lauder Barns Borders 271 F10
Laugharne = Talacharn Carms 74 C4
Laughern Hill Worcs 116 F5
Laughterton Lincs 188 F4
Laughton E Sus 23 C8
Laughton Leics 136 F3
Laughton Lincs 155 C11
Laughton Lincs 188 B4
Laughton Common E Sus 23 C7
Laughton Common S Yorks 187 D8
Laughton en le Morthen S Yorks 187 D8
Launcells Corn 24 F2
Launcells Cross Corn 24 F3
Launceston Corn 12 D2
Launcherley Som 44 E4
Laund Lancs 195 C10
Launton Oxon 102 G2
Laurencekirk Aberds 293 F9
Laurieston Dumfries 237 C8
Laurieston Falk 279 F8
Lavendon M Keynes 121 G8
Lavenham Suff 107 B8
Laverackloch Moray 301 C11
Laverhay Dumfries 248 D4
Laverlaw Borders 261 B7
Laverley Som 44 F5
Lavernock V Glam 59 F7
Laversdale Cumb 239 E11
Laverstock Wilts 47 G7
Laverstoke Hants 48 D3
Laverton Glos 99 D11
Laverton N Yorks 214 E4
Laverton Som 45 C9
Lavington Sands Wilts 46 B4
Lavister Wrex 166 D5
Lavrean Corn 5 D10
Law Hill S Lnrk 268 E6
Lawers Perth 285 D10
Lawers Perth 285 E11
Lawford Essex 107 E11
Lawford Som 42 F6
Lawford Heath Warks 119 C9
Lawhill Perth 286 F3
Lawhitton Corn 12 E3
Lawkland N Yorks 212 F5
Lawkland Green N Yorks 212 F5
Lawley Telford 132 B3
Lawn Swindon 63 C7
Lawnhead Staffs 150 E6
Lawns W Yorks 197 C10
Lawnswood W Yorks 205 F11
Lawnt Denb 165 B8
Lawrence Hill Newport 59 B10
Lawrence Weston Bristol 60 D4
Lawrenny Pembs 73 D8
Lawrenny Quay Pembs 73 D8
Lawshall Suff 125 G7
Lawshall Green Suff 125 G7
Lawton Hereford 115 F8
Lawton Shrops 131 G10
Lawton-gate E Ches 168 D4
Lawton Heath End E Ches 168 D3
Laxey I o M 192 D5
Laxfield Suff 126 C5
Laxfirth Shetland 313 H6
Laxfirth Shetland 313 J6
Laxford Bridge Highld 306 E7
Laxo Shetland 313 G6
Laxobigging Shetland 312 F6
Laxton E Yorks 199 B9
Laxton Northants 137 D8
Laxton Notts 172 B2
Laycock W Yorks 204 E6
Layer Breton Essex 88 B6
Layer de la Haye Essex 89 B7
Layer Marney Essex 88 B6
Layerthorpe York 207 C8
Layham Suff 107 C10
Laymore Dorset 28 G5
Layters Green Bucks 85 G7
Laytham E Yorks 207 F10
Layton Blkpool 202 F2
Lazenby Redcar 225 B11
Lazonby Cumb 230 D6
Le Skerne Haughton Darl 224 B6
Lea Derbys 170 D4
Lea Hereford 98 G3
Lea Lancs 202 G5
Lea Lincs 188 D4
Lea Shrops 131 B8
Lea Shrops 131 F7
Lea Wilts 62 B3
Lea Bridge London 67 B11
Lea by Backford W Ches 182 G5
Lea End Worcs 117 B10
Lea Forge E Ches 168 F2
Lea Green Mers 183 C8
Lea Hall W Mid 134 F2
Lea Heath Staffs 151 D10
Lea Line Hereford 98 G3
Lea Marston Warks 134 E4
Lea Town Lancs 202 G5
Lea Valley Herts 85 B11
Lea Yeat Cumb 212 B5
Leabrooks Derbys 170 E6
Leac a Li W Isles 305 J3
Leacainn W Isles 305 H3
Leachkin Highld 300 E6
Leacnasaide Highld 299 B7
Leadburn Midloth 270 D4
Leaden Roding Essex 87 C9
Leadendale Staffs 151 B8
Leadenham Lincs 173 E7
Leadgate Cumb 231 C10
Leadgate Durham 242 G4
Leadgate T & W 242 F4
Leadhills S Lnrk 259 G9
Leadingcross Green Kent 53 C11
Leadmill Derbys 186 E2
Leadmill Flint 166 C2
Leafield Oxon 82 B4
Leafield Wilts 61 F11
Leagrave Luton 103 G10
Leagreen Hants 19 C11
Leake Lincs 174 F6
Leake N Yorks 225 G8
Leake Commonside Lincs 174 E5
Leake Fold Hill Lincs 174 E6
Lealholm N Yorks 226 D5
Lealholm Side N Yorks 226 D5
Lealt Argyll 275 D7
Lealt Highld 298 C5
Leam Derbys 186 F2
Leamington Hastings Warks 119 D8
Leamoor Common Shrops 131 F8
Leamore W Mid 133 C9
Leamside Durham 234 B2
Leanach Argyll 275 D11
Leanachan Highld 290 F4
Leanaig Highld 300 D5
Leapgate Worcs 116 C6
Leargybreck Argyll 274 F6
Lease Rigg N Yorks 226 E6
Leasey Bridge Herts 85 C11
Leasgill Cumb 211 C9
Leasingham Lincs 173 F9
Leasingthorne Durham 233 F11
Leason Swansea 56 C3
Leasowe Mers 182 C3
Leatherhead Sur 51 B7
Leatherhead Common Sur 51 B7
Leathern Bottle Glos 80 E2
Leathley N Yorks 205 D10
Leaths Dumfries 237 C9
Leaton Shrops 149 F9
Leaton Telford 150 G2
Leaton Heath Shrops 149 F9
Leaveland Kent 54 C4
Leavenheath Suff 107 D9
Leavening N Yorks 216 G5
Leaves Green London 68 G2
Leavesden Green Herts 85 E9
Leazes Durham 242 F5
Lebberston N Yorks 217 C11
Leburnick Corn 12 E3
Lechlade-on-Thames Glos 82 F2
Leck Lancs 212 D2
Leckford Hants 47 F11
Leckfurin Highld 308 D7
Leckgruinart Argyll 274 G3
Leckhampstead Bucks 102 D4
Leckhampstead W Berks 64 D2
Leckhampstead Thicket W Berks 64 D2
Leckhampton Glos 80 B6
Leckie Highld 299 C10
Leckmelm Highld 307 K6
Leckuary Argyll 275 D9
Leckwith V Glam 59 E7
Leconfield E Yorks 208 E6
Ledaig Argyll 289 F11
Ledburn Bucks 103 G8
Ledbury Hereford 98 D4
Ledcharrie Stirl 285 E9
Leddington Glos 98 E3
Ledgemoor Hereford 115 G8
Ledgowan Highld 299 D11
Ledicot Hereford 115 E8
Ledmore Angus 293 G7
Ledmore Highld 307 H7
Lednagullin Highld 308 C7
Ledsham W Ches 182 G5

Ledsham W Yorks 198 B3
Ledston W Yorks 198 B2
Ledston Luck W Yorks 206 G4
Ledstone Devon 8 F4
Ledwell Oxon 101 F8
Lee Argyll 288 G6
Lee Devon 40 D3
Lee Devon 40 D5
Lee Hants 32 D5
Lee Lancs 203 B7
Lee London 67 E11
Lee Northumb 241 F10
Lee Shrops 149 C8
Lee Bank W Mid 133 F11
Lee Brockhurst Shrops 149 D10
Lee Chapel Essex 69 B7
Lee Clump Bucks 84 E6
Lee Common Bucks 84 E6
Lee Gate Bucks 84 D5
Lee Ground Hants 33 F8
Lee Head Derbys 185 C8
Lee Mill Devon 8 D2
Lee Moor Devon 7 C11
Lee Moor W Yorks 197 B10
Lee-on-the-Solent Hants 33 G9
Lee-over-Sands Essex 89 C10
Leeans Shetland 313 J5
Leebotten Shetland 313 L6
Leebotwood Shrops 131 D9
Leece Cumb 210 F4
Leechpool Mon 60 B4
Leechpool Pembs 73 B7
Leeds Kent 53 C10
Leeds W Yorks 205 G11
Leedstown Corn 2 C4
Leeford Devon 41 D9
Leegomery Telford 150 G3
Leeholme Durham 233 E10
Leek Staffs 169 D7
Leek Wootton Warks 118 D5
Leekbrook Staffs 169 E7
Leeming N Yorks 214 B5
Leeming W Yorks 204 G6
Leeming Bar N Yorks 224 G5
Leemings Lancs 203 D10
Lees Derbys 152 B5
Lees Gtr Man 196 G3
Lees W Yorks 204 F6
Leesthorpe Leics 154 G5
Leeswood = Coed-Llai Flint 166 D3
Leetown Perth 286 E6
Leftwich W Ches 183 G11
Legar Powys 78 B2
Legbourne Lincs 190 E5
Legburthwaite Cumb 220 B6
Legerwood Borders 271 G11
Leggatt Hill W Sus 34 C6
Legsby Lincs 189 D10
Leicester Leicester 135 C11
Leicester Forest East Leics 135 C10
Leicester Grange Warks 135 E8
Leigh Devon 26 E2
Leigh Dorset 18 B6
Leigh Dorset 29 F10
Leigh Dorset 30 F3
Leigh Glos 99 F7
Leigh Gtr Man 195 G7
Leigh Kent 52 D4
Leigh Shrops 130 C6
Leigh Sur 51 D8
Leigh Wilts 81 G9
Leigh Worcs 116 G5
Leigh Beck Essex 69 C10
Leigh Common Som 30 B2
Leigh Delamere Wilts 61 D11
Leigh Green Kent 54 G2
Leigh-on-Sea Sthend 69 B10
Leigh Park Hants 22 B2
Leigh Sinton Worcs 116 G5
Leigh upon Mendip Som 45 D7
Leigh Woods N Som 60 E5
Leigham Plym 7 D10
Leighland Chapel Som 42 F4
Leighswood W Mid 133 C11
Leighterton Glos 80 G4
Leighton N Yorks 214 D3
Leighton Shrops 132 B2
Leighton Som 45 E8
Leighton = Tre'r llai Powys 130 B4
Leighton Bromswold Cambs 122 B2
Leighton Buzzard C Beds 103 F8
Leinthall Earls Hereford 115 D8
Leinthall Starkes Hereford 115 D8
Leintwardine Hereford 115 C8
Leire Leics 135 E10
Leirinmore Highld 308 C4
Leiston Suff 127 E8
Leitfie Perth 286 C6
Leith Edin 280 F5
Leithenhall Dumfries 248 D4
Leitholm Borders 272 G5
Lelant Corn 2 B2
Lelant Downs Corn 2 B2
Lelley E Yorks 209 G10
Lem Hill Worcs 116 C4
Lemington T & W 242 E5
Lemmington Hall Northumb 264 G4
Lempitlaw Borders 263 C7
Lemsford Herts 86 C2
Lenacre Cumb 212 B3
Lenborough Bucks 102 E3
Lenchwick Worcs 99 B10
Lendalfoot S Ayrs 244 F4
Lendrick Lodge Stirl 285 G9
Lenham Kent 53 C11
Lenham Forstal Kent 54 C2
Lenham Heath Kent 54 D2
Lennel Borders 273 G7
Lennoxtown E Dunb 278 F2
Lent Bucks 66 C2
Lent Rise Bucks 66 C2
Lenten Pool Denb 165 B8
Lenton Lincs 155 C10
Lenton Nottingham 153 B11
Lenton Abbey Nottingham 153 B10
Lentran Highld 300 E5
Lenwade Norf 159 F11
Leny Ho Stirl 285 G10
Lenzie E Dunb 278 G3
Lenziemill N Lnrk 278 G5
Leoch Angus 287 D7
Leochel-Cushnie Aberds 293 B7
Leominster Hereford 115 F9
Leomonsley Staffs 134 B2
Leonard Stanley Glos 80 E4
Leonardston Pembs 72 D6
Leorin Argyll 254 C4
Lepe Hants 20 B5
Lephin Highld 297 G7
Lephinchapel Argyll 275 D10
Lephinmore Argyll 275 D10
Leppington N Yorks 216 G5
Lepton W Yorks 197 D8
Lepton Edge W Yorks 197 D8
Lerigoligan Argyll 275 C9
Lerrocks Stirl 285 G11
Lerryn Corn 6 D2
Lerwick Shetland 313 J6
Lesbury Northumb 264 G6
Leschangie Aberds 293 B9
Leslie Aberds 302 G5
Leslie Fife 286 G6
Lesmahagow S Lnrk 259 B8
Lesnewth Corn 11 C8
Lessendrum Aberds 302 E5
Lessingham Norf 161 D7
Lessness Heath London 68 D3
Lessonhall Cumb 238 G6
Leswalt Dumfries 236 C2
Letchmore Heath Herts 85 F11
Letchworth Herts 104 E4
Letcombe Bassett Oxon 63 B11
Letcombe Regis Oxon 63 B11
Letham Angus 287 C9
Letham Falk 279 D7
Letham Fife 287 F7
Letham Perth 286 E4
Letham Grange Angus 287 C10
Lethem Borders 250 B5
Lethen Ho Highld 301 D9
Lethenty Aberds 303 E8
Lethenty Aberds 303 G7
Letheringham Suff 126 F5
Letheringsett Norf 159 B11
Lettaford Devon 13 E10
Lettan Orkney 314 B7
Letter Aberds 293 B9
Letterewe Highld 299 B9
Letterfearn Highld 295 C10
Letterfinlay Highld 290 D4
Lettermay Argyll 284 G5
Lettermorar Highld 295 G9
Lettermore Argyll 288 E6
Letters Highld 307 L6
Letterston = Treletert Pembs 91 F8
Lettoch Highld 292 B2
Lettoch Highld 301 F10
Lettoch Moray 302 F3
Lettoch Perth 291 G11
Letton Hereford 96 B6
Letton Hereford 115 C7
Letton Green Norf 141 B9
Lett's Green Kent 52 B3
Letty Brongu Bridgend 57 D11
Letty Green Herts 86 C3
Letwell S Yorks 187 D9
Leuchars Fife 287 E8
Leuchars Ho Moray 302 C2
Leumrabhagh W Isles 305 G5
Levalsa Meor Corn 5 F10
Levan Invclyd 276 F4
Leveneap Shetland 313 G6
Levedale Staffs 151 F7
Level of Mendalgief Newport 59 B10
Level's Green Essex 105 G9
Leven E Yorks 209 D8
Leven Fife 287 G7
Leven Seat W Loth 269 D8
Levencorroch N Ayrs 256 E2
Levenhall E Loth 281 G7
Levens Cumb 211 B9
Levens Green Herts 105 G7
Levenshulme Gtr Man 184 C5
Leventhorpe W Yorks 205 G8
Levenwick Shetland 313 L6
Lever-Edge Gtr Man 195 F8
Leverington Cambs 157 G8
Leverington Common Cambs 157 G8
Leverstock Green Herts 85 D9
Leverton Lincs 174 F6
Leverton W Berks 63 E10
Leverton Highgate Lincs 174 F6
Leverton Lucasgate Lincs 174 F6
Leverton Outgate Lincs 174 F6
Levington Suff 108 D4
Levisham N Yorks 226 G6
Levishie Highld 290 B6
Lew Oxon 82 D4
Lewannick Corn 11 E11
Lewcombe Dorset 29 F9
Lewdown Devon 12 D4
Lewes E Sus 36 E6
Leweston Pembs 91 G8
Lewisham London 67 D11
Lewiston Highld 300 G5
Lewistown Bridgend 58 B2
Lewknor Oxon 84 F2
Leworthy Devon 24 G4
Leworthy Devon 41 F7
Lewson Street Kent 70 G3
Lewth Lancs 202 F5
Lewthorn Cross Devon 13 F11
Lewtrenchard Devon 12 D5
Lexden Essex 107 G9
Ley Aberds 293 B7
Ley Corn 6 B3
Ley Som 41 F10
Ley Green Herts 104 G3
Ley Hey Park Gtr Man 185 D7
Ley Hill W Mid 134 D2
Leybourne Kent 53 B7
Leyburn N Yorks 224 G2
Leycett Staffs 168 F3
Leyfields Staffs 134 B4
Leyhill Bucks 85 E7
Leyhill S Glos 79 G11
Leyland Lancs 194 C4
Leylodge Aberds 293 B9
Leymoor W Yorks 196 D6
Leys Aberds 292 C6
Leys Aberds 303 D10
Leys Cumb 219 B11
Leys Perth 286 D6
Leys Staffs 169 F8
Leys Castle Highld 300 E6
Leys Hill Hereford 79 B9
Leys of Cossans Angus 287 C7
Leysdown-on-Sea Kent 70 E4
Leysmill Angus 287 C10
Leysters Hereford 115 E11
Leysters Pole Hereford 115 E11
Leyton London 67 B11
Leytonstone London 67 B11
Lezant Corn 12 F2
Lezerea Corn 2 C5
Leziate Norf 158 F3
Lhanbryde Moray 302 C2
Liatrie Highld 300 F2
Libanus Powys 95 F9
Libberton S Lnrk 269 G9
Libbery Worcs 117 F9
Liberton Edin 270 B5
Liceasto W Isles 305 J3
Lichfield Staffs 134 B2
Lick Perth 286 B2
Lickey Worcs 117 B9
Lickey End Worcs 117 C9
Lickfold W Sus 34 B6
Lickhill Worcs 116 C6
Lickleyhead Castle Aberds 302 G6
Liddaton Devon 12 E5
Liddel Orkney 314 H4
Liddesdale Highld 289 D9
Liddeston Pembs 72 D5
Liddington Swindon 63 C8
Liden Swindon 63 C7
Lidgate Suff 124 F4
Lidget S Yorks 199 G7
Lidget Green W Yorks 205 G8
Lidgett Notts 171 B10
Lidgett Park W Yorks 206 F2
Lidham Hill E Sus 38 D4
Lidlington C Beds 103 D9
Lidsey W Sus 22 C6
Lidsing Kent 69 G9
Lidstone Oxon 101 G7
Lieurary Highld 310 C4
Liff Angus 287 D7
Lifford W Mid 117 B11
Lifton Devon 12 D3
Liftondown Devon 12 D3
Light Oaks Staffs 168 E6
Lightcliffe W Yorks 196 B6
Lighteach Shrops 149 C10
Lightfoot Green Lancs 202 G6
Lighthorne Warks 118 F6
Lighthorne Heath Warks 119 F7
Lighthorne Rough Warks 118 F6
Lightmoor Telford 132 B3
Lightpill Glos 80 E4
Lightwater Sur 66 G2
Lightwood S Yorks 186 E5
Lightwood Shrops 132 E2
Lightwood Shrops 150 D3
Lightwood Staffs 169 G8
Lightwood Stoke 168 G6
Lightwood Green E Ches 167 G10
Lightwood Green Wrex 166 G5
Liglartrie S Ayrs 244 F6
Lilbourne Northants 119 B11
Lilburn Tower Northumb 264 E2
Lilford Gtr Man 195 G7
Lillesdon Som 28 C4
Lilleshall Telford 150 F4
Lilley Herts 104 F2
Lilley W Berks 64 D2
Lilliesleaf Borders 262 E2
Lillingstone Dayrell Bucks 102 D4
Lillingstone Lovell Bucks 102 C4
Lillington Dorset 29 E10
Lillington Warks 118 D6
Lilliput Poole 18 C6
Lilstock Som 43 E7
Lilybank Invclyd 276 G6
Lilyhurst Shrops 150 G4
Lilyvale Kent 54 F5
Limbrick Lancs 194 D6
Limbury Luton 103 G11
Lime Side Gtr Man 196 G2
Lime Street Worcs 98 E6
Lime Tree Park W Mid 118 B5
Limebrook Hereford 115 D7
Limefield Gtr Man 195 E10
Limehouse London 67 C11
Limehurst Gtr Man 196 G2
Limekiln Field Derbys 187 G7
Limekilnburn S Lnrk 268 E4
Limekilns Fife 279 E11
Limerigg Falk 279 G7
Limerstone I o W 20 E4
Limestone Brae Northumb 231 B11
Limington Som 29 C8
Limpenhoe Norf 143 C7
Limpenhoe Hill Norf 143 C8
Limpers Hill Wilts 45 G10
Limpley Stoke Wilts 61 G9
Limpsfield Sur 52 C2
Limpsfield Chart Sur 52 C2
Limpsfield Common Sur 52 C2
Linbriggs Northumb 251 B9
Linburn W Loth 270 B2
Linby Notts 171 E8
Linchmere W Sus 49 G11
Lincluden Dumfries 237 B11
Lincoln Lincs 189 G7
Lincomb Worcs 116 D6
Lincombe Devon 8 D4
Lincombe Devon 40 D3
Lindal in Furness Cumb 210 D5
Lindale Cumb 211 C8
Lindean Borders 261 C11
Linden Glos 80 B4
Lindfield W Sus 36 B4
Lindford Hants 49 F10
Lindifferon Fife 287 F7
Lindley N Yorks 205 D10
Lindley W Yorks 196 D6
Lindley Green N Yorks 205 D10
Lindores Fife 286 F6
Lindow End E Ches 184 F4
Lindrick Dale S Yorks 187 E8
Lindridge Worcs 116 D3
Lindsell Essex 106 F2
Lindsey Suff 107 C9
Lindsey Tye Suff 107 B9
Lindwell W Yorks 196 C5
Lineholt Worcs 116 D6
Lineholt Common Worcs 116 D6
Liney Som 43 F11
Linfitts Gtr Man 196 F3
Linford Hants 31 F11
Linford Thurrock 69 D7
Lingague I o M 192 E3
Lingards Wood W Yorks 196 E5
Lingbob W Yorks 205 F7
Lingdale Redcar 226 B3
Lingen Hereford 115 D7
Lingfield Darl 224 C6
Lingfield Sur 51 E11
Lingfield Common Sur 51 E11
Lingley Green Warr 183 D9
Lingley Mere Warr 183 D10
Lingreabhagh W Isles 296 C6
Lingwood Norf 143 B7
Linhope Borders 249 C10
Linhope Northumb 263 F11
Linicro Highld 298 C3
Link N Som 44 B3
Linkend Worcs 98 E6
Linkenholt Hants 47 B11
Linkhill Kent 38 B4
Linkinhorne Corn 12 G2
Linklater Orkney 314 H4
Linklet Orkney 314 A7
Linksness Orkney 314 E5
Linksness Orkney 314 F2
Linktown Fife 280 C5
Linley Shrops 131 E7
Linley Shrops 132 D3
Linley Brook Shrops 132 D3
Linley Green Hereford 116 G3
Linleygreen Shrops 132 D3
Linlithgow W Loth 279 F10
Linlithgow Bridge W Loth 279 F9
Linndhu Ho Argyll 289 D7
Linneraineach Highld 307 J6
Linns Angus 292 F3
Linnyshaw Gtr Man 195 G8
Linshiels Northumb 251 B9
Linsiadar W Isles 304 E4
Linsidemore Highld 309 K5
Linslade C Beds 103 F8
Linstead Parva Suff 126 B6
Linstock Cumb 239 F10
Linthorpe M'bro 225 B9
Linthurst Worcs 117 C9
Linthwaite W Yorks 196 E6
Lintlaw Borders 272 D6
Lintmill Moray 302 C5
Linton Borders 263 D7
Linton Cambs 105 B11
Linton Derbys 152 F5
Linton Hereford 98 F3
Linton Kent 53 D9
Linton N Yorks 213 G9
Linton Northumb 253 E7
Linton W Yorks 206 D3
Linton Heath Derbys 152 F5
Linton Hill Hereford 98 G3
Linton-on-Ouse N Yorks 215 G9
Lintridge Glos 98 E4
Lintz Durham 242 F5
Lintzford T & W 242 F4
Lintzgarth Durham 232 C4
Linwood Hants 31 F11
Linwood Lincs 189 D10
Linwood Renfs 267 C8
Lionacleit W Isles 297 G3
Lional W Isles 304 B7
Lions Green E Sus 23 B9
Liphook Hants 49 G10
Lipley Shrops 150 C4
Lippitts Hill Essex 86 F5
Liquo or Bowhousebog N Lnrk 269 D7
Liscard Mers 182 C4
Liscombe Som 41 G11
Liskeard Corn 6 C5
Liss Hants 34 B3
Liss Forest Hants 34 B3
Lissett E Yorks 209 B8
Lissington Lincs 189 E10
Lisson Grove London 67 C9
Listerdale S Yorks 187 C7
Listock Som 28 C4
Listoft Lincs 191 G8
Liston Essex 107 C7
Liston Garden Essex 106 B6
Lisvane Cardiff 59 C7
Liswerry Newport 59 B10
Litcham Norf 159 F7
Litchard Bridgend 58 C2
Litchborough Northants 120 G2
Litchfield Hants 48 C3
Litchurch Derbys 153 B7
Litherland Mers 182 B4
Litlington Cambs 104 C6
Litlington E Sus 23 E8
Litmarsh Hereford 97 B10
Little Abington Cambs 105 B10
Little Addington Northants 121 C9
Little Airmyn E Yorks 199 B8
Little Almshoe Herts 104 F3
Little Alne Warks 118 E2
Little Altcar Mers 193 F10
Little Ann Hants 47 E10
Little Arowry Wrex 167 G7
Little Asby Cumb 222 D3
Little Ashley Wilts 61 G10
Little Assynt Highld 307 G6
Little Aston Staffs 133 C11
Little Atherfield I o W 20 E5
Little Ayre Orkney 314 G3
Little-ayre Shetland 313 G5
Little Ayton N Yorks 225 C11
Little Baddow Essex 88 D3
Little Badminton S Glos 61 C10
Little Ballinluig Perth 286 B3
Little Bampton Cumb 239 F7
Little Bardfield Essex 106 E3
Little Barford Beds 122 F3
Little Barningham Norf 160 C2
Little Barrington Glos 82 C2
Little Barrow W Ches 183 G7
Little Barugh N Yorks 216 D5
Little Bavington Northumb 241 B11
Little Bayham E Sus 52 F6
Little Bealings Suff 108 B4
Little Beckford Glos 99 E9
Little Bedwyn Wilts 63 F9
Little Bentley Essex 108 F2
Little Berkhamsted Herts 86 D3
Little Billing Northants 120 E6
Little Billington C Beds 103 G8
Little Birch Hereford 97 E10
Little Bispham Blkpool 202 E2
Little Blakenham Suff 108 B2
Little Blencow Cumb 230 E5
Little Bloxwich W Mid 133 C10
Little Bognor W Sus 35 C8
Little Bolehill Derbys 170 E3
Little Bollington E Ches 184 D2
Little Bolton Gtr Man 184 B3
Little Bookham Sur 50 C6
Little Bosullow Corn 1 C4
Little Bourton Oxon 101 C9
Little Bowden Leics 136 F4
Little Boys Heath Bucks 84 F6
Little Bradley Suff 124 G3
Little Braithwaite Cumb 229 G10
Little Brampton Shrops 131 G7
Little Braxted Essex 88 C4
Little Bray Devon 41 F7
Little Brechin Angus 293 G7
Little Brickhill M Keynes 103 E8
Little Bridgeford Staffs 151 D7
Little Brington Northants 120 E3
Little Bristol S Glos 80 G2
Little Britain Warks 118 G2
Little Bromley Essex 107 F11
Little Bromwich W Mid 134 F2
Little Broughton Cumb 229 E7
Little Budworth W Ches 167 B9
Little Burstead Essex 87 G11
Little Bytham Lincs 155 F10
Little Cambridge Essex 106 F2
Little Canfield Essex 105 G11
Little Canford Poole 18 B6
Little Carleton Lancs 202 F2
Little Carlton Lincs 190 D5
Little Carlton Notts 172 D3
Little Casterton Rutland 137 B10
Little Catwick E Yorks 209 E8
Little Catworth Cambs 122 C2
Little Cawthorpe Lincs 190 E5
Little Chalfield Wilts 61 G11
Little Chalfont Bucks 85 F7
Little Chart Kent 54 D2
Little Chart Forstal Kent 54 D3
Little Chell Stoke 168 E5
Little Chester Derby 153 B7
Little Chesterford Essex 105 C10
Little Chesterton Oxon 101 G11
Little Cheverell Wilts 46 C3
Little Chishill Cambs 105 D8
Little Clacton Essex 89 B11
Little Clanfield Oxon 82 E3
Little Clegg Gtr Man 196 E2
Little Clifton Cumb 229 F7
Little Coates NE Lincs 201 F8
Little Colp Aberds 303 E7
Little Comberton Worcs 99 C9
Little Comfort Corn 12 E2
Little Common E Sus 38 F2
Little Common Lincs 156 D6
Little Common Shrops 115 B7
Little Common W Sus 34 C6
Little Compton Warks 100 E5
Little Corby Cumb 239 F11
Little Cornard Suff 107 D7
Little Cowarne Hereford 116 G2
Little Coxwell Oxon 82 G3
Little Crakehall N Yorks 224 G4
Little Cransley Northants 120 B6
Little Crawley M Keynes 103 B8
Little Creaton Northants 120 C4
Little Creich Highld 309 L6
Little Cressingham Norf 141 D7
Little Crosby Mers 193 G10
Little Cubley Derbys 152 B3
Little Dalby Leics 154 G5
Little Dawley Telford 132 B3
Little Dens Aberds 303 E10
Little Dewchurch Hereford 97 E10
Little Ditton Cambs 124 F3
Little Doward Hereford 79 B8
Little Downham Cambs 139 G10
Little Drayton Shrops 150 C3
Little Driffield E Yorks 208 B6
Little Drybrook Glos 79 D9
Little Dunham Norf 159 G7
Little Dunkeld Perth 286 C4
Little Dunmow Essex 106 G3
Little Durnford Wilts 46 G6
Little Eastbury Worcs 116 F6
Little Easton Essex 106 G2
Little Eaton Derbys 170 G5
Little Eccleston Lancs 202 E4
Little Ellingham Norf 141 D10
Little End Cambs 122 F3
Little End E Yorks 208 F2
Little End Essex 87 E8
Little Everdon Northants 119 F11
Little Eversden Cambs 123 G7
Little Faringdon Oxon 82 E2
Little Fencote N Yorks 224 G5
Little Fenton N Yorks 206 F6
Little Finborough Suff 125 G10
Little Fransham Norf 159 G8
Little Frith Kent 54 B2
Little Gaddesden Herts 85 C7
Little Gidding Cambs 138 G2
Little Gight Aberds 303 F8
Little Glemham Suff 126 F6
Little Glenshee Perth 286 D3
Little Gorsley Glos 98 F3
Little Gransden Cambs 122 F5
Little Green Cambs 104 B5
Little Green Notts 172 G2
Little Green Som 45 D8
Little Green Suff 125 C11
Little Green Wrex 167 G7
Little Grimsby Lincs 190 C4
Little Gringley Notts 188 E2
Little Gruinard Highld 307 L4
Little Habton N Yorks 216 D4
Little Hadham Herts 105 G8
Little Hale Lincs 173 G10
Little Hale Norf 141 B8
Little Hallam Derbys 171 G7
Little Hallingbury Essex 87 B7
Little Hampden Bucks 84 E5
Little Haresfield Glos 80 D4
Little Harrowden Northants 121 C7
Little Harwood Blkburn 195 B7
Little Haseley Oxon 83 E10
Little Hatfield E Yorks 209 E9
Little Hautbois Norf 160 E5
Little Haven Pembs 72 C5
Little Haven W Sus 51 G7
Little Hay Staffs 134 C2
Little Hayfield Derbys 185 D8
Little Haywood Staffs 151 E10
Little Heath E Ches 167 G11
Little Heath Herts 85 D8
Little Heath Herts 86 E3
Little Heath London 68 B3
Little Heath Staffs 151 F8
Little Heath Sur 66 G6
Little Heath W Berks 65 E7
Little Heath W Ches 166 B6
Little Heath W Mid 134 G6
Little Heck N Yorks 198 C5
Little Henham Essex 105 E10
Little Henny Essex 107 D7
Little Herbert's Glos 81 B7
Little Hereford Hereford 115 D11
Little Hill Hereford 97 F9
Little Hill Som 28 E3
Little Holbury Hants 32 G6
Little Honeyborough Pembs 73 D7
Little Hoole Moss Houses Lancs 194 C3
Little Horkesley Essex 107 E9
Little Hormead Herts 105 F8
Little Horsted E Sus 23 B7
Little Horton W Yorks 205 G9
Little Horton Wilts 62 G4
Little Horwood Bucks 102 E5
Little Houghton Northants 120 F6
Little Houghton S Yorks 198 G2
Little Hucklow Derbys 185 F11
Little Hulton Gtr Man 195 G8
Little Humber E Yorks 201 C8
Little Hungerford W Berks 64 E4
Little Ilford London 68 B2
Little Ingestre Staffs 151 E9
Little Inkberrow Worcs 117 F10
Little Irchester Northants 121 D8
Little Keyford Som 45 D9
Little Kimble Bucks 84 D4
Little Kineton Warks 118 G6
Little Kingshill Bucks 84 F5
Little Knowles Green Suff 124 F5
Little Langdale Cumb 220 E6
Little Langford Wilts 46 F4
Little Laver Essex 87 D8
Little Lawford Warks 119 B9
Little Layton Blkpool 202 F2
Little Leigh W Ches 183 F10
Little Leighs Essex 88 B2
Little Lepton W Yorks 197 E8
Little Leven E Yorks 209 D8
Little Lever Gtr Man 195 F9
Little Limber Lincs 200 E6
Little Linford M Keynes 102 C6
Little Load Som 29 C7
Little London Bucks 83 C10
Little London Bucks 84 D5
Little London Cambs 139 D8
Little London E Sus 23 B9
Little London Essex 105 F9
Little London Essex 106 D3
Little London Glos 80 B2
Little London Hants 47 D11
Little London Hants 48 B6
Little London Lincs 156 E4
Little London Lincs 157 E8
Little London Lincs 189 D10
Little London Lincs 190 F4
Little London Norf 140 D5
Little London Norf 160 C2
Little London Norf 160 C5
Little London Norf 160 E3
Little London Oxon 83 E8
Little London Powys 129 F10
Little London Shrops 131 F10
Little London Som 44 D6
Little London Suff 125 F10
Little London W Yorks 205 F10
Little London Worcs 116 C2
Little Longstone Derbys 185 G11
Little Lynturk Aberds 293 B7
Little Lyth Shrops 131 B9
Little Madeley Staffs 168 F3
Little Malvern Worcs 98 C5
Little Mancot Flint 166 B4
Little Maplestead Essex 106 E6
Little Marcle Hereford 98 D3
Little Marlow Bucks 65 B11
Little Marsden Lancs 204 F3
Little Marsh Bucks 102 G3
Little Marsh Norf 159 B10
Little Marsh Wilts 45 B11
Little Marton Blkpool 202 G2
Little Mascalls Essex 88 E2
Little Massingham Norf 158 E5
Little Melton Norf 142 B3
Little Merthyr Hereford 96 B5
Little Milford Pembs 73 C7
Little Mill Kent 53 D7
Little Mill Mon 78 E4
Little Milton Newport 59 B11
Little Milton Oxon 83 E10
Little Minster Oxon 82 C4
Little Missenden Bucks 84 F6
Little Mongeham Kent 55 C10
Little Moor Gtr Man 184 D6
Little Moor Lancs 203 E10
Little Moor End Lancs 195 B8
Little Morrell Warks 118 F6
Little Mountain Flint 166 C3
Little Musgrave Cumb 222 C5
Little Ness Shrops 149 F8
Little Neston W Ches 182 F3
Little Newcastle Pembs 91 F9
Little Newsham Durham 224 B2
Little Norlington E Sus 23 C7
Little Norton Som 29 D7
Little Oakley Essex 108 F4
Little Oakley Northants 137 F7
Little Odell Beds 121 F9
Little Offley Herts 104 F2
Little Onn Staffs 150 F6
Little Ormside Cumb 222 B4
Little Orton Cumb 239 F9
Little Orton Leics 134 B6
Little Ouse Norf 140 F2
Little Ouseburn N Yorks 215 G8
Little Overton Wrex 166 G5
Little Oxney Green Essex 87 D11
Little Packington Warks 134 G4
Little Parndon Essex 86 C6
Little Paxton Cambs 122 E3
Little Petherick Corn 10 G4
Little Pitlurg Moray 302 E4
Little Plumpton Lancs 202 G3
Little Plumstead Norf 160 G6
Little Ponton Lincs 155 C8
Little Posbrook Hants 33 G8
Little Poulton Lancs 202 F3
Little Preston Kent 53 B8
Little Preston W Yorks 206 G3
Little Raveley Cambs 122 B5
Little Reedness E Yorks 199 C10
Little Reynoldston Swansea 56 D3
Little Ribston N Yorks 206 C3
Little Rissington Glos 81 B11
Little Rogart Highld 309 J7
Little Rollright Oxon 100 E5
Little Ryburgh Norf 159 D9
Little Ryle Northumb 264 G2
Little Ryton Shrops 131 C9
Little Salisbury Wilts 63 G7
Little Salkeld Cumb 231 D7
Little Sampford Essex 106 E3
Little Sandhurst Brack 65 G10
Little Saredon Staffs 133 B8
Little Saxham Suff 124 E5
Little Scatwell Highld 300 D3
Little Scotland Gtr Man 194 E6
Little Sessay N Yorks 215 E9
Little Shelford Cambs 123 G9
Little Shoddesden Hants 47 D9
Little Shrewley Warks 118 D4
Little Shurdington Glos 80 B6
Little Silver Devon 26 F6
Little Silver Devon 40 E4
Little Singleton Lancs 202 F3
Little Skillymarno Aberds 303 D9
Little Skipwith N Yorks 207 F9
Little Smeaton N Yorks 198 D4
Little Smeaton N Yorks 224 E6
Little Snoring Norf 159 C9
Little Sodbury S Glos 61 C9
Little Sodbury End S Glos 61 C8
Little Somborne Hants 47 G11
Little Somerford Wilts 62 C3
Little Soudley Shrops 150 D4
Little Stainforth N Yorks 212 F6
Little Stainton Darl 234 G2
Little Stanmore London 85 G11
Little Stanney W Ches 182 G6
Little Staughton Beds 122 E2

344 Lit – Log

Little Steeping Lincs 174 C6
Little Stoke S Glos 60 C6
Little Stoke Staffs 151 C8
Little Stonham Suff 126 E2
Little Stretton Leics 136 C3
Little Stretton Shrops 131 E8
Little Strickland Cumb 221 B11
Little Studley N Yorks 214 E6
Little Stukeley Cambs 122 B4
Little Sugnall Staffs 150 C6
Little Sutton Lincs 157 E9
Little Sutton Shrops 131 G10
Little Sutton W Ches 182 F5
Little Swinburne Northumb 241 B10
Little Tarrington Hereford 98 C2
Little Tew Oxon 101 F7
Little Tey Essex 107 G7
Little Thetford Cambs 123 B10
Little Thirkleby N Yorks 215 D9
Little Thornage Norf 159 B11
Little Thornton Lancs 202 E3
Little Thorpe Durham 234 C4
Little Thorpe W Yorks 197 C7
Little Thurlow Suff 124 G3
Little Thurlow Green Suff 124 G3
Little Thurrock Thurrock 68 D6
Little Torboll Highld 309 K7
Little Torrington Devon 25 D7
Little Totham Essex 88 C5
Little Toux Aberds 302 D5
Little Town Cumb 220 B4
Little Town Lancs 203 F9
Little Town Warr 183 C10
Little Tring Herts 84 C6
Little Twycross Leics 134 B6
Little Urswick Cumb 210 E5
Little Vantage W Loth 270 C2
Little Wakering Essex 70 B2
Little Walden Essex 105 C10
Little Waldingfield Suff 107 B8
Little Walsingham Norf 159 B8
Little Waltham Essex 88 C2
Little Walton Warks 135 G9
Little Warley Essex 87 G10
Little Warton Warks 134 C5
Little Washbourne Glos 99 E9
Little Weighton E Yorks 208 G5
Little Weldon Northants 137 F8
Little Welland Worcs 98 D6
Little Welnetham Suff 125 E7
Little Welton Lincs 190 D4
Little Wenham Suff 107 D11
Little Wenlock Telford 132 B2
Little Weston Som 29 B10
Little Whitehouse I o W 20 C5
Little Whittingham Green Suff 126 B5
Little Wigborough Essex 89 B7
Little Wilbraham Cambs 123 F10
Little Wisbeach Lincs 156 C2
Little Wishford Wilts 46 F5
Little Witcombe Glos 80 B6
Little Witley Worcs 116 E5
Little Wittenham Oxon 83 G9
Little Wolford Warks 100 D5
Little Wood Corner Bucks 84 E6
Little Woodcote London 67 G9
Little Woolgarston Dorset 18 E5
Little Worthen Shrops 130 B6
Little Wratting Suff 106 B3
Little Wymington Beds 121 D9
Little Wymondley Herts 104 F4
Little Wyrley Staffs 133 B10
Little Wytheford Shrops 149 F11
Little Yeldham Essex 106 D5
Littlebeck N Yorks 227 D7
Littleborough Devon 26 E4
Littleborough Gtr Man 196 D2
Littleborough Notts 188 E4
Littlebourne Kent 55 B8
Littlebredy Dorset 17 D7
Littlebury Essex 105 D10
Littlebury Green Essex 105 D9
Littlecote Bucks 102 G6
Littlecott Wilts 46 C6
Littledean Glos 79 C11
Littledean Hill Glos 79 C11
Littledown Bmouth 19 C8
Littledown Hants 47 B10
Littleferry Highld 311 K2
Littlefield NE Lincs 201 F9
Littlefield Common Sur 50 C3
Littlefield Green Windsor 65 D11
Littlegain Shrops 132 D5
Littleham Devon 14 E6
Littleham Devon 24 C6
Littlehampton W Sus 35 G8
Littlehempston Devon 8 C6
Littlehoughton Northumb 264 F6
Littlemill Aberds 292 D5
Littlemill E Ayrs 257 F11
Littlemill Highld 301 D9
Littlemill Northumb 264 F6
Littlemoor Derbys 170 C5
Littlemoor Dorset 17 E9
Littlemore Oxon 83 E8
Littlemoss Gtr Man 184 B6
Littleover Derby 152 C6
Littleport Cambs 139 F11
Littler W Ches 167 B10
Littlestead Green Oxon 65 D8
Littlestone-on-Sea Kent 39 C9
Littlethorpe Leics 135 D10
Littlethorpe N Yorks 214 F6
Littleton Bath 60 G5
Littleton Dorset 30 G5
Littleton Hants 48 G3
Littleton Perth 286 D6
Littleton Som 44 G3
Littleton Sur 50 D3
Littleton Sur 66 F5
Littleton W Ches 166 B6
Littleton Wilts 62 G2
Littleton Common Sur 66 E5
Littleton Drew Wilts 61 C10
Littleton-on-Severn S Glos 60 B5
Littleton Panell Wilts 46 C4
Littleton-upon-Severn S Glos 79 G9
Littletown Durham 234 C2
Littletown I o W 20 C6
Littletown W Yorks 197 C8
Littlewick Green Windsor 65 D10
Littlewindsor Dorset 28 G6
Littlewood Staffs 133 B9
Littlewood Green Warks 117 E11
Littleworth Beds 103 C11
Littleworth Glos 80 E4
Littleworth Glos 100 D2
Littleworth Oxon 82 F4
Littleworth Oxon 83 D9
Littleworth Oxon 83 G10
Littleworth S Yorks 187 B10
Littleworth Staffs 151 E8
Littleworth Staffs 151 G10
Littleworth W Sus 35 C11
Littleworth Warks 118 E4
Littleworth Wilts 63 G7
Littleworth Worcs 117 E9
Littleworth Worcs 117 G7
Littleworth Common Bucks 66 B2
Littleworth End Warks 134 D3
Littley Green Essex 87 B11
Litton Derbys 185 F11
Litton N Yorks 213 E8
Litton Som 44 C5
Litton Cheney Dorset 17 C7
Litton Mill Derbys 185 G11
Liurbost W Isles 304 F5
Livermead Torbay 9 C8
Liverpool Mers 182 C4
Liverpool Airport Mers 182 E6
Liversedge W Yorks 197 C8
Liverton Devon 14 F2
Liverton Redcar 226 B4
Liverton Mines Redcar 226 B4
Liverton Street Kent 53 C11
Livesey Street Kent 53 C8
Livingshayes Devon 27 G7
Livingston W Loth 269 B11
Livingston Village W Loth 269 B10
Lix Toll Stirl 285 D9
Lixwm Flint 181 G11
Lizard Corn 2 G6
Llaingoch Anglesey 178 E2
Llaithddu Powys 129 G11
Llampha V Glam 58 D2
Llan Powys 129 C7
Llan-dafal Bl Gwent 77 E11
Llan eurgain = Northop Flint 166 B2
Llan Ffestiniog Gwyn 164 G2
Llan-mill Pembs 73 C10
Llan-non = Llanon Ceredig 111 D10
Llan-y-pwll Wrex 166 E5
Llanaber Gwyn 146 F2
Llanaelhaearn Gwyn 162 G5
Llanafan Ceredig 112 C3
Llanafan-fawr Powys 113 F9
Llanallgo Anglesey 179 D7
Llananno Powys 113 C11
Llanarmon Gwyn 145 B8
Llanarmon Dyffryn Ceiriog Wrex 148 C3
Llanarmon Mynydd-mawr Powys 148 D2
Llanarmon-yn-Ial Denb 165 D11
Llanarth Ceredig 111 F8
Llanarth Mon 78 C5
Llanarthne Carms 93 G10
Llanasa Flint 181 E10
Llanbabo Anglesey 178 D5
Llanbad Rhondda 58 C3
Llanbadarn Fawr Ceredig 128 G2
Llanbadarn Fynydd Powys 114 B2
Llanbadarn-y-Garreg Powys 96 B2
Llanbadoc Mon 78 E5
Llanbadrig Anglesey 178 C5
Llanbeder Newport 78 G5
Llanbedr Gwyn 145 D11
Llanbedr Powys 96 B2
Llanbedr Powys 96 G4
Llanbedr-Dyffryn-Clwyd Denb 165 D10
Llanbedr Pont Steffan = Lampeter Ceredig 93 B11
Llanbedr-y-cennin Conwy 164 B3
Llanbedrgoch Anglesey 179 E8
Llanbedrog Gwyn 144 C6
Llanberis Gwyn 163 C9
Llanbethery V Glam 58 F4
Llanbister Powys 114 C2
Llanblethian = Llanfleiddan V Glam 58 E3
Llanboidy Carms 92 G4
Llanbradach Caerph 77 G10
Llanbrynmair Powys 129 C7
Llancadle = Llancatal V Glam 58 F4
Llancaiach Caerph 77 F10
Llancarfan V Glam 58 E5
Llancatal = Llancadle V Glam 58 F4
Llancayo Mon 78 E5
Llancloudy Hereford 97 G9
Llancowrid Powys 130 E3
Llancynfelyn Ceredig 128 E2
Llandaff Cardiff 59 D7
Llandaff North Cardiff 59 D7
Llandanwg Gwyn 145 D11
Llandarcy Neath 57 B8
Llandawke Carms 74 C3
Llanddaniel Fab Anglesey 179 G7
Llanddarog Carms 75 B8
Llanddeiniol Ceredig 111 C11
Llanddeiniolen Gwyn 163 B8
Llandderfel Gwyn 147 B9
Llanddeusant Anglesey 178 D4
Llanddeusant Carms 94 G5
Llanddew Powys 95 E11
Llanddewi Swansea 56 D3
Llanddewi-Brefi Ceredig 112 F3
Llanddewi Fach Mon 78 F4
Llanddewi Rhydderch Mon 78 C5
Llanddewi Skirrid Mon 78 B4
Llanddewi Velfrey Pembs 73 B10
Llanddewi Ystradenni Powys 114 D2
Llanddewi'r Cwm Powys 95 B10
Llanddoged Conwy 164 C4
Llanddona Anglesey 179 F9
Llanddowror Carms 74 C3
Llanddulas Conwy 180 F6
Llanddwywe Gwyn 145 E11
Llanddyfynan Anglesey 179 F8
Llandecwyn Gwyn 146 B2
Llandefaelog Powys 95 E10
Llandefaelog Fach Powys 95 E10
Llandefaelog-tre'r-graig Powys 96 F2
Llandefalle Powys 96 D2
Llandegai Gwyn 179 G9
Llandegfan Anglesey 179 G9
Llandegla Denb 165 E11
Llandegley Powys 114 E2
Llandegveth Mon 78 F4
Llandegwning Gwyn 144 C5
Llandeilo Carms 94 G2
Llandeilo Graban Powys 95 C11
Llandeilo'r Fan Powys 95 E7
Llandeloy Pembs 91 F7
Llandenny Mon 78 E6
Llandenny Walks Mon 78 E5
Llandevaud Newport 78 G6
Llandevenny Mon 60 B2
Llandewi Ystradenny Powys 114 D2
Llandilo Pembs 92 F2
Llandilo-yr-ynys Carms 93 G9
Llandinabo Hereford 97 F10
Llandinam Powys 129 F10
Llandissilio Pembs 92 G2
Llandogo Mon 79 E8
Llandough V Glam 58 E3
Llandough V Glam 59 E7
Llandovery = Llanymddyfri Carms 94 E5
Llandow = Llandw V Glam 58 E2
Llandre Carms 94 C3
Llandre Ceredig 128 F2
Llandrillo Denb 147 B10
Llandrillo-yn-Rhôs Conwy 180 E4
Llandrindod Wells Powys 113 E11
Llandrinio Powys 148 F5
Llandruidion Pembs 90 G5
Llandudno Conwy 180 E3
Llandudno Junction = Cyffordd Llandudno Conwy 180 F3
Llandudoch = St Dogmaels Pembs 92 B3
Llandw = Llandow V Glam 58 E2
Llandwrog Gwyn 163 D7
Llandybie Carms 75 B10
Llandyfaelog Carms 74 C6
Llandyfan Carms 75 B10
Llandyfriog Ceredig 92 C6
Llandyfrydog Anglesey 178 D6
Llandygwydd Ceredig 92 C4
Llandynan Denb 165 F11
Llandyrnog Denb 165 B10
Llandysilio Powys 148 F5
Llandyssil Powys 130 D3
Llandysul Ceredig 93 C8
Llanedeyrn Cardiff 59 C8
Llanedi Carms 75 D9
Llanedwen Anglesey 163 B8
Llaneglwys Powys 95 D11
Llanegryn Gwyn 110 B2
Llanegwad Carms 93 G10
Llaneilian Anglesey 179 C7
Llanelian yn-Rhôs Conwy 180 F5
Llanelidan Denb 165 E10
Llanelieu Powys 96 E3
Llanellen Mon 78 C4
Llanelli Carms 56 B4
Llanelltyd Gwyn 146 F4
Llanelly Mon 78 C2
Llanelly Hill Mon 78 C2
Llanelwedd Powys 113 G10
Llanelwy = St Asaph Denb 181 G8
Llanenddwyn Gwyn 145 E11
Llanengan Gwyn 144 D5
Llanerch Powys 130 E6
Llanerch Emrys Powys 148 E4
Llanerchymedd Anglesey 178 E6
Llanerfyl Powys 129 B10
Llaneuddog Anglesey 179 D7
Llanfabon Caerph 77 G10
Llanfachraeth Anglesey 178 E4
Llanfachreth Gwyn 146 E5
Llanfaelog Anglesey 178 G4
Llanfaelrhys Gwyn 144 D4
Llanfaenor Mon 78 B6
Llanfaes Anglesey 179 F10
Llanfaes Powys 95 F10
Llanfaethlu Anglesey 178 D4
Llanfaglan Gwyn 163 C7
Llanfair Gwyn 145 D11
Llanfair Caereinion Powys 130 B2
Llanfair Clydogau Ceredig 112 G2
Llanfair-Dyffryn-Clwyd Denb 165 D10
Llanfair Kilgeddin Mon 78 D4
Llanfair Kilgheddin Mon 78 D4
Llanfair-Nant-Gwyn Pembs 92 D3
Llanfair Talhaiarn Conwy 180 G6
Llanfair Waterdine Shrops 114 B4
Llanfairfechan Conwy 179 F11
Llanfairpwll-gwyngyll Anglesey 179 G8
Llanfairyneubwll Anglesey 178 F3
Llanfairynghornwy Anglesey 178 C4
Llanfallteg Carms 73 B11
Llanfallteg West Carms 73 B10
Llanfaredd Powys 113 G11
Llanfarian Ceredig 111 B11
Llanfechain Powys 148 E3
Llanfechan Powys 113 G9
Llanfechell Anglesey 178 C5
Llanferres Denb 165 C11
Llanfflewyn Anglesey 178 D5
Llanfigael Anglesey 178 E4
Llanfihangel-ar-arth Carms 93 D9
Llanfihangel-Crucorney Mon 96 G6
Llanfihangel Glyn Myfyr Conwy 165 F7
Llanfihangel-helygen Powys 113 E10
Llanfihangel Nant Bran Powys 95 E8
Llanfihangel-nant-Melan Powys 114 F3
Llanfihangel Rhydithon Powys 114 D3
Llanfihangel Rogiet Mon 60 B2
Llanfihangel Tal-y-llyn Powys 96 F2
Llanfihangel Tor y Mynydd Mon 79 E7
Llanfihangel-uwch-Gwili Carms 93 G9
Llanfihangel-y-Creuddyn Ceredig 112 B3
Llanfihangel-y-pennant Gwyn 128 B3
Llanfihangel-y-pennant Gwyn 163 F8
Llanfihangel-yng-Ngwynfa Powys 147 F11
Llanfihangel yn Nhowyn Anglesey 178 F4
Llanfilo Powys 96 E2
Llanfleiddan = Llanblethian V Glam 58 E3
Llanfoist Mon 78 C3
Llanfor Gwyn 147 B8
Llanfrechfa Torf 78 G4
Llanfrothen Gwyn 163 G10
Llanfrynach Powys 95 F11
Llanfwrog Anglesey 178 E4
Llanfwrog Denb 165 D10
Llanfyllin Powys 148 F2
Llanfynydd Carms 93 F11
Llanfynydd Flint 166 D3
Llanfyrnach Pembs 92 E4
Llangadfan Powys 147 G10
Llangadog Carms 74 D6
Llangadog Carms 94 F4
Llangadwaladr Anglesey 162 B5
Llangadwaladr Powys 148 C3
Llangaffo Anglesey 162 B6
Llangain Carms 74 B5
Llangammarch Wells Powys 95 B8
Llangan V Glam 58 D3
Llangarron Hereford 97 G10
Llangasty Talyllyn Powys 96 F2
Llangathen Carms 93 G11
Llangattock Powys 78 B2
Llangattock Lingoed Mon 97 G7
Llangattock nigh Usk Mon 78 D4
Llangattock-Vibon-Avel Mon 79 B7
Llangedwyn Powys 148 E3
Llangefni Anglesey 179 F7
Llangeinor Bridgend 58 B2
Llangeitho Ceredig 112 F2
Llangeler Carms 93 D7
Llangendeirne Carms 75 C7
Llangennech Carms 75 E9
Llangennith Swansea 56 C2
Llangenny Powys 78 B2
Llangernyw Conwy 164 B5
Llangeview Mon 78 E5
Llangewydd Court Bridgend 57 E11
Llangian Gwyn 144 D5
Llangloffan Pembs 91 E8
Llanglydwen Carms 92 F3
Llangoed Anglesey 179 F10
Llangoedmor Ceredig 92 B3
Llangollen Denb 166 G2
Llangolman Pembs 92 F2
Llangors Powys 96 F2
Llangorwen Ceredig 128 G2
Llangovan Mon 79 D7
Llangower Gwyn 147 C8
Llangrannog Ceredig 110 G6
Llangristiolus Anglesey 178 G6
Llangrove Hereford 79 B8
Llangua Mon 97 F7
Llangunllo Powys 114 C4
Llangunnor Carms 74 B6
Llangurig Powys 113 B8
Llangwm Conwy 165 G7
Llangwm Mon 78 E6
Llangwm Pembs 73 D7
Llangwnnadl Gwyn 144 C4
Llangwyfan Denb 165 B10
Llangwyfan-isaf Anglesey 162 B4
Llangwyllog Anglesey 178 F6
Llangwyryfon Ceredig 111 C11
Llangybi Ceredig 112 G2
Llangybi Gwyn 162 G6
Llangybi Mon 78 F5
Llangyfelach Swansea 56 B6
Llangyndeyrn Carms 75 C7
Llangynhafal Denb 165 C10
Llangynidr Powys 77 B11
Llangyniew Powys 130 B2
Llangynin Carms 74 B2
Llangynog Carms 74 B4
Llangynog Powys 147 D11
Llangynwyd Bridgend 57 D11
Llanhamlach Powys 95 F11
Llanharan Rhondda 58 C4
Llanharry Rhondda 58 C4
Llanhennock Mon 78 G5
Llanhilleth Bl Gwent 78 E2
Llanhowel Pembs 90 F6
Llanidloes Powys 129 G9
Llaniestyn Gwyn 144 C5
Llanifyny Powys 129 G7
Llanigon Powys 96 D4
Llanilar Ceredig 112 C2
Llanilid Rhondda 58 C3
Llanilltud Fawr = Llantwit Major V Glam 58 F3
Llanio Ceredig 112 F2
Llanion Pembs 73 E7
Llanishen Cardiff 59 C7
Llanishen Mon 79 E7
Llanllawddog Carms 93 F9
Llanllechid Gwyn 163 B10
Llanllowell Mon 78 F5
Llanllugan Powys 129 C11
Llanllwch Carms 74 B5
Llanllwchaiarn Powys 130 E2
Llanllwni Carms 93 D9
Llanllwyd Shrops 130 G3
Llanllyfni Gwyn 163 E7
Llanmadoc Swansea 56 C2
Llanmaes Cardiff 58 D6
Llanmaes V Glam 58 F3
Llanmartin Newport 59 B11
Llanmerwig Powys 130 E3
Llanmihangel V Glam 58 E3
Llanmiloe Carms 74 D3
Llanmorlais Swansea 56 C4
Llannefydd Conwy 181 G7
Llannerch-y-môr Flint 181 F11
Llannon Carms 75 D8
Llannor Gwyn 145 B7
Llanon Pembs 90 E6
Llanon = Llan-non Ceredig 111 D10
Llanover Mon 78 D4
Llanpumsaint Carms 93 F8
Llanreath Pembs 73 E7
Llanreithan Pembs 91 F7
Llanrhaeadr Denb 165 C9
Llanrhaeadr-ym-Mochnant Powys 148 D2
Llanrhian Pembs 90 E6
Llanrhidian Swansea 56 C3
Llanrhos Conwy 180 E3
Llanrhyddlad Anglesey 178 D4
Llanrhystud Ceredig 111 D10
Llanrosser Hereford 96 D5
Llanrothal Hereford 79 B7
Llanrug Gwyn 163 C8
Llanrumney Cardiff 59 C8
Llanrwst Conwy 164 C4
Llansadurnen Carms 74 C3
Llansadwrn Anglesey 179 F9
Llansadwrn Carms 94 E3
Llansaint Carms 74 D5
Llansamlet Swansea 57 B7
Llansanffraid Glan Conwy Conwy 180 F4
Llansannan Conwy 164 B6
Llansannor V Glam 58 D3
Llansantffraed Ceredig 111 D10
Llansantffraed Powys 96 G2
Llansantffraed Cwmdeuddwr Powys 113 D9
Llansantffraed-in-Elwel Powys 113 G11
Llansantffraid-ym-Mechain Powys 148 E4
Llansawel Carms 94 D2
Llansawel = Briton Ferry Neath 57 C8
Llansilin Powys 148 D4
Llansoy Mon 78 E6
Llanspyddid Powys 95 F10
Llanstadwell Pembs 72 D6
Llansteffan Carms 74 C5
Llanstephan Powys 96 C2
Llantarnam Torf 78 G4
Llanteems Mon 96 G6
Llanteg Pembs 73 C11
Llanthony Mon 96 F5
Llantilio Crossenny Mon 78 C5
Llantilio Pertholey Mon 78 B4
Llantood Pembs 92 C3
Llantrisant Anglesey 178 E5
Llantrisant Mon 78 F5
Llantrisant Rhondda 58 C4
Llantrithyd V Glam 58 E4
Llantwit Neath 57 B9
Llantwit Fardre Rhondda 58 B5
Llantwit Major = Llanilltud Fawr V Glam 58 F3
Llanuwchllyn Gwyn 147 C7
Llanvaches Newport 78 G6
Llanvair Discoed Mon 78 G6
Llanvapley Mon 78 C5
Llanvetherine Mon 78 B5
Llanveynoe Hereford 96 E6
Llanvihangel Crucorney Mon 96 G6
Llanvihangel Gobion Mon 78 D4
Llanvihangel-Ystern-Llewern Mon 78 C6
Llanwarne Hereford 97 F10
Llanwddyn Powys 147 F10
Llanwenarth Mon 78 C3
Llanwenog Ceredig 93 B9
Llanwern Newport 59 B11
Llanwinio Carms 92 F5
Llanwnda Gwyn 163 D7
Llanwnda Pembs 91 D8
Llanwnnen Ceredig 93 B10
Llanwnog Powys 129 E10
Llanwrda Carms 94 E4
Llanwrin Powys 128 C5
Llanwrthwl Powys 113 E9
Llanwrtud = Llanwrtyd Wells Powys 95 B7
Llanwrtyd Wells = Llanwrtud Powys 95 B7
Llanwyddelan Powys 129 C11
Llanyblodwel Shrops 148 E4
Llanybri Carms 74 C4
Llanybydder Carms 93 C10
Llanycefn Pembs 91 G11
Llanychaer Pembs 91 D9
Llanycil Gwyn 147 C8
Llanycrwys Carms 94 B2
Llanymawddwy Gwyn 147 F8
Llanymddyfri = Llandovery Carms 94 E5
Llanymynech Powys 148 E5
Llanynghenedl Anglesey 178 E4
Llanynys Denb 165 C10
Llanyrafon Torf 78 G4
Llanyre Powys 113 E10
Llanystumdwy Gwyn 145 B9
Llanywern Powys 96 F2
Llawhaden Pembs 73 B9
Llawnt Shrops 148 C5
Llawrdref Bellaf Gwyn 144 D5
Llawr-y-glyn Powys 129 E8
Llay Wrex 166 D4
Llechcynfarwy Anglesey 178 E5
Llecheiddior Gwyn 163 G7
Llechfaen Powys 95 F11
Llechfraith Gwyn 146 F3
Llechryd Caerph 77 D10
Llechryd Ceredig 92 C4
Llechrydau Powys 148 C4
Llechwedd Conwy 180 F3
Lledrod Ceredig 112 C2
Llenmerewig Powys 130 E3
Llethrid Swansea 56 C4
Llettyrychen Carms 75 E7
Llidiad Nenog Carms 93 D10
Llidiardau Gwyn 147 B7
Llidiart-y-parc Denb 165 G10
Llithfaen Gwyn 162 G5
Lloc Flint 181 F10
Llong Flint 166 C3
Llowes Powys 96 C3
Lloyney Powys 114 B4
Llugwy Powys 128 D4
Llundain-fach Ceredig 111 F11
Llwydarth Bridgend 57 C11
Llwydcoed Rhondda 77 E7
Llwyn Denb 165 C9
Llwyn Shrops 130 G5
Llwyn-derw Powys 129 G8
Llwyn-du Mon 78 B3
Llwyn-hendy Carms 56 B4
Llwyn-on Village M Tydf 77 C8
Llwyn-tg Carms 75 D9
Llwyn-y-brain Carms 73 C11
Llwyn-y-go Shrops 148 E6
Llwyn-y-groes Ceredig 111 F11
Llwyn-yr-hwrdd Pembs 92 E4
Llwyncelyn Ceredig 111 F8
Llwyndafydd Ceredig 111 F7
Llwynderw Powys 130 C4
Llwynduris Ceredig 92 C4
Llwyndyrys Gwyn 162 G5
Llwyneinion Wrex 166 F3
Llwyngwril Gwyn 110 B2
Llwynhendy Carms 56 B4
Llwynmawr Wrex 148 B4
Llwynygog Powys 129 E7
Llwynypia Rhondda 77 G7
Llynclys Shrops 148 E5
Llynfaes Anglesey 178 F6
Llys-y-frôn Pembs 91 G10
Llysfaen Conwy 180 F5
Llyswen Powys 96 D2
Llysworney V Glam 58 E3
Llywel Powys 95 E7
Llywernog Ceredig 128 G4
Load Brook S Yorks 186 D3
Loan Falk 279 F9
Loandhu Highld 301 B8
Loanend Northumb 273 E8
Loanhead Aberds 302 D6
Loanhead Midloth 270 B5
Loanhead Perth 286 D5
Loanreoch Highld 300 B6
Loans S Ayrs 257 C8
Loans of Tullich Highld 301 B8
Loansdean Northumb 252 G5
Lobb Devon 40 F3
Lobhillcross Devon 12 D5
Lobley Hill T & W 242 E6
Lobthorpe Lincs 155 E9
Loch a Charnain W Isles 297 G4
Loch a' Ghainmhich W Isles 304 F4
Loch Baghasdail W Isles 297 K3
Loch Choire Lodge Highld 308 F6
Loch Eil Highld 290 F2
Loch Euphoirt W Isles 296 E4
Loch Head Dumfries 236 E5
Loch Head Dumfries 245 E11
Loch Loyal Lodge Highld 308 E6
Loch nam Madadh W Isles 296 E5
Loch Sgioport W Isles 297 H4
Lochailort Highld 295 G9
Lochaline Highld 289 E8
Lochanhully Highld 301 G9
Lochans Dumfries 236 D2
Locharbriggs Dumfries 247 G11
Lochassynt Lodge Highld 307 G6
Lochavich Ho Argyll 275 B10
Lochawe Argyll 284 E5
Lochbuie Argyll 289 G8
Lochbuie Ho Argyll 289 G8
Lochcallater Lodge Aberds 292 E3
Lochcarron Highld 295 B10
Lochdhu Highld 310 E4
Lochdochart House Stirl 285 E8
Lochdon Argyll 289 F9
Lochdrum Highld 300 B2
Lochead Argyll 275 E11
Lochead Argyll 275 F8
Lochearnhead Stirl 285 E9
Lochee Dundee 287 D7
Lochend Edin 280 G5
Lochend Highld 300 F5
Lochend Highld 310 C6
Lochend Ho Stirl 277 B11
Locherben Dumfries 247 D11
Lochetive Ho Highld 284 C5
Lochfoot Dumfries 237 B10
Lochgair Argyll 275 D10
Lochgarthside Highld 291 B7
Lochgelly Fife 280 C3
Lochgilphead Argyll 275 E9
Lochgoilhead Argyll 284 G6
Lochhill Moray 302 C2
Lochhussie Highld 300 D4
Lochinch Castle Dumfries 236 C3
Lochindorb Lodge Highld 301 F9
Lochinver Highld 307 G5
Lochlane Perth 286 E2
Lochletter Highld 300 G4
Lochluichart Highld 300 C3
Lochmaben Dumfries 248 G3
Lochmore Cottage Highld 310 E4
Lochmore Lodge Highld 306 F7
Lochnell Ho Argyll 289 F10
Lochore Fife 280 B3
Lochorodale Argyll 255 F7
Lochportain W Isles 296 D5
Lochran Perth 280 B2
Lochranza N Ayrs 255 B10
Lochs Crofts Moray 302 C3
Lochside Aberds 293 G9
Lochside Highld 301 D8
Lochside Highld 308 D4
Lochside Highld 310 F2
Lochside S Ayrs 257 E8
Lochslin Highld 311 L2
Lochstack Lodge Highld 306 E7
Lochton Aberds 293 D9
Lochty Angus 293 G7
Lochty Fife 287 G9
Lochty Perth 286 E4
Lochuisge Highld 289 D9
Lochurr Dumfries 247 F7
Lochwinnoch Renfs 267 D7
Lochwood Dumfries 248 D3
Lochwood Glasgow 268 B3
Lochyside Highld 290 F3
Lockengate Corn 5 C10
Lockerbie Dumfries 248 G4
Lockeridge Wilts 62 F6
Lockeridge Dene Wilts 62 F6
Lockerley Hants 32 B3
Lockhills Cumb 230 B6
Locking N Som 43 B11
Locking Stumps Warr 183 C10
Lockinge Oxon 64 B2
Lockington E Yorks 208 D5
Lockington Leics 153 D9
Lockleaze Bristol 60 D6
Lockleywood Shrops 150 D3
Locks Heath Hants 33 F8
Locksbottom London 68 F2
Locksbrook Bath 61 G8
Locksgreen I o W 20 C4
Lockton N Yorks 226 G6
Lockwood W Yorks 196 D6
Loddington Leics 136 C5
Loddington Northants 120 B6
Loddiswell Devon 8 F4
Loddon Norf 143 D7
Loddon Ingloss Norf 142 D6
Lode Cambs 123 E10
Lode Heath W Mid 134 G3
Loders Dorset 16 C5
Lodge Green N Yorks 223 F9
Lodge Green W Mid 134 G5
Lodge Hill Corn 6 C4
Lodge Hill W Mid 133 G10
Lodge Hill W Yorks 197 C9
Lodge Lees Kent 55 D8
Lodge Moor S Yorks 186 D3
Lodge Park Worcs 117 D10
Lodgebank Shrops 149 D11
Lodsworth W Sus 34 C6
Lodsworth Common W Sus 34 C6
Lodway Bristol 60 D4
Lofthouse N Yorks 214 E2
Lofthouse W Yorks 197 B10
Lofthouse Gate W Yorks 197 C10
Loftus Redcar 226 B4
Logan E Ayrs 258 E3
Logan Mains Dumfries 236 E2
Loganlea W Loth 269 C9
Loggerheads Denb 165 C11

Log – Lub 345

Loggerheads Staffs 150 B4
Logie Argus 293 G8
Logie Fife 287 E8
Logie Moray 301 D10
Logie Coldstone Aberds 292 C6
Logie Hill Highld 301 B7
Logie Newton Aberds 302 F6
Logie Pert Angus 293 G8
Logiealmond Lodge Perth 286 D3
Logierait Perth 286 B3
Login Carms 92 G3
Logmore Green Sur 50 D6
Loidse Mhorsgail W Isles 304 F3
Lolworth Cambs 123 E7
Lomeshaye Lancs 204 F2
Lôn Gwyn 147 C7
Lon-las Swansea 57 B8
Lonbain Highld 298 D6
Londesborough E Yorks 208 D3
London Apprentice Corn 5 E10
London Beach Kent 53 F11
London Colney Herts 85 E11
London End Cambs 121 D11
London Fields W Mid 133 E8
London Minstead Hants 32 E3
Londonderry N Yorks 214 B6
Londonderry W Mid 133 F10
Londonthorpe Lincs 155 B9
Londubh Highld 307 L3
Lonemore Highld 299 B7
Lonemore Highld 309 L7
Long Ashton N Som 60 E5
Long Bank Worcs 116 C5
Long Bennington Lincs 172 G4
Long Bredy Dorset 17 C7
Long Buckby Northants 120 D2
Long Buckby Wharf Northants 120 D2
Long Clawson Leics 154 D4
Long Common Hants 33 E8
Long Compton Staffs 151 E7
Long Compton Warks 100 E5
Long Crendon Bucks 83 D11
Long Crichel Dorset 31 E7
Long Cross Wilts 45 G9
Long Dean Wilts 61 D11
Long Ditton Sur 67 F7
Long Drax N Yorks 199 B7
Long Duckmanton Derbys 186 G6
Long Eaton Derbys 153 C9
Long Gardens Essex 106 D6
Long Green Suff 125 B11
Long Green W Ches 183 G7
Long Green Worcs 98 E6
Long Hanborough Oxon 82 C6
Long Itchington Warks 119 D8
Long John's Hill Norf 142 B4
Long Lane Telford 150 F2
Long Lawford Warks 119 B9
Long Lee W Yorks 205 E7
Long Load Som 29 C7
Long Marston Herts 84 B5
Long Marston N Yorks 206 C6
Long Marston Warks 100 B3
Long Marton Cumb 231 G9
Long Meadow Cambs 123 E10
Long Meadowend Shrops 131 G8
Long Melford Suff 107 B7
Long Newton Glos 80 G6
Long Newton E Loth 271 C10
Long Oak Shrops 149 E7
Long Park Hants 48 G2
Long Preston N Yorks 204 B2
Long Riston E Yorks 209 E8
Long Sandall S Yorks 198 F6
Long Sight Gtr Man 196 F2
Long Stratton Norf 142 E3
Long Street M Keynes 102 B5
Long Sutton Hants 49 D8
Long Sutton Lincs 157 E8
Long Sutton Som 29 B7
Long Thurlow Suff 125 D10
Long Whatton Leics 153 E9
Long Wittenham Oxon 83 G8
Longbar N Ayrs 266 E6
Longbarn Warr 183 C10
Longbenton T & W 243 D7
Longborough Glos 100 F3
Longbridge Plym 7 D10
Longbridge W Mid 117 B10
Longbridge Warks 118 E5
Longbridge Deverill Wilts 45 E11
Longbridge Hayes Stoke 168 E5
Longbridgemuir Dumfries 238 D3
Longburgh Cumb 239 F8
Longburton Dorset 29 E11
Longcause Devon 8 C5
Longcliffe Derbys 170 D2
Longcot Oxon 82 G3
Longcroft Cumb 238 F6
Longcroft Falk 278 F5
Longcross Devon 12 F4
Longcross Sur 66 F3
Longdale Cumb 222 D2
Longdales Cumb 230 C6
Longden Shrops 131 B8
Longden Common Shrops 131 C8
Longdon Staffs 151 G11
Longdon Worcs 98 D6
Longdon Green Staffs 151 G11
Longdon Heath Worcs 98 D6
Longdon Hill End Worcs 98 D6
Longdon on Tern Telford 150 F2
Longdown Devon 14 C3
Longdowns Corn 2 C6
Longdrum Angus 292 G4
Longfield Kent 68 F6
Longfield Shetland 313 M5
Longfield Wilts 45 B11
Longfield Hill Kent 68 F6
Longfleet Poole 18 C6
Longford Derbys 152 B4
Longford Glos 98 G6
Longford Kent 52 B4
Longford London 66 D4
Longford Shrops 150 C2
Longford Telford 150 F4
Longford W Mid 135 G7
Longford Warr 183 C10
Longfordlane Derbys 152 B4
Longforgan Perth 287 E7
Longformacus Borders 272 D3
Longframlington Northumb 252 C4
Longham Dorset 19 B7
Longham Norf 159 F8
Longhaven Aberds 303 F11
Longhedge Wilts 45 E10
Longhill Aberds 303 D9
Longhirst Northumb 252 F6
Longhope Glos 79 B11
Longhope Orkney 314 G3
Longhorsley Northumb 252 E4
Longhoughton Northumb 264 G6
Longhouse Bath 61 G8
Longlands Cumb 229 D11
Longlands London 68 E2
Longlane Derbys 152 B5
Longlane W Berks 64 E3
Longlevens Glos 99 G7
Longley W Yorks 196 C5
Longley W Yorks 196 F6
Longley Estate S Yorks 186 C5
Longley Green Worcs 116 G4
Longleys Perth 286 C6
Longmanhill Aberds 303 C7
Longmoor Camp Hants 49 G9
Longmorn Moray 302 D2
Longmoss E Ches 184 G5
Longnewton Borders 262 D3
Longnewton Stockton 225 B7
Longney Glos 80 C3
Longniddry E Loth 281 F8
Longnor Shrops 131 C9
Longnor Staffs 151 G7
Longnor Staffs 169 C9
Longnor Park Shrops 131 C9
Longparish Hants 48 E2
Longpark Cumb 239 E10
Longpark E Ayrs 257 B10
Longport Stoke 168 F5
Longridge Glos 80 D5
Longridge Lancs 203 F8
Longridge Staffs 151 F8
Longridge W Loth 269 C9
Longridge End Glos 98 G6
Longrigg N Lnrk 278 G6
Longriggend N Lnrk 278 G6
Longrock Corn 1 C5
Longscales N Yorks 205 B10
Longsdon Staffs 169 E7
Longshaw Gtr Man 194 G4
Longshaw Staffs 169 F9
Longside Aberds 303 E10
Longsight Gtr Man 184 B5
Longslow Shrops 150 B3
Longsowerby Cumb 239 G9
Longstanton Cambs 123 D7
Longstock Hants 47 F11
Longstone Corn 2 B2
Longstone Corn 11 G7
Longstone Edin 280 G4
Longstone Pembs 73 D10
Longstone Som 28 B5
Longstowe Cambs 122 G6
Longstreet Wilts 46 C6
Longthorpe P'boro 138 D3
Longthwaite Cumb 230 G4
Longton Lancs 194 B3
Longton Stoke 168 G6
Longtown Cumb 239 D9
Longtown Hereford 96 F6
Longtownmail Orkney 314 F4
Longview Mers 182 C6
Longville in the Dale Shrops 131 E10
Longway Bank Derbys 170 E4
Longwell Green S Glos 61 E7
Longwick Bucks 84 D3
Longwitton Northumb 252 F3
Longwood Shrops 132 B2
Longwood W Yorks 196 D6
Longwood Edge W Yorks 196 D6
Longworth Oxon 82 F5
Longyester E Loth 271 B10
Lonmay Aberds 303 D10
Lonmore Highld 298 E2
Looe Corn 6 E5
Looe Mills Corn 6 C4
Loose Kent 53 C9
Loose Hill Kent 53 C9
Loosegate Lincs 156 D6
Loosley Row Bucks 84 E4
Lopcombe Corner Wilts 47 F9
Lopen Som 28 E6
Lopen Head Som 28 E6
Loppergarth Cumb 210 D5
Loppington Shrops 149 D9
Lopwell Devon 7 C9
Lorbottle Northumb 252 B2
Lorbottle Hall Northumb 252 B2
Lord's Hill Soton 32 D5
Lords Wood Medway 69 G9
Lordsbridge Norf 157 G11
Lordshill Common Sur 50 E4
Lordswood Soton 32 D6
Lornty Perth 286 C5
Loscoe Derbys 170 F6
Loscoe W Yorks 198 C2
Loscombe Dorset 16 B6
Losgaintir W Isles 305 J2
Lossiemouth Moray 302 B2
Lossit Argyll 254 B2
Lossit Lodge Argyll 274 G5
Lostford Shrops 150 C2
Lostock Gtr Man 195 F7
Lostock Gralam W Ches 183 F11
Lostock Green W Ches 183 G11
Lostock Hall Lancs 194 B4
Lostock Junction Gtr Man 195 F7
Lostwithiel Corn 6 D2
Loth Orkney 314 C6
Lothbeg Highld 311 H3
Lothersdale N Yorks 204 D5
Lothianbridge Midloth 270 C6
Lothmore Highld 311 H3
Lottisham Som 44 G5
Loudwater Bucks 84 G6
Loudwater Herts 85 F9
Loughborough Leics 153 F10
Loughor Swansea 56 B5
Loughton Essex 86 F6
Loughton M Keynes 102 D6
Loughton Shrops 132 G2
Lound Lincs 155 F11
Lound Notts 187 D11
Lound Suff 143 D10
Loundsley Green Derbys 186 G5
Lount Leics 153 F7
Lour Angus 287 C8
Louth Lincs 190 D4
Lovat Highld 300 E5
Lovaton Devon 7 B10
Love Clough Lancs 195 B10
Love Green Bucks 66 C4
Lovedean Hants 33 E11
Lover Wilts 32 C2
Loversall S Yorks 187 B9
Loves Green Essex 87 E10
Lovesome Hill N Yorks 225 F7
Loveston Pembs 73 D9
Lovington Som 44 G5
Low Ackworth W Yorks 198 D3
Low Alwinton Northumb 251 B10
Low Angerton Northumb 252 G3
Low Barlings Lincs 189 G9
Low Barugh S Yorks 197 F10
Low Bentham N Yorks 212 F2
Low Biggins Cumb 212 D2
Low Blantyre S Lnrk 268 D3
Low Borrowbridge Cumb 222 E2
Low Bradfield S Yorks 186 C3
Low Bradley N Yorks 204 D6
Low Braithwaite Cumb 230 C4
Low Bridge Wilts 62 E3
Low Brunton Northumb 241 C10
Low Burnham N Lincs 199 G9
Low Burton N Yorks 214 C4
Low Buston Northumb 252 B6
Low Catton E Yorks 207 C10
Low Clanyard Dumfries 236 F3
Low Common Norf 142 E2
Low Compton Gtr Man 196 F2
Low Coniscliffe Darl 224 C5
Low Cotehill Cumb 239 G11
Low Coylton S Ayrs 257 F10
Low Crosby Cumb 239 F10
Low Dalby N Yorks 217 B7
Low Dinsdale Darl 224 C6
Low Eighton T & W 243 F7
Low Ellington N Yorks 214 C4
Low Etherley Durham 233 F9
Low Fell T & W 243 F7
Low Fold W Yorks 205 F10
Low Fulney Lincs 156 E5
Low Garth N Yorks 226 D4
Low Gate N Yorks 214 F5
Low Gate Northumb 241 E10
Low Geltbridge Cumb 240 F2
Low Grantley N Yorks 214 E4
Low Green N Yorks 205 B10
Low Green Suff 125 E7
Low Green W Yorks 205 F10
Low Greenside T & W 242 E4
Low Habberley Worcs 116 B6
Low Ham Som 28 B6
Low Hauxley Northumb 253 C7
Low Hawsker N Yorks 227 D8
Low Hesket Cumb 230 B5
Low Hesleyhurst Northumb 252 D3
Low Hill W Mid 133 C8
Low Hutton N Yorks 216 F5
Low Knipe Cumb 230 G6
Low Laithe N Yorks 214 G3
Low Laithes S Yorks 197 G11
Low Leighton Derbys 185 D8
Low Lorton Cumb 229 F9
Low Marishes N Yorks 216 D6
Low Marnham Notts 172 B4
Low Mill N Yorks 226 F3
Low Moor Lancs 203 E10
Low Moor W Yorks 197 B7
Low Moorsley T & W 234 B2
Low Moresby Cumb 228 G5
Low Newton Cumb 211 C8
Low Newton-by-the-Sea Northumb 264 E6
Low Prudhoe Northumb 242 E4
Low Risby N Lincs 200 E2
Low Row Cumb 229 C9
Low Row Cumb 240 E3
Low Row N Yorks 223 F9
Low Salchrie Dumfries 236 C2
Low Smerby Argyll 255 E8
Low Snaygill N Yorks 204 D5
Low Street Norf 141 B10
Low Street Thurrock 69 D7
Low Tharston Norf 142 D3
Low Thornley T & W 242 E5
Low Torry Fife 279 D10
Low Town Shrops 132 E4
Low Toynton Lincs 190 G3
Low Valley S Yorks 198 G2
Low Valleyfield Fife 279 D10
Low Walton Cumb 219 C9
Low Waters S Lnrk 268 E4
Low Westwood Durham 242 F4
Low Whinnow Cumb 239 G8
Low Whita N Yorks 223 F10
Low Wood Cumb 210 C6
Low Worsall N Yorks 225 C7
Low Wray Cumb 221 E7
Lowbands Glos 98 E5
Lowbridge House Cumb 221 E10
Lowca Cumb 228 G5
Lowcross Hill W Ches 167 E7
Lowdham Notts 171 F11
Lowe Shrops 149 C10
Lowe Hill Staffs 169 D7
Lowedges S Yorks 186 E4
Lower Achachenna Argyll 284 E4
Lower Aisholt Som 43 F8
Lower Allscot Shrops 132 D4
Lower Altofts W Yorks 197 C11
Lower Amble Corn 10 G5
Lower Ansty Dorset 30 G3
Lower Ardtun Argyll 288 G5
Lower Arncott Oxon 83 B10
Lower Ashtead Sur 51 B7
Lower Ashton Devon 14 E2
Lower Assendon Oxon 65 C8
Lower Badcall Highld 306 E6
Lower Ballam Lancs 202 G3
Lower Bartle Lancs 202 G5
Lower Basildon W Berks 64 D6
Lower Bassingthorpe Lincs 155 D9
Lower Bearwood Hereford 115 F7
Lower Bebington Mers 182 E4
Lower Beeding W Sus 36 B2
Lower Benefield Northants 137 F9
Lower Bentley Worcs 117 D9
Lower Beobridge Shrops 132 E5
Lower Berry Hill Glos 79 C9
Lower Binton Warks 118 G2
Lower Birchwood Derbys 170 E6
Lower Bitchet Kent 52 C5
Lower Blandford St Mary Dorset 30 F5
Lower Blunsdon Swindon 81 G10
Lower Bobbingworth Green Essex 87 D8
Lower Bockhampton Dorset 17 C10
Lower Boddington Northants 119 G9
Lower Bodham Norf 160 B2
Lower Bodinnar Corn 1 C4
Lower Bois Bucks 85 E7
Lower Bordean Hants 33 C11
Lower Boscaswell Corn 1 C3
Lower Bourne Sur 49 E10
Lower Bradley W Mid 133 D9
Lower Brailes Warks 100 D6
Lower Breakish Highld 295 C8
Lower Bredbury Gtr Man 184 C6
Lower Breinton Hereford 97 D9
Lower Broadheath Worcs 116 F6
Lower Brook Hants 32 B4
Lower Broughton Gtr Man 184 B4
Lower Brynamman Neath 76 C2
Lower Brynn Corn 5 C9
Lower Buckenhill Hereford 98 E2
Lower Buckland Hants 20 B2
Lower Bullingham Hereford 97 D10
Lower Bullington Hants 48 E3
Lower Bunbury E Ches 167 D9
Lower Burgate Hants 31 D11
Lower Burrow Som 28 C6
Lower Burton Hereford 115 F8
Lower Bush Medway 69 F7
Lower Cadsden Bucks 84 E4
Lower Caldecote C Beds 104 B3
Lower Cam Glos 80 E2
Lower Canada N Som 43 B11
Lower Carden W Ches 167 E7
Lower Catesby Northants 119 F10
Lower Cator Devon 13 F9
Lower Caversham Reading 65 E8
Lower Chapel Powys 95 D10
Lower Chedworth Glos 81 C9
Lower Cheriton Devon 27 G10
Lower Chicksgrove Wilts 46 G3
Lower Chute Wilts 47 C10
Lower Clapton London 67 B11
Lower Clent Worcs 117 B8
Lower Clicker Corn 6 C5
Lower Clopton Warks 118 F3
Lower Common Hants 48 E6
Lower Common Hants 65 G9
Lower Common Mon 78 B2
Lower Common Mon 78 E4
Lower Common Shrops 131 B9
Lower Copthurst Lancs 194 C5
Lower Cotburn Aberds 303 D7
Lower Cousley Wood E Sus 53 G7
Lower Cox Street Kent 69 G10
Lower Cragabus Argyll 254 C4
Lower Creedy Devon 26 G4
Lower Croan Corn 10 G6
Lower Crossings Derbys 185 E8
Lower Cumberworth W Yorks 197 F8
Lower Cwm-twrch Powys 76 C3
Lower Daggons Hants 31 E9
Lower Darwen Blkburn 195 B7
Lower Dean Beds 121 D11
Lower Dean Devon 8 C4
Lower Dell Highld 292 B2
Lower Denby W Yorks 197 F8
Lower Denzell Corn 5 B7
Lower Deuchries Aberds 302 D6
Lower Diabaig Highld 299 C7
Lower Dicker E Sus 23 C9
Lower Dinchope Shrops 131 G9
Lower Dowdeswell Glos 81 B8
Lower Down Shrops 130 G6
Lower Drift Corn 1 D4
Lower Dunsforth N Yorks 215 G8
Lower Durston Som 28 B3
Lower Earley Wokingham 65 E9
Lower East Carleton Norf 142 C3
Lower Eastern Green W Mid 118 B5
Lower Edmonton London 86 G4
Lower Egleton Hereford 98 B2
Lower Elkstone Staffs 169 D9
Lower Ellastone Staffs 169 G10
Lower End Bucks 83 D11
Lower End Bucks 102 E4
Lower End C Beds 103 D8
Lower End C Beds 103 G9
Lower End Glos 81 E7
Lower End Northants 120 F6
Lower End Northants 120 G5
Lower End Northants 121 E7
Lower End Oxon 82 B4
Lower Everleigh Wilts 47 C7
Lower Eythorne Kent 55 D9
Lower Failand N Som 60 E4
Lower Faintree Shrops 132 F3
Lower Falkenham Suff 108 D5
Lower Farringdon Hants 49 F8
Lower Feltham London 66 E5
Lower Fittleworth W Sus 35 D8
Lower Forge Shrops 132 F4
Lower Foxdale I o M 192 E3
Lower Frankton Shrops 149 C7
Lower Freystrop Pembs 73 C7
Lower Froyle Hants 49 E9
Lower Gabwell Devon 9 B8
Lower Gledfield Highld 309 K5
Lower Godney Som 44 E3
Lower Goldstone Kent 71 G9
Lower Gornal W Mid 133 E8
Lower Grange W Yorks 205 G8
Lower Gravenhurst C Beds 104 D2
Lower Green Essex 88 E2
Lower Green Essex 105 E8
Lower Green Essex 106 E4
Lower Green Gtr Man 184 B2
Lower Green Herts 104 E3
Lower Green Kent 52 E5
Lower Green Kent 52 E6
Lower Green Norf 159 B9
Lower Green Staffs 133 B8
Lower Green Suff 124 D4
Lower Green Sur 66 F6
Lower Green W Berks 63 G11
Lower Green Warks 119 D10
Lower Grove Common Hereford 97 F11
Lower Hacheston Suff 126 F6
Lower Halistra Highld 298 D2
Lower Halliford Sur 66 F5
Lower Halstock Leigh Dorset 29 F8
Lower Halstow Kent 69 F11
Lower Hamswell S Glos 61 E8
Lower Hamworthy Poole 18 C6
Lower Hardres Kent 55 C7
Lower Hardwick Hereford 115 F8
Lower Harpton Powys 114 E5
Lower Hartlip Kent 69 G10
Lower Hartshay Derbys 170 E5
Lower Hartwell Bucks 84 C3
Lower Hatton Staffs 150 B6
Lower Hawthwaite Cumb 210 B4
Lower Haysden Kent 52 D5
Lower Hayton Shrops 131 G10
Lower Hazel S Glos 60 B6
Lower Heath E Ches 168 C5
Lower Hempriggs Moray 301 C11
Lower Heppington Kent 54 C6
Lower Hergest Hereford 114 F5
Lower Herne Kent 71 F7
Lower Heyford Oxon 101 G9
Lower Heysham Lancs 211 G8
Lower Higham Kent 69 E8
Lower Highmoor Oxon 65 B8
Lower Holbrook Suff 108 E3
Lower Holditch Dorset 28 G4
Lower Holloway London 67 B10
Lower Holwell Dorset 31 E9
Lower Hook Worcs 98 C6
Lower Hookner Devon 13 E10
Lower Hopton Shrops 149 E7
Lower Hopton W Yorks 197 D7
Lower Hordley Shrops 149 D7
Lower Horncroft W Sus 35 D8
Lower Horsebridge E Sus 23 C9
Lower House Halton 183 D8
Lower Houses W Yorks 197 D7
Lower Howsell Worcs 98 B5
Lower Illey Worcs 133 G9
Lower Island Kent 70 F6
Lower Kersal Gtr Man 195 G10
Lower Kilburn Derbys 170 F5
Lower Kilcott Glos 61 B9
Lower Killeyan Argyll 254 C3
Lower Kingcombe Dorset 17 B7
Lower Kingswood Sur 51 C8
Lower Kinnerton W Ches 166 C4
Lower Kinsham Hereford 115 E7
Lower Knapp Som 28 B4
Lower Knightley Staffs 150 E6
Lower Knowle Bristol 60 E5
Lower Langford N Som 60 G3
Lower Largo Fife 287 G8
Lower Layham Suff 107 C10
Lower Ledwyche Shrops 115 C10
Lower Leigh Staffs 151 B10
Lower Lemington Glos 100 E4
Lower Lenie Highld 300 G5
Lower Lode Glos 99 E7
Lower Lovacott Devon 25 B8
Lower Loxhore Devon 40 F6
Lower Lydbrook Glos 79 B9
Lower Lye Hereford 115 D8
Lower Machen Newport 59 B8
Lower Maes-coed Hereford 96 E6
Lower Mains Clack 279 B9
Lower Mannington Dorset 31 F9
Lower Marsh Som 30 C2
Lower Marston Som 45 E9
Lower Meend Glos 79 E9
Lower Menadue Corn 5 D10
Lower Merridge Som 43 G8
Lower Mickletown W Yorks 198 B2
Lower Middleton Cheney Northants 101 C10
Lower Midway Derbys 152 E6
Lower Mill Corn 3 B10
Lower Milovaig Highld 296 F7
Lower Milton Som 44 D4
Lower Moor Wilts 81 G8
Lower Moor Worcs 99 B9
Lower Morton S Glos 79 G10
Lower Mountain Flint 166 D4
Lower Nazeing Essex 86 D5
Lower Netchwood Shrops 132 E2
Lower Netherton Devon 14 G3
Lower New Inn Torf 78 F4
Lower Ninnes Corn 1 C5
Lower Nobut Staffs 151 C10
Lower North Dean Bucks 84 F5
Lower Norton Warks 118 E4
Lower Nyland Dorset 30 C2
Lower Ochrwyth Caerph 59 B8
Lower Odcombe Som 29 D8
Lower Oddington Glos 100 F4
Lower Ollach Highld 295 B7
Lower Padworth W Berks 64 F6
Lower Penarth V Glam 59 F7
Lower Penn Staffs 133 D7
Lower Pennington Hants 20 C2
Lower Penwortham Lancs 194 B4
Lower Peover W Ches 184 G2
Lower Pexhill E Ches 184 G5
Lower Pilsley Derbys 170 C6
Lower Pitkerrie Highld 311 L2
Lower Place Gtr Man 196 E2
Lower Place London 67 C8
Lower Pollicot Bucks 84 C2
Lower Porthkerry V Glam 58 F5
Lower Porthpean Corn 5 E10
Lower Quinton Warks 100 B3
Lower Rabber Hereford 114 G5
Lower Race Torf 78 E3
Lower Radley Oxon 83 F8
Lower Rainham Medway 69 F10
Lower Ratley Hants 32 C4
Lower Raydon Suff 107 D10
Lower Rea Glos 80 B4
Lower Ridge Devon 28 G2
Lower Ridge Shrops 148 C6
Lower Roadwater Som 42 F4
Lower Rochford Worcs 116 D2
Lower Rose Corn 4 E5
Lower Row Dorset 31 G8
Lower Sapey Worcs 116 E3
Lower Seagry Wilts 62 C3
Lower Sheering Essex 87 C7
Lower Shelton C Beds 103 C9
Lower Shiplake Oxon 65 D9
Lower Shuckburgh Warks 119 E9
Lower Skelty Swansea 56 C6
Lower Slackstead Hants 32 B5
Lower Slade Devon 40 D4
Lower Slaughter Glos 100 G3
Lower Solva Pembs 87 G11
Lower Soothill W Yorks 197 C9
Lower Soudley Glos 79 D11
Lower Southfield Hereford 98 C3
Lower Stanton St Quintin Wilts 62 C2
Lower Stoke Medway 69 D10
Lower Stoke W Mid 119 B7
Lower Stondon C Beds 104 D3
Lower Stone Glos 79 G11
Lower Stonnall Staffs 133 C11
Lower Stow Bedon Norf 141 E9
Lower Stratton Som 28 D6
Lower Stratton Swindon 63 B7
Lower Street E Sus 38 E2
Lower Street Norf 160 B5
Lower Street Norf 160 C3
Lower Street Norf 160 F6
Lower Street Suff 108 E3
Lower Street Suff 124 G5
Lower Strensham Worcs 99 C8
Lower Stretton Warr 183 E10
Lower Studley Wilts 45 B11
Lower Sundon C Beds 103 F10
Lower Swainswick Bath 61 F9
Lower Swanwick Hants 33 F7
Lower Swell Glos 100 F3
Lower Sydenham London 67 E11
Lower Tadmarton Oxon 101 D8
Lower Tale Devon 27 G9
Lower Tasburgh Norf 142 D3
Lower Tean Staffs 151 B10
Lower Thorpe Northants 101 B10
Lower Threapwood Wrex 166 G6
Lower Thurlton Norf 143 D8
Lower Thurnham Lancs 202 C5
Lower Thurvaston Derbys 152 B4
Lower Todding Hereford 115 B8
Lower Tote Highld 298 C5
Lower Town Devon 27 E8
Lower Town Hereford 98 C2
Lower Town Pembs 91 D9
Lower Town W Yorks 204 G6
Lower Town Worcs 117 F7
Lower Trebullett Corn 12 F2
Lower Tregunnon Corn 11 E10
Lower Treworrick Corn 6 B4
Lower Tuffley Glos 80 C4
Lower Turmer Hants 31 F10
Lower Twitchen Devon 24 D5
Lower Twydall Medway 69 F10
Lower Tysoe Warks 100 B6
Lower Upham Hants 33 D8
Lower Upnor Medway 69 E9
Lower Vexford Som 42 F6
Lower Wainhill Oxon 84 E3
Lower Walton Warr 183 D10
Lower Wanborough Swindon 63 C8
Lower Weacombe Som 42 E6
Lower Weald M Keynes 102 D5
Lower Wear Devon 14 D4
Lower Weare Som 44 C2
Lower Weedon Northants 120 F2
Lower Welson Hereford 114 G5
Lower Westholme Som 44 E5
Lower Westhouse N Yorks 212 E3
Lower Westmancote Worcs 99 D8
Lower Weston Bath 61 F8
Lower Whatcombe Dorset 30 G4
Lower Whatley Som 45 D8
Lower Whitley W Ches 183 F10
Lower Wick Glos 80 F2
Lower Wick Worcs 116 G6
Lower Wield Hants 48 E6
Lower Willingdon E Sus 23 E9
Lower Winchendon or Nether Winchendon Bucks 84 C2
Lower Withington E Ches 168 B4
Lower Wolverton Worcs 117 G8
Lower Woodend Aberds 293 B8
Lower Woodend Bucks 65 B10
Lower Woodford Wilts 46 G6
Lower Woodley Corn 5 B10
Lower Woodside Herts 86 D2
Lower Woolston Som 29 B11
Lower Woon Corn 5 C10
Lower Wraxall Dorset 29 G9
Lower Wraxall Som 44 F6
Lower Wraxall Wilts 61 G10
Lower Wych W Ches 167 G7
Lower Wyche Worcs 98 C5
Lower Wyke W Yorks 197 B7
Lower Yelland Devon 40 G3
Lower Zeals Wilts 45 G9
Lowerford Lancs 204 F3
Lowerhouse E Ches 184 F6
Lowerhouse Lancs 204 G2
Lowertown Corn 2 D5
Lowertown Corn 5 C11
Lowertown Devon 12 E5
Lowes Barn Durham 233 C11
Lowesby Leics 136 B4
Lowestoft Suff 143 E10
Loweswater Cumb 229 G8
Lowfield S Yorks 186 D5
Lowfield Heath W Sus 51 E9
Lowford Hants 33 E7
Lowgill Cumb 222 F2
Lowgill Lancs 212 G3
Lowick Cumb 210 B5
Lowick Northants 137 G9
Lowick Northumb 264 B2
Lowick Bridge Cumb 210 B5
Lowick Green Cumb 210 B5
Lowlands Torf 78 F3
Lowmoor Row Cumb 231 F8
Lowna N Yorks 226 G3
Lownie Moor Angus 287 C8
Lowood Borders 262 B2
Lowsonford Warks 118 D3
Lowther Cumb 230 G6
Lowthertown Dumfries 238 D6
Lowtherville I o W 21 F7
Lowthorpe E Yorks 217 G11
Lowton Gtr Man 183 B10
Lowton Som 27 D11
Lowton Common Gtr Man 183 B10
Lowton Heath Gtr Man 183 B10
Lowton St Mary's Gtr Man 183 B10
Loxbeare Devon 26 D6
Loxford London 68 B2
Loxhill Sur 50 F4
Loxhore Devon 40 F6
Loxhore Cott Devon 40 F6
Loxley S Yorks 186 D4
Loxley Warks 118 G5
Loxley Green Staffs 151 C11
Loxter Hereford 98 C4
Loxton N Som 43 B11
Loxwood W Sus 50 G4
Loyter's Green Essex 87 C8
Loyterton Kent 70 G3
Lozells W Mid 133 F11
Lubachlaggan Highld 300 B3
Lubachoinnich Highld 309 K4
Lubberland Shrops 116 B2
Lubcroy Highld 309 J3
Lubenham Leics 136 F4
Lubinvullin Highld 308 C5

346 Luc – Mar

Lucas End Herts 86 E4
Lucas Green Lancs 194 C5
Lucas Green Sur 50 B2
Luccombe Som 42 E2
Luccombe Village I o W 21 F7
Lucker Northumb 264 C5
Luckett Corn 12 G3
Lucking Street Essex 106 E6
Luckington Wilts 61 C10
Lucklawhill Fife 287 E8
Luckwell Bridge Som 42 F2
Lucton Hereford 115 E8
Ludag W Isles 297 K3
Ludborough Lincs 190 B3
Ludbrook Devon 8 E3
Ludchurch Pembs 73 C10
Luddenden W Yorks 196 B4
Luddenden Foot W Yorks 196 C4
Ludderburn Cumb 221 G8
Luddesdown Kent 69 F7
Luddington N Lincs 199 D10
Luddington Warks 118 G3
Luddington in the Brook Northants 138 G2
Lude House Perth 291 G10
Ludford Lincs 190 D2
Ludford Shrops 115 C10
Ludgershall Bucks 83 B11
Ludgershall Wilts 47 C9
Ludgvan Corn 2 C2
Ludham Norf 161 F7
Ludlow Shrops 115 C10
Ludney Lincs 190 B5
Ludney Som 28 E5
Ludstock Hereford 98 D3
Ludstone Shrops 132 E6
Ludwell Wilts 30 C6
Ludworth Durham 234 C3
Luffenhall Herts 104 F5
Luffincott Devon 12 C2
Lufton Som 29 D8
Lugar E Ayrs 258 E3
Lugate Borders 271 G8
Lugg Green Hereford 115 E9
Luggate Burn E Loth 282 G2
Luggiebank N Lnrk 278 G5
Lugsdale Halton 183 D8
Lugton E Ayrs 267 E8
Lugwardine Hereford 97 C11
Luib Highld 295 C7
Luibeilt Highld 290 G4
Lulham Hereford 97 C8
Lullenden Sur 52 E2
Lullington Derbys 152 G5
Lullington Som 45 C9
Lulsgate Bottom N Som 60 F4
Lulsley Worcs 116 F4
Lulworth Camp Dorset 18 E2
Lumb Lancs 195 C10
Lumb Lancs 195 D9
Lumb W Yorks 196 C4
Lumb W Yorks 197 E7
Lumb Foot W Yorks 204 F6
Lumburn Devon 12 G5
Lumbutts W Yorks 196 C3
Lumby N Yorks 206 G5
Lumley W Sus 22 B3
Lumley Thicks Durham 243 G8
Lumloch E Dunb 268 B2
Lumphanan Aberds 293 C7
Lumphinnans Fife 280 C3
Lumsdaine Borders 273 B7
Lumsden Aberds 302 G4
Lunan Angus 287 B10
Lunanhead Angus 287 B8
Luncarty Perth 286 E4
Lund E Yorks 208 D5
Lund N Yorks 207 G9
Lund Shetland 312 C7
Lundal W Isles 304 E3
Lundavra Highld 290 G2
Lunderton Aberds 303 E11
Lundie Angus 286 D6
Lundie Highld 290 B3
Lundin Links Fife 287 G8
Lundwood S Yorks 197 F11
Lundy Green Norf 142 E4
Lunga Argyll 275 C8
Lunna Shetland 312 G6
Lunning Shetland 312 G7
Lunnister Shetland 312 F5
Lunnon Swansea 56 D4
Lunsford Kent 53 B7
Lunsford's Cross E Sus 38 E2
Lunt Mers 193 G10
Luntley Hereford 115 F7
Lunts Heath Halton 183 D8
Lupin Staffs 152 F2
Luppitt Devon 27 F11
Lupridge Devon 8 E4
Lupset W Yorks 197 D10
Lupton Cumb 211 C11
Lurg Aberds 293 C8
Lurgashall W Sus 34 B6
Lurignich Argyll 289 D11
Lurley Devon 26 E6
Lusby Lincs 174 B4
Luscott Shrops 131 D11
Luson Devon 8 F2
Luss Argyll 277 C7
Lussagiven Argyll 275 E7
Lusta Highld 298 D2
Lustleigh Devon 13 E11
Lustleigh Cleave Devon 13 E11
Luston Hereford 115 E9
Lusty Som 45 G7
Luthermuir Aberds 293 G8
Luthrie Fife 287 F7
Lutley W Mid 133 G8
Luton Devon 14 F4
Luton Devon 27 G9
Luton Luton 103 G11
Luton Medway 69 F9
Lutsford Devon 24 D3
Lutterworth Leics 135 G10
Lutton Devon 7 D11
Lutton Devon 8 C3
Lutton Lincs 157 D8
Lutton Northants 138 F2
Lutton Gowts Lincs 157 E8
Lutworthy Devon 26 D3
Luxborough Som 42 F3
Luxley Glos 98 G3
Luxted London 68 G2
Luxton Devon 28 E2
Luxulyan Corn 5 D11
Luzley Gtr Man 196 G3
Luzley Brook Gtr Man 196 F2
Lyatts Som 29 E8
Lybster Highld 310 F6
Lydbury North Shrops 131 F7
Lydcott Devon 41 F7
Lydd Kent 39 C8
Lydd on Sea Kent 39 C9
Lydden Kent 55 D9
Lydden Kent 71 F11
Lyddington Rutland 137 D7
Lyde Orkney 314 E3
Lyde Shrops 130 C6
Lyde Cross Hereford 97 C10
Lyde Green Hants 49 B8
Lyde Green S Glos 61 D7
Lydeard St Lawrence Som 42 G6
Lydford Devon 12 E6
Lydford Fair Place Som 44 G5
Lydford-on-Fosse Som 44 G5
Lydgate Derbys 186 F4
Lydgate Gtr Man 196 G3
Lydgate W Yorks 196 B2
Lydham Shrops 130 E6
Lydiard Green Wilts 62 B5
Lydiard Millicent Wilts 62 B5
Lydiard Plain Wilts 62 B5
Lydiard Tregoze Swindon 62 C6
Lydiate Mers 193 G11
Lydiate Ash Worcs 117 B9
Lydlinch Dorset 30 E2
Lydmarsh Som 28 F5
Lydney Glos 79 E10
Lydstep Pembs 73 F9
Lye W Mid 133 G8
Lye Cross N Som 60 G3
Lye Green Bucks 85 E7
Lye Green E Sus 52 G4
Lye Green Warks 118 D3
Lye Green Wilts 45 B10
Lye Head Worcs 116 C5
Lye Hole N Som 60 G4
Lyewood Common E Sus 52 F4
Lyford Oxon 82 G5
Lymbridge Green Kent 54 E6
Lyme Green E Ches 184 G6
Lyme Regis Dorset 16 C2
Lymiecleuch Borders 249 C9
Lyminge Kent 55 E7
Lymington Hants 20 B2
Lyminster W Sus 35 G8
Lymm Warr 183 D11
Lymore Hants 19 C11
Lympne Kent 54 F6
Lympsham Som 43 C10
Lympstone Devon 14 E5
Lynbridge Devon 41 D8
Lynch Hants 48 D4
Lynch Som 42 D2
Lynch Hill Hants 48 D3
Lynch Hill Slough 66 C2
Lynchat Highld 291 C9
Lynchgate Shrops 131 F7
Lyndale Ho Highld 298 D3
Lyndhurst Hants 32 F4
Lyndon Rutland 137 C8
Lyndon Green W Mid 134 F2
Lyne Borders 270 G4
Lyne Sur 66 F4
Lyne Down Hereford 98 E2
Lyne of Gorthleck Highld 300 G5
Lyne of Skene Aberds 293 B9
Lyne Station Borders 260 B6
Lyneal Shrops 149 C8
Lyneal Mill Shrops 149 C9
Lyneal Wood Shrops 149 C9
Lyneham Oxon 100 G5
Lyneham Wilts 62 D4
Lynemore Highld 301 G10
Lynemouth Northumb 253 E7
Lyness Orkney 314 G3
Lynford Norf 140 E6
Lyng Norf 159 F11
Lyng Som 28 B4
Lyngate Norf 160 C5
Lyngford Som 28 B2
Lynmore Highld 301 F10
Lynmouth Devon 41 D8
Lynn Staffs 133 C11
Lynn Telford 150 F5
Lynnwood Borders 261 G11
Lynsore Bottom Kent 55 D7
Lynsted Kent 70 G2
Lynstone Corn 24 F2
Lynton Devon 41 D8
Lynwilg Highld 291 B10
Lynworth Glos 99 G9
Lyons T & W 234 B3
Lyon's Gate Dorset 29 F11
Lyon's Green Norf 159 G8
Lyons Hall Essex 88 B2
Lyonshall Hereford 114 F6
Lypiatt Glos 80 D6
Lyrabus Argyll 274 G3
Lytchett Matravers Dorset 18 B4
Lytchett Minster Dorset 18 C5
Lyth Highld 310 C6
Lytham Lancs 193 B11
Lytham St Anne's Lancs 193 B10
Lythbank Shrops 131 B9
Lythe N Yorks 226 C6
Lythes Orkney 314 H4
Lythmore Highld 310 C4

M

Maam Argyll 284 F5
Mabe Burnthouse Corn 3 C7
Mabie Dumfries 237 B11
Mabledon Kent 52 E5
Mablethorpe Lincs 191 D8
Macclesfield E Ches 184 G6
Macclesfield Forest E Ches 185 G7
Macduff Aberds 303 C7
Mace Green Suff 108 C2
Machan S Lnrk 268 E5
Macharioch Argyll 255 G8
Machen Caerph 59 B8
Machrie N Ayrs 255 D9
Machrie Hotel Argyll 254 C4
Machrihanish Argyll 255 E7
Machroes Gwyn 144 D6
Machynlleth Powys 128 C4
Machynys Carms 56 B4
Mackerel's Common W Sus 35 B8
Mackerye End Herts 85 B11
Mackham Devon 27 F11
Mackney Oxon 64 B5
Mackside Borders 262 G4
Mackworth Derbys 152 B6
Macmerry E Loth 281 G8
Madderty Perth 286 E3
Maddington Wilts 46 E5
Maddiston Falk 279 F8
Maddox Moor Pembs 73 C7
Madehurst W Sus 35 E7
Madeley Staffs 168 G3
Madeley Telford 132 C3
Madeley Heath Staffs 168 F3
Madeley Heath Worcs 117 B9
Madeley Park Staffs 168 G3
Madeleywood Telford 132 C3
Maders Corn 12 G2
Madford Devon 27 E10
Madingley Cambs 123 E7
Madjeston Dorset 30 B4
Madley Hereford 97 D8
Madresfield Worcs 98 B6
Madron Corn 1 C5
Maen-y-groes Ceredig 111 F7
Maenaddwyn Anglesey 179 E7
Maenclochog Pembs 91 F11
Maendy V Glam 58 D4
Maenporth Corn 3 D7
Maentwrog Gwyn 163 G11
Maer Corn 24 F2
Maer Staffs 150 B5
Maerdy Carms 94 G2
Maerdy Conwy 165 G8
Maerdy Rhondda 77 F7
Maes-bangor Ceredig 128 G3
Maes-glas Newport 59 B9
Maes Glas = Greenfield Flint 181 F11
Maes Llyn Ceredig 93 C7
Maes Pennant Flint 181 F11
Maes-Treylow Powys 114 D5
Maes-y-dre Flint 166 C2
Maesbrook Shrops 148 E5
Maesbury Shrops 148 D6
Maesbury Marsh Shrops 148 D6
Maesgeirchen Gwyn 179 G9
Maesgwyn-Isaf Powys 148 G3
Maesgwynne Carms 92 G4
Maeshafn Denb 166 C2
Maesllyn Ceredig 93 C7
Maesmynis Powys 95 B10
Maesteg Bridgend 57 C10
Maesybont Carms 75 B9
Maesycoed Rhondda 58 B5
Maesycrugiau Carms 93 C9
Maesycwmmer Caerph 77 G11
Maesygwartha Mon 78 C2
Maesymeillion Ceredig 93 B8
Maesypandy Powys 129 D9
Maesyrhandir Powys 129 E11
Magdalen Laver Essex 87 D8
Maggieknockater Moray 302 E3
Maggots End Essex 105 F9
Magham Down E Sus 23 C10
Maghull Mers 193 G11
Magor Mon 60 B2
Magpie Green Suff 125 B11
Mahaar Dumfries 236 B2
Maida Vale London 67 C9
Maiden Bradley Wilts 45 F10
Maiden Head N Som 60 F5
Maiden Law Durham 233 B9
Maiden Newton Dorset 17 B7
Maiden Wells Pembs 73 F7
Maidenbower W Sus 51 F9
Maidencombe Torbay 9 B8
Maidenhall Suff 108 C3
Maidenhead Windsor 65 C11
Maidenhead Court Windsor 66 C2
Maidenpark Falk 279 E9
Maidens S Ayrs 244 B6
Maiden's Green Brack 65 E11
Maiden's Hall Northumb 252 D6
Maidensgrave Suff 108 B5
Maidensgrove Oxon 65 B8
Maidenwell Corn 11 G8
Maidenwell Lincs 190 F4
Maidford Northants 120 G2
Maids Moreton Bucks 102 D4
Maidstone Kent 53 B9
Maidwell Northants 120 B4
Mail Shetland 313 L6
Mailand Shetland 312 C8
Mailingsland Borders 270 G4
Main Powys 148 F3
Maindee Newport 59 B10
Maindy Cardiff 59 D7
Mainholm S Ayrs 257 E9
Mains Cumb 229 G7
Mains of Airies Dumfries 236 C1
Mains of Allardice Aberds 293 F10
Mains of Annochie Aberds 303 E9
Mains of Ardestie Angus 287 D9
Mains of Arnage Aberds 303 F9
Mains of Auchoynanie Moray 302 E4
Mains of Baldoon Dumfries 236 D6
Mains of Balhall Angus 293 G7
Mains of Ballindarg Angus 287 B8
Mains of Balnakettle Aberds 293 F8
Mains of Birness Aberds 303 F9
Mains of Blackhall Aberds 303 G7
Mains of Burgie Moray 301 D10
Mains of Cairnbrogie Aberds 303 G8
Mains of Cairnty Moray 302 D3
Mains of Clunas Highld 301 E8
Mains of Crichie Aberds 303 E9
Mains of Daltulich Highld 301 E7
Mains of Dalvey Highld 301 F11
Mains of Dellavaird Aberds 293 E9
Mains of Drum Aberds 293 D10
Mains of Edingight Moray 302 D5
Mains of Fedderate Aberds 303 E8
Mains of Flichity Highld 300 G6
Mains of Hatton Aberds 303 D9
Mains of Hatton Aberds 303 E7
Mains of Inkhorn Aberds 303 F9
Mains of Innerpeffray Perth 286 F3
Mains of Kirktonhill Aberds 293 G8
Mains of Laithers Aberds 302 E6
Mains of Mayen Moray 302 E5
Mains of Melgund Angus 287 B9
Mains of Taymouth Perth 285 C11
Mains of Thornton Aberds 293 F8
Mains of Towie Aberds 303 E7
Mains of Ulbster Highld 310 E7
Mains of Watten Highld 310 D6
Mainsforth Durham 234 E2
Mainsriddle Dumfries 237 D11
Mainstone Shrops 130 F5
Maisemore Glos 98 G6
Maitland Park London 67 C9
Major's Green W Mid 118 B2
Makeney Derbys 170 G5
Malacleit W Isles 296 D3
Malborough Devon 9 G9
Malcoff Derbys 185 E9
Malden Rushett London 67 G7
Maldon Essex 88 D4
Malehurst Shrops 131 B7
Malham N Yorks 213 G8
Maligar Highld 298 C4
Malinbridge S Yorks 186 D4
Malinslee Telford 132 B3
Malkin's Bank E Ches 168 D3
Mallaig Highld 295 F8
Mallaig Bheag Highld 295 F8
Malleny Mills Edin 270 B3
Malling Stirl 285 G9
Mallows Green Essex 105 F9
Malltraeth Anglesey 162 B6
Mallwyd Gwyn 147 G7
Malmesbury Wilts 62 B2
Malmsmead Devon 41 D9
Malpas Corn 4 G6
Malpas Newport 78 G4
Malpas W Berks 64 E6
Malpas W Ches 167 F7
Malswick Glos 98 F4
Maltby Lincs 190 E4
Maltby S Yorks 187 C8
Maltby Stockton 225 C9
Maltby le Marsh Lincs 191 E7
Malting End Suff 124 G4
Malting Green Essex 107 G9
Maltings Angus 293 G9
Maltman's Hill Kent 54 E2
Malton N Yorks 216 E5
Malvern Common Worcs 98 C5
Malvern Link Worcs 98 B5
Malvern Wells Worcs 98 C5
Mambeg Argyll 276 D4
Mamble Worcs 116 C3
Mamhilad Mon 78 E4
Man-moel Caerph 77 E11
Manaccan Corn 3 E7
Manadon Plym 7 D9
Manafon Powys 130 C2
Manais W Isles 296 C7
Manar Ho Aberds 303 G7
Manaton Devon 13 E11
Manby Lincs 190 D5
Mancetter Warks 134 D6
Manchester Gtr Man 184 B4
Manchester Airport Gtr Man 184 D4
Mancot Flint 166 B4
Mancot Royal Flint 166 B4
Mandally Highld 290 C4
Manea Cambs 139 F9
Maney W Mid 134 D2
Manfield N Yorks 224 C4
Mangaster Shetland 312 F5
Mangotsfield S Glos 61 D7
Mangrove Green Herts 104 G2
Mangurstadh W Isles 304 E2
Manhay Corn 2 C5
Manian-fawr Pembs 92 B3
Mankinholes W Yorks 196 C3
Manley Devon 27 E7
Manley W Ches 183 G8
Manley Common W Ches 183 G8
Manmoel Caerph 77 E11
Mannal Argyll 288 E1
Mannamead Plym 7 D9
Mannerston W Loth 279 F10
Manningford Abbots Wilts 46 B6
Manningford Bohune Wilts 46 B6
Manningford Bruce Wilts 46 B6
Manningham W Yorks 205 G9
Mannings Heath W Sus 36 B2
Mannington Dorset 31 F9
Manningtree Essex 107 E11
Mannofield Aberdeen 293 C11
Manor London 68 B2
Manor Bourne Devon 7 F9
Manor Estate S Yorks 186 D5
Manor Hill Corner Lincs 157 F8
Manor House W Mid 135 G7
Manor Park Bucks 84 C4
Manor Park E Sus 37 C7
Manor Park London 68 B2
Manor Park Notts 153 C11
Manor Park S Yorks 186 D5
Manor Park Slough 66 C3
Manor Park W Ches 167 B11
Manor Park W Yorks 205 D9
Manor Parsley Corn 4 F4
Manor Royal W Sus 51 F9
Manorbier Pembs 73 F9
Manorbier Newton Pembs 73 F8
Manordeilo Carms 94 F3
Manorhill Borders 262 C5
Manorowen Pembs 91 D8
Man's Cross Essex 106 D5
Mansegate Dumfries 247 G9
Mansel Lacy Hereford 97 B8
Manselfield Swansea 56 D5
Mansell Gamage Hereford 97 C7
Manselton Swansea 57 B7
Mansergh Cumb 212 C2
Mansewood Glasgow 267 C11
Mansfield E Ayrs 258 G4
Mansfield Notts 171 C8
Mansfield Woodhouse Notts 171 C8
Manson Green Norf 141 C10
Mansriggs Cumb 210 C5
Manston Dorset 30 D4
Manston Kent 71 F10
Manston W Yorks 206 F3
Manswood Dorset 31 F7
Manthorpe Lincs 155 B8
Manthorpe Lincs 155 F11
Mantles Green Bucks 85 F7
Manton N Lincs 200 G2
Manton Notts 187 F9
Manton Rutland 137 C7
Manton Wilts 63 F7
Manton Warren N Lincs 200 F2
Manuden Essex 105 F9
Manwood Green Essex 87 C8
Manywells Height W Yorks 205 F7
Maperton Som 29 B11
Maple Cross Herts 85 G8
Maple End Essex 105 D11
Maplebeck Notts 172 C2
Mapledurham Oxon 65 D7
Mapledurwell Hants 49 C7
Maplehurst W Sus 35 C11
Maplescombe Kent 68 G5
Mapleton Derbys 169 F11
Mapperley Derbys 170 G6
Mapperley Nottingham 171 G9
Mapperley Park Nottingham 171 G9
Mapperton Dorset 16 B6
Mapperton Dorset 18 B4
Mappleborough Green Warks 117 D11
Mappleton E Yorks 209 E10
Mapplewell S Yorks 197 F10
Mappowder Dorset 30 F2
Mar Lodge Aberds 292 D2
Maraig W Isles 305 H3
Marazanvose Corn 4 E6
Marazion Corn 2 C2
Marbhig W Isles 305 G6
Marbrack Dumfries 246 E3
Marbury E Ches 167 F9
March Cambs 139 D8
March S Lnrk 259 G11
Marcham Oxon 83 F7
Marchamley Shrops 149 D11
Marchamley Wood Shrops 149 C11
Marchington Staffs 152 C2
Marchington Woodlands Staffs 152 D2
Marchroes Gwyn 144 D6
Marchwiel Wrex 166 F5
Marchwood Hants 32 E5
Marcross V Glam 58 F2
Marden Hereford 97 B10
Marden Kent 53 E8
Marden T & W 243 C9
Marden Wilts 46 B5
Marden Ash Essex 87 E9
Marden Beech Kent 53 E8
Marden Thorn Kent 53 E9
Marden's Hill E Sus 52 G3
Mardleybury Herts 86 B3
Mardu Shrops 130 G5
Mardy Mon 78 B4
Mardy Shrops 148 C5
Marefield Leics 136 B4
Mareham le Fen Lincs 174 C3
Mareham on the Hill Lincs 174 B3
Marehay Derbys 170 F5
Marehill W Sus 35 D9
Maresfield E Sus 37 C7
Maresfield Park E Sus 37 C7
Marfleet Hull 200 B6
Marford Wrex 166 D5
Margam Neath 57 D9
Margaret Marsh Dorset 30 D4
Margaret Roding Essex 87 C9
Margaretting Essex 87 E11
Margaretting Tye Essex 87 E11
Margate Kent 71 E11
Margery Sur 51 C9
Margnaheglish N Ayrs 256 C2
Margreig Dumfries 237 B10
Margrove Park Redcar 226 B3
Marham Norf 158 G4
Marhamchurch Corn 24 G2
Marholm P'boro 138 C2
Marian Flint 181 F9
Marian Cwm Denb 181 F9
Marian-glas Anglesey 179 E8
Marian y de = South Beach Gwyn 145 C7
Marian y mor = West End Gwyn 145 C7
Mariandyrys Anglesey 179 E10
Marianglas Anglesey 179 E8
Mariansleigh Devon 26 C2
Marine Town Kent 70 E2
Marionburgh Aberds 293 C9
Marishader Highld 298 C4
Marjoriebanks Dumfries 248 G3
Mark Dumfries 236 D3
Mark Dumfries 237 C7
Mark S Ayrs 236 B2
Mark Som 43 D11
Mark Causeway Som 43 D11
Mark Cross E Sus 23 C7
Mark Cross E Sus 52 G5
Mark Hall North Essex 87 C7
Mark Hall South Essex 87 C7
Markbeech Kent 52 E3
Markby Lincs 191 F7
Markeaton Derbys 152 B6
Market Bosworth Leics 135 C8
Market Deeping Lincs 138 B2
Market Drayton Shrops 150 C3
Market Harborough Leics 136 F4
Market Lavington Wilts 46 C4
Market Overton Rutland 155 F7
Market Rasen Lincs 189 D10
Market Stainton Lincs 190 F2
Market Warsop Notts 171 B9
Market Weighton E Yorks 208 E3
Market Weston Suff 125 B9
Markethill Perth 286 D6
Markfield Leics 153 G9
Markham Caerph 77 E11
Markham Moor Notts 188 G2
Markinch Fife 286 G6
Markington N Yorks 214 F5
Markland Hill Gtr Man 195 F7
Markle E Loth 281 F11
Mark's Corner I o W 20 C5
Marks Gate London 87 G7
Marks Tey Essex 107 G8
Marksbury Bath 61 G7
Markyate Herts 85 B9
Marl Bank Worcs 98 C5
Marland Gtr Man 195 E11
Marlas Hereford 97 F8
Marlborough Wilts 63 F7
Marlbrook Hereford 115 G10
Marlbrook Worcs 117 C9
Marlcliff Warks 117 G11
Marldon Devon 9 C7
Marle Green E Sus 23 B9
Marle Hill Glos 99 G9
Marlesford Suff 126 F6
Marley Kent 55 C10
Marley Kent 55 C7
Marley Green E Ches 167 F9
Marley Heights W Sus 49 G11
Marley Hill T & W 242 F6
Marley Pots T & W 243 F9
Marlingford Norf 142 B2
Marloes Pembs 72 D3
Marlow Bucks 65 B10
Marlow Hereford 115 B8
Marlow Bottom Bucks 65 B11
Marlow Common Bucks 65 B10
Marlpit Hill Kent 52 D2
Marlpits E Sus 38 E2
Marlpool Derbys 170 F6
Marnhull Dorset 30 D3
Marnoch Aberds 302 D5
Marnock N Lnrk 268 B4
Marple Gtr Man 185 D7
Marple Bridge Gtr Man 185 D7
Marpleridge Gtr Man 185 D7
Marr S Yorks 198 F4
Marr Green Wilts 63 G8
Marrel Highld 311 H4
Marrick N Yorks 223 F11
Marrister Shetland 313 G7
Marros Carms 74 D2
Marsden T & W 243 E9
Marsden W Yorks 196 E4
Marsden Height Lancs 204 F3
Marsett N Yorks 213 B8
Marsh Bucks 84 D4
Marsh Devon 28 E3
Marsh W Yorks 196 D6
Marsh W Yorks 204 F6
Marsh Baldon Oxon 83 F9
Marsh Benham W Berks 64 F2
Marsh Common S Glos 60 C5
Marsh End Worcs 98 D6
Marsh Gate W Berks 63 F10
Marsh Gibbon Bucks 102 G2
Marsh Green Devon 14 C6
Marsh Green Gtr Man 194 F5
Marsh Green Kent 52 E2
Marsh Green Staffs 168 D5
Marsh Green Telford 150 G2
Marsh Green W Ches 183 F8
Marsh Houses Lancs 202 C5
Marsh Lane Derbys 186 F6
Marsh Lane Glos 79 D9
Marsh Mills Som 43 F7
Marsh Side Norf 176 E3
Marsh Street Som 42 E3
Marshall Meadows Northumb 273 D9
Marshall's Cross Mers 183 C8
Marshall's Elm Som 44 G3
Marshall's Heath Herts 85 B11
Marshalsea Dorset 28 G5
Marshalswick Herts 85 D11
Marsham Norf 160 E3
Marshaw Lancs 203 C7
Marshborough Kent 55 B10
Marshbrook Shrops 131 F8
Marshchapel Lincs 190 B5
Marshfield Newport 59 C9
Marshfield S Glos 61 E9
Marshfield Bank E Ches 167 D11
Marshgate Corn 11 C9
Marshland St James Norf 139 B10
Marshmoor Herts 86 D2
Marshside Kent 71 F8
Marshside Mers 193 D11
Marshwood Dorset 16 B3
Marske N Yorks 224 E2
Marske-by-the-Sea Redcar 235 G8
Marston Hereford 115 F7
Marston Lincs 172 G5
Marston Oxon 83 D8
Marston Staffs 150 G6
Marston Staffs 151 D8
Marston W Ches 183 F11
Marston Warks 119 B8
Marston Warks 134 E4
Marston Wilts 46 B3
Marston Bigot Som 45 E9
Marston Doles Warks 119 F9
Marston Gate Som 45 D9
Marston Green W Mid 134 F3
Marston Hill Glos 81 F10
Marston Jabbett Warks 135 F7
Marston Magna Som 29 C9
Marston Meysey Wilts 81 F10
Marston Montgomery Derbys 152 B2
Marston Moretaine C Beds 103 C9
Marston on Dove Derbys 152 D4
Marston St Lawrence Northants 101 C10
Marston Stannett Hereford 115 F11
Marston Trussell Northants 136 F3
Marstow Hereford 79 B9
Marsworth Bucks 84 C6
Marten Wilts 47 B9
Marthall E Ches 184 F4
Martham Norf 161 F9
Marthwaite Cumb 222 G2
Martin Hants 31 D9
Martin Kent 55 D10
Martin Lincs 173 D10
Martin Lincs 174 B2
Martin Dales Lincs 173 C11
Martin Drove End Hants 31 C9
Martin Hussingtree Worcs 117 E7
Martin Mill Kent 55 D10
Martin Moor Lincs 174 C2
Martindale Cumb 221 B8
Martinhoe Devon 41 D7
Martinhoe Cross Devon 41 D7
Martin's Moss E Ches 168 C4
Martinscroft Warr 183 D11
Martinstown Dorset 17 D8
Martinstown or Winterbourne St Martin Dorset 17 D8
Martlesham Suff 108 B4
Martlesham Heath Suff 108 B4
Martletwy Pembs 73 C8
Martley Worcs 116 E5
Martock Som 29 D7
Marton Cumb 210 D4
Marton E Ches 168 B5
Marton E Yorks 209 F9
Marton Lincs 188 E4
Marton M'bro 225 B10
Marton N Yorks 215 G8
Marton N Yorks 216 C4
Marton Shrops 130 C5
Marton Shrops 149 E8
Marton W Ches 167 B10
Marton Warks 119 D8
Marton Green W Ches 167 B10
Marton Grove M'bro 225 B9
Marton-in-the-Forest N Yorks 215 F11
Marton-le-Moor N Yorks 215 E7
Marton Moor Warks 119 D8
Marton Moss Side Blkpool 202 G2
Martyr Worthy Hants 48 G4
Martyr's Green Sur 50 B5
Marwick Orkney 314 D2
Marwood Devon 40 F4
Mary Tavy Devon 12 F6
Marybank Highld 300 D4
Marybank Highld 301 B7
Maryburgh Highld 300 D5
Maryfield Aberds 293 D7
Maryfield Corn 7 D8
Maryhill Glasgow 267 B11
Marykirk Aberds 293 G8
Maryland Mon 79 D8
Marylebone Gtr Man 194 F5
Marypark Moray 301 F11
Maryport Cumb 228 D6

Maryport Dumfries 236 F3
Maryton Angus 287 B10
Maryton Angus 287 B7
Marywell Aberds 293 D11
Marywell Aberds 293 D7
Marywell Angus 287 C10
Masbrough S Yorks 186 C6
Mascle Bridge Pembs 73 D7
Masham N Yorks 214 C4
Mashbury Essex 87 C11
Masongill N Yorks 212 D3
Masonhill S Ayrs 257 E9
Mastin Moor Derbys 187 F7
Mastrick Aberdeen 293 C10
Matchborough Worcs 117 D11
Matching Essex 87 C8
Matching Green Essex 87 C8
Matching Tye Essex 87 C8
Matfen Northumb 242 C2
Matfield Kent 53 E7
Mathern Mon 79 G8
Mathon Hereford 98 B4
Mathry Pembs 91 E7
Matlaske Norf 160 C3
Matley Gtr Man 185 B7
Matlock Derbys 170 C3
Matlock Bank Derbys 170 C3
Matlock Bath Derbys 170 D3
Matlock Bridge Derbys 170 D3
Matlock Cliff Derbys 170 D4
Matlock Dale Derbys 170 D3
Matshead Lancs 202 E6
Matson Glos 80 B4
Matterdale End Cumb 230 G3
Mattersey Notts 187 D11
Mattersey Thorpe Notts 187 D11
Matthewsgreen Wokingham 65 F10
Mattingley Hants 49 B8
Mattishall Norf 159 G11
Mattishall Burgh Norf 159 G11
Mauchline E Ayrs 257 D11
Maud Aberds 303 E9
Maudlin Corn 5 C11
Maudlin Dorset 28 F5
Maudlin W Sus 22 B5
Maudlin Cross Dorset 28 F5
Maugersbury Glos 100 F4
Maughold I o M 192 C5
Mauld Highld 300 F4
Maulden C Beds 103 D11
Maulds Meaburn Cumb 222 B2
Maunby N Yorks 215 B7
Maund Bryan Hereford 115 G11
Maundown Som 27 B9
Mauricewood Midloth 270 C4
Mautby Norf 161 G9
Mavesyn Ridware Staffs 151 F11
Mavis Enderby Lincs 174 B5
Maviston Highld 301 D9
Maw Green E Ches 168 D2
Mawbray Cumb 229 B7
Mawdesley Lancs 194 E3
Mawdlam Bridgend 57 E10
Mawgan Corn 2 D6
Mawgan Porth Corn 5 B7
Mawla Corn 4 F4
Mawnan Corn 3 D7
Mawnan Smith Corn 3 D7
Mawsley Northants 120 B6
Mawson Green S Yorks 198 D6
Mawthorpe Lincs 191 G7
Maxey P'boro 138 B2
Maxstoke Warks 134 F4
Maxted Street Kent 54 E6
Maxton Borders 262 C4
Maxton Kent 55 E10
Maxwellheugh Borders 262 C6
Maxwelltown Dumfries 237 B11
Maxworthy Corn 11 C11
May Bank Staffs 168 F5
May Hill Mon 79 C8
May Hill Village Glos 98 G4
Mayals Swansea 56 C6
Maybole S Ayrs 257 G8
Maybury Sur 50 B4
Maybush Soton 32 E5
Mayer's Green W Mid 133 E10
Mayes Green Sur 50 F6
Mayeston Pembs 73 E8
Mayfair London 67 C9
Mayfield E Sus 37 B9
Mayfield Midloth 271 C7
Mayfield Northumb 243 B7
Mayfield Staffs 169 F11
Mayfield W Loth 269 B8
Mayford Sur 50 B3
Mayhill Swansea 56 C6
Mayland Essex 88 E6
Maylandsea Essex 88 E6
Maynard's Green E Sus 23 B9
Mayne Ho Moray 302 C2
Mayon Corn 1 D3
Maypole Kent 68 E4
Maypole Kent 68 G3
Maypole Kent 71 G8
Maypole Mon 79 B7
Maypole Scilly 1 G4
Maypole Green Essex 107 G9
Maypole Green Norf 143 D8
Maypole Green Suff 125 F8
Maypole Green Suff 126 D5
May's Green N Som 59 G11
Mays Green Oxon 65 C8
May's Green Sur 50 B5
Mayshill S Glos 61 C7
Maythorn S Yorks 197 F7
Maythorne Notts 171 D11
Maywick Shetland 313 L5
Mead Devon 13 G11
Mead Devon 24 D2
Mead End Hants 19 B11
Mead End Hants 33 E11
Mead End Wilts 31 C8
Mead Vale Sur 51 D9
Meadgate Bath 45 B7
Meadle Bucks 84 D4
Meadow Green Hereford 116 F4
Meadow Hall S Yorks 186 C5
Meadow Head S Yorks 186 E4
Meadowbank Edin 280 G5
Meadowbank W Ches 167 B11
Meadowend Essex 106 C4
Meadowfield Durham 233 D10
Meadowfoot N Ayrs 266 F4
Meadowley Shrops 132 E3
Meadowmill E Loth 281 G8
Meadows Nottingham 153 B11
Meadowtown Shrops 130 C6
Meads E Sus 23 F10
Meadside Oxon 83 G9
Meadwell Devon 12 E4
Meaford Staffs 151 B7
Meagill N Yorks 205 B9
Meal Bank Cumb 221 F10
Meal Hill W Yorks 197 F7
Mealabost Bhuirgh W Isles 304 C6
Mealabost W Isles 304 E6
Mealasta W Isles 304 F1
Mealrigg Cumb 229 B8
Mealsgate Cumb 229 C10
Meanwood W Yorks 205 F11
Mearbeck N Yorks 212 G6
Meare Som 44 E3
Meare Green Som 28 B4
Meare Green Som 28 C3
Mearns Bath 45 B7
Mearns E Renf 267 D10
Mears Ashby Northants 120 D6
Measborough Dike S Yorks 197 F11
Measham Leics 152 G6
Meath Green Sur 51 E9
Meathop Cumb 211 C8
Meaux E Yorks 209 F7
Meaver Corn 2 F5
Meavy Devon 7 B10
Medbourne Leics 136 E5
Medbourne M Keynes 102 D6
Medburn Northumb 242 C4
Meddon Devon 24 D3
Meden Vale Notts 171 B9
Medhurst Row Kent 52 D3
Medlam Lincs 174 D4
Medlar Lancs 202 F4
Medlicott Shrops 131 E8
Medlyn Corn 2 C6
Medmenham Bucks 65 C10
Medomsley Durham 242 G4
Medstead Hants 49 F7
Meer Common Hereford 115 G7
Meer End W Mid 118 C4
Meerbrook Staffs 169 C7
Meerhay Dorset 29 G7
Meers Bridge Lincs 191 D7
Meersbrook S Yorks 186 E5
Meesden Herts 105 E8
Meeson Telford 150 E3
Meeson Heath Telford 150 E3
Meeth Devon 25 F8
Meethe Devon 25 C11
Meeting Green Suff 124 F4
Meeting House Hill Norf 160 D6
Meggernie Castle Perth 285 C9
Meggethead Borders 260 E5
Meidrim Carms 92 G5
Meifod Denb 165 D8
Meifod Powys 148 G3
Meigle N Ayrs 266 B3
Meigle Perth 286 C6
Meikle Earnock S Lnrk 268 E4
Meikle Ferry Highld 309 L7
Meikle Forter Angus 292 G3
Meikle Gluich Highld 309 L6
Meikle Obney Perth 286 D4
Meikle Pinkerton E Loth 282 F4
Meikle Strath Aberds 293 F8
Meikle Tarty Aberds 303 G9
Meikle Wartle Aberds 303 F7
Meikleour Perth 286 D5
Meinciau Carms 75 C7
Meir Stoke 168 G6
Meir Heath Staffs 168 G6
Melbourn Cambs 105 C7
Melbourne Derbys 153 D7
Melbourne E Yorks 207 E11
Melbourne S Lnrk 269 G11
Melbury Abbas Dorset 30 D5
Melbury Bubb Dorset 29 F9
Melbury Osmond Dorset 29 F9
Melbury Sampford Dorset 29 F9
Melby Shetland 313 H3
Melchbourne Beds 121 D10
Melcombe Som 43 G9
Melcombe Bingham Dorset 30 G3
Melcombe Regis Dorset 17 E9
Meldon Devon 13 C7
Meldon Northumb 252 G4
Meldreth Cambs 105 B7
Meldrum Ho Aberds 303 G8
Melfort Argyll 275 B9
Melgarve Highld 290 D6
Meliden = Gallt Melyd Denb 181 E9
Melin Caiach Caerph 77 F10
Melin-y-coed Conwy 164 C4
Melin-y-ddôl Powys 129 B11
Melin-y-grug Powys 129 B11
Melin-y-Wig Denb 165 F8
Melinbyrhedyn Powys 128 D6
Melincourt Neath 76 E4
Melincryddan Neath 57 B8
Melinsey Corn 3 B10
Melkington Northumb 273 G7
Melkinthorpe Cumb 231 F7
Melkridge Northumb 240 E6
Melksham Wilts 62 G2
Melksham Forest Wilts 62 G2
Mell Green W Berks 64 D3
Mellangaun Highld 307 L3
Mellangoose Corn 2 D5
Melldalloch Argyll 275 F10
Mellguards Cumb 230 B4
Melling Lancs 211 E11
Melling Mers 193 G11
Melling Mount Mers 194 G2
Mellingey Corn 10 G4
Mellis Suff 126 C2
Mellis Green Suff 125 C11
Mellon Charles Highld 307 K3
Mellon Udrigle Highld 307 K3
Mellor Gtr Man 185 D7
Mellor Lancs 203 G9
Mellor Brook Lancs 203 G8
Mells Som 45 D8
Mells Suff 127 B8
Mells Green Som 45 D8
Melmerby Cumb 231 D8
Melmerby N Yorks 213 B11
Melmerby N Yorks 214 D6
Melon Green Suff 124 F6
Melplash Dorset 16 B5
Melrose Borders 262 C2
Melsetter Orkney 314 H2
Melsonby N Yorks 224 D3
Meltham W Yorks 196 E6
Meltham Mills W Yorks 196 E6
Melton E Yorks 200 B3
Melton Suff 126 G5
Melton Constable Norf 159 C10
Melton Mowbray Leics 154 F5
Melton Ross N Lincs 200 E5
Meltonby E Yorks 207 C11
Melvaig Highld 307 L2
Melverley Shrops 148 F6
Melverley Green Shrops 148 F6
Melvich Highld 310 C2
Membland Devon 7 F11
Membury Devon 28 G3
Memsie Aberds 303 C9
Memus Angus 287 B8
Mena Corn 5 C10
Menabilly Corn 5 E11
Menadarva Corn 4 G2
Menagissey Corn 4 F4
Menai Bridge = Porthaethwy Anglesey 179 G9
Mendham Suff 142 G5
Mendlesham Suff 126 D2
Mendlesham Green Suff 125 E11
Menethorpe N Yorks 216 F5
Mengham Hants 21 B10
Menheniot Corn 6 C5
Menherion Corn 2 B6
Menithwood Worcs 116 D4
Menna Corn 5 E8
Mennock Dumfries 247 B8
Menston W Yorks 205 E9
Menstrie Clack 278 B6
Mentmore Bucks 84 B6
Menzion Borders 260 E3
Meoble Highld 295 G9
Meole Brace Shrops 149 G9
Meols Mers 182 C2
Meon Hants 33 G8
Meonstoke Hants 33 D10
Meopham Kent 68 F6
Meopham Green Kent 68 F6
Meopham Station Kent 68 F6
Mepal Cambs 139 G8
Meppershall C Beds 104 D2
Merbach Hereford 96 B6
Mercaton Derbys 170 G3
Merchant Fields W Yorks 197 B7
Merchiston Edin 280 G4
Mere E Ches 184 E2
Mere Wilts 45 G10
Mere Brow Lancs 194 D2
Mere Green W Mid 134 D2
Mere Green Worcs 117 E9
Mere Heath W Ches 183 G11
Mereclough Lancs 204 G3
Merehead Wrex 149 B9
Meresborough Medway 69 G10
Mereside Blkpool 202 G2
Meretown Staffs 150 E5
Mereworth Kent 53 C7
Mergie Aberds 293 E9
Meriden Herts 85 F10
Meriden W Mid 134 G4
Merkadale Highld 294 B5
Merkland Dumfries 237 B9
Merkland N Ayrs 256 B2
Merkland S Ayrs 244 E6
Merkland Lodge Highld 309 G4
Merle Common Sur 52 D2
Merley Poole 18 B6
Merlin's Bridge Pembs 72 C6
Merlin's Cross Pembs 73 E7
Merridale W Mid 133 D7
Merridge Som 43 G8
Merrie Gardens I o W 21 E7
Merrifield Devon 8 F6
Merrifield Devon 24 G3
Merrington Shrops 149 E9
Merrion Pembs 72 F6
Merriott Dorset 16 B6
Merriott Som 28 E6
Merriottsford Som 28 E6
Merritown Dorset 19 B8
Merrivale Devon 12 F6
Merrivale Hereford 98 G2
Merrow Sur 50 C4
Merry Field Hill Dorset 31 G8
Merry Hill Herts 85 G10
Merry Hill W Mid 133 D7
Merry Lees Leics 135 B9
Merry Meeting Corn 11 G7
Merry Oak Soton 32 E6
Merrybent Darl 224 C4
Merryhill Green Wokingham 65 E9
Merrylee E Renf 267 D11
Merrymeet Corn 6 B5
Mersham Kent 54 F5
Merstham Sur 51 C9
Merston W Sus 22 C5
Merstone I o W 20 E6
Merther Corn 5 G7
Merther Lane Corn 5 G7
Merthyr Carms 93 G7
Merthyr Cynog Powys 95 D9
Merthyr-Dyfan V Glam 58 F6
Merthyr Mawr Bridgend 57 F11
Merthyr Tydfil M Tydf 77 D8
Merthyr Vale M Tydf 77 F9
Merton Devon 25 E8
Merton London 67 E9
Merton Norf 141 D8
Merton Oxon 83 B9
Merton Park London 67 F9
Mervinslaw Borders 262 G5
Meshaw Devon 26 D3
Messing Essex 88 B5
Messingham N Lincs 199 G11
Mesty Croft W Mid 133 E9
Mesur-y-dorth Pembs 87 E11
Metal Bridge Durham 233 E11
Metfield Suff 142 G5
Metherell Corn 7 B8
Metheringham Lincs 173 C9
Methersgate Suff 108 B5
Methil Fife 281 B7
Methilhill Fife 281 B7
Methlem Gwyn 144 C3
Methley W Yorks 197 B11
Methley Junction W Yorks 197 B11
Methley Lanes W Yorks 197 B11
Methlick Aberds 303 F8
Methven Perth 286 E4
Methwold Norf 140 E4
Methwold Hythe Norf 140 E4
Mettingham Suff 143 F7
Metton Norf 160 B3
Mevagissey Corn 5 G10
Mewith Head N Yorks 212 F4
Mexborough S Yorks 187 B7
Mey Highld 310 B6
Meyrick Park Bmouth 19 C7
Meysey Hampton Glos 81 F10
Miabhag W Isles 305 H2
Miabhag W Isles 305 J3
Miabhig W Isles 304 E2
Mial Highld 299 B7
Michaelchurch Hereford 97 F10
Michaelchurch Escley Hereford 96 E6
Michaelchurch on Arrow Powys 114 G4
Michaelston-le-Pit V Glam 59 E7
Michaelston-y-Fedw Newport 59 C8
Michaelstow Corn 11 F7
Michealston-super-Ely Cardiff 58 D6
Michelcombe Devon 8 B3
Micheldever Hants 48 F4
Michelmersh Hants 32 B4
Mickfield Suff 126 E2
Mickle Trafford W Ches 166 B6
Micklebring S Yorks 187 C8
Mickleby N Yorks 226 C6
Micklefield Bucks 84 G5
Micklefield W Yorks 206 G4
Micklefield Green Herts 85 F8
Mickleham Sur 51 C7
Micklehurst Gtr Man 196 G3
Mickleover Derby 152 C6
Micklethwaite Cumb 239 G7
Micklethwaite W Yorks 205 E8
Mickleton Durham 232 G5
Mickleton Glos 100 C3
Mickletown W Yorks 197 B11
Mickley Derbys 186 F4
Mickley N Yorks 214 D5
Mickley Shrops 150 C2
Mickley Green Suff 124 F6
Mickley Square Northumb 242 E3
Mid Ardlaw Aberds 303 C9
Mid Auchinleck Invclyd 276 G6
Mid Beltie Aberds 293 C8
Mid Calder W Loth 269 B11
Mid Cloch Forbie Aberds 303 D7
Mid Clyth Highld 310 F6
Mid Garrary Dumfries 237 B7
Mid Holmwood Sur 51 D7
Mid Lambrook Som 28 D6
Mid Lavant W Sus 22 B5
Mid Letter Argyll 284 G4
Mid Main Highld 300 F4
Mid Murthat Dumfries 248 D3
Mid Urchany Highld 301 E8
Mid Walls Shetland 313 H4
Mid Yell Shetland 312 D7
Midanbury Hants 33 E7
Midbea Orkney 314 B4
Middle Assendon Oxon 65 B8
Middle Aston Oxon 101 F9
Middle Balnald Perth 286 B4
Middle Barton Oxon 101 F8
Middle Bickenhill W Mid 134 G4
Middle Bockhampton Dorset 19 B9
Middle Bourne Sur 49 E10
Middle Bridge N Som 60 D3
Middle Burnham Som 43 D10
Middle Cairncake Aberds 303 E8
Middle Chinnock Som 29 E7
Middle Claydon Bucks 102 F4
Middle Cliff Staffs 169 E8
Middle Crackington Corn 11 B9
Middle Drums Angus 287 B9
Middle Duntisbourne Glos 81 D7
Middle Green Bucks 66 C4
Middle Green Som 27 D10
Middle Green Suff 124 D4
Middle Handley Derbys 186 F6
Middle Harling Norf 141 F9
Middle Herrington T & W 243 G9
Middle Hill Pembs 73 C7
Middle Hill Staffs 133 B9
Middle Kames Argyll 275 E10
Middle Littleton Worcs 99 B11
Middle Luxton Devon 28 E2
Middle Madeley Staffs 168 F3
Middle Maes-coed Hereford 96 E6
Middle Marwood Devon 40 F4
Middle Mayfield Staffs 169 G10
Middle Mill Pembs 87 F11
Middle Quarter Kent 53 F11
Middle Rainton T & W 234 B2
Middle Rasen Lincs 189 D9
Middle Rigg Perth 286 G4
Middle Rocombe Devon 9 B8
Middle Side Durham 232 F4
Middle Stoford Som 27 C11
Middle Stoke Devon 13 G9
Middle Stoke Medway 69 D10
Middle Stoke W Mid 119 B7
Middle Stoughton Som 44 D2
Middle Strath W Loth 279 G8
Middle Street Glos 80 E3
Middle Taphouse Corn 6 C3
Middle Town Scilly 1 F4
Middle Tysoe Warks 100 C6
Middle Wallop Hants 47 F9
Middle Weald M Keynes 102 D5
Middle Wick Glos 80 F2
Middle Winterslow Wilts 47 G8
Middle Woodford Wilts 46 F6
Middlebie Dumfries 238 B6
Middlecave N Yorks 216 E5
Middlecliffe S Yorks 198 F2
Middlecott Devon 13 D10
Middlecott Devon 24 F6
Middlecott Devon 26 F3
Middlecroft Derbys 186 G6
Middlefield Falk 279 E7
Middleforth Green Lancs 194 B4
Middleham N Yorks 214 B2
Middlehill Corn 6 B5
Middlehill Wilts 61 F10
Middlehope Shrops 131 F9
Middlemarsh Dorset 29 F11
Middlemoor Devon 12 G5
Middlemuir Aberds 303 D9
Middlemuir Aberds 303 E8
Middlemuir Aberds 303 G9
Middleport Stoke 168 F5
Middlerig Falk 279 F8
Middlesbrough M'bro 234 G5
Middlesceugh Cumb 230 C4
Middleshaw Cumb 211 B11
Middlesmoor N Yorks 213 E11
Middlestone Durham 233 E11
Middlestone Moor Durham 233 E10
Middlestown W Yorks 197 D9
Middlethird Borders 272 G3
Middlethorpe York 207 D7
Middleton Aberds 293 B10
Middleton Argyll 288 E1
Middleton Cumb 212 B2
Middleton Derbys 169 C11
Middleton Derbys 170 D3
Middleton Essex 107 D7
Middleton Gtr Man 195 F11
Middleton Hants 48 E2
Middleton Hereford 115 D10
Middleton Hrtlpl 234 E6
Middleton I o W 20 D2
Middleton Lancs 202 B4
Middleton Midloth 271 D7
Middleton N Yorks 204 E5
Middleton N Yorks 205 D8
Middleton N Yorks 216 B5
Middleton Norf 158 F3
Middleton Northants 136 F6
Middleton Northumb 252 F3
Middleton Northumb 264 B4
Middleton Perth 286 C5
Middleton Perth 286 F2
Middleton Perth 286 G5
Middleton Shrops 115 B10
Middleton Shrops 130 D5
Middleton Shrops 148 D6
Middleton Suff 127 D8
Middleton Swansea 56 D2
Middleton W Yorks 197 B10
Middleton Warks 134 D3
Middleton Baggot Shrops 132 E2
Middleton Cheney Northants 101 C9
Middleton Green Staffs 151 B9
Middleton Hall Northumb 263 D11
Middleton-in-Teesdale Durham 232 F4
Middleton Junction Gtr Man 195 G11
Middleton Moor Suff 127 D8
Middleton of Rora Aberds 303 E10
Middleton-on-Leven N Yorks 225 D9
Middleton-on-Sea W Sus 35 G7
Middleton on the Hill Hereford 115 E10
Middleton-on-the-Wolds E Yorks 208 D4
Middleton One Row Darl 225 C7
Middleton Place Cumb 219 G11
Middleton Priors Shrops 132 E2
Middleton Quernhow N Yorks 214 D6
Middleton St George Darl 224 C6
Middleton Scriven Shrops 132 F3
Middleton Stoney Oxon 101 G10
Middleton Tyas N Yorks 224 D4
Middletown Cumb 219 D9
Middletown N Som 60 E3
Middletown Powys 148 G6
Middletown Warks 117 E11
Middlewich E Ches 167 B11
Middlewick Wilts 61 E11
Middlewood Corn 11 F11
Middlewood E Ches 184 E6
Middlewood S Yorks 186 C4
Middlewood Green Suff 125 E11
Middleyard Glos 80 E4
Middlezoy Som 43 G11
Middridge Durham 233 F11
Midelney Som 28 C6
Midfield Highld 308 C5
Midford Bath 61 G9
Midgard Borders 262 F3
Midge Hall Lancs 194 C4
Midgehole W Yorks 196 B3
Midgeholme Cumb 240 F4
Midgham W Berks 64 F5
Midgham Green W Berks 64 F5
Midgley W Yorks 196 B4
Midgley W Yorks 197 E9
Midhopestones S Yorks 186 B2
Midhurst W Sus 34 C5
Midland Orkney 314 F3
Midlem Borders 262 D2
Midlock S Lnrk 259 E11
Midmar Aberds 293 C8
Midmuir Argyll 289 G11
Midpark Argyll 255 B11
Midplaugh Aberds 302 E5
Midsomer Norton Bath 45 C7
Midton Invclyd 276 F4
Midtown Highld 307 L3
Midtown Highld 308 C5
Midtown of Buchromb Moray 302 E3
Midtown of Glass Aberds 302 E4
Midville Lincs 174 D5
Midway E Ches 184 E6
Midway Som 45 D7
Miekle Toux Aberds 302 D5
Migdale Highld 309 K6
Migvie Aberds 292 C6
Milarrochy Stirl 277 C8
Milber Devon 14 G3
Milborne Port Som 29 D11
Milborne St Andrew Dorset 18 B2
Milborne Wick Som 29 C11
Milbourne Northumb 242 B4
Milbourne Wilts 62 B2
Milburn Aberds 302 E5
Milburn Aberds 302 F6
Milburn Cumb 231 F9
Milbury Heath S Glos 79 G11
Milby N Yorks 215 F8
Milch Hill Essex 106 G4
Milcombe Corn 6 D4
Milcombe Oxon 101 E8
Milden Suff 107 B9
Mildenhall Suff 124 C4
Mildenhall Wilts 63 F8
Mile Cross Norf 160 G4
Mile Elm Wilts 62 F3
Mile End Cambs 140 G2
Mile End Devon 14 G2
Mile End Essex 107 F9
Mile End Glos 79 C9
Mile End London 67 C11
Mile End Suff 124 G6
Mile Oak Brighton 36 F2
Mile Oak Kent 53 E7
Mile Oak Shrops 148 D6
Mile Oak Staffs 134 C3
Mile Town Kent 70 E2
Milebrook Powys 114 C6
Milebush Kent 53 D9
Mileham Norf 159 F8
Miles Green Staffs 168 F4
Miles Green Sur 50 B3
Miles Hill W Yorks 205 F11
Miles Platting Gtr Man 184 B5
Milesmark Fife 279 D11
Miles's Green W Berks 64 F4
Milfield Northumb 263 C10
Milford Derbys 170 F5
Milford Devon 24 C2
Milford Powys 129 E11
Milford Shrops 149 E8
Milford Staffs 151 E9
Milford Sur 50 E2
Milford Wilts 31 B11
Milford Haven Pembs 72 D6
Milford on Sea Hants 19 C11
Milkhouse Water Wilts 63 G7
Milkieston Borders 270 F4
Milkwall Glos 79 D9
Milkwell Wilts 30 C6
Mill Bank W Yorks 196 C4
Mill Brow Gtr Man 185 D7
Mill Common Norf 142 C6
Mill Common Suff 143 G8
Mill Corner E Sus 38 C4
Mill Dam N Yorks 212 F3
Mill End Bucks 65 C9
Mill End Cambs 124 F3
Mill End Glos 81 C10
Mill End Herts 85 G8
Mill End Herts 104 E6
Mill End Green Essex 106 F2
Mill Farm Aberds 303 C8
Mill Green Cambs 106 B2
Mill Green Essex 87 E10
Mill Green Hants 64 G4
Mill Green Herts 86 D2
Mill Green Norf 142 G2
Mill Green Shrops 150 D3
Mill Green Staffs 107 C9
Mill Green Suff 125 F9
Mill Green Suff 126 F2
Mill Green W Mid 133 C11
Mill Hall Dumfries 237 E8
Mill Hill Blkburn 195 B7
Mill Hill E Sus 23 D10
Mill Hill Essex 88 G4
Mill Hill Glos 79 D10
Mill Hill Gtr Man 195 F8
Mill Hill Kent 55 C11
Mill Hill Lincs 175 B8
Mill Hill London 86 G2
Mill Hill Suff 125 G7
Mill Hills Suff 108 B5
Mill Hirst N Yorks 214 G3
Mill Lane Hants 49 C9
Mill Meads London 67 C11
Mill of Brydock Aberds 302 D6
Mill of Chon Stirl 285 G8
Mill of Haldane W Dunb 277 E8
Mill of Kingoodie Aberds 303 G8
Mill of Lynebain Aberds 302 F4
Mill of Muiresk Aberds 302 E6
Mill of Rango Orkney 314 E2
Mill of Sterin Aberds 292 D5
Mill of Uras Aberds 293 E10
Mill Park Argyll 255 G8
Mill Place N Lincs 200 F3
Mill Shaw W Yorks 205 G11
Mill Side Cumb 211 C8
Mill Street Kent 53 B7
Mill Street Norf 159 F11
Mill Street Suff 107 D9
Mill Throop Bmouth 19 B8
Milland W Sus 34 B4
Millarston Renfs 267 C9
Millbank Aberds 303 E11
Millbank Highld 310 C5
Millbank Kent 71 F8
Millbeck Cumb 229 F11
Millbounds Orkney 314 C5
Millbreck Aberds 303 E10
Millbridge Sur 49 E10
Millbrook C Beds 103 D10
Millbrook Corn 7 E8
Millbrook Devon 41 G9
Millbrook Gtr Man 185 B7
Millbrook Soton 32 E5
Millburn S Ayrs 257 D10
Millcombe Devon 8 F6
Milldale Staffs 169 E10
Millden Lodge Angus 293 F7
Milldens Angus 287 B9
Millend Glos 80 D3
Millend Glos 80 F3
Millendreath Corn 6 E5
Millerhill Midloth 270 B6
Miller's Dale Derbys 185 G10
Miller's Green Derbys 170 E3
Miller's Green Essex 87 D9
Millersneuk E Dunb 278 G3
Millerston Glasgow 268 B2
Millfield P'boro 138 C3
Millfield T & W 243 F9
Millgate Lancs 195 D11
Millgate Norf 160 D3
Millgillhead Cumb 229 G7
Millhalf Hereford 96 B5
Millhall Kent 53 B8
Millhayes Devon 27 E10
Millhayes Devon 28 G2
Millhead Lancs 211 E9
Millheugh S Lnrk 268 E5
Millhill Devon 12 G5
Millholme Cumb 221 G11
Millhouse Argyll 275 F10
Millhouse Cumb 230 D3
Millhouse Green S Yorks 197 G8
Millhousebridge Dumfries 248 F4
Millhouses S Yorks 186 E4
Millhouses S Yorks 198 G2
Millikenpark Renfs 267 C8
Millin Cross Pembs 73 C7
Millington E Yorks 208 C2
Millington Green Derbys 170 F3
Millmeece Staffs 150 C6
Millmoor Devon 27 E10
Millness Cumb 211 C10
Millom Cumb 210 C3
Millook Corn 11 B9
Millow C Beds 104 C4
Millpool Corn 2 C3
Millpool Corn 11 G8
Millport N Ayrs 266 E3
Millquarter Dumfries 246 G4
Milltack Aberds 303 D7
Millthorpe Derbys 186 F4
Millthorpe Lincs 156 C2
Millthrop Cumb 222 G3
Milltimber Aberdeen 293 C10
Milltown Aberds 292 C4
Milltown Corn 6 B2
Milltown Corn 6 D2
Milltown Derbys 170 C5
Milltown Devon 40 F5
Milltown Highld 301 E9
Milltown of Aberdalgie Perth 286 E4
Milltown of Auchindoun Moray 302 E3
Milltown of Craigston Aberds 303 D7
Milltown of Edinvillie Moray 302 E2
Milltown of Kildrummy Aberds 292 B6
Milltown of Rothiemay Moray 302 E5
Milltown of Towie Aberds 292 B6
Millwall London 67 D11
Milnathort Perth 286 G5
Milner's Heath W Ches 167 C7
Milngavie E Dunb 277 G11
Milnquarter Falk 278 F6
Milnrow Gtr Man 196 E2
Milnsbridge W Yorks 196 D6
Milnshaw Lancs 195 B9
Milnthorpe Cumb 211 C9
Milnthorpe W Yorks 197 D10
Milnwood N Lnrk 268 D4
Milo Carms 75 B9
Milson Shrops 116 C2
Milstead Kent 54 B2
Milston Wilts 47 D7
Milthorpe Northants 101 B11

Milton Angus 287 C7
Milton Angus 292 E6
Milton Cambs 123 E9
Milton Cumb 211 C10
Milton Cumb 240 E3
Milton Derbys 152 D6
Milton Dumfries 236 D4
Milton Dumfries 237 B10
Milton Dumfries 247 G8
Milton Fife 287 E8
Milton Glasgow 267 B11
Milton Highld 299 E7
Milton Highld 300 D3
Milton Highld 300 E5
Milton Highld 300 F4
Milton Highld 301 B7
Milton Highld 301 E7
Milton Highld 310 D7
Milton Kent 69 E7
Milton Moray 292 B3
Milton Moray 302 C5
Milton N Som 59 G10
Milton Notts 188 G2
Milton Oxon 83 G7
Milton Oxon 101 E8
Milton Pembs 73 E8
Milton Perth 286 F3
Milton Powys 114 G4
Milton Ptsmth 21 B9
Milton S Yorks 197 G11
Milton Som 29 C7
Milton Stirl 285 G9
Milton Stoke 168 E6
Milton W Dunb 277 G8
Milton Wilts 45 G11
Milton Abbas Dorset 30 G4
Milton Bridge Midloth 270 C4
Milton Bryan C Beds 103 E9
Milton Clevedon Som 45 F7
Milton Coldwells Aberds 303 F9
Milton Combe Devon 7 B9
Milton Common Oxon 83 E11
Milton Coombe Devon 7 B9
Milton Damerel Devon 24 E5
Milton End Glos 80 C2
Milton End Glos 81 E10
Milton Ernest Beds 121 F10
Milton Green Devon 12 F4
Milton Green W Ches 167 D7
Milton Heights Oxon 83 G7
Milton Hill Devon 14 F4
Milton Hill Oxon 83 G7
Milton Keynes M Keynes 103 D7
Milton Keynes Village M Keynes 103 D7
Milton Lilbourne Wilts 63 G7
Milton Malsor Northants 120 F4
Milton Morenish Perth 285 D10
Milton of Auchinhove Aberds 293 C7
Milton of Balgonie Fife 287 G7
Milton of Buchanan Stirl 277 C8
Milton of Campfield Aberds 293 C8
Milton of Campsie E Dunb 278 F3
Milton of Corsindae Aberds 293 C8
Milton of Cullerlie Aberds 293 C9
Milton of Cultoquhey Perth 286 E2
Milton of Cushnie Aberds 293 B7
Milton of Dalcapon Perth 286 B3
Milton of Drimmie Perth 286 B5
Milton of Edradour Perth 286 B3
Milton of Gollanfield Highld 301 D7
Milton of Lesmore Aberds 302 G4
Milton of Logie Aberds 292 C6
Milton of Machany Perth 286 F3
Milton of Mathers Aberds 293 G9
Milton of Murtle Aberdeen 293 C10
Milton of Noth Aberds 302 G5
Milton of Tullich Aberds 292 D5
Milton on Stour Dorset 30 B3
Milton Regis Kent 70 F2
Milton Street E Sus 23 E8
Milton under Wychwood Oxon 82 B3
Miltonduff Moray 301 C11
Miltonhill Moray 301 C10
Miltonise Dumfries 236 B3
Milverton Som 27 B10
Milverton Warks 118 D6
Milwich Staffs 151 C9
Milwr Flint 181 G11
Mimbridge Sur 66 G3
Minard Argyll 275 D10
Minard Castle Argyll 275 D10
Minchington Dorset 31 E7
Minchinhampton Glos 80 E5
Mindrum Northumb 263 C8
Minehead Som 42 D3
Minera Wrex 166 E3
Mineshope Corn 11 B9
Minety Wilts 81 G8
Minffordd Gwyn 145 B11
Minffordd Gwyn 146 G4
Minffordd Gwyn 179 G9
Mingarrypark Highld 289 C8
Mingoose Corn 4 F4
Miningsby Lincs 174 C4
Minions Corn 11 G11
Minishant S Ayrs 257 G8
Minllyn Gwyn 147 G7
Minnes Aberds 303 G9
Minngearraidh W Isles 297 J3
Minnigaff Dumfries 236 C6
Minnonie Aberds 303 C7
Minnow End Essex 88 C2
Minnygap Dumfries 248 D2
Minshull Vernon E Ches 167 C11
Minskip N Yorks 215 G7
Minstead Hants 32 E3
Minsted W Sus 34 C5
Minster Kent 70 E3
Minster Kent 71 G10
Minster Lovell Oxon 82 C4
Minsterley Shrops 131 C7
Minsterworth Glos 80 B3
Minterne Magna Dorset 29 G11
Minterne Parva Dorset 29 G11
Minting Lincs 189 G11
Mintlaw Aberds 303 E10
Minto Borders 262 E3
Minto Kames Borders 262 E3
Minton Shrops 131 E8
Mintsfeet Cumb 221 G10
Minwear Pembs 73 C8
Minworth W Mid 134 E3
Mirbister Orkney 314 E2
Mirehouse Cumb 219 B9
Mireland Highld 310 C7
Mirfield W Yorks 197 D8
Miserden Glos 80 D6
Misery Corner Norf 142 F5
Miskin Rhondda 58 C4
Miskin Rhondda 77 F8
Misselfore Wilts 31 C8
Misson Notts 187 C11
Misterton Leics 135 G11
Misterton Notts 188 C3
Misterton Som 29 F7
Misterton Soss Notts 188 B3
Mistley Essex 108 E2
Mistley Heath Essex 108 E2
Mitcham London 67 F9
Mitchel Troy Mon 79 C7
Mitcheldean Glos 79 B11
Mitchell Corn 5 E7
Mitchell Hill Borders 260 C3
Mitchellslacks Dumfries 247 D11
Mitchelston Borders 271 F9
Mitcheltroy Common Mon 79 D7
Mite Houses Cumb 219 F11
Mitford Northumb 252 F5
Mithian Corn 4 E4
Mithian Downs Corn 4 F4
Mitton Staffs 151 F7
Mitton Worcs 99 E8
Mixbury Oxon 102 E2
Mixenden W Yorks 196 B5
Mixtow Corn 6 E2
Moat Cumb 239 C10
Moats Tye Suff 125 F10
Mobberley E Ches 184 F3
Mobberley Staffs 169 G8
Moblake E Ches 167 G11
Mobwell Bucks 84 E5
Moccas Hereford 97 C7
Mochdre Conwy 180 F4
Mochdre Powys 129 F11
Mochrum Dumfries 236 E5
Mockbeggar Hants 31 F11
Mockbeggar Kent 54 E6
Mockbeggar Medway 69 E8
Mockerkin Cumb 229 G7
Moclett Orkney 314 B4
Modbury Devon 8 E3
Moddershall Staffs 151 B8
Model Village Derbys 187 G8
Model Village Warks 119 E8
Modest Corner Kent 52 E5
Moel Tryfan Gwyn 163 D8
Moel-y-crio Flint 165 B11
Moelfre Anglesey 179 D8
Moelfre Conwy 181 G7
Moelfre Powys 148 D3
Moffat Dumfries 248 B3
Moffat Mills N Lnrk 268 C5
Mogador Sur 51 C8
Moggerhanger C Beds 104 B2
Mogworthy Devon 26 D5
Moira Leics 152 F6
Moity Powys 96 C3
Mol-chlach Highld 294 D6
Molash Kent 54 C4
Mold Flint 166 C2
Moldgreen W Yorks 197 D7
Molehill Green Essex 105 G11
Molehill Green Essex 106 G4
Molescroft E Yorks 208 E6
Molesden Northumb 252 G4
Molesworth Cambs 121 B11
Molinnis Corn 5 D10
Moll Highld 295 B7
Molland Devon 26 B4
Mollington Oxon 101 B8
Mollington W Ches 182 G5
Mollinsburn N Lnrk 278 G4
Monachty Ceredig 111 E10
Monachylemore Stirl 285 F8
Monar Lodge Highld 300 E2
Monaughty Powys 114 D4
Monboddo House Aberds 293 F9
Mondaytown Shrops 130 B6
Mondynes Aberds 293 F9
Monemore Stirl 285 D9
Monevechadan Argyll 284 G5
Monewden Suff 126 F4
Money Hill Leics 153 F7
Moneyacres E Ayrs 267 E8
Moneydie Perth 286 E4
Moneyhill Herts 85 G8
Moneyrow Green Windsor 65 D11
Moneystone Staffs 169 F9
Mongleath Corn 3 C7
Moniaive Dumfries 247 E7
Monifieth Angus 287 D8
Monikie Angus 287 D8
Monimail Fife 286 F6
Monington Pembs 92 C2
Monk Bretton S Yorks 197 F11
Monk End N Yorks 224 D5
Monk Fryston N Yorks 198 B4
Monk Hesleden Durham 234 D5
Monk Sherborne Hants 48 B6
Monk Soham Suff 126 D4
Monk Street Essex 106 F2
Monken Hadley London 86 F3
Monkerton Devon 14 C5
Monkhide Hereford 98 C2
Monkhill Cumb 239 F8
Monkhill W Yorks 198 C3
Monkhopton Shrops 132 E2
Monkland Hereford 115 F9
Monkleigh Devon 25 C7
Monkmoor Shrops 149 G10
Monknash V Glam 58 E2
Monkokehampton Devon 25 F9
Monks Eleigh Suff 107 B9
Monk's Gate W Sus 36 B2
Monks Heath E Ches 184 G4
Monks Hill Kent 53 E11
Monks Kirby Warks 135 G9
Monks Orchard London 67 F11
Monk's Park Wilts 61 F11
Monks Risborough Bucks 84 E4
Monkscross Corn 12 G3
Monkseaton T & W 243 C8
Monkshill Aberds 303 E7
Monksilver Som 42 F5
Monkspath W Mid 118 B2
Monksthorpe Lincs 174 B6
Monkston Park M Keynes 103 D7
Monkswood Midloth 270 C6
Monkswood Mon 78 E4
Monkswood W Yorks 206 F2
Monkton Devon 27 G11
Monkton Kent 71 G9
Monkton Pembs 73 E7
Monkton S Ayrs 257 D9
Monkton T & W 243 E8
Monkton V Glam 58 E2
Monkton Combe Bath 61 G9
Monkton Deverill Wilts 45 F11
Monkton Farleigh Wilts 61 F10
Monkton Heathfield Som 28 B3
Monkton Up Wimborne Dorset 31 E8
Monktonhall E Loth 280 G6
Monkwearmouth T & W 243 F9
Monkwood Hants 49 G7
Monkwood Green Worcs 116 E6
Monmarsh Hereford 97 B10
Monmore Green W Mid 133 D8
Monmouth Mon 79 C8
Monmouth Cap Mon 97 F7
Monnington on Wye Hereford 97 C7
Monreith Dumfries 236 E5
Monreith Mains Dumfries 236 E5
Montacute Som 29 D7
Montcliffe Gtr Man 195 E7
Montcoffer Ho Aberds 302 C6
Montford Argyll 266 C2
Montford Shrops 149 G8
Montford Bridge Shrops 149 F8
Montgarrie Aberds 293 B7
Montgomery Powys 130 D4
Montgomery Lines Hants 49 C11
Monton Gtr Man 184 B3
Montpelier Bristol 60 E5
Montrave Fife 287 G7
Montrose Angus 287 B11
Montsale Essex 89 F8
Monwode Lea Warks 134 E5
Monxton Hants 47 E10
Monyash Derbys 169 B11
Monymusk Aberds 293 B8
Monzie Perth 286 E2
Monzie Castle Perth 286 E2
Moodiesburn N Lnrk 278 G3
Moolham Som 28 E5
Moon's Green Kent 38 B5
Moon's Moat Worcs 117 D11
Moonzie Fife 287 F7
Moor Som 28 D6
Moor Allerton W Yorks 205 F11
Moor Common Bucks 84 G4
Moor Crichel Dorset 31 F7
Moor Cross Devon 8 D2
Moor Edge W Yorks 205 F7
Moor End Bucks 84 G4
Moor End C Beds 103 G9
Moor End Cambs 105 B7
Moor End Durham 234 C2
Moor End E Yorks 208 F2
Moor End Glos 99 G9
Moor End Lancs 202 E3
Moor End N Yorks 207 F7
Moor End N Yorks 215 G7
Moor End S Yorks 197 G9
Moor End W Yorks 196 B5
Moor End W Yorks 206 D4
Moor End Worcs 117 F8
Moor End York 207 B9
Moor End Field N Yorks 215 F8
Moor Green Herts 104 F6
Moor Green Staffs 169 G7
Moor Green W Mid 133 G11
Moor Green Wilts 61 F11
Moor Hall W Mid 134 D2
Moor Head W Yorks 197 B8
Moor Head W Yorks 197 E8
Moor Monkton N Yorks 206 B6
Moor Monkton Moor N Yorks 206 B6
Moor of Balvack Aberds 293 B8
Moor of Granary Moray 301 D10
Moor of Ravenstone Dumfries 236 E5
Moor Park Cumb 229 D7
Moor Park Hereford 97 C9
Moor Park Herts 85 G9
Moor Park Sur 49 D11
Moor Row Cumb 219 C10
Moor Row Cumb 229 B10
Moor Side Lancs 202 F5
Moor Side Lancs 202 G4
Moor Side Lincs 174 D2
Moor Side W Yorks 197 B7
Moor Side W Yorks 204 F6
Moor Street Kent 69 F10
Moor Top W Yorks 197 C7
Mooradale Shetland 312 F6
Mooray Wilts 46 G3
Moorby Lincs 174 C3
Moorclose Cumb 228 F5
Moorclose Gtr Man 195 F11
Moorcot Hereford 115 F7
Moordown Bmouth 19 C7
Moore Halton 183 E9
Moorend Cumb 239 G8
Moorend Derbys 170 F2
Moorend Dumfries 239 C7
Moorend Glos 80 C5
Moorend Glos 80 E2
Moorend Gtr Man 185 D7
Moorend S Glos 61 D7
Moorend Cross Hereford 98 B4
Moorends S Yorks 199 D7
Moorfield Derbys 185 C8
Moorgate Norf 160 C3
Moorgate S Yorks 186 C6
Moorgreen Hants 33 D7
Moorgreen Notts 171 F7
Moorhaigh Notts 171 C8
Moorhall Derbys 186 G4
Moorhampton Hereford 97 B7
Moorhaven Village Devon 8 D3
Moorhayne Devon 28 F2
Moorhead W Yorks 205 F8
Moorhey Gtr Man 196 G2
Moorhole S Yorks 186 E6
Moorhouse Cumb 239 F8
Moorhouse Cumb 239 G7
Moorhouse Notts 172 B3
Moorhouse S Yorks 198 E3
Moorhouse Bank Sur 52 C2
Moorhouses Lincs 174 D3
Moorland or Northmoor Green Som 43 G10
Moorledge Bath 60 G5
Moorlinch Som 43 F11
Moorsholm Redcar 226 C3
Moorside Corn 30 D3
Moorside Durham 233 B7
Moorside Gtr Man 195 G9
Moorside Gtr Man 196 F3
Moorside W Ches 182 F3
Moorside W Yorks 197 B8
Moorside W Yorks 205 F10
Moorstock Kent 54 F6
Moorswater Corn 6 C4
Moorthorpe W Yorks 198 E3
Moortown Devon 12 B2
Moortown Devon 12 G6
Moortown Devon 25 C8
Moortown Hants 31 G11
Moortown I o W 20 E4
Moortown Lincs 189 B9
Moortown Telford 150 F2
Moortown W Yorks 206 F2
Morangie Highld 309 L7
Morar Highld 295 F8
Moravian Settlement Derbys 153 B8
Môrawelon Anglesey 178 E3
Morayhill Highld 301 E7
Morborne Cambs 138 E2
Morchard Bishop Devon 26 F3
Morchard Road Devon 26 G3
Morcombelake Dorset 16 C4
Morcott Rutland 137 C8
Morda Shrops 148 D5
Morden Dorset 18 B4
Morden London 67 F9
Morden Green Cambs 104 C5
Morden Park London 67 F8
Mordiford Hereford 97 D11
Mordington Holdings Borders 273 D8
Mordon Durham 234 F2
More Shrops 130 E6
More Crichel Dorset 31 F7
Morebath Devon 27 C7
Morebattle Borders 263 E7
Morecambe Lancs 211 G8
Moredon Swindon 62 B6
Moredun Edin 270 B5
Morefield Highld 307 K6
Morehall Kent 55 F8
Morelaggan Argyll 284 G6
Moreleigh Devon 8 E5
Morenish Perth 285 D9
Moresby Cumb 228 G5
Moresby Parks Cumb 219 B9
Morestead Hants 33 B8
Moreton Dorset 18 D2
Moreton Essex 87 D8
Moreton Hereford 115 E10
Moreton Mers 182 C3
Moreton Oxon 82 E6
Moreton Oxon 83 E11
Moreton Staffs 150 F5
Moreton Staffs 152 D2
Moreton Corbet Shrops 149 E11
Moreton-in-Marsh Glos 100 E4
Moreton Jeffries Hereford 98 B2
Moreton Morrell Warks 118 F6
Moreton on Lugg Hereford 97 B10
Moreton Paddox Warks 118 G6
Moreton Pinkney Northants 101 B11
Moreton Say Shrops 150 C2
Moreton Valence Glos 80 D3
Moretonhampstead Devon 13 D11
Moretonwood Shrops 150 C2
Morfa Carms 56 B4
Morfa Carms 75 C9
Morfa Ceredig 110 G6
Morfa Gwyn 144 C3
Morfa Bach Carms 74 C5
Morfa Bychan Gwyn 145 B10
Morfa Dinlle Gwyn 162 D6
Morfa Glas Neath 76 D5
Morfa Nefyn Gwyn 162 G3
Morfydd Denb 165 F10
Morgan's Vale Wilts 31 C11
Morganstown Cardiff 58 C6
Moriah Ceredig 112 B2
Mork Glos 79 D9
Morland Cumb 231 G7
Morley Derbys 170 G5
Morley Durham 233 F8
Morley E Ches 184 E4
Morley W Yorks 197 B9
Morley Green E Ches 184 E4
Morley Park Derbys 170 F5
Morley St Botolph Norf 141 D11
Morley Smithy Derbys 170 G5
Morleymoor Derbys 170 G5
Mornick Corn 12 G2
Morningside Edin 280 G3
Morningside N Lnrk 268 D6
Morningthorpe Norf 142 E4
Morpeth Northumb 252 F6
Morphie Aberds 293 G9
Morrey Staffs 152 F2
Morridge Side Staffs 169 E8
Morrilow Heath Staffs 151 B9
Morris Green Essex 106 E4
Morriston = Treforys Swansea 57 B7
Morristown V Glam 59 E7
Morston Norf 177 E8
Mortehoe Devon 40 D3
Morthen S Yorks 187 D7
Mortimer W Berks 65 G7
Mortimer West End Hants 64 G6
Mortimer's Cross Hereford 115 E8
Mortlake London 67 D8
Mortomley S Yorks 186 B4
Morton Cumb 230 D4
Morton Cumb 239 G9
Morton Derbys 170 C6
Morton I o W 21 D8
Morton Lincs 155 E11
Morton Lincs 172 C5
Morton Lincs 188 C4
Morton Norf 160 F2
Morton Notts 172 E2
Morton S Glos 79 G10
Morton Shrops 148 E5
Morton Bagot Warks 118 E2
Morton Common Shrops 148 E5
Morton Mains Dumfries 247 D9
Morton Mill Shrops 149 E11
Morton-on-Swale N Yorks 224 G6
Morton Spirt Warks 117 G10
Morton Tinmouth Durham 233 G9
Morton Underhill Worcs 117 F10
Morvah Corn 1 B4
Morval Corn 6 D5
Morven Lodge Aberds 292 C5
Morvich Highld 295 C11
Morvich Highld 309 J7
Morville Shrops 132 E3
Morville Heath Shrops 132 E3
Morwellham Quay Devon 7 B8
Morwenstow Corn 24 E2
Mosborough S Yorks 186 E6
Moscow E Ayrs 267 G9
Mose Shrops 132 E5
Mosedale Cumb 230 E3
Moseley W Mid 133 D8
Moseley W Mid 133 G11
Moseley Worcs 116 F6
Moses Gate Gtr Man 195 F8
Mosley Common Gtr Man 195 G8
Moss Argyll 288 E1
Moss Highld 289 C8
Moss S Yorks 198 E5
Moss Wrex 166 E4
Moss Bank Halton 183 D8
Moss Bank Mers 183 B8
Moss Edge Lancs 202 D4
Moss Edge Lancs 202 E4
Moss End Brack 65 E11
Moss End E Ches 183 F11
Moss Houses E Ches 184 G5
Moss Lane E Ches 184 G6
Moss Nook Gtr Man 184 D4
Moss Nook Mers 183 C8
Moss of Barmuckity Moray 302 C2
Moss of Meft Moray 302 C2
Moss Pit Staffs 151 E8
Moss Side Cumb 238 G5
Moss Side Gtr Man 184 B4
Moss-side Highld 301 D8
Moss Side Lancs 193 G11
Moss Side Lancs 194 C4
Moss Side Lancs 202 G3
Moss Side Mers 182 B6
Moss-side Moray 302 D5
Mossat Aberds 292 B6
Mossbank Shetland 312 F6
Mossbay Cumb 228 F5
Mossblown S Ayrs 257 E10
Mossbrow Gtr Man 184 D2
Mossburnford Borders 262 F5
Mossdale Dumfries 237 B8
Mossedge Cumb 239 D11
Mossend N Lnrk 268 C4
Mosser Mains Cumb 229 F8
Mossfield Highld 300 B6
Mossgate Staffs 151 B8
Mossgiel E Ayrs 257 D11
Mosshouses Borders 262 B2
Mosside Angus 287 B8
Mossley E Ches 168 C5
Mossley Gtr Man 196 G3
Mossley Brow Gtr Man 196 G3
Mossley Hill Mers 182 D5
Mosspark Glasgow 267 C10
Mosstodloch Moray 302 D3
Mosston Angus 287 C9
Mosstown Aberds 303 C10
Mossy Lea Lancs 194 E4
Mosterton Dorset 29 F7
Moston E Ches 168 C2
Moston Gtr Man 195 G11
Moston Shrops 149 D11
Moston W Ches 182 G6
Moston Green E Ches 168 C2
Mostyn Flint 181 E11
Mostyn Quay Flint 181 E11
Motcombe Dorset 30 B5
Mothecombe Devon 8 F2
Motherby Cumb 230 F4
Motherwell N Lnrk 268 D5
Motspur Park London 67 F8
Mottingham London 68 E2
Mottisfont Hants 32 B4
Mottistone I o W 20 E4
Mottram in Longdendale Gtr Man 185 B7
Mottram Rise Gtr Man 185 B7
Mottram St Andrew E Ches 184 F5
Mott's Green Essex 87 B8
Mott's Mill E Sus 52 F4
Mouldsworth W Ches 183 G8
Moulin Perth 286 B3
Moulsecoomb Brighton 36 F4
Moulsford Oxon 64 C5
Moulsham Essex 88 D2
Moulsoe M Keynes 103 C8
Moultavie Highld 300 B6
Moulton Lincs 156 E6
Moulton N Yorks 224 E4
Moulton Northants 120 D5
Moulton Suff 124 E3
Moulton V Glam 58 E5
Moulton W Ches 167 B11
Moulton Chapel Lincs 156 F5
Moulton Eaugate Lincs 156 F6
Moulton Park Northants 120 E5
Moulton St Mary Norf 143 B7
Moulton Seas End Lincs 156 D6
Moulzie Angus 292 F4
Mounie Castle Aberds 303 G7
Mount Corn 4 D5
Mount Corn 6 B2
Mount Highld 301 E9
Mount W Yorks 196 D5
Mount Ambrose Corn 4 G4
Mount Ballan Mon 60 B3
Mount Batten Plym 7 E9
Mount Bovers Essex 88 G4
Mount Bures Essex 107 E8
Mount Canisp Highld 301 B7
Mount Charles Corn 5 B10
Mount Charles Corn 5 E10
Mount Cowdown Wilts 47 C9
Mount End Essex 87 E7
Mount Ephraim E Sus 23 B7
Mount Gould Plym 7 D9
Mount Hawke Corn 4 F4
Mount Hermon Corn 2 F6
Mount Hermon Sur 50 B4
Mount Hill S Glos 61 E7
Mount Lane Devon 12 B3
Mount Pleasant Bucks 102 E3
Mount Pleasant Corn 5 C10
Mount Pleasant Derbys 152 D6
Mount Pleasant Derbys 152 F5
Mount Pleasant Derbys 170 F4
Mount Pleasant Devon 27 G11
Mount Pleasant Durham 233 E11
Mount Pleasant E Ches 168 D4
Mount Pleasant E Sus 23 E7
Mount Pleasant E Sus 36 D6
Mount Pleasant Flint 182 G2
Mount Pleasant Hants 19 B11
Mount Pleasant Kent 71 F10
Mount Pleasant London 85 G8
Mount Pleasant M Tydf 77 F9
Mount Pleasant Neath 57 B9
Mount Pleasant Norf 141 E9
Mount Pleasant Pembs 73 D8
Mount Pleasant Shrops 149 G9
Mount Pleasant Stockton 234 G4
Mount Pleasant Stoke 168 G5
Mount Pleasant Suff 106 B4
Mount Pleasant T & W 243 E7
Mount Pleasant W Yorks 197 C8
Mount Pleasant Warks 135 F7
Mount Pleasant Worcs 99 D10
Mount Pleasant Worcs 117 E10
Mount Sion Wrex 166 E3
Mount Skippett Oxon 82 B5
Mount Sorrel Wilts 31 C8
Mount Tabor W Yorks 196 B5
Mount Vernon Glasgow 268 C3
Mount Wise Corn 7 E9
Mountain Anglesey 178 E2
Mountain W Yorks 205 G7
Mountain Air Bl Gwent 77 D11
Mountain Ash = Aberpennar Rhondda 77 F8
Mountain Bower Wilts 61 D10
Mountain Cross Borders 270 F2
Mountain Street Kent 54 C5
Mountain Water Pembs 91 G8
Mountbenger Borders 261 D8
Mountbengerburn Borders 261 D8
Mountblow W Dunb 277 G9
Mounters Dorset 30 D3
Mountfield E Sus 38 C2
Mountgerald Highld 300 C5
Mountjoy Corn 5 C7
Mountnessing Essex 87 F10
Mounton Mon 79 G8
Mountsolie Aberds 303 D9
Mountsorrel Leics 153 F11
Mousehill Sur 50 E2
Mousehole Corn 1 D5
Mousen Northumb 264 C4
Mousley End Warks 118 D4
Mouswald Dumfries 238 C3
Mouth Mill Devon 24 B3
Mow Cop E Ches 168 D5
Mowbreck Lancs 202 G4
Mowden Darl 224 B5
Mowden Essex 88 C3
Mowhaugh Borders 263 E8
Mowmacre Hill Leicester 135 B11
Mowshurst Kent 52 D3
Mowsley Leics 136 F2
Moxby N Yorks 215 F11
Moxley W Mid 133 D9
Moy Argyll 255 E8
Moy Highld 290 E6
Moy Highld 301 F7
Moy Hall Highld 301 F7
Moy Ho Moray 301 C10
Moy Lodge Highld 290 E6
Moyles Court Hants 31 F11
Moylgrove = Trewyddel Pembs 92 C2
Muasdale Argyll 255 C7
Much Birch Hereford 97 E10
Much Cowardne Hereford 98 B2
Much Cowarne Hereford 98 B2
Much Dewchurch Hereford 97 E9
Much Hadham Herts 86 B5
Much Hoole Lancs 194 C3
Much Hoole Moss Houses Lancs 194 C3
Much Hoole Town Lancs 194 C3
Much Marcle Hereford 98 E3
Much Wenlock Shrops 132 C2
Muchalls Aberds 293 D11
Muchelney Som 28 C6
Muchelney Ham Som 28 C6
Muchlarnick Corn 6 D4
Muchrachd Highld 300 F2
Muckairn Argyll 289 F11
Muckernich Highld 300 D5
Mucking Thurrock 69 C7
Muckle Breck Shetland 312 G7
Muckleford Dorset 17 C8
Mucklestone Staffs 150 B4
Muckleton Norf 158 B6
Muckleton Shrops 149 E11
Muckletown Aberds 302 G5
Muckley Shrops 132 D2
Muckley Corner Staffs 133 B11
Muckley Cross Shrops 132 D2
Muckton Lincs 190 E5
Muckton Bottom Lincs 190 E5
Mudale Highld 308 F5
Mudd Gtr Man 185 C7
Muddiford Devon 40 F5
Muddlebridge Devon 40 G4
Muddles Green E Sus 23 C8
Mudeford Dorset 19 C9
Mudford Som 29 D9
Mudford Sock Som 29 D9
Mudgley Som 44 D2
Mugdock Stirl 277 F11
Mugeary Highld 294 B6
Mugginton Derbys 170 G3
Muggintonlane End Derbys 170 G3
Muggleswick Durham 232 B6
Mugswell Sur 51 C9
Muie Highld 309 J6
Muir Aberds 292 E2
Muir of Alford Aberds 293 B7
Muir of Fairburn Highld 300 D4
Muir of Fowlis Aberds 293 B7
Muir of Kinellar Aberds 293 B10
Muir of Miltonduff Moray 301 D11
Muir of Ord Highld 300 D5
Muir of Pert Angus 287 D8
Muircleugh Borders 271 F10
Muirden Aberds 303 D7
Muirdrum Angus 287 D9
Muiredge Fife 281 B7
Muirend Glasgow 267 C11
Muirhead Angus 287 D7
Muirhead Fife 286 G6
Muirhead Fife 287 F8
Muirhead N Lnrk 268 B3
Muirhead S Ayrs 257 C8
Muirhouse Edin 280 F4
Muirhouse N Lnrk 268 D5
Muirhouselaw Borders 262 D4
Muirhouses Falk 279 E10
Muirkirk E Ayrs 258 D5
Muirmill Stirl 278 E4
Muirshearlich Highld 290 E3
Muirskie Aberds 293 D10
Muirtack Aberds 303 F9
Muirton Aberds 303 D7
Muirton Highld 301 C7
Muirton Perth 286 E5
Muirton Perth 286 F3
Muirton Mains Highld 300 D4
Muirton of Ardblair Perth 286 C5
Muirton of Ballochy Angus 293 G8
Muiryfold Aberds 303 D7
Muker N Yorks 223 F8
Mulbarton Norf 142 C3
Mulben Moray 302 D3
Mulberry Corn 5 B10
Mulfra Corn 1 C5
Mulindry Argyll 254 B4
Mulla Shetland 313 G6
Mullardoch House Highld 300 F2
Mullenspond Hants 47 D9
Mullion Corn 2 F5

Mullion Cove Corn 2 F5
Mumbles Hill Swansea 56 D6
Mumby Lincs 191 G8
Mumps Gtr Man 196 F2
Mundale Moray 301 D10
Munderfield Row Hereford 116 G2
Munderfield Stocks Hereford 116 G2
Mundesley Norf 160 B6
Mundford Norf 140 E6
Mundham Norf 142 D6
Mundon Essex 88 E5
Mundurno Aberdeen 293 B11
Mundy Bois Kent 54 D2
Munerigie Highld 290 C4
Muness Shetland 312 C8
Mungasdale Highld 307 K4
Mungrisdale Cumb 230 E3
Munlochy Highld 300 D6
Munsary Cottage Highld 310 E6
Munsley Hereford 98 C3
Munslow Shrops 131 F10
Munstone Hereford 97 C10
Murch V Glam 59 E7
Murchington Devon 13 D9
Murcot Worcs 99 C11
Murcott Oxon 83 B9
Murcott Wilts 81 G7
Murdieston Stirl 278 B3
Murdishaw Halton 183 E9
Murieston W Loth 269 C11
Murkle Highld 310 C5
Murlaggan Highld 290 D2
Murlaggan Highld 290 E5
Murra Orkney 314 F2
Murrayfield Edin 280 G4
Murrayshall Perth 286 E5
Murraythwaite Dumfries 238 C4
Murrell Green Hants 49 B8
Murrell's End Glos 98 E4
Murrell's End Glos 98 G5
Murrion Shetland 312 F4
Murrow Cambs 139 B7
Mursley Bucks 102 F6
Murston Kent 70 G2
Murthill Angus 287 B8
Murthly Perth 286 D4
Murton Cumb 231 G10
Murton Durham 234 B3
Murton Northumb 273 F9
Murton Swansea 56 D5
Murton T & W 243 C8
Murton York 207 C8
Murton Grange N Yorks 215 B10
Murtwell Devon 8 D5
Musbury Devon 15 C11
Muscliff Bmouth 19 B7
Muscoates N Yorks 216 C3
Muscott Northants 120 E2
Musdale Argyll 289 G11
Mushroom Green W Mid 133 F8
Musselburgh E Loth 280 G6
Musselwick Pembs 72 D4
Mustard Hyrn Norf 161 F8
Muston Leics 154 B6
Muston N Yorks 217 D11
Mustow Green Worcs 117 C7
Muswell Hill London 86 G3
Mutehill Dumfries 237 E8
Mutford Suff 143 F9
Muthill Perth 286 F2
Mutley Plym 7 D9
Mutterton Devon 27 G8
Mutton Hall E Sus 37 C9
Muxton Telford 150 G4
Mwdwl-eithin Flint 181 F11
Mwynbwll Flint 165 B11
Mybster Highld 310 D5
Myddfai Carms 94 F5
Myddle Shrops 149 E9
Myddlewood Shrops 149 E9
Myddyn-fych Carms 75 C10
Mydroilyn Ceredig 111 F9
Myerscough Lancs 202 F5
Myerscough Smithy Lancs 203 G8
Mylor Bridge Corn 3 B8
Mylor Churchtown Corn 3 B8
Mynachdy Cardiff 59 D7
Mynachdy Rhondda 77 F8
Mynachlog-ddu Pembs 92 E2
Mynd Shrops 115 C7
Myndd Llandegai Gwyn 163 B10
Myndtown Shrops 131 F7
Mynydd Bach Ceredig 112 B4
Mynydd-bach Mon 79 G7
Mynydd-Bach Swansea 57 B7
Mynydd-bach-y-glo Swansea 56 B6
Mynydd Bodafon Anglesey 179 D7
Mynydd Fflint = Flint Mountain Flint 182 G2
Mynydd Gilan Gwyn 144 E5
Mynydd-isa Flint 166 C3
Mynydd-llan Flint 181 G11
Mynydd Marian Conwy 180 F5
Mynydd Mechell Anglesey 178 D5
Mynyddislwyn Caerph 77 G11
Mynyddygarreg Carms 74 D6
Mynytho Gwyn 144 C6
Myrebird Aberds 293 D9
Myrelandhorn Highld 310 D6
Myreside Perth 286 E6
Myrtle Hill Carms 94 E5
Mytchett Sur 49 B11
Mytchett Place Sur 49 C11
Mytholm W Yorks 196 B3
Mytholmes W Yorks 204 F6
Mytholmroyd W Yorks 196 B4
Mythop Lancs 202 G3
Mytice Aberds 302 F4
Myton Warks 118 E6
Myton Hall N Yorks 215 F8
Myton-on-Swale N Yorks 215 F8
Mytton Shrops 149 F8

N

Na Gearrannan W Isles 304 D3
Naast Highld 307 L3
Nab Hill W Yorks 197 D7
Nab Wood W Yorks 205 F8
Nab's Head Lancs 194 B6
Naburn York 207 D7
Naccolt Kent 54 E4
Nackington Kent 55 C7
Nacton Suff 108 C4
Nadderwater Devon 14 C3
Nafferton E Yorks 209 B7
Nag's Head Glos 80 F5
Naid-y-march Flint 181 F11
Nailbridge Glos 79 B10
Nailsbourne Som 28 B2
Nailsea N Som 60 D3
Nailstone Leics 135 B8
Nailsworth Glos 80 F5
Nailwell Bath 61 G8
Nairn Highld 301 D8
Nalderswood Sur 51 D8
Nance Corn 4 G3
Nanceddan Corn 2 C2
Nancegollan Corn 2 C4
Nancemellin Corn 4 G2
Nancenoy Corn 2 D6
Nancledra Corn 1 B5
Nangreaves Lancs 195 D10
Nanhoron Gwyn 144 C5
Nanhyfer = Nevern Pembs 91 D11
Nannau Gwyn 146 E4
Nannerch Flint 165 B11
Nanpantan Leics 153 F10
Nanpean Corn 5 D9
Nanquidno Corn 1 D3
Nanstallon Corn 5 B10
Nant Carms 74 B6
Nant Denb 165 D11
Nant Alyn Flint 165 B11
Nant-ddu Powys 77 B8
Nant-glas Powys 113 E9
Nant Mawr Flint 166 C3
Nant Peris = Old Llanberis Gwyn 163 D10
Nant Uchaf Denb 165 D8
Nant-y-Bai Carms 94 C5
Nant-y-Bwch Bl Gwent 77 C10
Nant-y-cafn Neath 76 D4
Nant y Caws Shrops 148 D5
Nant-y-ceisiad Caerph 59 B8
Nant-y-derry Mon 78 D4
Nant-y-felin Conwy 179 G11
Nant-y-ffin Carms 93 E11
Nant-y-gollen Shrops 148 D4
Nant-y-moel Bridgend 76 G6
Nant-y-pandy Conwy 179 G11
Nant-y-Rhiw Conwy 164 D4
Nanternis Ceredig 111 F7
Nantgaredig Carms 93 G9
Nantgarw Rhondda 58 B6
Nantglyn Denb 165 C8
Nantgwyn Powys 113 B9
Nantithet Corn 2 E5
Nantle Gwyn 163 E8
Nantmawr Shrops 148 E5
Nantmel Powys 113 D10
Nantmor Gwyn 163 F10
Nantserth Powys 113 C9
Nantwich E Ches 167 E11
Nantycaws Carms 75 B7
Nantyffyllon Bridgend 57 C11
Nantyglo Bl Gwent 77 C11
Nantyronen Station Ceredig 112 B3
Napchester Kent 55 D10
Naphill Bucks 84 F4
Napleton Worcs 99 B7
Napley Staffs 150 B4
Napley Heath Staffs 150 B4
Nappa N Yorks 204 C3
Nappa Scar N Yorks 223 G9
Napton on the Hill Warks 119 E9
Narberth = Arberth Pembs 73 C10
Narberth Bridge Pembs 73 C10
Narborough Leics 135 D10
Narborough Norf 158 G4
Narfords Som 28 F3
Narkurs Corn 6 D6
Narracott Devon 24 D5
Narrowgate Corner Norf 161 F8
Nasareth Gwyn 163 E7
Naseby Northants 120 B3
Nash Bucks 102 E5
Nash Hereford 114 E6
Nash Kent 55 B9
Nash London 68 G2
Nash Newport 59 C10
Nash Shrops 116 C2
Nash Som 29 E8
Nash End Worcs 132 G5
Nash Lee Bucks 84 D4
Nash Mills Herts 85 E9
Nash Street E Sus 23 C8
Nash Street Kent 68 F6
Nashend Glos 80 D5
Nashes Green Hants 49 D7
Nassington Northants 137 D11
Nast Hyde Herts 86 D2
Nastend Glos 80 D3
Nasty Herts 105 G7
Natcott Devon 24 C3
Nateby Cumb 222 D5
Nateby Lancs 202 E5
Nately Scures Hants 49 C8
Natland Cumb 211 B10
Natton Glos 99 E8
Naughton Suff 107 B10
Naunton Glos 100 G2
Naunton Worcs 99 D7
Naunton Beauchamp Worcs 117 G9
Navant Hill W Sus 34 B6
Navenby Lincs 173 D7
Navestock Heath Essex 87 F8
Navestock Side Essex 87 F9
Navidale Highld 311 H4
Navity Highld 301 C7
Nawton N Yorks 216 C3
Nayland Suff 107 E9
Nazeing Essex 86 D6
Nazeing Gate Essex 86 D6
Nazeing Long Green Essex 86 E6
Nazeing Mead Essex 86 D5
Neacroft Hants 19 B9
Nealhouse Cumb 239 G8
Neal's Green Warks 134 G6
Neames Forstal Kent 54 B5
Neap Shetland 313 H7
Near Hardcastle N Yorks 214 F2
Near Sawrey Cumb 221 F7
Nearton End Bucks 102 F6
Neasden London 67 B8
Neasham Darl 224 C6
Neat Enstone Oxon 101 G7
Neat Marsh E Yorks 209 G9
Neath = Castell-nedd Neath 57 B8
Neath Abbey Neath 57 B8
Neath Hill M Keynes 103 C7
Neatham Hants 49 E8
Neatishead Norf 160 E6
Neaton Norf 141 C8
Nebo Anglesey 179 C7
Nebo Ceredig 111 D10
Nebo Conwy 164 D4
Nebo Gwyn 163 E7
Nebsworth Warks 100 C3
Nechells W Mid 133 F11
Necton Norf 141 B7
Nedd Highld 306 F6
Nedderton Northumb 252 G6
Nedge Hill Som 44 C5
Nedge Hill Telford 132 B4
Nedging Suff 107 B9
Nedging Tye Suff 107 B10
Needham Norf 142 G4
Needham Green Essex 87 B9
Needham Market Suff 125 G11
Needham Street Suff 124 D4
Needingworth Cambs 122 C6
Needwood Staffs 152 E3
Neen Savage Shrops 116 B3
Neen Sollars Shrops 116 C3
Neenton Shrops 132 F2
Nefod Shrops 148 B6
Nefyn Gwyn 162 G4
Neighbourne Som 44 D6
Neight Hill Worcs 117 F8
Neilston E Renf 267 D9
Neinthirion Powys 129 B9
Neithrop Oxon 101 C8
Nelly Andrews Green Powys 130 B5
Nelson Caerph 77 F10
Nelson Lancs 204 F3
Nelson Village Northumb 243 B7
Nemphlar S Lnrk 269 G7
Nempnett Thrubwell N Som 60 G4
Nene Terrace Lincs 138 B5
Nenthall Cumb 231 B11
Nenthead Cumb 231 C11
Nenthorn Borders 262 B5
Neopardy Devon 13 B11
Nep Town W Sus 36 D2
Nepcote W Sus 35 F10
Nepgill Cumb 229 F7
Nerabus Argyll 254 B3
Nercwys Flint 166 C2
Nerston S Lnrk 268 D2
Nesbit Northumb 263 C11
Ness Orkney 314 C4
Ness W Ches 182 F4
Nesscliffe Shrops 149 F7
Nessholt W Ches 182 F4
Nesstoun Orkney 314 A7
Neston W Ches 182 F3
Neston Wilts 61 F11
Netchells Green W Mid 133 F11
Netham Bristol 60 E6
Nethanfoot S Lnrk 268 F6
Nether Alderley E Ches 184 F4
Nether Blainslie Borders 271 G10
Nether Booth Derbys 185 D10
Nether Broughton Leics 154 D3
Nether Burrow Lancs 212 D2
Nether Burrows Derbys 152 B5
Nether Cassock Dumfries 248 C6
Nether Cerne Dorset 17 B9
Nether Chanderhill Derbys 186 G4
Nether Compton Dorset 29 D9
Nether Crimond Aberds 303 G8
Nether Dalgliesh Borders 249 B7
Nether Dallachy Moray 302 C3
Nether Edge S Yorks 186 E4
Nether End Derbys 186 G3
Nether End Leics 154 G4
Nether End W Yorks 197 F8
Nether Exe Devon 26 G6
Nether Glasslaw Aberds 303 D8
Nether Hall Leicester 136 B2
Nether Handley Derbys 186 F6
Nether Handwick Angus 287 C7
Nether Haugh S Yorks 186 B6
Nether Headon Notts 188 F2
Nether Heage Derbys 170 E5
Nether Heyford Northants 120 F3
Nether Hindhope Borders 263 G7
Nether Horsburgh Borders 261 B8
Nether Howecleuch S Lnrk 260 G2
Nether Kellet Lancs 211 F10
Nether Kidston Borders 270 G4
Nether Kinmundy Aberds 303 E10
Nether Kirton E Renf 267 D9
Nether Langwith Notts 187 G8
Nether Leask Aberds 303 F10
Nether Lenshie Aberds 302 E6
Nether Loads Derbys 170 B4
Nether Monynut Borders 272 C4
Nether Moor Derbys 170 B5
Nether Padley Derbys 186 F3
Nether Park Aberds 303 D10
Nether Poppleton York 207 B7
Nether Row Cumb 230 D2
Nether Savock Aberds 303 E10
Nether Shiels Borders 271 F8
Nether Silton N Yorks 225 G9
Nether Skyborry Shrops 114 C5
Nether St Suff 125 E8
Nether Stowe Staffs 152 G2
Nether Stowey Som 43 F7
Nether Street Essex 87 C9
Nether Street Herts 86 B6
Nether Urquhart Fife 286 G5
Nether Wallop Hants 47 F10
Nether Warden Northumb 241 D10
Nether Wasdale Cumb 220 E2
Nether Welton Cumb 230 B3
Nether Westcote Glos 100 G4
Nether Whitacre Warks 134 E4
Nether Winchendon or Lower Winchendon Bucks 84 C2
Nether Worton Oxon 101 E8
Nether Yeadon W Yorks 205 E10
Netheravon Wilts 46 D6
Netherbrae Aberds 303 D7
Netherbrough Orkney 314 E3
Netherburn S Lnrk 268 F6
Netherbury Dorset 16 B5
Netherby Cumb 239 C9
Netherby N Yorks 206 D2
Netherclay Som 28 C3
Nethercote Oxon 101 C9
Nethercote Warks 119 E10
Nethercott Devon 12 B3
Nethercott Devon 40 F3
Nethercott Oxon 101 G9
Nethercott Som 42 G6
Netherdale Shetland 313 H3
Netherend Glos 79 E9
Netherfield E Sus 38 D2
Netherfield M Keynes 103 D7
Netherfield Notts 171 G10
Nethergate Norf 159 D11
Netherhampton Wilts 31 B10
Netherland Green Staffs 152 C2
Netherlaw Dumfries 237 E9
Netherlay Dorset 28 F6
Netherlee E Renf 267 D11
Netherley Aberds 293 D10
Netherley Mers 182 D6
Netherley W Yorks 196 E4
Nethermill Dumfries 248 F2
Nethermills Moray 302 D5
Nethermuir Aberds 303 E9
Netherne on-the-Hill Sur 51 B9
Netheroyd Hill W Yorks 196 D6
Netherplace E Renf 267 D10
Netherraw Borders 262 E3
Netherseal Derbys 152 G5
Netherstoke Dorset 29 F8
Netherthird E Ayrs 258 F3
Netherthong W Yorks 196 F6
Netherthorpe Derbys 186 G6
Netherthorpe S Yorks 187 E8
Netherton Aberds 303 E8
Netherton Angus 287 B9
Netherton Corn 11 G11
Netherton Cumb 228 D6
Netherton Devon 14 G3
Netherton Glos 81 E11
Netherton Hants 47 B11
Netherton Hereford 97 F10
Netherton Mers 193 G11
Netherton N Lnrk 268 E5
Netherton Northumb 251 B11
Netherton Oxon 82 F6
Netherton Perth 286 B5
Netherton Shrops 132 G4
Netherton Stirl 277 F11
Netherton W Ches 183 F8
Netherton W Mid 133 F8
Netherton W Yorks 196 E6
Netherton W Yorks 197 D9
Netherton Worcs 99 C9
Netherton of Lonmay Aberds 303 C10
Nethertown Cumb 219 D9
Nethertown Highld 310 B7
Nethertown Lancs 203 F10
Nethertown Staffs 152 F2
Netherwitton Northumb 252 E4
Netherwood E Ayrs 258 D5
Nethy Bridge Highld 301 G10
Netley Hants 33 F7
Netley Hill Soton 33 E7
Netley Marsh Hants 32 E4
Nettacott Devon 14 B4
Netteswell Essex 87 C7
Nettlebed Oxon 65 B8
Nettlebridge Som 44 D6
Nettlecombe Dorset 16 B6
Nettlecombe I o W 20 F6
Nettleden Herts 85 C8
Nettleham Lincs 189 F8
Nettlestead Kent 53 C7
Nettlestead Suff 107 B11
Nettlestead Green Kent 53 C7
Nettlestone I o W 21 C8
Nettlesworth Durham 233 B11
Nettleton Glos 80 C6
Nettleton Lincs 200 G6
Nettleton Wilts 61 D10
Nettleton Green Wilts 61 D10
Nettleton Hill W Yorks 196 D5
Nettleton Shrub Wilts 61 D10
Nettleton Top Lincs 189 B10
Netton Wilts 46 F6
Neuadd Carms 94 G3
Nevendon Essex 88 G2
Nevern = Nanhyfer Pembs 91 D11
Nevilles Cross Durham 233 C11
New Abbey Dumfries 237 C11
New Aberdour Aberds 303 C8
New Addington London 67 G11
New Alresford Hants 48 G5
New Alyth Perth 286 C6
New Arley Warks 134 F5
New Arram E Yorks 208 E6
New Ash Green Kent 68 F6
New Balderton Notts 172 E4
New Barn Kent 68 F6
New Barnet London 86 F3
New Barnetby N Lincs 200 E5
New Barton Northants 121 E7
New Basford Nottingham 171 G9
New Beaupre V Glam 58 E4
New Beckenham London 67 E11
New Bewick Northumb 264 E3
New-bigging Angus 286 C6
New Bilton Warks 119 B9
New Bolingbroke Lincs 174 D4
New Bolsover Derbys 187 G7
New Boston Mers 183 B9
New Botley Oxon 83 D7
New Boultham Lincs 189 G7
New Bradwell M Keynes 102 C6
New Brancepeth Durham 233 C10
New Bridge Wrex 166 G3
New Brighton Flint 166 B3
New Brighton Mers 182 C4
New Brighton W Sus 22 B3
New Brighton W Yorks 197 B9
New Brighton W Yorks 205 F8
New Brighton Wrex 166 E3
New Brimington Derbys 186 G6
New Brinsley Notts 171 E7
New Brotton Redcar 235 G9
New Broughton Wrex 166 E4
New Buckenham Norf 141 E11
New Buildings Bath 45 B7
New Buildings Dorset 18 E5
New Bury Gtr Man 195 F8
New Byth Aberds 303 D8
New Catton Norf 160 G4
New Charlton London 68 D2
New Cheltenham S Glos 61 E7
New Cheriton Hants 33 B9
New Clipstone Notts 171 C9
New Costessey Norf 160 G3
New Coundon Durham 233 E10
New Cowper Cumb 229 B8
New Crofton W Yorks 197 D11
New Cross Ceredig 112 B2
New Cross London 67 D11
New Cross Oxon 65 D9
New Cross Som 28 D6
New Cross Gate London 67 D11
New Cumnock E Ayrs 258 G4
New Deer Aberds 303 E8
New Delaval Northumb 243 B7
New Delph Gtr Man 196 F3
New Denham Bucks 66 C4
New Downs Corn 1 C3
New Downs Corn 4 E4
New Duston Northants 120 E4
New Earswick York 207 B8
New Eastwood Notts 171 F7
New Edlington S Yorks 187 B8
New Elgin Moray 302 C2
New Ellerby E Yorks 209 F9
New Eltham London 68 E2
New End Lincs 190 G2
New End Warks 118 E2
New End Worcs 117 F11
New England Essex 106 C4
New England Lincs 175 D8
New England P'boro 138 C3
New England Som 28 E4
New Farnley W Yorks 205 G10
New Ferry Mers 182 D4
New Fletton P'boro 138 D3
New Fryston W Yorks 198 B3
New Galloway Dumfries 237 B8
New Gilston Fife 287 G8
New Greens Herts 85 D10
New Grimsby Scilly 1 F3
New Ground Herts 85 C7
New Hainford Norf 160 F4
New Hall Hey Lancs 195 C10
New Hartley Northumb 243 B8
New Haw Sur 66 G5
New Headington Oxon 83 D9
New Heaton Northumb 273 G7
New Hedges Pembs 73 E10
New Herrington T & W 243 G8
New Hinksey Oxon 83 E8
New Ho Durham 232 D3
New Holkham Norf 159 B7
New Holland N Lincs 200 C5
New Holland W Yorks 205 F7
New Horwich Derbys 185 E8
New Houghton Derbys 171 B7
New Houghton Norf 158 D5
New House Kent 68 E6
New Houses Gtr Man 194 G5
New Houses N Yorks 212 E6
New Humberstone Leicester 136 B2
New Hunwick Durham 233 E9
New Hutton Cumb 221 G11
New Hythe Kent 53 B8
New Inn Carms 93 D9
New Inn Devon 24 F6
New Inn Mon 79 E7
New Inn Pembs 91 E11
New Inn Torf 78 F4
New Invention Shrops 114 B5
New Invention W Mid 133 C9
New Kelso Highld 299 E9
New Kingston Notts 153 D10
New Kyo Durham 242 G5
New Ladykirk Borders 273 F7
New Lanark S Lnrk 269 G7
New Lane Lancs 194 E2
New Lane End Warr 183 B10
New Langholm Dumfries 249 G9
New Leake Lincs 174 D6
New Leeds Aberds 303 D9
New Lodge S Yorks 197 F10
New Longton Lancs 194 B4
New Luce Dumfries 236 C3
New Malden London 67 F8
New Marske Redcar 235 G8
New Marston Oxon 83 D8
New Marton Shrops 148 C6
New Micklefield W Yorks 206 G4
New Mill Aberds 293 E9
New Mill Borders 262 G2
New Mill Corn 1 C5
New Mill Corn 4 F6
New Mill Cumb 219 E11
New Mill Herts 84 C6
New Mill W Yorks 197 F7
New Mill Wilts 63 G7
New Mills Borders 271 F10
New Mills Corn 5 E7
New Mills Derbys 185 D7
New Mills E Ches 184 E3
New Mills Glos 79 E10
New Mills Hereford 98 D4
New Mills = Felin Newydd Powys 129 C11
New Milton Hants 19 B10
New Mistley Essex 108 E2
New Moat Pembs 91 F11
New Moston Gtr Man 195 G11
New Ollerton Notts 171 B11
New Oscott W Mid 133 E11
New Pale W Ches 183 G8
New Park N Yorks 205 B11
New Parks Leicester 135 B11
New Passage S Glos 60 B4
New Pitsligo Aberds 303 D8
New Polzeath Corn 10 F4
New Quay = Ceinewydd Ceredig 111 F7
New Rackheath Norf 160 G5
New Radnor Powys 114 E4
New Rent Cumb 230 D5
New Ridley Northumb 242 F3
New Road Side N Yorks 204 E5
New Road Side W Yorks 197 B7
New Romney Kent 39 C9
New Rossington S Yorks 187 B10
New Row Ceredig 112 C4
New Row Lancs 203 F8
New Row N Yorks 226 C2
New Sarum Wilts 46 G6
New Sawley Derbys 153 C9
New Scarbro W Yorks 205 G10
New Sharlston W Yorks 197 C11
New Silksworth T & W 243 G9
New Skelton Redcar 226 B3
New Smithy Derbys 185 E9
New Southgate London 86 G3
New Springs Gtr Man 194 F6
New Sprowston Norf 160 G4
New Stanton Derbys 153 B9
New Stevenston N Lnrk 268 D5
New Street Kent 68 G6
New Street Staffs 169 E9
New Swanage Dorset 18 E6
New Swannington Leics 153 F8
New Thirsk N Yorks 215 C8
New Thundersley Essex 69 B9
New Totley S Yorks 186 F4
New Town Bath 45 B9
New Town Bath 60 G5
New Town Dorset 30 C3
New Town Dorset 30 D6
New Town Dorset 31 D7
New Town Dorset 31 F7
New Town E Loth 281 G8
New Town E Sus 37 C7
New Town Edin 280 G4
New Town Edin 280 G5
New Town Glos 99 E10
New Town Kent 53 B7
New Town Kent 68 E4
New Town Lancs 203 F8
New Town Luton 103 G11
New Town Medway 69 G8
New Town Oxon 100 F5
New Town Reading 65 E8
New Town Shetland 312 E6
New Town Som 29 D11
New Town Som 29 D9
New Town Som 44 D3
New Town Soton 33 E7
New Town Swindon 63 C7
New Town T & W 234 B2
New Town T & W 243 E8
New Town W Berks 64 D6
New Town W Mid 133 B11
New Town W Mid 133 E9
New Town W Sus 35 B11
New Town W Yorks 198 C3
New Town Wilts 46 C6
New Town Wilts 63 E9
New Tredegar Caerph 77 E10
New Trows S Lnrk 259 B8
New Ulva Argyll 275 E8
New Village E Yorks 209 G7
New Village S Yorks 198 F5
New Walsoken Cambs 139 B9
New Waltham NE Lincs 201 G9
New Well Powys 113 B11
New Wells Powys 130 D3
New Whittington Derbys 186 F5
New Wimpole Cambs 104 B6
New Winton E Loth 281 G8
New Woodhouses Shrops 167 G9
New Works Telford 132 B3
New Wortley W Yorks 205 G11
New Yatt Oxon 82 C5
New York Lincs 174 D2
New York N Yorks 214 G3
New York T & W 243 C8
New Zealand Wilts 62 D4
Newall W Yorks 205 D10
Newall Green Gtr Man 184 D4
Newark Orkney 314 B7
Newark P'boro 138 C4
Newark-on-Trent Notts 172 E3
Newarthill N Lnrk 268 D5
Newball Lincs 189 F9
Newbarn Kent 55 F7
Newbarns Cumb 210 E4
Newbattle Midloth 270 B6
Newbie Dumfries 238 D5
Newbiggin Cumb 210 F5
Newbiggin Cumb 211 D11
Newbiggin Cumb 219 G11
Newbiggin Cumb 230 F5
Newbiggin Cumb 231 B7
Newbiggin Cumb 231 F8
Newbiggin Durham 232 B5
Newbiggin Durham 232 F4
Newbiggin Durham 233 B8
Newbiggin N Yorks 213 B9
Newbiggin N Yorks 223 G9
Newbiggin-by-the-Sea Northumb 253 F8
Newbiggin Hall Estate T & W 242 D6
Newbiggin-on-Lune Cumb 222 D4
Newbigging Aberds 303 G7
Newbigging Angus 287 D8
Newbigging Borders 262 F6
Newbigging Edin 280 F2
Newbigging S Lnrk 269 F10
Newbiggings Orkney 314 B6
Newbold Derbys 186 G5
Newbold Gtr Man 196 E2
Newbold Leics 136 B5
Newbold Leics 153 F8
Newbold Heath Leics 135 B8
Newbold on Avon Warks 119 B9
Newbold on Stour Warks 100 B4
Newbold Pacey Warks 118 F5
Newbold Verdon Leics 135 C8
Newbolds W Mid 133 C8
Newborough P'boro 138 B4
Newborough Staffs 152 D2
Newbottle Northants 101 D10
Newbottle T & W 243 G8
Newbourne Suff 108 C5
Newbridge Bath 61 F8
Newbridge Caerph 78 F2
Newbridge Ceredig 111 F10
Newbridge Corn 1 C4
Newbridge Corn 4 G5
Newbridge Corn 7 B7
Newbridge Dumfries 237 B11
Newbridge E Sus 52 G3
Newbridge Edin 280 G2
Newbridge Hants 32 D3
Newbridge I o W 20 D4
Newbridge Lancs 204 F3
Newbridge N Yorks 216 B6
Newbridge Oxon 82 E6
Newbridge Pembs 91 E8
Newbridge Shrops 148 D6
Newbridge W Mid 133 D7
Newbridge Wrex 166 G3
Newbridge Green Worcs 98 D6
Newbridge-on-Usk Mon 78 G5
Newbridge-on-Wye Powys 113 F10
Newbrough Northumb 241 D9
Newbuildings Devon 26 G3
Newburgh Aberds 303 D9
Newburgh Aberds 303 G9
Newburgh Borders 261 F8
Newburgh Fife 286 F6
Newburgh Lancs 194 E3
Newburn T & W 242 D5
Newbury Kent 54 B2
Newbury W Berks 64 F3
Newbury Wilts 45 E10
Newbury Park London 68 B2
Newby Cumb 231 G7
Newby Lancs 204 D2
Newby N Yorks 205 D11
Newby N Yorks 212 E4
Newby N Yorks 215 F7
Newby N Yorks 225 C10
Newby N Yorks 227 G10
Newby Bridge Cumb 211 B7
Newby Cote N Yorks 212 E4
Newby East Cumb 239 F11
Newby Head Cumb 231 G7
Newby West Cumb 239 G9
Newby Wiske N Yorks 215 B7
Newcastle Bridgend 58 D2
Newcastle Mon 78 B6
Newcastle Shrops 130 G4
Newcastle Emlyn = Castell Newydd Emlyn Carms 92 C6
Newcastle-under-Lyme Staffs 168 F4
Newcastle upon Tyne T & W 242 E6
Newcastleton or Copshaw Holm Borders 249 F11
Newchapel Powys 129 G9
Newchapel Staffs 168 E5
Newchapel Sur 51 E11
Newchapel = Capel Newydd Pembs 92 D4
Newchurch Bl Gwent 77 C11

350 New – Nor

Newchurch Carms 93 G7
Newchurch Hereford 115 G7
Newchurch I o W 21 D7
Newchurch Kent 54 G5
Newchurch Lancs 195 C10
Newchurch Mon 79 F7
Newchurch Powys 114 G4
Newchurch Staffs 152 E2
Newchurch in Pendle Lancs 204 F2
Newcott Devon 28 F2
Newcraighall Edin 280 G6
Newdigate Sur 51 E7
Newell Green Brack 65 E11
Newenden Kent 38 B4
Newent Glos 98 F4
Newerne Glos 79 E10
Newfield Durham 233 E10
Newfield Durham 242 G6
Newfield Highld 301 B7
Newfield Stoke 168 E6
Newford Scilly 1 G4
Newfound Hants 48 C5
Newgale Pembs 90 G6
Newgarth Orkney 314 E2
Newgate Lancs 194 F4
Newgate Norf 177 E9
Newgate Corner Norf 161 G8
Newgate Street Herts 86 D4
Newgrounds Hants 31 E11
Newhailes Edin 280 G6
Newhall Derbys 152 E5
Newhall E Ches 167 F10
Newhall Green Warks 134 F5
Newhall House Highld 300 C6
Newhall Point Highld 301 C7
Newham Lincs 174 E3
Newham Northumb 264 D5
Newhaven Derbys 169 C11
Newhaven Devon 24 C5
Newhaven E Sus 36 G6
Newhaven Edin 280 F5
Newhay N Yorks 207 G9
Newhey Gtr Man 196 E2
Newhill Fife 286 F6
Newhill Perth 286 G5
Newhill S Yorks 186 B6
Newhills Aberdeen 293 C10
Newholm N Yorks 227 C7
Newhouse Borders 262 F2
Newhouse N Lnrk 268 C5
Newhouse Shetland 313 G6
Newhouses Borders 271 G10
Newick E Sus 36 C6
Newingreen Kent 54 F6
Newington Edin 280 G5
Newington Kent 55 F7
Newington Kent 69 G11
Newington Kent 71 F11
Newington London 67 D10
Newington Notts 187 C11
Newington Oxon 83 F10
Newington Shrops 131 G8
Newington Bagpath Glos 80 G4
Newland Cumb 210 D6
Newland E Yorks 199 B10
Newland Glos 79 D9
Newland Hull 209 G7
Newland N Yorks 199 C7
Newland Oxon 82 C5
Newland Worcs 98 B5
Newland Bottom Cumb 210 C5
Newland Common Worcs 117 E8
Newland Green Kent 54 D2
Newlandrig Midloth 271 C7
Newlands Borders 250 E2
Newlands Borders 262 E2
Newlands Cumb 229 G10
Newlands Cumb 230 D2
Newlands Derbys 170 F6
Newlands Dumfries 247 F11
Newlands Glasgow 267 C11
Newlands Highld 301 E7
Newlands Moray 302 D3
Newlands Northumb 242 F3
Newlands Notts 171 C9
Newlands Staffs 151 E11
Newlands Corner Sur 50 D4
Newlands of Geise Highld 310 C4
Newlands of Tynet Moray 302 C3
Newlands Park Anglesey 178 E3
Newlandsmuir S Lnrk 268 E2
Newliston Edin 280 G2
Newliston Fife 280 C5
Newlot Orkney 314 E5
Newlyn Corn 1 D5
Newmachar Aberds 293 B10
Newmains N Lnrk 268 D6
Newman's End Essex 87 C8
Newman's Green Suff 107 C7
Newman's Place Hereford 96 B5
Newmarket Glos 80 F4
Newmarket Suff 124 E2
Newmarket W Isles 304 E6
Newmill Borders 261 G11
Newmill Corn 1 C5
Newmill Moray 302 D4
Newmill of Inshewan Angus 292 G6
Newmillerdam W Yorks 197 D10
Newmills Corn 11 D11
Newmills Fife 279 D10
Newmills Highld 300 C6
Newmills of Boyne Aberds 302 D5
Newmiln Perth 286 D5
Newmilns E Ayrs 258 B2
Newmore Highld 300 B6
Newmore Highld 300 D5
Newnes Shrops 149 C7
Newney Green Essex 87 D11
Newnham Cambs 123 F8
Newnham Glos 79 C11
Newnham Hants 49 C8
Newnham Herts 104 D4
Newnham Kent 54 B3
Newnham Northants 119 F11
Newnham Warks 118 E3
Newnham Bridge Worcs 116 D2
Newpark Fife 287 F8
Newpool Staffs 168 D5
Newport Corn 12 D2
Newport Devon 40 G5
Newport Dorset 18 C3
Newport E Yorks 208 G3
Newport Essex 105 E10
Newport Glos 79 F11
Newport Highld 311 G5
Newport I o W 20 D6
Newport Newport 59 B10
Newport Norf 161 F10
Newport Som 28 C4
Newport Telford 150 F4
Newport = Trefdraeth Pembs 91 D11
Newport-on-Tay Fife 287 E8
Newport Pagnell M Keynes 103 C7
Newpound Common W Sus 35 B9
Newquay Corn 4 C6
Newsam Green W Yorks 206 G3
Newsbank E Ches 168 B4
Newseat Aberds 303 E10
Newseat Aberds 303 F7
Newsells Herts 105 D7
Newsham Lancs 202 F6
Newsham N Yorks 215 C7
Newsham N Yorks 224 C2
Newsham Northumb 243 B8
Newsholme E Yorks 199 B8
Newsholme Lancs 204 C2
Newsholme W Yorks 204 F6
Newsome W Yorks 196 E6
Newstead Borders 262 C3
Newstead Northumb 264 D5
Newstead Notts 171 E8
Newstead Staffs 168 G5
Newstead W Yorks 197 E11
Newstreet Lane Shrops 150 B2
Newtake Devon 14 G3
Newthorpe N Yorks 206 G5
Newthorpe Notts 171 F7
Newthorpe Common Notts 171 F7
Newtoft Lincs 189 D8
Newton Argyll 275 D11
Newton Borders 262 E3
Newton Borders 262 F2
Newton Bridgend 57 F10
Newton C Beds 104 C4
Newton Cambs 105 B8
Newton Cambs 157 G8
Newton Cardiff 59 D8
Newton Corn 5 C11
Newton Cumb 210 E4
Newton Derbys 170 D6
Newton Dorset 30 E3
Newton Dumfries 239 C7
Newton Dumfries 248 E4
Newton Gtr Man 185 B7
Newton Hereford 96 C5
Newton Hereford 96 E6
Newton Hereford 115 D7
Newton Hereford 115 G10
Newton Highld 301 C7
Newton Highld 301 E7
Newton Highld 306 F7
Newton Highld 310 E7
Newton Lancs 202 F2
Newton Lancs 202 G4
Newton Lancs 203 C9
Newton Lancs 211 E11
Newton Lincs 155 B10
Newton Mers 182 D2
Newton Moray 301 C11
Newton Norf 158 F6
Newton Northants 137 G7
Newton Northumb 242 E2
Newton Notts 171 G11
Newton Perth 286 D2
Newton S Glos 79 G10
Newton S Lnrk 259 C10
Newton S Lnrk 268 C3
Newton S Yorks 198 G5
Newton Shetland 312 E5
Newton Shetland 313 K5
Newton Shrops 132 D4
Newton Shrops 149 C8
Newton Som 42 F6
Newton Staffs 151 D10
Newton Suff 107 C8
Newton Swansea 56 D6
Newton W Ches 166 B6
Newton W Ches 167 D8
Newton W Ches 183 F8
Newton W Loth 279 F11
Newton W Mid 133 E10
Newton Warks 119 B10
Newton Wilts 32 C2
Newton Abbot Devon 14 G3
Newton Arlosh Cumb 238 F5
Newton Aycliffe Durham 233 G11
Newton Bewley Hrtlpl 234 F5
Newton Blossomville M Keynes 121 G8
Newton Bromswold Northants 121 D9
Newton Burgoland Leics 135 B7
Newton by Toft Lincs 189 D9
Newton Cross Pembs 91 F7
Newton Ferrers Devon 7 F10
Newton Flotman Norf 142 D4
Newton Green Mon 79 G8
Newton Hall Durham 233 B11
Newton Hall Northumb 242 D2
Newton Harcourt Leics 136 D2
Newton Heath Gtr Man 195 G11
Newton Hill W Yorks 197 C10
Newton Ho Aberds 302 G6
Newton Hurst Staffs 151 D11
Newton Ketton Darl 234 G2
Newton Kyme N Yorks 206 E5
Newton-le-Willows Mers 183 B9
Newton-le-Willows N Yorks 214 B4
Newton Longville Bucks 102 E6
Newton Mearns E Renf 267 D10
Newton Morrell N Yorks 224 D4
Newton Morrell Oxon 102 F2
Newton Mulgrave N Yorks 226 B5
Newton of Ardtoe Highld 289 B8
Newton of Balcanquhal Perth 286 F5
Newton of Balcormo Fife 287 G9
Newton of Falkland Fife 286 G6
Newton of Mountblairy Aberds 302 D6
Newton of Pitcairns Perth 286 F4
Newton on Ayr S Ayrs 257 E8
Newton on Ouse N Yorks 206 B6
Newton-on-Rawcliffe N Yorks 226 G6
Newton on the Hill Shrops 149 E9
Newton on the Moor Northumb 252 B5
Newton on Trent Lincs 188 G4
Newton Park Argyll 266 B2
Newton Park Mers 183 C9
Newton Peveril Dorset 18 B4
Newton Poppleford Devon 15 D7
Newton Purcell Oxon 102 E2
Newton Regis Warks 134 B5
Newton Reigny Cumb 230 E5
Newton Rigg Cumb 230 E5
Newton St Boswells Borders 262 C3
Newton St Cyres Devon 14 B3
Newton St Faith Norf 160 F4
Newton St Loe Bath 61 G8
Newton St Petrock Devon 24 E6
Newton Solney Derbys 152 D5
Newton Stacey Hants 48 E2
Newton Stewart Dumfries 236 C6
Newton Tony Wilts 47 E8
Newton Tracey Devon 25 B8
Newton under Roseberry Redcar 225 C11
Newton Underwood Northumb 252 F4
Newton upon Derwent E Yorks 207 D10
Newton Valence Hants 49 G8
Newton with Scales Lancs 202 G4
Newton Wood Gtr Man 184 B6
Newtonairds Dumfries 247 G9
Newtongrange Midloth 270 C6
Newtonhill Aberds 293 D11
Newtonhill Highld 300 E5
Newtonia E Ches 167 B11
Newtonmill Angus 293 G8
Newtonmore Highld 291 D9
Newtown Argyll 284 G4
Newtown Bl Gwent 77 C11
Newtown Bucks 85 E7
Newtown Caerph 78 G2
Newtown Cambs 121 D11
Newtown Corn 2 D3
Newtown Corn 11 F11
Newtown Cumb 229 B7
Newtown Cumb 239 F9
Newtown Cumb 240 E2
Newtown Derbys 185 E7
Newtown Devon 26 B3
Newtown Dorset 29 G7
Newtown E Ches 184 E6
Newtown Falk 279 E9
Newtown Glos 79 E11
Newtown Glos 80 D3
Newtown Glos 99 E8
Newtown Gtr Man 194 F5
Newtown Gtr Man 195 G9
Newtown Hants 21 B8
Newtown Hants 32 C4
Newtown Hants 32 E3
Newtown Hants 33 D8
Newtown Hants 33 E10
Newtown Hants 33 F7
Newtown Hants 49 F8
Newtown Hants 49 G10
Newtown Hants 64 G3
Newtown Hereford 97 E10
Newtown Hereford 98 C2
Newtown Highld 290 C5
Newtown I o W 20 C4
Newtown I o M 192 E4
Newtown Mers 183 B7
Newtown Norf 143 B10
Newtown Northumb 252 C2
Newtown Northumb 263 C11
Newtown Northumb 264 D2
Newtown Oxon 65 C9
Newtown Poole 18 C6
Newtown Powys 130 E2
Newtown Rhondda 77 F9
Newtown Shrops 132 C2
Newtown Shrops 149 C9
Newtown Shrops 149 E8
Newtown Som 28 E3
Newtown Som 43 F9
Newtown Staffs 133 C9
Newtown Staffs 168 C6
Newtown Staffs 169 C9
Newtown W Ches 183 F8
Newtown W Mid 133 F11
Newtown Wilts 30 B6
Newtown Wilts 63 G10
Newtown Worcs 116 F5
Newtown Worcs 117 E7
Newtown-in-St Martin Corn 2 E6
Newtown Linford Leics 135 B10
Newtown St Boswells Borders 262 C3
Newtown Unthank Leics 135 C9
Newtyle Angus 286 C6
Newyears Green London 66 B5
Nextend Hereford 114 F6
Neyland Pembs 73 D7
Niarbyl I o M 192 E3
Nib Heath Shrops 149 F8
Nibley Glos 79 D11
Nibley S Glos 61 C7
Nibley Green Glos 80 F2
Nibon Shetland 312 F5
Nicholashayne Devon 27 D10
Nicholaston Swansea 56 D4
Nidd N Yorks 214 G6
Niddrie Edin 280 G5
Nigg Aberdeen 293 C11
Nigg Highld 301 B8
Nigg Ferry Highld 301 C7
Nightcott Som 26 B5
Nilig Denb 165 D8
Nimble Nook Gtr Man 196 G2
Nimlet S Glos 61 E8
Nimmer Som 28 E4
Nine Ashes Essex 87 E9
Nine Elms London 67 D9
Nine Elms Swindon 62 B6
Nine Maidens Downs Corn 2 B5
Nine Mile Burn Midloth 270 D3
Nine Wells Pembs 90 G5
Ninebanks Northumb 241 G7
Nineveh Worcs 116 C3
Nineveh Worcs 116 E2
Ninewells Glos 79 C9
Ninfield E Sus 38 E2
Ningwood I o W 20 D3
Ningwood Common I o W 20 D3
Ninnes Bridge Corn 2 B2
Nisbet Borders 262 D5
Nisthouse Orkney 314 E3
Nisthouse Shetland 313 G7
Nithbank Dumfries 247 D9
Niton I o W 20 F6
Nitshill Glasgow 267 C10
No Man's Heath W Ches 167 F8
No Man's Heath Warks 134 B5
No Man's Land Corn 6 D5
No Man's Land Hants 33 B8
Noah's Arks Kent 52 B5
Noah's Green Worcs 117 E10
Noak Bridge Essex 87 G11
Noak Hill Essex 87 G11
Noak Hill London 87 G8
Nob End Gtr Man 195 F9
Nobland Green Herts 86 B5
Noblethorpe S Yorks 197 F9
Nobold Shrops 149 G9
Nobottle Northants 120 E3
Nob's Crook Hants 33 C7
Nocton Lincs 173 C9
Noctorum Mers 182 D3
Nodmore W Berks 64 D2
Noel Park London 86 G4
Nog Tow Lancs 202 G6
Nogdam End Norf 143 C7
Noke Oxon 83 C8
Noke Street Medway 69 E8
Nolton Pembs 72 B5
Nolton Haven Pembs 72 B5
Nomansland Devon 26 E4
Nomansland Herts 85 C11
Nomansland Wilts 32 D3
Noneley Shrops 149 D9
Noness Shetland 313 L6
Nonikiln Highld 300 B6
Nonington Kent 55 C9
Nook Cumb 211 C10
Noon Nick W Yorks 205 F8
Noonsbrough Shetland 313 H4
Noonsun E Ches 184 F4
Noonvares Corn 2 C3
Noranside Angus 292 G6
Norbiton London 67 F7
Norbreck Blkpool 202 E2
Norbridge Hereford 98 C4
Norbury Derbys 169 G10
Norbury E Ches 167 F9
Norbury London 67 F10
Norbury Shrops 131 E7
Norbury Staffs 150 E5
Norbury Common E Ches 167 F9
Norbury Junction Staffs 150 E5
Norbury Moor Gtr Man 184 D6
Norby N Yorks 215 C8
Norby Shetland 313 H3
Norchard Worcs 116 D6
Norcote Glos 81 E8
Norcott Brook W Ches 183 E10
Norcross Blkpool 202 E2
Nordelph Norf 139 C11
Nordelph Corner Norf 141 C10
Norden Dorset 18 E4
Norden Gtr Man 195 E11
Norden Heath Dorset 18 E4
Nordley Shrops 132 D3
Norham Northumb 273 F8
Norham West Mains Northumb 273 F8
Nork Sur 51 B8
Nork Sur 67 G8
Norland Town W Yorks 196 C5
Norleaze Wilts 45 C11
Norley Devon 25 G8
Norley W Ches 183 G9
Norley Common Sur 50 E4
Norleywood Hants 20 B3
Norlington E Sus 36 E6
Normacot Stoke 168 G6
Norman Cross Cambs 138 E3
Norman Hill Glos 80 F3
Normanby N Lincs 199 D11
Normanby N Yorks 216 C4
Normanby Redcar 225 B10
Normanby-by-Spital Lincs 189 D7
Normanby by Stow Lincs 188 E5
Normanby le Wold Lincs 189 B10
Normandy Sur 50 C2
Norman's Bay E Sus 23 D11
Norman's Green Devon 27 G9
Normanston Suff 143 E10
Normanton Derby 152 C6
Normanton Leics 172 G4
Normanton Lincs 172 F6
Normanton Notts 172 E2
Normanton Rutland 137 B8
Normanton W Yorks 197 C11
Normanton Wilts 46 E6
Normanton le Heath Leics 153 G7
Normanton on Soar Notts 153 E10
Normanton-on-the-Wolds Notts 154 C2
Normanton on Trent Notts 172 B3
Normanton Spring S Yorks 186 E6
Normanton Turville Leics 135 D9
Normoss Lancs 202 F2
Norney Sur 50 E2
Norr W Yorks 205 F7
Norrington Common Wilts 61 G11
Norris Green Corn 7 B8
Norris Green Mers 182 C5
Norris Hill Leics 152 F6
Norristhorpe W Yorks 197 C8
Norseman Orkney 314 E3
North Acton London 67 C8
North Anston S Yorks 187 E8
North Ascot Brack 66 F2
North Aston Oxon 101 F9
North Ayre Shetland 312 F6
North Baddesley Hants 32 D5
North Ballachulish Highld 290 G2
North Barrow Som 29 B10
North Barsham Norf 159 C8
North Batsom Som 41 G10
North Beer Corn 12 C2
North Benfleet Essex 69 B9
North Bersted W Sus 22 C6
North Berwick E Loth 281 D11
North Bitchburn Durham 233 E9
North Blyth Northumb 253 G8
North Boarhunt Hants 33 E10
North Bockhampton Dorset 19 B9
North Bovey Devon 13 E10
North Bradley Wilts 45 C11
North Brentor Devon 12 E5
North Brewham Som 45 F8
North Brook End Cambs 104 C5
North Broomage Falk 279 E7
North Buckland Devon 40 E3
North Burlingham Norf 161 G7
North Cadbury Som 29 B10
North Cairn Dumfries 236 B1
North Camp Hants 49 C11
North Carlton Lincs 188 F6
North Carlton Notts 187 E9
North Carrine Argyll 255 G7
North Cave E Yorks 208 G3
North Cerney Glos 81 D8
North Chailey E Sus 36 C5
North Charford Wilts 31 D11
North Charlton Northumb 264 E5
North Cheam London 67 F8
North Cheriton Som 29 B11
North Cliff E Yorks 209 D10
North Cliffe E Yorks 208 F3
North Clifton Notts 188 G4
North Close Durham 233 E11
North Cockerington Lincs 190 C5
North Coker Som 29 E8
North Collafirth Shetland 312 E5
North Common S Glos 61 E7
North Common Suff 125 B9
North Connel Argyll 289 F11
North Cornelly Bridgend 57 E10
North Corner Corn 3 F7
North Corner S Glos 61 C7
North Corriegills N Ayrs 256 C2
North Corry Highld 289 D10
North Cotes Lincs 201 G11
North Country Corn 4 G3
North Court Som 41 F11
North Cove Suff 143 F9
North Cowton N Yorks 224 E5
North Craigo Angus 293 G8
North Crawley M Keynes 103 C8
North Cray London 68 E3
North Creake Norf 159 B7
North Curry Som 28 B4
North Dalton E Yorks 208 C4
North Darley Corn 11 G11
North Dawn Orkney 314 F4
North Deighton N Yorks 206 C3
North Denes Norf 161 G10
North Dronley Angus 287 D7
North Drumachter Lodge Highld 291 F8
North Duffield N Yorks 207 F9
North Dykes Cumb 230 D6
North Eastling Kent 54 B3
North Elham Kent 55 E7
North Elkington Lincs 190 C3
North Elmham Norf 159 E9
North Elmsall W Yorks 198 E3
North Elmshall W Yorks 198 E3
North Elphinestone E Loth 281 G7
North End Bath 60 G6
North End Beds 103 B9
North End Beds 121 F10
North End Bucks 102 F4
North End Bucks 102 F6
North End Cumb 239 F8
North End Devon 27 D10
North End Dorset 30 B4
North End Durham 233 C11
North End E Yorks 209 C9
North End E Yorks 209 E9
North End E Yorks 209 G11
North End Essex 87 B11
North End Essex 106 D5
North End Hants 31 D10
North End Hants 33 B9
North End Hants 64 G2
North End Leics 153 F11
North End Lincs 174 G2
North End Lincs 189 B8
North End Lincs 190 C5
North End Lincs 190 D6
North End Lincs 191 D7
North End Lincs 201 G10
North End London 67 B9
North End London 68 D4
North End N Lincs 200 C6
North End N Som 60 F2
North End Norf 141 E10
North End Northumb 252 C4
North End Ptsmth 33 G11
North End Som 28 B3
North End W Sus 35 F10
North End W Sus 35 G7
North End W Sus 51 F11
North End Wilts 81 G8
North Erradale Highld 307 L2
North Evington Leicester 136 C2
North Ewster N Lincs 199 G10
North Fambridge Essex 88 F5
North Fearns Highld 295 B7
North Featherstone W Yorks 198 C2
North Feltham London 66 E6
North Feorline N Ayrs 255 E10
North Ferriby E Yorks 200 B3
North Finchley London 86 G3
North Flobbets Aberds 303 F7
North Frodingham E Yorks 209 C8
North Gluss Shetland 312 F5
North Gorley Hants 31 E11
North Green Norf 141 B10
North Green Norf 142 F4
North Green Suff 126 B6
North Green Suff 126 E6
North Green Suff 127 D7
North Greetwell Lincs 189 G8
North Grimston N Yorks 216 F6
North Halley Orkney 314 F5
North Halling Medway 69 F8
North Harrow London 66 B6
North Hayling Hants 22 C2
North Hazelrigg Northumb 264 C3
North Heasley Devon 41 G8
North Heath W Berks 64 E3
North Heath W Sus 35 C9
North Hill Corn 11 F11
North Hillingdon London 66 C5
North Hinksey Oxon 83 D7
North Hinksey Village Oxon 83 D7
North Ho Shetland 313 J5
North Holmwood Sur 51 D7
North Houghton Hants 47 G10
North Howden E Yorks 207 G11
North Huish Devon 8 D4
North Hyde London 66 D6
North Hykeham Lincs 172 B6
North Hylton T & W 243 F8
North Kelsey Lincs 200 G4
North Kelsey Moor Lincs 200 G5
North Kensington London 67 C8
North Kessock Highld 300 E6
North Killingholme N Lincs 200 D6
North Kilvington N Yorks 215 B8
North Kilworth Leics 136 G2
North Kingston Hants 31 G11
North Kirkton Aberds 303 D11
North Kiscadale N Ayrs 256 D2
North Kyme Lincs 173 E11
North Laggan Highld 290 D4
North Lancing W Sus 35 F11
North Landing E Yorks 218 E4
North Lee Bucks 84 D4
North Lees N Yorks 214 E6
North Leigh Kent 54 D6
North Leigh Oxon 82 C5
North Leverton with Habblesthorpe Notts 188 E3
North Littleton Worcs 99 B11
North Looe Sur 67 G8
North Lopham Norf 141 G10
North Luffenham Rutland 137 C8
North Marden W Sus 34 D4
North Marston Bucks 102 G5
North Middleton Midloth 271 D7
North Middleton Northumb 264 E2
North Millbrex Aberds 303 E8
North Molton Devon 26 B2
North Moreton Oxon 64 B5
North Mosstown Aberds 303 D10
North Motherwell N Lnrk 268 D4
North Moulsecoomb Brighton 36 F4
North Mundham W Sus 22 C5
North Muskham Notts 172 D3
North Newbald E Yorks 208 F4
North Newington Oxon 101 D8
North Newnton Wilts 46 B6
North Newton Som 43 G9
North Nibley Glos 80 F2
North Oakley Hants 48 C4
North Ockendon London 68 C5
North Ormesby M'bro 234 G6
North Ormsby Lincs 190 C3
North Otterington N Yorks 215 B7
North Owersby Lincs 189 C9
North Perrott Som 29 F7
North Petherton Som 43 G9
North Petherwin Corn 11 D11
North Pickenham Norf 141 B7
North Piddle Worcs 117 G9
North Poorton Dorset 16 B6
North Port Argyll 284 E4
North Poulner Hants 31 F11
North Queensferry Fife 280 E2
North Radworthy Devon 41 G9
North Rauceby Lincs 173 F8
North Reddish Gtr Man 184 C5
North Reston Lincs 190 E5
North Rigton N Yorks 205 D11
North Ripley Hants 19 B9
North Rode E Ches 168 B5
North Roe Shetland 312 E5
North Row Cumb 229 E10
North Runcton Norf 158 F2
North Sandwick Shetland 312 D7
North Scale Cumb 210 F3
North Scarle Lincs 172 B5
North Seaton Northumb 253 F7
North Seaton Colliery Northumb 253 F7
North Sheen London 67 D7
North Shian Argyll 289 E11
North Shields T & W 243 D9
North Shoebury Sthend 70 B2
North Shore Blkpool 202 F2
North Side Cumb 228 F6
North Side P'boro 138 D5
North Skelmanae Aberds 303 D9
North Skelton Redcar 226 B3
North Somercotes Lincs 190 B6
North Stainley N Yorks 214 D5
North Stainmore Cumb 222 B6
North Stifford Thurrock 68 C6
North Stoke Bath 61 F8
North Stoke Oxon 64 B6
North Stoke W Sus 35 E8
North Stoneham Hants 32 D6
North Street Hants 31 D11
North Street Hants 48 G6
North Street Kent 54 B4
North Street Medway 69 E10
North Street W Berks 64 E6
North Sunderland Northumb 264 C6
North Synton Borders 261 E11
North Tamerton Corn 12 B2
North Tawton Devon 25 G11
North Thoresby Lincs 190 B3
North Tidworth Wilts 47 D8
North Togston Northumb 252 C6
North Town Devon 25 F8
North Town Hants 49 C11
North Town Som 29 B10
North Town Som 44 E5
North Town Windsor 65 C11
North Tuddenham Norf 159 G10
North Walbottle T & W 242 D5
North Walney Cumb 210 F3
North Walsham Norf 160 C5
North Waltham Hants 48 D5
North Warnborough Hants 49 C8
North Water Bridge Angus 293 G8
North Waterhayne Devon 28 F3
North Watford Herts 85 F10
North Watten Highld 310 D6
North Weald Bassett Essex 87 E7
North Weirs Hants 32 G3
North Wembley London 67 B7
North Weston N Som 60 D3
North Weston Oxon 83 D11
North Wheatley Notts 188 D3
North Whilborough Devon 9 B7
North Whiteley Moray 302 E4
North Wick Bath 60 F5
North Widcombe Bath 44 B5
North Willingham Lincs 189 D11
North Wingfield Derbys 170 B6
North Witham Lincs 155 E8
North Woolwich London 68 D2
North Wootton Dorset 29 E11
North Wootton Norf 158 E2
North Wootton Som 44 E5
North Wraxall Wilts 61 D10
North Wroughton Swindon 63 C7
Northacre Norf 141 D9
Northall Bucks 103 G9
Northall Green Norf 159 G9
Northallerton N Yorks 225 G7
Northam Devon 24 B6
Northam Soton 32 E6
Northampton Northants 120 E5
Northaw Herts 86 E3
Northay Devon 28 G5
Northay Som 28 E3
Northbeck Lincs 173 G9
Northborough P'boro 138 B3
Northbourne Bmouth 19 B7
Northbourne Kent 55 C10
Northbridge Street E Sus 38 C2
Northbrook Dorset 17 C11
Northbrook Hants 33 D9
Northbrook Hants 48 F4
Northbrook Oxon 101 G9
Northbrook Wilts 46 C4
Northchapel W Sus 35 B7
Northchurch Herts 85 D7

Northcote Devon 27 G11
Northcott Corn 24 F2
Northcott Devon 12 C2
Northcott Devon 27 E9
Northcott Devon 27 F10
Northcourt Oxon 83 F8
Northdown Kent 71 E11
Northdyke Orkney 314 D2
Northedge Derbys 170 B5
Northend Bath 61 F9
Northend Bucks 84 G2
Northend Essex 89 E7
Northend Essex 105 D10
Northend Warks 119 G7
Northenden Gtr Man 184 C4
Northern Moor Gtr Man 184 C4
Northfield Aberdeen 293 C11
Northfield Borders 262 D3
Northfield Borders 273 B8
Northfield E Yorks 200 B4
Northfield Edin 280 G5
Northfield Highld 301 B7
Northfield M Keynes 103 C7
Northfield Northants 137 E7
Northfield Som 43 F9
Northfield W Mid 117 B10
Northfields Hants 33 B7
Northfields Lincs 137 B10
Northfleet Kent 68 E6
Northfleet Green Kent 68 E6
Northgate Lincs 156 D3
Northgate Som 27 B9
Northgate W Sus 51 F9
Northhouse Borders 249 B10
Northiam E Sus 38 B4
Northill C Beds 104 B2
Northington Glos 80 D2
Northington Hants 48 F5
Northlands Lincs 174 E4
Northlea Durham 243 G10
Northleach Glos 81 C10
Northleigh Devon 15 B9
Northleigh Devon 40 G6
Northlew Devon 12 B6
Northmoor Devon 24 D4
Northmoor Oxon 82 E6
Northmoor Corner Som 43 G10
Northmoor Green or Moorland Som 43 G10
Northmuir Angus 287 B7
Northney Hants 22 C2
Northolt London 66 C6
Northop = Llan-eurgain Flint 166 B2
Northop Hall Flint 166 B3
Northorpe Lincs 155 F11
Northorpe Lincs 156 B4
Northorpe Lincs 188 B5
Northorpe W Yorks 197 C8
Northover Som 29 C8
Northover Som 44 F3
Northowram W Yorks 196 B6
Northpark Argyll 275 G11
Northport Dorset 18 D4
Northpunds Shetland 313 L6
Northrepps Norf 160 B4
Northside Aberds 303 D8
Northside Orkney 314 D2
Northton Aberds 293 C9
Northtown Orkney 314 G4
Northtown Shetland 313 M5
Northumberland Heath London 68 D4
Northville Torf 78 F3
Northway Devon 24 C5
Northway Glos 99 E8
Northway Som 27 B10
Northway Swansea 56 D5
Northwich W Ches 183 G11
Northwick S Glos 60 B5
Northwick Som 43 D11
Northwick Worcs 116 F6
Northwold Norf 140 D5
Northwood Derbys 170 C3
Northwood I o W 20 C5
Northwood Kent 71 F11
Northwood London 85 G9
Northwood Mers 182 B6
Northwood Shrops 149 C9
Northwood Staffs 168 G5
Northwood Stoke 168 F5
Northwood Green Glos 80 B2
Northwood Hills London 85 G9
Norton Devon 9 E7
Norton Devon 24 B3
Norton E Sus 23 E7
Norton Glos 99 G7
Norton Halton 183 E9
Norton Herts 104 E4
Norton I o W 20 D2
Norton Mon 78 B6
Norton N Som 59 G10
Norton Northants 120 E2
Norton Notts 187 G9
Norton Powys 114 D6
Norton S Yorks 186 E5
Norton S Yorks 198 D4
Norton Shrops 131 B11
Norton Shrops 131 G9
Norton Shrops 132 C4
Norton Stockton 234 G4
Norton Suff 125 D9
Norton Swansea 56 D3
Norton Swansea 56 D6
Norton W Mid 133 G7
Norton W Sus 22 B6
Norton W Sus 22 D5
Norton Wilts 61 C11
Norton Worcs 99 B10
Norton Worcs 117 G7
Norton Ash Kent 70 G3
Norton Bavant Wilts 46 E2
Norton Bridge Staffs 151 C7
Norton Canes Staffs 133 B10
Norton Canon Hereford 97 B7
Norton Corner Norf 159 D11
Norton Disney Lincs 172 D5
Norton East Staffs 133 B10
Norton Ferris Wilts 45 F9
Norton Fitzwarren Som 27 B11
Norton Green Herts 104 G4
Norton Green I o W 20 D2
Norton Green Staffs 168 E6
Norton Green W Mid 118 C3
Norton Hawkfield Bath 60 G5
Norton Heath Essex 87 E10
Norton in Hales Shrops 150 B4
Norton-in-the-Moors Stoke 168 E5
Norton-Juxta-Twycross Leics 134 B6
Norton-le-Clay N Yorks 215 E8
Norton Lindsey Warks 118 E4
Norton Little Green Suff 125 D9
Norton Malreward Bath 60 F6
Norton Mandeville Essex 87 E9
Norton-on-Derwent N Yorks 216 E5
Norton St Philip Som 45 B9
Norton sub Hamdon Som 29 D7
Norton Subcourse Norf 143 D8
Norton Woodseats S Yorks 186 E5
Norton's Wood N Som 60 E2
Norwell Notts 172 C3
Norwell Woodhouse Notts 172 C2
Norwich Norf 142 B4
Norwick Shetland 312 B8
Norwood Derbys 187 E7
Norwood Dorset 29 F8
Norwood End Essex 87 D9
Norwood Green London 66 D6
Norwood Green W Yorks 196 B6
Norwood Hill Sur 51 E8
Norwood New Town London 67 E10
Norwoodside Cambs 139 D8
Noseley Leics 136 D4
Noss Highld 310 D7
Noss Shetland 313 M5
Noss Mayo Devon 7 F11
Nosterfield N Yorks 214 C5
Nosterfield End Cambs 106 C2
Nostie Highld 295 C10
Notgrove Glos 100 G2
Nottage Bridgend 57 F10
Notter Corn 7 C7
Notting Hill London 67 C8
Nottingham Nottingham 153 B11
Nottington Dorset 17 E9
Notton W Yorks 197 E10
Notton Wilts 62 F2
Nounsley Essex 88 C3
Noutard's Green Worcs 116 D5
Nova Scotia W Ches 167 B10
Novar House Highld 300 C6
Novers Park Bristol 60 F5
Noverton Glos 99 G9
Nowton Suff 125 E7
Nox Shrops 149 G8
Noyadd Trefawr Ceredig 92 B5
Noyadd Wilym Ceredig 92 C4
Nuffield Oxon 65 B7
Nun Appleton N Yorks 207 F7
Nun Hills Lancs 195 C11
Nun Monkton N Yorks 206 B6
Nunburnholme E Yorks 208 D2
Nuncargate Notts 171 E8
Nunclose Cumb 230 B5
Nuneaton Warks 135 E7
Nuneham Courtenay Oxon 83 F9
Nuney Green Oxon 65 D7
Nunhead London 67 D11
Nunney Som 45 D8
Nunney Catch Som 45 E8
Nunnington N Yorks 216 D3
Nunnykirk Northumb 252 E3
Nunsthorpe NE Lincs 201 F9
Nunthorpe M'bro 225 C10
Nunthorpe York 207 C8
Nunton Wilts 31 B11
Nunwick N Yorks 214 E6
Nup End Bucks 84 B5
Nup End Herts 86 B2
Nupdown S Glos 79 F10
Nupend Glos 80 D3
Nupend Glos 80 F4
Nuper's Hatch Essex 87 G8
Nuppend Glos 79 E10
Nuptown Brack 65 E11
Nursling Hants 32 D5
Nursted Hants 34 C3
Nursteed Wilts 62 G4
Nurston V Glam 58 F5
Nurton Staffs 132 D6
Nurton Hill Staffs 132 D6
Nut Grove Mers 183 C7
Nutbourne W Sus 22 B3
Nutbourne W Sus 35 D9
Nutbourne Common W Sus 35 D9
Nutburn Hants 32 C5
Nutcombe Sur 49 G11
Nutfield Sur 51 C10
Nuthall Notts 171 G8
Nuthampstead Herts 105 E8
Nuthurst W Sus 35 B11
Nuthurst Warks 118 C3
Nutley E Sus 36 B6
Nutley Hants 48 E6
Nuttall Gtr Man 195 D9
Nutwell S Yorks 198 G6
Nybster Highld 310 C7
Nye N Som 60 G2
Nyetimber W Sus 22 D5
Nyewood W Sus 34 C4
Nyland Som 44 C3
Nymet Rowland Devon 26 F2
Nymet Tracey Devon 26 G2
Nympsfield Glos 80 E4
Nynehead Som 27 C10
Nythe Som 44 G2
Nythe Swindon 63 B7
Nyton W Sus 22 B6

O

Oad Street Kent 69 G11
Oadby Leics 136 C2
Oak Bank Gtr Man 195 F10
Oak Cross Devon 12 B6
Oak Hill Stoke 168 G5
Oak Hill Suff 109 B7
Oak Tree Darl 225 C7
Oakall Green Worcs 116 E6
Oakamoor Staffs 169 G9
Oakbank W Loth 269 B11
Oakdale Caerph 77 F11
Oakdale N Yorks 205 B11
Oakdale Poole 18 C6
Oake Som 27 B11
Oake Green Som 27 B11
Oaken Staffs 133 C7
Oakenclough Lancs 202 D6
Oakengates Telford 150 G4
Oakenholt Flint 182 G3
Oakenshaw Durham 233 D10
Oakenshaw Lancs 203 G10
Oakenshaw W Yorks 197 B7
Oakerthorpe Derbys 170 E5
Oakes W Yorks 196 D6
Oakfield Herts 104 F3
Oakfield I o W 21 C7
Oakfield Torf 78 G4
Oakford Ceredig 111 F9
Oakford Devon 26 C6
Oakfordbridge Devon 26 C6
Oakgrove E Ches 168 B6
Oakgrove M Keynes 103 D7
Oakham Rutland 137 B7
Oakham W Mid 133 F9
Oakhanger E Ches 168 E3
Oakhanger Hants 49 F9
Oakhill Som 44 D6
Oakhill W Sus 51 G7
Oakhurst Kent 52 C4
Oakington Cambs 123 E8
Oaklands Carms 74 B6
Oaklands Herts 86 B2
Oaklands Powys 113 G10
Oakle Street Glos 80 B3
Oakleigh Park London 86 G3
Oakley Beds 121 G10
Oakley Bucks 83 C10
Oakley Fife 279 D10
Oakley Glos 99 G9
Oakley Hants 48 C5
Oakley Oxon 84 E3
Oakley Poole 18 B6
Oakley Staffs 150 B4
Oakley Suff 126 B3
Oakley Court Oxon 64 B6
Oakley Green Windsor 66 D2
Oakley Park Powys 129 F9
Oakley Park Suff 126 B3
Oakley Wood Oxon 64 B6
Oakmere W Ches 167 B9
Oakridge Glos 80 E6
Oakridge Hants 48 C6
Oakridge Lynch Glos 80 E6
Oaks Shrops 131 C8
Oaks Green Derbys 152 C3
Oaks in Charnwood Leics 153 F9
Oaksey Wilts 81 G7
Oakshaw Ford Cumb 240 B2
Oakshott Hants 34 B2
Oakthorpe Leics 152 G6
Oakwell W Yorks 197 B8
Oakwood Derby 153 B7
Oakwood London 86 F3
Oakwood Northumb 241 D10
Oakwood W Yorks 206 F2
Oakwood Warr 183 C11
Oakwoodhill Sur 50 F6
Oakworth W Yorks 204 F6
Oape Highld 309 J4
Oare Kent 70 G4
Oare Som 41 D10
Oare W Berks 64 E4
Oare Wilts 63 G7
Oareford Som 41 D10
Oasby Lincs 155 B10
Oath Som 28 B5
Oathill Dorset 28 F6
Oathlaw Angus 287 B8
Oatlands Glasgow 267 C11
Oatlands N Yorks 205 C11
Oatlands Park Sur 66 G5
Oban Argyll 289 G10
Oban Highld 295 G10
Oban W Isles 305 H3
Obley Shrops 114 B6
Oborne Dorset 29 D11
Obthorpe Lincs 155 F11
Obthorpe Lodge Lincs 156 F2
Occlestone Green W Ches 167 C11
Occold Suff 126 C3
Ocean Village Soton 32 E6
Ochiltree E Ayrs 258 E2
Ochr-y-foel Denb 181 F9
Ochtermuthill Perth 286 F2
Ochtertyre Perth 286 E2
Ochtow Highld 309 J4
Ockbrook Derbys 153 B8
Ocker Hill W Mid 133 E9
Ockeridge Worcs 116 E5
Ockford Ridge Sur 50 E3
Ockham Sur 50 B5
Ockle Highld 289 B7
Ockley Sur 50 F6
Ocle Pychard Hereford 97 B11
Octon E Yorks 217 F10
Octon Cross Roads E Yorks 217 F10
Odam Barton Devon 26 D2
Odcombe Som 29 D8
Odd Down Bath 61 G8
Oddendale Cumb 221 C11
Odder Lincs 188 G6
Oddingley Worcs 117 F8
Oddington Glos 100 F4
Oddington Oxon 83 C9
Odell Beds 121 F9
Odham Devon 25 G7
Odie Orkney 314 D6
Odiham Hants 49 C8
Odsal W Yorks 197 B7
Odsey Cambs 104 D5
Odstock Wilts 31 B10
Odstone Leics 135 B7
Offchurch Warks 119 D7
Offenham Worcs 99 B11
Offenham Cross Worcs 99 B11
Offerton Gtr Man 184 D6
Offerton T & W 243 F8
Offerton Green Gtr Man 184 D6
Offham E Sus 36 E5
Offham Kent 53 B7
Offham W Sus 35 F8
Offleyhay Staffs 150 D5
Offleymarsh Staffs 150 D5
Offleyrock Staffs 150 D5
Offord Cluny Cambs 122 D4
Offord D'Arcy Cambs 122 D4
Offton Suff 107 B11
Offwell Devon 15 B9
Ogbourne Maizey Wilts 63 E7
Ogbourne St Andrew Wilts 63 E7
Ogbourne St George Wilts 63 E8
Ogden W Yorks 205 G7
Ogdens Hants 31 E11
Ogil Angus 292 G6
Ogle Northumb 242 B4
Ogmore V Glam 57 F11
Ogmore-by-Sea = Aberogwr V Glam 57 F11
Ogmore Vale Bridgend 76 G6
Okeford Fitzpaine Dorset 30 E4
Okehampton Devon 13 B7
Okehampton Camp Devon 13 C7
Oker Derbys 170 C3
Okewood Hill Sur 50 F6
Okle Green Glos 98 F5
Okraquoy Shetland 313 K6
Okus Swindon 62 C6
Olchard Devon 14 F3
Old Northants 120 C5
Old Aberdeen Aberdeen 293 C11
Old Alresford Hants 48 G5
Old Arley Warks 134 E5
Old Balornock Glasgow 268 B2
Old Basford Nottingham 171 G8
Old Basing Hants 49 C7
Old Belses Borders 262 E3
Old Bewick Northumb 264 E3
Old Bexley London 68 E3
Old Blair Perth 291 G10
Old Bolingbroke Lincs 174 B4
Old Boston Mers 183 B9
Old Bramhope W Yorks 205 E10
Old Brampton Derbys 186 G4
Old Bridge of Tilt Perth 291 G10
Old Bridge of Urr Dumfries 237 C9
Old Buckenham Norf 141 E11
Old Burdon T & W 243 G9
Old Burghclere Hants 48 B3
Old Byland N Yorks 215 B11
Old Cambus Borders 272 B6
Old Cardinham Castle Corn 6 B2
Old Carlisle Cumb 229 B11
Old Cassop Durham 234 D2
Old Castleton Borders 250 E2
Old Catton Norf 160 G4
Old Chalford Oxon 100 F6
Old Church Stoke Powys 130 E5
Old Clee NE Lincs 201 F9
Old Cleeve Som 42 E4
Old Colwyn Conwy 180 F5
Old Coppice Shrops 131 B9
Old Corry Highld 295 C8
Old Coulsdon London 51 B10
Old Country Hereford 98 C4
Old Craig Aberds 303 G9
Old Craig Angus 292 G4
Old Crombie Aberds 302 D5
Old Cryals Kent 53 E7
Old Cullen Moray 302 C5
Old Dailly S Ayrs 244 D6
Old Dalby Leics 154 E3
Old Dam Derbys 185 F10
Old Deer Aberds 303 E9
Old Denaby S Yorks 187 B7
Old Ditch Som 44 D4
Old Dolphin W Yorks 205 G8
Old Down S Glos 60 B6
Old Duffus Moray 301 C11
Old Edlington S Yorks 187 B8
Old Eldon Durham 233 F10
Old Ellerby E Yorks 209 F9
Old Fallings W Mid 133 C8
Old Farm Park M Keynes 103 D8
Old Felixstowe Suff 108 D6
Old Field Shrops 115 B9
Old Fletton P'boro 138 D3
Old Fold T & W 243 E7
Old Ford London 67 C11
Old Forge Hereford 79 B9
Old Furnace Torf 78 E3
Old Gate Lincs 157 E8
Old Glossop Derbys 185 C8
Old Goginan Ceredig 128 G3
Old Goole E Yorks 199 C8
Old Gore Hereford 98 F2
Old Graitney Dumfries 239 D8
Old Grimsby Scilly 1 F3
Old Hall Powys 129 G8
Old Hall Green Herts 105 G7
Old Hall Street Norf 160 C6
Old Harlow Essex 87 C7
Old Hatfield Herts 86 D2
Old Heath Essex 107 G10
Old Heathfield E Sus 37 C9
Old Hill W Mid 133 F9
Old Hills Worcs 98 B6
Old Hunstanton Norf 175 G11
Old Hurst Cambs 122 B5
Old Hutton Cumb 211 B11
Old Johnstone Dumfries 248 D6
Old Kea Corn 4 G6
Old Kilpatrick W Dunb 277 G9
Old Kinnernie Aberds 293 C9
Old Knebworth Herts 104 G4
Old Langho Lancs 203 F10
Old Laxey I o M 192 D5
Old Leake Lincs 174 E6
Old Leckie Stirl 278 C3
Old Lindley W Yorks 196 D5
Old Linslade C Beds 103 F8
Old Llanberis = Nant Peris Gwyn 163 D10
Old Malden London 67 F8
Old Malton N Yorks 216 E5
Old Marton Shrops 148 C6
Old Mead Essex 105 F10
Old Micklefield W Yorks 206 G4
Old Mill Corn 12 G3
Old Milton Hants 19 C10
Old Milverton Warks 118 D5
Old Monkland N Lnrk 268 C4
Old Nenthorn Borders 262 B5
Old Netley Hants 33 F7
Old Neuadd Powys 129 F11
Old Newton Suff 125 E11
Old Oak Common London 67 C8
Old Park Corn 6 B4
Old Park Telford 132 B3
Old Passage S Glos 60 B5
Old Perton Staffs 133 D7
Old Philpstoun W Loth 279 F11
Old Polmont Falk 279 F8
Old Portsmouth Ptsmth 21 B8
Old Quarrington Durham 234 D2
Old Radnor Powys 114 F5
Old Rattray Aberds 303 D10
Old Rayne Aberds 302 G6
Old Romney Kent 39 B8
Old Shirley Soton 32 E5
Old Shoreham W Sus 36 F2
Old Snydale W Yorks 198 C2
Old Sodbury S Glos 61 C9
Old Somerby Lincs 155 C9
Old Stillington Stockton 234 G3
Old Storridge Common Worcs 116 G4
Old Stratford Northants 102 C5
Old Struan Perth 291 G10
Old Swan Mers 182 C5
Old Swarland Northumb 252 C5
Old Swinford W Mid 133 G8
Old Tame Gtr Man 196 F3
Old Tebay Cumb 222 D2
Old Thirsk N Yorks 215 C8
Old Tinnis Borders 261 D9
Old Toll S Ayrs 257 E9
Old Town Cumb 211 C11
Old Town Cumb 230 C5
Old Town E Sus 23 F9
Old Town E Sus 38 F2
Old Town E Sus 38 F4
Old Town E Yorks 218 F3
Old Town Edin 280 G5
Old Town Herts 104 F4
Old Town Scilly 1 G4
Old Town Swindon 63 C7
Old Town W Yorks 196 B3
Old Trafford Gtr Man 184 B4
Old Tree Kent 71 G8
Old Tupton Derbys 170 B5
Old Warden C Beds 104 C2
Old Warren Flint 166 C4
Old Way Som 28 D5
Old Weston Cambs 121 B11
Old Wharf Hereford 98 D4
Old Whittington Derbys 186 G5
Old Wick Highld 310 D7
Old Wimpole Cambs 122 G6
Old Windsor Windsor 66 E3
Old Wingate Durham 234 D3
Old Wives Lees Kent 54 C5
Old Woking Sur 50 B4
Old Wolverton M Keynes 102 C6
Old Woodhall Lincs 174 B2
Old Woodhouses Shrops 167 G9
Old Woodstock Oxon 82 B6
Oldany Highld 306 F6
Oldberrow Warks 118 D2
Oldborough Devon 26 F3
Oldbrook M Keynes 103 D7
Oldbury Kent 52 B5
Oldbury Shrops 132 E4
Oldbury W Mid 133 F9
Oldbury Warks 134 E6
Oldbury Naite S Glos 79 G10
Oldbury-on-Severn S Glos 79 G10
Oldbury on the Hill Glos 61 B10
Oldcastle Mon 96 G6
Oldcastle Heath W Ches 167 F7
Oldcotes Notts 187 D9
Oldcroft Glos 79 D10
Oldend Glos 80 D3
Oldfallow Staffs 151 G9
Oldfield Cumb 229 F7
Oldfield Shrops 132 F3
Oldfield W Yorks 196 E6
Oldfield W Yorks 204 F6
Oldfield Worcs 116 E6
Oldfield Brow Gtr Man 184 D3
Oldfield Park Bath 61 G8
Oldford Som 45 C9
Oldfurnace Staffs 169 G8
Oldhall Renfs 267 C10
Oldhall Green Suff 125 F7
Oldhall Ho Highld 310 D6
Oldham Gtr Man 196 F2
Oldham Edge Gtr Man 196 F2
Oldhamstocks E Loth 282 G4
Oldhurst Cambs 122 B6
Oldington Shrops 132 D4
Oldland S Glos 61 E7
Oldland Common S Glos 61 E7
Oldmeldrum Aberds 303 G8
Oldmixon N Som 43 B10
Oldshore Beg Highld 306 D6
Oldshoremore Highld 306 D7
Oldstead N Yorks 215 C10
Oldtown Aberds 293 C7
Oldtown Aberds 302 G5
Oldtown Highld 309 L5
Oldtown of Ord Aberds 302 D6
Oldwalls Swansea 56 C3
Oldway Swansea 56 D5
Oldway Torbay 9 C7
Oldways End Devon 26 B5
Oldwhat Aberds 303 D8
Oldwich Lane W Mid 118 C4
Oldwood Worcs 115 D11
Olgrinmore Highld 310 D4
Olive Green Staffs 152 F2
Oliver's Battery Hants 33 B7
Ollaberry Shetland 312 E5
Ollag W Isles 297 G3
Ollerbrook Booth Derbys 185 D10
Ollerton E Ches 184 F3
Ollerton Notts 171 B11
Ollerton Shrops 150 D2
Ollerton Fold Lancs 194 C6
Ollerton Lane Shrops 150 D3
Olmarch Ceredig 112 F2
Olmstead Green Essex 106 C2
Olney M Keynes 121 G7
Olrig Ho Highld 310 C5
Olton W Mid 134 G2
Olveston S Glos 60 B6
Olwen Ceredig 93 B11
Ombersley Worcs 116 E6
Ompton Notts 171 B11
Omunsgarth Shetland 313 J5
Onchan I o M 192 E4
Onecote Staffs 169 D9
Onehouse Suff 125 F10
Onen Mon 78 C6
Onesacre S Yorks 186 C3
Ongar Hill Norf 157 E11
Ongar Street Hereford 115 D7
Onibury Shrops 115 B9
Onich Highld 290 G2
Onllwyn Neath 76 C4
Onneley Staffs 168 G3
Onslow Village Sur 50 D3
Onthank E Ayrs 267 G8
Onziebust Orkney 314 D4
Openshaw Gtr Man 184 B5
Openwoodgate Derbys 170 F5
Opinan Highld 299 B7
Opinan Highld 307 K3
Orange Lane Borders 272 G5
Orange Row Norf 157 E10
Orasaigh W Isles 305 G5
Orbiston N Lnrk 268 D4
Orbliston Moray 302 D3
Orbost Highld 298 E2
Orby Lincs 175 B7
Orchard Hill Devon 24 B6
Orchard Leigh Bucks 85 E7
Orchard Portman Som 28 C2
Orcheston Wilts 46 D5
Orcop Hereford 97 F9
Orcop Hill Hereford 97 F9
Ord Highld 295 D8
Ordale Shetland 312 C8
Ordhead Aberds 293 B8
Ordie Aberds 292 C6
Ordiequish Moray 302 D3
Ordiqhill Aberds 302 D5
Ordley Northumb 241 F10
Ordsall Gtr Man 184 B4
Ordsall Notts 187 E11
Ore E Sus 38 E4
Oreston Plym 7 E10
Oreton Shrops 132 G3
Orford Suff 109 B8
Orford Warr 183 C10
Organford Dorset 18 C4
Orgreave S Yorks 186 D6
Orgreave Staffs 152 F3
Oridge Street Glos 98 F5
Orlandon Pembs 72 D4
Orlestone Kent 54 G3
Orleton Hereford 115 D9
Orleton Worcs 116 D3
Orleton Common Hereford 115 D9
Orlingbury Northants 121 C7
Ormacleit W Isles 297 H3
Ormathwaite Cumb 229 F11
Ormesby Redcar 225 B10
Ormesby St Margaret Norf 161 G9
Ormesby St Michael Norf 161 G9
Ormiclate Castle W Isles 297 H3
Ormidale Lodge Argyll 275 F11
Ormiscaig Highld 307 K3
Ormiston Borders 262 G2
Ormiston E Loth 271 B8
Ormsaigbeg Highld 288 C6
Ormsaigmore Highld 288 C6
Ormsary Argyll 275 F8
Ormsgill Cumb 210 E3
Ormskirk Lancs 194 F2
Ornsby Hill Durham 233 B9
Orpington London 68 F3
Orrell Gtr Man 194 F4
Orrell Mers 182 B4
Orrell Post Gtr Man 194 G4
Orrisdale I o M 192 C4
Orrock Fife 280 D4
Orroland Dumfries 237 E9
Orsett Thurrock 68 C6
Orsett Heath Thurrock 68 D6
Orslow Staffs 150 F6
Orston Notts 172 G3
Orthwaite Cumb 229 E11
Ortner Lancs 202 C6
Orton Cumb 222 D2
Orton Northants 120 B6
Orton Staffs 133 D7
Orton Brimbles P'boro 138 D3
Orton Goldhay P'boro 138 D3
Orton Longueville P'boro 138 D3
Orton Malborne P'boro 138 D3
Orton-on-the-Hill Leics 134 C6
Orton Rigg Cumb 239 G8
Orton Southgate P'boro 138 E2
Orton Waterville P'boro 138 D3
Orton Wistow P'boro 138 D2
Orwell Cambs 123 G7
Osbaldeston Lancs 203 G8
Osbaldeston Green Lancs 203 G8
Osbaldwick York 207 C8
Osbaston Leics 135 C8
Osbaston Shrops 148 E6
Osbaston Telford 149 F11
Osbaston Hollow Leics 135 B8
Osbournby Lincs 155 B11
Oscroft W Ches 167 B8
Ose Highld 298 E3
Osea Island Essex 88 D6
Osehill Green Dorset 29 F11
Osgathorpe Leics 153 F8
Osgodby Lincs 189 C9
Osgodby N Yorks 207 G8
Osgodby N Yorks 217 C11
Osgodby Common N Yorks 207 F8
Osidge London 86 G3
Oskaig Highld 295 B7
Oskamull Argyll 288 E6
Osleston Derbys 152 B4
Osmaston Derby 153 C7
Osmaston Derbys 170 G2
Osmington Dorset 17 E10
Osmington Mills Dorset 17 E10
Osmondthorpe W Yorks 206 G2
Osmotherley N Yorks 225 F9
Osney Oxon 83 D8
Ospisdale Highld 309 L7
Ospringe Kent 70 G4
Ossaborough Devon 40 E3
Ossemsley Hants 19 B10
Osset Spa W Yorks 197 D9
Ossett W Yorks 197 C9
Ossett Street Side W Yorks 197 C9
Ossington Notts 172 C3
Ostend Essex 88 F6
Ostend Norf 161 C7
Osterley London 66 D6
Oswaldkirk N Yorks 216 D2
Oswaldtwistle Lancs 195 B8
Oswestry Shrops 148 D5
Otby Lincs 189 C10
Oteley Shrops 149 C8
Otford Kent 52 B4
Otham Kent 53 C9
Otham Hole Kent 53 C10
Otherton Staffs 151 G8
Othery Som 43 G11
Otley Suff 126 F4
Otley W Yorks 205 D10
Otter Ferry Argyll 275 E10
Otter Ho Argyll 275 F10
Otterbourne Hants 33 C7
Otterburn N Yorks 204 B3
Otterburn Northumb 251 E9
Otterburn Camp Northumb 251 D9
Otterden Place Kent 54 C2
Otterford Som 28 E2
Otterham Corn 11 C9
Otterham Quay Kent 69 F10
Otterham Station Corn 11 D9
Otterhampton Som 43 E8
Ottershaw Sur 66 G4
Otterspool Mers 182 D5
Otterswick Shetland 312 E7
Otterton Devon 15 D7
Otterwood Hants 32 G6
Ottery St Mary Devon 15 B8
Ottinge Kent 55 E7
Ottringham E Yorks 201 C9
Oughterby Cumb 239 F7
Oughtershaw N Yorks 213 C7
Oughterside Cumb 229 C8
Oughtibridge S Yorks 186 C4
Oughtrington Warr 183 D11
Oulston N Yorks 215 E10
Oulton Cumb 238 G6
Oulton Norf 160 D2
Oulton Staffs 150 E5
Oulton Staffs 151 B8
Oulton Suff 143 D10
Oulton W Yorks 197 B11
Oulton Broad Suff 143 E10
Oulton Grange Staffs 151 B8
Oulton Heath Staffs 151 B8
Oulton Street Norf 160 D3
Oultoncross Staffs 151 C8
Oundle Northants 137 F10
Ounsdale Staffs 133 E7
Ousby Cumb 231 E8
Ousdale Highld 311 G4
Ousden Suff 124 F4
Ousefleet E Yorks 199 C10
Ousel Hole W Yorks 205 E8
Ouston Durham 243 G7
Ouston Northumb 241 G7
Ouston Northumb 242 C3
Out Elmstead Kent 55 C8
Out Newton E Yorks 201 C11
Out Rawcliffe Lancs 202 E4
Outcast Cumb 210 D6
Outer Hope Devon 8 G3
Outertown Orkney 314 E2
Outgate Cumb 221 F7
Outhgill Cumb 222 E5
Outhill Warks 118 D2
Outhills Aberds 303 D10

352 Out – Pen

Outlands Staffs 150 C5
Outlane W Yorks 196 D5
Outlane Moor W Yorks 196 D5
Outlet Village W Ches 182 G6
Outmarsh Wilts 61 G11
Outwell Norf 139 C10
Outwick Hants 31 D10
Outwood Gtr Man 195 F9
Outwood Som 28 B4
Outwood Sur 51 D10
Outwood W Yorks 197 C10
Outwoods Leics 153 F8
Outwoods Staffs 150 F5
Outwoods Staffs 152 E4
Outwoods Warks 134 G4
Ouzlewell Green W Yorks 197 B10
Ovenden W Yorks 196 B5
Ovenscloss Borders 261 C11
Over Cambs 123 C7
Over Glos 80 B4
Over S Glos 60 C5
Over W Ches 167 B10
Over Burrow Lancs 212 D2
Over Burrows Derbys 152 B5
Over Compton Dorset 29 D9
Over End Cambs 137 E11
Over End Derbys 186 G3
Over Green W Mid 134 E3
Over Haddon Derbys 170 B2
Over Hulton Gtr Man 195 F7
Over Kellet Lancs 211 E10
Over Kiddington Oxon 101 G8
Over Knutsford E Ches 184 F3
Over Langshaw Borders 271 G10
Over Monnow Mon 79 C8
Over Norton Oxon 100 F6
Over Peover E Ches 184 G3
Over Silton N Yorks 225 G9
Over Stowey Som 43 F7
Over Stratton Som 28 D6
Over Tabley E Ches 184 E2
Over Town Lancs 195 B11
Over Wallop Hants 47 F9
Over Whitacre Warks 134 E5
Over Worton Oxon 101 F8
Overa Farm Stud Norf 141 F9
Overbister Orkney 314 B6
Overbury Worcs 99 D9
Overcombe Dorset 17 E9
Overend W Mid 133 G9
Overgreen Derbys 186 G4
Overleigh Som 44 F3
Overley Staffs 152 F3
Overley Green Warks 117 F11
Overmoor Staffs 169 F7
Overpool W Ches 182 F5
Overs Shrops 131 D7
Overscaig Hotel Highld 309 G4
Overseal Derbys 152 F5
Overslade Warks 119 C9
Oversland Kent 54 B5
Oversley Green Warks 117 F11
Overstone Northants 120 D6
Overstrand Norf 160 A4
Overthorpe Northants 101 C9
Overthorpe W Yorks 197 D8
Overton Aberdeen 293 B10
Overton Aberds 293 B9
Overton Dumfries 237 C11
Overton Glos 80 C2
Overton Hants 48 D4
Overton Invclyd 276 G5
Overton Lancs 202 B4
Overton N Yorks 207 B7
Overton Shrops 115 C10
Overton Staffs 151 B10
Overton Swansea 56 D3
Overton W Ches 183 F8
Overton W Yorks 197 D9
Overton = Owrtyn Wrex 166 G5
Overton Bridge Wrex 166 G5
Overtown Lancs 212 D2
Overtown N Lnrk 268 E6
Overtown Swindon 63 D7
Overtown W Yorks 197 D11
Oving Bucks 102 G5
Oving W Sus 22 C6
Ovingdean Brighton 36 G5
Ovingham Northumb 242 E3
Ovington Durham 224 C2
Ovington Essex 106 C5
Ovington Hants 48 G5
Ovington Norf 141 C8
Ovington Northumb 242 E3
Owen's Bank Staffs 152 D4
Ower Hants 32 D4
Owermoigne Dorset 17 D11
Owl End Cambs 122 B4
Owlbury Shrops 130 E6
Owlcotes Derbys 170 B6
Owler Bar Derbys 186 F3
Owlerton S Yorks 186 D4
Owlet W Yorks 205 F9
Owlpen Glos 80 F4
Owl's Green Suff 126 D5
Owlsmoor Brack 65 G11
Owlswick Bucks 84 D3
Owlthorpe S Yorks 186 E6
Owmby Lincs 200 G5
Owmby-by-Spital Lincs 189 D8
Ownham W Berks 64 E2
Owrtyn = Overton Wrex 166 G5
Owslebury Hants 33 C8
Owston Leics 136 B5
Owston S Yorks 198 E5
Owston Ferry N Lincs 199 G10
Owstwick E Yorks 209 G11
Owthorne E Yorks 201 B10
Owthorpe Notts 154 C3
Owton Manor Hrtlpl 234 F5
Oxborough Norf 140 C4
Oxclose S Yorks 186 E6
Oxclose T & W 243 F7
Oxcombe Lincs 190 F4
Oxcroft Derbys 187 G7
Oxcroft Estate Derbys 187 G7
Oxen End Essex 106 F3
Oxen Park Cumb 210 B6
Oxenhall Glos 98 F4
Oxenholme Cumb 211 B10
Oxenhope W Yorks 204 F6
Oxenpill Som 44 E2
Oxenton Glos 99 E9
Oxenwood Wilts 47 B10
Oxford Oxon 83 D8
Oxford Stoke 168 E5
Oxgang E Dunb 278 G3
Oxgangs Edin 270 B4
Oxhey Herts 85 F10
Oxhill Durham 242 G5
Oxhill Warks 100 B6
Oxlease Herts 86 D2
Oxley W Mid 133 C8
Oxley Green Essex 88 C6
Oxley's Green E Sus 37 C11
Oxlode Cambs 139 F9
Oxnam Borders 262 F5
Oxnead Norf 160 E4
Oxshott Sur 66 G6
Oxspring S Yorks 197 G9
Oxted Sur 51 C11
Oxton Borders 271 E9
Oxton Mers 182 D3
Oxton N Yorks 206 E6
Oxton Notts 171 E10
Oxton Rakes Derbys 186 G4
Oxwich Swansea 56 D3
Oxwich Green Swansea 56 D3
Oxwick Norf 159 D8
Oykel Bridge Highld 309 J3
Oyne Aberds 302 G6
Oystermouth Swansea 56 D6
Ozleworth Glos 80 G3

P

Pabail Iarach W Isles 304 E7
Pabail Uarach W Isles 304 E7
Pabo Conwy 180 F4
Pace Gate N Yorks 205 C8
Pachesham Park Sur 51 B7
Packers Hill Dorset 30 E2
Packington Leics 153 G7
Packmoor Staffs 168 E5
Packmores Warks 118 D5
Packwood W Mid 118 C3
Packwood Gullet W Mid 118 C3
Padanaram Angus 287 B8
Padbury Bucks 102 E4
Paddington London 67 C9
Paddington Warr 183 D10
Paddlesworth Kent 55 F7
Paddlesworth Kent 69 G7
Paddock Kent 54 C3
Paddock W Yorks 196 D6
Paddock Wood Kent 53 E7
Paddockhaugh Moray 302 D2
Paddockhill E Ches 184 F4
Paddockhole Dumfries 248 G6
Paddolgreen Shrops 149 C10
Padfield Derbys 185 B8
Padgate Warr 183 D10
Padham's Green Essex 87 F10
Padiham Lancs 203 G11
Padney Cambs 123 C10
Padog Conwy 164 E4
Padside N Yorks 205 B9
Padside Green N Yorks 205 B9
Padson Devon 13 B7
Padstow Corn 10 F4
Padworth W Berks 64 F6
Padworth Common Hants 64 G6
Paganhill Glos 80 D4
Page Bank Durham 233 D10
Page Moss Mers 182 C6
Pagelsham Eastend Essex 88 G6
Page's Green Suff 126 D2
Pagham W Sus 22 D5
Paglesham Churchend Essex 88 G6
Paglesham Eastend Essex 88 G6
Paibeil W Isles 296 E3
Paible W Isles 305 J2
Paignton Torbay 9 C7
Pailton Warks 135 G9
Painleyhill Staffs 151 C10
Pains Hill Sur 52 C2
Painscastle Powys 96 B3
Painshawfield Northumb 242 E3
Painsthorpe E Yorks 208 B2
Painswick Glos 80 D5
Painter's Forstal Kent 54 B3
Painter's Green Herts 86 B3
Painters Green Wrex 167 G8
Painthorpe W Yorks 197 D10
Paintmoor Som 28 F4
Pairc Shiaboist W Isles 304 D4
Paisley Renfs 267 C9
Pakefield Suff 143 E10
Pakenham Suff 125 D8
Pale Gwyn 147 B9
Pale Green Essex 106 C3
Palehouse Common E Sus 23 B7
Palestine Hants 47 E9
Paley Street Windsor 65 D11
Palfrey W Mid 133 D10
Palgowan Dumfries 245 G9
Palgrave Suff 126 B2
Pallaflat Cumb 219 C9
Pallington Dorset 17 C11
Pallion T & W 243 F9
Pallister M'bro 225 B10
Palmarsh Kent 54 G6
Palmer Moor Derbys 152 C2
Palmers Cross Staffs 133 C7
Palmers Cross Sur 50 E4
Palmer's Flat Glos 79 D9
Palmer's Green Kent 53 E7
Palmers Green London 86 G4
Palmersbridge Corn 11 F9
Palmerstown V Glam 58 F6
Palmersville T & W 243 C7
Palmstead Kent 55 D7
Palnackie Dumfries 237 D10
Palnure Dumfries 236 C6
Palterton Derbys 171 B7
Pamber End Hants 48 B6
Pamber Green Hants 48 B6
Pamber Heath Hants 64 G6
Pamington Glos 99 E8
Pamphill Dorset 31 G7
Pampisford Cambs 105 B9
Pan I o W 20 D6
Pan Orkney 314 G3
Panborough Som 44 D3
Panbride Angus 287 D9
Pancakehill Glos 81 C9
Pancrasweek Devon 24 F3
Pancross V Glam 58 F4
Pandy Gwyn 128 C2
Pandy Gwyn 146 F4
Pandy Gwyn 147 D7
Pandy Mon 96 G6
Pandy Powys 129 C8
Pandy Wrex 148 B3
Pandy Wrex 166 G6
Pandy Tudur Conwy 164 C5
Pandy'r Capel Denb 165 E9
Panfield Essex 106 F4
Pangbourne W Berks 64 D6
Panhall Fife 280 C6
Panks Bridge Hereford 98 B2
Pannal N Yorks 206 C2
Pannal Ash N Yorks 205 C11
Pannel's Ash Essex 106 C5
Panpunton Powys 114 C5
Panshanger Herts 86 C3
Pant Denb 166 E2
Pant Flint 181 G10
Pant Gwyn 144 C4
Pant M Tydf 77 D9
Pant Powys 129 C11
Pant Shrops 148 E5
Pant Wrex 166 D5
Pant Wrex 166 F3
Pant-glâs Powys 128 D5
Pant-glas Gwyn 163 F7
Pant-glas Shrops 148 C5
Pant-lasau Swansea 57 B7
Pant Mawr Powys 129 G7
Pant-pastynog Denb 165 C8
Pant-teg Carms 93 F9
Pant-y-Caws Carms 92 F3
Pant-y-crûg Ceredig 112 B3
Pant-y-dwr Powys 113 B9
Pant-y-dwr Powys 113 C9
Pant-y-ffridd Powys 130 C3
Pant-y-pyllau Bridgend 58 C2
Pant-y-Wacco Flint 181 F10
Pant-yr-awel Bridgend 58 B2
Pantasaph Flint 181 F11
Pantdu Neath 57 C9
Panteg Ceredig 111 E9
Panteg Torf 78 F4
Pantersbridge Corn 6 B3
Pantgwyn Carms 93 F11
Pantgwyn Ceredig 92 B4
Pantmawr Cardiff 58 C6
Panton Lincs 189 F11
Pantperthog Gwyn 128 C4
Pantside Caerph 78 F2
Pantyffynnon Carms 75 C10
Pantygasseg Torf 78 F3
Pantymwyn Flint 165 C11
Panxworth Norf 161 G7
Papcastle Cumb 229 E8
Papermill Bank Shrops 149 D11
Papigoe Highld 310 D7
Papil Shetland 313 K5
Papley Northants 138 F2
Papley Orkney 314 G4
Papple E Loth 281 G11
Papplewick Notts 171 E8
Papworth Everard Cambs 122 E5
Papworth St Agnes Cambs 122 E5
Papworth Village Settlement Cambs 122 E5
Par Corn 5 E11
Paradise Glos 80 C5
Paradise Green Hereford 97 B10
Paramoor Corn 5 F9
Paramour Street Kent 71 G9
Parbold Lancs 194 E3
Parbrook Som 44 F5
Parbrook W Sus 35 B9
Parc Gwyn 147 C7
Parc Erissey Corn 4 G3
Parc-hendy Swansea 56 B4
Parc Mawr Caerph 77 G10
Parc-Seymour Newport 78 G6
Parc-y-rhôs Carms 93 B11
Parchey Som 43 F10
Parciau Anglesey 179 E7
Parcllyn Ceredig 110 G4
Pardown Hants 48 D5
Pardshaw Cumb 229 G7
Pardshaw Hall Cumb 229 F8
Parham Suff 126 E6
Park Corn 10 G6
Park Devon 14 B2
Park Dumfries 247 E10
Park Som 44 G3
Park Swindon 63 C7
Park Barn Sur 50 C3
Park Bottom Corn 4 G3
Park Bridge Gtr Man 196 G2
Park Broom Cumb 239 F10
Park Close Lancs 204 E3
Park Corner Bath 45 B9
Park Corner E Sus 23 C8
Park Corner E Sus 52 F4
Park Corner Oxon 65 B7
Park Corner Windsor 65 C11
Park End Beds 121 G9
Park End Cambs 123 E11
Park End M'bro 225 B10
Park End Northumb 241 B9
Park End Som 43 G7
Park End Staffs 168 E3
Park End Worcs 116 C5
Park Gate Dorset 30 F2
Park Gate Hants 33 F8
Park Gate Kent 55 D7
Park Gate Suff 124 F4
Park Gate W Yorks 197 E8
Park Gate Worcs 117 C8
Park Green Essex 105 F9
Park Hall Shrops 148 C6
Park Head Cumb 231 C7
Park Head Derbys 170 E5
Park Head W Yorks 197 F7
Park Hill Glos 79 F9
Park Hill Kent 54 G3
Park Hill Mers 194 G3
Park Hill N Yorks 214 F6
Park Hill Notts 171 E11
Park Hill S Yorks 186 D5
Park Lane Staffs 133 B7
Park Lane Wrex 149 B8
Park Langley London 67 F11
Park Mains Renfs 277 G9
Park Mill W Yorks 197 E9
Park Royal London 67 C7
Park Street Herts 85 E10
Park Street W Sus 50 G6
Park Town Luton 103 G11
Park Town Oxon 83 D8
Park Village Northumb 240 E5
Park Village W Mid 133 C8
Park Villas W Yorks 206 F2
Park Wood Kent 53 C9
Park Wood Medway 69 G10
Parkend Glos 79 D10
Parkend Glos 80 C3
Parkengear Corn 5 F8
Parker's Corner W Berks 64 E6
Parker's Green Herts 104 F6
Parker's Green Kent 52 D6
Parkeston Essex 108 E4
Parkfield Corn 6 B6
Parkfield S Glos 61 D7
Parkfield W Mid 133 D8
Parkfoot Falk 278 F6
Parkgate Cumb 229 B10
Parkgate Dumfries 248 F2
Parkgate E Ches 184 G3
Parkgate Essex 87 B11
Parkgate Kent 53 G11
Parkgate S Yorks 186 B6
Parkgate Sur 51 E8
Parkgate W Ches 182 F3
Parkhall W Dunb 277 G9
Parkham Devon 24 C5
Parkham Ash Devon 24 C5
Parkhead Cumb 230 C2
Parkhead Glasgow 268 C2
Parkhead S Yorks 186 E4
Parkhill Aberds 303 E10
Parkhill Invclyd 277 G7
Parkhill Ho Aberds 293 B10
Parkhouse Mon 79 E7
Parkhouse Green Derbys 170 C6
Parkhurst I o W 20 C5
Parklands W Yorks 206 F3
Parkmill Swansea 56 D4
Parkneuk Aberds 293 F9
Parkneuk Fife 279 D11
Parkside C Beds 103 G10
Parkside Cumb 219 B10
Parkside Durham 234 B4
Parkside N Lnrk 268 D6
Parkside Staffs 151 D8
Parkside Wrex 166 D5
Parkstone Poole 18 C6
Parkway Hereford 98 D4
Parkway Som 29 C9
Parkwood Springs S Yorks 186 D4
Parley Cross Dorset 19 B7
Parley Green Dorset 19 B7
Parliament Heath Suff 107 C9
Parlington W Yorks 206 F4
Parmoor Bucks 65 B9
Parnacott Devon 24 F4
Parney Heath Essex 107 E10
Parr Mers 183 C8
Parr Brow Gtr Man 195 G8
Parracombe Devon 41 E7
Parrog Pembs 91 D10
Parsley Hay Derbys 169 C10
Parslow's Hillock Bucks 84 E4
Parson Cross S Yorks 186 C5
Parson Drove Cambs 139 B7
Parsonage Green Essex 88 D2
Parsonby Cumb 229 D8
Parsons Green London 67 D9
Parson's Heath Essex 107 F10
Partick Glasgow 267 B11
Partington Gtr Man 184 C2
Partney Lincs 174 B6
Parton Cumb 228 G5
Parton Cumb 239 G7
Parton Dumfries 237 B8
Parton Glos 99 G7
Parton Hereford 96 B5
Partridge Green W Sus 35 D11
Partrishow Powys 96 G5
Parwich Derbys 169 E11
Pasford Staffs 132 D6
Passenham Northants 102 D5
Passfield Hants 49 G10
Passingford Bridge Essex 87 F8
Passmores Essex 86 D6
Paston Norf 160 C6
Paston P'boro 138 C3
Paston Green Norf 160 C6
Pasturefields Staffs 151 D9
Patchacott Devon 12 B5
Patcham Brighton 36 F4
Patchetts Green Herts 85 F10
Patching W Sus 35 F9
Patchole Devon 40 E6
Patchway S Glos 60 C6
Pategill Cumb 230 F6
Pateley Bridge N Yorks 214 F3
Paternoster Heath Essex 88 C6
Path Head T & W 242 E5
Path of Condie Perth 286 F4
Pathe Som 43 G11
Pather N Lnrk 268 E5
Pathfinder Village Devon 14 C2
Pathhead Aberds 293 G9
Pathhead E Ayrs 258 G4
Pathhead Fife 280 C5
Pathhead Midloth 271 C7
Pathlow Warks 118 F3
Pathstruie Perth 286 F4
Patient End Herts 105 F8
Patmore Heath Herts 105 F8
Patna E Ayrs 257 G10
Patney Wilts 46 B5
Patrick I o M 192 D3
Patrick Brompton N Yorks 224 G4
Patricroft Gtr Man 184 B3
Patrington E Yorks 201 C10
Patrington Haven E Yorks 201 C10
Patrixbourne Kent 55 B7
Patsford Devon 40 F4
Patterdale Cumb 221 B7
Pattiesmuir Fife 279 E11
Pattingham Staffs 132 D6
Pattishall Northants 120 G3
Pattiswick Essex 106 G6
Patton Shrops 131 E11
Patton Bridge Cumb 221 F11
Paul Corn 1 D5
Paulerspury Northants 102 B4
Paull E Yorks 201 B7
Paul's Green Corn 2 C4
Paulsgrove Ptsmth 33 F10
Paulton Bath 45 B7
Paulville W Loth 269 B9
Pave Lane Telford 150 F5
Pavenham Beds 121 F9
Pawlett Som 43 E10
Pawlett Hill Som 43 E9
Pawston Northumb 263 C9
Paxford Glos 100 D3
Paxton Borders 273 E8
Payden Street Kent 54 C2
Payhembury Devon 27 G9
Paynes Green Sur 50 F6
Paynter's Cross Corn 7 C7
Paynter's Lane End Corn 4 G3
Paythorne Lancs 204 C2
Payton Som 27 C10
Peacehaven E Sus 36 G6
Peacehaven Heights E Sus 36 G6
Peacemarsh Dorset 30 B4
Peak Dale Derbys 185 F9
Peak Forest Derbys 185 F10
Peak Hill Lincs 156 F5
Peakirk P'boro 138 B3
Pean Hill Kent 70 G6
Pear Ash Som 45 G9
Pear Tree Derby 153 C7
Pearsie Angus 287 B7
Pearson's Green Kent 53 E7
Peartree Herts 86 C2
Peartree Green Essex 87 F9
Peartree Green Hereford 97 E11
Peartree Green Soton 32 E6
Peartree Green Sur 50 F3
Peas Acre W Yorks 205 E8
Peas Hill Cambs 139 D8
Pease Pottage W Sus 51 G9
Peasedown St John Bath 45 B8
Peasehill Derbys 170 F6
Peaseland Green Norf 159 F11
Peasemore W Berks 64 D3
Peasenhall Suff 127 D7
Peaslake Sur 50 E5
Peasley Cross Mers 183 C8
Peasmarsh E Sus 38 C5
Peasmarsh Som 28 E4
Peasmarsh Sur 50 D3
Peaston E Loth 271 B8
Peastonbank E Loth 271 B8
Peat Inn Fife 287 G8
Peathill Aberds 303 C9
Peatling Magna Leics 135 E11
Peatling Parva Leics 135 F11
Peaton Shrops 131 G10
Peatonstrand Shrops 131 G10
Peats Corner Suff 126 E3
Pebmarsh Essex 107 E7
Pebsham E Sus 38 F3
Pebworth Worcs 100 B2
Pecket Well W Yorks 196 B3
Peckforton E Ches 167 D8
Peckham London 67 D10
Peckham Bush Kent 53 D7
Pecking Mill Som 44 F6
Peckingell Wilts 62 E2
Peckleton Leics 135 C9
Pedair-ffordd Powys 148 E2
Pedham Norf 160 G6
Pedlars End Essex 87 D8
Pedlar's Rest Shrops 131 G9
Pedlinge Kent 54 F6
Pedmore W Mid 133 G8
Pednor Bottom Bucks 84 E6
Pednormead End Bucks 85 E7
Pedwell Som 44 F2
Peebles Borders 270 G5
Peel Borders 261 B10
Peel I o M 192 D3
Peel Lancs 202 G3
Peel Common Hants 33 G9
Peel Green Gtr Man 184 B2
Peel Hall Gtr Man 184 D4
Peel Hill Lancs 202 G3
Peel Park S Lnrk 268 E2
Peene Kent 55 F7
Peening Quarter Kent 38 B5
Peggs Green Leics 153 F8
Pegsdon C Beds 104 E2
Pegswood Northumb 252 F6
Pegwell Kent 71 G11
Peinaha Highld 298 D4
Peinchorran Highld 295 B7
Peingown Highld 298 B4
Peinlich Highld 298 D4
Peinmore Highld 298 E4
Pelaw T & W 243 E7
Pelcomb Pembs 72 B6
Pelcomb Bridge Pembs 72 B6
Pelcomb Cross Pembs 72 B6
Peldon Essex 89 B7
Pelhamfield I o W 21 C7
Pell Green E Sus 52 G6
Pellon W Yorks 196 B5
Pelsall W Mid 133 C10
Pelsall Wood W Mid 133 C10
Pelton Durham 243 G7
Pelton Fell Durham 243 G7
Pelutho Cumb 229 B8
Pelynt Corn 6 D4
Pemberton Carms 75 E8
Pemberton Gtr Man 194 G5
Pembles Cross Kent 53 D11
Pembre = Pembrey Carms 74 E6
Pembrey = Pembre Carms 74 E6
Pembridge Hereford 115 F7
Pembroke Pembs 73 E7
Pembroke Dock = Doc Penfro Pembs 73 E7
Pembroke Ferry Pembs 73 E7
Pembury Kent 52 E6
Pempwell Corn 12 F3
Pen-allt Hereford 97 F11
Pen-bedw Pembs 92 D4
Pen-bont Rhydybeddau Ceredig 128 G3
Pen-caer-fenny Swansea 56 B4
Pen-clawdd Swansea 56 B4
Pen-common Powys 76 D6
Pen-gilfach Gwyn 163 C9
Pen-groes-oped Mon 78 D4
Pen-lan Swansea 56 B6
Pen-Lan-mabws Pembs 91 F7
Pen-llyn Anglesey 178 E4
Pen-lon Anglesey 162 B6
Pen Mill Som 29 D9
Pen-onn V Glam 58 F5
Pen-Rhiw-fawr Neath 76 C2
Pen-rhos Wrex 166 E3
Pen-sarn Gwyn 145 D11
Pen-sarn Gwyn 162 G6
Pen-twyn Caerph 78 E2
Pen-twyn Carms 75 C9
Pen-twyn Mon 79 D8
Pen-twyn Torf 78 E3
Pen-Uchar Plwyf Flint 181 G11
Pen-y-Ball Top Flint 181 F11
Pen-y-banc Carms 93 G8
Pen-y-banc Carms 94 G2
Pen-y-bank Caerph 77 E10
Pen-y-Bont Bl Gwent 78 D2
Pen-y-bont Carms 92 F6
Pen-y-bont Gwyn 128 C4
Pen-y-bont Gwyn 146 D2
Pen-y-bont Powys 148 E4
Pen y Bont ar ogwr = Bridgend Bridgend 58 C2
Pen-y-Bryn Gwyn 145 B9
Pen-y-bryn Gwyn 146 F3
Pen-y-bryn Pembs 92 C3
Pen-y-Bryn Powys 130 C3
Pen-y-Bryn Shrops 148 B6
Pen-y-bryn Wrex 166 G3
Pen-y-cae Bridgend 58 C2
Pen-y-cae Neath 57 D9
Pen-y-cae Powys 76 C4
Pen-y-cae-mawr Mon 78 F6
Pen-y-cefn Flint 181 F10
Pen-y-clawdd Mon 79 D7
Pen-y-coed Shrops 148 E5
Pen-y-coedcae Rhondda 58 B5
Pen-y-Darren M Tydf 77 D9
Pen-y-fai Bridgend 57 E11
Pen-y-fai Carms 75 E7
Pen-y-fan Carms 56 B4
Pen-y-fan Mon 79 D8
Pen-y-felin Flint 165 B11
Pen-y-ffordd Denb 181 F8
Pen-y-ffordd Flint 181 E10
Pen y Foel Shrops 148 E5
Pen-y-garn Carms 93 E11
Pen-y-garn Ceredig 128 F2
Pen-y-garnedd Anglesey 179 F8
Pen-y-gop Conwy 164 G6
Pen-y-graig Gwyn 144 C3
Pen-y-groes Carms 75 C9
Pen-y-groeslon Gwyn 144 C4
Pen-y-Gwryd Hotel Gwyn 163 D11
Pen-y-lan Cardiff 59 D7
Pen-y-lan Newport 59 B9
Pen-y-lan V Glam 58 D3
Pen-y-maes Flint 181 F11
Pen-y-Myndd Carms 75 E7
Pen-y-Park Hereford 96 C5
Pen-y-rhiw Rhondda 58 B5
Pen-y-stryt Denb 165 E11
Pen-y-wern Shrops 114 B6
Pen-yr-englyn Rhondda 76 F6
Pen-yr-heol Bridgend 58 C2
Pen-yr-heol Mon 78 C6
Pen-yr-Heolgerrig M Tydf 77 D8
Penallt Mon 79 C8
Penally = Penalun Pembs 73 F10
Penalt Hereford 97 F11
Penalun = Penally Pembs 73 F10
Penare Corn 5 G9
Penarlâg = Hawarden Flint 166 B4
Penarron Powys 130 F2
Penarth V Glam 59 E7
Penarth Moors Cardiff 59 E7
Penbeagle Corn 2 B2
Penbedw Flint 165 B11
Penberth Corn 1 E4
Penbidwal Mon 96 G6
Penbodlas Gwyn 144 C5
Penboyr Carms 93 D7
Penbryn Ceredig 110 G5
Pencader Carms 93 D8
Pencaenewydd Gwyn 162 G6
Pencaerau Neath 57 B8
Pencaitland E Loth 271 B8
Pencarnisiog Anglesey 178 G5
Pencarreg Carms 93 B10
Pencarrow Corn 11 E8
Penceiliogi Carms 75 E8
Pencelli Powys 95 F11
Pencoed Bridgend 58 C3
Pencombe Hereford 115 G11
Pencoyd Hereford 97 F10
Pencoys Corn 2 B5
Pencraig Anglesey 179 F7
Pencraig Hereford 97 G11
Pencraig Powys 147 D10
Pencroesoped Mon 78 D4
Pencuke Corn 11 C9
Pendas Fields W Yorks 206 F3
Pendeen Corn 1 C3
Pendeford W Mid 133 C7
Penderyn Rhondda 77 D7
Pendine = Pentwyn Carms 74 D2
Pendlebury Gtr Man 195 G9
Pendleton Gtr Man 184 B4
Pendleton Lancs 203 F11
Pendock Worcs 98 E5
Pendoggett Corn 10 F6
Pendomer Som 29 E8
Pendoylan V Glam 58 D5
Pendre Bridgend 58 C2
Pendre Gwyn 110 C2
Pendre Powys 95 F10
Pendrift Corn 11 G8
Penegoes Powys 128 C5
Penelewey Corn 4 G6
Penenden Heath Kent 53 B9
Penffordd Pembs 91 G11
Penffordd Lâs = Staylittle Powys 129 E7
Pengam Caerph 77 F11
Penge London 67 E11
Pengegon Corn 2 B5
Pengelly Corn 11 E7
Pengenffordd Powys 96 E3
Pengersick Corn 2 D3
Pengold Corn 11 C8
Pengorffwysfa Anglesey 179 C7
Pengover Green Corn 6 B5
Penguithal Hereford 97 G10
Pengwern Denb 181 F8
Penhale Corn 2 F5
Penhale Corn 5 D8
Penhale Jakes Corn 2 D4
Penhallick Corn 3 F7
Penhallick Corn 4 G3
Penhallow Corn 4 E5
Penhalurick Corn 2 B6
Penhalvean Corn 2 B6
Penhelig Gwyn 128 D2
Penhill Devon 40 G4
Penhill Swindon 63 B7
Penhow Newport 78 G6
Penhurst E Sus 23 B11
Peniarth Gwyn 128 B2
Penicuik Midloth 270 C4
Peniel Carms 93 G8
Peniel Denb 165 C8
Penifiler Highld 298 E4
Peninver Argyll 255 E8
Penisa'r Waun Gwyn 163 C9
Penistone S Yorks 197 G8
Penjerrick Corn 3 C7
Penketh Warr 183 D9
Penkhull Stoke 168 G5
Penkill S Ayrs 244 D6
Penknap Wilts 45 D11
Penkridge Staffs 151 G8
Penleigh Wilts 45 C11
Penley Wrex 149 B8
Penllech Gwyn 144 C4
Penllergaer Swansea 56 B6
Penllwyn Caerph 77 F11
Penllwyn Ceredig 128 G3
Penllyn V Glam 58 D3
Penmachno Conwy 164 E3
Penmaen Caerph 77 F11
Penmaen Swansea 56 D4
Penmaen Rhôs Conwy 180 F5
Penmaenan Conwy 180 F2
Penmaenmawr Conwy 180 F2
Penmaenpool Gwyn 146 F3
Penmark V Glam 58 F5
Penmarth Corn 2 B6
Penmayne Corn 10 F4
Penmon Anglesey 179 E10
Penmore Mill Argyll 288 D6
Penmorfa Ceredig 110 G6
Penmorfa Gwyn 163 G8
Penmynydd Anglesey 179 G8
Penn Bucks 84 G6
Penn W Mid 133 D7
Penn Bottom Bucks 84 G6
Penn Street Bucks 84 F6
Pennal Gwyn 128 C4
Pennan Aberds 303 C8
Pennance Corn 4 G4
Pennant Ceredig 111 E10
Pennant Conwy 164 D5
Pennant Denb 147 C10
Pennant Denb 165 E8
Pennant Powys 129 D7
Pennant Melangell Powys 147 D10
Pennar Pembs 73 E7
Pennar Park Pembs 72 E6
Pennard Swansea 56 D5
Pennerley Shrops 131 D7
Pennington Cumb 210 D5
Pennington Gtr Man 183 B11
Pennington Hants 20 C2

Pen – Pon 353

Pennington Green Gtr Man 194 F6
Pennorth Powys 96 F2
Pennsylvania Devon 14 C4
Pennsylvania S Glos 61 E8
Penny Bridge Cumb 210 C6
Penny Green Derbys 187 F8
Penny Hill Lincs 157 D7
Penny Hill W Yorks 196 D5
Pennycross Argyll 289 G7
Pennycross Plym 7 D9
Pennygate Norf 160 E6
Pennygown Argyll 289 E7
Pennylands Lancs 194 F3
Pennymoor Devon 26 E5
Pennypot Kent 54 G6
Penny's Green Norf 142 D3
Pennytinney Corn 10 F6
Pennywell T & W 243 F9
Penparc Ceredig 92 B4
Penparc Pembs 91 E7
Penparcau Ceredig 128 G1
Penpedairheol Caerph 77 F10
Penpedairheol Mon 78 E4
Penpergym Mon 78 C4
Penperlleni Mon 78 E4
Penpethy Corn 11 D7
Penpillick Corn 5 D11
Penplas Carms 74 B5
Penpol Corn 3 B8
Penpoll Corn 6 E2
Penponds Corn 2 B4
Penpont Corn 11 G7
Penpont Dumfries 247 E8
Penpont Powys 95 F9
Penprysg Bridgend 58 C3
Penquit Devon 8 E2
Penrallt Gwyn 145 B7
Penrallt Powys 129 F9
Penrhôs Mon 78 C6
Penrherber Carms 92 D5
Penrhiw Caerph 78 G2
Penrhiw-llan Ceredig 93 C7
Penrhiw-pal Ceredig 92 B6
Penrhiwceiber Rhondda 77 F8
Penrhiwgarreg Bl Gwent 78 E2
Penrhiwtyn Neath 57 B8
Penrhos Anglesey 178 E3
Penrhos Gwyn 144 C6
Penrhos Hereford 114 F6
Penrhos Mon 78 C6
Penrhos Powys 76 C3
Penrhos-garnedd Gwyn 179 G9
Penrhosfeilw Anglesey 178 E2
Penrhyd Lastra Anglesey 178 C6
Penrhyn Bay =
Bae-Penrhyn Conwy 180 E4
Penrhyn Castle Pembs 92 B2
Penrhyn-coch Ceredig 128 G2
Penrhyn side Conwy 180 E4
Penrhyndeudraeth Gwyn 146 B2
Penrhynside Conwy 180 E4
Penrhys Rhondda 77 F8
Penrice Swansea 56 D3
Penrith Cumb 230 E6
Penrose Corn 10 G3
Penrose Corn 11 F7
Penrose Hill Corn 2 D4
Penruddock Cumb 230 F4
Penryn Corn 3 C7
Pensarn Carms 74 B6
Pensarn Conwy 181 F7
Pensax Worcs 116 D4
Pensby Mers 182 E3
Penselwood Som 45 G9
Pensford Bath 60 G6
Pensham Worcs 99 C8
Penshaw T & W 243 G8
Penshurst Kent 52 E4
Pensilva Corn 6 B5
Pensnett W Mid 133 F8
Penston E Loth 281 G8
Penstone Devon 26 G3
Penstraze Corn 4 F5
Pentewan Corn 5 F10
Pentiken Shrops 130 G4
Pentir Gwyn 163 B9
Pentire Corn 4 C5
Pentirvin Shrops 130 C6
Pentlepoir Pembs 73 D10
Pentlow Essex 106 B6
Pentlow Street Essex 106 B6
Pentney Norf 158 G4
Penton Corner Hants 47 D10
Penton Grafton Hants 47 D10
Penton Mewsey Hants 47 D10
Pentonville London 67 C10
Pentowin Carms 74 B3
Pentraeth Anglesey 179 F8
Pentrapeod Caerph 77 E11
Pentre Carms 75 C8
Pentre Denb 165 D10
Pentre Flint 165 C11
Pentre Flint 166 B4
Pentre Flint 166 C2
Pentre Flint 166 D2
Pentre Powys 129 F11
Pentre Powys 130 B4
Pentre Powys 130 E5
Pentre Powys 147 D11
Pentre Powys 148 G3
Pentre Rhondda 77 F7
Pentre Shrops 148 D4
Pentre Shrops 149 F7
Pentre Wrex 148 B2
Pentre Wrex 166 G3
Pentre-bâch Ceredig 93 B11
Pentre-bach Powys 95 E8
Pentre Berw Anglesey 179 G7
Pentre-bont Conwy 164 E2
Pentre Broughton Wrex 166 E4
Pentre Bychan Wrex 166 F4
Pentre-cefn Shrops 148 D4
Pentre-celyn Denb 165 E11
Pentre-Celyn Powys 129 B7
Pentre-chwyth Swansea 57 B7
Pentre Cilgwyn Wrex 148 B4
Pentre-clawdd Shrops 148 C5
Pentre-coed Shrops 149 B7
Pentre-cwrt Carms 93 D7
Pentre Dolau-Honddu
Powys 95 C9
Pentre-dwr Swansea 57 B7
Pentre-Ffwrndan Flint 182 G3
Pentre-galar Pembs 92 E3
Pentre-Gwenlais Carms 75 B10
Pentre Gwynfryn Gwyn 145 D11
Pentre Halkyn Flint 182 G2
Pentre Hodre Shrops 114 B6
Pentre Isaf Conwy 164 B5
Pentre Llanrhaeadr
Denb 165 C9
Pentre Llifior Powys 130 D2
Pentre-llwyn-llwyd
Powys 113 G9
Pentre-llyn Ceredig 112 C2
Pentre-llyn cymmer
Conwy 165 E7
Pentre Maelor Wrex 166 F5
Pentre Meyrick V Glam 58 D3
Pentre-newydd Shrops 148 B5
Pentre-Piod Torf 78 E3
Pentre-Poeth Carms 75 E8
Pentre-poeth Newport 59 B9
Pentre-rhew Ceredig 112 G3
Pentre-tafarn-y-fedw
Conwy 164 C4
Pentre-ty-gwyn Carms 94 D6
Pentre-uchaf Conwy 180 F5
Pentrebach Carms 94 E6
Pentrebach M Tydf 77 E9
Pentrebach Rhondda 58 B5
Pentrebach Swansea 75 D10
Pentrebane Cardiff 58 D6
Pentrebeirdd Powys 148 G3
Pentrecagal Carms 92 C6
Pentredwr Denb 165 F11
Pentref-y-groes
Caerph 77 F11
Pentrefelin Anglesey 178 C6
Pentrefelin Carms 93 G11
Pentrefelin Ceredig 94 B2
Pentrefelin Conwy 180 G4
Pentrefelin Denb 166 G2
Pentrefelin Gwyn 145 B10
Pentrefoelas Conwy 164 E5
Pentregat Ceredig 111 G7
Pentreheyling Shrops 130 E4
Pentrellwyn Ceredig 93 C8
Pentre'r beirdd Powys 148 G3
Pentre'r Felin Conwy 164 B4
Pentre'r-felin Denb 165 B10
Pentre'r-felin Powys 95 E8
Pentreuchaf Gwyn 145 B7
Pentrich Derbys 170 E5
Pentridge Dorset 31 D8
Pentrisil Pembs 91 E11
Pentwyn Caerph 77 E10
Pentwyn Cardiff 59 C8
Pentwyn = Pendine
Carms 74 D2
Pentwyn Berthlwyd
Caerph 77 F10
Pentwyn-mawr Caerph 77 F11
Pentyrch Cardiff 58 C6
Penuchadre V Glam 57 G11
Penuwch Ceredig 111 E11
Penwartha Corn 4 E5
Penwartha Coombe Corn 4 E5
Penweathers Corn 4 G6
Penwithick Corn 5 D10
Penwood Hants 64 G2
Penwortham Lane
Lancs 194 B4
Penwyllt Powys 76 B5
Penybanc Carms 75 C10
Penybedd Carms 74 E6
Penybont Ceredig 128 F2
Penybont Powys 114 E2
Penybontfawr Powys 147 E11
Penybryn Caerph 77 F10
Penycae Wrex 166 F3
Penycaerau Gwyn 144 D3
Penycwm Pembs 90 G6
Penydre Swansea 75 E11
Penyfeidr Pembs 91 F7
Penyffordd Flint 166 C4
Penyffridd Gwyn 163 D8
Penygarn Torf 78 E3
Penygarnedd Powys 148 E2
Penygelli Powys 130 E2
Penygraig Rhondda 77 G7
Penygraigwen Anglesey 178 D6
Penygroes Gwyn 163 E7
Penygroes Pembs 92 D3
Penymynydd Flint 166 C4
Penyraber Pembs 91 D9
Penyrheol Caerph 58 B6
Penyrheol Swansea 56 B5
Penyrheol Torf 78 F3
Penysarn Anglesey 179 C7
Penywaun Rhondda 77 E7
Penzance Corn 1 C5
Peopleton Worcs 117 G8
Peover Heath E Ches 184 G3
Peper Harow Sur 50 E2
Pepper Hill Som 43 F7
Pepper Hill W Yorks 196 B6
Peppercombe Devon 24 C5
Peppermoor Northumb 264 F6
Pepper's Green Essex 87 C10
Pepperstock C Beds 85 B9
Per-ffordd-llan Flint 181 F10
Perceton N Ayrs 267 G7
Percie Aberds 293 D7
Percuil Corn 3 C9
Percy Main T & W 243 D8
Percyhorner Aberds 303 C9
Perham Down Wilts 47 D9
Periton Som 42 D3
Perivale London 67 C7
Perkhill Aberds 293 C7
Perkinsville Durham 243 G7
Perlethorpe Notts 187 G11
Perran Downs Corn 2 C3
Perran Wharf Corn 3 B7
Perranarworthal Corn 3 B7
Perrancoombe Corn 4 E5
Perranporth Corn 4 E5
Perranuthnoe Corn 2 D2
Perranwell Corn 3 B7
Perranwell Corn 4 E5
Perranwell Station Corn 3 B7
Perranzabuloe Corn 4 E5
Perrott's Brook Glos 81 D8
Perry Devon 26 F5
Perry Kent 55 B9
Perry W Mid 133 E11
Perry Barr W Mid 133 E11
Perry Beeches W Mid 133 E11
Perry Common W Mid 133 E11
Perry Crofts Staffs 134 C4
Perry Green Essex 106 G6
Perry Green Herts 86 B6
Perry Green Som 43 F9
Perry Green Wilts 62 B3
Perry Street Kent 68 E6
Perry Street Som 28 F4
Perryfields Worcs 117 C8
Perryfoot Derbys 185 E10
Perrymead Bath 61 G9
Perrystone Hill Hereford 98 F2
Perrywood Kent 54 B4
Pershall Staffs 150 C6
Pershore Worcs 99 B8
Pert Angus 293 G8
Pertenhall Beds 121 D11
Perth Perth 286 E5
Perthcelyn Rhondda 77 F9
Perthy Shrops 149 C7
Perton Hereford 97 C11
Perton Staffs 133 D7
Pertwood Wilts 45 F11
Pested Kent 54 C4
Peter Tavy Devon 12 F6
Peterborough P'boro 138 D3
Peterburn Highld 307 L2
Peterchurch Hereford 96 D6
Peterculter Aberdeen 293 C10
Peterhead Aberds 303 E11
Peterlee Durham 234 C4
Peter's Finger Devon 12 D3
Peter's Green Herts 85 B10
Peters Marland Devon 25 E7
Petersburn N Lnrk 268 C5
Petersfield Hants 34 C2
Petersham London 67 E7
Peterston-super-Ely
V Glam 58 D5
Peterstone Wentlooge
Newport 59 C9
Peterstow Hereford 97 G11
Petertown Orkney 314 F3
Peterville Corn 4 E4
Petham Kent 54 C6
Petherwin Gate Corn 11 D11
Petrockstow Devon 25 F8
Petsoe End M Keynes 103 B7
Pett E Sus 38 E5
Pett Bottom Kent 54 E6
Pett Bottom Kent 55 C7
Pett Level E Sus 38 E5
Pettaugh Suff 126 F3
Petteridge Kent 53 E7
Pettinain S Lnrk 269 G9
Pettings Kent 68 G6
Pettistree Suff 126 G5
Petton Devon 27 C8
Petton Shrops 149 D8
Petts Wood London 68 F2
Petty Aberds 303 F7
Petty France S Glos 61 B9
Pettycur Fife 280 D5
Pettymuick Aberds 303 G9
Pettywell Norf 159 E11
Petworth W Sus 35 C7
Pevensey E Sus 23 E10
Pevensey Bay E Sus 23 E11
Peverell Plym 7 D9
Pewsey Wilts 63 G7
Pewsey Wharf Wilts 63 G7
Pewterspear Warr 183 E10
Phantassie E Loth 281 F11
Pharisee Green Essex 106 G2
Pheasants Bucks 65 B9
Pheasant's Hill Bucks 65 B9
Pheasey W Mid 133 D11
Pheonix Green Hants 49 B9
Phepson Worcs 117 F8
Philadelphia T & W 243 G8
Philham Devon 24 C3
Philiphaugh Borders 261 D10
Phillack Corn 2 B3
Philleigh Corn 3 B9
Phillip's Town Caerph 77 E10
Philpot End Essex 87 B10
Philpstoun W Loth 279 F10
Phocle Green Hereford 98 F2
Phoenix Green Hants 49 B9
Phoenix Row Durham 233 F9
Phorp Moray 301 D10
Pibsbury Som 28 B6
Pibwrlwyd Carms 74 B6
Pica Cumb 228 G6
Piccadilly S Yorks 187 B7
Piccadilly Warks 134 D4
Piccadilly Corner Norf 142 F5
Piccotts End Herts 85 D9
Pickburn S Yorks 198 F4
Picken End Worcs 98 C6
Pickering N Yorks 216 C5
Pickering Nook Durham 242 F5
Picket Hill Hants 31 F11
Picket Piece Hants 47 D11
Picket Post Hants 31 F11
Pickford W Mid 134 G5
Pickford Green W Mid 134 G5
Pickhill N Yorks 214 C6
Picklenash Glos 98 F4
Pickles Hill W Yorks 204 F6
Picklescott Shrops 131 D8
Pickletillem Fife 287 E8
Pickley Green Gtr Man 195 G7
Pickmere E Ches 183 F11
Pickney Som 27 B11
Pickstock Telford 150 E4
Pickup Bank Blkburn 195 C8
Pickwell Devon 40 E3
Pickwell Leics 154 G5
Pickwick Wilts 61 E11
Pickwood Scar W
Yorks 196 C5
Pickworth Lincs 155 C10
Pickworth Rutland 155 G9
Picton Flint 181 E10
Picton N Yorks 225 D8
Picton W Ches 182 G6
Pict's Hill Som 28 B6
Piddinghoe E Sus 36 G6
Piddington Bucks 84 G4
Piddington Northants 120 G6
Piddington Oxon 83 B10
Piddlehinton Dorset 17 B10
Piddletrenthide
Dorset 17 B10
Pidley Cambs 122 B6
Pidney Dorset 30 F2
Piece Corn 2 B5
Piercebridge Darl 224 B4
Piercing Hill Essex 86 F6
Pierowall Orkney 314 B4
Piff's Elm Glos 99 F8
Pig Oak Dorset 31 G8
Pigdon Northumb 252 F5
Pightley Som 43 F8
Pigstye Green Essex 87 D10
Pike End W Yorks 196 D4
Pike Hill Lancs 204 G3
Pike Law W Yorks 196 D4
Pikehall Derbys 169 D11
Pikeshill Hants 32 F3
Pikestye Hereford 97 B10
Pilford Dorset 31 G8
Pilgrims Hatch Essex 87 F9
Pilham Lincs 188 C5
Pilhough Derbys 170 C3
Pill N Som 60 D4
Pill Pembs 72 D6
Pillaton Corn 7 C7
Pillaton Staffs 151 G8
Pillerton Hersey Warks 100 B6
Pillerton Priors Warks 100 B5
Pilleth Powys 114 D5
Pilley Glos 81 B7
Pilley Hants 20 B2
Pilley S Yorks 197 G10
Pilley Bailey Hants 20 B2
Pillgwenlly Newport 59 B10
Pilling Lancs 202 D4
Pilling Lane Lancs 202 D3
Pillmouth Devon 25 C7
Pillowell Glos 79 D10
Pillows Green Glos 98 F5
Pillwell Dorset 30 D3
Pilmuir Borders 261 G11
Pilning S Glos 60 B5
Pilrig Edin 280 F5
Pilsbury Derbys 169 C10
Pilsdon Dorset 16 B4
Pilsgate P'boro 137 B11
Pilsley Derbys 170 C6
Pilsley Derbys 186 G2
Pilsley Green Derbys 170 C6
Pilson Green Norf 161 G7
Piltdown E Sus 36 C6
Pilton Devon 40 G5
Pilton Edin 280 F4
Pilton Northants 137 G10
Pilton Rutland 137 C8
Pilton Som 44 E5
Pilton Green Swansea 56 D2
Piltown Som 44 F5
Pimhole Gtr Man 195 E10
Pimlico Herts 85 D9
Pimlico Lancs 203 E10
Pimlico London 67 D9
Pimlico Northants 102 C2
Pimperne Dorset 29 F9
Pimperne Dorset 30 F6
Pin Green Herts 104 F4
Pin Mill Suff 108 D4
Pinchbeck Lincs 156 D4
Pinchbeck Bars Lincs 156 D3
Pinchbeck West Lincs 156 E4
Pincheon Green S Yorks 199 D7
Pinckney Green Wilts 61 G10
Pincock Lancs 194 D5
Pineham Kent 55 D10
Pineham M Keynes 103 C7
Pinehurst Swindon 63 B7
Pinfarthings Glos 80 E5
Pinfold Lancs 193 E11
Pinfold Hill S Yorks 197 G9
Pinfoldpond C Beds 103 E8
Pinford End Suff 124 F6
Pinged Carms 74 E6
Pingewood W Berks 65 F7
Pinhoe Devon 14 C5
Pink Green Worcs 117 D11
Pinkett's Booth W Mid 134 G5
Pinkie Braes E Loth 281 G7
Pinkney Wilts 61 B11
Pinkneys Green
Windsor 65 C11
Pinksmoor Som 27 D10
Pinley W Mid 119 B7
Pinley Green Warks 118 D4
Pinminnoch Dumfries 236 D2
Pinminnoch S Ayrs 244 E5
Pinmore S Ayrs 244 E6
Pinmore Mains S Ayrs 244 E6
Pinnacles Essex 86 D6
Pinner London 66 B6
Pinner Green London 85 G10
Pinnerwood Park
London 85 G10
Pin's Green Worcs 98 B6
Pinsley Green E Ches 167 F9
Pinstones Shrops 131 F9
Pinvin Worcs 99 B9
Pinwall Leics 134 C6
Pinwherry S Ayrs 244 F5
Pinxton Derbys 171 E7
Pipe and Lyde Hereford 97 C10
Pipe Aston Hereford 115 C9
Pipe Gate Shrops 168 G2
Pipe Ridware Staffs 151 F11
Pipehill Staffs 133 B11
Pipehouse Bath 45 B9
Piperhall Argyll 266 D2
Piperhill Highld 301 D8
Piper's Ash W Ches 166 B6
Piper's End Worcs 98 E6
Piper's Hill Worcs 117 D9
Piper's Pool Corn 11 E11
Pipewell Northants 136 F6
Pippacott Devon 40 F4
Pippin Street Lancs 194 C5
Pipps Hill Essex 69 B7
Pipsden Kent 53 G9
Pipton Powys 96 D3
Pirbright Sur 50 B2
Pirbright Camp Sur 50 B2
Pirnmill N Ayrs 255 C9
Pirton Herts 104 E2
Pirton Worcs 99 B7
Pisgah Ceredig 112 B3
Pisgah Stirl 285 G11
Pishill Oxon 65 B8
Pishill Bank Oxon 84 G2
Pismire Hill S Yorks 186 C5
Pistyll Gwyn 162 G4
Pit Mon 78 D5
Pitagowan Perth 291 G10
Pitblae Aberds 303 C9
Pitcairngreen Perth 286 E4
Pitcalnie Highld 301 B8
Pitcaple Aberds 303 G7
Pitch Green Bucks 84 E3
Pitch Place Sur 49 F11
Pitch Place Sur 50 C3
Pitchcombe Glos 80 D5
Pitchcott Bucks 102 G5
Pitcher's Green Suff 125 F8
Pitchford Shrops 131 C10
Pitcombe Som 45 G7
Pitcorthie Fife 280 D2
Pitcorthie Fife 287 G9
Pitcot Som 45 D7
Pitcot V Glam 57 G11
Pitcox E Loth 282 F2
Pitcur Perth 286 D6
Pitfancy Aberds 302 E5
Pitfichie Aberds 293 B8
Pitforthie Aberds 293 F10
Pitgair Aberds 303 D7
Pitgrudy Highld 309 K7
Pithmaduthy Highld 301 B7
Pitkennedy Angus 287 B9
Pitkevy Fife 286 G6
Pitkierie Fife 287 G9
Pitlessie Fife 287 G7
Pitlochry Perth 286 B3
Pitmachie Aberds 302 G6
Pitmain Highld 291 C9
Pitmedden Aberds 303 G8
Pitminster Som 28 D2
Pitmuies Angus 287 C9
Pitmunie Aberds 293 B8
Pitney Som 29 B7
Pitrocknie Perth 286 C6
Pitscottie Fife 287 F8
Pitsea Essex 69 B8
Pitses Gtr Man 196 G2
Pitsford Northants 120 D5
Pitsford Hill Som 42 G6
Pitsmoor S Yorks 186 D5
Pitstone Bucks 84 B6
Pitstone Green Bucks 84 B6
Pitstone Hill Bucks 85 C7
Pitt Hants 33 B7
Pitt Court Glos 80 F3
Pittachar Perth 286 E2
Pittendreich Moray 301 C11
Pittentrail Highld 309 J7
Pittenweem Fife 287 G9
Pitteuchar Fife 280 B5
Pittington Durham 234 C2
Pittodrie Aberds 302 G6
Pitton Swansea 56 D2
Pitton Wilts 47 G8
Pitts Hill Stoke 168 E5
Pittswood Kent 52 D6
Pittulie Aberds 303 C9
Pittville Glos 99 G9
Pity Me Durham 233 B11
Pityme Corn 10 F5
Pityoulish Highld 291 B11
Pixey Green Suff 126 B4
Pixham Sur 51 C7
Pixham Worcs 98 B6
Pixley Hereford 98 D3
Pixley Shrops 150 D3
Pizien Well Kent 53 C7
Place Newton N Yorks 217 E7
Plaidy Aberds 303 D7
Plaidy Corn 6 E5
Plain-an-Gwarry Corn 4 G3
Plain Dealings Pembs 73 B9
Plain Spot Notts 171 E7
Plain Street Corn 10 F5
Plains N Lnrk 268 B5
Plainsfield Som 43 F7
Plaish Shrops 131 D10
Plaistow London 68 C2
Plaistow London 68 E2
Plaistow W Sus 50 G4
Plaistow Green Essex 106 F6
Plaitford Wilts 32 D3
Plaitford Green Hants 32 C3
Plank Lane Gtr Man 194 G6
Plans Dumfries 238 D3
Plantation Bridge Cumb 221 F9
Plantationfoot Dumfries 248 E4
Plardiwick Staffs 150 E6
Plas-canol Gwyn 145 F11
Plas Coch Wrex 166 E4
Plas Dinam Powys 129 F10
Plas Gogerddan Ceredig 128 G2
Plas Llwyngwern Powys 128 C5
Plas Meredydd Powys 130 D3
Plas Nantyr Wrex 148 B3
Plas-yn-Cefn Denb 181 G8
Plasau Shrops 149 E7
Plashet London 68 C2
Plashett Carms 74 D3
Plasiolyn Powys 129 C11
Plasnewydd Powys 129 D9
Plaster's Green Bath 60 G4
Plastow Green Hants 64 G4
Platt Kent 52 B6
Platt Bridge Gtr Man 194 G6
Platt Lane Shrops 149 B10
Platts Common S Yorks 197 G11
Platt's Heath Kent 53 C11
Plawsworth Durham 233 B11
Plaxtol Kent 52 C6
Play Hatch Oxon 65 D8
Playden E Sus 38 C6
Playford Suff 108 B4
Playing Place Corn 4 G6
Playley Green Glos 98 E5
Plealey Shrops 131 B8
Pleamore Cross Som 27 D10
Plean Stirl 278 D6
Pleasant Valley Pembs 73 D10
Pleasington Blkburn 194 B6
Pleasley Derbys 171 C8
Pleasleyhill Notts 171 C8
Pleck Dorset 30 D3
Pleck Dorset 30 E2
Pleck W Mid 133 D9
Pleck or Little Ansty
Dorset 30 G3
Pleckgate Blkburn 203 G9
Pledgdon Green Essex 105 F11
Pledwick W Yorks 197 D10
Plemstall W Ches 183 G7
Plenmeller Northumb 240 E6
Plâs Berwyn Denb 165 G11
Pleshey Essex 87 C11
Plockton Highld 295 B10
Plocrapol W Isles 305 J3
Plot Gate Som 44 G4
Plot Street Som 44 F5
Plough Hill Warks 134 E6
Ploughfield Hereford 97 C7
Plowden Shrops 131 F7
Ploxgreen Shrops 131 C7
Pluckley Kent 54 D2
Pluckley Thorne Kent 54 E2
Plucks Gutter Kent 71 G9
Plumbland Cumb 229 D9
Plumbley S Yorks 186 E6
Plumford Kent 54 B4
Plumley E Ches 184 F2
Plump Hill Glos 79 B11
Plumpton Cumb 230 D5
Plumpton E Sus 36 E5
Plumpton Northants 101 B11
Plumpton End
Northants 102 B4
Plumpton Foot Cumb 230 D5
Plumpton Green E Sus 36 D5
Plumpton Head Cumb 230 E6
Plumstead London 68 D3
Plumstead Norf 160 C2
Plumstead Common
London 68 D3
Plumstead Green Norf 160 C2
Plumtree Notts 154 C2
Plumtree Green Kent 53 D10
Plumtree Park Notts 154 C2
Plungar Leics 154 C5
Plush Dorset 30 G2
Plusha Corn 11 E11
Plushabridge Corn 12 G2
Plusterwine Glos 79 F9
Plwmp Ceredig 111 G7
Plymouth Plym 7 E9
Plympton Plym 7 D10
Plymstock Plym 7 E10
Plymtree Devon 27 G9
Pobgreen Gtr Man 196 F4
Pochin Houses Caerph 77 E11
Pocket Nook Gtr Man 183 B10
Pockley N Yorks 216 B2
Pocklington E Yorks 208 D2
Pockthorpe Norf 141 D8
Pockthorpe Norf 158 D6
Pockthorpe Norf 159 E10
Pockthorpe Norf 159 F11
Pode Hole Lincs 156 E4
Podimore Som 29 C8
Podington Beds 121 E8
Podmoor Worcs 117 C7
Podmore Norf 159 G9
Podmore Staffs 150 B5
Podsmead Glos 80 B4
Poffley End Oxon 82 C5
Pogmoor S Yorks 197 F10
Point Corn 3 B8
Point Clear Essex 89 C9
Pointon Lincs 156 C2
Pokesdown Bmouth 19 C8
Pol a Charra W Isles 297 K3
Polbae Dumfries 236 B4
Polbain Highld 307 H4
Polbathic Corn 7 D7
Polbeth W Loth 269 C10
Polborder Corn 7 C7
Polbrock Corn 5 B10
Polchar Highld 291 C10
Pole Elm Worcs 98 B6
Pole Moor W Yorks 196 D5
Polebrook Northants 137 F11
Polegate E Sus 23 D9
Poles Highld 309 K7
Pole's Hole Wilts 45 C10
Polesden Lacey Sur 50 C6
Poleshill Som 27 C9
Polesworth Warks 134 C5
Polgear Corn 2 B5
Polgigga Corn 1 E3
Polglass Highld 307 J5
Polgooth Corn 5 E9
Poling W Sus 35 G8
Poling Corner W Sus 35 F8
Polkerris Corn 5 E11
Poll Hill Mers 182 E3
Polla Highld 308 D3
Polladras Corn 2 C4
Pollard Street Norf 160 C6
Pollhill Kent 53 C11
Pollie Highld 309 H7
Pollington E Yorks 198 D6
Polliwilline Argyll 255 G8
Polloch Highld 289 C9
Pollok Glasgow 267 C10
Pollokshields Glasgow 267 C11
Polmadie Glasgow 267 C11
Polmarth Corn 2 B6
Polmassick Corn 5 F9
Polmear Corn 5 E11
Polmont Falk 279 F8
Polmorla Corn 10 G5
Polnessan E Ayrs 257 G10
Polnish Highld 295 G9
Polopit Northants 121 B10
Polpenwith Corn 2 D6
Polpeor Corn 2 B2
Polperro Corn 6 E4
Polruan Corn 6 E2
Polsham Som 44 E4
Polsloe Devon 14 C4
Polstead Suff 107 D9
Polstead Heath Suff 107 C9
Poltalloch Argyll 275 D9
Poltesco Corn 2 F6
Poltimore Devon 14 B5
Polton Midloth 270 C5
Polwarth Borders 272 E4
Polwheveral Corn 2 D6
Polyphant Corn 11 E11
Polzeath Corn 10 F4
Pomeroy Derbys 169 B10
Pomphlett Plym 7 E10
Ponciau Wrex 166 F3
Pond Close Som 27 B10
Pond Park Bucks 85 E7
Pond Street Essex 105 D9
Ponde Powys 96 D2
Ponders End London 86 F5
Pondersbridge Cambs 138 E5
Pondtail Hants 49 C10
Pondwell I o W 21 C8
Poniou Corn 1 B4
Ponjeravah Corn 2 D6
Ponsanooth Corn 3 B7
Ponsford Devon 27 F8
Ponsonby Cumb 219 D11
Ponsongath Corn 3 F7
Ponsworthy Devon 13 G10
Pont Corn 6 E2
Pont Aber Carms 94 G4
Pont Aber-Geirw Gwyn 146 D5
Pont-ar-gothi Carms 93 G10
Pont ar Hydfer Powys 95 F7
Pont-ar-llechau Carms 94 G4
Pont Cyfyng Conwy 164 D2
Pont Cysyllte Wrex 166 G3
Pont Dolydd Prysor
Gwyn 146 B4
Pont-faen Powys 95 E9
Pont-Faen Shrops 148 B5
Pont Fronwydd Gwyn 146 E6
Pont-gareg Pembs 92 C2
Pont-Henri Carms 75 D7
Pont Hwfa Anglesey 178 E2
Pont iets = Pontyates
Carms 75 D7
Pont-Llogel Powys 147 F10
Pont-newydd Carms 74 D6
Pont-newydd Flint 165 B11
Pont Pen-y-benglog
Gwyn 163 C10
Pont Rhyd-goch Conwy 163 C11
Pont-Rhyd-sarn Gwyn 147 D7
Pont Rhyd-y-berry
Powys 95 D9
Pont Rhyd-y-cyff
Bridgend 57 D11
Pont-rhyd-y-groes
Ceredig 112 C4
Pont Rhydgaled Powys 128 G6
Pont-Rhythallt Gwyn 163 C8
Pont-rug Gwyn 163 C8
Pont Senni =
Sennybridge Powys 95 F8
Pont Siôn Norton
Rhondda 77 G9
Pont-siôn Ceredig 93 B8
Pont-Walby Neath 76 D5
Pont-y-blew Shrops 148 B6
Pont-y-gwaith Rhondda 77 G8
Pont-y-pant Conwy 164 E3
Pont y Pennant Gwyn 147 E8
Pont-y-rhyl Bridgend 58 B2
Pont-y-wal Powys 96 D2
Pont yr Afon-Gam
Gwyn 164 G2
Pont-yr-hafod Pembs 91 F8
Pont-Ystrad Denb 165 C9
Pontamman Carms 75 C10
Pontantwn Carms 74 C6
Pontardawe Neath 76 E2
Pontarddulais Swansea 75 E9
Pontarfynach =
Devils Bridge Ceredig 112 B4
Pontarsais Carms 93 F8
Pontblyddyn Flint 166 C3
Pontbren Araeth Carms 94 G3
Pontbren Llwyd Rhondda 76 D6
Pontcanna Cardiff 59 D7
Pontdolgoch Powys 129 E10
Pontefract W Yorks 198 C3
Ponteland Northumb 242 C5
Ponterwyd Ceredig 128 G4
Pontesbury Shrops 131 B7
Pontesbury Hill Shrops 131 B7
Pontesford Shrops 131 B8
Pontfadog Wrex 148 B4
Pontfaen Pembs 91 E10
Pontgarreg Ceredig 110 G6
Ponthen Shrops 148 F6
Ponthir Torf 78 G4
Ponthirwaun Ceredig 92 B5
Pontiago Pembs 91 D8
Pontithel Powys 96 D3
Pontllanfraith Caerph 77 F11
Pontlliw Swansea 75 E10
Pontllyfni Gwyn 162 E6
Pontlottyn Caerph 77 D10
Pontneddfechan Powys 76 D6
Pontnewydd Torf 78 F3
Pontnewynydd Torf 78 E3

354 Pon – Ram

Pontrhydfendigaid Ceredig 112 D4
Pontrhydyfen Neath 57 C9
Pontrhydyrun Torf 78 F3
Pontrilas Hereford 97 F7
Pontrobert Powys 148 G2
Ponts Green E Sus 23 B11
Pontshill Hereford 98 G2
Pontsticill M Tydf 77 C9
Pontwgan Conwy 180 G3
Pontyates = Pont-iets Carms 75 D7
Pontyberem Carms 75 C8
Pontyclun Rhondda 58 C4
Pontycymer Bridgend 76 G6
Pontyglasier Pembs 92 D2
Pontymister Caerph 78 G2
Pontymoel Torf 78 E3
Pontypool Torf 78 E3
Pontypridd Rhondda 58 B5
Pontywaun Caerph 78 G2
Pooksgreen Hants 32 E5
Pool Corn 4 G3
Pool W Yorks 205 D10
Pool Head Hereford 115 G11
Pool Hey Lancs 193 D11
Pool o' Muckhart Clack 286 G4
Pool Quay Powys 148 G5
Poolbrook Worcs 98 C5
Poole N Yorks 198 B3
Poole Poole 18 C6
Poole Som 27 C10
Poole Keynes Glos 81 F8
Poolend Staffs 169 D7
Poolestown Dorset 30 D2
Poolewe Highld 307 L3
Pooley Bridge Cumb 230 G5
Pooley Street Norf 141 G11
Poolfold Staffs 168 D5
Poolhead Shrops 149 C9
Poolhill Glos 98 F4
Poolmill Hereford 97 G11
Poolsbrook Derbys 186 G6
Poolside Moray 302 E4
Poolstock Gtr Man 194 G5
Pooltown Som 42 F3
Pootings Kent 52 D3
Pope Hill Pembs 72 C6
Pope's Hill Glos 79 C11
Popeswood Brack 65 F10
Popham Devon 41 G8
Popham Hants 48 E5
Poplar London 67 C11
Poplar Grove Lincs 190 B6
Poplars Herts 104 G5
Popley Hants 48 C6
Porchester Nottingham 171 G9
Porchfield I o W 20 C4
Porin Highld 300 D3
Poringland Norf 142 C5
Porkellis Corn 2 C5
Porlock Som 41 D11
Porlock Weir Som 41 D11
Porlockford Som 41 D11
Port Allen Perth 286 E6
Port Ann Argyll 275 E10
Port Appin Argyll 289 E11
Port Arthur Shetland 313 K5
Port Askaig Argyll 274 G5
Port Bannatyne Argyll 275 G11
Port Brae Fife 280 C5
Port Bridge Devon 9 D7
Port Carlisle Cumb 238 E6
Port Charlotte Argyll 254 B3
Port Clarence Stockton 234 G5
Port Dinorwic = Y Felinheli Gwyn 163 B8
Port Driseach Argyll 275 F10
Port Dundas Glasgow 267 B11
Port e Vullen I o M 192 C5
Port Edgar Edin 280 F2
Port Ellen Argyll 254 C4
Port Elphinstone Aberds 293 B9
Port Erin I o M 192 F2
Port Erroll Aberds 303 F10
Port-Eynon Swansea 56 D3
Port Gaverne Corn 10 E6
Port Glasgow Invclyd 276 G6
Port Henderson Highld 299 B7
Port Hill Oxon 65 B7
Port Isaac Corn 10 E5
Port Lamont Argyll 275 F11
Port Lion Pembs 73 D7
Port Logan Dumfries 236 E2
Port Mead Swansea 56 B6
Port Mholair W Isles 304 E7
Port Mor Highld 288 B6
Port Mulgrave N Yorks 226 B5
Port Nan Giùran W Isles 304 E7
Port nan Long W Isles 296 D4
Port Nis W Isles 304 B7
Port of Menteith Stirl 285 G9
Port Quin Corn 10 E5
Port Ramsay Argyll 289 E10
Port St Mary I o M 192 F3
Port Solent Ptsmth 33 F10
Port Sunlight Mers 182 E4
Port Sutton Bridge Lincs 157 E9
Port Talbot Neath 57 D9
Port Tennant Swansea 57 C7
Port Wemyss Argyll 254 B2
Port William Dumfries 236 E5
Portachoillan Argyll 255 B8
Portash Wilts 46 G3
Portavadie Argyll 275 G10
Portbury N Som 60 D4
Portchester Hants 33 F10
Portclair Highld 290 B6
Porteath Corn 10 F5
Portencalzie Dumfries 236 B2
Portencross N Ayrs 266 F3
Porterfield Renfs 267 B9
Porter's End Herts 85 B11
Portesham Dorset 17 D8
Portessie Moray 302 C4
Portfield Argyll 289 G9
Portfield Som 28 B6
Portfield W Sus 22 B5
Portfield Gate Pembs 72 B6
Portgate Devon 12 D4
Portgordon Moray 302 C3
Portgower Highld 311 H4
Porth Corn 4 C6
Porth Rhondda 77 G8
Porth Colmon Gwyn 144 C3
Porth Kea Corn 4 G6
Porth Navas Corn 3 D7
Porth Tywyn = Burry Port Carms 74 E6
Porth-y-felin Anglesey 178 E2
Porth-y-waen Shrops 148 E5
Porthallow Corn 3 E7
Porthallow Corn 6 E4
Porthcawl Bridgend 57 F10
Porthcothan Corn 10 G3
Porthcurno Corn 1 E3
Portheiddy Pembs 90 E6
Porthgain Pembs 90 E6
Porthgwarra Corn 1 E3
Porthhallow Corn 3 E7
Porthill Shrops 149 G9
Porthill Staffs 168 F5
Porthilly Corn 10 F4
Porthkerry V Glam 58 F5
Porthleven Corn 2 D4
Porthllechog = Bull Bay Anglesey 178 C6
Porthloo Scilly 1 G4
Porthmadog Gwyn 145 B11
Porthmeor Corn 1 B4
Porthoustock Corn 3 E8
Porthpean Corn 5 E10
Porthtowan Corn 4 F3
Porthyrhyd Carms 75 B8
Porthyrhyd Carms 94 D4
Portico Mers 183 C7
Portincaple Argyll 276 C4
Portington Devon 12 F4
Portington E Yorks 207 G11
Portinnisherrich Argyll 275 B10
Portinscale Cumb 229 G11
Portishead N Som 60 D3
Portkil Argyll 276 E5
Portknockie Moray 302 C4
Portland Som 44 F3
Portlethen Aberds 293 D11
Portlethen Village Aberds 293 D11
Portlevorchy Highld 306 D7
Portling Dumfries 237 D10
Portloe Corn 3 B10
Portlooe Corn 6 E4
Portmahomack Highld 311 L3
Portmeirion Gwyn 145 B11
Portmellon Corn 5 G10
Portmore Hants 20 B2
Portnacroish Argyll 289 E11
Portnahaven Argyll 254 B2
Portnalong Highld 294 B5
Portnaluchaig Highld 295 G8
Portnancon Highld 308 C4
Portnellan Stirl 285 E8
Portnellan Stirl 285 F8
Portobello Edin 280 G6
Portobello T & W 243 F7
Portobello W Mid 133 D9
Portobello W Yorks 197 D10
Porton Wilts 47 F7
Portpatrick Dumfries 236 D2
Portrack Stockton 225 B9
Portreath Corn 4 F3
Portree Highld 298 E4
Portscatho Corn 3 B9
Portsea Ptsmth 33 G10
Portsea Island Ptsmth 33 G11
Portskerra Highld 310 C2
Portskewett Mon 60 B4
Portslade Brighton 36 F3
Portslade-by-Sea Brighton 36 G3
Portslade Village Brighton 36 F3
Portsmouth Ptsmth 21 B9
Portsmouth W Yorks 196 B2
Portsonachan Argyll 284 E4
Portsoy Aberds 302 C5
Portswood Soton 32 E6
Porttanachy Moray 302 C3
Portuairk Highld 288 C6
Portvasgo Highld 308 C5
Portway Dorset 18 D2
Portway Glos 98 E5
Portway Hereford 97 B9
Portway Hereford 97 D9
Portway Som 28 B6
Portway Som 44 F3
Portway W Mid 133 F9
Portway Worcs 117 C11
Portwood Gtr Man 184 C6
Portwrinkle Corn 7 E7
Posenhall Shrops 132 C3
Poslingford Suff 106 B5
Posso Borders 260 C6
Post Green Dorset 18 C5
Post Mawr = Synod Inn Ceredig 111 G8
Postbridge Devon 13 F9
Postcombe Oxon 84 F2
Postling Kent 54 F6
Postlip Glos 99 F10
Postwick Norf 142 B5
Pot Common Sur 50 E2
Potarch Aberds 293 D8
Potash Suff 108 D2
Potbridge Hants 49 C8
Potholm Dumfries 249 F9
Potmaily Highld 300 F4
Potman's Heath Kent 38 B5
Potsgrove C Beds 103 F9
Pott Row Norf 158 E4
Pott Shrigley E Ches 184 F6
Potten End Herts 85 D8
Potten Street Kent 71 F9
Potter Brompton N Yorks 217 D9
Potter Heigham Norf 161 F8
Potter Hill Leics 154 E4
Potter Hill S Yorks 186 B4
Potter Somersal Derbys 152 B2
Potter Street Essex 87 D7
Pottergate Street Norf 142 E3
Potterhanworth Lincs 173 B9
Potterhanworth Booths Lincs 173 B9
Potterne Wilts 46 B3
Potterne Wick Wilts 46 B4
Potternewton W Yorks 206 F2
Potters Bar Herts 86 E3
Potters Brook Lancs 202 C5
Potters Corner Kent 54 E3
Potter's Cross Staffs 132 G6
Potters Crouch Herts 85 D10
Potter's Forstal Kent 53 D11
Potter's Green E Sus 37 C8
Potter's Green W Mid 135 G7
Potters Hill N Som 60 F4
Potters Marston Leics 135 D9
Pottersheath Herts 86 B2
Potterspury Northants 102 C5
Potterton Aberds 293 B11
Potterton W Yorks 206 F4
Pottery Field W Yorks 206 G2
Potthorpe Norf 159 E8
Pottington Devon 40 G5
Potto N Yorks 225 E9
Potton C Beds 104 B4
Pouchen End Herts 85 D8
Poughill Corn 24 F2
Poughill Devon 26 F5
Poulner Hants 31 F11
Poulshot Wilts 46 B3
Poulton Glos 81 E10
Poulton Mers 182 C4
Poulton Mers 182 E4
Poulton W Ches 166 D5
Poulton-le-Fylde Lancs 202 F2
Pound Som 28 D6
Pound Bank Worcs 98 B5
Pound Bank Worcs 116 C4
Pound Green E Sus 37 C8
Pound Green Hants 48 B5
Pound Green I o W 20 D2
Pound Green Suff 124 G4
Pound Green Worcs 116 B5
Pound Hill W Sus 51 F9
Pound Street Hants 64 G3
Poundbury Dorset 17 C9
Poundffald Swansea 56 C5
Poundfield E Sus 52 G4
Poundford E Sus 37 C9
Poundgate E Sus 37 B7
Poundgreen Wokingham 65 F7
Poundland S Ayrs 244 F5
Poundon Bucks 102 F2
Poundsbridge Kent 52 E4
Poundsgate Devon 13 G10
Poundstock Corn 11 B10
Pounsley E Sus 37 C8
Poverest London 68 F3
Povey Cross Sur 51 E9
Pow Green Hereford 98 C4
Powburn Northumb 264 F3
Powder Mills Kent 52 D5
Powderham Devon 14 E5
Powers Hall End Essex 88 B4
Powerstock Dorset 16 B6
Powfoot Dumfries 238 D4
Powhill Cumb 238 F6
Powick Worcs 116 G6
Powler's Piece Devon 24 D5
Powmill Perth 279 B10
Pownall Park E Ches 184 E4
Powntley Copse Hants 49 E8
Poxwell Dorset 17 E10
Poyle Slough 66 D4
Poynings W Sus 36 E3
Poyntington Dorset 29 D11
Poynton E Ches 184 E6
Poynton Telford 149 F11
Poynton Green Telford 149 F11
Poyntzfield Highld 301 C7
Poyston Pembs 73 B7
Poyston Cross Pembs 73 B7
Poystreet Green Suff 125 F9
Praa Sands Corn 2 D3
Pratling Street Kent 53 B8
Pratt's Bottom London 68 G3
Praze Corn 2 B3
Praze-an-Beeble Corn 2 B4
Predannack Wollas Corn 2 F5
Prees Shrops 149 C11
Prees Green Shrops 149 C11
Prees Heath Shrops 149 B11
Prees Higher Heath Shrops 149 B11
Prees Lower Heath Shrops 149 C11
Prees Wood Shrops 149 C11
Preesall Lancs 202 D3
Preesall Park Lancs 202 D3
Preesgweene Shrops 148 B5
Preeshenlle Shrops 148 C6
Pren-gwyn Ceredig 93 C8
Prenbrigog Flint 166 C3
Prendergast Pembs 73 B7
Prendergast Pembs 90 G6
Prendergest Borders 273 D8
Prendwick Northumb 264 G2
Prenteg Gwyn 163 G9
Prenton Mers 182 D4
Prescot Mers 183 C7
Prescott Devon 27 E9
Prescott Glos 99 F9
Prescott Shrops 132 G3
Prescott Shrops 149 E8
Presdales Herts 86 C5
Preshome Moray 302 C4
Press Derbys 170 B5
Pressen Northumb 263 B8
Prestatyn Denb 181 E9
Prestbury E Ches 184 F6
Prestbury Glos 99 G9
Presteigne Powys 114 E6
Presthope Shrops 131 D11
Prestleigh Som 44 E6
Prestolee Gtr Man 195 F9
Preston Borders 272 D5
Preston Brighton 36 F4
Preston Devon 14 G3
Preston Dorset 17 E10
Preston E Loth 281 F11
Preston E Loth 281 G7
Preston E Yorks 209 G9
Preston Glos 81 E8
Preston Glos 98 E3
Preston Herts 104 G3
Preston Kent 70 G4
Preston Kent 71 G8
Preston Lancs 194 B4
Preston London 67 B7
Preston Northumb 264 D5
Preston Rutland 137 C7
Preston Shrops 149 G10
Preston T & W 243 D8
Preston Torbay 9 C7
Preston Wilts 62 D4
Preston Wilts 63 E9
Preston Bagot Warks 118 D3
Preston Bissett Bucks 102 F3
Preston Bowyer Som 27 B10
Preston Brockhurst Shrops 149 E10
Preston Brook Halton 183 E9
Preston Candover Hants 48 E6
Preston Capes Northants 119 G11
Preston Crowmarsh Oxon 83 G10
Preston Deanery Northants 120 F5
Preston Fields Warks 118 D3
Preston Grange T & W 243 C8
Preston Green Warks 118 D3
Preston Gubbals Shrops 149 F9
Preston-le-Skerne Durham 234 G2
Preston Marsh Hereford 97 B11
Preston Montford Shrops 149 G8
Preston on Stour Warks 118 G4
Preston-on-Tees Stockton 225 B8
Preston on the Hill Halton 183 E9
Preston on Wye Hereford 97 C7
Preston Pastures Worcs 100 B3
Preston Plucknett Som 29 D8
Preston St Mary Suff 125 G8
Preston-under-Scar N Yorks 223 G11
Preston upon the Weald Moors Telford 150 F3
Preston Wynne Hereford 97 B11
Prestonfield Edin 280 G5
Prestonmill Dumfries 237 D11
Prestonpans E Loth 281 G7
Prestwich Gtr Man 195 G10
Prestwick Northumb 242 C5
Prestwick S Ayrs 257 D9
Prestwold Leics 153 E11
Prestwood Bucks 84 E5
Prestwood Staffs 133 F7
Prestwood Staffs 169 G10
Prey Heath Sur 50 B3
Price Town Bridgend 76 G6
Prickwillow Cambs 139 G11
Priddy Som 44 C4
Pride Park Derbys 153 B7
Priest Down Bath 60 G6
Priest Hutton Lancs 211 E10
Priest Weston Shrops 130 D5
Priestacott Devon 24 F6
Priestcliffe Derbys 185 G10
Priestcliffe Ditch Derbys 185 G10
Priestfield W Mid 133 D8
Priestfield Worcs 98 C6
Priesthaugh Borders 249 C11
Priesthill Glasgow 267 C10
Priesthorpe W Yorks 205 F10
Priestley Green W Yorks 196 B6
Prieston Borders 262 D2
Priestside Dumfries 238 D4
Priestthorpe W Yorks 205 F8
Priestwood Brack 65 F11
Priestwood Kent 69 G7
Priestwood Green Kent 69 G7
Primethorpe Leics 135 E10
Primrose T & W 243 E8
Primrose Corner Norf 160 G6
Primrose Green Norf 159 F11
Primrose Hill Bath 61 F8
Primrose Hill Lancs 193 F11
Primrose Hill London 67 C9
Primrose Hill W Mid 133 F8
Primrose Valley N Yorks 218 D2
Primrosehill Herts 85 E9
Primsland Worcs 117 E8
Prince Hill E Ches 168 G2
Prince Royd W Yorks 196 D6
Princes End W Mid 133 E9
Princes Gate Pembs 73 C10
Prince's Marsh Hants 34 B3
Princes Park Mers 182 D5
Princes Risborough Bucks 84 E4
Princethorpe Warks 119 C8
Princetown Caerph 77 C10
Princetown Devon 13 G7
Prinsted W Sus 22 B3
Printstile Kent 52 E5
Prion Denb 165 C9
Prior Muir Fife 287 F9
Prior Park Northumb 273 E9
Prior Rigg Cumb 239 D11
Priors Frome Hereford 97 D11
Priors Halton Shrops 115 B9
Priors Hardwick Warks 119 F9
Priors Marston Warks 119 F9
Prior's Norton Glos 99 G7
Priors Park Glos 99 E7
Priorslee Telford 150 G4
Priorswood Som 28 B2
Priory Pembs 72 D6
Priory Green Suff 107 C8
Priory Heath Suff 108 C3
Priory Wood Hereford 96 B5
Prisk V Glam 58 D4
Pristacott Devon 25 B8
Priston Bath 61 G7
Pristow Green Norf 142 F2
Prittlewell Sthend 69 B11
Privett Hants 21 B7
Privett Hants 33 B11
Prixford Devon 40 F4
Probus Corn 5 F7
Proncy Highld 309 K7
Prospect Cumb 229 C8
Prospect Village Staffs 151 G10
Prospidnick Corn 2 C4
Provanmill Glasgow 268 B2
Prowse Devon 26 F4
Prudhoe Northumb 242 E3
Prussia Cove Corn 2 D3
Ptarmigan Lodge Stirl 285 G7
Pubil Perth 285 C8
Publow Bath 60 G6
Puckeridge Herts 105 G7
Puckington Som 28 D5
Pucklechurch S Glos 61 D7
Pucknall Hants 32 B5
Puckrup Glos 99 D7
Puckshole Glos 80 D4
Puddaven Devon 8 C5
Pudding Pie Nook Lancs 202 F6
Puddinglake W Ches 168 B2
Puddington Devon 26 E4
Puddington W Ches 182 G4
Puddle Corn 5 D11
Puddlebridge Som 28 E4
Puddledock Kent 52 C3
Puddledock Kent 68 E4
Puddledock Norf 141 E11
Puddletown Dorset 17 C11
Pudleigh Som 28 E4
Pudleston Hereford 115 F11
Pudsey W Yorks 196 B2
Pudsey W Yorks 205 G10
Pulborough W Sus 35 D8
Pulcree Dumfries 237 D7
Pule Hill W Yorks 196 B5
Puleston Telford 150 E4
Pulford W Ches 166 D5
Pulham Dorset 30 F2
Pulham Market Norf 142 F3
Pulham St Mary Norf 142 F4
Pullens Green S Glos 79 G10
Pulley Shrops 131 B9
Pullington Kent 53 G10
Pulloxhill C Beds 103 E11
Pulverbatch Shrops 131 C8
Pumpherston W Loth 269 B11
Pumsaint Carms 94 C3
Puncheston = Cas -Mael Pembs 91 F10
Puncknowle Dorset 16 D6
Punnett's Town E Sus 37 C10
Purbrook Hants 33 F11
Purewell Dorset 19 C9
Purfleet Thurrock 68 D5
Puriton Som 43 E10
Purleigh Essex 88 E4
Purley London 67 G10
Purley on Thames W Berks 65 D7
Purlogue Shrops 114 B5
Purlpit Wilts 61 F11
Purls Bridge Cambs 139 F9
Purn N Som 43 B10
Purse Caundle Dorset 29 D11
Purslow Shrops 131 G7
Purston Jaglin W Yorks 198 D2
Purtington Som 28 F5
Purton Glos 79 E11
Purton W Berks 64 D3
Purton Wilts 62 B5
Purton Common Wilts 62 B5
Purton Stoke Wilts 81 G9
Purwell Herts 104 F4
Pury End Northants 102 B4
Pusey Oxon 82 F5
Putley Hereford 98 D2
Putley Common Hereford 98 D2
Putley Green Hereford 98 D3
Putloe Glos 80 D3
Putney London 67 D8
Putney Heath London 67 E8
Putney Vale London 67 E8
Putnoe Beds 121 G11
Putsborough Devon 40 E3
Putson Hereford 97 D10
Puttenham Herts 84 C5
Puttenham Sur 50 D2
Puttock End Essex 106 C6
Puttock's End Essex 87 B9
Putton Dorset 17 E9
Puxey Dorset 30 E3
Puxley Northants 102 C5
Puxton N Som 60 G2
Pwll Carms 75 E7
Pwll Powys 130 C3
Pwll-clai Flint 181 G11
Pwll-glas Denb 165 E10
Pwll-Mawr Cardiff 59 D8
Pwll-melyn Flint 181 G11
Pwll-trap Carms 74 B3
Pwll-y-glaw Neath 57 C9
Pwllcrochan Pembs 72 E6
Pwllgloyw Powys 95 E10
Pwllheli Gwyn 145 B7
Pwllmeyric Mon 79 G8
Pwllypant Caerph 59 B7
Pye Bridge Derbys 170 E6
Pye Corner Devon 14 B4
Pye Corner Kent 53 D11
Pye Corner Newport 59 B10
Pye Corner S Glos 60 D6
Pye Green Staffs 151 G9
Pye Hill Notts 170 E6
Pyecombe W Sus 36 E3
Pyewipe NE Lincs 201 E9
Pyle I o W 20 F5
Pyle Swansea 56 D5
Pyle = Y Pîl Bridgend 57 E10
Pyle Hill Sur 50 B3
Pylehill Hants 33 D7
Pyleigh Som 42 G6
Pylle Som 44 F6
Pymore or Pymoor Cambs 139 F9
Pype Hayes W Mid 134 E2
Pyrford Sur 50 B4
Pyrford Green Sur 50 B4
Pyrford Village Sur 50 B4
Pyrland Som 28 B2
Pyrton Oxon 83 F11
Pytchley Northants 121 C7
Pyworthy Devon 24 G4

Q

Quabbs Shrops 130 G4
Quabrook E Sus 52 G2
Quadring Lincs 156 C4
Quadring Eaudike Lincs 156 C4
Quags Corner W Sus 34 C5
Quainton Bucks 84 B2
Quaker's Yard M Tydf 77 F9
Quaking Houses Durham 242 G5
Quality Corner Cumb 219 B9
Quarhouse Glos 80 E5
Quarley Hants 47 E9
Quarmby W Yorks 196 D6
Quarndon Derbys 170 G4
Quarndon Common Derbys 170 G4
Quarr Hill I o W 21 C7
Quarrelton Renfs 267 C8
Quarrendon Bucks 84 B4
Quarriers Village Invclyd 267 B7
Quarrington Lincs 173 G9
Quarrington Hill Durham 234 D2
Quarry Bank W Mid 133 F8
Quarry Heath Staffs 151 G8
Quarry Hill Staffs 134 C4
Quarrybank W Ches 167 B8
Quarryford E Loth 271 B11
Quarryhead Aberds 303 C9
Quarryhill Highld 309 L7
Quarrywood Moray 301 C11
Quarter S Lnrk 268 E4
Quartley Devon 27 B7
Quatford Shrops 132 E4
Quatquoy Orkney 314 E3
Quatt Shrops 132 F5
Quebec Durham 233 C9
Quebec W Sus 34 C3
Quedgeley Glos 80 C4
Queen Adelaide Cambs 139 G11
Queen Camel Som 29 C9
Queen Charlton Bath 60 F6
Queen Dart Devon 26 D4
Queen Oak Dorset 45 G9
Queen Street Kent 53 D7
Queen Street Wilts 62 B4
Queenborough Kent 70 E2
Queenhill Worcs 99 D7
Queen's Bower I o W 21 E7
Queen's Corner W Sus 34 B5
Queen's Head Shrops 148 D6
Queen's Park Beds 103 B10
Queen's Park Blkburn 195 B7
Queen's Park Essex 87 F11
Queen's Park Northants 120 E5
Queen's Park W Ches 166 B6
Queensbury London 67 B7
Queensbury W Yorks 205 G8
Queensferry Edin 280 F2
Queensferry Flint 166 B4
Queenslie Glasgow 268 B3
Queenstown Blkpool 202 F2
Queensville Staffs 151 E8
Queenzieburn N Lnrk 278 F3
Quemerford Wilts 62 F4
Quendale Shetland 313 M5
Quendon Essex 105 E10
Queniborough Leics 154 G2
Quenington Glos 81 E10
Quernmore Lancs 202 B6
Queslett W Mid 133 E11
Quethiock Corn 6 C6
Quhamm Shetland 312 G6
Quholm Orkney 314 E2
Quick Gtr Man 196 G3
Quick Edge Gtr Man 196 G3
Quicks Green W Berks 64 D5
Quidenham Norf 141 F10
Quidhampton Hants 48 C4
Quidhampton Wilts 46 G6
Quilquox Aberds 303 F9
Quina Brook Shrops 149 C10
Quinbury End Northants 120 G2
Quindry Orkney 314 G4
Quinton Northants 120 G5
Quinton W Mid 133 G9
Quintrell Downs Corn 5 C7
Quixhill Staffs 169 G10
Quoditch Devon 12 B4
Quoig Perth 286 E2
Quoisley E Ches 167 F8
Quoit Corn 5 C8
Quordon or Quorn Leics 153 F11
Quothquan S Lnrk 259 B11
Quoyloo Orkney 314 D2
Quoynee Highld 310 D6
Quoyness Orkney 314 F2
Quoys Shetland 312 B8
Quoys Shetland 313 G6

R

Raasay Ho Highld 295 B7
Rabbit's Cross Kent 53 D9
Rableyheath Herts 86 B2
Raby Cumb 238 G5
Raby Mers 182 F4
Racecourse Suff 108 C3
Racedown Hants 47 E9
Rachan Mill Borders 260 C4
Rachub Gwyn 163 B10
Rack End Oxon 82 E6
Rackenford Devon 26 D5
Rackham W Sus 35 E9
Rackheath Norf 160 G5
Rackley Som 43 C11
Racks Dumfries 238 C2
Rackwick Orkney 314 B4
Rackwick Orkney 314 G2
Radbourne Derbys 152 B5
Radcliffe Gtr Man 195 F9
Radcliffe Northumb 253 C7
Radcliffe on Trent Notts 154 B2
Radclive Bucks 102 E3
Radcot Oxon 82 F3
Raddery Highld 301 D7
Raddington Som 27 B8
Raddon Devon 26 G6
Radernie Fife 287 G8
Radfall Kent 70 G6
Radfield Kent 70 G2
Radford Bath 45 B7
Radford Nottingham 171 G9
Radford Oxon 101 G8
Radford W Mid 134 G6
Radford Worcs 117 F10
Radford Semele Warks 118 E6
Radfordbridge Oxon 101 G8
Radipole Dorset 17 E9
Radlet Som 43 F8
Radlett Herts 85 F11
Radley Oxon 83 F8
Radley Green Essex 87 D10
Radley Park Oxon 83 F8
Radlith Shrops 131 B8
Radmanthwaite Notts 171 C8
Radmoor Shrops 150 E2
Radmore Green E Ches 167 D9
Radmore Wood Staffs 151 D11
Radnage Bucks 84 F3
Radnor Corn 4 G4
Radnor Park W Dunb 277 G9
Radstock Bath 45 C7
Radstone Northants 101 C11
Radway Warks 101 B7
Radway Green E Ches 168 E3
Radwell Beds 121 F10
Radwell Herts 104 D4
Radwinter Essex 106 D2
Radwinter End Essex 106 D2
Radyr Cardiff 58 C6
Raehills Dumfries 248 E3
Raera Argyll 289 G10
Rafborough Hants 49 B11
Rafford Moray 301 D10
Raga Shetland 312 D6
Ragdale Leics 154 F3
Ragdon Shrops 131 E9
Raggalds W Yorks 205 G7
Ragged Appleshaw Hants 47 D10
Raginnis Corn 1 D5
Raglan Mon 78 D6
Ragmere Norf 141 E11
Ragnal Wilts 63 E10
Ragnall Notts 188 G4
Rahane Argyll 276 D4
Rahoy Highld 289 D8
Raigbeg Highld 301 G8
Rails S Yorks 186 D3
Rain Shore Gtr Man 195 D11
Rainbow Hill Worcs 117 F7
Rainford Mers 194 G3
Rainford Junction Mers 194 G3
Rainham London 68 C4
Rainham Medway 69 F10
Rainhill Mers 183 C7
Rainhill Stoops Mers 183 C8
Rainow E Ches 185 F7
Rainowlow E Ches 185 F7
Rainsough Gtr Man 195 G10
Rainton Dumfries 237 D8
Rainton N Yorks 215 D7
Rainton Bridge T & W 234 B2
Rainton Gate Durham 234 B2
Rainworth Notts 171 D9
Raisbeck Cumb 222 D2
Raise Cumb 231 B10
Rait Perth 286 E6
Raithby Lincs 190 E4
Raithby by Spilsby Lincs 174 B5
Rake W Sus 34 B4
Rake Common Hants 34 B3
Rake End Staffs 151 F11
Rake Head Lancs 195 C10
Rakes Dale Staffs 169 G9
Rakeway Staffs 169 G8
Rakewood Gtr Man 196 E2
Raleigh Devon 40 G5
Ralia Lodge Highld 291 D9
Rallt Swansea 56 C4
Ram Carms 93 B11
Ram Alley Wilts 63 G8
Ram Hill S Glos 61 D7
Ram Lane Kent 54 D3
Ramasaig Highld 297 G7
Rame Corn 2 C6
Rame Corn 7 F8
Rameldry Mill Bank Fife 287 G7
Ramnageo Shetland 312 C8
Rampisham Dorset 29 G9
Rampside Cumb 210 F4
Rampton Cambs 123 D8
Rampton Notts 188 F3
Ramsbottom Gtr Man 195 D9

Ramsburn Moray 302 D5
Ramsbury Wilts 63 E9
Ramscraigs Highld 311 G5
Ramsdean Hants 34 C2
Ramsdell Hants 48 B5
Ramsden London 68 F3
Ramsden Oxon 82 B5
Ramsden Worcs 99 B8
Ramsden Bellhouse Essex 88 G2
Ramsden Heath Essex 88 F2
Ramsden Wood W Yorks 196 C2
Ramsey Cambs 138 F5
Ramsey Essex 108 E4
Ramsey I o M 192 C5
Ramsey Forty Foot Cambs 138 F6
Ramsey Heights Cambs 138 F5
Ramsey Island Essex 89 D7
Ramsey Mereside Cambs 138 F5
Ramsey St Mary's Cambs 138 F5
Ramseycleuch Borders 261 G7
Ramsgate Kent 71 G11
Ramsgill N Yorks 214 E2
Ramshaw Durham 232 B5
Ramshaw Durham 233 F8
Ramsholt Suff 108 C6
Ramshorn Staffs 169 F9
Ramsley Devon 13 C8
Ramslye Kent 52 F5
Ramsnest Common Sur 50 G2
Ranais W Isles 304 F6
Ranby Lincs 190 F2
Ranby Notts 187 E11
Rand Lincs 189 F10
Randwick Glos 80 D4
Ranfurly Renfs 267 C7
Rangag Highld 310 E5
Rangemore Staffs 152 E3
Rangeworthy S Glos 61 B7
Rankinston E Ayrs 257 G11
Rank's Green Essex 88 B3
Ranmoor S Yorks 186 D4
Ranmore Common Sur 50 C6
Rannerdale Cumb 220 B3
Rannoch Lodge Perth 285 B9
Rannoch Station Perth 285 B8
Ranochan Highld 295 G10
Ranskill Notts 187 D11
Ranton Staffs 151 E7
Ranton Green Staffs 150 E6
Ranworth Norf 161 G7
Rapkyns W Sus 50 G6
Raploch Stirl 278 C5
Rapness Orkney 314 B5
Rapps Som 28 D4
Rascal Moor E Yorks 208 F2
Rascarrel Dumfries 237 E9
Rashielee Renfs 277 G9
Rashiereive Aberds 303 G9
Rashwood Worcs 117 D8
Raskelf N Yorks 215 E9
Rassal Highld 299 E8
Rassau Bl Gwent 77 C11
Rastrick W Yorks 196 C6
Ratagan Highld 295 D11
Ratby Leics 135 B10
Ratcliff London 67 C11
Ratcliffe Culey Leics 134 D6
Ratcliffe on Soar Leics 153 D9
Ratcliffe on the Wreake Leics 154 G2
Ratford Wilts 62 E3
Ratfyn Wilts 47 E7
Rathen Aberds 303 C10
Rathillet Fife 287 E7
Rathmell N Yorks 204 B2
Ratho Edin 280 G2
Ratho Station Edin 280 G2
Rathven Moray 302 C4
Ratlake Hants 32 C6
Ratley Warks 101 B7
Ratling Kent 55 C8
Ratlinghope Shrops 131 D8
Ratsloe Devon 14 B5
Rattar Highld 310 B6
Ratten Row Cumb 230 B3
Ratten Row Cumb 230 C2
Ratten Row Lancs 202 E4
Ratten Row Norf 157 G10
Rattery Devon 8 C4
Rattlesden Suff 125 F9
Rattray Perth 286 C5
Raughton Cumb 230 B3
Raughton Head Cumb 230 B3
Raunds Northants 121 C9
Ravelston Edin 280 G4
Ravenfield S Yorks 187 B7
Ravenglass Cumb 219 F11
Ravenhead Mers 183 C8
Ravenhills Green Worcs 116 G4
Raveningham Norf 143 D7
Raven's Green Essex 108 G2
Ravenscar N Yorks 227 E9
Ravenscliffe Stoke 168 E4
Ravenscliffe W Yorks 205 F9
Ravenscraig Invclyd 276 F5
Ravensdale I o M 192 C4
Ravensden Beds 121 G11
Ravenseat N Yorks 223 E7
Ravenshall Staffs 168 F3
Ravenshead Notts 171 E9
Ravensmoor E Ches 167 E10
Ravensthorpe Northants 120 C3
Ravensthorpe P'boro 138 C3
Ravensthorpe W Yorks 197 C8
Ravenstone Leics 153 G8
Ravenstone M Keynes 120 G6
Ravenstonedale Cumb 222 E4
Ravenstown Cumb 211 D7
Ravenstruther S Lnrk 269 F8
Ravenswood Village Settlement Wokingham 65 G10
Ravensworth N Yorks 224 D2
Raw N Yorks 227 D8
Raw Green S Yorks 197 F9
Rawcliffe E Yorks 199 C7
Rawcliffe York 207 C7
Rawcliffe Bridge E Yorks 199 C7
Rawdon W Yorks 205 F10
Rawdon Carrs W Yorks 205 F10
Rawfolds W Yorks 197 C7
Rawgreen Northumb 241 F10
Rawmarsh S Yorks 186 B6
Rawnsley Staffs 151 G10
Rawreth Essex 88 G3
Rawreth Shot Essex 88 G3
Rawridge Devon 28 F2
Rawson Green Derbys 170 F5
Rawtenstall Lancs 195 C10
Rawthorpe W Yorks 197 D7
Rawyards N Lnrk 268 B5
Raxton Aberds 303 F8
Raydon Suff 107 D11
Raygill N Yorks 204 D4
Raylees Northumb 251 E10
Rayleigh Essex 88 G4
Rayne Essex 106 G4
Rayners Lane London 66 B6
Raynes Park London 67 F8
Reabrook Shrops 131 C7
Reach Cambs 123 D11
Read Lancs 203 G11
Reader's Corner Essex 88 E2
Reading Reading 65 E8
Reading Street Kent 54 G2
Reading Street Kent 71 F11
Readings Glos 79 B10
Ready Token Glos 81 E10
Readymoney Corn 6 E2
Reagill Cumb 222 B2
Rearquhar Highld 309 K7
Rearsby Leics 154 G3
Reasby Lincs 189 F9
Rease Heath E Ches 167 E10
Reaster Highld 310 C6
Reaulay Highld 299 D7
Reawick Shetland 313 J5
Reawla Corn 2 B4
Reay Highld 310 C3
Rechullin Highld 299 D8
Reculver Kent 71 F8
Red Ball Devon 27 D9
Red Bridge Lancs 211 D9
Red Bull E Ches 168 D4
Red Bull Staffs 150 B4
Red Dial Cumb 229 B11
Red Hill Bmouth 19 B7
Red Hill Hants 34 E2
Red Hill Hereford 97 D10
Red Hill Kent 53 C7
Red Hill Leics 135 D10
Red Hill Pembs 72 B6
Red Hill W Yorks 198 B2
Red Hill Warks 118 F2
Red Hill Worcs 117 G7
Red House Common E Sus 36 C5
Red Lake Telford 150 G3
Red Lodge Suff 124 C3
Red Lumb Gtr Man 195 D10
Red Pits Norf 159 D11
Red Post Corn 24 F3
Red Rail Hereford 97 F10
Red Rice Hants 47 E10
Red Rock Gtr Man 194 F5
Red Roses Carms 74 C2
Red Row Northumb 253 D7
Red Scar Lancs 203 G7
Red Street Staffs 168 E4
Red Wharf Bay Anglesey 179 E8
Redberth Pembs 73 E9
Redbourn Herts 85 C10
Redbournbury Herts 85 C10
Redbourne N Lincs 189 B7
Redbourne N Lincs 200 G3
Redbridge Dorset 17 D11
Redbridge London 68 B2
Redbridge Soton 32 E5
Redbrook Mon 79 C8
Redbrook Wrex 167 G8
Redburn Highld 300 C5
Redburn Highld 301 E9
Redburn Northumb 241 E7
Redcar Redcar 235 G8
Redcastle Angus 287 B10
Redcastle Highld 300 E5
Redcliff Bay N Som 60 D2
Redcroft Dumfries 237 B9
Redcross Worcs 117 C7
Reddicap Heath W Mid 134 D2
Redding Falk 279 F8
Reddingmuirhead Falk 279 F8
Reddish Gtr Man 184 C5
Reddish Warr 183 D11
Redditch Worcs 117 D10
Rede Suff 124 F6
Redenhall Norf 142 G5
Redenham Hants 47 D10
Redesdale Camp Northumb 251 D8
Redesmouth Northumb 251 G9
Redford Aberds 293 F9
Redford Angus 287 C9
Redford Dorset 29 F10
Redford Durham 233 E7
Redford W Sus 34 B5
Redfordgreen Borders 261 F9
Redgorton Perth 286 E4
Redgrave Suff 125 B10
Redheugh Angus 292 G6
Redhill Aberds 293 C9
Redhill Aberds 302 F6
Redhill Herts 104 E6
Redhill N Som 60 G4
Redhill Notts 171 F9
Redhill Shrops 131 B9
Redhill Shrops 150 G4
Redhill Staffs 150 D6
Redhill Sur 51 C9
Redhill Telford 150 G4
Redhills Cumb 230 F6
Redhills Devon 14 C4
Redhouse Argyll 275 G9
Redhouses Argyll 274 G4
Redisham Suff 143 G8
Redland Bristol 60 D5
Redland Orkney 314 D3
Redland End Bucks 84 E4
Redlands Dorset 17 E9
Redlands Som 44 G3
Redlands Swindon 81 G11
Redlane Som 28 E2
Redlingfield Suff 126 C3
Redlynch Som 45 G8
Redlynch Wilts 32 C2
Redmain Cumb 229 E8
Redmarley D'Abitot Glos 98 E5
Redmarshall Stockton 234 G3
Redmile Leics 154 B5
Redmire N Yorks 223 G10
Redmonsford Devon 24 D4
Redmoor Corn 5 C11
Redmoss Aberds 303 F8
Rednal Shrops 149 D7
Rednal W Mid 117 B10
Redpath Borders 262 B3
Redpoint Highld 299 C7
Redruth Corn 4 G3
Redscarhead Borders 270 G4
Redstocks Wilts 62 G2
Redtye Corn 5 C10
Redvales Gtr Man 195 F10
Redwick Newport 60 C2
Redwick S Glos 60 B4
Redwith Shrops 148 E6
Redworth Darl 233 G10
Reed Herts 105 D7
Reed End Herts 104 D6
Reed Point Lincs 174 E2
Reedham Lincs 174 D2
Reedham Norf 143 C8
Reedley Lancs 204 F2
Reedness E Yorks 199 C9
Reeds Beck Lincs 174 B2
Reeds Holme Lancs 195 C10
Reedsford Northumb 263 C9
Reedy Devon 14 D2
Reen Manor Corn 4 E5
Reepham Lincs 189 G8
Reepham Norf 159 E11
Reeth N Yorks 223 F10
Reeves Green W Mid 118 B5
Refail Powys 130 C3
Regaby I o M 192 C5
Regil Bath 60 G4
Regoul Highld 301 D8
Reiff Highld 307 H4
Reigate Sur 51 C9
Reigate Heath Sur 51 C8
Reighton N Yorks 218 D2
Reighton Gap N Yorks 218 D2
Reinigeadal W Isles 305 H4
Reisque Aberds 293 B10
Reiss Highld 310 D7
Rejerrah Corn 4 D5
Releath Corn 2 C5
Relubbus Corn 2 C3
Relugas Moray 301 E9
Remenham Wokingham 65 C9
Remenham Hill Wokingham 65 C9
Remony Perth 285 C11
Rempstone Notts 153 E11
Remusaig Highld 309 J7
Rendcomb Glos 81 D8
Rendham Suff 126 E6
Rendlesham Suff 126 G6
Renfrew Renfs 267 B10
Renhold Beds 121 G11
Renishaw Derbys 186 F6
Renmure Angus 287 B10
Rennington Northumb 264 F6
Renshaw Wood Shrops 132 B6
Renton W Dunb 277 F7
Renwick Cumb 231 C7
Repps Norf 161 F8
Repton Derbys 152 D6
Reraig Highld 295 C10
Reraig Cot Highld 295 B10
Rerwick Shetland 313 M5
Rescassa Corn 5 G9
Rescobie Angus 287 B9
Rescorla Corn 5 D10
Resipole Highld 289 C9
Reskadinnick Corn 4 G2
Resolfen = Resolven Neath 76 E4
Resolis Highld 300 C6
Resolven = Resolfen Neath 76 E4
Restalrig Edin 280 G5
Reston Borders 273 C7
Reston Cumb 221 F9
Restronguet Passage Corn 3 B8
Restrop Wilts 62 B5
Resugga Green Corn 5 D10
Reswallie Angus 287 B9
Retallack Corn 5 B8
Retew Corn 5 D8
Retford Notts 188 E2
Retire Corn 5 C10
Rettendon Essex 88 F3
Rettendon Place Essex 88 F3
Revesby Lincs 174 C3
Revesby Bridge Lincs 174 C4
Revidge Blkburn 195 B7
Rew Devon 9 G9
Rew Devon 13 G11
Rew Dorset 29 F11
Rew Street I o W 20 C5
Rewe Devon 14 B4
Rexon Devon 12 D4
Rexon Cross Devon 12 D4
Reybridge Wilts 62 F2
Reydon Suff 127 B9
Reydon Smear Suff 127 B9
Reymerston Norf 141 B10
Reynalton Pembs 73 D9
Reynoldston Swansea 56 C3
Rezare Corn 12 F3
Rhadyr Mon 78 E5
Rhaeadr Gwy = Rhayader Powys 113 D9
Rhandir Conwy 180 G4
Rhandirmwyn Carms 94 C5
Rhayader = Rhaeadr Gwy Powys 113 D9
Rhedyn Gwyn 144 C5
Rhegreanoch Highld 307 H5
Rhemore Highld 289 D7
Rhencullen I o M 192 C4
Rhenetra Highld 298 D4
Rhes-y-cae Flint 181 G11
Rhewl Denb 165 C10
Rhewl Denb 165 F11
Rhewl Shrops 148 C6
Rhewl Wrex 149 B7
Rhewl-fawr Flint 181 E10
Rhewl-Mostyn Flint 181 E11
Rhian Highld 309 H5
Rhicarn Highld 307 G5
Rhiconich Highld 306 D7
Rhicullen Highld 300 B6
Rhidorroch Ho Highld 307 K6
Rhiews Shrops 150 B2
Rhifail Highld 308 E7
Rhigolter Highld 308 D3
Rhigos Rhondda 76 D6
Rhilochan Highld 309 J7
Rhippinllwyd Ceredig 92 C5
Rhippinllwyd Ceredig 110 G6
Rhiroy Highld 307 L6
Rhitongue Highld 308 D6
Rhivichie Highld 306 D7
Rhiw Gwyn 144 D4
Rhiwabon = Ruabon Wrex 166 G4
Rhiwbebyll Denb 165 B10
Rhiwbina Cardiff 59 C7
Rhiwbryfdir Gwyn 163 F11
Rhiwceiliog Bridgend 58 C3
Rhiwderin Newport 59 B9
Rhiwen Gwyn 163 C9
Rhiwfawr Neath 76 C2
Rhiwinder Rhondda 58 B4
Rhiwlas Gwyn 147 B8
Rhiwlas Gwyn 163 B9
Rhiwlas Powys 148 C3
Rhode Som 43 G9
Rhode Common Kent 54 B5
Rhodes Gtr Man 195 F11
Rhodes Minnis Kent 55 E7
Rhodesia Notts 187 F9
Rhodiad Pembs 90 F5
Rhonadale Argyll 255 D8
Rhondda Rhondda 77 F7
Rhonehouse or Kelton Hill Dumfries 237 D9
Rhoose V Glam 58 F5
Rhos Carms 93 D7
Rhôs Neath 76 E2
Rhôs Denb 165 C10
Rhos Powys 148 F5
Rhôs Common Powys 148 F5
Rhos-ddû Gwyn 144 B5
Rhos-fawr Gwyn 145 B7
Rhos-goch Powys 96 B3
Rhos Haminiog Ceredig 111 E10
Rhos-hill Pembs 92 C3
Rhos Isaf Gwyn 163 D7
Rhôs Lligwy Anglesey 179 D7
Rhôs-on-Sea Conwy 180 E4
Rhos-y-brithdir Powys 148 E2
Rhos-y-garth Ceredig 112 C2
Rhos-y-gwaliau Gwyn 147 C8
Rhos-y-llan Gwyn 144 B4
Rhos-y-Madoc Wrex 166 G4
Rhos-y-meirch Powys 114 D5
Rhosaman Carms 76 C2
Rhosbeirio Anglesey 178 C5
Rhoscefnhir Anglesey 179 F8
Rhoscolyn Anglesey 178 F3
Rhoscrowther Pembs 72 E6
Rhosddu Wrex 166 E4
Rhosdylluan Gwyn 147 D7
Rhosesmor Flint 166 B2
Rhosfach Pembs 92 F2
Rhosgadfan Gwyn 163 D8
Rhosgoch Anglesey 178 D6
Rhosgoch Powys 96 B3
Rhosgyll Gwyn 163 G7
Rhoshirwaun Gwyn 144 D3
Rhoslan Gwyn 163 G7
Rhoslefain Gwyn 110 B2
Rhosllanerchrugog Wrex 166 F3
Rhosmaen Carms 94 G2
Rhosmeirch Anglesey 179 F7
Rhosneigr Anglesey 178 G4
Rhosnesni Wrex 166 E5
Rhosrobin Wrex 166 E4
Rhossili Swansea 56 D2
Rhosson Pembs 90 F4
Rhostrehwfa Anglesey 178 G6
Rhostryfan Gwyn 163 D7
Rhostyllen Wrex 166 F4
Rhoswiel Shrops 148 B5
Rhosybol Anglesey 178 D6
Rhosycaerau Pembs 91 D8
Rhosygadair Newydd Ceredig 92 B4
Rhosygadfa Shrops 148 C6
Rhosygilwen Pembs 92 C4
Rhosymedre Wrex 166 G3
Rhosyn-coch Carms 92 G5
Rhu Argyll 275 G9
Rhu Argyll 276 E5
Rhuallt Denb 181 F9
Rhubodach Argyll 275 F11
Rhuddall Heath W Ches 167 C9
Rhuddlan Ceredig 93 C9
Rhuddlan Denb 181 F8
Rhue Highld 307 K5
Rhulen Powys 96 B2
Rhunahaorine Argyll 255 C8
Rhyd Ceredig 92 C5
Rhyd Gwyn 163 G10
Rhyd Powys 129 C9
Rhyd-Ddu Gwyn 163 E9
Rhyd-Rosser Ceredig 111 D11
Rhyd-uchaf Gwyn 147 B8
Rhyd-y-Brown Pembs 91 G11
Rhyd-y-clafdy Gwyn 144 B6
Rhyd-y-cwm Shrops 130 G3
Rhyd-y-foel Conwy 180 F6
Rhyd-y-fro Neath 76 D2
Rhyd-y-gwin Swansea 75 E11
Rhyd-y-gwystl Gwyn 145 B8
Rhyd-y-meirch Mon 78 D4
Rhyd-y-meudwy Denb 165 E10
Rhyd-y-pandy Swansea 75 E11
Rhyd-y-sarn Gwyn 163 G11
Rhyd-yr-onen Gwyn 128 C2
Rhydaman = Ammanford Carms 75 C10
Rhydargaeau Carms 93 F8
Rhydcymerau Carms 93 D11
Rhydd Worcs 98 B6
Rhydd Green Worcs 98 B6
Rhydding Neath 57 B8
Rhydfudr Ceredig 111 D11
Rhydgaled Conwy 165 C7
Rhydgaled = Chancery Ceredig 111 B11
Rhydlewis Ceredig 92 B6
Rhydlios Gwyn 144 C3
Rhydlydan Conwy 164 E5
Rhydlydan Powys 129 E11
Rhydmoelddu Powys 113 B11
Rhydness Powys 96 C2
Rhydowen Carms 92 F3
Rhydowen Ceredig 93 B8
Rhydspence Hereford 96 B4
Rhydtalog Flint 166 D2
Rhydwen Gwyn 146 F4
Rhydwyn Anglesey 178 D4
Rhydycroesau Powys 148 C4
Rhydyfelin Carms 92 D5
Rhydyfelin Ceredig 111 B11
Rhydyfelin Powys 129 E11
Rhydyfelin Rhondda 58 B5
Rhydygele Pembs 91 G7
Rhydymain Gwyn 146 E6
Rhydymwyn Flint 166 B2
Rhydywrach Carms 73 B11
Rhyl Denb 181 E8
Rhymney Caerph 77 D10
Rhyn Wrex 148 B6
Rhynd Fife 287 E8
Rhynd Perth 286 E5
Rhynie Aberds 302 G4
Rhynie Highld 301 B8
Ribbesford Worcs 116 C5
Ribble Head N Yorks 212 D5
Ribblehead N Yorks 212 D5
Ribbleton Lancs 203 G7
Ribby Lancs 202 G4
Ribchester Lancs 203 F8
Riber Derbys 170 D4
Ribigill Highld 308 D5
Riby Lincs 201 F7
Riby Cross Roads Lincs 201 F7
Riccall N Yorks 207 F8
Riccarton E Ayrs 257 B10
Richards Castle Hereford 115 D9
Richborough Port Kent 71 G10
Richings Park Bucks 66 D4
Richmond London 67 E7
Richmond N Yorks 224 E3
Richmond S Yorks 186 D6
Richmond Hill W Yorks 206 G2
Richmond's Green Essex 106 F2
Rich's Holford Som 42 G6
Rickard's Down Devon 24 B6
Rickarton Aberds 293 E10
Rickerby Cumb 239 F10
Rickerscote Staffs 151 E8
Rickford N Som 44 B3
Rickinghall Suff 125 B10
Rickleton T & W 243 G7
Rickling Essex 105 E9
Rickling Green Essex 105 F10
Rickmansworth Herts 85 G9
Rickney E Sus 23 D10
Riddell Borders 262 E2
Riddings Derbys 170 E6
Riddlecombe Devon 25 E10
Riddlesden W Yorks 205 E7
Riddrie Glasgow 268 B2
Ridgacre W Mid 133 G10
Ridge Bath 44 B5
Ridge Dorset 18 D4
Ridge Hants 32 D4
Ridge Herts 86 E2
Ridge Lancs 211 G9
Ridge Som 28 F3
Ridge Wilts 46 G3
Ridge Common Hants 34 C2
Ridge Green Sur 51 D10
Ridge Hill Gtr Man 185 B7
Ridge Lane Warks 134 E5
Ridge Row Kent 55 E8
Ridgebourne Powys 113 E11
Ridgehill N Som 60 G4
Ridgemarsh Herts 85 G8
Ridgeway Bristol 60 D6
Ridgeway Derbys 170 E5
Ridgeway Derbys 186 E6
Ridgeway Kent 54 E5
Ridgeway Newport 59 B9
Ridgeway Pembs 73 D10
Ridgeway Som 45 D8
Ridgeway Staffs 168 E5
Ridgeway Cross Hereford 98 B4
Ridgeway Moor Derbys 186 E6
Ridgewell Essex 106 C4
Ridgewood E Sus 23 B7
Ridgmont C Beds 103 D9
Ridgway Shrops 131 F7
Ridgway Sur 50 B4
Riding Gate Som 30 B2
Riding Mill Northumb 242 E2
Ridley Kent 68 G6
Ridley Northumb 241 E7
Ridley Stokoe Northumb 250 F6
Ridleywood Wrex 166 E6
Ridlington Norf 160 C6
Ridlington Rutland 136 C6
Ridlington Street Norf 160 C6
Ridsdale Northumb 251 G10
Riechip Perth 286 C4
Riemore Perth 286 C4
Rienachait Highld 306 F5
Rievaulx N Yorks 215 B11
Rift Orkney 314 E4
Riffin Aberds 303 E7
Rifle Green Torf 78 D3
Rift House Hrtlpl 234 E5
Rigg Dumfries 239 D7
Riggend N Lnrk 278 G5
Rigsby Lincs 190 F6
Rigside S Lnrk 259 B9
Riley Green Lancs 194 B6
Rileyhill Staffs 152 F2
Rilla Mill Corn 11 G11
Rillaton Corn 11 G11
Rillington N Yorks 217 E7
Rimac Lincs 191 C7
Rimington Lancs 204 D2
Rimpton Som 29 C10
Rimswell E Yorks 201 B10
Rimswell Valley E Yorks 201 B10
Rinaston Pembs 91 F9
Rindleford Shrops 132 D4
Ring o' Bells Lancs 194 E3
Ringasta Shetland 313 M5
Ringford Dumfries 237 D8
Ringing Hill Leics 153 F9
Ringinglow S Yorks 186 E3
Ringland Newport 59 B11
Ringland Norf 160 G2
Ringles Cross E Sus 37 C7
Ringlestone Kent 53 B11
Ringlestone Kent 53 B9
Ringley Gtr Man 195 F9
Ringmer E Sus 36 E6
Ringmore Devon 8 F3
Ringorm Moray 302 E2
Ring's End Cambs 139 C7
Ringsfield Suff 143 F8
Ringsfield Corner Suff 143 F8
Ringshall Herts 85 C7
Ringshall Suff 125 G10
Ringshall Stocks Suff 125 G10
Ringstead Norf 176 E2
Ringstead Northants 121 B9
Ringtail Green Essex 87 B11
Ringwood Hants 31 F11
Ringwould Kent 55 D11
Rinmore Aberds 292 B6
Rinnigill Orkney 314 G3
Rinsey Corn 2 D3
Rinsey Croft Corn 2 D4
Riof W Isles 304 E3
Ripe E Sus 23 C8
Ripley Derbys 170 E5
Ripley Hants 19 B9
Ripley N Yorks 214 G5
Ripley Sur 50 B5
Riplingham E Yorks 208 G5
Ripon N Yorks 214 E6
Ripper's Cross Kent 54 E3
Rippingale Lincs 155 D11
Ripple Kent 55 D10
Ripple Worcs 99 D7
Ripponden W Yorks 196 D4
Rireavach Highld 307 K5
Risabus Argyll 254 C4
Risbury Hereford 115 G10
Risby E Yorks 208 G6
Risby Lincs 189 C10
Risby Suff 124 D5
Risca Caerph 78 G2
Rise E Yorks 209 E9
Rise Carr Darl 224 B5
Rise End Derbys 170 D3
Rise Park London 87 G8
Rise Park Nottingham 171 F9
Riseden E Sus 52 G6
Riseden Kent 53 F8
Risegate Lincs 156 D4
Riseholme Lincs 189 F7
Risehow Cumb 228 E6
Riseley Beds 121 E10
Riseley Wokingham 65 G8
Rishangles Suff 126 D3
Rishton Lancs 203 G10
Rishworth W Yorks 196 D4
Rising Bridge Lancs 195 B9
Rising Sun Corn 12 G3
Risingbrook Staffs 151 E8
Risinghurst Oxon 83 D9
Risley Derbys 153 B9
Risley Warr 183 C10
Risplith N Yorks 214 F4
Rispond Highld 308 C4
Rivar Wilts 63 G10
Rivenhall Essex 88 B4
Rivenhall End Essex 88 B4
River Kent 55 E9
River W Sus 34 C6
River Bank Cambs 123 D10
Riverhead Kent 52 B4
Rivers' Corner Dorset 30 E3
Riverside Cardiff 59 D7
Riverside Plym 7 D8
Riverside Stirl 278 C6
Riverside Worcs 117 D10
Riverside Docklands Lancs 194 B4
Riverton Devon 40 G6
Riverview Park Kent 69 E7
Rivington Lancs 194 E6
Rixon Dorset 30 E3
Rixton Warr 183 C11
Roa Island Cumb 210 G4
Roach Bridge Lancs 194 B5
Roaches Gtr Man 196 G3
Roachill Devon 26 C4
Road Green Norf 142 E5
Road Weedon Northants 120 F2
Roade Northants 120 G5
Roadhead Cumb 240 C2
Roadmeetings S Lnrk 269 F7
Roadside Highld 310 C5
Roadside of Catterline Aberds 293 F10
Roadside of Kinneff Aberds 293 F10
Roadwater Som 42 F4
Roag Highld 298 E2
Roast Green Essex 105 E9
Roath Cardiff 59 D7
Roath Park Cardiff 59 D7
Rob Roy's House Argyll 284 F5
Roberton Borders 261 G10
Roberton S Lnrk 259 D10
Robertsbridge E Sus 38 C2
Robertstown Moray 302 E2
Robertstown Rhondda 77 E8
Roberttown W Yorks 197 C7
Robeston Back Pembs 73 B9
Robeston Cross Pembs 72 D5
Robeston Wathen Pembs 73 B9
Robeston West Pembs 72 D5
Robhurst Kent 54 G2
Robin Hill Staffs 168 D6
Robin Hood Derbys 186 G3
Robin Hood Lancs 194 E4
Robin Hood W Yorks 197 B10
Robin Hood's Bay N Yorks 227 D9
Robinhood End Essex 106 D4
Robins W Sus 34 B4
Robinson's End Warks 134 E6
Roborough Devon 7 C10
Roborough Devon 25 D9
Robroyston Glasgow 268 B2
Roby Mers 182 C6
Roby Mill Lancs 194 F4
Rocester Staffs 152 B2
Roch Pembs 91 G7
Roch Gate Pembs 91 G7
Rochdale Gtr Man 195 E11
Roche Corn 5 C9
Roche Grange Staffs 169 C7
Rochester Medway 69 F8
Rochester Northumb 251 D8
Rochford Essex 88 G5
Rochford Worcs 116 D2
Rock Caerph 77 F11
Rock Corn 10 F4
Rock Devon 28 G3
Rock Neath 57 C9
Rock Northumb 264 E6
Rock Som 28 C4
Rock W Sus 35 E10
Rock Worcs 116 C4
Rock End Staffs 168 D5
Rock Ferry Mers 182 D4
Rockbeare Devon 14 C6
Rockbourne Hants 31 D10
Rockcliffe Cumb 239 E9
Rockcliffe Dumfries 237 D10
Rockcliffe Flint 182 G3
Rockcliffe Lancs 195 C11
Rockcliffe Cross Cumb 239 E8
Rockfield Highld 311 L3
Rockfield Mon 79 C7
Rockford Devon 41 D9
Rockford Hants 31 F11
Rockgreen Shrops 115 B10
Rockhampton S Glos 79 G11
Rockhead Corn 11 E7
Rockhill Shrops 114 B5
Rockingham Northants 137 E7
Rockland All Saints Norf 141 D9
Rockland St Mary Norf 142 C6
Rockland St Peter Norf 141 D9
Rockley Notts 188 G2
Rockley Wilts 63 E7
Rockley Ford Som 45 C8
Rockness Glos 80 F4
Rockrobin E Sus 52 G6
Rocks Park E Sus 37 C7
Rocksavage Halton 183 E8
Rockstowes Glos 80 F3
Rockville Argyll 276 C4
Rockwell End Bucks 65 B9
Rockwell Green Som 27 C10
Rocky Hill Scilly 1 G4
Rodbaston Staffs 151 G8
Rodborough Glos 80 E4
Rodbourne Swindon 62 C6
Rodbourne Wilts 62 C2
Rodbourne Bottom Wilts 62 C2
Rodbourne Cheney Swindon 62 B6
Rodbridge Corner Essex 107 C7
Rodd Hereford 114 E6
Rodd Hurst Hereford 114 E6
Roddam Northumb 264 E2
Rodden Dorset 17 E8
Roddymoor Durham 233 D9
Rode Som 45 C10
Rode Heath E Ches 168 D3
Rode Hill Som 45 C10
Rodeheath E Ches 168 B5
Roden Telford 149 F11
Rodford S Glos 61 C7
Rodgrove Som 30 C2
Rodhuish Som 42 F4
Rodington Telford 149 G11
Rodington Heath Telford 149 G11
Rodley Glos 80 C2
Rodley W Yorks 205 F10
Rodmarton Glos 80 F6
Rodmell E Sus 36 F6
Rodmer Clough W Yorks 196 B3
Rodmersham Kent 70 G2
Rodmersham Green Kent 70 G2
Rodney Stoke Som 44 C3
Rodsley Derbys 170 G2
Rodway Som 43 F9
Rodway Telford 150 F3
Rodwell Dorset 17 F9
Roe Cross Gtr Man 185 B7
Roe End Herts 85 B8
Roe Green Gtr Man 195 G9
Roe Green Herts 86 D2
Roe Green Herts 104 E6
Roe Lee Blkburn 203 G9
Roebuck Low Gtr Man 196 F3
Roecliffe N Yorks 215 F7
Roedean Brighton 36 G4

Roehampton London 67 E8
Roesound Shetland 312 G5
Roestock Herts 86 D2
Roffey W Sus 51 G7
Rogart Highld 309 J7
Rogart Station Highld 309 J7
Rogate W Sus 34 C4
Roger Ground Cumb 221 F7
Rogerstone Newport 59 B9
Rogerton S Lnrk 268 D2
Roghadal W Isles 296 C6
Rogiet Mon 60 B3
Rogue's Alley Cambs 139 B7
Roke Oxon 83 G10
Rokemarsh Oxon 83 G10
Roker T & W 243 F10
Rollesby Norf 161 F8
Rolleston Leics 136 C4
Rolleston Notts 172 E2
Rolleston-on-Dove Staffs 152 D4
Rollestone S Yorks 186 E5
Rollestone Wilts 46 E5
Rollestone Camp Wilts 46 E5
Rolls Mill Dorset 30 E3
Rolston E Yorks 209 D10
Rolstone N Som 59 G11
Rolvenden Kent 53 G10
Rolvenden Layne Kent 53 G11
Romaldkirk Durham 232 G5
Roman Hill Suff 143 E10
Romanby N Yorks 225 G7
Romannobridge Borders 270 F3
Romansleigh Devon 26 C2
Rome Angus 293 G7
Romesdal Highld 298 D4
Romford Dorset 31 F9
Romford Kent 52 E6
Romford London 68 B4
Romiley Gtr Man 184 C6
Romney Street Kent 68 G4
Rompa Shetland 313 L6
Romsey Hants 32 C5
Romsey Town Cambs 123 F9
Romsley Shrops 132 G5
Romsley Worcs 117 B9
Romsley Hill Worcs 117 B9
Ronachan Ho Argyll 255 B8
Ronague I o M 192 E3
Rondlay Telford 132 B4
Ronkswood Worcs 117 G7
Rood End W Mid 133 F10
Rook End Essex 105 E11
Rook Street Wilts 45 G10
Rookby Cumb 222 C6
Rookhope Durham 232 C4
Rooking Cumb 221 B8
Rookley I o W 20 E6
Rookley Green I o W 20 E6
Rooks Bridge Som 43 C11
Rooks Hill Kent 52 C5
Rook's Nest Som 42 G5
Rooksey Green Suff 125 G8
Rooksmoor Glos 80 E4
Rookwith N Yorks 214 B4
Rookwood W Sus 21 B11
Roos E Yorks 209 G11
Roose Cumb 210 F4
Roosebeck Cumb 210 F5
Roosecote Cumb 210 F4
Roost End Essex 106 C4
Rootham's Green Beds 122 F2
Rooting Street Kent 54 D3
Rootpark S Lnrk 269 E9
Ropley Hants 48 G6
Ropley Dean Hants 48 G6
Ropley Soke Hants 49 G7
Ropsley Lincs 155 C9
Rora Aberds 303 D10
Rorandle Aberds 293 B8
Rorrington Shrops 130 C5
Rosarie Moray 302 E3
Roscroggan Corn 4 G3
Rose Corn 4 E5
Rose-an-Grouse Corn 2 B2
Rose Ash Devon 26 C3
Rose Green Essex 107 F8
Rose Green Suff 107 C9
Rose Green Suff 107 D8
Rose Green W Sus 22 D6
Rose Grove Lancs 204 G2
Rose Hill Bucks 66 C2
Rose Hill Derbys 153 B7
Rose Hill E Sus 23 B7
Rose Hill Gtr Man 195 F8
Rose Hill Lancs 204 G2
Rose Hill Oxon 83 E8
Rose Hill Suff 108 C3
Rose Hill Sur 51 D7
Rose Valley Pembs 73 E8
Roseacre Kent 53 B9
Roseacre Lancs 202 F4
Rosebank E Dunb 278 G3
Rosebank S Lnrk 268 F6
Rosebery Midloth 270 D6
Rosebrae Moray 301 C11
Rosebrough Northumb 264 D4
Rosebush Pembs 91 F11
Rosecare Corn 11 B9
Rosedale Herts 86 E4
Rosedale Abbey N Yorks 226 F4
Roseden Northumb 264 E2
Rosedinnick Corn 5 B8
Rosedown Devon 24 C3
Rosefield Highld 301 D8
Rosehall Highld 309 J4
Rosehall N Lnrk 268 C4
Rosehaugh Mains Highld 300 D6
Rosehearty Aberds 303 C9
Rosehill Blkburn 195 C8
Rosehill Corn 4 E5
Rosehill Corn 5 C10
Rosehill Gtr Man 184 D3
Rosehill London 67 F9
Rosehill Pembs 72 B5
Rosehill Shrops 150 C3
Rosehill T & W 243 D8
Roseisle Moray 301 C11
Roseland Corn 6 C5
Roselands E Sus 23 E10
Rosemarket Pembs 73 D7
Rosemarkie Highld 301 D7
Rosemary Lane Devon 27 E11
Rosemelling Corn 5 D10
Rosemergy Corn 1 B4
Rosemount Perth 286 C5
Rosenannon Corn 5 B9
Rosenithon Corn 3 E8
Roser's Cross E Sus 37 C9
Rosevean Corn 5 D10
Rosevear Corn 2 E5
Roseville W Mid 133 E8
Rosevine Corn 3 B9
Rosewarne Corn 2 B4
Rosewarne Corn 4 G2
Rosewell Midloth 270 C5
Roseworth Stockton 234 G4
Roseworthy Corn 2 B4
Roseworthy Corn 4 F5
Roseworthy Barton Corn 2 B4
Rosgill Cumb 221 B10
Rosherville Kent 68 E6
Roshven Highld 289 B9
Roskear Croft Corn 4 G3
Roskhill Highld 298 E2
Roskill House Highld 300 D6
Roskorwell Corn 3 E7
Rosley Cumb 230 B2
Roslin Midloth 270 C5
Rosliston Derbys 152 F4
Rosneath Argyll 276 E5
Ross Borders 273 C9
Ross Dumfries 237 E8
Ross Northumb 264 B4
Ross Perth 285 E11
Ross Green Worcs 116 E5
Ross-on-Wye Hereford 98 G2
Rossett Wrex 166 D5
Rossett Green N Yorks 206 C2
Rossie Ochill Perth 286 F4
Rossie Priory Perth 286 D6
Rossington S Yorks 187 B10
Rosskeen Highld 300 C6
Rossland Renfs 277 G8
Rossmore Poole 19 C7
Roster Highld 310 F6
Rostherne E Ches 184 E2
Rostholme S Yorks 198 F5
Rosthwaite Cumb 220 C5
Rosthwaite Cumb 220 G4
Roston Derbys 169 G10
Rosudgeon Corn 2 D3
Rosyth Fife 280 E2
Rotchfords Essex 107 E8
Rotcombe Bath 44 B6
Rothbury Northumb 252 C3
Rotherbridge W Sus 35 C7
Rotherby Leics 154 F3
Rotherfield E Sus 37 B9
Rotherfield Greys Oxon 65 C8
Rotherfield Peppard Oxon 65 C8
Rotherham S Yorks 186 C6
Rotherhithe London 67 D11
Rothersthorpe Northants 120 F4
Rotherwas Hereford 97 D10
Rotherwick Hants 49 B8
Rothes Moray 302 E2
Rothesay Argyll 275 G11
Rothiebrisbane Aberds 303 F7
Rothiemay Crossroads Moray 302 E5
Rothiemurchus Lodge Highld 291 C11
Rothienorman Aberds 303 F7
Rothiesholm Orkney 314 D6
Rothley Leics 153 G11
Rothley Northumb 252 F2
Rothley Plain Leics 153 G11
Rothley Shield East Northumb 252 E2
Rothmaise Aberds 302 F6
Rothwell Lincs 189 B11
Rothwell Northants 136 G6
Rothwell W Yorks 197 B10
Rothwell Haigh W Yorks 197 B10
Rotsea E Yorks 209 C7
Rottal Angus 292 G5
Rotten End Essex 106 F4
Rotten End Suff 127 D7
Rotten Green Hants 49 B9
Rotten Row W Berks 64 E5
Rotten Row W Mid 118 B3
Rottingdean Brighton 36 G5
Rottington Cumb 219 C9
Rotton Park W Mid 133 F10
Roud I o W 20 E6
Rough Bank Gtr Man 196 E2
Rough Close Staffs 151 B8
Rough Common Kent 54 B6
Rough Haugh Highld 308 E7
Rough Hay Staffs 152 E4
Rougham Norf 158 E6
Rougham Suff 125 E8
Rougham Green Suff 125 E8
Roughbirchworth S Yorks 197 G9
Roughburn Highld 290 E5
Roughcote Staffs 168 G6
Roughlee Lancs 204 E2
Roughley W Mid 134 D2
Roughmoor Som 28 B2
Roughmoor Swindon 62 B6
Roughrigg N Lnrk 278 G6
Roughsike Cumb 240 B2
Roughton Lincs 174 C2
Roughton Norf 160 B4
Roughton Shrops 132 E5
Roughton Moor Lincs 174 C2
Roughway Kent 52 C6
Round Bush Herts 85 F10
Round Green Luton 103 G11
Round Maple Suff 107 C9
Round Oak Shrops 131 G7
Round Oak W Mid 133 F8
Round Spinney Northants 120 D5
Round Street Kent 69 F7
Roundbush Essex 88 E5
Roundbush Green Essex 87 C9
Roundham Som 28 F6
Roundhay W Yorks 206 F2
Round's Green W Mid 133 F9
Roundshaw London 67 G10
Roundstonefoot Dumfries 248 B4
Roundstreet Common W Sus 35 B9
Roundswell Devon 40 G4
Roundthorn Gtr Man 184 D4
Roundthwaite Cumb 222 E2
Roundway Wilts 62 G4
Roundyhill Angus 287 B7
Rous Lench Worcs 117 G10
Rousdon Devon 15 C11
Rousham Oxon 101 G9
Routenburn N Ayrs 266 C3
Routh E Yorks 209 E7
Rout's Green Bucks 84 F3
Row Corn 11 F7
Row Cumb 211 B8
Row Cumb 231 E8
Row Ash Hants 33 E8
Row Brow Cumb 229 D7
Row Green Essex 106 G4
Row Heath Essex 89 B10
Row-of-trees E Ches 184 F4
Row Town Sur 66 G4
Rowanburn Dumfries 239 B10
Rowanfield Glos 99 G8
Rowardennan Stirl 277 B7
Rowarth Derbys 185 D8
Rowbarton Som 28 B2
Rowberrow Som 44 B3
Rowde Wilts 62 G3
Rowden Devon 13 B8
Rowden N Yorks 205 B11
Rowe Head Cumb 210 D5
Rowen Conwy 180 G3
Rowfoot Northumb 240 E5
Rowford Som 28 B2
Rowhedge Essex 107 G10
Rowhill Sur 66 G4
Rowhook W Sus 50 G6
Rowington Warks 118 D4
Rowington Green Warks 118 D4
Rowland Derbys 186 G2
Rowlands Castle Hants 34 E2
Rowlands Gill T & W 242 F5
Rowland's Green Hereford 98 D3
Rowledge Sur 49 E10
Rowlestone Hereford 97 F7
Rowley E Yorks 208 G5
Rowley Shrops 130 B6
Rowley Green London 86 F2
Rowley Hill W Yorks 197 E7
Rowley Park Staffs 151 E8
Rowley Regis W Mid 133 F9
Rowley's Green W Mid 134 G6
Rowling Kent 55 C9
Rowly Sur 50 E4
Rownall Staffs 169 F7
Rowner Hants 33 G9
Rowney Green Worcs 117 C10
Rownhams Hants 32 D5
Rowrah Cumb 219 B11
Rowsham Bucks 84 B4
Rowsley Derbys 170 B3
Rowstock Oxon 64 B3
Rowston Lincs 173 D9
Rowthorne Derbys 171 C7
Rowton Shrops 149 G7
Rowton Telford 150 F2
Rowton W Ches 166 C6
Rowton Moor W Ches 166 C6
Roxburgh Borders 262 C5
Roxburgh Mains Borders 262 D5
Roxby N Lincs 200 D2
Roxby N Yorks 226 B5
Roxeth London 66 B6
Roxton Beds 122 G3
Roxwell Essex 87 D10
Royal British Legion Village Kent 53 B8
Royal Leamington Spa Warks 118 D6
Royal Oak Darl 233 G10
Royal Oak Lancs 194 G2
Royal Oak N Yorks 218 D2
Royal Tunbridge Wells = Tunbridge Wells Kent 52 F5
Royal's Green E Ches 167 G10
Roybridge Highld 290 E4
Royd S Yorks 197 G8
Royd Moor S Yorks 197 G8
Royd Moor W Yorks 198 E2
Roydhouse W Yorks 197 E8
Roydon Essex 86 D6
Roydon Norf 141 G11
Roydon Norf 158 E4
Roydon Hamlet Essex 86 D6
Royds Green W Yorks 197 B11
Royston Glasgow 268 B2
Royston Herts 105 C7
Royston S Yorks 197 E11
Royston Water Som 28 E2
Royton Gtr Man 196 F2
Ruabon = Rhiwabon Wrex 166 G4
Ruaig Argyll 288 E2
Ruan High Lanes Corn 3 B10
Ruan Lanihorne Corn 5 G7
Ruan Major Corn 2 F6
Ruan Minor Corn 2 F6
Ruarach Highld 295 C11
Ruardean Glos 79 B10
Ruardean Hill Glos 79 B10
Ruardean Woodside Glos 79 B10
Rubery Worcs 117 B9
Rubha Ghaisinis W Isles 297 G4
Rubha Stoer Highld 306 F5
Ruchazie Glasgow 268 B3
Ruchill Glasgow 267 B11
Ruckcroft Cumb 230 C6
Ruckhall Hereford 97 D9
Ruckinge Kent 54 G4
Ruckland Lincs 190 F4
Rucklers Lane Herts 85 E9
Ruckley Shrops 131 C10
Rudbaxton Pembs 91 G9
Rudby N Yorks 225 D9
Ruddington Notts 153 C11
Ruddle Glos 79 C11
Rudford Glos 98 G5
Rudge Shrops 132 D6
Rudge Som 45 C10
Rudge Heath Shrops 132 D5
Rudgeway S Glos 60 B6
Rudgwick W Sus 50 G5
Rudhall Hereford 98 F2
Rudheath W Ches 183 G11
Rudheath Woods W Ches 184 G2
Rudhja Garbh Argyll 289 E11
Rudley Green Essex 88 E4
Rudloe Wilts 61 E10
Rudry Caerph 59 B7
Rudston E Yorks 217 F11
Rudyard Staffs 169 D7
Ruewood Shrops 149 D9
Rufford Lancs 194 D3
Rufforth York 206 C6
Ruffs Notts 171 F8
Rugby Warks 119 B10
Rugeley Staffs 151 F10
Ruggin Som 27 D11
Ruglen S Ayrs 245 C7
Rugley Northumb 264 G5
Ruilick Highld 300 E5
Ruishton Som 28 C3
Ruisigearraidh W Isles 296 C5
Ruislip London 66 B5
Ruislip Common London 66 B5
Ruislip Gardens London 66 B5
Ruislip Manor London 66 B6
Ruiton W Mid 133 E8
Ruloe W Ches 183 G9
Rumach Highld 295 G8
Rumbling Bridge Perth 279 B10
Rumbow Cottages Worcs 117 B8
Rumburgh Suff 142 G6
Rumbush W Mid 118 B2
Rumer Hill Staffs 133 B9
Rumford Corn 10 G3
Rumford Falk 279 F8
Rumney Cardiff 59 D8
Rumsam Devon 40 G5
Rumwell Som 27 C11
Runcorn Halton 183 E8
Runcton W Sus 22 C5
Runcton Holme Norf 140 B2
Rundlestone Devon 13 G7
Runfold Sur 49 D11
Runhall Norf 141 B11
Runham Norf 143 B10
Runham Norf 161 G9
Runham Vauxhall Norf 143 B10
Running Hill Head Gtr Man 196 F4
Running Waters Durham 234 C2
Runnington Som 27 C10
Runsell Green Essex 88 D3
Runshaw Moor Lancs 194 D4
Runswick Bay N Yorks 226 B6
Runwell Essex 88 G2
Ruscombe Glos 80 D4
Ruscombe Wokingham 65 D9
Ruscote Oxon 101 C8
Rush Green Essex 89 B11
Rush Green Herts 86 C5
Rush Green Herts 104 G4
Rush Green London 68 B4
Rush Green Norf 141 B11
Rush-head Aberds 303 E8
Rush Hill Bath 61 G8
Rushall Hereford 98 E2
Rushall Norf 142 G3
Rushall W Mid 133 C10
Rushall Wilts 46 B6
Rushbrooke Suff 125 E7
Rushbury Shrops 131 E10
Rushcombe Bottom Poole 18 B5
Rushden Herts 104 E6
Rushden Northants 121 D9
Rushenden Kent 70 E2
Rusher's Cross E Sus 37 B10
Rushey Mead Leicester 136 B2
Rushford Devon 12 F4
Rushford Norf 141 G8
Rushgreen Warr 183 D11
Rushington Hants 32 E5
Rushlake Green E Sus 23 B10
Rushland Cross Cumb 210 B6
Rushley Green Essex 106 D5
Rushmere C Beds 103 F8
Rushmere Suff 143 F9
Rushmere St Andrew Suff 108 B4
Rushmere Street Suff 108 B4
Rushmoor Sur 49 E11
Rushmoor Telford 150 G2
Rushmore Hants 33 E11
Rushmore Hill London 68 G3
Rushock Hereford 114 F6
Rushock Worcs 117 C7
Rusholme Gtr Man 184 B5
Rushton Dorset 18 D3
Rushton N Yorks 217 C9
Rushton Northants 136 G6
Rushton Shrops 132 B2
Rushton W Ches 167 C9
Rushton Spencer Staffs 168 C6
Rushwick Worcs 116 G6
Rushy Green E Sus 23 C7
Rushyford Durham 233 F11
Ruskie Stirl 285 G10
Ruskington Lincs 173 E9
Rusland Cumb 210 B6
Rusling End Herts 104 G4
Rusper W Sus 51 F8
Ruspidge Glos 79 C11
Russ Hill Sur 51 E8
Russel Highld 299 E8
Russell Hill London 67 G10
Russell's Green E Sus 38 E2
Russell's Hall W Mid 133 F8
Russell's Water Oxon 65 B8
Russel's Green Suff 126 C5
Rusthall Kent 52 F5
Rustington W Sus 35 G9
Ruston N Yorks 217 C9
Ruston Parva E Yorks 217 G11
Ruswarp N Yorks 227 D7
Ruthall Shrops 131 F11
Rutherford Borders 262 C4
Rutherglen S Lnrk 268 C2
Ruthernbridge Corn 5 B10
Ruthin Denb 165 D10
Ruthin V Glam 58 D3
Ruthrieston Aberdeen 293 C11
Ruthven Aberds 302 E5
Ruthven Angus 286 C6
Ruthven Highld 291 D9
Ruthven Highld 301 F8
Ruthven House Angus 287 C7
Ruthvoes Corn 5 C8
Ruthwaite Cumb 229 D10
Ruthwell Dumfries 238 D3
Ruxley London 68 E3
Ruxton Hereford 97 F11
Ruxton Green Hereford 79 B8
Ruyton-XI-Towns Shrops 149 E7
Ryal Northumb 242 C2
Ryal Fold Blkburn 195 C7
Ryall Dorset 16 C4
Ryall Worcs 99 C7
Ryarsh Kent 53 B7
Rychraggan Highld 300 F4
Rydal Cumb 221 D7
Ryde I o W 21 C7
Rydens Sur 66 F6
Rydeshill Sur 50 C3
Rydon Devon 14 G3
Rye E Sus 38 C6
Rye Common Hants 49 C9
Rye Foreign E Sus 38 C5
Rye Harbour E Sus 38 D6
Rye Park Herts 86 C5
Rye Street Worcs 98 D5
Ryebank Shrops 149 C10
Ryecroft S Yorks 186 B6
Ryecroft W Yorks 205 F7
Ryecroft Gate Staffs 168 C6
Ryeford Glos 80 E4
Ryehill E Yorks 201 B8
Ryeish Green Wokingham 65 F8
Ryelands Hereford 115 F9
Ryeworth Glos 99 G9
Ryhall Rutland 155 G10
Ryhill W Yorks 197 E11
Ryhope T & W 243 G10
Rylah Derbys 171 B7
Rylands Notts 153 B10
Rylstone N Yorks 204 B5
Ryme Intrinseca Dorset 29 E9
Ryther N Yorks 207 F7
Ryton Glos 98 E4
Ryton N Yorks 216 D5
Ryton Shrops 132 C5
Ryton T & W 242 E5
Ryton Warks 135 F7
Ryton-on-Dunsmore Warks 119 C7
Ryton Woodside T & W 242 E4

S

Sabden Lancs 203 F11
Sabine's Green Essex 87 F8
Sackers Green Suff 107 D8
Sacombe Herts 86 B4
Sacombe Green Herts 86 B4
Sacriston Durham 233 B10
Sadberge Darl 224 B6
Saddell Argyll 255 D8
Saddell Ho Argyll 255 D8
Saddington Leics 136 E3
Saddle Bow Norf 158 F2
Saddle Street Dorset 28 G5
Saddlescombe W Sus 36 E3
Sadgill Cumb 221 D9
Saffron Walden Essex 105 D10
Saffron's Cross Hereford 115 G10
Sageston Pembs 73 E9
Saham Hills Norf 141 C8
Saham Toney Norf 141 C8
Saighdinis W Isles 296 E4
Saighton W Ches 166 C6
Sain Dunwyd = St Donats V Glam 58 F2
Sain Tathon = St Athan V Glam 58 F4
St Abbs Borders 273 B8
St Abb's Haven Borders 273 B8
St Agnes Corn 4 E4
St Agnes Scilly 1 H3
St Albans Herts 85 D10
St Allen Corn 4 E6
St Andrews Fife 287 F9
St Andrew's Major V Glam 58 E6
St Andrew's Wood Devon 27 F9
St Annes Lancs 193 B10
St Anne's Park Bristol 60 E6
St Ann's Dumfries 248 E3
St Ann's Nottingham 171 G9
St Ann's Chapel Corn 12 G4
St Ann's Chapel Devon 8 F3
St Anthony Corn 3 C9
St Anthony-in-Meneage Corn 3 D7
St Anthony's T & W 243 E7
St Anthony's Hill E Sus 23 E10
St Arvans Mon 79 F8
St Asaph = Llanelwy Denb 181 G8
St Athan = Sain Tathon V Glam 58 F4
St Augustine's Kent 54 C6
St Austell Corn 5 E10
St Austins Hants 20 B2
St Bees Cumb 219 C9
St Blazey Corn 5 E11
St Blazey Gate Corn 5 E11
St Boswells Borders 262 C3
St Breock Corn 10 G5
St Breward Corn 11 F7
St Briavels Glos 79 E9
St Briavels Common Glos 79 E8
St Bride's Pembs 72 C4
St Brides Major = Saint-y-Brid V Glam 57 G11
St Bride's Netherwent Mon 60 B2
St Brides-super-Ely V Glam 58 D5
St Brides Wentlooge Newport 59 C9
St Budeaux Plym 7 D8
St Buryan Corn 1 D4
St Catherine Bath 61 E9
St Catherine's Argyll 284 G5
St Catherine's Hill Dorset 19 B8
St Chloe Glos 80 E4
St Clears = Sanclêr Carms 74 B3
St Cleer Corn 6 B5
St Clement Corn 4 G6
St Clether Corn 11 E10
St Colmac Argyll 275 G11
St Columb Major Corn 5 C8
St Columb Minor Corn 4 C6
St Columb Road Corn 5 D8
St Combs Aberds 303 C10
St Cross Hants 33 B7
St Cross South Elmham Suff 142 G5
St Cyrus Aberds 293 G9
St David's Perth 286 E3
St David's = Tyddewi Pembs 90 F5
St Day Corn 4 G4
St Decumans Som 42 E5
St Dennis Corn 5 D9
St Denys Soton 32 E6
St Devereux Hereford 97 E8
St Dials Torf 78 G3
St Dogmaels = Llandudoch Pembs 92 B3
St Dominick Corn 7 B8
St Donat's = Sain Dunwyd V Glam 58 F2
St Edith's Wilts 62 G3
St Endellion Corn 10 F5
St Enoder Corn 5 D7
St Erme Corn 4 E6
St Erney Corn 7 D7
St Erth Corn 2 B3
St Erth Praze Corn 2 B3
St Ervan Corn 10 G3
St Eval Corn 5 B7
St Ewe Corn 5 F9
St Fagans Cardiff 58 D6
St Fergus Aberds 303 D10
St Fillans Perth 285 E10
St Florence Pembs 73 E9
St Gennys Corn 11 B8
St George Bristol 60 E6
St George Conwy 181 F7
St George in the East London 67 C10
St George's Gtr Man 184 B4
St Georges N Som 59 G11
St George's Telford 150 G4
St George's V Glam 58 D5
St George's Hill Sur 66 G5
St George's Well Devon 27 F8
St Germans Corn 7 D7
St Giles Lincs 189 G7
St Giles London 67 C10
St Giles in the Wood Devon 25 D8
St Giles on the Heath Devon 12 C3
St Giles's Hill Hants 33 B7
St Gluvias Corn 3 C7
St Godwalds Worcs 117 D9
St Harmon Powys 113 C9
St Helen Auckland Durham 233 F9
St Helena Warks 134 C5
St Helens Cumb 228 E6
St Helen's E Sus 38 E4
St Helens I o W 21 D8
St Helens Mers 183 B8
St Helen's S Yorks 197 F11
St Helen's Wood E Sus 38 E4
St Helier London 67 F9
St Hilary Corn 2 C3
St Hilary V Glam 58 E4
St Ibbs Herts 104 F3
St Illtyd Bl Gwent 78 E2
St Ippollytts Herts 104 F3
St Ishmael's Pembs 72 D4
St Issey Corn 10 G4
St Ive Corn 6 B6
St Ive Cross Corn 6 B6
St Ives Cambs 122 C6
St Ives Corn 2 A2
St Ives Dorset 31 G10
St James Dorset 30 C5
St James London 67 C9
St James Norf 160 E5
St James South Elmham Suff 142 G6
St James's End Northants 120 E4
St Jidgey Corn 5 B8
St John Corn 7 E8
St John's E Sus 52 G4
St John's I o M 192 D3
St John's Kent 52 B4
St John's Kent 52 E5
St Johns London 67 D11
St John's Sur 50 B3
St John's W Yorks 206 F4
St Johns Warks 118 C5
St John's Worcs 116 G6
St John's Chapel Devon 25 B8
St John's Chapel Durham 232 D3
St John's Fen End Norf 157 G10
St John's Highway Norf 157 G10
St John's Park I o W 21 C8
St John's Town of Dalry Dumfries 246 G4
St John's Wells Aberds 303 F7
St John's Wood London 67 C9
St Judes I o M 192 C4
St Julians Herts 85 D10
St Julians Newport 59 B10
St Just in Roseland Corn 3 B9
St Just Corn 1 C3
St Justinian Pembs 90 F4
St Katharines Wilts 63 G9
St Katherine's Aberds 303 F7
St Keverne Corn 3 E7
St Kew Corn 10 F6
St Kew Highway Corn 10 F6
St Keyne Corn 6 C4
St Lawrence Corn 5 B10
St Lawrence Essex 89 E7
St Lawrence I o W 20 F6
St Lawrence Kent 71 F11
St Leonard's Bucks 84 D6
St Leonards Dorset 31 G10
St Leonards E Sus 38 F3
St Leonards S Lnrk 268 E2
St Leonard's Street Kent 53 B7
St Levan Corn 1 E3
St Luke's Derby 152 B6
St Luke's London 67 C10
St Lythans V Glam 58 E6
St Mabyn Corn 10 G6
St Madoes Perth 286 E5
St Margaret South Elmham Suff 142 G6
St Margaret's Hereford 97 E7
St Margarets Herts 86 C5
St Margarets London 67 E7
St Margaret's at Cliffe Kent 55 E11
St Margaret's Hope Orkney 314 G4
St Mark's Glos 99 G8
St Mark's I o M 192 E3
St Martin Corn 2 E6
St Martin Corn 6 E5
St Martins Perth 286 D5
St Martin's Shrops 148 B6
St Martin's Moor Shrops 148 B6
St Mary Bourne Hants 48 C2
St Mary Church V Glam 58 E4
St Mary Cray London 68 F3
St Mary Hill V Glam 58 D3
St Mary Hoo Medway 69 D10
St Mary in the Marsh Kent 39 B9
St Marychurch Torbay 9 B8
St Mary's Orkney 314 F4
St Mary's Bay Kent 39 B9
St Maughans Mon 79 B7
St Maughans Green Mon 79 B7
St Mawes Corn 3 C8
St Mawgan Corn 5 B7
St Mellion Corn 7 B7
St Mellons Cardiff 59 C8
St Merryn Corn 10 G3
St Mewan Corn 5 E9
St Michael Caerhays Corn 5 G9
St Michael Church Som 43 G10
St Michael Penkevil Corn 5 G7
St Michael South Elmham Suff 142 G6
St Michaels Kent 53 F11
St Michaels Torbay 9 C7
St Michaels Worcs 115 D11
St Michael's Hamlet Mers 182 D5
St Michael's on Wyre Lancs 202 E5
St Minver Corn 10 F5
St Monans Fife 287 G9
St Neot Corn 6 B3
St Neots Cambs 122 E3
St Newlyn East Corn 4 D6
St Nicholas Herts 104 F5
St Nicholas Pembs 91 D7
St Nicholas V Glam 58 E5
St Nicholas at Wade Kent 71 F9
St Nicholas South Elmham Suff 142 G6
St Nicolas Park Warks 135 E7
St Ninians Stirl 278 C5
St Olaves Norf 143 D9
St Osyth Essex 89 B10
St Osyth Heath Essex 89 B10
St Owens Cross Hereford 97 G10
St Pancras London 67 C10
St Paul's Glos 80 B4
St Paul's Cray London 68 F3

St Paul's Walden Herts 104 G3
St Peter South Elmham Suff 142 G6
St Peter The Great Worcs 117 G7
St Peter's Glos 99 G8
St Peters Kent 71 F11
St Peter's T & W 243 E7
St Petrox Pembs 73 F7
St Pinnock Corn 6 C4
St Quivox S Ayrs 257 E9
St Ruan Corn 2 F6
St Stephen Corn 5 E8
St Stephens Corn 7 D8
St Stephen's Corn 12 D2
St Stephens Herts 85 D10
St Teath Corn 11 E7
St Thomas Devon 14 C4
St Thomas Swansea 57 C7
St Tudy Corn 11 F7
St Twynnells Pembs 73 F7
St Veep Corn 6 E2
St Vigeans Angus 287 C10
St Vincent's Hamlet Essex 87 G9
St Wenn Corn 5 C9
St Weonards Hereford 97 G9
St Winnow Corn 6 D2
St y-Nyll V Glam 58 D5
Saint Hill Devon 27 F9
Saint Hill W Sus 51 F11
Saint y Brid = St Brides Major V Glam 57 G11
Saintbridge Glos 80 B5
Saintbury Glos 100 D2
Saint's Hill Kent 52 E4
Saith ffynnon Flint 181 F11
Salcombe Devon 9 G9
Salcombe Regis Devon 15 D9
Salcott-cum-Virley Essex 88 C6
Salden Bucks 102 F6
Sale Gtr Man 184 C3
Sale Green Worcs 117 F8
Saleby Lincs 191 F7
Salehurst E Sus 38 C2
Salem Carms 94 F2
Salem Ceredig 128 G3
Salem Corn 4 G4
Salen Argyll 289 E7
Salen Highld 289 C8
Salendine Nook W Yorks 196 D6
Salenside Borders 261 E11
Salesbury Lancs 203 G9
Saleway Worcs 117 F8
Salford C Beds 103 D8
Salford Gtr Man 184 B4
Salford Oxon 100 F5
Salford Ford C Beds 103 D8
Salford Priors Warks 117 G11
Salfords Sur 51 D9
Salhouse Norf 160 G6
Saligo Argyll 274 G3
Salisbury Wilts 31 B10
Salkeld Dykes Cumb 230 D6
Sallachan Highld 289 C11
Sallachy Highld 295 B11
Sallachy Highld 309 J5
Salle Norf 160 E2
Salmans Kent 52 E4
Salmonby Lincs 190 G4
Salmond's Muir Angus 287 D9
Salmonhutch Devon 14 B2
Salperton Glos 99 G11
Salperton Park Glos 81 B9
Salph End Beds 121 G11
Salsburgh N Lnrk 268 C6
Salt Staffs 151 D9
Salt Coates Cumb 238 G5
Salt End E Yorks 201 B7
Salt Hill Slough 66 C3
Salta Cumb 229 B7
Saltaire W Yorks 205 F8
Saltash Corn 7 D8
Saltburn Highld 301 C7
Saltburn-by-the-Sea Redcar 235 G9
Saltby Leics 155 D7
Saltcoats Cumb 219 F11
Saltcoats E Loth 281 E9
Saltcoats N Ayrs 266 G4
Saltcotes Lancs 193 B11
Saltdean Brighton 36 G5
Salter Lancs 212 G2
Salter Street W Mid 118 C2
Salterbeck Cumb 228 F5
Salterforth Lancs 204 D3
Salters Heath Hants 48 B6
Salters Lode Norf 139 C11
Saltershill Shrops 150 D2
Salterswall W Ches 167 B10
Salterton Wilts 46 F6
Saltfleet Lincs 191 C7
Saltfleetby All Saints Lincs 191 C7
Saltfleetby St Clement Lincs 191 C7
Saltfleetby St Peter Lincs 190 D6
Saltford Bath 61 F7
Salthouse Cumb 210 F4
Salthouse Norf 177 E9
Saltley W Mid 133 F11
Saltmarsh Newport 59 C11
Saltmarshe E Yorks 199 C9
Saltness Orkney 314 G2
Saltness Shetland 313 J4
Saltney Flint 166 B5
Salton N Yorks 216 D4
Saltrens Devon 25 C7
Saltwell T & W 243 E7
Saltwick Northumb 242 B5
Saltwood Kent 55 F7
Salum Argyll 288 E2
Salvington W Sus 35 F10
Salwarpe Worcs 117 E7
Salwayash Dorset 16 B5
Sambourne Warks 117 E11
Sambourne Wilts 45 E11
Sambrook Telford 150 E4
Samhla W Isles 296 E3
Samlesbury Lancs 203 G7
Samlesbury Bottoms Lancs 194 B6
Sampford Arundel Som 27 D10
Sampford Brett Som 42 E5
Sampford Chapple Devon 25 G10
Sampford Courtenay Devon 25 G10
Sampford Moor Som 27 D10
Sampford Peverell Devon 27 E8
Sampford Spiney Devon 12 G6
Sampool Bridge Cumb 211 B9
Samuel's Corner Essex 70 B3
Samuelston E Loth 281 G9
Sanachan Highld 299 E8
Sanaigmore Argyll 274 F3
Sanclêr = St Clears Carms 74 B3
Sancreed Corn 1 D4
Sancton E Yorks 208 F4
Sand Highld 307 K4
Sand Shetland 313 J5
Sand Som 44 D2
Sand Gate Cumb 211 D7
Sand Hole E Yorks 208 F2
Sand Hutton N Yorks 207 B9
Sand Side Cumb 210 C4
Sand Side Lancs 202 C4
Sandaig Highld 295 E9
Sandal W Yorks 197 D10
Sandal Magna W Yorks 197 D10
Sandale Cumb 229 C10
Sandavore Highld 294 G6
Sandbach E Ches 168 C3
Sandbach Heath E Ches 168 C3
Sandbank Argyll 276 E3
Sandbanks Kent 70 G4
Sandbanks Poole 18 D6
Sandborough Staffs 152 F2
Sandbraes Lincs 200 G6
Sandend Aberds 302 C5
Sanderstead London 67 G10
Sandfields Glos 99 G8
Sandfields Neath 57 C8
Sandfields Staffs 134 B2
Sandford Cumb 222 B4
Sandford Devon 26 G4
Sandford Dorset 18 D4
Sandford Hants 31 G11
Sandford I o W 20 E6
Sandford N Som 44 B2
Sandford S Lnrk 268 G4
Sandford Shrops 148 E6
Sandford Shrops 149 C11
Sandford W Yorks 205 F11
Sandford Worcs 99 B7
Sandford Batch N Som 44 B2
Sandford Hill Stoke 168 G6
Sandford on Thames Oxon 83 E8
Sandford Orcas Dorset 29 C10
Sandford St Martin Oxon 101 F8
Sandfordhill Aberds 303 E11
Sandgate Kent 55 G7
Sandgreen Dumfries 237 D7
Sandhaven Aberds 303 C9
Sandhaven Argyll 276 E3
Sandhead Dumfries 236 E2
Sandhill Bucks 102 F4
Sandhill Cambs 139 F11
Sandhill S Yorks 198 F2
Sandhills Dorset 29 E11
Sandhills Dorset 29 G9
Sandhills Mers 182 C4
Sandhills Oxon 83 D9
Sandhills Sur 50 F2
Sandhills W Yorks 206 F3
Sandhoe Northumb 241 D11
Sandhole Argyll 275 D11
Sandholme E Yorks 208 G2
Sandholme Lincs 156 B6
Sandhurst Brack 65 G10
Sandhurst Glos 98 G6
Sandhurst Kent 38 B3
Sandhurst Cross Kent 38 B3
Sandhutton N Yorks 215 C7
Sandiacre Derbys 153 B9
Sandilands Lincs 191 E8
Sandilands S Lnrk 259 B9
Sandiway W Ches 183 G10
Sandleheath Hants 31 E10
Sandling Kent 53 B9
Sandlow Green E Ches 168 B3
Sandness Shetland 313 H3
Sandon Essex 88 E2
Sandon Herts 104 E6
Sandon Staffs 151 C8
Sandonbank Staffs 151 D8
Sandown I o W 21 E7
Sandown Park Kent 52 E6
Sandpit Dorset 28 G6
Sandpits Glos 98 F6
Sandplace Corn 6 D5
Sandridge Herts 85 C11
Sandridge Wilts 62 F2
Sandringham Norf 158 D3
Sands Bucks 84 G4
Sands End London 67 D9
Sandsend N Yorks 227 C7
Sandside Cumb 210 D6
Sandside Cumb 211 C9
Sandside Orkney 314 F2
Sandside Ho Highld 310 C3
Sandsound Shetland 313 J5
Sandtoft N Lincs 199 F8
Sandvoe Shetland 312 D5
Sandway Kent 53 C11
Sandwell W Mid 133 F10
Sandwich Kent 55 B10
Sandwich Bay Estate Kent 55 B11
Sandwick Cumb 221 B8
Sandwick Orkney 314 H4
Sandwick Shetland 313 L6
Sandwith Cumb 219 C9
Sandwith Newtown Cumb 219 C9
Sandy C Beds 104 B3
Sandy Carms 75 E7
Sandy Bank Lincs 174 E3
Sandy Carrs Durham 234 C3
Sandy Cross E Sus 37 C9
Sandy Cross Sur 49 D11
Sandy Down Hants 20 B2
Sandy Gate Devon 14 C5
Sandy Haven Pembs 72 D5
Sandy Lane W Yorks 205 F8
Sandy Lane Wilts 62 F3
Sandy Lane Wrex 166 G5
Sandy Way I o W 20 E5
Sandybank Orkney 314 C5
Sandycroft Flint 166 B4
Sandyford Dumfries 248 E6
Sandyford Stoke 168 E5
Sandygate Devon 14 G3
Sandygate I o M 192 C4
Sandygate S Yorks 186 D4
Sandyhills Dumfries 237 D10
Sandylake Corn 6 C2
Sandylands Lancs 211 G8
Sandylands Som 27 C10
Sandylane Swansea 56 D5
Sandypark Devon 13 D10
Sandysike Cumb 239 D9
Sangobeg Highld 308 C4
Sangomore Highld 308 C4
Sanham Green W Berks 63 F10
Sankey Bridges Warr 183 D9
Sankyns Green Worcs 116 E5
Sanna Highld 288 C6
Sanndabhaig W Isles 297 G4
Sanndabhaig W Isles 304 E6
Sannox N Ayrs 255 C11
Sanquhar Dumfries 247 B7
Sansaw Heath Shrops 149 E10
Santon Cumb 220 E2
Santon N Lincs 200 E2
Santon Bridge Cumb 220 E2
Santon Downham Suff 140 F6
Sapcote Leics 135 E9
Sapey Bridge Worcs 116 F4
Sapey Common Hereford 116 E4
Sapiston Suff 125 B8
Sapley Cambs 122 C4
Sapperton Derbys 152 C3
Sapperton Glos 80 E6
Sapperton Lincs 155 C10
Saracen's Head Lincs 156 D6
Sarclet Highld 310 E7
Sardis Carms 75 D9
Sardis Pembs 73 D10
Sarisbury Hants 33 F8
Sarn Bridgend 58 C2
Sarn Flint 181 F10
Sarn Powys 130 E4
Sarn Bach Gwyn 144 D6
Sarn Meyllteyrn Gwyn 144 C4
Sarnau Carms 74 B4
Sarnau Ceredig 110 G6
Sarnau Gwyn 147 B9
Sarnau Powys 95 E10
Sarnau Powys 148 F4
Sarnesfield Hereford 115 G7
Saron Carms 75 C10
Saron Carms 93 D7
Saron Denb 165 C8
Saron Gwyn 163 B8
Saron Gwyn 163 D7
Sarratt Herts 85 F8
Sarratt Bottom Herts 85 F8
Sarre Kent 71 G9
Sarsden Oxon 100 G5
Sarsden Halt Oxon 100 G5
Sarsgrum Highld 308 C3
Sasaig Highld 295 E8
Sascott Shrops 149 G8
Satley Durham 233 C8
Satmar Kent 55 F9
Satran Highld 294 B6
Satron N Yorks 223 F8
Satterleigh Devon 25 C11
Satterthwaite Cumb 220 G6
Satwell Oxon 65 C8
Sauchen Aberds 293 B8
Saucher Perth 286 D5
Sauchie Clack 279 C7
Sauchieburn Aberds 293 G8
Saughall W Ches 182 G5
Saughall Massie Mers 182 D3
Saughton Edin 280 G4
Saughtree Borders 250 D3
Saul Glos 80 D2
Saundby Notts 188 D3
Saundersfoot Pembs 73 E10
Saunderton Bucks 84 E3
Saunderton Lee Bucks 84 F4
Saunton Devon 40 F3
Sausthorpe Lincs 174 B5
Saval Highld 309 J5
Savary Highld 289 E8
Saveock Corn 4 F5
Saverley Green Staffs 151 B9
Savile Park W Yorks 196 C5
Savile Town W Yorks 197 C8
Sawbridge Warks 119 D10
Sawbridgeworth Herts 87 B7
Sawdon N Yorks 217 B8
Sawley Derbys 153 C9
Sawley Lancs 203 D11
Sawley N Yorks 214 F4
Sawood W Yorks 204 G6
Sawston Cambs 105 B9
Sawtry Cambs 138 G3
Sawyer's Hill Som 27 C11
Sawyers Hill Wilts 81 G8
Saxby Leics 154 F6
Saxby Lincs 189 D8
Saxby W Sus 35 G7
Saxby All Saints N Lincs 200 D3
Saxelbye Leics 154 E4
Saxham Street Suff 125 E11
Saxilby Lincs 188 F5
Saxlingham Norf 159 B10
Saxlingham Green Norf 142 D4
Saxlingham Nethergate Norf 142 D4
Saxlingham Thorpe Norf 142 D4
Saxmundham Suff 127 E7
Saxon Street Cambs 124 F3
Saxondale Notts 154 B3
Saxtead Suff 126 D5
Saxtead Green Suff 126 E5
Saxtead Little Green Suff 126 D5
Saxthorpe Norf 160 C2
Saxton N Yorks 206 F5
Sayers Common W Sus 36 D3
Scackleton N Yorks 216 E2
Scadabhagh W Isles 305 J3
Scaftworth Notts 187 C11
Scagglethorpe N Yorks 216 E6
Scaitcliffe Lancs 195 B9
Scaladal W Isles 305 G3
Scalan Moray 292 B4
Scalasaig Argyll 274 D4
Scalby E Yorks 199 B10
Scalby N Yorks 227 G10
Scald End Beds 121 F10
Scaldwell Northants 120 C5
Scale Hall Lancs 211 G9
Scale Houses Cumb 231 B7
Scaleby Cumb 239 E11
Scalebyhill Cumb 239 E10
Scales Cumb 210 E5
Scales Cumb 230 F2
Scales Cumb 231 C7
Scales Lancs 202 G5
Scalford Leics 154 E5
Scaling Redcar 226 C4
Scaliscro W Isles 304 F3
Scallasaig Highld 295 D10
Scallastle Argyll 289 F8
Scalloway Shetland 313 K6
Scalpay W Isles 305 J4
Scalpay Ho Highld 295 C8
Scalpsie Argyll 255 B11
Scamadale Highld 295 F9
Scamblesby Lincs 190 F3
Scamland E Yorks 207 E11
Scammadale Argyll 289 G10
Scamodale Highld 289 B10
Scampston N Yorks 217 D7
Scampton Lincs 189 F7
Scaniport Highld 300 F6
Scapa Orkney 314 F4
Scapegoat Hill W Yorks 196 D5
Scar Orkney 314 B6
Scar Head Cumb 220 G5
Scarborough N Yorks 217 B10
Scarcewater Corn 5 E8
Scarcliffe Derbys 171 B7
Scarcroft W Yorks 206 E3
Scarcroft Hill W Yorks 206 E3
Scardroy Highld 300 D2
Scarff Shetland 312 E4
Scarfskerry Highld 310 B6
Scargill Durham 223 C11
Scarinish Argyll 288 E2
Scarisbrick Lancs 193 E11
Scarness Cumb 229 E10
Scarning Norf 159 G9
Scarrington Notts 172 G2
Scarth Hill Lancs 194 F2
Scarthingwell N Yorks 206 F5
Scartho NE Lincs 201 F9
Scarvister Shetland 313 J5
Scarwell Orkney 314 D2
Scatness Shetland 313 M5
Scatraig Highld 301 F7
Scatwell Ho Highld 300 D3
Scawby N Lincs 200 F3
Scawsby S Yorks 198 G5
Scawthorpe S Yorks 198 F5
Scawton N Yorks 215 C10
Scayne's Hill W Sus 36 C5
Scethrog Powys 96 F2
Scholar Green E Ches 168 D4
Scholemoor W Yorks 205 G8
Scholes Gtr Man 194 F5
Scholes S Yorks 186 B5
Scholes W Yorks 197 B7
Scholes W Yorks 197 F7
Scholes W Yorks 204 F6
Scholes W Yorks 206 F3
Scholey Hill W Yorks 197 B11
School Aycliffe Durham 233 G11
School Green Essex 106 E4
School Green I o W 20 D2
School Green W Ches 167 C10
School Green W Yorks 205 G8
School House Dorset 28 G5
Schoolgreen Wokingham 65 F8
Schoolhill Aberds 293 D11
Scilly Bank Cumb 219 B9
Scissett W Yorks 197 E8
Scleddau Pembs 91 E8
Sco Ruston Norf 160 E5
Scofton Notts 187 E10
Scole Norf 126 B2
Scole Common Norf 142 G2
Scolpaig W Isles 296 D3
Scone Perth 286 E5
Sconser Highld 295 B7
Scoonie Fife 287 G7
Scoor Argyll 274 B5
Scopwick Lincs 173 D9
Scoraig Highld 307 K5
Scorborough E Yorks 208 D6
Scorrier Corn 4 G4
Scorriton Devon 8 B4
Scorton Lancs 202 D6
Scorton N Yorks 224 E5
Scot Hay Staffs 168 F4
Scot Lane End Gtr Man 194 F6
Scotbheinn W Isles 296 F4
Scotby Cumb 239 G10
Scotch Corner N Yorks 224 E4
Scotches Derbys 170 F4
Scotforth Lancs 202 B5
Scotgate W Yorks 196 E6
Scothern Lincs 189 F8
Scotland Leics 136 D3
Scotland Leics 153 E7
Scotland Lincs 155 C10
Scotland W Berks 64 F5
Scotland End Oxon 100 E6
Scotland Gate Northumb 253 G7
Scotland Street Suff 107 D9
Scotlands W Mid 133 C8
Scotlandwell Perth 286 G5
Scots' Gap Northumb 252 F2
Scotsburn Highld 301 B7
Scotscalder Station Highld 310 D4
Scotscraig Fife 287 E8
Scotston Aberds 293 F9
Scotston Perth 286 C3
Scotstoun Glasgow 267 B10
Scotstown Highld 289 C10
Scotswood T & W 242 E5
Scotswood Windsor 66 F2
Scott Willoughby Lincs 155 B11
Scottas Highld 295 E9
Scotter Lincs 199 G11
Scotterthorpe Lincs 199 G11
Scottlethorpe Lincs 155 E11
Scotton Lincs 188 B5
Scotton N Yorks 206 B2
Scotton N Yorks 224 F3
Scottow Norf 160 E5
Scoughall E Loth 282 E2
Scoulag Argyll 266 D2
Scoulton Norf 141 C9
Scounslow Green Staffs 151 D11
Scourie Highld 306 E6
Scourie More Highld 306 E6
Scousburgh Shetland 313 M5
Scout Dike S Yorks 197 G8
Scout Green Cumb 221 D11
Scouthead Gtr Man 196 F3
Scowles Glos 79 C9
Scrabster Highld 310 B4
Scraesburgh Borders 262 F5
Scrafield Lincs 174 B4
Scragged Oak Kent 69 G10
Scrainwood Northumb 251 B11
Scrane End Lincs 174 G5
Scrapsgate Kent 70 E2
Scraptoft Leics 136 B2
Scrapton Som 28 E3
Scratby Norf 161 F10
Scrayingham N Yorks 216 G4
Scredda Corn 5 E10
Scredington Lincs 173 G9
Screedy Som 27 B9
Scremby Lincs 174 B6
Scremerston Northumb 273 F10
Screveton Notts 172 G2
Scrivelsby Lincs 174 B3
Scriven N Yorks 206 B2
Scronkey Lancs 202 D4
Scrooby Notts 187 C11
Scropton Derbys 152 C3
Scrub Hill Lincs 174 D2
Scruton N Yorks 224 G5
Scrwgan Powys 148 E3
Scuddaborg Highld 298 C3
Scuggate Cumb 239 C10
Sculcoates Hull 209 G7
Sculthorpe Norf 159 C7
Scunthorpe N Lincs 199 E11
Scurlage Swansea 56 D3
Sea Som 28 E4
Sea Mill Cumb 210 F5
Sea Mills Bristol 60 D5
Sea Mills Corn 10 G4
Sea Palling Norf 161 D8
Seaborough Dorset 28 F6
Seabridge Staffs 168 G4
Seabrook Kent 55 G7
Seaburn T & W 243 F10
Seacombe Mers 182 C4
Seacox Heath Kent 53 G8
Seacroft Lincs 175 C9
Seacroft W Yorks 206 F3
Seadyke Lincs 156 B6
Seafar N Lnrk 278 G5
Seafield Highld 311 L3
Seafield Midloth 270 C5
Seafield S Ayrs 257 E8
Seafield W Loth 269 B10
Seaford E Sus 23 F7
Seaforth Mers 182 B4
Seagrave Leics 154 F2
Seagry Heath Wilts 62 C3
Seaham Durham 234 B4
Seahouses Northumb 264 C6
Seal Kent 52 B4
Sealand Flint 166 B5
Seale Sur 49 D11
Seamer N Yorks 217 C10
Seamer N Yorks 225 C9
Seamill N Ayrs 266 F4
Searby Lincs 200 F5
Seasalter Kent 70 F5
Seascale Cumb 219 E10
Seathorne Lincs 175 B9
Seathwaite Cumb 220 C4
Seathwaite Cumb 220 F4
Seatle Cumb 211 C7
Seatoller Cumb 220 C4
Seaton Corn 6 E6
Seaton Cumb 228 E6
Seaton Devon 15 C10
Seaton Durham 243 G9
Seaton E Yorks 209 D9
Seaton Kent 55 B8
Seaton Northumb 243 B8
Seaton Rutland 137 D8
Seaton Burn T & W 242 C6
Seaton Carew Hrtlpl 234 F6
Seaton Delaval Northumb 243 B8
Seaton Ross E Yorks 207 E11
Seaton Sluice Northumb 243 B8
Seatown Aberds 302 C5
Seatown Aberds 303 D11
Seatown Dorset 16 C4
Seaureaugh Moor Corn 2 B6
Seave Green N Yorks 225 E11
Seaview I o W 21 C8
Seaville Cumb 238 G5
Seavington St Mary Som 28 E6
Seavington St Michael Som 28 D6
Seawick Essex 89 C10
Sebastopol Torf 78 F3
Sebay Orkney 314 F5
Sebergham Cumb 230 C3
Sebiston Velzian Orkney 314 D2
Seckington Warks 134 B5
Second Coast Highld 307 K4
Second Drove Cambs 139 F10
Sedbergh Cumb 222 G3
Sedbury Glos 79 G8
Sedbusk N Yorks 223 G7
Seddington C Beds 104 B3
Sedgeberrow Worcs 99 D10
Sedgebrook Lincs 155 B7
Sedgefield Durham 234 F3
Sedgeford Norf 158 B4
Sedgehill Wilts 30 B5
Sedgemere W Mid 118 B4
Sedgley W Mid 133 E8
Sedgley Park Gtr Man 195 G10
Sedgwick Cumb 211 B10
Sedlescombe E Sus 38 D3
Sedlescombe Street E Sus 38 D3
Sedrup Bucks 84 C3
Seed Kent 54 B2
Seed Lee Lancs 194 C5
Seedley Gtr Man 184 B4
Seend Wilts 62 G2
Seend Cleeve Wilts 62 G2
Seend Head Wilts 62 G2
Seer Green Bucks 85 G7
Seething Norf 142 D6
Seething Wells London 67 F7
Sefton Mers 193 G11
Segensworth Hants 33 F8
Seggat Aberds 303 E7
Seghill Northumb 243 C7
Seifton Shrops 131 G9
Seighford Staffs 151 D7
Seilebost W Isles 305 J2
Seion Gwyn 163 B8
Seisdon Staffs 132 E6
Seisiadar W Isles 304 E7
Selattyn Shrops 148 C5
Selborne Hants 49 G8
Selby N Yorks 207 G8
Selgrove Kent 54 B4
Selham W Sus 34 C6
Selhurst London 67 F10
Selkirk Borders 261 D11
Sellack Hereford 97 F11
Sellack Boat Hereford 97 F11
Sellafirth Shetland 312 D7
Sellan Corn 1 C4
Sellibister Orkney 314 B7
Sellick's Green Som 28 D2
Sellindge Kent 54 F6
Selling Kent 54 B4
Sells Green Wilts 62 G3
Selly Hill N Yorks 227 D7
Selly Oak W Mid 133 G10
Selly Park W Mid 133 G11
Selmeston E Sus 23 D8
Selsdon London 67 G10
Selsey W Sus 22 E5
Selsfield Common W Sus 51 G10
Selside Cumb 221 F10
Selside N Yorks 212 D5
Selsley Glos 80 E4
Selsmore Hants 21 B10
Selson Kent 55 B10
Selsted Kent 55 E8
Selston Notts 171 E7
Selston Common Notts 171 E7
Selston Green Notts 171 E7
Selwick Orkney 314 F2
Selworthy Som 42 D2
Sem Hill Wilts 30 B5
Semblister Shetland 313 H5
Semer Suff 107 B9
Semington Wilts 61 G11
Semley Wilts 30 B5
Sempringham Lincs 156 C2
Send Sur 50 B4
Send Grove Sur 50 C4
Send Marsh Sur 50 B4
Senghenydd Caerph 77 G10
Sennen Corn 1 D3
Sennen Cove Corn 1 D3
Sennybridge = Pont Senni Powys 95 F8
Serlby Notts 187 D10
Serrington Wilts 46 F5
Sessay N Yorks 215 D9
Setchey Norf 158 G2
Setley Hants 32 G4
Seton E Loth 281 G8
Seton Mains E Loth 281 F8
Setter Shetland 312 E6
Setter Shetland 313 H5
Setter Shetland 313 J7
Setter Shetland 313 L6
Settiscarth Orkney 314 E3
Settle N Yorks 212 G6
Settrington N Yorks 216 E6
Seven Ash Som 43 G7
Seven Kings London 68 B3
Seven Sisters = Blaendulais Neath 76 D4
Seven Springs Glos 81 B7
Seven Star Green Essex 107 F8
Sevenhampton Glos 99 G10
Sevenhampton Swindon 82 G2
Sevenoaks Kent 52 C4
Sevenoaks Common Kent 52 C4
Sevenoaks Weald Kent 52 C4
Severn Beach S Glos 60 B4
Severn Stoke Worcs 99 C7
Severnhampton Swindon 82 G2
Sevick End Beds 121 G11
Sevington Kent 54 E4
Sewards End Essex 105 D11
Sewardstone Essex 86 F5
Sewardstonebury Essex 86 F5
Sewell C Beds 103 G9
Sewerby E Yorks 218 F3
Seworgan Corn 2 C6
Sewstern Leics 155 E7
Sexhow N Yorks 225 D9
Sezincote Glos 100 E3
Sgarasta Mhor W Isles 305 J2
Sgiogarstaigh W Isles 304 B7
Sgiwen = Skewen Neath 57 B8
Shab Hill Glos 80 B6
Shabbington Bucks 83 D11
Shackerley Shrops 132 B6
Shackerstone Leics 135 B7
Shacklecross Derbys 153 C8
Shackleford Sur 50 D2
Shackleton W Yorks 196 B3
Shacklewell London 67 B10
Shacklford Sur 50 D2
Shade W Yorks 196 C2
Shadforth Durham 234 C2
Shadingfield Suff 143 G8
Shadoxhurst Kent 54 F3
Shadsworth Blkburn 195 B8
Shadwell Glos 80 F3
Shadwell London 67 C11
Shadwell Norf 141 G8
Shadwell W Yorks 206 F2
Shaffalong Staffs 169 E7
Shaftenhoe End Herts 105 D8
Shaftesbury Dorset 30 C5
Shafton S Yorks 197 E11
Shafton Two Gates S Yorks 197 E11
Shaggs Dorset 18 E3
Shakeford Shrops 150 D3
Shakerley Gtr Man 195 G7
Shakesfield Glos 98 E3
Shalbourne Wilts 63 G10
Shalcombe I o W 20 D3
Shalden Hants 49 E7
Shalden Green Hants 49 E7
Shaldon Devon 14 G4
Shalfleet I o W 20 D4
Shalford Essex 106 F4
Shalford Som 45 G8
Shalford Sur 50 D4
Shalford Green Essex 106 F4
Shalloch Moray 302 D3
Shallowford Devon 25 B11
Shallowford Devon 41 E8
Shallowford Staffs 151 D7
Shalmsford Street Kent 54 C5
Shalstone Bucks 102 D2
Shamley Green Sur 50 E4
Shandon Argyll 276 D5
Shandwick Highld 301 B8
Shangton Leics 136 D4
Shankhouse Northumb 243 B7
Shanklin I o W 21 E7
Shannochie N Ayrs 255 E10
Shannochill Stirl 277 B10
Shanquhar Aberds 302 F5
Shanwell Fife 287 E8
Shanzie Perth 286 B6
Shap Cumb 221 B11
Shapridge Glos 79 B11
Shapwick Dorset 30 G6
Shapwick Som 44 F2
Sharcott Wilts 46 B6
Shard End W Mid 134 F3
Shardlow Derbys 153 C8
Shareshill Staffs 133 B8
Sharlston W Yorks 197 D11
Sharlston Common W Yorks 197 D11
Sharmans Cross W Mid 118 B2
Sharnal Street Medway 69 E9
Sharnbrook Beds 121 F9
Sharneyford Lancs 195 C11
Sharnford Leics 135 E9
Sharnhill Green Dorset 30 F2
Sharoe Green Lancs 202 G6
Sharow N Yorks 214 E6
Sharp Street Norf 161 E7
Sharpenhoe C Beds 103 E11
Sharperton Northumb 251 C11
Sharples Gtr Man 195 E8
Sharpley Heath Staffs 151 B9
Sharpness Glos 79 E11
Sharp's Corner E Sus 23 B9
Sharpsbridge E Sus 36 C6
Sharpstone Bath 45 B9
Sharpthorne W Sus 51 G11
Sharptor Corn 11 G11
Sharpway Gate Worcs 117 D9
Sharrington Norf 159 B10
Sharrow S Yorks 186 D4
Sharston Gtr Man 184 D4
Shatterford Worcs 132 G5
Shatterling Kent 55 B9
Shatton Derbys 185 E11
Shaugh Prior Devon 7 C10
Shavington E Ches 168 E2
Shaw Gtr Man 196 F2
Shaw Swindon 62 B6
Shaw W Berks 64 F3
Shaw W Yorks 204 F6
Shaw Wilts 61 F11
Shaw Common Glos 98 F3
Shaw Green Herts 104 E5
Shaw Green Lancs 194 D4
Shaw Green N Yorks 205 C11
Shaw Heath E Ches 184 F3
Shaw Heath Gtr Man 184 D5
Shaw Lands S Yorks 197 F10
Shaw Mills N Yorks 214 G5
Shaw Side Gtr Man 196 F2
Shawbank Shrops 131 G9
Shawbirch Telford 150 G2

358 Sha – Smi

Shawbury Shrops 149 E11
Shawclough Gtr Man 195 E11
Shawdon Hall Northumb 264 G3
Shawell Leics 135 G10
Shawfield Gtr Man 195 E11
Shawfield Staffs 169 C9
Shawfield Head N Yorks 205 C11
Shawford Hants 33 C7
Shawford Som 45 C9
Shawforth Lancs 195 C11
Shawhead Dumfries 237 B10
Shawhead N Lnrk 268 C4
Shawhill Dumfries 238 D6
Shawlands Glasgow 267 C11
Shawsburn S Lnrk 268 E5
Shawton S Lnrk 268 F3
Shawtonhill S Lnrk 268 F3
Shay Gate W Yorks 205 F8
Sheandow Moray 302 F2
Shear Cross Wilts 45 E11
Shearington Dumfries 238 D2
Shearsby Leics 136 E2
Shearston Som 43 G9
Shebbear Devon 24 F6
Shebdon Staffs 150 D5
Shebster Highld 310 C4
Sheddens E Renf 267 D11
Shedfield Hants 33 E9
Sheen Staffs 169 C10
Sheep Hill Durham 242 F5
Sheepbridge Derbys 186 G5
Sheepdrove W Berks 63 D10
Sheeplane C Beds 103 E8
Sheepridge Bucks 65 B11
Sheepridge W Yorks 197 D7
Sheepscar W Yorks 206 G2
Sheepscombe Glos 80 C5
Sheepstor Devon 7 B11
Sheepwash Devon 25 F7
Sheepwash Northumb 253 F7
Sheepway N Som 60 D3
Sheepy Magna Leics 134 C6
Sheepy Parva Leics 134 C6
Sheering Essex 87 C8
Sheerness Kent 70 E2
Sheerwater Sur 66 G4
Sheet Hants 34 C3
Sheet Shrops 115 C10
Sheets Heath Sur 50 B2
Sheffield Corn 1 D5
Sheffield S Yorks 186 D5
Sheffield Bottom W Berks 65 F7
Sheffield Green E Sus 36 C6
Sheffield Park S Yorks 186 D5
Shefford C Beds 104 D2
Shefford Woodlands W Berks 63 E11
Sheigra Highld 306 C6
Sheildmuir N Lnrk 268 D5
Sheinton Shrops 132 C2
Shelderton Shrops 115 B8
Sheldon Derbys 169 B11
Sheldon Devon 27 F10
Sheldon W Mid 134 G3
Sheldwich Kent 54 B4
Sheldwich Lees Kent 54 B4
Shelf Bridgend 58 C2
Shelf W Yorks 196 B6
Shelfanger Norf 142 G2
Shelfield W Mid 133 C10
Shelfield Warks 118 E2
Shelfield Green Warks 118 E2
Shelfleys Northants 120 F4
Shelford Notts 171 G11
Shelford Warks 135 F8
Shell Worcs 117 F9
Shell Green Halton 183 D8
Shelland Suff 125 E10
Shellbrook Leics 152 F6
Shelley Essex 87 E9
Shelley Suff 107 D10
Shelley W Yorks 197 E8
Shelley Woodhouse W Yorks 197 E8
Shellingford Oxon 82 G4
Shellow Bowells Essex 87 D10
Shellwood Cross Sur 51 D8
Shelsley Beauchamp Worcs 116 E4
Shelsley Walsh Worcs 116 E4
Shelthorpe Leics 153 F10
Shelton Beds 121 D10
Shelton Norf 142 E4
Shelton Notts 172 G3
Shelton Shrops 149 G9
Shelton Stoke 168 F5
Shelton Green Norf 142 E4
Shelton Lock Derby 153 C7
Shelton under Harley Staffs 150 B6
Shelve Shrops 130 D6
Shelvin Devon 27 G11
Shelvingford Kent 71 F8
Shelwick Hereford 97 C10
Shelwick Green Hereford 97 C10
Shenfield Essex 87 G10
Shenington Oxon 101 C7
Shenley Herts 85 E11
Shenley Brook End M Keynes 102 D6
Shenley Church End M Keynes 102 D6
Shenley Fields W Mid 133 G10
Shenley Lodge M Keynes 102 D6
Shenley Wood M Keynes 102 D6
Shenleybury Herts 85 E11
Shenmore Hereford 97 D7
Shennanton Dumfries 236 C5
Shennanton Ho Dumfries 236 C5
Shenstone Staffs 134 C2
Shenstone Worcs 117 C7
Shenstone Woodend Staffs 134 C2
Shenton Leics 135 C7
Shenval Highld 300 G4
Shenval Moray 302 G2
Shenvault Moray 301 E10
Shepeau Stow Lincs 156 G6
Shephall Herts 104 G5
Shepherd Hill W Yorks 197 C9
Shepherd's Bush London 67 C8
Shepherd's Gate Norf 157 F11
Shepherd's Green Oxon 65 C8
Shepherd's Hill Sur 50 G2
Shepherd's Patch Glos 80 E2
Shepherd's Port Norf 158 C3
Shepherdswell or Sibertswold Kent 55 D9
Shepley W Yorks 197 F7
Shepperdine S Glos 79 F10
Shepperton Sur 66 F5
Shepperton Green Sur 66 F5
Shepreth Cambs 105 B7
Shepshed Leics 153 F9
Shepton Beauchamp Som 28 D6
Shepton Mallet Som 44 E6
Shepton Montague Som 45 G7
Shepway Kent 53 C9
Sheraton Durham 234 D4
Sherberton Devon 13 G8
Sherborne Bath 44 B5
Sherborne Dorset 29 D10
Sherborne Glos 81 C11
Sherborne St John Hants 48 B6
Sherbourne Warks 118 E5
Sherbourne Street Suff 107 C9
Sherburn Durham 234 C2
Sherburn N Yorks 217 D9
Sherburn Grange Durham 234 C2
Sherburn Hill Durham 234 C2
Sherburn in Elmet N Yorks 206 G5
Shere Sur 50 D5
Shereford Norf 159 D7
Sherfield English Hants 32 C3
Sherfield on Loddon Hants 49 B7
Sherfin Lancs 195 B9
Sherford Devon 8 G5
Sherford Dorset 18 C4
Sherford Som 28 C2
Sheriff Hill T & W 243 E7
Sheriff Hutton N Yorks 216 F3
Sheriffhales Shrops 150 G5
Sheriff's Lench Worcs 99 B10
Sheringham Norf 177 E11
Sherington M Keynes 103 B7
Sheringwood Norf 177 E11
Shermanbury W Sus 36 D2
Shernal Green Worcs 117 E8
Shernborne Norf 158 C4
Sherrard's Green Worcs 98 B5
Sherrardspark Herts 86 C2
Sherriffhales Shrops 150 G5
Sherrington Wilts 46 F3
Sherston Wilts 61 B11
Sherwood Nottingham 171 G9
Sherwood Green Devon 25 C9
Sherwood Park Kent 52 E6
Shettleston Glasgow 268 C2
Shevington Gtr Man 194 F4
Shevington Moor Gtr Man 194 E4
Shevington Vale Gtr Man 194 F4
Sheviock Corn 7 D7
Shewalton N Ayrs 257 B8
Shibden Head W Yorks 196 B5
Shide I o W 20 D5
Shiel Aberds 292 B4
Shiel Bridge Highld 295 D11
Shield Row Durham 242 G6
Shieldaig Highld 299 B8
Shieldaig Highld 299 D8
Shieldhall Glasgow 267 B10
Shieldhill Dumfries 248 F2
Shieldhill Falk 279 F7
Shieldhill S Lnrk 269 G10
Shielfoot Highld 289 C8
Shielhill Angus 287 B8
Shielhill Invclyd 276 G4
Shifford Oxon 82 E5
Shifnal Shrops 132 B4
Shilbottle Northumb 252 B5
Shilbottle Grange Northumb 252 B6
Shildon Durham 233 F10
Shillford E Renf 267 D8
Shillingford Devon 27 C8
Shillingford Oxon 83 G9
Shillingford Abbot Devon 14 D4
Shillingford St George Devon 14 D4
Shillingstone Dorset 30 E4
Shillington C Beds 104 E2
Shillmoor Northumb 251 B9
Shilton Oxon 82 D3
Shilton Warks 135 G8
Shilvington Northumb 252 G5
Shimpling Norf 142 G3
Shimpling Suff 125 G7
Shimpling Street Suff 125 G7
Shincliffe Durham 233 C11
Shiney Row T & W 243 G8
Shinfield Wokingham 65 F8
Shingay Cambs 104 B6
Shingham Norf 140 C5
Shingle Street Suff 109 C7
Shinner's Bridge Devon 8 C5
Shinness Highld 309 H5
Shipbourne Kent 52 C5
Shipdham Norf 141 B9
Shipdham Airfield Norf 141 B9
Shipham Som 44 B2
Shiphay Torbay 9 B7
Shiplake Oxon 65 D9
Shiplake Bottom Oxon 65 C8
Shiplake Row Oxon 65 D9
Shiplate N Som 43 B11
Shiplaw Borders 270 F4
Shipley Derbys 170 G6
Shipley Northumb 264 F4
Shipley Shrops 132 D6
Shipley W Sus 35 C10
Shipley W Yorks 205 F8
Shipley Bridge Sur 51 E10
Shipley Common Derbys 171 G7
Shipley Shiels Northumb 251 E7
Shipmeadow Suff 143 F7
Shipping Pembs 73 D10
Shippon Oxon 83 F7
Shipston-on-Stour Warks 100 C5
Shipton Bucks 102 F5
Shipton Glos 81 B8
Shipton N Yorks 207 B7
Shipton Shrops 131 E11
Shipton Bellinger Hants 47 D8
Shipton Gorge Dorset 16 C5
Shipton Green W Sus 22 C4
Shipton Lee Bucks 102 G4
Shipton Moyne Glos 61 B11
Shipton Oliffe Glos 81 B8
Shipton on Cherwell Oxon 83 B7
Shipton Solers Glos 81 B8
Shipton-under-Wychwood Oxon 82 B3
Shiptonthorpe E Yorks 208 E3
Shirburn Oxon 83 F11
Shirdley Hill Lancs 193 E11
Shire Oak W Mid 133 C11
Shirebrook Derbys 171 B8
Shirecliffe S Yorks 186 C4
Shiregreen S Yorks 186 C5
Shirehampton Bristol 60 D4
Shiremoor T & W 243 C8
Shirenewton Mon 79 G7
Shireoaks Derbys 185 E9
Shireoaks Notts 187 E9
Shires Mill Fife 279 D10
Shirkoak Kent 54 F2
Shirl Heath Hereford 115 F8
Shirland Derbys 170 D6
Shirlett Shrops 132 D3
Shirley Derbys 170 G2
Shirley Hants 19 B9
Shirley London 67 F11
Shirley Soton 32 E6
Shirley W Mid 118 B2
Shirley Heath W Mid 118 B2
Shirley holms Hants 19 B11
Shirley Warren Soton 32 E5
Shirrell Heath Hants 33 E9
Shirwell Devon 40 F5
Shirwell Cross Devon 40 F5
Shiskine N Ayrs 255 E10
Shitlington Dorset 18 C2
Shobdon Hereford 115 E8
Shobley Hants 31 F11
Shobnall Staffs 152 E4
Shobrooke Devon 26 G5
Shoby Leics 154 F3
Shocklach W Ches 166 F6
Shocklach Green W Ches 166 F6
Shoeburyness Sthend 70 C2
Sholden Kent 55 C11
Sholing Soton 32 E6
Sholing Common Soton 33 E7
Sholver Gtr Man 196 F3
Shoot Hill Shrops 149 G8
Shootash Hants 32 C4
Shooters Hill London 68 D2
Shootersway Herts 85 D7
Shop Corn 10 G3
Shop Corn 24 E2
Shop Devon 24 E5
Shop Corner Suff 108 E4
Shopford Cumb 240 C3
Shopnoller Som 43 G7
Shopp Hill W Sus 34 B6
Shopwyke W Sus 22 B5
Shore Gtr Man 196 D2
Shore W Yorks 196 B2
Shore Bottom Devon 28 G2
Shore Mill Highld 301 C7
Shoreditch London 67 C10
Shoreditch Som 28 C2
Shoregill Cumb 222 E5
Shoreham Kent 68 G4
Shoreham Beach W Sus 36 G2
Shoreham-by-Sea W Sus 36 F2
Shores Green Oxon 82 D5
Shoresdean Northumb 273 F9
Shoreside Shetland 313 J4
Shoreswood Northumb 273 F8
Shoreton Highld 300 C6
Shorley Hants 33 B9
Shorncliffe Camp Kent 55 F7
Shorncote Glos 81 F8
Shorne Kent 69 E7
Shorne Ridgeway Kent 69 E7
Shorne West Kent 69 E7
Short Cross W Mid 133 G9
Short Green Norf 141 F11
Short Heath Derbys 152 G6
Short Heath W Mid 133 C9
Short Heath W Mid 133 E11
Short Street Wilts 45 D10
Shortacombe Devon 12 D6
Shortacross Corn 6 D5
Shortbridge E Sus 37 C7
Shortfield Common Sur 49 E10
Shortgate E Sus 23 B7
Shorthampton Oxon 100 G6
Shortheath Hants 49 F9
Shortheath Sur 49 E10
Shorthill Shrops 131 B8
Shortlands London 67 F11
Shortlanesend Corn 4 F6
Shortlees E Ayrs 257 B10
Shortmoor Devon 28 G2
Shortmoor Dorset 29 G7
Shorton Torbay 9 C7
Shortroods Renfs 267 B9
Shortstanding Glos 79 C9
Shortstown Beds 103 B11
Shortwood Glos 80 F4
Shortwood S Glos 61 D7
Shorwell I o W 20 E5
Shoscombe Bath 45 B8
Shoscombe Vale Bath 45 B8
Shotatton Shrops 149 E7
Shotesham Norf 142 D5
Shotgate Essex 88 G3
Shotley Northants 137 D8
Shotley Suff 108 D4
Shotley Bridge Durham 242 G3
Shotley Gate Suff 108 E4
Shotleyfield Northumb 242 G3
Shottenden Kent 54 C4
Shottermill Sur 49 G11
Shottery Warks 118 G3
Shotteswell Warks 101 B8
Shottisham Suff 108 C6
Shottle Derbys 170 F4
Shottlegate Derbys 170 F4
Shotton Durham 234 D4
Shotton Durham 234 F3
Shotton Flint 166 B4
Shotton Northumb 242 B6
Shotton Northumb 263 C8
Shotton Colliery Durham 234 C3
Shotts N Lnrk 269 C7
Shotwick W Ches 182 G4
Shouldham Norf 140 B3
Shouldham Thorpe Norf 140 B3
Shoulton Worcs 116 F6
Shover's Green E Sus 53 G7
Shraleybrook Staffs 168 F3
Shrawardine Shrops 149 F8
Shrawley Worcs 116 E6
Shreding Green Bucks 66 C4
Shrewley Warks 118 D4
Shrewley Common Warks 118 D4
Shrewsbury Shrops 149 G9
Shrewton Wilts 46 E5
Shripney W Sus 22 C6
Shrivenham Oxon 63 B8
Shropham Norf 141 E9
Shroton or Iwerne Courtney Dorset 30 E5
Shrub End Essex 107 G9
Shrubs Hill Sur 66 F3
Shrutherhill S Lnrk 268 F5
Shucknall Hereford 97 C11
Shudy Camps Cambs 106 C2
Shulishadermor Highld 298 E4
Shulista Highld 298 B4
Shuna Ho Argyll 275 C8
Shurdington Glos 80 B6
Shurlock Row Windsor 65 E10
Shurnock Worcs 117 E10
Shurrery Highld 310 D4
Shurrery Lodge Highld 310 D4
Shurton Som 43 E8
Shustoke Warks 134 E4
Shut Heath Staffs 151 E7
Shute Devon 15 B11
Shute Devon 26 G5
Shute End Wilts 31 B11
Shutford Oxon 101 C7
Shuthonger Glos 99 D7
Shutlanger Northants 120 G4
Shutt Green Staffs 133 B7
Shutta Corn 6 E5
Shuttington Warks 134 B5
Shuttlesfield Kent 55 E7
Shuttlewood Derbys 187 G7
Shuttleworth Gtr Man 195 D10
Shutton Hereford 98 F3
Shwt Bridgend 57 D11
Siabost bho Dheas W Isles 304 D4
Siabost bho Thuath W Isles 304 D4
Siadar W Isles 304 C5
Siadar Iarach W Isles 304 C5
Siadar Uarach W Isles 304 C5
Sibbaldbie Dumfries 248 F4
Sibbertoft Northants 136 G3
Sibdon Carwood Shrops 131 G8
Sibford Ferris Oxon 101 D7
Sibford Gower Oxon 101 D7
Sible Hedingham Essex 106 E5
Sibley's Green Essex 106 F2
Sibsey Lincs 174 E5
Sibsey Fen Side Lincs 174 E4
Sibson Cambs 137 D11
Sibson Leics 135 C7
Sibster Highld 310 D7
Sibthorpe Notts 172 F3
Sibthorpe Notts 188 G2
Sibton Suff 127 D7
Sibton Green Suff 127 C7
Sicklesmere Suff 125 E7
Sicklinghall N Yorks 206 D3
Sid Devon 15 D8
Sidbrook Som 28 B3
Sidbury Devon 15 C8
Sidbury Shrops 132 F3
Sidcot N Som 44 B2
Sidcup London 68 E3
Siddal W Yorks 196 C6
Siddick Cumb 228 E6
Siddington E Ches 184 G4
Siddington Glos 81 F8
Siddington Heath E Ches 184 G4
Side of the Moor Gtr Man 195 E8
Sidemoor Worcs 117 C9
Sidestrand Norf 160 B5
Sideway Stoke 168 G5
Sidford Devon 15 C8
Sidlesham W Sus 22 D5
Sidlesham Common W Sus 22 C5
Sidley E Sus 38 F2
Sidlow Sur 51 D9
Sidmouth Devon 15 D8
Sidway Staffs 150 B5
Sigford Devon 13 G11
Sigglesthorne E Yorks 209 D9
Sighthill Edin 280 G3
Sighthill Glasgow 268 B2
Sigingstone = Tresigin V Glam 58 E3
Signet Oxon 82 C2
Sigwells Som 29 C10
Silchester Hants 64 G6
Sildinis W Isles 305 G4
Sileby Leics 153 F11
Silecroft Cumb 210 C2
Silfield Norf 142 D2
Silford Devon 24 B6
Silian Ceredig 111 G11
Silk Willoughby Lincs 173 G9
Silkstead Hants 32 C6
Silkstone S Yorks 197 F9
Silkstone Common S Yorks 197 G9
Silloth Cumb 238 G4
Sills Northumb 251 C8
Sillyearn Moray 302 D5
Siloh Carms 94 D4
Silpho N Yorks 227 G9
Silsden W Yorks 204 D6
Silsoe C Beds 103 D11
Silton Dorset 30 B3
Silver End Essex 88 B4
Silver End W Mid 133 F8
Silver Green Norf 142 E5
Silver Hill E Sus 38 B2
Silver Knap Som 29 C11
Silver Street Glos 80 E3
Silver Street Kent 69 G11
Silver Street Som 27 C11
Silver Street Som 44 G4
Silver Street Worcs 117 B11
Silverburn Midloth 270 C4
Silverdale Lancs 211 E9
Silverdale Staffs 168 F4
Silverdale Green Lancs 211 E9
Silvergate Norf 160 D3
Silverhill E Sus 38 E3
Silverhill Park E Sus 38 E4
Silverknowes Edin 280 F4
Silverley's Green Suff 126 B5
Silvermuir S Lnrk 269 F8
Silverstone Northants 102 C3
Silverton Devon 27 G7
Silverton W Dunb 277 F8
Silvertonhill S Lnrk 268 E4
Silvertown London 68 D2
Silverwell Corn 4 F4
Silvington Shrops 116 B2
Silwick Shetland 313 J4
Sim Hill S Yorks 197 G9
Simister Gtr Man 195 F10
Simmondley Derbys 185 C8
Simm's Cross Halton 183 D8
Simm's Lane End Mers 194 G4
Simonburn Northumb 241 C9
Simonsbath Som 41 F9
Simonsburrow Devon 27 D10
Simonside T & W 243 E8
Simonstone Lancs 203 G11
Simonstone N Yorks 223 G7
Simprim Borders 272 F6
Simpson M Keynes 103 D7
Simpson Pembs 72 B5
Simpson Cross Pembs 72 B5
Simpson Green W Yorks 205 F9
Sinclair's Hill Borders 272 E6
Sinclairston E Ayrs 257 F11
Sinclairtown Fife 280 C5
Sinderby N Yorks 214 C6
Sinderhope Northumb 241 G8
Sinderland Green Gtr Man 184 C2
Sindlesham Wokingham 65 F9
Sinfin Derby 152 C6
Sinfin Moor Derby 153 C7
Singdean Borders 250 C3
Single Hill Bath 45 B8
Singleborough Bucks 102 E5
Singleton Lancs 202 F3
Singleton W Sus 34 E5
Singlewell Kent 69 E7
Singret Wrex 166 D4
Sinkhurst Green Kent 53 E10
Sinnahard Aberds 292 B6
Sinnington N Yorks 216 B4
Sinton Worcs 116 E6
Sinton Green Worcs 116 E6
Sion Hill Bath 61 F8
Sipson London 66 D5
Sirhowy Bl Gwent 77 C11
Sisland Norf 142 D6
Sissinghurst Kent 53 F9
Sisterpath Borders 272 F5
Siston S Glos 61 D7
Sithney Corn 2 D4
Sithney Common Corn 2 D4
Sithney Green Corn 2 D4
Sittingbourne Kent 70 G2
Six Ashes Staffs 132 F5
Six Bells Bl Gwent 78 E2
Six Hills Leics 154 E2
Six Mile Bottom Cambs 123 F11
Sixhills Lincs 189 D11
Sixmile Kent 54 E6
Sixpenny Handley Dorset 31 D7
Sizewell Suff 127 E9
Skaigh Devon 13 C8
Skail Highld 308 E7
Skaill Orkney 314 F5
Skaill Orkney 314 C4
Skaill Orkney 314 E2
Skares E Ayrs 258 F2
Skateraw E Loth 282 F4
Skaw Shetland 312 B8
Skaw Shetland 312 G7
Skeabost Highld 298 E4
Skeabrae Orkney 314 D2
Skeeby N Yorks 224 E4
Skeete Kent 54 E6
Skeffington Leics 136 C4
Skeffling E Yorks 201 D11
Skegby Notts 171 C7
Skegby Notts 188 G3
Skegness Lincs 175 C9
Skelberry Shetland 313 G6
Skelberry Shetland 313 M5
Skelbo Highld 309 K7
Skelbo Street Highld 309 K7
Skelbrooke S Yorks 198 E4
Skeldyke Lincs 156 B6
Skelfhill Borders 249 C11
Skellingthorpe Lincs 188 G6
Skellister Shetland 313 H6
Skellorn Green E Ches 184 E6
Skellow S Yorks 198 E4
Skelmanthorpe W Yorks 197 E8
Skelmersdale Lancs 194 F3
Skelmonae Aberds 303 F8
Skelmorlie N Ayrs 266 B3
Skelmuir Aberds 303 E9
Skelpick Highld 308 D7
Skelton Cumb 230 D4
Skelton E Yorks 199 B9
Skelton N Yorks 223 E11
Skelton Redcar 226 B3
Skelton York 207 B7
Skelton-on-Ure N Yorks 215 F7
Skelwick Orkney 314 B4
Skelwith Bridge Cumb 220 E6
Skendleby Lincs 174 B6
Skendleby Psalter Lincs 190 G6
Skene Ho Aberds 293 C9
Skenfrith Mon 97 G9
Skerne E Yorks 208 B6
Skerne Park Darl 224 C5
Skeroblingarry Argyll 255 E8
Skerray Highld 308 C6
Skerricha Highld 306 D7
Skerryford Pembs 72 C6
Skerton Lancs 211 G9
Sketchley Leics 135 E8
Sketty Swansea 56 C6
Skewen = Sgiwen Neath 57 B8
Skewes Corn 5 B9
Skewsby N Yorks 216 E2
Skeyton Norf 160 D4
Skeyton Corner Norf 160 D5
Skiag Bridge Highld 307 G7
Skibo Castle Highld 309 L7
Skidbrooke Lincs 190 C6
Skidbrooke North End Lincs 190 B6
Skidby E Yorks 208 G6
Skilgate Som 27 B7
Skillington Lincs 155 D7
Skinburness Cumb 238 F4
Skinflats Falk 279 E8
Skinidin Highld 298 E2
Skinner's Bottom Corn 4 F4
Skinners Green W Berks 64 F2
Skinnet Highld 308 C5
Skinningrove Redcar 226 B4
Skipness Argyll 255 B9
Skippool Lancs 202 E3
Skiprigg Cumb 230 B3
Skipsea E Yorks 209 B9
Skipsea Brough E Yorks 209 C9
Skipton N Yorks 204 C5
Skipton-on-Swale N Yorks 215 D7
Skipwith N Yorks 207 F9
Skirbeck Lincs 174 G4
Skirbeck Quarter Lincs 174 G4
Skirethorns N Yorks 213 G9
Skirlaugh E Yorks 209 F8
Skirling Borders 260 B3
Skirmett Bucks 65 B9
Skirpenbeck E Yorks 207 B10
Skirwith Cumb 231 E8
Skirza Highld 310 C7
Skitby Cumb 239 D10
Skitham Lancs 202 E4
Skittle Green Bucks 84 E3
Skulamus Highld 295 C8
Skullomie Highld 308 C6
Skyborry Green Shrops 114 C5
Skye Green Essex 107 G7
Skye of Curr Highld 301 G9
Skyfog Pembs 90 F6
Skyreholme N Yorks 213 G11
Slack Derbys 170 C4
Slack W Yorks 196 B3
Slack W Yorks 196 D5
Slack Head Cumb 211 D9
Slackcote Gtr Man 196 F3
Slackhall Derbys 185 E9
Slackhead Moray 302 C4
Slackholme End Lincs 191 G8
Slacks of Cairnbanno Aberds 303 E8
Slad Glos 80 D5
Sladbrook Glos 98 F5
Slade Devon 27 F10
Slade Devon 40 D4
Slade Kent 54 C2
Slade Pembs 72 B6
Slade End Oxon 83 G9
Slade Green London 68 D4
Slade Heath Staffs 133 B8
Slade Hooton S Yorks 187 D8
Sladen Green Hants 48 C2
Slades Green Worcs 99 E7
Sladesbridge Corn 10 G6
Slaggyford Northumb 240 G5
Slaidburn Lancs 203 C10
Slaithwaite W Yorks 196 E5
Slaley Derbys 170 D3
Slaley Northumb 241 F11
Slamannan Falk 279 G7
Slape Cross Som 43 F10
Slapewath Redcar 226 B2
Slapton Bucks 103 G8
Slapton Devon 8 G6
Slapton Northants 102 B2
Slate Haugh Moray 302 C4
Slateford Edin 280 G4
Slatepit Dale Derbys 170 B4
Slattocks Gtr Man 195 F11
Slaugham W Sus 36 B3
Slaughter Hill E Ches 168 D2
Slaughterbridge Corn 11 D8
Slaughterford Wilts 61 E10
Slawston Leics 136 E5
Slay Pits S Yorks 199 F7
Sleaford Hants 49 F10
Sleaford Lincs 173 F9
Sleagill Cumb 221 B11
Sleap Shrops 149 D9
Sleapford Telford 150 F2
Sleapshyde Herts 86 D2
Sleastary Highld 309 K6
Slebech Pembs 73 B8
Sledge Green Worcs 98 E6
Sledmere E Yorks 217 G8
Sleeches Cross E Sus 52 G5
Sleepers Hill Hants 33 B7
Sleet Moor Derbys 170 E6
Sleetbeck Cumb 240 B2
Sleight Dorset 18 B5
Sleights N Yorks 227 D7
Slepe Dorset 18 C4
Sliabhna h-Airde W Isles 296 F3
Slickly Highld 310 C6
Sliddery N Ayrs 255 E10
Slideslow Worcs 117 C9
Sligachan Hotel Highld 294 C6
Sligneach Argyll 288 G4
Sligrachan Argyll 276 C3
Slimbridge Glos 80 E2
Slindon Staffs 150 C6
Slindon W Sus 35 F7
Slinfold W Sus 50 G6
Sling Glos 79 D9
Sling Gwyn 163 B10
Slingsby N Yorks 216 E3
Slioch Aberds 302 F5
Slip End C Beds 85 B9
Slip End Herts 104 D5
Slippery Ford W Yorks 204 E6
Slipton Northants 121 B9
Slitting Mill Staffs 151 F10
Slochd Highld 301 G8
Slockavullin Argyll 275 D9
Slogan Moray 302 E3
Sloley Norf 160 E5
Sloncombe Devon 13 D10
Sloothby Lincs 191 G7
Slough Slough 66 D3
Slough Green Som 28 C3
Slough Green W Sus 36 B3
Slough Hill Suff 125 G7
Sluggan Highld 301 G8
Sluggans Highld 298 E4
Slumbay Highld 295 B10
Sly Corner Kent 54 G3
Slyfield Sur 50 C3
Slyne Lancs 211 F9
Smailholm Borders 262 B4
Small Dole W Sus 36 E2
Small End Lincs 174 D6
Small Heath W Mid 134 F2
Small Hythe Kent 53 G11
Small Way Som 44 G6
Smallbridge Gtr Man 196 D2
Smallbrook Devon 14 B3
Smallbrook Glos 79 E9
Smallburgh Norf 160 E6
Smallburn Aberds 303 E10
Smallburn E Ayrs 258 D5
Smalldale Derbys 185 E11
Smalldale Derbys 185 F9
Smalley Derbys 170 G6
Smalley Common Derbys 170 G6
Smalley Green Derbys 170 G6
Smallfield Sur 51 E10
Smallford Herts 85 D11
Smallholm Dumfries 238 B4
Smallmarsh Devon 25 C10
Smallrice Staffs 151 C9
Smallridge Devon 28 G4
Smallshaw Gtr Man 196 G2
Smallthorne Stoke 168 E5
Smallwood E Ches 168 C4
Smallwood Worcs 117 D10
Smallwood Green Suff 125 F8
Smallwood Hey Lancs 202 D3
Smallworth Norf 141 G10
Smannell Hants 47 D11
Smardale Cumb 222 D4
Smarden Kent 53 E11
Smarden Bell Kent 53 E11
Smart's Hill Kent 52 E4
Smaull Argyll 274 G3
Smeatharpe Devon 27 E11
Smeaton Fife 280 C5
Smeeth Kent 54 F5
Smeeton Westerby Leics 136 E3
Smelthouses N Yorks 214 G3
Smercleit W Isles 297 K3
Smerral Highld 310 F5
Smestow Staffs 133 E7
Smethcott Shrops 131 D9
Smethwick W Mid 133 F10
Smethwick Green E Ches 168 C4
Smirisary Highld 289 B8
Smisby Derbys 152 F6
Smite Hill Worcs 117 F7
Smith End Green Worcs 116 G5
Smith Green Lancs 202 C5
Smithaleigh Devon 7 D11
Smithbrook W Sus 34 C6
Smithfield Cumb 239 D10
Smithies S Yorks 197 F11
Smithincott Devon 27 E9
Smithley S Yorks 197 G11
Smith's End Herts 105 D8

Smith's Green E Ches 168 E3
Smiths Green E Ches 184 G4
Smith's Green Essex 105 G11
Smith's Green Essex 106 C3
Smithston Aberds 302 G5
Smithstown Highld 299 B7
Smithton Highld 301 E7
Smithwood Green Suff 125 G8
Smithy Bridge Gtr Man 196 D2
Smithy Gate Flint 181 F11
Smithy Green E Ches 184 G2
Smithy Green Gtr Man 184 D5
Smithy Houses Derbys 170 F5
Smithy Lane Ends Lancs 194 E2
Smock Alley W Sus 35 D9
Smockington Leics 135 F9
Smoky Row Bucks 84 D4
Smoogro Orkney 314 F3
Smug Oak Herts 85 E10
Smyrton S Ayrs 244 G4
Smythe's Green Essex 88 B6
Snagshall E Sus 38 C3
Snaigow House Perth 286 C4
Snailbeach Shrops 131 C7
Snails Hill Som 29 E7
Snailswell Herts 104 E3
Snailwell Cambs 124 D2
Snainton N Yorks 217 C8
Snaisgill Durham 232 F5
Snaith E Yorks 198 C6
Snape N Yorks 214 C5
Snape Suff 127 F7
Snape Green Lancs 193 E11
Snape Hill Derbys 186 F5
Snape Hill S Yorks 198 G2
Snapper Devon 40 G5
Snaresbrook London 67 B11
Snarestone Leics 134 B6
Snarford Lincs 189 E9
Snargate Kent 39 B7
Snarraness Shetland 313 H4
Snatchwood Torf 78 E3
Snave Kent 39 B8
Sneachill Worcs 117 G8
Snead Powys 130 E6
Snead Common Worcs 116 D4
Sneads Green Worcs 117 D7
Sneath Common Norf 142 F3
Sneaton N Yorks 227 D7
Sneatonthorpe N Yorks 227 D8
Snedshill Telford 132 B4
Sneinton Nottingham 153 B11
Snelland Lincs 189 E9
Snelston Derbys 169 G11
Snetterton Norf 141 E9
Snettisham Norf 158 C3
Sneyd Green Stoke 168 F5
Sneyd Park Bristol 60 D5
Snibston Leics 153 G8
Snig's End Glos 98 F5
Snipeshill Kent 70 G2
Sniseabhal W Isles 297 H3
Snitter Northumb 252 C2
Snitterby Lincs 189 C7
Snitterfield Warks 118 F4
Snitterton Derbys 170 C3
Snitton Shrops 115 B11
Snittongate Shrops 115 B11
Snodhill Hereford 96 C6
Snodland Kent 69 G7
Snods Edge Northumb 242 G3
Snow End Herts 105 E8
Snow Hill E Ches 167 E10
Snow Hill W Yorks 197 C10
Snow Lea W Yorks 196 D5
Snow Street Norf 141 G11
Snowden Hill S Yorks 197 G9
Snowdown Kent 55 C8
Snowshill Glos 99 E11
Snydale W Yorks 198 D2
Soake Hants 33 E11
Soar Anglesey 178 G5
Soar Carms 94 F2
Soar Devon 9 G9
Soar Gwyn 146 B2
Soar Powys 95 E9
Soar-y-Mynydd Ceredig 112 G5
Soberton Hants 33 D10
Soberton Heath Hants 33 E10
Sockbridge Cumb 230 F6
Sockburn Darl 224 D6
Sockety Dorset 29 F7
Sodom Denb 181 G9
Sodom Shetland 313 G7
Sodom Wilts 62 C4
Sodylt Bank Shrops 148 B6
Soham Cambs 123 C11
Soham Cotes Cambs 123 B11
Soho London 67 C9
Soho Som 45 D7
Soho W Mid 133 F10
Solas W Isles 296 D4
Soldon Cross Devon 24 E4
Soldridge Hants 49 G7
Sole Street Kent 54 D5
Sole Street Kent 69 F7
Solfach = Solva Pembs 90 G5
Solihull W Mid 118 B2
Solihull Lodge W Mid 117 B11
Sollers Dilwyn Hereford 115 F8
Sollers Hope Hereford 98 E2
Sollom Lancs 194 D3
Solva = Solfach Pembs 90 G5
Somerby Leics 154 G5
Somerby Lincs 200 F5
Somercotes Derbys 170 E6
Somerdale Bath 61 F7
Somerford Dorset 19 C9
Somerford E Ches 168 B4
Somerford Staffs 133 B7
Somerford Keynes Glos 81 G8
Somerley W Sus 22 D4
Somerleyton Suff 143 D9
Somers Town London 67 C9
Somers Town Ptsmth 21 B8
Somersal Herbert Derbys 152 B2
Somersby Lincs 190 G4
Somersham Cambs 123 B7
Somersham Suff 107 B11
Somerton Newport 59 B10
Somerton Oxon 101 F9
Somerton Som 29 B7
Somerton Suff 124 G6
Somerton Hill Som 29 B7
Somerwood Shrops 149 G11
Sompting W Sus 35 G11
Sompting Abbotts W Sus 35 F11
Sonning Wokingham 65 D9
Sonning Common Oxon 65 C8
Sonning Eye Oxon 65 D9
Sontley Wrex 166 F4
Sookholme Notts 171 B8
Sopley Hants 19 B9
Sopwell Herts 85 D11
Sopworth Wilts 61 B10
Sorbie Dumfries 236 E6
Sordale Highld 310 C5
Sorisdale Argyll 288 C4
Sorley Devon 8 F4
Sorn E Ayrs 258 D3
Sornhill E Ayrs 258 C2
Sortat Highld 310 C6
Sotby Lincs 190 F2
Sothall S Yorks 186 E6
Sots Hole Lincs 173 C10
Sotterley Suff 143 G9
Soudley Shrops 131 E9
Soudley Shrops 150 D4
Soughley S Yorks 197 G7
Soughton = Sychdyn Flint 166 B2
Soulbury Bucks 103 F7
Soulby Cumb 222 C4
Soulby Cumb 230 F5
Souldern Oxon 101 E10
Souldrop Beds 121 E9
Sound E Ches 167 F10
Sound Shetland 313 H5
Sound Shetland 313 J6
Sound Heath E Ches 167 F10
Soundwell S Glos 60 D6
Sour Nook Cumb 230 C3
Sourhope Borders 263 E8
Sourin Orkney 314 C4
Sourlie N Ayrs 266 G6
Sourton Devon 12 C6
Soutergate Cumb 210 C4
South Acre Norf 158 G6
South Acton London 67 D7
South Alkham Kent 55 E8
South Allington Devon 9 G10
South Alloa Falk 279 C7
South Ambersham W Sus 34 C6
South Anston S Yorks 187 E8
South Ascot Windsor 66 F2
South Ashford Kent 54 E4
South Auchmachar Aberds 303 E9
South Baddesley Hants 20 B3
South Ballachulish Highld 284 B4
South Balloch S Ayrs 245 D8
South Bank Redcar 234 G6
South Bank York 207 C7
South Barrow Som 29 B10
South Beach Northumb 243 B8
South Beach = Marian-y-de Gwyn 145 C7
South Beddington London 67 G9
South Benfleet Essex 69 B9
South Bents T & W 243 E10
South Bersted W Sus 22 C6
South Blainslie Borders 271 G10
South Bockhampton Dorset 19 B9
South Bramwith S Yorks 198 E6
South Brent Devon 8 D3
South Brewham Som 45 F8
South Bromley London 67 C11
South Broomage Falk 279 E7
South Broomhill Northumb 252 D6
South Burlingham Norf 143 B7
South Cadbury Som 29 B10
South Cairn Dumfries 236 C1
South Carlton Lincs 189 F7
South Carlton Notts 187 E9
South Carne Corn 11 E10
South Cave E Yorks 208 G4
South Cerney Glos 81 F8
South Chailey E Sus 36 D5
South Chard Som 28 F4
South Charlton Northumb 264 E5
South Cheriton Som 29 C11
South Church Durham 233 F10
South Cliffe E Yorks 208 F3
South Clifton Notts 188 G4
South Clunes Highld 300 E5
South Cockerington Lincs 190 D5
South Common Devon 28 G4
South Cornelly Bridgend 57 E10
South Corriegills N Ayrs 256 C2
South Corrielaw Dumfries 248 G5
South Cove Suff 143 G9
South Creagan Argyll 289 E11
South Creake Norf 159 B7
South Crosland W Yorks 196 E6
South Croxton Leics 154 G3
South Croydon London 67 G10
South Cuil Highld 298 C3
South Dalton E Yorks 208 D5
South Darenth Kent 68 F5
South Denes Norf 143 C10
South Down Hants 33 C7
South Down Som 28 E2
South Duffield N Yorks 207 G9
South Dunn Highld 310 D5
South Earlswood Sur 51 D9
South Elkington Lincs 190 D3
South Elmsall W Yorks 198 E3
South Elphinstone E Loth 281 G7
South End Beds 103 B10
South End Bucks 103 F7
South End Cumb 210 G4
South End E Yorks 209 E9
South End Hants 31 D10
South-end Herts 86 B6
South End N Lincs 200 C6
South End Norf 141 E9
South Erradale Highld 299 B7
South Fambridge Essex 88 F5
South Farnborough Hants 49 C11
South Fawley W Berks 63 C11
South Ferriby N Lincs 200 C3
South Field E Yorks 200 B4
South Field Windsor 66 D3
South Flobbets Aberds 303 F7
South Garth Shetland 312 D7
South Garvan Highld 289 B11
South Glendale W Isles 297 K3
South Gluss Shetland 312 F5
South Godstone Sur 51 D11
South Gorley Hants 31 E11
South Gosforth T & W 242 D6
South Green Essex 89 B8
South Green Essex 87 G11
South Green Kent 69 G11
South Green Norf 157 F10
South Green Norf 159 G11
South Green Suff 126 B3
South Gyle Edin 280 G3
South-haa Shetland 312 E5
South Hackney London 67 C11
South Ham Hants 48 C6
South Hampstead London 67 C9
South Hanningfield Essex 88 F2
South Harefield London 66 B5
South Harrow London 66 B6
South Harting W Sus 34 D3
South Hatfield Herts 86 D2
South Hayling Hants 21 B10
South Hazelrigg Northumb 264 C3
South Heath Bucks 84 E6
South Heath Essex 89 B10
South Heighton E Sus 23 E7
South-heog Shetland 312 E5
South Hetton Durham 234 B3
South Hiendley W Yorks 197 E11
South Hill Corn 12 G2
South Hill N Som 43 B10
South Hill Pembs 72 C4
South Hinksey Oxon 83 E8
South Hole Devon 24 C2
South Holme N Yorks 216 D3
South Holmwood Sur 51 D7
South Hornchurch London 68 C4
South Huish Devon 8 G3
South Hykeham Lincs 172 C6
South Hylton T & W 243 F9
South Kelsey Lincs 189 B8
South Kensington London 67 D9
South Kessock Highld 300 E6
South Killingholme N Lincs 201 D7
South Kilvington N Yorks 215 C8
South Kilworth Leics 136 G2
South Kirkby W Yorks 198 E2
South Kirkton Aberds 293 C9
South Kiscadale N Ayrs 256 D2
South Knighton Devon 14 G2
South Knighton Leicester 136 C2
South Kyme Lincs 173 F11
South Lambeth London 67 D10
South Lancing W Sus 35 G11
South Lane S Yorks 197 F9
South Leigh Oxon 82 D5
South Leverton Notts 188 E3
South Littleton Worcs 99 B11
South Lopham Norf 141 G10
South Luffenham Rutland 137 C8
South Malling E Sus 36 E6
South Marston Swindon 63 B7
South Merstham Sur 51 C9
South Middleton Northumb 263 E11
South Milford N Yorks 206 G5
South Millbrex Aberds 303 E8
South Milton Devon 8 G4
South Mimms Herts 86 E2
South Molton Devon 26 B2
South Moor Durham 242 G5
South Moreton Oxon 64 B5
South Mundham W Sus 22 C5
South Muskham Notts 172 D3
South Newbald E Yorks 208 F4
South Newbarns Cumb 210 F4
South Newington Oxon 101 E8
South Newsham Northumb 243 B8
South Newton Wilts 46 G5
South Normanton Derbys 170 D6
South Norwood London 67 F10
South Nutfield Sur 51 D10
South Ockendon Thurrock 68 C5
South Ormsby Lincs 190 F5
South Ossett W Yorks 197 D9
South Otterington N Yorks 215 B7
South Owersby Lincs 189 C9
South Oxhey Herts 85 G10
South Park Sur 51 D8
South Pelaw Durham 243 G7
South Perrott Dorset 29 F7
South Petherton Som 28 D6
South Petherwin Corn 12 E2
South Pickenham Norf 141 C7
South Pill Corn 7 D8
South Pool Devon 8 G5
South Poorton Dorset 16 B6
South Port Argyll 284 E4
South Quilquox Aberds 303 F8
South Radworthy Devon 41 G9
South Rauceby Lincs 173 F8
South Raynham Norf 159 E7
South Reddish Gtr Man 184 C5
South Reston Lincs 190 E6
South Ruislip London 66 B6
South Runcton Norf 140 B2
South Scarle Notts 172 C4
South Shian Argyll 289 E11
South Shields T & W 243 D9
South Shore Blkpool 202 G2
South Side Durham 233 F8
South Side Orkney 314 D5
South Somercotes Lincs 190 C6
South Stainley N Yorks 214 G6
South Stainmore Cumb 222 C6
South Stanley Durham 242 G5
South Stifford Thurrock 68 D6
South Stoke Oxon 64 C6
South Stoke W Sus 35 F8
South Stour Kent 54 F4
South Street E Sus 36 D5
South Street Kent 54 B5
South Street Kent 68 G6
South Street Kent 69 G10
South Street Kent 70 F6
South Street London 52 B2
South Tawton Devon 13 C9
South Tehidy Corn 4 G3
South Thoresby Lincs 190 F6
South Tidworth Wilts 47 D8
South Tottenham London 67 B10
South Town Devon 14 E5
South Town Hants 49 F7
South Twerton Bath 61 G8
South Ulverston Cumb 210 D6
South View Hants 48 C6
South Voxter Shetland 313 G5
South Walsham Norf 161 G7
South Warnborough Hants 49 D8
South Weald Essex 87 G9
South Weirs Hants 32 G3
South Weston Oxon 84 F2
South Wheatley Corn 11 C10
South Wheatley Notts 188 D3
South Whiteness Shetland 313 J5
South Widcombe Bath 44 B5
South Wigston Leics 135 D11
South Willesborough Kent 54 E4
South Willingham Lincs 189 E11
South Wimbledon London 67 E9
South Wingate Durham 234 E4
South Wingfield Derbys 170 D5
South Witham Lincs 155 F8
South Wonford Devon 24 F5
South Wonston Hants 48 F3
South Woodford London 86 G6
South Woodham Ferrers Essex 88 F4
South Wootton Norf 158 E2
South Wraxall Wilts 61 G10
South Yardley W Mid 134 G2
South Yarrows Highld 310 E7
South Yeo Devon 25 G8
South Zeal Devon 13 C9
Southall London 66 C6
Southam Cumb 219 C9
Southam Glos 99 F9
Southam Warks 119 E8
Southampton Soton 32 E6
Southay Som 28 D6
Southborough Kent 52 E5
Southborough London 67 F7
Southborough London 68 F2
Southbourne Bmouth 19 C8
Southbourne W Sus 22 B3
Southbrook Wilts 45 G10
Southburgh Norf 141 C9
Southburn E Yorks 208 C5
Southchurch Sthend 70 B2
Southcoombe Oxon 100 F6
Southcote Reading 65 E7
Southcott Corn 11 B9
Southcott Devon 24 D6
Southcott Wilts 47 B7
Southcourt Bucks 84 C4
Southcrest Worcs 117 D10
Southdean Borders 250 B4
Southdene Mers 182 B6
Southdown Bath 61 G8
Southdown Corn 7 E8
Southease E Sus 36 F6
Southend Argyll 255 G7
Southend Bucks 65 B9
Southend Glos 80 F2
Southend London 67 E11
Southend Oxon 83 E9
Southend W Berks 64 D2
Southend W Berks 64 E5
Southend Wilts 63 E7
Southend-on-Sea Sthend 69 B11
Southerhouse Shetland 313 K5
Southerly Devon 12 D6
Southern Cross Brighton 36 F3
Southern Green Herts 104 E6
Southernby Cumb 230 D3
Southernden Kent 53 D11
Southerndown V Glam 57 G11
Southerness Dumfries 237 D11
Southery Norf 140 E2
Southey Green Essex 106 E5
Southfield Northumb 243 B7
Southfields London 67 E9
Southfields Thurrock 69 C7
Southfleet Kent 68 E6
Southford I o W 20 F6
Southgate Ceredig 111 B11
Southgate London 86 G3
Southgate Norf 159 C7
Southgate Norf 160 E2
Southgate Swansea 56 D5
Southgate W Sus 51 F9
Southill C Beds 104 C3
Southill Dorset 17 E9
Southington Hants 48 D4
Southlands Dorset 17 F9
Southleigh Devon 15 C10
Southmarsh Som 45 G8
Southmead Bristol 60 D5
Southminster Essex 89 F7
Southmoor Oxon 82 F5
Southoe Cambs 122 E3
Southolt Suff 126 D3
Southorpe P'boro 137 C11
Southover Dorset 17 C8
Southover E Sus 36 F6
Southover E Sus 37 B11
Southowram W Yorks 196 C6
Southport Mers 193 D10
Southpunds Shetland 313 L6
Southrepps Norf 160 B5
Southrey Lincs 173 B10
Southrop Glos 81 E11
Southrop Oxon 101 E7
Southrope Hants 49 E7
Southsea Ptsmth 21 B8
Southsea Wrex 166 E4
Southstoke Bath 61 G8
Southtown Norf 143 B10
Southtown Orkney 314 G4
Southtown Som 28 D4
Southtown Som 44 F5
Southville Devon 8 G4
Southville Torf 78 F3
Southwaite Cumb 230 C4
Southwark London 67 D10
Southwater W Sus 35 B11
Southwater Street W Sus 35 B11
Southway Plym 7 C9
Southway Som 44 E4
Southwell Dorset 17 G9
Southwell Notts 172 E2
Southwick Hants 33 F10
Southwick Northants 137 E10
Southwick Som 43 D11
Southwick T & W 243 F9
Southwick W Sus 36 F2
Southwick Wilts 45 B10
Southwold Suff 127 B10
Southwood Derbys 153 E7
Southwood Hants 49 B10
Southwood Norf 143 B7
Southwood Som 44 G5
Southwood Worcs 116 E4
Soval Lodge W Isles 304 F5
Sowber Gate N Yorks 215 B7
Sower Carr Lancs 202 E3
Sowerby N Yorks 215 C8
Sowerby W Yorks 196 C4
Sowerby Bridge W Yorks 196 C5
Sowerby Row Cumb 230 D3
Sowley Green Suff 124 G4
Sowood W Yorks 196 D5
Sowood Green W Yorks 196 D5
Sowton Devon 14 C5
Sowton Barton Devon 14 D2
Soyal Highld 309 K5
Soyland Town W Yorks 196 C4
Spa Common Norf 160 C5
Spacey Houses N Yorks 206 C2
Spalding Lincs 156 E4
Spaldington E Yorks 207 G11
Spaldwick Cambs 122 C2
Spalford Notts 172 B4
Spanby Lincs 155 B11
Spango Invclyd 276 G4
Spanish Green Hants 49 B7
Sparham Norf 159 F11
Sparhamhill Norf 159 F11
Spark Bridge Cumb 210 C6
Sparkbrook W Mid 133 G11
Sparkford Som 29 B10
Sparkhill W Mid 133 G11
Sparkwell Devon 7 D11
Sparl Shetland 312 G5
Sparnon Corn 1 E3
Sparnon Gate Corn 4 G3
Sparrow Green Norf 159 G9
Sparrow Hill Som 44 C2
Sparrowpit Derbys 185 E9
Sparrow's Green E Sus 52 G6
Sparsholt Hants 48 G2
Sparsholt Oxon 63 B10
Spartylea Northumb 232 B3
Spath Staffs 151 B11
Spaunton N Yorks 226 G4
Spaxton Som 43 F8
Spean Bridge Highld 290 E4
Spear Hill W Sus 35 D10
Spearywell Hants 32 B4
Speckington Som 29 C9
Speed Gate Kent 68 F5
Speedwell Bristol 60 E6
Speen Bucks 84 F4
Speen W Berks 64 F3
Speeton N Yorks 218 E2
Speke Mers 182 E6
Speldhurst Kent 52 E5
Spellbrook Herts 87 B7
Spelsbury Oxon 101 G7
Spelter Bridgend 57 C11
Spen W Yorks 197 B7
Spen Green E Ches 168 C4
Spencers Wood Wokingham 65 F8
Spennells Worcs 116 C6
Spennithorne N Yorks 214 B2
Spennymoor Durham 233 E11
Spernall Warks 117 E11
Spetchley Worcs 117 G7
Spetisbury Dorset 30 G6
Spexhall Suff 143 G7
Spey Bay Moray 302 C3
Speybank Highld 291 C10
Speybridge Highld 301 G10
Speyview Moray 302 E2
Spillardsford Aberds 303 D10
Spilsby Lincs 174 B6
Spindlestone Northumb 264 C5
Spinkhill Derbys 187 F7
Spinney Hill Northants 120 E5
Spinney Hills Leicester 136 C2
Spinningdale Highld 309 L6
Spion Kop Notts 171 B9
Spirthill Wilts 62 D3
Spital Mers 182 E4
Spital Windsor 66 D3
Spital Hill S Yorks 187 C10
Spital in the Street Lincs 189 D7
Spital Tongues T & W 242 D6
Spitalbrook Herts 86 D5
Spitalfields London 67 C10
Spitalhill Derbys 169 F11
Spithurst E Sus 36 D6
Spittal Dumfries 236 D5
Spittal E Loth 281 F9
Spittal E Yorks 207 C11
Spittal Highld 310 D5
Spittal Northumb 273 E10
Spittal Pembs 91 G9
Spittal Stirl 277 D10
Spittal Houses S Yorks 186 B5
Spittal of Glenmuick Aberds 292 E5
Spittal of Glenshee Perth 292 F3
Spittalfield Perth 286 C5
Spittlegate Lincs 155 C8
Spixworth Norf 160 F4
Splatt Corn 10 F4
Splatt Corn 11 D10
Splatt Devon 25 F10
Splatt Som 43 F8
Splayne's Green E Sus 36 C6
Splott Cardiff 59 D7
Spofforth N Yorks 206 C3
Spon End W Mid 118 B6
Spon Green Flint 166 C3
Spondon Derby 153 B8
Spooner Row Norf 141 D11
Spoonleygate Shrops 132 D6
Sporle Norf 158 G6
Spotland Bridge Gtr Man 195 E11
Spott E Loth 282 F3
Spratton Northants 120 C4
Spreakley Sur 49 E10
Spreyton Devon 13 B9
Spriddlestone Devon 7 E10
Spridlington Lincs 189 E8
Spring's Alley Oxon 84 F3
Spring Bank Cumb 229 G10
Spring Cottage Leics 152 F6
Spring End N Yorks 223 F9
Spring Gardens Som 45 D9
Spring Green Lancs 204 E4
Spring Grove London 67 D7
Spring Hill Gtr Man 196 F2
Spring Hill Lancs 195 B8
Spring Hill W Mid 133 D7
Spring Park London 67 F11
Spring Vale S Yorks 197 G9
Spring Valley I o M 192 E4
Springbank Glos 99 G8
Springboig Glasgow 268 C3
Springbourne Bmouth 19 C8
Springburn Glasgow 268 B2
Springfield Argyll 275 F11
Springfield Caerph 77 F11
Springfield Dumfries 239 D8
Springfield Essex 88 D2
Springfield Fife 287 F7
Springfield Gtr Man 194 F5
Springfield Highld 300 C6
Springfield M Keynes 103 D7
Springfield Moray 301 D10
Springfield W Mid 133 D8
Springfield W Mid 133 F9
Springfield W Mid 133 G11
Springfields Stoke 168 G5
Springhead Gtr Man 196 G3
Springhill E Renf 267 D10
Springhill I o W 20 B6
Springhill N Lnrk 269 D7
Springhill Staffs 133 B11
Springhill Staffs 133 C9
Springholm Dumfries 237 C10
Springkell Dumfries 239 B7
Springside N Ayrs 257 B9
Springthorpe Lincs 188 D5
Springwell Essex 105 C10
Springwell T & W 243 F7
Springwell T & W 243 F9
Springwells Dumfries 248 E3
Sproatley E Yorks 209 G9
Sproston Green W Ches 168 B2
Sprotbrough S Yorks 198 G4
Sproughton Suff 108 C2
Sprouston Borders 263 B7
Sprowston Norf 160 G4
Sproxton Leics 155 E7
Sproxton N Yorks 216 C2
Sprunston Cumb 230 B3
Spunhill Shrops 149 C8
Spurlands End Bucks 84 F5
Spurstow E Ches 167 D9
Spurtree Shrops 116 D2
Spynie Moray 302 C2
Spyway Dorset 16 C6
Square and Compass Pembs 91 E7
Squires Gate Blkpool 202 G2
Sraid Ruadh Argyll 288 E1
Srannda W Isles 296 C6
Sronphadruig Lodge Perth 291 F9
Stableford Shrops 132 D5
Stableford Staffs 150 B6
Stacey Bank S Yorks 186 C3
Stackhouse N Yorks 212 F6
Stackpole Pembs 73 F7
Stackpole Quay Pembs 73 F7
Stacksford Norf 141 E11
Stacksteads Lancs 195 C10
Stackyard Green Suff 107 B9
Staddiscombe Plym 7 E10
Staddlethorpe E Yorks 199 B10
Staddon Devon 24 C3
Staddon Devon 24 G5
Staden Derbys 185 G9
Stadhampton Oxon 83 F10
Stadhlaigearraidh W Isles 297 H3
Stadmorslow Staffs 168 D5
Staffield Cumb 230 C6
Staffin Highld 298 C4
Stafford Staffs 151 E8
Stafford Park Telford 132 B4
Stafford's Corner Essex 89 B7
Stafford's Green Dorset 29 C10
Stagbatch Hereford 115 F9
Stagden Cross Essex 87 C10
Stagehall Borders 271 G9
Stag's Head Devon 25 B11
Stagsden Beds 103 B9
Stagsden West End Beds 103 B9
Stain Highld 310 C7
Stainburn Cumb 228 F6
Stainburn N Yorks 205 D10
Stainby Lincs 155 E8
Staincliffe W Yorks 197 C8
Staincross S Yorks 197 E10
Staindrop Durham 233 G8
Staines Sur 66 E4
Staines Green Herts 86 C3
Stainfield Lincs 155 D11
Stainfield Lincs 189 G10
Stainforth N Yorks 212 F6
Stainforth S Yorks 198 E6
Staining Lancs 202 F3
Stainland W Yorks 196 D5
Stainsacre N Yorks 227 D8
Stainsby Derbys 170 B6
Stainsby Lincs 190 G4
Stainton Cumb 211 B10
Stainton Cumb 230 F5
Stainton Cumb 239 F9
Stainton Durham 223 B11
Stainton M'bro 225 C9
Stainton N Yorks 224 F2
Stainton S Yorks 187 C9
Stainton by Langworth Lincs 189 F9
Stainton le Vale Lincs 189 C11
Stainton with Adgarley Cumb 210 E5
Staintondale N Yorks 227 F9
Stair Cumb 229 G10
Stair E Ayrs 257 E10
Stairfoot S Yorks 197 F11
Stairhaven Dumfries 236 D4
Staithes N Yorks 226 B5
Stake Hill Gtr Man 195 F11
Stake Pool Lancs 202 D4
Stakeford Northumb 253 F7
Stakenbridge Worcs 117 B7
Stalbridge Dorset 30 D2
Stalbridge Weston Dorset 30 D2
Stalham Norf 161 D7
Stalham Green Norf 161 E7
Stalisfield Green Kent 54 C3
Stallen Dorset 29 D10
Stalling Busk N Yorks 213 B8
Stallingborough NE Lincs 201 E7
Stallington Staffs 151 B8
Stalmine Lancs 202 D3
Stalmine Moss Side Lancs 202 D3
Stalybridge Gtr Man 185 B7
Stambermill W Mid 133 G8
Stamborough Som 42 F4
Stambourne Essex 106 D4
Stambourne Green Essex 106 D4
Stamford Lincs 137 B10
Stamford Bridge E Yorks 207 B10
Stamford Bridge W Ches 167 B7
Stamford Hill London 67 B10
Stamfordham Northumb 242 C3
Stamperland E Renf 267 D11
Stamshaw Ptsmth 33 G10
Stanah Cumb 220 B6
Stanah Lancs 202 E3
Stanborough Herts 86 C2
Stanbridge C Beds 103 G9
Stanbridge Dorset 31 G8
Stanbridgeford C Beds 103 G9
Stanbrook Essex 106 F2
Stanbrook Worcs 98 B6
Stanbury W Yorks 204 F6
Stand Gtr Man 195 F9
Stand N Lnrk 268 B5
Standburn Falk 279 G8
Standeford Staffs 133 B8
Standen Kent 53 E11
Standen Hall Lancs 203 E10
Standen Street Kent 53 G10
Standerwick Som 45 C10
Standford Hants 49 G10
Standford Bridge Telford 150 E4
Standingstone Cumb 229 B11
Standingstone Cumb 229 E7
Standish Glos 80 D4
Standish Gtr Man 194 E5
Standish Lower Ground Gtr Man 194 F5
Standlake Oxon 82 E5
Standon Hants 32 B6
Standon Herts 105 G7
Standon Staffs 150 B6
Standon Green End Herts 86 B5

360 Sta – Str

Stane N Lnrk 269 D7
Stanecastle N Ayrs 257 B8
Stanfield Norf 159 E8
Stanford Stoke 168 E5
Stanford C Beds 104 C3
Stanford Kent 54 F6
Stanford Norf 141 E7
Stanford Shrops 148 G6
Stanford Bishop Hereford 116 G3
Stanford Bridge Worcs 116 D4
Stanford Dingley W Berks 64 E5
Stanford End Wokingham 65 G8
Stanford Hills Notts 153 E10
Stanford in the Vale Oxon 82 G4
Stanford-le-Hope Thurrock 69 C7
Stanford on Avon Northants 119 B11
Stanford on Soar Notts 153 E10
Stanford on Teme Worcs 116 D4
Stanford Rivers Essex 87 E8
Stanfree Derbys 187 G7
Stanground P'boro 138 D4
Stanhill Lancs 195 B8
Stanhoe Norf 158 B6
Stanhope Borders 260 D4
Stanhope Durham 232 D5
Stanhope Kent 54 E3
Stanion Northants 137 F8
Stank Cumb 210 E4
Stanklyn Worcs 117 C7
Stanks W Yorks 206 F3
Stanley Derbys 170 G6
Stanley Durham 242 G5
Stanley Lancs 194 F3
Stanley Notts 171 C7
Stanley Perth 286 D5
Stanley Shrops 132 G3
Stanley Shrops 132 G5
Stanley Staffs 168 E6
Stanley W Yorks 197 C10
Stanley Wilts 62 E3
Stanley Common Derbys 170 G6
Stanley Crook Durham 233 D9
Stanley Downton Glos 80 E4
Stanley Ferry W Yorks 197 C11
Stanley Gate Lancs 194 G2
Stanley Green E Ches 184 E5
Stanley Green Poole 18 C6
Stanley Green Shrops 149 B10
Stanley Hill Hereford 98 C3
Stanley Moor Staffs 168 E6
Stanley Pontlarge Glos 99 E9
Stanleytown Rhondda 77 G8
Stanlow Staffs 132 D5
Stanlow W Ches 182 F6
Stanmer Brighton 36 F4
Stanmore Hants 33 B7
Stanmore London 85 G11
Stanmore Shrops 132 E4
Stanmore W Berks 64 D3
Stanner Powys 114 F5
Stannergate Dundee 287 D8
Stanners Hill Sur 66 G3
Stannersburn Northumb 250 F6
Stanningfield Suff 125 F7
Stanningley W Yorks 205 G10
Stannington Northumb 242 B6
Stannington S Yorks 186 D4
Stanpit Dorset 19 C9
Stansbatch Hereford 114 E6
Stansfield Suff 124 G5
Stanshope Staffs 169 E10
Stanstead Suff 106 B6
Stanstead Abbotts Herts 86 C5
Stansted Kent 68 G6
Stansted Airport Essex 105 G11
Stansted Mountfitchet Essex 105 G10
Stanthorne W Ches 167 B11
Stanton Glos 99 E11
Stanton Mon 96 G6
Stanton Northumb 252 F4
Stanton Staffs 169 F10
Stanton Suff 125 C9
Stanton by Bridge Derbys 153 D7
Stanton-by-Dale Derbys 153 B9
Stanton Chare Suff 125 C9
Stanton Drew Bath 60 G5
Stanton Fitzwarren Swindon 81 G11
Stanton Gate Notts 153 B9
Stanton Harcourt Oxon 82 D6
Stanton Hill Notts 171 C7
Stanton in Peak Derbys 170 C2
Stanton Lacy Shrops 115 B9
Stanton Lees Derbys 170 C3
Stanton Long Shrops 131 E11
Stanton-on-the-Wolds Notts 154 C2
Stanton Prior Bath 61 G7
Stanton St Bernard Wilts 62 G5
Stanton St John Oxon 83 D9
Stanton St Quintin Wilts 62 D2
Stanton Street Suff 125 D9
Stanton under Bardon Leics 153 G9
Stanton upon Hine Heath Shrops 149 E11
Stanton Wick Bath 60 G6
Stantonbury M Keynes 102 C6
Stantway Glos 80 C2
Stanwardine in the Fields Shrops 149 E8
Stanwardine in the Wood Shrops 149 D8
Stanway Essex 107 G8
Stanway Glos 99 E11
Stanway Green Essex 107 G9
Stanway Green Suff 126 C4
Stanwell Sur 66 E5
Stanwell Moor Sur 66 E4
Stanwick Northants 121 C9
Stanwick-St-John N Yorks 224 C3
Stanwix Cumb 239 F10
Stanycliffe Gtr Man 195 F11
Stanydale Shetland 313 H4
Staoinebrig W Isles 297 H3
Stape N Yorks 226 G5
Stapehill Dorset 31 G9
Stapeley E Ches 167 F11
Stapenhill Staffs 152 E5
Staple Kent 55 B9
Staple Som 42 E6
Staple Cross Devon 27 C8
Staple Fitzpaine Som 28 D3
Staple Hill S Glos 61 D7
Staple Hill Worcs 117 C9
Staple Lawns Som 28 D3
Staplecross E Sus 38 C3
Staplefield W Sus 36 B3
Stapleford Cambs 123 G9
Stapleford Herts 86 B4
Stapleford Leics 154 F6
Stapleford Lincs 172 D5
Stapleford Notts 153 B9
Stapleford Wilts 46 F5
Stapleford Abbotts Essex 87 G8
Stapleford Tawney Essex 87 F8
Staplegrove Som 28 B2
Staplehay Som 28 C2
Staplehurst Kent 53 E9
Staplers I o W 20 D6
Staples Hill W Sus 35 B8
Staplestreet Kent 70 G5
Stapleton Bristol 60 D6
Stapleton Cumb 240 C2
Stapleton Hereford 114 D6
Stapleton Leics 135 D8
Stapleton N Yorks 198 D4
Stapleton N Yorks 224 C5
Stapleton Shrops 131 C9
Stapleton Som 29 C7
Stapley Som 27 E11
Staploe Beds 122 E2
Staplow Hereford 98 C3
Stapness Shetland 313 J4
Star Fife 287 G7
Star Pembs 92 E4
Star Som 44 B2
Star Hill Mon 79 E7
Stara Orkney 314 D2
Starbeck N Yorks 206 B2
Starbotton N Yorks 213 E9
Starcross Devon 14 E5
Stareton Warks 118 C6
Stargate T & W 242 E5
Starkholmes Derbys 170 D4
Starling Gtr Man 195 E9
Starlings Green Essex 105 E9
Starr's Green E Sus 38 D3
Starston Norf 142 G4
Start Devon 8 G6
Start Hill Essex 105 G10
Startforth Durham 223 B10
Startley Wilts 62 C2
Startop's End Bucks 84 C6
Starveall S Glos 61 B9
Starvecrow Kent 52 D5
Statenborough Kent 55 B10
Statford St Andrew Suff 127 E7
Statham Warr 183 D11
Stathe Som 28 B5
Stathern Leics 154 C5
Station Hill Cumb 229 B11
Station Town Durham 234 D4
Statland Common Norf 141 D10
Staughton Green Cambs 122 D2
Staughton Highway Cambs 122 E2
Staughton Moor Beds 122 E2
Staunton Glos 79 C8
Staunton Glos 98 F5
Staunton in the Vale Notts 172 G4
Staunton on Arrow Hereford 115 E7
Staunton on Wye Hereford 97 B7
Staupes N Yorks 205 B10
Staveley Cumb 211 B7
Staveley Cumb 221 F9
Staveley Derbys 186 G6
Staveley N Yorks 215 G7
Staveley-in-Cartmel Cumb 211 B7
Staverton Devon 8 C5
Staverton Glos 99 G7
Staverton Northants 119 E10
Staverton Wilts 61 G11
Staverton Bridge Glos 99 G7
Stawell Som 43 F11
Stawley Som 27 C9
Staxigoe Highld 310 D7
Staxton N Yorks 217 D10
Staylittle Ceredig 128 F2
Staylittle = Penffordd-Lâs Powys 129 E7
Staynall Lancs 202 E3
Staythorpe Notts 172 E3
Stead W Yorks 205 D8
Steam Mills Glos 79 B10
Stean N Yorks 213 E11
Steanbow Som 44 F5
Stearsby N Yorks 216 E2
Steart Som 29 B9
Steart Som 43 D9
Stebbing Essex 106 G3
Stebbing Green Essex 106 G3
Stechford W Mid 134 F2
Stede Quarter Kent 53 F11
Stedham W Sus 34 C5
Steel Northumb 241 F10
Steel Northumb 251 G9
Steel Bank S Yorks 186 D4
Steel Cross E Sus 52 G4
Steel Green Cumb 210 D3
Steel Heath Shrops 149 B10
Steele Road Borders 250 E2
Steelend Fife 279 C10
Steeleroad-end Borders 250 E2
Steen's Bridge Hereford 115 F10
Steep Hants 34 B2
Steep Lane W Yorks 196 C4
Steep Marsh Hants 34 B3
Steephill I o W 21 F7
Steeple Dorset 18 E4
Steeple Essex 88 E6
Steeple Ashton Wilts 46 B2
Steeple Aston Oxon 101 F9
Steeple Barton Oxon 101 G8
Steeple Bumpstead Essex 106 C3
Steeple Claydon Bucks 102 F3
Steeple Gidding Cambs 138 G2
Steeple Langford Wilts 46 F4
Steeple Morden Cambs 104 C5
Steeraway Telford 132 B3
Steeton W Yorks 204 E6
Stein Highld 298 D2
Steinmanhill Aberds 303 E7
Stella T & W 242 E5
Stelling Minnis Kent 54 D6
Stelvio Newport 59 B9
Stembridge Som 28 C6
Stembridge Swansea 56 C3
Stemster Highld 310 C5
Stemster Ho Highld 310 C5
Stenalees Corn 5 D10
Stenaquoy Orkney 314 C5
Stencoose Corn 4 F4
Stenhill Devon 27 E9
Stenhouse Dumfries 247 E8
Stenhouse Edin 280 G4
Stenhousemuir Falk 279 E7
Stenigot Lincs 190 E3
Stennack Corn 2 B5
Stenness Shetland 312 F4
Stenscholl Highld 298 C4
Stenso Orkney 314 D3
Stenson Derbys 152 D6
Stenton E Loth 282 G2
Stenton Fife 280 B5
Stentwood Devon 27 F10
Stenwith Lincs 154 B6
Stepaside Corn 5 F9
Stepaside Pembs 73 D10
Stepaside Powys 129 F11
Stepping Hill Gtr Man 184 D6
Steppingley C Beds 103 D10
Stepps N Lnrk 268 B3
Sterndale Moor Derbys 169 B10
Sternfield Suff 127 E7
Sterridge Devon 40 D5
Stert Wilts 46 B4
Sterte Poole 18 C6
Stetchworth Cambs 124 F2
Stevenage Herts 104 G4
Steven's Crouch E Sus 38 D2
Stevenston N Ayrs 266 G5
Stevenstone Devon 25 D8
Steventon Hants 48 D4
Steventon Oxon 83 G7
Steventon Shrops 115 C10
Steventon End Essex 105 C11
Stevington Beds 121 G9
Stewards Essex 87 D7
Steward's Green Essex 87 E7
Stewartby Beds 103 C10
Stewarton Argyll 255 F7
Stewarton E Ayrs 267 F8
Stewkley Bucks 103 F7
Stewkley Dean Bucks 102 F6
Stewley Som 28 D4
Stewton Lincs 190 D5
Steyne Cross I o W 21 D8
Steyning W Sus 35 E11
Steynton Pembs 72 D6
Stibb Corn 24 E2
Stibb Cross Devon 24 E6
Stibb Green Wilts 63 G8
Stibbard Norf 159 D9
Stibbington Cambs 137 D11
Stichill Borders 262 B6
Stick Hill Kent 52 E3
Sticker Corn 5 E9
Stickford Lincs 174 D5
Sticklepath Devon 13 C8
Sticklepath Devon 40 G5
Sticklepath Som 28 E4
Sticklepath Som 42 F4
Sticklinch Som 44 F5
Stickling Green Essex 105 E9
Stickney Lincs 174 D4
Stiff Street Kent 69 G11
Stiffkey Norf 177 E7
Stifford's Bridge Hereford 98 B4
Stileway Som 44 E3
Stillingfleet N Yorks 207 E7
Stillington N Yorks 215 F11
Stillington Stockton 234 G3
Stilton Cambs 138 F3
Stinchcombe Glos 80 F2
Stinsford Dorset 17 C10
Stiperstones Shrops 131 C7
Stirchley Telford 132 B4
Stirchley W Mid 133 G11
Stirkoke Ho Highld 310 D7
Stirling Aberds 303 E11
Stirling Stirl 278 C5
Stirtloe Cambs 122 D3
Stirton N Yorks 204 C5
Stisted Essex 106 G5
Stitchcombe Wilts 63 F8
Stitchin's Hill Worcs 116 G5
Stithians Corn 2 B6
Stittenham Highld 300 B6
Stivichall W Mid 118 B6
Stixwould Lincs 173 B11
Stoak W Ches 182 G6
Stobhill Northumb 252 G6
Stobhillgate Northumb 252 F6
Stobieside S Lnrk 258 B4
Stobo Borders 260 B5
Stoborough Dorset 18 D4
Stoborough Green Dorset 18 D4
Stobs Castle Borders 250 B2
Stobshiel E Loth 271 C9
Stobswood Northumb 252 E6
Stock Essex 87 F11
Stock Lancs 204 D3
Stock N Som 60 G3
Stock Green Worcs 117 F9
Stock Hill Suff 125 D9
Stock Wood Worcs 117 F10
Stockbridge Hants 47 G11
Stockbridge S Yorks 198 F5
Stockbridge W Sus 22 C5
Stockbridge W Yorks 205 E7
Stockbridge Village Mers 182 C6
Stockbury Kent 69 G10
Stockcross W Berks 64 F2
Stockend Glos 80 D4
Stocker's Head Kent 54 C3
Stockerston Leics 136 D6
Stockfield W Mid 134 G2
Stockheath Hants 22 B2
Stockholes Turbary N Lincs 199 F9
Stockiemuir Stirl 277 E10
Stocking Hereford 98 E2
Stocking Green Essex 105 D11
Stocking Pelham Herts 105 F9
Stockingford Warks 134 E6
Stockland Devon 28 G2
Stockland Bristol Som 43 E8
Stockland Green Kent 52 E5
Stockland Green W Mid 133 E11
Stockleigh English Devon 26 F5
Stockleigh Pomeroy Devon 26 G5
Stockley Wilts 62 F4
Stocklinch Som 28 D5
Stockport Gtr Man 184 C5
Stocks Green Kent 52 D5
Stocksbridge S Yorks 186 B3
Stocksfield Northumb 242 E3
Stockstreet Essex 106 G6
Stockton Hereford 115 E10
Stockton Norf 143 E7
Stockton Shrops 130 C5
Stockton Shrops 132 D4
Stockton Telford 150 F5
Stockton Warks 119 E8
Stockton Wilts 46 F3
Stockton Brook Staffs 168 E6
Stockton Heath Warr 183 D10
Stockton-on-Tees Stockton 225 B8
Stockton on Teme Worcs 116 D4
Stockton on the Forest York 207 B9
Stocktonwood Shrops 130 C5
Stockwell Devon 27 G7
Stockwell Glos 80 C6
Stockwell London 67 D10
Stockwell End W Mid 133 C7
Stockwell Heath Staffs 151 E11
Stockwitch Cross Som 29 C9
Stockwood Bristol 60 F6
Stockwood Dorset 29 F9
Stockwood Vale Bath 60 F6
Stodday Lancs 202 B5
Stodmarsh Kent 71 G8
Stody Norf 159 C11
Stoer Highld 307 G5
Stoford Som 29 E9
Stoford Wilts 46 F5
Stoford Water Devon 27 F9
Stogumber Som 42 F5
Stogursey Som 43 E8
Stoke Devon 24 C2
Stoke Hants 22 C2
Stoke Hants 48 C2
Stoke Medway 69 D10
Stoke Plym 7 D9
Stoke Suff 108 C3
Stoke W Mid 119 B7
Stoke Abbott Dorset 29 G7
Stoke Albany Northants 136 F6
Stoke Aldermoor W Mid 119 B7
Stoke Ash Suff 126 C2
Stoke Bardolph Notts 171 G10
Stoke Bishop Bristol 60 D5
Stoke Bliss Worcs 116 E3
Stoke Bruerne Northants 102 B4
Stoke by Clare Suff 106 C4
Stoke-by-Nayland Suff 107 D9
Stoke Canon Devon 14 B4
Stoke Charity Hants 48 F3
Stoke Climsland Corn 12 G3
Stoke Common Hants 33 C7
Stoke Cross Hereford 116 G2
Stoke D'Abernon Sur 50 B6
Stoke Doyle Northants 137 F10
Stoke Dry Rutland 137 D7
Stoke Edith Hereford 98 C2
Stoke End Warks 134 D3
Stoke Farthing Wilts 31 B9
Stoke Ferry Norf 140 D4
Stoke Fleming Devon 9 F7
Stoke Gabriel Devon 8 D6
Stoke Gifford S Glos 60 D6
Stoke Golding Leics 135 D7
Stoke Goldington M Keynes 102 B6
Stoke Green Bucks 66 C3
Stoke Hammond Bucks 103 F7
Stoke Heath Shrops 150 D3
Stoke Heath W Mid 135 G7
Stoke Heath Worcs 117 D8
Stoke Hill Devon 14 C4
Stoke Hill Hereford 98 B2
Stoke Holy Cross Norf 142 C4
Stoke Lacy Hereford 98 B2
Stoke Lane Hereford 116 G2
Stoke Lyne Oxon 101 F11
Stoke Mandeville Bucks 84 C4
Stoke Newington London 67 B10
Stoke on Tern Shrops 150 D2
Stoke-on-Trent Stoke 168 F5
Stoke Orchard Glos 99 F8
Stoke Park Suff 108 C3
Stoke Poges Bucks 66 C3
Stoke Pound Worcs 117 D9
Stoke Prior Hereford 115 F10
Stoke Prior Worcs 117 D8
Stoke Rivers Devon 40 F6
Stoke Rochford Lincs 155 D8
Stoke Row Oxon 65 C7
Stoke St Gregory Som 28 B4
Stoke St Mary Som 28 C3
Stoke St Michael Som 45 D7
Stoke St Milborough Shrops 131 G11
Stoke sub Hamdon Som 29 D7
Stoke Talmage Oxon 83 F11
Stoke Trister Som 30 B2
Stoke Wake Dorset 30 F3
Stoke Water Dorset 29 G7
Stoke Wharf Worcs 117 D9
Stokeford Dorset 18 D3
Stokegorse Shrops 131 G11
Stokeham Notts 188 F3
Stokeinteignhead Devon 14 G4
Stokenchurch Bucks 84 F3
Stokenham Devon 8 G6
Stokesay Shrops 131 G8
Stokesby Norf 161 G8
Stokesley N Yorks 225 D10
Stokoe Northumb 250 F6
Stolford Som 43 D8
Ston Easton Som 44 C6
Stondon Massey Essex 87 E9
Stone Bucks 84 C3
Stone Glos 79 F11
Stone Kent 38 B6
Stone Kent 68 E5
Stone S Yorks 187 D9
Stone Som 44 G5
Stone Staffs 151 C8
Stone Worcs 117 B7
Stone Allerton Som 44 C2
Stone Bridge Corner P'boro 138 C5
Stone Chair W Yorks 196 B6
Stone Cross E Sus 23 E10
Stone Cross E Sus 37 B8
Stone Cross E Sus 52 G6
Stone Cross Kent 52 F4
Stone Cross Kent 54 F4
Stone Cross Kent 55 B10
Stone Cross W Mid 133 E10
Stone-edge Batch N Som 60 E3
Stone Head N Yorks 204 E4
Stone Heath Staffs 151 B9
Stone Hill Kent 54 D2
Stone Hill Kent 54 F5
Stone Hill S Glos 60 E6
Stone Hill S Yorks 199 F7
Stone House Cumb 212 B5
Stone in Oxney Kent 38 B6
Stone Raise Cumb 230 B4
Stone Street Kent 52 C5
Stone Street Suff 107 D9
Stone Street Suff 143 G7
Stonea Cambs 139 E9
Stoneacton Shrops 131 E10
Stonebow Worcs 99 B8
Stonebridge Essex 70 B2
Stonebridge London 67 C8
Stonebridge N Som 43 B11
Stonebridge Norf 141 E8
Stonebridge Sur 51 D7
Stonebridge W Mid 134 G4
Stonebridge Green Kent 54 D2
Stonebroom Derbys 170 D6
Stonebyres Holdings S Lnrk 268 G6
Stonecloug h Gtr Man 195 F9
Stonecombe Devon 40 E6
Stonecrouch Kent 53 G7
Stonedge Borders 250 B3
Stoneferry Hull 209 G8
Stonefield Argyll 289 F11
Stonefield S Lnrk 268 D3
Stonefield Staffs 151 C7
Stonefield Castle Hotel Argyll 275 F9
Stonegate E Sus 37 B11
Stonegate N Yorks 226 D5
Stonegrave N Yorks 216 D3
Stonegravels Derbys 186 G5
Stonehall Kent 55 D9
Stonehall Worcs 99 B7
Stonehaugh Northumb 241 B7
Stonehaven Aberds 293 E10
Stonehill Sur 66 G4
Stonehills Hants 33 G7
Stonehouse Aberds 303 F8
Stonehouse Glos 80 D4
Stonehouse Northumb 240 F5
Stonehouse Plym 7 E9
Stonehouse S Lnrk 268 F5
Stonehouse Shrops 114 C6
Stonehouses Staffs 169 G7
Stoneleigh London 67 G8
Stoneleigh Warks 118 C6
Stoneley Green E Ches 167 E10
Stonely Cambs 122 D2
Stonepits Worcs 117 F10
Stonequarry W Sus 52 F2
Stoner Hill Hants 34 B2
Stones Green Essex 108 F3
Stonesby Leics 154 E6
Stonesfield Oxon 82 B5
Stonestreet Green Kent 54 F5
Stonethwaite Cumb 220 C5
Stoneton Warks 119 G9
Stonewells Moray 302 C2
Stonewood Kent 68 E5
Stoney Cross Hants 32 E3
Stoney Hill Worcs 117 C9
Stoney Middleton Derbys 186 F2
Stoney Royd W Yorks 196 C5
Stoney Stanton Leics 135 E9
Stoney Stoke Som 45 G8
Stoney Stratton Som 45 F7
Stoney Stretton Shrops 131 B7
Stoneyard Green Hereford 98 C4
Stoneybank E Loth 280 G6
Stoneybreck Shetland 313 N2
Stoneyburn W Loth 269 C9
Stoneycombe Devon 9 B7
Stoneycroft Mers 182 C5
Stoneyfield Gtr Man 195 E11
Stoneyfield Moray 301 D11
Stoneyford Derbys 170 F6
Stoneyford Devon 27 F8
Stoneygate Aberds 303 F10
Stoneygate Leicester 136 C2
Stoneyhills Essex 88 F6
Stoneykirk Dumfries 236 D2
Stoneylane Shrops 115 B11
Stoneywood Aberdeen 293 B10
Stoneywood Falk 278 E5
Stonganess Shetland 312 C7
Stonham Aspal Suff 126 F2
Stonnall Staffs 133 C11
Stonor Oxon 65 B8
Stonton Wyville Leics 136 D4
Stony Batter Hants 32 B3
Stony Cross Devon 25 B8
Stony Cross Hereford 98 B4
Stony Cross Hereford 115 D10
Stony Dale Notts 172 G2
Stony Gate T & W 243 G9
Stony Green Bucks 84 F5
Stony Heap Durham 242 G4
Stony Heath Hants 48 B5
Stony Houghton Derbys 171 B7
Stony Knaps Dorset 28 G5
Stony Littleton Bath 45 B8
Stony Stratford M Keynes 102 C5
Stonyfield Highld 300 B6
Stonyford Hants 32 D4
Stonyland Devon 25 B8
Stonymarsh Hants 32 B4
Stoodleigh Devon 26 D6
Stop-and-Call Pembs 91 D8
Stopes S Yorks 186 D3
Stopgate Devon 28 F2
Stopham W Sus 35 D8
Stopper Lane Lancs 204 D2
Stopsley Luton 104 G2
Stoptide Corn 10 F4
Stores Corner Suff 109 B7
Storeton Mers 182 E4
Storiths N Yorks 205 C7
Stormontfield Perth 286 E5
Stormore Wilts 45 D10
Stornoway W Isles 304 E6
Storridge Hereford 98 B4
Storrington W Sus 35 E9
Storrs Cumb 221 G7
Storrs S Yorks 186 D3
Storth Cumb 211 C9
Storwood E Yorks 207 E10
Stotfield Moray 302 B2
Stotfold C Beds 104 D4
Stottesdon Shrops 132 G3
Stoughton Leics 136 C2
Stoughton Sur 50 C3
Stoughton W Sus 34 E4
Stoughton Cross Som 44 D2
Stoul Highld 295 F9
Stoulton Worcs 99 B8
Stour Provost Dorset 30 C3
Stour Row Dorset 30 C4
Stourbridge W Mid 133 G8
Stourpaine Dorset 30 F5
Stourport on Severn Worcs 116 C6
Stourton Staffs 133 F7
Stourton W Yorks 206 G2
Stourton Warks 100 D5
Stourton Wilts 45 G9
Stourton Caundle Dorset 30 D2
Stourton Hill Warks 100 D6
Stout Som 44 G2
Stove Orkney 314 C6
Stove Shetland 313 L6
Stoven Suff 143 G8
Stow Borders 271 G9
Stow Lincs 155 B11
Stow Lincs 188 E5
Stow Bardolph Norf 140 B2
Stow Bedon Norf 141 D9
Stow cum Quy Cambs 123 E10
Stow Lawn W Mid 133 D8
Stow Longa Cambs 122 C2
Stow Maries Essex 88 F4
Stow-on-the-Wold Glos 100 F3
Stow Park Newport 59 B10
Stowbridge Norf 140 B2
Stowe Glos 79 D9
Stowe Hereford 96 B5
Stowe Lincs 156 G2
Stowe Shrops 114 C6
Stowe Staffs 152 G2
Stowe-by-Chartley Staffs 151 D10
Stowe Green Glos 79 D9
Stowell Glos 81 C9
Stowell Som 29 C11
Stowey Bath 44 B5
Stowfield Hereford 79 B9
Stowford Devon 12 B4
Stowford Devon 12 D4
Stowford Devon 24 E3
Stowford Devon 25 B10
Stowford Devon 41 E7
Stowgate Lincs 156 G3
Stowlangtoft Suff 125 D9
Stowmarket Suff 125 F10
Stowting Kent 54 E6
Stowting Common Kent 54 E6
Stowting Court Kent 54 E6
Stowupland Suff 125 F11
Straad Argyll 275 G11
Strachan Aberds 293 D8
Strachurmore Argyll 284 G5
Stradbroke Suff 126 C4
Stradishall Suff 124 G4
Stradsett Norf 140 C3
Stragglethorpe Lincs 172 E6
Straid S Ayrs 244 E4
Straight Soley Wilts 63 E10
Straith Dumfries 247 F8
Straiton Edin 270 B5
Straiton S Ayrs 245 C9
Straloch Aberds 303 G8
Straloch Perth 292 G2
Stramshall Staffs 151 B11
Strand Glos 80 C2
Strand London 67 C10
Strands Cumb 210 C3
Strang I o M 192 E4
Strangeways Gtr Man 184 B4
Strangford Hereford 97 F11
Stranghow Redcar 226 B3
Strangways Wilts 46 E6
Stranog Aberds 293 D10
Stranraer Dumfries 236 C2
Strata Florida Ceredig 112 D4
Stratfield Mortimer W Berks 65 G7
Stratfield Saye Hants 65 G7
Stratfield Turgis Hants 49 B7
Stratford C Beds 104 B3
Stratford Glos 99 D7
Stratford London 67 C11
Stratford Marsh London 67 C11
Stratford New Town London 67 C11
Stratford St Andrew Suff 127 E7
Stratford St Mary Suff 107 E10
Stratford Sub Castle Wilts 46 G6
Stratford Tony Wilts 31 B9
Stratford-upon-Avon Warks 118 F3
Strath Highld 299 B7
Strath Highld 310 D6
Strathallan Castle Perth 286 F3
Strathan Highld 295 F11
Strathan Highld 307 G5
Strathan Highld 308 C5
Strathan Skerray Highld 308 C6
Strathaven S Lnrk 268 G4
Strathavon Lo Moray 301 G11
Strathblane Stirl 277 F11
Strathcanaird Highld 307 J6
Strathcarron Highld 299 E9
Strathcoil Argyll 289 F8
Strathcoul Highld 310 D5
Strathdon Aberds 292 B5
Strathellie Aberds 303 C10
Strathgarve Lodge Highld 300 C4
Strathkinness Fife 287 F8
Strathmashie House Highld 291 D7
Strathmiglo Fife 286 F6
Strathmore Lodge Highld 310 E5
Strathpeffer Highld 300 D4
Strathrannoch Highld 300 B3
Strathtay Perth 286 B3
Strathvaich Lodge Highld 300 B3
Strathwhillan N Ayrs 256 B2
Strathy Highld 300 B6
Strathy Highld 310 C2
Strathyre Stirl 285 F9
Stratton Corn 24 F2
Stratton Dorset 17 C9
Stratton Glos 81 E8
Stratton Audley Oxon 102 F2
Stratton Chase Bucks 85 G7
Stratton-on-the-Fosse Som 45 C7
Stratton St Margaret Swindon 63 B7
Stratton St Michael Norf 142 E4
Stratton Strawless Norf 160 E4
Stravithie Fife 287 F9
Strawberry Bank Cumb 211 B8
Strawberry Hill E Sus 52 F5
Strawberry Hill London 67 E7
Strawberry Hill W Yorks 198 C2
Streat E Sus 36 D5
Streatham London 67 E10
Streatham Hill London 67 E10
Streatham Park London 67 E9
Streatham Vale London 67 E9
Streatley C Beds 103 F11
Streatley W Berks 64 C5
Street Cumb 222 D2
Street Lancs 202 C6
Street N Yorks 226 E4
Street Som 28 F5
Street Som 44 F3
Street Ash Som 28 E3
Street Ashton Warks 135 G9
Street Dinas Shrops 148 B6
Street End Hants 33 D9
Street End Kent 54 C6
Street End W Sus 22 D5
Street Gate T & W 242 F6
Street Houses N Yorks 206 D6
Street Lane Derbys 170 F5

Street Lydan Wrex 149 B8
Street of Kincardine Highld 291 B11
Street on the Fosse Som 44 F6
Streethay Staffs 152 G2
Streethouse W Yorks 197 C11
Streetlam N Yorks 224 F6
Streetly W Mid 133 D11
Streetly End Cambs 106 B2
Strefford Shrops 131 F8
Strelley Notts 171 G8
Strensall York 216 G2
Strensham Worcs 99 C8
Stretch Down Devon 26 E4
Stretcholt Som 43 E9
Strete Devon 8 F6
Stretford Gtr Man 184 C4
Stretford Hereford 115 F10
Stretford Court Hereford 115 F8
Strethall Essex 105 D9
Stretham Cambs 123 C10
Strettington W Sus 22 B5
Stretton Derbys 170 C5
Stretton Rutland 155 F8
Stretton Staffs 151 G7
Stretton Staffs 152 D5
Stretton W Ches 166 E6
Stretton Warr 183 E10
Stretton en le Field Leics 152 G6
Stretton Grandison Hereford 98 C2
Stretton-on-Dunsmore Warks 119 C8
Stretton-on-Fosse Warks 100 D4
Stretton Sugwas Hereford 97 C9
Stretton under Fosse Warks 135 G8
Stretton Westwood Shrops 131 D11
Strichen Aberds 303 D9
Strines Gtr Man 185 D7
Stringston Som 43 E7
Strixton Northants 121 E8
Stroat Glos 79 F9
Strode N Som 60 G4
Strom Shetland 313 J5
Stromeferry Highld 295 B10
Stromemore Highld 295 B10
Stromness Orkney 314 F2
Stronaba Highld 290 E4
Stronachlachar Stirl 285 F8
Stronachullin Lodge Argyll 275 F9
Stronchreggan Highld 290 F2
Stronchrubie Highld 307 H7
Strone Argyll 255 F7
Strone Argyll 274 G6
Strone Argyll 276 E3
Strone Highld 290 E3
Strone Highld 291 D9
Strone Highld 300 G5
Strone Invclyd 276 G5
Stronelairg Lodge Highld 291 C7
Stroneskar Argyll 275 C9
Stronmachair Stirl 285 G8
Stronmilchan Argyll 284 E5
Stronord Dumfries 236 C6
Stronsaul Argyll 276 F2
Strontian Highld 289 C10
Stronvar Stirl 285 E9
Strood Kent 53 G11
Strood Medway 69 F8
Strood Green Sur 51 D8
Strood Green W Sus 35 C8
Strood Green W Sus 50 G6
Strothers Dale Northumb 241 F11
Stroud Glos 80 D4
Stroud Hants 34 C2
Stroud Sur 50 F2
Stroud Green Essex 88 G5
Stroud Green Glos 80 D4
Stroud Green London 67 B10
Stroude Sur 66 F4
Strouden Bmouth 19 C8
Stroul Argyll 276 E4
Stroupster Highld 310 C7
Stroxton Lincs 155 C8
Stroxworthy Devon 24 D4
Struan Highld 294 B5
Struan Perth 291 G10
Strubby Lincs 191 E7
Structon's Heath Worcs 116 D5
Strugg's Hill Lincs 156 B5
Strumpshaw Norf 142 B6
Strutherhill S Lnrk 268 F5
Struthers Fife 287 G7
Struy Highld 300 F3
Stryd Anglesey 178 E2
Stryd y Facsen Anglesey 178 E4
Stryt-issa Wrex 166 F3
Stuartfield Aberds 303 E9
Stub Place Cumb 219 G11
Stubb Norf 161 E8
Stubbermere W Sus 22 B3
Stubber's Green W Mid 133 C10
Stubbings Windsor 65 C10
Stubbing's Green Suff 125 C11
Stubbington Hants 33 G9
Stubbins Lancs 195 D9
Stubbins Lancs 202 E6
Stubble Green Cumb 219 F11
Stubbles W Berks 64 D5
Stubbs Cross Kent 54 F3
Stubb's Green Norf 142 D5
Stubbs Green Norf 143 D7
Stubhampton Dorset 30 E6
Stubshaw Cross Gtr Man 194 G5
Stubton Lincs 172 F5
Stubwood Staffs 151 B11
Stuckgowan Argyll 285 G7
Stuckton Hants 31 E11
Stud Green E Ches 168 C2
Stud Green Windsor 65 D11
Studd Hill Kent 71 F7
Studdal Kent 55 D10
Studfold N Yorks 212 E6
Studham C Beds 85 B8
Studland Dorset 18 E6
Studley Warks 117 E11
Studley Wilts 62 E3
Studley Green Bucks 84 F3
Studley Green Wilts 45 B10
Studley Roger N Yorks 214 E5
Studley Royal N Yorks 214 E5
Stump Cross Essex 105 C10
Stumps Cross Glos 99 E11
Stuntney Cambs 123 B11
Stunts Green E Sus 23 C10
Sturbridge Staffs 150 C6
Sturford Wilts 45 E10
Sturgate Lincs 188 D5
Sturmer Essex 106 C3
Sturminster Common Dorset 30 E3
Sturminster Marshall Dorset 31 G7
Sturminster Newton Dorset 30 E3
Sturry Kent 71 G7
Stursdon Corn 24 E2
Sturton N Lincs 200 G3
Sturton by Stow Lincs 188 E5
Sturton le Steeple Notts 188 E3
Stuston Suff 126 B2
Stutton N Yorks 206 E5
Stutton Suff 108 E3
Styal E Ches 184 E4
Styants Bottom Kent 52 B5
Stydd Lancs 203 F9
Styrrup Notts 187 C10
Suainebost W Isles 304 B7
Suardail W Isles 304 E6
Succoth Aberds 302 F4
Succoth Argyll 284 G6
Suckley Worcs 116 G4
Suckley Green Worcs 116 G4
Suckley Knowl Worcs 116 G4
Suckquoy Orkney 314 H4
Sucksted Green Essex 105 F11
Sudborough Northants 137 G9
Sudbourne Suff 127 G8
Sudbrook Lincs 173 G7
Sudbrook Mon 60 B4
Sudbrooke Lincs 189 F8
Sudbury Derbys 152 C3
Sudbury London 67 C7
Sudbury Suff 107 C7
Sudden Gtr Man 195 E11
Suddie Highld 300 D6
Sudgrove Glos 80 D6
Suffield N Yorks 227 G9
Suffield Norf 160 C4
Sugnall Staffs 150 C5
Sugwas Pool Hereford 97 C9
Suisnish Highld 295 D7
Suladale Highld 298 D3
Sulaisiadar W Isles 304 E7
Sulby I o M 192 C4
Sulgrave Northants 101 B11
Sulgrave T & W 243 F8
Sulham W Berks 64 E6
Sulhampstead W Berks 64 F6
Sulhampstead Abbots W Berks 64 F6
Sulhampstead Bannister Upper End W Berks 64 F6
Sulhamstead W Berks 64 F6
Sulland Orkney 314 B5
Sullington W Sus 35 E9
Sullington Warren W Sus 35 E9
Sullom Shetland 312 F5
Sullom Voe Oil Terminal Shetland 312 F5
Sully V Glam 59 F7
Sumburgh Shetland 313 N6
Summer Bridge N Yorks 214 G4
Summer Heath Bucks 84 G2
Summer Hill E Sus 23 D9
Summer Hill W Mid 133 E9
Summerbridge N Yorks 214 G4
Summercourt Corn 5 D7
Summerfield Kent 55 B9
Summerfield Norf 158 B5
Summerfield Worcs 116 C6
Summerfield Park W Mid 133 F10
Summergangs Hull 209 G8
Summerhill Newport 59 B10
Summerhill Pembs 73 D11
Summerhill Staffs 133 B11
Summerhill Telford 150 F4
Summerhill Worcs 116 B6
Summerhill Wrex 166 E4
Summerhouse Darl 224 B4
Summerlands Cumb 211 B10
Summerlands Som 29 D8
Summerleaze Mon 60 B2
Summerley Derbys 186 F5
Summerscales N Yorks 205 C8
Summersdale W Sus 22 B5
Summerseat Gtr Man 195 E9
Summerston Glasgow 277 G11
Summerstown Bucks 102 G3
Summerstown London 67 E9
Summertown Oxon 83 D8
Summit Gtr Man 195 E10
Summit Gtr Man 196 D2
Summit Gtr Man 196 F2
Sun Green Gtr Man 185 B7
Sunbrick Cumb 210 E5
Sunbury Common Sur 66 E5
Sunbury-on-Thames Sur 66 F6
Sundayshill S Glos 79 G11
Sundaywell Dumfries 247 G8
Sunderland Argyll 274 G3
Sunderland Cumb 229 D9
Sunderland Lancs 202 B4
Sunderland T & W 243 F9
Sunderland Bridge Durham 233 D11
Sundhope Borders 261 D8
Sundon Park Luton 103 F11
Sundridge Kent 52 B3
Sundridge London 68 E2
Sunhill Glos 81 E10
Sunipol Argyll 288 D5
Sunk Island E Yorks 201 D9
Sunken Marsh Essex 69 C10
Sunningdale Windsor 66 F3
Sunninghill Windsor 66 F2
Sunningwell Oxon 83 E7
Sunniside Durham 233 D8
Sunniside T & W 242 F6
Sunniside T & W 243 G8
Sunny Bank Gtr Man 195 F10
Sunny Bower Lancs 203 G10
Sunny Hill Derby 152 C6
Sunnybrow Durham 233 E9
Sunnyfields S Yorks 198 F4
Sunnyhurst Blkburn 195 C7
Sunnylaw Stirl 278 B5
Sunnymead Oxon 83 D8
Sunnymeads Windsor 66 D4
Sunnymede Essex 87 G11
Sunnyside S Yorks 187 C7
Sunnyside W Sus 51 F11
Sunset Hereford 114 F6
Sunton Wilts 47 C8
Surbiton London 67 F7
Surby I o M 192 E3
Surfleet Lincs 156 D5
Surfleet Seas End Lincs 156 D5
Surlingham Norf 142 B6
Surrex Essex 107 G7
Suspension Bridge Norf 139 E10
Sustead Norf 160 B3
Susworth Lincs 199 G10
Sutcombe Devon 24 E4
Sutcombemill Devon 24 E4
Sutherland Grove Argyll 289 E11
Suton Norf 141 D11
Sutors of Cromarty Highld 301 C8
Sutterby Lincs 190 G5
Sutterton Lincs 156 B5
Sutterton Dowdyke Lincs 156 C5
Sutton Bucks 66 D4
Sutton C Beds 104 B4
Sutton Cambs 123 B8
Sutton Devon 8 G4
Sutton E Sus 23 F7
Sutton Kent 55 D10
Sutton Lincs 172 E5
Sutton London 67 G9
Sutton Mers 183 C8
Sutton N Yorks 198 B3
Sutton Norf 161 E7
Sutton Notts 154 B5
Sutton Notts 187 E11
Sutton Oxon 82 D6
Sutton P'boro 137 D11
Sutton Pembs 72 B6
Sutton S Yorks 198 E5
Sutton Shrops 132 F4
Sutton Shrops 149 D7
Sutton Shrops 149 G10
Sutton Shrops 150 C3
Sutton Som 44 G6
Sutton Staffs 150 E5
Sutton Suff 108 B6
Sutton Sur 50 D5
Sutton W Sus 35 D7
Sutton Abinger Sur 50 D6
Sutton at Hone Kent 68 E5
Sutton Bassett Northants 136 E5
Sutton Benger Wilts 62 D2
Sutton Bingham Som 29 E8
Sutton Bonington Notts 153 E10
Sutton Bridge Lincs 157 E9
Sutton Cheney Leics 135 C8
Sutton Coldfield W Mid 134 D2
Sutton Corner Lincs 157 D8
Sutton Courtenay Oxon 83 G8
Sutton Crosses Lincs 157 E8
Sutton Cum Lound Notts 187 E11
Sutton End W Sus 35 D7
Sutton Forest Side Notts 171 D8
Sutton Gault Cambs 123 B8
Sutton Green Sur 50 C4
Sutton Green W Ches 182 F5
Sutton Green Wrex 166 F6
Sutton Hall Shrops 132 C4
Sutton Heath Mers 183 C8
Sutton Hill Telford 132 C4
Sutton Holms Dorset 31 F9
Sutton Howgrave N Yorks 214 D6
Sutton in Ashfield Notts 171 D7
Sutton-in-Craven N Yorks 204 E6
Sutton in the Elms Leics 135 E10
Sutton Ings Hull 209 G8
Sutton Lakes Hereford 97 B10
Sutton Lane Ends E Ches 184 G6
Sutton Leach Mers 183 C8
Sutton Maddock Shrops 132 C4
Sutton Mallet Som 43 F11
Sutton Mandeville Wilts 31 B7
Sutton Manor Mers 183 C8
Sutton Marsh Hereford 97 C10
Sutton Mill N Yorks 204 E6
Sutton Montis Som 29 C10
Sutton on Hull Hull 209 G8
Sutton on Sea Lincs 191 E8
Sutton-on-the-Forest N Yorks 215 G11
Sutton on the Hill Derbys 152 C4
Sutton on Trent Notts 172 B3
Sutton Poyntz Dorset 17 E10
Sutton Row Wilts 31 B7
Sutton St Edmund Lincs 157 G7
Sutton St James Lincs 157 F7
Sutton St Michael Hereford 97 B10
Sutton St Nicholas Hereford 97 B10
Sutton Scarsdale Derbys 170 B6
Sutton Scotney Hants 48 F3
Sutton Street Suff 108 C6
Sutton under Brailes Warks 100 D6
Sutton-under-Whitestonecliffe N Yorks 215 C9
Sutton upon Derwent E Yorks 207 D10
Sutton Valence Kent 53 D10
Sutton Veny Wilts 45 E11
Sutton Waldron Dorset 30 D5
Sutton Weaver W Ches 183 F8
Sutton Wick Bath 44 B5
Sutton Wick Oxon 83 G7
Swaby Lincs 190 F5
Swadlincote Derbys 152 F6
Swaffham Norf 140 B6
Swaffham Bulbeck Cambs 123 E11
Swaffham Prior Cambs 123 E11
Swafield Norf 160 C5
Swaile's Green E Sus 38 C3
Swain House W Yorks 205 F9
Swainby N Yorks 225 E9
Swainshill Hereford 97 C9
Swainsthorpe Norf 142 C4
Swainswick Bath 61 F9
Swaithe S Yorks 197 G11
Swalcliffe Oxon 101 D7
Swalecliffe Kent 70 F6
Swallow Lincs 201 G7
Swallow Beck Lincs 173 B7
Swallowcliffe Wilts 31 B7
Swallowfield Wokingham 65 G8
Swallowfields Devon 8 C5
Swallowhurst Cumb 220 G2
Swallownest S Yorks 187 E7
Swallows Cross Essex 87 F10
Swalwell T & W 242 E6
Swampton Hants 48 C2
Swan Bottom Bucks 84 D6
Swan Green Suff 126 C5
Swan Green W Ches 184 G2
Swan Street Essex 107 F7
Swan Village W Mid 133 E9
Swanage Dorset 18 F6
Swanbach E Ches 167 G11
Swanbister Orkney 314 F3
Swanborough Swindon 81 G11
Swanbourne Bucks 102 F6
Swanbridge V Glam 59 F7
Swanland E Yorks 200 B3
Swanley Glos 80 F2
Swanley Kent 68 F4
Swanley Bar Herts 86 E3
Swanley Village Kent 68 F4
Swanmore Hants 33 D9
Swanmore I o W 21 C7
Swannay Orkney 314 D2
Swannington Leics 153 F8
Swannington Norf 160 F2
Swanpool Lincs 189 G7
Swanscombe Kent 68 E6
Swansea = Abertawe Swansea 56 C6
Swanside Mers 182 C6
Swanston Edin 270 B4
Swanton Abbott Norf 160 D5
Swanton Hill Norf 160 D5
Swanton Morley Norf 159 F10
Swanton Novers Norf 159 C10
Swanton Street Kent 53 B11
Swanwick Derbys 170 E6
Swanwick Hants 33 F8
Swanwick Green E Ches 167 F9
Swarby Lincs 173 G8
Swarcliffe W Yorks 206 F3
Swardeston Norf 142 C4
Swarister Shetland 312 E7
Swarkestone Derbys 153 D7
Swarland Northumb 252 C5
Swarraton Hants 48 F5
Swartha W Yorks 205 D7
Swarthmoor Cumb 210 D5
Swartland Orkney 314 D2
Swathwick Derbys 170 B5
Swaton Lincs 156 B2
Swavesey Cambs 123 D7
Sway Hants 19 B11
Swayfield Lincs 155 E9
Swaythling Soton 32 D6
Sweet Green Worcs 116 E2
Sweetham Devon 14 B3
Sweethaws E Sus 37 B8
Sweethay Som 28 C2
Sweetholme Cumb 221 B11
Sweethouse Corn 5 C11
Sweets Corn 11 B9
Sweetshouse Corn 5 C11
Sweffling Suff 126 E6
Swell Som 28 C5
Swelling Hill Hants 49 G7
Swepstone Leics 153 G7
Swerford Oxon 101 E7
Swettenham E Ches 168 B4
Swetton N Yorks 214 E3
Swffryd Caerph 78 F2
Swift's Green Kent 53 E11
Swiftsden E Sus 38 B2
Swilland Suff 126 G3
Swillbrook Lancs 202 G5
Swillington W Yorks 206 G3
Swillington Common W Yorks 206 G3
Swimbridge Devon 25 B10
Swimbridge Newland Devon 40 G6
Swinbrook Oxon 82 C3
Swincliffe N Yorks 205 B10
Swincliffe W Yorks 197 B8
Swincombe Devon 41 E7
Swinden N Yorks 204 C3
Swinderby Lincs 172 C5
Swindon Glos 99 G8
Swindon Staffs 133 E7
Swindon Swindon 63 C7
Swine E Yorks 209 F8
Swinefleet E Yorks 199 C9
Swineford S Glos 61 F7
Swineshead Beds 121 D11
Swineshead Lincs 174 G2
Swineshead Bridge Lincs 174 G2
Swinethorpe Lincs 172 B5
Swiney Highld 310 F6
Swinford Leics 119 B11
Swinford Oxon 82 D6
Swingate Notts 171 G8
Swingbrow Cambs 139 F7
Swingfield Minnis Kent 55 E8
Swingfield Street Kent 55 E8
Swingleton Green Suff 107 B9
Swinhoe Northumb 264 D6
Swinhope Lincs 190 B2
Swining Shetland 312 G6
Swinister Shetland 312 E5
Swinister Shetland 313 L6
Swinithwaite N Yorks 213 B10
Swinmore Common Hereford 98 C3
Swinnie Borders 262 F4
Swinnow Moor W Yorks 205 G10
Swinscoe Staffs 169 F10
Swinside Cumb 229 G10
Swinside Townfoot Borders 262 F6
Swinstead Lincs 155 E10
Swinton Borders 272 F6
Swinton Glasgow 268 C3
Swinton Gtr Man 195 G9
Swinton N Yorks 214 D4
Swinton N Yorks 216 E5
Swinton S Yorks 186 B6
Swinton Bridge S Yorks 187 B7
Swinton Hill Borders 272 F6
Swinton Park Gtr Man 195 G9
Swintonmill Borders 272 F6
Swiss Valley Carms 75 E8
Swithland Leics 153 G10
Swordale Highld 300 C5
Swordale Highld 309 K6
Swordland Highld 295 F9
Swordly Highld 308 C7
Sworton Heath E Ches 183 E11
Swyddffynnon Ceredig 112 D3
Swynnerton Staffs 151 B7
Swyre Dorset 16 D6
Sycamore Devon 28 F3
Sychdyn = Soughton Flint 166 B2
Sychtyn Powys 129 B9
Sydallt Wrex 166 D4
Syde Glos 81 C7
Sydenham London 67 E11
Sydenham Oxon 84 E2
Sydenham Som 43 F10
Sydenham Damerel Devon 12 F4
Syderstone Norf 158 C6
Sydling St Nicholas Dorset 17 B8
Sydmonton Hants 48 B3
Sydney E Ches 168 D2
Syerston Notts 172 F2
Syke Gtr Man 195 D11
Sykehouse S Yorks 198 D6
Sykes Lancs 203 C8
Syleham Suff 126 B4
Sylen Carms 75 D8
Symbister Shetland 313 G7
Symington Borders 271 F8
Symington S Ayrs 257 C9
Symington S Lnrk 259 B11
Symonds Green Herts 104 F4
Symonds Yat Hereford 79 B9
Symondsbury Dorset 16 C4
Synderford Dorset 28 G5
Synod Inn = Post Mawr Ceredig 111 G8
Synton Borders 261 E11
Synton Mains Borders 261 E11
Synwell Glos 80 G3
Syre Highld 308 E6
Syreford Glos 99 G10
Syresham Northants 102 C2
Syster Highld 310 C6
Syston Leics 154 G2
Syston Lincs 172 G6
Sytch Ho Green Shrops 132 E5
Sytch Lane Telford 150 E2
Sytchampton Worcs 116 D6
Sywell Northants 120 D6

T

Taagan Highld 299 C10
Tabley Hill E Ches 184 F2
Tabor Gwyn 146 F5
Tabost W Isles 305 G5
Tàbost W Isles 304 B7
Tachbrook Mallory Warks 118 E6
Tacker Street Som 42 F4
Tackley Oxon 101 G9
Tacleit W Isles 304 E3
Tacolneston Norf 142 D2
Tadcaster N Yorks 206 E5
Tadden Dorset 31 G7
Taddington Derbys 185 G10
Taddington Glos 99 E11
Taddiport Devon 25 D7
Tadhill Som 45 D7
Tadley Hants 64 G6
Tadley Oxon 64 B4
Tadlow Beds 104 B5
Tadlow C Beds 104 B5
Tadmarton Oxon 101 D7
Tadnoll Dorset 17 D11
Tadwick Bath 61 E8
Tadworth Sur 51 B8
Tafarn-y-bwlch Pembs 91 E11
Tafarn-y-gelyn Denb 165 C11
Tafarnau-bach Bl Gwent 77 C10
Taff Merthyr Garden Village M Tydf 77 F10
Taff's Well Rhondda 58 C6
Tafolwern Powys 129 C7
Tai Conwy 164 C3
Tai-bach Powys 148 D3
Tai-mawr Conwy 165 G7
Tai-morfa Gwyn 144 D5
Tai-nant Wrex 166 F3
Tai-Ucha Denb 165 D8
Taibach Neath 57 D9
Taigh a Ghearraidh W Isles 296 D3
Taigh Bhalaigh W Isles 296 D3
Tain Highld 309 L7
Tain Highld 310 C6
Tainlon Gwyn 162 E6
Tai'r-Bull Powys 95 F9
Tai'r-heol Caerph 77 G10
Tai'r-ysgol Swansea 57 B7
Tairbeart W Isles 305 H3
Tairgwaith Neath 76 C2
Takeley Essex 105 G11
Takeley Street Essex 105 G10
Tal-sarn Ceredig 111 F10
Tal-y-bont Ceredig 128 F3
Tal-y-Bont Conwy 164 B3
Tal-y-bont Gwyn 145 E11
Tal-y-bont Gwyn 179 G10
Tal-y-cafn Conwy 180 G3
Tal-y-coed Mon 78 B6
Tal-y-llyn Gwyn 128 B4
Tal-y-waenydd Gwyn 163 F11
Tal-y-wern Powys 128 C6
Talachar = Laugharne Carms 74 C4
Talachddu Powys 95 E11
Talacre Flint 181 E10
Talardd Gwyn 147 D7
Talaton Devon 15 B7
Talbenny Pembs 72 C4
Talbot Green Rhondda 58 C4
Talbot Heath Poole 19 C7
Talbot Village Poole 19 C7
Talbot Woods Bmouth 19 C7
Talbot's End S Glos 80 G2
Tale Devon 27 G9
Talerddig Powys 129 C8
Talgarreg Ceredig 111 G8
Talgarth Powys 96 E3
Talgarth's Well Swansea 56 D2
Talisker Highld 294 B5
Talke Staffs 168 E4
Talke Pits Staffs 168 E4
Talkin Cumb 240 F3
Talla Linnfoots Borders 260 E4
Talladale Highld 299 B9
Tallaminnoch S Ayrs 245 D10
Talland Corn 6 E4
Tallarn Green Wrex 166 G6
Tallentire Cumb 229 D8
Talley Carms 94 E2
Tallington Lincs 137 B11
Talmine Highld 308 C5
Talog Carms 92 F6
Talsarn Carms 94 F5
Talsarnau Gwyn 146 B2
Talskiddy Corn 5 B8
Talwrn Anglesey 179 F7
Talwrn Wrex 166 F3
Talybont-on-Usk Powys 96 G2
Talygarn Rhondda 58 C4
Talyllyn Powys 96 F2
Talysarn Gwyn 163 E7
Talywain Torf 78 E3
Tamanabhagh W Isles 304 F2
Tame Bridge N Yorks 225 D10
Tame Water Gtr Man 196 F3
Tamer Lane End Gtr Man 194 G6
Tamerton Foliot Plym 7 C9
Tamfourhill Falk 279 E7
Tamworth Staffs 134 C4
Tamworth Green Lincs 174 G5
Tan Hills Durham 233 B11
Tan Hinon Powys 129 F7
Tan-lan Conwy 164 C3
Tan-lan Gwyn 163 G10
Tan Office Suff 126 E2
Tan Office Green Suff 124 F5
Tan-y-bwlch Gwyn 163 G11
Tan-y-fron Conwy 165 C7
Tan-y-graig Anglesey 179 F8
Tan-y-graig Gwyn 144 B6
Tan-y-groes Ceredig 92 B5
Tan-y-mynydd Gwyn 144 C6
Tan-y-pistyll Powys 147 D11
Tan-yr-allt Denb 181 E9
Tan-yr-allt Gwyn 163 E7
Tancred N Yorks 206 B5
Tandem W Yorks 197 D7
Tanden Kent 54 F2
Tandlehill Renfs 267 C8
Tandridge Sur 51 C11
Tanerdy Carms 93 G8
Tanfield Durham 242 F5
Tanfield Lea Durham 242 G5
Tang N Yorks 205 B10
Tang Hall York 207 C8
Tangasdal W Isles 297 M2
Tangiers Pembs 73 B7
Tangley Hants 47 C10
Tanglwst Carms 92 E6
Tangmere W Sus 22 B6
Tangwick Shetland 312 F4
Tangy Argyll 255 E7
Tanhouse Lancs 194 F3
Tanis Wilts 62 G3
Tankersley S Yorks 197 G10
Tankerton Kent 70 F6
Tanlan Flint 181 E10
Tanlan Banks Flint 181 E10
Tannach Highld 310 E7
Tannachie Aberds 293 E9
Tannadice Angus 287 B8
Tanner's Green Worcs 117 C11
Tannington Suff 126 D4
Tannington Place Suff 126 D4
Tannochside N Lnrk 268 C4
Tansley Derbys 170 D4
Tansley Hill W Mid 133 F9
Tansley Knoll Derbys 170 C4
Tansor Northants 137 E11
Tanterton Lancs 202 G6
Tantobie Durham 242 G5
Tanton N Yorks 225 C10
Tanwood Worcs 117 C8
Tanworth-in-Arden Warks 118 C2
Tanyfron Wrex 166 E3
Tanygrisiau Gwyn 163 F11
Tanyrhydiau Ceredig 112 D4
Tanysgafell Gwyn 163 B10
Taobh a Chaolais W Isles 297 K3
Taobh a' Ghlinne W Isles 305 G5
Taobh a Thuath Loch Aineort W Isles 297 J3
Taobh a Tuath Loch Baghasdail W Isles 297 J3
Taobh Siar W Isles 305 H3
Taobh Tuath W Isles 296 C5
Taplow Bucks 66 C2
Tapnage Hants 33 E9
Tapton Derbys 186 G5
Tapton Hill S Yorks 186 D4
Tarbat Ho Highld 301 B7
Tarbert Argyll 255 B7
Tarbert Argyll 275 E7
Tarbert Argyll 275 G9
Tarbet Argyll 285 G7
Tarbet Highld 295 F9
Tarbet Highld 306 E6
Tarbock Green Mers 183 D7
Tarbolton S Ayrs 257 D10
Tarbrax S Lnrk 269 D10
Tardebigge Worcs 117 D10
Tardy Gate Lancs 194 B4
Tarfside Angus 292 F6
Tarland Aberds 292 C6
Tarleton Lancs 194 C3
Tarleton Moss Lancs 194 C2
Tarlogie Highld 309 L7
Tarlscough Lancs 194 E2
Tarlton Glos 81 F7
Tarn W Yorks 205 F9
Tarnbrook Lancs 203 B7
Tarnock Som 43 C11
Tarns Cumb 229 B8
Tarnside Cumb 221 G8
Tarporley W Ches 167 C9
Tarpots Essex 69 B9
Tarr Som 42 G6
Tarraby Cumb 239 F10
Tarrant Crawford Dorset 30 G6
Tarrant Gunville Dorset 30 E6
Tarrant Hinton Dorset 30 E6
Tarrant Keyneston Dorset 30 G6
Tarrant Launceston Dorset 30 F6
Tarrant Monkton Dorset 30 F6
Tarrant Rawston Dorset 30 F6
Tarrant Rushton Dorset 30 F6
Tarrel Highld 311 L2
Tarring Neville E Sus 36 G6
Tarrington Hereford 98 C2
Tarrington Common Hereford 98 D2
Tarryblake Ho Moray 302 E5
Tarsappie Perth 286 E5
Tarskavaig Highld 295 E7
Tarts Hill Shrops 149 B8
Tarves Aberds 303 F8
Tarvie Highld 300 D4
Tarvie Perth 292 G2
Tarvin W Ches 167 B7
Tarvin Sands W Ches 167 B7
Tasburgh Norf 142 D4
Tasley Shrops 132 E3
Taston Oxon 101 G7
Tat Bank W Mid 133 F9
Tatenhill Staffs 152 E4
Tatenhill Common Staffs 152 E3
Tathall End M Keynes 102 B6
Tatham Lancs 212 F2
Tathwell Lincs 190 E4
Tatling End Bucks 66 B4
Tatsfield Sur 52 B2
Tattenhall W Ches 167 D7
Tattenhoe M Keynes 102 E6
Tatterford Norf 159 D7
Tattersett Norf 158 C6
Tattershall Lincs 174 D2
Tattershall Bridge Lincs 173 D11
Tattershall Thorpe Lincs 174 D2
Tattingstone Suff 108 D2
Tattingstone White Horse Suff 108 D2
Tattle Bank Warks 118 E3
Tatton Dale E Ches 184 E2
Tatworth Som 28 F4
Taunton Gtr Man 196 G2
Taunton Som 28 C2
Taverham Norf 160 G3

362 Tav – Tib

Taverners Green Essex 87 B9
Tavernspite Pembs 73 C11
Tavistock Devon 12 G5
Taw Green Devon 13 B9
Tawstock Devon 25 B9
Taxal Derbys 185 F8
Tay Bridge Dundee 287 E8
Tayinloan Argyll 255 C7
Taymouth Castle Perth 285 C11
Taynish Argyll 275 E8
Taynton Glos 98 G4
Taynton Oxon 82 C2
Taynuilt Argyll 284 D4
Tayport Fife 287 E8
Tayvallich Argyll 275 E8
Tea Green Herts 104 G2
Tealby Lincs 189 C11
Tealing Angus 287 D8
Team Valley T & W 242 E6
Teams T & W 242 E6
Teanford Staffs 169 G8
Teangue Highld 295 E8
Teanna Mhachair W Isles 296 E3
Teasley Mead E Sus 52 F4
Tebay Cumb 222 E2
Tebworth C Beds 103 F9
Tedburn St Mary Devon 14 C2
Teddington Glos 99 E9
Teddington London 67 E7
Teddington Hands Worcs 99 E9
Tedsmore Shrops 149 D7
Tedstone Delamere Hereford 116 F3
Tedstone Wafer Hereford 116 F3
Teesville Redcar 225 B10
Teeton Northants 120 C3
Teffont Evias Wilts 46 G3
Teffont Magna Wilts 46 G3
Tegryn Pembs 92 E4
Teigh Rutland 155 F7
Teign Village Devon 14 E2
Teigncombe Devon 13 D9
Teigngrace Devon 14 G2
Teignmouth Devon 14 G4
Telford Telford 132 B3
Telham E Sus 38 E3
Tellisford Som 45 B10
Telscombe E Sus 36 G6
Telscombe Cliffs E Sus 36 G5
Templand Dumfries 248 F3
Temple Corn 11 G8
Temple Glasgow 267 B10
Temple Midloth 270 D6
Temple Wilts 45 E10
Temple Windsor 65 C10
Temple Balsall W Mid 118 B4
Temple Bar Carms 75 B9
Temple Bar Ceredig 111 G10
Temple Bar W Sus 22 B5
Temple Cloud Bath 44 B6
Temple Cowley Oxon 83 E8
Temple End Essex 106 C6
Temple End Suff 124 G3
Temple Ewell Kent 55 E9
Temple Fields Essex 87 C7
Temple Grafton Warks 118 G2
Temple Guiting Glos 99 F11
Temple Herdewyke Warks 119 G7
Temple Hill Kent 68 D5
Temple Hirst N Yorks 198 C6
Temple Normanton Derbys 170 B6
Temple Sowerby Cumb 231 F8
Templeborough S Yorks 186 C6
Templecombe Som 30 C2
Templehall Fife 280 C5
Templeman's Ash Dorset 28 G6
Templeton Devon 26 E5
Templeton Pembs 73 C10
Templeton W Berks 63 F11
Templeton Bridge Devon 26 E5
Templetown Durham 242 G4
Tempsford C Beds 122 G3
Ten Acres W Mid 133 G11
Ten Mile Bank Norf 140 D2
Tenandry Perth 291 G11
Tenbury Wells Worcs 115 D11
Tenby = Dinbych-y-Pysgod Pembs 73 E10
Tencreek Corn 6 E4
Tendring Essex 108 G2
Tendring Green Essex 108 F2
Tendring Heath Essex 108 F2
Tenston Orkney 314 E2
Tenterden Kent 53 G11
Terfyn Conwy 180 F6
Terfyn Gwyn 163 C9
Terhill Som 43 G7
Terling Essex 88 B3
Ternhill Shrops 150 C2
Terpersie Castle Aberds 302 G5
Terras Corn 5 E8
Terregles Banks Dumfries 237 B11
Terrible Down E Sus 23 B7
Terrick Bucks 84 D4
Terriers Bucks 84 G5
Terrington N Yorks 216 E3
Terrington St Clement Norf 157 E10
Terrington St John Norf 157 G10
Terryhorn Aberds 302 F4
Terry's Green Warks 118 C2
Terwick Common W Sus 34 C4
Teston Kent 53 C8
Testwood Hants 32 E5
Tetbury Glos 80 G5
Tetbury Upton Glos 80 F5
Tetchill Shrops 149 C7
Tetchwick Bucks 83 B11
Tetcott Devon 12 B2
Tetford Lincs 190 G4
Tetley N Lincs 199 E9
Tetney Lincs 201 G10
Tetney Lock Lincs 201 G10
Tetsworth Oxon 83 E11
Tettenhall W Mid 133 D7
Tettenhall Wood W Mid 133 D7
Tetworth Cambs 122 G4
Teuchan Aberds 303 F10
Teversal Notts 171 C7
Teversham Cambs 123 F9
Teviothead Borders 249 B10
Tewel Aberds 293 E10
Tewin Herts 86 C3
Tewin Wood Herts 86 B3
Tewitfield Lancs 211 E10
Tewkesbury Glos 99 E7
Teynham Kent 70 G3
Teynham Street Kent 70 G3
Thackley W Yorks 205 F9
Thackley End W Yorks 205 F9
Thackthwaite Cumb 229 G8
Thainston Aberds 293 F8
Thakeham W Sus 35 D10
Thame Oxon 84 D2
Thames Ditton Sur 67 F7
Thames Haven Thurrock 69 C8
Thames Head Glos 81 F7
Thamesmead London 68 C3
Thanington Kent 54 B6
Thankerton S Lnrk 259 B11
Tharston Norf 142 E3
Thatcham W Berks 64 F4
Thatto Heath Mers 183 C8
Thaxted Essex 106 E2
The Aird Highld 298 D4
The Alders Staffs 134 C3
The Arms Norf 141 D7
The Bage Hereford 96 C5
The Balloch Perth 286 F2
The Bank E Ches 168 D4
The Banks Gtr Man 185 D7
The Banks Wilts 62 D4
The Barony E Ches 167 E11
The Barony Orkney 314 D2
The Barton Wilts 62 D5
The Batch S Glos 61 E7
The Beeches Glos 81 E8
The Bell Gtr Man 194 F4
The Bents Staffs 151 C10
The Blythe Staffs 151 D10
The Bog Shrops 131 D7
The Borough Dorset 30 E2
The Borough London 67 D10
The Bourne Sur 49 E10
The Bourne Worcs 117 F9
The Bows Stirl 285 G11
The Braes Highld 295 B7
The Brampton Staffs 168 F4
The Brand Leics 153 G10
The Bratch Staffs 133 E7
The Breck Orkney 314 F3
The Brents Kent 70 G4
The Bridge Dorset 30 E3
The Broad Hereford 115 E9
The Brook Suff 125 B11
The Brushes Derbys 186 F5
The Bryn Mon 78 D4
The Burf Worcs 116 D6
The Butts Hants 49 F8
The Butts Som 45 D9
The Camp Glos 80 D6
The Camp Herts 85 D11
The Cape Warks 118 D5
The Chart Kent 52 C3
The Chequer Wrex 167 G7
The Chuckery W Mid 133 D10
The City Bucks 84 F3
The Cleaver Hereford 97 F10
The Close W Sus 22 C5
The Colony Oxon 100 D6
The Common Bath 60 G6
The Common Bucks 102 E5
The Common Dorset 30 E3
The Common Shrops 150 D3
The Common Suff 108 B2
The Common Swansea 56 C4
The Common W Sus 51 G7
The Common Wilts 47 G8
The Common Wilts 61 G11
The Common Wilts 62 C4
The Corner Kent 53 E8
The Corner Shrops 131 F8
The Cot Mon 79 F8
The Craigs Highld 309 K4
The Crofts E Yorks 218 E4
The Cronk I o M 192 C4
The Cross Hands Leics 134 C6
The Cwm Mon 79 G7
The Dell Suff 143 D9
The Delves W Mid 133 D10
The Den N Ayrs 266 E6
The Dene Durham 242 G4
The Dene Hants 47 C11
The Down Kent 53 F7
The Down Shrops 132 E3
The Downs Sur 50 F3
The Dunks Wrex 166 E4
The Eals Northumb 251 F7
The Eaves Glos 79 D10
The Fall W Yorks 197 B10
The Fence Glos 79 D8
The Flat Glos 80 B3
The Flatt Cumb 240 B3
The Flourish Derbys 153 B8
The Folly Herts 85 C11
The Folly S Glos 61 E8
The Fording Hereford 98 F3
The Forge Hereford 114 F6
The Forstal Kent 54 F4
The Forties Derbys 152 F6
The Four Alls Shrops 150 C3
The Fox Wilts 62 B6
The Foxholes Shrops 132 G2
The Frenches Hants 32 C4
The Frythe Herts 86 C2
The Garths Shetland 312 B8
The Gibb Wilts 61 D10
The Glack Borders 260 B6
The Gore Shrops 131 G11
The Grange N Yorks 225 F11
The Grange Norf 160 E2
The Green C Beds 85 B8
The Green Cambs 122 D5
The Green Cumb 210 C3
The Green Cumb 211 D7
The Green Essex 88 B3
The Green Hants 32 B3
The Green M Keynes 103 C7
The Green Norf 141 C11
The Green Norf 159 B11
The Green Northants 102 C5
The Green Oxon 101 F9
The Green S Yorks 197 G8
The Green Shrops 130 G6
The Green Warks 118 F4
The Green Wilts 45 G11
The Grove Dumfries 237 B11
The Grove Durham 242 G3
The Grove Herts 85 F9
The Grove Shrops 131 B7
The Grove Shrops 131 G8
The Grove Worcs 99 C7
The Gutter Derbys 170 F5
The Gutter Worcs 117 B9
The Hacket S Glos 61 B7
The Hague Derbys 185 C8
The Hall Shetland 312 D8
The Hallands N Lincs 200 C5
The Ham Wilts 45 C11
The Handfords Staffs 151 E7
The Harbour Kent 53 D10
The Haven W Sus 50 G5
The Headland Hrtlpl 234 E6
The Heath Norf 159 D8
The Heath Norf 160 E3
The Heath Norf 160 E4
The Heath Staffs 151 C11
The Heath Suff 108 D2
The Hem Shrops 132 B4
The Hendre Mon 79 C7
The Herberts V Glam 58 E3
The Hermitage Cambs 123 C7
The High Essex 86 C6
The Highlands E Sus 38 F2
The Hill Cumb 210 C3
The Hobbins Shrops 132 E4
The Hollands Staffs 168 D6
The Hollies Notts 172 E4
The Holmes Derbys 153 B7
The Holt Wokingham 65 D10
The Hook Worcs 98 C6
The Hope Shrops 115 B10
The Howe Cumb 211 B9
The Howe I o M 192 F2
The Humbers Telford 150 G3
The Hundred Hereford 115 E10
The Hyde London 67 B8
The Hyde Worcs 98 C6
The Hythe Essex 107 G10
The Inch Edin 280 G5
The Knab Swansea 56 D6
The Knap V Glam 58 F5
The Knapp Hereford 116 G3
The Knapp S Glos 79 G11
The Knowle W Mid 133 F9
The Laches Staffs 133 B8
The Lake Dumfries 237 E8
The Lakes Worcs 116 B5
The Lawe T & W 243 D9
The Lawns E Yorks 208 G6
The Leacon Kent 54 G3
The Leath Shrops 131 F11
The Lee Bucks 84 E6
The Lees Kent 54 C4
The Leigh Glos 99 F7
The Leys Staffs 134 C4
The Lhen I o M 192 B4
The Ling Norf 142 D6
The Lings Norf 141 B10
The Lings S Yorks 199 F7
The Linleys Wilts 61 F11
The Lunt W Mid 133 D9
The Manor W Sus 22 C4
The Marsh E Ches 168 C4
The Marsh Hereford 115 F9
The Marsh Powys 130 D6
The Marsh Shrops 150 D3
The Marsh Staffs 150 D6
The Marsh Suff 125 B11
The Marsh Suff 126 B2
The Marsh Wilts 62 C5
The Middles Durham 242 G6
The Mint Hants 34 B3
The Moor Flint 166 B4
The Moor Kent 38 B3
The Moors Hereford 97 E10
The Mount Hants 64 G2
The Mount Reading 65 E8
The Mumbles = Y Mwmbwls Swansea 56 D6
The Murray S Lnrk 268 E2
The Mythe Glos 99 E7
The Nant Wrex 166 E3
The Narth Mon 79 D8
The Neuk Aberds 293 D9
The Node Herts 104 G4
The Nook Shrops 149 C11
The Nook Shrops 150 E3
The North Mon 79 D8
The Oval Bath 61 G8
The Park Glos 99 G8
The Parks S Yorks 198 F6
The Pitts Wilts 31 B9
The Platt Oxon 83 E9
The Pludds Glos 79 B10
The Point Devon 14 E5
The Pole of Itlaw Aberds 302 D6
The Port of Felixstowe Suff 108 E5
The Potteries Stoke 168 F5
The Pound Glos 98 E4
The Quarry Glos 80 F2
The Quarry Shrops 149 G9
The Quarter Kent 53 E11
The Quarter Kent 53 G11
The Rampings Worcs 99 E7
The Rectory Lincs 156 G2
The Reddings Glos 99 G8
The Rhos Pembs 73 C8
The Rhydd Hereford 97 E9
The Riddle Hereford 115 E9
The Ridge Wilts 61 F11
The Ridges Wokingham 65 G10
The Ridgeway Herts 86 E3
The Riding Northumb 241 D10
The Riggs Borders 261 C8
The Rink Borders 261 C11
The Rise Windsor 66 F2
The Rock Telford 132 B3
The Rocks Kent 53 B8
The Rocks S Glos 61 C8
The Roe Denb 181 G8
The Rookery Herts 85 G10
The Rookery Staffs 168 D5
The Row Lancs 211 D9
The Rowe Staffs 150 B6
The Ryde Herts 86 D2
The Sands Sur 49 D11
The Scarr Glos 98 F4
The Shoe Wilts 61 E10
The Shruggs Staffs 151 C8
The Slack Durham 233 F8
The Slade W Berks 64 F4
The Smeeth Norf 157 G10
The Smithies Shrops 132 D3
The Spa Wilts 62 G2
The Spring Warks 118 C5
The Square Torf 78 F3
The Stocks Kent 38 B6
The Stocks Wilts 62 G2
The Straits Hants 49 F9
The Straits W Mid 133 E8
The Strand Wilts 46 B2
The Swillett Herts 85 F8
The Sydnall Shrops 150 C3
The Thrift Cambs 104 D6
The Throat Wokingham 65 F10
The Toft Staffs 151 F8
The Towans Corn 2 B3
The Town Scilly 1 F3
The Twittocks Glos 99 D7
The Tynings Glos 80 B6
The Vale W Mid 133 G11
The Valley E Ches 167 D11
The Valley Kent 54 C3
The Valley Leics 154 F4
The Valley Pembs 73 D10
The Vauld Hereford 97 B10
The Village Newport 78 G4
The Village W Mid 133 F7
The Village Windsor 66 E3
The Walshes Worcs 116 C6
The Warren Kent 54 E3
The Warren Wilts 63 F8
The Waterwheel Shrops 131 C7
The Weaven Hereford 97 E10
The Wells Sur 67 G7
The Wern Wrex 166 E3
The Willows NE Lincs 201 F8
The Wood Shrops 148 E6
The Wood Shrops 149 D9
The Woodlands Leics 136 D3
The Woodlands Suff 107 C11
The Woodlands Suff 108 D3
The Woods W Mid 133 D10
The Wrangle Bath 44 B4
The Wrythe London 67 F9
The Wyke Shrops 132 B4
The Wymm Hereford 97 B10
The Yeld Shrops 131 G11
Theakston N Yorks 214 B6
Thealby N Lincs 199 D11
Theale Som 44 D3
Theale W Berks 64 E6
Thearne E Yorks 209 F7
Theberton Suff 127 D8
Theddingworth Leics 136 F3
Theddlethorpe All Saints Lincs 191 D7
Theddlethorpe St Helen Lincs 191 D7
Thelbridge Barton Devon 26 E3
Thelnetham Suff 125 B10
Thelveton Norf 142 G3
Thelwall Warr 183 D10
Themelthorpe Norf 159 E11
Thenford Northants 101 C10
Theobald's Green Wilts 62 F4
Therfield Herts 104 D6
Thetford Lincs 156 F2
Thetford Norf 141 G7
Theydon Bois Essex 86 F6
Theydon Garnon Essex 87 F7
Theydon Mount Essex 87 F7
Thick Hollins W Yorks 196 E6
Thicket Mead Bath 45 B7
Thickthorn Hall Norf 142 B3
Thickwood Wilts 61 E10
Thimble End W Mid 134 E2
Thimbleby Lincs 190 G2
Thimbleby N Yorks 225 F9
Thinford Durham 233 E11
Thingley Wilts 61 E11
Thingwall Mers 182 E3
Thirdpart N Ayrs 266 F3
Thirlby N Yorks 215 C9
Thirlestane Borders 271 F11
Thirn N Yorks 214 B4
Thirsk N Yorks 215 C8
Thirtleby E Yorks 209 G9
Thistleton Lancs 202 F4
Thistleton Rutland 155 F8
Thistley Green Essex 88 B2
Thistley Green Suff 124 B3
Thixendale N Yorks 216 G6
Thockrington Northumb 241 B11
Tholomas Drove Cambs 139 B7
Tholthorpe N Yorks 215 F9
Thomas Chapel Pembs 73 D10
Thomas Close Cumb 230 C4
Thomastown Aberds 302 F5
Thomastown Rhondda 58 B4
Thompson Norf 141 D8
Thomshill Moray 302 D2
Thong Kent 69 E7
Thongsbridge W Yorks 196 F6
Thoralby N Yorks 213 B10
Thoresby Notts 187 G10
Thoresthorpe Lincs 191 F7
Thoresway Lincs 189 B11
Thorganby Lincs 190 B2
Thorganby N Yorks 207 E9
Thorgill N Yorks 226 F4
Thorington Suff 127 C8
Thorington Street Suff 107 D10
Thorlby N Yorks 204 C5
Thorley Herts 87 B7
Thorley I o W 20 D3
Thorley Houses Herts 105 G9
Thorley Street Herts 87 B7
Thorley Street I o W 20 D3
Thormanby N Yorks 215 E9
Thorn Devon 13 D9
Thorn Powys 114 E5
Thorn Hill S Yorks 186 C6
Thornaby on Tees Stockton 225 B9
Thornage Norf 159 B11
Thornborough Bucks 102 E4
Thornborough N Yorks 214 D5
Thornbury Devon 24 F6
Thornbury Hereford 116 F2
Thornbury S Glos 79 G10
Thornbury W Yorks 205 G9
Thornby Cumb 239 G7
Thornby Northants 120 B3
Thorncliff W Yorks 197 E8
Thorncliffe Staffs 169 D8
Thorncombe Dorset 28 G5
Thorncombe Dorset 30 G5
Thorncombe Street Sur 50 E4
Thorncote Green C Beds 104 B3
Thorncross I o W 20 E4
Thorndon Suff 126 D2
Thorndon Cross Devon 12 C6
Thorne Corn 24 G2
Thorne S Yorks 199 E7
Thorne Coffin Som 29 D8
Thorne Moor Devon 12 D3
Thorne St Margaret Som 27 C9
Thornehillhead Devon 24 D6
Thornend Wilts 62 D3
Thorner W Yorks 206 E3
Thornes Staffs 133 C11
Thornes W Yorks 197 D10
Thorney Bucks 66 D4
Thorney Notts 188 G5
Thorney P'boro 138 C5
Thorney Som 28 C6
Thorney Close T & W 243 G9
Thorney Crofts E Yorks 201 C8
Thorney Green Suff 125 E11
Thorney Hill Hants 19 B9
Thorney Island W Sus 22 C3
Thorney Toll P'boro 138 C6
Thorneywood Notts 171 G9
Thornfalcon Som 28 C3
Thornford Dorset 29 E10
Thorngrafton Northumb 241 D7
Thorngrove Som 43 G11
Thorngumbald E Yorks 201 B8
Thornham Norf 176 E2
Thornham Fold Gtr Man 195 F11
Thornham Magna Suff 126 C2
Thornham Parva Suff 126 C2
Thornhaugh P'boro 137 C11
Thornhill Cardiff 59 C7
Thornhill Cumb 219 D10
Thornhill Derbys 185 E11
Thornhill Dumfries 247 D9
Thornhill Soton 33 E7
Thornhill Stirl 278 B3
Thornhill Torf 78 F3
Thornhill W Yorks 197 D9
Thornhill Wilts 62 D5
Thornhill Edge W Yorks 197 D8
Thornhill Lees W Yorks 197 D8
Thornhill Park Hants 33 E7
Thornhills W Yorks 197 C7
Thornholme E Yorks 218 G2
Thornicombe Dorset 30 G5
Thornielee Borders 261 B10
Thornley Durham 233 D8
Thornley Durham 234 D3
Thornliebank E Renf 267 D10
Thornly Park Renfs 267 C9
Thornroan Aberds 303 F8
Thorns N Yorks 223 E7
Thorns Suff 124 F4
Thorns Green Ches 184 E3
Thornseat S Yorks 186 C2
Thornsett Derbys 185 D8
Thornthwaite Cumb 229 F10
Thornthwaite N Yorks 205 B9
Thornton Angus 287 C7
Thornton Bucks 102 D5
Thornton E Yorks 207 D11
Thornton Fife 280 B5
Thornton Lancs 202 E2
Thornton Leics 135 B9
Thornton Lincs 174 B2
Thornton M'bro 225 C9
Thornton Mers 193 G10
Thornton Northumb 273 F9
Thornton Pembs 72 D6
Thornton W Yorks 205 G8
Thornton Curtis N Lincs 200 D5
Thornton Heath London 67 F10
Thornton Hough Mers 182 E4
Thornton in Craven N Yorks 204 D4
Thornton in Lonsdale N Yorks 212 E3
Thornton-le-Beans N Yorks 225 G7
Thornton-le-Clay N Yorks 216 F3
Thornton-le-Dale N Yorks 216 C6
Thornton le Moor Lincs 189 B9
Thornton-le-Moor N Yorks 215 B7
Thornton-le-Moors W Ches 182 G6
Thornton-le-Street N Yorks 215 B8
Thornton Rust N Yorks 213 B9
Thornton Steward N Yorks 214 B3
Thornton Watlass N Yorks 214 B4
Thorntonhall S Lnrk 267 D11
Thorntonloch E Loth 282 G4
Thornton Park Northumb 273 F8
Thornwood Common Essex 87 D7
Thornydykes Borders 272 F2
Thoroton Notts 172 G3
Thorp Gtr Man 196 F2
Thorp Arch W Yorks 206 D4
Thorpe Cumb 230 F5
Thorpe Derbys 169 E11
Thorpe E Yorks 208 D5
Thorpe Lincs 191 E7
Thorpe N Yorks 213 G10
Thorpe Norf 143 D8
Thorpe Notts 172 F3
Thorpe Sur 66 F4
Thorpe Abbotts Norf 126 B3
Thorpe Acre Leics 153 E10
Thorpe Arnold Leics 154 E5
Thorpe Audlin W Yorks 198 D3
Thorpe Bassett N Yorks 217 E7
Thorpe Bay Sthend 70 B2
Thorpe by Water Rutland 137 D7
Thorpe Common Suff 108 D5
Thorpe Constantine Staffs 134 B5
Thorpe Culvert Lincs 175 C7
Thorpe Edge W Yorks 205 F9
Thorpe End Norf 160 G5
Thorpe Fendykes Lincs 175 C7
Thorpe Green Essex 108 G3
Thorpe Green Lancs 194 C5
Thorpe Green Suff 125 G8
Thorpe Green Sur 66 F4
Thorpe Hamlet Norf 142 B4
Thorpe Hesley S Yorks 186 B5
Thorpe in Balne S Yorks 198 E5
Thorpe in the Fallows Lincs 188 E6
Thorpe Langton Leics 136 E4
Thorpe Larches Durham 234 F3
Thorpe Latimer Lincs 156 B2
Thorpe-le-Soken Essex 108 G3
Thorpe le Street E Yorks 208 E2
Thorpe le Vale Lincs 190 C2
Thorpe Lea Sur 66 E4
Thorpe Malsor Northants 120 B6
Thorpe Mandeville Northants 101 B10
Thorpe Market Norf 160 B4
Thorpe Marriot Norf 160 F3
Thorpe Morieux Suff 125 G8
Thorpe on the Hill Lincs 172 B6
Thorpe on The Hill W Yorks 197 B10
Thorpe Row Norf 141 B9
Thorpe St Andrew Norf 142 B5
Thorpe St Peter Lincs 175 C7
Thorpe Salvin S Yorks 187 E8
Thorpe Satchville Leics 154 G4
Thorpe Street Suff 125 B10
Thorpe Thewles Stockton 234 G4
Thorpe Tilney Lincs 173 D10
Thorpe Underwood N Yorks 206 B5
Thorpe Underwood Northants 136 G5
Thorpe Waterville Northants 137 G10
Thorpe Willoughby N Yorks 207 G7
Thorpe Wood N Yorks 207 G7
Thorpeness Suff 127 F9
Thorpland Norf 140 B2
Thorrington Essex 89 B9
Thorverton Devon 26 G6
Thoulstone Wilts 45 D10
Thrandeston Suff 126 B2
Thrapston Northants 121 B9
Thrashbush N Lnrk 268 B5
Threapland Cumb 229 D9
Threapland N Yorks 213 G9
Threapwood Staffs 169 G8
Threapwood W Ches 166 F6
Three Ashes Hants 64 G6
Three Ashes Hereford 97 G10
Three Ashes Shrops 115 B7
Three Ashes Som 45 D7
Three Bridges Argyll 284 F4
Three Bridges Lincs 190 D6
Three Bridges W Sus 51 F9
Three Burrows Corn 4 F4
Three Chimneys Kent 53 F10
Three Cocked Hat Norf 143 D8
Three Cocks = Aberllynfi Powys 96 D3
Three Crosses Swansea 56 C5
Three Cups Corner E Sus 37 C10
Three Fingers Wrex 167 G7
Three Gates Dorset 29 F10
Three Hammers Corn 11 D10
Three Holes Norf 139 C10
Three Holes Cross Corn 10 G6
Three Leg Cross E Sus 53 G7
Three Legged Cross Dorset 31 F9
Three Maypoles W Mid 118 B2
Three Mile Cross Wokingham 65 F8
Three Oaks E Sus 38 E4
Three Sisters Denb 165 C9
Threehammer Common Norf 160 E6
Threekingham Lincs 155 B11
Threelows Staffs 169 F9
Threemile Cross Wokingham 65 F8
Threemilestone Corn 4 G5
Threemiletown W Loth 279 F11
Threepwood Borders 271 G10
Threewaters Corn 5 B10
Threlkeld Cumb 230 F2
Threshers Bush Essex 87 D7
Threshfield N Yorks 213 G9
Thrigby Norf 161 G9
Thringarth Durham 232 G4
Thringstone Leics 153 F8
Thrintoft N Yorks 224 G6
Thriplow Cambs 105 B8
Throapham S Yorks 187 D8
Throckenholt Lincs 139 B7
Throcking Herts 104 E6
Throckley T & W 242 D5
Throckmorton Worcs 99 B9
Throop Dorset 18 C2
Throphill Northumb 252 F4
Thropton Northumb 252 C2
Throsk Stirl 279 C7
Througham Glos 80 D6
Throughgate Dumfries 247 G9
Throwleigh Devon 13 C9
Throwley Kent 54 B3
Throwley Forstal Kent 54 C3
Throxenby N Yorks 217 B10
Thrumpton Notts 153 C10
Thrumpton Notts 188 E2
Thrumster Highld 310 E7
Thrunton Northumb 264 G3
Thrupe Som 44 D6
Thrupp Glos 80 E5
Thrupp Oxon 82 F3
Thrupp Oxon 83 B7
Thruscross N Yorks 205 B9
Thrushelton Devon 12 D4
Thrussington Leics 154 F2
Thruxton Hants 47 D9
Thruxton Hereford 97 E8
Thrybergh S Yorks 187 B7
Thulston Derbys 153 C8
Thunder Bridge W Yorks 197 E7
Thunder Hill Norf 161 F8
Thundergay N Ayrs 255 C9
Thunder's Hill E Sus 23 C9
Thundersley Essex 69 B9
Thundridge Herts 86 B5
Thurcaston Leics 153 G11
Thurcroft S Yorks 187 D7
Thurdon Corn 24 E3
Thurgarton Norf 160 C3
Thurgarton Notts 171 F11
Thurgoland S Yorks 197 G9
Thurlaston Leics 135 D10
Thurlaston Warks 119 C9
Thurlbear Som 28 C3
Thurlby Lincs 156 F2
Thurlby Lincs 172 C6
Thurlby Lincs 191 F7
Thurleigh Beds 121 F11
Thurlestone Devon 8 G3
Thurloxton Som 43 G9
Thurlstone S Yorks 197 G8
Thurlton Norf 143 D8
Thurlton Links Norf 143 D8
Thurlwood E Ches 168 D4
Thurmaston Leics 136 B2
Thurnby Leics 136 C2
Thurne Norf 161 F8
Thurnham Kent 53 B10
Thurnham Lancs 202 C5
Thurning Norf 159 D11
Thurning Northants 137 G11
Thurnscoe S Yorks 198 F3
Thurnscoe East S Yorks 198 F3
Thursby Cumb 239 G8
Thursford Norf 159 C9
Thursford Green Norf 159 C9
Thursley Sur 50 F2
Thurso Highld 310 C5
Thurso East Highld 310 C5
Thurstaston Mers 182 E2
Thurston Suff 125 D8
Thurston Clough Gtr Man 196 F3
Thurston End Suff 124 G5
Thurstonfield Cumb 239 F8
Thurstonland W Yorks 197 E7
Thurton Norf 142 C6
Thurvaston Derbys 152 B2
Thurvaston Derbys 152 B4
Thuxton Norf 141 B10
Thwaite N Yorks 223 F7
Thwaite Suff 126 D2
Thwaite Flat Cumb 210 E4
Thwaite Head Cumb 220 G6
Thwaite St Mary Norf 142 E6
Thwaites W Yorks 205 E7
Thwaites Brow W Yorks 205 E7
Thwing E Yorks 217 E11
Tibbermore Perth 286 E4
Tibberton Glos 98 G5
Tibberton Telford 150 E3
Tibberton Worcs 117 F8
Tibenham Norf 142 F2
Tibshelf Derbys 170 C6
Tibshelf Wharf Notts 171 C7

Tibthorpe E Yorks 208 B5
Ticehurst E Sus 53 G7
Tichborne Hants 48 G5
Tickencote Rutland 137 B9
Tickenham N Som 60 E3
Ticket Wood Devon 8 G4
Tickford End M Keynes 103 C7
Tickhill S Yorks 187 C9
Tickleback Row Brack 65 E11
Ticklerton Shrops 131 E9
Tickmorend Glos 80 F4
Ticknall Derbys 153 E7
Tickton E Yorks 209 E7
Tidbury Green W Mid 117 B11
Tidcombe Wilts 47 B9
Tiddington Oxon 83 E11
Tiddington Warks 118 F4
Tidebrook E Sus 37 B10
Tideford Corn 6 D6
Tideford Cross Corn 6 C6
Tidenham Glos 79 F9
Tidenham Chase Glos 79 F9
Tideswell Derbys 185 F11
Tidmarsh W Berks 64 E6
Tidmington Warks 100 D5
Tidnor Hereford 97 D11
Tidpit Hants 31 D9
Tidworth Wilts 47 D8
Tiers Cross Pembs 72 C6
Tiffield Northants 120 G3
Tifty Aberds 303 E7
Tigerton Angus 293 G7
Tigh-na-Blair Perth 285 F11
Tighnabruaich Argyll 275 F10
Tighnacachla Argyll 274 G3
Tighnafiline Highld 307 L3
Tighness Argyll 284 G6
Tigley Devon 8 C5
Tilbrook Cambs 121 D11
Tilbury Thurrock 68 D6
Tilbury Green Essex 106 C4
Tilbury Juxta Clare Essex 106 C5
Tile Cross W Mid 134 F3
Tile Hill W Mid 118 B5
Tilegate Green Essex 87 D8
Tilehouse Green W Mid 118 B3
Tilehurst Reading 65 E7
Tilekiln Green Essex 105 G10
Tiley Dorset 29 F11
Tilford Sur 49 E11
Tilford Common Sur 49 E11
Tilford Reeds Sur 49 E11
Tilgate W Sus 51 G9
Tilgate Forest Row W Sus 51 G9
Tilkey Essex 106 G6
Tilland Corn 6 C6
Tillathrowie Aberds 302 F4
Tillers' Green Glos 98 E3
Tilley Shrops 149 D10
Tilley Green Shrops 149 D10
Tillicoultry Clack 279 B8
Tillietudlem S Lnrk 268 F6
Tillingham Essex 89 E7
Tillington Hereford 97 B9
Tillington Staffs 151 E8
Tillington W Sus 35 C7
Tillington Common Hereford 97 B9
Tillislow Devon 12 C3
Tillworth Devon 28 G4
Tilly Down Hants 47 D10
Tilly Lo Aberds 293 C7
Tillyarblet Angus 293 G7
Tillybirloch Aberds 293 C8
Tillycorthie Aberds 303 G9
Tillydrine Aberds 293 D8
Tillyfour Aberds 293 B7
Tillyfourie Aberds 293 B8
Tillygarmond Aberds 293 D8
Tillygreig Aberds 303 G8
Tillykerrie Aberds 303 G8
Tillynaught Aberds 302 C5
Tilmanstone Kent 55 C10
Tilney All Saints Norf 157 F11
Tilney cum Islington Norf 157 G11
Tilney Fen End Norf 157 G10
Tilney High End Norf 157 F11
Tilney St Lawrence Norf 157 G10
Tilsdown Glos 80 F2
Tilshead Wilts 46 D4
Tilsmore E Sus 37 C9
Tilsop Shrops 116 C2
Tilstock Shrops 149 B10
Tilston W Ches 167 E7
Tilstone Bank W Ches 167 D9
Tilstone Fearnall W Ches 167 C9
Tilsworth C Beds 103 G9
Tilton on the Hill Leics 136 B4
Tilts S Yorks 198 F5
Tiltups End Glos 80 F4
Tilty Essex 105 F11
Timberden Bottom Kent 68 G4
Timberhonger Worcs 117 C8
Timberland Lincs 173 D10
Timbersbrook E Ches 168 C5
Timberscombe Som 42 E3
Timble N Yorks 205 C9
Timbold Hill Kent 54 B2
Timbrelham Corn 12 E3
Timperley Gtr Man 184 D3
Timsbury Bath 45 B7
Timsbury Hants 32 C4
Timsgearraidh W Isles 304 E2
Timworth Suff 125 D7
Timworth Green Suff 125 D7
Tincleton Dorset 17 C11
Tindale Cumb 240 F4
Tindale Crescent Durham 233 F9
Tindon End Essex 106 E2
Tingewick Bucks 102 E3
Tingley W Yorks 197 B9
Tingon Shetland 312 E4
Tingrith C Beds 103 E10
Tingwall Orkney 314 D3
Tinhay Devon 12 E3
Tinkers End Bucks 102 F5
Tinshill W Yorks 205 F11
Tinsley S Yorks 186 C6
Tinsley Green W Sus 51 F9
Tintagel Corn 11 D7
Tintern Parva Mon 79 E8
Tintinhull Som 29 D8
Tintwistle Derbys 185 B8
Tinwald Dumfries 248 G2
Tinwell Rutland 137 B10
Tipner Ptsmth 33 G10
Tippacott Devon 41 D9
Tipper's Hill Warks 134 F5
Tipperty Aberds 302 C6
Tipperty Aberds 303 G9
Tipple Cross Devon 12 D3
Tipps End Norf 139 D10
Tip's Cross Essex 87 E9
Tiptoe Hants 19 B11
Tipton W Mid 133 E8
Tipton Green W Mid 133 E9
Tipton St John Devon 15 C7
Tiptree Essex 88 B5
Tiptree Heath Essex 88 B5
Tir-y-berth Caerph 77 F11
Tir-y-dail Carms 75 C10
Tirabad Powys 95 C7
Tiraghoil Argyll 288 G5
Tircanol Swansea 57 B7
Tirdeunaw Swansea 57 B7
Tirinie Perth 291 G10
Tirley Glos 98 F6
Tirley Knowle Glos 98 F6
Tiroran Argyll 288 G6
Tirphil Caerph 77 E10
Tirril Cumb 230 F6
Tirryside Highld 309 H5
Tisbury Wilts 30 B6
Tisman's Common W Sus 50 G5
Tissington Derbys 169 E11
Titchberry Devon 24 B2
Titchfield Hants 33 F8
Titchfield Common Hants 33 F8
Titchfield Park Hants 33 F8
Titchmarsh Northants 121 B10
Titchwell Norf 176 E3
Titcomb W Berks 63 F11
Tithby Notts 154 B3
Tithe Barn Hillock Mers 183 B9
Tithebarn Staffs 169 G9
Titley Hereford 114 E6
Titlington Northumb 264 F4
Titmore Green Herts 104 F4
Titsey Sur 52 C2
Titson Corn 24 G2
Tittenhurst Windsor 66 F3
Tittensor Staffs 151 B7
Titterhill Shrops 131 G10
Tittle Row Windsor 65 C11
Tittleshall Norf 159 E7
Titton Worcs 116 D6
Titty Hill W Sus 34 B5
Tiverton Devon 27 E7
Tiverton W Ches 167 C9
Tivetshall St Margaret Norf 142 F3
Tivetshall St Mary Norf 142 F3
Tividale W Mid 133 E9
Tivington Som 42 D2
Tivington Knowle Som 42 E2
Tivoli Cumb 228 G5
Tivy Dale S Yorks 197 F9
Tixall Staffs 151 E9
Tixover Rutland 137 C9
Toab Orkney 314 F5
Toab Shetland 313 M5
Toad Row Suff 143 F10
Toadmoor Derbys 170 E4
Tobermory Argyll 289 D7
Toberonochy Argyll 275 C8
Tobha Beag W Isles 296 D5
Tobha Mor W Isles 297 H3
Tobhtarol W Isles 304 E3
Tobson W Isles 304 E3
Toby's Hill Lincs 191 C7
Tocher Aberds 302 F6
Tockenham Wilts 62 D4
Tockenham Wick Wilts 62 C4
Tockholes Blkburn 195 C7
Tockington S Glos 60 B6
Tockwith N Yorks 206 C5
Todber Dorset 30 C4
Todding Hereford 115 B8
Toddington C Beds 103 F10
Toddington Glos 99 E10
Toddington W Sus 35 G8
Toddlehills Aberds 303 E10
Todd's Green Herts 104 F4
Todenham Glos 100 D4
Todhill Angus 287 D8
Todhills Cumb 239 E9
Todhills Durham 233 E10
Todlachie Aberds 293 B8
Todmorden W Yorks 196 C2
Todpool Corn 4 G4
Todrig Borders 261 F10
Todwick S Yorks 187 E7
Toft Cambs 123 F7
Toft Lincs 155 F11
Toft Shetland 312 F6
Toft Warks 119 C9
Toft Hill Durham 233 F9
Toft Hill Lincs 174 C2
Toft Monks Norf 143 E8
Toft next Newton Lincs 189 D8
Toftrees Norf 159 D7
Tofts Highld 310 C7
Toftshaw W Yorks 197 B7
Toftwood Norf 159 G9
Togston Northumb 252 C6
Tokavaig Highld 295 D8
Tokers Green Oxon 65 D8
Tokyngton London 67 C7
Tolastadh a Chaolais W Isles 304 E3
Tolastadh bho Thuath W Isles 304 D7
Tolborough Corn 11 F9
Tolcarne Corn 2 B5
Tolcarne Corn 2 C5
Tolcarne Wartha Corn 2 B5
Toldish Corn 5 D8
Tolgus Mount Corn 4 G3
Tolhurst E Sus 53 G7
Toll Bar Mers 183 C7
Toll Bar Rutland 137 B10
Toll Bar S Yorks 198 F5
Toll End W Mid 133 E9
Toll of Birness Aberds 303 F10
Tolladine Worcs 117 F7
Tolland Som 42 G6
Tollard Farnham Dorset 30 D6
Tollard Royal Wilts 30 D6
Tollbar End W Mid 119 B7
Toller Fratrum Dorset 17 B7
Toller Porcorum Dorset 17 B7
Toller Whelme Dorset 29 G8
Tollerford Dorset 17 B7
Tollerton N Yorks 215 G10
Tollerton Notts 154 C2
Tollesbury Essex 89 C7
Tollesby M'bro 225 B10
Tolleshunt D'Arcy Essex 88 C6
Tolleshunt Knights Essex 88 C6
Tolleshunt Major Essex 88 C5
Tollie Highld 300 D5
Tolm W Isles 304 E6
Tolmers Herts 86 E4
Tolpuddle Dorset 17 C11
Tolskithy Corn 4 G3
Tolvaddon Downs Corn 4 G3
Tolvah Highld 291 D10
Tolworth London 67 F7
Tom an Fhuadain W Isles 305 G5
Tomaknock Perth 286 E2
Tomatin Highld 301 G8
Tombreck Highld 300 F6
Tombui Perth 286 B2
Tomchrasky Highld 290 B4
Tomdoun Highld 290 C3
Tomich Highld 300 B6
Tomich Highld 300 G3
Tomich House Highld 300 E5
Tomintoul Aberds 292 D3
Tomintoul Moray 292 B3
Tomlow Warks 119 E9
Tomnaven Moray 302 F4
Tomnavoulin Moray 302 G2
Tomperrow Corn 4 G5
Tompkin Staffs 168 E6
Tompset's Bank E Sus 52 G2
Tomsleibhe Argyll 289 F8
Tomthorn Derbys 185 F9
Ton Mon 78 F5
Ton Breigam V Glam 58 D3
Ton-Pentre Rhondda 77 F7
Ton-teg Rhondda 58 B5
Ton-y-pistyll Caerph 77 F11
Tonbridge Kent 52 D5
Tonderghie Dumfries 236 F6
Tondu Bridgend 57 E11
Tone Som 27 C10
Tone Green Som 27 C11
Tonedale Som 27 C10
Tong Kent 53 D10
Tong Shrops 132 B5
Tong W Yorks 205 G10
Tong Forge Shrops 132 B5
Tong Green Kent 54 C3
Tong Norton Shrops 132 B5
Tong Park W Yorks 205 F9
Tong Street W Yorks 205 G9
Tonge Leics 153 E8
Tonge Corner Kent 70 F2
Tonge Fold Gtr Man 195 F8
Tonge Moor Gtr Man 195 E8
Tongham Sur 49 D11
Tongland Dumfries 237 D8
Tongue Highld 308 D5
Tongue End Lincs 156 F3
Tongwell M Keynes 103 C7
Tongwynlais Cardiff 58 C6
Tonmawr Neath 57 B10
Tonna = Tonnau Neath 57 B9
Tonnau = Tonna Neath 57 B9
Tontine Lancs 194 G4
Tonwell Herts 86 B4
Tonypandy Rhondda 77 G7
Tonyrefail Rhondda 58 B4
Toot Baldon Oxon 83 E9
Toot Hill Essex 87 E8
Toot Hill Staffs 169 G9
Toothill Hants 32 D5
Toothill Swindon 62 C6
Toothill W Yorks 196 C6
Tooting Graveney London 67 E9
Top End Beds 121 E10
Top Green Notts 172 F3
Top Lock Gtr Man 194 F6
Top o' th' Lane Lancs 194 C5
Top o' th' Meadows Gtr Man 196 F3
Top of Hebers Gtr Man 195 F11
Top Valley Nottingham 171 F9
Topcliffe N Yorks 215 D8
Topcliffe W Yorks 197 B9
Topcroft Norf 142 E5
Topcroft Street Norf 142 E5
Topham S Yorks 198 D6
Topleigh W Sus 34 D6
Toppesfield Essex 106 D4
Toppings Gtr Man 195 E8
Toprow Norf 142 D3
Topsham Devon 14 D5
Torbeg N Ayrs 255 E10
Torboll Farm Highld 309 K7
Torbothie N Lnrk 269 D7
Torbreck Highld 309 J7
Torbrex Stirl 278 C5
Torbryan Devon 8 B6
Torbush N Lnrk 268 D6
Torcross Devon 8 G6
Torcroy Highld 291 D9
Tore Highld 300 D6
Torfrey Corn 6 E2
Torgyle Highld 290 B5
Torinturk Argyll 275 G9
Torkington Gtr Man 184 D6
Torksey Lincs 188 F4
Torlum W Isles 296 F3
Torlundy Highld 290 F3
Tormarton S Glos 61 D9
Tormisdale Argyll 254 B2
Tormitchell S Ayrs 244 E6
Tormore Highld 295 E8
Tormore N Ayrs 255 D9
Tornagrain Highld 301 E7
Tornahaish Aberds 292 C4
Tornapress Highld 299 E8
Tornaveen Aberds 293 C8
Torness Highld 300 G5
Toronto Durham 233 E9
Torpenhow Cumb 229 D10
Torphichen W Loth 279 G9
Torphin Edin 270 B4
Torphins Aberds 293 C8
Torpoint Corn 7 E8
Torquay Torbay 9 C8
Torquhan Borders 271 F8
Torr Devon 7 E11
Torr Devon 8 C2
Torra Argyll 254 B4
Torran Argyll 275 C9
Torran Highld 298 E5
Torran Highld 301 B7
Torrance E Dunb 278 G2
Torrans Argyll 288 G6
Torranyard N Ayrs 267 G7
Torre Som 42 E4
Torre Torbay 9 C8
Torridon Highld 299 D9
Torridon Ho Highld 299 D8
Torries Aberds 293 B8
Torrin Highld 295 C7
Torrisdale Highld 308 C6
Torrisdale Castle Argyll 255 D8
Torrisdale-Square Argyll 255 D8
Torrish Highld 311 H3
Torrisholme Lancs 211 G9
Torroble Highld 309 J5
Torroy Highld 309 K5
Torrpark Corn 11 D10
Torry Aberdeen 293 C11
Torry Aberds 302 F4
Torryburn Fife 279 D10
Torsonce Borders 271 G9
Torsonce Mains Borders 271 G9
Torterston Aberds 303 E10
Torthorwald Dumfries 238 B2
Tortington W Sus 35 F8
Torton Worcs 116 C6
Tortworth S Glos 80 G2
Torvaig Highld 298 E4
Torver Cumb 220 G5
Torwood Falk 278 E6
Torwoodlee Mains Borders 261 B11
Torworth Notts 187 D11
Tosberry Devon 24 C3
Toscaig Highld 295 B9
Toseland Cambs 122 E4
Tosside N Yorks 203 B11
Tostock Suff 125 E9
Tot Hill Hants 64 G3
Totaig Highld 295 C10
Totaig Highld 298 D2
Totardor Highld 294 B5
Tote Highld 298 E4
Tote Hill Hants 32 C4
Tote Hill W Sus 34 C5
Totegan Highld 310 C2
Totford Hants 48 F5
Totham Hill Essex 88 C5
Totham Plains Essex 88 C5
Tothill Lincs 190 E6
Totland I o W 20 D2
Totley S Yorks 186 F4
Totley Brook S Yorks 186 E4
Totley Rise S Yorks 186 E4
Totmonslow Staffs 151 B9
Totnell Dorset 29 F10
Totnes Devon 8 C6
Totnor Hereford 97 E11
Toton Notts 153 C10
Totronald Argyll 288 D3
Totscore Highld 298 C3
Tottenham London 86 G4
Tottenham Hale London 67 B10
Tottenhill Norf 158 G2
Tottenhill Row Norf 158 G2
Totteridge Bucks 84 G5
Totteridge London 86 G2
Totternhoe C Beds 103 G9
Totteroak S Glos 61 C8
Totterton Shrops 131 F7
Totties W Yorks 197 F7
Tottington Gtr Man 195 E9
Tottington Norf 141 D7
Tottlebank Cumb 210 C6
Tottleworth Lancs 203 G10
Totton Hants 32 E5
Touchen End Windsor 65 D11
Toulston N Yorks 206 E5
Toulton Som 43 G7
Toulvaddie Highld 311 L2
Tournaig Highld 307 L3
Toux Aberds 303 D9
Tovil Kent 53 C9
Tow House Northumb 241 E7
Tow Law Durham 233 D8
Towan Corn 10 G3
Towan Cross Corn 4 F4
Toward Argyll 266 B2
Towcester Northants 102 B3
Towednack Corn 1 B5
Tower End Norf 158 F3
Tower Hamlets Kent 55 E10
Tower Hill Devon 12 C3
Tower Hill E Ches 184 F6
Tower Hill Essex 108 E5
Tower Hill Herts 85 E8
Tower Hill Mers 194 G2
Tower Hill Sur 51 D7
Tower Hill W Mid 133 E11
Tower Hill W Sus 35 B11
Towerage Bucks 84 G4
Towerhead N Som 44 B2
Towersey Oxon 84 D2
Towie Aberds 292 B6
Towie Aberds 302 G5
Towie Aberds 303 C8
Towiemore Moray 302 E3
Town Barton Devon 14 C2
Town End Bucks 84 F3
Town End Cambs 139 D8
Town End Cumb 211 B7
Town End Cumb 211 C8
Town End Cumb 212 C2
Town End Cumb 220 D6
Town End Cumb 221 E8
Town End Cumb 221 F7
Town End Cumb 231 F8
Town End Derbys 185 F11
Town End E Yorks 207 C10
Town End Mers 183 D7
Town End W Yorks 196 D5
Town Fields W Ches 167 B10
Town Green Gtr Man 183 B9
Town Green Lancs 194 F2
Town Green Norf 161 G7
Town Head Cumb 220 D6
Town Head Cumb 221 E8
Town Head Cumb 222 C2
Town Head Cumb 222 C3
Town Head Cumb 231 F7
Town Head Cumb 231 F8
Town Head Cumb 231 G8
Town Head Cumb 231 G9
Town Head Derbys 185 F11
Town Head N Yorks 204 B2
Town Head N Yorks 212 F5
Town Head Staffs 169 F8
Town Head W Yorks 204 D6
Town Kelloe Durham 234 D3
Town Lane Gtr Man 183 B11
Town Littleworth E Sus 36 D6
Town of Lowton Mers 183 B10
Town Park Telford 132 B3
Town Row E Sus 52 G5
Town Street Glos 98 F6
Town Yetholm Borders 263 D8
Townend Derbys 185 E9
Townend Staffs 151 B9
Townend W Dunb 277 F8
Townfield Durham 232 B5
Towngate Cumb 230 B6
Towngate Lincs 156 G2
Townhead Argyll 275 G11
Townhead Cumb 229 D7
Townhead Cumb 230 D6
Townhead Cumb 231 E8
Townhead Dumfries 237 E8
Townhead N Lnrk 268 B4
Townhead Northumb 251 E9
Townhead S Ayrs 244 C6
Townhead S Yorks 186 E4
Townhead S Yorks 197 G7
Townhead of Greenlaw Dumfries 237 C9
Townhill Fife 280 D2
Townhill Swansea 56 C6
Townhill Park Hants 33 E7
Townlake Devon 12 G4
Townland Green Kent 54 G2
Town's End Bucks 102 G2
Town's End Dorset 18 B3
Town's End Dorset 18 E5
Town's End Dorset 29 F9
Towns End Hants 48 B5
Towns End Som 30 D2
Town's End Som 45 D7
Townsend Bath 44 B5
Townsend Bucks 84 D2
Townsend Devon 25 B10
Townsend Herts 85 D10
Townsend Oxon 63 B11
Townsend Pembs 72 D4
Townsend Som 44 C4
Townsend Stoke 168 F6
Townsend Wilts 46 B3
Townsend Wilts 46 B4
Townsend Fold Lancs 195 C10
Townshend Corn 2 C3
Townwell S Glos 79 G11
Towthorpe E Yorks 217 G8
Towthorpe York 207 B8
Towton N Yorks 206 F5
Towyn Conwy 181 F7
Toxteth Mers 182 D5
Toynton All Saints Lincs 174 C5
Toynton Fen Side Lincs 174 C5
Toynton St Peter Lincs 174 C6
Toy's Hill Kent 52 C3
Trabboch E Ayrs 257 E10
Traboe Corn 2 E6
Trabrown Borders 271 F10
Tracebridge Som 27 C9
Tradespark Highld 301 D8
Tradespark Orkney 314 F4
Trafford Park Gtr Man 184 B3
Traigh Ho Highld 295 F8
Trallong Powys 95 F9
Trallwn Rhondda 77 G9
Trallwn Swansea 57 B7
Tram Inn Hereford 97 E9
Tramagenna Corn 11 E7
Tranch Torf 78 E3
Tranent E Loth 281 G8
Tranmere Mers 182 D4
Trantlebeg Highld 310 D2
Trantlemore Highld 310 D2
Tranwell Northumb 252 G5
Trapp Carms 75 B11
Traprain E Loth 281 F11
Trap's Green Warks 118 D2
Trapshill W Berks 63 G11
Traquair Borders 261 C8
Trash Green W Berks 65 F7
Travellers' Rest Carms 74 B5
Trawden Lancs 204 F4
Trawscoed Powys 95 E11
Trawsfynydd Gwyn 146 B4
Trawsnant Ceredig 111 D11
Tre-Aubrey V Glam 58 E4
Tre-Beferad V Glam 58 F3
Tre-boeth Swansea 57 B7
Tre-derwen Powys 148 F4
Tre-Forgan Neath 76 D3
Tre-gagle Mon 79 D8
Tre-Gibbon Rhondda 77 E7
Tre Gwyr = Gowerton Swansea 56 B5
Tre-gynwr Carms 74 B6
Tre-hill V Glam 58 E5
Tre-Ifor Rhondda 77 D7
Tre-lan Flint 165 B11
Tre-Mostyn Flint 181 F10
Tre-pit V Glam 58 E2
Tre-Taliesin Ceredig 128 E3
Tre-vaughan Carms 93 G8
Tre-wyn Mon 96 G6
Treadam Mon 78 B5
Treaddow Hereford 97 G10
Treal Corn 2 F6
Trealaw Rhondda 77 G8
Treales Lancs 202 G4
Trearddur Anglesey 178 F3
Treaslane Highld 298 D3
Treath Corn 3 D7
Treator Corn 10 F4
Trebanog Rhondda 77 G8
Trebanos Neath 76 E2
Trebarber Corn 5 C7
Trebartha Corn 11 F11
Trebarwith Corn 11 D7
Trebarwith Strand Corn 10 D6
Trebeath Corn 11 D11
Trebell Green Corn 5 C11
Treberfydd Powys 96 F2
Trebetherick Corn 10 F4
Trebilcock Corn 5 C9
Treble's Holford Som 43 G7
Treborough Som 42 F4
Trebudannon Corn 5 C7
Trebullett Corn 12 F2
Treburgett Corn 11 F7
Treburgie Corn 6 C4
Treburley Corn 12 F3
Treburrick Corn 10 G3
Trebyan Corn 5 C11
Trecastle Powys 95 F7
Trecenydd Caerph 58 B6
Trecott Devon 25 G10
Trecwn Pembs 91 E9
Trecynon Rhondda 77 E7
Tredannick Corn 10 G6
Tredaule Corn 11 E10
Tredavoe Corn 1 D5
Treddiog Pembs 91 F7
Tredegar Bl Gwent 77 D10
Trederwen Powys 148 F5
Tredethy Corn 11 G7
Tredington Glos 99 F8
Tredington Warks 100 C5
Tredinnick Corn 1 C4
Tredinnick Corn 5 D10
Tredinnick Corn 6 B3
Tredinnick Corn 6 D4
Tredinnick Corn 10 G4
Tredogan V Glam 58 F5
Tredomen Caerph 77 G10
Tredomen Powys 96 E2
Tredown Devon 24 D2
Tredrizzick Corn 10 F5
Tredunnock Mon 78 G5
Tredustan Powys 96 E2
Tredworth Glos 80 B4
Treen Corn 1 B4
Treen Corn 1 E3
Treesmill Corn 5 D11
Treeton S Yorks 186 D6
Tref y Clawdd = Knighton Powys 114 C5
Trefaes Gwyn 144 C5
Trefanny Hill Corn 6 D4
Trefasser Pembs 91 D7
Trefdraeth Anglesey 178 G6
Trefdraeth = Newport Pembs 91 D11
Trefecca Powys 96 E2
Trefechan Ceredig 111 A11
Trefechan M Tydf 77 D8
Trefechan Wrex 166 F3
Trefeglwys Powys 129 E9
Trefeitha Powys 96 E2
Trefenter Ceredig 112 D2
Treffgarne Pembs 91 G9
Treffynnon Pembs 90 F6
Treffynnon = Holywell Flint 181 F11
Trefgarn Owen Pembs 91 F7
Trefil Bl Gwent 77 C10
Trefilan Ceredig 111 F11
Trefin = Trevine Pembs 90 E6
Treflach Shrops 148 D5
Trefnanney Powys 148 F4
Trefnant Denb 181 G9
Trefonen Shrops 148 D5
Trefor Anglesey 178 E5
Trefor Gwyn 162 F5
Treforda Corn 11 E7
Treforest Rhondda 58 B5
Treforgan Ceredig 92 B4
Treforys = Morriston Swansea 57 B7
Trefriw Conwy 164 C3
Trefrize Corn 12 F2
Tregada Corn 12 E2
Tregadgwith Corn 1 D4
Tregadillett Corn 12 E2
Tregaian Anglesey 178 F6
Tregajorran Corn 4 G3
Tregamere Corn 5 C8
Tregardock Corn 10 E6
Tregare Mon 78 C6
Tregarland Corn 6 D5
Tregarlandbridge Corn 6 D4
Tregarne Corn 3 E7
Tregaron Ceredig 112 F3
Tregarrick Mill Corn 6 D4
Tregarth Gwyn 163 B10
Tregath Gwyn 163 B10
Tregatillian Corn 5 C8
Tregatta Corn 11 D7
Tregavarah Corn 1 D4
Tregear Corn 2 E5
Tregeare Corn 11 D10
Tregeiriog Wrex 148 C3
Tregele Anglesey 178 C5
Tregellist Corn 10 F6
Tregeseal Corn 1 C3
Tregew Corn 3 C8
Tregidden Corn 3 E7
Treginnis Pembs 90 G4
Treglemais Pembs 90 F6
Tregole Corn 11 B9
Tregolls Corn 2 B6
Tregolwyn = Colwinston V Glam 58 D2
Tregona Corn 5 B7
Tregonce Corn 10 G4
Tregonetha Corn 5 C9
Tregonna Corn 10 G4
Tregonning Corn 5 D7
Tregony Corn 5 G8
Tregoodwell Corn 11 E8
Tregorden Corn 10 G6
Tregorrick Corn 5 E10
Tregoss Corn 5 C9
Tregoyd Powys 96 D4
Tregoyd Mill Powys 96 D3
Tregreenwell Corn 11 E7
Tregrehan Mills Corn 5 E10
Tregroes Ceredig 93 C8
Tregullon Corn 5 C11
Tregunna Corn 10 G5
Tregurrian Corn 5 B7
Tregurtha Downs Corn 2 C2
Tregyddulan Pembs 91 D7
Tregynon Powys 129 D11
Trehafod Rhondda 77 G8
Trehafren Powys 129 E11
Trehan Corn 7 D8
Treharris M Tydf 77 F9
Trehemborne Corn 10 G3
Treherbert Rhondda 76 F6
Trehunist Corn 6 C6
Trekeivesteps Corn 11 G10
Trekenner Corn 12 F2
Trekenning Corn 5 C8
Treknow Corn 11 D7
Trelales = Laleston Bridgend 57 F11
Trelan Corn 2 F6
Trelash Corn 11 C9
Trelassick Corn 5 E7
Trelawnyd Flint 181 F9
Trelech Carms 92 E5
Treleddyd-fawr Pembs 90 F5
Treleigh Corn 4 G4
Treletert = Letterston Pembs 91 F8
Trelew Corn 3 B8
Trelewis M Tydf 77 F10
Treligga Corn 11 E7
Trelights Corn 10 F5
Trelill Corn 10 F6
Trelion Corn 5 E8
Treliske Corn 4 F6
Trelissick Corn 3 B8
Treliver Corn 5 B9
Trellech Mon 79 D8
Trelleck Grange Mon 79 E7
Trelogan Flint 181 E10
Treloquithack Corn 2 D5
Trelowia Corn 6 D5
Trelowth Corn 5 E9
Trelystan Powys 130 C5
Tremadog Gwyn 163 G9
Tremail Corn 11 D9
Tremain Ceredig 92 B4
Tremaine Corn 11 D10
Tremains Bridgend 58 D2
Tremar Corn 6 B5
Trematon Corn 7 D7
Trematon Castle Corn 7 D8
Tremayne Corn 2 B4
Trembraze Corn 6 B5
Tremedda Corn 1 B5
Tremeirchion Denb 181 G9
Tremethick Cross Corn 1 C4
Tremore Corn 5 C10
Tremorebridge Corn 5 C10
Tremorfa Cardiff 59 D8
Trenance Corn 4 C6
Trenance Corn 5 B7
Trenance Corn 5 C9
Trenance Corn 10 G4
Trenant Corn 6 B4
Trenant Corn 10 G5
Trenarren Corn 5 F10
Trenay Corn 6 B3
Trench Telford 150 G3
Trench Green Oxon 65 D7
Trench Wood Kent 52 D5
Trencreek Corn 4 C6
Trencrom Corn 2 B2
Trendeal Corn 5 E7
Trenear Corn 2 C5
Treneglos Corn 11 D10
Trenerth Corn 2 B4
Trenewan Corn 6 E3
Trengune Corn 11 C9
Trenhorne Corn 11 F11
Treningle Corn 5 B10
Treninnick Corn 4 C6
Trenoon Corn 2 F6
Trenoweth Corn 3 C7
Trent Dorset 29 D9
Trent Vale Stoke 168 G5
Trentham Stoke 168 G5

Trentishoe Devon 40 D6
Trentlock Derbys 153 C9
Trenwheal Corn 2 C4
Treoes V Glam 58 D2
Treopert = Granston Pembs 91 E7
Treorchy = Treorci Rhondda 77 F7
Treorci = Treorchy Rhondda 77 F7
Treowen Caerph 78 F2
Treowen Powys 130 E2
Trequite Corn 10 F6
Tre'r-ddôl Ceredig 128 E3
Trer Ilai = Leighton Powys 130 B4
Trerhyngyll V Glam 58 D4
Trerise Corn 2 F6
Trerose Corn 3 D7
Trerulefoot Corn 6 D6
Tresaith Ceredig 110 G5
Tresamble Corn 3 B7
Tresarrett Corn 11 G7
Tresavean Corn 2 B6
Tresawle Corn 5 F7
Tresawsen Corn 4 F5
Trescoll Corn 5 C10
Trescott Staffs 132 D6
Trescowe Corn 2 C3
Tresean Corn 4 D5
Tresevern Croft Corn 2 B6
Tresham Glos 80 G3
Tresigin = Sigingstone V Glam 58 E3
Tresillian Corn 5 F7
Tresimwn = Bonvilston V Glam 58 E5
Tresinney Corn 11 E8
Tresinwen Pembs 91 C7
Treskerby Corn 4 G4
Treskillard Corn 2 B5
Treskilling Corn 5 D10
Treskinnick Cross Corn 11 B10
Treslothan Corn 2 B5
Tresmeer Corn 11 D10
Tresowes Green Corn 2 D3
Tresoweshill Corn 2 D4
Tresparrett Corn 11 C8
Tresparrett Posts Corn 11 C8
Tressady Highld 309 J7
Tressait Perth 291 G10
Tresta Shetland 312 D8
Tresta Shetland 313 H5
Treswell Notts 188 F3
Treswithian Corn 4 G2
Treswithian Downs Corn 4 G2
Trethellan Water Corn 2 B6
Trethevy Corn 11 D7
Trethewell Corn 3 B9
Trethewey Corn 1 E3
Trethillick Corn 10 F4
Trethomas Caerph 59 B7
Trethosa Corn 5 E8
Trethowel Corn 5 E10
Trethurgy Corn 5 D10
Tretio Pembs 90 F5
Tretire Hereford 97 G10
Tretower Powys 96 G3
Treuddyn Flint 166 D3
Trevadlock Corn 11 F11
Trevail Corn 4 D5
Trevalga Corn 11 D7
Trevalgan Corn 1 A5
Trevalyn Wrex 166 D5
Trevance Corn 10 G4
Trevanger Corn 10 F5
Trevanson Corn 10 G5
Trevarrack Corn 1 C5
Trevarren Corn 5 C8
Trevarrian Corn 4 B6
Trevarrick Corn 5 G9
Trevarth Corn 4 G4
Trevaughan Carms 73 B11
Trevaughan Carms 93 G7
Treveal Corn 1 A5
Trevegean Corn 1 D3
Treveighan Corn 11 F7
Trevellas Corn 4 E4
Trevelmond Corn 6 C4
Trevelver Corn 10 G5
Trevemper Corn 4 D6
Treven Corn 11 D7
Trevena Corn 2 D4
Trevenen Corn 2 D5
Trevenen Bal Corn 2 D5
Trevenning Corn 11 F7
Treveor Corn 5 G9
Treverbyn Corn 5 D10
Treverbyn Corn 6 B4
Treverva Corn 3 C7
Trevescan Corn 1 E3
Trevethin Torf 78 E3
Trevia Corn 11 E7
Trevigro Corn 6 B6
Trevilder Corn 10 G6
Trevilla Corn 3 B8
Trevilson Corn 4 D6
Trevine Corn 10 F5
Trevine = Trefin Pembs 90 E6
Treviscoe Corn 5 D8
Treviskey Corn 2 B6
Trevithal Corn 1 D5
Trevoll Corn 4 D6
Trevone Corn 10 F3
Trevor Wrex 166 G3
Trevor Uchaf Denb 166 G2
Trevorrick Corn 10 G4
Trevowah Corn 4 D5
Trevowhan Corn 1 B4
Trew Corn 2 D4
Trewalder Corn 11 E7
Trewarmett Corn 11 D7
Trewartha Corn 2 B2
Trewartha Corn 3 B10
Trewassa Corn 11 D8
Treween Corn 11 E10
Trewellard Corn 1 C3
Trewen Corn 11 E11
Trewen Corn 11 E7
Trewen Mon 79 G7
Trewennack Corn 2 D5
Trewennan Corn 11 E7
Trewern Powys 148 G5
Trewetha Corn 10 E6
Trewethen Corn 10 F6
Trewethern Corn 10 F6
Trewey Corn 1 B5
Trewidland Corn 6 D5
Trewindle Corn 6 C2
Trewint Corn 6 C5
Trewint Corn 11 B9
Trewint Corn 11 E10
Trewithian Corn 3 B9
Trewithick Corn 11 D11
Trewollock Corn 5 G10
Trewoodloe Corn 12 G2
Trewoofe Corn 1 D4
Trewoon Corn 2 F5
Trewoon Corn 5 E9
Treworga Corn 5 G7
Treworgan Common Mon 78 D6
Treworlas Corn 3 B9
Treworld Corn 11 C8
Trewornan Corn 10 G5
Treworrick Corn 6 B4
Treworthal Corn 3 B9
Trewyddel = Moylgrove Pembs 92 C2
Trewyn Devon 24 G4
Treyarnon Corn 10 G3
Treyford W Sus 34 D4
Trezaise Corn 5 D9
Trezelah Corn 1 C5
Triangle Glos 79 E8
Triangle Staffs 133 B11
Triangle W Yorks 196 C4
Trickett's Cross Dorset 31 G9
Triffleton Pembs 91 G9
Trillacott Corn 11 D11
Trimdon Durham 234 E3
Trimdon Colliery Durham 234 D3
Trimdon Grange Durham 234 D3
Trimingham Norf 160 B5
Trimley Lower Street Suff 108 D5
Trimley St Martin Suff 108 D5
Trimley St Mary Suff 108 D5
Trimpley Worcs 116 B5
Trims Green Herts 87 B7
Trimsaran Carms 75 E7
Trimstone Devon 40 E3
Trinafour Perth 291 G9
Trinant Caerph 78 E2
Tring Herts 84 C6
Tring Wharf Herts 84 C6
Tringford Herts 84 C6
Trinity Angus 293 G8
Trinity Devon 27 F7
Trinity Edin 280 F4
Trinity Fields Staffs 151 D8
Trisant Ceredig 112 B4
Triscombe Som 43 F7
Trislaig Highld 290 F2
Trispen Corn 4 E6
Tritlington Northum 252 E6
Troan Corn 5 D7
Trochry Perth 286 C3
Trodigal Argyll 255 E7
Troearhiwgwair Bl Gwent 77 D11
Troedrhiwdalar Powys 113 G9
Troedrhiwffenyd Ceredig 93 C8
Troedrhiwfuwch Caerph 77 E10
Troedyraur Ceredig 92 B6
Troedyrhiw M Tydf 77 E9
Trofarth Conwy 180 G5
Trolliloes E Sus 23 C10
Tromode I o M 192 E4
Trondavoe Shetland 312 F5
Troon Corn 2 B5
Troon S Ayrs 257 C8
Trooper's Inn Pembs 73 C7
Trosaraidh W Isles 297 K3
Trossachs Hotel Stirl 285 G9
Troston Suff 125 C7
Trostre Carms 56 B4
Trostrey Common Mon 78 E5
Troswell Corn 11 C11
Trotshill Worcs 117 F7
Trotten Marsh W Sus 34 B4
Trottiscliffe Kent 68 G6
Trotton W Sus 34 C4
Trough Gate Lancs 195 C11
Troutbeck Cumb 221 E8
Troutbeck Cumb 230 F3
Troutbeck Bridge Cumb 221 F8
Trow Green Glos 79 D9
Troway Derbys 186 F5
Trowbridge Cardiff 59 C8
Trowbridge Wilts 45 B11
Trowell Notts 153 B9
Trowle Common Wilts 45 B10
Trowley Bottom Herts 85 C9
Trows Borders 262 C5
Trowse Newton Norf 142 B4
Troy Town Kent 52 D2
Troy Town Kent 54 E5
Troy Town Medway 69 F8
Troydale W Yorks 205 G10
Truas Corn 11 D7
Trub Gtr Man 195 F11
Trudoxhill Som 45 E8
True Street Devon 8 C6
Trueman's Heath Worcs 117 B11
Trull Som 28 C2
Trumaisgearraidh W Isles 296 D4
Trumfleet S Yorks 198 E6
Trumpan Highld 298 C2
Trumpet Hereford 98 D3
Trumpington Cambs 123 F8
Trumpsgreen Sur 66 F3
Trunch Norf 160 C5
Trunnah Lancs 202 E2
Truro Corn 4 G6
Truscott Corn 12 D2
Trusham Devon 14 E3
Trusley Derbys 152 B5
Trussall Corn 2 D5
Trussell Corn 11 D10
Trusthorpe Lincs 191 E8
Truthan Corn 4 E6
Truthwall Corn 2 C2
Trwstllewelyn Powys 130 D3
Tryfil Anglesey 178 E6
Trysull Staffs 133 E7
Trythogga Corn 1 C5
Tubbs Mill Corn 5 G9
Tubney Oxon 82 F6
Tubslake Kent 53 G9
Tuckenhay Devon 8 D6
Tuckermarsh Devon 7 B8
Tuckerton Som 28 B3
Tuckhill Shrops 132 F5
Tucking Mill Bath 61 G9
Tuckingmill Corn 4 G3
Tuckingmill Corn 11 F7
Tuckingmill Wilts 30 B6
Tuckton Bmouth 19 C8
Tuddenham Suff 108 B3
Tuddenham Suff 124 C4
Tuddenham St Martin Suff 108 B3
Tudeley Kent 52 D6
Tudeley Hale Kent 52 D6
Tudhay Devon 28 G4
Tudhoe Durham 233 D11
Tudhoe Grange Durham 233 E11
Tudor Hill W Mid 134 D2
Tudorville Hereford 97 G11
Tudweiliog Gwyn 144 B4
Tuebrook Mers 182 C5
Tuesley Sur 50 E3
Tuesnoad Kent 54 E2
Tuffley Glos 80 C4
Tufnell Park London 67 B9
Tufton Hants 48 D3
Tufton Pembs 91 F10
Tugby Leics 136 C5
Tugford Shrops 131 F11
Tughall Northumb 264 D6
Tulchan Lodge Angus 292 F3
Tullecombe W Sus 34 B4
Tullibardine Perth 286 F3
Tullibody Clack 279 B7
Tullich Argyll 284 F4
Tullich Highld 299 E9
Tullich Highld 300 G6
Tullich Muir Highld 301 B7
Tulliemet Perth 286 B3
Tulloch Aberds 293 F9
Tulloch Aberds 303 F8
Tulloch Highld 290 E5
Tulloch Perth 286 E4
Tulloch Castle Highld 300 C5
Tulloch-gribban Highld 301 G9
Tullochgorm Argyll 275 D10
Tullochroisk Perth 285 B11
Tullochvenus Aberds 293 C7
Tulloes Angus 287 C9
Tullybannocher Perth 285 E11
Tullybelton Perth 286 D4
Tullycross Stirl 277 D9
Tullyfergus Perth 286 C6
Tullymurdoch Perth 286 B5
Tullynessle Aberds 293 B7
Tulse Hill London 67 E10
Tumble = Y Tymbl Carms 75 C8
Tumbler's Green Essex 106 F6
Tumby Lincs 174 D2
Tumby Woodside Lincs 174 D3
Tummel Bridge Perth 285 B11
Tumpy Green Glos 80 E2
Tumpy Lakes Hereford 97 B10
Tunbridge Hill Medway 69 E10
Tunbridge Wells = Royal Tunbridge Wells Kent 52 F5
Tunga W Isles 304 E6
Tungate Norf 160 D5
Tunley Bath 45 B7
Tunley Glos 80 E6
Tunnel Hill Worcs 98 C6
Tunnel Pits N Lincs 199 G8
Tunshill Gtr Man 196 E2
Tunstall E Yorks 209 G12
Tunstall Kent 69 G11
Tunstall Lancs 212 E2
Tunstall N Yorks 224 F4
Tunstall Norf 143 B8
Tunstall Staffs 150 D5
Tunstall Stoke 168 E5
Tunstall Suff 127 G7
Tunstall T & W 243 G9
Tunstead Derbys 185 G10
Tunstead Gtr Man 196 G4
Tunstead Norf 160 E5
Tunworth Hants 49 D7
Tupsley Hereford 97 C10
Tupton Derbys 170 B5
Tur Langton Leics 136 E4
Turbary Common Poole 19 C7
Turf Hill Gtr Man 196 E2
Turfdown Corn 5 B11
Turfholm S Lnrk 259 B8
Turfmoor Devon 28 G3
Turfmoor Shrops 149 F7
Turgis Green Hants 49 B7
Turin Angus 287 B9
Turkdean Glos 81 B10
Turkey Island Hants 33 E9
Turkey Island W Sus 34 D3
Turkey Tump Hereford 97 F10
Turleigh Wilts 61 G10
Turleygreen Shrops 132 F5
Turlin Moor Poole 18 C5
Turmer Hants 31 F10
Turn Lancs 195 D10
Turnalt Argyll 275 C9
Turnastone Hereford 97 E7
Turnberry S Ayrs 244 B6
Turnchapel Plym 7 E9
Turnditch Derbys 170 F3
Turner Green Lancs 203 G8
Turner's Green E Sus 23 B10
Turner's Green E Sus 52 G6
Turner's Green W Berks 64 F4
Turner's Green Warks 118 D3
Turners Hill W Sus 51 F10
Turners Puddle Dorset 18 C2
Turnerwood S Yorks 187 E8
Turnford Herts 86 E5
Turnhouse Edin 280 G3
Turnhurst Stoke 168 E5
Turnstead Milton Derbys 185 E8
Turnworth Dorset 30 F4
Turrerich Perth 286 D2
Turriff Aberds 303 D7
Tursdale Durham 234 D2
Turton Bottoms Blkburn 195 D8
Turves Cambs 138 D6
Turves Green W Mid 117 B10
Turvey Beds 121 G8
Turville Bucks 84 G3
Turville Heath Bucks 84 G2
Turweston Bucks 102 D2
Tushielaw Borders 261 F8
Tutbury Staffs 152 D4
Tutnall Worcs 117 C9
Tutnalls Glos 79 E10
Tutshill Glos 79 G8
Tutt Hill Kent 54 D3
Tuttington Norf 160 D4
Tutts Clump W Berks 64 E5
Tutwell Corn 12 F3
Tuxford Notts 188 G2
Twatt Orkney 314 D2
Twatt Shetland 313 H5
Twechar E Dunb 278 F4
Tweedale Telford 132 C4
Tweeddaleburn Borders 270 E5
Tweedmouth Northumb 273 E9
Tweedsmuir Borders 260 E3
Twelve Heads Corn 4 G5
Twelve Oaks E Sus 37 C11
Twelvewoods Corn 6 B4
Twemlow Green E Ches 168 B3
Twenties Kent 71 F10
Twenty Lincs 156 E3
Twerton Bath 61 G8
Twickenham London 67 E7
Twigworth Glos 98 G6
Twineham W Sus 36 D3
Twineham Green W Sus 36 C3
Twinhoe Bath 45 B8
Twinstead Essex 107 D7
Twinstead Green Essex 106 D6
Twiss Green Warr 183 B11
Twist Devon 28 G3
Twiston Lancs 204 E2
Twitchen Devon 41 G9
Twitchen Shrops 115 B7
Twitchen Mill Devon 41 G9
Twitham Kent 55 B9
Twitton Kent 52 B4
Two Bridges Devon 13 G8
Two Bridges Glos 79 D11
Two Burrows Corn 4 F4
Two Dales Derbys 170 C3
Two Gates Staffs 134 C4
Two Mile Ash M Keynes 102 D6
Two Mile Ash W Sus 35 B10
Two Mile Hill Bristol 60 E6
Two Mile Oak Cross Devon 8 B6
Two Mills W Ches 182 G5
Two Pots Devon 40 E4
Two Waters Herts 85 D9
Twr Anglesey 178 E2
Twycross Leics 134 C6
Twydall Medway 69 F9
Twyford Bucks 102 F3
Twyford Derbys 152 D6
Twyford Dorset 30 D5
Twyford Hants 33 C7
Twyford Leics 154 G4
Twyford Lincs 155 E8
Twyford Norf 159 E10
Twyford Oxon 101 D9
Twyford Shrops 148 D6
Twyford Wokingham 65 D9
Twyford Worcs 99 B10
Twyford Common Hereford 97 D10
Twyn-Allws Mon 78 C3
Twyn Shôn-Ifan Caerph 77 G11
Twyn-y-Sheriff Mon 78 D6
Twyn-yr-odyn V Glam 58 E6
Twynholm Dumfries 237 D8
Twyning Glos 99 D7
Twyning Green Glos 99 D8
Twynllanan Carms 94 G5
Twynmynydd Carms 75 C11
Twynyrodyn M Tydf 77 D9
Twywell Northants 121 B9
Ty-coch Swansea 56 C6
Ty-draw Conwy 164 D5
Ty-draw Swansea 57 C7
Ty-fry Mon 78 F6
Ty-hen Carms 92 G6
Ty-hen Gwyn 144 C3
Ty-isaf Carms 56 B4
Ty Llwyn Bl Gwent 77 D11
Ty-mawr Anglesey 179 D7
Ty Mawr Carms 93 C10
Ty-mawr Conwy 181 F7
Ty Mawr Cwm Conwy 164 F6
Ty-nant Conwy 165 G7
Ty-nant Gwyn 147 D8
Ty-Newydd Ceredig 111 D10
Ty Rhiw Rhondda 58 C6
Ty-Sign Caerph 78 G2
Ty-uchaf Powys 147 E10
Tyberton Hereford 97 D7
Tyburn W Mid 134 E2
Tyby Norf 159 D11
Tycroes Carms 75 C10
Tycrwyn Powys 148 F2
Tydd Gote Lincs 157 F9
Tydd St Giles Cambs 157 F8
Tydd St Mary Lincs 157 F8
Tyddewi = St Davids Pembs 90 F5
Tyddyn Powys 129 F9
Tyddyn Angharad Denb 165 F9
Tyddyn Dai Anglesey 178 C6
Tyddyn-mawr Gwyn 163 G9
Tye Hants 22 C2
Tye Common Essex 87 G11
Tye Green Essex 87 C10
Tye Green Essex 87 D7
Tye Green Essex 87 F11
Tye Green Essex 105 D11
Tye Green Essex 105 G10
Tye Green Essex 106 G5
Tyegate Green Norf 161 G7
Tyersal W Yorks 205 G9
Tyganol V Glam 58 E4
Tyla Mon 78 C2
Tylagwyn Bridgend 58 B2
Tyldesley Gtr Man 195 G7
Tyle Carms 94 F3
Tyle-garw Rhondda 58 C4
Tyler Hill Kent 70 G6
Tylers Causeway Herts 86 D3
Tylers Green Bucks 84 G6
Tyler's Green Essex 87 D8
Tyler's Green Sur 51 C11
Tyler's Hill Bucks 85 E7
Tylorstown Rhondda 77 F8
Tylwch Powys 129 G9
Tyn-lon Gwyn 163 D7
Ty'n-y-bryn Rhondda 58 B4
Tyn-y-celyn Wrex 148 B3
Tyn-y-coed Shrops 148 D4
Ty'n-y-coedcae Caerph 59 B7
Tyn-y-cwm Swansea 75 E10
Tyn-y-fedwen Powys 148 C2
Ty'n-y-ffordd Denb 181 G8
Tyn-y-ffridd Powys 148 C2
Ty'n-y-garn Bridgend 57 E11
Tyn-y-graig Powys 113 G10
Ty'n-y-groes Conwy 180 G3
Ty'n-y-maes Gwyn 163 C10
Tyn-y-pwll Anglesey 178 D6
Ty'n-yr-eithin Ceredig 112 E3
Tynant Rhondda 58 B5
Tyncelyn Ceredig 112 E2
Tyndrum Stirl 285 D7
Tyne Dock T & W 243 D9
Tyne Tunnel T & W 243 D8
Tyneham Dorset 18 E3
Tynehead Midloth 271 D7
Tynemouth T & W 243 D9
Tynewydd Ceredig 92 B4
Tynewydd Neath 76 D4
Tynewydd Rhondda 76 F6
Tyning Bath 45 B7
Tyninghame E Loth 282 F2
Tynron Dumfries 247 E8
Tyntesfield N Som 60 E4
Tyntetown Rhondda 77 F9
Tynyfedw Conwy 165 B7
Tynygongl Anglesey 179 E8
Tynygraig Ceredig 112 D3
Tynyrwtra Powys 129 F7
Tŷ'r-felin-isaf Conwy 164 C5
Tyrells End C Beds 103 E9
Tyrell's Wood Sur 51 B7
Tyrie Aberds 303 C9
Tyringham M Keynes 103 B7
Tyseley W Mid 134 G2
Tythecott Devon 24 D6
Tythegston Bridgend 57 F11
Tytherington E Ches 184 F6
Tytherington S Glos 61 B7
Tytherington Som 45 D9
Tytherington Wilts 46 E2
Tytherleigh Devon 28 G4
Tytherton Lucas Wilts 62 E2
Tyttenhanger Herts 85 D11
Tywardreath Corn 5 E11
Tywardreath Highway Corn 5 D11
Tywyn Conwy 180 F3
Tywyn Gwyn 110 C2

U

Uachdar W Isles 296 F3
Uags Highld 295 B9
Ubberley Stoke 168 F6
Ubbeston Green Suff 126 C6
Ubley Bath 44 B4
Uckerby N Yorks 224 E4
Uckfield E Sus 37 C7
Uckinghall Worcs 99 D7
Uckington Glos 99 G8
Uckington Shrops 131 B11
Uddingston S Lnrk 268 C3
Uddington S Lnrk 259 C9
Udimore E Sus 38 D5
Udley N Som 60 G3
Udny Green Aberds 303 G8
Udny Station Aberds 303 G9
Udston S Lnrk 268 D3
Udstonhead S Lnrk 268 F4
Uffcott Wilts 62 D6
Uffculme Devon 27 E9
Uffington Lincs 137 B11
Uffington Oxon 63 B10
Uffington Shrops 149 G10
Ufford P'boro 137 C11
Ufford Suff 126 G5
Ufton Warks 119 E7
Ufton Green W Berks 64 F6
Ufton Nervet W Berks 64 F6
Ugadale Argyll 255 E8
Ugborough Devon 8 D3
Ugford Wilts 46 G5
Uggeshall Suff 143 G8
Ugglebarnby N Yorks 227 D7
Ughill S Yorks 186 C3
Ugley Essex 105 F10
Ugley Green Essex 105 F10
Ugthorpe N Yorks 226 C5
Uidh W Isles 297 M2
Uig Argyll 276 E2
Uig Argyll 288 D3
Uig Highld 296 F7
Uig Highld 298 C3
Uigen W Isles 304 E2
Uigshader Highld 298 E4
Uisken Argyll 274 B4
Ulaw Aberds 303 G9
Ulbster Highld 310 E7
Ulcat Row Cumb 230 G4
Ulceby Lincs 190 G6
Ulceby N Lincs 200 E6
Ulceby Skitter N Lincs 200 E6
Ulcombe Kent 53 D10
Uldale Cumb 229 D10
Uley Glos 80 F3
Ulgham Northumb 252 E6
Ullapool Highld 307 K6
Ullcombe Devon 28 F2
Ullenhall Warks 118 D2
Ullenwood Glos 80 B6
Ulleskelf N Yorks 206 E6
Ullesthorpe Leics 135 F10
Ulley S Yorks 187 D7
Ullingswick Hereford 97 B11
Ullington Worcs 100 B2
Ullinish Highld 294 B5
Ullock Cumb 229 G10
Ullock Cumb 229 G7
Ulnes Walton Lancs 194 D4
Ulpha Cumb 220 G3
Ulrome E Yorks 209 B9
Ulshaw N Yorks 214 B2
Ulsta Shetland 312 E6
Ulva House Argyll 288 F6
Ulverley Green W Mid 134 G2
Ulverston Cumb 210 D5
Ulwell Dorset 18 E6
Umberleigh Devon 25 C10
Unapool Highld 306 F7
Unasary W Isles 297 J3
Under Bank W Yorks 196 F6
Under the Wood Kent 71 F8
Under Tofts S Yorks 186 D4
Underbarrow Cumb 221 G9
Undercliffe W Yorks 205 G9
Underdale Shrops 149 G10
Underdown Devon 14 D3
Underhill London 86 F3
Underhill Wilts 45 G11
Underhoull Shetland 312 C7
Underling Green Kent 53 D9
Underriver Kent 52 C5
Underriver Ho Kent 52 C5
Underton Shrops 132 E3
Underwood Newport 59 B11
Underwood Notts 171 E7
Underwood Pembs 73 C7
Underwood Plym 7 D10
Undley Suff 140 G3
Undy Mon 60 B2
Ungisiadar W Isles 304 F3
Unifirth Shetland 313 H4
Union Cottage Aberds 293 D10
Union Mills I o M 192 E4
Union Street E Sus 53 G8
United Downs Corn 4 G4
Unstone Derbys 186 F5
Unstone Green Derbys 186 F5
Unsworth Gtr Man 195 F10
Unthank Cumb 230 B3
Unthank Cumb 230 D5
Unthank Cumb 231 C8
Unthank Derbys 186 F4
Unthank End Cumb 230 D5
Up Cerne Dorset 29 G11
Up End M Keynes 103 B8
Up Exe Devon 26 G6
Up Green Hants 65 G9
Up Hatherley Glos 99 G8
Up Holland Lancs 194 F4
Up Marden W Sus 34 E3
Up Mudford Som 29 D9
Up Nately Hants 49 C7
Up Somborne Hants 47 G11
Up Sydling Dorset 29 G10
Upavon Wilts 46 C6
Upchurch Kent 69 F10
Upcott Devon 24 D2
Upcott Devon 25 F11
Upcott Devon 25 F9
Upcott Devon 40 F3
Upcott Hereford 114 G6
Upcott Som 27 C11
Upend Cambs 124 F3
Upgate Norf 160 F2
Upgate Street Norf 141 E11
Upgate Street Norf 142 E5
Uphall Dorset 29 G9
Uphall W Loth 279 G11
Uphall Station W Loth 279 G11
Upham Devon 26 F5
Upham Hants 33 C8
Uphampton Hereford 115 E7
Uphampton Worcs 116 E6
Uphempston Devon 8 C6
Uphill N Som 43 B10
Uphill Manor N Som 43 B10
Uplands Glos 80 D5
Uplands Swansea 56 C6
Uplawmoor E Renf 267 D8
Upleadon Glos 98 F5
Upleadon Court Glos 98 F5
Upleatham Redcar 226 B2
Uplees Kent 70 G3
Uploders Dorset 16 C6
Uplowman Devon 27 D8
Uplyme Devon 16 C2
Upminster London 68 B5
Upnor Medway 69 E9
Upottery Devon 28 F2
Uppacott Devon 25 B9
Uppat Highld 311 J2
Uppend Essex 105 F9
Upper Affcot Shrops 131 F8
Upper Ardchronie Highld 309 L6
Upper Ardgrain Aberds 303 F9
Upper Ardroscadale Argyll 275 G11
Upper Arley Worcs 132 G5
Upper Armley W Yorks 205 G11
Upper Arncott Oxon 83 B10
Upper Astley Shrops 149 F10
Upper Aston Shrops 132 E6
Upper Astrop Northants 101 D10
Upper Badcall Highld 306 E6
Upper Bangor Gwyn 179 G9
Upper Basildon W Berks 64 D5
Upper Batley W Yorks 197 B8
Upper Battlefield Shrops 149 F10
Upper Beeding W Sus 35 E11
Upper Benefield Northants 137 F9
Upper Bentley Worcs 117 D9
Upper Bighouse Highld 310 D2
Upper Birchwood Derbys 170 E6
Upper Blainslie Borders 271 G10
Upper Boat Rhondda 58 B6
Upper Boddam Aberds 302 F6
Upper Boddington Northants 119 G9
Upper Bogrow Highld 309 L7
Upper Bogside Moray 302 D2
Upper Bonchurch I o W 21 F7
Upper Booth Derbys 185 D10
Upper Borth Ceredig 128 F2
Upper Boyndlie Aberds 303 C9
Upper Brailes Warks 100 D6
Upper Brandon Parva Norf 141 B10
Upper Breakish Highld 295 C8
Upper Breinton Hereford 97 C9
Upper Broadheath Worcs 116 F6
Upper Brockholes W Yorks 196 B5
Upper Broughton Notts 154 D3
Upper Broxwood Hereford 115 G7
Upper Bruntingthorpe Leics 136 F2
Upper Brynamman Carms 76 C2
Upper Buckenhill Hereford 97 E11
Upper Bucklebury W Berks 64 F4
Upper Bullington Hants 48 E3
Upper Burgate Hants 31 D11
Upper Burnhaugh Aberds 293 D10
Upper Bush Medway 69 F7
Upper Caldecote C Beds 104 B3
Upper Cam Glos 80 F3
Upper Canada N Som 43 B11
Upper Canterton Hants 32 E3
Upper Catesby Northants 119 F10
Upper Catshill Worcs 117 C9
Upper Chapel Powys 95 C10
Upper Cheddon Som 28 B2
Upper Chicksgrove Wilts 31 B7
Upper Church Village Rhondda 58 B5
Upper Chute Wilts 47 C9
Upper Clapton London 67 B10
Upper Clatford Hants 47 E11
Upper Coberley Glos 81 B7
Upper College Shrops 149 C11
Upper Colwall Hereford 98 C5
Upper Common Hants 48 D6
Upper Cotburn Aberds 303 D7
Upper Cotton Staffs 169 F9
Upper Coullie Aberds 293 B9
Upper Cound Shrops 131 C11
Upper Croxley Som 44 E4
Upper Cudworth S Yorks 197 F11
Upper Culphin Aberds 302 D6
Upper Cumberworth W Yorks 197 F8
Upper Cwm-twrch Powys 76 C3
Upper Cwmbran Torf 78 F3
Upper Dallachy Moray 302 C3
Upper Deal Kent 55 C11
Upper Dean Beds 121 D10
Upper Dean Devon 8 C4
Upper Denby W Yorks 197 D8
Upper Denby W Yorks 197 F8
Upper Denton Cumb 240 D4
Upper Derraid Highld 301 F10
Upper Diabaig Highld 299 C8
Upper Dicker E Sus 23 D9
Upper Dinchope Shrops 131 G9
Upper Dormington Hereford 97 D11
Upper Dounreay Highld 310 C4
Upper Dovercourt Essex 108 E4
Upper Dowdeswell Glos 81 B8
Upper Druimfin Argyll 289 D7
Upper Dunsforth N Yorks 215 G8
Upper Dunsley Herts 84 C6
Upper Eashing Sur 50 E3
Upper Eastern Green W Mid 134 G5

Upper Eathie Highld 301 C7
Upper Edmonton London 86 G4
Upper Egleton Hereford 98 C2
Upper Elkstone Staffs 169 D9
Upper Ellastone Staffs 169 G10
Upper Elmers End London 67 F11
Upper End Derbys 185 F9
Upper End Glos 81 C10
Upper End Glos 81 D8
Upper End Leics 154 G4
Upper Enham Hants 47 D11
Upper Farmcote Shrops 132 E5
Upper Farringdon Hants 49 F8
Upper Feorlig Highld 298 E2
Upper Fivehead Som 28 C4
Upper Forge Shrops 132 F4
Upper Framilode Glos 80 C3
Upper Froyle Hants 49 E9
Upper Gambolds Worcs 117 D9
Upper Gills Highld 310 B7
Upper Glenfintaig Highld 290 E4
Upper Godney Som 44 E3
Upper Goldstone Kent 71 G9
Upper Gornal W Mid 133 E8
Upper Gravenhurst C Beds 104 D2
Upper Green Essex 105 E8
Upper Green Mon 78 B5
Upper Green Suff 124 E4
Upper Green W Berks 63 G11
Upper Green W Yorks 197 B9
Upper Grove Common Hereford 97 F11
Upper Guist Norf 159 D10
Upper Hackney Derbys 170 C3
Upper Hale Sur 49 D10
Upper Halistra Highld 298 D2
Upper Halliford Sur 66 F5
Upper Halling Medway 69 G7
Upper Ham Worcs 99 D7
Upper Hambleton Rutland 137 B8
Upper Hamnish Hereford 115 F10
Upper Harbledown Kent 54 B6
Upper Hardres Court Kent 55 C7
Upper Hardwick Hereford 115 F8
Upper Hartfield E Sus 52 G3
Upper Hartshay Derbys 170 E5
Upper Haselor Worcs 99 C10
Upper Hatton Staffs 150 B6
Upper Haugh S Yorks 186 B6
Upper Hawkhillock Aberds 303 F10
Upper Hayesden Kent 52 E5
Upper Hayton Shrops 131 G10
Upper Heath Shrops 131 F11
Upper Heaton W Yorks 197 D7
Upper Hellesdon Norf 160 G4
Upper Helmsley N Yorks 207 B9
Upper Hengoed Shrops 148 C5
Upper Hergest Hereford 114 G5
Upper Heyford Northants 120 F3
Upper Heyford Oxon 101 F9
Upper Hill Glos 79 F11
Upper Hill Hereford 115 G9
Upper Hindhope Borders 251 B7
Upper Holloway London 67 B9
Upper Holton Suff 127 B8
Upper Hopton W Yorks 197 D7
Upper Horsebridge E Sus 23 C9
Upper Howsell Worcs 98 B5
Upper Hoyland S Yorks 197 G11
Upper Hulme Staffs 169 C8
Upper Hyde I o W 21 E7
Upper Ifold Sur 50 G4
Upper Inglesham Swindon 82 F2
Upper Inverbrough Highld 301 F8
Upper Kergord Shetland 313 H6
Upper Kidston Borders 270 G4
Upper Kilcott Glos 61 B9
Upper Killay Swansea 56 C5
Upper Killeyan Argyll 254 C3
Upper Kinsham Hereford 115 D7
Upper Knockando Moray 301 E11
Upper Lambourn W Berks 63 C10
Upper Landywood Staffs 133 B9
Upper Langford N Som 44 B3
Upper Langwith Derbys 171 B8
Upper Layham Suff 107 C10
Upper Leigh Staffs 151 B10
Upper Lenie Highld 300 G5
Upper Littleton N Som 60 G5
Upper Loads Derbys 170 B4
Upper Lochton Aberds 293 D8
Upper Lode Worcs 99 E7
Upper Longdon Staffs 151 G11
Upper Longwood Shrops 132 B2
Upper Ludstone Shrops 132 D6
Upper Lybster Highld 310 F6
Upper Lydbrook Glos 79 B10
Upper Lyde Hereford 97 C9
Upper Lye Hereford 115 D7
Upper Maes-coed Hereford 96 D6
Upper Marsh W Yorks 204 F6
Upper Midhope S Yorks 186 B2
Upper Midway Derbys 152 E5
Upper Milovaig Highld 297 G7
Upper Milton Oxon 82 B3
Upper Milton Som 44 D4
Upper Minety Wilts 81 G8
Upper Mitton Worcs 116 C6
Upper Moor Worcs 99 B9
Upper Moor Side W Yorks 205 G10
Upper Morton S Glos 79 G11
Upper Nash Pembs 73 E8
Upper Netchwood Shrops 132 E2
Upper Newbold Derbys 186 G5
Upper Nobut Staffs 151 B10
Upper North Dean Bucks 84 F4
Upper Norwood London 67 F10
Upper Norwood W Sus 34 D6
Upper Obney Perth 286 D4
Upper Ochrwyth Caerph 59 B8
Upper Oddington Glos 100 F4
Upper Ollach Highld 295 B7
Upper Padley Derbys 186 F2
Upper Pickwick Wilts 61 E11
Upper Pollicott Bucks 84 C2
Upper Poppleton York 207 C7
Upper Port Highld 301 G10
Upper Postern Kent 52 D6
Upper Quinton Warks 100 B3
Upper Race Torf 78 F3
Upper Ratley Hants 32 C4
Upper Ridinghill Aberds 303 D10
Upper Rissington Glos 82 B2
Upper Rochford Worcs 116 D2
Upper Rodmersham Kent 70 G2
Upper Sandaig Highld 295 D9
Upper Sanday Orkney 314 F5
Upper Sapey Hereford 116 E3
Upper Saxondale Notts 154 B3
Upper Seagry Wilts 62 C2
Upper Shelton C Beds 103 C9
Upper Sheringham Norf 177 E10
Upper Shirley London 67 G11
Upper Shirley Soton 32 E6
Upper Siddington Glos 81 F8
Upper Skelmorlie N Ayrs 266 B4
Upper Slackstead Hants 32 B5
Upper Slaughter Glos 100 G3
Upper Solva Pembs 90 G5
Upper Soudley Glos 79 C11
Upper Stanton Drew Bath 60 G6
Upper Staploe Beds 122 F2
Upper Stoke Norf 142 C5
Upper Stoke W Mid 135 G7
Upper Stondon C Beds 104 D2
Upper Stowe Northants 120 F2
Upper Stratton Swindon 63 B7
Upper Street Hants 31 D11
Upper Street Norf 142 G3
Upper Street Norf 160 B5
Upper Street Norf 160 E6
Upper Street Norf 160 F6
Upper Street Norf 161 F7
Upper Street Suff 108 E2
Upper Street Suff 124 G5
Upper Street Suff 126 G2
Upper Strensham Worcs 99 D8
Upper Studley Wilts 45 B10
Upper Sundon C Beds 103 F10
Upper Swainswick Bath 61 F9
Upper Swanmore Hants 33 D9
Upper Swell Glos 100 F3
Upper Sydenham London 67 E10
Upper Tankersley S Yorks 186 B4
Upper Tean Staffs 151 B10
Upper Threapwood W Ches 166 F6
Upper Thurnham Lancs 202 C5
Upper Tillyrie Perth 286 G5
Upper Tooting London 67 E9
Upper Tote Highld 298 D5
Upper Town Derbys 170 D3
Upper Town Derbys 170 E2
Upper Town Durham 233 D7
Upper Town Hereford 97 B11
Upper Town N Som 60 F4
Upper Town Suff 125 D8
Upper Town W Yorks 204 G6
Upper Town Wilts 62 D3
Upper Treverward Shrops 114 B5
Upper Tysoe Warks 100 C6
Upper Up Glos 81 F8
Upper Upham Wilts 63 D8
Upper Upnor Medway 69 E9
Upper Vobster Som 45 D8
Upper Walthamstow London 67 B11
Upper Wardington Oxon 101 B9
Upper Wardley W Sus 34 B4
Upper Weald M Keynes 102 D5
Upper Weedon Northants 120 F2
Upper Welland Worcs 98 C5
Upper Wellingham E Sus 36 E6
Upper Welson Hereford 114 G5
Upper Westholme Som 44 E5
Upper Weston Bath 61 F8
Upper Weybread Suff 126 B4
Upper Whiston S Yorks 187 D7
Upper Wick Glos 80 F2
Upper Wick Worcs 116 G6
Upper Wield Hants 48 F6
Upper Wigginton Shrops 148 B6
Upper Winchendon Bucks 84 C2
Upper Witton W Mid 133 E11
Upper Wolvercote Oxon 83 D7
Upper Wolverton Worcs 117 G8
Upper Woodend Aberds 293 B8
Upper Woodford Wilts 46 F6
Upper Woolhampton W Berks 64 F5
Upper Wootton Hants 48 C5
Upper Wraxall Wilts 61 E10
Upper Wyche Hereford 98 C5
Upperby Cumb 239 G10
Upperdale Derbys 185 G11
Uppermill Gtr Man 196 F3
Uppersound Shetland 313 J6
Upperthong W Yorks 196 F6
Upperthorpe Derbys 187 E7
Upperthorpe N Lincs 199 G9
Upperton E Sus 23 E10
Upperton Oxon 83 G11
Upperton W Sus 35 C7
Uppertown Derbys 170 C4
Uppertown Highld 300 F4
Uppertown Highld 310 B7
Uppertown Northumb 241 C9
Uppertown Orkney 314 G4
Upperwood Derbys 170 D3
Uppincott Devon 26 G5
Uppingham Rutland 137 D7
Uppington Dorset 31 F8
Uppington Shrops 132 B2
Upsall N Yorks 215 B9
Upsher Green Suff 107 C8
Upshire Essex 86 E6
Upstreet Kent 71 G8
Upthorpe Glos 80 E3
Upthorpe Suff 125 C9
Upton Bucks 84 C3
Upton Cambs 122 B3
Upton Corn 11 G11
Upton Corn 24 G2
Upton Cumb 230 D2
Upton Devon 8 G4
Upton Devon 27 G9
Upton Dorset 17 E10
Upton Dorset 18 C5
Upton E Yorks 209 C8
Upton Hants 32 D5
Upton Hants 47 B11
Upton I o W 21 C7
Upton Kent 71 F11
Upton Leics 135 D7
Upton Lincs 188 D5
Upton London 68 C2
Upton Mers 182 D3
Upton Mers 183 D7
Upton Norf 161 G7
Upton Northants 120 E4
Upton Notts 172 E2
Upton Notts 188 F2
Upton Oxon 64 B4
Upton Oxon 82 C2
Upton P'boro 138 C2
Upton Slough 66 D3
Upton Som 27 B7
Upton Som 29 B7
Upton W Ches 166 B6
Upton W Yorks 198 E3
Upton Warks 118 F2
Upton Wilts 45 G11
Upton Bishop Hereford 98 F2
Upton Cheyney S Glos 61 F7
Upton Cressett Shrops 132 E3
Upton Crews Hereford 98 F2
Upton Cross Corn 11 G11
Upton End C Beds 104 E2
Upton Field Notts 172 E2
Upton Green Norf 161 G7
Upton Grey Hants 49 D7
Upton Heath W Ches 166 B6
Upton Hellions Devon 26 G4
Upton Lea Bucks 66 C3
Upton Lovell Wilts 46 E2
Upton Magna Shrops 149 G11
Upton Noble Som 45 F8
Upton Park London 68 C2
Upton Pyne Devon 14 B4
Upton Rocks Halton 183 D8
Upton St Leonards Glos 80 C5
Upton Scudamore Wilts 45 D11
Upton Snodsbury Worcs 117 G8
Upton upon Severn Worcs 99 C7
Upton Warren Worcs 117 D8
Upwaltham W Sus 34 E6
Upware Cambs 123 C10
Upwell Norf 139 C9
Upwey Dorset 17 E9
Upwick Green Herts 105 G9
Upwood Cambs 138 G5
Uradale Shetland 313 K6
Urafirth Shetland 312 F5
Uragaig Argyll 274 D4
Urchfont Wilts 46 B4
Urdimarsh Hereford 97 B10
Ure Shetland 312 F4
Ure Bank N Yorks 214 E6
Urgashay Som 29 C9
Urgha W Isles 305 J3
Urgha Beag W Isles 305 H3
Urishay Common Hereford 96 D6
Urlar Perth 286 C2
Urlay Nook Stockton 225 C7
Urmston Gtr Man 184 C3
Urpeth Durham 242 G6
Urquhart Highld 300 D5
Urquhart Moray 302 C2
Urra N Yorks 225 E11
Urray Highld 300 D5
Ushaw Moor Durham 233 C10
Usk Mon 78 E5
Usselby Lincs 189 C9
Usworth T & W 243 F8
Utkinton W Ches 167 B8
Utley W Yorks 204 E6
Uton Devon 14 B2
Utterby Lincs 190 C4
Uttoxeter Staffs 151 C11
Uwchmynydd Gwyn 144 D3
Uxbridge London 66 C5
Uxbridge Moor London 66 C5
Uyea Shetland 312 D5
Uyeasound Shetland 312 C7
Uzmaston Pembs 73 C7

V

Vachelich Pembs 90 F5
Vadlure Shetland 313 J4
Vagg Som 29 D8
Vaila Hall Shetland 313 J4
Vaivoe Shetland 312 G7
Vale W Yorks 196 B2
Vale Down Devon 12 D6
Vale of Health London 67 B9
Valeswood Shrops 149 E7
Valley = Y Fali Anglesey 178 F3
Valley Park Hants 32 C6
Valley Truckle Corn 11 E7
Valleyfield Dumfries 237 D8
Valsgarth Shetland 312 B8
Valtos Highld 298 C5
Van Caerph 59 B7
Van Powys 129 F9
Vange Essex 69 B8
Vanlop Shetland 313 M5
Varchoel Powys 148 G4
Varfell Corn 2 C2
Varteg Torf 78 D3
Vassa Shetland 313 H6
Vastern Wilts 62 C5
Vatsetter Shetland 312 E7
Vatsetter Shetland 313 L5
Vatten Highld 298 E2
Vaul Argyll 288 E2
Vauxhall London 67 D10
Vauxhall Mers 182 C4
Vauxhall W Mid 133 F11
Vaynol Hall Gwyn 163 B8
Vaynor M Tydf 77 C8
Veensgarth Shetland 313 J6
Velator Devon 40 F3
Veldo Hereford 97 C11
Velindre Powys 96 D3
Vellanoweth Corn 2 C2
Vellow Som 42 F5
Velly Devon 24 C3
Veness Orkney 314 D5
Venn Devon 8 F4
Venn Green Devon 24 E5
Venn Ottery Devon 15 C7
Venngreen Devon 24 E5
Vennington Shrops 130 B6
Venn's Green Hereford 97 B10
Venny Tedburn Devon 14 B2
Venterdon Corn 12 G3
Vention Devon 40 E3
Ventnor I o W 21 F7
Venton Devon 7 D11
Ventongimps Corn 4 E5
Ventonleague Corn 2 B3
Venus Hill Herts 85 E8
Veraby Devon 26 B3
Vermentry Shetland 313 H5
Vernham Bank Hants 47 B10
Vernham Dean Hants 47 B10
Vernham Row Hants 47 B10
Vernham Street Hants 47 B11
Vernolds Common Shrops 131 G9
Verwood Dorset 31 F9
Veryan Corn 3 B10
Veryan Green Corn 5 G8
Vicarage Devon 15 D10
Vicarscross W Ches 166 B6
Vickerstown Cumb 210 F3
Victoria Corn 5 C9
Victoria S Yorks 197 F7
Victoria Dock Village Hull 200 B6
Victoria Park Bucks 84 C4
Victory Gardens Renfs 267 B10
Vidlin Shetland 312 G6
Viewpark N Lnrk 268 C4
Vigo W Mid 133 C10
Vigo Village Kent 68 G6
Vinegar Hill Mon 60 B2
Vinehall Street E Sus 38 C3
Vines Cross E Sus 23 B9
Viney Hill Glos 79 D11
Vinney Green S Glos 61 D7
Virginia Water Sur 66 F3
Virginstow Devon 12 C3
Viscar Corn 2 C6
Vobster Som 45 D8
Voe Shetland 312 E5
Voe Shetland 313 G6
Vogue Corn 4 G4
Vole Som 43 D11
Vowchurch Hereford 97 D7
Vowchurch Common Hereford 97 D7
Voxmoor Som 27 D10
Voxter Shetland 312 F5
Voy Orkney 314 E2
Vron Gate Shrops 130 B6
Vulcan Village Mers 183 C9

W

Waberthwaite Cumb 220 G2
Wackerfield Durham 233 G9
Wacton Hereford 116 F2
Wacton Norf 142 E3
Wacton Common Norf 142 F3
Wadbister Shetland 313 J6
Wadborough Worcs 99 B8
Wadbrook Devon 28 G4
Waddesdon Bucks 84 B2
Waddeton Devon 9 D7
Waddicar Mers 182 B5
Waddicombe Devon 26 B5
Waddingham Lincs 189 B7
Waddington Lancs 203 E10
Waddington Lincs 173 C7
Waddingworth Lincs 189 G11
Waddon Devon 14 F3
Waddon London 67 G10
Wade Hall Lancs 194 C4
Wadebridge Corn 10 G5
Wadeford Som 28 E4
Wadenhoe Northants 137 G10
Wades Green E Ches 167 C11
Wadesmill Herts 86 B5
Wadhurst E Sus 52 G6
Wadshelf Derbys 186 G4
Wadsley S Yorks 186 C4
Wadsley Bridge S Yorks 186 C4
Wadswick Wilts 61 F10
Wadwick Hants 48 C2
Wadworth S Yorks 187 B9
Waen Denb 165 B10
Waen Denb 165 C7
Waen Flint 181 G11
Waen Powys 129 E9
Waen Aberwheeler Denb 165 B9
Waen-fâch Powys 148 F4
Waen Goleugoed Denb 181 G9
Waen-pentir Gwyn 163 B9
Waen-wen Gwyn 163 B9
Wag Highld 311 G4
Wagbeach Shrops 131 C7
Wagg Som 28 B6
Waggersley Staffs 151 B7
Waggs Plot Devon 28 G4
Wain Lee Staffs 168 D5
Wainfelin Torf 78 E3
Wainfleet All Saints Lincs 175 D7
Wainfleet Bank Lincs 175 D7
Wainfleet St Mary Lincs 175 D8
Wainfleet Tofts Lincs 175 D7
Wainford Norf 142 E6
Waingroves Derbys 170 F6
Wainhouse Corner Corn 11 B9
Wainscott Medway 69 E8
Wainstalls W Yorks 196 B4
Waitby Cumb 222 D5
Waithe Lincs 201 G9
Wake Green W Mid 133 G11
Wake Hill N Yorks 214 E3
Wake Lady Green N Yorks 226 F3
Wakefield W Yorks 197 C10
Wakeley Herts 104 F6
Wakerley Northants 137 D9
Wakes Colne Essex 107 F7
Wakes Colne Green Essex 107 E7
Walberswick Suff 127 C9
Walberton W Sus 35 F7
Walbottle T & W 242 D5
Walby Cumb 239 E10
Walcombe Som 44 D5
Walcot Bath 61 F9
Walcot Lincs 155 B11
Walcot N Lincs 199 C11
Walcot Oxon 82 B4
Walcot Shrops 130 F6
Walcot Swindon 63 C7
Walcot Telford 149 G11
Walcot Worcs 99 B8
Walcot Green Norf 142 G2
Walcote Leics 135 G11
Walcote Warks 118 F2
Walcott Lincs 173 D10
Walcott Norf 161 C7
Walden N Yorks 213 C10
Walden Head N Yorks 213 C9
Walden Stubbs N Yorks 198 D5
Waldersey Cambs 139 C8
Waldershaigh S Yorks 186 B3
Walderslade Medway 69 G9
Walderton W Sus 34 E3
Walditch Dorset 16 C5
Waldley Derbys 152 B2
Waldridge Durham 243 G7
Waldringfield Suff 108 C5
Waldringfield Heath Suff 108 B5
Waldron E Sus 23 B8
Waldron Down E Sus 37 C8
Wales S Yorks 187 E7
Wales Som 29 C9
Wales Bar S Yorks 187 E7
Wales End Suff 106 B5
Walesby Lincs 189 C10
Walesby Notts 187 G11
Walesby Grange Lincs 189 C10
Waleswood S Yorks 187 E7
Walford Hereford 97 G11
Walford Hereford 115 C7
Walford Shrops 149 E8
Walford Som 28 B3
Walford Staffs 150 C6
Walford Heath Shrops 149 F8
Walgherton E Ches 167 F11
Walgrave Northants 120 C6
Walham Glos 98 G6
Walham Green London 67 D9
Walhampton Hants 20 B2
Walk Mill Lancs 204 G3
Walkden Gtr Man 195 G8
Walker T & W 243 E7
Walker Barn E Ches 185 G7
Walker Fold Lancs 203 E9
Walkerburn Borders 261 B9
Walkeringham Notts 188 C3
Walkerith Lincs 188 C3
Walkern Herts 104 F5
Walker's Green Hereford 97 B10
Walker's Heath W Mid 117 B11
Walkerville N Yorks 224 F4
Walkford Dorset 19 C10
Walkhampton Devon 7 B10
Walkington E Yorks 208 F5
Walkley S Yorks 186 D4
Walkmill Shrops 131 E7
Walkmills Shrops 131 D9
Wall Corn 2 B4
Wall Northumb 241 D10
Wall Staffs 134 B2
Wall Bank Shrops 131 E10
Wall End Cumb 210 C4
Wall End Kent 71 G8
Wall Heath W Mid 133 F7
Wall Hill Gtr Man 196 F3
Wall Mead Bath 45 B7
Wall Nook Durham 233 B10
Wall under Heywood Shrops 131 E10
Wallacestone Falk 279 F8
Wallaceton Dumfries 247 F8
Wallacetown S Ayrs 245 C7
Wallacetown S Ayrs 257 E8
Wallacetown Shetland 313 H5
Wallands Park E Sus 36 E6
Wallasey Mers 182 C4
Wallbank Lancs 195 D11
Wallbrook W Mid 133 E8
Wallcrouch E Sus 53 G7
Wallend London 68 C2
Waller's Green Hereford 98 D3
Walley's Green E Ches 167 C11
Wallingford Oxon 64 B6
Wallington Hants 33 F9
Wallington Herts 104 E5
Wallington London 67 G9
Wallington Heath W Mid 133 C9
Wallingwells Notts 187 E9
Wallis Pembs 91 F10
Wallisdown Poole 19 C7
Walliswood Sur 50 F6
Wallow Green Glos 80 F4
Wallridge Northumb 242 B3
Walls Shetland 313 J4
Wallsend T & W 243 D7
Wallston V Glam 58 E6
Wallsuches Gtr Man 195 E7
Wallsworth Glos 98 G6
Wallyford E Loth 281 G7
Walmer Kent 55 C11
Walmer Bridge Lancs 194 C3
Walmersley Gtr Man 195 E10
Walmgate Stray York 207 C8
Walmley W Mid 134 E2
Walmsgate Lincs 190 F5
Walnut Grove Perth 286 E5
Walnut Tree M Keynes 103 D7
Walnuttree Green Herts 105 G9
Walpole Som 43 E10
Walpole Suff 127 C7
Walpole Cross Keys Norf 157 F10
Walpole Highway Norf 157 G10
Walpole Marsh Norf 157 F9
Walpole St Andrew Norf 157 F10
Walpole St Peter Norf 157 F9
Walrow Som 43 D10
Walsal End W Mid 118 B4
Walsall W Mid 133 D10
Walsall Wood W Mid 133 C10
Walsden W Yorks 196 C2
Walsgrave on Sowe W Mid 135 G7
Walsham le Willows Suff 125 C9
Walshaw Gtr Man 195 E9
Walshford N Yorks 206 C4
Walsoken Cambs 157 G9
Walson Mon 97 G8
Walston S Lnrk 269 F11
Walsworth Herts 104 E4
Walters Ash Bucks 84 F4
Walter's Green Kent 52 E4
Walterston V Glam 58 E5
Walterstone Hereford 96 F6
Waltham Kent 54 D6
Waltham NE Lincs 201 G9
Waltham Abbey Essex 86 E5
Waltham Chase Hants 33 D9
Waltham Cross Herts 86 E5
Waltham on the Wolds Leics 154 D6
Waltham St Lawrence Windsor 65 D10
Waltham's Cross Essex 106 E3
Walthamstow London 67 B11
Walton Bucks 84 C4
Walton Cumb 240 E2
Walton Derbys 170 B5
Walton Leics 135 F11
Walton M Keynes 103 D7
Walton Mers 182 C5
Walton P'boro 138 C3
Walton Powys 114 F5
Walton Shrops 115 B9
Walton Som 44 F3
Walton Staffs 151 C7
Walton Staffs 151 D7
Walton Suff 108 D5
Walton Telford 149 F11
Walton W Yorks 197 D11
Walton W Yorks 206 D4
Walton Warks 118 G5
Walton Cardiff Glos 99 E8
Walton Court Bucks 84 C4
Walton East Pembs 91 G10
Walton Elm Dorset 30 D3
Walton Grounds Northants 101 E10
Walton Heath Hants 33 F10
Walton Highway Norf 157 G9
Walton in Gordano N Som 60 E2
Walton-le-Dale Lancs 194 B5
Walton Manor Oxon 83 D8
Walton-on-Thames Sur 66 F6
Walton on the Hill Staffs 151 E9
Walton on the Hill Sur 51 B8
Walton-on-the-Naze Essex 108 G5
Walton on the Wolds Leics 153 F11
Walton-on-Trent Derbys 152 F4
Walton Pool Worcs 117 B8
Walton St Mary N Som 60 E2
Walton Summit Lancs 194 B5
Walton Warren Norf 158 F4
Walton West Pembs 72 C5
Walwen Flint 181 F10
Walwen Flint 181 G11
Walwen Flint 182 F2
Walwick Northumb 241 C10
Walworth Darl 224 B4
Walworth London 67 D10
Walworth Gate Darl 233 G10
Walwyn's Castle Pembs 72 C5
Wambrook Som 28 F3
Wampool Cumb 238 G6
Wanborough Sur 50 D2
Wanborough Swindon 63 C8
Wandel Dyke S Lnrk 259 D11
Wandle Park London 67 F10
Wandon End Herts 104 G2
Wandsworth London 67 E9
Wangford Suff 127 B9
Wanlip Leics 154 G2
Wanlockhead Dumfries 259 G9
Wannock E Sus 23 E9
Wansford E Yorks 209 B7
Wansford P'boro 137 D11
Wanshurst Green Kent 53 D9
Wanson Corn 24 G1
Wanstead London 68 B2
Wanstrow Som 45 E8
Wanswell Glos 79 E11
Wantage Oxon 63 B11
Wants Green Worcs 116 F5
Wapley S Glos 61 D8
Wappenbury Warks 119 D7
Wappenham Northants 102 B2
Wapping London 67 C10
Warbleton E Sus 23 B10
Warblington Hants 22 B2
Warborough Oxon 83 G9
Warboys Cambs 138 G6
Warbreck Blkpool 202 F2
Warbstow Corn 11 C10
Warbstow Cross Corn 11 C10
Warburton Gtr Man 184 D2
Warburton Green Gtr Man 184 E3
Warcop Cumb 222 B4
Ward End W Mid 134 F2
Ward Green S Yorks 197 G10
Ward Green Suff 125 E10
Ward Green Cross Lancs 203 F8
Warden Kent 70 E4
Warden Northumb 241 D10
Warden Powys 114 E6
Warden Hill Glos 99 G8
Warden Point I o W 20 D2
Warden Street C Beds 104 C2
Wardhedges C Beds 103 D11
Wardhill Orkney 314 D6
Wardington Oxon 101 B9
Wardlaw Borders 261 F7
Wardle E Ches 167 D10
Wardle Gtr Man 196 D2
Wardle Bank E Ches 167 D10
Wardley Gtr Man 195 G9
Wardley Rutland 136 C6
Wardley T & W 243 E7
Wardley W Sus 34 B4
Wardlow Derbys 185 G11
Wardour Wilts 30 B6
Wardpark N Lnrk 278 F5
Wardrobes Bucks 84 E4
Wardsend E Ches 184 E6
Wardy Hill Cambs 139 G9
Ware Herts 86 C5
Ware Kent 71 G9
Ware Street Kent 53 B9
Wareham Dorset 18 D4
Warehorne Kent 54 G3
Waren Mill Northumb 264 C4
Warenford Northumb 264 D4
Warenton Northumb 264 C4
Wareside Herts 86 B5
Waresley Cambs 122 G4
Waresley Worcs 116 C6
Warfield Brack 65 E11
Warfleet Devon 9 E7
Wargate Lincs 156 C4
Wargrave Mers 183 C9
Wargrave Wokingham 65 D9
Warham Hereford 97 D9
Warham Norf 176 E6
Warhill Gtr Man 185 B7
Waring's Green W Mid 118 C2
Wark Northumb 241 B9
Wark Northumb 263 B8
Wark Common Northumb 263 B8
Warkleigh Devon 25 C10
Warkton Northants 121 B7
Warkworth Northants 101 C9
Warkworth Northumb 252 B6
Warlaby N Yorks 224 G6
Warland W Yorks 196 C2
Warleggan Corn 6 B3
Warleigh Bath 61 G9
Warley Essex 87 G9
Warley Town W Yorks 196 B5
Warley Woods W Mid 133 F10
Warlingham Sur 51 B11
Warmbrook Derbys 170 E3
Warmfield W Yorks 197 C11
Warmingham E Ches 168 C2
Warminghurst W Sus 35 D10
Warmington Northants 137 E11
Warmington Warks 101 B8

366 War – Wes

Warminster Wilts 45 D11
Warminster Common Wilts 45 E11
Warmlake Kent 53 C10
Warmley S Glos 61 E7
Warmley Hill S Glos 61 E7
Warmley Tower S Glos 61 E7
Warmonds Hill Northants 121 D9
Warmsworth S Yorks 198 G4
Warmwell Dorset 17 D11
Warnborough Green Hants 49 C8
Warndon Worcs 117 F7
Warners End Herts 85 D8
Warnford Hants 33 C10
Warnham W Sus 51 G7
Warningcamp W Sus 35 F8
Warninglid W Sus 36 B2
Warpsgrove Oxon 83 F10
Warren Dorset 18 C3
Warren E Ches 184 G5
Warren Pembs 72 F6
Warren S Yorks 186 B5
Warren Corner Hants 34 B2
Warren Corner Hants 49 D10
Warren Heath Suff 108 C4
Warren Row Windsor 65 C10
Warren Street Kent 54 C2
Warrenby Redcar 235 F7
Warren's Green Herts 104 F5
Warrington M Keynes 121 G7
Warrington Warr 183 D10
Warriston Edin 280 F5
Warsash Hants 33 F7
Warsill N Yorks 214 F4
Warslow Staffs 169 D9
Warsop Vale Notts 171 B8
Warstock W Mid 117 B11
Warstone Staffs 133 B9
Warter E Yorks 208 C3
Warthermarske N Yorks 214 D4
Warthill N Yorks 207 B9
Wartle Aberds 293 C7
Wartling E Sus 23 D11
Wartnaby Leics 154 E4
Warton Lancs 194 B2
Warton Lancs 211 E9
Warton Northumb 252 C2
Warton Warks 134 C5
Warton Bank Lancs 194 B2
Warwick Warks 118 E5
Warwick Bridge Cumb 239 F11
Warwick on Eden Cumb 239 F11
Warwick Wold Sur 51 C10
Warwicksland Cumb 239 B10
Wasbister Orkney 314 C3
Wasdale Head Cumb 220 D3
Wash Derbys 185 E9
Wash Common W Berks 64 G3
Wash Dyke Norf 157 F10
Wash Water W Berks 64 G3
Washall Green Herts 105 E8
Washaway Corn 5 B10
Washbourne Devon 8 E5
Washbrook Som 44 C2
Washbrook Suff 108 C2
Washbrook Street Suff 108 C2
Washerwall Staffs 168 F6
Washfield Devon 26 D6
Washfold N Yorks 223 E11
Washford Som 42 E5
Washford Worcs 117 D11
Washford Pyne Devon 26 E4
Washingborough Lincs 189 G8
Washingley Cambs 138 F2
Washington T & W 243 F8
Washington W Sus 35 E10
Washington Village T & W 243 F8
Washmere Green Suff 107 B8
Washpit W Yorks 196 F6
Washwood Heath W Mid 134 F2
Wasing W Berks 64 G5
Waskerley Durham 233 B7
Wasp Green Sur 51 D10
Wasperton Warks 118 F5
Wasps Nest Lincs 173 C9
Wass N Yorks 215 D11
Waste Green Warks 118 D4
Wastor Devon 8 F2
Watch House Green Essex 106 G3
Watchet Som 42 E5
Watchfield Oxon 63 B8
Watchfield Som 43 D10
Watchgate Cumb 221 F10
Watchhill Cumb 229 C9
Watchill Dumfries 238 D6
Watchill Dumfries 248 G3
Watcombe Torbay 9 B8
Watendlath Cumb 220 B5
Water Devon 13 E11
Water Lancs 195 B10
Water Eaton M Keynes 103 E7
Water Eaton Oxon 83 C8
Water End Beds 104 B2
Water End C Beds 103 D11
Water End C Beds 104 B5
Water End E Yorks 207 F11
Water End Essex 105 C11
Water End Hants 49 C7
Water End Herts 85 C8
Water End Herts 86 E2
Water Fryston W Yorks 198 B3
Water Garth Nook Cumb 210 F3
Water Houses N Yorks 213 F7
Water Newton Cambs 138 D2
Water Orton Warks 134 E3
Water Stratford Bucks 102 E3
Water Yeat Cumb 210 B5
Waterbeach Cambs 123 D9
Waterbeach W Sus 22 B5
Waterbeck Dumfries 238 B6
Waterdale Herts 85 E10
Waterden Norf 159 B7
Waterditch Hants 19 B9
Waterend Bucks 84 F3
Waterend Cumb 229 G8
Waterend Glos 80 C3
Waterend Herts 86 C2
Waterfall Staffs 169 E9
Waterfoot Argyll 255 D9
Waterfoot Cumb 230 G5
Waterfoot E Renf 267 D11
Waterfoot Lancs 195 C10
Waterford Hants 20 B2
Waterford Herts 86 C4
Watergate Corn 6 E4
Watergate Corn 11 E8
Watergore Som 28 D6
Waterhales Essex 87 F8
Waterham Kent 70 G5
Waterhay Wilts 81 G9
Waterhead Angus 292 F6
Waterhead Cumb 221 E7
Waterhead Devon 8 F3
Waterhead Dumfries 248 E5
Waterhead on Minnoch S Ayrs 245 E9
Waterheads Borders 270 E4
Waterheath Norf 143 E8
Waterhouses Durham 233 C9
Waterhouses Staffs 169 E9
Wateringbury Kent 53 C7
Waterlane Glos 80 E6
Waterlip Som 45 E7
Waterloo Blkburn 195 B7
Waterloo Corn 11 G8
Waterloo Derbys 170 C6
Waterloo Gtr Man 196 G2
Waterloo Highld 295 C8
Waterloo Mers 182 B4
Waterloo N Lnrk 268 E6
Waterloo Norf 126 B2
Waterloo Norf 143 E8
Waterloo Norf 160 F4
Waterloo Pembs 73 E7
Waterloo Perth 286 D4
Waterloo Poole 18 C6
Waterloo Shrops 149 C9
Waterloo Park Mers 182 B4
Waterloo Port Gwyn 163 C7
Waterlooville Hants 33 F11
Waterman Quarter Kent 53 E10
Watermead Glos 80 B5
Watermeetings S Lnrk 259 G11
Watermill E Sus 38 E2
Watermillock Cumb 230 G4
Watermoor Glos 81 E8
Waterperry Oxon 83 D10
Waterrow Som 27 B9
Water's Nook Gtr Man 195 F7
Waters Upton Telford 150 F2
Watersfield W Sus 35 D8
Watersheddings Gtr Man 196 F2
Waterside Aberds 292 B5
Waterside Aberds 303 G10
Waterside Blkburn 195 C8
Waterside Bucks 85 E7
Waterside Cumb 229 B10
Waterside Derbys 185 E8
Waterside E Ayrs 245 B10
Waterside E Ayrs 267 G9
Waterside E Dunb 278 G3
Waterside E Renf 267 D10
Waterside S Yorks 199 E7
Waterside Sur 51 D11
Waterside Telford 150 F2
Waterslack Lancs 211 D9
Waterstein Highld 297 G7
Waterstock Oxon 83 D10
Waterston Pembs 72 D6
Waterthorpe S Yorks 186 E6
Waterton Aberds 303 F9
Waterton Bridgend 58 D2
Watford Herts 85 F10
Watford Northants 120 D2
Watford Gap Staffs 134 C2
Watford Heath Herts 85 G10
Watford Park Caerph 58 B6
Wath Cumb 222 D3
Wath N Yorks 214 D6
Wath N Yorks 214 F2
Wath N Yorks 216 D3
Wath Brow Cumb 219 C10
Wath upon Dearne S Yorks 198 G2
Watherston Borders 271 F8
Watledge Glos 80 E4
Watley's End S Glos 61 C7
Watlington Norf 158 G2
Watlington Oxon 83 G11
Watnall Notts 171 F8
Watsness Shetland 313 H3
Watten Highld 310 D6
Wattisfield Suff 125 C10
Wattisham Suff 125 G10
Wattisham Stone Suff 125 G10
Wattlefield Norf 142 D2
Wattlesborough Heath Shrops 149 G7
Watton E Yorks 208 C6
Watton Norf 141 C8
Watton at Stone Herts 86 B4
Watton Green Norf 141 C8
Watton's Green Essex 87 F8
Wattston N Lnrk 268 B5
Wattstown Rhondda 77 G8
Wattsville Caerph 78 G2
Wauchan Highld 295 G11
Waulkmill Lodge Orkney 314 F3
Waun Gwyn 163 C9
Waun Powys 148 F4
Waun Beddau Pembs 90 F5
Waun Fawr Ceredig 128 G2
Waun-Lwyd Bl Gwent 77 D11
Waun-y-clyn Carms 75 E7
Waun y Gilfach Bridgend 57 D10
Waunarlwydd Swansea 56 B6
Waunclunda Carms 94 E3
Waunfawr Gwyn 163 D8
Waungilwen Carms 92 D6
Waungron Swansea 75 E9
Waunlwyd Bl Gwent 77 D11
Wavendon M Keynes 103 D8
Wavendon Gate M Keynes 103 D8
Waverbridge Cumb 229 B10
Waverton Cumb 229 B10
Waverton W Ches 167 C7
Wavertree Mers 182 D5
Wawcott W Berks 63 F11
Wawne E Yorks 209 F7
Waxham Norf 161 D8
Waxholme E Yorks 201 B10
Way Kent 71 F10
Way Village Devon 26 E5
Way Wick N Som 59 G11
Waye Devon 13 G11
Wayend Street Hereford 98 D4
Wayfield Medway 69 F9
Wayford Som 28 F6
Waymills Shrops 167 G9
Wayne Green Mon 78 B6
Way's Green W Ches 167 B10
Waytown Devon 24 C5
Waytown Devon 40 G5
Wdig = Goodwick Pembs 91 D8
Weachyburn Aberds 302 D6
Weacombe Som 42 E6
Weald Oxon 82 E4
Wealdstone London 67 B7
Wearde Corn 7 D8
Weardley W Yorks 205 E11
Weare Som 44 C2
Weare Giffard Devon 25 C7
Wearhead Durham 232 D3
Wearne Som 28 B6
Weasdale Cumb 222 E3
Weasenham All Saints Norf 158 E6
Weasenham St Peter Norf 159 E7
Weaste Gtr Man 184 B4
Weatherhill Sur 51 E10
Weatheroak Hill Worcs 117 C11
Weaverham W Ches 183 G10
Weavering Street Kent 53 B9
Weaverslake Staffs 152 F2
Weaverthorpe N Yorks 217 E9
Webbington Som 43 B11
Webheath Worcs 117 D10
Webscott Shrops 149 E9
Wecock Hants 33 E11
Wedderlairs Aberds 303 F8
Wedderlie Borders 272 E2
Weddington Kent 55 B9
Weddington Warks 135 E7
Wedhampton Wilts 46 B5
Wedmore Som 44 D2
Wednesbury W Mid 133 D9
Wednesbury Oak W Mid 133 E9
Wednesfield W Mid 133 C8
Weecar Notts 172 B4
Weedon Bucks 84 B4
Weedon Bec Northants 120 F2
Weedon Lois Northants 102 B2
Weeford Staffs 134 C2
Week Devon 8 C5
Week Devon 12 E5
Week Devon 25 B9
Week Devon 26 D2
Week Green Corn 11 B10
Week St Mary Corn 11 B10
Weeke Devon 26 F3
Weeke Hants 48 G3
Weekley Northants 137 G7
Weekmoor Som 27 B10
Weeks I o W 21 C7
Weel E Yorks 209 F7
Weeley Essex 108 G2
Weeley Heath Essex 108 G3
Weelsby NE Lincs 201 F9
Weem Perth 286 C2
Weeping Cross Staffs 151 E8
Weethley Warks 117 F11
Weethley Bank Warks 117 G11
Weethley Gate Warks 117 G11
Weeting Norf 140 F5
Weeton E Yorks 201 C11
Weeton Lancs 202 G3
Weeton N Yorks 205 D11
Weetwood W Yorks 205 F11
Weetwood Common W Ches 167 B8
Weetwood Hall Northumb 264 D2
Weir Essex 69 B10
Weir Lancs 195 B11
Weir Quay Devon 7 C8
Weirbrook Shrops 148 E6
Welborne Norf 159 G11
Welborne Common Norf 141 B11
Welbourn Lincs 173 E7
Welburn N Yorks 216 C3
Welburn N Yorks 216 F4
Welbury N Yorks 225 E7
Welby Lincs 155 B9
Welches Dam Cambs 139 F9
Welcombe Devon 24 D2
Weld Bank Lancs 194 D5
Weldon Northants 137 F8
Weldon Northumb 252 D4
Welford Northants 136 G2
Welford W Berks 64 E2
Welford-on-Avon Warks 118 G3
Welham Leics 136 E5
Welham Notts 188 E2
Welham Som 45 G7
Welham Green Herts 86 D2
Welhambridge E Yorks 207 G11
Well Hants 49 D9
Well Lincs 190 G6
Well N Yorks 214 C5
Well Bottom Dorset 30 D6
Well End Bucks 65 B11
Well End Herts 86 F2
Well Green Gtr Man 184 D3
Well Heads W Yorks 205 G7
Well Hill Kent 68 G3
Well Place Oxon 65 B7
Well Street Kent 53 B7
Well Town Devon 26 F6
Welland Worcs 98 C5
Welland Stone Worcs 98 D6
Wellbank Angus 287 D8
Wellbrook E Sus 37 B9
Welldale Dumfries 238 D5
Weller's Town Kent 52 E4
Wellesbourne Warks 118 F5
Wellheads Aberds 302 F4
Wellhouse W Berks 64 E4
Wellhouse W Yorks 196 E5
Welling London 68 D3
Wellingborough Northants 121 D7
Wellingham Norf 159 E7
Wellingore Lincs 173 D7
Wellington Cumb 219 E11
Wellington Hereford 97 B9
Wellington Som 27 C10
Wellington Telford 150 G3
Wellington Heath Hereford 98 C4
Wellington Hill W Yorks 206 F2
Wellisford Som 27 C9
Wellow Bath 45 B8
Wellow I o W 20 D3
Wellow NE Lincs 201 F9
Wellow Notts 171 B11
Wellow Wood Hants 32 C3
Wellpond Green Herts 105 G8
Wellroyd W Yorks 205 F10
Wells Som 44 D5
Wells Green E Ches 167 E11
Wells-Next-The-Sea Norf 176 E6
Wellsborough Leics 135 C7
Wellsprings Som 28 B2
Wellstye Green Essex 87 B10
Wellswood Torbay 9 C8
Welltown Corn 6 B2
Wellwood Fife 279 D11
Welney Norf 139 E10
Welsford Devon 24 C3
Welsh Bicknor Hereford 79 B9
Welsh End Shrops 149 B10
Welsh Frankton Shrops 149 C7
Welsh Harp London 67 B8
Welsh Hook Pembs 91 F8
Welsh Newton Hereford 79 B7
Welsh Newton Common Hereford 79 B8
Welsh St Donats V Glam 58 D4
Welshampton Shrops 149 B8
Welshpool Powys 130 B4
Welshwood Park Essex 107 F10
Welstor Devon 13 G10
Welton Bath 45 C7
Welton Cumb 230 C3
Welton E Yorks 200 B3
Welton Lincs 189 F8
Welton Northants 119 D11
Welton Hill Lincs 189 E8
Welton le Marsh Lincs 175 B7
Welton le Wold Lincs 190 D3
Welwick E Yorks 201 C10
Welwyn Herts 86 B2
Welwyn Garden City Herts 86 C2
Wem Shrops 149 D10
Wembdon Som 43 F9
Wembley London 67 B7
Wembley Park London 67 B7
Wembury Devon 7 F10
Wembworthy Devon 25 F11
Wemyss Bay Invclyd 266 B3
Wenallt Ceredig 112 C3
Wenallt Gwyn 146 F4
Wenallt Gwyn 165 G7
Wendens Ambo Essex 105 D10
Wendlebury Oxon 83 B9
Wendling Norf 159 G8
Wendover Bucks 84 D5
Wendover Dean Bucks 84 E5
Wendron Corn 2 C5
Wendy Cambs 104 B6
Wenfordbridge Corn 11 F7
Wenhaston Suff 127 B8
Wenhaston Black Heath Suff 127 C8
Wennington Cambs 122 B4
Wennington Lancs 212 E2
Wennington London 68 C4
Wensley Derbys 170 C3
Wensley N Yorks 213 B11
Wentbridge W Yorks 198 D3
Wentnor Shrops 131 E7
Wentworth Cambs 123 B9
Wentworth S Yorks 186 B5
Wenvoe V Glam 58 E6
Weobley Hereford 115 G8
Weobley Marsh Hereford 115 G8
Weoley Castle W Mid 133 G10
Wepham W Sus 35 F8
Wepre Flint 166 B3
Wereham Norf 140 C3
Wereham Row Norf 140 C3
Wereton Staffs 168 E3
Wergs W Mid 133 C7
Wern Gwyn 145 B10
Wern Powys 77 B10
Wern Powys 147 G9
Wern Powys 148 E5
Wern Powys 148 G5
Wern Shrops 148 C5
Wern Swansea 56 C4
Wern ddu Shrops 148 D4
Wern-Gifford Mon 96 G6
Wern-olau Swansea 56 B5
Wern Tarw Bridgend 58 C3
Wern-y-cwrt Mon 78 D5
Wern-y-gaer Flint 166 B2
Werneth Gtr Man 196 G2
Werneth Low Gtr Man 185 C7
Wernffrwd Swansea 56 C4
Wernlas Shrops 148 E6
Wernrheolydd Mon 78 C5
Wernyrheolydd Mon 78 C5
Werrington Corn 12 D2
Werrington P'boro 138 C3
Werrington Staffs 168 F6
Wervin W Ches 182 G6
Wescoe Hill N Yorks 205 D11
Wesham Lancs 202 G4
Wessington Derbys 170 D5
West Aberthaw V Glam 58 F4
West Acre Norf 158 F5
West Acton London 67 C7
West Adderbury Oxon 101 D9
West Allerdean Northumb 273 F9
West Allotment T & W 243 C8
West Alvington Devon 8 G4
West Amesbury Wilts 46 E6
West Anstey Devon 26 B5
West Appleton N Yorks 224 G4
West Ardhu Argyll 288 D6
West Ardsley W Yorks 197 B9
West Ardwall Dumfries 236 E2
West Arthurlie E Renf 267 D9
West Ashby Lincs 190 G3
West Ashford Devon 40 F4
West Ashling W Sus 22 B4
West Ashton Wilts 45 B11
West Auckland Durham 233 F9
West Ayton N Yorks 217 C9
West Bagborough Som 43 G7
West Bank Bl Gwent 78 D2
West Bank Halton 183 E8
West Barkwith Lincs 189 E11
West Barnby N Yorks 226 C6
West Barnes London 67 F8
West Barns E Loth 282 F3
West Barsham Norf 159 C8
West Bay Dorset 16 C5
West Beckham Norf 160 B2
West Bedfont Sur 66 E5
West Benhar N Lnrk 269 C7
West Bergholt Essex 107 F9
West Bexington Dorset 16 D6
West Bilney Norf 158 F4
West Blackdene Durham 232 D3
West Blackdown Devon 12 E5
West Blatchington Brighton 36 F3
West Bold Borders 261 B9
West Boldon T & W 243 E9
West Bourton Dorset 30 B3
West Bowling W Yorks 205 G9
West Bradford Lancs 203 E10
West Bradley Som 44 F5
West Bretton W Yorks 197 E9
West Bridgford Notts 153 B11
West Brompton London 67 D9
West Bromwich W Mid 133 E10
West Broughton Derbys 152 C2
West Buckland Devon 41 G7
West Buckland Som 27 C11
West Burnside Aberds 293 F8
West Burrafirth Shetland 313 H4
West Burton N Yorks 213 B10
West Burton W Sus 35 E7
West Butsfield Durham 233 C8
West Butterwick N Lincs 199 F10
West Byfleet Sur 66 G4
West Caister Norf 161 G10
West Calder W Loth 269 C10
West Camel Som 29 C9
West Carlton W Yorks 205 E10
West Carr Hull 209 G7
West Carr N Lincs 199 F8
West Chadsmoor Staffs 151 G9
West Challow Oxon 63 B11
West Charleton Devon 8 G5
West Chelborough Dorset 29 F8
West Chevington Northumb 252 D6
West Chiltington W Sus 35 D9
West Chiltington Common W Sus 35 D9
West Chinnock Som 29 E7
West Chirton T & W 243 D8
West Chisenbury Wilts 46 C6
West Clandon Sur 50 C4
West Cliff Bmouth 19 C7
West Cliff N Yorks 227 C7
West Cliffe Kent 55 E10
West Clyne Highld 311 J2
West Clyth Highld 310 F6
West Coker Som 29 E8
West Common Hants 32 G6
West Compton Dorset 17 C7
West Compton Som 44 E5
West Cornforth Durham 234 E2
West Cowick E Yorks 199 C7
West Cranmore Som 45 E7
West Cross Kent 53 G10
West Cross Swansea 56 D6
West Crudwell Wilts 80 G6
West Clyne Highld 311 J2
West Clyth Highld 310 F6
West Cullery Aberds 293 C9
West Curry Corn 11 C11
West Curthwaite Cumb 230 B2
West Darlochan Argyll 255 E7
West Dean W Sus 34 E5
West Dean Wilts 32 B3
West Deeping Lincs 138 B2
West Denant Pembs 72 C6
West Denton T & W 242 D5
West Derby Mers 182 C5
West Dereham Norf 140 C3
West Didsbury Gtr Man 184 C4
West Down Devon 40 E4
West Down Hants 47 F11
West Downs Corn 5 C10
West Drayton London 66 D5
West Drayton Notts 188 G2
West Dulwich London 67 E10
West Ealing London 67 C7
West Edge Derbys 170 C4
West Ella E Yorks 200 B4
West End Beds 121 E11
West End Beds 121 G9
West End Brack 65 E11
West End Caerph 78 F2
West End Cumb 239 F8
West End Dorset 30 G6
West End E Yorks 201 B9
West End E Yorks 208 G4
West End E Yorks 209 B9
West End E Yorks 209 G9
West End E Yorks 217 G11
West End Glos 80 F5
West End Hants 33 E7
West End Hants 33 F9
West End Hants 48 F6
West End Herts 86 D3
West End Kent 54 B2
West End Kent 71 F7
West End Lancs 195 B8
West End Lancs 211 G8
West End Leics 153 F8
West End Lincs 174 F5
West End Lincs 190 B5
West End Mon 78 F6
West End N Som 60 F3
West End N Yorks 205 B8
West End N Yorks 206 E6
West End N Yorks 207 F7
West End Norf 141 B8
West End Norf 161 G10
West End Oxon 64 B5
West End Oxon 82 E6
West End S Glos 61 B8
West End S Lnrk 269 F9
West End S Yorks 199 F7
West End Som 44 C5
West End Som 45 G7
West End Suff 143 G9
West End Sur 49 E10
West End Sur 66 G2
West End Sur 66 G6
West End W Sus 36 D2
West End W Yorks 197 B7
West End W Yorks 205 F10
West End Wilts 30 C6
West End Wilts 31 C7
West End Wilts 62 D3
West End Windsor 65 D10
West End Worcs 99 D11
West End = Marian-y-mor Gwyn 145 C7
West End Green Hants 65 G7
West-end Town V Glam 58 F3
West Ewell Sur 67 G8
West Farleigh Kent 53 C8
West Farndon Northants 119 G10
West Felton Shrops 148 D6
West Fenton E Loth 281 E9
West Ferry Dundee 287 D8
West Field N Lincs 200 D6
West Field York 207 C7
West Fields W Berks 64 F3
West Firle E Sus 23 D7
West Fleetham Northumb 264 D5
West Flodden Northumb 263 C10
West Garforth W Yorks 206 G3
West Ginge Oxon 64 B2
West Gorton Gtr Man 184 B5
West Grafton Wilts 63 G8
West Green Hants 49 B8
West Green London 67 B10
West Green S Yorks 197 F11
West Green W Sus 51 F9
West Greenskares Aberds 303 C7
West Grimstead Wilts 32 B2
West Grinstead W Sus 35 C11
West Haddlesey N Yorks 198 B5
West Haddon Northants 120 C2
West Hagbourne Oxon 64 B4
West Hagley Worcs 133 G8
West Hall Cumb 240 D3
West Hallam Derbys 170 G6
West Halton N Lincs 200 C2
West Ham Hants 48 C6
West Ham London 68 C2
West Hampstead London 67 B9
West Handley Derbys 186 F5
West Hanney Oxon 82 G6
West Hanningfield Essex 88 F2
West Hardwick W Yorks 198 D2
West Harling Norf 141 G9
West Harlsey N Yorks 225 F8
West Harnham Wilts 31 B10
West Harptree Bath 44 B5
West Harrow London 66 B6
West Harting W Sus 34 C3
West Harton T & W 243 E9
West Hatch Som 28 C3
West Hatch Wilts 30 B6
West Head Norf 139 B11
West Heath E Ches 168 C4
West Heath Hants 48 B5
West Heath Hants 49 B11
West Heath London 68 D3
West Heath W Mid 117 B10
West Helmsdale Highld 311 H4
West Hendon London 67 B8
West Hendred Oxon 64 B2
West Herrington T & W 243 G8
West Heslerton N Yorks 217 D8
West Hewish N Som 59 G11
West Hill Devon 15 C7
West Hill E Sus 38 E4
West Hill E Yorks 218 F3
West Hill London 67 E8
West Hill N Som 60 D3
West Hill Som 30 B2
West Hill Staffs 151 G9
West Hill W Sus 51 G10
West Hill Wilts 61 F11
West Hoathly W Sus 51 G11
West Holme Dorset 18 D3
West Holywell T & W 243 C8
West Horndon Essex 68 B6
West Horrington Som 44 D5
West Horsley Sur 50 C5
West Horton Northumb 264 C2
West Hougham Kent 55 E9
West Houlland Shetland 313 H4
West Houses Lincs 174 E4
West Howe Bmouth 19 B7
West Howetown Som 42 G2
West Huntington York 207 B8
West Huntspill Som 43 E10
West Hurn Dorset 19 B8
West Hyde Herts 85 G8
West Hynish Argyll 288 F1
West Hythe Kent 54 G6
West Ilkerton Devon 41 D8
West Ilsley W Berks 64 C3
West Itchenor W Sus 22 C3
West Jesmond T & W 243 D7
West Keal Lincs 174 C5
West Kennett Wilts 62 F6
West Kensington London 67 D8
West Kilbride N Ayrs 266 F4
West Kilburn London 67 C8
West Kingsdown Kent 68 G5
West Kingston W Sus 35 G9
West Kington Wilts 61 D10
West Kington Wick Wilts 61 D10
West Kinharrachie Aberds 303 F9
West Kirby Mers 182 D2
West Kirkby Mers 182 D2
West Knapton N Yorks 217 D7
West Knighton Dorset 17 D10
West Knoyle Wilts 45 G11
West Kyloe Northumb 273 G11
West Kyo Durham 242 G5
West Lambrook Som 28 D6
West Langdon Kent 55 D10
West Langwell Highld 309 J6
West Lavington W Sus 34 C5
West Lavington Wilts 46 C4
West Layton N Yorks 224 D2
West Lea Durham 234 B4
West Leake Notts 153 D10
West Learmouth Northumb 263 B9
West Leigh Devon 25 F11
West Leigh Hants 22 B2
West Leigh Som 42 G6
West Lexham Norf 158 F6
West Lilling N Yorks 216 F2
West Linton Borders 270 E2
West Liss Hants 34 B3
West Littleton S Glos 61 D9
West Lockinge Oxon 64 B2
West Looe Corn 6 E5
West Luccombe Som 41 D11
West Lulworth Dorset 18 E2
West Lutton N Yorks 217 F8
West Lydford Som 44 G5
West Lydiatt Hereford 97 C11
West Lyn Devon 41 D8
West Lyng Som 28 B4
West Lynn Norf 158 E2
West Mains Borders 271 F11
West Mains S Lnrk 268 E2
West Malling Kent 53 B7
West Malvern Worcs 98 B5
West Marden W Sus 34 E3
West Marina E Sus 38 F3
West Markham Notts 188 G2
West Marsh NE Lincs 201 E9
West Marton N Yorks 204 C3
West Mathers Aberds 293 G9
West Melbury Dorset 30 C5
West Melton S Yorks 198 G2
West Meon Hants 33 C10
West Meon Woodlands Hants 33 B10
West Merkland Highld 308 F3
West Mersea Essex 89 C8
West Milton Dorset 16 B6
West Minster Kent 70 E2
West Molesey Sur 66 F6
West Monkseaton T & W 243 C8
West Monkton Som 28 B3
West Moor T & W 243 C7
West Moors Dorset 31 G9
West Morden Dorset 18 B4
West Morriston Borders 272 G2
West Morton W Yorks 205 E7
West Mudford Som 29 C9
West Muir Angus 293 G7
West Myreriggs Perth 286 C6
West Ness N Yorks 216 D3
West Newham Northumb 242 B3
West Newton E Yorks 209 F9
West Newton Norf 158 D3
West Newton Som 28 B3
West Norwood London 67 E10
West Ogwell Devon 14 G2
West Orchard Dorset 30 D4

West Overton Wilts 62 F6
West Panson Devon 12 C2
West Park Hrtlpl 234 E5
West Park Hull 200 B5
West Park Mers 183 B7
West Park T & W 243 D9
West Park W Yorks 205 F11
West Parley Dorset 19 B7
West Pasture Durham 232 G4
West Peckham Kent 52 C6
West Pelton Durham 242 G6
West Pennard Som 44 F4
West Pentire Corn 4 C5
West Perry Cambs 122 D2
West Pontnewydd Torf 78 F3
West Poringland Norf 142 C5
West Porlock Som 41 D11
West Portholland Corn 5 G9
West Porton Renfs 277 G8
West Pulham Dorset 30 F2
West Putford Devon 24 D5
West Quantoxhead Som 42 E6
West Rainton Durham 234 B2
West Rasen Lincs 189 D9
West Ravendale NE Lincs 190 B2
West Raynham Norf 159 D7
West Retford Notts 187 E11
West Rounton N Yorks 225 E8
West Row Suff 124 B3
West Royd W Yorks 205 F9
West Rudham Norf 158 D6
West Ruislip London 66 B5
West Runton Norf 177 E11
West Saltoun E Loth 271 B9
West Sandford Devon 26 G4
West Sandwick Shetland 312 E6
West Scholes W Yorks 205 G7
West Scrafton N Yorks 213 C11
West Shepton Som 44 E6
West Side Bl Gwent 77 D11
West Side Orkney 314 C5
West Skelston Dumfries 247 F8
West Sleekburn Northumb 253 G7
West Somerton Norf 161 F9
West Southbourne Bmouth 19 C8
West Stafford Dorset 17 D10
West Stockwith Notts 188 C3
West Stoke Devon 13 G9
West Stoke Som 29 D7
West Stoke W Sus 22 B4
West Stonesdale N Yorks 223 E7
West Stoughton Som 44 D2
West Stour Dorset 30 C3
West Stourmouth Kent 71 G9
West Stow Suff 124 C6
West Stowell Wilts 62 G6
West Strathan Highld 308 C5
West Stratton Hants 48 E4
West Street Kent 54 C2
West Street Kent 55 C10
West Street Medway 69 D8
West Street Suff 125 C9
West Tanfield N Yorks 214 D5
West Taphouse Corn 6 C3
West Tarbert Argyll 275 G9
West Tarring W Sus 35 G10
West Third Borders 262 B4
West Thirston Northumb 252 D5
West Thorney W Sus 22 C3
West Thurrock Thurrock 68 D5
West Tilbury Thurrock 69 D7
West Tisted Hants 33 B11
West Tofts Norf 140 E6
West Tofts Perth 286 D5
West Tolgus Corn 4 G3
West Torrington Lincs 189 E10
West Town Bath 60 G4
West Town Devon 14 B3
West Town Devon 24 C4
West Town Hants 21 B10
West Town Hereford 115 E8
West Town N Som 60 F3
West Town Som 44 F4
West Town W Sus 36 D3
West Tytherley Hants 32 B3
West Tytherton Wilts 62 E2
West Vale W Yorks 196 C5
West View Hrtlpl 234 D5
West Village V Glam 58 E3
West Walton Norf 157 G9
West Walton Highway Norf 157 G9
West Watergate Corn 6 E4
West Watford Herts 85 F10
West Wellow Hants 32 D3
West Wemyss Fife 280 C6
West Wick N Som 59 G11
West Wickham Cambs 106 B2
West Wickham London 67 F11
West Williamston Pembs 73 D8
West Willoughby Lincs 173 G7
West Winch Norf 158 F2
West Winterslow Wilts 47 G8
West Wittering W Sus 21 B11
West Witton N Yorks 213 B11
West Woodburn Northumb 251 F9
West Woodhay W Berks 63 G11
West Woodlands Som 45 E9
West Worldham Hants 49 F8
West Worlington Devon 26 E3
West Worthing W Sus 35 G10
West Wratting Cambs 124 G2
West Wycombe Bucks 84 G4
West Wylam Northumb 242 E4
West Yatton Wilts 61 E11
West Yell Shetland 312 E6
West Yeo Som 43 G10
West Yoke Kent 68 F5
West Youlstone Corn 24 D3
Westacott Devon 40 G5
Westbere Kent 71 G7
Westborough Lincs 172 G5
Westbourne Bmouth 19 C7
Westbourne Suff 108 B2
Westbourne W Sus 22 B3
Westbourne Green London 67 C9
Westbrook Hereford 96 C5
Westbrook Kent 71 E10
Westbrook Sur 50 E3
Westbrook W Berks 64 E2
Westbrook Warr 183 C9
Westbrook Wilts 62 F3
Westbrook Green Norf 142 G2
Westbrook Hay Herts 85 D8
Westburn S Lnrk 268 C3
Westbury Bucks 102 D2
Westbury Shrops 131 B7
Westbury Wilts 45 C11
Westbury Leigh Wilts 45 C11
Westbury-on-Severn Glos 80 C2
Westbury on Trym Bristol 60 D5
Westbury Park Bristol 60 D5
Westbury-sub-Mendip Som 44 D4
Westby Lancs 202 G3
Westby Lincs 155 D9
Westcliff-on-Sea Sthend 69 B11
Westcombe Som 29 B7
Westcombe Som 45 F7
Westcot Oxon 63 B10
Westcote Glos 100 G4
Westcotes Leicester 135 C11
Westcott Bucks 84 B2
Westcott Devon 27 G8
Westcott Shrops 131 C8
Westcott Sur 50 D6
Westcott Barton Oxon 101 F8
Westcourt Wilts 63 G8
Westcroft M Keynes 102 E6
Westcroft W Mid 133 C8
Westdean E Sus 23 F8
Westdene Brighton 36 F3
Westdown Camp Wilts 46 D4
Westdowns Corn 11 E7
Westend Oxon 100 G6
Westend S Glos 79 G10
Westend Town Northumb 241 D7
Westenhanger Kent 54 F6
Wester Aberchalder Highld 300 G5
Wester Arboll Highld 311 L2
Wester Auchinloch N Lnrk 278 G3
Wester Auchnagallin Highld 301 F10
Wester Balgedie Perth 286 G5
Wester Brae Highld 300 C6
Wester Broomhouse E Loth 282 F3
Wester Craiglands Highld 301 D7
Wester Culbeuchly Aberds 302 C6
Wester Dalvoult Highld 291 B11
Wester Dechmont W Loth 269 B10
Wester Deloraine Borders 261 E8
Wester Denoon Angus 287 C7
Wester Ellister Argyll 254 B2
Wester Essendy Perth 286 C5
Wester Essenside Borders 261 E10
Wester Feddal Perth 286 G2
Wester Fintray Aberds 293 B10
Wester Galgantray Highld 301 E8
Wester Gospetry Fife 286 G5
Wester Gruinards Highld 309 K5
Wester Hailes Edin 270 B4
Wester Housebyres Borders 262 B2
Wester Kershope Borders 261 D9
Wester Lealty Highld 300 B6
Wester Lix Stirl 285 E9
Wester Milton Highld 301 D9
Wester Mosshead Aberds 302 F5
Wester Newburn Fife 287 G8
Wester Ord Aberds 293 C10
Wester Parkgate Dumfries 248 F2
Wester Quarff Shetland 313 K6
Wester Skeld Shetland 313 J4
Wester Strath Highld 300 D6
Wester Watten Highld 310 D6
Westerdale Highld 310 D5
Westerdale N Yorks 226 D3
Westerfield Shetland 313 H5
Westerfield Suff 108 B3
Westerfolds Moray 301 C11
Westergate W Sus 22 C6
Westerham Kent 52 C2
Westerhope T & W 242 D5
Westerleigh S Glos 61 D8
Westerleigh Hill S Glos 61 D8
Western Bank Cumb 229 B10
Western Downs Staffs 151 E8
Western Heights Kent 55 E10
Western Hill Durham 233 C11
Western Park Leicester 135 C11
Westerton Aberds 293 B9
Westerton Aberds 302 E5
Westerton Angus 287 B10
Westerton Durham 233 E10
Westerton Moray 302 D3
Westerton W Sus 22 B5
Westertown Aberds 303 F7
Westerwick Shetland 313 J4
Westfield Bath 45 C7
Westfield Cumb 228 F5
Westfield E Sus 38 D4
Westfield Hants 21 B10
Westfield Hereford 98 B4
Westfield Highld 310 C4
Westfield N Lnrk 278 G4
Westfield Norf 141 B9
Westfield Redcar 235 G7
Westfield S Yorks 186 E6
Westfield Sur 50 B4
Westfield W Loth 279 G8
Westfield W Yorks 197 C8
Westfield W Yorks 205 E9
Westfield Sole Kent 69 G9
Westfields Dorset 30 F2
Westfields Hereford 97 C9
Westfields of Rattray Perth 286 C5
Westford Som 27 C10
Westgate Durham 232 D4
Westgate N Lincs 199 F9
Westgate Norf 176 E4
Westgate Norf 177 E7
Westgate Hill W Yorks 197 B8
Westgate on Sea Kent 71 E10
Westgate Street Norf 160 E3
Westhall Aberds 302 G6
Westhall Suff 143 G8
Westhall Hill Oxon 82 C3
Westham Dorset 17 F9
Westham E Sus 23 E10
Westham Som 44 D2
Westhampnett W Sus 22 B5
Westhay Som 44 E2
Westhead Lancs 194 F2
Westhide Hereford 97 C11
Westhill Aberds 293 C10
Westhill E Yorks 209 F10
Westhill Highld 301 E7
Westhope Hereford 115 G9
Westhope Shrops 131 F9
Westhorp Northants 119 G10
Westhorpe Lincs 156 C4
Westhorpe Notts 171 E11
Westhorpe Suff 125 D10
Westhoughton Gtr Man 195 F7
Westhouse N Yorks 212 E3
Westhouses Derbys 170 D6
Westhumble Sur 51 C7
Westing Shetland 312 C7
Westington Glos 100 D2
Westlake Devon 8 E2
Westland Argyll 275 G11
Westland Green Herts 105 G8
Westlands Staffs 168 G4
Westlands Worcs 117 E7
Westlea Northumb 252 G6
Westlea Swindon 62 C6
Westleigh Devon 25 B7
Westleigh Devon 27 D9
Westleigh Gtr Man 194 G6
Westleton Suff 127 D8
Westley Shrops 131 B7
Westley Suff 124 E6
Westley Heights Essex 69 B7
Westley Waterless Cambs 124 F2
Westlington Bucks 84 C3
Westlinton Cumb 239 E9
Westmancote Worcs 99 D8
Westmarsh Kent 71 G9
Westmeston E Sus 36 E4
Westmill Herts 104 E3
Westmill Herts 105 F7
Westminster London 67 D10
Westmoor End Cumb 229 D8
Westmuir Angus 287 B7
Westness Orkney 314 D3
Westnewton Cumb 229 C8
Westnewton Northumb 263 C10
Westoe T & W 243 D9
Weston Bath 61 F8
Weston Devon 15 D9
Weston Devon 27 G10
Weston Dorset 17 G9
Weston Dorset 29 F8
Weston E Ches 168 E2
Weston E Ches 184 G5
Weston Halton 183 E8
Weston Hants 34 C2
Weston Hereford 115 F7
Weston Herts 104 E5
Weston Lincs 156 D5
Weston N Yorks 205 D9
Weston Northants 101 B11
Weston Notts 172 B3
Weston Pembs 73 C8
Weston S Lnrk 269 F10
Weston Shrops 114 C6
Weston Shrops 131 E11
Weston Shrops 148 D5
Weston Shrops 149 D11
Weston Soton 32 E6
Weston Staffs 151 D9
Weston Suff 143 F8
Weston W Berks 63 E11
Weston Bampfylde Som 29 C10
Weston Beggard Hereford 97 C11
Weston by Welland Northants 136 E5
Weston Colley Hants 48 F4
Weston Colville Cambs 124 G2
Weston Common Soton 33 E7
Weston Corbett Hants 49 D7
Weston Coyney Stoke 168 G6
Weston Ditch Suff 124 B3
Weston Favell Northants 120 E5
Weston Green Cambs 124 G2
Weston Green Norf 160 G2
Weston Green Sur 67 F7
Weston Heath Shrops 150 G5
Weston Hills Lincs 156 E5
Weston in Arden Warks 135 F7
Weston-in-Gordano N Som 60 E2
Weston Jones Staffs 150 E5
Weston Longville Norf 160 F2
Weston Lullingfields Shrops 149 E8
Weston Manor I o W 20 D2
Weston Mill Plym 7 D9
Weston-on-Avon Warks 118 G3
Weston-on-the-Green Oxon 83 B8
Weston-on-Trent Derbys 153 D8
Weston Park Bath 61 F8
Weston Patrick Hants 49 D7
Weston Point Halton 183 E7
Weston Rhyn Shrops 148 B5
Weston-sub-Edge Glos 100 C2
Weston-super-Mare N Som 59 G10
Weston Town Som 45 E8
Weston Turville Bucks 84 C5
Weston under Lizard Staffs 150 G6
Weston under Penyard Hereford 98 G2
Weston under Wetherley Warks 119 D7
Weston Underwood Derbys 170 G3
Weston Underwood M Keynes 121 G7
Westonbirt Glos 61 B11
Westoncommon Shrops 149 D8
Westoning C Beds 103 E10
Westonwharf Shrops 149 D8
Westonzoyland Som 43 G11
Westow N Yorks 216 F5
Westowe Som 42 G6
Westown Devon 27 E10
Westown Perth 286 E6
Westport Argyll 255 E7
Westport Som 28 D5
Westquarter Falk 279 F8
Westra V Glam 58 E6
Westridge Green W Berks 64 D5
Westrigg W Loth 269 B8
Westrip Glos 80 D4
Westrop Wilts 61 E11
Westrop Green W Berks 64 E4
Westrum N Lincs 200 F4
Westruther Borders 272 F2
Westry Cambs 139 D7
Westthorpe Derbys 187 F7
Westvale Mers 182 B6
Westville Devon 8 G4
Westville Notts 171 F8
Westward Cumb 229 C11
Westward Ho! Devon 24 B6
Westweekmoor Devon 12 C4
Westwell Kent 54 D3
Westwell Oxon 82 D2
Westwell Leacon Kent 54 D3
Westwells Wilts 61 F11
Westwick Cambs 123 D8
Westwick Durham 223 B11
Westwick Norf 160 D5
Westwick Row Herts 85 D9
Westwood Devon 14 B6
Westwood Devon 14 E5
Westwood Kent 55 D7
Westwood Kent 71 F11
Westwood Notts 171 E7
Westwood P'boro 138 D3
Westwood S Lnrk 268 E2
Westwood Wilts 45 B10
Westwood Wilts 46 G6
Westwood Heath W Mid 118 B5
Westwood Park Essex 107 E9
Westwood Park Gtr Man 184 B3
Westwoodside N Lincs 188 B3
Westy Warr 183 D10
Wetham Green Kent 69 F10
Wetheral Cumb 239 G11
Wetheral Plain Cumb 239 F11
Wetherby W Yorks 206 D4
Wetherden Suff 125 E10
Wetherden Upper Town Suff 125 D10
Wetheringsett Suff 126 D2
Wethersfield Essex 106 E4
Wethersta Shetland 312 G5
Wetherup Street Suff 126 E2
Wetley Rocks Staffs 169 F7
Wetmore Staffs 152 E5
Wettenhall E Ches 167 C10
Wettenhall Green E Ches 167 C10
Wettles Shrops 131 F8
Wetton Staffs 169 D10
Wetwang E Yorks 208 B4
Wetwood Staffs 150 C5
Wexcombe Wilts 47 B9
Wexham Street Bucks 66 C3
Weybourne Norf 177 E10
Weybourne Sur 49 D11
Weybread Suff 142 G4
Weybridge Sur 66 G5
Weycroft Devon 16 B2
Weydale Highld 310 C5
Weyhill Hants 47 D10
Weymouth Dorset 17 F9
Weythel Powys 114 F4
Whaddon Bucks 102 E6
Whaddon Cambs 104 B6
Whaddon Glos 80 C4
Whaddon Glos 99 G9
Whaddon Wilts 31 B11
Whaddon Wilts 61 G11
Whaddon Gap Cambs 104 B6
Whale Cumb 230 G6
Whaley Derbys 187 G8
Whaley Bridge Derbys 185 E8
Whaley Thorns Derbys 187 G8
Whaligoe Highld 310 E7
Whalley Lancs 203 F10
Whalley Banks Lancs 203 F10
Whalley Range Gtr Man 184 C4
Whalleys Lancs 194 F3
Whalton Northumb 252 G4
Wham N Yorks 212 G5
Whaplode Lincs 156 E6
Whaplode Drove Lincs 156 G6
Whaplode St Catherine Lincs 156 E6
Wharf Warks 119 G8
Wharfe N Yorks 212 F5
Wharles Lancs 202 F4
Wharley End C Beds 103 C8
Wharmley Northumb 241 D9
Wharncliffe Side S Yorks 186 C3
Wharram le Street N Yorks 217 F7
Wharram Percy N Yorks 217 G7
Wharton Hereford 115 F10
Wharton Lincs 188 C4
Wharton W Ches 167 B11
Wharton Green W Ches 167 B11
Whashton N Yorks 224 D3
Whasset Cumb 211 C10
Whatcombe Dorset 30 G4
Whatcote Warks 100 C6
Whatcroft W Ches 167 B11
Whateley Staffs 134 D4
Whatfield Suff 107 B10
Whatley Som 28 F5
Whatley Som 45 D8
Whatlington E Sus 38 D3
Whatmore Shrops 116 C2
Whatsole Street Kent 54 E6
Whatstandwell Derbys 170 E4
Whatton Notts 154 B4
Whauphill Dumfries 236 E6
Whaw N Yorks 223 E9
Wheal Alfred Corn 2 B3
Wheal Baddon Corn 4 G5
Wheal Busy Corn 4 G4
Wheal Frances Corn 4 E5
Wheal Kitty Corn 4 E4
Wheal Rose Corn 4 G4
Wheat Hold Hants 64 G5
Wheatacre Norf 143 E9
Wheatcroft Derbys 170 D5
Wheatenhurst Glos 80 D3
Wheathall Shrops 131 C9
Wheathampstead Herts 85 C11
Wheathill Shrops 132 G2
Wheathill Som 44 G5
Wheatley Devon 14 C4
Wheatley Hants 49 E9
Wheatley Oxon 83 D9
Wheatley S Yorks 198 G5
Wheatley W Yorks 196 B5
Wheatley Hill Durham 234 D3
Wheatley Hills S Yorks 198 G6
Wheatley Lane Lancs 204 F2
Wheatley Park S Yorks 198 F5
Wheaton Aston Staffs 151 G7
Wheddon Cross Som 42 F2
Wheedlemont Aberds 302 G4
Wheelbarrow Town Kent 55 D7
Wheeler End Bucks 84 G4
Wheelerstreet Sur 50 E2
Wheelock E Ches 168 D3
Wheelock Heath E Ches 168 D2
Wheelton Lancs 194 C5
Wheelton Lancs 194 C6
Wheelton Lancs 194 D5
Wheelton Lancs 194 D6
Wheen Angus 292 F5
Wheldale W Yorks 198 B3
Wheldrake York 207 D9
Whelford Glos 81 F11
Whelley Gtr Man 194 F5
Whelp Street Suff 107 B8
Whelpley Hill Herts 85 E7
Whelpo Cumb 230 D2
Whelston Flint 182 F2
Whempstead Herts 104 G6
Whenby N Yorks 216 F2
Whepstead Suff 124 F6
Wherry Town Corn 1 D5
Wherstead Suff 108 C3
Wherwell Hants 47 E11
Wheston Derbys 185 F10
Whetley Cross Dorset 29 G7
Whetsted Kent 53 D7
Whetstone Leics 135 D11
Whetstone London 86 G3
Whettleton Shrops 131 G8
Whicham Cumb 210 C2
Whichford Warks 100 E6
Whickham T & W 242 E6
Whickham Fell T & W 242 F6
Whiddon Devon 40 F5
Whiddon Down Devon 13 C9
Whifflet N Lnrk 268 C4
Whigstreet Angus 287 C8
Whilton Northants 120 E2
Whilton Locks Northants 120 E2
Whim Farm Borders 270 E4
Whimble Devon 24 G5
Whimple Devon 14 B6
Whimpwell Green Norf 161 D7
Whin Lane End Lancs 202 E3
Whinfield Darl 224 B6
Whinhall N Lnrk 268 B5
Whinmoor W Yorks 206 F3
Whinney Hill S Yorks 187 C7
Whinney Hill Stockton 225 B7
Whinnieliggate Dumfries 237 D9
Whinny Heights Blkburn 195 B7
Whinnyfold Aberds 303 F10
Whins of Milton Stirl 278 C5
Whins Wood W Yorks 205 F7
Whipcott Devon 27 D9
Whippendell Botton Herts 85 E9
Whippingham I o W 20 C6
Whipsiderry Corn 4 C6
Whipsnade C Beds 85 B8
Whipton Devon 14 C5
Whirley Grove E Ches 184 F5
Whirlow S Yorks 186 E4
Whisby Lincs 172 B6
Whissendine Rutland 154 G6
Whissonsett Norf 159 E8
Whisterfield E Ches 184 G4
Whistlefield Argyll 276 C2
Whistlefield Argyll 276 C4
Whistley Green Wokingham 65 E9
Whistlow Oxon 101 F9
Whiston Mers 183 C7
Whiston Northants 120 E6
Whiston S Yorks 186 D6
Whiston Staffs 151 G7
Whiston Staffs 169 F8
Whiston Cross Mers 183 C7
Whiston Cross Shrops 132 C5
Whitacre Heath Warks 134 E4
Whitbarrow Village Cumb 230 F4
Whitbeck Cumb 210 C2
Whitbourne Hereford 116 F4
Whitbourne Moor Wilts 45 D10
Whitburn T & W 243 E10
Whitburn W Loth 269 C8
Whitburn Colliery T & W 243 E10
Whitby N Yorks 227 C7
Whitby W Ches 182 F5
Whitbyheath W Ches 182 F5
Whitchurch Bath 60 F6
Whitchurch Bucks 102 G5
Whitchurch Cardiff 59 C7
Whitchurch Devon 12 G5
Whitchurch Hants 48 D3
Whitchurch Hereford 79 B9
Whitchurch Pembs 90 F5
Whitchurch Shrops 167 G8
Whitchurch Som 30 C2
Whitchurch Canonicorum Dorset 16 B3
Whitchurch Hill Oxon 64 D6
Whitchurch-on-Thames Oxon 64 D6
Whitcombe Dorset 17 D10
Whitcombe Som 29 C10
Whitcot Shrops 131 E7
Whitcott Keysett Shrops 130 G5
White Ball Som 27 D9
White Colne Essex 107 F7
White Coppice Lancs 194 D6
White Cross Bath 44 B5
White Cross Bath 44 B6
White Cross Corn 2 E5
White Cross Corn 5 D7
White Cross Hereford 97 C9
White Cross Som 43 D10
White Cross Wilts 45 G9
White Cross Hill Cambs 123 B9
White End Worcs 98 E5
White Gate Gtr Man 195 G11
White Gate Som 28 F4
White Grit Shrops 130 D6
White Hall Herts 104 G5
White Hill Bath 45 B8
White Hill W Yorks 204 E6
White Hill Wilts 45 G10
White Hills Northants 120 E4
White House Suff 108 B2
White Houses Notts 188 F2
White Lackington Dorset 17 B10
White Ladies Aston Worcs 117 G8
White-le-Head Durham 242 G5
White Lee W Yorks 197 B8
White Lund Lancs 211 G8
White Mill Carms 93 G9
White Moor Derbys 170 F5
White Ness Shetland 313 J5
White Notley Essex 88 B3
White Oak Kent 68 F4
White Ox Mead Bath 45 B8
White Pit Lincs 190 F5
White Post Kent 52 E4
White Post Notts 171 D10
White Rocks Hereford 97 G8
White Roding or White Roothing Essex 87 C9
White Stake Lancs 194 B4
White Stone Hereford 97 C11
White Waltham Windsor 65 D10
Whiteacen Moray 302 E2
Whiteacre Kent 54 D6
Whiteacre Heath Warks 134 E4
Whiteash Green Essex 106 E5
Whitebirk Blkburn 195 B8
Whitebog Highld 301 C7
Whitebridge Highld 290 B6
Whitebrook Mon 79 D8
Whiteburn Borders 271 F11
Whitebushes Sur 51 D9
Whitecairn Dumfries 236 D4
Whitecairns Aberds 293 B11
Whitecastle S Lnrk 269 G10
Whitechapel Lancs 203 E7
Whitechapel London 67 C10
Whitechurch Maund Hereford 97 B11
Whitecleat Orkney 314 F5
Whitecliff Glos 79 C9
Whiteclosegate Cumb 239 F10
Whitecote W Yorks 205 F10
Whitecraig E Loth 281 G7
Whitecraigs E Renf 267 D11
Whitecroft Glos 79 D10
Whitecrook W Dunb 267 B10
Whitecross Corn 2 C2
Whitecross Corn 6 E2
Whitecross Corn 10 G5
Whitecross Falk 279 F9
Whitecross Som 28 C6
Whitecross Staffs 151 E7
Whiteface Highld 309 L7
Whitefarland N Ayrs 255 C9
Whitefaulds S Ayrs 245 B7
Whitefield Aberds 303 G7
Whitefield Dorset 18 C4
Whitefield Gtr Man 195 F10
Whitefield Perth 286 D5
Whitefield Som 27 B9
Whitefield Lane End Mers 183 D7
Whiteflat E Ayrs 258 D2
Whiteford Aberds 303 G7
Whitegate W Ches 167 B10
Whitehall Blkburn 195 C7
Whitehall Bristol 60 E6
Whitehall Devon 27 E10
Whitehall Devon 40 F4
Whitehall Hants 49 C8
Whitehall Herts 104 E6
Whitehall W Sus 35 C10
Whitehall Village Orkney 314 D6
Whitehaven Cumb 219 B9
Whitehaven Shrops 148 E5
Whitehawk Brighton 36 G4
Whiteheath Gate W Mid 133 F9
Whitehill E Sus 37 B8
Whitehill Hants 49 G9
Whitehill Kent 54 B4
Whitehill Midloth 271 B7
Whitehill Moray 302 D5
Whitehill S Lnrk 268 D4
Whitehill Staffs 168 E3
Whitehills Aberds 302 C6
Whitehills S Lnrk 268 E2
Whitehills T & W 243 E7
Whiteholme Blkpool 202 E2
Whitehough Derbys 185 E8
Whitehouse Aberds 293 B8
Whitehouse Argyll 275 G9
Whitehouse Common W Mid 134 D2
Whitehouse Green W Berks 65 F7
Whiteinch Glasgow 267 B10
Whitekirk E Loth 281 E10
Whiteknights Reading 65 E8
Whiteknowes Aberds 293 C7
Whitelackington Som 28 D5
Whitelaw S Lnrk 268 G2
Whiteleaf Bucks 84 E4
Whiteleas T & W 243 E9
Whiteleaved Oak Glos 98 D5
Whitelee Borders 262 C3
Whitelee Northumb 250 B6
Whitelees S Ayrs 257 C9
Whiteley Bank I o W 21 E7
Whiteley Green E Ches 184 F6
Whiteley Village Sur 66 G5
Whitelye Mon 79 E8
Whitemans Green W Sus 36 B4
Whitemire Moray 301 D9
Whitemoor Corn 5 D9
Whitemoor Nottingham 171 G8
Whitemoor Warks 118 C5
Whitemore Staffs 168 C5
Whitenap Hants 32 C5
Whiteoak Green Oxon 82 C4
Whiteparish Wilts 32 C2
Whitepits Wilts 45 F10
Whiterashes Aberds 303 G8
Whiterigg Borders 262 C3
Whiterock Bridgend 58 D2
Whiterow Highld 310 E7
White's Green W Sus 34 B6
Whiteshill Glos 80 D4
Whiteshill S Glos 60 D6
Whiteside Northumb 240 D6
Whiteside W Loth 269 B9
Whitesmith E Sus 23 C8
Whitespots Dumfries 247 F10
Whitestaunton Som 28 E3
Whitestone Aberds 293 D8
Whitestone Devon 14 C3
Whitestone Devon 40 D3
Whitestone Warks 135 F7
Whitestones Aberds 303 D8
Whitestreet Green Suff 107 D9
Whitewall Common Mon 60 B2
Whitewall Corner N Yorks 216 E5
Whiteway Bath 61 G8
Whiteway Dorset 18 E3
Whiteway Glos 80 C6
Whiteway Glos 80 F4
Whitewell Aberds 303 C9
Whitewell Corn 11 E7
Whitewell Highld 291 C11
Whitewell Lancs 203 D9
Whitewell Wrex 167 G7
Whitewell Bottom Lancs 195 C10
Whiteworks Devon 13 G8
Whitfield Kent 55 D10
Whitfield Northants 102 D2
Whitfield Northumb 241 F7
Whitfield S Glos 79 G11
Whitfield Court Sur 50 B3
Whitfield Hall Northumb 241 F7
Whitford Devon 15 B11
Whitford = Chwitffordd Flint 181 F10
Whitgift E Yorks 199 C10
Whitgreave Staffs 151 D7
Whithaugh Borders 249 F11
Whithebeir Orkney 314 C5
Whithorn Dumfries 236 E6
Whiting Bay N Ayrs 256 D2
Whitington Norf 140 D4
Whitkirk W Yorks 206 G3

368 Whi – Woo

Whitland = Hendy-Gwyn Carms 73 B11
Whitlaw Borders 271 F9
Whitleigh Plym 7 C9
Whitletts S Ayrs 257 E9
Whitley Gtr Man 194 F5
Whitley N Yorks 198 C5
Whitley Reading 65 E8
Whitley S Yorks 186 C4
Whitley W Mid 119 B7
Whitley Wilts 61 F11
Whitley Bay T & W 243 C9
Whitley Bridge N Yorks 198 C5
Whitley Chapel Northumb 241 F10
Whitley Head W Yorks 204 E6
Whitley Heath Staffs 150 D6
Whitley Lower W Yorks 197 D8
Whitley Reed W Ches 183 E10
Whitley Row Kent 52 C3
Whitley Sands T & W 243 C9
Whitley Thorpe N Yorks 198 C5
Whitley Wood Reading 65 F8
Whitlock's End W Mid 118 B2
Whitminster Glos 80 D3
Whitmoor Devon 27 E9
Whitmore Dorset 31 F9
Whitmore Staffs 168 G4
Whitmore Park W Mid 134 G6
Whitnage Devon 27 D8
Whitnash Warks 118 E6
Whitnell Som 43 F8
Whitney Bottom Som 28 E4
Whitney-on-Wye Hereford 96 B5
Whitrigg Cumb 229 D10
Whitrigg Cumb 238 F6
Whitriggs Borders 262 F3
Whitsbury Hants 31 D10
Whitslaid Borders 271 G11
Whitsome Borders 273 E7
Whitsomehill Borders 273 F7
Whitson Newport 59 C11
Whitstable Kent 70 F6
Whitstone Corn 11 B11
Whittingham Northumb 264 G3
Whittingslow Shrops 131 F8
Whittington Glos 99 G10
Whittington Lancs 212 D2
Whittington Norf 140 D4
Whittington Shrops 148 C6
Whittington Staffs 133 G7
Whittington Staffs 134 B3
Whittington Staffs 150 C5
Whittington Warks 134 D5
Whittington Worcs 117 G7
Whittington Moor Derbys 186 G5
Whittleford Warks 134 E6
Whittle-le-Woods Lancs 194 C5
Whittlebury Northants 102 C3
Whittlesey Cambs 138 D5
Whittlesford Cambs 105 B9
Whittlestone Head Blkburn 195 D8
Whitton Borders 263 E7
Whitton Hereford 115 C8
Whitton London 66 E6
Whitton N Lincs 200 C2
Whitton Northumb 252 C3
Whitton Powys 114 D5
Whitton Shrops 115 C11
Whitton Stockton 234 G3
Whitton Suff 108 B2
Whittonditch Wilts 63 E9
Whittonstall Northumb 242 F3
Whittytree Shrops 115 B8
Whitway Hants 48 B3
Whitwell Derbys 187 F8
Whitwell Herts 104 G3
Whitwell I o W 20 F6
Whitwell N Yorks 224 F5
Whitwell Rutland 137 B8
Whitwell-on-the-Hill N Yorks 216 F4
Whitwell Street Norf 160 E2
Whitwick Leics 153 F8
Whitwood W Yorks 198 C2
Whitworth Lancs 195 D11
Whixall Shrops 149 C10
Whixley N Yorks 206 B4
Whoberley W Mid 118 B6
Wholeflats Falk 279 E8
Whome Orkney 314 G3
Whorlton Durham 224 C2
Whorlton N Yorks 225 E9
Whydown E Sus 38 F2
Whygate Northumb 241 B7
Whyke W Sus 22 C5
Whyle Hereford 115 E11
Whyteleafe Sur 51 B10
Wibdon Glos 79 F9
Wibsey W Yorks 205 G8
Wibtoft Leics 135 F9
Wichenford Worcs 116 E5
Wichling Kent 54 B2
Wick Bmouth 19 C8
Wick Devon 27 G11
Wick Highld 310 D7
Wick S Glos 61 E8
Wick Shetland 313 K6
Wick Som 28 B6
Wick Som 43 C10
Wick Som 43 E8
Wick V Glam 58 E2
Wick W Sus 35 G8
Wick Wilts 31 C11
Wick Worcs 99 B9
Wick Episcopi Worcs 116 G6
Wick Hill Brack 65 E11
Wick Hill Kent 53 E10
Wick Hill Wokingham 65 G9
Wick Rocks S Glos 61 E8
Wick St Lawrence N Som 59 F11
Wick Street Glos 80 D5
Wicken Cambs 123 C11
Wicken Northants 102 D4
Wicken Bonhunt Essex 105 E9
Wicken Green Village Norf 158 C6
Wickenby Lincs 189 E9
Wicker Street Green Suff 107 C9
Wickersley S Yorks 187 C7
Wickford Essex 88 G3
Wickham Hants 33 E9
Wickham W Berks 63 E11
Wickham Bishops Essex 88 C4
Wickham Green Suff 125 D11
Wickham Green W Berks 63 E11
Wickham Heath W Berks 64 F2
Wickham Market Suff 126 F6
Wickham St Paul Essex 106 D6
Wickham Skeith Suff 125 D11
Wickham Street Suff 124 G5
Wickham Street Suff 125 D11
Wickhambreaux Kent 55 B8
Wickhambrook Suff 124 G4
Wickhamford Worcs 99 C11
Wickhampton Norf 143 B8
Wickham's Cross Som 44 G4
Wickhurst Kent 52 D4
Wicklane Bath 45 B7
Wicklewood Norf 141 C11
Wickmere Norf 160 C3
Wickridge Street Glos 98 F6
Wickstreet E Sus 23 D8
Wickwar S Glos 61 B8
Widbrook Wilts 45 B10
Widcombe Bath 61 G9
Widdington Essex 105 E10
Widdrington Northumb 253 D7
Widdrington Station Northumb 252 E6
Widecombe in the Moor Devon 13 F10
Widegates Corn 6 D5
Widemarsh Hereford 97 C10
Widemouth Bay Corn 24 G2
Wideopen T & W 242 C6
Widewall Orkney 314 G4
Widewell Plym 7 C9
Widford Essex 87 D11
Widford Herts 86 B6
Widgham Green Cambs 124 F3
Widham Wilts 62 B5
Widley Hants 33 F11
Widmer End Bucks 84 F5
Widmerpool Notts 154 D2
Widmoor Bucks 66 B2
Widmore London 68 F2
Widnes Halton 183 D8
Wierton Kent 53 D9
Wig Powys 130 F2
Wig Fach Bridgend 57 F10
Wigan Gtr Man 194 F5
Wiganthorpe N Yorks 216 E3
Wigbeth Dorset 31 F8
Wigborough Som 28 D6
Wiggaton Devon 15 C8
Wiggenhall St Germans Norf 157 G11
Wiggenhall St Mary Magdalen Norf 157 G11
Wiggenhall St Mary the Virgin Norf 157 G11
Wiggenhall St Peter Norf 158 G2
Wiggens Green Essex 106 C3
Wiggington Staffs 134 B4
Wigginstall Staffs 169 C9
Wigginton Herts 84 C6
Wigginton Oxon 101 E7
Wigginton Shrops 148 B6
Wigginton Staffs 134 B4
Wigginton York 207 B7
Wigginton Bottom Herts 84 D6
Wigginton Heath Oxon 101 D7
Wigglesworth N Yorks 204 B2
Wiggonby Cumb 239 G7
Wiggonholt W Sus 35 D9
Wighill N Yorks 206 D5
Wighton Norf 159 B8
Wightwick Manor Staffs 133 D7
Wigley Derbys 186 G4
Wigley Hants 32 D4
Wigmarsh Shrops 149 D7
Wigmore Hereford 115 D8
Wigmore Medway 69 G10
Wigsley Notts 188 G5
Wigsthorpe Northants 137 G10
Wigston Leics 136 D2
Wigston Magna Leics 136 D2
Wigston Parva Leics 135 F9
Wigthorpe Notts 187 E9
Wigtoft Lincs 156 B5
Wigton Cumb 229 B11
Wigtown Dumfries 236 D6
Wigtwizzle S Yorks 186 B2
Wike W Yorks 206 E2
Wike Well End S Yorks 199 E7
Wilbarston Northants 136 F6
Wilberfoss E Yorks 207 C10
Wilberlee W Yorks 196 E5
Wilburton Cambs 123 C9
Wilby Norf 141 F10
Wilby Northants 121 D7
Wilby Suff 126 C4
Wilcot Wilts 62 G6
Wilcott Shrops 149 F7
Wilcott Marsh Shrops 149 F7
Wilcove Corn 7 D8
Wilcrick Newport 60 B2
Wild Mill Bridgend 58 C2
Wilday Green Derbys 186 G4
Wildboarclough E Ches 169 B7
Wilde Street Suff 124 B4
Wilden Beds 121 F11
Wilden Worcs 116 C6
Wildern Hants 33 E7
Wildernesse Kent 52 B4
Wilderspool Warr 183 D10
Wilderswood Gtr Man 194 E6
Wildhern Hants 47 C11
Wildhill Herts 86 D3
Wildmanbridge S Lnrk 268 E6
Wildmoor Hants 49 B7
Wildmoor Oxon 83 F7
Wildmoor Worcs 117 B9
Wildridings Brack 65 F11
Wildsworth Lincs 188 B4
Wildwood Staffs 151 E8
Wilford Nottingham 153 B11
Wilgate Green Kent 54 B3
Wilkesley E Ches 167 G10
Wilkhaven Highld 311 L3
Wilkieston W Loth 270 B2
Wilkin Throop Som 29 C11
Wilkinthroop Som 29 C11
Wilksby Lincs 174 C3
Will Row Lincs 191 D7
Willacy Lane End Lancs 202 F5
Willand Devon 27 E8
Willand Som 27 E11
Willand Moor Devon 27 E8
Willard's Hill E Sus 38 C2
Willaston E Ches 167 E11
Willaston Shrops 149 B11
Willaston W Ches 182 F4
Willen M Keynes 103 C7
Willenhall W Mid 119 B7
Willenhall W Mid 133 D9
Willerby E Yorks 208 G6
Willerby N Yorks 217 D10
Willersey Glos 100 D2
Willersley Hereford 96 B6
Willesborough Kent 54 E4
Willesborough Lees Kent 54 E4
Willesden London 67 C8
Willesden Green London 67 C8
Willesley Leics 152 G6
Willesley Wilts 61 B11
Willett Som 42 G6
Willey Shrops 132 D3
Willey Warks 135 G9
Willey Green Sur 50 C2
Willhayne Som 28 E4
Williamhope Borders 261 C10
William's Green Suff 107 C9
Williamscott Oxon 101 B9
Williamslee Borders 270 G6
Williamstown Rhondda 77 G8
Williamthorpe Derbys 170 B6
Willian Herts 104 E4
Willicote Pastures Worcs 100 B3
Willingale Essex 87 D9
Willingcott Devon 40 E3
Willingdon E Sus 23 E9
Willingham Cambs 123 C8
Willingham Suff 143 G8
Willingham by Stow Lincs 188 E5
Willingham Green Cambs 124 G2
Willington Beds 104 B2
Willington Derbys 152 D5
Willington Durham 233 D9
Willington Kent 53 C9
Willington T & W 243 D8
Willington Warks 100 D5
Willington Corner W Ches 167 B8
Willington Quay T & W 243 D8
Willisham Suff 125 G11
Willisham Tye Suff 125 G11
Willitoft E Yorks 207 F10
Williton Som 42 E5
Willoughbridge Staffs 168 G3
Willoughby Lincs 191 G7
Willoughby Warks 119 D10
Willoughby Hills Lincs 174 F4
Willoughby-on-the-Wolds Notts 154 D2
Willoughby Waterleys Leics 135 E11
Willoughton Lincs 188 C6
Willow Green W Ches 183 F10
Willow Green Worcs 116 F5
Willow Holme Cumb 239 F9
Willowbank Bucks 66 B5
Willows Gtr Man 195 F8
Willows Green Essex 88 B2
Willowtown Bl Gwent 77 C11
Willsbridge S Glos 61 E7
Willslock Staffs 151 C11
Willstone Shrops 131 D9
Willsworthy Devon 12 E6
Wilmcote Warks 118 F3
Wilmington Bath 61 G7
Wilmington Devon 15 B10
Wilmington E Sus 23 E8
Wilmington Kent 68 E4
Wilmington Green E Sus 23 D8
Wilminstone Devon 12 F5
Wilmslow E Ches 184 E4
Wilmslow Park E Ches 184 E5
Wilnecote Staffs 134 C4
Wilney Green Norf 141 G11
Wilpshire Lancs 203 G9
Wilsden W Yorks 205 F7
Wilsden Hill W Yorks 205 F7
Wilsford Lincs 173 G8
Wilsford Wilts 46 B6
Wilsford Wilts 46 F6
Wilsham Devon 41 D9
Wilshaw W Yorks 196 F6
Wilsic S Yorks 187 B9
Wilsill N Yorks 214 G3
Wilsley Green Kent 53 F9
Wilsley Pound Kent 53 F9
Wilsom Hants 49 F8
Wilson Hereford 97 G11
Wilson Leics 153 E8
Wilsontown S Lnrk 269 D9
Wilstead Beds 103 C11
Wilsthorpe Derbys 153 C9
Wilsthorpe Lincs 155 G11
Wilstone Herts 84 C6
Wilstone Green Herts 84 C6
Wilthorpe S Yorks 197 F10
Wilton Borders 261 G11
Wilton Cumb 219 C10
Wilton Hereford 97 G11
Wilton N Yorks 217 C7
Wilton Redcar 225 B11
Wilton Som 28 C2
Wilton Wilts 46 G5
Wilton Wilts 63 G9
Wilton Park Bucks 85 G7
Wiltown Devon 27 D11
Wiltown Som 28 C5
Wimbish Essex 105 D11
Wimbish Green Essex 106 D2
Wimble Hill Hants 49 D10
Wimblebury Staffs 151 G10
Wimbledon London 67 E8
Wimblington Cambs 139 E8
Wimbolds Trafford W Ches 182 G6
Wimboldsley W Ches 167 C11
Wimborne Minster Dorset 18 B6
Wimborne St Giles Dorset 31 E8
Wimbotsham Norf 140 B2
Wimpole Cambs 104 B6
Wimpson Soton 32 E5
Wimpstone Warks 100 B4
Winburgh Norf 141 B10
Wincanton Som 30 B2
Winceby Lincs 174 B4
Wincham W Ches 183 F11
Winchburgh W Loth 279 G11
Winchcombe Glos 99 F10
Winchelsea E Sus 38 D6
Winchelsea Beach E Sus 38 D6
Winchester Hants 33 B7
Winchestown Bl Gwent 77 C11
Winchet Hill Kent 53 E8
Winchfield Hants 49 C9
Winchfield Hurst Hants 49 C9
Winchmore Hill Bucks 84 G6
Winchmore Hill London 86 G4
Wincle E Ches 169 B7
Wincobank S Yorks 186 C5
Wind Hill Cumb 210 E5
Wind Hill Pembs 73 F9
Winder Cumb 219 B10
Windermere Cumb 221 F8
Winderton Warks 100 C6
Windhill Highld 300 E5
Windhill S Yorks 198 G3
Windhill W Yorks 205 F9
Windhouse Shetland 312 D6
Winding Wood W Berks 63 E11
Windle Hill W Ches 182 F4
Windlehurst Gtr Man 185 D7
Windlesham Sur 66 G2
Windley Derbys 170 F4
Windmill Corn 10 G3
Windmill Flint 181 G11
Windmill Flint 182 G2
Windmill Hill Bristol 60 E5
Windmill Hill E Sus 23 C10
Windmill Hill Halton 183 E9
Windmill Hill Kent 69 F10
Windmill Hill Som 28 D4
Windmill Hill W Yorks 197 D11
Windmill Hill Worcs 99 B8
Windrush Glos 81 C11
Windsor N Lincs 199 E9
Windsor Windsor 66 D3
Windsor Green Suff 125 G7
Windsoredge Glos 80 E4
Windwhistle Som 28 F5
Windy Arbor Mers 183 D7
Windy Arbour Warks 118 C5
Windy Hill Wrex 166 E4
Windy Nook T & W 243 E7
Windy-Yett E Ayrs 267 E9
Windydoors Borders 261 B10
Windygates Fife 287 G7
Windyharbour E Ches 184 G4
Windyknowe W Loth 269 B9
Windywalls Borders 263 C7
Wineham W Sus 36 C2
Winestead E Yorks 201 C9
Winewall Lancs 204 E4
Winfarthing Norf 142 F2
Winford I o W 21 E7
Winford N Som 60 F4
Winforton Hereford 96 B5
Winfrith Newburgh Dorset 18 E2
Wing Bucks 103 G7
Wing Rutland 137 C7
Wingate Durham 234 D4
Wingates Gtr Man 195 F7
Wingates Northumb 252 D4
Wingerworth Derbys 170 B5
Wingfield C Beds 103 F10
Wingfield S Yorks 186 B6
Wingfield Suff 126 B4
Wingfield Wilts 45 B10
Wingfield Green Suff 126 B4
Wingfield Park Derbys 170 E5
Wingham Kent 55 B8
Wingham Green Kent 55 B8
Wingham Well Kent 55 B8
Wingmore Kent 55 D7
Wingrave Bucks 84 B5
Winkburn Notts 172 D2
Winkfield Brack 66 E2
Winkfield Place Brack 66 E2
Winkfield Row Brack 65 E11
Winkhill Staffs 169 E9
Winkhurst Green Kent 52 D3
Winklebury Hants 48 C6
Winkleigh Devon 25 F10
Winksley N Yorks 214 E5
Winkton Dorset 19 B9
Winlaton T & W 242 E5
Winlaton Mill T & W 242 E5
Winless Highld 310 D7
Winllan Powys 148 E4
Winmarleigh Lancs 202 D5
Winmarleigh Moss Lancs 202 D4
Winnal Hereford 97 E9
Winnal Common Hereford 97 E9
Winnall Hants 33 B7
Winnall Worcs 116 D6
Winnard's Perch Corn 5 B8
Winnersh Wokingham 65 E9
Winnington Staffs 150 B4
Winnington W Ches 183 G10
Winnington Green Shrops 148 G6
Winnothdale Staffs 169 G8
Winscales Cumb 228 F6
Winscombe N Som 44 B2
Winsdon Hill Luton 103 G11
Winsford Som 42 G2
Winsford W Ches 167 B10
Winsh-wen Swansea 57 B7
Winsham Devon 40 F3
Winsham Som 28 F5
Winshill Staffs 152 E5
Winsick Derbys 170 B6
Winskill Cumb 231 D7
Winslade Devon 24 D5
Winslade Hants 49 D7
Winsley N Yorks 214 G4
Winsley Wilts 61 G10
Winslow Bucks 102 F5
Winslow Mill Hereford 98 D2
Winson Glos 81 D9
Winson Green W Mid 133 F10
Winsor Hants 32 E4
Winstanley Gtr Man 194 G5
Winstanleys Gtr Man 194 F5
Winster Cumb 221 G8
Winster Derbys 170 C2
Winston Durham 224 B2
Winston Suff 126 E3
Winston Green Suff 126 E3
Winstone Glos 81 D7
Winswell Devon 25 E7
Winter Gardens Essex 69 C9
Winter Well Som 28 C3
Winterborne Bassett Wilts 62 E6
Winterborne Came Dorset 17 D10
Winterborne Clenston Dorset 30 G4
Winterborne Herringston Dorset 17 D9
Winterborne Houghton Dorset 30 G4
Winterborne Kingston Dorset 18 B3
Winterborne Monkton Dorset 17 D9
Winterborne Monkton Wilts 62 E6
Winterborne Muston Dorset 18 B3
Winterborne Stickland Dorset 30 G4
Winterborne Tomson Dorset 18 B3
Winterborne Whitechurch Dorset 30 G4
Winterborne Zelston Dorset 18 B3
Winterbourne Kent 54 B5
Winterbourne S Glos 60 C6
Winterbourne W Berks 64 E3
Winterbourne Abbas Dorset 17 C8
Winterbourne Bassett Wilts 62 E6
Winterbourne Dauntsey Wilts 47 G7
Winterbourne Down S Glos 61 D7
Winterbourne Earls Wilts 47 G7
Winterbourne Gunner Wilts 47 F7
Winterbourne Steepleton Dorset 17 D8
Winterbourne Stoke Wilts 46 E5
Winterbrook Oxon 64 B6
Winterburn N Yorks 204 B4
Winterfield Bath 45 B7
Winterhay Green Som 28 D5
Winterhead N Som 44 B2
Winteringham N Lincs 200 C2
Winterley E Ches 168 D2
Wintersett W Yorks 197 D11
Wintershill Hants 33 D8
Winterton N Lincs 200 D2
Winterton-on-Sea Norf 161 F9
Winthorpe Lincs 175 B9
Winthorpe Notts 172 D4
Winton Bmouth 19 C7
Winton Cumb 222 C5
Winton E Sus 23 E8
Winton Gtr Man 184 B3
Winton N Yorks 225 F8
Wintringham N Yorks 217 E7
Winwick Cambs 138 G2
Winwick Northants 120 C2
Winwick Warr 183 C10
Winwick Quay Warr 183 C10
Winyard's Gap Dorset 29 F7
Winyates Worcs 117 D11
Winyates Green Worcs 117 D11
Wirksworth Derbys 170 E3
Wirksworth Moor Derbys 170 E4
Wirswall E Ches 167 G8
Wisbech Cambs 139 B9
Wisbech St Mary Cambs 139 B8
Wisborough Green W Sus 35 B8
Wiseton Notts 188 D2
Wishanger Glos 80 D6
Wishaw N Lnrk 268 D5
Wishaw Warks 134 E3
Wisley Sur 50 B5
Wispington Lincs 190 G2
Wissenden Kent 54 E2
Wissett Suff 127 B7
Wistanstow Shrops 131 F8
Wistanswick Shrops 150 D3
Wistaston E Ches 167 E11
Wistaston Green E Ches 167 E11
Wiston Pembs 73 B8
Wiston S Lnrk 259 C11
Wiston W Sus 35 E10
Wiston Mains S Lnrk 259 C11
Wistow Cambs 138 G5
Wistow Leics 136 D2
Wistow N Yorks 207 F7
Wiswell Lancs 203 F10
Witcham Cambs 139 G9
Witchampton Dorset 31 F7
Witchford Cambs 123 B10
Witcombe Som 29 C7
Withacott Devon 24 D6
Witham Essex 88 C4
Witham Friary Som 45 E8
Witham on the Hill Lincs 155 F11
Witham St Hughs Lincs 172 C5
Withcall Lincs 190 E3
Withdean Brighton 36 F4
Witherenden Hill E Sus 37 B10
Withergate Norf 160 D5
Witheridge Devon 26 E4
Witheridge Hill Oxon 65 C7
Witherley Leics 134 D6
Withermarsh Green Suff 107 D10
Withern Lincs 190 E6
Withernsea E Yorks 201 B10
Withernwick E Yorks 209 E9
Withersdale Street Suff 142 G5
Withersdane Kent 54 D5
Withersfield Suff 106 B3
Witherslack Cumb 211 C8
Witherwack T & W 243 F9
Withial Som 44 F5
Withiel Corn 5 B9
Withiel Florey Som 42 G3
Withielgoose Corn 5 B10
Withielgoose Mills Corn 5 B10
Withington Glos 81 B8
Withington Gtr Man 184 C5
Withington Hereford 97 C11
Withington Shrops 149 G11
Withington Staffs 151 B10
Withington Green E Ches 184 G4
Withington Marsh Hereford 97 C11
Withleigh Devon 26 E6
Withnell Lancs 194 C6
Withnell Fold Lancs 194 C6
Withy Mills Bath 45 B7
Withybed Green Worcs 117 C10
Withybrook Som 45 D7
Withybrook Warks 135 G8
Withybush Pembs 73 B7
Withycombe Som 41 F11
Withycombe Som 42 E4
Withycombe Raleigh Devon 14 E6
Withyditch Bath 45 B8
Withyham E Sus 52 F3
Withymoor Village W Mid 133 F8
Withypool Som 41 F10
Withystakes Staffs 169 F7
Withywood Bristol 60 F5
Witley Sur 50 F2
Witnells End Worcs 132 G5
Witnesham Suff 126 G3
Witney Oxon 82 C5
Wittensford Hants 32 E3
Wittering P'boro 137 C11
Wittersham Kent 38 B5
Witton Angus 293 F7
Witton Norf 142 B6
Witton W Mid 133 E11
Witton Worcs 117 E7
Witton Bridge Norf 160 C6
Witton Gilbert Durham 233 B10
Witton Hill Worcs 116 E5
Witton-le-Wear Durham 233 E8
Witton Park Durham 233 E9
Wiveliscombe Som 27 B9
Wivelrod Hants 49 F7
Wivelsfield E Sus 36 C4
Wivelsfield Green E Sus 36 C5
Wivenhoe Essex 107 G10
Wivenhoe Cross Essex 107 G10
Wiveton Norf 177 E8
Wix Essex 108 F3
Wixford Warks 117 G11
Wixhill Shrops 149 D11
Wixoe Suff 106 C4
Woburn C Beds 103 E8
Woburn Sands M Keynes 103 D8
Wofferwood Common Hereford 116 G3
Wokefield Park W Berks 65 F7
Woking Sur 50 B4
Wokingham Wokingham 65 F10
Wolborough Devon 14 G3
Wold Newton E Yorks 217 E10
Wold Newton NE Lincs 190 B2
Woldhurst W Sus 22 C5
Woldingham Sur 51 B11
Woldingham Garden Village Sur 51 B11
Wolfclyde S Lnrk 260 B2
Wolferd Green Norf 142 D5
Wolferlow Hereford 116 E3
Wolferton Norf 158 D3
Wolfhampcote Warks 119 D10
Wolfhill Perth 286 D5
Wolf's Castle Pembs 91 F9
Wolfsdale Pembs 91 G8
Wolfsdale Hill Pembs 91 G8
Woll Borders 261 E11
Wollaston Northants 121 E8
Wollaston Shrops 148 G6
Wollaston W Mid 133 G7
Wollaton Nottingham 153 B10
Wollerton Shrops 150 C2
Wollerton Wood Shrops 150 C2
Wollescote W Mid 133 G8
Wollrig Borders 261 E11
Wolsingham Durham 233 D7
Wolstanton Staffs 168 F5
Wolstenholme Gtr Man 195 D11
Wolston Warks 119 B8
Wolsty Cumb 238 G4
Wolterton Norf 160 C3
Wolvercote Oxon 83 D7
Wolverham W Ches 182 F6
Wolverhampton W Mid 133 D8
Wolverley Shrops 149 C9
Wolverley Worcs 116 B6
Wolverstone Devon 27 G10
Wolverton Hants 48 B5
Wolverton Kent 55 E9
Wolverton M Keynes 102 C6
Wolverton Shrops 131 F9
Wolverton Warks 118 E4
Wolverton Wilts 45 G9
Wolverton Common Hants 48 B5
Wolvesnewton Mon 79 F7
Wolvey Warks 135 F8
Wolvey Heath Warks 135 F8
Wolviston Stockton 234 F5
Womaston Powys 114 E5
Wombleton N Yorks 216 C3
Wombourne Staffs 133 E7
Wombridge Telford 150 G3
Wombwell S Yorks 197 G11
Womenswold Kent 55 C8
Womersley N Yorks 198 D4
Wonastow Mon 79 C7
Wonderstone N Som 43 B10
Wonersh Sur 50 D4
Wonford Devon 14 C4
Wonson Devon 13 D9
Wonston Dorset 30 F2
Wonston Hants 48 F3
Wooburn Bucks 66 B2
Wooburn Green Bucks 66 B2
Wood Pembs 91 G7
Wood Som 28 D4
Wood Bevington Warks 117 G11
Wood Burcote Northants 102 B3
Wood Dalling Norf 159 D11
Wood Eaton Staffs 150 F6
Wood End Beds 103 B10
Wood End Beds 121 D11
Wood End Beds 121 F11
Wood End Bucks 102 E5
Wood End C Beds 103 C9
Wood End Gtr Man 196 F2
Wood End Hereford 98 C2
Wood End Herts 104 F6
Wood End W Mid 133 C8
Wood End W Mid 135 G7
Wood End Warks 118 C2
Wood End Warks 134 D4
Wood End Warks 134 F5
Wood End Windsor 66 E2
Wood End Green London 66 C5
Wood Enderby Lincs 174 C3
Wood Field Sur 51 B7
Wood Gate Staffs 152 D3
Wood Green Essex 86 E6
Wood Green London 86 G4
Wood Green Norf 142 E4
Wood Green W Mid 133 D9
Wood Green Worcs 116 D6
Wood Hall Essex 105 E9
Wood Hayes W Mid 133 C8
Wood House Lancs 203 C10
Wood Lane Shrops 149 C8
Wood Lane Staffs 168 E4
Wood Lanes E Ches 184 E6
Wood Norton Norf 159 D10
Wood Norton Worcs 99 B10
Wood Road Gtr Man 195 E9
Wood Row W Yorks 197 B11
Wood Seats S Yorks 186 B4
Wood Stanway Glos 99 E11
Wood Street Norf 161 E7
Wood Street Sur 50 C3
Wood Street Village Sur 50 C3
Wood Walton Cambs 138 G4
Woodacott Devon 24 F5
Woodacott Cross Devon 24 F5
Woodale N Yorks 213 D10
Woodbank Argyll 255 F7
Woodbank Shrops 131 F11
Woodbank W Ches 182 G5
Woodbastwick Norf 160 F6
Woodbeck Notts 188 F3
Woodborough Notts 171 F10
Woodborough Wilts 46 B6
Woodbridge Dorset 30 D5
Woodbridge Dorset 30 E2
Woodbridge Glos 81 C8
Woodbridge Northumb 253 F7
Woodbridge Suff 108 B5
Woodbridge Hill Sur 50 C3
Woodbridge Walk Suff 109 B7
Woodburn Common Bucks 66 B2
Woodburn Moor Bucks 84 G6
Woodbury Devon 14 D6
Woodbury Salterton Devon 14 D6
Woodchester Glos 80 E4
Woodchurch Kent 54 G2

Woodchurch Mers 182 D3
Woodcock Wilts 45 E11
Woodcock Heath Staffs 151 D11
Woodcock Hill Herts 85 G9
Woodcock Hill W Mid 133 G10
Woodcombe Som 42 D3
Woodcot Hants 33 G9
Woodcote London 67 G10
Woodcote Oxon 64 C6
Woodcote Sur 51 B8
Woodcote Telford 150 F5
Woodcote Green London 67 G9
Woodcote Green Worcs 117 C8
Woodcott Hants 48 C2
Woodcroft Glos 79 F8
Woodcutts Dorset 31 D7
Woodditton Cambs 124 F3
Woodeaton Oxon 83 C8
Wooden Pembs 73 D10
Woodend Cumb 219 C10
Woodend Cumb 220 F3
Woodend Cumb 229 F10
Woodend Cumb 229 G7
Woodend E Ches 185 D7
Woodend Essex 87 C9
Woodend Fife 280 B4
Woodend Northants 102 B2
Woodend Notts 171 C7
Woodend Staffs 152 D3
Woodend W Loth 279 F11
Woodend W Sus 22 B4
Woodend Green Essex 105 F11
Woodend Green Northants 102 B2
Woodend Ho Argyll 275 G11
Woodfalls Wilts 31 C11
Woodfield Glos 80 F2
Woodfield Oxon 101 G11
Woodfield S Ayrs 257 E8
Woodford Corn 24 E2
Woodford Devon 8 E5
Woodford Glos 79 F11
Woodford Gtr Man 184 E5
Woodford London 86 G6
Woodford Northants 121 B9
Woodford Plym 7 D10
Woodford Som 42 F5
Woodford Som 44 E4
Woodford Bridge London 86 G6
Woodford Green London 86 G6
Woodford Halse Northants 119 G10
Woodford Wells London 86 G6
Woodgate Devon 27 D10
Woodgate Norf 159 F10
Woodgate W Mid 133 G9
Woodgate W Sus 22 C6
Woodgate Worcs 117 D9
Woodgate Hill Gtr Man 195 E10
Woodgate Valley W Mid 133 G10
Woodgates End Essex 105 F11
Woodgates Green Worcs 116 C2
Woodgreen Hants 31 D11
Woodgreen Oxon 82 C5
Woodhall Herts 86 C2
Woodhall Invclyd 276 G6
Woodhall N Yorks 207 G9
Woodhall N Yorks 223 G9
Woodhall Hills W Yorks 205 F10
Woodhall Spa Lincs 173 C11
Woodham Bucks 84 B2
Woodham Durham 233 F11
Woodham Sur 66 G4
Woodham Ferrers Essex 88 F3
Woodham Mortimer Essex 88 E4
Woodham Walter Essex 88 D4
Woodhatch Sur 51 D9
Woodhaven Fife 287 E8
Woodhead Aberds 303 F7
Woodheads Borders 271 F10
Woodhey Gtr Man 195 D9
Woodhey Mers 182 D4
Woodhey Green E Ches 167 E9
Woodhill Essex 88 E3
Woodhill N Som 60 D3
Woodhill Shrops 132 G4
Woodhill Som 28 B5
Woodhorn Northumb 253 F7
Woodhouse Cumb 211 C10
Woodhouse Cumb 219 B9
Woodhouse Hants 47 D11
Woodhouse Leics 153 F10
Woodhouse N Lincs 199 F9
Woodhouse S Yorks 186 D6
Woodhouse W Yorks 196 C2
Woodhouse W Yorks 197 C11
Woodhouse W Yorks 205 F7
Woodhouse W Yorks 205 F11
Woodhouse Down S Glos 60 B6
Woodhouse Eaves Leics 153 G10
Woodhouse Green Staffs 168 C6
Woodhouse Mill S Yorks 186 D6
Woodhouse Park Gtr Man 184 D4
Woodhouselee Midloth 270 C4
Woodhouselees Dumfries 239 C9
Woodhouses Cumb 239 G8
Woodhouses Gtr Man 184 C3
Woodhouses Gtr Man 196 G2
Woodhouses Staffs 133 B11
Woodhouses Staffs 152 F3
Woodhouses W Ches 183 F8
Woodhurst Cambs 122 B6
Woodingdean Brighton 36 F5
Woodington Hants 32 C4
Woodkirk W Yorks 197 C9
Woodlake Dorset 18 C3
Woodland Cumb 210 B4
Woodland Devon 8 B5
Woodland Devon 8 D2
Woodland Durham 233 F7
Woodland Kent 54 E6
Woodland Head Devon 13 B11
Woodlands Aberdeen 293 B10
Woodlands Aberds 293 D9
Woodlands Aberds 303 G8
Woodlands Dorset 31 F9
Woodlands Dumfries 238 B3
Woodlands Gtr Man 185 B7
Woodlands Hants 32 E4
Woodlands Highld 300 C5
Woodlands Kent 68 G5
Woodlands London 67 D7
Woodlands N Yorks 206 C2
Woodlands S Yorks 198 F4
Woodlands Som 43 E7
Woodlands Som 44 F4
Woodlands W Yorks 196 B5
Woodlands Wokingham 65 C9
Woodlands Common Dorset 31 F9
Woodlands Park Windsor 65 D11
Woodlands St Mary W Berks 63 E10
Woodlane Shrops 150 D3
Woodlane Staffs 152 E2
Woodleigh Devon 8 F4
Woodlesford W Yorks 197 B11
Woodley Gtr Man 184 C6
Woodley Hants 32 C5
Woodley Wokingham 65 E9
Woodley Green Wokingham 65 E9
Woodleys Oxon 82 B6
Woodlinkin Derbys 170 F6
Woodloes Park Warks 118 D5
Woodmancote Glos 80 F3
Woodmancote Glos 81 D8
Woodmancote Glos 99 F9
Woodmancote W Sus 22 B3
Woodmancote W Sus 36 E2
Woodmancote Worcs 99 C8
Woodmancott Hants 48 E5
Woodmans Green E Sus 38 D3
Woodmansey E Yorks 209 F7
Woodmansgreen W Sus 34 B5
Woodmansterne Sur 51 B9
Woodmill Staffs 152 E2
Woodminton Wilts 31 C8
Woodnesborough Kent 55 B10
Woodnewton Northants 137 E10
Woodnook Lancs 195 B9
Woodnook Lincs 155 C8
Woodplumpton Lancs 202 G6
Woodram Som 28 D2
Woodrising Norf 141 C9
Woodrow Bucks 84 F6
Woodrow Cumb 229 B10
Woodrow Dorset 30 E3
Woodrow Dorset 30 F2
Woodrow Worcs 117 B7
Woodrow Worcs 117 D11
Woods Hereford 96 B5
Woods Bank W Mid 133 D9
Wood's Corner E Sus 23 B11
Woods End Gtr Man 184 B2
Wood's Green E Sus 52 G6
Woods Moor Gtr Man 184 D6
Woodsden Kent 53 G9
Woodseats Derbys 185 C7
Woodseaves Shrops 150 C3
Woodseaves Staffs 150 D5
Woodsend Pembs 72 C5
Woodsend Wilts 63 D8
Woodsetton W Mid 133 E8
Woodsetts S Yorks 187 E9
Woodsfield Worcs 98 B6
Woodsfold Lancs 202 F5
Woodsford Dorset 17 C11
Woodside Aberdeen 293 C11
Woodside Aberds 303 E10
Woodside Beds 121 G11
Woodside Brack 66 E2
Woodside C Beds 85 B9
Woodside Derbys 170 G5
Woodside Derbys 187 G7
Woodside Dumfries 238 B2
Woodside Durham 233 F9
Woodside E Ches 167 C10
Woodside Essex 87 E7
Woodside Fife 287 G8
Woodside Hants 20 C2
Woodside Herts 85 E10
Woodside Herts 86 D3
Woodside I o W 20 C6
Woodside London 67 F10
Woodside N Lincs 199 G8
Woodside Perth 286 D6
Woodside Shrops 130 G6
Woodside Telford 132 C3
Woodside W Ches 183 G8
Woodside W Mid 133 F8
Woodside W Yorks 196 B6
Woodside Green Essex 87 B8
Woodside Green Kent 54 C2
Woodside of Arbeadie Aberds 293 D9
Woodside Park London 86 G3
Woodspeen W Berks 64 F2
Woodspring Priory N Som 59 F10
Woodstock Kent 70 G2
Woodstock Oxon 82 B6
Woodstock Pembs 91 F10
Woodston P'boro 138 D3
Woodthorpe Derbys 187 G7
Woodthorpe Leics 153 F10
Woodthorpe Lincs 190 E6
Woodthorpe Notts 171 G9
Woodthorpe York 207 D7
Woodton Norf 142 E5
Woodtown Devon 24 C6
Woodtown Devon 25 B7
Woodvale Mers 193 E10
Woodville Derbys 152 F6
Woodville Dorset 30 C4
Woodville Feus Angus 287 C10
Woodwall Green Staffs 150 C5
Woodway Oxon 64 C4
Woodway Park W Mid 135 G7
Woodwell Northants 121 B9
Woodwick Orkney 314 D3
Woodworth Green E Ches 167 D9
Woody Bay Devon 41 D7
Woodyates Dorset 31 D8
Woofferton Shrops 115 D10
Wookey Som 44 D4
Wookey Hole Som 44 D4
Wool Dorset 18 D2
Woolacombe Devon 40 E3
Woolage Green Kent 55 D8
Woolage Village Kent 55 C8
Woolaston Glos 79 F9
Woolaston Common Glos 79 E9
Woolaston Slade Glos 79 E9
Woolaston Woodside Glos 79 E9
Woolavington Som 43 E10
Woolbeding W Sus 34 C5
Wooldale W Yorks 197 F7
Wooler Northumb 263 D11
Woolfall Heath Mers 182 C6
Woolfardisworthy Devon 26 F4
Woolfardisworthy or Woolsery Devon 24 C4
Woolfold Gtr Man 195 E9
Woolfords Cottages S Lnrk 269 D10
Woolford's Water Dorset 29 F11
Woolgarston Dorset 18 E5
Woolgreaves W Yorks 197 D10
Woolhampton W Berks 64 F5
Woolhope Hereford 98 D2
Woolhope Cockshoot Hereford 98 D2
Woolland Dorset 30 F3
Woollard Bath 60 G6
Woollaston Staffs 151 F7
Woollaton Devon 25 E7
Woollensbrook Herts 86 C5
Woolley Bath 61 F8
Woolley Cambs 122 C3
Woolley Corn 24 D3
Woolley Derbys 170 C5
Woolley W Yorks 197 E10
Woolley Wilts 61 G10
Woolley Bridge Gtr Man 185 B8
Woolley Green Wilts 61 G10
Woolley Green Windsor 65 C11
Woolmer Green Herts 86 B3
Woolmer Hill Sur 49 G11
Woolmere Green Worcs 117 E9
Woolmersdon Som 43 G9
Woolminstone Som 28 F6
Woolpack Corner Kent 53 F11
Woolpit Suff 125 E9
Woolpit Green Suff 125 E9
Woolpit Heath Suff 125 E9
Woolridge Glos 98 G6
Woolsbridge Dorset 31 F9
Woolscott Warks 119 D9
Woolsery or Woolfardisworthy Devon 24 C4
Woolsgrove Devon 26 G3
Woolsington T & W 242 D5
Woolstanwood E Ches 167 D11
Woolstaston Shrops 131 D9
Woolsthorpe Lincs 155 E8
Woolsthorpe by Belvoir Lincs 154 C6
Woolsthorpe-by-Colsterworth Lincs 155 E8
Woolston Corn 6 B5
Woolston Devon 8 G4
Woolston Shrops 131 F8
Woolston Shrops 148 E6
Woolston Som 29 B10
Woolston Som 42 F5
Woolston Soton 32 E6
Woolston Warr 183 D10
Woolston Green Devon 8 B5
Woolstone Glos 99 E9
Woolstone M Keynes 103 D7
Woolstone Oxon 63 B9
Woolton Mers 182 D6
Woolton Hill Hants 64 G2
Woolvers Hill N Som 59 G11
Woolverstone Suff 108 D3
Woolverton Som 45 C9
Woolwell Devon 7 C10
Woolwich London 68 D2
Woolwich Ferry London 68 D2
Woon Corn 5 D10
Woonton Hereford 115 E10
Woonton Hereford 115 G7
Wooperton Northumb 264 E2
Wooplaw Borders 271 G9
Woore Shrops 168 G2
Wooton Shrops 115 C11
Wooton Shrops 132 F5
Wootten Green Suff 126 C4
Wootton Beds 103 B10
Wootton Hants 19 B10
Wootton Hereford 97 D11
Wootton Hereford 114 G6
Wootton I o W 20 C6
Wootton Kent 55 D8
Wootton N Lincs 200 D5
Wootton Northants 120 F5
Wootton Oxon 82 B6
Wootton Oxon 83 E7
Wootton Shrops 115 B9
Wootton Shrops 148 D6
Wootton Staffs 150 D6
Wootton Staffs 169 F10
Wootton Bassett Wilts 62 C5
Wootton Bourne End Beds 103 B9
Wootton Bridge I o W 20 C6
Wootton Broadmead Beds 103 C10
Wootton Common I o W 20 C6
Wootton Courtenay Som 42 E2
Wootton Fitzpaine Dorset 16 B3
Wootton Green Beds 103 C9
Wootton Green W Mid 118 B4
Wootton Rivers Wilts 63 G7
Wootton St Lawrence Hants 48 C5
Wootton Wawen Warks 118 E3
Woottons Staffs 151 B11
Worbarrow Dorset 18 F3
Worcester Worcs 117 F7
Worcester Park London 67 F8
Wordsley W Mid 133 F7
Wordwell Suff 124 C6
Worfield Shrops 132 D5
Worgret Dorset 18 D4
Work Orkney 314 E4
Workhouse Common Norf 161 E7
Workhouse End Beds 122 G2
Workhouse Green Suff 107 D8
Workhouse Hill Essex 107 E9
Workington Cumb 228 F5
Worksop Notts 187 F9
Worlaby Lincs 190 F4
Worlaby N Lincs 200 E4
World's End Bucks 84 D5
Worlds End Hants 33 E10
World's End London 86 F4
World's End Suff 125 F9
Worlds End W Mid 134 G2
World's End W Sus 36 D4
Worle N Som 59 G11
Worlebury N Som 59 G10
Worleston E Ches 167 D11
Worley Glos 80 F4
Worlingham Suff 143 F8
Worlington Devon 40 G3
Worlington Suff 124 C3
Worlingworth Suff 126 D4
Wormadale Shetland 313 J5
Wormald Green N Yorks 214 G6
Wormbridge Hereford 97 E8
Wormbridge Common Hereford 97 E8
Wormegay Norf 158 G3
Wormelow Tump Hereford 97 E9
Wormhill Derbys 185 G10
Wormingford Essex 107 E8
Worminghall Bucks 83 D10
Wormington Glos 99 D10
Worminster Som 44 E5
Wormiston Ho Fife 287 G10
Wormit Fife 287 E7
Wormleighton Warks 119 G8
Wormley Herts 86 D5
Wormley Sur 50 F2
Wormley West End Herts 86 D4
Wormleybury Herts 86 D5
Worms Ash Worcs 117 C8
Worms Hill Kent 53 F8
Wormshill Kent 53 B11
Wormsley Hereford 97 B8
Wornish Nook E Ches 168 B4
Worplesdon Sur 50 C3
Worrall S Yorks 186 C4
Worrall Hill Glos 79 C10
Worsbrough S Yorks 197 G11
Worsbrough Bridge S Yorks 197 G11
Worsbrough Common S Yorks 197 F10
Worsbrough Dale S Yorks 197 G11
Worsham Oxon 82 C3
Worsley Gtr Man 195 G8
Worsley Hall Gtr Man 194 F5
Worsley Mesnes Gtr Man 194 G5
Worstead Norf 160 D6
Worsthorne Lancs 204 G3
Worston Devon 7 E11
Worston Lancs 203 E11
Worswell Devon 7 F10
Worten Kent 54 E3
Worth Kent 55 B10
Worth Som 44 D4
Worth W Sus 51 F9
Worth Abbey W Sus 51 G10
Worth Matravers Dorset 18 F5
Wortham Suff 125 B11
Worthen Shrops 130 C6
Worthenbury Wrex 166 F6
Worthing Norf 159 F9
Worthing W Sus 35 G10
Worthington Leics 153 E8
Worthy Som 41 D11
Worthybrook Mon 79 C7
Worting Hants 48 C6
Wortley Glos 80 G3
Wortley S Yorks 186 B4
Wortley W Yorks 205 G11
Worton N Yorks 223 G9
Worton Oxon 83 C7
Worton Wilts 46 B3
Wortwell Norf 142 G5
Wotherton Shrops 130 C5
Wothorpe P'boro 137 B10
Wotter Devon 7 C11
Wotton Glos 80 B4
Wotton Sur 50 D6
Wotton-under-Edge Glos 80 G3
Wotton Underwood Bucks 83 B11
Woughton on the Green M Keynes 103 D7
Wouldham Kent 69 G8
Woundale Shrops 132 E5
Wrabness Essex 108 E3
Wraes Aberds 302 F5
Wrafton Devon 40 F3
Wragby Lincs 189 F10
Wragby W Yorks 198 D2
Wragholme Lincs 190 B5
Wramplingham Norf 142 B2
Wrangaton Devon 8 D3
Wrangbrook W Yorks 198 E3
Wrangham Aberds 302 F6
Wrangle Lincs 174 E6
Wrangle Bank Lincs 174 E6
Wrangle Low Ground Lincs 174 E6
Wrangle Lowgate Lincs 174 E6
Wrangway Som 27 D10
Wrantage Som 28 C4
Wrawby N Lincs 200 F4
Wraxall Dorset 29 G9
Wraxall N Som 60 E3
Wraxall Som 44 F6
Wray Lancs 212 F2
Wray Common Sur 51 C9
Wraysbury Windsor 66 E4
Wrayton Lancs 212 E2
Wrea Green Lancs 202 G3
Wreaks End Cumb 210 B4
Wreath Som 28 F4
Wreay Cumb 230 B4
Wreay Cumb 230 G4
Wrecclesham Sur 49 D10
Wrekenton T & W 243 F7
Wrelton N Yorks 216 B5
Wrenbury E Ches 167 F9
Wrenbury cum Frith E Ches 167 F9
Wrench Green N Yorks 217 B9
Wreningham Norf 142 D3
Wrentham Suff 143 G9
Wrenthorpe W Yorks 197 C10
Wrentnall Shrops 131 C8
Wressle E Yorks 207 G10
Wressle N Lincs 200 F3
Wrestlingworth C Beds 104 B5
Wretham Norf 141 F8
Wretton Norf 140 D3
Wrexham Wrex 166 E4
Wreyland Devon 13 E11
Wribbenhall Worcs 116 B5
Wrickton Shrops 132 F2
Wrightington Bar Lancs 194 E4
Wright's Green Essex 87 B8
Wrights Green Warr 183 E10
Wrinehill Staffs 168 F3
Wringsdown Corn 12 D2
Wrington N Som 60 G3
Wrinkleberry Devon 24 C4
Writhlington Bath 45 C8
Writtle Essex 87 D11
Wrockwardine Telford 150 G2
Wrockwardine Wood Telford 150 G4
Wroot N Lincs 199 G8
Wrose W Yorks 205 F9
Wrotham Kent 52 B6
Wrotham Heath Kent 52 B6
Wroughton Swindon 62 C6
Wroughton Park M Keynes 103 D7
Wroxall I o W 21 F7
Wroxall Warks 118 C4
Wroxeter Shrops 131 B11
Wroxhall Warks 118 C4
Wroxham Norf 160 F6
Wroxton Oxon 101 C8
Wyaston Derbys 169 G11
Wyatt's Green Essex 87 F9
Wybers Wood NE Lincs 201 F8
Wyberton Lincs 174 G4
Wyboston Beds 122 F3
Wybunbury E Ches 168 F2
Wych Cross E Sus 52 G2
Wychbold Worcs 117 D8
Wychnor Staffs 152 F3
Wychnor Bridges Staffs 152 F3
Wyck Hants 49 F9
Wyck Rissington Glos 100 G3
Wycliffe Durham 224 C2
Wycoller Lancs 204 F4
Wycomb Leics 154 E5
Wycombe Marsh Bucks 84 G5
Wyddial Herts 105 E7
Wydra N Yorks 205 C10
Wye Kent 54 D5
Wyebanks Kent 54 C2
Wyegate Green Glos 79 D9
Wyesham Mon 79 C8
Wyfordby Leics 154 F5
Wyke Dorset 30 B3
Wyke Shrops 132 C2
Wyke Sur 50 C2
Wyke W Yorks 197 B7
Wyke Champflower Som 45 G7
Wyke Regis Dorset 17 F9
Wykeham Lincs 156 D5
Wykeham N Yorks 216 D6
Wykeham N Yorks 217 C9
Wyken Shrops 132 E5
Wyken W Mid 135 G7
Wykey Shrops 149 E7
Wykin Leics 135 D8
Wylam Northumb 242 E4
Wylde Hereford 115 D9
Wylde Green W Mid 134 E2
Wyllie Caerph 77 G11
Wylye Wilts 46 F4
Wymans Brook Glos 99 G8
Wymbush M Keynes 102 D6
Wymering Ptsmth 33 F10
Wymeswold Leics 154 E2
Wymington Beds 121 E9
Wymondham Leics 155 F7
Wymondham Norf 142 C2
Wymondley Bury Herts 104 F4
Wymott Lancs 194 C4
Wyndham Bridgend 76 G6
Wyndham Park V Glam 58 D5
Wynds Point Hereford 98 C5
Wynford Eagle Dorset 17 B7
Wyng Orkney 314 G3
Wynn's Green Hereford 98 B2
Wynyard Village Stockton 234 F4
Wyre Piddle Worcs 99 B9
Wysall Notts 154 D2
Wyson Hereford 115 D10
Wythall Worcs 117 B11
Wytham Oxon 83 D7
Wythburn Cumb 220 C6
Wythenshawe Gtr Man 184 D4
Wythop Mill Cumb 229 F9
Wyton Cambs 122 C5
Wyton E Yorks 209 G9
Wyverstone Suff 125 D10
Wyverstone Green Suff 125 D10
Wyverstone Street Suff 125 D10
Wyville Lincs 155 D7
Wyvis Lodge Highld 300 B4

Y

Y Bala = Bala Gwyn 147 B8
Y Bont Faen = Cowbridge V Glam 58 E3
Y Borth = Borth Ceredig 128 E2
Y Fali = Valley Anglesey 178 F3
Y Felinheli = Port Dinorwic Gwyn 163 B8
Y Ferwig Ceredig 92 B3
Y Ffôr Gwyn 145 B7
Y-Ffrith Denb 181 E8
Y Gors Ceredig 112 B2
Y Gribyn Powys 129 E8
Y Mwmbwls = The Mumbles Swansea 56 D6
Y Pîl = Pyle Bridgend 57 E10
Y Tymbl = Tumble Carms 75 C8
Y Waun = Chirk Wrex 148 B5
Yaddlethorpe N Lincs 199 F11
Yafford I o W 20 E4
Yafforth N Yorks 224 G6
Yair Borders 261 C11
Yalberton Torbay 9 D7
Yalding Kent 53 C7
Yanley N Som 60 F5
Yanworth Glos 81 C9
Yapham E Yorks 207 C11
Yapton W Sus 35 G7
Yarberry N Som 43 B11
Yarborough NE Lincs 201 F9
Yarbridge I o W 21 D8
Yarburgh Lincs 190 C5
Yarcombe Devon 28 F2
Yard Som 42 F5
Yarde Som 42 F5
Yardhurst Kent 54 E3
Yardley W Mid 134 F2
Yardley Gobion Northants 102 C5
Yardley Hastings Northants 121 F7
Yardley Wood W Mid 118 B2
Yardro Powys 114 F4
Yarford Som 28 B2
Yarhampton Worcs 116 D5
Yarhampton Cross Worcs 116 D5
Yarkhill Hereford 98 C2
Yarlet Staffs 151 D8
Yarley Som 44 D4
Yarlington Som 29 B11
Yarlside Cumb 210 F4
Yarm Stockton 225 C8
Yarmouth I o W 20 D3
Yarnacott Devon 40 G6
Yarnbrook Wilts 45 C11
Yarnfield Staffs 151 C7
Yarningale Common Warks 118 D3
Yarnscombe Devon 25 C9
Yarnton Oxon 83 C7
Yarpole Hereford 115 E9
Yarrow Borders 261 D9
Yarrow Northumb 250 F6
Yarrow Som 43 D11
Yarrow Feus Borders 261 D8
Yarrowford Borders 261 C10
Yarsop Hereford 97 B8
Yarwell Northants 137 D11
Yate S Glos 61 C8
Yate Rocks S Glos 61 C8
Yateley Hants 65 G10
Yatesbury Wilts 62 E5
Yattendon W Berks 64 E5
Yatton Hereford 115 D8
Yatton N Som 60 F2
Yatton Keynell Wilts 61 D11
Yaverland I o W 21 D8
Yawthorpe Lincs 188 C5
Yaxham Norf 159 G10
Yaxley Cambs 138 E3
Yaxley Suff 126 C2
Yazor Hereford 97 B8
Yeabridge Som 28 D6
Yeading London 66 C6
Yeadon W Yorks 205 E10
Yealand Conyers Lancs 211 E10
Yealand Redmayne Lancs 211 D10
Yealand Storrs Lancs 211 D9
Yealmbridge Devon 7 E11
Yealmpton Devon 7 E11
Yearby Redcar 235 G8
Yearngill Cumb 229 C8
Yearsley N Yorks 215 E11
Yeaton Shrops 149 F8
Yeaveley Derbys 169 G11
Yedingham N Yorks 217 D7
Yelden Beds 121 D10
Yeldersley Hollies Derbys 170 G2
Yeldon Beds 121 D10
Yelford Oxon 82 E5
Yelland Devon 40 G3
Yelling Cambs 122 E5
Yelsted Kent 69 G10
Yelvertoft Northants 119 B11
Yelverton Devon 7 B10
Yelverton Norf 142 C5
Yenston Som 30 C2
Yeo Mill Devon 26 B4
Yeo Vale Devon 24 C6
Yeoford Devon 13 B11
Yeolmbridge Corn 12 D2
Yeovil Som 29 D9
Yeovil Marsh Som 29 D8
Yeovilton Som 29 C8
Yerbeston Pembs 73 D9
Yesnaby Orkney 314 E2
Yetlington Northumb 252 B2
Yetminster Dorset 29 E9
Yett N Lnrk 268 D5
Yettington Devon 15 D7
Yetts o' Muckhart Clack 286 G4
Yew Green Warks 118 D4
Yew Tree Gtr Man 185 B7
Yew Tree W Mid 133 D10
Yewhedges Kent 54 B3
Yewtree Cross Kent 55 E7
Yieldshields S Lnrk 269 E7
Yiewsley London 66 C5
Yinstay Orkney 314 E5
Ynus-tawelog Swansea 75 D10
Ynys Gwyn 145 B11
Ynys-isaf Powys 76 C3
Ynys-meudwy Neath 76 D2
Ynys Tachwedd Ceredig 128 E2
Ynysboeth Rhondda 77 F9
Ynysddu Caerph 77 G11
Ynysforgan Swansea 57 B7
Ynysgyfflog Gwyn 146 G2
Ynyshir Rhondda 77 G8
Ynyslas Ceredig 128 E2
Ynysmaerdy Neath 57 B8
Ynysmaerdy Rhondda 58 C4
Ynysmeudwy Neath 76 D2
Ynystawe Swansea 75 E11
Ynyswen Powys 76 C4
Ynyswen Rhondda 77 F7
Ynysybwl Rhondda 77 G9
Ynysygwas Neath 57 C9
Yockenthwaite N Yorks 213 D8
Yockleton Shrops 149 G7
Yodercott Devon 27 E9
Yokefleet E Yorks 199 C10
Yoker W Dunb 267 B10
Yonder Bognie Aberds 302 E5
Yondertown Devon 7 D11
Yopps Green Kent 52 C6
York Lancs 203 G10
York York 207 C7
York Town Sur 65 G11
Yorkletts Kent 70 G5
Yorkley Glos 79 D10
Yorkley Slade Glos 79 D10
Yorton Shrops 149 E10
Yorton Heath Shrops 149 E10
Yottenfews Cumb 219 D10
Youlgrave Derbys 170 C2
Youlstone Devon 24 D3
Youlthorpe E Yorks 207 B11
Youlton N Yorks 215 G9
Young Wood Lincs 189 G10
Young's End Essex 88 B2
Youngsbury Herts 86 B5
Yoxall Staffs 152 F2
Yoxford Suff 127 D7
Yr Hôb = Hope Flint 166 D4
Ysbyty Cynfyn Ceredig 112 B5
Ysbyty Ifan Conwy 164 F4
Ysbyty Ystwyth Ceredig 112 C4
Ysceifiog Flint 181 G11
Ysgeibion Denb 165 D9
Yspitty Carms 56 B5
Ystalyfera Neath 76 D3
Ystrad Rhondda 77 F7
Ystrad Aeron Ceredig 111 F10
Ystrad-mynach Caerph 77 G10
Ystrad Uchaf Powys 129 C11
Ystradfellte Powys 76 C6
Ystradffin Carms 94 B5
Ystradgynlais Powys 76 C3
Ystradmeurig Ceredig 112 D4
Ystradowen Carms 76 C2
Ystradowen V Glam 58 D4
Ystumtuen Ceredig 112 B4
Ythanbank Aberds 303 F9
Ythanwells Aberds 302 F6
Ythsie Aberds 303 F8

Z

Zeal Monachorum Devon 26 G2
Zeals Wilts 45 G9
Zelah Corn 4 E6
Zennor Corn 1 B5
Zoar Corn 3 F7
Zouch Notts 153 E10

County and unitary authority boundaries

Ordnance Survey National Grid

The blue lines which divide the Navigator map pages into squares for indexing match the Ordnance Survey National Grid and correspond to the small squares on the boundary map below. Each side of a grid square measures 10km on the ground.

The National Grid 100-km square letters and kilometre values are indicated for the grid intersection at the outer corners of each page. For example, the intersection SE6090 at the upper right corner of page 215 is 60km East and 90km North of the south-west corner of National Grid square SE.

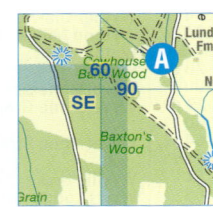

Using GPS with Navigator mapping

Since Navigator Britain is based on Ordnance Survey mapping, and rectified to the National Grid, it can be used with in-car or handheld GPS for locating identifiable waypoints such as road junctions, bridges, railways and farms, or assessing your position in relation to any of the features shown on the map.

On your receiver, choose British Grid as the location format and for map datum select Ordnance Survey (this may be described as Ord Srvy GB or similar, or more specifically as OSGB36). Your receiver will automatically convert the latitude/longitude co-ordinates transmitted by GPS into compatible National Grid data.

Positional accuracy of any particular feature is limited to 50–100m, due to the limitations of the original survey and the scale of Navigator mapping.

For further information see www.gps.gov.uk

Greater London

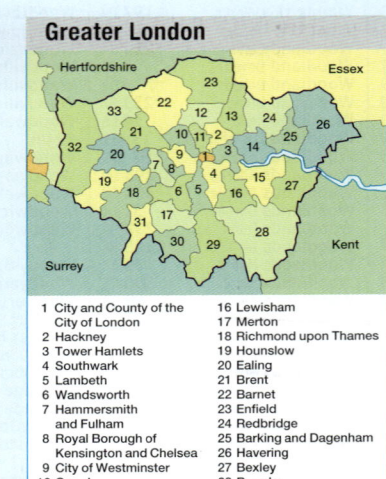

1. City and County of the City of London
2. Hackney
3. Tower Hamlets
4. Southwark
5. Lambeth
6. Wandsworth
7. Hammersmith and Fulham
8. Royal Borough of Kensington and Chelsea
9. City of Westminster
10. Camden
11. Islington
12. Haringey
13. Waltham Forest
14. Newham
15. Greenwich
16. Lewisham
17. Merton
18. Richmond upon Thames
19. Hounslow
20. Ealing
21. Brent
22. Barnet
23. Enfield
24. Redbridge
25. Barking and Dagenham
26. Havering
27. Bexley
28. Bromley
29. Croydon
30. Sutton
31. Kingston upon Thames
32. Hillingdon
33. Harrow

1 Central Scotland

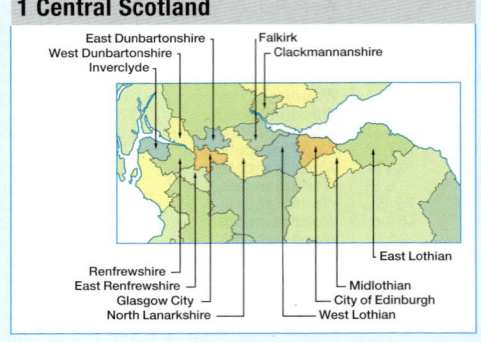

2 Northern England

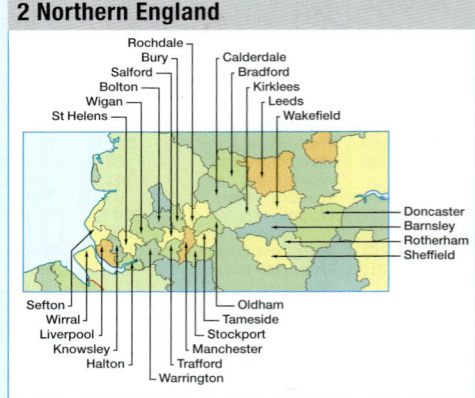

3 West Midlands

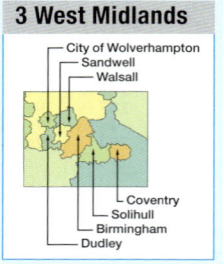

4 South Wales and Bristol area

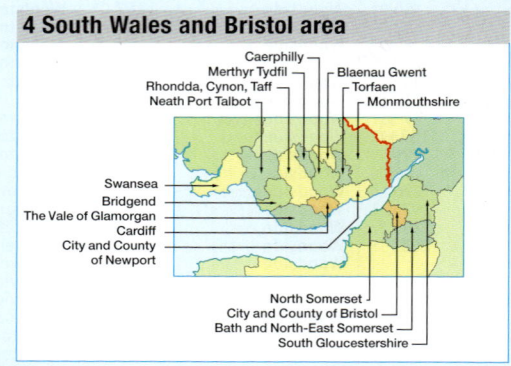

5 Thames Valley

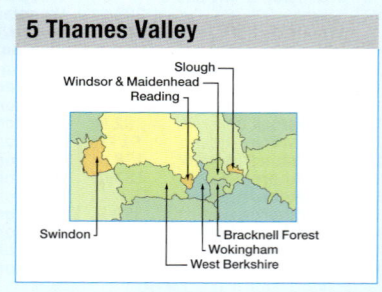